BRITANNICA

Book of the Year

1971

Encyclopædia Britannica, Inc.

WILLIAM BENTON

Publisner

Chicago, Toronto, London, Geneva, Sydney, Tokyo, Manila

© 1971

BY ENCYCLOPÆDIA BRITANNICA, INC.

Copyright Under International Copyright Union
All Rights Reserved Under Pan American And Universal Copyright Conventions
By Encyclopædia Britannica, Inc.
Library of Congress Catalog Number: 38–12082
International Standard Book Number: 0–85229–158–2

No part of this work may be reproduced or utilized in any form or by any means, electronic or
mechanical, including photocopying, recording, or by any information storage and retrieval system,
without permission in writing from the publisher.

BRITANNICA BOOK OF THE YEAR

(Trademark Reg. U.S. Pat. Off.)
Printed in U.S.A.

THE UNIVERSITY OF CHICAGO

The Britannica Book of the Year is published with the editorial advice
of the faculties of The University of Chicago

The Publisher's Message

Old Values and New Discoveries

ARIZONA REPUBLIC
Senators William Benton and Hubert Humphrey visit in Arizona. Humphrey was a board member of Encyclopædia Britannica, Inc., and Encyclopædia Britannica Educational Corp. in 1969 and 1970.

By its very nature, the *Britannica Book of the Year* acts as a coda—"a concluding passage, the function of which is to bring a composition or division to a cogent and well-proportioned close." But in the rush of events of our times, it has taken on an ever greater dimension: it provides an annual perspective, an insight that shapes the manner in which history is perceived.

Ever since Herodotus, the thrust of history was considered to be in the tidal heave of events. For centuries, even millennia, man studied the gathering forces through the long roll of the years and sought to describe them in terms of slow but irresistible movements. Thus, history was an epochal event, followed by another epochal event—not, as in our times, a day-to-day and year-by-year experience.

In taking an epochal view of our times, Arnold Toynbee has suggested that 300 years from now, the 20th century will be remembered not for its wars, nor for its conquest of distance or disease, not even for the splitting of the atom, but for "having been the first age, since the dawn of civilization, some five or six thousand years back, in which people dared to think it practicable to make the benefits of civilization available for the whole human race." In the year 2271, perhaps Albert Schweitzer will dominate a chapter heading for the 20th century while Winston Churchill shrinks to a footnote.

It is the hope of the editors that the *Britannica Book of the Year* will help bring its readers a historical perspective without tolling the long roll of centuries. This is not altogether simple. We must measure the pace of history—not as the tide heaves—but, in these fast-moving times, as the waves break, one upon the other. That puts a special responsibility on the *Book of the Year* not only to observe history with a sense of the perennial but to locate man in time and space. It is a deep satisfaction for me, in my 28th year as publisher of the Britannica, to share with you the manner in which we have achieved our hopes—both explicitly and implicitly—in this current volume for 1971.

On the more explicit level, you see history in two of our three feature articles through the eyes of men who have made it—President Park Chung Hee writing of his Republic of Korea; Harold Wilson, former prime minister of Great Britain, writing of the role of public opinion polls in government. The third major article is by Theodore H. White, America's outstanding historian of contemporary affairs, who—in a work of unique illumination and insight—describes and analyzes the American scene in 1970.

On the more implicit level, you will discern, I think, a change in the angle of vision that this generation has of its historical moment. No one dares assert that the prism has turned identically throughout the world, but there is everywhere a clear impatience with our sociological traditions, with the ambiguity of the past and the forces that gave it sustenance. Today's generation tells us it cannot live with the pragmatism or the ambiguities of the past; indeed, it goes further and gives us powerful evidence that it cannot live with the ambiguities of the present. It rejects the notion that civilization and progress grow by slow processes, like the building of a coral reef.

Yet the discontent of our young people is not a new phenomenon. Alexander Heard, chancellor of Vanderbilt University, reminds us that dissent and disruption marked many a 19th-century campus in the U.S. "Students have confounded their elders at least as far back as the time of Plato," Heard notes, recalling words of the Greek philosopher dating back 2,300 years:

What is happening to our young people? They disrespect their elders, they disobey their parents. They ignore the laws. They riot in the streets inflamed with wild notions. Their morals are decaying. What is to become of them?

The older generation does not have so sharp an appetite for doom or for catastrophe—having, perhaps, experienced it more personally and recently than its offspring—but neither does it reject learning from the mistakes of the past. In fact, I do not believe the "generation gap" is what it is cracked up to be by our children and grandchildren. They know nothing about the post-

World War I generation gap when I was in college. Scott Fitzgerald described that generation in *Echoes of the Jazz Age:*

> Scarcely had the staider citizens of the republic caught their breaths when the wildest of all generations, the generation which had been adolescent during the confusion of the war, bruskly shouldered my contemporaries out of the way and danced into the limelight.

When the girls bobbed their hair, it startled the oldsters more than when today's boys let theirs grow long. When girls started to smoke and carry flasks of whiskey to football games, the startled shock exceeded that of marihuana. Skirts became just as short as they are now. The new jazz music had more wallop of change than rock. Cheek-to-cheek dancing and the Charleston, for a sensational change in the mores of the young, cannot be matched today, nor can the universal acceptance of "necking" and "petting." I still remember my surprise at the first girl who would not kiss me. Yes, today's generation gap is overrated. And today's is captured by record albums, by *Playboy,* by the Yearbook, as the late teens and early 1920s never were until Fitzgerald wrote *This Side of Paradise.* Today's is embossed and exaggerated under the glare of the TV cameras which my generation was spared.

"From the past, we all have a heritage of error," said Adlai E. Stevenson, a Britannica director. "But we cannot dwell on the past, for the future is too challenging and too peremptory." And so we at *Britannica Book of the Year* endeavour to account for man's ever changing angle of vision in its own terms: "The earth," wrote Thomas Jefferson, "belongs to the living." This Yearbook is an account of how the living may come to possess the earth; it is an account of the questing sense of discovery of our civilization as we enter the '70s.

One of the historic things that the living now seem to be doing —as illustrated in the events of the past year—is turning from a predominantly scientific impulse to a more humanistic one. The change seems not only dramatic but perhaps ennobling: "A creative economy," said Emerson, "is the fuel of magnificence." Astonishingly, the shape of the change broke upon us virtually overnight and at the summit of a superlative scientific era. Just a year ago, we were celebrating man's first landing on the moon. It was the climax of what might fairly be called "The Golden Age of Physics," an era in which it seemed that physics would not only shape man's destiny but also rule his mind. So self-contained was this "golden age" that it offered its own sense of drama: it was exactly 24 years from one of the highest moments of physics—the exploding of the first atomic bomb in the New Mexico desert on July 16, 1945—to the launching of Apollo 11 on July 16, 1969. There seemed every reason to believe that this vast success with the moon would be followed by an enormous outpouring of wealth for NASA so that success could follow upon success. Indeed, the competition between the U.S. and the U.S.S.R. would seem to encourage that outpouring. Yet it did not happen. The U.S. cut back on its investment in space. It reduced its number of moon landings and rescheduled those that were left. (*See* our special report on the post-Apollo period.) The United States—having known two of the most distinguished moments in scientific history—suddenly decided to turn to more humanistic priorities, perhaps in an effort to restore—in Archibald MacLeish's words—the "precarious balance between the society and the self."

The widening field of vision that took place in 1970 is reflected in the Yearbook's special reports:

—The concern over drug abuse among the young;

—The rising clamour over consumer rights;

—The social changes represented by the activity of Women's Liberation groups;

—The emerging problems posed by explosive population growth.

Such reports recall the injunction of Edmund Burke that "a nation without means of reform is without means of survival."

And yet it must be said quickly that there is an international dimension to change or to reform—for example, Women's Lib; there are groups promoting it in eight Western European countries. In our special report on Women's Lib, giving a historical view of its struggle for recognition, you will find that medieval theologians argued that women had no soul and were more prone to sin than were men. And that Jean Jacques Rousseau—that philosopher of the liberated mind and spirit—did not extend his beneficence to women: he argued that they had their own peculiarly feminine rights and were not entitled to usurp those of men in the bargain. A good many people argued through the centuries that women were not capable of abstract thought or, for that matter, of taking on the responsibilities of government. (This argument rose again in the last year.) The vehicle of activism for Women's Lib was the civil rights movement. The militant young women who were for equal rights were for equal rights for everybody; they came to the conclusion that in the civil rights movement there was as deep a prejudice over sex as in society at large.

In the turn of the public temper, the most significant movement was in man's growing challenge to science and in particular the "immutability" of biological destiny. History, it has been said, is a fragment of biology. Plant life, animal life, even man himself are considered to be products of an inevitable biological evolution that started long before recorded history. So overwhelming was that process that it raised a passive submission in some and a sense of alarm in very few. Yet, in his *Politics,* Aristotle observed that the "neglect of an effective birth-control policy is a never-failing source of poverty which, in turn, is the parent of revolution and crime."

The biological process was so unchallenged for so long that it took on a certain inevitability; man seemed cowed by the conviction that he could do nothing about it. "Whether or not we find what we are seeking/Is idle, biologically speaking," wrote Edna St. Vincent Millay. Only in this last portion of the 20th century did the twin catastrophes of an ultimate biology—the biological drive toward procreation which would overpopulate the world, the drive toward war which would depopulate it—become intolerable. These twin drives had placed man in a position that was, to use Sir Winston Churchill's words, "both measureless and laden with doom." Julian Huxley among others began to suggest that evolution is now a cultural rather than a biological process, and that man has the fearful responsibility of guiding it. If the dark abyss is of his own making, so then is the obligation to avoid it.

In the past, man had worked against war—and famine and pestilence—in an effort to control the death rate; now he has begun to work on controlling the birthrate. Through it, he hoped to overcome the biological "inevitability" of overpopulation. Otherwise, the population of the world will quadruple—to 14.4 billion persons—in one man's lifetime. The urgency of the situation is such that the scientists are working for the human imperatives instead of submitting wordlessly to biological ones.

Beyond all this, I tend to see each *Britannica Book of the Year* as a personal document of the editors and the readers as well as a historical one. I have a moving personal response to much of the material included here, a response that leaves me—and, I hope, you—with a heightened sense of identity and involvement. For the Yearbook offers that sense of revelation that surrounds some very old ideas, as if the world of good and evil had just been rediscovered.

It is this personal sense of destiny that preoccupies us in the *Book of the Year.* We appreciate the vast range of interest of our readers in the topical; we provide for that. We know also that the scholar's interest is in the generic and the historical; we provide generously for that. The particular dimension that we hope to add—and, each year, to learn how better to add—is an enduring perspective of man's affairs. This is the particular vision of impassioned mankind's concern for all men. To this vision we shall continue to dedicate ourselves.

Wm Benton

How to Use the Book of the Year

THE *Britannica Book of the Year* is carefully planned for ready availability of reference material.

Three devices aid the reader to find information he seeks in the main section, which begins on page 65: first and most important, the Index; second, hundreds of cross-reference entries grouped alphabetically in the margins of the pages for quick and convenient information; and third, inserted frequently in or after articles, the suggestion to *"see also"* other specific articles for further related information.

The reader will be repaid richly if he learns more of the contents than just the answers to an occasional reference question about an event of the year. In the pages of this volume, including the special articles which begin on page 17, there are many features to be noted.

The first thing to catch the attention of the reader as he thumbs through the volume will be the many pictures and other illustrations. These include many of the outstanding news photographs of the year, gathered from all over the world, and they constitute a remarkable pictorial record of the year's events.

OTHER FEATURES OF SPECIAL INTEREST:

- A list of the authors of the articles in the *Book of the Year* ... starts on page 7.

- Calendar of major religious and national holidays scheduled or expected to occur in 1971 ... is on page 50.

- Chronology of 1970 — the major events of the past year listed day by day as they happened ... starts on page 51.

- Obituaries — sketches of scores of prominent individuals who died in 1970 ... starts on page 556.

- Biographies of many prominent living figures whose activities dominated the news in 1970 ... starts on page 130. Government officials are named in articles on their countries.

- Statistical data of all types, the latest available, appear in many articles.

Above all, remember to use the Index (starting on page 801) whenever you wish information in the *Book of the Year*. The alphabetical arrangement of the book enables a reader to find subjects easily; the Index tells not only where articles appear but often guides the reader to other related subjects.

Before using the Index be sure to read the instructions that precede it.

Contents

Editorial Staff

Editor: DEAN H. SCHOELKOPF

Managing Editor, London: J. E. DAVIS

Consulting Editor: Jacques Havet, Paris

Latin America Editor: Cesar A. Ramos, Mexico City

Classification Advisers: A. G. Armstrong, Morris Fishbein, M.D., Edwin W. Goodpaster, Jerome Holtzman, Miroslav Kriz, D. A. Pyke, M.D., M.R.C.P., John Kerr Rose, Harvey Sherman

Associate Editor: Daphne Daume

Copy Editors: Judy Booth, David Calhoun, Conrad Chyatte, Vanessa A. Clarke, R. M. Goodwin, Mary Alice Molloy, Allan Murray, Dorothy M. Partington, William Spector, Andrew Thomas, Basil H. Tripp

Art Director: Will Gallagher

Associate Art Director: David Ross-Robertson

Senior Picture Editor: James Sween

Picture Editors: Florence Scala; Elizabeth West, London

Layout Artist: Mark Cowans

Art Production: Durango Mendoza

Cartographers: Chris Leszczynski, Supervisor; William Karpa, Eugene Tiutko

Art Staff: Laurence Campbell, George Carlson, Martina Daker, Ramon Goas, Kenneth Hirte, Bernard Holliday, Edwin Huff, Dean Schultz, James Taylor

Geography Editor: Frank J. Sutley

Assistant Geography Editor: Olga A. Titelbaum

Geography Staff: William A. Cleveland, Supervisor; Sujata Banerjee, Juanita Bartholomew, Peggy L. Clark, Reynaldo S. G. Cruz, William A. Johnson, Gerald E. Keefe, Charlene R. Neidlinger, Marino P. PeBenito, David L. Schein, Joseph R. Sturgis, Daniel G. Welker, Janice F. Wesemann

Editorial Production Manager: J. Thomas Beatty

Production Coordinator: Lorene Lawson

Staff: John Atkinson, Necia Brown, Anthony R. Burrell, Barbara W. Cleary, Barbara Hurd, Patrick M. Joyce, Winifred Laws, Lynn K. McEwan, Steven Meyer, Richard O'Connor, Ruth Passin, Mary Reardon, Susan G. Recknagel, Julian Ronning, Madolynn Scheel, Elliott Major Singer, Carol Smith, Cheryl Trobiani, Valerie Walker, Anita K. Wolff

Proofreading Staff: Harry Sharp, Supervisor; Michana Buchman, Susan Alison Bush, Peggy Collins, Gerald M. Fisher, Marilyn Klein, Lila H. Morrow, Gwen I. Phelps, Salena Ehrich Rapp, Linda G. H. Schmidt

Copy Control: Felicité Buhl, Supervisor; Mary K. Finley, Recorder; Carol Du Bois, Barbara Grimm, Gurtha McDonald, Shirley Richardson
Barbara Chandler, Pat Woodgate, London

Index Staff: Frances E. Latham, Supervisor; Virginia Palmer, Assistant Supervisor; Grace R. Lord, Mary Reynolds, Rosalba Rueda

Editorial Assignments: Mary Hunt, Billie A. Moore, Allena McCorvey

Copy Correspondent: Judith Lukens

Executive Vice-President Editorial, Encyclopædia Britannica, Inc.: HOWARD L. GOODKIND

CONTRIBUTORS

Initials and names of contributors to the Britannica Book of the Year *with the articles written by them.*
The arrangement is alphabetical by initials.

A.D.Bu./El Salvador; Honduras
ALLEN D. BUSHONG. Associate
Professor of Geography, University of
South Carolina.

Ad.He./Medicine (*in part*)
ADELE HERWITZ. Executive Director,
International Council of Nurses, Geneva,
Switz.

A.Dr./Industrial Review (*in part*)
ALFRED DAWBER. Chairman and
Editorial Director, Emmott and Company,
Ltd.; Kennedy Press Ltd., technical
publishers, Manchester. Editor, *Textile
Manufacturer.* Compiler of *Mechanical World
Year Book; Electrical Year Book.*

Ad.T./Literature (*in part*)
ADRIEN THERIO. Professor of Lettres
Françaises, University of Ottawa. Author of
*L'Humour au Canada français; Soliloque en
hommage à une femme.*

A.D.Wi./Sweden
ALAN DAVID WILSON. Assistant
Editor, *Sweden Now.*

Ae.B./Literature (*in part*)
ANNIE J. M. BRIERRE. Literary
Critic, *Les Nouvelles Littéraires; La Revue des
Deux Mondes; France—U.S.A.* Author of
Ninon de Lenclos.

A.F.D./Merchandising (*in part*)
ALTON F. DOODY. Professor of
Marketing, College of Administrative
Science, Ohio State University. Author of
*Retailing Management; Marketing in
America: Settlement to Civil War* (vol. 1).

A.G./Malta
ALBERT GANADO. Lawyer, Malta.

**A.G.A./Investment, International; Trade,
International** (*in part*)
ALAN GORDON ARMSTRONG.
Lecturer, Department of Economics,
University of Bristol.

A.G.Bl./Music (*in part*)
ALAN GEOFFREY BLYTH. Music
Critic, London.

A.G.R./Religion (*in part*)
ARTHUR GUY REYNOLDS. Registrar
and Associate Professor of Church History,
Emmanuel College, Toronto.

A.J.A.M./Turkey
ANDREW JAMES ALEXANDER MAN-
GO. Orientalist and broadcaster.

A.J.Z./European Unity
ARNOLD J. ZURCHER. Professor
of Comparative Politics, Graduate
School of Arts and Sciences,
New York University.

Al.Ma./Engineering Projects (*in part*)
ALDO MARCELLO. Civil Engineer.

Al.Pa./Medicine (*in part*)
ALEXANDER PATON. Consultant
Physician, Birmingham Hospital Group,
Eng. Postgraduate Clinical Tutor,
University of Birmingham, Eng.

A.P.Kl./Religion (*in part*)
ALFRED PAUL KLAUSLER. Executive
Secretary, Associated Church Press.
Author of *Censorship, Obscenity and Sex;
Growth in Worship.*

A.R.A./Cricket
ARTHUR REX ALSTON. Broadcaster
and Journalist. Author of *Taking the Air;
Over to Rex Alston; Test Commentary;
Watching Cricket.*

Ar.C.B./Indonesia
ARNOLD C. BRACKMAN. Author
of *Indonesian Communism: A History;
Southeast Asia's Second Front: The Power
Struggle in the Malay Archipelago; The
Communist Collapse in Indonesia.*

A.R.G.G./Australia; Nauru
ANTHONY ROYSTON GRANT
GRIFFITHS. Lecturer in History, Flinders
University of South Australia.

A.R.W./Panama
ALMON ROBERT WRIGHT. Retired
Senior Historian, U.S. Department of State.

A.S./Museums and Galleries (*in part*)
ANDREW SZPAKOWSKI. Program
Specialist, Monuments and Museums
Section, UNESCO, Paris.

A.Sd./Swimming
ALBERT SCHOENFIELD. Editor,
Swimming World.

A.S.M./Medicine (*in part*)
ABRAHAM SAMUEL MARKOWITZ.
Director, Department of Experimental
Immunology, Hektoen Institute for Medical
Research; Professor of Microbiology,
University of Illinois Medical School.

A.Th./Libraries
ANTHONY THOMPSON. General
Secretary, International Federation of
Library Associations. Author of *Vocabularium
Bibliothecarii; Library Buildings of Britain
and Europe.*

A.Tl./Industrial Review (*in part*)
ARTHUR TATTERSALL. Textile Trade
Expert and Statistician, Manchester, Eng.

A.W.Bs./Japan
ARDATH WALTER BURKS. Professor
and Director, International Programs, Rutgers
University, New Brunswick, N.J. Author of
*The Government of Japan; East Asia: China,
Korea, Japan.*

A.W.O./Nicaragua
ARDEN W. OHL. Instructor of
Geography, Modesto (Calif.) Junior College.

A.W.Wo./Medicine (*in part*)
ALAN WALLER WOODRUFF. Wellcome
Professor of Clinical Tropical Medicine,
University of London; Physician, Hospital
for Tropical Diseases, London. Co-author of
Recent Advances in Tropical Medicine.

Ay.K./Literature (*in part*)
(THOMAS) ANTHONY KERRIGAN.
Editor and translator of *Selected Works of*
Miguel de Unamuno (10 vol.). Author of
At the Front Door of the Atlantic;
Co-translator of *Selected Poems* of Pablo
Neruda (1970).

B.Ar./Biography (*in part*); **Ireland**
BRUCE ARNOLD. Free-lance
Journalist and Writer, Dublin.

B.B.Mo./Medicine (*in part*)
BERTRAM B. MOSS, M.D. Clinical
Director, Division of Gerontology, Chicago
Medical School; Medical Administrator,
Jewish Home for Aged and Park View Home
for Aged. Author of *Caring for the Aged.*

B.C.N./Fuel and Power (*in part*)
BRUCE CARLTON NETSCHERT.
Director, National Economic Research
Associates, Inc., Washington, D.C. Author of
The Future Supply of Oil and Gas; Co-author of
Energy in the American Economy: 1850-1975.

Be.N./Track and Field Sports (*in part*)
BERT NELSON. Publisher, *Track and
Field News.*

B.Gr./Music (*in part*)
BENNY GREEN. Jazz Critic, *Observer,*
London; Record Reviewer, British Broad-
casting Corporation. Author of *The Reluctant
Art; Blame It on My Youth; 58 Minutes to
London; Jazz Decade.* Contributor to
Encyclopedia of Jazz.

B.L.Go./Religion (*in part*)
BRIAN LLEWELLYN GOLLAND.
General Secretary, The General Assembly of
Unitarian and Free Christian Churches,
London.

B.N.D./Trade, International (*in part*)
BARRIE NICHOLAS DAVIES. Director,
Statistical Division, Economic Commission
for Europe, Geneva.

C.C.O./Engineering Projects (*in part*);
Industrial Review (*in part*)
CARTER CLARKE OSTERBIND.
Director, Bureau of Economic and Business
Research, University of Florida.
Co-author of *Florida's Older People.*

Cd.H./Religion (*in part*)
CLIFFORD HAIGH. Editor, *The Friend,*
London.

C.E.N./Religion (*in part*)
C. EMIL NELSON. National Chief
Secretary and Colonel, Salvation Army,
U.S.A.

C.E.R./Timber
CHARLES EDGAR RANDALL.
Assistant Editor, *Journal of Forestry.* Author
of *Famous Trees; Our Forests.*

C.F.Sa./Biography (*in part*); **Finland**
CARL FREDRIK SANDELIN. Foreign
News Editor, Finnish News Agency.
President, Society of Swedish-speaking
Writers in Finland.

C.H.J./U.S. Supplement: *Church Membership
Table.*
CONSTANT HERBERT JACQUET, JR.
Director of Research Library and Research
Associate, National Council of Churches.
Editor, *Yearbook of American Churches.*

C.H.M.J.W./Philosophy (*in part*)
CHRISTIAN HENRI MARIE JOSEPH WENIN. Ordinary Professor of Philosophy, Université Catholique de Louvain, Belg. Academic Secretary, Institut supérieur de Philosophie. Author of *La Bibliothèque idéale.*

C.J.Ay./Motor Sports (*in part*)
CYRIL J. AYTON. Editor, *Motorcycle Sport,* London.

C.L.Be./Conservation (*in part*)
CHARLES LEOFRIC BOYLE. Lieutenant-Colonel, R.A. (ret'd). Chairman, Survival Service Commission, International Union for Conservation of Nature and Natural Resources, 1958–63; Secretary, Fauna Preservation Society, London, 1950–63.

C.L.F.W./Biological Sciences (*in part*)
CHRISTOPHER LEONARD FRANK WOODCOCK. Lecturer on Biology and Associate in Electron Microscopy, Department of Biology, Harvard University.

C.M.Jo./Bowling and Lawn Bowls (*in part*)
CLARENCE MEDLYCOTT JONES. Editor, *World Bowls; Lawn Tennis.* Author of *Winning Bowls; The Watney Book of Bowls.* Co-author of *Tackle Bowls My Way; Bryant on Bowls.*

Co.L./Biography (*in part*)
COLIN LEGUM. Commonwealth Correspondent, *Observer,* London. Author of *Must We Lose Africa?; Bandung, Cairo and Accra; Congo Disaster; Pan-Africanism—A Short Political Guide.* Co-author of *Attitude to Africa; South Africa: Crisis for the West; The Bitter Choice.* Editor of *Africa—A Handbook to the Continent.*

Co.S./Commercial Policies (*in part*)
CONSTANT CHUNG-TSE SHIH. Counsellor, Trade Policy Department, General Agreement on Tariffs and Trade (GATT), Switz.

C.U.L./Religion (*in part*)
CHAIM URI LIPSCHITZ. President, National Information Bureau for Jewish Life; Vice President, Mesivta Torah Vodaath; Managing Editor, *The Jewish Press.* Author of *Shield of Israel.*

Cy.W./Industrial Review (*in part*)
CYRIL WEEDEN. Assistant Director, Glass Manufacturers' Federation, London.

D.A.F./Archaeology (*in part*)
DAVID A. FREDRICKSON. Assistant Professor of Anthropology, Sonoma State College, Rohnert Park, Calif.

Da.J.R./Biography (*in part*); **Cinema** (*in part*)
DAVID JULIEN ROBINSON. Film Critic, *The Financial Times.* Author of *Buster Keaton; Hollywood in the Twenties; The Great Funnies—A History of Screen Comedy.*

D.A.S.J./Employment, Wages, and Hours
DUDLEY ANTHONY STEPHENSON JACKSON. Research Officer, Department of Applied Economics, University of Cambridge.

D.B.J.F./Football (*in part*)
DAVID BROUGH JAMES FROST. Rugby Union Correspondent, *The Guardian,* London.

D.Bo./Netherlands
DICK BOONSTRA. Member of the staff, Department of Political Science, Free University, Amsterdam.

D.D./Economics
DUDLEY DILLARD. Professor and Head, Department of Economics, University of Maryland. Author of *The Economics of John Maynard Keynes; Economic Development of the North Atlantic Community.*

Dd.H./Inter-American Affairs
DAVID HUELIN. Manager, Economic Intelligence Department, Bank of London and South America Ltd., London.

De.C./Industrial Design
DENNIS CHEETHAM. Lecturer in Liberal Studies, School of Graphics, City of Leicester Polytechnic, Eng.

D.F.C./Metallurgy
DONALD FREDERIC CLIFTON. Professor of Metallurgy, University of Idaho.

D.Fo./Migration, International (*in part*)
DAVID FOUQUET. Staff Writer, *Congressional Quarterly.*

D.H.C.P.-B./Sailing
DOUGLAS HEXTALL CHEDZEY PHILLIPS-BIRT. Associate Member of the Royal Institution of Naval Architects. Consulting naval architect. Yachting correspondent, *Observer,* London. Author of *Sailing Yacht Design; Motor Yacht and Boat Design; The Waters of Wight.*

D.J.Ro./Peru
DAVID JONATHAN ROBINSON. Economic Adviser, Petroleum Press Service, London.

D.K.Da./Bolivia (*in part*); **Uruguay**
DAVID KEITH DAVIES. Economic and Political Research Officer, Bank of London and South America Ltd., London.

D.K.R.P./Sporting Record
DAVID KEMSLEY ROBIN PHILLIPS. Contributor, *World Sports.* Editor, *World Sports Olympic Games Report.* Co-compiler of *Guinness Book of Olympic Records.*

D.L.Bi./Insurance (*in part*)
DAVID LYNN BICKELHAUPT. Professor of Insurance, College of Administrative Science, Ohio State University. Author of *Transition to Multiple-Line Insurance Companies.* Co-author of *General Insurance.*

D.L.McE./Dentistry
DONALD L. McELROY. Associate Dean, College of Dentistry, University of Illinois. Co-author of *Handbook of Oral Diagnosis and Treatment Planning.*

D.L.St./Psychology
DAVID LLOYD STREINER. Assistant Professor of Psychiatry (Psychology), McMaster University, Hamilton, Ont.

D.M.L.F./Canada
DAVID M. L. FARR. Professor of History, Carleton University, Ottawa. Author of *The Colonial Office and Canada, 1867–1887; Two Democracies; The Canadian Experience.*

D.P.B./Industrial Review (*in part*)
DONALD P. BURKE. Senior Editor, *Chemical Week.*

Du.C./Crime (*in part*)
DUNCAN CHAPPELL. Professor of Criminal Justice, State University of New York at Albany. Author of *The Police and the Public in Australia and New Zealand.*

E.A.J.D./Transportation (*in part*)
ERNEST ALBERT JOHN DAVIES. Editor, *Traffic Engineering and Control* (monthly); *Roads and Their Traffic; Traffic Engineering Practice.*

E.B.Br./Religion (*in part*)
EDWIN BLAINE BRONNER. Professor of History and Curator of the Quaker Collection, Haverford College, Haverford, Pa. Author of *William Penn's Holy Experiment.* Editor, *American Quakers Today; An English View of American Quakerism.*

E.B.Nn./Rubber
EDWIN BOHANNON NEWTON. Former Manager, Advanced Rubber Technology, B.F. Goodrich Company, Brecksville, O.

E.Di./Austria; Biography (*in part*)
ELFRIEDE DIRNBACHER. Austrian Civil Servant.

E.H.Ha./Vital Statistics
EVELYN HUNTINGTON HALPIN. Writer and consultant on vital statistics and accident prevention programs.

Ei.K./Cities and Urban Affairs (*in part*)
EISSE KALK. Research Officer, International Union of Local Authorities, The Hague, Neth.

Er.As./Horse Racing (*in part*)
ERIC ARTHUR ASTROM. Executive Secretary, National Association of Canadian Race Tracks; Editor, *Track Talk* (the Association's publication).

E.St./Medicine (*in part*)
ERWIN STENGEL. Emeritus Professor of Psychiatry in the University of Sheffield, Eng.

E.T.Ch./Medicine (*in part*)
EMIL THEODORE CHANLETT. Professor of Sanitary Engineering, School of Public Health, University of North Carolina. Contributor to *Air Pollution.*

Ev.R./Domestic Arts and Sciences
EVELYN GITA ROSE. Home economics consultant; Broadcaster; Food Historian; Vice-Chairman, Association of Home Economists of Great Britain; Cookery Editor, *Jewish Chronicle.* Contributor to *Home Economics; The Guardian,* London. Author of *More Fun with Your Food; The Jewish Home.*

E.W.M./Religion (*in part*)
ERIK W. MODEAN. Director, News Bureau, Lutheran Council in the U.S.A.

F.Br./Boxing
FRANK BUTLER. Sports Editor, *News of the World,* London.

F.Dd./Algeria
FRANÇOIS DURIAUD. Reuters correspondent, Algiers.

F.G./Biography (*in part*); **Italy**
FABIO GALVANO. London Correspondent, *Epoca,* Milan.

F.H.Ka./Religion (*in part*)
FREDERIK HERMAN KAAN. Secretary of the Department of Cooperation and Witness, World Alliance of Reformed Churches (Presbyterian and Congregational), Geneva, Switz.

F.H.Li./Religion (*in part*)
FRANKLIN HAMLIN LITTELL. Professor, Department of Religion, Temple University, Philadelphia, Pa. Author of *The Origins of Sectarian Protestantism; From State Church to Pluralism.*

F.H.Sk./Fuel and Power (*in part*); **Mining** (*in part*); **U.S. Supplement: Mining Table; Power: Mineral Fuels Table**
FRANK H. SKELDING. President, AMDEC Corp. (mineral consultants).

F.I.Or./Astronautics (*in part*)
FREDERICK I. ORDWAY. Director, Science and Technology Applications and Evaluation, Research Institute, Div. of Graduate Studies and Research, University of Alabama in Huntsville. Author of *Life in Other Solar Systems.* Co-author of *History of Rocketry and Space Travel; Basic Astronautics; International Missile and Spacecraft Guide.*

F.J.C.R./Medicine (*in part*)
FRANCIS JOHN CALDWELL ROE. Reader in Experimental Pathology, Institute of Cancer Research, University of London; Associate Pathologist, Royal Marsden Hospital, London. Author of *Biology of Cancer; The Prevention of Cancer*.

F.J.Se./Medicine (*in part*)
FREDRICK J. STARE, M.D. Professor of Nutrition and Chairman, Department of Nutrition, Harvard School of Public Health. Author of syndicated newspaper column "Food and Your Health."

F.N.He./Zoos and Botanical Gardens (*in part*)
FRANK NIGEL HEPPER. Principal Scientific Officer, Herbarium, Royal Botanic Gardens, Kew, Eng. Editor of *Flora of West Tropical Africa* (vol. ii and iii).

F.P.P./Fairs and Shows
FREDERICK P. PITTERA. Chairman, International Exposition Consultants Co. Member, Board of Trustees, New York Institute of Technology. Member, Board of Governors, National Business and Professional Council. Director, New Nations Exposition and Development Corporation. Author of *The Art and Science of International Fairs and Exhibitions; The Fairs of the United States and Canada*.

F.S.Rl./Biological Sciences (*in part*)
SIR FREDERICK STRATTEN RUSSELL. Director, Plymouth Laboratory, Marine Biological Association of the United Kingdom, 1945–65. Author of *The Medusae of the British Isles*. Co-author of *The Seas*.

F.W.N./Medicine (*in part*)
FRANK W. NEWELL. Professor of Ophthalmology, The University of Chicago. Author of *Ophthalmology, Principles and Concepts*. Editor, *American Journal of Ophthalmology*.

F.W.Rr./Meteorology
FRANCIS W. REICHELDERFER. Aeronautical and Marine Meteorology Consultant. Former Chief, Weather Bureau, U.S. Department of Commerce, Washington, D.C.

F.Wt./Biography (*in part*)
FRANK G. WRIGHT. Washington (D.C.) Correspondent, *Minneapolis Tribune*.

G.A.A./Dominican Republic
GUSTAVO ARTHUR ANTONINI. Associate Professor, Center for Latin American Studies, University of Florida.

Ga.Pa./Commercial Policies (*in part*)
GARDNER PATTERSON. Assistant Director General, Trade Policy Department, General Agreement on Tariffs and Trade (GATT), Switz. Author of *Discrimination in International Trade; Survey of United States International Finance; NATO: A Critical Appraisal*.

G.A.Po./Profits
GERALD A. POLLACK. Vice-President, First National City Bank, New York, N.Y. Author of *Perspectives on the U.S. International Financial Position*.

G.B.Sm./Philately and Numismatics (*in part*)
GLENN B. SMEDLEY. Governor, American Numismatic Association. President, Society of Paper Money Collectors.

G.C./Literature (*in part*)
GIOVANNI CARSANIGA. Lecturer in Italian, University of Sussex, Eng.

G.C.Cu./Jamaica
GLORIA CLARE CUMPER. Chairman, Council of Voluntary Social Services; Member, Judicial Services Commission, Kingston, Jamaica.

G.C.Ho./Merchandising (*in part*)
GRAHAM CHARLES HOCKLEY. Lecturer, Department of Economics, University College, Cardiff. Author of *Monetary Policy and Public Finance*. Co-author of *The Wealth of the Nation: The Balance Sheet of the United Kingdom, 1957–61*.

G.C.L./Ethiopia
GEOFFREY CHARLES LAST. Adviser, Imperial Ethiopian Ministry of Education and Fine Arts, Addis Ababa. Author of *A Regional Survey of Africa; A Geography of Ethiopia*. Co-author of *A History of Ethiopia in Pictures*.

Ge.We./Industrial Review (*in part*)
GEORGE WEBER. Editor-in-chief, *The Oil and Gas Journal*.

G.F.R./Industrial Review (*in part*)
GEORGE FRANK RAY. Senior Research Fellow, National Institute of Economic and Social Research, London.

G.J.Br./Medicine (*in part*)
GARY JULES BRAUNER, M.D. Chief Resident and Research Fellow in Dermatology, Massachusetts General Hospital and Harvard University.

G.O.K.B./Migration, International (*in part*)
GUNTHER O. K. BEIJER. Secretary General, European Center for Population Studies, The Hague. Author of *National Rural Manpower; Adjustment to Industry; Rural Migrants in Urban Setting; Some Aspects of Migration Problems in the Netherlands*.

Go.M./Industrial Review (*in part*)
GORDON MINNES. Secretary, Canadian Pulp and Paper Association.

G.P./Literature (*in part*)
GABRIEL PREIL. Writer. Hebrew and Yiddish poet. Author of *Israeli Poetry in Peace and War; Nof Shemesh Ukhfor* ("Landscape of Sun and Frost"); *Ner Mul Kokhavim* ("Candle Against the Stars"); *Mapat Erev* ("Map of Evening"); *Lieder* ("Poems"); *Haesh Vehadmama* ("The Fire and the Silence").

G.R.De./Economic Planning (*in part*)
GEOFFREY RICHARD DENTON. Reader in Economics, University of Reading, Eng. Co-author of *Economic Planning and Policies in Britain, France and Germany*. Editor of *Economic Integration in Europe*.

G.S.Mo./Zoos and Botanical Gardens (*in part*)
GEORGE SAUL MOTTERSHEAD. Director-Secretary, Chester Zoo, Chester, Eng.

G.U./Burma; Dependent States (*in part*); **Nepal**
GOVINDAN UNNY. Agence France-Presse Special Correspondent for India, Nepal and Ceylon.

Ha.E./Medicine (*in part*)
HAROLD ELLIS. Professor of Surgery, Westminster Medical School, University of London. Author of *Clinical Anatomy* (4th edition); *Anatomy for Anaesthetists* (2nd edition); *Lecture Notes in Surgery* (3rd edition); *Principles of Resuscitation; History of Bladder Stone*.

Ha.Fr./Contract Bridge
HAROLD FRANKLIN. Editor, *English Bridge Quarterly*. Bridge Correspondent, *Yorkshire Post; Yorkshire Evening Post*. Broadcaster. Author of *Best of Bridge on the Air*.

H.A.Ru./Medicine (*in part*)
HOWARD A. RUSK, M.D. Chairman, Department of Rehabilitation Medicine, New York University Medical Center, New York City. Contributing Editor, the *New York Times*. Author of *Rehabilitation Medicine*.

H.A.Ta./Transportation (*in part*)
HAROLD ANTHONY TAYLOR. Air Transport Editor, *Flight International*, London, 1964–69.

H.B./Hockey (*in part*); **Ice Skating; Skiing**
HOWARD BASS. Winter Sports Correspondent, *The Daily Telegraph*, London; *The Christian Science Monitor*, Boston. Author of *The Sense in Sport; This Skating Age; The Magic of Skiing; Winter Sports*.

H.C.Cl./Literature (*in part*)
HENRY CUMMINGS CAMPBELL. Chief Librarian, Toronto Public Library, Toronto.

H.D.M./Engineering Projects (*in part*)
HORACE DENTON MORGAN. Senior Partner, Sir William Halcrow and Partners, London.

H.Du./Historic Buildings
HIROSHI DAIFUKU. Chief, Section for the Development of the Cultural Heritage, UNESCO, Paris.

He.B.H./Food (*in part*)
HENRY BERNARD HAWLEY. Consultant, Human Nutrition and Food Science, Sherborne, Eng.

H.E.Ku./Molecular Biology (*in part*)
HERBERT E. KUBITSCHEK. Senior Physicist, Division of Biological and Medical Research, Argonne National Laboratory. Author of *Introduction to Research with Continuous Cultures*.

H.Go./Chess
HARRY GOLOMBEK. British Chess Champion, 1947, 1949, and 1955. Chess Correspondent, *The Times* and *Observer*, London. Author of *Penguin Handbook on the Game of Chess; Modern Opening Chess Strategy*.

H.H.Sa./Propaganda
HOWLAND H. SARGEANT. President, Radio Liberty Committee. Author of *The Representation of the United States Abroad*.

Hi.S./Housing
HIDEHIKO SAZANAMI. Chief, Urban Facilities Research Group, Building Research Institute, Ministry of Construction, Tokyo. Author of *Housing in Metropolitan Areas*.

H.J.Kl./Prisons and Penology
HUGH JOHN KLARE. Secretary, Howard League for Penal Reform, London. Author of *Anatomy of Prison*. Editor of *Changing Concepts of Crime and Its Treatment*.

H.Ko./Communist Movement
HANS KOHN. Emeritus Professor of History, City College of New York. Author of *Prologue to Nation-States: the French and German Experiences 1789-1815*.

H.L.En./Conservation (*in part*)
HERBERT LEESON EDLIN. Publications Officer, Forestry Commission of Great Britain. Author of *Trees, Woods and Man; Wayside and Woodland Trees; Man and Plants; What Wood is That?; Guide to Tree Planting and Cultivation*.

H.M.F.M./Industrial Review (*in part*)
HUGH MICHAEL FINER MALLETT. Editor, *Weekly Wool Chart*, Bradford, Eng.

Ho.S./Literature (*in part*)
HOWARD SERGEANT. Lecturer and writer. Editor of *Outposts*, London. Author of *The Cumberland Wordsworth; Tradition in the Making of Modern Poetry*.

H.R.Mo./Music (*in part*)
HAZEL ROMOLA MORGAN. Assistant to Administrative Manager, International Sales Division, E.M.I. Records, London.

H.R.Sh./Agriculture (*in part*); **Food** (*in part*); **U.S. Supplement:** *Principal Crops Table*
HARVEY R. SHERMAN. Environmental Policy Division, Legislative Reference, Library of Congress.

H.Sa./Biological Sciences (*in part*)
HAROLD SANDON. Formerly Professor of Zoology, University of Khartoum, Sudan. Author of *The Protozoan Fauna of the Soil; The Food of Protozoa; An Illustrated Guide to the Fresh-water Fishes of the Sudan; Essays on Protozoology.*

H.S.N./Fisheries
HAROLD STANLEY NOEL. Editor, *World Fishing*, London.

H.-T.Ch./China; Taiwan
HUNG-TI CHU. Expert in Far Eastern Affairs. UN Area Specialist and Chief of Asia-Africa Section and Trusteeship Council Section, 1946–67; Professor of Government, Texas Tech University, Lubbock, 1968–69.

H.Y.S.P./India
HOLENARASIPUR Y. SHARADA PRA-SAD. Director of Information, Prime Minister's Secretariat, New Delhi.

I.H.M./Alcoholic Beverages (*in part*)
IRVING H. MARCUS. Editor-Publisher, *Wines and Vines*. Author of *Dictionary of Wine Terms.*

I.Ka./Mathematics
IRVING KAPLANSKY. George Herbert Mead Distinguished Service Professor, Department of Mathematics, The University of Chicago.

I.Pr./Stock Exchanges (*in part*)
IRVING PFEFFER. Professor of Insurance and Finance, Graduate School of Business Administration, University of California at Los Angeles. Author of *Insurance and Economic Theory; The Financing of Small Business.*

I.S.F./Development, Economic
IRVING S. FRIEDMAN. The Economic Adviser to the President of the International Bank for Reconstruction and Development. Author of *Exchange Controls and The International Monetary System; U.S. Foreign Economic Policy.*

ITU/Telecommunications (*in part*)
INTERNATIONAL TELECOMMUNICATION UNION, Geneva.

Ja.C.C./Molecular Biology (*in part*)
JAMES CLINTON COPELAND. Associate Geneticist, Division of Biological and Medical Research, Argonne National Laboratory, Argonne, Ill.

Ja.E.M./Motor Sports (*in part*)
JAMES EDWARD MARTENHOFF. Boating Editor, *Miami* (Fla.) *Herald.* Author of *How to Buy a Better Boat; Handbook of Skin and Scuba Diving.*

J.Ag./Horse Racing (*in part*)
JOSEPH C. AGRELLA. Turf Editor, *Chicago Sun-Times.* Author of *Ten Commandments for Professional Handicapping.*

Ja.G.S./Medicine (*in part*)
JAMES G. SHAFFER. Associate Dean and Professor of Microbiology, the Chicago Medical School. Author of *Amebiasis: A Biomedical Problem.*

J.A.Kr./Chemistry (*in part*)
JAMES ALISTAIR KERR. Lecturer, University of Birmingham, Eng.

Ja.Ma./Television and Radio (*in part*)
JAMES MAGEE. Communications Consultant, Geneva.

J.A.O'L./Biography (*in part*)
JEREMIAH ALOYSIUS O'LEARY. Latin America Correspondent, *Washington Evening Star*, Washington, D.C. Author of *Dominican Action—1965.*

Ja.R.E./Belgium
JAN ROBERT ENGELS. Editor, *P.V.V. Flitsen* (Journal of the Belgian Party for Freedom and Progress).

J.B.A./Religion (*in part*)
JACOB BERNARD AGUS. Rabbi, Beth El Congregation, Baltimore, Md. Visiting Professor of Religion, Temple University, Philadelphia, Pa. Author of *The Evolution of Jewish Thought; The Meaning of Jewish History.*

J.B.Be./Industrial Review (*in part*);
Transportation (*in part*)
JOHN BERESFORD BENTLEY. Editor, *Air-Cushion Vehicles.* Publisher, *Hoverfoil News.*

J.Be./Baseball
JACK BRICKHOUSE. Vice President and Manager of Sports, WGN Continental Broadcasting Company.

J.B.Kr./Medicine (*in part*)
JOSEPH BARNETT KIRSNER, M.D. Louis Block Professor of Medicine, The University of Chicago School of Medicine.

J.B.St./Religion (*in part*)
J. BUROUGHS STOKES. Manager, Committees on Publication, the First Church of Christ, Scientist, Boston.

J.C.Y./Chemistry (*in part*)
JOHN COLIN YOUNG. Lecturer in Chemistry, University College of Wales.

Je.Ho./Basketball (*in part*);
Biography (*in part*); **Football** (*in part*)
JEROME HOLTZMAN. Sportswriter, *Chicago Sun-Times.* Columnist, *Sporting News.*

J.E.McK./Sociology
JAMES EDWARD McKEOWN. Professor of Sociology, University of Wisconsin-Parkside, Kenosha, Wis. Co-editor of *The Changing Metropolis.* Author of *Study Guide for Economics; Study Guide for Sociology.* Co-author of *A Study of Integrated Living in Chicago.*

J.E.Pa./Literature (*in part*)
JOSÉ EMILIO PACHECO. Associate Editor, *La Cultura en México.* Author of *Morirás lejos; Antología del modernismo.*

Je.Wi./Medicine (*in part*)
JELIA C. WITSCHI. Assistant in Nutrition, Department of Nutrition, Harvard School of Public Health.

J.F.Ba./Biography (*in part*)
JOHN FREDERICK BARTON. Diplomatic Correspondent, United Press International, Washington, D.C.

J.F.Ss./Veterinary Medicine
J. FREDERICK SMITHCORS. Associate Editor, American Veterinary Publications, Inc., Santa Barbara, Calif. Author of *Evolution of the Veterinary Art; The American Veterinary Profession.*

J.G.M./Consumer Expenditures
JAMES GEORGE MORRELL. Chairman, James Morrell and Associates Ltd.; Economic Adviser to a number of leading companies; Economic Editor, *Management Today.*

J.G.S.M./Gardening (*in part*)
JOHN GRAHAM SCOTT MARSHALL. Horticultural Consultant.

J.H.Bo./Biological Sciences (*in part*)
JEFFERY HUGH BOSWALL. Producer of Sound and Television Programs, British Broadcasting Corporation Natural History Unit, Bristol, Eng.

J.J.A./Bowling and Lawn Bowls (*in part*)
JOHN J. ARCHIBALD. Sportswriter, the *St. Louis Post-Dispatch.* Author of *Bowling for Boys and Girls.*

J.J.Ac./Fuel and Power (*in part*)
JOSEPH JOHN ACCARDO. Washington Columnist.

J.J.Gm./Advertising (*in part*)
JARLATH JOHN GRAHAM. Editor, *Advertising Age.*

J.J.Sm./Paraguay
JOHN JERVIS SMITH. Research Officer, Economic Intelligence Department, Bank of London and South America Ltd., London.

J.K./Biography (*in part*); **Israel**
JON KIMCHE. Editor, *The New Middle East.* Expert on Middle East Affairs, *Evening Standard*, London. Author of *The Second Arab Awakening: The Middle East, 1914–1969.*

J.Ki./Museums and Galleries (*in part*)
JOSHUA B. KIND. Associate Professor of Art History, Northern Illinois University, De Kalb. Author of *Rouault; Titian.*

J.Kn./France
JEAN MARCEL KNECHT. Assistant Foreign Editor, *Le Monde*, Paris. Formerly Permanent Correspondent in Washington and Vice-President of the Association de la Presse Diplomatique Française.

J.K.R./Agriculture (*in part*)
JOHN KERR ROSE. Senior Specialist in Natural Resources and Conservation, Legislative Reference Service, Library of Congress, Washington, D.C.

J.L.Re./Oceanography
JOSEPH LEE REID. Research Oceanographer, Scripps Institution of Oceanography, La Jolla, Calif. Author of *Intermediate Waters of the Pacific Ocean.*

J.Me./Religion (*in part*)
JOHN MEYENDORFF. Professor of Church History and Patristics, St. Vladimir's Seminary; Professor of History, Fordham University, New York City; Adjunct-Professor of Religion, Columbia University. Author of *The Orthodox Church.*

J.M.Ka./Religion (*in part*)
JOSEPH M. KITAGAWA. Professor of History of Religions and Dean of the Divinity School, The University of Chicago. Author of *Religions of the East; Religion in Japanese History.*

J.M.Th./Toys and Games
JOHN MICHAEL THEWLIS. Industrial Journalist.

J.N.B./Religion (*in part*)
JOHN NICHOLLS BOOTH. Unitarian Universalist clergyman. Co-founder Japan Free Religious Association. Author of *The Quest for Preaching Power; Introducing Unitarian Universalism.*

Jn.M./Social Services
JOHN MOSS. Barrister-at-Law. Author of *Hadden's Health and Welfare Services Handbook.* Editor of *Local Government Law and Administration.*

J.No./Theatre (*in part*)
JULIUS NOVICK. Assistant Professor of English, New York University, New York City; Guest Lecturer, Drama Division of the Juilliard School. Dramatic Critic for the *Village Voice* and *The Humanist.* Contributor to *The Nation*; the *New York Times.* Author of *Beyond Broadway: The Quest for Permanent Theatres.*

Jo.A./Religion (*in part*)
JOSEPH ANDERSON. Assistant to the Council of Twelve Apostles, Church of Jesus Christ of Latter-day Saints (Mormons), Salt Lake City, Utah.

Jo.A.A./Libya
JOHN ANTHONY ALLAN. Lecturer in Geography, School of Oriental and African Studies, University of London.

Jo.A.K./New Zealand
JOHN ARNOLD KELLEHER. Editor, the *Dominion*, Wellington, N.Z.

Jo.B.W./Cycling
JOHN BORLAND WADLEY. Editor, *International Cycle Sport*.

Jo.H.S./Nuclear Energy
JOHN H. STUMPF. Special Projects Editor, Atomic Industrial Forum, Inc.

Jo.N./Mountaineering
JOHN NEILL. Chemical Engineer. Author of Climbers' Club Guides: *Cwm Silyn and Tremadoc, Snowdon South*; Alpine Club Guide: *Selected Climbs in the Pennine Alps*.

J.T.B./Cinema (*in part*)
JOHN TEAL BOBBITT. Writer and Producer of Encyclopædia Britannica Films: *The Bill of Rights of the United States; The Congress; The Constitution of the United States; The Declaration of Independence by the Colonies; The Supreme Court*.

Ju.W./Alcoholic Beverages (*in part*)
JULIUS WILE. Senior Vice-President, Julius Wile Sons & Co., Inc., New York City. Vice-President, New England Distillers, Inc., Teterboro, N.J. Vice-Chairman, Wine Conference of America. Lecturer on wines, School of Hotel Administration, Cornell University.

J.W.Ma./Alcoholic Beverages (*in part*)
JOHN WILLIAM MAHONEY. Director, Society of Friends of Wine, London. Author of *A Guide to Good Wine* (Introduction); *Wines; Spirits and Liqueurs; The Labelling of Wines and Spirits; A Brief History of the Wine and Spirit Trade in England*.

J.W.Mw./Chronology
JOSEPH W. MARLOW. Lawyer.

Jy.L./Postal Services (*in part*)
JERRY LIPSON. Reporter, *Chicago Daily News*.

K.de la B./Arctic Regions
KENNETH de la BARRE. Director, Montreal Office, Arctic Institute of North America.

K.F.C./Philately and Numismatics (*in part*)
KENNETH FRANCIS CHAPMAN. Editor, *Stamp Collecting*; Philatelic Correspondent, *The Times*, London. Author of *Good Stamp Collecting; Commonwealth Stamp Collecting*.

K.F.Cv./Yugoslavia
KRSTO FRANJO CVIIĆ. Leader Writer and East European Correspondent, *The Economist*, London.

K.H.W./Religion (*in part*)
KENNETH H. WOOD. Editor, *The Review and Herald*. Author of *Meditations for Moderns*. Co-author of *His Initials Were F.D.N.*

K.I./Congo, Democratic Republic of the; Dependent States (*in part*); **Equatorial Guinea; Kenya; Malawi; Rhodesia; Tanzania; Uganda; Zambia**
KENNETH INGHAM. Professor of History, University of Bristol, Eng. Author of *Reformers in India; A History of East Africa*.

K.K.Mi./Basketball (*in part*)
KEITH KIRKMAN MITCHELL. Lecturer, Department of Physical Education, Leeds University; Hon. General Secretary, Amateur Basket Ball Association.

K.L.O./Rowing
KEITH LANGFORD OSBORNE. Editor, *Rowing*, 1961–63. Hon. Editor, *British Rowing Almanack*, 1961–.

K.R.P./Literature (*in part*)
KARIN ROSAMUND PETHERICK. Crown Princess Louise Lecturer in Swedish, University College, London.

K.Sm./Albania; Biography (*in part*); **Bulgaria; Economic Planning** (*in part*); **Hungary; Intelligence Operations; Mongolia; Poland; Political Parties; Romania**
KAZIMIERZ MACIEJ SMOGORZEWSKI. Writer on contemporary history. Founder and Editor, *Free Europe*, London. Author of *The United States and Great Britain; Poland's Access to the Sea*.

L.C.Ba./Industrial Review (*in part*)
LESLIE CHARLES BATEMAN. Manager, Tariffs and Trade Regulations Section, International Department, British Steel Corporation, London.

L.C.Br./Cities and Urban Affairs (*in part*)
LEWIS CHARLES BRAITHWAITE. Research Associate, Centre for Urban and Regional Studies, University of Birmingham, Eng.

L.Ch./Fuel and Power (*in part*)
LUCIEN CHALMEY. Adviser, Union Internationale des Producteurs et Distributeurs d'Énergie Électrique, Paris.

L.Dn./Biography (*in part*)
LYLE WILLIAM DENNISTON. Supreme Court Reporter, *Evening Star*, Washington, D.C.

L.F.R.W./Afghanistan; Iran; Pakistan
LAURENCE FREDERIC RUSHBROOK WILLIAMS, Fellow of All Souls College, Oxford University, 1914–21; Professor of Modern Indian History, Allahabad, India, 1914–19. Author of *India Under the Company and the Crown; The State of Pakistan; What About India?; Kutch in History and Legend*. Editor of *Handbook to India, Pakistan, Burma, and Ceylon*.

L.H./Biography (*in part*); **South Africa**
LOUIS HOTZ. Formerly editorial writer, the *Johannesburg (S.Af.) Star*. Co-author and contributor to *The Jews in South Africa: A History*.

L.H.Jo./Telecommunications (*in part*)
LAURENCE HENRY JOHN. Producer, Science Unit, British Broadcasting Corporation (radio).

L.H.No./Geology
LAURENCE H. NOBLES. Professor of Geology and Dean, College of Arts and Sciences, Northwestern University, Evanston, Ill.

L.Ke./Cooperatives
LOTTE KENT. Editor, *Cooperative News Service*, International Cooperative Alliance, London.

L.M.Gd./Antarctica
LAURENCE M. GOULD. Professor of Geology, University of Arizona. Chairman, Committee on Polar Research, National Academy of Sciences. Author of *Cold: The Record of an Antarctic Sledge Journey*.

L.M.M./Seismology
LEONARD M. MURPHY. Chief, Seismology Division, Coast and Geodetic Survey, Environmental Science Services Administration, U.S. Department of Commerce, Washington, D.C.

L.O.T./Tennis
LANCELOT OLIVER TINGAY. Lawn Tennis Correspondent, *The Daily Telegraph*, London.

L.R.Bu./Education
LEONARD RALPH BUCKLEY. Formerly Assistant Editor, *The Times Educational Supplement*, London.

M.A.G./Literature (*in part*)
MICHAEL A. GONZALEZ. Research student preparing Ph.D. thesis on the Mexican novel.

M.A.K./Economy, World; Payments and Reserves, International
MIROSLAV A. KRIZ. Vice-President, First National City Bank, New York City. Author of *The Price of Gold; Gold in World Monetary Affairs Today; Gold: Barbarous Relic or Useful Instrument?*

Ma.Ka./Music (*in part*)
MAUD KARPELES. Hon. President, International Folk Music Council, Kingston, Ont. Author of *Cecil Sharp: His Life and Works; Folk Songs from Newfoundland*. Editor of *Journal of the International Folk Music Council*, vol. i–xiii and xvi; *English Folk Songs from the Southern Appalachians*.

M.B.Su./Biography (*in part*)
MARK BARRY SULLIVAN. Staff Correspondent, Washington Bureau, *Time* magazine. Contributor, Time-Life Library of America series.

M.By./Transportation (*in part*)
MICHAEL BAILY. Shipping and Transport Correspondent, *The Times*, London.

M.C.G.I./Medicine (*in part*)
MARTIN C. G. ISRAËLS. Director, Department of Clinical Haematology, University and Royal Infirmary, Manchester. Author of *Atlas of Bone Marrow Pathology; Diagnosis and Treatment of Blood Diseases*.

M.C.MacD./Agriculture (*in part*); **Transportation** (*in part*)
MALCOLM CHARLES MacDONALD. Director, Econtel Research Ltd., London. Editor, *Factual Series; Business Cycle Series*.

M.Ct./Laos
MAX COIFFAIT. Correspondent, Agence France-Presse, Vientiane, Laos.

M.D.Bu./Publishing (*in part*)
M. DALLAS BURNETT. Associate Professor of Communications, Brigham Young University, Provo, Utah.

M.F.B.B./Parks
MERVYN FRANCIS BERNARD BELL. Secretary, Countryside Commission, London.

M.F.F./Income, National
MICHAEL FREDERICK FULLER. Lecturer in Economic and Social Statistics, Eliot College, University of Kent at Canterbury.

M.Fi./Medicine (*in part*)
MORRIS FISHBEIN. Editor of *Medical World News*. Emeritus Professor, The University of Chicago; University of Illinois, College of Medicine. Author of *Modern Home Remedies and How to Use Them; Handy Home Medical Adviser; Concise Medical Encyclopedia*.

M.F.S./Switzerland
MELANIE F. STAERK. Editor, *Unesco Press*, Swiss National Commission for UNESCO.

12 Contributors

Mi.F./Historical Studies
MICHEL FRANÇOIS. Member of the
French Institute (Académie des
Inscriptions et Belles-Lettres). Director,
École nationale des chartes. Secretary
General, International Committee of
Historical Sciences, Paris.

**M.Mr./Botswana; Burundi;
Commonwealth of Nations; Dependent
States** (*in part*); **Ghana; Lesotho; Maldives;
Mauritius; Nigeria; Rwanda; Swaziland**
MOLLY MORTIMER. Writer on
Commonwealth and International Affairs.
Author of *Trusteeship in Practice; Kenya.*

M.M.Tu./Race Relations (*in part*)
MELVIN MARVIN TUMIN. Professor
of Sociology and Anthropology, Princeton
University. Author of *Social Class and
Social Change in Puerto Rico; Social
Stratification; Crimes of Violence in the U.S.*

M.N.Y./Religion (*in part*)
M. NORVEL YOUNG. President,
Pepperdine University, Los Angeles. Editor,
Twentieth Century Christian and *Power for
Today.* Author of *Churches of Today.*

Mo.M./Greece
MARIO (S.) MODIANO. Athens
Correspondent, *The Times*, London.

M.Pan./Prices
MILIVOJE PANIĆ. Senior Economic
Adviser, National Economic Development
Office, London.

M.Pl./Industrial Review (*in part*)
MAURICE PLATT. Consulting Engineer.
Formerly Director of Engineering, Vauxhall
Motors, Ltd. Author of *Elements of Automo-
bile Engineering.*

M.Pu./Mexico; Spain
MANUEL PULGAR. Senior Economic
Research Officer, Bank of London and South
America Ltd., London.

M.R.-R./Literature (*in part*)
MARCEL REICH-RANICKI. Literary
critic, *Die Zeit.* Author of *Deutsche Literatur
in West und Ost; Literarisches Leben in
Deutschland; Wer schreibt, provoziert;
Literatur der kleinen Schritte; Die
Ungeliebten.*

M.R.S./Astronautics (*in part*)
MITCHELL R. SHARPE. Science writer.
Author of *Living in Space: The Environment
of the Astronaut; Yuri Gagarin, First Man in
Space; Satellites and Probes, the Development
of Unmanned Space Flight.* Co-author of
Applied Astronautics; Basic Astronautics.

M.Sn./Literature (*in part*)
MOSHE STARKMAN. Essayist in Yiddish
and Hebrew, Bibliographer. President,
Yiddish P.E.N. Club, N.Y. Editor,
*Hemshekh Anthology of American Yiddish
Poetry.*

M.S.R./Biography (*in part*); **Malaysia;
Singapore**
MAHINDER SINGH RANDHAWA.
Sub-editor, *The Straits Times*, Kuala Lumpur,
Malaysia.

Mu.L./Advertising (*in part*)
MURRAY LEASK. Director, McCann-
Erickson, Paris.

M.W.Wo./Religion (*in part*)
REVEREND MAX W. WOODWARD.
British Secretary, World Methodist
Council.

Mx.B./Vatican City State
MAX BERGERRE. Deputy Director,
Vatican Affairs Department, Agence France-
Presse, Rome.

Mx.H./Biography (*in part*)
MAX HARRELSON. Chief of United
Nations Bureau, The Associated Press.

My.B.B./Fiji; Tonga; Western Samoa
MARY BEATRICE BOYD. Senior Lec-
turer in History, Victoria University of
Wellington, N.Z.

N.Cr./Biography (*in part*); **Germany** (*in part*)
NORMAN CROSSLAND. Bonn
Correspondent, *The Guardian*, London.

N.D.McW./Track and Field Sports (*in part*)
NORRIS DEWAR McWHIRTER.
Television commentator, British Broadcasting
Corporation, London. Co-compiler, *Guinness
Book of Records.*

N.H.K./Religion (*in part*)
NATHAN HOMER KNORR. President,
Watch Tower Bible and Tract Society of
Pennsylvania.

Ni.B./Literature (*in part*)
NIELS BARFOED. Editor of *Vindrosen.*
Literary Critic, *Politiken*, Copenhagen.
Author of *Den tøvende dag* (poems);
Ajourføringer (essays on literature).

N.M.H./Law (*in part*)
NEVILLE MARCH HUNNINGS. Senior
Research Officer, British Institute of Inter-
national and Comparative Law, London.
Author of *Film Censors and the Law.*

N.R.U./Commodities, Primary
NORMAN RICHARD URQUHART.
Assistant Vice-President, in charge of
Commodity Section, Economics
Department, First National City Bank,
New York City.

N.Si./Horse Racing (*in part*)
NOEL SIMPSON. Managing Director,
Sydney Bloodstock Proprietary Ltd.,
Sydney, Austr.

O.F.K./Norway
OLE FERDINAND KNUDSEN.
Editor, *Norway Exports*, Oslo.

O.H.H./Guatemala
OSCAR H. HORST. Professor of
Geography, Western Michigan University.

O.K./Industrial Review (*in part*)
ORLAND BENJAMIN KILLIN. Asso-
ciate Professor of Industrial Education and
Technology, Eastern Washington State
College.

O.Me./Tourism (*in part*)
OLIVIER MOSSÉ. Marketing Specialist,
International Union of Official Travel
Organisations (IUOTO), Geneva.

O.Pl./Medicine (*in part*)
OGLESBY PAUL, M.D. Chief, Division
of Medicine, Passavant Memorial Hospital,
Chicago, Ill. Professor of Medicine,
Northwestern University Medical
School, Chicago.

**Ot.P./Czechoslovakia; Union of Soviet
Socialist Republics**
OTTO PICK. Reader in International
Relations, University of Surrey.

O.Tr./Biography (*in part*); **Theatre** (*in part*)
OSSIA TRILLING. Vice-President,
International Association of Theatre Critics.
Co-editor and contributor, *International
Theatre.* Contributor, *The Times*, London.

P.A.H./Religion (*in part*)
THE REV. PETER ANTHONY
HEBBLETHWAITE, S.J. Editor, *The
Month.* Author of *Bernanos; The Council
Fathers and Atheism; Understanding the
Synod.*

P.A.St./Astronomy
PETER ALBERT STRITTMATTER.
Staff member, Institute of Theoretical
Astronomy, Cambridge; Visiting Research
Associate, University of California,
San Diego.

P.A.W.-T./Golf
PERCY AINSWORTH WARD-
THOMAS. Golf Correspondent,
The Guardian, Manchester.

P.Bs./Art Sales (*in part*)
PIERRE BERÈS. Managing Director,
Hermann Publishing Company, Paris.
Founder and Editor in Chief, *Sciences.* Expert
in rare books.

P.B.St./Publishing (*in part*)
PHYLLIS B. STECKLER. Project
Director, CCM Information Corporation.
Editor, *How To Run a Paperback Bookshop;
The College Bluebook; Transdex Bibliographic
Service.*

Pe.B./Medicine (*in part*)
PETER BEEDLE. Assistant Secretary,
Home Office, London.

P.F.Y./Mining (*in part*)
PAUL FREDERICK YOPES. Mining
Engineer, Bureau of Mines, U.S. Department
of the Interior, Washington, D.C.

P.Gl./Religion (*in part*)
PAUL GLIKSON. Secretary, Division of
Jewish Demography and Statistics, Institute
of Contemporary Jewry, The Hebrew University, Israel.

**Ph.D./Cameroon; Central African Republic;
Chad; Congo, People's Republic of the;
Dahomey; Dependent States** (*in part*); **Gabon;
Ivory Coast; Malagasy Republic; Mali;
Mauritania; Niger; Senegal; Togo; Tunisia;
Upper Volta**
PHILIPPE DECRAENE. Member of
editorial staff, *Le Monde*, Paris. Editor in
Chief, *Revue française d'Études politiques
africaines.* Research assistant at the Centre
d'Études des Relations Internationales de
l'Institut d'Études Politiques de Paris.
Author of *Le Panafricanisme; Tableau des
Partis Politiques Africains.*

Ph.K./Biography (*in part*)
PHILIP KOPPER. Free-lance writer,
Washington, D.C.

P.J.T./Medicine (*in part*)
PETER JOHN TAYLOR. Physician in
charge, Information and Advisory Service,
T.U.C. Centenary Institute of Occupational
Health, London School of Hygiene and
Tropical Medicine, University of London.
Author of *Absenteeism—Causes and Control.*

P.Md./Biography (*in part*); **Iraq; Jordan;
Kuwait; Lebanon; Middle East; Oman;
Saudi Arabia; Southern Yemen; Syria;
United Arab Republic; Yemen**
PETER (JOHN) MANSFIELD. Former
Middle East Correspondent, *Sunday Times*,
London. Free-lance writer on Middle East
affairs.

P.M.Ha./Cities and Urban Affairs (*in part*)
PHILIP MORRIS HAUSER. Professor of
Sociology and Director, Population Research
Center, The University of Chicago. Editor of
Urbanization in Latin America.

P.M.Re./Industrial Review (*in part*)
PHILIP MORTON ROWE. Press Officer,
British Man-Made Fibres Federation,
Manchester.

Pr.K./Sudan
PETER KILNER. Editor, *Arab Report
and Record*.

P.Sh./Tourism (*in part*)
PETER SHACKLEFORD. Research
Officer, International Union of Official
Travel Organisations (IUOTO), Geneva.

P.Ss./Insurance (*in part*)
PERCY STEBBINGS. Insurance
Correspondent of *Investors' Chronicle*;
Post Magazine, London.

P.V.-P./Biography (*in part*)
PIERRE VIANSSON-PONTÉ. Political
News Editor, *Le Monde*, Paris. Author of *Les
Gaullistes*; *The King and His Court*.

P.W.Ga./Industrial Review (*in part*)
PETER WILLIAM GADDUM. Chairman,
H. T. Gaddum and Company Ltd., Silk
Merchants, Macclesfield, Cheshire, Eng.
President, International Silk Association.
Author of *Silk—How and Where It Is
Produced*.

P.W.He./Cosmetics; Fashion and Dress
PHYLLIS WEST HEATHCOTE. Paris
Correspondent on women's topics,
The Guardian, Manchester.

P.Wi./Biography (*in part*); **Dance** (*in part*)
PETER WILLIAMS. Editor, *Dance and
Dancers*.

P.W.Mi./Biological Sciences (*in part*)
PETER WALLACE MILES. Professor of
Zoology, University of Zambia, Lusaka.

R.A.Kl./Medicine (*in part*)
ROBERT A. KLOBNAK. Director,
Department of Public Relations, American
Osteopathic Association.

Ra.Pa./Philippines
RAFAEL PARGAS. Computer Operator,
National Geographic Society, Washington,
D.C.

Ra.R./Dependent States (*in part*); **Guyana;
Trinidad and Tobago**
RANDOLPH RICHARD RAWLINS.
Journalist and broadcaster.

R.B.Gt./Medicine (*in part*)
ROBERT BENJAMIN GREENBLATT,
M.D. Professor and Chairman, Department
of Endocrinology, Medical College of
Georgia, Augusta. Author of *Office
Endocrinology*; *The Hirsute Female*; *Ovulation*.

R.B.Le./Colombia; Ecuador
RAYMOND BASIL LEWRY. Senior
Research Officer, Bank of London and South
America Ltd., London.

R.C.Pe./Industrial Review (*in part*)
ROBIN CHARLES PENFOLD. Public
relations executive, Carl Byoir and
Associates Ltd., London. Author of *A
Journalist's Guide to Plastics*.

R.D.A.G./United Nations (*in part*)
RICHARD D. A. GREENOUGH. Chief
English writer, Press Division, UNESCO,
Paris. Author of *Africa Prospect*; *Children's
Progress*.

R.d'E./Brazil
RAUL d'ECA. Formerly Fulbright Visiting
Lecturer on American History, University of
Minas Gerais, Belo Horizonte, Braz. Co-
author of *Latin American History*.

**R.D.Ho./Andorra; Liechtenstein; Luxem-
bourg; Monaco; San Marino**
ROBERT DAVID HODGSON.
Geographer, U.S. Department of State,
Washington, D.C. Author of *The Changing
Map of Africa*.

R.E.E.H./Religion (*in part*)
REUBEN ELMORE ERNEST HARK-
NESS. Emeritus Professor of History
of Christianity, Crozer Seminary, Chester,
Pa. Emeritus Professor of History of World
Religions, History of Christianity, Baptist
History, Ellen Cushing Junior College,
Bryn Mawr, Pa.

R.E.St./Electronics
ROBERT E. STOFFELS. Director, EAX
Operations, Automatic Electric Laboratories.
Author of *The Simple Truth About
Semiconductor Electronics*.

R.F.G.C./Religion (*in part*)
RALPH FORMAN GODLEY CALDER.
Secretary, Overseas Appointments
Bureau, Christian Education Movement,
London.

R.F.Mi./Philately and Numismatics (*in part*)
RICHARD F. MILLER, Professor of
English, Eastern Washington State College.

R.F.Sa./Anthropology
RICHARD FRANK SALISBURY.
Professor of Anthropology, McGill University.
Author of *From Stone to Steel*; *Vunamami:
Economic Transformation in a Traditional
Society*.

R.G.Bu./Medicine (*in part*)
RICHARD GEOFFREY BURWELL.
Professor of Orthopaedics, Institute of
Orthopaedics, London.

R.H.Be./Hockey (*in part*)
RICHARD HERBERT BEDDOES.
Sports Columnist, the *Toronto Globe and
Mail*.

R.H.Tr./Stock Exchanges (*in part*)
ROBERT H. TRIGG. Manager,
Institutional Research, New York Stock
Exchange.

R.H.W.D./Literature (*in part*)
R. H. W. DILLARD. Associate Professor
of English, Hollins College, Va. Author of
*The Day I Stopped Dreaming About
Barbara Steele and Other Poems* (1966);
News of the Nile (1970).

R.Hy./Peace Movements
RICHARD HATHAWAY. Dean, Adult
Degree Program; Teaching Faculty, History
and International Studies, Goddard College,
Plainfield, Vt.; Member, Board of Editors,
Current.

Ri.W./Biography (*in part*); **Liberia;
United States**
RICHARD WORSNOP. Writer, Editorial
Research Reports, Washington, D.C.

R.J.B./Archaeology (*in part*)
ROBERT J. BRAIDWOOD. Professor of
Old World Prehistory, the Oriental
Institute and the Department of
Anthropology, The University of Chicago.

R.J.Fe./Motor Sports (*in part*)
ROBERT JOSEPH FENDELL. New
York Editor, *Automotive News*. Automobile
Columnist for *Action*. Scriptwriter for
Speed Sport News syndicated radio
series.

R.J.Fo./Fuel and Power (*in part*)
ROBERT JOHN FOWELL. Research
Associate, Department of Mining
Engineering, University of Newcastle upon
Tyne, Eng.

R.J.Le./Industrial Review (*in part*)
RICHARD JOHN LEDWITH. Con-
sultant, The International Paint Company,
Surrey, Eng.

R.J.Ra./Defense
ROBERT JOHN RANGER. Visiting
Lecturer in Strategic Studies, Queen's
University, Kingston, Ont.

R.L.A./Biography (*in part*)
ROBERT LOUIS ASHER. Member,
Editorial Page Staff, *Washington Post*.
Contributor to *Ten Blocks from the
White House*.

R.L.F./Religion (*in part*)
ROBERT LOUIS FRIEDLY. Director,
Office of Communication, Christian Church
(Disciples of Christ), Indianapolis, Ind.

R.L.Hi./Molecular Biology (*in part*)
ROBERT LEE HILL. Professor and
Chairman, Department of Biochemistry,
Duke University Medical Center,
Durham, N.C.

R.L.Hs./Hockey (*in part*)
RICHARD LYNTON HOLLANDS.
Hockey Correspondent. Editor, *Hockey
News*, London. Co-author of *Hockey*.

R.L.R./Religion (*in part*)
ROGER LEWIS ROBERTS. Editorial
Consultant, *Church Times*, London.

R.L.Ro./Chile
ROBERT L. ROSS. Vice-President,
Adela Investment Co., Washington, D.C.

R.M.Gn./Horse Racing (*in part*)
ROBERT MARSHALL GOODWIN.
Assistant Editor, London, *Encyclopædia
Britannica*.

R.M.Sm./Economic Planning (*in part*)
RAMASWAMY MEENATCHI SUN-
DRUM. Director, Development Programs
Study Group, World Bank. Author of
*Long-Term Projections for Economic and
Social Development*.

Rn.C./Cuba; Haiti; Portugal
ROBIN CHAPMAN. Economic Research
Officer, Bank of London and South America
Ltd., London.

R.N.S./United Nations (*in part*)
RICHARD N. SWIFT. Professor of
Politics, New York University, New York
City. Author of *International Law: Current
and Classic*. Former Editor of *Annual
Review of United Nations Affairs*.

Ro.Ch./Engineering Projects (*in part*)
ROBERT CHAUSSIN. Government
Civil Engineer, S.E.T.R.A. (Service d'études
Techniques des Routes et autoroutes),
Bagneux, France.

Ro.E.S./Costa Rica; Venezuela
ROBERT EDWARD STENT. Economic
and Political Research Officer, Bank of
London and South America Ltd., London.

Ro.Go./Vietnam (*in part*)
ROBERT GORALSKI. NBC News
Pentagon Correspondent.

Ro.P.H./U.S. Supplement: *Major Legislation
Table*
ROBERT PIERPONT HEY. Staff
Correspondent, Washington Bureau,
The Christian Science Monitor.

R.Pn./Alcoholic Beverages (*in part*)
RENÉ PROTIN. Director, International
Vine and Wine Office, Paris.

R.R.No./Biological Sciences (*in part*)
RONALD RICHARDS NOVALES.
Professor of Biological Sciences,
Northwestern University, Evanston, Ill.
Member, Editorial Board, *American Zoologist.*

R.S.Mi./Engineering Projects (*in part*)
RAYMOND SPENCER MILLARD.
Deputy Director, Road Research Labora-
tory, Ministry of Transport, Crowthorne,
Berkshire, Eng.

R.V.M./Religion (*in part*)
ROBERT V. MOSS. President, United
Church of Christ, New York City; President,
American Association of Theological Schools,
1966–68. Author of *The Life of Paul;
We Believe; As Paul Sees Christ.*

R.W.Cr./Television and Radio (*in part*)
RUFUS WILLIAM CRATER. Editorial
Director, *Broadcasting*, New York City.

R.W.Fe./Fuel and Power (*in part*)
RONALD WHITAKER FERRIER.
Company Historian, British Petroleum.

R.W.Sm./Religion (*in part*)
REUBEN WILLIAM SMITH. Assistant
Professor of Islamic History, The University
of Chicago.

R.W.T./Religion (*in part*)
RONALD WILLIAM THOMSON.
Assistant General Secretary, Baptist Union
of Great Britain and Ireland. Author of
*Heroes of the Baptist Church; William Carey;
The Service of Our Lives; A Pocket History
of the Baptists.*

S.Aa./Denmark
STENER AARSDAL. Economic Editor,
Børsen. Press Officer, Chamber of Commerce,
Copenhagen.

Sa.H./Literature (*in part*)
SAMUEL JOHN HAZO. Director,
International Poetry Forum, and Professor,
Duquesne University, Pittsburgh, Pa.
Author of *Blood Rights; My Sons in God;
The Quiet Wars.*

S.A.P./Ceylon
SIDNEY ARNOLD PAKEMAN.
Historian. Author of *Ceylon.*

S.B.P./Physics
STUART BEAUMONT PALMER.
Lecturer, Department of Applied Physics,
University of Hull.

Se.H./Political Science
SERGE HURTIG. Director of Studies
and Research, Fondation Nationale des
Sciences Politiques; Professor, Paris Institute
of Political Studies. Former Secretary
General, International Political Science
Association.

S.E.S./Germany (*in part*)
STEPHAN E. SCHATTMANN.
Economist, London.

Sh.P./Barbados; Race Relations (*in part*)
SHEILA CAFFYN PATTERSON.
Research Fellow, Centre for Multi-Racial
Studies, University of Sussex, Brighton.
Author of *Colour and Culture in South
Africa; The Last Trek; Dark Strangers;
Immigrants in Industry.*

Si.P./Words and Meanings, New (*in part*)
SIMEON POTTER. Emeritus Professor
of English Language and Philology,
University of Liverpool. Author of *Our
Language; Language in the Modern World;
Modern Linguistics; Changing English.*

S.J.N./Geography
SALVATORE JOHN NATOLI.
Educational Affairs Director, Association of
American Geographers. Co-author of
Dictionary of Basic Geography.

S.Mi./Architecture; Art Exhibitions
SANDRA MILLIKIN. Assistant Curator
of Drawings, Royal Institute of British
Architects, London.

S.M.Mc./Philosophy (*in part*)
STERLING M. McMURRIN.
E. E. Ericksen Distinguished Professor and
Dean of the Graduate School, University of
Utah. Co-author of *A History of Philosophy.*

S.Mu./Biography (*in part*)
STEPHANIE MULLINS. Historian.

Sn.H./Morocco
STEPHEN HUGHES. Reuters
Correspondent, Morocco.

S.Pa./Furs
SANDY PARKER. Fur Editor,
Women's Wear Daily.

S.S.G./Medicine (*in part*)
SYDNEY S. GELLIS, M.D. Professor
and Chairman, Department of Pediatrics,
Tufts University School of Medicine, and
Pediatrician-in-chief, Tufts-New England
Medical Center, Boston. Author of *Current
Pediatric Therapy*. Editor, *Year Book of
Pediatrics.*

S.Tf./Television and Radio (*in part*)
SOL TAISHOFF. President, Editor and
Publisher, *Broadcasting*, Washington, D.C.

St.F.B./Horse Racing (*in part*)
STANLEY F. BERGSTEIN. Executive
Secretary, Harness Tracks of America Inc.;
Vice President, United States Trotting
Association.

T.B.F./Medicine (*in part*)
THOMAS B. FITZPATRICK. Edward
Wigglesworth Professor of Dermatology and
Head, Department of Dermatology, Harvard
Medical School; Chief, Dermatology Service,
Massachusetts General Hospital, Boston.

T.C.J.C./Industrial Review (*in part*)
THOMAS CHARLES JOHN COGLE.
Technical Editor, *Electrical Review*, London.

**T.J.S.G./Cambodia; Korea; Southeast Asia;
Thailand; Vietnam** (*in part*)
THAYIL JACOB SONY GEORGE.
Assistant Editor, *Far Eastern Economic
Review*, Hong Kong. Author of *Krishna
Menon, a Biography.*

T.L.T.L./Medicine (*in part*)
THOMAS LOFTUS TOWNSHEND
LEWIS. Obstetric Surgeon, Guy's Hospital;
Surgeon, Queen Charlotte's Maternity
Hospital; Surgeon, Chelsea Hospital for
Women. Author of *Progress in Clinical
Obstetrics and Gynaecology;* (jointly) *The
Queen Charlotte's Textbook of Obstetrics.*

T.M.R./Savings and Investment
TADEUSZ MIECZYSLAW
RYBCZYNSKI. Economist, Lazard
Brothers, London.

Tm.S./Gardening (*in part*)
TOM STEVENSON. Garden Columnist,
*Baltimore News American; Washington
Post; Washington Post-Los Angeles Times
News Service*. Author of *Pruning Guide for
Trees, Shrubs and Vines; Lawn Guide;
Gardening for the Beginner.*

To.S./Literature (*in part*)
TORBJØRN STØVERUD. W.P. Ker
Senior Lecturer in Norwegian, University
College, London.

T.R.Sh./Speleology
TREVOR ROYLE SHAW. Commander,
Royal Navy. Vice-President, British
Speleological Association.

T.Sc./Alcoholic Beverages (*in part*)
TILMAN SCHMITT. Brewery Engineer.
Editor of *Brauwelt; Brauwissenschaft.*

T.W./Biography (*in part*)**; Football** (*in part*)
TREVOR WILLIAMSON. Sports sub-
editor, *The Daily Telegraph*, London.

T.W.Ho./Cinema (*in part*)
THOMAS W. HOPE. Editor and
Publisher, *Hope Reports.*

T.W.Me./Engineering Projects (*in part*)
T. W. MERMEL. Assistant to
Commissioner for Research and Chief,
General Engineering Division, Bureau of
Reclamation, U.S. Department of the
Interior, Washington, D.C. Chairman,
Committee on World Register of Dams,
International Commission on Large Dams.
Author of *Register of Dams in the United
States.*

Va.K./Iceland
VALDIMAR KRISTINSSON. Editor of
Fjármálatidindi, Reykjavik.

V.F.Ra./Tobacco
VIVIAN FOSTER RAVEN. Editor,
Tobacco, London.

V.G.C.B./Photography
VICTOR GORDON CHARLES
BLACKMAN. Staff photographer, *Daily
Express*, London. Columnist, *Amateur
Photographer.*

V.J.P./Cyprus
VERNON JOHN PARRY. Reader in
the History of the Near and Middle East,
School of Oriental and African Studies,
University of London. Contributor to *New
Cambridge Modern History; Cambridge
History of Islam; Encyclopaedia of Islam.*

V.L.A./Labour Unions
VICTOR LEONARD ALLEN. Reader in
Industrial Relations, University
of Leeds. Author of *Power in Trade
Unions; Trade Union Leadership; Trade
Unions and the Government; Militant Trade
Unionism; International Bibliography of
Trade Unionism.*

V.R.Lu./Somalia
VIRGINIA R. LULING. Historian.

V.W.P./Crime (*in part*)**; Police** (*in part*)
VIRGIL W. PETERSON. Executive
Director, Chicago Crime Commission.
(1942–1970), Retired. Author of *Gambling—
Should It Be Legalized?; Barbarians in
Our Midst.*

W.A.Ha./Publishing (*in part*)
WILLIAM A. HACHTEN.
Professor, School of Journalism, University
of Wisconsin.

W.A.Ka./Publishing (*in part*)
WILLIAM A. KATZ. Professor, School
of Library Science, State University of
New York. Author of *Introduction to
Reference Magazines for Libraries.*

Wa.Ls./Art Sales (*in part*)
WILMA LAWS. Journalist, London.
Member, International Association of Art
Critics.

W.B.Mi./Religion (*in part*)
WILLIAM B. MILLER. Manager,
Department of History, United
Presbyterian Church, U.S.A.

W.Bn./Argentina
WILLIAM BELTRÁN. Economic
Research Officer, Economic Intelligence
Department, Bank of London and South
America Ltd., London.

W.C.Bo./Motor Sports (*in part*)
WILLIAM CHARLES BODDY. Editor,
Motor Sport. Full Member, Guild of Motoring
Writers. Author of *The Story of Brooklands;
The 200 Mile Race; The World's Land Speed
Record; Continental Sports Cars; The Sports
Car Pocketbook; The Bugatti Story.*

W.D.E./Industrial Review (*in part*)
WILLIAM DUNLOP EWART. Editor
and Director, *Fairplay International
Shipping Journal.* Author of *Marine
Engines; Atomic Submarines; Hydrofoils
and Hovercraft; Building a Ship.*

W.D.Hd./Law (*in part*)
WILLIAM D. HAWKLAND. Provost
and Professor of Law, School of Law,
State University of New York, Buffalo.
Author of *Sales Under Uniform Commercial
Code; Cases on Bills and Notes; Commercial
Paper; Transactional Guide of the Uniform
Commercial Code; Cases on Sales and Security.*

W.D.Hi./Telecommunications (*in part*)
WILLIAM DALE HICKMAN, JR.
Washington (D.C.) News Correspondent,
McGraw-Hill Publications. Author of
*Talking Moons, the Story of Communications
Satellites.*

W.D.McC./Money and Banking
WARREN D. McCLAM. Economist,
Bank for International Settlements,
Basel, Switz.

W.Ei./Populations and Areas (*in part*)
WARREN WOLFF EISENBERG.
Legislative Assistant to Rep. William J.
Green.

W.H.Is./Gambia, The; Sierra Leone (*in part*)
(WILLIAM) HAROLD INGRAMS.
Former Adviser on Overseas Information,
Colonial Office, London. Author of
*Arabia and the Isles; Hong Kong; Seven
Across the Sahara; Uganda; The Yemen
Imams: Rulers and Revolution.*

WHO/Medicine (*in part*)
WORLD HEALTH ORGANIZATION,
Geneva.

W.H.Ta./Religion (*in part*)
WINSTON HOWARTH TAYLOR.
Director, Washington Office, Commission on
Public Relations and United Methodist
Information. Author of *Angels Don't Need
Public Relations; Ending Racial Segregation
in the Methodist Church; Toward an Inclusive
Church.*

W.H.Ts./Biography (*in part*); **United
Kingdom**
WILLIAM HARFORD THOMAS.
Managing Editor, *The Guardian,* London and
Manchester.

Wi.D./Television and Radio (*in part*)
WILLIAM I. DUNKERLEY, JR.
Assistant Secretary, American Radio
Relay League.

W.Le./Government Finance
WILFRED LEWIS, JR. Chief Economist,
National Planning Association. Author of
*Federal Fiscal Policy in the Postwar
Recessions.*

W.L.We./ Literature (*in part*)
WILLIAM LESLIE WEBB. Literary
Editor, *The Guardian,* London and
Manchester.

W.P./Religion (*in part*)
WILLIAM ASHWORTH PRATT.
Director, Salvation Army International
Information Services, London.

W.P.Ja./Industrial Review (*in part*)
W. PINCUS JASPERT. Technical
editorial consultant. European Editor,
North American Publishing Company,
Philadelphia, Pa. Member, Society of
Photographic Scientists and Engineers.
Editor of *Encyclopaedia of Type Faces.*

W.So./Africa
WALLACE SOKOLSKY. Associate
Professor, History Department, Bronx
Community College, the New School for
Social Research, New York University,
Division of Adult Education. Co-author of
*Contemporary Civilization; African National-
ism in the Twentieth Century.*

W.Te./Dance (*in part*)
WALTER TERRY. Dance Critic, *Saturday
Review.* Author of *The Dance in America;
The Ballet Companion; Miss Ruth: The
"More Living Life" of Ruth St. Denis.*

W.Vö./Religion (*in part*)
WALTER ALFRED VÖLKNER.
Minister, Evangelical Lutheran Church of
Tanzania, Northern Diocese, Kibaya,
Tanzania.

Y.S./Bowling and Lawn Bowls (*in part*)
YRJÖ SARAHETE. Secretary, Fédération
Internationale des Quilleurs, Helsinki,
Fin.

AUTHORS OF THE SPECIAL REPORTS IN THE 1971 BOOK OF THE YEAR

ASTRONAUTICS

After Apollo, What?

Rudy P. Abramson
Washington Bureau
The Los Angeles Times

CONSERVATION

Alaskan Dilemma

Thomas M. Brown
Anchorage Daily News
Anchorage, Alaska

DEFENSE

The International Arms Trade

Lord Chalfont
Former British Minister of State
Foreign and Commonwealth Office

GERMANY

West Germany's Ostpolitik

Philip Windsor
Reader in International Relations
London School of Economics and Political Science

IRELAND

The Two Irelands

Bruce Arnold
Author and Journalist
Dublin, Ireland

LAW

The Chicago Conspiracy Trial

J. Anthony Lukas
The New York Times Magazine
Author: *The Barnyard Epithet and Other Obscenities*

MEDICINE

Drugs and Youth

Dr. Leonide Goldstein
Bureau of Research
New Jersey Neuropsychiatric Institute

MERCHANDISING

Protecting the Consumer

Dr. Colston E. Warne
President
Consumers Union of U.S.

POPULATIONS AND AREAS

The Population Crisis

Paul R. Ehrlich, Professor of Biological Sciences
and Anne H. Ehrlich, Senior Research Assistant
Stanford University

RELIGION

The New English Bible

Basil Willey
Emeritus Professor of English Literature
Cambridge University

SOCIOLOGY

The Largest Minority

Eva Figes
British Novelist
Author: *Patriarchal Attitudes*

TRANSPORTATION

Skyjacking: Can It Be Stopped?

Jerry Hannifin
Washington Bureau
Time Magazine

UNION OF SOVIET SOCIALIST REPUBLICS

Intellectual Dissent in the Soviet Union

Karel van het Reve
Professor of Russian Literature
University of Leyden (Netherlands)

KOREA:
Building a Nation
by PRESIDENT PARK CHUNG HEE

THE YEAR A.D. 1971 in the Western calendar marks the 4,304th year of Korea's nationhood according to the traditional Tanggi system of chronology. Yet it is only 26 years since Korea's modern liberation from colonialism and barely 23 years since the Republic of Korea held its first representative election in 1948.

Thus, if the term "newly emerging nation" is applied to all independent nations that were liberated from colonial rule following the end of World War II, Korea doubtless counts as a newly emerging nation. But considering Korea's centuries-old existence as a nation-state, one must realize that Korea is fundamentally different from what nowadays are known as the newly emerging nations; i.e., those transformed for the first time in the present century from a nomadic state or a tribal society into unified countries.

In its beginnings Korea was a divided country, split between the kingdoms of Koguryo (37 B.C.–A.D. 668), Paekche (18 B.C.–A.D. 660), and Silla (57 B.C.–A.D. 935). In A.D. 676 the rulers of Silla unified the three kingdoms, and Korea remained as a single nation thereafter. Several titular revolutions took place, however, which toppled corrupt and incompetent dynasties. Silla was replaced by Koryo in 935 and Koryo by the Yi dynasty in 1392. Except for these instances, Korea has maintained its coherent system as a unified nation-state throughout its history—until it was sundered into north and south sections in 1945.

Taking advantage of Korea's strategic peninsular location in Northeast Asia, the peoples of the North Asian hinterland attempted to use Korea as a beachhead for their advance toward the sea. The insular people of Japan, on the other hand, wished to secure Korea as an outpost for their forays onto the continent. Hence, Korea was frequently invaded. Yet during their long history, Koreans have been known as a particularly peace-loving people who never provoked alien nations or waged a war of invasion.

Minor raids aside, Korea has suffered from nine major invasions in the past 2,000 years. The first attack, by the Han dynasty of China (206 B.C.–A.D. 221), went on for several hundred years. Korea was later invaded by the Sui dynasty (589–618), the T'ang dynasty (618–906), once by the Khitan (907–1125), once by the Yuan (1280–1368), twice by Japan, and once by the Ch'ing (1644–1912). The Chinese, the Mongols, the Manchu, and the Japanese all have intruded into Korea for centuries. Whenever they trod on Korean soil, many Koreans were killed and much farmland was ravaged.

It might be surmised that such frequent invasions would have ended the nation's existence or, at the least, eroded its national spirit, language, and culture. During each invasion thousands of Koreans were mercilessly slaughtered. Yet their survivors maintained our nation-state intact, in terms of both racial homogeneity and cultural uniqueness. This in itself is a miracle of human history.

Consider the Mongols who once swept across all Asia and into Eastern Europe, or the desert Arabs after the rise of Islam. Despite their rapid expansion and vast domains, both of these empires declined. Compared with them, we have shown a much stronger viability and indomitability. In modern times the government of prewar imperial Japan made systematic attempts for over 30 years to eliminate Korean unity and culture. Yet in the end the Japanese subversion of Korea's identity proved as ephemeral as raindrops on lotus leaves.

In fact, the ordeals of Korea served as a stimulus, for its people displayed marvelous powers of recuperation. During the Japanese invasion by Toyotomi Hideyoshi—about 380 years ago—the Korean population decreased to four million. According to the census conducted 200 years later during the reign of King Yungjo (1724–76), however, the population had recovered to the level of seven million.

Today the people of the Republic of Korea alone number 35 million. Add some 15 million in Communist North Korea and the total of 50 million demonstrates more than a threefold increase in the last 60 years. It is likely that the population will increase to 80 million in 30 years' time.

Cultural creativity and native inventiveness were surely major factors in Korea's stubborn survival. The people of Korea could always derive consolation and pride from their extraordinary, living heritage.

Koreans absorbed diverse strands of Chinese culture. In earlier days Korea imported both its spiritual and its material culture from the Han dynasty. During the Period of the Three Kingdoms, Buddhism as well as T'ang culture were introduced to Korea. The Koryo dynasty of ancient Korea first assimilated Sung culture, with which succeeding generations blended influences from the Yuan, Ming, and Ch'ing dynasties. Korea refined these Chinese cultures, in many cases developing standards higher than those of the originals.

Silla and Koryo not only produced eminent Buddhist leaders of international reputation, but also reinforced Buddhist theory. Later, Koreans of the Yi dynasty (1392–1910) put Confucian studies in a new context, developed the native Sil-Hak (Practical Science), and met the rising influence of Western thought and Christianity. It is no exaggeration to say that the spiritual culture of Korea became a reservoir where various streams of Eastern culture joined.

The development of classical music in Korea is a good example, channeling the best of musical styles originating in the western Asian regions, the Chinese mainland, Mongolia, and Manchuria. Korea suffered considerable cultural loss in war and through the Confucian-oriented cultural policies of the Yi rulers. Yet, as historical remains prove, the Korean culture served in many ways as the melting pot of various Asian cultural traditions. Korea's originality developed through the process of acculturation in many fields, the arts as well as science and technology.

Korea invented the world's first movable metal type for printing, in 1234, more than 200 years before Gutenberg's invention of Western type. Koreans invented a rain gauge during the reign of King Sejong the Great (1419–50), the fourth king of the Yi dynasty. The Koryo celadon glaze pottery of the 15th and 16th centuries is still unmatched in its outstanding quality. The world's first ironclad warships were built by Adm. Yi Sunsin (1545–98).

Above all, a national alphabet known as Hangul, invented by King Sejong in the 15th century, represents the superb creativity of the Korean people. This alphabet is one of the most outstanding inventions of mankind. Designed in a remarkably scientific system of vowel and consonant notation, it was planned by King Sejong to replace Chinese ideographs, as an aid to popular literacy. It is regarded as the essence of Korean culture.

When we reflect upon the remote past of our long history, we come to realize that Koreans are truly a self-reliant, democratic people with a highly developed culture and that Korea is, in its historic essence, a peace-loving nation, though often compelled to defend itself against invasions.

The Korean national spirit finds its roots in the ancient founding principle of the nation known as *hongik ingan,* or "the welfare of the masses," as well as the knightly ethic of the United Silla period known as *hwarang-do chongsin,* the *hwarang* spirit. The term *hongik ingan,* which may be translated as "give much help to the multitude," was the creed of the mythological Tangun, the legendary founder of the nation. It implies that both the individual and the state have the obligation to help others, making men in all walks of life brethren in the true sense. This philosophy finds a consistent expression in today's peaceful democracy.

The *hwarang-do* was a collective movement of young men in Silla who devoted themselves to the cultivation of knighthood and comradeship based upon a common creed, the knights errant of Korean chivalry. This young elite made inspection tours to the provinces and reported their findings on people's living conditions to the government. They recommended talent, commended merit, and punished injustice.

In developing personality, the *hwarang* movement emphasized the cultivation of benevolence, wisdom, filial piety, and loyalty. As a device of early political education, it nourished a spirit of generosity and an awareness of individual as well as social rights. Unlike the Japanese samurai, who overstressed their rigid concept of battle and death, the *hwarang* preferred the combination of the pen and the sword. The ideal personality of those Silla people was partially expressed in the two aspects of the Sokkuram Stone Cave Temple—dignity and grace.

The rise and decline of dynasties during more than 4,000 years of history provided Koreans with valuable lessons. The nation flourished whenever the *hongik ingan* and *hwarang* spirit prevailed, but it declined whenever these deteriorated. For instance, they flourished when Silla accomplished the unification of the three ancient kingdoms into one state, whereas they were deficient when the Yi dynasty was deprived of its sovereignty by the Japanese.

The 2,000 years up to the end of the 19th century were a period of defensive resistance against foreign invasions; they also represented a vigorous national creativity. But the last 100 years, from the late 19th century to the middle of the 20th, were marked by darkness and filled with suffering. Korea was not successful in its early attempts at modernization. The Korean people brought to culmination their "national disgrace" by surrendering to the Japanese imperialists on Aug. 29, 1910. And during the 35 years of Japanese rule we were never free from Japanese exploitation.

We had our enlightenment movements initiated by pioneer thinkers, and we often struck out against foreign domination—as in the Samil Independence Movement (March 1, 1919), in which the people fought vainly against armed Japanese gendarmes with their bare fists. Yet our politicians were mostly corrupt and inefficient, and enlightenment movements ended without fruitful results. Nor was the Samil Independence Movement able to restore the nation's sovereignty, due to the absence of favourable conditions within the country and abroad.

We obtained our freedom from foreign rule only following Japan's surrender to the Allies in World War II. Yet from the moment of liberation the land was divided and Korea's high hopes were shattered, then disappeared completely with the Communist invasion of June 25, 1950.

But for Koreans the ordeal of the 1950s was not a useless one. The harsher our trials became, the more rigorously the nation examined itself as to their causes. Such self-examination gradually awakened the majority of Koreans to the need for seeking their own self-reliance, independence, prosperity, and peace. The first fruit of this awakening was the April 19, 1960, student revolution, a campaign of national salvation that aimed to eliminate the rule of the Liberal Party, a symbol of corruption and inefficiency in modern Korea. Then came the May 16, 1961, military revolution, a decisive step toward national reconstruction.

Nine years have since elapsed. Now, as we move ahead into the 1970s, our role and our perspective have changed. After a hundred years of deteriorating domestic politics and brutal foreign invasion, modern Korea has shaken off the memory of past hardships to find a new kind of excellence in its dramatic social and economic reconstruction. For the military revolution of 1961 enabled the country, for the first time, to set itself single-mindedly on the path of concerted recovery.

Today when one looks over the rising city of Seoul one is amazed to see a forest of new steel and concrete skyscrapers in a city that slumbered through past years as a dusty ex-Japanese colonial capital. With its new enterprises, banks, communications, hotels, industries, and cultural centres, Seoul has become one of the world's metropolises, a five-million-strong city of hope nestling below the venerable scarred mountains that have historically guarded it from invasion. In the shadows of new girders and construction cranes nestle the palaces and monuments of former times.

New six-lane highways link Seoul with Pusan in the south and other centres of the country. (It can be said that 63% of Korea's population is now served by the Seoul–Pusan artery.) The new steel and chemical plants in the Ulsan-Pusan and the Seoul-Inch'on complexes are symbols of a rising economy, just as the recently founded research centre in the Korean Institute of Science and Technology bears witness to Korea's commitment to the future. The national product increased by 222% between 1961, the year of the military revolution, and 1969. Perhaps an even more dramatic index of Korea's rise as an economic power is the fact that exports, which totaled a mere $20 million in 1959, rose to fully $700 million in 1969.

We Koreans have a brilliant history and tradition. But we should interpret the unfortunate aspects of our history as more valuable and worthy, for it is the examination of our unfortunate recent past rather than the boasts about the glories of our ancient history that gives a strong impetus to our self-awakening.

At the threshold of the 1970s, a decade in which we are determined to attain tremendous goals of national reconstruction—self-reliance, independence, prosperity, and the eventual unification of our divided homeland—let us reflect upon the past 100 years of continued deterioration, confusion, suffering, and misery. Let us evaluate our present and speculate on the prospects of our future.

TRIALS AND AWAKENING

The Tides of Imperialism. In international politics, power tends to flow from the higher to the lower planes. In the age of imperialism, in particular, several dominant currents flowed toward what political scientists like to call power vacuums. A nation situated in a power vacuum is liable to become an arena of competition among powerful nations. Such a power vacuum was responsible for the Korean people's tragedy, in which they lost

Seoul, the capital and largest city in South Korea, is the nation's political, cultural, and industrial centre. Since the end of the Korean War in 1951, the city has made great progress.

the national sovereignty they had maintained for over 4,000 years and were driven into a state of subjugation and stagnation. In the mid-19th century, when Korea still slumbered in national seclusion, its shores were battered by the tides of imperialism, reinforced by the Anglo-Russian rivalry that lasted throughout the 19th century.

The occupation of Komun Island (Port Hamilton) by a British fleet in April 1885 signaled the first recognition by the world powers of the importance of the Korean peninsula. The British occupation, a swift move designed to counter the secret agreement between Russia and Korea on concessions in Yonghung Bay (Port Lagarett), came to an end two years later with the explanation by the Korean government that the accord was not a formal one. The Port Hamilton incident might well have marked the decisive moment for Korea to turn its eyes toward the outside world, but the royal court did not sufficiently grasp the meaning of the incident or the warning it contained.

Concurrently with the onslaught of European imperialism, another tidal wave swept across the Korean peninsula. This was the turmoil resulting from the collision of the policies of Ch'ing China and imperial Japan, which had been engaged in a dangerous confrontation over Korea. It was inevitable that Japan, advancing on the Asian continent after having completed its domestic reorganization, would enter into a bitter contest with China over hegemony in Korea.

Japan, which grasped the essence of international politics in its own development as a modern nation-state, did not oppose the tide of European imperialism. Instead, it allowed the tide to flow by rather than engulf it and, indeed, formed a substream in that current. Japan made its debut on the Korean peninsula under the guise of promoting "Korean independence." It first sought to sever the traditional relationship between the Ch'ing and Korea. The initial result of this Korean policy was the Ganghwa Treaty of 1876, which provided that Korea should open its ports to the outside world for the first time.

Ch'ing China also made a persistent effort to retain its suzerainty over Korea, that special arrangement between the two countries which Western scholars term "vassal relations." The confrontation between the Ch'ing and Japan continued for over ten years with now one side, then the other, gaining the advantage. The two countries began a war for supremacy in Korea, ending in a one-sided victory for Japan in 1895 with China expelled from the peninsula. Japan demanded "special concessions"

from the Korean government as compensation. It intervened in Korea's domestic affairs by placing so-called consultants in every agency of the Korean government, and by this means secured actual power.

However, the real struggle among the imperialist powers was yet to begin. Russia, its European borders secured by its alliance with France, initiated the contest with an advance into Asia. It forced Japan to return to China the Liaotung Peninsula, obtained in accordance with the Shimonoseki Treaty (1895) after the Sino-Japanese War. Encouraged by its successful occupation of Manchuria following the Boxer Rebellion, Russia started to challenge Japan's "special privileges" on the Korean peninsula.

The Russian intervention caused a series of upheavals in Korean political circles. A Korean queen was killed by a group of Japanese assassins, and the emperor moved to the Russian legation for safety. On Jan. 30, 1902, Great Britain, abandoning its traditional policy of noninterference, allied itself with Japan and intervened in Korea to check Russia's southward expansion.

U.S. Pres. Theodore Roosevelt criticized the Korean people for not even so much as clenching their fists to promote their own national interests. However, it may well have been that no matter how firmly the Koreans clenched their fists, it was too late for them to save their nation. After the Russo-Japanese War had swept across the Korean peninsula, scarcely a vestige of an independent Korea remained.

We were powerless. What could be found in Korea in the age of imperialism was a power vacuum. Neither the Korean government nor its ruling class possessed the capability of mobilizing the people for the nation's defense. The caste-ridden ruling class curried foreign favour in its own struggles. This served only to aggravate frictions between the world powers involved.

This desperate state of affairs, however, did not extinguish the spirit of self-reliance which the Korean people had demonstrated down through their long history. Not all of the people continued to remain in deep sleep. In the shock and confusion of the 20-odd years from the dawn of enlightenment to the loss of national sovereignty, one group of pioneers possessed a penetrating knowledge of history and reality and found lessons therein. Retaining the hope of their forefathers, they strove for a new, bright future.

The Pioneers of Modernization. Long after Western society had realized itself in the Renaissance and the Reformation and had liberated itself from feudalism, Korea remained fast asleep. Only after the two foreign invasions in the middle part of the Yi dynasty era—by the Japanese in 1592 and by the Manchus in

People fill the streets in Seoul to celebrate the liberation of Korea from Japanese occupation on Aug. 15, 1945.

1636—did our leaders awaken to the need for modernity and modern national defense. Two great scholars lived at that time—Yi Hwang (Toige, 1501–70) and Yi I (Yulgok, 1536–84)—whose Confucian learning surpassed that of their Chinese contemporaries. Their thought, however, was highly speculative in nature and aloof from reality.

It was the school of Practical Science (Sil-Hak) that first proposed to reform the metaphysical propensity of Confucianism by research into practical problems. This school, expanding its scope by absorbing knowledge from China and broadening contact with European thought, carried the first torch lit for national modernization. Scholars of the Practical Science school made a strenuous effort to embody their theories in state policy and to utilize them for national projects. But the political situation existing at that time prevented the government from accepting their ideas.

Although Practical Science failed to achieve any great political results, it offered many plans for a better society, including reforms in government, taxation, education, and national defense. Its spirit was subsequently incorporated into the social reform initiated by Christianity, introduced into Korea from China in the early part of the 19th century.

Confucianism, long the supreme principle of government, had made too rigid a distinction between the aristocrats and the common people. It regarded knowledge of the Chinese classics as the ultimate status symbol and discriminated greatly against women. The principle of equality advocated by the Christian religion, therefore, found ready acceptance among the oppressed commoners and women. The Korean version of the Bible, written entirely in the Hangul alphabet, facilitated the rapid propagation of Christianity, and the religion contributed to the increased awareness of human rights. Because Christianity contradicted traditional Confucian thought, however, government leaders for a long time severely oppressed Christians, and the overall effect of Christianity was minimal.

The modernization drives launched by Practical Science scholars and Christians failed because feudalistic politicians either opposed or neglected them. Thus the Korean people lost a precious opportunity to reform their society before they were drawn into the whirlpool of imperialist encroachment.

The reform movements up to that time had rejected excesses, advocating only gradual social renovation in the face of merciless oppression. However, as the Korean government, unable to counter the imperialist threat, simply assumed a flattering attitude toward it, Korean pioneers, anxious about their national survival, attempted more radical social reform. Two epoch-making incidents dramatized this movement—the Gapsin Political Incident and the Tonghak (Donghak) Revolution.

The Gapsin Incident of Oct. 27, 1884, was brought about by the Kaehwa Tongnip party (the Independence Club) led by Kim Okgyun (1851–94) and other progressive young patriots. Unlike the conservative politicians in power, these men correctly grasped the international situation and felt the need for modernization. They aimed at eradicating the conservative faction that was dependent on China. Drawing a lesson from the experience of Japan, which had achieved rapid development, these progressives were convinced that modernization alone could guarantee national survival.

The 14-point reform policy they put forth made it clear that they intended to bring tributary diplomacy to an end and to restore Korea's national prestige. They demanded that the tyranny of the nobility be eliminated and that the people be guaranteed equal rights. They proposed that, in the interests of economy, government systems be simplified, asserting at the same time that government discipline should be strictly enforced by eradicating fraudulent practices and punishing corrupt officials. They advocated the establishment of modern police and military systems, proposed a modern political system based on government by consensus, a modern social welfare policy for the poor, and amnesty for political offenders. In short, their aim was to organize a modern democratic government based on nationalism and self-reliance.

This great step forward, however, was tragically frustrated within three days. Aided by Japanese betrayal and Chinese intervention, the conservatives were able to crush the young revolutionaries. If a movement aims to secure an abundant living for the masses, then it is necessary that the masses be awakened to the need for modernization. But only a few pioneers realized this, while the thinking of the masses was still governed by premodern consciousness. This being the case, the reform movement initiated by Kim Okgyun and his party, poorly planned, failed to gain popular support. Furthermore, the engineers of the Gapsin Incident were negligent in that they trusted Japan excessively and failed to anticipate Chinese intervention.

Ten years later, on March 21, 1894 (the 31st year of King Kojong's reign, 1864–1907), Jeon Bongjun (1854–95) and his followers rose up against the government in Kobu, Chollado Province, in what is known as the Tonghak Revolution. In contrast to the Gapsin Incident, this was an unprecedented spontaneous popular revolt. And whereas the Kaehwa Tongnip group had sought Western-style modernization, the Tonghak Revolution aspired to modernize on the basis of Oriental thought. The ideological basis for the revolt was the religion called Tonghak (later called Chondokyo), among whose tenets was the doctrine that God and man are equal or, rather, that God resides within man. It was named Tonghak (Eastern Learning) to set it in opposition to Christianity, which was then called Sohak (Western Learning). In fact, however, Tonghak adopted much of the Christian doctrine, along with strains of Confucianism, Buddhism, and Taoism. Two of its conspicuous concepts were a strong national dedication to prevent the nation from being overrun by the European powers and Japan, and a populist call for universal equality, directed at helping commoners suffering under the tyranny of the nobility.

Tonghak won a large number of converts, especially among farmers, but it was hated by the ruling class and subjected to ruthless persecution as a heretical religion. Its founder was executed. In spite of these atrocities, its believers eventually broke out in rebellion and won a considerable, if short-lived, influence on a new spirit of reform throughout the country. But the royal court, to its disgrace, responded with a campaign of subjugation, requesting Chinese assistance which, in turn, invited Japanese intervention. Within a year, the peasants' revolution was over.

The 12-point reform proposal that the Tonghak "rebels" put forth was a far more ardent expression of desire for modernization than the policy pursued by the leaders of the Gapsin Incident. They called for a purge of corrupt officials and for the punishment of dishonest wealthy people and the Yangban (aristocracy). They advocated liberation of serfs, and their demand for permission for widows to remarry indicates that they planned not only political but also social reform. They demanded the abolition of various taxes and the exemption of the poor people from the repayment of loans. They called for land reform. And they tried to maintain the national identity by professing a desire to cooperate with the government, calling for the punishment of those who collaborated with the Japanese.

The Tonghak Revolution failed, first of all, because of poor leadership, a failure to understand the political situation, and an inability to organize and train the masses. The second cause of its failure was the intervention by neighbouring imperialist powers. It is sad that the modern awakening of the peasantry was trampled down by China and, especially, by the armed intrusion of modernized Japan. Nevertheless, the nationalistic and democratic spirit with which the farmers had defied the aggressive schemes of neighbouring powers, and their zeal for social reform, remained vividly in the minds of the people and provided a strong foundation for subsequent modernization movements.

Although these two reform attempts failed, the conservative government was stimulated to make some changes. A reformist Cabinet was appointed with Kim Hongjip (1842–96) as the prime minister. The new Cabinet undertook reform of the political, economic, and social systems on a broad scale. The so-called Gabo Kyongjang (Gabo Reform) had as its main features:

1. Establishment of a basis for independence.
2. Revision of the royal household law to clarify the succession and the limits of royal kinship.
3. Consultation with Cabinet ministers by the king; the queen and members of her family should not intervene in affairs of state.
4. Separate administration of the royal household.
5. Definition of the jurisdiction for each agency of the government.
6. Legal system of tax collection.
7. Systematized tax collection and government expenditures.
8. Economies in the royal household.
9. Introduction of a budget system.
10. Revision of and limitation of authority of local government systems.
11. Education of able youths abroad.
12. Establishment of a modern military system.

13. Revision of the civil and criminal codes.
14. Appointment of competent persons to government positions regardless of their family lineage.

Korea's modernization really began with the Gabo Reform, which was a direct reflection of the spirit manifested in the Gapsin Incident and the Tonghak Revolution. However, the reform policy was enforced by the coercive force of the Japanese troops occupying Korea rather than by the Korean government acting on its own. For this reason the people did not pin many hopes on it, and no substantial results were achieved—except for the employment of Japanese consultants in the Korean government. Since this paved the way for Japan's imperialist aggression, it led the Korean people to view later attempts at modernization with suspicion.

Despite this, the Korean pioneers, yearning for the modernization of their country, became ever more convinced such a movement demanded the voluntary participation of an awakened people. The Tongnip Hyophoe (Independence Association) was formed in 1896 under the leadership of Seo Jaepil (1864–1951), who exiled himself to the United States after the Gapsin Incident and returned home later. The association was the first popular nationwide modernization movement, without any foreign influence behind it, quite different from both the Gapsin Incident and the Gabo Reform. Nor was it a class struggle spearheaded by the lower classes, as in the case of the Tonghak Revolution. As a result, the association won a following and support among young students.

Seo founded the *Tongnip Shinmun* (*The Independent*), written entirely in Hangul, in 1896, in the conviction that the cooperation of the masses was essential for any successful modernization movement. Through its editorial columns, he emphasized the defense of national sovereignty through national unity. He asserted the importance of mass education to an independent country, and he launched an enlightenment movement covering all fields of national life, including the improvement of clothing, food, and housing, the elimination of superstitions and superstitious practices, and the betterment of sanitation and hygiene. In the political field, he insisted that the government must discard its reliance on foreign countries and must put democracy

Below, great damage was inflicted on Seoul during its occupation by Communist forces in 1950 and again in 1951.
Right, thousands of South Korean civilians flee battle areas during the Korean War.

into practice by guaranteeing civil rights. At the same time, he assailed the government and the world powers, the former for its impotence and the latter for their aggressive moves.

Seo also launched a large-scale civil rights movement through the Tongnip Hyophoe. The Independence Gate was erected to symbolize a stronger self-reliant attitude. At a mass rally on Chongno Avenue, Seoul, on Oct. 29, 1898, Seo attacked the government for its subservient attitude and adopted a six-point reform proposal, which Kojong (who had proclaimed himself emperor in 1897) was asked to implement immediately. In three months the association expanded its membership to more than 10,000.

Youthful leaders such as Yun Chiho, Yi Sangjae, and Syngman Rhee took part in the activities of the Independence Association with impressive zeal. However, there were many obstacles hindering the association's activities. Reactionary forces, now determined to crush the activities of the Independence Association, formed the Hwangguk Hyophoe (Imperial Association) to head off reform proposals to the emperor. Thousands of hoodlums gathered to assault the association's mass rally. When the Independence Association expanded its civil rights movement, the conservatives resorted to even more oppressive measures: the Independence Association was ordered to disband and its leading figures were arrested. The civil rights movement subsequently began to decline.

It should be remembered that the imperialist powers, Japan, Great Britain, and Russia, worked very effectively to ensure the emergence of the conservatives as an organized political force, opposing the modernization movement. After the Independence Association disbanded, the pioneers were unable to develop another well-organized movement. If any of the several reform attempts—those golden opportunities for national modernization—had been successful, we would not have experienced the tragedy and disgrace of losing our sovereignty.

It is needless to point out that an incessant struggle to galvanize our people was fought by our patriots, who displayed a defiant energy at home and abroad. Worthy of mention are the Heungsadan Movement led by An Chang Ho (1878–1938) and others, the press activities of Chang Jiyeon (1864–1921) and other journalists, the martyrdom of Min Yeonghwan (1861–1905) and other patriots, the suicide of emissary Yi Jun (1859–1907) at The Hague peace conference, the assassination of Hirobumi Ito by

South Korean marines in full battle dress set up mortar positions in Seoul in support of the military action that toppled Prime Minister John M. Chang, May 16, 1961.

UPI COMPIX

An Jungkeun (1878–1910), the operations of independence forces in every part of the country, and the efforts of teachers to educate the people to govern themselves.

But the masses, having lived under a tyrannical feudal rule for so long, were accustomed more to resignation than to resistance. The politicians in power, blind to the course of history, cared only for themselves, and the imperialist powers cleverly utilized the politicians' stupidity. Eventually, the Ulsa Treaty was concluded with Japan in 1905, paving the way for Japan's formal annexation of Korea on Aug. 29, 1910. The pioneers of modernization were arrested, imprisoned, or driven underground. Some went into exile. However, the seeds these abortive reform movements had sown started to grow. The nation's will to independence intensified.

The Declaration of an Independent People. From 1910 until their liberation in 1945, the Korean people underwent a severe trial. Japanese colonial policy, keynoted by harsh military oppression from beginning to end, paid no heed to world opinion, much less to the principles of humanitarian justice. It suppressed all antagonistic ideologies and activities and even attempted to annihilate our national culture. Yet the more merciless the Japanese colonial rule of Korea became, the more firmly did our spirit of self-reliance develop into organized resistance.

Even in the darkness of the period around 1910, several rays of light could be discerned. The struggle for the recovery of the nation's sovereignty now moved outside Korea. Organized in the United States were the Heungsadan (1913) and the Tongjiwhoe (1914), while the Bumindan (1912) came into being in Manchuria. After the end of World War I, the Korean independence movement became very animated.

Conspicuous among overseas activities in and after 1919 were the Korean Students' Conference on Independence held in Japan, the independence movement in China with the French concession in Shanghai as its centre, and the submission of an appeal for Korean independence by an assembly of Korean residents in the United States. The Korean press was still in its infancy at that time, but it was resolute in denouncing political and social elements that it regarded as detrimental to independence. The birth of a national press had coincided with the downfall of the nation itself. Therefore Korean journalists were acutely aware of their mission to reflect the national spirit.

The ideal of civil rights was an undercurrent of the independence movement. It was only natural that nationalistic resistance was first generated by the people's indignation at the loss of their civil rights. The conviction gradually took root among them that to serve their country was to sacrifice themselves not for a king, as they had believed before, but for the Korean people as a whole. Thus they realized the restoration of the people did not mean the revival of a dynasty.

The enlightenment or new culture movement propagated such concepts. Herein lies the special nature of the modernization movement undertaken during the Japanese rule. The only method of resistance for the Koreans after they had lost their independence was to launch a new culture movement. Korean leaders remaining at home after 1910 engaged mostly in cultural and religious activities. But, ultimately, this became the vanguard of the independence movement. As the combination of cultural enlightenment and national pride penetrated into the minds of the people, a large-scale nationwide resistance became possible.

On March 1, 1919, an unprecedented wave of anti-Japanese demonstrations took place, in a concerted resistance movement that erupted in every part of the country and gradually spread to embrace all the people. The scale of the movement can be judged by the following figures: 1,442 rallies were held mobilizing 2,051,448 persons; 7,509 were killed; and another 46,306 were arrested by the Japanese police. These figures are only estimates. Nonetheless, they suggest how extensively people participated in the March 1 Independence Movement.

The movement was elaborately planned well in advance by patriots in exile and a few leaders at home. A group of 33 leaders of the major religions—Chondokyo (represented by Son Byeonghi, 1861–1922), Christianity, and Buddhism—drew up the "Declaration of Korea Independence" and placed their signatures on it. "We hereby proclaim this to the world and to our posterity, demand our just right of national survival, and appeal to mankind's sense of justice." The declaration made the nation's will to independence clear to all by reiterating that Japan's annexation of Korea was contrary to universal justice.

The movers of the March 1 uprising were a nationalist elite, who, influenced by Japan and the United States, had developed a modern consciousness and a firm belief in nationalism, but students also played an important role. Woodrow Wilson's Fourteen Points, set down as the basis of a World War I peace settlement, provided the direct impetus for the March 1 movement—most notably, the American president's principle of national self-determination.

Korea was moving with the times. During World War I, liberation movements had broken out among the oppressed peoples in Ireland, Egypt, Turkey, India, and China. After the war, many countries in Central and Eastern Europe regained or attained independence under this principle, Czechoslovakia, Poland, and Yugoslavia among them. Whether President Wilson had Korea in mind or not, his doctrine of national self-determination greatly encouraged the Korean people to free themselves. Their leaders moved resolutely because they believed that justice and the trend of world thinking supported them.

Yet how many instances have there been in world history of such an idealistic expression of spirit in the face of tyranny? I recall only the American Declaration of Independence of 1776. Although 1919, unlike 1776, did not achieve a nation's independence, I am confident that the Korean movement was not inferior in terms of vigour and the loftiness of its ideals. And, notably, the March 1 declaration called for a nonviolent response to tyranny. It emphasized true coexistence, stressing that one should be neither an aggressor nor the victim of aggression. The leaders of the March 1 movement instructed the people only to "demonstrate their free will" and "even though this is our national demand for justice, humanity, survival and prosperity, we should be careful not to antagonize anyone." While reaffirming a belief in orderly action, they told the people to "demonstrate the nation's just intentions to the last man and to the last minute."

We, the present generation, have many things to learn from our grandfathers, who could confidently express their nationalism even under the oppressive political and economic yoke of imperial Japan. It is hoped that foreigners, when evaluating Korea's recent awakening, will not overlook the idealism of 1919 merely because of its lack of immediate result.

As the March 1 movement erupted in large-scale nationwide demonstrations of nonviolence, the Japanese tried to suppress it with torture and massacre. But repression was not so easy, and the Japanese government had to change its policy to one of governance through cultural domination. If Japan had respected justice somewhat more, Korean-Japanese relations could have been normalized much earlier and Japan might have avoided its tragic defeat in World War II.

Although March 1 failed to achieve its political objective of restoring independence, it nevertheless renewed world understanding of Korea's situation. It also led directly to the establishment of the Provisional Government of the Republic of Korea in Shanghai. This marked a revolutionary turning point in the independence movement. Previously, to Koreans, independence had meant the restoration of the Yi dynasty. Now the sole aim was to be the establishment of a republican form of government. All subsequent independence movements, including the armed resistance in Manchuria, were carried out in the name of the provisional government in Shanghai.

A more valuable result, however, was the people's realization that the only way to achieve independence was to build up their own strength. The colonial policy of Japan, which aimed to exploit Korea in order to alleviate the depression that gripped

AUTHENTICATED NEWS INTERNATIONAL

San Dong mine, largest single tungsten mine in the world, is responsible for 90% of South Korea's tungsten production. South Korea produces about 20% of the tungsten output in the free world.

Japan following World War I, severely impoverished the Koreans' lives. Its adverse impact on the rural populace was especially devastating. The policy of civil appeasement was nothing but a disguise to conceal the vicious nature of Japan's colonial policy. In order to counter this increased exploitation effectively, independence movements both at home and abroad gradually resorted to armed resistance.

Journalists also grew more active after 1920, receiving wide support among the people. It was in this period that Koreans for the first time developed full-fledged magazines and private newspapers such as the *Dong-a Ilbo* and the *Chosun Ilbo*. In spite of continuous Japanese interference, these periodicals acted as spokesmen for the nation. It was in the press that the national spirit of resistance manifested itself as an organized force. The journalists of that time were the symbolic vanguard of the struggle for independence, the standard-bearers for civil rights, and the spokesmen for the people's aspirations.

At the same time, new movements began to bear fruit in various other fields. In literature and the arts an effort was made to produce works on the theme of democratic ideals and to assimilate modern European thought. The new culture spread to women's and children's movements and extended to the campaign for a "new mode of life," the encouragement of sports, "the movement to recover the national language" led by the Korean Language Society, and the campaign to increase productivity.

However, such efforts were doomed to frustration as Japan's aggressive ambitions became more pronounced. After the Japanese took over Manchuria and began their invasion of China, Korea was forced to accept a policy of assimilation aimed at converting the peninsula into a forward military base. The Japanese also conscripted Korean youth, thus denying them a school education. Between the mid-1930s and the liberation in 1945,

The Ulsan Oil Refinery, constructed in 1962 at the Ulsan industrial complex on the southeast coast, has an annual crude oil capacity of 115,000 tons.

we were even faced with an attempt to destroy our language.

All efforts directed to modernization, even though conducted in a disguised and secret form, disappeared like water bubbles. The national awakening was brought to a halt. "Now the land is lost to others. Does spring come to a stolen field?" This poem aptly describes the painful feeling of a people who had lost their country. They had to wait until the summer of 1945 before spring could come to the field again.

THE WILL TO FREEDOM

The Price of Liberation. The joy felt by Koreans on Aug. 15, 1945, is indescribable. Although the liberation from Japan was not achieved by the Koreans themselves, the excitement they felt, as a people who throughout had maintained their national pride, was tremendous. Proud of their old cultural tradition, they could not but harbour a sense of indignation because Korea had been ruled by a Japan that had itself benefited greatly from Korean culture. The liberation, therefore, was all the more exciting—a time of justice regained after years of enormous humiliations and sacrifices.

Contrary to the people's expectations, however, the nation was again to experience a period of harsh trials, as if the fates disapproved of its premature joy. Indeed, what awaited was not the glory of independence rebuilt, but tragic division and the menace of Communism. The division of the nation along the 38th parallel, originally a postwar military arrangement to speed the surrender of Japanese troops, turned out to be a decisive hindrance to unification. The confrontation between the U.S. and the U.S.S.R., which jointly occupied Korea, sacrificed Korea's interests to the cold war.

Immediately after Japan accepted the Potsdam Declaration, the Japanese governor-general in Korea selected such prominent Korean figures as Lyuh Woon-hyung, An Jaehong, and Song Jinwu to take over authority and maintain public safety. These men soon contacted other associates and organized a Preparatory Committee for Nation-Building. The Preparatory Committee was not at all content to function as a mere arm of the Japanese administration. It quickly expanded, set up a Students Corps and a Public Safety Corps, and prepared to establish a foundation for taking over the reins of government.

The committee, the only political body in the nation at the

Several men work on a gasoline-powered cart in Chicol village. Powered tools and vehicles are replacing the older types of agricultural equipment in most parts of the country.

PETER FEBBRORIELLO FROM NANCY PALMER

KEYSTONE

Perched on a mast, a fisherman mends his nets. In 1959 fish and other raw materials comprised 83% of the nation's export dollar, but by 1969 manufactured goods rose to 79% of all exports.

time, was a mixture of various resistance forces—conservatives and reformists, leftists and rightists, moderates and radicals—having managed to assemble, though not cohesively, representatives of various sectors of society, including intellectuals and students. The postwar history of Korea might well have been much different had these political leaders shown a positive capacity to take over power. Eventually, however, the Preparatory Committee collapsed because its members were involved in internal strife, intensified by the implications of the country's division along the 38th parallel.

Meanwhile, U.S. troops, whose arrival the entire nation had awaited so expectantly, belatedly landed in Inch'on on September 8 and went to Seoul the next day. The Japanese flag, which had flown over Korea for 35 years, was lowered for good that afternoon. Lieut. Gen. John R. Hodge, commanding the U.S. 24th Army Corps, and Adm. Thomas C. Kinkaid, commander of the U.S. 7th Fleet, accepted the surrender of Japanese forces south of the 38th parallel.

The U.S. Army, which lacked concrete plans for Korean administration, prescribed in the surrender documents that Japanese civil and military officers should continue to perform their normal duties, unless dismissed by the commanding general of the Allied forces. It was later learned that General Hodge, who finally reached the decision to set up a military government, had originally considered the idea of extending the rule of the Japanese governor-general. This idea could not be put into practice because of pressure from Gen. Douglas MacArthur, who read the minds of the Korean people correctly, but General Hodge still chose to retain the existing Japanese administrative network.

Unprepared themselves, the Korean people and their leaders were unable to oppose these measures of the U.S. military government. Japanese colonial rule had reduced them to a state of paralysis. In addition, the unity of the Preparatory Committee began to weaken, and frustrated conservatives and moderates gradually left it. As leaders who had first rallied around the committee began to abandon it, political groups and factions multiplied, with the confrontation between radical and conservative growing ever more fierce.

Extreme social unrest arose for the want of a stable political force. The disorderly and rude withdrawal policy adopted by the Japanese government-general, the inflation born of the excessive issuance of paper money, the market confusion resulting from the theft of stored goods, the paralysis of administrative functions due to the departure of experienced personnel, and the destruction or suspension of operations at production plants formerly operated by the Japanese, all contributed to the chaos. A sense of frustration caused by Korea's artificial division made the situation even worse.

By contrast, the Soviet occupation in North Korea quickly handled the problems related to Japanese surrender, took over administrative power, and immediately set up a military government. The methods employed by the Soviets were entirely different from those of the U.S. authorities. Soon after its arrival, the Soviet Army launched a movement to enlist the support of native nationalists to fill the social and political vacuum.

There existed no real Communist foundation in North Korea at the time, and those few Communists released from prisons after the liberation had not received proper Communist training. Most of those who labeled themselves Communists were in fact radical nationalists. The Soviet occupation authorities therefore decided that it was still too early for them to carry out a socialist revolution with a Communist force as its core. As a provisional measure, they attempted to mobilize conservative nationalist forces and to combine leftists and rightists to take over power from the Japanese. The full-fledged socialist revolution was to be carried out later, once its organizational basis was established.

By the middle of November 1945, dual ruling systems had been established in each of the five northern provinces: a Communist Party chapter and a government administration. The Soviet occupation forces appointed Kim Il Sung, a former Soviet Army captain, as the Communist Party chief and, the following February, as chairman of the North Korean People's Committee, thus completing the groundwork for the eventual emergence of a Stalinist-type government in North Korea.

People in the South, disillusioned by political confusion and division, saw a dim ray of hope in the return of Syngman Rhee and other leaders of the Korean provisional government-in-exile. Fifteen key members of the provisional government, including the venerable Kim Koo (1876–1949), returned home to an enthusiastic welcome from the people. Contrary to public expectation, however, the U.S. military government made it clear that these leaders had returned in an "individual capacity." This attitude reflected the basic U.S. policy of not recognizing the provisional government as legitimate. It might also be that the U.S. military government still hoped to form a single, authentic political force throughout South and North Korea.

As—contrary to U.S. expectations—the 38th parallel division gradually came to be permanent, General Hodge proposed to the commander of the Soviet occupation forces in P'yongyang, Lieut. Gen. I. M. Chistiakov, that a political conference be held in Seoul. General Chistiakov refused on the grounds that "the unification problem is a matter that should be solved by the U.S. and the Soviet governments." Now worried about the existence of the parallel, the U.S. was compelled to take measures to solve the problem. At the Moscow foreign ministers' conference held in December 1945, a five-year trusteeship plan for Korea was proposed by U.S. Secretary of State James F. Byrnes and was generally approved. Agreement was reached on four important matters, including the establishment of a U.S.-U.S.S.R. Joint Commission for the eventual founding of a provisional government for Korea, as proposed by Soviet Foreign Secretary Vyacheslav M. Molotov.

As soon as the U.S.-Soviet trusteeship agreement became known, the Korean people expressed their opposition en masse. On Dec. 31, 1945, endless columns of demonstrators, left and right alike, took to the streets in protest—an intense expression of national indignation by a people firmly determined to regain their sovereignty.

Quite contrary to general expectations, however, the Communists suddenly supported the Moscow agreement, reportedly following a secret directive from Moscow. The Central People's Committee in North Korea sent a message of gratitude for the trusteeship agreement. From this time on, trusteeship became not only a political issue but also a decisive factor accelerating Korea's ideological split.

The U.S.-U.S.S.R. Joint Commission, which met in 1946 and again in 1947, got nowhere. While the U.S. delegation stressed "freedom of expression," the Soviets insisted obstinately on the "eradication of all reactionary elements." While the U.S. side contended that political organizations opposed to trusteeship should also be consulted by the Joint Commission, the Soviets insisted that only those parties that supported trusteeship, *i.e.*, only the leftists of the so-called People's Front, could be consulted. The Soviet stand clearly revealed Moscow's plans for Korea. This was confirmed by the Soviet delegate, who emphasized that "Korea can never be used as a base for an attack on the Soviet Union, but should become a country close and friendly to the Soviet Union."

After the Joint Commission had virtually broken down, acting U.S. Secretary of State Robert A. Lovett proposed in a memorandum sent to Foreign Secretary Molotov that a unified government be established in Korea through general elections in proportion to population, held throughout South and North Korea under UN supervision. The Soviet Union refused to agree. When Secretary of State George Marshall brought the Korean question to the UN, Soviet delegate Andrei Gromyko, erroneously interpreting art. 107 of the UN Charter, opposed the U.S. move. He held it was "illegal to refer a problem resulting from the war, on the solution of which the big powers had already reached an agreement, to the General Assembly."

After the Korean issue was voted a subject for discussion, the Soviet Union, early in 1948, began to propagandize in favour of a simultaneous U.S. and Soviet troop withdrawal from Korea. To anyone not familiar with the situation in North Korea at that

U.S. Pres. John F. Kennedy speaks with R.O.K. Pres. Park Chung Hee during his state visit to the U.S. in 1961.

time, the Soviet proposal might have seemed to be based on the principle of national self-determination. In reality, the Soviet Union had already established a regime headed by Kim Il Sung in the North. Therefore, the Soviet proposal was aimed at capitalizing on what would be a power vacuum in South Korea following the withdrawal of the U.S. troops, enabling it to take over the South without striking a blow.

When the U.S. delegate proposed to the General Assembly a resolution for free elections throughout Korea, under UN supervision, to be held by the end of March 1948, the Soviet delegate suggested instead that "representatives of both south and north Korea be invited to the debate on the Korean question" and that "both the U.S. and Soviet troops be withdrawn simultaneously from Korea." Since it was not clear how the qualifications of such

continued on page 784

1970: Introduction to the Politics of Change

by THEODORE H. WHITE

IT IS HISTORY'S CUSTOM, rarely broken except in time of war, to open each year quietly. All across the Western world, the season of Christmas lulls the striving of men—princes and presidents, generals and businessmen, lawmakers and desperadoes alike pause, dreaming that plans will work as hoped, that clouds will vanish with spring.

History has run this way at least back to the time of the Romans who, at the dark winter solstice, celebrated the holiday of Saturnalia just before their Senate called them back to political attention in January. January is the month of good resolutions when statesmen and leaders are most apt to warm themselves with the illusion that will and wisdom may control events.

The year 1970 was no exception to this ancient custom. The 1960s had delivered to newspaper headlines and television images a group of problems so perplexing, yet so well known, that they had become worn household furnishings for thoughtful men. The quiet weeks of early January thus seemed comfortably familiar: talks on nuclear disarmament were about to begin in Europe between Soviets and Americans; and the United States was scheduled to resume conversations with China in Warsaw. In Paris, Americans and Vietnamese were still talking, as they had for 18 months, about *how* to talk about peace—but the fighting was at a two-year low, and troops were coming home. In the Middle East, Egyptians and Israelis still volleyed sporadically across the Suez Canal. In Africa, 30 months of agony for Biafra was guttering out in Nigerian victory, and no major civil strife threatened black Africa anywhere. At home, in the U.S., the students, having disgorged from campus to streets for the fall Moratorium in 1969, were quiet. Political fashion was marking environment as the prime issue of the winter months. Foreboding hung over the stock market, yet in January it was enjoying a deceptive upswing. All in all, the fevers of 1969 seemed momentarily in January 1970 to be held in check—if no better, the fevers seemed no worse.

By the end of 1970, the year's turbulence had erased this tranquil January pause from recollection. But even at the end of the year, it was still too early to give 1970 an identity of its own in history. No supreme event had slashed the year with its signature as Pearl Harbor had slashed 1941, the Marshall Plan 1948, the Kennedy assassination 1963. Undercurrents of mood and passion, rather than grand events, gave 1970 its character. Traditional emotional and theoretical controls in society were slipping their grip—neither antique calls to patriotism nor the most sophisticated economic theory brought anticipated response; nor did increasing education bring increasing tolerance. Men, women, and youngsters; great states and corporate entities; historic communities and races—all seemed breaking away from the categories by which conventional politics sorted them out. There were, thus, few neat endings or climaxes in 1970. Rather, the year was full of beginnings, both terrifying and promising—beginnings in which men groped for a sense of control, for new ideas to manage the Politics of Change. It was clearly a year of introduction to a new decade, as obscure in prospect as had been the revolution of the 1930s.

All around the globe the postwar settlements of 1945 were clearly obsolete. Such great powers as Germany and Japan were, bit-by-bit, setting out to dismantle the structures built on their defeat. The ability of the United Nations, celebrating its 25th anniversary, to influence the grand diplomatic perspectives of the great powers never had been less. And in the U.S., after a quarter century of unprecedented prosperity, the self-expression fostered by that prosperity had created a domestic Conflict of Cultures that overshadowed all politics.

Somehow deep undercurrents and grand events all linked. The precise bonds and sequences between them would have to wait upon the analysis of historians decades hence with their greater clarity of view. But the coarse dynamics were already visible. For 25 years the great drives in world politics had come from a few clearly identifiable sources—the U.S., the U.S.S.R., and China. To these in 1970 were now decisively added the drives of Japan, Germany, the Arab world. Not only that. For a quarter century, in the overall game of thrust and parry between the superpowers, the U.S.S.R. and the U.S., the U.S. and its allies had generally led the thrusting, and the Soviets responded. In 1970, it was the U.S.S.R., with its client states and allies, who forced the thrust—and the U.S. parried. In the decade of the 1950s, Richard M. Nixon, then vice-president, had been one of the world's most aggressive and vocal cold-warriors, at the peak of U.S. strength. In 1970, as president of a weakened, divided U.S., Richard Nixon had become the world's chief peace seeker. In doing so, he was authentically expressing the will of the American people; and his world diplomacy, more than that of any other U.S. president of this century, was cramped by the imperatives of his shaky domestic front.

The interlinking of the domestic and global fronts could be traced through any number of patterns. But it is best to begin with the pattern of the great war in Vietnam as the year unfurled it.

VIETNAM: TAPS FOR LOST BATTALIONS

The great retreat in Vietnam had begun almost immediately with Mr. Nixon's first months in the presidency. The war burdened and cramped all his planning. Shortly after his election and before his inauguration, he had been briefed on its pressures and dimensions, and he had told friends privately, "Unless we can find some means of de-escalating the arms race, unless we can do that, we're not going to be able to save our system. Our economic system, our freedoms will be lost unless we can reduce the arms burden." He had come to office with 549,000 U.S. troops stretched thin over 900 miles of swamp, jungle, and paddy along the crescent of Indochina. The war was costing a minimum of $20 billion a year. Some 44,200 Americans had died; more bomb tonnage had been dropped than in all of World War II; U.S. hospitals had nursed 293,529 wounded; no one knew how many more would be crippled for life.

What lay before Mr. Nixon was a task of exquisite proportions: how to withdraw from the strange and bungled U.S. commitment in Southeast Asia, without acknowledging defeat. For the U.S. was not yet ready to accept defeat. However bitter the experience, however costly in lives of youth, the country-at-large was not yet ready to dip the U.S. flag and sue for terms. Yet, on the other hand, it wanted out. Republicans and Democrats, Wall Street and Faculty Club, rich and poor—all wanted out. And thus the country was divided into two new unidentified but real parties—a party that wished to get out, immediately, at whatever cost, including acknowledgment of defeat; and another party that wanted to get out "as fast as possible," to which the president belonged.

But what was "fast as possible"? And how far did "getting out" go?

In 1969, the president had announced a Guam Doctrine, soon to be known as the Nixon Doctrine. Vaguely shaped and worded, the Nixon Doctrine was a major turning in 25 years of American history—the U.S., the president felt, must retain its presence and interests in Asia; but the main burden of defense, of fighting, would lie with the Asian nations themselves; the U.S. would withdraw to a position of low-profile support and diplomacy. More harshly translated, "the question of implementing a low-posture policy," said one eminent member of the State Department's policy planning staff, "is one of relinquishing power." In Vietnam, specifically, the doctrine bound the president to reducing U.S. troops in that country while turning the main burden of combat over to the South Vietnamese in the program called Vietnamization. From the peak of 549,000 troops in early 1969, the U.S. total fell to 543,000 during the year, then to 472,-000 (beginning 1970), then to 434,000 (spring 1970). The process was a slow-motion, grand-scale Dunkirk, the first strategic retreat under fire in U.S. history since George Washington had yielded Eastern seaports to the British in the Revolutionary War. But the slowness of the pace hushed those who quietly supported the president, and infuriated those who opposed him.

By mid-April 1970, therefore, the president had decided to quicken the pace of withdrawal. Television had become his favorite means of communication with his nation, a direct channel, he hoped, to the hearts of his countrymen. Thus, on the evening of April 20, composed and lucid, he announced the most far-reaching step yet in his strategy of withdrawal without surrender; 150,000 more troops would be brought home by spring of 1971, reducing U.S. forces to half the field strength when he took office. All was going well in Vietnam, he said—as other presidents had reported over the previous decade.

Yet events in the squirming politics of Southeast Asia, of which Americans had so long been so ignorant, were to betray his hopes—and the aftershock was to ripple first through the press; then explode in blood and violence on a hundred campuses; then into the first serious Constitutional attempt in generations to remove from the president, as commander in chief, his power over the unlimited use of U.S. troops.

The Move into Cambodia. It was in distant Cambodia that an unnoticed rustling of the racial politics of Indochina set in motion the chain of events that was to end in this massive challenge to the authority of a U.S. president by his own people. There in Cambodia, from his bucolic capital of Phnom Penh, a hereditary monarch, Prince Norodom Sihanouk, had for years permitted use of his country by North Vietnamese Communists as sanctuary and assault base for their war in South Vietnam. The gay and unstable monarch left Phnom Penh for France on January 6, leaving behind a country that seemed securely locked

in the embrace of Communist diplomacy. Within weeks, his government had turned him out in absentia; on March 18 his army substituted a new premier, Gen. Lon Nol, who forthwith demanded evacuation of all Communist troops and bases from his occupied country. Within days, the Communist occupants of the country, who had been installed by invitation of the deposed monarch, had wheeled from the South Vietnam front against the fragile new regime in Phnom Penh.

The map of Indochina and the troop movements left little doubt as to the perspectives. If the shaky new Cambodian government fell, then Communist forces would occupy all Cambodia, secure both sanctuaries in the interior and main ports of entry on the coast, then emerge stronger than ever, frustrating Mr. Nixon's grand plan of phased withdrawal and Vietnamization.

U.S. military decisions were swift and secret—but absolutely baffling to the U.S. public. Having been told so definitely by their president only ten days earlier that all was going well in Vietnam, that another 150,000 men were soon to come home, they now watched on April 30 as the president, alternately sitting between the flags at his desk, and then again rising to give a map lecture with his pointer on a chart of Indochina, declared: U.S. troops, that morning, April 30, had crossed the borders of South Vietnam to invade Cambodia.

The action itself, seen in retrospect, was one of the most successful of the long Vietnam war. Conceived as a spoiling rearguard counterthrust in a strategic retreat, it was neatly executed.

American troops, 31,000 strong, swept through the long-inviolate Communist sanctuaries in the enclaves styled Parrot's Beak and Fishhook, captured or killed 11,349 of the enemy, wiped out or captured 25,000 weapons, 15 million rounds of assorted ammunition, plus miscellaneous equipment and supplies of uncounted tonnage; and, within 60 days, all U.S. troops were, as promised, back within South Vietnam, their casualties minimal. As seen from the end of the year, the thrust had, most of all, achieved a larger purpose. The unstable new government of Lon Nol, with a life expectancy of only a few weeks when the Communist offensive began, had survived until year's end, to open a new, apparently permanent southern front to burden the enemy.

It was the abrupt nature of the action itself, multiplied by its covering rhetoric, that touched off the totally unexpected domestic political explosion in the U.S. Mr. Nixon's television talk had inflated what was a tactical raid into a major strategic stroke —the invasion, he promised, would find, demolish, and erase the ever-elusive enemy headquarters in the South, COSVN. His sound was that of the bugle call that rallies to arms—to which sound Americans in other times had responded as if by Pavlovian reflex. In the politics of change, however, the automatic response of traditional patriotism was a thing of the past. Translated into the politics of 1970, the call meant that Mr. Nixon, rather than withdrawing, was expanding the war, taking on new enemies, engaging the country, without consent of Congress, in an exertion that might see no end. And to no group in the country did his call come with more shivering impact than to its youth, who would have to fight such a war.

Insurrection on the Campus. It was spring season, a time when in other years, U.S. students might sweep dormitories in panty raids, swallow goldfish, or unhook trolley cars. But the new generation of college students had learned to pour its vernal exuberance into politics; and the apparent extension of the war into Cambodia was a gamble with their lives. Their roar of outrage came almost immediately, as accident linked military adventure abroad to massacre at home.

It was Mr. Nixon who, with complete innocence, provided the linkage in a blurted outburst of unthinking emotion. Like all presidents, he had found his first military initiative, his first gamble with lives, a tormenting emotional experience. Passing through the Pentagon on Friday night (May 1) of the upsetting week, he had been tape-recorded by the press in a moment of passion. Such moments of naked emotional response had been long characteristic of his early career. Somehow, in the campaign of 1968 he had overcome this emotional frailty. Now, goaded by questioners, he declared his pride in the young Americans fighting and dying in the Cambodian raid ("They stand tall and they are proud.") and then, in a whiplash of exasperation at campus protesters, he denounced "these bums . . . blowing up the campuses . . . burning up the books."

Contagions of emotion are even harder to define than the links of historic decision. Whether or not the president's emotion influenced the events of Monday, May 4, is just such a mystery of emotional contagion. That Monday, however, on the hilly campus of Kent (O.) State University, after a weekend of student trashings, burnings, and riots, a unit of abominably commanded National Guardsmen fired point-blank into a knot of protesting students, killing four and wounding nine. At once and for the next few weeks, learning was suspended from coast to coast. A score of colleges had immediately protested the invasion of Cambodia; on the morrow of the Kent killings their protest exploded exponentially. From Yale to Wisconsin to Stanford, schools began to close down—80 colleges on strike two days after the Kent killings, 200 by week's end, 400 by the beginning of the following week. The president, so the students insisted, had called them all "bums," and the campus proletariat of 7.8 million students, the largest activist political bloc in the country, was out in protest—examinations canceled; strike centers and political action headquarters organized from coast to coast; parents and students alike pouring into Washington to lobby their senators and congressmen for resistance. Some 250 members of the State Department signed a manifesto to denounce the policy they were supposed to shape; politicians thundered, editorialists denounced, intellectuals mourned. "Whirl is King, and Richard Nixon is First Minister," wrote Richard Rovere in *The New Yorker*.

Somehow, no matter how effective his command of troops in the field had been, Mr. Nixon had momentarily lost control of the tides of opinion at home; and with it, possibly, his authority as president.

Two Months of Deep Trouble. April already had been a bad month for the national leader. After two spectacularly successful landings on the moon, the U.S.'s Apollo 13 had ruptured in flight and, on April 17, its astronauts were perilously brought back to earth after an aborted effort. On April 8 the president had failed for a second time to persuade the Senate to confirm the appointment of a Southern judge to the Supreme Court. (Said one White House aide, "the Carswell rejection got to him—even the Republicans he relied on, people he trusted, turned against him in the Senate. It was a question to him whether anybody could govern the country with the machinery he had.") The ferocity of press attacks and student outbursts after the Cambodia-Kent episodes unsettled him to a point only his intimates could judge. Said another White House aide, in a remarkable insight into the White House mood at its spring low, "they'd driven one president from office, they'd broken Johnson's will. Were they going to break another president?—they had him on the edge of nervous breakdown."

Finally, as if reflecting the nation's total uncertainty, in a momentary loss of faith in both the system's general validity and the enterprise system of planning, the New York Stock Exchange, in its worst week in 40 years, broke wide open. It had been sinking since March, losing approximately $100 billion in value in the spring months; and then, on Thursday, May 21 (trading 16,713,-000 shares), and Tuesday, May 26 (17,036,060 shares), the market plunged to an eight-year low (631.16 on the Dow-Jones average)—and $164 billion had been erased from stock market values since January 1.

Superimposed on this general unrest, there came in May its most pointed formulation—the McGovern-Hatfield Bill, the most serious Constitutional challenge to a president in a generation. Introduced by Senators George McGovern of South Dakota and Mark Hatfield of Oregon, it ordered the president to reduce troop force in Vietnam to 280,000 by April 1971 and to zero by the end of that year. In effect, the Senate, having authorized the president by its Tonkin Gulf Resolution of 1964 (by a vote of 88–2) to make war, was now withdrawing that authority and directing surrender. ("Every Senator in this chamber is partly responsible for sending 50,000 young Americans to an early grave," said McGovern later, in the climactic debate of September; and then, expressing the guilt and sorrow of uncounted millions of Americans, he continued, "and in one sense this chamber literally reeks of blood.")

If the outburst of U.S. student opinion in the spring, coincident with an open rupture in the president's own Cabinet, followed by the stock market break in May, was to be capped by depriving the president of his authority in world diplomacy—then, indeed, 1970 would become a revolutionary year. Could Mr. Nixon recover his authority in time to cope with the growing tensions of the Middle East? How far would student unrest carry? Could it dominate the fall elections as it mobilized for the political contest? How authentically did this administration speak for the American people?

One could not help but recall Gen. Charles de Gaulle's gloomy remark on France's posture in the mid-1950s. There are only two kinds of powers in the world, de Gaulle had said—first-class powers and second-class powers. Second-class powers are those whose domestic politics are governed by the larger forces of foreign policy, and France was, alas, a second-class power. First-class powers, however, are those whose foreign policy is governed by domestic politics. The U.S. was a first-class power. But in 1970, Americans were questioning not only the role of the U.S. in the world but the very nature and purpose of government. So we must pass to a consideration of what was happening inside the U.S. before we can resume the 1970 story of the U.S. role in the outer world.

THE DOMESTIC FRONT: QUESTIONING OLD VALUES

It was probably not too much to say that the U.S. had invented the 20th century. From the probing of the inner atom to the landing on the moon, America had led. In the war against fascism, in the spread of education, in the institution of television, in the sharing of wealth among common people—always the U.S. had been foremost. And it was thus the U.S. that was uniquely confronted with new problems on the fringes of the unknown it had explored—pollution of air and waters by excess of abundance, performance of traditional politics in the presence of television, the explosive political potential of highly educated masses.

For a generation, several all-embracing lines of common philosophy had shaped the spectacular energy of the American people. Their commitment to collective security against Communist aggression had led to the growth of an enormous military-industrial complex—and the imposition of a permanent draft, unknown in U.S. history before. At home, a mastery of modern economics had made the government the chief fostering force of a booming free-enterprise system; yet economists could offer no solution to creeping inflation.

Above all, the U.S.'s secular faith in education and science had created an establishment of learning which in numbers of students and faculty, as well as in intellectual creativity, was entirely new. Not since the Roman Catholic Church imposed its mandates on medieval culture and politics had Western civilization known so potent a community of learned men. But whereas the church saw its very adversary in change, which Roman Catholic traditions sought to restrain, the U.S. community of learning saw change as its own mission. This community was the herald of novelty; and, linked with the communications media, which carried its message, it formed what may be called the Academic-Media Complex: Universities provided ideas, surveys, critiques, and reference points for the executive, the Congress, the social structure. They offered fresh news and observations that the media found fascinating. Arthur Schlesinger has said, "Marx held that power was control of the means of production; in our day, power is control of the means of communication." Together, Academia and Media, in the Academic-Media Complex, were, at the very least, as potent a disrupter of conventional politics as the long-recognized military-industrial complex.

This new force rested as much on sheer weight of numbers as on the magic of ideas for a nation seeking new ideas; and there is no better starting point than to measure the mass and momentum of its critical constituents. From 1,350,000 students in all U.S. colleges and universities in 1939, the students of the campus proletariat had grown year by year until, in October 1970, their number was estimated by the U.S. Office of Education as 7.8 million. When one added to their numbers the teachers, administrators, and custodial staff who served them in 2,551 recognized schools, colleges had become the largest industry in the nation. Fifty percent of all American youngsters applied, and were admitted, to some institution of higher learning. Of all Americans between the ages of 18 and 21, no less than 36 out of every 100 were permanently in attendance at a school of higher learning. So vast an experiment had never been tried before.*

There could be no doubt that this campus proletariat had developed to what physicists called critical mass. The nationwide upheaval after the Cambodian invasion and the Kent killings might be either a crest that would fade, as did the black urban upheavals of 1965–68—or it might be a foretaste of even greater turbulence to come. "No episode or series of episodes had a higher impact in all of our history than the events of last April and May," said Clark Kerr, chairman of the Carnegie Commission on Higher Education. The statement was exaggeration, of course, but a survey conducted by the commission did report that some form of organized dissent had developed at 57% of all the nation's colleges and universities and that normal academic activities had been entirely closed down at 21% of them. Moreover, outbursts of violence had been most intense and dramatic at the most renowned and famous institutions, those whose leadership names attract the elite of the aspiring young. Thus, as hard hats and construction workers clashed with students in New York's streets, as National Guard units or state police occupied a score of campuses from coast to coast, as a nationwide organization of students prepared to plunge into fall politics in a hundred congressional and senatorial campaigns, it seemed, in early summer, that the conventional politics of the fall elections would be dominated, for the first time, by a nation's attitude toward the role and passions of its own children.

Yet figures of riots, raids, and demonstrations gave little sense of the political significance of the academic insurrection. In their key area of protest, the war in Vietnam, the students and professors were joined by millions of general sympathizers—businessmen, parents, pacifists, concerned citizens who felt this war was the greatest blunder in U.S. history. But the academic restlessness had far greater meaning than simple antiwar protest. It arose from a questioning of values; a foretaste of cultural revolution was delivered with each new swing of college fashion, with each new formulation of amorphous grievance.

A Critical View of Technology. Fundamentally—or so it seemed to contemporaries in 1970—Academia was questioning the values of the U.S.'s technological society. It is the quality of the trained mind to probe—to probe and probe again until what is accepted as truth is shattered, and a new truth erected that must be probed once again. The scientists, engineers, economists, professors, and administrators spawned by Academia had been critically important contributors to a society where the

* In 1970, the experiment in mass education was pressed yet further. Students had rioted and seized buildings in New York in 1969, demanding that the City University system adopt an open-admission policy that, in effect, would guarantee a college education to everyone regardless of qualification or capacity for college education. Accepting this demand, the city saw the number of incoming freshmen in the city system jump from 19,559 in September 1969 to 35,395 in September 1970. It was too early to tell whether this explosive increase in a single locality would become a nationwide trend—or whether the precedent would become binding on the dominant liberal philosophy of American politics.

FRANK JOHNSTON FROM CAMERA 5

Pres. Richard M. Nixon still held the support of a majority of Americans at the close of 1970 despite a year of crisis both at home and abroad.

WIDE WORLD

Civil Service Commission officials inspect files kept on 1.5 million Americans favorably mentioned in publications of dissent. It also was reported in 1970 that the Army kept extensive files on dissenting civilians.

basic problems of production had been long since overcome. Now, moved by conscience, vision, or parochial ambitions, they continued to probe: Why did pockets of injustice and deprivation still exist in the bosom of abundance? With the ever growing resources of the nation and technology, how should such resources be shared? What was the proper relation of government to the common welfare? And, as Academia drew up the nation's agenda for probing and questioning, it created both intellectual and street drama—which, when translated to the nation by the communications media, stimulated entirely new political shock waves.

What hitherto had been the questioning of philosophers now became hard political controversy, the stuff of a new order of lawsuits, the talk of parlors and barrooms. Was an automobile company responsible or not to every one of its customers for the pistons, axles, steering drives of cars that left its factories? Courts wrestled with such questions all across the country and one could sense a new consumer jurisprudence developing. Was it wise to continue the great space adventure at the same rhythm and pace? In 1970 the government, responding, slashed the space budget, subtly transforming the moon race with the Soviets from a sprint to a lope. Did the U.S. have to match other nations in developing a supersonic transport (SST) plane? Under the new pressures, Congress debated at length the massive $290 million developmental appropriation for the SST and left moot the question whether ever, in our time, the U.S. would develop such a plane. All such individual issues, each shrill of protest against the engulfing technology of the future, were orchestrated, however, into the prime political fashion of the early year—environment, ecology, pollution.

The Environment Issue. If there were any other unifying political theme on which all Americans could agree, beyond their desire to end the Vietnam war, it was the issue of environment.

The problem of how Americans might live within the beauty of their continent, without spoiling it, had nagged even at the earliest settlers—but such concern had come and gone in generational surges. The war had interrupted the last such surge of

concern, in the New Deal, a generation earlier; the postwar boom had then smothered carefree Americans with a glut of goods and technologies; and thus, when that brilliant seminal book *Silent Spring* had been published by Rachel Carson in 1962, few could see it as the spark of a new surge of such political force as exploded in 1970. But, from 1962 on, the ravage of the U.S.'s environment became a cause that first flickered, then flared as traditional conservationists, nature lovers, and students of ecology fanned the public's attention to a score of local outrages. In January 1969 it had ignited finally as a nationwide issue: an offshore oil well had punctured an underwater pool of oil off the coast of California. Nightly, television showed filth smearing the waterfront of Santa Barbara, beautiful blue-black grebes dying with feathers gummed by the ooze of crude petroleum, a community defiled by technical irresponsibility and indifference.

Through 1969 the legions of the concerned had grown, and the Academic-Media complex fed that concern. By year-end, as television networks made pollution Theme Number One, as the year-end issues of the great periodicals—*Time, Life, Look, Newsweek, Fortune*—made environment the signal stories of their covers, the issue had reached the status of a holy cause. Senators and congressmen, governors and legislators, clubwomen and industrialists, students and fishermen, young and old raised their chorus as in crusade. Just as national defense had been the sacred issue of the 1950s and education the sacred issue of the 1960s, so environment promised to be the sacred issue of the 1970s.

One should pause to separate the reality of the environment issue from its politics.

What was happening in the world of reality was becoming clear in 1970—the fountains of postwar abundance and technology were disgorging along with their conveniences such impossibly large burdens of waste that the two ancient containers of man's life on earth, the air and the water, could no longer absorb them. And by 1970 most concerned students of the subject had arrived at understanding solid enough to know that the problems could be divided into two sharp families of aggravation. One was scientific, the other aesthetic, and both probably required government action of a scope and intrusion into daily lives not attempted since the days of the New Deal.

Scientifically, the chief polluting parameter could be traced back to man's hunger for more energy. Man has been an energy-consuming animal since the first peasant yoked the first ox to a plow and used ox energy to turn earth. But all energy—except for water power—results from a combustion of fuel, whether the fuel is grain that animals eat (which leaves manure behind), or nuclear fissile particles (which leave radiation and thermal pollution behind), or coal (which leaves soot behind), or petroleum (which leaves unburned hydrocarbons and sulfur compounds behind). All consumption of fuel for energy leaves behind a waste product to pollute man's life. This condition is worldwide, as true in Germany and Japan as in the U.S.; but, since Americans' appetite for energy is greater than that of any other society, Americans found themselves overwhelmed by the residues of their giant appetite.

Two forms of energy consumption were the chief contributors to the scientific problem. The first was energy consumption in the family auto at the touch of the gas pedal. From 31 million automobiles registered in the U.S. in 1945, the figure had grown to over 104 million registrations in 1970. Moreover, such automobiles, with higher-compression engines, higher-acceleration capacity, higher use, burned four times as much gasoline. Behind them they left the acrid-ochre shawls of gray-green-greasy smog that smudged the skies of New York, Los Angeles, Phoenix, Chicago, and Boston. The second expression of energy-appetite—for electric energy at the switch—had exploded even more spectacularly. By 1969 the U.S. was consuming 1,552 billion kilowatt hours of electricity, or 5.7 times as much as the 271 billion kilowatt hours in 1945. Whether it was oil or coal the power plants burned, they vomited filth into the air. In the single city of New York, an estimated 3,090,000 tons of sulfur, nitrate, and carbon compounds fell in 1970 over rich and poor, tenement blocks and penthouse gardens alike; of this total, power plants generated 525,000 tons. Scientifically, the problem suggested no easy escape from pollution until man harnessed the energy of the sun; the problem could be solved only by political decision on how much more Americans must pay for clean air if power producers were forced to police their pollutants.

Aesthetically, the problem pollution posed to politics was even more difficult. It rose from man's self-indulgence as a comfort-loving consumer. Americans wanted green lawns, mosquito-free evenings by the beach, easily disposable containers, attractive packages, snowmobiles, power boats. For two decades, U.S. technology had moved to satisfy this appetite, with spray cans that fizzed DDT or Chlordane, or detergents or shaving cream; with nonbiodegradable plastic containers; with packages and wrappings that became mountains of urban refuse. By 1970, urban centers and surrounding suburban belts weltered in the filth of their appetites. Eyes, ears, noses of Americans were insulted daily, as nature was defiled and nature's healing powers were overwhelmed.

Americans, like gorillas who defecate in their own nests until the nests are unbearable and then move on, were defecating in their own habitat—and trying to move on. Except that there was nowhere to move to. U.S. prosperity had given Americans unprecedented leisure time. By 1970, it was estimated, the average workingman had 140 days off work each year and most tried to "get away from it all," on vacations and weekends. Except that "it" followed them. Rivers and bays smelled, noise roared in once quiet sylvan retreats, junkyards lined great highways, bulldozers ripped open the sanctuaries of nature.

A Plan for Pollution Control. All this had been happening for years, but in 1970 national recognition reached the level of political consciousness. The protection of their environment had seized the imagination of all Americans in a rare moment of national political unanimity. And so, when Mr. Nixon moved in late summer to offer both strategy and mechanism for attacking the problem in one of the major achievements of his administration, the nation accepted his actions without either a murmur of dissent or a round of applause. Paradoxically, what the literate public had been demanding loudest—a decisive reorganization of government mechanisms for protecting America from Americans —was accepted almost without notice.

Specifically, by the end of the year, the federal government had reorganized the tangle of conflicting, overlapping, incomprehensible bureaucracies that dealt with environment into three major bodies. A master agency, called the Environmental Protection Agency (EPA), clustered all controls of air, water, pesticides, solid wastes, and radiation hazards into one national policing body that would—so its charter ran—have authority over all states, industries, and municipalities in controlling pollution. Another agency—the Council on Environmental Quality—would supervise the federal government itself; all projects, plans, proposals that might affect American environment would pass under its scrutiny; and its three members would advise the president on the perspectives that lay before the country for the next quarter century. These two agencies would, so the theory ran, control U.S. industrial effluvia within the thin membrane of air and moisture that holds the nation's activity on the earth's surface. The third agency was called NOAA—the National Oceanic and Atmospheric Agency. It would be a superior scientific agency, clustering half a dozen hitherto separate bureaus in one overall body with jurisdiction over ocean depths and upper atmosphere, along with all the creatures that live in them. This agency would be scientific in essence, its mission to explore how badly the outer envelope of air and water had already been poisoned; what could be done to sanitize it; to learn what resources man could, in the future, extract from the depths and the air; and how, eventually, man might control or modify the interaction of global energies that shape the weather.

On paper, at the end of the year, the U.S. for the first time had a master plan for control of its environment. Whether this master plan would work, whether the new agencies would develop a vitality, a constituency, a congressional base of their own, no one could tell. All depended on the education of the American people in the dangers of their living habits—and on the effective pressure they could put on Congress and executive to appropriate the money the new agencies needed to make control of man's environment more than a dream.

Government at Work. The reorganization of America's environmental-control machinery was one of those rare achievements which a historian could note as a solid departure point.

But U.S. politics in 1970 provided few other such solid points of achievement. After environment, the administration's largest domestic achievement was perhaps its slow progress in liquidating the draft. In 1969 the president had limited draft call-up to 19-year-olds and made their choice a lottery. In 1970, as its operation was transferred from 76-year-old Gen. Lewis B. Hershey to 45-year-old Curtis W. Tarr, the draft was, for the first time in 20 years, beginning to make sense; and millions of young Americans found themselves released from the haphazard threat of conscription and death. By year-end it was clear that, if all went well in Vietnam, in a few years the draft would be abolished entirely. The postal strike, too, had left behind a landmark of legislation. The ancient, inefficient, politics-ridden system of postal delivery descended from Benjamin Franklin was to be abolished—the postmaster general to be removed from the Cabinet, and the nation's mails to be transferred by August 1971 to an independent corporation called the U.S. Postal Service.

Political partisans could rattle off other lists of achievements— or shortfalls—of the federal government. But for a historian the indecisive quality of the year could best be recaptured by noting the continuing unresolved debates that preoccupied the ever-

Ruins of a townhouse on New York City's W. 11th Street after the explosion that killed three members of the radical Weatherman group who had been using the premises for a bomb factory.

RICHARD BALAGUR FROM NANCY PALMER AGENCY

lasting struggle between hostile Congress and weakened president. The nature of the Supreme Court was one such continuing debate —Senate and president deadlocked as he sought to restrict the court's dynamics of moral intervention and appoint individuals who, he asserted, would bring it back to the older tradition of strict construction of the Constitution. The long debate over how Americans should elect their president—whether by mass plebiscite or some revision of the electoral college system to retain the states as voting communities—resulted in no action. The president's most far-reaching domestic proposal—that the federal government establish a new welfare system that guaranteed a minimal annual income to all Americans, white or black, North or South, working or nonworking—faced a long series of congressional roadblocks. The debate over school integration ebbed to its lowest intensity in years. Legally and technically, in 1970, the separate school systems for black and white in the Southern states were virtually abolished—16 years after the Supreme Court's order for "deliberate speed." But the more complex and explosive question of how, practically, in such unified school systems, one distributed black and white children through classrooms remained unresolved—in the rural South and on the inner frontiers of Northern cities. Passionately, Senate and House debated national defense, focusing their arguments on the newest lethal instruments of holocaust, the ABM and the MIRV systems; but no new agreed-on defense posture emerged. In September, the McGovern-Hatfield restriction on presidential powers was defeated 55 to 39. As an obligato, one noticed faint sounds of a new isolationism in Congress—and a debate whether, for the first time in 25 years, the U.S. would restrict world trade by closing threatened domestic markets to foreign competition.

Curiously, however, none of these ongoing debates of hard substance could compare, in public concern, with the murky, unshaped issue that came to dominate the forum of conventional politics by the autumn season of elections.

This was the issue crudely defined as Law and Order. In the bizarre political confrontation over this issue, one could scarcely separate the participants into players and bystanders, certainly not into Republicans and Democrats. Nor did the words "repression," "permissiveness," "campus rioters," "crime in the streets," "pornography" give a more precise sense of what the issue was all about. Americans were becoming more and more afraid of each other, torn further and further apart in their view of what government should, or should not, do either to expand their freedoms or to protect their children and safety. The common culture

on which their politics rested seemed to be crumbling. Political leaders of both parties groped trying to make the issue clear.

THE CLASH OF CULTURES

One has to begin the discussion of this new issue with the fact of violence—not the ineradicable animal violence of thuggery, abnormality, industrial conflict, and crime, but a new kind of political violence: In 1970, for the first time, the skein of traditional American politics was ripped by the first activity of a true, terrorist revolutionary movement.

Encapsulated in dogma and wild rhetoric, isolated even on the extreme left, the members of this revolutionary movement might number a few hundred or a few thousand. No one knew for sure. Nor could anyone trace the fissures and cleavages between its feuding sectarians. One tightly organized element was, clearly, the Black Panthers; the other, more violent, element was clearly white youths, organized in underground collectives of various nomenclature, of whom the most paranoid were those joined in the sect called Weatherman. No cohesive doctrine bound these terrorists together; and the Weatherman group spurned both black revolutionaries and white working-class masses alike, believing that simple chaos would usher in their opportunity for making a perfect new brotherhood of the American people. What was startling about the new revolutionaries, however, was their power to kill and terrify. Never before had U.S. politics known groups so ready, in their fanatic cruelty, to maim and injure innocents, to perpetrate wanton murder, arson, and brutalities, all absolved by the bleak morality of programless nihilism.

It was on March 6 that the full nature of terrorist activity burst on national attention. On that day in New York, a quiet brownstone house on sedate and fashionable W. 11th St. exploded —and its neighbors learned that a crude but effective bomb-making factory had been operating in their midst. Three dead bodies were found in the ruins, and two young women fled. It was the nature of the bomb makers that perplexed. Violence by Black Panthers could be understood—the grief and depersonalization of blacks in America had created a fringe of catatonic hate that, though frightening, was understandable. But the Weatherman bomb makers of W. 11th St. were college students, well bred, well nursed, swaddled by middle-class comfort and conventions; and they had been preparing to sacrifice human lives. Nor were they alone—it was clear that the most desperate white militants were young people of such background. They had repudiated American civilization, and they were on the move.

Senators Walter Mondale (left) and Birch Bayh inspect a dormitory at Jackson (Miss.) State College where two youths were killed when police opened fire on a group of demonstrators.

UPI COMPIX

The week after the 11th St. explosion, threats caused evacuation, on the single day of March 13, of no less than 15,000 people from their places of work in Manhattan; two weeks later two more people were blown up at a bomb-making factory in lower Manhattan. By December the nationwide count of the FBI read: 3,000 bombings during the year, 50,000 threatened bombings causing search or evacuation of buildings.

On August 7, black militants invaded a courtroom in San Rafael, Calif., and seized Superior Court Judge Harold J. Haley at gunpoint. In the fracas of their escape, the judge as well as three others were killed, and three more people (including two court officials) were wounded. Terror cut another notch on public opinion less than three weeks later when a research associate of the University of Wisconsin was killed in the bombing of the university's mathematics research center in Madison—and no phrase of remorse came from those who had done the deed.

It was true, of course, that dozens of centers of industry and communications were bombed during the year. It was true, further, that terror was an international disease, for the dynamics of irrationality in 1970 took on an epidemic cast. From South America to Canada, from the U.S.S.R. to the Middle East, kidnappings and murders, airplane hijackings and the violence of zealots pocked the record as fanatics found the blood of innocents the best material with which to stencil their causes on broad general opinion. Yet in the U.S. terrorism came, somehow, to be associated with a new generation of youth, and the universities that taught them. From California to Boston, the action seemed to center on campus. In Boston, cradle of America's greatest university, Harvard, the action began in spring with the burning of one university building to the ground in May, and climaxed with a bomb, placed in the desk of an army colonel, in October. In California, it was alleged that a University of California assistant professor, Angela Davis, had bought guns with which Judge Haley had been kidnapped by black militants.

The Growing Drug Menace. Such a wave of senseless violence had never before been known in America. In the popular mind, however, it was webbed inextricably with another youth phenomenon of 1970—the rise to central attention of a menacing national epidemic, euphemistically called the "drug culture."

No set of figures could adequately measure either the menace or the movement of narcotic infection through American life and civilization. Indeed, most figures contradicted each other. Some figures held that of New York's population either 25,000 or 50,000 or 100,000 were confirmed hard-drug addicts. In October 1969, the National Institute of Mental Health estimated that 5 million Americans had used or experimented with marihuana, the introductory drug of youngsters; in March 1970 that figure was raised to 8 million people; in June the estimate was raised again to 20 million. In June, the Army released figures of its investigation of drug use by troops; the figures could be interpreted as showing a rise in drug sampling from 1.2% of all troops in 1969 to 2.4% in 1970. Other guesses and estimates quickly followed. By August, new data could be read to indicate that perhaps three out of ten soldiers had been sampling marihuana and hard drugs; by November, another frightening survey of a cross section of soldiers at Fort Bragg, N.C., purportedly showed six out of ten sampling drugs.

The truth was that no official agency knew how widespread was drug use in the U.S., or how rapidly the scourge was progressing. Drugs were an element in a culture that at every opportunity urged Americans to escape. Television advertising had popularized a score of pill-popping escape avenues—from the sleeping pill that seduced one to sleep, to the headache pill that soothed away the migraine. Increasingly, Americans of every class and race were popping pills that promised release from reality; drugs were only the morbid extremity of the escape spectrum; and though no one could be precise about the drug culture, the impact on popular thinking was profound.

The story began with the use of marihuana ("pot" in common language, or *Cannabis sativa* in scientific terminology), a medic-

BURK UZZLE FROM MAGNUM

Mourner at the funeral of a student slain at Kent State University holds a poster with a picture taken on the campus just moments after National Guard troops stopped shooting.

inal herb, native to India, which by the 19th century had become a common comfort in Mexico and Cuba. For decades, the smoking of pot had been used as a stimulant among ghetto Americans of the South and the Mexican border before being outlawed by Congress in the 1930s. By the early 1960s, despite the ban, marihuana had penetrated the life of middle-class U.S., particularly into the culture of youth and college students. Marihuana—a form of escape that, its users insist, is no worse than alcohol—led millions on, however, to hard drugs, addictives and hallucinogens. By 1970 the U.S. had become the world's greatest market for such hard addictives, and the world's drug trade filtered heroin, morphine, and cocaine through its ports in greater quantity than any known since the East India Co. had poisoned China with Persian and Indian opium. The results could be read in death. In New York City, for example, with the best municipal statistics in the country, it was clear: Deaths from heroin had risen in the ten years to 1970 from approximately 199 in 1960 to approximately 1,100 in 1970; and, among teen-agers (from 1964 to 1969) from only 39 to about 225.

It was the vulnerability of the very young to the drug epidemic that amplified the alarm. True enough, drugs incubated crime in the streets as addicts snatched purses, mugged, robbed, and stole to support their habit. This, somehow, the general society accepted as part of the general climate of violence in the U.S. But it was the ravage of the drug culture, as it worked its way down the age scale to infect high school and even grammar school children, that cut at the hearts of parents of every class.

Neither science nor legislation held out much hope. Although in October Congress passed, and the president signed, the harshest drug-control bill of U.S. history—a bill that permitted narcotics agents to violate any home under a disturbing special "no-knock" provision for search and seizure—few believed that laws alone would solve the problem. At the dark frontier of the menace, debate raged: Was addiction to hard drugs (as distinct from moderate stimulants like marihuana) a disease as incurable as cancer? Amenable only to such draconian measures as those that guard cattle from foot-and-mouth disease? If the U.S. really did want to cope with the drug epidemic, would the hard-hooked

BURT GLINN FROM MAGNUM

Members of labor and veterans' organizations express
support of Pres. Richard M. Nixon's policies.
In a number of instances pro- and antiadministration
groups clashed in the streets.

CATHERINE URSILLO FROM NANCY PALMER AGENCY

addicts and pushers of hard drugs have to be isolated from
society, as are human bearers of typhoid, or animal bearers of
foot-and-mouth disease? At whatever cost to traditional liberties?

Pornography Becomes an Issue. Oddly joined to the grave
issues of terror and drugs was the third in the trinity of matters
that seemed most to bother Americans of traditional culture—
the frivolous issue of pornography. In 1967 Congress had authorized then-Pres. Lyndon Johnson to choose a Commission on
Obscenity and Pornography. In September 1970, the commission
reported not to Lyndon Johnson but to his successor, Mr. Nixon,
and made the matter a subject of public debate.

The details of the October debate on the pornography report,
and Mr. Nixon's repudiation of that document, are of little moment. More important is that certain American cities, namely
San Francisco, New York, and Los Angeles, had become centers
for traffic in films, pictures, books, and demonstrations describing
or portraying the arts of intercourse. Millions of Americans felt
that the instruction of their children in the ways of love was their
private right—and not to be invaded by either profit makers or
government instruction.

Yet the commission, as its major recommendation, urged that
the federal government begin a "massive sex education effort."
"Its purpose," said the majority of the commission, "should be to
contribute to healthy attitudes and orientations to sexual relationships so as to provide a sound foundation for our society's basic
institution of marriage and family." With vehement protests
from a minority of the commission, the majority report discussed
whether "these materials (pornography) also appear to serve to
increase and facilitate constructive communication about sexual
matters within marriage." The constitutional injunctions of freedom, and the Declaration's faith in "the pursuit of happiness,"
never had conceived that liberties of such privacy and intimacy
would become matters of national politics; yet in 1970, the national government was urged to a decisive stand.

Thus, grotesquely, on the peripheral issue of pornography the
strange new philosophical debate was most tightly focused. What
is the role of government in modern society? What is the relationship of the individual to that government? What restraints is government empowered to put on the private liberties of individuals
to preserve the tranquillity and privacy of other individuals from
disruption? Street violence, riot, demonstrations, drug use, pornography all raised the same question—could laws succeed in
binding men and women to a common code of behavior, when
the ethics and culture that had hitherto bound them in familiar
patterns was torn as never before?

An afterglance at earlier history was necessary to understand
the unworded premises of this new debate. For almost two cen-

turies Americans had prided themselves on being freest of all
peoples to come and go, worship and congregate, think and speak,
vote and choose, build and pollute without interference from
government authority.

But that freedom of the individual had rested on the stern code
of individual self-restraint that the Protestant dissenters had
brought with them from England when the new nation was
aborning. America had flourished for three centuries under what
may be called the "Emersonian" code, a code in which the key
words "duty," "self-restraint," "loyalty," "work," "good citizenship" needed no explanation, and covered all behavior from lowly
family pieties to the higher patriotism. This older code of U.S.
culture still prevailed in 1970 in small towns throughout the nation, in the Midwest, in the Allegheny belt and the Rocky
Mountain states. But though it still prevailed in such areas, it
nursed a growing sense of outrage at the New Culture that had
begun to flourish in the decade of the 1960s in the East Coast
cities, in Los Angeles and San Francisco, and in the Academic-
Media Complex.

Values of the New Culture. The New Culture had been born
of the exuberance of energy in the U.S. that emerged triumphant
after World War II. Riding the surge of in-rolling wealth, American scholars, artists, and leaders were free, with excess energy
and resources, to experiment at every level of life. By 1970, the
U.S. flashed with the colors and costuming that the New Culture
had brought to art and style. U.S. architecture and design were
marvels of the world, whether in the grace of new suburban
houses of worship or the dazzle of window walls in the towers
of congested metropoles. With expanding freedom to explore, the
U.S. had become the world's center of art, of drama, of music,
of science.

The essence of the New Culture was, however, self-expression
not self-restraint, the right of the individual to set up his own
values, whether or not government or society approved. Pagan
and statist values seemed inexplicably mixed in the New Culture.
On the one hand it demanded totally free pursuit of individual
happiness; on the other hand it insisted that government expand
its activities by a quantum jump where conscience insisted on a
rectification of social grievances.

The first rumblings against the New Culture, when voiced by
Barry Goldwater in 1964, had seemed manic in their intensity.
By 1970, as politicians of both parties modernized Goldwater's
social ululations, the resistance of the old to the new had become
what demographers Richard M. Scammon and Ben J. Wattenberg
called "The Social Issue," recognized as one of the main themes
of the fall political campaign.

Difficult as it is to summarize the record of the contending cultures, one must nonetheless attempt to draw the balance sheet of 1970 as the one side warned of "repression" and the other side of "revolution." And, in so doing, there could be no doubt of the direction of flow of life in the U.S.

In New York State, center of the New Culture, the state legislature approved the U.S.'s first civilized legislation on abortion, making a woman's personal choice the determinant of whether a new child be brought into the world. In Mississippi, the first legal mixed marriage between races was openly registered. Congress authorized overwhelmingly and the president approved the expenditure of $267 million to coordinate national birth-control planning. The austere U.S. Navy formally declared its sailors free to wear beards, dress as they chose off duty, drink beer aboard ship; the Army formally abolished for its troops the bugle's morning call to reveille. Congress passed a national voting rights act, lowering the age of voters in federal elections to 18. Spokeswomen of the Women's Liberation movement seized attention everywhere. From coast to coast, the Gay Liberation Front openly paraded, demanding in public that homosexuals' individual way of life be respected by all and freed of legal persecution. Venereal disease rates rose to a 25-year high.

The ferment of change invaded even the Roman Catholic Church: some priests openly questioned the rules of celibacy. In California 315 nuns left the church en bloc to seek God's work in their own way; the familiar Douai Bible was replaced with a new translation; and the National Council of Catholic Bishops altered its sanctions for Catholics marrying men or women of other faiths.

The mainstream of U.S. culture continued to record its accustomed triumphs. Neglected in the U.S. penchant for self-flagellation and alarm, such victories accepted as commonplace were nonetheless to be remembered. In 1970 came the report that, for the first time in history, there had not been a single recorded American death from polio the year before; the National Institute of Dental Health forecast that by the end of the decade, new techniques would all but end tooth decay. For the first time since aviation accident records began in 1938, not a single airline passenger lost his life in a regularly scheduled domestic flight. What had been a dream of U.S. agronomists only ten years before was now a reality—"miracle rice" and·"miracle wheat" were stimulating a Green Revolution in the peasant Asia of hunger. For leadership in this work, American Norman E. Borlaug was awarded the Nobel Peace Prize. And U.S. laboratories promised another revolution as cassette and tape devices suggested that, in another decade, home visuals of movies, drama, orchestra, or television recordings might become as familiar as books.

These forces of culture, provocative and resistant, played over a nation of healthy biological growth and rhythm of expansion. The data of the census of 1970 were still too raw to permit complete interpretation. The census said that the country had grown from 179 million in population in 1960 to a final count of 204,-765,770 on November 30. For generations, however, the census had recognized three geographic groupings of U.S. population—rural people, city people, and suburbanites. Gradually, ever since the war, the proportion of suburban Americans to the whole had grown, and grown again. Preliminary census figures showed that Americans who lived in suburbs were now, finally, the largest single bloc of the U.S. population—their number had grown 25% between 1960 and 1970 to a 74.9 million total, surpassing, for the first time, both city Americans (62.2 million) and rural Americans (63.2 million). Suburbs are inhabited, generally, by middle-class citizens who wish to escape the grind of very rich against very poor in the big cities, yet are unwilling to live away from the excitement and leadership opportunities those big cities alone provide. It was in the suburbs, the fastest-growing family of communities, that the Clash of Cultures, the ferment of values cut most sharply.

How to govern such ferment and energy, how to make of such a Clash of Cultures an epochal reexamination of human values, might at any time have challenged the wisest community of men in history. Yet, by late fall, when the U.S., already weary of war and disturbed by its children, turned to face the matter of its culture as formulated by Spiro T. Agnew in the phrase "law and order" and by the Democrats as "the social issue," another more homely concern had intervened:

If the banner of the New Culture might have been anachronistically worded, "Man Cannot Live by Bread Alone," by the end of the year millions of ordinary Americans recognized that the pursuit of bread is, nonetheless, still essential. By fall, such millions were wondering where their bread would come from— for the U.S. economy was undergoing its sharpest, most baffling fallaway since World War II.

THE ECONOMY: A GRIM RECESSION

Economists are scholars who offer as a science their efforts to translate men's work, greed, and product into graphs and figures. Theoretically, they offer models of past human behavior that scientifically forecast future human behavior. Wise governments seek from economists guidance in offering lures or imposing restraints by which they try to force their economies to adjustments politically necessary. This science, or art, of economics is generally considered to have reached its highest mastery in the U.S.—and, indeed, in 1970, was so recognized when a Nobel Prize was awarded to economist Paul Samuelson.

Yet the arts, or sciences, of the economists could only describe what was happening to the U.S. economy in 1970—they could not explain it. Two sets of figures spanned their dilemma. By the end of the year 6% of job-seeking Americans were unemployed —roughly 4.6 million persons, or more than had been out of work in nine years. At the same time, the devastating inflation of previous years continued but little abated—in 1970, the U.S. dollar lost roughly 6% of its value; and dollars saved in bonds, and at banks, were worth only 65% of their purchasing power a decade before. Generally, in times of inflation, overemployment and overtime pay ease the pain of rising prices for the masses of working people. The recession of 1970 was, however, almost unique in the contradictory phenomenon of simultaneously *rising* unemployment and *rising* prices.

The story of the year's business traced once again the familiar pattern of old ideas failing to grip new reality. The economic year had begun grimly. The administration, pursuing the best wisdom of the community of economists, continued in the analysis that had set inflation as the most serious domestic threat to economic good health. On February 2, Mr. Nixon had presented his first budget to the nation. The president had recognized—and all economists, right, left, and center, agreed with him—that the chief thrust behind the inflationary surge of the previous five years had been the Vietnam war: the huge expenditures on defense and space; and the unwillingness of the Johnson administration to face up to the costs of these national exertions with taxes. Balancing foreign and domestic needs, Mr. Nixon therefore offered the nation in February a budget of $200.8 billion, which cut defense and space appropriations by $6 billion and transferred almost that much money to social welfare programs at home. A balanced budget is one of the standard recommendations of economists in inflationary situations, but the administration moved yet further in the path of classic economics as it sought to stem inflation. Tightening the mechanisms of credit, the government sought to choke pressure of domestic demand from consumers and industry by throttling the flow of easy money and credit to the economy. By spring, the government itself was paying 8% on its own short-term notes (the highest rates since the Civil War) and U.S. industries were paying 9, 10, or 11% on long-term borrowing.

One could judge the results of administration policy in any number of ways. Traditionally, the collective judgment of investors is reflected in the stock market, where the commonest measure of reaction and anticipation is the hallowed Dow-Jones

UPI COMPIX

Junior high school students in a St. Louis suburb demonstrate against smog caused by automobiles. The environment issue was one of the few that united a large majority of Americans in 1970.

average of 30 major industrial stocks. That average had reached a peak of 985.21 in December 1968—a near all-time high. It had sagged steadily through the first year of the Nixon administration, dipping to 809 at the beginning of 1970. It held rather steadily at that figure until spring and then, declining continuously, hit the bleak month of May when, in 20 days of trading, it lost 105 points to hit an average of 631.16, an eight-year low. No less than $250 billion of paper value had been wiped out since the peak of 1968. The crash of May reflected in part the nation's fear that the Cambodian expedition might result in a greatly enlarged war; when that near-panic reaction passed, the stock market gradually recovered to an index of approximately 750, where it hovered uncertainly for the rest of the year until, rising in a burst of exuberance in December, it soared to a close of 838.92.

A Mood of Uncertainty. Yet the traditional index scarcely reflected the tone and mood of those who direct U.S. industry and finance. That tone was one of baffled uncertainty, jolted at each turn of heralded recovery by some new event or development. It was not simply that industrial production had, by November, fallen to its lowest level since late 1967. It was that the pillars of the financial establishment themselves were being shaken. In June the Penn Central Railroad, largest in the nation, was forced into receivership; the shock rippled through the community. In summer, Lockheed Aircraft Corp., largest defense contractor in the nation, found itself on the edge of insolvency. Great airlines and new conglomerates alike were rumored on the edge of bankruptcy. In September the president of the American Association of Stock Exchange Firms predicted that 50 brokerage firms would disappear in the next six months; the financial industry found itself, too, being forced to the wall. And though the government, from midsummer on, began steadily to increase the nation's money supply, to ease the liquidity crisis, no great turnaround in production could be detected, and none in consumer buying or unemployment. Only the stock market's sudden December surge indicated a quick response to the administration's efforts.

Warily, the predominant opinion of the financial community held that the slack and recession of 1970 were transitory and, as so often before, if not in 1971, then in 1972, or 1973, the boom would resume and the bulls would frolic once more.

Gloomily, a tiny minority of pessimists questioned this prevailing thought: had the "mystique of investment" been ruptured? U.S. business, said pessimists, had always unknowingly operated from under the guns of a fortress—a U.S. government

that understood modern business and whose economic thinking fostered investment. The U.S. had become the mecca of world capital, the haven of timid investors around the world whose savings seemed safer when transferred to the custody of U.S. finance than invested under their own unpredictable governments. If the U.S. government did not know how to shelter investors and capital against inflation and disruption, where else in the world could investors go?

Thus the investment climate at the end of 1970—a heavy year-end influx of savings into the market from U.S. institutions, but a cautious wait-and-see attitude on the part of world finance, hitherto a buttress of rising bull markets.

The Working People. For ordinary people, workingmen and women and their families, such long-range thinking was metaphysics. In 1970 more such ordinary people were hurting than in many years.

The first of their hurts was unemployment. Unemployment is one of the folk perils of industrial society. The psychic scar of the depression of the 1930s, when one-third of all Americans were unemployed, as transmitted by daddy-stories, had made unemployment, second only to war, the chief manipulator of the U.S. mood. Unemployment in the U.S. had begun in 1970 at a rate of 3.5% (2.5 million unemployed). It had risen steadily to a December rate of 6%. Much of the unemployment was due to the federal cut of $6 billion in defense and space expenditures. The million Americans left unemployed by that inexorable decision were joined by the hundreds of thousands of construction workers left jobless by the slump in the housing industry, to which in summer and fall were added unemployed, direct and indirect, made idle by the General Motors strike—perhaps another half-million; to which were added several million made surplus by the general slump. Statistically, those hurt most by the general rollback in jobs were, of course, the most vulnerable—women (1,557,000 unemployed), teen-agers (1,235,000), and blacks (788,000). Most vocal, however, were upper-level executives and white-collar workers and, particularly, the troop of recent graduates of universities who had expected greeting, salaries, and expanding careers from industry immediately on graduation.

If unemployment was the shaft of hurt to directly affected families, it was not what perplexed the economic scientists most. Unemployment can be cured almost anywhere by modern economic techniques—either by government-induced production or by the subtler, corrosive means of inflation. Yet inflation, if the government chose to go that course, was eventually crueler to ordinary people. Already inflation was a far greater curse to the majority of common people than unemployment was to the minority of those left jobless. Month by month, as the government tried to grip the problem, inflation continued—at an average annual rate of approximately 6%. Yet it was not just the single year that weighed on private hopes. It was the continuous, persistent rise in cost of living and erosion of commercial values over the previous five years that unsettled Americans trying to plan their lives in dollar figures.

Inflation is the subtle thief of economic values, the hidden tax that injures the weakest most, the ultimate denial of thrift and savings, of sober investment. In inflation, the spender, not the saver, is the wise man; the speculator, not the builder, the one who succeeds most. Inflation eats away at the honor and integrity of civil servants, expected to remain decent and judicial as they try, on shrinking salaries, to match the standards of the vulgar who get rich. Inflation eats away at the responsibility of trade unions, whose organized power leads them to protect their members against the menace by extortionate demands of overcompensation. In periods of inflation, the most miserable victims are always the unorganized and the weak—the aged living on savings that melt in value yearly, widows on government pension reduced to penury, the poor dependent on welfare and Social Security. These in the U.S., as everywhere, were the chief victims of inflation. Yet by 1970 inflation was a creeping, corrosive threat to the life-style of the middle class too. The extermination of the middle class by inflation in Weimar Germany and Nationalist China was the prelude to political disaster in both those countries. In the U.S., the threat to the middle class was nowhere remotely as serious—yet the menace was there. It was there in the prices posted in the supermarket; in the rising lust of middle-class families for country real estate; in their slow acceptance that their children could no longer be educated at private colleges out of earnings but must, like the children of the poor, be educated by dipping into savings or borrowing against the future.

Seen from a larger perspective, the peculiar *nature* of the U.S. inflation was as noteworthy as its persistence. Most economists clung to orthodox analysis—that the root cause of inflation was U.S. exertion in Vietnam. But at the outer fringe of speculation simmered the thought that this explanation was inadequate—and that the new inflation reflected a new society. Old societies had dealt in the economy of goods, of materials, of production distributed over markets. Classically, one could cure inflation in such a society either by tightening money or increasing supply to meet demand—more wheat, more bread, more houses, more steel, paper, or copper brought prices of such things down. But the new economy, resting on productivity, had made hard products less and less important in the budget of everyday living. Services were more important. Slowly, the ratio of expenditure-on-goods to expenditure-on-services in the U.S. economy had shrunk. And the most intractable component in the rise in cost of living of 1960–70 was the rise in cost of services. Where prices of goods had risen, for the average family, by 27.7% in 13 years, prices of services had risen by 58.5%. Not only the plumber's charge, the taxi fare, the barber's tab, and the doctor's bill were rising but middle-class Americans now used a score of professional personal services once reserved for the very rich. They used psychiatrists and beauticians, lawyers, accountants, tax-advisers. They voraciously demanded services at vacation places. Above all, they demanded more services from the state—in sanitation, in schooling, in policing, in child care.

Long-Range Problems Appear. Were the battle against inflation as simple as it had been at other times when quantity controlled the price of bread, shirts, or carriages, U.S. thinking and the Nixon administration might easily have mastered the matter. But the essence of the Nixon administration was not innovation but the orderly, housekeeping quality of mind of its leader. This mind and leadership had rung up large credit in the fields of environment and draft management, even larger credit in foreign affairs. Its greatest shortfall lay in management of the economy; it had accepted the best conventional ideas; they had not worked; and the administration lacked fresh ideas of its own—as did the academic critics who pounced on its shortcomings.

Of the same order of magnitude as the conundrum of inflation in the economics of 1970 was the perplexing change in the relation of the U.S. economy to the outer world. From the Marshall Plan on, it had been the good-willed assumption of the U.S. that its economic strength was so great no other nation could threaten it. From this assumption, the U.S. for 25 years had encouraged other nations in the Western orbit to share its markets and raw materials; faith held that free trade was in the best interests of the strongest trading nation in the world, the U.S.

This old assumption rubbed against contradictory reality in 1970. U.S. industry realized that whether it was in electronics or playshoes, supersonic aircraft or textiles, its domestic market, and thus U.S. wage scales, were under threat not only of traditionally underpaid foreign workers but of rival and brilliant technologies abroad. Though U.S. foreign trade registered the healthiest surplus in four years in June (an excess of exports over imports estimated at $3 billion), the surplus rested heavily on raw materials such as coal, grains, farm products, and return on previous investment; and was well below the $5 billion annually needed to sustain the nation's international commitments. At home, the pinch on such domestic industries as television, shoes, and clothing was so great that for the first time since the war protectionists found champions in Congress—and Congress spent its last month,

WIDE WORLD

Long lines of unemployed jam the State Employment Security Department office in Seattle, Wash., a city particularly hard hit by large cutbacks in aerospace and defense spending.

December, considering whether it would, selectively but decisively, close the U.S.'s open market to all comers. Similarly, the authority and flexibility of U.S. capital around the globe found growing restrictions from other systems of politics. Raw material producers from Chile to the oil-laden Middle Eastern principalities prepared to curb U.S. access to their resources—and Western European industrial states continued to consider restriction of U.S. industrial enterprise within their borders.

Such new facts, as always, were records of problems and challenges. But a historian, surveying the sweep and busyness of U.S. productive life, would have to record that an old fact still outweighed all the new: Despite the recession of 1970, Americans lived on a plateau of well-being no other nation could match. One in 11 homes now had a swimming pool; four out of five homes had cars; of these, one in every three had two or more cars; four out of five homes boasted television; and one of three had color television. Despite rising tuition costs, more Americans sent children to college than ever before; despite fiscal crisis, U.S. airlines introduced to service Boeing's 747, the new airbus; and U.S. ingenuity flooded marts with every sort of new gadget from magic plastics to trash compactors.

Thus, summarizing: the rhythm of U.S. expansion had sharply broken in 1970; whether it was a break in expectations or a break in the system, no one could yet say; millions were unemployed, but few hungered; the economic year had begun with uncertainty and ended with uncertainty. And, thus stalemated in direction and perspective at home, it was probably from the outer world that the next impelling thrust to the U.S. economy could be expected.

It is well then to look at this outer world.

THE WORLD SCENE: MIDEAST CONFRONTATION

Nothing tempts the talents of historians more than the flow of international affairs. Great events are carved in collisions of arms, the lives of heroes, the names of treaties signed in gilded halls or wasted ruins. Time itself weeds out from historians' attention the village Cromwells who lie in unmarked graves, Napoleons who rose no higher than garrison commanders, revolutionary riots crushed by local police, visionaries smothered by public indifference. The remaining names, dates, and upheavals give a grand clarity to the forces that have shaped the world.

Yet the world scene, as it offers itself to men who must act in it, does not show that way at all. Each day, from dawn to dusk and around the clock, the great gray brooding hulk of the State

Department building in Washington receives some 400,000 words by cable and radio. No one knows how much of this is read as the bulk of wordage is routed to desks of hundreds of officers who sift it for significance. Perhaps no more than 10 or 15 cables a day require interrupting the routine of the secretary of state; and it is a crisis year if the president must be awakened in his sleep more than four or five times for emergency.

The sorting of this enormous traffic in development and episode is the work of professionals who know that most reportage, in six months, will fade to meaninglessness. And they recognize that even the episodes over which they pause must be divided into those that are simple markers, those that require response, and those that cluster on distant horizons as thrusts of such major dimensions as will some day change the policy of every other nation on earth.

There is no better way of tracing the traffic of nations in 1970 than just this diplomatic exercise of separating the episodes of the year into markers, responses, and historic thrusts.

The Markers of Change. In 1970 the world offered its usual number of attention-catching episodes that were to be noted simply as markers of the passage of time:

• Charles de Gaulle, foremost patriot of France, died. His death marked the close of a 30-year career through which he had stalked as the flamboyant personal custodian of France's pride and nationhood. Though the Gallic glories he championed—whether in arms, or arts, or science, or cuisine—continuously lost luster during the generation he dominated, he left behind, paradoxically, a nation more self-confident than at any time in this century.

Elections around the world brought other markers—chiefly in Britain and in Chile.

• In Britain, upsetting all polling prediction, the Labour government of Harold Wilson was turned out on June 18 and Edward Heath installed by a Conservative margin of 330 to 287 (Labour) in the House of Commons. Traditionally the Conservatives had chosen as their leaders men of land, or industrial ownership, or family heritage, who spoke sometimes for the best, sometimes for the most stubborn in the old squirearchy. Heath, a man of lower middle-class origin and banking background, spoke for the newer elements of the Conservatives, the business and administrative executive class. But his early efforts to cope with the riddle of British industrial and diplomatic stagnation gave no clue to ultimate judgment on his efforts.

• More exciting was the election on September 4 of Salvador Allende Gossens as president of Chile, one of Latin America's most stable democracies. Allende, an avowed Marxist, had ac-

cepted openly the support of the Chilean Communist Party in his campaign to rid Chile of U.S. and other "imperialisms." How much of his campaign was rhetoric and how much program no one could easily tell. But the great nations with interests in Chile seemed prepared to give him large latitude, waiting to see whether responsibility would guide his actions, or revolutionary theory lead him to a position of outright enmity.

• In Canada came another disturbing marker, the kidnapping of two officials and the murder of one (Quebec's minister of labor) by separatist terrorists in the French-speaking province of Quebec. However nationalist the Quebec terrorists might seem in their own eyes, their cruelty could not help but be seen as a spillover from the terror that was infecting the U.S. The Canadian government's response was, however, much stiffer than the American. Its imposition of martial law on the province of Quebec on October 16 was an invocation of such wartime powers as breached all peacetime tradition of civil liberty.

• On September 28, U.A.R. dictator Gamal Abd-al-Nasser died. The 52-year-old Arab leader was the first charismatic leader that Islamic culture had cast on the world scene since the days of Saladin of Egypt eight centuries before. Nasser's death was more than a simple marker; stricken in full career, at the height of the Middle East crisis, he had set in motion a train of events with which the world would have to grapple for decades.

Few other episodes around the globe could be seen as major markers. Over the vast expanse of Latin America, no major initiative, except in Chile, seemed likely to involve the great powers. The doctrine of urban guerrilla warfare seemed most advanced in the cities of Latin America—but its menace was that of an intellectual infection, which might, by contagion, influence or confirm the madness of other idiot fanatics around the world. Military dictators in several Latin-American states seemed to be masquerading the iron rigidity of their rule in a newer more populist rhetoric of "anti-imperialism." But Cuba, seedbed of Latin-American revolution, in its 12th year under Fidel Castro, seemed further than ever from having attained the promised workers' paradise. With the shortfall of Cuba's sugar crop came further tightening of its economy, and rationing was extended even to cigars and cigarettes. At the end of July, Castro drew a bleak picture for his people—"The enemy will say our difficulties are growing and he will be right; the enemy will say we have problems of inefficiency and he will be right; only through the will of the people will our problems be solved."

Black Africa, too, was quiescent, neutralized by the indifference of the great powers. Chinese diplomats prowled through two black states, Zambia and Tanzania, but their efforts seemed less noteworthy than what was being achieved by the black states themselves, blessed momentarily by the benign neglect of great power imperialism. The Congo, Nigeria, Togo, and other significant African states were slowly reestablishing order and progress after years of fratricidal war. They seemed too busy—and successful—in their efforts to draw the attention of any power other than the UN. It was in Africa, especially in the stimulation of its economy by the UN Development Program under Paul Hoffman, that the UN seemed closest to fulfilling the high hopes that had given it birth.

The Response in the Middle East. Most episodes that mark unpredictable major responses are too obscure at their initiation to be noted carefully. They usually happen only in a conjunction of circumstances that have long been incubating violence—as the assassination of Archduke Francis Ferdinand at Sarajevo in 1914, for example, which brought to bursting the thunderheads of the Triple Alliance and the Central Powers.

In 1970, only two such obscure episodes triggered off unpredictable responses by major world powers.

The first, as we have seen, was the palace coup in Cambodia that removed Prince Sihanouk—and eventually enlarged itself into Mr. Nixon's Cambodian invasion, the revolt of U.S. opinion in the spring and summer, and the profound constitutional threat to the president's leadership in the U.S. Senate.

Police disperse a crowd of rioters in downtown Asbury Park, N.J., one of the few U.S. cities that experienced an outbreak of racial violence during the year.

WIDE WORLD

Immeasurably graver, however, were the skirmishes in the Middle East—for there the Soviet Union and the U.S. were arrayed in full force against each other, and came closer to outright confrontation and world devastation than at any time since the missile crisis of 1962.

Two regional forces, Arab nationalism and the Israelite renaissance, had been arrayed in the Middle East since the close of World War II—forces with no formulas of nationhood, little tradition of self-government, scanty experience in diplomacy. The Israelis, an in-gathering of Jewish people to their ancestral home on the tawny hills of Judea, had created out of faith their own new state in the mandated areas of Palestine by 1948. Grown to 2.8 million in number by 1970, the Israeli state faced out on an enemy Arab world of 80 million—a civilization still struggling to define itself in nation-states. Five centuries of imperialism—Turkish, British, French—had robbed the Arab communities of leadership, statesmanship, or experience; and the fragile Arab states left behind by the ebb of imperialism had, in their domestic turbulence, found only a single unifying theme: extermination of the Israeli state in their midst. Among Arabs, seeking national identity to erase memory of the abuse and humiliation of past masters, Israel could easily be described as the last symbol of Western imperialism. Yet the Israelis, whose century-long return to the homeland of the Jews had been so long encouraged by world opinion, now had life, roots, and presence of their own in the Middle East—nor did they propose to unravel the history of that century, or be exterminated as had so many million of their kind in Hitler's Europe.

Three wars between these regional forces in 20 years had punctuated the uneasy Middle East basin. In 1948, when the British mandate ended, the Israelis had established by arms the borders of a Jewish state. In 1956, allied with the British and French, their armor had punched to the Suez Canal—and withdrawn only after an armistice guaranteed by the UN. In 1967, with the repudiation of that guarantee, U.A.R. armor had moved on the Israeli border and the Arab states had mobilized for final kill when again, in a spastic and brilliant response, the Israelis had cleared their military frontiers from the Golan Heights to the Jordan to the Suez Canal, simultaneously defeating Syrians, Jordanians, and Egyptians in the Six-Day War.

None of these earlier wars had taken place in a diplomatic vacuum. The contestants had been armed variously by the arsenals of the U.S.S.R., Czechoslovakia, France, or Britain. Both sides had continuously found the sponsorship of senior powers. By 1970, however, the lesser powers had withdrawn from the game—and it was clearly becoming an arena of confrontation between the superpowers, the U.S.S.R. and the U.S. Israel's only hope of survival—short of using atomic weapons—lay in the diplomatic patronage and arms supply of the U.S. The Arabs' only hope of redemption of conquered territory and ultimate annihilation of Israel lay in the Soviet Union—their chief armorer and diplomatic sponsor.

Imperceptibly, the early months of 1970 changed in quality in the Middle East. The truce and cease-fire that had ended the war of 1967 had been broken as early as 1968. Local U.A.R. sniping had escalated to shelling, drawing local Israeli response of sharper and sharper quality until Israeli warplanes were striking at will not only along the entire Suez Canal but deep within the U.A.R., on the outskirts of its major cities.

Such probing at its vitals could not long be tolerated and so, by early 1970, the U.A.R. had invited the Soviet Union to take over, in effect, its air defenses. By February, when Nasser publicly announced the nature of the commitment by Moscow, the Soviet presence in force was already established. Four thousand Soviet military advisers were believed to be retraining and reequipping the U.A.R. Army—their number was to grow through the year to an estimated 10,000, added to 4,000 Soviet civilian advisers. On April 18 came the first encounter between the Israeli Air Force and the Soviet Air Force; by May, three squadrons of Soviet MiG-21s, manned by 100 Soviet pilots, were providing

CATHERINE URSILLO FROM NANCY PALMER AGENCY

Large crowds gather at a rally in Washington on May 9 to protest what appeared to be an expansion of the war in Southeast Asia and the student deaths at Kent State a few days earlier.

the U.A.R. with interior air cover; and by July, in a direct clash the Israelis shot down four Soviet pilots. Simultaneously, the Soviets began to build a shelter belt of missile sites along the U.A.R. side of the Suez Canal; and their Mediterranean fleet had grown strong enough to challenge the hitherto total hegemony in the Mediterranean of the massive U.S. 6th Fleet.

By midsummer, despite the delivery of U.S. planes and war matériel to Israel, it was obvious that escalation of armament on both sides could settle nothing. Tweaked by the emotions of their clients, the superpowers were inching their way to outright collision in a war that might destroy the world—and which neither wanted.

Historically, perhaps the largest act of the Nixon administration may yet be recorded as its response to the tumescent crisis of the Middle East in July. If successful its response might rank with Truman's acceptance of confrontation in Korea in 1950, or John Kennedy's frustration of Soviet penetration of the Caribbean in the missile crisis of 1962. The Nixon response, devised by Secretary of State William Rogers, was a masterfully prepared solicitation of all involved in the Middle East to support a 90-day cease-fire. During the truce Israelis and Arabs would refrain from hostile acts or military buildups and negotiate, through a UN intermediary, a permanent settlement of disputes. For the first time, implicit in the acceptance of such a cease-fire, would be Arab recognition of Israel's right to survival, and Israel's acknowledgment that the larger part of its conquests of 1967 must be given up.

Two events disrupted, and almost shattered, the cease-fire of August 7.

The first was the deliberate violation of what the U.S. State Department called "categorical commitments" that neither side would take advantage of the halt in shooting along the canal. Soviets and the U.A.R. had rushed instantly on the morrow of the cease-fire to beef up their missile strength along the canal; within 60 days an estimated 50 batteries of SAM 2 and SAM 3 rockets had been installed, to make the Soviet-U.A.R. defenses of the canal the densest concentration of antiaircraft fire in the world, surpassing even the defenses of Hanoi. Secretly furious at this Soviet violation, vehement in direct cables to Moscow, the president was nonetheless publicly silent. Privately feeling that the Soviets had betrayed him personally and were testing his will, he seemed determined not to let Moscow underestimate him again as the next event developed.

This second event was larger and sharper, and brought the world to the edge of war. What had hitherto been ignored in Middle East negotiations—whether with Arab states, Israel, the UN or the U.S.S.R.—was the invisible presence of the Arab Palestinians. The refugees and their children, having fled from Palestine in 1948 to wait each year for the extermination of the Israeli state, had waited long. Their numbers had grown from 600,000 to approximately a million; their grievances had marinated to hate in refugee camps; and their presence disturbed every state of their dispersion in the Middle East.

Furious at the indifference of the world to their desire to wipe out the Israeli state, shocked by the war weariness of a U.A.R. that was willing to discuss Israeli survival, a handful of Palestinian Arabs decided to blaze their cause on world opinion by terror. In a four-day period (September 6–9), Palestinian hijackers seized four international passenger planes in midair; kidnapped 700 passengers; isolated them in a Jordanian desert hideout; and defied the world and any Arab leadership that contemplated negotiation. Most ominous was their outright challenge to the sovereignty of Jordan, the last Arab state with which the U.S. maintained friendly communication. Jordan had been for years the chief base of the Palestinian Liberation Front, and now leaders of the front called for an uprising against the authority of King Husain. For ten days, from Amman, Jordan's capital, to the Syrian border, Jordanian regulars and Palestinian guerrillas bloodied the sands with civil war.

One must see the events of September as a wild swirl of confusion in which half-formed states and nervous armies milled about seeking a jugular to strike.

Within this confusion came the decision of the Syrian government to move armored columns south across the Jordanian border to support the Palestinian insurrectionaries. With full diplomatic support from the U.S. government, the Israelis mobilized armor to counter in a preventive strike, to keep Syrians and Palestinians from converting Jordan into a base of assault. Coordinate with this Israeli mobilization, as Arabs in Amman continued to kill each other, came an alert to all U.S. forces. The 6th Fleet steamed east through the Mediterranean; in Europe, U.S. NATO divisions earmarked battalions for an airlift and a swoop on Amman; in the U.S., the Strike Command earmarked home strategic forces for dispatch to global war. If the Soviets moved to back the Syrians, cataclysm was imminent. In a complete recovery of nerve, Mr. Nixon was preparing not for a limited raid, as in Cambodia, but for a war that might involve the Soviet Union, and thus the fate of the U.S.

In history, those things that do not happen are sometimes more important than events that do. What happened was nothing. Under the U.S. threat and the restraint of Soviet diplomacy, Syrian armor was called back; the Jordanian Army recovered control of most of its real estate; the Israeli mobilization was ended; and so, too, the partial U.S. mobilization. The full nature of the Soviets' role in stilling the threat is unknown; what role Nasser played is also unknown—he was to die, of a heart attack, under emotional stress, two weeks after the outbreak of civil war in Jordan. Behind him, however, Nasser left the inescapable impression that he, and the U.A.R., had suffered long enough from war with the Israelis and were prepared to seek settlement. The Israelis, too, were prepared for peace to the extent, as voiced by their chief warrior, Gen. Moshe Dayan, of giving up the Sinai Desert and the West Bank of the Jordan.

On November 6, the Nixon/Rogers cease-fire was renewed. At the end of the year, it still persisted, and negotiations seemed imminent between Israelis and Arabs. In the Middle East, impending cataclysm had shrunk to a condition of less than normal tension; and U.S. diplomacy had scored a first success for peace in many years. An observer might pinch himself to determine whether the apparent quiet was a dream—but there it was.

Great Thrusts, New and Old. Beyond these two major shock episodes—Cambodia and the Middle East—were those shaping thrusts, still unformed, that observers would have to study on the horizon of the future. Of these thrusts, two were most significant.

• In Asia, the thrust lay in 1970 with Japan. Underlying this thrust were the spectacular vigor and mastery of technology that the Japanese economy was developing. In mass, speed, and momentum, history had never seen growth remotely resembling that of Japanese industry. Almost devoid of raw materials at home, the Japanese seemed determined to overcome this handicap by skill and spirit alone. From the shattered sockets of hardstands, furnaces, and rolling mills that, in 1946, had produced only a half-million tons of steel, the Japanese, by 1970, had rebuilt or expanded a capacity that in the current fiscal year would pour an estimated 101 million tons. Japan in 1969 produced more than half the entire world's ship tonnage, more than 21 times the 463,682 tons of the U.S., whose navy 25 years before had erased Japan from the high seas. Whether in textiles, electronics, or automobiles, the rhythm of Japanese growth surpassed belief. Where the U.S. in the 1960s had added an increment of 4% a year to its industrial capacity, the Japanese had averaged a growth rate of 12% a year. Already the third largest industrial nation (by product), Japan, in the opinion of some analysts, might surpass the U.S. as the world's first power in industry by the turn of the century.

Parallel with this industrial growth, and dependent on it, was an inescapable change in the quality of Japanese politics. Having forever abjured war and war-making institutions in their postwar constitution, the Japanese now displayed a disturbing pre-echo of their war-making samurai past. Their self-defense force was now a real army. Patriot demands for larger control of their own security recalled Japanese militarism of the 1930s, when Japanese "security" insisted on larger and larger intrusion into China, until Japanese security required control of all Asia in the Greater East Asia Co-Prosperity Sphere. (It was the reluctance of Americans to acquiesce in the Japanese formulations of security needs that had called forth the attack on Pearl Harbor.) By fall of 1970, Japanese emissaries to the United States were courteously requesting that the U.S. share with them their secret data on nuclear technology and nuclear arms. And the nuclear nonproliferation treaty, which the Japanese had signed six years before, was still unratified.

  • The politics of change brought recognition of a similar, familiar thrust in Europe. Long before 1970, West Germany had emerged as the most vigorous economic force in Western Europe. Now, in 1970, West Germany under the leadership of Chancellor Willy Brandt moved to liquidate the ambiguities of diplomacy that had framed its sovereignty since the war. After months of protracted negotiation, on August 12 Brandt journeyed to Moscow to sign a treaty recognizing the conquests of the Red Army and its clients in Eastern Europe as permanent; and renounced forever the use of arms in settlement of disputes between the U.S.S.R. and Germany.

The Germans still needed the support of Americans. The 300,-000 U.S. troops, stationed with nuclear arms along the Thuringian ridges, were still so vital to them that Germans, chief among all European allies, were willing to pay a large part of the cost that kept Americans there. But in forward diplomacy, the Germans had clearly struck out on their own, shrugging off paternal U.S. guidance. There seemed little inclination in the Brandt diplomacy to break Germany's ties with the Common Market of Western Europe. Rather, it was as if the Germans had quietly glided into the position of leading partner in the West European alliance, assuming the role that had once been Britain's and that de Gaulle had sought, and failed to create, for France. What Germans apparently wanted, at this moment, was freedom of maneuver through the great belt of Eastern European states that lay between them and the Soviets—using the strength of the U.S. and the Western allies as base for the thrust. For this Germany was willing to make the first down payment required by the Soviets. On December 7, after direct negotiations with the Polish Communists, Germany accepted "forever" the Oder-Neisse wartime line as the permanent frontier between an eventually reunified Teutonic state and the Slavs. Communist harassment of access to Berlin continued, but West Germans still were disposed to overlook it. The Germans in 1970 had advanced Europe, and thus the world, a step on the road to peace.

  • China remained a mystery as it always had been for Westerners. The year had begun auspiciously as China consented to talk with the U.S. at Warsaw. Yet, after two quick meetings, the 135th and 136th in their long dialogue of the deaf, the Chinese halted the talks as a response to the invasion of Cambodia. Within China, a major resumption of civilized living took place —college students were invited back to classes for the first time since the abolition of all formal higher education in the Cultural Revolution that began in 1965. No famine or other disaster struck the Chinese in 1970—but of what else was happening in the world's largest single culture, the West knew but little. U.S. efforts to probe the mystery continued as Mr. Nixon, pursuing his policy of tentative rapprochement, directed the State Department to permit any American, with the slightest pretext of interest, to visit China. Other nations also tried to make contact. Both Canada and Italy recognized China. The UN, for the first time in 20 years of debate, voted by 51 to 49 that mainland China be invited to join, but it was still short of the two-thirds vote needed for membership.

  • Little more could be made of development in the Soviet Union. Soviet movement into the Middle East crisis has been noted. The steady spread of the Soviet Navy reached into the Indian Ocean; the Soviet effort to overtake the U.S. in nuclear missiles was, during the course of the year, well publicized. But one could make out only vaguely what was going on within the closed society of the Soviet Union. The ferment of Soviet intellectuals, as compared to the frenzy of U.S. intellectuals, was modest yet noteworthy in context; and was duly noted by the naming of Aleksandr Solzhenitsyn as Nobel Prize writer of the year. The style of Soviet diplomacy persisted in incubating schizophrenia among those who had to deal with it. After a full year of negotiations with the Soviets on nuclear disarmament, U.S. negotiators still were uncertain whether the conversations were meaningless, or whether Moscow did share their desire, seriously, to de-escalate the arms race.

  • A citizen of the third world, viewing the U.S. from afar, might find America almost as mysterious—not for lack of testimony but from the confusion of many voices. Questioned and suspected by its traditional allies, criticized and denounced by a majority of the world's thinkers, the U.S. image in the world of word makers and ideologues never had been lower.

The U.S. thrust in the outer world might be feebler than at any time since 1945, yet it persisted. The U.S., said Mr. Nixon, would not abandon NATO. The U.S., he reaffirmed, would not yield to Soviet pressure in the Middle East. The Nixon Doctrine

AUTHENTICATED NEWS INTERNATIONAL

Rival groups seeking an immediate end to the war in Vietnam (above) and advocating a military victory (right) demonstrate in Washington in April 1970.

PICTORIAL PARADE

could be interpreted as withdrawal from the active mood of U.S. diplomacy since World War II—but that withdrawal would clearly be selective, and set its own pace.

In Vietnam, where pressure for withdrawal was greatest, the president on October 7 made the most far-reaching proposal yet to end U.S. involvement in the long war—a call for standstill cease-fire on every front and an Indochina peace conference in Paris as prelude to ultimate total liquidation of U.S. troop presence in Southeast Asia. The proposal brought no movement in negotiations. The Communists rested on their hard-core position—no cease-fire or any other military settlement was acceptable until *after* a political settlement. This political settlement, as defined by the Communists, was that any new government chosen in South Vietnam must exclude specific, named individuals proscribed by them. Unless the U.S. accepted such purge terms, the war must go on. Some U.S. government might ultimately accept such terms, but Mr. Nixon was not yet ready to do so. To continue his slow, deliberate liquidation of the war on minimal U.S. terms, he would therefore have to continue to accept inflation, unrest, and death all the while he sought to restore the drive ("the lift of a driving dream," he called it) of U.S. politics—and the authority of the U.S. presidency that had been so shaken.

This was his purpose in the fall elections as he sought the confidence of the American people. Yet rarely has so clear a purpose been presented so poorly to the vote of a democracy as in November.

THE ELECTION: NO CLEAR-CUT DECISION

In true democracies, elections are the occasion for vox populi to roar. The people—so the folklore goes—shuffle to the polls in their millions and from the count of their numbers their will emerges. Politicians and soothsayers, psephologists and analysts then disgorge instant analysis as they shred the figures for clues to the movement of power, the response of opinion to challenge and propaganda. Such instant analysis is part of the political game, too, for after a tightly contested election, the *impression* the people get of what they did is quite as important as what they *actually* did.

Instant analysis, however, usually treats election returns as an event in itself, as a permanent portrait of a nation, self-drawn from life. Yet election returns, especially when they are close, are much more like the single frame of a motion picture, a static snap lifted from a sequence of motion. Voting results make sense only when one understands the peaks and dips of the surges behind them.

Thus, the technical voting results of the 1970 elections can be simply told: Approximately 56 million Americans voted on November 3, roughly 45.3% of the voting-age population of the country; despite the turbulence of 1970, it was the lowest percentage turnout in a midterm election in 12 years. All 435 seats of the House of Representatives were at stake, and in Congress the Democrats gained nine seats net, to give them a margin in the 92nd Congress of 255 to 180. Thirty-five governorships were at stake, and here the Democrats gained no less than 11 governors to make their nationwide gubernatorial margin 29 to 21. Thirty-five Senate seats were at stake. In this contest, the Democrats lost 3 seats net, the Republicans gained one and Independents (both Conservative) carried off two—setting the structure of the incoming Senate as 54 Democrats, 44 Republicans, 2 Independents.

The trouble with this technical score is that it gives only the net tallies of a political battle that had been one of the most hotly contested, yet most poorly defined, of recent years. And one must look back at the sway of political movement through summer and fall months to invest such results with meaning.

The political season had begun in earnest in late summer, after the primary contests within the two parties had been settled. Republican primaries had been generally lackluster since the president had, himself, chosen the key Republican candidates

to carry his banners for the year. Democratic primaries, particularly in the East, had been marked by the effort of the insurgents of the New Politics to carry off their party's nominations in traditional urban strongholds. If any novelties could be detected in these primaries, they were two: first, the flagrant and extravagant use of television to make candidates out of unknowns almost overnight. And, second, the activity of the students who, in the peak of post-Kent passion, seemed to be exploding into a hundred campaigns from coast to coast. But as both parties squared off to face each other in August and September, the issues as we have seen them were ready for debate: The shock of the Cambodian adventure was wearing off and troops were coming home; a perplexing yet pleasing cease-fire had been established in the Middle East under Nixon's leadership; unemployment and inflation were both rising; and the August strokes of terrorism— the killing of Judge Haley, the bombings at the University of Wisconsin—still scarred emotions. How would the two parties translate such issues into political terms?

A New Kind of Campaign. Presidential elections in the quaternary years have a dramatic outline. They are formal contests for seizure of power. Midterm elections, however, resemble more guerrilla campaigns. The sitting administration is under assault. The rival party, having no national responsibility, attacks on all fronts at every level. Normally, the administration in power carries on its defense by pretending a lofty above-the-battle preoccupation with national responsibilities, while covertly bracing its supporters with money, publicity, "nonpartisan visits," and political ammunition. "We view with dismay . . ." is traditionally the chant of the out-party, while the in-party thunders, "We point with pride to . . . ."

The campaign of 1970 was structured entirely otherwise, and it was in September that the administration decided on a midterm strategy almost unique in recent political history. It would make the midterm elections a nationwide referendum on the president's years in power—and it would do so by going on the attack. The war in Vietnam was being wound down, the Middle East was temporarily at peace, the odious draft was being liquidated, for the first time a reasonable environment control mechanism had been blueprinted. But instead of making these achievements the subject of the familiar litany "We point with pride to," the administration inexplicably adopted the opposition's traditional chant, "We view with dismay." "Our president," said a White House aide sadly in midcampaign, "is really a centrist in his policies; but when it comes to politics, he's a hard-rock, right-wing tactician."

On September 9, in the president's Oval Office, it was decided that the early effort of the Republican campaign would, thus, be led by Vice-President Agnew, while the president, after his planned European trip, would return in October to give it the uplift of statesmanship. It was quite the most important assignment given a vice-president in recent years—and from the initial Agnew brand the campaign was never thereafter to recover.

Agnew is a familiar type in U.S. political history—the character who, instantly, makes the blood of the opposition boil. As Harold Ickes had been for Roosevelt, as Richard Nixon had been for Eisenhower, as Robert Kennedy had been for John F. Kennedy, Agnew now was for Nixon—the reflex hate-focus of the opposition. A man of considerable eloquence, Agnew, when he thrust, thrust for the exposed underbelly—and, occasionally, the blows were low. His early campaign theme was quite simple: revolution and terror were abroad in the country; "radical-liberals" condoned terrorism with their "permissive" philosophy; most radical-liberals were Democrats; therefore, they must be purged. The campaign proceeded against the backdrop of the U.S.'s cultural confusion, as we have seen. Terror, drugs, pornography, the culture itself were legitimate themes for political discussion. Such themes might have been used to unify people, or to rally the Old Culture against the New around a nonpartisan center. Instead, in Agnew's rendition, Republicans stood for law and order, Democrats for riot and unrest; Republicans for virtue,

Democrats for radicalism; Republicans for parent groups, Democrats for student rioters.

Stimulated by such rhetoric, disturbed like most Americans by the turbulence of the spring months, the Democrats moved to compete on "the social issue" as if by wordless command. Liberal Democrats sprouted flags in their lapels, addressed audiences in veterans' caps, on some occasions wore their war medals in public, thumped away so hard at law and order, and campus unrest as to leave little room on their flank for Republican candidates to maneuver except by exaggeration and overkill. Moving from left to center by herd instinct, Democrats forced Republicans further to the right; by mid-October, Republican efforts to outfrighten Democrats had made such senatorial races as Utah, Indiana, Illinois, and California, which earlier had been considered reasonable Republican prospects for victory, into contests in which the tide ran with the Democrats.

In October, too, came that irresistible surge of joblessness which is the folk terror of workingmen and their families. In January, at the beginning of the election year, when unemployment stood at only 3.5%, Mr. Nixon had opined to Republican congressional leaders that if, by fall, unemployment had risen to 5%, the party would be in real trouble. By the end of September unemployment had reached 5.5% and was still rising. In some California centers, hard squeezed by cutbacks in the defense and space industries, unemployment had reached 11%, the highest rate since the great depression. By late October, polls and surveys showed Republican hopes of emerging from the election with any substantial victory to be shrinking daily. At the grassroots level, it appeared that U.S. politics were parodying one of the more successful cigarette advertisements of the season, saying "Which Do You Want, Safe Jobs or Safe Streets?"

The closing weeks of the campaign were marked by Mr. Nixon's personal intervention, on a scale more extravagant than any previous president defending his record in an off year. Visiting 22 states, flying 17,241 miles in 23 days, the president, rather than explaining his own creditable record or explaining joblessness and other problems in realistic terms, took up the Agnew theme of attack in his "gloves-off style." A vicious, rock-throwing brawl in San Jose, Calif., in which student militants actually attempted to assault the president, gave solid justification to his emotions. But his final dramatic appeal to the nation on television, a badly filmed and edited version of a campaign speech on the over beaten theme of law and order, lacked presidential quality and unifying thought. Mr. Nixon was followed immediately in the nation's view by Sen. Edmund Muskie of Maine. An intraparty coup by Democratic political veterans had given Muskie the money, time, and opportunity to speak for his entire party against Nixon—and Muskie, knowing his own presidential aspirations hung on the quality of his response, made the most of it. Speaking gravely, simply, and directly from a living room in Maine, he offered the theme of trust—mutual trust of Americans for Americans, trust in the nation and one's neighbors, and branded the Republicans' theme flatly, "That is a lie . . . and the American people know it is a lie."

The campaign had, by this point, election eve, lost all quality as a national referendum. For weeks it had been degenerating into a state-by-state, district-by-district, *mano-a-mano* series of contests, swayed by local issues and local personalities; and it was in this manner that Americans voted.

What the Results Meant. There remained then the analysis of the contradictory election results for national meaning: What true shifts of power had taken place within the nation? How much room for maneuver would the administration have? Had the nation restrained or enlarged the president's ability to direct affairs?

From the state-by-state results, the following could be read:

• In the House of Representatives: standoff, with a faint Democratic tilt. Though the Republicans lost nine seats, this was far less than the normal off-year loss of sitting administrations, which, in the past 35 years, has averaged just under 40.

WIDE WORLD

Pres. Richard M. Nixon's limousine moves through a hostile crowd at San Jose, Calif. The jeering demonstrators were predominantly students. A few hurled rocks and eggs at the president's car.

There would be little change in the balance of congressional forces.

• In the Senate, the president's administration had fallen short of its dreamed-of majority. With 44 seats in the Senate, however, Republican strength there had risen to its highest in 14 years; and the character of the men elected promised the president slightly enlarged authority and support in the conduct of foreign relations; of war and defense policy; and probably of confirmations in disputed nominations of high rank.

• In the nationwide, state-by-state, issue-by-issue, *mano-a-mano* contests for control of governors and legislatures, Democrats scored a most remarkable success. No less than 14 statehouses shifted control and the Democrats registered a net gain of 11. In the industrial Midwest—Wisconsin, Minnesota, Ohio, Pennsylvania; in the South—Arkansas and Florida; in the Rocky Mountain states—Idaho, New Mexico—the Democrats emerged once more, after the shattering ordeal of 1968, as masters of executive power. With the control of statehouses went those major, solid bases of patronage and prestige that are the building blocks of presidential campaigns and delegate control.

• The most substantial victory of the Democrats in 1970 was not, however, their conquest of statehouses but reestablishment of party cohesion. The viciousness of the intraparty struggle of 1968 had left the Democrats almost as shattered as had been the Republicans after the Goldwater campaign of 1964. Raddled and riven by three groups—the traditionalists, the Southerners, and the ideological insurgents of the New Politics—the future of the Democratic Party in the spring of 1970 had seemed less promising than the maiden voyage of the "Titanic." Scandal and contempt had smeared the traditionalists in their big-city states; national media reviled them as being the voice of yesterday. In the South, Republican victories, the threat of George Wallace, along with the intransigence of Northern liberals over party loyalty, had threatened to reduce the Democratic Party to an all-black minority. Finally, their access to the press and intellectual ferment had made the insurgents, particularly in such states as New York, Connecticut, Wisconsin, and Massachusetts, seem like the voice of the future.

The elections confounded all predictions of the imminent collapse of the world's oldest political party. The major victories of the Democrats were victories of men of the moderate center—Humphrey of Minnesota, Kennedy of Massachusetts, Muskie of Maine, Proxmire and Lucey of Wisconsin, Jackson of Washington, Tunney of California, Gilligan of Ohio, Stevenson of Illinois. In the South, equally noteworthy was the election of four fresh Democrats to governorships: West in South Carolina, Askew in Florida, Bumpers in Arkansas, Carter in Georgia. All four were, in parochial Southern terms, relative liberals—moderates who perceived that the Democratic Party in the South must henceforth include black citizens and give them some voice in policy and choice. The victories of the Northern traditionalists and Southern moderates were promise of a 1972 convention of compromise and conciliation.

Remarkably, wherever the insurgents had captured the machinery and nominations of the Democratic Party in the primaries, their candidacies conspicuously failed to mobilize basic Democratic resources against Republicans. The democracy of New York State, where the insurgents were most powerful, was reduced from normal chaos to total anarchy. In Connecticut, the Rev. Joseph Duffy, who had mounted the ablest insurgent campaign in the East, fell sharply below expectations in his race for the Senate—Republican Lowell Weicker scored 443,000 votes, Duffy no more than 360,000, while Democratic breakaways gave discredited outgoing candidate Thomas Dodd no less than 260,000. In the House races nationally, Democratic candidates lifted their margins by a noteworthy average 3% over their congressional totals two years earlier. But where the most colorful messengers of the New Politics had captured upset nominations in spring, traditional Democratic districts produced sharply reduced margins in the fall elections. In the 3rd Massachusetts, Father Robert Drinan led his Republican rival by only 5 points where in 1968 the Democratic margin over the Republican had been 19. In the 7th California, Ronald V. Dellums led by 14 points—as against 33 points in 1968. In the 19th New York, Bella Abzug led by 9 points, as against 20 in 1968.

• If the promising new harmony was the greatest gain of the Democrats, their greatest threat came not from Mr. Nixon but from another potentially historic development: the rise of an intelligent and educated leadership of American conservatives.

American conservatives had, hitherto, fallen into two categories: the parade of primitive men which had run from Pitchfork Ben Tilman, through Senators Bilbo and Eastland, to Goldwater and Wallace; or the chain of striped-pants, thin-lipped elitists that has run from Henry Cabot Lodge down through Herbert Hoover to Robert Taft, Sr.

The most significant individual victory of 1970 was, therefore, the election of a new kind of conservative, James Buckley, as senator from the most liberal state in the Union, New York. The victorious Conservative Party of New York is the private intellectual property of the Buckley family of Connecticut. It is, not, however, their intellectual panache that intrigues one, as much as their ability to perceive what bothers ordinary people—a quality rare in conservatives. In less than a decade— from 1962 to 1970—the rhythm of Conservative growth in New York State had gone from 141,877 votes in 1962 to 510,023 in 1966, to 1,139,402 in 1968, to 2,139,000 (and victory) in the candidacy of Buckley in 1970. This victory was achieved by shearing through the nerve ends of the lower classes, by raising issues of culture and order as more important than issues of bread and butter. This issue was apparently sharper in the congested multilayered cities of the East than in the one-industry factory towns of the Midwest such as Akron, Cleveland, Kenosha, Moline, and Detroit. The spectacular victory of the Conservatives in urban New York opened an entire new flank of menace for the Democrats—and it would be surprising if, in future years, Conservative Party influence did not spread to adjacent New Jersey, Pennsylvania, and Connecticut.

Year-End. Their blurred and inconclusive results were probably the most significant report that the elections gave the American people of themselves—and the year ended as it had begun, in a deceptive calm. Confused and divided in January, Americans had remained so through a year of shock and challenge.

The spring and summer turbulence on the campus had hushed.

No one could measure the calm statistically, yet it could be felt both negatively and positively. The anticipated army of student participants in the fall elections, expected to reach 100,000, simply had failed to materialize. In spring, student leaders had expected to sway at least 100 congressional elections, but their final effort reached no more than 50 campaigns; only in five races across the country did student-backed challengers succeed in ousting an incumbent.

A score of explanations could be given for the gradual return of calm to the intellectual centers of the nation: the Kent State massacre had chilled many of the young; even more had been alienated by the atrocities of the psychopathic terrorists; by fall, at lesser universities, administrators of federal aid had begun to pinch off scholarships for more violent demonstrators; changes in regulations in late December released hundreds of thousands of young men from the draft forever. University administrators reported quiet, study, and work—so much so that many college libraries reported the sharpest upsurge in demand for books in four years. Yet no one would guarantee a continuance of tranquillity beyond the months immediately approaching. Perhaps more indicative of student mood than anything else was a footnote on student taste: The year had begun with students trooping to see the filmed documentary of the carnival of drugs and rock that had been the 1969 Woodstock Festival. In December, students took to their heart a movie called *Love Story,* an old-fashioned, tenderly scripted, hearts-and-flowers romance of college, which drew their tears as sincerely as similar movies of love-and-loss had drawn the tears of their parents.

The standard readings of public opinion gave no clue to any sharp movement of general feeling in the closing weeks of the year. The war in Vietnam went on, casualties falling steadily, with troop numbers reduced by December 31 to 335,800. Opinion polls still set the war in Vietnam close to the top of the concerns of American people—yet the war had all but disappeared from public debate by year-end. The rub of inflation still wore away at savings, and unemployment still was rising at year-end. Yet, paradoxically, the market in December had recovered all its losses for the year, and then gained in an upsurge that carried it to 838.92 on the Dow-Jones average, 30 points higher than its opening 12 months before. The president had recovered his nerve, authority, and leadership in foreign affairs—but public approval of the way he was doing his job slipped to 52% in the Gallup poll of December, the lowest mark since he took office.

The deadlock that had paralyzed U.S. politics since the beginning of the Vietnam war therefore continued; and Congress, called back after the election to finish its housekeeping chores, milled about aimlessly. There remained less than two years in which, either at home or abroad, Richard Nixon must set a direction by which people might judge him for reelection. The elections had neither harmed nor helped him, but he remained the most vulnerable president of recent times, as he had been since the day he took office. Elected by the tiniest of margins in 1968, with a minority of the popular vote, he was the first incoming president in generations without a working majority in either House or Senate, and confronted with a predominantly hostile press. How he might make his purpose clear, or transmit the larger outline of his visions clearly to the American people, certainly would determine his fate in the next election—and, if he were successful, also might change the character of the coming decade.

Yet the problem was not his alone. If he lacked the skill to describe his course, so too did his rivals, the Democrats, likewise barren of any formulation of issues that might cleave the American people with clear options of choice. In the Politics of Change, both parties seemed anachronistically primitive, trying to diagnose what bothered a restless nation in words and ideas rapidly becoming obsolete. Thus, neither could convincingly promise Americans at year-end that sense of control over events or destiny that once they had expected so naturally from their government—and that now eluded its grasp.

OPINION POLLS:
Their Role in Government

by HAROLD WILSON

In December 1965, I was discussing the latest developments in the Vietnamese war with Pres. Lyndon Johnson. I felt it right to tell him of a telegram I had received that morning from 60 Labour members of Parliament protesting against the course of events there. We discussed a recent statement by the government of India. I told him of views expressed by some of the non-aligned African countries at the Commonwealth Conference. The attitude of France came up. A demarche by Romania. Then the president said, or I thought he said, "Have you seen what the Poles are saying?"

I rapidly tried, but failed, to recall some weighty pronouncement by Mr. Gomulka or Mr. Rapacki. But the president pulled a folded sheet of notepaper from his pocket and read the details of the latest public opinion poll. As I recall them, some 70% were stated to be "opposed" to the president's policies, but the detailed figures went on to show that 43% or so felt he should pull out of the war and 44% that he should escalate the fighting. The poll obviously had worried him, most of all because the almost equal division of his critics left him stranded in the centre, without any clear guidance about the direction the American public, at that moment in time, wanted him to take.

That incident raised the whole question of whether governments should, or whether they even can, trim their policies to the shifts of public opinion as so recorded. I shall try to answer in the light of British experience over recent years, with particular reference to my period as prime minister from 1964 to 1970.

Since the general election of June 18, 1970, the British public opinion poll organizations have been undergoing an agonizing reappraisal. In every previous general election, and in many parliamentary by-elections, they had been remarkably accurate in forecasting the outcome. In 1970 four of the five polls forecast a clear Labour majority, some indicating a landslide. Only one, the Opinion Research Centre, on the very last day, forecast a marginal Conservative victory, and then only as a result of adjusting the figures actually recorded to allow for a differential turnout of each party's supporters on polling day and of reinterviewing some of those polled earlier. As it turned out, 1970 was the British pollsters' Dewey-Truman experience of 1948. Edward Heath was perfectly fair in his euphoric speech to the annual conference of his party supporters, when he said:

> I find today that the world is divided into two groups—those who are proudly boasting that their opinion poll was at any rate within six points of where we got to, even though they said we . . . were going to lose, and those who are still busy writing and publishing books proving in fact that we lost.

Disenchantment with the polls has revived proposals that the publication of poll results should be forbidden by law for a given period before an election. This was actually recommended by the all-party Speaker's conference on electoral reform a few years ago, but on the government's advice the House of Commons rejected it. It is unlikely to occur. For one thing, private polls would continue to be taken; rumours about their results would circulate and might even lead to speculation on security markets.

Polls as a Guide to Government. One by-product of the pollsters' self-examination has been the reopening of a public debate on the role of the public opinion polls, not only in forecasting elections but in influencing decisions of government. In attempting to form a judgment on that question, I begin by stating certain general principles.

First, *a government cannot govern, and should not seek to govern, by relating its policies to public opinion poll results,* whatever its judgment of their accuracy. To do so is hardly more sophisticated or all that certain to be a better guide to policy than an earlier practice of governments based on scrutiny of the entrails of a recently slaughtered chicken.

Not only does the value of polls depend on the precise way in which questions are put, but the polls frequently record highly volatile changes in public opinion—or in a broader, more indefinable public mood. A slavish following of their dictates would involve violent lurchings of policy, for violent swings in public opinion on particular issues can be brought about by a sudden, perhaps shocking, turn in events or be induced by a well-managed publicity campaign. While over recent years British public opinion has moved steadily against supporting United States policy in Vietnam, the polls, no doubt correctly, recorded a seismic convulsion when Britain received the first reports of the 1966 massacre of rebellious Buddhists by South Vietnamese troops at Da Nang. In such circumstances, government by public opinion poll would have required a British administration broadly supporting American policy to have reversed all its policies, a reversal that would not have been justified unless it could be shown that disasters such as Da Nang were an endemic and inevitable consequence of American involvement in Vietnam.

It is not only a question of sudden and shocking events. Public opinion can be swung by a successful campaign, be it morally just or unjust, or even by the tone of public comment in the principal communications media. The unscrupulous public relations campaign launched against Britain and other countries on the issue of Biafra made a profound impression, first on some of its more gullible targets in the communications field and then, through them, on public opinion and Parliament.

A different kind of pressure, a dedicated and documented campaign against homelessness in Britain, had a marked effect on opinion, and here administrators and ministers were moved. But not by the polls; by the facts. And even without the work of pressure lobbies, good or bad, public opinion—including political attitudes—can be swayed by the tone of public comment, especially where facts and comment are stated by partisan journals or other than neutral radio and television commentators.

Nor is this all. Expressions of public opinion made in response to poll questions frequently relate to a single issue. A government would be wrong to respond automatically to disapproval for, in terms of administration and policy, such an issue can rarely be considered in isolation. A policy of, say, nationalization or denationalization of an individual industry, or the introduction or amendment of a particular form of tax, or an element in monetary policy may be condemned by the public opinion poll results, but to scrap the policy might endanger the government's entire industrial or economic or financial policy. One has only to consider the consequence of such political response in the field of taxation. It is certain that public opinion polls in any country would show a large majority in favour of reducing or abolishing each and every form of tax in a nation's fiscal armoury. It is almost equally probable that there would be strong majorities in favour of increasing most forms—certainly the more popular forms—of public social expenditure. To follow public opinion polls here would be a prescription for national bankruptcy.

It is true that much depends on the form in which the question is put on the doorstep. A more helpful and responsible picture would be presented if the question set a given increase or reduction in taxation against given charges in government expenditure, as: "Would you be willing to see your income tax raised by a shilling in the pound if it led to the building of X more schools?" or "Would you accept the ending of public aid to the employment service if it led to this or that stated reduction in one or another tax?" But politicians would not agree with the choices posed. Probably the most useful questions are those, frequently put, that ask those who are interviewed to list tax cuts in order of their choice or to rank items in order of preference for increases or reductions in social spending.

Nor is it simply a matter of consistency in a given area of policy. Opinions on particular issues may lead to the destruction of the central strategy of national policy. The interrelation of defense and economic policy is but one example; the effect of decisions about trading with particular countries on diplomacy, defense, and trade is another.

The second principle is this: *if a government has embarked on a policy it believes to be right, it should stick to it despite hostile, short-term reactions*. At some time—and in the case of governments that have inherited crisis conditions, all the time—every government worthy of the name has to introduce measures involving deep political unpopularity and hostility. It may take years for the results of the policy to become manifest. To retreat at the first whiff of psephological grapeshot is not only cowardly, but may be the means of inflicting on the nation long-term hardship, even national decline. A government that is, for example, fighting to convert a record deficit in its balance of international payments into a record surplus—which was the task of Britain's government from 1964 to 1970—has to take many unpopular measures. Even if the need for the measures is accepted initially, months and years of "freeze and squeeze" can cause first apathy and then political hostility.

Again, sudden setbacks to a developing policy can cause sharp reactions that are reflected in the polls. To take one example, in the spring of 1967 we were almost within sight of balancing our overseas trade and payments when the Middle East war and the closure of the Suez Canal inflicted great damage on us—a major factor in forcing devaluation upon us later in the year, after three years of determined struggle to maintain the parity of the pound sterling. The immediate reaction of public opinion, as measured in the polls, illustrates what I have said in drawing a distinction between an expression of *opinion* or *judgment* on a particular issue and the more indefinable public mood or feeling, which may indeed derive from subjective causes. When devaluation was forced on us in 1967, the public opinion polls showed the country almost equally divided on the specific question of whether we were "right" to devalue. But questions on political support showed a strong swing away from the government to the Conservative opposition.

Again, in the following spring, when the chancellor of the Exchequer introduced the toughest budget in our peacetime history to ensure the transfer of resources from domestic consumption to the needs of overseas trade, public opinion polls recorded an extremely high number of electors who regarded it as "fair." But the political mood, as shown in "voting intention," was still strongly antigovernment. A majority of the electorate felt that we should not have got into a situation where such a budget was necessary, however "fair" it was as between one section of the community and another.

When the electorate feels that, however right—or inevitable—a particular decision may have been, the government should not have "landed the country" in the situation that required such a decision, or when it feels that the government does not know what it is doing from one moment to another, is striking an uncertain note in its public pronouncements, or appears divided in its counsels, then the polls—and above all the "voting intention" —show a strong and hostile trend. That does not necessarily mean that the particular decision was wrong, or that the totality of

the continuing, unpopular, policy was misconceived. Time may be required. In the year between May 1969 and May 1970, a Conservative lead of 21.5 points was converted into a Labour lead of 7.5 points according to the Gallup Poll in the *Daily Telegraph;* that was the year when Britain moved decisively into surplus, and more people were prepared not only to acknowledge that our policies had been justified, but even to give retrospective credit to a government that was willing to incur certain and continuing unpopularity to get the country right.

The third principle is more briefly stated. *He is a poor democratic leader, of any political party, in any country, who needs public opinion polls to tell him what is likely to be the popular reaction to particular policies.* Poll records may be useful on specific issues, especially human and sociological questions that fall outside the main range of political controversy, but a prime minister or opposition leader can usually forecast the short- and medium-term reaction, both of the public and of his supporters in Parliament. In those cases where I was wrong in my forecast, I was nearly always too pessimistic. What is more surprising is that commentators and politicians should think that the reaction had not been foreseen, and sometimes discounted. I was always amused to see headlines "Shock for Wilson" when the newspapers published a poll's finding. In almost every case the Cabinet had foreseen the inevitability of the reaction before the decision was taken. That did not mean the decision was wrong.

The Uncertain Electoral Barometer. Following that statement of broad principles about the relation of government to statistical samples measuring public opinion, it is right to assess the true role and value of the public opinion industry. Naturally I confine myself to British experience.

First, there is their general task of recording the standing of the government, of the opposition—or alternative government—and of the parties' respective leaders. Britain's polls are in the main published monthly, apart from a feverish period of weekly returns in 1964, and, provided that not too much weight is placed on individual monthly figures, they are widely regarded as a reasonably accurate assessment of the parties' standing. Their findings have been broadly substantiated, too, by the results of town and country local elections and of by-elections held to fill parliamentary vacancies. But neither the polls nor such electoral contests necessarily express how a government would fare in a general election; both tend to exaggerate antigovernment feeling.

To this certificate of accuracy I would make two qualifications. The question usually asked is, "If there were a general election tomorrow, how would you vote?" Except once in every four or five years, there is not going to be an election tomorrow, and in the early months and years of a Parliament such a question must appear remote and the answer to it must be correspondingly impressionistic.

The other discount is a seasonal one. It is widely accepted that a government in Britain is least popular in the winter. While people do not actually blame cold weather on the government—even a Labour government—gloomy skies and cold inevitably affect the public's sense of well-being. Moreover, winter imposes its own seasonal taxation, requiring that more coins be inserted in the gas or electricity heating meter, more payments made for coal or central heating—and leaving emptier pockets and less to spend on other things. Correspondingly, polls have shown some swing back to the government in the late summer and early autumn. This has been held to be due to the effects on personal well-being of fine weather and holidays and to the fact that during the three months when Parliament is not sitting the government is more free from daily criticism.

A special case regarding the role of the public opinion polls relates to the duty, which under British constitutional practice falls upon the prime minister, of deciding the date of a general election, within the five-year limit to the life of a Parliament laid down by statute. The view was sometimes expressed during the lifetime of the previous government, mainly by the then opposition, that the prime minister should not have this freedom, and that Britain should follow the United States and certain other countries in having an immutable electoral timetable. It was held that, given the accepted accuracy of the polls, the government of the day could choose a moment when public opinion seemed favourable, with a virtual certainty of victory. Since June 1970, this view has not been so forcefully advanced.

From my own experience, I would discount the dependence a prime minister is supposed to place on the polls in deciding the election date. In 1966 I chose March 31. This was the first March election in Britain since 1880, when Disraeli's government was defeated. But I had a special necessity forced upon me in that our parliamentary majority, 3 in a House of 630, was the smallest since our modern party system developed. For most of the winter of 1965–66 it was, due to death, down to 2, and one lost by-election would have reduced it to 1. The polls were undoubtedly favourable to an early election, but the main factor was the difficulty we were likely to face in the coming months in getting necessary and controversial legislation through the House of Commons with a minuscule majority.

But the polls are not without influence. For although the decision is that of the prime minister alone, not the government, he is wise to consult his senior colleagues. In a sense, therefore, the main relevance of the polls is in creating a consensus that the date he has penciled in his diary is the right one—unless, most unusually, he flies in the face of the evidence the polls produce. It is a lonely responsibility. The outlook is serious enough for a prime minister who chooses the earlier option between dates and loses, if many of his colleagues and parliamentary supporters— all of whose seats are at risk—think that the government would have fared better by "soldiering on." But woe betide the premier who, faced with auspicious omens, postpones the election—and then goes down when public opinion changes.

I suffered some of these comments, though not lethally, at various times in 1965. In late January the foreign secretary lost a by-election in a traditionally safe Labour district, thus reducing our majority from 5 to 3, and polls soon reflected a swing against us. The press almost unanimously forecast the government's early demise. When our poll ratings improved in the spring, I was widely criticized for not having held the election in March. Since a full month's notice is usually given, this would have meant pressing the electoral button some three weeks or so after our disastrous by-election defeat, when the odds against our survival —as assessed by the polls, the betting shops, and the press— were overwhelming. Again, in September of that year, the death of the then (Conservative) speaker and the necessity of replacing him by a Labour MP, which appeared certain to reduce our majority still further, was taken as a signal that our end was near. When the polls swung sharply in our favour in October, and still more so in November, I was dismissed by most commentators as a bungling amateur for not having called the election for October—i.e., announced it in that gloomy September when our electoral prospects were almost universally discounted.

In 1970 it was not the improvement in the polls that decided the date. One of the considerations in my mind when I set the date in March 1966 was the degree of freedom I should have to settle on a spring election four years later if, as I then expected, I should want to do so. The polls had improved steadily from October 1969 through the winter and early spring. It was not, however, until April 22 that the first of our five polls, Harris, crossed the line from a Tory lead to one of just 2% for Labour. I had decided in principle several days earlier in favour of a spring election, and had begun to consult my colleagues. It was not the polls that settled the issues; the voting in the boroughs was a more decisive test. What the polls, followed by the municipal voting, did was to convince more members, in the Cabinet and throughout the parliamentary party, that June was right. Before I finally announced the date—though my senior colleagues knew my intention—pressure from party and press was such that I should have been thought mad if I had decided to wait until later in the year. On past experience, therefore, polls have been a help

but no more, their value being limited to the fact that they carry others with the prime minister in his decision. It is likely, perhaps, that they will have less effect in the future. For if the election of June 1970 proved anything in this context, it was to show that the number who stayed at home, and their division between the parties they would probably have supported had they voted, decided the outcome. Furthermore, there was the evidence of a shift, of last-minute doubts, in the last day or two, after the principal polls had canvassed their last sample voter.

Opinion and Issues. Having dealt with this specific problem, on which so much learned rubbish has been written, it is right to seek to measure the influence of public opinion polls on the work of government and Parliament, that is, on individual issues and acts of policy. Here I would divide the issues and policies between those that involve major decisions of government and the vast number of other issues, some of which involve government initiative before Parliament is called upon to decide, but many of which, the so-called human issues or "issues of conscience," are usually left by the government to a free vote by individual members of Parliament, in most cases irrespective of party.

On the main issues of public policy, the striking fact is the sweeping changes in public opinion that occur over a period of time, even if one discounts short-run swings due, perhaps, to the volatility of human opinion or—rarely—doubtful representativeness of the sample in a particular month. Significant changes in trend may be caused by a simple change in the external facts, or by boredom, or by changes in the style of reporting or commentating on those facts, or by less definable shifts in what I have called the public mood.

To take specific examples:

First, the question of whether Britain should renew its application to join the European Common Market. Taking the figures published by National Opinion Polls (NOP), in July 1966, 62% said "Yes," 18% "No," with 20% "Don't Knows," to the question "Should Britain try to join the Common Market?" In November I announced a new British initiative aimed at seeking entry if conditions proved favourable. To a question that said "Should Britain now try to join the Common Market?" 58% answered "Yes," 17% "No," and 25% were recorded as "Don't Know." The fall may have been due to the inclusion of the word "now" in the question. Alternatively, it may have been that the anti-Common Market propaganda, called out of hibernation by my announcement, was more effective than that of the pro-European organizations and press. By May 1967, despite an overwhelming vote in all parties in Parliament in support of the government's firm decision to apply for membership, public opinion had shifted. Asked to record approval or disapproval of the decision of government and Parliament to try and join the Market, 37% approved, 41% disapproved, and 22% expressed no opinion.

Later in the year, after Pres. Charles de Gaulle had interposed his veto (and after the devaluation of sterling), even a vague question by NOP asking whether joining the Market would help to solve Britain's problems resulted in a majority of 50–31 saying that it would *not*, with 19% expressing no view. On a "harder" question, 51% felt that Britain should withdraw its application to join and 36% said we should press on with it. Boredom? A xenophobic reaction to the general? A post-devaluation feeling that the problems were too deep-seated to be eased by entry— indeed, that entry might aggravate them? It is hard to be dogmatic. In March 1970, with the road into Europe appearing open once again, the poll showed no less than 64–22 against joining, and in October 1970, after the change of government, it was 61– 24 against joining. One interesting fact that appears with a change of government, say from Labour to Conservative, is that although the new government may be pursuing, on a given issue, broadly the same policy as its predecessor, more of those who declare themselves Conservative appear to support the policy, while more of those who declare themselves Labour move into opposition to it. The attitude, at any rate in the early days of a new government, appears to be, "If my government thinks it's right, then maybe I should support it."

But these long-term shifts from one year to another make the task of government difficult, and inevitably lead to demands from the government's supporters for a better effort in public relations and "education" of the public. On Rhodesia, strong support in 1965 and early 1966 for the Labour government against the illegal declaration of independence was followed by very divided responses to subsequent polls until, after the negotiations with Ian Smith on board HMS "Tiger" in December 1966, the public swung much more unitedly to a judgment that the fault lay mainly with the Rhodesians. In recent years there has again been strong support for the government, both in maintaining economic sanctions and in refusing to use military force. But there were considerable periods when a slavish following of opinion as recorded in the polls would have made any consistency of policy or firmness of purpose impossible, and would have wrought havoc in the United Nations and in the Commonwealth.

On Vietnam, British policy of qualified support for President Johnson's policies at first carried majority support in the main polls. By July 1966 the figures, according to NOP as published in the *Daily Mail*, were 43% for, 45% against. By November 1967 the figures were 66–21 against. It should be observed that those opposing the policy included none who would have favoured a more vigorous prosecution of the war; the vast majority were in favour of the U.S. pulling out and of British government dissociation from United States policy.

On a highly controversial domestic issue, immigration, there has been little change in basic public attitudes. A very large percentage of supporters of each of the three parties, usually in the higher 80s, has demanded much tougher controls on immigration from the Commonwealth, with a strong majority in favour of repatriation. A great deal of this has been based on colour prejudice, worked up by unscrupulous politicians who have been able to exploit deep social problems in the inner areas of a number of Britain's cities and industrial towns. This is not a case where it can be said that public opinion, as measured by the polls, has failed to give a clear lead or has changed from time to time; the message has been clear throughout. But this is manifestly one of the areas of policy where government itself has to give not only a lead, but leadership, even if this opens up electoral advantages to those who have not been above exploiting this issue.

In Britain all major legislation on public policy is introduced into Parliament by the government. But back-bench members of all parties are able, within certain limits set by the parliamentary timetable, to introduce bills, many of which refer to "human" issues. Many of these involve matters of conscience, such as those concerned with abortion-law reform, the laws relating to homosexuality and divorce, changes in the law on Sunday observance, control of the liquor trade, and cruelty to animals.

It is probably the case that public opinion polls are more helpful to the legislator in these areas than in the great issues involving governments. But many of the sponsors of these private members' bills are crusaders, willing to fly in the face of public opinion for some great principle—and sometimes individually paying the price in a subsequent election. One of the most controversial issues settled by a private member's bill was the abolition of the death penalty. Capital punishment was suspended for five years by an act of 1965 and powers were given to make this permanent unless either House passed a contrary resolution. The issue was ultimately decided in December 1969, when the death penalty was finally abolished. But throughout the 30 years and more that this was a live parliamentary issue, public opinion was almost certainly consistently in favour of retaining it. When Parliament voted for the second reading of the abolition bill in December 1964, 67% were shown by an NOP poll to support retention. In September 1966—just after the brutal murder of three policemen—82% were recorded by the same poll as favouring its reintroduction, and in December 1969, on the eve of Parliament's final act of abolition, 84% in a Harris poll showed that they

were opposed to what Parliament was doing. These figures were repeatedly quoted in the House by those opposing abolition, but this was clearly a case where most members felt that it was their duty to move out ahead of public opinion, whatever their constituents' views.

To sum up, most legislators, and all press writers on public affairs, would regret the disappearance of the polls from our political scene. But very many MPs and others active in public life regard them as only one means, and not necessarily the principal one, of keeping in touch with public thinking.

How to Live with the Polls. Every household likes to have a clinical thermometer in the medicine cupboard. It is sometimes reassuring—or, to a hypochondriac, occasionally disappointing. The same is true of the polls, which are also capable of registering feverish fluctuations. But a doctor does not base his diagnosis, still less his treatment, solely on the measurement of the expansion of a sliver of mercury. Nor does, or should, a politician. But just as a patient, treating himself, can be panicked into unwise courses by misreading his thermometer, or relying on it to tell him more than it is designed to do, so the politician can be misled by an undue reliance on psephological mercury.

It has not been my practice to comment on poll reports, whether the results they showed were favourable or unfavourable to my party. But it has always been my view that the importance of public opinion polls has been not so much in what they portray as in what they cause—including the hypochondriacal reaction. In the autumn of 1969 I had to take the long trail from the Commons chamber to the House of Lords, on one of the procedural occasions required by our constitutional practice. The party leaders process, two by two. Reginald Maudling, who in the absence of Mr. Heath was leading the Conservative Party, said that I must be pleased at the recent trend to Labour in the polls. I gathered that he was not. I said that I paid little attention to polls; their principal importance was in the effect they created. For example, when I was leader of the opposition, one poll, less pro-Labour than its predecessors, had started a process of backbiting and diminution of the authority of the leadership.

Polls, then, can hearten or depress and, less frequently, inform. The politicians may be influenced by them and no doubt can exploit them; the statesman will study them to see what, if any, message they have for him. But Rudyard Kipling, the poet of British imperialism, might well have had in mind the statesman—be he legislator, prime minister, or president—when he wrote in "If,"

> If you can meet with Triumph and Disaster
> And treat those two imposters just the same . . . .

If so, it was wise advice; how much more should it relate to the lesser triumphs and disasters of public opinion poll measurements.

The statesman's conclusions, then, might be: *Accord to the polls interest, but not idolatry. Seek not to ban their publication, whether on election eve or at any other time. Regard them as an honest attempt to record the state of public opinion, at one moment in time, on one issue of political importance; or, less reliably, as an assessment not of opinion but of that indefinable phenomenon, the public mood on the broad political situation—a factor in, not a determinant of, policy. Scrutinize the form of the question and the detail of the answer. Insist that publication of the results be frank and fair, not influenced—whether in selection, omission, or slant—by the editorial or proprietorial prejudices of those who control publication, for public opinion polls constitute a public service. And service means they should be a servant, not a purported master, of the process of democratic decision making.*

Treat them, then, with respect, as you would give to any honest and expert professional assessment of facts that you have to take into account. And then recognize that you were elected, as legislator, as an executive, to exercise a judgment—not on what is expedient, or electorally rewarding, but a judgment on what is right.

BRITANNICA

Book of the Year

1971

1971 Calendar

1970 Chronology of major international events

1970

JANUARY	FEBRUARY	MARCH	APRIL
S M T W T F S	S M T W T F S	S M T W T F S	S M T W T F S
1 2 3	1 2 3 4 5 6 7	1 2 3 4 5 6 7	1 2 3 4
4 5 6 7 8 9 10	8 9 10 11 12 13 14	8 9 10 11 12 13 14	5 6 7 8 9 10 11
11 12 13 14 15 16 17	15 16 17 18 19 20 21	15 16 17 18 19 20 21	12 13 14 15 16 17 18
18 19 20 21 22 23 24	22 23 24 25 26 27 28	22 23 24 25 26 27 28	19 20 21 22 23 24 25
25 26 27 28 29 30 31		29 30 31	26 27 28 29 30

MAY	JUNE	JULY	AUGUST
S M T W T F S	S M T W T F S	S M T W T F S	S M T W T F S
1 2	1 2 3 4 5 6	1 2 3 4	1
3 4 5 6 7 8 9	7 8 9 10 11 12 13	5 6 7 8 9 10 11	2 3 4 5 6 7 8
10 11 12 13 14 15 16	14 15 16 17 18 19 20	12 13 14 15 16 17 18	9 10 11 12 13 14 15
17 18 19 20 21 22 23	21 22 23 24 25 26 27	19 20 21 22 23 24 25	16 17 18 19 20 21 22
24 25 26 27 28 29 30	28 29 30	26 27 28 29 30 31	23 24 25 26 27 28 29
31			30 31

SEPTEMBER	OCTOBER	NOVEMBER	DECEMBER
S M T W T F S	S M T W T F S	S M T W T F S	S M T W T F S
1 2 3 4 5	1 2 3	1 2 3 4 5 6 7	1 2 3 4 5
6 7 8 9 10 11 12	4 5 6 7 8 9 10	8 9 10 11 12 13 14	6 7 8 9 10 11 12
13 14 15 16 17 18 19	11 12 13 14 15 16 17	15 16 17 18 19 20 21	13 14 15 16 17 18 19
20 21 22 23 24 25 26	18 19 20 21 22 23 24	22 23 24 25 26 27 28	20 21 22 23 24 25 26
27 28 29 30	25 26 27 28 29 30 31	29 30	27 28 29 30 31

THE YEAR 1971 of the Christian Era corresponds to the year of Creation 5731-5732 of the Jewish calendar; to the year 1390-1391 of the Muslim hegira; to the 195th year of the United States; and to the 203rd year of the *Encyclopædia Britannica*.

1971

JANUARY	FEBRUARY	MARCH	APRIL
S M T W T F S	S M T W T F S	S M T W T F S	S M T W T F S
1 2	1 2 3 4 5 6	1 2 3 4 5 6	1 2 3
3 4 5 6 7 8 9	7 8 9 10 11 12 13	7 8 9 10 11 12 13	4 5 6 7 8 9 10
10 11 12 13 14 15 16	14 15 16 17 18 19 20	14 15 16 17 18 19 20	11 12 13 14 15 16 17
17 18 19 20 21 22 23	21 22 23 24 25 26 27	21 22 23 24 25 26 27	18 19 20 21 22 23 24
24 25 26 27 28 29 30	28	28 29 30 31	25 26 27 28 29 30
31			

MAY	JUNE	JULY	AUGUST
S M T W T F S	S M T W T F S	S M T W T F S	S M T W T F S
1	1 2 3 4 5	1 2 3	1 2 3 4 5 6 7
2 3 4 5 6 7 8	6 7 8 9 10 11 12	4 5 6 7 8 9 10	8 9 10 11 12 13 14
9 10 11 12 13 14 15	13 14 15 16 17 18 19	11 12 13 14 15 16 17	15 16 17 18 19 20 21
16 17 18 19 20 21 22	20 21 22 23 24 25 26	18 19 20 21 22 23 24	22 23 24 25 26 27 28
23 24 25 26 27 28 29	27 28 29 30	25 26 27 28 29 30 31	29 30 31
30 31			

SEPTEMBER	OCTOBER	NOVEMBER	DECEMBER
S M T W T F S	S M T W T F S	S M T W T F S	S M T W T F S
1 2 3 4	1 2	1 2 3 4 5 6	1 2 3 4
5 6 7 8 9 10 11	3 4 5 6 7 8 9	7 8 9 10 11 12 13	5 6 7 8 9 10 11
12 13 14 15 16 17 18	10 11 12 13 14 15 16	14 15 16 17 18 19 20	12 13 14 15 16 17 18
19 20 21 22 23 24 25	17 18 19 20 21 22 23	21 22 23 24 25 26 27	19 20 21 22 23 24 25
26 27 28 29 30	24 25 26 27 28 29 30	28 29 30	26 27 28 29 30 31
	31		

1972

JANUARY	FEBRUARY	MARCH	APRIL
S M T W T F S	S M T W T F S	S M T W T F S	S M T W T F S
1	1 2 3 4 5	1 2 3 4	1
2 3 4 5 6 7 8	6 7 8 9 10 11 12	5 6 7 8 9 10 11	2 3 4 5 6 7 8
9 10 11 12 13 14 15	13 14 15 16 17 18 19	12 13 14 15 16 17 18	9 10 11 12 13 14 15
16 17 18 19 20 21 22	20 21 22 23 24 25 26	19 20 21 22 23 24 25	16 17 18 19 20 21 22
23 24 25 26 27 28 29	27 28 29	26 27 28 29 30 31	23 24 25 26 27 28 29
30 31			30

MAY	JUNE	JULY	AUGUST
S M T W T F S	S M T W T F S	S M T W T F S	S M T W T F S
1 2 3 4 5 6	1 2 3	1	1 2 3 4 5
7 8 9 10 11 12 13	4 5 6 7 8 9 10	2 3 4 5 6 7 8	6 7 8 9 10 11 12
14 15 16 17 18 19 20	11 12 13 14 15 16 17	9 10 11 12 13 14 15	13 14 15 16 17 18 19
21 22 23 24 25 26 27	18 19 20 21 22 23 24	16 17 18 19 20 21 22	20 21 22 23 24 25 26
28 29 30 31	25 26 27 28 29 30	23 24 25 26 27 28 29	27 28 29 30 31
		30 31	

SEPTEMBER	OCTOBER	NOVEMBER	DECEMBER
S M T W T F S	S M T W T F S	S M T W T F S	S M T W T F S
1 2	1 2 3 4 5 6 7	1 2 3 4	1 2
3 4 5 6 7 8 9	8 9 10 11 12 13 14	5 6 7 8 9 10 11	3 4 5 6 7 8 9
10 11 12 13 14 15 16	15 16 17 18 19 20 21	12 13 14 15 16 17 18	10 11 12 13 14 15 16
17 18 19 20 21 22 23	22 23 24 25 26 27 28	19 20 21 22 23 24 25	17 18 19 20 21 22 23
24 25 26 27 28 29 30	29 30 31	26 27 28 29 30	24 25 26 27 28 29 30
			31

RELIGIOUS, NATIONAL, AND OTHER MAJOR HOLIDAYS

U.S. Legal Public Holidays

In 1971, in accordance with a 1968 law, dates for observance of four major legal holidays will fall on Monday:
Washington's Birthday, Feb. 15 (3rd Monday in February)
Memorial Day, May 31 (last Monday in May)
Columbus Day, Oct. 11 (2nd Monday in October)
Veterans Day, Oct. 25 (4th Monday in October)

January 1971
1 New Year's Day
1 Cameroon, Haiti, Sudan
4 Burma
11 Chad
26 Australia, India

February
4 Ceylon
6 New Zealand
14 St. Valentine's Day
23 Shrove Tuesday, Mardi Gras
24 Ash Wednesday
25 Kuwait
27 Dominican Republic
27 Muslim New Year (1391)

March
3 Morocco
6 Ghana
11 Purim (Feast of Lots)
11 Denmark
12 Mauritius
15 Ides of March
17 St. Patrick's Day
17 Ireland
23 Pakistan
25 Greece

April
1 April Fool's Day
4 Hungary, Senegal
4 Palm Sunday
9 Good Friday
10 Pesach (Passover), 1st day
11 Easter Sunday
14 Pan American Day
17 Syria
18 Easter (Eastern Orthodox)
26 Tanzania
27 Sierra Leone, Togo
29 Japan
30 Israel
30 Netherlands

May
1 International Labour Day
9 Czechoslovakia
11 Laos
14 Paraguay
17 Norway
20 Ascension Day
24 Commonwealth Day, U.K.
25 Argentina, Jordan
26 Guyana
27 Afghanistan
30 Pentecost
30 Shabuoth (Feast of Weeks), 1st day
31 South Africa

June
1 Tunisia
2 Italy
10 Portugal
11 Nepal
11 Philippines
12 Sovereign's Birthday, U.K.
17 Iceland
23 Luxembourg
24 Midsummer Day
30 Congo (Kinshasa)

July
1 Burundi, Canada, Rwanda, Somali Republic
4 United States
5 Venezuela
6 Malawi
12 Orangemen's Day, N.Ire.
14 France, Iraq

[August–December]
18 Spain
20 Colombia
21 Belgium
22 Poland
23 Ethiopia, U.A.R.
26 Liberia, Maldives
28 Peru

August
1 Dahomey, Switzerland
2 Jamaica
6 Bolivia
7 Ivory Coast
9 Singapore
10 Ecuador
15 Korea
17 Gabon, Indonesia
23 Romania
25 Uruguay
31 Malaysia, Trinidad and Tobago

September
1 Libya
6 Swaziland
6 Labor Day, U.S. and Canada
7 Brazil
9 Bulgaria
15 Costa Rica, El Salvador, Guatemala, Honduras, Nicaragua
16 Mexico
18 Chile
20 Rosh Hashana (Jewish New Year, 5732)
21 Malta
22 Mali
23 Saudi Arabia
26 Yemen
29 Yom Kippur (Day of Atonement)
30 Botswana

October
1 Cyprus, Nigeria
2 Guinea
4 Sukkoth (Feast of Tabernacles), 1st day
4 Lesotho
9 Uganda
10 China
14 Malagasy
21 Ramadân, 1st day
24 United Nations Day
24 Zambia
26 Austria, Iran
29 Turkey
31 Halloween

November
1 Algeria, Vietnam
3 Panama
7-8 U.S.S.R.
9 Cambodia
11 Sweden
22 Lebanon
25 Thanksgiving Day, U.S.
28 Mauritania
28 First Sunday in Advent
29 Yugoslavia
30 Barbados

December
1 Central African Republic
5 Thailand
6 Finland
11 Upper Volta
12 Kenya
13 Hanukkah (Feast of Lights), 1st day
18 Niger
25 Christmas Day
31 New Year's Eve

JANUARY

1

Israeli jets knocked out Jordan's East Ghor Canal on the east bank of the Jordan River for the third time in a year.

Family Law Reform Act lowering the age of legal majority from 21 to 18 went into effect in the U.K.

U.S. Vice-Pres. Spiro T. Agnew made a 24-hour visit to South Vietnam while on a ten-nation Asian tour.

2

Nigerian federal troops claimed they had cut the secessionist state of Biafra into three sections.

International Monetary Fund (IMF) announced the completed allocation of the first distribution of Special Drawing Rights to member nations.

U.S. Health, Education, and Welfare Secy. Robert H. Finch announced his department had dropped its controversial blacklisting of some prominent scientists.

New Year's cease-fires observed separately by allied and Communist forces ended in South Vietnam.

3

Israeli commandos were reported to have captured, dismantled, and airlifted to their lines a Soviet-built radar installation during their raid on a U.A.R. position in the Gulf of Suez on Dec. 26, 1969.

African nationalist guerrillas from Zambia staged their first infiltration raid on Rhodesia since mid-1968.

New constitution promulgated in the Congo (Brazzaville) created a Congolese Workers' Party whose chairman was automatically head of the state and changed the country's name to the People's Republic of the Congo.

Lebanese protest filed with the UN Security Council accused Israel of unjustified aggression and kidnapping in a raid on a Lebanese village.

4

New China News Agency accused the U.S.S.R. of preparing for war with China.

UN Secy.-Gen. U Thant urged Biafra to submit to a call for talks by the Organization of African Unity (OAU).

5

Israel filed a complaint with the UN Security Council that 19 guerrilla attacks against Israel in ten days had emanated from Lebanon.

United Mine Workers official Joseph A. Yablonski, his wife and daughter were found slain in their Clarksville, Pa., home.

6

Soviet Communist Party newspaper *Pravda* charged China with slandering the U.S.S.R. and preparing for war.

Nixon administration reported France had agreed to cooperate in halting illegal production of heroin in Marseilles.

8

Murder charges in connection with an alleged massacre at My Lai, South Vietnam, in March 1968 were made against two more U.S. soldiers.

9

Price of gold on the free market fell below the official price of $35 an ounce.

South Vietnamese Pres. Nguyen Van Thieu said the withdrawal of all U.S. combat troops from South Vietnam in 1970 was "impossible and impractical."

10

U.K. Prime Minister Harold Wilson urged workers to avoid wage demands that would endanger Britain's economic recovery.

11

Nigeria reported the capture of Owerri, the last Biafran stronghold.

Kansas City Chiefs defeated the Minnesota Vikings, 23 to 7, to win the U.S. professional football championship.

12

Biafra capitulated to the federal Nigerian government, ending the 31-month-old civil war.

Cuban Prime Minister Fidel Castro admitted that heavy rains and other difficulties would prevent the realization of the goal of a ten million-ton sugar harvest planned for 1970.

Details of the U.S.S.R. rejection of the U.S. Middle East peace proposal of October 1969 on the grounds that it was "pro-Israeli" were disclosed.

14

Nigerian leader Maj. Gen. Yakubu Gowon refused to accept aid from countries and agencies that had been "hostile" to Nigeria during the civil war.

Eisaku Sato was reelected prime minister of Japan.

U.S. Senate subcommittee opened hearings on the potential dangers of oral contraceptives.

U.S. Supreme Court set Feb. 1, 1970, as the deadline for school desegregation in six states.

15

Nixon administration announced agreement with Florida officials prohibiting the construction of an international jetport near Everglades National Park.

Soviet sources said Communist Party General Secy. Leonid I. Brezhnev had admitted serious economic difficulties prevented success of the 1965 economic plan.

16

Federal reports confirmed a slowing in the U.S. economy in spite of little evidence that inflation was slackening.

18

Clashes erupted between supporters of left- and right-wing parties in Dacca, East Pakistan.

Israeli jets bombed military targets near Cairo as part of a week-long offensive against the U.A.R. interior.

19

Second session of the 91st U.S. Congress convened in Washington, D.C.

U.S. Pres. Richard M. Nixon nominated U.S. Court of Appeals Judge G. Harrold Carswell to the Supreme Court seat left vacant by the resignation of Justice Abe Fortas in May 1969.

U.S. Supreme Court ruled that the Selective Service System lacked authority to accelerate the induction of persons violating draft regulations.

20

U.S. Federal Reserve Board announced increases in the interest rates payable on savings deposits.

U.S. and China resumed formal ambassadorial talks in Warsaw after a two-year suspension.

Albania and China announced the signing of an agreement to expand their trade.

Canadian Prices and Incomes Commission called for strong sanctions against companies making unnecessary price increases.

Israeli armoured troops crossed into Jordan in a 23-hour operation against Arab guerrillas.

18

Iraqi government announced it had crushed a right-wing, military-civilian coup.

21

Chicago coroner's jury ruled as justifiable the deaths of two Black Panther Party leaders during a police raid in December 1969.

Three men were arrested in Cleveland, O., in connection with the Yablonski murders.

North Vietnam refused to publish the names of captured U.S. pilots declaring they were "criminals," not prisoners of war.

French Defense Minister Michel Debré announced that France had agreed to sell Libya 100 combat aircraft rather than the 50 originally reported.

22

Pres. Nixon's State of the Union message to Congress focused on domestic problems, particularly environmental pollution.

West German Chancellor Willy Brandt sent a letter to East German Premier Willi Stoph proposing negotiations between the two countries.

Israeli troops were airlifted to Shadwan island at the start of a 30-hour drive to neutralize U.A.R. military installations in the Gulf of Suez.

23

Israeli High Court ruled that a person could be registered as Jewish by nationality without belonging to the Jewish faith.

Okinawan workers ended a five-day strike to protest the dismissal of workers at U.S. military bases.

Israeli task force on island of Shadwan . . . January 22

WIDE WORLD

French Foreign Minister Maurice Schumann completed two days of meetings in London with Prime Minister Wilson and Foreign Secy. Michael Stewart that focused on U.K. entry into the EEC.

24

Greek government announced an agreement to resume trade relations with Albania, one of a series of policy changes establishing closer ties with the Communist trading bloc.

26

Pres. Nixon vetoed as inflationary the 1970 appropriations for the Departments of Labor and Health, Education, and Welfare.

EEC Council of Ministers approved a plan to provide short-term assistance to members with balance of payments problems.

28

U.S. House of Representatives failed to override Pres. Nixon's veto of two appropriation bills.

Lubomir Strougal succeeded Oldrich Cernik as premier of Czechoslovakia.

Prime Minister Wilson and Pres. Nixon completed two days of talks in Washington, D.C.

30

Pres. Nixon stressed the goal of an economic slowdown in 1970 in his first economic report to Congress and discussed U.S. policy on Vietnam, the Middle East, and nuclear arms control at a formal press conference.

UN Security Council resolution condemned South Africa's presence in South West Africa.

Lesotho Prime Minister Chief Leabua Jonathan declared a state of emergency and ordered the arrest of his opponent, Ntsu Mokhehle, who had claimed victory in Lesotho's first parliamentary election since independence.

U.S. command in Saigon announced that U.S. jets had bombed an antiaircraft installation inside North Vietnam two days earlier.

Soviet Foreign Minister Andrei A. Gromyko and West German Secy. of State Egon Bahr met in Moscow to discuss the possibility of a mutual renunciation of force.

31

Ten-day restraining order issued by a U.S. District Court prevented a nationwide railroad shutdown.

French Pres. Georges Pompidou and West German Chancellor Brandt concluded a summit meeting in Paris.

Soviet Premier Aleksei N. Kosygin hinted in a letter to Pres. Nixon that the U.S.S.R. would increase military aid to the U.A.R. if the U.S. continued to deliver arms to Israel.

FEBRUARY

1

Israeli and Syrian tank and artillery units fought a two-hour battle along the Golan Heights frontier.

Pope Paul VI said that priestly celibacy was a fundamental principle of the Roman Catholic Church and could not be questioned.

China pledged support of the Arab struggle against Israel.

U.S.S.R. and West Germany formally signed an agreement under which Soviet natural gas would be exchanged for West German pipe.

North Vietnam warned its people to be prepared to continue fighting for "many years."

2

Pres. Nixon submitted to Congress a federal budget for fiscal 1971 that included a $1.3 billion surplus.

Costa Rican election returns indicated a substantial victory for former Pres. José Figueres Ferrer and his National Liberation Party.

3

Nixon administration sent Congress a new farm bill modifying the system of price supports.

4

Pres. Nixon urged adoption of a three-point proposal on Middle East problems in his reply to a letter from Soviet Premier Kosygin.

5

Pres. Nixon, administration members, and ten mayors met in Indianapolis, Ind., at the first session of the president's Council for Urban Affairs held outside Washington, D.C.

Allied and Communist forces in South Vietnam began observing separate Tet truces.

Pathet Lao and North Vietnamese spurned the proposal of Laotian Premier Prince Souvanna Phouma to neutralize the Plaine des Jarres.

6

West German and Polish representatives ended two days of talks in Warsaw aimed at improving political relations.

Inter-American Economic and Social Council ministerial meeting in Caracas, Venezuela, agreed to form a permanent trade negotiating committee.

U.S. Sen. Fred R. Harris (Dem., Okla.) resigned as chairman of the Democratic National Committee.

EEC and Yugoslavia signed a full-scale trade pact, the first such agreement between the EEC and an Eastern European nation.

U.A.R. frogmen sank an Israeli supply ship in Eilat Harbour; Israeli jets retaliated by sinking a U.A.R. vessel in the Gulf of Suez.

7

U.S. Secy. of State William P.

Rogers arrived in Rabat, Mor., to begin a ten-nation tour of Africa.

Five-nation Arab summit meeting to map strategy against Israel began in Cairo.

Roman Catholic marchers in ten Northern Ireland cities defied the two-day-old Public Order Act, which established conditions for demonstrations.

Italian Premier Mariano Rumor and his minority government resigned in an effort to force creation of a new coalition.

8

Governors of four Southern U.S. states met in Mobile, Ala., to discuss strategy against court-ordered school desegregation plans.

10

U.K. Prime Minister Wilson issued a government White Paper on the probable results of British entry into the EEC.

Arab terrorist grenades killed one Israeli and wounded 11 persons in an attack at a Munich, W.Ger., airport.

Pres. Nixon presented a national program to control air and water pollution in his first special message to Congress.

Canadian business leaders agreed to accept price controls for the balance of 1970.

11

U.S. bombers attacked Communist gun positions inside Cambodia.

Jordanian troops and Palestinian commandos clashed around Amman in fighting precipitated by a government decree restricting commando activities.

12

U.S. urged that the Big Four discuss limiting arms shipments to the Middle East and appealed for restoration of the cease-fire.

North Vietnamese launched a major offensive in northeastern Laos.

Israeli jets attacked a scrap metal processing plant near Cairo, reportedly killing 70 civilians.

13

EEC and Israel completed a five-year preferential trade agreement.

U.S. Defense Secy. Melvin R. Laird concluded a three-day visit to South Vietnam.

Four hundred U.S. volunteers sailed for Cuba to help harvest sugarcane.

14

Indian Prime Minister Indira Gandhi issued an ordinance renationalizing 14 private banks; the previous bank nationalization law had been ruled unconstitutional.

16

EEC Executive Commission annual report, released in Brussels, stressed the need for greater collaboration with the U.S.

Canadian provincial premiers agreed to adopt various anti-inflationary restraints.

17

Geneva Disarmament Conference reconvened.

18

U.S. Senate voted to cut off federal funds to all school districts where residential patterns resulted in de facto school segregation.

U.S. embassy in Manila was attacked by an estimated 2,000 youths, who had broken from a massive peaceful demonstration.

Pres. Nixon submitted a foreign policy message to Congress, outlining a "new strategy for peace" in the '70s.

Chicago jury acquitted seven defendants of charges of conspiring to incite a riot during the 1968 Democratic national convention but convicted five of the seven of seeking to incite a riot through individual acts.

19

U.S. Commissioner of Baseball Bowie Kuhn suspended Denny McLain, Detroit Tigers pitcher, for his alleged role in a bookmaking operation.

Canadian External Affairs Minister Mitchell Sharp asserted Canada's claim to jurisdiction over the waters of the Northwest Passage and other Arctic areas.

20

Chile agreed to sell $11 million worth of foodstuffs to Cuba despite the embargo imposed by members of the Organization of American States (OAS) in 1964.

21

North Vietnamese troops captured the Laotian government's last stronghold in the Plaine des Jarres.

23

Guyana changed its status from a parliamentary state within the Commonwealth of Nations to a cooperative republic.

French Pres. and Mme Pompidou arrived in the U.S. for a state visit; 3,500 persons rallied at the Washington Monument protesting French Middle East policy.

Georgia Gov. Lester G. Maddox signed legislation preventing the court-ordered transfer of teachers and students to achieve racial balance in the state's schools. Louisiana Gov. John J. McKeithen had signed a similar law the previous day.

Unified Command of Palestinian guerrilla groups denied claims by the Popular Front for the Liberation of Palestine that the PFLP was responsible for the February 21 crash of a Swiss airliner in which 47 persons were killed.

24

EEC finance ministers' meeting in Paris concluded agreement on broad plans for economic and monetary union by 1980.

Hawaii state legislature approved a bill legalizing abortions on demand.

25

U.S. Supreme Court held that the one man-one vote principle applied to school board and other local elections.

Military court in Saigon convicted two members of the South Vietnamese House of Representatives of dealings with Communists.

Reported expansion of the U.S. military role in Laos was criticized in the U.S. Senate.

26

U.S. Defense Secy. Laird said no U.S. troops were engaged in Laos and that U.S. air strikes there were directed only at North Vietnamese supply lines to South Vietnam.

Preliminary figures revealed that the U.S. government's index of "leading" economic indicators for January 1970 had made the sharpest drop since the 1957 recession.

California Gov. Ronald Reagan declared a state of emergency in Santa Barbara after a night of student rioting in which a Bank of America branch office was burned.

Israel reported that its jets had shot down three U.A.R. MiG-21 interceptors after attacking missile sites near Cairo.

U.S. Marine Corps command in Saigon announced that five Marines had been charged with murdering 16 South Vietnamese women and children while on patrol south of Da Nang.

Pres. Nixon proposed to revise or eliminate 57 federal programs to save at least $2 billion a year.

27

U.S., U.K., and France accepted a U.S.S.R. proposal for talks on the future status of Berlin.

Pres. Nixon asked Congress for a revision of the legislation dealing with transportation strikes.

General Agreement on Tariffs and Trade (GATT) members ended their 26th general assembly in Geneva.

Amended charter of the OAS, providing for a General Assembly as its supreme organ, went into effect.

Guatemalan Foreign Minister Alberto Fuentes Mohr was kidnapped in Guatemala City.

28

Italian Acting Premier Rumor abandoned efforts to form a centre-left coalition government.

MARCH

1

Austrian Socialist Party won an unexpected victory in National Assembly elections.

2

Rhodesia declared itself a republic, dissolving its last ties with the British crown.

French Pres. Pompidou accused Chicago authorities of having been "accomplices" in the Chicago demonstration against French Middle East policy; Pres. Nixon flew to New York City to substitute for Vice-Pres. Agnew at a dinner honouring Pres. Pompidou.

U.S. Supreme Court ruled that the five-year statute of limitations on federal prosecutions applies to young men failing to register for the draft at age 18.

4

Pres. Nixon signed special legislation blocking a nationwide railroad strike.

U.K. announced it would return to its NATO defense assignment in West Germany a brigade withdrawn as an economy measure in 1968.

5

Nuclear nonproliferation treaty went into effect.

U.S. Justice Department filed a suit to invalidate the reelection of W. A. Boyle as president of the United Mine Workers and to hold a federally supervised election.

Lawrence F. O'Brien was elected chairman of the Democratic National Committee.

OAU Council of Ministers meeting in Addis Ababa, Eth., passed a resolution urging assistance to African liberation movements.

6

Pres. Nixon reported he had asked the U.S.S.R. and the U.K. to initiate efforts to restore the terms of the 1962 Geneva agreements on Laos.

U.S. diplomat Sean M. Holly was kidnapped in Guatemala by members of the Rebel Armed Forces guerrilla group.

7

Malaysia and Thailand signed an agreement in Bangkok, Thailand, permitting their troops to combat Communist guerrillas in each other's territory.

8

El Salvador's National Conciliation Party retained its majority in congressional elections.

White House task force urged major changes in the administrative structure of and the concepts behind U.S. foreign aid.

9

Laotian Premier Prince Souvanna Phouma agreed to discuss a Pathet Lao five-point peace plan.

10

Israeli Knesset approved a bill establishing the legal definition of a Jew in Israel as one born of a Jewish mother, or a convert to the faith.

New York City police speculated that a Greenwich Village town house demolished by explosions four days earlier had been used as a bomb factory by members of the Weatherman faction of Students for a Democratic Society (SDS).

WIDE WORLD

W. A. Boyle, president of the United Mine Workers of America . . . March 5

11

Iraq agreed to recognize the autonomy of the Kurdish people, ending over eight years of warfare.

Brazilian revolutionaries kidnapped Nobuo Okuchi, Japanese consul general in São Paulo.

12

Curtis W. Tarr was nominated by Pres. Nixon as director of the Selective Service System.

U.S. Senate approved an amendment to the Voting Rights Act of 1965, lowering the voting age to 18 years.

Canadian Finance Minister Edgar J. Benson submitted a budget for the 1970–71 fiscal year and announced that consumer credit curbs would be introduced.

13

U.S. Central Intelligence Agency Director Richard Helms was reported to have confirmed that the CIA was active in Laos under cover of the Agency for International Development (AID).

Consultation on Church Union submitted preliminary plans to unite nine Protestant denominations into a single church.

14

"Columbia Eagle," U.S. freighter bound for Thailand, was seized by two crewmen and forced to sail into Cambodian waters.

Japan World Exposition, Expo 70, opened in Osaka.

16

U.S. State Department announced the removal of most of the restrictions on travel to China by U.S. citizens.

Cambodia demanded the removal of Communist troops from its border areas in talks requested by the North Vietnamese and Viet Cong after demonstrators had sacked their embassies in Cambodia.

Chief minister of West Bengal, India, resigned to protest the widespread use of violence in the state by the Marxist Communist Party of India.

Finnish legislative elections resulted in the end of the majority held by the Socialist parties.

Israel told the UN Security Council that Israeli attacks the day before on an army camp, power station, and road inside Syria were "self-defense measures."

17

Guyanan National Assembly elected former Supreme Court Justice Raymond Arthur Chung as first president of the Cooperative Republic of Guyana.

U.S. Army accused 14 officers, including Maj. Gen. Samuel W. Koster, superintendent of the U.S. Military Academy, of involvement in suppression of information about the alleged 1968 massacre at My Lai.

U.S. exercised its UN Security Council veto for the first time on a resolution to condemn the U.K. for not forcibly overthrowing the Rhodesian government.

18

Postal workers in New York City went on strike to protest lack of congressional action on pay legislation.

Cambodian Chief of State Prince Norodom Sihanouk was overthrown in a bloodless coup while in Moscow for meetings with Soviet leaders.

UN Security Council approved a resolution condemning Rhodesia.

U.S. Federal Reserve Board Chairman Arthur F. Burns announced a relaxation of monetary policy.

19

Philippine military officials denied charges made by Sen. Stuart Symington (Dem., Mo.) that the U.S. had provided cash assistance to the Philippines contingent in Vietnam.

U.S. government confirmed the U.S. had agreed to sell eight fighter jets to Libya.

East German Premier Stoph and West German Chancellor Brandt conferred in Erfurt, E.Ger., at the first meeting of the heads of the postwar German states.

20

U.A.R. newspapers confirmed the reported arrival in the U.A.R. of Soviet SAM-3s (surface-to-air missiles) and personnel to operate them.

21

Guatemalan Congress officially declared Col. Carlos Arana Osorio president-elect.

Alexander Dubcek, Czechoslovak ambassador to Turkey and Communist Party first secretary during the reform movement of 1968, was reported to have been suspended from party membership.

Cheng Heng, Cambodian National Assembly president, was sworn in as acting chief of state.

22

New Cambodian leadership urged the U.K. and the U.S.S.R. to reactivate the International Control Commission established for Cambodia by the 1954 Geneva Conference.

23

U.S. Secy. of State Rogers announced that the U.S. had postponed a decision on Israel's request to purchase 125 jet fighters.

Pres. Nixon ordered federal troops into New York City to help handle the mail.

French shopkeepers staged a nationwide protest of government policies.

Foreign ministers of 24 Islamic nations began their first conference on cooperation in Jidda, Saudi Arabia.

U.S. Supreme Court ruled that welfare recipients have a constitutional right to formal hearings before their benefits are terminated.

24

Pres. Nixon pledged the government's continued efforts to eliminate de jure segregation.

25

U.S. and U.S.S.R. resumed formal talks on the Middle East after a three-month lapse.

Clashes broke out in Lebanon between Palestinian commandos and civilians opposed to the guerrillas' presence.

"Sick-out" begun by federal air traffic controllers delayed or canceled about 1,000 flights throughout the U.S.

26

Dominican Republic released 20 political prisoners in exchange for Lieut. Col. Donald J. Crowley, a U.S. air attaché kidnapped two days earlier by Dominican revolutionaries.

U.S. Federal Communications Commission (FCC) said it would prohibit new combinations of radio and television ownership in any urban area.

U.S., U.K., French, and U.S.S.R. representatives met in West Berlin to discuss the problems of Berlin for the first time in 11 years.

27

Israeli pilots claimed they shot down five U.A.R. MiG-21 jets over the Suez Canal in one of a series of recent raids to prevent establishment of SAM-2 installations.

Washington authorities reaffirmed the U.S. policy not to widen the Vietnam war and said that the first major South Vietnamese operation inside Cambodia, launched with U.S. air support, had occurred without their prior knowledge.

28

New Italian coalition Cabinet headed by Mariano Rumor was sworn in.

Paraguayan consul in Ituzaingó, Arg., was released after the Argentine government refused to meet kidnappers' demands.

Dahomey's military government suspended the national elections begun March 9 because of continuing unrest.

29

Cambodian government reported that Vietnamese Communists were intensifying their military activity inside Cambodia.

30

Laotian government troops recaptured Sam Thong, a strategic base seized two weeks earlier by North Vietnamese forces.

31

Canadian government banned commercial fishing in Lake Erie, one week after imposing the same ban on Lake St. Clair.

Lesotho Prime Minister Jonathan ordered King Moshoeshoe II into exile.

Earthquakes were recorded in Turkey for the fourth straight day.

APRIL

1

Cambodia denounced all foreign incursions into its territory.

France proposed an international conference on Vietnam, Laos, and Cambodia.

Labour contract covering U.S. table-grape pickers for the first time was signed in Los Angeles.

Communist forces launched a major assault throughout South Vietnam, ending a six-month-long general lull.

2

U.S. grand jury in Chicago indicted 12 members of the Weatherman faction of the SDS on charges of conspiring to cross state lines to incite to riot in October 1969.

Massachusetts Gov. Francis W. Sargent signed a bill providing that servicemen from that state did not have to fight in an undeclared war.

Israeli and Syrian air and ground forces clashed for eight hours.

3

Pres. Nixon signed the Water Quality Improvement Act of 1970.

Japan Air Lines jet was flown to P'yongyang, North Korea, after attempts to trick its nine sword-carrying hijackers into disembarking at Seoul, South Korea, failed.

4

South Korean ships sank a North Korean boat apparently attempting to land agents in South Korea.

Five hundred additional British troops were flown into Northern Ireland following a week of disturbances.

5

Count Karl von Spreti, West German ambassador to Guatemala, was found slain after the Guatemalan government refused to grant demands of his kidnappers.

Israeli Cabinet rejected a bid for peace negotiations allegedly made by U.A.R. Pres. Gamal Abd-al-Nasser to World Jewish Congress Pres. Nahum Goldmann.

6

West Germany ordered a drastic downgrading of its diplomatic relations with Guatemala.

7

Prime Minister Wilson pledged to keep British troops in Northern Ireland as long as necessary.

8

Hijacked U.S. ship "Columbia Eagle" was released by Cambodia.

U.S. Senate rejected the nomination of Judge Carswell to the U.S. Supreme Court.

U.A.R. claimed that two Israeli jets had bombed an elementary school, killing 30 children.

Laotian Premier Prince Souvanna Phouma replied to a Pathet Lao peace plan by calling for peace talks preceded by a cease-fire.

9

Pres. Nixon signed legislation imposing a contract negotiated in December 1969 on U.S. railroads and four shopcraft unions.

U.S. Senate passed a resolution calling on Pres. Nixon to propose to the U.S.S.R. an immediate mutual suspension of the deployment of all nuclear strategic weapons.

U.S. announced it would not recognize yesterday's proposed legislation extending Canadian claims to jurisdiction over Arctic waters.

10

Greek Prime Minister Georgios Papadopoulos announced the restoration of some constitutional rights suspended in 1967.

11

Bodies of Vietnamese civilian residents of Cambodia were seen floating down the Mekong River.

Apollo 13 spacecraft with U.S. astronauts James A. Lovell, Jr., Fred W. Haise, Jr., and John L. Swigert, Jr., a last-minute substitute, was launched from Cape Kennedy, Fla., and headed for a planned moon landing.

West German Chancellor Brandt concluded his eight-day visit to the U.S.

12

Florida Gov. Claude R. Kirk, Jr., capitulated to a federal district court, ending his week-long defiance of orders to desegregate Manatee County public schools.

Recovery of the Apollo 13 spacecraft in the Pacific . . . April 17

COURTESY, NASA

Israeli authorities reported increasing acts of violence by Arab guerrillas in the Gaza Strip.

Greek military tribunal returned guilty verdicts against 27 of 34 persons charged with sedition.

13

Oxygen tank in the service module section of the Apollo 13 spacecraft exploded.

Soviet Communist Party General Secy. Brezhnev announced "substantial corrective changes" in economic areas.

Pres. Nixon signed the controversial education aid bill.

14

Cambodian Premier Lon Nol issued a world appeal for arms.

Pres. Nixon named Adm. Thomas H. Moorer to succeed Gen. Earle G. Wheeler as chairman of the Joint Chiefs of Staff and nominated U.S. Court of Appeals Judge Harry A. Blackmun to the Supreme Court.

Clifford Dupont was named the first president of the Rhodesian Republic.

U.K. Chancellor of the Exchequer Roy Jenkins presented a budget for fiscal 1970–71 that permitted tax reductions and an easing of credit restraints.

Sweden announced it would apologize for the racially biased insults shouted by demonstrators as Jerome H. Holland delivered his credentials as U.S. ambassador to Sweden.

French government introduced two measures aimed at curbing public disorders.

15

Council of Europe Committee of Ministers condemned Greece for repeated violations of the European Convention on Human Rights.

U.S. House of Representatives Republican Leader Gerald R. Ford (Mich.) called for an investigation into whether Justice William O. Douglas should be removed from the Supreme Court.

Legislation providing a 6% pay raise for postal, civil service, and military personnel was signed by Pres. Nixon.

16

U.S. and U.S.S.R. reopened strategic arms limitation talks (SALT) in Vienna.

Dominican Republic Pres. Joaquín Balaguer turned over the powers of his office temporarily to campaign for reelection.

17

Soviet Ambassador to the UN Yakov A. Malik said that a Geneva conference on Southeast Asia was "unrealistic," in an apparent contradiction of his earlier statement suggesting such a conference.

Jordanian King Husain I asked the U.S. to recall its ambassador to Jordan in protest of the decision of U.S. Assistant Secy. of State Joseph J. Sisco to drop Jordan from his tour of Middle East capitals

UPI COMPIX
U.S. combat troops attack Communist sanctuaries in Cambodia . . . April 30

because of violent anti-U.S. demonstrations in Amman.

Apollo 13 spacecraft splashed down in the Pacific Ocean.

19

Communist forces captured the town of Saang, about 20 mi. S of Phnom Penh, Cambodia.

20

Pres. Nixon announced the planned withdrawal of 150,000 more U.S. troops from South Vietnam by spring 1971.

Cambodian Premier Lon Nol sent Pres. Nixon a personal appeal for extensive military assistance.

21

Bruno Kreisky was sworn in as chancellor of Austria.

Two days of ceremonies commemorating the centenary of Lenin's birth opened in Moscow.

22

Canadian House of Commons voted unanimously to extend pollution controls over 100 mi. of offshore Arctic waters.

Australian Prime Minister John Gorton announced plans to withdraw one of Australia's three battalions from South Vietnam.

Earth Day observances focused attention on environmental problems in communities throughout the U.S.

23

Pres. Nixon issued an executive order ending the granting of some draft deferments.

Rifles and ammunition captured from Communist forces in South Vietnam were sent to Cambodia.

The Gambia was proclaimed a republic within the British Commonwealth.

24

China launched its first earth satellite.

Polish and West German repre-

sentatives concluded their third round of talks in Warsaw.

Deputy Premier Chiang Ching-kuo of Taiwan was shot at by a Taiwanese national while visiting in New York City.

26

Official results of the Colombian presidential election of April 19 gave the victory to Misael Pastrana Borrero.

27

Cambodia assured South Vietnam that it would protect Vietnamese civilians living in Cambodia and cooperate with South Vietnamese repatriation efforts.

Hanoi radio reported that Communist leaders from North and South Vietnam and Laos had met with Prince Sihanouk.

28

Indonesian Foreign Minister Adam Malik announced an Asian nation conference on Cambodia would be held in May despite formal opposition from the U.S.S.R., China, and North Vietnam.

U.A.R. claimed its troops had inflicted heavy damage on Israeli positions along the Suez Canal.

29

Israel officially confirmed that U.S.S.R. pilots were flying operational support missions for the U.A.R.

Official transcripts of the inquest into the death of Mary Jo Kopechne were released along with a statement by the presiding judge that he could not accept as true key parts of the testimony of U.S. Sen. Edward M. Kennedy (Dem., Mass.).

South Vietnamese troops opened a ground offensive into the Parrot's Beak area of Cambodia, backed by U.S. air and logistical support.

30

Pres. Nixon announced that U.S. combat troops were moving into Cambodia in an offensive against Communist border sanctuaries.

MAY

1

U.S. and South Vietnamese forces launched an offensive into the Fishhook area of Cambodia.

Formation of a three-man civilian presidential commission to replace the ruling military commission in Dahomey was announced.

Uganda Pres. Milton Obote announced the immediate nationalization of banks and various businesses involved in import-export trade.

3

Israeli patrol killed 21 Al Fatah guerrillas attempting to infiltrate across the Jordon.

4

Four students were killed and at least nine wounded when National Guardsmen suddenly fired into a group of antiwar demonstrators at Kent (O.) State University.

Soviet Premier Kosygin held a rare press conference to denounce Pres. Nixon's decision to send U.S. troops into Cambodia and resume bombing of North Vietnam.

U.S. Defense Department announced the termination of the heavy bombing raids on targets in North Vietnam begun on May 1.

Viet Cong and North Vietnamese forces cut off the highway between Phnom Penh and Saigon 29 mi. from the Cambodian capital.

5

Irish Prime Minister John Lynch dismissed two Cabinet ministers on charges of attempting to supply arms to Roman Catholics in Northern Ireland.

U.S. Federal Reserve Board reduced the margin requirement on stock purchases as stock price averages dropped to their lowest figures since Aug. 9, 1963.

Prince Sihanouk announced the formation of a Cambodian government-in-exile in Peking.

6

U.S. Interior Secy. Walter J. Hickel, in a letter to Pres. Nixon, charged that continued attacks on the motives of young people would solidify their hostility.

Viet Cong and North Vietnamese boycotted the Paris peace talks to protest the renewed U.S. bombing of North Vietnam.

7

White House announced U.S. troops had captured a major abandoned Communist base in the Fishhook area of Cambodia.

U.S. House of Representatives rejected a proposal to cut off funds for U.S. combat efforts in Cambodia on July 1 as student antiwar groups began intensive lobbying in Washington, D.C.

Pres. Nixon assured a meeting of university presidents that verbal attacks by administration members on students would cease.

8

South Vietnamese troops turned back North Vietnamese attacks near the Demilitarized Zone; 64 towns and bases in South Vietnam were shelled in a coordinated Communist attack.

South Vietnamese Pres. Thieu said his country would not be bound by the June 30 time limit set on U.S. operations in Cambodia.

U.S. Sen. George McGovern (Dem., S.D.) announced formation of a Committee to End the War to seek public support for congressional efforts to bar funds for military use in Cambodia, repeal the Tonkin Gulf Resolution, and require total U.S. troop withdrawal from South Vietnam by mid-1971.

Pres. Nixon discussed U.S. involvement in Cambodia and the domestic reaction to it at a televised news conference.

Construction workers disrupted student antiwar demonstrations in New York City's Wall Street.

9

Hastily organized protest of U.S. actions in Cambodia drew a crowd estimated at up to 100,000 in Washington, D.C.; Pres. Nixon visited demonstrators at the Lincoln Memorial shortly before dawn.

U.S. and South Vietnamese flotilla began a thrust up the Mekong into Cambodia; U.S. and South Vietnam established a naval blockade of 100 mi. of Cambodian coastline.

10

Brandeis University (Waltham, Mass.) student strike centre reported that 448 U.S. universities and colleges were on strike or closed.

11

EEC foreign ministers meeting in Brussels agreed to begin membership negotiations with the U.K., Ireland, Denmark, and Norway on June 30.

Pres. Nixon met with 45 state and territorial governors to discuss Southeast Asia policies and campus turmoil.

12

U.S. Senate confirmed unanimously the nomination of Judge Blackmun to the Supreme Court.

Six black men were killed and at least 60 other persons wounded in clashes with Augusta, Ga., police.

First withdrawal of U.S. troops from Cambodia was reported.

14

Finnish Pres. Urho Kekkonen ap-

pointed a caretaker government after six weeks of negotiations for a new government had failed.

15

South Africa was expelled from the International Olympic Committee.

Two black youths were killed and nine others wounded when police fired into a crowd outside a women's dormitory at Jackson (Miss.) State College.

16

Israeli planes attacked and sank two U.A.R. military vessels at a Red Sea naval base in reprisal for two U.A.R. naval attacks.

French Pres. Pompidou called for public calm in the wake of a series of bomb and arson attacks against police stations, public buildings, and homes of politicians.

Joaquín Balaguer was elected to a second four-year term as president of the Dominican Republic.

17

U.S. military sources reported the capture of part of the Communists' Central Office for South Vietnam (COSVN); Cambodian troops recaptured the city of Kompong Cham, penetrated the previous day by North Vietnamese and Viet Cong forces.

Meeting of foreign ministers of 11 Asian nations in Jakarta, Indon., recommended a new international conference on Indochina and the reactivation of the International Control Commission in Cambodia.

Israeli military sources admitted that increased air and artillery strikes along the Suez Canal in recent days were intended to frustrate reinforcement of U.A.R. missile sites.

18

U.K. Prime Minister Wilson ordered the dissolution of Parliament on May 29 and general elections on June 18.

U.S. Federal Reserve Board Chairman Burns and Housing and Urban Development Secy. George Romney, in separate speeches, called for federal wage and price guidelines.

Pravda editorial charged China with seeking the total domination of Asia.

China announced cancellation of ambassadorial talks with the U.S. scheduled for May 20 in Warsaw.

19

UN Security Council approved a resolution condemning Israel for its 32-hour retaliatory drive against Arab guerrilla bases in Lebanon on May 12–13.

Communist forces shelled more than 60 allied positions in South Vietnam as Viet Cong broadcasts called for stepped-up activity to mark the 80th anniversary of the birth of the late North Vietnamese Pres. Ho Chi Minh while South Vietnam and its allies concluded a 24-hour cease-fire to mark the birth of Buddha.

JOHN P. FILO, "TARENTUM (PA.) VALLEY DAILY NEWS"

National Guardsmen fire on antiwar demonstrators at Kent State University . . . May 4

Cuban Prime Minister Castro confirmed that despite massive efforts the sugar harvest would fall short of ten million tons.

20

South Vietnamese troops opened a new offensive in Cambodia.

Noontime rally and parade around New York's City Hall in support of Pres. Nixon and his Indochina policy drew a crowd of construction workers, longshoremen, and office workers estimated at from 60,000 to 150,000.

U.A.R. Pres. Nasser confirmed that U.S.S.R. pilots were flying armed U.A.R. planes; Soviet Premier Kosygin acknowledged the U.S.S.R. was providing "extensive aid" to Arab nations to help them "successfully defend their legitimate national rights."

Israeli Foreign Minister Abba Eban arrived in Washington to press Israel's request to purchase U.S. aircraft.

21

Chinese Communist Party Chairman Mao Tse-tung called for a world revolution against "U.S. imperialism" in a statement read at a mass rally in Peking.

U.S. Defense Department announced that intelligence reports indicated that COSVN had been moved beyond the 21-mi. limit set on U.S. ground operations in Cambodia.

West German Chancellor Brandt and East German Premier Stoph held their second meeting in Kassel, W.Ger.

22

Israeli school bus was ambushed

by Arab guerrillas near the Lebanese border; 12 persons were killed.

23

Portugal and Spain signed an agreement extending the Iberian friendship treaty at the conclusion of a state visit to Spain by Portuguese Premier Marcello Caetano.

Civil rights marchers rallied in Atlanta, Ga., at the conclusion of a 110-mi. "march against repression."

24

Laotian troops were reported to have begun a counterattack against recent advances by the North Vietnamese and Pathet Lao.

China and North Vietnam signed an agreement providing more economic and military aid for North Vietnam in 1970.

25

U.S. Treasury Department requested an increase in the national debt ceiling to $395 billion.

New York Stock Exchange prices recorded their largest single-day decline since the assassination of Pres. John F. Kennedy, Nov. 22, 1963.

26

Indonesian Pres. Suharto met with Pres. Nixon at the White House to discuss the Cambodian situation.

Canadian postal union officials ordered the first of a planned series of 24-hour strikes to rotate among Canadian cities and aimed at forcing government agreement on wage demands.

27

Lebanese government agreed to enforce curbs on Palestinian commando activities.

Cambodia and South Vietnam signed documents in Saigon under which South Vietnam would provide direct military assistance to Cambodia.

NATO Ministerial Council meeting ended in Rome with the issuance of a communiqué inviting Warsaw Pact and other interested nations to explore a mutual, balanced reduction of forces in Central Europe.

U.S. stock-exchange indicators recorded the largest gains ever posted for a single day.

29

Mme Sirimavo Bandaranaike was sworn in as Ceylon's prime minister following the victory of her three-party leftist coalition in national elections.

Canadian Prime Minister Pierre Elliott Trudeau concluded a 19-day tour of Pacific nations intended to dramatize Canada's interest in that area.

31

U.A.R. War Minister Gen. Muhammad Fawzi disclosed that U.A.R. forces had been reduced along the Suez Canal to protect them from Israeli attacks while training for a "war of liberation."

Massive earthquake struck the mountain region of northern Peru.

Canadian Finance Minister Benson announced the suspension of the fixed exchange rate on the Canadian dollar.

JUNE

1

Flooding of rivers in Romania, Yugoslavia, and Hungary was reported to have reached record levels.

Thailand agreed to provide direct military assistance to Cambodia.

2

U.S. and U.S.S.R. resumed talks in Washington, D.C., on the Middle East.

University of Wisconsin scientists announced the first complete synthesis of a gene.

3

Delegation of U.S. congressmen, governors, and White House aides departed Washington, D.C., on an inspection trip to South Vietnam and Cambodia.

4

Tonga became an independent kingdom and member of the British Commonwealth.

El Salvador and Honduras agreed to the establishment of a 1.8-mi. demilitarized zone along their border.

5

U.S.S.R. accused China of interfering in the internal affairs of the nations of South and Southeast Asia.

French Foreign Minister Schumann attended the meeting of the Western European Union, ending France's 15-month boycott.

North Korea claimed it sank a U.S. spy ship within its territorial waters; South Korea reported one of its naval vessels guiding fishermen was shelled and seized in its waters by North Korean ships.

U.S. Labor Department reported that unemployment had reached 5% of the work force in May.

Canadian Prices and Incomes Commission called for a 6% limit on wage increases.

6

Stockholm police began a 40-hour sick-in protesting the Swedish government's refusal to discuss demands concerning salaries and working conditions.

Pres. Nixon announced that Health, Education, and Welfare Secy. Finch would become counselor to the President and nominated Undersecy. of State Elliot L. Richardson to succeed Finch.

7

Constitutional amendment to limit the number of foreigners in

each Swiss canton except Geneva to 10% of the population was narrowly defeated in a national referendum.

8

Military commanders assumed presidential power in Argentina, forcing the resignation of Pres. Juan Carlos Onganía.

U.S. intelligence sources were reported to have revised upward estimates of Communist strength in Cambodia and parts of South Vietnam on the basis of captured documents.

9

North Korea made public a document proposing a five-point program for the reunification of Korea.

Central Committee to act as supreme political authority for ten Palestinian groups was formed.

Jordanian King Husain was the target of another assassination attempt while traveling to Amman to cope with a crisis brought on by clashes between Palestinian guerrillas and Jordanian troops.

10

U.S. military attaché in Amman, Maj. Robert Perry, was shot to death by commandos; a truce was declared in fighting between guerrillas and Jordanian troops.

Pres. Nixon named Secy. of Labor George P. Shultz as director and Casper W. Weinberger as deputy director of a new Office of Management and Budget, which replaced the Bureau of the Budget; John D. Ehrlichman as executive director of a new Domestic Council; and Undersecy. of Labor James D. Hodgson as Shultz's successor.

Resignation of James E. Allen, Jr., U.S. commissioner of education and critic of certain administration policies, was announced.

Revised version of the Nixon administration's welfare reform program was submitted to Congress.

11

NATO defense ministers authorized a comprehensive review of defense needs for the 1970s.

Communist forces were reported to have seized Cambodia's famous Angkor ruins.

U.S. Senate rejected a proposal by Sen. Robert C. Byrd (Dem., W.Va.) to endorse presidential authority to retain troops in Cambodia.

West German Ambassador to Brazil Ehrenfried von Holleben was kidnapped in Rio de Janeiro by terrorists who demanded the release of 40 political prisoners.

12

UN Security Council endorsed a Finnish proposal for periodic Cabinet-level meetings of member states to strengthen the UN's peacekeeping role.

Israeli commandos were reported to have staged two raids against U.A.R. positions on the Suez Canal and Gulf of Suez; U.A.R. reported

smashing two Israeli attempts to cross the canal.

13

Pres. Nixon named a nine-member commission to explore campus violence and student grievances.

Publication of Britain's major newspapers was resumed following a four-day strike.

14

West German coalition parties suffered setbacks in parliamentary elections in three states.

Elections to the Supreme Soviet were held throughout the U.S.S.R.

15

U.S. Supreme Court ruled that men who objected to war for purely moral and ethical reasons were entitled to draft exemptions as conscientious objectors.

16

Turkish government declared martial law in Istanbul and Kocaeli Province following labour riots.

Trial of Charles Manson and three women charged with the Sharon Tate murders of August 1969 began in Los Angeles.

17

Presidents of the two Congos met aboard a yacht in the Congo River to demonstrate their countries' reconciliation.

Pres. Nixon announced several supplementary anti-inflation measures as he appealed for wage and price restraints but ruled out mandatory controls in a television address.

18

Conservative Party won an upset victory in U.K. parliamentary elections.

Highway 1 from Phnom Penh to Saigon was closed when Communist forces staged a mine and mortar attack on the village of Koki Thom, Cambodia.

Brig. Gen. Roberto Marcelo Levingston was sworn in as president of Argentina.

Venezuela and Guyana agreed to a 12-year moratorium on their border dispute.

19

Edward Heath replaced Harold Wilson as U.K. prime minister.

Soviet spacecraft Soyuz 9 returned to earth concluding record-breaking 17-day flight.

U.S. Air Force announced that multiple warheads had been deployed on some U.S. intercontinental missiles.

20

China deferred plans to resume Chinese-U.S. ambassadorial talks in Warsaw.

21

Penn Central Transportation Co. was granted authority to reorganize under U.S. bankruptcy laws.

Brazil defeated Italy, 4–1, to win the ninth World Cup soccer championship in Mexico City.

22

Pres. Nixon signed legislation extending the Voting Rights Act of 1965 but asked for a prompt court test of the constitutionality of lowering the voting age to 18 by statute instead of by constitutional amendment.

Japan declared its intention to allow the automatic extension of its security pact with the U.S.

Ecuador Pres. José María Velasco Ibarra announced he was assuming dictatorial powers.

23

West Germany and Poland reached agreement on a broad economic cooperation pact in Warsaw.

25

U.S. Commerce Secy. Maurice H. Stans announced the administration would support legislation limiting textile imports following the collapse of negotiations with Japan

Victims of Peru earthquake . . . May 31

UPI COMPIX

for voluntary restrictions on its textile exports.

U.S. presented a new Middle East peace proposal calling for a 90-day cease-fire and indirect negotiations conducted by UN mediator Gunnar V. Jarring.

Major report on Canadian foreign policy called for a balance between Canada's involvement with the U.S. and its relations with other nations.

Cambodian government decreed the general mobilization of all citizens between the ages of 18 and 60.

26

Bernadette Devlin, Northern Ireland Roman Catholic activist and member of the U.K. Parliament, began serving a six-month prison term for her role in rioting in Londonderry in August 1969.

27

Cambodian forces were reported to have abandoned the last of four northeastern provinces.

Cambodian National Assembly extended wartime powers to Premier Lon Nol.

Chile Pres. Eduardo Frei Montalva declared a six-month state of emergency in Santiago Province.

29

U.S. ground troops completed their withdrawal from Cambodia.

Israeli Prime Minister Golda Meir stated opposition to the temporary cease-fire proposal in the new U.S. Middle East peace plan.

30

U.S. Senate adopted, after 34 days of debate, the Cooper-Church amendment to the foreign military sales bill, barring spending of funds for future U.S. military operations in Cambodia without congressional approval.

U.S. Congress completed action to override Pres. Nixon's veto of the bill extending the Hill-Burton hospital aid program.

EEC and delegations from the U.K., Ireland, Denmark, and Norway formally opened membership negotiations in Luxembourg.

OAS General Assembly unanimously adopted a resolution condemning terrorism and political kidnapping.

JULY

1

David K. E. Bruce was named by Pres. Nixon to head the U.S. delegation at the Paris peace talks.

Carlos Arana Osorio was sworn in as president of Guatemala.

Franco Maria Malfatti of Italy succeeded Jean Rey of Belgium as president of the EEC Executive Commission.

2

Queen Elizabeth II outlined the program of the new Conservative government in her speech from the throne at the opening of Parliament.

3

Portugal recalled its ambassador to the Vatican and delivered a formal protest of Pope Paul VI's meeting two days earlier with three leaders of independence movements in Portugal's African territories.

U.S.S.R. Communist Party Central Committee approved a report condemning mismanagement of the agricultural program and calling for increased meat and grain production.

4

British troops searched house-to-house for weapons in the Falls Road district of Belfast, N. Ire., after five civilians had been killed in rioting.

Honor America Day celebrations to mark Independence Day were held in Washington, D.C.

5

Luis Echeverría Álvarez was elected president of Mexico in national elections.

British royal family began a ten-day tour of Canada.

6

Coalition government of Italian Premier Rumor resigned in an internal dispute.

Israeli Army chief of staff Maj. Gen. Haim Bar-Lev reported three Israeli planes had been shot down in the past six days by missiles fired by crews including Soviet personnel.

7

Pres. Nixon invoked emergency powers to halt a strike against three U.S. railroads.

Two members of the U.S. House of Representatives fact-finding team that toured the Indochina war area condemned conditions in a South Vietnamese prison on Con Son island.

8

U.K. appealed to Geneva Conference nations to help reactivate the International Control Commission for Laos.

Pres. Nixon proposed a comprehensive program to provide self-determination for American Indians.

9

U.S. Defense Secy. Laird stated that the U.S.S.R. had been continuing to deploy intercontinental ballistic missiles since the start of the SALT talks.

Pres. Nixon called for a major reorganization of federal agencies concerned with environmental problems.

Bolivian Pres. Alfredo Ovando Candía dismissed Gen. Juan José

KEYSTONE
British troops battle rioters in Belfast, N.Ire. . . . July 4

Torres as commander in chief of the armed forces.

10

Roman Catholic Bishop James Walsh entered Hong Kong after being imprisoned in China as a spy for 12 years.

U.S. Internal Revenue Service announced that private schools practicing racial discrimination would lose their tax-exempt status.

Iceland Minister of Justice and Industry Johann Hafstein was named acting prime minister following the death of Prime Minister Bjarni Benediktsson.

Jordan and the Palestinian commandos signed a new accord in Amman.

12

Montreal police defused a 150-lb. dynamite bomb outside the Bank of Montreal in one of a series of bomb investigations.

13

Soviet news agency Tass reported that the 24th Communist Party Congress would be postponed until March 1971.

14

New Cabinet headed by Ahti Karjalainen was formed ending Finland's three-month political crisis.

Pres. Nixon and members of his Cabinet and staff discussed domestic problems with 12 governors in Louisville, Ky.

15

Supreme Soviet reappointed the entire U.S.S.R. government.

South Vietnamese forces began the second coordinated drive in four days into northeastern South Vietnam.

U.S. Senate passed and sent to Pres. Nixon the Newspaper Preservation Act.

16

Prince Charles and Princess Anne

of Britain began an informal three-day visit to Washington, D.C.

British government declared a state of emergency following the start of a nationwide dock strike.

17

Body of former Argentine Pres. Pedro Eugenio Aramburu, found seven weeks after he had been kidnapped, was identified.

U.S.S.R.-U.A.R. communiqué calling for a political settlement in the Middle East was issued at the conclusion of Pres. Nasser's 18-day visit to Moscow.

18

Pres. Nixon warned Congress of the need to impose limits on its spending.

20

Pres. Nixon held an impromptu news conference to discuss pending trade legislation, opposition to a coalition government in South Vietnam, and the Middle East situation.

British government announced it would consider defensive arms sales to South Africa.

22

U.S. agreed to strengthen South Korea's armed forces and defense industries before any substantial troop withdrawal from South Korea.

Palestinian commandos hijacked a Greek passenger jet and demanded the release of seven Arab guerrillas held in Greece.

Cambodian Premier Lon Nol arrived in Bangkok for talks with Thai Prime Minister Thanom Kittikachorn.

23

Tear gas bombs thrown from the visitors' gallery forced the evacuation of the U.K. House of Commons.

U.S. grand jury in Detroit indicted 13 Weatherman faction members on conspiracy to commit bombing charges.

UN Security Council approved an Afro-Asian resolution tightening its 1963 arms embargo against South Africa.

Northern Ireland government banned public parades for six months.

Sultan Sa'id bin Taimur, of Oman, was deposed by his son, Qabus bin Sa'id, in a palace coup.

U.A.R. Pres. Nasser announced acceptance of the U.S. plan for a three-month Middle East cease-fire.

24

U.S. Defense Department announced approximately 6,000 U.S. military personnel would be withdrawn from the Philippines by July 1, 1971.

Brazilian Pres. Emílio G. Médici denounced the activities of vigilante "death squads" said to be composed of policemen.

Chief U.S. negotiator Gerald C. Smith formally presented a U.S. proposal on arms limitation at the SALT talks in Vienna.

Moroccan voters approved a new constitution effectively ending the five-year state of emergency.

25

Anthony Barber was named U.K. chancellor of the Exchequer.

26

Jordan announced its acceptance of the U.S. Middle East cease-fire plan; Syria, Iraq, and Arab guerrilla organizations rejected the plan.

27

António Salazar, Portuguese chief of state for 40 years, died in Lisbon.

Negotiations on a West German-U.S.S.R. renunciation of force treaty began in Moscow.

Chinese Premier Chou En-lai endorsed Sino-French relations in an interview broadcast on French television.

28

U.S. government announced a federal budget deficit of $2.9 billion for the fiscal year ended June 30, 1970.

Presidential commission report recommending a radical reorganization of the U.S. Defense Department was made public.

Peruvian Pres. Juan Velasco Alvarado promulgated a new national industrial reform law.

29

New York City Mayor John V. Lindsay placed the city on alert as a temperature inversion along the U.S. East Coast sent pollution levels above the danger point; Tokyo, Sydney, and other major cities also experienced pollution crises.

U.S. Treasury Secy. David M. Kennedy denied charges that his department was making a general investigation of readers of library books on explosives.

Pres. Nixon signed the District of Columbia crime control bill.

30

Pres. Nixon held a news conference in which he discussed domestic issues and stated that Israel's security would not be endangered by the U.S.

Israel claimed that it shot down four U.A.R. planes over the Suez Canal.

31

Israeli Cabinet decided to accept the U.S. formula for a limited cease-fire after a week-long debate.

Lieut. Gen. Odd Bull resigned as UN Middle East truce supervisor and was replaced by Maj. Gen. Ensio Siilasvuo of Finland.

AUGUST

1

British Army announced new security measures for its forces in Northern Ireland.

2

First Boeing 747 jetliner to be hijacked was met in Havana by Cuban Prime Minister Castro.

3

Canadian provincial premiers met for their 11th annual conference aboard a cruiser on Lake Winnipeg, Manitoba.

Pres. Nixon said in Denver, Colo., that Charles Manson was "guilty" of the Sharon Tate murders; a defense request for a mistrial was turned down in Los Angeles.

U.S. Poseidon missile was successfully test-fired from under water for the first time in the Atlantic in the presence of an uninvited Soviet trawler.

Hurricane Celia struck the Texas coast of the Gulf of Mexico.

4

Right-wing Gahal faction resigned from the Israeli Cabinet to protest Israel's acceptance of the U.S. Middle East peace plan.

5

Black Panther Party co-founder Huey P. Newton was freed on bail from an Oakland, Calif., jail after a reversal of his 1968 conviction for voluntary manslaughter was upheld.

Conference of Arab foreign and defense ministers opened in Tripoli, Libya, after a two-day delay caused by a boycott of the meeting by Iraq and Algeria.

6

U.S. and Spain signed an agreement providing for the continued U.S. use of bases in Spain for five years.

U.S. House of Representatives gave final congressional approval to a bill creating an independent postal agency.

Emilio Colombo was sworn in as premier of a new Italian coalition Cabinet.

7

Ninety-day truce went into effect on the Israeli-U.A.R. front along the Suez Canal.

Misael Pastrana Borrero was sworn in as president of Colombia.

Ghanaian three-man Presidential Commission was dissolved with the resignation of its members.

California Judge Harold J. Haley and his three kidnappers were killed in an escape attempt at the San Rafael courthouse.

10

Bolivian Pres. Ovando Candía named a new Cabinet including all but one of the members of the Cabinet that had resigned on August 4.

First annual report of the U.S. Council on Environmental Quality recommending action on proposed environmental legislation was sent to Congress by Pres. Nixon.

U.S. House of Representatives approved a constitutional amendment, first introduced in 1923, that would prohibit discrimination on the basis of sex.

Pres. Nixon signed a bill extending unemployment insurance coverage.

Body of U.S. diplomat Dan A. Mitrione was found in Montevideo, 11 days after he had been kidnapped by Uruguayan Tupamaro terrorists.

11

Tokyo metropolitan council passed a supplementary budget to be used to combat smog and pollution.

Nixon administration rejected the recommendations of the Commission on Obscenity and Pornography even though the report had not been released.

12

British troops and Ulster police sealed off Catholic areas of Londonderry to quell disturbances following a Protestant rally.

Iraq and Syria issued statements reaffirming their opposition to U.A.R. involvement in Middle East peace efforts.

U.S.S.R.-West German treaty on the renunciation of force was signed in Moscow.

13

U.S. House of Representatives overrode Pres. Nixon's August 11 veto of an education appropriations bill but failed to override his veto of bill funding housing, space, and other programs.

14

Israeli jets attacked Jordanian Army posts for the first time since the August 7 cease-fire in reprisal for alleged army assistance of guerrilla activities.

SALT talks in Vienna adjourned with the announcement that they would resume in Helsinki, Fin., in November.

Yugoslavia and the Vatican resumed full diplomatic relations after an interval of nearly 18 years.

16

Pakistani Pres. Agha Muhammad Yahya Khan announced postponement of general elections until December because of flooding in East Pakistan.

Federal warrant was issued for black militant Angela Davis in connection with the San Rafael courthouse deaths.

17

Pathet Lao reported a breakdown in efforts to establish peace talks with the Laotian government.

Suleiman Franjieh was elected to succeed Charles Helou as president of Lebanon.

Israeli Foreign Minister Eban took strong exception to remarks made the previous day by U.S. De-

Shrimp boat fleet wrecked by Hurricane Celia . . . August 3

WIDE WORLD

fense Secy. Laird that Israeli charges of U.A.R. truce violations were "difficult to prove or disprove."

Agreement by which Switzerland would help the U.S. track down money held in Swiss banks for illegal purposes was announced.

Pres. Nixon signed a bill extending the Defense Production Act although he objected to the provisions authorizing him to freeze wages, prices, and rents.

18

U.S. Senate overrode Pres. Nixon's veto of the education appropriations bill, and the bill became law.

U.S. Liberty ship and its cargo of nerve gas were sunk in deep water off the Florida coast despite strong public protest.

John W. Gardner, chairman of the National Urban Coalition, announced the formation of Common Cause, a citizens' lobby for governmental reforms.

19

U.S. Senate defeated the second proposal in a week designed to limit extension of the Safeguard antiballistic missile system.

Israel published photographs to support its charges of a U.A.R. missile buildup in the Suez Canal truce zone.

U.S. and Cambodia concluded a military assistance agreement in Phnom Penh.

Pres. Nixon requested that the U.S. Senate ratify the 1925 Geneva protocol against the use of chemical and biological weapons in war.

20

Cambodian and Communist troops clashed about seven miles from Phnom Penh.

Mexican Pres. Gustavo Díaz Ordaz and U.S. Pres. Nixon agreed on a proposed treaty providing for settlement of all current and future border disputes.

21

Warsaw Pact endorsed the new U.S.S.R.-West German treaty.

22

North Korea rejected the proposal for reunification made August 15 by South Korean Pres. Park Chung Hee.

U.S. Vice-Pres. Agnew began a tour intended to reassure four Asian nations of continued U.S. support.

23

Israeli Cabinet named Foreign Minister Eban its chief delegate to proposed UN peace talks.

24

Research building at the Univer-

sity of Wisconsin in Madison was destroyed and one person killed in an early morning explosion.

25

Peace talks aimed at settling the Middle East dispute opened at UN headquarters in New York City.

26

"Women's Strike" for Equality" demonstrations marked the 50th anniversary of women's suffrage in the U.S.

27

U.A.R. reported it had filed its first formal charge of Israeli ceasefire violations, including the movement of troops into the Suez Canal truce zone.

U.S. economic indicators published for July showed a strong advance.

28

Czechoslovak Communist Party First Secy. Gustav Husak said that the nation's crisis had been "eliminated."

U.S. State Department announced that Thailand planned to withdraw all its troops from South Vietnam.

31

Desegregated classes began for the first time in more than 200 school districts across the southern U.S.

Indonesian Amboinese separatists seized the Indonesian embassy at The Hague, Neth.

Edward Akufo-Addo was elected president of Ghana.

SEPTEMBER

1

Jordanian King Husain escaped an assassination attempt in Amman.

U.S. Senate defeated an amendment proposed by Senators McGovern (Dem., S.D.) and Mark Hatfield (Rep., Ore.) to withdraw all U.S. troops from Indochina by the end of 1971.

U.S.S.R. Ministry of Justice, abolished in 1956, was restored.

2

National Aeronautics and Space Administration (NASA) canceled two of six planned U.S. Apollo program moon landings.

3

U.S. reported that its "latest evidence" confirmed U.A.R. cease-fire violations and appealed to the U.S.S.R. and U.A.R. to refrain from any further violations.

North Vietnamese chief negotiator Xuan Thuy returned to the Paris peace talks.

Panamanian rejection of three draft treaties on the status of the Canal Zone was announced by the U.S. State Department.

UN Conference of the Committee on Disarmament ended its 1970 session with the approval of a draft treaty banning nuclear weapons from the ocean floor.

Indonesian Pres. Suharto began a state visit to the Netherlands that had been postponed two days because of disturbances in The Hague.

OAU summit conference in Addis Ababa ended after adopting resolutions on arms sales to South Africa, decolonization, and the Middle East.

4

Marxist candidate Salvador Allende Gossens won a plurality in Chilean presidential election.

U.A.R. rejected as untrue U.S. and Israeli charges of cease-fire violations.

Mexican Pres. Díaz Ordaz warned during a state visit to the U.S. against U.S. protectionist trade policies toward Latin America.

Canadian postal strike ended.

5

UN Security Council condemned Israeli attacks on Arab guerrilla bases in Lebanon.

Cease-fire was announced after four days of clashes between the Jordanian troops and Palestinian forces attempting to strengthen ties with Iraq.

6

Plenary session of the Chinese Communist Party Central Committee announced plans for a fourth National People's Congress.

Malagasy Republic Pres. Philibert Tsiranana's Social Democratic Party won an overwhelming majority in parliamentary elections.

Israel announced its withdrawal from the UN peace talks.

Arab commandos hijacked three jetliners bound for New York from Europe and demanded the release of commandos held in Israel, Switzerland, West Germany, and the U.K. in exchange for the passengers; a fourth hijacking attempt failed.

7

U.S. strength in Vietnam fell below 400,000 for the first time since January 1967.

8

Second cease-fire in four days was first announced in Jordan and then called off by commandos.

International Committee of the Red Cross was selected to seek the release of airline passengers held in Jordan by Arab commandos.

9

Arab commandos hijacked a British jetliner and landed it near two others in the Jordanian desert.

10

Summit conference of 54 nonaligned nations ended in Lusaka,

Zambia, with the adoption of resolutions dealing with Middle Eastern, southern African, and Southeast Asian problems.

Third cease-fire in Jordanian fighting was announced.

U.S. Vice-Pres. Agnew began a six-state political campaign with an attack on "radic-libs."

11

Arab commandos added new demands for a "national authority" to Jordanian peace plans.

Pres. Nixon ordered the use of federal armed guards on overseas flights of U.S. airlines.

12

Arab commandos blew up three hijacked airliners in the Jordanian desert; all but 54 passengers and crew to be held as "prisoners of war" were released.

U.S. Secy. of State Rogers announced the U.S. was planning to resume aid to Israel.

15

Strike by United Automobile Workers began against the General Motors Corp.

U.S. officials reported Israeli violations of the Middle East ceasefire.

Pres. Nixon sent to Congress his program to overhaul U.S. foreign aid.

Fourth cease-fire in Jordan in two weeks was announced; King Husain dismissed Abdel Monem Rifai, prime minister since June 27, upon learning that the truce gave commandos control of the cities.

U.A.R. Foreign Minister Mahmoud Riad said the U.S. Middle East peace initiative was "dead."

UN General Assembly opened its 25th session; Edvard Hambro of Norway was elected president.

Canadian federal-provincial conference on constitutional reform ended in Ottawa.

16

North Korea proposed a "confederation" with South Korea that would precede eventual reunification.

Jordanian King Husain announced formation of a military government headed by Brig. Gen. Muhammad Daoud; Central Committee of the Palestine Liberation Organization (PLO) rejected the new government and ordered its units to fortify their positions.

17

Jordanian troops attacked two Palestinian refugee camps in clashes with commandos throughout Amman.

Viet Cong presented an eight-point peace proposal at the Paris peace talks.

20

Israeli Prime Minister Meir concluded a five-day visit to the U.S.

UPI COMPIX

Arab commandos blow up hijacked airliners . . . September 12

French Premier Jacques Chaban-Delmas defeated reformist Jean-Jacques Servan-Schreiber in a Bordeaux by-election.

Jordanian broadcast said Syrian tanks had crossed into northwestern Jordan to link up with commando units.

First general election under Sweden's new constitutional reform resulted in the loss of the absolute majority held by the Social Democrats.

U.S. Secy. of State Rogers warned that Syrian intervention in Jordan raised the danger of a wider war.

21

Pres. Nixon named retired Air Force Lieut. Gen. Benjamin O. Davis, Jr., to the new post of head of civil aviation security in the Transportation Department.

Yugoslav Pres. Marshal Tito announced plans for a collective leadership to succeed him.

22

Formal emergency meeting in Cairo of Arab chiefs of state was put off, and envoys headed by Sudanese Pres. Gafaar al-Nimeiry were sent to Jordan to persuade King Husain and PLO leader Yasir Arafat to attend.

Tun Abdul Razak succeeded Tunku Abdul Rahman as prime minister of Malaysia.

Pres. Nixon signed a bill giving the District of Columbia a nonvoting delegate in the U.S. House.

23

"Brownouts" occurred along the U.S. East Coast as a prolonged heat wave taxed low power reserves.

Jordanian forces pushed back a large commando force headed by Syrian tanks.

24

Luna 16, Soviet unmanned spacecraft, returned from the moon with rock samples.

Jordanian Prime Minister Daoud resigned abruptly and disappeared in Cairo.

Second threat in a week of a U.S. rail strike was averted with an agreement to resume negotiations.

Canadian Prime Minister Trudeau completed a Cabinet revision in which Donald Macdonald succeeded Defence Minister Léo Cadieux.

25

PLO leader Arafat announced he would meet with Arab League envoys.

Nationwide cease-fire was agreed to by Jordanian military government and the PLO as government troops held most of Amman and encircled commando units in the north.

U.S., Chile, Peru, and Ecuador concluded meetings in Buenos Aires, Arg., on fishing rights without reaching agreement.

26

Street fighting erupted in Belfast after a soccer game.

South Vietnamese Vice-Pres. Nguyen Cao Ky reversed his decision to address a pro-war rally in Washington, D.C., on October 3.

King Husain announced a new military-civilian government headed by Ahmed Toukan.

U.S. Commission on Campus Unrest issued a report warning of growing crisis.

27

Pres. Nixon arrived in Rome at the start of a five-nation European tour.

28

U.A.R. Pres. Nasser suffered a fatal heart attack after Cairo airport ceremonies ending the Arab summit meeting.

Largest brush fire in California history raged near the Mexican border.

Pres. Nixon canceled U.S. naval demonstrations planned to emphasize the U.S. presence in the Mediterranean.

29

Last hijack hostages in Jordan

were released as part of a deal for the release of Arab terrorists held in Britain, West Germany, and Switzerland.

U.S. Senate failed to invoke cloture on a constitutional amendment for direct presidential elections.

Censure motion brought against Australian Prime Minister Gorton was defeated in Parliament.

30

Pres. Nixon arrived in Belgrade at the start of a two-day visit to Yugoslavia, the first by a U.S. president.

U.S. Commission on Obscenity and Pornography released its controversial report.

U.S.S.R. denounced U.S. charges it was building a submarine missile base in Cuba.

U.K. Labour Party annual meeting opened in Blackpool and endorsed U.K. entry into the EEC.

OCTOBER

1

Emotional demonstrations held throughout the Arab world marked the funeral of U.A.R. Pres. Nasser in Cairo.

Niger Pres. Hamani Diori was reelected to a third term without opposition.

Chairman Mao presided over Chinese National Day ceremonies in Peking.

2

UN General Assembly heard Cuba's offer to negotiate bilateral agreements to extradite hijackers.

UN Middle East mediator Jarring suspended his peace-seeking mission.

3

Pres. Nixon declared in Spain a "new era" in relations between Spain and the U.S., and met with Prime Minister Heath and Queen Elizabeth II during a five-hour visit to Britain.

U.A.R.-U.S.S.R. communiqué said

---

the two countries would continue to seek peace in the Middle East.

4

Pres. Nixon met in Ireland with the U.S. delegation to the Paris peace talks.

U.S. Commission on Campus Unrest issued its second report in four days, describing the Kent State shooting, like that at Jackson State, as "unwarranted."

5

British government publicized a bill to regulate industrial-union relations.

French-Canadian separatists kidnapped British diplomat James R. Cross in Montreal.

6

Right-wing Bolivian Army Chief of Staff Gen. Rogelio Miranda seized presidential power immediately following the resignation of Pres. Ovando Candía.

7

Left-wing Gen. Torres ousted Gen. Miranda and named himself president of Bolivia.

Pres. Nixon proposed a five-point Indochina peace plan.

China and North Vietnam announced a new economic and military aid agreement.

Communiqué ending three days of Polish-West German talks in Bonn said negotiations on normalizing relations had reached an advanced stage.

8

U.S.S.R. Foreign Ministry denied any involvement in Middle East cease-fire violations.

Nobel Prize for Literature was awarded to Soviet novelist Aleksandr I. Solzhenitsyn.

9

Cambodia was proclaimed officially the Khmer Republic.

Big Four representatives met to discuss the problems of Berlin.

10

Fiji became independent in ceremonies presided over by Britain's Prince Charles.

Pierre Laporte, Quebec labour minister, was kidnapped from his Montreal home by French-Canadian separatists.

12

UN Conference on Trade and Development (UNCTAD) agreed to a plan to give trade preferences to less developed nations.

Pres. Nixon announced the planned withdrawal of 40,000 troops from South Vietnam by Christmas of 1970.

U.S. Commission on Civil Rights reported that there had been a "major breakdown" in the enforcement of civil rights legislation.

Pres. Nixon vetoed legislation limiting campaign spending on television and radio time.

13

Canada and China established diplomatic relations.

French Pres. Pompidou and Soviet Pres. Nikolai V. Podgorny signed in Moscow an agreement for political and economic cooperation.

14

North Vietnam officially rejected Pres. Nixon's five-point Indochina peace plan.

UN General Assembly began a special ten-day session commemorating its 25th anniversary.

U.S., U.S.S.R., and China exploded nuclear devices within hours of each other.

U.S. Congress began a month-long election-time recess after completing action to establish a National Railroad Passenger Corp.

Zambian Pres. Kenneth Kaunda began a tour of Western nations at the head of an OAU mission seeking withdrawal of support for South Africa and Portugal.

15

U.A.R. Acting Pres. Anwar al-Sadat was elected president in a national plebiscite.

U.K. White Paper announced a government reorganization creating two new ministries, the Department of Trade and Industry and the Department of the Environment.

Two Lithuanians accomplished the first successful hijacking of a Soviet airliner; the stewardess was killed.

Baltimore Orioles won the baseball World Series by defeating the Cincinnati Reds, 9–3, in the fifth game.

Pres. Nixon signed the Organized Crime Control and Urban Mass Transportation acts.

16

Canadian Prime Minister Trudeau invoked the War Measures Act for the first time in peacetime to deal with the Quebec kidnappings.

EEC warned it would consider retaliation if the U.S. adopted pending trade legislation.

Ohio grand jury indicted 25 persons, none of them National Guardsmen, on charges connected with the Kent State disturbances in May.

Italian troops were sent into Reggio Calabria after a renewal of violence that began in the summer when the rival city of Catanzaro was chosen the capital of the Calabria region.

17

Warsaw Pact troops concluded five days of military exercises in East Germany.

Indian Prime Minister Gandhi permitted an opposition coalition to form a new government in Uttar Pradesh, which had been placed under presidential rule October 2.

Heavy fighting between government troops and commandos was reported in northern Jordan.

Testimony by U.S. State and Defense Department officials that the U.S. had been secretly arming and training Ethiopian troops since 1960 was disclosed.

18

Body of Quebec Labour Minister Laporte was found near Montreal.

21

Nobel Peace Prize was awarded to Norman E. Borlaug of the U.S.

Jordanian authorities announced that Iraqi troops had begun to withdraw from Jordan.

U.S. Air Force plane carrying two U.S. generals landed in Soviet Armenia instead of its intended Turkish destination.

Pope Paul VI condemned police torture of political prisoners in a statement clearly alluding to the practice in Brazil.

22

Pres. Nixon and Soviet Foreign Minister Gromyko held a lengthy conference in Washington.

State of emergency was declared in Chile after the fatal shooting of Army Commander Gen. René Schneider Chereau.

23

Pres. Nixon addressed the UN General Assembly.

24

Chilean Congress chose Salvador Allende president of Chile.

Japanese Prime Minister Sato and Pres. Nixon agreed in Washington to resume textile-trade negotiations.

25

Former French Premier Maurice Couve de Murville concluded a private visit to China.

South Vietnamese forces opened the second of two new offensives into Cambodia.

Montreal Mayor Jean Drapeau won a landslide reelection in heavily guarded voting.

26

NASA engineers joined Soviet scientists for discussions in Moscow on standardized spacecraft docking systems.

Statement endorsing U.S. Sen. Charles E. Goodell (Rep., N.Y.), attacked by Vice-Pres. Agnew as a "radical-liberal" who "has left his party," was signed by 18 Republican senators.

Argentina, Belgium, Italy, Japan, and Somalia were elected nonpermanent members of the UN Security Council.

27

Canada announced the sale of 98 million bu. of wheat to China.

Four agreements were announced in the negotiations for U.K. entry into the EEC.

British government announced the "mini-budget," which called for cuts in taxes, subsidies, and public spending.

28

Jordanian King Husain appointed a new Cabinet, headed by Wasfi al-Tal as prime minister.

U.K. White Paper pledged the country would keep a small military force in Southeast Asia and increase its NATO contribution.

29

U.S. charged the U.S.S.R. had violated a 1968 agreement by not allowing prompt consular access to three detained U.S. Army officers.

Laotian government accepted a Pathet Lao formula for peace talks.

East and West Germany announced they would resume talks on normalizing relations.

30

Four-hour street battle marked a fresh outbreak of violence in Belfast.

31

Pres. Nixon called for the end of "appeasement" of "thugs and hoodlums" in a campaign speech in Phoenix, Ariz., two days after objects were thrown at him following a rally in San Jose, Calif.

Tanzanian Pres. Julius Nyerere won reelection overwhelmingly.

South Vietnamese Pres. Thieu reiterated his strong opposition to a coalition government with the Communists.

NOVEMBER

1

Polish diplomat Zygfryd Wolniak and three Pakistanis were killed when a van ran into a reception line for Polish Pres. Marshal Marian Spychalski at Karachi International Airport.

Jack the Ripper was reported in a *Sunday Times* of London story to have been Edward, duke of Clarence, a grandson of Queen Victoria.

2

Canadian Prime Minister Trudeau introduced legislation to replace the War Measures Act in dealing with the Quebec crisis.

SALT talks resumed in Helsinki.

3

Mixed results in U.S. midterm elections produced Republican gains in the Senate and Democratic gains in the House of Representatives and state governorships.

4

UN General Assembly adopted a resolution calling for a three-month extension of the Middle East cease-fire and the resumption of peace talks.

U.S. announced plans to withdraw its division from the Korean demilitarized zone.

Ivory Coast Pres. Félix Houphouët-Boigny called for an African summit conference on South Africa.

EEC Executive Commission submitted to the Council of Ministers its draft of medium-term economic policies based on the Werner plan of Luxembourg Prime Minister Pierre Werner.

5

Ecuadorian Air Force Commander Cesar Rohon Sandoval was reportedly relieved of his duties following unsatisfactory accounts of his kidnapping on October 27.

U.S. military sources reported a massive supply buildup in southern North Vietnam.

Israeli Prime Minister Meir concluded a visit to London that included discussions of a U.K. peace plan calling for Israeli withdrawal from Arab areas.

Vatican issued instructions ending experimentation with the Roman Catholic liturgy.

British municipal workers ended their six-week strike for higher wages.

6

Italy and China announced agreement to establish diplomatic relations; Taiwan and Italy severed ties.

Two bombs exploded in the Tel Aviv central bus station, killing one person in the first Arab terrorist attack in an urban Israeli area in a year.

7

U.S.S.R. marked the 53rd anniversary of the Bolshevik Revolution with a Red Square parade; U.S. downgraded its attendance to protest the continued detention of U.S. military personnel.

8

U.A.R., Libya, and the Sudan agreed in Cairo to work toward a tripartite federation.

East German Pres. Walter Ulbricht warned that a reduction in West German presence in Berlin would have to precede talks on eased access to the city.

Combined force of Cambodian and South Vietnamese troops reportedly launched an offensive south of Phnom Penh.

9

U.S. Supreme Court refused to hear a suit based on a Massachusetts law challenging the constitutionality of the Vietnam war.

North Vietnamese and Viet Cong forces launched an offensive near Kompong Cham.

Ethiopian Emperor Haile Selassie concluded his first official visit to Italy since the Italian take-over of Ethiopia in 1935.

10

U.S.S.R. released the two U.S. Army generals, a U.S. major, and a Turkish colonel held since their plane landed in Soviet Armenia on October 21.

French Pres. Pompidou announced that "France is a widow" with the death the previous evening of former Pres. Charles de Gaulle.

11

General Motors Corp. and the United Automobile Workers agreed on a new contract to end an eight-week strike.

12

Chilean Pres. Allende announced his decision to reestablish diplomatic relations with Cuba.

Major U.S. banks lowered their prime rate from 7.5 to 7.25%; Bank of Canada made effective its fourth bank rate reduction in six months, down to 6%.

U.S.S.R. Foreign Minister Gromyko during a visit to Italy met with Pope Paul VI.

13

Argentine workers concluded the third of a series of general strikes protesting government economic and social policies.

Cyclone and tidal wave inflicted massive damage on the Ganges River Delta area of East Pakistan.

UN General Assembly approved an amendment rejecting accreditation of the South African delegation.

Guatemalan Pres. Arana imposed a 30-day state of siege to combat terrorism.

Bloodless coup by rightist Syrian Army officers headed by Defense Minister Gen. Hafez al-Assad deposed the government of Nureddin al-Attassi.

Unarmed U.S. plane was shot down over North Vietnam.

14

Pakistan and China signed an economic cooperation pact.

Guatemalan planes fired on Salvadorean fishing boats off the Guatemalan Pacific coast.

15

South Vietnamese Vice-Pres. Ky began an unofficial visit to the U.S.

Brazilian Alliance for National Renewal party increased its ruling majority in congressional and state elections.

16

Jordanian King Husain disclosed that he had rejected an Israeli proposal for bilateral peace talks amid rumours that such talks had been occurring secretly.

U.S. Congress began its first lame duck session in 20 years.

17

Luna 17, Soviet unmanned spacecraft, landed a "Lunokhod," a self-propelled, eight-wheel vehicle, on the moon.

EEC Executive Commission approved a draft proposal of a five-year transition for full U.K. adoption of EEC rules.

18

Nobelist Linus Pauling maintained that relatively large doses of vitamin C could ward off the common cold.

West German-Polish treaty renouncing force and recognizing the Oder-Neisse line as Poland's western border was initialed in Warsaw.

19

U.S. House of Representatives passed and sent to the Senate a trade bill imposing import quotas on textiles and shoes.

U.S. Senate completed congressional action on a bill continuing basic farm support programs.

20

U.S. Senate Finance Committee rejected for the second time the administration's welfare reform plan.

U.S. Army court-martial acquitted S. Sgt. David Mitchell of murder charges in connection with the 1968 My Lai incident.

Simple majority of the UN General Assembly approved UN membership for China for the first time, 16 votes short of the two-thirds majority required.

21

U.S. planes carried out heavy bombing of military targets in North Vietnam, Laos, and Cambodia.

Australian senatorial elections resulted in drops in popular support for both the ruling Liberal and opposition Labor parties.

22

Guinean Pres. Sékou Touré charged that Portuguese forces had invaded and attacked the capital, Conakry.

23

U.S. Senate failed to override Pres. Nixon's veto of the bill to limit political broadcast spending.

U.S. Defense Secy. Laird described a commando-style U.S. raid attempted on November 21 to free U.S. prisoners of war in North Vietnam.

Pope Paul VI issued a decree barring cardinals over age 80 from voting for a new pope.

U.S.S.R. and China signed a one-year trade agreement in Peking.

North Vietnamese and Viet Cong forces directed a new Cambodian assault south of Phnom Penh.

Lithuanian seaman was forced to return to his Soviet fishing vessel after boarding a U.S. Coast Guard cutter off Martha's Vineyard, Mass., seeking asylum in the U.S.

25

Soviet Foreign Minister Gromyko visited East Berlin for talks with Pres. Walter Ulbricht.

Japanese writer Yukio Mishima committed ritual suicide in Tokyo in protest against Japan's "spinelessness."

Paris peace talks were boycotted by North Vietnam and the Viet Cong in protest against the U.S. resumption of bombing of North Vietnam.

U.S. Interior Secy. Hickel was dismissed by Pres. Nixon.

27

Syria agreed to join Libya, the Sudan, and the U.A.R. in the proposed Arab federation.

Soviet novelist Solzhenitsyn said he would not attend the Nobel Prize ceremonies in Stockholm as planned.

Knife-wielding assailant dressed as a priest attempted to assassinate Pope Paul VI shortly after his arrival in the Philippines, the third country on his ten-day trip to Asia and Oceania.

White House announced presidential adviser Daniel P. Moynihan would return to his post at Harvard University rather than become ambassador to the UN as had been rumoured.

Four East German seamen jumped their Cuba-bound ship off the Florida coast and were picked up by a small boat.

East and West Germany resumed talks in East Berlin on normalizing relations.

28

Israeli patrol vessel sank a U.A.R. launch in the Gulf of Suez.

29

Ivory Coast Pres. Houphouët-Boigny won a third term in unopposed voting.

Pope Paul VI broadcast a "message to Asia" warning against militant atheism and visited Pago Pago on his way from the Philippines to Western Samoa.

30

U.S. Federal Reserve Board cut its discount rate for the second time in three weeks to 5.5%.

Southern Yemen changed its name to the People's Democratic Republic of Yemen.

U.S. 1970 census final report, indicating changes in congressional representation in 14 states, was presented to Pres. Nixon.

DECEMBER

1

Italian Pres. Giuseppe Saragat signed a bill to legalize divorce.

Canadian House of Commons approved legislation to replace the War Measures Act.

West German honorary consul in San Sebastian, Spain, Eugen Beihl, was kidnapped by Basque separatists.

Second inflation alert was issued by the U.S. Council of Economic Advisers.

2

NATO Defense Planning Commit-

JOHN-PIERRE REY FROM LIAISON AGENCY

Funeral of Gen. Charles de Gaulle . . . November 12

tee adopted plans for improvements in conventional forces in Central Europe and the Middle East to counter growing Soviet strength.

3

Pope Paul VI concluded a three-day visit to Australia and was welcomed in Jakarta by Indonesian Pres. Suharto.

U.S. Senate rejected an administration request for funding for further development of a supersonic transport (SST) plane.

British diplomat Cross was freed unharmed in Montreal after his kidnappers had been flown to Cuba.

4

Lesotho King Moshoeshoe II ended an eight-month exile in the Netherlands.

Pope Paul VI addressed a message of unity to all Chinese from Hong Kong and concluded his Asian tour with a two-hour stop in Ceylon.

U.S. House of Representatives investigating panel approved a report recommending against the impeachment of Supreme Court Justice Douglas.

Irish government threatened to assume emergency powers to control a "secret conspiracy" of lawlessness.

5

Pres. Nixon called on Congress to reverse its rejection of SST funds.

7

Polish-West German treaty to end aggression was signed in Warsaw.

Swiss Ambassador to Brazil Giovanni Enrico Bucher was kidnapped in Rio de Janeiro.

British electrical workers began "working to rule" to press wage demands, thereby causing nationwide power shortages.

Awami League of East Pakistan won a majority of National Assembly seats in Pakistan's first direct general elections.

8

U.S. State Department issued a report urging implementation of a modernization plan to permit greater creativity in U.S. diplomacy.

10

Big Four representatives held their final meeting of the year on the future status of Berlin.

U.S. and South Vietnamese delegates to the Paris peace talks called for an immediate prisoner of war exchange.

Pres. Nixon, at his first news conference in four months, warned he would order further bombing of North Vietnam if needed to protect

U.S. troops, and discussed other issues, including U.S. policy toward China, the U.S.S.R., and the Middle East, campus unrest, and economic policy.

Federal court injunction ended 18-hour nationwide railroad strike.

12

North Vietnam denounced Pres. Nixon's warning of possible bombing as a threat to expand the war.

14

Pres. Nixon nominated former Texas Gov. John B. Connally, a Democrat, to succeed Treasury Secy. Kennedy.

Spanish government granted police emergency powers because of intensifying protests against the conduct of the military trial in Burgos of 15 Basque separatists charged with banditry and other terrorist acts as well as the murder of a police official in 1968.

15

Polish workers protesting the announcement of substantial increases in food prices began rioting in Gdansk and other Baltic coast cities.

South Vietnamese troops were reported to have been airlifted to Kompong Cham in answer to a personal appeal from Cambodian Premier Lon Nol to South Vietnamese Pres. Thieu.

Two Congos formally resumed diplomatic relations.

Venera 7, Soviet unmanned spacecraft, landed on Venus.

16

Pres. Nixon vetoed legislation extending manpower training programs, rather than reorganizing them as he had requested.

International convention calling for "severe punishment" for hijacking of civilian aircraft was signed by 50 nations meeting at The Hague.

U.S. Army was charged with having conducted surveillance of prominent Illinois civilians.

Ethiopian government declared a state of emergency in parts of Eritrea because of increased guerrilla activity.

17

North Vietnamese delegation to the Paris peace talks called on the U.S. to suggest a "reasonable deadline" for the withdrawal of U.S. troops from South Vietnam.

U.S. Defense Department issued new antidiscrimination directives following release of a report of unrest among black troops stationed in West Germany.

18

SALT sessions in Helsinki recessed; both sides agreed to meet in Vienna in March.

Report of an eight-year study by a U.S. Senate subcommittee called the F-111 fighter-bomber program a major "fiscal blunder."

19

Guinean Pres. Touré charged Portuguese troops were massed at Guinea's border and called on the UN to safeguard its independence.

South Korean Pres. Park named Paik Too Chin to replace Chung Il Kwon as prime minister.

20

Polish Communist Party First Secy. Wladyslaw Gomulka and other key members of his 14-year regime resigned; Edward Gierek was named first secretary.

21

Two U.S. Coast Guard officers who ordered the return of a Lithuanian defector were reprimanded and allowed to retire.

U.S. Supreme Court upheld the constitutionality of legislation lowering the voting age to 18 for federal elections but maintained the right of states to set qualifications for state and local elections.

Cambodian troops were reported to have begun a drive to reopen the highway from Phnom Penh to the Gulf of Siam.

U.S. command in Tokyo confirmed the planned withdrawal of 12,000 U.S. troops from Japan by mid-1971.

22

East Germany removed obstructions that had blocked traffic between West Germany and West Berlin for four days.

U.S. Congress approved a military aid bill for Cambodia including a ban on the use of U.S. ground forces and began a Christmas recess with the fate of much major legislation unresolved.

North Vietnam released a "definitive" list of its U.S. prisoners of war.

23

California Supreme Court ordered the release of César Chávez, farm workers' union organizer, pending appeal of a contempt charge resulting from his refusal to end a nationwide lettuce boycott.

Polish Premier Jozef Cyrankiewicz was named president of Poland and replaced as premier by Piotr Jaroszewicz.

Roman Catholic-Jewish conference ended in Rome with agreement to join forces against all forms of discrimination.

Bolivian government freed French Marxist writer Régis Debray, serving a 30-year sentence for guerrilla activities.

24

Leningrad court sentenced to death two Jews charged with attempted hijacking and gave prison terms to nine other defendants.

25

Allied forces in South Vietnam ended their 24-hour Christmas truce; Viet Cong continued their

72-hour truce although several clashes were reported.

Basque separatists released West German diplomat Beihl.

Israeli Knesset and religious and secular leaders in various countries urged reductions in the harsh sentences given Soviet Jews convicted of attempted hijacking in Leningrad.

26

Pres. Nixon signed into law 20 pieces of legislation passed by Congress in recent days.

27

Indian Prime Minister Indira Gandhi dissolved Parliament, citing its opposition to reform programs.

28

U.A.R. Pres. Sadat ordered an end to government appropriation of private property.

Three men suspected of the kidnapping and murder of Quebec Labour Minister Laporte were arrested near Montreal.

Spanish court-martial found 15 Basque separatists guilty of terrorist acts; six received death sentences.

Israeli Cabinet voted to reopen indirect peace talks at the UN.

29

U.S. stock market averages reached their highest levels for 1970 in heavy trading.

Appeals for clemency for the six Basques sentenced to death in Spain were made by various governments and private organizations.

Arab guerrillas in Jordan, Syria, and Lebanon stepped up attacks against Israel; U.A.R. Pres. Sadat ordered a state of war readiness.

30

U.S. Navy F-14 fighter-plane prototype crashed during a test flight from Calverton, N.Y.

Paris peace talks ended their second full year with both sides agreeing there had been no progress.

Spanish Chief of State Gen. Francisco Franco commuted to 30-year prison terms the death sentences of six Basque separatists.

Benjamin Sheares was elected president of Singapore.

31

U.S. House of Representatives completed action on a bill authorizing pay raises for federal employees, approved a military sales bill including the Cooper-Church amendment, and passed a resolution continuing funding of the SST for three months; the Senate completed action on federal food stamp legislation.

Soviet court commuted the death sentences of two Soviet Jews and reduced the prison terms of three others charged with attempted hijacking. (J. W. Mw.)

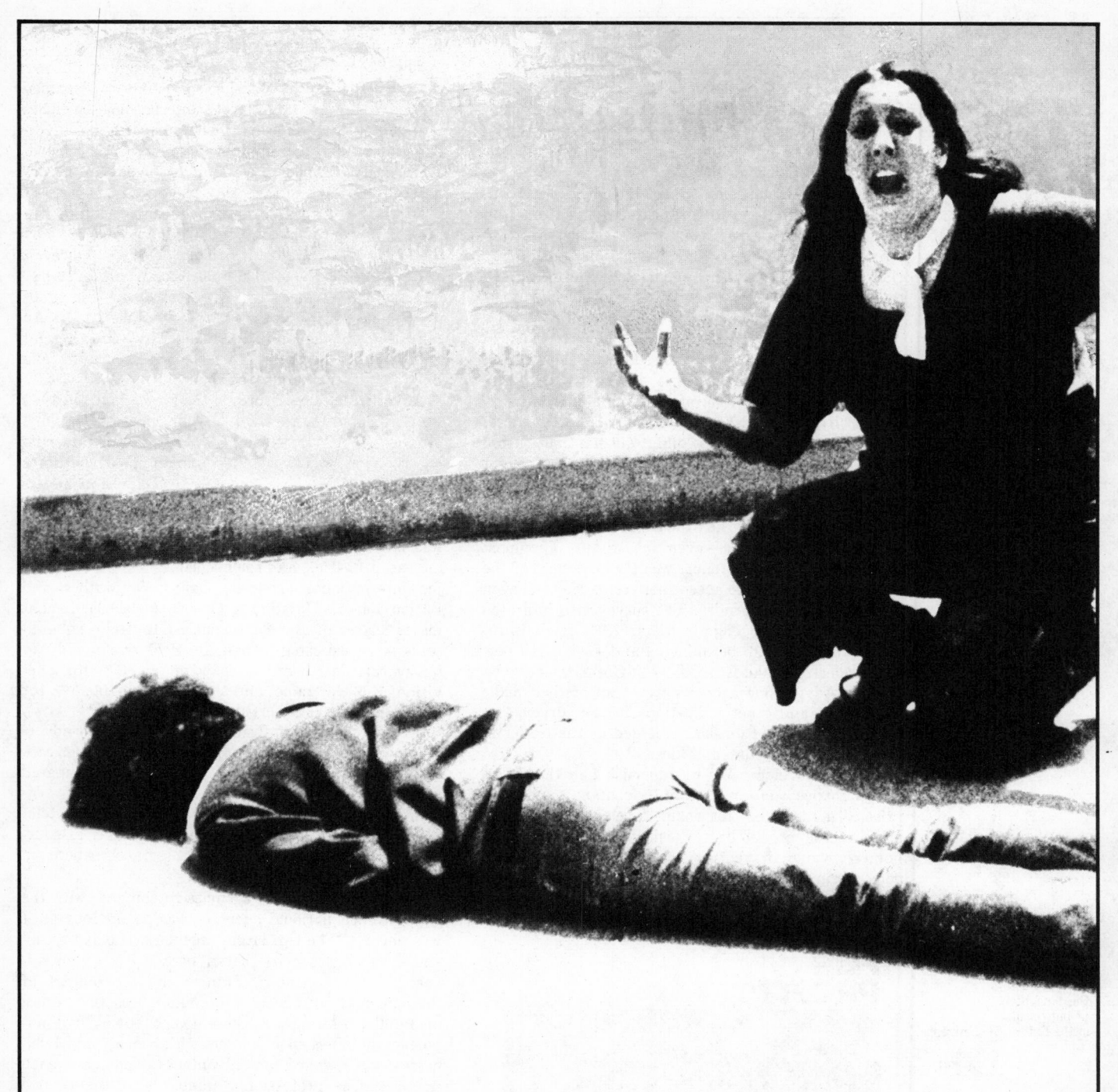

1970: a year of violence

Advertising

Europe. The Pan-European thinking that was evident in 1970 in the opening of negotiations for an expanded European Economic Community also manifested itself in advertising at the European meeting of the International Advertising Association, held in Copenhagen. It was decided to form a secretariat to act on behalf of European advertising agencies and to strengthen activities of the association outside the U.S. All major advertising agencies in Europe agreed that their future lay in products conceived for the whole European market.

A survey on the European consumer prepared by the *Reader's Digest* and presented at the Copenhagen meeting strongly indicated the breakdown of European national differences on all economic fronts. Although living standards and the pace of material progress were shown to differ substantially from country to country, those things most often bought and/or desired were very similar: a home; a car; television sets; all labour-saving devices; convenience foods; soft drinks, at the expense of wine; and coffee, at the expense of tea—even in Britain. The most startling aspect of the report was the eagerness of the European consumer to accept material advances, even at the price of uniformity. The survey also indicated a sharp drop in language barriers: 28% of all Europeans were found to be bilingual and 42% of all persons under 25 spoke English, 32% German, and 29% French. Advertising agencies were expected to make use of this and other indications in the survey that the postwar generation had emerged as the leader in fashion, music, leisure, and ideas.

General developments in advertising in the different countries were not seen to contain many surprises. In the U.K., the main development was the growing use of colour television, with 65% of all homes owning or renting colour sets. The cost of colour transmission, however, was almost prohibitive, so that advertisements were seldom seen in colour on Independent Television.

The Swiss Publicity Association founded its own school in Biel but advertising opportunities remained limited to a few large, truly international agencies represented in Switzerland. The lack of good advertising media and the problems posed by three national languages continued to prohibit expansion of the industry in Switzerland.

Of the total advertising expenditure spent in Europe, 31% was spent by West Germany and 25% by the U.K. Norwegian advertising agencies, however, again set the pace for Europe. Agency turnover had increased an average of 12% a year during the 1960s and increased 15% in the first six months of 1970. An estimated 45% of all advertising expenditures went to newspapers. Norway, like Denmark, Sweden, and Belgium, had no commercial television.

Advertising expenditures in the Netherlands in 1970 were expected to rise by 4% while the gross national product (GNP) increased 8%. Volume of advertising, however, was expected to remain unchanged since media rates also rose about 4%. Television advertising was expected to be introduced in Belgium in mid-1971. The level of media space or time purchased was fixed at 18%. Advertising rates for newspapers increased 10–15% and for magazines 3–5%. Two major international agencies, Ogilvy & Mather and Batten Barton Durstine & Osborn (BBDO), bought major shares of Benelux agencies. In Italy expenditures were expected to rise in 1970 due mainly to heavy rate increases; rates were up 30% for television, 16% for radio, and a more reasonable 4% for press and cinema advertising.

The percentage of France's GNP spent on advertising was the lowest in Europe and spending per capita was also relatively low, $10.50 in 1968 compared with $25 in West Germany. The two brief segments of advertising permitted on state-owned television and the lack of national coverage discouraged advertising at the levels seen elsewhere in Europe.

The need for outside agencies to compete with the giant French national agencies was as obvious as it was difficult. The two largest agencies, Havas Conseil and Publicis Conseil, shared over 20% of all advertising investment in France, and the billings of their nearest rival were $40 million less than those of Publicis. Moreover, these two agencies had important holdings in other French agencies and businesses, which gave them advantages over non-French agencies. The professional standards of the French agencies, however, did not meet those of the non-French agencies with offices in Paris, such as Young & Rubicam, Ted Bates & Co., McCann-Erickson, and J. Walter Thompson Co. While these agencies primarily serviced their international clients, all had succeeded in obtaining good French clients. Nonetheless, the prestige of Havas was certainly one of the major assets of a new network formed when Havas joined the three-year-old partnership of Needham, Harper & Steers of the U.S. and S. H. Benson of the U.K. The new Benson Needham Univas had $300 million in billings and representation in 93% of the free world's advertising markets.　　(Mu. L.)

North America. It seemed certain that 1970 would be the tenth consecutive year in which advertising volume in the U.S. increased over the previous year. But not even the most optimistic forecaster was predicting a gain of the magnitude of the 7.7% increase

COURTESY, FRIENDS OF ANIMALS, INC.

Advertisement produced by the Friends of Animals, Inc., protests the slaughter of baby seals in the Gulf of St. Lawrence.

MURDER FOR PROFIT

photo by Brian Davies

The baby seal in the photo was one of 50,000 killed in the Gulf of St. Lawrence, one of over half a million seals clubbed, speared, shot, gaffed during the 1970 Canadian-Norwegian slaughter in the Atlantic.

Don't believe furriers who would persuade you that Friends of Animals has been "misleading" you, that any slaughter anywhere is done for the benefit of the seals.

I, Alice Herrington, testify that on March 21, 1970—the second day of the Canadian season on seals—I saw the same brutal massacre against which Friends of Animals, of which I am president, has been protesting for years. As the bubble-domed helicopter flew low over the first day's kill, I saw mother seals nuzzling the skinless corpses of their babies. Standing ten feet away from the killers on the ice floes, twenty miles out in the Gulf, I saw baby seals clubbed twice, and then sliced open. Other babies were battered as many as fourteen times while the mothers watched in terror and stress.

If You Are One Who Cannot Be Indifferent to the Suffering of Other Creatures

YOU CAN HELP

First—by refusing to garb yourself in the agony of another, by refusing to buy the skins of wildlife.

Second—by causing this advertisement to be inserted in your local newspaper. (A mat will be sent upon your request to Friends of Animals. See coupon below.)

Third—by sending a tax-deductible contribution to Friends of Animals, Inc., a non-profit organization that intends to pound on the world's conscience until sentient men and women everywhere are made aware of the unnecessary cruelty and destruction being inflicted upon animals. Your contribution will be used to plead for those creatures who cannot speak for themselves but who dumbly implore your pity.

Friends of Animals, Inc.
11 WEST 60TH STREET
NEW YORK, N.Y. 10023

☐ Enclosed is my tax-deductible contribution to help stop the slaughter of marine mammals.

☐ Send me a mat of this advertisement so that I can place this advertisement in my local paper at my own expense (also tax-deductible).

NAME
ADDRESS
CITY　　STATE　　ZIP

Aden:
see Southern Yemen

of 1969, when total dollar volume was $20.4 billion. One substantial dent in advertising expenditures in the last quarter of 1970 was caused by the prolonged strike at General Motors, which began at the time of year when advertising expenditures by car makers were usually their heaviest. Although there was no question that advertising expenditures were off in other hard-goods lines, expenditures in the packaged-goods field held up very well during 1970. While total expenditures for 1970 would be greater than for 1969, the percentage gain was set by the cautious at 2–4%.

Dollar volumes for 1970 for all but one of the seven major media, outdoor advertising, were predicted to be down from the 1969 figures and the combined volume for all seven seemed likely to dip from the previous year's total of $9,950,000,000 to about $9.1 billion in national advertising dollars (local advertising dollars were not included in the figures).

Newspapers anticipated a national ad volume for 1970 of $1,080,000,000, down from $1.1 billion in 1969, a drop of 1.8%. Network television, usually a substantial gainer each year, saw 1970 as a $1,650,-000,000 year in contrast with a $1.7 billion year in 1969; spot television predicted a slip-off from $1.3 billion in 1969 to $1.2 billion in 1970. Magazines dropped out of the "billion dollar" category in 1970, expecting a volume of $930 million in contrast with $1,240,000,000 in 1969. Business publications expected a volume of $807.4 million, a decline of 0.5% from the $811.8 million total for 1969. Network radio expected a $37 million volume in 1970, compared with $40 million in 1969, a drop of 7.5%; spot radio would be up, moving from $332 million in 1969 to $360 million in 1970, an increase of 8.4%. Outdoor advertising antic-ipated a $190 million year, in contrast with a $168 million year in '69, or a gain of 13%. Direct mail dollar volume slipped from $2.9 billion in 1969 to $2,850,000,000 in 1970.

A number of events during 1970 kept the issue of consumerism very much alive. In a unanimous decision handed down in May, the United States Supreme Court ruled that under present law a citizen had the right to prevent a direct mail advertiser from sending him anything at home. This sweeping ruling was looked on as being particularly inimical to direct mail advertisers. Ironically, it came about as the re-sult of a 1967 law aimed at banning the use of the mails to smut peddlers. The court broadened the scope of the law to include anything the homeowner might wish to consider "erotically arousing and sexually provocative," whether it be a dry goods catalog, a department store circular, or a solicitation for a maga-zine subscription.

In July 1970 the Federal Trade Commission de-cided on a test case to establish tough ground rules to govern the promotion of preselected winner sweep-stakes. Maintaining that McDonald's Corp. had awarded only $13,000 in prizes in its "McDonald's $500,000 Sweepstakes," the FTC said that hence-forth promotions of this sort must disclose to con-sumers the odds for winning each prize, and that sweepstakes promoters must award all the prizes that are advertised.

Early in the year the Nixon administration served notice on the advertising industry that unless it worked strenuously to effect better and "more visible" forms of self regulation it was in for troubled times. As if in response to this warning, a number of self-regulation plans were advanced by segments of the

LONDON "DAILY EXPRESS" FROM PICTORIAL PARADE

Model carries a transparent sandwich board advertising the film "More" down London's Oxford Street in February 1970.

industry. Probably the most ambitious, and certainly the most talked about, was unveiled in the fall by Victor Elting, new chairman of the American Adver-tising Federation. Elting's plan called for the estab-lishment of an Advertising Review Council, with a budget of $1.5 million, to review complaints or in-quiries from any legitimate group or person and, if voluntary compliance was not made to its rulings, to publicize the abuse and its findings, in order to direct public scorn at the violators, and call on all media to refuse to carry the offending ads. Because present laws treated such an agreement among media as restraint of trade, the Elting proposal called on Congress to grant an exemption from antitrust legis-lation.

In 1970 the FTC issued complaints against Coca-Cola Co. for misrepresenting the nutritional value of its Hi-C fruit drink; and against Standard Oil Co. of California for falsifying the antipollution poten-tial of the F-310 additive in its Chevron gasoline. The complaints were not in themselves unusual—the FTC issued a number of such complaints each year, including complaints in 1970 that the advertising for a toy racing car and a dancing doll were deceptive and exploited the gullibility of children, and that tele-vision advertising for Zerex antifreeze was false and misleading. In the Hi-C and Chevron cases, however, for the first time the FTC proposed that each ad-vertiser would be required in all its advertising for the next year to state that previous ads for these products had been found by the FTC to be false, misleading, and deceptive. The advertising community maintained that the decision was unfair.

After a six-year battle, in March Congress finally passed a bill banning cigarette advertising from the nation's airwaves after Jan. 1, 1971. The bill also called on cigarette companies to beef up the health warning on all packages. Congress also made it quite clear that it would not look favourably on simply switching cigarette advertising dollars from radio and television to other media, particularly if they happened to be youth oriented. Nevertheless, by October it seemed fairly certain that as much as $30 million of the $200 million formerly spent on cigarette ads in broadcasting would find its way into outdoor advertising. Plans were also being made to sponsor sports events that—together with the sponsor's name—would be telecast. In December the FTC accepted a proposal whereby eight major U.S. manufacturers agreed to voluntarily include tar and nicotine yield information in their ads.

Ethnic groups were insisting that stereotypes of their people not be used in advertising. Frito-Lay, which for some time had used a cartoon character called the "Frito bandito," finally advised the protesting Mexican-American groups that it had instructed its agency to prepare new commercials.

The quality of much of the advertising employed in the 1970 election campaign, which often used misleading information and smear and scare tactics, was generally regarded as having done more harm

COURTESY, DOYLE DANE
BERNBACH, INC.

Advertisement created
for Volkswagen
of America, Inc., by Doyle
Dane Bernbach, Inc.

After 30 Volkswagens, Father Bittman still believes.

than good. In many cases those employing the most offensive advertising lost their races. As a result of strong criticism of the tactics used, *Advertising Age* and other responsible voices in the industry called for a set of ethical and moral standards for the advertising of political candidates and issues in future elections.

The 125 largest advertisers in the U.S. nudged their media and promotion investment upward a modest 2.9% in 1969 for a total of $4,970,000,000, compared with $4,830,000,000 in 1968. Procter & Gamble continued its longtime leadership by edging its advertising upward 2% to an estimated $275 million, as compared with $270 million the year before. Second once again was General Motors, despite the cutback of its total investment from $214 million in 1968 to $171.5 million in 1969. The next eight members of the top ten, in decreasing order of investment, were General Foods, Sears, Roebuck, Colgate-Palmolive, Bristol-Myers, Ford Motor Co., American Home Products, Warner-Lambert, and American Telephone & Telegraph. Five of these eight increased their

investments but the investment of General Foods was down from $154 million to $151 million, Colgate-Palmolive from $122 million to $121 million, and Ford from $119,150,000 to $112,132,000.

The 663 advertising agencies covered in the *Advertising Age* annual agency billings survey had total billings of $9.9 billion in 1969, a healthy increase of 11% over the $8.9 billion reported in 1969 by 600 agencies. There were 66 agencies in the over-$25 million billing group, ten more than in 1968, and the largest agency once again was J. Walter Thompson, whose worldwide billing total soared from $636.8 million in 1968 to $736 million in 1969. The other top billing agencies and their 1969 billings were: Young & Rubicam ($522.9 million); McCann-Erickson ($511.1 million); Ted Bates ($375.1 million); BBDO ($356.2 million); Leo Burnett Co. ($355.9 million); Doyle Dane Bernbach (DDB; $269.9 million); Foote, Cone & Belding ($265.5 million); Ogilvy & Mather International ($229.8 million); and Grey Advertising ($228.1 million).

According to the American Association of Advertising Agencies, agency profits showed a "modest improvement" in 1969 because of "a slight decrease in total payroll, which was tempered by a slight increase in overhead costs." Based on gross income, including commissions, service charges, and fees, the average net profit percentage in 1969 increased to 4.03%, up from 3.97%. Advertising agencies did a considerable amount of belt tightening in 1970, particularly in the last half, when the General Motors strike caused an almost complete cutback in massive automobile campaigns and in salaries and personnel at agencies handling General Motors accounts. The biggest account switch of 1970 was that of Miles Laboratories' "Alka-Seltzer" from Doyle Dane Bernbach to Wells, Rich, Green. DDB had acquired the account only in July 1969 and had produced for the product two of the most talked about television commercials of the year, one of an actor flubbing his line about spicy meatballs, and "Groom's First Meal," which won a Gold Lion award at the Cannes International Advertising Film Festival.

Advertising revenue for Canadian media in 1970 was expected to show the lowest annual growth rate of the past decade, gaining an estimated 5.5% to $983 million, compared with a rate of almost 7% for the preceding ten years. The estimated revenue increases for 1970 for the various media were: daily newspapers, up 5% to $253 million; television, up 6% to $131 million; radio, up 7% to $104 million; magazines, weekly newspapers, and business and farm publications, up 5% to $132 million.

In September Canadian Consumer and Corporate Affairs Minister S. Ronald Basford suggested that limits on ad expenditures might have to be imposed by the government unless the industry cut out "advertising overkill." In June, in response to criticism by federal authorities, major cigarette manufacturers agreed to stop advertising and offering cash prizes or major gifts with their various brands after July 1. To compensate, they turned more heavily to sponsorship of major sporting events, including car and snowmobile racing, curling matches, horse races, and tennis tournaments. In May the Canadian Radio-Television Commission announced new regulations calling for increased Canadian content in both television and radio programs.   (J. J. GM.)

See also Industrial Review; Merchandising; Telecommunications; Television and Radio.

Aerospace Industry:
see Astronautics;
Defense; Industrial
Review; Transportation

**Afars and Issas,
French Territory of
the:**
see Dependent States

Afghanistan

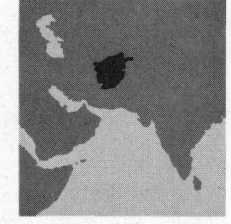

A constitutional monarchy in central Asia, Afghanistan is bordered by the U.S.S.R., China, West Pakistan, and Iran. Area: 250,775 sq.mi. (649,508 sq.km.). Pop. (1970 est.): 17,124,583, including Pathans, Tadzhiks, Uzbeks, Hazaras. Cap. and largest city: Kabul (metro. area pop., 1970 est., 488,844). Language: Persian and Pashto. Religion: Muslim. King, Mohammad Zahir Shah; prime minister in 1970, Noor Ahmad Etemadi.

As expected, the elections held in the summer of 1969 for the House of the People and for one-third of the House of Elders produced little change in the composition of Parliament. Since political parties were not legalized in time for the elections, most of the candidates were men of local prominence and were again chosen for their personal prestige rather than their political views. Only about 50% of the electorate voted; except in times of national crisis political life is so highly localized that interest in central institutions remains minimal. This was generally true throughout 1970, although in Kabul and its environs live broadcasts of the proceedings in Parliament, which resulted in the confirmation (as required by the 1964 constitution) of Prime Minister Noor Ahmad Etemadi and his new Cabinet, attracted large crowds of listeners.

Progress in establishing a modern type of administration throughout the country to replace traditional tribal institutions was steady rather than spectacular. The personal popularity of the king and his firm support of the prime minister ensured growing respect for the central government, but this did not prevent occasional outbreaks of severe intertribal hostilities.

An important factor in the modernizing process to which the king had committed himself was the steady improvement of communications with the outside world. Several international airlines called regularly at Kabul, and the road from the capital to the Khyber Pass carried increasingly heavy traffic in both directions. The tourist industry received a great impetus both from the erection on the road between Kabul and Paghman of a luxury hotel with spectacular views, and from the readiness with which the Afghan diplomatic posts in many countries granted tourist visas.

External communications were stimulated by a marked improvement in relations with Pakistan. The Afghan government showed increasing interest in the economic success of the Regional Cooperation for Development program (RCD), which was being vigorously pursued by Pakistan, Iran, and Turkey; a visit to Kabul by the Pakistan finance minister, Nawab Mozaffar Ali Khan Qizilbash, led to a scheme for technical aid in the fields of irrigation, seeds, and fertilizers to help Afghanistan achieve agricultural self-sufficiency as part of its policy of decreasing its reliance on external aid. (L. F. R. W.)

AFGHANISTAN
Education. (1968–69) Primary, pupils 472,487, teachers 10,245; secondary, pupils 68,595, teachers 2,501; vocational, pupils 7,833; teacher training, students 7,724; vocational and teacher training, teachers 778; higher (including 2 universities), students 4,320, teaching staff (1967–68) 612.
Finance. Monetary unit: afghani, with a par value of 45 afghanis to U.S. $1 (108 afghanis = £1 sterling) and a free rate (Sept. 14, 1970) of 84 afghanis to U.S. $1 (200 afghanis = £1 sterling). Budget (1969–70 est.): revenue 6,796,000,000 afghanis; expenditure 7,419,000,000 afghanis (excluding development expenditure financed by foreign aid). Money supply: (March 1970) 7,011,000,000 afghanis; (March 1969) 5,931,000,000 afghanis.
Foreign Trade. (1968–69) Imports: 9,266,798,000 afghanis; exports 5,348,316,000 afghanis. Import sources: U.S.S.R. 38%; Japan 10%; India 9%; West Germany 9%; U.S. 8%; China 7%. Export destinations: U.S.S.R. 37%; India 22%; U.K. 10%; Pakistan 8%; U.S. 6%. Main exports: fresh fruit 22%; dried fruit 15%; natural gas 13%; karakul (Persian lamb) skins 12%; wool 10%; cotton 8%; carpets 6%.
Transport and Communications. Roads (motorable; 1968) c. 6,700 km. Motor vehicles in use (1968): passenger 29,200; commercial (including buses) 17,800. Air traffic (1968): 95,770,000 passenger-km.; freight 5,375,000 net ton-km. Telephones (Jan. 1969) c. 10,000. Radio receivers (Dec. 1967) 248,000.
Agriculture. Production (in 000; metric tons; 1969; 1968 in parentheses): rice (1967) 345, (1966) 337; wheat (1967) 2,200, (1966) 2,033; corn 785 (773); barley (1967) 375, (1966) 375; cotton, lint 30 (24); sugar, raw value (1969–70) c. 18, (1968–69) c. 18; wool, greasy (1968) c. 27, (1967) c. 25. Livestock (in 000; 1968–69): cattle 3,605; sheep 21,668 (including c. 6,000 karakul); horses (1967–68) c. 277.
Industry. Production (in 000; metric tons; 1968–69): coal 125; electricity (kw-hr.) 325,000; cement 86; salt 41; cotton yarn 0.4; cotton fabrics (m.) 50,000.

Africa

A decade after Africa's momentous year of independence (1960) the continent in 1970 continued to experience the benefits and difficulties of freedom. The year's most dramatic event occurred early when the Nigerian government won a military victory over secessionist Biafra on January 13.

In 1960, a total of 17 countries, including Nigeria, the Congo (Kinshasa), and former French dependencies cut their colonial ties. At the time, there were predictions of utopia or chaos for the new states, but after ten years neither had been realized. In recent years, numerous coups, tribal disputes, border frictions, and economic problems had plagued the continent. No nation, however, petitioned during this era for a return to colonial status.

As in previous years, Africans displayed both an assertive nationalism and a recognition of their dependence upon outside countries. But while economically tied to foreigners for capital, trade, and skills,

Homeless Ibo refugees cluster in a makeshift camp shortly after the surrender of Biafra to federal government forces.

TERENCE SPENCER, "LIFE" MAGAZINE © TIME INC.

A nomadic family rests
at a waterhole
in Mauritania near
the Spanish Sahara border.
Nomads apparently
are unaffected
by the tripartite agreement
made in September 1970
between Mauritania,
Morocco, and Algeria
concerning the ownership
of the Spanish Sahara
and its phosphate reserves.

they could maneuver with increasing ability for aid from sources other than their former colonial governors. For example, the building of Algeria's $600 million iron and steel complex was being done by French, West German, Soviet, and Italian concerns. Zambia, having taken over 51% of the copper companies' assets on January 1 but being unable, by itself, to mine copper, distributed new prospecting concessions to Canadian, U.S., and Japanese companies. And while an upward-turning economy in the Congo (Kinshasa) might, in part, be ascribed to the return of approximately 45,000 Belgians, concessions were also given to an international consortium to mine copper in Katanga. Nigeria, formerly a British colony, was able to suppress Biafran secession with both British and Soviet aid. And Chinese funds and labour were being used in the construction of the Tanzam railroad between Tanzania and Zambia.

Nigeria. The breakaway of Biafra which had begun in May 1967 ended with the capture of Owerri on January 10. Relief for the defeated Biafrans was quickly begun. Original estimates of death by starvation (several hundred thousand) were revised downward to between 20,000 and 50,000. At the peak of relief operations in March more than three million people were receiving emergency aid. Nigeria's chief of state, Maj. Gen. Yakubu Gowon, described his nation's victory as a triumph of Nigerian unity. The war had cost the country approximately $800 million in a land where per capita income was $70–$80 per year. Yet in Gowon's words the war had contributed to the objective of asserting "the ability of the black man to build a strong, progressive and prosperous modern state." Gowon promised that there would be no policy of vindictiveness but that high-echelon Biafran leaders would be barred from holding office. In September, reconciliation was achieved with the four countries that had recognized Biafra: Tanzania, Zambia, Gabon, and Ivory Coast. Former Biafran leader Gen. Odumegwu Ojukwu took refuge in the Ivory Coast.

Biafra's high oil revenues, which in 1969 amounted to $100 million and which had been a factor in emboldening the region to secede, were taken over by the Nigerian government. The government encouraged Anglo-Dutch (Shell-British Petroleum) in April to announce expansion of operations by $160 million. Concessions were granted to U.S., West German, Japanese, and Nigerian companies. Hoping to expand revenue fivefold by 1975, Gowon outlined a plan at

the tenth anniversary celebrations that would make the economy self-sufficient in four years. As declared on Dec. 2, 1969, the government required that within ten years of the granting of a business concession, 75% of the managerial staff and all the low-skilled workers were to be Nigerian. Gowon said on October 1 that he did not expect a return to civilian rule before 1976.

Coups d'etat. During the decade of independence, some 25 successful coups and many more unsuccessful attempts at seizing power took place throughout the continent. Their causes, a compound of frustrated expectations of rapidly improving living standards, dissatisfaction with party disputes, ineffectual leadership, different economic philosophies, and concentration of power in the armed forces, were not easily overcome. Individual circumstances varied.

In Uganda, where a would-be assassin shot and wounded Pres. Milton Obote on Dec. 19, 1969, the opposition Democratic Party was banned. In the Congo (Brazzaville) four persons received capital sentences for their part in an attempted coup on Nov. 8, 1969, aimed at bringing back former president Fulbert Youlou, ousted in 1963. On March 24, 1970, more than 60 persons were reported killed in an attempt to overthrow the government.

In Dahomey, after 17 months of rule, the regime of Émile Zinsou was superseded by the military rule of the Army chief of staff, Lieut. Col. Maurice Kouandete (Dec. 10, 1969). Elections were held throughout the country in March, but they were attended by violence and the government annulled them. A constitutional coup occurred in Lesotho subsequent to the electoral defeat, on January 27, of Prime Minister Chief Leabua Jonathan. With the words, "I have seized power and I am not ashamed of it . . . in my conscience I know that the majority of the people are behind me," Chief Jonathan imprisoned 30 leaders of the opposition Congress Party and drove King Moshoeshoe II into temporary exile.

Guinean forces repulsed an invasion of the country in November. Pres. Sékou Touré claimed that the invaders included Portuguese forces and white mercenaries, who presumably were attempting to destroy the bases of guerrillas active in neighbouring Portuguese Guinea. A United Nations mission sent to Guinea reported that the invading force was led by regular white Portuguese officers and included mostly African troops from Portuguese Guinea. Lisbon denied any responsibility for the raid.

Unsuccessful plots against their respective governments were reported by Morocco (February 18), Somalia (April 27), and the Sudan (August 20). Earlier in the year, the Sudanese government put down an uprising of 30,000 Ansaris led by the imam al-Mahdi. He was killed. In Togo the official newspaper reported on August 9 that 27 people, including Ghanaians and Dahomeans, had been arrested in an abortive coup. Twenty-seven people were tried, and in November four were acquitted and the remainder sentenced to terms of six months to 20 years.

Nationalism. Continuing to seek their identities, African states displayed nationalism in a variety of ways. Kenya, on May 9, proclaimed Swahili to be the official, national language, and a plan to adopt a national dress was proposed. In Uganda, Ghana, Malawi, and Tanzania, Asian businessmen who did not secure licenses were to lose their holdings. Ghana compelled approximately 200,000 African "foreigners" to leave the country. Libya saw the British (March

May Day parade in Algeria features workers with saws rather than military might. Under the leadership of Houari Boumédienne the nation has adopted dynamic programs of economic and political development.

MARC RIBOUD FROM MAGNUM

31) and U.S. troops (June 11) leave their military bases. The government of Zanzibar, piqued by the exclusiveness of residents of Asian ancestry, forced girls of Persian descent to marry members of the Cabinet.

To knit its people together more firmly, Ivory Coast announced plans for a nationwide educational television system. On June 17, the formerly estranged presidents of the two Congos ended their countries' disaffection by reconciling their differences at a meeting in the middle of the river that forms the boundary. In July nonwhites in South Africa were barred from participating in a Beethoven music competition on the ground that it was not "their" music. Zambians acted as hosts to the third Afro-Asian Conference of 54 nonaligned nations in early September. In his opening address to the conference, Zambian Pres. Kenneth Kaunda (*see* BIOGRAPHY) called on the nonaligned nations to work together in order to gain strength against the world's major powers. He also warned that a crisis was developing in regard to the minority white regimes in southern Africa.

The conference adopted resolutions in support of the Palestine liberation movement against Israel, and other such movements in Southeast Asia and southern Africa. It also proposed sanctions in regard to southern Africa, if the countries in the region did not conform to a UN resolution on decolonization and racial discrimination. These included: a trade embargo against Portugal, Rhodesia, and South Africa; severance of diplomatic relations with Portugal and South Africa; and refusal of landing rights and port facilities to aircraft and ships going to or returning from South Africa, Portugal, and Rhodesia. The conference also pledged more material support to liberation movements in southern Africa, to be channeled through the Organization of African Unity. Lesotho and Swaziland, both heavily dependent economically on South Africa, expressed reservations about the resolution.

Zambia's Trade Ministry drafted laws that would ban miniskirts, wigs, and skin-lightening creams. One-party-state elections were held during the year in Senegal, Cameroon, Congo (Kinshasa), Tanzania, and Kenya (December 1969).

The Economy. Per capita income for 11 African countries, as reported by the UN Economic Commission for Africa, was between $300–$400 per year; for 13 countries it was $100–$200 per year; and in 17 countries it was less than $100 per year. Most Africans still lived in a subsistence economy, but they and their leaders wanted the products of modern industrialism. Needing external capital and skills, many thought, nonetheless, that they were prisoners of a "neocolonial" economy. Consequently, several countries nationalized portions of their industry. In May, 60%

of the banks, insurance companies, and important industries and plantations of Uganda were nationalized, though the fishing industry employing 30,000 was being developed through external assistance.

In Libya the property of Italians was confiscated on July 21. Earlier in the month the country's oil-importing and distributing companies were nationalized. The U.S.-owned Occidental Petroleum Co. reluctantly signed an agreement on September 3, raising the oil tax rate, and other companies followed. In effect, the new agreements gave Libya and the companies a 75–25 split on oil revenues. Ironically, while drilling for oil, Occidental uncovered in Libya a basin of underground water "equal to the flow of the Nile for a thousand years."

On July 21, Algeria notified France in a unilateral revision of a 1965 accord that royalty taxes on French-owned property would be raised by 50% retroactive to January 1969. Earlier in the summer, Algeria launched a four-year development plan calling for the investment of $5 billion. In the Congo (Kinshasa) Pres. Joseph Mobutu, although he had nationalized the copper companies in December 1966, traveled to the U.S., in part to solicit involvement by private industry in his country. An economic boom in the Congo raised government receipts by 44% in 1969 and reserves to $250 million.

Ghana and Kenya, however, which had also nationalized several industries, were faced with economic pressures. Pres. Jomo Kenyatta of Kenya ordered employers to increase their work force by 10% to meet the unemployment problem. Ghana's prime minister, Kofi Busia, continued to seek refinancing of the country's large foreign debt of $800 million. Both lands pressed their search for oil, with Ghana making its first offshore strike in June. Economically successful in Tanzania were the *ujamaas* (agricultural cooperatives) to which many people flocked. Tanzania found no inconsistency in accepting a $10 million loan from Italy to build the Kilimanjaro International Airport and using Chinese labour and money to build the Tanzam railroad. The railroad, involving 6,000 Chinese workers and an interest-free loan of $412 million from the Peking government, was being built so as to give Zambia an outlet for its copper other than through the white-dominated southern African states. On May 7, the Somalian government declared the nationalization of banks and oil companies with compensation. Symbolic of Africa's interest in financial matters was the selection of an economist to be premier of Tunisia.

Southern Africa. No major change occurred in the European-dominated southern lands. Rhodesia became a republic on March 2, and held its first election on April 10. Prime Minister Ian Smith's party won all

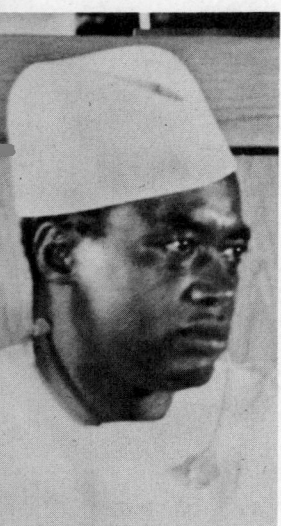

KEYSTONE

Pres. Kenneth Kaunda
of Zambia
chairs the Organization
of African Unity
heads of states meeting
at Addis Ababa
in September 1970.

Fang Yi (centre), minister
of the Commission
for Economic Relations
with Foreign Countries
in the government
of the People's Republic
of China, and two other
members of the Chinese
delegation attend
inauguration ceremonies
for the Tanzam Railway
in Dar es Salaam,
Tanzania, Oct. 26, 1970.

seats. Under the new Land Tenure Act, the whites in Rhodesia were allocated one-half of the land despite the fact that they were outnumbered 20–1 by black Africans. Protest came from the Roman Catholic Church, which feared that interracial worship would be prevented. Funds for education of the black Africans, which to a large degree had been channeled through mission schools, were to be reduced.

In South Africa results of the general elections held on April 22 showed a loss by the Nationalist Party government of 9 seats to the more liberal United Party and a gain of 4 from the ultrarightist Reconstituted Nationalists. Black nations continued to oppose South Africa's regime and received a promise of $200,000 from the World Council of Churches in September to aid guerrilla warfare. The Conservative government of Britain, however, decided to resume arms sales to South Africa, ostensibly to protect the sea route around the Cape. In July, France supplied South Africa with the first of three submarines. Efforts to isolate the South Africans economically were rebuffed by Japanese interests, which negotiated to build a $428 million iron ore export harbour. The world's sports community, however, stung South Africa by banning it from the 1972 Olympic Games (May 15), Davis Cup tennis competition (March 23), and international track and field meets for two years (August 31).

Signs that not all South African whites agreed with the government's racial separation policies were seen in protests by church and student groups. The Supreme Court in September again acquitted 19 Africans accused of terrorism who had been arrested in 1969, freed in February 1970, and rearrested. Despite millionaire Harry Oppenheimer's observation that discrimination against African labour was "economic suicide," white mine workers threatened to strike if black workers were trained for skilled jobs, even in the black "homelands."

In the fight against African guerrillas operating in the colonies of Angola and Mozambique the Portuguese government admitted that heavy casualties resulted from an attack in February in Mozambique near the Zambian frontier. Also during the year a Portuguese revolutionary group sabotaged a freighter used in ferrying supplies to Africa.

Miscellany. An International Congress of African People met in Atlanta, Ga., in September and heard many expressions of black solidarity. U.S. Secretary

of State William Rogers conducted a 15-day tour of the African continent, the first by a U.S. official of his stature. "We want no military allies, no spheres of influence, no big power competition in Africa," he said. In October it was revealed that the U.S. had had an agreement to protect Ethiopia since 1960.

In Tanzania a law easing the restrictions on polygamy was passed. In South Africa, although they had acted as extras in the motion picture *Zulu*, 500 Zulus were not permitted to see the film. Forty-six years after his last visit to Italy, Ethiopian Emperor Haile Selassie, in a dramatic gesture, laid a wreath on the tomb of Italy's unknown soldier. The French, who had assisted the government of Chad for several years in its fight against an Arab rebellion in the north of that country, said that they would quit Chad in 1971.

Death came to U.A.R. Pres. Gamal Abd-al-Nasser, to Abdullah Khalil, formerly prime minister of the Sudan, and to Belkacem Krim, a former Algerian rebel leader. (*See* OBITUARIES.)   (W. So.)

See also Dependent States; Migration, International; Refugees; articles on the various political units.

ENCYCLOPÆDIA BRITANNICA FILMS. *Life in the Sahara* (1953); *Egypt and the Nile* (1954); *East Africa (Kenya, Tanganyika, Uganda)* (1962); *The Suez Canal* (1962); *Continent of Africa (Lands Below the Sahara)* (1963); *The Republic of South Africa* (1963); *West Africa (Nigeria)* (1963); *The Nile Valley and Its People* (1964); *Oasis* (1965); *Africa: Living in Two Worlds* (1970); *Boy of Botswana* (1970); *City Boy of the Ivory Coast* (1970); *A Family of Liberia* (1970); *Two Boys of Ethiopia* (1970); *Youth Builds a Nation in Tanzania* (1970).

Agriculture

Whereas the world agricultural situation in 1969 had been characterized by the Food and Agriculture Organization of the United Nations (FAO) as stagnant, that of 1970 could be described as one of renewed but limited progress. In 1970, unlike 1965–68, the increases were largest where they were most needed. Some of the developed areas, especially Western Europe and North America, produced somewhat less than in 1969, while the big increases were in India, the U.S.S.R., and perhaps China. Rice, the staple food of the Far East, was in surplus, and sugar was exported by India. Even some areas in Latin America and Africa experienced a degree of progress. Fittingly enough, the 1970 Nobel Peace Prize went to U.S. agriculturist Norman E. Borlaug (*see* BIOGRAPHY), who had been instrumental in developing high-yield grains that had contributed to improved production in the less developed countries.

Yet widespread skepticism remained that the Green Revolution, which in one form had led to the planting of new varieties of wheat and rice on an estimated 34 million ac. in Asia, would serve the food needs of the rapidly growing population for very long. One estimate was that an annual expenditure of $11 billion by governments, industry, and private sources would be required to expand the global food supply to meet needs in 1979. In April a total of $122.6 million was approved for World Food Program projects in 22 countries.

NORTH AMERICA

United States. Farmers and the wider public were reminded in 1970 of the complex and sometimes fragile chain of conditions on which the abundant productivity of modern agriculture depends. The southern corn leaf blight, a blackish-brown rot, spread north

MARION KAPLAN

into the Corn Belt, turning a promising corn crop into a mediocre one. By early autumn blight damage to the corn crop was officially confirmed. With feed-grain prices sure to rise, farmers began to slow down production of red meats, poultry, and eggs, and many wondered whether to plant corn in 1971 and how much resistant seed would be available. Current supplies were ample, however; because of earlier expansion, hog prices had declined as much as 80% from summer peaks and broilers were selling below cost.

Overall, livestock provided the major contribution to the still comparatively favourable situation; crops were held in check not only by fortuitous circumstances, but also by official programs designed to keep prices up. Export markets proved unexpectedly large, particularly for soybeans and feed grains. Fears were expressed over rising protectionist sentiment and the possibility that it might lead other countries to retaliate against such products in the future.

Farm numbers declined to 2,895,000 at the beginning of the year, down 28% from a decade earlier. Average farm size increased, as did income per farm. Unionization made a major breakthrough as the long boycott against California grapes ended with recognition of the union by the growers. The public became more aware of possible conflicts between a quality environment and pollution resulting from such agricultural activities as fertilization and the use of pesticides and herbicides. Chicago lost its last claim to be "hog butcher for the world" when that market was discontinued in May and Peoria, Ill., became the new live-hog price-basing point. The Chicago stockyards announced plans to discontinue the handling of all farm animals on Feb. 1, 1971.

Crops. U.S. farmers' intentions in March 1970 were to plant 6.4 million more acres to major crops than in 1969, but because of poor weather the acreage finally planted totaled about 300 million, only 1 million ac. above a year earlier. Acreage to be harvested was indicated at 289 million, up 1%. As late as early August prospects nearly equaled the record 1969 outturn, but after mid-August a major crop, corn (maize), was heavily damaged by a widespread infection of southern leaf blight (Race T strain of *Helminthosporium maydis*). The July 1 prospects had indicated a record corn crop of 4,819,999,000 bu., compared with 4,577,-864,000 bu. in 1969, but the November report showed a total of only 4,103,973,000 bu. for an average yield of 70.8 bu. per ac. This was 10% below 1969 and 15%, or 716 million bu., less than the July estimate. There continued to be unanswered questions about the feeding quality of the corn, as well as about seed-corn supplies for 1971 planting and whether the blight would persist.

Acreage planted to oats, barley, and grain sorghums was reduced, but those crops were less problem ridden than corn; total feed-grain production was estimated at about 159 million tons, 9% below 1969. The sorghum grain crop was an indicated 707,778,000 bu., about 5% below 1969. Production of oats was estimated at 891,310,000 bu., 6% below the 1969 crop. Barley was estimated at 410,255,000 bu., down 2%. In late autumn the production index for feed grains was 112 (1957–59 = 100), compared with 123 for the preceding year.

The production index for food grains (wheat, rye, and rice) was 122, compared with 130 in 1969. The total crop of 46 million tons was down 6%. Acreage harvested was 46,804,000, compared with 51,017,000 in 1969, largely as a result of acreage reductions under

official programs. The total wheat crop was estimated at 1,360,182,000 bu., 7% less than a year earlier. The average yield of 31.2 bu. per ac. exceeded the record 30.7 bu. of 1969. The average winter wheat yield was 33.6 bu. per ac., also a new record, but because of acreage reductions, production, at 1,108,941,000 bu., was the lowest since 1966. Spring wheat other than durum totaled 201,205,000 bu., about the same as in 1969. The durum wheat crop, at 50,036,000 bu., was less than half that of the preceding year.

The hay and forage crop index was estimated at 116, down from 117 in 1969. Total hay acreage was 62,728,000, increased from 61,838,000 ac. harvested in 1969. The total crop was indicated at 126,432,000 tons, compared with 127,127,000 tons a year earlier. Alfalfa accounted for 73,877,000 tons and clover and timothy for 23,927,000 tons. Preliminary indications were that the record high oilseed index of 196, set in 1969, would be exceeded by 2%, with production reaching 40.7 million tons. The 1970 soybean crop was estimated at a record 1,134,151,000 bu. from 41,-619,000 ac. Cottonseed production was expected to rise by 4%, and the prospective peanut crop was up 16% to 2,926,775,000 lb. Flaxseed acreage was up 12%, but late planting, frost, and some dry weather reduced the crop to an estimated 30,877,000 bu., compared with 36,448,000 bu. in 1969. The index of cotton production was 85, compared with 82 a year earlier. The crop was estimated at 10,618,400 bales (480 lb. each), compared with 10,015,000 bales in 1969. World cotton production also rose; the total was estimated at 51,968,000 bales, including 16,518,000 bales from Communist countries.

The production index for the U.S. 1970 sugar crop declined to 170 from the 1969 record of 175. Sugarcane acreage was 9% above the previous year and production was indicated at 25,278,000 tons, 12% more than in 1969. Sugar-beet acreage and production both fell, however; the sugar-beet crop was forecast at 26,127,000 tons. Production of maple syrup totaled 1,105,000 gal., compared with 1,032,000 gal. a year earlier.

Production of all types of tobacco was indicated at about 1,873,742,000 lb., compared with 1,806,656,000 lb. in 1969. Acreage was reduced to 905,000 from 922,-000. Production of flue-cured types rose to 1,160,909,-000 lb., but Burley declined to 552 million lb. Cigar binder increased about 20%.

Fresh vegetable supplies from winter and spring crops fell moderately in 1970, largely because of heavy rains and freezing in Florida. Summer and fall supplies were about 2% above 1969; onions, cabbage, and celery were short but carrots were abundant and

Table I. Index Numbers of Volume of Agricultural Production
Average 1952–56 = 100

Region	Total agricultural production			Per capita food production		
	1969*	1968	1948–52	1969*	1968	1948–52
Western Europe	145	145	84	129	130	87
North America	125	126	93	105	107	99
Latin America	149	147	87	100	102	97
Oceania	163	166	90	121	129	102
Far East (excl. China and Japan)	154	148	87	108	106	94
Near East (excl. Israel)	159	157	82	106	108	90
Africa (excl. South Africa)	142	142	88	94	97	97
Eastern Europe and U.S.S.R.	169	174	82	142	148	87
Other developed countries (Japan, South Africa, and Israel)	168	166	81	143	143	87
All above regions	148	147	87	112	114	93

*Preliminary.
Source: Food and Agriculture Organization of the United Nations, *The State of Food and Agriculture, 1970* (1970).

melons were up 4%. Principal vegetables for processing were expected to be 2% below 1969. Estimated potato production was 323,485,000 cwt., compared with 311,903,000 cwt. the preceding year. Sweet potato production, indicated at 13,797,000 cwt., was 6% below the 1969 crop. The 1970 dry edible bean harvest of some 17,922,000 cwt. was 5% below 1969. Dry field peas totaled 4,413,000 cwt., down 8% in spite of increased acreage.

The total crop of seven major deciduous fruits was 13% below 1969. The indicated 149,895,000 bu. of apples was 6% below 1969. Peaches were down by 17%, pears by 23%, and grapes by 22%. California prunes and plums were up 46 and 84%, respectively, but outside California the crop was 47% below a year earlier. The 1970 strawberry crop was down 2.5%; imports of fresh strawberries rose 12% and of frozen strawberries, 13%. Cranberry production was indicated at 3% above 1969. The first forecast of pecan production was 152.5 million lb., 32% less than the 1969 crop. Almonds, filberts, and walnuts were all expected to be more abundant. Incomplete reports indicated a record 1970–71 citrus crop, 19% above a year earlier. Total oranges would substantially exceed the 185,860,000 boxes of 1969–70, with Florida producing an estimated 168 million boxes.

Livestock. The composite livestock index stood at 124, compared with 118 a year earlier. Meat animals reached an index of 130, compared with 122 in 1969; dairy products were stable at 98; and poultry and eggs rose to 147 from 139. The value of livestock and poultry at the beginning of 1970 was a record $23.5 billion, 16% higher than a year earlier. Meat animals accounted for $22,896,000,000 of the total. With livestock numbers up and supplies of concentrate feeds per animal unit reduced, however, it appeared that sharp readjustments in the livestock industry were near at hand.

Cattlemen added about 2.5 million head to their herds during 1969, the sharpest increase in recent years. The Jan. 1, 1970, inventory was 112,330,000 head. The beef herd, at 91,135,000 head, was 2,866,000 above Jan. 1, 1969, while the dairy herd fell 2% to 21,195,000. All cattle and calves had an average value of $180, compared with $158 a year earlier. With a larger calf crop and reduced slaughter of cows and calves, a further buildup in numbers appeared likely. About 6% more fat cattle moved to market in the first half of the year, and numbers marketed were expected to remain above the 1969 figures. Prices of fat stock held rather firm. Despite large numbers of young cattle potentially available, fattening of cattle for 1971 marketing faced considerable uncertainty, chiefly involving feed prices and the high price of feeder cattle that could not be marketed for many months.

With a slower decline in milk cow numbers and a larger rise in output per cow, milk production for 1970 was expected to be slightly above the 116,200,000,000 lb. of 1969. Consumption of some products, such as cheese, low-fat fluid milk, nonfat dry milk, and frozen desserts, increased, but the forecast was for a continued decline in per capita consumption of milk in all dairy products.

The 56.7 million hogs on farms on Dec. 1, 1969, represented a 6% drop from a year earlier. They were valued at $39 per head, compared with $30.50. The June to November 1969 pig crop had been reduced 7%, and this, combined with generally higher hog prices and favourable feeding ratios in 1969, encouraged a 12% increase in the 1970 spring pig crop. Be-

ginning in July, hog prices broke sharply—the November price was $18 per hundredweight, $6–$7 below a year earlier; corn prices rose, and the feeding ratio became much less favourable. Nevertheless, it appeared that hog numbers would remain high until mid-1971. Hog numbers in September were 13% above a year earlier, and autumn farrowing intentions were up 13%.

There were 20,422,000 head of sheep and lambs on farms and ranches at the beginning of 1970, a reduction of 4% from a year earlier. The average value of stock sheep rose from $22 to $24.70. The 1970 lamb crop totaled 13.4 million head, 2% less than a year earlier; even with the higher lambing rate evident in 1970, the inventory was expected to continue falling for the 11th year in a row. Feeder lamb prices continued strong, but fat lamb prices declined sharply from $31.75 per hundredweight in March to $27 in April. Shorn wool production of 161.9 million lb. (greasy basis) was 2% below 1969 and 39% below 1960, and prices were seriously depressed.

At 431,533,000, the Jan. 1, 1970, inventory of chickens was 3% above a year earlier. The laying flock in September totaled 315 million hens, up about 2%. Production of 5,833,000,000 eggs during the first seven months was 1% above the corresponding period of 1969. Prices early in the year were favourable, and some shell eggs from Spain appeared in U.S. markets. Output of broiler meat in federally inspected plants during January–July was 14% above a year earlier. Wholesale prices during January–August averaged 25.7 cents per pound, a drop of 17%, and the U.S. Department of Agriculture (USDA) recommended that broiler marketings in the first quarter of 1971 be reduced 8% from the record 1970 level. There were 6,674,000 turkeys on farms in January 1970. The 1970 turkey crop was estimated at 115 million birds, 8% more than in 1969.

The 1970 U.S. honey crop was of average size, well below the record 283,268,000 lb. harvested by 4,762,000 bee colonies in 1969. Larger honey harvests in 1970 were indicated in several major producing countries, however, and the world total might approach the 1969 record of 978 million lb. from reporting countries.

Farm Prices, Costs, Income, and Finances. In October 1970 prices received by U.S. farmers stood at a composite index of 274 (1910–14 = 100), compared with 277 a year earlier. The price index for all crops was 229 against 215 in October 1969. All crop groups except tobacco were up. Livestock and products, at 313, were down from 329 a year earlier, with only dairy products showing an increase; much of the decline was related to the sharp break in hog prices. Earlier in the year some products had been substantially lower in price; Idaho farmers burned potatoes in a giant "potatobake" to dramatize their protest.

The parity index of production costs paid by farmers for commodities and services, interest, taxes, and wages reached a new record high of 394 in October 1970, up from 377 a year earlier. An increase of 4% in the cost of production goods was broadly based, with all items affected except motor supplies. Farmers reduced expenditures for new farm machinery so drastically that farm equipment makers referred to 1970 as "the year of the locust." Some 5,264,000 persons were employed in farming late in September 1970, of whom 3,728,000 were "family" labour and 1,536,000 were "hired." The composite per-hour wage rate was $1.46 on October 1, compared with $1.37 a year earlier; farmhands were receiving an average of $325 per month, with housing and other allowances.

The parity ratio, an overall measure of farmers' purchasing power, was 75 in October 1970, the lowest since 1933. The farmer's share of the retail all-food "market basket" was approximately 38%, compared with a 1969 average of 41%. In July the index of retail food costs was 133.4 (1957–59 = 100), up from 126.7 a year earlier; meanwhile, the more inclusive consumer price index had increased from 128.2 to 135.7.

Cash receipts from farm marketings during the first half of 1970 were at a seasonally adjusted annual rate of about $49 billion, compared with $47.2 billion in 1969. With government payments of about $3.8 billion and allowances for housing and food consumed on the farm added, gross income came to about $56 billion. Cash receipts in 1969 totaled about $18,790,000,000 from crops and $28,439,000,000 from livestock and products. Production expenses in 1970 rose to an estimated $32,880,000,000, leaving a residual net realized income approximating the $16.2 billion of 1969.

The estimated value of U.S. farm assets in 1969 was $298 billion, of which real estate accounted for more than two-thirds. Farmland values rose 4% during the year ended March 1, 1970, to a national average of $193 per acre, the smallest advance in seven years. Farm mortgage debt increased to $28,407,000,000, compared with $27,139,000,000 a year earlier. Non-real-estate loans outstanding amounted to $18,502,-000,000, up from $17,219,000,000 in the preceding year.

Trade and Stocks. Total value of U.S. agricultural exports in 1969–70 was $6,646,300,000, 16% more than in 1968–69 and the third highest on record. Commercial sales for dollars were at a new record level of over $5.6 billion. Animals and animal products averaged only 6% higher than the previous year, but fats were up 33%. Exports of all oilseeds and products rose 35% and cottonseed and soybean oils increased 85%. Agricultural shipments from the U.S. to a single country exceeded the billion dollar level for the first time as commercial sales to Japan reached $1,089,-000,000, up 30% from 1968–69. Soybeans and feed grains accounted for a large part of the total. U.S. food and fibre exports to the EEC rose 6% to $1,383,-000,000 in 1969–70. Products not subject to EEC's variable import levies, including fruits, vegetables, and oilseeds, showed gains averaging about 15%. U.S. imports of agricultural products reached a record $5,-481,000,000 in 1969–70, a gain of 11% over the previous year. The value of competitive (supplementary)

"THE DAILY PANTAGRAPH"
The dark area on the shank and at the base of this ear of corn indicates the presence of southern corn leaf blight, which threatened the 1970 U.S. corn crop.

agricultural imports, at $3,373,000,000, was 10% higher than in 1968–69, while complementary imports increased by 13% to $2,108,000,000. Cocoa beans, soluble coffee, crude rubber, and spices all registered large gains.

The problems associated with superabundant stocks were not so acute in 1970, and some served as reserves under stress. Even some Commodity Credit Corporation stocks were moved into the market to dampen the overemphasis on shortages. The 880 million-bu. carryover of wheat was perhaps the most troublesome reserve in view of the large surplus in Canada. Feedgrain reserves declined to about 47 million tons and the cotton carry-over of 6 million bales was the smallest since 1953.

Legislation and Administration. Major new farm legislation was enacted late in 1970 to replace the expiring, once-extended, much criticized Food and Agriculture Act of 1965. A highlight of the long, complex Agricultural Act of 1970 was an acreage "set-aside" principle for corn and other feed grains, wheat, and cotton for the next three crop years instead of the old acreage "diversion" programs. After setting aside the required portion of his basic allotment and meeting conservation base requirements, the farmer would be generally unrestricted with regard to crops planted.

Table II. Cotton Production of the Principal Producing Countries

In 000 500-lb. bales

Country	Indicated 1970	1969	Average 1964–68	Average 1960–64
Argentina	550	640	483	552
Brazil	2,800	3,100	2,540	2,235
China	6,900	6,800	6,580	5,040
Colombia	600	590	421	335
Greece	435	510	366	377
India	5,200	5,100	4,860	4,741
Iran	550	710	582	494
Mexico	1,600	1,750	2,345	2,206
Pakistan	2,600	2,475	2,116	1,656
Peru	400	390	507	632
Spain	200	265	356	427
Sudan	950	950	858	675
Syria	700	685	714	656
Turkey	1,800	1,835	1,710	1,091
U.S.S.R.	9,500	8,900	8,980	7,370
U.A.R.	2,200	2,350	2,161	2,037
United States	10,429	10,015	11,641	14,795

Source: U.S. Department of Agriculture, Foreign Economic Service.

Table III. Orange (including Tangerine) Production in Principal Producing Countries

In 000 boxes

Country	1969*	1968	Average 1960–64
Algeria	13,200	12,900	11,647
Argentina	34,329	32,723	21,540
Brazil	56,790	51,096	27,020
Greece	14,708	11,171	7,646
Israel	29,416	26,550	16,536
Italy	51,336	52,778	30,650
Japan	86,105	89,213	38,314
Mexico	29,510	28,313	23,478
Morocco	25,700	22,670	15,493
South Africa	14,883	14,706	13,939
Spain	65,878	54,529	51,191
Turkey	14,172	16,755	8,522
United States	248,873	237,042	145,937

*Preliminary.
Source: U.S. Department of Agriculture.

AUTHENTICATED NEWS
INTERNATIONAL

A caravan of Canadian-made farm equipment begins tour of five Midwestern U.S. states to explore potential markets for machinery manufactured in Manitoba and Saskatchewan.

Table IV. Honey Production in Specified Countries

In 000,000 lb.

Country	1969*	Average 1960–64
Argentina	44	47
Australia†	29	41
Austria	13	10
Brazil	16	17
Canada	53	35
Chile	12	14
China	38	6
France	23	32
Germany, West	40	26
Guatemala	5	5
Italy	15	15
Japan	15	15
Mexico	79	60
New Zealand	11	12
Spain	22	20
Turkey	36	20
United Kingdom	9	8
United States	283	253
U.S.S.R.	226	234
Yugoslavia	8	8

*Preliminary.
†Crop year beginning July of previous year.
Source: U.S. Department of Agriculture.

Title I of Public Law 480, which provides for foreign currency and dollar credit sales of agricultural commodities to friendly countries, was extended to the end of 1973, as was Title II authorizing the donation of agricultural commodities outside the U.S. for specified purposes.

Miscellaneous legislation included authority for lease and transfer of tobacco acreage allotments; extension of marketing and order programs for apples to additional states; an amendment to the Bankhead-Jones Farm Tenant Act authorizing financial assistance for recreational developments within resource/conservation projects; a three-year extension of health services for domestic migrant agricultural workers; and extension and expansion of school lunch programs, child nutrition programs, and special milk programs for children.

Canada. Faced with a domestic wheat glut and an oversupplied world market, Canada in 1970 took major steps toward reducing production. In February a one-year program was announced providing a cash incentive for as many as 188,000 farmers in a designated region to hold wheat land out of production. Early indications were that the program would cost about $80 million and that 120,000 farmers participated. Wheat plantings in 1970 were the smallest since 1914, when the prairie wheat area was only 9.3 million ac. Preliminary estimates were that land in summer fallow had been increased to 46.9 million ac., compared with 28.8 million ac. in 1969. Acres devoted to all wheat were reduced by 51%. Uncommonly cold and wet weather seriously delayed planting, particularly in Saskatchewan, but otherwise the growing season was fairly normal; average wheat yields dipped slightly, to 26.5 bu. per ac. from 27.4 bu. in 1969, but were well above the 21.2 bu. average for 1959–68.

As of September, Canadian officials hoped to export 700 million bu. of grain in 1970–71, exceeding the previous record of 685 million bu. set in 1963–64. Wheat would account for about 500 million bu. of the total. Included would be some part of the overdue obligation of the U.S.S.R. to take an additional 128 million bu. of wheat under an agreement negotiated in 1966. Whether these estimates would prove out remained to be seen, but smaller crops in some important exporting areas provided encouragement. Also, with less corn available, it appeared that more wheat might be used for animal feedstuffs, especially in Western Europe. Preliminary estimates were for a

world wheat crop of 10,280,604,000 bu., compared with 10,753,600,000 bu. in 1969. Shipments of wheat grain by the five major exporters (U.S., Canada, Australia, Argentina, and France) in 1969–70 totaled 36.9 million metric tons (1,354,483,000 bu.), an increase of 8.6% over the previous year. Carry-over stocks in exporting countries amounted to 68,099,000 tons, compared with 58,472,000 tons a year earlier. Prices rose somewhat in late summer, but later there were reports of a renewed wheat-price war.

The decline in wheat sales had resulted in a drop of about one-fifth in total farm cash receipts in the Prairie Provinces after 1967, and there was some expansion in other crops and diversification into livestock. Barley acreage was increased to 9.5 million from 9 million in 1969, and preliminary estimates indicated production of 424 million bu. Acreage of rapeseed, of which Canada was the world's major producer, was greatly increased; the prospective crop was 71.6 million bu., compared with 33.4 million bu. in 1968. Official plans were to have Canada's whole rapeseed crop switched to new erucic-acid-free varieties by 1972. Livestock production was stimulated by the grain surplus. The June 1, 1970, estimate showed hog numbers at 7,086,000, up 23% from a year earlier and the highest total since 1943. Milk production rose early in the year, but heavy penalties for overquota deliveries of manufacturing milk and heavy culling of the dairy herd reduced the supply later.

LATIN AMERICA

Latin America's agriculture registered both gains and losses in 1970. An improved Mexican wheat harvest was offset by reduced wheat and livestock production in Argentina. Drought and the effects of disease brought the outlook for Brazil's important coffee crop to a new low. Cuba, on the other hand, harvested a record sugar crop, although possibly at severe cost to other sectors of its economy. Land-reform programs in Mexico, Chile, Colombia, and other Latin-American countries continued, in some cases with evidence of renewed vigour.

Mexico. Severe heat and drought conditions continued into 1970, reducing Mexico's crops of cotton and some important foods substantially. Poor pasture conditions and water shortages in major livestock areas, particularly Chihuahua, Coahuila, and Durango, forced cattlemen to cut back herds, raising the prospect of substantial increases in exports of both meat and live cattle. Early indications pointed to a 1970–71 cotton crop of no more than 1.6 million bales, compared with 1,750,000 bales a year earlier. Several factors were responsible, among them drought in the Altamira region and a combination of pink bollworm infestation and inefficient irrigation in the Mexicali district. Exports of Mexican cotton for 1971 were expected to be the lowest in two decades.

Adverse weather was expected to reduce the 1970–71 corn crop; production in 1969–70, at 6.5 million metric tons, had been some 2 million tons less than a year earlier. Wheat, grown mostly under irrigation in the northwestern coastal states of Sonora and Sinaloa, totaled about 2.2 million tons in 1969–70, about 18% more than in 1968–69; irrigation and the increased use of new varieties were credited. The 1969–70 rice crop of 371,000 metric tons (rough basis) was only slightly above the preceding year and sugar production was down 8%. The livestock industry continued to suffer the effects of drought and poor pasture conditions; heavy slaughter resulted in higher exports of boneless beef and shipments of live cattle rose 18%. Exports of horticultural crops in 1969–70 were the highest on record; tomato exports were up 27% and fresh strawberry exports were doubled.

Central America. Record levels of coffee production and a good outturn of sugar in major producing Central American countries in 1969–70 tended to offset generally poor cotton and rice crops. Favourable growing conditions raised estimates for El Salvador's coffee production to 2.4 million bags (132.3 lb. each), equal to the previous record set in 1967–68. Nicaragua's 1969–70 coffee crop was a record 605,000 bags, and Honduras, with an estimated 500,000 bags, expected to increase exports above the $18 million estimated for 1969. Sugar production in Guatemala, at an estimated 218,000 short tons, was 11% above 1968–69, and production in Nicaragua, El Salvador, and Costa Rica reached new records.

Exports of bananas from the Central American nations in 1970 were forecast at 2,441,000 metric tons, an increase of about 11% over actual exports in 1969. Supplies in Guatemala were forecast at 20% above a year earlier, and an estimated exportable supply of 725,000 tons in Costa Rica was 12% above 1969. Production of the important banana crop in Honduras suffered a setback as a result of tree damage caused by Hurricane Francelia in September 1969; indications were that 1970 exports would be 30 to 40% below those of a year earlier.

LONDON "DAILY EXPRESS" FROM PICTORIAL PARADE

Engineers in the Dominican Republic test the Ford DNT tractor. It is designed to help mechanize the small farm in less developed countries and costs roughly the price of a pair of oxen.

South America. Sales of farm products helped raise Brazil's export earnings 22% in 1969, and a further gain of about 10% was expected in 1970. Nevertheless, midyear drought severely affected five northeastern states. Brazil's limited capacity to increase agricultural output through traditional farming methods was demonstrated by a Ministry of Agriculture survey of soils of the western two-thirds of the country. The survey found that while 467 million ac. had good potential, only 24 million ac. could be cultivated profitably using present practices.

The first estimate of Brazil's 1970–71 coffee crop was for only 10 million bags, about half the 1969–70 crop and far below the 27,580,000-bag average for the period 1962–66. The very short crop reflected severe freeze damage that struck Paraná in July 1969, as well as prolonged drought in São Paulo. In late January, *Hemeleia vastatrix*, or coffee rust, was discovered in Bahia state, and this first appearance of the fungus disease in Latin America was soon followed by the discovery of affected trees in pockets over a 45,000-sq.mi. area. Although none was discovered in São Paulo and Paraná, Brazil's most important producing states, and

Table V. Poultry Meat Production in Selected Countries*
In 000,000 lb.

Country	1969†	1968	1967	Average 1955–59
Belgium-Luxembourg	194	200	223	95
France	1,280	1,199	1,129	511
Germany, West	508	463	450	172
Italy	1,197	1,173	829	215
Netherlands	540	470	441	96
Total EEC	3,719	3,505	3,071	1,089
Austria	81	80	76	4
Canada	903	807	818	428
Denmark	145	142	146	58
Greece	125	113	102	36
Japan	741	606	529	—
Poland	265	251	236	109
Spain	628	566	567	—
United Kingdom	1,246	1,160	1,062	455
United States	9,728	9,145	9,410	5,480

*On ready-to-cook basis (70% of live weight).
†Preliminary.
Source: U.S. Department of Agriculture, Foreign Agricultural Service.

Table VI. Egg Production in Specified Countries
In 000,000

Country	1969*	1968	1967
Argentina	2,940	2,880	2,640
Australia	2,380	2,328	2,554
Belgium-Luxembourg	3,900	3,438	3,083
Brazil	9,670	9,480	8,750
Canada	5,655	5,436	5,306
Czechoslovakia	3,410	3,270	3,110
France	11,200	10,800	10,300
Germany, East	4,050	4,046	3,995
Germany, West	14,400	14,076	13,802
Hungary	2,600	2,792	2,750
Italy	10,281	9,450	10,465
Japan	27,565	24,390	23,307
Mexico	5,657	5,375	5,356
Netherlands	4,370	3,969	3,695
Poland	6,400	6,315	6,348
Romania	3,200	3,113	2,900
U.S.S.R.	37,000	35,522	33,921
United Kingdom†	15,036	14,814	14,916
United States	68,700	69,324	70,161

*Preliminary.
†Year beginning June 1 of year shown.

Table VII. Milk Cows and Milk Production in Specified Countries

	Number of milk cows in 000			Milk production in 000,000 lb.		
Country	1969*	1968	Average 1961–65	1969*	1968	Average 1961–65
Australia	2,700	2,794	3,190	16,574	15,353	15,244
Austria	1,115	1,115	1,122	7,330	7,401	6,743
Belgium	1,072	1,065	1,024	9,128	9,283	8,664
Canada	2,584	2,616	2,930	18,698	18,362	18,404
Denmark	1,233	1,295	1,428	10,752	11,292	11,713
France	9,700	9,758	9,409	65,624	67,117	54,162
Germany, West	5,878	5,865	5,852	48,977	48,768	45,368
Greece	470	481	434	1,217	1,239	1,159
Ireland	1,655	1,607	1,373	8,101	8,094	6,458
Italy	3,520	3,479	3,448	20,062	20,474	21,872
Netherlands	1,903	1,830	1,701	17,582	16,997	15,597
New Zealand	2,304	2,233	2,007	14,547	13,493	12,302
Norway	453	470	568	4,030	4,105	3,666
Sweden	802	851	1,180	7,035	7,275	8,446
Switzerland	904	929	926	6,993	7,103	6,837
United Kingdom	4,432	4,399	4,202	26,784	26,477	24,791
United States	12,689	13,038	16,195	116,200	117,234	125,660

*Preliminary.
Source: U.S. Department of Agriculture, Foreign Agricultural Service.

COURTESY, "FOREIGN AGRICULTURE"

Irrigation is just one of the methods being utilized by Brazilian farmers to upgrade their agriculture.

A record sorghum harvest and an above-average corn crop raised Argentina's grain production to an estimated 21,072,000 metric tons for 1969–70, exceeding the previous record of 20,109,000 tons set in 1934–35. Below-average wheat, rye, barley, and oats crops were offset as farmers shifted to coarse grains. The corn crop, estimated at 9,440,000 metric tons, was nearly 38% larger than a year earlier and the largest since 1940–41. Production of grain sorghum in 1969–70 was estimated at a record 3.5 million metric tons, 40% more than in the preceding year. The role of wheat in the nation's economy continued to be uncertain in view of declining world prices, the vulnerability of yields to Argentina's erratic weather, and the shift to other crops. At midyear the Argentine government announced tax concessions on cattle deliveries at the Buenos Aires and Rosario markets for June and July. This attempt to reduce domestic beef prices followed previous efforts to lower demand by restricting the sale of beef to two days a week in public eating places and establishing maximum margins for retail beef sales—actions so severely criticized as to cause the resignation of the minister of agriculture. Domestic beef prices rose as much as 35% in the first half of 1970, and the Economic Ministry proposed that Argentina consider importation.

Reduced production of both crops and livestock in 1969–70 indicated a bleak outlook for Uruguay's agriculture. The livestock industry, still recovering from the disastrous 1965 drought, continued to feel the effects of a four-month strike of packinghouse workers in 1969. Cattle numbers, estimated at 8.4 million, were still far below the average of the early 1960s. Prospects for Paraguay's agriculture in 1970 were favourable. The outlook for the corn crop was a record 260,000 metric tons, and increases were expected for tobacco, soybeans, castor beans, rice, and sugar. Chile appeared to make modest gains. The 1969–70 corn crop rose sharply over a year earlier, and corn yields improved more than 20%. Chile's 1969–70 rice harvest also rose. Damage resulting from the severe 1968 drought in the Central Valley continued to hold food prices at high levels, however.

Acceleration of Colombia's nine-year-old agrarian reform program appeared to be under way in June, when INCORA, the reform institute, announced expropriation of some 60,000 ac. of land belonging to about 50 owners in the Cauca Valley, south of Bogotá. The action was challenged by the landowners, however, and the dispute remained unresolved. Total agricultural production in Peru rose to an index of 142 (1952–56 = 100) in 1969, and prospects for 1970 appeared favourable. The corn crop, estimated at 640,000 metric tons, was about 7% above 1968–69. Emergency food relief was rushed to Peru following the devastating earthquake in early June; damage was especially heavy in the north-central portions of the country. Total agricultural output in Bolivia rose to an index of 187 in 1969. The 1969–70 rice crop was estimated at 62,000 metric tons, compared with 58,000 tons a year earlier. The 1969 index of total agricultural production for Ecuador also rose; increased production of corn and coffee in 1970 appeared to be offset by smaller sugar and rice crops. In Venezuela, increases in sugar, coffee, and rice were offset by a reduced corn crop in 1970.

Cuba. Cuba's 1969–70 sugar production, estimated at 9.4 million short tons, was the largest on record, but still short of the goal sought by Prime Minister Fidel Castro. Weather conditions, transport dif-

the affected region accounted for less than 10% of total production, the government promptly appropriated $9 million for eradication. All coffee trees in a 40-mi.-wide area running 500 mi. from Rio de Janeiro to beyond Belo Horizonte were to be destroyed. Fear that the rust would spread to other Latin-American countries prompted the convening of the Inter-American Institute of Agricultural Sciences in Costa Rica in July to consider methods of combating the disease. In October the Brazilian Coffee Institute reported that sample tests showed up to 30% of coffee trees were affected by *broca*, a disease attacking the green beans.

The USDA's second estimate of the 1970–71 world coffee crop was for 57,048,000 bags, about 13% below the 65,310,000 bags produced in 1969–70 and nearly 17% below the 1962–66 average. The sharp decline was attributed almost entirely to the reduced crop in Brazil. South American new crop production, at an estimated 21,167,000 bags, amounted to only 38% of the world total, compared with 55% for the years 1962–66. Production continued to rise in Africa, and that continent's estimated output of 19,401,000 bags for 1970–71 accounted for nearly 34% of world production. Total world coffee exports in 1969 were estimated at 53,751,000 bags, with South America accounting for about 50.6%.

There was increasing evidence throughout the 1969–70 coffee year that the coffee economy had shifted from one of overproduction and depressed prices to one of tightening supplies and higher prices. The International Coffee Organization, in an attempt to hold prices within an agreed range, increased the 1969–70 export quotas above the initial 46 million-bag limit to 51,760,000 bags. Import demand in 1969–70 substantially exceeded new exportable production, resulting in a working-down of accumulated stocks, particularly in Brazil. Wholesale green coffee prices at New York for the first eight months of 1970 rose to new ten-year highs. The International Coffee Organization, whose meetings early in 1970 had reached an impasse because of disputes over export quotas, as well as a U.S.-Brazilian dispute over Brazil's exports of soluble coffee, met in London in mid-August to negotiate quotas for the 1970–71 coffee year. The initial quota was set at 54 million bags, a compromise between the 48 million-bag proposal by Brazil and the 58 million bags proposed by several consuming countries. After the average composite price of all coffees held above 52 cents per pound for 17 days in early October, the council released an additional 2 million bags into the market.

World Production and Trade of Principal Grains

In 000 metric tons

	Wheat			Barley			Oats			Rye			Corn (Maize)			Rice		
	Production 1948-52 average	1969	Imports− Exports+ 1966-69 average	Production 1948-52 average	1969	Imports− Exports+ 1966-69 average	Production 1948-52 average	1969	Imports− Exports+ 1966-69 average	Production 1948-52 average	1969	Imports− Exports+ 1966-69 average	Production 1948-52 average	1969	Imports− Exports+ 1966-69 average	Production 1948-52 average	1969	Imports− Exports+ 1966-69 average
World total	171,148	317,485	−59,286* / +50,054*	59,325	132,653	−6,709* / +6,668	61,719	c.54,100	−1,287* / +1,203*	36,966	31,109	−681* / +711*	139,516	263,698	−26,965* / +27,054*	167,335	294,650	−7,122* / +7,033*
EUROPE Austria	348	950	−40 / +11*	210	935	−166	274	288	−35	343	440	−39	120	698	−177 / +1*	—	—	−37*
Belgium	525	772	−654† / +161*†	244	552	−513† / +58*†	483	273	−76† / +1*†	221	73	−15† / +3*†	3	3§	−1,016† / +197†	—	—	−45† / +7*†
Bulgaria	1,776	2,569	−197* / +433*	332	905	−18* / +1*	148	162	−2*	240	c.28	—	720	2,415	−47* / +206*	37	c.40	−22* / +4‡
Czechoslovakia	1,493	3,149	−1,210*	1,046	2,245	−147* / +19*	961	914	−7*	1,110	670	−116*	316	480	−236* / +3*	—	—	−73* / +3*
Denmark	285	429	−12 / +23*	1,708	5,194	−334* / +229	922	755	−34 / +11	365	126	−30	—	—	−203	—	—	−7*
Finland	263	520	−43 / +10*	201	855	−16*	718	1,146	+9*	201	141	−25 / +2*	—	—	−18	—	—	−15*
France	7,791	14,535	−603 / +4,066	1,534	9,347	−3* / +2,607	3,392	2,349	+98	573	319	+24	452	5,660	−515 / +1,702	46	107	−116 / +33
Germany, East	1,243	1,987	−1,203* / +2‡	593	c.2,067	−165*	1,188	841	—	2,516	c.1,480	−37*	5	2§	−347*	—	—	−34*
Germany, West	2,669	6,000	−1,895* / +164*	1,402	5,130	−1,448* / +25*	2,523	2,976	−425 / +24	3,066	2,886	−76 / +8	20	287§	−2,314* / +73	—	—	−149 / +20*
Greece	894	c.1,701	−2* / +346*	211	447	−15 / +45*	119	c.120	—	47	c.8	—	225	c.421	−233*	39	108§	−4* / +15*
Hungary	1,909	3,585	−227* / +96*	654	909	−42*	216	86	—	732	236	−17* / +11*	c.2,081	4,820	−45* / +27*	40	50	−28* / +3*
Ireland	327	357	−225	163	776	−30	616	286§	−14	4	1§	—	—	—	−125	—	—	−2* / +1*
Italy	7,170	9,537	−1,200* / +26	258	292	−997	495	491	−229 / +2*	123	71	−1*	2,306	4,506	−4,502* / +54	723	862	−8* / +147
Netherlands	324	677	−971* / +400	201	389	−195 / +134	419	338	−72 / +83	455	207	−59 / +30	26	—	−2,174* / +115*	—	—	−69 / +18*
Norway	58	16§	−352 / +1*	109	506	−71	170	c.130	−11	2	c.5	−39	—	—	−94	—	—	−6*
Poland	1,833	c.4,714	−1,293	1,061	1,939	−370 / +57	2,238	c.2,660	−6* / +6*	6,374	8,167	−45* / +36*	c.4	13	−237*	—	—	−63*
Portugal	499	82	−316	96	56	−7*	124	94	—	162	164	−3*	421	570	−334 / +1*	114	181	−30*
Romania	2,778	4,345	+791*	412	615	+4*	369‖	c.155	—	177‖	c.50	+22*	2,495‖	7,680	−444* / +1*	35‖	60§	−30*
Spain	3,625	4,692	−19 / +280*	1,909	3,877	−262	519	533	−1*	482	348	—	520	1,577	−2,416	280	404	−2* / +79
Sweden	677	917	−57 / +238	231	1,523	−3 / +108*	804	1,133	+160	258	178	−34 / +17	—	—	−44	—	—	−12*
Switzerland	260	345	−410	55	131	−398	68	34	−157	34	44	−1	6	24§	−199	—	—	−25* / +1*
U.S.S.R.	35,759¶	93,393§	−3,581* / +4,148*	6,354¶	28,904§	+452*	13,005¶	11,639§	+9*	17,961¶	14,120§	+278*	5,751‖	8,828§	−261* / +183*	202¶	1,063§	−311* / +4*
United Kingdom	2,397	3,373	−4,184 / +10*	2,061	8,698	−268 / +634	2,852	1,334	−21 / +8‡	52	11	−10*	—	—	−3,487	—	—	−115
Yugoslavia	2,171	4,882	−468 / +1*	323	459	+69*	286	308	+2	248	135	—	3,078	7,816	−1* / +463	5	.31	−22*
ASIA Burma	4¶	73§	...	—	—	—	—	—	—	—	—	—	30‖	c.65§	−11* / +87	5,481	8,350	+673*
Cambodia	—	—	—	—	—	—	—	—	—	—	—	—	57	118	−78‡ / +91*	1,635‖	2,503	−75‡ / +168*
China	15,913‖	27,000§	−4,966*	c.12,360	c.18,000§	+1*	c.1,540	c.2,000	—	—	—	—	c.14,082	25,000§	−30*	58,188‖	91,000§	−543 / +1,132*
India	6,087	18,652	−5,497	2,384	2,424	−2*	—	—	—	—	—	—	2,165	c.6,000	—	33,383	c.63,000	+3*
Indonesia	—	—	—	—	—	—	—	—	—	—	—	—	1,535¶	c.3,400	+74*	9,441¶	16,580	−426*
Iran	1,879‖	c.4,000	−250* / +95*	767	864	+5*	—	—	—	—	—	—	6¶	c.35§	−27*	424	c.1,046	−19* / +1*
Iraq	448	1,189	−143* / +9*	722	1,250	+67*	—	—	—	—	—	—	14	4§	−1*	203	293	−1‡
Japan	1,375	758	−4,040*	2,020	494	−561*	119	c.86	−19*	6	c.1§	−80*	57	c.46	−4,234*	12,736	17,504	−531*
Korea, South	139	c.366	−804	c.846	2,066	−55*	4	—		c.36	27		14	63§	−8* / +10*	c.3,385	5,527	−135* / +10*
Lebanon	51	33	−242*	25	12§	−44* / +2‡	2	c.2◇	−5‡	—	—	—	12	4§	−55‡ / +1‡	—	—	−24‡ / +1‡
Malaysia	—	—	−272*	—	—	—	—	—	−4*	—	—	—	8□	c.10§	−78*	670□	1,250§	−349* / +21*
Pakistan	3,685	6,711	−1,439*	150	115	—	—	—	—	—	—	—	384	654	−104‡	12,399	c.21,267	−108* / +135
Philippines	—	—	−487*	—	—	—	—	—	−2‡	—	—	—	695	1,786	−25‡	2,767	4,997	−100 / +14*
Syria	761	1,004	−210* / +2*	321	627	+52*	6	3§	+3*	—	—	—	31	8§	−5* / +1*	13	8§	−38*
Thailand	—	—	−41*	—	—	—	—	—	—	—	—	—	31	c.1,700	−2* / +1,263*	6,846	10,772§	+1,262
Turkey	4,770	10,593	−138	2,270	3,740	—	326	c.480	—	500	c.825	+7*	747	c.1,100	—	109	205§	−3* / +1*
Vietnam, South	—	—	—	—	—	—	—	—	—	—	—	—	30¶	32§	−4*	2,395□	5,115	−557
AFRICA Algeria	996	1,534§	−701* / +16*	808	538§	−37* / +18*	137	42§	−3*	—	—	—	6	7§	−7*	—	6§	−2*
Kenya	101	162§	−10* / +45*	8	6§	—	5	1§	—	—	—	—	93◇	1,682◇	−50* / +140	c.6	19§	−2* / +1*
Morocco	786	c.1,469	−532 / +1*	1,483	2,206	−11* / +3*	51	c.25§	+1*	4	c.2§	—	302	450	−10* / +5*	8¶	38§	−77 / +4*
South Africa	555◇	1,350◇	−285	41‖◇	18◇	−2*	79‖	146	−6*	10‖	6	−1*	2,400◇	4,799◇	−99* / +1,437	c.6	c.2▲	−77 / +1*
Tunisia	452	c.350	−273 / +32*	218	c.80	−41 / +6*	14	6▲	−1*	—	—	—	—	—	−19*	—	—	−2*
United Arab Republic	1,111	1,518§	−1,479* / +1*	123	105	+1*	—	—	—	—	—	—	1,378	2,297§	−166* / +1*	971	2,586§	+531
NORTH AND CENTRAL AMERICA Canada	13,443	18,623	+10,011	4,245	8,238	+811	6,220	5,728	+91	469	419	+162	388	1,864	−685 / +2*	—	—	−41*
Mexico	534	c.2,200	+146	160	180§	−8	47	c.66§	−3*	—	—	—	3,090	c.8,600	−6 / +948	173	c.300	−4* / +15*
United States	31,065	39,704	−25 / +17,041+	5,843	9,084	−164 / +662	18,970	13,789	−36 / +148	524	798	−21 / +71	74,308	116,282	−25 / +14,351+	1,925	4,141	−2* / +1,754
SOUTH AMERICA Argentina	5,175	5,700	+3,179	656	523	+120*	743	381	+208*	526	377	+9*	2,839	6,900	−1* / +3,654*	137	345	+53*
Bolivia	37□	60	−30*	39¶	57§	—	2¶	11▲	−1*	—	—	—	163□	250	—	20¶	68§	−1*
Brazil	498	1,088	−2,487*	15	29§	−30*	9	26§	−14*	17	19§	—	5,841	10,808	−6* / +737	2,921	5,600	+136
Chile	928	1,214	−373*	79	80	+1*	80	95	—	5	10	—	68	154	−33‡	75	37	−21*
Colombia	124	80	−216*	50	76	−26*	—	—	—	—	—	—	733	796	−4* / +1*	248	c.720	—
Peru	146	149	−531*	208	174	−14*	c.2	c.1§	—	—	—	—	275	590§	−3‡ / +1‡	191	299	−35‡
Uruguay	469	430	+75‡	23	41	—	44	73§	−1‡ / +6‡	—	—	—	141	129	—	41	104§	+35*
Venezuela	5¶	1§	−667*	—	—	—	—	—	−8*	—	—	—	303	736§	−44*	41	245§	−4* / +49*
OCEANIA Australia	5,161	10,713	+6,105	531	1,789	−1* / +335	560	1,669	+296	12	20§	—	126	168	−1* / +2*	63	221§	−2* / +96
New Zealand	139	457	−80*	49	233	—	49	55	−1*	—	—	—	—	36§	−1*	—	—	−4*

Note: (—) indicates quantity nil or negligible; (. . .) indicates quantity not known; (c.) indicates provisional or estimated. *1966-68 average. †Belgium-Luxembourg economic union. ‡1966-67 average.
§1968. ‖Average of 4 years. ¶Average of 3 years. ⊙1950. δ1965. □Average of 2 years. ◇Farms and estates only. ▲1966. +Incl. foreign aid shipments.

Sources: FAO Production Yearbook 1969; FAO Trade Yearbook 1969; FAO Monthly Bulletin of Agricultural Economics and Statistics.

(M. C. Mac D.)

ficulties, labour shortages, and antiquated and inefficient mills were blamed by the prime minister, who indicated that some officials in charge of sugar production would be replaced. The government's recruitment of a reported 400,000 labourers over the ten-month harvest period was costly in terms of its effect on other sectors of the economy. In a July 26 address, Castro stated that milk production had been reduced by a quarter and that production and delivery of cement, fertilizer, and other industrial products had declined sharply. Some 5.5 million tons of sugar from the 1970 harvest was earmarked for export to Communist bloc countries, principally the U.S.S.R.

The USDA's preliminary estimate for the 1969–70 world sugar harvest was 79,671,000 short tons (raw value), an increase of about 6% above the 1968–69 record of 75.3 million short tons. In addition to Cuba's record crop, South American production was up about 6% and African production rose slightly to an estimated 4,985,000 tons. A record cane harvest raised India's production 20% above the previous year. Substantial declines were registered for South American and African exporting nations, however, and this accounted for the generally lower volume of trading. Although the International Sugar Council had agreed to hold sugar export quotas for 1970 at 90% of basic export tonnages set by the International Sugar Agreement, a rise in prices by mid-July led the council to distribute an additional 125,000 metric tons to exporters to maintain price stability. Additional quantities were authorized in October and November.

WESTERN EUROPE

Western Europe in 1970 was troubled both by problems of agricultural production and by those of organization and surpluses. The European harvest was reported to be almost universally poor. The wheat crop of about 43.6 million metric tons was 4% smaller than in 1969, while barley, at 36.2 million tons, was down 7%. Even the Western European apple crop was 13% smaller than that of the previous year. Observers continued to wonder when, if ever, the EEC would sort out its farm policy and control burdensome surpluses of some products such as butter.

United Kingdom and Ireland. In Britain the harvest was better than on the continent. A large acreage of fall-sown winter wheat developed ahead of an uncommonly dry summer. Spring sown crops, especially barley and sugar beets, were not so fortunate, and later harvests were below those of 1969. Generally higher market prices and a reduction in deficiency payments under the guaranteed price program resulted. The wheat crop totaled 4,148,000 metric tons, compared with 3,373,000 tons in 1969, while barley declined to 7,819,000 tons from 8,698,000. Food-grain imports in 1969–70 rose as much as 10% over the previous year.

Livestock presented a mixed picture in 1970. Not only were livestock products imported in large amounts, but three breeds of cattle, Limousin, Simmental, and MRI, were brought from the continent for testing to improve production. Livestock markets were boycotted for a week in May as farmers expressed their dissatisfaction with the terms of the 1970 Price Review. Beef production was expected to increase by 30,000 short tons in 1970, but 1969 had been a poor year. Despite a 6.5% decline in dairy cow numbers in the year ended March 31, milk production rose 1% to a record 2,205,000,000 gal. Swine breeding herds were even smaller than in 1969, when numbers

had declined to the lowest level since World War II.

With agricultural productivity increasing about 6% a year, the farm workers, who constituted some 3% of Britain's labour force, requested a 37% increase in basic pay; this would raise farm costs more than £100 million yearly. Net agricultural income for the year was approximately £600 million, compared with a target of £650 million and a revised 1969–70 figure of £528 million. The Price Review determinations allowed an additional £54 million in price guarantees, together with an extra £25 million for fertilizer, capital grants, and incentives for brucellosis eradication. The problem of mounting costs continued, however, and some 60% of farmers sampled reported cutting back on expenditures.

A third attempt was made to gain admission to the EEC. While estimates of the possible effects on agriculture varied widely, it was generally felt that farm production might rise 3 to 10% but would be partly offset by higher costs. Net income would be higher, although distribution of gains and losses would differ widely among commodities, types of farming, and regions. Costs of food would increase 18 to 26%, with expenditures on food rising by some 15 to 22%.

Early season crops in Ireland were good in 1970. Cattle production declined in 1969 to 1,260,000 head, and live cattle exports totaled 570,000 head, compared with 625,000 in 1968. Hog output set a new record of more than 2 million and milk production continued near 7 billion lb. About 20% of the government's 1970–71 budget, or £95.8 million, was earmarked for agriculture. An official White Paper on the implications of EEC membership estimated that in seven years agricultural output would increase 30 to 40% in volume and even more in value. Membership would mean elimination of price supports and export subsidies, and food prices would increase 11 to 16%.

EEC Countries. Though production of several important crops declined moderately in the EEC countries in 1970, the area continued to produce and hold surpluses of several major agricultural items, notably soft wheat and butter. The butter situation was still considered serious; in September it was reported that almost $1 billion had been spent over 12 months to reduce the surplus from about 400,000 metric tons to 150,000 tons. Though at least 300,000 dairy cows had been used for beef, butter production was exceeding consumption at a rate of about 170,000 tons per year. Approximately $700 million had been spent in 1968–69 for price support measures and export subsidies for grain, and still higher expenditures were anticipated in 1969–70. Proposals for structural reforms in the agriculture of the EEC appeared to be stalled, although agreement was reached on the framework for future financing.

The intensive but modernized agriculture of the Netherlands continued to develop. Broiler numbers were up by about 15% in the second half of 1969, and poultry meat exports rose 7%. Laying hen numbers rose 20%, and egg exports were nearly 15% above the 1968 level. Red-meat production also showed gains, as did milk cow numbers and milk production.

West German grain crops all showed declines in 1970; total production fell from 17 million tons in 1969 to less than 16 million tons. Reduction in the number of small farms continued at the rate of about 4% per year, and a new program was set up to bring industry to the rural areas. The agricultural budget for 1970 totaled about $1,941,000,000, compared with $1,391,000,000 in the previous year.

POPPERFOTO FROM
PICTORIAL PARADE

Farmers demonstrate
for better prices
outside the Ministry
of Agriculture in London
before the start
of farm Price Review talks
Feb. 2, 1970.

France also suffered a cutback in most grain crops in 1970, particularly wheat, which declined to 12,936,-000 tons from 14,535,000. Barley, oats, and rye were less seriously reduced, and in September it was reported that corn production was up 25%. Beef supplies increased somewhat, but livestock production in general deteriorated in relation to demand. Farm prices rose between 2 and 12.5% as part of the EEC agricultural price realignment. The reference target price for milk ex-dairy was raised from $4.15 per hundredweight to $4.46. It was not clear to what degree this was related to farm unrest.

The 1970 Italian wheat crop of 9.5 million tons was almost as large as the 9,536,000-ton crop of 1969. The long, hot summer suggested that 1970 might be a vintage year for wine. Italy's almond crop was forecast at 37,000 tons, 61% above 1969. Some fruit crops set new records, and as much as 100,000 tons (mostly pears and peaches) were destroyed because of high costs and low prices to farmers. Italy displaced Spain as the leading olive oil producer with 420,000 tons, against 358,000 tons for Spain and 150,000 tons for Greece. Both cattle and beef were imported to meet demand, and some cheese was imported from the U.S.

Other Countries. Agricultural production remained generally prosperous in other European countries. The European Free Trade Association (EFTA) marked its tenth anniversary; Iceland was admitted, changing the Outer Seven to eight, but with the U.K., Ireland, Denmark, and Norway seeking admission to the EEC, the organization's future was problematical. Denmark seemed to be the most eager of the applicants, not only because, as an efficient producer of livestock products, it found EFTA's exclusion of agricultural goods from the tariff-free schedule discriminatory, but also because its important farm exports had been increasingly squeezed out of the EEC countries, especially West Germany. On the other hand, special bilateral trade agreements between EFTA members had been permitted, and the one between Denmark and the U.K. accounted for more than half of all Danish agricultural exports. The highly important Danish barley crop dropped to 4,857,000 metric tons in 1970, compared with 5,255,000 tons in 1969. Poultry production increased about 20% in the first half of 1970.

A new agricultural price act with overproduction penalties became effective in Finland in April 1970. Dairy herds were severely culled to obtain a slaughter premium of $120 per cow. A soil bank program took 222,000 ac. out of production in 1969, at a compensation of about $24 per acre. Austria developed a surplus of wheat and efforts were made to shift some acreage to feed grains. Modernization of Greek agriculture proceeded, particularly in the livestock and fruit sectors. The Greek dried fruit crop was estimated at 224,000 tons, near the level of 1969.

The important Spanish wheat crop totaled only 4 million tons, compared with 4,691,000 tons in 1969; the barley crop also declined, from 3,855,000 tons to 3.1 million. Of a large 1970 world almond crop indicated at 168,000 tons, Spain produced 35,000 tons, surpassed only by the U.S. (71,500 tons) and Italy. The world filbert crop also was large, with Spain providing 29,000 tons of the 334,600-ton total. The orange crop rose despite severe drought, and new markets were being sought in late 1970.

AFRICA

Early reports of good harvests in most African nations in 1970 encouraged the view that gains made in 1969 would be sustained. Above-average cereal crops in North and West Africa reduced the need for imports, and the 1969–70 output of such export crops as coffee and cocoa in West Africa assured continuation of export earnings. The important South African corn and sorghum crops appeared to have recovered from the 1969 drought. Some areas of South Africa were stricken by drought at midyear, to the disadvantage of livestock herds, and the Rhodesian corn crop was reduced by lack of moisture. Total agricultural output in Africa in 1969 was about 2% greater than a year earlier and 28% higher than the 1957–59 base period. However, because of population increases, per capita food production in 1969 was 2% below the 1957–59 period.

North Africa. Cereal crops harvested in the May–July 1970 season in the Maghreb were above average. Total production of more than 4 million metric tons of grain in Morocco was 25% above 1969. Wheat, estimated at 2,039,000 tons, exceeded the previous year's harvest by 400,000 tons, and corn production rose to an estimated 333,000 metric tons, compared with only 240,000 tons a year earlier. Preliminary indications pointed to a 1970 wheat harvest in Algeria equal to the 1.5 million tons of 1968. Tunisia's wheat crop recovered from four years of drought, and production rose sharply to an estimated 450,000 tons. Tunisia's 1970 olive harvest was expected to reach 500,000 tons, a fivefold increase over 1969, but its citrus production, at an estimated 82,000 tons, was unchanged. Morocco's orange crop was 13% above the preceding year, while Algerian citrus production showed a slight improvement. Flood damage to Tunisia's date trees in 1969 resulted in an extremely poor 1970 harvest; Tunisia continued to plant about 10,000 new trees annually in artesian-fed oases in the Sahara.

In Libya several important crops were reduced in 1970 by inadequate rainfall.

The Algerian government announced plans to reapportion agricultural lands in the north, where a survey revealed that 3% of the landowners controlled 25% of the arable land; under the new plan, holdings would be limited to a size that could be farmed by a single family. The government also continued to encourage the conversion of vineyards to other crops as marketing difficulties made wine production less profitable. The Tunisian government's collective farm movement, strongly resisted by that country's farmers, was officially deemphasized. The Libyan government allocated $560 million for agricultural development, of which $78.5 million was earmarked for agricultural settlement projects.

Cotton production in the U.A.R. rose 17% to an estimated 2,350,000 bales (480 lb. each). Acreage was increased to 1,680,000 and average yields improved 6%. Production of an estimated 975,000 tons of cottonseed was 17% above a year earlier. Sudan's cotton production, estimated at 1.1 million bales, represented a slight increase. Wheat production in the U.A.R. for 1969–70 was estimated at 1,518,000 metric tons and the 1968–69 corn crop at 2,297,000 tons. Development of additional agricultural land in the U.A.R. was being delayed by the financial demands of the military buildup, as well as by the dangerous proximity of some potentially arable areas to the Suez Canal. The productivity of some areas of the lower Nile delta was reportedly being reduced as an indirect effect of the Aswan Dam; salt was being deposited over large areas of the delta by encroaching seawater, which was no longer held back by the full flow of the river.

West Africa. Both export and subsistence crops showed improvement in 1969–70. Rice production in ten West African nations increased 6% over the 2,002,000 tons of 1968–69. The important millet and sorghum crops were improved, and corn production was modestly higher. Cotton and oil palm production continued to be encouraged. In Liberia two plantations

totaling 5,750 ac. had been planted to hybrid palm trees, some of which had begun to produce. The International Institute of Tropical Agriculture at Ibadan, Nigeria, was dedicated in April. Jointly supported by the Ford and Rockefeller foundations, the institute's primary concern was the production of local-consumption crops such as rice, cassava, and yams.

Ivory Coast coffee production of 4.3 million bags was considerably above that of a year earlier. Nigeria's 1969–70 peanut crop, damaged by late rains, was estimated at 1,355,000 metric tons, compared with 1,455,000 tons in 1968–69. Senegal's 1969–70 peanut crop was reported at 885,000 tons, an improvement over drought-reduced production of only 815,000 tons a year earlier; acreage was cut back 19% because of low prices set by the government, and large quantities were reported to have been smuggled into The Gambia, where prices were higher. Production of bananas and plantains in West Africa as a whole was above that of the preceding year.

The harvest of Ghana's important cocoa bean crop was estimated at 417,000 metric tons in 1969–70, marking recovery from the rain-damaged harvest of only 338,000 tons a year earlier. Nigeria's cocoa bean harvest, at 230,000 tons, also indicated recovery from the poor 1968–69 output, and prospects were favourable in the Ivory Coast. The USDA forecast a 1970–71 world cocoa harvest of 1,387,400 metric tons, about 2% less than the estimated 1,420,200 realized in 1969–70 and approximately equal to the 1967–68 harvest. The forecast for Ghana's 1970–71 crop was 406,000 tons and Nigeria's was estimated at 254,000 tons, although reports of heavy rainfall cast doubt on Nigerian production. Ivory Coast production was forecast at 160,000 tons.

Following four consecutive deficit years that had reduced world stocks to very low levels, 1969–70 production was expected to exceed consumption requirements. U.S. cocoa bean grindings in 1969 totaled 268,484 metric tons, 8% less than in 1968; the U.K. grind fell to 90,000 tons from 91,500, and most other

Table VIII. Cattle and Buffalo Numbers in Major Producing Areas

In 000

Area	Estimated 1970*	1969*	Average 1961–65
North America	171,000	167,300	150,500
Canada	11,828	11,475	11,332
Mexico	28,000	27,500	19,337
United States	112,330	109,885	103,892
South America	196,000	195,600	168,700
Argentina	52,500	52,000	43,341
Brazil	91,115	92,276	78,718
Colombia	20,359	19,576	15,780
Uruguay	8,500	8,400	...
Venezuela	7,226	7,000	6,580
Western Europe	89,500	88,700	83,400
France	21,886	22,093	20,020
Germany, West	14,286	14,061	13,115
Italy	10,280	10,067	9,292
United Kingdom	12,311	12,094	11,610
Eastern Europe	34,200	34,700	33,000
Poland	...	11,049	9,697
Yugoslavia	5,078	5,305	5,509
U.S.S.R.	95,000	95,700	83,500
Africa	134,200	133,600	128,100
South Africa	12,251	11,780	12,514
Asia	426,100	424,900	395,500
Iran	5,960	5,855	4,782
Japan	3,650	3,458	3,327
Philippines	6,050	5,970	4,849
Turkey	15,265	15,018	13,783
Oceania	30,900	29,600	25,300
Australia	21,500	20,598	18,357
New Zealand	8,950	8,605	6,646
World total†	1,176,900	1,170,100	1,068,000

*Preliminary.
†Includes allowance for any missing data for countries shown and for other producing countries not shown.
Source: U.S. Department of Agriculture.

Table IX. Hog Numbers in Major Producing Areas

In 000

Area	Estimated 1970*	1969*	Average 1961–65
North America	81,200	84,000	76,100
Canada	6,458	5,695	5,220
Mexico	11,000	10,698	9,170
United States	56,743	60,632	55,544
South America	79,600	80,500	66,700
Argentina	4,000	3,900	3,388
Brazil	64,000	65,640	53,126
Western Europe	81,900	76,500	66,300
Denmark	8,350	7,769	7,284
France	10,622	10,020	8,908
Germany, West	19,323	18,732	16,933
Italy	9,224	7,300	4,787
Spain	6,400	6,129	5,870
United Kingdom	8,135	7,969	7,098
Eastern Europe	47,700	47,600	47,000
Germany, East	...	9,523	8,654
Hungary	4,950	5,334	6,216
Poland	...	14,356	13,080
Yugoslavia	5,566	5,093	5,815
U.S.S.R.	56,100	49,000	59,800
Africa	5,500	5,500	5,100
South Africa	1,289	1,240	...
Asia	173,200	172,100	122,400
Japan	6,400	5,429	3,474
Philippines	12,000	12,000	9,236
Taiwan	...	3,011	2,917
Oceania	3,100	3,100	2,500
Australia	2,300	2,253	1,567
World total†	528,300	518,300	445,900

*Preliminary.
†Includes allowance for any missing data for countries shown and for other producing countries not shown.
Source: U.S. Department of Agriculture, Foreign Agricultural Service.

Table X. Sheep Numbers in Major Producing Areas

In 000

Area	Estimated 1970*	1969*	Average 1961–65
North America	30,400	30,900	37,200
Canada	598	602	911
Mexico	8,200	7,986	6,064
United States	20,422	21,238	29,023
South America	124,600	126,400	121,100
Argentina	47,400	47,500	48,127
Brazil	25,000	24,585	19,997
Peru	14,500	15,000	14,454
Uruguay	19,900	21,700	21,860
Western Europe	76,900	77,500	79,400
France	9,681	9,506	8,876
Greece	7,700	7,800	8,765
Italy	8,160	8,206	7,956
Spain	18,800	18,962	20,574
United Kingdom	19,254	19,667	20,689
Eastern Europe	43,500	44,500	42,800
Bulgaria	...	9,652	10,070
Romania	...	14,298	12,217
Yugoslavia	8,968	9,730	10,232
U.S.S.R.	131,000	140,600	133,900
Africa	132,600	133,100	134,000
South Africa	39,850	40,350	39,759
Asia	252,000	250,700	218,600
Iran	35,000	34,000	21,445
Turkey	37,000	36,587	32,863
Oceania	242,000	234,600	211,500
Australia	182,000	174,602	160,924
New Zealand	60,000	59,937	50,536
World total†	1,033,300	1,038,300	978,500

*Preliminary.
†Includes allowance for any missing data for countries shown and for other producing countries not shown.
Source: U.S. Department of Agriculture, Foreign Agricultural Service.

European nations reported similar declines. Imports into the U.S. in 1969 fell to 221,941 tons from 231,869. New York wholesale prices for Accra (African) cocoa averaged 45.7 cents per pound in 1969, compared with 34.4 cents a year earlier. Bahia (Brazilian) cocoa prices at New York averaged 43.5 cents per pound, a sharp increase over the 33 cent average of 1968. Prices in the early months of 1970 fell sharply, but in the third quarter, December cocoa futures in New York rose from approximately 26.5 cents to 35.5 cents.

East Africa. Early reports of good harvests throughout East Africa pointed to continued agricultural growth in the region. A 2½% decline in regional corn production and a slightly reduced sugar harvest were offset by substantial increases in other important crops. Cotton production was 15% above a year earlier, and forecasts for the 1970–71 coffee crop were excellent. Efforts to establish an East African Common Market between Kenya, Tanzania, and Uganda were advanced in late 1969 with the conclusion of a five-year trade agreement with the EEC. Achievement of an economic community operating along lines similar to those of the EEC was seen as a possibility by 1983.

Kenya experienced better-than-average production in 1969–70. The reduced corn crop was offset by larger outturns of sugar, cotton, citrus, coffee, and tea. The corn harvest fell to an estimated 1.4 million metric tons from 1,542,000 tons a year earlier, but even under these circumstances Kenya led the region in corn production. An additional grain storage facility was completed at Nairobi, adding about 18,000 tons of storage capacity to the country's granaries. Tea production was forecast at 90 million lb. for 1970, 13% more than a year earlier. The new development plan published in December 1969 allotted about 20% of planned expenditures to agriculture.

Ethiopia's 1969–70 production of sorghum and millet was estimated at 1.3 million metric tons, a slight increase over the 1968–69 crop. The National Coffee Board was unable to fill its national coffee quotas and proposed stockpiling at emergency purchase centres. A program was inaugurated to inoculate cattle against rinderpest.

The Uganda cotton crop was estimated at 380,000 bales (480 lb. each) in 1969–70, an increase over the 350,000 bales of the preceding year. Tanzania's cotton crop rose to an estimated 325,000 bales and production in Mozambique to an estimated 200,000 bales. Production in Malawi was unchanged. Uganda's cottonseed production rose to an estimated 185,000 short tons, and production of 158,000 tons in Tanzania was sharply above a year earlier. Tanzania's wheat crop showed a modest gain over the 1,150,000 tons of 1968–69. An excellent cotton crop and a slightly larger rice crop continued that country's gradual improvement. Cyclone Louise in late March reduced the sugar crop on Mauritius to an estimated 605,000 tons, compared with 737,000 tons produced in 1969. Exports of vanilla beans from the Malagasy Republic in 1969 rose 14% to 2,420,000 lb.

Tanzania's sisal production of 438.7 million lb. in 1969–70 was a slight increase over a year earlier. World sisal production was estimated at 1,329,900,000 lb., compared with 1,332,600,000 lb. in 1968. World production of all hard fibres (sisal, abaca, and henequen) continued to decline in 1969–70. Abaca production, dominated by the Philippines, was reported at 167.8 million lb., and henequen, chiefly from Mexico,

NOVOSTI FROM SOVFOTO

A Soviet dairy farm in Kazakhstan. In July 1970 the Soviet government announced creation of an $8 billion yearly subsidy to increase the prices paid to farmers for meat and dairy products while keeping the cost to the consumer the same.

was estimated at 283.5 million lb. Hard fibre prices continued to be depressed by increasing competition from synthetic fibres. Producers appeared to be conforming to export quotas agreed to under an informal arrangement that went into effect in 1968.

Central and South Africa. After two consecutive years of below-average production, unusually favourable weather and improved yields in South Africa combined to produce a 1969–70 corn crop estimated at 6.4 million metric tons. The new crop, 40% larger than the drought-damaged crop of 1968–69, was the second largest harvest on record. Corn supplies for export in the 1970–71 marketing year were forecast at nearly 2 million tons. Sorghum production also recovered after two poor years; production for 1969–70 was estimated at 500,000 metric tons, which would provide a surplus for exports or carry-over of 215,000 tons. The new sorghum crop was more than twice that of 1968–69. Expanded acreage and unusually good weather in the Orange Free State and Transvaal failed to offset severe drought in Cape Province, holding the

Table XI. Centrifugal Sugar Production in Principal Producing Countries			
In 000 short tons, raw value			
Country	Forecast 1970–71	1969–70	1968–69	Average 1961–66
---	---	---	---	---
Argentina	1,051	1,059	1,006	1,053
Australia	2,554	2,387	2,927	1,943
Brazil	5,500	5,153	4,804	4,121
China	2,300	2,200	2,200	1,236
Colombia	764	774	740	440
Cuba	6,500	9,400	5,200	5,094
Czechoslovakia	850	850	1,005	1,142
Denmark	341	335	375	346
Dominican Republic	1,100	1,080	975	808
France	2,696	3,000	2,623	2,225
Germany, East	650	650	815	847
Germany, West	2,280	2,330	2,177	1,894
India	5,000	5,542	4,640	3,788
Indonesia	800	700	750	686
Iran	654	642	568	206
Italy	1,440	1,472	1,422	1,136
Jamaica	450	422	429	537
Mauritius	650	627	737	660
Mexico	2,808	2,616	2,765	2,043
Netherlands	827	845	793	595
Peru	882	816	716	880
Philippines	2,300	2,100	1,760	1,709
Poland	1,885	1,683	1,880	1,688
South Africa	1,650	1,788	1,659	1,206
Spain	970	876	815	565
Taiwan	819	668	834	1,004
Turkey	719	600	778	610
United Kingdom	1,166	1,030	1,075	978
U.S.S.R.	10,500	9,500	11,111	8,443
United States	5,900	5,706	5,904	5,047
U.S. dependencies*	500	460	483	964
Yugoslavia	498	545	433	340
World total	79,164	79,671	75,385	62,746

*Puerto Rico and Virgin Islands of the U.S.
Source: U.S. Department of Agriculture, Foreign Agricultural Service.

Table XII. Coffee Production (Green) in Principal Producing Countries			
In 000 bags, 132.3 lb. each			
Country	1970–71*	1969–70	1968–69	Average 1962–66
---	---	---	---	---
Angola	3,300	3,400	3,100	2,919
Brazil	10,000	19,000	16,500	27,580
Cameroon	1,200	1,200	1,100	906
Colombia	8,200	8,100	7,900	7,860
Congo (Kinshasa)	1,150	1,100	1,000	1,005
Costa Rica	1,300	1,400	1,260	1,028
Ecuador	1,000	700	1,000	808
El Salvador	2,000	2,500	1,900	1,886
Guatemala	1,800	1,750	1,740	1,814
India	1,250	1,100	1,300	1,055
Indonesia	2,200	2,200	2,000	2,016
Ivory Coast	4,100	4,600	3,400	3,457
Kenya	875	815	800	687
Malagasy Republic	900	830	900	902
Mexico	3,200	3,050	2,850	2,611
Peru	950	940	860	802
Philippines	800	785	735	667
Tanzania	1,000	800	950	535
Uganda	2,900	2,700	3,335	2,568
Venezuela	800	750	750	814
Total North America	11,439	11,802	10,692	10,556
Total South America	21,167	29,732	27,262	38,000
Total Africa	19,401	18,944	18,215	15,834
Total Asia and Oceania	5,041	4,832	4,702	4,143
World total	57,048	65,310	60,871	68,534

*Second estimate.
Source: U.S. Department of Agriculture, Foreign Agricultural Service.

wheat harvest to about 1.2 million tons, unchanged from a year earlier. Widespread drought reduced corn yields in Rhodesia, and the 1969–70 corn crop was estimated at no more than 700,000 tons, 40% below the record 1.2 million of 1968–69. The wheat and rice crops, both largely produced under irrigation, were not expected to be affected.

South African sugar production was estimated at 1,788,000 short tons in 1970, a partial recovery from the preceding year but less than the 1968 harvest of 2,009,000 tons. Rhodesia's 150,000-ton sugar harvest represented a return to the 1968 level. Rhodesia's cotton harvest was 240,000 bales (480 lb. each), an increase over the 200,000 bales produced a year earlier. In South Africa production was down 10%.

Flue-cured tobacco production in Rhodesia in 1970 was expected to be little changed from the 132 million lb. produced a year earlier. The flue-cured tobacco target for 1971 and 1972 was set at 100 million lb., with producer prices guaranteed at the equivalent of 32 U.S. cents per pound, compared with 29 cents for the 1969 and 1970 crops. Growers were critical of a cut in direct supports for the tobacco crop, but the budgetary move was considered necessary because of the increased costs of stockpiling, the export market having been severely limited by the British embargo. South Africa, a growing producer in recent years, exported 28.2 million lb. of unmanufactured tobacco in 1969, a 25% increase over 1968.

South Africa's cattle herds numbered 12,251,000 head in 1970, an increase from 11,780,000 head a year earlier. Hog numbers, at 1,289,000 head, were moderately higher. Sheep numbers declined to 39,850,000 head from 40,350,000; wool production in 1970 was estimated at 320 million lb., compared with 352 million lb. in 1969. Fruit production included 14,883,000

boxes of oranges, 2,828,000 boxes of grapefruit, and 485,000 boxes of lemons.

EASTERN EUROPE AND THE U.S.S.R.

Overall, agriculture in this broad, diverse area appeared to rebound substantially in 1970 from the setbacks of 1969, thanks largely to new grain production records in the U.S.S.R. As measured by meat supplies, livestock continued to be a major problem, especially in Eastern Europe where earlier droughts had substantially reduced feed-grain supplies. Livestock numbers at the beginning of 1970 were generally lower than in most recent years, and considerably higher meat prices were reported in some urban areas. Plans for 1970 had called for an increase of 8.5% in agricultural output in the Soviet Union and moderate to strong increases for Eastern Europe.

Eastern Europe. As of September, much of Eastern Europe appeared to have had a difficult year. Yugoslavia's 1970 wheat crop was down perhaps a fifth from the record 4,880,000 metric tons harvested in 1969, and midseason indications were that feed-grain production would be reduced about 10%. Prospects were that some wheat imports would be required. With approximately 71 million plum trees of bearing age, Yugoslavia, the world's largest producer, harvested a record plum crop in 1969; brandy output reached a new high of 143 million qt. Livestock had declined about 5% in 1969 and did not make a major recovery in 1970, but demand was strong. A three-year trade agreement to ensure Yugoslavia more favourable conditions for exports of baby beef to the EEC became effective in May.

Romania and some nearby areas were hard hit by early summer floods. About 6% of the agricultural land of Romania was flooded in May; more than 1.7 million ac. of crops were affected and 30,000 to 40,000 head of livestock were lost. Much crop area was replanted only to be flooded again. The 1971–75 plan called for a 28–31% increase in overall agricultural production.

Hungary, which made a strong agricultural recovery in 1969, was also hurt by floods. The wheat crop declined to 3 million tons against 3,579,000 tons in 1969, and the barley crop was off by about 20%. To counteract livestock product shortages, the numerical limit on livestock raised on household plots was rescinded for farmers who would contract to market through their collectives. Producer prices for livestock products were increased some 10% as of Jan. 1, 1970. Farm investment was reported to be up 30%.

Preliminary forecasts indicated that Czechoslovakia and East Germany, where output declined sharply in 1969, would lag again in 1970. Some reports indicated grave delay in the Czechoslovak grain harvest. Compulsory deliveries at lower prices were abolished in East Germany. Bonus prices for sales above the contracted level apparently caused excessive slaughter of herds in Czechoslovakia in 1969, and that country announced plans to step up imports of livestock products from non-Communist countries. Exports of oriental-type tobacco from Bulgaria declined further in 1970; the 1969 crop was seriously affected by disease on about one-fifth of the total acreage.

Poland was said to be experiencing another farm crisis, with local food riots reported. Following a severe winter and late spring, floods, drought, and wet harvests contributed to the shortages. The wheat crop was not much smaller than in 1969, and the barley crop of 2 million tons was moderately larger, but

Table XIII. World Cocoa Production in Leading Areas*

In 000 metric tons

Area	Forecast 1970–71	1969–70	1968–69	Average 1962–66
North and Central America	79.6	89.3	68.8	83.4
Dominican Republic	30.0	43.0	21.0	34.0
Mexico	25.0	24.0	23.0	21.6
South America	259.0	282.1	265.0	206.7
Brazil	155.0	185.0	166.2	127.9
Ecuador	60.0	55.0	53.0	40.3
Africa	1,909.7	1,011.7	865.9	928.9
Cameroon	105.0	105.0	103.8	81.0
Ghana	406.0	417.0	338.9	453.7
Ivory Coast	160.0	180.0	142.7	108.9
Nigeria	254.0	230.0	195.0	215.0
Asia and Oceania	39.1	30.8	37.1	27.4
New Guinea and Papua	29.0	27.0	27.2	16.3
World total	1,387.4	1,420.2	1,236.8	1,246.4

*Crop year, October 1 to September 30.
Source: U.S. Department of Agriculture, Foreign Agricultural Service.

Table XIV. Tea Production in Principal Producing Areas

In 000,000 lb.

Area	Forecast 1970	1969*	1968	1967	Average 1961–65
World total†	2,341	2,330	2,276	2,165	1,971
Asia†	1,908	1,903	1,898	1,816	1,706
Ceylon	478	484	496	487	478
India	890	873	885	848	788
Indonesia	80	89	91	74	98
Japan	198	198	187	188	177
Pakistan	68	66	62	65	57
Taiwan	58	58	54	54	43
U.S.S.R.	125	127	119	121	96
Africa	251	239	208	179	131
South America	57	61	51	49	39

*Preliminary.
†Excluding China.
Source: U.S. Department of Agriculture, Foreign Agricultural Service.

the important rye crop declined 26% to 6.1 million tons. Even rapeseed production was reported to be below the purchase level planned by the state. Hog numbers in June 1970 were about 5% below a year earlier. Cattle raisers were given a reduction in land taxes in 1969 if they guaranteed to deliver young cattle fattened to above-quota weights in 1970.

U.S.S.R. The 1970 Soviet grain harvest was delayed, but early and incomplete reports indicated good to excellent crops. Whereas the grain harvest of 1969 had been about 5% smaller than in 1968, that of 1970 might possibly exceed previous records. Wheat accounted for much of the gain. One preliminary estimate put wheat production in a range of 90 million to 100 million gross metric tons, compared with 79.2 million tons in 1969 and a 1966 record of 100.5 million tons. The total for all grains was estimated at 170 million–180 million tons, compared with 161.1 million tons in 1969. The outlook for corn was favourable, but the barley harvest totaled 25.9 million tons, compared with 26.8 million tons a year earlier. With an estimated 1970 rye crop of 11.5 million tons, 17% above that of 1969, the U.S.S.R. accounted for more than a third of the world rye crop of 27,282,000 tons.

Sunflower seed, sugar beets, and potatoes were expected to exceed the reduced production of 1969, although it was uncertain whether sunoil exports, which had fallen by 8% in 1969, would be restored to earlier levels. Sugar-beet production had declined by one-fourth in 1969–70, to 71 million tons, as a result of cloudy, cool summer weather and the appearance of harmful insects and diseases. Cotton, largely of the upland type grown under irrigation, was seeded early but might not have exceeded the 8.8 million-bale crop of 1969. Official plans called for an increase in production to about 10.9 million bales, largely by increasing per-acre yield.

Livestock numbers rose, though livestock products, especially meat supplies, continued to be a significant problem. After three years of decline, hog numbers on state and collective farms in July 1970 were 25% above a year earlier. Poultry numbers rose by about a fifth. Cattle, sheep, and goats were slightly more numerous, a trend that was expected to continue for some time. The state announced that it would pay an average of 20% more for milk and cream, retroactive to May 1970, and that returns to producers for production of several livestock products in excess of plan quotas would rise 50%. It was hoped that annual state purchases of meat and poultry would reach nearly 16 million tons by 1975, compared with 11.9 million tons in 1968. For the short term, however, imports of butter and poultry from Western Europe and of beef and mutton from Australia and New Zealand were increased.

Fertilizer production in 1970 was expected to reach a record 46 million tons, about 6% of which was reported to be of complex, high quality. Production of new tractors was estimated to be no more than was needed for replacement. For the 1971–75 period, planned agricultural investment was to be increased over the current period by 70% for the state farms and 50% for the collectives. Additional investments were scheduled for industries supporting agriculture. Announced targets called for an annual average production of 195 million tons of grain, possibly reaching 210 million tons in the final year. Total agricultural output was to increase by 4.3% per year, compared with approximately 2.8% per year in 1965–69.

MIDDLE EAST AND INDIA

Middle East. Weather and war in this area clouded the agricultural picture in 1970. The crops of several countries on or near the Mediterranean were damaged by drought. The important Turkish wheat crop amounted to only 7.5 million metric tons, compared with 8.3 million tons in 1969, and imports would almost certainly be required. The barley crop of 3.5 million tons was moderately smaller than that of the preceding year. New efforts were made to deal with the mounting tobacco surplus by stimulating exports, which had declined 23% from the record 202 million-lb. level of 1967. Self-sufficiency had been achieved in vegetable oils and some olive oil was exported. The EEC reduced or set zero-duty quotas for 1970 on Turkish raisins, figs, and filberts. The 1970 dried-fig crop of 55,000 tons was reported to be the largest since 1966, and the raisin crop of 135,000 tons, 36% above 1969, was a record.

Completing its first decade of independence, Cyprus showed a considerable improvement in agriculture, especially citrus; the agricultural index reached 209 (1957–59 = 100) in 1969, but drought damaged some crops in 1970. Syria proceeded with construction of a dam on the Euphrates that would provide irrigation water for 1.5 million ac.; completion was scheduled for 1973. Saudi Arabia reported discovery of underground water resources sufficient to support considerable irrigated agriculture. Famine was reported in Yemen in midsummer. Iraq's important barley crop totaled 700,000 tons, slightly smaller than in 1969. Wheat was thought sufficient to meet domestic needs.

Israel's wheat crop declined to 125,000 tons from 145,000 tons in 1969, but the 1970 cotton crop was reported to be 5% larger and both fibre and seed would be exported in substantial amounts. Vegetable exports of 50,000 tons were planned for 1970–71, compared with 42,300 tons in 1969–70. Plans called for the investment of about $30 million per year to increase agricultural output, especially of industrial crops. Citrus would be increased moderately, with emphasis on grapefruit and mandarin oranges.

Iran harvested a good wheat crop of 3.8 million tons, slightly smaller than in 1969 but larger than the 3,418,000-ton average of 1964–68. The barley crop equaled the 1.2 million tons of 1969. The 409,000-ton

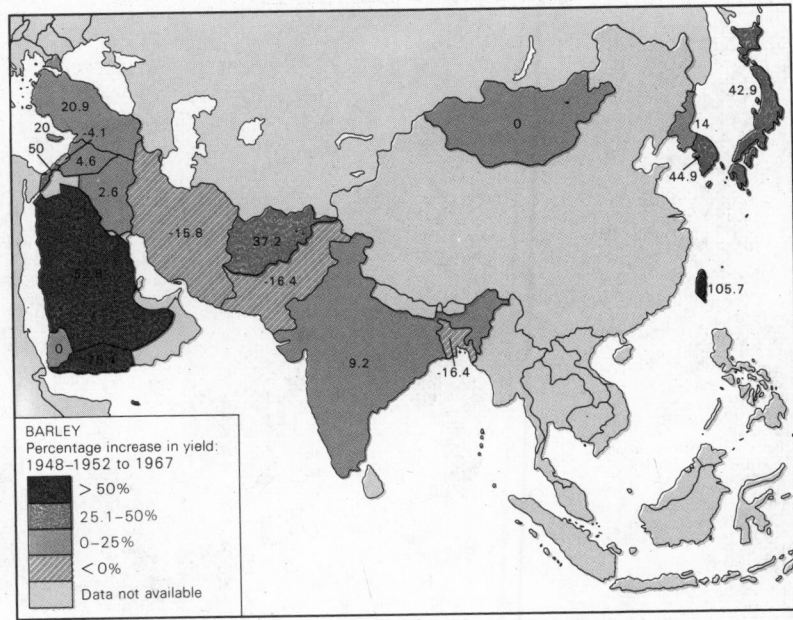

BARLEY
Percentage increase in yield:
1948–1952 to 1967

- \> 50%
- 25.1–50%
- 0–25%
- < 0%
- Data not available

dried fruit crop was the largest since 1963 and the pistachio crop was a record. Rice production reached a record level of about 200,000 tons, primarily as a result of acreage expansion. Iran embarked on a fourth development plan, 1968–69 to 1972–73; a growth rate of 5% was being attempted, compared with 3.4% achieved under the third plan.

Pakistan. An abundant wheat harvest of 7,329,000 tons far surpassed the 4,654,000-ton average of 1964–68. Favourable weather, increased use of fertilizers, and the planting of more than 3 million ac. to new high-yielding Mexpak types were contributing factors. The 1969–70 rice crop totaled 21,266,000 tons, compared with 20,084,000 tons in 1968–69 and a 1963–67 average of only 17,745,000 tons. Some 72,100 ac. were sown with new varieties, out of a total rice acreage of 27.3 million. Tea production rose to 68 million lb. Wheat and vegetable oils continued to be imported, mostly from the U.S. Some 2,800 sq.mi. of land in East Pakistan were affected by the disastrous cyclone and tidal wave of November 1970, and an estimated 600,-000 tons of rice were destroyed.

India. A dry winter caused renewed food-supply worries, and there was some increase in prices before the rains came in late winter. The wheat crop was a record 20 million tons, surpassing even the previous year when new records were set for rice, wheat, grain sorghums, millet, sugarcane, peanuts, vegetables, and fruits. The barley crop was an abundant 3 million tons, compared with 2,424,000 tons in 1969, and the 1969–70 rice harvest was 61,560,000 tons, compared with 59,701,000 tons a year earlier. Millets, some of them new hybrids, and sorghums yielded increasingly well in the drier areas. Sugar crops, mostly sugarcane, yielded 4 million tons in 1969–70, against 3.5 million tons in 1968–69.

A complicated tangle of weather conditions and human factors resulted in a tight supply of edible fats and oils. It was estimated at midyear that production would be about 1 million tons below the 8.5 million-ton target. Some 135,000 tons were requested from the U.S. under the Public Law 480 program for 1970–71, as well as 3 million tons of food grains for buffer stocks. The 1970–71 cotton crop was estimated at 6.1 million bales. All cotton markets in India were closed for two weeks in August to protest their take-

COURTESY, "FOREIGN AGRICULTURE"

A man inspects a stalk of pearl millet in India. Because it has unique merits as a dryland crop and is nutritious for both man and his livestock, millet is becoming increasingly important in India.

over by the Indian government. Indian cashew production was raised to 105,000 tons in 1970 to offset the higher prices of African nuts.

The struggle to increase agricultural export items continued. India produced about one-third of the world's tea, which accounted for about 40% of its agricultural exports. Domestic use was increasing sharply, however, and the value of tea exports had declined from $278 million in 1963 to $160 million in 1969. The Indian Tea Board assisted in launching a massive promotion campaign for Indian tea in Britain. Jute products accounted for about one-third of India's exports of manufactured goods, but very little raw jute was exported and supplies were reported to be short. Tobacco production and exports did not expand as planned. Exports of black pepper increased but ginger exports fell. India was seeking to initiate an international pepper agreement through the FAO.

With grain crops at record levels, the availability of adequate storage and timely transportation became major problems. Restrictions on interstate movement of grain were lifted. Domestic "grain bank" procurement and imports provided a reserve of at least 6.5 million tons as of June 30. The procurement target for autumn cereals for 1970–71 was 5.5 million tons, mostly rice. The 1969–74 five-year plan called for self-sufficiency in food production by 1974, and if the projected 5% annual growth rate was achieved, food-grain production would total 129 million tons by the end of the period. Agricultural credit availability was increased, some of it provided by the International Development Association. In spite of the remarkable progress achieved, India's central problem remained one of improving the food-to-population ratio. At the same time, agrarian unrest appeared to be increasing as the Green Revolution failed to benefit the poorer farmers.

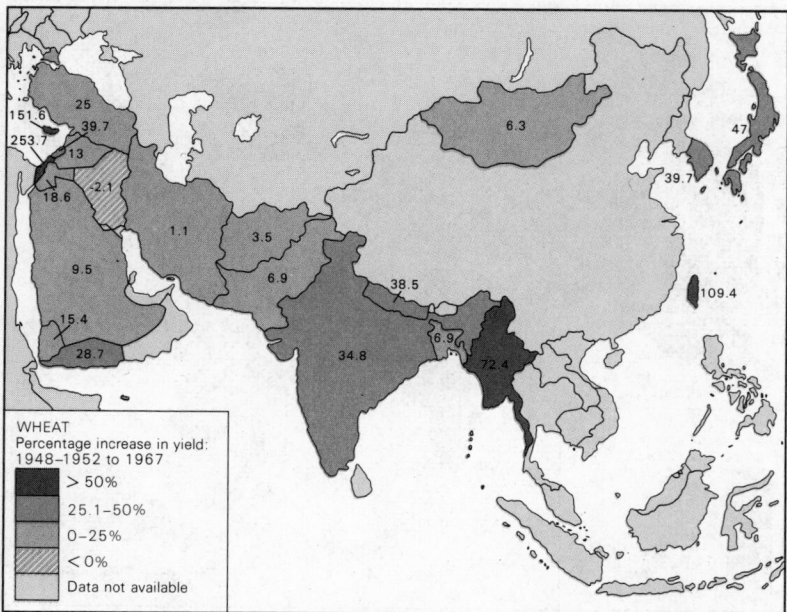

WHEAT
Percentage increase in yield: 1948–1952 to 1967

- > 50%
- 25.1–50%
- 0–25%
- < 0%
- Data not available

FAR EAST

In many areas of the Far East, the food situation seemed to have eased as compared with the mid-1960s. Substantial surpluses developed in the case of a few items, such as rice in Japan. Rice production in the Far East totaled 162 million metric tons in 1969, about 4% above the preceding year.

In Japan production of major crops in 1970 continued the downward trend of 1969 and 1968. The wheat crop amounted to only 494,000 tons against 758,000 tons in 1969, and barley totaled 572,000 tons, compared with 812,000 tons in the preceding year. Rice, already in troublesome surplus, yielded 17,505,000 tons in 1969, against 18,061,000 in 1968. About 12.5 million tons were used to fill domestic requirements. In February 1970 a program was adopted for diverting rice land to other crops and to public uses. Rice carry-over on Oct. 30, 1970, was estimated at 6 million tons, but prices were held at levels approximately two to three times as high as the world market price.

Production of livestock products in Japan continued to gain in 1970. Dairy cattle increased to 1,750,000 head as of February 1970 from 1,663,000 a year earlier. Brood sow numbers at the end of 1969 were up 22%. Imports of agricultural commodities increased, especially wheat, feed grains, soybeans, cotton, tallow, and leaf tobacco. The value of agricultural imports in 1969 totaled $3.7 billion. Wheat imports reached a record of nearly 160 million bu. in the fiscal year ended March 30, 1970, and feed-grain imports rose by about 20%. Beef imports increased by 37% in 1969.

Largely because of its excellent rice crop, South Korea accounted for one-eighth of the overall gain in agricultural output of the Far East in 1969. Rice totaled 5,582,000 tons, compared with 4,350,000 tons in 1968. Early indications were that 1970 was another good crop year, although floods in some areas late in October damaged the rice crop.

China's agricultural situation was described as an upsurge but not a "leap." Based on very limited information, the 1970 harvests of wheat and early rice were good and weather conditions seemed to favour intermediate and late rice and coarse grains. The wheat crop was estimated at 23 million tons, compared with 22.3 million tons in 1969. With the possible exception of rapeseed, oilseed production in 1969–70 was unexceptional. It was not clear to what extent new, higher-yielding varieties of wheat and rice were being used. Food rationing was eased in 1969; the rural economy received increased attention and small plots were again somewhat emphasized. Adequate incentives for high production continued to be a problem, however.

After several years of very substantial agricultural growth, Taiwan experienced a decline in farm output of about 5% in 1969, partly as a result of typhoon damage, a severe cost-price squeeze, and migration to cities of some labour needed on small farms. Mechanization was encouraged and some degree of restructuring of the agricultural economy was planned. Farmers would be encouraged to shift from rice production to more profitable fruits and vegetables and to livestock, especially swine. The pineapple crop was smaller in 1970 than in 1969, and the canned pack was reduced about one-fifth.

Agricultural productivity in the Philippines improved in 1969, but a difficult food-cost spiral was reported in March. The 1969–70 sugar crop was estimated at 2,105,000 tons, 20% more than a year earlier. Largely because of increased acreage planted to high-yielding varieties, rice in 1969–70 was estimated at 3,347,000 tons, up 16%. Copra sales, almost suspended between February and June 1970, were resumed under a new export tax, set at 10% on copra and 8% on coconut oil and meal. It was estimated that 1970 production could rise 10% over the 1969 level, chiefly because of increased acreage and better weather.

Malaysia expanded its cultivated area and increased production of rice, oil palm, natural rubber, and broilers. Thailand anticipated a sugar surplus of some 110,000 tons, with substantial quota exports to the U.S. and under the International Sugar Agreement. Exports of tobacco and corn also rose. Larger rice crops in several areas resulted in a cutback in world trade. Thailand's 1969–70 rice crop was 13,410,000 tons, compared with 11,190,000 tons the previous year. Production in Burma rose to 8,350,000 tons, and in South Vietnam, to 5,115,000 tons. South Vietnamese agriculture appeared to be recovering from the decline that began in 1963, and possible self-sufficiency in rice was envisioned for 1971.

Indonesia harvested a large rice crop of 16,923,000 tons in 1969–70, compared with 16,231,000 tons a year earlier, but imports of rice and wheat would still be required. Tobacco, a major export crop, yielded a record 287 million lb., 18% larger than in the preceding year.

OCEANIA

Overall, agriculture in Australia and New Zealand appeared not to have made gains in 1969–70. Wheat production was reduced in Australia, largely because of market adjustments, and most other crops suffered from adverse weather. Drought conditions in major farm areas lowered New Zealand's output. Meat production rose in both countries, but the declining market for wool, combined with drought in Australian wool-producing areas, resulted in a poor year for that product.

Australia. Australia produced 10,835,000 metric tons of wheat (398.1 million bu.) in 1969–70, a 27% reduction from the preceding year. Drought in Queensland and Western Australia affected both yields

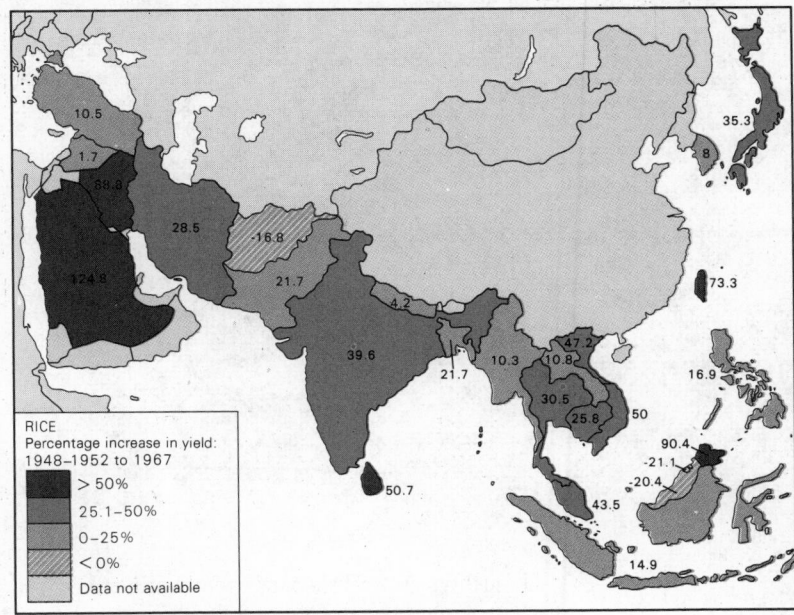

RICE
Percentage increase in yield:
1948–1952 to 1967

- > 50%
- 25.1–50%
- 0–25%
- < 0%
- Data not available

COURTESY, "FOREIGN AGRICULTURE"

A farmer cultivates a small rice field in Japan where since 1967 rice production has exceeded consumption.

AUTHENTICATED NEWS
INTERNATIONAL

Mice forage in stored wheat on a farm in northwest Victoria, Australia, during a plague of the rodents in March 1970. Hundreds of square miles were afflicted when unusually favourable weather conditions resulted in a heavy increase in the normal mouse population.

and quality. Australia's new wheat delivery quota system became effective with the 1969–70 crop. Under this system, advance payments of U.S. $1.23 per bushel for 1969–70-crop wheat were limited to deliveries of 357 million bu. to the Wheat Board. A guaranteed price of $1.62 per bushel applied to the first 200 million bu. exported. Australia's wheat stocks on July 1, 1970, were estimated by the USDA at 12,-227,000 metric tons, the highest on record. Although the early outlook was for a crop of only about 225 million bu. in 1970–71, the chairman of the Australian Wheat Board forecast exportable supplies for the 1970–71 marketing year at 13.2 million tons. Exports in the July 1969–June 1970 period had totaled 6,820,000 metric tons, compared with 4,891,000 tons a year earlier.

Barley production for 1969–70 was estimated at 1,789,000 metric tons, a 20% increase over a year earlier. Oat production, at 1,604,000 tons, was reduced slightly, but the rice harvest, at 305,000 tons, was up 19%. Drought in Queensland lowered sorghum 50% to an estimated 220,000 tons, while corn rose 32% to 231,000 tons. Severe drought cut sugar production 20% to 2,373,000 short tons. At 150,000 bales (480 lb. each), cotton was down slightly from a year earlier but still more than double the 1963–67 average.

Australian cattle numbers rose 4% to an estimated 21.5 million head in 1970, as strong domestic and foreign demand continued to encourage the livestock and meat industry. Hog numbers were up slightly to 2.3 million and sheep numbers rose to 182 million head from 174,062,000. Total meat production in 1969 was estimated at 3,903,000,000 lb.; beef and veal production accounted for 2,056,000,000 lb., one-third of which was exported. In May, the U.S. temporarily banned further imports of mutton from Australia, charging that Australia's inspection system was not equal to that applying to meat produced in the U.S. Canada imposed a similar ban on Australian mutton in June and added beef in July, but the ban on beef was lifted at mid-September.

Australian wool production rose to 2,043,400,000 lb. in 1969–70, an increase of nearly 5% from a year earlier. The year ended June 30, 1970, was reported to have been disastrous for Australia's 100,000 sheep farmers. Wool prices fell to 38.3 U.S. cents per pound, the lowest level since 1948, and drought-plagued Queensland producers were said to have suffered losses amounting to 27% of their annual income. Despite these reverses, the 1970–71 wool clip was expected to rise about 2% to an estimated 2,086,800,000 lb. World wool production in 1970 (including the 1970–71 season in the Southern Hemisphere) was estimated by the USDA at 6,214,000,000 lb. (greasy basis); this represented a slight reduction from a year earlier, but most of the decline occurred in southern Africa. Prices of Australian and New Zealand wools in world markets averaged 71.1 cents per pound in the first half of 1970, compared with 76.3 cents in 1969 and 80.1 cents in 1968, and relatively large world supplies in 1970–71 were expected to prevent any significant improvement. Prices of Australian wool broke sharply in the first three months of the 1970–71 season; average prices fell nearly 10 cents per pound (greasy basis), the lowest level since 1946–47. Australia exported 1,363,000,000 lb. of raw wool in the first ten months of the 1969–70 trade year, compared with 1,304,000,000 lb. a year earlier.

Australian agriculture appeared to be facing a turning point in the 1970s. The growth of mining and industry had reduced its relative importance in the economy, to the point where it accounted for only 10% of the gross national product in the year ended June 30, 1970. At the same time, agricultural products, which had provided 57% of the value of total exports in 1968–69, remained crucial to the country's balance of payments. Wheat, wool, and dairy products, especially, faced increasing competition in world markets, and overproduction was a persistent problem. Both industry and government were attempting to bring production into line with demand, but the outlook remained gloomy. The minister of primary industry reported that Australian farmers could expect their net incomes to fall steadily by some 3% per year.

New Zealand. Total agricultural production in 1969–70 was held to year-earlier levels by drought. Net farm income rose 6% to an estimated $386 million, chiefly because of buoyant foreign demand. Cattle numbers rose more than 4% to 8,950,000 head in 1970; hog numbers declined slightly and sheep numbers held even. Total production of meat was estimated at 2,153,000,000 lb. in 1969, compared with 2,093,000,000 lb. a year earlier. Milk production, at 14,547,000,000 lb., was up nearly 8%, and butter production rose to 586 million lb. from 541 million. New

Table XV. Production of Meats in Principal Producing Countries
In 000,000 lb., carcass-meat basis

Country	Beef and veal 1969*	Beef and veal 1968	Beef and veal Average 1961–65	Pork (excluding lard) 1969*	Pork (excluding lard) 1968	Pork (excluding lard) Average 1961–65	Mutton, lamb, and goat meat 1969*	Mutton, lamb, and goat meat 1968	Mutton, lamb, and goat meat Average 1961–65
Argentina	6,063	5,613	4,913	410	416	384	428	467	344
Australia	2,056	1,993	1,941	359	330	257	1,488	1,465	1,310
Belgium-Luxembourg	564	545	482	776	772	508	16	8	6
Brazil	3,472	3,417	3,095	1,243	1,288	1,022	121	118	106
Canada	1,915	1,990	1,618	1,096	1,181	1,002	16	20	30
Colombia	909	874	837	...	...	95	5	5	5
Denmark	404	457	357	1,493	1,577	1,465	4	7	3
France	3,424	3,578	3,159	2,537	2,765	2,370	262	265	238
Germany, West	2,844	2,734	2,540	3,902	4,755	3,979	24	24	28
Italy	1,764	1,728	1,388	1,209	952	887	93	93	86
Japan	474	353	400	1,113	1,147	647	3	3	5
Mexico	1,251	1,174	1,046	549	545	453	124	124	129
Netherlands	627	628	590	1,296	1,308	923	17	19	18
New Zealand	830	760	614	82	84	94	1,241	1,249	1,038
Poland	...	1,172	878	...	1,958	1,826	...	...	58
South Africa	864	880	998	148	142	115	381	342	281
Spain	560	536	410	950	924	608	284	289	276
U.S.S.R.	10,130	10,120	6,520	6,750	6,780	6,250	1,760	1,760	1,870
United Kingdom	1,920	1,997	1,978	2,036	1,895	1,796	453	543	559
United States	21,843	21,610	17,862	12,949	13,063	11,863	548	602	755
Yugoslavia	787	760	533	834	890	844	148	138	117

*Preliminary.
Source: U.S. Department of Agriculture, Foreign Agricultural Service.

Zealand's 1970 wool clip was forecast at 740 million lb., a slight increase from a year earlier.

New Zealand's farm exports continued to provide the mainstay of the country's economy. Agricultural products accounted for NZ$836 million, or 87% of total exports in the year ended June 30, 1969. Wool, lamb, butter, and beef and veal constituted more than half of all farm products sold abroad. Nearly all categories of agricultural exports except dairy products gained in 1969. Exports of meat and meat products in 1969 rose to $413.6 million from $332.9 million and wool exports rose to $270 million from $225 million. Even so, lower prices in 1970 threatened to reduce export earnings. Of particular concern was the renewed effort by the U.K. to join the EEC. New Zealand's export trade had diversified in the post-World War II period, but the U.K. continued to absorb high percentages of New Zealand lamb, cheese, and butter, and alternatives, especially for butter, were limited.   (J. K. R.; H. R. SH.)

See also Commercial Policies; Commodities, Primary; Conservation; Cooperatives; Fisheries; Food; Gardening; Industrial Review; Prices; Tobacco.

ENCYCLOPÆDIA BRITANNICA FILMS. *Antibiotics* (1952); *The Story of Rice* (1952); *The Story of Sugar* (1953); *The Middle States* (1955); *Milk* (1955); *Meat—From Range to Market* (1956); *The Wheat Farmer* (1956); *The Corn Farmer* (1960); *DNA: Molecule of Heredity* (1960); *Seed Germination* (1960); *Wheat Country* (1960); *Wheat Rust* (1960); *The Cotton Farmer* (1963); *Cattleman—A Rancher's Story* (1964); *The Dairy Farmer* (1965); *The Great Plains —Land of Risk* (1966); *Interior West: The Land Nobody Wanted* (1966); *The Orange Grower* (1967); *The Sheep Rancher* (1967); *Midwest—Heartland of the Nation* (1968); *Produce—From Farm to Market* (1968); *Problems of Conservation—Soil* (1969).

Albania

A people's republic in the western part of the Balkan Peninsula, Europe, Albania is on the Adriatic Sea, bordered by Greece and Yugoslavia. Area: 11,100 sq.mi. (28,748 sq.km.). Pop. (1969 est.): 2,075,000. Cap. and largest city: Tirane (pop., 1967 est., 169,300). Language: literary Albanian and two spoken dialects, Gheg in the north, Tosk in the south. Religion: Muslim, Orthodox, Roman Catholic. First secretary of the Albanian (Communist) Party of Labour in 1970, Enver Hoxha; president of the Presidium of the People's Assembly, Haxhi Leshi; chairman of the Council of Ministers (premier), Mehmet Shehu.

During 1970 Enver Hoxha continued making speeches against the "two imperialist great powers," meaning the U.S. and the U.S.S.R., but following the appearance of the Soviet Navy in the Mediterranean he held out an olive branch to Yugoslavia and even an olive twig to Greece. Speaking late in May at Tropoje, near the Yugoslav border, he said that, ideological differences notwithstanding, Albania wanted to improve trade and other relations with Yugoslavia and to foster friendship. Belgrade newspapers gave prominence to this speech, while noting that Hoxha's cautious step followed a slight thaw in Sino-Yugoslav relations. President Tito did not reply to Hoxha until August 7, when he addressed a large meeting at Zabljak. "We should also like to have good relations with Albania," he said. "We have no other interests in regard to Albania and have always wished our relations to be as good as possible."

Greece and Albania had never concluded a peace treaty ending the 1940 war (when Albania was a satellite of Fascist Italy), and Greece still had claims on certain areas in southern Albania. Nevertheless, at the end of May an Albanian trade delegation arrived in Greece to negotiate an agreement with the Athens Chamber of Commerce. The agreement called for $1.5 million in trade, with Albania sending crude petroleum and by-products to Greece in exchange for industrial goods and raw materials. Albania also turned to Western Europe, establishing diplomatic relations with Denmark and Switzerland in July and concluding modest trade agreements with a score of countries.

China, however, remained Albania's best friend. On October 16 it granted Albania a long-term, interest-free loan of 1 billion leks (a fifth of Albania's yearly revenue) for the construction of 30 major industrial plants, to be built during the fifth five-year plan (1971–75). An Albanian delegation of some 70 members, led by Abdyl Kellezi, a deputy premier, took part in the Peking celebrations of the 21st anniversary of the foundation of the Chinese People's Republic.

The new five-year plan was introduced by Hoxha under the slogan "Actions through concentrated blows," and a drive was begun for decentralization and more initiative and responsibility at all levels of the party. A great effort was being made to develop foreign tourism. During 1970 only one 400-room hotel was open to foreigners at Durres, but a few more were being built along the Adriatic coast.

On September 20 a new National Assembly of 214 members was elected. It was announced that 100% of the electors had voted for the official candidates of the Democratic Front.   (K. SM.)

ALBANIA

Education. (1966–67) Primary, pupils 380,786, teachers 14,000; secondary, pupils 17,171, teachers 990; vocational, pupils 12,827, teachers 514; teacher training, students 3,949, teachers 161; higher (including University of Tirane with 5,237 full-time students in 1967–68), students 11,361, teachers 472.

Finance. Monetary unit: lek, with an official exchange rate of 5 leks to U.S. $1 (12 leks = £1 sterling) and a tourist rate of 12.5 leks to U.S. $1 (30 leks = £1 sterling). Budget (1968 est.): revenue 4,-025,000,000 leks; expenditure 3,985,000,000 leks.

Foreign Trade. (1964) Imports U.S. $98 million; exports U.S. $66 million. Import sources: China 63%; Czechoslovakia 10%; Poland 8%; East Germany 5%. Export destinations: China 40%; Czechoslovakia 19%; East Germany 10%; Poland 10%. Main exports: fuels, minerals, and metals (including petroleum, iron ore, chrome ore, and copper) 54%; foodstuffs (including wine and fruit) 21%; timber, wool.

Transport and Communications. Roads (motorable; 1960) 3,100 km. Motor vehicles in use (1960 est.): passenger 1,900; commercial (including buses) 3,400. Railways: (1968) 205 km.; traffic (1967) 146 million passenger-km., freight 123 million net ton-km. Shipping (1969): merchant vessels 100 gross tons and over 10; gross tonnage 36,407; traffic (1966) goods loaded *c.* 1.3 million metric tons, unloaded *c.* 500,000 metric tons. Telephones (Dec. 1963) 10,150. Radio receivers (Dec. 1968) 150,000. Television receivers (Dec. 1967) 1,200.

Agriculture. Production (in 000; metric tons; 1968; 1967 in parentheses): wheat *c.* 180 (215); corn *c.* 220 (*c.* 260); rye *c.* 7 (*c.* 7); oats (1967) *c.* 16, (1966) *c.* 16; barley *c.* 8 (*c.* 8); cottonseed *c.* 16 (*c.* 14); sugar, raw value (1969–70) *c.* 16, (1968–69) *c.* 16; potatoes (1967) *c.* 31, (1966) *c.* 31; tobacco (1967) *c.* 13, (1966) *c.* 13; timber (cu.m.; 1967) *c.* 1,540, (1966) *c.* 1,540. Livestock (in 000; Dec. 1968): sheep *c.* 1,625; cattle *c.* 430; pigs *c.* 148; goats (Dec. 1966) *c.* 1,200; poultry (Oct. 1966) *c.* 1,746.

Industry. Production (in 000; metric tons; 1968): lignite *c.* 434; crude oil 1,046; petroleum products (1967) 480; electricity (kw-hr.; 1967) 589,000; chrome ore (oxide content; 1967) 127; iron ore (1968) *c.* 400; copper ore (metal content) 6; cement 22; cotton fabrics (m.; 1965) 28,200.

Aircraft:
see Defense; Industrial Review; Transportation

Air Forces:
see Defense

Alcoholic Beverages

Beer. World production of beer rose to 605 million hectolitres (hl.) in 1969, an increase of 6% over the previous year. The rates of increase for Africa (16.8%), Central and South America (12.4%), and Asia (11.7%) were appreciably higher than in those regions accounting for the bulk of beer production— Western Europe (5.5% increase), Eastern Europe (4.4%), North America (4%), and Oceania (7.4%). Among individual countries the U.S. had the highest production (140 million hl.), followed by West Germany (with West Berlin, 84 million hl.), the U.K. (54 million hl.), the U.S.S.R. (36 million hl.), and Japan, which with 27 million hl. accounted for 70% of all Asian production. Aside from these five, no single country surpassed the 22 million hl. produced by the world's largest brewery concern, Anheuser-Busch Inc., with headquarters in St. Louis, Mo.

That further expansion of beer consumption was still possible even in countries already having a very high per capita intake was shown in West Germany, where the per capita consumption rose to almost 136 litres in 1969, compared with just over 129 litres in 1968. This was achieved by energetic promotion of beer's all-round appeal, for example as an ideal thirst-quencher, a relaxer, an essential ingredient of social jollity, and an ideal beverage to accompany any meal.

German brewers were convinced that the increased popularity of beer was due to its claim to "purity," an important consideration in a beverage whose flavour and degree of strength made it suitable for drinking in comparatively large quantities. There was considerable competition in justifying this claim, which was not, for example, compatible with the use of unmalted grain. West Germany's EEC partners were not drawn into this dispute, and for that matter West Germany accounted for two-thirds of total EEC beer production. In an expanded Common Market, which in 1970 again became a possibility, the already complicated problems of integration would extend to the brewery sector. Quite apart from differences in fiscal systems, the highest rate of tax currently applicable to beer within the EEC would be far exceeded by the heavy duty levied on it in the U.K. and Denmark.

The most important brewery mergers of 1970 were those of the two largest Danish concerns, Carlsberg and Tuborg (sharing about 85% of Denmark's production), and of the French Société Européenne de Brasseries and Kronenbourg under the leadership of the glass and container firm of Bussois-Suchon-Neuvesel. The latter merger resulted in a group producing 8–9 million hl. of beer annually (40–45% of total French production).

In West Germany the tobacco firm of Reemtsma further extended its brewery interests, which now embraced Dortmunder-Union and subsidiaries, Henninger-Bräu-Frankfurt, Hannen-Brauerei-Willich, the Bavaria-St. Pauli-Brauerei of Hamburg, and Lindener-Gilde Bräu of Hanover. Following the lead of Allied Breweries and Watney Mann, Bass Charrington of Britain acquired a controlling interest in an important EEC brewery—in this case Brasserie Lamot, the fifth largest Belgian producer.

Technical research again concentrated on the development of enzyme preparations that permitted unmalted barley and other cheap raw materials to be used. It was possible to obtain preisomerized hop ex-

tracts so pure that they could produce the requisite degree of bitterness in unhopped beer by addition immediately before filtration. This enabled the utilization rate for hop extract to be increased to 80–90%, compared with 20–25% by conventional hopping.

The building of new breweries raised the question of what was the most economic size. With the existing state of brewing technology, building costs could in general be amortized by a year's production of 600,000 to 1 million hl. (T. Sc.)

Spirits. Almost without exception, world demand for spirits in 1970 continued its upward trend. A notable defaulter was the U.K., where increased taxation was responsible for a 5% decline. New distilleries for rum, gin, vodka, whiskies, and some brandies were opened in the U.S., Canada, Scotland, Japan, Africa, Central and South America, and a number of European countries, and plans for others were announced. The current tendency was for brand owners with worldwide distribution to manufacture locally, where their product allowed it, in order to reduce transport costs, avoid discriminatory taxation and nontariff obstacles, and to obtain local goodwill.

In Scotland fears of overproduction of Scotch whiskey were allayed; total production was again below the peak figures reached in 1965–66. Stocks as of March 31, 1970, were estimated to include 760 million proof gallons over three years old, or $10\frac{3}{4}$ years' supply. Exports in 1969 were below the 1968 figure but, after adjustment for abnormal stocking up in the U.S. in 1968 (due to fears of a dock strike), 1969 showed an overall increase in most markets. Distillers in the U.S. proceeded with their plans to launch a new light whiskey, to compete with Scotch, in mid-1972. Japan entered the export market with whiskies, gins, and sake, and seemed likely to become a formidable competitor.

The tendency toward state monopoly, closer official control, or even nationalization continued in some countries, particularly in Africa and South America. Discrimination by state monopolies in favour of homemade products, sometimes contrary to international agreements, aroused complaint. In France, where the problem of alcoholism was acute in the non-wine-growing areas of the north, the government announced proposed legislation for a compulsory maximum alcohol/blood level for drivers, thus joining many other European countries where such regulations already existed.

Little further progress was made internationally toward agreed definitions of spirits or codes of practice for their manufacture, but the international associations of wine and spirit merchants pressed for prohibition of the use of synthetic spirits, either for consumption or for use on the human body in such products as perfumes.

Large British and European firms continued to strengthen their mutual trading links so as to have access rights to each other's markets, whether or not the U.K. joined the EEC. (J. W. Ma.)

Apparent consumption of distilled spirits in the U.S. in 1969 reached a record high of 362.7 million gal., 5% above 1968. Per capita consumption rose 4% to 1.8 gal., while consumption per drinker remained at 3.8 gal. Prohibition was eliminated in 63 areas in 12 U.S. states by local option. Consumer expenditure for alcoholic beverages in 1969 was $20.6 billion, compared with $19.7 billion in 1968. Federal excise tax on alcoholic beverages totaled $4,765,-312,000, 74.3% of which was accounted for by distilled spirits. During fiscal 1970, U.S. agents seized 5,228 stills producing illicit spirits.

A total of 917,457,041 gal. of distilled spirits was produced in the U.S. in fiscal 1970, 7.1% less than in 1969. This included industrial alcohol. Whiskey production was down 11.1% to 160,038,765 tax gallons. Brandy decreased 11.4% to 14,785,232 tax gallons, and rum increased 1.5% to 1,028,972 gal. Total bottlings rose 2.5% to 311,683,192 gal. Vodka exceeded gin bottlings by 33.7%, and production of bottled cocktails continued to rise significantly. Production of bourbon, the largest selling type of distilled spirit in the United States, decreased 8.2% to 116,-168,537 gal.

At 90,340,151 tax gallons, total imports of spirits into the U.S. were up 9.9% in 1969. Tequila imports rose 10.7%. U.S. distilled spirits exports rose 24% to 3,973,257 gal.

Public revenue from alcoholic beverage taxes in Canada increased 7.5% to Can$847,060,000 in fiscal 1969. Consumption of spirits in the same period was unchanged at 22,916,000 imperial gallons. Production rose 8.7% to 76,824,000 imperial tax gallons; imports rose 10% and exports, 4%.   (JU. W.)

Wine. The 1970 harvest was superior in quantity to that of 1969. According to provisional estimates, it amounted to around 280 million hl. while that of the preceding year had reached 272 million hl. France had a large harvest, 16.5 million hl. greater than that of 1969. The other major Mediterranean producers, Italy, Spain, and Portugal, maintained production at only a fair average. However, in every region the wine harvests were gathered in ideal weather conditions and the fruit was mostly healthy, promising wines of a very high quality. For some, 1970 was predicted to be a great vintage.

In France, production was excellent, both in quality and quantity, thanks to especially favourable weather conditions. Total production amounted to 66.5 million hl. or an increase of 34% over the previous year, making it a harvest well above the average. Alcoholic content was mostly from 0.5 to 1.5% higher. In Bordeaux there was an abundant harvest, notably for

red wines. The quality was expected to be either very good or excellent, according to the district and vintage. In Burgundy the result was equally satisfactory, while the 1970 Beaujolais grape growths produced exceptional first drawings and were expected to provide remarkable old wines. In Mâcon, 1970 was certainly the best vintage since 1950, while in the Rhône Valley the red wines were of very fine colour and very good alcoholic content, ranging from 11.5 to 13 or 13.5%. In Champagne, the harvest was a record in quantity and had all the characteristics of superior quality.

The Italian vines remained very healthy throughout the year. Sufficient humidity in the winter, and a satisfactory amount of sunshine in the summer, resulted in a harvest that was very good from every point of view. Nearly 70 million hl. were produced, some of them classed among the best Italian wines since World War II, comparable with the great vintages of 1961, 1964, and 1967. In Trentino and Alto Adige the harvest was quite outstanding. The white wines, in particular, had seldom been so successful. In Emilia-Romagna, the harvest was equally good, in both quantity and quality. In Tuscany, the 1970 Chiantis were among the best in the vine-growing history of the region. However, a decrease of 20% from the previous year was registered in Apulia, and 25% in Sicily and Sardinia.

The 1970 harvest in Spain, amounting to around 25 million hl., or roughly the same amount as 1969, gave wines with outstanding qualities and an above-average alcoholic content. The fine weather also produced Portuguese wines of excellent quality.   (R. PN.)

A 1970 California grape crop of 2.7 million tons, down from 3.6 million tons the year before and well below the record 3,975,000 tons harvested in 1965, resulted in limited availability of many wine variety grapes, and the highest prices ever paid by California wineries for grapes. In a number of north coast counties, an early spring warm spell brought out buds that were killed later by a bitter frost. Quality, however, was good, an extremely warm summer brought the grapes to early maturity, and, for the first time in six years, the California grape harvest was without any

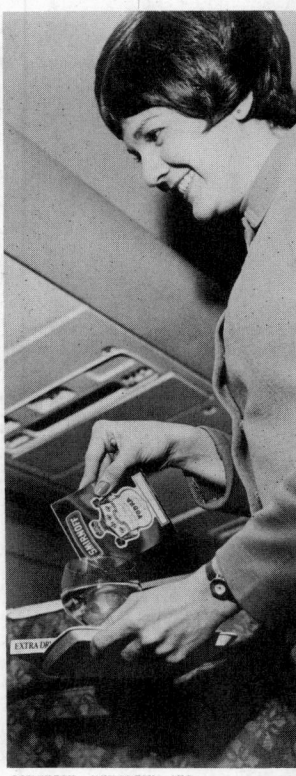

COURTESY, HEUBLEIN, INC.

A stewardess serves vodka from an aluminum-foil packet. Heublein, Inc., was offering the packets of cocktails and liquors for a two-year test aboard both domestic and international airlines.

Table I. Estimated Consumption of Beer in Selected Countries				
In litres* per capita of total population				
Country	1965	1966	1967	1968
Belgium†	140	140	140	140
Czechoslovakia	130.0	132.0	129.3	132.8
Germany, West	122.1	125.8	127.2	129.4
Australia‡	109.1	110.0	113.1	116.8
Luxembourg	127.1	128.7	121.4	116.1
New Zealand	103.1	107.2	109.9	110.4
Austria	92.1	98.8	102.6	98.2
United Kingdom	91.5	90.4	93.2	96.5
Denmark	78.5	88.7	91.5	94.4
Germany, East	80.6	81.7	84.5	86.3
Ireland	62.3	63.5	62.2	85.1
Switzerland	74.0	74.8	76.2	73.7
Canada§	67.7	67.6	69.5	71.0
United States	60.2	62.1	63.2	65.2
Sweden	40.4	43.3	45.5	51.8
Hungary	44.2	46.4	49.9	51.2
Netherlands‖	37.2	39.0	44.3	45.4
France	39.2	40.4	40.8	40.0
Venezuela	32	33	35	35
Spain	23.4	26.4	30.4	32.9
Finland	25.1	27.8	29.9	32.6
Norway	27.9	28.8	30.0	32.5
Colombia	37.9	35	30	31
Poland	24.0	25.6	27.7	28.9
Bulgaria	20.1	22.8	25.5	27.6

*One litre=1.0567 U.S. quarts=0.8799 imperial quart.
†Including so-called "household beer."
‡Years ending June 30.
§Years ending March 31.
‖Excluding ships' supplies.

Table II. Estimated Consumption of Potable Distilled Spirits in Selected Countries				
In litres* of 100% pure spirit per capita of population				
Country	1965	1966	1967	1968
Poland	2.6	2.8	3.0	3.3
Cyprus	1.51	1.56	1.56	2.85
United States	2.46	2.55	2.67	2.82
Yugoslavia	2.6	2.6	2.6	2.6
Germany, West	2.73	2.35	2.23	2.59
Sweden	2.70	2.65	2.70	2.55
Spain	2.5	3	2.3	2.3
Canada†	1.79	2.03	2.16	2.26
France‡	2.49	2.52	2.5	2.2
Germany, East	1.9	2.2	2.2	2.2
Austria	2.20	1.9	1.8	2
Hungary	1.50	1.75	1.86	1.95
Bulgaria	1.6	1.6	1.7	1.8
Italy	1.40	1.50	1.60	1.8
Luxembourg	1.23	1.41	1.14	1.8
Switzerland	1.91	1.84	1.8	1.8
Netherlands	1.89	1.44	1.63	1.76
Peru	0.8	1.0	1.5	1.7
Czechoslovakia	1.08	1.28	1.32	1.64
Norway	1.33	1.36	1.42	1.47
Finland	1.4	1.4	1.4	1.4
Ireland	1.97	1.79	1.97	1.19
Belgium	1.12	0.94	0.96	1.10
South Africa	1.11	1.14	1.11	1.07
Australia§	0.93	0.78	0.78	1.04

†Years ending March 31.
‡Including alcohol-based aperitifs and liqueur wines.
§Years ending June 30.

Table III. Estimated Consumption of Wine in Selected Countries				
In litres* per capita of total population				
Country	1965	1966	1967	1968
Italy	111.0	111.8	109.7	114.2
France†	120.0	116.0	113.0	113.0
Portugal	108.6	131.1	92.3	93.2
Argentina	85.8	80.2	82.8	87.5
Spain	63.0	66.5	61.0	62.1
Chile	42.4	54.8	44.6	48.9
Switzerland‡	38.3	39.1	38.5	38.6
Greece	39.2	38.7	36.7	36.7
Luxembourg	30.1	34.9	33.8	35.9
Hungary	32.8	30.4	34.2	34.8
Austria	29.8	30.0	31.9	29.7
Romania	29.2	31.7	20.0	26.9
Yugoslavia	25.0	26.2	26.5	26.3
Uruguay	30.3	30.3	25.0	25
Bulgaria	20.7	20.0	18.5	21.7
Czechoslovakia	15.6	14.5	18.6	15.8
Germany, West	16.8	15.5	15.6	15.3
U.S.S.R.	9.8	9.3	8.9	12.0
Belgium	11.2	9.7	10.6	11.9
Cyprus	12	8.2	10.4	11.2
South Africa	8.7	8.4	9.2	9.1
Australia§	5.6	6.1	6.8	7.7
Sweden	4.3	4.6	5.0	5.3
Poland	4.5	4.7	5.0	5.0
Germany, East	4.2	4.4	4.7	4.6

†Excluding cider (20.4 litres per capita in 1966).
‡Excluding cider (annual average 8.3 litres per capita, 1965–68).
§Years ending June 30.

Source: Produktschap voor Gedistilleerde Dranken, *Hoeveel Alcoholhoudende Dranken Worden er in de Wereld Gedronken?*

CENTRAL PRESS FROM
PICTORIAL PARADE

British sailors, wearing black arm bands to mourn the passing of an almost 300-year-old tradition, collect their last daily free rum "tot" at the Royal Naval Dockyards in Chatham, Kent, July 31, 1970.

field labour problems. California vintners had to content themselves with a comparatively small crush of 1.5 million tons, against almost 2 million tons processed in 1969. Outside California, the crop and crush for 1970 was average in tonnage and a bit above average in quality, especially in upstate New York.

During fiscal 1970, the U.S. wine industry set a new sales record for the 16th year in a row. Volume moved up 10.5% to 222 million gal., with table wine sales (up 16.6%) accounting for 104 million gal. This very satisfactory gain faded, however, against the 123.6% increase (from 4.9 to 10.8 million gal.) made by the light "special natural wines" that were finding a wide market among young adults. The U.S. public also purchased a record 27.7 million gal. of wine produced in other countries.　　　　　　　　　　　　(I. H. M.)

Algeria

A republic on the north coast of Africa, Algeria is bounded by Morocco, Mauritania, Mali, Niger, Libya, and Tunisia. Area: 919,591 sq.mi. (2,381,743 sq.km.). Pop. (1970 est.): 13,547,000. Cap. and largest city: Algiers (pop., 1970 est., 1,839,000). Language: Arabic, Berber, French. Religion: Muslim. President in 1970, Col. Houari Boumédienne.

In 1970 Algeria launched its first four-year development plan, aimed at laying the foundations for an economic boom that some experts foresaw for the 1980s. The plan called for total investments of $5,280,000,000 and an average annual production growth rate of 9%. The annual output of oil, currently accounting for about 70% of the country's export earnings, was expected to increase from 45 million tons to about 50 million in 1970 and to 65 million in 1973. Foreign currency restrictions and import quotas were tightened during the summer to gather maximum resources for financing the plan. The main problem, however, was not money but personnel. Despite a continuing education drive, which included setting up a number of technological institutes, the country was still expected to be short in 1973 of approximately 14,000 of the technical personnel required.

Algeria put pressure on French oil-producing companies, nationalized a number of non-French pro-

ducers, and undertook to coordinate its oil policies with Libya and Iraq. Unfruitful negotiations with France, lasting seven months and aimed at fixing higher oil prices, resulted on July 21 in the unilateral imposition of new tax reference prices upon French oil-producing companies, which were responsible for about two-thirds of the total Algerian output. This would have the effect of forcing the French companies to increase their tax payments by about 50% and was seen by the French as a violation of the Franco-Algerian oil treaty of July 1965; the two countries, however, agreed to resume talks a few weeks later and to discuss a scheduled revision of the entire treaty. The Algerian authorities were determined to put an end to a situation that, according to their calculations, had enabled French companies to make an average revenue of $9.60 per ton of crude oil over the past five years, while Algeria was receiving less than $4.

Simultaneously, Algeria strengthened its own national oil concern, Sonatrach, which took over the assets of the Algerian subsidiaries of Anglo-Dutch Shell and the U.S.-owned Phillips. Construction of another refinery began at Arzew in western Algeria, and work continued on a second gas liquefaction plant at Skikda in the east. In June, Algeria was the host at ministerial meetings of both the Organization of Petroleum Exporting Countries (OPEC) and the Organization of Arab Petroleum Exporting Countries (OAPEC). The Algerians believed that producers should take the offensive against foreign oil companies and no longer restrict themselves to the role of a trade union for the defense of oil prices.

The architect of these policies, Belaid Abdessalam, kept the portfolio of industry and energy in the first ministerial reorganization announced by President Boumédienne after five years in power. Six men

---

ALGERIA

Education. (1967–68) Primary, pupils 1,485,390, teachers (public only) 30,666; secondary, pupils 116,-077, teachers (public only) 4,735; vocational, pupils 38,877, teachers (public only) 2,603; teacher training, students 5,439, teachers (public only) 325; higher (including 3 universities), students 9,720.

Finance. Monetary unit: dinar, with a par value of 4.94 dinars to U.S. $1 (11.85 dinars = £1 sterling). Budget (1969 est.) balanced at 3,890,000,000 dinars.

Foreign Trade. (1968) Imports 4,022,675,000 dinars; exports 4,097,891,000 dinars. Import sources: France 57%; U.S. 8%; West Germany 6%; Italy 6%. Export destinations: France 55%; West Germany 13%; Italy 6%; U.K. 5%. Main exports: crude oil 69%; wine 9%.

Transport and Communications. Roads (1965) 35,541 km. Motor vehicles in use (1968): passenger 117,000; commercial (including buses) 88,500. Railways: (1968) 3,951 km.; traffic (1969) 954 million passenger-km., freight 1,337,000,000 net ton-km. Air traffic (1968): 362,692,000 passenger-km.; freight 3,747,000 net ton-km. Shipping (1969): merchant vessels 100 gross tons and over 7; gross tonnage 19,456. Telephones (Dec. 1968) 156,038. Radio receivers (Dec. 1967) 650,000. Television receivers (Dec. 1967) c. 100,000.

Agriculture. Production (in 000; metric tons; 1968; 1967 in parentheses): wheat 1,534 (1,266); barley 538 (340); oats 42 (26); potatoes 272 (204); dates c. 148 (148); figs 45 (44); oranges 412 (381); tomatoes (1967) 69, (1966) 80; onions (1967) c. 39, (1966) 39; tobacco 4.6 (4.6); olive oil (1969) c. 22, (1968) c. 18; wine 1,005 (682). Livestock (in 000; Nov. 1968): sheep c. 7,300; goats (Nov. 1966) 1,800; cattle c. 890; asses (Nov. 1967) 255; horses (Nov. 1967) 113; camels (Nov. 1966) 175.

Industry. Production (in 000; metric tons; 1969): crude oil 43,806; natural gas (cu.m.) 2,985,000; electricity (excluding most industrial production; kw-hr.; 1968) 1,305,000; iron ore (metal content; 1968) 1,664; phosphate rock (1968) 361.

joined the 23-member Cabinet for the first time, but all the key ministers retained their posts. Boumédienne also initiated a thorough diplomatic reshuffle, following his announcement late in 1969 that all Algerian ambassadors but one, appointed a few months earlier, would be replaced.

Meanwhile, efforts to implement a regional development policy in preparation for a series of nationwide reforms were continued, notably in education and agriculture. The planned "agrarian revolution," as outlined in a draft issued during the course of the year, had a triple aim: to limit the size of privately owned estates; ban landholding by those with other sources of income; and distribute the land thus recovered to destitute peasants who were to be regrouped within cooperatives. Official statistics showed that 25% of the privately owned land was occupied by 16,000 farmers owning more than 50 ha. each (1 ha. = 2½ ac.), while 300,000 peasants with plots of less than 5 ha. each shared 10%. Privately owned land accounted for about two-thirds of the nation's total cultivable land, the rest being farmed either as self-managed estates or as cooperatives.

In foreign affairs, a spectacular Algerian diplomatic achievement was a settlement of the border dispute with Morocco, reached at a meeting between Boumédienne and King Hassan II at Tlemcen, western Algeria, in May. The two leaders decided to create a joint military commission to delineate the border, as well as a joint committee to study the exploitation in common of the rich iron ore deposits near Tindouf, in that part of the Algerian Sahara over which they had gone to war in 1963. Algeria and Morocco, together with Mauritania, also took steps to unify their policies on the Spanish Sahara, calling for decolonization of that phosphate-rich territory when their leaders met in Mauritania in mid-September. (F. Dd.)

Andorra

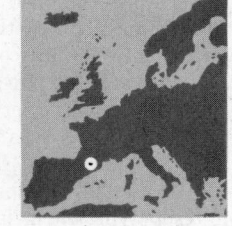

An autonomous principality of Europe, Andorra is in the Pyrenees Mountains between Spain and France. Area: 175 sq.mi. (453 sq.km.). Pop. (1970 est.): 19,500. Cap.: Andorra la Vella (Catalan) or Andorra la Vieja (Spanish) (pop., 1970 parish est., 7,600). Language: chiefly Catalan. Religion: predominantly Roman Catholic. Co-princes: the president of the French Republic and the bishop of Urgel, Spain, represented by their *vegeurs* (provosts) and *batlles* (prosecutors). An elected Council General of 24 members elects

ANDORRA
Education. (1967–68) Primary, pupils 804, teachers 30; secondary, pupils 181, teachers 11.
Finance. Monetary units: French franc and Spanish peseta. No income tax, death duty, or customs; public treasury is funded by 3% levy on gasoline and liquor. Exchange and deposit banking is important.
Foreign Trade. (1969) Imports from France Fr. 130,520,000 (U.S. $25.1 million), from Spain, 868,-682,000 pesetas (U.S. $12,410,000). Tourism (1968) c. 800,000 visitors.
Communications. Radio receivers (Dec. 1968) 5,900. Television receivers (Dec. 1968) 1,600.
Agriculture and Industry. Production: cereals, potatoes, tobacco, wool. Livestock (in 000; 1968): sheep c. 25; cattle c. 3; horses c. 1.

the first syndic (*sindic procurador general de les valls d'Andorra*); in 1970, Francesc Escudé-Ferrero.

Following the general elections of December 1969, First Syndic Escudé and Subsyndic Eduardo Rosell Pujal were reelected for a three-year period by the new Council General. The new bishop of Urgel took up his duties as co-prince, replacing the bishop of Lerida, who had served in the position temporarily.

On April 23, 1970, a decree issued by the *vegeurs* granted the right to vote to female citizens of the principality for the first time in history. The decree put into effect a bill passed by the Council General on July 12, 1969. The right to vote, however, was restricted to Andorran nationals, *i.e.*, female members of families resident in the principality for at least two generations. The decree did not confer eligibility on women to be elected to the Council General or to be chosen as first syndic. It would result in the doubling of the electorate, from approximately 1,500 to nearly 3,000 voters, and according to an unnamed official "will bring about great changes in the politics of Andorra." (R. D. Ho.)

Antarctica

The 11th plenary session of the Scientific Committee on Antarctic Research (SCAR) of the International Council of Scientific Unions (ICSU) was held in Oslo, Aug. 17–22, 1970. All 12 signatory nations to the Antarctic Treaty were represented, along with eight delegates from affiliated international scientific unions. Immediately preceding the meeting, SCAR sponsored a symposium on Antarctic Geology and Solid Earth Geophysics. The sixth Consultative Meeting of Antarctic Treaty Nations was held in Tokyo, Oct. 15–17, 1970. The agenda included discussions on regulation of Antarctic pelagic sealing, agreed measures for the conservation of Antarctic fauna and flora, specially protected areas, environmental pollution, historical monuments, and tourism in Antarctica. The 22nd meeting of the International Whaling Commission took place in London, June 22–26, 1970, and reported that, in the 1969–70 whaling season, 3,001 fin, 5,856 sei, and 3,090 sperm whales were harvested in Antarctic waters.

Six SCAR nations made preliminary plans for launching a joint interdisciplinary research program to include drilling through the Ross Ice Shelf, a floating mass of fresh ice up to 1,500 ft. thick and larger in area than France. Field studies by a team of earth scientists from 11 nations showed that the geographic South Pole of 450 million years ago had gradually moved northward a distance of 5,500 mi. and was now situated in the Algerian Sahara Desert; it was believed that the movement was due to sliding action of the earth's crust. Studies of the 1967–69 volcanic eruptions on Deception Island off the Antarctic Peninsula suggested that further volcanic activity could be expected, and that eruptions profoundly altered the local ecological environment; only the local penguins appeared to be unaffected. Uruguay applied for membership in SCAR and planned to establish stations in Antarctica along with a corresponding research program, both being prerequisites for membership.

Scientific Programs. The Antarctic Treaty celebrated its tenth anniversary in 1970 and had another 20 years to go. Of the 12 treaty nations, 10 had stations in the Antarctic and sub-Antarctic. Norway and Belgium, while not maintaining stations at present, had done so in the past and continued their active interest in the area by participating in the programs of other nations.

Argentina. The Argentine Antarctic Institute continued its program of Antarctic research at seven bases in Antarctica, all but one located on the Antarctic Peninsula. A new atmospheric physics laboratory constructed near General Belgrano Base investigated a large fissure in the Filchner Ice Shelf to determine its possible effect on the base, which was located on the shelf. The Teniente Matienzo Base was temporarily closed and a new one established nearby, while Sobral Base was deactivated. Damage to the icebreaker "San Martin" cut short Argentina's involvement with the U.S. and Norway in the International Weddell Sea Oceanographic Expedition.

Australia. The Australian National Antarctic Research Expedition (ANARE) implemented a research program centred at its two main bases on the continent: Casey and Mawson. A geologic, mapping, and glaciologic party surveyed a rocky outcrop 190 mi. S of Mawson Base. Scientists at Amery Ice Shelf Base continued measurements of ice movement and accumulation, and 11 men wintered at the newly reoccupied Davis Station. Australian and U.S. scientists aboard the U.S. research ship "Eltanin" conducted a 60-day oceanographic study in the seas between Australia and Antarctica. The Australian government issued a license to harvest 1,900 tons of whale meat from the Antarctic for use as food for pets. Fifty-eight Australians received the British Polar Medal for service in Antarctica between 1959 and 1967.

Belgium. Belgians joined with South Africans in an airborne ice-profiling program in Antarctica. Belgium's Otter aircraft crashed near Sanae Base early in the field season, thereby curtailing a major part of the planned effort.

Chile. A broad research program was carried out at Chile's three permanent bases on the Antarctic Peninsula, with the support of helicopters, light aircraft, and ships. The base on Deception Island was abandoned. The meteorological facility at Presidente Frei Base underwent extensive refurbishing and expansion.

France. The French Antarctic program was focused at their only base on the continent, Dumont d'Urville, with lesser programs on the sub-Antarctic islands of Crozet, Amsterdam, and Kerguelen. The wintering complement at Dumont d'Urville Station was composed of 15 scientists and 12 support personnel. The chartered Danish ship "Thala Dan" ran into heavy sea ice in its attempt to resupply the base and arrived 24 days late. Much of the planned summer construction program was delayed because of the late arrival of supplies.

Japan. The 11th Japanese Antarctic Research Expedition (JARE) was launched from Japan's main Showa Base, where 28 members wintered over. A ten-man over-snow traverse, with aircraft support, was launched to the Yamato Mountains to lay a glaciological grid for ice-strain measurements. The discovery of thick morainal deposits suggested the former existence of rugged sub-ice structure with a thin ice cover in this region. At Showa Station, new research programs on atmospheric electricity and infrasonic sound waves were introduced. Garth Morgan (Australia) and Herman Friis (U.S.) participated with the Japanese as exchange scientists and conducted studies on oceanography and geology while aboard the icebreaker "Fuji." While evacuating Showa Base on February 25,

the "Fuji" became beset in heavy sea ice. Before Soviet and U.S. help could arrive, the "Fuji" freed herself on March 18.

New Zealand. The New Zealand Antarctic research program was centred in and around Scott Base, Vanda Station, and Campbell Island. Over 80 personnel participated in the summer scientific program. Mrs. Pam Young again accompanied her husband Euan Young to Cape Bird where they studied the behaviour of penguins and skua gulls. Two extensive deposits of peridot, a semiprecious stone, were discovered on Ross Island. Earthquakes originating in the Antarctic continent were thought to be quite rare; however, New Zealand scientists reported that small earthquakes, believed to have originated in the Terra Nova Bay region, were recorded on seismographs at Vanda Station.

On Dec. 1, 1969, representatives of several nations gathered at Scott Base to formally commemorate the tenth anniversary of the Antarctic Treaty. On New Year's Day, in a whiteout caused by blowing snow, a Rugby match was played at Scott Base before a small crowd of New Zealanders and startled Americans. Three New Zealanders and a U.S. admiral introduced cricket at the South Pole and discussions were under way for holding the first full cricket match. The British Polar Medal was awarded to 29 members of New Zealand Antarctic expeditions.

Norway. While Norway did not maintain bases in Antarctica, its scientists continued studies of Antarctic bottom waters while participating in the International Weddell Sea Oceanographic Expedition.

South Africa. The 11th South African National Antarctic Expedition was composed of 18 members, four of whom wintered at Borga Base, some 350 km. S of the main Sanae Base. Geologic investigations and mapping of the nearby Kirwan Escarpment were continued and a radio-echo ice sounding program was initiated. Geologic maps of part of Queen Maud Land were compiled and published. For the first time, a member of the expedition was killed when he fell into a snow-covered crevasse between Sanae and Borga bases. In addition to resupplying bases, the vessel "RSA" served as a platform for marine geophysical studies in the southern Indian Ocean.

United Kingdom. The British Antarctic Survey (BAS) used three ships, helicopters, and small aircraft in resupplying the main Halley Bay Base on the continent and seven other bases on the Antarctic Peninsula and sub-Antarctic islands. A small group undertook topographic and geologic surveys of the Shackleton Range and were evacuated to Halley Bay Station by U.S. aircraft. Four field parties, operating from Stonington and Fossil Bluff bases, conducted geologic, glaciological gravity, and magnetic surveys in the vicinity of the Eklund Islands. A 15-man group traveled from Stonington Island to King George VI Sound, conducting geologic and geophysical studies en route. Two glaciologists conducted investigations in an area south of Fossil Bluff Station.

U.S.S.R. The 15th Soviet Antarctic Expedition (SAE) was supported by the scientific research ships "Professor Vize" and "Ob," and its broad research program was centred at four bases on the Antarctic continent: Mirnyy, Vostok, Molodezhnaya, and Novolazarevskaya. Lesser programs were carried out at Bellingshausen Station, which is situated 200 mi. from the U.S. Hallett Station. Altogether 225 personnel wintered on Soviet bases in Antarctica, along with one exchange scientist each from the U.S., Argentina, Cuba, and East Germany; two Soviet scientists wintered on bases of other nations.

A 14-man traverse over 1,500 km. from Mirnyy to Vostok stations provided new information on the rock structure underlying East Antarctica. Along the coastal stations, the physical and biological properties of near-shore ice were studied and techniques were developed for recording oscillations of ice floes caused by distant storms. From a new facility at Molodezhnaya Station rockets were launched weekly to an altitude of 60 mi. for meteorological and upper atmospheric studies. The most powerful radio station in Antarctica was being constructed at Molodezhnaya Station and, for the first time, all Soviet stations received real-time weather data from space satellites.

United States. The U.S. Antarctic Research Program included 66 individual field projects in biology, earth science, and atmospheric sciences. Around 200 scientists and technicians representing 47 institutions and government agencies participated; about 30 remained for the winter along with around 200 support personnel. Studies were carried on throughout Antarctica. Three U.S. exchange scientists joined foreign expeditions, while 14 foreign scientists accompanied U.S. expeditions.

A highlight of the summer field season was the discovery of a bed of fossil bones of several types of vertebrates, including amphibians and reptiles, in a site in the Transantarctic Mountains. All appear to be remnants of now extinct creatures that lived during the Triassic period, more than 200 million years ago. The discovery established beyond further question the former existence of the great southern continent of Gondwanaland. For the first time a group of five women scientists participated in the U.S. Antarctic field program, under the leadership of Lois Jones, a geochemist. They conducted geologic studies in the ice-free dry valleys about 70 mi. W of McMurdo Station. British and U.S. scientists joined in a continuing program of profiling the ice sheet of Antarctica using airborne radio-echo sounding techniques.

The research vessel "Eltanin" made six cruises into the Central and Southern Pacific Ocean, Tasman Sea, and South Indian Ocean and the trawler "Hero" made eight cruises into the seas bordering the southern tip of South America and the Antarctic Peninsula.

Other Activities. In a new specially constructed ship, Lindblad Travel Inc. launched three tourist excursions to Antarctica carrying nearly 200 passengers, who paid up to $5,000 each for cruises lasting 12–19 days. The New Zealand Transport Ministry revealed plans for building a luxury hotel to accommodate 90 people on the Ross Ice Shelf. Scandinavian Airlines System announced that it was considering the extension of its air route from South Africa to New Zealand via Antarctica. Max Conrad (U.S.) became the first solo pilot to land at the South Pole. However, his plane crashed at the South Pole shortly after takeoff for Punta Arenas, Chile. A few hours later, Thor Tjontveit and Einar Pedersen (Norway) also arrived at the South Pole and successfully flew on to Punta Arenas via McMurdo Station.   (L. M. Gɒ.)

See also Geography; Oceanography.

Anthropology

The most striking revisions of previous theories regarding the spread of peoples around the world emerged from a 1969 conference in Fiji on "Culture History in the Pacific Area" and from recent archaeological and linguistic work in that region. Radiocarbon dates of sites in northern Australia and New Guinea, obtained principally by J. P. and C. White, dated into the terminal Pleistocene, between 20,000 and 30,000 before present (B.P.). The characteristic "waisted" and often edge-ground axes found there are the oldest ground axes in the world. These axes are also found on the island of New Britain, indicating that by that time southeast Asian man had the ability to cross open water.

If these early inhabitants are tentatively identified,

WIDE WORLD
Thor Heyerdahl, at the helm of "Ra II," waves to his wife and daughter aboard a Barbados government tug as the papyrus vessel sails into Carlisle Bay, July 12, 1970.

as J. P. Golson has done, with speakers of non-Austronesian languages, then Melanesian speakers (one branch of the Austronesian family, which spreads from Madagascar and Taiwan to Hawaii and Easter Island) must have arrived in the Southwest Pacific at a later date. Their arrival presumably antedates the diversification of languages within the Eastern Oceanic subgroup, which seems to have occurred, along with the population of islands as far away from Asia as Fiji, around 4,000 years ago.

Other Melanesian language subgroups with much greater internal diversity and presumably greater age have been identified in inland areas of New Guinea. The first occurrences of pig bone there date from about 6500 B.P., suggesting that the newcomers were already agriculturalists. Presumably they had adequate means of water transport before that date, possibly even contemporaneously with the emerging agriculturalists of southwest Asia. The widespread distribution of somewhat similar "Lapita ware" pottery in the Southwest Pacific around 3000 B.P., and the subsequent voyaging and peopling of Polynesia, seem now to fall into place as part of a history of Southeast Asia and the islands much longer than had been suspected.

In his second attempt in as many years, the Norwegian anthropologist Thor Heyerdahl succeeded in sailing from Safi, Mor., to Barbados in a papyrus boat. Designed according to ancient Egyptian tomb drawings, the "Ra II" was built by four of the Bolivian Indians who still use reed boats on Lake Titicaca. Heyerdahl made the voyage to provide evidence for his controversial theory that the high Indian civilizations of Middle and South America were founded by Egyptians who crossed the Atlantic in ancient times. The first "Ra" was abandoned in 1969 when its hull became waterlogged some 600 mi. from its destination.

Apart from its use in historical reconstruction, linguistic anthropology has been receiving increasing attention. In partnership with linguists, anthropologists have considered how social factors—class, situation, or the roles involved—affect the language used. Most recently, interest in bilingualism has been reinforced by work on situations in Europe and America where people speaking language or dialect A at home and in childhood learn language or dialect B later as a public, polite, or adult language. William Labov's work on black dialects in New York, and their relation to standard American, has been outstanding.

To date, however, most of this work has been aimed at furthering linguistic analysis and has treated social factors as features to be included in the analysis of language. Robbins Burling tried to reverse this situation in his *Man's Many Voices*, in which he compiles the sociolinguistic findings and recent ethnological work on semantic categories to show how such findings contribute to cultural theory. In effect, his message is a cultural one: the importance for individuals of maintaining distinct cultural identities at many levels, and of the constant (and patterned) innovations in all behaviour, linguistic and other, that go along with this search.

The social consequences of the tendency for subgroups within wider population aggregates to maintain their cultural identities was the subject of a seminal work, *Ethnic Groups and Boundaries* by Fredrik Barth. Why, he asks, amid a whole range of interactions, do people choose to label their partners for some of them by ethnic labels? In Norwegian fjord villages, for example, everyone goes to the same schools, does the same jobs, and in public speaks the same language, but many domains of interaction revolve around whether a person is categorized as *folk* (Norwegian) or *finn* (Lapp). Why do people draw such boundaries around people they feel to be "their own kind" and exclude people they define as "foreign"? And what are the consequences? Very generally, even the act of defining a stranger as a "foreigner" establishes a code within which interaction can take place. Labeling of some kind is inevitable in social life. The extreme generality of the ethnic label, however, means that only a very few characteristics are common to all "foreigners." They achieve high symbolic importance and are consciously manipulated as rallying points of cultural identity, even though they would often be relatively insignificant in an analysis of the internal structure of the culture.

By contrast, Eric Wolf, in his *Peasant Wars of the Twentieth Century,* sees the existence of culturally distinct subgroupings within modern society as something of an anachronism. They exist, but only because the rewards of social life have been preempted by a limited elite, usually urban based, which fragments the large agricultural mass of society. In these terms, the first 70 years of the 20th century have seen a worldwide peasant reaction, spurred in large part by new means of communication. It has meant the breakdown of closed communities and, at the same time, a rejection of the subservient status that urban capitalist wealth has typically forced on the rural dweller.

On a much less grandiose canvas, however, Emilio Willems, in an article in the *American Anthropologist,* sketched a thousand years of life in a peasant village near Cologne, Ger., in a way that questions whether large-scale urban society does inevitably imply the disruption of "peasant society." Although the village is now part of metropolitan Cologne, traditional costumes and ceremonials are still in evidence and are felt to be a matter of local pride. Local endogamy is practiced, and the presence of the same 20 family names has been common for a hundred years. The reason, Willems hints, is that agricultural prosperity, particularly during the 18th century, gave the community a structure and a degree of cultural self-respect and identity that have persisted despite the engulfing urban spread.

Agricultural prosperity and urban poverty were not popular themes in the 1960s, but, increasingly, anthropological studies were describing agricultural communities where modern facilities were being incorporated easily into "traditional" contexts and where agriculture was prosperous. A monograph of the Society for Applied Anthropology, entitled *Urban Anthropology,* points up the reverse—wealth, despite the myth, is no longer to be found in the cities. Urban problems are no longer those of "urbanizing" unsophisticated peasant immigrants, but of constructing a viable new urban life-style when productive work is lacking, modern facilities are expensive and overused, and "traditional" facilities are unavailable. The emergence of the culturally distinct community within the city as a topic of anthropological research may well be a reflection of this social reality.   (R. F. SA.)

See also Archaeology.

ENCYCLOPÆDIA BRITANNICA FILMS. *Remnants of a Race* (1955); *American Indians of Today* (1957); *Indian Family of Long Ago* (1957); *Indians of Early America* (1957); *Eskimo Family* (1959); *Cave Dwellers of the Old Stone Age* (1960); *Eskimo in Life and Legend (The Living Stone)* (1960); *Prehistoric Man in Northern Europe* (1961); *The Egyptologists* (1967).

Archaeology

Eastern Hemisphere. Few if any large-scale or long-range archaeological field programs were begun in the Old World during 1970. Various older field expeditions continued to work, although generally on a somewhat reduced scale. A few new excavations of small size were undertaken, and surface surveys (without the heavy commitment in expense, staff, and gear characteristic of full excavations) tended to become more numerous. The situation was, of course, a direct result of political instability in many parts of the world, of tightened financial circumstances, and of xenophobia—often prompted by the outrages of the growing illicit antiquities trade. Some agreement had been reached between the respective governments for the return of antiquities illicitly acquired and exported from Mexico into the United States, but such arrangements did not yet exist as regards Old World countries. Twice during the year the serious probability arose that permission for U.S. archaeological work in Turkey would be denied because two American fine arts museums accepted gifts of illicitly acquired antiquities, reputedly coming from Turkey.

Very few outstanding discoveries were reported during the year. One so-called archaeological effort burst like a toy balloon. After blasts of publicity, a fundamentalist-backed organization that proposed to "uncover and identify an *ancient wooden structure of immense size* that may well be the remains of Noah's ark" was refused permission to renew work in the politically sensitive region of Mount Ararat, where the Iranian, Soviet, and Turkish frontiers join. At the same time came news of a second radiocarbon age determination (by a UCLA laboratory) on previously taken specimens of the wood in question. This age determination, which closely conformed to that of an earlier determination (by a British laboratory), suggested timber felled around A.D. 700.

If a find of the year were to be suggested, it would probably be the excellent series of Greek frescoes that Mario Napoli exposed in some 109 tombs adjacent to the temples of Paestum in the Salerno district, Italy. It was claimed that these were the only examples of truly classical Greek wall paintings yet found. The themes depicted range from games honouring the dead to mythological scenes. The tombs date to *c.* 340–310 B.C., and were those of Lucanians, tribes that overwhelmed the Greeks of Paestum about 400 B.C. The paintings themselves indicate that Greek artists were still available, however.

Pleistocene Prehistory. North of Beirut in Lebanon, Ralph Solecki of Columbia University undertook the salvage clearance of caves that would be destroyed in new highway construction. Considerable quantities of artifacts resembling those of the Mousterian were recovered. Nearby, Jacques Tixier of the French Centre National de la Recherche Scientifique continued his excavations on the old and essentially undescribed site of Ksar Akil. Otto Bader of the Academy of Sciences of the U.S.S.R., continuing his clearance of the Upper Paleolithic site of Sungir, encountered more burials. These included the skeletons of two boys, buried head to head in one grave, along with thinned and straightened mammoth tusk spears, lances, daggers, needles, and a horse figurine. Sungir is probably the northernmost substantial occurrence of Upper Paleolithic material (*c.* 25,000 years ago),

COURTESY, ROYAL GREEK EMBASSY

Skeletons believed to be those of Plataean soldiers were unearthed in a mass grave on the Plain of Marathon northeast of Athens in April 1970. The Plataeans died turning back the Persians of Darius I almost 2,500 years ago in the Battle of Marathon.

and Bader's report of a broad-spectrum food supply, with evidence of small animals, fish, and birds as well as reindeer, horse, and mammoth, was of interest.

The Near East. In the U.A.R. archaeological activity was almost entirely restricted to the urban environs of such cities as Cairo and Luxor, where security could be assured. The Oriental Institute of the University of Chicago continued to glean new historical information from its careful study of temple reliefs at Medinet Habu. A detailed report of the cosmic-ray absorption examination of the second of the great pyramids at Giza, that of Khafre, indicated that inner chambers such as those in the pyramids of Khufu and Sneferu do not exist.

Surprisingly, there was considerable archaeological activity in Israel although it was understandably concentrated along the Mediterranean littoral; *i.e.*, in Philistia. The American Schools of Oriental Research and the Hebrew Union College-Jewish Institute of Religion programs, both of which involved large numbers of student volunteers, were active. The American Schools began one of the few new longer-range projects of the year: a resumption of work at Tell el Hesi, begun by Sir Flinders Petrie in 1890 and continued by F. J. Bliss in 1891–93. It was on this large mound, believed to have been the site of the biblical Eglon, that Petrie's pioneering studies in the value of potsherds were first made.

At Gezer the Hebrew Union College completed its clearance of a monumental city gate of the time of Solomon and also encountered a cave burial of the mid-15th century B.C. A. Biran, Israeli director of antiquities, continued his excavations at Tel Dan, where he exposed a city gate of very large size. B. Rothenberg's analysis of the excavations of sites in the Wadi Timna, once reputed to be the location of King Solomon's mines, indicated the clear presence of an Egyptian temple and of artifacts of about the 14th–12th centuries B.C., several hundred years too early for Solomon.

Few expeditions worked in Syria or Iraq. At Qasr al-Hayr Sharqi, northeast of Palmyra, Oleg Grabar continued his clearances of this early Islamic site. In Iraq government archaeologists exposed broad areas of the two uppermost levels of Tell al-Fakhar, southwest of Kirkuk, recovering the walls of a palace and many cuneiform tablets of the mid-2nd millennium B.C. Most of the long-established foreign and national expeditions were at work in Turkey, and salvage ex-

COURTESY, CHARLES C. KOLB

These moldmade figurines from the Classic Teotihuacán period made in the generalized "Princess" style were recovered from Mexico's Teotihuacán sites.

cavations proceeded in the region to be flooded by a dam on the upper Euphrates.

Iran, a relatively vast country with numerous sites, tended to absorb the activities of many archaeologists displaced from other, less peaceful countries of the Near East. Perhaps especially noteworthy were the new French exposures of additional monumental buildings of the Persian kings' capital at Susa and the finding there of a pair of Darius' inscriptions. For several years an Italian institute had been at work on a vast city site, Shahr-i-Sokhta in Seistan (east central Iran), with exceptionally well-preserved materials and building plans. The occupation appears to have been before c. 2000 B.C., and there were hints that the site was a centre of trade in lapis lazuli. At Altyn-Tepe, in the Turkmen Soviet Socialist Republic, Vadim Masson excavated an important 3rd–2nd millennium B.C. site, including a temple with features recalling Mesopotamia.

The Greco-Roman Regions. The "News Letter from Greece" (*American Journal of Archaeology,* vol. 74, no. 3, pp. 261–284 [July 1970]) suggested no very startling discoveries. An extensive prehistoric settlement was being examined near Marathon, as well as a small mound with the burials of young adult males, possibly Plataeans, Athenian allies in the famous battle. At Mycenae a building complex discovered in 1968 was cleared further; more clay idols and some carved ivory heads appeared, and one room was taken to have been a cult room. The prehistoric exposures in the important Franchthi cave were enlarged, and more evidence of the transition from food-gathering to food-producing ways of life in early Greece appeared. The foundations of a building found in the Athenian agora were identified as those of the Stoa of the Basileus, the site of Socrates' trial.

Fine examples of Scythian gold and silver vessels and ornaments, with decoration suggesting Greek craftsmanship, appeared in a grave in the Ukraine. On Cyprus a Polish expedition at New Paphos reported the recovery of a well-preserved series of sculptures and a polychrome mosaic of the slaying of the Minotaur. A new Etruscan site was identified at Porto Clementino, 62 mi. N of Rome. On the basis of recent excavations and topographical studies on the Palatine Hill in Rome, G. Carettoni identified structures he believed to be the house of the emperor Augustus and the temple of Apollo. The Augustus house is a relatively simple affair (*cf.* Suetonius, that Augustus was satisfied with a house "scarcely fit for a private citizen"), but fragments of fine painting and terra-cotta came from the terrace below the temple.

Late Prehistoric and Historic Europe. S. Bokonyi's study of animal bones recovered several years earlier from the remarkable site of Lepenski Vir, in the Iron Gate gorge of the Danube, Yugoslavia, revealed that the dog was the only domesticated animal of the two earliest phases. These two phases were both "villages" and dated sometime before c. 5500 B.C. In the following, third phase, cattle, sheep, and a few pigs were kept. In England salvage archaeology revealed traces of circular roofed timber structures within a large henge (circular Bronze Age monument) at Durrington. Excavation on the largest British henge, at Marden, also revealed the traces of timber structures, and it was suggested that these larger henges demote Stonehenge to the position of "a 'parish church' as it were—even if [its] sophistication . . . means that it must be accounted as a very 'royal' parish church."

Asia. General claims continued to be made for a very early appearance of plant domestication at Spirit Cave in northern Thailand, but detailed descriptions of the botanical evidence were not yet available. A prehistoric village site in northeast Thailand, Non Nok Tha, was reported to have yielded rice dating from c. 3500–2500 B.C. (R. J. B.)

Western Hemisphere. Despite cutbacks in funding, more than 500 and perhaps as many as 1,000 field expeditions were active in the New World during 1970. Increasing numbers of field projects were being carried out to test explicit hypotheses generated by ecological and general systems theory, as illustrated in *Anthropological Archaeology in the Americas,* edited by Betty J. Meggers, which provides eight papers demonstrating the so-called "new archaeology." The selections are consistently grounded in ecological theory and provide a broad spectrum of current research problems and methods. Most of the papers either describe prehistoric settlement systems or attempt to explain changes that took place in them.

Technical Studies. Leslie B. Davis, Montana State University, dated approximately 1,300 obsidian specimens from 145 prehistoric sites in the northwestern Plains by the hydration method, in which the hydration rim that forms naturally on obsidian is measured to determine age. In California, Clement W. Meighan, UCLA, and C. Vance Haynes, Jr., Southern Methodist University (Texas), reported an obsidian hydration study that helped to resolve controversy concerning the Borax Lake site in Lake County. The findings suggested that the site was initially utilized during the Palaeo-Indian period about 12,000 years ago, with subsequent major occupation between 6,000 and 8,000 years ago.

An application of X-ray fluorescence spectroscopy to obsidian samples from sources throughout Mexico and Guatemala and to a large number of specimens from the San Lorenzo Tenochtitlán sites in Veracruz was reported by Michael D. Coe and R. Cobean of Yale University. The analysis demonstrated that extensive exchange or procurement systems involving obsidian existed as early as the Ojochi phase (1450–1350 B.C.) of the Early Formative and continued throughout the long occupation of the San Lorenzo Tenochtitlán sites.

A systematic survey using a recording magnetometer was conducted by A. E. Wilson, Canadian National Historic Sites Service, on the winter ice pan at the head of Chaleur Bay, Quebec, to survey the site of the 1760 Battle of Restigouche, the last major naval engagement between French and British forces in the Seven Years' War. Approximately 22 French ships were sunk or scuttled during the battle. Magnetic anomalies provided precise information regarding the location of both unknown and previously recorded wrecks.

Far North. A large artifact assemblage, dated A.D. 400 or 500 and representing a non-Eskimo, possibly Indian culture, was recovered in the Brooks Range of Alaska during investigations at the Onion Portage site on the Kobuk River by Douglas D. Anderson, Brown University, Providence, R.I. Edwin S. Hall, Jr., Ohio State University, excavated a large Eskimo inland encampment on the shore of Tukuto Lake in the Etivluk drainage. He determined that the site was probably first utilized slightly before A.D. 1800 and abandoned shortly after A.D. 1900. Investigation revealed that bows and arrows were the primary hunting tools, even after the introduction of the rifle, and that these traditional hunting techniques, rather than

COURTESY, UNIVERSITY OF PENNSYLVANIA MUSEUM

Baskets of broken pottery from the excavation of Phoenician levels at Sarafand in southern Lebanon. These fragments, first uncovered in April 1970, make up the first large body of evidence needed to piece together the origins of Phoenician culture.

the rifle, probably brought about the early 20th-century decline in numbers of caribou.

Coastal Studies. Investigations in the Bella Bella region of British Columbia, directed by James J. Hester, University of Colorado, focused on changes in utilization of the environment that might provide a means for describing cultural phases. Faunal analysis suggested a transition from the use of land animals to maritime mammalian forms such as seal, porpoise, and whale. Efforts were being made to determine whether such changes resulted from cultural or environmental factors. David Sawbridge, University of Victoria, B.C., initiated a study of ecological succession on shell middens at the mouth of Knight Inlet, Vancouver Island, designed to test the hypothesis that vegetation can serve as an indicator of age on Northwest Coast sites.

Herbert Mills, Nassau County (N.Y.) Museum of Natural History, conducted a study of Wading River Marsh, Long Island, in an effort to reconstruct the local environment during the period of prehistoric occupation. Preliminary results indicated that an early shallow bay was eventually filled by deposition, so that open water was replaced by marsh and tidal creeks. The major prehistoric human occupation was believed to have taken place during a period when extensive mud flats supported an abundant population of soft clams.

Interior United States. A late Middle Period buffalo pound located south of Gillette, Wyo., in the Powder River basin was investigated by George C. Frison, University of Wyoming. The pound, dated about A.D. 250, was almost entirely man-made, consisting of two fence lines in an arroyo meander leading to a restraining structure where the animals were killed. In southwestern Idaho, L. D. Agenbroad, Chadron (Neb.) State College, reported the investigation of a buffalo jump dated by artifact analysis at nearly 2000 B.C. That buffalo drives may have even greater antiquity was suggested by summary work done by B. Galdikas, UCLA, who found that fossil bison and mammoth became extinct at approximately the same time. On the basis of differences in faunal remains, he proposed that while both Clovis and Folsom man stalked individual animals or small groups, Folsom man developed a drive technique for taking bison that was unknown to the earlier Clovis hunters.

Christy G. Turner II and Nancy T. Morris of Arizona State University reported on fragmented human bone excavated in 1964. The bone was demonstrated to have been the remains of a massacre of at least 30 individuals of both sexes and all ages, who were killed, crudely dismembered, violently mutilated, and probably cannibalized about A.D. 1700. The massacre occurred 10 mi. S of the Hopi villages. Available information suggested that the remains were those of villagers taken captive by other Hopi warriors, referred to in the legendary account of the destruction of Awatobi Pueblo that occurred 10 to 12 generations ago. The alleged purpose was to prohibit the return of Spanish missionaries to Hopi country after the Pueblo Revolt of 1680, as well as to retaliate against Awatobians for witchery practiced on other Hopi villagers.

Mexico. The Teotihuacán mapping project, directed by René Millon, University of Rochester, N.Y., completed the archaeological survey of the city. In addition to maps summarizing field data, publication would include maps showing hypothetical reconstruction of all substantial buildings that existed during the late phases of the Teotihuacán sequence. C. C. Kolb, Bryn Mawr (Pa.) College, reported on an analysis of nearly 3,000 fragmentary and complete figurines dating from the Classic Teotihuacán period (*c.* 200 B.C.–A.D. 750), recovered from 7 excavated and 126 surface surveyed rural Classic sites. The range of rural figurine types was strikingly limited in comparison with the types found in the urban centre, and this was interpreted as reflecting a peasant orientation toward the metropolis.

In a substantial review paper, Paul Tolstoy, Queens (N.Y.) College, and Louise I. Paradis, Yale University, proposed a revision of the Preclassic sequence in the Valley of Mexico. They pointed out that resemblances between Veracruz, Oaxaca, and the Valley of Mexico appear to be very close, although it is premature to accept the view that an Olmec empire was responsible.

Following survey and test excavations in the state of Guerrero, Robert E. Greengo, University of Washington, reported that there was an early to middle Preclassic occupation in the northern part of the state closely affiliated with those of Morelos and the Valley of Mexico. A number of attributes in the figurine complex appeared to represent indigenous variations on a general Preclassic theme, however. Reconnaissance and testing were carried out on the coast of Oaxaca by D. L. Brockington, University of North Carolina; preliminary findings indicated that, from at least middle Preclassic times through the Postclassic, the coastal cultures produced distinctive ceramics related to those from the Valley of Oaxaca and Tabasco. M. Jorrin, also of the University of North Carolina, located nearly 70 stone monuments, many of them carved, in a survey of a portion of Oaxaca.

British Honduras. Excavations at Altun Ha, reported by D. M. Pendergast, Royal Ontario Museum, yielded a claw-shaped bead of a gold-copper alloy occurring as part of an Early Classic offering. Stratigraphic evidence and radiocarbon dating placed the offering at or prior to A.D. 500. Stylistic elements indicated a source for the bead in the Coclé culture of central Panama. The Altun Ha discovery provides evidence of trade ties, however tenuous, linking the Maya

A gilded lead leaf, above, probably from a ceiling decoration in the bedchamber of Henry VIII's palace (c. 1500), is among the discoveries in excavations at the Royal Naval College in London, below.

"THE GUARDIAN," LONDON

with southern Central America at an unexpectedly early time.

South America. One of the major interpretive problems of Peruvian archaeologists concerns the character of the Middle Horizon expansion in the Central Andes, which occurred during the period A.D. 600–1000. Rapid developments took place, involving conquest and the spread of a culture that brought sweeping changes to nearly all of Peru, although the diversity of regional cultures gave rise to varied patterns of assimilation. The first step toward understanding the processes involved is to unravel the chronology, usually achieved by analysis of ceramic styles. A sophisticated methodology has been developed toward this end and, in addition to the study of new finds, older museum collections are constantly being reexamined. Allison C. Paulsen presented a reanalysis of field notes of the 1952 Columbia University expedition to Pinilla in the Ica Valley, demonstrating that each of two key burials had its own individually associated grave lot. This allowed a redefinition, carried out by Patricia J. Lyon, of the Pinilla style of the Middle Horizon and the distinguishing of all vessels of this style from the preceding Ica-Pachacamac style.

Where earlier workers tended to lump archaeological manifestations in the northern highlands of Ecuador into a single broad horizon, Alice Francisco, University of California, Berkeley, distinguished a temporal sequence of three ceramic styles in the Carchi region. The Capulí style, earliest in the sequence, had received relatively little attention, primarily because commercial collectors in the region had focused upon the middle, Piartal style, thus distorting its importance. The final, Tuza style was associated with a new mode of manufacture involved in the production of flat-bottomed vessels.

Early Man. The earliest known date for human remains in South America was reported by Richard S. MacNeish, Robert S. Peabody Foundation for Archaeology, Andover, Mass., and associates from UCLA. Crude unifacial tools, choppers, and a burin were recovered in association with extinct sloths and cameloids in a buried stratum in a cave located in the Ayacucho Valley of highland Peru. The latest of three occupation zones yielded a radiocarbon date of 12,200 B.C., so that older dates might well be forthcoming. The complex as a whole was unique among tool assemblages of early man in the Americas, and the absence of projectile points in the complex tended to confirm the hypothesis that the earliest horizon in South America belongs to a preprojectile-point stage.   (D. A. F.)

See also Anthropology.

ENCYCLOPÆDIA BRITANNICA FILMS. *Carbon Fourteen* (1953); *The Egyptologists* (1967).

Architecture

The outstanding architectural event of 1970 was Japan's Expo 70 exhibition at Osaka. With its theme "Progress and Harmony for Mankind," it followed the high architectural standard set by Canada's Expo 67 at Montreal three years earlier. As had become traditional with international expositions in this century, Expo 70 was a proving ground for new ideas in architecture, planning, and environmental technology. The central feature was the theme pavilion and Festival Plaza, a multilevel circulation area covered by a vast space-frame roof designed by architect Kenzo Tange

and engineer Yoshikatsu Tsuboi. The *Architectural Review,* in an issue devoted entirely to Expo 70, described this roof as the one astonishing architectural achievement of the show. The spectacular and monumental structure was also hailed as providing fruitful new ideas for the treatment of central spaces in towns of the future. The street furniture and fountains were other outstanding features, providing practical ideas for existing urban areas.

Many of the national, industrial, and commercial pavilions were outstanding examples of exhibition architecture. The British pavilion, by Powell and Moya, consisted of four connected exhibition galleries suspended from steel masts. The plywood walls were faced with aluminum foil and painted white. The whole was "advertised" by a gigantic balloon coloured to resemble the Union Jack. The United States pavilion made use of an adventurous form of construction. It was sunk into the ground with a minimum of visible external walling. The vast oval interior was covered with an air-supported roof of translucent vinyl-coated fibreglass. The architects for this were Davis, Brody, Chermayeff, Geismar, and de Harak.

Canada's pavilion was among the more spectacular constructions, consisting of a vast mirror-faced truncated pyramid designed by architects Erickson and Massey. Built around a courtyard, it exploited visual fascination in the multiple reflections from the building's surface and the interior pool.

The Swiss exhibit was not a building at all but rather a stylized aluminum "tree" 68 ft. high standing in the middle of an empty paved area and festooned with 32,000 electric lamps. The trunk of the tree was made of aluminum-clad lattice steel columns, and the main branches were box beams to which extruded aluminum bars were attached, thus creating a complex filigree effect. The structure broadcast electronic music and emitted cool air in hot weather. The architect was Willi Walter, in collaboration with Charlotte Schmid and Paul Leber.

The Netherlands pavilion by J. B. Bakema and Carel Weeber was cubic in form to house a film display that occupied the whole interior. The steel structure had wall surfaces of asbestos sheet, painted silver above and blue and orange below, with all the external angles rounded. The Czechoslovak pavilion consisted of two single-story buildings linked by a continuous roof, which was the dominating feature of the building. The roof was formed by a grid of lattice steel beams faced with oil-stained plywood and supported by tubular steel columns. The walls were of glass, stiffened by fins set at right angles, and the floor consisted of black ceramic tiles both inside and out. The architects were V. Palla, V. Rudis, A. Jencek, and J. Jiricny.

Some of the commercial and industrial pavilions erected by various Japanese groups were even more exciting. The Takara exhibit was one of the most successful architectural fantasies, consisting of a steel-pipe framework in which cubic stainless steel capsules were inserted to house the exhibits. The architect for this was Kisho Kurokawa. The pavilion of the Fuji group was claimed to be the world's largest pneumatic structure. Designed by Yutaka Murata, it was built up in an arched shape like a covered wagon and constructed out of 16 inflated vinyl-and-rubber tubes painted yellow and red on the outside. The Sumitomo pavilion was a sort of science-fiction structure consisting of nine circular capsules, some glazed and some opaque, set at different levels in a steel framework,

Archery:
see Sporting Record

connected by bridges and escalators. The architect was Sachio Otani.

School and University Architecture. Once again, throughout the world, many of the more forward-looking architectural productions were commissioned by schools and universities. The British firm of Howell, Killick, Partridge, and Amis was responsible for three new college buildings at Cambridge University. At Downing College they designed new combination rooms, kitchens, and offices to harmonize with the famous 19th-century Greek Revival exteriors by William Wilkins. The new extension was a precast concrete structure with large double-glazed windows and was linked to the old Greek Revival hall by a low, plain connecting wing. A new residential block and dining hall were added to Darwin College. The structure was built of cavity brick walls and featured an octagonal dining hall raised above an open car park. The hall was of brick with an impressive pine ceiling supported on reinforced concrete beams. Blundell Court, a new residential building at Sidney Sussex College, designed by the same firm, followed the traditional Cambridge pattern of stacks of study-bedrooms and sets of rooms for the fellows of the college. The structure was of brick and reinforced concrete. With these new buildings, Cambridge continued to uphold its reputation as the centre for modern architecture in Britain.

Another outstanding new university residence, designed by James Stirling, was Andrew Melville Hall, University of St. Andrews, Scot. The spectacular view across the Scottish mountains and the North Sea was exploited fully, and all student rooms in the residence were focused toward it. The hall consisted of precast concrete units forming a central core with two rambling projecting wings. When fully developed, the project was to comprise two dormitory complexes grouped on adjacent crests with each pair symmetrically mirrored about a common central service yard.

Hull University, Yorkshire, was the first British university to acquire a specially built studio exclusively for the use of its drama department. Named the Gulbenkian Centre, the building consisted of a theatre and television studio and was designed by Peter Moro and Partners. The structure was of board-marked concrete with red brick panels and a projecting copper-clad roof.

A new departure in school design was exemplified by the Butler County Community Junior College, El Dorado, Kan., by architects Schaefer, Schirmer, and Eflin. It was to consist of a dozen or more individual buildings, ten of which had been built by 1970; they would be linked by steps, ramps, and landscaped terraces designed to provide informal areas for discussion and relaxation. Brick plinths and tile-hung walls clothed a steel frame.

The campus of the University of California at San Diego had a new and magnificent focal point—the Central University Research Library. Designed by William L. Pereira and Associates, it consisted of a vast concrete structure that cantilevered five levels over a narrow podium to create a treelike shape. One feature of the design was that even on the widest horizontal level a student was never more than two minutes away from any other part of the building. Another excellent new library was the Goddard Library at Clark University, Worcester, Mass. Designed by John Johansen, it was intended to resemble a gigantic "box of books" with myriad shapes protruding from the central core.

COURTESY, JAPAN INFORMATION CENTRE

The Canadian pavilion at Japan's Expo 70 is sheathed in mirrored slopes to suggest the ice, mountains, and prairie sky of the Canadian landscape.

Office Buildings. High-rise office buildings continued to dominate city buildings as urban land values shot up everywhere. The skyline of the City of London, where not so long ago the dome of St. Paul's Cathedral had been the highest point, was taking on a new look with an increasing number of tall office buildings. While nothing to compare with the giants of New York and other U.S. cities, they nevertheless seemed to dwarf some of the City's narrow streets and old historic churches. Among the best of the year's new buildings in the City were the Commercial Union building and the P & O building, both by Gollins, Melvin, Ward and Partners. These were built facing one another across a common plaza. Each building is a square tower rising from a podium, and the site planning was arranged to allow for incorporation of the high-level pedestrian walkways envisaged in the City of London development plan. Basement parking space was another feature. The Commercial Union tower was 387 ft. high, and the P & O 191 ft. Both buildings were of similar construction, with a central reinforced concrete core enclosed in curtain walling. The new Stock Exchange headquarters by Llewelyn-Davies and Partners was completed and became another prominent part of the City's skyline.

In Boston the First National Bank's new headquarters was taking shape. Designed by architects Campbell, Aldrich and Nulty, its novel design featured the first six stories set back to leave room for a plaza and the next eight stories bulging out to make up the lost space. Above the bulge, the building continued straight up in the normal way. Situated near the new Government Center, the bank promised to be a novel addition to the new skyline of this historic city. The Government Center with its new city hall and vast pedestrian plaza continued to excite comment in architectural circles.

In Nairobi, Kenya, a new office building for the Agricultural Development Corporation, designed by Richard Hughes, featured a double-height shopping complex running under the building and opening into a central courtyard. The ten floors of offices were linked to a cluster of three concrete towers containing elevators, stairs, and cloakrooms. The reinforced-concrete structure was placed outside the curtain wall and used to suspend precast concrete sunbreakers.

A new addition to the San Francisco skyline was the Aetna Life and Casualty building by Welton Becket and Associates. This was an octagonal tower of steel sheathed with dark granite and bronze-tinted windows. Also exciting comment in San Francisco was the proposed pyramid-shaped skyscraper headquarters of Transamerica Corp.

Religious Architecture. Again in San Francisco, the new Roman Catholic cathedral by P. Belluschi and P. L. Nervi was nearing completion. The vast cru-

Commercial Union building in London by Gollins, Melvin, Ward and Partners. The site, a plaza facing the new P & O building, would feature high-level pedestrian walkways and underground parking.

COURTESY, GOLLINS, MELVIN, WARD AND PARTNERS

ciform concrete edifice was described by the *Architectural Review* as "an extraordinary exercise in enclosing the smallest amount of space with the greatest amount of wall."

Another new Roman Catholic church, that of St. Verene, near Friedrichshafen, W.Ger., built to replace a neo-Gothic structure, was designed by architects Hans Kammerer, Walter Belz, and Hans-Ulrich Schroeder. It featured shed-roofed towers grouped around a central congregational area. Construction was of reinforced concrete, and the interior was skylit. The new Roman Catholic church of St. Antonius in Wildegg, Switz., was designed in a castle-like form by architect Justus Dahinden in order to harmonize with its surroundings. The design sought to enclose in a minimum volume the formation people fall into when they attend Mass in an open field. Although it was a large church, the interior was nevertheless "domestic" in atmosphere, due to the low walls and the large expanse of boarded timber roof. The first joint Anglican-Roman Catholic church to be built in England was under construction at Cippenham, near Slough. The architects were W. S. Hattrell and Partners. The plan was a square divided unequally into sections by sliding folding doors; the doors also formed corridors in order to ensure access when more than one section was being used at the same time.

A new ecumenical centre was erected in Rotterdam, Neth., as a gift to the Dutch people from the churches in West Germany, a gesture of penance for the destruction of Rotterdam during World War II. Much of the construction was done by West German volunteer workers. The building was designed by Rietveld, van Dillen, and van Tricht and consisted of a perfect cube supported on four service and stair towers.

Other Buildings. The new town hall at Bukoba, Tanzania, by Richard Hughes was modest in scale, in keeping with the relatively poor township on the shores of Lake Victoria for which it was designed. It was built mainly of brick and concrete for ease of maintenance.

A new department store for Tokyo, the Ichi-Ban-Kan, was designed as a prismatic structure by Minoru Takeyama. In New York a new building for the Feigen Gallery on E. 79th Street was the first U.S. commission for the leading Austrian architect Hans Hollein. It featured a gleaming 18-ft.-high stainless steel column at the entrance and an excellent flowing interior.

The Acorn housing project, a low-cost scheme in West Oakland, Calif., was designed by Burger and Coplans. It was built by a black contractor and had a 50% black population. The dwellings were of timber frame construction that could be built rapidly and cheaply and consisted of three-story blocks of flats joining rows of two-story family houses. The whole had an "international style" air to it and was reminiscent of some of the German projects produced in the late 1920s and early 1930s by pioneers of modern architecture such as Ludwig Mies van der Rohe and Walter Gropius.

A new addition to Boston's Logan International Airport by Kubitz and Pepi comprised a bold geometric interpretation of the standard boarding-finger plan. At New York's Kennedy International Airport the new British Overseas Airways Corp. terminal by Robert Matthew Johnson-Marshall was completed, only to be severely damaged by fire a few months later.

The Cincinnati Reds baseball team had a new stadium. The Riverfront Stadium by Heery and Heery-Alexander and Rothschild was a four-level structure built over a triple-level parking deck. It was the first major league stadium to use Astroturf on the infield.

The Royal Institute of British Architects awarded its Royal Gold Medal for 1970 to Sir Robert Matthew. The American Institute of Architects similarly honoured R. Buckminster Fuller (recipient of the RIBA medal two years before).   (S. Mi.)

See also Cities and Urban Affairs; Engineering Projects; Housing; Industrial Review.

ENCYCLOPÆDIA BRITANNICA FILMS. *The Living City* (1953); *Art of the Middle Ages* (Humanities Course) (1962); *Athens: The Golden Age* (Humanities Course) (1962); *Chartres Cathedral* (Humanities Course) (1962); *The Louvre* (1966); *The Medieval Mind* (1969).

Arctic Regions

Despite the accelerated resource-exploration activities in both the Soviet and North American Arctic regions in 1970, the surge of actual development and production failed to materialize. There was growing concern over legal and jurisdictional questions and over the protection of the delicate northern environment and its native peoples.

To assist with shipping in the polar basin, the U.S. government announced plans to construct up to four new 11,000-ton icebreakers at an estimated cost of $50 million each. The Soviet Union disclosed its intention to construct two nuclear icebreakers to be used off the north coast of Siberia. The first was to be completed by 1975. The new series of icebreakers, to be called "Arktika," would be twice as powerful as the "Lenin," the Soviet Union's first nuclear icebreaker, which completed her 11th year of service during 1970. It was thought that the new icebreakers would help extend the shipping season off the Soviet Arctic coast from the present $4\frac{1}{2}$ to 6 months. In January the Soviet Union declared a ban on all shipping within 30 mi. of the Komandorski Islands, the islands closest to Alaska's Aleutian chain. The ban was announced in order to protect seals, and apparently extended the Soviet claim from a 12-mi. limit to 30 mi. in that area.

The Canadian Northwest Territories held centennial celebrations throughout 1970. One of the main events was a visit by Queen Elizabeth II, Prince Philip, Prince Charles, and Princess Anne to the Territories during the summer. On April 1 the Canadian federal government completed the transfer of responsibilities for the administration of government services in the eastern Arctic to the government of the Northwest Territories. In April the Canadian Defence Department announced that a permanent headquarters for the Canadian Forces would be established at Yellowknife, N.W.T., to coordinate the increasing military activity in Canada's northern regions.

In the spring the Canadian government introduced two measures to prevent pollution in the waters of the far north, the Northern Inland Waters Bill and the Arctic Waters Pollution Prevention Bill. The legislation provided for the comprehensive management of northern freshwater resources and for stringent regulations governing ship design, construction, navigational procedures and aids, and pollution liability applicable to all commercial shipping operating within a specified control zone. The two bills, and a letter to the United Nations, extended Canada's territorial sea limits to 12 mi. and claimed jurisdiction over waters up to 100 nautical miles from its Arctic coastline.

In May the Canadian government announced a

sweeping research program designed to accelerate both development and conservation in Canada's North. The four-point program, which was placed under the direction of the Department of Indian Affairs and Northern Development, embodied northern land use regulations, Arctic land use research, a task force on conservation, and comprehensive trials of tracked vehicles designed especially for operating over tundra.

Resources. The Humble Oil and Refining Co. reported in May that it had let a contract for the design of tankers in the 250,000-deadweight-ton class, although no decision had been reached on the construction of icebreaker tankers for transporting Alaskan oil. The second voyage of the U.S. supertanker "Manhattan" took place during April and May. The "Manhattan," which had accomplished the historic west- and eastbound passages through the Arctic Islands in 1969, restricted its voyage in 1970 to the waters of Baffin Bay and the eastern half of the Canadian Arctic Archipelago.

The construction of the trans-Alaska pipeline system (TAPS) continued to be delayed. Although hundreds of miles of Japanese-made pipe were stacked at Valdez and Fairbanks, permission to construct an approximately 400-mi. gravel road to haul the pipe from the Yukon River across the Brooks Range to Prudhoe Bay had not been granted. At stake was a pool of oil that had been conservatively valued at $60 billion. (*See* CONSERVATION: *Special Report.*)

Early in the year the secretary of Tyumen Province in the U.S.S.R. stated that western Siberia contained a giant oil field comparable to the one at Prudhoe Bay, and that production of 700 million bbl. annually by 1975 had been forecast. It was estimated that Soviet reserves of natural gas, much of it in the Tyumen area, were now the largest in the world. Production had fallen far short of planned targets, however, and the U.S.S.R. was attempting to arrange large gas sales to Western Europe in exchange for pipe and other needed equipment.

In January, Canada officially entered the Arctic oil sweepstakes when Imperial Oil Ltd. announced the discovery of a large oil field at Atkinson Point in the Mackenzie Delta, Northwest Territories. The discovery led to speculation that an ice-free harbour would be built somewhere between the Alaska North Slope and the Mackenzie Delta area, probably on Herschel Island. The Canadian government increased its stake in Panarctic Oils Ltd. to maintain a 45% equity interest in the Arctic oil and gas exploration consortium. The Dominion Bureau of Statistics announced in June that petroleum industry expenditures for exploration, development, and production in the Yukon, Northwest Territories, and Arctic Islands in 1969 totaled Can$86.7 million, nearly double those of the previous year.

Science and Technology. Because oil-prospecting activities on the North Slope had scattered the grizzly bear population of that region, the state of Alaska eliminated the 1970 spring hunting season. The state also curtailed the hunting of polar bears. This was a direct result of an international conference held during 1970 in Morges, Switz., where it was disclosed that the world polar bear population was incapable of maintaining itself in the face of new hunting techniques using light aircraft and snowmobiles.

One of the most important polar bear denning areas in the world was discovered 100 mi. S of Churchill, Man. It was estimated that about 60 female bears reared young in dens in this region during the year,

and the area was ranked with such major denning areas as Wrangel Island in the U.S.S.R., Kong Karls Land north of Norway, and Southampton Island in the Canadian Arctic.

In March 1970, the Soviet periodical *Water Transport* reported that the high latitude air expedition "North 22," organized by the Arctic and Antarctic Scientific Research Institute of Leningrad, was operational. For several years members of these expeditions, which used drifting ice stations as bases, had accumulated a vast amount of scientific material concerning the nature of the central Arctic Basin. One of the objectives of the 1970 program was to establish a new drift station north of Wrangel Island.

A scientist at the University of Copenhagen reported that a computer-aided analysis of a 4,000-ft. core of ice drilled from the Greenland Ice Cap indicated that the climate of the Arctic Islands was getting colder and that this would probably affect the overall climate of the Northern Hemisphere.

Early in 1970 the Canadian federal government decided to spend an additional Can$500,000 on the further development of the "Alexbow," a Canadian-designed ice plow that would lift ice out of a ship's path rather than crushing it. During the year an Edmonton, Alta., transportation firm ordered a prototype air-cushion trailer capable of moving 25 tons of oil and mineral drilling equipment over Arctic tundra areas. (K. DE LA B.)

See also **Geography.**

ENCYCLOPÆDIA BRITANNICA FILMS. *The Arctic—Islands of the Frozen Sea* (1959); *The Face of the High Arctic* (1959); *High Arctic—Life on the Land* (1959); *The High Arctic Biome* (1961); *Life on the Tundra* (1965).

Argentina

The republic of Argentina, occupying the southeastern section of South America, is bounded by Bolivia, Paraguay, Brazil, Uruguay, Chile, and the Atlantic Ocean. It is the second largest Latin-American country, after Brazil, with an area of 1,072,156 sq.mi. (2,776,884 sq.km.), excluding 481,177 sq.mi. of Antarctic and South Atlantic island areas. Pop. (1970 est.): 24,352,000. Cap. and largest city: Buenos Aires (pop., 1970 est., 3.6 million). Language: Spanish. Religion: mainly Roman Catholic. Presidents in 1970, Juan Carlos Onganía until June 8 and, from June 18, Brig. Gen. Roberto Marcelo Levingston.

Domestic Affairs. Argentina's political pattern in 1970 was dominated by the consequences of a change in its military leadership. On June 8, after almost four years as president, Juan Carlos Onganía—leader of the revolution proclaimed in 1966—was quietly deposed by the heads of the three armed services: Lieut. Gen. Alejandro Lanusse, Adm. Pedro Gnavi, and Brig. Carlos Rey. Forming a military junta, they ordered the immediate closing of the foreign exchange market and announced changes in the revolutionary charter that empowered them to make all decisions of national importance.

On June 13 the junta nominated as president Brig. Gen. Roberto Marcelo Levingston (*see* BIOGRAPHY), a former chief of army intelligence (under Pres. Arturo Frondizi) and later military attaché in the U.S. Taking office on June 18, Levingston appointed as economy and labour minister Carlos Moyano Llerena, who at once devalued the currency by 12.5% (from 3.50 to 4 new pesos to the U.S. dollar) and reopened the foreign exchange market.

Areas:
see Populations and Areas; *see also the individual country articles*

KEYSTONE

Brig. Gen. Roberto Marcelo Levingston, new president of Argentina by appointment of the military chiefs of staff.

Ongania's downfall could be partly explained by the gradual erosion of public confidence in his administration. Although he contrived to ride the political and social storms of mid-1969, persistent labour unrest and the soaring cost of living had appreciably weakened his position by the beginning of 1970. These troubles, coupled with reactions to his inept handling of the challenge presented by the kidnapping and murder of ex-Pres. Pedro Aramburu, finally unseated him.

Giving more specific reasons for its take-over, the junta emphasized Ongania's lack of preparations to restore representative government. Instead, his first priorities had been to forge a united labour front under the Confederación General de Trabajo (CGT) and to complete the revolution's economic and social phases before tackling the all-important "political plan."

The composition of the new administrative team provoked much comment. Moyano, former adviser to Adalbert Krieger Vasena (author of the 1967 stabilization plan), stood for the policy that local businessmen and international investors hoped would continue, but Aldo Ferrer, minister of public works and services, was a recognized advocate of industrial development at the expense, if necessary, of rigid stabilization. This evidence of a counterweight to Moyano's policy was followed by wage increases (blanket and selective) for all workers in the private sector and state enterprises, which confirmed a growing belief that the new regime preferred inflationary risks to public unrest.

Its central aim, however, was a planned approach to the restoration of democratic government. On September 29 Levingston assembled all provincial governors to announce a five-year program for "the progressive normalization of institutions." Within that period, he said, the government would reform the constitution, create "three or four" political parties to replace those dissolved on June 28, 1966 (when the armed forces deposed Pres. Arturo Illía), activate economic development, promote social and educational reforms, and, finally, call presidential and congressional elections. Describing as "irreversible" the dissolution of pre-1966 political parties, Levingston said that the new ones would reflect "all currents of popular opinion in a politically tolerant climate."

His announcement provoked anger and dismay throughout the political spectrum except from followers of ex-President Frondizi. The Peronistas (strongest of the country's political groupings) demanded a short-term plan to permit all traditional parties to take part in the next elections. Other party leaders openly denounced the government's proposals; the CGT, with which it had envisaged a political dialogue, promptly called a nationwide 24-hour strike for October 9, to be followed by protest demonstrations on October 22; and bomb outrages on October 3 in Buenos Aires, Rosario, Santa Fé, and Tucumán were officially blamed on political extremists.

The government was reportedly taken aback by these unmistakable symptoms of widespread opposition to its "political plan." In late August the outlook for its proposed dialogue with the CGT's newly reelected executive council had been clouded by the brutal assassination of José Alonso, leader of the garment workers' union and former secretary-general of the CGT. By early October it had become clear that organized labour and the traditional political parties had been deeply disillusioned by the plan and were in no mood to cooperate.

The Economy. Progress was satisfactory despite the change in political management and an accelerating rate of inflation—11.2% in the first eight months of 1970, against 3.6% in the same period of 1969—caused mainly by rises in the price of beef and other primary consumer goods. The gross domestic product grew by 5.8% from January to June, less than the 7.1% achieved in the first half of 1969 but well in line with the 5.5% target for the year. By lowering the target (from 6.7% for 1969) the government hoped to curb inflationary pressures.

Argentina's economic strength clearly lay in foreign trade. January–June exports, worth $947 million against $877 million in January–June 1969, largely reflected bumper 1969–70 harvests of grain and oilseeds. Imports rose less than in 1969, partly because of the lower economic growth rate and partly because of higher import costs resulting from devaluation.

Major projects under way included the El Chocón-Cerros Colorados hydroelectric-irrigation complex (planned capacity: 600,000 kw. by 1973; 1.2 million kw. by 1978). As part of its second stage, another hydroelectric plant was to be built between 1972 and 1978 at Planicie Banderita on the Neuquén River. In June, Industrias Dow Argentina (a Dow Chemical subsidiary) began construction of its $100 million petrochemical plant at Bahía Blanca.　　(W. Bn.)

ENCYCLOPÆDIA BRITANNICA FILMS. *Argentina (People of the Pampa)* (1957).

ARGENTINA

Education. (1967) Primary, pupils 3,206,625, teachers 158,858; secondary, pupils 189,754, teachers 29,093; vocational, pupils 454,743, teachers 64,653; teacher training, students 203,-399, teachers 24,357; higher (including 14 universities), students 264,048, teaching staff 16,307.

Finance. Monetary unit: new peso (introduced on Jan. 1, 1970; 1 new peso = 100 old pesos), with an exchange rate of 4 new pesos to U.S. $1 (9.60 new pesos = £1 sterling). Gold, SDRs, and foreign exchange, central bank: (March 1970) U.S. $501 million; (March 1969) U.S. $712 million. Budget (1969 est.): revenue 9,773,000,000 new pesos; expenditure 205 million new pesos. Gross national product: (1968) 61.1 billion new pesos; (1967) 52,150,000,000 new pesos. Money supply: (March 1970) 15,260,000,000 new pesos; (March 1969) 14,020,000,000 new pesos. Cost of living (Buenos Aires; 1963 = 100): (May 1970) 366; (May 1969) 325.

Foreign Trade. (1969) Imports 5,516,320,000 new pesos; exports 5,642,130,000 new pesos. Import sources: U.S. 22%; Brazil 11%; West Germany 11%; Italy 7%; U.K. 6%. Export destinations: Italy 14%; Netherlands 10%; U.K. 10%; U.S. 9%; Brazil 8%; Chile 5%; Spain 5%; West Germany 5%. Main exports: cereals 26%; meat 19%; hides and skins 6%.

Transport and Communications. Roads (1968) 215,304 km. Motor vehicles in use (1968): passenger 1,152,300; commercial 652,-400. Railways: (1968) 42,000 km.; traffic (1969) 14,128,000,000 passenger-km., freight 12,948,000,000 net ton-km. Air traffic (1968): 1,748,777,000 passenger-km.; freight 40,058,000 net ton-km. Shipping (1969): merchant vessels 100 gross tons and over 319; gross tonnage 1,-217,646. Telephones (Dec. 1968) 1,599,861. Radio receivers (Dec. 1968) 9 million. Television receivers (Dec. 1968) 2.5 million.

Agriculture. Production (in 000; metric tons; 1969; 1968 in parentheses): wheat 5,700 (5,-740); corn 6,900 (6,560); sorghum 2,579 (2,-033); barley 523 (556); oats c. 381 (490); potatoes 2,339 (1,967); sugar, raw value (1969–70) 978, (1968–69) 936; linseed 520 (510); sunflower seed 876 (940); cotton, lint 96 (72); oranges 1,029 (816); apples 436 (470); wine (1968) 1,951, (1967) 2,817; tobacco 52 (62); beef and veal (1968) 2,579, (1967) 2,564; cheese (1968) c. 180, (1967) 157; wool, greasy (1968) 174, (1967) 190; quebracho extract (1968) 123, (1967) 119. Livestock (in 000; June 1969): cattle c. 51,600; sheep c. 47,600; pigs c. 3,900; horses (June 1968) c. 3,700; chickens (1968–69) c. 33,000.

Industry. Index of manufacturing (1963 = 100): (1969) 151; (1968) 140. Fuel and power (in 000; 1969): crude oil 18,096 metric tons; coal 521 metric tons; natural gas 5,328,000 cu.m.; electricity (excluding most industrial production) 15,225,000 kw-hr. Production (in 000; metric tons; 1969): cement 4,347; crude steel 1,698; cotton yarn 76; passenger cars (including assembly; units): 156; commercial vehicles (including assembly; units) 60.

Art Exhibitions

Gallery-going became more and more popular in 1970 as exhibitions proliferated everywhere. The days of the enormous loan retrospectives seemed to be numbered, since the insurance costs and transportation risks involved in lending tended to make many museums more reluctant to send works of art long distances. But this gave new impetus to the organization of smaller exhibitions, concentrating on single aspects of artists or small groups of artists. More galleries experimented with mixed-media exhibitions making use of the wonders of modern technology.

One of the largest and most magnificent exhibitions of the year was, fittingly, the exhibition at the Metropolitan Museum of Art in New York entitled "19th-Century America." It was the third of the Met's centenary exhibitions. (Others were the New York School show held in the autumn of 1969 and, in 1970, "The Year 1200," devoted to art of the period 1180–1220.) The exhibition included architecture, painting, sculpture, and the decorative arts. The painting and sculpture section included many significant works in the history of American art. Works included portraits by Gilbert Stuart and J. S. Copley, landscapes of the Hudson River School, the famous "Gross Clinic," and many portraits by Thomas Eakins, paintings by Winslow Homer, and sculpture by Hiram Powers and John Rogers. The furniture section was equally impressive, ranging from the utilitarian everyday furniture of the early settlers to magnificent pieces from the Federal period and early pioneers of the modern movement, including the Green brothers and Gustave Stickley. Decorative pieces included some splendid glass objects by Louis Comfort Tiffany.

An exhibition entitled "Masterpieces of Painting from the Museum of Fine Arts, Boston," ran concurrently at the Met. Part of the joint centennial celebrations of the Met and Boston's Museum of Fine Arts, it included a fine selection of masterpieces from the Boston collection.

"The Reality of Appearance" was the title of an exhibition devoted to "The Trompe l'Oeil Tradition in American Painting" at the Whitney Museum of American Art, New York, from mid-May to mid-July. It focused on the work of William Harnett, J. F. Peto, and John Haberle. It was shown earlier in the year at the National Gallery, Washington, D.C., and was scheduled to go on to San Francisco and Detroit.

Frederick R. Spencer (1806–75) was the subject of an exhibition sponsored by the Munson-Williams-Proctor Institute and the Oneida Historical Society of Utica, N.Y., at Foundation Elms, Utica. This lesser-known American painter was particularly notable for his fine portraits. The Munson-Williams-Proctor Institute also mounted a memorial retrospective of the work of the 20th-century American artist Charles Burchfield. The University of Maryland Art Gallery exhibited 48 drawings and paintings by the 19th-century French artist Thomas Couture, with a section devoted to his American pupils.

One of the outstanding college collections in the U.S., that of the Smith College Museum of Art, Northampton, Mass., toured the U.S. during 1970 while the college prepared to build a new museum to house it. The exhibition was entitled "Nineteenth- and Twentieth-Century Paintings from Smith Col-

A.F.P. FROM PICTORIAL PARADE

"The Dance," a painting from the exhibition of works by Henri Matisse held at the Grand Palais in Paris, April 20 through September 21.

lege" and consisted largely of French and American works.

"Selections from the Collection of Nathan Cummings" were on view at the National Gallery and at the Metropolitan Museum of Art in the summer. This outstanding modern collection included works by Daumier, Manet, Pissarro, Degas, Monet, and Kandinsky. Other modern art exhibitions included a retrospective of the work of the Romanian sculptor Constantin Brancusi at the Art Institute of Chicago and two Van Gogh exhibitions, one at Philadelphia and another at Columbus, O. "The Morton D. May Collection of 20th-Century German Masters" was on view at the Marlborough-Gerson Gallery in New York in the winter and later in the year at the City Art Museum, St. Louis, Mo. One of the most remarkable private collections devoted to German Expressionism, the May collection contained works by Max Beckmann, Max Pechstein, Erich Heckel (*see* Obituaries), Ernst Kirchner, and others. Many of the same German artists were included in the first museum exhibition in the U.S. to be devoted to the work of Die Brücke, the pioneering group of 20th-century German Expressionists. The exhibition was assembled by the Cornell University Art Museum and was shown also at Rochester, N.Y.

The Fogg Museum in Cambridge, Mass., celebrated the bicentenary of the Italian artist Giambattista Tiepolo with an exhibition of 104 drawings by Tiepolo and his circle, mainly from American collections. The exhibition included problem drawings as well as typical examples from his middle and later years.

In a very different spirit was "N-Dimensional Space," held at the Finch College Museum of Art, New York, in the spring. Subtitled "An exhibition of holograms and lasers with an historical examination of this incredible new technology," the show included holograms by Robert Indiana, Bruce Nauman, and George Ortman. A studio was established in Ann Arbor, Mich., by a scientist and two artists to encourage artists to experiment in holography. "Art and Technology," an exhibition in the U.S. pavilion at Expo 70 in Osaka, Jap., comprised the works of nine American artists: Roy Lichtenstein, Claes Oldenburg, Robert Rauschenberg, Tony Smith, Andy Warhol, Robert Whitman, Rockne Krebs, Newton Harrison, and Boyd Mefferd.

The work of American Pop artists was attracting renewed attention everywhere, and attempts were

NISHAN BICHAJIAN, COURTESY,
CENTER FOR ADVANCED VISUAL
STUDIES, MASSACHUSETTS
INSTITUTE OF TECHNOLOGY

Cybernetic sculpture
by Wen-Ying Tsai
from the show
"Explorations"
at the Smithsonian's
National Collection
of Fine Arts.

made to evaluate their contribution to modern art. The Pasadena (Calif.) Art Museum organized a major exhibition of the work of Andy Warhol, concentrating on the serial aspect of his production: multiple flower images, soup cans, etc. The show traveled to Chicago, Eindhoven, Neth., Paris, and London and was to conclude its tour at the Whitney Museum during April 1971. Meanwhile, visitors to the Whitney in April 1970 were treated to a retrospective of the work of Jim Dine, including painting, assemblages, drawings, and prints by this celebrated pioneer of "happenings."

In May the Tate Gallery, London, featured the work of three Los Angeles artists, Larry Bell, Robert Irwin, and Doug Wheeler. The show consisted of three complete environments, dealing with the limits of perception and illusion. In the summer the Tate held a retrospective of the work of Claes Oldenburg, the American Pop artist best known for his giant hamburgers. The exhibition was organized by the Museum of Modern Art, New York. Two London exhibitions dealt with English Pop Art: the Richard Hamilton retrospective at the Tate and a David Hockney show at the Whitechapel. The retrospective, which was also shown in the Netherlands and Switzerland, covered 20 years of Hamilton's work. The Hayward Gallery, London, held a Frank Stella show in August. Sponsored by the Arts Council, the exhibition consisted of 38 large paintings covering the last 12 years of Stella's output. They were all antiabstract Expressionist, showing

Stella's interest in flat pattern making and acid high-keyed colour.

In the autumn the Arts Council exhibited an "International Survey of Kinetic Art" at the Hayward Gallery. "Legible City," an exhibition devoted to the exploration of printed words in the urban environment, was mounted at the Institute of Contemporary Arts, London, from mid-October to December. It was "designed to take a searching and thoroughly irreverent look at London, Britain's largest and wordiest urban specimen." The Institute of Contemporary Arts continued to put on shows that excited comment. In the spring it exhibited 347 erotic engravings done by Picasso in 1968.

Early in 1970 the Hayward Gallery was the setting for a large Rodin show. Many of the less familiar pieces of sculpture and a number of drawings were included in this Arts Council exhibition. All 34 paintings by Thomas Gainsborough in the royal collection were on display at the Queen's Gallery, Buckingham Palace. This exquisite small show consisted predominantly of portraits. The National Portrait Gallery, London, held an amusing exhibition entitled "Drawn and Quartered: The World of the British Newspaper Cartoon." Also in 1970, large crowds queued at the same gallery to see Pietro Annigoni's controversial portrait of Queen Elizabeth II. The Victoria and Albert Museum held a large centennial exhibition devoted to Charles Dickens in the summer. Another fine Dickens exhibition was mounted by the Pierpont Morgan Library in New York.

One of the more exciting shows of the year was the long-awaited Museum of Modern Art exhibition of the work of Hector Guimard, the French art nouveau architect famous for designing the Paris Métro stations. It brought together furniture, drawings, photographs, and decorative objects and could be seen at the Museum of Modern Art from March to May and then in San Francisco and Toronto. It was scheduled to go on to the Musée des Arts Décoratifs in Paris in early 1971. The Busch-Reisinger Museum, Cambridge, Mass., explored German art nouveau in an exhibition of Jugendstil, linked with a survey of art nouveau printing and book design held concurrently at the Houghton Library, Harvard. The Villa Stuck, Munich, showed "Illustrations of the Jugendstil in Munich."

Several important exhibitions were held in Paris during the year. The Grand Palais paid tribute to 82-year-old Marc Chagall with a large exhibition of his work, concentrating on the familiar subjects repeated in his paintings. At the same time the Galerie Vision Nouvelle showed the 105 poetic engravings of the Bible on which Chagall worked from 1930 to 1956. An exhibition of highly coloured canvases by the Flemish Expressionists was presented at the Orangerie in the early spring. Included were works by James Ensor, Frits Van den Berghe, Constant Permeke, and Henri Evenepoel. In March the Institut Néerlandais in Paris exhibited 19 paintings and many drawings by the Dutch artist Pieter Saenredam (1597–1665), known for his mathematically precise interiors of Dutch churches.

Two important exhibitions of African art were held in 1970. The International Exhibitions Foundation circulated a large exhibition of African sculpture sponsored by the ambassadors of 34 African nations, which was seen in several U.S. cities. It included the great bronze seated figure of a man of Ife, probably a king, moved from its permanent shrine on the Niger River and described as perhaps "the most remarkable work

"The Great American Pastime," a satiric comment by Tomiyo Sasaki at the Montreal Museum of Fine Arts, includes exaggerated papier-mâché figures and a real colour television set.

GARRY FAIRBAIRN—CANADIAN PRESS

of art ever found in Africa south of the Sahara." In January the Museum of Art of the Carnegie Institute, Pittsburgh, Pa., held a show drawn from the Jay C. Leff Collection of Black African Art.

The Mount Trust Collection of Chinese Art was exhibited at the Victoria and Albert Museum during the winter. The collection, formed by Vivian Bulkeley-Johnson, includes a wide range of ceramic and bronze wares from the earliest periods to the Ch'ing dynasty. The China House Gallery of the China Institute in New York held an exhibition of nearly 100 Chinese painted enamels drawn from private collections.

An exhibition entitled "1,000 Years of Art in Poland" was held at the Royal Academy, London, in the winter. It introduced Londoners to many unfamiliar aspects of the development of Polish art. The largest exhibition organized by Polish museums outside Poland, the show included particularly fine textiles, glass, silver, and armour from the Renaissance and Baroque periods, as well as a section devoted to painting and sculpture of the 20th century.

One of the most important exhibitions of modern art held in Italy was the large show devoted to Giorgio de Chirico in the Palazzo Reale, Milan. His personal surrealistic vision was represented by paintings, drawings, etchings, and some pieces of sculpture. In Florence a small exhibition of drawings in the Loggia Rucellai included fine works by Baccio Bandinelli, Guercino, and Aniello Falcone, as well as many by lesser-known artists. Also in Florence, the Gabinetto Disegni e Stampe of the Uffizi held an exhibition of drawings by Raphael and other Italian artists from the Museé des Beaux-Arts, Lille, France.

"Late Gothic in Cologne and on the Lower Rhine" at the Kunsthalle, Cologne, W.Ger., covered the range of Rhenish art at the end of the Middle Ages. The great late-15th-century painting "Martyrdom of St. Ursula," which gives one of the earliest views of Cologne, was lent by the Victoria and Albert Museum. Many other exhibits came from churches in the Rhineland. The collection of 71 paintings and 49 drawings by Dutch and Flemish masters belonging to the Essen publisher Herbert Girardet was shown at the Wallraf-Richartz Museum in Cologne in February and March.

In Spain an exhibition of 17th-century Italian painting was held at the Casón of the Buen Retiro, Madrid, in April and May. Two hundred canvases were assembled, a number from provincial museums and churches. The National Gallery in Prague, Czech., celebrated the centenary of Matisse's birth with an exhibition of 14 paintings and 7 drawings. Works were lent from the collections of the Hermitage, Leningrad, and the Pushkin Museum, Moscow. (S. Mɪ.)

See also Museums and Galleries; Photography.

Encyclopædia Britannica Films. *The Louvre* (1965); *Michelangelo* (1965); *Meaning in Modern Painting* (1967); *The Artist at Work—Jacques Lipchitz Master Sculptor* (1968); *Henry Moore—The Sculptor* (1969); *Siqueiros— "El Maestro"* (1969); *Richard Hunt—Sculptor* (1970); *Interpretations* (1970).

Art Sales

The steady rise in salesroom prices of the last few years was not maintained in 1970 except for works of the very highest category. Sotheby's of London reported only a marginal increase in total turnover for the season, £25,356,484 as against £25,082,520 in 1968–69, although they had added such sidelines as "railwayana" and racehorses. Christie's, however,

made a 31% increase in turnover with a total of £19,999,956, a remarkable achievement in a difficult year. Both these firms included "bought-in" lots in their totals, a practice questioned by the London press during the year. However, it was argued that since auctioneers acted for the vendors and received commission on unsold items, these were part of their business and turnover.

Parke-Bernet in New York, although owned by Sotheby's, did not follow this practice. Their season's total of $38,534,966, an increase of 23% over the previous year, did not include any bought-in lots. However, many items had failed to reach their reserve price, particularly in the spring and early summer sales. It was estimated that if Parke-Bernet had included all bought-in lots their total would have been 20% higher.

In spite of the trend, huge prices were paid for celebrated works. A world record auction price of $5,540,000 was paid at Christie's on November 27 for Velázquez' portrait of his assistant, Juan de Pareja, traditionally called "The Slave of Velázquez." The purchaser was the Wildenstein Gallery of New York City. Alec Wildenstein, vice-president of the gallery, said that his great-grandfather had wanted the picture and that, rumours to the contrary, the gallery would keep it. An art investment company, Artemis, based in Luxembourg, paid £430,500 at Christie's for a small painting by Georges Seurat entitled "Les Poseuses." A world record price for a pastel by Degas was paid at Parke-Bernet's when "Danseuse sur la pointe (Premier sujet)" went for $550,000.

Also at Parke-Bernet's, the previous world record prices for four painters' work were broken with the sale of "Le Cyprès et l'arbre en fleurs" by Van Gogh for $1.3 million, "Fête des fleurs à Nice" by Henri Matisse for $230,000, "Portrait aux bras levés" by Kees van Dongen for $92,500, and "Paysage Charbonneux" by Jean Dubuffet for $61,000. In Paris, Rheims and Laurin sold a painting by Georges Braque, "Nature morte: pommes et pichet," at the Palais Galliéra for Fr. 266,000. Ader and Picard sold "La Bouteille de rhum," signed and dated 1911 by Picasso, for Fr. 1,130,000. A world auction record for a U.S. artist was set when Thomas Eakins' "Cowboys of the Badlands" brought $210,000 at Parke-Bernet.

Other modern works reached new values; $150,000 was paid for "Femme de Venise I," a bronze by Alberto Giacometti, at Parke-Bernet's, and $60,000 for a large painting by Andy Warhol of "Campbell Soup Can with Peeling Label." In London £16,000 was paid at Sotheby's for "Good Friday, Daisy Nook" by L. S. Lowry, and £18,500 for "Dog, 1952" by Francis Bacon. Among old masters, Rembrandt's "Portrait of an Old Man, said to be Harmen Gerritsz van Rijn" was sold for £315,000 at Christie's. Sotheby's sold a fine miniature of a lady by Hans Holbein the Younger for £21,000.

The new rush for well-known watercolours was notable. Sotheby's sold a large one of Lake Geneva and Mont Blanc by J. M. W. Turner for £31,000. Another by Turner, of Ely Cathedral, which Christie's had sold in 1937 for 630 guineas, fetched 10,000 guineas. Phillips, Son and Neale, London, sold a pastel by Édouard Vuillard, "A View of Ventimille," for £2,000. Among prints, Christie's sold an etching by Giorgio Morandi, "Grande natura morta con la lampada a destra," signed and dated 1928, for £1,785. In Cologne, Kunsthaus Lempertz sold a signed lithograph by Marc Chagall for DM. 5,500, and a painting dated 1663 by Qu. G. van Brekelenkam, "Die Fisch-verkäuferin," for DM. 50,000.

A historic diamond was sold in New York: the 43.38-carat Nassak stone, once set in the eye of a Hindu statue near Bombay, was bought by Edward Hand, owner of a New York trucking firm, for $500,-000; he described it as "a bargain." The Mancini pearls, a pair of pearl and diamond drop earrings, were sold by Christie's in Geneva for SFr. 320,000.

Silver suffered a severe drop in value, especially English 18th-century pieces which had risen dramatically in 1968–69. Nevertheless, a record price of £78,000 was paid at Christie's for an unequaled Charles I inkstand. Unusual French glass paperweights continued to change hands at high prices in London. In March a world record price was made with the sale at Sotheby's of a Clichy lily-of-the-valley weight for £8,500. The fashion for Tiffany glass objects continued to grow. Parke-Bernet's sold a Tiffany wisteria lamp for $16,000. (WA. Ls.)

Book Sales. Among medieval books sold during 1969–70, a fine copy of Schedel's *Chronica*, 1493, in contemporary pigskin, brought the high price of 50,000 kroner at the sale in Oslo (October 1969) of the library of Jonas Skjøngaard. Another very early printed book, the *Opera* of Lactantius, published at Subiaco near Rome in 1465, was bought by a U.S. firm, the House of El Dieff, for £22,000 at Christie's in July 1970.

The Sassoon collection of Hebrew printed books, sold at Sotheby's (June 1970), brought £121,414 for

UPI COMPIX

Auctioneer at Christie's in London solicits bids for the Velázquez portrait of Juan de Pareja (right) on Nov. 27, 1970. Selling price for the painting was a record $5,540,000.

186 lots. The two top prices of £11,000 were for copies on vellum of the Bible printed at Bologna in 1482, the second appearance of any part of the Hebrew Bible, and an imperfect imprint from Hijar, *c.* 1490. In July 1970 Sotheby's sold an Armenian Bible on vellum, illuminated at Isfahan, for £8,580. The Kevorkian Foundation's sale of Oriental manuscripts held at Sotheby's in December 1969 included a Persian miniature of the early 14th century, a single leaf from the "Demotte" *Shah-Nama* of Firdausi, bought for £30,000 by the U.S. dealer M. Mahboubian.

An English poem of 63 lines in the hand of John Donne, found among papers of the duke of Manchester, was sold at Sotheby's on June 23, 1970, for £23,000; it was first published in the 1633 edition of Donne's poems as "A Letter to the Lady Carey and Mrs. Essex Riche." This was the longest piece of work in his hand known to have survived.

In Marburg, W.Ger. (November 1969), a series of

Association Football:
see Football

18 letters and 15 postcards written by Franz Kafka to Felix Weltsch brought DM. 56,000. The following month, when the third part of the Rothschild collection of autographs was sold in Paris, a 1,065-page manuscript by Jean-Paul Sartre, on Cuban affairs, fetched Fr. 16,000 and a series of 11 letters written by Stéphane Mallarmé, Fr. 40,000. Other autographs sold in Paris included (June 1970) a letter by Descartes (Fr. 13,500), another by Dostoevski, and a receipt signed by Ambroise Paré (Fr. 4,500).

The second work to be printed in Pennsylvania, Thomas Budd's *Good Order Established . . .* , 1685, reached $26,000 at Parke-Bernet's in October 1969. Also at Parke-Bernet's, on Jan. 20, 1970, the second printed draft of the Constitution of the United States, Philadelphia, Sept. 12, 1787, four leaves, was sold for $160,000.

A collection of 3,750 books and pamphlets printed in the reign (1702–14) of Queen Anne, formed by Peter Smithers, the author of *Life of Joseph Addison* (1954), was sold at Sotheby's on Nov. 24, 1969, for £67,000. The next stroke of the auctioneer's hammer on the same day disposed of a single work, a remarkable copy of Audubon's *Birds of America*, which crossed the Atlantic at £90,000. The *fermiers généraux* illustrated edition of La Fontaine's *Contes et Nouvelles*, 1762, bound in contemporary morocco with Madame du Barry's coat of arms, went for Fr. 91,000 in Paris on April 27, 1970.

Two royal libraries were auctioned in June 1970. Rare books from the library of the Belgian reigning family were sold at Sotheby's, while in Hamburg, W.Ger., Hauswedel displayed the first portion of the library of King Ernest Augustus of Hanover. In London, Humboldt and Bonpland's *Voyage aux régions équinoxiales du nouveau continent*, 1805–25, 29 vol. only, brought £5,000; Berleze's *Iconographie de genre Camellia*, 1841–43, £4,600; and a complete *Topographia* of M. Zeiller, £6,000.

Scientific and medical books did very well. A sale at Sotheby's (October 1969) of the Royal Medical Society of Edinburgh's library featured a copy of James Parkinson's *Essay on the Shaking Palsy*, 1817, which fetched £2,000. Also at Sotheby's (June 1970) a first edition of I. P. Semmelweiss' work on puerperal fever, *Die Ätiologie, der Begriff und die Prophylaxis des Kindbettfiebers*, 1861, brought £1,200. (P. Bs.)

Astronautics

After the Apollo 11 and Apollo 12 lunar landing triumphs of 1969, the year 1970 was one of retrenchment and disappointment. In the United States, a single attempt at landing another Apollo on the moon failed, the budget of the National Aeronautics and Space Administration (NASA) was tightened to a seven-year low, and a general feeling of apathy grew as the country became increasingly concerned with its unpopular Indochina war and growing internal problems. In the Soviet Union a single Soyuz was orbited and, although it broke world endurance records, it did not appear to mark a major advance or turning point in the country's space program. The successful retrieval of lunar rock and soil samples by the unmanned Luna 16 spacecraft in September, an important technological feat, may have served notice that the U.S.S.R. did not plan early manned flights to the moon. The Soviets provided additional evidence of this in November when they soft-landed Luna 17 on the moon and then deployed from it Lunokhod 1, a vehicle controlled from the earth that moved on its own power over the lunar surface and performed various experiments. At best, 1970 was a year of transition; at worst, the beginning of what hopefully would be only a short-term pause in astronautical progress.

Reduced budgets in the U.S. space program (under $3.3 billion) contributed significantly to a critical situation in that nation's aerospace industry. Cutbacks in the defense program and in the commercial aviation field hit at the same time, compounding the difficulties facing aerospace scientists, engineers, technicians, and support personnel. From a civilian employment of well over 400,000 at the height of the Apollo program, about 250,000 had been laid off and had had to seek jobs elsewhere. Such space-oriented communities as the Cocoa-Melbourne-Orlando complex in Florida; Huntsville, Ala.; and Seattle, Wash., were particularly hard hit. And in Cambridge, Mass., the entire NASA Electronics Research Center was ordered closed. The lamentable situation was highlighted when NASA Administrator Thomas O. Paine announced that he would resign and return to private industry.

The Soviet Union continued a relatively cautious program. In January Boris N. Petrov, a leading scientist, announced that due to budget reductions the Soviet space program would continue at a modest pace and that as far as lunar exploration was concerned, "prime emphasis . . . will go to unmanned spacecraft." The only country to announce a significant increase in space spending during the year was West Germany. For the five-year period ending Dec. 31, 1974, it planned to spend $422.4 million, $104 million more than during the preceding five years. Within its budget were joint programs with the French (the Symphonie communications satellite) and the U.S. (the Helios solar probe). Overall, 1970 space expenditures (national programs, European Space Research Organization [ESRO], and European Launcher Development Organization [ELDO]) dropped from $310 million in 1969 to $297 million in 1970. France operated within its lowest budget in four years.

Shortages in funding devoted to space flight helped provide incentives for Western European organizations such as ELDO and ESRO to seek ways of cooperating with the U.S. In midyear meetings at Bonn, W.Ger., and Brussels, European experts deliberated over U.S. post-Apollo programs, particularly plans for space shuttles and space stations, and agreed to consider further a NASA offer of cooperation. ESRO Director Hermann Bondi predicted that all European space organizations could be combined into a consortium, which would work closely with NASA. During a meeting in Venice, Italy, in September, and at the International Astronautical Federation Congress in Constance, W.Ger., in October, similar sentiments were expressed. At the practical, industrial working level, Messerschmitt-Bölkow-Blohm of West Germany and the British Aircraft Corp. began assisting North American Rockwell Corp. engineers in studies of designs for a space shuttle.

Manned Space Flight. The Apollo lunar exploration program was beset with difficulties, uncertainties, and cutbacks during 1970. The only flight undertaken was Apollo 13, which began on April 11 as the giant Saturn V launch vehicle roared to life at Cape Kennedy, Fla. Only minutes later, Apollo 13, with spacecraft commander James A. Lovell, Jr. (*see* BIOGRAPHY), lunar module pilot Fred W. Haise, Jr., and command module pilot John L. Swigert, Jr., aboard,

was inserted into orbit around the earth; about $2\frac{1}{2}$ hours after launch the still-attached S IVB third stage was reignited to provide the final boost toward the moon.

The transposition maneuver (removing the lunar module, code-named Aquarius, from the S IVB adapter) was carried out efficiently, and soon Apollo 13 was coasting toward the moon on a path so accurate that the first planned course adjustment was cancelled. Later in the mission, the craft underwent a hybrid transfer maneuver to facilitate landing in the difficult Fra Mauro region of the moon; to do this, the service module's propulsion system provided a 15-ft.-per-sec. velocity change designed to lower the command module's closest approach to the moon from 210 to 59 nautical miles and place the craft on a "non-free-return" trajectory. This meant that should no further propulsive maneuver be made during the flight, the craft would not swing around the moon and return directly to the earth on a "free-return" trajectory but instead would miss our planet by 2,950 mi. (However, a shift back to a free-return trajectory was within the capability of both the service module propulsion system and the lunar module descent stage propulsion system.) So accurate was the hybrid transfer that a scheduled course correction was canceled.

April 12, the day after launch, passed without incident. Early on the evening of April 13, the astronauts pressurized the lunar module Aquarius, and Lovell and Haise passed from the command module (named Odyssey) through the connecting tunnel while checking all systems for the forthcoming landing. Suddenly, as Lovell was moving through the tunnel on his way back from Aquarius to Odyssey, a loud explosion was heard. All three astronauts quickly gathered in Odyssey to study the instruments in an effort to determine what had happened. Noting that one of the main electrical systems aboard was degrading, Swigert radioed the information to the earth, quickly turning a routine flight into one of the most exciting episodes in space history.

Within eight seconds of the explosion, pressure in one of the service module's two cryogenic oxygen tanks had dropped to zero. Together with the cryogenic hydrogen tanks, they fed the required supplies to the craft's three fuel cells which were needed for the generation of electrical power, oxygen for breathing, and drinking water.

About an hour after the accident, mission control in Houston announced that "we are now looking toward an alternate mission, swinging around the moon and using the lunar module power systems because of the situation that has developed here this evening." The astronauts were to move into Aquarius, which would serve as a lifeboat, while the disabled Apollo 13 swung around the moon and headed homeward. All thoughts of a lunar landing had long since been abandoned.

The anxiety for the safety of the astronauts was felt in every corner of the globe, and millions of persons remained glued to television and radio sets as the perilous journey unfolded. Still three days away from the earth, the astronauts moved into the lunar module Aquarius, which they powered up before shutting down the command module Odyssey to conserve the latter's emergency battery power for the atmospheric reentry maneuver at the end of the mission. Only the command module could pass through the earth's atmosphere; the lunar module would have to be discarded, along with the service module, before

UPI COMPIX

Drawing of the Soviet Union's Lunokhod 1 leaving the landing stage of Luna 17, which landed on the moon Nov. 17, 1970. Movement of the unmanned, eight-wheeled vehicle is controlled by radio from earth.

Table I. Major Satellites and Space Probes Launched Oct. 21, 1969–Sept. 30, 1970

Name/country/ launch vehicle/ scientific designation	Launch date, lifetime*	Physical characteristics				Experiments	Initial orbital data			
		Weight (kg.)†	Shape	Diameter	Length or height		Perigee (km.)†	Apogee (km.)†	Period (min.)	Inclination to Equator (degrees)
GRS-A (Azur)/W. Ger./ Scout/1969-97A	11/8/69	79 (157)	Cylinder with truncated end cone	75 cm. (30 in.)	1.1 m. (44.4 in.)	Investigation of variations in energy and intensity of charged particles in Van Allen radiation belt	386 (238.5)	3,116 (1,954.6)	125.5	103.0
Apollo 12/U.S./Saturn V/ 1969-99A	11/14/69 11/24/69	48,380 (96,795)	Cylinder with conical end	3 m. (12 ft.)	9 m. (36.7 ft.)	Second manned lunar landing in Apollo program	Landed on moon after 110 hr. 20 min. flight and orbit of moon			
Skynet A/U.K./Thor-Delta/ 1969-101A	11/22/69	143 (285)	Cylinder	135 cm. (54 in.)	50 cm. (32 in.)	Communications satellite for U.K. defense forces	35,795 (21,556)	35,885 (22,792)	1,438.8	2.4
Intercosmos 2/U.S.S.R./ B-1/1969-110A	12/26/69 6/7/70	‡	Octagon with hemispherical ends	108 cm. (42 in.).	178 cm. (70 in.)	Investigations of the ionosphere with instruments supplied by scientists of the U.S.S.R. and Eastern Europe	205 (128)	1,096 (685)	98.5	48.4
Intelsat 3 (F-6)/U.S./Thor-Delta/ 1970-003A	1/14/70	1,160 (322)	Cylinder	140 cm. (56 in.)	103 cm. (41 in.)	Communications satellite	35,782 (21,469)	35,791 (21,475)	1,436.1	0.4
ITOS 1/U.S./Thor-Delta/ 1970-008A	1/23/70	337 (675)	Box-shape with three solar cell panels	‡	‡	Weather satellite capable of taking nighttime pictures of earth's cloud cover	1,432 (890)	1,478 (919)	115	102
Sert 2/U.S./Thor-Agena O/ 1970-009A	2/4/70	1,650 (3,300)	Cylinder with two solar cell panels	1.5 m. (60 in.)	10.4 m. (35 ft.)	Continuously operate ion thrusters in space for six months	988 (620)	1,010 (627)	105.2	99.1
Ohsumi/Japan/Lambda I V/ 1970-011A	2/11/70	11.5 (24)	Truncated cone	40 cm. (16 in.)	70 cm. (28 in.)	Charged particle counters, beacon transmitter	525 (326)	5,136 (3,191)	116.1	31.4
Molniya 1 (13)/U.S.S.R./‡/ 1970-013A	2/19/70	1,100 (2,200)	Cylinder with conical ends	1.2 m. (4 ft.)	3.6 m. (12 ft.)	Communications satellite	335 (208)	39,309 (24,425)	703.4	65.3
DIAL (WIKA)/W. Ger./Diamant B/1970-017A	3/10/70	126 (253)	Octagon with cylindrical centre	95 cm. (37 in.)	155 cm. (46 in.)	Scientific studies of space near earth	308 (191)	1,613 (1,002)	104.3	5.4
Meteor 3/U.S.S.R./A-1/ 1970-019A	3/17/70	‡	Cylinder with two solar cell panels	1.5 m. (5 ft.)	4.8 m. (16 ft.)	Weather satellite	537 (334)	633 (393)	96.3	81.1
Natosat 1/Nato/Thor-Delta/ 1970-021A	3/20/70	263 (535)	Cylinder	1.4 m. (4.4 ft.)	0.8 m. (2.4 ft.)	Communications satellite for NATO forces	34,421 (21,393)	36,619 (22,759)	1,410	0.3
Nimbus 4/U.S./Thor-Agena D/ 1970-025A	4/8/70	745 (1,489)	Octagon with two solar cell panels	1.5 m. (5 ft.)	2.9 m. (9.5 ft.)	Weather satellite	1,087 (676)	1,098 (682)	107.1	99.9
Vela/U.S./Titan IIIC/ 1970-027A	4/8/70	385 (770)	26-sided polygon	140 cm. (56 in.)	115 cm. (46 in.)	Search for evidence of nuclear testing in space	111,077 (66,646)	111,568 (66,940)	6,697.7	32.8
Vela/U.S./Titan IIIC/ 1970-027B	4/8/70	385 (770)	26-sided polygon	140 cm. (56 in.)	115 cm. (46 in.)	Search for evidence of nuclear testing in space	110,828 (66,497)	111,731 (67,039)	6,694	32.6
Apollo 13/U.S./Saturn V/ 1970-029A	4/11/70 4/17/70	43,385 (96,800)	Cylinder with conical end	3 m. (12 ft.)	9 m. (36.7 ft.)	Aborted lunar landing mission	Swung around moon and returned to earth			
Intelsat 3(F-7)/U.S./Thor-Delta/ 1970-032A	4/23/70	120 (322)	Cylinder	140 cm. (56 in.)	102.5 cm. (41 in.)	Communications satellite	35,738 (22,211)	35,773 (22,233)	1,436.1	0.2
Meteor 4/U.S.S.R./‡/ 1970-037A	4/28/70	‡	Cylinder with two solar cell panels	1.5 m. (5 ft.)	4.8 m. (16 ft.)	Weather satellite	636 (395)	743 (462)	98.2	81.2
Soyuz 9/U.S.S.R./A-2/ 1970-041A	6/1/70 6/19/70	6,660 (13,320)	Two spheres in tandem with a cylinder and two solar cell panels	3.1 m. (9.8 ft.)	10.7 m. (34.3 ft.)	Manned spacecraft endurance test	236 (147)	249 (155)	89.3	51.6
Meteor 5/U.S.S.R./A-1/ 1970-047A	6/23/70	‡	Cylinder with two solar cell panels	1.5 m. (5 ft.)	4.8 m. (16 ft.)	Weather satellite	830 (516)	888 (552)	102	81.2
Molniya 1(14)/U.S.S.R./A-2e/ 1970-049A	6/26/70	1,100 (2,200)	Cylinder with conical ends	1.2 m. (4 ft.)	3.6 m. (12 ft.)	Communications satellite	468 (291)	39,233 (24,378)	704.5	65.4
Intercosmos 3/U.S.S.R./B-1/ 1970-057A	8/7/70	‡	Octagon with hemispherical ends and two solar cell panels	108 cm. (42 in.)	178 cm. (70 in.)	Investigations of the ionosphere with instruments supplied by scientists of Soviet bloc nations	200 (120)	1,192 (715)	98.7	48.4
Venera 7/U.S.S.R./Proton/ 1970-060A	8/17/70	1,200 (2,600)	Cylinder with spherical end	3 m. (12 ft.)	1.2 m. (4 ft.)	Probe to Venus	To enter orbit around the sun			
Luna 16/U.S.S.R./Proton/ 1970-072A	9/12/70 9/24/70	1,360 (3,000)	Two-stage functional structure	4.3 m. (14 ft.)	4.3 m. (14 ft.)	Landed on moon and returned rock samples to earth	Landed on moon on September 20			

*All dates are in universal time (UT).
†English units in parentheses: weight in pounds, apogee and perigee in statute miles.
‡Not available.

(M. R. S.)

the outer atmosphere was reached. In the meantime, however, the lunar module would be their home.

When the astronauts first transferred into and activated Aquarius, Apollo 13 was about 20 hours from the moon. Plans were made for transferring out of the hybrid trajectory and onto the free-return trajectory, a maneuver that was executed in the early morning hours of April 14. At mission control teams of experts worked to check out all feasible maneuvers and situations in flight simulators, feeding every plan and contingency through computers. Leaders from all parts of the world voiced concern, and from Soviet Premier Aleksei N. Kosygin came the message that "the Soviet Government has given orders to all citizens and members of the armed forces to use all necessary means to render assistance in the rescue of the American astronauts." Four Soviet ships began moving toward the planned recovery area, while French and British warships also moved to the rescue. Radio contact with the Apollo 13 was lost during the evening of April 14 as the craft swung behind the moon, passing at an altitude of 164 mi. at the closest approach. Soon afterward the spacecraft started along its return path home. Meanwhile, the long-since-discarded S IVB third stage crashed onto the moon—it had followed an independent trajectory—as part of a planned experiment to cause an artificial moonquake to aid scientists in understanding the nature of the lunar interior. When the astronauts learned from Houston of the stage's impact, they radioed back "Well, at least something worked on this flight . . . I'm sure glad we didn't have an LM impact, too!"

About two hours later the descent stage propulsion system of the lunar module was ignited for 5 seconds at 10% throttle, 21 seconds at 40% throttle, and almost 4 minutes at full throttle. This added 585 mph to Apollo 13's velocity, thereby cutting by 10 hours the length of the homeward journey and assuring a splashdown in the Pacific Ocean south of Samoa. On board the spacecraft drinking water and oxygen stores remained sufficient, as did cooling water. However, the lunar module's lithium hydroxide cartridges that removed carbon dioxide from the air would only last about 50 hours, and those from the command module were not designed to fit Aquarius. Therefore, engineers on the ground devised a makeshift adapter scheme, radioing to Apollo 13 instructions on how to attach the cartridges from the command module to the lunar module hoses. The job was done, and the astronauts reported "OK, our do-it-yourself lithium hydroxide unit is complete."

During the morning of April 15, Apollo 13 entered the region of gravitational influence of the earth, at a distance from the earth's surface of 216,277 mi. Calculations showed that the speeded-up trajectory needed an additional refinement, and so the lunar module descent propulsion system was again ignited. The adjustment was successful, and the flight wore on, with the cold, weary astronauts fitfully sleeping between receiving instructions on spacecraft separation and reentry maneuvers they would soon undergo upon approaching the earth. The first step was to jettison the service module, leaving the command and lunar modules joined together in a configuration never previously flown. Valuable photos of the damaged service module were snapped by the astronauts, who remarked, "And there's one whole side of that spacecraft missing. . . . Right by the high-gain antenna, the whole panel is blown out, almost from the base to the engine. . . . Looks like a lot of debris is just

hanging out of the side near the S-band antenna."

The astronauts then moved out of the lunar module and back into Odyssey, powering up the life-support systems that had been shut down in order to conserve them for reentry. The two modules then were separated, as pressure in the connective tunnel was permitted to force them apart. The command module, with the astronauts inside, continued onward, entered the earth's atmosphere, and splashed down on target, 142 hr. 54 min. and 41 sec. from the time the huge Saturn V had roared to life. The astronauts had no lasting ill effects from their ordeal.

After the accident NASA quickly established the Apollo 13 Review Board under the chairmanship of Edgar M. Cortright. Charged with the responsibility of reviewing the "circumstances surrounding the accident to the spacecraft . . . in order to establish the probable cause or causes of the accident and assess the effectiveness of the recovery actions," it spent approximately two months of careful investigation and deliberation before publishing its exhaustive report. The board concluded that "All indications are that an electrically initiated fire in oxygen tank No. 2 in the service module (SM) was the cause of the accident." The members felt that "the accident was not the result of a chance malfunction in a statistical sense, but rather resulted from an unusual combination of mistakes, coupled with a somewhat deficient and unforgiving design."

Among other findings, it was determined that the tank in question contained two protective thermostatic switches on the heater assembly "which were inadequate and would subsequently fail [they accidentally welded closed] during ground test operations at Kennedy Space Center." Moreover, an incident occurred at the contractor's plant that caused the tank to be jarred, causing the fill tube assembly to become loose. It was even learned that the contractor did not change the tank heater assembly switches to be compatible with a 65-v. power supply, leaving them to operate on 28 v. as with earlier models. "The thermostatic switch discrepancy was not detected by NASA, NR [North American Rockwell Corp.], or Beech [Beech Aircraft Corp.] in their review of documentation, nor did tests identify the incompatibility of the switches with the ground support equipment at KSC, since neither qualification nor acceptance testing required switch cycling under load as should have been done. It was a serious oversight in which all parties shared."

Once the failed switches could no longer function as protective thermostats, the heater tube assembly reached such a high temperature (about 1,000° F) that a short circuit was created, igniting the teflon insulation. This burned toward and then through the tank. High-pressure oxygen rushed out into Bay 4, pressurized it, and blew off the side panel of the service module. The oxygen tank system was damaged, resulting in oxygen and power loss in the command module.

At the end of August NASA announced that future Apollo command and service modules would be modified so as "to enhance their potential use in an emergency mode." Among the modifications were the installation of a 400-amp-hr. battery in the service module that could be used as an alternative power source should the primary system fail. Also, a third oxygen tank was to be added to bolster the service module's oxygen system.

In the face of budget cuts NASA not only reduced personnel in its own organization and forced reduc-

COURTESY, NASA

Apollo 13's damaged service module after being jettisoned. An entire panel on the SM was blown away by the apparent explosion of an oxygen tank, forcing crew members to use the lunar module as a lifeboat in their emergency return to earth.

tions on its many contractors and subcontractors, but it also scaled down its entire manned space flight program and in early September canceled a pair of Apollos, 15 and 19. Since the saving on the two flights involved only operational costs—the hardware had already been paid for—lunar scientists called it "chicken feed" and warned of a "national disaster." One leading scientist said that "It's like buying a Rolls Royce and then not using it because you claim you can't afford the gas."

As the U.S. lost interest in the space frontier it had played such a leading role in penetrating, the superbly trained cadre of astronauts began to be concerned about its future. Apollo 8 veteran Frank Borman left NASA to become a vice-president of Eastern Air Lines. One of the seven original Mercury astronauts and a two-time space traveler, L. Gordon Cooper, Jr., left NASA at the end of July to become president of a convention exhibit firm. Others remained with NASA but no longer stayed on flight status. Apollo 11 commander Neil A. Armstrong became deputy associate administrator for aeronautics at NASA's Office of Advanced Research and Technology, while Donn F. Eisele moved to the Langley Research Center, Hampton, Va., as technical assistant for manned flight in the Space Systems Research Division. In an effort to provide the best, most imaginative planning for the 1970s amid a climate of public antipathy and dwindling resources, NASA in March transferred space pioneer Wernher von Braun from his post as director of its George C. Marshall Space Flight Center, Huntsville, to the agency headquarters, in Washington, D.C., where he was to serve as deputy associate administrator.

Despite the restricted moon exploration program, work continued during 1970 on the lunar roving vehicle (LRV), which was to be used to transport two Apollo astronauts across the moon's surface. The four-wheel vehicle was designed to be about 10 ft. 7 in. long and nearly 6 ft. wide, and was to have a 7½-ft. wheelbase. Weighing approximately 400 lb., it was to carry the astronauts, their life-support systems, about 100 lb. of scientific gear, and up to 70 lb. of lunar soil and rock samples. With a lifetime of 54 hours, it was expected to be able to travel a total distance of approximately 75 mi. On Oct. 28, 1969, the Boeing Co. was selected as prime contractor for the LRV, with an obligation to deliver four flight-qualified vehicles beginning in late 1971.

Despite lunar program uncertainties, the post-Apollo Skylab development program continued, and

planners looked forward to the development of larger space stations that might become operational in the mid-1970s as well as space bases for the 1980s. (See Special Report.)

On June 1 the Soviet Union resumed its manned orbital flights following eight months of inactivity. Soyuz 9 was launched with a crew of Vostok 3 veteran Andrian G. Nikolayev and flight engineer Vitaly I. Sevastyanov. The two cosmonauts remained in orbit a record-breaking length of time, almost 18 days, before undergoing a successful reentry and landing sequence. According to Soviet medical releases, the men adapted themselves completely to the weightless condition after three days of flight, and then maintained their physical fitness by taking regular exercises. The flight continued without a hitch, and on June 15 the cosmonauts broke the U.S. Gemini 7 endurance record of 13 days 18 hr. and 35 min. set in December 1965.

The principal aim of the Soyuz 9 flight was to determine the effects on man of prolonged space flight, so as to be able to plan and execute space station and perhaps planetary exploration missions in future years. Of great importance was the need to determine whether man could operate extensively in the weightless environment, or if he would have to be provided with artificial gravity—either temporarily or permanently. Geological survey and meteorological observations were also conducted.

Although the flight was termed fully successful by the Soviets, the two cosmonauts experienced some difficulties with their eyesight, including an inability to perceive accurately colours—especially purple, light blue, and green. Eye coordination muscles were affected by the prolonged absence of gravity, although it was not readily apparent why.

At the end of their approximately 17⅔-day flight the cosmonauts complained of a "heavy body" feeling, and experienced a craving for "earth food." During post-flight medical examinations, they were found to have lost weight and to have developed an "instability" of their cardiovascular systems. U.S. space medical experts were particularly interested in the Soyuz 9 flight, which was more than twice as long in time as the Apollo earth-moon-earth flight and about four days longer than the record Gemini mission. Before firm plans could be made for flights to such distant objectives as Mars and for long space-station missions, it was absolutely essential to gain an understanding of how long an average astronaut can endure the zero-gravity experience without having his performance impaired and perhaps even suffering permanent physical damage.

Space Carrier Vehicles. The Saturn V carrier that launched the Apollo 13 spacecraft in April successfully performed its mission, although a study of data showed that its S II second stage suffered from excessive vibration, causing an early shutdown of the centre engine. To compensate for loss of thrust, the four outer engines burned for 34 seconds longer than planned, and the third (S IVB) stage functioned 12 seconds longer. Otherwise, the carrier's performance was virtually perfect; the premature cutoff of the engine due to the vibration did not affect the mission in any way.

When NASA canceled Apollos 15 and 19, it had to contend with the problem of what to do with the already-built Saturn Vs that were to launch them. As the U.S. Navy does with nonoperational ships, NASA decided to do with its huge carrier rockets:

continued on page 115

AFTER APOLLO, WHAT?

By Rudy Abramson

During the 1960s the widely publicized national commitment to put an American on the moon before the end of the decade, and also before the Soviet Union did so, gave the United States' space program such urgency and purpose that Congress was moved to appropriate, in peak years, more than $5 billion for the U.S. National Aeronautics and Space Administration (NASA). But as the manned space effort entered the 1970s, it was under relentless reassessment. The increasingly asked question was where should space rank in the scheme of national priorities. The answer was clear. Space exploration, as a national activity, was regarded as far less important than it had been a few years before.

By the time of Apollo 11's spectacular fulfillment of the lunar landing goal, the social problems of the U.S. were being pressed upon the public conscience as never before; there was a nationwide quest to improve the quality of life. Inflation had become the country's most persistent headache, aside from the war in Vietnam itself, and there was a seemingly sudden public conviction that environmental pollution was a national disgrace.

In this new atmosphere, it was seriously questioned whether the manned space program—the country's most celebrated single undertaking of the 1960s—was squandering limited technological talent and resources. Congress, exerting its authority more than it had in many years, began taking a tougher attitude toward nearly all high-cost engineering development programs—even those said to be vital to the national defense. Instead of justifying manned space flight as an unavoidable area of competition with the Soviet Union, public officials talked more seriously of substantive cooperation with the U.S.S.R., thus endorsing the idea of making space exploration an international pursuit.

By fiscal 1971—beginning July 1, 1970—NASA's budget had been reduced to a little more than $3 billion. Project Apollo was nearing its end; unmanned space projects were being postponed; both government and industry payrolls associated with space projects were being reduced.

The once-held dream of some officials to follow up the Apollo moon program with a similar commitment to land men on Mars had long since evaporated. A new blueprint, altogether different from the space plan of the 1960s, had solidified a year after the first moon landing. There would be no single objective like the moon landing deadline. The goal of the new approach was to develop a broad capability that could be used for practical returns: such a capability would embrace scientific research in earth orbit, and continued exploration of the moon and beyond.

Although disagreement remained over how fast the manned space program should progress and how much the U.S. could afford to spend, the general direction for the 1970s appeared to be charted. Envisioned was a new family of space transportation vehicles, designed for repeated use: a shuttle craft to operate routinely between the ground and low earth orbit; a so-called "space tug" to move such heavy objects as space stations or scientific observatories from one orbit to another or to haul cargo between the surface of the moon and a space station in lunar orbit; and a nuclear-powered shuttle for long-distance moving, such as sending a space station from earth orbit to lunar orbit, or starting a scientific payload on its way to neighbouring planets from earth orbit.

Development of the earth-to-orbit shuttle—which would also be used by the U.S. Air Force—emerged in 1970 as the first key step in developing the new post-Apollo manned space program. Close behind the shuttle in NASA's plans was a permanent space station capable of supporting a dozen or more scientists and engineers in earth orbit.

Skylab. But the slowdown in space spending has already produced a gap between the end of the Apollo moon flights and the first orbital missions of the shuttle. The bridge between these two generations is a program called Skylab. A forerunner of the permanent space station, Skylab will consist of the third stage of a Saturn V moon rocket converted into an earth orbital workshop where teams of three astronauts will work for periods up to 56 days. Carrying scientific experiments in the fields of astronomy, space physics, biology, oceanography, water management, agriculture, forestry, geology, geography, and ecology, Skylab is scheduled for launch in late 1972.

The workshop will be divided into two "stories," with living quarters and recreational facilities for the astronauts apart from the laboratory work area. Mounted outside the vehicle will be a solar telescope, which the astronauts will use to study portions of the sun's electromagnetic spectrum not visible to earthbound observatories. With the workshop, telescope equipment, and docking hardware, Skylab will stretch 117 ft. in length and have a wingspan of 90 ft. after its massive solar panels unfold to convert the sun's energy into electricity for the station.

During a lifetime of about eight months, Skylab will be used by three different astronaut teams. A day after a Saturn V lofts the workshop into an orbit about 270 nautical miles high, three astronauts, in an Apollo command module, will be launched by a smaller Saturn I booster. Afterward, they will rendezvous and dock with the workshop. Then, in a comfortable "shirt-sleeve" environment, these first visitors will live in Skylab for 28 days before returning to earth. This 28-day mission will break the previous endurance record of $17\frac{2}{3}$ days set by two Soviet cosmonauts in 1970. About two months later, a second team will fly to the laboratory for a mission lasting 56 days. A 56-day visit by the third crew will begin about a month after the second team has descended in its Apollo spacecraft.

A prime objective of the three flights is to find whether there are still unsuspected hazards in prolonged exposure to weightlessness. Through Skylab, the information will be available soon enough to use in the design of the permanent space station. If surprising physiological problems do arise from long-term weightlessness, then it might be necessary to design a permanent station that will be in constant rotation so as to produce artificial gravity.

Medical and physiological experiments will be assigned top priority on the first Skylab visit. The second crew will have solar astronomy as its number one assignment. The third will emphasize earth resources work, and will use instruments aboard the laboratory—mainly cameras—to see how well orbital observatories, manned or unmanned, can detect natural resources, identify crop diseases, and aid planners in land management.

Skylab is to be launched at a greater inclination to the Equator than any previous U.S. manned space vehicle. As a result, its earth resources cameras will be able to cover any area of the United States and most of the most heavily populated regions of the entire earth. U.S. astronauts had previously passed over the United States along a path cutting across southern California, Texas, the Gulf of Mexico, and Florida.

Because a backup Skylab is being assembled against the possibility of losing the first in a launch failure, NASA might have the opportunity of orbiting a second workshop. The first—including the cost of the backup—is expected to cost approximately $2 billion. Depending on how many changes are made, a second Skylab could be flown at a relatively low cost. A decision as to whether to fly the second workshop is expected in the summer or fall of 1971.

Apollo Cutback. Whether or not a second Skylab is launched, it would not be able to span the gap completely between Apollo and the new programs. As the budget pinch began, NASA had already dropped one of its planned moon landings. It also decided to convert a Saturn V third stage into Skylab before launch, rather than using Saturn Is and outfitting an expended upper stage as a crude workshop after it had reached orbit.

As the financial pressure became more intense, NASA decided to cut further into Apollo to keep the plans for the shuttle and space station alive. It speeded the layoff of space contractor employees and decided to mothball rocket test facilities in Mississippi and to suspend production of the Saturn V.

An earlier plan had been to fly Apollo missions through 17 and then take a year's break from exploring the moon to conduct the Skylab before concluding the Apollo program with two flights in 1974. But a cutback of two flights by NASA meant that there would be two flights to the moon in 1971, two in 1972, and then Skylab, which would be completed in June 1973. After that, the U.S. would have no manned space activity until the shuttle was ready in 1976 or 1977—unless there was a decision to fly a second Skylab. By cutting the number of moon flights, NASA officials expected that they would be able to save a total of $600 million to $900 million for work on the shuttle and space station.

Both of the scientific advisory panels consulted on the decision urged NASA to go ahead and fly its lunar missions through Apollo 19. Instead of cutting back exploration of the moon, they argued, the Skylab program should be postponed.

In a letter to NASA Administrator Thomas O. Paine, Nobel laureate Charles H. Townes, chairman of the Space Science Board, and John W. Findlay, chairman of the Lunar and Planetary Missions Board, explained the reasoning of the scientific community:

"It should be recognized," they said, "that any reduction in the number of missions will seriously threaten the ability of the total Apollo program to answer first-order scientific questions. We are concerned that a further reduction in the present Apollo may well lead to our inability to answer these questions and that the consequences of such failure for the future of the agency and, we believe, for large-scale science in this country, are incalculable."

Shuttle Program. The shuttle program NASA hopes to get approved in Congress in 1971 could cost, by the agency's own estimates, more than $6 billion. Some skeptics put the figure much higher than that. But in spite of this cost the prime motive behind the shuttle concept is to reduce for all time the cost of sending men and equipment into orbit. It may be able to reduce Saturn V's freight rate of $1,000 per pound to $20 to $50 per pound; besides that, it will be able to haul cargo from space down to earth, which conventional rockets cannot do because they are lost after launch.

Designers are aiming for a shuttle that will operate much in the fashion of a commercial airliner. It must be capable of being readied for launch in a period of two hours and must be able to make at least 100 round trips from earth to orbit without major refurbishment.

The shuttle NASA wants to build consists of two vehicles—a booster and an orbiter. Launched vertically like other rockets, the booster will carry the smaller orbiter piggyback-style to an altitude of about 200,000 ft., where they will separate. The booster will descend and, powered by jet engines, fly back to the launch base under control of a two-man crew. The orbiter will then continue on to an altitude of 100 mi. or more.

Though the orbiter will be much smaller than the powerful booster that pushes it off the ground, it will be about the size of a Boeing 707 jetliner. NASA has told contractors working on preliminary design that the shuttle must have a cargo compartment 15 ft. in diameter and 60 ft. in length. A shuttle of these dimensions will be able to carry as many as a dozen passengers and make the transit to and from orbit gently enough for middle-aged scientists to make the trip as comfortably as professional astronauts. Returning from orbit, it will land at the same base where it took off, touching down on an ordinary runway.

Capable of operating at altitudes up to 600 nautical miles, the shuttle will have a payload up to 50,000 lb. Since it will be used by the U.S. Air Force as well as NASA, its design will probably be somewhat influenced by military requirements. As preliminary design studies progressed, the space agency and the Air Force disagreed about whether the orbiter should have fixed wings or be delta-shaped to give it increased maneuverability on reentry, as the Air Force wanted.

While the shuttle is basically a transportation system to ferry satellites and carry men and supplies to and from a space station, it will have the ability to operate in orbit for a week and, therefore, can serve as a small space station-observatory until a bona fide space station is in operation. Engineers working on the shuttle believe that it can eventually replace all rocket launchers. In so doing the shuttle will cut the cost of building spacecraft by as much as a third according to some estimates. This will be possible because the spacecraft will no longer require elaborate protection against the crushing forces of rocket launches. Early NASA estimates were that the shuttle would pay for itself in five to six years, assuming 30 flights per year.

Despite these impressive characteristics of the shuttle and also the appeal of having a permanent space station in orbit, both of these programs for the next decade in space had their opponents. Rep. Joseph Karth (Dem., Minn.), chairman of the House Science and Astronautics Committee's Space Science and Applications Subcommittee, believes that much more research is needed before a commitment is made to go ahead.

Even with this kind of opposition, the House of Representatives and Senate space committees authorized $160 million for shuttle-space station work in fiscal 1971.

Space Tug and Nuclear Shuttle. While priority was being given the earth-to-orbit shuttle and the space station, preliminary work was also under way on the space tug and the nuclear shuttle. Preliminary feasibility studies on the tug were due from contractors early in 1971. Early concepts foresaw the tug as a vehicle capable of operating in either the manned or unmanned mode. As a manned vehicle it would be able to carry a payload of 5,000 to 10,000 lb. from a lunar orbiting space station down to the moon's surface. Unmanned, it might land as much as 70,000 lb. on the moon to aid in the buildup of a lunar outpost. It could support a manned expedition—three astronauts—as long as 28 days on the lunar surface.

NASA's grand design calls for the tug to come into operation about two years after the nonnuclear earth-to-orbit shuttle. A nuclear-powered shuttle would then be ready soon after that. The latter would be able to boost a payload of about 175,000 lb. from earth orbit to a low orbit around the moon.

Permanent Space Station. NASA invested approximately $6 million in fiscal 1970 on space station studies. It had $30 million to continue the work in fiscal 1971.

Under the present concept, the first "permanent" station would be designed for a lifetime of ten years. It would be laid out with the care and long-range planning that goes into a major research facility on earth. The station would have a crew of three or four astronauts in charge of its operation, with the rest of its residents working full-time on research projects.

The first station, like Skylab, will be a trailblazer for bigger and better things to come if NASA's present strategy is accepted. After the permanent space station, scientists hoped to establish a space base where dozens or even a hundred or more men would work at pursuits ranging from pure science to the manufacturing of materials that can be better managed without the burden of gravity.

continued from page 112

mothball them, making them part of "a national resource of heavy-lift rocket capability." It was not certain what would become of these Saturns, but presumably they would be used to orbit Skylab orbital workshops in the mid-1970s.

While high-cost, single-use "throwaway" Saturn Vs were being used to propel Apollos and Skylabs to their lunar or orbital destinations, sooner or later economy and practicality would demand the introduction of reusable craft. Accordingly, NASA started the space shuttle program, craft capable of delivering to orbit up to 50,000 lb. of crew, passengers, and cargo, and then of returning to earth.

For U.S. Air Force missions, TRW Systems developed an unusual DART (decomposed ammonia radioisotope thruster) propulsion system, which could be fired to change a spacecraft's orientation. The decomposing isotope generates heat that is applied to the ammonia propellant, which then expands as a gas-producing thrust. A DART weighs about 6 lb. Meanwhile, the 250,000-lb.-thrust Air Force-developed XLR 129-P-1 reusable rocket engine successfully passed its final review tests in August. The engine could provide the basic technology for the space shuttle. Pratt & Whitney, Aerojet-General Corp., and North American Rockwell's Rocketdyne Division all had study contracts to design 400,000-lb.-thrust staged combustion cycle rocket engines for the shuttle, and the XLR 129-P-1 represented an important step toward that goal.

In mid-June, the Europa I carrier made its first flight with all three stages performing and separating according to plan. However, it failed to place an experimental (575-lb.) Italian satellite into orbit because the protective shrouding apparently did not separate and the craft reentered the atmosphere prematurely. The flight was the last one for Europa I from Woomera, Austr.; Europa II flights were scheduled from Kourou in French Guiana. Europa II, with a fourth stage for orbiting geostationary telecommunications satellites, was under development during 1970, and by midyear ELDO had authorized work to begin on a Europa III—a two-stage configuration with a liquid hydrogen-liquid oxygen second stage.

Unmanned Satellites and Interplanetary Probes. Japan became the fourth nation to launch a satellite into orbit using its own rocket booster. The Ohsumi, launched on February 11 from the Kagoshima Space Centre, weighed 50.8 lb. and transmitted data for about 12 hours before going silent on its fifth or sixth orbit. Launched by a Lambda IV booster, it represented Japan's fifth attempt to do so since 1966. The satellite cost only $330,000. With much more élan, the Chinese launched their first satellite on April 24, becoming the fifth nation to do so. Using a booster derived from the two-stage Soviet SS IV (Sandal) ballistic missile, China orbited a 380-lb. satellite from a launching site at Shuang-cheng-tzu, approximately 1,000 mi. W of Peking. It transmitted brief telemetered signals on performance of components, as well as bursts of the Chinese revolutionary song "The East Is Red." The satellite went silent in May.

Several other nations announced plans to launch satellites in the future. Brazil revealed that it would develop a communications satellite for launch by a U.S. booster into a synchronous orbit sometime in 1976. It would be preceded by three test satellite launchings. The Netherlands announced that it would

NOVOSTI FROM SOVFOTO
The U.S.S.R.'s Luna 16 landed on the moon September 20 and scooped up lunar soil by means of a retractable boring mechanism before returning to earth. The mission was the first successful unmanned retrieval of lunar soil.

launch the Astronautical Netherlands Satellite from the Western Test Range in the U.S. by a Scout booster in August 1974. And Japan said that it would orbit its own communications satellite between 1975 and 1984, a number of meteorological satellites between 1975 and 1976, and a navigational satellite in 1977 or 1978. Likewise, India undertook an ambitious ten-year space program that envisioned a 2,640-lb. communications satellite to be orbited by 1980.

West Germany continued to demonstrate its growing competence in the design and manufacture of scientific satellites. On Nov. 8, 1969, the 159-lb. GRS-A (Azur) was launched by NASA for West Germany from the Western Test Range in California. Azur was designed to study the earth's radiation belt, the aurorae, and solar particles. In all, it carried seven scientific experiments. For some reason the satellite ceased transmitting on the night of June 28, 1970; however, most of its mission had been accomplished by that date. On March 10, another West German satellite, DIAL, was launched by a French Diamant B booster from France's new launching centre at Kourou. Oscar 5, a 39-lb. radio satellite built by a group of Australian amateur radio operators, was orbited piggyback with the U.S. ITOS 1 on January 23.

Launching activity in the U.S. slackened during the year, reflecting the general decline in the space program. On Nov. 22, 1969, a Thor-Delta launched the Skynet A military communications satellite for the United Kingdom. It was placed into an equatorial, synchronous orbit. On January 15 an Intelsat 3 was launched from Cape Kennedy by a Long Tank Thor-Delta booster. Weighing 320 lb. the communications satellite had 1,200 channels for audio and visual relay. On January 23, ITOS 1 (Improved Tiros Operational System) was orbited from the Western Test Range by a Thor-Delta N booster. This improved weather satel-

Table II. Satellites in Orbit and Probes in Space as 1970 Began

Nation	Number of satellites	Number of probes
U.S.	290	18
U.S.S.R.	75	14
U.K.	3	..
France	5	..
Canada	3	..
West Germany	1	..
Australia	1	..
ESRO	3	..

KEYSTONE

Soviet spacecraft
Soyuz 9 before takeoff.
Cosmonauts Andrian
Nikolayev and Vitaly
Sevastyanov established
a new space endurance
record, surpassing the 1965
record of U.S. astronauts
James Lovell and Frank
Borman aboard Gemini 7.

lite carried sensors to take infrared pictures of the earth's cloud cover at night and to measure cloud top and surface temperatures. Other sensors measured proton fluxes from the sun and the amount of heat radiated from the earth.

Sert 2 was launched on February 4 from the Western Test Range by a Thor-Agena D. The satellite was to test an ion propulsion engine that had a thrust of only 0.006 lb. During its first six months of flight, the ion engine was burned continuously. On March 31, Explorer 1, the first U.S. satellite, decayed from orbit and burned as a meteor south of Easter Island. It had been launched on Jan. 31, 1958. On November 30 the third Orbiting Astronomical Observatory failed to achieve orbit, and the $83 million scientific payload was destroyed.

Natosat 1 (NATO A), a communications satellite for NATO, was launched by NASA on March 20 by a Thor-Delta into an equatorial, synchronous orbit from Cape Kennedy. NASA also performed a piggyback launch on April 8 when it launched the Nimbus 4 weather satellite and Topo A by a Thor-Agena D from the Western Test Range. The Nimbus carried new sensing instruments. Among other things, the satellite measured the temperature and moisture content of the atmosphere at various altitudes and interrogated approximately 30 weather balloons drifting at a constant altitude through the atmosphere to learn more about wind velocities. The piggyback spacecraft on the launch was Topo A, an experimental topographical mapping satellite launched for the U.S. Army.

April 23 saw the successful launching of another Intelsat 3 from Cape Kennedy by a Thor-Delta booster. It was the seventh and next to last in the series of Intelsat 3s built for the Communications Satellite Corp. (Comsat) and launched by NASA. The final satellite, launched on July 23, was a failure.

The Soviet Union scored a technological triumph on September 20 when Luna 16 landed on the moon in the Sea of Fertility. The unmanned probe had been launched on September 12 by the large Proton booster. Luna 16 spent one day on the moon collecting rock samples and drilling core specimens with a 13.6-in. drill. All operations were observed and controlled remotely from the earth by scientists who observed them via television. Samples of rocks and soil were stored in a hermetically sealed container within the probe. Upon receiving the command from earth on September 21, the ascent stage of the vehicle lifted off and back into lunar orbit before being placed on a trajectory to the earth. The descent stage remained on the moon, telemetering data on radiation and temperature from on-board sensors.

In November the U.S.S.R. achieved an even more impressive triumph when Luna 17 landed on the moon and deployed Lunokhod 1, the first self-propelled vehicle to move across the lunar surface. Luna 17 was launched on November 11 and soft-landed in the Sea of Rains on November 17. Three hours after the landing, the Lunokhod 1, which resembled an eight-wheeled bathtub with a top that opened like a clamshell, rolled off the spacecraft and began its operations. Controlled from the earth and powered by solar energy, the moon rover rolled about 300 ft. across the Sea of Rains. According to Soviet scientists it took pictures and measured "the mechanical properties of the lunar soil." Neither Luna 17 nor Lunokhod 1 was designed to return to the earth.

Not so successful, however, was a Soviet mission to Venus in August. Two probes designed to study the planet's atmosphere were launched from Tyuratam on August 17 and 22. The 2,610.7-lb. Venera 7 was successfully placed on a trajectory to Venus on the first date. Venera 8, on the other hand, failed to leave earth orbit on the latter date; its engine did not burn long enough to reach escape velocity, and the Soviets redesignated the probe Cosmos 359.

Sounding Rockets. The year 1969 ended with an unusual scientific payload being boosted into the lower fringes of space by a Canadian-built Black Brant VB rocket from Wallops Island, Va. On November 9 an infrared telescope was boosted to a height of 175 mi. The instrumentation was surrounded by a cooling unit of boiling liquid helium that kept its temperature at −450° F. The experiment was flown to search for cosmic radiation, which may have originated at the beginning of the universe approximately 10,000,000,000 years ago.

In 1970 reddish orange clouds visible for hundreds of miles were seen along the east coast of the U.S.; they resulted from a series of seven sounding rockets launched from Wallops Island on January 14. These Nike-Apache and Nike-Cajun rockets released clouds of sodium and trimethylaluminum into the atmosphere at altitudes between 25 and 125 mi. Solar radiation on the clouds produced colours that permitted tracking by cameras. The purpose was to study the winds at high altitudes.   (M. R. S.; F. I. Or.)

See also Astronomy; Defense; Industrial Review; Meteorology; Telecommunications; Television and Radio.

Encyclopædia Britannica Films. *Earth Satellites: Explorers of Outer Space* (1958); *Rockets: How They Work* (1958); *First Men into Space* (1962); *Frontiers in Space* (1962); *A Trip to the Planets* (1963); *The Van Allen Radiation Belts* (1963); *Space Probes—Exploring Our Solar System* (1964); *You and the Aerospace Future* (1966).

Astronomy

Astronomy, no less than politics, is subject to violent swings of the pendulum. While the previous two years saw a veritable flood of new discoveries and theories, 1970 was a period, if not of peace, then at least of retrenchment and reform. It was, perhaps, no coincidence that 1970 was also the year when the International Astronomical Union (IAU) General Assembly met in Brighton, Eng. At those triennial gatherings astronomers from throughout the world meet to discuss recent results, to separate established fact from the more speculative suggestions, and to set goals for future research. There are also meetings organized by the various IAU commissions to allow discussion of particular problems. Under these circumstances it was to be expected that considerable upheavals should occur in the newer branches of the subject. As it happened, however, it became clear that substantial revision might also be required in the approach even to some of the supposedly "well understood" aspects of astronomy. Among these are the evolution and composition of stars.

Stellar Evolution. The aim of stellar evolution studies is to predict the way in which the structure of a star of given mass and initial chemical composition will change with time. The results may be compared simply by observation, using the star's luminosity and surface temperature, or, in more detail, by using the theory of stellar atmospheres (*see* below) to predict the star's entire spectrum. If the composition can be determined by alternative means—usually spectroscopically—the problem can be inverted and the observations used to determine the mass, age, and internal structure of the stars. Alternatively, if the age and mass are known reasonably accurately—as, for example, for the sun—the observed luminosity and surface temperature can, in principle, be used to determine the initial helium abundance, a quantity that cannot be determined spectroscopically for most cool stars. The initial helium abundance is an extremely important parameter since it can furnish important constraints on conditions prevailing in the early phases of the "big bang" cosmologies. Unfortunately, almost all old stars (that is, those that should best indicate initial conditions) are cool, and the helium abundance is accordingly difficult to determine except from stellar evolution calculations. The theory is thus not only of importance in understanding the way in which stars evolve but also provides a powerful tool for determining ages of star clusters, compositions of stars, and even conditions in the early phases of an evolutionary (as opposed to steady-state) universe.

The basic input to the calculations, apart from the stellar mass, is the initial chemical composition of a star, mainly hydrogen and helium but with a smattering of other elements that for convenience are referred to collectively as "metals." The distribution of elements within this last group had generally been assumed to be the same as in the sun and to be fairly unimportant. For a given composition it was necessary to compute the opacity, the nuclear energy generation rates, and the equation of state, after which the structure calculation could proceed. The theory had until recent months been deemed satisfactory, largely, perhaps, because of the plausible results obtained for the sun. Recently, however, the number of independent tests of the theory increased and confidence in it waned rather drastically.

In one such test J. Davis and his collaborators, working 5,000 ft. below ground in a South Dakota mine, attempted to detect solar neutrinos. Through late 1970 they had failed to measure unambiguously any neutrino flux from the sun at a level greater than one-half that predicted by the "best solar models" computed by J. Bahcall and his collaborators at the California Institute of Technology. In fairness it must be stated that the experiment and its interpretation are extremely complex. Nonetheless, this discrepancy became sufficiently well established to indicate that our knowledge of the internal structure of the sun was not as complete as had been supposed. Further suggestions that all was not well came from the mass-luminosity relation derived by O. J. Eggen (Mt. Stromlo Observatory, near Canberra, Austr.) for the main sequence stars in the Hyades cluster. His results suggested luminosities at a given mass almost twice those predicted from theory. This same phenomenon manifested itself in Cepheid variable stars and, even more dramatically, in the fact that certain star clusters in our galaxy appear, on the basis of stellar evolution theory, to have ages in excess of that of the universe as determined from Hubble's law of expansion.

These and other discrepancies can all be reduced, according to results obtained by K. Fricke, R. Stobie, and P. Strittmatter (Cambridge University), if current estimates of opacity are too high. In this context it is noteworthy that 1970 saw a series of papers suggesting major revisions of the existing opacity results. In particular, it became apparent from the work of T. Carson (University of St. Andrews, Scot.) that the individual abundances of the elements can be of

COURTESY, MOUNT WILSON AND PALOMAR OBSERVATORIES

Observations by rocket disclosed that galaxy NGC 5128, distinguished by a dark band of dust, is emitting intense X-ray energy at a rate that cannot be explained by known processes.

major importance. For example, using standard abundances the element neon was shown to be the dominant opacity source in certain ranges of temperature and density frequently encountered in stellar interiors. For most stars, however, the neon abundance is uncertain to a factor of ten. Similarly, improved laboratory experimental technique resulted in substantially altered absorption line strengths for iron. The estimated solar iron abundance was altered correspondingly and, consequently, the opacity in the central regions of the sun.

It thus became apparent that, due to uncertainties in opacity alone, substantial systematic errors had probably been introduced into the results of stellar evolution calculations. While the qualitative features of the theory should, of course, remain unchanged, little weight could be attached to the absolute values of quantities derived from the theory. Thus, agreement with the independent derivations could not be expected. On the other hand, within the framework of the theory, relative values, for example of cluster ages, should still be capable of determination. That these systematic errors should have remained hidden for so long served to emphasize both the extreme complexity of the calculations and the great difficulty in providing independent observational tests. A minimum condition for an improvement in the situation was that the relative distribution of "metals" should be more accurately determined.

Stellar Atmospheres. Apart from the sun, the only direct way to obtain information on the composition of a star is by studying its spectrum. In conjunction with a model stellar atmosphere, the strengths of absorption lines in the spectrum can furnish information about the surface abundances of individual elements. Whether this provides any indication of the initial abundances in the interior has been a longstanding subject for debate. Considerable progress was made during the last year in resolving this problem, however. L. Aller and S. Chapman had suggested in the 1950s that in very stable atmospheres the heavier elements might sink under the influence of gravitation, thus becoming deficient in the surface layers. This proposal was modified and extended by G. Michaud (California Institute of Technology) to take into account the effect of radiation pressure on the various atoms and ions in the atmosphere. An element in a particular state of ionization may thus "sink" or "swim" according to whether gravity or radiation pressure is the dominant force acting on it,

COURTESY SKY PUBLISHING CORP.

Comet Bennett, photographed on April 5, 1970, will not be seen again for at least 500 years.

thus causing apparent deficiencies in some and enhancements in other species. In this manner Michaud was able to account for a number of the abundance anomalies found in the peculiar A stars, in particular the apparent deficiency of helium and excess of manganese. These stars are, in general, slow rotators and possess substantial magnetic fields, both of which properties should help ensure the stability of the surface layers.

Although this separation process required further study, it received strong support from the following general arguments. Among main sequence stars those in a state of rapid rotation or without strong magnetic fields are generally free of abundance peculiarities, their atmospheres presumably being too unstable. Among the peculiar stars there is a tendency for elements to show anomalous behaviour when they are neutral and can consequently diffuse more rapidly through the ambient medium. It is, however, from the spectra of white dwarf stars that the most dramatic support may be adduced. These stars have very high gravities but low luminosity; settling of heavy elements should, therefore, be favoured. The spectroscopic information accumulated by J. L. Greenstein (Mount Wilson and Palomar Observatories) indicated that, in the absence of atmospheric convection, only hydrogen, the lightest element, is present in detectable quantities in most white dwarfs. The evidence that separation of elements occurs thus seems overwhelming.

Clearly, for such stars abundances determined from stellar atmospheres give no indication of the interior composition. Lest it be thought, however, that no hope remains of determining interior compositions and, hence, opacity, two qualifying remarks should be made. First, it is clear that not all abundance anomalies can be explained in terms of this mechanism. Several recent discoveries have indicated that some must be due to nuclear processes. Second, most stars are in moderate rotation or have convective outer layers, thus preventing separation; their spectra are generally normal, and their surface abundances should give a

reasonable indication of the interior composition.

Before leaving the subject of stellar surfaces, one remarkable discovery must be recorded. J. C. Kemp and J. B. Swedlund (University of Oregon) and J. D. Landstreet and J. R. Angel (Columbia University) detected a net circular polarization in the continuum radiation from a peculiar white dwarf star. If interpreted as due to the influence of a magnetic field, the required field strength is $\sim 10^7$ gauss, more than two orders of magnitude greater than any previously measured value. Such a field strength may readily be understood if a main sequence star with a field strength of $\sim 10^2$ gauss contracts to white dwarf densities. This discovery provided additional confirmation that magnetic fields and peculiar spectra go hand in hand. It also came as a welcome relief to those who hoped to account for the large ($\gtrsim 10^{10}$ gauss) magnetic fields required in most models of pulsars.

Pulsars. After the frenetic activity of the past two years, 1970 was a period of relative calm in the pulsar field. On the observational side, improvements were made in both the quality and quantity of measurements. No entirely new phenomena were detected, although a sharp change in period, similar to that previously noted in the Vela pulsar, was observed in great detail in the Crab pulsar. J. Scargle and E. Harlan at the Lick Observatory, on Mt. Hamilton, California, were even able to show that the "wisps" of gas in the nebula surrounding the pulsar underwent changes that appeared to originate near the pulsar at the time of period change.

On the theoretical side little progress was made in understanding the mechanism giving rise to the pulsed emission, although the idea of a rotating neutron star with a magnetic field inclined to the rotation axes was generally accepted as the starting point for all models. An ingenious proposal to account for the rapid period changes observed in the Vela and Crab pulsars was put forward by G. Baym, C. Pethick, and D. Pines (University of Illinois) and M. Ruderman (Columbia University). They pointed out that in the interior of

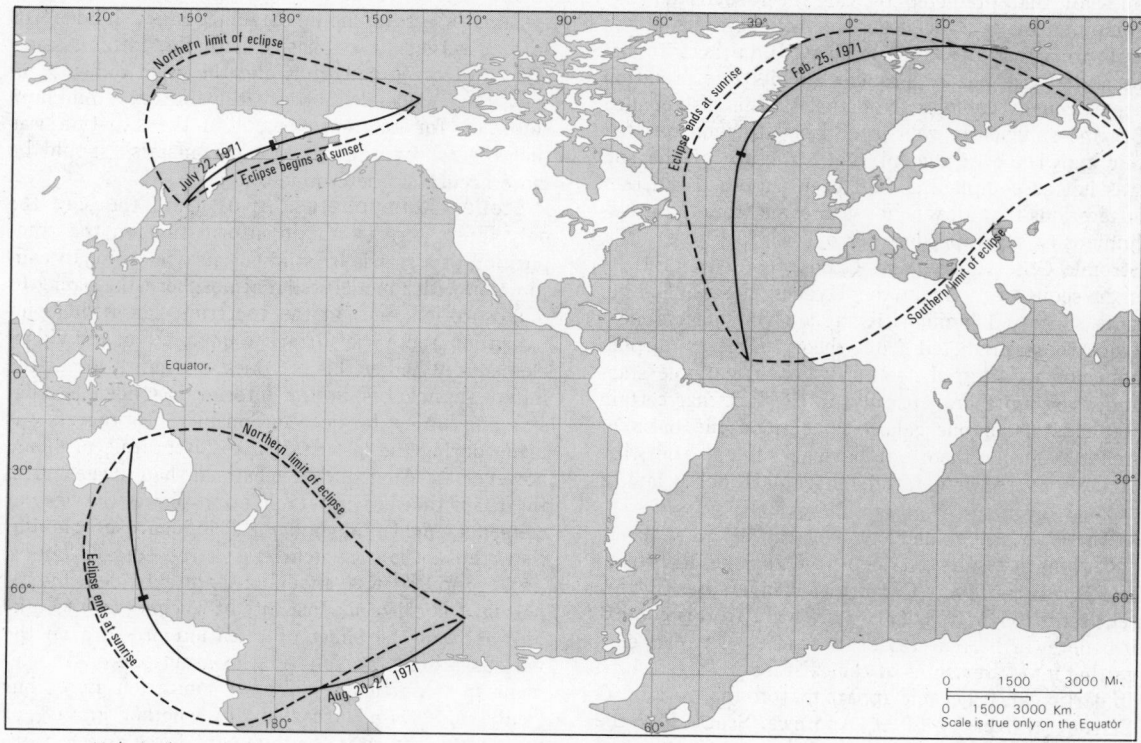

a pulsar, neutron superfluidity and proton superconductivity are serious possibilities. The surface layers, on the other hand, probably form a solid mantle. As the rotation rate of the neutron star decreases because of magnetic braking, the centrifugal force on the mantle is reduced. Due to its solid nature, however, the mantle will not adjust smoothly to the new equilibrium configuration. Eventually the stresses set up in the mantle become too large, and it fractures, giving rise to a "starquake." The moment of inertia of the mantle is thus reduced, and it accordingly spins faster, together with the field lines and proton fluid. The superfluid neutrons, which provide the main bulk of the star, are not, however, tied to the field and interact only weakly with the other material. It therefore takes some time (about one to two years) for the various components to reach co-rotation. Such a sequence of events accounts nicely for both the sudden increase in rotation rate and subsequent slower decrease observed in detail in the Crab pulsar.

Galaxies, Quasars, and Cosmology. The centre of our galaxy was the subject of continuing investigation in the infrared region of the spectrum during the past year. F. J. Low and his collaborators at Rice University, making observations from high-flying aircraft, showed that the infrared spectrum continues to rise steeply to a wavelength of at least 70 μ (1 μ = 0.001 mm.) and that the main source is at most 10 parsecs in diameter (1 parsec = 19.2 trillion mi.) and is probably varying. They also obtained evidence that the spectrum of the Seyfert galaxy NGC 1068 has a similar shape to a wavelength of at least 70 μ. If this is confirmed, the infrared emission would exceed 2×10^{46} ergs/sec. orders of magnitude greater than the total radiated at all other wavelengths or by normal spiral galaxies. Working at shorter wavelengths (10 μ), both the Rice group and W. A. Stein and F. C. Gillett at the University of California demonstrated that this emission varies in a time scale of months or less.

This combination of high luminosity and rapid variations places severe restrictions on the emission mechanism and indicates that a coherent (maser-like) radiation process must be responsible. The energy requirements alone demand that even with complete efficiency an energy equivalent of at least 10^8 solar masses must be converted into infrared emission during the lifetime of these objects. This is uncomfortably close to the entire mass at present in the nuclear regions as determined from a study of the rotation law in the spiral regions of these galaxies. To resolve these difficulties, Low suggested that the nuclei of galaxies may be sites of matter and antimatter creation. This has the advantage of not requiring the conversion of mass presently in place. When the matter and antimatter meet, they annihilate and produce electron-positron pairs, gamma rays, and neutrinos. The energy in pairs and gamma rays can then be converted into infrared radiation at relatively high efficiency.

By far the most dramatic discovery in quasar research was the redshift measurement of $z = 2.877$ for the quasar 4C 05.34 by R. Lynds and D. Wills at Kitt Peak National Observatory near Tucson, Ariz. The previous record was $z = 2.38$ for 5C 02.56. The new measurement indicated that the apparent dearth of objects with redshifts exceeding 2 is not due to the presence of obscuring material at these epochs, as had been suggested earlier, but rather to a real decline in the number of quasars per unit volume of space.

Finally, it should be pointed out that even if the quasar redshifts are cosmological in the sense of Hubble's law, scientists remain far from obtaining an accurate distance determination either for them or for galaxies. After more than 30 years of effort, the value of Hubble's constant (the factor relating redshift to distance) is not known to an accuracy better than 30%. The reason, of course, is the difficulty in finding independent distance indicators. For example, at the IAU Symposium, S. V. Clube (Royal Greenwich Observatory in England) submitted evidence that the RR Lyrae stars were, in fact, intrinsically fainter than had been supposed. If adopted, his suggestion could result not only in a decrease in estimates of the size of our galaxy but also of the entire distance scale of the universe. An improvement could, of course, be made if the structure and, hence, luminosity of RR Lyrae stars were better determined, which conveniently brings us back to our starting point. Astronomy, clearly, is a bootstrap operation.

A group of U.S. scientists announced on December 1 that they had discovered 17 amino acids in a meteorite that had fallen in Australia in 1969. The finding provided strong evidence that conditions suitable for the possible evolution of life exist beyond the earth.

New Telescopes. In view of these great uncertainties in even some of the more established branches of astronomy, it is most gratifying to be able to record the commissioning or construction, during the last year or so, of a number of large observational facilities. For radio work, a large synthesis telescope was commissioned at Westerbork, Neth., in 1970, while a telescope for similar work was under construction in Cambridge, Eng. Near Bonn, W.Ger., a fully steerable radio dish 300 ft. in diameter, the largest in the world, was commissioned in late 1970.

For optical astronomy construction of large (approximately 150-in. aperture) telescopes was in progress at the European Southern Observatory, La Silla, Chile; the Cerro Tololo Inter-American Observatory, La Serena, Chile; the Anglo-Australian Observatory, Siding Spring, Austr.; and the Kitt Peak National Observatory. (P. A. ST.)

See also Astronautics.

Australia

A federal parliamentary state and a realm of the Commonwealth of Nations, Australia occupies the smallest continent and, with the island state of Tasmania, is the sixth largest country in the world. Area: 2,967,909 sq.mi. (7,686,849 sq.km.). Pop. (1969 est.): 12,295,300. Cap.: Canberra (pop., 1970 est., 130,250). Largest city: Sydney (metro. pop., 1969 est., 2,712,600). Queen, Elizabeth II; governor-general in 1970, Sir Paul Hasluck; prime minister, John Grey Gorton.

Domestic Affairs. In 1970 Prime Minister Gorton and the Liberal-Country Party (LCP) government faced lively opposition from the Australian Labor Party (ALP). During a debate on water resources the speaker, Sir William Aston, had to suspend the sitting of the House of Representatives because of disorder. Two ALP members were suspended for 24 hours for refusing to withdraw "unparliamentary" statements. During the visit of Canada's prime minister, Pierre Trudeau, Gorton narrowly survived censure after some members of his party threatened to vote with the ALP on a motion that accused the government of breaking agreements with the states over offshore mineral rights legislation. In May the federal government

Athletics:
see Baseball; Basketball; Bowling and Lawn Bowls; Boxing; Cricket; Cycling; Football; Golf; Hockey; Ice Skating; Rowing; Skiing; Sporting Record; Swimming; Tennis; Track and Field Sports

was forced by public opinion to stop its attempt to direct the Australian Broadcasting Commission to reduce its expenditure on current affairs programs, which, government members believed, were biased and politically prejudiced against the LCP. Considerable tension was generated within the community by the government's Vietnam policy.

Although the government passed strong legislation by which it could compel youths to register for national service, and prevent adults from trying to dissuade them, it was reluctant to use its powers in 1970. Delegates to the Victorian State ALP annual conference signed a declaration affirming their intention to defy the National Service Act, and A. C. Holding, the leader of the Victorian State ALP opposition, dared the Commonwealth to prosecute. Donald A. Dunstan, who became premier of South Australia in June, said on national television that he would refuse to register for national service if he were 20 years old. Prominent leaders of the Methodist church, the Rev. Allan Walker and the Rev. D. A. Trathern, publicly urged 20-year-olds not to register. The Rev. Trathern, headmaster of Newington College, a leading Sydney public school, was dismissed and then reinstated over his letter to the *Sydney Morning Herald* in which he urged 20-year-olds to give their loyalty to "God, rather than Caesar." A moratorium was held in May to show how public opinion stood on the question of withdrawing Australian troops from Vietnam and repealing the National Service Act. Students, unionists, schoolchildren, academics, clergy, housewives, and businessmen turned the day into the biggest antiwar demonstration in Australia's history.

The year saw a reexamination of Australia's traditional views on the desirability of a high level of immigration. In July the minister for immigration, Phillip R. Lynch, called for a five-point study to evaluate the current migration policy. Lynch believed that Australia would have to continue to attract a large number of migrants, but that in the future the implications of immigration would have to be related more closely to total progress, including nonmaterial and environmental considerations.

The leader of the opposition, E. Gough Whitlam, faced serious divisions within the ALP during 1970. The most important breach was between himself and the Victorian branch of the ALP. The Victorian branch asked the party executive to instruct Whitlam to desist from making any unilateral interpretation of federal policy, and from taking any action that

would imply that he had the status and prerogative to deal with the internal affairs of state branches. It was subsequently found that the Victorian state executive was controlled by an outside clique whose aim was revolutionary change. In September the ALP federal executive took control of the branch and appointed an advisory council to carry out reforms.

There was an important extension of Australia's social services in March. The government introduced a national health scheme that gave increased benefits to contributors. This new scheme was timely in view of the report of Justice John A. Nimmo, deputy president of the Commonwealth Conciliation and Arbitration Commission. He found in his inquiry into health insurance that there was a considerable amount of appalling social and economic distress in a country he had previously regarded as affluent. Nimmo discovered that there were about a million Australians living below a miserably poor "poverty line."

Work on the West Gate Bridge being built across the Lower Yarra River at Melbourne was halted by disaster. On October 15 a 384-ft. span collapsed into the river. (*See* DISASTERS.)

Foreign Affairs. Papua-New Guinea supplanted Vietnam as the chief problem area for Australian diplomats in 1970. In December 1969 the administrator of Papua-New Guinea, D. O. Hay, was faced with riots in the town of Rabaul, on the island of New Britain, in the Trust Territory of New Guinea. The Mataungan Association, a powerful native group, opposed with force the establishment of a multiracial local government council on the Gazelle peninsula. Local government officials were beaten, and it was necessary for the police commissioner in Port Moresby, Papua, to fly 72 policemen to Rabaul, where they patrolled the streets, armed with batons and tear gas.

The political temperature in Papua-New Guinea increased after Gough Whitlam had spent 15 days in the territory gaining material to provide a basis for ALP policy on the question of independence. Whitlam visited the Keravat prison, where the Mataungan leaders were serving six-month sentences for their part in the riots, and, although he said that violence should be forgotten as a way to oppose a multiracial council, the leading businessmen and copra planters deplored his intervention. The management of Bali Plantations Ltd. feared that visits like Whitlam's would prevent any chances of increased Australian investment in the area, and sent a telegram to the prime minister asking for the government's views.

AUSTRALIA

Education. (1967) Primary, pupils 1,798,521, teachers 62,200; secondary, pupils 847,818, teachers 48,100; vocational, pupils 153,600; higher (including 14 universities), students 153,-000, teaching staff (at universities only) 6,044.

Finance. Monetary unit: Australian dollar, with a par value of A$0.89 to U.S. $1 (A$2.14 = £1 sterling). Gold, SDRs, and foreign exchange, official and banks: (June 1970) U.S. $1,380,000,-000; (June 1969) U.S. $1,362,000,000. Commonwealth budget (1969–70 est.): revenue A$6,875,-000,000; expenditure A$6,322,000,000. Gross national product: (1968–69) A$26.6 billion; (1967–68) A$23,720,000,000. Money supply: (April 1970) A$5,204,000,000; (April 1969) A$4,865,000,000. Cost of living (1963 = 100): (Jan.–March 1970) 122; (Jan.–March 1969) 118.

Foreign Trade. (1969) Imports A$3,626,900,-000; exports A$3,765,100,000. Import sources: U.S. 25%; U.K. 22%; Japan 12%; West Germany 6%. Export destinations: Japan 25%; U.S. 14%; U.K. 12%. Main exports: wool 21%; meat

9%; wheat 9%; iron ore 6%; nonferrous metals 6%.

Transport and Communications. Roads (1968) 860,359 km. (including 212,193 km. classified roads). Motor vehicles in use (1969): passenger 3,523,344; commercial (including buses) 949,191. Railways (government; 1968): 40,466 km.; freight traffic 20,490,000,000 net ton-km. Air traffic (1968): 7,296,819,000 passenger-km.; freight 217,197,000 net ton-km. Shipping (1969): merchant vessels 100 gross tons and over 321; gross tonnage 893,613; traffic (1968) goods loaded 43,426,000 metric tons, unloaded 31,187,000 metric tons. Telephones (Dec. 1968) 3,392,436. Radio licenses (Dec. 1969) 2,634,382. Television licenses (Dec. 1969) 2,657,148.

Agriculture. Production (in 000; metric tons; 1969; 1968 in parentheses): wheat 10,713 (14,-647); oats 1,669 (1,713); barley 1,814 (1,585); sorghum (1968) 433, (1967) 269; corn 168 (172); potatoes 691 (669); sugar, raw value (1969–70) c. 2,275, (1968–69) 2,769; apples 396 (374); oranges 261 (257); wine (1968) 195,

(1967) 189; wool, greasy (1968–69) 886, (1967–68) 803; milk (1968–69) 6,866, (1967–68) 7,-035; butter (1968–69) 201, (1967–68) 196; beef and veal (1968–69) 939, (1967–68) 905; mutton and lamb (1968–69) 677, (1967–68) 670. Livestock (in 000; March 1969): sheep 174,602; cattle 20,772; pigs 2,289; horses (March 1968) c. 475; chickens (1968–69) c. 22,700.

Industry. Fuel and power (in 000; metric tons; 1969): coal 46,088; lignite 23,284; crude oil 2,007; manufactured gas (cu.m.; 1967–68) 3,470,000; electricity (kw-hr.) 51,183,000. Production (in 000; metric tons; 1969): iron ore (65% metal content) 39,100; bauxite 7,920; pig iron 6,106; crude steel 7,031; zinc 246; aluminum 126; copper 101; lead 190; tin 4.2; nickel ore (metal content; 1968) 4.6; sulfuric acid 1,862; cement 4,306; cotton yarn 29; wool yarn 25; gold (troy oz.; 1968) 797; passenger cars (including assembly; units) 371; commercial vehicles (including assembly; units) 78. Dwelling units completed (1969) 136,000.

Six months later Gorton himself visited Papua-New Guinea and found that the groups that opposed the government were still far from peaceful. The crucial issue was the date of independence. Whitlam pledged the ALP, if it took office, to grant home rule by 1972 and independence by 1976. The prime minister, on the other hand, announced that the Australian government had decided to give the ministerial members of the local House of Assembly power to direct the budget of the territory. Power over the judiciary, foreign affairs, trade relations, defense, and civil aviation were retained by Australia, but Gorton's announcement represented a major transfer of power.

Gorton intended to help the territory take a major step along the road to self-government, but he could not predict future developments. He said that the Australian government did not wish to remain in the territory against the wishes of the people, nor did Australia wish to leave the territory against their wishes. As a result of his tour, Gorton's original idea of Papua-New Guinea as a homogeneous whole had been shaken to such an extent that he began to think that different parts of the territory might progress toward independence at different rates. He found that the highland people (who made up the majority of the population) were opposed to self-government in 1972 or at any fixed date. In the coastal areas—Wewak, Lae, Madang—opinion was divided, but most of the people did not want self-government until a time of their own choosing. Bougainville, one of the Solomon Islands, was the most radical area, and a demand for a referendum there on the secession question was refused.

In July the government began to make plans for reorganizing Australian defense in the post-Vietnam war period. For the needs of the Vietnam war, Australia conscripted 8,000 men for a two-year cycle—one year spent on training, the next year spent in Vietnam. In the post-Vietnam war period the government intended to call up 16,000 men each year for one year's service, a second year not being insisted upon unless an emergency arose. In response to the situation in Cambodia, the minister for external affairs, William McMahon, announced in June that the Cabinet had refused to grant the new Cambodian government arms, ammunition, and military equipment. Australia did, however, extend a special and immediate grant to Cambodia of A$500,000 that was spent on dual purpose items such as trucks and trailers.

All told, the government provided over A$200 million for external aid during 1970–71. The basis on which financial assistance to Papua-New Guinea was provided was changed in accord with the arrangements to transfer budgetary responsibility to local ministers. Increased aid was given to Indonesia, South Vietnam, Cambodia, Thailand, and the islands in the South Pacific. The government also proposed to contribute U.S. $10 million to the special funds of the Asian Development Bank over the period 1971–74.

On April 22 Gorton announced that Australia would phase out troops in line with the U.S. government's withdrawal from Vietnam; the Australian task force would be reduced by about 1,000 in November, when the 8th Battalion and its support companies, which were due to leave Vietnam, would not be replaced. This decision followed the increasing self-reliance of the Saigon government's forces under the vietnamization program. On the site vacated by the 8th Battalion, Australia was to provide instructors and other aid for a South Vietnamese training centre for junior leaders.

COURTESY, AUSTRALIAN NEWS AND INFORMATION BUREAU

Above, Khancoban Dam, part of the new A$800 million Snowy Mountains Scheme in southeastern Australia. Below, view across the Botanic Gardens to the Sydney Opera House, which neared completion in 1970.

The Economy. In 1969–70 the economy of Australia achieved a high rate of growth. Despite the trials and setbacks in rural industry, the gross national product increased by $5\frac{1}{2}\%$. The number of wage and salary earners rose by 4%. Although wool prices fell sharply throughout the world, there was an increase of 24% in the total value of Australian exports. On the negative side, the consumer price index rose at an accelerating rate throughout the year, reaching an annual rate of growth of 5%. The demand for labour increased until the job vacancies were well above the number of registered applicants for work, despite immigration and the entry of more and more married women into the work force. Average weekly earnings rose by about 8% and consumer spending by 9.6%.

To try to reduce the possibility of inflation, the federal treasurer, Leslie Bury, introduced a precautionary budget in August 1970, which, while in no sense trying to slow down the rate of growth, sought to ensure that the budget would not add impetus to demand in general. The major feature was the attempt of the government to provide substantial income tax relief to those in the lower and middle income groups. In doing this, Bury was concerned both to relieve the inequality that had developed and to stimulate initiative, thus promoting conditions significant for future economic growth. The government was concerned that rising incomes had led to a relatively rapid rise in personal income taxation, so it decided to reduce by 10% the amount payable on taxable incomes up to A$10,000 a year. To balance the reduction in personal income taxation, the government simultaneously increased air navigation charges, company tax, sales tax, excise and customs duty on motor fuel, and, most controversial of all, introduced for the first time excise duty on wine.

The economic position of the states caused considerable tension between the state and federal governments. At the beginning of the financial year 1969–70, the states' total public debt stood at A$10,676,000,000, compared with the Commonwealth debt of A$204 million. The states attempted to recover some lost ground by introducing a receipts tax duty at the rate of one cent in A$10, but this was declared invalid by the High Court. In February 1970, Gorton offered to give the states an additional A$12 million and agreed to discuss the possibility of assuming responsibility for A$1 billion of the states' debts. In addition, the government introduced a federal receipts duty bill, only to find it rejected by the Senate. Drought in Queensland cut back rural production by A$157 million. In the December 1969 quarter there was a fall of A$155 million in net capital inflow compared with 1968.

Since the wool industry was a vital component in the Australian economy, there was considerable controversy over a decision to lift the 40-year-old embargo on the export of Merino rams. The secretary of the Embargo Committee, F. S. Coventry, said that, with artificial breeding methods, 300 rams could produce 900,000 sheep in one year, and the effect on the Australian wool and meat industry would be disastrous.

On March 9 the Reserve Bank of Australia introduced higher trading bank deposit and lending rates to curb inflationary trends in the economy. J. G. Phillips, the governor of the Reserve Bank, announced that the maximum overdraft rate chargeable by trading banks would be increased by 0.5% to 8.25%, the highest in many years. (A. R. G. G.)

See also Dependent States.

ENCYCLOPÆDIA BRITANNICA FILMS. *Australia* (1959); *Changing Matilda: The New Australia* (1965).

Austria

A republic of central Europe, Austria is bounded by Germany, Czechoslovakia, Hungary, Yugoslavia, Italy, Switzerland, and Liechtenstein. Area: 32,374 sq.mi. (83,850 sq.km.). Pop. (1970 est.): 7,384,189. Cap. and largest city: Vienna (pop., 1969 est., 1,644,976). Language: predominantly German. Religion: 89% Roman Catholic. President in 1970, Franz Jonas; chancellors, Josef Klaus and, from April 21, Bruno Kreisky.

The outstanding political event in Austria in 1970 was the victory of the Socialist Party of Austria (SPÖ) in the general election of March 1, resulting in the formation of a purely Socialist government for the first time in Austrian history. In its election campaign the SPÖ took every opportunity to present a modern, forward-looking image. It adopted a clearly non-Communist stance and in its new chairman, the former foreign minister, Bruno Kreisky (*see* BIOGRAPHY), was able to put forward a particularly well-known and well-liked politician as prospective chancellor. Of 4,635,026 valid votes cast, the SPÖ received 2,235,061, the Austrian People's Party (ÖVP) 2,078,010, and the Austrian Freedom Party (FPÖ) 254,292; this gave the SPÖ 81 seats (74 in the 1966 election), the ÖVP 79 (85), and the FPÖ 5 (6). No seats went to the Communists, right-wing extremists, or other splinter groups.

Entrusted with the formation of the new government, Kreisky first initiated talks with the ÖVP. These led to nothing, however, and on April 21 an entirely Socialist Cabinet was formed. On April 27 the government reaffirmed the main points of its program, which included proposals for reform in practically every field. On May 15 a start was made with setting up the various reform boards whose task would be to prepare draft legislation.

The first test for the Kreisky government came at the end of May, when the West German magazine *Der Spiegel* attacked some of its members for their past Nazi connections. The minister for agriculture, Hans Öllinger, who had been in the SS, resigned and was succeeded by Oskar Weihs. This was followed by a controversy between the SPÖ leadership and Simon Wiesenthal, head of the Jewish Documentation Centre, whom the former accused of exercising a form of private justice that would not be tolerated in a court of law. A later allegation by *Der Spiegel,* that

a secret agreement had been reached between the SPÖ and the FPÖ guaranteeing support for the former SPÖ minority government, was energetically denied by both parties.

On June 25 the Constitutional Court declared the election results in three Vienna constituencies void because of unlawful manipulation; 16 members lost their seats as a result. By-elections were held on October 4, as a result of which the ÖVP lost one seat in the National Assembly and the FPÖ gained one.

An ÖVP conference in May formally elected Hermann Withalm to succeed Josef Klaus, who had resigned as party chairman in March. Karl Schleinzer became the new secretary-general. Internal squabbles showed that the ÖVP had not yet gotten over its defeat and was still unused to its unaccustomed role in opposition.

At the end of July, Austria sent a memorandum on European security to 32 foreign governments, proposing that a conference on this subject be held in Helsinki, Fin., or Vienna. At the same time, Austria made known its interest in obtaining a seat in the UN Security Council. Foreign Minister Rudolf Kirchschläger restated the government's opinion that a neu-

AUSTRIA

Education. (1967–68) Primary, pupils 836,670, teachers 37,784; secondary, pupils 139,582, teachers 9,055; vocational, pupils 222,518, teachers 12,646; teacher training, students 4,939, teachers 542; higher (including 6 universities), students 53,737, teaching staff 5,561.

Finance. Monetary unit: schilling, with a par value of 26 schillings to U.S. $1 (62.40 schillings = £1 sterling). Gold, SDRs, and foreign exchange, central bank: (June 1970) U.S. $1,369,000,000; (June 1969) U.S. $1,254,000,000. Budget (1970 est.): revenue 92,248,000,000 schillings; expenditure 101,223,000,000 schillings. Gross national product: (1969) 323 billion schillings; (1967–68) 295.1 billion schillings. Money supply: (March 1970) 66,240,000,000 schillings; (March 1969) 60,820,000,000 schillings. Cost of living (1963 = 100): (June 1970) 128; (June 1969) 122.

Foreign Trade. (1969) Imports 73,460,000,000 schillings; exports 62,723,000,000 schillings. Import sources: EEC 56% (West Germany 41%, Italy 7%); Switzerland 8%; U.K. 7%. Export destinations: EEC 41% (West Germany 24%, Italy 10%); Switzerland 9%; U.K. 6%; U.S. 5%. Main exports: machinery 19%; iron and steel 13%; textile yarns and fabrics 8%; timber 7%; chemicals 6%; paper and board 5%.

Transport and Communications. Roads (1968) 93,273 km. (including 411 km. expressways). Motor vehicles in use (1968): passenger 1,053,321; commercial 107,392. Railways: state (1968) 5,924 km.; private (1967) 635 km.: traffic (state only; 1969) 6,294,000,000 passenger-km.; freight 8,726,000,000 net ton-km. Air traffic (1969): 428 million passenger-km.; freight 8,925,000 net ton-km. Telephones (Dec. 1968) 1,242,785. Radio receivers (Dec. 1968) 2,071,000. Television receivers (Dec. 1968) 1,129,000.

Agriculture. Production (in 000; metric tons; 1969; 1968 in parentheses): wheat 950 (1,045); rye 440 (413); barley 935 (770); oats 288 (324); corn 698 (399); potatoes 2,941 (3,473); sugar, raw value (1969–70) 349, (1968–69) 293; apples 347 (342); wine (1968) 317, (1967) 332; meat (1968) 497, (1967) 477; timber (cu.m.; 1968) 11,200, (1967) 11,500. Livestock (in 000; Dec. 1968): cattle 2,433; sheep 126; pigs 3,094; horses (Dec. 1967) 66; goats (Dec. 1967) 88; chickens 11,291.

Industry. Fuel and power (in 000; metric tons; 1969): lignite 3,840; crude oil 2,768; natural gas (cu.m.) 1,483,000; electricity (kw-hr.) 26,358,000 (71% hydroelectric in 1968); manufactured gas (Vienna only; cu.m.) 650,000. Production (in 000; metric tons; 1969): iron ore (30% metal content) 3,982; pig iron 2,816; crude steel 3,926; magnesite (1968) 1,547; aluminum 131; copper 19; lead 7; zinc 15; cement 4,558; paper (1968) 842; nitrogenous fertilizers (N content; 1968–69) 256; cotton yarn 21; woven cotton fabric 19; wool yarn 14; rayon fibres (1968) 63.

tral (*i.e.,* nonaligned) state need not be excluded from pursuing an active policy in the interests of peace or from adopting a stance on international problems.

At the end of November 1969, the South Tirol People's Party had voted (583–492) to accept the Italian proposals for autonomy. The dispute involving the South Tirol, an area within Italy populated largely by persons of Austrian descent, had troubled Austrian-Italian relations for many years. On Nov. 30, 1969, however, the Italian and Austrian foreign ministers agreed that the Italian proposals should be carried out, that Austria should formally declare the dispute ended, and that Italy should withdraw its veto on Austria's admittance to the EEC. In December the government placed a declaration to this end before Parliament, but it was strongly opposed and was adopted only by the narrow margin of 83 to 79.

During 1969–70 the Austrian economy experienced boom conditions. Unemployment was at its lowest since 1945, and the labour force included 77,000 foreign workers. There were practically no strikes. In 1969 the gross national product reached a record 323 billion schillings. (E. Dɪ.)

Barbados

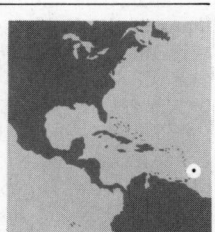

The parliamentary state of Barbados is a member of the Commonwealth of Nations and occupies the most easterly island in the southern Caribbean Sea. Area: 166 sq.mi. (430 sq.km.). Pop. (1969 est.): 252,900, predominantly Negro. Cap. and largest city: Bridgetown (pop., 1969, 12,300). Language: English. Religion: Christian, with Anglicans in the majority. Queen, Elizabeth II; governor-general in 1970, Sir Winston Scott; prime minister, Errol Walton Barrow.

A three-year development plan, launched in December 1969, provided a framework for expanding the island's economy, which in 1970 continued to depend on sugar and the thriving tourist industry. Some progress was being made with agricultural diversification and fishery development. In the manufacturing sector the plan allotted ECar$750,000 a year for building industrial estates which, together with increased activity in the construction and service industries, could help to reduce the 13% unemployment rate.

Social welfare developments included the introduction in April 1970 of a national insurance scheme to give 98,000 contributors old-age pensions. On May Day the Barbados Workers' Union called for implementation of International Labour Organization conventions (already ratified by the government) on

freedom of association and the right to organize and bargain collectively.

Trinidad's racial disturbances, culminating with its Black Power riots in April, prompted the Barbados government to pass a public order act and quash a proposal to hold a Black Power conference in Barbados in July. The island's interest in strengthening regional trade links was acknowledged in January when Barbados became the headquarters of the newly created Caribbean Development Bank.

(Sʜ. P.)

Baseball

The Baltimore Orioles followed third baseman Brooks Robinson (*see* Bɪᴏɢʀᴀᴘʜʏ) to baseball's biggest jackpot in 1970. The Orioles eliminated the Cincinnati Reds in five games to win the World Series. It was the same number of games in which the Orioles had lost the Series to the New York Mets in 1969. Robinson collected nine hits, including two home runs, and jolted the vaunted Cincinnati offense with superb defensive play. He was voted the Series' most valuable player.

Baltimore had won the American League pennant by winning three straight over the Minnesota Twins in the divisional play-offs. The scores were 10–6, 11–3, and 6–1. Cincinnati captured National League honours in a similar manner, ousting the Pittsburgh Pirates in the play-offs by 3–0, 3–1, and 3–2.

Minor league umpires worked the first game of the Cincinnati-Pittsburgh play-off series after the major league arbiters voted to strike in the wake of a salary dispute. Major league umpires asked $5,000 per man for the play-offs and $10,000 for the World Series. They settled for $3,000 and $7,000, respectively, moments before the second game of the play-offs was to get under way, pending further negotiations in which any agreement would become retroactive to the 1970 post-season games.

BARBADOS
Education. (1966–67) Primary, pupils 40,712, teachers 1,163; secondary, pupils 25,136, teachers 1,074; vocational, pupils 2,362, teachers 141; teacher training, students 300, teachers 30; higher, students 373, teaching staff 85.
Finance and Trade. Monetary unit: East Caribbean dollar, with a par value of ECar$2 to U.S. $1 (ECar $4.80 = £1 sterling). Budget (1969–70 est.): revenue ECar$27,768,000; expenditure ECar$62,061,000. Foreign trade (1968): imports ECar$168,067,000 (27% from U.K., 21% from U.S., 13% from Canada); exports ECar$73,509,000 (40% to U.K., 18% to U.S.). Main exports: sugar 40%; shellfish 10%; molasses 5%.
Agriculture. Sugar production, raw value (metric tons); (1969–70) 173,000 (1968–69) 142,000.

Table I. Final Major League Standings, 1970

American League
Eastern Division

Club	W.	L.	Pct.	G.B.	Balt.	N.Y.	Bos.	Det.	Clev.	Wash.	Cal.	Chi.	K.C.	Mil.	Minn.	Oak.
Baltimore	108	54	.667	—	—	11	13	11	14	12	7	9	12	7	5	7
New York	93	69	.574	15	7	—	8	11	10	10	7	11	9	7	6	
Boston	87	75	.537	21	5	10	—	9	12	12	5	8	7	5	7	
Detroit	79	83	.488	29	7	7	9	—	11	9	6	6	6	8	4	6
Cleveland	76	86	.469	32	4	8	6	7	—	11	6	6	8	7	6	7
Washington	70	92	.432	38	6	8	6	9	7	—	5	8	6	7	6	2

Western Division

Club	W.	L.	Pct.	G.B.	Minn.	Oak.	Cal.	K.C.	Mil.	Chi.	Balt.	Bos.	Clev.	Det.	N.Y.	Wash.
Minnesota	98	64	.605	—	—	13	10	13	13	12	7	5	6	8	5	6
Oakland	89	73	.549	9	5	—	10	11	10	16	5	5	5	6	6	10
California	86	76	.531	12	8	8	—	10	12	12	5	7	6	6	5	7
Kansas City	65	97	.401	33	5	7	8	—	12	11	0	5	4	6	1	6
Milwaukee	65	97	.401	33	5	8	6	6	—	11	5	7	5	4	3	5
Chicago	56	106	.346	42	6	2	6	7	7	—	3	4	6	6	5	4

Ties: Milwaukee 1, New York 1.

National League
Eastern Division

Club	W.	L.	Pct.	G.B.	Pitt.	Chi.	N.Y.	St.L.	Phil.	Mon.	Atl.	Cin.	Hou.	L.A.	S.D.	S.F.
Pittsburgh	89	73	.549	—	—	10	12	12	14	9	6	4	6	6	6	4
Chicago	84	78	.519	5	8	—	7	7	9	13	4	7	6	9	7	
New York	83	79	.512	6	6	11	—	12	13	8	6	4	6	5	6	
St. Louis	76	86	.469	13	6	11	6	—	10	11	5	3	6	5	8	5
Philadelphia	73	88	.453	15½	4	9	5	8	—	7	5	5	8	5	9	8
Montreal	73	89	.451	16	9	5	10	7	11	—	6	5	4	4	6	

Western Division

Club	W.	L.	Pct.	G.B.	Cin.	L.A.	S.F.	Hou.	Atl.	S.D.	Chi.	Mon.	N.Y.	Phil.	Pitt.	St.L.
Cincinnati	102	60	.630	—	—	13	9	15	13	8	5	7	8	7	8	9
Los Angeles	87	74	.540	14½	5	—	9	10	12	11	6	8	7	6	6	7
San Francisco	86	76	.531	16	9	9	—	8	11	13	5	6	6	4	8	7
Houston	79	83	.488	23	3	8	10	—	9	14	5	8	6	4	6	7
Atlanta	76	86	.469	26	5	6	7	9	—	9	8	6	6	7	6	7
San Diego	63	99	.389	39	7	5	4	9	7	—	3	6	3	6	4	

Source: *The Sporting News.*

Pitcher Denny McLain of Detroit, who had posted 31 wins in 1968, became baseball's biggest newsmaker in 1970. He was suspended three different times. On April 1, baseball commissioner Bowie Kuhn (*see* BIOGRAPHY) suspended McLain until July 1 for his involvement with gamblers. When McLain returned to the Tigers, he saw action in 14 games and his record was 3–5 at the time the Detroit management suspended him for seven days for throwing buckets of ice water on two sportswriters. Kuhn then suspended McLain for the remainder of the season, charging that he had been carrying a gun. Kuhn announced the end of the suspension shortly before the World Series and revealed that McLain, along with infielders Don Wert and Elliott Maddox and pitcher Norm McRae, had been traded to the Washington Senators in an eight-player deal. The Senators gave up pitchers Joe Coleman and Jim Hannan and infielders Ed Brinkman and Aurelio Rodriguez.

Another major post-season trade saw the St. Louis Cardinals send celebrated slugger Richie Allen to the Los Angeles Dodgers for infielder Ted Sizemore and minor league catcher Bob Stinson. Allen hit 34 home runs and drove in 101 runs in 1970 even though injuries allowed him to play only one game in the final seven weeks.

In October 1969 Allen had been secured by the Cardinals in a deal that sent outfielder Curt Flood to the Philadelphia Phillies. Flood elected not to play baseball in 1970, instead deciding to test the reserve clause, which binds a professional baseball player to his original team. On August 12, in a U.S. district court in New York, Judge Irving Ben Cooper ruled against Flood in his antitrust suit, upholding the defense argument that federal antitrust laws do not apply to baseball as a result of Supreme Court decisions in 1953 and 1957. Flood's attorneys announced that they would appeal the ruling. In November Flood signed a one-year contract with the Washington Senators, who gave up utility man Greg Goossen, first baseman Gene Martin, and pitcher Jeff Terpko to the Phillies in exchange.

Milwaukee rejoined the big league baseball ranks on March 31 after an absence of four years when the Seattle Pilots became the Milwaukee Brewers of the American League. A bankruptcy court approved the franchise move by the Pilots, who were beset with financial woes during their one-year stay in the league. The Milwaukee group paid $10.8 million.

The National League unveiled two dazzling new parks: Riverfront Stadium in Cincinnati and Three Rivers Stadium in Pittsburgh. Fittingly, the occupants, the Reds and the Pirates, each won a divisional title.

Hank Aaron of the Atlanta Braves slammed his 3,000th hit, the ninth player to do so, and Willie Mays of the San Francisco Giants joined Aaron in the select group shortly thereafter. The Chicago Cubs' Ernie Banks hit his 500th home run. Only eight others, including Mays and Aaron, had reached that plateau.

Tom Seaver of the New York Mets struck out ten successive San Diego batters on April 22 for a new major league record. He registered 19 strikeouts in all to tie another record. Four major league pitchers registered no-hit, no-run games: Dock Ellis of Pittsburgh, Clyde Wright of the California Angels, Bill Singer of the Dodgers, and rookie Vida Blue of the Oakland Athletics.

Hoyt Wilhelm of Atlanta, a much-traveled major league pitcher since 1952, pitched in his record 1,000th game on May 10, two months before his 47th birthday. The Cardinals' Vic Davalillo came through with 24 pinch-hits to tie the major league record. The National League endurance record owned by Billy Williams of the Cubs came to an end on September 3 as Williams sat out after playing in 1,117 consecutive games.

The Hall of Fame at Cooperstown, N.Y., inducted four new members: Ford Frick, Lou Boudreau, Jesse Haines, and Earle Combs. Jim Bouton (*see* BIOGRAPHY) wrote a controversial baseball book, *Ball Four,* recounting his experiences as a pitcher with the New York Yankees and Seattle Pilots.

Major Leagues. Baltimore won Eastern Division honours in the American League by 15 games over the runner-up New York Yankees. The Orioles produced three 20-game winners: Mike Cuellar (24–8), Dave McNally (24–9), and Jim Palmer (20–10). Baltimore finished the regular season with 11 straight wins, ran that streak to 14 with a three-game sweep in the play-offs, and boosted it to 17 in the first three games of the World Series. Minnesota took the Western Division by nine games, with Oakland second.

Cincinnati's margin in the Western Division of the National League was 14½ games. Los Angeles was the runner-up. The closest race in divisional play came in the National League East, where Pittsburgh survived a blistering stretch fight to outlast the Cubs by five games and the Mets by six.

A capacity crowd of 51,531 showed up for the first game of the World Series in Cincinnati's new Riverfront Stadium. Baltimore erased a 3–0 Cincinnati lead to win, 4–3. A home run by Brooks Robinson in the seventh inning shattered a 3–3 tie. Earlier John ("Boog") Powell and Elrod Hendricks homered for the Orioles, while Lee May hit one out for the Reds. The winner on a five-hitter was Jim Palmer, the loser Gary Nolan. A controversial play developed with Cincinnati batting in the sixth inning. Bernie Carbo attempted to score from third on Ty Cline's high chopper in front of the plate. As catcher Hendricks jumped out to field the ball, plate umpire Ken Burkhart moved between Carbo and Hendricks. Burkhart was flattened as Hendricks made a desperate lunge to tag Carbo, who represented the lead run. Even as he fell, Burkhart called Carbo out, precipitating a lengthy argument.

Baltimore also staged a big rally to capture the second game. The Orioles trailed, 4–0, after three innings, and then used a five-run fifth to triumph,

UPI COMPIX
Curt Flood of the St. Louis Cardinals. In August a federal judge ruled against his suit that challenged the legality of baseball's reserve clause.

UPI COMPIX
Cincinnati Reds' catcher Johnny Bench is too late with the tag as Baltimore Orioles' Boog Powell scores in the final game of the World Series. Baltimore won to take the series 4–1 over Cincinnati.

6–5. Powell slammed a home run in the fourth to set the stage for the Orioles' explosion. Baltimore collected six hits in the fifth, with the key blow a two-run double by Hendricks which dissolved a 4–4 deadlock. Cincinnati homers by Bobby Tolan and Johnny Bench went for naught. The winner in relief of Baltimore starter Mike Cuellar was Tom Phoebus. The loser in relief of Cincinnati starter Jim McGlothlin was Milt Wilcox.

Dave McNally pitched and batted the Orioles to victory in game three, 9–3, as the Series switched to Baltimore following an off-day. A crowd of 51,773 saw McNally become the first pitcher in World Series history to hit a grand slam home run. It came in the sixth inning and boosted the Orioles' lead to 8–1. Frank Robinson and Don Buford also homered for Baltimore. McNally surrendered nine hits in going the distance. The losing pitcher was Tony Cloninger. Brooks Robinson, who sparkled defensively for the third successive Series game, jolted Cloninger with a two-run first-inning double to put the Orioles ahead to stay.

Baltimore's bid for a four-game sweep was thwarted when Lee May's three-run eighth-inning home run off reliefer Eddie Watt rubbed out a 5–3 deficit and brought Cincinnati a 6–5 victory in the fourth contest. Clay Carroll earned the win in relief. Pete Rose also homered for the Reds. Brooks Robinson continued his sensational performance for Baltimore with four hits, including his second home run of the Series.

The Orioles won the Series, four games to one, by rolling over Cincinnati, 9–3, in the fifth game. The Reds got to Oriole starter Mike Cuellar for a 3–0 lead in the top of the first inning, but Cuellar pitched shutout baseball the rest of the game, yielding a total of six hits. Frank Robinson's two-run homer off loser Jim Merritt in the bottom of the first narrowed Baltimore's deficit to 3–2. Singles by Mark Belanger and Paul Blair drove in two more runs in the second and the Orioles never were headed. They collected 15 hits off six Cincinnati pitchers.

Baltimore thus wound up with 18 wins in its last 19 games of 1970, and its most convincing showing since a four-game World Series sweep of the Dodgers in 1966. Brooks Robinson and Blair totaled nine hits apiece during the Series, and the Orioles as a team racked up ten home runs, a record for a five-game Series.

Rico Carty won the National League batting title with an average of .366, highest in the majors since 1957 when Ted Williams hit .388. The American League batting race, however, went to the final day before being decided. Alex Johnson of the California Angels got two hits in his final three at-bats to finish with an average of .3289, thus beating out three-time titlist Carl Yastrzemski, the Boston slugger, who had completed his season a day earlier with a final average of .3286.

Frank Howard of Washington led the American League in home runs with 44, and in runs batted in with 126. In pitching the league produced seven 20-game winners. In addition to the Baltimore triumvirate of Cuellar, McNally, and Palmer, they were Jim Perry (24–12) of Minnesota, Clyde Wright (22–12) of California, Fritz Peterson (20–11) of the New York Yankees, and Sam McDowell (20–12) of Cleveland. McDowell paced the strikeout department with 304.

In the National League, Bob Gibson of St. Louis turned in his fifth 20-game season with a record of

UPI COMPIX

Brooks Robinson of the Baltimore Orioles makes a diving catch on a line drive by Cincinnati Reds' Johnny Bench during the third game of the World Series.

23–7. San Francisco's Gaylord Perry, a brother to Minnesota's 24-game winner, Jim, also reached the coveted circle with 23–13. Ferguson Jenkins of the Cubs posted his fourth 20-game year in succession with a 22–16 mark. The fourth 20-game winner in the league was Cincinnati's Jim Merritt (20–12). Tom Seaver of the Mets led in strikeouts with 283. Johnny Bench of the Reds captured the home run title with 45 and also paced the runs batted in category with 148.

The Most Valuable Player awards went to "Boog" Powell of the Orioles in the American League and to Johnny Bench of the Reds in the National. The Cy Young Awards for best pitchers were given to Jim Perry of the Twins in the American League and to the Cardinals' Bob Gibson in the National. Rookie-of-the-year honours went to Thurman Munson, a New York Yankee catcher, in the American League and to Carl Morton, a Montreal Expo pitcher, in the National.

Table II. Minor League Champions, 1970

League	Won pennant	Won play-offs
	Class AAA	
American Association	East—Omaha	Omaha
	West—Denver	
International	Syracuse	Syracuse
Pacific Coast	North—Spokane	Spokane
	South—Hawaii	
Mexican	North—Mexico City Reds	Veracruz
	South—Veracruz	
	Class AA	
Eastern	Waterbury	No play-off
Southern	Columbus, Ga.	No play-off
Texas	East—Memphis	Albuquerque
	West—Albuquerque	
	Class A	
California	1st half—Bakersfield	No play-off
	2nd half—Bakersfield	
Carolina	1st half—Winston-Salem	Winston-Salem
	2nd half—Burlington, N.C.	
Florida State	East—Miami	Miami
	West—St. Petersburg	
Mexican Center	1st half—Madero	No play-off
	2nd half—Madero	
Mexican Southeast	1st half—Puerto Mexico	Puerto Mexico
	2nd half—Campeche	
Midwest	1st half—Quincy	Quincy
	2nd half—Quad Cities	
New York–Pennsylvania	Auburn	No play-off
Northern	Duluth	No play-off
Northwest	North—Lewiston*	No play-off
	South—Coos Bay-North Bend	
Western Carolinas	1st half—Greenville	No play-off
	2nd half—Greenville	
	Rookie	
Appalachian	Bluefield	No play-off
Gulf Coast	White Sox	No play-off
Pioneer	Idaho Falls	No play-off

Note: The Junior World Series was resumed in 1970, with Syracuse, International League champions, beating Omaha, winners in the American Association, four games to one.
*Declared champion on basis of regular-season play with Coos Bay-North Bend.
Source: *The Sporting News.*

UPI COMPIX
Uniform of Detroit Tigers' Denny McLain hangs in his locker. In 1970 McLain was suspended for half of the season for contributing to a bookmaking operation; then later for the remainder of the season for carrying a gun.

Frank Alfano's infield single with the bases loaded and none out in the 15th decided the issue in the week-long, double elimination tournament. The winner in relief was Jim Barr, who shut out the Seminoles over the last eight innings.

The American Association of College Baseball Coaches named a 1970 collegiate all-American team. It included Doug Howard of Brigham Young University at first base; Dave Yates of the University of Delaware at second base; Mike Schmidt of Ohio University at shortstop; Pete Duncan of Washington State at third base; Sam Ewing of the University of Tennessee, Steve Mikulic of the University of Arizona, and Gene Hiser of the University of Maryland in the outfield; Arnold Holtberg of Princeton as catcher; and Brent Strom of Southern California and Burt Hooton of the University of Texas as pitchers.

In Little League competition Wayne, N.J., defeated Campbell, Calif., 2–0 in the World Series championship game. A two-run double by Dave Shaver gave Wayne the triumph. Chinandega, Nic., beat Highland, Ind., 3–0 for third place. (J. BE.)

The National League defeated the American League, 5–4, in 12 innings in the 41st annual All-Star game in Cincinnati. Jim Hickman of the Cubs singled home the Reds' Pete Rose from second for the winning run. A home run by the Giants' Dick Dietz in the ninth inning had triggered a three-run rally by the Nationals to send the game into extra innings. A crowd of 51,838 watched the National League win the classic for the eighth straight time. The winner was Claude Osteen of the Dodgers, the loser Clyde Wright of the Angels. With their victory the Nationals had a record in the All-Star game of 23 wins against 17 losses and 1 tie.

Mid-season managerial changes found Bob Lemon replacing Charlie Metro at Kansas City and Charlie Fox taking over for Clyde King at San Francisco. In a late season shift Chuck Tanner was named manager of the Chicago White Sox, replacing Don Gutteridge. In post-season announcements, Dick Williams took over John McNamara's job at Oakland, and Billy Martin moved in for Mayo Smith at Detroit.

Amateur. Southern California ruled the college baseball World Series for the sixth time in 1970. The Trojans won the National Collegiate Athletic Association (NCAA) title by stopping Florida State, 2–1, in the 15-inning championship game. Second baseman

Basketball

United States. *Collegiate.* The University of California at Los Angeles (UCLA) continued to dominate U.S. college basketball despite the loss by graduation of All-America centre Lew Alcindor. With a balanced attack—none of their starters was among the nation's top 50 scorers—the UCLA Bruins finished the season with a 28–2 won-and-lost record and for an unprecedented fourth successive year won top honours in the National Collegiate Athletic Association (NCAA) tournament.

The Bruins accomplished this principally as a result of superior team play. All five of their starters averaged more than 10 points per game. Sidney Wicks, a 6-ft. 8-in. forward, led in scoring with an average of 18.6 points a game. Other starters were John Vallely, a guard and the only senior on the squad, 16.3 points; Henry Bibby, guard, 15.6; Curtis Rowe, forward, 15.3; and Steve Patterson, who replaced Alcindor as centre, 12.5.

The Bruins played their usual fast-break style accompanied by a "pressure" defense. As a team they made half of their field goal attempts, and all of their regulars made good on at least 48% of their shots. For the season, UCLA averaged 91.9 points per game, compared with 73.4 for their opponents.

Going into NCAA tournament play, Kentucky was the favourite. It had lost only one of its 26 regular-season games and was ranked first in the nation in the final regular weekly polls conducted by the Associated Press (AP) and the United Press International (UPI).

Kentucky won its first tournament game, defeating Notre Dame 109–99, but was then upset by Jacksonville (Fla.) University 106–100 in the finals of the Mideast Regional which, in effect, was an NCAA quarterfinal. It was a stunning victory for Jacksonville's Dolphins, who then advanced to the finals with a 91–83 triumph over St. Bonaventure. UCLA, in the meantime, was advancing easily, eliminating Utah State 101–79 in the quarterfinals and New Mexico State 93–77 in the semifinals.

Jacksonville and UCLA then met in the climactic championship game. Jacksonville, which had a distinct height advantage, opened up an early 22–13 lead and

Hank Aaron of the Atlanta Braves connects for his 3,000th career hit in a game against Cincinnati on May 17. Aaron was the ninth player in major league history to reach the 3,000-hit mark.

UPI COMPIX

was being paced by Artis Gilmore, a 7-ft. 2-in. centre who scored 14 of those points. UCLA then changed its defense. The result was that Gilmore was held to two baskets thereafter and was held scoreless for a stretch of 16 minutes.

The Bruins took the lead and went ahead to stay at 37–36 with 1 minute 20 seconds remaining in the first half. The go-ahead goal was scored by Bibby, after receiving a perfect pass from Vallely. Wicks was especially brilliant in the game. He guarded Gilmore, blocking 5 of his shots and forcing him to miss 20 of his 29 field goal attempts. Moreover, Wicks, though six inches shorter, outrebounded Gilmore 18–16. The game, which had a final score of 80–69, was UCLA's 24th consecutive tournament victory, an NCAA record. In the National Invitational Tournament (NIT) Marquette defeated St. John's 65–53.

Pete (Pistol Pete) Maravich of Louisiana State, a talented and record-breaking shot-maker, was the nation's most highly publicized college player. He broke his own records while winning the NCAA's major division scoring championship, setting new standards in the two major categories, most points in one season and most points throughout a college career. For the season, Maravich scored 1,381 points on 522 field goals (also a record) and 337 free throws. He played in 31 games, giving him a game average of 44.5 points, another record. He scored 69 points in a game against Alabama, the highest total scored by an individual in one game for the season and the fourth highest in major division history.

Maravich led the nation's scorers in each of his three varsity seasons at Louisiana State, increasing his totals and accuracy each year. He scored 1,138 points as a sophomore (43.8 average); 1,148 as a junior (44.2) average; and the aforementioned 1,381 points as a senior. This gave him a career total of 3,667 points, breaking the previous career high of 2,973 set by Oscar Robertson. Maravich's career average of 44.2 was 10.4 points better than the previous mark, also held by Robertson.

Maravich's sensational play overshadowed the largest group of high scorers in NCAA history. Austin Carr of Notre Dame was second to Maravich with 1,108 points, a 38.1 average, and Rick Mount of Purdue finished third with a 35.4 average. Calvin Murphy of Niagara, who like Maravich was finishing a brilliant three-year collegiate career, was eighth with an average of 29.4 points and had a career total of 33.1, third best in NCAA history.

Players chosen on the first-string All-American team, as published in the *Official NCAA Basketball Guide*, were: Rick Mount of Purdue; Bob Lanier, St. Bonaventure; Calvin Murphy, Niagara; Maravich, Louisiana State; and Dan Issel, Kentucky. The second team consisted of Austin Carr, Notre Dame; Jimmy Collins, New Mexico State; John Roche, South Carolina; Charlie Scott, North Carolina; and Sidney Wicks, UCLA.

Philadelphia College of Textiles and Science, with no starters taller than 6 ft. 5 in. and none averaging as much as 20 points, won the NCAA college division tournament, defeating Tennessee State 76–65 in the championship game. Philadelphia Textile finished the season with a 29–2 record and with a 28-game winning streak. John Rinka of Kenyon, for the second season in a row, won the college division scoring title with 942 points, an average of 41 per game.

Professional. The New York Knickerbockers, stressing defense and always trying to hit the open man on offense, won their first National Basketball Association (NBA) championship by defeating the Los Angeles Lakers in a memorable seven-game play-off. With the series tied after six games, the Knicks won the seventh and final game 113–99, bringing to an end 23 years of championship frustration.

Willis Reed, a 6-ft. 10-in. centre who was the Knicks' individual star (*see* BIOGRAPHY), suffered a serious hip and thigh injury in the fifth game. His absence in the sixth contest helped the Lakers to gain a 135–113 victory and tie the series. Reed received medication before the seventh game and played for the first 27 minutes. He scored New York's first two baskets, his only points of the game, and was an inspirational force in the victory.

Reed's second goal broke a 2–2 tie and triggered a surge that sent the Knicks ahead 9–2. They led 38–24 at the end of the first quarter, 69–42 at half time, and 94–69 going into the final quarter, when they easily withstood a final Laker rally. Walt Frazier led the Knicks in scoring with a brilliant 36-point performance, sinking 12 of 17 field goal attempts and scoring on each of his 12 free throws.

Coached by William (Red) Holzman, a one-time player who emphasized fundamentals, the Knicks finished their regular season with a record of 60 victories and 22 defeats. They dominated the Eastern Division race from the outset, winning their first 5 games and then, after a loss, winning 18 more in a row, a league record. This gave them a 23–1 record, and they led the division thereafter. The Milwaukee Bucks, paced by rookie star Lew Alcindor, finished second in the East with a 56–26 record. Baltimore finished third and Philadelphia fourth.

The Atlanta Hawks won the NBA's Western Division championship with a 48–34 record, finishing two

WIDE WORLD

Sidney Wicks of UCLA goes up for the ball against Jacksonville's Artis Gilmore at College Park, Md. The Bruins' 80–69 victory over Jacksonville gave them their fourth straight NCAA championship.

Table I. Major College Champions, 1970

League	Team and location	League record	All games
Eastern (Ivy)	Pennsylvania (Philadelphia)	14–0	25–2
Yankee	Massachusetts (Amherst)	8–2	18–7
	Connecticut (Storrs)	8–2	14–9
Atlantic Coast	South Carolina (Columbia)	14–0	25–3
Southeastern	Kentucky (Lexington)	17–1	26–2
Southern	Davidson (N.C.)	10–0	22–5
Ohio Valley	Western Kentucky (Bowling Green)	14–0	22–3
Intercollegiate (Big Ten)	Iowa (Iowa City)	14–0	20–5
Mid-American	Ohio Univ. (Athens)	9–1	20–5
Big Eight	Kansas State (Manhattan)	10–4	20–8
Missouri Valley	Drake (Des Moines, Ia.)	14–2	22–7
Southwest	Rice (Houston, Tex.)	10–4	14–11
Western A.C.	Texas (El Paso)	10–4	17–8
AAWU (Pacific Eight)	UCLA (Los Angeles, Calif.)	12–2	28–2
West Coast	Santa Clara (Calif.)	11–3	23–6
	Pacific (Stockton, Calif.)	11–3	21–6

Table II. NBA Final Standings and Play-offs, 1970

Eastern Division				Western Division			
Team	W	L	Pct.	Team	W	L	Pct.
New York	60	22	.732	Atlanta	48	34	.585
Milwaukee	56	26	.683	Los Angeles	46	36	.561
Baltimore	50	32	.610	Chicago	39	43	.476
Philadelphia	42	40	.512	Phoenix	39	43	.476
Cincinnati	36	46	.439	Seattle	36	46	.439
Boston	34	48	.415	San Francisco	30	52	.366
Detroit	31	51	.378	San Diego	27	55	.329

Play-offs

Eastern semifinals	Western semifinals
Milwaukee 4, Philadelphia 1	Atlanta 4, Chicago 1
New York 4, Baltimore 3	Los Angeles 4, Phoenix 3
Eastern finals	Western finals
New York 4, Milwaukee 1	Los Angeles 4, Atlanta 0

Championship series

New York defeated Los Angeles 4 games to 3
New York 124, Los Angeles 112
Los Angeles 105, New York 103
New York 111, Los Angeles 108 (overtime)
Los Angeles 121, New York 115 (overtime)
New York 107, Los Angeles 100
Los Angeles 135, New York 113
New York 113, Los Angeles 99

JOHN ZIMMERMAN,
LIFE MAGAZINE © TIME INC.

New York's Willis Reed eludes the taller Lew Alcindor of Milwaukee during the NBA Eastern Division play-off game in New York City April 13. The Knicks edged the Bucks 112–111 to take a 2–0 lead in the play-off series.

games ahead of the Los Angeles Lakers who were crippled by injuries much of the season. Laker star Wilt Chamberlain ruptured a tendon in his right knee and missed 70 games. Chicago and Phoenix finished in a third place tie, both qualifying for play-off positions.

New York defeated Baltimore in seven games and Milwaukee eliminated Philadelphia in five games in the Eastern Division semifinals. A seventh-game 127–114 victory over Baltimore kept the Knicks alive. Milwaukee had an easy time whipping Philadelphia and in one game, in which nine play-off records were set, beat the 76ers by a whopping 156–120 score. Alcindor had scoring totals of 36, 33, 33, 33, and 46 in this series.

In the Western Division semifinals, the Atlanta Hawks eliminated Chicago in five games, using mostly a tight defense that minimized the effectiveness of Chet Walker and Bob Love, Chicago's high-scoring forwards. With Chamberlain working his way back into the lineup, Los Angeles rallied to beat the Phoenix Suns. Phoenix won three of the first four games in this series but failed in three subsequent attempts to gain the necessary fourth victory.

The Lakers, reaching the peak of their game, whipped Atlanta in four straight in the Western Division finals, a remarkable achievement. In so doing, they became the first club in NBA history to win seven consecutive play-off games. New York, in the meantime, eliminated Milwaukee in five games in the Eastern Division finals. The classic seven-game New York v. Los Angeles series followed.

Jerry West of Los Angeles, a ten-year NBA veteran, won the league's individual scoring title with 2,309 points, a 31.2 average. It was West's first such championship. Alcindor of Milwaukee was second with a 28.8 average; Elvin Hayes of San Diego, third, with 27.5; and Billy Cunningham, Philadelphia, fourth, with 26.1.

The league's top individual honour was won by Reed of the Knicks, who was selected its most valu-

able player. Reed, who had finished second in the balloting for this award the previous season, was a close winner over Jerry West of Los Angeles. Lew Alcindor of Milwaukee, selected rookie of the year, was third in the most valuable player voting.

The NBA's cumulative attendance was 5,146,858, the league's first season over 5 million and an 11.6% increase over the previous season in which 14 clubs also competed. That professional basketball was making large strides as a spectator sport was also demonstrated when the NBA signed a new three-year television contract with the American Broadcasting Company for a reported $17 million.

The Indiana Pacers won the championship in the rival American Basketball Association (ABA), defeating the Los Angeles Stars four games to two. Subsequently, there was considerable discussion of the possibility of a merger between the established NBA and the comparatively new ABA, but the leagues were still operating independently of each other when the 1970–71 season began.   (JE. HO.)

World Amateur. The final of the 1969–70 European Cup for men was played before 5,000 spectators at Sarajevo, Yugos., when Ignis, Varese, representing Italy, defeated Moscow's Red Army Club, T.S.S.K.A., in a tremendous game by 79–74. The climax of the European Cup Winners' Cup took place when the Fides Club of Naples, Italy, played JA Vichy of France. The first round, played at Vichy, resulted in a 64–60 win for the home club. In the second leg in Naples, Fides won 87–65, giving them the cup. The European Cup for women went once more to Daugava Riga, of the U.S.S.R.; the Soviet women gained their ninth victory when they beat TS Wisla, Krakow, of Poland 61–45 and 59–42.

The 1970 world championships took place in Yugoslavia. The elimination rounds were played at Sarajevo, Split, and Karlovac, and the finals in Ljubljana. The U.S.S.R., Yugoslavia (which qualified for the final round by being the host country), and the United States were the seeded competitors. At Sarajevo, the U.S. was undefeated and, with Czechoslovakia, went through to the final pool. At Split, Brazil, playing brilliantly, ousted Italy from first place and qualified with Italy for the finals. At Karlovac, the U.S.S.R. had no trouble in heading its group, and Uruguay, in second place, accompanied them to Ljubljana.

The championship round, played as a league, provided exciting basketball. Brazil defeated the U.S.S.R. 66–64, and then Czechoslovakia beat Brazil 72–71 to gain its first victory in the final round. The real surprise came, however, when the Italians defeated the U.S. 66–64. Then Yugoslavia tussled with the U.S. in a match the Yugoslavians had to win to secure the title. In an atmosphere of intense emotion Yugoslavia triumphed 70–63. The world championships were, in effect, over and the championship crown was Yugoslavia's. The final standings were: Yugoslavia, Brazil, U.S.S.R., Italy, U.S., Czechoslovakia, Uruguay, Cuba, Panama, Canada, Korea, Australia, and the United Arab Republic.

Basketball was honoured on May 14 when René Maheu, director general of UNESCO, presented the International Fair Play Trophy Pierre de Coubertin for 1969 to Francisco Buscato, a player of Badalona, Spain, because of his actions on Dec. 25, 1969, when he refused to take advantage of an opponent's injury in a game against Real Madrid.   (K. K. MI.)

ENCYCLOPÆDIA BRITANNICA FILMS. *Basic Elementary Basketball Skills* (1967); *Playing Better Basketball* (1967).

Beekeeping:
see Agriculture

Beer:
see Alcoholic
Beverages

Belgium

A constitutional monarchy on the North Sea coast of Europe, Belgium is bordered by the Netherlands, West Germany, Luxembourg, and France. Area: 11,784 sq.mi. (30,514 sq.km.). Pop. (1970 est.): 9,660,754. Cap.: Brussels (pop., 1970 est., 164,013). Largest city: Antwerp (pop., 1970 est., 230,184). Language: French and Dutch. Religion: predominantly Roman Catholic. King, Baudouin I; prime minister in 1970, Gaston Eyskens.

Renewed efforts were made during 1970 to establish cultural autonomy for the Flemish and Walloon communities. An all-party conference, presided over by the prime minister, led to a consensus on the need for restructuring Belgium on a basis of broad regionalism, recognizing the three cultural communities (the Flemish, the Walloon, and the bilingual French- and Dutch-language community in Brussels), which should be granted real autonomy in a number of fields. Agreement was reached also on the reorganization and modernization of the country's institutions. Viewpoints on Brussels could not be reconciled, however. The Brussels French-language delegates insisted on the incorporation in the bilingual Brussels conurbation of six Flemish boroughs where French-speaking inhabitants had enjoyed certain administrative facilities since 1963. In some instances they now outnumbered the Dutch-speaking inhabitants. All Flemish politicians firmly rejected this request.

Though the deadlock on Brussels could not be broken, the government drew up new proposals aimed at a national compromise that would preserve Belgian unity on new foundations. The proposals were submitted to Parliament on Feb. 18, 1970. Some 15 points received parliamentary approval, including the transfer of power to supranational authorities; the creation of federations of boroughs and conurbations, and the first step toward the administrative reorganization of the municipalities. When, however, the first "community" articles (relating to cultural autonomy) were voted upon, just before the summer recess, the constitutional quorum (two-thirds of the members present) was not attained. The government's compromise proposals suffered a further heavy blow when municipal elections on October 11 resulted in considerable gains for French-language parties in the Brussels area. Prime Minister Eyskens nevertheless decided to maintain his proposals and began talks with various groups. A new compromise was worked out, and by the end of the year all "community" articles in the constitution had been approved by both houses of Parliament, putting an end to a legislative battle that had lasted 16 years.

The other main item in the government program, planning and economic decentralization, was approved by Parliament, but it ran into difficulties on the language question, especially the limits of the Brussels economic area. A second bill, tacked on as a corollary to the economic decentralization measure, specifically mentioned that the six disputed Flemish boroughs would come under the Economic Council for Flanders. The Walloon Social Christian leader, Léon Servais, warned, however, that the ministers belonging to his group would resign if the second bill was enacted before guarantees for the minorities had been included in the constitution.

A dispute on harbour policy arose from a decision by the minister of public works to build a new sea lock at Zeebrugge for ships of up to 125,000 tons deadweight. Harbour interests at Antwerp and Ghent were disturbed but were given assurances. Walloon politicians and the Walloon Economic Council objected to the investment at Zeebrugge and sought compensation to further economic expansion in their region.

During wildcat strikes in January in the Limburg mines, in protest against the social programming worked out by employers and trade unions, independent workers' committees were set up, but the authorities refused to negotiate with them. At a subsequent economic and social conference, organized at the request of the trade unions, a formula was agreed upon for a guaranteed monthly wage, the preservation of purchasing power, and social security charges.

Legal status was granted to the two sections of both Brussels and Louvain (Leuven) universities, which thus became independent. The government also decided to create a complete university at Antwerp.

Although economic activity weakened, industry was working at full capacity at midsummer. The total of unemployed fell to 20,528 (10,544 fewer than at the corresponding period in 1969). The price index rose by 4.1%. (JA. R. E.)

BELGIUM

Education. (1967–68) Primary, pupils 1,015,563, teachers 47,902; secondary, pupils 300,101, teachers 40,074; vocational (1966–67), pupils 487,889, teachers 47,956; teacher training, students 24,847, teachers 6,089; higher (at 4 universities), students 59,172, teaching staff 5,489.

Finance. Monetary unit: Belgian franc, with a par value of BFr. 50 to U.S. $1 (BFr. 120 = £1 sterling). Gold, SDRs, and foreign exchange, central bank: (June 1970) U.S. $2,290,000,000; (June 1969) U.S. $2,024,-000,000. Budget (1969 est.): revenue BFr. 265,071,-000,000; expenditure BFr. 303,439,000,000. Gross national product: (1968) BFr. 1,036,000,000,000; (1967) BFr. 975 billion. Money supply: (May 1970) BFr. 400 billion; (May 1969) BFr. 382 billion. Cost of living (1963 = 100): (June 1970) 128; (June 1969) 124.

Foreign Trade. (Belgium-Luxembourg economic union; 1969) Imports BFr. 498.2 billion; exports BFr. 501.6 billion. Import sources: EEC 57% (West Germany 23%, France 16%, Netherlands 14%); U.S. 8%; U.K. 7%. Export destinations: EEC 67% (West Germany 23%, France 21%, Netherlands 19%); U.S. 7%. Main exports: iron and steel 6%; machinery 10%; motor vehicles 9%; nonferrous metals 9%; textile yarns and fabrics 8%; chemicals 8%.

Transport and Communications. Roads (1968) 91,758 km. (including 335 km. expressways in 1967). Motor vehicles in use (1968): passenger 1,806,464; commercial 270,026. Railways: (state only; 1968) 4,282 km.; traffic (1969) 8,237,000,000 passenger-km., freight 7,369,000,000 net ton-km. Air traffic (1969): 2,206,000,000 passenger-km.; freight 177,710,000 net ton-km. Shipping (1969): merchant vessels 100 gross tons and over 228; gross tonnage 1,051,882. Navigable inland waterways in regular use (1968) 1,589 km. Telephones (Dec. 1968) 1,839,457. Radio receivers (Dec. 1968) 3.2 million. Television receivers (Dec. 1968) 1,894,000.

Agriculture. Production (in 000; metric tons; 1969; 1968 in parentheses): wheat 772 (855); oats c. 273 (315); barley 552 (574); rye 73 (87); potatoes 1,478 (1,566); apples c. 300 (175); flax fibre 18 (18); sugar, raw value (1969–70) c. 685, (1968–69) 586; meat (1968) 628, (1967) 571; fish catch (1968) 68, (1967) 64.

Industry. Fuel and power (in 000; 1969): coal 13,-200 metric tons; manufactured gas (1968) 4,247,000 cu.m.; electricity 29,134,000 kw-hr. Production (in 000; metric tons; 1969): pig iron 11,217; crude steel 12,876; copper 301; lead 112; zinc 262; tin 4.5; sulfuric acid 1,837; cement 6,270; cotton yarn 75; cotton fabrics 71; wool yarn 81.

AGNELLI, GIOVANNI

Fiat, the giant Italian automobile manufacturer, in 1970 saw the first automobiles go off the assembly line at its plant in the Soviet Union. Begun in 1967, the Fiat plant was one of the largest in the U.S.S.R. to be financed by a Western nation. Also during the year Fiat more than doubled its financial interest in the French auto firm Citroën. Behind these decisions was one of Italy's leading industrialists, Giovanni Agnelli, the chairman of the board of Fiat. They were typical of the farsighted ventures that had marked Agnelli's tenure as head of Fiat and had built it into one of Italy's largest industrial concerns.

Born in Turin on March 12, 1921, the son of the founder of Fiat, Agnelli lost both his parents as a youth and was raised in large part by his grandfather. He obtained a degree in law from the University of Turin and then served with distinction in World War II. After the war he began working at Fiat, becoming managing director in 1963 and chairman of the board in 1966.

To all his activities, and particularly at Fiat, Agnelli brought vast and well-established international connections and a progressive feeling for the human values of work. He was active in promoting public welfare programs in many parts of the world, especially in Turin.

During the centennial celebrations of the unification of Italy, held in 1961, Agnelli presided over the international labour exhibition, in which more than 30 nations, including the U.S. and the Soviet Union, participated. He also became a prime mover in initiating plans to establish an international training centre for less developed countries under the sponsorship of the International Labour Office. Among Agnelli's other positions were membership on the international committee of the Chase Manhattan Bank, N.A., and membership on the board of directors of the Atlantic Community Development Group for Latin America.   (F. G.)

AGNEW, SPIRO THEODORE

Woodrow Wilson's vice-president, Thomas Marshall, said that "what this country needs is a really good five-cent cigar," but after his time U.S. vice-presidents remained remarkably unquotable. Spiro Agnew changed all that. In 1970 alone he produced "vicars of vacillation," "hopeless, hysterical hypochondriacs of history," "nattering nabobs of negativism," and "pusillanimous pussyfooters," among others. Republican faithful flocked to fund-raising dinners where he appeared, not merely to hear the Word but to find out how euphonically he would phrase it.

Agnew became something of a folk figure to both friends and enemies. His likeness appeared on T-shirts and buttons. A California doctor founded a thriving business by making Spiro Agnew watches, patterned after the Mickey Mouse watches of an earlier generation (Agnew said he didn't mind if the profits went to charity). The GOP National Committee sent records of his speeches to campaign contributors.

There was, of course, a more serious side to his activities, which as the November election grew closer consisted largely of crossing and recrossing the country in support of Nixon-favoured candidates. It was then that he coined "radic-lib"—short for "radical-liberal." He never precisely defined who the radic-libs were, but by implication they included everyone to the left of Nixon and, most especially, Democratic aspirants to crucial Senate seats. Even one Republican was tarred by the radic-lib brush—Charles Goodell, the liberal senator from New York.

Goodell ran third in a three-way race, but the overall effect of Agnew's hard-hitting tactics was not so clear. The states where he had campaigned most intensively went both ways. Certainly he aroused strong feelings. Media pundits—among his favourite targets—pointed out that, by crystallizing public resentment against such targets as the dissident young, he was further polarizing an already divided country. Yet early in the year a Gallup poll found he was the third most admired American—after Nixon and the Rev. Billy Graham.

Not all Agnew's duties were political. He made two Far Eastern tours, the first of which was the subject of a USIA propaganda film. Born Nov. 9, 1918, Agnew spent most of his life in and around Baltimore. He was governor of Maryland before becoming vice-president.

AKUFO-ADDO, EDWARD

Ghana completed its return to civilian and democratic rule in August 1970 when it elected its chief justice, Edward Akufo-Addo, as president. The military leaders went back to their barracks, from which they had emerged in 1966 to stage a successful coup against Pres. Kwame Nkrumah, still in exile in Guinea. The new president, a bitter opponent of Nkrumah, was the chairman of the constitutional commission appointed by the military junta to restore parliamentary democracy to Ghana. By his own recommendations, the president's post was nonexecutive; effective power resided with the prime minister, K. A. Busia.

For a time in the 1940s, Akufo-Addo had worked in political alliance with the young Kwame Nkrumah in the anticolonial movement, the United Gold Coast Convention, but he later broke with Nkrumah's brand of radicalism. Strongly opposed to British colonialism, he was still conservative in his outlook, a great admirer of the British model of democracy and a respecter of the traditionalism of the tribal chiefs.

Ghana's new president was born in Akwapim in 1906 and was educated at Oxford University in England, where he read mathematics. He then went on to read law at the Middle Temple, London, and was called to the bar in 1940. On his return home he quickly established a flourishing legal practice in Accra. He was a close collaborator of Ghana's grand old man of nationalist politics, J. B. Danquah, to whom he was related by marriage. He served briefly as a member of the colonial Legislative Council, but in 1948 was exiled for a period after riots in the capital. After his release he took a strong political line against Nkrumah. In 1962 he agreed to serve as a Supreme Court judge but, after only two years, he was dismissed when he and two fellow judges acquitted three politicians accused of attempting to assassinate Nkrumah. He was made chief justice after the army coup.   (Co. L.)

ALFVÉN, HANNES OLOF GÖSTA

A relatively unsung Swedish astrophysicist, Hannes Alfvén shared the 1970 Nobel Prize for Physics with Louis Néel (*q.v.*) of France. Alfvén was honoured for "fundamental work in magnetohydrodynamics with fruitful applications in different parts of plasma physics."

Plasma, which is believed to make up 99% of the universe, is a form of matter distinct from solids, liquids, or normal gases. It is a gaseous state that is electrically neutral in the aggregate but which contains ions, free electrons, and neutral particles, and is electrically conductive. Magnetohydrodynamics (MHD) is the study of plasmas in magnetic fields, and Alfvén is credited as being the preeminent pioneer in this field.

As early as 1942 he theorized that plasma in space would create electromagnetic waves when passing through magnetic fields. His theories were confirmed by spacecraft monitors, and the waves that have been observed bear his name. His work is considered critical to the eventual harnessing of the enormous energy produced by the thermonuclear explosion of a hydrogen bomb. "Without Alfvén's work, man's attempt to control the fusion process probably could not have started," according to one scientist.

For many years Alfvén's contributions were generally overlooked, and he was even at times "without honour in his own country." He condemned Swedish nuclear development—one reactor that was built in spite of him did not work—and left the country. Offered posts abroad, he went to the Soviet Union but left after two months for the University of California in San Diego, where he joined the faculty and taught half of each year. Under a pseudonym he published a science fiction novel, *The Great Computer*.

Having made peace with the Swedish government, Alfvén spent the other half of the year at the Royal Institute of Technology in Stockholm. He began his teaching career there in 1940, served as a professor of electronics from 1945 to 1963, and taught plasma physics from 1963 to 1967. Alfvén was born May 30, 1908, and educated at Uppsala.   (Ph. K.)

ALLENDE GOSSENS, SALVADOR

The first Marxist ever to be elected president of a democratic country by the free vote of the people, Salvador Allende Gossens became president of Chile on Nov. 3, 1970. He had emerged as the front-runner by a small plurality in a three-man race on September 4 with rightist Jorge Alessandri and Christian Democrat Radomiro Tomic. His plurality was enough to send him into the constitutionally required runoff election in the Chilean Congress with Alessandri on October 24. Although it is a Chilean tradition that the man with the most popular votes is confirmed by the vote of the 200-member Congress, Allende's victory was made even more certain by the speed with which Tomic and another Christian Democrat leader, Bernardo Leighton, moved to give him their support. Of the 200 votes, Allende received 153.

Allende's victory was a surprise not only to his enemies but to himself and his coalition, Unidad Popular, which was made up of Socialists, Communists, left-wing Christian Democrats, and dissident Radicals. He had lost three previous attempts to win a Chilean presidential election, and all predictions were that he would be nosed out by the 74-year-old Alessandri.

Allende had campaigned on a Marxist platform calling for wholesale nationalization of big businesses and industry and for immediate resumption of diplomatic relations with Cuba. However, he occupied himself in preinauguration days trying to soften his image in an attempt to forestall any effort to defeat him in the runoff or bar him from office by force. He gave the shocked Christian Democrats assurances that he would not interfere with Chile's democratic institutions, with the professionalism of the armed forces, or with the freedom of the press.

Allende was born in Santiago on July 26,

1908, and was trained as both a physician and a lawyer. But he spent his entire adult life in politics. Despite his personal wealth he became a leftist early in his career and after the mid-1930s was the leader of the Socialist parties. In Chilean politics the Socialists follow the Peking-line of Marxist thought as compared with the Soviet-oriented Communist Party.   (J. A. O'L.)

ANNE ELIZABETH ALICE LOUISE, PRINCESS

Soon after Princess Anne began to carry out formal engagements on her own, it became clear that she was entering—perhaps more decisively than her brother Prince Charles—the magic circle composed of those members of the royal family who enjoy the particular favour of the British people. As the princess undertook engagements of increasing diversity, she gave special pleasure, not only by her youth and good looks but by her clothes, her vivacity, her quick sympathy, and her interest in all kinds of machinery. Even her occasional tart rejoinders were welcomed as contributing to the impression of a vivid personality.

It was probably more difficult for Princess Anne to find what she really wanted to do and what, in her position, she could do than it would be for her younger brothers. She had often felt disadvantaged by being a girl and the second child, particularly in her earliest years when, with her only sibling the heir to the throne, she inevitably felt somewhat unregarded. A recurrence of this feeling may have contributed to the "glumness" widely commented upon during her and Prince Charles' visit to the White House in July 1970, during which, according to at least one reporter, she was upstaged by her brother. Other factors were the crowds, the reporters, the heat, and the effect of the flight from Canada (where they had been on a formal tour with their parents) on someone appallingly prone to air sickness. Her courageous recovery was a good deal more noteworthy than the initial lapse.

Born on Aug. 15, 1950, at Clarence House, London, her parents' home until Princess Elizabeth became queen in 1952, Princess Anne was brought up in the traditional royal-nursery-and-governess regime until she was sent (1963–68) as a boarder to Benenden School, near Cranbrook in Kent. There she received expert riding tuition and began to learn dressage. She did well in competitions and would like to be a successful rider because "if I'm good at it, I'm good at it—and not because I'm Princess Anne." She also enjoyed sailing, dancing, and pop music and to some extent shared Prince Charles' dramatic talent.   (S. Mu.)

ARAFAT, YASIR

Leader of Al Fatah, the largest organization of Palestinian guerrillas, Yasir Arafat suffered a considerable loss of authority during 1970 as a result of the clashes between the guerrillas and the Jordanian Army. These conflicts took place in June and September. On both occasions extremist groups and his own rank and file forced Arafat into a confrontation he had not sought. In June he emerged with considerable credit and with his leadership position greatly strengthened. But September proved a catastrophe. At first, Arafat was disowned by his own men and the extremist Popular Front for the Liberation of Palestine (PFLP), which had helped foment the conflict by hijacking airliners to Jordan. When Arafat did enter the battle against King Husain (q.v.), he was disowned by his two principal deputies, who agreed to a peace settlement despite Arafat's opposition. During the height of the crisis Arafat's leadership clearly broke down. He

Spiro Theodore Agnew
STEVE NORTHRUP FROM CAMERA 5

CENTRAL PRESS FROM PICTORIAL PARADE
Princess Anne

Yasir Arafat
WIDE WORLD

later regained some of it, but his position as head of the Palestinian resistance movement was under a strong challenge, especially from PFLP leader George Habash (q.v.).

Arafat was born in Jerusalem on Feb. 17, 1929, to a family of landowners and traders in Ramallah, north of Jerusalem. During the war of 1948 in which Israel took control of Palestine, Arafat and his family left Palestine for Jordan and Lebanon. Arafat graduated from Cairo University and in the late 1950s served in the Egyptian Army. He went to Beirut, Lebanon, in 1959 to join a large conglomeration of companies, which he represented in Kuwait. After several more industrial jobs, Arafat began in the early 1960s to concern himself seriously with Palestinian politics.

Dissatisfied with Ahmed Shukairy's management of the Palestine Liberation Organization, Arafat helped organize Al Fatah in 1965. His group took control of the Palestine Liberation Organization in 1969, and until the events of 1970 Arafat enjoyed a strong position as leader of the Palestinian guerrilla movement.   (J. K.)

ARANA OSORIO, CARLOS

In 1970 Carlos Arana Osorio gained the distinction of being the first president in the history of Guatemala to succeed by free election after a predecessor had completed his full term. He won the March election fairly and squarely from two opponents and in July was sworn in to succeed Julio César Méndez Montenegro, who had been freely elected four years before. Arana, an army colonel with a record of combating Communist guerrillas, was the law-and-order candidate. His victory by more than 40,000 votes indicated that many Guatemalans were revolted by the murders, kidnappings, and other acts of violence perpetrated by the Fuerzas Armadas Rebeles, the leftist urban guerrillas.

Arana himself was almost personally responsible for eliminating the rural guerrillas. He was the colonel in command of the army operations in the Zacapa region that virtually destroyed the FAR as an effective force in the countryside. Born July 17, 1918, in Barberena, he had been a career military man since his graduation from Guatemala's military academy in 1939. He became personally involved in the fight against the guerrillas when his son-in-law was killed by the leftists. In July 1966 Arana led his ranger-trained Indian soldiery into northeastern Guatemala and began an eye-for-an-eye campaign that wiped out the guerrillas in less than two years.

His enemies began to call him the "assassin colonel," and President Méndez, a certified liberal, made him ambassador to Nicaragua mainly to get him out of the way. It was from that post that he returned to Guatemala in 1970 to win the election handily, despite the opposition of liberals and Marxists. His candidacy was backed by the coalition of the National Liberation Movement and the Institutional Democratic Party and his message was conservative. Not rich himself, he was supported by the business interests of Guatemala, as well as by the peasants, to whom he promised security.

Until he ran for president, Arana had no involvement in politics and none with public administration. Realizing his limitations, he surrounded himself with a Cabinet and technical advisers more at home than he with the details of the national economy.

(J. A. O'L.)

AXELROD, JULIUS

When Julius Axelrod, chief of pharmacology at the National Institute of Mental Health (NIMH), won the 1970 Nobel Prize for Medicine or Physiology, it was the fifth time in as many years that the prize had gone to an American. He shared the citation with British biophysicist Sir Bernard Katz and Ulf von Euler, a Swedish physiologist (qq.v.). All three scientists were honoured for their independent explorations into neural chemistry and mechanics.

Aware of von Euler's work on the carrier of nerve impulses, Axelrod discovered the substance that inhibits a nerve impulse after its job is done. Noradrenalin, which von Euler discovered to be a key neurotransmitter, can either be reabsorbed by nerve endings or neutralized by an enzyme that Axelrod identified: catechol-o-methyl transferase. The role of the inhibiting enzyme, which Axelrod studied in depth, is critical to the understanding of the entire nervous system. It has proved useful in dealing with the effects of certain depressants and stimulants and in research on hypertension and schizophrenia.

Born in New York City on May 30, 1912, Axelrod began his career hampered by poverty and prejudice. Unable to enter medical school because of Jewish quotas, he took a master's degree in chemical pharmacology at New York University in 1941 after getting a bachelor of science degree from the City College of New York. He worked as a commercial chemist in New York and lost the sight of one eye when a bottle of ammonia exploded in his laboratory. He joined the National Heart Institute in Bethesda, Md., in 1949 and six years later moved to NIMH. At that time he matriculated at George Washington University in nearby Washington, D.C., to earn a doctorate in six months. (PH. K.)

BACHARACH, BURT

Innovative and prolific, Burt Bacharach was a composer of singular stature in the popular music world. One index of his success: two 1970 Academy Awards—for the best movie score, *Butch Cassidy and the Sundance Kid,* and for the best song of the year, "Raindrops Keep Fallin' on My Head." Another index: money in such amounts that

Newsweek called him an "outrageously wealthy man." His assets included a racing stable, a music publishing house, a $640,000 piece of A & M Records, 2% royalties from a musical that had grossed $8 million on Broadway alone, and income from Scepter Records amounting to $1.5 million a year (which he shared with lyricist Hal David). And he performed for $35,000 a week.

The milestones of Bacharach's success were legion. He had scored films as diverse as the crazily comic *What's New, Pussycat?* and the disturbingly moving *Alfie.* He took a crack at musical comedy and came up with the fabulously successful *Promises, Promises.*

Among his songs were "Walk On By," "Magic Moments," "Do You Know the Way to San Jose?," "What the World Needs Now Is Love," and "Trains and Boats and Planes."

Son of newspaper columnist Bert Bacharach, Burt was born May 12, 1929, in Kansas City, Mo., grew up in Forest Hills, N.Y., and attended McGill University in Montreal. After serving in the Army, he continued his formal music training, at Tanglewood's Berkshire Music Festival and in Santa Barbara, Calif., where he studied under Darius Milhaud. Meanwhile, he started accompanying such singers as Vic Damone, the Ames Brothers, and Polly Bergen. In 1958 he began working with Marlene Dietrich as accompanist, conductor, and arranger.

Wearing several musical hats was part of his recipe. He orchestrated his work, conducted the recording sessions, and supervised the "mixing." He insisted on live recording sessions with singers, soloists, and instrumentalists rather than the piecemeal approach that was the rule in the modern recording industry. Still, he was an artist of his time. "I don't think Burt Bacharach would have been possible in the '30s," said the venerable Richard Rodgers. "He's not interested in the 32-bar form or in 8-bar phrases. And I think it's healthy." (PH. K.)

BANDARANAIKE, SIRIMAVO RATWATTE DIAS

Sirimavo Bandaranaike became the world's first woman prime minister after leading Ceylon's Sri Lanka Freedom Party to victory at the polls in July 1960. She had become the party's president following the assassination (September 1959) of its leader, her husband Solomon Bandaranaike, and she maintained that her success then was largely a public tribute to his memory. But her return to power in the elections of May 1970, when she polled more than 20,000 votes in her own constituency and her party won 91 seats in the House of Representatives, was a triumph entirely her own.

Of aristocratic origin, she was born at Ratnapura, Ceylon, on April 17, 1916, the elder daughter of the *ratemahatmaya* or chief of the district; although a Buddhist, she was educated in Roman Catholic convents. Conveying in her unobtrusive social life something of the old ethic governing the behaviour of Asian women, she nevertheless became leader of a deeply radical party, working in parliamentary alliance with Trotskyist and Communist groups. Her concern for social justice was probably fostered during the years after her marriage (1940) when she was prominent in the Lanka Mahila Samitya, a women's organization for social work. In her first ministry (1960–65) she nationalized private schools, U.S. and British petroleum works, and the distributive section of the rubber industry; she also introduced improved health and education services. A very popular act was her increase of the rice ration to 1,800 g. per

week. This was halved by the government (1965–70) of Dudley Senanayake, but Mme Bandaranaike promised to restore it. She also planned to nationalize at least some sectors of the tea industry.

Mme Bandaranaike became minister of planning by her own choice; by custom, as prime minister, she was also minister of defense. She clearly considered that Ceylon's safety would be best preserved by a policy of neutrality, and she attended conferences of nonaligned countries in Belgrade, Yugos. (1961), and Lusaka, Zambia (1970). In 1962 she was hostess in Colombo to a similar conference concerned with the solution of the Sino-Indian border dispute. In furtherance of her policy she planned to make Ceylon a "free, sovereign, and independent" republic, probably in 1971; Ceylon would also seek contacts with Eastern Europe and North Vietnam. (S. Mu.)

BARBER, ANTHONY PERRINOTT LYSBERG

British Conservative Party chairman—and as such architect of the electoral victory of June 1970—Anthony Barber seemed to epitomize the enigmatic character of the Heath administration. First charged with the conduct of Britain's negotiations to join the EEC, Barber was, as a result of Iain Macleod's death, almost immediately (July 25) transferred to the post of chancellor of the Exchequer. As such, and because of his closeness to Prime Minister Edward Heath, he was potentially the most influential member of the Cabinet.

Yet, although it was certainly too early to judge, Barber's personal appearance, public performances, and even the opportunist success of his career contributed to an impression that he was somewhat lightweight. His famous gaffe (Nov. 3, 1969), when he uncritically followed the *Daily Express*'s attempt to discredit the Labour chancellor's trade figures, caused many to think him lacking in basic mathematical aptitude.

Privately unshockable and willing to discuss all viewpoints, he still expressed some of the more traditionally right-wing Tory opinions. A quick rather than a weighty debater, he lacked Macleod's power to dominate the House of Commons and failed to make a forceful impression at the formal opening of the EEC negotiations. Yet later performances with the Six showed him quick to learn.

Born on July 4, 1920, at Hessle, near Hull, Barber shared Heath's grammar school and Oxford background. In World War II he served in the artillery and with the RAF and was a prisoner of war from 1942 to 1945. As member of Parliament for Doncaster (1951–64) he worked in the Whips' Office (1955–57), as private parliamentary secretary to Prime Minister Harold Macmillan (1958–59), and as economic and then financial secretary to the Treasury (1959–63). From 1965 he had been MP for Altrincham, and in 1967 disputes between Heath and Edward du Cann led to Barber replacing the latter as party chairman. (S. Mu.)

BENTON, WILLIAM

Publisher William Benton won new honours both at home and abroad in 1970 for his contributions to education. On April 15 he received an award for distinguished service in international education from the Institute of International Education and the Reader's Digest Foundation. He was the only individual to receive such an award, given in "recognition of outstanding contributions to the development of international understanding through creative and practical support of educational, cultural and technical exchange programs." A month later Benton, a former U.S. senator, traveled with former Vice-Pres. Hubert H. Humphrey to Israel, where the Weizmann Institute of Science conferred honorary fellowships on them. Benton had been active in the educational field both as publisher of the *Encyclopædia Britannica* and as a former U.S. delegate to the UN Educational, Scientific and Cultural Organization (UNESCO). He had been publisher of the encyclopaedia for 28 years.

At Expo 70 in Osaka, Jap., 71 works especially chosen from Benton's collection of 20th-century American paintings were exhibited. To quote from the foreword of the catalog for the exhibit, the loan was "a very personal gesture of friendship for the Japanese people on the part of a man whose greatest interests lie in world education and international understanding." In 1969 Benton had proposed that the wide use of English in Japan be recognized by the establishment of an International Institute of Intercommunication in that country. He was the co-recipient (with Humphrey) of the Kajima Peace Award from Japan's Kajima Institute of International Peace.

Benton also was the subject of a biography, *The Lives of William Benton* by Sidney Hyman, published in February 1970 by the University of Chicago Press.

Benton was born in Minneapolis, Minn., April 1, 1900, and was graduated from Yale in 1921. After seven years as a partner of Chester Bowles in the New York advertising agency of Benton and Bowles, he had become a millionaire and left to enter public service. He became a vice-president of the University of Chicago in 1937. In partnership with the university in 1943, he became publisher and chairman of the *Encyclopædia Britannica*. He served as assistant secretary of state under Pres. Harry S. Truman, was appointed to the U.S. Senate from Connecticut in 1949, and was elected in 1950 to a two-year term. He traveled widely and wrote extensively. His books included *The Voice of the Kremlin, This Is the Challenge,* and *The Voice of Latin America.*

(Mx. H.)

BIG BIRD

Big Bird, an unlikely bundle of false feathers and shaggy pants on the order of 7 ft. tall, was one of the more influential educators in America in 1970. Possessor of an inquisitive five-year-old's mentality, he—together with the Cookie Monster, Oscar the Grouch, and other assorted Muppets and humans—was a star of "Sesame Street," the most instructive series in the history of children's television.

Launched late in 1969, the experimental program won a host of awards the following year. It achieved instant success among its potential audience of 12 million preschool children in 182 cities across the country. Most noteworthy of all, it accomplished its primary goal: to educate the kids, not just to amuse or pacify them. One preliminary test demonstrated that basic learning skills of young viewers were increased two and a half times by the program.

In essence, "Sesame Street" comprised a primary educational curriculum compiled around the most whiz-bang proven techniques of electronic communication. One hour-long show might include a short documentary film about dairy farming, a de facto lesson in the laws of perspective, songs, conversations, and 30 vocabulary words (usually with the same initial) flashed to viewers in 65-seconds-plus animated comparisons of the square and triangle.

Joan Ganz Cooney, head of Children's Television Workshop (until April 1970 a division of National Educational Televi-

WIDE WORLD
Burt Bacharach and his wife, Angie Dickinson

Big Bird from "Sesame Street," and Susan
BILL PIERCE. TIME MAGAZINE © TIME INC.

KEYSTONE
Anthony Perrinott Lysberg Barber

sion), which produces the program, said four years of planning and experimentation went into the project. With the help of teachers, psychiatrists, and media technicians—and with $8 million from the Carnegie Corporation, the Ford Foundation, the U.S. Office of Education, and Project Head Start—Mrs. Cooney identified the specific goals and methods for "Sesame Street." It was decided to concentrate on the alphabet and numbers, basic reasoning skills, vocabulary, and information about the world at large. Advertising men were especially helpful in identi-

fying ways to hold children's attention: snappy animation, bright dialogue, imaginative films, songs, skits, captivating characters, and a Pogo-stick pace.

The show's human cast is "the most naturally integrated" in all television, according to *Variety*'s critic. This was done to appeal especially to minority-race children in urban ghettos. The program was banned for a time in Mississippi, but a study showed that 90% of the youngsters in Brooklyn's black Bedford-Stuyvesant section watched regularly.

(Ph. K.)

BLACKMUN, HARRY ANDREW

Perhaps few men had wanted to become an associate justice of the U.S. Supreme Court more than Harry A. Blackmun. And probably no man who made it came as close as he did to missing the opportunity. Considered once but passed over by Pres. Richard Nixon in the summer of 1969, Blackmun was not even considered when the president made a second try, in January 1970, to fill the vacant seat on the highest court. But after two Senate rejections of Southern nominees (Clement F. Haynsworth, Jr., of South Carolina and G. Harrold Carswell of Florida), the president said he had no choice but to turn to the North. Harry Blackmun of Minnesota was the choice.

Fully satisfied this time, the Senate confirmed the nomination by a vote of 94 to 0 on May 12. Within less than a month, Blackmun was installed at the Supreme Court in the seat that had stood vacant for more than 13 months after Justice Abe Fortas resigned. His first written utterance as a member of the court, in the controversial field of obscenity law, aligned him closely with Chief Justice Warren E. Burger.

That alignment seemed to follow a pattern. Blackmun and Burger attended the same kindergarten and grade school in St. Paul. Blackmun was best man at Burger's wedding in 1933. The two were associated when Blackmun was on the legal staff of the Mayo Clinic in Rochester, Minn., and Burger was on its board of trustees. The new justice had obviously come highly recommended by Burger. Although President Nixon had made much of his demand for judges with a "strict" judicial philosophy, he did not even ask Blackmun about his views before he submitted the nomination. In Blackmun, the court had received one of its most unabashed admirers. Blackmun openly spoke of having "an attitude of sanctity" about the highest tribunal.

Born Nov. 12, 1908, in Nashville, Ill., Blackmun graduated summa cum laude in mathematics from Harvard College in 1929 and received his law degree from Harvard in 1932. His first job out of law school was clerking for John B. Sanborn, a member of the U.S. Court of Appeals for the 8th Circuit. Twenty-six years later Blackmun succeeded Sanborn on that court and served on it for more than ten years.   (L. DN.)

BORLAUG, NORMAN ERNEST

The winner of the 1970 Nobel Peace Prize was Norman E. Borlaug, a U.S. agronomist and an agricultural Horatio-at-the-bridge in the fight against world famine. Borlaug was honoured for a quarter century of work that centred around a research station in Campo Atizapan, Mex. There he developed strains of grain that increased yields in several countries dramatically. Wheat production in Mexico multiplied sixfold in the time he worked with the Mexican government; "dwarf" wheat imported in the mid-1960s was responsible for a 60% increase in Pakistan and India.

"Dr. Borlaug, as the prime mover in the 'green revolution,' has made it possible for the developing countries to break away from hunger and poverty," a Nobel committee spokesman said. "Through his improvement of wheat and rice plants, [he] has created a technological breakthrough which makes it possible to abolish hunger in the developing

countries in the course of a few years."

The new laureate was not so sure that his work had fertilized a panacea. "We have only delayed the world food crisis for another 30 years," he told newsmen. "If the world population continues to increase at the same rate, we will destroy the species" *Homo sapiens*. A number of observers agreed. Some noted that the ability of presently agrarian nations to support ever growing populations could spawn internal pressures leading to international crises of the first magnitude. Other demographers argued that burgeoning man would use up the planet's resources and make it uninhabitable through pollution.

Borlaug was director of the Rockefeller Foundation's International Maize and Wheat Improvement Center in Mexico, where he had worked since 1944. He was born on a 50-ac. farm in Cresco, Ia., on March 25, 1914, studied plant biology and forestry at the University of Minnesota, and earned a doctorate in plant pathology there in 1941. He preferred fieldwork to office chores and the travel entailed in overseeing several research centres around the world, and modestly suggested that his Mexican colleagues should share his honour. He was selected for the $78,000 Peace Prize over 33 other nominees, including the UN and the World Council of Churches.   (PH. K.)

BOURASSA, (JEAN) ROBERT

Economist Robert Bourassa seemed to be the golden boy of Canadian politics early in 1970; he won a heated fight for the leadership of Quebec's Liberal Party in January and then was elected premier of the province. Later in the year the outlook was less bright, as radical terrorism broke out in Quebec and Prime Minister Pierre Trudeau imposed martial law throughout the nation. Under the circumstances, the province's economic problems and Bourassa's plans for its recovery were receiving little attention.

Born July 14, 1933, in Montreal, Bourassa won the Governor-General's Medal in 1956 when he was first in his class at the University of Montreal Law School. Following studies in law and economics at Oxford and Harvard, he became a fiscal adviser to the Department of National Revenue in Ottawa and taught economics and fiscal law at the university. In 1966 Bourassa was elected to the Quebec provincial assembly.

Two months after Bourassa's selection as Liberal Party leader in 1970, National Unionist Premier Jean-Jacques Bertrand called for elections on April 29. At first this seemed a brilliant stroke, since the Liberals were still disunited. But Bourassa launched an aggressive campaign, insisting that the province was going broke under Bertrand's leadership. While Bertrand blamed any and all economic ills in Quebec on the national government, Bourassa outlined a recovery program for the province. He pledged to attract outside capital and to bring 100,000 jobs to Quebec within a year.

Meanwhile, the separatist Parti Québécois was calling for political independence from the rest of Canada. Two predominantly rural parties, the Créditistes and the electorally untried New Democrats, were also active in the hustings. The April balloting gave Bourassa's Liberal Party 44% of the province-wide vote and a majority of assembly seats. The Parti Québécois received almost one-fourth of the popular vote but only 7 seats in the 108-member house, while the National Union, which had dominated Quebec politics for the better part of four decades, received one-fifth of the vote and 17 seats. Commentators throughout Canada interpreted the result as a local mandate against secession, a view that may have led

some extremist separatists to launch their private reign of terror.   (PH. K.)

BOUTON, JAMES

A professional baseball pitcher for 12 years, most of them with the New York Yankees, Jim Bouton gained national prominence in 1970 with the publication of *Ball Four*. Almost immediately, the book leaped to the best-seller lists and at year's end approached the 150,000 mark in hard-cover sales, believed to be an unprecedented total for a sports book.

Many of the persons within the baseball Establishment, especially the players, were critical of Bouton, insisting he had betrayed confidences. Bowie Kuhn, the baseball commissioner, in midsummer summoned Bouton to his office ". . . and warned him against future writings of this kind."

Bouton presented the public with a previously unavailable view of baseball players. Wrote a reviewer in the *New York Times:* "Mr. Bouton leaves very little for you to imagine. He tells you things you never dreamed of when your father took you to the old ball game." The book gave glimpses of the sex life and carousing of the players, told how some of them, Bouton included, were peeping toms, and how the players often joked about their wives in clubhouse conversations. Bouton also revealed the cheating and chicanery of some club officials.

The book received wide serious acclaim as a realistic social document. Many reviewers were convinced that it was beneficial to baseball because Bouton revealed the players as people instead of mere cardboard heroes. Asked why he wrote the book, Bouton said: "I did it for one reason: to share with others some of the fun I've had in baseball." The book was done with considerable warmth and wit and was described by one critic as "the funniest baseball since Ring Lardner."

Bouton was born on March 8, 1939, in Newark, N.J., the oldest of three sons. He attended Western Michigan University and began his professional baseball career in 1958 when he signed a $30,000, three-year bonus contract with the New York Yankees. He had two outstanding seasons, 21–7 in 1963 and 18–13 in 1964, both pennant-winning years for the Yankees. He retired from baseball near the end of the 1970 season when he took a job as a television sports announcer in New York City.   (JE. HO.)

BRANDT, WILLY

As the first Socialist in 39 years to hold the chancellorship of West Germany, Willy Brandt might have been expected to head a government concerned with domestic reforms. But while revaluation of the mark had been the principal campaign issue and the first act of the new government when it took office in October 1969, the main thrust of Brandt's efforts in 1970 was in foreign affairs.

Before the first quarter of the year was ended, international dialogues had begun on four fronts: West Germany and the U.S.S.R. were discussing a treaty calling for mutual renunciation of force and the acceptance of present European borders; the Brandt government and Polish officials were meeting regularly to discuss normalizing relations and agreement on Poland's western frontier; the Big Four powers had met to discuss the status of Berlin for the first time since 1959; and Brandt and East German Premier Willi Stoph had held a day of "useful" talks. The East German effort was the least successful, ending after a second, chilly meeting in May. The Soviet discussions, however, were rewarding. Agreement on the treaty, which Brandt signed in Moscow in August, opened the way for similar negotiations with other Communist bloc nations and a fresh series of talks on trade agreements. The Polish negotiations also bore fruit in the form of a nonaggression treaty, signed in December, establishing the Oder-Neisse line as Poland's boundary. In the same month, Brandt told the West German Cabinet that the outlook for a great power agreement on the status of Berlin had improved.

But the move toward the East created serious problems at home. The opposition Christian Democratic Union charged Brandt with selling out to the U.S.S.R. and refused to send a delegate to the Moscow negotiations. In addition, in June the Social Democrat-Free Democrat coalition parties lost ground in state elections that some viewed as plebiscites on Brandt's foreign policy.

Born Herbert Ernst Karl Frahm in Lübeck on Dec. 18, 1913, Brandt assumed his present name when he fled from the Nazis in 1933 to Norway, and later to Sweden, where he earned a living as a journalist. He returned to Germany in 1945 with Norwegian nationality, resumed German citizenship in 1947, and rejoined the Social Democratic Party. He was elected governing mayor of West Berlin in 1957, and achieved an international reputation as an able politician who kept cool in times of crisis. As chairman of the Social Democratic Party since 1964, he had suffered two bitter electoral defeats as candidate for the chancellorship and served as foreign minister for three years.   (N. Cr.)

BREWSTER, KINGMAN, JR.

Rioting was more evident than scholarship on U.S. campuses in 1970, when arson seemed a gruesome intramural game and when students at two colleges were killed in the name of "law and order." In the midst of this turmoil, Yale University emerged as an oasis of cooperation between educators and students. Kingman Brewster, Jr., the 17th president of the 269-year-old university, was largely responsible.

There was, indeed, considerable continuing dissent over a broad range of issues on the New Haven campus. In the spring of 1970 the situation was made more volatile by a Black Panther murder-conspiracy trial in New Haven that attracted activists from around the country. Brewster's administration fostered open discussion among students and faculty, permitted nonviolent demonstrations, and briefly suspended classes for a mass rally. Yale went so far as to prepare simple food and shelter for out-of-towners. When 12,000 people gathered for the rally, Panthers joined undergraduates as marshals to keep the peace. Though there were scattered incidents, the city and the campus were remarkably free from violence.

While these events were the most dramatic of Brewster's seven-year administration, they typified his approach. "Kingman is visible," as one associate put it—visible to the undergraduates, available to dissidents, and in touch with the entire college community. A university administration must be held accountable, and students should be consulted in matters that affect them, but beyond that he believed the faculty "must have an ultimate, exclusive voice" in setting academic standards, deciding faculty appointments, and governing the university. Some of his policies—he admitted women to the undergraduate body and radically liberalized admissions policies for men—angered more than a few Old Blues. Nonetheless, the annual fund drive raised more money than any similar appeal in the history of Yale or any other U.S. university.

Brewster was born in Longmeadow, Mass., June 17, 1919. He received an A.B.

from Yale in 1941, served in the Navy, and received a law degree from Harvard in 1948. He subsequently taught at the Harvard Law School before returning to Yale as provost and professor in 1961. He was elected president of the university two years later.   (Ph. K.)

BROWN, CHRISTY

Christy Brown, touted as the latest Dubliner to follow in the Joyce-Behan tradition of Irish lyricism, wrote better with his left foot than many people do with both hands. That was one reason he became a literary celebrity in 1970—he had severe cerebral palsy and typed with his toes.

Born June 10, 1932, the 10th of 22 children in a slum family, Brown was considered hopelessly handicapped. One day when he was five, a sister was writing on a slate, and he clutched a piece of chalk in his toes. He began to draw with it on the floor; his left foot, it appeared, was his single functional extremity. With the help of medical therapists, Brown learned to speak intelligibly. At 18 he began his autobiography, with the help of one of the dozen siblings who had survived the ravages of a squalid household. The first draft was "a veritable forest of seven and eight syllable words,"

James Bouton
WIDE WORLD

Brown recalled. Three drafts and more than three years later it was published as *My Left Foot.*

Brown resumed writing, and the result, published in the U.S. in 1970, was *Down All the Days,* which received mixed reviews. One critic called it a "tough but lyrical panorama of the booze, fornication and heartbreak that teemed around him in '30s and '40s Dublin." *Time*'s critic saw it as "more memoir than first novel," though he did recognize "a native gift" salted with "O'Portnoyesque sexual gropings." That critic reserved his severest attack for the mawkish dust jacket blurb: "This Barnumesque hawking freak-show tone manages to degrade the book and insult the limited but quite legitimate talents of the author."

Brown, who made little of his disability in public, did not appear troubled by it all. The subject of a well-received television documentary and with a biographical movie in process, Brown invested some of the profits from *Down All the Days* in a new electric typewriter. Some of the rest he

Kingman Brewster, Jr.
WIDE WORLD

Norman Ernest Borlaug
WIDE WORLD

parted with in the Stone Boat, a neighbourhood pub that he patronized with regularity. He also held a brush with facility, and his paintings were exhibited in Dublin, Zürich, Switz., and Stockholm.   (PH. K.)

BURNS, ARTHUR FRANK

Arthur Burns stepped into the chairmanship of the U.S. Federal Reserve Board in February 1970, at a critical period in the nation's economic history. Appointed by Pres. Richard Nixon to succeed the retiring William McChesney Martin, Jr., a Democrat, Republican Burns was closely tuned to the administration's attempt to bring inflation under control without bringing on a recession. Burns had been chief White House economic adviser during Nixon's first year in office.

Burns's favourite slogan under pressure was "don't panic." He kept a steady hand at the Fed, allowing a moderate expansion of the nation's money supply. Before year's end he was pointing to signs of lessening inflationary pressures and an upturn in the economy. At the same time, critics complained that his tight-money policies had driven interest rates to their highest levels in a hundred years and that unemployment was rising.

Burns was born April 27, 1904, in Eastern Galicia, then a region of the Austro-Hungarian Empire and now a part of the Soviet Ukraine. His father emigrated to the U.S. when his son was nine, and later young Arthur learned his father's trade of paperhanging, however. He applied for admission to Columbia University and made such an impressive appearance at his initial interview that he was admitted and was given a scholarship as well, even though enrollment for the school year had closed. Burns chose economics as his specialty and later, as an assistant professor at Rutgers University, became a pioneer in the field of business cycles.

As chairman of Pres. Dwight Eisenhower's Council of Economic Advisers, he warned that a recession in 1960 was on the way and advised a loosening of spending and credit policies. Vice-President Nixon,

who was running against John F. Kennedy for president, agreed but could not persuade the administration to follow Burns's advice. Later Nixon said privately that the recession that year had cost him the election.

As chairman of the Fed, Burns headed an independent body officially separated from administration or congressional interference. But Burns, like Nixon, was cautious in monetary affairs, a free trader, opposed to big government, and for such administration-backed measures as federal-state revenue sharing.   (M. B. Su.)

BUTKUS, RICHARD

One of the new glamour positions that has emerged in the increasingly violent and popular world of professional football is that of middle linebacker. It is a position manned by husky, bruising men who direct their team's defense. They must have the strength of a lineman and also the agility to defend against short passes. Some professional coaches regard the middle linebacker position equal in importance to that of a quarterback.

By the late 1960s, one such middle linebacker, Dick Butkus of the Chicago Bears, was generally acclaimed as the best in the National Football League. Butkus was chosen four times, by unanimous consent, as the NFL's all-pro middle linebacker and had been selected to play in six Pro Bowl games.

Butkus was born on Dec. 9, 1942, in Chicago. He started playing football in grade school on Chicago's South Side and continued at Chicago Vocational High School, where he was so outstanding that he received an estimated 50 to 60 scholarship offers from colleges and universities. He played both fullback and linebacker as a schoolboy and in his senior year at Vocational figured, directly or indirectly, in approximately 70% of his team's tackles.

Butkus attended the University of Illinois, where he won even more honours. He was a virtually unanimous All-American choice during his junior and senior years there, and in 1964, as a senior, was chosen by both the Associated Press and the United Press International as the season's outstanding college lineman. That same year the College Football Coaches Association selected him as the college player of the year.   (JE. HO.)

CARR, ROBERT

Thirty years of continuous experience with the problems of industrial relations, both on the factory floor and in politics, brought Robert Carr to the Department of Employment and Productivity as the minister in Edward Heath's new Conservative Party government. Charged with achieving reforms in trade-union law and industrial relations, Carr was given potentially the most controversial job in the Cabinet, and one that seemed likely to be even more difficult because of the threat of labour unrest. He had been in office only a few days when a national dock strike began. The strike marked the beginning of a governmental policy of resistance to inflationary wage increases in which Carr was to show both coolness and firmness.

Born Nov. 11, 1916, Carr attended Cambridge University and graduated with a degree in metallurgy. He then went into his family's metal manufacturing business, where he rose from a factory foreman to a director of the company. Elected to the House of Commons in 1950, he made his first speech on industrial relations. At that time he said, "I believe most deeply that a man will never find satisfaction in his leisure unless he has first found satisfaction in his work." In the mid-1950s Carr served as a parliamentary secretary to the Ministry of Labour before returning to his family business as company chairman. He took a hand in shaping Conservative Party industrial policy at that time, and ten years later was the principal author of the Conservative policy document, *Fair Deal at Work*.

Carr's defense of the Heath administration's industrial relations bill was based on his belief in the importance of having a set of good rules for both management and the trade unions. He denied that the legislation was either pro-employer or antiunion, claiming that it constituted a fair deal for all.   (W. H. Ts.)

CHÁVEZ, CÉSAR ESTRADA

Few gave César Chávez much chance of success when he began a farm workers' strike against California grape growers in 1965. Farm workers are not covered under federal labour laws, and they have remained largely unorganized. Not that they do not have grievances. Farm work is seasonal and

César Chávez
CURT GUNTHER FROM CAMERA 5

Chi Cheng
WIDE WORLD

CAMERA PRESS FROM PIX
John Cranko

sporadic, and field hands often move in family groups following harvests. Pay is low, hours are long, and the work is hot, hard, and dusty. Living conditions in migrant workers' camps are often substandard. Average migrant family income in the U.S. is less than $1,600 a year. Many of the three million hired farm workers in the U.S. are, like Chávez, of Mexican ancestry.

Chávez, who headed the United Farm Workers Organizing Committee, turned the grape strike into more than just a labour confrontation. Under his direction it became "La Causa," almost a religious movement. Initially it gained limited support from workers in the San Joaquin grape-growing area, but it was not until Chávez conceived the idea of a national consumer boycott in 1968 that it started to gain momentum.

Publicized by news of Chávez' fasts, supported nationally by the AFL-CIO and the United Auto Workers and locally by picket lines of housewives in front of supermarkets, Chávez' boycott began to work. Sales of table grapes fell off from New Hampshire to Honolulu in support of the "Chicanos," Chávez' people.

In July 1970, in the face of declining sales, California grape growers finally capitulated. A substantial wage increase was granted, and one of the most agonizing and unusual of labour disputes was over. Chávez said, however, that this was only "the end of the beginning." Late in August his union struck lettuce growers in California's Salinas Valley, and before the year was over Chávez had been jailed for failing to call off a boycott against a lettuce grower who had signed with a rival union. He was released on Christmas Eve pending further court hearings.

Born March 31, 1927, near Yuma, Ariz., Chávez was the son of an impoverished migrant farm worker; he attended dozens of schools but never got as far as the eighth grade. He began full-time efforts to organize farm workers in 1962, but he was not well known outside California until the boycott. His goal was the organization of all farm workers, and he vowed "to stay with it if it takes a lifetime."   (M. B. Su.)

CHI CHENG
Beginning in 1969 Chi Cheng, a 26-year-old late bloomer from Taiwan, developed into the world's fastest and most versatile woman in track and field. Over one stretch of 121 races, she lost only 2. At the end of 1970 she held 11 Asian, 6 U.S., and 4 world records. Two of her world records were set in June 1970 in the same meet—the Portland, Ore., Rose Festival, where she ran as a member of the Los Angeles Track Club. At that tournament Miss Chi did the 100-yd. dash in 10.1 sec., breaking the old record by 0.2 sec., and the 220-yd. dash in 22.7 sec., 0.2 of a second faster than the old mark. In July she lowered the record for the 200-m. dash to 22.4.

Miss Chi blossomed as a runner after coming to the U.S. from her Chinese island homeland in 1963 to enroll as a student at California State Polytechnic College and to run for Vince Reel, track coach at nearby Claremont-Mudd College. Reel first saw her in 1960, when she performed as a 16-year-old for Nationalist China (Taiwan) in the Olympic Games. Even though she was last in her heat in the hurdles, Reel liked what he saw—a girl unusually tall and lanky for a Chinese (5′ 7½″) and so full of desire that her teammates called her "the Iron Girl." Reel got a closer look in 1962, when he was sent to Taiwan by the U.S. Department of State to prepare the Nationalist Chinese team for the Asian games. He talked

her into coming to Los Angeles to complete her education and to train in earnest, with her government paying the cost.

She failed to qualify for any of the finals at the 1964 Olympics. But in 1968, at the Mexico City Olympics, running with pulled muscles in both legs, she qualified for the finals in the 100-m. dash, placing seventh, and the hurdles. Her third-place finish in the hurdles won a bronze medal; and she thus became the only Asian woman to win a medal that year in track. After the Olympics she improved steadily, a situation that put Reel in a quandary trying to decide what she should specialize in for the 1972 Olympic Games. On December 27, Reel and Miss Chi were married in T'ai-pei.

In 1970 she posted the year's best marks in six different U.S. events—the 100- and 220-yd. dashes, the hurdles, the long (broad) jump, the pentathlon, and, most recently, the quarter-mile run, which she took up just to improve her time in the 220. In each event she beat the best U.S. women at their specialties.   (F. Wт.)

COLOMBO, EMILIO
Italy was plunged into a government crisis in 1970 when the coalition government of Premier Mariano Rumor resigned on July 6. After a month of searching for a new leader, Pres. Giuseppe Saragat chose Emilio Colombo, a Christian Democrat who had been serving as minister of finance. Colombo took office on August 6 after succeeding in forming a centre-left coalition Cabinet consisting of 16 Christian Democrats, 6 Socialists, 4 Unitary Socialists (official name of the Social Democrats), and 1 Republican.

Colombo was born April 11, 1920, in Potenza. After graduating with a degree in law from Rome University, he became interested in politics. In 1946 he was elected a deputy to the postwar Constituent Assembly and two years later was elected to the Chamber of Deputies. Reelected in 1953, he was appointed minister of agriculture and forestry by Premier Antonio Segni. He became minister of foreign trade in 1958 and then served as minister of industry and commerce from 1959 to 1963. In that post his name was linked with the nationalization of the electrical industry. He also had a primary role in the preparation of agreements in Brussels that introduced the second phase of the European Common Market.

After his reelection to Parliament in 1963, Colombo was appointed minister of finance. To create the basis for a new expansion of the economy, he applied measures to balance public expenditures with revenue and to defend monetary stability.

As premier, Colombo hoped to resolve the issue that had caused the Rumor government to fall: the feud between the Socialists and the Unitary Socialists over the former's collaboration with the Communist Party. Colombo committed himself to a strong national anti-Communist stand but allowed the Socialists to join with the Communists in local administrations where his centre-left group did not have a majority.   (F. G.)

CORNFELD, BERNARD
One day in May 1970 Bernard Cornfeld fell from power. And if that event went unnoticed by many persons, it was only because they were not current with the new generation of swinging financiers. For "Bernie," as friends and enemies alike called him, was big indeed. Starting from scratch in the mid-1950s, he had built his Investors Overseas Services and its Fund of Funds into an organization that employed 20,000 persons and boasted a million·customers in 26 countries (including six heads of state

and persons behind the iron curtain) and assets of some $2 billion.

As a member of the jet set, 42-year-old Bernie was also a big swinger. Corporate headquarters was a lavish villa on the shores of Switzerland's Lake Geneva. Bernie's female employees were miniskirted and looked like beauty queens. His legendary entertainment efforts included an estimated $100,000 for his 1969 Christmas party.

It was not always so. Born in Istanbul, Aug. 17, 1927, Cornfeld arrived in the U.S. at the age of four during the depths of the depression. He attended tuition-free Brooklyn College, campaigned for Socialist Norman Thomas for president in 1948, then went into social work in Philadelphia. But capitalism beckoned and Bernie found he was a natural mutual fund salesman. After a vacation in Europe he decided he liked it enough to set up shop there. He started selling U.S. securities door-to-door on the installment plan, and the approach—new in Europe—was an immediate success. Cornfeld branched out into insurance, banking, and real estate. Estimates of his personal wealth reached $100 million.

But the prosperity of Cornfeld's financial conglomerate was tied to the U.S. securities markets. Early in 1970 prices on the New York exchanges fell, and the value of Cornfeld's Fund of Funds dropped $200 million. His customers did not panic, but his financial partners did as the value of their investment dropped from an earlier high of more than $30 a share to $2. Cornfeld cut overhead and costs but it was too late. With operating capital depleted and confidence gone, the IOS board fired him as chief executive officer. Out but not down, he remained the largest single IOS stockholder, regained a seat on the board, and at year's end was planning a proxy fight to try to establish control.   (M. B. Su.)

CRANKO, JOHN
To be responsible for direction of two West German ballet companies, in Stuttgart and Munich, and to bring one of them to the position of a principal European company with a great transatlantic reputation, would seem enough of a feat for one year. But then in addition to create a major full-length work, *The Taming of the Shrew*, and several shorter ones, including *Poème de l'Extase* for Margot Fonteyn, might seem almost impossible. But all this John Cranko did between the spring of 1969 and that of 1970.

Even before his Stuttgart company went on its first triumphant tour to the U.S., thus establishing itself as a company of international importance, it had been developing a personality and reputation of its own. Cranko's success at Stuttgart was not surprising since, while in England, first with the Sadler's Wells Theatre Ballet and later in other branches of the theatre, he had shown that he had an inventive and original mind.

Born in the South African town of Rustenberg on Aug. 15, 1927, Cranko joined the Cape Town University Ballet School at the age of 15 and there, in 1942, created his first work to Igor Stravinsky's *Soldier's Tale*. Four years later he went to Britain to join the Sadler's Wells, primarily as a dancer though in that year, 1946, he created a popular pas de trois, *Tritsch-Tratsch*.

After several other creations of growing importance, Cranko's real breakthrough came in 1951 with his *Pineapple Poll*, a ballet set to music by Sir Arthur Sullivan. This lighthearted work of great choreographic ingenuity achieved a lasting popularity. After several more works for Sadler's Wells and the Covent Garden company, which joined to become known as the Royal Ballet, Cranko moved temporarily to the lighter theatre with his revue *Cranks,* originally put on in London and later equally successful in New York.

Cranko also produced opera, including Benjamin Britten's *A Midsummer Night's Dream,* and more ballets for the New York City Ballet, the Paris Opéra, and other companies. Through all this he returned continually to the Royal Ballet to mount works such as Britten's full-length *The Prince of the Pagodas* and Mikis Theodorakis' *Antigone.* In 1961, however, Cranko left Britain to take up his assignment in Stuttgart. (P. Wɪ.)

DAVIES, JOHN EMERSON HARDING

Although he arrived late in politics, being elected an MP for the first time in June 1970, John Davies found himself with a seat in the Cabinet within weeks of reaching Westminster. In the reshuffle that followed the death of Iain Macleod in late July, he became minister of technology and then, in October, minister of the newly formed Department of Trade and Industry. Both his experience and his political beliefs fitted him for a place in Edward Heath's Cabinet. His knowledge of management of big business was linked with an outspoken conviction in the virtues of private enterprise and the misguidedness of government interference.

He set out his philosophy in uncompromising terms in speeches at the Conservative conference at Blackpool in October, when he argued the case for disengagement by the government from policies of intervention that he said stultified management. Though an effective platform speaker, he was less successful in adjusting to the Commons, which gave him an unusually rough hearing in a debate on November 4 when he expressed his attitude to subsidies: "National decadence is the consequence of treating us all, the whole country, as though we were all lame ducks. The vast majority lives and thrives in a bracing climate and not in a soft, sodden morass of subsidized incompetence."

Born in London on Jan. 8, 1916, and trained as an accountant, Davies joined the Anglo-Iranian Oil Co. in 1946. By 1962, at the age of 45, he had become vice-chairman and managing director of Shell-Mex and BP Ltd., then the biggest oil marketing and distributing organization in Western Europe. There was some surprise when he moved to a less highly paid job as director general of the Confederation of British Industry in 1965, but it was in this role that he came into close contact with political and trade-union leaders. By 1969 his political ambitions had crystallized and he gave up his CBI job to seek a seat in Parliament. (W. H. Ts.)

DAVIS, ANGELA YVONNE

In August 1970 four gunmen abducted a judge from his San Rafael, Calif., courtroom in one of the year's most brutal and bizarre cases of violence. Soon afterward, at a roadblock shootout, three of the men were killed by police fire. But their hostage, Superior Court Judge Harold J. Haley, 65, also was killed, by a burst of fire from a shotgun the group had attached to his neck with adhesive tape. The kidnapping of Haley was an attempt by a group of radical revolutionaries to publicize the cause of the "Soledad Brothers," three inmates of Soledad prison charged with murdering a guard.

Police investigating the case quickly discovered that four of the guns used by the abductors were registered in the name of Angela Davis, and a warrant was issued for her arrest. Under California law a person who abets a murderer before the act is as culpable as the killer himself, and although Miss Davis was not seen in the area at the time of the abduction, she was promptly charged with murder. The FBI placed her on its "most wanted" list, and a nationwide search was undertaken after she dropped from sight.

Angela Davis, 26, was described by friends as quite literally "black and beautiful." The daughter of a middle-class Southern black family, she was a good student in high school at Birmingham, Ala., and later obtained scholarships and studied at Brandeis University, the Sorbonne, and the Institute for Social Research in Frankfurt, W.Ger. After receiving honours she returned to the U.S. to study philosophy at the University of California in San Diego. There she became interested in Marxism and joined the Communist Party. Later that proved to be the reason for her dismissal from a teaching job at UCLA.

Friends said that she was bitter over the dismissal, and Miss Davis began to show more interest in revolutionary causes and groups. This led to her involvement in the case of the Soledad Brothers. She gave speeches and helped raise money for a legal defense fund for the men, who claimed they were really the victims of a racial incident.

Two months after the murder, acting on a tip, police picked up Miss Davis in a New York City motel room, registered under an assumed name. Extradited to California, she was booked on charges of murder, kidnapping, and criminal conspiracy on December 22 in the Marin County Jail, not far from the scene of Judge Haley's kidnapping. (M. B. Sᴜ.)

DAYAN, MOSHE

A major shift in the foreign policy of Israel took place in 1970 as the nation's approach changed from insistence on direct negotiations and a peace settlement with the Arab world to a more pragmatic effort to reach a partial settlement with the United Arab Republic. Instrumental in formulating this new policy was Israel's minister of defense, Moshe Dayan.

One of Dayan's most important suggestions was that Israel withdraw about 20 mi. from the Suez Canal as the first step in a general demilitarization of that region. Despite opposition from Foreign Minister Abba Eban and a majority of the Cabinet, Dayan won the support of Prime Minister Golda Meir (*q.v.*) and the Cabinet on November 29. In December he traveled to the United States to discuss the Middle East situation with Pres. Richard Nixon. Dayan thus emerged at the end of 1970 as one of the major shapers of Israel's foreign policy.

Dayan was born May 20, 1915, in Degania "A," the first kibbutz to be established in Palestine. He spent his youth working as a farmer on Nahalal cooperative, which his parents had founded. He joined the Haganah, the Jewish defense force, and was arrested by the British authorities in 1939. After two years in prison he volunteered for service with the Australians during the invasion of Syria, then under Vichy French control, was seriously wounded and lost his left eye.

During Israel's war of independence in 1948, Dayan was appointed commander of the Jerusalem area. His personal contact with the Jordanian commander helped pave the way for an armistice. He served as chief of the general staff from 1953 to 1958 and was largely responsible for the successful Sinai campaign of 1956. From 1959 to 1964 he served as minister of agriculture but resigned because of differences within the Labour Party to join David Ben-Gurion in forming the Rafi Party. Dayan was not happy with this breach and used every opportunity to heal it. His chance came on the eve of Israel's Six-Day War against the Arab nations in June 1967. At that time, there was a sudden popular demand that Dayan be included in the Cabinet. As a result, he was appointed minister of defense on June 1, 1967, and led Israel to its victory in the war. (J. K.)

DOUGLAS-HOME, SIR ALEXANDER FREDERICK

Few British governments have had former prime ministers in the Cabinet, but Sir Alec Douglas-Home, who became foreign and Commonwealth secretary in the new Conservative Party government in June 1970, had been the last Conservative prime minister, in 1963 and 1964. In terms of years in Parliament and in government, Sir Alec was by far the most experienced of Prime Minister Edward Heath's Cabinet. He entered the House of Commons in 1931, and in the years immediately before World War II served as parliamentary private secretary (or personal aide) to Prime Minister Neville Chamberlain, accompanying him on the visit to Adolf Hitler at Munich.

In 1951 Sir Alec moved to the House of Lords when he succeeded to an ancient Scottish title as 14th earl of Home. He moved up quickly in the Conservative governments of the 1950s, becoming foreign secretary in 1960. His leadership in the Conservative Party was confirmed when he was chosen to succeed Harold Macmillan as prime minister in 1963. To do this he had to renounce his earldom for his lifetime in order to return to the Commons to lead the government. After narrowly losing the 1964 general election, he made way for Edward Heath as leader of the Conservative Party.

Born July 2, 1903, Sir Alec was educated at Eton and Oxford University. A substantial Scottish landowner, enjoying fishing and shooting on his estates, he was in the old tradition of Tory aristocracy. Yet he was no amateur. It was typical of his professionalism that when he was ill for some months in 1940 he used the time to study Marxism.

As foreign secretary he quickly showed that he intended to act more independently of the prime minister than some of his recent predecessors. Indeed, his prompt statement of intent to resume the sale of arms to South Africa was found embarrassingly impetuous by some of his colleagues. In his foreign policy he emphasized the importance of Britain joining the Common Market as a way of making British influence felt, and he looked for greater European self-reliance for defense through NATO. (W. H. Ts.)

ECHEVERRÍA ÁLVAREZ, LUIS

Mexico's new president in 1970, Luis Echeverría Álvarez, was the archetypical organization man of Mexico's ruling party, the Institutional Revolutionary Party (PRI), which had made Mexico the success story of Latin America in the half century it had held control. PRI rewards loyal party members, and when PRI nominates a candidate for president, he is as good as elected. Echeverría had been a solid party member since 1946, and PRI would not have chosen him if he had not been cast in the mold of the successful presidents who had gone before.

Echeverría was born in Mexico City on Jan. 17, 1922, when Mexico was just beginning to emerge from the bloody era of the 1910 revolution. In a sense, he and PRI grew up together. There is nothing quite like PRI anywhere else in Latin America. It is an all-encompassing political entity, with room for campesinos and factory workers, planters and soldiers, Communists and white-collar workers. Operating on a system of patronage, PRI has a cradle-to-grave structure that can reward or ignore, and it has evolved into what has been called a unique system of consensual democracy. It is a native product of Mexico and Mexico has thrived under it.

Echeverría's bloodlines are mestizo, as any successful Mexican politician's must be, with roots in Jalisco, San Luis Potosí, Sonora, and Oaxaca. He received his degree as licenciado, or lawyer, from the National University in 1945 and immediately launched into party work, holding a series of party and government offices. His major leap forward came in 1958 when he became undersecretary of Gobernacion, similar to a European ministry of interior. The secretary of Gobernacion was Gustavo Díaz Ordaz, and when Díaz resigned to become the PRI candidate for the presidency in 1963, Echeverría moved up to take his place. In July 1970 Echeverría was elected to succeed Díaz as president, and on December 1 he assumed office.

The new president was very friendly to the U.S., but like all Mexican presidents he was unalterably opposed to intervention in the affairs of one nation by another—a kind of genetic reaction to the loss of Mexican territory to the U.S. in the 19th century. It was for this reason that Mexico maintained relations with Cuba, even though there was no secret about the distaste Mexican leaders felt for the Castro government. Echeverría inherited few problems with the U.S., however. Such outstanding questions as that of the international boundary near Juarez had been solved, and while the narcotics traffic and the use of the Gulf of Lower California were potential irritants, on the whole Echeverría took office at a time when relations between the two countries were extremely good. (J. A. O'L.)

EHRLICH, PAUL

Once a researcher in the quiet of the laboratory, by 1970 Paul Ehrlich had become the angry man of the ecology movement. A professor of biology and former director of graduate studies for the department of biological sciences at Stanford University, Ehrlich burst on the public scene with *The Population Bomb* (1968), a book that became the bible of those who believe we must act now to head off overpopulation.

As of 1970, the book had sold almost a million copies in paperback and had made its author one of the leading figures in the battle to save the environment. Campuses clamoured for him as a speaker; he became a frequent guest on nationally televised interview programs; he was on the move 18 hours a day, traveling 80,000 mi. a year to spread his message.

The message was simple enough. "Over the next few centuries we must reduce the number of people on the planet to well under one billion." "Even if we prevented all unwanted children . . . we would still have a severe population problem." "We must move from an economic system based on growth, production, consumption and waste to one that emphasizes stability, quality of capital

WIDE WORLD
Angela Yvonne Davis

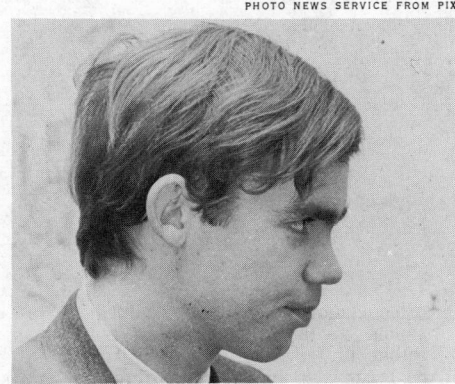

Dwight David Eisenhower II
PHOTO NEWS SERVICE FROM PIX

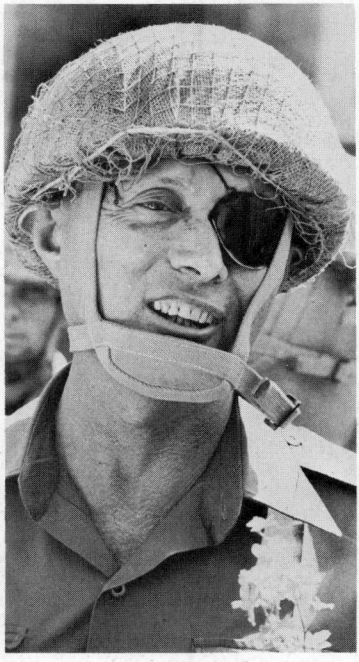

Moshe Dayan
GAMMA FROM PIX

goods, recycling of resources." "The population has been increasing faster than the food supply since 1958." Some critics called Ehrlich an alarmist. He agreed. "After all, I'm alarmed," he said. "I'm scared."

To further the cause, Ehrlich helped organize an activist group called Zero Population Growth. Formed in 1969, it grew to a membership of more than 8,000 in 1970. Its program included legalized abortion, a maximum of two children in a family, government support of birth control, and tax incentives for smaller families.

Ehrlich was born May 29, 1932, in Philadelphia, received his B.A. from the University of Pennsylvania in 1953 and his Ph.D. from the University of Kansas in 1957. In 1959 he joined the Stanford faculty as assistant professor of biological sciences, attaining the rank of full professor in 1966. (F. Wt.)

EHRLICHMAN, JOHN DANIEL

One observer described John D. Ehrlichman as "both an individualist and a Middle American with a curiously vulnerable core that from time to time explodes in bursts of impatience with some of the trends in contemporary America and that seems constantly at war with the part of him which is compassionate and easy-going." This set of qualities evidently appealed to U.S. Pres. Richard Nixon, whom Ehrlichman served as campaign organizer, presidential assistant for domestic affairs, and, from June 10, 1970, executive director of the Domestic Council.

Ehrlichman's appointment to head the Domestic Council, designed as a counterpart of the National Security Council, was not unexpected. Soon after the 1968 presidential election, Nixon directed him to set up a domestic policy-making group similar to the NSC. Many Washington observers asserted that Ehrlichman had become one of the

most influential White House aides in history.

Ehrlichman regarded himself as a "traffic manager" of competing approaches to domestic problems. In this capacity, he played a key role in fashioning administration policy on such issues as student unrest, school desegregation, and purchase of national park lands. The welfare reform plan proposed by President Nixon was pieced together by Ehrlichman from the sharply differing proposals of presidential aides Arthur Burns and Daniel Moynihan.

Ehrlichman had been associated with the president since 1960, when he acted as an advance man for Nixon's first presidential campaign. In 1962 he was in charge of scheduling for Nixon's unsuccessful campaign for governor of California. During the 1968 presidential race, Ehrlichman was responsible for all logistics on Nixon's 50,000-mi. nationwide tour. In the process he developed a reputation for strict punctuality that kept the Nixon campaign always on schedule.

Ehrlichman was born in Tacoma, Wash., on March 20, 1925. In 1948 he graduated from the University of California at Los Angeles, where he was a classmate of H. R. Haldeman, another Nixon aide. Ehrlichman also held a law degree from Stanford. During World War II he was a first lieutenant in the Army Air Corps. (Ri. W.)

EISENHOWER, DWIGHT DAVID, II

At a time when—at least if one believed the media—the world of youth was dominated by radical ideology, long hair, love beads, and pot, David Eisenhower, the grandson of one U.S. president and the son-in-law of another, seemed to symbolize the "straight," old-fashioned young American that Middle America longed to believe was still in the majority. Nor was his father-in-law slow to capitalize on that fact. In an election year, David was in great demand as a speaker for Republican candidates.

Yet despite—or perhaps because of—the symbolism, there was a question as to whether David was truly a part of his generation. He and his wife, Julie Nixon Eisenhower, had declined to attend David's commencement ceremony at Amherst in June 1970 because they objected to the speaker (liberal journalist I. F. Stone) and because of the possibility of student demonstrations. Earlier, they had forgone Julie's graduation from Smith for similar reasons.

Dwight David Eisenhower II was born on March 31, 1948, at West Point, N.Y., to Capt. and Mrs. John S. D. Eisenhower. He graduated from Phillips Exeter Academy before entering Amherst. The only grandson of Pres. Dwight D. Eisenhower (Camp David, the presidential retreat in Maryland, was named for him), he was a frequent guest at the White House, where he first met Julie, the younger daughter of then Vice-Pres. Richard Nixon. Years later, when they were both college students, they met again, became engaged, and were married on Dec. 22, 1968.

In October 1970 David both followed and broke with family tradition by entering Naval Officers Candidate School at Newport, R.I. Both his father and grandfather had been Army men, but President Nixon had served in the Navy in World War II. The Navy was not all David and his father-in-law had in common. Both were avid baseball fans. David threw out the first ball at the Washington Senators' opening game in April—a task traditionally performed by the president—and he worked for the Senators during the summer as team statistician. Committed to remain in the Navy for three years, he said he had "no idea" what he would do after that. There was speculation, however, that he would choose a political career. (RI. W.)

FIGUERES FERRER, JOSÉ

Elected president of Costa Rica for four years early in 1970, José Figueres Ferrer was an uncompromising enemy of both Communists and right-wing dictatorships. This was the third time Don Pepe, as he was affectionately known to his countrymen, had been president of the tidy little democracy where there was no army and where more money was spent on teachers than on policemen. He had led an irregular army that prevented the ouster of the duly elected president in 1948 and had ruled Costa Rica until the elected official could assume charge. He also was elected in the usual free Costa Rican election of 1953.

As president and leader of the National Liberation Party, Figueres was one of the few democratically elected presidents in Latin America. He had mellowed from his youthful days when, as a vigorous democratic militant, he had counted among his mortal enemies such dictators as Anastasio Somoza of Nicaragua and Rafael Trujillo of the Dominican Republic. In 1970 Don Pepe was not only constitutional president of the republic but also a prosperous lawyer and planter and a respected voice in hemispheric councils. In Costa Rica he was regarded as the father and guardian of the country's democratic way of life.

Figueres was born Sept. 25, 1906, at San Ramón in the upland coffee country of Costa Rica. He spent many years studying economics and engineering in the U.S., and

John Gardner
WIDE WORLD

Wladysław Gomułka
ELLIOTT ERWITT FROM MAGNUM

often claimed that his real education was gained by random reading in the Boston Public Library. In the '30s and early '40s he became an implacable enemy of Caribbean dictators. The so-called Caribbean Legion, with which he was associated, gave arms, money, and men to exiles trying to bring the dictators down. In 1948 he fought the Costa Rican Army and Communist commandos to preserve the presidency for Otilio Ulate.

Elected to the office himself in 1953, he had to fight off invaders backed by Nicaragua. Figueres was an early supporter of Fidel Castro, but broke with him when the Cuban revealed his Marxist colours. Openly pro-U.S., Figueres regarded Costa Rica as a pilot project for the future growth of democracy in Latin America. (J. A. O'L.)

FRANJIEH, SULEIMAN

Elected president of Lebanon Aug. 17, 1970, by a one-vote margin, 60-year-old Suleiman Franjieh was typical of the society he represented. He was born on June 14, 1910, in a small village to a family that was the undisputed leader of the farmer-business community in the area. Franjieh completed his studies in Beirut and joined the family business at age 20. He developed a flair for banking and insurance and drew rich rewards from his highly specialized knowledge. Unlike the majority of successful Lebanese businessmen, however, he made no attempt at first to become involved in politics. He left this to his older brother, Hamid Franjieh, a distinguished lawyer who played a major part in Lebanon's struggle for independence in 1945 and then became the country's first foreign minister. In 1956, however, Hamid suffered an acute attack of poliomyelitis and had to retire from politics.

Despite family pressure, Franjieh refused to step into the position vacated by his brother as a deputy to Parliament and continued to devote himself to the family business. But in 1960 he changed his mind and ran for his brother's former seat. He won and was subsequently appointed minister of trade and economics in the new govern-

RUSSELL REIF FROM PICTORIAL PARADE
Betty Friedan

ment. He won a considerable reputation as a banker of repute and integrity and as the country's ablest financial brain. He was, however, a surprise nomination in the confused situation that preceded the presidential election in 1970. His opponent was Elias Sarkis, the nominee of Gen. Fuad Chehab, a former president and reputedly the most powerful man in the country.

Franjieh's success, though narrow, reflected the consensus for which he stood. He had the support of Christians and Muslims, of the right and the left, and he reflected this in the government that he formed after his election. In place of the customary politicians and representatives of powerful interests, Franjieh formed a Cabinet composed of experts and experienced officials. He reasserted Lebanon's independence in relation to the Palestinian guerrillas and also in restoring quiet on Lebanon's border with Israel. (J. K.)

FRIEDAN, BETTY

There were those (mostly men) who called Betty Friedan the Pandora of the U.S. women's liberation movement, for it was her book *The Feminine Mystique,* published in 1963, that first brought to popular attention the frustrations of the modern American woman trying to conform to the traditional image of housewife and mother. There were also those (mostly women) who considered her to be the movement's Joan of Arc. As leader of the National Organization for Women (NOW), she was a leading spirit in the national women's strike called on Aug. 26, 1970, and she was in the forefront of battles to strike down discrimination against women in such areas as employment.

For all that Mrs. Friedan's views had seemed radical in 1963, when the lustre was only beginning to fade from the '50s dream of suburbia, NOW in 1970 found itself at the right of the women's liberation spectrum. Drawing its strength largely from white, middle-class, often professional women, it concentrated on removing legal disabilities based on sex—a stance that led some observers to call it the NAACP of

Elliott Gould
WIDE WORLD

women's lib. NOW, for example, strongly favoured the proposed women's rights amendment to the U.S. Constitution that would forbid discrimination on account of sex.

All this seemed very old-fashioned to those women—especially younger ones—who demanded more radical solutions. Some said that true equality between the sexes would be possible only when society was totally restructured. "We're the real radicals," Mrs. Friedan told a *New York Times* interviewer when asked about these criticisms. "We're changing things."

Despite these differences of opinion, most women's groups did cooperate on August 26. The day was more demonstration than strike, but the eminent seriousness of most of the participants signaled that many of America's women meant what they said about claiming what they considered to be their rightful place in society.

Mrs. Friedan was born Betty Goldstein on Feb. 4, 1921, in Peoria, Ill., and graduated from Smith College, Northampton, Mass. After a period as a working girl living in Greenwich Village, she married Carl Friedan (they were divorced in 1969) and raised three children in the suburbs.

GARAUDY, ROGER

A member of the French Communist Party since 1932 and its leading intellectual, Roger Garaudy faced a dilemma at the end of 1970: how to remain a Communist although rejected by the party. Since 1956 he had been one of ten members of its Politburo, the supreme executive council. A doctor of letters and professor in the faculty of letters at the University of Clermont-Ferrand (1962–65), he had been considered the French party's chief theoretician. And in 1970 he was booed at the party's 19th congress in Nanterre and removed from the Politburo and from the Central Committee.

Behind this episode lay a story of destalinization that went too far, or at least too far for the French Communist leaders to stomach. Garaudy was born July 17, 1913, in Marseilles, and attended the University of Paris. After joining the party, he moved

up through the hierarchy. He faithfully followed the party line at the time of the Hitler-Stalin pact of 1939, when the party was outlawed and its activists were hunted down, and was active in the Resistance during the German occupation. After the war he was a deputy from 1945 to 1951 and again from 1956 to 1958. From 1959 to 1962 he was a senator.

Among all Communist leaders, his qualifications and university experience made him a natural choice to take charge of the party intellectuals. An ardent Stalinist, hostile to Titoism and the various other heresies, he gained the reputation of being the most intelligent but also the most dogmatic and sectarian of Communist philosophers.

The change came around 1958–60. In an essay entitled "D'un réalisme sans rivages," Garaudy attacked Stalinism and put the case for liberalization of Communist thought, a rapprochement with Christians, and an "open" and evolving Marxism. Moving "from anathema to dialogue" (the title of one of his books), he led the Centre d'Études et de Recherches Marxistes, which he directed, toward a liberal Communism and a humanist Marxism.

It could not last. As long as Maurice Thorez, the all-powerful leader of the French Communists, was alive, he had been protected. But Thorez was dead, and Garaudy's outspoken protests against the Soviet invasion of Czechoslovakia were too much. Reduced to an ordinary party member, he still called himself a better Communist and a better Marxist than those responsible for his dismissal.   (P. V.-P.)

GARDNER, JOHN WILLIAM

When Illinois Constitutional Convention officials told former Health, Education, and Welfare Secretary John W. Gardner he could not give a speech he had written at their invitation—because of its content—he flew back to Washington and gave it to the press. The noise over his "muzzling" only increased the attention paid his thesis that there was a "growing crisis of confidence in our leadership." It also demonstrated Gardner's skill at identifying problems that touch inner chords of Americans of all classes and political stripes and for mobilizing remedial action in Washington.

In the fall of 1970, he turned those talents to a new vehicle for dealing with the problems of politics and government, a national citizens' organization. Common Cause, as it was called, emerged from the Urban Coalition Action Council, a surprisingly effective lobby Gardner also headed. The purpose of Common Cause was to mobilize public opinion and energy behind the kinds of goals the Urban Coalition lobbied for privately. In Gardner's words: "It is a new, independent, nonpartisan organization for those Americans who want to help in the rebuilding of this nation. . . . One of our aims will be to revitalize politics and government. . . . We want public officials to have literally millions of American citizens looking over their shoulders." Gardner's efforts were endorsed widely and received for him the description in the *New York Times* of "the paradigm of the concerned private citizen."

Born in Los Angeles on Oct. 8, 1912, Gardner took degrees at Stanford and the University of California prior to teaching psychology. During World War II he served as a U.S. Marine Corps officer with the Office of Strategic Services. He joined the Carnegie Corporation of New York in 1946 and became its president in 1955. He received the Presidential Medal of Freedom in 1964 and a year later became Pres. Lyndon B. Johnson's HEW secretary, a post he held nearly three years.   (Ph. K.)

GOMULKA, WLADYSLAW

The 14-year reign of Wladyslaw Gomulka as head of the Communist Party in Poland ended suddenly and dramatically on December 20 as the 65-year-old leader resigned in the wake of bloody rioting over government-imposed price increases. The official announcement of the resignation stated that it was because of ill health, but most observers believed that the rioting had toppled the veteran politician. Pres. Marian Spychalski and three top aides of Gomulka lost their positions of power in the party at the same time. Gomulka was replaced by Edward Gierek, a party leader from the Katowice area.

Ironically, Gomulka's downfall came at the end of what had appeared to be one of his most successful years. He had pushed through a new system of managing the Polish economy, and his country had signed a treaty with West Germany that, in substance, recognized the Oder-Neisse line as Poland's boundary. The treaty was, to a great extent, Gomulka's personal triumph, marking the first time since 1949 that there had been fruitful Polish-West German talks.

Gomulka was born on Feb. 6, 1905, at Bialobrzegi, near Krosno, in the then Austrian part of Poland. He joined the illegal Communist Party of Poland in 1926 and was arrested twice, in 1932 and again shortly after his return from the Soviet Union where he spent the years 1934–35 at the International Lenin School near Moscow. Escaping at the outbreak of World War II, he remained in German-occupied Poland and started his activity as an independent Communist organizer.

In November 1943 Gomulka was made secretary-general of the Polish Workers' Party, which then numbered about 8,000 members. On Dec. 31, 1944, he was appointed deputy premier of the Soviet-supported provisional government formed in Lublin, and in November 1945 he was appointed minister of the former German lands east of the Oder-Neisse line. Under pressure from Stalin, Gomulka was successively dismissed from the post of party secretary-general, removed from the government, expelled from the party, and arrested. Rehabilitated after Stalin's death, he was co-opted to the party Central Committee and, on Oct. 21, 1956, elected as its first secretary on a wave of national popularity following the Poznan riots earlier in that year.   (K. Sm.)

GOULD, ELLIOTT

Elliott Gould, who attracted hardly any attention at all when he was married to one of America's superstars, came into his own in 1970 as the anti-idol of an iconoclastic generation. And "Mr. Streisand" succeeded in Barbra's adopted medium, film.

His first hit was the comic sociosexual comment *Bob & Carol & Ted & Alice,* in which he almost won an Oscar for playing an awkward show-biz attorney who almost tries wife-swapping. Next came *M*A*S*H,* a brutal antiwar, anti-Establishment black-comedy-in-technicolor about a combat hospital in the Korean War. In *Getting Straight,* Gould played a reasonably maladjusted, reasonably radical graduate student in a riot-torn university. He considered it his best work to date. His one unabashed box office flop was *Move,* a confusing sexual sketch. It did gain Gould a *Playboy* picture spread and the distinction of being the first Playmate with a hairy back.

WIDE WORLD

Edward Richard George Heath

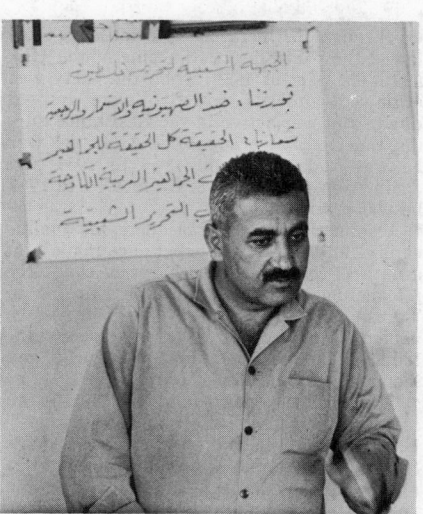

BRUNO BARBEY FROM MAGNUM

George Habash

Billy Graham
SAHM DOHERTY FROM CAMERA 5

Born in Brooklyn, N.Y., on Aug. 29, 1938, Elliott Goldstein received prodigy treatment from a doting mother who enrolled him in elocution lessons before he was nine. The name change occurred before his debut on a local TV show at nine or ten. After a checkered career in and out of show business he auditioned to understudy the lead in the Broadway musical *I Can Get It for You Wholesale*. He got the part, not the backup role, but an unknown named Barbra Streisand stole the show. "Marriage to Barbra was a fantastic experience," Gould recalled. "It had a lot of chocolate soufflé and things like that, but it was also like a bath of lava." They separated after seven years and the birth of a son named Jason.

Meanwhile, Gould appeared on the London stage, toured the U.S. in *The Fantasticks,* and starred in a TV special. He won raves for his New York performance in Jules Feiffer's short-lived *Little Murders.* Then came a film part in *The Night They Raided Minsky's* and, at last, *B & C & T & A* and his big break. Not satisfied with Hollywood alone, he talked of playing an archaeologist in a feature directed by the Swedish master Ingmar Bergman. (Ph. K.)

GOWON, YAKUBU

Nigeria's head of state, Maj. Gen. Yakubu Gowon, emerged from a bitter civil war that ended in January 1970 as the undisputed leader of Africa's most populous country. His prestige stood so high that there was widespread support for his announcement, made on the tenth anniversary of Nigeria's independence (Oct. 1, 1970), that the Army would remain in power for another six years in order to give the country a chance to recover from the civil war and to develop national political parties. But the general remained opposed to military rule. "I hope I am speaking the mind of my fellow military leaders elsewhere in Africa when I say that our military government is purely a corrective one," he said, "and our aim is to lay the foundation for a stable civilian government."

When Gowon took power after the second military coup in August 1966, he was a largely unknown lieutenant colonel not yet 32 years old, and completely apolitical. His success was due to the skill with which he won the Army's loyalty, the firmness with which he handled the older politicians, and his single-mindedness in fighting to reestab-

lish the unity of Nigeria after the abortive attempt at secession by the Ibo people in the breakaway republic of Biafra.

Gowon was born Oct. 19, 1934, of Christian parents belonging to the minority Pankshin tribe on the Benue Plateau. He was educated by Christian missionaries before going to a government secondary school. On leaving school he joined the Army, was sent to Britain's premier military establishments—Sandhurst, Eaton Hall, and the Young Officers' Courses at Hythe and Warminster—and was the first Nigerian to be appointed adjutant general of the Army. He served with the UN forces in the former Belgian Congo during the post-independence disturbances there. He had been back in the country for barely 36 hours when the first Army coup occurred in January 1966. Although he was not a party to it, he played a leading role in helping to maintain discipline among the troops, and after the second coup he was chosen head of federal military government and commander in chief of the armed forces.   (Co. L.)

GRAHAM, BILLY

Newsweek called Billy Graham "the president's preacher," *Life,* "an American Rasputin." Either way, he was the most influential clergyman in the United States in 1970. Moreover, his power did not rest solely on personal relationships with presidents but on his immense public following. That, of course, might have a direct bearing on his easy access to the White House, whoever the tenant.

A frequent preacher at White House religious observances since Harry Truman first received him in 1949, it was Graham who counseled Dwight Eisenhower on instituting the annual Prayer Breakfast. Friendly but not intimate with the more urbane John Kennedy, Graham became a White House regular again under Lyndon Johnson. Having known Richard Nixon's parents as evangelical Quakers at California revivals, he had played golf with Nixon when Nixon was a junior senator. The friendship apparently thrived over the years, though Graham avoided publicly endorsing Nixon for the presidency in 1960 and '68. However, in Nixon's final television ad blitz in 1968, widespread use was made of news service reports that Graham had voted for Nixon by absentee ballot.

The evangelist's position as a sort of White House chaplain-on-retainer was made manifest at Honor America Day, July 4, 1970. Graham was the spiritual headliner at the morning's event, a prayer meeting on the steps of the Lincoln Memorial that drew a crowd of only several thousand people. A worldwide Christian celebrity who preached to royalty and commoners on every continent, Graham was more accustomed to praying with hundreds of thousands of the faithful at his 200 crusades a year. Such numbers were indicative of Graham's standing as the second "most admired" American; a 1969 Gallup Poll found he fit into the nation's esteem between the president and the vice-president.

Born in Charlotte, N.C., Nov. 7, 1918, and ordained as a Southern Baptist, Graham launched his public pastorate by radio from Chicago in 1943. By 1970 his weekly broadcasts were carried by 900 stations, his televised crusades by 235 channels, his magazine *Decision* circulated four million copies a month, and he received nearly 50,000 letters a week.   (Ph. K.)

HABASH, GEORGE

When four passenger airliners were hijacked to the Middle East in September 1970, it soon became known that a Palestinian guerrilla organization, the Popular Front for the Liberation of Palestine (PFLP), was responsible. Leading this organization throughout the year was a physician turned full-time politician, George Habash.

Habash was born in 1925, in a village near Haifa. He attended school in Jerusalem and then was chosen by U.S. missionaries as one of ten Christian boys to receive a higher education. During the 1948 war in which Israel established its control over Palestine, Habash fought on the Arab side. He was not satisfied with the Arab conduct of the war and afterward withdrew to Beirut, Lebanon, to study for a medical degree. From 1950 to 1956 he practiced medicine in Beirut and then moved to Jordan.

His practice was not very successful, and Habash gradually devoted more and more of his time to political agitation. By 1965 he had decided to give all his time to politics. He joined Yasir Arafat (*q.v.*) and Naif Hawatmeh to form a secret Palestinian guerrilla movement, which they called Al Fatah. They started by recruiting Palestinian Arabs for underground and intelligence work in Israel. But after Israel's triumph over the Arabs in the Six-Day War of 1967, dissension broke out, and Habash and Hawatmeh rejected Arafat's leadership and formed the PFLP. Habash's main criticism of Arafat was that he was opposed to any political ideology for the guerrillas, while Habash favoured a Marxist-Leninist line. Hawatmeh later broke with Habash in favour of a Maoist orientation.

During the hijacking crisis and subsequent civil war in Jordan, Habash was in North Korea, with which he appeared to have close ties. When he returned to Jordan in late October, however, he was reelected chairman of the PFLP. His dramatic flair for publicity, as illustrated in the hijacking policy, helped him increase the membership in his movement as it began to attract recruits from Al Fatah. (J. K.)

HALL, PETER REGINALD FREDERICK

Unsure as a boy whether he wanted to be a conductor or a theatrical director, Peter Hall found the solution to his dilemma in 1970 with his appointment as co-director, together with Colin Davis, of the Royal Opera House, Covent Garden, an appointment to be taken up in 1971. Meantime, this many-sided virtuoso had created something of a directorial revolution on the British dramatic and operatic stage ever since he left Cambridge University and student dramatics and took charge in 1960 of what was to become the Royal Shakespeare Theatre in Stratford. It was he who understood that Shakespearean actors needed modern plays in which to extend their powers and created the second London home of the Royal Shakespeare Company at the Aldwych Theatre in 1961.

Born at Bury St. Edmunds, Suffolk, on Nov. 22, 1930, the son of a railway stationmaster, Hall spent his childhood traveling free on his father's trains to watch theatrical productions at Cambridge, where he later attended the Perse School and graduated from St. Catharine's College. His university activities included directing Shakespeare and modern dramatists. After working in repertory theatre in England, he became head of the London Arts Theatre, where he made theatrical history with the English premiere of *Waiting for Godot* in 1955.

Hall formed his own company, the International Playwrights' Theatre, in 1957, the year in which he also directed his first opera (*The Moon and Sixpence*) at Sadler's Wells. He made his debut at Stratford in 1956 with *Love's Labour's Lost* and in 1957 directed

Cymbeline. He resigned as managing director of the Royal Shakespeare Company in 1968, but remained a co-director. Among his outstanding stage productions during those years were *The Wars of the Roses* in 1964, *Hamlet* in 1965, and Harold Pinter's *The Homecoming,* which won him a New York critics' Tony Award in 1967.

Hall made his film debut in 1968 when he directed Henry Livings' *Work Is a Four-Letter Word.* This was followed by *A Midsummer Night's Dream, Three into Two Won't Go,* and, in 1970, *Perfect Friday.* His principal operatic productions were *Moses and Aaron* and *The Magic Flute* at Covent Garden, where he staged the world premiere of Sir Michael Tippett's *The Knot Garden* in December 1970. (O. Tr.)

HAMBRO, EDVARD

To preside over its milestone 25th session, the UN General Assembly elected Edvard Hambro of Norway, a second-generation diplomat whose experience went back to the League of Nations. When he took the chair as president on Sept. 15, 1970, he was following in the footsteps of his father, the late Carl Hambro, who was the last president of the League of Nations assembly from 1939 to 1946. At the time of his election, Hambro was 59 years old and was Norway's permanent representative at UN headquarters.

Hambro is a firm believer in the UN and in the Charter, which he had helped to draft. In his inaugural speech, he noted that "perfectionists" at times have insisted on revision of the Charter, but he added that "experience of 25 years has shown that the Charter has proved sufficiently flexible to adapt to the ever changing needs and situations." He said the success of the organization depends upon the support and concern of men and women all over the world. "Those who observe the United Nations from the outside may have experienced deeper disappointments over the past 25 years than those of us who work within the organization. It is our task to rekindle the enthusiasm of public opinion."

Born in Oslo on Aug. 22, 1911, Hambro got his first taste of international affairs as a 22-year-old law student when he received a fellowship for study at the League of Nations. Although most of his adult life had been spent in diplomacy, he also served in the Norwegian Storting (parliament) and held teaching posts in widely scattered institutions, including Northwestern University in Evanston, Ill., Cambridge, and the University of California at Berkeley. At one time he was acting chief of the UN legal section and he served as administrative head of the International Court of Justice for seven years. (Mx. H.)

HEATH, EDWARD RICHARD GEORGE

Had the Conservative Party not won the 1970 British general election, Edward Heath might well have been displaced from its leadership. It was understandable, therefore, that he claimed the result as a "famous victory."

Although he had rarely shown in politics the authority he conveyed in the television program (June 28, 1970) on his musical activities, he at least convinced *The Times* (Oct. 27, 1970) that he found it "natural" to be prime minister. The paper's claim that he had overcome his communication problem was based on impressive speeches made to the Conservative Party conference (October 10) and to the UN (October 23), but it remained to be seen whether he had acquired the adroitness to resume, on more equal terms, his parliamentary duel with Harold Wilson.

Heath was a new portent in the Tory firmament; he arrived without the help of wealth or influence and was the first leader to be chosen (July 1965) by straightforward election. All his successes resulted from hard work and meticulous planning, with every detail taken into account. His government's apparent inertia in some fields stemmed, however, not from overcaution but from a doctrinaire policy of laissez-faire. In fact he had remarkable nerve, and his handling of the Palestinian hijacking crisis showed a firm and cool touch. He conducted politics as he sailed: "All the time you're going out to win." He won the Sydney to Hobart race (December 1969) by setting an unconventional but carefully calculated course; on this analogy, although his ship of state appeared to be headed for multiple collision, he might yet ultimately triumph.

Born at Broadstairs in Kent on July 9, 1916, the son of a carpenter who later became a builder, Heath was educated at a Ramsgate grammar school and at Balliol College, Oxford, where he won the college organ scholarship and became president of the Oxford Union. Emerging from World War II with the rank of lieutenant colonel, he entered the civil service and then worked in a merchant bank. As MP for Bexley from February 1950, he served in the Whips' Office (1951–55) and as government chief whip (1959–59). He was minister of labour (1959–60), lord privy seal (1960–63) in charge of (unsuccessful) negotiations for Britain to join the EEC, and secretary of state for industry, trade, and regional development (1963–64). (S. Mu.)

HERTZOG, ALBERT

After serving for ten years in the South African Nationalist government as minister of posts and telegraphs and also of health, Albert Hertzog was dismissed from the Cabinet in 1968. In 1969 he was expelled from the ruling party because he had disagreed openly with the program of Prime Minister B. J. Vorster and was heading a group in opposition to the party leadership.

Ultraconservative in his views, Hertzog considered that the position and traditions of the Afrikaners, the white descendants of early Dutch settlers, were endangered by government policies. He was critical of what he regarded as concessions to "English liberalism." He disapproved of the encouragement of certain types of immigration, the official attitude on racially mixed sports, and the establishment of diplomatic relations with black African states. He was opposed to the introduction of television, believing it to be a social evil likely to undermine the Afrikaners' moral standards.

Hertzog's differences with the government came to a head toward the end of 1969 when he formed a new party, the Herstigte Nasionale Party (Reconstituted Nationalist Party), based on "Christian-National" and Calvinist principles and emphasizing the dominance in the nation of the Afrikaner. Three other members of Parliament, who had been expelled or had resigned from the Nationalist Party, joined the HNP. Supported by a newspaper Hertzog had founded and by a countrywide organization, the party nominated 80 candidates for the general election in April 1970, which the government held primarily to test the strength of the breakaway movement. All the party's candidates, including Hertzog, were heavily defeated.

Born in Bloemfontein on July 4, 1899,

Hertzog was educated at South African, British, and Dutch universities and practiced as a lawyer. He was the eldest son of J. B. M. Hertzog, a former general and prime minister (1924–39) who played a historic role as the leader of Afrikaner nationalism and founder, in 1914, of the Nationalist Party and, in 1934 (with Jan Christiaan Smuts), of the United Party.   (L. H.)

HICKEL, WALTER JOSEPH

Nobody expected it when he was named secretary of the interior, but in 1970 Walter Hickel turned out to be the rebel of Pres. Richard Nixon's Cabinet and the first Cabinet member in 18 years to be fired. Initially, Hickel had sounded like an exploiter of the nation's resources. He was opposed to water quality standards that "hinder industrial development," did not believe in "conservation for conservation's sake," and felt that "a tree looking at another tree really doesn't do anything."

Once in office, however, Hickel started taking on many of the interest groups that had helped put Nixon in the White House. He urged adoption of strong legislation requiring oil companies to clean up accidental oil spills in offshore waters at their own expense. He shut down wells around the Union Oil Co.'s spill in the Santa Barbara Channel, hauled the Chevron Oil Co. into court to face 900 violation counts, and took the initiative in saving the Everglades from a proposed jetport. He launched a lawsuit against U.S. Steel for alleged pollution, banned the use of 16 pesticides on government land, and moved against commercial signs on public lands.

As if that were not enough, in May, at the height of student demonstrations against the U.S. move into Cambodia, Hickel wrote a letter to Nixon and allowed it to be leaked to the public. He accused the administration of lacking concern for the young and asked that Vice-Pres. Spiro Agnew's tirades against students be toned down. Washington was agog at Hickel's political impudence and the White House did little to quiet speculation that Hickel would not remain long as secretary. Hickel, however, resisted all efforts to get his resignation and finally was dismissed on November 25. Probably the best summation of his conduct in office was his own parting statement: "I had to do it my way."

Born in Ellinwood, Kan., on Aug. 18, 1919, Hickel set out at 16 to make his fortune in Australia. Instead, he arrived in Alaska in 1940 with 37 cents in his pocket. Soon he had built a house and sold it, setting the pattern that led to a construction business valued at $14 million. Hickel became the first elected Republican governor of Alaska in 1966 in his first bid for elective office.   (F. WT.)

HILLERY, PATRICK JOHN

On July 6, 1970, just a week before the crucial Orangeman's Day celebrations in Northern Ireland, Paddy Hillery, Irish minister for external affairs, told an astonished press conference in Dublin that he had just come back from the Falls Road in Belfast, scene of some of the most severe of the Ulster rioting. "I went," he said, "with the purpose of relieving the tension in the North of Ireland." He was in the Falls Road for only 90 minutes. He was recognized by only a few people, and he did not identify himself. He traveled in a private car, and he told neither the British nor the Northern Ireland government. In view of the tense situation

that prevailed, the news created a sensation. It was also possible that it reassured the worried and nervous Catholics in the North and that it served as a warning, if only of the unpredictable nature of the South's reaction.

It was also typical of Hillery himself. He made quite clear on this occasion, as he had done previously, that the practical needs of the situation far outweighed more delicate diplomatic considerations. It was simply a visit to reassure a beleaguered minority.

A mild, good-natured man, Hillery came from Clare in the far west, where he was born May 2, 1923. He attended University College, Dublin, and served as a doctor in Clare after qualifying in the '40s. He held several government posts before being appointed minister for external affairs in 1969.

With Ireland actively seeking EEC membership, placing the responsibility for negotiating on the shoulders of this friendly country doctor did not seem the most promising of decisions. But Hillery took over smoothly from Frank Aiken, who had served from 1951 to 1954 and from 1957 to 1969, and quickly convinced the EEC of Ireland's determination to enter. He was firm and outspoken in setting forth Ireland's attitude during key periods of the crisis in the North, although he was in no real position to make positive proposals and his contribution, like that of Prime Minister John Lynch, was inevitably more emotional than practical. As Lynch's position became increasingly tenuous during the year, Hillery appeared to many to be a likely successor.   (B. AR.)

HUMPHREY, HUBERT HORATIO

Rested, restless and buoyant as ever, former Vice-Pres. Hubert Humphrey rolled up his sleeves and made a political comeback in 1970, returning to the U.S. Senate and perhaps gaining another chance to rekindle his dashed presidential hopes of 1968.

There was no hiding his famed campaign gusto as Humphrey moved out in June from a 17-month recess that had been his only out-of-office interlude since 1945. Even as the year began, he had rationalized his defeat at the hands of Richard Nixon as a welcome opportunity to tone up for a fresh crack at public life. "I was running dry," he said, "I'm sure I was. I knew I needed new ideas."

He hammered on inflation, interest rates, and the problems of the cities as he campaigned for the Minnesota seat being vacated by former Democratic presidential rival Eugene J. McCarthy. Outlining his view of a U.S. senator's role, Humphrey said, "I hear a call to leadership that will not tolerate mindless and senseless violence, and at the same time, I've heard the voices of compassion and tolerance and justice." While making the familiar promise to serve a full term in the Senate, Humphrey noted that, in all candor, he would not "turn away" from another presidential nomination.

Born May 27, 1911, in Wallace, S.D., Humphrey attended the Denver (Colo.) College of Pharmacy from 1932 to 1933 and worked as a pharmacist before earning a B.A. at the University of Minnesota in 1939 and an M.A. in 1940 from the University of Louisiana. He taught political science and held a variety of jobs before becoming mayor of Minneapolis on a reform ticket. In 1948 he was elected to the U.S. Senate, where he became one of the leading voices of liberalism.

In 1960 he made an unsuccessful try for the Democratic presidential nomination and, four years later, became vice-president. In 1968, after Pres. Lyndon Johnson announced

that he would not run again, Humphrey won the party nomination but lost the election to Nixon. During his time out of office he returned to teaching—at Macalester College in St. Paul and the University of Minnesota in Minneapolis—and held a position with *Encyclopædia Britannica*.   (R. L. A.)

HUNTLEY, CHESTER ROBERT

After nearly 14 years as half of the most famous team in broadcast journalism, Chet Huntley retired from television in the summer of 1970. Canceling a $300,000-a-year contract two years before it expired, Huntley went back home to Montana to be the anchor man of Big Sky, a projected $15 million, 15,000-ac. resort, to be developed for summer and winter recreation.

Apparently Huntley felt he was getting stale. "I don't know what I believe any more," he said. "The noise . . . the clamoring for attention . . . the divisions in our society. . . . When you deliver it night after night you start feeling almost responsible for it. . . . Maybe where there's clarity of air, there's clarity of thought."

That the veteran newsman found events overwhelming was understandable. At the time he quit, 17 million viewers were watching him six nights a week. For many of them, "The Huntley-Brinkley Report" was the primary source of information about the nation and the world. With David Brinkley he had covered eight national political conventions, four presidential elections, two presidential funerals, two manned moon expeditions, the initial exploration of space, innumerable riots, and several wars. Huntley's unflappable and objective reason and Brinkley's wry observations had created a unique chemistry. NBC considered Huntley irreplaceable, per se, and when he left, it changed the format of its national news show.

However objective he may have been on the air, Huntley gave vent to a couple of startling personal opinions upon his retirement. Commenting to an interviewer on Pres. Richard Nixon—in remarks he later claimed were misquoted—he said, "The shallowness of the man overwhelms me; the fact that he is President frightens me." He also criticized Vice-Pres. Spiro Agnew for "appealing to the most base of elements. . . . I resent being lumped in with his Eastern Establishment effete intellectuals. I've had more cow manure on my boots than he ever thought about."

Huntley was born in Cardwell, Mont., Dec. 10, 1911, and received a B.A. from the University of Washington in 1934. His broadcasting career began at radio station KPCB in Seattle, Wash. He moved on to Spokane, Wash., then to Portland, Ore., and Los Angeles before joining CBS there in 1939. He switched to ABC in 1951 and NBC in 1955, moving to New York the next year.   (PH. K.)

HUSAIN IBN TALAL

King Husain I of Jordan in 1970 was confronted by the Palestinian-Jordanian civil war he had always hoped to avoid. It was provoked by Palestinian guerrilla extremists on the one hand and by senior Jordan Army officers of Bedouin origin loyal to the throne on the other. Following earlier clashes, various agreements between the government and the Palestinian refugee organizations had broken down, but a full-scale conflict had been avoided. The situation worsened as a result of Jordan's acceptance and the guerrillas' rejection of the U.S. peace proposals for the Middle East and also because of the Palestinian hijacking of three Western civilian planes to an airfield in Jordan.

Under strong pressure from the Army to bring the guerrillas under control, on September 15 the king brought matters to a head by appointing Gen. Habis al-Majali military governor and commander in chief of the armed forces. In the eight days of fighting that followed, Husain and the Army gained the upper hand over the guerrillas, but they were unable to win control of the whole country. Finally, strong pressure from other Arab states induced Husain to reach a compromise agreement with the Palestinian leader Yasir Arafat and to accept a measure of Arab League control of the government of his country. In a further agreement with Arafat in October, Husain formally agreed that Jordan was the principal base for the Palestinian struggle against Israel.

Born in Amman on Nov. 14, 1935, Husain was educated at Harrow School and the Royal Military Academy at Sandhurst in England. In 1951 his grandfather, King Abdullah, was assassinated before his eyes, and he became king the following year after his father, King Talal, had been declared mentally ill. Although receptive to new ideas, Husain maintained strong convictions concerning his family's hereditary right to rule. Of proved personal courage, he sometimes showed rashness and haste in his political decisions, and his strongly pro-Western sympathies caused him increasing difficulties because of the growth of anti-Western feelings among his Palestinian subjects and other Arab nations. (P. Md.)

POPPERFOTO FROM PICTORIAL PARADE

Husain ibn Talal

PAUL CONKLIN FROM PIX

Walter Joseph Hickel

JENKINS, CLIVE

Estimates in 1970 indicated that four out of ten British workers were in the white-collar category. Britain's traditional trade unions, oriented toward blue-collar occupations, did not apply to many of these workers. Into this largely unexploited territory early in the 1960s moved a garrulous, flamboyant Welshman, Clive Jenkins. In 1961, when (at the age of 34) he became general secretary of the Association of Supervisory Staffs, Executives, and Technicians, the union had a membership of approximately 20,000. In the next ten years Jenkins increased its membership more than sixfold, and changed its name to the Association of Scientific, Technical and Managerial Staffs.

With a panache that did not always win him friends, Jenkins set about unionizing white-collar workers everywhere. In his drive for members he sometimes found himself in conflict with older established unions. And the variety of the industries and occupations from which he drew his members could cause him to become engaged in a bewildering number of disputes and negotiations at the same time.

Jenkins was born May 2, 1926, a railway worker's son, in the South Wales steel town of Port Talbot. After attending schools in Port Talbot he worked in several metal manufacturing occupations before becoming a leader in the union movement. He maintained a left-wing position in the labour movement, and his distaste for capitalist society as materialist and corrupt was at the heart of his political beliefs. Jenkins was one of the union leaders who vociferously opposed Britain's application to join the EEC. In September–October 1970 he visited North Vietnam. (W. H. Ts.)

KARJALAINEN, AHTI

When Ahti Karjalainen became prime minister of Finland on July 15, 1970, it came as no surprise to those who knew the intricacies of that country's domestic politics. His Centre Party had been defeated in the general election in March; its representation in Parliament had fallen from 50 to 37 seats, and it had accordingly announced its unwilling-

Patrick John Hillery

WIDE WORLD

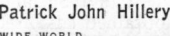

Hubert Horatio Humphrey

Chester Robert Huntley

WIDE WORLD

ness to participate in the new Cabinet. But the leaders of the party, which for decades had played a leading role in the Finnish government, knew how to play their cards.

After months of unsuccessful talks, during which the Social Democrats and Conservatives failed to form a government, Pres. Urho Kekkonen turned to Karjalainen. A five-party coalition was formed in which the Centre Party received four portfolios and a fifth went to an expert minister close to the party. By comparison, the Social Democratic Party, the largest group in Parliament (51 seats), also had five ministers in the new Cabinet.

Karjalainen was now 47, eight years older than when, as the youngest prime minister in Finland's history, he had headed a government for the first time in 1962–63. He was born Feb. 10, 1923, the son of a farmer, and when, as a student, he first became interested in politics, the Agrarian (later Centre) Party was a natural choice. After receiving a political science degree from the University of Helsinki in 1946, he worked as secretary of information at the party headquarters. In 1950 he became secretary to Prime Minister Kekkonen, then heading his first Cabinet, and he served Kekkonen in five governments.

Kekkonen became president in 1956, and a year later Karjalainen obtained his first Cabinet post as minister of finance in a caretaker government. From that time he was a fixture in most governments, usually as foreign minister or minister in charge of foreign trade. He became a member of the board of the Bank of Finland in 1958, was secretary and chairman of the advisory Economic Council, and was elected to Parliament in 1966. Karjalainen was a staunch advocate of Kekkonen's policy of neutrality and of friendship toward both the Soviet Union and the West, and had been mentioned as Kekkonen's possible successor.

(C. F. Sa.)

KATZ, SIR BERNARD

A German-born biophysicist and head of the department of physiology at University College, London, Sir Bernard Katz shared a 1970 Nobel Prize for Medicine or Physiology with Swedish physiologist Ulf von Euler and Julius Axelrod, a U.S. pharmacologist (*qq.v.*). The three scientists were honoured for their independently conducted basic research into the mechanics and biochemistry of nerve impulses. "Their discoveries concerning these regulatory mechanisms in the nervous system are found fundamental in neurophysiology and neuropharmacology," the Royal Caroline Institute of Stockholm said in its citation, "and have greatly stimulated the search for remedies against nervous and mental disturbances."

While von Euler and Axelrod's work involved the release of noradrenalin and its inhibition by an enzyme, Katz's research concerned a different neurotransmitter, acetylcholine, which is released at nerve-muscle junctions. He discovered how the substance is released by neural impulse: in a sudden burst of thousands of molecules that make muscles contract. He worked with the large nerve cells of squid and with frogs to study the shotgun-like emanations of neurotransmitter particles, which carry information infinitesimal distances between nerves and the muscles they govern. He declined to discuss the practical applications of his discoveries with reporters. "All I have to say is that I hope that this will lead to

understanding the nervous system as a whole."

Born in Leipzig, March 26, 1911, Sir Bernard was trained at the university there and earned a medical degree when he was 23. In 1935 he fled the Nazis and settled in London, where he began the research that ultimately won him a share in the award. For four years he performed neuromuscular research at University College, before accepting a Carnegie grant to work in Australia. He returned to University College in 1950 and remained there for most of his career. A naturalized British subject, he was knighted in 1969. (Ph. K.)

KAUNDA, KENNETH DAVID

Zambia's Pres. Kenneth Kaunda emerged as a major international figure in 1970 when he was elected chairman of the Organization of African Unity and, subsequently, chairman of the nonaligned group of nations following their summit meeting in his capital, Lusaka. In October he embarked on a political crusade to halt what he regarded as a dangerous drift toward racial conflict in southern Africa. He led a delegation of African foreign ministers to Rome, Bonn, London, New York, and Paris to urge Western governments to observe a total arms embargo on South Africa, to withhold NATO and other arms from Portugal, which still held colonial African territories, and to withdraw support from the Cahorabassa hydroelectric project in Portuguese-ruled Mozambique.

Kaunda's crusade was dictated partly by his personal philosophy of nonviolence and belief in nonracial societies and partly by the strategic location of his country along the frontiers of Rhodesia, South West Africa, and Portuguese-ruled Angola and Mozambique. Kaunda's parents had been Church of Scotland mission teachers in the Northern Province of present-day Zambia, where their son, Kenneth David, was born on April 28, 1924. His education in mission schools fortified his fundamental Christian ideas and later, in India, he studied Mohandas Gandhi's philosophy of nonviolence. Trained as a teacher, he was deeply offended by the racialism of colonial society, and at 21 he joined the anticolonial movement. He helped establish the United National Independence Party, which became the ruling party after Zambia achieved independence in 1964, with Kaunda as its first president.

Kaunda was at first reluctant to become too directly involved in supporting the increasingly active African guerrilla movements in Angola and Mozambique, mainly because of his own antipathy to violence. He helped formulate the 1969 Lusaka Manifesto, which offered a nonviolent program for constitutional change in the white-ruled states of southern Africa. When this appeal failed, however, he began more openly to champion the cause of the "liberation movements." An outspoken opponent of Communism, he was willing to accept Chinese help when the Western countries refused to support construction of a railway line from landlocked Zambia to the sea. (Co. L.)

KREISKY, BRUNO

When the Socialist Party of Austria (SPÖ) emerged from the general election of March 1, 1970, as the strongest party, with 81 seats out of 165, it fell to Bruno Kreisky, as its chairman, to form the new government. Since the SPÖ's majority was only relative, Kreisky first tried to negotiate a coalition. This came to nothing, however, and on April 21 he formed a minority government drawn exclusively from the SPÖ.

Only twice before in Austria's history had the head of government been a social

democrat, and on both occasions (1918–20 and 1945) the political circumstances had been exceptional. Kreisky thus became the first social democrat to accede to the federal chancellorship under normal conditions, and also the first to preside over a purely Socialist government.

From 1953 until 1959 Kreisky had been state secretary in the Ministry of Foreign Affairs under a succession of coalition governments. As such, he took part in the negotiations that culminated in 1955 in the signing of the four-power treaty that reestablished Austria as an independent state. From 1959 until 1966 he was foreign minister. During this period, Austria became a member of the European Free Trade Association and also sought neighbourly relations with Eastern European states. Considering Austria's neutrality to be a purely military matter, Kreisky intensified his country's collaboration with international organizations.

Kreisky was born in Vienna on Jan. 22, 1911. He studied jurisprudence and political economy and graduated as doctor of law from the University of Vienna. In 1938, persecuted by the Gestapo because of his political beliefs and Jewish birth, he fled to Sweden, where he engaged in journalism and business. From 1956 onward he was a member of the Austrian Parliament, and in 1959 he was elected deputy chairman of the SPÖ. Following the party's decisive defeat in the 1966 general election, he took the lead in an intraparty reform movement. Narrowly elected chairman in 1967, he was reelected with increased majorities in 1968 and 1970. (E. Di.)

KUHN, BOWIE KENT

Previously a Wall Street attorney and also the legal counsel for the National League, Bowie Kuhn was given on Feb. 4, 1969, a one-year term as baseball commissioner pro tempore by the major league club owners. By August he had so impressed the owners that they met again and signed him to a new seven-year contract.

In the months after his election, Kuhn helped settle a severe pension dispute between the owners and players and thus averted a player strike. He also forced some club owners to sell their interests in Las Vegas gambling casinos. Almost immediately Kuhn was being compared favourably to Judge Kenesaw M. Landis, baseball's first commissioner. Later in 1970 Kuhn came in for some criticism for his method of disciplining pitcher Denny McLain and for his attack on *Ball Four*, an outspoken baseball book by Jim Bouton (*q.v.*).

A descendant of the legendary frontiersman Jim Bowie and of two Maryland governors, Bowie Kent Kuhn was born in Takoma Park, Md., on Oct. 28, 1926. Though not athletic, he developed an early interest in baseball and while still in high school spent one summer vacation working inside the scoreboard at the old Griffith Stadium, then the home of the Washington Senators.

Kuhn graduated from Princeton University and then studied law at the University of Virginia. He subsequently joined the law firm of Willkie, Farr, and Gallagher in New York City, partly because this firm had among its clients the National League and several individual baseball clubs.

For almost 20 years prior to his appointment as commissioner, he was among the National League's attorneys. In this capacity he successfully defended the National League's franchise shift from Milwaukee to Atlanta, a transfer legally challenged by Milwaukee and Wisconsin interests.

(Je. Ho.)

William Moses Kunstler
MICHAEL ABRAMSON
FROM BLACK STAR

Bruno Kreisky
AUTHENTICATED NEWS INTERNATIONAL

Kenneth David Kaunda
AUTHENTICATED NEWS INTERNATIONAL

WIDE WORLD
Bowie Kent Kuhn

KUNSTLER, WILLIAM MOSES

For most of a decade, it had seemed inevitable that William Kunstler would one day lead the Movement against the Establishment. The "movement" at first was the Negro rights revolution and then it was the antiwar and "youth-culture" revolution. The "establishment" was the nation's courts, less and less sympathetic as the causes defended by lawyers like Kunstler became more and more disruptive. In 1970 the confrontation came in Chicago, in the conspiracy trial of the "Chicago 7" with Kunstler for the defense.

A late convert to the ranks of civil liberties lawyers, the New York attorney had begun volunteering to defend blacks in 1961 because he felt the law was "a profession that can be used in some way for social advancement." By 1970 he had begun to urge active disruption in the courts as a last-resort protest against what he called "political repression." At the Chicago trial, in which "New Left" and self-styled radical political leaders were charged with stirring up a riot during the 1968 Democratic national convention, the boisterous conduct of Kunstler, other lawyers, and their clients (often in response to rulings by trial judge Julius J. Hoffman) led to 175 charges of contempt. Kunstler himself was given the longest prison sentence in modern history for a lawyer convicted of contempt: four years and 13 days. The objective of such tactics, Kunstler was to say in public lectures and articles, was to show that "the mechanisms of society are not responding to serious grievances."

The man who had often warned that indifference to wrongs would "radicalize protest" had, he said himself, become personally radicalized. In the process, William Kunstler had become the best-known legal defender of the nation's new-style revolutionaries. Over the years, his clients had included H. Rap Brown, Stokely Carmichael, Rep. Adam Clayton Powell, Jr., black freedom riders in the South, white priests who destroyed draft records to protest the war in Vietnam, and 25 persons indicted in connection with the May 1970 disorders at Kent (O.) State University. His role in the Chicago conspiracy trial had made Kunstler a popular campus lecturer, but his tough rhetoric often led authorities to try to ban his appearances.

All this was a far cry from the William Kunstler who, as a newly graduated lawyer, had gone to work for Macy's department store and been assigned to write a manual for department managers.

A native of New York City, Kunstler was born July 7, 1919. He graduated from Yale and served in World War II before enrolling at Columbia Law School.   (L. Dn.)

LELOIR, LUIS FREDERICO

The 1970 Nobel Prize for Chemistry was awarded to an Argentine biochemist, Luis Frederico Leloir, for his investigations into the ways that complex sugars are broken down into simpler carbohydrates. A Nobel official said Leloir's "work and the work inspired by him has given us real knowledge in wide fields of biochemistry, where earlier we had to resort to vague hypotheses."

In general terms, Leloir's complex studies filled gaps in the understanding of the transformations of sugar. Specifically, he discovered sugar nucleotides, the group of organic substances that enable the natural synthesis of carbohydrates which can be stored in the body and reconverted into energy. In the course of his experiments he synthesized the body sugar glycogen and proved that it could not be created in the body without enzymes from the liver.

Scion of an aristocratic Argentine family, Leloir was born in Paris on Sept. 6, 1906. He earned a medical degree at the University of Buenos Aires in 1932.

After working at the Cambridge University biochemical laboratory for a year, he returned to Argentina and studied fatty acid oxidation at the Institute of Physiology. In 1943 the government of Juan Perón purged the institute, and Leloir spent the next two years in the United States, doing research at Washington University in St. Louis and at Columbia University's College of Physicians and Surgeons.

Returning to Buenos Aires, he received financial support from a businessman and established the Institute of Biochemical Research. For a time, his organization was hamstrung by a shortage of funds; later, however, some assistance was received from the Rockefeller Foundation and the National Institutes of Health.   (Ph. K.)

LEVINGSTON, ROBERTO MARCELO

Plucked from the relative obscurity of the Argentine military mission in Washington, Brig. Gen. Roberto Marcelo Levingston became president of Argentina on June 18, 1970, by appointment of the chiefs of the three armed forces of the republic. They had just ousted another army general, Juan Carlos Onganía. The details of Levingston's selection were not made public, but observers believed the military leaders chose him because they regarded him as being—unlike Onganía—a team player.

Onganía, a taciturn and ascetic cavalry officer who took over after another bloodless military coup in 1966, had made the mistake of cutting himself off from the military chiefs, especially from the army commander, Lieut. Gen. Alejandro Lanusse. The Army-Navy-Air Force junta was determined to share in the rule of Argentina, and Levingston became their man. The advent of Levingston was also rooted in the decision of the armed forces chiefs that military rule could not be continued indefinitely, as Onganía seemed to wish. Given Argentina's many internal difficulties, the military wanted to build up political support by offering Argentines some kind of concrete timetable for the return to constitutional government.

Although never forgetting where his power base lay, Levingston proved to be a surprisingly vigorous chief executive. He began to steer Argentina away from the free enterprise policies of Onganía and to follow the corporate state policies advocated by nationalists. He also broke the wage-price freeze Onganía had imposed and authorized pay increases, obviously intended to build the sort of political base the officer corps wanted before it would permit free elections.

Levingston was born on Jan. 10, 1920, in the provincial city of San Luis and entered Argentina's military college at the age of 18. On graduation he joined the cavalry, the elite branch of the Argentine Army, and rose rapidly through the ranks. He became chief of staff of the Cavalry Corps and was chief of intelligence during the presidency of Arturo Frondizi. He was serving as Argentina's representative on the Inter-American Defense Board in Washington when he was notified of his recall to Argentina after the ouster of Onganía.   (J. A. O'L.)

LON NOL

Soft-spoken Gen. Lon Nol of Cambodia had been known as a man of few words and reserved gestures, but in 1970 he proved also to be a man of swift, decisive action. On March 18 he overthrew Prince Norodom Sihanouk, at a time when Sihanouk was out of the country seeking Soviet and Chinese support for his efforts to get North Vietnamese forces to withdraw from Cambodia. Vowing that Sihanouk's cult of personality had been ended, Lon Nol named Cheng Heng as head of state instead of himself.

An ardent anti-Communist, Lon Nol was relatively unknown abroad until the coup, but he was thought to have been instrumental in sparking the civil disturbances that led up to it. The coup came at a time of increasing fear that the Vietnam war might spread from the border areas and engulf the entire country. It was preceded by several days of rioting in normally placid Phnom Penh, during which the North Vietnamese embassy and Viet Cong consulate were sacked.

Unlike most military leaders in Asia, Lon Nol had had extensive experience as a magistrate, civil administrator, and policeman as well as a soldier. He was best known in Cambodia for his campaigns against North Vietnamese guerrillas before the Geneva Conference of 1954, which ended French colonial rule in Indochina. Reserved and pragmatic, Lon Nol was frequently compared to Indonesian President Suharto, who also came to power in an anti-Communist coup.

Lon Nol was born Nov. 13, 1913, in the province of Prey Veng in southern Cambodia, and served as magistrate in the tribunal at Siem Réap, near the famous ruins of Angkor Wat. In 1937 he joined the administrative service, becoming a provincial governor ten years later, director of the administrative service in 1949, and head of the national police in 1951. He joined the Army in 1952 as a lieutenant colonel and fought against the Communist Viet Minh. Rising rapidly through the ranks, he became commander in chief of the Royal Armed Forces in 1960, deputy premier in 1963, and premier in 1966. He resigned in 1967 after being injured in an automobile crash, but in 1968 he returned to the Cabinet as defense minister. He became premier again in August 1969, retaining his defense portfolio as well.   (J. F. Ba.)

LOVELL, JAMES ARTHUR, JR.

When James Lovell blasted off in April as commander of the three-man crew on the Apollo 13 mission to the moon, he figured he was "as good a target for the law of averages as anyone." He had already logged 572 hours in space, more than any other man alive. "Of course when you train to fly a mission you never think that 'it' will happen to you," he said. "Emotionally you feel that it won't happen to you, that it won't be your wristwatch that breaks down."

But on the Apollo 13 it did happen. Part way to the moon an oxygen tank exploded—and, after 22 flights without serious incident, the U.S. manned space program suddenly no longer was routine. People throughout the world hung on every move as the astronauts, aided by their crews on the ground, struggled to return safely to earth. To preserve the life-support systems of their Odyssey command module, the crew moved into the fragile Aquarius lunar landing craft, rode it on an orbit around the moon, and headed home. Near the earth's atmosphere, they shifted back to Odyssey and made a normal splashdown in the Pacific Ocean recovery area.

To many people, Apollo 13, which was to have been the United States' third landing on the moon, was a failure. But not to Lovell. "I look back on it as a triumph: a triumph of teamwork, initiative and ingenuity, on the ground and in the spacecraft," he said. "Just by getting back under these critical circumstances, we did prove something about the American capacity for accomplishment under stress: you can do it if you have to do it. That was the primary accomplishment—and the triumph—of Apollo 13."

Lovell, 42, did not expect to go into space again. His 715 hours up there was "enough, or ought to be," he said. Almost half of those hours came in December 1965 during the Gemini 7 mission, which Lovell shared with Frank Borman. Lovell also flew on Gemini 12 in November 1966 and, in December 1968, was the command module pilot on Apollo 8, man's first flight around the moon.

Born in Cleveland, O., on March 25, 1928, Lovell moved as a boy to Wisconsin, where he attended high school and two years of college. He graduated from the U.S. Naval Academy in 1952 and served as a test pilot before joining the manned space program.   (F. Wt.)

LYNCH, JOHN MARY

In the early hours of May 6, 1970, in a crisis situation unparalleled in the Republic of Ireland's history, Prime Minister John Lynch sacked two senior Cabinet ministers. The action had more to do with ending internal divisions in the face of the disorders in Northern Ireland than with the arms conspiracy charge that led to the subsequent trial. In weathering the crisis and all that followed, Lynch revealed himself in a new light.

Lynch had always been represented as a politician who accepted the responsibilities of power unwillingly. When he became *taoiseach* (prime minister) in November 1966 he was a compromise choice. This element of compromise had always been present in his political character. He managed to combine the pragmatism of his immediate predecessor, Sean Lemass, with the idealism of Fianna Fail's founder, Eamon de Valera. The combination weakened his decisiveness, however, and encouraged divisions in the party.

But behind the mild-mannered, unassuming man from Cork, there was a politician who believed firmly enough in his peaceful policy toward Northern Ireland to take on the toughest element in his own party and remove it from power. He dragged the details of party strife into the open in a way that shocked the country, and every time he was challenged, he appealed for a vote of confidence and won. When the trial brought a verdict of not guilty against the former minister for finance, Charles Haughey, and a further challenge for leadership, Lynch was firm in rejecting it. In December, faced with an alleged conspiracy involving threats of kidnapping and robbery, he did not hesitate to declare a state of emergency.

Yet the outward personality remained unchanged. Jack Lynch went through a year of challenge and crisis with a look of hurt surprise. His voice remained quiet and he often fumbled his words as he announced his decisions, but it was always Lynch who made the announcement.

Lynch was born in Cork on Aug. 15, 1917. A lawyer by profession, he entered politics as a member of the opposition in 1948 and worked closely with de Valera. After Fianna Fail came to power in 1951, he was a parliamentary secretary (1951–54), minister for the Gaelic-speaking districts (March–June 1957), and minister for education. From there he went to Industry and Commerce and Finance before taking over as party leader and prime minister.   (B. Ar.)

MALFATTI, FRANCO MARIA

The first Italian appointed to the presidency of the European Economic Community (EEC), Franco Maria Malfatti began his two-year term in Brussels in July 1970. Prior to his appointment he had been Italy's minister for post and telecommunications, the latest in a series of public offices held by the 43-year-old Christian Democrat.

Malfatti was born at Contigliaro, near Rome, on June 13, 1927. He began his career as a writer, contributing to various periodicals and magazines. His interest in politics soon took him to high positions within the Christian Democratic Party: he became a member of the executive committee and leader of the party's Office of Cultural Activities. He also remained active in business, becoming manager of a publishing company.

In 1958 Malfatti was elected to the Chamber of Deputies from the constituency of

Perugia; he was reelected in 1963 and in 1968. His first official part in the government was as undersecretary of industry in the first and third centre-left coalitions of Premier Aldo Moro. During the government of Premier Giovanni Leone, Malfatti was made undersecretary for foreign affairs.

Malfatti achieved his first Cabinet-level position in August 1969 when he was appointed minister for state-subsidized industries in the government led by Premier Mariano Rumor. He became minister for post and telecommunications early in 1970. Malfatti succeeded Jean Rey of Belgium as president of the EEC.   (F. G.)

MANSHOLT, SICCO LEENDERT

During 1970 Sicco Mansholt, vice-president of the European Commission and author of a controversial plan for radically restructuring Western European agriculture, visited Paris, Rome, Bonn, and even London and Dublin, trying to convince the farmers of member and potential member countries of the EEC that, being a farmer himself, he was naturally the farmers' friend. The Mansholt Plan had been strongly criticized among the Community's member states, especially in France with its hundreds of thousands of uneconomic small farms.

Mansholt had submitted his plan to the EEC Council of Ministers in December 1968. Its short-term goal was to put an end to the troublesome surpluses, especially in dairy products, that had plagued the EEC. Its long-run aims could be summarized as follows: (1) The number of persons employed in agriculture should be reduced from ten million to five million during 1970–80; half of those abandoning farming would become state pensioners while the other half should find work in industry or elsewhere. (2) In order to maintain the current prices for agricultural products and make farmers' incomes even with those of other trades, it would be necessary to increase the size of farms considerably and to introduce specialization and cooperative leadership. (3) About three million hectares, or 10% of the Community's arable land, should be transferred to other uses. (4) The number of dairy cows in the Community should be reduced from 21 million to 18 million (the 1956 figure) and beef output should be increased.

Mansholt was born on Sept. 13, 1908, near Groningen, Neth. Having graduated from the State Agricultural University of Wageningen, he worked as a farmer in the Netherlands and in Java, where he directed a tea plantation from 1934 to 1937. During the German occupation he took an active part in the resistance movement. After the liberation, he joined the Labour Party and was elected burgomaster of Wieringermeer. From June 1945 to August 1953, and again in 1956–58, he served as Dutch minister of agriculture, fisheries, and food. In 1958 he became vice-president of the EEC Commission, later combined with the executives of the European Coal and Steel Community and Euratom into the European Commission.   (K. Sm.)

MAUDLING, REGINALD

One of the hottest seats in Britain's new Conservative Party government was that of home secretary. It went to Reginald Maudling, who (had things turned out only a little differently) might have been the prime minister. At the Home Office, he took over governmental responsibility for troubled Northern Ireland and domestic issues as explosive as race, immigration, crime, law and order, demonstrations, and drugs.

Maudling was one of the younger generation of members of Parliament who a few

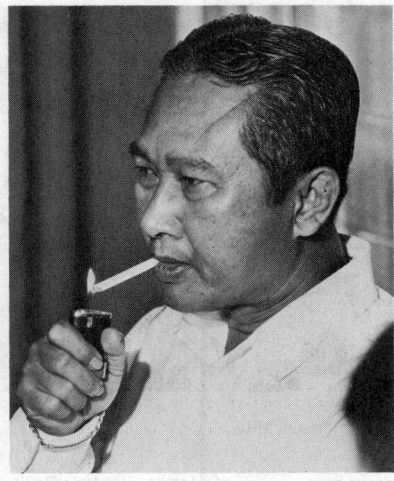

WIDE WORLD
Lon Nol

© KARSH, OTTAWA FROM RAPHO GUILLUMETTE
James Arthur Lovell, Jr.

Sicco Leendert Mansholt
WIDE WORLD

John Mary Lynch
CAMERA PRESS FROM PIX

CAMERA PRESS FROM PIX
Franco Maria Malfatti

FRED WARD FROM BLACK STAR
John Newton Mitchell

Martha Elizabeth Beall Mitchell
WIDE WORLD

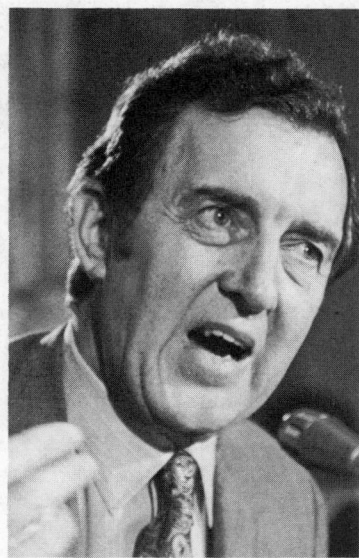

WIDE WORLD
Edmund Sixtus Muskie

KEN REGAN FROM CAMERA 5
Golda Meir

The epitome of the professional soldier—quiet, dignified, aloof from politics—he was regarded as a middle-of-the-roader in a country that had been dominated by the right wing since 1964. In army circles Médici established a reputation as a man of forceful character and few words and, as a product of the staff system and the military caste, he knew how to give orders as well as how to carry them out. But he was so self-effacing and so little known outside the Army that character judgments were difficult to make. Some said that the name "Garrastazú," inherited from his Basque ancestors, was as good a guide as any to Médici's personality; it means "persistence."

Médici was born Dec. 4, 1905, at Bagé in the cattle-raising state of Rio Grande do Sul. His early army service was in the cavalry and intelligence arms, and as a youth he formed a lifelong friendship with Costa e Silva. He was commanding the Brazilian Military Academy at Agulhas Negras at the time of the 1964 coup, and threw in immediately with the victorious rebels. He spent the next two years as military attaché in Washington, becoming an advocate of closer relations between Brazil and the U.S.

When Costa e Silva became president in 1966, he appointed Médici head of the National Intelligence Service, where he served until early 1969. Médici was commander of the 3rd Army in Rio Grande do Sul when Costa e Silva was stricken and the military chiefs began looking among the ranks for a successor. Médici made no secret of the fact that he would prefer the anonymity of army life and the chance to watch his favourite football team to the drudgery of the presidency. Nevertheless, he believed, with most Brazilians, that the nation was marked for world greatness—a sense of destiny that typifies the top level of Brazil's present-day leadership. (J. A. O'L.)

MEIR, GOLDA

In 1970 the outbreak of a series of serious military engagements on Israel's borders increased Israeli Prime Minister Golda Meir's burden of frustration and the conflict of interests that her lifelong and devoted service to Zionism had always laid upon her. When traveling for World Zionism in the late 1920s and the 1930s she frequently had to leave her two children, and she was clearly aware of their and her own sacrifice. Now, desperately anxious to launch housing and social welfare programs, she had to appropriate an ever increasing proportion of Israel's budget to defense. Always conscious of the human aspect of war ("I am never in a group when someone . . . has not a son at the war"), she was obliged to prepare stringently against renewed, more widespread conflict.

Nevertheless, her attitude toward peace negotiations had modified since she became prime minister. At first opposed to outside mediators, she later expressed willingness to enter indirect negotiations with the Arabs under UN auspices. In September Israel withdrew from the talks mediated by Gunnar Jarring on the ground that the U.A.R. had violated the agreed cease-fire, but it decided to rejoin them in December.

A sturdily-built, essentially archetypal figure, careless of fashion but finding her pleasures in reading, music, domestic pursuits, and her family, Golda Meir was born in Kiev, Russia, on May 3, 1898. She emigrated with her family to Milwaukee, Wis., in 1906 and settled in Palestine with her Russian-born husband in 1921. After three years in a kibbutz (1921–24), she became increasingly involved in politics and Jewish trade-union organizations. Her husband did not share her interests, and the marriage broke up in 1945. He later died. In 1946 she

years earlier had been regarded as a likely future prime minister. He was born March 7, 1917, and educated at Oxford University. Elected to Parliament with a safe seat in 1950, he caught the eye of the Conservative leaders of that time, having spent five years in the Conservative Party research department. He advanced rapidly in the Conservative governments of the 1950s, getting his first Cabinet job at the age of 40. Trade and finance were his specialties, but he was not always successful. His negotiations for a European free trade area in 1957 failed, and his attempt to break out of the stop-go economic cycle when he was chancellor of the Exchequer (1962–64) was overwhelmed by the calamitous balance of payments deficit of 1964. Even so, after the Conservatives had lost the election of 1964 Maudling was thought likely to win the succession to the Conservative leadership. He was narrowly beaten by Edward Heath, but continued to occupy a leading place in the party while it was in opposition.

Maudling achieved a reputation as a sound, reasonable, unflappable man of high intelligence. But to his party rank and file he seemed to lack something in fire. His reputation for moderation was accompanied by firmness, however, and this showed itself in his unambiguous rejection of extremist racial views, and an early indication that if extremists were to win control of the government in Northern Ireland, the British government would be prepared to intervene by direct rule. (W. H. Ts.)

MÉDICI, EMÍLIO GARRASTAZÚ

The third army officer to serve as president of Brazil since the 1964 military coup, Gen. Emílio Garrastazú Médici was chosen by the armed forces in October 1969, after illness incapacitated Pres. Artur da Costa e Silva. Even in Brazil, Médici was a virtual unknown until the military rulers of Latin America's largest and most populous nation selected him for the presidency.

became the director of the political department of the Jewish Agency for Israel. She was minister of labour from 1949 to 1956, when she became foreign minister, retiring to become secretary-general of the Mapai (Labour) Party in 1966. Following the death of Prime Minister Levi Eshkol, she was persuaded that it was her duty to accept office, and she became prime minister on March 17, 1969.   (S. Mu.)

MITCHELL, JOHN NEWTON

Every home-front crisis for U.S. Pres. Richard Nixon—and there were many in 1970—was also a crisis for Attorney General John Mitchell, who had come to be the administration's domestic "crisis manager." As the president's most important adviser on the government's most controversial domestic policies, Mitchell never once was given reason to doubt the president's confidence and reliance.

Of the year's home-front troubles, two most vexed the president, and in both he had come to the crisis depending on Mitchell's advice. The first was the Senate's rejection of Supreme Court nominee G. Harrold Carswell, who had been a Mitchell selection. The other was the nationwide student uprising that followed the entry of U.S. troops into Cambodia. From most accounts, it was Mitchell who had advised that the domestic response to that strategy could be managed. Yet, as those crises developed, it was to Mitchell that the president turned again, and in time the difficulties seemed to become manageable. The attorney general produced another Supreme Court nominee (Harry A. Blackmun) who was approved unanimously, and he advised a government-wide attempt to widen communication with the nation's students.

Meanwhile, Mitchell did not lack controversy in his own Department of Justice. He continued the pursuit of domestic militants and revolutionaries, revived the failing government machinery for monitoring "subversion," claimed full personal power under the Constitution to use wiretapping and eavesdropping in internal security cases, demanded some of the notes and work materials of newsmen who had interviewed militant suspects, persuaded Congress to approve the pretrial detention of "dangerous" suspects, and continued to insist on priority of the "neighbourhood school" over total desegregation of every school in the South.

Through all this Mitchell was a highly visible public figure, but he remained primarily a private man, almost eager to be anonymous. At times it seemed that Mrs. Mitchell (q.v.), the former Martha Beall, had become the "personality" Mitchell himself did not want to be. She emerged as the most quotable Cabinet wife, and the quotes were often provocative and sometimes controversial.

Born on Sept. 5, 1913, in Detroit, Mitchell moved to the New York City area as a child. He clerked in the firm of James H. Caldwell, one of the nation's first bond attorneys, while still a law student at Fordham, and within five years of his 1937 graduation became a partner in the firm. It was merged with Richard Nixon's law firm on Jan. 1, 1967, an event that marked the beginning of Mitchell's close personal association with Nixon.   (L. Dn.)

MITCHELL, MARTHA ELIZABETH BEALL

The most flamboyant nonworking member of Pres. Richard Nixon's official family was Attorney General John Mitchell's wife, Martha, whose fame rested on her indefatigable jaw.

During 1970 she became notorious for discussing public issues in a manner unheard of among politicians' wives. Her pronouncements included suggestions that radicals be sent to some Communist country—"preferably Russia, Cuba's too close"; that street demonstrations are tantamount to "revolution"; and that intellectuals and academics are "destroying our country."

Her most famous pronouncement grew out of the administration's unsuccessful efforts to put a Southerner on the Supreme Court. When fellow Arkansan Sen. J. William Fulbright voted against the confirmation of G. Harrold Carswell, Mrs. Mitchell telephoned the locally influential *Arkansas Gazette* at 2 A.M. to demand that the paper "crucify" Fulbright. Soon afterward, apparently to seek a little insulation from the press, Mrs. Mitchell hired a public relations aide. Her new assistant, however, was married to a television newsman whose boss said he could not work as long as his wife was associated with such a controversial figure. The couple left Washington.

Attempting to explain Mrs. Mitchell's actions, *Parade* magazine suggested she had "reached the age of life, 52, when some of her statements may be attributed to hormonal change rather than sound, rational reasoning." Those who knew her as a child, however, described her as having always been a "talker." Mrs. Mitchell blamed her outbursts on her "thin skin." She found it hard, she said, "to take the criticism of my husband, my poor husband." And the attorney general? He took to answering reporters' queries with: "I love her. That's all I have to say."

Born in Pine Bluff, Ark., on Sept. 2, 1918, Martha Elizabeth Beall earned a degree at the University of Miami (Fla.) and taught in Mobile, Ala., for a year. In 1946 she was married to Clyde Jennings whom she had met while both were working in Washington during the war. She and Jennings were divorced in August 1957 and she married John Mitchell, a divorced Manhattan lawyer, that December. It was no secret that she preferred life in Rye, N.Y., to Washington and looked forward to her husband's return to his $250,000-a-year practice.   (Ph. K.)

MUSKIE, EDMUND SIXTUS

During 1970 Sen. Edmund Muskie of Maine established himself as the front-runner for the Democratic Party nomination for president in 1972. In 1968 he had been Hubert Humphrey's running mate on the ticket that lost to Richard Nixon and Spiro Agnew. Pollsters and politicians agreed that Muskie was a popular, new face during that campaign and his support continued to grow after the election.

Evidence that the Democratic Party was turning to him for leadership was the fact that he was chosen to give the rebuttal to President Nixon's partisan election-eve national television speech. Muskie's talk, an appeal to the electorate to disclaim Republican political rhetoric about violence and the law and order issue and replace it with a call for progress based on patience and reason, was considered an important success.

Muskie was born March 28, 1914, in Rumford, Me. His father, a Polish immigrant tailor, anglicized the family name from Marciszewski. He earned a Phi Beta Kappa key at Bates College, and a law degree from Cornell University in 1939. After practicing law in Maine, he was in 1954 elected the state's first Democratic governor in 20 years. In 1958 he became the first popularly elected Democratic senator in the state's history.

In Congress he was associated with liberal movements and causes and, in particular,

was an early backer of antiwater pollution and clean air legislation. He gained a reputation as an expert on federal-state relations and the problems of the cities.

At the end of 1970 Muskie was organizing a staff and planning an extensive speaking schedule in anticipation of the 1972 presidential election campaign. His chief rival for the nomination figured to be fellow senator Edward Kennedy of Massachusetts. But Kennedy, once the front-runner, was badly hobbled in 1969 by circumstances surrounding an automobile accident, and Muskie, as the polls indicated, moved well ahead in popularity.   (M. B. Su.)

NAKASONE, YASUHIRO

Yasuhiro Nakasone, Japan's new defense agency director general, recommended a mutually attractive plan to enable his government to share more fully the costs and use of some 122 U.S. military bases and facilities on Japanese soil. Early in 1970 he proposed to U.S. Ambassador Armin H. Meyer that the two countries consider a transfer of the U.S. bases to Japanese ownership and let the U.S. use them as needed. The idea was attractive to the U.S. because of Pres. Richard Nixon's intentions to reduce American military involvement in the Far East and to cut overall military spending. It was attractive to the Japanese because of rising nationalistic feeling there.

A number of details had to be worked out, however, and this process took months, mainly because of complex postwar treaties between the two nations. The agreements required the U.S. to defend Japan from outside aggression; in return for this protection, Japan would provide bases for the support of other mutual allies, such as South Korea.

Coincidentally, Nakasone lent significant strength to the nuclear nonproliferation treaty, for which the U.S. had been trying to marshal international support. He declared that Japan "should not now, or in the future, build its own nuclear weapons." Formerly an advocate of developing a Japanese nuclear capability, Nakasone signed the nonproliferation treaty for his country.

Nakasone changed his mind about nuclear weapons for several reasons, among them Japan's geographic vulnerability and the astronomical costs involved in developing such weapons. Also, he believed that China's imminent entry into the "nuclear club" would result in a "triangular stalemate" between China, the U.S.S.R., and the U.S.

Nakasone was born May 27, 1918, and educated at Tokyo Imperial University. A member of the House of Representatives and former director general of the Science and Technology Agency, he at various times chaired the Joint Committee on Atomic Energy and the Special Committee on Scientific Technology. In 1970 he held the Cabinet-level office of minister of state.   (Ph. K.)

NÉEL, LOUIS EUGÈNE FÉLIX

A leading scientist in the field of magnetism, Louis Néel of the University of Grenoble shared the 1970 Nobel Prize for Physics with Swedish astrophysicist Hannes Alfvén (q.v.). The Swedish Royal Academy of Sciences cited Néel "for fundamental work and discoveries concerning antiferromagnetism and ferrimagnetism which have led to important applications in solid state physics."

In the 1930s, Néel began theorizing about those atomic mechanics of magnetism that differ from the most common form, ferro-

LIAISON AGENCY
Paul VI

WIDE WORLD
Richard Milhous Nixon

Joyce Carol Oates
WIDE WORLD

bodia and that the operation had been a success. Addressing a nationwide television audience on October 7, Nixon asked North Vietnam and the Viet Cong to agree to a standstill cease-fire throughout Indochina. On another foreign policy front the president made a five-nation European tour in the fall to demonstrate his administration's continuing concern with maintaining adequate international security in the Mediterranean.

On the domestic front, strained relations with Congress crippled the president's legislative program. Nixon achieved one major objective when he signed on August 12 a bill to replace the Post Office Department with the U.S. Postal Service, an independent federal agency. Congress also passed another key Nixon measure, the District of Columbia crime-control bill. On the other hand, the president vetoed four fund bills in 1970, and Congress overrode two of the vetoes—those of the hospital-construction authorization bill and of the Office of Education appropriations bill.

Nixon's most humiliating defeat at the hands of Congress in 1970 was the Senate's rejection of the nomination of Judge G. Harrold Carswell of Florida to the Supreme Court. The president accused the Senate of regional discrimination and pledged that his next nominee to the court would "fulfill the criteria of a strict constructionist. . . ." That nominee turned out to be Judge Harry A. Blackmun of the U.S. Court of Appeals, who was confirmed by the Senate virtually without dissent.

In November Nixon fired Walter Hickel as secretary of the interior. Relations between the two had reportedly become strained, and Hickel had publicly criticized Nixon's handling of student dissent. Rogers Morton, the GOP national chairman, was named as Hickel's successor.

Nixon campaigned actively for a number of Republican congressional candidates in the 1970 elections. Although some of those he supported won, many others lost, and the president again was faced with a Democratic majority in both houses.

Born on Jan. 9, 1913, in Yorba Linda, Calif., Nixon was graduated from Whittier College and from Duke University Law School. After serving in the Navy during World War II, he won election in 1946 as a U.S. representative from California. He was elected to the U.S. Senate four years later, and in 1952 won election as vice-president on the ticket headed by Dwight D. Eisenhower. Nixon was defeated by John F. Kennedy in the presidential election of 1960. (RI. W.)

OATES, JOYCE CAROL

The 1970 National Book Award for fiction was won by Joyce Carol Oates for *Them,* the epic biography of a family through three decades—from the depression to the 1967 riots—in Detroit. In a prefatory note to the book she declared: "This is a work of history in fictional form—that is, in personal perspective." However, it is a kind of fiction akin to the recent factual "novels" of Truman Capote and Norman Mailer.

Miss Oates described having had a student at the University of Detroit who, in the course of their friendship, told the teacher her life story. That became the framework for the novel. "My initial feeling about her life was, 'This must be fiction, this can't all be real!'" the author recalled. "My permanent feeling was 'This is the only kind of fiction that is real.'"

A critic endorsed her hybrid form: "Although rooted in case history, *Them* is fiction in the purest sense: data; perception, feeling transformed by language and imagi-

magnetism, in which electrons line up (or spin) in the same direction. He deduced that there are some substances in which alternating groups of atoms orient their electrons in opposite directions, thus neutralizing the net magnetic effect. Later he discovered that in ferrimagnetic substances a preponderance of the electrons are uniformly oriented, but that some atoms take a reverse alignment, resulting in a weak magnetic effect. He also demonstrated how the magnetic properties of many substances can be modified or controlled by temperature.

The most widespread applications of Néel's work are found in solid-state devices, such as computers and tape recorders, in which information is recorded and stored by the use of minute magnetic particles.

Born in Lyons, France, Nov. 22, 1904, Néel attended the École Normale Supérieure in Paris, earning a doctorate in 1932. In 1937 he succeeded Pierre Weiss to a chair at the University of Strasbourg, where he worked until he moved to the University of Grenoble in 1946. At Grenoble he served

as director of the Laboratory for Electrostatics and the Physics of Metals (the Fourier Institute), director of the Centre for Nuclear Studies, and director of the Polytechnic Institute of Grenoble.

(PH. K.)

NIXON, RICHARD MILHOUS

In his first state of the union message, Jan. 22, 1970, U.S. Pres. Richard Nixon asserted that "the major immediate goal of our foreign policy is to bring an end to the war in Vietnam." To this end, he announced on April 20 that 150,000 additional U.S. troops would be withdrawn from Vietnam by the spring of 1971. Only ten days later, however, Nixon ordered U.S. forces into Cambodia to clear out sanctuaries used by the North Vietnamese and the Viet Cong. The Cambodian venture touched off a wave of student strikes on college campuses and protest demonstrations in several cities. Criticism of the president diminished when he announced on June 30 that all U.S. ground forces had been removed from Cam-

nation into a new existence with a vitality that can even survive critical explanation." Another wrote: "On the surface the book is hard, cold and terrifying. Its core, however, is mellow with sympathy for the struggle of its major characters. The result is Urban Gothic."

Judging by the volume of her work, Miss Oates seemed to have an insatiable drive to write. *Them* was her third novel in three consecutive years to be nominated for the National Book Award. In 1968 *A Garden of Earthly Delights* was in the running, and in the following year, *Expensive People*. Since first breaking into print as an undergraduate at Syracuse University, Miss Oates had won many honours, among them a Guggenheim Fellowship and several O. Henry Prize citations.

Born in Lockport, N.Y., June 16, 1938, Miss Oates earned her master's degree in English at the University of Wisconsin, where she met her husband, Raymond Joseph Smith, then a doctoral candidate. In 1961 they moved to Detroit, where she taught until 1967. Miss Oates and her husband in 1970 were both professors at the University of Windsor, across the river from Detroit in Ontario.   (Ph. K.)

O'BRIEN, LAWRENCE FRANCIS

The Democratic Party—out of the White House, out of money, and scrambling for a national image in the important off-year elections—turned to an old pro with some new ideas for chairman of its National Committee in 1970: Larry O'Brien, a man who had served all three Democratic presidential candidates in the 1960s. O'Brien could not claim total victory in November—the Democrats lost slightly in the Senate, gained slightly in the House, and made strong inroads among the governorships—but the party on November 4 was far healthier than the disordered, demoralized loser of two years before.

The change in chairmanship from Sen. Fred R. Harris of Oklahoma to O'Brien, a former chairman, took place in characteristically chaotic style. When word went out in late February that O'Brien was the preference of titular party leader Hubert Humphrey, the hoped-for consensus of party leaders failed to jell, and O'Brien—eyeing the dispute, not to mention a party debt of nearly $9 million—rejected the post. After a two-day deadlock, the committee's executive committee finally settled unanimously on a second offer to O'Brien, who then dropped regular duties with his new public relations firm in New York to begin revamping the political organization.

Known before as a "nuts and bolts" organizer who had concentrated on power blocs, patronage, and precinct work, O'Brien changed his style to what he termed the "new form of the game of American politics . . . Issues and Image." He set out to take issue with Pres. Richard Nixon on national topics, and fought to counter the president's easy access to television through demands for equal time. And he worked the circuit in an uphill fight for campaign funds.

Lawrence O'Brien was born July 7, 1917, in Springfield, Mass., and received an LL.B. from Northeastern University, Boston, in 1942. He worked in real estate and public relations from 1943 to 1960, meanwhile becoming active in Democratic politics. In 1960 he directed John F. Kennedy's successful presidential campaign and then became special assistant to both Presidents Kennedy and Johnson. He served as postmaster general from 1965 to 1968, when he headed the presidential campaign for Humphrey.   (R. L. A.)

ORR, ROBERT GORDON

At 22 years of age and with only five seasons as a professional, Bobby Orr of the Boston Bruins might have seemed a premature choice as the best all-around hockey player in the game's history. Yet many responsible hockey officials, including Clarence Campbell, president of the National Hockey League (NHL), insisted that such was the case. "I've seen all the greats except Cyclone Taylor," said Campbell, an NHL pioneer, "and Bobby Orr is the best I've ever seen."

Campbell was moved to this accolade after the 1969–70 season when Orr, a husky defenseman, won four of the NHL's prized trophies: the James Norris Memorial Trophy, as the outstanding defenseman; the Conn Smythe Trophy, for the outstanding player in the Stanley Cup play-offs; the Art Ross Trophy, for leading the league in scoring; and the Hart Trophy, as the league's most valuable player. Additionally, Orr set NHL records for the regular season for most goals, 33, and most assists, 87, by a defenseman.

That Robert Gordon Orr should score such an unprecedented sweep in his fourth professional season was not as surprising as it might seem. Bobby, born on March 20, 1948, at Parry Sound, Ont., was a child hockey prodigy. The Boston Bruins of the NHL had scouted him by the time he was 12.

Orr's prowess was such that at 12, when he should have been entering Pee Wee hockey, he was playing with older boys in the bantam division. When Orr was 16, *Maclean's,* a national magazine in Canada, ran a cover colour photo of him with an accompanying headline: "How Hockey's Sixteen Year Old Is Groomed for Stardom—Has Boston Captured the NHL's Next Super-Star?"

Orr did, indeed, sign with the Bruins and was an immediate sensation. He won the Calder Memorial Trophy for 1966–67, given annually to the NHL's best rookie, and, in addition, was named to the NHL's second-string All-Star team. He was chosen the league's outstanding defenseman every season afterward. By the start of the 1970–71 campaign he had grown to a burly 199 lb. with "arms and forearms the size of a heavyweight boxer." He led the Bruins to a Stanley Cup championship in 1970, their first such title in 29 years.   (Je. Ho.)

PASTRANA BORRERO, MISAEL

Installed as president of Colombia on Aug. 7, 1970, Misael Pastrana Borrero faced a difficult four years. The margin by which he won the election had been narrow, and his legislative support was so weak as to constitute a ready-made prescription for parliamentary paralysis.

The 47-year-old chief executive of Colombia, one of the few Latin-American nations functioning as a democracy, defeated the aging former dictator Lieut. Gen. Gustavo Rojas Pinilla by about 60,000 votes in the April 19 election. Pastrana had been the official Conservative Party candidate, but he was unable to present a solid front to the voters because two other Conservatives, Evaristo Sourdis and Belisario Betancur, insisted on running. Under Colombia's unique National Front system, the two major political parties, the Liberals and Conservatives, alternate in holding the presidency. Because of the Conservative split, Pastrana got more support from the opposition Liberal Party than from his own. (Rojas' following was outside the National Front arrangement.)

In the Congress, Pastrana could count on only 57 votes in the 118-man Senate and 92 in the 210-member Chamber of Deputies. This meant that Pastrana would have to rule by coalition with the Liberals and dissident Conservatives, at the cost of some compromise. He had two major advantages, however: the backing of former president Carlos Lleras Restrepo and the admiration and respect of the U.S. government. Rojas, on the other hand, was feared by the armed forces and inspired no confidence in Washington.

Pastrana was born Nov. 14, 1923, in the rural town of Neiva. His father was a politician, and although Pastrana was undeniably of the political elite he was not a member of Colombia's social and economic top drawer. He was not wealthy and was still making payments on his $35,000 house in Bogotá. A lawyer and an economist by profession, Pastrana had also been a judge, a business executive, and Colombia's ambassador to the U.S. He was colourless as Colombian politicians go, lacking the oratorical skill that is virtually a must in Latin politics. A democrat and believer in the free enterprise system, he had the backing of big business and of U.S. companies doing business in Colombia.   (J. A. O'L.)

PAUL VI

Seemingly undaunted by the attempt of a Bolivian artist dressed as a priest to assassinate him on his arrival in Manila, Pope Paul VI remained on schedule throughout a busy, obviously exhausting tour of the Far East in late November and early December 1970. Traveling farther from Rome than any other Roman Catholic pontiff (and thereby breaking his own record), Paul VI covered over 28,000 mi. to eight places in nine days.

The purpose of the trip was apparent in his message to Asia, delivered in English and broadcast throughout Asia in Chinese, Japanese, and French, in which he called for an alliance of all faiths to counter militant godlessness, and in his message of "unity and love" to all Chinese people, delivered in Hong Kong. The trip began with a stop in Dacca, East Pakistan, added as a gesture of concern for those stricken by a massive cyclone and tidal wave. At all stops the pontiff participated in religious ceremonies that crossed many denominational lines.

Earlier in the year, on May 29, the pope celebrated the 50th anniversary of his ordination to the priesthood in a formal but simple style in St. Peter's Basilica. The anniversary, and the obvious fatigue the pope displayed by the end of his trip, pointed up his age, 73 in September. These facts and the content of his one major ruling during the year, that cardinals over 80 could not take part in the election of a new pope, gave credence to speculation that Paul VI was considering following his own request that bishops and parish priests resign at age 75.

In other matters during the year, Paul VI became the first pontiff to visit nearby Sardinia; expressed his distress at the passing of a divorce law by the Italian Parliament; reiterated his stand against legalized abortion; criticized the torture of prisoners in Brazil; sent aid to Christians in the Nigerian civil war; and personally pleaded for release of U.S. prisoners of war in North Vietnam and kidnapped diplomats and passengers of hijacked airplanes in South America and the Middle East.

Born Giovanni Battista Montini on Sept.

26, 1897, in Concesio, Italy, Paul VI was crowned pontiff on June 30, 1963.

(J. F. Ba.)

PELÉ

Rated by many as the world's finest association football (soccer) player, the Brazilian Negro Pelé played a major part in his country's victory in the World Cup competition in Mexico in June. For Pelé it was his fourth World Cup finals appearance, and for Brazil its third championship, thus allowing it to retain the Jules Rimet Trophy. In the final 4–1 triumph over Italy, Pelé scored one goal and was instrumental in setting up two others.

Born Edson Arantes do Nascimento in Três Corações, Minas Gerais, Braz., on Oct. 21, 1940, Pelé, as he was soon nicknamed, started his footballing career with the Bauru Athletic Club. In 1957, however, he joined his present club, Santos. Within a year his outstanding talent had been recognized, and he was selected for Brazil's victorious World Cup squad to play in the finals in Sweden in 1958. He played in all but the first match and so collected a winner's medal at the age of 17.

Pelé was regularly included on Brazil's national team thereafter, and when the World Cup finals again came around in 1962 in Chile he was an automatic selection. But he played only in the first match, during which he scored, and part of the second, before a pulled muscle put him out of the tournament.

The 1966 World Cup finals were a tragedy for both Pelé and Brazil. He played in the opening and was injured. After missing the second contest he was included in the lineup for the third, against Portugal, even though he was not yet fully fit. Brazil lost the game and was eliminated from the tournament.

In 1967, despite Brazil's loss in the World Cup, the Italians were prepared to offer £500,000 ($1.2 million) for Pelé's services on the soccer field. However, the Santos club, to which he was under contract, rejected the offer because of Pelé's proven drawing power with Brazilian soccer fans. He played for Brazil regularly, and passed another milestone in 1969 when he scored his 1,000th goal in the Maracanã Stadium in Rio de Janeiro.

(T. W.)

PEROT, H(ENRY) ROSS

Perhaps only a rich Texan would have tried, but H. Ross Perot went to Southeast Asia early in 1970 to ransom U.S. prisoners of war and end the Indochina conflict single-handed. Had he succeeded, people would have pretended not to be surprised, because the self-made billionaire had not failed often.

The son of a cotton broker, Perot learned his first business lessons watching his father trade horses around Texarkana, Tex., where he had been born in 1930. By the time he was six he was in business himself, breaking horses at a dollar a head. An Eagle Scout and a hustler, he received a commission to the U.S. Naval Academy and graduated in the middle of the class of '53. After completing his first tour of duty, he resigned and joined the computer sales staff at IBM in Dallas.

Perot did so well at IBM that the giant corporation put a ceiling on the commissions salesmen could earn in a year. Perot ran into the ceiling at mid-January. Bored by sitting around the office, he hatched the idea of a software computer firm—one that would sell computer programs (not the machines themselves) and teach clients how to use them. Starting with $1,000 in capital, he lured several colleagues from IBM and incorporated Electronic Data Systems Corp. on June 27, 1962, his 32nd birthday. Six years later, when the company went public, it was worth well over $600,000, and it continued to double its business annually. Perot owned 81% of the stock.

Fortune magazine wrote: "In the history of American business, probably no other man ever made so much money so fast." Neither was he reluctant to spend it—on causes he supported. He gave $2.5 million for experimental public school programs benefiting black and Mexican-American Texans; gave $1 million to the Boy Scouts; and paid for a statewide antidrug program. In the fall of 1969 he organized United We Stand and spent $2 million for ads supporting Pres. Richard Nixon's Indochina policy. Later he tried to fly a hundred tons of food, medical supplies, and gifts to U.S. prisoners of war for Christmas. When he was rebuffed by Hanoi (the material was later mailed in through the Soviet Union), Perot offered his good offices to investigate POW conditions in South Vietnam and negotiate a peace settlement.

(Ph. K.)

POMPIDOU, GEORGES JEAN RAYMOND

One does not run ten thousand metres like a hundred yards and the marathon is not a sprint. This was the metaphor that French Pres. Georges Pompidou habitually invoked in reply to those who accused him of going too slowly, of being overcautious, and of not seeking the limelight. Unlike his predecessor Charles de Gaulle, who had tried to direct the wind, Pompidou was content to avoid storms, and de Gaulle's death in November 1970 brought the contrast between the two men forcibly to the public mind. Yet it was clear that the period of comparative calm that had followed de Gaulle's quest for grandeur was no mean achievement.

Pompidou had been elected on a platform of Gaullism without de Gaulle, and as far as circumstances permitted he continued to apply the Gaullist principles—national independence in foreign policy, economic expansion with stability. His more open approach made it possible to contemplate entrance of the U.K. into the EEC. It also considerably widened the base of his regime by winning support from right-wing liberals and from the centre.

The independent course in foreign policy was symbolized by Pompidou's two major trips of the year—to Washington and Moscow. His visit to the U.S., from February 23 to March 2, was marred by demonstrations of Jewish groups protesting France's sale of Mirage fighters to Libya. He and his wife Claude were jostled by demonstrators in the lobby of a Chicago hotel, and when Mme Pompidou returned home she was reported to be very angry. The situation was saved when Pres. Richard Nixon made a personal apology and an unscheduled appearance at a dinner in Pompidou's honour.

The eight-day trip to the U.S.S.R. began on October 6, when Pompidou was welcomed at the Moscow airport not only by the Soviet president and premier but also by Communist Party secretary L. I. Brezhnev —the first time Brezhnev had made such a gesture toward a Western non-Communist leader.

Pompidou was born on July 5, 1911, at Montboudif in the Cantal. In 1958 de Gaulle

Georges Jean Raymond Pompidou

A.F.P. FROM PICTORIAL PARADE

R. NORMAN MATHENY FROM THE "CHRISTIAN SCIENCE MONITOR"

Willis Reed

H. Ross Perot

DENNIS BRACK FROM BLACK STAR

made him director of the Cabinet during the transition between the Fourth and Fifth Republics and in April 1962 appointed him premier. He was dismissed after the disturbances of May 1968, but when de Gaulle staked his office on a referendum in 1969 and lost, Pompidou returned to stand successfully for the presidency. (P. V.-P.)

RAZAK BIN HUSSEIN, TUN ABDUL

The long-time heir apparent of Malaysian Prime Minister Tunku Abdul Rahman, Tun Abdul Razak became the nation's second prime minister on Sept. 22, 1970. Probably best known to his people for his qualities as an administrator, Razak served as a district officer and a state *mentri besar* (chief minister) before entering politics. Not afraid to innovate and to cut through red tape, he was the prime mover behind the remarkable organizational effort that went into producing the successful five-year plans for national and rural development.

The significant progress achieved in national development was to a large extent due to Razak's genius in setting up a National Operations Room. From this operations centre, which was duplicated on a smaller scale in every state and district, Razak kept constant watch on the performances of each government agency. Scheduled and surprise inspection trips took him thousands of miles each year to every corner of East and West Malaysia. Often working 16 hours a day and living modestly, he expected and received similar service from his subordinates.

Born on March 11, 1922, the son of a member of the Malayan civil service and territorial chief of Pahang state, Razak attended the elite Malay College in Kuala Kangsar. At 17 he entered the Malay Administrative Service and was later sent to Raffles College in Singapore (now the University of Singapore) for higher studies. He was awarded a scholarship in 1947 to study law at Lincoln's Inn in London and was called to the bar in 1951.

Razak entered politics in 1950, and the following year he was appointed an unofficial member of the Federal Council. He was elected to Parliament at the first national elections in 1955 and was returned at every subsequent election. Among his administrative posts were those of minister of education, minister of defense, and minister of national and rural development. After May 1969, following the civil disturbances in Malaysia, he headed the National Operations Council and, as director of operations, was in effect the principal government executive during the most critical 16 months of Malaysia's history. (M. S. R.)

REED, WILLIS

In his second day as a professional basketball player, Willis Reed, a 6 ft. 10 in. centre, approached Eddie Donovan, who was then the New York Knicks' head coach.

"Coach," Reed said, "could I borrow a rule book?" "A rule book?" Donovan replied in amazement. "Yes," said Reed. "I want to read it."

In all of his years in basketball no one had ever asked Donovan for a rule book, and Donovan was still telling of this incident six years later, after Reed—by then one of the game's superstars—had led the Knicks to their first National Basketball Association (NBA) championship. The Knicks won the title on May 8, 1970, when they defeated the Los Angeles Lakers in the NBA's seventh and final play-off game.

Reed only scored four points in that final contest but, typically, was the inspirational force behind the triumph. He had injured his right hip and thigh in the fifth play-off game against Los Angeles and sat out the sixth game, which the Knicks lost. Then, limping, he returned for the seventh game. He scored the Knicks' first two baskets and played the first 28 minutes. By the time he was withdrawn, the Knicks were safely ahead.

It was the climax to a sensational season for Reed, who won virtually all of the NBA's individual honours. He was chosen the most valuable player in the mid-season All Star game, when he led the East to victory, and then, at the season's end, won the Podoloff Cup, given annually to the league's most valuable player. Though not an unusually high scorer—he averaged only 21.7 points per game during the regular season—Reed was the Knicks' individual star and team captain. He was the indispensable man and helped fuse the squad together with his spectacular teamwork and defensive play.

Reed was born at Hico, La., on June 25, 1942. During his senior year in high school, at Lillie, La., he stood 6 ft. 7 in., and received a scholarship offer from Grambling College, which he accepted. He emerged as a collegiate star at Grambling and upon graduation was drafted by the New York Knicks. (Je. Ho.)

REICH, CHARLES

In a widely discussed book written during the year by Yale University law professor Charles Reich, the author attempted a scholarly analysis of the meaning, purpose, and future of the continuing revolution of the young. Hippie culture, flower people, freaky clothes, rock music, a campus culture, and dropping out were features of this revolution, which to many was particularly disturbing since it seemed to have no direction or future. However, in his book, *The Greening of America,* Reich argued that modern man is actually entering into a significant new phase of his existence.

Reich described three such phases, which he named Consciousness I, II, and III. In Consciousness I, man is a freedom-loving, Jeffersonian-type free spirit, akin to the mood of the U.S. in its early years. But he argued that this stage eventually led to repression, bondage, and World War II. Consciousness II emerged then as the (false) hope of improvement; it emphasized the attainment of a better quality of life through use of institutional organization. Consciousness III, Reich explained, is the next natural and continuing step in man's evolvement, a total transformation into a new society that stresses a dedication to life style, simplicity, love, and comradeship. Such a society is always in a stage of becoming, eager for any and all experience. Reich maintained that many young people were entering or were already in Consciousness III.

As the movement takes hold, Reich wrote, the world will green and flourish like a garden. Consciousness III, he says, leads to a "childlike, breathless sense of wonder."

Reich gathered much of the descriptive material on the culture of the new generation from observations of campus life about him. Before joining the Yale faculty in 1960, he had been a law clerk for U.S. Supreme Court Justice Hugo Black and an attorney for the Washington, D.C., law firm of Arnold, Fortas & Porter. Reich was born May 20, 1928, in New York City. He was graduated from Oberlin College and received his law degree from Yale.

Reaction to the book was mixed. Young readers who felt that they were part of it thought it gave their movement meaning and reason for being. Reich became their most articulate spokesman. But others received it unfavourably. "The entire scheme is a delusive reduction of things to an unreal but orderly form," said the *New York Times* book reviewer. Reich would probably consider that a typical comment from a Consciousness II member. (M. B. Su.)

REUBEN, DAVID

As never before—or so it seemed—U.S. publishers were busy popularizing sex in 1970. And the readers were loving every word of it.

First there was *Human Sexual Inadequacy,* an authoritative study of sexual dysfunction based on the clinical studies of William Masters and Virginia Johnson. The detailed, scientific work was too deep for many, but a summary for laymen was published and *Reader's Digest* issued a condensed version that was simpler still. More popular was a "how to" manual, *The Sensuous Woman,* which told distaff amateurs how to be just that. Published anonymously, it was soon claimed by Joan Garrity, a New York career girl.

But the leader of the pack, which sold 700,000 copies in less time than *Homo sapiens* takes to gestate, was *Everything You Always Wanted to Know About Sex—But Were Afraid to Ask,* written by a West Coast psychiatrist, David Reuben. His libidinal Baedeker was serialized in a leading women's magazine, circulated by four major book clubs, and marketed in 22 countries. The movie rights were reportedly sold for $1 million.

Reuben said he began writing after vacationing at a Mexican resort. "We'd see the honeymoon couples come in. They'd be laughing, dancing and sitting so close together that they'd only be using one chair. The next morning, we'd see them at breakfast—angry, discouraged." His literary purpose, then, was to describe human sexuality in clear, straightforward terms that would prepare the uninitiated for its complexities. However, a number of qualified scientists and commentators questioned the book's accuracy. Masters and Johnson were reported to have said privately that Reuben was wrong a third of the time. He declined to defend his theses or to reveal his source data, other than to say that he read medical journals and gleaned a good deal from private patients.

Born in 1934, the son of a Hungarian immigrant and lawyer, Reuben graduated from grammar school at 12 and from the University of Illinois medical school at 23. He served as chief of neuropsychiatry at Walter Air Force Base Hospital and was a research associate at Harvard before going to San Diego, Calif., where he ran a clinic. (Ph. K.)

RICHARDSON, ELLIOT LEE

By protocol, the U.S. secretary of health, education, and welfare ranks tenth in the president's Cabinet—two places from the last. And, by expectation, his department, filled with more "New Deal" social programs than any other, would seem fairly low in priority in a Republican government. But with Elliot Richardson as the secretary in the Nixon administration, this was not the case. Richardson's place seemed to be wherever the administration had a major, but delicate, assignment.

He had come into the Nixon government as undersecretary of state, where his main assignment was to reform the internal machinery of the State Department while accommodating the professionalism and pride of the nation's permanent foreign service. By most reckoning, he did so.

After 18 months he was shifted to the HEW secretaryship for two new, but still delicate, assignments. The first was to reform the operations of a department that had resisted every secretary's efforts in that direction. The second was to rescue the Nixon administration's welfare program from its deep legislative trouble. Even amid those assignments, he was drafted temporarily to return to diplomacy. In October, Richardson was sent to Cairo to represent the president at the funeral of U.A.R. Pres. Gamal Abd-al-Nasser.

This was the third time the precise, patrician Bostonian had been recruited to Washington. In 1953 he had joined the legislative staff of Sen. Leverett Saltonstall (Rep., Mass.). After returning to private law practice in Boston, he was called back to the capital by Pres. Dwight Eisenhower to serve as an assistant secretary in HEW.

A native of Boston, Richardson was born July 20, 1920. He graduated with honours from Harvard and then, after service in World War II, returned to Harvard Law School, where he rose to the editorship of the *Law Review*. After law clerkships with Judge Learned Hand and Justice Felix Frankfurter, he began aiming toward politics. In 1959, following his first stint at HEW, he was appointed U.S. attorney in Boston, and there, too, he was handed an assignment of delicacy—prosecuting Bernard Goldfine, a close friend of Eisenhower's presidential assistant Sherman Adams. He ran unsuccessfully for Massachusetts state attorney general in 1962, was elected lieutenant governor of the state in 1964 and, in 1966, state attorney general.   (L. Dn.)

RIPPON, (AUBREY) GEOFFREY

The death of Iain Macleod (*see* OBITUARIES) soon after the formation of Britain's new Conservative Party government brought Geoffrey Rippon the job of leading negotiations for Britain's application to join the European Economic Community (EEC). But for that Rippon would no doubt have remained for at least a year or two as minister of technology, the position first allotted to him in Edward Heath's Cabinet after the general election. Yet in many respects Rippon seemed so well qualified for the role of "Mr. Europe," as his job was nicknamed, that he might well have been a first choice. Few Conservative members of Parliament had shown more sustained interest than Rippon in the growth of a united Europe. He served as leader of Conservative delegations to the Council of Europe and to the Western European Union and as president of the British section of the Council of European Municipalities. There could be no doubt about his commitment to bringing the application for British entry to the EEC to a successful conclusion.

Rippon was born May 28, 1924, and graduated from Oxford University. He was elected a local councillor in the London suburb of Surbiton when he was 21, and at 26 was mayor of Surbiton. Then he went to the London County Council, and at 34 was leader of the Conservative opposition there. He was elected to Parliament in 1955, and after moving through a number of junior posts reached the Cabinet in 1963.

During the years of the Labour government, Rippon was the Conservative spokesman on defense matters, gaining a reputation for hawkish views. He achieved a reputation for being a tough, hard bargainer, and in negotiations with the EEC nations made it clear that Britain would insist on fair terms for entry.   (W. H. Ts.)

ROBINSON, BROOKS

It was the sixth inning of the third game of the 1970 World Series. Johnny Bench, the Cincinnati catcher, was at bat and slammed a drive down the third base line. Brooks Robinson of the Baltimore Orioles made a diving stop, scrambled to his feet, and threw Bench out. As the crowd cheered, Dick Moss, the attorney for the Major League Baseball Players Association, turned to Marvin Miller, director of the players' union, and said: "Brooks is so good it's unfair to the rest of the players."

This statement was made somewhat in jest but it illustrated, nonetheless, Robinson's unique stature in major league baseball. Many considered him to be the best fielding third baseman in the game's history. Even Casey Stengel, when he was managing the New York Mets in the early 1960s, paid tribute to Robinson's skills and admitted: "That Robinson feller does some things at third base that I don't believe Pie Traynor did."

Seldom had one player dominated a World Series as did Robinson in 1970 when he led Baltimore to victory in five games over Cincinnati. He turned in a half dozen outstanding fielding plays, all of which brought standing ovations. In addition, he was one of the most effective batsmen with 9 hits in 21 at-bats for a .429 average. He also drove in six runs, almost all of them in crucial situations.

It could be said that Brooks Robinson was born to play baseball. Born in Little Rock, Ark., on May 18, 1937, he was a sandlot infielder. Robinson attended Central High School in Little Rock, which did not have a baseball team. He competed and won all-state honours on the school's football and basketball teams and drew the attention of major league scouts while performing in the American Legion junior baseball program with the M. M. Eberts Post No. 1, which he led to two state championships. The Baltimore Orioles signed him for a $4,000 bonus in 1955, and subsequently sent him to the minor leagues for more experience. He returned to major league competition in 1957. During his career he had set numerous fielding records, and for 11 years had been selected (by player vote) for the *Sporting News* Gold Glove award.   (Je. Ho.)

SADAT, ANWAR AL-

When Gamal Abd-al-Nasser died on Sept. 28, 1970, the United Arab Republic faced the formidable problem of choosing a successor to its long-time leader. On October 15 Anwar al-Sadat, the nation's vice-president, was elected president, polling more than 90% of the votes in a national referendum. His election had been virtually assured when he was unanimously selected as the candidate by the Arab Socialist Union Higher Executive Committee and the National Assembly. After the death of Abd-al-Hakim Amer in 1967 and the resignation of Zakaria Mohieddin in 1968, Sadat became Nasser's most trusted lieutenant. Because he lacked his predecessor's charisma and stature, however, Sadat was expected to share power with others to a much greater extent than Nasser had.

Born Dec. 25, 1918, in the Al Minufiyah Governorate of the Nile Delta, Sadat graduated as an army officer from the Cairo Military Academy in 1938. At the Manqabad

garrison in Upper Egypt he met and became associated with Nasser and others of the future revolutionary Free Officers. During World War II he worked secretly against the British occupation of Egypt and in 1942 was arrested by the British for spying. In 1943 he escaped but was again arrested in 1945 on a charge of participating in an assassination attempt against Wafd Party leader Nahas Pasha. Released on that charge, he joined the magazine *al-Musawwar*.

In 1950 Sadat was readmitted to the Army and at once became part of Nasser's Free Officers movement. By accident he took no part in the Nasser-led military coup that overthrew the monarchy in 1952, but it was he who announced the revolution over Radio Cairo and he later served on the court that tried the leaders of the old regime. Sadat served as speaker of the National Assembly from 1961 to 1969 and was vice-president of the U.A.R. from 1964 to 1966 and again in 1969 and 1970.   (P. Md.)

SAMUELSON, PAUL ANTHONY

Paul Samuelson, a U.S. professor and writer of the most widely read and influential economics textbook in the modern world, won the 1970 Nobel Memorial Prize in Economics. "By his many contributions, Samuelson has done more than any other contemporary economist to raise the level of scientific analysis in economic theory," said the Nobel committee in making the citation. His "extensive production, covering nearly all areas of economic theory, is characterized by an outstanding ability to derive important new theorems and to find new applications for existing ones."

The main body of his prolific output was published in 1966 in *The Collected Scientific Papers of Paul A. Samuelson*, which comprised nearly a million words and covered 130 specific topics. The text for which he was most famous, *Economics: An Introductory Analysis*, had introduced hundreds of thousands of undergraduates to what has been called the "dismal science." First published in 1948, it had gone through eight editions and had been translated into 14 languages. One economics writer observed that the book had "made him a household word in the academic community and a millionaire as well."

Samuelson was known as a "liberal" economist, basing his theories on those of the great British economist John Maynard Keynes, and his overall thesis called for the federal government to adjust fluctuations in the economy. In domestic political terms this was confirmed by his support of the economic and fiscal policies of Presidents Lyndon Johnson and John Kennedy, whom he advised. Conversely, he was an outspoken critic of Pres. Richard Nixon's economic approach.

Samuelson was born in Gary, Ind., May 15, 1915, and graduated from the University of Chicago before his 20th birthday. He took his master's and doctor's degrees at Harvard, where he won the David A. Wells Prize. In 1940 he joined the faculty of the Massachusetts Institute of Technology, where he continued to occupy a special chair. His theoretical adversary, Milton Friedman of the University of Chicago, wrote that he "has been the leader in creating a great center of economic study and research at MIT, raising a run-of-the-mill department to one of the premier departments in the world." Samuelson had been an adviser to the U.S. Treasury, the Federal Reserve Board, and the Rand Corporation. He was a fellow of the British Academy and of the American Academy of Arts and Sciences and a past president of the International Economics Association.   (Ph. K.)

Anwar al-Sadat
UPI COMPIX

John Schlesinger
MICHAEL CHILDERS FROM CAMERA 5

George Pratt Shultz
PAUL CONKLIN FROM PIX

SCHLESINGER, JOHN

Midnight Cowboy, which won three Oscars (best film, best director, best script) in 1970, besides six British Film Academy Awards, and a nice assortment of other prizes, was by any measure the most successful film of 1969. The fact that John Schlesinger started shooting it the day after he had received spectacularly disapproving notices for *Far from the Madding Crowd* made him, he said, a little wiser—perhaps a little more skeptical—about the nature of success in movies.

Schlesinger was born in London, on Feb. 16, 1926. As an Oxford undergraduate he made two amateur films, and in 1956 he began to direct film items for BBC-TV's "Tonight" (1956–57) and "Monitor" (1958), first attracting notice with a series of shorts on art subjects. Between directing TV commercials he made the prizewinning short *Terminus* (1960) for British Transport Films.

In his first feature film, *A Kind of Loving* (1962), Schlesinger applied a documentary and analytical approach to the problems of a young marriage threatened by specifically contemporary class pressures. The hero of *Billy Liar* (1963) also suffers from the deracinating effects of modern welfare society, but Schlesinger adapted his style to the Keith Waterhouse and Willis Hall play, reflecting the hero's mythomania with elements of visual fantasy. With less conviction, *Darling* (1965) moved to another area of British life, the world of glamour in which the heroine is a success in material terms but a human failure. After this came *Far from the Madding Crowd,* in which Hardy's characters were realized less convincingly than the Victorian countryside. *Midnight Cowboy* (1969), Schlesinger's only American film, was in several respects his best—often overdecorated, but deeply re-

sponsive to the central relationship between its two heroes, social outcasts who find their only dignity in their friendship for each other. Perhaps because Schlesinger enjoyed the outsider's privileged view, his vision of contemporary American urban life was shrewd and vivid. In 1970 Schlesinger was working on *Bloody Sunday,* scripted by the film critic Penelope Gilliatt. (DA. J. R.)

SERVAN-SCHREIBER, JEAN-JACQUES

In 1969 Jean-Jacques Servan-Schreiber decided that he was no longer content to be a collaborator with politicians or to comment on their doings as a journalist, but that he wished to enter French politics on his own account. In 1970 his political career had a promising beginning and an unpromising—though perhaps not a final—ending.

Ambitious and controversial, Servan-Schreiber persuaded the small and long-established Radical Party, a liberal, lay party with socialist leanings, to accept his services as secretary-general of its political bureau. He drafted and published a "manifesto," *Ciel et Terre,* which became a best seller. In April he received worldwide publicity when he personally arranged the release of Communist composer Mikis Theodorakis (*q.v.*) from a Greek prison, and in June, after a barnstorming campaign, he won a National Assembly seat, formerly held by the Gaullists, in a by-election at Nancy.

His prospects seemed bright, and there was talk that he might even succeed in uniting France's fragmented non-Communist left and centre—a task that politicians had been attempting unsuccessfully since World War II. Then, in the fall, he chose to run against Premier Jacques Chaban-Delmas in a by-election in Bordeaux, where the premier was mayor and which he had represented as a deputy for more than 20 years. The

attempt was a failure. Servan-Schreiber gained only 16% of the vote—far short of the 30% that he himself had set as the mark of success. In the process he alienated politicians of all stripes, from the Gaullists to the Communists. Later in the year he again attracted attention when he described the public mourning for Charles de Gaulle as "excessive," and when the policy of "regional liberation" for France, which he advocated at the Radical Party congress in December, was widely debated.

Previously, Servan-Schreiber had been best known outside France as the author of the best-selling *Le Défi américain* (*The American Challenge*), which had warned Europe that it must unite and modernize if it was to avoid becoming an economic colony of the U.S. He was born on Feb. 13, 1924, the son of the owner and one of the founders of an economic daily, *Les Echos.* After graduating from the École Polytechnique in 1943, he joined the Free French as a fighter pilot. In 1953 he founded a weekly, *L'Express,* which became the chief organ of the liberal left and which he subsequently transformed into a newsmagazine on the model of *Time.* (P. V.-P.)

SHULTZ, GEORGE PRATT

A rare accolade went to George P. Shultz when U.S. President-elect Richard Nixon appointed him secretary of labour in 1968—he was praised by both management and labour. Unknown to the public, Shultz had long been highly regarded in union, industrial, government, and academic circles as an accomplished economist, labour mediator, and expert on manpower displacement and unemployment. No stranger to Washington, he had served as an economic consultant under the Eisenhower, Kennedy, and Johnson administrations.

Shultz's high standing with the president was underscored by his appointment, effective July 1, 1970, to head the newly organized Office of Management and Budget, successor to the old Bureau of the Budget. In announcing formation of the OMB, Nixon indicated that it would work closely with the Domestic Council headed by John D. Ehrlichman (*q.v.*). The council, the president said, "will be primarily concerned with *what* we do; the Office of Management and Budget will be primarily concerned with *how* we do it, and *how well* we do it."

Shultz advocated an economy directed by market forces, not governmental manipulation, and he believed that the rate of growth in the money supply is a major determinant of economic activity. At the same time, he said, "I've got to think that the budget and the tax system are important." He had been the first administration official to speak out publicly against the unusually tight monetary policies of the Federal Reserve Board in 1969.

A memo signed by Shultz and transmitted to the president in June 1970 described the growing frustrations of blue-collar workers. "Living in close proximity to the poor and near-poor," Shultz wrote, such workers "rub up against . . . severe social tensions in their daily lives. . . . Observing the welfare programs for the poor, they feel excluded and forgotten." The implication of the memo was that it would be good politics for the Republican Party to build a constituency among blue-collar workers.

Born Dec. 13, 1920, in New York City, Shultz received a B.A. in economics from

Norodom Sihanouk
WIDE WORLD

"THE TIMES," LONDON, FROM PICTORIAL PARADE
Maggie Smith

ascribe infallibility to them. So it was not a matter of critical theological importance that in 1962 Smith declared, "Man does not belong on the moon," saying he based his position on scripture.

Born in Salt Lake City, Utah, on July 19, 1876, Smith graduated from Latter-day Saints College in 1897 and performed his missionary service in Britain. He returned to Utah and joined the church historian's office in 1901 as a staff member. Five years later he was "sustained" as assistant church historian, and became church historian in 1921. He was ordained as an apostle in 1910 by his father, who was the sect's sixth president, became president of the Council of the Twelve Apostles in 1951, and was elevated to the rank of counselor in 1965.

Active in temporal affairs, Smith was a director of Zions First National Bank and the Beneficial Life Insurance Co., and a trustee of Brigham Young University. He was also the author of several books on Mormon history and doctrine. Married three times, he was the father of 11 children. In July, on the 123rd anniversary of Brigham Young's discovery of Salt Lake Valley, he was visited by U.S. Pres. Richard Nixon.   (PH. K.)

SMITH, MAGGIE
In the British theatre 1970 was without doubt "Maggie Smith year." A most talented actress, Miss Smith began the year in splendid style by appearing in the National Theatre's *The Three Sisters* and *The Beaux' Stratagem* in Los Angeles in February. In March she won the best-actress-of-the-year award from the U.K. Society of Film and Television Arts for her part in the film *The Prime of Miss Jean Brodie*. That same role also won her the U.S. Academy Award for best actress the following month. Immediately afterward she appeared in the title role of Ingmar Bergman's adaptation of Henrik Ibsen's *Hedda Gabler* at the National Theatre in London, proving once again, as she had already done when playing Desdemona opposite Sir Laurence Olivier, that her comic talent could be extended with equal ease to tragedy.

Born Dec. 28, 1934, in Ilford, Essex, Miss Smith attended school in Oxford and made her acting debut with the Oxford University Drama Society in 1952 as Viola in Shakespeare's *Twelfth Night*. After playing in Shakespeare and other classics at Oxford and appearing at the Edinburgh Festival, she played on the stage in New York in 1956, scoring a hit there in *New Faces of 1956*. She made her London stage debut in *Share My Lettuce* in 1957. After that her stage, film, and television credits were numerous. She joined the Old Vic in 1959, and also acted in the London commercial theatre, receiving the *Evening Standard* best actress award for her roles in Peter Shaffer's *The Private Ear* and *The Public Eye*. The 1963 Variety Club best actress award went to her for the lead in *Mary, Mary*.

Miss Smith joined Britain's National Theatre in 1963 and also appeared at the Chichester Festival, notably in *Miss Julie* and *The Country Wife*. Her motion-picture roles included *The Pumpkin Eater* and *Oh, What a Lovely War*. Among her many television credits were performances in *Man and Superman* and *Home and Beauty*.
      (O. TR.)

SOLZHENITSYN, ALEKSANDR ISAEVICH
Twice in a dozen years the Nobel Prize for Literature has gone to a Russian recognized at the time as one of the world's greatest living writers: to Boris Pasternak in 1958 and to Aleksandr I. Solzhenitsyn in 1970. The works of both men were proscribed in

Princeton in 1942 and a Ph.D. in industrial economics from Massachusetts Institute of Technology in 1949. From 1962 until his appointment as secretary of labour, he served as dean of the University of Chicago's Graduate School of Business.   (RI. W.)

SIHANOUK, NORODOM
Successively Cambodia's king, premier, and head of state, and also Khmer nationalist and Buddhist socialist, corrupt oligarch and incompetent administrator, a windbag and a pedestrian journalist, Norodom Sihanouk finally in 1970 lost his hold over some of his people. Alarmed by the prospect of an eventual U.S. disengagement from Vietnam and by the renewal of North Vietnamese activities in Cambodia, in March he left France, where he had been since early in the year, for Moscow and Peking in an effort to bring pressure on North Vietnam to cease its activities in his country. He was talking to Soviet leaders when on March 18, at Phnom Penh, Gen. Lon Nol, commander of the Cambodian armed forces, overthrew him.

After the coup, the Soviet Union visibly was not too keen to shelter Sihanouk, and he went to China, where he was received with open arms. On May 5 he announced in Peking the formation of a royal government of national union based on a "United National Front of Kampuchea," concluding his three-hour speech by proclaiming his alliance not only with China but also with North Vietnam, North Korea, and the Pathet Lao movement. This alliance would have the aim of "fighting against American imperialism." The response of the new Cambodian regime was to sentence Sihanouk to death. In August, in his first contact with the West since having been overthrown, Sihanouk notified *Time* magazine that he had instructed his people to find and return Robert Anson, a missing *Time* correspondent. Anson subsequently was released.

Sihanouk was born on Oct. 31, 1922, at Phnom Penh, the son of Norodom Suramarit, a Khmer nobleman who in 1920 married Princess Kossamak Nearireak, the daughter of Prince Sisowath, the king of

Cambodia from 1904 to 1927. When Sisowath's son, Monivong, died in 1941, he was succeeded as king by the 18-year-old Sihanouk. After World War II the young king's aim was to terminate peacefully the French protectorate, an aim that he brought about after France's retreat from Indochina in 1954. He founded the so-called Socialist People's Community Party in January 1955, won in February a referendum approving its program, and on March 2 abdicated in favour of his father, becoming himself the head of government.

When his father died on April 3, 1960, Sihanouk refused to ascend the throne again, agreeing instead to serve as head of state. After the involvement of the United States in Vietnam it became exceedingly difficult for him to maintain his policy of neutrality. On May 3, 1965, he broke off diplomatic relations with the U.S. but did not conceal his misgivings about the result of a Communist victory in Vietnam.   (K. SM.)

SMITH, JOSEPH FIELDING
A great-nephew of Joseph Smith, founder of the Mormon Church, Joseph Fielding Smith was, at age 93, "ordained and set apart as tenth president and prophet, seer, and revelator" of the Church of Jesus Christ of Latter-day Saints on Jan. 23, 1970. His elevation to succeed the late David O. McKay as leader of 2.8 million Mormons was expected, since Smith was the senior member of the Council of the Twelve Apostles. However, the sect deemed it a matter of divine will, not simply an observance of the traditional rules of succession. Though Smith had not announced any major revelations since taking office, spokesmen believed the thrust of his administration would be to develop more fully the church's existing educational activities. Consequently, religious study programs in cooperation with secular high schools and colleges were being expanded while the traditional missionary program was to be enlarged by at least 100% in the next few years.

While Mormons believe God reveals his will through church leaders, they do not

their native country, and neither man appeared in Stockholm to receive the award. Solzhenitsyn excused himself from the ceremonies "for personal reasons." It was not clear whether the Soviet authorities refused to permit him to leave or whether he feared they would not permit him to return.

Solzhenitsyn was born Dec. 11, 1918, in Rostov, the scion of an intellectual Cossack family. He was wounded in World War II and twice decorated for bravery, but in 1945, after slurring Stalin in a personal letter, he was sentenced to eight years at forced labour. He was officially rehabilitated after Stalin's death, and in 1962, during the period of destalinization under Premier Nikita S. Khrushchev, his first major work, *One Day in the Life of Ivan Denisovich,* was published.

The book's grim picture of Siberian prison life in the Stalinist era served Khrushchev's purposes, and its author was widely acclaimed both inside and outside the Soviet Union. After Khrushchev's fall, however, criticism of the regime became unacceptable. Solzhenitsyn's work was banned, and in the U.S.S.R. it circulated only illegally, in manuscript or through the underground press.

The manuscripts of two major novels, *The First Circle* and *The Cancer Ward*—both based on the author's experiences—were smuggled out of the Soviet Union without Solzhenitsyn's authorization and published in the West. To Westerners accustomed to post-Joycean writing they seemed old-fashioned, cast—like Pasternak's *Dr. Zhivago*—in the form of the 19th-century novel. Yet they were profound and powerful works, and, partly because of their merit, partly because they afforded an inside view of the Soviet Union, they became best sellers.

This only exacerbated Solzhenitsyn's position at home. Expelled from the Writers' Union, he lived quietly near Moscow, protected from outsiders by friends such as the cellist Mstislav Rostropovich. Late in 1970 Rostropovich wrote an impassioned letter in Solzhenitsyn's defense, addressed to several Soviet publications. None published it, although it appeared in Western newspapers.

(PH. K.)

SOUVANNA PHOUMA

Laotian Premier Souvanna Phouma spent most of 1970 in an active, but vain, search for a peaceful settlement to his wartorn nation's problems. With Communist forces led by his half brother, Prince Souphanouvong, holding the Plaine des Jarres and nearby critical areas, Souvanna Phouma declared a state of emergency and very nearly fell from power as a result.

The premier angrily stormed from the Laotian Parliament when opposition members claimed such a move was excessive, and dared them to oust him from power. He prevailed, but only narrowly.

His efforts toward peace began early in the year. On January 31 he announced that he would permit Vietnamese Communists to keep on using the Ho Chi Minh Trail provided an estimated 50,000 North Vietnamese forces were withdrawn from the rest of Laos. The Communists responded by sending 6,000 soldiers, led by tanks, to recapture the strategic Plaine des Jarres and a vital nearby airstrip. Souvanna Phouma then asked Britain and the Soviet Union to reconvene the 1962 Geneva conference on Indochina, but to no avail.

Meanwhile, renewed fighting had aroused fears in the U.S. that American forces might become as involved in Laos as they had in Vietnam. On March 6, U.S. Pres. Richard Nixon confirmed that the U.S. had increased military aid and air operations in Laos, but he claimed the involvement was still small.

On the same day Souphanouvong demanded that the U.S. halt its bombing in Laos and withdraw any forces it might have there. He also suggested that a coalition government be formed, leading to the eventual election of a neutralist government of national union. On March 9 Souvanna Phouma agreed to permit the Communists to send a messenger to Vientiane with the proposals. Negotiations between the two princes continued throughout the year, but with little progress. Souvanna Phouma visited Europe in October.

Souvanna Phouma was born Oct. 7, 1901, nephew of King Sisavang Vong. After studying engineering and public works in France, he entered government service in 1931 in the Public Works Service of Indochina, becoming minister for public works in Laos in 1950. He was then successively premier (1951–54), minister of national defense (1955–56), premier (1956–58), ambassador to France, and premier again from 1962.

(J. F. BA.)

SUZMAN, HELEN

When Mrs. Helen Suzman was elected from the wealthy Johannesburg constituency of Houghton in 1970, it marked the third time in her parliamentary career of 17 years that she had become the sole representative of the Progressive Party in the South African House of Assembly.

Mrs. Suzman won reelection on a liberal platform with a greatly increased majority while all other Progressive candidates lost. It was recognition of her record as the most consistent and determined opponent of South Africa's policy of racial separation (apartheid). In a legislature of 170 members, 168 of them men, she earned the reputation of being "a tireless minority of one" and spokesman of the voteless nonwhite people comprising more than 80% of the South African population.

In and out of Parliament Helen Suzman defended the cause of the Africans in particular and fought against laws that she considered unjust, such as the enforced removal of communities under the group areas legislation. She championed the principles of civil liberty and worked for the abolition of capital punishment. (South Africa had one of the highest execution rates in the world.) On many of these issues she clashed with the official opposition as well as with the government. She called herself "a voice of dissent in a conformist society."

Born in Germiston, Transvaal, on Nov. 7, 1917, the daughter of Samuel and Freda Gavronsky, Helen Suzman graduated from the University of the Witwatersrand and lectured there in economics and economic history. Entering Parliament as a member of the United Party (the opposition) in 1953, she was one of a group of parliamentarians who in 1959 left that party because of policy differences and formed the liberal Progressive Party. In 1966, in recognition of her fight against racial discrimination, she was presented with a scroll of honour by the World Council of Synagogues.

(L. H.)

THANG, TON DUC

The oldest living member of the Vietnamese Communist Party, Ton Duc Thang, 82, succeeded his longtime friend, Ho Chi Minh, as president of North Vietnam late in 1969, but did not assume Ho's political power. Thang, who spent 15 years in prison for murder, apparently was a figurehead president, while real political power was divided among other leaders in the Communist Party hierarchy.

Thang was born into a middle-class farm family on Aug. 20, 1888, in Longxuyen Province, now part of South Vietnam. He

graduated in 1910 from the École Industrielle de l'Extrême-Orient in Saigon, where he organized student strikes. After working as a mechanic in Saigon, he went into self-imposed exile in France, where he was drafted into the French Navy. His unit was sent to Sevastopol where the French joined other nations in trying to put down the Russian Revolution.

At Sevastopol, Thang participated in a mutiny led by André Marty, who later became a high-ranking official in the French Communist Party, and as a result was expelled from the French Navy. He returned to Indochina, became active in the League of Revolutionary Vietnamese Youth formed by Ho Chi Minh, and rose swiftly to become a member of the league's central committee. Thang was arrested in 1929 on charges of sedition and complicity in murder, and was sentenced to 20 years' imprisonment on Poulo Condore, a prison island, where he remained until released by his colleagues in August 1945, when the Vietnamese Communists seized power in North Vietnam.

From that time Thang played a continuously important but not dominant role in Vietnamese Communist Party affairs. He was the first person to receive the Gold Star Medal, the highest decoration bestowed by North Vietnam, was awarded the Stalin Peace Prize in 1955, and was presented with the Order of Lenin in October 1967 in recognition of his role in the Sevastopol mutiny.

(J. F. BA.)

THEODORAKIS, MIKIS

On April 13, 1970, a private aircraft landed at Paris' Le Bourget airport, bringing from Athens its owner, Jean-Jacques Servan-Schreiber (*q.v.*), and Mikis Theodorakis, a talented Greek composer and member of the Greek Communist Party. Servan-Schreiber, a prominent French journalist and politician, had arrived in Athens two days before, called on Prime Minister Georgios Papadopoulos, and explained that he would like to help Greece by stopping the attempt of the Scandinavian states formally to suspend Greece from the Council of Europe.

He advised Papadopoulos that he should soften his policy at home, which would help Servan-Schreiber convince his friend Olof Palme, the Swedish prime minister, that the suspension demand should be dropped. He even foresaw a possibility of an official visit to Athens by the Swedish statesman, but the price would be to free Theodorakis and to let him go abroad. Papadopoulos agreed. Shortly after snatching Theodorakis from Greece in a blaze of international publicity, Servan-Schreiber won a seat in the National Assembly. Palme, of course, never planned a visit to Athens.

In June Theodorakis arrived in London to conduct a concert of his own works—some of them written recently in Greek prisons—at the Royal Albert Hall. At the press conference he was asked if he was still a Communist. "Of course," he replied. "Every good Greek must be a Communist." He expressed doubts, however, about the call to arms formulated by Andreas Papandreou, leader of the Pan-Hellenic Liberation Movement. "I believe," said Theodorakis, "we have many other means to overthrow the colonels."

Theodorakis was born on July 28, 1925, on the island of Chios, and studied composition at the conservatories of Athens and Paris. Among his more ambitious composi-

Aleksandr Trifonovich Tvardovski
PICTORIAL PARADE

WAYNE MILLER FROM MAGNUM
John Wayne

tions were *Alhambra: The Honeymoon* (1962), a sinfonietta for guitar and piano; *Oedipus Tyrannos* (1964), a cantata for string orchestra; and the oratorio *March of the Spirit.* He was best known, however, for the score of the motion picture *Zorba, the Greek.* Theodorakis joined the Greek Communist Party during the German occupation of Greece. In 1964 he was elected to the Chamber of Deputies. Arrested in 1967, he was amnestied in January 1968 and then rearrested and sent to a concentration camp at Oropos, 31 mi. N of Athens.   (K. Sm.)

TORRES GONZALES, JUAN JOSÉ

A general in the Bolivian Army, Juan José Torres became the "strongman" president of that turbulent Andean nation after a coup d'etat and a countercoup in October 1970. In a wild period of 72 hours, Bolivian Pres. Alfredo Ovando Candía was ousted by rightist Gen. Rogelio Miranda, who in turn was overthrown by left-wing nationalist Torres. Ovando and Miranda successively sought refuge in the embassy of Argentina as the 49-year-old Torres took charge of Bolivia. He thus became the 183rd president of the nation in 145 years of independence.

Torres bluffed Miranda into vacating the presidency by astute use of the radio, of three Bolivian Air Force planes that buzzed the palace threateningly, and through the demonstrations of militant labour unions and students in La Paz. Miranda had almost the entire strength of the armed forces behind him but gave up without firing a shot when it seemed to him that Torres was threatening civil war.

Torres was born March 5, 1921, in Cochabamba and attended the Autonomous National University at Sucre before entering the Army in 1941. During his youth he was a member of the conservative Bolivian Socialist Falange Party. Later in life, Torres became increasingly leftist and inclined toward socialism but he remained primarily an ardent nationalist. He served as minister of labour in the government of Lieut. Gen. René Barrientos Ortuño.   (J. A. O'L.)

TORRIJOS HERRERA, OMAR

Panama had a president for window dressing in 1970, but the country's strongman was Gen. Omar Torrijos Herrera, 41-year-old commander of the paramilitary Guardia Nacional. Torrijos came to prominence in the military coup of October 1968. For a time he shared power with Col. Boris Martínez, but he soon sent his former ally packing into exile. After December 1969, when he dramatically overcame an effort by younger officers to unseat him, his rule was undisputed.

The young general was a husky, crewcut man with little formal education but with overwhelming self-confidence and flair. He virtually declared war against Panama's traditional oligarchs, the 400 or so families that had controlled the country's finances and commerce since its birth. He was equally fearless in openly espousing birth control despite the opposition of conservative churchmen.

Torrijos was not a sophisticated man, and this might well prove to be his greatest handicap in his efforts to alleviate the plight of the Panamanian poor—meaning most of the people. He did not hesitate to tax the rich as no Panamanian leader had ever dared to do before, but how well he spent the money would be decided by the technicians around him. He was Panamanian to the core in his belief that his country's location at the crossroads of the two Americas was its greatest asset, and he did not intend to sell it cheaply. Under Torrijos the three treaties that the U.S. had been attempting to negotiate with Panama concerning the old canal, the U.S. military bases, and the proposed sea-level canal were once again at the starting point.

Torrijos was born Feb. 13, 1929, in Santiago de Veraguas. He joined the Guardia in 1952 and rose through the ranks, taking many courses in the military schools of the U.S., Venezuela, and El Salvador. He was a lieutenant colonel when he and Martínez ousted Pres. Arnulfo Arias after only 11 days in office. The big challenge to his regime came in December 1969 when he was in Mexico and Col. Amado Sanjur and Col. Ramira Silvera announced they had seized control. Several Guardia units remained loyal to Torrijos, however, and Torrijos flew to the city of David, assembled loyal followers, and dramatically headed toward Panama City, leading a cavalcade of cars that became a victory parade.   (J. A. O'L.)

TRUDEAU, PIERRE ELLIOTT

Although Canadian Prime Minister Pierre Trudeau made a name for himself as somewhat of a swinger during his first two years in office, the popular French-Canadian showed he could be very tough indeed when faced with a crisis. In October 1970 members of a French-Canadian separatist group called Le Front de Libération du Québec (FLQ) kidnapped British trade official James R. Cross from his home in Montreal and held him hostage.

Two weeks after Cross's abduction, FLQ members kidnapped Pierre Laporte, Quebec's minister of labour. He was murdered, and Canadians were shocked to learn that he had been strangled by twisting the chain attached to a religious medal around his neck. Cross continued to be held prisoner while the FLQ demanded a ransom of $500,000 in gold bullion, release of political prisoners, and safe passage to Cuba.

Trudeau responded by invoking the War Measures Act, used only twice before in Canadian history and never in peacetime. It suspends civil rights for a period of six months while a state of possible "insurrection" exists. Canadian troops rounded up suspected FLQ members, confiscated relatively small quantities of guns and explosives, and searched for Cross.

Trudeau said that the use of the War Measures Act was distasteful to him. As a long-time defender of civil liberties, he had been in the forefront of the fight for an ever wider range of freedoms. He was born Oct. 18, 1919, in Montreal and attended universities there and also in London and Paris. A one-time law professor at the University of Montreal, he served as justice minister in the Canadian government before being elected prime minister with a large Liberal Party majority in 1968. In that office he acted to reduce Canadian participation in NATO, cut the federal bureaucracy, took steps leading to the recognition of Communist China, and in the domestic area attempted to curb inflation.

Only the third prime minister (out of 15) to be a French-Canadian, Trudeau was believed to be making progress in bringing French- and English-speaking Canadians closer together, but the Cross and Laporte affairs set that effort back. In November police discovered Cross's whereabouts in Montreal and he was freed in return for safe passage to Cuba for the kidnappers. The following month three suspects were seized and charged with the kidnapping and murder of Laporte.   (M. B. Su.)

TSIEN HSUE-SHEN

On April 24, 1970, the first Chinese satellite began orbiting the earth to intermittent strains of "The East Is Red," theme song of the nation's Cultural Revolution. Credit for China's successful first venture into space was believed in the West to be mainly due to Tsien Hsue-shen, once a colonel in the U.S. Air Force and later a member of the Central Committee of the Chinese Communist Party.

Born in Shanghai in 1909, Tsien Hsue-shen graduated from Chiao-tung University in 1934 and then went to the Massachusetts Institute of Technology on a grant and took a master's degree in aeronautical engineering.

Later, he attended the California Institute of Technology, where he became an assistant professor of aeronautics. During World War II he directed the rocket division of the U.S. National Defense Scientific Advisory Board and in 1945, with the rank of colonel, headed a team sent to investigate rocket developments in Germany. After the war he went back to China, but being found too young for a senior university post he returned to the U.S. and became head of the Guggenheim Jet Propulsion Center at the California Institute of Technology. In 1950 he again set out for China—now under Communist rule—dispatching in advance to Shanghai via Hong Kong a large consignment of scientific documents. On orders from the U.S. Department of State he was arrested at his home in Altadena, Calif. Following the Sino-U.S. agreement of Sept. 10, 1955, on the repatriation of nationals of the two countries, Tsien was allowed to leave and returned to China under a deportation order. There he became head of a team of rocket experts many of whom had comparable backgrounds of experience gained outside China.

TVARDOVSKI, ALEKSANDR TRIFONOVICH

In February 1970 Aleksandr T. Tvardovski, a poet of high repute, resigned from the editorship of *Novy Mir* ("New World"). Founded in 1925 by Anatoli V. Lunacharski, then people's commissar for education, *Novy Mir* had become the leading Soviet literary journal and—as far as possible under a totalitarian political system—a liberal one. At the time of the Stalinist purges its editors had to lie low, but *Novy Mir* became brilliant again when Tvardovski was appointed its editor in 1950.

In 1954, a year after Stalin's death, *Novy Mir* published Ilya G. Ehrenburg's *Thaw,* in which he described the tragedy of an artist under Stalinism. Tvardovski was dismissed, but in 1956 his successor, Konstantin M. Simonov, published Vladimir D. Dudintsev's novel *Not by Bread Alone,* indicting the hypocrisy in Soviet life. Simonov in turn had to go, but in 1958, by order of Premier Nikita S. Khrushchev, Tvardovski returned to the editorship and was given considerable scope.

In 1962 Tvardovski received from Aleksandr I. Solzhenitsyn (*q.v.*), then an unknown writer, the manuscript of his labour camp memoir entitled *One Day in the Life of Ivan Denisovich.* Recognizing in its author a great Russian prose writer—but also recognizing the incriminating character of the work—Tvardovski asked Khrushchev for permission to publish it. Khrushchev agreed, and Solzhenitsyn became famous overnight. But in October 1964 Khrushchev fell from power. Tvardovski soon came under fire, especially since he continued to defend Solzhenitsyn against official ostracism and persecution. Finally, after four key members of his editorial staff had been dismissed, Tvardovski gave up the struggle and resigned his post. Nevertheless, his reputation as a poet was such that he did not fall entirely from favour, and on his 60th birthday he was awarded the Order of the Red Banner "for services in the development of Soviet poetry."

Tvardovski was born on June 21, 1910, at Zagorye, near Smolensk, and graduated in 1939 from the Moscow Institute of History and Philosophy. In 1940 he joined the Communist Party of the Soviet Union, and during World War II he served as war correspondent. By 1954 more than 3.6 million copies of his works had been published in the Soviet Union in 15 different languages.

(K. Sm.)

ULBRICHT, WALTER ERNST KARL

Since Walter Ulbricht had become East Germany's head of state in 1960, his efforts to win international recognition of East Germany as a sovereign state had met with considerable success, particularly in the nonaligned world. By 1970 he had got even the West German government to accept the existence of two German states. In fact, it was Ulbricht who initiated the action that led to meetings between East German Premier Willi Stoph and West German Chancellor Willy Brandt in March and May.

In August, Ulbricht made use of the "basically new situation" in Europe to ask the U.S., the U.K., and France to recognize East Germany and to support UN membership for both East and West Germany. The "new situation" was the establishment of the U.S.S.R.-West German treaty to renounce force. A statement issued by the East German Cabinet noted that the countries of the North Atlantic Alliance had agreed with West Germany's action and that "it follows logically that these countries should now normalize their relations with the German Democratic Republic."

Ulbricht was born in Leipzig on June 30, 1893. At the age of 15 he was a member of the Socialist Workers' Youth Movement and when he was 19 joined the Social Democratic Party. He campaigned against World War I and, as an infantryman, escaped from a train to the Western Front, was caught, and spent some time in prison for desertion. He joined the Communist Party in 1919 and after visiting the Lenin School in Moscow took over a senior post in the organizational department of the German Communist Party.

Ulbricht fled to Paris when Hitler came to power in 1933 and in 1938 took up permanent residence in Moscow, where he helped form the National Committee for a Free Germany. He returned to Berlin on April 30, 1945, at the head of a group of functionaries whose job was to lay the foundations for the revival of Communism in the Soviet Zone. A loyal servant of Moscow, he managed to survive purges in which many of his former comrades perished and skillfully adapted himself to changes of power in the Kremlin and to revisions of Communist ideology.

(N. Cr.)

VON EULER, ULF SVANTE

Ulf von Euler, a Swedish physiologist and professor at the Royal Caroline Institute, was one of three scientists to share the 1970 Nobel Prize for Medicine or Physiology. The others to share the prestigious award, which carries a $78,000 honorarium, were Julius Axelrod of the U.S. National Institute of Mental Health and Sir Bernard Katz, a German-born biophysicist at University College, London (*qq.v.*). All three were honoured for their independent study of nerve impulses.

In the 1940s von Euler made his most dramatic discovery when he determined the identity of the key impulse-carrier in the sympathetic nervous system—noradrenalin, which he found in small granules stored in nerve fibres near the muscles they control. The sympathetic nervous system governs involuntary actions, such as breathing, blood vessel dilation, and reaction to external stimuli. Noradrenalin is found principally in peripheral nerves, though there is some evidence that it may also exist in the brain itself. The enzyme that inhibits its action and its method of reabsorption by nerve tissue were revealed by Axelrod.

Born in Stockholm, Feb. 7, 1905, von Euler received his M.D. from the Royal

Caroline Institute in 1930 and taught there for the next 40 years. His many previous honours included the Swedish Order of the North Star and the Stouffer Prize for his work related to hypertension and arteriosclerosis. In 1929 his father shared the Nobel Prize for Chemistry, and the physiologist himself was a member of the medical prize committee from 1953 to 1960. In 1966 he became president of the Nobel Foundation, but he did not participate in the selection of the 1970 science laureates. (Ph. K.)

WALKER, PETER EDWARD

Not many people set out to make a fortune as a preliminary to going into politics, and succeed in doing it, but that was the story told of Peter Walker, at 38 the youngest minister in the new Cabinet formed after the British general election in June 1970. Walker was born March 25, 1932, and while still a schoolboy he was said to have been advised by a Tory elder statesman, Leopold Amery, to make money first in order to secure his personal independence.

At the age of 20 Walker started his own firm of insurance brokers. At 24, with Edward du Cann, who for a time was chairman of the Conservative Party organization, he launched a highly successful unit trust. After that, with the financier Jim Slater, he formed the Slater-Walker investment bank. By the time he became a minister he was believed to be a millionaire.

But politics rather than money was his first interest. While still at school in the London suburbs, he became chairman of the local Young Conservatives. He was elected to Parliament in 1961, and during the years the Conservatives were in opposition he became a close confidant of Edward Heath, who picked him for the key domestic post of minister of housing and local government, a department that later was converted into the Ministry for the Environment.

Walker was dedicated to the philosophy of private enterprise, but he headed a department that was largely concerned with government intervention through local authorities and planning controls. One of his first acts was to introduce the principle of fair rents—with rent rebates for those too poor to afford the economic rent—for privately owned housing as well as local authority housing. (W. H. Ts.)

WAYNE, JOHN

After 40 years in Hollywood, a big kid from Iowa finally made it as the gruff and tough guy. Marion Michael Morrison won an Oscar in 1970, although it was under the name of John Wayne that he had snarled and scrapped his way to stardom.

Born on May 26, 1907, he went west from a town called Winterset, played professional football, and hired on in Hollywood as a prop boy at 20. In 1931 he got his first starring credit, in *The Big Trail,* which was notable for having been shot in wide screen. Westerns remained his forte—John Ford's 1939 classic *Stagecoach, Red River* nine years later, and in 1960 *The Alamo,* which Wayne also produced and directed. Even when he played an outlaw (*Three Godfathers*), he remained the heroic, straightshooting, two-fisted All-American, with a heart as pure as Ma's apple pie and just as crusty.

His basic character was remarkably adaptable, as World War II proved when he rode *Flying Tigers* instead of mustangs.

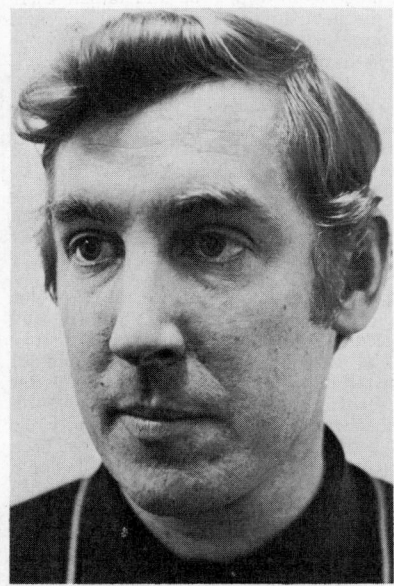

Des Wilson
CAMERA PRESS FROM PIX

DENNIS BRACK FROM BLACK STAR
Leonard Freel Woodcock

Finally there came a character—Rooster Cogburn, the one-eyed, salty-tongued, drunken bounty hunter in *True Grit*—whom many critics immediately identified as Wayne with a larger-than-life eye patch. Wayne presented a bravura parody of his Model A character, and it won him the Academy Award.

Off screen, Wayne was known for his ultraconservative politics, a devotion sometimes reflected in his work, as when he made an anti-Communist-conspiracy movie called *Big Jim McLain* during Sen. Joe McCarthy's heyday. In 1969 he starred in *The Green Berets,* the single contemporary Vietnam war film.

In "the business" as well as on screen, "Duke" Wayne showed a rare talent to survive and thrive. One of the few stars of the giant studios' golden age to hold his rank in the era of independents, he had widespread financial interests. He was among the first to see the tax benefits of deferred earnings. While some stars in the 1950s demanded a share of a film's gross income or net profits, Wayne made a three-film deal that guaranteed him $2 million in salary, spread over 20 years.   (Ph. K.)

WILLIAMS, ERIC
One of the many black leaders of Caribbean governments to cope with "Black Power" militancy during 1970 was Eric Williams, prime minister of Trinidad and Tobago. Riots rocked his island nation for a week in the spring as mobs demonstrated against high unemployment, inflation, and the fact that a white minority controlled most of the island's wealth. The crisis was complicated when half of the 720-man Army mutinied against an unpopular commander.

Williams declared a state of emergency and asked for military matériel from Venezuela and the U.S. Meantime, his loyal Coast Guard and police force isolated the dissident soldiers who had captured an arsenal where most of the island's arms were stored.

Ultimately, peace was restored, but not before four persons had died and the nation's schisms were revealed. As in Bermuda, Jamaica, and elsewhere in the English-speaking West Indies, dissident black citizens continued to rally around extremist banners to oppose their own elected, so-called "Afro-Saxon" governments. Williams' response to the crisis was to fire the unpopular commander, which ended the Army mutiny, and to announce an ambitious new five-year program of housing construction and rural development.

Born in Trinidad Sept. 25, 1911, Williams was educated at Oxford University. After receiving his doctorate he went to the U.S. where he taught sociology and political science at Howard University in Washington, D.C. In 1948 he was appointed to the Caribbean Commission, a group concerned with the economic and social development of the Caribbean colonies. In 1955 he began the organization of the People's National Movement, which dominated island politics and engineered independence from the U.K. in 1962.

As the first prime minister of independent Trinidad and Tobago, Williams practiced what has been called "empirical socialism," which stresses social services, improved education, and economic development through the cautious attraction of foreign investment capital.   (Ph. K.)

WILSON, DES
In less than five years Des Wilson made Shelter, a national campaign for the homeless, one of the best-known charities in Britain, and in the process made himself one of the nation's best-known charity organizers. Joining Shelter in 1966 as publicity adviser at the age of 25, he became its director during the following year. In 1970 he announced his decision to move to another job before he ran out of ideas. In that time, Shelter had raised nearly £3 million and helped to rehouse approximately 5,000 families.

Wilson was, at times, criticized for seeking personal publicity. It was true that the Shelter campaigns were accompanied by a torrent of words from him, in newspapers, on television and on the radio, and in speeches throughout the country. But Wilson frankly conceded that that was his manner of operation. "From the word go," he wrote, "the emphasis has been on publicity. I've not hesitated to allow myself to be pushed forward as a public personality."

Wilson was a campaigner with passion. Shelter became known for its scalding series of pamphlets, posters, and newspaper advertisements, with headings such as "Home Sweet Hell." From the start Wilson pitched into the complacency of official statistics which acknowledged fewer than 20,000 homeless in the whole of Britain. In his first research report in 1966 he wrote, "My research confirms that thousands of families are fighting for their very existence in appalling housing conditions and that many are falling through the net of the welfare state."

A native of New Zealand, Wilson was born March 5, 1941. He left school at 15 to become a newspaper reporter and reached England via Australia in 1960. On leaving Shelter, he was to have been appointed director of the watchdog Consumer Council. That organization died when the Conservative government withdrew its grant, however, and Wilson joined the staff of *The Observer* as a columnist on social issues.
          (W. H. Ts.)

WOODCOCK, LEONARD FREEL
Until Walter Reuther's sudden death in a plane crash in May 1970, it had appeared that Leonard Woodcock would never gain national prominence as a U.S. labour figure. Although a top-ranking union vice-president, Woodcock, at 59, had been considered too close to Reuther's own age to succeed him as president of the United Automobile Workers upon his anticipated retirement in 1974. After a brief internal political struggle, Woodcock took charge of the 1.4 million member union and promptly faced the challenge of negotiating a new, three-year contract with Detroit automakers.

Negotiations dragged on through the summer and by September it was obvious that both the union's members and General Motors, selected as the "target company" for settlement, were itching for a showdown and strike.

The principal issue was money; inflation had badly eroded the pay increases of the last contract. Woodcock demanded unlimited cost-of-living increases and a settlement that GM said would amount to a 45% wage increase over three years. Woodcock also pushed hard for "30 and out," a demand that workers be allowed to retire at $500 a month anytime after serving 30 years in the plants.

Under the new agreement, reached November 11 after a two-month shutdown of GM's 145 plants, Woodcock accomplished most of his money goals, including a 20% raise over the life of the contract, and compromised on the retirement issue. GM negotiators acknowledged that Woodcock was every bit as tough a bargainer as Reuther, and UAW members applauded their new leader's nerve.

Regarded as an intellectual in the labour movement, Woodcock was a mild appearing yet completely frank man with a keen and incisive mind leavened with a dash of wit. Like Reuther, he was a social activist, and under his leadership the union was likely to change little in direction or tone, or to return to the AFL-CIO, which Reuther left in 1968 because, he said, it was too conservative on social matters.

Born Feb. 15, 1911, in Providence, R.I., Woodcock was a Socialist (like Reuther) in his youth, later left the party and was an early organizer for the UAW in auto plants in the 1930s. His career was stopped twice by tuberculosis, once in 1936, when he was stricken for a year, and again in 1969, when his recovery was more rapid.   (M. B. Su.)

Biological Sciences

One of many indications that the 1970s would see a major reorientation of the biological sciences was the establishment of the Council for Biology in Human Affairs, under the direction of Jacob Bronowski, at the Salk Institute for Biological Studies, San Diego, Calif. The council was planned as "an international organization which will study the present and future social and humanistic implications of discoveries in the life sciences." The need for such an organization stemmed from a growth of awareness—not only of the horrors of biological warfare but of the delicacy of the balance between good and evil in many aspects of modern biology, notably those involving possibilities of tampering with the human personality (the various brain sciences; drugs and food additives; genetic engineering; transparent surgery; etc.).

The most striking aspect of this awareness was the explosive growth of concern for the terrestrial environment. Even in the late 1960s this was still commonly regarded as the stamping ground of nature-loving faddists, but in 1970 it became a favourite theme for politicians and publicists of all kinds. Ecology, formerly the Cinderella of the sciences, suddenly became the heir apparent to nuclear physics as the politically dominant science, assuming the social responsibilities and ethical problems that go with the rank. Public policies that science shows to be desirable or even essential usually are expensive and clash with important private interests. In attempting to save the world from pollution, mismanagement, and destructive exploitation, ecologists must be prepared to plunge themselves into the polluted waters of politics at all levels.

The year saw some fine achievements to their credit. The success of the International Biological Program, planned to end in 1971, justified the formation of two new international organizations to continue its work, namely the semipermanent Man and Biosphere (MAB) program and the Special Committee on the Problems of the Environment (SCOPE). Also, the brilliant successes of the antilocust campaigns in recent years were noteworthy for their dependence on close cooperation between numerous states in a part of the world where political animosities were strong (see *Entomology,* below). This cooperation was extended to deal with other pests of international significance, starting with the armyworm moth and weaverbird (*Quelea*). Control efforts for the latter would have to be international since, unlike most widely distributed species of organisms, this bird exists as a single continuous population covering almost the whole of Africa.

The spectacular news items, however, continued to be new variations and developments of the nature of the genetic code, the replication and transcription of deoxyribonucleic acid (DNA) through ribonucleic acid (RNA) to protein synthesis by the ribosomes, and the continued spread of the influence of the principles and techniques of molecular biology into other branches of biology (*see* MOLECULAR BIOLOGY). This work was accompanied by notable advances in cell surgery and in biochemistry.   (H. SA.)

Botany. Work in many laboratories continued to be directed toward an understanding of the relationship between chloroplasts and the rest of the cell. While one factor that could limit the degree of autonomy of the chloroplast was known to be the amount of coded information (in the form of DNA strands) each chloroplast contained, it was not known whether this quantity was in the form of a single nonrepeating sequence or of a number of reiterated sequences. In 1970, the first reports on the complexity of chloroplast DNA appeared and provided evidence that in *Lactuca* (lettuce) and *Euglena* the chloroplast DNA was extensively reiterated. Thus it appeared probable that the coding capacities of these DNAs were more akin to that of a large virus than to that of a bacterium. Evidence also was accumulated, both from DNA/RNA hybridization and from inhibitor studies, to indicate that chloroplast DNA contained the sequences coding for chloroplast ribosomal RNA. It was not possible, however, to obtain unequivocal data to show that any particular enzyme was coded for and synthesized inside the chloroplast.

The recently developed scanning electron microscope (SEM) was applied to a wider range of problems in botanical research than in previous years, and promised to become a major tool in the study of microtopography. It was found that certain plant tissues were sufficiently moist to conduct electrons without the need for the metal coating used previously in work on pollen grains and other surfaces, and that the water was retained for a sufficient time to allow the specimen to be photographed in its (presumably) natural state. It also was possible to obtain good results with tissues fixed and soaked in glycerin. Scanning electron microscopy was used to study the leaf surfaces of the insectivorous plants *Pinguicula grandifolia* and *Dionaea muscipula* (Venus's-flytrap), the morphology of the shoot apex of *Tropaeolum,* the fungi living symbiotically in the "fungus gardens" of Attine ants, the state of chloroplasts in in vitro preparations, the cell surfaces of plant tissue callous cultures, the structure of cereal pollen, and the occurrence of *Endosporites* in fossilized lycopsid sporangia.

A group of algal taxonomists showed that the class Xanthophyceae contained a group of genera that shared a number of characteristics not normally associated with the Xanthophyceae. They proposed the formation of a new algal class, the Eustigmatophyceae, to be distinguished from the Xanthophyceae by a number of features, particularly of the motile cell.

As perhaps expected, the analysis of the moon rock samples collected during the Apollo 11 and 12 missions showed no evidence of life, botanical or otherwise. In addition, no deleterious or toxic effects were reported when whole plants and tissue cultures of pine, corn, rice, soybean, sunflower, tobacco, *Haplopappus,* and *Euphorbia* were challenged with moon soil. In fact, several species, including ferns, liverworts, and sunflower and tobacco cultures responded with marked increases in mass and pigmentation. The relationship between these results and the inorganic content of the moon soil was still under investigation.

The mechanism by which certain blue-green algae perform gliding and creeping movements (four centimetres per hour was recorded in 1% agar) had long puzzled botanists. In 1970, arrays of fibrils were observed in the walls of freeze-etched and sectioned algae, *Oscillatoria princeps,* and the suggestion was made that waves of deformation of these arrays when acting against a solid substrate could cause such movements. Although no direct evidence was found to support this hypothesis, circumstantial evidence included observations that the algal filaments were only able to move when in contact with a solid substratum and that the gliding movements were always associated with a right-handed rotation.

During the year, the first step in the development of a method of raising hybrid plants by fusing single somatic (nonreproductive) cells was reported. Plant protoplasts (cells freed from their walls) were isolated in sucrose solution and then transferred to sodium nitrate solution, which conditioned the cell membranes for fusion. Most of the fusion experiments were between protoplasts of the same species, but some fusion between *Avena sativa* (oat) and *Zea mays* (corn) protoplasts was reported. It was clear that much further work would be required before the production of whole, functioning hybrid plants from cultured cells became possible. (C. L. F. W.)

Marine Biology. In 1970 further studies of the physiology of larval fish supplied knowledge useful for fish rearing. It was found in Loch Ewe, Scotland, that from April to July the change in light intensity was such that the time available for feeding by larval plaice increased from 12 to 20 hours, and that for metamorphosed plaice, from 16 to 24 hours. Late spawned larvae might thus have an advantage and grow faster. In a number of species of larval fish studied, the retina in the eye at first had only cones, the rods developing later. Sole larvae could feed in the dark soon after hatching; plaice larvae only at metamorphosis.

In some deep-sea fish the ventral photophores have chambers, in which light is produced, with strongly reflecting walls. These open into structures with reflecting surfaces that distribute the light after passing through a layer of coloured tissue. It was found that this coloured tissue acts as a filter allowing blue-green light to pass. In such fish as *Argyropelecus*, the light emitted from the photophores would thus match the colour of the daylight at depths at which they live, and help camouflage by reducing the shadows on their ventral surfaces. In other fish, such as *Pachystomias*, there are also large photophores close to the eyes covered with tissue transmitting only red light, to which its retinal pigments are probably very sensitive. The fish would thus be well fitted for hunting or avoiding the red or brown animals that live in the middle depths of the ocean.

The silver layers in fish, principally guanin, were known to function as light reflectors in scales and tapetum. But it was found that when such layers occur lining the body cavity, and surrounding the swim bladder, kidney, heart, and eyes, they have another function. It was shown for the swim bladder that the silver layer acts as a relatively impermeable barrier, especially to nitrogen, oxygen, and carbon dioxide. Its permeability was only one-hundredth that of connective tissue.

A school of fish, *Lutianus monostigma,* was kept under almost daily observation for four months in a shallow reef environment off the Aldabra Islands, British Indian Ocean Territory. During the whole of this time the school remained within a limited home range. The structure of the school varied according to the strength of the current. It broke up in the morning and evening, probably because of the fish's crepuscular feeding habits. The fright reactions of the school were studied in relation to the intensity of the fright. Another Indian Ocean fish, *Siphania argentea,* lives usually within the interradial spaces of the sea urchin *Astropyga radiata,* whose coloration it resembles. When all the space is filled, those fish that are left

out form a dense group around the urchin to resemble a large urchin. Another fish, *Plutosus anguillaris,* also forms groups so dense that the individuals touch each other.

A remarkable sex change was discovered in a Red Sea fish, *Anthias squamipinnis*. If female fish are kept together in an aquarium without a male, one of them gradually will change sex. After two weeks it has developed the typical colour pattern and behaviour of the male. If the male is removed, another is produced; thus, in one year 20 females were turned into 20 males. Females will not change sex if they can see a male, although separated from it by a glass plate. In nature 90% are females, the few males each taking up their individual territories; thus the greater part of the population can be reproducing females.

Eight tuna tagged in California were recaptured two to four years later near Japan, a migration of some 4,500 mi. Two tagged off Japan were caught off California within a year.

The starfish *Marthasterias glacialis* continually secretes a sterol-glycoside containing ester sulfate; amounts of this less than 0.1 μg induce a behavioural response in the whelk *Buccinum undatum. Platynereis dumerilii* is a polychaete that swarms in a so-called "nuptial dance" coincident with lunar phases. It was found that the exciting substance that incites the nuptial dance is present in the body surface and the coelomic fluid but not in the genital products. It is emitted by both males and females.

Mature female lobsters, *Homarus,* release a sex attractant substance, or pheromone, during the molt period. It was found that different kinds of hair on the limbs and mouthparts of the lobster are associated with chemoreception. Such hairs lack tanning distally, and this would afford a route through which chemicals could permeate.

A remarkable symbiotic advantage was shown between the commensal polynoid worm *Arctonoë vittata* and the keyhole limpet *Diodora aspera*. If the tube feet of a starfish *Pisaster* touched the mantle of the limpet, the worm bit the starfish, but it would not do this if isolated from the limpet. If denied access to sand, the burrowing polychaete *Nephtys* is stimulated to swim by increased pressure, while decrease of pressure inhibits swimming.

It was found that young *Octopus cyanea,* about one centimetre long, soon established "homes" on the bottom, chiefly in gastropod shells. They defended them against members of their own species. They always took their prey, mainly crabs, home to eat. Their method of capture of prey and morning and evening activities were typically adult. It was confirmed that octopuses use their beaks and radulas to eat their food, and do not use external digestion as was once supposed. The tropical gastropods *Cymatium* fed on mollusks, and *Bursa* ate polychaetes and sipunculids. A paralyzing fluid is first expelled from the mouth, and *Cymatium* then bites pieces from its prey by means of its strong jaws and radula, while *Bursa* swallows worms whole.

A remarkable film showed the mating behaviour of the giant octopus, *Octopus dofleini martini.* Its spermatophores, each over one metre long, contain ropes of up to 10^{10} spermatozoa in the proximal portion. The distal end is placed into the mantle cavity of the female by the hectocotylized arm. Mating lasts two to three hours. For the first time the squid *Sepioteuthis sepioidea* was reared from egg to adult in the laboratory, fed on mysids of which, when five days old, it could eat 50 a day. The squids mature five months after hatching. Rearing of squid could prove of value to physiologists who use its giant axon for neurological research. (F. S. Rl.)

Zoology. A number of interesting findings involving animal behaviour appeared during 1970. Among these was new evidence for homing behaviour in salamanders. Radioactive tags in the form of tantalum wires three–five millimetres long were injected into the abdomens of salamanders of the species *Plethodon jordani.* A scintillation radiation detection system, accompanied by direct observation under subdued lantern light at night, was used to follow the animals' movements. The study was conducted in North Carolina by D. M. Madison of the University of Maryland and C. R. Shoop of the University of Rhode Island. Homing movements were clearly demonstrated in these animals, and the authors concluded that this species has a well-developed homing orientation mechanism, presumably associated with olfaction.

The first report of a side-swimming cetacean, *Platanista gangetica,* the "blind" dolphin of the muddy waters of the Ganges, Indus, and Brahmaputra river systems in India and Pakistan, was made by investigators from California. Although the dolphin is not totally blind, its eye is usually not visible externally, being concealed in the skin. Three specimens, captured remarkably free of injuries, were observed swimming in clear water. They swam on their sides in either a clockwise or counterclockwise direction, and a pectoral flipper either touched the bottom or trailed about two–three centimetres above it. The tail was kept higher than the head in this unique mode of swimming, never before seen in members of this order of mammals. A study of the dolphin's skull disclosed that flanges of the maxillary bones may act as acoustic baffles to direct returning sonic pulses into a narrow beam, thereby facilitating echolocation, the ability of an animal to fix its position by emitting sounds and then receiving them back after they rebound from objects in the environment.

Noel and Helen Snyder of the University of South Florida found that if one member of a clump of the sea urchin *Diadema antillarum* is crushed, the other members flee a metre or so from the site in great "alarm," mounted on their ventral spines. The Snyders could not readily explain why this species of urchin should be so sensitive to its own juices except to assume that such movement might help avoid predation. The failure of the juices from other species of urchins to initiate the response was attributed to their poor taxonomic relationship to *Diadema antillarum.*

Still another behavioural study lent support to the view that there is a correlation between taxonomic position and nesting behaviour in crocodilians. Early work had indeed suggested such a correlation, but later work seemed not to support it. Most recently, however, A. E. Greer of the Harvard Museum of Comparative Zoology found that crocodilians can be divided into two groups, hole nesters and mound nesters. Presumably the common Eusuchian ancestor was a hole nester, using the primitive mode of nesting. It gave rise early to the family Gavialidae, also hole nesters, and to the subfamily Crocodylinae, which gave rise to a number of crocodilians with both types of nesting habits. Presumably the mound nesting line of the genus *Crocodylus* gave rise to other mound nesting groups, including the alligators, which are presumed to be mound nesters, although complete information was lacking. Greer's study made it appar-

KEYSTONE

A specialist dissects dinosaur eggs discovered in May 1970 by a joint Soviet and Mongolian paleontology expedition in the Gobi Desert.

ent that there is some correlation between nesting behaviour and taxonomic position among crocodilians, even though the genus *Crocodylus* cannot be characterized firmly as either hole or mound nesting.

There were also reports of changes in the known distributions of animals. S. H. Hopkins and J. D. Andrews called attention to an apparently large (1,000-mi.) increase in the range of a brackish-water clam, *Rangia cuneata,* which had been thought to be extinct on the East Coast of the U.S. since the Pleistocene and restricted to Gulf Coast estuaries. The reappearance of this clam in estuaries on the East Coast from Florida to Maryland was probably the result of either an invasion from the Gulf Coast or the explosion of a small, undiscovered population surviving since the Pleistocene in East Coast rivers. Whichever explanation was correct, it was also probable that the East Coast population was capable of surviving lower temperatures than was the Gulf Coast population.

Another distributional finding of importance concerned the occurrence of *Neopilina* in the South Atlantic Ocean. This primitive mollusk, of the class Monoplacophora, had been reported previously in the Pacific and Indian oceans. Its presence in the Atlantic supported the view that this group, once thought to be extinct, may be fairly widely distributed at abyssal ocean depths.

Another report tended to dispel the common belief that there are no semiterrestrial shrimps and prawns. L. G. Abele of Florida State University observed a semiterrestrial shrimp, *Merguia rhizophorae,* along the Atlantic coast of Panama. This shrimp resides on mangroves or driftwood and has a well-developed walking or leaping ability and certain appendages (pereiopods) that are more robust than those of most marine shrimps and that can support the body on land.

In the field of parasitology, S. C. Ayala and D. Lee of the Agricultural Experiment Station of the University of California at Berkeley reported the first case of the probable transmission of malaria by an insect other than a mosquito. In this case, the malaria organism, *Plasmodium mexicanum,* was transmitted by the sandflies *Lutzomyia vexatrix* and *L. stewarti.* The vertebrate host was *Sceloporus occidentalis,* the western fence lizard. (R. R. No.)

Entomology. In July 1970 the 25th anniversary of

the Anti-Locust Research Centre was the occasion of an international study conference in London. Delegates were told by the centre's director, Peter T. Haskell, that the 1967–68 upsurge in populations of the desert locust, *Schistocerca gregaria,* over an area extending from West Africa to the Red Sea had been successfully suppressed. By the beginning of 1970 no hopper bands were being reported. The future emphasis in research on locust control, said Haskell, would be to find more selective methods of killing the insects in order to replace the broad spectrum of insecticides currently in use.

Meanwhile, research workers throughout the world continued to seek methods for the control of individual species of insect pests. One possibility that received much attention was the use of pheromones —the secretions released by insects that modify the behaviour of other individuals of the same species. It was thought that if pheromones could be identified and manufactured, they might be used to confuse the behaviour of a pest species or lure it to insecticidal traps.

Teams at the Zoecon Corp. in California and at the U.S. Department of Agriculture's Boll Weevil Research Laboratory in Mississippi isolated from the feces of the male boll weevil four terpenes that attracted the female. When synthesized, the compounds were effective only when they were the correct stereoisomers, and when they were mixed in the correct proportions.

At the same time, a surprising feature of reports by several workers was that pheromones could attract more than one species. Thus W. L. Roelofs and J. P. Tette of Cornell University found that cis-11-tetradecenyl acetate was a sex attractant for males of two tortricid leaf-roller moths, *Argyrotaenia velutiana* and *Choristoneura rosaceana.* But they also found that the trans isomer was a strong repellent under field conditions. They postulated that when the same compound was a sex pheromone of more than one species, sexual isolation of each species was achieved by combination of the attractant with secondary substances in the natural secretion that repelled all but the "right" species.

A different class of pheromone is the "alarm" pheromone that in ants alerts the workers to attack prey or enemies. R. A. and R. L. Metcalf of the University of Illinois reported that 2-heptanone, the natural alarm pheromone in *Iridomyrmex* and *Conomyrma* species, could be replaced by other compounds of similar nature and molecular shape. One compound, hexanoylchloride, had the curious effect, however, of provoking violent combat between workers of the same nest.

The internal hormones of insects also continued to excite interest. Juvenile hormone, the compound that controls the development of insects by delaying the onset of maturity, can be synthesized or replaced by similar compounds. When a synthetic preparation was applied to the eggs of insects such as the plant-sucking bug, *Oncopeltus fasciatus,* the treated insects appeared to develop normally until the time when they should have become adults. At this stage they molted to become supernumerary giant larvae, or forms intermediate between larva and adult. Light was shed on the physiological mechanism underlying this phenomenon when L. M. Riddiford of Harvard University found a way to reverse the effect of the treatment. In immature insects, juvenile hormone is released from a pair of glands, the corpora allata, that lie just behind the brain. If these glands were extir-

pated just before the final molt, the treated insects became normal adults. Thus the result of the treatment of the eggs with the hormone had been to cause abnormal activity in the insect's own endocrine system. The treatment had not, for instance, altered any long-term "programming" of the molting tissues themselves.

Other workers found a remarkable link between the susceptibility of insects to insecticides and their "circadian rhythms"—the periodicity of activities that many insects show in every 24 hours. H. Rothert of the Max von Pettenkofer Institute, West Berlin, found that the susceptibility of the vinegar fly, *Drosophila,* to parathion was closely linked with diurnal variations in the activity of the fly. Such variations are induced by the regime of light and dark periods in which the insect is reared, and when the time of peak activity was manipulated by altering the regime, the time of maximum susceptibility changed accordingly. W. N. Sullivan and co-workers at the U.S. Department of Agriculture laboratories at Beltsville, Md., independently discovered the same phenomenon and, as a result of their work, were able to report that the most effective time to attack cockroaches and houseflies with household insecticides was about 4 P.M.

For many years, a familiar story in textbooks of entomology had been the way in which dark variants of the peppered moth, *Biston betularia,* gradually replaced its lighter forms in northern England after the Industrial Revolution. The light-coloured individuals, so it was argued, had been too easily visible to predatory birds in the soot-grimed environments of the north. Some interesting new results obtained at the Institute of Forestry Research in Vienna threw doubt on this interpretation. E. Jahn and C. Holzschuh found that when they bred the nun moth, *Lymantria monacha,* under various kinds of environmental stress, such as high density, poor nutrition, or continuous exposure to parathion, the melanized (dark) variants had a selective advantage and came to predominate over the lighter forms, without any intervention by predators. On the other hand, the dark forms were more susceptible to polyhedrosis diseases, and this probably explained why, in otherwise suitable environments, it was the light-coloured individuals that had the advantage.   (P. W. Mi.)

Ornithology. The major event in 1970 was the 15th International Ornithological Congress, held in the Netherlands in September. Perhaps the most significant of the discussions concerned the mounting threat of chemical pollution, and specifically the effect of organochlorine insecticides on birdlife. The highest residue levels of these persistent toxic chemicals were being found in bodies of birds that eat other birds or fish, or that feed on marine plankton, including the goshawk, osprey, and great crested grebe in Europe, and the peregrine falcon, bald eagle, and brown pelican in North America.

As eggs of the bobwhite quail (*Colinus virginianus*) approach hatching, the embryos inside signal to one another. The signaling results in "bringing on" the less developed embryos and the "holding back" of the more advanced ones so that all will hatch together—within, say, an hour—and be able to move off with their mother together. Clicking and vocal sounds were recorded on tape by Margaret A. Vince of Cambridge University. Eggs in close proximity in an incubator hatched together; singles, all of the same age, hatched over a two-day period.

Roosting birds generally have two requirements:

COURTESY, WAITE AGRICULTURAL
RESEARCH INSTITUTE

A novel means of sectioning whole insects by embedding them first in agar was developed at the Waite Agricultural Research Institute in Australia. This example shows the internal organs of a male cricket.

protection from predators and shelter from adverse weather. But W. R. Seifried of the Percy FitzPatrick Institute of African Ornithology, University of Cape Town, suggested that with communal roosting there is a third and probably overriding requirement: the need to convey information about the availability of food. The nightly aggregation acts as an information centre. Birds that have fed well the previous day leave the roost purposefully in the morning. Those that fed badly tag along behind and thus are guided to favourable feeding grounds.

Further work on the jockey behaviour of the northern carmine bee-eater (*Merops nubicus nubicus*) and a summary of previous observation showed that this bird has been known to use four species of domestic mammal, and nine species of wild bird, as "beaters." The bird waits for its steed to flush a grasshopper and then sallies forth to capture the prey thus usefully exposed. Particularly favoured steeds are the kori or giant bustard (*Ardeotis kori*) and the Arabian bustard (*Ardeotis arabs*).

The ornithological effect of Hurricane Gladys was analyzed by E. L. Mills in the *Nova Scotia Bird Society News Letter*. Gladys originated in the Caribbean, crossed Cuba and Florida, wandered up the East Coast of North America to Cape Hatteras, N.C., made a circuit out to sea, and eventually dumped a mixed bag of land and sea birds, including tens of thousands of laughing gulls (*Larus atricilla*) and 1,000-odd black skimmers (*Rhynchops nigra*), on the coast of Nova Scotia. The gulls must have returned south either at a high altitude or well offshore as they were not observed, but the skimmers were seen passing down the littoral of first Nova Scotia and then New England for six weeks afterward.

Studies on the biology of the edible-nest swiftlets of Southeast Asia, carried out by Lord Medway, suggested that if the populations were to be maintained on a sustained yield basis, changes would be necessary in the rules governing the collection of nests. The species nidificates in huge totally dark caves where the birds find their way by echolocation. However, the sensitivity afforded by the calls used for this purpose is insufficient for the location of prey, but does allow nocturnal flighting to distant daytime feeding sites.

The singing of duets by pairs of mated tropical boubou shrikes was reported on by T. and B. I. Hooker. Each pair has a number of duet patterns or "songs." Either partner can initiate a duet. Duetting occurs throughout the year between members of an established pair occupying and defending a territory. The birds probably pair for several seasons, if not for life. Duetting helps to maintain the bond between family groups in dense vegetation, and is used in joint aggressive vocal display during territorial disputes.

The use of tools by birds (indeed by any animal except man) is very rare. It was therefore of particular interest to record that wild brown-headed nuthatchers (*Sitta pusilla*) were observed using bits of bark scale to pry pieces of bark off trunks and limbs of trees to get at insects. In Britain a captive bare-eyed cockatoo, when offered a dead matchstick, would hold it in the claw and quite deliberately use it to scratch the throat area immediately below the bill.

An important reference book published during the year was *An Atlas of Speciation in African Passerine Birds* by B. P. Hall and R. E. Moreau, published by the trustees of the British Museum (Natural History). It was the first attempt to show the continu-

DOUGLAS FISHER

A northern carmine bee-eater rides an Arabian bustard, using it as a "beater" to flush grasshoppers for it to dart forth and capture.

ing process of evolution in a continental avifauna by plotting on one map the distribution of species believed to be immediately descended from a common ancestor. The distribution of nearly 1,000 species was depicted.

E. T. Gilliard's *Birds of Paradise and Bower Birds* dealt with a group of birds in which "arena displays" have evolved to a degree of elaboration unique in the animal kingdom. The author theorized that in the course of evolution of these birds the use of external objects, often brightly coloured ones, to decorate the bower acquired the function of secondary sexual characteristics, and that, associated with this, there was a tendency for males to lose their conspicuous plumage.

(J. H. Bo.)

See also Conservation; Gardening; Medicine.

ENCYCLOPÆDIA BRITANNICA FILMS. *How Pine Trees Reproduce—Pine Cone Biology* (1963); *Life Between Tides* (1963); *Life Story of the Hummingbird* (1963); *Life Story of the Oyster* (1963); *Life Story of the Sea Star* (1963); *The Marine Biologist* (1963); *Metamorphosis—Life Story of the Wasp* (1963); *Life Story of a Water Flea* (*Daphnia*) (1965); *Life Story of the Ladybird Beetle* (1965); *Message from a Dinosaur* (1965); *Army Ants: Study In Social Behavior* (1966); *Discovering the Forest* (1966); *Experimenting with Animals* (*White Rats*) (1966); *The Fish in a Changing Environment* (1966); *Flowering Plants* (1966); *Food from the Sun* (1966); *Green Plants and Sunlight* (1966); *Life Story of a Grasshopper* (1966); *The Marsh Community* (1966); *A Plant Through the Seasons* (*Apple Tree*) (1966); *Trees and Their Importance* (1966); *Chromosomes of Man* (1967); *Life Story of a Social Insect: The Ant* (1967); *Looking at Mammals* (1967); *Monarch Butterfly Story* (2nd ed., 1967); *Photosynthesis* (2nd ed., 1967); *Water for Living Things* (1967); *Insect Parasitism—The Alder Woodwasp and Its Enemies* (1968); *The Ears and Hearing* (2nd ed., 1969); *Muscle: Chemistry of Contraction* (1969); *Muscle: Dynamics of Contraction* (1969); *Muscle: Electrical Activity of Contraction* (1969); *The Origin of Life—Chemical Evolution* (1969); *Radioisotopes: Tools of Discovery* (1969); *Theories on the Origin of Life* (1969); *Succession on Lava* (1970).

Bolivia

A landlocked republic in central South America, Bolivia is bordered by Brazil, Paraguay, Argentina, Chile, and Peru. Area: 424,162 sq.mi. (1,098,581 sq.km.). Pop. (1969 est.): 4.5 million, of whom more than 50% were Indian. Language: officially Spanish. Religion: Roman Catholic. Legal and judicial cap.: Sucre (pop., 1966 est., 59,701). Seat of government and largest city: La Paz (pop., 1966 est., 362,298). Presidents in 1970, Gen. Alfredo Ovando Candía and, from October 7, Gen. Juan José Torres Gonzales.

In 1970 the left-wing forces of Bolivian nationalism that General Ovando Candía had tried to harness to his economic program, against growing resistance

CAMERA PRESS FROM PIX

Gen. Juan José Torres Gonzales took over the presidency of Bolivia in October 1970 after ousting a military triumvirate that had forced the resignation of the previous president, Ovando Candía.

from conservative elements in the Army, finally found expression. After a week of political convulsions the left-wing General Torres (*see* BIOGRAPHY) took over the presidency on October 7.

Since late September Ovando had been under strong pressure from right-wing officers headed by Gen. Rogelio Miranda—who had supplanted Torres in July as effective chief of the armed forces—to resign in favour of a military triumvirate with the declared aim of restoring constitutional rule and preparing for elections. On October 6 Miranda occupied the presidential palace in La Paz; Ovando resigned and was given asylum in the Argentine embassy. This right-wing coup provoked an outcry from organized forces of the left—mineworkers, peasants, students, and political parties. Rallying round Torres, they swept him into power the next day, causing Miranda, in turn, to obtain asylum first in the Paraguayan and then in the Argentine embassy.

At his first international press conference on October 10 the new president said that Bolivia would recognize Cuba in line with a policy of establishing relations with all countries, and called on the Organization of American States to turn itself into a body "responding more to the real problems" of its Latin-American members. Torres promised to honour Ovando's pledge to compensate the U.S.-owned Bolivian Gulf Oil Co., after whose nationalization in October 1969 Ovando had agreed to pay $70 million, half of the compensation claimed by the U.S. parent company.

Outlining his attitude to external aid, Torres said that it would have to be multilateral but warned that foreign investment would be subject to a law which "while guaranteeing private capital in a state economy will progressively nationalize foreign capital and also allow the people to participate in investments."

The policy he thus envisaged was plainly calculated to cement the allegiance of his left-wing support from outside the Army; however, his first Cabinet (of five military officers and nine civilians) contained none of the more extreme Marxist elements. It also excluded Col. Samuel Gallardo, commander of the so-called "revolutionary army" that had mobilized support for the Torres coup.

The country's economic position gradually improved in 1970. According to the official figures total investments had slumped from $28 million in 1968 to $7 million in 1969, and the nationalization of the Bolivian Gulf Oil Co. had seemed to foreshadow a further worsening. Early in 1970, however, the resumption of U.S. military aid was followed by international loans for industrial, agricultural, and public works projects. During the first quarter of 1970 the world price of tin (Bolivia's economic mainstay) was 17% higher than in the same quarter of 1969, and in May the Banco Central's international reserves stood at $49.9 million, representing a rise of $16.6 million over the preceding 12 months.

All the nation's tin mines were operating profitably; Bolivia's first tin smelter was being built at Vinto, where a Japanese firm declared itself interested in setting up an antimony refinery; and there was some talk of developing a petrochemical industry. Meanwhile, the oil industry's prospects were brightened by the resumption of shipments to the U.S. and an agreement with Camba (a firm backed by the Spanish government) to market Bolivian oil abroad. In the manufacturing sector, diversification continued to make progress.

Significant evidence of an economic rapprochement with the Soviet Union was the signing of a commercial treaty between the two countries. Bolivia received a Soviet loan of $28 million and agreed to supply large quantities of tin to the Soviet Union.

(D. K. DA.; X.)

BOLIVIA
Education. (1967) Primary, pupils 556,280, teachers (1965) 17,841; secondary, pupils 102,321, teachers (1965) 3,921; vocational, pupils 10,903, teachers (1965) 1,404; teacher training, students 7,989, teachers (1965) 461; higher (including 7 universities), students 13,312.
Finance. Monetary unit: peso boliviano, with a selling rate of 11.88 pesos to U.S. $1 (28.51 pesos = £1 sterling). Gold, SDRs, and foreign exchange, central bank: (June 1970) U.S. $51.3 million; (June 1969) U.S. $45.9 million. Budget (1969 rev. est.) balanced at 1,265,300,000 pesos. Gross national product: (1969) 10,468,000,000 pesos; (1968) 9,625,000,000 pesos. Money supply: (March 1970) 1,321,300,000 pesos; (March 1969) 1,225,300,000 pesos. Cost of living (La Paz; 1963 = 100): (Feb. 1970) 149; (Feb. 1969) 144.
Foreign Trade. Imports (1968) U.S. $151.7 million; exports (1969) U.S. $209.2 million. Import sources: U.S. 42%; West Germany 13%; Japan 11%; Argentina 7%; U.K. 5%. Export destinations (1968): U.K. 45%; U.S. 35%; Argentina 5%. Main exports: tin 49%; antimony 5%; tungsten 5%; silver 5%.
Transport and Communications. Roads (1968) 24,985 km. (including 11,324 km. all-weather). Motor vehicles in use (1968): passenger 14,500; commercial (including buses) 24,900. Railways (1967) 3,560 km. Air traffic (1968): 61.4 million passenger-km.; freight 1,380,000 net ton-km. Telephones (Jan. 1969) c. 32,300. Radio receivers (Dec. 1965) 525,000.
Agriculture. Production (in 000; metric tons; 1967; 1966 in parentheses): corn c. 250 (271); wheat c. 60 (c. 70); barley (1968) 57, (1967) 56; potatoes c. 670 (635); cassava 149 (c. 170); citrus fruit (1968) 38, (1967) c. 38; sugar, raw value (1969–70) c. 117, (1968–69) c. 111; rubber (exports) c. 3 (3).
Industry. Production (in 000; metric tons; 1968): crude oil 1,897; electricity (kw-hr.) 672,000 (86% hydroelectric); cement 71; tin concentrates (metal content; 1969) 30; gold (troy oz.) 68; other metal ores (exports; metal content) lead 22, antimony 11, zinc 11, tungsten 2.3, copper 6.9, silver 0.16.

Botswana

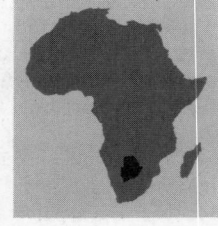

A landlocked republic of southern Africa, Botswana, a member of the Commonwealth of Nations, is bounded by South Africa, South West Africa, and Rhodesia. Area: 220,000 sq.mi. (570,000 sq.km.). Pop. (1969 est.): 623,000, almost 99% African. Capital: Gaborone (pop., 1969 est., 14,000). Largest city: Serowe (pop., 1969 est., 34,186). Language: English (official) and Tswana. Religion: about 85% pagan. President in 1970, Sir Seretse Khama.

The October 1969 elections returned Sir Seretse Khama's Botswana Democratic Party to power with an overwhelming victory of 24 out of 31 seats against

BOTSWANA
Education. (1968) Primary, pupils 78,963, teachers 1,791; secondary, pupils 2,299, teachers 131.
Finance and Trade. Monetary unit: South African rand (R 1 = U.S. $1.40; R 1.714 = £1 sterling). Budget (1969–70 est.): revenue R 21,404,000; expenditure R 20,394,000. Foreign trade (1968): imports R 23,231,000 (65% from South Africa in 1966); exports R 7,491,000 (18% to South Africa in 1966). Main exports (1967): meat 42%; hides and skins 18%; meat extract 14%; other meat products 11%; live cattle 5%.

the three opposition parties. This enabled Seretse Khama to emphasize Botswana's role as "a bridge across the ideological rift" in Africa, acceptance of the conviction that Botswana could coexist as part of the white-dominated southern African complex and that change in the region could come "by peaceful means." The political situation was, however, complicated by the continued presence of more than 4,000 refugees for settlement, and others in transit from Zambia, Rhodesia, Angola, and South Africa. The government maintained strict regulations against refugee political activities.

Discord over refugee and terrorist activities reached a wider international field when the U.S. government voted $4.8 million to build an international highway linking Zambia and Botswana over the Zambezi River. Following the South African government's statement that Botswana and Zambia had no common frontier, the Botswana government expressed the view that there was a common though undefined boundary at Kazungula. Access by ferry between the two countries had long been established by grace of South Africa. South Africa's objection to improved means of communication was based on fear of its use by terrorist groups returning to southern Africa via Zambia and Botswana, unless the area were recognized to be under South African control.   (M. Mr.)

Bowling and Lawn Bowls

The World Bowling Cup, the most important amateur singles bowling tournament in the world, again in 1970 drew bowlers from throughout the world. The new tournament entry record, 34 nations, reflected the importance of this competition. The finals took place in Tokyo, and the outcome was revolutionary: the winner, Graydon Robinson of Canada; runner-up, Ut Lenavat of Thailand; third, José Damian of Panama; fourth, Jan Kozaki of Australia; fifth, S. P. Loh of Singapore; and sixth, Edmond Clauws of Belgium; all men were from relatively "new" bowling countries —remarkable evidence of the growth of the sport. Since the participants were amateurs, no prize money was involved, the winner receiving a free trip to Copenhagen in November 1970 to defend his crown.

Another recent highlight was the Fifth American Championships, held in Puerto Rico in November 1969. Eleven countries from both North and South America entered. As in previous tournaments U.S. bowlers dominated, finishing 1–2–3 in the individual contest. The winners were: men's teams of five, (1) Mexico, 5,528, (2) Puerto Rico, 5,493, (3) U.S., 5,489; men's doubles, (1) Puerto Rico, 2,356, (2) U.S., 2,298, (3) Colombia, 2,297; men's teams of eight, (1) U.S., 11,996, (2) Venezuela, 11,626, (3) Mexico, 11,459; men's all events, (1) David Beck, U.S., 5,435, (2) Bruce Sherman, U.S., 5,415, (3) Edward Jackson, U.S., 5,358; ladies' teams of five, (1) U.S., 5,272, (2) Puerto Rico, 5,087, (3) Mexico, 4,965; ladies' doubles, (1) U.S., 2,170, (2) U.S., 2,151, (3) Puerto Rico, 2,112; ladies' teams of four, (1) U.S., 4,210, (2) Venezuela, 4,075, (3) Mexico, 3,928; ladies' all events, (1) Annese Dunleavy, U.S., 4,387, (2) Rosemary Losee, U.S., 4,358, (3) Irene Monteroso, U.S., 4,353.

For the eighth time Miami, Fla., sponsored and conducted the Tournament of the Americas, held in July 1970. The winners were: men's singles, Eddie Garofalo, Puerto Rico, 3,057; men's doubles, Canada, 3,547; men's all events, Arnaldo Gonzalez, Costa Rica,

7,040; women's singles, Joan Holm, U.S., 2,801; women's doubles, U.S., 3,546; women's all events, Joan Holm, U.S., 6,951; mixed doubles, Bermuda, 2,370; mixed foursomes, Bermuda, 4,347.

The most important Asian bowling event, the annual Asian International Bowling Tournament, took place in December 1969 in Hong Kong. The winners of this tournament were: men's teams of five, Malaysia, 5,579; men's doubles, Malaysia, 2,292; men's singles, O. B. Lim, Malaysia, 1,165; men's all events, A. Hooi, Malaysia, 3,470; women's teams of five, Malaysia, 3,032; women's doubles, Japan, 2,105; women's singles, S. Stone, Malaysia, 1,090; women's all events, K. Fujii, Japan, 3,207.   (Y. S.)

United States. Sons of famous athletes seldom achieve the heights of their fathers in that particular sport, but the events of 1970 indicated that bowling may produce such a rarity. Nelson Burton, Jr., of St. Louis, Mo., 28-year-old son of Nelson Burton, a member of the American Bowling Congress (ABC) Hall of Fame, was one of the dominant figures in 1970, and he made a strong bid to become Bowler of the Year.

With just a handful of Professional Bowlers Association (PBA) tournaments remaining, the junior Burton was the only man to have won as many as four such meets. He was the champion at Toledo, O.; Denver, Colo.; El Paso, Tex.; and Fort Worth, Tex. In addition, Burton bowled a 684 series in the Classic Division doubles event of the ABC tournament in Knoxville, Tenn., and, with partner Dave Soutar, of Detroit, Mich., contributing 747, gained a share of another title with a 1,431 doubles total. Burton's other successes included an 869 series in a doubles tournament in St. Louis, the third highest ABC-sanctioned score in history. His 34 strikes were a record for a three-game series.

Other champions in the ABC tournament in the professionals' Classic Division were: singles, Glenn Allison, Whittier, Calif., 730; team, Merchant Enterprises, New York, N.Y., 3,154; all events, Bob Strampe, Detroit, Mich., 2,043. In the Regular Division the winners were: doubles, Dick Selgo and Don Bredehoft, Toledo, O., 1,371; singles, Jack Yoder, Fort Wayne, Ind., 744; team, Hamm's, Minneapolis, Minn., 3,243; all events, Mike Berlin, Muscatine, Ia., 2,004.

The winner of the Masters Tournament, held on the same lanes as the ABC meet, was left-handed Don Glover, of Bakersfield, Calif. He was defeated in a four-game match in one of the early rounds by Bob Strampe, 898–862, but in the championship final of the double-elimination tournament, Glover downed Strampe, 821–800 and 916–877.

One of Burton's chief contenders for 1970 Bowler-of-the-Year honours was Don Johnson, of Akron, O., who within an eight-day period in April won the PBA tournament in New Orleans, La., and the $25,000 first prize in the PBA's Firestone Tournament of Champions, in Akron. Johnson captured the Firestone by bowling a 299 game in the nationally televised final.

In the 29th annual All-Star Tournament, held in Northbrook, Ill., the winner was Bobby Cooper, of Houston, Tex., who outdistanced the field by the equivalent of 629 pins. Billy Hardwick, of Louisville, Ky., who had included the All-Star among his seven major victories en route to 1969 Bowler-of-the-Year honours, placed second.

The Woman's International Bowling Congress (WIBC) tournament produced a rare repeat champion as Gloria Bouvia, Portland, Ore., and Judy Cook,

Kansas City, Mo., won the Open Division doubles title for the second successive year. Their score was 1,256. Dotty Fothergill, a left-hander from North Attleboro, Mass., was a triple winner in the WIBC meet, held in Tulsa, Okla. Her team won the Open Division crown with 3,034, and Miss Fothergill won the singles title with 695 and the all events with 1,984.

The 1969–70 duckpin season was highlighted by the rolling of the highest game ever shot by a man or woman, a 253 by Mrs. Geraldine Gravino, Warwick, R.I. The champions of the National Duckpin Bowling Congress tournament were: men—team, Kahlua Hut, Washington, D.C., 2,054; doubles, Tony Zagryn and Adolph Petro, Cheshire, Conn., 867; singles, Travis Cook, West Hartford, Conn., 473; all events, Paul Popowyck, Taunton, Mass., 1,319. Women—team, Johnny's New & Used Cars, Baltimore, Md., 1,843; doubles, Nancy Skidmore and Martha Reed, Silver Spring, Md., 872; singles, Patricia Price, Hartford, Conn., and Lori LaBlanc, Collinsville, Conn., each 431; all events, Jean Harris, Washington, D.C., 1,213. Mixed-team, Pinlanders, Baltimore, Md., 1,899; doubles, Jean Stewart, Joppa, Md., and Adolph Petro, Cheshire, Conn., 876. (J. J. A.)

Lawn Bowls. England decided in 1970 to stage the second World Championship series in 1972, the first having taken place at Kyeemagh, Austr., in 1966. The cost of staging such championships was estimated conservatively at £55,000 ($132,000), a figure that caused the U.S. to back down after applying to stage a series in 1970. English officials delayed for many months while trying to encourage commercial sponsorship, or at least a guarantee against loss. Finally, the English Bowling Association won support from the 34 constituent counties, who undertook to raise the money internally. The application to the International Bowling Board was then made and accepted; Worthing, an English seaside resort, was chosen as the site, and the date was fixed for early June 1972.

A total of 14 countries entered the Commonwealth Games bowls events, staged at the Balgreen Club in the suburbs of Edinburgh. There the heavy greens proved something of a handicap to bowlers from hotter climates where the greens run fast. The singles gave England's David Bryant yet another opportunity to demonstrate his immense superiority to the rest of the world's bowlers. Beaten only by Bob Motroni, who had the advantage of a home green, Bryant won all his other 12 matches to make his record in Commonwealth Games and World Championship singles 39 victories out of 41 contests, all matches being played outside his home country. Victory gave Bryant his third Commonwealth Games gold medal—he also won the fours in 1962—while in the pairs Norman King of England, a lead in the 1958 title-winning four, took a second gold medal by partnering Peter Line to the pairs championship. Despite these English victories the major sensation in the tournament was Hong Kong. Using new tactical ideas, Sacko Delgado, Abdul Kitchell, Robert da Silva, and George Souza lost only once in taking the fours and winning the first gold medal for Hong Kong in the history of the games.

The first International Women's Lawn Bowls Championships ever staged took place in Sydney during December 1969. Gladys Doyle of Papua-New Guinea won the singles, while South Africa won the pairs, triples, and fours, thereby taking the team trophy.

The Australian Championships were staged in Brisbane. Mervyn Davey won the singles from an entry

COURTESY, AMERICAN BOWLING CONGRESS

Don Glover, 1970 ABC Masters champion, clears the pin deck with a powerful strike ball.

exceeding 1,000. The South African singles title went to a left-hander, Tom Harvey. His grandfather and father had both won international bowling honours, but this third-generation bowler surpassed them both. The game continued to flourish in Australia and South Africa where, unfortunately, the demise of the *South African Bowling Magazine* after a lifetime of 35 years emphasized the worldwide difficulty of survival of independent magazines.

In New Zealand, an intensive bowls country, Phil Skoglund dominated the scene. It appeared that Papua-New Guinea might soon become a major power. The country's chief club laid a special quarter-sized green where youngsters aged ten or even younger were being taught to play. (C. M. Jo.)

Boxing

Joe Frazier (Philadelphia) was accepted as official heavyweight champion of the world by all U.S. states and by Europe and the Orient when he stopped Jimmy Ellis (Louisville, Ky.) in four rounds at Madison Square Garden in New York City on February 16. The confusion over the heavyweight situation had begun after Muhammad Ali (Cassius Clay) had made his last appearance in March 1967, defending his world title successfully against Zora Folley, and had then declined on conscientious grounds to join the U.S. armed forces upon being drafted; following this, most states refused to recognize Ali as champion. The World Boxing Association accepted Ellis as the new champion after he had won a series of elimination bouts, while New York and six other states recognized Frazier. Though Frazier was accepted officially, boxing fans throughout the world continued to support Ali because he had never lost his title in a fight. After nearly three years in the boxing wilderness, Ali was given permission to fight again in the state of Georgia. On October 26 at Atlanta he met a leading contender for the title, Jerry Quarry, and defeated him decisively on a technical knockout in the third round. He then defeated another contender, Oscar Bonavena, by a technical knockout in the 15th round.

After his victory over Ellis, Frazier successfully defended his title by knocking out Bob Foster (U.S.) in the second round at Detroit on November 18. Among the heavyweights in Europe, José Urtain (Spain) won the European title by knocking out Peter Wieland (W.Ger.) in seven rounds and successfully defended his championship against another West German, Jurgen Blin, with a victory on points. Meanwhile, in Britain, Henry Cooper regained the British heavyweight championship by outpointing Jack Bodell. This victory settled a controversy that had arisen from a dispute between Cooper and the British Boxing Board of Control late in 1969, when the board declined to recognize a proposed match between Cooper and Jimmy Ellis as being for the world heavyweight championship, Cooper gave up his British championship in protest. Later in the year Cooper defeated Urtain to regain the European heavyweight crown.

Bob Foster continued to dominate the light-heavyweight division and successfully retained his world championship by stopping Roger Rouse (U.S.) in three rounds and Mark Tessman (U.S.) in ten. After successfully defending his middleweight crown against Tom Bethea (U.S.), Nino Benvenuti of Italy lost it in November to Carlos Monzon of Argentina in a 12th-round knockout. Carmelo Bossi of Italy outpointed defender Freddie Little of the U.S. to win the junior middleweight championship. José Napoles, former Cuban welterweight champion who transferred to Mexico, knocked out Ernie Lopez (U.S.) in 15 rounds, but surprisingly lost the title to Billy Backus (U.S.).

The lightweight title changed hands when Ismael Laguna (Pan.) stopped Mando Ramos (U.S.) in the tenth round. Laguna later retained the championship, stopping Ishimatsu Suzuki (Jap.) in 13 rounds. A dispute then arose when the World Boxing Council ordered Laguna to defend the title against Ramos, the former champion. Instead, Laguna agreed to put the championship up against Ken Buchanan (Scot.) in Puerto Rico. Buchanan, holder of the British title, caused a surprise by outpointing the champion. The World Boxing Association (WBA) and New York State recognized Buchanan as the new champion, but the World Boxing Council (WBC) declared the title vacant. The British Boxing Board of Control, which worked in union with the WBC, declined to recognize Buchanan as champion. In junior lightweight competition Yoshiaki Numata of Japan won the WBC title by outpointing defending champion Rene Barrientos of the Philippines. The WBA version was retained by Japan's Hiroshi Kobayashi in a 15-round decision over Antonio Amaya of Panama.

The featherweight championship also changed hands. After Johnny Famechon (Austr.) had retained it with a 14-round knockout against Masahiko "Fighting" Harada (Jap.) in Tokyo, the Australian was surprisingly outpointed by Vicente Saldivar (Mex.) in Rome. Saldivar was then the victim of an upset 13th-round knockout by Kuniaki Shibata of Japan on December 11 in Tijuana, Mex. Shozo Saijo (Jap.), recognized as featherweight champion by the WBA, retained this version of the title, outpointing Godfrey Stevens (Chile) and Frankie Crawford (U.S.).

Ruben Olivares of Mexico remained top bantamweight. He knocked out Alan Rudkin (Eng.) in two rounds at Los Angeles and outpointed fellow Mexican Chucho Castillo. Then, surprisingly, in a return match he lost his title to Castillo, who won in 14 rounds when Olivares retired with a cut eye. The flyweight situation remained unsettled. Chartchai Chionoi of Thailand, the WBC champion, outpointed Efren Torres (Mex.) but then lost to Erbito Salavarria of the Philippines. WBA champion Bernabe Villacampo of the Philippines lost his title in Bangkok to Berkrerk Chartvanchai of Thailand who, in turn, was defeated by Masao Ohba of Japan.

Spain and Italy dominated boxing in Europe. Although José Urtain lost his heavyweight title late in the year to Henry Cooper of England, Spain claimed

WIDE WORLD

Muhammad Ali slams a hard right to the head of Jerry Quarry during their scheduled 15-round fight in Atlanta October 26. In the third round Ali opened a deep cut over Quarry's left eye, and the fight was stopped. Ali was declared the winner by technical knockout.

champions in Miguel Velazquez and José Legra, a former Cuban. Velazquez won the vacant lightweight title with a victory on points over Ken Buchanan in Madrid. He retained this championship by stopping Carmelo Cosio (Italy) in 11 rounds. Legra took over the featherweight championship from Tomaso Galli (Italy) with a victory on points. Italy claimed three European champions; Piero del Papa outpointed Yvan Preberg (Yugos.) in a light-heavyweight title fight; in the bantamweight division Franco Zurlo outpointed Mimoun Ben Ali (Spain) and later stopped Francisco Martinez (Spain) in four rounds and gained a win on points against E. Farinelli (Italy); Fernando Atzori hung onto the flyweight crown with a 12-round knockout against Franco Sperati (Italy).

In other European championship fights Tom Bogs (Den.) retained the middleweight title for Scandinavia with victories against Les McAteer and Chris Finnegan, but then lost it to Carlos Duran (Italy), while Austria retained the welterweight title when Johann Orsolics stopped Klaus Klein (W.Ger.) in nine rounds and outpointed Carmelo Bossi (Italy). Orsolics later surrendered the crown to Ralph Charles of England, who knocked him out in 12 rounds.

In Commonwealth competition Alan Rudkin retained the bantamweight title, stopping Johnny Clark (Eng.) in 12 rounds. Johnny McCluskey (Scot.) won the vacant flyweight championship, outpointing Harry Hayes (Austr.), while Percy Hayles (Jam.) retained the lightweight title, outpointing Jeff White (Austr.). Eddie Avoth of Wales won the light-heavyweight crown with a sixth-round victory over Trevor Thornberry of Australia.   (F. Br.)

Boxing Champions
As of Dec. 31, 1970

Division	World	Europe	Commonwealth	Britain
Heavyweight	Joe Frazier, U.S.	Henry Cooper, Eng.	Henry Cooper, Eng.	Henry Cooper, Eng.
Light heavyweight	Bob Foster, U.S.	Piero del Papa, Italy	Eddie Avoth, Wales	Eddie Avoth, Wales
Middleweight	Carlos Monzon, Arg.	Carlos Duran, Italy	Bunny Sterling, Jam.	Bunny Sterling, Jam.
Junior middleweight	Carmelo Bossi, Italy	José Hernandez, Spain	...	...
Welterweight	Billy Backus, U.S.	Ralph Charles, Eng.	Ralph Charles, Eng.	Ralph Charles, Eng.
Junior welterweight	Nicolino Loche, Arg.* Bruno Arcari, Italy	René Roque, Fr.	...	...
Lightweight	Ken Buchanan, Scot.*	Miguel Velazquez, Spain	Percy Hayles, Jam.	Ken Buchanan, Scot.
Junior lightweight	Hiroshi Kobayashi, Jap.* Yoshiaki Numata, Jap.	...	...	...
Featherweight	Kuniaki Shibata, Jap. Shozo Saijo, Jap.*	José Legra, Spain	vacant	Jimmy Revie, Eng.
Bantamweight	Chucho Castillo, Mex.	Franco Zurlo, Italy	Alan Rudkin, Eng.	Alan Rudkin, Eng.
Flyweight	Erbito Salavarria, Phil. Masao Ohba, Jap.*	Fernando Atzori, Italy	John McCluskey, Scot.	John McCluskey, Scot.

*Recognized as champions only by World Boxing Association.

Brazil

A federal republic in eastern and central South America, Brazil is bounded by the Atlantic Ocean and all the countries of South America except Ecuador and Chile. Area: 3,286,470 sq.mi. (8,511,965 sq.km.). Pop. (1969 est.): 93 million, including (1960 census) Caucasians 60%; mulattoes 26%; Negroes 11%; Amerindians 2%; Asians 1%. Principal cities (metro. pop., 1969 est.): Brasília (cap.) 450,000; Rio de Janeiro 4.4 million; São Paulo 5.8 million. Language: Portuguese. Religion: 93% Roman Catholic. President in 1970, Gen. Emílio Garrastazú Médici.

Domestic Affairs. On Oct. 30, 1969, a total of 58 amendments to the 1967 constitution went into effect. Among them, one authorized the president, after consultation with the National Security Council, to abrogate any or all provisions of the Institutional acts issued since act number 5. (This act, signed in December 1968, gave the chief executive special sweeping powers, including the right to "recess" the national and local legislative bodies for periods to be determined by him.) Another provided that the term of office of the president and vice-president was to be five years after March 15, 1974. One other amendment provided for a new apportioning of the federal deputies to be elected by the people. This was to be done on the basis of the number of registered electors and not on the basis of population as before. The constitution as amended provided also that the Congress should meet annually from March 31 to November 30.

Addressing the nation over radio and television, President Médici (*see* BIOGRAPHY) announced his Cabinet members and promised to continue the policies of his two predecessors. Shortly after that, during his first press conference, the president declared that it was too early to even consider revoking act number 5. He affirmed, however, that it was his intention to "redemocratize" the nation before the end of his term. The act, he added, did not impede the regular evolution of democracy in Brazil: Congress was in session and elections were being held as provided by the laws. The act, he said, had in fact helped to "maintain" and "perfect" democracy in the country for juridical forms were not the most important factor in a society in rapid change such as Brazil. What mattered was the way in which justice was carried out.

Early in 1970 it was announced that elections for federal and state senators, deputies, and municipal officials would be held on November 15. The results were a clear victory for President Médici and his supporters. In the first nationwide congressional elections in four years, the pro-government Alliance for National Renewal increased its already sizable majority in the Chamber of Deputies. It also won a majority of the Senate seats (two-thirds of the total) that were at stake.

In May the minister of justice declared that by 1974 conditions were expected to be such as to allow again total freedom of political action. However, as unrest throughout the country continued, new suspensions of political rights were announced from time to time.

These strong measures of the administration, along with alleged police brutality in handling political prisoners, were criticized sharply in some newspapers in other countries. Government officials in Brazil and abroad replied that there were no political prisoners in the country, only persons convicted of common criminal acts or awaiting trial for such acts. The criticism of the Brazilian authorities abroad also included responsibility for alleged inhuman treatment of the Indian population, which was estimated at about 100,000 living mostly in the northwestern regions. Although admitting that there had been some criminal action against certain Indian groups on the part of a

"MANCHETE" FROM PICTORIAL PARADE

Gen. Emílio Garrastazú Médici pledged to "redemocratize" Brazil during his term as president.

"MANCHETE" FROM PICTORIAL PARADE

Above, Ehrenfried von Holleben, West German ambassador to Brazil, talks to newsmen after his release by terrorist kidnappers. Below, police reenactment shows how kidnappers' truck intercepted the ambassador's limousine.

"MANCHETE" FROM PICTORIAL PARADE

BRAZIL

Education. Primary (1967), pupils 11,182,746, teachers 395,149; secondary (1968), pupils 2,318,456, teachers 134,070; vocational (1968), pupils 542,418, teachers 43,798; teacher training (1968), students 344,815, teachers 33,272; higher (including 43 universities; 1967), students 215,322, teaching staff 39,556.

Finance. Monetary unit: cruzeiro, with an exchange rate (as devalued Sept. 18, 1970) of 4.705 cruzeiros to U.S. $1 (11.292 cruzeiros = £1 sterling). Gold, SDRs, and foreign exchange, official: (May 1970) U.S. $973 million; (May 1969) U.S. $392 million. Budget (1970 est.): revenue 15,874,000,000 cruzeiros; expenditure 16,474,000,000 cruzeiros. Gross national product: (1967) 73,839,000,000 cruzeiros; (1966) 53,216,000,000 cruzeiros. Money supply: (June 1969) 23,578,000,000 cruzeiros; (June 1968) 17,976,000,000 cruzeiros. Cost of living (São Paulo; 1963 = 100): (April 1970) 1,013; (April 1969) 833.

Foreign Trade. Imports (1969) 8,883,200,000 cruzeiros; exports (1968) 4,873,900,000 cruzeiros. Import sources (1968): U.S. 32%; West Germany 11%; Argentina 7%; U.K. 5%. Export destinations (1968): U.S. 33%; West Germany 8%; Argentina 6%; Italy 6%; Netherlands 5%. Main exports (1968): coffee 41%; raw cotton 7%; iron ore 6%.

Transport and Communications. Roads (1969) 1,024,000 km. (including 64,000 km. main roads). Motor vehicles in use (1968): passenger 1,537,000; commercial (including buses) 953,900. Railways: (1966) 31,961 km.; traffic (1968) 13,803,000,000 passenger-km., freight 21,974,000,000 net ton-km. Air traffic (1969): 3,932,000,000 passenger-km.; freight 152,375,000 net ton-km. Shipping (1969): merchant vessels 100 gross tons and over 414; gross tonnage 1,381,458. Telephones (Dec. 1968) 1,560,701. Radio receivers (Dec. 1969) c. 5,575,000. Television receivers (Dec. 1969) c. 6 million.

Agriculture. Production (in 000; metric tons; 1969; 1968 in parentheses): corn 10,808 (12,814); rice 5,600 (6,652); cassava (1968) 29,203, (1967) 27,268; potatoes c. 1,300 (1,606); sweet potatoes (1968) 2,120, (1967) 2,226; wheat 1,088 (856); cotton, lint 720 (596); coffee (1968) 1,057, (1967) 1,507; cocoa (1967–68) 147, (1966–67) 173; bananas (1967) 5,236, (1966) c. 4,626; oranges (1968) 2,933, (1967) 2,701; sisal (1968) 328, (1967) 319; tobacco (1968) 258, (1967) 243; peanuts 611 (754); sugar, raw value (1969–70) c. 4,800, (1968–69) 4,270; dry beans (1968) 2,420, (1967) 2,554; soybeans 936 (654); rubber c. 23 (23); timber (cu.m.; 1968) 162,800, (1967) c. 160,400; fish catch (1967) 419, (1966) 393. Livestock (in 000; Dec. 1968): cattle 92,276; horses (Dec. 1967) 9,244; pigs 65,640; sheep 24,606; goats (Dec. 1966) 13,957; chickens 271,699.

Industry. Fuel and power (in 000; 1968): coal 2,364 metric tons; crude oil (1969) 8,340 metric tons; natural gas (1969) 1,248,000 cu.m.; electricity 38,181,000 kw-hr. (80% hydroelectric). Production (in 000; metric tons; 1969): pig iron 4,917; crude steel 3,717; bauxite (1968) 314; iron ore (metal content; 1968) 17,084; manganese ore (metal content; 1968) 922; gold (troy oz.; 1968) 170; cement 7,822; wood pulp (1968) c. 636; paper (1967) 773; passenger cars (including assembly; units) 243; commercial vehicles (including assembly; units) 109.

few government officials in 1967, the government maintained that it had ordered an investigation and that judicial action had been taken against the persons responsible for such acts.

The administration showed special interest in the development of the northern and northwestern states, particularly in the sparsely inhabited Amazon basin. A program of national assistance was adopted for the area, including the construction of roads.

Apparently the criticism leveled at the Brazilian authorities abroad led the International Red Cross to send a three-physician mission to Brazil in May to investigate conditions. During its meeting in May the National Conference of Bishops of Brazil petitioned the government to order a thorough investigation of alleged police brutality against political prisoners, some of whom were said to be Roman Catholic priests. At the same time a pastoral letter was issued by the bishops criticizing acts of violence, approving the government measures to punish those found guilty of such acts, and specifically repudiating the charges against the Brazilian authorities in foreign newspapers of alleged cruel treatment of the Indians. However, the fifth assembly of the Lutheran World Federation, which had been scheduled to meet at Pôrto Alegre, was transferred to another country as a consequence of the published accusations. The leaders of the Brazilian Lutheran Church protested against this action.

The situation was aggravated by new kidnappings of foreign diplomatic officials. On March 11 the Japanese consul general in São Paulo was kidnapped. The demand of the kidnappers for the liberation of five prisoners to be sent to Mexico City with some children was met by the government. The consul was freed four days later. The following month an attempt to kidnap the U.S. consul at Pôrto Alegre failed. But on June 11 West Germany's ambassador to Brazil, Ehrenfried von Holleben, was kidnapped. The demand of the kidnappers for the release of 40 prisoners was promptly met. The prisoners were flown to Algiers five days later, and the ambassador was released. On December 7 the Swiss ambassador, Giovanni Bucher, was kidnapped by terrorists who demanded the release of 70 prisoners. At year's end, the Brazilian government had agreed to the release of 51.

The nation was deeply disturbed by news of the kidnapping of the Brazilian consul at Montevideo, Uruguay, on July 31. The Uruguayan authorities refused to meet the kidnappers' demands and the Brazilian government addressed repeated requests to the Uruguayan authorities for prompt action.

The Economy. The financial and economic conditions of the country continued to improve, according to all the information available. Exports were expected to total $2.2 billion in 1969. Exports of manufactured goods were said to have increased more than 80% over the previous year. The balance of payments was estimated at $190 million during the first nine months of 1969 as against a deficit of $4 million in the identical period of 1968. The cost of living was said to have increased at the rate of 22.9% in 1969 as against 22.4% during the previous year. It was estimated that the gross national product for 1970 would be 9% over the 1969 figure.

The authorities continued to adhere to the policy of devaluing the cruzeiro as often as the economic conditions of the country indicated. After Dec. 19, 1969, the rate officially established was 4.32–4.35 cruzeiros to $1; after successive devaluations on March 10,

1970, July 10, and July 24, it was changed again on September 18 to 4.69–4.72 to $1.

Foreign Relations. At a session of the General Assembly of the Organization of American States held at Washington, D.C., in June, Brazil proposed that political kidnapping and air piracy be declared to constitute a threat to the peace and security of the American continents. Such a declaration would allow the eventual invocation of the Rio Security Pact, which called for the use of intercontinental armed forces to deal with such threats. The proposal was rejected by the assembly, although political terrorism was declared a "common crime" subject to the penalties provided by the laws of each country.

Brazil continued its refusal to sign the nuclear nonproliferation treaty of 1968, which was considered by the Brazilian authorities as impeding the development of its commercial nuclear energy industry. The ministry of foreign affairs was totally transferred to Brasília, the new capital, where on April 21 the new Itamaraty palace was solemnly inaugurated.

The country experienced an immense exhilaration with the triumph of the Brazilian team in the association football (soccer) World Cup tournament. The final victory on June 21 at Mexico City marked the third world championship for the Brazilians. This entitled them to keep permanently the Jules Rimet Trophy. (R. D'E.)

ENCYCLOPÆDIA BRITANNICA FILMS. *The Amazon—People and Resources of Northern Brazil* (1957); *Brazil—People of the Highlands* (1957).

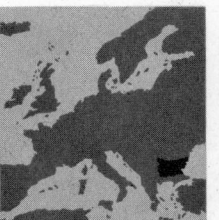

Bulgaria

A people's republic of Europe, Bulgaria is situated on the eastern Balkan Peninsula along the Black Sea, bordered by Romania, Yugoslavia, Greece, and Turkey. Area: 42,823 sq.mi. (110,912 sq.km.). Pop. (1967 est.): 8,310,200. Cap. and largest city: Sofia (pop., 1967 est., 825,200). Language: chiefly Bulgarian. First secretary of the Bulgarian Communist Party and chairman of the Council of Ministers (premier) in 1970, Todor Zhivkov; chairman of the Presidium of the National Assembly, Georgi Traikov.

The year 1970, the last of the fifth five-year plan for national development, was the occasion for an outpouring of speeches in which Bulgarian leaders emphasized the transformation of the national economy since World War II. Among the evidences of progress, industrial production in 1970 was said to be 33 times greater than that of 1939. Between that year and 1969 generation of electric power had risen from 266 million to 17,232,000,000 kw-hr.; the extraction of coal (mainly brown) from 2.2 million to 31.2 million metric tons; the production of steel from 6,000 to 1,512,000 tons; and that of cement from 225,000 to 3,552,000 tons. The first atomic power station was under construction at Kozlodu, on the Danube River.

As a result of the country's industrial development, the proportion of total manpower employed in agriculture fell from 81.9% in 1948 to 39.1% in 1968, but agricultural production increased both in total volume (the wheat harvest rose from 2,003,000 tons in 1939 to 2,549,000 in 1968) and in yield per hectare (from 13.1 kg. in 1939 to 24 in 1968). Collectivization of agriculture had been completed in 1958, and by 1969 more than 84,000 tractors and 15,000 combine-harvesters were in operation on collective farms. In April 1970, however, the plenary session of the

Central Committee of the Bulgarian Communist Party decided that further concentration on agriculture and animal husbandry was necessary. The existing collective farms would be merged into huge "agrarian-industrial complexes" of from 20,000 to 50,000 ha., each specializing in one kind of high-quality crop or one kind of livestock.

In foreign relations a delicate situation had been created by Bulgarian historians debating the problem of Macedonia, part of which was included in Yugoslavia but which many Bulgarians believed was inhabited by ethnic Bulgars. In August 1969 President Tito of Yugoslavia had denounced "the absurd tittle-tattle about the nonexistence of the Macedonian nation." In December 1969 Bulgarian Foreign Minister Ivan Bashev, while visiting in Belgrade, had declared to Mirko Tepavac, the Yugoslav state secretary for foreign affairs, that the Macedonians are ethnically related to Bulgarians. The Yugoslav press commented caustically about Bashev's statement and speculated as to the purpose of his visit. Tepavac advanced the hypothesis that perhaps some other socialist country was behind the Bulgarian claim. In 1970 Zhivkov and Tito exchanged letters concerning a possible Bulgarian-Yugoslav summit meeting, including joint renunciation of all territorial claims, but no definite conclusions were reached.

On September 11 and 12, at Ruse and Giurgiu, Zhivkov and Pres. Nicolae Ceausescu of Romania discussed the joint building of a power station on the Danube at Islaz-Somovit. They agreed to sign a new 20-year treaty of friendship and mutual aid to replace the Bulgarian-Romanian treaty of Jan. 16, 1948.

(K. Sm.)

Burma

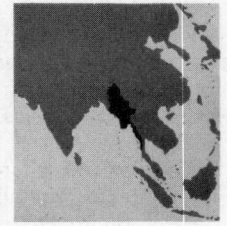

A republic of southeast Asia, Burma is on the Indochinese Peninsula, bordered by East Pakistan, India, Tibet, China, Laos, and Thailand. Area: 261,789 sq.mi. (678,034 sq. km.). Pop. (1970 est.) 27.6 million. Cap. and largest city: Rangoon (pop., 1969 census, 1,733,000). Language: Burmese 66%. Religion: Buddhist 84%. Chairman of the Revolutionary Council and prime minister in 1970, Gen. Ne Win.

Two significant events during late 1969 and 1970 helped the Burmese Revolutionary Council, led by Gen. Ne Win, to consolidate its hold on the Burmese people: the fourth Seminar on a Draft Constitution, in November 1969; and the second anniversary meeting of the Central People's Peasants' Council (CPPC), held in February–March 1970. The seminar decided to postpone indefinitely work on a democratic constitution and agreed to support the one-party system and a unitary form of state. The majority of participants from all parts of the country, including the various ethnic groups, rejected the federal system as totally unacceptable. They called for the transformation of the Burma Socialist Program Party into a mass party and underlined socialism and nonalignment as fundamental aims of the government.

The CPPC anniversary meeting, hailed as a historic occasion, began on February 25 and ended on March 2 with a mammoth rally in Rangoon. Gen. Ne Win, in a message to the participants, underlined the basic unity between the Burmese Way to Socialism Program and the CPPC and noted that during its first year the latter had brought a certain measure of prosperity to the peasants. The meeting agreed to uphold the five-point program: training and education; solidarity of rural bodies; organized management of the rural economy; a peasant-worker alliance; and the setting up of more regional bodies.

The Burmese economy plodded along its chosen socialist path with no apparent gains in growth or productivity. An International Monetary Fund report termed the economy merely stagnant, but economic experts, basing their judgments on statistics, felt that there was deterioration all around. Exports of the country's major crop, rice, had declined from $171 million in 1963 to $63 million in 1969. Total exports during the same period dropped from $270 million to $128 million. Foreign aid from the U.S. and the U.S.S.R. was negligible. The government of West Germany signed an agreement in May to grant a loan of DM. 32 million at favourable terms for erecting a complete textile finishing plant. The plant was to be constructed, together with a spinning and weaving plant with 40,000 spindles and 600 looms, near Paleik, in central Burma. At about the same time, Ne Win visited Japan where he discussed with Prime Minister Eisaku Sato increased cooperation in trade and economic relations. He specifically asked Japan to buy

BULGARIA
Education. (1967–68) Primary, pupils 1,095,645, teachers 49,451; secondary, pupils 117,247, teachers 6,879; vocational, pupils 264,499, teachers 15,826; teacher training, students 333, teachers 15; higher (including Sofia University with 13,036 students), students 91,691, teaching staff 6,893.
Finance. Monetary unit: lev, with an official exchange rate of 1.17 leva to U.S. $1 (2.81 leva = £1 sterling) and a tourist rate of 2 leva to U.S. $1 (4.80 leva = £1 sterling). Budget (1970 est.): revenue 5,235,-000,000 leva; expenditure 5,225,000,000 leva.
Foreign Trade. (1969) Imports U.S. $1,750,000,-000; exports U.S. $1,801,000,000. Main import sources (1968): U.S.S.R. 52%; East Germany 8%; Czechoslovakia 5%. Main export destinations (1968): U.S.S.R. 55%; East Germany 7%; Czechoslovakia 5%. Main exports (1968): machinery 25%; tobacco and cigarettes 13%; wines and spirits 6%; clothing 6%; metals 6%.
Transport and Communications. State roads (1968) 29,821 km. (including 2,389 km. main roads). Motor vehicles in use (1961): passenger c. 9,300; commercial c. 20,400. Railways: (1968) 4,157 km.; traffic (1969) 6,062,000,000 passenger-km., freight 12,619,000,000 net ton-km. Air traffic (1968): 132,-910,000 passenger-km.; freight 2,860,000 net ton-km. Shipping (1969): merchant vessels 100 gross tons and over 124; gross tonnage 638,167. Telephones (Dec. 1968) 378,152. Radio receivers (Dec. 1968) 2,245,000. Television receivers (Dec. 1968) 621,000.
Agriculture. Production (in 000; metric tons; 1969; 1968 in parentheses): wheat 2,569 (2,549); corn 2,415 (1,768); barley 905 (807); oats c. 162 (76); dry peas (1968) 28, (1967) 83; sunflower seed 545 (459); cotton, lint (1968) 10, (1967) 19; sugar, raw value (1969–70) c. 196, (1968–69) 165; tomatoes (1968) 701, (1967) 715; grapes (1968) 1,336, (1967) 923; apples (1968) 427, (1967) 413; tobacco 96 (115); wool, greasy (1968) 29, (1967) 27; meat (1968) 387, (1967) 359. Livestock (in 000; Jan. 1969): sheep 9,652; cattle 1,297; goats (Jan. 1968) 384; pigs 2,140; horses (Jan. 1968) 224; asses (Jan. 1968) 301; poultry 24,874.
Industry. Index of industrial production (1963 = 100): (1969) 199; (1968) 181. Fuel and power (in 000; metric tons; 1969): coal 370; lignite 28,613; crude oil 325; electricity (kw-hr.) 17,228,000. Production (in 000; metric tons; 1969): iron ore (32% metal content) 2,687; manganese ore (metal content; 1968) 12; copper concentrates (metal content) 32; lead concentrates (metal content) 83; pig iron 1,122; crude steel 1,515; copper (1968) 36; lead 95; zinc 76; cement 3,551; sulfuric acid 498; soda ash (1968) 225; cotton yarn 71; cotton fabrics (m.) 335,000; wool yarn 23; woolen fabrics (m.) 25,000.

more Burmese timber and minerals to reduce the current trade imbalance in Japan's favour. While in Japan, Ne Win took part in the Burma Day celebrations at Expo 70 in Osaka.

Insurgency from Communist guerrilla forces and ethnic minorities within the country continued but remained within manageable limits. Externally, the fear of China still loomed large, since China could intervene among the border rebels if it chose; in November, however, a Burmese ambassador arrived in Peking after a three-year hiatus. The other threat came from former prime minister U Nu, who allegedly entered Burma from Thailand in October to carry on his attempt to foment rebellion. But the army and the people rallied behind the general, and the threat from U Nu and his supporters was not taken seriously. Ne Win also took the bold step of releasing another batch of 900 political prisoners, many of them former followers of U Nu, in September.

Relations with Burma's other big neighbour, India, continued to improve. During two visits to New Delhi, Ne Win had cordial talks with Prime Minister Indira Gandhi. Minor differences in border demarcation were resolved, a new trade agreement was accomplished, and both leaders agreed to take joint steps against Naga and Mizo rebels who were passing through Burmese territory to receive training and arms in China with the intention of menacing Indian security.

(G. U.)

Encyclopædia Britannica Films. *Burma, People of the River* (1957).

BURMA
Education. (1967–68) Primary, pupils 2,791,190, teachers 50,449; secondary, pupils 586,306, teachers 15,321; vocational, pupils 3,662, teachers 304; teacher training, students 3,155, teachers 180; higher (including universities of Mandalay and Rangoon), students 28,890, teaching staff 2,339.
Finance. Monetary unit: kyat, with a par value of 4.76 kyats to U.S. $1 (11.43 kyats = £1 sterling). Gold, SDRs, and foreign exchange, official: (June 1970) U.S. $103.6 million; (June 1969) U.S. $139.2 million. Budget (1969–70 est.): revenue 8,907,000,000 kyats; expenditure 9,019,000,000 kyats. National income: (1966–67) 7,283,000,000 kyats; (1965–66) 7,058,-000,000 kyats. Money supply: (Sept. 1969) 2,480,000,-000 kyats; (Sept. 1968) 2,372,000,000 kyats.
Foreign Trade. (1969) Imports 531.1 million kyats; exports 599 million kyats. Import sources (1968): Japan 24%; U.K. 15%; Netherlands 8%; West Germany 7%; Czechoslovakia 5%; U.S. 5%. Export destinations (1968): India 17%; Ceylon 9%; Japan 9%; Indonesia 8%; U.K. 7%; Mauritius 6%; Denmark 6%; West Germany 6%. Main exports: rice 53%; teak 25%.
Transport and Communications. Roads (1968) c. 25,000 km. (including c. 13,000 km. all-weather). Motor vehicles in use (1968): passenger 28,900; commercial (including buses) 29,100. Railways (1968): 4,290 km.; traffic 2,398,000,000 passenger-km., freight 802 million net ton-km. Air traffic (1969): 114.6 million passenger-km.; freight 1,830,000 net ton-km. Shipping (1969): merchant vessels 100 gross tons and over 34; gross tonnage 50,326. Telephones (Dec. 1968) 22,080. Radio receivers (Dec. 1968) 388,000.
Agriculture. Production (in 000; metric tons; 1969; 1968 in parentheses): rice c. 8,350 (8,023); rubber (exports; 1968) 9, (1967) c. 6; sesame (1968) 83, (1967) 83; peanuts (1968) c. 336, (1967) 389; dry beans (1967) c. 140, (1966) c. 140; cotton, lint (1968) c. 11, (1967) 21; jute 23 (21); tobacco c. 43 (c. 54); sugar, raw value (1969–70) c. 228, (1968–69) c. 208; timber (cu.m.; 1967–68) 4,800, (1966–67) 5,200. Livestock (in 000; March 1969): cattle c. 6,850; buffaloes (March 1967) 1,372; pigs 1,400; goats (March 1967) 682.
Industry. Production (in 000; metric tons; 1969): cement 182; crude oil (1968) 728; electricity (excluding most industrial production; kw-hr.) 409,000; lead concentrates (metal content; 1968) 11; zinc concentrates (metal content; 1968) 4.5; tin concentrates (metal content; 1968) 0.3.

Burundi

A republic of eastern Africa, Burundi is bordered by the Congo, Rwanda, and Tanzania. Area: 10,747 sq.mi. (27,834 sq.km.). Pop. (1969 est.): 3,475,000, mainly Hutu, Tutsi, and Twa. Cap. and largest city: Bujumbura (pop., 1970 est., 110,000). Language: Kirundi and French. Religion: Roman Catholic 40%; Protestant 5%; animist 55%. President in 1970, Michel Micombero.

President Micombero's Unity and National Progress Party was strengthened in July 1970, when the party's Political Bureau adopted a new charter. According to this document, the president became party secretary-general, with a five-man executive of the Central Committee to implement party congress directives and Central Committee decisions. The biannual congress consisted of the Central Committee, with provincial and local representation.

In December 1969 Micombero met with Pres. Joseph Mobutu of the Congo (Kinshasa) and Pres. Grégoire Kayibanda of Rwanda. They instructed their foreign ministers to work toward economic and cultural integration of the three countries.

Though Chinese influence, aimed at using the country as a gateway to the Congo and at arming the Tutsi refugees against Rwanda, was not entirely eradicated, there was a general shift toward the West, with a preponderance of Belgian military and technical aid (France also signed a treaty of military assistance in April). This culminated in the visit to Burundi in July of Baudouin I, king of the Belgians. Micombero, in welcoming the king, emphasized Belgian aid in every sector of the economy, public and private, and assured foreign investors of safety and stability. International aid for 1970 included $380,000 from the International Development Association for transport. The UN Development Program allocated $719,000 to develop fisheries in Lake Tanganyika.

The refugee problem complicated local politics; the majority of 73,000 refugees in Burundi were Tutsi from Rwanda. For its six refugee settlements, Burundi was granted the largest single allocation by the UN High Commissioner for Refugees for 1970.

(M. Mr.)

BURUNDI
Education. (1967–68) Primary, pupils 170,915, teachers 4,308; secondary, pupils 3,297, teachers 323; vocational, pupils 2,126, teachers 204; teacher training, students 2,175, teachers 213; higher (including University of Bujumbura), students 281, teaching staff 85.
Finance. Monetary unit: Burundi franc, with a par value of BurFr. 1.75 to Belgian Fr. 1 (BurFr. 87.50 = U.S. $1; BurFr. 210 = £1 sterling). Gold, SDRs, and foreign exchange, central bank: (March 1970) U.S. $8.7 million; (March 1969) U.S. $2,270,000. Budget (1968 est.): revenue BurFr. 1,843,200,000; expenditure BurFr. 1,804,700,000.
Foreign Trade. (1969) Imports BurFr. 1,889,000,-000; exports BurFr. 1,039,000,000. Import sources (1968): Belgium-Luxembourg 26%; Japan 12%; West Germany 12%; U.S. 7%; Iran 6%; France 5%; U.K. 5%. Export destinations (1968): U.S. 72%; Belgium 11%. Main exports: coffee 79%; cotton 10%.
Transport and Communications. Roads (1968) c. 6,000 km. (including 80 km. with improved surface). Telephones (Jan. 1969) c. 3,200.
Agriculture. Production (in 000; metric tons; 1968; 1967 in parentheses): cassava c. 875 (c. 875); corn (1967) c. 112, (1966) 110; sweet potatoes 752 (747); dry beans 121 (123); dry peas 36 (37); coffee (1967) 18, (1966) 14.

Business Management:
see Employment, Wages, and Hours; Industrial Review; Merchandising

Business Review:
see Economy, World

Butter:
see Agriculture

Cambodia

A republic of Southeast Asia, Cambodia is the south-west part of the Indochinese Peninsula. Area: 69,898 sq.mi. (181,035 sq.km.). Pop. (1970 est.): 6,818,200, including (est.) Cambodian 85%; Vietnamese 8%; Chinese 6%. Cap.: Phnom Penh (pop., 1970 est., 468,900). Language: Cambodian and French. Religion: Buddhism. Chiefs of state in 1970, Prince Norodom Sihanouk until March 18 and Cheng Heng from March 21; premier, Gen. Lon Nol.

The dawn of 1970, Cambodia's year of reckoning, found Prince Norodom Sihanouk (*see* BIOGRAPHY) preparing to visit France on his first holiday in three years. He was not to return. Taking advantage of his long absence from the country, his ministers decided to challenge him. They began on March 8 by organizing anti-Vietnamese demonstrations in the country in an obvious attempt to arouse popular sentiment in their favour; the Vietnamese are, historically, racial enemies of the Khmers (the predominant people of Cambodia), and approximately 600,000 of them, mostly traders and technicians, were living in Cambodia. The Phnom Penh embassies of North Vietnam and the Provisional Revolutionary Government of South Vietnam (Viet Cong) were sacked on March 11 by crowds led by soldiers. The next day the Cabinet cabled Sihanouk that the demonstrations represented the legitimate indignation of the people over his allegedly pro-Communist policies and that it had now decided on radical changes in the government's foreign and military policies. It then served an ultimatum on the North Vietnamese and the Viet Cong authorities that they should withdraw all guerrilla troops from Cambodian territory in two days.

The coup de grace came on March 18. As all airports remained closed, the National Assembly met, surrounded by armoured cars. Its historic decision was later announced by its president, Cheng Heng: "The National Assembly and the Council of the Kingdom, meeting in joint session, have withdrawn, conforming to the constitution, in a unanimous vote, their confidence from Prince Norodom Sihanouk in his position of Chief of State." The Assembly chose Cheng Heng as the new provisional head of state, a job reduced in status to one of formal significance only. Lieut. Gen. Lon Nol (*see* BIOGRAPHY) continued as premier, and Prince Sisowath Sirik Matak (a cousin of Sihanouk), reputedly the strong man of the Cabinet and the brain behind the coup, remained first deputy premier (in July he became the sole deputy premier). On October 5 the Cambodian Parliament voted unanimously to proclaim the nation a republic, effective November 1. Thus, after more than 1,000 years, the monarchy was ended.

At first, the new leadership found considerable support. Although Sihanouk had great popularity among the peasants, the urban elites were against him. So were students and teachers, frustrated by the lack of opportunities under a one-man rule. The government's popularity, however, waned as the military situation quickly deteriorated. The Cambodian Army, numbering barely 35,000, was ill-trained and ill-equipped. The government survived only because of aid from the South Vietnamese Army. On April 30 U.S. Pres. Richard Nixon announced that U.S. troops would also march into Cambodia for the limited purpose of destroying Communist sanctuaries along the border with South Vietnam. What developed was an all-out allied offensive, the Americans officially staying within 21.7 mi. of the border. The war rapidly enveloped previously unaffected areas of Cambodia as Communist troops, estimated by Sihanouk before his ouster at 40,000, were driven out of their border sanctuaries and pushed west and north. They gained control of vast areas in the south and southwest, as well as in the north and east. At one stage the government was reportedly resigned to conceding half the country to the Communists. Not entirely facetiously, Premier Lon Nol began to be referred to as the mayor of Phnom Penh.

U.S. troops withdrew from Cambodia by July 1 as scheduled. South Vietnam continued to maintain a

UPI COMPIX

Cambodian Premier Lon Nol applauds during a parade celebrating Cambodia's becoming a republic.

South Vietnamese Rangers' armoured personnel carriers rumble back into Vietnam after a sweep into Cambodia. A Vietnamese farmer pays no attention.

UPI COMPIX

CAMBODIA

Education. (1967–68) Primary, pupils 934,292, teachers 20,048; secondary, pupils 99,574, teachers 3,886; vocational, pupils 5,787, teachers 464; teacher training (1966–67), students 1,751, teachers 104; higher (including 10 universities), students 8,929, teaching staff 874.

Finance. Monetary unit: riel, with a rate of exchange (following devaluation of Aug. 18, 1969) of 55.54 riels to U.S. $1 (133.30 riels = £1 sterling). Budget (1969 est.): revenue 6,250,000,000 riels; expenditure 7,565,-000.000 riels.

Foreign Trade. (1968) Imports 4,060,000,000 riels; exports 3,110,000,000 riels. Import sources: France 31%; Japan 21%; Singapore 10%; Hong Kong 6%; China 6%. Export destinations: South Vietnam 17%; Hong Kong 11%; China 10%; France 8%; Singapore 8%. Main exports (1967): rice 42%; rubber 25%; corn 5%.

Transport and Communications. Roads (1967) 10,826 km. (including 2,600 km. all-weather). Motor vehicles in use (1968): passenger 23,100; commercial 10,700. Railways: (1968) 655 km.; traffic (1969) 170 million passenger-km., freight 71 million net ton-km. Air traffic (1968): 50,890,000 passenger-km.; freight 1,152,000 net ton-km. Inland waterway (Mekong River; 1968) *c.* 1,400 km. Telephones (Jan. 1969) 7,315. Radio receivers (Dec. 1968) 1 million. Television receivers (Dec. 1967) *c.* 20,000.

Agriculture. Production (in 000; metric tons 1969; 1968 in parentheses): rice 2,503 (3,251); corn 118 (154); rubber 51 (47); bananas (1968) 189, (1967) 193; dry beans (1968) 32, (1967) 29; jute 15 (6). Livestock (in 000; Dec. 1968): cattle *c.* 1,920; buffalo (Dec. 1967) 856; pigs *c.* 1,100.

WIDE WORLD
Bodies of Vietnamese residents of Cambodia, victims of racist demonstrations, float down the Mekong River in April 1970.

large presence, while Thailand played a marginal role. As if in retaliation for the Lon Nol government's earlier repression of the Vietnamese minority in the country, South Vietnamese troops plundered the Cambodian villages they overran and indulged in hectic raping and looting. They supervised the evacuation to South Vietnam of part of Cambodia's Vietnamese population which had been confined to detention camps in Phnom Penh.

Meanwhile, Prince Sihanouk in Peking received unexpectedly strong support from the Chinese government. Chairman Mao himself publicly received him; full military and economic assistance was promised. Diplomatic circles concluded that China was motivated by a desire to undercut the Soviet Union on the one hand and, on the other, to prop up Sihanouk and Cambodia as an eventual Indochinese counterbalance to independence-prone North Vietnam. Keeping Peking as his headquarters, Sihanouk traveled to North Vietnam and North Korea and kept up a barrage of letters and press statements to win support for his cause.

On May 5 Sihanouk announced the formation of a parallel government, under the auspices of the National United Front of Kampuchea, with himself as the head of state, Samdech Penn Nouth as premier, and Sarim Chhak, Hu Nim, Khieu Samphan, and Hou Yuon as principal ministers. In Cambodia the last three had been leaders of the underground Khmer Rouge movement whom Sihanouk had hounded while in power and who had then been reported as killed by government troops. The government-in-exile was recognized by 18 countries as of September, but the list did not include the Soviet Union and India. In July the government in Phnom Penh put Sihanouk and all his men on trial in absentia. The prince and some of his leading ministers were sentenced to death, his wife and mother-in-law to life imprisonment. Sihanouk ridiculed the trial, arguing that the Lon Nol government was unconstitutional and that he alone was the legal head of state.

A direct consequence of the war that finally caught up with Cambodia was the complete shattering of the economy. Tourism and the rubber industry, two of the principal exchange earners, were ruined. The big rubber plantations were razed by allied bombings. Rice exports were seriously affected as paddies turned into battlegrounds. The Cambodian riel plummeted to more than 100 to the U.S. dollar against the official

rate of 35. The U.S. Agency for International Development estimated that the Cambodian government would need $230 million in outside support to keep the economy functioning through 1971. Late in the year President Nixon asked Congress for a supplemental appropriation of $255 million for military and economic aid to Cambodia.

Meanwhile, the fighting continued without definitive results. In November the South Vietnamese launched a major offensive in the southeast. Action around the temple complex of Angkor, which had occurred at various times during the year, was reported again in November. (T. J. S. G.)

WIDE WORLD
Cache of rifles captured during the offensive by U.S. and South Vietnamese troops against Communist sanctuaries in Cambodia.

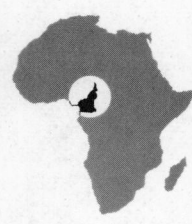

Cameroon

A federal republic of west equatorial Africa on the Gulf of Guinea, Cameroon borders on Nigeria, Chad, the Central African Republic, the Congo (Brazzaville), Gabon, and Equatorial Guinea. Area: 183,591 sq.mi. (475,500 sq.km.). Pop. (1969 est.): 5,680,000, mainly Negro. Cap.: Yaoundé (pop., 1970 est., 178,-000). Largest city: Douala (pop., 1970 est., 250,000). Language: Bantu, Sudanic, French, and English. Religion: mainly animism or tribal beliefs; some Christian and Muslim. President in 1970, Ahmadou Ahidjo.

On March 28 Ahmadou Ahidjo was reelected president with 97.89% of the votes cast. Nevertheless, the opposition in Cameroon continued to provide considerable difficulties for the president.

In August Ernest Ouandie, leader of the illegal opposition party, the Union of the Cameroon Peoples (UPC), was taken prisoner by government forces. A few days later, Albert Ndongmo, bishop of Nkongsamba, was likewise arrested on his return from Rome and accused of participating in a plot against the head of state. The cases of Ouandie and Ndongmo focused attention not only upon the ten-year-old state of emergency that permitted preventive arrest and detention but even more upon the persistence of discontent among the Bamiléké population.

Two medical attendants were killed and two others wounded in July in an armed attack on a clinic at Loum in the southwest of the country. Two weeks later, approximately 30 Nigerian nationals were reported to have been killed by Cameroonian customs officials in a pitched battle. The report was immediately denied by the Presidency Office. Nigerian fishermen who claimed to have witnessed the incident

thought that the officials had mistaken the men for smugglers and had therefore opened fire on them, but it was not clear whether this was in fact a straightforward border incident or whether there was a political side to the matter.

President Ahidjo enjoyed a double prestige success in January with the tenth anniversary of his country's independence and the summit conference of the African, Malagasy, and Mauritian Common Organization (OCAMM). Early in the same month, agreements concerning cultural and economic cooperation were signed at Yaoundé between Cameroon and Equatorial Guinea. The president of Equatorial Guinea, Francisco Macías Nguma, paid an official visit to Cameroon and stayed to attend the independence day celebrations. (Ph. D.)

CAMEROON
Education. (1966–67) Primary, pupils 773,680, teachers (including preprimary) 16,421; secondary, pupils 32,300, teachers 1,451; vocational, pupils 11,058; teacher training, students 2,151; higher (including university at Yaoundé), students 1,804, teaching staff 166.
   Finance. Monetary unit: CFA franc, with a parity of CFA Fr. 50 to the French franc (CFA Fr. 277.71 = U.S. $1; CFA Fr. 666.50 = £1 sterling). Federal budget (1968–69 est.) balanced at CFA Fr. 27.5 billion (including capital expenditure of CFA Fr. 2.9 billion).
   Foreign Trade. (1969) Imports CFA Fr. 53 billion; exports CFA Fr. 58,570,000,000. Import sources (1968): France 53%; West Germany 9%; U.S. 6%; U.K. 5%. Export destinations (1968): France 34%; Netherlands 21%; West Germany 11%; U.S. 10%. Main exports: cocoa 38%; coffee 20%; aluminum 10%; cotton 7%; timber 5%.
   Transport and Communications. Roads (1968) *c.* 10,600 km. Motor vehicles in use (1967): passenger 23,700; commercial (including buses) 25,500. Railways: (1968) 868 km.; traffic (1969) 170 million passenger-km., freight 254 million net ton-km. Telephones (Jan. 1969) *c.* 5,000. Radio receivers (1969) *c.* 210,000.
   Agriculture. Production (in 000; metric tons; 1968; 1967 in parentheses): corn *c.* 370 (*c.* 338); coffee 55 (*c.* 66); sweet potatoes (1967) *c.* 306, (1966) 308; cassava (1967) *c.* 750, (1966) 774; cocoa (1967–68) *c.* 94, (1966–67) *c.* 86; bananas (1967) *c.* 115, (1966) *c.* 117; peanuts 125 (148); rubber (exports) 13 (21); cotton, lint (1969) 27, (1968) 25; millet and sorghum 460 (271); palm kernels (1967) *c.* 38, (1966) *c.* 37; palm oil (1967) *c.* 39, (1966) *c.* 39; timber (cu.m.) *c.* 7,100 (*c.* 7,000). Livestock (in 000; Dec. 1968): cattle *c.* 2,000; pigs *c.* 370; sheep *c.* 1,600; goats (Dec. 1966) *c.* 2,375; chickens (Dec. 1966) 7,000.
   Industry. Aluminum production (1968) 45,000 metric tons.

Canada

Canada is a federal parliamentary state and member of the Commonwealth of Nations covering North America north of conterminous United States and east of Alaska. Area: 3,851,809 sq.mi. (9,976,196 sq.km.). Pop. (1970 est.): 21,324,000, including (1961) British 43.8%; French 30.4%; other European 22.6%; Indian and Eskimo 1.2%. Cap.: Ottawa (metro. pop., 1969 est., 527,000). Largest city: Montreal (metro. pop., 1969 est., 2,553,-000). Language (1961): English only 67.4%; French only 19.1%; both 12.2%; neither 1.3%. Religion: Roman Catholic 45.7%; Protestant 47.7%. Queen, Elizabeth II; governor-general in 1970, Roland Michener; prime minister, Pierre Elliott Trudeau.

Canada, normally one of the most stable countries in the Western world, experienced an outbreak of political terrorism in late 1970. Reflecting the ferment that had characterized Quebec since it embarked on the road to modernization a decade earlier, the outburst drew support from deeply felt nationalist aspirations found in the province. The crisis, which resulted in the murder of a prominent Quebec Cabinet minister and the temporary suspension of civil liberties in Canada, provided a severe test for the two-year-old government of Pierre Elliott Trudeau (*see* Biography). Faced with the agonizing decision of dealing firmly with Quebec revolutionaries and thereby running the risk of estranging opinion in his native province, Trudeau showed no hesitation in upholding the authority of legitimate government.

The crisis began with a political kidnapping in Montreal when British trade commissioner James R. Cross was abducted from his home on the morning of October 5. His kidnappers subsequently revealed that they were members of Le Front de Libération du Québec (FLQ) and that they wished a substantial ransom. Their demands included the release of 23 "political prisoners" who had been convicted earlier of crimes of violence carried out for the sake of Quebec independence; safe conduct of these prisoners to Cuba or Algeria; and the payment of $500,000 in gold. The FLQ had been in existence since 1963; a collection of autonomous secret cells, loosely linked by certain individuals, it had as its objective the independence of Quebec and the overthrow of existing governments at provincial and federal levels. Its size was unknown but was believed to be very small. Its leaders, mostly young persons, were determined revolutionaries, some of whom had been trained abroad in the use of terrorist methods. These had been its chief preoccupation in Quebec, where a series of armed robberies, thefts, and bomb explosions had occurred intermittently since the appearance of the movement.

Two weeks of anxiety followed the kidnapping of the British diplomat, during which time a second abduction occurred. On October 10 Pierre Laporte, minister of labour in the provincial Cabinet, was seized by a group of armed men in front of his home. The Quebec government, under a new premier, Robert Bourassa (*see* BIOGRAPHY), attempted to negotiate with the FLQ, refusing to consider its original demands but offering to let the kidnappers leave Canada safely if they would surrender their prisoners. As tension increased, there were rumours of plots to blow up public buildings and to assassinate leading political figures.

Early in the morning of October 16 the Trudeau government, acting at the request of the Quebec government and the municipal authorities in Montreal, proclaimed a state of emergency in Canada under the War Measures Act of 1914. The emergency powers assumed by the federal government outlawed the FLQ and any other organization relying on violence or force to achieve its ends. The police were given sweeping authority to carry out searches of property and arrest persons without warrants. At the same time, military protection was provided for Quebec and federal officials, especially in the Montreal area.

A day later the FLQ struck back by brutally murdering Laporte and leaving his body, perhaps as an act of provocation, near the Canadian Forces military base at Saint-Hubert, south of Montreal. Over 400 persons—students, newspapermen, teachers, union organizers, artists, and others—were detained by police, but only one—a 19-year-old youth—admitted taking part in the kidnapping of Laporte. By early November most of the detainees had been released, although about 65 were to be brought to trial on various charges of subversion and related activities.

The extensive manhunt for Cross continued, however, and on December 3 the house where he was being held, in a residential section of Montreal, was surrounded by police. His captors then offered to bargain, and Cross was released unharmed in return for safe conduct to Havana for three terrorists and four members of their families.

Prime Minister Trudeau, well-known as a critic of authoritarian government during the regime of the late Premier Maurice Duplessis of Quebec, was understandably defensive in announcing the stringent security restrictions. The government had assumed powers more sweeping than the situation required, but it had no ready alternative. The emergency powers would be replaced within a month by regulations specifically drafted to meet the terrorist menace in Quebec. This legislation, the Public Order (Temporary Measures) Act, was introduced into the Commons on November 2 and passed by that body on December 1. It continued the earlier ban on the FLQ, but provided that persons arrested would have to be charged within three days or, in special circumstances, within a week, rather than the 21 days allowed under the War Measures Act. Rights to counsel, to trial by jury, and the use of normal rules of evidence were also guaranteed to accused persons. The right of the police to search, seize, or make arrests without warrant in the search for subversive elements in Quebec was also spelled out.

Most commentators recognized that the violence of a few in Quebec symbolized the continuing social and economic problems in the province, associated with the rapid transformation of Quebec's institutions following long years of stagnation and the need to provide a diversified and growing economic system. The sluggish state of the economy in 1970 had exacerbated the discontent that was inherent in many areas of Quebec society. It was clearly necessary that both Ottawa and the provincial government deal as vigorously as possible with Quebec's special difficulties.

Domestic Affairs. The House of Commons sat for 152 days during the 1969–70 session, which began on Oct. 23, 1969, adjourned for approximately three months during the summer, and concluded on October 7, 1970. The session was the second of the 28th Parliament, which had been elected on June 25, 1968. Trudeau's Liberal Party held 154 seats for most of the year, losing one when a Toronto member defected to the Conservatives in September and winning one from the Créditistes in a November by-election. The Conservative Party, with 73 seats counting this addition, continued to be led by Robert Stanfield, who seemed increasingly confident in his role.

The 1969–70 session, while approving 60 pieces of legislation, was not a session of exciting debate or momentous achievement. Many hours were devoted

MARC RIBOUD FROM MAGNUM

René Lévesque, leader of the Parti Québecois, which received 23% of the vote in elections held in April 1970.

CANADA

Education. (1967–68) Primary, pupils 3,836,476, teachers (including preprimary) 152,121; secondary, pupils 1,324,727, teachers 98,591; vocational, pupils 129,317; higher (including 46 principal universities), students 449,902, teaching staff (full time) 24,219.

Finance. Monetary unit: Canadian dollar, with a free rate (Sept. 14, 1970) of Can$1.02 to U.S. $1 (Can$2.42 = £1 sterling). Gold, SDRs, and foreign exchange, official; (June 1970) U.S. $3,811,000,000; (June 1969) U.S. $2,639,000,000. Budget (1968–69 actual): revenue Can$10,191,136,000; expenditure Can$10,767,249,000. Gross national product: (1969) Can$78.1 billion; (1968) Can$71,450,000,000. Money supply: (May 1970) Can$12.8 billion; (May 1969) Can$13,210,000,000. Cost of living (1963 = 100): (June 1970) 126; (June 1969) 122.

Foreign Trade. (1969) Imports Can$14,202,000,000; exports Can$14,870,000,000. Import sources: U.S. 73%; U.K. 6%; EEC 6%. Export destinations: U.S. 71%; U.K. 7%; EEC 6%. Main exports: motor vehicles 22%; machinery 11%; nonferrous metals 8%; metal ores 8%; newsprint 8%; timber 7%; wood pulp 5%.

Transport and Communications. Roads (1968) 806,281 km. (including 2,611 km. expressways). Motor vehicles in use (1968): passenger 6,159,600; commercial (including buses) 1,587,200. Railways: (1968) 69,470 km.; traffic (1969) 4,080,000,000 passenger-km., freight 139,340,000,000 net ton-km. Air traffic (1968): 12,044,454,000 passenger-km.; freight 301,687,000 net ton-km. Shipping (1969): merchant vessels 100 gross tons and over 1,278; gross tonnage 2,450,944; goods loaded (1969) 69,752,000 metric tons, unloaded 50,850,000 metric tons. Telephones (Dec. 1968) 8,821,000. Radio receivers (Dec. 1968) 14.1 million. Television receivers (Dec. 1968) 6.1 million.

Agriculture. Production (in 000; metric tons; 1969; 1968 in parentheses): wheat 18,623 (17,686); oats 5,728 (5,591); barley 8,238 (7,084); rye 419 (331); corn 1,864 (2,062); potatoes 2,288 (2,409); rapeseed 841 (440); linseed 781 (500); tobacco 100 (99); butter 159 (152); cheese 98 (90); beef and veal (1968) 976, (1967) 892; pork (1968) 537, (1967) 537; timber (cu.m.; 1967) 107,600, (1966) c. 109,000; fish catch (1968) 1,490, (1967) 1,303. Livestock (in 000; Dec. 1968): cattle 11,483; sheep 620; horses (June 1968) 363; pigs 5,697; chickens (June 1969) 83,269.

Industry. Labour force (excluding agriculture; May 1970) 7,907,000. Unemployment: (May 1970) 6.1%, (May 1969) 4.7%. Index of industrial production (1963 = 100): (1969) 144; (1968) 137. Fuel and power (in 000; metric tons; 1969): coal 7,849; lignite 1,832; crude oil 55,450; natural gas (cu.m.) 62,409,000; electricity (kw-hr.) 190,511,000 (77% hydroelectric in 1968). Mineral and metal production (in 000; metric tons; 1969): iron ore (shipments; 55% metal content) 34,852; crude steel 9,324; copper ore (metal content) 500; nickel ore (metal content; 1969) 239; zinc ore (metal content) 1,194; lead ore (metal content) 300; aluminum (exports) 804; asbestos (1968) 1,448; gold (troy oz.) 2,433; silver (troy oz.) 41,915; uranium oxide (1968) 3.4. Other production (in 000; metric tons; 1969): wood pulp 18,125; newsprint 7,945; sulfuric acid 2,173; synthetic rubber 199; passenger cars (units) 1,036; commercial vehicles (units) 317. Dwelling units completed (1969) 195,800.

MARC RIBOUD FROM MAGNUM

Troops stand guard in Quebec during Canada's emergency invocation of the War Measures Act following FLQ terrorist kidnappings of two officials in October.

ning of the third session of Parliament on October 8, Donald S. Macdonald, formerly government leader of the House of Commons and responsible for the passage of legislation through the chamber, became minister of national defense in succession to Léo Cadieux. Macdonald was succeeded in the delicate task of managing the House by Allan J. MacEachen, who moved from the Department of Manpower and Immigration. Otto Lang of Saskatchewan became minister of manpower and immigration while retaining responsibility for the Canadian Wheat Board.

A series of meetings between federal ministers and the heads of the provincial governments was held during 1970. On the whole, significant achievement was lacking, although the conferences undoubtedly performed a useful function in the interchange of information and viewpoints. The first was held in Ottawa on February 16 and 17, and was devoted to a consideration of the federal government's plans for fighting inflation. The premiers agreed to restrain spending, lending, and borrowing as far as possible and to establish rent review boards in the municipalities under their jurisdiction. Inflation also occupied a second conference, in Winnipeg, Man., on June 5 and 6, when approval was given to the federal government's guideline of a 6% maximum for wage and salary increases. This conference was the first to be attended by Bourassa, who pressed for adjustments in equalization payments for his province and won an additional grant of $100 million from the federal treasury.

A third conference, on the revision of the constitution, took place in Ottawa on September 14 and 15, with most of the sessions in camera. After several years of constitutional discussion without notable achievement, the September meeting failed to excite expectations, and this proved to be justified. Trudeau's interventions in the discussions suggested that he now felt less sense of urgency in approaching constitutional change than he had when the antifederalist Union Nationale government was in power in Quebec. The April 29 election of a Liberal administration under Bourassa had seemed to remove some of the pressures for revision in the Canadian federal system.

The Union Nationale government, under Jean-Jacques Bertrand, had gone into the Quebec election bitterly divided over Bertrand as its leader and with differing viewpoints on many questions of policy, especially Quebec's place in the Canadian federal system. Against the Union Nationale were three other parties: the Liberals, led since January by Bourassa, a 36-year-old economist from Montreal; the Parti Québecois (separatist), with a former Liberal, René Lévesque, as its head; and the Ralliement Créditiste, a branch of the federal party running in a provincial election for the first time. The Union Nationale lost a shattering 39 seats, holding only 17 seats in an assembly of 108 members. Twelve ministers in the Bertrand Cabinet were defeated. The Parti Québecois, while winning 24% of the popular vote, gained only 7 seats and saw Lévesque defeated in his bid for election. The Ralliement Créditiste took 12 seats. The Liberals, who had campaigned on a strongly federalist position and had promised swift action to cure unemployment, won 72 seats, a gain of 25 from their previous standing. Bourassa assumed office on May 12, the youngest man ever to become premier of Quebec.

General elections were also held in the three Maritime Provinces. An election on May 11 in Prince Edward Island resulted in a victory for the Liberal government of 36-year-old Alex Campbell, in power since

to an examination of the government's White Paper on taxation reform, tabled by Finance Minister Edgar Benson on Nov. 7, 1969. While the government did not agree that all income should be taxed on an equal basis, as had been recommended by a 1967 royal commission, it announced its support of the principle of a capital gains tax as a means of ensuring that the total income of the wealthy was brought within the tax system. To compensate for this levy, the White Paper suggested that the rate on top income earners be reduced from the present 82 to 51%. At the same time, it proposed that approximately 10% of Canada's 7.7 million taxpayers be dropped from the tax rolls.

The legislative output of the second session was diverse. The Canada Elections Act was amended to lower the voting age for federal elections from 21 to 18 years, to allow 18-year-olds to stand for Parliament, and to permit the placing of political party labels on ballots. An amendment to the Criminal Code provided for the sealing of criminal records five years after completion of sentence for individuals whose cases were recommended by the parole board. Another measure approved was intended to outlaw literature promoting or inciting hatred between groups. An International Development Research Centre to look into problems of aid and economic growth in the developing world was sanctioned by Parliament. Later, it was announced that the organization would be headed by former prime minister Lester B. Pearson.

As in so many legislative bodies in North America in 1970, the pressing problems of pollution and the safeguarding of the environment were given much consideration. In anticipation of an increase in commercial shipping in the Arctic Archipelago as a result of oil discoveries in eastern Alaska, a bill was approved laying down pollution controls for Canada's Arctic waters. The government also announced an extension of Canada's territorial water boundaries from 3 to 12 mi., allowing for new regulations to govern the inshore fisheries. The U.S. protested both these moves and the Japanese government also made representations against the Canadian acts. Toward the end of the session the Commons gave final approval to the Canada Water Act, which created water quality management agencies across Canada.

One reorganization of the Trudeau Cabinet occurred during the year. In September, just before the begin-

1966. In the other two provinces sitting governments were turned out. The New Brunswick election on October 26 saw Louis Robichaud's government, in power since 1960, defeated by a rejuvenated Conservative Party under Richard Hatfield. In Nova Scotia, which went to the polls on October 13, George Smith's Conservative government, facing its first electoral test since Smith succeeded Robert Stanfield as premier in 1967, was upset by the Liberals under Gerald Regan, a Halifax lawyer.

Foreign Affairs. The Trudeau government unveiled a comprehensive statement of its views on an appropriate foreign policy for Canada in 1970. Tabled in the House of Commons on June 25 by Mitchell Sharp, the secretary of state for external affairs, the study comprised six position papers, collectively entitled *Foreign Policy for Canadians*. The papers provided a reasoned discussion of Canada's external policies in the past and suggested how they should be adapted to meet the challenges offered by a dynamic international situation. Canada's basic national aims were defined as the preservation of an independent political entity, the maintenance of an expanding prosperity, and a constructive contribution to the needs of humanity.

In commenting on the papers, Sharp said that they were conceptual in character and marked an attempt to set out broad principles of foreign policy in a way that had never been done before in official statements in other countries. One of the purposes of the papers, he remarked, was "to invite the public to think about foreign policy not as something apart from domestic policy but simply as a means of pursuing national policy by other means in the international environment." There was no paper on relations with the U.S., he went on, because the subject was so "overwhelming" to the Canadian viewpoint that it was difficult to express it under a single heading. Sharp denied charges that the papers represented a rejection of the internationalist approach embodied in the diplomacy of Pearson. "We are trying to avoid having too reactive a foreign policy —too much improvisation," he said. "What we are seeking are guides to policy . . . certain objectives that we pursue in a very uncertain world, and we shouldn't simply be reacting to events outside."

The Pacific region was described as offering a great potential for the expansion of Canadian trade, especially to the resource industries of western Canada. In the Western Hemisphere, Canada must "accept its full responsibility" through a series of coordinated programs designed to strengthen links with the Latin-American countries. Full membership in the Organization of American States was rejected for "the immediate future." Canada's historic involvement with Europe was stressed as needing to be continued in spite of the greater interest to be shown in the Pacific basin and Latin America. In international development the government promised "a steady and increasing flow of resources" to official development assistance. In the UN, Canada promised to continue traditional objectives such as peacekeeping and limiting the arms race, while undertaking new initiatives in such areas as satellite systems, the use of the seabed, and the preservation of the environment.

Although few specific objectives were mentioned in the review, one—the establishment of diplomatic relations with China—was brought about late in 1970. Following talks in Stockholm that lasted almost two years, the Canadian and Chinese governments announced agreement on the subject on October 13. Sharp, in making the announcement in Ottawa, said that the

MARC RIBOUD FROM MAGNUM

Prime Minister
Pierre Elliott Trudeau
(left) leaves the funeral
of Quebec Labour Minister
Pierre Laporte, who was
kidnapped and slain
by FLQ terrorists.

Canadian government did not consider it "appropriate either to endorse or to challenge the Chinese government's position on the status of Taiwan." The Nationalist Chinese ambassador left Canada on the day the decision was announced, and shortly afterward a team of officials from the Department of External Affairs flew to China to begin the task of setting up the Canadian embassy.

Canada reacted strongly to the presence of Soviet fishing vessels on the continental shelf area of its Pacific coast in 1970. A series of incidents occurred in which Canadian vessels were brushed, and there was much agitation among west coast fishermen over the alleged depletion of fishery resources by the Soviets. A stiff protest was handed to the Soviet Union on July 28 over sideswiping incidents. At the next Law of the Sea conference, to be held in 1971, Canada was expected to press for new territorial limits on the continental shelf.

In March a Canadian delegation took part in a conference of 26 French-language countries at Niamey in Niger, where a new international organization, designed to enhance scientific and cultural cooperation among French-language states, was called into being. It was agreed that nonsovereign governments could participate in the activities of the organization provided approval was secured from their national governments. Four provinces participated under this arrangement: Quebec, Ontario, Manitoba, and New Brunswick.

The transfer of natural resources to the U.S. was a major issue in Canadian-American relations in 1970. The U.S. decision, announced on March 10, to reduce oil imports from Canada into the area east of the Rockies from the February level of over 550,000 to 395,000 bbl. a day was regarded in Canada as an indication that the U.S. desired a comprehensive arrangement for the purchase of energy resources from Canada. It was apparent that the U.S. was more interested in buying gas than oil from Canada, while Canada was probably more anxious to dispose of oil. On September 29 the Canadian government agreed to the export to the U.S. of an additional 6.3 trillion cu.ft. of natural gas over the next 15 to 20 years, an increase of 50%. Ottawa announced that, even with this increase, gas exports to the U.S. represented less than 1% of Canada's estimated gas-producing potential. The increased exports of Canadian gas were accompanied by a relaxation in the U.S. controls on oil imports. It was apparent, however, that a coordinated

CANADIAN PRESS

COURTESY, BRITISH INFORMATION SERVICE

FLQ kidnap victims:
top, Pierre Laporte;
above, James R. Cross.

energy-sharing arrangement was still some distance in the future.

Another energy source, uranium, was also in the headlines in 1970. In March the sale of 25.5% of the shares of Denison Mines Ltd., Canada's largest uranium producer, to a U.S. firm was halted by an order of the Canadian Cabinet. Subsequently, amendments to the Atomic Energy Act were proposed that set a 33% maximum on the total foreign ownership of Canadian uranium properties of proven productive capacity. The U.S. was invited to assist Canada's plans for a countrywide communications system based on satellite transmission when the Hughes Aircraft Co. was awarded a $30 million contract in September to build three satellites.

The Economy. The Canadian economy performed less impressively in 1970 than in the two preceding years. Growth in real output for the year was expected to be 3% in terms of 1969 dollars, compared with 4.8% in 1968 and 1969. The gross national product was expected to reach Can$82,876,000,000 for the year. The saving factor was a substantial increase in exports, led by the sale of automobiles and parts to the U.S. Grain sales were also excellent, with buoyant markets being experienced in Britain, Western Europe, and China. Commodity exports to all countries for the first nine months of 1970 rose 14.7% to a high of $12,-477,100,000, and sales to the U.S. amounted to $8,136,-600,000, an increase of 6.2% over the comparable period in 1969. On the other hand, Canadian imports rose by only 1.8% in the first nine months of the year, standing at $10,549,500,000 at the end of September.

The resultant record-breaking surplus, combined with very large capital inflows from the U.S., impelled the government on May 31 to release the Canadian dollar from its fixed rate of 1% on either side of 92.5 U.S. cents. The adoption of a floating dollar rate represented an upward revaluation of the currency and reflected the great pressure on federal reserves that had been created by the exceptional foreign trade patterns. The Canadian dollar soon rose to a point near parity with the U.S. dollar, stabilizing at about 98.5 U.S. cents.

Unemployment was severe in 1970. On a seasonally adjusted basis it was expected to run at 6.6% of the labour force for the year, the highest rate since 1961. Over 500,000 persons were unemployed in June, normally a good month, and it was expected that the figure in the depth of winter might rise to 750,000. As a compensating factor, the Trudeau government's determined fight against inflation began to show results. The general price index did not fall, but it rose less rapidly. On an annual basis the rate of increase was about 3%, compared with 5% in 1969.

The federal budget, brought down on March 12, attempted to reconcile the conflicting demands of inflation and unemployment. No new taxes or changes in tariff duties were announced, the first time since 1913 that no proposals had been made in these areas. Revenues for the 1970–71 fiscal year were expected to reach $13,150,000,000 while expenditures were estimated at $12.9 billion. A surplus was therefore predicted, although subsequent demands on the federal treasury whittled most of it away by the end of the year.   (D. M. L. F.)

ENCYCLOPÆDIA BRITANNICA FILMS. *Canada: The Atlantic Provinces* (1958); *Canada: The Industrial Provinces* (1958); *Canada: The Pacific Provinces* (1958); *Canada: The Prairie Provinces* (1958); *The St. Lawrence Seaway* (1959); *Canada's Royal Canadian Mounted Police* (1963); *The Legend of the Magic Knives* (1970).

Central African Republic

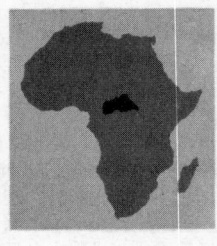

The landlocked Central African Republic is bounded by Chad, Sudan, the Congo republics, and Cameroon. Area: 240,540 sq.mi. (623,000 sq. km.). Pop. (1969 est.): 1,518,-000, chiefly Mandja-Baya, Banda, Mbaka, and Azande. Cap. and largest city: Bangui (pop., 1968, 298,579). Official language: French. Religion: mainly animist. President and premier in 1970, Jean Bedel Bokassa.

In June and August, President Bokassa made several changes in his government, but little was known outside about the internal development of the Central African Republic during 1970.

In the field of foreign affairs, the year was characterized by considerable tension in relations between the Central African Republic and France, and by a marked turn toward the Communist world on the part of the Bangui leaders. Relations between Paris and Bangui, already cool as a result of the expulsion of approximately 40 French technicians working in the diamond mines in November 1969, became progressively more bitter. In July Bokassa protested a speech made by the French ambassador, Albert de Schonen, on the occasion of the French national holiday. Time and again French technical assistants were accused of subversive activities and expelled from the country, and there were also frequent attacks upon the French press. Finally, the Bangui government took the unprecedented step of declaring the French ambassador persona non grata.

In October technical assistants working in the Central African Republic's agricultural services were returned to France. During the same period, invited by the Nigerian government to attend the celebrations marking the tenth anniversary of Nigeria's independence, Bokassa made violently anti-French statements and accused the African, Malagasy, and Mauritian Common Organization (OCAMM), of which his country was a member, of being "in the pay of France."

At the same time, Bokassa, whose accession to power in 1966 had been marked by the expulsion of Chinese Communists from Bangui and the severing of

CENTRAL AFRICAN REPUBLIC
Education. (1967–68) Primary, pupils 153,324, teachers 2,706; secondary, pupils 5,205, teachers 204; vocational, pupils 1,090, teachers 81; teacher training, students 129, teachers 17. The University of Bangui opened in 1970.
Finance. Monetary unit: CFA franc, with a parity of CFA Fr. 50 to the French franc (CFA Fr. 277.71 = U.S. $1; CFA Fr. 666.50 = £1 sterling). Budget (1969–70 est.): revenue CFA Fr. 10,749,000,000; expenditure CFA Fr. 11,450,000,000.
Foreign Trade. (1968) Imports CFA Fr. 9,802,000,-000; exports CFA Fr. 8,816,000,000. Import sources: France 54%; West Germany 10%; Italy 7%; U.S. 5%. Export destinations: France 38%; U.S. 32%; Israel 17%; Italy 5%. Main exports: diamonds 52%; cotton 23%; coffee 14%.
Agriculture. Production (in 000; metric tons; 1968; 1967 in parentheses): cassava 1,000 (1,000); peanuts 75 (70); sweet potatoes 42 (40); bananas (1967) *c.* 170, (1966) *c.* 170; coffee 9 (9); cotton, lint 22 (18). Livestock (in 000; 1966–67): cattle 450; pigs (1968–69) *c.* 26; sheep *c.* 113; goats *c.* 520; chickens *c.* 900.
Industry. Diamond production (1968) 609,000 metric carats.

all links with Peking, became lavish in his praise of the countries of the East. On April 19 he announced that the Central African Republic had recognized East Germany, and in May relations were established with Albania, Czechoslovakia, and Hungary. In July Bokassa paid an 11-day official visit to the U.S.S.R., and an agreement for economic and technical cooperation was signed. (Ph. D.)

Ceylon

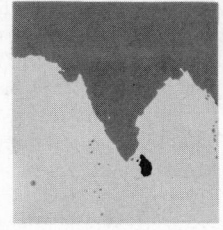

An Asian parliamentary state of the Commonwealth of Nations, Ceylon occupies an island off the southeast coast of peninsular India. Area: 25,332 sq.mi. (65,610 sq.km.). Pop. (1968 est.): 11,992,000, including Sinhalese about 70%; Tamils 22%; Moors 6%. Cap. and largest city: Colombo (pop., 1968 est., 558,500). Language: Sinhalese (official), Tamil, and English. Religion: mainly Buddhism, with Hindu, Christian, and Muslim minorities. Queen, Elizabeth II; governor-general in 1970, William Gopallawa; prime ministers, Dudley Senanayake and, from May 29, Mme Sirimavo Bandaranaike.

The major event of 1970 was the landslide victory, at a general election on May 27, of a left-wing coalition under Mme Sirimavo Bandaranaike (see BIOGRAPHY) over Dudley Senanayake's United National Party (UNP) that had governed Ceylon since 1965 (and for the first 8 of its 22 years of independence). Mme Bandaranaike's own Sri Lanka Freedom Party (SLFP) won 91 of the 151 elected seats in the House of Representatives, giving it a clear parliamentary majority, but the country's key labour unions were con-

CAMERA PRESS FROM PIX

Mme Sirimavo Bandaranaike, elected prime minister of Ceylon for the second time, prays in the shrine room of the Temple of the Tooth in Kandy.

trolled by SLFP's two opposition partners—the Trotskyist Lanka Sama Samaja Party (LSSP), which won 19 seats, and the pro-Moscow Communist Party (CCP), which won six seats. Forming a coalition, all three fought the election as the United Front, and it was as prime minister of a United Front government that Mme Bandaranaike took office. Appointments to her 21-strong Cabinet included three Trotskyists (LSSP) and the general secretary of the CCP.

In the election the UNP obtained 1,879,996 of the 4,953,769 votes cast, 62,647 more than the SLFP. But its previous 72 seats were reduced to only 17. The new government was thus the first since independence to win more than a two-thirds majority.

The landslide surprised many observers; recalling the UNP's clear majority in local elections in late 1969, they had expected a close contest. While the factors favouring Mme Bandaranaike were not easy to understand, voters were probably influenced by the United Front's pledge to restore the rice ration—halved by Senanayake in 1966 because of the burden it imposed on the economy (since the rice was distributed at a price far below the cost of importing it).

The new government's program, as outlined by the governor-general when opening Parliament on June 14, could only be described as revolutionary. It promised a new constitution to make Ceylon a "free, sovereign, and independent" republic, thus ending its Commonwealth link with Britain. The government's aim was to create a socialist democracy. Banks, foreign trade, and the mainly British-owned agency houses (which managed tea, coconut, and rubber plantations) were to be nationalized; measures were to be taken "to end the present domination of the daily press by capitalist monopolies"; and administrative services were to be drastically reformed.

In June the prime minister convened all members of the House of Representatives and announced that a constituent assembly would frame the new constitution. Stressing that its authority derived from the people, not from the British crown, Mme Bandaranaike said that the assembly would comprise the members of the House of Representatives, but not the Senate. The House of Representatives duly passed the necessary resolution; with some reservations the opposition parties agreed to participate; and the task of drafting the constitution (which was expected to take some months) fell to the LSSP finance minister.

The Constituent Assembly met at the end of July. Such was the parliamentary interest in its subsequent deliberations that few other items in the government's

CEYLON

Education. (1967–68) Primary, secondary, and vocational, pupils 2,594,072, teachers 94,113; teacher training, students 5,570, teachers 438; higher (including 3 universities; 1966–67), students 16,098, teaching staff 1,064.

Finance. Monetary unit: Ceylonese rupee, with a par value of CRs. 5.95 to U.S. $1 (CRs. 14.29 = £1 sterling). Gold, SDRs, and foreign exchange, official: (June 1970) U.S. $41 million; (June 1969) U.S. $39 million. Budget (1968–69 est.): revenue CRs. 2,338,-509,171; expenditure CRs. 2,356,780,000. Gross national product: (1968) CRs. 10,596,000,000; (1967) CRs. 9,052,000,000. Money supply: (Feb. 1970) CRs. 1,865,000,000; (Feb. 1969) CRs. 1,866,000,000. Cost of living (Colombo; 1963 = 100): (June 1970) 127; (June 1969) 120.

Foreign Trade. (1969) Imports CRs. 2,543,445,-000; exports CRs. 1,916,000,000. Import sources: U.K. 17%; China 11%; U.S. 8%; India 8%; Japan 7%; West Germany 6%. Export destinations: U.K. 20%; China 13%; U.S. 8%; U.S.S.R. 5%. Main exports: tea 61%; rubber 22%; coconut products 12%.

Transport and Communications. Roads (1968) 20,955 km. Motor vehicles in use (1968): passenger 84,678; commercial 30,388. Railways: (1968) 1,500 km.; traffic (1967–68) 2,701,000,000 passenger-km., freight 336 million net ton-km. Air traffic (1968): 97,118,000 passenger-km.; freight 2.9 million net ton-km. Telephones (Dec. 1968) 57,598. Radio receivers (Dec. 1968) 400,000.

Agriculture. Production (in 000; metric tons; 1969; 1968 in parentheses): rice 1,478 (1,347); cassava (1968) 346, (1967) 346; sweet potatoes (1968) 76, (1967) 73; onions (1968) 35, (1967) 38; tea (1968) 225, (1967) 221; rubber 143 (149); copra (1967) 191, (1966) 212. Livestock (in 000; June 1969): cattle c. 1,700; sheep c. 25; buffaloes (June 1967) 765; goats (June 1967) 580; pigs c. 129; chickens c. 6,600.

Industry. Production (in 000; metric tons; 1969): cement 283; graphite (exports; 1968) 11; electricity (kw-hr.; 1968) 650,000.

program were tackled—except in the field of foreign affairs where Senanayake's pro-Western orientation was radically changed with the establishment, in June, of diplomatic relations with North Korea, North Vietnam, and East Germany and the suspension, in July, of relations with Israel. The government also implemented its pledge to double the previous rice ration.

(S. A. P.)

Chad

A landlocked republic of central Africa, Chad is bounded by Libya, Sudan, the Central African Republic, Cameroon, Nigeria, and Niger. Area: 490,-750 sq.mi. (1,271,000 sq.km.). Pop. (1969): 3,510,-000, including Saras, Arabs, and other Africans. Cap. and largest city: Fort-Lamy (pop., 1967 est., 118,000). Official language: French. Religion: Muslim and animist. President and premier in 1970, François Tombalbaye.

The killing of 11 French soldiers in an ambush in the Tibesti region in October marked the lowest point of the deteriorating situation at Fort-Lamy. The advantages of the French intervention, increasingly unpopular in both France and Africa, seemed clear only to President Tombalbaye.

French forces in Chad, which had numbered approximately 2,500 men in 1969, were reduced to 1,900 in 1970. There was talk of repatriating the entire corps during 1971, leaving only about 900 men to maintain permanent installations at Fort-Lamy and a few dozen French officers and enlisted men attached to the Chad National Army as technical aides. However, these plans were put in doubt by the ambush, which aroused a large body of opinion in France hostile to the policing operation. Hostility was increased by Tombalbaye's refusal to acknowledge the extent of the conflict and his dismissal of the Chad National Liberation Front as mere "bandits."

Those responsible for French policy justified their action by reference to military assistance agreements signed at the time Chad became independent. However, these provided for joint action by France and Chad together with Congo (Brazzaville) and the Central African Republic, and neither of the last two showed any intention of participating in the conflict. The geographic location of Chad in the centre of an area of political instability lent some support to the view that an extension of the Chad conflict might lead to a deterioration of the situation in central Africa as a whole.

Nevertheless, the reasons for the French and Chadian forces' apparent inability to restore order remained unclear. Interference by foreign powers, in-

cluding Algeria and Libya, could not entirely account for this; nor was such interference proved. The cohesion of the rebel forces as an organized movement was in itself open to doubt. (PH. D.)

Chemistry

Physical and Inorganic. *Lasers in Studies of Fast Photochemical Reactions.* Until recently the resolution of events in flash photolysis and luminescence studies was restricted to the microsecond (10^{-6}) and nanosecond (10^{-9}) ranges. The application of laser techniques, however, made it possible to study flash photolysis of transient species lasting a few nanoseconds and emission processes in the picosecond (10^{-12}) range.

Spectroscopic monitoring of the transient species produced by the laser flashes involved two different approaches. In the first, the absorption spectrum of the transient was measured against a continuum of background light from the spark produced by passing the red portion of a ruby laser through an inert gas. The second device consisted of the conventional method of building up pictures from a series of spectra taken at a preselected delay after the excitation flash. The delay unit in this case was based on the speed of light and involved passing part of the laser beam through an optical delay system before it entered the reaction vessel. Typical studies by these new methods included absorption spectra of electronically excited singlet states of triphenylene in benzene solution and the decay rates of singlet and triplet states of 1,2-benzanthracene in various solvents.

Anomalous Water. Although anomalous water was first reported several years ago, only recently had Western scientists begun to take seriously and to investigate thoroughly the claim by Soviet chemist Boris V. Deryagin that he had prepared a new form of water. Called variously anomalous water, orthowater, polywater, and superwater, the material was readily prepared in milligram quantities by placing a beaker containing a large number of fine capillary tubes of silica or borosilicate glass (diameters 1–10 μ) in a desiccator containing a second beaker of saturated aqueous potassium sulfate. The desiccator was evacuated and left undisturbed over a period of a few days to several months, whereupon anomalous water could be observed, under a microscope, to have formed in the capillaries.

The properties that distinguished this substance from ordinary water were its low freezing range (below $-10°$ C), its high density (above 1.4), and its high viscosity and refractive index. Several research groups in the U.S. and U.K. confirmed the preparation of anomalous water and concentrated on examining its spectroscopic properties. Thus, the nuclear magnetic resonance spectrum of a 1-mg. sample at 100 MHz. and the mass spectrum indicated no differences from water and led to the conclusions that although the liquid had gel properties it contained only the elements of water. On the other hand, infrared and Raman studies of nonvolatile samples revealed that they contained ordinary water plus a component that modified the vibrational properties of the O—H bond, leading to the suggestion that anomalous water contained an unusually short O—H—O bond with an energy corresponding to 125 to 210 kilojoules per gram molecule.

Ion-Selective Electrodes. The National Bureau of

CHAD
Education. (1966–67) Primary, pupils 172,485, teachers 2,136; secondary, pupils 7,993, teachers 265; vocational, pupils 502, teachers (1965–66) 30; teacher training, students 594, teachers 29.
Finance. Monetary unit: CFA franc, with a parity of CFA Fr. 50 to the French franc (CFA Fr. 277.71 = U.S. $1; CFA Fr. 666.50 = £1 sterling). Budget (1969 est.) balanced at CFA Fr. 12.6 billion. Cost of living (Fort-Lamy; 1963 = 100): (May 1970) 141; (May 1969) 130.
Foreign Trade. (1968) Imports CFA Fr. 9,494,-000,000; exports CFA Fr. 6,824,000,000. Import sources: France 43%; Nigeria 10%; West Germany 9%; U.S. 9%; Italy 8%. Export destinations: France 64%; Belgium 9%; Congo (Kinshasa) 5%; Japan 5%. Main export cotton 85%.

Cheese:
see Agriculture

Chemical Industry:
see Industrial Review

Standards, Washington, D.C., published the papers presented at a 1969 conference on ion-selective electrodes which highlighted the recent progress in this area of chemistry. The development of electrodes that were selective to a specific ion dated back to the hydrogen-responsive glass electrode, but recent advances had been made with electrodes involving different materials. Ion-selective electrodes could be classified into four main types: (1) solid-state electrodes based on a membrane consisting of a single crystal or discs compacted of the active material; (2) heterogeneous membrane electrodes with the active material dispersed in an inert binder or matrix; (3) liquid ion exchange membranes incorporating the selected ion attached to a large organic molecule insoluble in water; and (4) glass electrodes specific for cations (ions that migrate toward the cathode).

Commercial electrodes of the solid-state type were available for F^-, Cl^-, Br^-, I^-, and S^{2-} ions, and these were based on insoluble silver salts in the forms of discs sealed onto the bottom of a tube. The F^- ion-selective electrode depended on single crystals of lanthanum, neodymium, or praseodymium fluoride. The heterogeneous membrane electrodes, specific for Cl^-, Br^-, I^-, and S^{2-}, contained the active material dispersed in inert binders such as polyvinyl chloride, polystyrene, or silicone rubber. The most important liquid ion-exchange electrode was that for the Ca^{++} ion which utilized the Ca^{++} salt of didecylphosphoric acid dissolved in di-n-acetylphenyl-phosphonate.

Alkali Metal Ion Complexes of Macrocyclic Polyethers. Scientists at the E. I. du Pont de Nemours & Co., Wilmington, Del., led by C. J. Pedersen, discovered a new class of organometallic compounds containing the interesting feature of a coordinated alkali metal ion. The first such compound was prepared from the macrocyclic (containing an atomic ring structure of a large size) polyether, 2,3,11,12-dibenzo-1,4,7,10,13,16-hexaoxacyclooctadeca-2, 11-diene; this polyether formed a complex with Na^+ or K^+ in which the six oxygen atoms were virtually planar with the alkali metal ion in the centre, as shown in the figure. This type of structure, confirmed by X-ray crystallographic analysis carried out by Mary R. Truter and co-workers at the ARC Unit of Structural Chemistry, London, was named a "crown compound."

The crown compounds were likened to the transition metal cation coordination spheres that had been used as templates for assembling macrocycles from simple organic compounds while they were around the cation. The latter were adequately accounted for by the ligand field model (a molecular orbital theory that allows for delocalization of certain of the central metal's electrons into the ligand orbitals). In contrast, it was believed that in the crown compounds the heterocyclic oxygen atoms of the macromolecules chelated the alkali metals by electrostatic attraction enhanced by the fit of the ring diameter with the metal ion size. (To chelate is to combine with a metal and form a ring that contains five or six atoms holding a central metallic ion in a coordination complex.)
(J. A. Kr.)

Organic. Much interesting work appeared during the year on the nature of the various reactive intermediates in organic chemistry. The long-standing controversy over the structure of certain carbonium ions, such as the norbornyl cation, appeared to be subsiding with the development of ^{13}C nuclear mag-

netic resonance spectroscopy. G. A. Olah showed that the ^{13}C chemical shift provided direct experimental evidence of the degree of the "nonclassical" character of these ions, prepared by solvolysis (chemical reaction of a solvent and a dissolved substance) of the appropriate alcohol in antimony pentafluoride/sulfuryl chlorofluoride mixtures. At $-150°$ C the norbornyl cation was found to exist largely in the "corner-protonated-cyclopropane" form **1**; at higher temperatures the rate of 1,2 hydrogen shift around the cyclopropane ring increased. Cyclopropylcarbinol and cyclobutanol both gave the same cation, thought to be either **2** or **3**, with **4** also participating. By the same spectroscopic technique the structure **5** was confirmed for the intermediate bromonium ion formed in the addition of bromine to ethylene. The first stable ion with this structural feature to be isolated resulted from the reaction of adamantylideneadamantane with bromine in carbon tetrachloride. The product **6** was precipitated as a reasonably stable yellowish solid, insoluble in organic solvents.

New evidence was also presented for the formation of vinyl cations, which may be produced in the solvolysis of vinyl halides and similar compounds, and by the protonation (addition of a proton) of acetylenes. Treatment of either geometrical isomer **7** or **8** with silver acetate in acetic acid gave the same mixture of products, including the corresponding *cis* and *trans* acetates and the ring-expanded product **9**, thus indicating the linear cyclopropyl vinyl cation **10** as the common intermediate. Reaction of t-butylacetylene with hydrogen chloride also gave products consistent with 1,2 methyl shift having occurred in the t-butylvinyl cation **11**.

The chemistry of nitrenium ions $R_2N:^+$, isoelectronic (having the same number of electrons) with carbonium ions except for a lone pair of electrons rather than a third bonding pair, was further clarified. Methanolysis of the N-chloroazabicycloheptane **12** (X = Cl), gave the nitrenium ion, which yielded products from rearrangement to the carbonium ion **13** and also the parent amine **12** (X = H). The latter resulted from spin-inversion that transformed the initial singlet (spin of zero) nitrenium ion into a triplet; homolytic hydrogen abstraction from the solvent, characteristic of a species containing unpaired electrons, gave rise to the amine.

Conditions were found in which the nucleophilic (affinity for an atomic nucleus) properties of some anions (ions that migrate toward the anode) could be exploited in situations which had previously been experimentally inaccessible though conceptually simple. Sodium borohydride was shown to reduce many organic halides to the corresponding hydrocarbons in dimethylsulfoxide or sulfolane. Lithium bis (trimethylsilyl) amide in tetrahydrofuran at $-78°$ C reacted with ethyl acetate to give essentially quantitative yields of lithio ethyl acetate. This intermediate was not rapidly attacked by the solvent at this temperature, permitting application in the synthesis of β-hydroxy esters from aldehydes and ketones:

$$LiCH_2CO_2C_2H_5 + R_2C=O \rightarrow$$
$$R_2C(OLi)CH_2CO_2C_2H_5$$

Trialkylboranes, which were already well known for their many reactions of synthetic value proceeding by molecular or ionic pathways, were found in 1970 to enter also into free radical chain reactions with α,β-unsaturated carbonyl compounds. Alkyl radicals, generated from the organoborane thermally,

WIDE WORLD
Luis F. Leloir, winner of the 1970 Nobel Prize for Chemistry.

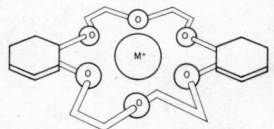

"Crown compound" of alkali metal ion complexes of macrocyclic polyethers.

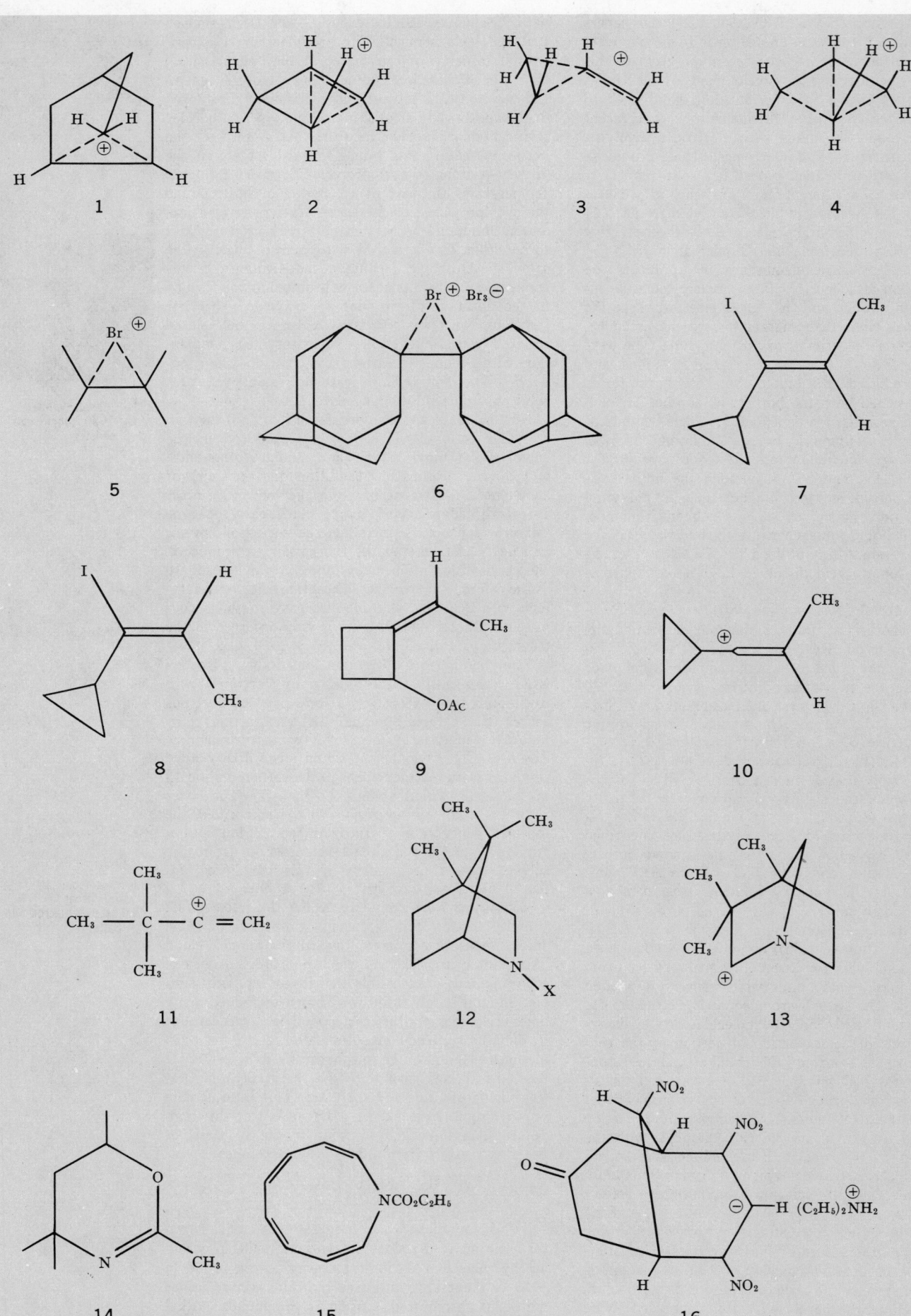

photolytically, or by reaction with oxygen or an organic peroxide, attacked the terminal carbon atom of the conjugated system:

$$R\cdot + \;>C=CH\cdot C=O \rightarrow R-\underset{|}{C}-\overset{\cdot}{C}H\cdot \underset{|}{C}=O \leftrightarrow$$

$$R-\underset{|}{C}-CH=\underset{|}{C}-\overset{\cdot}{O}$$

The radical chain was then propagated by homolytic displacement of an alkyl radical from the trialkylborane with formation of an enol borinate. At the completion of the reaction the enol borinate could be hydrolyzed to release the new carbonyl compound:

$$R-\underset{|}{C}-CH=\underset{|}{C}-\overset{\cdot}{O} + BR_3 \rightarrow$$

$$R-\underset{|}{C}-CH=\underset{|}{C}-O-BR_2 + R\cdot$$

$$\downarrow H_2O$$

$$R-\underset{|}{C}-CH_2\cdot \underset{|}{C}=O$$

1,4 addition of an acyl group and a metal atom to similar conjugated systems was achieved by reaction with the complex formed from an alkyl-lithium and nickel carbonyl at −50° C:

$$(CH_3)_2C = CH\cdot COCH_3 +$$
$$[C_4H_9CONi(CO_3)]^- \; Li^+ \rightarrow$$
$$C_4H_9CO\cdot C(CH_3)_2CH_2COCH_3.$$

This procedure provided the most convenient route to the 1,4-dicarbonyl system.

Dihydro-oxazines such as **14** also found synthetic application. This compound was hydrolyzed by aqueous hydrobromic acid to give acetic acid, but unlike the acid itself the methyl group could be metalated by reaction with an alkyl lithium and then subjected to a variety of transformations before the acid function was finally exposed. (Metalation is the process of attaching a metal atom to a carbon atom of an organic molecule.)

N-carbethoxyazacyclononatetraene, **15**, a possible 10 π-electron analogue of pyrrole, was prepared, but seemed to have no aromatic stability. The origin of the red colour produced with acetone and base in the time-honoured test for trinitrobenzene was elucidated. The intense colour was associated with salts of the type **16**, which were isolated and characterized.

(J. C. Y.)

See also Industrial Review; Molecular Biology; Physics.

ENCYCLOPÆDIA BRITANNICA FILMS. *Preface to Chemistry* (1954).

Chess

The world champion, Boris Spassky, was chosen as sportsman of 1969 by the Soviet sports journalists. First place in an international tournament at Skopje, Yugos., in August 1969 was shared by V. Hort (Czech.) and M. Matulovic (Yugos.). The Yugoslav grand master D. Janosevic, who had done badly at Skopje, redeemed himself by winning first prize at Vrsac, Yugos. In October the European zonal tournament no. 3 was played in Athens. First was Matulovic and equal second were Hort and R. Hubner

(W.Ger.). The Northern Open championship at Linköping, Swed., was won by O. Jakobsen (Den.). Two more European zonal tournaments were played in October and November 1969. In the European zonal tournament no. 1 at Praia da Rocha, Port., there was a triple tie for first among D. Minic and S. Gligoric (both Yugos.) and M. Filip (Czech.). First in European zonal tournament no. 2 at Raach, Aus., was W. Uhlmann (E.Ger.).

The Danish grand master Bent Larsen won first

Caro-Kann defense (played on Board Two in the match Rest of the World v. U.S.S.R. at Belgrade, March 29, 1970).

White R. Fischer	Black T. Petrosian	White R. Fischer	Black T. Petrosian
1 P — K4	P — QB3	21 P — B5	Kt X Kt
2 P — Q4	P — Q4	22 P X Kt	B X KP
3 P X P	P X P	23 P X P	B — KB3
4 B — Q3(a)	Kt — QB3	24 P X P	B X P(B2)
5 P — QB3	Kt — B3	25 Kt — B3	B X B
6 B — KB4	B — Kt5(b)	26 Kt X B	Kt — B3
7 Q — Kt3	Kt — QR4	27 Kt — Kt6ch	B X Kt
8 Q — R4ch	B — Q2	28 B X B(h)	K — K2
9 Q — B2	P — K3	29 Q — B5	K — Q1
10 Kt — B3	Q — Kt3	30 QR — K1	Q — B4ch
11 P — QR4(c)	R — B1	31 K — R1	R — B1
12 QKt — Q2	Kt — B3(d)	32 Q — K5	R — QB2
13 Q — Kt1	Kt — KR4(e)	33 P — QKt4	Q — B3(i)
14 B — K3	P — KR3	34 P — B4	P X P
15 Kt — K5(f)	Kt — B3	35 B — B5	R(B1) — B2
16 P — R3	B — Q3	36 R — Q1ch	R(KB2) — Q2
17 O — O	K — B1(g)	37 B X R	R X B
18 P — KB4	B — K1	38 Q — Kt8ch	K — K2(j)
19 B — KB2	Q — B2	39 R(Q1) — K1ch	resigns
20 B — R4	Kt — KKt1		

(a) An old-fashioned line: the modern continuation is 4 P — QB4, but Fischer is known to have a predilection for this steady form of the attack. (b) Likewise old fashioned and also a little passive; better is 6 ..., P — KKt3. (c) So as to prevent Black from freeing his position by exchanges with B — QKt4. (d) Threatening Kt — QKt5; hence White's next move, removing the queen from the indirect threat by Black's rook. (e) He should have prepared to castle by 13 ..., B — K2. (f) Threatening 16 Kt X P, K X Kt; 17 B — Kt6ch. (g) This does not solve the problem of the safety of the king; O — O was still the best move even though by now White is in a position to mount a very strong king-side attack. (h) Fischer has conducted the whole attack in exemplary style; now he has established a winning position since not only is Black weak on the white squares but his king is still in deadly danger. (i) If 33 ..., Q X BP; 34 Q — Q6ch. (j) Or 38 ..., Q — B1; 39 R X Rch; 40 Q — Q6.

Queen's pawn, Grunfeld defense (played on first board in the match U.S.S.R. v. United States at the Siegen Olympiad, September 1970)

White B. Spassky	Black R. Fischer	White B. Spassky	Black R. Fischer
1 P — Q4	Kt — KB3	21 Kt — B5	P X P
2 P — QB4	P — KKt3	22 P X P	P — QKt4
3 Kt — QB3	P — Q4	23 Kt — K4(e)	B X P
4 P X P	Kt X P	24 Kt — Kt5	B X Bch(f)
5 P — K4	Kt X Kt	25 R X B	R — Q3(g)
6 P X Kt	B — Kt2	26 R — K1	Q — Kt3
7 B — QB4	P — QB4	27 Kt — K4	R — Q5
8 Kt — K2	Kt — B3	28 Kt — B6ch	K — R1
9 B — K3	O — O	29 Q X P	R — Q3(h)
10 O — O	Q — B2	30 Q — K4	R — KB1
11 R — B1	R — Q1(a)	31 P — Kt5	R — Q7
12 P — KR3	P — Kt3	32 Kt — KB1	Q — B2(i)
13 P — B4	P — K3	33 R X R	Kt X R
14 Q — K1	Kt — R4	34 Q — Q4	R — Q1
15 B — Q3	P — B4(b)	35 Kt — Q5dis ch	K — Kt1
16 P — Kt4(c)	P X KP	36 R — B2	Kt — B5
17 B X P	B — Kt2	37 R — K2	Q — Q3
18 Kt — Kt3	Kt — B5	38 R — K8ch	K — B2
19 B X B(d)	Q X B	39 Kt — B8ch1	resigns
20 B — B2	R — B3		

(a) Thus far as in a game between the same two players at Santa Monica, 1966; now Spassky played 12 Q — K1, P — K3; 13 P — B4, Kt — R4; 14 B — Q3, P — B4; 15 R — Q1, P — Kt3; 16 Q — B2, P X QP; 17 B X P, B X B; 18 P X B, B — Kt2; 19 Kt — Kt3, Q — B2; 20 P — Q5, BP X P; 21 P X P, Q X KP; 22 P — B5, after which White had a winning attack. Clearly, in order to prevent Black from producing a prepared variation, White now varies with a move that prepares for P — KB4 without allowing his opponent to play B — Kt5. (b) As he played in the Santa Monica game. It would seem that he dislikes the line 15 ..., B — Kt2; on account of 16 P — B5, but this would have given him better prospects than in the game. (c) A dashing and logical follow-up of his 12th move; slower, but also good and on a parallel with his Santa Monica game, was 16 Q — B2, followed by R — Q1. (d) With 19 B — B2, B X B; 20 Q X B, Kt — Q7; 21 Q X Pch, K — R1; 22 KR — Q1, Kt — B6ch; 23 K — R1, he would win a pawn but Black would have distinct counterplay along the long white diagonal after 23 ..., Kt — R5. (e) A fine pawn sacrifice to preserve the initiative and enable him to establish a strong bind on Black's king side. (f) The exchange of bishops leaves Black's king too vulnerable; he should have let the pawn go and played 24 ..., B — B3. (g) Not a good plan of defense; better was R — K1 and better still was the abandonment of the pawn by Q — Q4. (h) Against 29 ..., R — Q8 White has the stunning 30 Q — B7, and if 30 ..., R X Rch; 31 K — Kt2, Q — B6ch; 32 K — Kt3, Q — K6ch; 33 K — R4, R X Pch; 34 K X R, Q — R8ch; 35 R — R2, Q — B8ch; 36 K — R4, Q — K8ch; 37 K — Kt5. (i) A better chance of defense lay in Kt — Q3; now White finishes off the game in brilliant style.

prize in the strongest tournament of 1969 at Palma de Mallorca, Spain, with 12 points. There was a quadruple tie for first at the Belgrade international tournament among Gligoric, B. Ivkov (Yugos.), Matulovic, and L. Polugaievsky (U.S.S.R.). The former world champion, M. Botvinnik (U.S.S.R.), seventh, announced that this was his last big tournament. In December Nona Gaprindashvili (U.S.S.R.) won the European ladies' championship at Vrnjacka Banja, Yugos. An international tournament at Tbilisi, U.S.S.R., ended in a tie between M. Tal and B. Gurgenidz (both U.S.S.R.).

The U.S. championship tournament, held at the turn of the year at New York, was also the U.S. zonal tournament. S. Reshevsky won the title. A play-off for the U.S.S.R. championship between T. Petrosian and Polugaievsky was won by Petrosian by $3\frac{1}{2}$–$1\frac{1}{2}$. L. Portisch (Hung.) won the annual Hastings tournament in January, and M. Taimanov (U.S.S.R.) was an easy winner of the Hoogoven international tournament in the Netherlands. In February a young Icelander, G. Sigurjonsson, scored a surprise victory in an international tournament at Reykjavik, Ice. At Malaga, Spain, Pal Benko (U.S.) and B. Kurajica (Yugos.) tied for first place. A strong double-round tournament was held at Lugano, Switz., in March. Larsen was first with $9\frac{1}{2}$. At Budapest Paul Keres (U.S.S.R.) was an easy first.

At Belgrade, March 29–April 5, there took place the match of the century, as it subsequently became known, between teams of ten representing the U.S.S.R. and the Rest of the World. The U.S.S.R. scored a narrow victory by $20\frac{1}{2}$–$19\frac{1}{2}$. In April the Clare Benedict international team tournament was played in England for the first time; Spain was first. Bobby Fischer (U.S.) won a strong tournament at Rovinj-Zagreb, Yugos. A four-round quadrangular event at Leiden, Neth., was won by Spassky. The European team championship finals took place in May at Kapfenberg, Aus., and the U.S.S.R. won easily with $52\frac{1}{2}$ points. The first game to be played in outer space was conducted by Soviet cosmonauts in Soyuz 9 on June 11.

L. Kavalek (U.S.) was first in an international tournament at Caracas, Venez. A. Planinc (Yugos.) won first prize in the Varna International Tournament in Bulgaria. Polugaievsky and Spassky tied for first place in the IBM tournament at Amsterdam. Larsen was first in the Canadian Open at St. John's, Nfd., and Fischer was an overwhelming first at Buenos Aires. In August R. G. Wade won the British championship at Coventry. The U.S.S.R. retained the world team championship at the 19th Chess Olympiad at Siegen, W.Ger., in September.   (H. Go.)

FREDERIC OHRINGER FROM
NANCY PALMER

Salvador Allende Gossens, newly elected president of Chile, speaks at a victory news conference September 5.

Child Welfare:
see Education; Social
Services

Chile

A republic extending along the southern Pacific coast of South America, Chile has an area of 292,256 sq. mi. (756,945 sq.km.), not including its Antarctic claim between 53° and 90° W. It is bounded by Argentina, Bolivia, and Peru. Pop. (1970 est.): 9,780,100. Cap. and largest city: Santiago (pop. of greater Santiago, 1970 metro. est., 2,586,200). Language: Spanish. Religion: predominantly Roman Catholic. Presidents in 1970, Eduardo Frei Montalva and, from November 3, Salvador Allende Gossens.

On October 24, Salvador Allende Gossens (see BIOGRAPHY), a Socialist Party senator, was elected

president of Chile by a special session of both houses of the Congress. The vote was 153 in favour of Allende, 35 for Jorge Alessandri, abstentions 7. Allende had received the highest number of votes in the nationwide presidential elections on September 4 but had failed to obtain an absolute majority. According to the constitution, if no candidate receives an absolute majority, the Congress must choose between the two candidates with the highest number of votes.

The presidential election dominated the year's events. Six parties originally presented separate candidates, but a process of elimination and alliance-forming reduced the number to three. Jorge Alessandri, a political independent and former president, represented a conservative group, including the National Party and the Democratic Radicals. Allende, running for the fourth consecutive time, led a coalition of six left-wing parties, including the Socialist Party, of which he was a founder, the Radical Party, the Communist Party, the MAPU (a dissident Christian Democratic group), and two minor parties headed by Rafael Tarud. The third candidate was Radomiro Tomic of the ruling Christian Democratic Party, a former Chilean ambassador to the United States.

The election results were close. Allende received

CHILE

Education. (1968) Primary, pupils 1,937,925, teachers (1967) 54,900; secondary, pupils 128,167, teachers 10,242; vocational (1967), pupils 68,848, teachers 7,398; teacher training, students 6,582, teachers 1,000; higher (including 8 universities), students (1967) 57,146, teaching staff (1965) 8,835.

Finance. Monetary unit: escudo, with (Sept. 14, 1970) a banks' free market exchange rate (for trade and some invisible operations) of 12.30 escudos to U.S. \$1 (29.41 escudos = £1 sterling) and a brokers' market rate (for most other transactions) of 14.40 escudos to U.S. \$1 (34.30 escudos = £1 sterling). Gold, SDRs, and foreign exchange, central bank: (May 1970) U.S. \$442.9 million; (May 1969) U.S. \$252.2 million. Budget (1970 est.): revenue 17,465,000,000 escudos; expenditure 17,250,000,000 escudos. Gross national product: (1968) 42,904,000,000 escudos; (1967) 31,814,000,000 escudos. Money supply: (March 1970) 7,177,000,000 escudos; (March 1969) 5,047,000,000 escudos. Cost of living (Santiago; 1963 = 100): (June 1970) 596; (June 1969) 459.

Foreign Trade. (1968) Imports U.S. \$742.7 million; exports U.S. \$932.9 million. Import sources: U.S. 38%; West Germany 11%; Argentina 11%; U.K. 6%. Export destinations: U.S. 22%; U.K. 15%; Japan 13%; Netherlands 12%; West Germany 8%; Italy 6%; Argentina 5%. Main exports: copper 78%; iron ore 8%.

Transport and Communications. Roads (1968) 54,520 km. Motor vehicles in use (1968): passenger 130,225; commercial 111,721. Railways (1968): 8,408 km.; traffic (principal railways) 2,085,000,000 passenger-km., freight 2,637,000,000 net ton-km. Air traffic (1969): 729.6 million passenger-km.; freight 39,512,000 net ton-km. Shipping (1969): merchant vessels 100 gross tons and over 133; gross tonnage 287,992. Telephones (Jan. 1969) 312,042. Radio receivers (Dec. 1968) c. 1,375,000. Television receivers (Dec. 1969) c. 200,000.

Agriculture. Production (in 000; metric tons; 1969; 1968 in parentheses): wheat 1,214 (1,220); barley 80 (157); oats 95 (163); corn 154 (321); sugar, raw value (1969–70) c. 191, (1968–69) 188; potatoes 603 (725); dry beans 47 (65); onions (1967) 104, (1966) 156; apples (1968) c. 66, (1967) c. 65; wine (1967) c. 489, (1966) 474; wool, greasy (1967) c. 23, (1966) c. 24; timber (cu.m.; 1968) 6,300, (1967) 6,300; fish catch (1968) 1,376, (1967) 1,053. Livestock (in 000; 1968–69): cattle c. 2,850; sheep c. 6,700; pigs c. 1,120; horses (1967–68) c. 530.

Industry. Production (in 000; metric tons; 1969): coal 1,533; crude oil 1,742; electricity (kw-hr.) 7,084,-000; iron ore (65% metal content) 11,605; pig iron 484; crude steel 601; copper 398; nitrate of soda (1968) 623; iodine (1968) 2; molybdenum (metal content; 1968) 3.9; silver (troy oz.; 1968) 3,757; gold (troy oz.; 1968) 53; woven cotton fabrics (m.) c. 113,000; fish meal (1968) 235.

a plurality with 1,075,616 votes (36.7%), while Alessandri finished second with 1,036,278 (35.3%), and Tomic last with 824,849 (28%). Nearly 85% of the total electorate voted. Alessandri won a plurality in Santiago and among the women voters, but Allende overcame this with support from male voters outside the capital city. Allende's narrow victory left open the possibility of alternative political solutions since his backers only controlled approximately 80 votes in the Congress, well below the number needed for a majority. Although the Chilean Congress had always elected the candidate receiving the plurality in the direct popular elections, Allende needed Christian Democratic support in order to win. This support was given in return for several modifications to the constitution designed to ensure continuity in the country's democratic traditions. This Statute of Guarantees included guarantees on the right to vote, freedom of the press, freedom of opinion, and freedom of education; it also tacitly made it illegal to create a militia, as was feared by the Chilean armed forces.

The election campaign was carried out normally. The main issues centred on economic and social reform. Both Allende and Tomic proposed similar programs of accelerated reform, including a more radical agrarian reform, nationalization of basic industry, and control over foreign trade. Alessandri offered a platform of accepting the reforms already carried out by President Frei but not going beyond them. The campaign was occasionally affected by extremist violent action, at first by the leftist Movimiento de la Izquierda Revolucionaria and later by rightist groups. Shortly before the congressional confirmation of President Allende, extremists fatally shot the Army commander, Gen. René Schneider. Martial law was declared and tight security measures were in force at the time the Congress voted.

The economy, which had been growing slowly during the first eight months of the year, was adversely affected by public reaction to the election results. A crisis of confidence was caused by fears of wholesale expropriations of privately owned businesses and of possible political repression. This crisis was reflected in a sudden emigration, particularly of wealthy people, technicians, and those in professions. Industrial production temporarily fell about 9%, and sales in many appliance and other industries declined by 80%.

Allende's economic program, published in November, included short-term measures designed to spur the economy. The long-term emphasis was on socialization, including nationalization of the private banks and the U.S.-owned share of the copper industry.

Prior to the elections, the Christian Democratic government nationalized the Compañía Chilena de Electricidad of the U.S.-owned South American Power Company. CORFO, the government development corporation, bought out the U.S.-owned shares for $81 million, most of it payable over 25 years, and assumed responsibility for the company's liabilities.

Chile's balance of payments showed a surplus of nearly $120 million on commercial account during the first eight months of the year, partially reflecting continued high prices for copper on the international market. Inflation, however, continued unabated. During the first eight months of the year, the rate of price increases had reached 29.5%, similar to the inflation registered during all of 1969. A drought, which adversely affected agricultural production during 1969 and 1970, was partially responsible for this acceleration in price increases.　　　　　(R. L. Ro.)

China

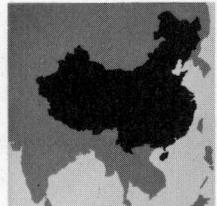

The most populous country in the world and the third largest in area, China is bounded by the U.S.S.R., Mongolia, North Korea, North Vietnam, Laos, Burma, India, Bhutan, Sikkim, Nepal, Pakistan, and Afghanistan. From 1949 the country has been divided into the People's Republic of China (Communist) on the mainland and on Hainan and other islands, and the Republic of China (Nationalist) on Taiwan (see TAIWAN). Area: 3,691,501 sq.mi. (9,560,988 sq.km.), including Tibet but excluding Taiwan. Pop. of the People's Republic (1970 est.): 827 million, of whom about 94% are Han. Cap.: Peking (metro. pop., 1967–68 est., 7 million). Largest city: Shanghai (metro. pop., 1968 est., 10 million). Language: Chinese (Mandarin dialect). Chairman of the Communist Party in 1970, Mao Tse-tung; premier, Chou En-lai.

Domestic Affairs. After the turbulence and disruptions of the Great Proletarian Cultural Revolution in 1966–69, and following the convocation of the long-postponed ninth congress of the Chinese Communist Party in April 1969, the rulers on the mainland of China began in 1970 to seek a return to more normal conditions in internal affairs and international relations. The party congress formally purged former chief of state Liu Shao-ch'i and his "revisionist" followers, reshaped the ruling organs of the party by centralizing the power of control in the 21-member Politburo (with a standing committee of only 5 members), proclaimed the victory of Maoism and Mao himself as the successor to Marx and Lenin in Communist ideology, and acclaimed Mao and his heir-designate, Defense Minister Lin Piao, as the supreme leaders of the party and government.

The rebuilding of the party at the provincial and subprovincial levels and the reorganization of the state administrative organs proved, however, to be an arduous and slow process. Although factional violence was brought under control, only one of the three-way alliance revolutionary committees (the armed forces, the Red Guards, and remnants of the party hierarchy) had been transformed into a regular party committee (in Hunan province in south central China) by late 1970. The shattered government structure remained without a legal head of state.

However, steps to rebuild the political and administrative apparatus were taken during the year. In March the first meeting of the State Council, or cabinet, since the start of the Cultural Revolution in 1966 was held, indicating an important move toward resumption of normal governmental activities. In order to simplify the administrative structure, superfluous ministries and agencies were combined or eliminated. From August 23 to September 6, the second plenary session of the Central Committee of the ninth party congress was held; it comprised 279 members (170 full members and 109 alternates, including 118 military officers). In a communiqué "the plenary session proposed to the Standing Committee of the National People's Congress that necessary preparations be made so that the Fourth National People's Congress will be convened at an appropriate time." The National People's Congress, the highest organ of state, consisted of more than 2,000 deputies with terms of four years and was supposed to meet annually, according to the constitution. The first congress met in 1954 to adopt the constitution and elect Mao as the first chairman

Mass celebration in Peking October 1 marks the 21st anniversary of the People's Republic of China.

CAMERA PRESS FROM PIX

KEYSTONE
Former Cambodian
chief of state
Prince Norodom Sihanouk
with Chairman
Mao Tse-tung.
After his ouster from
Cambodia, Sihanouk set
up a government-in-exile
and received strong support
from China.

of the People's Republic. The second congress in 1959 elected Liu Shao-ch'i to succeed Mao as chairman, and five years later the third congress in December 1964–January 1965 reelected Liu.

It was understood that the fourth congress would be a newly elected body. The work of choosing delegates, however, required preparation and could not be easily carried out before the completion of the party structure at local levels. The mere fact that the communiqué made no mention of party reconstruction indicated that the task of rebuilding regional, provincial, and county party committees continued to face important obstacles. However, during the observance of the 21st anniversary of Communist rule in China on October 1, Mao and Lin Piao were given new titles as, respectively, the supreme and deputy supreme commanders of "the Whole Nation and the Whole Army." The new designation was regarded as an indication of Mao's acceptance of election as chief of state, with Lin as deputy chief, at the coming meeting of the National People's Congress.

On April 25 China launched its first satellite into orbit around the earth. The launching enhanced the nation's political and technological prestige, indicating that it had the ability to build a missile for nuclear warheads. After a lapse of more than a year, Peking reportedly detonated on October 14 a nuclear device of about three megatons in the atmosphere in Sinkiang Autonomous Region. It was the 11th explosion detected by the United States since China began its nuclear testing in October 1964. In early November China renewed its bid for a world summit conference on the complete prohibition and thorough destruction of nuclear weapons.

Rebuilding the Party. Prior to the Cultural Revolution the Communist Party represented authority in the country. After the collapse of the civilian party apparatus during the Cultural Revolution, the revolutionary committees dominated by military leaders carried out the functions of government in the provinces and special municipalities. At the beginning of 1970 these leaders started a campaign for rebuilding the party organization from the bottom up and for reasserting party control at all levels.

Before October 1 intensive efforts were made to rebuild party organs at lower levels; party committees were reconstituted in farm collectives, local industrial enterprises, and administrative organs throughout the country. But the task was far from complete by the end of the year, and only about 30 new party committees at the county (*hsien*) level, the basic unit,

had reportedly been established. Since China contained more than 2,000 counties, a great deal remained to be done.

Although excesses in factionalism were brought under control, an inevitable rivalry continued between Maoist partisans and officials who had been a part of the old power structure. The question of the relationship of the emerging party organs to the present revolutionary committees and especially to the military remained a difficult and crucial issue.

Social and Economic Developments. A drive against class enemies, which included capitalist tendencies, corruption, theft, embezzlement, and any other acts of opposition to the Maoist social order, was launched in early 1970. At the same time, the people were urged to make necessary preparations against imperialist wars by intensifying army and militia training, constructing air raid shelters and tunnels, and stockpiling food and strategic materials. In conjunction with programs for stockpiling food and strategic materials and developing regional self-sufficiency, a new austerity campaign was inaugurated. These measures reflected not only Peking's concern with possible threats of war but also its continuing need to tighten its political and economic control.

Following Mao's instructions that youths should go to the countryside to do agricultural work, thousands of former Red Guards and young students were being moved from the cities into rural areas. According to press reports, the young people in the cities showed reluctance in accepting rural assignments and many of those who did go to the countryside became restless. Many of them managed to escape back to the cities where some banded together to commit robberies, while others tried to enter Hong Kong illegally. Consequently, in Kwangtung Province, adjacent to the New Territories of Hong Kong, it became a major offense to attempt to flee to the British colony. To curb such crimes as well as arson, rape, and various others, harsh penalties were introduced. In an effort to restore social order, mass trials and executions in various parts of the country were reported.

The wounds inflicted on the economy by the Cultural Revolution were being gradually healed, and good harvests in various parts of the nation were reported in 1970. But China continued its substantial wheat purchases from Canada and Australia. After the failure of the 1958 Great Leap Forward to achieve rapid economic growth, production statistics and other specific economic information were not made available to outsiders. The post-Cultural Revolution economic program appeared to be a pragmatic one, with primary emphasis on agriculture and small rural manufactures. The March meeting of the State Council considered plans for a huge campaign to increase production of grain and cotton during 1970. In a speech on the eve of celebrations of Communist China's 21st anniversary on October 1, Premier Chou stated that the economic effort for 1970 was aimed at laying the foundation for the fourth five-year plan (1971–75). However, the results of the third five-year plan (1965–70) had never been published.

Educational Reform. At the start of the Cultural Revolution all schools were closed, pending the institution of an educational reform program to transform old political, economic, and social institutions in accordance with Mao's egalitarian ideology. The educational policy advanced by Mao was to "enable those receiving an education to develop morally, intellectually and physically and to become labourers with socialist consciousness and culture." Most primary and secondary schools resumed operation on the new Maoist basis in 1968. Colleges and universities did not reopen until September 1970.

Under the new system, education was primarily for members of the proletariat and not for members of the former bourgeoisie. Primary and secondary schooling was reduced from 12 to 9 years, with 5 years of primary and 4 years at full secondary schools. There were also numerous half-work and half-study secondary schools with courses of shorter duration. The period of higher education was also reduced from four or more to two or three years. Instead of centralizing education in the Ministry of Education and the Ministry of Higher Education, the government decentralized the basic unit of educational administration to local bodies. The admissions policy and curriculum of the universities were drastically revised, putting class background ahead of academic achievement and emphasizing technical subjects over liberal arts courses. Students were admitted into colleges on the basis of ideology and labour experience, and preference in admission was given to children of labourers, peasants, and soldiers. The college curriculum was oriented toward meeting the needs of economic production. The curricula of primary and secondary schools consisted mainly of the Chinese language, the study of Mao's thought, physical and military training, and instruction in science.

Foreign Relations. During the Cultural Revolution Mao's personal obsessions and domination of policy formation resulted in China's isolation from the outside world. After the ninth party congress, however, Mao could no longer rule the country with an iron fist, and a more pragmatic group appeared to have assumed the leadership in lifting China's self-imposed diplomatic isolation.

In January, tension between China and the Soviet Union was eased with the end of the border clashes. At China's initiative, and in response to a conciliatory attitude by the U.S., the Warsaw ambassadorial talks between Peking and Washington were resumed. In February, Chinese economic and technical missions visited Zambia, Tanzania, and Yemen, while a Cuban trade delegation and the new ambassador from Tanzania arrived in Peking. Following the appointment in March of the first Chinese ambassador to North Korea since 1967, Chou En-lai paid an official visit from April 5 to 7 to that country. Apart from a brief visit to Hanoi after Ho Chi Minh's death, this was Chou's first journey outside China since 1966.

During the spring and summer a large number of official foreign visitors and some foreign correspondents were received in Peking. The diplomatic missions included Albania, Czechoslovakia, France, North Korea, North Vietnam, Romania, Somalia, and Sudan. By the end of the summer more than half of China's embassies in 45 countries left under the control of chargés d'affaires during the Cultural Revolution were once again manned by ambassadors. In late October, China, Tanzania, and Zambia ceremonially inaugurated at Dar es Salaam the construction of a 1,116-mi. railroad with Chinese financial and technical assistance. The projected rail line linked Zambia's copper mine area with Dar es Salaam.

China's relations with Yugoslavia and Romania were greatly improved, partly owing to their neutral stand in the ideological dispute between the Soviet Union and China. Yugoslavia, formerly branded revisionist by Peking, inaugurated a shipping link with China in early 1970 and also upgraded its diplomatic mission in Peking to full ambassadorial status in June. This was followed by an exchange of ambassadors between Peking and Belgrade. At China's invitation a Romanian delegation headed by Vice-Pres. Emil Bodnaras visited China in June and was received by Mao. China agreed to give Romania $21 million in aid for reconstruction after Romania's disastrous floods.

The most significant diplomatic event of the year was Canada's recognition of the Communist regime in Peking as the sole legal government of China on October 13, following nearly two years of negotiations

---

CHINA
Education. Primary (1959–60), pupils 90 million, teachers (1964) *c.* 2.6 million; secondary (1958–59), pupils 8,520,000; vocational (1958–59), pupils 850,000; teacher training, students (1958–59) 620,000; higher (1962–63), students 820,000.
Finance. Monetary unit: jen min piao or people's bank dollar, also called the yuan, with an official exchange rate of 2.46 yuan to U.S. $1 (5.90 yuan = £1 sterling). Budget (1960 est.; latest published) balanced at 70,020,000,-000 yuan. Gross domestic product (1965 est.) 130 billion yuan.
Foreign Trade. (1968) Imports *c.* U.S. $1.9 billion; exports *c.* U.S. $1,750,000,000. Import sources: Japan *c.* 21%; West Germany *c.* 8%; U.K. *c.* 5%. Export destinations: Hong Kong *c.* 25%; Japan *c.* 13%; U.K. *c.* 5%. Main exports: textiles and clothing, metal ores and nonferrous metals, rice, tea, coal.
Transport and Communications. Roads (1966) *c.* 550,000 km. (including *c.* 200,000 km.

with improved surface). Motor vehicles in use (1967): passenger *c.* 50,000; commercial *c.* 300,-000. Railways: (1966) *c.* 36,000 km.; traffic (1959) 45,670,000,000 passenger-km., freight 265,260,000,000 net ton-km. Air traffic (1960): 63,882,000 passenger-km.; freight 1,967,000 net ton-km. Inland waterways (including Yangtze River; 1966) *c.* 160,000 km. Shipping (1969): merchant vessels 100 gross tons and over 237; gross tonnage 791,893. Telephones (1951) 255,-000. Radio receivers (Dec. 1966) *c.* 8 million. Television receivers (Dec. 1965) *c.* 100,000.
Agriculture. Production (in 000; metric tons; 1968; 1967 in parentheses): rice *c.* 91,000 (*c.* 92,000); corn *c.* 25,000 (*c.* 25,000); wheat *c.* 27,000 (*c.* 28,000); barley *c.* 18,000 (*c.* 16,000); potatoes *c.* 30,000 (*c.* 30,000); soybeans (1969) *c.* 10,920, (1968) *c.* 10,670; peanuts (1969) *c.* 2,400, (1968) *c.* 2,200; cotton, lint *c.* 1,474 (*c.* 1,518); jute *c.* 495 (*c.* 480); rapeseed *c.* 1,070 (*c.* 1,120); sugar, raw value (1969–70) *c.* 3,400, (1968–69) *c.* 3,400; tobacco (1969) *c.* 776,

(1968) *c.* 848; tea *c.* 160 (*c.* 160); pears *c.* 890 (*c.* 880); oranges (1967) *c.* 650, (1966) *c.* 600; timber (cu.m.; 1967) *c.* 147,000, (1966) *c.* 136,-000; fish catch (1960) 5,800, (1959) 5,020. Livestock (in 000; 1968–69): cattle *c.* 62,300; sheep *c.* 70,300; pigs *c.* 215,000; goats *c.* 56,000; buffalo *c.* 30,000; horses *c.* 7,600; asses *c.* 11,000.
Industry. Fuel and power (in 000; 1968): coal (including lignite) *c.* 300,000 metric tons; coke *c.* 15,000 metric tons; crude oil *c.* 15,000 metric tons; electricity (1960) *c.* 58,500,000 kw-hr. Production (in 000; metric tons; 1968): iron ore (metal content) *c.* 20,900; pig iron *c.* 19,000; crude steel *c.* 15,000; lead *c.* 100; copper *c.* 100; bauxite *c.* 380; aluminum *c.* 90; tungsten concentrates (oxide content) *c.* 10; cement *c.* 9,000; sulfuric acid (1966) *c.* 2,500; chemical fertilizers (1966) *c.* 5,500; cotton yarn (1960) 1,633; woven cotton fabrics (m.; 1966) *c.* 5,900,000; paper (1968) 3,400.

UPI COMPIX

Chinese militia women stage a simulated attack across a river during army training exercises held early in 1970.

regime, while China supported Sihanouk's government-in-exile. On May 20 Mao issued a rare personal statement on Cambodia and U.S. imperialism, accusing the United States of "treacherously engineering the reactionary coup d'etat by the Lon Nol-Sirik Matak clique," attacking the U.S. invasion of Cambodia, and reiterating China's support of Sihanouk's exiled government. Although Peking's statements in relation to Cambodia and Taiwan became more harsh, they implied no military action in the region.

Sino-Soviet Negotiations. On the initiative of Premier Aleksei N. Kosygin, the Sino-Soviet negotiations on border disputes began in Peking on Oct. 20, 1969, but recessed in December, when the Soviet chief delegate returned to Moscow ostensibly to attend a meeting of the Supreme Soviet. The announcement soon afterward that the Sino-American ambassadorial talks would resume in January 1970 reportedly set off a flurry of consultations in the capitals of the Soviet bloc countries, while China and the Soviet Union renewed their exchange of polemics.

After consultation in Moscow, the Soviet delegate returned to Peking on January 2, but fundamental differences prevented an early agreement even on the scope of the negotiations. Apparently Peking wanted to limit the discussions to questions relating to the frontier, sought Soviet acknowledgment in principle that the Russians had gained much of their Far Eastern territory through unequal treaties in the 19th century, and insisted on the withdrawal of Soviet forces from the border area. On the other hand, Moscow wanted to expand the talks to include trade, political, and cultural matters, and refused to discuss the question of legitimacy of Soviet territorial control along the border. Moscow feared that withdrawing its troops without a political agreement would leave Soviet border areas exposed to Chinese inroads.

In the meantime, an increase in Soviet troops near the Chinese border and the campaign for war preparedness in China were reported. When the Soviet Union celebrated the 100th anniversary of Lenin's birth on April 22 with a message from the Soviet leader, Leonid I. Brezhnev, calling for unity in the Communist world but criticizing the nationalistic policy of the Chinese leadership, Peking marked the occasion with a series of articles charging that the present Soviet leaders had betrayed Lenin. In reply, Soviet broadcasts made a fierce personal attack on Mao. This was followed by a lengthy editorial in the Soviet newspaper *Pravda* on May 18, attacking Communist China and Mao for "imperialism's malicious anti-Soviet and anti-Communist campaign."

After the cancellation of Sino-American talks in Warsaw, however, there was a notable decrease in Peking's criticism of Moscow. But in the summer the talks on the border issues came to a halt with the return of the chief Soviet negotiator to Moscow. In mid-August Leonid F. Ilyichev, a Soviet deputy foreign minister, arrived in Peking as the new negotiator. While the negotiations on the overall border and political issues remained deadlocked, both the Soviet Union and China seemed reluctant to break off the talks. Also, after a break of more than three years, ambassadorial relations between Peking and Moscow were resumed in November; a one-year trade pact was signed in the same month.   (H. T. Ch.)

See also Communist Movement; Propaganda; Taiwan.

in Stockholm. Canada and China later agreed to exchange ambassadors within six months. Peking thus scored a victory in winning the recognition of a NATO member in the Western Hemisphere, and it was the first time since 1964, when France took the step, that a major country had extended such recognition. Canada also yielded to Peking's request to break diplomatic ties with Nationalist China. Early in November Italy followed Canada's precedent by recognizing the Peking regime and breaking diplomatic ties with Nationalist China.

In its diplomatic activities Peking indicated its interest in UN membership and claim to Nationalist China's seat therein. Canada's secretary of state for external affairs declared that Canada would vote to seat Communist China in the world organization and would work to that end. Tanzanian Pres. Julius Nyerere and Foreign Minister Maurice Schuman of France made a strong appeal to the 25th anniversary session of the UN General Assembly for the admission of Communist China. Eighteen nonaligned and Communist countries sponsored a resolution urging the expulsion of Nationalist China and admission of Communist China. For the first time, a majority of the General Assembly voted in favour of seating Peking; the vote was 51–49, with 25 abstentions. However, the assembly also voted to consider this as an "important" question requiring a two-thirds majority for adoption.

Sino-American Ambassadorial Talks. The U.S. began toward the end of 1969 to relax trade and travel restrictions with China, moving toward an accommodation of differences and the improvement of relations between the two countries. Following preliminary meetings between Chinese and U.S. diplomats in Warsaw, the Sino-American ambassadorial talks, first begun in 1958 and broken off in January 1968, resumed at the 135th session on Jan. 20, 1970. A second meeting took place on February 20, but, following the dramatic events of March in Cambodia and the invasion of Cambodia by U.S. and South Vietnamese forces in April, the session scheduled for May 20 was postponed indefinitely.

On March 18 a coup d'etat in Cambodia deposed Prince Norodom Sihanouk while he was leaving the Soviet Union for China. The U.S. recognized the new

ENCYCLOPÆDIA BRITANNICA FILMS. *China: A Portrait of the Land* (1967); *China's Industrial Revolution* (1967); *China's Villages in Change* (1967).

Cinema

The Lumière brothers showed their films to the world's first paying cinema audience on Dec. 28, 1895; thus, 1970 could be considered the 75th anniversary of motion pictures. The occasion was commemorated by many exhibitions, most notably by a massive celebration in Paris presented by the Cinémathèque Française. The year also marked the end of a decade of change perhaps more far-reaching than at any other time in the history of the cinema, including the change-over to talking pictures. The new waves of the early 1960s, the new forms and purposes of communication developed by directors such as Alain Resnais, Jean-Luc Godard, and Michelangelo Antonioni had created a cinema appropriate to a decade of striking political and social upheaval.

At another level, still further large-scale revolution was inevitable with the forcibly changed economics of the cinema. In Britain at the end of World War II the weekly audience numbered about 30 million: by 1969 it was barely 4.7 million, with new competition on the way from large-scale colour television. The pattern of declining audiences was evident in every film-producing country where television had developed on any scale.

By 1970, practically all the great old Hollywood companies had been taken over by big finance groups. As a symbol of the fall of the old empires, the legendary properties of Metro-Goldwyn-Mayer—furnishings, costumes, scenery, and properties from half a century of U.S. movies—were put up for sale at a colourful but melancholy auction.

With the decline of the old commercial cinema, however, a new generation had arisen, which—perhaps reacting against television as the medium of their parents—embraced the cinema as its natural medium of communication in a way no earlier generation had ever done. The rise of the "underground" cinema in many parts of the world—the noncommercial production and exhibition of low-budget, private films, deliberately discarding the technical standards and values of the commercial cinema and using the medium as a direct, vital, natural means of communication for social, political, or aesthetic ideas—was sporadic but determined, and perhaps indicated the future.

The year's main technical advance was the rapid movement toward the widespread use of the video-cassette, which would make screen material more readily available for home use than ever before. It was not yet possible to predict the ultimate effect of the development upon film economics and film methods.

In the choice of themes and methods, no new general tendency could be discerned, apart from the fairly widespread attempt to appeal to the young people who made up the largest part of the audience. The general relaxation of censorship and other social restrictions continued unabated; by the end of 1970, very little remained that could not be said or shown on the screen, at least in the English-speaking world. Total nudity in films had become commonplace. *Women in Love* was the first British film to make the final concession to frontal male nudity; the Swedish cinema had depicted most forms of conventional sexual activity (*The Language of Love*); and four-letter Anglo-Saxon terminology was no longer taboo. The effect of the relaxation, far from ushering in an era of total license, seemed to be a general loss of interest in pornography for its own sake; certainly, the mass of such material produced in the U.S. in 1970 appeared to make less and less appeal to the popular market.

This climate necessarily produced revisions in censorship approaches, particularly in the English-speaking countries. A new system of film classification introduced in Britain from June 1970 raised the age limit of the "X" certificate, which previously excluded persons under 16 years of age, to 18 years. A new classification "AA" forbade certain films to those under 14, while at the other end of the scale the "A" certificate, formerly prohibiting entrance to children unaccompanied by an adult, became merely an advisory classification, warning parents of the possible unsuitability of a film for children under 14. Similarly, beginning in March the U.S. raised the limit from 16 to 17 years for admission to "X" films, though retaining the "R" category to signify that young people under 17 might be admitted only if accompanied by an adult. "GP" replaced "M" as the designation for films calling for parental discretion.

In Britain, a curious sidelight on the censorship question was the seizure by the police of a copy of Andy Warhol's *Flesh* together with the projector and records of the theatre showing it (the Open Space Theatre). The case was withdrawn, but the British police continued to evince suspicion of the underground cinema.

The English-Speaking Cinema. *U.S.* Although the U.S. still claimed one of the world's higher per capita rates of cinema attendance, and box-office takings showed a marked improvement in 1969–70 (largely due to increased prices), the revolution in Hollywood was complete. Apart from the family-controlled Disney studios and, for the time being at least, Columbia and Twentieth Century-Fox, by the end of 1970 all the major studios had come under new control. Attempting to make the industry more responsive to the desires of its audience, the new managements had by and large noted the recent unprofitability of the traditional multimillion dollar products, together with large takings from certain low-budget productions such as *Easy Rider;* the immediate trend seemed to be to stabilize production at moderate budget levels. The short-term effect of this tended toward a moderation of salaries and the prices of literary properties; a general move away from the studios toward location shooting; and a reconsideration of themes and subjects.

Two audiences for the moment proved fairly stable among the uncertainties of the changing box office: the blacks and the teen-age section of the population. Inevitably this resulted in a spate of films with black stars (Jim Brown, Sidney Poitier) and racial problem stories—among them *Watermelon Man,* directed by one of Hollywood's few black directors, Melvin Van Peebles. Another, Ossie Davis, directed the successful *Cotton Comes to Harlem.*

Joseph Heller's novel *Catch-22,* which first appeared in 1961, was at once a recollection of World War II and a prediction of the dissenting mood of the late 1960s. Without any concessions or betrayal of the original text, Mike Nichols' screen version made Heller's character—a touchstone of sanity in a crazy world of war—an archetypal hero of our time. Robert Altman's *M*A*S*H*—significantly scripted by Ring Lardner, Jr., for many years blacklisted by the film industry because of his allegedly far left sympathies—

Annual Cinema Attendance		
Country	Total in 000	Per capita
Afars and Issas	300	4
Algeria	27,000	2.2
American Samoa	100	2
Andorra	200	18
Angola	2,800	0.5
Antigua	130	2
Australia	37,500	3
Austria	57,700	8
Bahamas	1,300	9
Bahrain	1,200	6
Barbados	1,200	5
Belgium	39,500	4
British Honduras	2,000	18
British Solomon Is.	100	0.6
British Virgin Is.	400	9
Brunei	2,300	21
Bulgaria	119,900	14
Burma	209,000	8
Burundi	500	0.2
Cambodia	20,000	3
Canada	99,000	5
Canal Zone	500	8
Cape Verde Islands	300	1.3
Cayman Islands	80	9
Ceylon	50,900	4
Chad	800	0.2
Chile	69,400	8
Colombia	85,400	4
Comoro Islands	20	0.1
Congo (Brazzaville)	1,700	2
Cook Islands	300	13
Cyprus	8,300	14
Czechoslovakia	118,800	8
Denmark	33,900	7
Ecuador	15,100	3
Equatorial Guinea	480	1.7
Faeroe Islands	200	6
Falkland Islands	20	10
France	215,700	4
French Guiana	400	10
Germany, East	99,200	6
Germany, West	243,000	4
Ghana	11,800	1.5
Greenland	400	11
Guam	500	6
Hong Kong	95,600	25
Hungary	96,800	9
Iceland	2,300	1.2
India	1,825,000	4
Iraq	8,300	1
Israel	57,500	22
Italy	567,000	11
Jamaica	3,600	2
Japan	335,100	3
Jordan	6,100	3
Korea, South	173,200	6
Laos	1,100	0.4
Liberia	900	0.8
Luxembourg	2,000	6
Malta	3,300	10
Martinique	2,100	7
Mauritius	7,200	9
Mexico	344,200	8
Monaco	200	7
Morocco	18,200	1.3
Netherlands	34,300	3
New Caledonia	1,000	11
New Hebrides	250	3
New Zealand	26,000	10
Pakistan	225,000	2
Poland	163,100	5
Portugal	29,700	3
Portuguese Guinea	200	0.4
Réunion	800	2
Romania	209,200	11
Ryukyu Islands	4,200	4
St. Kitts-Nevis-Anguilla	70	1
San Marino	200	11
São Tomé and Príncipe	80	1.4
Senegal	5,200	1.5
Seychelles	100	2
Singapore	25,900	14
Spain	393,900	12
Spanish Sahara	400	8
Swaziland	100	0.3
Sweden	32,600	4
Switzerland	40,000	7
Taiwan	868,100	66
Tunisia	7,700	1.7
U.S.S.R.	4,502,800	19
U.A.R.	70,000	2.3
United Kingdom	265,000	5
United States	7,000,000	7
Western Samoa	300	2
Yugoslavia	104,900	5

Note: Figures given are most recent available.
Source: *UNESCO Statistical Yearbook* (1968).

COURTESY, 20TH CENTURY-FOX
Duke (Tom Skerritt) toasts Painless (John Schuck) in the Last Supper scene from "M*A*S*H."

aimed at the same goal as *Catch-22* but employed different means. Masquerading as a farcical comedy of military life and cultivating calculatedly execrable taste, it succeeded in reducing the conventions and paraphernalia of war to total idiocy. The movie also helped advance the career of one of its stars, Elliott Gould (*see* Biography), who became one of Hollywood's most sought after actors. It is hard to resist the temptation to put alongside those two films Franklin Schaffner's *Patton*, which started out looking like a Hollywood celebration of military glory but appeared to end as the revelation of a military maniac. That this result was not entirely accidental was suggested by the appearance on the writing credits of the name of Francis Ford Coppola, one of the most progressive young Hollywood directors as well as a writer and producer.

Another group of films was dedicated to demonstrations and campus revolts. Stuart Hagmann's *The Strawberry Statement* related an incident similar to the revolt at Columbia University, but its radical message was much weakened by concessions to commercial cliché. Richard Rush's *Getting Straight* approached the campus problem with detached comedy and an apparent principle of making love *and* war. Paul Williams' *The Revolutionary* coolly detailed the radicalization of a student. Haskell Wexler's *Medium Cool* lay somewhere between the commercial cinema and the underground. Wexler, a photographer, created a fictional story around footage shot by him in Chicago at the 1968 Democratic Party convention demonstrations. A less aggressive declaration of the ideals of the protest generation was *Woodstock*, Michael Wadleigh's flamboyant but sympathetic record of the great three-day pop music festival held at Woodstock, N.Y.

Michelangelo Antonioni's first picture made in the U.S., *Zabriskie Point*, hardly belonged with this group of films; but it hardly belonged anywhere else, either. The film received remarkably unfavourable notices in the U.S. Critics insisted on seeing it as a realistic impression of contemporary America, rather than as an individual and apocalyptic vision of the explosion of a contemporary consumer society, eroded by fear, prejudice, and violence.

One of the biggest commercial successes of 1970 was a Western that rather obliquely addressed the young dissenting generation. George Roy Hill's *Butch Cassidy and the Sundance Kid* was a fairly accurate reconstruction of two of the more amiable turn-of-the-century outlaws, treated with a quirky humour reminiscent of François Truffaut's *Jules et Jim;* it conveyed a sense of the pathos of innocents caught up in a web of violence and crime. The post-*Bonnie and Clyde* vogue for reconstructing the careers of gangsters of the 1920s and 1930s was continued in Roger Corman's *Bloody Mama*, based on the life of Kate ("Ma") Barker and her homicidal brood.

To prove that the old fashions of Hollywood were not quite dead, there were several big new musicals in 1970: Herbert Ross's *Goodbye Mr. Chips*, Gene Kelly's *Hello, Dolly!*, and Joshua Logan's *Paint Your Wagon*. None of them enjoyed enthusiastic critical receptions, but *Paint Your Wagon* achieved some success as a result of the popularity of Lee Marvin's recording of "Wand'rin' Star."

Several Hollywood veterans had successes during the year. At 71, Henry Hathaway directed an unashamedly old-fashioned, marvelously accomplished Western, *True Grit*, that earned its veteran star John Wayne (*see* Biography) an Academy Award. Alfred Hitchcock based *Topaz* on an actual historical event, a spy drama of the 1962 Cuban missile crisis. This sacrifice of an element of control over his story left him seemingly ill at ease.

Other notable U.S. movies included *Joe*, the story of a factory worker and his encounters with both the executive and hippie worlds; *Five Easy Pieces*, about a man who has rejected his overrefined classical music background to work in the California oil fields and who cannot fit into either world; *Diary of a Mad Housewife*, concerned with the frustrations of an educated woman; and *Tora! Tora! Tora!*, a much-criticized spectacular about the Japanese attack on Pearl Harbor, Hawaii.

The U.S. Academy of Motion Picture Arts and Sciences presented its annual Academy Awards in April. Best movie was *Midnight Cowboy,* while John Wayne was voted best actor for his role in *True Grit.* Maggie Smith won the best actress award for her part in *The Prime of Miss Jean Brodie,* while Goldie Hawn was named best supporting actress for *Cactus Flower.* Best supporting actor was Gig Young in *They Shoot Horses, Don't They?,* and John Schlesinger (*see* BIOGRAPHY) won the best director honour for *Midnight Cowboy.*

Britain. The withdrawal of U.S. investment left the British cinema in perhaps the most severe crisis of its history. Production dwindled, and unemployment mounted throughout the industry. Confidence was further shaken when the first films to emerge from Bryan Forbes's ambitious program as head of production at the reorganized ABPC-EMI proved, one after the other, severe disappointments, both artistically and commercially.

Expensive costume pictures such as Charles Jarrott's *Anne of the Thousand Days* and Ken Hughes's *Cromwell*—like most of their kind, unimaginatively pedantic in writing and unadventurously tasteful in design—were clearly unlikely to solve the industry's problems. Meanwhile, there was a vogue for literary adaptations. D. H. Lawrence provided subjects for Ken Russell's showy *Women in Love* and Christopher Miles's more modest and authentically Lawrentian *The Virgin and the Gipsy,* with its sensitive central performance by Joanna Shimkus. The U.S. director Delbert Mann made an unadventurous *David Copperfield* to commemorate the Dickens centenary. In Bryan Forbes's screen version, Jean Giraudoux' *The Madwoman of Chaillot* proved to have become badly dated. Tony Richardson, however, made an excellent *Hamlet,* with Nicol Williamson as the prince.

John Boorman returned to Britain after two U.S. films to make one of the most original films of the year, *Leo the Last,* a bizarre allegory about a would-be liberal, a European princeling whose conscience is stirred by the wretchedness of his neighbours in the London district of Notting Hill. His efforts to help or to identify himself with their lot, however, inevitably bring disaster.

Two of the most notable British films of the year were small-scale works. *Kes,* directed by Ken Loach from a story about a "difficult" child, concerned a boy from a broken home who was unable to fit into the inflexible ways of school life but who found a new self-respect and maturity through his experiences in training a kestrel. *Bronco Bullfrog,* Barney Platts-Mills's first feature film, was made on a budget of £17,000 and employed a cast of nonactors, mainly youngsters from London's East End. With enormous warmth and humour, and a complete freedom from patronage, it related the difficulties of growing up in the environment of the British urban working class in the 1970s.

Canada. Robin Spry's first feature film, *Prologue,* attracted a good deal of attention following its various festival showings. A casual but controlled study of dropout life in North America, it was built, like Haskell Wexler's *Medium Cool,* around scenes shot at the 1968 Democratic Party convention demonstrations in Chicago, but with fewer concessions to commercial habits and more genuine insight into the state of mind of a generation.

Western Europe. *France.* The directors who came to the fore at the end of the 1950s as the *nouvelle vague* continued in prominence. François Truffaut re-ceived poor critical reviews for his *La Sirène du Mississippi* but recovered his form with *L'Enfant sauvage,* an atmospheric re-creation of a true historical incident. The director himself played the 18th-century Parisian physician who established an understanding with a child found wild and wandering in the forests.

Jean-Luc Godard seemed to have withdrawn further into the problems of political cinema, *Le Vent d'Est* (*Wind from the East*) proving no more comprehensible than *Le Gai Savoir.* Claude Chabrol directed two psychological thrillers of brilliant style: *Que La Bête meure,* about the hunting down of a hit-and-run driver by the father of one of his victims, and *Le Boucher,* set in a village menaced by a series of mysterious murders.

Among directors of the older generation, Georges Franju directed a characteristically poetic adaptation, at once tender and violent, of Émile Zola's *La Faute de l'abbé Mouret.* Robert Bresson's *Une Femme douce* took a Dostoevski story—the young wife of a pawn-broker commits suicide, leaving her obtuse husband to ponder the failure of their relationship—and turned it into a typically Bressonian subject, exquisitely poised, delicate, and muted.

Costa-Gavras' *Z,* a political thriller about contemporary Greece, took everyone by surprise by proving one of 1970's biggest box-office successes. The same director and writer (Jorge Semprun) followed it with *L'Aveu,* the obverse of the political coin. Based on Artur London's memoirs, the film was a concentrated, restrained, and terrifying reconstruction of the methods employed in the Prague, Czech., show trials of 1962.

Italy. Of the directors who emerged in the 1960s, the most strikingly successful in 1970 was Bernardo Bertolucci, who seemed entirely to have overcome his phase of Godardian imitation (*Partner*). *The Spider's Stratagem* and *The Conformist* presented two aspects

Jack Nicholson plays a once-promising pianist turned oil field worker in the 1970 film "Five Easy Pieces."

COURTESY, COLUMBIA PICTURES INDUSTRIES, INC.

COURTESY, 20TH CENTURY-FOX

Barbra Streisand marches with Walter Matthau in a scene from the musical comedy hit "Hello, Dolly!"

Cresta (Candice Bergen) avoids Isaac Cumber (Donald Pleasence) after recognizing him as a gunrunner to the Cheyenne in this scene from "Soldier Blue."

FROM THE MOTION PICTURE "SOLDIER BLUE," © 1970 BY AVCO EMBASSY PICTURES COPP.

of the same historical situation. In the first, a young man returns to the small town where his father was killed by Fascist assassins in the 1930s. Seeking answers to various mysteries surrounding the man's death, he uncovers a web of deceit and intrigue. The *Conformist* was about the self-torment of a Fascist philosophy lecturer, delegated to murder a left-wing professor; Jean-Louis Trintignant played the assassin with extraordinary integrity. Both films were marked by a forceful, elliptical narrative drive and powerful visual style.

Other Italian directors also turned to historical themes. Based on the recollections of Emilio Lussu, Francesco Rosi's *Uomini contro* examined the role of the Italian Army in World War I. Among the year's commercial successes was Vittorio de Sica's *Sunflower*—an Italian woman's search for her husband, who had disappeared on the Russian front—a saccharine romance quite unworthy of a former master of the Italian neorealist cinema. Made in West Germany with an international cast, Luchino Visconti's *The Damned* (*La caduta degli dei*) was a magnificent panorama of the decadence of Nazi Germany, a Wagnerian drama of a dynastic family of armament manufacturers. From this Visconti moved on to the smaller canvas of an adaptation of Thomas Mann's *Death in Venice*.

West Germany. The young German avant-garde seemed more determinedly in pursuit of personal extravagance. Jean-Marie Straub presented Corneille's *Othon*, in costume, but against the background of present-day Rome. Werner Herzog's *Even Dwarfs Started Small* was a bizarre piece of show-off that never progressed beyond the initial novelty of using only dwarfs and midgets as actors. Werner Schroeter's *Eika Kappa*, a fantastic seriocomic excursion through the grand-opera universe, was more original in conception and treatment.

A group of films shown at the Berlin Festival, however, demonstrated that some young German directors were working in more traditional forms. Roland Gall's *Wie ich ein Neger wurde* related the eroding effects of German society in the 1930s, as revealed in experiences at a boys' summer camp. Rainer Werner Fassbinder's *Warum läuft Herr R. Amok?* was a casual, chilling study of an explosion in the humdrum surface of a man's life.

Sweden. In *A Passion*, also called *The Passion of Anna*, Ingmar Bergman returned to his current favourite location, the tiny island of Fårö, and his preoccupation with the haunted nights of lonely souls. Four people are caught up in close, tormenting emotional involvements and the deceits and lies that unite and divide them. Around the group, the community of the little island devises its own forms of cruelty and persecution.

Other Swedish directors showed a more outgoing interest in social problems. Lasse Forsberg's *Misshandlingen* (*Mistreatment*) dealt forcefully with the treatment of the insane in Sweden, illustrated by the plight of a young radical arrested after a casual street brawl and confined in a mental hospital. In *You Are Lying*, Vilgot Sjöman, director of the *I Am Curious* films, examined the inadequacy of penal detention, viewed through the experiences of a young alcoholic.

Spain. Paying a rare visit to his native country, Luis Buñuel produced a small, characteristic masterpiece in *Tristana*. Adapted from a novel by Perez Galdos, it was a mordant tale of a beautiful young girl and her aged guardian.

Eastern Europe. *U.S.S.R.* Creative film making seemed to continue at a low ebb in the Soviet Union. The only feature films noted internationally during 1970 were Lev Kulidjanov's leadenly pedantic adaptation of *Crime and Punishment*, and Sergei Bondarchuk's massive interpretation of *Waterloo*, a co-production with the Italian company of Dino de Laurentiis. As in the director's earlier *War and Peace*, the sheer weight of economic resources expended in lavish display and spectacle seemed to have stifled any creative effort.

Poland. The outstanding Polish film of 1970 was *Landscape After the Battle*, directed by Andrzej Wajda. In this haunting and powerful study of people in a displaced persons' camp after World War II, Wajda looked again at the world of his great films of the 1950s (*A Generation, Kanal*, and *Ashes and Diamonds*) from the new perspectives of a changed cinema and a matured vision.

Hungary. The Hungarian cinema was the most vital in Eastern Europe. Since 1963 a new generation of directors such as Istvan Szabo, Istvan Gaal, Ferenc Kosa, Ferenc Kardos, and Janos Rosza had emerged to join the slightly senior generation of Miklos Jancso, Andras Kovacs, and Peter Bacso, creating a style and cinema quite new to Eastern Europe in the frankness of its historical criticism and political discussion. Outstanding productions of this school were Jancso's *The Red and the White, The Roundup*, and *The Confrontation*, Kovacs' *Cold Days*, Kosa's *Ten Thousand Suns*, Szabo's *The Father*, and Gaal's *The Green Years*.

In 1970 the best films of this new wave included Gaal's *The Falcons*, an austerely beautiful allegory about conflicts of humanism and authoritarianism; Szabo's *Love Film*, a richly textured panorama of the years after World War II, reflected through the memories and emotions of a boy and girl separated after the 1956 revolution; and Imre Gyogyossy's *Palm Sunday*, a poetic reconstruction of an incident from the collapse of the Hungarian Republic of Councils (1919) that developed a cinematic equivalent of a folk culture.

Africa. The continent's emergent nations were making strenuous efforts to find their voices, cinematically speaking, but in 1970 only Shadi Abdelsalam's *The Night of Counting the Years* from the United Arab

Republic achieved real international status. Reconstructing the story of the discovery in the 1880s of a great cache of ancient graves that had long provided the livelihood of a remote desert tribe, it created its own poetic world out of the dunes, the lonely monuments of ancient Egypt, the black cloaks of the tribesmen whipped by the wind, and at the same time revealed a strong contemporary sense of a national culture and destiny.

Asia. *Japan.* The most significant film from the new Japanese cinema was Yoshishige Yoshida's *Eros + Massacre,* a complex philosophical inquiry into the connections between sexual and political revolution. It combined a modern love story and a real historical event—the killing of a Japanese anarchist half a century ago.

Akira Kurosawa's first colour film, *Dodeska-Den,* was a kind of *Lower Depths* set in a mythical modern Tokyo. Down-and-outs in a sordid shantytown live out a variety of dreams and fantasies. Kurosawa employed images and colours with brilliant and often disturbing nonrealistic effect.

India. Satyajit Ray returned in 1970 to his favourite theme of the confrontation of old and new India, with *Days and Nights in the Forest,* the story of four men who set out from Calcutta in a car, in search of relaxation and a little erotic excitement. (DA. J. R.)

Nontheatrical. The most spectacular showcase of nontheatrical film technique during the year took place at Japan's Expo 70, the international exposition held at Osaka. As at most recent international expositions, the fresh and daring use of film was the principal feature of the show. A number of the techniques introduced at the Canadian exposition of 1967 were repeated or refined at the Osaka exhibits, one of the main ones being the projection of multitudes of images on vast screens.

Among outstanding exhibits was the film produced for the Fuji group by Kroiter, Britten, and Low in collaboration with Japanese film maker Ichiikowa. It achieved an exceptional quality of image by filming in the new 15-sprocket 70-mm. horizontal format called IMAX and by projecting on a huge screen using a rolling loop mechanism and 25-kw. lamp.

Complete involvement of the viewer in multiple sights and sounds was accomplished by the Dutch producer Jan Vriiman, in the exhibit in the Netherlands pavilion. This show used fifteen 35-mm. film loops, ten slide projectors, and a carefully designed building to project a vastly varied and swiftly changing array of images and sounds throughout the three stories of a great pavilion, to the accompaniment of an eight-channel stereo sound track.

Trends in U.S. nontheatrical films indicated continued growth despite a slump in both the educational and the business markets for films, equipment, and services. According to an official report, there was an increase of 7% in customer spending in 1969, reaching the record level of $1,044,000,000. This was about the same as the increase of the preceding year. In the major markets, business and industry showed an increase in spending of 9%, schools and colleges spent a modest 5% more, and government agencies made an increase of only 3%.

This moderate increase in spending was not reflected in the number of nontheatrical motion pictures produced during the year. They rose only 3%, with 14,200 titles released as compared with 13,750 during the preceding year. The number of films produced for community agencies enjoyed a striking growth of 50%, while the number of films produced for business and industry increased by 6% and films for government declined 5%.

In the field of education, no increase was reported in the number of 16-mm. films released for distribution. This lack of growth probably reflected a general reduction in budgets by educational film producers in response to an anticipated slump in the market. The production of 8-mm. or short film titles, which were largely used in education and industrial training, continued the dramatic rise of recent years, climbing from 2,300 titles in 1968 to 3,100 in 1969.

(J. T. B.; T. W. Ho.)

See also Photography; Television and Radio.

ENCYCLOPÆDIA BRITANNICA FILMS. *New Tools for Learning* (1952); *The Unique Contribution* (1959); *Project Discovery: A Demonstration in Education* (1965); *Let Them Learn* (1967); *Growing* (1969)—a completely computer-animated film.

Cities and Urban Affairs

With each successive year it has become increasingly difficult to distinguish urban affairs from those of the population in general. In 1970 most people lived in urban areas, and those who did not were dependent on cities for their economic well-being and for services. Two of the most frequently mentioned problems of cities were only the most apparent manifestations of major world crises. The poverty of inner-city areas and the ghettos of underprivileged minorities reflected the poverty of vast areas of the world and the disparity between rich and poor nations. Urban pollution and overcrowding constituted the leading edge of the worldwide environmental crisis.

The Urban Environment. A long-standing problem received world attention in the course of 1970: the pollution of the biosphere—land, water, and air—became the subject of the day when big cities like Tokyo and New York were covered with a poisonous smog for days and weeks and when a major river like the Rhine was polluted to the extent that several million fish were killed. The continuing process of deterioration in the human environment, caused by an overemphasis on such priorities of contemporary society as economic growth, the indiscriminate use of technological inventions, the increase in motor traffic, and continuing urbanization, had reached critical proportions.

Certainly air pollution was one of the most acute problems facing the cities. During a late summer heat spell the East Coast of the United States was blanketed by smog that at times reached dangerous levels, and the situation was made worse by power shortages that necessitated cutbacks in air conditioning. Sydney, Austr., experienced smog that was described as smelling like rotten eggs. According to press reports, the air pollution in Osaka, Jap., was bad enough on July 29 to kill 16 rabbits belonging to a primary school; the children survived, but some 20% of them suffered from dizziness and nausea. Similar effects were reported in Tokyo. Some cities planned "pollution alerts" that, in extreme instances, included shutting down factories and banning automobiles. However, the effects of smog were by no means confined to short-term critical periods. Air pollution was reportedly killing the famous trees along Rome's Appian Way, and in Buenos Aires the chemicals in the air turned paint gray.

Since automobile exhaust was one of the major con-

Circuses:
see Fairs and Shows

tributors to urban air pollution, the proliferation of urban expressways came under increasing attack from environmentalists. There were, of course, other evils connected with expressway building, not the least of which were the breaking up of neighbourhoods and the elimination of refuges for the pedestrian.

At the Greater London Council elections a new party fought a number of seats under the slogan "Homes Before Roads," and such persistent criticisms were made of the road proposals in the Greater London Development Plan that the government set up an official inquiry into the plan, which started on October 6. Since London had a reputation as one of the best governed cities in the world, this was a sad commentary on the state of city planning everywhere.

According to a draft report of the London Region Environment Group of the Royal Institute of British Architects, if the Greater London Development Plan were accepted, the future of London would be determined by the private car at the expense of public-transport users and pedestrians. The GLC was accused of starting from the assumption that the demand for road space should be satisfied wherever possible, without questioning whether this served the best interests of the population as a whole. "It becomes apparent that the pedestrian is having to make concessions in every case to the car driver. Underpasses for pedestrians are likely to become more common. Apart from the considerable difficulties of policing these, is it to become a permanent feature of life in London that to reach one part of a community—say, a group surgery, or school, or church, or shops—on foot, it will be necessary to go underground, or climb over a bridge to do so?" As an alternative, the group suggested the construction of subway lines that went from point to point on the city's periphery rather than funneling into the centre, restriction of commuter cars in inner London, the establishment of clearways and lanes for buses only, and shopping areas solely for pedestrians. In Tokyo an experiment was begun in which some of the more crowded districts were reserved on certain days for pedestrian use only.

Another aspect of environmental pollution that was receiving increased attention during the year was that of noise. A number of doctors expressed the opinion that hearing impairment and loss could be caused

not only by long-term, continuous exposure to high noise levels, as in some factories, but also by the steadily rising level of background noise familiar to all city dwellers. The psychic damage resulting from such noise also came under investigation. In light of these findings, growing attention was being focused on the problem of aircraft noise in general and the proposed supersonic transport (SST), with its accompanying sonic boom, in particular.

The problem of airport expansion and placement had been growing increasingly critical for some years, as both air traffic and the residential areas around airports grew more congested. The complexities of the situation were exemplified in Chicago, where O'Hare International, the world's busiest airport, was becoming obsolete less than 15 years after it had been opened and where the once open space around it was being engulfed in suburban sprawl. A possible solution was put forward in the form of an airport in Lake Michigan, just off the city's shoreline, to be built by a polder-type construction. The plan was opposed by the airline pilots, who feared the hazards of lake fogs and possible conflicts with the O'Hare traffic patterns, and by conservation groups who claimed that it posed threats of lake pollution, increased traffic congestion, and elimination of the city's beaches and lakefront recreational areas. The alternative seemed to be an airport inconveniently far away in the countryside, and it was noted that airline passengers still seemed to prefer the delays and overcrowding at National Airport in Washington, D.C., to Dulles International, a $15 taxi ride away.

The SST was an especially interesting case in that it represented a still-untried technology, the effects of which could only be conjectured. In the U.S. the Nixon administration's request for funds for continued work on the SST was approved by the House of Representatives and rejected by the Senate. A further attempt to get the measure past the Senate by parliamentary maneuvering was blocked by a filibuster, and in the last days of the session the two houses agreed to fund the project at a level of $210 million a year until March 31, 1971, when another effort would be made to reach a final decision. Proponents of the SST, testifying at legislative hearings, had argued that the supersonic plane represented progress and would provide jobs in the depressed aerospace industry. Opponents had pleaded that this was one instance in which a pollution-threatening technology could be stopped before it became an integral—and inseparable —part of the system.

In Britain, where the British-French SST, the Concorde, was nearer completion, the problem was more immediate. Within the next two or three years, 50 supersonic flights were planned to determine whether supersonic flight over populated areas would be acceptable. Already doubts were being expressed. In February a *Guardian* editorial asked "whether millions of people on the ground should be expected to put up with the disturbance of some bangs, so that a few hundred air passengers can get to their destination a couple of hours earlier."

Such questions of pollution and congestion were both symptomatic of and contributing factors to the larger question of whether the city was still a viable form for the ordering of human life. The whole economic and social system of which the city was a product was called into question. Thus the economist E. J. Mishan spoke of the "myth" of economic growth. The reason for the myth, he said, was that gross na-

World's 25 Most Populous Cities

Rank	City and country	City proper — Most recent census	City proper — Estimate	City proper — Year	Metropolitan — Estimate	Metropolitan — Year
1	Tokyo, Japan	8,893,094*	9,013,222	1970	23,123,355	1970
2	New York, U.S.	7,771,730†	—	—	11,900,000	1969
3	Shanghai, China‡	—	—	—	10,000,000	1967-68
4	London, U.K.§	—	—	—	7,703,410	1969
5	Peking, China‡	—	—	—	7,060,000	1967-68
6	Moscow, U.S.S.R.	6,942,000†	—	—	7,061,000†	1970
7	Greater Bombay, India	4,152,056	5,700,358	1970	5,700,358	1970
8	São Paulo, Brazil	3,164,804	5,000,000	1966	5,684,706	1968
9	Cairo, U.A.R.	4,219,853‖	4,961,000	1970	5,925,400	1970
10	Jakarta, Indonesia	2,973,052	4,500,000	1968	4,349,950	1967
11	Seoul, S. Korea	3,793,280‖	3,972,000	1967	. . .	. . .
12	Delhi-New Delhi, India	2,359,408	3,772,457	1970	3,772,457	1970
13	Buenos Aires, Argentina	2,966,634	3,600,000	1970	7,866,000	1967
14	Leningrad, U.S.S.R.	3,513,000†	—	—	3,950,000†	1970
15	Mexico City, Mexico	2,832,133	3,483,649	1969	7,005,855	1970
16	Madrid, Spain	2,259,931	3,381,406	1970	2,926,374	1965
17	Chicago, U.S.	3,322,855†	—	—	6,892,509†	1970
18	Tientsin, China	2,693,831¶	3,278,000	1958	3,800,000	1958
19	Rio de Janeiro, Brazil	3,223,408	. . .	. . .	. . .	. . .
20	Calcutta, India	2,927,289	3,158,838	1970	5,074,668	1968
21	Osaka, Japan	3,156,222*	3,018,175	1969	14,548,613	1969
22	Teheran, Iran	2,719,730‖	2,840,494	1967	3,250,000	1970
23	Los Angeles, U.S.	2,781,829†	—	—	6,974,103†	1970
24	Rome, Italy	2,188,160	2,731,397	1970	. . .	. . .
25	Paris, France	2,590,771¶	. . .	. . .	8,196,746ọ	1968

*1965. †1970 census. ‡Municipality. §Greater London. ‖1966. ¶1953. ọ1968 census.
Ranking based on latest estimates of city proper population. Most recent census refers to 1960 or 1961, except as footnoted. Berlin, both sectors combined 1970 population 3,218,156, is excluded due to the political as well as physical division of the city.

tional product "tots up the values of all man-made goods, while assiduously ignoring all the man-made bads that are produced simultaneously." (L. C. BR.)

Throughout the urban United States, the onset of the new decade led to reevaluation of "the urban crisis" and speculation about the urban future. The 46th annual Congress of Cities of the National League of Cities, held in December 1969, followed this course, as indicated in its theme, "Cities in the '70s." As set forth by congress participants, who included mayors of the major as well as the smaller cities of the nation, the principal problems facing the cities included: physical problems, such as environmental pollution, insufficient and inadequate housing, air and surface traffic congestion, insufficient recreational facilities, and deficient mass transportation; economic problems, such as poverty, unemployment, underemployment, consumer protection, and inflation; social problems, such as the revolt of the blacks, the revolt of youth, crime and delinquency, alcoholism and drug addiction, controversial welfare provisions, and inadequate medical care; and problems of governance, such as "home rule" for cities, inadequate schools, rising needs for governmental services, deficient city revenues, and fragmented political control within metropolitan areas.

Speculation on the future contained little that was hopeful. Projections of existing trends indicated that there was little prospect that the urban crisis would abate during the '70s or in the foreseeable future. Central cities would gain increasing proportions of blacks as suburbs remained predominantly white; continued white racism would be met with growing black pressures for separatism and control; the gap between generations would widen rather than narrow. There was little evidence that the physical, economic, social, and governmental problems would be solved; unrest would lead to greater manifestations of alienation and violence; and increased disorder would lead to increased suppression—and possibly a repressive society. The National Commission on the Causes and Prevention of Violence (Milton Eisenhower, chairman) held forth the prospect of future American cities as "places of terror" in which citizens would live in armed "fortresses."

As a number of the participants in the congress saw it, the only hope for the future of American cities lay in changes in national priorities. Chief among these, as called for by New York's Mayor John Lindsay and others, was the need to "halt the growth of the military budget and turn our priorities toward home." Whitney Young, executive director of the National Urban League, agreed with Lindsay and added: "The national priority of life in space must be replaced by the national priority of making cities livable . . . the top national priority must be elimination of poverty and racism and the revitalization of the city." The fiscal magnitude of such a change was indicated by Lindsay, who, after estimating that the cities faced a revenue gap of $250 billion in the '70s, called on the federal government to share revenues with the cities, beginning with a contribution of $5 billion in 1970.

The events of the year provided no basis for greater optimism. Although no major riots comparable to previous disorders in Watts, Detroit, or Chicago occurred during the year, disruptions and violence in perhaps an even more sinister form were manifest. At a hearing before a Senate panel, Eugene T. Rossides, assistant secretary of the treasury for enforcement and operations, reported that during the 15-month period from Jan. 1, 1969, to April 15, 1970, the U.S. experienced 4,330 bombings, 1,475 unsuccessful bombing attempts, and 35,129 threatened bombings. The bombings were responsible for 43 deaths, 384 injuries, and a loss of $21.8 million in property damage. In New York City alone, Police Commissioner Howard R. Leary testified, there were 368 bombings between January 1969 and June 1970—more than twice the total in the preceding eight years. Even the New York City police headquarters was bombed. The specific sources of the bombings were in the main unknown, but they undoubtedly had their origin in the frustrations of some combination of minority groups, in extreme leftist and rightist political groups, and in organized crime. There could be no question but that the great increase in bombings was attributable to increasing alienation and frustration with "the Establishment" and a growing belief that social change could not be accomplished by working within the system. (*See* CRIME.)

While racial riots were less prominent in 1970 than in preceding years, it would be dangerous to interpret this fact as indicating that discontent and anger were abating within the black community. On the contrary, as Whitney Young stated, the likelihood was that "the revolution of rising expectations" had changed to a "revolution of rising resentment." Some riots, racial in character, did occur in a number of cities, among them Miami, Fla.; Augusta, Ga.; New Brunswick and Asbury Park, N.J.; Peoria and Cairo, Ill.; Kansas City, Mo.; Lima, O.; and Hartford, Conn. Moreover, there was increasing evidence of guerrilla tactics, including accelerated sniper activities, directed especially toward policemen.

Cities were beset with violence from sources other than minority-group alienation. The Weatherman faction of the Students for a Democratic Society, after their violent "days of rage" in Chicago in 1969, went underground with avowed intent to harass and to wreak destruction on the Establishment. Widespread disruption and violence on college campuses often led to counterviolence, as when construction workers—the so-called hard hats—attacked student and other "peace" demonstrators in Manhattan. The "generation gap" also produced disorders, as well as flagrant violations of narcotics laws. Moreover, there was no indication that the rising tide of common crimes and gang warfare was abating. At the same time, evidence mounted that growing violence and threats of violence were being met with increasingly repressive measures.
(P. M. HA.)

UPI COMPIX
Hugh J. Addonizio, former mayor of Newark, N.J. He and other city officials were convicted of conspiracy and extortion of money from a company doing business with the city.

New York City firemen battle blazes on Sutter Avenue in the Brownsville section of Brooklyn. A wave of arson and looting, triggered by large accumulations of uncollected garbage, swept the neighbourhood in mid-June.

THE "NEW YORK TIMES"

JULIAN ZUKMAN FROM KEYSTONE

Above, townhouse in New York's Greenwich Village after bombs being made by members of SDS Weatherman faction exploded accidentally. Below, policeman inspects damage in the Socony Mobil Building, one of three New York office buildings hit by bombs on March 12, 1970.

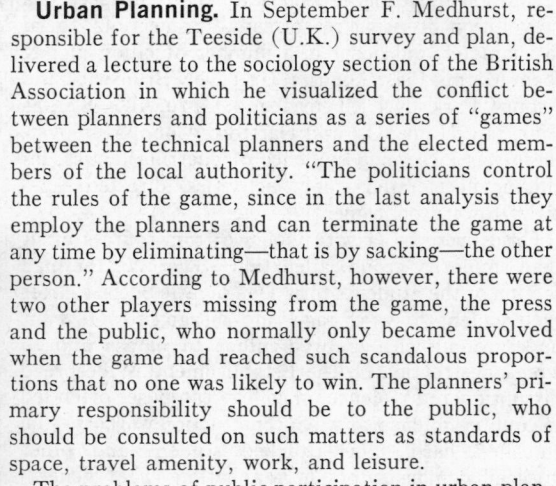

UPI COMPIX

Urban Planning. In September F. Medhurst, responsible for the Teeside (U.K.) survey and plan, delivered a lecture to the sociology section of the British Association in which he visualized the conflict between planners and politicians as a series of "games" between the technical planners and the elected members of the local authority. "The politicians control the rules of the game, since in the last analysis they employ the planners and can terminate the game at any time by eliminating—that is by sacking—the other person." According to Medhurst, however, there were two other players missing from the game, the press and the public, who normally only became involved when the game had reached such scandalous proportions that no one was likely to win. The planners' primary responsibility should be to the public, who should be consulted on such matters as standards of space, travel amenity, work, and leisure.

The problems of public participation in urban planning were epitomized by the experience of two neighbourhood groups protesting similar road schemes in London. One group, in Acklam Road, threatened in the last resort to lie down in the road, and they won their battle. The other, Gilda Court group went through proper channels and lost. The *Guardian* epitomized the matter in an editorial: "A situation in which broken glass works better than democracy is intolerable."

A 1970 report published by the Civic Trust announced that 1,000 conservation areas had been designated throughout Great Britain under the Civic Amenities Act of 1967, the thousandth being the centre of the historic town of Shrewsbury. Of these, 395 were in cities and town centres, 475 in villages, and 130 in the suburbs of London, and they varied from one or two buildings and the surrounding landscape to the whole of Hampstead Garden Suburb. The Civic Trust predicted that 3,000 conservation areas might eventually be designated.

Local authorities in Britain were sharply criticized for failing to face their obligations with regard to the preservation of listed buildings of architectural or historic interest. According to one survey, 16s. 9d. (about $2) was the average amount spent by the local authorities in England and Wales on each listed building. However, in February Lord Kennet, then the joint parliamentary secretary to the Ministry of Housing and Local Government, said the annual loss of historic buildings during the preceding three years had been reduced by over a third. In 1966 more than 400 listed buildings had been destroyed; in 1969 the number was 266.

The advent of the 1970s brought an opportunity for reassessment of progress in the New Towns program. A number of books were published, including Ray Thomas' *Aycliffe to Cumbernauld*, a study of seven older New Towns outside London. According to Thomas, the New Towns outside London had had only a limited success in the regional context. They had assisted "the growth point strategy," but they had not made, and were not making, "an adequate contribution to housing the truly under-privileged."

In January a special report by F. Zweig, commissioned by the Urban Research Bureau, was published on the award-winning British New Town of Cumbernauld in central Scotland. It was once regarded as a triumph of town planning, with complete pedestrian-vehicle segregation and a density of 48 persons per acre, but Zweig considered it a "streetless city" with an inadequate social life and increasing risk of crime. Paradoxically, by excluding cars from the town centre and yet providing a garage and parking space in every home, the planners had inflated car ownership to the highest level in Scotland. The result was "a lack of involvement in community affairs," since the citizens preferred to drive elsewhere rather than to walk downtown.

Fifteen New Towns had been built in Britain in less than 20 years, and a million people were living in them. Of special interest were the conclusions of two doctors, quoted in *The New Story* by Frank Shaffer, on the medical record of Harlow. "Our survey has shown that the creation of a new town, with full social and economic planning, results in an improvement in general health, both subjective and objective. About nine-tenths of the new population are satisfied with their environment and the one-tenth who are dissatisfied would be dissatisfied wherever they were. Full satisfaction with environment is a product of time."

(L. C. BR.)

Municipal Government. During 1970 municipal governments all over the world continued to show a capacity to adapt themselves to the demands of a society in rapid evolution. Such demands included the need for increased and better services at the local level, ranging from education to street lighting and sewage disposal, but they were also increasingly expressed in the call for more opportunities for participation by citizens in local affairs and for the preservation or creation of an environment fit to live in. Local authorities were increasingly aware of these demands and tried to develop policies to meet them.

Reform of Local Government. One such policy was the adoption of drastic reforms in the overall structure of local government, introduced in a growing number of countries. In recent years it had been thought that various forms of cooperation and gradual amalgamation would solve the problems posed by enlargement of scale and the demand for more efficient services. However, it was clear that certain limits had been reached, concerning, for example, complexity of local governmental structure and available finances and personnel.

In Scandinavia, Denmark followed the Swedish example of an overall amalgamation of existing municipalities into new units of local government that were larger in size, had more financial and other powers, and were generally better equipped for their new tasks. On April 1, 1970, the number of municipalities was reduced from some 1,100 to 280 and the number of counties (*amter*) from 23 to 13. At the same time, the distinction between boroughs and rural districts was abolished, and a transfer of certain tasks from the central to the local level took place. The Swedish reform, the second within 20 years, which had reduced the number of local authorities from some 1,000 to 282, was still in progress and was expected to be completed by 1974. In Finland plans were submitted that, following a reorganization of the comprehensive school system, would lead to the creation of 350–400 municipalities with at least 8,000 inhabitants each.

In the United Kingdom the Labour government adopted many of the recommendations proposed by the Royal Commission on Local Government, whose report had been issued in June 1969. A White Paper issued in February 1970 proposed the division of England into 56 government areas, 51 of which would have unitary authorities responsible for the provision of all services and would contain a population of between 250,000 and one million. Five metropolitan areas would have a two-tier structure of government, with functions divided between a metropolitan authority and metropolitan district authorities, the former (larger) ones covering such tasks as planning, transportation, and education. Local councils would be created (in place of the existing borough, urban, and rural district councils and the parishes) that would have advisory powers and would have to be consulted on matters of immediate local interest.

The new Conservative government did not take a definite position, but was generally believed to be in favour of the reform proposals. A vigorous opposition campaign was mounted by the Rural District Councils Association, whose very existence was at stake, since the territory of its member authorities would be encompassed by the new unitary authorities. A campaign fund was created in an attempt to prevent the implementation of the reform proposals, which, it was held, would make local government "too remote from the people."

Yet another royal commission delivered its report in the United Kingdom in 1970. The Wheatley Commission on the reform of the local government structure in Scotland recommended setting up a new two-tier structure whereby the existing 397 cities, districts, and burghs would be amalgamated into 37 new authorities (called districts) with an average population of 50,000 to 150,000 inhabitants. The existing 33 counties would be transformed into 7 regions, responsible for planning, police, social work, and health. The district authorities would exercise local planning functions and be responsible for housing improvement and libraries. "Community Councils" would be set up within these districts, designed to express the views of the local community on matters affecting it. It was interesting to note that in three parts of the United Kingdom, proposals were submitted for either a one-tier local government structure (England outside London) or a two-tier structure (Scotland and Wales). Both solutions were defended on the grounds of democracy and efficiency and both were challenged on the same basis.

The same complexity and diversity of local government structures were to be found in the various Länder (states) of West Germany, where a series of reform proposals was made by experts' committees. In general they had one element in common: they explicitly

and implicitly seemed to accept 8,000 inhabitants as the minimum population size for viable local government units. A similar figure was used in the Scandinavian reforms.

Local government reform proposals were contemplated in other areas of the world as well. In the Philippines the joint local government reform commission was charged to conduct a comprehensive study into the need for a new system of local government administration. In Pakistan the ten-year-old multitier system of basic democracies was scrapped altogether by the new government because of its rigid control and the indirect nature of its elections. In its place a two-tier structure of directly elected councils at the union (lower) and district (higher) levels was installed. In urban areas, town committees, municipal committees, and city corporations might be set up. The first general elections for the new local councils were due to be held before April 1971.

Interest in the United States focused on metropolitan areas rather than on statewide reform schemes. In the course of 1970 a number of city-county consolidations took place (as in previous years), but more far-reaching proposals were formulated by the Committee for Economic Development (CED), composed of 200 leading businessmen and educators. The CED recommended the creation of a two-level system of local government, including an area-wide level containing one or more counties and a local level comprising "community districts." These proposals for a "metropolitan federation" were the first that went clearly in the direction of an overall reform of the structure of municipal government in metropolitan areas since the creation, a few years earlier, of voluntary and advisory metropolitan-area-wide councils of elected officials.

The growing importance of reform of local government systems was also reflected in a study being undertaken by the United Nations' Public Administration Division, which would evaluate experiences over the past 25 years, with reference to new arrangements for decentralization of responsibilities for major development programs and the promotion of citizen participation in them.

Citizen Participation. One of the most pressing demands of contemporary society was for more participation of citizens in affairs that concerned them directly. These demands were often most clearly expressed at the local level. Increasingly, local authorities were responding positively and were taking initiatives to promote such participation. These initiatives ranged from improving existing channels of information and communication and creating new forms of two-way communication to the promotion of active participation by citizen groups in the decision-making process. Information and complaint centres were being created in those areas where urban renewal was to take place; hearings and referenda were held to give citizens a chance to express their own desires; social counselors and community-development officers were appointed to obtain more direct information on the citizens' demands and problems. In certain areas of local government (sports, education, culture), functional councils, to whom specific tasks were delegated, were appointed.

During 1970 the installation of local "ombudsmen" was proposed in the U.K. These officials would thoroughly investigate citizens' complaints of maladministration, including unnecessary delays, nepotism, arbitrariness, and cases where the proper administration of a rule had caused an injustice. The London borough

KEYSTONE
Pedestrians stroll on the main street of the Shinjuku district of Tokyo. Traffic was barred from the centre of the city on Sundays during the summer of 1970.

FOX PHOTOS FROM PICTORIAL PARADE

Lauderdale Tower (centre), the City of London School for Girls (left), and Defoe House (right). These three buildings are part of the Barbican Project, a 32-ac. urban renewal development being undertaken by the City of London.

of Camden started a postcard scheme, enabling citizens to register their complaints by filling in prepaid postcards.

In Sweden a law was introduced that would give local authorities the right to subsidize political parties to undertake research on municipal questions. It was recognized that democracy is realized through political parties, which, therefore, should not be prevented by lack of economic resources from doing informative and opinion-creating work.

Increasingly, however, citizens were choosing to undertake action outside the existing channels of communication and representation—for example, through citizen action groups. Many such groups were formed to protest against the deterioration of neighbourhoods, particularly with regard to the pollution of the environment, poor housing conditions, and the need for better services. Thus, in several French cities, *associations de quartier* were created by citizen groups and private organizations with the aim of defending the interests of their neighbourhoods and promoting more participation by citizens in their affairs. In the Netherlands and Sweden, less institutionalized and more spontaneous action groups sprang up in those cities and rural areas where environment was threatened or where town planning did not appear to take into account the desires and demands of the citizens themselves.

In the U.K. and the U.S. the call for neighbourhood government received more and more support. In Britain the Association of Neighbourhood Councils was created with the object of pressuring the national government to set up elected neighbourhood or urban parish councils inside cities and large towns. These councils would have the power to provide any amenities that local ratepayers were prepared to pay for,

and would have the right to be consulted by higher levels of government. In the U.S. people in several cities took the initiative in improving communications between city hall and the neighbourhoods. Information and service centres were installed, and "mini" city halls and mobile city halls were being operated experimentally. The Los Angeles City Charter Commission prepared a draft charter that would enable citizens to create a neighbourhood organization with an elected board and an appointed "neighbourman." A limited form of neighbourhood government was attempted in New York City, where 31 community school boards were elected directly and given certain distinct powers.

More general measures that could improve the capacity and willingness of citizens to take a direct interest in their own affairs were the elaboration of an educational and information system directed toward these needs. In this context, the experiences with local radio stations in Britain were significant. In the course of 1970, 12 new stations were announced by the government, bringing the total to 20. After initial hesitation, the local government associations supported this innovation, which proved to be of great value in achieving more consciousness of local affairs among citizens and providing channels for their views and complaints.

Human Environment. Although rarely the immediate cause of pollution, local government was called upon by many to develop the human environment in accordance with the needs of the inhabitants, to save what natural resources could be saved, and in general to involve citizens more directly in the decisions that determined their own environment. Measures to control pollution were taken at the local level in virtually all industrially developed countries, but usually in an ad hoc manner, since air and water pollution do not respect administrative boundaries—and, indeed, not even national boundaries, as was evident from the pollution of the Rhine.

A spectacular plan was launched in France, where a new city, Vaudreuil, with an eventual 150,000 inhabitants, was scheduled for construction in the lower Seine region outside Paris. The aim was to make Vaudreuil the world's first urban centre without noise or pollution. Traffic arteries, conduits for smoke from factories, and refuse conduits would all go underground. Gases would be burned off at the source, and the burning of refuse would provide part of the energy for the future city's central heating system.

In several existing cities, measures were taken to reduce pollution and noise from traffic. The city of Lyons, France, was considering the introduction of a "silent" overhead rapid rail transit system. In Moscow a ten-seater electric minibus was tried out by municipal transport services. A similar experiment was taking place in Koblenz, W.Ger., where a battery-powered city bus, a coproduct of several German firms, joined the fleet of the municipally owned transport company. The city of Vienna reconverted its buses from diesel fuel to a mixture of diesel and liquid gas. The town of Orange, Calif., used natural gas as fuel for six of its public motor vehicles in an effort to reduce both air pollution and costs.

Campaigns against litter were mounted in several countries and cities. A national no-litter week started in London and then moved across the U.K. The use of paper and plastic bags for refuse collection was encouraged in such cities as New York, where Mayor Lindsay also called upon 14 bottling firms to reintroduce deposit bottles to ease the enormous disposal problems caused by nondeposit, nonreturnable containers. As part of a national litter-prevention campaign, the city of Rodney, N.Z., introduced "talking" litter bins that called on pedestrians to use them.

Concerned citizens took action in several towns to prevent the undue expansion or attraction of such polluting industries as oil refineries, steel factories, and aluminum plants. However, the possibilities of local government action of this kind were limited, since the necessary legal prerequisites were often lacking. Moreover, reliable data on the extent of pollution were seldom available. In the Netherlands, the Rijnmond Authority, operating in the Greater Rotterdam area, put a fully automated monitoring network into operation to trace the degree of air pollution in the heavily industrialized port area. In Britain the Open University initiated a spare-time course to train private citizens to set up laboratories for testing the quality of the air throughout the country in the framework of a massive test program.

The Urban Scene. While preventing further pollution was one of the tasks of public authorities at different levels of government, it was increasingly realized that environmental problems would have to be put in the context of the overall environment in which they occurred—the "urban crisis" experienced by many cities. It was not surprising, therefore, that new research centres were created in a number of countries to study in more detail the problems facing municipal government. In Canada the Canadian Council on Urban and Regional Research was to sponsor the groundwork needed for setting up a comprehensive urban information service available to all local authorities. In Austria the Association of Austrian Towns, the City of Vienna, and the Academy of Sciences founded the Institute of Urban Research. In Finland a large research project, "Urban Research '70," was launched by six research institutes under supervision of the Association of Finnish Cities. With financial aid from the West German government, four research divisions of the Municipal Research Centre in West Berlin started an interdisciplinary research project on the aims, theory, and instruments of urban development.

In the U.S. the Advisory Commission on Intergovernmental Relations issued a report, *Urban America and the Federal System,* that summarized the findings of a series of separate reports previously issued by the commission. The report called for restoration of fiscal balance between national, state, and local government, the formation of national and state policies, and the reconstruction of state constitutions and statutes with respect to local government. The newly created National Committee on Urban Growth Policy also emphasized the need for a national policy. Among other recommendations, the committee urged federal support in the creation of 110 new urban communities. The National League of Cities and the U.S. Department of Housing and Urban Development agreed on the elaboration of the "urban observatory" concept, which would link the resources available at the universities to local governmental action. There were experimental observatories in six metropolitan areas.

On October 15 the U.K. government announced the creation of a new ministry, the Department of the Environment, formed by the merger of three former ministries—Housing and Local Government, Transport, and Public Building and Works. The new secretary of state for the environment was to coordinate the work of three subdivisions, including a reorganized Ministry for Local Government and Development.

(EI. K.)

See also Architecture; Crime; Historic Buildings; Housing; Parks; Police; Transportation.

ENCYCLOPÆDIA BRITANNICA FILMS. *The Living City* (1953); *Health in Our Community* (1959); *Megalopolis—Cradle of the Future* (1962); *Chicago—Midland Metropolis* (1963); *Operation Bootstrap* (1968); *Problems of Conservation—Air* (1968); *The House of Man, Part II—Our Crowded Environment* (1969); *Manuel from Puerto Rico* (1969); *The South: Roots of the Urban Crisis* (1969); *Chicano from the Southwest* (1970); *The Garbage Explosion* (1970); *The Industrial City* (1970); *Linda and Billy Ray from Appalachia* (1970); *The Rise of the American City* (1970); *What Is a Community?* (1970).

Colombia

A republic in northwestern South America, Colombia is bordered by Panama, Venezuela, Brazil, Peru, and Ecuador and has coasts on both the Caribbean Sea and the Pacific Ocean. Area: 439,734 sq.mi. (1,138,914 sq.km.). Pop. (1968 est.): 19,829,185. Cap.: Bogotá (pop., 1968, 1,984,599). Language: Spanish. State religion: Roman Catholic (90%). Presidents in 1970, Carlos Lleras Restrepo and, from August 7, Misael Pastrana Borrero.

In 1970, against a continuing background of healthy economic expansion, the political pressures for social reform were strengthened by the outcome of presidential and congressional elections held on April 19. Misael Pastrana Borrero (*see* BIOGRAPHY), the National Front's presidential candidate, won 1,614,419 votes, against 1,557,782 cast for Gustavo Rojas Pinilla, representing the Alianza Nacional Popular (Anapo). Two other contenders, Belisario Betancur and Evaristo Sourdis, polled 805,891 votes between them.

Supporters of the narrowly defeated Rojas Pinilla, alleging electoral fraud, staged demonstrations which threatened to get out of hand, and a state of siege was imposed from April 21 until May 15. President Lleras appealed to all four candidates to restore political harmony by upholding public order, supporting vigorous social policies, and enabling the country's institutions to function democratically. Their response foreshadowed the congressional alignment of their parties.

Pastrana, backing the president's appeal, asked the people to participate in a "Great Social Front." Rojas Pinilla, whose program was a judicious mixture

THE "NEW YORK TIMES"

Billboard sponsored by a group of businessmen in downtown Bogotá reads, "Another child? Think about it in time." Persistent work by medical and social groups has overcome much of the traditional opposition to family planning in Colombia.

of traditional Roman Catholicism, social reform, and nationalism, said that there could be no dialogue with the National Front unless the government freed political prisoners, accepted Anapo's basic ideology, and recognized that electoral fraud had been widespread. Betancur reaffirmed his determination to oppose the National Front, but Sourdis hinted that his party might be willing to cooperate with it. Lleras ordered a recount and promised to hand over power on August 7 to the winning candidate.

Pastrana's victory was officially confirmed shortly before the new Congress assembled on July 20, and he was duly sworn in on August 7. He had earlier reached an understanding with Sourdis that gave the National Front an effective majority of 18 in the Senate and 14 in the House of Representatives. Since the constitutional reforms of December 1968 enabled ordinary legislation to be carried by a simple (instead of a two-thirds) majority, it was generally believed that the new administration would be able to carry out its program.

This, as Pastrana defined it before taking office, was to continue and develop many of the policies successfully pursued by the Lleras government, which had ensured a solid improvement in exchange reserves, a healthier balance of payments, greater diversification of exports, a reduced rate of inflation, and faster economic growth. Under strong pressure from Anapo, Pastrana's government was expected to lay greater emphasis on agrarian and social reform as distinct from industrial expansion. Anapo persisted in claiming that Rojas Pinilla had won the election and would therefore refuse to recognize Pastrana's presidency.

Efforts to reunite the Conservative Party (the Liberal Party's partner in the National Front, which had governed the country since 1958) made some progress, but newspapers committed to the Liberal Party carried articles suggesting that differences had developed over its future leadership. There were also insistent rumours of a split in Anapo, stemming from a proposal that María Eugenia Rojas de Moreno Díaz, a daughter of Rojas Pinilla, should stand as the party's candidate in the 1974 presidential election. Confirming this proposal, her husband later said it had been dropped at the request of Rojas Pinilla.

The economy continued to gain strength. In 1970 the gross national product was expected to increase by 7% (compared with 6.5% in 1965, the best year of the previous decade). From January to May the balance of payments surplus ($49 million in 1968 and $59.1 million in 1969) grew to $82.3 million, while net exchange reserves rose (despite higher imports) from $96.6 million in January to a record peak of $183.5 million on June 2. Manufacturing output in 1969, stimulated by adequate imports of raw materials and capital goods together with extensive credit facilities, rose by 7.5%, and in 1970 the monthly average of reimbursable imports was expected to reach $65 million (against $60 million in 1969). With a fiscal surplus of 1,484,000,000 pesos on June 30, Colombia seemed likely to achieve its fifth consecutive budget surplus. Efforts to contain internal inflation were reasonably successful. The cost of living index, which rose by 8.7% in 1969, registered a 3.8% increase in the first half of 1970.   (R. B. LE.)

ENCYCLOPÆDIA BRITANNICA FILMS. *Colombia and Venezuela* (1961).

Commercial Policies

The lull in new international commercial policy activity that followed the conclusion of the Kennedy Round of trade negotiations in 1967 had ended by mid-1969 as the world began grappling with a series of most complicated policy issues. Although the world trading system, which had been laboriously constructed, gave a good account of itself in 1969–70 in the sense that world trade continued to expand at a high rate, the pressures on the system were great and protectionist influences were stronger than at any time since the early 1930s.

Those who believed that the world's welfare—economic and political—was best served by reducing, rather than raising, barriers to trade did not lack opportunities to argue their case. Matters before the General Agreement on Tariffs and Trade (GATT), the negotiations of the European Economic Community (EEC) on enlargement and preferential trade agreements, and the efforts of many nations, the United Nations Conference on Trade and Development (UNCTAD), and the Organization for Economic Cooperation and Development (OECD) to establish a program of preferences for less developed nations were not without their challenges and difficulties. Influencing all of these was the continuing debate in the U.S. over new trade legislation.

National Commercial Measures. While the rate of expansion in U.S. production and imports, thanks to stringent monetary and fiscal policies, was sharply curtailed in 1969, high and sustained inflationary pressures became even more marked than in preceding years in continental Europe and in Japan. The high

---

COLOMBIA
Education. (1966) Primary, pupils 2,408,489, teachers 67,764; secondary, pupils 320,287, teachers 21,332; vocational, pupils 129,562, teachers 8,567; teacher training, students 63,549, teachers 4,627; higher (including 34 universities), students 49,930, teaching staff 8,190.
Finance. Monetary unit: peso, with a free rate (Sept. 14, 1970) of 18.60 pesos to U.S. $1 (44.37 pesos = £1 sterling). Gold, SDRs, and foreign exchange, central bank: (June 1970) U.S. $280 million; (June 1969) U.S. $164 million. Budget (1970 est.): revenue 11,030,800,000 pesos; expenditure 12,132,500,000 pesos. Gross national product: (1968) 94,380,000,000 pesos; (1967) 82,050,000,000 pesos. Money supply: (Feb. 1970) 18,796,000,000 pesos; (Feb. 1969) 15,612,000,-000 pesos. Cost of living (Bogotá; 1963 = 100): (May 1970) 199; (May 1969) 185.
Foreign Trade. (1968) Imports 10,349,000,-000 pesos; exports 7,431,000,000 pesos. Import sources: U.S. 50%; West Germany 9%; Spain 6%; U.K. 5%. Export destinations: U.S. 42%; West Germany 13%; Netherlands 8%. Main exports: coffee 61%; crude oil 4%.
Transport and Communications. Roads (1967) c. 45,000 km. (including 7,200 km. with improved surface). Motor vehicles in use (1968): passenger 141,100; commercial (including buses) 123,200. Railways: (1966) 3,483 km.; traffic (1969) 274 million passenger-km., freight 1,166,-000,000 net ton-km. Air traffic (1969): 1,743,-000,000 passenger-km.; freight 65,313,000 net ton-km. Shipping (1969): merchant vessels 100 gross tons and over 47; gross tonnage 206,084. Telephones (Dec. 1968) 817,423. Radio receivers (Dec. 1968) 2,210,000. Television receivers (Dec. 1968) c. 500,000.
Agriculture. Production (in 000; metric tons; 1969; 1968 in parentheses): rice c. 720 (784); wheat c. 80 (130); corn 796 (845); barley c. 110 (c. 85); potatoes 1,000 (900); cassava (1968) 900, (1967) 850; coffee c. 474 (480); bananas (1968) 770, (1967) 764; cotton, lint 125 (120); cane sugar, raw value (1969–70) c. 750, (1968–69) c. 709; sugar, panela (1969–70) c. 650, (1968–69) c. 660; tobacco 44 (43). Livestock (in 000; Dec. 1968): cattle c. 16,600; sheep c. 2,031; pigs c. 2,209; goats (Dec. 1966) c. 765; horses (Dec. 1967) 1,000; poultry (Oct. 1968) c. 25,000.
Industry. Fuel and power (in 000; 1969): crude oil 10,688 metric tons; natural gas 1,338,-000 cu.m.; coal (1968) c. 3,000 metric tons; electricity (excluding most industrial production) 6,520,000 kw-hr. Production (in 000; metric tons; 1969): crude steel (ingots) 206; gold (troy oz.; 1968) 237; salt (1968) 505; cement 2,400.

COURTESY, AUSTRALIAN INFORMATION SERVICE

Container ship is unloaded at White Bay terminal in Sydney. Government officials expressed concern that the United Kingdom's expected entry into the EEC would seriously disrupt Australia's traditional pattern of foreign trade.

demand in industrial countries brought with it a record level of exports of primary producing countries. In 1969 world exports increased by nearly 10% in volume and by 14% in value, which was the highest rate since the Korean War boom. Parallel to this were several developments serving to facilitate the adjustment of payments imbalances in certain major countries and to lessen the strains on the international monetary system. Consequently, there were only a few cases in which a trading nation was compelled to take defensive action by tightening payments regulations or trade restrictions.

On the other hand, perhaps owing to the general sense of insecurity while the policies of major nations were in the melting pot, the improvement in the international payments situation was not accompanied by many important steps toward trade liberalization. One notable feature was an increased propensity for governments to use import surcharges and import deposit systems, which required importers to deposit funds equal to a given percent of their goods before they were released from customs. The deposit was usually repayable after six months. The various formal and informal arrangements for voluntary restraints on exports (cotton textiles, meat, steel) were substantially unchanged, and import impediments maintained by industrial countries in connection with domestic agricultural policies remained entrenched.

Late in 1969 Austria introduced temporary measures designed to contain domestic price rises follow-ing the revaluation of the West German mark, including temporary duty reductions on some 70 products, lower equalization levies, and more liberal licensing of some durable goods from Japan and Eastern Europe. Denmark liberalized a number of agricultural commodities imported and undertook a substantial relaxation of remaining restrictions, particularly on imports from Eastern European countries. Commercial policy measures taken by France from mid-1969 included the extension of most of the 1969 import liberalization to French overseas *départements*, the reduction of tariff quotas for a number of products (silk and cotton piece goods), and the liberalization of additional imports from Eastern Europe and China.

With the introduction of a floating rate for the mark at the end of September 1969, West Germany introduced a temporary levy on agricultural imports and, subsequently, a temporary subsidy on agricultural exports. The rates were increased in October and the measures remained in force until the end of 1969. A 4% special turnover tax was imposed on most exports prior to the changes in the exchange rate and remained in force until the revaluation of the mark on October 27.

Japan freed several products from quantitative restrictions during 1969–70 and stated that it planned to free additional items earlier than the 1971–72 dates previously envisaged. Many products, however, remained subject to such restrictions. In October 1969 the U.K. renewed for a further year the import deposit system introduced in November 1968 but reduced the rate from 50 to 40% of import value. This was further reduced to 30% in April 1970 and to 20% in July, pending the termination of the policy in December.

The Greek import deposit system remained in force and the withholding period was extended from two to four months for a number of products. In December 1969 Spain also instituted an import deposit policy, requiring importers to lodge a peseta deposit equal to 20% of import value to be held by the Bank of Spain for six months; the scheme was scheduled to expire at the end of 1970. Israel introduced a similar import deposit requirement in January 1970 in conjunction with a wide range of other measures designed to stabilize the domestic economy and meet intensified balance of payments difficulties. The deposit, applied at the rate of 50% of import value on all goods subject to customs duty of 30% or over, was to be refunded after six months. In addition, in August an import surcharge of 20% was placed on the major part of imports.

Algeria placed a number of additional products under quantitative restriction in 1969 and reserved the importation of certain essential products to specified agencies. Argentina introduced a number of modifications in its import duties; for example, in June 1970 duties on certain equipment not available from local production were lowered by 20% or reduced to zero. Chile substantially reduced its import deposit rates. The import prohibitions that had been in force in Peru since March 1968 were expanded in September 1969 by some 150 items. Ecuador's monetary stabilization surcharge was raised for all categories of imports in May 1970. To supplement quantitative restrictions applied for balance of payments reasons, Yugoslavia also made use of an import surcharge of 5%, for a period of nine months until July 1971. Ghana also imposed an import surcharge in the autumn of 1970. The European Free Trade Association (EFTA) was enlarged to include Iceland.

Colonies: *see* Dependent States
Comecon: *see* Economic Planning
Commerce: *see* Commercial Policies; Consumer Expenditures; Economy, World; Merchandising; Trade, International

Policies of Industrial Nations. Tensions between major trading countries tended to increase during 1969–70. In the United States, where EEC policies had been criticized for some time, there was a gradual but accelerated concretization of proposals for counteraction. Many U.S. spokesmen considered the EEC's agricultural and preferential trade policies to be increasingly protectionist and discriminatory. Specific points of grievance included the practice of giving border rebates of the value-added tax on exports and an electronics components agreement between London, Bonn, and Paris, which threatened to damage U.S. export interests substantially. For its part, the EEC expressed increasing concern about the strong protectionist overtones of proposals before the U.S. Congress, and criticized both the failure to abolish the American Selling Price (ASP) system, as had been agreed during the Kennedy Round, and new proposals to restrict noncotton textiles.

Although the Japanese government had begun a gradual removal of its remaining import restrictions, the common feeling in the U.S. and Europe was that the present degree of protectionism was incompatible with Japan's position as a leading industrial nation enjoying fairly free access to the vast U.S. market and gaining better footholds in European markets. The rapidly expanding Japanese exports of textiles (and of other goods) to the U.S. were seized upon by U.S. industry and organized labour as justification for additional protection; serious attempts were made by the U.S. to induce the Japanese to accept voluntary restraints on exports of wool and man-made fibre products. In the background was the European fear that the products thus denied entry to the U.S. would be diverted to European markets.

Some found the efforts of the U.S. to formulate its long-term trade policies disappointing: the administration continued to profess adherence to the principles of free and expanding world trade but appeared to be unable to resist clamours for protection against rising imports. In November 1969 Pres. Richard Nixon had sent Congress a trade bill calling for authority to make modest reductions in U.S. tariffs, eliminate ASP, extend the 1962 Trade Expansion Act to include duties and restrictions in retaliation for unfair limitations on U.S. agricultural exports, and liberalize the criteria for adjusting assistance to industries and workers adversely affected by imports. Another bill introduced in April 1970 by the chairman of the House Ways and Means Committee, Wilbur D. Mills (Dem., Ark.), provided for quota restrictions on textile, apparel, and footwear imports and limited them to the 1967–69 level, but permitted the president to negotiate agreements allowing imports above that level.

The bill as passed by the House in November established import quotas on textiles and nonrubber footwear and provided for the introduction of quota restrictions on other imports. The administration had thrown its support behind quotas for textile items, but the House bill was considerably more restrictive than President Nixon had wanted. Protracted talks were held with the Japanese in the hope that Japan would voluntarily limit its textile exports to the U.S. Such restraint was strongly opposed by the Japanese textile industry, however, and no agreement was reached.

The trade bill died in the Senate during the last-minute rush toward adjournment. The fact remained that it had received strong support from a number of interest groups, and there was growing concern that rising protectionist sentiment in the U.S. could lead to legislation that would bring about the disintegration of the international trading system built around GATT or even a trade war. At the end of July senior representatives of the U.S., the EEC, Japan, and the U.K. met at the GATT headquarters in Geneva to consult informally on the situation. In September trade negotiations opened between the EEC and Japan.

EEC Expansion and Association. By April 1970 the EEC had achieved the effective completion of the Common Market when agreement had been reached, inter alia, on the financing of the common agricultural policy and the common organization of agricultural markets. The way was clear for "strengthening" and "enlargement" of the grouping. In preparation for negotiations for the accession of new members (applications for entry had been lodged by the U.K., Denmark, Norway, and Ireland), in the spring the member states discussed certain points, such as the transitional period for adjustment by new members, and continued discussion of such problems as the EEC attitude toward sterling and the British balance of payments, and toward EFTA countries not wishing to become full members of the EEC.

This latter point raised difficult problems. Primarily, preferential arrangements between the Six and any other countries, unless they were to lead in a reasonable time to a free-trade area or a customs union, would be incompatible with GATT. In addition, the likelihood of any wide range of tariff reductions on a most-favoured-nation basis, such as would be needed to lessen the impact of the separation between the new entrants and the nonentrants, appeared remote because of the general disinclination on the part of the major trading nations to embark on new tariff negotiations.

On the British side, there was deep concern over the contribution that would be required to finance the Community's common agricultural policy, and a desire to safeguard insofar as possible the vital interests of such Commonwealth suppliers as New Zealand farmers and Caribbean sugar growers. Other Commonwealth countries, notably Australia, bemoaned their likely loss of privileged access to the British market.

When the negotiations officially opened at the end of June the Six reaffirmed their position: solutions must be sought through transitional arrangements, not through changes in existing rules; such measures must be of defined duration and preceded by initial significant tariff reductions; increase in mutual access for industrial products must be adequately synchronized with the achievement of the enlarged agricultural common market; and the transitional period must be the same for all four prospective entrants and the accession treaties should enter into force on the same date.

As soon as actual negotiations got under way in September, the British presented rather concrete proposals regarding the transitional period. These envisaged a one-year initiation period after accession, a 40% cut in industrial tariffs by both sides at the end of that period, followed by two 30% reductions at intervals of one year. The same rhythm would be followed in aligning the U.K. tariff with the EEC common external tariff. A six-year transitional period, however, was proposed for agriculture. In December, however, the British dropped their insistence on separate periods and submitted a second proposal envisioning a single five-year transitional period for harmonizing agriculture, industry, taxation, and the movement of capital. It was noted, however, that the U.K. would probably need more than five years (possibly eight) before it would be able to bear its full share in financing the common agricultural policy. The parties concerned seemed earnest about the negotiations and the British and West Germans, in particular, made public pronouncements on the need to complete them before 1972.

In 1969 the EEC negotiated a new Yaoundé Convention to renew its association agreement with 18 African countries, and new association agreements with three East African countries (Kenya, Tanzania, and Uganda) and with Morocco and Tunisia. Preferential trade agreements were signed in June 1970 with Israel and Spain and negotiations for similar agreements with the U.A.R. and Lebanon started in September 1970. By the summer of 1970 the EEC had thus entered into agreements involving reciprocal trade preferences with 27 countries. Of these countries, Greece, Turkey, and Spain were known to be desirous of eventually becoming EEC members. The Yaoundé agreement and those with Morocco and Tunisia were said to be aimed at introducing free trade gradually between these countries and the EEC; in the view of the parties involved these arrangements had special historical justifications. The Mediterranean and East African countries considered the arrangements desirable because their economies and exports closely resembled those of the associate countries in the region (Morocco and Tunisia), with which they had to compete in the European markets.

These preferential agreements met with severe criticism from other countries. The matter came to a head at GATT meetings where the controversy centred around the so-called Mediterranean Policy of the EEC, which some called a "grand design," and its trade manifestations, which, in the view of several countries, directly contravened the basic principles and rules of GATT and could have a serious adverse effect on their exports.

International Organizations. After years of discussion, in various international forums, the proposed generalized system of tariff preferences for less developed countries began to take shape. Working under general guidelines laid down by the OECD in May 1970, the more developed countries concluded that it would not be possible to arrive at agreement on a single system of preferences or on essential elements that all individual plans should uniformly embody. They therefore proceeded to formulate schemes that were harmonized as much as possible and could be expected to yield comparable results. Specific problems related to the concern that the burden might not be equitably shared among the more developed countries and to the "reverse preferences" received by EEC countries and Britain from particular less developed countries. In September 1970 the OECD countries transmitted their individual proposals, and consultations with less developed nations took place in the Special Committee on Preferences of UNCTAD.

An interesting and important development during 1969–70 was the growing interest of the Eastern European countries in participating in the multilateral trading system. Romania and Hungary were both actively seeking full membership in GATT. Also to be noted was the increasing attention being paid in GATT to the trade problems of the less developed countries, particularly the possibilities offered by a reduction of

trade barriers aimed at increasing trade among themselves. Other activities of GATT were an arrangement to further regulate trade in certain dairy products, which entered into force May 14, 1970, and a general agreement that the arrangement regarding International Trade in Cotton Textiles, negotiated in 1962, should be extended for three more years from Sept. 30, 1970.

The tariff reductions negotiated during the Kennedy Round were originally scheduled for application by steps between 1968 and 1972. In many cases, however, the concessions were applied ahead of schedule and in some cases (Argentina, Canada, Iceland, Ireland, and Switzerland) had been fully applied by 1970.

(GA. PA.; CO. S.)

See also Agriculture; Commodities, Primary; Development, Economic; Payments and Reserves, International; Trade, International.

Commodities, Primary

Less developed countries, relying on agricultural products for exports, found it difficult in 1970 to increase trade with industrial nations. Until they made more progress in attracting new industries, it appeared that the less developed nations would take a relatively small share of exports from North America, Europe, and Japan. For the most part, the less developed countries were largely shippers of agricultural products, the demand for which in the 1960s rose more slowly than did demand for industrial products. This trend was expected to continue. As prosperity increases, the additional purchasing power created does not result in much additional consumption of coffee, tea, cocoa, spices, and similar products.

Also, many of the commodities grown in the less developed countries were faced with increased competition from man-made products. This was particularly true of rubber and the natural fibres, such as cotton and wool. The market for cotton produced in less de-

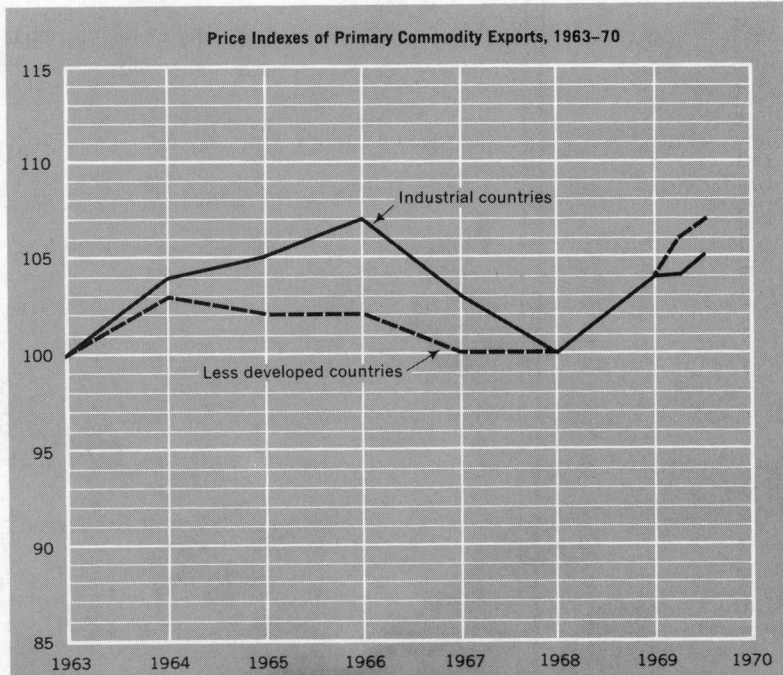

Price Indexes of Primary Commodity Exports, 1963–70

Industrial countries

Less developed countries

Note: Industrial countries: North America, Western Europe, Australia, New Zealand, Japan, South Africa. Less developed countries: Latin America, rest of Africa, rest of Asia, rest of Oceania.

Source: United Nations, *Monthly Bulletin of Statistics.*

**Table 1. Indexes of World Production* of
Agricultural, Fishery, and Forestry Products**

1952–56 average=100

Item	1959	1963	1967	1968	1969
Total production	116	128	142	147	147
Agriculture	116	128	143	147	148
Fisheries	116	138	170	176	173
Forestry	111	115	125	127	130
Population	110	119	129	132	134
Per capita production	105	107	110	111	109
Agriculture	106	108	111	112	110
Fisheries	105	116	132	134	128
Forestry	101	97	97	97	97

*Excluding China and other Asian centrally planned countries.
Source: Food and Agriculture Organization of the
United Nations, *The State of Food and Agriculture*
(1970).

**Table II. Indexes of World Production of
Certain Raw Materials**

1963 average=100

Raw material	1960	1964	1967	1968	1969
Coal*	94	103	105	105	108
Crude petroleum	81	108	135	147	158
Cement	83	110	129	138	144
Pig iron†	88	113	130	138	150
Crude steel	87	113	129	137	148
Copper (smelter)‡	93	105	102	117	127
Zinc‡§	88	108	119	133	145
Lead‡§	94	103	110	115	126
Tin‖	102	98	122	129	122
Aluminum‡§	85	113	146	156	174
Natural rubber	96	108	119	125	136

*Including coal equivalent of brown coal and
lignite.
†Including ferroalloys.
‡Excluding the U.S.S.R., East Germany, and North
Korea.
§Excluding Czechoslovakia and Romania.
‖Excluding the U.S.S.R. and Eastern Europe.
Source: United Nations, *Monthly Bulletin of Sta-
tistics* (November 1970).

veloped countries was almost wholly dependent upon
the protection afforded by U.S. cotton acreage restrictions. Lifting of those curbs would enable U.S. cotton
growers to meet all world needs at prices with which
other world cotton producers could not compete.

In addition, there were other agricultural products,
such as sugar, where special pricing arrangements and
trade barriers operated against the less developed
countries. In fact, some observers believed that sugar-
producing countries might be in a better position if the
world sugar market were completely free. While prices
would drop to very low levels, less developed countries
would be able to increase greatly the volume of their
sales.

One way in which less developed countries could
boost their agricultural exports would be by increasing
meat production. World demand for meat was growing
faster than production in the northern countries. Also,

Table III. Changes in International Prices of Selected Major Primary Commodities

Commodity, unit, country of origin, and market	Wholesale price in U.S. dollars				
	1962	1967	1968	1969	July 1970
Beef (100 lb.) U.K. (London)	29.19	32.74	35.42	37.04	40.50
Butter (100 lb.) New Zealand (London)	37.50	36.60	32.14	32.14	33.75
Cocoa (100 lb.) Ghana (N.Y.)	21.00	29.07	34.40	45.59	32.52
Coffee (100 lb.) Brazil (N.Y.)	34.30	37.93	37.48	40.27	54.60
Copper (100 lb.) U.K. (London)	29.23	51.10	56.09	66.54	61.81
Copra (100 lb.) Philippines (London)	7.28	9.28	10.42	9.23	9.35
Cotton (100 lb.) U.A.R. (Liverpool)	41.84	53.24	58.66	63.20	63.40
Hides (100 lb.) Argentina (London)	23.84	25.26	19.58	23.74	22.86
Jute (short tons) Pakistan (London)	279.00	310.00	291.00	315.00	302.00
Lead (100 lb.) U.K. (London)	7.00	10.28	10.91	13.14	13.62
Newsprint (short tons) Canada (Quebec)	116.70	122.40	124.00	128.20	131.40
Peanuts (100 lb.) Nigeria (London)	7.75	8.11	7.49	9.38	10.22
Petroleum (bbl.) Venezuela (La Cruz)	2.80	2.80	2.80	2.80	2.80*
Rice (100 lb.) Thailand (Bangkok)	6.93	9.34	9.14	8.30	6.31†
Rubber (100 lb.) Malaysia (Singapore)	25.56	17.70	17.33	22.81	17.39
Sugar (100 lb.) Caribbean (N.Y. for exp.)	2.98	2.06	1.98	3.45	3.86
Tea (100 lb.) Ceylon-India (N.Y.)	51.70	45.93	46.00	42.60	45.80
Tin (100 lb.) Malaysia (Penang)	109.70	147.00	138.60	153.40	155.20
Tobacco (100 lb.) U.S. (U.S.)	62.20	65.00	66.50	69.33	70.59
Wheat (bu.) Canada (Ft. William)	1.82	1.90	1.82	1.76	1.68
Wool (100 lb.) Australia (Sydney)	51.10	51.00	51.80	49.60	41.50
Zinc (100 lb.) U.K. (London)	8.43	12.34	11.91	12.69	13.50

*April 1970.
†May 1970.
Source: International Monetary Fund, *International Financial Statistics*.

some less developed countries had great mineral
wealth, providing them with a future in which they
might become important markets for the products of
industrial nations. Nevertheless, neither agricultural
nor mineral exports were likely to provide enough additional employment to permit those countries to develop into important consumers. Therefore, it appeared that the less developed countries must
become industrialized before they would be able to absorb some of the surplus labour that was drifting to
the developed nations in search of employment. Policies that would encourage industries to open branch
plants in the less developed countries in order to arrest the flow of migrants in their direction were being
considered in some industrialized countries.

Trends in World Production. For the first time in
12 years, combined world production of agricultural,
fishery, and forest products in 1969 showed no increase, according to UN Food and Agriculture Organization (FAO) estimates (*see* Table I). This stability
compared with a 4% rise in 1968 and a 1958–68 average growth of nearly 3% per year. A 2% increase in
forestry production and a very slight upturn in agricultural output were offset by a 2% drop in fishery
production, which in preceding years had risen much
faster than the other two sectors.

The actual situation, however, might have been
better than was indicated by the statistics. For example, the small increase in agricultural output largely
reflected reduced production in the developed countries where surpluses, not shortages, were the problem. Although the 3% increase in agricultural production in the less developed countries was below that in
recent years, the fastest growth, as was true in 1967
and 1968, was in the Far East (excluding Japan and
China), the region where in the past the food problem
had been most serious and where governments and
farmers of many countries had worked hard to boost
agricultural output. The 4% increase in food production in the Far East, while below that in 1968, was
still higher than the longer-term trend. Even more
noteworthy was the 4% increase in food-importing
countries that were making determined efforts to increase their cereal output, such as Ceylon, Indonesia,
South Korea, Malaysia, and Pakistan.

In the other less developed regions, agricultural
production results were less favourable. Recovery of
output in Latin America, which in large areas had
been plagued by a drought since late 1967, was only
about 2%, though there was a wide variation among
countries. Output in the less developed countries of
the Middle East also increased about 2%, somewhat
less than the longer-term rate of growth. But in view
of the instability of agricultural production in that region, too much importance should not be attached to
data for a single year. However, countries in the Middle East experienced some difficulty in spreading the
use of high-yielding cereal varieties. In Africa, overall food production showed little or no change, owing
to the impact of adverse weather on the cereal and
olive crops of Morocco, Algeria, and Tunisia.

On a per capita basis, food production declined in
each of the less developed regions except the Far East.
Even in that region successive increases in output
since the poor crops of 1965 and 1966 only brought
food production per capita back to the level of the
early 1960s. Despite the decline in per capita output,
food intake per person in the less developed countries
did not necessarily fall, as shortages might have been
made up from imports and stocks. Nevertheless, the

data on production clearly indicated the stubbornness of the food problem faced by the less developed countries and the importance of efforts to overcome it.

Looking at the developed regions, total agricultural production in 1969 fell by between 1 and 3%, except in Western Europe where it remained at the 1968 level. This was in strong contrast with the rising longer-term trend in those regions at rates ranging between 1.9 and 3.6% per year, and the 3% increase for developed countries achieved in 1968. An exception to the trend in the developed countries was the 5% rise in South Africa. Reductions of agricultural output in the developed countries in 1969 were partly deliberate, following the renewed and more wide-spread accumulation of surplus food stocks that had started a few years earlier.

Among other primary commodities—excluding agricultural, fishery, and forest products—crude petroleum, pig iron, crude steel, and cement were still involved in 1969 with problems of surpluses and excess capacity, reflecting sizable increases in the output of those items (*see* Table II). Similarly, except for tin, sizable increases occurred in the production of non-ferrous metals. The output of natural rubber also moved up markedly as a result of increased world needs, only a small part of which were met from government stockpiles. However, synthetic rubber with its somewhat lower price continued to meet the bulk of the world's new rubber requirements; it accounted for more than 75% of the total new rubber consumption in the U.S. But with rising wage rates in developed countries adding to costs of producing synthetic rubber, the competitive position of natural rubber improved.

Prices and Terms of Trade. Trends in primary commodity prices during recent years are shown in Table III. Although there was considerable variation among the various products, rises exceeded declines in 1969. The prices of beef, cocoa, coffee, copper, hides, lead, peanuts, rubber, sugar, tin, tobacco, and zinc showed the largest advances. Declines were particularly noticeable for copra, tea, wheat, and wool. In 1970, prices of cocoa, copper, lead, hides, and wool weakened markedly, as did coffee late in the year. These declines reflected increasing production (larger International Coffee Agreement quotas for coffee), as well as economic recessions in some of the major developed countries.

The value of world exports of agricultural, fishery, and forest products combined increased by about 5% in 1969. As in 1968, a sizable share of the increase (the largest since 1964) was due to the continued rapid growth in forest exports. Although the expansion in agricultural and fishery products was smaller, a number of individual commodities showed large rises in value, particularly meat, cocoa, and natural rubber. As the accompanying chart shows, prices of commodity exports by less developed countries in 1969 were on a par with prices of exports from developed countries. In early 1970, the advantage shifted to the less developed countries, reflecting in part considerably higher prices for copper, coffee, cattle, and oilseeds.

Overall, the 4% increase in the value of exports of agricultural products in 1969 was also largely a reflection of higher prices, since the total volume of trade was unchanged. Although this increase was noteworthy in view of the near stagnancy in the overall value of agricultural trade in recent years, it was well below the growth in world trade in all commodities which in 1969 rose by 14%.

Looking at the principal agricultural commodities, the value of world exports in 1969 was estimated at $24.4 billion, 4% above 1968. Although the 1969 level was only 1% above the earlier peak figure of 1966, the rate of increase in 1969 compared favourably with the average increase of 3% per year during the period 1961–63 to 1968, the 5% drop in 1967, and the unchanged situation in 1968.

The increased value of agricultural trade in 1969 resulted more from higher prices than from the volume of trade, which was about the same as in 1968. The only products for which there was a significant increase in volume were rubber and meat, up 22 and 4%, respectively. The upturn in prices of agricultural export products in 1969 was a reversal of the trend of the previous four years. The largest price increases were recorded for sugar, meat, cocoa, wool, and rubber.

Where export commodity prices fell, it was generally because of ample supplies rather than declining demand. Possible exceptions were wheat and rice, where lower prices were caused by reduced import demand as well as by a rise in exportable supplies. The pressure of wheat supplies was so great that the International Grains Arrangement could not keep prices from falling below specified floors until late 1969. Falling prices of rice reflected a similar situation, and exports were increasingly aided by subsidies.

World trade in fishery products in 1969 featured a substantial rise in export prices, caused by both shortages in supply and improved demand. Fishery exports rose by nearly 10% in value despite a somewhat lower volume of shipments.

Showing an 11% increase in export value, world trade in forest products in 1969 continued its dynamic growth. Although still relatively less important for less developed regions, recent growth was particularly rapid. In 1969, export earnings of the less developed countries of the Far East from this source rose 13% and those of the less developed African countries by 15%. Forest products accounted for 21 and 11%, respectively, of the combined value of agricultural, fishery, and forest products from those two regions.

Prices for forest products entering trade in 1969 were mostly firm, especially for chemical pulp. North American prices for sawn softwood, after rising to unprecedented high levels in early 1969, fell sharply thereafter.

Commodity Policies. *National Policies.* In November 1970, Canada announced a new policy applicable to producing, marketing, and exporting wheat and other major grains and oilseeds. The new program emphasized increased aggressiveness in finding and keeping overseas grain markets, and also stressed improving the efficiency of grain production, storage, and selling within Canada. Under the program in effect during 1970, grain production was held down, and farmers were rewarded for taking land out of wheat or out of production entirely. The new program would reward farmers for selling grains during good export years by a scheme of income compensation effective when foreign sales were slow.

The U.S. Senate on Nov. 19, 1970, passed the Agricultural Act of 1970, signed by Pres. Richard Nixon a few days later. This new law provided price support programs for key farm commodities for three years following Dec. 31, 1970, when the 1965 Food and Agriculture Act expired. It called for a new market-oriented policy under which U.S. farmers would put more stress on seeking new markets and

COURTESY, "FOREIGN AGRICULTURE"

Danish bacon awaits shipment to foreign markets. A worldwide pork shortage continued during 1970, and Denmark, the world's leading exporter, was forced to turn down many attractive offers for its pork products.

supplying customers at competitive prices. Emphasis would be placed on such crops as feed grains, food grains, and soybeans, products in which U.S. farmers had a comparative production advantage. Under a provision in the new law, a farmer would set aside his share of the national land diversion requirement and then be free to plant whatever he liked on his remaining acres (except rice, peanuts, sugar, tobacco, or extra-long-staple cotton, which were covered by separate legislation).

The Agricultural Act of 1970 also allowed competitive pricing for U.S. products in world markets. For wheat, the minimum price support loan rate was to be $1.25 per bushel, and for corn the minimum would be $1 per bushel, with other feed grains pegged accordingly on their feeding value. Cotton price support loans were to be 90% of the average world price for the two preceding years, and the U.S. secretary of agriculture could adjust support loan prices following periods of exceptionally high prices to keep U.S. cotton competitive.

For the first time in 40 years, the government of India in 1970 established a National Commission on Agriculture to make a comprehensive assessment of the progress being made by Indian agriculture and to determine ways to improve this segment of the economy. Specifically, the new group was to examine and report on the present condition of agriculture and the rural economy and make recommendations for the improvement of agriculture and the promotion of the welfare and prosperity of the people.

Australia, in an attempt to revive its wool industry (which produced 20% of that country's total export earnings and accounted for 45% of the world's total raw wool exports), established a Wool Commission in late 1970. This commission started a flexible reserve price system to counteract falling wool prices, thereby bringing to an end the Australian "free auction system" for wool, referred to as a model of wool marketing in years past. In recent years, however, the auction system had been under attack from Australian wool growers, not only because of the drop in wool prices to a 22-year low but also because of rising costs. Under the new system, a bidder from the commission either forced up the price to a predetermined minimum during a wool auction or else bought wool with the intention of selling it later when supplies were smaller.

Pres. Salvador Allende Gossens of Chile created a special government-labour commission to carry out the complete nationalization of the copper industry in that country. Prime targets were the three U.S. mining companies: Anaconda Co. and Kennecott Cop-

per Corp., whose properties were already partially nationalized, and the Cerro Corp. According to President Allende, "we shall nationalize the major copper interest in accordance with Chilean law, with compensation, but we will not pay exorbitant indemnizations to anyone."

International Policies. The International Coffee Organization (ICO), meeting in London, on Aug. 31, 1970, set International Coffee Agreement (ICA) initial overall export quotas for the 1970–71 coffee year (October–September) at 54 million bags (1 bag = 132.3 lb.). Owing to the concern of ICA importing members that sharp increases in prices might occur, the ICO also set up a special reserve of 4 million bags, in two lots of 2 million bags each, to be distributed pro rata to all ICA exporting members should the composite price of the four main types of green coffee remain at or above 52 cents per pound for a specified period of time. Likewise, in the event of sharp declines in coffee prices, overall quotas could be reduced by as much as three million bags pro rata, again in two lots.

On Oct. 22, 1970, initial 1970–71 overall export quotas of 54 million bags were boosted to 56 million because the composite price had remained above the 52-cent trigger point for the required 15 marketing days. Also, an additional 328,000 bags were distributed to Robusta producers and 542,000 bags to producers of unwashed Arabicas (mainly Brazil), the prices of these two types having surpassed their respective ceilings for the required period. Thus, at the end of October 1970 the effective ICA overall quotas had risen to 56,870,000 bags, well above the 1969–70 final quotas of 51,760,700 bags and considered more than enough to supply the requirements of the importing countries.

As available supplies increased, green coffee prices weakened. On Dec. 17, 1970, the ICO ordered a cut of 2 million bags to 54,870,000 bags in the ICA export quotas, following a 15-day period in which the composite price averaged 48.85 cents, or 1.15 cents below the point at which the ICO imposes quota reductions.

The International Sugar Organization (ISO) on Nov. 18, 1970, set 1971 initial export quotas under the International Sugar Agreement (ISA) at 95% of basic export tonnages, or about 7,850,000 metric tons (including 1,150,000 for the U.S.S.R.). The ISO stated that 1970 ISA quotas would not be boosted above their current level of 90% even if prices warranted such action under the ISA. Therefore, the ISO suspended art. 48 (2) (b) of the ISA, which had called for 100% quotas if the prevailing world sugar price exceeded 4 cents per pound. During most of the last quarter of 1970, the world price was above 4 cents per pound. This price strength partly reflected 1970 ISA shortages of 853,300 metric tons, of which only 445,000 tons were reallocated. Because prices continued to hold above 4 cents per pound, the ISO on Dec. 30, 1970, announced that the normal procedures of the ISA should be followed and that export quotas would thus have to be 100% of basic export tonnages at the start of 1971.

The International Wheat Council, in reporting on the world wheat situation in early November 1970, stated that there had been a marked rise in world wheat prices at the beginning of 1970–71. This price improvement resulted from a better balance between supply and demand brought about by a number of factors. These included measures taken by several major exporting countries (particularly Canada and the

U.S.) to cut down production, an increase in world trade, and reduced corn production, particularly in the U.S.

The four member nations of the Intergovernmental Council of Copper Exporting Countries (CIPEC) reportedly agreed in December 1970 to cut copper production to maintain world prices for the metal. The four—Chile, Zambia, the Congo (Kinshasa), and Peru —were quite dependent on foreign exchange earned by selling copper in world markets. They produced about 40 to 45% of the non-Communist world's primary copper and accounted for about 80% of its exports. From a high of more than 80 cents a pound in April 1970, the CIPEC countries saw their selling prices for copper decline to about 47 cents at the year's end. (N. R. U.)

See also Agriculture; Commercial Policies; Development, Economic; Food; Payments and Reserves, International; Trade, International.

Commonwealth of Nations

In 1970 the number of full members of the Commonwealth rose from 28 to 31 with the accession of three Pacific countries—Tonga on June 4, Western Samoa (the first independent non-Commonwealth state to join) on August 28, and Fiji on October 10. Members at the end of the year included: United Kingdom, Australia, Barbados, Botswana, Canada, Ceylon, Cyprus, Fiji, The Gambia, Ghana, Guyana, India, Jamaica, Kenya, Lesotho, Malawi, Malaysia, Malta, Mauritius, New Zealand, Nigeria, Pakistan, Sierra Leone, Singapore, Swaziland, Tanzania, Tonga, Trinidad and Tobago, Uganda, Western Samoa, and Zambia.

British plans for resuming arms sales to South Africa aroused unusually bitter opposition from several African leaders who threatened either to leave the Commonwealth or to call for Britain's expulsion at the Commonwealth Prime Ministers' Conference in Singapore on Jan. 14–22, 1971. The choice of Singapore reflected an earlier preoccupation with an area where Britain (as reaffirmed at a SEATO meeting in July) stood committed to partnership with Australia, New Zealand, Singapore, and Malaysia in a five-power Commonwealth defense force. For the Conservative government elected on June 18, this policy interlocked with that of safeguarding the Cape of Good Hope route to the Far East (by honouring the Simonstown naval agreement) at a time when Soviet naval strength in the Indian Ocean and the growth of ideological divisions in Africa together posed a political challenge to Western interests. For Britain's African critics, however, the real threat to the Commonwealth was not political ideology but racialism—a point made very plainly in verbal exchanges over arms sales during the UN's 25th anniversary session in October. Pres. Kenneth Kaunda (*see* BIOGRAPHY) of Zambia had earlier expressed African feelings when he said he found Britain's military arguments about arming South Africa "ridiculous to say the least."

Africa. The ending in mid-January of Nigeria's civil war prefaced a continuing period of rehabilitation in this most populous of African states. In the same area Ghana's civilian government, grappling with the formidable legacy of the country's earlier departure from democratic rule, found that measures to expel aliens and limit foreign enterprise failed to solve its persistent financial problems, while The Gambia—

which on April 24 became a republic within the Commonwealth—faced up to the reality of Senegal's retreat from moves toward their political union.

In 1970, however, it became clearer than ever that the continent's ideological fulcrum was on the fringe of the white-dominated southern bloc: South Africa, Portuguese Africa, and Rhodesia (which declared itself a republic on March 2). A Chinese interest-free loan to Tanzania and Zambia of about $406 million for building the Tanzam railway was announced in July, and this project, scheduled for completion in 1975, was formally inaugurated by Kaunda on October 26. China was also helping Tanzania to build a naval base at Dar es Salaam and in October was reportedly expected to supply MiG fighters for a new Tanzanian Air Force.

Kenya and Uganda, committed to "africanization," continued to expel Asians (a process that had badly strained Britain's capacity to absorb immigrants) and to nationalize foreign-owned enterprises. Kenya embarked in July on a "tripartite" system to raise by 10% the proportion of Africans in employment and obtained an International Development Association loan of $6.1 million to improve farming skills; at the same time, £25 million ($60 million) of British aid (of which £13.5 million represented the cancellation of previous debts) included £3 million for buying out British-owned farms. In Uganda about half the Asian population was deprived of citizenship; the state also acquired a 60% share in private business concerns "to be paid for out of future profits" and simultaneously abolished the right to strike.

On June 15 the UN sanctions committee reported that Rhodesia's total 1969 exports, valued at $336 million, were still 30% below the 1965 (pre-rebellion) level but 42% higher than in 1968; the committee also noted that European immigration remained substantial and that cases of suspected sanctions-breaking had increased. On September 2 a Commonwealth committee recommended that the sanctions be continued. Malawi's close partnership with the southern bloc was demonstrated in May by South African Prime Minister B. J. Vorster's visit to Pres. H. K. Banda (his first to a black African state) and by the opening of a rail link to the Mozambique coast for potential exports of Malawi's hitherto untapped bauxite reserves.

Other Countries. From Indian elections in March, Indira Gandhi's government emerged with a greatly reduced majority, suggesting a political trend to the right. In May, however, Ceylon's pro-Western government was routed at the polls by a left-wing coalition led by Mme Sirimavo Bandaranaike (*see* BIOGRAPHY), pledged to secession from the Commonwealth and closer ties with Communist countries. Malaysia (under its new prime minister, Tun Abdul Razak; *see* BIOGRAPHY) remained free from racial outbreaks. In Pakistan a general election due to be held in October was postponed until December 7 because of heavy floods; that disaster paled into insignificance, however, beside the cyclone and tidal wave that struck the coastal and island areas of East Pakistan in November, killing hundreds of thousands. Australia and New Zealand took a more serious interest in their aboriginal and Polynesian minorities and, while strengthening their regional links, remained anxious about the economic impact of Britain's potential membership in the European Economic Community.

Canadian Prime Minister Pierre Trudeau also visited Commonwealth countries in the Pacific, but Canada's strongest economic links (reinforced by its aid

Common Market: *see* Commercial Policies; European Unity; *see also* Index *for information on specific common markets*

BEN ROTH AGENCY
"White man's burden"
—Abu, "Indian Express,"
New Delhi.

program) continued to be with the Caribbean area, where an April revolt by Black Power extremists in Trinidad suggested a new danger to political stability. On February 23 Guyana became the first Commonwealth country in the Caribbean area to assume republican status—as a "cooperative republic."

Economic Affairs. Financial and technical aid continued to play a major part in the framework of Commonwealth cooperation. In September an official forecast of British aid to the third world countries (predominantly to Commonwealth members) put this at £224 million for 1970, rising to £229 million in the financial year 1970–71.

On September 17–18 Commonwealth finance ministers met in Cyprus and reviewed the aid pattern; they agreed that the trend toward state control of industry and commerce in recipient countries made it desirable to draw up a code for the foreign investor.   (M. Mr.)

See also articles on the various political units.

Communist Movement

The year 1970 marked, on the whole, a period of stabilization within the Communist movement, which in the two preceding years had been badly shaken by the Soviet invasion of Czechoslovakia (Aug. 20, 1968) and by the Soviet clash with China at several places along the Sino-Soviet frontier (1969). Both situations were on the road to "normalization" in 1970. At the same time, there was a consolidation of the domestic situation in China with the apparent termination of the Cultural Revolution.

The scars of the Czechoslovakian invasion and the Sino-Soviet dispute were not yet healed in 1970, but the relative stabilization allowed the Communist powers, especially the U.S.S.R., to play a more active role in world politics. The closer ties sought by France and West Germany with the Soviet Union strengthened the latter's position in Europe. As far as China was concerned, recognition of the Mao Tse-tung regime by Canada in mid-October 1970 and by Italy in November was a strong indication of China's return to the community of nations.

April 22, 1970, was the centenary of the birth of Lenin, the only 20th-century socialist leader recognized by all Communist parties as the true heir of Marx. On April 21 and 22, in the presence of most Communist leaders from both East and West, Leonid I. Brezhnev, the general secretary of the Soviet party, paid a glowing tribute to Lenin's "gigantic figure" and called for Communist unity and for improvement

Communications:
see
Telecommunications;
Television and Radio

of the Soviet economy. He attacked Western civilization as "a society without ideals," and at the same time opposed the trend toward a more positive interpretation of Stalinism. Some observers had predicted that Brezhnev would establish himself as the one leader of the U.S.S.R., but on July 15 the Supreme Soviet reelected Premier Aleksei N. Kosygin and Pres. Nikolai V. Podgorny, thus keeping intact the collective leadership established in October 1964.

The Quest for Independent Foreign Policies. The pattern of cooperation without monolithic control, established by the Communist and workers' parties that met in Moscow in June 1969, continued to be valid during 1970. Albania and Yugoslavia had not participated in the conference and remained outside the Warsaw Pact, Albania as the self-proclaimed defender of Communist "orthodoxy." Following the example of China, however, Albania abandoned its policy of isolation. Despite the fact that for years Albania had bitterly attacked "revisionism," especially in Yugoslavia, which in many ways had been the leader of "revisionism" in the Communist camp, there was in 1970 a rapprochement between the two countries. Albania also sought cultural exchanges with the U.A.R. and Turkey and tried to improve its relations with Greece.

A similar policy of seeking improved relations was followed by Yugoslavia. It adhered to its position as a neutralist nation outside all the power blocs, eager for good relations everywhere. Yugoslavia took the leading role in the conference of nonaligned nations that met in early September 1970 in Lusaka, Zambia. As its leading elder statesman, President Tito demanded the withdrawal of all foreign forces from Indochina and the end of Israeli occupation of Arab territories conquered in the Six-Day War of 1967. He welcomed the attendance of the provisional revolutionary government of South Vietnam. But Tito was also eager to meet U.S. Pres. Richard Nixon during his European tour in September–October, although their discussion apparently changed Tito's policy as little as Nixon's 1969 visit to Romania had influenced the fundamental policy of that country.

Romania maintained its membership in the Warsaw Pact, but within the framework of that alliance it followed its own independent foreign policy. It participated only halfheartedly in the military cooperation of the Warsaw Pact states. In October 1970 seven member countries held military maneuvers in East Germany, but whereas about 100,000 men from the Soviet Union and its Eastern European allies took part, Romania sent only a 300-man staff contingent. Similarly, although Romania participated in the Council for Mutual Economic Assistance (Comecon), it did not join the other member states in establishing an international investment bank in Moscow.

On the occasion of the 25th UN General Assembly in October, Pres. Nicolae Ceausescu was the only head of a Communist nation present. The Romanians recognized Prince Norodom Sihanouk's Cambodian government-in-exile in Peking (which Moscow did not), and in June it sent a delegation led by Emil Bodnaras to China, where it was received with considerable fanfare. Bodnaras declared that the establishment of the Communist regime in China was not only a turning point in the history of the 20th century, but represented a shift in the world balance of power second only to the Russian Revolution. Notably, this visit to Peking took place within a policy framework that also included visits by Ceausescu to Moscow, Paris, and Washington and by Premier Ion Gheorghe Maurer to Bonn. Yet with all Romania's insistence on sovereignty, it "normalized" its relationship with the Soviet Union in 1970. In May the U.S.S.R. agreed to supply Romania with a nuclear reactor for peaceful uses, and on July 7 a 20-year pact of friendship and cooperation between the two countries was signed in Bucharest.

The Soviet Position in Europe. In 1970 the West German government, under Chancellor Willy Brandt, a Social Democrat, and Foreign Minister Walter Scheel, a liberal, took the initiative in relaxing tensions in Europe. Recognizing that an improvement in its relations with Moscow was the precondition for entering into friendly relations with Poland and Czechoslovakia, West Germany's immediate neighbours, the West German government declared its willingness to regard the existing post-1945 frontiers in Eastern Europe as inviolable. The West Germans expected, in return, Soviet and East German recognition of the freedom of and security of access to West Berlin, 110 mi. behind the East German border.

The Moscow talks, which began on July 27, ended in a treaty initialed on August 7 by the foreign ministers of the Soviet Union and West Germany, although final ratification depended on the outcome of talks among the U.S., the U.S.S.R., Britain, and France on the future of Berlin. In a statement made after his return from Moscow, Scheel declared that West Germany had acted "in careful consultation with, and support from, our Western Allies. This treaty is designed to "provide a constructive beginning for cooperation" between West Germany and the U.S.S.R. A similar pact between West Germany and Poland was initialed by the Polish and West German foreign ministers in Warsaw on November 18.

West Germany was not alone in seeking a rapprochement between Eastern and Western Europe. In October 1970 French Pres. Georges Pompidou visited the Soviet Union for a week and was received with the greatest honours. Many observers saw an element of competition at work and wondered whether a European détente would be based on the cooperation of the Soviet Union with West Germany or with France. Officially, however, both Brandt and Pompidou emphasized their readiness to cooperate fully in the interests of universal peace.

If Soviet relations with Yugoslavia and Romania remained difficult in 1970, the relationship of the Soviet Union with the other members of the Warsaw Pact was much more "normal" from the Soviet point of view. On May 6 Brezhnev and Kosygin visited Prague and, together with the first secretary of the Czechoslovak Communist Party, Gustav Husak, and Czechoslovak Premier Lubomir Strougal, signed a treaty of friendship and cooperation. Its preamble followed the so-called Brezhnev doctrine by declaring that the "support, the strengthening and the protection of socialist acquisitions, which were achieved through heroic efforts and sacrifice-filled toil by the people of the two countries, are the joint international duty of the socialist countries," thus providing an after-the-fact justification for the Soviet military presence in Czechoslovakia, since official Soviet theory regarded the events of 1968 as a threat to socialism. Art. 2 of the treaty confirmed the will of both nations to contribute to the further development of economic integration among the members of Comecon.

In Czechoslovakia, Husak steered a middle of the road course. Most of the Communists involved in the "liberal" movement of 1968, including former party chief Alexander Dubcek, were expelled from the party or went into exile. On the other hand, there was no judicial persecution, as some liberals had feared. In August 1970 hardly any demonstrations were held on the second anniversary of the Soviet occupation and, to judge from appearances, the Czechs and Slovaks had, though with many misgivings, accepted the situation. But in Poland there was bitter protest against the policies of Wladyslaw Gomulka, which toppled him from power.

By and large, the people of the Eastern European countries were preoccupied with their own economic problems and gave little evidence of striving for greater participation in public affairs. The Soviet Union could count on the full cooperation of East Germany, Poland, Hungary, Czechoslovakia, and Bulgaria. On the other hand, while remaining safely under the Soviet umbrella, these countries could and did display nationalistic tendencies. These local nationalisms, and the trend toward building up cultural and economic ties with countries outside Eastern Europe, gained strength during the year and would probably gain even more if Soviet relations with West Germany and France continued to improve.

Communist Movements in Asia. In China the year was mostly devoted to domestic consolidation. The control of the party over the Red Guards was restored. The anarchistic tendencies of the Red Guards were to be directed into more constructive channels by bringing back the Communist Youth League, with emphasis on building up the new "socialist" countryside. Army representatives began to occupy leading positions in the revolutionary committees, which had dominated the scene from 1967 to 1969, and the trend seemed to be toward restoring the administrative apparatus that was largely destroyed in the Cultural Revolution. On September 9 China announced its intention of convening the National People's Congress, which had not met in full session since the third congress was held in December 1964–January 1965. It was expected to appoint a successor to the deposed head of state, Liu Shao-ch'i.

With domestic pacification, the government tried to resume its foreign policy. The foreign office took up its "normal" activity, and a number of ambassadors and military attachés returned to their posts abroad. In September the Soviet government named a new ambassador to China, the first since April 1967, when Sergei G. Lapin had been recalled as a result of violent anti-Soviet demonstrations. The new appointee was Vasily S. Tolstikov, secretary of the Communist

Leonid Brezhnev (left), general secretary of the Communist Party in the U.S.S.R., officiates at ceremony honouring Kharkov tractor factory in April 1970.

TASS FROM SOVFOTO

BEN ROTH AGENCY
—Ranan Lurie.

Party in Leningrad and a member of the party Central Committee and of the Presidium of the Supreme Soviet. At the same time China sent a deputy foreign minister, Liu Hsin-chuan, as ambassador to Moscow. Brezhnev's speeches during his tour of the Soviet Central Asian republics in September were characterized by restraint as regards China. On the state level, at least, Chinese relations with the Soviet Union appeared less tense.

Cabinet-level delegations from Tanzania, Zambia, Sudan, and the Congo (Brazzaville) visited Peking. Premier Chou En-lai, who was also acting foreign minister, sent greetings to Poland's Premier Josef Cyrankiewicz on the occasion of Poland's National Day, celebrating that country's liberation from German rule. In receiving André Bettencourt, the French minister of planning and land development, Chou expressed the hope for "enhancing the mutual understanding and friendly relations" between the two countries. "China," he said, "has always stood for the establishment and development of relations between countries of different social systems on the basis of . . . peaceful coexistence." While Premier Pompidou was visiting Moscow in early October, a former French premier, the Gaullist Maurice Couve de Murville, spent two weeks as a private visitor in China. Even relations between China and Yugoslavia—the target of bitter ideological attacks for years—began to improve. China sent a new ambassador to Poland, where, prior to 1968, irregular talks had been held between the Chinese and U.S. ambassadors. Those talks were resumed early in the year, but were broken off by China after the U.S. invasion of Cambodia.

North Korea and North Vietnam continued their efforts to maintain a neutralist attitude in the competition between the U.S.S.R. and China for influence on Asian Communist governments. On July 1 the North Vietnamese attended the 11th congress of the Japanese Communist Party, which had long been in disagreement with Maoism, and the Lenin centenary celebrations in Moscow were attended by Choi Yong Kun, North Korea's head of state, and Le Duan, first secretary of the North Vietnamese party. China, on the other hand, became the protector of Prince Sihanouk's Cambodian government-in-exile and of the efforts toward cooperation among the Communist forces of Vietnam, Laos, and Cambodia.

In two officially nonaligned Asian countries, the ruling party entered into a coalition with the pro-Moscow (and more conservative) branch of the local Communist Party. Indian Prime Minister Indira Gandhi won the September election in Kerala state in a coalition with the Communist Party. Similarly, the Sri Lanka Freedom Party, under Mme Sirimavo Bandaranaike, won the May election in Ceylon with Communist help, and the Communists entered the governmental coalition. As a result, Ceylon broke diplomatic relations with Israel and granted full recognition to East Germany, North Korea, North Vietnam, and the Viet Cong provisional government.

Communism in Latin America. In Cuba, Fidel Castro used his televised speech of July 26, 1970 (commemorating the start of the Cuban revolution), to explain the country's difficult economic situation—due, as he himself recognized, to the economic and administrative shortcomings of his highly personal regime. His relationship to Moscow improved, though it was hardly intimate. One sore spot in Soviet-Cuban relations had long been Castro's insistence on supporting revolutionary guerrilla movements within Latin-American countries where Moscow was attempting to establish friendly relations with the regimes in power. Marxist or leftist-nationalist regimes appeared elsewhere in Latin America, but, although the circumstances differed in each case, none of them seemed to have arisen as the result of direct influence by Moscow, Peking, or Havana.

In Peru the reigning military junta, which had come to power in October 1968, was distinguished from the older type of Latin-American military regime by its competent concern with the economy and education. It started its reign by nationalizing a U.S.-owned oil field and refinery and by seizing and distributing large landholdings among the poor peasants. The government owed its mass support to its extreme nationalism, which had led to a deterioration of its relations with the U.S. and to the establishment of diplomatic and economic ties with Soviet bloc countries.

Similar nationalist regimes, opposed above all to U.S. "imperialism," arose in 1970 in two quite different countries, backward and poor Bolivia and relatively advanced and democratic Chile. In Chile, headed since 1964 by the Christian Democratic Party under Eduardo Frei Montalva, the presidential elections of Sept. 4, 1970, resulted in a plurality for Salvador Allende, a Marxist. His election was confirmed by the National Congress in October. In Chile students and intellectuals had been the chief movers in the direction of socialism, but in Bolivia this task was assumed by a leftist air force general, Juan José Torres, who took power on October 7 after overthrowing a rightist military government. He promised Bolivia a "popular nationalist government" resting on four pillars, the peasant farmers, the workers, the students, and the armed forces. These developments strengthened feelings among several Latin-American states—Chile, Peru, Bolivia, Venezuela, and Ecuador—that the boycott imposed on Cuba by the Organization of American States should be ended.   (H. Ko.)

See also China; Czechoslovakia; Defense; Intelligence Operations; and articles on the various countries.

Encyclopædia Britannica Films. *Hungary and Communism: Eastern Europe in Change* (1964); *China: A Portrait of the Land* (1967); *China's Industrial Revolution* (1967); *China's Villages in Change* (1967).

Congo, Democratic Republic of the

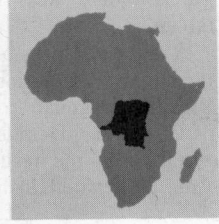

A country of equatorial Africa, the Congo is bounded by the Central African Republic, Sudan, Uganda, Rwanda, Burundi, Tanzania, Zambia, Angola, the Congo (Brazzaville), and the Atlantic Ocean. Area: 905,559 sq.mi. (2,345,409 sq.km.). Pop. (1969 est.): 16,586,000. Cap. and largest city: Kinshasa (metro. pop., 1969, 1,052,520). Language: French; Bantu dialects, mainly Swahili and Lingala. Religion: mainly fetishism. President in 1970, Joseph Mobutu.

The disappointing diplomatic exchanges between the Congo and its African neighbours during the previous 12 months took a turn for the better in 1970. There had been a foretaste of this change when President Mobutu met the presidents of Burundi and Rwanda in Rwanda on Dec. 19, 1969. The three leaders adopted a resolution confirming their "joint" determination to strengthen the "mutual understanding" among their countries and to achieve integration in the "economic, technical, and cultural spheres." Three

CONGO, DEMOCRATIC REPUBLIC OF THE
Education. (1966–67) Primary, pupils 2,193,200, teachers 56,718; secondary, pupils 85,093; vocational, pupils 28,951; teacher training, students 33,636; secondary, vocational, and teacher training, teachers 7,149; higher (including 3 universities; 1967–68), students 5,827, teaching staff 812.
Finance. Monetary unit: zaire, with an official exchange rate of 0.50 zaire to U.S. $1 (1.20 zaires = £1 sterling) and a free market rate (Sept. 14, 1970) of 0.62 zaire to U.S. $1 (1.48 zaires = £1 sterling). Gold, SDRs, and foreign exchange, central bank: (March 1970) U.S. $197 million; (March 1969) U.S. $134,-270,000. Budget (1970 est.) balanced at 215 million zaires. Money supply: (March 1970) 156,560,000 zaires; (March 1969) 149,510,000 zaires. Cost of living (Kinshasa; 1963 = 100): (Dec. 1969) 383; (Dec. 1968) 339.
Foreign Trade. (1968) Imports 160.4 million zaires; exports 287.3 million zaires. Import sources: Belgium-Luxembourg 24%; U.S. 17%; West Germany 10%; France 10%; Japan 7%; U.K. 7%; Italy 7%; Netherlands 6%. Export destinations: Belgium-Luxembourg 51%; Italy 11%; France 9%; U.S. 7%; West Germany 7%; U.K. 7%. Main exports (1967): copper 59%; coffee 6%; diamonds 5%; palm oil 5%; tin 5%.
Transport and Communications. Roads (1968) 141,298 km. Motor vehicles in use: passenger (1968) c. 46,100; commercial (including buses; 1967) 23,200. Railways (1968): 5,164 km.; traffic 619 million passenger-km., freight 1,959,000,000 net ton-km. Air traffic (1968): 330,881,000 passenger-km.; freight 10,-727,000 net ton-km. Shipping (1969): merchant vessels 100 gross tons and over 6; gross tonnage 28,817. Inland waterways (including Congo River; 1968) c. 13,500 km. Telephones (Dec. 1968) c. 23,919. Radio receivers (Dec. 1968) c. 60,000. Television receivers (Dec. 1968) c. 7,000.
Agriculture. Production (in 000; metric tons; 1968; 1967 in parentheses): rice 187 (166); corn c. 250 (297); sweet potatoes and yams (1967) c. 310, (1966) c. 306; cassava (1967) c. 8,000, (1966) 8,116; palm oil (1967) c. 178, (1966) c. 168; palm kernels (1967) c. 107, (1966) c. 102; rubber (exports; 1969) c. 36, (1968) 40; cotton, lint 12 (8); coffee (1969) c. 66, (1968) c. 60; peanuts c. 115 (c. 113); sugar, raw value (1969–70) c. 44, (1968–69) c. 42; timber (cu.m.; 1967) c. 11,450, (1966) c. 11,500. Livestock (in 000; Dec. 1968): cattle c. 740; sheep 564; goats (Dec. 1966) 1,325; pigs c. 440.
Industry. Production (in 000; metric tons; 1968): coal 71; copper 167; zinc 63; tin 1.9; cobalt ore (metal content) 10; manganese ore (metal content) 187; gold (troy oz.) 170; diamonds (metric carats; 1967) 13,153; electricity (kw-hr.) 2,756,000.

weeks later, the celebration of the tenth anniversary of the independence of Cameroon on January 10 provided an opportunity for Mobutu to meet the presidents of Chad and the Central African Republic and for the three to give public expression to a reconciliation of their nations, which had been estranged since December 1968. This was followed with an announcement by the foreign minister of the Central African Republic that diplomatic relations with the Congo would be resumed on January 24.

In spite of indications in April of heightened tension between the Congo and its western neighbour, the People's Republic of the Congo, Mobutu's campaign of reconciliation took a step forward in this quarter also when he met Pres. Marien Ngouabi on board ship in the Congo River on June 16 to sign an agreement restoring relations, broken off in October 1968, between the two countries. The agreement specified the resumption of diplomatic relations, the renewal of telephonic and telegraphic communications, and the reopening of river traffic between Kinshasa and Brazzaville.

Outside Africa a similar atmosphere of goodwill prevailed. In November 1969 Mobutu visited Belgium, together with his foreign minister, Cyrille Adoula. The president took the opportunity to emphasize his desire for Belgian participation in the economic revival of the Congo and to give assurances regarding the security of foreign investment.

In August 1970 Mobutu visited the U.S., where he again maintained that the nationalization of foreign assets in the Congo formed no part of his policy. When asked how the fate of the Belgian mining company, Union Minière, nationalized in 1966, could be reconciled with this statement, he claimed that the company had refused to obey the laws of the country but had subsequently admitted the justice of the charges laid against it and was now preparing to resume mining activities.

The way had been prepared for this new move in September 1969 when, after mediation by the president of the World Bank, the government of the Congo had proposed terms of compensation for the Union Minière, and these had been accepted by the company. This turn of affairs was a blow to the Lonrho company, which had hoped to take over some of the former commitments of the Union Minière and to build the Katanga–West Coast railway.

National elections took place late in the year. In October Mobutu was reelected without opposition to a new seven-year term as president. Only 158 votes were cast against him. A new legislature was elected in November, the candidates all running unopposed as members of the ruling Popular Movement of the Revolution. Early in December Mobutu announced a major reshuffle of his Cabinet, involving the dismissal of eight ministers.

In August the U.S. firm Goodyear Tire and Rubber Co. announced that it planned to build the first tire plant in the Congo. To be constructed in Kinshasa, the plant was expected to produce 184,000 tires per year. Its estimated cost of $16 million would be the largest foreign investment in consumer-product manufacturing in the Congo.

In June the nation celebrated the tenth anniversary of its independence from Belgium with elaborate ceremonies, highlighted by a visit from King Baudouin of the Belgians. Toward year's end, however, relations with Belgium deteriorated as a result of the nationalization issue. (K. I.)

Comoro Islands: see Dependent States
Computer Technology: see Electronics

Congo, People's Republic of the

A people's republic of equatorial Africa, the Congo is bounded by Gabon, Cameroon, the Central African Republic, the Congo (Kinshasa), Angola, and the Atlantic Ocean. Area: 134,749 sq.mi. (349,000 sq.km.). Pop. (1968 est.): 870,000, mainly Bantu Negroes; Europeans 11,000. Cap. and largest city: Brazzaville (pop., 1962 est., 135,632). Language: French and Bantu dialects. Religion: mostly pagan, with a strong Christian minority. President in 1970, Maj. Marien Ngouabi.

Renamed the People's Republic of the Congo on Dec. 31, 1969, the country chose a new flag that featured the hammer and sickle. However, "Les Trois Glorieuses" eventually became the new national anthem, rather than the Communist "Internationale" as had been expected previously.

Under the new constitution, the president of the newly created Parti Congolais du Travail (Congolese Workers' Party), elected by the party congress for a five-year term, would also be head of state. He would appoint the vice-president of the Council of State, which replaced the government, and could dismiss him after consultation with the Central Committee. He would also appoint and dismiss the other members of the Council of State on the advice of its vice-president. No national assembly was provided for. The single party was headed by a Central Committee of 41 members and an 8-man Political Bureau.

These profound changes proved insufficient to restore stability, and announcements of attempted coups and political trials followed in rapid succession. In March President Ngouabi announced the crushing of a coup planned by elements in the Army: three military men were executed, including a chief adjutant of the gendarmerie. Subsequently, the National Gendarmerie was replaced by a People's Militia. In August the National People's Army chief of staff was suspended, shortly before Ngouabi announced that he had thwarted a further plot. In September, for

WIDE WORLD

Pres. Marien Ngouabi, whose government in Brazzaville withstood an attempted coup in March 1970.

the third time in one year, the national radio announced yet another plot and a former minister of public works was sentenced to ten years at hard labour.

After 28 months at loggerheads, a somewhat spectacular reconciliation took place in June between President Ngouabi and Pres. Joseph Mobutu of the neighbouring Democratic Republic of the Congo, resulting in the resumption of river traffic between Brazzaville and Kinshasa.　　　　　(PH. D.)

CONGO, PEOPLE'S REPUBLIC OF THE

Education. (1967–68) Primary, pupils 207,595, teachers 3,474; secondary, pupils 18,243, teachers 597; vocational, pupils 2,437, teachers 281; teacher training (1966–67), students 408, teachers 30; higher, students 1,110, teaching staff 83.

Finance. Monetary unit: CFA franc, with a parity of CFA Fr. 50 to the French franc (CFA Fr. 277.71 = U.S. \$1; CFA Fr. 666.50 = £1 sterling). Budget (1970 est.) balanced at CFA Fr. 18.1 billion.

Foreign Trade. (1968) Imports CFA Fr. 24,060,-000,000; exports CFA Fr. 12,190,000,000. Import sources: France 58%; West Germany 10%; U.S. 5%. Export destinations: West Germany 25%; Netherlands 19%; Belgium-Luxembourg 14%; France 12%; Israel 6%; South Africa 6%. Main exports: timber 51%; diamonds 31%.

Transport and Communications. Roads (1966) 10,842 km. (including 243 km. with improved surface). Motor vehicles in use (1968): passenger 7,235; commercial 5,585. Railways: (1968) 785 km.; traffic (1969) 143 million passenger-km., freight 488 million net ton-km. Air traffic (1968): 61,229,000 passenger-km.; freight 5,289,000 net ton-km. Telephones (Dec. 1968) 9,287. Radio receivers (Dec. 1968) 62,000. Television receivers (Dec. 1968) 500.

Agriculture. Production (in 000; metric tons; 1968; 1967 in parentheses): cassava 400 (400); coffee 1.8 (1.9); peanuts 17 (17); palm kernels (exports; 1967) 2.8, (1966) 4; palm oil (1967) 5.6, (1966) 6.8. Livestock (in 000; 1968–69): sheep c. 34; cattle (1966–67) 28; pigs 17.

Congregational Churches: see Religion

Conservation

The U.S. landing on the moon in July 1969 crystallized man's thoughts on the conservation of his own world. Once men had stepped outside it and returned safely, it became easier to consider the world as a finite environment, having no resources, except solar radiation, available from elsewhere. At the same time, the confirmation of the moon as a sterile satellite, devoid of both air and water and utterly unable to support life, brought home the continuing need to conserve soil, water, air, plants, and animal life on our own globe to prevent their deterioration to a similar state of lifelessness.

People began to pay more attention to the risk that air, land, and sea could all become so seriously polluted, through growing human chemical activity, that the pace of life might slacken. The consumption of fossil fuel—coal, natural gas, and oil—had already raised the proportion of carbon dioxide gas in the air over industrial districts and great cities packed with automobiles. Once this happened globally, the forests and farmlands would gain new values, beyond their production of timber and food. Only the green leaf of the growing plant can lower this carbon dioxide content on any worthwhile scale, by fixing the carbon element and releasing the vital oxygen gas that man and all animals must breathe. Though the world's oceans were still treated as convenient dumping grounds for every sort of discarded oil, noxious chemical, or dangerous radioactive waste, it was increasingly realized that there were limits to the pollution that they could neutralize. No nation could opt out of the harmful consequences of poisoned seas that might, for example, cease to support fish. Significantly, the U.S. celebrated an Earth Day on April 22, 1970, when, with the support of Pres. Richard Nixon, demonstrations were held on a nationwide scale to remind people of the perils of polluted air, water, and land.

Murray Mitchell, a U.S. government scientist, calculated that increasing carbon dioxide in the air could eventually lead to a warming up of the world's atmosphere, followed by the melting of polar ice caps, higher ocean levels, and coastal flooding. On the other hand, conservationists could increase carbon dioxide fixation rates by raising irrigated crops on substantial sunlit areas hitherto arid and sterile.

The Council on Environmental Quality, created by the U.S. National Environmental Policy Act, in its first report to Congress, in August 1970, said that, in addition to its threat to human life, the total costs of air pollution in the United States amount to many billions of dollars a year. "Acute episodes of [air] pollution in London, New York and other cities have been marked by dramatic increases in death and illness rates, especially among the elderly and those with preexisting respiratory or cardiac conditions," the report said.

At the end of July a devastating outbreak of smog crippled New York City. A heat wave, combined with a succession of windless days, trapped fumes and stale air so that they were unable to rise and spread normally. Smoky particles arising from reactions between air, moisture, and the combustion of gasoline and heavier hydrocarbon oils hung over buildings like a dark blanket. At the same time, the failure of a major electric power generator crippled air-conditioning plants, making it impossible for people to improve the murky air within their dwellings. Similar fouling of the atmosphere, together with pollution of coastal waters, was reported from Tokyo, West Germany, and the Milan-Turin-Genoa industrial triangle of northern Italy. By contrast, London began to reap the benefits of stringent "clean air" legislation, and plans were advanced to convert the Thames from its old status of an "open sewer" to a clear inland lagoon, protected from the sea by a tidal barrage.

The Alaskan oil strikes resulted in fears of a conservation crisis in Arctic North America. This had political implications since the region is shared between Canada and the U.S. Queen Elizabeth II, during her visit to Yellowknife, N.W.T., in July, echoed world opinion when she said: "In this North-West Territory, vast tracts of land and water are still unspoiled. This places a particularly heavy responsibility upon the authorities to plan and manage its development, not only for the benefit of Canada, but as a vital part in the balance of nature throughout the world." Meanwhile, oil companies and conservationists formed two opposing camps whose interests appeared irreconcilable. Transport of oil south called for a major pipeline, serviced by an all-weather road system. The alternative outlet by huge tankers cruising through the Northwest Passage posed the hazard that any mishap could release crude oil at zero temperatures, where it would never disintegrate through biochemical action but would foul the seas for all time. On land the main difficulty was the permafrost, a layer of frozen earth just below the surface that remains rockhard the whole year round if left undisturbed. Engineering operations could so disturb the critical balance of heat gain and loss that hard roads, blasted through this frozen earth, would deteriorate into quagmires. (*See* Special Report.)

European Conservation Year, sponsored by the Council of Europe, opened with a conference at Strasbourg, France, in February 1970. Seventeen member nations, with ten observers, met to consider ameliorative measures in one of the world's most densely populated and technically developed regions.

Starting from the basis that "Nature is the provider of resources and amenities for man's material prosperity, physical and mental well-being, and spiritual life," the conference suggested that these resources must be used rationally and with proper planning "because of growing populations and technical progress." This demanded a scientific ecological approach, with the aim of maintaining as much diversity as possible, because diversity helps to ensure the stability of the environment and enhance its quality. The application of these principles to the highly industrialized countries of Europe involved not only planning of the natural environment but also elimination or, where possible, reutilization of modern society's by-products and waste, and control of the use of poisonous substances.

To put these principles into effect, the strengthening, development, and better coordination of existing international organizations would be needed, and the conference urged the Council of Europe to convene a European ministerial conference with the following tasks: to review and promote coordination of the programs of the existing intergovernmental organizations; to instruct these organizations to secure agreed-upon standards for European industry in such areas as, for example, the manufacture of pesticides, vehicle exhaust systems, and aircraft engines; and to promote the harmonization of national legislation relating to the environment. More ambitiously, the proposed conference would probably be asked to examine the possibility of setting up a "political authority at European level" to guide the management of the continent's natural environment, bringing in countries not in membership with the Council of Europe; and also to study the proposal for a European fund to combat pollution.

Many believed that the Council of Europe should also be charged to draw up a protocol to its Human Rights Convention "guaranteeing the right of every individual to enjoy a healthy and unspoiled environment, including clean air and water, freedom from undue noise and other nuisances," and reasonable access to coast and countryside.

At the national level the conference urged all governments to declare publicly during 1970 their policy aims for the environment. Besides the necessary planning legislation, these were expected to include the training of adequate staff both to enforce and advise; and practical steps to reclaim and reuse derelict land, particularly for recreation and wildlife. The conference recommended that unspoiled areas of all types, including the solitudes vulnerable even to small developments, be safeguarded immediately.

Land and Forests. The United Nations Food and Agriculture Organization (FAO) reassessed the forest potential of Latin America at a Regional Consultation on the Development of Forest, Pulp and Paper Industries, held in Mexico City during May. The region holds one-quarter of the world's natural forest, with three times the world's average area of forest per inhabitant. Yet it was a net importer of forest produce, paying a bill of $200 million a year. Virtually all the region's 2.2 billion ac. of forest are of broad-leaved trees, whose hardwood timbers enjoyed only limited demand. By contrast, the 50 million ac. of native conifers, including pines in Mexico, Guatemala, Honduras, and Nicaragua and the *Araucarias* of Brazil, Chile, and Argentina, had been overcut and reserves were fast becoming depleted. A tremendous expansion of conifer plantations was urgently needed to supply the growing paper, packaging, and timber industries, expected to double their intake of wood during the next ten years. Fast-growing pines from the southern United States and selected *Eucalyptus* species from Australia were leading candidates for extensive planting by many governments.

Wilhelm Knabe, a West German scientist engaged in fume-damage and soil-fertility protection research in the province of North Rhine-Westphalia, listed contrasting types of man-made ground offered to conservationists for the establishment of man-made forests. Sometimes surface soil had simply been scraped off, leaving infertile compacted subsoil lacking humus, mineral nutrients, drainage, and aeration. Alternatively, waste from mining and quarrying was just dumped to form slag heaps, often with high conical forms that increased wind exposure. Other industrial waste minerals had been disintegrated by severe

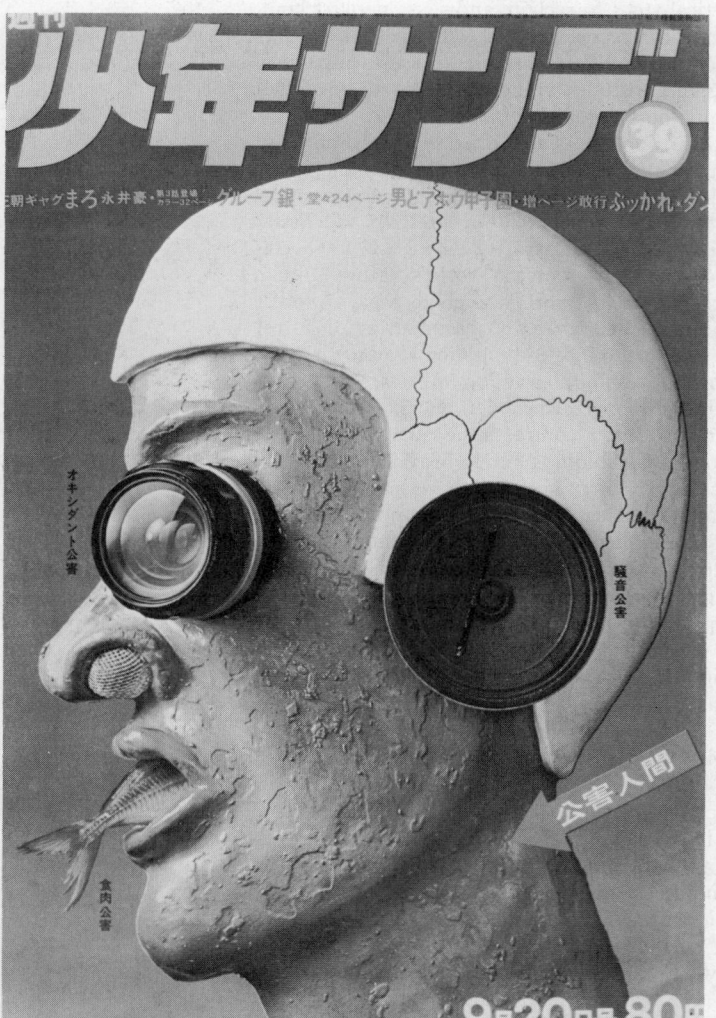

SYEUS MOTTEL FROM NANCY PALMER AGENCY

POPPERFOTO FROM PICTORIAL PARADE

少年サンデー

Top, New York City's Pageant Players dramatize the problem of polluted air by wearing gas masks to an ecology rally in April. Left, cover of the September 20 issue of the weekly magazine "Shonen Sunday" features a "polluted man" to illustrate the effects of a deteriorating environment on the inhabitants of Japan. Above, "Fritillaria meleagris," which grows only in certain riverside pastures along the upper Thames River, faces extinction because of the inroads of man. Opposite, a militant ecology group protests plans by the Pacific Gas and Electric Co. to run power lines through a park near Oakland, Calif.

KEYSTONE

mechanical treatment or had undergone chemical reactions by fire, acids, or alkalies; in extreme cases the substratum itself was a waste synthetic substance, unknown in nature. Dredged sand and silt from watercourses or the seabed might also be presented as a suitable medium for afforestation, though heavily polluted by salt. Domestic waste, built up into rubbish piles, might include industrial by-products of high toxicity, and could vary markedly with place and time. To reclaim such sites, the forester must have full information on the origins of all components of the "made" ground, and be ready to ameliorate it by drainage, cultivation, fertilization, or covering-over with normal soil.

In April the U.S. government suspended the use of the leading herbicide 2,4,5-T, previously regarded by chemists as a major tool for the economic control of unwanted woody growth. This trichlorophenol compound was in general use throughout the world as a selective weed killer helpful to forestry and agriculture, and had also been extensively employed as a defoliant by U.S. forces operating in Vietnam. Aerial spraying there was followed by deaths among both wildlife and domestic animals, and a suspected increase in deformities among babies born to Vietnamese mothers. Experts believed that the harmful side effects arose from impurities in 2,4,5-T, but counseled the substitution of safer, if less efficient, chemical weed killers.

The FAO announced a $2 million development project to increase rice production on the coastal lowlands of Guinea. This region of high (100-in.) rainfall, with a good temperature regime, had been of little use because it is subject to seasonal floods from delta rivers inland, and to the incursion of salt water from the sea. Hurza Engineering Co. of Chicago tackled the engineering problems of establishing seasonally dry fields, free of salt. FAO plant breeders supplied modern high-yielding strains of rice, some of which had already proved their worth in the Philippines.

The government of Somalia published proposals for the protection and conservation of the country's few surviving forests. Regions described by 19th-century travelers as open parkland teeming with elephants, antelopes, and wild asses had deteriorated into semidesert. Increasing population had led to the felling of trees for firewood or building timber, and the cutting of their foliage to provide fodder for sheep and goats. Overgrazing and fires lit to improve rough pastures had completed the wreck of the old savanna woodlands. The remedy proposed was the creation of nature reserves for picturesque semidesert trees and plants and outstanding animals to attract tourists and so boost Somalia's revenue. Other Arab states to the north also felt the need to conserve their semidesert regions.

Water. Recent developments in the assessment and control of water resources were outlined in papers presented to a symposium at Washington, D.C., in February, to celebrate the centennial of U.S. national weather services and the golden anniversary of the American Meteorological Society. The emphasis was on "nowcasting," implying the immediate evaluation of any weather situation by computerized techniques rather than forecasting by slower methods. Max A. Kohler of Silver Spring, Md., described a new means of gauging the depth of snowfall by monitoring natural gamma radiation from the soil; this could be detected by both hand-held and airborne sensors. William C.

Ackermann of the Illinois State Water Survey stressed the need for forecasts of water quality as well as its simple physical quantity. For example, accidental pollution had to be reported promptly to users downstream even though several days might elapse before slow river flow brought polluted water to their intakes, so that alternative supplies might be organized.

The water pollution problem existed in all parts of the U.S., particularly in the Northeast and in the Great Lakes region, according to a report of the U.S. Council on Environmental Quality. A national effort to reduce water pollution was imperative, the council said, and it maintained that such an effort would require institutional and management changes, would possibly bring some changes in the products people consume, and would lead to higher prices for some products. In May the U.S. Federal Water Quality Administration announced a policy to control thermal pollution in Lake Michigan by forbidding the discharge into the lake of any water more than one degree Fahrenheit warmer than the lake water temperature at the point of discharge. In July the U.S. government sued eight industrial firms on charges of dumping mercury into lakes and rivers, while in August the Chevron Oil Co. was fined $1 million by the government for allowing an oil spill from an offshore well to pollute the Gulf of Mexico. In December, President Nixon ordered implementation of a section of an 1899 law requiring industrial plants discharging

continued on page 223

RALPH CRANE, "LIFE" MAGAZINE © TIME INC.

ALASKAN DILEMMA

By Thomas M. Brown

In the bitterly cold February of 1968, a drilling rig operating under contract to Atlantic Richfield Co. struck oil more than 8,000 ft. below the tundra of Alaska's remote northern rim, at an inhospitable place called Prudhoe Bay. The discovery was quickly proved to be the biggest ever in North America, with reserves that in 1970 were estimated at 12,000,000,000–15,000,000,000 bbl. of recoverable oil. It confronted the sprawling, sparsely peopled (population 302,173) 49th state with two possibilities: on the one hand, great wealth much needed by a poor state; on the other, the destruction of the wilderness environment that makes Alaska unique.

In short, two valuable resources—oil and wilderness—were placed in direct conflict. That conflict had not eased in the succeeding three years. Indeed, as of 1970 a satisfactory resolution was not in sight. Oil development continued—but not at the pace oil industry and state officials would like. A start on the controversial 800-mi. trans-Alaska pipeline had been delayed repeatedly. Conservation groups maintained their unrelenting pressure, but the environmental controls were not as strict as they would like. Even the most sincere attempts by industry at development without despoliation often ran afoul of the unusual conditions of the Arctic, and the degradation of the landscape continued.

Bonanza. There was tremendous pressure for rapid development of the Prudhoe Bay oil fields: the industry was anxious to retrieve its $2 billion investment in the area, known as the North Slope, and to reap the potentially great profits that would follow, and the state government urgently needed the money. Other dividends would include a favourable effect on the national economy and alleviation of the nation's dependence on the unstable Middle East for much of its crude oil. Many Alaskans favoured rapid exploitation of the fields—even at the expense of the environment—because of the economic effect it would have on the state. Alaska receives a royalty of $12\frac{1}{2}\%$ on every barrel of oil produced and exacts a severance tax of between 3 and 8% per barrel, depending on well productivity. The state's share in the bonanza has been estimated at $4 billion–$6 billion over the 15–30-year life of the field.

Alaska has an abundance of problems to spend it on. Since becoming a state in 1959, Alaska has lived a largely hand-to-mouth existence. It has little in the way of a domestic economy, suffers from a high cost of living (up to 85% above the U.S. average) because of its remoteness and harsh climate, and historically has been dependent on the federal government for six of every ten dollars spent within its borders. There has never been enough money to deal with the appalling poverty in rural areas, which particularly afflicts the state's first residents, the Indians, Eskimos, and Aleuts who constitute about 20% of the population. Education, though generously supported within the context of the funds available, has lagged. Social services are mediocre. Even the most elementary facilities—sewers, pure drinking water, hospitals, and roads—are more often than not lacking.

Alaskans got their first taste of what oil might eventually mean in September 1969, when they sold ten-year leases on 450,000 ac. of North Slope land at an average price of about $2,000 an acre—a windfall of $900 million, or almost six times

the state budget for the 1969–70 fiscal year. The state legislature celebrated in 1970 by passing a $314 million general fund budget—double the previous year's authorized expenditures and as much as $100 million above the state's anticipated income from normal revenues.

Despite its preoccupation with economics, however, the Alaska legislature also demonstrated a dawning awareness of the ecological problems presented by the prospect of oil development. It established an Environmental Quality Control Commission with authority to veto projects (subject to the governor's concurrence) that it determined would significantly alter the environment without some offsetting benefit to society; established a Pesticide Control Board; amended the Water Quality Control Act to remove a water pollution exemption for placer mining; and established three state parks totaling one million acres. A bill banning oil lease sales and drilling in Bristol Bay on Alaska's west coast was vetoed by Gov. Keith H. Miller.

There appeared to be a growing awareness among Alaskans generally that their desire to improve living standards through exploitation of oil was frequently in direct conflict with the requirements of prudent conservation. That message was being driven home by conservation groups throughout the country. Wilderness—true, unpopulated, untrammeled wilderness—is fast vanishing from the earth. The last big piece of it in the United States is Alaska—and much of Alaska's remaining true wilderness lies on the North Slope and in the magnificent, but little-known, Brooks Range south of the oil development area. Conservationists have set a high priority on preserving as much of it as possible, and the bulletin of one influential conservation organization, the Sierra Club, has predicted that Alaska will become "the conservation battleground of the century."

And there is more at stake than protection of the North Slope alone, for the manner in which the North Slope is developed will set a critical precedent. About half of Alaska's land mass and the vast offshore acreage are underlain with geologic formations that the oil industry considers promising. It is reasonable to expect that some will be productive—and

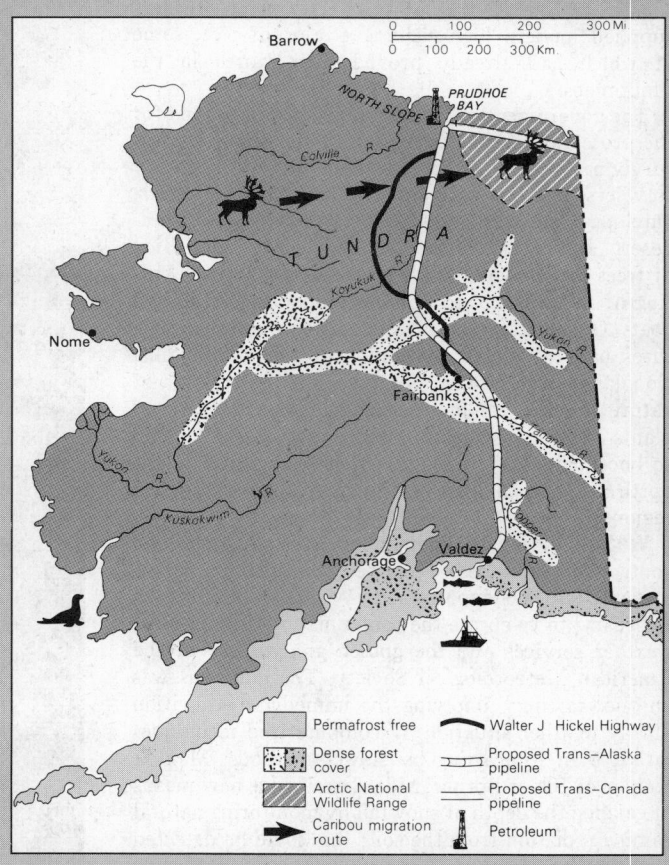

Permafrost free — Walter J. Hickel Highway
Dense forest cover — Proposed Trans-Alaska pipeline
Arctic National Wildlife Range — Proposed Trans-Canada pipeline
Caribou migration route — Petroleum

some are of significantly greater importance to the quality of life in Alaska than the North Slope. Bristol Bay and the Gulf of Alaska, with their rich fisheries, are two examples. The way the North Slope oil fields are developed could have a decisive influence on how oil discoveries in the rest of the state are managed.

The Fragile Arctic. The North Slope runs north from the spiny peaks of the Brooks Range to the Beaufort Sea, a distance that varies from roughly 40 to 150 mi. Near the foothills it is a rolling plateau, gouged by streams and rivers, fairly well drained and quite dry in the summer. Along the ocean the plateau tapers into a broad, utterly flat plain that is poorly drained and pocked by thousands of lakes. It is in the plain area that oil was found.

Winter descends on the North Slope in October and soon the plain is white in the wan twilight, with patches of black lake ice showing where the cold winds scour off the snow. For $2\frac{1}{2}$ months the sun never edges above the horizon. The plain is monotonously flat, with no landmarks in the conventional sense: no trees, no bushes, no hills, no rise in the land of more than a couple of feet for as far as the eye can see, scarcely any snowdrifts, for there is little for snow to drift against. It is cold, sometimes −65° F, and when the wind blows hard and drives the snow in stinging pellets, a man can barely make out his fingertips.

The Brooks Range lies to the south, a jumble of forbidding peaks of great variety and stunning beauty. Fewer than 200 persons inhabit this formidable expanse, the largest virgin wilderness in the United States—and perhaps the world. Yet even in this frozen wilderness life exists. A dozen species of birds remain. Hundreds of thousands of caribou inhabit the north and south slopes. Wolves persist, as do Dall sheep in the high crags and polar bears on the coast.

There is no spring in the usual sense and summer comes suddenly late in May. Light returns, and the ice in the rivers goes out in a cacophony that can be heard for 20 mi. The caribou, most of which have spent the winter on the more temperate southern slopes of the Brooks Range, move back through the mountains to the North Slope. The ice melts on the slope lakes in June, the top few inches of tundra melt, and billions of mosquitoes appear. The permafrost beneath keeps the surface water from sinking in. The ground is wet and spongy and travel for man is difficult.

The oilmen who have worked in this wilderness, where frostbite is a constant hazard in winter and snow can fall in July, frequently scoff at the environmentalists' contention that the Arctic ecology is fragile. They opt for the adjective "hostile." Yet it is precisely because it is so extreme that the Arctic is peculiarly vulnerable to man's intrusions. Because it receives so little sunlight, the Arctic is very poor in plant life. There are about 435 plant species in the Alaskan Arctic—a fraction of the number found in the great forests of the temperate and tropic zones. This, in turn, means that there is relatively little energy available in the form of food for plant-eating animals, and for the meat-eating animals that feed on the plant eaters.

Thus the food chains, through which the sun's energy is transferred from plants to animals, are short. The resulting food web, composed of the various food chains, is simple. Plant growth is slow. Animal populations per acre are sparse, since each animal requires a large area for sustenance.

The strength of an ecosystem is directly related to its complexity. A tropical rain forest is a complex ecosystem and therefore a tough one. The Arctic has one of the simplest ecosystems, and hence one of the most fragile. Relatively slight disturbances can have significant effects.

Finally, the comparatively low level of solar radiation ensures the existence of permafrost, which is the cause of almost every major engineering problem in the Arctic. Permafrost, as defined by the U.S. Geological Survey, is "rock or soil material . . . that has remained below 0 degrees C. (32 degrees F.) continuously

THE "NEW YORK TIMES"

Sections of pipe lie piled in readiness north of Fairbanks, Alaska, pending government approval for an 800-mi. oil pipeline extending from the Arctic coast to Valdez. Conservationists fear the pipeline will cause irreparable damage to the environment.

for two or more years." It can be any kind of frozen subsurface material, including gravel and solid rock, and some of it remains stable when thawed, presenting no particular engineering problems. But much permafrost is of the so-called "ice-rich" variety—usually silty soil with a high frozen-water content. Such permafrost underlies much of the North Slope and many areas along the proposed route of the pipeline that the Alyeska Pipeline Service Co. (formerly the Trans-Alaska Pipeline System [TAPS]) wants to build.

On the North Slope the vegetative cover of the tundra insulates the ground, and normally only a foot or so of surface soil thaws during the summer. The permafrost beneath remains frozen solid. But disturbing the mat of soil and vegetation exposes the permafrost to warm summer air and sunlight and can quickly cause trouble, for, when thawed, ice-rich permafrost becomes an unstable slurry of watery, oozing mud. The Geological Survey has found that "the simple passage of a tracked vehicle that destroys the vegetation mat is enough . . . to cause the top of the permafrost layer to thaw. This thawing can cause differential settlement of the surface of the ground, drainage problems, and severe frost action. Once the equilibrium is upset, the whole process can feed on itself and be practically impossible to reverse."

The Invasion by Man. The vulnerability of this environment was demonstrated during World War II, when the federal government dispatched crews to explore the 23 million-ac. Naval Petroleum Reserve No. 4 (NPR 4), located roughly between Prudhoe Bay and Barrow. A base was built inland at Umiat and the Arctic was invaded, for the first time, by heavy tracked vehicles. The crews left trash and garbage and countless miles of bulldozer trails all across NPR 4. Unsightly junk heaps still stand at Umiat. The bulldozer trails exposed the permafrost and eroded into gullies, draining lakes and changing the character of surrounding areas. Thousands of oil drums left floating in the shallow lakes are only now rusting through, polluting the lakes and, on occasion, killing birds.

More refuse was left during the construction of Distant Early Warning Line radar stations in the 1950s, and some of the federal government's mistakes were repeated by the state of Alaska in the winter of 1968–69 when Highway Department crews built a winter road to help supply the oil fields. Development of the North Slope oil fields by private enterprise poses the same kind of threat on a much larger scale. Compared with the federal and state governments, the performance of the oil industry has been good. Still, there has been unnecessary damage, and even techniques that would leave little trace in more temperate regions cause harm here.

Some of the worst environmental abuses occurred before the Prudhoe Bay strike, when geophysical exploration crews, working under contract to the oil companies, were roaming the Arctic searching for promising subsurface geologic structures. They sometimes traveled across the tundra in tracked vehicles in the summer months, damaging the fragile vegetative mat and leaving a web of trails over hundreds of miles. They frequently set up winter camps on frozen lakes, drained oil from machines onto the ice, and left oil drums and heaps of garbage to bob on the lakes in the summer. They also did seismic surveying, a technique that involves planting widely spaced dynamite charges below the surface of the ground, detonating them simultaneously, and recording the resulting underground shock waves. In some instances, the vegetative cover of the tundra was removed in a straight line for ten miles to allow strings of charges to be set, and these trails have eroded into water-filled ditches several feet deep. Sometimes the wire used to detonate the charges was left lying on the tundra, where it became a trap for unwary caribou. A bulldozer operator for one geophysical firm carved his company's initials into the tundra in letters a hundred feet high. The Atlantic Richfield (ARCO) discovery triggered a race by other leaseholders to explore their holdings, and soon dozens of geophysical teams were roaming the slope, shooting their seismic charges and leaving a trail of powder boxes, detonating wire, oil drums, garbage, and polluted lakes.

At the same time, the major oil companies themselves were beginning to learn some hard but valuable lessons about Arctic engineering. What was more, with conservation organizations throughout the U.S. taking an active interest in the North Slope, the companies soon realized that unusual concern for the environment would have to be demonstrated if they were to be allowed to develop their discovery. Led by ARCO and British Petroleum (BP), they began instituting development practices that were by far the most sophisticated—and least harmful environmentally—of any ever employed on a mass scale in the American Arctic.

Instead of haphazard bulldozer trails, the oil companies began constructing $200,000-a-mile all-weather gravel roads, made five feet thick to insulate the underlying permafrost. Instead of merely scraping the frozen tundra smooth for a winter runway, they built airfields 5,000 ft. long, 150 ft. wide, and 5 ft. thick. Drilling rigs were put on gravel pads so they could be operated in the summer without thawing the permafrost. BP began collecting the refuse from its drilling sites at one location for disposal. ARCO sent cleanup crews out to collect refuse. Pressure was put on the geophysical crews to clean up after themselves. The oil companies agreed not to dispatch tracked vehicles across the tundra before freeze-up in the fall or after breakup in the spring, and ARCO began transporting drilling rigs from one site to another by helicopter. It would be hard to find a cleaner industrial site anywhere than ARCO's Prudhoe Bay camp.

Yet even these exemplary practices were not without their environmental drawbacks. Conservationists wondered whether the network of roads, airfields, and drilling pads might not prove to be a monument as enduring—and not nearly as attractive—as the Pyramids. They also were concerned that the removal of millions of cubic yards of gravel from rivers might damage them irreparably.

Pipelines and Tankers. Disturbed as they were about some of the things happening on the North Slope, there was little the conservationists could do except complain. There were no apparent legal soft spots. So they concentrated on the trans-Alaska pipeline that the Alyeska Pipeline Service Co. wanted to build.

When first announced in early 1969, the 800-mi., 48-in.-diameter pipeline, with an estimated cost of $900 million, was described as the most expensive privately financed construction project in history. By late 1970 the estimated cost had doubled

and the project was not only the biggest ever but also one of the most controversial. It had become, for many persons, symbolic of the entire question of conservation versus development. And since most of the pipeline route lay over federal land and its construction required approval of the secretary of the interior, the conservationists had a chance to influence the way it was built.

The pipeline project worried the environmental protection groups on a number of counts. The oil industry insisted that it could bury 95% of the pipeline, thereby preventing it from becoming an eyesore and a barrier to caribou migrations. The conservationists were skeptical about the practicality of burying a huge pipeline, carrying oil at a temperature of about 160° F, in permafrost. What would happen when the permafrost melted? Furthermore, the pipeline would contain some 200,000 gal. of oil per mile, and a major break could deluge the surrounding countryside. They were also skeptical of the pipeline proponents' argument that TAPS was requesting a right-of-way only 100 ft. wide by 800 mi. long, or about 15 sq.mi.—not much in a state that embraced 586,000 sq.mi. of real estate. The conservationists maintained that a much larger area would be affected: an access road would have to be constructed, and an enormous amount of gravel would have to be dug from pits along the way to be used during construction.

The Interior Department was also concerned with these questions, and it was insisting on satisfactory answers before issuing a pipeline construction permit. In late 1970, then Secretary Walter J. Hickel said that as far as his department was concerned, the most important unanswered questions were how the pipeline would be constructed in permafrost areas and its final design specifications. Hickel was believed to have been nearing an agreement on the pipeline when he was fired by Pres. Richard Nixon.

Despite its drawbacks, the pipeline might well be the lesser of two evils. The most commonly discussed alternative involved giant icebreaking tankers like the SS "Manhattan" or extraordinarily expensive submarine tankers that would cross the Northwest Passage across the top of Alaska to east coast markets. The Humble Oil and Refining Co. spent about $40 million converting the 115,000-ton "Manhattan" into a 1,005-ft. icebreaker, and the "Manhattan" successfully transited the passage in the summer of 1969 (though she returned home with a hole in her hull described as "big enough to drive a truck through"). Humble engineers concluded that it would be technically possible to build tankers that could withstand the rigours of the passage, where ice pressure ridges 100 ft. thick are encountered. The question was whether the ships, which naturally would be much more expensive than their conventional counterparts, could carry oil at a competitive price. Nonetheless, the tanker method apparently was gaining favour as costs of the proposed pipeline skyrocketed. Submarine tankers, proposed by General Dynamics, would cost far more than icebreakers, but presumably would be both safer and faster.

In questioning the advisability of Arctic tanker operations, conservationists cited studies demonstrating the slow decomposition of oil in cold water, which meant that a spill would be more persistent than in warmer waters. Almost certainly, such a spill would have disastrous effects on the Arctic marine food chain. Nor were the pipeline and Arctic tanker operations the only threats that oil posed to Alaska. Other potential trouble spots were tanker operations off Valdez, which has an ecologically delicate estuary important for its commercial fish runs and its population of sea otters, and possible offshore drilling operations, especially in the important Bristol Bay and Gulf of Alaska areas.

In short, it had become clear that no matter how much care is exercised in developing the Arctic, the face of the land will be changed and there will be some environmental damage. The crucial question was how much damage was acceptable. There was no consensus on that.

waste into navigable waterways to obtain permits. The Army Corps of Engineers was to be responsible for issuing the permits upon recommendation of the Environmental Protection Agency.

On the global scale, Roger Revelle of Harvard University calculated that only one-third of the earth's total land surface was capable, for hydrological reasons, of supporting crops, the actual figure being 10×10^9 ac. The limiting circumstances are that rainfall, plus storage by the soil, must exceed loss through evaporation and transpiration (loss of moisture through plant leaves) during that part of the year when temperatures are above freezing. The actual cultivated area was only one-fifth of the theoretical potential. Nevertheless, 10% of all cultivated land, or 300 million ac., was artificially irrigated and represented a man-made extension into hitherto sterile climatic zones. Revelle estimated that this irrigated area would be doubled during the next ten years.

In a pamphlet entitled "Managing Forested Watersheds," the Forest Service of the U.S. Department of Agriculture, besides restating well-known principles, drew attention to phreatophytes, or "well plants." These are deep-rooted plants of low economic value, which form dense thickets along floodplains and river banks in the southwestern U.S., tapping the groundwater and transpiring it rapidly. Their replacement by shallow-rooted grasses provides pasture and lessens the drain on water supplies.

In South Africa, S. P. Botha, minister of water affairs and forestry, announced legislation to protect river sources by control of catchment areas under both private and public ownership. Unplanned uses of watersheds had been followed by soil erosion, leading in turn to the sludging up of dams downstream that were vital for both water storage and power supply. Correct treatment of catchments, whether by afforestation or thick bush covers to ensure silt-free outflows, was vital to South Africa's water-saving and hydroelectric power programs.

Throughout April an exceptional series of avalanches demonstrated the need to conserve the Alpine environment shared by France, Switzerland, Austria, and Italy. The worst of these disasters demolished a boys' sanatorium at Plateau d'Assy, in the French Alps, killing 72 persons. The basic cause was held to be an exceptionally heavy winter snowfall, up to 20 ft. deep on the upper slopes, which brought about instability as soon as spring thaws began, followed by landslides at situations previously considered safe. Defenses mustered by the Swiss against the ever-present threat of the "white death" descending from slopes above their villages included daily monitoring of snowfall and the use of explosives—including bombs dropped by aircraft—to trigger off dangerous slides at known and foreseen times.

In England the Thames Conservancy, a public authority that controls the country's largest watershed and supplies London with two-thirds of its needs, announced a $20 million project to increase underground water storage by an entirely new method. The upper Thames flows over porous chalk rock beds that are normally saturated. If these are pumped partially dry during a hot summer, they will fill up again during the wet, cold winter that follows. A series of 100 deep boreholes that were being dug would increase available supplies by 100 million gal. a day. The Thames itself would carry this flow downstream to London, without the expense of new reservoirs, pipes, or pumping stations. The basic idea of using existing underground storage, currently occupied by "dead" or "fossil" water, could be applied in many situations where similar physical conditions occur.

The government of the Soviet Union announced its intention of diverting three major north-flowing rivers feeding the Arctic Ocean—the Pechora, the Ob, and the Yenisei—southward through a series of giant canals to the landlocked Caspian and Aral seas. This water could thus be used to irrigate the steppes, in a warm climate, rather than the sterile tundra. The potential benefits to food production were immense. Meteorologists speculated about the long-term effects of such a diversion on world climate. Fresh water from those rivers raises the freezing point of the Arctic seas and, if its supply were diminished, the polar ice cap might shrink. This could, in theory, release vast quantities of water from cold storage for free circulation and profoundly affect weather patterns across Europe, Asia, and North America. World sea levels might conceivably rise through the shrinkage of the ice cap. On the other hand, less water would reach the world's "free seas" because both the Caspian and the Aral seas are completely landlocked.

In Australia a noteworthy development was the start of major construction work in a completely new region for irrigation and river control. The Ord River, which flows north from the Kimberley Plateau in Western Australia to the Timor Sea, taps a region with a reasonable rainfall in the southern summer around January, followed by many arid months. After pilot trials with a small dam and demonstration farm, the new Ord River Dam was planned. It was to rise 220 ft. above the existing riverbed at a narrow gorge, and hold back a lake covering 286 sq.mi. and containing 4.6 million ac-ft. of water. The annual yield of 1 million ac-ft. would irrigate 178,000 ac. of black-soil country, two-thirds being in Western Australia and the remaining one-third in the Northern Territory. Cotton and sorghum would be the main crops grown, and beef cattle would be fattened. There would also be a substantial yield of hydroelectric power, though part of this would have to be used to pump some of the water up to the more fertile areas.

In southeast Europe the Bulgarian Academy of Agricultural Sciences announced a long-term program to raise the country's irrigated area to 8.5 million ac., equivalent to 70% of the total arable acreage. In the north, more water was to be drawn from the Danube, along the frontier with Romania, but all this water had to be pumped up to the higher levels that existed on the Bulgarian side. About 100 mi. to the south, gravitational flow was feasible in the basin of the Maritsa River, and a great South Bulgarian Canal was being excavated to run east for 190 mi. from Pazardzhik to Karnobat. Fed by winter rains from surrounding mountain ranges, this canal would have a flow capacity of 2,000 cu.ft. per sec., and water would be led off at eight separate points to irrigate a total area of 1,250,000 ac. (H. L. EN.)

Wildlife. In November 1969 representatives of 44 countries attended the tenth General Assembly of the International Union for Conservation of Nature and Natural Resources (IUCN) in New Delhi, India. The assembly was inaugurated by India's prime minister, Indira Gandhi, who called for "a massive campaign . . . to educate our people in the first principles of nature conservation" and for "long term vision" rather than "considerations of immediate economic gain." Following the retirement of E. J. H. Berwick, Gerardo

Budowski (Venez.), coming from two years' service in ecology and conservation with UNESCO, was appointed director general from April 1970. Harold J. Coolidge (U.S.) was elected to a second term as president. Peter Scott (U.K.) was appointed chairman of the Survival Service Commission (SSC), through which the "Red Data Books" of threatened species of wildlife were published.

On Dec. 5, 1969, President Nixon signed the Endangered Species Conservation Act. Besides other far-reaching measures for the preservation of wildlife, this act prohibited the importation into the U.S. of any wildlife (or parts thereof) threatened with extinction throughout the world—even if such wildlife enjoyed no protection in its native country. Importation of wildlife could be restricted to certain points of entry, by land, air, or sea.

In January 1970 the ban by Kenya on importation of wildlife skins for commercial purposes came into effect, after which only the skins of wild animals shot legally under control measures could be used in manufactures. This followed the realization that thousands of leopards were being killed in Kenya by poachers from the north and their skins taken to Somalia, to be reexported to Kenya for the local market.

In Natal, S.Af., the decline in the crocodile population was alleviated by the release of 500 specimens reared in a hatchery at the Ndumu game reserves. These reptiles, previously regarded as vermin, had been protected in Natal since April 1969, following the realization of their value, when young, in maintaining the life balance in ponds by eating insects and snails and, when adult, by devouring large predatory fish and by acting as scavengers of decomposing carcasses.

On returning to Rwanda after four years, Dian Fossey found a reduction in the population of mountain gorillas (an endangered species) from 50 to 20 individuals and a similar reduction in other animals, except elephants and buffalo. She attributed the decrease to invasion of the area for illegal cattle grazing.

The meeting of the International Whaling Commission, held in June, showed cynical disregard for conservation of the Antarctic whaling stock by fixing the quota for the 1970–71 season at 2,700 blue whale units, the same as for the previous season. This catch could certainly not be achieved and was therefore no true restriction whatever. The increasing catch of the sperm whale also caused concern to conservationists.

In Queensland, Austr., where marine turtles and their eggs enjoyed full protection except for some slight use by aboriginals, Robert Bustard, reporting on his investigations for the World Wildlife Fund, estimated the combined female breeding of green, flatback, and loggerhead turtles there to be not less than 75,000. Costa Rica also took steps to protect turtles by establishing a national park at Tortuguero, the biggest nesting site of the green turtle in the Caribbean. Nevertheless, the world situation of marine turtles and of other sea life remained critical. Jacques-Yves Cousteau, returning from a world exploration of the oceans in his ship "Calypso," declared that life in the oceans had decreased by 40% since 1950 because of pollution and overfishing. "The human species will not survive if the oceans die," warned Cousteau.

In July the Council of Europe called on governments to standardize control of the use of pesticides, particularly the requirements to be met by manufacturers in the nature and presentation of their products,

Construction Industry:
see Engineering
   Projects; Housing;
   Industrial Review

Consumer Affairs:
see Merchandising

stipulating that marketing should be authorized only when the results of chemical, physical, toxicologic, and biological studies had been submitted.

At the 15th International Ornithological Congress held in August in the Netherlands, D. Snow (U.K.) advocated that a list of specimens of endangered birds that were in museums should be published, so that those specimens could be used for scientific work everywhere and the unnecessary collection of rare birds avoided.

During September, at a world meeting of the International Council for Bird Preservation (ICBP) in Texel, Neth., reports were received from 40 countries on the growing and almost uncontrolled traffic in wild birds. Noting that the importation of birds of prey had been controlled in the U.K. from July 1, the conference advocated restrictions on the importation of birds in every country to named places of entry and urged that all containers of birds should be labeled with the numbers and the species they held. The effects of pollution, the continued decrease in birds of prey, particularly of the peregrine falcon in the U.S., and the killing of small migratory birds in Europe were also discussed and action suggested. In Britain, the Royal Society for the Protection of Birds estimated that the death toll of seabirds around the coasts of the British Isles might amount to 200,000 during the year, from oil and other pollution. Between 1967 and 1969 guillemots had declined by 24%. Nearly half the guillemots and one-quarter of the razorbills had not returned to their cliff breeding ledges in the Irish Sea. J. Sultana (Malta) said that his country was a black spot for European birds, owing to uncontrolled and indiscriminate shooting, especially of migratory birds, for sport and collections and because of the trapping of wild birds for caging. But, said Sultana, there was one encouraging development in that the island of Comino had been made a bird sanctuary, and he made a powerful appeal that the pool at Ghadira, the only marshy area in Malta, which was saved from road building in 1967, should be made a nature reserve and that a field study centre should be established there.

At the end of September the International Fur Trade Federation, after discussion with the Survival Service Commission of IUCN, recommended a total ban on the skins of the La Plata otter, giant otter, clouded leopard, snow leopard, and tiger, and a three-year ban on the leopard and cheetah. A joint survey into the use of the skins of South American cats feared to be becoming rare, such as the jaguar, ocelot, and margay cat, was started under the field directorship of Paul Leyhausen (W.Ger.), chairman of the SSC Cat Group.   (C. L. BE.)

See also Arctic Regions; Biological Sciences; Disasters; Engineering Projects; Fuel and Power; Historic Buildings; Medicine; Mining; Oceanography; Parks; Timber.

ENCYCLOPÆDIA BRITANNICA FILMS. *Nature's Plan* (1953); *Look to the Land* (1954); *Succession—From Sand Dune to Forest* (1960); *The Cave Community* (1961); *The High Arctic Biome* (1961); *The Community* (1962); *The Grasslands* (1962); *The Temperate Deciduous Forest* (1962); *The Tropical Rain Forest* (1962); *What Is Ecology?* (1962); *The Pond and the City* (1964); *The House of Man: Our Changing Environment* (1965); *Waterfowl: A Resource in Danger* (1965); *Trees and Their Importance* (1966); *Water for Living Things* (1967); *The Everglades: Conserving a Balanced Community* (1968); *Problems of Conservation—Air* (1968); *The House of Man, Part II—Our Crowded Environment* (1969); *Problems of Conservation—Forest and Range* (1969); *Problems of Conservation—Minerals* (1969); *Problems of Conservation—Water* (1969); *The Garbage Explosion* (1970); *Problems of Conservation—Our Natural Resources* (1970); *Problems of Conservation—Soil* (1970); *Problems of Conservation—Wildlife* (1970).

Consumer Expenditures

In almost all the Western industrialized countries, the year 1970 was marked by quite exceptionally rapid growth of wages, leading to very substantial increases in costs and prices. Inevitably the value of consumer expenditure also rose at an above-average rate. In the countries of the Organization for Economic Cooperation and Development (OECD) as a whole, consumer expenditure rose by 9% in value and 4% in volume, compared with 8.8 and 4.4% in 1969. In the primary producing countries the dampening effect of a shallow recession in the U.S. on commodity prices, which had risen sharply in 1969, affected consumer expenditure only toward the end of the year. Total spending on consumer goods and services in the non-Communist world rose by some 8% in 1970, as much as in the previous year.

While the problems in most industrialized countries were similar, developments were by no means synchronized. In France and the U.S. deflationary measures taken in 1969 reduced the rate of spending in 1970. In Italy and West Germany, on the other hand, the wage explosion came later and consumer expenditure and the rate of price inflation accelerated in 1970.

The situation in West Germany was especially interesting. Wages began to move upward sharply in the final quarter of 1969, and by the beginning of 1970 hourly earnings in manufacturing were already 13% higher than at the beginning of 1969. At the same time, measures of monetary restraint were beginning to slow down the rate of growth of output, so that unit labour costs were rising sharply. Additional measures, including a temporary income tax surcharge, were taken during the year and productivity growth slowed further, but wages continued to bound ahead. Revaluation of the mark in October 1969 had cheapened imports, thus shielding consumers from the full effect of rising costs. Even so, retail prices rose by 4½% in 1970, compared with less than 3% in 1969 and less than 2% in each of the preceding two years. Growth of wage incomes led to a 13% increase in consumer expenditure, compared with 10% in 1969 and only 5½% in 1968. The acceleration in prices, however, kept the increase in volume of consumer expenditure down to 8½%, less than 1% above 1969.

Developments in Italy were somewhat similar. Widespread strikes at the end of 1969 had led to a very inflationary wage settlement, and further large increases by midyear brought the index of hourly wage rates in manufacturing to 22% above the corresponding level in 1969. Productivity continued to rise rapidly, however, so that costs did not increase as sharply as wages. Retail prices rose by 5½%, compared with 2½ and 1½% in 1969 and 1968, respectively. Overall consumer expenditure increased by 14% in current prices and 8% in constant prices, both appreciably faster than in recent years. An unsettled political environment led to some delay in the adoption of effective measures to cool the overheated economy, but by the end of the year the temperature seemed to have been reduced a little.

In most countries, both developed and less developed, retail prices rose faster in 1970 than in 1969. Canada and France were exceptions. The measures of economic restraint taken by the Canadian government in 1969 reduced the rate of growth of output in 1970 and increased the level of unemployment. In addi-

UPI COMPIX

Mrs. Doris Behre, testifying before the U.S. Senate Consumer Subcommittee, shows that a one-eighth-ounce jar of chives at 69 cents would cost $88.32 for one pound if sold at the same rate.

tion, from May the exchange rate of the dollar was permitted to float; it promptly moved upward, which also had a deflationary effect. As a result, the 3½% increase in retail prices was less than in either of the two preceding years. The increase in consumer expenditure—6% in value and 2½% in volume—was well below that of 1968 and 1969.

The French devaluation of August 1969 showed signs of being one of the most successful of such changes in recent years. Following devaluation, "stabilization" measures were immediately taken to check the growth of domestic spending, and by the end of 1969 the trade balance was back to equilibrium. During the first half of 1970 it proved possible to take selective measures of relaxation, including easing of credit for the purchase of durable consumer goods. In 1970 as a whole the volume of consumer expenditure rose by 4%, compared with 7.2% in 1969. Nevertheless, an inflationary problem remained. The growth of wages accelerated a little and retail prices rose by 5% in 1970, compared with 6½% in the previous year.

Many countries had used tighter monetary policies in 1969 to curb excessive growth of demand, and in general these were continued in 1970. However, a wide variety of supplementary measures was also adopted. In Belgium introduction of the value-added tax (VAT), due in January 1970, was deferred for 12 months, partly on the ground that such an increase in indirect taxation would aggravate inflation in an already overheated economy. In the event, Belgium was relatively successful in containing inflation without much slowing down of the growth of output. In 1970 both prices and the volume of consumer expenditure rose by around 4%, about the same as in 1969.

The Belgian government may well have noted the experience of the Netherlands, where introduction of the VAT in 1969 so accentuated inflationary pressure that the retail price index rose by 7%, necessitating imposition of a price freeze by the government that had very limited success in curbing wage demands. Both Sweden and Denmark resorted to price freezes during 1970. In Sweden, where wages and prices grew rapidly and the balance of payments was weak, the freeze on food prices was expanded in October to include goods and services for a six-month period. In Denmark where again a new VAT had aggravated an already severe inflationary situation, a general price freeze was imposed from September.

By contrast, indirect tax increases formed the basis of measures taken in Italy to check the growth of consumer, expenditure. In this the government may have been mindful of the results obtained by increasing indirect taxes in the U.K. between 1965 and 1969, when the growth of consumption volume had been slowed and resources were diverted into exports. During this period the volume of consumer expenditure in the U.K. rose at an average annual rate of only 2%, compared with 3½% a year in the seven preceding years. This slowdown, however, was achieved at the cost of a steep acceleration in prices and mounting wage demands, which burst out in the autumn of 1969.

In 1970 wages and salaries rose by 10%, despite cuts in employment. Retail prices rose by 6%, compared with 5½% in the previous year, but the volume of consumer expenditure rose by 3%, the biggest increase since 1964.

Japan had persistently experienced faster increases in retail prices than other industrialized countries, so the 6% increase in 1970 was not far out of the ordinary. Despite a combination of monetary and fiscal restraints on the economy, consumer expenditure—following record wage awards—remained strong.

Growth of national income in the U.S.S.R. had slowed to 6% in 1969, and there were no signs of a reversal of the trend in 1970. Production of consumer goods continued to grow faster than production of capital goods. Eastern Europe was not exempt from inflationary problems. They were particularly acute in Czechoslovakia, where output and consumption remained high despite the upheavals of political reorganization, but where wage and price controls had to be reinforced. Economic reforms led to a recovery of growth in Hungary. Consumer expenditure in Poland was still being affected by the sharp dip in production growth in 1969.

Early in 1970 the monetary squeeze, which had brought the U.S. economy to the brink of a major recession, was eased. The volume of output fell a little between the third quarter of 1969 and the first quarter of 1970. It began to rise again in the second half and, with higher utilization rates, price inflation eased. The growth of personal incomes slowed during this "mini-recession," but the volume as well as the value of consumer expenditure continued to rise. Spending gathered strength in the second half of 1970; for the year as a whole it increased 7½% in value and 3% in volume.

Slowing and, in some quarters, actual decline of U.S. output growth affected world trade and commodity prices, although consumer expenditure in many of the primary producing and less developed countries reflected the previous year's boom rather than later, more depressing trends. In Australia employment, wages, and spending continued to rise while retail prices only gradually accelerated. In South Africa consumer expenditure slowed from the 10% growth of the previous year but remained strong. The end of the civil war in Nigeria led to an acute price inflation, but increased oil production substantially raised income from exports. Inflation remained endemic in many Latin-American countries, and the volume of consumer expenditure changed little. Among the poorest areas of the world, food production rose faster than population in 1969 only in the

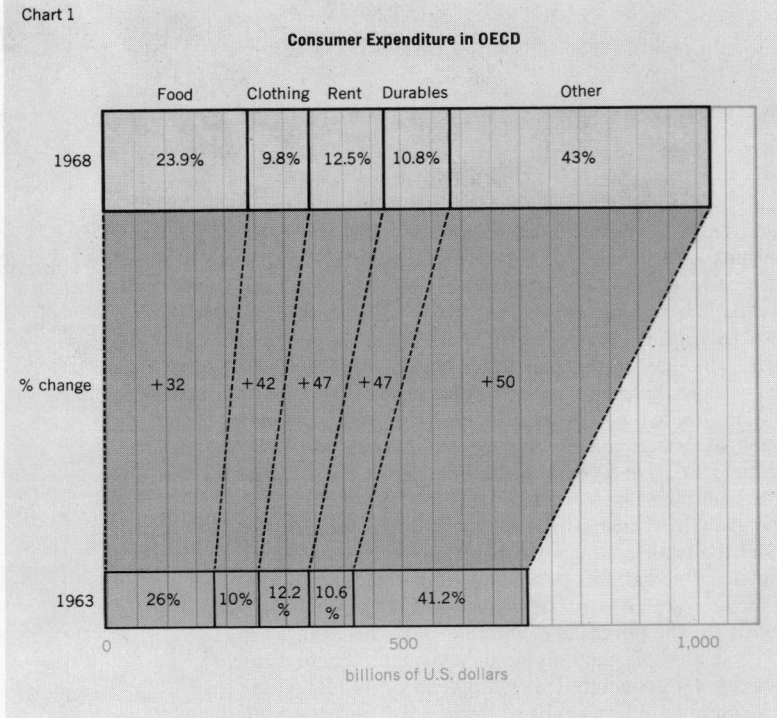

Chart 1

Consumer Expenditure in OECD

billions of U.S. dollars

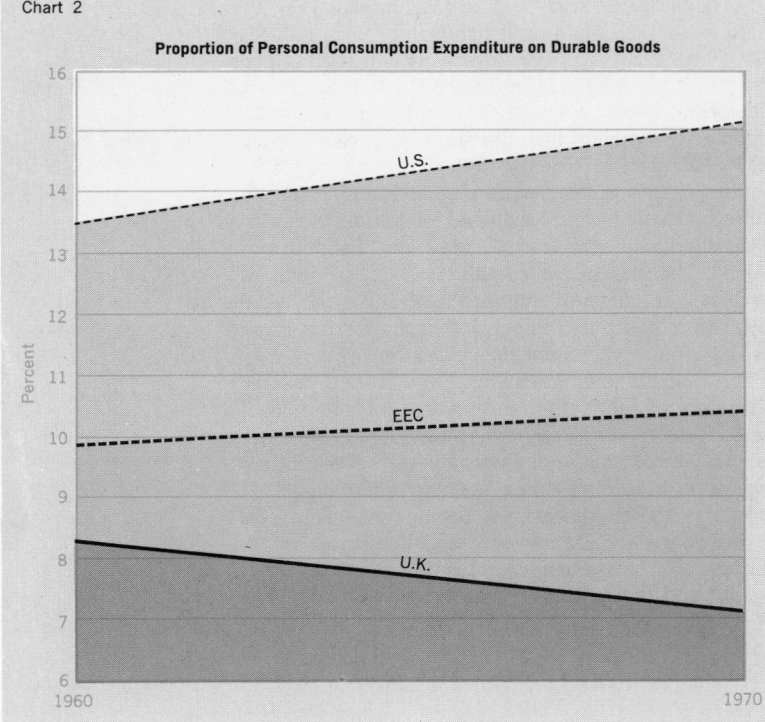

Chart 2

Proportion of Personal Consumption Expenditure on Durable Goods

Table I. Consumer Expenditure in Current Prices

% change from previous year

Region	1967	1968	1969	1970
North America	+ 5.8	+ 8.9	+ 8.0	+ 7.4
EEC	+ 6.4	+ 7.0	+10.4	+11.0
U.K.	+ 4.6	+ 7.4	+ 6.4	+ 9.0
Japan	+13.8	+15.1	+14.0	+16.0
All OECD*	+ 6.4	+ 7.2	+ 8.8	+ 9.0

*Including others.

Table II. Consumer Expenditure at 1963 Prices

% change from previous year

Region	1967	1968	1969	1970
North America	+3.1	+5.2	+3.6	+2.9
EEC	+3.6	+4.0	+6.2	+5.7
U.K.	+2.0	+2.8	+1.1	+3.2
Japan	+9.6	+9.6	+9.2	+9.0
All OECD*	+3.6	+4.9	+4.4	+4.0

*Including others.

Far East. In India agricultural incomes continued to grow in 1970 and industrial production rose quite sharply. Prices began to move upward after two years of near stability, but there was an increase in the volume of per capita consumer expenditure.

The proportion of income that must be spent on food declines as income rises. This is true within countries, between countries, and between periods of time. The latter is illustrated in Chart 1 for the OECD countries combined. The converse is true for durable goods and rent and housing. Spending on services, especially those connected with leisure activities and travel (included in "other" in the chart), was increasing rapidly in the wealthiest countries.

Chart 2 shows how the proportion spent on durables changed during the 1960s in three regions. The high level already reached in the EEC countries by 1960 reflected much faster growth in car ownership than in the U.S. or the U.K. In the U.K. restrictions on credit and high rates of taxation took their toll. The durables proportion in the U.S. tended to level off after 1965 but remained very high. (J. G. M.)

Contract Bridge

In 1970 the United States regained the Bermuda Bowl, the world bridge championship, which it last held in 1954. It did so in Stockholm in June in a tournament that was like *Hamlet* without the prince; the famous Italian Blue Team first won the Bermuda Bowl in 1957 and, with only two changes of personnel in 13 years, had retained the title. When it surrendered the title, it was by an act of abdication after the 1969 victory.

Since the defending champion was Italy, and not the players Pietro Forquet, Benito Garozzo, Walter Avarelli, Giorgio Belladonna, Massimo D'Alelio, and Camillo Pabis Ticci, Italy had the right to be represented in the championship play-off. The team it was able to select was a poor substitute for its illustrious predecessors and took an undistinguished last place behind the United States, Taiwan, Norway, and Brazil. Taiwan was runner-up for the second consecutive year, a splendid performance by relative newcomers.

The central character in the winning team, the new world champions, was Ira Corn, a prominent Dallas, Tex., industrialist and a bridge enthusiast. Corn decided in 1968 that he would create an American team that could regain the world championship. He engaged six young bridge experts, Bill Eisenberg from New York, Bobby Goldman from Philadelphia, Bob Hamman and Mike Lawrence from California, and James Jacoby and Robert Wolff from Texas. He brought them to Dallas where their new occupation was to train to be world bridge champions.

With salaries of up to $25,000 and various incentive schemes, they were free to talk, think, and live bridge. A computer was provided to help them test their theories of bidding. A retired lieutenant colonel of the U.S. Air Force, Joe Musumeci, was hired as team coach and administrator.

In 1969 four of the Dallas Aces, the name under which they played, won places on the North American team for the Bermuda Bowl—and gave an undistinguished performance in the championship. In 1970 the results of two years' work began to tell and the Aces swept the board in the U.S. and qualified with ease to be the North American representatives. In the absence of the Italian Blue Team they found no serious challenge at Stockholm. In the qualifying pool they over-

whelmed all four opponents. Taiwan took second place and so qualified for the final, a series of four short matches against the United States.

Taiwan threatened a surprise when they won the first match 13–7. The United States won the second match 18–2 and one hand in the third match virtually put an end to the contest (*see* box).

Except with the help of an inspired view of the trump position, six spades would be expected to go down. North gave declarer an unexpected chance when he opened a low diamond. West, however, feared that the diamond lead was a singleton (unlikely) and played the ace, subsequently going one down.

At the other table Jacoby and Wolff also tried to play in six clubs but when North–South sacrificed in six hearts, Wolff bid seven clubs on the East hand, gambling on the heart void with his partner. After a heart lead, seven clubs, an excellent contract, was made with the help of the diamond finesse. The United States team went on to win the third match 20–minus 2, making sure of the championship with one match still to play, and it won this last by 19 points to 1.

Corn's ambition achieved, the Dallas Aces were in a position to cash in on their success. But another man and his ambition now appeared on the scene. When Taiwan took second place in the 1969 world championship, an untried team was playing the system of a U.S.-based Chinese, C. C. Wei. The team had had a two-week indoctrination in his methods, based on the Precision Club bidding system, and had gone on to outplay opponents with greater experience and superior playing techniques; then in Stockholm in 1970 Taiwan, again playing the Precision Club and taking second place, once more outplayed opponents with far greater international experience. Wei, therefore, decided that in the right hands his system might possibly beat the world. He persuaded some young U.S. experts to give it a trial and at the first attempt a Precision Club team won one of the two major U.S. championships, the Springold Cup, beating three top U.S. teams on its way to the final and in the final comprehensively defeating no less than the new world champions, the Dallas Aces.

The Precision Club team would now have the chance to qualify as the North American representa-

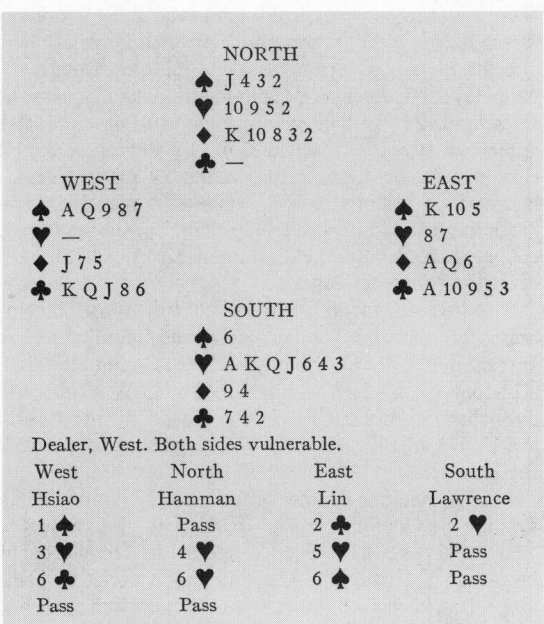

NORTH
♠ J 4 3 2
♥ 10 9 5 2
♦ K 10 8 3 2
♣ —

WEST
♠ A Q 9 8 7
♥ —
♦ J 7 5
♣ K Q J 8 6

EAST
♠ K 10 5
♥ 8 7
♦ A Q 6
♣ A 10 9 5 3

SOUTH
♠ 6
♥ A K Q J 6 4 3
♦ 9 4
♣ 7 4 2

Dealer, West. Both sides vulnerable.

West	North	East	South
Hsiao	Hamman	Lin	Lawrence
1 ♠	Pass	2 ♣	2 ♥
3 ♥	4 ♥	5 ♥	Pass
6 ♣	6 ♥	6 ♠	Pass
Pass	Pass		

tives for the next Bermuda Bowl. And the Dallas Aces would have to battle with them in the coming year not only for the championship but in the struggle to persuade the bridge-playing and bridge-reading public that theirs was the system to adopt.

Also at Stockholm in June Mrs. B. Brier and W. von Zedwitz of the U.S. (14,239 points) won the world Pairs Olympiad; Mrs. R. Markus (U.K.) and George Catzeflis (Switz.) were a close second (14,101 points).   (HA. FR.)

Cooperatives

Structural changes in the international cooperative movement were consolidated during 1970, and new proposals for further integration of the consumer movement were accepted in a number of countries. The importance of cooperation in the social and economic development of the less developed countries was recognized by several governments.

In Denmark the plan for amalgamation of the cooperative wholesale society and the retail societies into one national society was considered by the annual congress held in June. A proposal for a national society in the Netherlands was rejected, but 8 of the 17 regional societies agreed to come under the management of CO-OP Nederland. In the U.K. amalgamation of societies continued, and a move toward central control within the British consumer movement was approved by the congress held in May. It was agreed to transfer the Co-operative Union's Trade Advisory Services to the Co-operative Wholesale Society.

On February 23 Guyana proclaimed itself a "co-operative republic." Cooperation was declared to be the means for establishing social and economic democracy in the country. A bank was opened on the first day of the republic to channel funds to various cooperative ventures.

Pres. Kenneth Kaunda of Zambia outlined a change in government policy, from agricultural cooperatives to service and general-purpose cooperatives. The Co-operative Fertilizers International, organized in 1967 by U.S. cooperatives to assist Indian cooperatives in setting up a fertilizer plant, was to receive substantial loans from the U.S. and British governments. The U.S. government promised to advance $15 million through the Agency for International Development and the British government, $16.8 million through the Ministry of Overseas Development. Indian cooperatives and the Indian government and its agencies agreed to provide $110 million. In Ceylon a Royal Commission on Cooperation made 29 major recommendations about the cooperative movement. The most important proposed the setting up of a national cooperative development council to coordinate cooperative development.

The International Cooperative Alliance. To commemorate the 75th anniversary of the founding of the International Cooperative Alliance in London in 1895, a history of the ICA, written by W. P. Watkins, was published in August 1970. The postal authorities in the U.K. and Belgium issued postage stamps to mark the occasion.

At the meeting of the ICA Central Committee in London in October, it was decided to designate the years 1971–80 as the "Co-operative Development Decade." The program would include a series of planning studies geared to specific cooperative projects in less developed countries; fund-raising drives in

member movements and increased contributions to the ICA Development Fund; increased exchange of information among member movements on the promotion of cooperatives in less developed countries; and intensive collaboration with UN agencies. A committee was set up including representatives from the ICA and several other interested organizations to identify and prepare appropriate projects for making better use of available resources and to coordinate the experiences of intergovernmental organizations in providing technical assistance.

A seminar on "Cooperative Management for the Seventies" took place in Madison, Wis., in September, the first time such a seminar had been held outside Europe. A European symposium on "The Contribution of the Cooperative Movement to the Integration of Rural Families into Modern Society" took place in Milan in September. The first meeting of the newly established ICA Working Party of the Cooperative Press was held near Vienna in December. This was followed by a conference, organized by the Vienna Development Institute, the ICA, and the Austrian cooperative movement, to consider the role of the cooperative press in providing information about cooperative progress in less developed countries.

The work of the ICA Regional Office and Education Centre for South East Asia was considered at the meeting of the Advisory Council for South East Asia, held in Seoul, Korea, in May. At the earlier Agricultural Sub-Committee meeting it had been decided to set up a working group for promotion of trade in agricultural commodities. A proposal was accepted to conduct a survey of agricultural marketing projects, financed by the ICA, the Central Union of Agricultural Cooperatives of Japan, and the cooperative movements in Southeast Asia in membership with the ICA, in order to accelerate the development of cooperative agricultural marketing.

"Cooperative Management" was the subject of a seminar organized by the Regional Office and the Cooperative Union of Singapore, held in Singapore in April. A commodity conference on "Fruits and Vegetables and Feedingstuffs" met in Tokyo in May under the auspices of the Regional Office, the Central Union of Agricultural Cooperatives of Japan, and the Institute for the Development of Agricultural Cooperation. It was followed by a regional seminar on "Marketing of Fruit and Vegetables Through Cooperatives." The second housing seminar in Southeast Asia, organized by the ICA Regional Office and financed by the Swedish cooperative movement to consider "Development of Housing Cooperatives in South-East Asia," was held in Kuala Lumpur, Malaysia, from October 19 to November 3.

A number of seminars were organized throughout the year in the four African countries in membership with the ICA, Kenya, Tanzania, Uganda, and Zambia. Seminars were held for cooperative education secretaries, cooperative teachers, and cooperative committeemen, as well as on problems of cooperative marketing. Several women's cooperative seminars, financed by the Swedish International Development Authority and women cooperators in the Nordic countries, took place in Kenya, Tanzania, and Uganda. The Latin American Technical Institute for Cooperative Integration introduced a uniform bookkeeping and stockkeeping system in some consumer societies in Brazil, Guatemala, Colombia, and Ecuador.

The ICA Insurance Committee reported progress in cooperative insurance at a meeting in Columbus,

Copper:
see Mining

Corn:
see Agriculture

O., in May. Proposals for collaboration between co-operative insurance societies were discussed. The Insurance Development Bureau allocated $24,000 to assist insurance cooperatives in less developed countries and $6,000 to provide scholarships for cooperative insurance students. A seminar for cooperative construction and housing societies, organized by the Committee of Workers' Co-operative Productive and Artisanal Societies of the ICA in collaboration with the Housing Committee, was held in Paris in May to discuss modern management methods and the development of prefabrication and industrialization in the building industry.

The ICA Housing Committee meeting in London in September discussed collaboration with UN agencies and other international nongovernmental organizations, with special reference to a study of nonprofit and cooperative housing undertaken by the Committee on Housing of the Economic Commission for Europe (ECE). The annual meeting of the International Cooperative Housing Development Association received a report on "Interim Technical Assistance to the Government of Tanzania." Following a feasibility study carried out in 1969 to develop cooperative housing in East Africa, a pilot scheme was initiated in Tanzania and the construction of the first 60 dwellings was begun.

At the annual meeting of the Cooperative Wholesale Committee in London, it was reported that nonfood sales had increased from $16.5 million in 1968 to $31.1 million in 1969. The largest increase was registered in textiles, while food sales decreased during the same period. At a joint meeting of members of the Cooperative Wholesale Committee and the Committee on Retail Distribution, held in London in September, it was decided to amalgamate the two committees under the name of INTER-COOP.

Membership and Trade. At the end of 1970, the number of cooperative federations in membership with the ICA totaled 141 in 59 countries. The latest available statistics showed a further decrease in the total number of societies in membership with the ICA, from 593,712 in 1967 to 533,467 in 1968. Membership within these societies fell from 255.5 million in 1967 to 255 million in 1968. The apparent decline was partly due to amalgamations and partly to the fact that some of the societies had not supplied statistical data for the period under review. The largest membership was again reported by the U.S.S.R. (over 57 million), followed by India (over 54 million). Of the total membership, the greatest proportion was in consumer societies (44.21%), followed by credit societies (30.09%), agricultural societies (13.98%), miscellaneous societies (6.25%), building and housing societies (2.75%), workers' productive and artisanal societies (2.13%), and fisheries societies (0.59%).

At the end of 1969, 29 cooperative organizations and 22 banks from 21 different countries were shareholders in the International Cooperative Bank. Assets rose from £36,790,000 in 1968 to £55,070,000 in 1969.

A barter arrangement was concluded between the National Federation of Industrial Cooperatives of India and Centrosoyus, U.S.S.R., under which the National Federation would supply nylon and woolen knitwear in exchange for sunflower-seed oil from the Soviet Union. The National Agricultural Cooperative Marketing Federation of India and UNICOOP Japan concluded a trade agreement during the year.

(L. KE.)

Cosmetics

A noticeable change in the type of new product being given the "hard-sell" treatment by cosmetics firms in 1970 suggested an all-out attempt to regain the custom of the older woman. Over the preceding decade, emphasis had been on "looks"—in a word, on makeup. In 1970 there was a return to the earlier concept of skin care. A great deal was heard about the "pH" factor in products—an acid/alkaline balance which, when correctly proportioned, was said by specialists in the field to produce "the flawless complexion." Another essential property claimed for the pH factor in preparations was the control of skin bacteria.

Preoccupation with the face beneath the makeup was the 1970 message from such leading beauty firms as Revlon ("Moon Drops Face Care Collection"), Elizabeth Arden ("Directional Collection"), and Orlane (Rosée Démaquillante Cleansing Gel, "with a pH of 5–6 suitable for all types of skin"). Packaging, too, showed signs of greater simplicity, aimed, it would seem, at the more thoughtful taste of the older woman. Revlon's Moon Drops Face Care preparations were marketed in workmanlike roll-on containers, swivel sticks, and plastic packs.

A survey of beauty and toilet products carried out in 1970 revealed that 85% of women use lipstick, 92% use talcum powder, and 80% use smooth-on fragrance in one of its many forms. The survey also showed that use of these three top-selling products begins in the 12–13 age group and continues up to the 60- and 70-year-olds.

In line with the vogue for "unisex" clothes, the French firm Roger et Gallet promoted their famous Extra-Vieille Jean-Marie Farina Eau de Cologne in Britain as a unisex toilet water. In her unremitting search for up-to-the-minute ideas and gimmicks, in cosmetics as well as in clothes, Britain's Mary Quant introduced a new range of stick-fast makeup preparations labeled "Make-up to Make love in." "Love," Miss Quant is reported to have said, "is the destroyer of the beautiful face." Available in medium, dark, and bronze shades, Mary Quant's Colour Stick was said to have long-lasting adhesive properties. The range also included a stubbornly clinging eye tint.

Water-colour eye shadow, first marketed in the top and medium price ranges, was made available in cheaper brands. Mixed with a drop of water and painted on, these shadows could be applied in either intense or subtle shades. They were said to be proof against caking, fading, and streaking. "Beauty Without Cruelty Cosmetics," founded by Lady Dowding in 1959 within the framework of the Beauty Without Cruelty campaign, continued to make progress. The 1970 price list included 50 animal product-free beauty and hygiene aids prepared from nut, plant, and fruit oils blended with flower essences.   (P. W. HE.)

See also Fashion and Dress.

Costa Rica

A Central American republic, Costa Rica lies between Nicaragua and Panama and has coastlines on the Caribbean Sea and the Pacific Ocean. Area: 19,650 sq.mi. (50,900 sq.km.). Pop. (1969 est.): 1,685,170, including white and mestizo 97.6%. Cap. and largest

city: San José (pop., 1969 est., 203,148). Language: Spanish. Religion: predominantly Roman Catholic. Presidents in 1970, José Joaquín Trejos Fernández and, from May 8, José Figueres Ferrer.

Maintaining its traditional stability, Costa Rica continued in 1970 to strengthen its domestic economy, while a change of government removed a political stumbling block to closer cooperation with its four fellow members of the Central American Common Market (CACM). In the general election on February 1, José Figueres Ferrer (*see* BIOGRAPHY) of the Partido de Liberación Nacional emerged as president (an office he had filled from 1954 to 1958) with an absolute majority, and his party won 32 of the Legislative Assembly's 57 seats. Figueres took office on May 8 and, armed with a majority in Congress, later secured ratification of the San José Protocol. This belated endorsement of an agreement signed on June 1, 1968, by all five CACM governments paved the way for cooperation within an economic framework to which Costa Rica's neighbours were already committed. Another midyear development of significance was an agreement with the U.S.S.R. to exchange commercial representatives. Among the trade deals envisaged was an exchange of Costa Rican primary products for Soviet capital equipment.

Agriculture remained the mainstay of the economy. In 1969, although crops and communications suffered badly from Hurricane Martha in November, the gross domestic product grew by 7.7%. In April 1970 severe floods did extensive damage to banana plantations, housing, and transport in the Caribbean region, but the outlook for coffee exports was promising. The export quota for the 1969–70 crop was 1,370,000 quintals (1 quintal = 220.46 lb.) of which 1,060,000 were sold at an average price of $45 per quintal against $37 for the 1968–69 crop. Mainly

because of higher prices, 1969–70 coffee exports were expected to be worth $15 million more than the previous season's shipments.

Industrial development continued with the opening of new processing and manufacturing plants. The growth of industrial output in the first half of 1970 represented a 12.2% increase in the period from June 1969 to June 1970 against a 5.9% increase in the preceding 12 months. On preliminary estimates the value of manufactured exports in the first half of 1970 was $23.9 million, 13.3% more than in the first half of 1969.

The 1970 budget estimates put revenue at 753.8 million colones and expenditure at 809 million colones. How much had been allocated for investment was unclear, but it was officially stated that public investment over the four-year period 1969–72 would absorb 1,421,000,000 colones, about 80% more than was actually invested during the preceding four years. By June 30 Costa Rica had obtained external loans totaling $31 million for highway and other communications projects, industrial development, and farm research.

In terms of its per capita income ($387) and economic growth rate, Costa Rica compared favourably with its Central American neighbours. The combination of public investment, supported by external loans, with foreign funds for private investment was expected to sustain the momentum of economic development. (Ro. E. S.)

COSTA RICA

Education. (1966–67) Primary, pupils 296,058, teachers 10,742; secondary, pupils 47,823, teachers 2,570; vocational (public only), pupils 3,788, teachers 209; teacher training, students 1,759, teachers 22; higher (including University of Costa Rica), students 7,502, teaching staff 653.

Finance. Monetary unit: colón, with a par value of 6.625 colones to U.S. $1 (15.90 colones = £1 sterling). Gold, SDRs, and foreign exchange, central bank: (June 1970) U.S. $30,370,000; (June 1969) U.S. $30.9 million. Budget (1969 est.): revenue 624.5 million colones; expenditure 720 million colones. Gross national product: (1968) 4,935,000,000 colones; (1967) 4,486,000,000 colones. Money supply: (March 1970) 1,007,400,000 colones; (March 1969) 915 million colones. Cost of living (San José; 1963 = 100): (May 1970) 116; (May 1969) 111.

Foreign Trade. (1969) Imports 1,616,200,000 colones; exports 1,279,300,000 colones. Import sources (1968): U.S. 38%; West Germany 8%; El Salvador 8%; Guatemala 7%; Japan 7%; Nicaragua 6%. Export destinations (1968): U.S. 47%; Nicaragua 8%; West Germany 6%; El Salvador 5%; Guatemala 5%. Main exports: bananas 30%; coffee 29%.

Transport and Communications. Roads (1968) *c.* 10,000 km. (including *c.* 5,000 km. all-weather and 660 km. of Pan-American Highway). Motor vehicles in use (1968): passenger 33,700; commercial (including buses) 17,900. Railways (1968): 703 km.; traffic 71 million passenger-km. Air traffic (1969): 122.6 million passenger-km.; freight 10,650,000 net ton-km. Telephones (Jan. 1969) 50,093. Radio receivers (Dec. 1969) *c.* 106,000. Television receivers (Dec. 1967) 66,000.

Agriculture. Production (in 000; metric tons; 1968; 1967 in parentheses): coffee 77 (83); bananas 703 (512); sugar, raw value (1969–70) 167, (1968–69) 144. Livestock (in 000): cattle (1968–69) 1,435; horses (1967–68) *c.* 109; pigs (1966–67) 243.

Industry. Electricity production (1968) 833 million kw-hr. (92% hydroelectric).

Cricket

All the major cricket-playing countries except the West Indies were engaged in competition between September 1969 and August 1970. India played six tests, three each against New Zealand and Australia, while Pakistan played three against New Zealand. South Africa played four tests against Australia, and England played five against a Rest of the World XI.

The major event of the year, in which politics played an unsavoury part, was the cancellation of a South African tour of England. The English Test and County Cricket Board, despite threats of violence, damage to grounds, and disruption of matches by organized protesters against South Africa's racial separation policy, stood firm till the government at the 11th hour brought pressure to compel them to abandon the tour. In exchange, a series was hastily arranged against a Rest of the World XI, captained by G. S. Sobers, which included four other West Indians, four South Africans, and representatives of Australia, India, and Pakistan. This brilliant team won four of the five tests, but England, captained by R. Illingworth, won one test and was rarely outplayed. Sobers made 588 runs, including two 100s and three 50s, and took the most wickets (21, including a spell of six for 21). C. H. Lloyd (W.I.) and E. J. Barlow (S.Af.) each made two centuries, and R. B. Kanhai (W.I.) and R. G. Pollock (S.Af.) scored one each. Barlow also took 20 wickets, including a spell of seven for 64 that contained a hat trick and four wickets in five balls. Other good bowling performances were by Intikhab Alam (Pak.) six for 113, and M. J. Procter (S.Af.) five for 46.

For England, G. Boycott, B. W. Luckhurst, and B. L. D'Oliveira each scored a century, but the batsman of the series was Illingworth, who scored 476 runs, including two 90s and four other 50s in nine innings. In the third test at Edgbaston, D'Oliveira made 110 and 81. M. C. Cowdrey recovered from his achilles tendon injury in 1969 to play in four tests and made three 50s, while K. W. R. Fletcher (four 50s) also performed well. J. A. Snow (19 wickets) was the backbone of the bowling, followed by Illingworth (11 wickets). The best individual performance was seven for 83 by P. Lever in his first and only test.

South Africa v. Australia. Australia under W. M. Lawry suffered humiliating defeat in South Africa, losing all four tests by wide margins. South Africa, under A. Bacher, had a fine batting side, fielded brilliantly, and had a formidable fast bowling partnership of Procter and P. M. Pollock, who took 26 and 15 wickets, respectively, at low cost. Medium-paced support came from Barlow and T. L. Goddard, and South Africa had little need to use spin. South Africa's leading batsmen were R. G. Pollock and B. A. Richards, each of whom made more than 500 runs in seven innings. Pollock made the record South African score of 274 in the second test, in which Richards made 140. Barlow made two centuries and one 50, and B. L. Irvine one century and two 50s. In contrast Australian batsmen rarely mastered the fast bowling, and only two bowlers, A. N. Connolly (20 wickets) and J. W. Gleeson (19 wickets), showed international class. Australia's major bowling disappointment was the total eclipse of G. D. McKenzie, who took only one wicket in the series.

South Africa won the first test at Cape Town by 170 runs. South Africa made 382 (Barlow 127, A. A. Mallett five for 126) and 232 (G. Pollock 50, Connolly five for 47); Australia made 164 (K. D. Walters 73) and 280 (Lawry 83). South Africa won the second test at Durban by an innings and 129 runs. South Africa scored 622 for nine declared (G. Pollock 274, Richards 140); Australia replied with 157 (A. P. Sheahan 62) and 336 (K. R. Stackpole 71, Walters 74, I. R. Redpath not out 74). South Africa won the third test at Johannesburg by 307 runs, making 279 (Irvine 79, Richards 65, G. Pollock 52) and 408 (Barlow 110, G. Pollock 87, Irvine 73, Gleeson five for 125); and Australia scored 202 (Walters 64, P. Pollock five for 39) and 178 (Redpath 66). South Africa won the fourth test at Port Elizabeth by 323 runs, scoring 311 (Richards 81, Barlow 73, Connolly six for 47) and 470 for eight declared (Richards 126, Irvine 102, Bacher 73, D. Lindsay 60); Australia made 212 (Sheahan 67, Redpath 55) and 246 (Procter six for 73).

India v. New Zealand. New Zealand, on the way home from touring England in 1969, drew a three-match series with India. After India had won the first test and New Zealand the second, India was in a hopeless position in the third when rain saved them from defeat. The batting of both sides was slow and defensive. India relied on slow bowling and New Zealand on fast medium, and the latter team's fielding was far superior.

India won the first test at Bombay by 60 runs. India, under the nawab of Pataudi, made 156 and 260 (Pataudi 67); New Zealand, under G. T. Dowling, replied with 229 (B. E. Congdon 78) and 127 (B. S. Bedi six for 42). New Zealand won the second test at Nagpur by 167 runs, scoring 319 (M. G. Burgess 89, Dowling 69, Congdon 64) and 214 (G. M. Turner 57, S. Venkatdraghavan six for 74) to India's 257 (S. Abid Ali 63) and 109 (H. J. Howarth five for 34). The third test at Hyderabad was drawn. New Zealand made 181 (B. A. G. Murray 80, E. A. S. Prasanna

SPORT & GENERAL FROM PICTORIAL PARADE

During the fourth test match at Headingley, G. Sobers (captain, Rest of the World) just reaches his wicket to avoid being run out as A. Knott (England wicketkeeper) breaks the wicket.

five for 51) and 175 for eight declared (Dowling 60), to which India replied with 89 and 76 for seven.

Pakistan v. New Zealand. New Zealand moved on to Pakistan and won a three-match rubber 1–0. The cricket was more positive than in India, and Dowling and his travel-weary team deservedly triumphed. Burgess and Turner each made a century and Howarth (slow left arm) was the outstanding bowler. For Pakistan, captained by Intikhab Alam, the most successful batsmen were Asif Iqbal, Sadiq Mohammad, and Younis Ahmed, while Pervez Sajjad, with 22 wickets, was the leading bowler. The first test at Karachi was drawn. Pakistan made 220 (Sadiq 69, Howarth five for 80) and 283 for eight declared (Younis 62), and New Zealand 274 (D. R. Hadlee 56, Murray 50, Muhammad Nazir seven for 99) and 112 for five (Pervez five for 33). New Zealand won the second test at Lahore by five wickets. Pakistan made 114 and 208 (Shafquat Rana 95) to New Zealand's 241 (Murray 90, B. F. Hastings not out 80, Pervez seven for 74) and 82 for five. The third test at Dacca was drawn. New Zealand scored 273 (Turner 110, Burgess 59, Intikhab five for 92) and 200 (Burgess 119 not out, Intikhab five for 91) to Pakistan's 290 for seven declared (Asif Iqbal 92, Shafquat Rana 65) and 51 for four (R. S. Cunis four for 20).

India v. Australia. India entertained Australia, which was en route to South Africa, in a five-match series. After holding their own for three tests, the Indians collapsed in the last two and Australia, despite political and nationalistic disturbances, deservedly won the rubber 3–1. All the leading Australian batsmen played at least one good innings, and I. M. Chappell, Stackpole, Walters, and Sheahan each scored one century. The most successful bowlers were Mallett, McKenzie, and Connolly.

Australia won the first test at Bombay by eight wickets. India made 271 (Pataudi 95, Mankad 74, McKenzie five for 69) and 137; and Australia replied with 345 (Stackpole 103, Redpath 77, Prasanna five for 121) and 67 for two. The second test at Kanpur was drawn. India made 320 (F. M. Engineer 77, Mankad 64) and 312 for seven declared (G. R. Vishwanath 137, Mankad 68); Australia scored 348 (Sheahan 114, Redpath 70, Walters 53) and 95 for no wicket (Lawry 56 not out). India won the third test at New Delhi by seven wickets. Australia scored 296 (Chappell 138, Stackpole 61) and 107 (Lawry not out 49, Bedi five for 37, Prasanna five for 42) against India's 223 (Mankad 97, Mallett six for 64) and 181 for three (Wadekar not out 91). Australia won the fourth test at Calcutta by ten wickets. India got 212 (Vishwanath 54, McKenzie six for 67) and 161 (Wadekar 62), and Australia 335 (Chappell 99, Walters 56, Bedi seven for 98) and 42 for no wicket. Australia won the fifth test at Madras by 77 runs. Australia made 258 (Walters 102) and 153 (Redpath 63, Prasanna six for 74); India made 163 (Pataudi 59, Mallett five for 91) and 171 (Vishwanath 59, Wadekar 55, Mallett five for 53).

County and National Cricket. For the first time since 1913 Kent, captained by Cowdrey, won the county championship, with Glamorgan, the defending champions, second and Lancashire third. Kent's success was remarkable because they had contributed five players to the England XI. In another fine summer four batsmen—Turner, R. T. Virgin, J. B. Bolus, and Boycott—all made more than 2,000 runs and four men, all slow bowlers, took more than 100 wickets—D. J. Shepherd, F. J. Titmus, N. Gifford, and R. N. S. Hobbs. Lancashire won the Gillette Cup, beating Sussex by six wickets, and retained the John Player Sunday League title, with Kent second and Derbyshire third. Sobers easily headed the batting averages and T. W. Graveney, in his last season in English cricket before taking up an appointment as coach in Queensland, was second. The leading all-rounders were Sobers, Mushtaq Mohammad, P. M. Walker, A. W. Greig, and Intikhab. The first four made more than 1,000 runs and took over 50 wickets, and Intikhab's figures were 923 runs and 86 wickets.

In Australia, Victoria won the Sheffield Shield, and Otago won the Plunket Shield in New Zealand. In South Africa, Transvaal and Western Province shared the Currie Cup, and in the West Indies Trinidad won the Shell Shield. (A. R. A.)

Crime

John Linley Frazier in Santa Cruz County (Calif.) jail after his arraignment on five counts of murder in the slayings of Victor Ohta, three members of Ohta's family, and Ohta's secretary.

WIDE WORLD

In 1970, governments perplexed and disillusioned by burgeoning crime rates appeared ever less impressed by theoretical explanations and justifications of the state of crime and ever more concerned to discover pragmatic solutions to the problems of crime control. Leading this development was the United States, which experienced throughout the 1960s "unusual increases in crime and criminal behavior" (J. Edgar Hoover, *Uniform Crime Reports 1969*). The new and growing demands this increase placed upon law enforcement agencies was recognized in the far-reaching survey made of crime in the U.S. by a commission appointed in 1968 by Pres. Lyndon B. Johnson.

Implementation of many of the recommendations made by this commission gathered considerable momentum in 1970. Congressional appropriations totaling $268 million for fiscal 1970, compared with $63 million in fiscal 1969, included substantial funds for applied research promising immediate benefits in such fields as communications, detection, and apprehension. Longer term benefits were intended to emerge from extensive programs to upgrade recruiting standards and training schedules for law enforcement personnel.

U.S. government concern about crime was also reflected in the continuing spate of research reports produced in 1970 by official commissions investigating violence, pornography, and allied ills. The National Commission on the Causes and Prevention of Violence concluded in its final report that violence was "corroding the central political processes" of U.S. society. The commission urged a doubling of investment in the prevention of crime and the administration of justice and recommended a national policy limiting the availability of handguns.

This latter recommendation appeared to provoke as much public controversy as a subsequent proposal, made by a majority of members of the National Commission on Obscenity and Pornography, that the government should not interfere with the freedom of adults to view, read, or obtain obscene or pornographic material. In the opinion of these members, there was no evidence that such material caused crime or other forms of depravity. In 1969 a similar view seems to have motivated an Obscenity Laws Working Party, sponsored by the Arts Council of Great Britain, to propose that restrictive laws should be dismantled for an experimental period of five years in the U.K. Despite these recommendations, it appeared most unlikely that either the U.S. or U.K. governments would, at least in the immediate future, follow Denmark and repeal the majority of obscenity laws. Meanwhile, Danish experience continued to suggest that depravity and corruption were not inevitable adjuncts of law reform in this area.

A worldwide trend to liberalize abortion laws continued throughout 1970. The state of South Australia, for instance, introduced new legislation on abortion modeled upon the U.K. Abortion Act of 1967. In Britain, the influx of women from other countries seeking abortions—estimated at 4,000 annually—led critics to claim that the U.K. was becoming the abortion centre of the West. However, reform of U.S. abortion laws during 1970, particularly in New York State, seemed likely to stop much of this traffic.

International trafficking in drugs, and the growing incidence of drug abuse in many Western countries, continued to receive close attention and study by national and international agencies. Emphasis upon civil rather than criminal law processes to deal with the problems of drug abuse was called for by an increasing number of experts. Citing as support the failure in the U.S. of draconian measures to deter drug use and abuse, these experts pointed to the need for far more treatment facilities for drug-dependent persons.

Heated debate concerning the drug marijuana raged in many countries in 1970. Concluding that moderate consumption of marijuana produced no obvious harmful effects upon users, Canadian and British commissions studying drug problems, while not recommending legalization of marijuana, urged substantial reductions in the penalties imposed for the use of the drug and suggested that legislative and allied controls over marijuana be divorced entirely from those related to other narcotics.

The liberal approach of the Dutch toward homosexuals was also viewed with interest. Some countries, including the U.K., subsequently reformed their laws to reflect changed attitudes toward homosexuality. In 1970 active campaigns to further this liberal trend were launched in, among other countries, the U.S., Australia, and New Zealand. Canada, following the lead set by the U.K. Sexual Offences Act, 1967, reformed its law during 1969, so that homosexual acts between consenting adults in private were no longer criminal offenses.

The fourth UN Congress on the Prevention of Crime and the Treatment of Offenders was held at Kyoto, Jap., on August 17–26. The congress, held for the first time in Asia, was attended by over 1,100 participants from 82 countries. One interesting finding of the congress was that the rapid changes in patterns of crime over the previous 25 years contrasted sharply with the relatively slow changes in criminal law and penal codes. A nine-member ad hoc group of delegates considered the problems of hijacking; several speakers urged a new law to make the seizure of aircraft in the air an international crime. A summation of the current progress in criminal justice research and development took place at the sixth International Congress on Criminology, which met in Madrid, Spain, in September. (Du. C.)

Major Crimes. Bombings created a major crime problem in 1970. In the U.S., in the 15-month period from Jan. 1, 1969, through March 1970, there were 4,330 actual bombings resulting in over 40 deaths and property damage of $21.8 million, 1,475 attempted bombings, and 35,129 bomb threats. On July 23, 1970, a federal grand jury in Detroit indicted 13 leaders of the Weatherman faction of Students for a Democratic Society (SDS) on charges of conspiring to bomb and kill. The indictment attempted to link a Weatherman meeting in Flint, Mich., in December 1969 with bomb making in New York City and an arms cache found in Chicago. In the wreckage of a town house blown up on March 6 in New York City's Greenwich Village, police discovered 60 sticks of dynamite, some blasting caps, and three bodies of persons later identified as Weatherman members. After another explosion shattered a Lower East Side apartment on March 28, police found several live bombs, bomb-making materials, firearms, Black Panther party literature, and a map showing the sites of police stations and firehouses.

A thunderous explosion ripped the old Federal Office Building in Minneapolis, Minn., on August 17, and on August 24, at 3:45 A.M., a bomb ripped through the six-story, reinforced concrete building of the Army Mathematics Research Center on the University of Wisconsin campus in Madison, killing a research assistant and injuring four other persons. On September 2, the FBI announced it had initiated a nationwide search for four young men, reportedly admirers of Cuban Prime Minister Fidel Castro, who were charged with the Madison bombing. Early on the morning of October 14 an explosion ripped through the Center for International Affairs at Harvard University. On December 5 an explosion at the Humble Oil and Refining Co. plant in Linden, N.J., injured 30 persons.

On Jan. 5, 1970, the bodies of Joseph A. Yablonski, defeated candidate in a bitterly disputed election for president of the United Mine Workers union, his wife and daughter were found in the Yablonski home in Clarksville, Pa. A federal grand jury in Cleveland, O., indicted three men on charges of conspiracy to kill Yablonski and, because Yablonski was to have been a witness before a federal grand jury investigating election fraud charges, of obstructing justice and also depriving Yablonski of his civil rights. A later indictment accused Silous Huddleston, president of a UMW local, of "directing" the others in carrying out the slaying.

California Superior Court Judge Harold J. Haley and three of his kidnappers were killed and three persons wounded on August 7, when police blocked a commandeered van outside the Marin County Hall of Justice in San Rafael. The kidnappers were three San Quentin convicts, James D. McClain, William Arthur Christmas, and Ruchell Magee, and Jonathan

P. Jackson, brother of one of the "Soledad Brothers," three black prisoners charged with murdering a white guard at California's Soledad prison. Jackson had slipped the kidnappers' guns into Judge Haley's courtroom. On August 16 a warrant was issued for black militant Angela Davis (*see* BIOGRAPHY) after evidence showed that she had purchased the shotgun used to kill Judge Haley. Miss Davis was arrested in New York City on October 13.

After a trial filled with courtroom disruptions, on Feb. 18, 1970, a Chicago jury acquitted seven defendants of conspiring to incite a riot during the 1968 Democratic national convention. (*See* LAW: *Special Report.*) Late in the year hearings were held on whether the presiding judge or federal marshals had improperly influenced the jury during its deliberations. The trial of seven of eight persons charged with conspiracy to damage the Seattle, Wash., Federal Building (the "Seattle 8") began in Tacoma on November 23.

At Ann Arbor, Mich., on August 19, John Norman Collins, a former college student, was convicted of the first-degree murder of Karen Sue Beineman, one of seven young women killed in the Ann Arbor area in 1967–69. The first-degree murder trial of Charles Manson and three women members of his hippie "family" for the slayings of actress Sharon Tate and six other persons in August 1969 began in Los Angeles on June 16 and for the rest of the year was marked by disruptions by the defendants, including those prompted by a remark by Pres. Richard Nixon that Manson was "guilty," and by the disappearance of a defense lawyer in December.

Black militant H. Rap Brown was placed on the FBI's most wanted list on May 5, 1970, after he failed to appear for trial in Ellicott City, Md., on charges stemming from a riot in Cambridge, Md., in 1967. In March 1970 two of Brown's friends were killed when a bomb exploded in their automobile about a mile from the Bel Air, Md., courthouse, where Brown had failed to appear for his scheduled trial.

Martin Sweig, former chief administrative aide to U.S. House Speaker John W. McCormack (Dem., Mass.), was found guilty of one count of perjury in a New York federal court in 1970, but was acquitted of

WIDE WORLD

Arthur G. Barkley holds a pistol in the cockpit of the TWA 727 he hijacked from Phoenix, Ariz., June 4. He was rushed and subdued but not before he shot the captain, Dale C. Hupe, in the abdomen.

WIDE WORLD

A policeman inspects a car damaged by a bomb blast that destroyed much of the Army Mathematics Research Center and killed a staff member at the University of Wisconsin in Madison on Aug. 24, 1970.

JIM KEAN

Above, James McClain points a pistol at Judge Harold Haley while keeping a grip on the shotgun taped to the judge's neck during an attempted escape from the Marin County (Calif.) courthouse. At right, police converge on the getaway van seconds after the shooting stopped. Four persons including Judge Haley and McClain were killed.

conspiring to use the prestige of Speaker McCormack's office to defraud government agencies and for personal gain. Nathan M. Voloshen, a Washington lobbyist, pled guilty to the conspiracy charge. Unusual legal issues came to light in Alexandria, Va., on July 30, 1970, when a technician, Mario Jaime Escamilla, of Santa Barbara, Calif., was charged, under special maritime laws that apply to ships at sea, with killing Bennie Lightsy, of Louisville, Ky., leader of a research team, on Fletcher's Ice Island floating about 325 mi. from the North Pole. A key question was whether Escamilla could be tried in a U.S. court since it had not been decided previously that an iceberg is a "ship at sea."

The longest criminal trial in Japan's history ended on Jan. 28, 1970, when 110 defendants were found not guilty and 93 found guilty of the crime of "rioting" on May Day 1952. The presiding judge and five colleagues had devoted all of their time since 1952 to this single case. Chinese authorities began waging a vigorous campaign against crime, black market activities, and persistent political disorders by staging mass rallies throughout the Canton area at which alleged criminals were given short trials and executed.

The bodies of wealthy eye surgeon Victor M. Ohta, his wife, two sons, and secretary were found by firemen in the swimming pool of his burning mountaintop home near Santa Cruz, Calif., on October 19. A typewritten note declaring World War III on anyone misusing the environment was found signed with the names of the four knights on Tarot fortune-telling cards. With help from the area's sizable hippie community, police arrested John Linley Frazier for the murders on October 23. In Fresno, Calif., William E. Thoresen III, son of the president of the Great Western Steel Company, was shot to death on June 10, during a quarrel with his wife, Louise. Mrs. Thoresen was acquitted of murder charges at her trial in November where she testified she had killed her husband in self-defense after he told her he had hired a man to kill his brother Richard in 1965.

On August 31 Rome police reported that Marquis Camillo Casati-Stampa di Soncino, owner of a famous stable of trotting horses, had returned to his home from a hunting trip, killed his wife and her young lover, and then committed suicide. The drama touched off a national scandal when the Communist press charged that the marquis had enjoyed tax privileges for many years.

Traffic in narcotics has grown tremendously since 1960. U.S. authorities indicated that while there were not more than 100,000 heroin users in the entire U.S. at that time, in 1970 there were 100,000 in New York City alone, where for the first six months of 1970, narcotics arrests increased 79.2% over the same period in 1969.

On July 7, 1970, a Harlem boy became the 102nd teen-ager in New York City to die of drug-related causes in 1970; during the same period 322 adult addicts had died of drug-related causes. Widespread use of marijuana was reflected in the numerous arrests of youths from prominent U.S. families, including: John P. Cahill, son of New Jersey Gov. William T. Cahill; Curtis Howard Sitterson, son of Chancellor J. Carlyle Sitterson of the University of North Carolina; Michael M. Hollings, son of U.S. Sen. Ernest F. Hollings of South Carolina; Theodore Rosenberg, son of New York State Supreme Court Justice Samuel R. Rosenberg; Robert F. Kennedy, Jr., son of the late U.S. senator; and his cousin, Robert Sargent Shriver III.

Reports from Hong Kong in July 1970 revealed a 28% increase in crime over a five-year period and showed a link between crime and the use of drugs by young people. In 1969 persons under 21 committed 59% of the murders, 32% of the serious assaults, 65% of the robberies, and 85% of the common sexual offenses.

Canada's largest city, Montreal, by the end of 1969 had a crime rate 153% above the 1960 level. Major crimes in 1969 totaled 41,675, an increase of 10% over 1968; bank robberies jumped from 95 in 1968 to 192 in 1969 and armed robberies from 815 to 1,388, or a 70% increase. The 1969 robbery rate in Montreal of 117.3 per 100,000 inhabitants was three times the national level. A report on the administration of justice in Quebec province pointed up the low crime solution rate, the few arrests made in Montreal compared with the national average, and the apparent ease with which criminals escaped from Quebec jails.

Of Montreal's 34 murders in 1969, 7 were described by police as gangland-type slayings.

Several countries were plagued by assassinations and political kidnappings in 1970. Canadian Prime Minister Pierre Elliott Trudeau invoked the War Measures Act on October 16 after Quebec separatist groups kidnapped British diplomat James R. Cross and Quebec Minister of Labour Pierre Laporte. In Guatemala, Foreign Minister Alberto Fuentes Mohr and U.S. diplomat Sean M. Holly were kidnapped and released in exchange for political prisoners, but West German Ambassador Count Karl von Spreti was slain after the government refused to grant his kidnappers' demands. In late July and early August, Uruguayan Tupamaros guerrillas kidnapped four persons, including the chief U.S. police adviser to Uruguay, Dan A. Mitrione, whose body was found August 10. In Brazil a Japanese diplomat, the West German ambassador, and the Swiss ambassador were kidnapped during the year. The commander in chief of the Chilean Army, Gen. René Schneider Chereau, was fatally wounded by a gunman on October 22. (*See* articles on individual countries.)

The incidence of airline hijackings dropped noticeably following the adoption of strict security measures after Palestinian terrorists took over three aircraft bound for New York from European cities on September 6. (*See* TRANSPORTATION: *Special Report.*) Nonetheless, the first successful hijacking of a U.S.S.R. airliner occurred on October 15. U.S. Marine Corporal Raffaele Minichiello was convicted in Rome in November 1970 on various Italian charges stemming from his hijacking of a Trans World Airlines jet from California to Rome in October 1969. Minichiello was also wanted on U.S. kidnapping and hijacking charges.

London police announced on August 27 that machine guns, other firearms, and explosives had been seized in 150 simultaneous raids throughout England. The raids, described as the largest such operation in England, were made under 1968 legislation controlling the licensing of traders in firearms, and under the Explosive Substances Act of 1883.

On July 23, 1970, a demonstrator hurled two gas bombs of the type used by British troops to quell violence in Northern Ireland into a packed House of Commons chamber. (V. W. P.)

See also Law; Police; Prisons and Penology.

Firemen examine the ruins of some of the 24 Denver school buses dynamited in a parking lot Feb. 5, 1970.

WIDE WORLD

Cuba

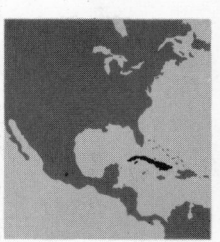

The socialist republic of Cuba occupies the largest island in the Greater Antilles of the West Indies. Area: 42,827 sq.mi. (110,922 sq.km.), including several thousand small islands and cays. Pop. (1967 est.): 7,937,200, including (1953) white 72.8%; mestizo 14.5%; Negro 12.4%. Cap. and largest city: Havana (pop., 1967 est., 1,008,500). Language: Spanish. Religion: predominantly Roman Catholic. President in 1970, Osvaldo Dorticós Torrado; prime minister, Fidel Castro.

Although political stability was maintained, 1970 brought severe economic setbacks that led to administrative changes. When the July sugar crop fell short of Castro's 10 million-ton target by 1.5 million tons, he dismissed three ministers: José Llanusa (education), Francisco Padrón (sugar), and Manuel Luzardo García (commerce). Llanusa's successor was Maj. Belarmino Castilla, previously responsible for technical and vocational training throughout Cuba, while Padrón was replaced by Marcos Lage Coello, a former university administrator, and Luzardo by Capt. Serafín Fernández Rodríguez, a junior Army officer who had been in charge of military food supplies. Other Cabinet changes were expected, and the fact that two ministries went to Army officers suggested an increasingly military regime.

In a speech on July 26 Castro called the 8.5 million-ton sugar crop a major disaster. In the hope of achieving his target, he said, vital economic projects had been neglected; products whose output had declined since 1968 included cement (23%), steel rods (38%), fertilizers (32%), tires (50%), milk (25%), and unspecified foodstuffs.

Blaming himself for these failures, Castro said Cuba was reaping the consequences of mistakes caused

CUBA
Education. (1967–68) Primary, pupils 1,273,581, teachers 43,714; secondary, pupils 177,133, teachers 11,286; vocational, pupils 50,181, teachers 3,637; teacher training, students 22,977, teachers (1966–67) 1,438; higher (including 3 universities), students 37,-326, teaching staff 4,499.
Finance. Monetary unit: peso, officially at par with the U.S. dollar (2.40 pesos = £1 sterling). Budget (1966) balanced at 2,718,000,000 pesos.
Foreign Trade. (1967) Imports 1,001,000,000 pesos; exports 717 million pesos. Import sources (1968 est.): U.S.S.R. 61%; China 7%; France 6%. Export destinations (1968 est.): U.S.S.R. 44%; China 9%; Spain 6%; Czechoslovakia 6%; East Germany 5%. Main exports (1966) sugar and products 85%.
Transport and Communications. Roads (1968) c. 13,300 km. (including 1,144 km. of the Central Highway). Motor vehicles in use (1965): passenger 162,-000; commercial (including buses) 103,700. Railways (1968) 14,740 km. (including 9,528 km. plantation). Shipping (1969): merchant vessels 100 gross tons and over 200; gross tonnage 277,206. Telephones (Jan. 1969) c. 242,000. Radio receivers (Dec. 1969) c. 1,325,000. Television receivers (Dec. 1968) c. 575,000.
Agriculture. Production (in 000; metric tons; 1968; 1967 in parentheses): rice 182 (94); corn c. 127 (c. 120); cassava (1967) c. 200, (1966) c. 200; sweet potatoes (1967) c. 230, (1966) c. 240; sugar, raw value (1969–70) c. 8,300, (1968–69) c. 4,352; coffee (1969) c. 30, (1968) c. 30; oranges c. 130 (123); tobacco c. 45 (45). Livestock (in 000; 1968–69): cattle c. 7,250; pigs c. 1,940; sheep c. 270; goats (1966–67) c. 220.
Industry. Production (in 000; metric tons; 1968): crude oil 104; petroleum products c. 4,050; electricity (kw-hr.; 1967) 4,488,000; chrome ore (oxide content; 1967) c. 11; manganese ore (metal content; 1967) 27; nickel ore (metal content; 1967) 32.

Crops:
see Agriculture

Cross-country:
see Sporting Record

KEYSTONE
Prime Minister
Fidel Castro
donates blood for Peruvian
earthquake victims.

by inexperience and virtually admitted that living conditions were the worst in his 11 years of rule. Economic planning for the 1970s, he explained, had counted on attainment of the sugar target, which was prevented by bad weather, faulty equipment, and low productivity; it was, therefore, imperative to reform the administrative machinery. Incentives to increase the workers' productivity were clearly to be moral rather than material. It was officially admitted that economic prosperity could not be expected before 1975. To achieve it by then, Cubans were asked for a further effort.

The gross national product in 1969 (by an unofficial U.S. reckoning) was $2.8 billion, $200 million less than in 1968; but nickel exports, valued at $55 million for 1969, were expected to rise again in 1970. Strict sugar rationing continued.

Despite Castro's economic setbacks his personal authority remained unchallenged. Still enormously popular with the general public, he had the Communist Party's support and the complete loyalty of the Army —an estimated force of 200,000–300,000 men that was rated the best trained and best equipped in Latin America. Nevertheless, symptoms of popular dissent (to which Castro admitted) included passive resistance among workers and some degree of internal terrorism. Successive raiding parties from the Bahamas, organized by the Alpha-66 group of Cuban exiles

UPI COMPIX
In Boston, young people
board buses to Canada.
From there they went
by boat to Cuba to help
harvest the sugar crop.

based in Miami, were speedily liquidated. Their incursions provoked strong diplomatic protests to the U.S. and U.K.

The U.S. showed no sign of relaxing its economic blockade of Cuba; mutual relations failed to improve; and rumours of an impending rapprochement were categorically denied by both sides. On May 20 Castro announced the severance of all remaining links with the U.S. government. This put an end to the agreed airlift of Cuban refugees to Miami, which began in 1961 and was estimated to have evacuated more than 300,000 people since 1965.

On September 24 the regime handed over to the U.S. government a U.S. Army private who had hijacked a Trans World Airlines plane to Cuba on August 24. He was the first U.S. citizen (80 had landed in Cuba) ever extradited for this offense, but the U.S. Department of State said that his return did not herald any thaw in mutual relations.

Cuba's relations with the Soviet Union remained on the cordial footing established in August 1968, when Castro had declared his support for the Soviet invasion of Czechoslovakia. In 1970 Cuba continued to depend entirely on Soviet economic assistance. Estimated to be running at an annual rate of $400 million, this had raised Cuba's total debt to about $3 billion— excluding Soviet military aid and sugar imports under the 1964 support price agreement. In May and June negotiations took place in Moscow for a renewal of the 1964 trade and aid agreement, previously extended on a provisional annual basis; there were no reports of a successful outcome to these talks. Cuba also sought a mutual defense treaty, which the Soviet government declined to negotiate—possibly fearing adverse U.S. reaction.

During the year, however, there were several indications of Moscow's positive interest in military links with the Castro regime: the first Soviet long-range army transport aircraft to arrive in the Western Hemisphere landed in Cuba; while Soviet naval units were in Cuban ports, the Soviet defense minister, Marshal A. A. Grechko, visited Havana; and when the Cuban defense minister, Maj. Raúl Castro, returned from a six-week trip to Moscow, it was reported that Cuba would offer repair facilities to the Soviet Navy. On September 25 Washington warned Moscow against building a nuclear submarine base near the Cuban port of Cienfuegos, although the Soviets denied any attempt to do so.   (Rn. C.)

ENCYCLOPÆDIA BRITANNICA FILMS. *The West Indies* (1965).

Cycling

After two years of split world championships with the professional and amateur title races organized in separate countries, there was a return to a combined meeting for the 1970 series, which was held at Leicester, Eng. (August 6–16). This was the first time in nearly half a century that Great Britain had been host country.

Leading up to the world championships were the Commonwealth Games at Edinburgh (July 16–25). Australian and New Zealand riders were the most successful at this tournament, each country winning two of the six Commonwealth titles, with Britain and Canada taking the others. In the sprint event two Australian rivals, John Nicholson and Gordon Johnson, worked their way impressively through to the "two up" final, which went to Nicholson as he won both matches by close margins.

Johnson, however, got his gold medal by joining forces with his countryman, Ron Jonker, to finish first in the tandem race (a new event for the Commonwealth Games) ahead of the Canadian pair, Barry Harvey and Jocelyn Lovell. Lovell had been regarded as the likely winner of the 1,000-m. time trial, but he had to be content with the bronze medal behind Harry Kent (N.Z.), whose time of 1 min. 8.69 sec. was a new Games record, and Leslie King (Trinidad). Whereas Kent won this short but severe test by 1.71 sec., his compatriot Bruce Biddle was successful in winning the 102-mi. road race by only 0.01 sec. from Australia's Ray Bilney after a tremendous duel in pouring rain. Lovell finally secured his gold medal in the 10-mi. track championship. The U.K.'s one success was by Ian Hallam, impressive winner of the 4,000-m. individual pursuit.

At the world championships, one of the runners-up in the Commonwealth Games was to provide the sensation of the tournament. Despite a fall in the early round of the world sprint, Gordon Johnson fought his way through to the final to beat a former titleholder, Santa Galardoni (Italy), in two straight matches. Having turned professional just after the Commonwealth Games, Johnson thus won Australia's first professional sprint title in 50 years. Johnson's compatriot John Nicholson rode strongly in the amateur event to reach the semifinal, where he met his match in Daniel Morelon (France), who went on to win his fourth championship in five years.

Hallam and Kent also reproduced their fine Edinburgh form at Leicester, but each finished second to the present or a previous titleholder of the respective championships. Kent (1 min. 9.21 sec.) lost to Denmark's Niels Fredborg (1 min. 8.82 sec.) in the 1,000-m. time trial, and Hallam lost to Xavier Kurmann (Switz.) in the 4,000-m. pursuit. It was, however, in pursuit racing that Great Britain took its only gold medal of the series, Hugh Porter dominating the 5,000-m. professional event to win the final comfortably from Lorenzo Bosisio (Italy).

Biggest total of victories in the tournament went to the U.S.S.R. and West Germany, each of which had seven gold medalists. The high totals resulted from victories in team contests, four Soviets winning the 100-km. road team time trial and four Germans taking the similar type of competition over 4,000 m. on the track. The West Germans' other championships were won by Jurgen Barth and Rainer Muller (tandem) and E. Rudolph (100-km. professional motor-paced).

Soviet cyclists were supreme in the women's events, winning with Anna Konkina (37-mi. road), Tamara Garkuschina (3,000-m. pursuit), and Galina Careva (sprint). In finishing third in the pursuit race Beryl Burton (U.K.) took her 13th world championship medal to equal the record total held by male competitor Arie Van Vliet (Neth.).

Although not among the winners in the world championships, Eddy Merckx (Belg.) competed in the road race and gave valuable team support to his victorious compatriot Monséré. Yet Merckx was unquestionably the greatest professional road rider of the year, dominating the competition to an even greater extent than in 1969. The Belgian was in form early in the season for the eight-day race from Paris to Nice, which lived up to its name of the "Race to the Sun" by starting off in bad weather and finishing under the bluest of Mediterranean skies. Merckx won 2 of the 11 stages

KEYSTONE
Hugh Porter of Great Britain pedals toward victory and a gold medal in the 5,000-m. professional pursuit during the world cycling championships in Leicester, Eng., Aug. 10, 1970.

and had a comfortable final lead over Luís Ocana (Spain), who later in the year was to score several notable successes, including the 19-day Tour of Spain. Merckx was the favourite in the Milan–San Remo race (March 19), the first big international event of the year in Italy, which he had already won three times. On this occasion, however, a native hero emerged in Michele Dancelli, convincing winner of the classic after a lone breakaway that had huge roadside crowds wild with enthusiasm, this being the first Italian victory in the event since 1953.

Three weeks later Merckx was back on home roads to win the four-day Tour of Belgium (April 6–9) in atrocious weather conditions, and from there he went on to crush the opposition in the Paris–Roubaix race, the last 40 mi. of which is over deliberately chosen narrow unkept cobbled roads. All this was building up to Merckx's two main objectives of the season, the tours of Italy and France. He won the Tour of Italy (May 17–June 6) with a final lead of 3 min. 14 sec. over Felice Gimondi (Italy), Martin Vandenbossche (Belg.) finishing third.

Twenty-one days later, Merckx started the Tour de France, the race that he had won in 1969 to become the first Belgian victor since 1939 thanks to forceful riding that earned six stage victories. It was expected that Merckx would be less aggressive in the 1970 Tour, but he was even more so, winning eight stages (equaling the 1930 record of Charles Pelissier of France) and winning the race by 12 min. 51 sec. from new professionals Joop Zoetemelk (Neth.) and Gösta Pettersen (Swed.). Earlier in the season Merckx had won the one-day Flèche Wallonne race in the Belgian Ardennes. Other "classic" race winners were: Liège–Bastogne–Liège, Roger De Vlaeminck (Belg.); Tour of Flanders, Eric Leman (Belg.); Bordeaux–Paris, Herman Van Springel (Belg.); Paris–Tours, Jurgen Tschan (W.Ger.); Tour of Lombardy, Franco Bitossi (Italy); Grand Prix des Nations Time Trial, Herman Van Springel.

Following the cancellation of the Tour de l'Avenir in France, the "Peace Race" (Warsaw–Berlin–Prague) again became the most important multistage amateur event, victory going to Ryzard Szurkowski (Pol.).

Curling:
see Sporting Record
Currency:
see Money and Banking
Cybernetics:
see Electronics

Eastern Europeans also dominated the two main British events, the 14-day Tour of Britain (won by Jiri Mainus, Czech.) and the two-day Tour of Scotland (Wojech Matusiak, Pol.).   (Jo. B. W.)

Cyprus

An island republic and a member of the Commonwealth of Nations, Cyprus is in the eastern Mediterranean. Area: 3,572 sq.mi. (9,251 sq.km.). Pop. (1969 est.): 630,000, including Greeks 77%; Turks 18%. Cap. and largest city: Nicosia (pop., 1969 est., 114,-000). Language: Greek and Turkish. Religion: Greek Orthodox 77%; Muslim 18.3%. President in 1970, Archbishop Makarios III.

Negotiations between the Greek and Turkish Cypriots on the administrative structure of a united and independent Cyprus made no headway in 1970, and a new challenge to the Makarios policy came from the National Front, a right-wing Greek Cypriot movement that wanted immediate *enosis* (union with Greece). Using terrorist tactics, it created tensions that came to a head in the spring, when an unsuccessful attempt on the president's life on March 8 was quickly followed by the assassination of his former minister of the interior and defense, Polycarpos Georghadjis. In November four Greek Cypriots, including a policeman and a constable, were sentenced to 14 years' imprisonment for the attack on Makarios. All four had pleaded not guilty to the charges. There were suggestions that Georghadjis, who was shot dead on March 15 near Nicosia, might also have been involved. Throughout most of the preindependence campaign against British rule, Georghadjis had been a prominent member of the militant EOKA (Union with Greece) resistance movement.

The political atmosphere in which the shootings occurred had been building up since the National Front emerged a year earlier to revive the demand for *enosis*.

CYPRUS
Education. (1967–68) Primary, pupils 72,394, teachers 2,202; secondary, pupils 31,466, teachers 1,292; vocational, pupils 4,143, teachers 236; higher, students 339, teaching staff 27.
Finance. Monetary unit: pound, at par with the pound sterling (C£1 = U.S. $2.40). Budget (1969 est.): revenue C£27,390,000; expenditure C£24.6 million. Gold, SDRs, and foreign exchange, monetary authorities: (June 1970) U.S. $168.4 million; (June 1969) U.S. $160.3 million.
Foreign Trade. (1969) Imports C£85,780,000; exports C£39,980,000. Import sources: U.K. 31%; Italy 10%; West Germany 8%; U.S. 5%; Greece 5%; France 5%. Export destinations: U.K. 40%; West Germany 16%; Italy 7%; U.S.S.R. 6%. Main exports: citrus fruit 18%; copper 16%; potatoes 12%; iron pyrites 8%.
Transport and Communications. Roads (1968) 7,591 km. (including 3,309 km. with improved surface). Motor vehicles in use (1968): passenger 42,400; commercial 13,500. Air traffic (1969): 70.9 million passenger-km.; freight 1,640,000 net ton-km. Shipping (1969): merchant vessels 100 gross tons and over 134; gross tonnage 770,463. Telephones (Dec. 1968) 33,396. Radio receivers (Dec. 1968) 147,000. Television receivers (Dec. 1968) 32,000.
Agriculture. Production (in 000; metric tons; 1968; 1967 in parentheses): oranges 99 (c. 89); grapefruit 58 (51); wheat (1967) c. 97, (1966) 56; potatoes (1967) c. 139, (1966) 134; olives 15 (c. 17); grapes 168 (c. 146). Livestock (in 000; 1968–69): sheep 405; cattle 39.
Industry. Production (in 000; metric tons; 1968): asbestos 19; copper ore (exports; metal content) 22; chromium ore (oxide content) 12; cement (1969) 246; electricity (excluding most industrial production; kw-hr.; 1969) 508,000.

After attacking several members of the Makarios government, it was declared illegal and embarked on a terrorist campaign.

On January 16 Makarios (just back from a trip to East Africa) flew to Athens for talks with the Greek government, after which both parties condemned the terrorist acts and reaffirmed their determination to work for "the consolidation of peaceful coexistence" between the island's two communities. A roundup of hidden arms was followed on January 29 by the passage of a law authorizing the police to detain suspects for three months without trial, and in February the Greek prime minister, Georgios Papadopoulos, categorically denied that the National Front enjoyed "any kind of support" from his government. But the terrorism continued; in May about 60 people, including a number of policemen, were arrested after an attack by masked men on the main police station at Limassol.

Despite the prevailing tension, the island's first elections since independence took place without incident. Held on July 5, they gave 15 of the 35 Greek Cypriot seats in the House of Representatives to the moderate right-wing Unified Party, led by Glafkos Clerides (president of the House) and committed to broad support of the Makarios policy. Nine seats went to AKEL (the pro-Communist front), seven to the Progressive Front (pledged to secure *enosis* through "the free self-determination of the Cypriot people"), and the other four were equally divided between two left-wing groups, the socialist Democratic Centre Union and the Independents. All 15 of the parliamentary seats allocated to the Turkish Cypriots were held by adherents of the community's leader, Rauf Denktash.

The elections were followed by the resumption of intercommunal talks between Clerides and Denktash. Both sides stood committed to the idea of a united and independent Cyprus, but there were intractable differences over the nature and extent of the autonomous powers sought by the Turkish Cypriots, notably on the question of whether or not the Turkish Cypriot police should retain exclusive control in Turkish Cypriot areas. The Athens and Ankara governments continued to declare their devotion to a peaceful settlement and insisted on the need to avoid a breakdown of direct negotiations between the island's two communities. On August 17, however, the third round of protracted negotiations ended with the release of a joint report in which Clerides and Denktash again confirmed their failure to agree.   (V. J. P.)

Czechoslovakia

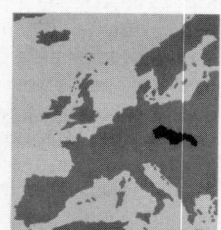

A federal socialist republic of central Europe, Czechoslovakia lies between Poland, the U.S.S.R., Hungary, Austria, and Germany. Area: 49,371 sq.mi. (127,870 sq.km.), including Slovakia 18,922 sq.mi. Pop. (1969 est.): 14,-418,175 (Slovakia 4.5 million), including (1966) Czech 66%; Slovak 29%. Cap. and largest city: Prague (pop., 1970 est., 1,103,350). First secretary of the Communist Party of Czechoslovakia in 1970, Gustav Husak; president, Ludvik Svoboda; premiers, Oldrich Cernik and, from January 28, Lubomir Strougal.

Throughout 1970 the Czechoslovak situation could be compared to a tug-of-war between the hard-line enemies of reform on the one hand and Gustav Husak, the Communist Party's first secretary, on the other. The issue at stake was not the continuation, or even salvaging, of the real substance of the reforms proposed in 1968, but Husak's desire to slow up the purges, which were decimating the country's most competent cadres, and his reluctance to sanction the staging of political show trials. Husak was only partially successful, although he enjoyed the confidence and trust of the Soviet leadership.

The first gain for the old guard came at the beginning of the year. In January it was announced that Alexander Dubcek's conduct in 1968 would be investigated; at the same time, eight resignations from the Communist Party's Central Committee were announced. Oldrich Cernik, a somewhat equivocal survivor from 1968, was replaced as premier by Lubomir Strougal and was expelled from the party in December. Strougal, who had been minister of the interior in the pre-Dubcek era, was the obvious challenger to Husak's authority. On the other hand, his rise coincided with the removal of the party leader in Slovakia, Stefan Sadovsky, reportedly for his failure to back Husak's policies with sufficient vigour.

Dubcek himself arrived in Ankara on January 26 to take up his post as ambassador to Turkey. On March 21 his suspension from the Communist Party was announced, and in June he was recalled from Turkey, expelled from the party, and consigned to provincial obscurity in Slovakia. Dubcek's fate had been decided when the Soviet tanks entered Prague in August 1968; his subsequent tribulations were merely symptomatic

CZECHOSLOVAKIA

Education. (1967–68) Primary, pupils 2,109,183, teachers 97,505; secondary, pupils 107,685, teachers 6,477; vocational, pupils 267,483, teachers 13,159; teacher training, students 8,941, teachers 462; higher (including 9 universities), students 134,033, teaching staff 19,232.

Finance. Monetary unit: koruna, with an official exchange rate of 7.20 koruny to U.S. $1 (17.28 koruny = £1 sterling) and a tourist rate of 16.20 koruny to U.S. $1 (38.74 koruny = £1 sterling). Budget (1969 est.) balanced at 156.3 billion koruny.

Foreign Trade. (1968) Imports 22,155,000,000 koruny; exports 21,638,000,000 koruny. Import sources: U.S.S.R. 34%; East Germany 13%; Poland 8%; Hungary 6%. Export destinations: U.S.S.R. 34%; East Germany 11%; Poland 8%; Hungary 6%. Main exports: machinery 49%; manufactured goods 18%; metals, minerals, and fuels 18%.

Transport and Communications. Roads (1968) 145,948 km. (including 73,249 km. main roads). Motor vehicles in use (1968): passenger 556,400; commercial 162,100. Railways: (1968) 13,317 km. (including 2,389 km. electrified); traffic (1969) 18,570,000,000 passenger-km., freight 56,667,000,000 net ton-km. Air traffic (1969): 850 million passenger-km.; freight 12,-878,000 net ton-km. Shipping (1969): merchant vessels 100 gross tons and over 10; gross tonnage 74,877. Telephones (Dec. 1968) 1,789,373. Radio receivers (Dec. 1968) 3,827,000. Television receivers (Dec. 1968) 2,712,000.

Agriculture. Production (in 000; metric tons; 1969; 1968 in parentheses): wheat 3,149 (3,153); barley 2,245 (2,113); oats 914 (869); rye 670 (769); corn c. 480 (453); potatoes c. 5,020 (6,526); sugar, raw value (1969–70) c. 716, (1968–69) c. 861; beef and veal (1968) 376, (1967) 345; pork (1968) 596, (1967) 574. Livestock (in 000; Jan. 1969): cattle 4,249; pigs 5,136; sheep 906; chickens 31,060.

Industry. Index of industrial production (1963 = 100): (1969) 144; (1968) 136. Production (in 000; metric tons; 1969): coal 27,221; brown coal 79,336; electricity (kw.-hr.) 42,900,000; iron ore (30% metal content) 1,568; pig iron 7,044; steel 10,819; cement 6,687; sulfuric acid 1,033; nitrogenous fertilizers (1968) 264; superphosphates (1967) 244; cotton yarn 100; cotton fabrics (m.) 500,000; woolen fabrics (m.) 48,000; rayon and acetate yarn 22; rayon and acetate fibres 48; passenger cars (units) 132; commercial vehicles (units) 46. Dwellings completed (1969) 83,000.

of the general line pursued by his successors. The most significant purge occurred within the Communist Party itself. Dubcek's colleagues were removed systematically from positions of influence, and through the summer the purge was taken to the grass roots by calling in party membership cards, interviewing suspect individuals, and denying new cards to unsatisfactory members. The expulsion rate was 22% of those interviewed. Of the 150 members of the Central Committee, 64 were expelled.

In January the discovery of Trotskyist conspiracies and Western-inspired espionage plots was announced. This was particularly ominous in view of the fact that the new amendments to the Criminal Code came into force at the beginning of the year. New crimes, such as the export of books or records described as harmful to the republic, were added to the calendar, and the penal provisions became more rigorous. The rehabilitation of the victims of the Stalinist era was slowed to a bureaucratic crawl, and the authorities sharply reduced the number of permits issued for travel abroad.

The most severe restrictions, however, were applied in the cultural sphere. Many of the journalists, writers, academics, and intellectuals who supported the 1968 reform program were removed from their posts and compelled to take up menial jobs in the provinces. Some writers were tried on charges of subversion or of uttering slander about the alliance with the Soviet Union. The Czechoslovak Writers' Union was virtually cut off from official funds, and royalties were paid only to authors who supported the new order. The autonomy of the Czechoslovak Academy of Sciences was practically abolished in July.

In the field of foreign policy, both Husak and Strougal gave a cautious welcome to the Soviet-West German treaty on the renunciation of force in August. This was preceded by a new trade agreement between Czechoslovakia and West Germany in June, which provided for an extension of trade between the two countries. However, the major exercise in foreign policy was the signing of yet another Soviet-Czechoslovak treaty of friendship, cooperation, and mutual assistance.

The draft treaty was discussed with Andrei A. Gromyko, the Soviet minister of foreign affairs, during his visit to Prague in March. In May, Leonid I. Brezhnev, general secretary of the Soviet Communist Party, himself went to Prague to sign the treaty, which legitimized the presence of Soviet troops in Czechoslovakia. The treaty also incorporated the essence of the so-called Brezhnev doctrine, stating that the "support, the strengthening and the protection of socialist acquisitions, which were achieved through heroic efforts and sacrifice-filled toil by the people of the two countries, are the joint international duty of the socialist countries."

Even this did not appear to satisfy the hard-line opposition, which continued to look to Strougal. In the second half of October, the dismissal of the Czech minister of the interior, Josef Groesser, was followed by the removal of Gen. Otakar Rytir, the chief liaison officer with the Soviet forces in Czechoslovakia. It was reported that they were implicated in a move to complain to the Soviet leaders about Husak's alleged liberalism. The first secretary seemed to have survived yet again, no doubt largely because his Soviet comrades still regarded him as their safest bet in Prague. (OT. P.)

See also Economic Planning; Propaganda.

WIDE WORLD

Alexander Dubcek, Czechoslovakia's deposed leader who later became ambassador to Turkey, strolls on a quiet street in Ankara. On March 21, 1970, he was removed from active Communist Party ranks, and on June 24 he was dismissed as ambassador.

Dahomey

A republic of West Africa, Dahomey is located north of the Gulf of Guinea and is bounded by Togo, Upper Volta, Niger, and Nigeria. Area: 43,483 sq.mi. (112,-620 sq.km.). Pop. (1970 est.): 2,718,000, mainly Dahomean and allied tribes. Cap.: Porto-Novo (pop., 1970 est., 87,000). Largest city: Cotonou (pop., 1970 est., 139,000). Language: French and local dialects. Religion: animist, with Christian and Muslim minorities. Heads of government in 1970, three-member military directorate and, from May 1, chairman of the Presidential Council, Hubert Maga.

The presidential election that was to have taken place in Dahomey between March 9 and 31 came to grief as a result of numerous incidents, particularly around Parakou, electoral stronghold of Hubert Maga, a former president. On March 28, the ruling military directorate temporarily suspended voting. There was a movement toward secession among Maga's supporters in the north, and on April 3, Lieut. Col. Paul Émile de Souza announced the official annulment of the election.

The results obtained by the presidential candidates in their respective electoral strongholds—Maga in the north, Justin Ahomadegbe in the southwest, and Sourou Migan Apithy in the southeast—as well as the presence of former president Émile Zinsou, running as a fourth candidate, made the crisis particularly difficult to unravel. Maga and Ahomadegbe proposed the formation of a collective Presidential Council.

At the beginning of May a charter, or "fundamental state law," was adopted to rule public life pending a general election and the institution of a constitutional regime. This named the Presidential Council as supreme organ of state. The three-man council would meet when summoned by its president, who would also be head of state and supreme commander of the armed forces, or when called by two of its members. Decisions were to be unanimous, but if one member refused his consent three times, a majority decision could be taken. Maga, president of Dahomey from 1960 to 1963, became first president of the council on the basis of a rotational system whereby Ahomadegbe would become president in May 1972 and Apithy in May 1974. (Ph. D.)

DAHOMEY

Education. (1967–68) Primary, pupils 139,734, teachers 3,445; secondary, pupils 13,354, teachers 470; vocational, pupils 727, teachers (public only) 69; teacher training, students 129, teachers 18; higher, students 115, teaching staff (1965–66) 5.

Finance. Monetary unit: CFA franc, with a parity of CFA Fr. 50 to the French franc (CFA Fr. 277.71 = U.S. \$1; CFA Fr. 666.50 = £1 sterling). Budget (1969 est.): receipts CFA Fr. 6,864,000,000; expenditure CFA Fr. 8,336,000,000.

Foreign Trade. (1968) Imports CFA Fr. 12,210,-000,000; exports CFA Fr. 5,510,000,000. Import sources: France 50%; Netherlands 11%; Italy 7%; West Germany 5%; U.K. 5%. Export destinations: France 51%; West Germany 16%; Belgium-Luxembourg 8%; Japan 5%. Main exports (1967): palm oil 40%; cotton 10%; palm nuts and kernels 9%.

Agriculture. Production (in 000; metric tons; 1968; 1967 in parentheses): cassava c. 1,142 (c. 1,120); peanuts c. 20 (c. 27); cottonseed c. 13 (c. 7); sweet potatoes (1967) c. 604, (1966) c. 587; corn c. 200 (c. 230); millet and sorghum (1967) c. 78, (1966) c. 76; palm oil (1967) c. 30, (1966) 30; palm kernels (1967) c. 40, (1966) 30. Livestock (in 000; 1968–69): cattle c. 450; pigs 350; sheep c. 560.

Dairy Products:
see Agriculture

Dams:
see Engineering Projects

Dance

Front-page ballet news in 1970 was the defection of Natalia Makarova, the most celebrated dancer of Leningrad's Kirov Ballet, who asked for asylum in Great Britain where she was dancing with the Kirov. Subsequently she joined the American Ballet Theatre and made her New York debut with the company December 22 in *Giselle*. The reason for her defection was artistic and not political, for she said that, at 30, she was destined for nothing but the old-time classics and that she wanted new challenges. In New York, she danced her first *Coppélia* and, most important, the dramatic lead in Antony Tudor's modern ballet *Lilac Garden*. Another defector was Aleksandr Filipov (from Igor Moiseyev's youth ballet troupe), who also joined the American Ballet Theatre.

In the U.S., 1970 was the 30th anniversary of the American Ballet Theatre. To its repertory, the company added a lavish new production of the Fokine-Stravinsky *Petrouchka*, a new work to a Duke Ellington score by black choreographer Alvin Ailey, other novelties, and pure modern dance works—José Limón's *The Moor's Pavane* and *The Traitor*—theretofore performed only by modern dancers.

The New York City Ballet highlighted the Christmas season with the 500th New York performance of its celebrated production of Tchaikovsky's *The Nutcracker*. Earlier in the year, the company produced an entirely new Balanchine-Stravinsky *Firebird*, with settings and new costumes by painter Marc Chagall; teen-aged Gelsey Kirkland danced the title part. Jerome Robbins created his second all-Chopin ballet, *In the Night* (Chopin nocturnes; the first, *Dances at a Gathering*, was done the preceding year). At the company's summer headquarters at Saratoga Springs, a working rehearsal of Robbins' newest pure dance work, *Goldberg Variations* (Bach), was shown to the public. Other novelties included Balanchine's *Who Cares?* (Gershwin music) and modest-size ballet pieces by the youthful John Clifford. Suzanne Farrell left the company, along with her husband, dancer Paul Mejia, and both joined Maurice Béjart's Ballet of the Twentieth Century in Belgium.

Of the younger, but major, U.S. companies, the City Center Joffrey Ballet produced a major new staging of *Petrouchka*, which was not as well received as the American Ballet Theatre's production, and leading choreographer Gerald Arpino created an instant hit with a new rock ballet, *Trinity*. Seasons in the spring and fall were, of course, held at the City Center. Eliot Feld's American Ballet Company, resident at the Brooklyn Academy of Music, featured new works by the prolific Feld, among them *Early Songs* (Richard Strauss), *A Poem Forgotten* (Riegger), *Cortège Parisien* (Chabrier), and *The Consort* (Elizabethan and supplemental music). Bruce Marks, a star dancer with the American Ballet Theatre and occasional guest artist for Feld, made his debut as a choreographer with *Clockwise* (Jean Francaix).

The Harkness Ballet was reorganized in 1970 around the somewhat smaller supplementary group called the Harkness Youth Dancers and moved its chief scene of operations to Europe. The Boston Ballet celebrated the 100th anniversary of the Saint-Léon-Leo Delibes *Coppélia* with a new production presented in a theatre on the site of the U.S. premiere of the ballet. Other non-New York ballet troupes active during the year included the San Francisco Ballet, the Atlanta (Ga.) Ballet, Ballet West (with headquarters in Salt Lake City, Utah), the Pennsylvania Ballet, the Pittsburgh Ballet, and the Birmingham (Ala.) Ballet. The first black classical ballet company, the Harlem Dance Theatre, founded by Arthur Mitchell, a principal with the New York City Ballet, and directed by Mitchell and Karel Shook, had its first extended engagement, one week at the Jacob's Pillow Dance Festival in Lee, Mass.

European choreographer Milko Sparemblek was appointed the new ballet director of the Metropolitan Opera, a post resigned by Dame Alicia Markova. Sparemblek staged a new production of Gluck's *Orfeo ed Euridice*. A debut at the Met was that of Donald Saddler, who choreographed the classical ballet in Act II of Offenbach's *La Périchole*. Saddler also choreographed the dances for the successful revival of the 1925 musical *No, No, Nanette*, which returned Ruby Keeler to the stage after a 41-year absence.

Dame Margot Fonteyn, making frequent guest appearances in various parts of the world, danced with the Boston Ballet with American Richard Cragun of the Stuttgart Ballet as her partner, and with the National Ballet of Washington, D.C., in a new full-length *Cinderella* choreographed by Ben Stevenson of the Harkness Ballet. (W. TE.)

The 1970s began with a clear change of direction in British ballet. Many of the recommendations outlined in the Arts Council's *A Report on Opera and Ballet in the United Kingdom* became effective—particularly with regard to consolidation, regional development, and encouragement in the contemporary field.

When Sir Frederick Ashton retired from the artistic directorship of the Royal Ballet in July 1970, his successors—Kenneth MacMillan and John Field—amalgamated the two sections of the Royal Ballet. The two companies that had previously worked independently under the name of the Royal Ballet, one usually in London and the other on tour, were merged into one company of about 125 dancers. This was divided into two parts, the larger of which was to play at Covent Garden during the winter and tour only the major provincial centres in the early summer. Meanwhile, the company's touring function would be undertaken by a group of some 25 dancers, which would take smaller and more modern works on tour. All dancers would be interchangeable between the two groups.

Before these changes were made, the Royal Ballet's Covent Garden company mounted two new works: Rudi van Dantzig's *The Ropes of Time* (to Jan Boerman's electronic score), especially for Rudolf Nureyev, and Ashton's *Lament of the Waves* (to Gérard Masson's *Dans Le Deuil des vagues II*). After a year that included a tour to Vienna and another New York season, the final performance before Ashton's retirement was a gala event entitled *In Tribute to Sir Frederick Ashton,* organized by the company to include 37 extracts spanning 40 years of creativity.

The smaller Royal Ballet, during its last year as a separate unit, mounted four new works and one revival: David Drew's *From Waking Sleep* (Alan Hovhaness score), Geoffrey Cauley's *Lazarus* (Ernest Bloch score) and *Symphonie Pastorale* (based on André Gide's story to Martinu music), and Ashton's

MARTHA SWOPE

Natalia Makarova, the Soviet ballerina who defected from the Kirov Ballet in September, and Ivan Nagy in the American Ballet Theatre's production of "Giselie" given in New York City, Dec. 22, 1970.

Creatures of Prometheus. This latter was performed first in Bonn as part of the Beethoven bicentenary celebrations in the composer's native city. The revival was Ninette de Valois' *Job* (Vaughan Williams score), which was one of the first important British ballets when it was created in the 1930s.

The London Festival Ballet was to become mainly responsible for touring with the classics. Recent additions to the classical repertory included *Coppélia* (produced by Jack Carter) and Minkus' *Don Quixote* (revived by Witold Borkowski). A revival of Fokine's *Scheherazade* restored the work to its former greatness, and Ronald Hynd created *Dvorak Variations* (to Dvorak's *Symphonic Variations*).

The most important feature of ballet in Britain was the development and growing popularity of companies with a more contemporary outlook. Ballet Rambert had sold-out London seasons and successful tours of Europe and the Middle East. The newest addition to the company's work was a program for children, *Bertram Batell's Sideshow* (a form of danced revue created by dancers in the company). For more adult audiences, Norman Morrice created *Blind-Sight* (to Bob Downes's jazz score), Christopher Bruce his *Living Space* (to words by Robert Cockburn), John Chesworth his *Four According* (Grazyna Bacewicz music), and Anna Sokolow revived her *Opus 65* (Teo Macero jazz score) about youthful protest and violence, first created in New York in 1965.

The other contemporary company, London Contemporary Dance Theatre, had by now established itself as a vital part of the British dance scene. In this company, based on the school and technique of Martha Graham, the accent was on creation. Many workshop performances were given, with some of the works taken into the repertory. These included Robert Cohan's *Cell* (Ronald Lloyd music), William Louther's *Vesalii Icones* (Peter Maxwell Davies score), and *In the Playground of the Zodiac* (George Quincey score). The company's London home, The Place, became the centre for avant-garde dance in Britain.

Regional development in ballet centred on Glasgow and Manchester. The Scottish Theatre Ballet, formerly Western Theatre Ballet, established a permanent residence in Glasgow, while still touring Britain. Recent creations included: Peter Darrell's full-length *Beauty and the Beast* (Thea Musgrave score) and *Herodias* (Mallarmé poem, Hindemith score),

Yuri Shumilin goes aloft in the show-stopping finale to "Gopak" in the Moiseyev Dance Company presentation.

COURTESY, HUROK CONCERTS, INC.

and also a revival of Bournonville's dances for Rossini's *William Tell*.

Northern Dance Theatre, only a year old, was formed to serve Manchester and the northwest region. This group of ten dancers was directed by Laverne Meyer who created *Brahms Sonata* (F minor Sonata). Other works included Clover Roope's *The Dreamers* (to Peter Maxwell Davies' *Leopardi Fragments*) and *The Predators* (to a Ronald Lloyd electronic tape). Revivals were Frank Staff's *Peter and the Wolf* (Prokofiev) and Andrée Howard's *Death and the Maiden* (Schubert).

Ballet for All, the Royal Ballet's demonstration theatre group, continued its work of taking ballet to places where large companies could not perform. In 1970 it celebrated the centenary of *Coppélia* with a full evening program giving the history of the ballet and its development.

In the most active dance year that London had ever known there were also visits from the Dutch National Ballet (with Nureyev as guest), the Antonio Gades Spanish Ballet, the Polish State Ballet, the Polish Mime Theatre, the Paul Taylor Dance Company, the Kathakali Dance Company, the Kirov Leningrad State Ballet, and the American Ballet Theatre, to name but a few.

In Europe the main activity was in the Netherlands and in West Germany. The Dutch National Ballet revived three works by Balanchine—*Concerto Barocco* (Bach), *Four Temperaments* (Hindemith), and *Apollo* (Stravinsky). Rudi van Dantzig, the company's artistic director, added to his famous *Monument for a Dead Boy* (Boerman electronic score) two works—*Moments* (Webern music) and *Epitaph* (Ligeti's *Atmospheres* and *Volumnia*). The Netherlands Dance Theatre increased its repertory of works by Glen Tetley with *Imaginary Film* (to Arnold Schoenberg's *Incidental Music for a Film Scene* and *Five Orchestral Pieces*) and *Mutations* (Karlheinz Stockhausen music). Hans van Manen, co-director with Tetley, created *Squares* (Satie's *Trois Gymnopédies*) and *Situation* (to records of sounds for amateur film makers).

The Württemberg State Ballet in Stuttgart, directed by John Cranko (*see* BIOGRAPHY), had risen to become one of the most important European companies. It gave its first New York season and U.S. tour in 1970. Its most important recent creations were Cranko's full-length *The Taming of the Shrew* (Stolze music based on Scarlatti), his *Poème de l'extase* (Scriabin music) created for Margot Fonteyn, and *Brouillards* (Debussy music).

The Royal Swedish Ballet gave the Stockholm premiere of Kenneth MacMillan's *Romeo and Juliet* in December 1969, and their Ballet Fortnight in June 1970 included José Limón's *There Is a Time* (based on the text from Ecclesiates), *Missa Brevis* (music by Kodaly), a new production of Glen Tetley's *Ricercare*, Balanchine's *Allegro Brillante*, and Robbins' *Les Noces*.   (P. Wi.)

See also Music; Theatre.

Defense

Despite limited progress in the U.S.-U.S.S.R. strategic arms limitation talks (SALT), there was a general spread of violence in 1970. The two superpowers edged closer to indirect confrontation in the Middle East, while the Soviets built up forces along their border with China. The war in Vietnam expanded into a second Indochina war, and guerrilla movements continued to spread. The most ominous phenomenon was the rise of radical movements and urban guerrillas engaged in increasingly random violence. Attacks on aircraft, chiefly by the Palestinian guerrillas, and hijackings by the Palestinians and by individuals became a matter of grave international concern. By June 90 persons had been killed in such incidents, including 23 over the previous 18 months. The Tokyo Convention on hijacking had proved totally inadequate, and a UN conference on air law, held at The Hague late in 1970, approved a much stronger convention providing for the extradition or prosecution of hijackers and eliminating any exemptions based on the political motives of the hijacker.

The kidnapping of diplomats who were then exchanged for political prisoners, which had become widespread in Latin America, took a more serious turn in April when the West German ambassador to Guatemala was killed after the government refused ransom demands. In October the British trade commissioner to Montreal, James Cross, and the Quebec labour minister, Pierre Laporte, were kidnapped by Quebec separatists, and Laporte was subsequently murdered. The Trudeau government invoked the Emergency War Measures Act, previously reserved for wartime, on grounds that a potential state of insurrection existed in Quebec. (*See* CANADA.) Under these circumstances, existing concepts of defense against external aggression might well have to be modified to provide protection against internal subversion and revolutionary movements.

DISARMAMENT

The entry into force on March 5 of the nuclear nonproliferation treaty, following its simultaneous ratification (Nov. 24, 1969) by the U.S. and the U.S.S.R., constituted a major step forward in arms control, complementing the start of SALT. Under the treaty, those signatories without nuclear weapons promised not to seek them; in return, they obtained unhindered access to nuclear technology and supplies of fissile material, which would be available under safeguards to be established by the International Atomic Energy Authority (IAEA).

The six Euratom members (France, West Germany,

Carla Hubbard, Jennifer Laird, and Ricarda McDonald perform in the National Ballet School's production of the new ballet "Sisters" at the National Arts Centre in Ottawa, June 15–16, 1970.

COURTESY, NATIONAL ARTS CENTRE

the U.K., and the Benelux countries) insisted that their organization act as IAEA's inspecting agent for them. West Germany and the Netherlands had joined with the U.K. to establish, in March, a consortium for manufacturing enriched uranium by the gas centrifuge process, and they wanted this inspected by Euratom as well, although the U.K. preferred direct IAEA inspection. Japanese ratification was conditional on a safeguards agreement not less favourable than Euratom's. Negotiations with the IAEA made good progress during the summer, and these problems seemed resolvable. Those posed by potential nuclear powers that had not signed the treaty remained, however. In order of probability, they were India, Israel, South Africa, Brazil, and Argentina. Australia had signed but had not ratified.

The Conference of the Committee on Disarmament at Geneva, Switz., made limited progress on a seabed treaty, limitation of chemical and biological weapons (CBW), and a comprehensive nuclear test-ban treaty, but resurrection of the unrealistic general and complete disarmament concept by the eight new members suggested a reversion to propaganda.

The joint U.S.-U.S.S.R. draft treaty of Oct. 7, 1969, on the peaceful uses of the seabed prohibited emplacement on the ocean floor of nuclear or other weapons of mass destruction, including chemical, bacteriological, and radiological weapons or dual-purpose weapons with some conventional capability. Discussion in the UN General Assembly had concentrated on inspection procedures and the extent of the ban. The Canadians, therefore, suggested inspection where reasonable doubt of violation could not be removed by unilateral observation. In July nine of the nonaligned members proposed that negotiations looking toward a more comprehensive limitation on military uses of the seabed should continue. Both amendments were embodied in the September 1, 1970, draft, which was approved by the General Assembly's First Committee in December.

The central issue in controlling chemical and biological weapons was whether to deal with them together or separately. The Soviet draft prohibited both types with only self-inspection. It omitted toxins, included in the British draft, which also provided for a complaints procedure involving the UN, in view of the extreme difficulties of effective inspection against biological weapons. These difficulties made the West even more insistent on effective verification, including on-site inspection, of a ban on chemical weapons, while the 12 nonaligned states advocated a ban on both weapons with reasonable national and international verification.

Meanwhile, Canada, the U.K., and the U.S. renounced biological weapons while Japan and Brazil ratified the 1925 Geneva Protocol banning the use of asphyxiating gases in war. Different interpretations were placed on the protocol; the General Assembly's December 1969 resolution said it included tear gases and herbicides, but the U.S. and the U.K. disagreed. The problem was that some gases intended to be incapacitating could be lethal under exceptional circumstances. The U.S. used a range of incapacitating agents in Vietnam and the U.K. used the allegedly nonlethal CS gas in Northern Ireland, though as an internal police matter the latter action was not affected by the protocol.

The slim chance of a comprehensive nuclear test-ban treaty depended on the outcome of SALT. The detection issue, however, was clarified by Sweden and Canada. In December 1969 they persuaded the Gen-

UPI COMPIX

Pres. Richard M. Nixon points to a map of Cambodia during his televised speech to the nation April 30. He announced that U.S. ground troops had entered Cambodia to wipe out Communist headquarters for all military operations against South Vietnam.

eral Assembly to ascertain, through the secretary-general, the willingness of states to participate in a detection club, guaranteeing the availability of specified seismological records. The poor response led them to submit two working papers in August, which the U.K. extrapolated to mean that adding 14 long-period arrays (bringing the total to 25) could reduce the size of detectable explosions from 100 to 10 kilotons.

During the preliminary SALT negotiations, held at Helsinki, Fin., from Nov. 17 to Dec. 22, 1969, the U.S. and U.S.S.R. reached agreement on the general range of subjects to be discussed and how this was to be done. After the chairman of each delegation (Gerard C. Smith, director of the U.S. Arms Control and Disarmament Agency, and Vladimir S. Semyonov, Soviet deputy foreign minister) had read a short prepared paper, the members would discuss the points raised with their opposite numbers. This provided a new form of constructive dialogue, forcing the Soviet government to pay greater attention to the scientific aspects of limiting the strategic arms race and lessening the previous considerable gap between their understanding of these problems and that of the Americans.

In his February 18 foreign policy message (see *United States*, below), Pres. Richard Nixon outlined the three possible U.S. strategies: limiting numbers of strategic weapons only; adding restrictions on capabilities, in which case verification would become crucial; or reducing offensive forces regardless of capabilities. A special April 7 NATO Council meeting on SALT confirmed the U.S. administration's intention to leave the subject of nuclear weapons in Europe for discussion at NATO-Warsaw Pact preparatory talks for a European security conference, if such a conference materialized. The Soviet view that all weapons capable of hitting the superpowers, including U.S. tactical nuclear weapons in Europe and aircraft carriers, should be included in SALT would be sidestepped after initial exploration.

When SALT opened in Vienna on April 16, the U.S. tabled three alternative proposals: (1) a total freeze with on-site inspection; (2) a limit on intercontinental ballistic missiles (ICBMs) and antiballistic missiles (ABMs), dependent on unilateral verification; and (3) some combination of these two. The second, limited approach comprised a gross numerical ceiling on offensive forces, plus a ban on ABMs or a limit on their deployment to the areas around Washington and

Deaths:
see Vital Statistics; *see also biographies of prominent persons who died in 1970, listed under* Obituaries

Debts, National:
see Government Finance

Moscow. It would trade a Soviet halt in deployment of the SS-9 ICBM for an end to U.S. deployment of the Safeguard ABM. The first, comprehensive version added to this a ban on U.S. MIRV (multiple independently targeted reentry vehicle) and Soviet MRV (multiple reentry vehicle) testing, reductions in strategic forces, and possible limits on Soviet medium range ballistic missiles (MRBMs) in Eastern Europe and U.S. tactical nuclear weapons in Europe.

This proposal was too far reaching to be acceptable, so on July 9 President Nixon instructed his delegation to seek a limited agreement, with gross numerical limits on ICBMs, submarine launched ballistic missiles (SLBMs), and long-range bombers (reckoned as worth one ICBM), plus an ABM freeze at a low level about equivalent to the existing 64–67 Soviet launchers. The more complicated MIRV and MRV problem would be tackled later. The formal U.S. proposal of July 24, the most important of the first session and christened the Vienna Plan, was for a freeze or reduction of offensive and defensive missiles, without restricting major improvements. Delivery vehicles would be fixed at not more than 2,000 (the current U.S. total was 2,260 less 360 obsolete bombers, against 1,650 for the U.S.S.R.). Each power could vary the mix as it desired, with ABMs held at less than 100 launchers or confined to the two capitals.

Ideally, the U.S. wanted to limit SS-9 deployment, though this was not essential. A MIRV moratorium was impossible because it required on-site inspection (although this was disputed in the U.S.), which the Soviets rejected. They also rejected a ban on MRV and MIRV testing, claiming it would freeze the U.S. lead in MIRV technology. Despite heavy U.S. pressure, the Soviet response was still unclear by the August adjournment, although in 1969 they had concentrated on the danger that Safeguard could expand into a heavy ABM, impairing their assumed destruction capability. Ironically, this had been the basis of former U.S. Defense Secretary Robert S. McNamara's original attempts to persuade them to enter SALT in 1967.

By the time the second session had opened in Helsinki (which was to alternate with Vienna as a site of SALT) in November, it was accepted that SALT would continue for years, possibly becoming an institutionalized strategic seminar. However, a number of developments had occurred that underlined the need for an early agreement to slow down technical innovations. On the U.S. side, the MIRV system had completed its two-year trials and the Mark 12, with three 200-kiloton warheads, would be fitted to 20 Minuteman IIIs by fiscal 1971. This virtually eliminated any chance of a moratorium. The U.S. now had sufficient knowledge to install MIRV without further tests—which could be unilaterally detected with some degree of success—and continuous on-site inspection would

be required to verify whether MIRVs were installed in any particular missiles.

On August 3 a U.S. submarine successfully test-fired a Poseidon missile with the Mark 3 MIRV (ten 50-kiloton warheads) and some form of terminal guidance system, a forerunner of the advanced ballistic reentry system designed to reduce the circular error probability—the radius of the circle within which 50% of the warheads could be expected to fall—from the existing half to one-quarter of a mile to 750 ft. Fears of a disarming first strike against the opposing strategic forces thus increased, since accuracy, measured in terms of circular error probability, was five times more important than the yield of the warheads in attacking silo-based missiles. This explained U.S. interest in the ultralong-range underwater ballistic missile system, a submarine mounting 20 missiles with the range of Minuteman (6,000 mi.) and with MIRVs. The Soviet Union had gone ahead with at least 60 additional siloes for the SS-9 and was testing an MRV for it, though not yet a MIRV. These changes were more serious than the successful U.S. test of its ABM, since ABM deployment was easily monitorable via reconnaissance satellites and in any case the defense was apparently being rapidly outstripped by sophisticated offenses.

NATO

The North Atlantic Treaty Organization faced two interrelated problems during the year: whether it should participate in the European security conference proposed by the Warsaw Pact, and the extent of possible U.S. troop reductions in Europe. The NATO ministerial meetings in November and December 1969 discussed the Pact's October 31 communiqué, proposing a conference guaranteeing European security via renunciation of the threat or use of force, plus the development of economic and social cooperation between East and West. NATO's four preconditions for participation were: (1) inclusion of the U.S. and Canada; (2) mutual and balanced force reductions, developed out of the balanced force reductions concept proposed at NATO's Reykjavik (Ice.) meeting on June 27, 1968 (these two points were accepted by the Pact foreign ministers' meeting in Budapest, Hung., on June 21–22); (3) acceptance of the principles of territorial integrity and (4) of nonintervention in the internal affairs of states.

The two latter points ran counter to the Brezhnev doctrine, enunciated after the 1968 invasion of Czechoslovakia, which permitted Pact intervention when Communist governments (i.e., one-party dictatorships favourable to the U.S.S.R.) were threatened. The NATO ministerial meeting held in Rome in May suggested partial balanced force reductions preserving the Pact's 3:1 superiority, plus the old concepts of notification of maneuvers and the exchange of observers and observer posts. The U.K., West Germany, France, the Benelux countries, and Canada favoured starting discussions on a security conference because not doing so gave the Soviets the diplomatic initiative. Against this, the U.S. insisted on the need for adequate preparation.

Through much of the year there were signs that political and economic pressures could force the Nixon administration to bring back a sizable number of the 250,000 U.S. troops in Europe. It was pointed out that two out of three brigades in each of the four divisions could be based in the U.S., leaving their heavy equipment in West Germany, and returned if

COURTESY, UNITED STATES AIR FORCE

A PARD (Pilot Airborne Recovery Device) is tested for the U.S. Air Force by Goodyear Aerospace Corp. The ballute (balloon and parachute combination) will hold a downed pilot above small-arms fire from the ground until he can be rescued in midair.

These are two of the Special Purpose Individual Weapons (SPIW) being developed by the U.S. Army. They can be used to shoot finned steel darts and 40-mm. antipersonnel grenades.

UPI COMPIX

necessary following the pattern of Exercise Reforger I in 1969, when 12,000 soldiers were airlifted across the Atlantic in a week. Unfortunately, unofficial reports suggested that the resulting maneuvers were chaotic. However, Canada's replacement of its mechanized battle group and CF-104 Starfighters by an air-transportable battalion group assigned to the Allied Command Europe Mobile Force, permitting a 50% reduction of Canadian forces in Europe by 1971, encouraged the U.S. to follow suit.

On November 30, however, U.S. Defense Secretary Melvin Laird announced that the U.S. did not plan to make substantial cuts in its forces in Europe before the end of fiscal 1972, and on December 3 President Nixon, in a statement read before the NATO foreign ministers' meeting in Brussels, pledged that the U.S. would not reduce its forces in Europe "unless there is reciprocal action from our adversaries." The foreign ministers of the U.S., the U.K., and West Germany all expressed opposition to a European security conference, although U.S. Secretary of State William Rogers suggested that exploratory talks on mutual and balanced force reductions might be held. Some hardening of attitude was noted at the ministerial meetings, exemplified by the adoption of proposals for strengthening the West's conventional forces.

On the crucial Northern and Central front, the NATO (including France)-Warsaw Pact balance was: 620,000 NATO to 585,000 Soviet and 315,000 Pact troops; 5,500 NATO to 8,000 Soviet and 6,000 Pact main battle tanks; and 1,750 NATO versus 3,300 Soviet and 1,900 Pact fighter-bombers and fighters.

In tactical nuclear weapons, there were 7,000 warheads (mostly U.S. but including British and French) on 2,250 delivery vehicles owned by the following nonnuclear powers under the two-key system which required approval of both the warhead and the vehicle owner before use: West Germany, Belgium, the Netherlands, Italy, Greece, and Canada (until the end of 1971).

UNITED STATES

President Nixon's February 18 report to Congress, *U.S. Foreign Policy for the Seventies,* foreshadowed major changes in the U.S. strategic posture in accordance with the move from an era of confrontation to one of negotiations. The U.S. would abandon its blanket commitment to oppose Communism through global military alliances. Its allies would have to provide the major part of their own defense, since U.S. aid would be forthcoming only against clear Communist aggression and would be proportional to the victim's efforts plus its capacity to absorb assistance.

Although the invasion of Cambodia appeared to undermine this new policy before it had started, most other indications were that it would form the basis for U.S. long-range defense planning in the 1970s. The most important single step was the reduction in strategic requirements from the ability—never actually achieved—to fight two major wars and one minor war simultaneously to one major war (implicitly European) and one minor (probably Asian). This change implied major alterations in the number and types of forces needed, as suggested by the reports of two presidential commissions.

The first, under former defense secretary Thomas Gates, reported February 21 on the draft. This had become a major domestic political issue, since the armed forces expansion from roughly 2.5 million to

AUTHENTICATED NEWS INTERNATIONAL

A high performance XM-808 combat vehicle charges up a slope at a Lockheed Missiles & Space Co. test course. The XM-808 Twister has two separate four-wheel drive bodies, each with its own engine, which are joined by a flexible yoke.

3.5 million men between 1965 and 1968 had been accomplished mostly by adding draftees, who comprised one-quarter to one-third of the men in Vietnam. Criticism of the Selective Service System on grounds of discrimination had been exacerbated by the insensitivity of its head, Lewis B. Hershey, who retired in February and was succeeded by Curtis W. Tarr. A new system of draft by lottery was introduced, and paternity and occupational deferments were eliminated on April 23, but neither these changes nor a reduction in call-up (to 163,500 in 1970) seemed likely to remove the political unrest.

The Gates Commission suggested a largely volunteer force of 2.5 million men needing 250,000 true volunteers a year; a further 75,000 conscripts would be provided by a form of draft that would include an incentive to volunteer and a means of emergency expansion. The gross cost would be $3.3 billion, reduced to a net $2.7 billion if the higher tax revenue that would be derived from increased pay was taken into account; $315 per month was suggested as basic pay instead of the current $115. Reaction was mixed. The services feared that instead of receiving reasonably representative and well-qualified recruits, they might become composed of blacks and the less well educated, with a Southern officer corps. The Army would lose most, but the Air Force and Navy believed that many of their skilled volunteers were selecting a less unpleasant alternative to the Army. President Nixon accepted the commission's basic recommendations but implemented them slowly. He requested a two-year extension of the draft law, due to expire on June 30, 1971; offered a 20% pay raise to enlisted men with less than two years of service plus other increases; and indicated a target of 2.9 million men for 1971. Meanwhile, the services themselves were attempting to eliminate outmoded disciplinary procedures and otherwise make military life more tolerable.

The second commission, the Fitzhugh panel, concluded its review of the Pentagon's operations on July 28 by commenting that it was amazed the system worked at all in its existing form. The panel's 113 recommendations came under six main headings. (1) The Pentagon should be functionally divided into three groups, for resource management, evaluation, and operations, each under a deputy secretary of defense. (2) The director, defense research and engineering, should be replaced by three assistant secretaries responsible for, respectively, research, development, and testing and evaluation. (3) There should be prototype testing before purchase, which would eliminate total package procurement. (4) The existing seven

AUTHENTICATED NEWS
INTERNATIONAL
Nuclear attack submarine
"Trepang" heads out
to sea from the shipyard
of Electric Boat Division,
General Dynamics,
at Groton, Conn. It was
the first sea trial
of the U.S. Navy's 88th
nuclear submarine.

service commands should be consolidated into three: strategic, tactical, and logistics. (5) Direct operational control should be exercised by a unified force commander who would come under a deputy secretary for operations. (6) The Joint Chiefs of Staff should revert to their proper role as chiefs of their own services and principal military advisers to the president. The Joint Chiefs naturally opposed these reductions in their power, but with the president and the secretary of defense supporting the broad lines of the proposals, they seemed likely to be implemented.

In large measure, this was because the costs of manpower and equipment were increasing in a domestic climate more critical of military spending. Secretary Laird's fiscal 1971 budget of $73,790,000,-000—$4,680,000,000 below fiscal 1970—reflected these pressures. Strategic forces accounted for approximately $10 billion, a figure likely to rise in view of technological innovations such as MIRV and ABM. The 490 Minuteman I missiles would be replaced by the Minuteman III, 10 of which were deployed with the Mark 12 MIRV on July 1, 1970. Of the 41 Polaris submarines, 10 would retain the A-3 missiles (2,880-mi. range); the remainder would be converted to Poseidon missiles. Of the remaining $65 million in the budget, about half went to salaries; hence, the planned elimination of 1.7 million defense jobs, including 600,000 servicemen. At $17 billion, spending on Vietnam was about half the level when President Nixon took office.

Cost overruns on 27 major projects totaled $20 billion, including the F-111 fighter-bomber (123%), the SRAM missile (250%), and the DD963 destroyer (97%). The C-5A Galaxy transport, with a 56.6% overrun, demonstrated the dependence of major defense contractors on the government and the dangers of making low initial bids to secure orders. Lockheed was to have received high profits on the second and third production runs to compensate for excess costs on the first, but the order for 120 was cut to 81. Lockheed wrote off $290 million, but it needed $200 million in immediate authorization and an eventual total of $430 million in order to keep supplying the

government—which bought 90% of its products. Nevertheless, some new projects secured preliminary funding. The Air Force was to obtain the F-15 air superiority fighter and the AWACS (airborne warning and control system) and OTH (over-the-horizon) radars; the B-1 bomber for 1978; and the A-X ground-support aircraft. The Navy received authorization for a new carrier, the "Eisenhower," although carriers continued to be attacked as unnecessarily costly.

The planned expansion of the Safeguard ABM system was approved by a Senate vote of 52–47 on August 12, compared with the 51–49 vote on initial deployment in 1969. The increased administration majority reflected greater acceptance of its arguments on the uncertainty of Soviet intentions, the need for a bargaining card in SALT, and fears that without ABM more offensive weapons might be needed. Estimates for completion of the second phase rose to $10.7 billion in 1969 dollars, against the original $9.1 billion, as a result of inflation, stretchout, and design changes. Warheads added $200 million. Two improvements were modification of the long-range Spartan for use against submarine-launched ballistic missiles and research on the hard-site ABM.

The administration reduced the chemical and biological warfare program, estimated to have cost $550 million in fiscal 1969. President Nixon's statement of Nov. 25, 1969, was expanded on Feb. 14, 1970, to include toxins in his ban on the production and use of biological weapons, and late in the year the Army made public detailed plans for destroying its biological weapons stocks. On August 19 the president fulfilled his promise to send the Geneva Protocol of 1925 to the Senate for ratification, with the interpretation that it did not ban the use of CS or of tear gases or defoliants. Nevertheless, on April 15 he had banned the compound 2,4,5-T, which was said to have caused fetal deformities when it was used in the U.S. defoliation program in Vietnam.

Disposal of existing chemical weapons proved difficult. The Army had to remove 12,000 tons of VX and GB (Sarin) nerve gases plus mustard gas from Okinawa before the island was returned to Japan in 1972. Plans to ship this to Oregon were canceled in May, following protests from those along the route. In December it was announced that the gas would be stored on Johnston Island. Within the U.S. deteriorating propellants in rockets with gas warheads, which had been coffined in concrete in 1968, threatened a dangerous explosion, and plans were made to dump them off Florida. Eleven shiploads of ordinance, including four of CS gas, had already been carefully scuttled in deep water, but this time there was widespread opposition. The operation was finally carried out on August 18. It was announced that the Rocky Mountain Arsenal would build two detoxification plants to burn the remaining CS.

UNITED KINGDOM

Following the surprise Conservative victory in the June elections, the new government began to reassert Britain's role as a major overseas power. As defined by the new defense secretary, Lord Carrington, Conservative policy differed from that of the Labour government in four main areas: Anglo-French nuclear cooperation; Malaysia; the Persian Gulf; and South Africa. The economic constraints embodied in the 1970–71 defense budget, presented in February, remained, however. At £2,380 million (5.1% of GNP) it was about the same as in the previous year.

During the debate on the budget, the then defense secretary, Denis Healey, emphasized NATO's dependence on early recourse to tactical nuclear weapons, refuting allegations that the reserves (48,000 first-line Territorial and Army Volunteer Reserves and 60,000 regulars) were too low by claiming that more conventional forces were irrelevant. He revealed that Lord Mountbatten, when chief of the Defence Staff, had advised him that NATO's role was to stop small attacks, forcing a major invasion that would have to be met by nuclear weapons. This reinforced the argument for nuclear cooperation with France, but the Conservatives' initial feelers met with a cool response.

Britain's strategic deterrent consisted of four submarines carrying 16 Polaris A-3 missiles with triple warheaded MRVs; three submarines were in service and a fourth was refitting. The RAF Strike Command provided tactical nuclear support with 50 Vulcan bombers carrying Blue Steel air-to-surface missiles, 35 Buccaneers, and 160 F-4 Phantoms ordered from the U.S., though these would not all be based in the U.K. at any one time. The Lightning had become the standard interceptor; 100 were in the U.K., 30 in West Germany, and one squadron was in Singapore. Canberras and Hunters were being replaced as ground-attack aircraft by the V/STOL (vertical/short takeoff and landing) Harriers. Bloodhound and Tigercat surface-to-air missiles provided antiaircraft defense. The Navy's antisubmarine warfare program centred on the Valient-class nuclear hunter-killer submarines; the third of the seven due by 1972 became operational during the year. Three guided-missile destroyers, with two more to come, combined with the two attack ships and the two commando carriers to form the nucleus of a useful *force d'intervention.* The two strike carriers, "Eagle" and "Ark Royal," would be withdrawn by the end of 1972.

Britain was committed to defend Malaysia against external aggression under the 1957 Anglo-Malaysian Defence Agreement, due to lapse in 1971. The Conservatives wanted to replace it with a five-power (U.K., Australia, New Zealand, Malaysia, and Singapore) arrangement for defense against external guerrilla attack, comprising British, Australian, and New Zealand battalions in the 28th Commonwealth Brigade based in Singapore, together with an air defense network and a Commonwealth naval task force. British personnel in Malaysia had already been reduced to about 30,000, one-third the 1968 figure, but it was planned to retain the jungle warfare school at Lahore. Exercise Bersatu Padu (Perfect Unity) in April–June airlifted a brigade from the U.K. to Singapore while about 80 warships were concentrated in the area.

The 6,000 men in the Persian Gulf were due to be withdrawn by the end of 1971. Of the three local powers, Saudi Arabia's attitude was uncertain while the other two wanted Britain out, Iran because it regarded the Gulf as its natural sphere of influence while its enemy, Iraq, wanted to use its 85,000 troops to annex Kuwait. Like the other oil sheikhdoms of Bahrain, Qatar, Abu Dhabi, and Oman, Kuwait wanted British protection against internal and external threats. The failure of the Federation of Arab Amirates suggested that a residual British presence might be retained, comprising the Sharjak base for reinforcements, plus training and officering the local forces, especially the Trucial Oman Scouts.

The new foreign secretary, Sir Alec Douglas-Home, stressed South Africa's strategic importance to the U.K., since the closing of the Suez Canal had forced over half Britain's oil imports to use the cape route. South Africa was already using this as an argument for its diplomatic acceptance as a NATO ally, and it also tried to force the issue on the question of arms supplies and the 1955 agreement on the Simonstown naval base. This allowed Britain to use the base in time of war, even if it did not involve South Africa, in return for naval cooperation (which continued) and arms supplies. The supplies in question were 12 antisubmarine vessels, but when the Labour government refused to modernize them, South Africa threatened to reconsider the agreement and suggested that it wished to place larger arms orders, including 20 Nimrod antisubmarine aircraft, 4 frigates, and Buccaneer dive-bombers. The bombers might violate the 1963 Security Council resolutions governing British policy on arms supplies to South Africa, which forbade those suitable for internal use. Intense Commonwealth and African diplomatic pressure forced Sir Alec to say that South African applications could be considered only on their individual merits.

The British Army of the Rhine remained at 53,500 men, with two armoured and four infantry brigades. The Chieftain tank with its 120-mm. gun replaced the Centurion in eight armoured regiments, and the Swingfire SP antitank missile was introduced. Tactical nuclear firepower was supplied by three regiments with Honest John missiles and 203-mm. guns. The only fighting was, tragically, in Northern Ireland. (*See* IRELAND: *Special Report.*) By July the emergency British garrison of 7,500 had been reinforced by 3,700 men, leaving the U.K. without effective reserves. In December the force was cut back to 6,000 men.

FRANCE

Although France remained aloof from NATO, the reinterpretation of its flexible-response strategy as a range of appropriate responses, both nuclear and non-nuclear, brought its strategic concept and NATO's more closely into line. This suggested that France would coordinate its planning with the organization of which it was still a member, without reassigning forces to it.

There were more delays in the nuclear weapons program as a result of cost overruns. The Mirage IVA jet bombers, equipped for low-level penetration with 60-kiloton atomic bombs, received the A.S.-2 180-mi. range air-to-ground missile. "Le Redoutable," the first of three nuclear submarines carrying M-112 250-kiloton warhead missiles, was unlikely to become operational before the end of 1971, instead of 1970. A second, "Le Terrible," was launched, but an 83% rise in costs led to postponement of the nuclear hunter-killer submarine intended as an escort. Cost of the intermediate range ballistic missile (IRBM) program, based on the Saphir missile with an initial range of 1,500 mi. (to be extended to 1,700 mi.), increased by 75%. The number was therefore cut from 27 to 18, with the first squadron of 9 due to become operational in 1971. The 25-kiloton tactical nuclear missile Pluton, with a 75-mi. range, was not expected to enter service until 1973. In February work on ICBMs and MRVs was virtually suspended. Nevertheless, France continued with its nuclear testing program to develop miniaturized warheads for the MRBMs and SLBMs. Two tests of one-megaton devices, on July 3 and August 5 at Mururora in the Pacific, established that H-bomb warheads would be available by 1972. Six routine tests were also held

A Poseidon missile is test-launched from the submarine "James Madison" at the U.S. Air Force's eastern test range on Aug. 3, 1970.
COURTESY, UNITED STATES AIR FORCE

LONDON "DAILY EXPRESS" FROM PICTORIAL PARADE

The first prototype of the West German VAK 191B subsonic vertical takeoff tactical strike fighter (VTOL) rolls out at the Bremen works of VFW-Fokker. It is powered by one Rolls-Royce thrust turbofan engine and two lift jets.

including the first of an operational 200–400-kiloton device.

What he regarded as excessive emphasis on the nuclear *force de frappe* led Adm. André Patou to resign as chief of staff of the French Navy on April 6. The nominal issue was cancellation of the refit for the cruiser "Colbert," but the real source of Patou's disaffection was the imminent need to cancel the MRBM program and end the draft in order to fund naval cover for the missile submarines. Minister of Defense Michel Debré countered on June 7 by announcing that France would build two more such submarines in the late 1970s. The admiral's comments were strengthened by the extreme weakness of the French Army. Selective military service of 12 to 15 months provided 328,000 men. Three mechanized, one air portable, and one Alpine division, plus 56,000-strong forces for local defense, were stationed in France. French troops in Africa totaled 12,500, comprising 600 in Ivory Coast, 2,200 in Senegal, 2,500 in Chad, 400 in Gabon, and 2,000 in Malagasy, plus a garrison of 4,400 in the French Territory of the Afars and Issas and 400 troops in Algeria.

France continued as a major arms exporter. The most noticed agreement was that of January 21, selling 5 trainer-interceptors and 110 Mirage IIIs worth more than $400 million to Libya for delivery between 1971 and 1975. Doubts as to whether their ultimate destination might not be the U.A.R. were reinforced by the arrest of the dozen or so pilots of the Libyan Air Force. Other deals included 30 Mirage III-EB interceptor-trainers to Spain ($90 million), 16 Mirage III-EBs to Brazil, and 30 AML scout cars to the Congo (Kinshasa). Despite this, the defense budget, at $5,874,000,000, amounted to 4.4% of GNP. Although less than West Germany's in absolute terms, it represented the highest percentage of GNP spent on defense among the EEC countries.

WEST GERMANY

At $5,560,100,000, the 1970–71 defense budget was 6.8% above that for 1969–70. The major changes envisaged by Chancellor Willy Brandt's government were set out in the Defense Ministry's White Paper on the Bundeswehr, published on May 20. Defense Minister Helmut Schmidt had appointed a special planning group, under Theo Sommer, assistant editor of *Die Zeit,* to examine the implications of possible U.S. troop reductions in Europe and the rising cost for West Germany of military manpower and equip-

ment. The basic conclusion was the need to preserve the balance of power in Europe while securing, through political means, a stable settlement with the East, as exemplified by the Soviet-West German treaty renouncing the use of force, signed on August 12.

For the Bundeswehr, the central problem remained the difficulty of securing enough long-term regular officers and men to handle increasingly complex weapons systems. It was still 2,600 officers and 25,000 NCOs short, while long-term soldiers comprised only 50% of the total establishment. Pay raises and promotions, plus $68 million for better accommodations by 1976, were recommended. There were now more conscripts eligible for military service than the Bundeswehr needed to maintain its fixed strength of 460,000, so the 18 months' compulsory service would probably be reduced to 15 months.

The basic concept was a shift toward a small, mobile, professional army, plus a larger Territorial Army of short-service troops providing quickly mobilizable reserves. Regrouping would therefore occur; in the North German plain the 11 panzer (armoured) brigades would be increased to 13½ and the 12 panzer-grenadier (armoured infantry) brigades to 16. This would partly compensate for Canada's withdrawal of 5,000 of its 10,000 troops and their change from a mechanized to an air-mobile role. West Germany agreed to buy British military goods offsetting 80% of the U.K.'s costs in returning the VI Brigade (4,500 men) to West Germany, together with the 36th Heavy Air Defence regiment and 18 RAF squadrons. In the more defensible central and southern areas, the number of reconnaissance brigades would be reduced from six to two to create three panzer regiments; the three airborne and two mountain brigades would be retained. The reservists, totaling 1.5 million (540,000 for direct mobilization), would be exercised more frequently.

There were also matériel changes. Development of the joint U.S.-West German main battle tank was canceled; the German Leopard with a 105-mm. gun, 1,840 of which were in service, would replace the 1,460 M-48A2 Patton tanks. The Leopard chassis would carry a new 34-mm. antiaircraft system instead of the projected 30-mm. antiaircraft armoured weapons system. Orders for the MRCA (multirole combat aircraft) would be cut from 800 to 420 by stretching the F-104G Starfighter to 1980, and 50 more F-104Gs were ordered; as of April 1, Starfighter losses totaled 118, with 57 pilots killed. Deliveries began on the 88 Phantom II RF4-E fighter-bombers ordered at a cost of $6,260,000, as did construction under license of 80 U.S. Sikorsky CH-53G helicopters.

The Navy had four projected frigates canceled because of an 80% rise in costs, leaving it with three guided missile destroyers, eight destroyers, and six frigates, plus coastal forces. Nuclear weapons delivery systems, under the two-key system, included 18 squadrons of F-104Gs, the Phantoms, 203-mm. artillery, 11 battalions of Honest John and 4 battalions of Sergeant missiles, plus 3 battalions of Pershing medium-range missiles. West German arms sales included 40 Noratlas transports to Greece and Cobra 2000 antitank missiles to Argentina.

SOUTHEAST AND EAST ASIA

Fighting in South Vietnam dropped to a relatively low level, but the conflict spread to Cambodia and Laos. The U.S. adopted a long-haul, low-cost strategy based on vietnamization, plus the residual U.S. presence for up to 15 years advocated by the British expert on guerrilla warfare, Sir Robert Thompson, and presidential adviser Henry Kissinger. This meant reducing U.S. forces and casualties to a domestically acceptable level while strengthening the South Vietnamese Army (ARVN) and local defense forces, thus forcing Hanoi to negotiate. David Bruce, former ambassador to the U.K., was named as ambassador to the Paris peace talks, which had been without a top-level U.S. negotiator, but the talks seemed further than ever from being productive. Elsewhere in the area, President Nixon's new foreign policy set in motion U.S. withdrawals from Thailand and South Korea.

By the time of President Nixon's April 20 speech, his first 150,000-man cutback in South Vietnam had been completed, enabling him to announce a further reduction of 150,000 by the spring of 1971. Secretary Laird later emphasized that more than 50,000 of these would be back by October 15. By November actual U.S. troops in Vietnam numbered 368,000, and the eventual aim seemed to be about 250,000, comprising two infantry divisions and one armoured regiment plus air support. The vietnamization program seemed reasonably successful, as evidenced by the ARVN's good performance in Cambodia. It had expanded from 700,000 to 1,186,000 men, comprising 481,000 regulars and 705,000 paramilitary forces.

Against them were 85,000 North Vietnamese and 40,000 Viet Cong regular forces plus 100,000 VC irregulars, with infiltration from North Vietnam at a level of 10,000–30,000 per month. The Communists were still feeling the effects of the 1968 Tet offensive,

Approximate Strengths of Regular Armed Forces of the World

Country	Military personnel in 000s Army	Navy	Air force	Aircraft carriers	Warships Submarines*	Cruisers	Destroyers/ frigates	Total ships	Aircraft Bombers†	Fighters	Defense expenditure as % of GNP
I. NATO											
Belgium	70.0	4.4	20.5	—	—	—	—	—	80 FB	—	3.0
Canada	35.3	17.0	41.0	—	4	—	20	24	50 FB	75	2.5
Denmark	27.0	7.0	10.5	—	6	—	6	12	48 FB	48	2.6
Germany, West	326.0	36.0	104.0	—	11	—	17	28	420 FB	80	3.5
Greece	118.0	18.0	23.0	—	2	—	12	14	108 FB	—	5.1
Italy	295.0	45.0	73.0	—	10	4	20	34	100 FB	200	2.9
Netherlands	80.0	20.0	21.2	—	7	2	18	27	100 FB	36	3.7
Norway	23.5	8.6	9.0	—	15	—	5	20	64 FB	20	3.8
Portugal	150.0	18.0	17.5	—	5	—	14	19	40 FB	20	6.1
Turkey	390.0	37.5	50.0	—	10	—	10	20	100 FB	180	4.6
United Kingdom	190.0	87.0	113.0	4	21, 3N 3 FBMS	1	72	104	200 FB, 170 B	150	5.1
United States	1,363.0	988.0‡	810.0	20	39, 44N 41 FBMS	10	224	378	1,400 FB, 540 SB	1,240	8.6
II. OTHER EUROPEAN											
Albania	35.0	4.0	2.5	—	4	—	—	4	70 FB	—	—
Austria	45.0	—	4.0	—	—	—	—	—	13 FB	—	1.2
Finland	34.0	2.0	3.0	—	—	—	3	3	30 FB	—	1.6
France	328.0	72.0	106.0	4	20	2	46	72	210 FB, 45 B	150	4.4
Spain	210.0	39.3	32.6	—	4	1	26	31	80 FB	86	2.1
Sweden	44.5	12.1	15.4	—	20	1	15	36	200 FB	420	4.0
Switzerland	19.5	—	8.0	—	—	—	—	—	150 FB	100	2.2
Yugoslavia	200.0	18.0	20.0	—	5	—	5	10	150 FB	160	5.3
III. WARSAW PACT											
Bulgaria	130.0	7.0	12.0	—	2	—	—	2	66 FB	122	2.8
Czechoslovakia	150.0	—	18.0	—	—	—	—	—	270 FB, 60 B	290	5.6
Germany, East	92.0	16.0	21.0	—	—	—	3	3	—	275	5.9
Hungary	90.0	1.5	10.0	—	—	—	—	—	12 B	140	3.4
Poland	195.0	22.0	25.0	—	5	—	3	8	120 FB, 60 B	450	5.0
Romania	165.0	8.0	8.0	—	—	—	—	—	—	200	2.9
U.S.S.R.	2,000.0‡	475.0	480.0	—	290, 80 N 25 FBMS	26	200	621	2,000 FB, 725 B 140 SB	5,300	8.5
IV. FAR EAST AND OCEANIA											
Australia	45.0	17.4	22.6	1	4	—	13	18	60 FB, 12 B	—	4.0
Burma	130.5	6.2	6.5	—	—	—	1	1	12 FB	—	4.7
Cambodia	120.0	1.5	2.3	—	—	—	—	—	—	24	5.9
China‡	2,450.0	150.0	180.0	—	33	—	13	46	500 FB, 150 B	1,000	10.0
India	800.0	40.0	90.0	1	4	2	19	26	180 FB, 45 B	210	3.5
Indonesia	275.0	40.0	50.0	—	6	1	30	37	55 B	130	2.3
Japan	179.0	38.0	42.0	—	10	—	28	38	200 FB	175	0.8
Korea, North	370.0	13.0	30.0	—	4	—	—	4	60 FB, 70 B	110	24.9
Korea, South	570.0	19.0	23.0	—	—	—	10	10	115 FB	75	4.0
Laos	65.0	0.4	1.8	—	—	—	—	—	—	—	11.0
Malaysia	40.0	3.2	4.5	—	—	—	2	2	30 FB	—	3.6
New Zealand	5.7	2.9	4.5	—	—	—	1	1	20 FB, 8 B	—	1.9
Pakistan	300.0	9.5	15.0	—	1	—	7	8	308 FB, 48 B	10	3.4
Philippines	18.0	6.0	9.0	—	—	—	1	1	20 FB	2	1.5
Taiwan	387.5	34.0	65.0	—	3	—	15	18	90 FB	283	9.2
Vietnam, North	425.0	3.2	4.5	—	—	—	—	—	10 B	130	21.3
Vietnam, South	420.0	38.0	23.0	—	—	—	2	2	100 FB	20	13.6
V. MIDDLE EAST, AFRICA, AND LATIN AMERICA											
Algeria	53.0	2.0	2.0	—	—	—	—	—	30 B	140	5.8
Argentina	85.0	35.0§	17.0	1	2	3	14	20	25 FB	45	2.6
Brazil	120.0	44.3§	30.0	1	4	2	18	25	18 FB	16	2.6
Chile	38.0	15.0	8.0	—	2	2	5	9	—	25	1.7
Colombia	50.0	8.0	6.0	—	—	—	10	10	—	2	2.0
Congo (Kinshasa)	37.5	0.1	0.6	—	—	—	—	—	—	17	2.0
Cuba	90.0	7.5	12.0	—	—	—	2	2	20 FB	165	6.1
Ethiopia	41.0	1.4	3.0	—	—	—	—	—	18 B	16	2.2
Iran	135.0	9.0	17.0	—	—	—	6	6	112 FB	20	6.6
Iraq	85.0	2.0	7.5	—	—	—	—	—	86 FB, 18 B	105	10.0
Israel‖	61.5/275.0	4.5/8.0	9.0/17.0	—	4	—	2	6	223 FB, 12 B	10	25.1
Jordan	58.0	0.2	2.0	—	—	—	—	—	20 FB	18	18.0
Mexico	54.0	7.6	6.0	—	—	—	5	5	15 FB	—	...
Nigeria	180.0	2.0	3.0	—	—	—	1	1	—	—	5.9
Peru	35.5	10.1	9.0	—	4	2	5	11	10 FB, 20 B	60	3.2
S. Africa	32.3	3.5	8.0	—	1	—	8	9	44 FB	74	2.4
Syria	75.0	1.7	10.0	—	—	—	—	—	120 FB	90	14.4
United Arab Republic	250.0	14.0	20.0	—	12	—	5	17	270 FB, 43 B	150	13.3

Note: Data exclude paramilitary, security, and irregular forces. Naval data exclude vessels of less than 100 tons standard displacement.
*Nuclear hunter-killers (N), fleet ballistic missile submarines (FBMS).
†Medium and heavy bombers (B), fighter-bombers (FB), and strategic bombers (SB).
‡Approximate.
§Includes Marine Corps.
‖Second figure is fully mobilized strength.
Sources: Institute for Strategic Studies, 18 Adam Street, London, *The Military Balance, 1970-71, Strategic Survey 1969-70.*

which had cost them 500,000 men killed and wounded. In retrospect, Tet apparently had failed to have the expected decisive effect on the U.S., and the Communists had been forced to fall back on protracted warfare. Their main targets were the South Vietnamese administrative structure—and U.S. public opinion. One hundred American deaths per week was seen as a critical level for influencing the U.S., but the toll was frequently lower. Moreover, the North Vietnamese had been frustrated in both their general autumn offensive against Saigon in 1969 and the May campaign against towns. The Americans and South Vietnamese had developed appropriate skills for dealing with guerrilla tactics. Search-and-destroy operations were abandoned in favour of holding and clearing the countryside.

To compensate for their losses in South Vietnam the Communists sent 40,000 additional men to Cambodia, which they planned to use as a base for their next major attack. This violated the implicit agreement whereby Prince Sihanouk was allowed to rule the nominally neutral country while permitting the North Vietnamese and VC to use it as a sanctuary and to use the Ho Chi Minh Trail and, until July 1967, the port of Sihanoukville. Sihanouk's inability to govern effectively, plus his absence in Moscow, led to a coup on March 18, after which he formed a Communist puppet government in exile. The new government, under Gen. Lon Nol, quickly appealed for help against the Communists, who were advancing on the capital, Phnom Penh. President Nixon announced the U.S. response on April 30: an incursion limited to 30 km. from the South Vietnamese border, with all forces withdrawn by July 1. Despite his talk of searching for COSVN (the Central Office for South Vietnam), the real target was the supply dumps the enemy had been accumulating in the Parrot's Beak and Fishhook areas. The operation succeeded. More than 10 million lb. of small arms ammunition, 14 million lb. of rice, and 22,000 weapons were captured or destroyed. The 4,000 tons of ammunition captured or destroyed compared with the Communists' monthly expenditure of 330 tons. Losses were U.S., 339 killed and 1,500 wounded; South Vietnam, 860 killed and 3,600 captured; Communists, 11,400 killed and 2,300 captured.

With the arrival of the monsoon in July, the U.S. concentrated on the Mekong Delta, while one-third of the North Vietnamese troops destined for that area were switched to Cambodia. The Communists controlled Cambodia's four northeastern provinces, but these contained less than 10% of the population. Fighting continued within 20 mi. of Phnom Penh, with the ARVN aiding the poorly equipped government forces.

With U.S. casualties in Vietnam sharply lowered, the question of the prisoners of war being held in the North assumed increasing importance. On November 21, while U.S. fighter-bombers struck at air defense and supply targets in the North, a small U.S. commando force staged a raid on a prisoner of war camp at Son Tay, 23 mi. from Hanoi. The operation was technically successful and the raiders escaped, but the camp was found to be unoccupied.

In November limited U.S. air strikes in the North were reported, allegedly in retaliation for North Vietnamese attacks on U.S. reconnaissance planes. At his December 10 press conference President Nixon threatened to resume general bombing in the North if U.S. forces remaining in Vietnam were endangered.

The 1962 Laos settlement was virtually a dead letter. Unofficial—though openly acknowledged—U.S. aid to the right-wing elements continued, including B-52 bomber raids. These failed to prevent the Communists, with 67,000 North Vietnamese regulars and 25,000 Pathet Lao, from controlling the strategic Plaine des Jarres and the North Vietnamese frontier. In August the Thai prime minister, Thanom Kittikachorn, announced that most of the 11,000-man Thai division in South Vietnam would be recalled to bring the Army up to its 110,000-man strength and to secure the Thai frontiers with Laos and Cambodia. Of the 42,000 Americans stationed in Thailand, 10,000 were scheduled for withdrawal in the next year.

Another combatant in South Vietnam, South Korea, found itself facing a cutback of 20,000 of the 53,000 U.S. troops stationed on its territory in the next 18 months. This would leave 30 South Korean divisions (560,000 men) and one U.S. division to face North Korea's 370,000-man Army and 700 aircraft. Following Secretary Laird's July meeting with South Korean Defense Minister Chung Nai Hyuk, a compensatory $1 billion, five-year modernization program was announced, in addition to the current $140 million per month of military assistance. Despite U.S. estimates that this would suffice as long as the U.S. provided air superiority and tactical nuclear weapons in reserve, the Korean government expected to recall some of its 50,000 troops in South Vietnam. Although they were traditional enemies, South Korea and Japan seemed likely to cooperate in defense matters; in August 54 Japanese F-104J fighter-bombers arrived in Korea for joint exercises.

Japan's reemergence as a regional power had been signaled by the Nixon-Sato communiqué of Nov. 21, 1969, whereby the U.S. agreed to return Okinawa to Japan by 1972. The U.S. also agreed to remove all nuclear weapons from the island and to request Japanese consent for their return or for the use of U.S. troops on Okinawa against third states. In exchange the Japanese agreed to indefinite extension of the 1951 treaty allowing the U.S. to retain its military installations on Japanese territory—excluding 24 Mace-B missiles and poison gas. The fourth Japanese five-year defense plan, for 1972–76, was being prepared by the new director of the National Self-Defense Agency, Yasuhiro Nakasone (*see* BIOGRAPHY), who supported the concept of autonomous Japanese capability for local defense, including the Ryukyu Islands, in cooperation with the U.S.

The percentage of Japan's GNP spent on defense rose 18% in 1970, from 0.84 to 1.12. Defense expenditure totaled $1,580,000, and this was expected to reach $3,540,000 by 1975. Increasing Soviet air and naval activity near Japan led to the allocation of greater resources to the Navy and Air Force in the 1970 budget. The Navy was to expand from 130,000 to 200,000 men and would receive a new 4,700-ton destroyer, 2 destroyer escorts, and one submarine, plus 11 Neptune antisubmarine aircraft. The Air Force was reequipping with 150 F-4 Phantoms, largely manufactured in Japan under license. Four prototypes of the Japanese XT-2 supersonic fighter were ordered. The Army, which remained at 179,000 men (13 divisions), was being modernized. All the services were overofficered to facilitate expansion.

U.S.S.R.

Official defense appropriations for 1970, at 17.9 billion rubles ($39.8 billion), were only 200 million rubles above 1969, indicating that the Communist Party was satisfied with the defense situation. Total military spending, including the cost of nuclear warheads, research and development expenditure on advanced weapons systems, and military elements of the space program, was estimated at $51.7 billion, about the same as in the previous year and representing only a slightly higher percentage of GNP—8.5—than U.S. defense spending. However, Soviet strategic policy became increasingly ambiguous in three areas: the strategic relationship with the U.S., with the Middle East, and with China. Previously, its aim had been seen as parity with the U.S. both in strategic weapons and in the role of a global, rather than a regional, superpower, implying a commitment to stability. The Soviets now appeared willing to take greater risks to increase their influence, though how far their motives were defensive rather than expansionist remained uncertain.

In strategic weapons the Soviet Union was ahead of the U.S. in numbers and behind in deliverable warheads. It had 1,300 ICBMs, including 800 SS-11 missiles, compared with the U.S.'s 1,000 Minuteman Is, IIs, and IIIs, and 280 SLBMs (about 120 in older submarines carrying three missiles each) to the U.S.'s 656 Polaris A2s and A3s. The figure of 2,000 Soviet deliverable warheads to the U.S.'s 4,652 was misleading, however, because 2,250 of the U.S. warheads were in aging strategic bombers, against only 420 for the U.S.S.R. Omitting the bombers, the U.S. superiority in warheads dropped from about 2.3:1 to about 5:3. Since the introduction of MRV and MIRV would change these ratios back in favour of the U.S., the Soviets' traditional emphasis on quantitative superiority could explain their continued production of the SS-9 (Scarp), despite U.S. fears that its 25-megaton payload, the largest of any ICBM, could represent a first-strike capability.

The crash production of five to ten a year of the Yankee (Y)-class Polaris-type submarines firing the SS-N-6 missile could be explained by the increasing vulnerability of silo-based missiles. The Moscow ABM network remained frozen at 67 launchers for the Galosh missile, but the nationwide network of ABM radars, nicknamed henhouses, continued to expand. Linked with the Tallin Line air defense network and its SAM-5 Griffon missiles by improved computers, these could increase Soviet ABM capability appreciably. The Soviets might, like the Americans, be taking time to adjust to the concepts of sufficiency and the goal of parity, but increased doubts about their intentions remained.

The rapid growth of Soviet influence in the Mediterranean after 1967 reflected the immediate need to support the U.S.S.R.'s Arab allies and the military requirements for defense against U.S. forces; hence the acquisition of a navy to track and destroy carriers in conjunction with land-based aircraft, while antisubmarine vessels, including the helicopter carriers "Moscow" and "Leningrad," assisted nuclear hunter-killer submarines in neutralizing Polaris submarines. The naval forces were also developed into symbols of the Soviet presence, exerting significant political influence in conjunction with the nominally civilian merchant marine. The latter had expanded to the sixth largest in the world (over 12 million tons, growing at 1 million tons a year), while the fishing fleet, which included intelligence-gathering ships, was the third largest. Anchorages were established in Libya, Tunisia, and the U.A.R., and the former French naval

WIDE WORLD

One of two Soviet submarines that entered the Caribbean Sea May 8, 1970. The destination of the conventionally powered vessels was unknown.

base of Mers-el-Kebir in Algeria was taken over. Developing U.S. style afloat-support techniques, the Soviets established a base in Cuba and became active in the Gulf of Mexico, where their Y-class submarines carried more missiles than Nikita Khrushchev had tried to install in Cuba. For Lenin's birthday, April 22, the Soviets mounted Operation Ocean. About 100 ships, including the "Leningrad," maneuvered around Norway and the Baltic; the 45-strong Mediterranean squadron mounted an antisubmarine warfare exercise; and the Indian (15 ships) and Pacific (25 ships) squadrons showed the flag in over 36 countries.

The Army's major activity was strengthening the defenses of Siberia, which contained three-quarters of the Soviet Union's coal reserves and four-fifths of its hydroelectric power, against China. The commander in chief of the new Central Asian military district was General Tolabko, a rocket specialist, whose forces had risen from 14 understrength divisions in 1965 to 36 divisions. Together with the 30 divisions of the Far Eastern military district and the Mongolian forces, they constituted about one-third of the Soviet total of 157 divisions. Their equipment included the new mobile Scaleboard solid-fuel missile, firing a one-megaton warhead over 500 mi., and extra air-portable Frog 30-mi. missiles. Warsaw Pact units were reportedly included. Meanwhile, the 31 Soviet divisions in Eastern Europe, continuing their dual function of keeping Communist governments in power and providing defense against a Western attack, practiced in Exercise Dvina. During March 11–15 several divisions under Marshal Andrei A. Grechko, the Soviet defense minister, conducted maneuvers, including simulated nuclear strikes and the air landing of an entire division (9,000 men) behind enemy lines.

CHINA

In contrast to China's worldwide diplomatic initiatives, the Soviet-Chinese border talks made little progress. The People's Liberation Army (PLA) consolidated its hold on the government as precautions against war with the U.S.S.R. increased. Both sides built up their forces along the border, with China's nuclear capability becoming increasingly important. The full extent of the clashes along the 4,150-mi. frontier slowly became apparent. There had been 16, starting at Damansky (Chen-Pao) Island in the Ussuri River on March 2 and 14–15, 1969, and extending to Suifen-ho later in the month. The Sinkiang border was the site of five conflicts near Chuguchak, on April 16, 17, and 25 and on May 10 and 20. There were five on the Amur River: on May 12–15 near Hu-Ma, May 14 near Ai-hui, May 25 near Blagoveshchensk, and May 28 and July 8 near Goldinsky. A medium-scale battle on the border in December was rumoured but unconfirmed.

Talks to ease the tension started in Peking on Oct. 20, 1969, adjourned on December 14, and resumed on January 5, between Deputy Foreign Ministers Chia Kuan-hua and Vasily Kuznetsov. The latter's replacement by the less influential Leonid Ilyichev in July, officially because of illness, suggested declining Soviet confidence in the negotiations. They were reported to have led to an April agreement on a mutual withdrawal of 30-mi. depth along the frontier, and in July China reopened talks with the U.S.S.R. on navigation of the border rivers in Heilungkiang province. The fundamental disagreement remained, however; China wanted a preliminary disengagement pact followed by negotiations on a broad range of ideological and territorial issues, whereas the U.S.S.R. wanted disengagement linked to acceptance of the territorial status quo. China disputed this, especially in Sinkiang, where it estimated it had lost 20,000 sq.mi. through unequal treaties with czarist Russia, as well as Soviet-claimed islands in the Amur and Ussuri rivers, totaling 1,000 sq.km.

Contrasting with this stalemate was China's diplomatic reemergence. (*See* CHINA.) The switch from internal to external preoccupations reflected the PLA's move into key positions of government; about half the members of the Politburo Central Committee and most of the heads of provincial, state, and county committees were PLA men, and Huang Yuang Sheng, the PLA chief of staff, was spoken of as Mao's successor. The P'eng Teh-huai and Lo Jui-yching factions were purged for advancing theories that emphasized the importance of weapons. Training emphasized the Korean-style tactics of a people's war. Troops were withdrawn from farm work and positions opposite Taiwan to their strategic reserve positions. Inner Mongolia was divided into three military regions, Lanchou, Peking, and Shen-Yang, defending possible invasion corridors in depth. Chinese forces in the border areas totaled 814,000, comprising 15 divisions (180,000 men) in the Sinkiang and Lanchou military regions and 32 divisions (384,000 men) in the Peking and Shen-Yang regions, each reinforced by 125,000 border troops and militia. With reinforcements, China could muster one million men against 30 Soviet divisions (270,000 men) on the frontier, although the Soviets were massively superior in artillery, armour, air power, missiles, and nuclear weapons. This explained the widespread Chinese civil defense precautions, including underground complexes in Peking, Canton, and Shanghai.

The Chinese nuclear deterrent thus became increasingly important. It could offset China's qualitative conventional inferiority in the event of a major Soviet incursion, but it might also provide the incentive for a Soviet strike to wipe out China's nuclear capability while it was still vulnerable. The idea had been widely discussed but seemed less and less possible. Parts of the nuclear testing facility in Sinkiang had been moved to Tibet. Other major installations in the east were at Haiyen, Paotou, and Lanchou, site of the vital gaseous diffusion plant producing enriched uranium for thermonuclear weapons. Persistent reports that the Chinese had developed the alternative gas centrifuge techniques which are easier to protect, emphasized the difficulties in guaranteeing the success of a preemptive attack. U.S. estimates of China's nuclear capability had been revised back upward to those current in 1967. Secretary Laird's February re-

port estimated that China would have 80–100 IRBMs with 200–500-kiloton warheads by the early 1970s. A large ICBM launch facility under construction since 1965 had been completed, and by 1973–75 it could mount 10–25 soft ICBMs able to deliver a three megaton warhead 6,000 mi. They would be followed by solid-fueled ICBMs in hard siloes. These forecasts were strengthened by the launching of the first Chinese satellite on April 25. Broadcasting the song "The East Is Red," it weighed about 380 lb., which meant that its launcher was equivalent to a 1,500-mi.-range IRBM. Though China's stockpile included only a few dozen weapons, its missile and nuclear weapons programs seemed to be recovering from the Cultural Revolution.

INDIA AND PAKISTAN

India's 1969–73 defense plan had been designed to meet potential threats from Pakistan and China. Accordingly, the 1970–71 defense budget of $1,466,-000,000 provided for consolidation and reequipment of all three services. Army strength remained at about 800,000. Any attack from the 50,000 Chinese troops in Tibet could be held by ten mountain divisions deployed forward in the Himalayas, where the terrain favoured the defense along the line reached by the Chinese in their 1962 attack. There were a further 13 infantry and 1 armoured divisions, plus 1 armoured, 6 infantry, and 2 parachute independent brigades, with trained reserves totaling 100,000 including a Territorial Army of 44,000. Although the Kashmir issue remained unresolved, the possibility of another war with Pakistan decreased with the demarcation of the Kutch-Sind border.

Counterinsurgency operations continued to be successful. By early 1970, 700 Mizos had been killed, 3,400 had surrendered, and 16,000 had been resettled. The Nagas had lost 2,370 killed and 2,600 captured, and in March a further 200 surrendered. Of the 1,600 thought to have been in China, only 700 had returned, 500 of whom were killed or captured.

The biggest changes were in the Air Force, where standardization was essential if the 45-squadron target was to represent effective capability. This meant purchasing Soviet and French planes and missiles, with arrangements for the maximum degree of Indian manufacture under license to build up the aircraft industry. India had already produced over 200 Gnat light fighters and the domestically designed Kiran trainer, which replaced the 50 Vampires as reserves. Lack of a suitable power plant continued to limit the Marut HF-24 1-A to a speed of Mach 1.05, but two squadrons were in service as fighter-bombers and work started on the improved model. Preliminary studies were under way for a ground attack successor for delivery in 1977.

The main fighter was the improved MiG-21F, 60% locally produced with Soviet assistance under an April agreement; 120 older MiG-21s were already in service in six squadrons. The two squadrons of Mystère IV F-Bs were phased out as the first four squadrons of Soviet Su-7B fighter-bombers became operational. A total of 140 had been ordered, with options on a further 60. These would also replace the 50 obsolete Canberra B-1 light bombers. License agreements with Nord-Aviation resulted in production of the AS-30 air-to-surface and S-11 antitank missiles. Work continued on the air defense network around New Delhi, using the Soviet SAM-2 Guideline

continued on page 256

THE INTERNATIONAL ARMS TRADE

By Lord Chalfont

UPI COMPIX

Dock workers load one of 24 self-propelled howitzers aboard the "Etrog" in Cleveland, O., July 8, 1970. The howitzers, destined for the Israeli Army, were loaded under heavy armed guard.

To be of any real value, an analysis of international arms trade must consider three broad aspects of the question: the extent and pattern of armaments transactions; political, economic, and strategic issues that arise from them; and the desirability of bringing them under some kind of international control.

Structure of the Arms Trade. The arms trade can no longer be regarded as a simplistic moral issue, to be discussed with emotive references to "merchants of death" and similar undesirable phenomena. In the 1920s and 1930s there was some justification for this approach. The press conducted vigorous campaigns against private manufacturers of arms, and the very mention of Sir Basil Zaharoff and Sir Charles Craven was enough to produce a conditioned reflex among the leaders and supporters of the peace movement, which was then at its strongest. A number of official inquiries were made into the activities of private dealers in armaments, notably in the United Kingdom and the United States, and there were loud but unsuccessful demands that they should be brought under state control.

Since then the picture has changed. In countries like the Soviet Union where private enterprise—at least of an overt kind—does not exist, the manufacture and sale of arms is firmly in the hands of the government. World War II, with its insatiable demand for new and advanced weapons, brought about a similar situation in both capitalist and mixed economies. Private armaments firms have come to depend almost entirely on government contracts, and for all practical purposes, governments are now responsible for the international arms trade.

Private arms dealers do exist—especially in countries where the economy is not centrally controlled. Their activities are, however, peripheral to the main problem. Whatever view one may take of a man who is prepared to make money out of a private traffic in weapons, it is not individuals but governments that are ultimately responsible; and if governments find it difficult to control such private transactions, there is nothing to prevent them from putting an end to the current practice of selling surplus armaments to private dealers.

The principal problem, thus, is one of arms transactions between governments. It is important to make another distinction if the arms trade is to be approached from the point of view of its effect on international security and stability: in the existing international structure certain arms transactions are clearly inevitable and, within the limitations of current international philosophy, admissible. So long as military alliances exist, it would be unrealistic to criticize the exchange of weapons among allies (except in certain specified categories such as that covered by the nuclear nonproliferation treaty [NPT]). It is, therefore, irrelevant in arms control terms to become concerned with the sale by the United States of arms to Japan, Canada, or the European allies of NATO; or by the Soviet Union to China, North Korea, or the countries of the Warsaw Pact.

The important area for examination is that which concerns the less developed countries of the third world and especially those in which there is an inherent danger of conflict likely to be exacerbated by competitive arms sales. The most significant areas are the Middle East and North Africa, South Asia, Southeast Asia, southern Africa, and Latin America.

The next significant categorization is that of weapons types. Nuclear weapons are in a category of their own. The NPT, which came into force in 1969, is designed to prohibit the supply of nuclear weapons to those countries that do not already possess them. Although two of the existing nuclear powers have not signed the treaty, one, France, has declared publicly that it will act in this respect as though it had; the other, China, has little incentive to disseminate a nuclear capability outside its own frontiers and is in too early a stage of nuclear weapons development to do so effectively. Unless there is some significant development (such as a total breakdown of the strategic arms limitation talks between the Soviet Union and the United States), the possibility of the growth of an international trade in nuclear arms on any significant scale is remote. It is important to make two points in this respect. One is that in certain areas of potential conflict, failure to obtain the nonnuclear weapons that it thought necessary for its defense might provoke a government into acquiring nuclear weapons. In this context one might point to the Middle East and South Asia, both areas of great military sensitivity and centres of political confrontation in which neither Israel nor India, both of whom have a highly developed nuclear capability, are signatories of the NPT. The second point is that there are many apparently "nonnuclear" weapons—jet aircraft, heavy guns, mortars—that could be used as part of a nuclear delivery system, leaving the country that received them with the need only to equip them with nuclear warheads.

At the other end of the scale of weapons, there is the problem of the "unsophisticated" weapon. It is difficult to draw any universally applicable distinction between sophisticated and unsophisticated weapons—much depends on factors such as the standard of training, command, and organization in the armed forces of the countries buying the weapons. It is also difficult to establish the scale of the trade in such weapons as rifles, pistols, tanks, and artillery. Obviously these are important in the arms control context, and of even greater importance in the field of internal security. They would have to be included in any effective agreement on the international arms trade. But it is in the field of the more obviously sophisticated weapons that the real issues of international stability and security arise—modern aircraft, warships, and missiles.

Thus, the nucleus of the problem of international arms trade concerns the supply, on a government-to-government basis, of advanced nonnuclear weapons to the less developed countries of the third world. The next aspect to examine is the pattern of this supply. The principal supplying countries are the United States, the Soviet Union, the United Kingdom, Sweden, France, West Germany, and Canada. A study of the arms trade from 1945 to 1965, compiled by John L. Sutton and Geoffrey Kemp and published by the Institute for Strategic Studies, London, brought up to date by more recent information, indicates the scale and pattern of the supplies.

Since the end of World War II more than 5,000 combat jet aircraft have been delivered to the less developed world. It is a traffic that continues on an increasing and virtually uncontrolled scale. Between 200 and 250 warships—a term covering major naval vessels such as cruisers, destroyers, frigates, and submarines—have been delivered to the Middle East, South Asia, Southeast Asia, and southern Africa. Over 3,000 guided missiles of various kinds (antiaircraft, antitank, surface-to-surface) have been sold to the third world. An indication of the continued scope and scale of this kind of traffic is reflected in the list of major identified arms agreements published in September 1970 by the Institute for Strategic Studies. (*See* Table.) It shows that the quantitative flow of weapons continues unabated, and that the sophistication of the equipment is increasing.

Controlling the Arms Trade: Arguments in Favour. In examining the arguments for control or reduction of this traffic, the obvious and apparently overriding one concerns the effect of arms on political and military stability. The supply of arms to an area of potential conflict is inevitably a destabilizing factor. The situation in the Middle East demonstrates the truth

of this proposition. The tripartite declaration issued by Britain, France, and the United States in 1950 was, predictably, a total failure. Instead of trying to defuse the situation by controlling or eliminating the supply of arms into the area, it initiated an abortive attempt to maintain a military balance between two sides. What actually happened in the Middle East was that the Soviet Union, which was not a party to the tripartite declaration of 1950, began to supply arms on an increasing scale to the Arabs. This led inevitably to an increase of arms to Israel from the West; the general flow of weapons into the area increased; the danger that they might be used increased in proportion; and a conflict that began as a local struggle between Arabs and Israelis has become one of the most sensitive areas in the superpower confrontation.

The most dangerous implication of this Middle East arms race concerns the possible use of nuclear weapons. If the Israelis should begin to believe that Soviet arms supplies were giving the Arabs a decisive superiority, they would come at once under an almost irresistible temptation to redress the balance by manufacturing nuclear weapons—a development for which their industrial, scientific, and economic base already provides them with a firm and attractive platform. Apart from the temptation to frighten the lives out of the Arabs once and

Major Arms Supplies to Less Developed Countries
(July 1969 to June 1970)

Recipient	Primary supplier	Approximate date of agreement	Name of system	Approximate numbers	Primary role	Approximate cost to recipient ($000,000)	Expected date of delivery
Middle East and North Africa							
Abu Dhabi	Britain	August 1969	Hunter 76/76A	12	fighter-bomber/ reconnaissance/ trainer	n.a.	1970–
Algeria	France	July 1969	Fouga Magister	28	armed jet trainer	9.6	n.a.
	France	August 1969	SA-330 Puma	15	helicopter	n.a.	n.a.
Iran	Italy	1970	CH-47C Chinook	22	helicopter	n.a.	n.a.
	Britain	May 1970	Rapier and ancillary systems	—	surface-to-air missile	112.8	n.a.
Israel	United States	1969	SP howitzers	—		n.a.	1970
Jordan	Britain	March 1970	Hunter FGA-73	4	fighter-bomber	n.a.	n.a.
Lebanon	France	October 1969	Crotale	—	surface-to-air missile	n.a.	1971–
Libya	United States	August 1969	C-130 Hercules	6	transport	n.a.	1970-71
	France	January 1970	Mirage IIID/E/R; 5	110	trainer/interceptor	400+	1971-75
	Soviet Union	1969-70	armour and artillery	n.a.		n.a.	n.a.
Muscat and Oman	Britain	April 1970	Skyvan 3-M	1	tactical transport	n.a.	1970
Qatar	Britain	January 1970	Tigercat	—	surface-to-air missile	n.a.	n.a.
	Britain	October 1969	Hunter	6	fighter-bomber	n.a.	n.a.
Saudi Arabia	Britain	1969	air-cushion vehicles	n.a.	coast-guard duties	12	n.a.
U.A.R.	Soviet Union	1969-70	SA-3 Goa	80 launchers	surface-to-air missile	n.a.	1970
	Soviet Union	1969-70	MiG-21	150	fighter-bomber	n.a.	1970
	Soviet Union	1969-70	Su-7	16+	fighter-bomber	n.a.	1970
South Asia							
India	Britain	1970	Westland Sea King	4	helicopter	4.8	n.a.
	Britain	1970	Canberra B. Mk. 15/16	12	bomber	n.a.	n.a.
Pakistan	China	1970	W-class submarine	2/3		grant aid	n.a.
Southeast Asia							
Thailand	United States	November 1969	OV-10A Bronco	16	counterinsurgency aircraft	n.a.	1970–
	Britain	October 1969	frigate	1		16.8	n.a.
Latin America							
Argentina	Britain	February 1970	Type 42 guided-missile destroyer (with Sea Dart SAM)	2		} 72	1973-75
			Westland WG-13	2	helicopter		
	Britain	1970	Canberra B.2/T.4	12	bomber	21.5	n.a.
	West Germany	January 1970	Cobra 2000	n.a.	antitank missile	n.a.	n.a.
	United States	May 1970	A-4F Skyhawk	16	attack aircraft	5	n.a.
Brazil	France	May 1970	Mirage IIIE/B	16	interceptor, trainer		1972
	Britain	August 1969	submarine	2		n.a.	n.a.
Chile	Britain	1969-70	Leander-class frigate	2			
			Oberon-class submarine	2		} 74	1973
			Seacat		antiaircraft missile		
			helicopters				
	Britain	1970	Hunter FGA.71	4	fighter	n.a.	n.a.
	United States	April 1970	Beechcraft 99A	9	light transport	7.1	mid-1970
Dominican Republic	United States	1970	Hughes OH-6A	7	helicopter	grant aid	n.a.
Ecuador	Britain	1970	HS.478.2A	2	transport	n.a.	late 1970
Mexico	United States	1969	Beechcraft Musketeer Sports	20	trainer	0.5	1969-70
Nicaragua	United States	1970	Hughes OH-6A	4	helicopter	grant aid	n.a.
Peru	United States	March 1970	C-130 Hercules	6	transport	n.a.	n.a.
	Canada	March 1970	DHC-5 Buffalo	16	utility transport	60	1971-72
Africa south of the Sahara							
Congo (Kinshasa)	France	December 1969	AML	30	scout car	n.a.	n.a.
	Italy	1969	SF-260	12	trainer	n.a.	n.a.
Ivory Coast	France	1969	SA-330 Puma	1	helicopter	n.a.	n.a.
Kenya	Britain	October 1969	Beagle Bulldog	5	primary trainers	n.a.	n.a.
	Britain	1970	BAC-167	6	light-strike	n.a.	n.a.
Nigeria	Soviet Union	1969	MiG-15s	n.a.	fighter	n.a.	1969
South Africa	France	1970	SA-330 Puma	n.a.	helicopter	n.a.	1970–

n.a.=no figures available.
Note: This table lists major agreements both on a firm-to-government and on a government-to-government basis, and covers both credit and cash sales. Costs to recipients may include spares, support, etc., and reflect the value of goods taken in part exchange where applicable. Payees may include subcontractors in the purchasing country, as well as prime contractors in the supplying country. No licensing agreements are included.
Source: Institute for Strategic Studies, London, *The Military Balance 1970-1971*.

for all, the economic arguments must be compelling. Israel spends, according to reliable estimates, roughly 25% of its gross national product on armaments—a vast sum for a comparatively small country (Britain spends between 5 and 6%). It is inevitable that some Israeli advisers will argue that defense can be bought more cheaply by reducing the size of conventional forces and relying on the deterrent power of a small but allegedly effective nuclear striking force. Such a force would probably tempt the Arabs to embark on one of two equally perilous courses—either to launch a preemptive military operation against Israel before its nuclear striking force could become effective; or, with the help of some outside power, to acquire a nuclear capability of their own. In either case a new dimension in the conflict would have been reached—one in which the superpowers would inevitably become involved. This is the classic danger of the supply of arms to areas of potential conflict—it does not promote balance or stability, but provokes an ascending spiral of armaments with the virtual certainty that sooner or later they will be used.

This argument can be applied with equal validity to any area with the possible exception, for special geopolitical reasons, of Latin America. It was summed up in the *Report on Arms Control and Disarmament* prepared in December 1965 by the National Citizens Commission, Washington, D.C., under the general direction of Jerome Wiesner, once scientific adviser to the president of the United States. In one of its most cogent sections the report states:

> Intense conventional arms races are taking place in several areas of the world at great cost to the participants, at the risk of the peace and tranquility of other regions and at the risk of appalling destruction should war break out . . . the international traffic in arms which makes these buildups possible . . . is already regulated in the major exporting countries. With minor exceptions armaments do not enter the world market without the active consent of the government concerned, both sellers and purchasers. But there is, at present, very little coordination or agreement concerning the types of weapons to be supplied and the types of clients that may receive them . . . consequently the major arms suppliers should refrain from the further introduction of sophisticated weapons such as bombers, tanks, and submarines into underdeveloped areas. The past record of the United States and the Soviet Union is bad.

Apart from some of the familiar semantic difficulties about sophisticated and unsophisticated weapons, it would be difficult to arrive at a more succinct statement of the case against an uncontrolled international traffic in arms. Just as it is difficult to distinguish between sophisticated and unsophisticated weapons (indeed it is doubtful whether either word has any real meaning when applied to armaments), so it is virtually impossible to distinguish effectively between offensive and defensive weapons. It can be argued, for example, that a surface-to-air missile, "defensive" in the sense that it was designed to destroy attacking aircraft, is "offensive" when used against enemy fighters that are themselves engaged in shooting down attacking bombers. Similarly, a fighter ground-attack aircraft, "offensive" enough in itself, might rightly be looked upon as defensive if it were knocking out an invading tank force. But the most questionable distinction is that which some have attempted to draw between weapons that can be used for riot control, or internal security, and those that cannot, as in the controversy over the supply of arms to South Africa. The proposition, for example, that an advanced fighter-bomber is irrelevant to police activities is patent nonsense to anyone who has seen one of these machines flying low to frighten and disperse a crowd; and anyone who in the 1940s saw the Royal Indian Navy frigates brought alongside the harbour in Bombay to fire their guns into the rioting crowds is unlikely to be impressed by arguments that warships could not be used to enforce South Africa's racial policy. Even those weapons like submarines, which clearly have no direct role in riot control, have a considerable value if outside powers or international organizations attempt to intervene in racial or political situations that have become outrageous and intolerable to world opinion.

Possible Methods of Control. What can be done to bring under control the trade in advanced weapons systems between the industrial countries and the third world? Perhaps the ideal arrangement would be a central coordinating body, consisting of representatives from all those countries that supply or import arms. All projected arms deals would be examined by this body, which would make mandatory recommendations to the governments concerned. The general considerations governing its decisions would include the political conditions in the area concerned, the existing military balance there, and the existence of military alliances or treaties.

Other forms of control, such as registration with an international body of all arms transactions, or an effective export licensing system enforced by international actions, have been considered, but none so far has been taken seriously by the international community. Is any attempt to regulate, limit, or control the arms race likely to meet with success? There are formidable difficulties in the way of any effective measures, however modest, to apply arms control measures to the international traffic. The first such difficulty is that the supply of military equipment is a powerful extension of modern diplomacy. Both the Soviet Union and the United States provide a large proportion of their foreign aid in the form of arms sales. In the Soviet Union the supply of arms is regarded as a traditional and legitimate way of spreading and consolidating Soviet influence. Second, the sale of arms is an important source of foreign exchange to many of the supplying countries. When the British government compensated for its idealism in appointing a minister responsible for disarmament by engaging an arms salesman shortly afterward, Denis Healey, then British minister of defense, explained to the House of Commons in February 1966:

> While the government attaches the highest importance to making progress in the field of arms control and disarmament, we must also take what practical steps we can to ensure that this country does not fail to secure its rightful share of this valuable commercial market.

Apart from the preoccupations of the supplying countries, many recipient countries also have their own reasons for resisting any international regulation of the arms trade. They would regard it as an example of the desire of the great powers to arrange the affairs of the world over their heads and as an unwarrantable interference with their legitimate right of self-defense. The strength of their feelings on this subject gives rise to the kind of paradox described by Dean Rusk, then U.S. secretary of state, in a television interview in 1965:

> I recall that at the United Nations General Assembly, when they were voting *unanimously* for disarmament, 70 members were at that moment asking us [the United States] for military assistance.

Even if the major arms suppliers decided to sacrifice the economic and strategic advantages of arms sales, and even if the recipient countries of the less developed world were persuaded to accept some form of control or registration, there would remain the problem of dealing with other arms producers who would be unlikely to agree to any form of control. These would probably include China; Switzerland and India (which would resent attempts to interfere with their commercial activities); and such countries as Algeria and the United Arab Republic, which are rapidly learning to imitate the great powers in providing arms to other countries in pursuit of their own political aims.

Conclusion. The international arms trade is an undesirable phenomenon, distorting the economies of less developed countries, creating instability in some areas, and exacerbating it where it already exists. In the present international structure the chances of controlling it seem small. The one way of getting an acceptable plan into the area of international discussion might be to include a section on international arms control in existing draft treaties on general and complete disarmament; but any serious negotiation on these draft treaties seems as remote now as it has ever been.

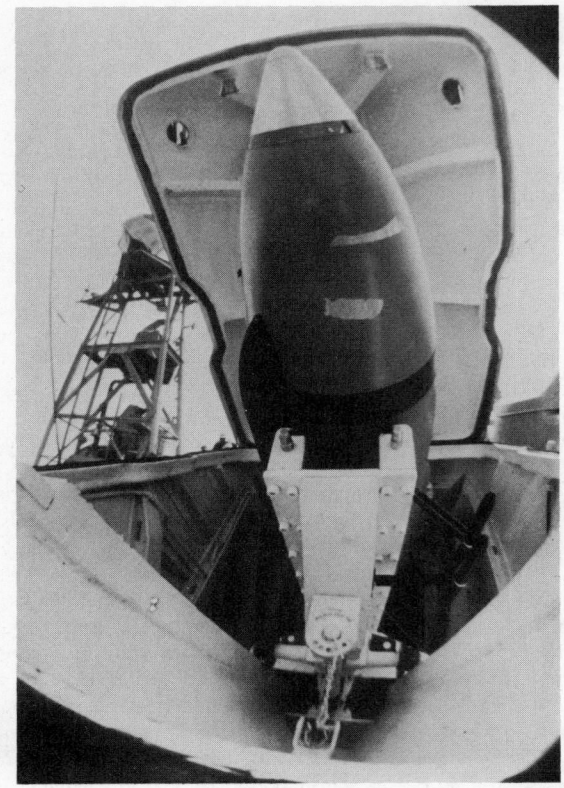

KEYSTONE

A Gabriel missile is on its launcher aboard a Saar missile boat. The boat is Israel's answer to the Soviet-made Komar and Ossa gunboats used by the U.A.R.

continued from page 252

missiles that were also being supplied to the U.A.R. and North Vietnam.

The Navy's future role was defined as antisubmarine warfare and the establishment of a small submarine force. The old aircraft carrier "Vikrant" and its 35 Sea Hawk attack aircraft were to be laid up. Soviet naval equipment proved unsatisfactory; the four F-class submarines continued to give trouble and the first two of the six Petya-class 1,000-ton destroyer escorts ordered had to put in for repairs at Hong Kong en route from Vladivostok. The preference for British vessels was reinforced by the successful launching of a Leander-class frigate built under license in the Mazaga docks at Bombay.

Nevertheless, the overall effect was a marked increase in Soviet influence. Prime Minister Indira Gandhi's December 1969 denials of this were unconvincing, since Foreign Minister Dinesh Singh and the Foreign Ministry's influential permanent secretary, T. N. Kaul, were pro-Soviet, as was her personal secretary, Sundar Haksar. The Soviets elaborated their concept of an Asian regional security organization as being pan-Asian, including the U.S.S.R., the U.S., and all Asian states.

With China's satellite launching, the development of India's nuclear weapons option became a major political issue, and in the parliamentary debate of April 28 the defense minister was heavily attacked for not having even authorized an official study of the costs involved. In May a committee was established to report to the Cabinet on the subject. The U.S. Atomic Energy Commission estimated that it would take India two years and $450 million to produce a bomb. A conference of scientists, academics, and politicians demanded a ten-year program to produce a 2,500-mi.-range IRBM with a nuclear warhead by 1970, and the right-wing Jan Sangh Party started campaigning openly for an Indian bomb in preparation for the 1972 election.

Pakistan's defense budget rose again to $625 million, an increase of $83 million or 15%. The Army had 300,000 men, including 25,000 Azad Kashmir troops, for a total of 11 infantry divisions and 2 armoured divisions. The Air Force had 270 combat aircraft of seven different types, predominantly 112 elderly F-86 Sabre fighter-bombers and 80 Chinese-supplied MiG-19s. The combat performance of the latter below 20,000 ft. had proved superior to India's early MiG-21s, and in April discussions were held with an important Chinese mission on the supply of more MiG-19s, I1-28 bombers (to add to the 16 Pakistan already had), and T-59 tanks.

MIDDLE EAST

The death of U.A.R. Pres. Gamal Abd-al-Nasser on September 28 removed the one Arab leader with the authority to secure acceptance of peace with Israel. Paradoxically, this had seemed closer as the result of a four-phase escalation and expansion of the limited Arab-Israeli conflict. In the first phase, from January to April, Israel's attempts to prevent the U.A.R. military buildup along the Suez Canal by bombing around Cairo proved so successful that the U.S.S.R. committed Soviet manned fighters and SAM-3 missiles to the U.A.R.'s defense. The second phase, from May to June, saw a dual expansion, with increasingly heavy fighting on all Israel's borders and threats of a direct confrontation between the two superpowers. The establishment of a 90-day U.A.R.-Israeli cease-fire created the third phase, in which an intensified search for diplomatic solutions was undermined from two directions: Soviet violations suggested that they discounted a settlement while making the U.S. ability to guarantee one less credible. The hijacking of four airliners by Palestinian guerrillas in early September began the fourth phase, which saw King Husain fighting the guerrillas to regain his precarious control of Jordan.

The initial Israeli escalation sought to topple Nasser by emphasizing the U.A.R.'s vulnerability. On December 26, 1969, an Israeli raid on Ras Ghareb captured one of the latest Soviet radar installations, the P-12 used to guide the 300-km.-range SAM-2 missiles. A second radar was seized in a January 22 raid on Shadwan Island, in which two U.A.R. MTBs were sunk. Starting on January 7 Israel bombed military installations around Cairo, beginning 25 mi. away, moving to within 10 mi., and then flying over the city. Civilian casualties inevitably occurred, notably 70 at Elkhanka on February 12 and 46 schoolchildren on April 8, creating popular unity instead of discord. These losses had to be set against the constant guerrilla attacks on Israeli civilians, including the May 22 bazooka attack on an Israeli school bus by the Popular Front for the Liberation of Palestine (PFLP) close to the Israeli-Lebanon border, in which eight children, three teachers, and the driver were killed.

The U.A.R. Air Force could not halt the Israeli raids; between March 25 and 27 alone, it lost nine MiG-21s. It lacked trained pilots, having only about 100, with 100 in reserve, for its 150 MiG-21s, whose endurance of 20 minutes made interception difficult in any case. Its 105 Su-7B fighter-bombers were failures as fighters, and the older MiG-15s and MiG-17s (about 165) were quite outclassed. Israel had a minimum of two crews per aircraft, while its 36 F-4E Phantoms, living up to their reputation as the world's best fighter-bomber, combined with 60 Mirage III-Cs to give Israel effective air superiority. The 67 A-4E

Skyhawks, 30 Mystère IV As, and 30 Ouragan fighter-bombers, though older, proved effective in skilled hands.

At the end of January Nasser visited Moscow to request further aid. The U.A.R.'s continued inability to handle the Soviets' equipment led them, like the U.S. in Vietnam, to shift from providing advisers to committing their own combat forces, though covertly. With 100 MiG-21Js and SAM-3 missile batteries, they sent 5,000 additional Soviets, bringing the total in the U.A.R. to 20,000. Each SAM-3 battery comprised eight missiles paired on mobile launchers, plus radar guidance equipment and mobile antiaircraft batteries. The SAM-3 was designed for use against low-flying aircraft (above 300 ft.) and had a slant range of 15 mi. The U.A.R.'s 250 SAM-2s, intended to intercept high-level bombers flying between 3,000 and 80,000 ft., had been largely nullified by Israeli knowledge of their guidance systems, gained from captured missiles, and by low-level attacks. The SAM-3 could thus change the strategic balance in the U.A.R.'s favour, providing a defensive umbrella under which Soviet siege howitzers could be brought up to bomb the main Israeli defenses along the Suez Canal, the Bar-Lev Line.

Israel tried to prevent this missile buildup by bombing up to 12 hours a day by mid-June. Deep-penetration raids into the U.A.R. ceased in late April, as Soviet pilots started to fly patrols outside the tacitly recognized combat zone 32 mi. from the canal. Despite attempts to avoid a direct clash, two were shot down on July 27. This, together with Israel's loss of 2 of the original 50 Phantoms ordered from the U.S. to SAM-3s on June 30, created some incentive for talks. So did clashes with Syria on the Golan Heights, which were continuous from May onward. Guerrilla activity also increased. Iraq's March settlement of its five-year war with the Kurdish rebels released 20,000 troops, and 3,000 were sent to Jordan to help the Palestinians. There were constant Israeli attacks on bases used by the guerrillas, including those around Mount Hebron in Lebanon. The U.A.R.'s one former British Z-class destroyer was sunk on May 16.

By July 1 President Nixon, describing the Middle East as being like the Balkans before World War I, was saying that the military balance would be preserved, though without making any specific commitments as to how. But Phantom deliveries increased, together with deliveries of advanced electronics countermeasures and the Shrike missile that homed in on the SAM-2 and 3 radar ground controls. The U.S. also sought a cease-fire, a halt to the escalation, and negotiations leading to a settlement. With Soviet help, the U.A.R., Jordan, and Israel were persuaded to accept a 90-day cease-fire, which prohibited any significant military reinforcements within the 32-mi. combat zone on either side of the canal. The Soviets immediately violated it by moving 10 SAM-3 batteries into the zone and starting to construct 30 more protected sites and to rebuild 20 destroyed by Israeli bombing. After initial denials, the U.S. confirmed this but was unable to halt it, though President Nixon adopted a much more assertive policy during his October visit to the Mediterranean and the 6th Fleet. On September 6 Israel abandoned the indirect peace talks being held at the UN under the auspices of special envoy Gunnar Jarring.

The Palestinian guerrillas had opposed any halt in hostilities, and the fanatical PFLP, under George Habash, prevented any resumption of talks by hijacking 4 airliners, with over 300 passengers, between September 6 and 9. A fifth attempt on an El-Al plane

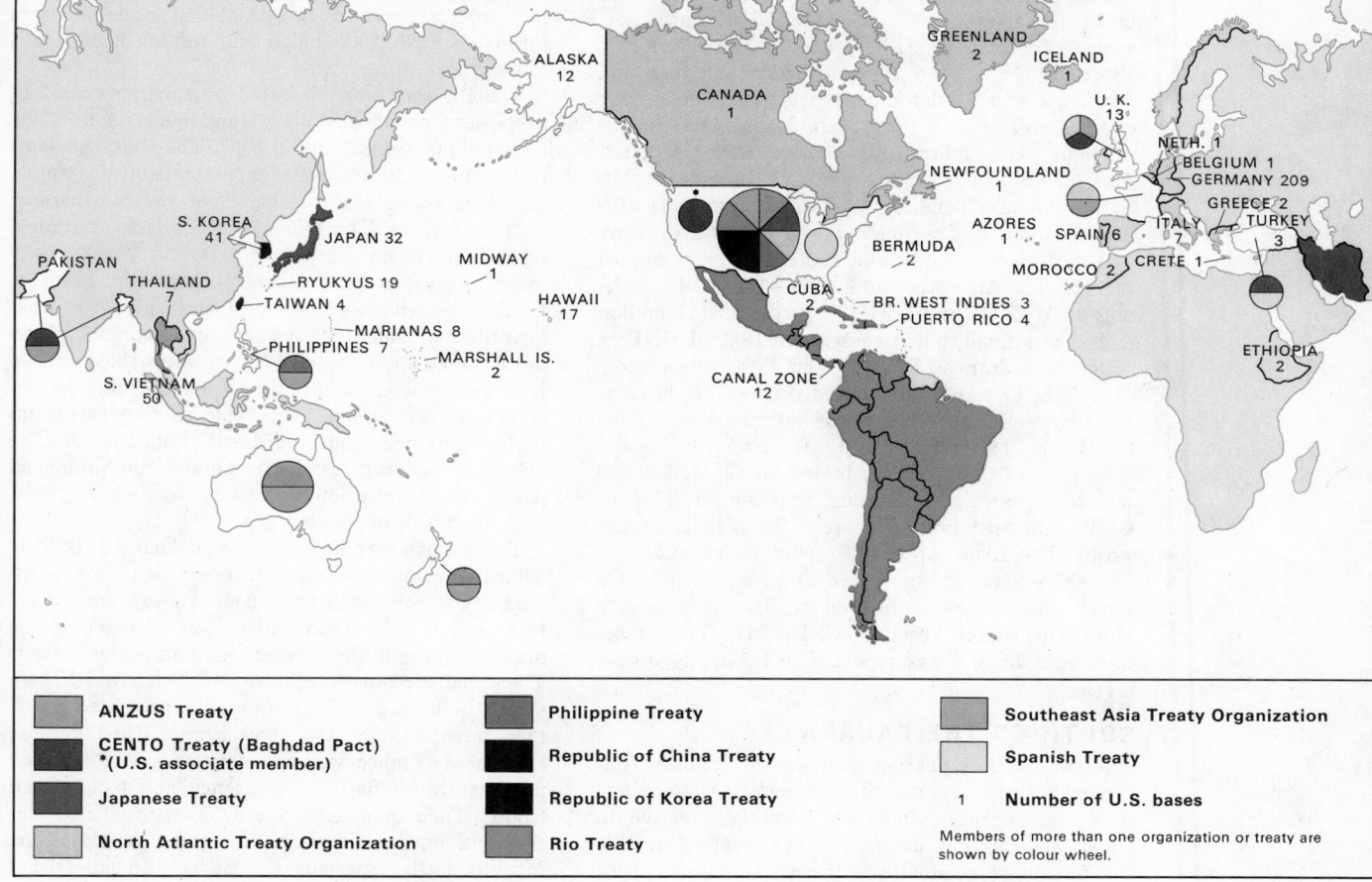

ANZUS Treaty

CENTO Treaty (Baghdad Pact)
*(U.S. associate member)

Japanese Treaty

North Atlantic Treaty Organization

Philippine Treaty

Republic of China Treaty

Republic of Korea Treaty

Rio Treaty

Southeast Asia Treaty Organization

Spanish Treaty

1   Number of U.S. bases

Members of more than one organization or treaty are shown by colour wheel.

was defeated and a hijacker was killed. One of the hijacked planes, a 747 jumbo jet, was diverted to Cairo and blown up at once. The other three were taken to a World War II landing strip in Jordan, where the 284 passengers were held as hostages. The guerrillas' shifting demands finally boiled down to the release of ten guerrillas imprisoned for hijackings (6 in West Germany, 3 in Switzerland, and 1 in the U.K.), plus some Palestinians held by Israel. This was arranged by late September and the hostages were released; the three aircraft were destroyed, bringing the damage—with the 747—to $52 million.

The PFLP action brought to a head the issue of who governed in Jordan, King Husain or the guerrillas. A military Cabinet was established, whose strongest member, Gen. Habis al-Majali, determined to crush the guerrillas. They were already being attacked by the king's traditional supporters, the Bedouins, who composed most of the Army. On September 17 the 58,000-man Army, equipped with 310 tanks and 130 armoured cars, launched a full-scale attack against 20,000 guerrillas, of whom 6,000 Al Fatah and 1,000 PFLP members had light arms. Syrian attempts to aid them were defeated, and after ten days of fighting the guerrillas in Jordan were largely destroyed, total casualties being estimated at 1,500–5,000. President Nasser secured a cease-fire and an agreement on mutual withdrawal from Amman, but the effort killed him. His successor, Anwar al-Sadat (*see* BIOGRAPHY), was reputed to be a hard-liner on Israel.

The state of permanent limited war in the Middle East was reflected by rises in already high defense budgets. The U.A.R.'s, at $1,272,000,000, was $467 million above the previous year's and nearly twice that of 1968–69. The 250,000-man Army comprised 3 armoured, 4 mechanized infantry, and 4 infantry divisions plus 15 artillery brigades, with just over 1,250 tanks, 150 amphibious tanks, and 906 armoured personnel carriers. The artillery had 1,500 guns of 122, 130, and 152 mm., 150 self-propelled assault guns, and 50 Frog-3 and Samlet short-range surface-to-surface missiles. All these figures were higher than in the previous year, indicating yet more Soviet supplies. The 20,000-man Air Force had 415 combat aircraft. Syrian defense spending was estimated at $221 million, up about 10%, providing for a 75,000-man Army with 700 medium tanks and 600 armoured personnel carriers. The Air Force had 90 MiG-21s and 40 Su-7s, plus 80 MiG-15s and MiG-17s. Jordan's $117 million budget was small, but it constituted 18% of GNP; a second squadron of F-104A Starfighter interceptors (18 aircraft) was being formed. Planes lost in combat before the cease-fire were estimated at 50 for the U.A.R., 15 for Syria, and 8 for Israel.

Israel's 1970–71 defense budget of $1,075,000,000 was 25% above the preceding year and, at 25% of GNP, remained proportionately the highest in the world. The Army of 61,500 could be expanded to 275,000 when fully mobilized and had about 1,000 tanks, plus 300 self-propelled artillery pieces, with more being supplied by the U.S. The MD-660 surface-to-surface missile was reported to be nearly operational.

SOUTH OF THE SAHARA

The end of the Nigerian civil war in January contrasted with continuing military operations elsewhere in Africa. France, which was especially active in Chad, was the only external power involved outside the remaining colonial territories. The last British

troops to be stationed permanently on the continent left Libya in March 1970. With the closing of Wheelus Air Force Base in Libya in June, the U.S. had only 1,750 men in Africa, at the Kagnew Communications Station in Eritrea. Spain maintained troops in the Spanish Sahara (10,000), Ceuta (8,000), and Melilla (9,000). Civil war in Sudan continued, as did guerrilla warfare in Portuguese Africa and Southern Rhodesia.

The Nigerian federal government defeated Biafra surprisingly quickly after the attack on the last town, Owein, started. By Dec. 24, 1969, the Onitsha-Onugu road was cleared, creating a flood of refugees, and the Awka-Onitsha road fell on Jan. 2, 1970, enabling the 1st and 3rd federal divisions to link up and operate under coordinated command. One quarter of the remaining 2,000 sq.mi. of Biafra and 500,000 Biafrans were cut off. Using medium artillery (Soviet 122-mm. guns), the government forces punched a gap for their British Saladin and Ferret armoured cars to advance the remaining 25 mi. to Uli airstrip, which was taken on January 10. Gen. Odumegwu Ojukwu, the rebel leader, fled in one of the last planes out of Biafra, handing over the leadership to Maj. Gen. Philip Effiong. The latter's formal surrender was accepted by Gen. Yakubu Gowon, head of the federal government, on January 15.

The next day Gowon announced that all relief would have to be channeled through the National Rehabilitation Commission and denounced Joint Church Aid and the Vatican for interfering in Nigeria's internal affairs. Despite difficulties in getting supplies through, an international commission of observers found no evidence of genocide, as distinct from the expected looting and sporadic violence which led to the 3rd Division's being withdrawn on January 25. There was no guerrilla warfare and no attempts were made to form a government in exile. Total casualties were estimated at 200,000 killed and wounded, with two million dead of starvation.

The Biafrans were defeated by superior numbers, firepower (including artillery), and light armour. They had held out since May 30, 1967. The Ibos, the dominant tribe of Biafra, were understandably fearful of further massacres at the hands of the Northerners and Westerners. The federal Army's lack of trained manpower (it expanded from 9,000 to 90,000 men) meant the absence of fire control or coordination; attacks were launched piecemeal and only after vast quantities of ammunition had been accumulated via a primitive supply system. French arms shipments to Biafra prolonged the war for 15 months, and the Nigerian Air Force was never able to stop them; up to 40 flights per night landed at Uli until it fell. The Nigerian jets were totally unsuitable for prolonged patrol and interception, and 19 out of their 20 losses were the result of accidents.

The French war in Chad was nicknamed its little Vietnam. France's domino theory was that a Communist government in Chad could cause Communism to spread to Cameroon and Gabon, threatening the uranium mines in the Ayadez region of eastern Niger. The socialist regimes in Sudan and Libya, which were sympathetic to the Chad insurgents, presented a further threat. Under the 1960 Franco-Chad defense agreement, France was spending about £20 million per year to support 2,500 French and 6,000 Chad troops. Their opponents, the 3,000-strong Chad National Liberation Front, represented a revolt of the Muslim north, especially the Borkou-Ennedi-Tibesti region, against Pres. François Tombalbaye's non-Muslim government in the south. When the rainy season ended in October 1969, Tombalbaye's French military adviser, Gen. Edouard Cortadellas (a veteran of Indochina and Algeria), directed three operations in west, east, and central Chad that brought total casualties for the year to 122 French Legionnaires and 360 Chad troops killed as against 1,100 guerrillas.

The major French gains came through diplomacy. In January Libya agreed to stop aiding the Chad guerrillas in return for the sale of French Mirage jets. The Sudanese government, meanwhile, became increasingly preoccupied with its six-year-old civil war against the three southern provinces, where the predominantly Christian Negro population opposed Arab Muslim rule. In July the Sudanese head of state, Maj. Gen. Gafaar al-Nimeiry, visited the Chad capital, Fort-Lamy, symbolizing an improvement in relations. The French felt able to make some withdrawals from Chad, including part of the 2nd Parachute Regiment.

Following the death of Portuguese Premier António Salazar, his effective successor, Marcello Caetano, formally assumed office. Caetano's policy was to retain Portugal's African empire by reorganizing the armed forces, making marginal political reforms, and developing its considerable mineral wealth. Portugal had 125,000 troops, including local enlistees, stationed in Africa out of a total Army of 182,000. Its defense budget, at $356.2 million, constituted 6% of its GNP. Only two nominal divisions, both heavily understrength, were in Portugal, together with the antisubmarine warfare elements of the 16,500-man Navy. Most of the Air Force was in Africa; its main elements were 60 medium transports, 3 light strike jet squadrons, and 50 Alouette II and III helicopters, plus 4,000 paratroopers.

In Portuguese Guinea 25,000 Portuguese troops were fighting 10,000 guerrillas. The countryside was insecure, and in July there was a concerted attack by guerrillas based in Senegal and Guinea. Senegal had been forced to limit the guerrillas' activities in April after the Portuguese had shelled Senegalese villages. An invasion of Guinea in November was said by a UN team to have been carried out chiefly by Portuguese-led troops, although Portugal denied it.

The 57,000 Portuguese troops in Angola were protecting oil exports, worth £7 million yearly, against two mutually hostile groups of guerrillas. In the north the 4,000 members of the União dos Populações de Angola (UPA) were supplied from their sanctuary in the Congo (Kinshasa). To the east the 3,000-strong Movimento Popular de Libertação de Angola (MPLA) operated hit-and-run raids from the Congo (Brazzaville) and Zambia.

The Mozambique guerrilla movement (FRELIMO) had been weakened by the assassination of its leader, Eduardo Mondlane, in 1969. His successor, Samora Machel, had been driven back into the northernmost areas of Cuba Delgado and Niassa. FRELIMO had about 7,000 men, plus an equal number in reserve in Tanzania and Zambia, against 43,000 Portuguese troops. In June the Portuguese launched Operation Gordian Knot to clear the area of the projected £130 million Cahorabassa Dam on the borders of Mozambique, Rhodesia, and Zambia. The dam would supply these three countries and South Africa with power and water, and South Africa provided a battalion of troops and air reconnaissance for the operation. A

UPI COMPIX

Soviet three-stage rocket, called "Savage" by NATO, rolls past St. Basil's Cathedral in Moscow on Nov. 7, 1970, during the annual parade celebrating the Bolshevik Revolution.

total of 300 guerrillas were killed and 35 tons of arms were captured.

In Rhodesia the guerrillas began to infiltrate three-man groups into the urban areas of Bulawayo and Salisbury, since the earlier large raids had been made too costly by the Rhodesian defenses. Rhodesia had established a patrol line from Lake Kariba to Mozambique with 30-man camps at five-mile intervals, supported by mobile strike forces. These defenses had accounted for 175 guerrillas since 1966, at a cost of 14 defenders killed. South African aid included 500 troops and paramilitary forces (compared with Rhodesia's 3,400-man Army and 6,400 paramilitary personnel). Air support included Mirage fighter-bombers and Super-Frelon helicopters, including some fitted with an experimental French 20-mm. cannon (used in Chad), which created a 400-m. lethal zone. Two guerrilla attacks on Victoria Falls and Kariba in January were ineffective, but they led Rhodesian Prime Minister Ian Smith to threaten to cut power and transport vital to Zambia's Copper Belt if Zambia continued to permit the guerrillas to use it as a base. Zimbabwe African People's Union (ZAPU), the main guerrilla group, had been effectively immobilized by April as a result of internal feuds.

South Africa's assistance to the Portuguese and Rhodesian regimes was part of its new "outward-looking" policy, which based its security on a buffer zone of friendly states to the north, including those with cooperative black rulers. In November 1969 a plan was put forward for a major increase in South Africa's defense forces, including an air base in Lilongwe in Malawi complementing those at Katino Mulilo in the Caprivi Strip and at Walvis Bay. The 1970–71 defense budget of $360 million was still only 2.5% of GNP. The Army comprised 10,000 regulars and 22,300 citizen forces under training at any one time, plus 58,000 commandoes. The Air Force had 5,000 regulars and 3,000 citizen forces. Crotale surface-to-air missiles were on order from France, which has supplied over £200 million worth of arms to South Africa since 1968. (R. J. Ra.)

See also Astronautics; Vietnam.

Denmark

A constitutional monarchy of north central Europe lying between the North and Baltic seas, Denmark includes the Jutland Peninsula and 100 inhabited islands in the Kattegat and Skagerrak straits. Area (excluding Faeroe Islands and Greenland): 16,629 sq.mi. (43,069 sq.km.). Pop. (1970 est.): 4,905,822. Cap. and largest city: Copenhagen (pop., 1969 est., 833,027). Language: Danish. Religion: the Danish Lutheran Church is the established church. King, Frederik IX; prime minister in 1970, Hilmar Baunsgaard.

The cautious optimism prevailing at the beginning of 1970 with regard to the Danish economy was rapidly reversed when forecasts early in the year predicted an increase in the balance of payments deficit. In spite of urgent financial policies designed to cool the overheated economy, later forecasts estimated a deficit of anything from 4 billion kroner—equivalent to about 4% of the gross national product—to as much as 7.5 billion kroner for the year.

The new pay-as-you-earn income tax system having failed to produce the expected decline in consumption, various indirect taxes were raised in the spring, and the value-added tax was increased from $12\frac{1}{2}$ to 15% from July. A severe credit squeeze was introduced, and the central bank rate of 9% meant that commercial credit would cost at least 12%. Restrictions were placed upon public-sector spending in the spring, and the provisional state budget for 1971–72 incorporated cuts in expenditure of about 1 billion kroner.

In addition to these stringent financial controls, the government planned to introduce an incomes policy toward the end of the year. Prime Minister Baunsgaard, in his opening speech when the Folketing reconvened in October, envisaged a policy embracing all sections of the community and in accordance with principles of social justice. A partial price freeze on services effective until February 1971 was introduced, and it was hoped that agreement could be reached with employers' and employees' organizations on a prices and incomes structure for the following 12 months or more.

One government proposal was to abolish the system of automatic wage regulation linked with a consumer price index, which had been in force for many years. The trade unions replied that, while they would accept an alternative system that provided compensation to wage earners for price increases, they were unwilling to give up the principle of inflation insurance. Economic experts estimated that an increase in real wages of 25 øre an hour resulted in a cost to the employer of 100 øre (1 krone), the difference being swallowed up in price, tax, and cost increases. In the early autumn, a system was introduced whereby the government paid one "portion" of automatic wage increases directly to the employers, to help cope with the wage-price-cost inflationary spiral by preventing an equivalent rise in the price index.

Economic experts predicted that private incomes could not rise for the next two years: one-half of the estimated growth in production would be needed to reduce the balance of payments deficit, and almost all the rest would be taken up by the public sector. In light of this, Prime Minister Baunsgaard appealed to all sections of the community to cooperate in the establishment of an incomes policy in addition to strict financial policies. It was hoped to achieve a policy based to a large degree on voluntary sacrifices and cooperation. The government also planned to

Demonstrating students occupy Copenhagen University, March 9, 1970, to protest a watered-down bill giving students more influence in university matters.

NORDISK PRESSEFOTO FROM PICTORIAL PARADE

DENMARK
Education. (1967–68) Primary, pupils 506,014; secondary, pupils 185,287; primary and secondary, teachers 41,652; vocational, pupils 128,256; teacher training (normal), students 70; higher (including 4 universities with 33,163 students), students 58,204, teaching staff (1965–66) 6,423.

Finance. Monetary unit: Danish krone, with a par value of 7.50 kroner to U.S. \$1 (18 kroner = £1 sterling). Gold, SDRs, and foreign exchange, central bank: (June 1970) U.S. \$341.1 million; (June 1969) U.S. \$371.4 million. Budget (1969–70 rev. est.): revenue 29,048,000,000 kroner; expenditure 28,162,000,-000 kroner. Gross national product: (1968) 92,950,-000,000 kroner; (1967) 84,760,000,000 kroner. Money supply: (April 1970) 29,740,000,000 kroner; (April 1969) 28,070,000,000 kroner. Cost of living (1964 = 100): (April 1970) 142; (April 1969) 135.

Foreign Trade. (1969) Imports 28,601,000,000 kroner; exports 22,639,000,000 kroner. Import sources: EEC 34% (West Germany 19%); Sweden 16%; U.K. 14%; U.S. 8%. Export destinations: EEC 23% (West Germany 13%); U.K. 20%; Sweden 16%; U.S. 9%; Norway 7%. Main exports: machinery 21%; meat and meat preparations 18% (including bacon 7%); dairy products 6%.

Transport and Communications. Roads (1966) 61,630 km. (126 km. expressways in 1968). Motor vehicles in use (1968): passenger 955,300; commercial 254,200. Railways: state (1968) 2,354 km.; private (1967) 1,124 km.; traffic (state only; 1968): 3,224,-000,000 passenger-km., freight 1,380,000,000 net ton-km. Air traffic (including Danish part of international operations of Scandinavian Airlines System; 1968): 1,202,400,000 passenger-km.; freight 55.4 million net ton-km. Shipping (1969): merchant vessels 100 gross tons and over 1,194; gross tonnage 3,490,334. Telephones (including Faeroe Islands and Greenland; Dec. 1968) 1,516,802. Radio licenses (Dec. 1968) 1,566,-000. Television licenses (Dec. 1968) 1,210,000.

Agriculture. Production (in 000; metric tons; 1969; 1968 in parentheses): wheat 429 (465); barley 5,194 (5,047); oats c. 755 (863); rye 126 (131); potatoes 663 (866); sugar, raw value (1969–70) c. 311, (1968–69) 341; apples (1968) c. 190, (1967) c. 195; butter 144 (160); cheese 108 (106); pork 742 (773); beef and veal 258 (265); fish catch (1968) 1,467, (1967) 1,070. Livestock (in 000; July 1969): pigs 8,023; cattle 3,002; sheep 90; horses (July 1967) 42; chickens 18,911.

Industry. Production (in 000; metric tons; 1969): pig iron 232; crude steel 482; cement 2,600; superphosphates (1968) 778; nitrogenous fertilizers (1968–69) 62; manufactured gas (cu.m.) 416,000; electricity (net; excluding most industrial production; kw-hr.) 16,226,000. Merchant vessels launched (100 gross tons and over; 1969) 598,000 gross tons.

introduce legislation prohibiting increases in dividends and imposing heavier capital gains taxes. Land values in Denmark had almost doubled during the previous few years.

Danish exports continued to rise in 1970, with industry carrying the main burden; agricultural exports rose only marginally, largely due to more favourable prices. However, imports rose considerably faster than exports, and invisible earnings from shipping, tourism, and so on were far from sufficient to close the gap. Thus, there was an estimated deficit of 4 billion kroner in 1970, or even 7.5 billion according to some sources. These forecasts took into consideration a marginal improvement in the early autumn, that is, a slight decrease in the growth of the deficit, but it was too early to predict whether this would be of permanent significance.

Denmark continued to "knock at the door of the Common Market," with the sole reservation that it wished to join the EEC in company with the U.K. Denmark did not ask for any special transitional period for agriculture and was disturbed to learn that Britain had. The ghost of the Nordek plan for a Nordic customs union was occasionally raised by opponents of the EEC as an alternative solution, but the average Dane had virtually forgotten it. However, individuals as well as business and government circles were anxious to maintain the close cooperation with other northern countries that had been so successful within the EFTA framework.

It was decided to reduce the minimum voting age from 21 to 20. Also on the domestic front, a council was established to deal with problems of environment and pollution; together with more serious concerns, this led to a violent debate on the subject of beer cans. Drug taking among young people was a growing problem. While severe sentences were imposed upon professional dealers, a policy of rehabilitation rather than punishment was pursued with regard to individual consumers. Demonstrations at the World Bank and International Monetary Fund annual meeting in Copenhagen in September became riots when gasoline bombs were thrown and the offenders were dealt with rather heavy-handedly by the police. Considerable debate followed in the mass media, but interest seemed to fade after the Copenhagen newspaper *Politiken* published an opinion poll indicating about 85% support for the police.   (S. Aa.)

Encyclopædia Britannica Films. *Scandinavia—Norway, Sweden, Denmark* (1962).

Dentistry

A device originally designed to examine soil from the moon's surface was being modified at the University of Chicago's Zoller Dental Clinic to study tooth enamel density. The instrument consisted of a radioactive isotope, a radiation detector, and a radiation counter. When the isotope emitted a stream of beta particles aimed at the crowns of teeth, the particles striking the calcium in tooth enamel bounced back and were counted by the detector. The counter recorded the data from all areas of the tooth and then printed out a model indicating those areas from which there were less than normal amounts of radiation backscatter. As reported by Frank Besic, a professor at the Zoller Clinic, the enamel of normal teeth is equally dense; therefore, the radiation would be similar from all areas. Thus, low amounts of back-scatter radiation

indicate areas where dissolution of the enamel is beginning to take place. These areas ordinarily develop into cavities. Sometimes backscatter radiation is low due to abnormal and poorly formed enamel, while in other cases low calcium concentration will be found in surfaces of the teeth ordinarily immune to dental decay.

The radiation dose absorbed by a patient in the above procedure is much less than the amount one would receive during routine dental radiographs and, according to Besic, it is definitely not detrimental to the patient. If the equipment were mass produced, it could sell for a sum of $2,000. The use of this device might allow the dental profession to practice true preventive dentistry in that early detection of susceptible areas would guide the dentist in the use of fluoride therapy to prevent serious dental decay.

Further studies indicated that dental decay might be a reversible process. Thus, incipient dental cavities should be afforded the opportunity to remineralize under optimum oral conditions, such as more effective tooth brushing, removal of cariogenic (cavity-producing) plaque, and reduction in the consumption of sucrose and other refined carbohydrates. Studies demonstrated that incipient enamel cavities could be remineralized to a high degree through the application of an artificial calcifying solution. Stephen Wei and Theodore Koulourides of the universities of Iowa and Alabama, respectively, found that enamel was remineralized to the point that it demonstrated an almost complete recovery of calcium and phosphorus and had a chemical composition near that of normal enamel, with a similarity in hardness. In recent years it had been demonstrated that the hardness of softened enamel could be restored if demineralization had not passed a critical limit. It was also found that traces of fluoride can improve the remineralizing capacity of a synthetic solution containing calcium and phosphorus.

If the findings from a large-scale clinical trial of a plastic sealant confirm the success of pilot tests, a material developed at the Eastman Dental Center, Rochester, N.Y., may be applied to tooth surfaces in order to prevent decay. The treatment consisted of applying a thin adhesive sealant to thoroughly clean teeth. An ultraviolet light beam was then directed onto the coated teeth. As a result of this action, the sealant was hardened into an almost invisible film. In its initial trial the material provided complete protection against dental decay in 200 pits and fissures on the grinding surfaces of what were judged to be healthy teeth. Approximately 42% of untreated or control areas on the opposite side of the same patients' mouths developed tooth decay. In the projected study researchers hoped that some of the following factors might become more clear: (1) the amount of time required to apply the sealant under normal conditions; (2) the length of time on the average that the sealant would remain on the teeth; and (3) the effect on areas from which the sealant was lost. If the long-term results of the test indicated favourable results, the dental profession might have another tool for the practice of preventive dentistry.   (D. L. McE.)

Dependent States

In 1970 two of Britain's Pacific dependencies, Fiji and Tonga, chose to become independent within the Commonwealth and Fiji joined the UN. The British

"NEW YORK TIMES"

Portuguese soldiers pause near a coffee plantation in Angola. Actual contact with nationalist guerrillas was rare as the war entered its tenth year in 1970.

prime minister, Edward Heath, speaking at the 25th anniversary session of the UN General Assembly on October 23, recalled that the UN began with 51 members and that Fiji's admission on October 13 brought the number to 127. Of the 76 new members, he pointed out, no fewer than 27 were former British dependencies whose applications had been sponsored by the U.K.

Britain's remaining 22 colonies (excluding the British Antarctic Territory and Rhodesia) covered an area of almost 34,000 sq.mi. and were largely made up of approximately 1,500 small islands round the globe. Their total population was estimated at something over five million, of whom about four-fifths lived in Hong Kong—a self-liquidating responsibility in the sense that a treaty provided for the reversion to China in 1997 of the island's hinterland, without which the U.K. could not support the teeming offshore community. In 1970 such were the colonial remnants of the former British empire (which had 650 million inhabitants when the UN was inaugurated in 1945). The task of steering each separate colony to a stable and internationally acceptable future posed a variety of complex problems.

Although most of these dependencies were at a definitive stage on the way to noncolonial status, only a few (notably Bermuda) could claim to be individually viable. The majority had chosen to exercise their right of self-determination by rejecting complete independence; they preferred to remain associated with Britain on a basis that gave them internal autonomy while relying on the U.K. for external defense and economic aid. Some in the Caribbean area were caught up in regional rivalries; Gibraltar, British Honduras, and the Falkland Islands remained the subject of foreign jurisdictional claims; and Diego Garcia in the British Indian Ocean Territory, one of the lesser-known islands, suddenly acquired international significance with the news in November that the British and U.S. governments were planning its joint development as a strategic defense base. Thus, the overall

pattern was one that ruled out any quick or comprehensive solution to the problems of responsible decolonization.

One of these problems was emphasized afresh in November when Anguilla rejected the conclusion of the Wooding Commission, a predominantly West Indian Commonwealth body, that its only viable future lay in continued membership in the St. Kitts-Nevis-Anguilla federation (from which the 6,000 Anguillans had proclaimed their secession in February 1969). The commission was set up in December 1969 and sat for almost 11 months. Every alternative to Anguilla's continuance in the three-island federation (including a reversion to crown colony status; separate independence; the maintenance of the status quo; association with some other state; and administration by other Caribbean countries, the Commonwealth, or the UN) was examined and rejected. The commission held the St. Kitts government partly to blame for Anguilla's grievances and recommended new safeguards for the island's legitimate interests within the federal framework. Its findings were unanimous but found no favour with the Anguillans.

This illustrated the difficulty of making independence viable for three small islands of kindred stock, language, and constitutional background without violating the basic right of self-determination. In contrast, the essential conflict in Britain's disputes with Spain over Gibraltar, with Guatemala over British Honduras, and with Argentina over the Falkland Islands was between the expressed wishes of old-established colonies and the claims to sovereignty over them put forward by neighbouring foreign states. In every case, however, the British position (maintained in UN debates and specifically reaffirmed to the Anguillans despite London's disappointment at their rejection of the Wooding report) was that independence would neither be denied to those who wanted it nor forced upon those who did not want it.

Anglo-Spanish contacts on Gibraltar took place at intervals throughout the year; there was no sustained dialogue, but the sovereignty dispute remained a live issue. In June the Spanish foreign minister, Gregorio López Bravo, described it as a "small but important problem." He was speaking in the context of a Spanish policy aimed at closer European cooperation (Spain had just signed a preferential trade agreement with the EEC countries). In August Maj. Robert Peliza, Gibraltar's chief minister, went to London for bilateral talks at which he was assured that Britain would stand by its pledge not to change the existing relationship without the approval of Gibraltar's inhabitants. Peliza continued to press for Gibraltar's total integration in the U.K. and was reported to be showing increasing frustration over Britain's apparent refusal to consider this step.

In October, despite earlier talk of a "new climate" in Anglo-Spanish relations (a phrase used by the British ambassador to Madrid to describe López Bravo's much-publicized hope of a rapprochement), the Spanish government again raised the colonial issue with the UN. Interviewed in October by the Madrid daily *A.B.C.* after a meeting in New York with the British foreign secretary, Sir Alec Douglas-Home, López Bravo said there would be no real improvement in mutual relations without "a definite solution of the Gibraltar problem in the only way possible for any Spaniard." His words were seen as a clear restatement of the Spanish claim to sovereignty, and the stalemate continued. Spain, however, apparently saw advantages in keeping the issue on ice (possibly having more to do with its own colonial problem in Spanish Sahara than with its European policy). This impression was strengthened by a minor concession in November to the "besieged" Gibraltarians in the form of an announcement that workers on the Rock who wished to visit their families in Algeciras would be allowed to cross the bay in British craft (since the elimination of the ferry service in July 1969 they had been forced to travel via Tangier).

There were no direct exchanges between Britain and Guatemala on the latter's territorial claim to British Honduras; a clear indication of the colony's refusal to sever the British link was the overwhelming victory of the ruling People's United Party at elections in December 1969.

In mid-July representatives of the British and Argentine governments met in London to discuss the promotion of direct communications between the Falkland Islands and the Argentine mainland. The advantages of opening direct links (surface, air, and telecommunications) were acknowledged in a joint communiqué that described the talks as "amicable." It was agreed to continue them at two further meetings, to be held in Buenos Aires, Arg., and Port Stanley, in the Falkland Islands. The central issue of the sovereignty dispute was not on the London agenda, but for the first time in any such exchanges the British team included three delegates from the Falklands. When they were originally invited by the previous foreign secretary, Michael Stewart, the islanders suspected that the Labour government saw the communications talks as a means of paving the way for a transfer of sovereignty. Their fears on this score were apparently allayed, if not dispelled, by the knowledge that Sir Alec Douglas-Home had consistently supported their case for staying British.

Africa. *French Africa.* In the French Territory of the Afars and Issas (formerly French Somaliland) a member of the Somali Liberation Front was sentenced in June to perpetual forced labour for throwing a bomb that injured 18 Europeans in Djibouti. The Somalia government, after condemning his action, sought UN support for an offer to cooperate with France in giving the colony independence.

Portuguese Africa. While antiguerrilla operations in Mozambique, Angola, and Portuguese Guinea were reportedly costing Portugal $216 million a year, the Pan-African governments waged a diplomatic offensive to secure the withdrawal of European participation in Portugal's Cahorabassa hydroelectric project. This involved the construction in Mozambique of Africa's largest dam, twice the size of the Kariba on the Rhodesia-Zambia frontier and 70% bigger than the U.A.R.'s Aswan barrage. It was designed to generate 3,600 Mw., of which more than half would go to South Africa. The project was central to Portuguese hopes of building up a strong colonial economy, and the Organization of African Unity (OAU) condemned it as a bid to consolidate white supremacy.

At Addis Ababa, Eth., in March the OAU Council of Ministers, after considering a Zambian claim that Portugal intended to settle a million Europeans in the Tete district where the dam was being built, called for steps to dissuade the West German Siemens company from carrying out a $36 million electrical contract (a small but vital part of the $307.2 million main contract of which West German firms held almost one-third). Pres. Kenneth Kaunda of Zambia later urged Bonn to end all West German participation. When

these pressures were resisted, Cahorabassa became almost as much of an irritant as Rhodesia to African relations with Western governments.

In July Lisbon officially denied any plan to encourage a huge influx of white immigrants into Mozambique. At the same time, Portuguese troops removed 24,000 Africans from Tete Province; the immediate aim was to counter the risks of sabotage by guerrillas of the Front for the Liberation of Mozambique (FRELIMO); during another antiguerrilla offensive, launched in September, there were unconfirmed reports of South African troops helping the Portuguese in this area.

FRELIMO's appointment in May of Samora Moisès Machel as president and Marcelino dos Santos as vice-president coincided with a significant shift of strategic policy by three of the main resistance groups (including FRELIMO) in Mozambique, Angola, and Portuguese Guinea; in a concerted bid for wider political support they promoted an international conference in Rome that took place in early July and attracted delegates from 64 countries. The final communiqué of the conference called for the "military, economic, and political isolation of Portugal" and for "concrete aid to the liberation movements." After an audience granted by Pope Paul VI to guerrilla leaders (which provoked a protest by Portugal to the Vatican), FRELIMO's vice-president urged that all the resistance groups work more closely with the OAU. The defection of an important FRELIMO official, Miguel Murupa, formerly in charge of the organization's foreign relations, was reported in December. He was said to have joined the Psychological Warfare Department of the Portuguese Army.

On November 22 Pres. Sékou Touré of Guinea called for UN military help to fight off "an invasion by Portuguese and other mercenaries." The Security Council immediately sent a UN mission to Conakry to investigate the situation; denials of Portuguese complicity came from the Lisbon government and from Gen. António Spínola, governor of Portuguese Guinea. (*See* GUINEA.)

In December, Portugal's premier, Marcello Caetano, announced that his government planned to give more local autonomy to the Portuguese African territories, especially to Angola and Mozambique. He said that the territories would become "autonomous regions within the Portuguese unitary state." Caetano firmly rejected the possibility that Portugal would grant independence to these areas and maintained that his country's policy was one of "racial brotherhood."

Spanish Africa. In May and June Mauritania, Morocco, and Algeria, at a series of meetings between their heads of government, agreed to cooperate in pressing for the decolonization of Spanish Sahara. Like Spain they professed their support in principle for settling by referendum under UN auspices the future of all Spanish Moroccan enclaves. Of these, however, Spanish Sahara, with a population of some 40,000 nomads, was the chief object of contention because of its mineral wealth. Since 1958, when this Spanish "province" was created by merging the two Atlantic coastal enclaves of Río de Oro and Saguia al Hamra, vast deposits of phosphate ore had been discovered at Bu-Craa in the latter area: production was scheduled to begin in 1971, and the prospect of developing other mineral deposits (including possible oil reserves in Río de Oro) gave Madrid a strong in-

continued on page 266

DEPENDENT STATES

Territory	Political status	Area (sq.mi.)	Population (1968–70)	Capital	Population of capital*	Government officials
AFRICA						
Afars and Issas	French overseas territory	8,880	81,000	Djibouti	...	High commissioner, D. Ponchardier
Angola	Portuguese overseas province	481,400	5,466,600	Luanda	339,938	Governor-general, Lieut. Col. Rebocho Vaz
Bouvet Island	Norwegian dependency	23	—	—	—	—
British Indian Ocean Territory	British colony	85	2,000	—	—	Commissioner, Bruce Greatbatch
Cape Verde Islands	Portuguese overseas province	1,557	244,800	Praia (São Tigao)	13,142	Governor, Cmdr. Rosado do Sacramento Monteiro
Comoro Islands	French overseas territory	863	270,962	Moroni (Grande Comore)	14,000	High commissioner, Antoine Colombani
Mozambique	Portuguese overseas province	303,073	7,596,100	Lourenço Marques	60,924	Governor-general, Eduardo de Arantes e Oliveira
Portuguese Guinea	Portuguese overseas province	13,948	530,000	Bissau	55,958	Governor, Gen. António Sebastião Ribeiro Spínola
Réunion	French overseas département	970	447,341	Saint-Denis	67,805	Prefect, Jean Vaudeville
St. Helena	British colony	119	4,829	Jamestown	1,475	Governor, D. A. Murphy; Administrators, Brig. H. McDonald (Ascension), J. Fleming (Tristan da Cunha)
São Tomé and Príncipe	Portuguese overseas province	372	66,000	São Tomé (São Tomé)	5,714	Governor, Lieut. Col. A. da Silva Sebastião
Seychelles	British colony	107	51,396	Victoria (Mahé)	14,000	Governor, Bruce Greatbatch
South West Africa (Namibia)	†	317,827	615,000	Windhoek	66,810	Administrator, J. G. H. van der Wath
Spanish Sahara	Spanish African province	102,700	64,588	El Aaíun	18,212	Governor-general, Gen. José María Pérez de Lema y Tejero
ANTARCTICA						
Australian Antarctic Territory	Australian external territory	2,472,000	—	—	—	—
British Antarctic Territory‡	British colony	650,000	96	—	—	High commissioner, Sir Cosmo Haskard
French Southern and Antarctic Lands	French overseas territory	202,916	177	—	—	Administrator, Pierre Rolland
Peter I Island	Norwegian dependency	96	—	—	—	—
Queen Maud Land	Norwegian dependency	...	—	—	—	—
Ross Dependency	New Zealand dependency	160,000	—	—	—	—
ASIA						
Bahrain	British-protected sheikhdom	256	198,200	Manama	93,300	Sheikh, Isa bin Sulman al-Khalifah British political agent, A. J. D. Stirling
Bhutan	Indian-protected kingdom	18,000	770,000	Thimphu	...	Druk gyalpo (king), Jigme Dorji Wangchuk
Brunei	British-protected sultanate	2,226	137,600	Bandar Seri Begawan	20,463	Sultan, Hassanal Bolkiah Mu'izzadin Waddaulah High commissioner, A. R. Adair
Christmas Island	Australian external territory	52	3,439	—	—	Official representative, Brig. L. D. King
Cocos (Keeling) Islands	Australian external territory	5.5	607	—	—	Official representative, C. W. Suthern
Hong Kong	British colony	400	4,089,000	Victoria	646,800	Governor, Sir David Trench
Macao	Portuguese overseas province	6	260,000	Macao	169,299	Governor, José Manuel Nobre de Carvalho
Neutral Zone	Disputed area claimed by Iraq and Saudi Arabia	7,000	...	—	—	—
Portuguese Timor	Portuguese overseas province	5,763	590,000	Dili	10,753	Governor, Brig. Gen. José Nogueira Valente Pires
Qatar	British-protected sheikhdom	4,400	100,000	Doha	22,500	Sheikh, Ahmad bin Ali bin Abdullah al-Thani British political agent, E. F. Henderson
Ryukyu Islands	U.S. civil administration	848	989,000	Naha City (Okinawa)	298,000	High commissioner, Lieut. Gen. James B. Lampert Civil administrator, Robert A. Fearey
Sikkim	Indian-protected kingdom	2,744	191,000	Gangtok	9,000	Chogyal (king), Palden Thondup Namgyal Principal administrative officer, R. N. Haldipur
Trucial States	7 Arab sheikhdoms under British protection	32,278	135,000	—	—	Sheikh for each state British political agents, C. N. Treadwell, J. L. Bullard
EUROPE						
Faeroe Islands	Self-governing integral part of the realm of Denmark	540	38,000	Thorshavn	10,188	Head of local government, K. Djurhuus
Gibraltar	British colony (self-governing)	2.25	28,407	—	—	Governor, Fleet Adm. Sir Varyl Begg; Chief minister, Maj. Robert Peliza
Guernsey	British crown dependency	30	48,433	St. Peter Port	15,804	Lieutenant governor, Vice-Adm. Sir Charles Mills; Bailiff, Sir William Arnold
Isle of Man	British crown possession	221	49,734	Douglas	19,517	Lieutenant governor, Sir Peter Stallard
Jan Mayen	Norwegian territory	144	36	—	—	—
Jersey	British crown dependency	45	64,500	St. Helier	26,594	Lieutenant governor, Air Chief Marshal Sir John Davis; Bailiff, Sir Robert Le Masurier
Svalbard	Norwegian territory	23,957	2,900	—	—	Administrator, Frederik Beichmann
NORTH AMERICA						
Antigua	British associated state (self-governing)	171	63,000	St. John's	21,396	Governor, Sir Wilfred E. Jacobs; Premier, Vere Cornwall Bird
Bahamas	British colony (self-governing)	5,382	168,209	Nassau (New Providence)	100,553	Governor, Sir Francis Cumming-Bruce; Prime minister, Lynden O. Pindling
Bermuda	British colony (self-governing)	20	53,000	Hamilton (Great Bermuda)	2,127	Governor, Lord Martonmere; Government leader, Sir Henry Tucker
British Honduras	British colony (self-governing)	8,866	122,000	Belize	42,273	Governor, Sir John Paul; Prime minister, George C. Price
British Virgin Islands	British colony	59	10,500	Road Town (Tortola)	2,183	Administrator, J. S. Thomson
Canal Zone	U.S. territory leased from Panama	647	51,249	Balboa Heights	190	Governor, Maj. Gen. Walter P. Leber
Cayman Islands	British colony	100	10,652	Georgetown (Grand Cayman)	4,146	Administrator, A. C. Long

Territory	Political status	Area (sq.mi.)	Population (1968–70)	Capital	Population of capital*	Government officials
Corn Islands	U.S. territory leased from Nicaragua	4	...	—	—	Administrator, U.S. State Department
Dominica	British associated state (self-governing)	290	74,000	Roseau	12,500	Governor, Louis Cools-Lartigue; Premier, E. O. Le Blanc
Greenland	Integral part of the realm of Denmark	840,000	47,000	Godthaab	6,104	Official representative, N. O. Christenson
Grenada	British associated state (self-governing)	133	105,000	St. George's	8,644	Governor, Hilda L. Bynoe; Premier, Eric M. Gairy
Guadeloupe	French overseas *département*	687	325,965	Basse-Terre	15,458	Prefect, J. Deleplanque
Martinique	French overseas *département*	421	332,000	Fort-de-France	99,031	Prefect, Pierre Beziau
Montserrat	British colony	40	12,300	Plymouth	3,500	Administrator, D. R. Gibbs; Chief minister, Austin Bramble
Navasa Island	U.S. unincorporated territory	2	—	—	—	
Netherlands Antilles	Self-governing integral part of the realm of the Netherlands	385	220,091	Willemstad (Curaçao)	43,547	Governor, B. M. Leito; Prime minister, G. C. Sprockel
Puerto Rico	U.S. commonwealth	3,421	2,689,932	San Juan	455,421	Governor, Luis A. Ferré
St. Kitts-Nevis-Anguilla§	British associated state (self-governing)	138	56,000	Basseterre	15,742	Governor, Sir Frederick Phillips; Premier, Robert L. Bradshaw
St. Lucia	British associated state (self-governing)	238	110,000	Castries	5,100	Governor, Sir Frederick J. Clarke; Premier, John G. M. Compton
Saint Pierre and Miquelon	French overseas territory	93	5,500	Saint Pierre (Saint Pierre)	...	Governor, J. J. Buggia
St. Vincent	British associated state (self-governing)	150	89,129	Kingstown	17,258	Administrator, Hywel George; Chief minister, R. M. Cato
Swan Islands	U.S. unincorporated territory	1	...	—	—	Administrator, Federal Aviation Administration
Turks and Caicos Islands	British colony	166	6,000	Cockburn Town (Grand Turk)	2,339	Governor, Sir Francis Cumming-Bruce; Administrator, R. E. Wainwright
Virgin Islands of the U.S.	U.S. organized unincorporated territory	133	74,033	Charlotte Amalie (St. Thomas)	29,351	Governor, Melvin H. Evans

OCEANIA

Territory	Political status	Area (sq.mi.)	Population (1968–70)	Capital	Population of capital*	Government officials
American Samoa	U.S. organized unincorporated territory	80	27,769	Fagatogo (Tutuila)	1,613	Governor, John M. Haydon
Ashmore and Cartier Islands	Australian external territory	77	—	—	—	—
British Solomon Islands	British protectorate	11,500	161,525	Honiara (Guadalcanal)	11,389	High commissioner for the Western Pacific, Sir Michael Gass
Canton and Enderbury Islands	Governed in common by U.K. and U.S.	27	—	—	—	British high commissioner for the Western Pacific, Sir Michael Gass; U.S. administrator, Federal Aviation Administration
Central and Southern Line Islands	British dependency	36	—	—	—	High commissioner for the Western Pacific, Sir Michael Gass
Cook Islands	Self-governing territory of New Zealand	93	21,260	Rarotonga	10,853	High commissioner, L. J. Davis; Prime minister, Albert Henry
French Polynesia	French overseas territory	1,543	103,000	Papeete (Tahiti)	22,278	Governor, Pierre Angeli
Gilbert and Ellice Islands	British colony	283	53,517	Tarawa Island	12,642	High commissioner for the Western Pacific, Sir Michael Gass; Resident commissioner, Sir John Field
Guam	U.S. organized unincorporated territory	212	70,000	Agaña	2,556	Governor, Carlos G. Camacho
Heard and McDonald Islands	Australian external territory	113	—	—	—	—
Howland, Baker, and Jarvis Islands	U.S. unincorporated territory	3	—	—	—	Administrator, U.S. Department of the Interior
Johnston and Sand Islands	U.S. unincorporated territory	‖	—	—	—	Administrator, U.S. Department of the Navy
Kingman Reef	U.S. unincorporated territory	‖	—	—	—	Administrator, U.S. Department of the Navy
Midway Islands	U.S. unincorporated territory	2	...	—	—	Administrator, U.S. Department of the Navy
New Caledonia	French overseas territory	7,358	100,579	Nouméa	41,853	Governor, Jean Risterrucci
New Guinea	Australian trust territory	93,500	1,695,000	Port Moresby (on Papua)	56,206	Administrator, D. O. Hay
New Hebrides	British/French condominium	5,700	83,000	Vila	3,072	British high commissioner, Sir Michael Gass; French high commissioner, Jean Risterrucci
Niue Island	New Zealand territory	100	5,302	—	—	Resident commissioner, S. D. Wilson
Norfolk Island	Australian external territory	14	1,377	—	—	Administrator, Roger B. Nott
Palmyra Island	U.S. unincorporated territory	4	—	—	—	Administrator, U.S. Department of the Interior
Papua	Australian external territory	90,000	620,000	Port Moresby	56,206	Administrator, D. O. Hay
Pitcairn Island	British colony	19	90	Adamstown		Governor, Sir Robert Foster
Tokelau Islands	New Zealand territory	4	1,745	—	—	Administrator (high commissioner in Western Samoa), R. B. Taylor
Trust Territory of the Pacific Islands (Caroline, Mariana [except Guam], and Marshall Islands)	U.S. trust territory	699	102,250	Saipan	9,214	High commissioner, W. R. Norwood
Wake Island	U.S. unincorporated territory	3	1,763	—	—	Administrator, Federal Aviation Administration
Wallis and Futuna	French overseas territory	98	9,000	Matautu (Uvea)	...	Administrator, André Duc Dufayard

SOUTH AMERICA

Territory	Political status	Area (sq.mi.)	Population (1968–70)	Capital	Population of capital*	Government officials
Falkland Islands	British colony	6,200	2,109	Stanley	1,110	Governor, Sir Cosmo Haskard
French Guiana	French overseas *département*	34,750	48,000	Cayenne	19,668	Prefect, P. Bonteiller
Surinam	Self-governing integral part of the realm of the Netherlands	63,064	389	Paramaribo	110,867	Governor, J. H. E. Ferrier; Minister-president, J. Sedney

*Most recent available figure.
†On Oct. 27, 1966, the UN General Assembly adopted a resolution to terminate South Africa's mandate and put South West Africa under the direct responsibility of the UN. South Africa considers the resolution illegal and has stated that it intends to continue its jurisdiction over the territory.
‡Includes some territory claimed by Argentina and Chile.
§Following Anguilla's attempted secession from St. Kitts-Nevis in January 1969, a British commissioner was appointed to administer the island pending settlement of its future status.
‖Less than 0.5 sq.mi.
A dash (—) indicates none or negligible; three dots (...) indicate not available.

continued from page 263

terest in retaining control of the whole colony. After offering to hold the proposed referendum in 1971, it set out to persuade the nomads that their best interests lay in cooperating with Spain (which promised to share with them the rewards of its mineral invest-

ments) rather than with their Arab neighbours (whose demands for decolonization left unanswered the question of how they proposed to divide the territory).

Caribbean. The constitutional pattern of British dependencies in the Caribbean area, comprising the colonies of the Bahamas, British Honduras, the British Virgin Islands, the Cayman Islands, Montserrat, and the six associated states of the eastern Caribbean (Antigua, Dominica, Grenada, St. Lucia, St. Kitts-Nevis-Anguilla, and St. Vincent), remained unaltered in 1970 except for the situation created by Anguilla's rejection of the Wooding report recommending its return to the three-island federation. On November 9 the Anguillan leader, Ronald Webster, in a letter to *The Times* (London), asked the British government to lift the island out of its "constitutional limbo" by giving it internal self-government while retaining control of its foreign affairs and exercising reserve powers in fiscal matters as long as Anguilla was aided by grants from the U.K. This was tantamount to a declaration that Anguilla would consider itself a British colony until London either accepted Webster's terms or used force to implement the Wooding report. Since neither alternative was contemplated, Britain seemed likely to renew its search for a workable solution by way of talks with Robert Bradshaw, premier of St. Kitts-Nevis-Anguilla. Bradshaw, whose government had welcomed the report, said he would do nothing further pending discussions with London.

The growth of the Black Power movement was widely regarded as a major if still largely potential threat both to orderly government throughout the area and to the tourist industry which most of the dependencies were developing. To meet the threat, Grenada's premier, Eric Gairy, introduced strict law-and-order legislation following the April riots in nearby Trinidad. In October Black Power demonstrations took place in the Virgin Islands before and during a visit by Prince Charles.

A new move to strengthen regional trade was the creation in January, with British and Canadian backing, of the Barbados-based Caribbean Development Bank. Within the Caribbean Free Trade Area

Above, the dam site of the Cahorabassa hydroelectric project on the Zambezi River in northern Mozambique. Right, South African workers begin the first stage of the five-year project.

LONDON "DAILY EXPRESS" FROM PICTORIAL PARADE

(CARIFTA), however, the six associated states and Montserrat continued to complain that while they were forced to pay high prices for imports from richer members there had been no significant increase in their own agricultural exports to the area. A delegation from the British Virgin Islands visited London in November for negotiations that were expected to result in the government buying out two British companies—the Anegada Development Corporation and Wickham's Cay Ltd.—operating as property developers under a concession granted in 1967. St. Lucia's banana crop was damaged by a tropical storm, but none of the British islands suffered seriously from hurricanes. However, in August the French dependency of Martinique was struck by Hurricane Dorothy, which caused 42 deaths and left 7,000 homeless. The sinking in July of the St. Kitts-Nevis ferry with the loss of some 200 lives was a major disaster.

In an effort to revive the island's faltering sugar industry, the government of Puerto Rico in August expropriated 12,000 ac. of sugarcane lands and a mill owned by the Aguirre Co. The company, citing economic difficulties, had closed the mill the previous month. Puerto Rican nationalist activities during the year largely centred around the opposition of the inhabitants of Culebra to the continued use of their island by the U.S. Navy as a gunnery range.

Persian Gulf. British efforts to breathe life into the Federation of Arab Amirates (Bahrain, Qatar, and the seven Trucial States) were patiently pursued but ran into difficulties, largely created by a local conflict of interests (commercial and strategic) and the persistent failure of the member states to agree on political and administrative aspects of their association. In October the British government's special adviser on the area, Sir William Luce, was understood to

AUSTRALIAN EXTERNAL TERRITORY

PAPUA

Education. (1968) Primary, pupils 65,035, teachers 1,733; secondary, pupils 5,140, teachers 213; vocational, pupils 1,160, teachers 88; teacher training, students 533, teachers 48; higher (University of Papua and New Guinea), students 595, teaching staff 92.

Finance and Trade. Monetary unit: Australian dollar (A$0.89 = U.S. $1; A$2.14 = £1 sterling). Budget (1968–69): revenue A$51,627,-000 (including A$23,001,787 grant by Australian government); expenditure A$51,470,000. Foreign trade (1968–69): imports A$56,035,000; exports A$11,429,000. Import sources (1967–68): Australia 63%; Japan 8%; U.S. 6%; U.K. 5%. Export destinations (1967–68): Australia 79%; U.S. 11%. Main exports (1967–68): copra 25%; rubber 17%.

Agriculture. Production (in 000; metric tons): copra (1967) 16, (1966) 15; rubber (1969) c. 6.2, (1968) 5.7.

AUSTRALIAN TRUST TERRITORY

NEW GUINEA

Education. (1968) Primary, pupils 144,572, teachers 4,009; secondary, pupils 9,181, teachers 408; vocational, pupils 2,165, teachers 131; teacher training, students 959, teachers 107.

Finance and Trade. Monetary unit: Australian dollar. Budget (1968–69) balanced at A$98,015,532 (including A$64,269,499 grant by Australian government). Foreign trade (1967–68): imports A$84,244,000; exports A$58,905,-000. Import sources: Australia 55%; Japan 12%; U.S. 7%; U.K. 5%. Export destinations: Australia 36%; U.K. 33%; U.S. 9%; West Germany 8%; Japan 5%. Main exports: coffee beans 19%; cocoa 20%; copra 19%; coconut oil 12%.

Transport. Shipping (1969): merchant vessels 100 gross tons and over 33; gross tonnage 17,833.

Agriculture. Production (in 000; metric tons; 1967; 1966 in parentheses): copra 101 (100); coconut oil (exports) 24 (22); cocoa (1967–68) 24, (1966–67) 21; coffee c. 16 (c. 6); timber (including Papua; cu.m.; 1967–68) 4,364, (1966–67) 4,347. Livestock (in 000; March 1967): cattle c. 32; pigs (March 1969) c. 6; horses c. 1.

Industry. Gold production (1967–68) 26,360 troy oz.

BRITISH COLONIES AND PROTECTORATES

ANTIGUA

Education. Primary and secondary, pupils (1966–67) 17,027; teachers (1963–64) 470; teacher training (1963–64), students 50, teachers 3.

Finance and Trade. Monetary unit: East Caribbean dollar (ECar$2 = U.S. $1; ECar$4.80 = £1 sterling). Budget (1967 est.): revenue ECar$13,759,496; expenditure ECar$12,632,803. Foreign trade (1967): imports ECar$39,094,190 (29% from U.S., 23% from U.K., 10% from Trinidad and Tobago); exports ECar$4,968,599 (21% to Canada, 9% to U.S., 5% to U.K., 5%

to Puerto Rico). Main export petroleum products 85%. Tourism (1969) 59,790 visitors.

BAHAMA ISLANDS

Education. (1966–67) Primary, pupils 37,716, teachers 825; secondary, pupils 11,622, teachers 498; higher, students 203, teaching staff 29.

Finance and Trade. Monetary unit: Bahamian dollar, at par (from Feb. 2, 1970) with the U.S. dollar (B$2.40 = £1 sterling). Budget (1969 est.): revenue B$78,705,719; expenditure B$78,-265,363. Foreign trade (1968): imports B$179,-186,000 (67% from U.S., 11% from U.K., 7% from Canada); exports B$51,782,000 (73% to U.S., 7% to U.K.). Main exports: cement 15%; rum 9%; pulpwood 7.6%; salt 5%. Tourism (1968): visitors 1,072,200; gross receipts (1965) c. U.S. $60 million.

Transport and Communications. Shipping (1969): merchant vessels 100 gross tons and over 136; gross tonnage 376,132. Telephones (Jan. 1969) 36,513. Radio receivers (Dec. 1968) 125,000. Television receivers (Dec. 1964) c. 4,500.

BERMUDA

Education. (1966–67) Primary, pupils 9,067, teachers 384; secondary, pupils 3,460, teachers 223; vocational, pupils 454, teachers 52.

Finance and Trade. Monetary unit: Bermuda dollar, at par (from Feb. 6, 1970) with the U.S. dollar. Budget (1969 est.): revenue Ber£11,512,-991; expenditure Ber£11,680,637. Foreign trade (1968): imports Ber£52,758,000 (including Ber £22,309,000 for free-port area); exports Ber £27,521,415. Import sources: U.S. 46%; U.K. 22%; Canada 9%; Export destinations (1967): U.K. 22%; Australia 13%; U.S. 12%; Netherlands 11%; France 8%; Japan 7%. Main exports: drugs and medicines 77%; currency 7%; petroleum products 6%. Tourism (1968): visitors 331,400; gross receipts U.S. $63 million.

Transport and Communications. Shipping (1969): merchant vessels 100 gross tons and over 29; gross tonnage 354,923. Telephones (Dec. 1968) 26,436. Radio receivers (Dec. 1967) 25,-000. Television receivers (Dec. 1968) 13,000.

BRITISH HONDURAS

Education. (1966–67) Primary, pupils 28,019, teachers 965; secondary, pupils 2,642, teachers 188; vocational, pupils 283, teachers 16; teacher training, students 79, teachers 6; higher, students 115, teaching staff 17.

Finance and Trade. Monetary unit: British Honduras dollar (BH$1.67 = U.S. $1; BH$4 = £1 sterling). Budget (1969 actual): revenue BH$13,786,000; expenditure BH$13,250,840 (capital budget BH$12,870,835). Foreign trade (1968): imports BH$44,200,780; exports BH $25,294,350. Import sources (1967): U.S. 34%; U.K. 30%; Jamaica 7%; Netherlands 5%. Export destinations (1967): U.K. 38%; U.S. 29%; Mexico 13%; Canada 10%. Main exports (1967): sugar 39%; citrus fruits and products 17%; mahogany 5%.

BRITISH SOLOMON ISLANDS

Education. (1968) Primary, pupils 21,644, teachers 1,166; secondary, pupils 749, teachers 36; vocational, pupils 299, teachers 25; teacher training, students 110, teachers 11.

Finance and Trade. Monetary unit: Australian dollar. Budget (1969 est.) balanced at A$9,265,340 (including U.K. grant-in-aid A$2,-331,584). Foreign trade (1969): imports A$8,-543,654 (44% from Australia, 19% from U.K., 6% from U.S., 6% from Japan); exports A$6,-475,370 (43% to U.K., 39% to Japan, 13% to Australia). Main exports: copra 54%; timber 38%.

BRITISH VIRGIN ISLANDS

Education. (1967–68) Primary and secondary, pupils 2,585, teachers 128.

Finance and Trade. Monetary unit: U.S. dollar (U.S. $2.40 = £1 sterling). Budget (1968 est.): revenue U.S. $2,558,461 (including U.K. financial aid U.S. $864,259); expenditure U.S. $3,176,465. Foreign trade (1968): imports U.S. $6,599,000; exports U.S. $145,000. Main exports: fish 54%; livestock 32%; fruit 6%.

CAYMAN ISLANDS

Education. (Public only; 1967–68) Primary, pupils 1,185, teachers 39; secondary, pupils 366, teachers 23.

Finance and Trade. Monetary unit: Jamaica dollar (Jam$0.83 = U.S. $1; Jam$2 = £1 sterling). Budget (1968 actual): revenue Jam$1,-392,268; expenditure Jam$1,195,328. Foreign trade (1968): imports Jam$5,351,412; exports Jam$16,246. Main exports (1967): rope 22%; turtle shell 14%. Tourism (1968): visitors 19,-411; gross receipts c. Jam$2.4 million.

Transport. Shipping (1969): merchant vessels 100 gross tons and over 29; gross tonnage 18,818. About 950 persons were employed as seamen in 1969.

DOMINICA

Education. Primary, pupils (1968–69) 19,224, teachers (1963–64) 459; secondary, pupils (1965–66) 1,452, teachers (1963–64) 83; vocational (1963–64), pupils 350, teachers 16.

Finance and Trade. Monetary unit: East Caribbean dollar. Budget (1968 est.): revenue ECar$10,519,917; expenditure ECar$10,053,484. Foreign trade (1967): imports ECar$17,316,000 (33% from U.K., 14% from U.S., 12% from Canada, 10% from Trinidad and Tobago, 7% from Netherlands); exports ECar$10,848,000 (86% to U.K.). Main export bananas 76%.

FALKLAND ISLANDS

Education. Primary and secondary (1968), pupils 381, teachers 40.

Finance and Trade. Monetary unit: Falkland Island pound, at par with the pound sterling (FI£1 = U.S. $2.40). Budgets: (colony: 1969–70) revenue FI£426,559, expenditure FI£480,393; (dependencies; 1969–70) revenue FI£23,000 (including U.K. grant FI£11,000), expenditure FI£23,000. Foreign trade: (colony; 1968) imports FI£598,839, exports FI£841,671 (mainly wool); (dependencies) imports (1967) FI£12,-491, exports (1966) FI£1,368,361 (mainly whale and seal oil).

GIBRALTAR

Education. (1967–68) Primary, pupils 3,268, teachers 134; secondary, pupils 1,758, teachers 105; vocational, pupils 74, teachers 12.

Finance and Trade. Monetary unit: Gibraltar

favour its perseverance, with attempts to promote a viable federation while implementing the U.K.'s existing plan for military withdrawal by the end of 1971. In November, however, there were signs that Bahrain (the most advanced of the nine member states, with half of their total 200,000 population) intended to withdraw from the federation and might seek UN membership in 1971. Iran was reported to have settled its differences with Bahrain over offshore oil concessions in the Gulf but in November was still pressing its claim to possession of two small islands that Britain regarded as belonging to Trucial states; the latter were themselves quarrelling over which had the right to sign oil concessions sought by rival U.S. petroleum interests. As the year ended, the future of the federation remained uncertain.

pound, at par with the pound sterling. Budget (1969 est.): revenue Gib£2,396,930; expenditure Gib£2,410,762. Foreign trade (1969): imports Gib£8.9 million (48% from U.K., 19% from EEC); exports Gib£900,000 (23% from EEC, 18% from U.K.). Tourism (1968) 306,010 arrivals.

Transport. Shipping (1969): merchant vessels 100 gross tons and over 15; gross tonnage 44,474. Ships entered (1968) vessels totaling 12,175,000 net registered tons; goods loaded (1968) 4,000 metric tons, unloaded 237,000 metric tons.

GILBERT AND ELLICE ISLANDS
Education. (1968) Primary, pupils 13,292, teachers 589; secondary, pupils 533, teachers 31; vocational, pupils 119, teachers (1967) 5; teacher training, students 88, teachers 12.

Finance and Trade. Monetary unit: Australian dollar. Budget (1968 est.): revenue A$3,857,520; expenditure A$3,595,650. Foreign trade (1968): imports A$4,133,000 (60% from Australia, 11% from U.K.); exports A$6,827,000 (63% to Australia, 24% to New Zealand, 12% to U.K.). Main exports: phosphates 84%; copra 14%.

GRENADA
Education. (1966–67) Primary, pupils 28,402, teachers 690; vocational, pupils 432, teachers 9; secondary, pupils 2,770, teachers 119; teacher training, students 77; teachers 11.

Finance and Trade. Monetary unit: East Caribbean dollar. Budget (1969 est.) balanced at ECar$21,309,540 (including ECar$4,044,000 aid and grants). Foreign trade (1968): imports ECar$26,346,000; exports ECar$9,962,000. Import sources: U.K. 33%; U.S. 10%; Canada 10%; Netherlands 5%. Export destinations: U.K. 64%; West Germany 10%; Netherlands 9%; U.S. 5%. Main exports: bananas 40%; cocoa 21%; nutmeg 25%; mace 7%.

HONG KONG
Education. (1967–68) Primary, pupils 696,176, teachers 21,388; secondary, pupils 219,686; vocational, pupils 11,939; secondary and vocational, teachers 8,875; higher (including 2 universities with 4,908 students in 1968–69), students 11,230, teaching staff 1,291.

Finance and Trade. Monetary unit: Hong Kong dollar (HK$6.06 = U.S. $1; HK$14.55 = £1 sterling). Budget (1969–70 est.): revenue HK$2,171,610,400; expenditure HK$2,118,195,830. Foreign trade (1969): imports HK$14,893,000,000 (23% from Japan, 18% from China, 13% from U.S., 8% from U.K.); exports HK $13,197,000,000 (35% to U.S., 11% to U.K., 7% to Japan, 6% to West Germany). Main exports: clothing 29%; plastic manufactures 9%; textile yarns and fabrics 9%; electrical equipment 8%. Tourism (1968): visitors arrived 618,400; gross receipts U.S. $160 million.

Transport and Communications. Roads (1969) 996 km. Railways (1968) 35 km. Shipping (1969): merchant vessels 100 gross tons and over 126; gross tonnage 707,748. Ships entered (1968) vessels totaling 27,813,000 net registered tons; goods loaded (1969) 3 million metric tons, unloaded 9,811,000 metric tons. Telephones (Dec. 1968) 426,540. Radio licenses (Dec. 1968) 639,000. Television licenses (Dec. 1968) 164,000.

MONTSERRAT
Education. (1967–68) Primary, pupils 2,969, teachers 113; secondary, pupils 263, teachers 18; vocational, pupils 15, teachers 1.

Finance and Trade. Monetary unit: East Caribbean dollar. Budget (1969 est.) balanced at ECar$4,037,180. Foreign trade (1967): imports ECar$6,923,900; exports ECar$500,000. Main exports: fruit and vegetables 52%; cotton 48%.

ST. HELENA
Education. (1966–67) Primary, pupils 753; secondary, pupils 409; primary and secondary, teachers 60; teacher training (1964–65), students 31, teachers 6.

Finance and Trade. Monetary unit: pound sterling (£1 = U.S. $2.40). Budget (1969 est.): revenue £511,580; expenditure £563,515. Foreign trade (1968): imports £376,000 (61% from U.K., 28% from South Africa); exports £15,000 (73% to U.K., 20% to South Africa).

ST. KITTS-NEVIS-ANGUILLA
Education. (1966–67) Primary, pupils 11,932, teachers 278; secondary, pupils 4,756, teachers 245; vocational, pupils 473, teachers 6.

Finance and Trade. Monetary unit: East Caribbean dollar. Budget (1969 est.) balanced at ECar$20.4 million. Foreign trade (1966): imports ECar$15,817,508; exports ECar$8,614,875. Main export sugar 88%.

ST. LUCIA
Education. (1967–68) Primary, pupils 19,709, teachers 606; secondary, pupils 4,705, teachers 191; higher, students 32, teaching staff 14.

Finance and Trade. Monetary unit: East Caribbean dollar. Budget (1970 est.) balanced at ECar$18,517,000. Foreign trade (1968): imports ECar$29,452,000 (31% from U.K., 14% from U.S., 12% from Trinidad and Tobago, 11% from Canada, 6% from Netherlands Antilles, 5% from Barbados); exports ECar$12,553,000 (82% to U.K., 7% to Barbados). Main exports: bananas 82%; copra 11%; coconut oil 5%. Tourism (1969): visitors 25,382; gross receipts ECar $7.2 million.

ST. VINCENT
Education. (1966–67) Primary, pupils 26,992, teachers 1,038; secondary, pupils 2,638, teachers 102; teacher training, students 257, teachers 13.

Finance and Trade. Monetary unit: East Caribbean dollar. Budget (1969 est.) balanced at ECar$9,245,896. Foreign trade (1967): imports ECar$15,808,000 (31% from U.K., 16% from Trinidad and Tobago, 12% from Canada, 11% from U.S.); exports ECar$6,891,000 (57% to U.K., 14% to Trinidad and Tobago, 9% to U.S., 7% to Barbados). Main exports: bananas 49%; arrowroot 16%; copra 14%.

SEYCHELLES
Education. (1967) Primary, pupils 8,108, teachers 356; secondary, pupils 1,659, teachers 110; vocational, pupils 192, teachers 9; higher, students 46, teaching staff 3.

Finance and Trade. Monetary unit: Seychelles rupee, valued at SRs. 5.56 to U.S. $1 (SRs. 13.33 = £1 sterling). Budget (1969 est.): revenue SRs. 16,326,832 (excluding grant-in-aid, valued at SRs. 1,693,334); expenditure SRs. 19,375,034. Foreign trade (1968): imports SRs. 33,875,000 (28% from U.K., 6% from South Africa, 6% from India); exports SRs. 14,196,000 (39% to India, 36% to U.S., 7% to U.K.). Main export cinnamon oil and bark 50%.

TURKS AND CAICOS ISLANDS
Education. (1968) Government primary, pupils 1,665.

Finance and Trade. Monetary unit: Jamaica dollar. Ordinary budget (1968 actual): revenue £512,168; expenditure £532,173. Foreign trade (1968): imports £443,000; exports £63,000. Main exports: crayfish 92%; salt 8%.

BRITISH CROWN DEPENDENCIES

GUERNSEY
Education. (1968) Primary and secondary, pupils 8,470.

Finance and Trade. Monetary unit: pound sterling. Budget (1968): revenue £5,731,177 (including £156,089 for Alderney); expenditure £5,001,535 (including £188,945 for Alderney).

Foreign trade included with U.K. Main exports: tomatoes, flowers, stone. Tourism (1968) 233,343 passengers arrived.

ISLE OF MAN
Education. (1968–69) Primary, pupils 3,996; secondary, pupils 3,292; vocational, pupils 1,940.

Finance and Trade. Monetary unit: pound sterling. Budget (1970–71 est.): revenue £10.2 million; expenditure £11.6 million. Foreign trade included with U.K. Tourism (1969) 532,808 passengers arrived.

Transport. Roads (1968) c. 800 km. Motor vehicles in use (1968): passenger and commercial 15,663; motorcycles 1,875. Railways (1968) 110 km.

Agriculture. Livestock (in 000; 1968): cattle 31; sheep 120; pigs 4; poultry 117.

JERSEY
Education. (1969) Primary and secondary, pupils 10,220.

Finance and Trade. Monetary unit: Jersey pound, at par with the pound sterling. Budget (1969): revenue £13,071,992; expenditure £10,143,901. Foreign trade included with U.K. Main exports: potatoes, tomatoes, cattle. Tourism (1969) 238,711 passengers arrived.

BRITISH-FRENCH CONDOMINIUM

NEW HEBRIDES
Education. British establishments only (1967): primary, pupils 9,499, teachers 359; secondary, pupils 55, teachers 5; vocational, pupils 153, teachers 10; teacher training, students 70, teachers 5. French establishments only (1966): primary, pupils 5,280; secondary, pupils 93; teacher training, students 25.

Finance. Currency: Australian dollar and New Hebrides franc (NHFr. 89.76 = U.S. $1; NHFr. 215.44 = £1 sterling; NHFr. 100.54 = A$1). Condominium budget (1969 est.) balanced at A$2,859,107. British administration budget (1969–70 est.) balanced at A$2,266,788. French administration budget (1969 est.) balanced at A$3,442,314.

Foreign Trade. (1968) Imports A$9,080,643; exports A$10,432,050. Import sources: Australia 45%; France 15%; Japan 10%; Hong Kong 6%. Export destinations: France 47%; Japan 23%; U.S. 16%; Venezuela 6%. Main exports: copra 53%; fish 23%; manganese ore 14%.

Agriculture and Industry. Production (in 000; metric tons): copra (1967) 42, (1966) 35; manganese ore (metal content; 1968) 14.

BRITISH-PROTECTED STATES

BAHRAIN
Education. (1967–68) Primary, pupils 36,179, teachers (public only) 1,099; secondary, pupils 9,022; vocational, pupils 728; teacher training, students 157; higher, students 40; teacher training and higher, teaching staff 34.

Finance and Trade. Monetary unit: Bahrain dinar, with a par value of 0.48 dinar to U.S. $1 (1.14 dinars = £1 sterling). Budget (1969 est.): revenue 12,750,000 dinars; expenditure 12,580,000 dinars. Foreign trade (1968): imports 52,021,000 dinars (24% from U.K., 16% from Japan, 12% from U.S., 5% from India, 5% from Pakistan); exports (excluding oil) 18,494,000 dinars (57% to Saudi Arabia, 8% to Qatar, 6% to Abu Dhabi, 6% to Iran, 5% to Dubai). Main export petroleum products.

Industry. Production (in 000; metric tons): crude oil (1969) 3,795; petroleum products (1968) 11,080.

BRUNEI
Education. (1968–69) Primary, pupils 26,706, teachers 1,143; secondary, pupils 7,969, teachers 405; vocational, pupils 72, teachers 7; teacher training, students 540, teachers 22.

Finance and Trade. Monetary unit: Brunei

Indian Ocean. A notable reminder of growing Soviet naval activity in the Indian Ocean was the disclosure in November of a British-U.S. agreement to develop a strategic base on the island of Diego García in the British Indian Ocean Territory. Although the details remained secret, a U.S. Department of Defense spokesman noted that Soviet naval activity in the area had tripled since 1968. The joint project provoked press criticism from Moscow and a formal protest from India.

French Dependencies. In the context of British and U.S. defense plans, a speech by the French defense minister, Michel Debré, during a visit to Réunion in August appeared significant. Describing the Indian Ocean as a region where the U.S.S.R., China, and the U.S. were seeking to extend their influence, Debré

dollar, with a par value of Br$3.06 to U.S. $1 (Br.$7.35 = £1 sterling). Budget (1969 est.): revenue Br$220,335,000; expenditure Br$246 million. Foreign trade (1968): imports Br$209,-731,625; exports Br$281,420,981. Import sources: U.K. 26%; U.S. 17%; Singapore 14%; Japan 10%; Thailand 5%. Export destination Sarawak 98%. Main export crude oil 95%.

Agriculture. Production (in 000; metric tons): rice (1967) 2, (1966) 3; rubber (exports; 1968) 0.1, (1967) 0.4. Livestock (in 000; Dec. 1966): cattle 2; pigs 6; goats *c.* 4.

Industry. Production (1968): crude oil 5,978,-000 metric tons; natural gas 213 million cu.m.

QATAR

Education. (1967–68) Primary, pupils 11,871, teachers 624; secondary, pupils 2,106, teachers 150; vocational, pupils 256, teachers 42; teacher training, students 103, teachers 15.

Finance and Trade. Monetary unit: Qatar/Dubai riyal, with a par value of 4.76 riyals to U.S. $1 (11.43 riyals = £1 sterling). Foreign trade (1967): imports 476,895,000 riyals (19% from Switzerland, 17% from Japan, 14% from U.K., 8% from U.S.); exports (excluding oil) 59,482,000 riyals. Main export crude oil.

Industry. Crude oil production (1969) 17,-341,000 metric tons.

TRUCIAL STATES

Education. Primary and secondary (1968), pupils *c.* 11,500 (including Dubai with *c.* 4,160 pupils and Sharjah with *c.* 3,230 pupils).

Finance and Trade. Monetary units: Abu Dhabi, Bahrain dinar; other states, Qatar/Dubai riyal. Budgets: Abu Dhabi (1968 actual) revenue 73.7 million dinars, expenditure 73.5 million dinars; other states (1967 est.) *c.* 3 million dinars. Foreign trade, Dubai (1968): imports 761,080,800 riyals; exports 95,760,000 riyals. Import sources: Japan 17%; U.K. 16%; Switzerland 12%; U.S. 9%; Pakistan 7%; India 5%. Export destinations (1967): Persian Gulf states 63%; Ceylon 10%; Saudi Arabia 8%; Oman 7%. Main export (excluding oil; 1967) dry fish 8%; reexports (entrepôt trade) account for 92% of total. Foreign trade, Abu Dhabi (1969) imports 59.3 million dinars (32% from U.K., 18% from U.S., 7% from Dubai). Main export crude oil.

Industry. Crude oil production (1969) 28,-548,000 metric tons.

DANISH REALM

FAEROE ISLANDS

Education. (1966–67) Primary, pupils 6,282; secondary, pupils 1,191; primary and secondary, teachers 299; vocational, pupils 1,032, teachers 88; teacher training, students 80, teachers 12; higher, students 6, teaching staff 4.

Finance and Trade. Monetary unit: Danish krone (7.50 kroner = U.S. $1; 18 kroner = £1 sterling). Foreign trade (1968): imports 211,-288,000 kroner; exports 154,110,000 kroner. Import sources: Denmark 63%; Norway 15%; U.K. 7%; Sweden 5%. Export destinations: Spain 17%; Denmark 15%; Italy 14%; U.K. 13%; Greece 8%; Norway 6%; Brazil 5%; Sweden 5%; U.S. 5%. Main exports fish and products 81%.

Transport. Shipping (1969): merchant vessels 100 gross tons and over 110; gross tonnage 36,-327.

Agriculture and Industry. Fish catch (1968) 166,300 metric tons. Livestock (in 000; June 1967): sheep 69; cattle 2. Electricity production (1968–69) 63 million kw-hr. (89% hydroelectric).

GREENLAND

Education. (1966–67) Primary, pupils 7,795; secondary, pupils 712; primary and secondary, teachers 553; teacher training, students 16, teachers (1965–66) 4.

Finance and Trade. Monetary unit: Danish krone. Foreign trade (1968): imports 358,056,-000 kroner (90% from Denmark, 7% from Venezuela); exports 87,576,000 kroner (61% to Denmark, 32% to U.S.). Main exports: fish and products 79%; minerals 11%.

Agriculture. Fish catch (metric tons; 1968) 34,000, (1967) 45,000. Sheep (Nov. 1967) 25,-000.

Industry. Production (in 000; metric tons; 1968): coal 27; cryolite 67; electricity (kw-hr.) 62,800.

FRENCH OVERSEAS DÉPARTEMENTS AND TERRITORIES

COMORO ISLANDS

Education. (1969) Primary, pupils 12,691, teachers (1967) 277; secondary, pupils 1,007, teachers (1967) 42.

Finance and Trade. Monetary unit: CFA franc, with a parity of CFA Fr. 50 to the French franc (CFA Fr. 277.71 = U.S. $1; CFA Fr. 666.50 = £1 sterling). Budget (1969 est.) balanced at CFA Fr. 1,269,000,000. Foreign trade (1968): imports CFA Fr. 1,763,000,000; exports CFA Fr. 1,008,200,000. Import sources (1965): France 47%; Malagasy Republic 17%; Cambodia 10%; Thailand 7%; Argentina 6%. Export destinations (1965): France 47%; U.S. 28%; Malagasy Republic 6%. Main exports: essential oils 42%; vanilla 35%; copra 17%.

FRENCH GUIANA

Education. (1966–67) Primary, pupils 6,739, teachers (including preprimary) 237; secondary, pupils 1,747; vocational, pupils 574; secondary and vocational, teachers 138.

Finance and Trade. Monetary unit: franc, at par with the French (metropolitan) franc (Fr. 5.55 = U.S. $1; Fr. 13.33 = £1 sterling). Budget (1969 est.) balanced at Fr. 61,256,396. Foreign trade (1968): imports Fr. 256,974,000 (74% from France, 9% from U.S.); exports Fr. 17,008,000 (74% to U.S., 18% to France). Main exports: shrimps 69%; timber 18%.

FRENCH POLYNESIA

Education. (1966–67) Primary, pupils 24,984, teachers 827; secondary, pupils 3,645, teachers 213; vocational, pupils 550, teachers 57; teacher training, students 40, teachers 6.

Finance. Monetary unit: CFP franc, with a parity of CFP Fr. 18.18 to the French franc (CFP Fr. 100.99 = U.S. $1; CFP Fr. 242.36 = £1 sterling). Budget (1968) balanced at CFP Fr. 3,072,000,000.

Foreign Trade. (1969) Imports CFP Fr. 10,-368,000,000 (56% from France, 18% from U.S.); exports CFP Fr. 1,303,000,000 (81% to France, 7% to Italy). Main exports: coconut oil 19%; vanilla 5%. Tourism (1967): visitors 23,600; gross receipts U.S. $4.7 million.

FRENCH TERRITORY OF THE AFARS AND ISSAS

Education. (1967–68) Primary, pupils 4,121, teachers 109; secondary, pupils 475, teachers 27; vocational, pupils 197, teachers 10.

Finance. Monetary unit: Djibouti franc, with a par value of DjFr. 214.39 to U.S. $1 (DjFr. 38.60 = 1 French franc; DjFr. 514.54 = £1 sterling). Budget (1969 est.) balanced at DjFr. 2,227,000,000.

Foreign Trade. (1968) Imports DjFr. 8,195,-000,000; exports DjFr. 817 million. Import sources (1967): Iran 24%; France 18%; U.K. 12%; Ethiopia 7%. Export destinations (1966): France 66%; Aden 5%. There is a transit trade through Djibouti for Ethiopia. Main exports: hides, cattle, coffee.

Transport. Ships entered (1967) vessels totaling 9.6 million net registered tons; goods loaded (1967) 101,000 metric tons; unloaded 1,455,000 metric tons.

GUADELOUPE

Education. (1966–67) Primary, pupils 65,065, teachers (including preprimary) 1,857; secondary, pupils 15,334; vocational, pupils 2,696; secondary and vocational, teachers 705; teacher training, students 101, teachers 9; higher, students 174, teaching staff 8.

Finance and Trade. Monetary unit: local franc, at par with the French (metropolitan) franc. Budget (1969 est.) balanced at Fr. 362,-849,695. Foreign trade (1968): imports Fr. 504,825,000 (70% from France, 9% from U.S.); exports Fr. 187,876,000 (71% to France, 17% to U.S., 7% to West Germany). Main exports: sugar 52%; bananas 35%; rum 8%.

MARTINIQUE

Education. (1966–67) Primary, pupils 66,664, teachers (including preprimary) 2,356; secondary, pupils 23,422; vocational, pupils 1,821; secondary and vocational, teachers 1,077; teacher training, students 1,325, teaching staff 21.

Finance and Trade. Monetary unit: local franc, at par with the French (metropolitan) franc. Budget (1968 est.) balanced at Fr. 287 million. Foreign trade (1969): imports Fr. 538,169,000 (71% from France, 6% from U.S.); exports Fr. 196,949,000 (82% to France). Main exports: bananas 62%; sugar 11%; rum 10%; canned fruit 6%.

NEW CALEDONIA

Education. (1968) Primary, pupils 21,863, teachers 893; secondary, pupils 3,295, teachers 183; vocational, pupils 941, teachers 86; teacher training, students 35, teachers 16; higher, students 63, teaching staff 10.

Finance. Monetary unit: CFP franc. Budget (1970 est.) balanced at CFP Fr. 4,750,000,000.

Foreign Trade. (1968) Imports CFP Fr. 8,350,000,000; exports CFP Fr. 10,164,000,000. Import sources (1970): France 45%; Australia 17%; West Germany 5%. Export destinations: Japan 44%; France 32%; West Germany 6%. Main exports: nickel castings 42%; nickel matte 26%; nickel 31%.

Transport and Communications. Ships entered (1965) vessels totaling 1,351,000 net registered tons; goods loaded (1966) 1,425,000 metric tons, unloaded 821,000 metric tons. Telephones (Dec. 1968) 6,573. Radio receivers (Dec. 1968) 16,000.

Industry. Production (in 000; metric tons; 1968): iron ore (metal content) 103; nickel ore (metal content) 160; electricity (kw-hr.) 643,-000.

RÉUNION

Education. (1968–69) Primary, pupils 119,180, teachers 3,785; secondary, pupils 10,405, teachers 455; vocational, pupils (1966–67) 964, teachers (1965–66) 54; teacher training (1966–67) students 295, teachers 25; higher (1966–67), students 365, teaching staff 26.

Finance and Trade. Monetary unit: CFA franc. Budget (1969) balanced at CFA Fr. 10.3 billion (including French aid CFA Fr. 1,937,-000,000). Foreign trade (1968): imports CFA Fr. 31,097,000,000 (66% from France, 13% from Malagasy Republic); exports CFA Fr. 11,385,000,000 (85% to France). Main exports: sugar 79%; essential oils 13%; rum 5%.

SAINT-PIERRE AND MIQUELON

Education. (1967–68) Primary, pupils 1,155, teachers (1966–67) 63; secondary, pupils 235; vocational, pupils 142; secondary and vocational (1966–67), teachers 47.

Finance. Monetary unit: CFA franc. Budget (1969 est.) balanced at CFA Fr. 762,705,000.

Foreign Trade. (1968) Imports CFA Fr. 1,952,690,000; exports CFA Fr. 720,959,000 (including ship's stores CFA Fr. 465,106,000). Import sources: Canada 57%; France 30%. Export destinations: U.S. 82%; France 14%. Main

said the French position was one of disengagement "since we do not believe that world peace can be established by conflict or agreement between these great powers alone, but only if all participate in preserving the equilibrium."

British Dependencies. Agreement on a new constitution for the Seychelles group of islands was reached at a London conference in March. James Mancham, leader of the Seychelles Democratic Party, had asked for "Channel Islands status"; after the conference he declared himself "more than happy" with an amended constitution that increased internal autonomy, left external defense and internal security in British hands, and provided for elections under a full-scale minis-

exports (excluding ship's stores): fresh and frozen fish 83%; dried fish 8%; fish meal 6%.

INDIAN-PROTECTED STATES

BHUTAN

Education. (1967–68) Primary, pupils 12,542, teachers 271; secondary, pupils 2,183, teachers 138; vocational, pupils 105, teachers 8.

Finance and Trade. Monetary unit: Indian rupee (Rs. 7.50 = U.S. $1; Rs. 18 = £1 sterling). Budget (1968–69) balanced at *c.* Rs. 11 million. Five-year development plan (1966–71) total expenditure (est.) Rs. 200 million; development aid from India (including aid to Sikkim; 1968–69) Rs. 50 million. About 95% of external trade is with India. Main exports (1963–64): timber Rs. 1,250,000; coal Rs. 220,000.

SIKKIM

Education. (1963) Primary and secondary, pupils 11,620.

Finance and Trade. Monetary unit: Indian rupee. Budget (1967–68 est.): revenue *c.* Rs. 12.5 million. Third five-year development plan (1966–71) Rs. 90 million (all financed by India); development aid from India (including aid to Bhutan; 1968–69) Rs. 50 million. Foreign trade is mainly with India. Main exports (excluding barter; 1960 est.): cardamom Rs. 5 million; oranges Rs. 1.4 million; potatoes Rs. 400,-000.

NETHERLANDS OVERSEAS TERRITORIES

NETHERLANDS ANTILLES

Education. (1967–68) Primary, pupils 44,238, teachers 1,270; secondary, pupils 10,294, teachers 412; vocational, pupils 2,810, teachers 153; teacher training (1966–67), students 311.

Finance. Monetary unit: Netherlands Antilles guilder or florin, with a parity of 0.52 Netherlands Antilles guilder to the Netherlands guilder (1.89 Netherlands Antilles guilders = U.S. $1; 4.53 Netherlands Antilles guilders = £1 sterling). Budget (central; 1968 est.): revenue 69,-252,924 Netherlands Antilles guilders; expenditure 69,206,226 Netherlands Antilles guilders. Cost of living (Curaçao; 1963 = 100): (April 1970) 110; (April 1969) 106.

Foreign Trade. (1968) Imports 1,258,697,-000 Netherlands Antilles guilders; exports 1,129,-631,000 Netherlands Antilles guilders. Import sources: Venezuela 72%; U.S. 10%. Export destinations: U.S. 43%; U.K. 5%. Main export petroleum products 97% (from crude oil imports, accounting for 77% of imports).

Transport and Communications. Roads (1967) 1,183 km. (Curaçao 541 km.; Aruba 380 km.; Bonaire 209 km.; St. Maarten 53 km.). Motor vehicles in use (1968): passenger 29,100; commercial 5,600. Ships entered (1967) vessels totaling 85,917,000 gross registered tons; goods loaded (1968) *c.* 38.7 million metric tons, unloaded *c.* 46 million metric tons. Telephones (Jan. 1969) 24,920. Radio receivers (Dec. 1966) 121,-000. Television receivers (Dec. 1966) *c.* 25,000.

Industry. Production (in 000; metric tons; 1968): petroleum products 36,380; phosphate rock (exports) 93; electricity (kw-hr.; 1967) 1,144,000.

SURINAM

Education. (1964–65) Primary, pupils 71,397, teachers 2,052; secondary, pupils 10,252, teachers 463; vocational, pupils 1,430, teachers 78; teacher training, students 1,583, teachers 150; higher, students 667, teaching staff 74.

Finance. Monetary unit: Surinam guilder or florin, with a parity of 0.52 Surinam guilder to the Netherlands guilder (1.89 Surinam guilders = U.S. $1; 4.53 Surinam guilders = £1 sterling). Budget (1969 est.): revenue 164.2 million Surinam guilders; expenditure 167.2 million Surinam guilders.

Foreign Trade. (1968) Imports 188.9 million Surinam guilders; exports 218.5 million Surinam guilders. Import sources: U.S. 36%; Netherlands 16%; U.K. 7%; West Germany 6%; Japan 6%. Export destinations: U.S. 50%; Netherlands 10%; West Germany 9%; Norway 8%; Canada 5%. Main exports: bauxite and alumina 70%; aluminum 16%; rice 5%.

Transport and Communications. Roads (1968) *c.* 1,560 km. Motor vehicles in use (1968): passenger 10,900; commercial 3,000. Railways (1968) 134 km. Ships entered (1966) vessels totaling 3,906,000 net registered tons; goods loaded (1968) *c.* 4.6 million metric tons, unloaded (1967) *c.* 730,000 metric tons. Telephones (Dec. 1968) 9,600. Radio receivers (Dec. 1968) 88,000. Television receivers (Dec. 1966) 16,000.

Agriculture. Production (in 000; metric tons; 1968; 1967 in parentheses): oranges *c.* 11 (11); grapefruit 6 (6); sugar, raw value (1967–68) *c.* 20, (1966–67) 18; coffee *c.* 0.4 (*c.* 0.4); rice 118 (112); bananas *c.* 25 (25). Livestock (in 000; Jan. 1967): cattle 47; goats 8; sheep 4; pigs (Nov. 1968) *c.* 13.

Industry. Production (in 000; metric tons; 1968): bauxite 5,660; aluminum 43; stone 66; gold (troy oz.) 4.7; electricity (kw-hr.) 1,076,-000 (72% hydroelectric).

NEW ZEALAND TERRITORIES

COOK ISLANDS

Education. (1967) Primary, pupils 5,172, teachers 309; secondary, pupils 603, teachers 45; teacher training, students 20, teachers 6.

Finance and Trade. Monetary unit: New Zealand dollar (NZ$0.89 = U.S. $1; NZ$2.14 = £1 sterling). Budget (1968–69 est.): revenue NZ$1,749,000 (excluding grant-in-aid NZ$2 million); expenditure NZ$3,749,000. Foreign trade (1967): imports NZ$2,991,307; exports NZ$1,-777,369. Main exports: fruit juice 51%; clothing 22%; citrus fruit 9%; copra 6%.

NIUE ISLAND

Education. (1967) Primary, pupils 1,442, teachers 80; secondary, pupils 263, teachers 15; teacher training, students 12, teachers 7.

Finance and Trade. Monetary unit: New Zealand dollar. Budget (1968–69): revenue NZ$809,453 (excluding grant NZ$900,000); expenditure NZ$1,766,969. Foreign trade (1968): imports NZ$693,323; exports NZ$56,832. Main exports: copra, sweet potatoes, bananas.

PORTUGUESE OVERSEAS TERRITORIES

ANGOLA

Education. (1966) Primary, pupils 264,836, teachers 5,898; secondary, pupils 17,320, teachers 766; vocational, pupils 15,884, teachers 874; teacher training, students 997, teachers 78; higher, students 754, teaching staff 112.

Finance and Trade. Monetary unit: Angola escudo, at par with the Portuguese escudo (28.75 escudos = U.S. $1; 69 escudos = £1 sterling). Budget (1968 est.) balanced at 5,164,787,000 escudos. Foreign trade (1969): imports 9,261,-182,000 escudos; exports 9,390,424,000 escudos. Import sources: Portugal 37%; West Germany 10%; U.S. 10%; U.K. 9%; France 5%; Japan 5%. Export destinations: Portugal 37%; U.S. 16%; Netherlands 11%; West Germany 8%; Japan 5%. Main exports: coffee 34%; diamonds 20%.

Transport. Roads (1967) *c.* 48,000 km. Motor vehicles in use (1968): passenger 64,400; commercial (including buses) 24,300. Railways (1967): 3,256 km.; traffic 151 million passenger-km., freight 2,164,000,000 net ton-km. Ships entered (1967) vessels totaling 4,239,000 net registered tons; goods loaded (1969) 8,307,000 metric tons, unloaded 1,496,000 metric tons.

Agriculture. Production (in 000; metric tons; 1968; 1967 in parentheses): dry beans *c.* 64 (*c.* 64); cotton, lint 14 (9); sisal *c.* 66 (*c.* 59); sugar, raw value (1969–70) *c.* 70, (1968–69) 67; coffee (1969) *c.* 201, (1968) *c.* 190; palm oil (1967) *c.* 35, (1966) *c.* 35; palm kernels (exports; 1967) *c.* 20, (1966) 17; fish catch (1968) 293, (1967) 292. Livestock (in 000; Dec. 1968): sheep *c.* 164; goats (Dec. 1966) *c.* 370; cattle *c.* 1,200; pigs *c.* 317.

Industry. Production (in 000; metric tons; 1969): crude oil 511; cement 383; iron ore (60–65% metal content) 5,479; diamonds (metric carats; 1968) 1,667; salt (1968) 72; fish meal (1968) 46.

CAPE VERDE ISLANDS

Education. (1967–68) Primary, pupils 19,680, teachers 381; secondary, pupils 2,134, teachers 91; vocational, pupils 564, teachers 34.

Finance and Trade. Monetary unit: Cape Verde escudo, at par with the Portuguese escudo. Budget (1968 est.) balanced at 118,952,000 escudos. Foreign trade (1969): imports 418,801,-000 escudos (49% from Portugal, 22% from Angola); exports 44,606,000 escudos (66% to Portugal, 12% to U.S., 5% to Portuguese Guinea). Main exports: bananas 23%; fish products 17%; fish 13%.

Transport. Ships entered (1968) vessels totaling 6,637,000 net registered tons; goods loaded (1968) *c.* 40,000 metric tons, unloaded *c.* 650,000 metric tons.

GUINEA

Education. (1966–67) Primary, pupils 17,805, teachers 497; secondary, pupils 417, teachers 21; vocational, pupils 643, teachers 30.

Finance and Trade. Monetary unit: Guinea escudo, at par with the Portuguese escudo. Budget (1967 est.): revenue 308,115,000 escudos; expenditure 296,853,000 escudos. Foreign trade (1968): imports 506,652,000 escudos (64% from Portugal, 5% from U.K.); exports 87,474,-000 escudos (75% to Portugal, 16% to West Germany). Main exports: peanuts 60%; coconuts 22%.

Agriculture. Production (in 000; metric tons; 1967; 1966 in parentheses): peanuts *c.* 65 (*c.* 65); palm kernels (exports) *c.* 11 (*c.* 9); palm oil *c.* 8 (*c.* 8). Livestock (in 000; 1966–67): cattle *c.* 240; pigs *c.* 104; sheep *c.* 61; goats *c.* 170.

MACAO

Education. (1966–67) Primary, pupils 35,520, teachers 916; secondary, pupils 9,177, teachers 562; vocational, pupils 2,276, teachers 123; teacher training, students 114, teachers 26.

Finance and Trade. Monetary unit: patacá (1 patacá = 4.75 escudos; 6.05 patacás = U.S. $1; 14.53 patacás = £1 sterling). Budget (1969 est.) balanced at 49,103,000 patacás. Foreign trade (1969): imports 303,236,000 patacás; exports 170,610,000 patacás. Import sources: Hong Kong 68%; China 26%. Export destinations: West Germany 23%; Hong Kong 18%; France 11%; U.S. 7%; Portugal 7%; Angola 6%; Mozambique 6%. Main exports: textiles 58%; animal products 8%; chemicals 8% (chiefly transit trade).

Transport. Ships entered (1966) vessels totaling 5,279,462 net registered tons; goods loaded (1967) 45,000 metric tons, unloaded 287,000 metric tons.

MOZAMBIQUE

Education. (1966) Primary, pupils 468,983, teachers 5,781; secondary, pupils 10,092, teachers 697; vocational, pupils 12,977, teachers 804; teacher training, students 903, teachers 86; higher, students 697, teaching staff 134.

Finance and Trade. Monetary unit: Mozambique escudo, at par with the Portuguese escudo. Budget (1970 est.): revenue 6,452,000,000 escudos; expenditure 6,451,000,000 escudos. Foreign trade (1968): imports 6,740,137,000 escudos; exports 4,420,172,000 escudos. Import sources: Portugal 33%; South Africa 12%; U.K. 10%; West Germany 8%; Iraq 6%; Japan 5%;

terial system. At these elections, held in November, Mancham's party won 10 of the 15 seats; the other

Pacific. *British Pacific Territories.* Tonga (on

271

Dependent States

Mancham's party won 10 of the 15 seats; the other five went to the People's United Party, which shared his view that the colony should retain the closest possible links with Britain. During the year a $12 million airfield was built in the Seychelles (which Britain regarded as an increasingly important staging post).

Pacific. *British Pacific Territories.* Tonga (on June 4) and Fiji (on October 10) became independent within the Commonwealth. Tonga, with a population of less than 100,000, considered itself too small to seek admission to the UN, but Fiji, with over 500,000 people, was admitted by acclamation on October 13. (*See* FIJI.)

U.S. 5%. Export destinations: Portugal 36%; U.S. 10%; South Africa 10%; U.K. 6%. Main exports: cashew nuts 16%; cotton 14%; sugar 9%; tea 7%; copra 6%.

Transport. Roads (1967) 37,525 km. Motor vehicles in use (1966): passenger 55,800; commercial (including buses) 13,200. Railways: (1967) 3,522 km.; traffic (1966) 238 million passenger-km., freight 2,408,000,000 net ton-km. Ships entered (1968) vessels totaling 16,956,000 net registered tons; goods loaded (1968) 9,624,-000 metric tons, unloaded 4,576,000 metric tons.

Agriculture. Production (in 000; metric tons; 1969; 1968 in parentheses): cotton, lint c. 45 (c. 44); sisal (1968) 32, (1967) 31; sugar, raw value (1969–70) c. 225, (1968–69) 214; copra (exports; 1967) 57, (1966) 41; bananas (1967) c. 25, (1966) c. 25; tea (1968) 14, (1967) 14. Livestock (in 000; Dec. 1968): cattle c. 1,200; sheep c. 97; goats (Dec. 1966) c. 435; pigs c. 130; asses (Dec. 1967) c. 16.

Industry. Production (in 000; metric tons; 1968): petroleum products 767; cement 286; electricity (kw-hr.) 167,000.

SÃO TOMÉ AND PRÍNCIPE ISLANDS

Education. (1967–68) Primary, pupils 7,525, teachers 237; secondary, pupils 643, teachers 39; vocational, pupils 177, teachers 11.

Finance and Trade. Monetary unit: Guinea escudo. Budget (1967 est.): revenue 115,088,000 escudos; expenditure 125,310,000 escudos. Foreign trade (1969): imports 224,856,000 escudos (46% from Portugal, 26% from Angola, 5% from West Germany, 5% from Netherlands); exports 248,279,000 escudos (43% to Netherlands, 32% to Portugal, 6% to Denmark, 6% to Poland). Main exports: cocoa 80%; copra 11%.

Agriculture. Production (in 000; metric tons; 1967; 1966 in parentheses): copra 5.4 (5.5); bananas c. 5 (c. 5); cocoa (1967–68) 10, (1966–67) 10; palm kernels (exports) c. 3.5 (c. 3.5); palm oil 1.2 (1.4). Livestock (in 000; Dec. 1966): cattle 3; sheep 2; pigs 4; goats 1.

TIMOR

Education. (1966–67) Primary, pupils 20,534, teachers 385; secondary, pupils 879, teachers 64; vocational, pupils 14, teachers 3; teacher training, students 83, teachers 8.

Finance and Trade. Monetary unit: Timor escudo, at par with the Portuguese escudo. Budget (1967 est.): revenue 150,452,000 escudos; expenditure 138,676,000 escudos. Foreign trade (1968): imports 153,271,000 escudos (38% from Portugal, 14% from Macao, 13% from Singapore, 9% from Mozambique, 5% from U.K.); exports 55,352,000 escudos (27% to Denmark, 25% to Netherlands, 9% to Portugal, 9% to Norway, 9% to Singapore, 9% to U.S.). Main exports: coffee 85%; copra 7%.

Agriculture. Production (in 000; metric tons; 1967; 1966 in parentheses): corn c. 20 (16); rice 7 (12); sweet potatoes 13 (13); copra 1.7 (2.3); coffee 6.6 (2.1). Livestock (in 000; 1966–67): goats 211; pigs 178; buffalo 117; horses c. 94; cattle 44; sheep 54.

SOUTH AFRICAN LEAGUE OF NATIONS MANDATE

SOUTH WEST AFRICA (NAMIBIA)

Education. (1966) Primary and secondary, pupils 93,491, teachers 2,970.

Finance and Trade. Monetary unit: South African rand, with a par value of R 0.71 to U.S. $1 (R 1.71 = £1 sterling). Budget (1966–67): revenue R 115,370,000; expenditure R 113,047,-000. Foreign trade included in the South African customs union. Main exports: diamonds and other minerals (1966) R 128 million; karakul pelts (1967) R 14.5 million.

Agriculture. Production (in 000; metric tons; 1968; 1967 in parentheses): beef and veal c. 60 (c. 60); corn c. 10 (c. 10); millet (1967) c. 13, (1966) c. 13; butter c. 2 (2); fish catch 983 (740). Livestock (in 000; 1968–69): cattle c.

2,450; sheep c. 3,900; goats (1966–67) c. 1,600; horses (1967–68) c. 35.

Industry. Production (in 000; metric tons; 1968): lead ore (metal content) 61; zinc ore (metal content) 60; copper ore (1966) 37; tin concentrates (metal content) 0.7; silver 0.042; diamonds (metric carats) 1,552; electricity (kw-hr.; 1963) 188,000.

SPANISH OVERSEAS PROVINCE

SPANISH SAHARA

Education. (1967–68) Primary, pupils 2,146, teachers 64; secondary, pupils 1,606, teachers 40.

Finance and Trade. Monetary unit: Spanish peseta (70 pesetas = U.S. $1; 168 pesetas = £1 sterling). Budget (1969 est.) balanced at 250 million pesetas. Foreign trade (1968): imports 210,350,000 pesetas; exports negligible.

Agriculture and Industry. Livestock (in 000; 1966–67): camels 38; goats 54; sheep 9. Electricity production (1968) 5,120,000 kw-hr. Phosphate mining is planned to begin in 1971; estimated initial annual production 3 million metric tons.

UNITED STATES DEPENDENCIES

AMERICAN SAMOA

Education. (1967–68) Primary, pupils 7,215, teachers 312; secondary and vocational, pupils 2,284, teachers 98.

Finance and Trade. Monetary unit: U.S. dollar. Budget (1969 est.) balanced at $11.1 million (including U.S. grant $7.1 million). Foreign trade (with U.S. only; 1968): imports $12,924,-000; exports $23,576,000. Main exports: canned tuna 89%; pet food 6%; frozen fish 5%.

GUAM

Education. (1967) Primary (including pre-primary), pupils 14,912, teachers 499; secondary, pupils 8,772, teachers 376; higher, students 1,597, teaching staff 100.

Finance and Trade. Monetary unit: U.S. dollar. Budget (1968 est.): revenue $36,240,734 (including U.S. grants $3,988,825); expenditure $38,983,569. Foreign trade (with U.S. only; 1969): imports $45,539,000; exports $4,146,000. Main exports: transshipped foodstuffs and scrap metal.

Agriculture and Industry. Main crops: corn, sweet potatoes, lemons, cassava. Industrial production (1968): stone 508,000 metric tons; electricity (excluding most industrial production) 597 million kw-hr.

PANAMA CANAL ZONE

Education. (1966–67) Primary, pupils 8,717, teachers 299; secondary and vocational, pupils 5,503, teachers 229; higher, students 1,390, teaching staff 73.

Finance. Monetary unit: U.S. dollar. Budgets (1969): Canal Zone government, revenue $38,-769,000, expenditure $43,386,000; Panama Canal Co., revenue $166,513,000, expenditure $158,-686,000.

Traffic. (1968–69) Total number of oceangoing vessels passing through the canal 13,150; total cargo tonnage 101,391,132; tolls collected U.S. $87,457,895. Nationality and number of commercial vessels using the canal: Liberian 1,569; U.S. 1,549; British 1,460; Norwegian 1,325; West German 1,162; Japanese 1,072; Panamanian 661; Greek 564; Swedish 487; Netherlands 479; Danish 393.

PUERTO RICO

Education. (1967–68) Primary, pupils 476,048, teachers 14,524; secondary and vocational, pupils 242,614, teachers 9,976; higher (including 4 universities), students 47,725, teaching staff 3,500.

Finance. Monetary unit: U.S. dollar. Central government budget (1968–69): revenue $961,-013,994; expenditure $924,456,790. Gross national product (1968–69) $4,093,100,000; (1967–68) $3,701,200,000. Cost of living (1963 = 100): (May 1970) 122; (May 1969) 119.

Foreign Trade. (1968–69) Imports $2,337,-517,000 (78% from U.S.); exports $1,535,473,-000 (87% to U.S.). Main exports (1965–66): clothing 23%; sugar 9%; tobacco 8%; chemicals 7%; petroleum products 6%; electrical machinery and equipment 5%. Tourism (1968–69): visitors 1,067,500; gross receipts U.S. $229 million.

Transport and Communications. Roads (1968) c. 10,000 km. Motor vehicles in use (1968): passenger 383,300; commercial (including buses) 67,800. Shipping traffic (1967–68) goods unloaded 26,848,000 tons. Telephones (Dec. 1968) 248,415.

Agriculture. Production (in 000; metric tons; 1968; 1967 in parentheses): bananas 112 (106); coffee (1969) 12, (1968) 12; sugar, raw value (1969–70) c. 435, (1968–69) 439; tobacco 5.1 (5.6); pineapples (1967) 56, (1966) 65; oranges 31 (30); grapefruit 11 (10); sweet potatoes 24 (23); milk c. 362 (361); beef and veal 17 (18). Livestock (in 000; Jan. 1969): cattle 507; pigs 194; chickens (Jan. 1967) 3,518.

Industry. Production (in 000; metric tons; 1968): sand and gravel 14,648; stone 6,683; cement (1969) 1,527; electricity (kw-hr.) 6,182,-000.

RYUKYU ISLANDS

Education. (1967–68) Primary, pupils 144,781, teachers 4,565; secondary, pupils 118,148; teachers 4,734; vocational, pupils 12,837, teachers 739; higher (including 3 universities), students 7,040, teaching staff 534.

Finance and Trade. Monetary unit: U.S. dollar. Budget (1969): revenue $130,325,000 (including U.S. grant $14,332,000 and Japanese grant $26,904,000); expenditure $126,521,000. Foreign trade (1969): imports $371,635,000; exports $87,471,000. Import sources (1967): Japan 78%; U.S. 15%. Export destinations (1967): Japan 76%; U.S. 8%. Main exports: sugar 51%; canned pineapple 14%; scrap metal 5%.

Agriculture. Production (in 000; metric tons; 1967; 1966 in parentheses): rice 12 (12); pineapple 85 (88); sweet potatoes (1968) 119, (1967) 101; sugarcane (1969–70) c. 200, (1968–69) 212; fish catch (1968) 35, (1967) 29. Livestock (in 000; Dec. 1968): cattle 28; pigs 174; goats 31; chickens 1,383.

VIRGIN ISLANDS, U.S.

Education. (1967–68) Primary, pupils 10,086, teachers 347; secondary and vocational, pupils 4,459, teachers 276; higher, students 1,333, teaching staff 40.

Finance and Trade. Monetary unit: U.S. dollar. Budget (1968–69 est.): revenue (including grant-in-aid) $70,492,569; expenditure $59,576,-266. Foreign trade (1969): imports $327,193,000 (49% from U.S.); exports $199,951,000 (87% to U.S.). Tourism (1967): visitors 554,434; gross receipts c. $75 million.

Industry. Production (1968): stone 332,000 metric tons; electricity 258 million kw-hr.

UNITED STATES TRUST TERRITORY

CAROLINE, MARIANA, AND MARSHALL ISLANDS

Education. (1966–67) Primary, pupils 26,069, teachers 1,061; secondary, pupils 3,230, teachers 220; vocational, pupils 121, teachers 16; teacher training, students 1,082.

Finance and Trade. Monetary unit: U.S. dollar. Budget (1968 est.) balanced at $24,680,000 (including U.S. grant $24 million). Foreign trade (1968): imports $13.6 million (50% from U.S., 28% from Japan); exports $3 million (27% to Japan). Main exports: copra 83%; scrap metal 10%.

Agriculture. Production (in 000; metric tons; 1967; 1966 in parentheses): copra 11 (13); bananas c. 2 (c. 2). Livestock (in 000; June 1967): cattle 9; pigs 22; goats 5; poultry 200.

Australian External Territories. As one of the last remaining trust territories, Papua-New Guinea became the object of demands for "decolonization" by the UN Trusteeship Council, and for immediate independence by the U.S.S.R. Resisting these pressures, Australia's governor-general refused in March to set an arbitrary date for independence against the wishes of the people. In 1970 ministerial responsibilities in the territory were enlarged, and the House of Assembly was given a greater say in budgetary matters; at the end of 1969 the territory had 93 local government councils covering 90% of the estimated population. The slow growth of political institutions, however, was dictated by the knowledge that time would be needed to encourage the development of a real national outlook.

U.S. Territories. The Ryukyu Islands, which the U.S. in 1969 agreed to return to Japan in 1972, continued to be the subject of negotiations between the two countries. The talks mainly dealt with the eventual disposition of the U.S. assets on the islands. In June Japan agreed to purchase a major part of the U.S. civil assets. Discussions also were held concerning the military assets, most of which the U.S. would continue to use after 1972.

Indian-Protected States. *Bhutan.* Bhutan's relations with India became closer in 1970 following visits to the Himalayan kingdom by Indian Pres. V. V. Giri and Indian Foreign Minister Danesh Singh. During Giri's visit (the first by an Indian head of state) King Jigme Dorji Wangchuk dispelled a widely held Bhutanese suspicion that India was blocking the country's efforts to join the UN. The king noted that India was not only in full agreement with these efforts but had decided to sponsor Bhutan's application. This was later confirmed by Danesh Singh when he toured the country in May. It was agreed that three ranking Bhutanese officials should join the Indian UN delegation in September to try to gain support for the application, to be presented at the 1971 session.

There were no serious incursions by the Chinese Army during the year, but the Chinese threat from the Tibetan border remained real. India continued to assist in Bhutanese Army training, and the Indian Border Roads Organization (DANTAK) completed more than 625 mi. of roads through strategic areas. Indian economic aid, amounting to approximately $26.6 million during the second five-year plan, was to be increased during the third plan (1971–75) to an estimated $49.3 million.

Sikkim. The fourth general election for the State Council took place peacefully in April and the 18 elected and 6 nominated councillors were sworn in on June 19. Of the elected seats, the National Party won seven, the National Congress five, the State Congress four, and Independents (pro-National Party) two. The fact that the leading National Party campaigned for revision of the Indo-Sikkimese treaty was considered significant, although the council itself had limited powers and relations with India did not come within its scope. Bhutan's intention to join the UN made some Sikkimese feel their own status more keenly; while India "guided" Bhutan in foreign affairs and defense, Sikkim's foreign affairs, defense, and communications were controlled by India. The chogyal, who maintained a tight grip on the State Council and general administration of the country, remained silent on this issue.

The cancellation through bad weather of a scheduled visit in April by President Giri of India caused widespread disappointment among the Sikkimese. The chogyal and his advisers had hoped during the visit to banish Indian fears on the issue of treaty revision and also to obtain more economic aid. India, which entirely financed Sikkim's first and second development plans, announced an outright grant of about $10 million for the third plan, which was being implemented. It was also spending large sums on defense, a geologic survey, the construction of border roads, and the resettlement of Tibetan refugees.

Economic Aid. Aid by the U.K. to its dependent territories, mainly channeled through Colonial Development and Welfare (CD & W) schemes and the Commonwealth Development Corporation, totaled about £15 million in 1970. The CD & W legislation, under which approximately £500 million had been disbursed since 1929 (£341 million since 1946), came to an end on March 31, and future aid was to be administered under the general authority of the Overseas Aid Act. Of the £7.5 million devoted in 1969–70 to CD & W projects in 22 dependencies, more than £6 million was spent in the Caribbean, a record total for that area. Plans for the continuing expansion of the British aid program, announced in November, revealed greater emphasis on agricultural and rural development. There was also a shift toward greater reliance on private investment in a pledge by the British government to make 1% of the gross national product its aid target for 1975. Among specific British aid projects due for completion in 1971 was the building of Belmopan, the new capital of British Honduras (for which Britain had provided a total of some £5 million). Many of the remaining dependencies, notably in the Caribbean, shared the misgivings of Commonwealth countries over the effect on their export economies of Britain's prospective EEC membership.   (PH. D.; K. I.; M. MR.; RA. R.; G. U.; X.)

See also Africa; Portugal; South Africa; United Nations.

Development, Economic

During 1969, the latest year for which figures were available, the combined gross domestic product (GDP) of the less developed countries grew at a rate of 6.7%, substantially higher than the average of about 5.5% for the period 1961–68. Furthermore, during 1961–68 the average growth rate of per capita income had been only 2.5% (due largely to the growth rate of population, which was also 2.5%), but in 1969 per capita income increased by an encouraging 4.1%. However, the average figures conceal wide regional variations. For example, per capita income rose only 1.7% in Africa during 1969, while the less developed countries in east Asia showed an improvement of 7.1%. "Less developed countries" in general refers to all Asian countries except Japan and the Sino-Soviet countries, all African countries except South Africa, all of Latin America, and Cyprus, Greece, Malta, Portugal, Spain, Turkey, and Yugoslavia. The group covers about 1,700,000,000 people, or more than 70% of the world's population outside the Sino-Soviet countries.

Food production, a major concern in many less developed countries, continued to advance. There was increasing evidence that this improvement reflected a permanent technological change, but the Green Revolution was still in its early stages and, at least for the next few years, a number of the less developed countries would need food imports. More-

Dermatology:
see Medicine

over, the higher agricultural output was still creating problems, involving such matters as taxation of the increased output and relations between owners and farmers. The rapidly rising population, with growth rates in many less developed countries of 3% or more per year, continued to lend urgency to the food problem, as well as to the more general question of how to raise the abysmally low living standards prevailing for a majority of mankind. (*See* POPULATIONS AND AREAS: *Special Report.*)

Financial Position of Less Developed Countries. The export earnings of less developed countries rose by about 9.8% in 1969, compared with an average increase of 7.6% during 1961–69. The 1969 rise was relatively small for Latin America (6.6%), but was substantial for Asia (10.1%) and Africa (11.1%). Apart from the petroleum-producing countries, Korea, Israel, Mexico, and Taiwan experienced relatively large gains in exports. India's exports, which had remained rather stagnant for some years, rose by 4.6% in 1969, and were especially large for nontraditional, manufactured, and semimanufactured products. Latin America's exports grew by only 6.6% in 1969, although Argentina and Mexico registered gains of 17.7 and 14%, respectively. (*See* Table II.)

Domestic savings are a major source of finance for investment in the less developed countries. In the 1960s domestic savings financed 85% of total investment—a major achievement since a high savings rate accomplished at low levels of income means a heavy sacrifice. In 1961–68 average capital formation from savings in the less developed countries, expressed as a percentage of gross national product (GNP equals GDP plus net factor payments on foreign investments), was 16%, and varied from about 13.1% in east Asia, 13.3% in south Asia, 13.1% in Africa, and 13% in the Middle East to 17.6 and 20.9% in Latin America and southern Europe, respectively. The average for industrialized countries in the same period was 22%. For a number of less developed countries the proportion of savings out of additional income (usually called the marginal savings ratio) was higher than the average savings/income ratio, suggesting that the average savings ratio over time was continuing to rise.

Helped by the inflow of foreign resources, gross investment in most less developed countries was higher than domestic savings. Expressed as a percentage of GNP for the period 1961–68, the average for all less developed countries was 18.4%, a figure that again conceals wide regional variations (for example, 23.8% in southern Europe and 15.6% in Africa).

Official Financial Assistance. External capital tends to seek out those investment projects that meet high technical, economic, and financial standards, but the lack of managerial, organizational, and technical expertise continued to hamper many less developed countries in the preparation of projects. Individual developed countries as well as international organizations therefore provided technical assistance to less developed countries in order to increase the latter's portfolio of projects and facilitate the inflow of foreign capital. In 1968 technical assistance disbursements by members of the Development Assistance Committee (DAC) of the Organization for Economic Cooperation and Development (OECD) reached a record $1.5 billion, 11% above 1967. In 1969, however, the disbursements rose by only $20 million.

According to preliminary estimates by the DAC, the flow of official capital from DAC member coun-

KEYSTONE

An agriculturist from the West German Organization for Economic Aid to less developed countries discusses the use of a machete with a farmer in Bolivia.

tries to less developed countries and to multilateral institutions, net of amortization, amounted to approximately $7.2 billion in 1969, roughly the same as in 1968. (*See* Table III.) Official assistance thus had increased by some $164 million over 1967 and was about $728 million higher than in 1966. The flow of official aid from France rose from $874 million in 1968 to $965 million in 1969. Official assistance from West Germany, after rising to $595 million in 1968, fell back to $544 million, approximately the same level as in 1967. The flow of official aid from Japan amounted to $811 million in 1969, compared with $679 million in the preceding year. Official assistance from the United States declined from $3,607,000,000 in 1968 to $3,328,000,000 in 1969. The official flow of funds from the United Kingdom remained constant at $429 million.

While the volume of official assistance remained at about the same level in 1969 as in 1968, the terms of this assistance, according to preliminary DAC data, improved slightly. Average interest rates on loans extended by DAC members rose to 3.7% in 1967, then dropped to about 3.3% in 1968 and to 2.8% in 1969. The average maturity period of bilateral loans, which had shortened from 28.4 years

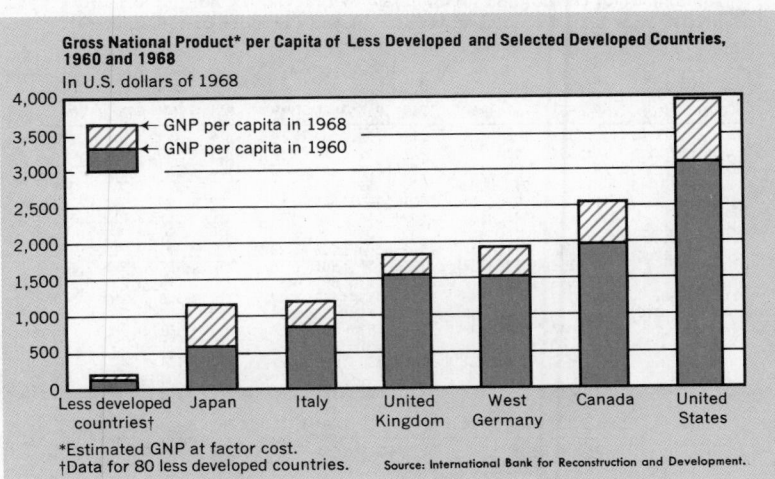

Gross National Product* per Capita of Less Developed and Selected Developed Countries, 1960 and 1968

In U.S. dollars of 1968

GNP per capita in 1968
GNP per capita in 1960

*Estimated GNP at factor cost.
†Data for 80 less developed countries.   Source: International Bank for Reconstruction and Development.

Table I. Selected Economic Indicators for Less Developed and Industrialized Countries, Regional Summary

Average annual rates of growth (%), 1961–69

Region	Total GDP	Agricultural production	Manufacturing production	Population	GDP per capita	Total gross investment	Gross investment (Shares in GNP %)	Savings (Shares in GNP %)
Less developed countries*								
1961–65	5.1	2.3	8.4	2.6	2.5	6.4	18.4	15.9
1968	5.9	3.0	9.2	2.5	3.3	9.5	18.6	15.8
1969†	6.7	...	...	2.5	4.1	...	...	...
Africa								
1961–65	4.3	2.2	9.7	2.4	1.9	2.5	15.4	12.4
1968	4.8	1.7	8.9	2.4	2.3	3.7	15.9	14.4
1969†	4.1	...	...	2.4	1.7	...	...	...
Southern Europe								
1961–65	7.3	2.5	11.3	1.4	5.8	10.8	24.5	21.2
1968	4.9	2.0	7.4	1.4	3.4	5.8	22.9	19.8
1969†	7.3	...	...	1.5	5.7	...	...	...
East Asia								
1961–65	5.5	3.0	8.1	2.8	2.7	10.7	15.2	11.5
1968	7.8	4.2	17.0	2.8	4.9	19.5	19.5	16.1
1969†	10.0	...	...	2.7	7.1	...	...	...
Middle East								
1961–65	7.4	5.4	11.0	2.9	4.4	8.2	19.8	13.0
1968	9.2	7.7	14.2	2.7	6.3	17.2	19.7	13.3
1969†	8.7	...	...	2.7	5.9	...	...	...
South Asia								
1961–65	3.5	0.8	9.7	2.5	0.9	5.9	16.1	13.9
1968	5.3	4.7	3.5	2.5	2.7	10.5	15.7	13.0
1969†	6.3	...	...	2.5	3.7	...	...	...
Western Hemisphere								
1961–65	5.0	3.8	5.8	3.0	1.9	4.1	19.1	18.0
1968	5.9	-0.4	9.3	3.0	2.9	8.3	18.5	16.4
1969†	6.4	4.4	7.7	3.0	3.3	...	...	...
Industrialized countries‡								
1961–65	5.1	1.8	6.0	1.3	3.8	6.3	21.3	21.9
1968	5.4	2.7	6.7	1.0	4.4	7.1	21.6	22.2
1969†	4.9	...	...	0.9	4.0	...	...	...

*Less developed countries (74 countries and territories covering approximately 96% of GDP of all less developed areas): Africa—Algeria, Angola, Cameroon, Congo (Kinshasa), Ethiopia, Gabon, Ghana, Ivory Coast, Kenya, Libya, Malagasy Republic, Malawi, Mali, Mauritius, Morocco, Niger, Nigeria, Rhodesia, Senegal, Sudan, Tanzania, Togo, Tunisia, Uganda, United Arab Republic, Upper Volta, and Zambia (coverage 91%); south Asia—Burma, Ceylon, India, and Pakistan (coverage 100%); east Asia—Cambodia, Hong Kong, Indonesia, Korea, Malaysia, Philippines, Singapore, Taiwan, Thailand, and Vietnam (coverage 94%); southern Europe—Cyprus, Greece, Portugal, Spain, Turkey, and Yugoslavia (coverage 100%); Western Hemisphere—Argentina, Bolivia, Brazil, Chile, Colombia, Costa Rica, Dominican Republic, Ecuador, El Salvador, Guatemala, Guyana, Honduras, Jamaica, Mexico, Nicaragua, Panama, Paraguay, Peru, Trinidad and Tobago, Uruguay, and Venezuela (coverage 99%); Middle East—Iran, Iraq, Israel, Jordan, Lebanon, and Syria (coverage 78%).
†Preliminary.
‡Industrialized countries: Australia, Austria, Belgium, Canada, Denmark, Finland, France, Germany, Iceland, Ireland, Italy, Japan, Luxembourg, Netherlands, New Zealand, Norway, South Africa, Sweden, Switzerland, United Kingdom, and United States.
Source: World Bank.

Table II. Trade Balance of Less Developed Countries

In U.S. $000,000,000

Item	1964	1965	1966	1967	1968	1969
Less developed countries						
Exports (f.o.b.)	37.1	39.3	42.3	44.0	47.9	52.6
Imports (c.i.f.)	-41.0	-44.2	-48.0	-49.6	-53.5	-57.5
Trade balance	-3.9	-4.9	-5.7	-5.6	-5.6	-4.9
Excluding less developed countries of southern Europe*						
Exports (f.o.b.)	34.0	35.9	38.3	39.6	43.3	47.3
Imports (c.i.f.)	-35.2	-37.3	-39.9	-41.5	-45.0	-47.6
Trade balance	-1.2	-1.4	-1.6	-1.9	-1.7	-0.3
Excluding southern Europe and major petroleum exporters†‡						
Exports (f.o.b.)	26.2	27.5	29.4	29.7	32.3	35.6
Imports (c.i.f.)	-31.8	-33.4	-35.8	-37.2	-39.5	-42.4
Trade balance	-5.6	-5.9	-6.4	-7.5	-7.2	-6.8

*Greece, Portugal, Spain, Turkey, Yugoslavia.
†Iran, Iraq, Kuwait, Libya, Saudi Arabia, Venezuela.
‡Estimated figures from 1965 to 1969 because of lack of detailed data.
Source: International Monetary Fund, *International Financial Statistics* (August 1970).

Table III. Total Official and Private Flow of Long-Term Financial Resources (Net)* from DAC Countries to Less Developed Countries and Multilateral Agencies by Country

In U.S. $000,000

Country	Official flows 1964	1967	1968	1969	Private flows 1964	1967	1968	1969	Total flows 1964	1967	1968	1969
Australia	104	167	157	175	15	25	49	58	119	192	206	232
Austria	15	27	28	22	7	21	46	58	21	48	74	81
Belgium	71	99	93	121	93	66	150	127	164	164	243	248
Canada	128	213	214	295	14	59	94	68	142	272	308	364
Denmark	11	28	29	55	21	-3	45	94	32	25	74	149
France	831	826	874	965	529	516	846	777	1,361	1,341	1,720	1,742
Germany, West	423	547	595	544	283	594	1,028	1,446	706	1,141	1,623	1,990
Italy	40	156	150	(137)	197	131	401	(710)	237	287	550	(848)
Japan	211	583	679	811	79	214	391	452	290	798	1,070	1,263
Netherlands	49	113	134	146	69	115	142	214	118	228	276	360
Norway	17	15	24	38	6	15	35	37	23	30	59	75
Portugal	62	47	35	(38)	—	32	13	13	62	78	48	(51)
Sweden	33	60	71	121	34	61	57	92	67	121	129	212
Switzerland	9	4	19	24	101	130	223	95	110	134	242	119
United Kingdom	493	477	429	429	426	326	331	489	919	803	760	918
United States	3,445	3,722	3,607	3,328	1,326	1,922	2,204	1,317	4,771	5,644	5,811	4,645
Total	5,942	7,084	7,138	7,248	3,200	4,224	6,055	6,047	9,142	11,306	13,193	13,297

*Net of loan repayments and private capital repatriation.
Source: OECD, *Development Assistance 1969 and Recent Trends* (July 20, 1970).

in 1964 to 23.5 years in 1966 and remained roughly constant in 1967 and 1968, increased to 27.8 years in 1969. The share of grants in total flows of official assistance continued to decline; in 1969 it was about 54%, as compared with 63% in 1966 and 75% in 1961. (See Tables IV and V.)

Grant and loan disbursements of the multilateral organizations concerned with providing financial assistance to less developed countries (chiefly the World Bank, the International Development Association [IDA], the European Development Fund, the Inter-American Development Bank, the European Investment Bank, and various UN agencies) were higher in 1969 than in 1968—about $1.2 billion, compared with a little over $800 million (net of capital subscriptions, bond purchases, and repayments by less developed countries). Loan commitments of the World Bank and the IDA increased from nearly $1.8 billion in fiscal 1969 to nearly $2.3 billion in fiscal 1970. Because of tighter financial conditions in the capital markets, borrowing costs of the bank in fiscal 1970 averaged 7.69%, compared with 6.46% a year earlier. This was reflected in the bank's decision to raise its lending rate from 7 to 7¼% in August 1970. Even so, the bank was paying more for its newly borrowed funds than it charged to its borrowers.

In March 1968 the economically advanced member countries of the IDA, an affiliate of the World Bank that makes interest-free loans with a maturity period of 50 years and a service charge of 0.75%, had reached agreement on a second general replenishment of the association's resources at the rate of $400 million annually for three years, beginning in November 1968. However, the U.S. Congress did not complete action on this agreement during the 1968 session, and the replenishment did not come into force until July 1969. Because of this delay, it was necessary to begin negotiations for a third replenishment. In July 1970, 21 member countries of IDA, plus Switzerland, proposed making approximately $813 million per year available to IDA for lending on development projects. The first payment by the contributing countries was scheduled for Nov. 8, 1971. Ireland, Spain, and Yugoslavia, which had not contributed to the second replenishment, agreed to participate in the third.

By the end of 1968 the total outstanding debt of 81 less developed countries for which data were available had reached $53.4 billion, an increase of 11.3% over the end of 1967, and this figure was estimated to have reached $60 billion by the end of 1969. At the same time, debt service payments on public and publicly guaranteed external debt of these 81 countries rose by about $265 million in 1967 and by about $511 million in 1968 (see Table VI). This rapid expansion of debt service obligations imposed severe difficulties on a number of countries, and there was a danger that debt crises would become more widespread and more persistent in the future. Short-term solutions to the problem for countries already in difficulty had been sought in rescheduling or refinancing arrangements, but longer-term and more basic solutions were needed. These included increasing the magnitude and liberalizing the terms of future aid, together with implementation of economic policies that would strengthen the ability of countries to service foreign debt and ensure the effective use of all borrowed funds.

Private Capital Flows. The flow of private capital from DAC countries to less developed countries and

Table IV. Net Flow of Official Bilateral Capital to Less Developed Countries by Type
In U.S. $000,000

Item	1966	1967	1968	1969
Total official bilateral, *net	5,990	6,348	6,469	6,227
Bilateral grants and grant-like contributions	3,802	3,673	3,431	3,350
Grants as a percent of total bilateral	63	58	53	54

*Disbursements.
Source: OECD, Development Assistance 1969 and Recent Trends (July 20, 1970).

Table V. Average Financial Terms of Official Bilateral Loan Commitments

Country	Weighted average maturity years 1967	1968	1969	Weighted average interest rates (%) 1967	1968	1969
Total bilateral loans*	23.4	24.8	27.8	3.7	3.3	2.8
United States	28.2	30.0	35.0	3.6	3.5	2.7
United Kingdom	24.1	24.8	24.1	1.1	1.3	1.2
France	15.1	18.0	17.0	3.7	3.7	3.7
Germany, West	19.0	21.2	26.0	4.3	3.9	3.2
Italy	9.3	9.3	—	4.0	4.0	—
Japan	16.6	18.0	19.5	4.8	3.9	3.7

*Countries covered are members of the Development Assistance Committee of the OECD, listed in Table III.
Source: OECD, Statistical Tables for 1968 Annual Aid Review (July 1969) and Development Assistance 1969 and Recent Trends (July 20, 1970).

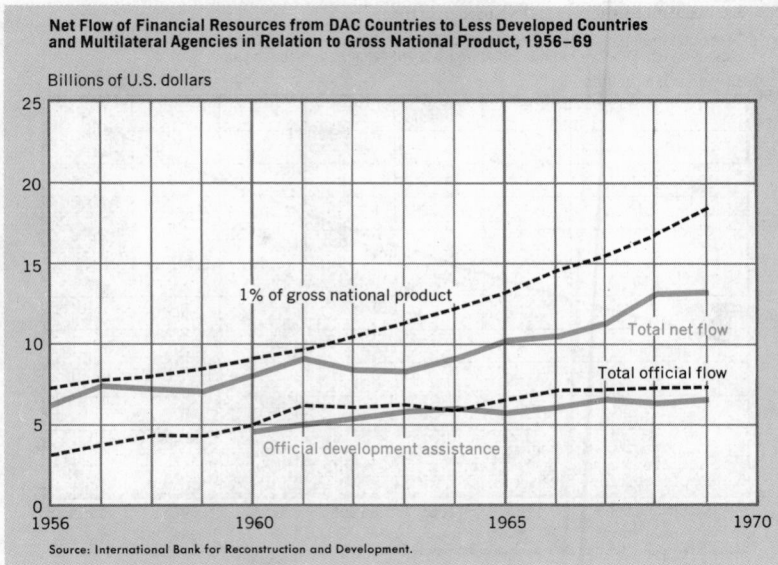

Net Flow of Financial Resources from DAC Countries to Less Developed Countries and Multilateral Agencies in Relation to Gross National Product, 1956–69

Billions of U.S. dollars

Source: International Bank for Reconstruction and Development.

multilateral institutions, net of amortization, reached $6.1 billion in 1968 and was tentatively estimated at $6 billion in 1969. Bilateral private capital flows remained at roughly the same level, but the sale of bonds net of redemptions by multilateral institutions in capital markets (other than to official institutions) rose. Private flows from the United States declined sharply in 1969, and for the first time in the post-World War II period another country—West Germany—surpassed the U.S. (See INVESTMENT, INTERNATIONAL.)

New Initiatives. During 1970 a number of international commissions examined the international development field. A report for the UN Committee for Development Planning was prepared by a group of experts under Jan Tinbergen, which had been working on guidelines for the Second United Nations Development Decade.

A study of the UN development system was carried out by Sir Robert Jackson at the request of Paul G. Hoffman, administrator of the UN Development Program, while in the U.S. Pres. Richard Nixon appointed a Presidential Task Force on International Development to formulate a new U.S. approach to aid for the 1970s. All of these reports expressed deep concern for the needs of the less developed countries and made recommendations as to how to increase the effectiveness of the efforts of the less developed countries themselves and of the aid provided by the richer nations.

After examining some of the objections raised against foreign aid, the various reports concluded that the effect on the balance of payments of donor nations was very limited, that economic aid does not lead to military entanglements, and that cases of corruption and mismanagement were relatively few. They agreed that assistance should be directed primarily at development and not at short-run political or economic objectives. In general, the reports stressed the desirability of increased use of multilateral institutions and emphasized the advantages of having the less developed countries operate within the framework of a development strategy, giving more emphasis to family planning programs, agriculture, and education.

Some of the richer countries took positive steps

to increase their aid contributions. Japan pledged a multi-billion-dollar foreign aid program in accordance with the recommendation by several international groups that industrialized countries devote 1% of their GNP to international assistance by 1975. The Canadian government announced that it intended not only to increase the amount of funds allocated to international development assistance during the coming years but to improve the quality of that assistance as well. The concessional financial terms of Canadian development aid were to be maintained, while steps would be taken toward removing restrictions on the procurement of goods purchased with aid funds. The proportion of Canadian assistance allocated to multilateral programs would be increased to about 25%. Most bilateral assistance would continue to be allocated to a small number of countries of special interest to Canada, but some 20% of bilateral aid would go to other less developed areas. In addition to Japan and Canada, the Netherlands, Norway, Sweden, and Great Britain also took steps toward

Table VI. External Public Debt Outstanding and Debt Service Payments of Less Developed Countries*
In U.S. $000,000

Year	Total	Africa	East Asia	Middle East	South Asia†	Southern Europe	Western Hemisphere‡
Debt outstanding Dec. 31							
1965	37,776	6,284	4,167	2,428	8,528	4,126	12,243
1966	42,698	7,349	4,632	3,149	10,147	4,328	13,093
1967	47,934	8,058	5,480	3,866	10,766	5,056	14,708
1968—Total	53,363	8,719	5,950	4,456	11,981	5,526	16,731
—Disbursed	39,958	6,942	4,770	3,233	9,153	3,949	11,911
—Undisbursed§	13,405	1,777	1,180	1,223	2,828	1,577	4,820
Service payments during							
1965	3,388	468	194	285	355	436	1,652
1966	3,897	474	225	358	428	440	1,970
1967	4,162	472	273	315	514	438	2,150
1968	4,673	625	310	411	540	488	2,298

Note: Items may not add to totals due to rounding.
*Includes 81 countries as follows: Africa—Botswana, Burundi, Cameroon, Central African Republic, Chad, Congo (Kinshasa), Dahomey, East African Community, Ethiopia, Gabon, Ghana, Guinea, Ivory Coast, Kenya, Lesotho, Liberia, Malagasy Republic, Malawi, Mali, Mauritania, Mauritius, Morocco, Niger, Nigeria, Rhodesia, Rwanda, Senegal, Sierra Leone, Somalia, Sudan, Swaziland, Tanzania, Togo, Tunisia, Uganda, United Arab Republic, Upper Volta, Zambia; east Asia—Indonesia, Korea, Malaysia, Philippines, Singapore, Taiwan, Thailand; Middle East—Iran, Iraq, Israel, Jordan, Lebanon, Syria; south Asia—Afghanistan, Ceylon, India, Pakistan; southern Europe—Cyprus, Greece, Malta, Spain, Turkey, Yugoslavia; Western Hemisphere—Argentina, Bolivia, Brazil, Chile, Colombia, Costa Rica, Dominican Republic, Ecuador, El Salvador, Guatemala, Guyana, Honduras, Jamaica, Mexico, Nicaragua, Panama, Paraguay, Peru, Trinidad and Tobago, Uruguay, Venezuela.
†Does not include suppliers' credits of India.
‡For Brazil, includes private debt and excludes undisbursed amounts.
§Due to a lack of information on amounts undisbursed for Ghana, Indonesia, Israel, and Lebanon, the entire amount outstanding is considered as disbursed.
Source: World Bank.

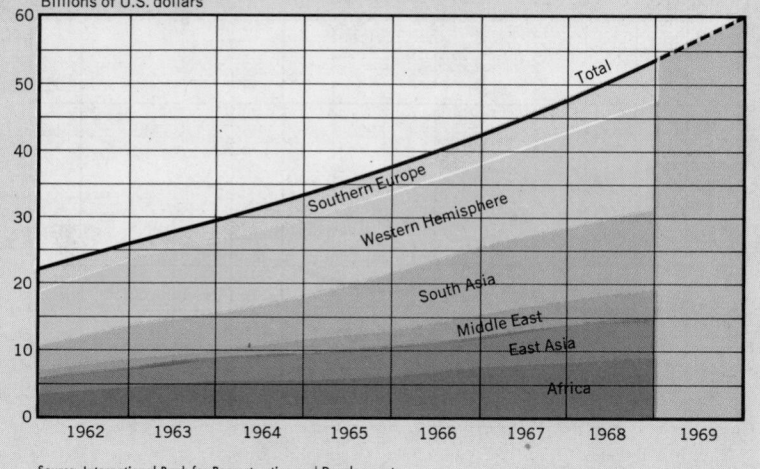

External Public Debt of Less Developed Countries

Debt outstanding of 81 less developed countries, or guaranteed by them, of maturity exceeding one year, including undisbursed, as of December 31 each year

Billions of U.S. dollars

Total · Southern Europe · Western Hemisphere · South Asia · Middle East · East Asia · Africa

1962 1963 1964 1965 1966 1967 1968 1969

Source: International Bank for Reconstruction and Development.

committing themselves to higher foreign aid targets. Increases from various countries, however, did little more than offset the substantial declines in U.S. contributions. The U.S. was still by far the largest contributor of foreign assistance, but it was among the lowest—if not the lowest—in terms of aid as a percentage of GNP.   (I. S. F.)

See also Agriculture; Commodities, Primary; Economic Planning; Industrial Review; Inter-American Affairs; Payments and Reserves, International; Trade, International.

Disasters

The loss of life and property in disasters during 1970 included the following. (*See also* METEOROLOGY.)

AVIATION

Jan. 13 Western Samoa. Samoan DC-3 airliner taking off from the Faleolo Airport in a heavy rainstorm plunged into a lagoon killing all 30 persons aboard.

Jan. 25 Poza Rica, Mex. Chartered Mexican twin-engine Convair 300 carrying newsmen assigned to cover the Mexican presidential elections crashed in heavy fog and burned on the side of Mesón Hill; of the 20 persons on board 19 were killed.

Feb. 15 Off Santo Domingo, Dom. Rep. Dominican DC-9 jetliner taking off from the International Airport and bound for San Juan, P.R., fell into the Caribbean killing all 102 persons aboard.

Feb. 21 Near Wüenlingen, Switz. Swiss Convair Coronado jet, 15 min. out of Zürich en route to Israel, crashed after an explosion on board; all 47 persons aboard were killed.

March 14 Off Belém, Braz. Brazilian twin turboprop Fairchild Hiller 227B on an approach to Belém International Airport ditched in the sea near the mouth of the Amazon River; of the 40 persons aboard 37 died.

April 1 Casablanca, Mor. Moroccan twin-engine Caravelle jetliner en route to Paris crashed as it approached Nouaseur Airport; of the 82 persons aboard 61 were killed.

April 21 Nueva Ecija, Phil. Philippine twin-engine Hawker Siddeley, ripped by an explosion in the tail section, fell near the village of Pant Bangan; all 36 persons aboard died.

May 2 Off St. Croix, W.I. Dutch chartered DC-9 jetliner en route to the Netherlands Antilles ran out of fuel and ditched in the Caribbean Sea killing 23 of the 60 persons aboard.

July 4 Near Arbucias, Spain. The worst air disaster in Spain's history occurred when a British Comet airliner carrying English vacationers crashed in mountainous terrain as it was coming in for a landing at Barcelona Airport; all 112 passengers and crewmen aboard were killed.

July 5 Toronto, Ont. Canadian DC-8 jetliner scheduled from Montreal to Los Angeles lost two engines on its landing approach to Toronto International Airport and plunged into a cornfield north of the airport killing all 109 persons aboard.

July 18 Off Keflavik, Iceland. Soviet turboprop Antonov-22 cargo plane on a mercy mission to Peru failed to make a scheduled stop at Halifax, N.S., and was believed lost in the North Atlantic with all 23 persons on board.

Aug. 6 Islamabad, Pak. Pakistani airliner crashed minutes after taking off from the airport, killing all 30 persons aboard.

Aug. 9 Near Cuzco, Peru. In the worst disaster in the airline history of Peru, a Peruvian Lockheed Electra turboprop en route from Cuzco to Lima with a full complement of passengers, including 51 U.S. teen-age students and 3 advisers, developed engine trouble soon after takeoff from Cuzco Airport and upon attempting a return to the airport plunged into a hillside and exploded, bringing death to 99 passengers and crewmen (the copilot survived).

Aug. 29 Assam State, India. Indian Fokker Friendship aircraft went down with 39 persons aboard; all were killed.

Oct. 2 Near T'ai-pei, Taiwan. U.S. Air Force C-130 transport plane crashed into a mountain and killed all 43 persons aboard.

Oct. 2 Silver Plume, Colo. Chartered U.S. Martin 440 carrying members of the Wichita State University football team lost power and in attempting to land on a highway smashed into Mt. Bethel; of the 40 persons aboard 31 died, including 14 team members.

Nov. 14 Huntington, W.Va. U.S. DC-9 jet, chartered for the Marshall University football squad, exploded in a wooded hollow as it approached the foggy rain-bound Tri-State Airport; all 75 persons aboard died, including 43 players and coaches of the Marshall team.

Nov. 27 Anchorage, Alaska. U.S. DC-8 airliner attempting to halt at takeoff fell back onto the icy runway, exploded and burned; of the 230 persons aboard 48 were killed.

Nov. 27 Central South Vietnam. U.S. Army C-123 transport went down in monsoon rains and heavy fog; all 79 persons aboard died.

Nov. 29 Central South Vietnam. U.S. Army C-123 transport, second plane in two days to crash in the same area, brought death to 44 of the 46 persons on board.

Dec. 7 Constanta, Rom. Romanian airliner en route from Tel Aviv crashed near the landing site at Lydda Airport killing 18 of the 27 persons on board.

FIRES AND EXPLOSIONS

Jan. 4 St. Roche de l'Achigan, Que. A weekend family reunion turned to tragedy when the home in which it was held caught fire and burned so rapidly that none of the 13 family members could escape.

Jan. 9 Marietta, O. Fire, presumably caused by a smoldering cigarette, blazed through a nursing home and brought death to 31 elderly patients.

Jan. 24 Eilat, Israel. A munitions explosion ripped through a military dock as soldiers unloaded arms and ammunition from an army truck; 18 men were killed and 42 seriously injured.

April 8 Osaka, Jap. Explosions set off by leaking gas at a subway construction site erupted into a crowded street tearing a hole 450 ft. long and 30 ft. wide; 27 buildings were destroyed, about 75 persons died, and more than 300 others were injured.

May 22 United Arab Republic. Brush fires ignited by the 118° F temperature reached on the hottest day in 60 years brought death to 41 persons and destroyed 660 homes.

Aug. 5 Minneapolis, Minn. An old three-story apartment building was swept by fire that started on a wooden back porch; 11 persons died and 4 others were injured seriously.

Sept. 13 Los Angeles, Calif. Predawn flames gutted a four-story downtown hotel and caused the deaths of 12 persons; 22 others were injured.

Sept. 25–30 Southern California. Brush and timber fires of five days' duration ravaged more than 200,000 ac. in Los Angeles, Ventura, and San Diego counties; 14 persons died and 1,500 buildings were burned with damage estimated at $175 million.

Nov. 1 Saint-Laurent-du-Pont, France. Flames caused by a discarded match raced through the plastic- and papier-mâché-decorated interior of an Alpine dance hall driving the occupants toward unopened exits where 142 young revelers perished; 4 of the seriously burned died later to bring the total fatalities to 146.

Nov. 5 Montreal, Que. Suburban home for the aged caught fire after an explosion in a basement furnace; 17 elderly persons died of asphyxiation; 17 other residents escaped.

Dec. 11 New York, N.Y. Three-story 19th-century building was ripped by a gas explosion and reduced to rubble by flames that brought death to 10 persons.

Dec. 20 Tucson, Ariz. Fire of unknown origin raced through the upper eight floors of the 11-story Pioneer International Hotel, trapping many of the 112 guests, 28 of whom perished in the flames; 27 others were injured.

MARINE

Jan. 18 Off southern Hokkaido, Jap. Sinking of a 2,302-ton collier brought death to 18 seamen.

Feb. 6 Off Middlesbrough, Eng. Scottish coastal ship, the 522-ton "Lairdsfield," capsized and sank in the Tees River estuary; all 10 crewmen were lost and presumed dead.

Feb. 27 Jaffna, Ceylon. Pilgrimage vessel sailing from Jaffna to Palaitivu capsized with 82 persons on board, 61 of whom drowned.

March 4 Cape Camaret, France. French submarine, the 850-ton "Eurydice," disappeared during diving maneuvers, possibly as a result of an inboard explosion; all 57 crewmen were lost.

April 9 Off Genoa, Italy. Storm-lashed 24,700-ton British ore carrier "London Valour" was crushed against a rocky breakwater killing 13 of the 57 crewmen on board.

June 12 China Sea. Philippine fishing boat "Baby Princess"

Diamonds:
see Mining

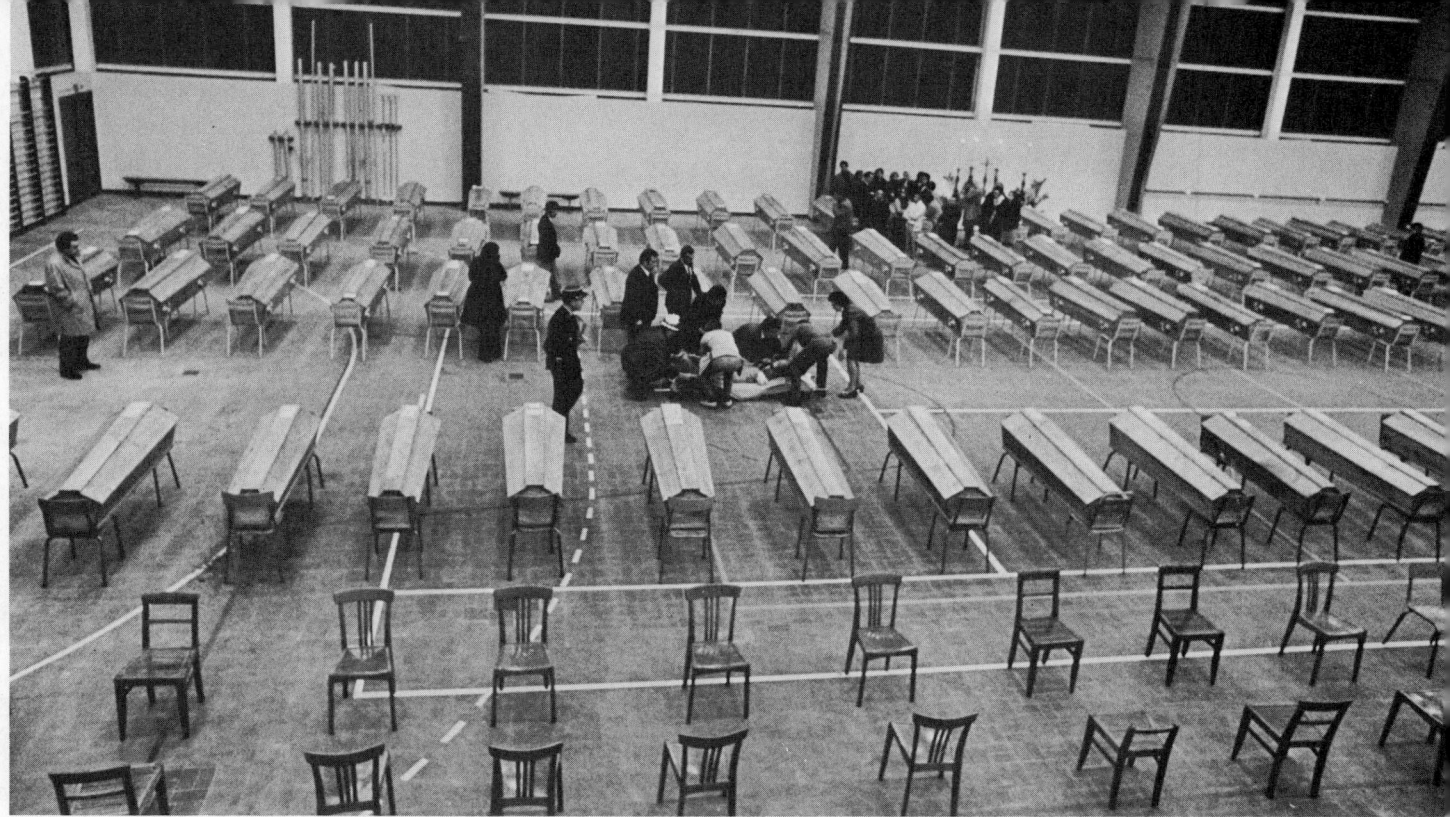

GAMMA FROM PHOTOREPORTERS

Coffins line the high school gymnasium in Saint-Laurent-du-Pont, France after a dance-hall fire which killed 146 young people in November 1970. In the centre relatives and officials attempt to identify one of the victims.

capsized in a violent storm 300 mi. SW of Manila; 22 persons were rescued, 22 others were devoured by sharks.

July 3 Dong Ha, S.Viet. South Vietnamese riverboat making a scheduled run on the Cua Viet River struck a floating mine, blew up, and killed 46 of the 50 civilian passengers.

July 5 English Channel. Under way in heavy fog, the West German freighter "Hagen" collided with the Greek ship "Bougaria" and sent it to the bottom; 17 "Bougaria" officers and crewmen were lost; 12 were rescued by the "Hagen."

July 5 Near Masulipatnam, India. Large cargo launch, in use as a ferry between two Krishna River towns, capsized and sank; about 150 persons were presumed drowned.

Aug. 1 Off Basseterre, St. Kitts I. Overcrowded with more than 200 passengers, the Caribbean ferryboat "Christena," on a 10-mi. trip from Basseterre to Charlestown on Nevis I., capsized and plunged the passengers into shark-infested waters; about 125 persons were believed to have perished.

Sept. 3 Tangadad, India. The flooded Krishna River claimed a boatload of festival goers on their way to a feast on a neighbouring island; at least 68 persons (many of them children) drowned.

Oct. 23 English Channel. Liberian-registered 42,000-ton oil tanker "Pacific Glory" collided with the Liberian tanker "Allegro" off the Isle of Wight; the burning "Pacific Glory" poured out 70,000 tons of oil into the sea, from which 30 Chinese crewmen were rescued; 13 others were dead or missing.

Nov. 5 Kristiansand, Nor. Working on the sprinkler system aboard the drydocked 19,180-ton Norwegian tanker "Pollo," more than 60 workmen were felled by leaking carbon dioxide gas; 12 men died, the others were hospitalized.

Dec. 15 Korea Strait. South Korean ferryboat, the 362-ton "Namyung-Ho," capsized because of an unbalanced cargo and flung its 278 crewmen and passengers into the icy waters; at least 261 persons perished.

Dec. 23 Off Jakarta, Indon. Two U.S. oil company ships, the "Northern Dancer," a 9-ton passenger vessel, and the 900-ton supply carrier "Aquadud," collided in the Java Sea; "Northern Dancer" sank and drowned 24 of its 42 passengers.

Dec. 23 NW of Pescara, Italy. Italian 500-ton fishing boat "Rodi" was shipwrecked during a storm in the Adriatic; all 22 crewmen perished.

MINING

April 4 Near Ostrava, Czech. Gas explosion ripped through the Paskov colliery and killed 26 miners; 3 others were missing.

June 6 Sharig, Pak. Explosion set off in a dynamite storeroom blasted a government-owned coal mine, killing 30 miners and officials; 20 others were injured.

Sept. 7 Sorrange, Pak. Cave-in caused by a gas explosion blocked the pit entrance to a coal mine and trapped the miners 150 ft. below the surface; 24 workers died and 10 others were missing.

Sept. 25 Lusaka, Zambia. Millions of tons of sand collapsed at the Mufulira copper mine, one of the world's largest, entrapping 89 mine workers in seas of mud and water; all perished.

Dec. 15 Sapporo, Jap. Gas explosion blasted through a coal mine; 19 miners were dead or missing and 11 others seriously injured.

Dec. 30 Wooton, Ky. Set off by a charge of explosives, a coal-dust explosion blasted through a coal mine entrapping 38 miners; all died.

MISCELLANEOUS

Feb. 13 Kumaon Hills, India. Man-eating tiger roaming a hilly area 50 mi. NE of New Delhi was reported to have killed 48 persons.

June 21 Rio de Janeiro, Braz. Celebration of Brazil's 4–1 victory over Italy in the World Cup soccer final game brought death to at least 44 persons; 1,800 others required hospitalization; more than 10 deaths and numerous injuries were reported elsewhere in Brazil.

Aug. 2 Baltimore, Md. State health authorities reported an outbreak of salmonella food poisoning at a city nursing home caused the deaths of 12 elderly patients; 60 others who were stricken recovered.

Oct. 15 Melbourne, Austr. Construction on the new West Gate Bridge was disrupted when a span of the structure collapsed and plunged 150 ft. into the Yarra River below, killing 34 workmen and injuring at least 18 others.

NATURAL

Jan. 4 Mendoza, Arg. Waters released from a collapsed earthen dam on the Mendoza River poured over the Andean city in a 3-ft.-high wave, leaving masses of slime and mud; at least 36 persons perished, hundreds were injured, and many more left homeless; property damage was around $25 million.

Jan. 16 Northern Morocco. Two weeks of torrential rain turned the Sebou Valley into an inland sea and completely inundated the city of Kenitra; at least 15 persons died and 100,000 others were left homeless; crop damage alone was estimated at $26 million.

Jan. 27–28 NE of Teheran, Iran. Avalanches of snow tumbled down from the Elburz Mountains onto a highway sweeping 150 vehicles into a deep ravine; a 50-hr. entombment in snow and near-zero weather brought death to at least 43 persons (including 39 in one bus); of the 1,000 others rescued, 100 were injured.

Feb. 10–12 Val d'Isère, France. A series of avalanches thundered off the 7,000-ft. crest of Le Dôme to cover an Alpine resort chalet where 200 young skiers were lodged; 42 youths were killed in the first avalanche, and an infant died in a later slide.

Feb. 24 Reckingen, Switz. Single giant avalanche swept over the small village and an army training camp; of the 48 persons buried beneath the tons of snow at least 30 perished.

March 28–31 Kutahya Prov., Turkey. Registering over 7 on the Richter scale, severe earthquakes in the Anatolia region centred in Kutahya Province and destroyed the town of Gediz and several villages; 1,087 persons died, at least 1,500 were injured, and another 90,000 left homeless.

April 7 Manila, Phil. Destructive earthquake shook the Manila area, killed 15 persons, and injured 200 others.

April 13 Near Dacca, Pak. A vicious tornado ripped through

POPPERFOTO FROM
PICTORIAL PARADE

Rescue workers search
in vain for survivors
of an avalanche
in the French Alps
that buried the boys' wing
of a children's
tuberculosis sanatorium
and killed 72 occupants
on April 16, 1970.

Lubbock, Tex.,
after a tornado struck
a 1.1-mi. path
through the centre
of the city and killed
26 persons
on May 11, 1970.

UPI COMPIX

six villages, killing 17 persons and injuring some 110 others.
April 16 Plateau d'Assy, France. Third major avalanche of
the year plunged down an Alpine slope and enveloped several buildings housing tubercular children and their nurses;
72 boys and staff members perished under the tons of snow
and debris.
April 18 Northern Texas. Tornadoes ripped through a 200-mi.
area in the Panhandle region tearing up 11 towns, including
a large trailer park where 300 homes were destroyed; at
least 25 persons died, hundreds more were injured, and property damage was estimated in the millions.
May 11 Lubbock, Tex. Second series of tornadoes in less than
a month struck the Texas plains, hitting hardest at Lubbock;
26 persons perished, 300 others were seriously injured, and
property damage amounted to more than $200 million.
May 14–31 Romania. Worst floods in centuries, triggered by
torrential rains and melting snow, inundated 37 of Romania's
39 districts, laying waste 1,000 villages and about 2 million
ac. of choice farmland in the valleys of the Danube River and
its tributaries; at least 226 persons died.
May 31 Peru. A devastating earthquake, registering about
7.8 on the Richter scale, centred 12 mi. offshore and traveled
inland to level towns and cities along the coastal mountain
areas; the official toll reached 66,794 dead or missing, with
800,000 persons homeless.
July 3–8 South Korea. Five days of ceaseless rain halted air,
rail, and road traffic along the east and southeast coastlines
and caused the deaths of at least 39 persons; 36 others were
injured, and 2,500 left homeless; property damage was estimated at $5.1 million.
July 22 Pernambuco State, Braz. Torrential rains caused
floods that killed 47 persons.
July 22 Near Badrinath, India. Flash flood poured over the
highway, engulfed a cluster of vehicles caught in a narrow
gorge, and swept away 25 buses carrying Hindu pilgrims from
"the Home of the Gods," as well as 5 taxis and an army
truck; 500 persons were believed dead.
July 30 Northeast Iran. A strong earthquake left scores of
villages in ruins throughout a rugged area of more than 20,000
sq.mi.; known dead numbered at least 176, with about 483
persons seriously injured and 10,000 homeless.
Aug. 1–9 Dacca, Pak. Floodwaters swirling knee-deep through
the streets of Dacca spread over vast areas of East Pakistan
to affect 10 million persons; at least 100 persons died, and
property damage, including standing crops, amounted to $150
million.

Aug. 4 Southern Texas. Hurricane Celia, spawned east of
Cuba, swept through the Caribbean off the tip of Florida
and struck the Corpus Christi area with a devastating force
of 160 mph; of the 32 persons dead, 5 died in Cuba, 14 in
Florida, and 13 in Texas; damage in Texas alone was estimated at more than $300 million.
Aug. 11–12 Recife, Braz. Floods caused by heavy rains
brought death to at least 123 persons.
Aug. 19 Eastern Caribbean Sea. Tropical Storm Dorothy
swirled across the Caribbean to lash the islands of Martinique, Dominica, and Guadeloupe with 70-mph winds and a
deluge of rain; 43 persons perished and hundreds were left
homeless.
Aug. 20 Ontario, Can. Freak storm, borne on 90-mph winds,
roared through the Lake Huron region almost destroying
the town of Lively; 10 persons died and hundreds were left
homeless.
Sept. 2 Central Luzon, Phil. Three days of torrential rains
caused flooding over much of Luzon Island, including Manila
and its suburbs; 24 persons died and thousands were left
homeless.
Sept. 8 Near Pyinmana, Burma. A flash flood raced down a
river and caught a crowd of 90 persons watching construction
work on a bridge; all were drowned.
Sept. 9 Central Arizona. Floods in Maricopa County caused
15 deaths and more than $1 million in damage.
Sept. 11 Venice, Italy. Sudden cyclone with a 125-mph wind
spun across the city of canals and killed 35 persons; more
than 200 others were injured, and damage amounted to about
$3.2 million.
Sept. 11 Northern Luzon, Phil. Typhoon Georgia raged inland
along the northern coast, ravaged the town of Casiguran, and
killed possibly 300 persons.
Sept. 15–17 South Korea. Torrential rains lashed the countryside, flooding more than 3,000 homes; 28 persons died, 35
were injured, and about 7,000 left homeless.
Sept. 27 Lete, Nepal. A landslide engulfed the Himalayan
village of Lete and killed 21 persons.
Sept. 30 Mexico City, Mex. A week of heavy rain caused eight
rivers to overflow, forcing thousands from their homes in the
area about the capital city; 35 persons perished.
Oct. 3–10 Puerto Rico. Week-long stationary tropical depression deluged the country with heavy rainfall, washing out
communication lines, roads, bridges, and railways as well as
towns and villages; at least 60 persons died; property damage amounted to about $100 million.
Oct. 5–9 Italian Riviera. Driving rains triggered floods that
swept through the heart of the port city of Genoa, inundated
villages for 50 mi. up and down the coast, and brought death
to at least 30 persons.
Oct. 12 Philippines. Typhoon Joan roared across the islands
killing at least 525 persons; 169 others were missing, and
912 injured.
Oct. 19 Philippines. Typhoon Kate, second of back-to-back
typhoons to hit the islands in a week, left 501 persons dead,
312 missing, and 76 injured.
Oct. 23 East Pakistan. Hurricane winds of 90 mph slashed
across nine districts and accompanying tidal waves washed
over the districts on the Bay of Bengal; 100 persons were
believed dead.
Oct. 26–30 South Vietnam. Severe floods swept five northern
provinces with Quang Ngai suffering the heaviest destruction; at least 237 persons were dead and more than 204,000
homeless.
Nov. 12 Northern Colombia. Month-long storms, abetted by
an earthquake, took the lives of more than 200 persons, with
460 others reported missing.
Nov. 12–13 East Pakistan. Possibly the greatest catastrophe
of the century came in the wake of gigantic, 30-ft., cyclone-driven tidal waves that hurtled in from the Bay of Bengal
to pound the Ganges-Brahmaputra delta, its dozens of offshore islands, and four coastal districts, affecting 3.3 million
persons in a 3,000 sq.mi. area. The official death toll was
close to 200,000 persons, with another 100,000 missing, but
it was believed a total of 500,000 may have perished; property damage was estimated at more than $2 billion; a $185
million reconstruction loan was proposed by the World Bank
as an addition to its current three-year $1.6 billion flood-control and economic development program.
Nov. 20 Luzon, Phil. Violent typhoon with winds of 125 mph
raged through the heavily populated island, wrecking the
harbour and airport facilities at Manila; 120 persons died,
60 others were missing, and more than 1,000 injured; property damage reached $80 million.
Dec. 9 Peru-Ecuador border. Earthquake registering 7.6 on
the Richter scale struck the Andes border area with such
force that many towns and villages were shattered; at least
50 persons were killed and about 600 others injured.
Dec. 12 Caldas, Col. Avalanches of mud and rocks tumbled
down the northwestern slopes of the Andes to block the rain-swollen Cauca River between the towns of Pintada and Supia;
the ensuing floodwaters swept away a roadside restaurant,
two crowded buses, more than 25 trucks and cars, and a
freight train; more than 100 persons died in the water and
debris.
Dec. 30 Neot Hakikar, Israel. Rockslide dumped tons of
debris on an army mess hall where a 40-man border patrol
was lunching; 20 soldiers were killed, another 4 missing, and
9 seriously injured.

RAILROAD

Feb. 1 General Pacheco Station, Arg. Worst train crash in Argentine history occurred when a cross-country express traveling at 65 mph rammed into the rear of a commuter train stalled on the Bartolomé Mitre tracks 18 mi. N of Buenos Aires; 141 persons died and 179 others were injured.

Feb. 16 Kaduna, Nig. Train wreck south of the town claimed the lives of at least 80 persons; an additional 52 injured passengers were killed when a truck transporting them to a hospital crashed.

Aug. 9 Plencia, Spain. Head-on collision of two trains at the Plencia station brought death to 40 persons and injured 136 others.

Aug. 22 Tamouh, U.A.R. Aswan-to-Cairo express train overturned and killed 13 persons; 54 others were injured.

Oct. 31 Near Johannesburg, S.Af. Crammed passenger train ran into the rear of an equally crowded commuter train, killing 13 persons and injuring more than 100 others.

Dec. 27 Belo Horizonte, Braz. Two passenger trains fell from the tracks and plunged into a ravine killing 17 persons and injuring 25 others.

TRAFFIC

March 6 Katmandu, Nepal. Swerving to avoid hitting a small girl, a speeding truck overturned and killed 14 persons riding on top of its load of cement; 14 other riders were hurt.

March 14 Pachuca, Mex. Pileup of a two-bus collision was smashed into and set afire by a truck loaded with industrial alcohol; 27 persons perished and 32 others were injured.

March 20 Ambato, Ec. A bus plunged through the guardrail of a bridge and into the Ambato River, killing 56 of the 107 passengers; 61 others were injured.

May 3 Near Managua, Nic. Truck and bus collision caused 13 deaths.

Aug. 21 S. Korea. Seoul-Pusan bus plunged over a 130-ft. cliff, killed 25 persons, and injured 22 others.

Sept. 18 Ceara State, Braz. Loaded with pilgrims returning from a religious festival, a truck suddenly lost its brakes, veered off a hilly curve and into a lake, bringing death to 19 pilgrims and injuring 33 others.

Oct. 14 Near Onyang, S.Kor. As it passed over an unmanned railroad crossing, a bus loaded with excursioning junior high school boys was struck by a train and pushed 100 yd. before bursting into flames; 52 boys and the driver were killed; 24 other students were injured.

Oct. 24 Near Bangkok, Thai. About 70 mi. SE of the city a truck smashed into a bus carrying Buddhist pilgrims and killed 27 persons.

Nov. 3 Takane, Jap. Construction minibus ran off the road and plunged into a reservoir, killing all 10 passengers.

Domestic Arts and Sciences

Home Economics. Education and family living were subjects that deeply concerned home economists throughout the world in 1970. Work in these fields was given special direction by close collaboration with two specialist agencies of the United Nations, the Food and Agriculture Organization (FAO) and UNESCO, through the International Federation of Home Economics (IFHE) centred in Paris. In conjunction with UNESCO, which had designated 1970 as International Education Year, the IFHE distributed questionnaires in English, Spanish, and French to its collective members, seeking information on the position of home economics in formal education in different parts of the world.

An indication of the growing importance of the profession was the new attitude to home economics education evidenced in many countries. In Britain a new four-year honours degree course was established at the University of Surrey, emphasizing the role of the home economist as an educator in the home and the community. In the United States there were signs of a change of thinking concerning the structure of home economics degree courses, reflected in a deeper study of the physical and social sciences, more emphasis on specialized areas of study, and less emphasis on the practical side of the subject.

The Home Economics Branch of the Nutrition Division of FAO announced a "Planning for Better Family Living" program to assist member nations in developing opportunities for their people to acquire the

COURTESY, VLADIMIR KAGAN

The "paper clip" lamp designed by Vladimir Kagan has a one-way mirror that makes the fluorescent bulb invisible when it is turned off.

knowledge, attitudes, and skills needed for sound planning in all aspects of family life. Assistance was pledged by the Home Economics Standing Committee of the International Council of Women, which held its triennial meeting in Bangkok, Thai., in February. Plans announced for the next three years included a program concentrating on nutrition as it affects the preschool child, the aging and the aged living alone, an evaluation of women's unpaid work in the home, and an investigation into the relationship between formal and informal home economics education.

The International Permanent Council of the IFHE, which met at Königstein, W.Ger., in July, reported an 8% rise in collective members. Recent progress included increased collaboration with international agencies, work on the documentation of home economics data and research, and a continuing inquiry into an acceptable international definition of the profession. In this connection, the Association of Home Economists of Great Britain had formulated and circulated the following definition: "Home economists are professional advisers on food, nutrition, shopping, textiles, household equipment and services, research and education, related to the home and the community."

Consumer education and protection involved many leading home economists. In the United States, Virginia Cutler, chairman of the family economics and

COURTESY, WHIRLPOOL CORP.

Whirlpool Trash Masher—
one of the first new major
household appliances
in 30 years—compresses
household trash
to one-quarter
of its original volume
in a heavy-duty
polyethylene bag.

home management department of Brigham Young University, Provo, Utah, was appointed chairman of the Major Appliance Consumer Action Panel (MACAP), set up by the home appliance industry to act as an ombudsman for consumer complaints.

In Great Britain home economists became more closely involved with the special needs of the disabled. *A Pilot Study of Disabled Housewives in Their Kitchens* was published by the Disabled Living Group, comparing movements and daily patterns of able-bodied and disabled housewives and investigating the problems and needs of the disabled housewife in her particular kitchen environment.

The truly international basis of the work of the home economist was underlined by a report in the *Bulletin* of the IFHE on the work of the home economist in Australia, South Africa, Swaziland, New Zealand, and Jamaica, compiled by four British home economists on a world tour. The special role of the home economist in translating the results of scientific research into terms of practical living was emphasized by an account of the work of home economists at Kasetsart University, Thailand, in the development of palatable forms of a protein evolved in the Institute of Food Research at the university and currently being used in a pilot feeding scheme for children.

Food Preparation. The purchase and preparation of food were made more convenient than ever before for both the domestic and the industrial consumer in 1970. At the same time, while food scientists continued their search for new means of increasing the world food supply, consumers in the more affluent countries became more and more concerned about the possible contamination of processed foods.

In all parts of the world, attempts were being made to develop protein, the nutrient in shortest supply, from such varied sources as leaves, oilseed residue, yeasts, and algae. In Great Britain textured vegetable protein (TVP), developed in the U.S. in 1968, was marketed for the first time and offered to caterers for inclusion in sausages and other processed foods. The first full season's large-scale experience with the new high-yield rice (IR8), which promised a fivefold increase in rice yields compared with native varieties, revealed difficulties in harvesting and deficiencies in eating qualities.

Controversy continued to rage over the question of cyclamates. After having relaxed its original ban to permit use of the artificial sweeteners in certain die-

tetic foods, the U.S. Food and Drug Administration again changed its mind and forbade the sale of any product containing cyclamates after September 1. California fruit packers protested to Washington over the February 1 deadline for the withdrawal from sale of cyclamate-sweetened canned goods, while Canadian producers were given until September 1. Saccharin was declared safe by the FDA, although studies of it were continuing. Another additive, monosodium glutamate, 47 million lb. of which were consumed annually in the U.S., had come under scrutiny when the National Academy of Sciences undertook to investigate its use, particularly in baby foods. An interim report indicated that it was safe for adults.

Considerable publicity was given during the year to a controversy over the nutritive qualities of dry breakfast cereals, U.S. sales of which amounted to many millions of dollars annually. Robert B. Choate, Jr., a nutrition crusader, testified before a Senate subcommittee that he had ranked the leading brands of dry cereals according to their nutritional content and had concluded that most of them consisted of "empty calories," with no more food value than alcohol or sugar. Furthermore, although a few fortified brands had been put on the market, it was the least nutritional ones that were most intensively advertised on television programs appealing to children. The breakfast cereal industry countered with statements by other scientists who insisted that Choate's evaluation was misleading and that, in any case, dry cereals were not meant to be consumed by themselves but with milk, fruit, and other foods added.

The market for convenience foods continued to grow, particularly in Europe. In Great Britain the U.S. firm of Pillsbury invested £750,000 in a bid to break into this lucrative sector with four refrigerated dough products. New products included a Grand Marnier flavoured dessert (Chambourcy), a kipper flavoured potato chip (Tudor Foods), and in Britain, where the canned milk pudding market alone was valued at £2 million, a canned dairy custard (Heinz). The highly competitive instant coffee market became even more of a battleground with the new granular instant coffee being introduced in quick succession by U.S. General Foods (Maxwell House) and the Swiss Nestlé (Nescafé); both companies invested a total of around $9.6 million in promoting their share of the £42 million ($100.8 million) market. In Europe, where the frozen food market was expected to triple in the ensuing decade, Nestlé and Unilever NV merged their frozen food interests in Italy, West Germany, and Austria, to share the burden of distribution costs.

In the U.S.S.R. ten sturgeon-breeding farms were established to safeguard the production of caviar, in danger of disappearing as massive pollution of the Volga threatened the beluga sturgeon with extinction. In Britain a renewed appetite for porridge was reported, with sales increasing 20% during the year. On the other hand, canteen diners were offered increasingly sophisticated fare when Gardner Merchant Industrial Caterers launched a £400,000 project to market over 100 frozen dishes, including *boeuf bourgignonne* and *coq au vin,* that could be speedily reheated in microwave and convection air ovens.

Greater convenience in shopping for food was offered to the housewife with a new system of marketing by computer (TeleMart, California), whereby a phoned grocery order was fed into an audio response computer that quoted prices and delivery times on

3,000 items. Greater speed in menu planning was also offered (for a price of $10,600) by a Honeywell kitchen computer featured in the Neiman-Marcus Christmas catalog.

Less futuristic but of more immediate importance to the housewife during a period of inflation was the introduction of so-called unit pricing by a number of U.S. supermarket chains, including Safeway Stores, the second largest in the country. Under this system, supermarkets posted the price of the products they sold by the ounce, pound, or other standard unit. For some years consumer advocates had complained that most packaged grocery products were put out in odd sizes that made comparison shopping impossible without complicated mathematical computations.

Cooking utensils were increasingly designed for the convenience of the cook. Although the new pots and pans looked beautiful, they were also more practical than ever before. In Sweden the ceramics industry established a quality-control system (VDN Fakta), linked to a coding system, that guaranteed the degree of resistance to cracking and the effect of various foods and dishwashing methods on glazed and patterned ceramics of all types. In Great Britain a growing number of manufacturers designed utensils with dishwashing performance particularly in mind. While a greater number of utensils were manufactured with existing hardbase nonstick finishes, the search for new materials continued; Phillips Petroleum was undertaking experiments with the plastic PPS (polyphenylsulfide).

Household Appliances. There was consolidation rather than innovation in household appliances in 1970, and standard models were increasingly marketed with features previously available only in luxury versions. Stoves of all kinds provided the major advances in design.

To take advantage of the growing use of convenience foods, which they could reheat more rapidly than conventional ovens, an increasing number of microwave ovens were introduced for domestic use. The Swedish Husqvarna 2000, rather like a helmeted spaceman in appearance, was a complete reassessment of microwave oven design. In the Philips (Eindhoven, Neth.) 1-kw. microwave oven, a frozen casserole for four could be reheated in $3\frac{1}{2}$ minutes.

Many electric ovens also incorporated new design features. An increasing number contained two ovens—one for everyday cooking, the other for entertaining and family weekend use. Many offered some method of self-cleaning. A new departure in cooking appliances was a glass ceramic range, made from material originally developed by the U.S. Corning Glass Works. This range, for which its designers predicted a profitable future, was characterized by the ability to conduct heat vertically rather than laterally, and had heating rings mounted on its underside.

In Britain, where electricity had begun to reassert its dominance in the fuel and appliance field, the North Eastern Gas Board forecast a boom in the sale of gas and gas appliances, following its linkup with Research Building Materials of Yorkshire to produce bathroom and kitchen units at prices a third cheaper than was possible with conventional building methods. The method used one-inch-thick brick slips bonded to stressed panel construction to achieve insulation 800% more effective than any other known building material. Greater U.S. influence of European appliance design was expected to follow the deal whereby the U.S. Westinghouse Electric Corp. acquired a ma-

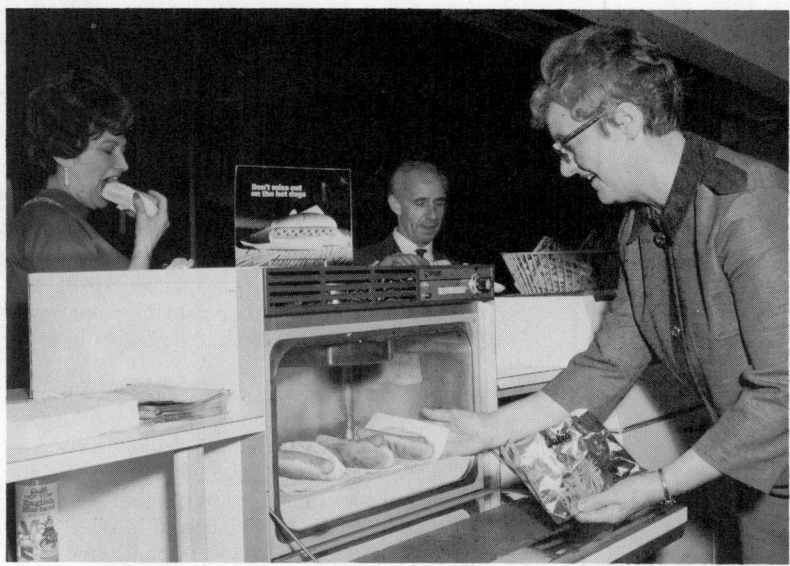

ART-WOOD PHOTOGRAPHY

A woman warms hot dogs in the 1-kw. microwave oven by Philips (Eindhoven, Neth.), which can heat a frozen casserole for four in 3½ minutes.

jority stake in the Belgian company of Ateliers et Constructions Électriques de Charleroi.

In freezers the trend was toward combined freezer-refrigerators, with Swedish, British, and Danish firms producing new models. In Britain, where one company announced a 50% increase in freezer sales during the year, the Swedish-owned Electrolux Co. forecast that British ownership would rise from 2 to 17% within five years. Sixty-two different models, priced from £43 to £218, were marketed by 24 companies of the Food Freezer Committee, many of them European in origin. Indeed, the Italian Indesit freezer was selected by the Consumer Association magazine *Which* as the best buy among freezers available in Britain.

Refrigerators were increasingly designed as pieces of furniture rather than as appliances. Finished in wood, or in colours to match cooking utensils, they were designed to fit over or under working surfaces, or to be wall hung or built into wooden cabinets. One U.S. model had castors that could be locked when the refrigerator was in position and unlocked when it was to be moved for housecleaning. During the first five months of the year, it was reported that British refrigerator exports to Europe had fallen by 21% from the previous year.

Many of the latest automatic washers incorporated solid-state electronic control modules to slow down washing action for smaller loads and to ensure even distribution of the load. There was also increasing sophistication in rinsing programs and spin speeds to ensure more effective laundering of the many new dress and furnishing fabrics. With the quality of the environment at the centre of public attention, the high phosphate content of most popular laundry detergents and other cleansing preparations became an issue among conservationists. According to the anti-phosphate forces, the phosphates, when discharged into a sewer system and then into a river or lake, caused an excessive growth of algae, leading to a decrease in the oxygen supply and eventual "death" of the body of water. A few U.S. localities passed laws that would prohibit the sale of phosphate-containing detergents within a specified period of time. Non-phosphate products were introduced, although most major manufacturers insisted that the time limits were too short to permit them to find substitutes that would perform satisfactorily and that could be used in modern washing machines. Some of the proposed substitutes were themselves under fire, and it was claimed that one, in particular, might be carcinogenic. Enzyme presoaks and additives, which were among the worst offenders as far as phosphates were concerned, were also criticized as possibly causing skin irritations. Despite this, the enzyme products consolidated their position on the market, and some washing machines incorporated a presoak period into their cycles.

Interior Decoration. Spatial simplicity and flexibility and a renewed interest in shape and form were the keynotes of interior decoration in 1970. Materials such as plastics and tubular steel, originally developed for industrial use, inspired designers in every field.

Preoccupation with shape was especially evident in seating design, where materials such as fibreglass, plexiglass, polyurethane foam, and Dacron were used to make "seating units" (as opposed to armchairs and couches) in nonstructural flexible shapes. Examples were the 30-ft.-long sack seating unit of Max Clendenning, Eero Aarnio's bright orange, upholstered foam pads, and the platform-mounted seating shapes designed by Tobia and Afra Scarpa for Cassina of Milan, which won the Compasso d'Oro awarded by the Italian Association for Industrial Design. Many seating units were designed to bypass conventional upholstery processes; an outstanding example was a chair (by OMK) of molded polyester foam, with a removable cover of wet-look plastic "Airskin" and a system of interlocking zippers allowing the chairs to be joined or left isolated as required.

Flexibility in furniture usage was especially notable in Italy, where interchangeable units allowed rooms to have multiple functions and created a strong feeling of spatial flexibility, a trend seen in modular systems such as Techno's "Graphis" and the shelving of CJFRA Mobili. Although there was much of interest to be found in Italian-designed interiors, Italy's two-year-old dominance, particularly in furniture design, began to be challenged by the Scandinavians. This was evident at the 12th International Furniture Fair at Cologne, W.Ger., where the Danish group exhibit of injection-molded plastic chairs in vivid colours, teamed with aluminum-framed tables and laminated wood armchairs, was in startling contrast to the classic teak and rosewood furniture that had established Scandinavian design during the 1950s. Plastics and metals also provided inspiration for new designs in West Germany, where Gunther Lambert produced an outstanding range of clear plastic furniture; in France, where Sentou designed unit furniture in plastic and tubular steel; and in Sweden, where Möbelfabrik used tubular steel for a range of chairs and tables made up from standard units, clipped together to act as supports for glass or wood.

From Italy came some of the most beautiful light fixtures of 1970, particularly those from Murano and Venice, examples being Mazzega's hanging lamp and the white glass bell shapes of Vistosi. Generally, however, the trend was toward more cleanly designed architectural fixtures allowing maximum flexibility in light intensity and direction. Trend setters included Swedish fixtures in plastic, steel enameled in car-body colours such as bitter chocolate and flaming orange, and Danish kits in perspex and polished aluminum that could be permutated to make 119 different lamps.

The tile dominated floor-covering design, whether in ceramic, vinyl, or carpet. Indeed, many body carpets were woven in tile designs or in bold geometric patterns producing the same effect. These patterns were used in the design of Italian ceramic tiles, and Italian influence could be seen in the tufted broadloom carpet that won the U.S. M-1 (Monsanto First) student design competition—a large-scale geometric pattern in sophisticated colours reminiscent of the rich reds, blues, and greens that dominated Italian interiors. Italian carpet designs were repeated in furnishing fabrics, either in clear brilliant colours or in dark and richly sombre shades.

Prints were to be found everywhere, especially in interiors designed for the young. Designs previously used in women's clothes were printed on such varied

CENTRAL PRESS FROM
PICTORIAL PARADE

The main hall
at the opening
on March 3, 1970,
of the "Daily Mail"
Ideal Home Exhibition
at Olympia, London.

materials as toweling, wallpaper, quilting, and oilcloth. Some manufacturers used prints, such as those of Marimekko of Finland, on cloth laminated to hard surfaces such as doors and to make screens or to hang as paintings. The effect had the same bright and informal appeal as pop posters and fantasy furniture.

While kitchen decor remained as diverse as in earlier years, there was a movement toward softer outlines, often achieved by relieving the starkness of kitchen appliances with hand-turned pine paneling. In kitchen-dining areas, the working area was often concentrated in a corridor, giving the dining area spaciousness that was enhanced by high-gloss paints sprayed on to give an auto-body finish. Following the Italian trend, "package deal kitchens" were increasingly marketed, and other complete kitchens were available in home assembly kits.   (Ev. R.)

See also Fashion and Dress; Food; Industrial Design; Merchandising: *Special Report*.

ENCYCLOPÆDIA BRITANNICA FILMS. *How to Make a Simple Loom and Weave* (1958); *How to Make a Starch Painting* (1958); *Lines in Relief—Woodcut and Block Printing* (1964); *Cloth—Fiber to Fabric* (1968).

Dominican Republic

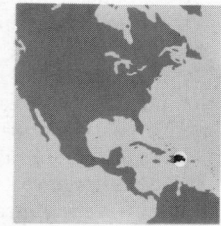

Covering the eastern two-thirds of the Caribbean island of Hispaniola, the Dominican Republic is separated from Haiti, which occupies the western third, by a rugged mountain range. Area: 18,720 sq.mi. (48,484 sq.km.). Pop. (1969 est.): 4,174,490, including European 28%; mestizo and mulatto 60%; Negro 11%. Cap. and largest city: Santo Domingo (pop., 1967 est., 577,-371). Language: Spanish. Religion: Roman Catholic. President in 1970, Joaquin Balaguer.

Political events focused on the May presidential election and dominated the course of the year's events in the Dominican Republic. President Balaguer and his Reformist Party ushered in 1970 on a rising tide of rural-based popular support. Yet the Dominican electorate continued to remain divided. Attempts at reconciliation between the incumbent Reformist Party and minority political groups proved futile because of basic ideological differences. Even within the Reformist Party, loyalty had been divided since Vice-Pres. Francisco Augusto Lora announced in 1969 his plans to enter the 1970 presidential race as the candidate of the Integrated Anti-Reelection Democratic Movement (MIDA).

The campaign period opened early in the year with pledges by the government to provide constitutional guarantees and equal opportunities for campaigning by all participating parties. The Independent Reelection Movement (MIR) immediately nominated Balaguer as their presidential candidate and the National Youth Movement (MNJ) quickly joined their ranks. In late February the Reformist Party at its national convention voted overwhelmingly to draft Balaguer for a second term.

The leftist-oriented Dominican Revolutionary Party (PRD), considerably weakened by the absence of viable leadership, decided to abstain from the coming presidential elections. By early April six additional parties had withdrawn from the presidential race, conceding that terrorist acts by both left- and right-wing groups had given rise to an unhealthy political climate that was not conducive to achieving free elections.

In an attempt to quiet rumours of political profiteering and to draw minority parties into the presidential race, President Balaguer announced that he would turn over his executive powers from April 16 to May 22 to the chief justice of the Supreme Court. This prompted a brief attempt by moderates of several political groups to rally around the middle-of-the-road National Conciliation Movement's dark-horse candidate, former president Héctor García-Godoy. However, his untimely natural death on April 20 left the only viable opposition movement without a candidate. In the election on May 16 the Reformist

WIDE WORLD

Tear gas routs Dominicans gathered in Santo Domingo on March 25, 1970, where a kidnapped U.S. military aide was to be exchanged for 20 prisoners linked to the "United Anti Re-election Command."

DOMINICAN REPUBLIC

Education. (1967–68) Primary, pupils 644,971, teachers (including preprimary) 11,681; secondary, pupils (including vocational and teacher training) 79,494, teachers (including teacher training) 3,344; higher, students 9,963, teaching staff 918.

Finance. Monetary unit: peso, at parity with the U.S. dollar (2.40 pesos = £1 sterling). Gold, SDRs, and foreign exchange, central bank: (June 1970) U.S. $34 million; (June 1969) U.S. $36.3 million. Budget (1968 est.): revenue 215.6 million pesos; expenditure 211.3 million pesos. Gross national product: (1968) 1,169,100,000 pesos; (1967) 1,084,400,000 pesos. Money supply: (June 1970) 156.5 million pesos; (June 1969) 128.5 million pesos. Cost of living (Santo Domingo; 1963 = 100): (June 1970) 103; (June 1969) 101.

Foreign Trade. (1969) Imports 211.3 million pesos; exports 184 million pesos. Import sources (1968): U.S. 55%; West Germany 7%; Japan 6%; Netherlands Antilles 5%. Export destination U.S. (1968) 89%. Main exports: sugar 51%; coffee 12%; cocoa 11%; bauxite 8%; tobacco 7%.

Transport and Communications. Roads (1968) *c.* 6,000 km. (including *c.* 2,500 km. main roads). Motor vehicles (1968): passenger 33,300; commercial (including buses) 18,100. Railways (1968) *c.* 220 km. (excluding *c.* 1,600 km. on sugar estates). Telephones (Jan. 1969) 35,735. Radio receivers (Dec. 1968) 155,-000. Television receivers (Dec. 1968) 75,000.

Agriculture. Production (in 000; metric tons; 1968; 1967 in parentheses): rice 211 (173); corn 40 (39); coffee (1969) *c.* 36, (1968) *c.* 32; sugar, raw value (1969–70) *c.* 1,016, (1968–69) *c.* 845; cassava (1967) 152, (1966) 153; peanuts (1969) 62, (1968) *c.* 47; sweet potatoes (1967) 97, (1966) 100; oranges *c.* 55 (*c.* 55); bananas (1967) 231, (1966) 238; tobacco (1969) *c.* 21, (1968) *c.* 16. Livestock (in 000; June 1969): cattle *c.* 1,150; pigs (June 1968) *c.* 1,275; horses *c.* 255; mules *c.* 85; asses *c.* 145; sheep *c.* 83; chickens *c.* 5,370.

Industry. Production (in 000; metric tons; 1968): bauxite 1,008; cement 328; electricity (kw-hr.) 701,-000.

Dominica: *see* Dependent States

Party polled 707,136 votes out of an estimated 1,852,404 total, assuring Balaguer a substantial victory.

During the first quarter of 1970 the tempo of student disturbances and terrorist acts heightened, in large measure because of the unconcealed animosity between leftist-oriented splinter groups and conservative factions within the military. Notwithstanding these acts of terrorism and increased political tensions in the capital and several of the larger provincial cities, the Balaguer regime by its moderate policies became the first democratically elected government to complete a full term of office within the past 40 years of Dominican history. (G. A. A.)

ENCYCLOPÆDIA BRITANNICA FILMS. *The West Indies* (1965).

Economic Planning

The uncertainties arising from speculation on exchange-rate adjustments, which had bedeviled planners in the industrialized countries in 1969, faded in 1970. The British balance of payments moved decisively into surplus in the summer and autumn of 1969 in a belated response to devaluation two years earlier; the French devaluation of August 1969 succeeded in restoring the equilibrium of French payments; and the West German revaluation of October 1969 finally relieved the strains in the international adjustment mechanism. Nevertheless, 1970 saw little real progress in the development of medium-term planning in the West. In the less developed countries, where planning was used as a device to promote both economic and social development, the newer plans—in contrast to the earlier ones—were placing increasing stress on the agricultural as opposed to the industrial sector, as well as on the growing problem of unemployment. The centrally planned economies of Eastern Europe continued to discuss methods of implementing "socialist economic integration."

Industrialized Countries. Among the three major Western European countries, only France proceeded with a formal five-year plan for the years 1971–75. Even this lacked conviction, since until an acceptable way could be found to control the inflation facing all three countries, there could be no real plan. The rate of inflation was higher in 1970 than at any time in the preceding 20 years. This was particularly worrisome for a country like Britain that had only a slow rate of growth, since the effect on cost per unit of output was much more serious than in countries with similar levels of inflation but faster growth. But even France and West Germany were finding that failure to control the monetary flows inhibited any real planning of the development of their economies in physical terms.

The *Rapport sur les principales options* for the sixth French plan was published early in 1970 and debated in the National Assembly in June. It outlined the consequences and problems of growth of the gross domestic product (GDP) at rates of 5.5, 6, and 6.5% annually in the years 1971–75. The Assembly somewhat predictably chose the 6% option, and this growth rate would form the basis for the detailed planning that was expected to result in the publication of the final version of the plan about the middle of 1971.

The plan emphasized the need to expand industrial output and raise the competitiveness of industry. For demographic reasons, the working population would be growing faster than during the fifth plan period. The shift of labour from agriculture and other declining sectors was also expected to continue to support the rapid expansion of manufacturing industry. Indeed, the plan was criticized by the left because the growth of output would not be rapid enough to prevent some increase in structural unemployment and a worsening in the relative position of the backward regions. The debate emphasized the problems of environment, participation, and the quality of life that had been prominent in France since the May 1968 disorders, and the plan was defended on the ground that these problems could be solved more easily within the context of rapid growth than by its sacrifice. Although public expenditure as a whole was planned to grow at the same rate as the GDP, public investment was expected to grow faster in an attempt to improve the social infrastructure.

No vestige was left of the notion, current in the third plan period and fashionable at one time in much of Western Europe, that plans could be self-fulfilling. The French government recognized that the implementation of the sixth plan would depend on whether the correct policies were being followed, and the budget of 1971 would begin the process of making the plan credible by showing how it was to be implemented. The major weakness from this point of view was that the likelihood of keeping the rate of inflation down even to West German levels seemed remote.

Despite a more favourable development of output relative to wage costs in West Germany, the government was very concerned over the accelerating rate of inflation. By mid-1970 the economy had reached the end of a long upswing, and the consequent pressure on wage levels gave rise to concern that these would exceed the growth of output for a year or two. Although the neoliberal and antiplanning ideology looked more and more out of date, the election of a Social Democratic government in 1969 had not led to any major developments in planning. The expected rate of growth for the early 1970s was 4.5%, lower than in either France or Italy, but there was no real plan for achieving this figure.

In Britain the movement into substantial balance of payments surplus made the forecasts in the last major planning document (*The Task Ahead*, February 1969) appear somewhat pessimistic during the first half of 1970. However, while it began to seem that the potential for growth by 1972 could be greater than the 3.3% per year indicated in *The Task Ahead*, actual growth remained very low indeed. Following the abandonment of the incomes policy in 1969, low growth of output began to be accompanied by an accelerating growth of earnings, with wage settlements in mid-1970 running at 15% or more. The economy thus faced the dilemma of low growth combined with rapid inflation, and this gave rise to grave doubts about how long the improvement in the balance of payments could be maintained.

With the return of a Conservative government in June 1970, the trend was away from formal medium-term planning. The intention of the government was to disengage itself as much as possible from economic intervention, and in pursuance of this policy the Ministry of Technology was merged with the Board of Trade, and the Industrial Reorganisation Corporation, the main instrument of the Labour government's industrial planning, was abolished. The intention was to rely on incentives to release the natural energies of businessmen and others. The autumn budget, which reduced taxation and public expenditure, was not a convincing implementation of this policy, but it was said to be only the first stage of policies that would progressively take effect through the next few years. There was little room in this context for any very formal approach to economic planning. The National Economic Development Council and its office remained in being, and ministers clearly found them a useful forum for discussing economic policy with representatives of business and trade unions. But even if the economic situation made a medium-term plan more feasible, it was unlikely that the new government would be interested in this method of promoting growth.

The EEC published its third medium-term policy program in 1970. This appeared at an earlier moment in the preparation of national plans than its predecessor in 1966. However, in view of the tentative nature of even the French plan for the early 1970s, it could not be more than a compilation of some very uncertain guesses about national growth rates for the 1970s.   (G. R. DE.)

Less Developed Countries. While earlier plans in the less developed countries had tended to stress the industrial sector, the plans of the later '60s began to place more emphasis on agriculture. A significant trend of the past few years was the concern of planners with the unemployment problem. High rates of industrial development achieved in the past decade were not accompanied by corresponding increases in industrial employment, because the less developed countries tended to imitate the capital-intensive industrial technology of the developed countries too closely. At the same time, the slower growth of the agricultural sector was not sufficient to provide a large increase in employment. These trends, combined with the rapid growth of the labour force, especially in urban areas, magnified the unemployment problem. Development plans, which had hitherto been concerned largely with the financial balancing of resources with expenditures, were becoming more concerned with ways of providing the growing labour force with adequate employment opportunities.

Significant developments occurred in two countries during the year. After four years in which planning was done on an annual basis, India, while continuing with its annual plans, adopted its fourth five-year plan. In Tanzania the second five-year plan was drawn up to promote development on the basis of Pres. Julius Nyerere's Arusha Declaration, which greatly extended the role of government in the economy. This plan was an exemplary one, with careful balancing of the long- and the short-term aspects in the choice of projects and with due emphasis on the social factors in development.

Economic planning is undertaken in the less developed countries primarily in connection with their efforts to promote economic and social development. For this purpose, planning is a technical device that can make such development efforts more effective. In one sense, a development plan is a blueprint for various government agencies to follow in their investment activities. In another sense, it is a way of looking intelligently into the future. It is also a way of choosing projects in various sectors and putting them together so as to have maximum impact on the country's development. Finally, particularly in mixed economies, it announces a set of government investment decisions, thereby increasing the climate of certainty and en-

BEN ROTH AGENCY

"Look Out!"
—Pierotti.

couraging the rest of the economy to undertake longer-term investments.

The plans drawn up by the less developed countries covered various periods—long-term plans covering a decade or two, medium-term plans covering about five years, and short-term plans covering one or two years. Because of their duration, the long-term plans were more concerned with mapping out the broad strategy of a country's development program; there was less emphasis on their implementation in detail, especially since the less developed countries did not generally have the political basis for continuity of decision-making over a long period. Medium-term plans were drawn in more detail and were more generally geared to actual implementation. In conditions of great uncertainty about the future, especially regarding the availability of resources for development, countries made their development plans for short periods, even as short as one year.

The drawing up of a development plan is a difficult undertaking, since such a project requires a considerable mass of data about the workings of the economy and many persons skilled in its analysis. Twenty years of experience, plus technical assistance from the developed countries and the UN, had greatly improved the less developed countries' stock of data and skilled personnel, and by 1970 most of these countries had some sort of development plan. However, the quality and effectiveness of a development plan depend essentially on its political backing and the planning organization through which it is expressed, and in this respect development plans varied greatly from country to country. In some countries such plans were still drawn largely for propaganda purposes or as bases for negotiating foreign assistance.

During the year a number of studies were made on the role of planning as a technique for promoting development, especially in an international framework. The 1969 report of the Pearson Commission on International Development, set up by the World Bank, was widely discussed. The UN adopted a resolution for the Second Development Decade, covering the '70s, which stressed the role of planning. The Centre for Development Planning of the UN Secretariat began a new periodical, the *Journal of Development Planning,* containing theoretical and practical studies of planning and summary descriptions of plans being followed in a number of countries.

To make development plans more effective in the future, the less developed countries would have to formulate longer-term development strategies and seek to draw up their medium-term plans on the basis of such strategies. Only in this way could they tackle some of their basic problems, such as unemployment, agricultural modernization, and social progress. At the same time, they needed more assistance from the developed countries, including measures that would make the availability of resources more certain so that they could plan more confidently over a longer period. In addition, more foreign assistance needed to be related to the development plan as a whole rather than to individual projects. (R. M. Sm.)

Centrally Planned Economies. The Council for Mutual Economic Assistance (CMEA, or Comecon) held its 24th session in Warsaw during May 12–14, 1970. The meeting was attended by delegations from all eight member states (the U.S.S.R., six Eastern European countries, and Mongolia), headed by the premiers rather than by the first (or general) secretaries of the Communist parties as had been the case at the special session of April 1969. The main object of the Warsaw session was to examine the present stage along the road toward "socialist economic integration," approved in principle a year earlier.

"We are all aware that realization of the many complicated undertakings of socialist integration is a long-term process," said Jozef Cyrankiewicz, the Polish premier, in his opening speech. Today, he went on, a single small or even medium-sized country is unable to resolve all the key scientific and technical problems connected with industrial development; this is why appropriate division of labour, economic specialization, and coordination among the Comecon countries were indispensable.

The Warsaw meeting heard and discussed a report of the Comecon Executive Committee (composed of deputy premiers), which met in Moscow in December 1969 and in February 1970. This report—not published—suggested a comprehensive long-term program for further strengthening and improving cooperation among the member countries. The session also heard reports from the chairmen of the national planning commissions on progress in the work of coordinating and dovetailing their respective 1971–75 development plans. This was the penultimate stage in the following procedure:

1. National planning commissions submit the drafts of their five-year plans to the Comecon secretariat in Moscow.

2. Specialized committees of the secretariat examine the drafts to sum up their respective supplies and demands in fuel and raw materials, as well as in agricultural and industrial goods.

3. Critical remarks on national plans are sent to the Moscow bureau of the Comecon Executive Committee.

4. After a collective effort of coordination of national plans, the latter are returned to the national planning commissions with appropriate recommendations.

5. Bilateral negotiations start between the governments and their planning commissions in order to prepare agreements—27 in all—stipulating precise quotas and values for goods and services to be exchanged.

6. Once the bilateral economic five-year agreements are signed—but not published—the respective party central committees and governments approve the development plans and submit them to their respective national assemblies for legislative enactment.

Such coordination of course limits the possibilities of "socialist division of labour" and slows down economic development. Multilateral trading within the area was the obvious answer, but this was linked with almost inextricable problems of prices and payments in national currencies, none of which was convertible even inside the Comecon area. An International Bank for Economic Cooperation with an authorized capital of 300 million "convertible" rubles (almost two-fifths guaranteed by the U.S.S.R.) had functioned in Moscow since January 1964, but it only settled accounts between the member states and accorded them short-term credits for approved foreign transactions. No surplus resulting from trade between two member states could be used to balance the deficit existing in the trade of one of them with a third member state.

Many member states, the U.S.S.R. excluded, had complained bitterly about the limited scope of the International Bank's activities. As a result, the 24th meeting of Comecon decided to create another financial institution, the International Investment Bank, with headquarters in Moscow and with authorized capital of 1 billion rubles. Of this, 70% was in "convertible" rubles, described as "collective currency of socialist countries," and 30% was in freely convertible currencies or in gold.

What was optimistically called the "convertible" ruble was actually the "new ruble," introduced on Jan. 1, 1961, and was simply a money of account for external trade within and outside the Comecon area. Its official gold content of 0.987421 g. was not related to the Soviet gold reserve, which remained a state secret. The introduction of the new ruble had resulted in a general exchange-rate adjustment among all Eastern European currencies involving dual rates of exchange, one for foreign trade and another for other transactions, mainly tourism and expenditure by diplomatic missions. Ten years later these exchange rates remained unchanged, and the Comecon countries were no closer to true convertibility and multilateralism than before. Poland, for instance, had three exchange rates for hard currencies: in foreign trade $1 was worth 4 zlotys; a tourist arriving in Warsaw exchanged his dollar at the bank for 24 zlotys; and a Pole receiving money from an American friend or relative obtained 72 zlotys per dollar. There was also an illegal black market price of more than 100 zlotys per dollar.

On July 10, in Moscow, the ministers of finance of seven Comecon member states signed the new bank's charter. Romania, still distrustful of "socialist integration," declared that it would study the possibilities of some form of participation in the bank's work. This stand was consistent with Romania's nonparticipation in such international trading organizations set up by Comecon as "Intermetal," "Interchem," and the Ball-Bearing Manufacturing Co-operative Organization. Romania objected to the rule that the new bank's board decisions would be taken by a 75% majority and not unanimously to preserve members' sovereignty. Vasily Garbuzov, the Soviet minister of finance, writing in *Pravda* on July 11, tried to appease Romania by stating that the 75% majority would apply only to the transactions of the bank and that a unanimous decision would be required to revise the charter, to increase the authorized capital, or to float a loan.

The chief purpose of the International Investment Bank was to supply medium- and long-term credits; usually 5 and 15 years, to projects connected with the international socialist division of labour, specialization and partnership in production, development of fuel and raw materials resources, and the construction of industrial plants vital to the economic growth of the member countries. Every member country was represented on the board with an equal voice, regardless of its contribution to the bank's authorized capital.

The 24th Comecon meeting recommended to the member countries and instructed its Executive Committee "that measures should be taken for the successful implementation of the work of drawing up a comprehensive program by the date laid down by the 23rd meeting"—a date that had not been made public. In addition, the meeting decided to set up an International Institute for Economic Problems of the World Socialist System.   (K. SM.)

See also Development, Economic; Government Finance.

Economics

As the new decade opened in 1970, economics was still dominated by the "new economics," which had begun with J. M. Keynes's *General Theory of Employment, Interest and Money* published in 1936. The prestige of economics as a discipline and the influence of economists on public policy may have reached a peak in the U.S. in the mid-1960s, immediately following the successful results of the 1964 tax cut which the new economists had advocated. Subsequently the discipline lost some influence as a result of persistent inflation and the apparent difficulty of curbing it by fiscal and monetary policies. In 1970 growing challenges to the mainstream were visible from conservative monetarism, led by Milton Friedman of the University of Chicago, and from a group of radical economists associated for the most part with the New Left.

In *The Political Economy of Prosperity* (1970), Arthur Okun, the last chairman of Pres. Lyndon Johnson's Council of Economic Advisers, reviewed the experience of the 1960s and projected a program of noninflationary prosperity for the 1970s. Okun viewed the unbroken expansion from 1961 to 1969 as the outstanding fact of economic history during the decade. The U.S. unemployment rate, which had stood at 7% when John F. Kennedy became president in 1961, was pushed below 4% by the stimulating effects of the 1964 tax cut. The expansion got out of control because of heavy spending on the war in Vietnam, but even this obstacle to noninflationary prosperity might have been surmounted, according to Okun, if Congress had not balked for two years at raising federal taxes to pay for increased military expenditures.

Inflation reached unacceptable rates in 1969 and 1970, and attempts to apply the brakes resulted in higher unemployment. As a partial solution, Okun proposed that in the future sharp changes in defense expenditures be met by appropriate changes in tax rates. He viewed as absurd trying to meet sudden increases in military spending by squeezing civilian social programs such as housing, education, health, and pollution. Okun recommended that the fiscal dividend (the annual increase in federal tax revenue from rising national income) be used to increase outlays on social needs in the public sector. He opposed a reduction in tax rates until these pressing social needs had been met.

Okun was prepared to accept a tradeoff of 4% unemployment for 2% annual price inflation. Some economists believed 4% unemployment was unnecessarily high. Melville Ulmer outlined a plan that he felt would keep unemployment at about 2% with virtually no inflation (*The Welfare State: U.S.A.: An Exploration In and Beyond the New Economics*, 1969). His plan involved extensive manpower training, improved job placement, and public employment of last resort, in combination with flexible fiscal policy. Instead of relying on short-term flexible tax rates, he proposed compulsory loans (refundable taxes) to curb inflation and refunds to stimulate demand when needed. Tax rates would be adjusted over longer periods as circumstances dictated. Either the Okun or Ulmer conditions would have represented a vast improvement over the actual state of affairs in 1970, when unemployment rose to 5.8% and the rate of inflation was almost as high.

The new monetarism, which gained wider support during 1970, emphasized the superiority of monetary policy over fiscal policy for controlling economic activity. For some years Friedman had championed the view that monetary policy is a more potent weapon for economic stabilization than fiscal policy. Economists in the Nixon administration were more sympathetic to monetarism than their predecessors under Kennedy and Johnson. Friedman espoused the rule that the money supply should expand at a constant annual rate, say between 3 and 5%. A fixed rule, he said, would yield better results than discretionary monetary policy by the central banking authorities, as well as better results than flexible fiscal policy. An important reason for rejecting discretionary monetary policy was the variable and sometimes lengthy time lag between changes in money supply and their impact on business. Even if the central bankers knew what to do, they would not know when to do it.

Friedman asserted that a change in money supply by itself has a potent effect on nominal (money) income and real income in the short run; that by itself it has important effects on nominal (money) income and prices in the long run; but it does not have, by itself, important long-run effects on real income and output. Long-term growth in real output depends on productivity and the operation of the free market.

Advocates of the new economics made several attempts during 1970 to respond critically to Friedman's monetarism. Nicholas Kaldor of Cambridge University described the new monetarism as a counterrevolution against the Keynesian revolution (*Lloyd's Bank Review*, July 1970) because it reverted to pre-Keynesian ways of thinking about the relations between money and business activity, namely, that the volume of demand (spending) in the economy is regulated by the supply of money and the velocity of its circulation, and that the level of expenditures can be regulated mainly by monetary policy. Kaldor's view was that the money supply accommodates itself to the needs of the economy, not the other way around. Even if one con-

WIDE WORLD
Paul A. Samuelson, winner of the 1970 Nobel Prize for Economics.

ceded the desirability of increasing the money supply at a constant rate, Kaldor doubted the feasibility of carrying it out because forces that make for changes in the demand for money would continue to operate in such a way that the banking authorities would be unable to keep the money supply on a smooth path of steady increase.

James Tobin of Yale, the 1970 president-elect of the American Economic Association, also challenged Friedman's views (*Quarterly Journal of Economics,* May 1970). He compared a Keynesian model of the economy with a Friedman model in order to test the consequences of changes in money supply. In Keynesian economics the role of money is clear. Starting with less than full employment, a reduction in taxes, for example, stimulates more spending for consumption and investment, which in turn increases the demand for money needed to turn over a larger volume of transactions. The money supply should be increased to accommodate the larger national income resulting from fiscal policy.

The causal sequence in Friedman's analysis is not so clear. He relies heavily on historical case studies, statistical regressions, and lead-lag sequences between changes in money and changes in income. Addressing himself specifically to the leads and lags in the timing sequence in a Keynesian and in a Friedman model of the economy, Tobin found "every single piece of observed evidence that Friedman reports on timing is consistent with the timing implications of the ultra-Keynesian model." In a reply, Friedman seemed to accept Tobin's analysis but rejected his inference that the findings cast doubt on the potency of monetary policy. Like many attempted confrontations in economic controversy, this one proved unsatisfactory.

Another challenge to the mainstream of economics came from a new radical economics. By 1970 a 1,000-member Union for Radical Political Economics had begun to publish a journal (*Review of Radical Political Economics*) and to hold conventions. At the annual meeting of the American Economic Association in New York in December 1969, a group of about 25 radical economists attempted to seize control of the business meeting in order to read a statement condemning the association. After some jostling for control of the microphone, Arthur MacEwan was permitted to read a statement containing the following passages:

> We have come to denounce the American Economic Association, and to denounce the dominant economics for which the AEA provides the organizational support . . . economists are the sycophants of inequality, alienation, destruction of environment, imperialism, racism, and the subjection of women. . . . But the economists do not merely praise the system; they also supply the tools—indeed they are the tools—instrumental to the elite's attainment of its unjust ends. . . . Our conflict is a basic conflict of interests. The economists have chosen to serve the *status quo*. We have chosen to fight it. (*The American Economic Review, Papers and Proceedings,* May 1970)

The "establishment" group in the American Economic Association was not insensitive to the issues that distressed the radicals. In the association's regular sessions papers were given on the economics of imperialism, increasing the supply of black economists, the market and price mechanism in socialist countries, the economy of cities, a radical approach to economics and the basis for a new curriculum, and the dynamics of income distribution. The *Journal of Economic Literature,* an organ of the American Economic Association, published a full-length survey article on "Radical Economics in America, 1970" (September 1970).

The literature of the radical economics was stronger in its criticisms of traditional economics than in constructing a new analytical framework for radical reform. Marxism was important but not dominant in the thinking of the radical economists. Some were anarchists rather than socialists, and many were neither. The aspect of Marx that was perhaps most appealing to them was the alienation of the workers under the juggernaut of capitalism. The most comprehensive radical work to appear was an English edition of the two-volume *Marxist Economic Theory* by the Belgian Ernest Mandel (1968).

Michael Zweig of the State University of New York at Stony Brook made one of the better statements about the content of radical economics ("New Left Critique of Economics" in David Mermelstein, ed., *Economics: Mainstream Readings and Radical Critiques,* 1970). He was highly critical of the concepts of equilibrium and competition, which are central in traditional economic theory. Criticism was directed at marginal, or incremental, analysis as a type of economics that tells what happens when not very much happens. Zweig says:

> Our charge against economics is precisely that it is at best not helpful to the construction of a decent society, and at worst supportive of the present order. Marginal analysis is legitimate only as long as the fundamental character of the thing being analyzed is legitimate. . . . The spirit of marginalism is ill suited to radical questioning of the precepts of economic and social arrangements.

Zweig was certainly correct in stating that marginal analysis is not useful for analyzing the revolutionary reconstruction of society. It was never intended for that purpose. In 1970 the positive theory of radical economics was still awaited.

The 1970 Nobel Memorial Prize in Economics was awarded to Paul A. Samuelson (*see* BIOGRAPHY) of the Massachusetts Institute of Technology for doing "more than any other contemporary economist to raise the level of scientific analysis in economic theory." Specific reference was made by the awarding committee to Samuelson's *Foundations of Economic Analysis* (1947), the original version of which was written under the title "The Operational Significance of Economic Theory," mainly when he was 22 years of age.

His contributions were to method as well as substance. Samuelson set out to derive theorems that were operationally meaningful in the sense that they represented hypotheses about empirical data that could be proven wrong. In the process he discovered analogous features in many different branches of economics, which he brought together into a more unified theory. In *Foundations of Economic Analysis* and in 200 scientific papers, he ranged widely over the pure theory of such seemingly divergent topics as price theory, income theory, taxation, international trade, business cycles, and money. His major contribution was in the synthesis of pure theory rather than in bold innovation.

In addition to being a great theoretician and a leader of the new economics, Samuelson was also the author of the best-selling textbook in elementary economics. His *Economics* (8th ed., 1970) was reported to have sold three million copies in 14 languages. A majority of college students who studied economic principles in the U.S. between 1950 and 1970 cut their teeth on Samuelson's text.   (D. D.)

See also Economy, World; Government Finance; Income, National; Merchandising; Money and Banking; Payments and Reserves, International; Trade, International.

Economy, World

The world economy in 1970 experienced a deep malaise—economic stagnation at high levels combined with a stubborn inflation of costs and prices. Accordingly, this article reviews this "stagflation," analyzes the politics of disinflation, and explores, in the light of the 1970 experience, how to live with inflation. The industrial countries, beset by domestic problems, also felt severe strains and stresses in their balances of payments, and inflation and business slowdown in industrial nations had adverse consequences on the volume and quality of their assistance to Latin America, Asia, and Africa.

Stagnation at High Levels. The dominant feature of the world economy in 1970 was the slowdown in the growth of output in the main industrial countries of North America and Europe. Even Japan, which remained the most rapidly growing large industrial economy in the world, slowed down a little. For the industrial world as a whole, the combined output—gross national products (GNPs) in real terms, that is, after correction for price increases—rose in 1970 by only 2.8%, as against 4.9% in 1969 (see Table I).

The cyclical positions of individual countries showed marked disparities (see Chart 1 and Table II). The most significant turnaround occurred in the U.S., which accounted for about one half of the world's output. GNP at current prices late in 1970 passed the trillion-dollar mark; but the landmark was illusory since, in real terms, GNP in the fourth quarter fell by 1.5% at an annual rate. While the General Motors strike was the main factor in this drop, declines in output and employment were also widespread among industries not directly affected by the strike. The fourth-quarter drop followed a modest GNP increase during the third quarter and a sideways movement during the second quarter. For the year as a whole, real output showed a small decline. Growth of output also weakened in Canada.

In both Europe and Japan, output rose at about the average rate of the past decade; but, in comparison with 1969, most countries experienced a slowdown in growth rates. Japan and West Germany, the second and third largest industrial countries in the world (apart from the U.S.S.R.), showed a weaker performance after periods of extraordinary boom. In Japan, the rise in output seemed to have fallen below its long-term trend. In West Germany, the slowdown became more pronounced during the second half of the year. In France, the economy, at a high level, moved sideways. Italy, where the economy was hampered by labour unrest in 1969, seemed to pick up renewed momentum. The United Kingdom was one of the few countries where output, sluggish in 1969, speeded up considerably in the second half of 1970.

Industrial production throughout the world remained stationary. In the U.S., it fell toward year-end to a two-year low. Elsewhere, it turned downward or flattened out—with the exception of Japan. In the perspective of previous years, however, industrial production everywhere remained close to record levels (see Chart 2).

This general slowdown in output growth during 1970 was an unusual phenomenon in the world economy for, ordinarily, while output accelerates in some countries, it decelerates in others. In the first half of 1970, the slowdown reflected mainly a deceleration (actually a small drop in the last quarter of 1969 and the first quarter of 1970) of economic activity in the U.S. The deceleration occurred earlier in the U.S. than in continental Europe and Japan because of differences in economic experience in earlier years. In the U.S., a peak in total output had been reached during the first half of 1966 but, following a short-lived and mild slowdown, the rapid expansion continued through mid-1969, after which the economy cooled off. In Canada, economic growth generally also eased in 1969. In the U.K., output growth had begun to slow down as far back as 1965. In West Germany, however, there had been a marked softening in the economy during 1966–67; a cyclical upswing in 1968 led to a gradual using up of excess capacity and, late in 1969 and in much of 1970, the country experienced an extraordinarily strong boom. In France, the disruption after the waves of strikes in mid-1968 was followed by a marked expansion of output, which came to a halt in early 1970. In Japan, the rapid expansion dated back to 1966.

During 1970, the growth of output in West Germany was held back by a shortage of capacity. Strikes in the U.S., the U.K. (where they were the worst since 1926), and Italy (where spasmodic strikes had partly political motives) interfered with output more than usually. To a decisive extent, however, output in the U.S., Canada, and most other industrial countries was held back because of demand that weakened as one nation after another found itself compelled to take restrictive steps in order to hold down inflation (see MONEY AND BANKING; GOVERNMENT FINANCE).

At the same time, total demand—of consumers as well as of businesses, including new outlays for plant and equipment—also weakened because it was inhibited by inflation. In the earlier phases of inflation,

Table I. Growth of Real Gross National Product in the Industrial World*

Area	Annual percent increases 1958–68	1969	1970
North America	4.7	3.0	0
Japan	11.1	12.3	11.5
Western Europe	4.9	6.1	5.0
European Economic Community	5.2	7.1	5.5
Overall increase	5.3	4.9	2.8

*Excluding the U.S.S.R., Eastern European countries, China, etc.
Source: Adapted from OECD, Economic Outlook (December 1970).

Table II. Growth of Real Gross National Product in the Principal Countries

Country	Annual percent changes 1958–68	1969	1970
Japan	11.1	12.3	11.5
Italy	5.7	4.8	6.5
France	5.4	7.9	5.8
Germany, West	5.0	8.0	4.5
Canada	4.8	5.0	2.8
United Kingdom	3.2	1.9	1.8
United States	4.7	2.8	—0.3
Major countries	5.4	4.8	2.5
Austria	4.4	6.4	6.5
Netherlands	5.3	5.3	5.5
Belgium	4.3	6.2	5.3
Sweden	4.5	5.8	5.0
Switzerland	4.8	5.8	4.5
Norway	4.8	3.9	4.3
Denmark	4.9	7.1	4.0
Other industrial countries*	4.7	5.9	5.0
Southern Europe†	5.9	7.1	6.3

Note: Arranged in descending order of growth of output within each group of countries in 1970.
*Including Finland, Iceland, Ireland, and Luxembourg in addition to the countries listed.
†Including Greece, Portugal, Spain, and Turkey.
Source: Adapted from OECD, Economic Outlook (December 1970).

it is true, consumers and businesses borrowed and spent freely in anticipation of rising prices; in the U.S., such euphoria prevailed in 1968. But, as inflation persisted and became increasingly severe, consumers as well as businesses found their buying power diminished through the rise in prices, their assets—equities, bonds, and tangible properties—reduced in value, and access to liquidity dried up. Retrenchment thus became a necessity.

As a result, the potential of the economy ceased to be utilized to the same extent as previously. In the second half of 1970, GNP in the U.S. was some 4–5% below its estimated potential. Unemployment increased from a seasonally adjusted 3.9% of the civilian labour force in January to 6% in December, the highest figure registered since 1961. It had been feared that unemployment among the black population would rise sharply; in fact, it increased rather moderately. The areas most affected were those parts of the country that had large concentrations of high-technology industries with close defense and aerospace links (parts of California, Seattle, Wash., the Boston area, and others). Wall Street was hit hard. Canada had 6.5% unemployment, with wide differences among regions. The trend was also upward in Japan and most Western European countries. In West Germany, with only 0.6% unemployment, employment of foreign workers exceeded two million.

Although the trends in output and employment differed from country to country, all countries experienced a severe inflation in 1970. Usually, there is inflation in one or several industrial countries; but in 1970—and this was the year's second characteristic feature—there were no islands of relative price stability. Moreover, the rate of price increases was, apart from war years, the highest in history.

The general price level in industrial countries rose during 1970 by 5.5%; the average rate in the first half of the 1960s was 3.5% (see Table III). In the U.S., where the price inflation was 2.1% in the early 1960s, the rate accelerated to 5.3%. In other major industrial countries, where price inflation had been much greater than in the U.S., it accelerated to 6%. In West Germany, prices surged at a whirlwind 7%, the highest rate in the industrial world. In most countries, however, the price rise seemed to have moderated during the second half of 1970; the Netherlands, Norway, and Switzerland were exceptions to this trend.

Generally throughout the industrial world, prices rose most in the service sectors and in construction; food prices generally increased roughly in line with the general price level although, in most countries, prices received by farmers rose distinctly less rapidly; and prices of manufactured goods rose the least—on the average by only 1–2.5% a year. For the first time in a decade, prices in world trade rose as fast as the general domestic price levels.

From Demand-Pull into Cost-Push Inflation. The fact that the price inflation was synchronized to an unusual extent did not necessarily mean that the causes were common. The circumstantial evidence reflected not only the spread of inflation at harsh, severe rates but also the fact that demand-pull inflation gave way increasingly to cost-push inflation. Demand-pull inflation, a state of the economy where the aggregate demand is expanding even though the resources of the economy—labour in particular—are virtually fully utilized, prevailed in 1968 and much of 1969 in the U.S. and France and in much of 1970

in several other major industrial countries, particularly West Germany and Japan. As more money chased an amount of goods and services that could not, for the time being, be increased, prices moved upward. Although profit margins declined and the interest rates rose to astonishing levels, a state of euphoria pervaded the economies and stock markets throughout the industrial world. Labour was hoarded, wage increases met with little resistance, and business investment was undertaken not only to economize on labour costs but also in the expectation that inflation would, in one way or another, validate almost any business judgment. Not too surprisingly, productivity declined.

Cost-push inflation, on the other hand, is a state

CHART 1.

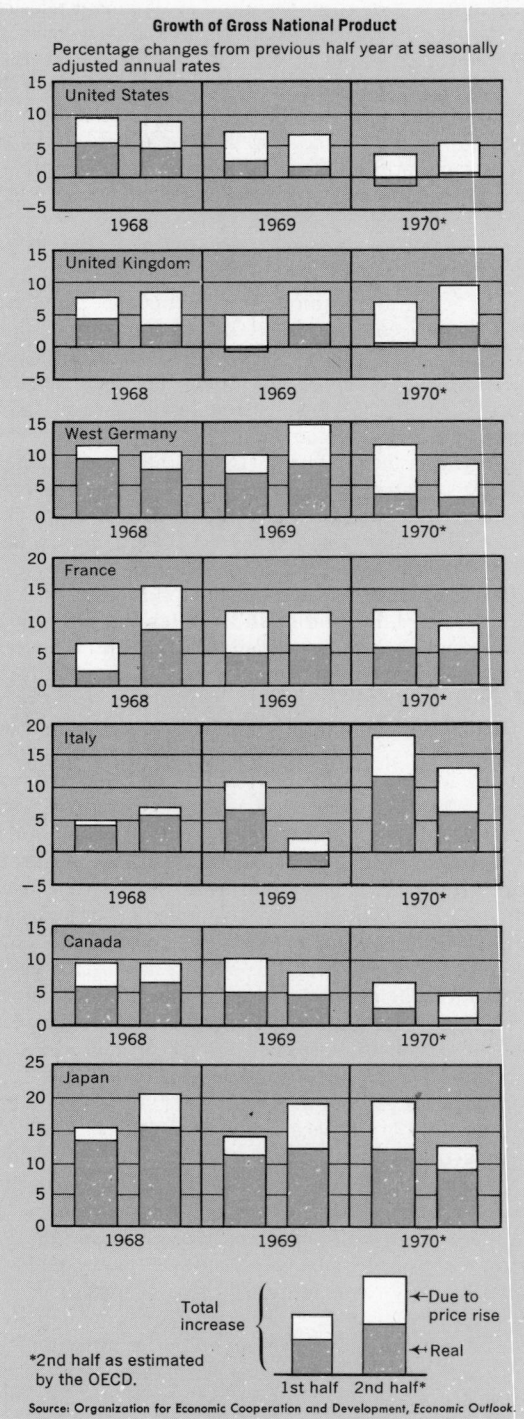

of the economy where cost pressures persist even though excess demand is slackening, real resources are not overstrained, unemployment is growing, and national output is stationary or even declining. Conditions of this sort prevailed during 1970 in the U.S., U.K., France, and, perhaps to a lesser extent, in Italy; toward the year-end, they appeared in West Germany. If anything, the trend toward wage increases seemed to have accelerated. The U.K. situation was probably the most serious, judging from the steepness of wage and price rises at a time when real resources were not overstrained.

To hold down excess demand, strong reliance was placed on monetary policy. Some countries also resorted to anti-inflationary fiscal steps—higher taxation and efforts to hold down the rise in government spending. Everywhere, however, monetary and fiscal restraint proved more difficult than had—perhaps too optimistically—been anticipated. For one thing, action that was recognized as necessary was, more often than not, delayed or adulterated because of political considerations; and, for another, domestic monetary restraint was partly offset by recourse to borrowings in the international Eurodollar market and tax increases were offset by dissaving or by extracting wage increases.

Although unemployment tended to rise, nearly all industrial countries experienced a veritable wage explosion in 1970. The typical figure for increases in hourly rates or earnings in manufacturing was of the order of 10–15%—one-and-a-half to three times the rate of only a few years before (see Chart 3). Particularly large increases occurred in Italy, Japan, Sweden, West Germany, and the U.K. (in that order).

The increases in hourly rates or in earnings in manufacturing were twice or three times as high as increases in productivity. Labour costs per unit of output thus shot up fast, particularly in Europe (see Table IV). Only in Japan, although wage inflation was little short of breathtaking, was productivity performance good and, as a result, wage costs per unit of output rose much less than in other industrial countries in 1970.

In the U.S., because of vigorous efforts to cut costs, productivity—after two years of stagnation—began to increase. Output per man-hour in the private nonfarm economy advanced at an annual rate of 5% in the third quarter. This gain was, however, associated with a rather large decline in man-hours, rather than with an appreciable increase in output, and could not, therefore, be regarded as a solid improvement resulting from such factors as innovation, increased use of capital, and a better educated labour force. Taken together, the output per man-hour and compensation movements indicated a third-quarter rise of 3% in labour costs per unit of output. Although this indi-

cated a much better performance than the 7% of early 1970 and all of 1969, the rise in unit labour costs was still too rapid because compensation continued, or accelerated, its swift advance and the nature of the productivity gains could not be regarded as permanent.

The impact of cost-push inflation became increasingly pronounced as the slowdown in the growth of output pushed up labour costs per unit. This was not, however, quite the same thing as saying that price inflation necessarily became more acute and more critical. With demand pressures eased, it became more difficult to pass along increased costs into increased prices; prices of manufactured goods showed much smaller increases than those of food or services. The inevitable consequence was a squeeze on industrial profits. In the U.S. in 1970, corporate profits represented the smallest portion of the GNP for any year since World War II and after-tax profits per unit of output were 34% below their peak in 1966. Not too surprisingly, the profit squeeze tended to retard investment in plant and equipment. The flattening in real investment reduced the pressure on economic resources and was, therefore, a stabilizing influence in the short run; but, for the long run, it was a self-aggravating condition in the economy, inimical to productivity and efficiency and, hence, to economic growth.

The Politics of Disinflation. The industrial countries also had in common the fact that the processes of curbing inflation and restoring noninflationary growth—mainly through monetary restrictions and, rather marginally, through tax increases and efforts to hold down government expenditures—were decidedly more prolonged, more arduous, and more painful than had been hoped in 1969 and early 1970. The sharp declines in Wall Street and on stock exchanges outside the U.S. had an adverse effect on both consumer and business confidence.

Furthermore, a common view of inflation in the U.S. and, perhaps to a lesser extent, in other industrial nations came increasingly to be questioned in 1970. Inflation used to be regarded as, fundamentally, a phenomenon that resulted from excessive expansion of money supplies—an aberration or failure of monetary policy-making. More often than not over the past half century, the central banks could invoke alleviating circumstances stemming from otherwise unmanageable deficits in government budgets or from governmental insistence on cheap money. For anti-inflation strategy to be successful, therefore, it was enough to put a brake on the excessive creation of money. Inflation would die a natural death if the authorities refused to finance it.

Table III. Price Trends in Industrial Countries*

Country	Annual percent increases 1958–68	1969	1970
Germany, West	2.8	3.5	7.0
Italy	3.5	4.1	6.3
United Kingdom	3.1	5.1	6.0
Japan	4.5	4.5	5.8
France	4.0	6.9	5.5
United States	2.1	4.7	5.3
Canada	2.5	4.7	4.0
Major countries excluding United States	3.7	4.8	6.0
Major countries	3.5	4.8	5.5

*As measured by deflators of gross national product.
Source: Adapted from OECD, *Economic Outlook* (December 1970).

Table IV. Unit Labour Costs in Manufacturing

Country	Annual percent changes 1968	1969	1970*
Germany, West	—3.1	2.5	14.1
United Kingdom†	1.2	5.5	9.5
Italy‡	—1.0	4.3	9.1
Canada†	1.6	4.9	8.4
Japan†	1.4	2.8	6.5
United States‡	3.8	4.0	5.8
France§	2.5	—2.3	3.8

*In descending order of percentage change in most recent quarterly data, compared with the corresponding period of 1969.
†Wage and salary costs, excluding fringe benefits and social security.
‡Labour costs, including fringe benefits and social security.
§Wage costs, excluding fringe benefits and social security.
Source: Adapted from OECD, *Economic Outlook* (December 1970).

The view that inflation is, fundamentally, a monetary phenomenon is a curiously old-fashioned thought. Evidently, money matters; but, judging from the current experience of the industrial nations, inflation is not merely a monetary phenomenon. In the highly intricate and complex economies of the world today, changes in output, employment incomes, and prices cannot be explained within the narrow framework of monetary theorizing. Realistically, inflation is a political and social phenomenon stemming, in democracies with competing political parties, from powerful and pervasive demands of three kinds: (1) demands for increasingly costly and extensive social services for the masses of people and for an increasingly costly and extensive economic infrastructure for an urbanized society; (2) demands for higher living standards by people who want more of the good things in life and with less waiting, population growth, and the expansion of industrialization to exert still further pressures on energy, food, and raw material resources; and (3) demands for higher wages by labour, endowed with strong political and economic power and prepared to take the necessary action to cut a larger slice of the national cake.

The motive force behind inflation is thus the success of modern society—achievements that lead to even higher expectations for the future. At the same time, society is passing through a moral crisis, evidenced in the disappearance of the cult of hard work and the questioning of such values as saving that used to be accepted as incontrovertible.

Central banks create money now dissociated from any gold cover; but they face an explosive dilemma: effective monetary restraint will hold down prices and wages only if there is unemployment, but monetary restraint cannot be tightened enough to bring about unemployment—at least within the fine limits of tolerance necessary to manage aggregate demand near full employment.

Furthermore, it has come to be believed that it is within the power of governments to keep the economy on a path of perpetual growth. A slowdown in the pace of expansion is resented with almost the same trauma as a depression in the economy was in earlier times. Even the word "recession," which started to be used as a euphemism for "depression," had an unacceptable opprobrium attached to it and governments avoided it scrupulously. The business slowdown in 1970 was described as a "pause," a "retardation," a "minirecession," a "growth recession," or some other equally inventive phrase.

Fears of recession receded as it became evident that no government was prepared, through monetary and fiscal restraint, to cut down the total demand for goods and services far enough to create a gap between actual and potential output, or to maintain a large margin of unused resources long enough to exert a downward pressure on prices and wages. Governments dependent on the popular vote felt unable to take the unpopular decisions necessary to halt inflation. Rightly or wrongly, people concluded that a major recession could not occur as a deliberate act of government but only from gross miscalculation.

The experience in the U.S. was particularly instructive. Beginning with early 1970, and more forcibly in the second half of the year in the aftermath of the Penn Central bankruptcy crisis, the monetary policy was reversed—a decision that was justifiable at a time when precautionary demands for liquidity were particularly strong. For the year as a whole, however, the money supply increased by 5%. Fiscal policy turned toward a more expansionist direction as the income tax surcharge was reduced at the end of 1969 and eliminated in mid-1970, and as a much larger deficit than had been originally anticipated appeared in the federal budget. True, the deficit was due, in large part, to the shortfall of revenues that resulted from the sluggishness in the economy, but pressure mounted for much larger spending in the fiscal year 1971–72.

The election campaign and its outcome in November 1970 gave rise to the view that the policy of refraining from greater monetary and fiscal stimulation had little political appeal. Statistics for December showed an unemployment rate of 6% of the civilian labour force, the highest figure in 9 years. Although the figure was not higher than in the first half of the 1960s, it was commonly believed that a jobless rate above 4% would drastically reduce Republican chances in 1972. The lure of 4%—arbitrary as the figure was—appeared strong. But to shoot for

Table V. Depreciation of Money

Country	Indexes of value of money (1959=100) 1964	Indexes of value of money (1959=100) 1969	Annual rates of depreciation (percent) '59–'69*	Annual rates of depreciation (percent) '68–'69	Annual rates of depreciation (percent) '69–'70†
Industrial countries					
Finland	79	61	4.8	2.2	2.5
Greece	93	83	1.9	2.3	2.9
Switzerland	87	74	3.0	2.5	3.0
Australia	92	78	2.4	2.8	3.4
Canada	93	78	2.4	4.3	3.6
Germany, West	89	78	2.4	2.6	3.6
Netherlands	86	67	3.8	6.9	3.8
Belgium	91	77	2.6	3.6	3.9
Austria	85	72	3.2	3.0	4.1
Spain	79	58	5.3	2.2	4.2
Luxembourg	93	81	2.1	2.2	4.3
Italy	80	70	3.6	2.5	4.6
South Africa	92	79	2.3	2.8	4.9
New Zealand	90	73	3.1	4.7	5.0
France	82	69	3.7	5.7	5.5
United States	94	79	2.2	5.1	5.6
United Kingdom	87	71	3.4	5.1	5.7
Denmark	81	59	5.1	3.2	6.2
Sweden	84	69	3.7	2.6	6.2
Turkey	82	57	5.5	4.8	6.5
Portugal	88	67	3.9	8.1	6.5
Japan	77	60	5.0	4.9	6.9
Ireland	85	68	3.8	6.9	7.1
Iceland	63	37	9.5	16.2	7.9
Norway	85	71	3.3	3.0	9.0
Less developed countries					
Honduras	92	81	2.1	2.6	0.2
Morocco	80	77	2.6	2.8	0.9
Thailand	94	83	1.9	2.1	1.0
Dominican Republic	86	85	1.6	1.0	1.4
Venezuela	98	90	1.1	2.3	1.6
Iran	84	78	2.4	3.0	2.2
Ecuador	83	67	3.8	6.0	3.0
El Salvador	100	96	0.4	−0.3	3.5
Guatemala	100	96	0.5	2.2	3.6
Bolivia	72	55	5.8	3.1	3.8
Mexico	90	77	2.5	2.8	4.4
Peru	69	39	9.0	5.9	4.4
Israel	75	60	4.9	2.4	4.5
Taiwan	75	63	4.6	4.8	4.6
India	80	56	5.6	0.8	4.6
Pakistan	87	70	3.6	3.1	5.0
Colombia	56	36	9.8	9.2	7.1
Jamaica	86	71	3.4	5.8	9.3
Argentina	36	13	18.4	7.1	10.1
Indonesia	5	‡	58.2	5.8	12.3
Philippines	67	56	5.7	2.8	13.3
South Korea	51	29	11.5	11.0	14.4
Brazil	11	2	31.4	18.8	16.5
Chile	35	11	19.7	23.4	24.3
South Vietnam	84	20	14.9	18.0	27.7

Note: Depreciation of money is measured by rates of decline in the domestic purchasing power of national currencies (as computed from reciprocals of official cost-of-living or consumer price indexes), not by rates of price inflation. For example, a rate of inflation of 100% is equivalent to a 50% rate of depreciation of buying power of money.
*Compounded annually.
†Based on average monthly data available for 1970 compared with corresponding period of 1969.
‡Less than one.
Source: First National City Bank, New York, N.Y.

it and for a target rate of real growth over the next two years of, say, 6% a year without endangering a satisfactory price performance—that is, inflation at the rate of perhaps 3% a year—seemed a risky undertaking. For in the past two decades, the U.S. economy experienced a rate of real growth of 6% on only two occasions—1950–51 in the wake of the Korean War and 1965–66. On both occasions, the end result was inflation—after a two- or three-year lag. An even more critical consideration is the fact that, in earlier periods, inflationary expectations were almost nonexistent; today, after half a decade of excess demand and at a time when price-cost pressures had merely begun to abate, it would not take too much to rekindle a new outburst of inflationary psychology.

The thought that there may well be political liability in inflation as well as in unemployment was sobering. The havoc wrought by the inflation of 1964–70 once again led to suggestions that the Employment Act of 1946 be amended to include explicit reference to the objective of general price stability. A change in the language would not, by itself, bring about a change in attitudes and policies; but it could, hopefully, make the nation more aware that its economic and political health also depended on reasonable price stability.

The U.S. experience was duplicated in much of the industrial world. In the U.K., with the consumer price index in November 1970 standing 8% above the previous year, the most urgent problem was, indeed, inflation. A "mini-budget" in late October announced a cut, beginning April 1971, in direct taxation in the hope that increased take-home pay would reduce the pressure for wage increases. The tax cut matched proposed reductions in government expenditures. Since aggregate demand could not be allowed to rise too fast lest demand pressures on the labour market aggravate the wage spiral, official policy was necessarily one of circumspection relying heavily on monetary restraint—a difficult undertaking after the expansion of money supply had been exceedingly rapid in the second and third quarters. The policy of circumspection encountered criticisms urging a strategy of going resolutely for growth in the hope that a faster growth would lower unit costs, reduce money wage demands, and thus temper price increases. But as official caution had serious political risks, the opposite strategy had serious economic risks even if they were more acceptable politically.

In West Germany's environment of a moderate slowdown in economic growth amid renewed inflation, the federal government was clearly reluctant to reduce domestic demand. Eventually, after much discussion, it introduced a stability program in July. Its main feature was the activation of the Stability and Growth Law requiring an advance payment of 10% on personal income and corporation tax liabilities.

The surcharge was to remain in force until June 1971 unless the government decided to shorten the period. Evidently, West Germany took no advantage of the U.S. experience that showed the effectiveness of a temporary surcharge of this nature to be limited. Nonetheless, the central bank reduced—in three steps —the official discount rate in circumstances where lower interest rates were indicated only by the need to prevent the West German market from acting as a magnet for foreign funds.

In France's slackened economy, the government—reasonably confident in the newly won strength of the franc—gradually eased the degree of domestic restraint. Awareness that a renewed period of snail's-pace growth—as in the mid-1960s—might perhaps provoke social unrest, and, hence, political difficulties, may well have been in the background of the search for reexpansion. Italy, which had more than its share of industrial troubles, nevertheless achieved in 1970 a growth rate of 6.5%. But the performance was regarded as well below potential and a wide-ranging economic decree-law was adopted to raise funds through stiffer taxes and social security contributions and use them to stimulate investment and to finance initial health service reforms.

In the U.S. as well as in much of Europe, it was feared that continued disinflation might bring about a sharp squeeze on the cash resources of many businesses and even a crisis of confidence if some large companies were to become bankrupt. A world that experienced the Penn Central collapse, distress calls from Wall Street, and cash stringencies of corporations in Europe was deeply concerned about corporate liquidity.

The Search for New Remedies. Since inflation could be contained only at costs regarded as politically and socially unacceptable in terms of growth and employment, the thought understandably emerged that conventional monetary and fiscal weaponry must be supplemented by other instruments. As 1970 drew to a close, more and more proposals were made for a wide range of measures that might be used to influence price and cost movements in the public interest—what had come to be called incomes policy.

The idea was by no means new. The difficulty was that there was no simple formula to inject considerations of the common interest into individual price and wage decisions. Among the many variants discussed, the range encompassed moral pressure, voluntary guideposts, and "jawboning" at one end, and compulsory arbitration of labour disputes and compulsory price and wage guidelines at the other. They included a policy of punitive taxes on employers granting inflationary wage increases or a policy of forced savings by employees receiving such increases. At a minimum, they aimed at an understanding among the participants in wage-price negotiations that wage and other cost increases should not exceed some rate that would take account of productivity growth and of past inflation but not allow for future inflation.

Aiming at substantial concentrations of private power, incomes policy required the exercise of high-level, sophisticated political leadership. Another difficulty was that labour—with hiring practices, work rules, and strike privileges that had developed in earlier decades—was unwilling to recognize that the world has changed. Moreover, people who had had little increase in real wages wanted to catch up in the inflationary merry-go-round with little regard to the consequences for the nation as a whole—not because of greed but because of fear of missing out.

Only a few countries ventured on this path in 1970. Finland and Norway froze both prices and incomes; Sweden, Denmark, and the Netherlands, prices only. In Canada and Ireland, the experiment lasted only a short time.

The U.S. administration issued two "inflation alerts," the second, in December, a little sharper than the first in August, pointed a finger at wage agreements and price actions in the automobile, construction, and a few other industries. It took direct action

A.F.P. FROM PICTORIAL PARADE
French Economic Affairs and Finance Minister Valéry Giscard d'Estaing presides in Paris May 20, 1970, at the ministerial meeting of the Organization for Economic Cooperation and Development (OECD).

in one area—oil, by allowing larger imports from Canada and larger production from federally leased offshore oil wells; and it threatened action in another area—construction wages. But the administration did not seek to quantify the price-wage standards or the guideposts, nor did it imply any program of backing these up if they were not respected. Its reluctance was justified by reference to past failures, for the guidelines that were enforced during the early 1960s were unable to withstand the renewed inflationary pressures during the second half of the decade. Significantly, however, the chairman of the Board of Governors of the Federal Reserve System, Arthur Burns, clearly and unequivocally identified "excessive wage increases" as by far the most important

single factor of the continuing rise in prices and advocated a "market-oriented" incomes policy.

In the U.K., wage guidance, "pauses," or "statutory freezes" were imposed on a number of occasions during the past 20 years, most recently in 1966–67, but were repeatedly allowed to lapse. In a country that was overtaxed but still overflooded with money, monetary caution continued to be indicated; but to cure the present inflation solely by restricting demand was regarded as likely to involve very high costs in terms of unemployment, bankruptcies, and falling output. Significantly, recourse to incomes policy was advocated by the governor of the Bank of England, Sir Leslie O'Brien.

No country pursued a consistent incomes policy long enough to permit proper judgment. Nevertheless, if a single conclusion could be drawn from past experience, it was that incomes policy could not be a substitute for effective monetary and fiscal restraints, only an adjunct to them. Where inflationary pressures originated from excess demand, incomes policy was wholly ineffective. But when monetary and fiscal restraints had stamped out excess demand and the economy operated below capacity, incomes policy might well have a chance at success. Another prerequisite for success appeared to be popular resistance to constant inflationary surrenders.

Strong emphasis was also put on other steps to hold down inflation: greater international competition through the reduction or removal of the remaining tariff and quota restrictions on imports; more domestic competition through the tightening of legislation on restrictive trade practices; and the need for selective action—such as manpower training and retraining, and relocation programs—to ease unemployment and alleviate its hardship. Help for the poor and the unfortunate must, over time, be made more effective, and, hence, possibly less burdensome.

At year-end, the trade-off between inflation and unemployment thus appeared as unresolved as ever. There were no signs that nations were ready to change their political habits and processes so that economic and financial policy-making could become less subject to politics. Governments sought economic reexpansion through reflation in the belief that the existence of unused resources allowed some leeway for such stimulation.

But the scope for stimulation and reexpansion was circumscribed. The thought that governmental fine-tuning could deal simultaneously with the slack in the economy and with cost-push inflation was not realistic. The malaise could be healed only if governments succeeded in dislodging the deeply embedded inflationary psychology. For too many people everywhere tended toward the fatalistic view that the economies—faced as they were, for the longer run, with an excess, not a deficiency, of demand and beset by strong cost-push forces—might have to live with inflation for a long time to come.

Living with Inflation. The 1970 experience thus added new dimensions and new urgency to the old problem of the depreciation of money. Unlike earlier years, there were no islands of price stability and, in industrial countries, the depreciation of money was the most pronounced since the Korean War (*see* Table V). The U.S. dollar lost 5.6% of its buying power in the 11 months ended November 1970, compared with losses of 5.1% in 1969, 4% in 1968, and 2.7% in 1967. When ranked by its rate of depreciation in 1970 with currencies of the industrial coun-

CHART 2.

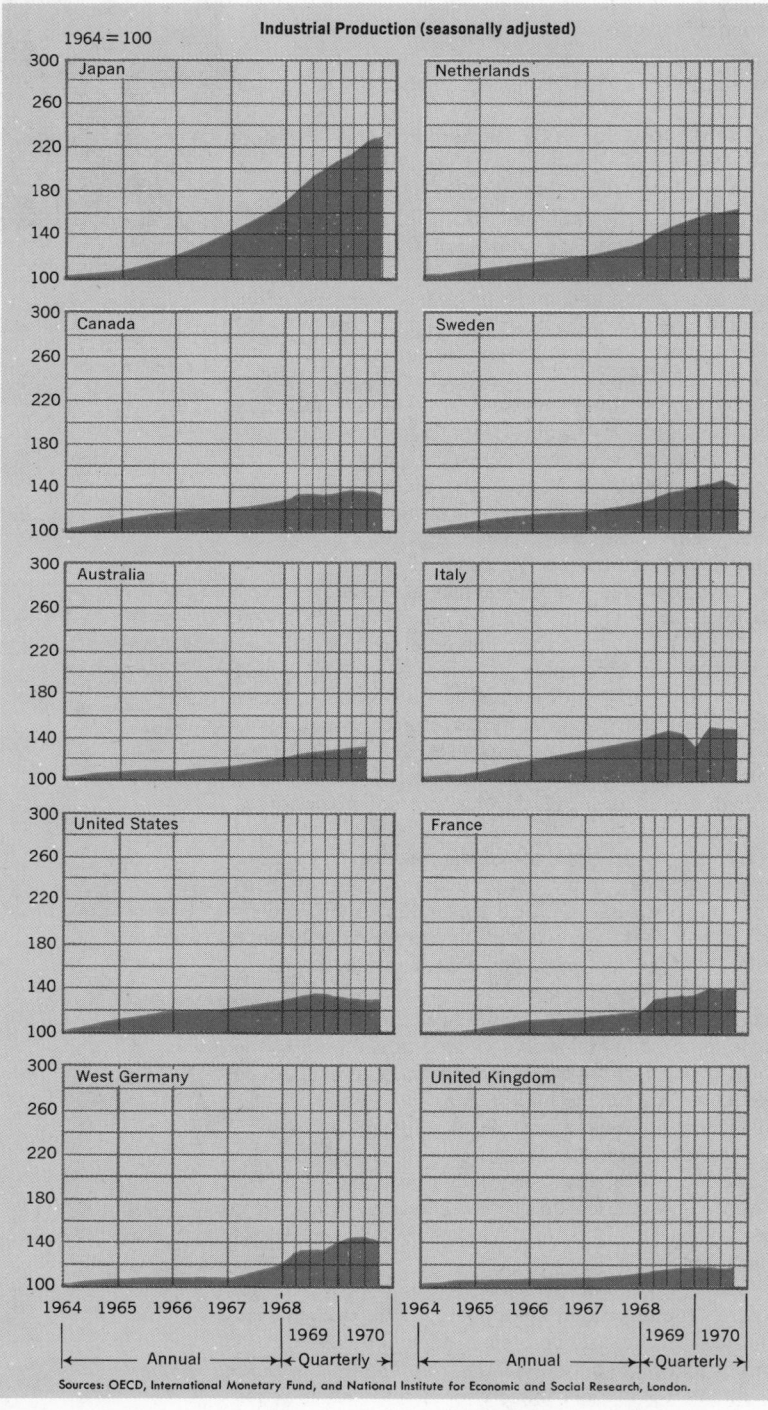

Industrial Production (seasonally adjusted)

1964 = 100

Japan · Netherlands · Canada · Sweden · Australia · Italy · United States · France · West Germany · United Kingdom

Sources: OECD, International Monetary Fund, and National Institute for Economic and Social Research, London.

tries, the dollar slipped to a point more than halfway down the list. Among Western European currencies, only the pound sterling, the Irish pound, the Norwegian and Danish kroner, and Swedish krona depreciated more than the dollar. The French franc improved its record modestly. The German mark suffered a relapse. The Canadian dollar fared distinctly better than the U.S. dollar. Elsewhere, the rates of shrinkage of currencies persisted.

Toward the year-end, there was evidence of a slow-down in the pace of the depreciation of money, particularly in the U.S. and Canada. But unless this improvement in price performance became more marked and widespread, the situation would remain serious. In the past, official expectations about the pace of inflation consistently understated the depreciation of money that occurred. This alone was enough to cast doubts on whether the slowdown in the rise of prices forecast at the year-end for 1971 would fully materialize. The last time the value of the U.S. dollar had not been eroded between one year and the next was in the mid-1950s.

If inflation is not vanquished—and, for reasons given earlier, vanquished at a cost, in terms of output and employment, acceptable to the popular vote —people have no choice but to live with it. Some countries—in Latin America in particular—have, of course, learned to live with inflation rates materially exceeding those that prevailed in 1970 in the U.S. and in much of Europe. But this art cannot be acquired rapidly.

The year set a record for attempts to provide protection against the loss of the buying power of money. Dramatic use was made of the so-called cost-of-living escalators—arrangements linking wage increases automatically to increases in prices (usually consumer prices). As rising prices robbed wage-earners of the gain from past wage increases, frustration and anger led, understandably, to a widespread clamour for the protection of real wages.

Not too surprisingly, savers and lenders of money also sought protection against the depreciation of money. For people have become uneasily aware that the longer they hold money, the less they will get for it. Human behaviour is, naturally, deeply affected by the realization that even at a 3% rate of annual depreciation—now regarded as the most hopeful expectation—the buying power of money is cut by one half in only 23 years. A 5% rate—typical for 1970— means halving the buying power in 14 years.

The realization that money is not worth saving except for the very short term brought about in 1970 the obvious reaction of a search for suitable hedges against inflation. "Equity kickers" (such as convertible bonds) and "variable annuities" (with assets invested in common stocks and with payments reflecting the results of such investments) became increasingly popular in the U.S. and abroad. To the surprise of many people, inflation in 1970 badly hit the common stocks (*see* STOCK EXCHANGES). Following a wave of speculation that had pushed prices of many stocks upward with little regard to actual or potential earnings, the U.S. stock markets in 1969 and the first half of 1970 took their most severe spill since World War II. In the second half of the year, they staged a notable recovery. The stock markets outside the U.S. remained generally poor. The obvious lesson is that common stocks are a hedge against inflation only if they meet the tests of profitability and quality. They do generally better in periods of milder infla-

tion than in those of severe pressures accompanied by a profit squeeze.

Agricultural land, forests, commercial properties, diamonds, stamps, coins, antiques, works of art, and even vintage cars remained steadily in demand on the strength of expectations that they would beat the depreciation of money. Basically, of course, they are speculation and not particularly helpful to a man of modest means without specialized knowledge.

There are some counselors of despair so overcome by the seemingly intractable depreciation of money

CHART 3.

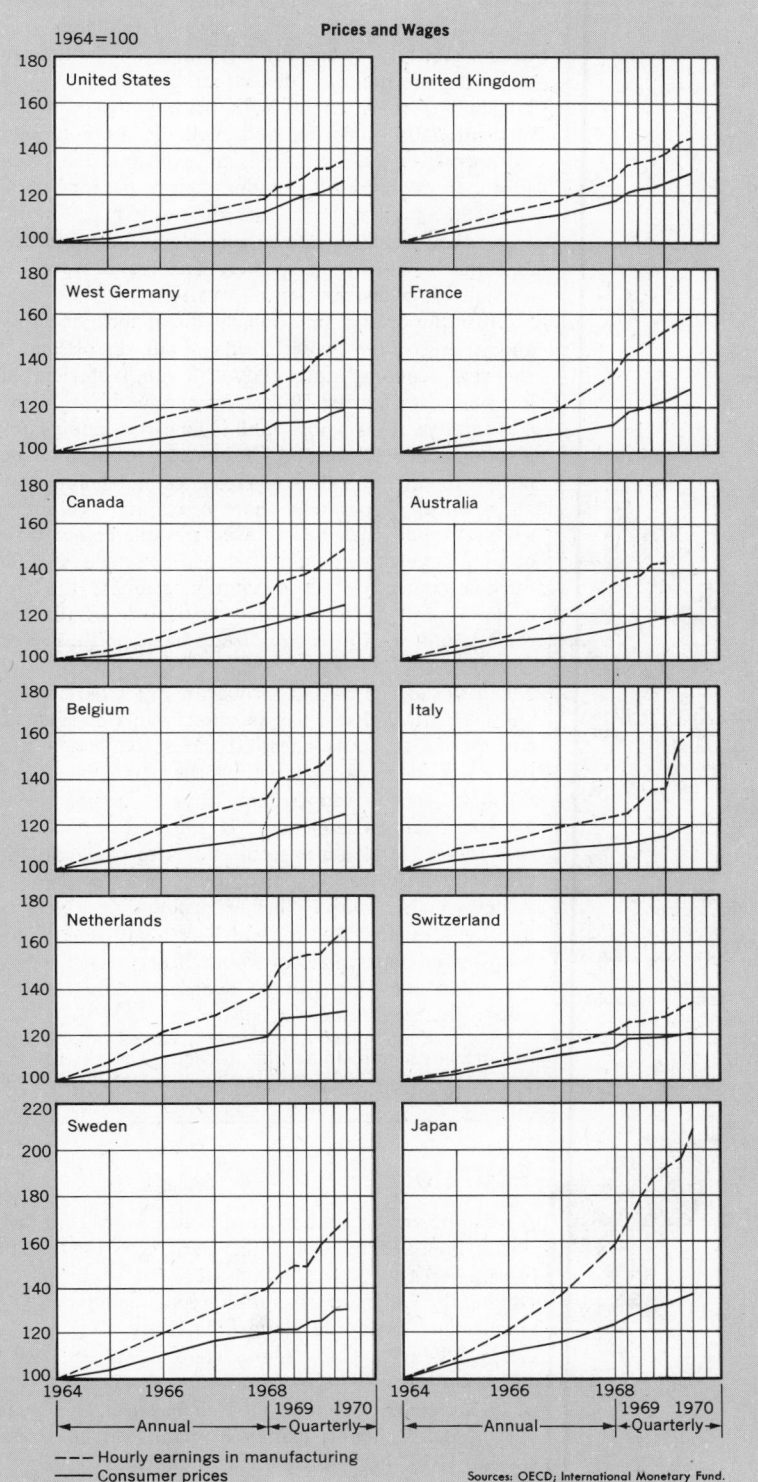

Prices and Wages

Sources: OECD; International Monetary Fund.

that they give up and say we must simply learn to live with inflation. Their ingenuity in inventing new devices and gimmicks to try to safeguard the buying power of money must not be underestimated. At the same time, however, experience shows that while some individuals can protect themselves up to a point, most people do not have equal ability, bargaining power, or luck at passing on to others the burden of the depreciation of money.

Living with inflation at anything near current rates would have profound consequences for society. In such an environment, income gains and the accumulation of wealth would come to depend less on work and saving and more on ingenuity and the exercise of political and economic power and influence; this would multiply social injustice and inequality and give rise to political discontent. Furthermore, arrangements to catch up with price increases would institutionalize inflation and make it more difficult to control. At the same time, rampant inflation would stimulate excessive indebtedness since debtors—governments as well as businesses and individuals—would repay their debts in money that would be worth less in terms of its buying power. The result would be a wholesale redistribution of wealth.

Most important, inflationary distortions of prices and interest rates would bring about distortions in the real economy and, above all, an inefficient allocation of resources. Uncertainty about future prices and interest rates would inhibit long-run lending for, if money depreciates rapidly, people cannot be expected to save and thus to create capital voluntarily. In a world desperately short of capital, voluntary savings would then be replaced by still higher taxes or by a government monopoly of investment capital. Such a course would, inevitably, strangle the free economy and undermine the very fabric of the free society and, with it, each citizen's basic political freedoms.

Our world has passed through many a dark valley and, at critical times, has repeatedly found regenerative power to spurt ahead. It must be hoped that there will be a reaction against the persistent depreciation of money and its cumulative economic, social, and political consequences. It must also be hoped that there will be purposeful efforts to safeguard individual initiative, responsibility, and freedom to achieve higher output, better productivity, and an improved quality of life, which is today one of the deep-seated aspirations of youth. But the malaise in the world economy will be overcome only through responsible government at all levels.   (M. A. K.)

See also Economics; Employment, Wages, and Hours; Income, National; Industrial Review; Labour Unions; Merchandising; Prices; Profits; Savings and Investment; Trade, International.

WIDE WORLD

José María Velasco Ibarra, president of Ecuador, assumed dictatorial powers June 22, 1970.

Ecuador

A republic on the west coast of South America, Ecuador is bounded by Colombia, Peru, and the Pacific Ocean. Area: 109,483 sq.mi. (283,561 sq.km.), including the Galápagos Islands (a dependency of 3,075 sq.mi.) and excluding claimed territory. Pop. (1969 est.): 5,890,000. Cap.: Quito (pop., 1969 est., 505,-577). Largest city: Guayaquil (pop., 1969 est., 754,-633). Language: Spanish, but Indians speak Quechuan and Jíbaro. Religion: mainly Roman Catholic. President in 1970, José María Velasco Ibarra.

A marked worsening of Ecuador's economic and

political difficulties, emphasized by an accumulation of budgetary problems and growing student unrest, led President Velasco to assume dictatorial powers on June 22. The developments that culminated in this step dated back to December 1969 when his government, already facing the prospect of a substantial deficit in the 1970 budget, was forced by smaller returns than expected from tax collections and bond sales to draw on 1970 revenue for the payment of salaries and other disbursements.

It did so with a pledge that public expenditure in 1970 would be cut by 1 billion sucres in equal monthly installments from March to December. In this way the estimated 1970 deficit was to be modestly reduced (by 400 million sucres to 2,538,000,000 sucres). By May 4, however, when Congress adjourned, no further action had been taken to cope with a budgetary situation in which preliminary estimates suggested that ordinary revenue would fall short of requirements for debt payments, education, and defense.

In mid-May Velasco attempted to solve this problem himself by promulgating four decrees. These provided for an emergency budget yielding 460 million sucres, the abolition of tax exemptions under the industrial development law and other laws, the imposition of sales and consumer taxes, and an increase in stabilization surcharges on imports.

The private sector of the economy, led by the influential Guayaquil Chamber of Commerce, reacted by petitioning Ecuador's Supreme Court to declare the decrees unconstitutional, whereupon Velasco announced that he would resign if the petition succeeded. On learning of the Supreme Court's intention to veto his measures on the ground that they infringed

ECUADOR

Education. (1967–68) Primary, pupils 897,539, teachers 23,673; secondary, pupils 84,984, teachers 7,278; vocational, pupils 49,629, teachers 3,269; teacher training, students 16,584, teachers 886; higher (including 9 universities), students 19,600, teaching staff 1,969.

Finance. Monetary unit: sucre, with a par value (following devaluation of Aug. 16, 1970) of 25 sucres to U.S. $1 (60 sucres = £1 sterling). Gold, SDRs, and foreign exchange, central bank: (June 1970) U.S. $64 million; (June 1969) U.S. $49.7 million. Budget (1969 est.) balanced at 5,147,000,000 sucres. Gross national product: (1968) 26,510,000,000 sucres; (1967) 24.4 billion sucres. Money supply: (May 1970) 4,072,000,-000 sucres; (May 1969) 3,571,000,000 sucres. Cost of living (Quito; 1963 = 100): (June 1970) 132; (June 1969) 128.

Foreign Trade. (1968) Imports U.S. $210.8 million; exports U.S. $207.6 million. Import sources: U.S. 46%; West Germany 13%; Italy 10%; Japan 7%; Venezuela 6%; U.K. 5%. Export destinations: U.S. 38%; West Germany 16%; Japan 16%; Italy 5%. Main exports: bananas 50%; cocoa 19%; coffee 16%.

Transport and Communications. Roads (1966) 18,345 km. Motor vehicles in use (1968): passenger 22,000; commercial (including buses) 34,300. Railways (1968): *c.* 1,900 km.; traffic 59 million passenger-km., freight 60 million net ton-km. Air traffic (1968): 263,414,000 passenger-km.; freight 5,174,000 net ton-km. Telephones (Jan. 1969) 88,000. Radio receivers (Dec. 1967) 801,000. Television receivers (Dec. 1967) 71,000.

Agriculture. Production (in 000; metric tons; 1968; 1967 in parentheses): bananas 2,693 (3,163); corn (1969) *c.* 210, (1968) 177; barley 96 (82); potatoes 353 (403); dry beans 28 (38); coffee (1969) *c.* 48, (1968) 66; cocoa 65 (76); rice (1969) 288, (1968) 218; cassava 125 (327); oranges 196 (194); sugar, raw value (1969–70) *c.* 264, (1968–69) 204. Livestock (in 000; 1968–69): cattle *c.* 2,400; sheep *c.* 1,830; pigs *c.* 1,300; horses *c.* 235; chickens (1967–68) *c.* 5,380.

Industry. Production (in 000; metric tons; 1968): petroleum products 972; crude oil (1969) 206; electricity (kw-hr.) *c.* 850,000; cement 434; gold (troy oz.) 8.6; silver (troy oz.) 135.

the right of Congress to legislate on tax and budgetary matters, the president declared himself supreme executive under the constitution of 1946.

Supported by the armed forces, he suspended Congress, reformed the Supreme Court, placed all foreign exchange dealings under the control of the Banco Central, and closed the university campuses in Quito, Guayaquil, Cuenca, and Loja.

In the wake of these midyear changes the Army, whose commander in chief, Gen. Nilo Alfredo Villagomez, was replaced by his chief of staff, Col. Julio Sacoto Montero, rounded up student leaders and left-of-centre politicians, while the police began a search for Vice-Pres. Jorge Zavalo Baquerizo and for the former president, Carlos Julio Arosemena Monroy. President Velasco announced that he would hand over power in 1972 and meanwhile would arrange a plebiscite for the purpose of seeking the country's approval of amendments to the 1946 constitution.

In the public uncertainty that prevailed, banks were inundated with customers anxious to withdraw their savings; one well-known bank was unable to meet its commitments and was closed for five months. On August 16 Ecuador's official exchange rate was altered from 18 to 25 sucres to the U.S. dollar. This was accompanied by a series of measures ending all exchange restrictions on international transactions except those relating to foreign loans and investments, and providing for tax allowances on exports, the abolition of stabilization surcharges on imports, the gradual elimination of prior import deposits over a $2\frac{1}{2}$-year period, and strict price controls on petroleum derivatives and products of prime necessity.

The new exchange rate, applicable within a 1% margin to all operations, was approved by the International Monetary Fund, which proposed to send a mission to Quito to negotiate a standby agreement to strengthen the country's international reserves. During the second half of 1969 these had climbed from their all-time low of $12.1 million in June to $39 million in December, thanks to higher banana exports and the advance payment of royalties and taxes by the Texaco-Gulf consortium. In the subsequent six months, however, they steadily declined and on June 22, 1970, stood at $24 million.

The country's relations with other members of the Andean Group (Bolivia, Chile, Colombia, and Peru) continued to improve. Early in the year the presidents of Ecuador and Colombia met at Rumichaca, where they pledged their governments to mutual cooperation in a number of development projects. From April 16 Ecuador was authorized to export 19 products, including bananas, coffee, and cacao, to the four other member countries of the group on a duty-free basis.

(R. B. Le.)

Education

Disaffected students continued to demand more control of their destinies in 1970. Some used their time to demonstrate against politicians and there were more ugly scenes on the campus. Politicians, in their turn, continued to disrupt the administration of education as they tried to press their social theories on it or to use campus unrest for their political advantage. There was, however, some evidence that the educational institutions were learning to live with their troubles, and the year was marked by more thinking about fundamentals than had sometimes been the case.

Student Unrest. The mood of the students, of course, did continue to claim attention. Leonid I. Brezhnev, the general secretary of the Soviet Communist Party, told a congress of the Komsomol (Young Communist League) in May that student upheavals in the West were an important symptom of the deepening crisis of capitalism. He saw such disturbances as a serious factor in the political struggle, but he urged Soviet students to maintain firm discipline. The first duty of youth was to follow Lenin's advice: "Firstly to study, secondly to study and thirdly to study."

In the U.S. the year was marred by widespread student demonstrations, in places over civil rights or local issues but more generally over the war in Vietnam. After a relatively quiet spring, Pres. Richard Nixon's April 30 announcement that U.S. troops had entered Cambodia sparked a sudden and spectacular upsurge in the campus antiwar movement. A wave of student demonstrations swept the country, and there were calls for a national student strike.

On May 4 at Kent State University in Ohio, one of several campuses where the National Guard had been brought in to restore order, guardsmen fired into a crowd of students, killing four and wounding several others. The exact sequence of events remained in dispute at year's end, but the immediate effect was to bring out hitherto uncommitted or inactive students and to plunge the country's higher educational system into chaos. For two weeks or more classes were canceled and demonstrations held as students and their elders agonized over the events. The killing of two students at nearly all-black Jackson (Miss.) State College by policemen had racial rather than antiwar overtones, but it added to the general furor.

With a great body of essentially middle-of-the-road students participating, the movement began to take a political direction. In the emotionalism of the moment, thousands of students pledged to work for antiwar candidates in the November election, and a few schools arranged to dismiss classes during the immediate preelection period. Commitment dwindled with time, however, and while more students than usual engaged in political activity, they were far from the hordes that had been envisaged in the spring.

The Cambodia-Kent State affair was the most spectacular instance of campus unrest during the year, but it was far from being the only one. Students at the Santa Barbara campus of the University of California burned a branch of the Bank of America during a riot in February. "Trashing"—property damage on or near campuses—became so common that it usually went unreported outside the local area. ROTC buildings and other campus institutions with government connections became favourite targets for bombing and arson, and in August a University of Wisconsin research assistant was killed in the bombing of a math centre where government work had been carried on. By fall this sporadic violence had spilled over into the larger society, and it was difficult to tell how much of the "revolutionary" and "urban guerrilla" activity was actually campus-connected.

Clearly the revolutionary activists formed only a small part of the U.S. college population, although polls revealed a continuum of opinion that included many nonactivist sympathizers. In an election year, however, campus protest could not long remain outside the political forum, and the fall campaign found many candidates using student protest as a whipping boy in their attempts to convince the electorate of their devotion to law and order.

WIDE WORLD

James E. Allen, Jr., talks to newsmen after being fired as U.S. commissioner of education. He said the post had "serious frustrations" but voiced surprise at being dismissed.

Ecumenical Movement:
see Religion

CAMERA PRESS FROM PIX

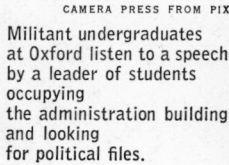

Militant undergraduates
at Oxford listen to a speech
by a leader of students
occupying
the administration building
and looking
for political files.

In the aftermath of Cambodia-Kent State, President Nixon named a Commission on Campus Unrest, chaired by former Pennsylvania governor William Scranton, to investigate causes and recommend solutions. The commission report, issued before the election, was on the whole evenhanded, laying the blame on extremist students and faculty, unprepared administrators, and overreacting peace officers and public. All sides were counseled to seek reconciliation and understanding, and the president in particular was urged to exert his moral leadership in what was seen as a crisis. Even this was brought into the political arena, however. Spokesmen for various factions castigated it for not placing all the fault on one group or another, and the president himself insisted that he was only one of many molders of public opinion. Meanwhile, positive action against disaffected students was in the air. Many university administrations began taking steps to meet possible future disorders, and the fall term opened in an atmosphere of uneasy calm.

The U.S. was not alone in experiencing student unrest. In Portugal, in February, fighting between striking and nonstriking students led the authorities at Lisbon University to close the faculty of law. In June some students at Belgrade (Yugos.) University went on a hunger strike in support of striking miners. May saw extensive demonstrations by students of the English-language universities in South Africa against the prosecution of some Africans under the Suppression of Communism Act. In August, Barney Pityana, president of the black South African Students' Association, announced that he had been refused a passport to take up a scholarship at Britain's Durham University.

After some relaxation of authoritarian attitudes toward them, the mood of West German students had become quieter, though there were indications of troubles ahead if the government's declared intention of making education a priority did not enable the universities to accommodate the growing number of potential students. In Finland there was pressure from students to replace the authoritarian university structure with a national system of university government that would give the students a voice in the election of university councils.

There was a sensation in France in March when Paul Ricoeur, dean of the faculty of letters at Nanterre and a declared supporter of university reform, resigned—because of ill health—and accused the government of leaving the academic authorities to shoulder responsibility for student troubles that should be solved politically. The following month Olivier Guichard, the minister of education, told the French National Assembly that a special unarmed force of police was being created to maintain order in the Paris universities. In June there was serious rioting on the campus at Grenoble after detectives had tried to arrest two students alleged to be agitators, and student strikes against the intervention of police on the campus subsequently interrupted examinations there.

In the U.K., Cambridge University students staged a violent demonstration against the Greek government at a hotel in the town in February, leading to some prison sentences. Keele University experienced vandalism and violence over several months, and the Staffordshire Education Committee decided to withhold its annual grant to the university until it was satisfied about discipline there. Disaffected students raiding administrative files at the University of Warwick in February discovered what they claimed to be political reports on a lecturer and on an applicant for entry. The University Assembly passed a vote of no confidence in the vice-chancellor, John Butterworth, and there was a nationwide agitation about confidential files. In May, Margaret Thatcher, the new minister of education and science, expressed the opinion that students and other demonstrators who occupied buildings should be liable to prosecution. This did not prevent Birmingham University students, in June, from disrupting a meeting of the senate; there had been continued protest at Birmingham over the case of Richard Atkinson, who had been involved in 1968 troubles at the university and whose appointment to a lectureship in sociology was vetoed by the university authorities.

A Change in Midstream. In Britain the year fell into two parts, neatly divided by the midsummer general election that put the Labour Party out of office and brought in the Conservatives. In the first part of the year there was generally clear sailing toward the Labour government goal of a comprehensive or nonselective secondary school system. In April the government suffered a defeat in Parliament over a bill that would have allowed it to coerce the few local authorities that still hesitated to reorganize their schools on the comprehensive principle. The Labour Party dismissed this as a procedural hitch and observers did not feel it was a major defeat.

Much anxiety did continue to be felt by the independent schools and those schools that, while independent of the local authorities, received a direct grant from the government in return for taking a quota of local authority pupils. The independent schools continued to see their future threatened by the government's egalitarian policies, while the direct-grant schools, traditionally grammar schools taking the most able pupils in their areas, felt that their whole nature would be changed by inclusion in the comprehensive system. In April the governors of Manchester Grammar School, the most famous of the direct-grant schools, announced that, if the recommendation of the commission was implemented by the government, the school would opt for independent status.

The climate was radically changed by the Conservative victory. In a circular to the local authorities, Margaret Thatcher reasserted the principle of local choice in the arrangements for secondary schools. Confusion followed as some local authorities abandoned or revised the comprehensive schemes on which they had embarked while others were all the more determined to carry theirs through. The National Union of Teachers, the largest association of primary and secondary school teachers, was sharply critical of Mrs. Thatcher, but the Joint Four associations of headmasters, headmistresses, assistant masters, and assistant mistresses—chiefly representing the grammar, direct-grant, and independent schools—supported her. Edward Short, her Labour predecessor, said that she was putting the clock back 50 years. Tory authorities, he declared, would continue to subject children to the eleven-plus (the procedure by which children were tested for academic or nonacademic schools) though that system had been condemned by every educationist of repute. Subsequently the general council of the Trades Union Congress urged its 150 affiliates to coordinate local moves in support of comprehensive schools.

Mrs. Thatcher was unperturbed, however. At the Conservative Party conference in October, she promised to do everything she could to encourage the direct-grant schools, which she saw as a bridge between a completely independent system and the state system, offering opportunities to pupils regardless of their parents' income or background. Noting that 5.3% of children were in independent schools, she declared that these schools were a valuable contribution to the national system and, more importantly, a safeguard against a state monopoly. "I would rather keep our secondary school system flexible," she said. "I am also concerned to see some variety of choice retained in the system."

Desegregation. In the U.S. the effort to end separate schooling for white and black pupils continued to be a major issue. The official picture was rosy. By the autumn of 1970 some 94% of the school systems in the South were classified as desegregated. In July the Justice Department had filed suits against the state of Mississippi and certain school districts in Florida, Arkansas, and South Carolina in what was described as a final push for desegregation, while in April Gov. Claude Kirk of Florida had yielded to a federal district court contempt order and allowed court-ordered integration to be carried out in the Manatee County public schools. In May President Nixon had asked Congress for $1.5 billion over two years to assist desegregation in the South and to help school districts in the North overcome racial divisions based on residence. The local authorities were to be given considerable latitude in how they spent the funds.

There was another picture, however. Earlier, there had been unsuccessful legislative moves by Southern conservatives in Washington to force all areas in the U.S. to desegregate at the same speed—a measure, it was pointed out, that would compel the federal authorities either to ease enforcement in the South or to face the well-nigh impossible task of abolishing the segregation resulting from housing patterns in the North. The difficulties of overcoming this so-called de facto segregation were underlined by the schemes put forward for integrating large cities, some of which would require bussing children long distances plus vast expenditures for the buses themselves. Although some smaller cities had introduced bussing successfully, it remained a highly emotional issue.

Meanwhile, the seamier side of Southern desegregation was brought out in testimony before a Senate subcommittee, in which it was claimed that black children entering some white schools were resegregated by class, that such children were denied the amenities they had enjoyed in all-black schools, and that black teachers, rather than being integrated into the system, had been fired. An Internal Revenue Service ruling denying tax exemption to private schools set up to avoid desegregation did little to discourage the overt support being given to such systems by local authorities.

In Britain the difficulty of achieving integration by school bus was becoming increasingly obvious to the few authorities still attempting it. It was reported from West Bromwich, for instance, that when children were transported to a school away from their neighbourhood, any link between home and school was broken; the parents made virtually no contact with the school to which their children were sent. The problems of coloured school dropouts also began to be aired. At a London conference on the subject in July, Richard Stokes, group personnel adviser to the Burton Group of companies, said that staff managers had failed to do anything to avoid discrimination while positive discrimination existed in many firms. The integration of different ethnic groups with different languages continued to present difficulties in Singapore, and the Malay Teachers Association was advocating a single school system with English as the main language of instruction.

The Cost Spiral. Efforts to achieve desegregation swelled the cost of education for some countries in 1970, but costs generally were soaring. In a record Norwegian budget of 23.7 billion kroner, education accounted for 2,696,000,000 kroner. In July, French Pres. Georges Pompidou said that in 1971 his country expected to spend more on education than on defense for the first time in its history. In Quebec the provincial budget for education was Can$792 million against $170 million in 1960. Italian parents were facing increases of 10 to 20% in the cost of school textbooks. At a Paris conference of the Organization for Economic Cooperation and Development in June it was reported that, if current trends continued, eight OECD states would be spending 10% of national income on education by 1980 and seven others would be spending 5 to 10%.

In the U.S. in August, President Nixon vetoed a $4.4 billion aid to education bill on the ground that it was more than he had asked for and that such spending was inflationary. The opposition suggested that his action was politically motivated and, as it turned out, his veto was overridden. The difficulties of finance as well as those of desegregation were evident factors in the unrest that became marked in 1970 in the U.S.

UPI COMPIX

Florida Gov. Claude Kirk talks with Manatee County school officials after he personally took control of the school system in an attempt to block a court-ordered integration plan.

World Education

Most recent official data

Country	1st level (primary) Students (full-time)	1st level Teachers (full-time)	1st level Total schools	General 2nd level (secondary) Students (full-time)	General 2nd level Teachers (full-time)	General 2nd level Total schools	Vocational 2nd level Students (full-time)	Vocational 2nd level Teachers (full-time)	Vocational 2nd level Total schools	3rd level (higher)* Students (full-time)	3rd level Teachers (full-time)	3rd level Total schools	Literacy % of population	Literacy Over age
Afghanistan	500,665	11,523	2,848	83,529	3,352	339	14,730	1,038	54	5,680	881	7	20.	7–12
Algeria	1,739,033	44,797	5,559	155,608	6,540	384	45,468	2,483	222	20,243	1,269	41	...	...
Angola	333,767	7,434	3,576	28,916	1,779	160	14,693	1,227	69	1,074	123	1	...	...
Argentina	3,600,787	188,245	25,849	211,537	31,947	940	519,079	71,583	2,269	465,686	47,038	1,302	91.5	...
Austria	599,954	24,656	4,018	475,314	26,999	2,055	224,698	12,177	1,052	59,990	6,734	66	100.	...
Bahrain	37,781	1,676	82	11,586	652	32	955	79	2	236	45	2	32.2	15
Barbados	44,630	1,725	131	21,315	925	35	80	19	2	472	62	3	96.	...
Bolivia	740,288	...	9,524	65,105	...	395	2,681	...	24	10,532	...	24	...	...
Botswana	82,214	2,037	280	3,049	157	10	809	...	16	303†	26†	2†	20.4	...
British Solomon Is.	14,798	1,268	395	897	53	7	140	26	1	162	18	1	...	...
Brunei	27,580	1,230	118	9,325	456	21	79	8	1	494	23	1	66.	10
Burma	3,070,970	48,656	14,539	644,979	15,401	1,413	4,164	361	20	43,784	2,891	30	68.	...
Burundi	182,444	4,852	970	3,701	328	18	1,202	152	13	3,293	356	20	...	...
Cambodia	989,464	22,465	5,699	119,988	3,990	172	5,798	510	107	10,198	1,299	10	...	...
Canada	4,056,948	...	...	1,640,330	260,908	17,047	181,511	13,226	381	345,966	24,537	232	...	...
Cape Verde Islands	19,680	381	257	2,059	85	5	569	34	2	—	—	—	...	...
Ceylon	2,380,000	57,447	8,184	401,000	35,965	1,555	1,662	75	3	19,018	1,376	29	71.9	...
Chad	178,894	2,596	877	8,724	186	33	383	52	2	758	43	3	14.	...
Chile	1,980,906	...	7,302	178,887	...	461	85,987	...	257	58,964	...	27	83.6	15
Colombia	3,021,473	81,552	30,265	522,074	20,883	2,920	141,137	5,644	1,381	164,086	8,026	328	72.9	15
Congo (Brazzaville)	228,578	3,712	883	25,428	672	54	2,594	315	32	2,369	155	7	30.5	...
Costa Rica	345,146	11,656	2,346	64,252	2,888	105	5,757	355	15	13,528	954	6	55.79	...
Cyprus	71,236	2,255	562	34,938	1,498	70	4,218	273	11	580	41	5	81.8	7
Denmark	535,063	41,461	2,460	221,629	3,663	209	94,411	...	193	58,272	7,901	49	100.	8
Dominica	19,818	481	58	1,533	81	4	70	4	1	—	—	—	86.5	15
El Salvador	531,309	13,501	2,891	60,870	2,635	300	25,983	559	113	9,895	...	10	55.	...
Ethiopia	513,981	10,403	1,844	88,861	3,399	84	7,204	508	74	6,225‡	533‡	24‡	...	...
Finland	413,586	18,755	5,110	387,717	20,494	1,150	101,917	9,164	845	56,726§	5,522	41	100.	7
France	5,346,298	225,274	68,116	3,032,904	194,107	9,256	825,214	39,722	2,076	700,868	29,794	180†	100.	7
Germany, West	6,136,006	192,067	28,498	2,060,244	91,445	4,272	2,018,916	34,805	5,091	597,777	57,530	3,350	...	...
Guatemala	484,745	13,009	4,924	63,078	5,122	364	19,541	2,957	388	18,316	...	90	...	...
Honduras	376,966	10,437	4,143	33,392	2,516	110	1,202	140	9	415,019	13,225	4,273	...	...
Hong Kong	723,467	21,625	1,437	204,190	8,079‖	302	12,994	8,079‖	24	12,416	601	15	...	...
Hungary	1,177,887	62,834	5,626	124,220	7,291	344	106,582	5,931	211	53,237	9,413	87	96.6	7
Iceland	27,500	1,320	195	15,500	1,230	130	5,000	550	50	2,200	250	6	100.	...
India	37,219,083	944,377	391,064	29,118,994	1,006,860	103,275	181,040	12,380	2,174	2,029,469	133,769	6,449	30.	...
Iran	2,916,255	89,320	15,776	897,443	25,890	2,298	23,335	2,050	164	76,543	3,268	204	28.12	10
Iraq	1,015,942	73,316	5,172	302,611	10,114	863	3,932	391	17	40,288	1,850	64	...	...
Ireland	528,217	15,640	4,307	181,043	...	903	4,364	...	107	21,849	...	34	100.	...
Israel	495,668	20,783‡	1,774‡	108,648	5,524‡	305‡	50,438‡	3,010‡	274‡	49,153	526†	54	89.6¶	...
Italy	4,796,593	223,806	39,261	3,157,583	244,217	11,981	250,760	22,510	1,987	842,131	27,831	858	91.6	6
Jamaica	480,169	...	1,273	40,641	1,775	58	4,127	239	11	4,906	492	10	57.28	15
Japan	9,403,193	361,149	25,013	9,244,605	431,292	16,155	1,414,324	48,916	8,024	1,618,189	90,151	852	...	...
Jordan♀	229,691	5,643	748	75,139	3,061	509	2,491	107	9	4,077	196	12	42.	15
Kenya	1,282,297	38,312	6,111	115,246	5,267	694	9,097	438	36	5,345	469	4	48.	...
Korea, South	5,757,153	101,340	6,030	1,706,513	43,817	2,352	316,637	11,783	662	194,796	10,270	168	93.3	11
Kuwait	115,683	6,337	235	13,773	1,215	22	3,558	397	18	4,260	722	5	48.	10
Laos	185,724	5,678	2,995	5,579	344	16	1,155	197	3	2,985	387	10	19.4	...
Lebanon	528,488	429,124	1,881	130,210	2,479	911	...	...	238	35,152	1,921	22	...	...
Lesotho	179,386	3,419	1,124	4,141	190	27	249	26	5	1,025	54†	8	...	...
Liberia	120,245	2,990	910	15,494	902	174	887	66	3	1,499	146	5	24.	...
Liechtenstein	2,412	89	14	689	33	4	—	—	—	70§	28§	1	100.	...
Luxembourg	36,035	1,597	337	10,086	541	23	5,212	379	37	365	78	3	...	...
Malaysia	1,689,707	53,486	6,313	575,366	22,200	1,070	17,316	592	87	18,722	1,336	26	54.6	...
Malta	55,297	2,546	164	12,074	886	28	2,608	157	6	1,602	287	4	...	...
Mauritius	146,490	4,405	337	42,444	1,940	141	714	48	11	612	41	2	...	...
Mexico	8,947,555	191,091	44,610	1,451,896‖	102,440‖	5,192‖	—	—	—	244,281	26,023§	301	...	...
Nauru	1,465	96	9	368	28	2	—	—	—	—	—	—	81.9	...
Nepal	448,754	17,563	6,880	94,731	4,060	959	4,500	131	29	15,331	1,005	45	11.8	...
Netherlands, The	1,509,319	37,777	8,879	537,281	34,907	1,664	390,502	35,000	1,982	153,548δ	15,500δ	337δ	100.	...
Netherlands Antilles	43,193	1,200	119	10,415δ	424δ	38δ	5,317	251	28	—	—	—	...	...
New Caledonia	23,933	950	255	3,448	252	17	1,136	87	4	44	26	2	88.8	15
New Guinea	149,026	4,743	1,177	10,672	503	36	2,974	190	48	1,103	142	10	18.2	10
New Zealand	514,774	18,769	2,584	...	9,541	...	1,681	804	7	28,123	2,310	16	100.	...
Nicaragua	278,752	7,391	2,063	38,149	1,751	152	3,722	272	29	11,453	699	26	50.8	...
Niger	84,248	1,965	673	5,587	253	23	137	21	1	548†	44†	4†	...	...
Norway	390,046	16,763	3,091	234,449	15,622	1,171	77,115	5,725	711	38,695	3,383	37	...	...
Pakistan	8,140,193	190,880	66,860	3,346,190	112,772	11,054	27,511	1,700	152	360,184	14,674	499	15.9	...
Papua	65,071	2,061	484	5,597	298	19	2,205	98	21	1,409	161	6	23.5	10
Peru	2,304,305	66,844	19,942	424,421	25,133	1,372	86,076	8,172	425	17,590†	2,001†	111†	46.9	6
Philippines	6,193,128	208,587	36,679	1,284,306	39,173	2,570	77,890	1,916	781	551,750	19,463	555	72.	...
Portugal	904,120	28,434	17,075	168,486	8,158	536	168,105	9,187	426	41,764	2,591	121	59.7	...
Réunion	108,630	4,112	398	27,086	1,172	61	1,802	168	6	637	54	3	...	...
Rhodesia	716,919	18,546	3,480	50,663	2,566	180	4,679	300	20	1,281	202	4	...	...
Romania	2,886,855	133,842	14,928	261,749	13,679	572	344,141	18,721	904	128,796	14,337	94	...	...
Ryukyu Islands	210,541	8,301	401	54,653	2,726	57	17,695	1,102	31	7,165	310	4	18.2	...
Singapore	365,956	12,263	427	144,181	6,971	122	3,997	384	9	10,750	757	5	76.7	10
Somalia	48,983	1,542	292	4,966	245	17	906	79	8	716	58	4	15.	...
South Africa□	3,466,021	78,388	13,089	412,530	18,442	1,234	49,842	1,804	184	93,637	12,702	86	...	...
Southern Yemen	105,158	3,493	645	12,305	681	70	701◇	120◇	10◇	—	—	—	...	...
Spain	4,390,000	128,407	126,337	1,210,249	36,628	2,775	300,798	18,060	725	260,752	14,590	285	...	...
Sudan	633,850	13,493‡	3,485‡	263,208	76,637‡	1,132‡	2,420	265	12	9,987	...	25	19.4	...
Sweden	631,267	31,600	4,500	391,642	41,250	263	174,058	...	775	121,393	1,078	57	...	...
Taiwan	2,428,041	57,935	2,275	872,277	32,244	702	155,947	7,308	141	184,743	9,470	95	...	...
Thailand	5,273,516	168,107	28,463	444,614	21,356	1,577	182,540	10,187	745	75,914	6,660	47	72.	...
Togo	206,283	3,689	905	16,688	556	63	2,072	157	29	332	33	2	44.	...
Turkey	4,908,743	126,106	37,200	965,697	24,146	2,057	222,507	9,268	1,098	222,503	11,001	203	48.72	...
Uganda	709,708	21,074	2,720	46,483	2,067	118	2,784	245	22	7,711	757	28	...	...
U.S.S.R.	39,058,000	1,449,000△	214,290	4,400,000	251,000	...	4,166,600◇	134,000	...	...	201,000	...	...	...
United Arab Republic	3,622,786	97,938	8,151	1,087,490	41,941	1,641	245,895	12,104	242	221,865	7,828	68	...	...
United Kingdom	5,816,258	201,686	28,456	3,587,163	192,584	6,948	288,535	50,070	936	339,675	42,713	254	...	...
United States	36,800,000	1,261,000§	85,779	14,800,000	1,014,000§	31,411	...	...	...	7,600,000	593,000§	2,525	97.6	14
Venezuela	1,726,129	51,040	10,681	288,060	12,401	652	147,031	6,756	389	86,463	8,967	55	...	...
Vietnam, South	2,406,264	45,077	7,425	632,221	16,260	782	22,893	1,103	259	47,670	1,066	9	80.	...
Western Samoa	29,419	869	140	9,619	408	63	95	11	1	319	29	2	97.5	10
Zambia	693,291	14,360	2,556	52,074	2,465	113	...	...	...	3,779	483	13	...	...

Note: Third level may include individual faculties within a university. *Includes teacher training at both 2nd and 3rd levels.
†Teacher training only. ‡Public only. §Includes part-time. ‖General and vocational combined. ¶Jewish population only.
♀Data refer to east bank of Jordan only. δTeacher training included in general secondary. □Not including Indian.
◇Includes teacher training. △Primary and secondary combined.

Office of Education. In June President Nixon removed Robert Finch from the office of secretary for health, education, and welfare and in the same month James E. Allen, Jr., who had been critical of the Nixon administration, was fired as commissioner of education (he was replaced by Sidney P. Marland, Jr., of New York in September).

Dissatisfaction led to the resignation of a number of senior officials. In a memorandum of complaint submitted when he gave up his job, James J. Gallagher, deputy commissioner for planning, research, and evaluation, alleged that the Office of Education received only perfunctory recognition in the making of national policy and that the administration had an uncertain commitment to educational research and development. He further alleged that "fiscal considerations and budget technicians often determine major educational policy decisions, no matter the rhetoric of the visible spokesmen for the administration."

The high cost of education prompted moves to ensure value for money, and a number of experiments in accountability were being made. These sometimes involved the employment of a private company. Thus the 800-pupil Banneker Elementary School in Gary, Ind., was taken over by Behavioral Research Laboratories of Palo Alto, Calif. The company was to employ the teachers and have charge of the curriculum and administration; for this it would receive $800 a year from the city for each student, with the proviso that the money would be refunded for any student below the national average of achievement after three years. The same company had a guaranteed-reading-performance contract for 23,000 students in Philadelphia. In Washington, D.C., a plan to improve pupils' reading standards envisaged paying the teachers, not on their qualifications or seniority, but on their ability to teach, as measured by the progress of their pupils. The plan was opposed by the local teachers' union.

Another experiment was sponsored by the U.S. Office of Economic Opportunity and developed by Christopher Jencks, associate professor of education at Harvard University and co-director of the Center for the Study of Public Policy. Parents of school-age children would be given a voucher equal to the cost of educating each child in their district's public schools. The parent would give the voucher to the school of his choice—private, public, or parochial—and the school would cash the voucher with the public authorities. A voucher agency would supervise the system, decide which schools were eligible, give the parents information about them, and make sure that the schools accepted a fair share of children belonging to local minority groups. It was argued that with all the schools thus placed on an equal footing, they would have to be efficient or close. The experiment was still in the discussion stage in 1970. Initial reactions from teachers' groups were hostile, but there was also responsible support for the project.

Teacher Unrest. If some thought accountability was a way to improve the schools, others preferred strikes and demonstrations. Increasingly teachers, parents, and even pupils were united in such actions. Thus, in July, pupils in Christchurch, N.Z., marched in support of their teachers' demands for better pay and better schools, while in May most elementary school children in Amsterdam took part in a one-day strike, called by an action committee of parents and teachers aggrieved at the state of education in the city. In France, April saw strikes against the authorities initiated by both parents and teachers, each supporting the other. The parents withheld their children from school in protest against increased boarding charges. The teachers demanded better conditions for themselves and their pupils, better schools and equipment, and more generous scholarships and grants.

In Australia and New Zealand there was some disillusionment over the recruitment of teachers from overseas. Teachers in New South Wales were angered by a poster campaign, conducted in Britain, that showed a man in cap and gown on a beach and invited British teachers to teach in the sun. The poster was reported to have prompted 1,300 inquiries in a week. New South Wales teachers retorted that they often did teach in the sun—there were not enough classrooms. In New Zealand it was the recruits—or at least some of them—who said they had been oversold. There were protests over shortages of equipment, a lack of free periods for preparation, and the imposition of subjects the newcomers were not qualified to teach, as well as complaints that promises made in London about accommodations were not kept.

Dissatisfaction among British teachers about their pay rumbled on through the year. In the early months there were sporadic strikes as the teachers campaigned for an interim increase. Then, after some adjustment had been made in their salaries, agitation began in earnest to set the scene for the next round of pay talks. Much was made in the late summer of a policy difference between the National Union of Teachers and the National Association of Schoolmasters. The NUT supported the official claim put to the employers by the teachers' representatives on the Burnham Committee, through which salaries were negotiated. The NAS, however, insisted that any money available should go to teachers of ability making a career in the profession (the practice of increasing the basic scale and thus giving extra pay to many young women who did not intend to stay in the profession had long been a bone of contention).

The NUT stigmatized the NAS as disruptive and decided to report it to the general council of the Trades Union Congress, to which both belonged, for nontrade-union practice. The NAS, however, was fortified by an inquiry into teachers' pay by the *Economist* Intelligence Unit, which concluded that salaries were rising rapidly enough and that starting levels were sufficiently competitive, but that expectations for the career teacher were poor. In the event, the employers countered with proposals to abolish the single basic scale, to which various allowances had been added, and to replace it with a series of scales to meet different qualifications and appointments.

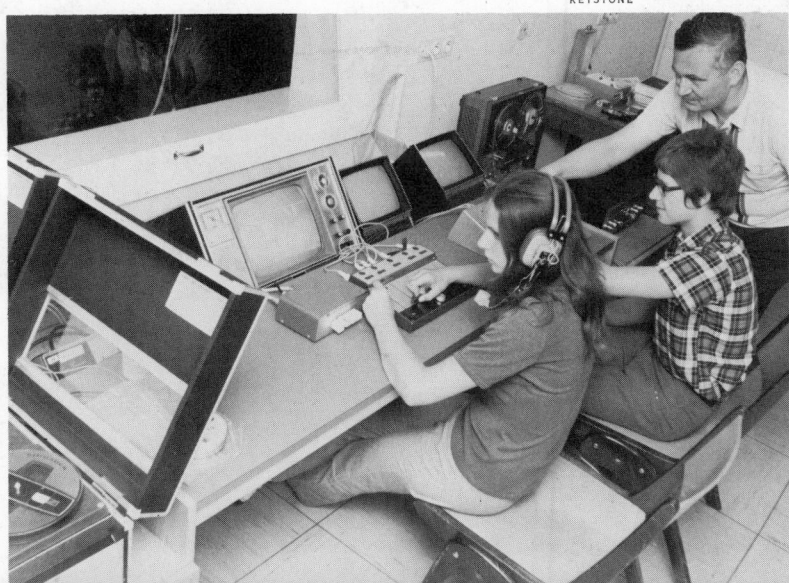

Students of Karl-Rehbein High School in Hanau, W.Ger., get instruction in the workings of their school's own television station.

KEYSTONE

Though it was emphasized that the proposals were not a formal offer, but merely an illustration of what might be done, it seemed evident that some grading of teachers was likely to emerge.

Other professional matters occupying British teachers in 1970 included moves toward compulsory union membership. The Association of Teachers in Technical Institutions was drawing up plans for a closed shop in colleges of further education, and there were similar demands for the schools. Fred Jarvis, deputy general secretary of the NUT, said in May, "There is a growing feeling in the profession that those who make no effort or sacrifice to win salary increases—of the kind union members made last year—should not reap the benefits won by others." Head teachers were increasingly incensed at the difficulties in which they were often placed because their assistants had won the right to withdraw from the supervision of school meals. There was also much discussion of a coming official inquiry into teacher training.

Some California teachers struck in April as negotiations between their union and the local authorities broke down. In Rhodesia there was anxiety among the church authorities after the government reduced its contribution toward the salaries of teachers in mission primary schools. It was reported that at least 6,000 mission teachers had been given notice, but the Ministry of Education announced that it planned to introduce a system in 1971 that would ensure the continuance of all African primary schools.

Old Problems and New Directions. That was a promise of fundamentals in a less developed country, but there was preoccupation with fundamentals elsewhere. In November 1969 the Quebec National Assembly had passed a bill giving Quebec parents the right to have their children educated in either English or French in the provincial schools. There was vigorous opposition to the bill by some French Canadians, who felt that the measure might mean the ultimate disappearance of French, and there were violent demonstrations against the bill, particularly in Montreal. In the same month the Canadian government announced that it would spend Can$50 million a year on a nationwide training scheme to promote bilingualism. Federal grants would be made to the provinces for the education of minority groups and for second-language teaching in the two mother tongues of the country.

Quarrels over language also continued in Belgium. In April a token stoppage of lectures in the French-language sections of Louvain University was ordered by the university authorities as a protest against the insufficiency of government grants for removing the French sections out of the Dutch-speaking area of Belgium to new quarters in the south. The decision to move was a concession to the Flemish after language riots had unseated the government in 1968. Some 13,000 students out of a total enrollment of 27,000 were involved.

There was much controversy in France over a government reform freeing lycée students from starting a second foreign language at 13, in addition to the one they had to start at 11. The first language chosen was usually English, and it was argued that if the French learned only English, other countries such as Italy, Germany, and Spain might follow suit and French would disappear as an international language. There were also protests from other governments, and it was pointed out that the reform violated a French-Italian cultural agreement under which each was to promote the use of the other's language.

The Inner London Education Authority was arranging to transmit on its educational television service a series of programs on the teaching of reading, designed for teachers who had not been trained in that subject. There had been concern over low standards of reading in the metropolis. At Nottingham University Keith Gardner, lecturer in the institute of education, was holding remedial courses in reading for undergraduates. He estimated that one in five read too badly to manage the complex material facing a university student. In Australia a short course in Australian usage and pronunciation was begun for Asian students at the University of New South Wales. Research was going on in experimental schools in Rio de Janeiro, Braz., to find faster ways of teaching read-

POPPERFOTO FROM PICTORIAL PARADE

KEYSTONE

Left, this youngster was one of a hundred pupils in London who took their parents to school to protest a teachers' strike Feb. 25, 1970. Above, London teachers on strike demonstrate in Trafalgar Square Jan. 30, 1970.

ing and writing. St. Louis, Mo., reported considerable success with intensive broadcast lessons designed to extend the vocabulary of schoolchildren.

Examinations, as usual, received much attention in 1970. In Britain teachers threatened to boycott the summer examinations in protest over pay, and some results were delayed by clerks striking for the same reason. The Portuguese Education Ministry had to cancel final tests in the high schools after it was discovered that copies of the questions had been leaked to the students. In India students at a number of colleges reacted violently when they were caught cheating, and in Manipuri, near Agra, a proctor was hacked to death. A thousand Italian graduates were indicted for obtaining degrees by false pretenses; agencies were said to exist in Rome and Milan that would write theses for the students.

There was continued dissatisfaction with the school examination system in Britain. A study by D. G. Bagg, admissions tutor at Manchester University Institute of Technology, concluded that the A level (sixth-form) examinations of the General Certificate of Education were a measure of the past and not a prediction for the future, and that the relationship between the university entrance examination and the final degree was very small indeed. Most attention centred on suggestions by working parties of the Schools Council that there be two new examinations for sixth-form pupils: a Q (qualifying) level of five subjects at 17, and a three-subject F (further) level at 18. The Standing Conference on University Entrance, the official mouthpiece of the universities on such matters, proposed that passes at O level (age 16) in the GCE no longer be an entrance requirement, and that the schools should be trusted to ensure that pupils destined for the universities received a broad and balanced education. A note of warning came from Jack Straw, president of the National Union of Students. Criticizing the attitude of "when in doubt set another examination," he said that the increasing tendency to subject sixth formers to ever increasing stress, like rats in an experimental labyrinth, could only exacerbate student unrest and disaffection.

In July the first, raw results of an ambitious program for a national assessment of educational progress in the U.S. were made public. Initiated by Francis Keppel, then U.S. commissioner of education, in 1963, the program had passed to the control of the Education Commission of the States, a body representing legislators and state school officials. It aimed to survey levels of knowledge for various age groups in a variety of subject areas, and was expected to be of great value in the planning of curricula.

Another topic claiming attention was the schooling of handicapped (exceptional) children. In Britain opinion had been hardening that more of these children should be taught in ordinary rather than separate, special schools. C. W. E. Cave, staff inspector for special schools in the Department of Education and Science, told delegates to a Manchester conference of the Joint Council for Handicapped Children in July that there would continue to be a place for special schools, but they must indeed offer something special—a situation that his visits to the schools suggested was not the case. In September, however, Britain's first all-age residential school for autistic children opened in Sussex. In Milwaukee, Wis., an experiment in giving intensive stimulation to the newly born babies of some mentally retarded mothers revealed an unexpected capacity on the part of the

THE "NEW YORK TIMES"

John Lowe, president of the student government at the Chicago Circle Campus of the University of Illinois, addresses the Illinois House of Representatives May 25, 1970, on the causes of student unrest.

babies for learning. More controversy attended an experiment in Omaha, Neb., in which drugs were given to hyperactive schoolchildren to increase their ability to concentrate. The drugs were administered under a doctor's care, and the program was supported by the president of the school board. Others, however, expressed fears that normal liveliness might be mistaken for abnormal hyperactivity and that the program, in general, tended to introduce drug dependence at an early age, increasing the likelihood of the child's experimenting with illegal drugs later on.

Politics and Policies. In the Communist countries, politicians continued to worry over the relationship of education to their policies. Soviet newspapers published warnings to parents who used personal influence, bribes, or other backdoor methods to get their children into universities, thus violating egalitarian Communist principles. In Czechoslovakia there was concern over the danger to children who learned at school that Communism was good and at home that it was bad. This, it was said, could harm their future as citizens of a socialist state. "The school gives the children a materialist, atheist, world outlook," declared Antonin Janec in the party newspaper *Rude Pravo*, "but in the family there is still a belief in God and churchgoing."

The importance of education to a nation was forcibly put by Lord Butler, master of Trinity College, Cambridge, in a lecture delivered in Delhi, India, in March. As the politician responsible for Britain's 1944 Education Act, Lord Butler was the architect of his own country's modern school system. "Your country and any country," he said, "would be wise to allow the education budget to be level with even that most sacred of items, the defence budget." He emphasized that for less developed countries, even more than for developed ones, knowledge was the key to the better life. He noted, also, that universities and other centres of higher education could no longer remain out of tune with the age of specialization; development of scientific and technological education was as vital for India as for other countries.

This could be described as the orthodox progressive view. It was sharply challenged later in the year in a paper written by Michael Huberman, a member of

© 1970 "CHICAGO DAILY NEWS"

"We find that the students did attack National Guard bullets with their bodies. . ."
—Fischetti, "Chicago Daily News."

the secretariat of UNESCO. The paper was intended for publication as a contribution to International Education Year, but was suppressed by UNESCO. Ironically, its suppression brought it more publicity than it might otherwise have received.

Huberman argued that education was presently based on the assumption that more could be learned in school than elsewhere and that, consequently, the way to compensate for social and economic inequality was to provide compulsory schooling for all. In practice, this did not work. Middle class children would consistently outdo working-class children because their schooling was an extension of their family and social environments. The system was self-justifying:

> Those who succeed in secondary and higher education are bound to succeed. They will pass more easily through an academic curriculum and academic examinations designed for their particular abilities. They will then receive superior certificates which will entitle them to high-level posts, without having proved that they can perform the necessary skills.

Besides being self-justifying, formal education in both developed and less developed countries was devouring funds needed for other purposes and was failing to achieve the results expected of it. So Huberman had some fundamental questions to ask:

> In fact, is it illegitimate to demand that the government also subsidise those young people who neither desire nor are eligible to take advantage of public education? Why should the state subsidise four years at the university for students while neglecting apprenticeships, independent study programmes, small community trade schools or even the purchase of small business by non-students?

In contrast to this sort of revolutionary talk, Lord Robbins, chairman of Britain's committee on higher education, declared in a debate in the House of Lords in July that it would be economic folly to limit student numbers. But Lord Todd had his own proviso to make in his presidential address to the British Association in September:

> Somehow or other we seem increasingly to equate higher education with traditional university education and to regard the obtaining of a B.A. or B.Sc. as the goal to which all must strive. This "degree fixation" has its roots in our own educational system but it has been powerfully reinforced by the argument that in the United States the educational system is such that far more people take college (i.e. university) degrees than in this country. There is much talk of a new system for British universities in which there would be a two-year general degree followed by a further two-year specialized degree for a selected group, and finally a restricted two-year doctorate group. Whatever system is finally adopted I hope we will bear in mind that we need far more technicians than scientists and technologists. If we train too many of the latter then many of them will have to follow the career of technician, for which their training was not designed and which they will tend to regard as inferior. The result will be a frustrated white-collar class, with all the dangers to society that such a class implies.

A few caveats of this kind were also voiced in the U.S., but the thrust was almost entirely in the direction of more education for more people. It seemed certain that within a few years the college degree would be what the high school diploma was now—the rule rather than the exception. In March the Carnegie Commission on Higher Education urged the country to undertake a program that would eliminate all barriers to college entrance by the year 2000, whether they were based on economics, race, place of residence, or quality of earlier education. Problems loomed, especially since the high schools themselves had not yet learned how to cope with universal attendance, but at least one noted university began to face the problem squarely. The City University of New York, long known for the high academic standards by which it had taught the children of earlier immigrants, began a policy of open admissions. In practice, this meant the acceptance of large numbers of minority group youth who were unprepared for college when measured by the conventional academic yardsticks.

The insufficiencies of the American educational system, which surfaced so glaringly at the college level, were explored by *Fortune* editor Charles Silberman in his thoughtful *Crisis in Education*. Silberman, who had participated in a 3½-year Carnegie Corporation study of U.S. schools, drew a dreary picture of the educational establishment: typically, the teacher's best energies were expended in maintaining discipline, while even the brightest pupil's interest and inquisitiveness were smothered by mindless routine. He saw some hope in the informal, "open-classroom" approach, practiced in a number of British primary schools and a few American ones, in which the young child learns naturally through play and projects that interest him. The method was strongly reminiscent of John Dewey's progressive education, which had fallen into ill repute in the 1950s—largely, Silberman felt, because poorly trained teachers had allowed it to devolve into a slipshod permissiveness. Obviously, teacher training was crucial to the informal approach as well, and some critics questioned whether widespread acceptance was possible at a time when the public temper seemed to be demanding greater economy and stricter discipline.

Searching criticism was also going on in Britain. In an article in *Parents and Schools* in July, P. J. Fitzgerald, professor of law at Kent University, drew attention to the neglect of the law of education. "What gives cause for alarm," he wrote, "is that the law of education is not taught and studied in law schools, is not dealt with frequently in the higher courts and is not the subject of scholarly works." Pointing to the effect that the law had had on education in the U.S.—in, for example, the cases about desegregation and school prayers—he contrasted the uncertainties that existed in Britain about the rights of parents and children and said that they would not be solved until the law, the lawyers, and the courts were brought into the centre of the educational scene.

Suggestions that existing chemistry degree courses were boring, especially for students with lively minds, were expressed by Colin Eaborn, professor at Sussex University, in the August issue of *Chemistry in Britain*. A major defect of the courses was that they gave the student little or no opportunity to exercise his originality, individuality, and creative ability. Eaborn suggested that, in his first year or at the start of his second year, the student be given a research problem that from then on would be his major concern. His work on it would decide his class of degree. These research projects should have a high probability of producing results of value and should involve a wide range of techniques, as well as drawing on substantial areas of chemistry.

Meanwhile, the universities in China were reopening after a long closure resulting from the Cultural Revolution. It was indicated that students would be selected from among workers, peasants, and soldiers who had distinguished themselves in the revolutionary movement. In April Queen Elizabeth II gave royal assent in person to a bill establishing the James Cook University of North Queensland, while in October the planning board was advertising for a vice-chancellor for the projected Murdoch University at Perth, expected to open in 1974. In September the council of the University College of Rhodesia confirmed the statutes of the new University of Rhodesia; this turned the former University College into a full university awarding its own degrees, instead of those of London and Birmingham, with which it had had a special relationship. The transition to full university status had been preceded by some months of demonstrations by students, who feared that the multiracial nature of the college might be ended. However, the original charter of the college, with its requirement that there should be no test of religious belief, race, individuality, or class, remained the basic instrument of incorporation.

In Britain the Open University, a new experiment in adult education that would employ broadcasting, correspondence courses, and a variety of other techniques for its home-based students, enrolled its first 25,000 undergraduates. London University announced some curtailment of its facilities for external degrees. There were fresh moves in Florence, Italy, to set up the European University proposed by the EEC. The project had been hanging fire, though a site had been made available in 1960. In South Africa, Rhodes University in Cape Province launched a £5 million fundraising campaign. J. M. Hyslop, the vice-chancellor, said that South African universities were being strangled by the government's tight-fisted policy and they could no longer wait for the government to wake up to the crisis.

McGill University in Montreal was also feeling a financial pinch. The administrators planned an economy program that included closing the agriculture faculty at Macdonald College and concentrating agricultural instruction on the main campus, closing the museums, shelving plans for more student residences, and withdrawing from intercollegiate sports competition. The moves were made necessary by a growing deficit and by some uncertainty about grants from the Quebec provincial government, which had given preferential treatment to the French-speaking University of Montreal. (L. R. Bu.)

See also Cinema; Libraries; Medicine; Museums and Galleries; Police; Race Relations.

Encyclopædia Britannica Films. *New Tools for Learning* (1952); *Should I Go to College?* (1957); *The Unique Contribution* (1959); *You Can Go a Long Way!* (1961); *George W. Beadle* ("Dialogue for This Decade") (1962); *Sterling McMurrin* ("Dialogue for This Decade") (1962); *Project Discovery: A Demonstration in Education* (1965); *How a Scientist Works* (1967); *The Humanities Films: Their Aims and Uses* (1967); *Project Discovery II: Let Them Learn* (1967); *Suzuki Teaches American Children and Their Mothers* (1967); *Teaching French with Films*, Parts I and II (1967); *Toward Inquiry—Teaching Earth Science* (1967); *The Schempp Case—Bible Reading in the Public Schools* (1969).

Electronics

Discussing electronics without discussing computers would be like discussing the internal-combustion engine without discussing automobiles. For not only has the computer industry been one of the main beneficiaries of modern-day electronics, but it has in turn served to stimulate the electronics industry to unimagined accomplishments.

Minicomputers. Of particular interest to the electronics industry and to the field of computers was the growth of minicomputers. Although still shunned by the giant of the computer industry, IBM, these machines increased in phenomenal numbers. Just a novelty only a few years ago, by 1970 they had become a more than $100 million annual business. About the size of a breadbox, these computers were, simply, small, low-cost versions of general-purpose data-processing computers. Although their capabilities were, of course, limited when compared with a huge million-dollar computer, their portability, versatility, and low cost (usually below $12,000) made them practical for thousands of new applications.

Minicomputers in 1970 employed essentially the same components as the larger machines; thus, their success was not due to a more advanced state of the art. But the overall state of the art was advancing, and this could only mean that the applications for, and the price of, the minicomputers would continue to drop. Experts in the field unhesitatingly predicted that before very many years the price of such a computer would be below $1,000.

Specific applications of minicomputers in 1970 included control of traffic in some parts of Massachusetts. The versatility of the system permitted virtually all traffic-control principles to be applied. In the Pacific Ocean a minicomputer was being applied to sonar testing. In the normal, manual way of conducting such tests, several days are required to collect and analyze data from hundreds of transducer elements. By using a minicomputer scientists can test these several hundred elements in a single "ping" of the system that

The prototype of a new long-range radar able to detect and analyze a target traveling faster than a bullet many miles away undergoes final tests at the Hughes Aircraft Co. in California.

KEYSTONE

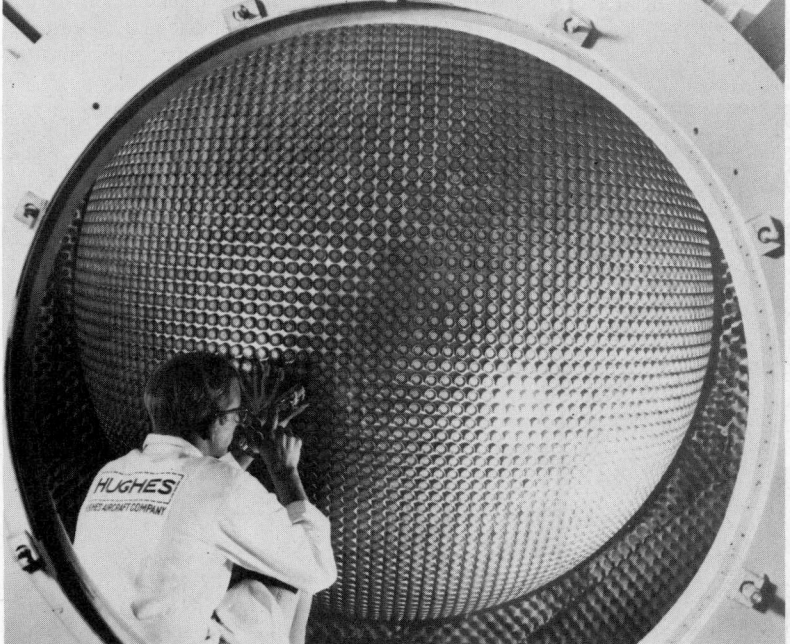

requires only about five seconds for acquisition, correlation, and printing of the data.

In California a new, 250-mph vehicle being developed under contract to the state Department of Transportation was being tested with the aid of a minicomputer. Telemetered data were being accepted at the rate of 32,000 readings per second, thus greatly shortening the test intervals. A minicomputer in Colorado was aiding in the refueling operations of a nuclear generating station, while in California a minicomputer was tied to a supermarket cash register to provide the check-out clerk with accurate price information. Finally, to bring these instruments home, minicomputers were being sold by some stores for general household applications. Not only would this machine balance the checkbook and do budgeting but it would also do all the necessary work associated with menu preparation.

Large Computers. All the excitement about minicomputers, however, did not mean that the importance or value of the large computers was going down. Already in the U.S. there was one computer for every 4,000 people (twice as many per capita as in any other nation), and the number promised to continue rising. Furthermore, as many members of large companies realized, computer time was one of the scarcest commodities within an organization. IBM recognized this fact and produced System 370, which is an extension (not a redesign) of System 360. To demonstrate the vast difference between these new machines and the minicomputers discussed earlier, it is only necessary to examine the price. The IBM 370–165, the larger of IBM's two new models, rented for $98,-715 per month, or sold for $4,674,160. Other firms, such as RCA, Honeywell, and Control Data, were also producing new equipment characterized by exceptional speed and complex microprogramming.

One of the areas that should be watched most closely in the next few years is the application of computers to the communications industry. For instance, Sylvania Electric Products, Inc., demonstrated a computer system that converts and processes speech immediately into digital information for subsequent transmission over communications lines. This "processed" data can be transmitted in approximately $\frac{1}{10}$ the bandwidth required for the transmission of unprocessed signals. And Bell Telephone Laboratories developed a system that works just the opposite;

UPI COMPIX

A supermarket checker uses a kind of "ray gun" to read the price on an item and ring it up. The system is designed to speed up check-outs and keep a constant inventory.

that is, it converts printed English to synthetic speech.

A rather recent use for large computers was time-sharing, a system that permits subscribers throughout the country to be tied in, via communications lines, to one large computer. By charging the user for only the actual processing time (usually seconds), the power of a huge computer can be utilized without too much expense by an engineer miles away.

Semiconductor Technology. The semiconductor industry, upon which most recent development in electronics has been based, did not rest on its laurels during the year. It continued its progress from transistor technology (with a packing density of about 100,000 components per cubic foot) to integrated circuit technology (with a packing density of ten million components per cubic foot), and was rapidly entering the era of MSI (medium-scale integration) and LSI (large-scale integration). As a general comparison, a silicon chip using integrated circuit technology contains the equivalent of approximately 10 transistors; one using MSI techniques, the equivalent of approximately 100 transistors; and one using LSI techniques, the equivalent of approximately 1,000 transistors. Such a chip, when mounted, is the size of a postage stamp or smaller.

Particularly noteworthy in 1970 was change in emphasis within the industry. Whereas in 1969 manufacturers were talking about both MSI and LSI with only slight emphasis on the former, by the end of 1970 they were so busy designing, producing, improving, and selling MSI devices that little was being said about LSI. The usage of microcircuits of this sort was increasing at 24% per year, and seemed likely to continue to do so for the next several years, despite the fact that the cost of developing a single MSI or LSI chip and putting it into operation was over $100,000.

One gets the impression from the various discussions of integrated circuits, MSIs, and LSIs that their great advantage is in the packing density. Actually that is only one of the advantages (and this one not so much because of size itself but because of the ability to save on interconnections); of equal importance is the improvement in reliability and maintainability afforded by these new devices.

One electronic device that began to appear in equip-

Dozens of aircraft paths build up on the display screen of a new computer, built by Goodyear Aerospace Corp., capable of sorting out aircraft on a potential collision course and showing them on the screen.

COURTESY, GOODYEAR AEROSPACE CORPORATION

ment was the light-emitting diode. It could be driven directly by transistors. It converts electricity directly into light, has very low power consumption, is inexpensive, and, most important, has a lifetime of the order of one million hours. This was far better than any existing light bulb. The diode, however, was not nearly as bright as a light bulb.

Memory Systems. For several years the manufacturers of integrated circuits had been promising high-performance memory systems (a most desirable goal, since up to half the cost of a computer is in the memory system). In 1970 these promises came true. Two integrated circuit technologies—bipolar and MOS (metal oxide semiconductor)—were being used to make semiconductor memories. The bipolar memories offered the fastest speeds, but the cost and power dissipation were higher. MOS systems, because of their high circuit-function density and higher yields, as well as lower costs, seemed the most likely candidates for large memories.

At the end of 1970 neither the bipolar nor the MOS systems were ready to take over from the firmly entrenched magnetic core memory, but that event seemed not too far off. For the time being the new systems were limited by their relatively small size, up to 8,192 bits in a module. (In the memories of large computers there must be, literally, millions of bits of information stored.) A significant advantage of the new systems over the magnetic cores was their faster access time. While even the fastest magnetic core memories had a cycle time on the order of $\frac{1}{2}$ microsecond (500 nanoseconds), the access time for the new semiconductor memories was about 100 nanoseconds, with future models expected to be able to operate at about 10 nanoseconds. Memory access time in a computer is important because it is directly related to the speed and power of the computer.

During the year plated wire memories, which consisted of an extremely thin conductive wire coated with magnetic film and sandwiched between the surfaces of a printed circuit board, received considerable publicity. This occurred not so much because those memories were a new technology but rather because they suddenly appeared to be a practical technology. The manufacturing problems were essentially solved, and the memories were appearing on the market. Plated wire memories, which promise high reliability, high speed, low power consumption, and small size, were being used in the Poseidon guidance system, as well as in telemetry data systems. Prices, also, were dropping, and it was predicted that by 1972 the market demand could approach $350 million.

The importance of memory systems was demonstrated by the large number of companies working on them and by the many types of memories under development. Many firms were conducting active research in the field of optical memories. The concept of these memory systems (perhaps they could be called entire computing systems) involved semiconductor technology, holography, and optical communication links. Bell Telephone Laboratories, working in a different field, announced a "bubble" memory that stores information in tiny magnetic spots that move through channels etched on a film. This memory, like the optical systems mentioned above, was, however, still several years away from commercial availability.

Lasers. At the time of its introduction in the early 1960s, the laser was touted as being the ideal instrument for many applications. And, indeed, the laser in 1970 was being used in many ways, from the welding of tiny semiconductors to the cutting of clothes patterns to the drilling of holes in wire-drawing dies. But the application that carried the most exciting promises—communications—had not satisfactorily materialized. It seemed likely that engineers were at that point where they understood the scientific side of the device but where certain practical problems simply defied solution. Research continued, but it appeared unlikely that anything spectacular would occur in the next months. The potential was still there, but by the end of 1970 it remained just potential, at least in the field of communications.

Applications. Probably the most clever and certainly one of the most sophisticated applications for electronics was an electronic timepiece announced by the Hamilton Watch Co. This device, called "a wrist computer programmed to tell time," was, in fact, just that. It contained three major components: a battery, a high-frequency quartz crystal, and a computer module. The computer module contained the equivalent of 3,474 transistors. The display, instead of rotating hands, utilized light-emitting diodes. A user had to press a "demand" button to illuminate the diode display. A single touch lighted the hours and minutes digits for $1\frac{1}{4}$ seconds. If a person kept his finger on the demand button, the hours and minutes disappeared and the digits counted off seconds.

On the more practical side was work being conducted in several countries on electronic pacemakers, devices implanted in a human body to regulate the heartbeats of certain medical patients. The implanted energy source (most often a small battery) must be changed approximately every year and a half. This battery change costs money, inconvenience, and some pain. In the U.S. there was experimentation with a system that converts energy from the human body itself to run the pacemaker. In France and the U.K. a plutonium-activated isotopic battery, which would never need changing during the lifetime of the patient, was under development. Two such plutonium-powered pacemakers were successfully implanted at the National Heart Hospital, London, in July.   (R. E. St.)

See also Industrial Review; Medicine; Telecommunications; Television and Radio.

A blind girl demonstrates a device developed by Stanford Research Institute that enables a blind person to read ordinary print. A scanner guided by her right hand feeds in signals that are translated into Braille-like touch signals read by her left hand.
WIDE WORLD

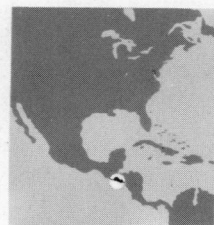

El Salvador

A republic on the Pacific coast of Central America and the smallest country on the isthmus, El Salvador is bounded on the west by Guatemala and on the north and east by Honduras. Area: 8,100 sq.mi. (21,000 sq.km.). Pop. (1970 est.): 3,480,115. Cap. and largest city: San Salvador (pop., 1969 est., 349,933). Language: Spanish. Religion: Roman Catholic. President in 1970, Col. Fidel Sánchez Hernández.

Repercussions from the brief but disruptive open conflict between El Salvador and Honduras in mid-1969 were evident in El Salvador in 1970. Diplomatic and trade relations between the two nations remained severed. However, a series of bilateral peace talks beginning late in January attempted to restore these relations. Held in San José, Costa Rica, the meetings were mediated by José A. Mora, former secretary-general of the Organization of American States (OAS). El Salvador and Honduras each sent three delegates. On June 4, the two countries accepted a plan to establish a demilitarized zone (DMZ) 1.8 mi. wide on either side of their common border; military planes of both nations would not be allowed within three miles of the outer edge of the DMZ. Costa Rica, Guatemala, and Nicaragua, the other participants in the San José talks, acted as "guarantors" of the agreement, which went into effect on July 16. The OAS supervised the withdrawal of Salvadorean and Honduran forces from the DMZ, but allowed each nation to maintain security patrols in certain defined places within the zone, and financed and appointed the military observers who were to see to it that the June 4 agreement was honoured.

The border closing made it imperative that El Salvador find alternative air and sea routes to carry on trade with Nicaragua and Costa Rica, which in prewar times had been accomplished by land across southern Honduras. By the end of 1970 these alternative routes were operating smoothly, but until then El Salvador lost valuable revenue.

The war necessitated the diversion of federal funds from economic enterprises to assist in the care of approximately 80,000 Salvadorean refugees from Honduras who returned to their native land. To offset these adversities brought on by the war, agricultural prospects improved markedly in 1970. The nation's leading agricultural commodity, coffee, increased in output at a time when world coffee prices were more favourable than in past years. Cotton, sugarcane, corn, sorghum, and beans also registered production increases.

Voting took place in March to elect members of the 52-seat Legislative Assembly. The incumbent National Conciliation Party (PCN) gained control of 34 seats; the principal opposition party, the Christian Democratic Party (PDC), won 16 seats. The right-wing Salvadorean Popular Party (PPS) and a new leftist group, the Nationalist Democratic Union (UDN), each won one seat.　　　　(A. D. Bu.)

EL SALVADOR

Education. (1967–68) Primary, pupils 473,449, teachers 12,736; secondary, pupils 48,378, teachers 2,081; vocational, pupils 17,885, teachers 591; teacher training, students 3,210, teachers 295; higher (including 2 universities), students 6,748, teaching staff 1,017.

Finance. Monetary unit: colón, with a par value of 2.50 colones to U.S. $1 (6 colones = £1 sterling). Gold, SDRs, and foreign exchange, central bank: (June 1970) U.S. $77.4 million; (June 1969) U.S. $56.5 million. Budget (1969 est.) balanced at 225,029,000 colones. Gross national product: (1969) 2,362,000,000 colones; (1968) 2,265,000,000 colones. Cost of living (1963 = 100): (June 1970) 109; (June 1969) 104.

Foreign Trade. (1969) Imports 536.2 million colones; exports 505.1 million colones. Import sources (1968): U.S. 29%; Guatemala 16%; Japan 8%; Honduras 7%; West Germany 6%; Venezuela 5%. Export destinations (1968): U.S. 20%; West Germany 20%; Guatemala 15%; Honduras 11%; Costa Rica 8%; Nicaragua 7%; Japan 7%. Main exports: coffee 44%; cotton 9%.

Transport and Communications. Roads (1966) 8,394 km. (including 625 km. of Pan-American Highway). Motor vehicles in use (1968): passenger 31,300; commercial (including buses) 15,900. Railways (1968) c. 700 km. Telephones (Jan. 1969) 36,842. Radio receivers (Dec. 1968) 398,000. Television receivers (Dec. 1967) 45,000.

Agriculture. Production (in 000; metric tons; 1969; 1968 in parentheses): rice c. 77 (72); corn c. 296 (258); sorghum (1968) 124, (1967) 108; coffee c. 138 (c. 114); cotton, lint c. 43 (43); sugar, raw value (1969–70) c. 166, (1968–69) 114. Livestock (in 000; 1968–69): cattle c. 930; pigs c. 300; horses c. 74; chickens c. 2,000.

Industry. Production: cement (1969) 142,000 metric tons; electricity (excluding most industrial production; 1968) 582,000,000 kw-hr.

Emigration:
see Migration, International

Employment, Wages, and Hours

One characteristic common to the world employment situation in 1970 was the increasing militancy of workers. A growing level of strike activity was apparent in developed economies, and in many less developed countries similar conflicts found expression in other, usually less institutionalized ways. The proportion of wages and salaries to other moneys in national incomes was thus an important variable, as seen in Table I.

For the developed market economies, the share of labour in national income was highest in the United Kingdom and lowest in Japan, an interesting fact in view of their contrasting growth performances. On average, the share of labour in the less developed economies was much lower than in the industrialized economies, reflecting their lower level of development and the fact that a great deal of output was by subsistence farmers with no defined wage costs. Even when their surplus of investable funds was greater, the third world economies had to cope with a far heavier burden of population growth than the developed economies. In nearly every country the share of labour in national income increased between 1953 and 1965. The Netherlands, Sweden, and Denmark experienced the largest increases, while the position of the U.S. changed very little.

Employment and Unemployment. The general growth in employment, and consequent reduction in unemployment, in 1968 and 1969 was due partly to increases in agricultural production followed by faster industrial growth in many less developed economies and to a widespread expansion in world trade. Population growth in the third world appeared to slacken very slightly, but remained nearly $2\frac{1}{2}$ times the rate of growth for the richer countries. (*See* Table II.)

Third World Economies. Although the good agricultural harvests of 1968 and 1969 stimulated employment growth in many less developed economies, in many others the situation remained serious as rapid population growth continued to press on the inadequate development of resources.

Table I. Share of Wages and Salaries in National Income

Country	Percent 1953	Percent 1965	Percentage points change
Industrial market:			
Australia	59.3	63.6	4.3
Austria	58.9	65.2	6.3
Belgium	53.7	60.8	7.1
Canada	64.5	68.9	4.4
Denmark	55.5	63.1	7.6
France	57.3	64.5	7.2
Germany, West	58.7	65.7	7.0
Japan	49.7	56.7	7.0
Netherlands	53.9	64.1	10.2
New Zealand	53.9	59.6	5.7
Norway	59.5	65.3	5.8
Sweden	62.6	71.0	8.4
Switzerland	61.2	64.0	2.8
United Kingdom	70.0	74.0	4.0
United States	68.4	69.8	1.4
Average	59.1	65.1	5.9
Third world:			
Ceylon	46.6	48.1	1.5
Colombia	39.4	44.3	4.9
Ecuador	47.1	51.2	4.1
Guyana	52.1	61.5	9.4
Honduras	42.4	51.3	8.9
Jamaica	58.3	61.4	3.1
Korea, South	25.1	30.8	5.7
Mauritius	54.1	58.1	4.0
Panama	68.7	69.0	0.3
Puerto Rico	67.2	71.5	4.3
Venezuela	57.9	56.8	−1.1
Average	50.8	54.9	4.1

Source: Calculated from United Nations, *Year Book of National Accounts* (1968).

The figures in Table III should be regarded with some caution, but they show that the average increase in recorded unemployment in the sample of third world countries in 1969 was under 1%. This average figure concealed a diversity of changes. In Singapore, for example, unemployment continued to fall, owing to the 20% annual rate of increase in industrial production supported by foreign investment. In mid-1970 restrictions on immigration and work permits were relaxed in an attempt to ease the labour shortage.

In South Korea, owing to the rapid expansion of agriculture and of industrial production stimulated by a substantial construction boom, unemployment continued to fall as real national product maintained its 15% growth rate. In Taiwan the 1969 harvest was very poor because of storm damage and, although industrial production and exports were expanding rapidly, the slackening of growth led to a considerable rise in unemployment.

In Ceylon, despite rapid industrial growth of over 10%, unemployment increased by 15% in 1969, adding to the already high level of some one-third of a million. Unemployment among university graduates continued to be a severe problem. In Pakistan, with a high rate of inflation, there was much labour unrest in 1969 as the trade unions tried to force reluctant employers to pay the minimum wage introduced at midyear. Despite good harvests in India in 1969, unemployment continued to grow.

Unemployment rose considerably in Chile in 1969 as industrial and agricultural growth was quite slow. Following the September 1970 election, in which a Marxist presidential candidate won a plurality of the popular vote, there was a huge capital flight from the country and a severe economic depression as purchases of consumer goods and house construction dwindled. In Greece, unemployment declined fairly steadily as industrial production, stimulated by an export boom, grew at over 10%. In Zambia, rapid economic growth in 1969 was accompanied by sudden and large increases in minimum wages, which reduced employment, particularly in commercial agriculture.

Industrial Market Economies. Although there was

a rapid rise in 1968 in the trade of the more developed economies, some were still being affected by the recession of 1967. Employment changes were, on average, negligible, and unemployment continued to rise, except in the U.S., Japan, West Germany, and the Netherlands, where expansion had begun earlier. But by 1969 the boom was widespread and the average decrease in unemployment was nearly 10%, with industrial employment tending to rise quite strongly (*see* Table IV). However, as measures of economic restraint began to take effect, it was likely that 1970 as a whole would see some general increase in unemployment.

In the U.S. there was a further slowing down of growth as the government, alarmed by the high rate of price inflation, cut public spending and imposed credit restrictions. By mid-1970 there had been a massive 41% rise in unemployment; the unemployment rate reached 5.8% of the labour force by November. Changes in unemployment in Canada were unusual because active immigration policies had increased the labour force by over 3% annually in the last five years. Thus, any slight slackening of employment growth resulted in a large increase in unemployment. Slower growth of output and further increases in unemployment were likely to continue. Japan's remarkably high growth rate did not slacken; employment continued to rise and unemployment to fall.

A rapid increase in imports into West Germany as domestic demand expanded faster than supply was responsible for a great deal of Europe's boom. The fall in West German unemployment from the high levels of 1967 was massive and the labour force was further augmented by foreign workers.

France, which had recovered from the 1968 unemployment during 1969, suffered a further increase in unemployment as the government attempted to re-

Table II. Employment, Unemployment, and Population

Changes for 1968 over 1967 (%)

Country	Employment General	Employment Manufacturing	Numbers unemployed	Population
Third world:				
Honduras, British	9.8	2.1	—	0.9
Korea, South	3.8	17.6	−15.9	2.3
Philippines	2.5	2.7	5.2	3.5
Puerto Rico	2.3	7.7	−3.1	1.0
Singapore	5.3	7.4	−15.1	1.6
Taiwan	4.7	−6.9	−23.4	2.4
Tanzania	0.9*	13.3	—	2.7
Trinidad	−1.4*	—	−1.9	1.1
Turkey	12.8*	15.4	—	2.5
Zambia	3.2	6.0	5.4	3.4
Average	4.4	7.3	−7.0	2.2
Industrial market:				
Australia	2.5	2.3	1.6	1.9
Austria	−0.9	−1.7	9.6	0.4
Belgium	−0.3	−1.3	20.4	0.4
Canada	2.2	−0.8	21.3	1.6
France	−1.5*	−2.3	29.5	0.8
Germany, West	0.3	3.1	−29.5	0.6
Italy	−0.2	2.0	0.7	0.8
Japan	1.7	0.4	−6.4	1.2
Netherlands	0.8	−1.0	−8.8	1.0
Norway	0.9	−0.6	44.7	0.9
Sweden	1.2	−3.2	4.9	0.6
United Kingdom	−0.7	−1.0	4.9	0.4
United States	2.0	1.7	−5.3	1.0
Average	0.6	−0.3	6.7	0.9
Planned economies:				
Bulgaria	1.6	1.2	—	0.7
Czechoslovakia	1.8	0.9	—	0.4
Germany, East	1.1	0.3	—	0
Hungary	2.0	4.1	—	0.4
Poland	0.1	3.6	—	1.1
Romania	2.2	4.3	—	2.3
Yugoslavia	0.6	−0.3	—	1.0
U.S.S.R.	2.5	3.7	—	1.0
Average	1.5	2.2	—	0.9

*Nonagricultural sector.
Sources: International Labour Office, *Yearbook of Labour Statistics* (1969); United Nations, *Monthly Bulletin of Statistics* (August 1970).

Table III. Unemployment: Third World

Change over previous year (%)

Country	1968	1969
Burma	−21.6	3.7
Ceylon	6.5	15.2
Cyprus	11.1	−14.8
Chile	2.7	16.6*
Ghana	5.0	−30.6*
Greece	−11.7	−9.8
Guyana	−14.5	−16.3
India	7.3	10.4
Korea, South	−15.9	−7.3*
Malaysia	9.0	—
Pakistan	−1.5	18.9
Puerto Rico	−3.1	−8.6
Sierra Leone	1.5	5.5
Singapore	−15.2	−9.5
Taiwan	−23.4	18.1
Zambia	5.4	18.5
Average	−3.7	0.7

*June 1968 to June 1969.
Source: International Labour Office, *Bulletin of Labour Statistics* (second quarter 1970).

Table IV. Employment in Manufacturing in Industrial Market Economies

Changes over previous year (%)

Country	Employment 1969	1970*	Unemployment 1969	1970*
Canada	2.5	−2.3	0	32.3
United States	2.0	−2.8	0.4	40.7
Japan	3.5	2.7	−3.4	−5.1
Austria	3.1	3.8	−5.6	−8.2
Belgium	3.3	1.1	−17.5	−17.9
France	1.9	2.2	−12.2	11.9
Germany, West	5.7	4.4	−44.8	−18.5
Ireland	6.1	3.2†	−2.7	28.6
Italy	3.1	2.4	−4.5	−10.8
Netherlands	0.9	0 †	−22.1	−14.0
Norway	1.1	3.3	−5.5	−26.3
Sweden	−0.8	−6.9	−10.5	−6.8
United Kingdom	1.4	−0.7	−0.7	9.1
Average	2.6	0.8	−9.9	1.2

*Second quarter over second quarter 1969.
†First quarter 1969 over first quarter 1968.
Source: Organization for Economic Cooperation and Development, *Main Economic Indicators* (September 1970).

strain expansion of domestic demand in order to preserve the benefits of the devaluation and improve the balance of trade. In Italy, gross national product expanded rapidly despite severe disruption caused by strikes in the second half of 1969, which cost about 2% of the year's output.

The Netherlands continued to enjoy a strong export-led boom, which caused a rapid drop in unemployment so that by the end of 1969 unfilled vacancies were 2½ times greater than the number of job seekers. Austria, too, had an accelerating growth of output due to an export boom, and this was clearly seen in the expansion of industrial employment. Belgium was in a similar position, but with the addition of a considerable investment boom. In Ireland, growth of output and employment in 1969 continued to be strong, but a growing proportion of firms were unable to increase output for lack of skilled labour.

In the U.K. continued cautious policies of economic restraint and a massive deflationary budget surplus resulted in a rise in unemployment in the second quarter of 1970. In the first quarter there were twice as many unemployed as there were job vacancies, and the position continued to deteriorate as unemployment rose to 2½% of the labour force. It should be noted, however, that the introduction of payments to laid-off workers and earnings-related unemployment benefits meant that the unemployed could afford to take longer in finding suitable jobs.

Centrally Planned Economies. In general, growth in the Communist countries continued to be rapid in 1969 (*see* Table V). Nearly all countries, however, experienced severe shortages of labour, and this intensified the search for methods of stimulating productivity.

The U.S.S.R. suffered a bad harvest in 1969 and delays in meeting construction targets caused by labour shortages. The expansion of employment was about 2%, but the productivity growth of 5% was considered insufficient, as rapidly rising money wages encountered a slow growth of supply. The labour shortage was so acute that in October 1969 it was decided that factories should dismiss "superfluous" labour and divide their wages among the remaining workers, but only in return for higher productivity.

Yugoslavia, the most decentralized and open of all the Communist economies, enjoyed the fastest rate of growth and suffered from the highest rate of inflation. While wages soared, unemployment remained a problem. Czechoslovakia, too, suffered from a high rate of growth of wages, but the rate of growth of output in 1969 was very slow and the need to stimulate the output of food and consumer goods was urgent. In Hungary, the demand for labour in 1969 was very strong as industry continued to utilize labour wastefully and investment was badly planned. By mid-1970, however, there were signs that economic reforms were beginning to have an effect.

In Poland, although the 1969 harvest was exceptionally unfavourable and industrial performance patchy, overall growth was rapid and employment and wages rose considerably. Bulgaria's fast economic growth was being threatened by labour shortages. Romania had also begun to suffer increasingly severe labour shortages, which necessitated more flexible incentive wage systems. The economy, however, was badly damaged by floods early in 1970.

Wages. *Industrial Market Economies.* The movement of money and real wages and of consumer prices is shown in Table VIII. The average rate of increase of money wages was accelerating: 7.8% in 1968, 9.1% in 1969, and about 12% in 1970. This acceleration was reflected quite strongly in real wage movements as the rate of price inflation lagged, although itself accelerating from 3.8% in 1968 to 4.4% in 1969 to an average of 5.3% in 1970. The higher rates of growth of wages were partly due to increasing pressures on labour markets, and partly to an upsurge of trade union militancy. (*See* LABOUR UNIONS.)

In the U.S., the policies of monetary and fiscal restraint and the consequent rise in unemployment caused a slowing down in the rate of growth of money wages. But, as an anti-inflationary policy, restraint appeared to be a conspicuous failure: prices continued to rise at a rate even more rapid than before, with real wages actually falling in the first half of 1970. Pressure on prices was especially strong during 1969 because money wages rose much faster than productivity, thus pushing up labour costs per unit of

Table V. Output, Employment, Wages, and Prices: Centrally Planned Economies

Change in 1969 over 1968 (%)

Country	Industrial output	Manufacturing employment	Average earnings	Consumer prices
Bulgaria	10.8	2.1	4.4	—
Czechoslovakia	2.5	—	6.3	3.7*
Hungary	2.7	2.8	3.5	1.3
Poland	9.1	3.7	4.4	1.3
Romania	9.1	5.6	—	—
U.S.S.R.	7.0	2.1†	5.0‡	—
Yugoslavia	11.4	3.6	15.5	10.8

*January 1969 to January 1970.
†Estimated by applying productivity growth rate of 4.8% to output growth.
‡Real income.
Source: International Labour Office, *Bulletin of Labour Statistics* (second quarter 1970); *Economist* Intelligence Unit *Reports* and *Annual Supplements* on individual countries.

Table VI. Weekly Hours of Work in Manufacturing

Country	1968	1969	Absolute change
Austria	43.7	43.7	0
Canada	40.3	40.0	−.3
Germany, West	43.0	43.8	.8
France	45.3	45.4	.1
Japan*	44.6	43.9	−.7
Ireland*	43.7	42.9	−.8
New Zealand	40.2	40.6	.4
Norway	36.7	35.6	−1.1
Switzerland	44.6	44.6	0
United Kingdom	45.8	45.7	−.1
United States	40.7	40.6	−.1
Average	42.6	42.4	−.2

*September of each year.
Source: International Labour Office, *Bulletin of Labour Statistics* (second quarter 1970).

output and reducing profit margins quite substantially.

Despite Canadian policies of monetary and fiscal restraint, there was no diminution in the rapid rate of increase of money wages, but requests by the government to employers at the beginning of 1970 to hold down price increases seemed to be having some effect on price inflation. As the trade unions refused to cooperate in the prices and incomes policy, the growth rate of real wages increased in 1970 and profit margins were reduced.

In Japan, the rapid rate of growth of exports and investments continued and real national product expanded by 13% in 1969. Productivity growth in industry remained high, and this led to considerable wage claims at the beginning of both 1969 and 1970 and to some acceleration in the rate of wage and price increases. But, relative to the rapid growth and persistently favourable balance of payments, inflation was not as crucial a problem for Japan as for most other countries.

In West Germany, the rate of money wage increase jumped from 4.4% in 1968 to 9.1% in 1969. The labour market was very strained, and a sudden increase in workers' militancy, with several wildcat strikes in the steel and engineering industries, was successful in obtaining wage increases of 10–12%. These set a pattern for other sectors to follow. However, as labour productivity was also rising rapidly, the wage spurt did not have much immediate effect on prices, and real wages increased considerably.

Wage increases remained high in France despite monetary and fiscal restraint following the devaluation of August 1969. A temporary general price freeze was imposed immediately after devaluation, and although this was later relaxed, the rate of price inflation diminished slightly so that the growth of real wages remained constant. The rate of price inflation, however, was still high and, in October 1969, a 3.8% increase in the minimum guaranteed wage was given in compensation for the increased cost of living.

Although the Netherlands government imposed a price freeze in April 1969, the measure had an impact only in the second half of the year. The rise in prices caused by the introduction of a value-added tax led to demands for wage increases, and money wages rose by 9.3% during the year. In September 1969 the government passed a wage control bill entitling it to freeze wages and invalidate collective agreements judged not to be in the best interests of the economy.

In Austria a sharp increase in wages was due largely to wage changes in the public sector. In Italy, between the second quarter of 1969 and the second quarter of 1970, wages—negotiated in an atmosphere of considerable militancy—had risen by 21%. In ad-

dition, the working week was to be reduced by four hours within three years, beginning with a decrease of one hour at the start of 1970.

In Sweden, where the demand for labour was very strong and immigration was rising, wage settlements during 1969 were quite generous. A 17% increase for a two-year period was given to the blue-collar workers in June. A year later the rate of price inflation had become so rapid that the government introduced a direct price freeze in an effort to reduce the next round of wage increases.

In Denmark, too, a price freeze was imposed as inflation accelerated and the balance of payments deteriorated alarmingly. Danish wages and prices were rising rapidly. Norway introduced a price freeze prior to the changeover to a value-added tax in January 1970. But the freeze was gradually lifted and the rate of wage increase accelerated with prices.

In the U.K., despite a slowing down in the rate of economic growth and high unemployment levels, the rate of wage increase continued to be high in 1969, accelerating still further in 1970. Government powers to defer wage increases expired at the end of 1969 and were not renewed. But even before this, wage increases in excess of the ceiling of $2\frac{1}{2}$–$4\frac{1}{2}$% had been granted in the public sector, and trade union pressure forced the private sector to exceed these increases.

Third World Economies. The growth of money wages in manufacturing in less developed economies continued to be rapid in 1968 and 1969, and in common with the rest of the world, price inflation ac-

Table VII. Money and Real Wages in Manufacturing and Consumer Prices: Third World

Changes over previous year (%)

Country	Money wages 1968	Money wages 1969	Real wages 1968	Real wages 1969	Prices 1968	Prices 1969
Brazil	28.6	—	3.5	—	24.2	23.2
Ceylon*	16.3	0	9.8	−6.8	5.9	7.3
Chile	34.2	38.3	5.9	8.9	26.6	27.0
Colombia	10.3	8.7	4.2	−2.4	5.8	11.4
Ghana	12.3	—	2.2	—	9.9	8.9
Greece	7.3	10.2	6.9	7.6	0.4	2.4
Guatemala	3.2	4.6	1.2	2.5	2.0	2.1
Korea, South	26.5	34.2	14.2	19.4	10.8	12.4
Mexico	5.2	2.3	2.8	−0.6	2.3	2.9
Philippines*	0.5	4.0	0	1.1	0.5	2.9
Puerto Rico	11.0	7.6	8.0	4.2	2.8	3.2
Sierra Leone	−6.9	—	−8.2	—	1.4	3.3
Taiwan	11.4	—	3.3	—	7.9	5.1
Tanzania	0.9	—	−2.4	—	3.4	1.0
Trinidad & Tobago*	1.6	3.9	−6.0	1.3	8.2	2.5
Average†	10.8	11.4	3.0	3.5	7.5	7.7

*Nonagricultural sector.
†Average of available statistics.
Sources: International Labour Office, *Bulletin of Labour Statistics* (second quarter 1970) and *Supplement to the Bulletin of Labour Statistics* (July and August 1970).

Table VIII. Money and Real Wages in Manufacturing and Consumer Prices: Industrial Market Economies

Changes over previous year (%)

Country	Money wages 1969	Money wages 1970*	Real wages 1969	Real wages 1970*	Prices 1969	Prices 1970*
Canada	8.3	8.5	3.6	4.5	4.5	3.7
United States	6.6	5.4	1.1	−0.6	5.4	6.1
Japan	16.4	17.3	10.7	9.0	5.2	7.6
Austria	5.8	11.9	2.4	7.4	3.4	4.1
Belgium	8.0	10.6	4.0	6.3	3.8	4.1
Denmark	11.5	—	7.5	—	3.7	5.7
France	11.3	10.6	4.6	4.6	6.4	5.8
Germany, West	9.1	12.7†	6.2	9.0†	2.7	3.5†
Ireland	12.8	12.5†	5.1	6.2†	7.3	5.9†
Italy	7.5	21.0	4.8	15.1	2.6	5.1
Netherlands	9.3	7.3	1.7	3.8	7.5	3.5
Norway	9.7	10.1	6.3	0.6	3.3	9.5
Sweden	8.1	16.4	5.3	9.1	2.7	6.7
Switzerland	4.7	6.0	2.1	2.9	2.5	3.0
United Kingdom	7.9	11.8	2.3	5.7	5.5	5.8
Average	9.1	11.6	4.5	6.0	4.4	5.3

*Second quarter 1970 over second quarter 1969.
†First quarter 1970 over first quarter 1969.
Source: Organization for Economic Cooperation and Development, *Main Economic Indicators* (September 1970).

THE "NEW YORK TIMES"

Longshoremen's hiring-hall practices for casual dock workers, as shown above, are being replaced with a computer system in the New York City area.

celerated (*see* Table VII). Minimum wages in Ceylon were held constant during 1969 in an effort to reduce the rate of price inflation, but with no success. In May 1970 a left-wing coalition won an overwhelming victory over the ruling United National Party, and increases in wages, together with statutory price control, were likely. In South Korea, the rapid advance of the economy was accompanied by even more rapid wage inflation, and unit labour costs were forcing a rapid rise in prices. Prices in Greece, after being stabilized by military decree in 1967, began to rise, and wages in the public sector and for the armed forces were increased considerably in 1969. In Chile price inflation in 1969 was 27%, and likely to be over 30% in 1970. Industrial relations deteriorated as trade unions pushed their wage claims vigorously.

In Trinidad and Tobago, a spurt of price inflation in 1968 led to a fall in real wages and to increased trade union militancy. This disturbed background of industrial relations set the scene for the army mutiny and the riots of April 1970; unemployment was about 15% of the labour force. Tanzania's 1967 policy of wage-price control appeared to be remarkably effective: in 1969 price inflation was down to 1%; manufacturing wages increased by only 0.9% in 1968.

Hours. Table VI gives data on weekly hours of work in industrial market economies. On average the working week shortened slightly during 1968–69. In Norway there was a marked shortening of the working week, as contractual hours were cut by 5.5% from 45 to 42.5 hours in mid-1968. There were decreases also in Japan and Ireland. Elsewhere there was little change, except for West Germany where the working week increased in response to the shortage of labour. The working week remained longest in the U.K. and shortest in Norway. (D. A. S. J.)

See also Economics; Economy, World; Income, National; Industrial Review; Prices.

ENCYCLOPÆDIA BRITANNICA FILMS. *Working Together* (1952); *Walter P. Reuther* ("Dialogue for This Decade") (1963); *The Industrial Revolution—Beginnings in the United States* (1968); *The Rise of Labor* (1968); *The Industrial Worker* (1969); *The Rise of Big Business* (1970).

Endocrinology:
see Medicine

Engineering Projects

Bridges. *Suspension Bridges.* Work began in 1970 on the Bosporus Bridge. Linking Europe and Asia across the Bosporus Strait in Turkey, this would be the longest bridge in the world outside the U.S., with a central span of 3,524 ft. Similar in conception to the Severn Bridge in the U.K., it had a number of original features; besides being longer and wider (width of deck, 110 ft.), the end spans (758 ft. and 837 ft. on the European and Asian banks, respectively) would not be suspended but carried by steel columns articulated at the top and at the foot, thus reducing flexion in the pylons and allowing the cables to join the anchorings at a more abrupt slope.

Two suspension bridges came into use in Canada: one, between Dartmouth and Halifax, N.S., had a 1,400-ft. central span flanked by two spans of 514 ft., and an orthotropic deck; the other, the Frontenac Bridge across the St. Lawrence at Quebec, was the largest in Canada, with spans of 617 ft., 2,190 ft., and 617 ft.

Cable-Stayed Bridges. In West Germany, following the opening in 1969 of the Ludwigshafen Bridge, consisting of a span of about 920 ft. suspended from a tetrapod pylon by two groups of cables, work began on a number of constructions of that type. The Duisburg Bridge across the Rhine, which set a new world record with a central span of 1,148 ft., had an all-welded deck comprising a triple-webbed caisson and an orthotropic plate. A second bridge over the Rhine, between Mannheim and Ludwigshafen, downstream from the Konrad Adenauer Bridge, consisted of two spans, a metal one of 944 ft. and a concrete one of 476 ft. Although of different materials, the spans were joined in such a way as to ensure continuity of moment. The new Düsseldorf Bridge (five spans of 169 ft. each, 845 ft., 246 ft.) was under construction alongside the old bridge and, after the latter was demolished, would be moved sideways to replace it.

Cable-stayed bridges were also completed or under construction in other parts of the world. The Leblanc-Papineau Bridge across the Rivière des Prairies between Laval and Montreal (295 ft., 790 ft., 295 ft.) had an orthotropic deck with space for six traffic lanes. The bridge over the Yodo River at Osaka, Jap., with a 709-ft. central span, had A-shaped pylons specially designed for stability in earthquakes.

Construction of the West Gate cable-stayed box girder bridge on the Lower Yarra at Melbourne, Austr., was halted in October when one of the side spans collapsed, killing 34 of the men working on it. A royal commission was set up to investigate the cause of the failure. (*See* DISASTERS.)

Other Metal Bridges. Among inclined-prop bridges under construction was one spanning a gorge on the Santiago River near Guadalajara, Mex. At a height of 425 ft., its overall length was 984 ft., with the points of attachment of the props to the deck 360 ft. apart. Similar in type was the Caronte Viaduct in France, which crossed the access channel to the Étang de Berre at a height of 150 ft.; its main structure, 984 ft. long, had an opening of 689 ft. between the prop bearings, and the points of attachment to the deck were 426 ft. apart.

While inclined-prop bridges were particularly suitable for spans at considerable heights, orthotropically decked box girder bridges were being increasingly adopted for long spans because of the need to limit deadweight. However, work on an outstanding example of this type, the Milford Haven road bridge on the Cleddau River, Wales, was interrupted when a section collapsed under construction. Following this accident, which cost four lives, and the subsequent Melbourne disaster, in November the British government began an independent inquiry into the design and construction of large box girder bridges. When completed, the Milford Haven bridge was to have the longest unsupported span in Europe (253 ft., 490 ft., 700 ft., 490 ft., three of 252 ft. each).

Another girder bridge of similar design was the new viaduct over the Danube at Vienna with three spans of 260 ft., 690 ft., and 390 ft., while in California the navigable channel of San Diego Bay was also being bridged by three girder spans (two of 660 ft., 560 ft.).

Prestressed Concrete Bridges. The successive cantilevering form of construction was being used for a number of large spans. However, in the U.S., construction of the Three Sisters Bridge over the Potomac was halted by court order when the piers were being erected because the design, which provided for a central span of 750 ft., was considered dangerous. The world record in this class of construction was still held by the Bendorf Bridge in West Germany with a span of 682 ft.

Other cantilevered viaducts notable for the length of their central spans included: the Kingston Bridge at Glasgow, Scot. (205 ft., 470 ft., 205 ft.), each of whose parallel components had a useful width of 68 ft.; and the Huccorgne Viaduct over the Mehaigne Valley, Belgium (246 ft.), also consisting of parallel caissons.

For very long structures, however, the form of construction using prefabricated voussoirs was preferred. This method was employed for the 8½-mi. bridge between Rio de Janeiro and Niterói, Braz., of which five miles was made up of 262-ft. caisson girders of uniform depth (to simplify prefabrication). In France the method was applied to several structures: at Tours (164 ft., seven of 230 ft. each, 164 ft.), Aramon (154 ft., five of 256 ft. each, 154 ft.), and Bourg-Saint-Andéol (147 ft., three of 256 ft. each, 154 ft.).

For spans of about 80 to 150 ft., the use of prefabricated, prestressed concrete girders remained the most economical form of construction, the current tendency being to eliminate crossbeams, as in the Weaver Valley Bridge, England, with 30 approach spans of 90 ft. each. For the erection of continuous structures with spans of between 100 and 200 ft., the use of self-launching centring proved economical where the overall length was sufficient to justify the cost of the equipment. This method was employed at Saag, Aus., on a viaduct comprising 50 spans of about 98 ft. each with twin caisson-section decks, and on the Incarville Viaduct, France, also with twin decks, each consisting of plates with two longitudinal trapezoidal ribs, but no crossbeams.   (Ro. Ch.)

Buildings. In 1970 various approaches were employed to provide improved housing for slum areas in the United States. One of the continuing problems was the dislocation of the residents in the area while the rebuilding was in process. An urban renewal concept by Frost Associates of New York City represented a novel approach to this problem. As reported in the *Architectural Forum,* it involved the concept of redeveloping one block at a time with a minimum dislocation of the existing residents. According to the concept, residential high-rise towers were to be built in the backyards of the existing homes to provide new residences for the families living in the immediate area. After the families were relocated in the new high-rise structure or structures, the existing outmoded tenements were to be replaced with nonresidential buildings that were to be uniformly no more than four stories in height. It was planned, additionally, that the roofs of these low-rise buildings would be made into recreational areas for the children so that they would not have to play in the streets.

The construction procedure called for the initiation of a project by locating a construction site where there was adequate space on a street near the end of a block. On this site could be constructed the first residential tower. If construction required the razing of a building, this would be done, but the relocation of families would be kept to a minimum. The foundation and the concrete core of the building, which would contain the elevators, stairs, and exit halls of the dwelling units, would be built first, as would the lobby space between the tower core and the street entrance. Around the top of the tower a structure would be built so that dwelling units could be hung below it. The plan specified further that the tower's dwelling units were to be built at an off-site location while the core was under construction. These units were to be built according to methods that would be most suitable for complete fabrication. The completed dwelling units would be delivered to the building site by trucks and would be lifted into place around the core by a derrick on top of the core. When the residential tower was completed, the families in the nearby tenements were to be moved into it. The businesses in the block were then to be relocated into vacant commercial spaces in the block, or nearby, so that the vacated buildings could be demolished and the new uniform buildings constructed. As the new low-rise structures were completed, the displaced businesses could be moved in along with new businesses that wished to locate in the area.

Plans to meet a variety of housing needs, such as the one proposed by Frost Associates, underlined the importance of industrialized systems for building construction. One of these reported on in 1970 was the Townland Building System. According to the *Apartment Construction News,* this system created synthetic land by providing pedestrian streets or walk-

Denmark's new suspension Lillebælt Bridge, linking Fyn and Jutland, is the longest bridge of its kind in Europe, with a main span of 1,968 ft. and side spans of 787 ft.

NORDISK PRESSEFOTO FROM PICTORIAL PARADE

LONDON "DAILY EXPRESS"
FROM PICTORIAL PARADE

The 1,200-ft.
Van Staden's Gorge Bridge
under construction near
Port Elizabeth, S.Af.,
was to be the largest
concrete arch bridge
in Africa upon
completion in mid-1971.

ways and backyards as high as 15 stories up in the air. The objective of this plan was to achieve the economics of high-rise construction and at the same time to provide the amenities of a town house. It was reported that the system consisted of two subsystems. The first comprised a long-span structural framework which contained precast concrete components. At three-story intervals there were to be spandrels supporting deck slabs. Within the structural framework there were to be three-story, metal-frame dwelling units. These three-story units were to be factory-built with preassembled utility cores. In front of each housing unit there was to be a pedestrian walkway and, in the back, an earthfill backyard.

Aside from unique projects such as those described, the major thrust of industrialized housing systems was to integrate mass-production techniques into building construction. Efforts to do this involved both on-site and off-site production. As these alternatives were pursued, the economies of large-scale off-site production appeared to outweigh the transportation costs. The U.S. Department of Housing and Urban Development (HUD), through its program "Operation Breakthrough," stimulated a great deal of interest in building systems in 1970. The purpose of HUD's program had been to speed up the construction of housing for low- and middle-income families by bringing the techniques of mass production into the construction field. Stirling Homex, a firm engaged in the manufacture of housing units, presented a system to HUD by means of which, it claimed, the unit was so completely finished at the factory that a family could move in immediately after the unit was installed on the construction site. Such an installation required about four hours. Every dwelling unit contained three or four modules, each 12 by 24 by 9 ft. The firm reported that a factory-built module could be completely ready for occupancy in 45 minutes. The company had three projects under way in New York State in 1970 in which the system was being used. In addition to the low-rise product, Stirling was developing a high-rise that would use the same type of modules. For such a building the steel beams and concrete flooring would be raised as a unit by use of an electronically controlled jacking system.

The condominium arrangement—individual ownership of a residential unit in a multiunit structure—continued to exert a significant influence on the design of residential buildings in the United States in 1970. It was reported in *Apartment Construction News* that the Miami, Fla., area was one of the strongest condominium apartment markets in the nation.

These developments were bringing forth interesting and imaginative structures and land-use plans. An example was Century 21, a 7,000-unit condominium project located only a short distance from the centre of Miami on a 160-ac. tract, almost completely surrounded by water. Only 40% of the land was to be covered by buildings. Each cluster or neighbourhood was designed to have a 27-story and 21-story building plus a limited number of town houses, which were to be placed between bays, lakes, and lagoons. The erection of the towers of multistory buildings involved the use of the Monroe slip form concrete system for core construction. (C. C. O.)

Dams. *Europe.* In Spain three important dams under construction were, on the Genil River, the Contreras concrete gravity dam (height 400 ft., volume 679,500 cu.yd., storage 712,800 ac-ft.) and the Iznajar concrete gravity dam (height 390 ft., volume 1,830,-000 cu.yd., storage 793,800 ac-ft.), and, on the Aguas Blancas River, the Quentar arch dam (height 436 ft., volume 230,000 cu.yd., storage 11,016,000 ac-ft.).

In the United Kingdom, the Llyn Brianne rockfill dam on the Towy River (height 300 ft., volume 2.5 million cu.yd.) was under construction. Romania had the Paltinul arch dam on the Doftana River (height 344 ft., volume 366,000 cu.yd., storage 48,600 ac-ft.) and the Vidra earthfill dam on the Lotru River (height 397 ft., volume 4,574,000 cu.yd., storage 275,400 ac-ft.) in the course of construction. The Krichim concrete gravity dam on the Vucha River in Bulgaria was being built, with a height of 338 ft. and a volume of 497,000 cu.yd., while in Yugoslavia, work was in progress on the Rama earthfill dam on the Rama River (height 328 ft., volume 1,050,000 cu.yd., storage 394,470 ac-ft.).

There was considerable activity in Turkey, where the Kozan rockfill dam, with a central clay core, on the Kilgen River (height 272 ft., volume 1,562,000 cu.yd.) was scheduled for completion in 1970. The dam area was known to be seismically active, and horizontally acting earthquake accelerations up to $0.15\,G$ were a factor in the design of the embankment, situated in a narrow limestone gorge. Other Turkish developments included a start in 1970 on the five years' work required to build the Adiguzel arch dam on the Buyuk Menderes River (height 675 ft., crest length 1,568 ft., volume 1,184,000 cu.yd., and storage capacity 1,864,625 ac-ft.).

Construction continued in the U.S.S.R. on the Inguri Dam, near the Black Sea, to be the world's highest concrete arch dam at 892 ft., and on the Nurek Dam on the Vakhsh River, near the border of Afghanistan, planned to be 1,017 ft. high, of earth. Two others under construction were the Charvakskaya earth and rockfill dam, on the Chirchik River (height 551 ft., crest length 2,499 ft., volume about 25 million cu.yd., storage 1,620,000 ac-ft.), and the Sayano-Shushenskaya arch dam on the Yenisei (height 774 ft., crest length 3,503 ft., volume about 12 million cu.yd., storage 25,353,000 ac-ft.).

Asia. The Reza Shah Kabir thin-arch multipurpose dam on the Karun River in Iran, begun in December 1969, was under construction (height 656 ft., crest length 1,247 ft., thickness at base 115 ft.). It was founded on limestone under 30 ft. of alluvium. Construction was continued in Pakistan on the Tarbela earth and rockfill dam on the Indus, the world's largest man-made mountain, with a height of 485 ft., a length of 9,000 ft., and a volume of 186 million cu.yd. Among dams under construction in India was the Cheruthoni concrete gravity dam on the river of that name (height 446 ft., crest length 2,136 ft., volume 2,353,000 cu.yd.).

In the Far East, Thailand had work in progress on the Sirikit earthfill dam on the Nan River (height 338 ft., crest length 2,560 ft., volume 13,097,500 cu.yd., storage 7,296,429 ac-ft.). In Malaysia, the Muda reinforced concrete buttress dam with short gravity wings (height 105 ft., crest length 720 ft.) neared completion and was of engineering interest because of an unusual arrangement of post-tensioned steel cables to anchor the dam to its foundations. Japanese work included the Shintoyone arch dam on the Onyu River (height 374 ft., volume 410,700 cu.yd.) and the Sameura concrete gravity dam on the Yoshino River (height 347 ft., volume 1,570,000 cu.yd., storage 256,000 ac-ft.).

North and South America. In the U.S. construction of the Auburn double-curvature arch dam on the North Fork of the American River was in its early stages. The dam's height was to be 680 ft., arch length 3,500 ft., and volume 6 million cu.yd. The Kentucky rockfill dam (1,420 ft. in length and 282 ft. high, with volume of approximately 3 million cu.yd.) was under construction. Also being built was the Grasshopper

Hollow earthfill dam (height 350 ft., volume 2.5 million cu.yd.). In 1970 approximately 270 dams were under construction in the U.S., and 400 more were projected. In Canada construction continued on the Mica rockfill dam on the Columbia River (height 800 ft., volume 42 million cu.yd.). It was scheduled for completion in 1973. On the Montreal River the Lower Notch Dam was under construction. Construction began in 1970 of the Manic 3 earthfill dam on the Manicouagan River (height 350 ft., volume 12 million cu.yd.).

In South America the Esmeralda rockfill dam, with an included impervious core, was under construction on the Batá River, Colombia (height 754 ft., volume 14,126,000 cu.yd.). In Brazil the Ilha Solteira earth and concrete gravity dam being built on the Paraná had a height of 262 ft., a crest length of 20,300 ft., and a volume of 32,838,000 cu.yd. The Mantaro River concrete gravity dam in Peru was completed in January 1970.

Australia. Three dams under construction were: the Ord River rockfill (height 330 ft., volume 2 million tons of rockfill, storage 4.6 million ac-ft.), to irrigate 178,000 ac.; the Copeton earth and rockfill dam on the Gwydir River (height 370 ft., crest length 4,870 ft., volume 10 million cu.yd., storage 1.1 million ac-ft.); and the Gordon double-curvature arch dam on the Gordon River (height 450 ft., volume 196,000 cu.yd., storage 10,080,000 ac-ft.).

Africa. Ceremonies in July marked completion of the Aswan High Dam (Sadd el Aali), U.A.R. (height 364 ft., crest length 12,565 ft., volume 55,809,000

Major World Dams Under Construction in 1970*

Name of dam	River	Country	Type†	Height (ft.)	Length of crest (ft.)	Volume content (000 cu.yd.)	Gross capacity of reservoir (000 ac-ft.)
Almendra	Tormes	Spain	AG	649	13,438	3,267	2,025
Auburn	N.F. American	U.S.	A	680	3,500	6,000	2,500
Ayvacik	Yesil	Turkey	A	551	1,715	1,464	689
Balimela	Sileru	India	E	230	15,200	29,627	3,097
Cahorabassa	Zambezi	Mozambique‡	A	525	994	589	129,389
Castaic	Castaic	U.S.	E	340	5,200	44,000	350
Charvakskaya	Chirchik	U.S.S.R.	ER	551	2,499	24,975	1,620
Chirkeyskaya	Sulak	U.S.S.R.	A	764	1,109	1,602	2,252
Don Pedro, New§	Tuolumne	U.S.	ER	585	1,900	16,760	2,030
Dworshak	N.F. Clearwater	U.S.	G	717	3,287	6,500	3,453
Emosson	Barberine	Switzerland	A	590	1,736	1,400	182
Gokcekaya	Sakarya	Turkey	A	518	1,529	850	737
Gran Suarna	Navia	Spain	A	499	1,150	882	567
Idikki	Periyar	India	MA	561	1,201	609	1,182
Ilha Solteira	Paraná	Brazil	EG	262	20,300	32,838	17,172
Inguri	Inguri	U.S.S.R.	A	892	2,198	4,967	891
Jayakwadi	Godavari	India	E	120	32,493	15,409	2,110
Kanev	Dnepr	U.S.S.R.	E	82	52,950	49,520	2,125
Kapchagay	Ili	U.S.S.R.	E	164	7,741	10,338	22,761
Keban	Euphrates	Turkey	RG	679	3,598	19,600	25,110
Khantayka	Khantayka	U.S.S.R.	RE	213	21,058	2,452	16,743
Kölnbrein	Malta	Austria	A	607	1,814	1,804	130
Krasnoyarsk	Yenisei	U.S.S.R.	G	407	3,493	5,685	59,425
Las Portas	Camba	Spain	G	498	1,587	977	609
Marimbondo	Grande	Brazil	EG	295	11,970	25,245	5,184
Melones, New§	Stanislaus	U.S.	ER	625	1,600	15,970	2,400
Mica	Columbia	Canada	R	800	2,600	42,000	20,000
Montanejos	Mijares	Spain	AG	492	820	163	203
Mratinje	Piva	Yugoslavia	A	722	853	1,019	749
Nurek	Vakhsh	U.S.S.R.	E	1,017	2,390	70,806	8,424
Reza Shah Kabir	Karun	Iran	A	656	1,247	n.a.	n.a.
Saratov	Volga	U.S.S.R.	E	131	4,130	19,034	10,854
Sayano-Shushenskaya	Yenisei	U.S.S.R.	A	774	3,503	11,916	25,353
Tachien	Tachia	Taiwan	A	591	951	562	188
Tarbela	Indus	Pakistan	ER	485	9,000	186,000	11,100
Toktogul	Naryn	U.S.S.R.	A	705	1,352	3,480	15,800
Ust-Ilim	Angara	U.S.S.R.	EG	344	11,695	17,090	48,100
Zeyskaya	Zeya	U.S.S.R.	G	371	2,312	10,456	55,080
MAJOR WORLD DAMS COMPLETED IN 1969 AND 1970*							
Aswan High (Sadd el Aali)	Nile	U.A.R.	ER	364	12,565	55,809	133,000
Talbingo	Tumut	Australia	R	530	2,300	18,500	747
Vilyuyskaya (1st stage)	Vilyuy	U.S.S.R.	ER	213	1,968	3,790	14,985

*Having a height exceeding 492 ft. (150 m.); or having a total volume content exceeding 20 million cu.yd. (15 million cu.m.); or forming a reservoir exceeding 12 million ac-ft. capacity.
†Type of dam: E=earth; R=rockfill; A=arch; G=gravity; MA=multiple arch.
‡Mozambique is a Portuguese possession.
§Replacement of present dam.
n.a.=data not available.

(T. W. Me.)

FOX PHOTOS
FROM PICTORIAL PARADE

This giant roundabout at White City forms part of West London's new Westway route, which is expected to carry 45,000 vehicles per day.

cu.yd., storage 133 million ac-ft.). In Morocco construction continued on the Assan Addakhil earthfill dam on the Ziz River (height 312 ft., crest length 2,575 ft., volume 7,580,000 cu.yd., storage 307,800 ac-ft.) and the Ait Adel earthfill dam on the Tessaout River (height 328 ft., volume 7,319,000 cu.yd., storage 162,000 ac-ft.). (AL. MA.)

Roads. In almost all countries road-building programs continued to gather impetus. A selection of some of the major projects completed during 1970 is detailed below. Overall, the amount spent on road building was broadly in the region of 1% of national income.

Europe. During 1969–70, an important new expressway between Corinth and Patras, in Greece, was opened to traffic. The work was done in three main stages. The section between Corinth and Akrata was opened in October 1969, the Patras–Diacophto section followed soon afterward, and the Diacophto–Akrata section was opened early in 1970.

Late in 1969, sections of two Swiss national roads were completed. One was the Wängi to Sankt Gallen section of the national road N1 (from Winterthur to Sankt Gallen); the others were the Trübbach–Sargans and the Grono–Castione sections of the N13 highway. The Trübbach–Sargans section linked up with the Sargans–Chur–Reichenau road and the Sargans–Zürich road (N3).

Several expressway sections were opened in West Germany. These were: 7.5 mi. of the Dortmund–Giessen motorway; 9.3 mi. of the Schleswig–Holstein motorway (bypassing the city of Neumünster); 6.2 mi. (from Stromberg to Rheinböllen) of the Krefeld–Ludwigshafen motorway; the Weinheim–Heidelberg section of the Frankfurt–Darmstadt–Heidelberg motorway, and the Wolfratshausen–Penzberg section of the Munich–Garmisch motorway.

In France an 8.7-mi. length of the Marseilles–Lyons motorway was opened between Sénas and Salon. The first section of the Paris–Rungis motorway (H6) was also opened to traffic; it was intended to relieve congestion of A6, which attracts traffic going to Orly International Airport.

The two new sections of the Brenner motorway were opened, one between Brenner Lake in Austria and the Italian border, and the other between the border and Terme del Brennero, Italy. Among other new expressway sections opened to traffic in Italy during the year were the Lauria North–Stazione Pollino (21 mi.), the Morano–Sibari (22 mi.), and the Sibari–Tarsia (3.3 mi.) sections of the Salerno–Reggio di Calabria motorway (A3); and the Turin/La Rotta–Marene (20 mi.) section of the Turin–Savona motorway (A6).

The U.K. approached the aim of 1,000 mi. of motorway by the early 1970s with 630 mi. completed and 350 mi. under construction. Among new lengths opened to traffic in 1970 were parts of the trans-Pennine route (M62) and the M6 approaching Scotland through the Lake District.

North and South America. In Peru, a 14-mi. toll road, the Pasamayo highway, was opened to traffic. Forming part of the Pan-American Highway, it began just north of Lima, near Ancón. The second stage of the Paseo de la Republica expressway was also opened. The completion of that stage meant that the expressway ran the full three miles from the National Sports Stadium in Lima to Miraflores.

In January 1970 the 41.6-mi. section (Los Andes–La Frontera) of the Valparaíso–Mendoza road from Chile to Argentina was completed. Part of it rose more than 10,000 ft. above sea level. The whole of the Pan-American Highway system in Chile was now paved.

It was announced in the U.S. that in 1967 (the latest year for which complete figures were available) 2,635 mi. of interstate expressway were built.

Africa. In South West Africa, construction since 1958 reached 1,345 mi. The work was well ahead of schedule, the 20-year plan envisaging only 1,245 mi. by the end of 1978. In South Africa itself, the Chrissiesmeer–Oshoek section of the Johannesburg–Swaziland road was tarred in late 1969.

Upper Volta completed two main projects in 1970, the road from Bobo Dioulasso to the border with Mali, and that from Ouagadougou to Pô, near the border with Ghana. The highway authorities in Nigeria built 51 mi. of road in the Idoma region.

Asia and Oceania. In Israel the 6.2-mi. Lod Airport–Ge'a road was opened, reducing traveling time between Tel Aviv and the airport. The 267-mi. four-lane Seoul–Pusan express highway in South Korea was completed in 1970. It replaced an old road, more than halving the journey time between the two cities.

The Ella–Wellawaya road in Ceylon was completed, connecting the northern and southern parts of Uva Province with the central and southern provinces. In New Zealand, the seaward lanes of the first section of the Wellington motorway, between Kaiwharawhara and Aotea Quay, were opened to traffic. (R. S. MI.)

Tunnels. An indication of the total value of tunneling being accomplished in 1970 was given during the Organization for Economic Cooperation and Development (OECD) conference on tunneling held in June in Washington, D.C. The total annual rate of expenditure on tunneling in the 20 participating countries was approximately $1 billion ($3 billion including mining). During the previous decade a total of at least 13,000 km. (430,000 km. including mining) of tunnels with an excavated volume of at least 300 million cu.m. (4 billion cu.m. including mining) were constructed. Demand was expected at least to double during the next decade.

In West Germany work started at Hamburg on a six-lane, triple-barreled, 2-mi. tunnel (estimated cost in 1968, $104 million) crossing under the Elbe River to form a major link in the European route E3 from

Stockholm to Lisbon. The first section of tunnel, 3,467 ft. long, extended under the river, and was formed by eight 53,000-ton precast-concrete sunken-tube units, each 433 ft. long, 137 ft. wide, 27.5 ft. high, and with external walls 4 ft. thick clad with ¼-in. sheet steel. The second section, 3,700 ft. long, started from the ventilation shaft on the north bank, rose at a 3.5% grade and was being bored through clay and marl by two 36-ft. diameter mechanical shields working under maximum air pressures of 22 psi (pounds per square inch). Each shield cost $3 million and was driven forward by 40 jacks exerting a total of 9,000 ton shove, and erected behind it iron liner segments 4 ft. by 7 ft. by 9 in. thick. The third and final section, 590 ft. long, was being built by the cut-and-cover method.

As part of the Spanish highway program, a second road tunnel, costing $14.5 million and 3.6 km. long, was being pushed through the Guadarrama mountain range on the route between Madrid and La Coruña. A fine seam of clay was encountered between the normal granite strata, on which the rock sometimes slipped. An articulated steel tunnel shield 3 m. long was kept in readiness to be moved quickly under any weakening tunnel section.

In the U.K. the Robbins tunneling machine boring the 31-ft. 7-in. internal diameter, 7,400-ft.-long second Mersey Tunnel holed through in March. Driving began on the 6,606-ft.-long pilot bore for the third Mersey Tunnel, using an 11-ft. diameter tunneling machine.

First-stage construction was in progress for the $45.6 million Hong Kong Cross Harbour Tunnel, a four-lane crossing to be formed by 15 sunken twin-tube sections 320 to 370 ft. long and 34 ft. in diameter. Completion was scheduled for 1972.

In many of the world's large cities during 1970 extensive lengths of tunnel were being constructed for new or existing subway systems. Work continued in Toronto on the 5-mi. Yonge Street extension scheduled for completion in 1972. Costing about $84 million, the project consisted of three lengths of bored twin tunnels and three new cut-and-cover stations. An interesting feature of the project was a station in construction under the Don River, which had been diverted over the workings during the construction period, using a specially constructed steel flume. In New York, the chief project in an extensive program of improvements was the 63rd Street East River tunnel, consisting of two lengths of immersed tube construction, each 750 ft. long, connected by a tunnel blasted under Welfare Island. The four 38-ft. by 38-ft. concrete tube sections were 375 ft. long, double-decked with two tracks on each level. The San Francisco BART (Bay Area Rapid Transit) system, costing about $1.3 billion, neared completion, construction of the subway line structures being more than 80% complete. Some 20 mi. of the 75-mi.-long system were underground. Rates of driving achieved by the tunneling machines were 364 ft. in one week in rock, and 363 ft. in one week in soft ground. The relative costs per foot were about $960 in rock and $1,850 in soft ground for the 18-ft. external diameter tunnel. In comparison, the costs of the Victoria Line, London, were about $384 per foot for a 13-ft. 6-in. external diameter tunnel driven through London clay.

The world record for rate of advance of bored and permanently lined tunnel was claimed by Edmund Nuttall, Sons & Co. Ltd., England, for their construction of 1,426 ft. in one week during December 1969.

This was achieved on a drive of the 12-mi. aqueduct tunnel, part of the Ely-Ouse flood protection scheme for the Essex River Authority. The tunnel was 8 ft. 4 in. in internal diameter, lined with precast concrete segments, and was driven by a tunneling machine made by Robert L. Priestly Ltd.

Extensive tunneling went on in many cities to meet demands for water supply and sewage disposal. As an example, in New York contracts totaling $222.6 million provided for a water supply project involving 13.7 mi., mostly of 24-ft. diameter tunnel deep under the city in hard rock.

In Japan, the $350 million Seikan rail tunnel, originally planned as a 23-mi. undersea link for conventional trains, was now expected to be 30 to 35 mi. long in order to provide the moderate grades needed for new high-speed trains. The tunnel passed 330 ft. below the ocean floor through badly faulted granite containing water-filled seams of broken rock.

(H. D. M.)

ENCYCLOPÆDIA BRITANNICA FILMS. *St. Lawrence Seaway* (1959): *The Panama Canal* (1961); *The Suez Canal* (1962); *Holland: Hold Back the Sea* (1967); *The Mississippi System: Waterway of Commerce* (1970).

Equatorial Guinea

The African republic of Equatorial Guinea consists of Río Muni, which is bordered by Cameroon on the north, Gabon on the east and south, and the Atlantic Ocean on the west; and the offshore islands of Fernando Po and Annobón. Area: 10,830 sq.mi. (28,050 sq.km.). Pop. (1969 est.): 286,000. Cap. and largest city: Santa Isabel, on Fernando Po (pop., 1965 est., 37,152). President in 1970, Francisco Macías Nguma.

In January 1970 President Macías made his first official visit abroad since the country became independent in October 1968. He spent several days in Cameroon, during which he attended that country's independence day celebrations. In August the president visited Nigeria and voiced the hope that relations between the two countries would become closer and more cordial. On the question of the treatment of the large number of Nigerian workers on the plantations of Fernando Po, a long-standing source of complaints from Nigeria, Macías stated that his government would draw up a new contract agreement to replace the harsh labour laws that had previously been in force.

After the period of tension in the early months of 1969, relations with Spain improved steadily, and Equatorial Guinea's economic and financial position was strengthened with Spanish assistance. Efforts to

EQUATORIAL GUINEA
Education. (1966–67) Primary, pupils 38,395, teachers 504; secondary, pupils 2,343, teachers 40; vocational (1965–66), pupils 464, teachers 35; teacher training, students 130, teachers 28.
Finance. Monetary unit: peseta Guineana, at par with the Spanish peseta (70 pesetas to the U.S. $1; 168 pesetas = £1 sterling). Budget (1969–70 est.): revenue 712.5 million pesetas; expenditure 1,139,000,000 pesetas.
Foreign Trade. (1966) Imports 1,278,000,000 pesetas (58% from Spain in 1965); exports 1,817,-000,000 pesetas (97% to Spain in 1965). Main exports (1965): cocoa 44%; coffee 21%; timber 19%.
Agriculture. Production (in 000; metric tons; 1968; 1967 in parentheses): coffee c. 6.6 (c. 6.6); cocoa (1968–69) 38; (1967–68) 33; palm kernels (exports) c. 2 (c. 1.7); palm oil c. 4 (c. 4). Livestock (in 000; 1967–68): sheep c. 27; cattle c. 3; pigs c. 6; goats c. 6; chickens c. 70.

establish links with other nations continued. On July 31 it was announced in Prague that Czechoslovakia and Equatorial Guinea had agreed to establish diplomatic relations at the ambassadorial level.   (K. I.)

Ethiopia

A constitutional monarchy of northeastern Africa, Ethiopia is bordered by Somalia, the French Territory of the Afars and Issas, Kenya, the Sudan, and the Red Sea. Area: 471,776 sq.mi. (1,221,900 sq.km.). Pop. (1968 est.): 24,140,200. Cap. and largest city: Addis Ababa (pop., 1968 est., 684,130). Language: Amharic (official) and English. Religion: Ethiopian Orthodox (Coptic) Christian 65%; Muslim 30%. Emperor, Haile Selassie I; prime minister in 1970, Aklilu Habte Wold.

Since the Ethiopian economy remained largely dependent on coffee, it benefited to some extent in 1970 from a blight that reduced coffee yields in Brazil. At the same time steps were being taken within the framework of the country's third five-year plan to diversify crops and exports. Agricultural development centred on various regional "package deal" projects—notably in the Awash Valley, Chilalo, and Wolamo districts south of Addis Ababa and in the Setit Humera region, northwest of Lake Tana along the Sudan border.

Other moves to strengthen the economy included proposals to reorganize the financial intermediaries in the government's development banking and investment structure. While a new investment code was being considered, new rates of income tax and land tax were approved to provide support for expanding

UPI COMPIX

Emperor Haile Selassie of Ethiopia opens a summit conference of the Organization of African Unity (OAU) in Addis Ababa Sept. 1, 1970.

ETHIOPIA

Education. (1967–68) Primary, pupils 452,457, teachers 9,525; secondary, pupils 71,467, teachers 3,062; vocational, pupils 6,251, teachers 533; teacher training, students 1,816, teachers 115; higher (at 2 universities), students 3,360, teaching staff 600.

Finance. Monetary unit: Ethiopian dollar, with a par value of Eth$2.50 to U.S. $1 (Eth$6 = £1 sterling). Gold, SDRs, and foreign exchange, central bank: (June 1970) U.S. $80.3 million; (June 1969) U.S. $63.9 million. Budget (1969–70 est.): revenue Eth$602 million; expenditure Eth$631 million. Money supply: (May 1970) Eth$456.9 million; (May 1969) Eth$406.8 million.

Foreign Trade. (1969) Imports Eth$388.3 million; exports Eth$298.6 million. Import sources (1968): U.S. 19%; Italy 18%; West Germany 11%; Japan 9%; U.K. 9%. Export destinations (1968): U.S. 43%; West Germany 8%; Saudi Arabia 7%; Italy 6%. Main exports: coffee 58%; hides and skins 9%; cereals 8%; oilseeds 8%.

Transport and Communications. Roads (1968) c. 23,000 km. (including 7,304 km. all-weather). Motor vehicles in use (1968): passenger 29,500; commercial 9,700. Railways (1968) 1,087 km. Air traffic (1969): 300 million passenger-km.; freight 17.4 million net ton-km. Telephones (Dec. 1968) 36,034. Radio receivers (Dec. 1968) c. 500,000. Television receivers (Dec. 1968) 6,000.

Agriculture. Production (in 000; metric tons; 1968; 1967 in parentheses): teff, millet, and sorghum 2,425 (2,396); corn (1969) 869, (1968) 849; barley c. 1,450 (1,430); wheat 755 (745); linseed c. 60 (c. 60); sunflower seed c. 35 (c. 33); sugar, raw value (1969–70) c. 103, (1968–69) c. 73; chick-peas c. 170 (174); lentils c. 100 (c. 95); sweet potatoes c. 239 (239); potatoes c. 145 (148); coffee c. 165 (c. 155). Livestock (in 000; 1968–69): cattle c. 25,900; sheep c. 12,600; goats (1967–68) c. 12,000; horses c. 1,390; mules c. 1,390; asses c. 3,850; camels (1967–68) c. 970; poultry c. 46,000.

Industry. Production (in 000; metric tons; 1966–67): cotton yarn 9.2; cotton fabrics (sq.m.) 58,000; cement 138; electricity (kw-hr.; 1967–68) 361,000.

social services, particularly education. U.S. military aid amounted to U.S. $12 million in 1970, bringing the total since 1953, when the U.S. base at Kagnew, Eritrea, was set up, to $159 million.

In the industrial sector a metal tool factory was opened in Addis Ababa with Polish assistance; a Greek-financed chemical detergent industry was to become operational in 1971; and, with Eth$800,000 from the UN Development Program, studies were initiated to determine the feasibility of exploiting geothermal power sources in the Rift Valley and the Afar Plain. In November the Lagadadi Dam, about 6 mi. E of Addis Ababa, began to provide a much-needed addition to the capital's water supply.

The seventh Organization of African Unity summit meeting was held in Addis Ababa on September 1, a notable result being Nigeria's reconciliation with the four African countries that had recognized the breakaway eastern state of Biafra. A UNESCO international committee charged with drafting an eight-volume history of Africa also met in Addis Ababa. Haile Selassie ended a series of state visits—to the U.S.S.R., France, and the U.A.R.—in Nairobi, Kenya, where on June 9 he and Pres. Jomo Kenyatta signed a border delimitation treaty establishing the two countries' 500-mi. frontier. In November he visited Italy, marking the complete reconciliation of the two countries 35 years after Mussolini's invasion. Among visitors to Ethiopia during the year was Pres. N. V. Podgorny of the U.S.S.R., with whom it was agreed to open an air service between Addis Ababa and Moscow. A visit from Pres. J. B. Bokassa of the Central African Republic led to mutual agreements on telecommunications links and cultural exchanges.

On October 12 Basilios, patriarch of the Ethiopian Orthodox Church, died at the age of 79. He was the first Ethiopian patriarch to be elected by the country's bishops and appointed by the emperor. From the 4th century until his appointment in 1959, this branch of the Coptic sect had been ruled from Alexandria in Egypt.   (G. C. L.)

European Unity

The year 1970 was marked by another of those surprising turnabouts in outlook that had characterized the European Community since its creation 22 years earlier. (Technically there were three Communities, the European Economic Community or Common Market, the European Coal and Steel Community, and the European Atomic Energy Community or Euratom, but for all practical purposes these were now one European Community.) Throughout most of 1969, even the more optimistic supporters of European unity had continued to regard the future as unpromising. In part, this was due to the unseemly but persistent quarrel among the six Community states over the cost of the Community agricultural policy, and to their insistence on maintaining national advantages unimpaired by any compromise in the interests of unity. Chiefly, however, the pessimistic outlook was inspired by the French position.

Despite the retirement of Pres. Charles de Gaulle, France had continued to oppose the admission of Britain and three other applicant states, Norway, Denmark, and Ireland, until certain major—and seemingly unlikely—actions had been taken by the Community's six member states. These were, first, adoption of a definitive system of financing agricultural support prices that would continue France's existing advantage over the other five states; and second, completion, by Dec. 31, 1969, of the 12-year "transitional" phase of the Community as required by the Treaty of Rome. Since it seemed unlikely that these conditions could be complied with on time (or complied with at all), only professional optimists were willing to predict a satisfactory future for this experiment in regional integration.

Early in December 1969, however, the pessimists were taken by surprise. Largely on France's initiative but with strong support from the new West German government of Chancellor Willy Brandt, a summit meeting of the six states was held at The Hague. There sufficient compromises were achieved, at least "in principle," to assure the French that their demands would be met. The "spirit of The Hague" was, moreover, tangible enough to carry Community negotiators successfully through subsequent rather trying sessions at Brussels, and these sessions led to decisions that ended the Community's transitional phase and provided a path, if not a highway, for future development. These decisions, in turn, persuaded the French to agree to negotiate with Britain and the other three candidate states. Negotiations for admitting these four states into the Community began in July 1970 following a formal meeting at Luxembourg on June 30, during which Britain formally reiterated its application for membership, originally made some years earlier; the other three applicant states reiterated their formal candidacy somewhat later. Thus the logjam that had hampered Community expansion was effectively broken.

Some fairly sharp bargaining characterized the post-Hague summit discussions. Italy sought and received concessions for price supports for certain commodities, notably wine and tobacco. West Germany demanded and received a pledge that a ceiling would be imposed on amounts the Community—and hence the individual states—would be required to spend on ambitious structural agricultural reform programs, such as that advocated by Sicco Mansholt (see BIOGRAPHY), which would benefit other states more than Germany. France received the most substantial concession—indefinite continuation of payments from the Community agricultural fund that amounted to about twice what it contributed.

Such concessions to national advantage notwithstanding, other decisions were taken during the post-Hague summit talks that would have the effect of strengthening the unity of the Community and advancing the cause of supranationalism. The negotiations produced a definitive plan for financing future Community operations that, in time, would make the Community less dependent on the various national exchequers and perhaps entirely independent of them. Under the existing system, practically all the agricultural levies (the import duties imposed on farm imports at the Community frontier) went to the Community treasury to finance the agricultural price-support program. Any deficit had to be made up by contributions from the member states. Between 1971 and 1975, the Community would put into effect a permanent plan for financing not only agriculture but other activities as well. Ninety percent of all agricultural levies and industrial tariff proceeds would be paid into the Community treasury. In addition, by 1975 the Community would receive a small percentage of the value-added tax which, it was anticipated, would be common to all member states by that time. The

amount to be contributed under this tax-sharing plan would be proportioned to the economic weight of each member state. By 1975 receipts from all these sources could total as much as $4 billion, and although the larger share of this amount would still be expended for farm subsidies, some of it would undoubtedly become available for expanding other Community activities.

Although the Community Council of Ministers would continue to draw up the budget and exercise initiative in determining what ideas and projects were to be supported, it was agreed that, by 1975, as much as $3\frac{1}{2}\%$ of the total budget could be redeployed by the European Parliament. Small though the percentage was, this was the first time that any really substantive authority had been committed to the Parliament, which had been little more than a debating society. Suggestions were also made to elect members of the Parliament directly and to enlarge it to accommodate new Community members, but decision on these proposals was postponed. In anticipation of the Community's expansion, the European Commission, only recently raised to 14 members, was reduced to 9; the full complement of 14 would be restored gradually as new members joined the Community. The reduction took place on the occasion of the installation, in July, of Franco Malfatti (see BIOGRAPHY), former Italian communications minister, as the new president of the Commission, in succession to Jean Rey of Belgium.

During 1970 there was additional discussion about various possible extensions of economic cooperation within the Community, such as the establishment of a common currency—or at least of national currencies with stabilized value ratios—and the chartering of industrial corporations on a Community-wide basis. Such discussions did not move far beyond the committee stage, however, and serious consideration was more likely after the issue of the Community's enlargement had been settled.

Although negotiations to add new states began in July, most observers believed that they would continue far into 1971. Meanwhile, some hard bargaining and jockeying for national advantage was expected to take place between the applicant states and the existing Community members. Britain asked that there be a lengthy transition period for the new members—something on the order of five years—while the Community wanted the transition period to be more nearly that number of months. All the new member states would probably have to accept the new budgetary formula and the Community agricultural price system. For each of the proposed new members there would be sacrifices. Thus Britain, which imported half its food, might experience an immediate cost-of-living increase, estimated at 5%, because of the high Community agricultural price supports. It would presumably have to sacrifice less expensive Commonwealth imports, such as cheaper New Zealand butter, as well as special Commonwealth economic ties and preferences. Moreover, the high Community import duties would place a strain on Britain's balance of payments unless it could greatly increase food production at home.

There were more subjective liabilities, as well. British statesmen disliked seeing their existing freedom of decision over national issues taken from their government and placed in forums in which Britain would merely share power—although this, of course, was the inevitable price of any sort of unification.

BEN ROTH AGENCY

"The European Effort" —Backes, "Kölnische Rundschau."

KEYSTONE

British Foreign and Commonwealth Secretary Sir Alec Douglas-Home (above) and West German Foreign Minister Walter Scheel (below) attended the initial meeting in Luxembourg June 30 on Britain's application to join the EEC.

KEYSTONE

British economists, mindful that Britain probably devotes a greater proportion of national income to welfare costs than any of its proposed partners, expressed the opinion that, after Britain joined the Community, British capital might seek investment in the partner states because the return there would be greater.

The three other applicants had somewhat similar concerns although, because their economies were so closely tied to Britain's, staying out if Britain entered would clearly be injurious if not disastrous. Of the three, Norway had perhaps the most unusual reason for hesitating. The 10% of its population engaged in agriculture enjoyed higher support prices than the very high ones guaranteed in the Common Market area, and the Norwegian farmers' lobby did not hesitate to remind Norway's prime minister of its concern. In any event, each of the three would undoubtedly follow Britain's lead in seeking to protect national interests and obligations against the possible adverse effects of accepting Community policy in certain areas, and of having to share decision-making discretion in Community forums in the future. Whatever the obstacles and the liabilities of joining the Community, however, they appeared to be outweighed by the long-run economic advantages of sharing in the expansive market provided by more than 200 million people.

EFTA and Nordek. As the negotiations between the EEC and the membership candidates proceeded, other non-Communist European multistate agencies took stock as to the effect on their future. The two most concerned were the European Free Trade Association, or EFTA, and the proposed Organization for Nordic Economic Cooperation, or Nordek. EFTA, created in 1959 as a less ambitious alternative to the EEC, consisted originally of seven states, grew to eight when Finland became an associate member, and expanded to nine on March 1, 1970, when Iceland joined. Plans for Nordek were laid in July 1969 by four Scandinavian states, Denmark, Norway, Sweden, and Finland, and the treaty establishing the agency came up for ratification a year later. Nordek was regarded as a means of extending traditional economic cooperation in Scandinavia, both directly among the states of that region and within EFTA, of which those states were also members. Finland declined to participate, however, and by the end of 1970 it appeared that Nordek, if not dead, was at least dormant until the EEC negotiations had been completed.

With the growing likelihood that Britain and at least two Scandinavian states would be absorbed by the European Community, suggestions that such groupings as EFTA were superfluous—and possibly even mischievous—were voiced with renewed vigour. France was especially emphatic about the need to liquidate EFTA now that the Community was about to be enlarged at the expense of EFTA membership. Sweden, Switzerland, and Austria, in particular, held back from seeking Community membership because the political implications of such an action might damage their traditional neutralism. The possibility remained that these states might be given "associate" status that would permit them to participate in Community trade arrangements, but French Foreign Minister Maurice Schumann, for one, insisted that any compromise of this kind would bring "chaos."

Others, however, were not so concerned. Sir John Coulson, EFTA secretary-general, suggested that, though EFTA might be dissolved, its member states would not all try to join the European Community.

EFTA members that for political reasons feared too intimate an identification with the Community might indeed seek a special free trade status in "association" with the Community. Other EFTA members, such as Portugal and Iceland, might also seek some sort of special arrangement with Brussels. Moreover, Nordek or some similar arrangement could satisfy a regional aspiration for somewhat more intimate economic cooperation without the political fears that Sweden and Finland, especially, might experience if they had to assume full membership in the wider European Community. Thus, observed Sir John, there might come into existence a kind of two- or three-tier arrangement of Western European states, all having some association or arrangement with Brussels. Meanwhile, EFTA would provide its members or prospective members with an insurance policy—a sort of fall-back position in the event that negotiations with the European Community collapsed.

Council of Europe. Of the remaining organizations for European cooperation, the Council of Europe at Strasbourg, France, retained its relative importance. During 1970 it again demonstrated its well-tested usefulness as a forum for discussion and for the working out of solutions to problems common to its European membership. This result was achieved by resolutions establishing guidelines for national legislation on a given subject or by drafting appropriate legislation or administrative regulations. Often the result was to mount a kind of transnational or continental attack on various problems, especially problems in education, public health, social welfare, and in other less politically sensitive areas.

Probably the Council's most publicized effort in this direction during 1970 occurred in February, when its Consultative Assembly and various committees provided a forum for the discussion of environmental problems—including urban decay and pollution—affecting all Europe. The sessions enjoyed the patronage of Prince Philip, himself a noted advocate of conservation and environmental protection, and of several noted scientists and conservationists. The resulting reports and resolutions stressed the desirability of concerted national action to limit environmental pollution, expand university training in such subjects as ecology and urban planning, and establish legal guidelines for regulation of the manufacture, sale, and use of certain pesticides.

Membership in the Council had been reduced to 17 at the end of 1969, when the Greek military regime withdrew. Following an intensive two-year investigation, one of the Council's committees had filed a lengthy report alleging that there was no evidence of growing democratization of the Greek regime, and offering evidence that the regime had been guilty of systematic ill treatment and even torture of political prisoners, in violation of art. 3 of the Council's statute, which requires each member state to accept the "principles of the rule of law" and to guarantee "the enjoyment by all persons within its jurisdiction of human rights and fundamental freedoms." Greece withdrew when it became apparent that a majority of the Council members, led by Britain, would vote to expel it. The decision to expel had been made despite a thinly veiled diplomatic effort by the U.S. to maintain Greek membership because of the possible adverse effects expulsion might have on NATO.

(A. J. Z.)

Evangelical Churches:
see Religion

Exchange Rates:
see Payments and Reserves, International

Exhibitions:
see Art Exhibitions; Fairs and Shows; Museums and Galleries; Photography

Expeditions, Scientific:
see Antarctica; Arctic Regions; Mountaineering; Oceanography; Speleology

Faeroe Islands:
see Dependent States

See also Commercial Policies; Defense; France; Payments and Reserves, International; Trade, International.

Fairs and Shows

Despite spiraling inflation, fairs and shows in 1970 continued to grow on an unprecedented scale. Attendance and revenues were generally higher in all sectors of this multibillion-dollar industry. Fairs open to the general public, numbering over 14,000 worldwide, attracted an estimated one billion persons, while some 950 trade and commercial fairs accounted for an additional 42 million visitors. Over two billion persons flocked to more than 16,500 amusement parks, aquariums, zoos, and similar tourist attractions. Revenues from admissions, rides, and shows were generally higher, but food and beverage income at parks and fairs slipped marginally.

The focal event of 1970 was Expo 70 at Osaka, Jap., the first world's fair on the Asian continent. The fair, which ran for 183 days (March 15 to September 13), set an attendance record of 64,218,770, as well as a new record for one day, 835,832 on September 5. The gates had to be closed on several occasions to avoid panic among the surging crowds. Sanctioned by the Bureau of International Expositions as a first-category universal exhibition, Expo 70 had begun inauspiciously. At first only a few foreign nations responded to Japanese Prime Minister Eisaku Sato's invitation to participate, and the advance ticket sale fell far short of expectations. Despite this slow start, however, all exhibit space was filled by opening day, and word-of-mouth praise attracted unprecedented throngs.

Over 115 pavilions of every description dotted the picturesque fair site, nestled among the Shenri Hills near Osaka. All were demolished or disassembled at the close of the fair except the Japan pavilion, the Japanese Gardens, the Steel Pavilion, the Japan Folk Crafts Museum, Expo Hall, and the Expo Museum of Fine Arts, which were retained as permanent fixtures. Moving sidewalks and assorted vehicles were used to move visitors around the fairgrounds to the exhibits, international shops, novelty stands, rides, and the more than 146 restaurants. A jet-powered roller coaster was an especially popular attraction. The fair's official emblem was a stylized cherry blossom. (See ARCHITECTURE.)

Philadelphia was selected as the site of a proposed $1.5 billion exposition designed as a showcase for the 200th anniversary of U.S. independence in 1976. Half of the cost would be borne by the federal government and the balance was to come from city, state, and private sources. The American Revolution Bicentennial Commission, which made the final selection, had also considered applications from Boston and Washington, D.C.

International Trade Fairs. Stringent policies applied by many governments in an effort to stem inflationary pressures, did not appear to hinder the vigorous growth of the world's trade and commercial fairs. Over 75% of the estimated 820 international trade fairs held in 76 countries reported sharp gains in exhibit space demands and buyer registrations. West German fairs closed the year with record-breaking results, as did those held in France, Italy, Great Britain, and Belgium. All exhibition facilities were booked to capacity, and several countries announced the construction of new exposition halls and convention centres. Among the special and general category commercial fairs reporting excellent business during the

Selected Major National and International Fairs, 1970

Country and date	Event and place	Attendance
Australia		
Sept. 24–Oct. 1	Perth Royal Show, Claremont	300,000
Austria		
Oct. 3–11	International Autumn Trade Fair, Graz	260,000
Oct. 6–13	International Autumn Trade Fair, Vienna	340,000
Belgium		
Sept. 12–27	International Trade Fair, Ghent	550,000
Bulgaria		
Sept. 20–29	26th International Trade Fair, Sofia	840,000
Canada		
Aug. 20–Sept. 2	Canadian National Exhibition, Toronto	3,171,000
Aug. 22–Sept. 2	Pacific National Exhibition, Vancouver, B.C.	1,167,030
Sept. 3–13	Quebec Provinciale Exhibition, Quebec	583,637
Colombia		
July 10–26	International Trade Fair, Bogotá	260,000
Cyprus		
Sept. 4–27	16th International Cyprus Fair, Nicosia	2,250,000
Czechoslovakia		
Sept. 5–14	International Trade Fair, Brno	1,225,000
El Salvador		
Nov. 7–29	International Fair of El Salvador, San Salvador	800,000
Finland		
Sept. 17–27	International Trade Fair, Helsinki	200,000
France		
Sept. 24–Oct. 5	International Trade Fair, Marseilles	1,620,000
Sept. 30–Oct. 11	International Trade Fair, Metz	1,400,000
Germany, East		
March 1–10	International Spring Fair, Leipzig	590,000
Germany, West		
Sept. 18–27	German Industries Fair, Berlin	800,000
April 4–12	17th German Camping Exhibition, Essen	370,000
Sept. 11–21	44th International Auto Show, Frankfurt	510,000
Greece		
Sept. 6–26	International Trade Fair, Thessaloniki	1,300,000
Hungary		
May 22–June 1	International Trade Fair, Budapest	700,000
Iraq		
Oct. 1–30	International Trade Fair, Baghdad	550,000
Israel		
June 2–16	International Trade Fair, Tel Aviv	200,000
Italy		
Sept. 10–23	34th International Levante Trade Fair, Bari	550,000
May 23–June 7	International Mediterranean Fair, Palermo, Sicily	406,000
May 16–31	International Trade Fair, Bologna	270,000
June 21–July 5	22nd International Trade Fair, Trieste	360,000
Japan		
March 15–Sept. 13	Expo 70 world's fair, Osaka	64,218,770
Kenya		
Sept. 29–Oct. 3	International Agricultural Show, Nairobi	110,000
Laos		
October	13th Annual That Luang Fair, Vientiane	400,000
Mozambique		
May 30–June 14	Agricultural, Commercial, and Industrial Fair, Lourenço Marques	350,000
Netherlands		
Oct. 2–13	Holidays, Travel, and Flower Exhibition, Rotterdam	340,000
New Zealand		
March 13–31	Easter Show, Auckland	600,000
Norway		
Aug. 19–30	North Sea Fair, Kristiansund	240,000
Poland		
June 14–23	International Trade Fair, Poznan	800,000
Portugal		
June 9–23	11th International Trade Fair, Lisbon	690,000
Romania		
Oct. 13–25	International Trade Fair, Bucharest	450,000
South Africa		
March 23–April 6	Rand Easter Show, Johannesburg	1,200,000
Spain		
July 1–12	5th International Samples Fair, Bilbao	300,000
May 4–17	48th International Samples Fair, Valencia	450,000
Oct. 3–18	30th National Samples Fair, Saragossa	310,000
Sweden		
May 9–18	53rd International Trade Fair, Göteborg	200,000
Switzerland		
April 11–21	54th Swiss Industries Fair, Basel	1,100,000
Sept. 12–27	Swiss Autumn Fair, Lausanne	280,000
Syria		
Aug. 25–Sept. 20	17th International Trade Fair, Damascus	1,260,000
Tanzania		
July	Saba Saba International Trade Fair, Dar es Salaam	700,000
Turkey		
Aug. 20–Sept. 20	39th International Trade Fair, Izmir	2,400,000
U.S.S.R.		
Sept. 10–24	International Chemistry in Industrial Construction and Agricultural Exhibition, Moscow	312,000
U. A. R.		
October	International Trade Fair, Cairo	340,000
United Kingdom		
Sept. 5–12	International Trade Fair, Brighton	150,000
Sept. 7–13	Aviation Exhibition and Flying Display, Farnborough	1,000,000
Oct. 14–24	International Motor Exhibition, London	600,000
United States		
Aug. 14–23	Wisconsin State Fair, West Allis	639,162
Aug. 22–30	Missouri State Fair, Sedalia	352,000
Aug. 7–15	Allentown Fair, Pa.	639,162
Aug. 29–Sept. 7	Oregon State Fair, Salem	420,519
Sept. 1–7	New York State Fair, Syracuse	601,478
Aug. 27–Sept. 7	Ohio State Fair, Columbus	2,219,170
Aug. 29–Sept. 7	Minnesota State Fair, St. Paul	1,332,734
Aug. 26–Sept. 7	Indiana State Fair, Indianapolis	1,009,426
Oct. 10–25	State Fair of Texas, Dallas	3,022,495
Sept. 25–Oct. 3	Mid-South Fair, Memphis, Tenn.	684,245
Uruguay		
Feb. 10–March 31	Industrial Fair, Montevideo	310,000
Yugoslavia		
April 18–26	International Spring Fair, Zagreb	1,300,000
Sept. 10–20	International Fall Fair, Zagreb	2,000,000

Source: Frederick P. Pittera, *Fairs of the World* (1970).

year were the International Hardware Trade Fair, London; the International Trade Fair, Casablanca, Mor.; the International Levante Trade Fair, Bari, Italy; and the Milan (Italy) Samples Fair. The number of U.S. Department of Commerce-sponsored trade fair centres overseas rose to 300 in 1970; the first such centre had been opened in London on June 26, 1961.

Fairs. Attendance at North American fairs rose more than 1.5% in 1970. Over 115 million persons visited one or more of the 3,200 U.S. and 800 Canadian fairs, and an additional 94 million were attracted to events held at fairground facilities during the off-season. Most of the approximately 200 larger fairs enjoyed good weather and 55% of them reported substantial increases in attendance, but many of the smaller U.S. county and Canadian district fairs experienced declines. Total gross revenues from North American state, county, district, and provincial fairs were estimated at well over $200 million. With front-gate admissions generally higher, U.S. and Canadian fairs spent an estimated $23 million for live talent, largely for free grandstand shows. European fairs also raised gate admissions, but Asian and Latin-American fairs held to lower prices.

Canada's National Exhibition at Toronto continued to lead the North American continent in attendance in 1970, although it did not draw as well as in the previous season. Some 3,171,000 persons visited the Toronto fair, while its closest contender, the State Fair of Texas at Dallas, reported its biggest year with 3,022,495 visitors. Moving into third position was Ohio's State Fair at Columbus with 2,219,170. Other general public fairs reaching or surpassing the one-million mark were the Minnesota State Fair, St. Paul; the Pacific National Exhibition, Vancouver, B.C.; the Indiana State Fair, Indianapolis; and the Royal Easter Show, Sydney, Austr.

Some 50 million persons attended the more than 260,000 retail and wholesale industrial shows held in the U.S. and Canada. Over $2.5 billion was spent by exhibitors to display their products and services at these events. At year's end an estimated $30 billion had been earmarked for new convention and exhibition facilities around the world, including over $8 billion in the U.S. and Canada. Boat and automobile shows continued to lead in attendance and sales, followed by sports, camping and recreational equipment, and home furnishing shows.

Amusement Parks. The world's more than 17,000 fun and recreation parks again emerged as the leaders among public attractions, in terms of both money and attendance. Over two billion adults and children patronized these facilities in 1970. In North America alone, 450 million persons visited over 2,000 parks, zoos, aquariums, and similar tourist attractions, spending an estimated $920 million. More than $70 million was invested in new equipment by U.S. and Canadian recreation parks, an increase of almost $19 million over 1969. Asia's kiddielands and fun parks had their best season during the year, with better-than-average business reported from Toshimaen Park, Tokyo; Lai Chi Kok Park, Hong Kong; and Wonderland Park, Singapore. In Sweden's fun parks more dance bands were engaged in an effort to attract younger crowds.

Carnivals, Rodeos, and Circuses. The carnival industry in North America, comprising approximately 410 carnivals, 265 independent show and ride operators, and over 2,000 concessionaires, grossed more

A portrait of the late Soviet cosmonaut Yuri Gagarin, first man to travel in space, looks down at the Soviet Union's exhibit of satellites and space vehicles at Asia's first world exposition, Expo 70.

WIDE WORLD

FOX PHOTOS FROM PICTORIAL PARADE

The 1970 Boat Show at Earls Court, London, opened Jan. 7, 1970. It was organized by the Ship and Boat Builders' National Federation and was sponsored by the "Daily Express."

than $452 million during 1970. Most units showed gains of from 17 to 25% in revenues. However, higher costs for labour and equipment were reflected in a lower profit ratio than in previous years. Ride prices were generally higher than in 1969. European carnivals also reported generally good business; the number of units rose by an estimated 10%, bringing the total on the continent to approximately 1,500 carnivals and 700 independent and show operators. The highest grosser among carnival and midway operators for a single engagement was the Conklin Shows unit at Canada's National Exhibition, Toronto, which grossed nearly $2 million in 19 days. Its founder, J. W. Conklin, died on Nov. 8, 1970.

More than 4,000 rodeo performers in the U.S. and Canada competed for over $5 million in prize money at more than 3,300 sanctioned and nonsanctioned events in 1970. A new prize-money record of $96,245 was established at the Houston (Tex.) Rodeo (February 27 to March 8). Previous efforts to promote rodeos in Europe had not been successful, but each year new attempts were made. The International Western Rodeo Association, which spent $1.5 million in 1970 to produce 200 rodeo performances in France, Switzerland, the Netherlands, West Germany, Austria, and Belgium, obtained only passive acceptance. Bloodless bullfights appeared here and there in North America, but the response was only fair. While the Florida legislature passed a special law legalizing such bullfights in that state, some other states banned these events altogether.

Over 660 circuses were active throughout the world in 1970, with the major units reporting their best season; gains ranged from 15 to 19% over 1969, and some units indicated increases of up to 30%. Indoor events showed higher revenues than tented shows. Atayde Bros. Circus (Mexico), Fossett Circus (Ireland), Circus Knie (Switzerland), Hamid-Morton (U.S.), and England's Chipperfield Circus all reported more bookings and capacity business on their tours. Mattel Inc., a toy-making concern, announced an agreement in principle to buy Ringling Bros.-Barnum & Bailey Combined Shows, Inc., which had previously expanded its activities to include two music publishing companies and a record company. The hockey-playing bears of the Moscow Circus on Ice appeared in the U.S. for the first time.

Livestock and Horse Shows. Thousands of livestock shows were held during the year, either as individual shows or in conjunction with agricultural and dairy shows and fairs. The world's great livestock shows reported an increase of over 20% in animal entries and a 15% rise in average gross sales. Some of the larger shows, such as Denver's National Western Stock Show, featured as many as 20,000 animal entries. The Royal Show at Trumpington near Cambridge, Eng., celebrated its 121st year.

Approximately 800 events were sanctioned by the American Horse Shows Association in North America, while over 4,000 nonsanctioned shows were held in the U.S. and Canada and an estimated 13,000 in other countries. The Pennsylvania Farm Show at Harrisburg and the show held in conjunction with the New York State Fair at Syracuse drew a record number of entries. (F. P. P.)

See also Art Exhibitions.

Fashion and Dress

The official demise of the mini-length hemline was decreed by fashion designers in 1970. Paris, London, Munich, Rome, Turin, and—more reluctantly—New York had all voted in their spring and fall shows for lengths that varied from just below the knee to ankle-long. In Europe it was the midi or mid-calf length that emerged in the fall as the more generally acceptable hemline. The maxi or ankle length had been adopted by a minority of younger fashion extremists in the winter of 1969–70 and, in London particularly, one saw the sorry sight of young women battling with the mud-clotted hems of long coats—the ungraciousness of which augured ill for the incoming trend. This unfortunate start, however, in no way hindered the growing urge for longer skirts. One Paris department store reported that midis were outselling minis by a ratio of three to one.

In the U.S. the outcome was more dubious. "Stop the midi" campaigns and protest marches were reminiscent of the (unsuccessful) resistance that had greeted Christian Dior's New Look in 1947. Predictably, men voiced strong objections to the disappearance of sightly legs. There were, however, more substantial reasons for the hesitancy with which American women approached the new length. The pinch of inflation and business recession made the purchase of a whole new wardrobe impractical for the vast majority of women. The militancy of the women's liberation movement—many of whose advocates, indeed, had made the freedom of the mini part of their credo —accorded poorly with the inhibiting effect of longer skirts. Finally, a long, warm autumn permitted women to wear summer clothes far longer than usual, putting off the day when a choice had to be made.

Women's Wear Daily, which publisher John Fairchild had made into the arbiter of U.S. fashion, staked its reputation on the "longuette" (although some felt that its hard-sell approach created more resentment than acceptance). Most of the higher-priced women's stores followed its lead, stocking minis only in the

junior department, if at all. Bonwit's, among others, urged its female employees to wear midis after August, and clerks were carefully instructed on how to overcome customer hesitancy. For whatever combination of reasons, the result was massive resistance. Midi coats sold reasonably well, possibly because they could be rationalized as "practical," but the response to other midi-length garments was so poor that by early October the *Wall Street Journal* was reporting deep trouble in the fashion industry.

The final verdict would not be known for many months, certainly not until after the midi had turned up in the after-Christmas sales. Some observers felt that the end result would be a new "conservative" length just below the knee. Many stores, compromising between high fashion and sales, seemed willing to settle for that, and they received backing from the Italians who, at the Samia Trade Fair in Turin in September, showed dresses at that length as well as at mid-calf. Nevertheless, the midi predominated in Seventh Avenue's spring lines. Its advocates, arguing from history, pointed out that it was already well established among fashion leaders and, in the end, the mass of women had always followed. The U.S., in fact, had been last to adopt the mini. For those who still championed the mini, a last bastion of support fell when its inventor, André Courrèges, showed midi-length hems in his fall collection.

For evening wear there was no equivocation in the matter of hemlines. From as early as 1969 everything was down to the ground—wide silk culottes, full-skirted gypsy dresses in ultrasoft materials, full sleeves, soft sashes, long scarves. "Everything is frail and everything floats," reported a London fashion editor. Reporting from Rome in the *International Herald Tribune,* Leonora Dodsworth said of Capucci's spring 1970 collection, "The evening dresses positively dripped with nostalgia."

The hemline controversy involved more than length; adjustment was needed in the shape of clothes. Jackets were radically shortened: the prototype suit launched by Dior in the fall showed a

This Cossack style outfit and white evening smoking dress are part of Manstyle International 71, a collection of fashions in terylene and crimplene for men shown at London's Piccadilly Hotel March 17, 1970.

UPI COMPIX

Falkland Islands: *see* Dependent States
Farming: *see* Agriculture

UPI COMPIX

spencer-short jacket cropped to the waist. A high-waisted effect was given by broad leather belting at a small, natural waistline, by high-placed patch pockets, and by high and important collars. When, in the fall, coats began to be worn, it was clear that here was the most successful image of the new look: close-fitting, small at the top, double-breasted, firmly belted at the waist, the new coats flared softly but without exaggeration to mid-calf—a welcome improvement on the dreary, bedraggled maxi. The cape staged a dramatic comeback in most of the fall collections and was heralded as the practical cover-up for all hem lengths. Dramatized accessories were seen as an essential adjunct to the longer skirt line, which, unless worn with a dash, risked the stigma of dowdiness. Shoulder bags, flowing scarves, wide and often clumsy-looking leather belts, dashing boots, exotic jewelry, bolder patterned fabrics were all called on to ward off the inherent menace.

The overall result of these various developments was a precious, covered-up, essentially feminine look that was accentuated in the winter by close-fitting, swathed headgear of all kinds—helmets, cloches, bonnets, snoods, caps, and, above all, head-and-ear covering, long-haired fur hats, from under which the face emerged, small, fragile, feminine. Boots, which continued to be worn, were given a lighter, more graceful look by the adoption of 5-cm. (2-in.) heels. In an interview with a Boston paper, New York designer Giorgio di Sant'Angelo summed up the new feminine look in fashion with a happy alliteration: "Exit the too tailored look, enter the frilly, fanciful, feminine female." And he added, "My things won't stand up without a woman inside them."

The favourite fabric of the designers was jersey—wool, silk, rayon, nylon. Jersey was reported to have accounted for 60% of the French ready-to-wear collections. Yves St. Laurent voted jersey "a wonderfully modern material." Fabric priorities listed in the fall by the Paris-based International Fashion Office (International Wool Secretariat) put broadcloth and jersey (particularly jacquard jersey) in the lead, followed by broadcloth and jersey reversibles, featherweight woolens, and tweed. Crepe and chiffon were favourite materials for later in the day. Colours listed by the office were smoky grays, muted tones, warm tones, black—a sophisticated range that was fully in line with the new elegance.

While reaction against constructed clothes and firm materials, as seen in the closing years of the 1960s, was basically responsible for the softness and femininity of 1970 styles, the influence of the hippie movement could not be ruled out. The exotic prints with their melee of colours, the jacquard and patchwork effects, the general look of casual softness with swathed heads and flowing draperies, peasant, gypsy, and "granny" looks, the bright wool ponchos worn by younger women, the vogue for fantastic and often garish jewelry, the long hair—all could be traced to the hippie syndrome.

By 1970 the trousered leg was "establishment." In the U.S., especially, it provided a refuge for women unwilling to take a stand on skirt length, and newspapers duly reported its acceptance as suitable attire for female employees by one conservative firm after another. The final accolade of respectability was given at the Ascot race meeting in England where, for the first time, women were admitted to the Royal Enclosure wearing trouser suits. A new trouser formula, and one that was in line with the midi hem-

KEYSTONE

Left, a maxiskirt from Ungaro features a slash to mid-thigh. Above, a metallic gold lace evening dress is from the first collection of London's Yugoslav-born Franka. Below, a miniskirted young lady considers the effect of a midiskirt, fashion's most visible controversy in 1970.

JOHN DOMINIS, LIFE MAGAZINE © TIME INC.

line, came with knickerbocker suits, plus fours, and gaucho pants.

The majority of young girls continued to wear their hair long and loose from a centre parting, and the straighter it was the better it suited the prevailing taste. Chignons with loose tendrils of hair on either side of the face, "à la Ingres," were often seen on formal occasions. Hair styling for older women was, on the whole, short, disciplined, unremarkable. The effort in 1969 to bring in waving and curls had met with little response. Older women continued to go hatless, while their daughters still favoured floppy hats.

Despite the return to more feminine styles, trendsetter Rudi Gernreich of California made a "statement for the '70s" that prophesied fewer clothes for the young, more and voluminous clothes for the old, and for everybody "a total unisex look through boldness." His models first appeared in identical slacks and halter outfits with head and eyebrows shaved. Later in the show they stripped to the skin. "This," said Rudi, "will simplify things—it will take our minds off how we look and enable us to concentrate on more important matters." Denouncing the new feminine look as unsuitable for modern life, Gernreich was one of the few major designers to show functionally designed, mini-length clothes in the fall. Another designer retaining the mini was Yves St. Laurent, who showed a spring boutique collection in a range of lengths, from micro-mini to maxi. "Length," said St. Laurent, "is no longer important. What is wonderful is the freedom to choose one's length."

With fashion in the balance, 1969–70 was a particularly difficult time for industries that had to look as far as 18 months ahead in styling: the ready-to-wear industry, lingerie, hosiery, and allied trades, and footwear. Was the longer hemline here to stay or was it a flash in the pan? Would the vogue for tights continue or would women revert to stockings? Had boots had their day? There had not been such a revolutionary change in the wind of fashion since Courrèges launched the miniskirt in 1965.

(P. W. HE.)

Fiji

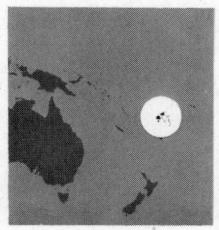

An independent parliamentary state and member of the Commonwealth of Nations, Fiji is an island group in the South Pacific Ocean, about 2,000 mi. E of Australia and 3,200 mi. S of Hawaii. Area: 7,707 sq.mi. (18,314 sq.km.), with two major islands, Viti Levu (4,010 sq.mi.) and Vanua Levu (2,137 sq.mi.), and several hundred smaller islands. Pop. (1970 est.): 526,765. Cap. and largest city: Suva (pop., 1970 est., 61,000). Language: English, Fijian, and Hindi. Religion: Christian and Hindu. Queen, Elizabeth II; governor-general in 1970, Sir Robert Foster; prime minister, Ratu Sir Kamisese Mara.

On October 10, exactly 96 years after the Deed of Cession to Great Britain, Fiji became the fourth new ministate in the South Pacific and the 30th member of the Commonwealth. Three days later it became the 127th member of the UN. Constitutional preparations for independence during the previous year had been marked by the willingness of the Fijian-based Alliance Party and the Indian-based National Federation Party

---

FIJI

Education. (1968) Primary, pupils 110,912; secondary, pupils 11,995; vocational, pupils 839; teacher training, students 294; teachers, all grades (1967) 3,588; higher (medical school), students 213. The University of the South Pacific at Suva opened in 1968; students 260, teaching staff 27.

Finance. Monetary unit: Fiji dollar, with a par value of F$0.87 to U.S. $1 (F$2.09 = £1 sterling). Budget (1969 est.): revenue F$63,430,000; expenditure F$64,271,000.

Foreign Trade. (1968) Imports F$68,402,000; exports F$49,118,000. Import sources: Australia 26%; U.K. 21%; Japan 13%; New Zealand 9%; U.S. 5%. Export destinations: U.K. 38%; U.S. 14%; Australia 11%; Canada 6%; New Zealand 5%. Main exports: sugar 64%; coconut products 13%; gold 9%. Tourism (1968): visitors 66,500; gross receipts (1967) U.S. $12.6 million.

Transport and Communications. Roads (1968) 2,316 km. Railways (private only; 1968) 710 km. Shipping (1969): merchant vessels 100 gross tons and over 18; gross tonnage 6,280. Ships entered (1968): vessels totaling 1,880,000 net registered tons; goods loaded 544,000 metric tons, unloaded 482,000 metric tons. Telephones (Dec. 1968) 14,507. Radio receivers (Dec. 1968) 40,000.

Agriculture. Production (in 000; metric tons; 1967; 1966 in parentheses): sweet potatoes c. 8 (c. 13); cassava c. 80 (c. 80); sugar, raw value (1969–70) c. 304, (1968–69) 400; copra 25 (26); bananas (exports) 1 (4). Livestock (in 000; Sept. 1968): horses 25; pigs 24; cattle (Sept. 1967) c. 155.

Industry. Production (in 000; 1968): cement 51 metric tons; gold 107 troy oz.; electricity 132,000 kw-hr.

---

to compromise. Awareness of Britain's anxiety to withdraw its commitments east of Suez, combined with a new spirit of confidence, had accelerated the final stages of decolonization.

After meetings in Suva and London, an agreement was reached to leave the thorny question of future electoral representation to a royal commission, which was expected to reach a decision in two or three years. Interim arrangements for the next election, due in October 1971, included equal representation in a lower house for Fijians (41.58% of the population and owners of 84% of the land) and Indians (50.12% of the population and the principal land users) and a complicated system of communal and cross voting. Provisions for the composition of a nominated upper house and for amending the constitution protected the special interests of the Fijians. (MY. B. B.)

Finland

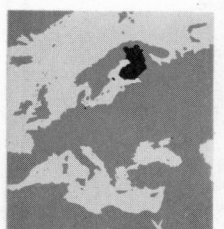

The republic of Finland is bordered on the north by Norway, on the west by Sweden and the Gulf of Bothnia, on the south by the Gulf of Finland, and on the east by the U.S.S.R. Area: 130,128 sq.mi. (337,032 sq.km.). Pop. (1970 est.): 4,695,118. Cap. and largest city: Helsinki (pop., 1970 est., 531,425). Language (1960): Finnish 92.4%; Swedish 7.4%. Religion: Lutheran 91.7%; Orthodox 1.6%. President in 1970, Urho Kaleva Kekkonen; prime ministers, Mauno Koivisto, Teuvo Aura from May 14, and, from July 15, Ahti Karjalainen.

In 1970 the essential problems of forming a stable coalition government—broadly enough based to avoid open conflict over price and wage issues—were dramatically illustrated by the outcome of the general election of March 15–16. The Socialists' parliamentary majority of 103–97 changed into a non-Socialist majority of 112–88, and the five-party Popular Front government headed by Mauno Koivisto promptly resigned. On May 14, after fruitless efforts to assem-

---

ble a new coalition that would reflect the evident swing away from the Socialists, the Koivisto government was succeeded by a caretaker government of civil servants with Teuvo Aura, mayor of Helsinki, as prime minister. This in turn was succeeded in July by another five-party coalition, broadly similar to Koivisto's, under 47-year-old Ahti Karjalainen (*see* BIOGRAPHY).

The new Cabinet included five Social Democrats, four members of the Centre Party, three Communists, two members of the Swedish Party, one of the Liberal Party, and two nonpolitical ministers (one of them close to the Centre Party). It had the support of 144 members of Parliament, with the possible exception of a few non-Socialist dissenters on controversial issues. After the March election the party strength of each group was: Social Democrats 51 (55 in the 1966 election); Conservatives 37 (26); Centre Party 37 (50); People's Democratic League (Communists) 36 (42); Rural Party 18 (1); Swedish Party 12 (12); Liberal Party 8 (8); and Christian League 1 (0). The Radical Socialist League, which won 6 seats in 1966, was wiped out.

The clear non-Socialist majority had been generally expected. The Socialist groups had been defeated at the 1968 municipal elections and lost further ground in 1970. The primary cause of their reverses, at a time when expanding trade and industrial activity placed Finland 15th among the world's richest na-

CAMERA PRESS FROM PIX

Ahti Karjalainen
became prime minister
of Finland July 15, 1970.

tions, was an emotional upsurge containing elements of anti-Communism. Most voters were reacting against the extension in recent years of the influence exerted by young Socialists through the mass media. As presented to television and radio audiences, their radical opinions seemed one-sided, which offended the Finnish sense of fair play. The Conservatives' victory therefore came as no surprise. Increased support for the small Rural Party had also been expected, although few people—with the possible exception of the party's leader, Veikko Vennamo—could have foreseen that its parliamentary strength would jump from 1 seat to 18. Vennamo had been able to stir up the grievances of small farmers and low-income groups. To prominent Finns and the Soviet press alike, he and his followers represented a movement incompatible with Finland's neutrality.

In its economic policy the new government followed the stabilization program of previous years, involving cautious price and wage increases. In September, however, the Communists advocated a departure from it that seemed likely to jeopardize a national solution of labour problems. In February the persistent disunity of the Communist Party led its "Stalinist" minority to approach the party's two governing bodies, the Central Committee and Politburo. Although the majority leader, Aarne Saarinen, remained party chairman, the "Stalinist" leader, Taisto Sinisalo, became second deputy chairman, while his group obtained 15 of the 35 seats on the Central Committee and 6 of the 16 in the Politburo. This internal split was seen as contributing to the Communist setback in the general election.

In 1970 Finland, which in March had decided not to sign the treaty creating a Nordic customs union (Nordek), declared its readiness to enter into talks at the ministerial level with members of the EEC, with which it hoped to negotiate a commercial relationship compatible with its neutrality. Foreign trade showed an increasing concentration on Western European markets, with the EEC and EFTA accounting for more than 67% of both imports and exports. The foreign trade deficit for the first eight months of 1970 was 557 million markkaa, against one of 151.6 million markkaa in the same period of 1969.

Throughout the year the proposition of a European security conference was kept in the forefront of Finnish diplomacy. The question was discussed during President Kekkonen's official visits to Moscow and Washington in July. In Moscow Kekkonen agreed to a 20-year extension of the Soviet-Finnish mutual friendship pact originally signed in 1948. (C. F. SA.)

FINLAND

Education. (1967–68) Primary, pupils 422,584, teachers (full time) 18,531; secondary, pupils 375,549, teachers 19,681; vocational, pupils 96,604, teachers 8,696; teacher training, students 2,177, teachers 381; higher (including 7 universities), students 51,775, teaching staff 5,023.

Finance. Monetary unit: markka, with a par value of 4.20 markkaa to U.S. \$1 (10.08 markkaa = £1 sterling). Gold, SDRs, and foreign exchange, central bank: (June 1970) U.S. \$359.6 million; (June 1969) U.S. \$253.3 million. Budget (1970 est.) balanced at 10,209,000,000 markkaa. Gross national product: (1968) 33,640,000,000 markkaa; (1967) 29.9 billion markkaa. Money supply: (June 1970) 3,627,000,000 markkaa; (June 1969) 2,731,000,000 markkaa. Cost of living (1963 = 100): (June 1970) 144; (June 1969) 141.

Foreign Trade. (1969) Imports 8,495,000,000 markkaa; exports 8,336,000,000 markkaa. Import sources: West Germany 16%; Sweden 15%; U.K. 13%; U.S.S.R. 13%; U.S. 5%. Export destinations: U.K. 18%; U.S.S.R. 14%; Sweden 13%; West Germany 10%; U.S. 6%. Main exports: paper 28%; timber 17%; wood pulp 13%.

Transport and Communications. Roads (1969) 71,870 km. (including 108 km. expressways). Motor vehicles in use (1969): passenger 643,057; commercial 101,778. Railways (1968): state 5,725 km.; private 29 km.; traffic 2,201,000,000 passenger-km., freight (1969) 6,027,000,000 net ton-km. Air traffic (1969): 587 million passenger-km.; freight 13,450,000 net ton-km. Navigable inland waterways (1967) c. 6,600 km. Shipping (1969): merchant vessels 100 gross tons and over 388; gross tonnage 1,330,488. Telephones (Dec. 1968) 1,009,336. Radio receivers (Dec. 1968) 1,727,-000. Television receivers (Dec. 1968) 927,000.

Agriculture. Production (in 000; metric tons; 1969; 1968 in parentheses): wheat 520 (516); rye 141 (134); barley 855 (718); oats 1,146 (1,064); potatoes 1,029 (908); sugar, raw value (1969–70) c. 55, (1968–69) c. 49; butter 101 (102); timber (cu.m.; 1968) 42,400, (1967) 41,100; fish catch (1968) 93, (1967) 74. Livestock (in 000; June 1969): cattle 2,153; sheep 168; pigs 792; horses 111; chickens 7,797.

Industry. Production (in 000; metric tons; 1969): iron ore (66% metal content) 588; pig iron 1,231; crude steel 907; copper 34; cement 1,759; plywood (cu.m.; 1967) 574; cellulose (1967) 4,083; mechanical wood pulp (1968) 1,748; chemical wood pulp (1968) 4,202; newsprint 1,297; other paper and board (1968) 2,383; electricity (kw-hr.) 19,936,000; manufactured gas (cu.m.) 67,000.

Fires:
see Disasters; Insurance

Fisheries

Large trawlers and purse seiners were built only on a limited scale during 1970, and the year appeared to be dominated by shrimp, for which the U.S. market continued to be insatiable. French, Polish, and Spanish shipyards shared large shrimp boat orders for the Middle East, Cuba, and South America, and expansion of the Mexican and U.S. fleets showed no sign of slackening. With Greenland, Iceland, and Norway also active in the Northern Hemisphere, and Australia and Southeast Asia in the Southern, shrimp catching was worldwide, suggesting the desirability of a close watch on stocks. A number of nations, especially Japan, continued to experiment with the artificial cultivation of suitable species.

It was also a boom year for scallops. A 200-mi. bed of the calico variety off Florida was the first commercial bed to be charted by submarine—the U.S. submersible "Aluminaut." For the first time scallops were shucked and processed on board by mechanized equipment. In northwest Scotland, discovery of a 45-mi. bed of large scallops and the smaller "queens" (similar to the calico scallop) led to the fitting out of a 300-boat fleet.

The prosperity of the U.S. shrimp and scallop fisheries was not shared by other American fleets. Government subsidies did little to stimulate investment by owners, for some of whom nothing short of a major injection of capital could be effective. The two new freezer factory trawlers, "Seafreeze Atlantic" and "Seafreeze Pacific," were not outstandingly successful. U.S. fisheries research also suffered from a major cutback favouring the retention of short-term cost-effective work at the expense of long-term effort.

In the U.K. building of middle-distance trawlers was almost at a standstill because of uncertainty about the best type of replacement for the large number of side trawlers approaching obsolescence. Most of these had been constructed during the building boom of the late 1950s, with the result that much of the fleet would be due for replacement over a short period. Following the loss at sea of three U.K. trawlers in one week in 1968, new safety recommendations were issued by a committee under Rear Adm. Sir Holland Martin. The most sweeping related to improved stability and higher bulwarks on side trawlers.

The continuing depression in the Icelandic and Norwegian herring purse seine fleet was alleviated somewhat by alternative catches of capelin and mackerel, which helped to keep the fish-meal plants supplied. There was, however, a marked swing from the specialized purse seiner back to the whitefish stern trawler, capable also of taking pelagic fish—especially herring—with the big midwater trawl, using the system developed by the Germans and French. This involved a greater dependence on *netzsonde*, an echo

NATIONAL FILM BOARD OF CANADA

Sardine fishermen utilize a special trap in Passamaquoddy Bay off New Brunswick. Fishing and other industries are attempting to revive the economy of this once prosperous province.

sounder mounted on the trawl, which enabled the skipper to "see" above and below his net and to set its depth accurately. The method also enabled a pelagic trawl to be skimmed above the bottom to take cod and haddock that were too high for the ground trawl. So important had this system become that it was made the subject of a special UN Food and Agriculture Organization conference in Reykjavik, Ice.

The world fish-meal market, still dominated by Peru, was marked by lower stocks, higher prices, and some uncertainty, the last resulting from fear that the higher prices would encourage users to increase the proportion of soy flour in their formula feeds. A small cloud on the horizon was the possibility of artificial production of protein, for example from raw petroleum. Two British scientists put forward the theoretical possibility of increasing the use of fish meal to feed pigs and poultry as an indirect means of obtaining protein in a form easier to handle than fresh fish. They named several species that were under-

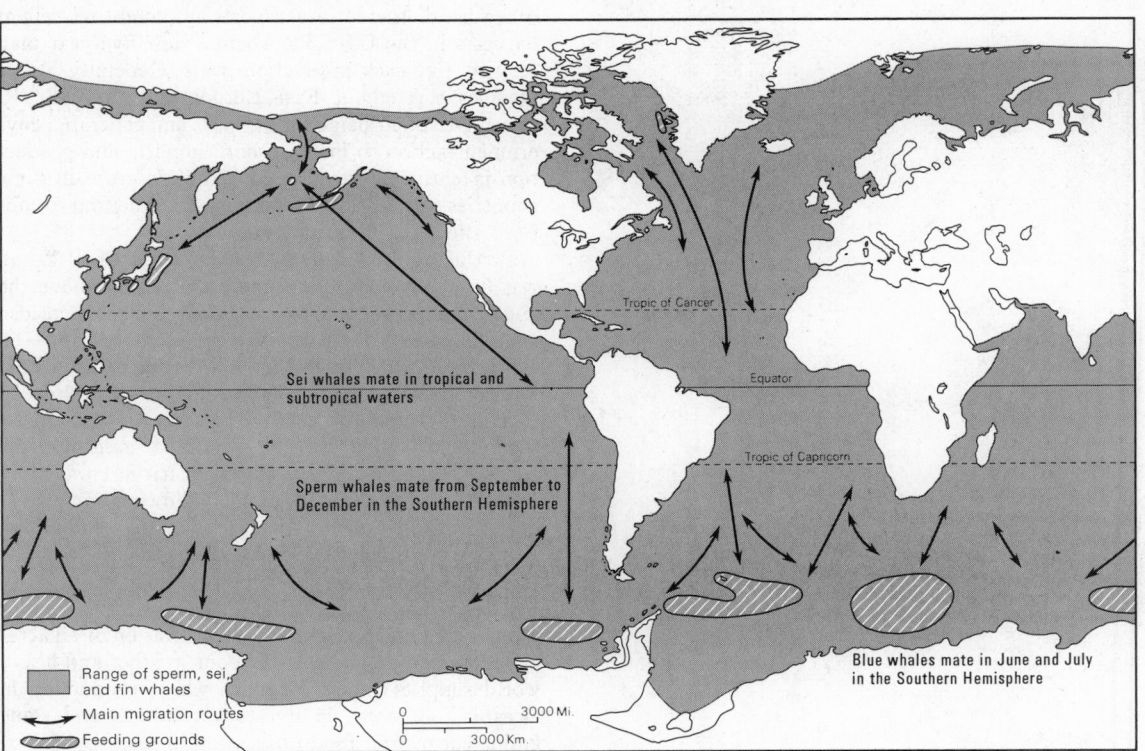

Sei whales mate in tropical and subtropical waters

Sperm whales mate from September to December in the Southern Hemisphere

Tropic of Cancer

Equator

Tropic of Capricorn

Blue whales mate in June and July in the Southern Hemisphere

Range of sperm, sei, and fin whales

Main migration routes

Feeding grounds

0   3000 Mi.
0   3000 Km.

Table I. Whaling: 1968-69 Season
Number of whales caught

Area and country	Blue whale	Fin whale	Humpback whale	Sei whale	Sperm whale	Others	Percentage assigned under quota agreement*
Antarctic: pelagic (open sea)							
Japan	...	1,821	...	3,495	...	42	47
Norway	...	...	...	...	...	...	23
U.S.S.R.	...	1,199	...	2,281	2,682	18	30
Total	...	3,020	...	5,776	2,682	60	...
Outside the Antarctic†	...	3,113	2	6,603	21,512	335	...

Note: No whaling operations from South Georgia during the 1968-69 season.
*Antarctic only.
†1967-68.
Source: Committee for Whaling Statistics, *International Whaling Statistics.*

fished but numerous enough to form the basis of such a fishery, among them Norway pout, silver smelt, and the common dab.

Although whitefish catches were down, demand was good and prices improved. The proportion of frozen fish continued to increase, as did movement of both fresh and frozen fish between countries. The major importers were the U.S., the U.K., West Germany, and Japan. The last-named, unable to catch enough for its fast-expanding needs, emerged as a considerable importer—a reversal of roles compared with a few years previously.

In the field of technical innovation, the Soviet Union completed fishing trials of the world's biggest fishing catamaran, "Experiment," and published a paper on the results. A major factor was the ability of this class to fish in weather that forced larger vessels into shelter. A fleet of these 131-ft. catamarans was to be built for the U.S.S.R.   (H. S. N.)

See also Food.

Table II. World Fisheries, by Country, Catch, and Value of Catch, 1968*†

Country	Catch in 000 metric tons	Value in U.S. $000
Argentina	223	13,551
Australia	103	62,089
Belgium	68	16,845
Brazil‡	419	76,956
Burma	396	77,632
Cambodia	171	43,985
Canada	1,490	169,134
Ceylon	144	64,269
Chile	1,376	27,387‡
Colombia‡	93	20,541
Cuba	66	28,830‡
Denmark	1,467	100,492
Finland	93	19,148
France	794	239,328
Germany, West	682	91,829
Ghana	102	23,692
Greece‡	85	35,234
Hong Kong	101	14,984
Hungary	30	43,282
India	1,526	186,200
Israel	26	14,222
Italy	363	183,675
Japan	8,670	1,952,851‡
Korea, South	841	112,454‡
Malaysia	407	93,234
Mexico	366	75,533
Netherlands	323	62,567
New Zealand‡	60	14,531
Norway	2,804	146,760
Pakistan	424	172,467
Peru	10,520	124,046‡
Philippines	945	369,463
Portugal‡	560	74,179
Ryukyu Islands	35	14,227
Senegal	194	24,091
Spain	1,503	313,794
Sweden	315	42,156
Taiwan	527	127,207
Thailand	1,089	193,722
Uganda	109	17,156
United Kingdom	1,040	154,261‡
United States	2,442	439,144‡
Venezuela	126	25,234

*Excludes whaling.
†Some double counting may occur.
‡1967.
Source: United Nations Food and Agriculture Organization, *Yearbook of Fishery Statistics,* vol. 26.

Food

Food Supplies. Harvests in 1970 appeared to set in motion again an upward trend in food production that had been slowed by agriculture's poor performance the previous year. The Food and Agriculture Organization (FAO) index of 1969 food production, at 150 (1952–56 = 100), was unchanged from 1968. The world index overall was not affected by an increase of three points in the index for the less developed regions of Latin America, the Near East (excluding Israel), the Far East (excluding Japan), and Africa (excluding South Africa), which was offset by a loss of one point in production among the more developed countries. The slowed rate of gain in total food production in 1969, when distributed among populations that continued to increase to an index of 145 above the 1952–56 average, resulted in a decrease in available per-capita food supplies for the people in the less developed regions.

Food Production. Although production of some major crops in North America and Europe was less than in 1969, there were impressive harvests of staple crops in many of the heavily populated less developed regions. In spite of some smaller crops, the U.S. and Canada continued to produce a surplus of grains, particularly wheat, in 1970. In Latin America, record sugar harvests were realized, and encouraging recoveries in cereal production were reported in Brazil, Argentina, Chile, and Mexico. West European countries harvested slightly smaller crops of grains in 1970, but supplies were more than adequate, and in the case of dairy products, overproduction continued to build surpluses. The European Economic Community (EEC) announced it would subsidize the slaughter of nearly 300,000 dairy cows and retire an additional 130,000 from milk production.

Throughout the East European countries floods and the effects of the severe 1969–70 winter reduced grain crops and helped to reduce meat supplies. On the other hand, there were reports of good-to-excellent harvests in the U.S.S.R., where a new five-year plan set new livestock production goals. Generally higher incomes throughout East Europe and the U.S.S.R. raised consumer demand for meat, and generated government action to increase both imports and production incentives. Drought reduced grain crops in some countries in the east Mediterranean, and war conditions affected output of some crops.

Production of 7,329,000 tons of wheat in Pakistan was 9% above 1969, and more than 50% above the 1964–68 average. India's wheat harvest was a record 20 million tons, a sharp increase from the 1964–68 average of 12.1 million tons. Impressive gains in East Pakistan's rice crops raised production to 21,266,000 tons, 20% above the 1963–67 average; a 61,560,000-ton rice harvest in India was a similar gain over the average. India's 4 million-ton sugar harvest was more than 10% above a year earlier, allowing for an export surplus. Abundant rice crops in the Philippines, Korea, and Indonesia raised production in the Far East 4% above 1969; although production in Japan was less than a year earlier, surpluses from earlier crops were on hand, requiring inauguration of an acreage reduction policy in 1970. Poor weather and heavy world supplies acted to reduce wheat production in Oceania, but gains in livestock products and some grains cut overall food production losses.

Trade. An increase in wheat trade, and strong demand for meat, fats, and oils held world trade in most agricultural products at high levels in 1969–70. Wheat exports rose to an estimated 1,800,000,000 bu. from 1,600,000,000 bu. a year earlier; shipments to East Europe, the U.S.S.R., Communist Asia, India, and Pakistan rose above year-earlier levels. Canada, the U.S., and Australia had 67% of the world trade, against 65% a year earlier. Heavy demand for meat in the U.S., the U.K., and the EEC, along with a leveling-off of production, held trade in beef and other meats at high levels. Rising incomes associated with industrial growth, particularly in Japan, added to the demand for meat. Reduced stocks of fats and oils in 1969, along with relatively static production, resulted in heavy demand and high prices for fats and oils; U.S. exports of soybeans in the September 1969–July 1970 period rose to 371 million bu., 43% more than in the same period a year earlier. Strong demand for feed grains in industrialized countries, particularly Japan, indicated increased trade on the order of 10% in 1969–70.

Rice exports, in particular, declined as demand for heavy food-aid shipments was filled by increased production in consuming countries. U.S. agricultural exports in 1969–70 were expected to exceed $6 billion, as compared with $5.7 billion a year earlier. Commercial sales for dollars were expected to account for 85% of total farm export values, as compared with 82% of a smaller total the year earlier. In 1969 some 17% of U.S. farm products were exported under the Food for Peace program.

High price supports in its system of variable levies insulated to a considerable degree the EEC countries from foreign competition. In the U.S. a number of bills to further restrict imports of agricultural commodities were not successful.

The Green Revolution. The improved outlook for food supplies was largely attributed to the Green Revolution—the widespread adoption of new varieties of wheat and rice in the Middle East, the Far East, North Africa, and, to a lesser extent, Latin America. Acreage planted to new high-yielding varieties was variously reported at 34 million and 40 million ac. Agricultural leaders and advisers, while crediting the improved varieties, tended to view their adoption as only one of the factors in increased productivity. Other "pre-conditions" in large measure explained the success obtained upon introduction of new varieties in these countries. These included the development of agricultural institutions, the existence of economic incentives for farmers to produce more, the development of agricultural industries to supply improved seed, fertilizers, machinery, and chemicals, the emergence of enlightened political leadership, and generally good weather worldwide.

In spite of the impressive record, there was a consensus that programs were needed to cope with "later generation" problems, which were predicted to appear once increased production exceeded local needs; these would include the need for new facilities, institutions, and mechanisms for harvesting, storing, processing, transporting, and marketing the excess production. More immediate, and even more disturbing, problems associated with unaccustomed productivity in some areas were identified. Successful adoption of new varieties required not only heavy inputs of fertilizer and chemicals but adequate water supplies, which more often than not meant irrigation. In addition, their promise of profits and their sub-

sidization by governments were seen by some as stimuli to farm consolidation, which in turn threatened dislocation of smaller farms and acceleration of the exodus of rural populations to already-overcrowded urban areas. The history of new varieties also showed their eventual susceptibility to local disease and the possibility of genetic erosion, the process by which primitive or "mongrel" strains are destroyed or lost as a result of the introduction of new hybrid varieties, threatening to remove the sources upon which future plant breeding would have to depend.

Population. As in previous years, population growth continued to hold per-capita gains in food supplies to very low levels. In the less developed regions net increases in population continued throughout the 1960s to add an average 2.6% more persons each year, while gains in food production averaged only 2.5%. Per capita production in 1969 in this part of the world was estimated by the FAO at an index of only 104 (1952–56 = 100); in Latin America and Africa, the 1969 index (97 and 98, respectively) showed a decline over previous years.

The second World Food Congress met in The Hague, Neth., in June to consider the overall food-population problem. Some 1,500 delegates from more than 100 countries discussed implementation of the FAO's Indicative World Plan for Agricultural Development, which estimated that by 1985 the developing countries would require $2\frac{1}{2}$ times as much food as in the plan's base year (1962). The Congress concluded that, if its various proposals were adopted, an average increase in the growth of food production in developing countries of 3.7% was feasible and was sufficient to assure adequate food supplies.

Development and Food Assistance. Strategy for aiding the economies of the developing countries continued in 1970 to shift from the individual-country approach that had been characteristic of most of the postwar period to an emphasis on the multilateral approach. U.S. Pres. Richard Nixon's message to the Congress in mid-September indicated U.S. policy for development assistance programs to be "a new partnership among nations in pursuit of a truly international development effort based upon a strengthened leadership role for multilateral development institutions." He also proposed legislation to create an

Hundreds of people wait at one of St. Louis' food stamp distribution centres Oct. 13, 1970. At midyear more than 14,000 households in the city were receiving stamps; strikes and rising unemployment in the fall swelled the number considerably.

UPI COMPIX

International Development Corporation to handle bilateral aid arrangements, and an International Development Institute to help build research and training competence in lower-income nations and to cooperate in international efforts dealing with population and employment problems.

One report on development aid indicated that in 1969, some $13.3 billion of net financial resources went to aid the economies of the less developed countries from the industrial nations, mainly those of North America and Europe, but including Australia and Japan. Although 1969 aid was slightly larger than a year earlier, it represented only 0.72% of the combined gross national products of the industrialized nations involved and included $4.3 billion of export credits. Increased development aid by the U.S.S.R. was noted. Agreement was reached among the 21 nations contributing to the World Bank's International Development Association to replenish IDA funds at the rate of $813 million per year for three years, beginning in November 1971; the second replenishment, in 1968, had been at the rate of $400 million per year. Agricultural development continued in 1970 to be a significant part of the total aid effort by international and national agencies, as well as private organizations. The UN Development Program announced in September approval of its 1,001st major preinvestment project to be aided since the Special Fund was established in 1959.

The Inter-American Development Bank reported that agricultural loans totaling $202.1 million represented 32% of the Bank's 1969 loans, bringing total agricultural loans to Latin-American countries in the decade to $833.8 million, or 24.3% of all Bank loans. The U.S. Agency for International Development continued to aid agricultural development in countries where local funds, generated by sales of U.S. surplus farm commodities, had accumulated. Combined lending by the World Bank and the International Development Association reached a record of nearly $1.8 billion in fiscal 1969, and Robert McNamara, the World Bank president, announced that development loans in the next five years would reach $11 to $12 billion. Efforts to improve tropical food crops continued at the International Institute of Tropical Research, near Ibadan, Nigeria, and its sister institute, the International Center for Tropical Agriculture, in Colombia.

The FAO in November 1969 announced a $300 million target for voluntary pledges to the World Food Program for 1971–72. The WFP target for 1969–70 was $200 million, and was over-subscribed by some $90 million. U.S. donations under its Food for Peace program in 1969 were reported at about $250 million; shipments of commodities in government-to-government programs of disaster relief and economic development totaled $103 million, and programs operated by voluntary relief agencies amounted to $153 million.

Food Consumption and Prices. Estimated per-capita consumption of major food items in the U.S. increased about 1% in 1970 over a year earlier, according to the U.S. Department of Agriculture (USDA). Increases of 2% in consumption of red meats (especially beef) and fish, a 3% increase in cheese consumption, and heavier use of chicken (7%), shortening (5%), and apples (10%), offset a 9% reduction in the use of veal, as well as reduced use of turkey, fluid milk, sweet potatoes, and cocoa. The USDA

estimate of per-capita consumption of major foods in 1969 included red meats, at 182 lb. (of which beef accounted for 110.5 lb.); 316 eggs (continuing a decline from 356 in 1957–59); 271 lb. of fluid milk and cream (as compared with 337 lb. per capita in 1957–59); 51.8 lb. of fats and oils; 79.1 lb. of fresh fruits; 97.9 lb. of fresh vegetables; 118.2 lb. of potatoes; 112 lb. of wheat flour; and 99.9 lb. of sugar.

Total food expenditures by U.S. consumers were expected to total about $113 billion in 1970, an increase of 7% over 1969. A Department of Agriculture report in August 1970 indicated that Americans spent an average of $518 per person for food in 1969, an increase of 4.6% from 1968. The percentage of disposable income spent for food, 16.7% in 1969, continued its downward trend.

Nevertheless, increasing food prices continued to generate consumer criticism. The U.S. retail food price index rose to 132.7 (1957–59 = 100) in June 1970, continuing its climb from 101.4 in 1960. The June food price index was 2 points above January, and 7.2 points above the average for 1969; the January–June retail food price increase of 1.5% compared with a 2.9% increase in prices of nonfood products. Total U.S. grocery store sales in 1968 were reported at $70 billion, an increase of nearly $4 billion over 1967 and $16 billion more than five years earlier. Sales of food by retail grocery stores in 1968 accounted for $50.8 billion, or 72.5% of total sales.

Retail food stores in 1970 continued to experiment with new computerized methods for checkout, inventory, and ordering operations. Simplified date marking on perishable grocery items was of major concern to retailers, consumers, and legislators. A system of open dating of grocery items was instituted by some of the larger chains, but widespread adoption of the practice was generally resisted by industry spokesmen, who claimed that open dating would result in increased prices and waste. A survey, however, indicated that open dating of grocery items was established practice in eight of nine European countries. Discount sale of food was adopted by several grocery retailer chains in an attempt to reduce prices as well as to placate critical buyers.

Sales and profits of U.S. food manufacturers increased 10% in 1969 over a year earlier. Sales totaled $83,362,000,000, and net profits (after taxes) were reported at $1,985,000,000. Dairy manufacturers' sales increased 13%, to $13,773,000,000, and profits increased 11%, to $308 million. Sales of bakery products declined to $5,272,000,000, and profits to $102 million, from 1968. The outlook for further gains in 1970 was clouded; the canned fruit and vegetable sector of the industry was reported to be plagued by problems of overproduction, and sugar refiners, faced with rising costs attributed to administration of the Sugar Act of 1948, were affected by food manufacturers' searches for lower-priced sugar substitutes.

The index of retail food prices of more than 40 countries reporting consumer price changes to the United Nations revealed only one (Kenya) with lower food prices in 1969 than in 1968. Nearly two-thirds had food price increases ranging from 3 to 6%; eight had increases over 6% and seven had less than a 3% rise. The 5% increase in U.S. retail food prices in 1969 from a year earlier equaled or exceeded those in most European countries, but was far less than inflation-triggered increases shown for most countries in Latin America, where a 25% increase was reported for São Paulo, Brazil, and a 31% increase was shown for Santiago, Chile. In Japan a rapid rise in retail food prices in the first half of 1970 resulted in the adoption of measures by the Cabinet to increase supplies and improve marketing.

In Sweden price increases of 5 to 6% between June 30 and mid-August 1970 resulted in Cabinet approval of a controversial decision to freeze some food prices, including bread and flour products, dairy products, and meat products. Food prices in Great Britain rose sharply in the first quarter of 1970, and supplies were temporarily threatened by a national dock strike in mid-July. Higher incomes, which generated heavier demand for meat, milk, eggs, and chicken in East European countries, moved the U.S.S.R. to contract for meat imports from Australia and New Zealand and the Polish, Hungarian, and Yugoslav governments to increase livestock delivery prices and offer incentives to farmers who increased beef and pork sales. Food price increases imposed in Poland late in the year led to rioting in several cities.

U.S. Developments. The paradox of hunger in the most affluent country in the world was not easily accepted by some, though by 1970 few could any longer doubt the reports of individual researchers and survey teams attempting to assess the problem. Overnourishment of an estimated 20 to 25% of Americans was a generally accepted finding by medical and nutritional specialists. Associated as it often was with poverty, undernourishment was less visible to the medical profession. Preliminary results of the first National Nutrition Survey, which got under way in 1969, indicated that as many as 15 million Americans might suffer from malnutrition. The survey revealed that non-poor Americans as well were malnourished in one or another respect: 10% of the population was apparently anemic; 8 to 20% suffered from deficiency of one or more vitamins; and percentages of the population having less than acceptable levels of other essential nutrients ranged from 9% (thiamine) to 19% (riboflavin). Other findings indicated growth retardation in 10% of children surveyed, and an estimated 5% of the total population with low iodine intake. Surveys of schoolchildren in widely scattered areas produced evidence of malnutrition that was not necessarily associated with either poverty or geography.

Against this backdrop of growing interest, several symposia and conferences were scheduled late in 1969 and congressional interest in the nutrition problem continued at a high level in 1970. The Senate Select Committee on Nutrition and Human Needs continued to hold hearings on a variety of hunger-related problems; its mission was extended through Jan. 31, 1971, by action of the Senate in February. In September the Democratic Study Group of the House of Representatives held a symposium on a national nutrition policy. The Food Stamp Program was expanded by administrative action in 1969 and early 1970 to accomplish the goal of an operating food stamp or commodity distribution program in every county in the country.

Senate and House versions of the Food Stamp bill to replace the one that was to expire at the end of 1970 differed widely. A compromise, passed on December 31, authorized $1,750,000,000 for fiscal 1971 and open-ended authorizations for the next two years. It set a ceiling of $106 per month for a family of four while requiring that all able-bodied adult registrants also register for work and accept jobs. The bill also provided for free stamps to families of four

ROBERT AZZI FROM NANCY PALMER AGENCY

At refugee camp in Jordan a Palestinian carries a sack of flour received from U.S. foreign aid shipment.

with incomes of less than $30 per month and eliminated a House-passed provision that states share up to 10% of the program's cost.

An estimated 21 million children participated in the school lunch and school breakfast programs in 1970, as compared with 19,125,000 a year earlier. Federal contributions to these programs in 1970 was estimated at $562.1 million; state and local contributions (including payments by children) totaled $1,795,000,000. Legislation to improve child nutrition programs included a bill approved in May that established eligibility standards by which children would be selected for free or reduced-price meals, and authorized advanced funding for the program.

Other aspects of nutrition received attention in 1970. In September the Food and Drug Administration announced it would set voluntary nutritional guidelines for processed foods. Criticism of the nutritional value of dry breakfast cereals produced a sharp and noisy controversy in July. In August the FDA undertook a review of the safety of hundreds of food additives. The FDA ban on cyclamates, an artificial sweetener, was extended to its use in all dietary foods and fruits in mid-August. Other additives, including monosodium glutamate and thyamine, were criticized as possibly dangerous to some consumers. (*See* DOMESTIC ARTS AND SCIENCES.)

In October the report of a study conducted at the University of Texas disclosed that ordinary white bread was so low in nutritional value that two-thirds of the laboratory rats living exclusively on it for a 90-day period died of malnutrition. The USDA came under attack for permitting the use of pesticides and herbicides considered dangerous to human food supplies and the feeding of antibiotics to meat animals was questioned for its possibly harmful effect on consumers.

As a precautionary measure, the FDA announced on December 15 that an estimated one million cans of tuna fish representing several major brands were being withdrawn from the market. On the basis of sample tests, it was established that 23% of all tuna packed in the U.S. in 1970 contained mercury in excess of the federally permitted minimum. Excessive amounts of mercury were also reported in frozen swordfish samples. Mercury poisoning reports had

WIDE WORLD

The Rev. Jesse Jackson of the Southern Christian Leadership Conference's Operation Breadbasket testifies before a Senate committee March 2, 1970. He said Pres. Richard M. Nixon's plan for a $1,600-per-year guaranteed income to poor families was cruelly inadequate.

been responsible also for the banning of fresh fish during the year in parts of the U.S. and in Sweden.

(H. R. Sh.)

Food Processing and Technology. Greater sophistication and the need to try and contain food prices, coupled with labour shortages, stimulated greatly the growth of highly automated giant food enterprises. Britain led in many of these developments. For example, the world's largest cocoa processing plant with an annual capacity of approximately 80,000 tons of beans and employing an entirely new chocolate process was constructed. A single flow-line plant to produce one million pies daily was commissioned at another factory. A completely automated, computer-controlled processing system was designed to select and apportion raw materials for 40 different soups from stocks of 44 solid or liquid ingredients. A similar system was introduced at a biscuit plant to apportion the ingredients to 17 dough-mixing machines, punched tapes supplying the recipes and process details to a computer. A new creamery, to process 100,000 gal. of milk daily, was commissioned; a computer monitored over 900 separate functions and closed-circuit television enabled a central controller to keep the entire plant under review. A modified Bell-Siro cheese maker was installed in Australia with a capacity of 10,000 lb. of cheese per hour. A machine was installed at a British factory to produce, from potato powder, fries of any desired dimensions at a rate of 1,400 three-ounce portions an hour.

Developments in aseptic filling of high-temperature, short-time processed products into cans and various laminates made available many ready-to-serve products that superseded some of the instant mixes, although the marketing of some innovations was curtailed by lack of shelf space in the supermarkets. It was noted that only 47 out of 4,197 new food preparations launched in the U.K. during the previous ten years were still on sale.

Consumption of instant coffee increased substantially in Europe, West Germany becoming the world's second largest user with a consumption exceeding 300,000 tons. The market for baby foods continued to expand and in Poland reached 15,000 tons compared with 4,000 tons three years previously. The staff at a 200-bed U.S. hospital was reduced by 50% after the introduction of total convenience food service. The first frozen meals school service was introduced in Britain. Some observers, however, noticed a trend away from complete convenience foods in parts of the U.S. This was attributed to more leisure and the desire of some housewives to contribute to the meal, causing a demand for part-baked bread and ready-to-bake cookies. The U.K. market for convenience foods was reported to be growing at an annual rate of 16%.

A U.S. company developed successfully a system using liquid Freon for direct-contact freezing. The Freon is recycled and cuts the freezing costs to about one-quarter compared with liquid nitrogen. The system was approved by the FDA and was installed by several leading processors. Canadian workers were able to freeze-dry cottage cheese by using liquid nitrogen for pre-freezing.

Fruit and Vegetables. British machines were developed for the mechanical harvesting of dwarf and broad beans, and progress was made in the mechanized harvesting of brussels sprouts. An automatic carrot topping machine with a capacity of 2.5 tons

Food Preparation:
see Domestic Arts and Sciences

per hour and a machine for the shelling of peas without damage were developed. A machine was designed in the U.S. to line up asparagus spears with the tips all in the same direction.

Protein-Rich Foods. Substantial expansion of the Polish dairy industries was reported, 30 new plants being commissioned. In India there was a substantial increase in school milk consumption. East Germany cut milk transportation costs by 70% through the installation of 25 mi. of sterilizable pipeline connecting production cooperatives with the processing plant. New joint ventures for the manufacture of recombined milk products were established in South East Asian countries by the Australian Dairy Produce Board. Further developments in the mechanized production of cheese were made in Australia, New Zealand, the U.S., the Netherlands, France, Italy, and the U.K. A direct acidification process made possible the production of mozzarella cheese in 5.5 minutes. Australian workers introduced a concentrated liquid nitrogen frozen starter in granular form that could be used for cheddar cheese-making. The world shortage of rennet continued to receive international attention. The British Agricultural Research Council announced the successful completion of cheese-making trials using a 50/50 rennet/pepsin preparation.

Meat production in the U.S.S.R. was up during the first quarter of the year by 9%, totaling 1,614,-000 tons. A shortage of meat for home consumption was reported from Argentina as a result of the demand from exporters. The New Zealand government introduced special inducements to encourage some diversion from milk to beef production. The American Meat Institute sponsored the development of a leaner pork to meet pressure from weight-conscious consumers. The West German Federal Institute for Meat Research issued a report, after several years' toxicological research on smoked meats, which discountenanced carcinogenicity hazards.

A Swedish whaling factory-ship was converted into the world's first floating fish-protein factory. Norway reported the commissioning of the largest floating fish-meal factory for operation in international waters. The Norwegian fish catch in 1969 was down by 250,-000 tons from the previous year. The British White Fish Authority also reported a decline in North Atlantic breeding stocks. U.S. fishery experts described the use of the television satellite Telstar to spot schools of fish. A tremendous increase in the production of cultured fish was reported from Japan. A petroleum yeast-derived feedstuff was developed to help meet a fish feed requirement approaching 500,-000 tons. The demand for seafoods, especially shrimp, continued to outstrip production. Shrimp, oyster, and mussel production was affected in Britain by oil slicks and oysters were severely depleted in the Gulf of Mexico by oil drilling operations. In the U.K., a method of gas-packaging fresh fish in a film, using an admixture of carbon dioxide and ethylene oxide, improved substantially the shelf life but Health Authority approval had to be obtained.

Oils and Fats Products. In Australia the polyunsaturated fatty acid content of milk fat was successfully increased by feeding encapsulated linseed oil to dairy cows. A new margarine that remained plastic in the refrigerator was developed in Sweden from an admixture of milk fat, soybean, and other polyunsaturated oils. Several new margarines, including a liquid margarine of high polyunsaturated fatty acid content, were developed. A U.S. company introduced a dried-egg preparation in which the natural fat and cholesterol were replaced by sunflower oil.

Food Production and Unconventional Products. The gap between world food requirements and available supplies continued to be tackled by improvements in productivity and nutritional quality, and by exploitation of novel protein resources. The Danish Meat Research Institute introduced a program to improve pig stock by raising specific pathogen-free pigs on a large scale. The use of caffeine as a pig feed supplement to improve live-weight gains and produce a leaner meat was proposed by Canadian workers.

The Philippines Atomic Reactor Center reported improvements in rice yield and quality in new genetic strains developed by using nuclear irradiation. The introduction of an infant feeding formula utilizing high-lysine corn was reported in the U.S. There was an increased demand for bread in less developed countries and much effort was devoted to its manufacture from indigenous cereals, especially cassava.

Progress in the production of a single-cell protein from natural gas and petroleum continued, and several international companies announced plans for animal feed production. New Zealand workers announced the development of a new protein food derived from wool, the production of leaf protein made progress in India, and in the U.S. a method of obtaining protein from alfalfa was developed. A British company announced the successful development of a fungal protein derived from starch. Another British company announced its intention to introduce meat analogues and convenience foods derived from spun soy protein. A factory for the production of high quality fish protein by isopropanol extraction was opened in Morocco and a joint U.S.-Swedish commercial enterprise was established to develop new foods based on fish protein.

(HE. B. H.)

See also Agriculture; Commodities, Primary; Fisheries; Prices.

ENCYCLOPÆDIA BRITANNICA FILMS. *Food and People* (1956); *Why Foods Spoil (Molds, Yeasts, Bacteria)* (1957); *Food from the Sun* (1965); *Plankton: Pastures of the Ocean* (1965); *Produce—From Farm to Market* (1968).

Football

Association Football (Soccer). The World Cup finals, in which Brazil performed brilliantly to win the Jules Rimet Trophy for the third time, were the focal point of 1970; practically everything in the soccer world was directed toward the Mexico tournament. Held at four centres—Mexico City, Puebla and Toluca, Guadalajara, and León—the finals followed the usual pattern of being played on a league system in which the 16 finalists were divided into four groups of four teams, the winner and runner-up of each group providing the eight quarter-finalists. The competition then continued on an elimination basis, and the two beaten semifinalists met for third place just before the final. Brazil certainly did not have the advantage of an easy draw, England, Romania, and Czechoslovakia being their opponents in Group 3 at Guadalajara. The other finalists were (Group 1) Mexico, Belgium, El Salvador, U.S.S.R.; (Group 2) Uruguay, Israel, Italy, Sweden; (Group 4) Peru, West Germany, Morocco, and Bulgaria.

Host country Mexico opened the finals on Sunday, May 31, with a goalless draw against the U.S.S.R. in the magnificent Aztec Stadium at Mexico City. Significantly, referee Kurt Tschenscher of West Germany

whistled for 61 infringements of the rules, and firm control set the pattern for the tournament: none of the matches got out of hand and no player was sent off the field. Two days later the other three groups got under way, Uruguay, England, and Peru winning. But it was obvious the following day when Brazil crushed Czechoslovakia 4–1 that they were living up to their reputation and that their 4–2–4 system was still highly effective. For Brazil, Pelé (*see* BIOGRAPHY) showed his master touches; Tostão (Eduardo Goncalves Andrade) and wingers Jairzinho (Jair Ventura Filho) and Roberto Rivelino—the latter sometimes operating in midfield—also demonstrated that they would trouble any defense. The small countries, El Salvador, Morocco, and Israel, provided no upsets, though Italy was held to a goalless draw by Israel.

By the end of the first week the pattern was clear, and the eight quarterfinalists could be determined. Brazil had beaten England, the defending champion, by a single goal from Jairzinho late in the match. The U.S.S.R., Italy, and West Germany topped Groups 1, 2, and 4 as Mexico somewhat surprisingly finished second to the Soviets. Uruguay, England, and Peru gained the other places in the last eight. The most prolific scorers in this phase of the contest were the West Germans and Brazilians. The former scored 10 times in their three games. Gerd Müller, their striker from Bayern Munich, registered hat tricks (three goals in one game) against Bulgaria and against Peru at León, and was leading scorer in all the matches played in Mexico with 10 goals. The new champions scored eight goals in their three fixtures, four coming from the gifted Jairzinho. In contrast, Italy led Group 2 on the strength of a single goal scored by Angelo Domenghini, against Sweden in the opening game.

In the quarterfinals the Italians showed what their attack could do when they defeated the Mexicans 4–1. Domenghini again led the way, Luigi Riva scored two more, and substitute Gianni Rivera added a fourth. Luis Gonzalez got Mexico's lone reply. Two of the quarterfinal contests went into overtime (30 minutes). In Mexico City the U.S.S.R. was holding Uruguay to a goalless draw when Victor Esparrago slotted the ball in to send the South Americans through to the semifinals in extra time. The other extra-time match was at Leon, where West Germany met England. England went into a two-goal lead through the efforts of the Tottenham pair, Alan Mullery and Martin Peters, but the Germans fought back with Franz Beckenbauer moving forward out of defense into a more attacking role. With 25 minutes of the second half gone, he scored the first goal and then Uwe Seeler added a second to tie the game and forced it into overtime. The decisive goal came from Müller after a few minutes, and West Germany thus qualified for the semifinals. In the all-South American game at Guadalajara, Brazil showed Peru the effectiveness of its attack, winning 4–2.

The Brazilians were then committed to another all-South American clash in the semifinals against the ultra-defensive Uruguayan squad. While Brazil swung into its familiar offensive rhythm, the Uruguayans played it hard and tough. Uruguay received a "gift goal" when a defensive error allowed Julio Morales to cross the ball for Luis Cubilla to tap it into the goal. But Brazil tied the score when seconds from the half-time break Tostão moved the ball from out on the left to create an opportunity for Clodoaldo Tavares Santana to crack it home.

Brazil had to wait until the last quarter hour of

CENTRAL PRESS FROM PICTORIAL PARADE

Chelsea left half Ron Harris (centre) and centre half John Dempsey (left) manage to keep out Leeds' Jackie Charlton, as he makes an airborne assault on the Chelsea goal during the F.A. Cup final replay at Old Trafford, Manchester, April 29, 1970. Chelsea won 2–1 in extra time.

the tactically absorbing duel for the flying Jairzinho to shoot home its second goal. Then in the final seconds Pelé, still the master footballer, slipped a pass to Rivelino to send Brazil into the final.

The other semifinal, at Mexico City, was a titanic struggle between West Germany and Italy, and was rated by most as the best game of the tournament. A composite blend of skill, flair, emotion, drama, and courage, the game was soccer entertainment at its most tingling, right to the 30th minute of extra time.

Italy was given a fine start when within seven minutes of the kickoff, Roberto Boninsegna scored. But the Germans were resilient and pounded away until Karl Schnellinger, their centre back, moved up just before the end of normal time to tie the score with a fierce drive; this was just reward for approximately 50 minutes of nonstop attacking, which saw Wolfgang Overath hit the bar and two brilliant saves by Enrico Albertosi from Uwe Seeler, who set a German record by earning his 95th cap during the tournament. Within four minutes of the beginning of the overtime period Müller had put the West Germans into the lead; then, within a similar period, Tarcisio Burgnich, the Italian back-four man, also moved forward to even the score. After another five minutes the Italians went in front again when Riva scored. Four minutes after the start of the second half of extra time, however, the irrepressible Müller scored his tenth goal of the tournament to put West Germany once more on even terms. But hardly had the cheers died away when they exploded again to herald Rivera's final goal that sent Italy through to its third championship match.

At the Aztec Stadium in Mexico City, on Sunday, June 21, the main question of the World Cup final was: could the Italian defense hold the quicksilver Brazilian forwards? The answer proved to be that they could not. The game ended with Brazil worthy winners by a score of 4–1. For the first 30 minutes or so of the game the magnificent Brazilians were matched by the Italians with their exceedingly close marking in defense. Perhaps significantly, Brazil opened its scoring through Pelé after 18 minutes with a perfectly timed header from a Rivelino pass. Casualness in defense led to the Italians' drawing even after 37 minutes when Boninsegna snapped up a lucky rebound to score. After 20 minutes of the second half Gerson Nunes scored for Brazil, and Jairzinho maintained his record of scoring in every round when a Gerson free kick was headed down by Pelé for the flying winger to crack home. The fourth goal again stemmed from Pelé. He passed the ball to his captain Carlos Alberto to thunder into the net as the Brazilians attacked until the final whistle.

European Cup. Feyenoord of Rotterdam became the first Dutch team to win a major European competition when it defeated Celtic of Glasgow 2–1 after extra time in the San Siro Stadium, Milan, Italy, on May 6. Celtic had looked likely to repeat its 1967 triumph when it swept into the lead with a thundering shot by Tommy Gemmell. But the Scots then relaxed and were caught by a high cross into the goal mouth which Feyenoord skipper Rinus Israel headed home to tie the match. Gradually, the Dutch began to dictate the pattern of the game, yet they were unable to add to their score before 90 minutes of play had elapsed. Thus, the overtime period was required. Celtic had substituted George Connelly for Bertie Auld just before the game was extended, but he was not able to bring the Scots the dominance in midfield

that they needed, and with four minutes of extra time remaining Ove Kindvall scored the crucial goal and brought the trophy to the Netherlands.

European Cup-Winners' Cup. Manchester City became the third English club to bring home this trophy by defeating Gornik Zabrze of Poland 2–1 in the final in Vienna on April 29. Manchester City led after 12 minutes with a goal from Neil Young, but lost halfback Mick Doyle with an ankle injury 4 minutes later. With young Ian Bowyer on the field as substitute, City continued to have the edge against the Polish side. Just before the end of the first half the English club went two up when H. Kostla, the Polish goalkeeper, conceded a penalty for a Rugby-style tackle on Young and Francis Lee scored from the spot. Midway through the second half, the Poles fought back to score through their veteran international, H. Oslizlo, but they never had enough penetration in attack on the slippery Prater Stadium pitch to ruffle the Manchester defense.

Inter-Cities' Fairs' Cup. Arsenal captured this trophy the night before Manchester City's triumph when, at their Highbury ground, north London, they defeated the Belgian team Anderlecht 3–0 to win the two-game final 4–3 on aggregate. In the first leg in Brussels on April 22, Anderlecht moved into a 3–0 lead with goals by Johann Devrindt and Jan Mulder (2) before Arsenal got the measure of them. Ignoring the usual tactic of closing up the game away from home, Arsenal persisted with its attacking policy and was rewarded when Ray Kennedy, a substitute, scored late in the game to cut the lead to two goals. In the second leg of the final, Arsenal took 20 minutes to settle down, and then Eddie Kelly gave them a lead at half time. In the second half the London club used controlled attacks and added to its score through goals by John Radford and Jon Sammels.

British Isles Championship. This tournament was played, as in 1968–69, at the end of the domestic season. Though officially England, Scotland, and Wales finished in a three-way tie, England scored the most goals. On the opening day, April 18, Scotland beat Northern Ireland 1–0 at Windsor Park, Belfast, with a goal scored by John O'Hare of Derby. Meanwhile, at Cardiff, England and Wales tied 1–1, a goal by Dick Krzywicki of Wales being equaled by one from Manchester City's Lee. England beat Northern Ireland the following Tuesday 3–1, led by Bobby Charlton of Manchester United on the occasion of gaining his 100th England cap. The following day the Scots were contained by the battling Welsh to a goalless draw at Hampden Park Stadium, Glasgow. In final matches Scotland and England fought out another goalless draw, again at Hampden, before 137,478 fans, while Wales, before a quarter of that number of people, beat Northern Ireland at Swansea with a goal from Ronnie Rees of Nottingham Forest.

Inter-Continental Club Championship. The long sorry story of violence in this competition for the right to be called world club champions continued when the European Cup holders, A. C. Milan, beat their South American counterparts, Estudiantes of Argentina, 4–2 on aggregate. The first leg in Milan on Oct. 8, 1969, was tough but gave no real indication of the rowdy affair that was to follow in Buenos Aires a fortnight later. The Italians triumphed in the first leg with goals by Angelo Sermani (2) and Nestor Combin, with the Argentines failing to score. In the return match Estudiantes went out determined to retain the trophy at any price, and fouls flew thick and

UPI COMPIX

Italian goalkeeper
Enrico Albertosi
lies stretched out
on the pitch after a shot
by Gerson Nunes of Brazil
entered the goal
during the final match
of the 1970 World Cup
soccer championships
in Mexico City
June 21, 1970.
Brazil won the coveted
championship 4–1.

fast. Chilean referee Domingo Massaro sent off the home side's Ramon Aguirre Suarez and Eduardo Manera, while Milan lost Combin and Pierino Prati with injuries. Estudiantes "set the Bocca stadium alight" by scoring twice after Luigi Rivera had opened the account for Milan. Conigliari and Aguirre Suarez were the Argentine scorers. Being two men short after the penalty dismissals, Estudiantes lost the edge and were then unable to pierce the tightly woven Milan defense.

After the game the Argentine football association suspended Manera for 20 league games and three years' internationals and Aguirre Suarez for 30 games and five years' internationals; Argentine goalkeeper Alberto Poletti was banned for life for his part in the game's becoming a shambles. (T. W.)

Rugby. *Rugby Union.* The 1969–70 period included a major tour of the British Isles by South Africa and a major tour of South Africa by New Zealand. In addition Scotland made short tours of Argentina and Australia, and the International Board decided to incorporate into the laws of the game the experimental law restricting kicking to touch between the 25-yd. lines.

The first activity of the period was Scotland's six-match tour of Argentina in September 1969. On this tour Scotland twice played the Argentine national team, losing on the first occasion 3–20 but winning the second match 6–3. Scotland won the other four matches of the tour and ended with a points record of 68 for and 46 against.

South Africa's tour of the British Isles lasted from the beginning of November 1969 until the end of January 1970. During this time the visitors played 25 matches, winning 16, drawing 4, and losing 5, with a point record of 345 for and 163 against. This was disappointing as compared with previous major tours by South Africa, especially in that the South Africans did not win any of the four international matches. They were beaten by Scotland 6–3 and by England 11–8, and they drew with Ireland 8–8 and with Wales 6–6. Several reasons were advanced for the South Africans' relative lack of success, the most obvious being that they were hounded both on and off the field by demonstrations against their country's racial policies. Hundreds of police had to be on duty both inside and outside most of the grounds on which the South Africans played, and plain-clothes police were stationed in all their hotels. In this atmosphere some of the players failed to find their normal form, and the team as a whole took a long time to settle down. In addition, South Africa lacked penetrative runners and hard defenders in midfield. The captain, Dawie de Villiers, played many fine games at scrum half, as did the vice-captain, Tommy Bedford, at no. 8.

The home international championship season was notable for the recovery made by France who, having finished last the previous season, now shared top position with Wales. France started its campaign by beating Scotland 11–9 at Murrayfield, and they followed this by defeating Ireland 8–0 in Paris. Since Wales lost 0–14 to Ireland in Dublin, France had high hopes of beating Wales at Cardiff; but this vital match ended in victory for Wales, 11–6. Wales, meanwhile, had beaten Scotland 18–9 at Cardiff and England 17–13 at Twickenham; thus, the position at the top of the standings depended on the last match of the championship season, that between France and England in Paris. If France could beat England, it would share the title with Wales; if England were to beat France, Wales would have the championship title to itself. In the game France gave a magnificent display of attacking Rugby in defeating England 35–13, the largest number of points ever scored against England in one match. Ireland, having lost to France and also to England (3–9 at Twickenham), recovered sufficiently to win both its matches in Dublin, 16–11 against Scotland and 14–0 against Wales, and so finished third. Scotland, having lost to France, Wales, and Ireland, managed to salvage something from its season by defeating England 14–5 at Murrayfield. For the English players, whose season began encouragingly with their first-ever victory over South Africa, the championship campaign was especially disappointing in that their 35–13 beating from France was their last match before arriving at their centenary season.

The home international championship included several unusual events. For the England-Ireland match at Twickenham the Irish selectors, faced with the late withdrawal of their left-wing three-quarter because of injury, recalled Tony O'Reilly, who had first played for Ireland in 1955 and had not played for them since 1963. The span of his international career, from 1955 to 1970, was the longest ever known in the history of Rugby. In the same game, England's victory, 9–3, owed a great deal to two astonishing, long dropped goals by the fullback and captain, Bob Hiller. In the England-Wales game, also at Twickenham, the French referee, R. Calmet, was accidentally knocked over. He broke a bone in a leg and had to be replaced by one of the touch judges, R. F. Johnson (England), who was already an international referee.

Apart from incorporating in the laws the former experimental law restricting kicking to touch between the 25-yd. lines, the International Board at its annual meeting in Edinburgh in March made no significant alterations to the character of the game. They did, however, set up a new standing committee to examine the implications of any changes in the laws that might be contemplated.

Scotland's tour of Australia took place in May and June. They played six matches, winning three and losing three, with a point record of 109 for and 94 against. One full international match was played, and Australia won this 23–3. The other teams who beat the Scots were New South Wales and Queensland.

New Zealand's tour of South Africa in June–September proved to be the customary battle of the Rugby giants. In their 24 matches the New Zealanders scored 669 points and had only 149 scored against them.

UPI COMPIX

Nebraska back Jeff Kinney crashes over Louisiana State's defense line during Orange Bowl action in Miami on New Year's Day, 1971. The Cornhuskers won 17–12.

They won all 20 of their ordinary games but failed in the four-match test series, losing it 1–3. The New Zealanders concentrated on playing the fast, open football that had made them so impressive during their 1967 tour of the British Isles. But, although this method of play proved highly successful, as well as entertaining, in the ordinary games, the New Zealanders found that under the pressures of test matches they made handling errors that were fatal against such quick loose forwards as J. H. Ellis and P. J. F. Greyling of South Africa. The scores in the test matches were 17–6 to South Africa at Pretoria, 9–8 to New Zealand at Cape Town, 14–3 to South Africa at Port Elizabeth, and 20–17 to South Africa at Johannesburg. New Zealand, captained by B. J. Lochore and including the veteran C. E. Meads, who played his 51st international match during the tour, used as many as 27 different players in the four tests. After the last test Dawie de Villiers, who had captained South Africa since 1965, announced his retirement from international Rugby.

Rugby League. The outstanding event of the 1969–70 period was the successful tour of Australia and New Zealand undertaken by Great Britain in June and July 1970. The British played 24 matches, winning 22, drawing 1, and losing 1, with a point record of 753 for and 288 against. They scored 165 tries and had only 36 scored against them. Their only defeat was by Australia in the first test of the tour, the Australians winning 37–15 at Brisbane. The British drew level in the test series by beating Australia 28–7 in the second test, at Sydney, and they won the series by triumphing in the third test of the three-match series 21–17, also at Sydney. In New Zealand the British won their three tests 19–15 at Wellington, 23–9 at Christchurch, and 33–16 at Auckland.

A triangular tournament took place in the north of England in October 1969. It involved England, France, and Wales, who finished in that order. The results were France 8, Wales 2; England 11, France 11; England 40, Wales 23. Wales got its revenge from France the following January by beating the French 15–11 at Perpignan, thus becoming the first Welsh team to win in France since 1936. The referee at Perpignan, R. Thomas, of Oldham, was knocked unconscious by the crowd as he left the field at the end of the match. (D. B. J. F.)

U.S. Football. Nebraska's Cornhuskers, for the first time, won the nation's mythical college football championship. The honour came in the final Associated Press (AP) poll taken after the Bowl games. Nebraska's no. 1 ranking was the result of Bowl upsets triggered by Notre Dame and Stanford. Notre Dame finished second in the final voting, with Texas third, Tennessee fourth, and Ohio State fifth.

At the conclusion of regular-season play, Texas was ranked no. 1. The Longhorns possessed a 30-game winning streak, longest among the schools playing a major schedule in the National Collegiate Athletic Association (NCAA). But Notre Dame's Irish began a series of climactic surprises by defeating Texas 24–11 in the Cotton Bowl at Dallas, Tex. Ohio State of the Big Ten, undefeated and untied and second in the ratings, would have soared to no. 1 with a victory over Stanford in the Rose Bowl at Pasadena, Calif., which began about an hour later. But the Buckeyes were flat and absorbed their first loss of the season, bowing to Stanford 27–17.

Nebraska was at the Orange Bowl in Miami, Fla., for a night game against Louisiana State University. Previously ranked third behind Texas and Ohio State, the Cornhuskers took the field with the knowledge that they might leap to no. 1 with a win over LSU. Nebraska did just that, battling to a 17–12 triumph to conclude its most successful season with a record of ten victories, no losses, and one tie.

The only blemish on Nebraska's otherwise flawless record was a 21–21 early-season tie with Southern California, which also inflicted Notre Dame's lone defeat. Only three of the 617 four-year schools that played major schedules went through the season unbeaten and untied. They were Dartmouth, 9–0, Arizona State, 11–0, and Toledo, 12–0. Arizona State and Toledo climaxed their seasons with Bowl victories, Arizona winning in the Peach Bowl and Toledo in the Tangerine Bowl.

As usual, there were many outstanding players, but the most honoured was Jim Plunkett, a senior quarterback from Stanford. Plunkett won the coveted Heisman Trophy as the nation's outstanding player. Two other quarterbacks, Joe Theismann of Notre Dame and Archie Manning of Mississippi, finished second and third, respectively.

The first Stanford player to win the Heisman, Plunkett set three major NCAA career records: (1) most yards gained total offense (rushing and passing) 7,887, becoming the first player to exceed 7,000 yd.; (2) most yards gained passing, 7,544; and (3) most yards total offense per game average, 254.4. The first two of these records were previously held by Steve Ramsey of North Texas State, 1967 through 1969; and the third by Johnny Bright of Drake, 1949 through 1951.

Chuck Hixson of Southern Methodist shattered the

Stanford's star quarterback, Jim Plunkett, sprints to a 22-yd. gain against Ohio State during the Rose Bowl game, Jan. 1, 1971. Stanford upset the Buckeyes 27–17 in a game highlighted by Plunkett's brilliant performance.

WIDE WORLD

NCAA's career record for pass completions with 642. Again Ramsey, with 491 completions, had been the previous record holder. Elmo Wright of Houston set a career mark of catching 34 touchdown passes; Bob Jacobs of Wyoming established a new career record for the most field goals, 37; Marv Bateman of Utah had a punting average of 45.7 yd., bettering the previous one-season record set by Bobby Joe Green of Florida in 1959; and Don McCauley of North Carolina rushed for 1,720 yd., improving on the previous record of 1,709 set in 1968 by O. J. Simpson of Southern California.

Attendance increased for the 17th consecutive season. Some of the increase was attributed to the fact that more than 50 of the major schools added an 11th game. Nonetheless, the overall gate, not counting postseason games, was 29,465,604, a remarkable gain of 6.66%. For the 13th successive season, Ohio State led in home attendance with 432,451 paid admissions, a per-game average of 86,490. Michigan and Purdue, also of the Big Ten, were second and third, with per-game averages of 79,361 and 68,018, respectively.

East. Dartmouth won the Ivy League title with a 7–0 conference record and was 9–0 overall. The Indians won their first four games by shutouts and, for the season, outscored their opponents 311 points to 42. As a reward, Dartmouth won the Lambert Trophy as the outstanding team in the East, and Bob Blackman, its veteran head coach, was offered a similar coaching position at Illinois in the Big Ten, which he accepted. Running back John Short was among the Dartmouth stars, setting a school rushing record by gaining 787 yd. from scrimmage.

Harvard and Yale tied for second place in the Ivy League, each with 5–2 records. Yale defeated Harvard in their traditional game, and at the season's end John Yovicsin resigned as the Harvard coach but remained with the school as the director of physical training and recreation. He was succeeded by Joe Restic. Jake Crouthamel, previously one of Blackman's assistants, was named the new head coach at Dartmouth.

Connecticut won the Yankee Conference title with a conference record of four victories, no losses, and one tie. Penn State, a perennial power, routed Navy 55–7 in its opener to run its winning streak to 31 games but then lost its next two games and finished with a 7–3 record.

Southwest. Texas won the Southwest Conference championship with a flawless 7–0 conference record by defeating Arkansas 42–7 in its final regular-season game. Quarterback Eddie Phillips, running back Steve Worster, defensive end Bill Atessis, and kicker Happy Feller were among the Texas stars. Arkansas was second in the conference with a 6–1 mark and Texas Tech third with 5–2. Louisville won top honours in the Missouri Valley Conference.

South. LSU, featuring an especially strong defense against rushing, won the Southeast Conference title with a 5–0 mark. Tennessee, which was not on the LSU schedule, was second, and Auburn third. LSU, which had not won an undisputed conference title since 1958, allowed an average of 52.2 yd. rushing. Wake Forest won the Atlantic Coast Conference championship, while William and Mary captured top honours in the Southern Conference.

Midwest. Ohio State, a perennial power, won the Big Ten title by defeating Michigan 20–9 in the final conference game for both teams. Michigan, which

was undefeated prior to its confrontation with Ohio State, finished in a second place conference tie with Northwestern, both with 6–1 records. Ohio State had one of the nation's leading rushers in John Brockington, who gained 1,041 yd. in the Buckeyes' nine regular-season games.

Notre Dame lost only once, bowing 38–28 to Southern California in its regular-season finale, the third time that USC had prevented the Irish from having a perfect season. Quarterback Joe Theismann, who completed 58% of his passes, directed an awesome Irish offense that was extremely well balanced and averaged 510.5 yd. during the regular season, 252.7 by passing and 257.8 by rushing. Nebraska won the Big Eight Conference title outright by defeating Oklahoma 28–21 in the final quarter of its last conference game. Quarterback Jerry Tagge, kicker Paul Rogers, and pass catchers Johnny Rodgers and Guy Ingles were among the Nebraska stars. Unbeaten and untied Toledo won the title in the Mid-American conference.

Pacific Coast. Stanford's Indians, led by All-American quarterback Jim Plunkett, won the Pacific Eight title with a 6–1 record, losing in the conference only to California, which finished in a four-way tie for second place with Washington, Oregon, and UCLA. Plunkett had outstanding receivers in Randy Vataha and Bob Moore. Arizona State, paced by quarterback Joe Spagnola, won the title in the Western Athletic Conference.

Small Colleges. Five NCAA teams that played a small-college schedule finished their regular-season schedules with perfect records. They were Arkansas State, Tennessee State, and Montana, all 10–0; St. Olaf of Northfield, Minn., 9–0; and Westminster of Fulton, Mo., 8–0.

Professional. The 1966 merger agreement between the National Football League (NFL) and the American Football League (AFL) was implemented in full in 1970. The 26 teams, 16 from the NFL and 10 from the comparatively new AFL, merged into one huge league, the National Football League, and were divided into conferences of 13 teams each, the National and American. For balance, three of the original NFL clubs, Baltimore, Pittsburgh, and Cleveland, were switched to the American. Each of the two conferences were then subdivided into three geographic divisions, the Eastern, Central, and West-

NFL Final Standings and Play-offs, 1970

AMERICAN CONFERENCE

Eastern Division

	W	L	T
Baltimore	11	2	1
*Miami	10	4	0
N. Y. Jets	4	10	0
Buffalo	3	10	1
Boston	2	12	0

Central Division

	W	L	T
Cincinnati	8	6	0
Cleveland	7	7	0
Pittsburgh	5	9	0
Houston	3	10	1

Western Division

	W	L	T
Oakland	8	4	2
Kansas City	7	5	2
San Diego	5	6	3
Denver	5	8	1

NATIONAL CONFERENCE

Eastern Division

	W	L	T
Dallas	10	4	0
N.Y. Giants	9	5	0
St. Louis	8	5	1
Washington	6	8	0
Philadelphia	3	10	1

Central Division

	W	L	T
Minnesota	12	2	0
*Detroit	10	4	0
Chicago	6	8	0
Green Bay	6	8	0

Western Division

	W	L	T
San Francisco	10	3	1
Los Angeles	9	4	1
Atlanta	4	8	2
New Orleans	2	11	1

*Fourth qualifier for play-offs.

Play-offs

American semifinals

Baltimore 17
Cincinnati 0

Oakland 21
Miami 14

American finals

Baltimore 27
Oakland 17

National semifinals

Dallas 5
Detroit 0

San Francisco 17
Minnesota 14

National finals

Dallas 17
San Francisco 10

Super Bowl

Baltimore 16
Dallas 13

Baltimore quarterback Johnny Unitas eludes Oakland defenseman Carleton Oats during the American Conference title game, Jan. 3, 1971. The Colts won 27–17 to qualify for the Super Bowl game.

WIDE WORLD

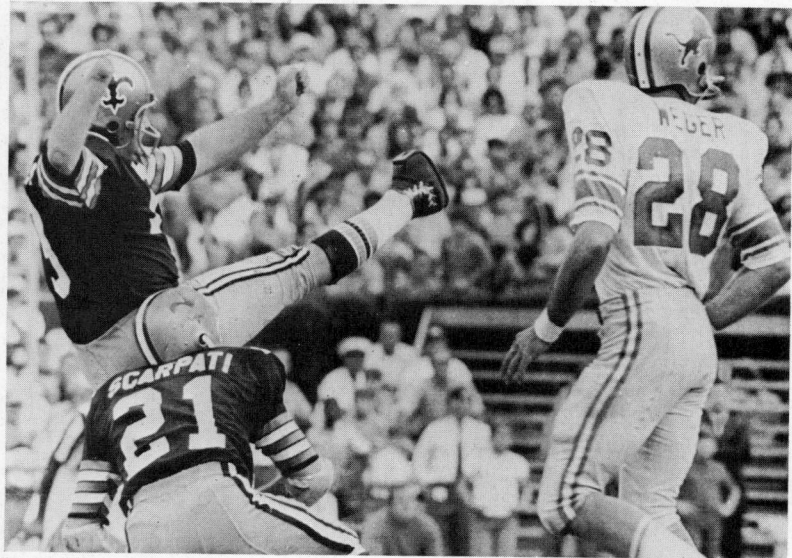

UPI COMPIX

New Orleans Saints' field goal expert Tom Dempsey scores against the Detroit Lions, Nov. 8, 1970. With two seconds remaining in the game, Dempsey, who was born without a right hand and with only half a right foot, kicked a record 63-yd. field goal to give the Saints a 19–17 victory.

UPI COMPIX

Rookie Jim O'Brien boots the winning field goal with five seconds remaining in the game to give the Baltimore Colts a 16–13 victory over the Dallas Cowboys in the Super Bowl, Jan. 17, 1971.

ern. The new arrangement included interconference games with each of the clubs playing a minimum three "crossover" opponents in the other conference.

The restructuring created six pennant races, which helped sustain spectator interest. Eight teams qualified for the play-offs, the six divisional champions and the second place team with the best won-and-lost record in each conference. Going into the final week of regular-season play, three teams had clinched play-off berths but the races were so close that ten other teams still had a chance for the remaining five play-off positions, an important factor that prevented noticeable late-season attendance drops.

Baltimore, again led by veteran quarterback Johnny Unitas, who was in his 15th professional season, dominated play in the Eastern Division of the American Conference after the co-favoured New York Jets lost Joe Namath, their star quarterback, because of an early-season injury. The Miami Dolphins, directed by former Baltimore coach Don Shula, gave the Colts their strongest challenge and qualified for the play-offs.

The Oakland Raiders, who were unable to win any of their first three contests, rallied behind the game-saving heroics of quarterback George Blanda, who accounted for five consecutive last-quarter victories with his field-goal kicking or passing. This streak enabled the Raiders to win the American's Western Division championship. For his efforts, the 43-year-old Blanda was voted the most valuable player in the American Conference and also the male athlete of the year.

The Cincinnati Bengals, coached by Paul Brown, won top honours in the American's Central Division. The Bengals won their regular-season opener, beating Oakland, then lost six in a row before executing a dramatic turnabout and finishing with seven successive victories.

The Dallas Cowboys, after floundering early in the season, also came on strong at the finish and won their last five games to capture the title in the National's Eastern Division. Duane Thomas, a rookie running back, paced the Dallas offense. Dallas also featured a highly publicized "Doomsday Defense" which allowed only 15 points in the last four regular-season games.

The Minnesota Vikings, who had the league's best

defense, led from start to finish in winning the National's Central Division championship. The Vikings' offense was undistinguished but their defense was superb, permitting only 14 touchdowns, fewest ever scored on a team through a 14-game schedule.

The San Francisco Forty-Niners won their first championship in 25 years of competition, finishing first in the National's Western Division. John Brodie, a 36-year-old quarterback chosen as the league's most valuable player, was the San Francisco star.

All play-off games were held within each conference, for the purpose of deciding a conference champion. Baltimore shut out Cincinnati 17–0, and Oakland edged Miami 21–14 in the American semifinals. The following week Baltimore won the title by eliminating Oakland 27–17. In the National semifinals, Dallas beat Detroit 5–0 and San Francisco ousted Minnesota 17–14. Dallas then defeated San Francisco 17–10 for the National championship, qualifying as Baltimore's opponent in the Super Bowl.

Baltimore won its first Super Bowl by defeating Dallas 16–13 with a field goal by rookie Jim O'Brien in the last ten seconds. Both teams showed strong defenses but were erratic on the attack. After throwing one touchdown pass, Unitas left the game in the second quarter with injured ribs, and Earl Morrall then quarterbacked the Colts to victory.

It was not a spectacular year for new records. The most sensational of them was a 63-yd. field goal by Tom Dempsey of the New Orleans Saints. Dempsey's kick came with only two seconds left to play and lifted his team to a 19–17 victory over Detroit. The previous professional field goal record, which stood for 17 years, was 56 yd., set by Bert Rechichar of the Baltimore Colts.

There were many coaching changes. At the season's end, George Allen was fired as head coach of the Los Angeles Rams and less than two weeks later was hired as the head coach and general manager of the Washington Redskins. Two coaches, Blanton Collier of Cleveland and Wally Lemm of Houston, finished the season and then retired. Fired or forced to resign were Tom Fears of New Orleans, Bill Austin of Washington, Clive Rush of Boston, Phil Bengtson of Green Bay, and Charlie Waller of San Diego. Professional football also lost one of its legendary figures with the death on September 3 of Vince Lombardi (*see* OBITUARIES).

Canadian Football. The Montreal Alouettes, last place finishers in 1969, defeated the Calgary Stampeders 23–10 to win the Grey Cup for 1970, symbolic of supremacy in the Canadian Football League. The Alouettes were third in the league's Eastern Conference, finishing behind Hamilton and Toronto, but defeated Hamilton in two successive play-off games to qualify for their first Grey Cup appearance since 1956. Calgary defeated Saskatchewan in the Western Conference play-offs. Moses Denson, a 25-year-old rookie running back, led the attack in the Grey Cup and was also Montreal's season-long star, averaging 7.1 yd. per carry.

Winners of the league's Schenley Awards were pass catcher Jim Young of British Columbia as the outstanding player, Ron Lancaster of Saskatchewan as the most valuable player, and Wayne Harris of Calgary as best lineman. Statistical leaders were Jack Abendschan of Saskatchewan in scoring with 116 points; Hugh McKinnis of Calgary, who rushed for 1,135 yd.; and Ron Lancaster of Saskatchewan and Gary Wood of Ottawa in passing. (JE. HƆ.)

France

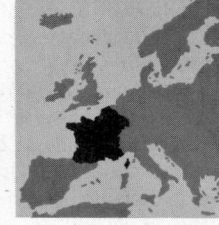

A republic of western Europe and head of the French Community, France is bounded by the English Channel, Belgium, Luxembourg, Germany, Switzerland, Italy, the Mediterranean Sea, Monaco, Spain, Andorra, and the Atlantic Ocean. Area: 210,038 sq.mi. (543,998 sq.km.), including Corsica. Pop. (1970 est.): 50,545,400. Cap. and largest city: Paris (pop., 1968, 2,590,771). Language: French. President in 1970, Georges Pompidou; premier, Jacques Chaban-Delmas.

During the first full year of his seven-year term of office, Georges Pompidou (*see* BIOGRAPHY) showed himself an able successor to Charles de Gaulle as he reaffirmed the role of the president of the republic in every field and maintained, in his own way, his predecessor's concept of French nationalism. Premier Chaban-Delmas also emerged with full honours from a difficult confrontation with Jean-Jacques Servan-Schreiber (*see* BIOGRAPHY), the dynamic secretary-general of the Radical Party who aimed to unite the non-Communist left against the Gaullist majority in order to provide a more forcible opposition in Parliament and, in the long term, an alternative government.

In June, Servan-Schreiber had achieved a striking by-election victory in Nancy, where he won the seat resigned by Roger Souchal, a Gaullist, or Union des Démocrates pour la République (UDR), deputy. Three months later in Bordeaux, Chaban-Delmas gained an easy victory in the first round (63.58%) over Servan-Schreiber (16.59%). Being a minister, Chaban-Delmas had to have a stand-in to represent his constituency in Parliament, and his seat, left vacant by the death on July 26 of Jacques Chabrat (UDR), was now filled by Jacques Valade, doyen of the faculty of science at the University of Bordeaux. The premier's personal standing was noticeably enhanced by this success and he expressed the intention of increasing his efforts to build the "new society." Servan-Schreiber continued his reformist activities with a view to the municipal elections of 1971 and the legislative elections in 1973.

Domestic Affairs. The death of Charles de Gaulle on Nov. 9, 1970, a year and a half after his resignation as first president of the Fifth Republic, brought striking testimony from throughout the world of his immense prestige and of the influence he had wielded in international affairs during the post-World War II era. French emotion at the loss of the living symbol of France's resurgence after the defeat of 1940, whose life's inspiration had been "a certain idea of France," was put into words by President Pompidou in his broadcast announcement to the nation: "General de Gaulle is dead. France is a widow."

In accordance with his wishes, de Gaulle was buried privately without state honours at Colombey-les-deux-Églises, on November 12. In contrast to the simple funeral ceremony, the requiem Mass at Notre Dame in Paris on the same day was attended by a gathering of sovereigns, heads of state and of government, and other notables such as had seldom been equaled in modern times. (*See* OBITUARIES.)

The canton elections for the formation of general councils took place on March 8 and 15, with 1,609 seats to be filled. The result showed new gains for the majority (with the UDR especially benefiting) and a further setback for the left-wing opposition (only the Communist and Socialist [Parti Socialiste Unifié, or PSU] parties made any advances). However, the vote did not show any landslide. The leading party generally consolidated its influence and was better prepared for the 1971 municipal elections.

The French Communist Party held its 19th congress in February, ousting Roger Garaudy (*see* BIOGRAPHY) from both Politburo and Central Committee. Marcel Waldeck Rochet, still inactive due to illness, was nonetheless reelected to the post of secretary-general, which he had held since 1964. Georges Marchais, 49, was elected deputy secretary-general.

Pompidou, whose chief aim was probably to make France a major modern industrial state, chose himself to write the summary of the report on the options for the sixth economic plan. "From 1970 to 1975," he wrote, "our industrial production must be increased almost by half and our foreign investment must be enlarged. At this price, and at this price only, can we ensure both the maintenance of France's role in the world and a satisfactory rise in the standard of living of our people."

On June 18, after four days' debate, the National

Foreign Aid:
see Development, Economic

Foreign Credits:
see Development, Economic; Payments and Reserves, International

Foreign Exchange:
see Payments and Reserves, International

Foreign Investments:
see Investment, International

Forests:
see Conservation; Timber

Formosa:
see Taiwan

FRANCE
Education. (1966–67) Primary, pupils 5,435,-061, teachers 177,800; secondary, pupils 2,534,-494; vocational, pupils 804,688; secondary and vocational, teachers 198,835; teacher training, students 31,293, teachers 2,063; higher (including 23 universities), students 531,750, teaching staff (universities only; 1964–65) 16,904.

Finance. Monetary unit: franc, with a par value of Fr. 5.55 to U.S. $1 (Fr. 13.33 = £1 sterling). Gold, SDRs, and foreign exchange, official: (June 1970) U.S. $4,447,000,000; (June 1969) U.S. $3,611,000,000. Budget (1971 est.): revenue Fr. 175,227,000,000; expenditure Fr. 175,102,000,000. Gross national product: (1968) Fr. 625.1 billion; (1967) Fr. 572.1 billion. Money supply: (Dec. 1969) Fr. 217,980,000,000; (Dec. 1968) Fr. 216,160,000,000. Cost of living (1963 = 100): (June 1970) 131; (June 1969) 124.

Foreign Trade. (1969) Imports Fr. 90,020,-000,000; exports Fr. 77,760,000,000. Import sources: EEC 50% (West Germany 22%, Belgium-Luxembourg 11%, Italy 10%, Netherlands 6%); U.S. 8%; U.K. 5%. Export destinations: EEC 47% (West Germany 20%, Belgium-Luxembourg 11%, Italy 10%, Netherlands 6%); U.S. 5%; Switzerland 5%. Main exports: machinery 18%; chemicals 11%; motor vehicles 9%; iron and steel 8%; cereals 6%; textile yarns and fabrics 6%. Tourism (1968): visitors 10.8 million; gross receipts U.S. $954 million.

Transport and Communications. Roads (1969) 784,739 km. (including 1,305 km. expressways). Motor vehicles in use (1969): passenger 11,860,000; commercial 1,766,000. Railways: (1968) 37,104 km.; traffic (state only; 1969) 39,057,000,000 passenger-km., freight 67,-205,000,000 net ton-km. Air traffic (1968): 9,-677,793,000 passenger-km.; freight 382,086,000 net ton-km. Navigable inland waterways in regular use (1967) 7,619 km.; goods traffic (1968) 13,235,000,000 ton-km. Shipping (1969): merchant vessels 100 gross tons and over 1,432; gross tonnage 5,961,963. Telephones (Dec. 1968) 7,-503,491. Radio licenses (Dec. 1968) 15,558,000. Television licenses (Dec. 1968) 9,252,000.

Agriculture. Production (in 000; metric tons; 1969; 1968 in parentheses): wheat 14,535 (14,-985); rye 319 (327); barley 9,347 (9,139); oats 2,349 (2,528); corn 5,660 (5,400); potatoes 8,824 (10,045); rice 107 (85); rapeseed 512 (454); tomatoes (1968) 529, (1967) 554; onions (1968) 195, (1967) 194; apples 3,618 (4,159); pears 441 (493); flax fibre 52 (51); sugar, raw value (1969–70) c. 2,720, (1968–69) 2,382; wine 5,266 (6,446); tobacco 48 (52); beef and veal (1968) 1,648, (1967) 1,607; pork (1968) 1,220, (1967) 1,240; milk 31,010 (31,-418); butter c. 540 (c. 575); cheese c. 730 (713); fish catch (1968) 794, (1967) 820. Livestock (in 000; Oct. 1968): cattle 22,093; sheep 9,506; horses 727; pigs 10,020; poultry c. 205,-000.

Industry. Index of production (1963 = 100): (1969) 142; (1968) 125. Fuel and power (in 000; 1969): coal (metric tons) 40,585; electricity (kw-hr.) 131,320,000; natural gas (cu.m.) 6,-519,000; manufactured gas (cu.m.; 1968) 6,577,-000. Production (in 000; metric tons; 1969): iron ore (32% metal content) 55,137; bauxite 2,711; pig iron 18,432; crude steel 22,512; aluminum 459; lead 132; zinc 254; cement 27,-696; cotton yarn 256; cotton fabrics 209; wool yarn 145; wool fabrics 65; rayon filament yarn 53; rayon staple fibre 74; nylon filament yarn 75; nylon staple fibre 82; sulfuric acid 3,527; nitrogenous fertilizers (1968–69) 1,372; passenger cars (units) 2,140; commercial vehicles (units) 298; petroleum products (1968) 69,503. Merchant shipping launched (100 gross tons and over; 1969) 818,000 gross tons.

POPPERFOTO FROM
PICTORIAL PARADE

A policeman kicks a tear
gas canister back toward
students rioting in Paris
after the trial
and imprisonment of two
left-wing editors
in May 1970.

on June 4 a compromise draft was passed by both chambers without difficulty. The law was aimed at left- and right-wing extremist groups that were active during the spring, both in Paris and in the provinces. At Nanterre, in March, 60 policemen and several dozen students were injured in scuffles, considerable damage was done at the Faculty of Law, and classes were suspended. In Grenoble, too, there were incidents on the university campus and the police had to intervene on several occasions. In May a series of bomb attacks and other acts of sabotage occurred in numerous localities.

Alain Geismar, leader of the Maoist Proletarian Left and a key figure in the 1968 disturbances, was sentenced to 18 months' imprisonment on October 22 for "direct provocation followed by violence and assault against officers of the peace." On November 24 the Court for State Security sentenced Geismar to a further two years for reconstituting a banned subversive organization.

Despite the demands of other sectors of the economy, Pompidou was giving absolute priority to a buildup of France's nuclear capacity. The general reorganization of defense, to be spread over some ten years, was conceived as a means of asserting France's independence and influence in world affairs by firmly establishing its nuclear deterrent capability. Of Fr. 93.5 billion authorized for military purposes for 1971–75 in a bill passed on October 8 by the National Assembly, one-third would be spent on strategic or tactical nuclear weapons. Allowing for predicted growth in the country's revenue, the military budget for 1975 would represent only about 3% of GNP (as against 5.6% ten years before and 3.44% in 1970). Nonetheless, the operational capacity of the armed forces would have increased significantly. In June, the National Assembly passed (439–1) a bill reducing the length of national service to one year.

On October 15 Chaban-Delmas asked for and won a vote of confidence from the National Assembly on his outline of social and economic policies designed to achieve the "new society" he had first proposed in September 1969. By a vote of 382–89 and three abstentions, the government was granted the "new lease of life it was looking for." The program was concerned chiefly with older people, the status of women, the humanization of the urban environment, and the democratization of culture.

A tragedy that shocked the nation occurred at Saint-Laurent-du-Pont, Isère, on the night of October 31–November 1, when 145 young people trapped in a blazing dance hall lost their lives (*see* DISASTERS).

The Council of Paris. Didier Delfour, a member of the Gaullist Union pour le Renouveau de Paris (URP), was elected president of the council on June 22, with 43 votes, on the third poll. The sole candidate of the left, Pierre Astier (Socialist), received 35 votes. Delfour succeeded Étienne Royer de Véricourt (Centrist). The council's decision that the Place de l'Étoile should be renamed Place Charles de Gaulle became effective on December 15.

University Reforms. In 1970 the University of Paris experienced the biggest organizational upheaval since its founding in 1215. The five faculties (letters, law, sciences, medicine, pharmacy) disappeared in October under the provisions of a bill on higher education proposed by former Education Minister Edgar Faure, and the single university, with its 190,000 students, gave way to 13 new, theoretically multidisciplinary, universities.

Assembly adopted, by a vote of 351–95, a bill calling for more rapid industrialization of the country. Shortly afterward (June 21), the Senate adopted the project, but by a much smaller majority of 109–88, with 82 abstentions.

Considering that the workers should be brought into this industrialization and should profit from it directly, the government adopted a series of measures affecting industrial relations. Profit-sharing by workers in the state-owned Renault concern was provided for in legislation calling for the free distribution of 500,000 shares (4% of the company's capital) to employees with at least five years' service; this applied to more than 45,000 of the nearly 85,000 workers. Renault's administrative council also was modified to permit participation by delegates of the worker-shareholders. The profit-sharing principle was to be extended to other nationalized industries.

As a result of wage agreements established for workers in various private and public concerns, including such large enterprises as Berliet, Peugeot, and Boussois-Souchon-Neuvesel, the average increase in wages in 1970 was estimated at 10%. The price rises set in December 1969 had to be taken into account in fixing wages and salaries and, while there were some serious confrontations, including the threat of strikes in the autumn, there were no pitched battles.

Noisy clashes reminiscent of May 1968 occurred when the National Assembly debated the government's *loi anti-casseurs* ("antismashers bill"), designed to combat "certain new forms of delinquency." However,

In the centre of Paris, Universities I to VII were created by dividing up the Sorbonne, the Panthéon-Assas law faculty, the science faculty in the *Halle aux vins* (the former wine market), the faculty of pharmacy, and the university hospital centres (CHU). Universities VIII (Vincennes) and IX (Dauphine) had been set up as experimental establishments by Faure in 1968. University X (Nanterre) was formed by combining the faculties of letters and law at Nanterre and the University Technological Institute of Ville-d'Avray. University XI (Orsay) was the unification of the faculty of sciences at Orsay, the Juridical Centre at Sceaux, and the CHU of Kremlin-Bicêtre. Two new universities, XII (Créteil and Saint-Maur) and XIII (Saint-Denis, Villetaneuse), were established.

The Paris faculty of medicine was also decentralized. A November bill sanctioned its division into 16 parts, together with the autonomy of ten CHUs and six more units for teaching and research.

Foreign Policy. Perhaps the least expected feature of the start of Pompidou's presidency was that he showed the same fascination with foreign policy as had de Gaulle. Pompidou, rather than the government, made all the major decisions. The high point of the year was his visit to the United States (February 23–March 4)—the first official visit by a French president in ten years. Private conversations between Pompidou and Pres. Richard Nixon were extremely friendly, but demonstrations by the U.S. Jewish community showed that Pompidou had not managed to dispel the hostility aroused by the sale of Mirage aircraft to Libya and the embargo on the supply of arms to Israel. However, Nixon was favourably disposed toward the argument that a French presence in the Mediterranean was preferable to that of the U.S.S.R.

Pompidou's concern that France should remain outside the blocs of either of the superpowers was shown by his visit to the U.S.S.R. (October 6–13) to strengthen the friendly ties established previously by de Gaulle and himself. The protocol and joint communiqué published at the end of his talks with Soviet leaders showed a desire to improve Franco-Soviet relations. France gave its support to the Soviet proposal for a European security conference. The two countries agreed to double the volume of trade between them during the next five years. Political relations were regularized by an agreement that the foreign ministers of the two countries, or their representatives, would meet every six months. Although there was no gesture of appeasement from the Soviets on the question of the status of Berlin, the French appeared satisfied with the many assurances given on the consequences of the Soviet-West German nonaggression treaty signed in August.

Franco-German relations continued to be characterized by great frankness and friendliness. In January the visit of West German Chancellor Willy Brandt to Paris gave French leaders the opportunity to express their full approval of the policy of détente with the East. This agreement was followed up in July with Pompidou's offer to Brandt of "political and moral" support at the time of his visit to Bonn for the regular discussions provided for by the Franco-German friendship treaty of 1963. "France supports you in your great undertaking of rapprochement with the East, and hails your courage and your sense of realism," he told Brandt. "This undertaking is of the greatest significance to the future of Europe."

Meanwhile, contacts with many other countries were established or renewed, most notably with the People's Republic of China. In July André Bettencourt, minister of Planning and Development, was received for two hours in Peking by Chairman Mao Tse-tung and his deputy, Lin Piao. It was the first time since the Cultural Revolution that Mao had received a Western statesman and the first time that a French minister had paid an official visit to Peking since former Cultural Affairs Minister André Malraux went there in 1965 as a personal envoy of de Gaulle. As a result, diplomatic and economic relations between France and China were expected to be strengthened.

British Entry into the EEC. Of major importance during the year was the relaxation in the French position on the opening of negotiations for the enlargement of the Common Market and on the possible entry of the main candidates (the United Kingdom, Denmark, Norway, and Ireland). The opening session of official negotiations between the Six and the U.K. took place in Luxembourg on June 30 and the first working session was held on July 21 in Brussels, a considerable advance on what had been achieved in previous years.

The official visit of the U.K. foreign minister, Sir Alec Douglas-Home, in mid-July to see his French counterpart, Maurice Schumann, and Premier Chaban-Delmas confirmed the wide area of agreement between London and Paris. "I am looking in vain for points of disagreement," remarked Schumann, who had opened the way for this improvement by a two-day visit to London in January to meet the British prime and foreign ministers (at that time Harold Wilson and Michael Stewart), roughly a year after the "Soames affair," which had marked the high point of Franco-British misunderstanding. "In the long run," Schumann declared, "there can be no Europe without Great Britain, for many reasons, and in particular because 30 years ago, if there had been no Great Britain, there would not today be a Europe worthy of that name."

Similarly, the crisis since February 1969 in relations between France and its six partners of the Western European Union ended on June 4–5 in Bonn, when France resumed its seat, left vacant for 15 months.

One of the five Israeli gunboats that disappeared from Cherbourg, France, on Christmas Day, 1969, is seen for the first time six days later steaming toward Israel only 40 mi. from Haifa.

WIDE WORLD

French foreign relations continued to follow de Gaulle's general policy of friendly contacts with both Eastern and Western countries. Thus, the spring brought in succession visits from the head of the Luxembourg government, Pierre Werner, from Polish Foreign Minister Stefan Jedrychowski, and from the Romanian Pres. Nicolae Ceausescu.

Schumann held talks on nuclear cooperation with Japanese Foreign Minister Kiichi Aichi before flying to Helsinki, Fin., where he was the guest of Pres. Urho K. Kekkonen. At the same time Pompidou played host to Lee Kuan Yew, prime minister of Singapore, and then, after returning from his visit to the Soviet Union at the end of October, to Pres. Tito of Yugoslavia and to Pres. Kenneth Kaunda of Zambia.

French Presence in the Mediterranean. In June, in two moves toward a strengthening of the French presence in the Mediterranean, Schumann visited Lisbon for three days of talks with Portuguese officials and Defense Minister Michel Debré was in Madrid for the signing on June 22 of a military agreement with Spain. Debré's visit had been planned in February when Spanish Foreign Minister Gregorio López Bravo had visited Paris to sign an agreement with the French government concerning the purchase of 30 Mirage III aircraft by Spain. The determination of France and Italy to take joint initiative in the Mediterranean marked the meeting in Paris later in the year between Italian Foreign Minister Aldo Moro and French leaders.

Other recent French activities with regard to the Mediterranean had included a confirmation of France's stand on the Arab-Israeli conflict, which included an embargo on arms shipments to Israel, a renewal of cooperation with Algeria, despite some difficulties during the summer of 1970, the sealing of the reconciliation with Tunisia, and overtures to the young Libyan republic, including an agreement to sell Libya as many as 100 Mirage military aircraft. It was natural that France should also seek to bring Morocco into this Franco-Arab collaboration in the Mediterranean and the decision to reestablish "all traditional relations" with Morocco, after a break of nearly four years as a result of the Ben Barka affair, was announced in December 1969.

The Economy. On August 4, almost a year after the devaluation of the franc, Finance Minister Valéry Giscard d'Estaing announced measures to ease exchange controls. These included a doubling of the individual annual foreign travel allowance, the abolition of the *carnet de change*, the document needed to obtain travelers' checks or foreign currency, and some relaxation of controls on exchanges of all but large movements of capital. On Aug. 8, 1969, net reserves in France had amounted to $1,290,000,000. One year later they were $3,670,000,000, showing a net gain of $2,380,000,000. On Oct. 20, 1970, the bank rate was lowered from $7\frac{1}{2}$ to 7%.　　　　(J. Kn.)

Fuel and Power

In the United States 1970 was the year of the great energy crisis. An unusually cold January in much of the nation placed severe demands on fuel supplies, but these were met without any sign of crisis. Before the year was out, however, the supply of coal, natural gas, and fuel oils had come to be seriously deficient, electric generating capacity was strained to the limit in some parts of the country, and efforts of fuel users to line up supplies for the coming year had become desperate.

The single most important factor in the crisis was the impact of efforts to reduce environmental pollution, especially the increasingly severe limitations on the sulfur content of fuels burned in the large metropolitan centres. In attempting to meet these limitations, fuel users turned to low-sulfur coal and low-sulfur oil (especially residual fuel oil) and to natural gas, which has no sulfur content. The result was a massive shift from established demand patterns. Under normal circumstances this shift might have been accommodated without serious trouble, but by an extraordinary series of coincidences supply problems due to wholly separate causes either existed or developed in each of the fuels.

In natural gas, the level of reserves dropped for the second year in a row, reflecting low levels of exploration, well drilling, and sales offerings as producers awaited U.S. Federal Power Commission (FPC) action on proposals for higher gas prices. The result was the virtual disappearance of the supply of new reserves to replace those being consumed and to support expanded consumption. Faced with this situation, gas pipelines and distribution companies in many parts of the country began refusing to accept new customers, especially industries, or to increase their commitments to existing customers.

In coal the situation was also adverse. Total coal resources were sufficient to meet conceivable needs for centuries, but only two-thirds of these resources were low in sulfur content (1% or less). The bulk of the U.S. coal markets, moreover, lay east of the Mississippi River, but only one-third of the total coal resources were in the eastern half of the country, and of those, only one-fifth were low in sulfur. Compounding the immediate supply problem was a combination of events that sharply curtailed the utilization of coal-mining capacity. Application of the provisions of the new Coal Mine Health and Safety Act, passed in 1969, caused the closing of many mines for substantial periods during the year. At the same time, there was a general shortage of coal mine labour, wildcat strikes occurred at many mines, and a shortage of railroad hopper cars developed. On top of this, the export demand for coal for metallurgical use (which also requires low sulfur content) sharply increased, still further limiting the available supply. As a result, many electric utilities operated virtually at the edge of coal famine. The Tennessee Valley Authority (TVA), for example, the nation's largest electric utility and largest coal consumer, saw its coal stockpiles reduced to a 10–12 day supply in contrast with a normal supply of two months.

In residual fuel oil, the switching by consumers to low-sulfur oil, in order to meet air pollution regulations, substantially outran the ability of the oil industry to meet the demand. The situation was complicated by the fact that U.S. refineries had for many years been reducing their residual fuel oil yields to very low levels in order to maximize gasoline output, so that the great bulk of U.S. consumption was being met by imports. The world supply of residual fuel oil naturally low in sulfur was limited, however, and in order to meet the growing demand the industry was investing in desulfurization equipment in the Caribbean refineries supplying the U.S. But with increases in demand on the order of 50%, the rate of increase in desulfurization capacity was inadequate. By the end of the year many established users as well as those attempting to switch to low-sulfur residual oil had no idea where their next year's supply was coming from or, indeed, if they would be able to get any at all.

For the electric utilities the combined effect of these fuel shortages was superimposed on difficulties arising from delays in completing nuclear generating units. Some delays were due to opposition to the plants on grounds of environmental protection; others reflected failure of equipment to be delivered on schedule; still others were caused by strikes at the construction sites.

In addition, many newly completed units experienced unusual difficulties in beginning operations. The net result of all this was to leave some utilities with almost no margin of available capacity over the expected peaks of electricity use caused by air conditioning during summer heat waves. The crisis came when a major heat wave occurred during the last week in July, in the course of which much of the U.S. East Coast experienced voltage reductions and requests to curtail usage, as utilities strove to keep their systems from being overloaded. The crisis was especially acute in New York City, which received help from as far away as Tennessee.

A second, unseasonal heat wave in late September caused even more serious problems in an area ranging from New York to Ohio and south to the Carolinas. Efforts to meet the surge in demand caused by air conditioning were hampered by widespread breakdowns at large generating stations, many of which had been operating at capacity during most of the summer. Voltage reductions proved insufficient to handle the crisis, and utility systems in New York City, Philadelphia, Washington, D.C., and other metropolitan areas were forced to cut service to selected residential and industrial areas. Unaffected systems throughout the eastern half of the country cooperated in making available their excess capacity and by this action prevented far more drastic cutbacks in service. The occasion was a dramatic demonstration of the value of multiple, large-capacity interconnections.

The combination of energy shortages and power crises prompted several government studies, some to provide the basis for short-term action to alleviate the expected fuel oil shortages during the 1970–71 heating season and others to concentrate on long-term reviews of all policies dealing with energy. Another result of the shortages was to push coal and oil prices up sharply, and the FPC indicated that oil industry demands for higher natural gas prices would receive sympathetic consideration.

Other energy developments in the U.S. included the following:

1. In February a Cabinet Task Force on Oil-Import Control, established in March 1969 to review the policy of limiting oil imports by means of quotas, issued its report. The Task Force recommended a drastic revision of import controls to establish them on a tariff basis that would be used to control the domestic price of crude oil. After White House review of the recommendation, the government announced in August that it was not accepting them but would continue import controls on a quota basis indefinitely. In December Pres. Richard Nixon announced that, in an effort to combat inflation, he had authorized an increase in import quotas for Canadian oil and had ordered the Department of the Interior to take over from the states the responsibility for gas and oil production on offshore federal lands.

2. Projects to import liquefied natural gas (LNG) continued to proliferate, with announcements that gas would be imported in this form from Venezuela, Algeria, and Libya. Some of this gas was intended for emergency use during the 1970–71 winter, and in March New York City received its first tanker load of LNG.

3. During the year preliminary tests were made concerning the results of an underground nuclear explosion set off in September 1969 to stimulate production from an otherwise noncommercial natural gas reservoir in Colorado. The findings were encouraging in that flow rates had been increased and radioactive contamination of the gas was within tolerable limits.

4. In February 1970 a serious fire on an offshore production platform in the Gulf of Mexico off Louisiana led to a potentially disastrous water pollution situation. During the four weeks it took to drill a well to shut off the burning gas wells on the platform, oil wells on the platform continued to leak into the sea. Favourable winds and tides kept onshore pollution to a minimum, however. In August the offending company was fined $1 million for the occurrence, the first such fine ever levied. In December three other companies were fined a total of $500,000 for failing to install safety devices on offshore wells in the Gulf. A fourth company, Shell, pleaded not guilty. At the time, Shell was fighting a fire on a drilling platform 10 mi. off the Louisiana coast that had begun with an explosion that killed at least two workmen.

Elsewhere in the world the international oil market was severely disrupted by a combination of unrelated events. During the first three-quarters of the year, the Libyan government, in a dispute with some of the oil companies operating within its territory, cut back allowable production by several hundred thousand barrels a day. In May the Trans-Arabian Pipeline, supplying one-half million barrels a day of crude oil from the Persian Gulf to the eastern Mediterranean, was damaged and then shut down when the Syrian government would not allow repairs until it was granted higher transit fees. The resultant loss of almost one million barrels a day in Mediterranean oil supply caused a heavy strain on tanker capacity to transport Persian Gulf oil around Africa. Spot tanker rates rose to near record levels, and prices of oil products in Europe climbed. An additional result was to make foreign crude oil on short-term charter movement more expensive than domestic crude oil at U.S. ports for the first time in memory.

Europe was provided solace for the long term, however, by a sensational discovery in the North Sea. On June 2 it was announced that a major oil discovery had been made in the extreme western portion of the Norwegian section of the North Sea, 185 mi. W of Norway and 200 mi. E of Scotland. The discovery, in 240 ft. of water, is separated from Norway by a deep submarine trench, which meant that the oil would be delivered either to Denmark or Britain.

The discovery demonstrated that significant oil occurrences could be found in the North Sea, where all previous discoveries had been natural gas. (It was shortly followed by other, smaller oil discoveries.) It was by far the largest find ever made in Europe. Initial estimates of more than 7,000,000,000 bbl. placed it among the largest oil fields of the world. This offered the hope that Europe might be able to reduce substantially its heretofore almost total reliance on Middle Eastern and African oil. (B. C. N.)

COAL

The global picture of the coal industry in 1970 was notable for the impact on coal exports of the continual growth in Japanese industry, especially the steel industry, from which producers in the U.S., Canada, and Australia all expected considerable returns. Among the major coal-producing areas and countries, the year was also marked by increased sales in the U.S., rising output per manshift in the European Economic Community (EEC), and falling overall output in the U.K.

In 1969, world hard coal production amounted to an estimated 2,077,300,000 metric tons, an increase of 20.7 million metric tons over the 1968 level but less than the record output of 2,097,000,000 metric tons achieved in 1966.

Trends in output followed those of 1968 with reductions in major Western countries balanced by increases in Eastern coal-producing areas. Production in Western Europe dropped by 5%, but Eastern European production (including the U.S.S.R.) showed an increase of 1.4%. The biggest advance shown in the 1969 estimates was for China, where the serious reversals of 1967 appeared to have been halted. Significant gains were recorded in Australia, due to increased exports to Japan.

It was reported in 1969 that the world's energy consumption by 1980 would be equivalent to 10,600,000,000 metric tons of coal, of which 20% would be supplied by coal. Coal consumption would remain about the same in terms of total tonnage.

U.S.S.R. With a total output of 599.1 million metric tons in 1969, the Soviet Union remained the world's leading coal producer. Production of hard coal was 459 million metric tons, showing a gain of 2.5% over the 1968 figure. The production of lignite increased by 1.4% to 140 million short tons.

In 1970 the Soviet government announced that production would be increased by an additional 230 million tons as a result of new development. Of this, 150 million tons would come from new pits and strip operations, and the remainder through expanding and modernizing existing sources.

United States. In 1970 the U.S. coal industry expected to exceed the 1969 sales level, the highest for 20 years, mainly because of a 5% increase in the demand from electrical power generating stations. These consumed a record 310 million short tons in 1969, and the forecast requirements for 1970 were put at 325 million short tons.

The expected 1970 consumption of bituminous coal was 582 million short tons, representing an increase of 3%, which was thought likely to exceed production. In the first half of 1970 total output was up by 16 million tons over the corresponding period in 1969. Bituminous coal production in 1969 was 555,440,000 short tons, an increase of 3.3 million over 1968. Production of anthracite, particularly vulnerable to competition from oil and gas, fell in 1969 by 6% to 10.8 million short tons.

Exports in the first half of 1970 totaled 33.2 million short tons, 42.6% going to Japan. For the year as a whole they were not expected to exceed the high levels of 1947 and 1957, but it seemed that 1970 might rank third highest in the history of U.S. coal exports.

European Economic Community (EEC). The five coal-producing nations of the EEC continued to suffer reductions of output in

PICTORIAL PARADE

New petroleum coke plant at Mizushima of Petrocokes, Ltd., an affiliate of Continental Oil Co. Petrocokes is the first company in Japan to produce calcined electrode-grade and steel-grade cokes.

1969. Belgium, with 13.2 million metric tons, experienced an 11.2% loss as compared with 1968. France (40,584,000 metric tons) lost 3.2%. Italy (306,000 metric tons) had a loss of 16.2%, and the Netherlands produced 5.6 million metric tons, 16% down. The average decline in production throughout the EEC was 2.3%. The relative stability of West Germany (111.6 million tons, a decline of only 0.34% from 1968) moderated the losses of the other four countries. In 1970 hard coal production was again expected to fall.

Underground output per manshift continued to improve. By January 1970, the EEC average was 3.415 metric tons, compared with 3.12 a year before. During the same period there was a reduction of 9% in the number of underground workers.

United Kingdom. During the financial year that ended March 28, 1970, total output was 147.4 million long tons, a reduction of 13.2 million from the previous year. This was mainly attributable to colliery closings, an unofficial strike in October 1969, and a lower rise in productivity than was expected. Output per manshift averaged 2.17 tons, an increase of only 2.1% over 1968–69 compared with a 9% increase during the previous financial year. Sales reached 157.9 million tons, which was 10.5 million tons in excess of production. As a result, undistributed stocks fell to 14.4 million tons by March 1970; by September stocks fell below 10 million tons, the lowest level for 13 years, and a severe shortage was forecast.

National Coal Board (NCB) deep-mined output was 139.8 million tons during the financial year 1969–70, with an additional 6.6 million tons coming from opencut operations. Licensed mines contributed 1 million tons. Only 19 NCB collieries, employing

10,521 men, were closed during the year, compared with 55 the year before, the lowest annual decline since 1961.

Because of the depleted reserves of prime coking coal, research was carried out into the blending of coals to provide cokes suitable for blast furnaces. A blending plant was opened for providing foundry coke from lower grade coals. Other plants were planned for the future. It was also reported that work on fluidized combustion of coal, aimed at reducing pollution and the high capital cost of large-scale boilers used in power stations, had reached the pilot plant stage. Exports increased in 1969 by nearly 30% to 3.5 million long tons; in the first half of 1970, however, they totaled 1.86 million metric tons, representing a gain of only 5.1% over the corresponding period in 1969.

Poland. In 1969, 135 million metric tons of hard coal were produced, an increase of 7 million tons over 1968. The production of lignite for the year was 25 million metric tons. The increased production in recent years was achieved by development of new mines and modernization, both below and above ground, of existing mines. Coal exports in the postwar period reached 500 million metric tons by September 1969, 50% of this going to Communist countries; 26,372,000 metric tons of coal were exported in 1969, a modest increase over 1968.

India. The 1969 output of 73.1 million metric tons was 2.3 million tons higher than in the preceding year. Capacity and production again exceeded consumption, and burdened operations with added costs, incurred by maintaining unused capacity and idle manpower; 54.3 million tons were produced by the private sector, 3.8 million by Singareni Collieries, and the remainder from government-owned operations. Four million tons of lignite were produced. Consumption of coking coal dropped, owing to labour disputes in the steel industry, though production remained the same at 16.5 million tons. Exports amounted to 320,223 metric tons, continuing the downward trend of previous years, though later there were hopes of increased trade with Japan.

Japan. In 1969, 44,689,000 metric tons of hard coal were produced, a decline of 1,880,000 compared with 1968. The industry was beset with geographic and geologic difficulties, making it cheaper to import than to use the limited indigenous resources. Imports increased steeply by 27% to just over 40 million tons, an import record for any country. The U.S. contributed 19.1 million and Australia 15.6 million tons. The Japanese steel industry, anxious to secure supplies of coking coal, completed contracts with the U.S., Australia, the U.S.S.R., Poland, and Canada. These accounted for more than 97% of the imports in 1969. In the first half of 1970 imports were running 25% above the level for the corresponding period in 1969.

Australia. A gain of 5.1 million long tons of black coal in 1969 represented an increase of 13% compared with 1968 production. The output of black coal was 45,402,000 long tons, with 22,859,000 long tons of lignite from Victoria. This advance arose from developing foreign markets and continued domestic demand. Coal exports increased by 3.7 million long tons to reach 16 million, 97% of it going to Japan. It was forecast that export records established in 1969 would be exceeded in 1970.

Africa. Coal output during 1969 was 56.9 million metric tons, of which 52 million were produced by South Africa. Rhodesia's output of 3 million tons was the only significant contribution from other African coal-producing nations. In South Africa the coal industry kept pace with the ever increasing demand, although the rate of expansion was slower than in the past few years. With an expanding demand, especially for anthracite, it was expected that production would increase steadily, though there was concern over the actual amount of workable reserves.

South America. Coal production in 1969 was 7.8 million metric tons, a gain of 100,000 tons, or 2.6%, over 1968. Colombia was the largest producer, with 3 million tons; Brazil produced 2.5 million, and Chile 1,650,000 metric tons. There had been no significant change for a number of years. Colombia investigated the possibility of developing an export market.

Canada. Production fell in 1969 to 10,672,000 short tons, from 11,008,000 in 1968. The reduction came largely from phasing out uneconomic mines in eastern Canada. Canada's coal industry, particularly that of western Canada, faced the 1970s with prospects of a successful future because of reserves of prime coking coal. Western Canadian coal companies already had contracts with the Japanese steel industry for 180 million tons of coking coal. Exports in 1969 totaled 1,450,000 short tons and imports from the U.S. 17.5 million short tons.

(R. J. Fo.)

ELECTRICITY

Total production of electricity continued to rise rapidly in most countries during 1970. Generally the increase was above an annual growth rate of 7.2%, that is, a doubling of production every ten years. The latest figures, for 1969, showed the following growth rates over the previous year in the major industrial countries: Japan +12.4%; France +11.1%; West Germany +10.2%; Canada +8.5%; U.S. +8.1%; U.S.S.R. +7.8%; and U.K. +6.4%.

Nuclear-Electric Power. During 1970 orders for nuclear power stations recovered from their recent slump. In the U.S., for example, 14 reactors with a total capacity of 14,000 Mw. were ordered during the first nine months, as compared with only 8 (8,060 Mw.) in all of 1969. Causing the recovery were price increases in fossil fuels used to generate electricity, sometimes more than 50% in less than a year, thus improving nuclear energy's competitiveness.

Among reactors ordered or under construction were 34 of between 1,000 Mw. and 1,200 Mw. With the exception of one in West Germany, all would be in the U.S. Twenty-one were the pressurized water reactor (PWR) type and 13 were the boiling water reactor (BWR) type. Although U.S. firms took the lion's share of the work for the nuclear components of these stations, European companies were successful in producing the turbogenerators to be powered by the heat from reactors.

All these high-capacity reactors were of the light-water type. Including those of less than 1,000-Mw. capacity, there were 140 such reactors in service, under construction, or on order throughout the world, with a total capacity of 98,700 Mw. Eighty-five of these, with a capacity of 59,000 Mw. in all (60%), were PWRs, and 55, total capacity 39,700 Mw. (40%), were BWRs. Nevertheless, the latter type of installation achieved some success in comparison with its rival, since, during the first five months of 1970, six reactors were ordered of each of the two types, but with a total capacity of 5,300 Mw. for BWRs and 4,800 Mw. for PWRs.

Five of the world's existing nuclear power stations each had a cumulative production exceeding 10,000,000,000 kw-hr. These were (in chronological order): Hanford, Wash. (PWR), U.S.; Yankee Rowe (PWR), U.S.; Hinkley Point (Magnox), U.K.; India Point (PWR), with 42% superheating by fuel oil, U.S.; and Dresden 1 (BWR), U.S.

According to the U.S. Atomic Energy Commission, the number of nuclear power stations under construction or projected in the U.S. in January 1970 was 109, with a total capacity of 81,254 Mw. Nuclear power in service during 1970 was expected to reach approximately 6,000 Mw. The first reactor of the 700–800 Mw. series became capable of sustaining a chain reaction on January 7. The most important nuclear energy order so far placed was that of the TVA, which consisted of four PWRs, two of 1,230 Mw. and two of 1,150 Mw. The TVA thus achieved the greatest capacity in service, under construction, or on order, with nine units totaling 10,500 Mw.

In the U.K., the Central Electricity Generating Board signed a contract for the Heysham, Lancashire, power station, which would consist of two AGR (advanced gas cooled) reactors of 625 Mw. each. The contract broke new ground, since it was not designed to cover the complete installation but only the nuclear sections (reactors, heat exchangers, and ventilation compressors); the conventional sections (turbogenerators and electric installations) were separately contracted.

In West Germany, work began in April on Brunsbüttel power station on the Elbe River. It was of BWR type with a capacity of 800 Mw. While not wishing to impede the use of nuclear energy, the government decided to strengthen safety measures and asked the Badische Anilin und Soda Fabrik to delay by two years the construction of the 2 × 660-Mw. nuclear power station that the firm wished to locate in the densely populated area of Ludwigshafen. The firm agreed to this delay. Similarly, a site was chosen in a sparsely populated region for the nitrogen-cooled breeder originally to have been built at Weisweiler, near Aachen.

Having given up its proposed natural uranium-graphite-gas series, Électricité de

Installed Capacity and Production of Electric Power in Selected Countries, 1969*				
	Hydroelectric power Operating plants		Total electric power	
Political division	Installed capacity (000 kw.)	Production (000,000 kw-hr.)	Installed capacity (000 kw.)	Production (000,000 kw-hr.)
World	...	...	...	4,191,900
Afghanistan	241.0	301	275	325
Algeria	340	563	639	1,305
Angola	214.3	333†	288.9	457
Argentina	543	1,496	5,836	17,851
Australia	3,136	7,694‡	12,095	44,531
Austria	4,821	18,185	7,056	25,714
Belgium	65‡	244‡	6,648†	26,460
Bolivia	144	581	222	672
Brazil	6,183	30,550	8,555	38,181
Bulgaria	771‡	1,304‡	3,462	15,451
Burma	103	344	260†‡	553
Cambodia	—	—	57‡	128.3
Cameroon	152	982	168.0§	1,016
Canada	24,961*	134,600*	35,933*‖	175,426*
Central African Republic	7§	—	9.8§	34.5‡
Ceylon	113†	410†	217	650
Chile	857	3,565	1,720	6,918
Colombia	1,315†	4,150*	2,120†	6,700*†
Costa Rica	179	766	236.6	833
Cuba	...	109†‡	1,255†	4,488†
Czechoslovakia	1,540	3,129	10,071	41,387
Denmark	—	21‡	3,920	12,097
Ecuador	117‡	320§	290	850
El Salvador	109‡	416‡	171	582
Ethiopia	91.9‡	233‡	...	361
Finland	2,093	10,489	4,635	17,834
France	14,512	50,342	34,133	117,925
Gabon	—	—	16†	74.1
Germany, East	...	1,197	11,673	63,231
Germany, West	4,741	16,760	47,054	198,913
Ghana	512‡	2,524‡	631	2,589
Greece	704.0†‡	1,354‡	1,605†	7,340
Guatemala	43	159	140†	535†
Guyana	—	—	80.8†	267
Honduras	32†‡	164	91	233†
Hong Kong	—	—	1,054	3,948
Hungary	21	89‡	2,601	13,155
Iceland	123‡	687	193	729
India	5,910	20,320	14,314	49,520
Indonesia	284†‡	917†	...	1,677†
Iran	309	855‡	1,089	5,008
Ireland	219‡	796†‡	1,230†‡	4,792‡
Israel	—	—	1,012	5,506
Italy	14,765	43,477	30,264	104,011
Jamaica	22	96‡	205†	1,068
Japan	17,815	74,570	52,650	270,611
Kenya	153	249	66.4	402
Korea, South	327‡	929‡	1,453	5,276†
Lebanon	198	763	374	1,036
Liberia	38.1	36	152.1	573
Libya	—	—	168.5	274
Luxembourg	925	719	1,153	2,043
Malagasy Rep.	28.7	102‡	82.4‖	152‖
Malawi	24.6	96.4‡	49.1	102.4‡
Malaysia:				
Malaya	139†	804	744	2,920
Sabah	—	—	30.8	68
Sarawak	—	—	39.4	88
Mauritius	16.4	47‡	101.4	127
Mexico	2,567.0	12,621	5,969	22,731
Morocco	323†	1,076‡	438†	1,538
Mozambique	66†‡	...	270†	292§
Netherlands	—	—	9,296	33,619
New Zealand	2,439	10,361	3,138	12,185
Nicaragua	57.4	220§	156.6	484
Nigeria	29‡	126‡	485	1,105
Norway	10,952†	60,030	11,085†	60,123
Pakistan	629†	1,753§	1,731	4,991†
Panama	...	...	123.7†	582†
Paraguay	45‡	6†	108.4	179
Peru	772§	3,121†	1,518†	4,880
Philippines	495‡	1,676‡	...	5,567§
Poland	486‡	1,055‡	11,591	55,520
Portugal	1,425	5,217	2,030	6,215
Rhodesia	705§	4,833‡	1,191§	5,576
Romania	831	1,562	5,611	27,828
Rwanda‡	21.3	46.8	22.5	48.1
Singapore	—	—	464	1,639
Spain	8,227	24,500	12,898†	45,900
Surinam	20.5‖	770	232.5‖	1,076
Sweden	10,423	48,771	13,731	56,237
Switzerland	8,940	29,402	9,500	30,552
Syria	—	—	216	773
Taiwan	721‡	3,864†	2,062	10,036
Tanzania	41.2§	...	71.6§	315
Thailand	303†‡	1,368†‡	687†	3,138
Trinidad and Tobago	—	—	253	1,119
Tunisia	32‡	33‡	262	678
Turkey	733	3,178	1,973	6,886
Uganda	150	729‡	165†	731‡
U.S.S.R.	27,035	104,040	142,504	638,661
U.A.R.	1,051‡	2,951‡	2,725	6,735
United Kingdom	2,164	4,446	59,628	223,302
United States	51,877	225,870	310,125	1,435,512
Uruguay	225†‡	1,314†	477†	1,944†
Venezuela	...	1,636†	2,455†	10,814
Vietnam, South	163†	—	438	808
Yugoslavia	2,605†	11,768	4,480†	20,641
Zambia	50†	...	262†	659

*Preliminary. †1967. ‡Public sector only, none in industry. §1966. ‖1965.

(F.H.Sk.)

France chose an enriched uranium and light-water reactor for the 800-Mw. station to be built at Fessenheim, on the Rhine River. The reactor (PWR) was ordered from the Schneider group on September 25.

Italy ordered an 800-Mw. BWR reactor for its fourth nuclear power station, on the Po River between Cremona and Piacenza. In Switzerland, Beznau, powered by a 350-Mw. PWR, reached full capacity in February 1970, seven months after coupling to the grid and producing 1,000,000,000 kw-hr. The Société Aar et Tessin applied in July 1970 for permission to build a light-water power station, with a capacity of 600-700 Mw., at Gösgen.

Three companies in Spain cooperated in the construction at Almaraz, Cáceres, near the Portuguese frontier, of a 2 × 500-Mw. station. In May the Swedish minister for industry decided to abandon plans for the Marviken BWR reactor, the capacity of which was to have been raised from 140 to 200 Mw. Experts calculated that the required safety provisions would make the reactor too costly.

An agreement was signed in April under which the U.S.S.R. would build four 440-Mw. pressurized water reactors in Czechoslovakia, with Czechoslovakian industry participating. This brought the total of reactors sold by the U.S.S.R. to neighbouring countries to 11. The Soviet Union had evolved this type of medium-capacity installation especially for export.

Work began in 1970 at Melkbosstrand, Cape Town, on South Africa's first nuclear power station, thought to be about 350-Mw. capacity. Elsewhere, the Indian prime minister, Mrs. Indira Gandhi, inaugurated the first Indian nuclear power station, consisting of two BWR groups of 200 Mw. each, at Tarapur, north of Bombay, in January. The Pakistan Atomic Energy Commission granted a Swiss firm, associated with a U.S. company, a contract to supply a 200-Mw. PWR-type reactor to be installed near Ishurdi on the Ganges River.

At Tai Paver, Taiwan, work began on the first nuclear power station there (BWR, with a 610-Mw. capacity). Australia sought bids for its first nuclear power station, of 500-Mw. capacity, at Jarvis Bay, New South Wales. After 1980 Australia's abundant uranium was to be used, which involved the problem of its enrichment.

According to the International Atomic Energy Agency the total number of power reactors in world service at the beginning of 1970 was 105. They were distributed over 15 countries and represented an overall capacity of 20,000 Mw.

Thermoelectricity. Despite the rising price of fossil fuels, their use increased more rapidly than that of nuclear energy, which was handicapped mainly by installation costs, and also by constructional delays. The period between the start of building and supply of power is much shorter for a conventional station, and several U.S. utilities were obliged by the rise in demand to abandon their nuclear projects and go back to conventional methods. In building new power stations, particularly the conventional kind, increasing account had to be taken of environmental problems.

The U.S.S.R., with four thermal stations of 2,400 Mw., decided to build another of 3,600 Mw., on the Dnieper River. The Soviet Union brought into operation the Slavianskaya station in the Donbass, an in-line group of 800 Mw.

A feature of conventional power production was the increasing importance of gas turbines in providing emergency supplies of power in the event of a breakdown, or to help in meeting peak demands. Their rate of development was in the region of 25% a year, because of the relatively low cost of installation and the high level of safety and availability. West Germany decided to install 12 Rolls-Royce-type gas turbines with a unit capacity of 80 Mw. in power stations at Marbach, near Stuttgart, and at Itzehoe, near Hamburg.

Hydroelectricity. The U.S.S.R. led in the number of hydroelectric projects. The tenth, and last, 500-Mw. group became operative at Krasnoyarsk, the world's most powerful station. The first group in the Djerdap project, on the Danube River, came into production in July. The installation consisted of a dam 1,200 m. long and 54 m. high, with two power stations, one on the Romanian side, the other in Yugoslavia. Each of these had six generator groups. In France, the Vallabrègues plant, on the Rhône, went into operation, raising potential annual output to 10,700,000,000 kw-hr. from the seven dams built on the river. Construction of a 600-Mw. station began at Lake Kariba, Zambia. The Aswan High Dam in the U.A.R. was inaugurated in July.

The TVA began construction of a pumped storage station at Racoon Mountain, 6 mi. W of Chattanooga, with a capacity of 1,350 Mw. in four groups of reversible turbopumps. It was scheduled to go into service in 1974-75. Because of difficulty in finding satisfactory sites, the high cost of financing such projects, and the extended construction period, this method of load equalization had tended to fall out of favour, gas turbines providing a cheaper and more practical solution.   (L. CH.)

GAS

Demand for natural gas in the U.S. continued strong in 1970, but the incentive for assuring an adequate supply of gas in future years faltered. The FPC moved toward allowing higher prices for gas at the wellhead in an effort to bolster incentive. But the commission admitted that it had to rely on industry figures on supply and thus sharpened the contention that the industry rather than the government was administering the price of gas. The FPC agreed to undertake its own survey to determine whether the industry was holding back on supply in an effort to force prices upward.

One problem in determining the availability of gas for the future was whether or not to include Alaska in the data. A wealth of gas existed in Alaska, but uncertainties as to its production and transportation clouded the question as to whether it could be counted on for future U.S. needs. Until recently, Alaskan gas was excluded in figures for proven reserves. There was strong support during the year for tapping Alaskan gas reserves, but there was opposition from those concerned about protecting the area's ecology. For example, heat transference from oil at 160° F passing through pipelines can disturb permafrost conditions unless pipeline designers can find an answer. Pipelines also can disrupt the natural movement of wildlife, and spillage is always a risk. Thus, plans to exploit the gas had to wait until the ecology issue was resolved. As a result, plans made for the oil-company-owned trans-Alaskan pipeline had to be shelved temporarily. (*See* CONSERVATION: *Special Report.*)

The uncertainty on gas pricing was evident in two FPC cases. After seven years of proceedings, producers in the Hugoton-Anadarko area (Texas Panhandle, Kansas,

western Oklahoma) agreed to reduce gas prices about $6.1 million annually and to refund $47 million to their pipeline customers. The area produced approximately 19% of the gas sold in interstate commerce and was the principal supplier for the Middle West. In the Permian Basin (southwestern Texas, southeastern New Mexico), the FPC found that producers received as much as nine cents more per 1,000 cu.ft. sold intrastate than for interstate sales. Part of the pricing problem arose from the relative ease in getting a price increase within a state as compared with obtaining one from the federal government, with the result that gas profits were often to be made within a state rather than in another state.

The FPC also moved to set new and higher rates without the refund requirement if rates were scaled down later. The proceeding would set rates on a national basis instead of the area-rate policy used in the 1960s. Meanwhile, individual states were dealing with a supply pinch that was aggravated by worries over a frigid winter and the increasing use of gas by electric power companies as a means of cutting down on air pollution. U.S. East Coast states asked for further use of offshore gas to ease the shortage, but, as with offshore oil, many pollution dangers continued to exist for coastal waters and the federal government instituted a go-slow-take-care approach. The FPC also took an easier regulatory posture aimed at boosting profits, encouraging research, and exempting smaller producers from regulation.

At the beginning of 1970, according to figures supplied by the American Gas Association (AGA), proved reserves in the U.S. were 275.1 trillion cu.ft., down 4.2% in a year. Production climbed 7% to a record 20.7 trillion cu.ft., while gross additions fell to 8.4 trillion cu.ft., compared with 13.7 trillion cu.ft. added to reserves in 1968. The AGA estimated that there were 1,227,000,-000,000,000 cu.ft. available in gas in addition to proved reserves. New discoveries in Alaska remained largely in the unproved category.

Some of the more than 40 million U.S. gas customers would undoubtedly derive benefits from discoveries that were made in 1970. These included a well producing 26.4 million cu.ft. a day for Union Oil Co. of California in Lea County, New Mexico, and Block 144 off the Louisiana coast, expected to produce about 50 million cu.ft. a day for Texas Gulf Sulphur Co., Standard Oil Co. (Indiana), and Skelly Oil Co., among others. Austral Oil Co., Inc., found that gas from its nuclear explosion-stimulated Project Rulison well was bringing forth new energy at a rate of 7.2 million cu.ft. a day, and with less of a concentration of dangerous tritium than predicted. Also, the U.S. Department of the Interior developed a new process for converting coal to nonpolluting pipeline gas.

Canada used 850,000,000,000 cu.ft. of natural gas in 1969 and estimated an increase to 935,000,000,000 cu.ft. for 1970. An additional 680,000,000,000 cu.ft. were slated for export to the U.S. Marketable reserves were estimated at nearly 52 trillion cu.ft. U.S. companies were seeking permission to purchase almost 10 trillion cu.ft. of the reserves from Canada over the next 20 to 25 years, in addition to current purchases. A consortium of the Canadian government and 20 private companies reported a major discovery of gas in the Canadian Arctic Islands.

In Latin America, the discovery of natural gas in the Gulf of Guayaquil off the coast of Ecuador was being evaluated in the hope that it might prove to be a major find. The Venezuelan Congress cleared the way for exploration of new areas by private companies for the first time in 13 years. One of the largest plants in the world for liquefying natural gas was proposed by a subsidiary of Standard Oil Co. (New Jersey) as a joint venture with the Venezuelan government. (J. J. Ac.)

In the U.K. 1970 was dominated by the program of converting gas appliances to work on natural instead of manufactured gas. As the program approached the planned maximum annual rate of more than two million customers, reports of inconvenience caused by the operation grew widespread. Accidents involving gas received much publicity, and the safety of natural gas as a fuel was questioned, prompting the government to set up an inquiry headed by Frank Morton, professor of chemical engineering at the University of Manchester, to investigate it. The inquiry vindicated the view of the gas industry that natural gas is a safe domestic fuel. It stated that the introduction of natural gas would remove the major hazard associated with manufactured gas, *i.e.*, carbon monoxide poisoning from unburned gas. It also concluded that the risk of fire and explosion was no greater with the new gas than with the old.

The British gas industry's large-scale development programs moved rapidly ahead, to the extent that natural gas accounted for more than half of all gas in supply by the middle of the year. The 2,000,000,000 cu.ft. per day of natural gas expected to be supplied toward the end of 1970 was equivalent to twice the average daily quantity of manufactured gas in supply before the North Sea gas finds in 1965. In the financial year 1969–70 sales rose by the record amount of 12.2% to a new peak of 5,264,000,000 therms. At the same time, the average price of gas fell to below the level of 1962–63.

Capital investment by the U.K. industry exceeded £200 million in 1969–70, well over half the total being invested in transmission and distribution pipelines. Nearly 500 mi. of large-diameter pipeline were added to the national transmission system for natural gas during the year, while about 700 mi. of high-pressure pipelines were added to the regional distribution systems.

The first phase of the national transmission system was completed in 1970, with natural gas pipelines reaching Scotland and South Wales for the first time. All 12 of the country's area gas boards thus had a natural gas supply on schedule. The national system totaled more than 1,500 mi. of large-diameter pipeline, and an additional 1,000 mi. were scheduled for completion before 1975.

Planning of a third coastal reception terminal began during the year. It would take supplies of natural gas from the North Sea's Viking field and any further discoveries in that area. Planning and construction work also moved ahead on the liquid natural gas storage centres at points on the extremities of the transmission system.

There were three new discoveries of natural gas in the British sector of the North Sea continental shelf—bringing the total of successful "wildcats" to 19 out of a total of 147 drilled since exploration started in December 1964. Although much of the drilling activity moved to waters off the Scottish coast after the big oil strike (Ekofisk) just over the median line in Norwegian territory, there was still optimism about further gas finds off British shores. The U.K. government issued a new round of exploration and production licenses to prospecting companies, who were interested not only in the North Sea but also in the Irish Sea and Cardigan Bay.

On the European continent 1970 was no-

UPI COMPIX
This ultraformer is the backbone of the processing units used to make lead-free gasoline at the American Oil Co.'s Texas City, Tex., refinery. With a crude oil running capacity of 241,000 bbl. a day, it is the world's largest producer of lead-free gasoline.

table for activity in international trading in natural gas. Italy, with its own new resources in the Adriatic, reached agreement in the summer to import nearly 600 million cu.ft. a day from the Netherlands. This followed an agreement with the U.S.S.R. in December 1969 to bring an equivalent amount of Siberian gas to Italy. Both deals were for 20-year periods. Italy also had an agreement with Libya to take 235 million cu.ft. a day of natural gas in liquid form from Marsa el Brega, and negotiations were continuing with the Algerians for possible new imports from that source. Italian production from the Adriatic reached 1,160,-000,000 cu.ft. a day in 1969 and was expected to reach a peak of 1,900,000,000 cu.ft. a day by 1975.

Sales of natural gas from the giant Groningen gas fields in the Netherlands increased by more than 50% in 1969 to 21,-733,000,000 cu.m. Exports, included in the total, jumped 74% and were expected to continue to grow. Groningen gas in 1970 accounted for 25% of overall energy consumption in the Netherlands, compared with 3% in 1963, four years after its discovery.

Spain's supplies of liquid natural gas from Algeria were due to start in 1970. The 390 million cu.ft. provided each day under this 15-year agreement would supplement the 110 million cu.ft. a day already being received from Libya. Further imports were planned, and exploration for internal resources continued.

Soviet gas exports rose 54% in 1969 to a record 94,000,000,000 cu.ft. Imports rose 36% to 72,000,000,000 cu.ft. All the imported gas came from Afghanistan, but in 1970 supplies from Iran were scheduled to start at an initial rate of more than 500 million cu.ft. a day. The Soviet Union continued to look for new export markets, and

The first cargo of crude oil from the Esso-BHP production in the Bass Strait is loaded at the terminal in Western Port Bay, Victoria, Austr., and is bound for the Adelaide refinery.

COURTESY, PETROLEUM INFORMATION BUREAU (AUSTRALIA)

negotiations began with Denmark. The U.S.S.R. also reported the discovery of over 500 trillion cu.ft. of solid natural gas in Siberia. The solid gas, usually found in permafrost zones at a depth down to 8,000 ft., is formed when a molecule of water collects around a molecule of gas under conditions of high pressure. Each cubic foot of the hydrate contains 200 cu.ft. of gas. A Soviet estimate put world reserves of solid natural gas at almost 1,800 trillion cu.ft.

Japan's imports of liquid natural gas from Alaska began in the autumn of 1969 at an annual rate of about a million tons a year (about 140 million cu.ft. a day). Shipments amounting to four times as much were to start in 1972 from Brunei, under the £650 million agreement with the Royal Dutch-Shell group. Additional gas imports to Japan were planned from Abu Dhabi, as well as from the U.S.S.R.

Three Australian cities, Brisbane, Melbourne, and Adelaide, were connected to use local natural gas supplies for the first time in 1969. The three large trunklines, totaling 850 mi. and connecting South Australia's Gidgealpa and Moonba gas fields, initially handled about 200 million cu.ft. a day. Two other fields, Daralingie and Toolachee, were located in the same area. Total reserves in the four fields were estimated at 2 trillion cu.ft.   (X.)

PETROLEUM

In the world petroleum industry two issues were outstanding in 1970. First, on the American continent, was that of conservation and pollution. Chief concerns were with the construction of the trans-Alaska pipeline and the Gulf of Louisiana spillages, while stricter regulations were introduced to control emissions from vehicle exhausts involving lead-free gasoline. In Japan also, which uses a high percentage of fuel oil for its energy requirements, closer attention was paid to atmospheric pollution and the construction of desulfurization plants. Second, increasing economic nationalism in some producing countries affected marketing, refinery operations, pricing, and supplies. The political difficulties in the Middle East were reflected in the continued closure of the Suez Canal and the Syrian objections to the repair of the Trans-Arabian Pipeline accidentally damaged in May. The most notable event was the discovery of the first commercial oil field in the North Sea (Norwegian section), Ekofisk, with a potential production of 225,000 bbl. a day by 1973. The prospecting company, Phillips Petroleum Co., in September reported a promising find in the British sector, 25 mi. W of the Ekofisk field, and in October British Petroleum made another major strike 110 mi. E of Aberdeen, Scot. A significant development was the discovery in 1969 of Indonesia's first offshore well. Following further exploration a field was proved, and production was expected by mid-1971.

Most major oil companies experienced a decline in the rate of return on capital investment and profits in the first half of 1970 due to higher tanker rates, shortages of Mediterranean crude oil, and higher operating costs. In the U.S. a consent decree permitting the merger of Sohio Petroleum Co. and BP Oil Corp., the principal U.S. operating subsidiary of the British Petroleum Co. Ltd., became final on January 1. On August 28, Atlantic Richfield Co. merged with Sinclair.

COURTESY, LOCKHEED AIRCRAFT CORPORATION

A steel capsule that will carry men from a ship to a seabed oil wellhead is slotted onto a chamber designed to fit permanently over the wellhead.

Reserves. At the beginning of 1970 total world proved and probable oil reserves amounted to 540,600,000,000 bbl., compared with 509,877,000,000 bbl. a year earlier. Of this, the Western Hemisphere's share amounted to 77,500,000,000 bbl., or 14.3%, and that of the Eastern Hemisphere was 463,100,000,000 bbl. The Middle East had the largest share of the world total with 332,800,000,000 bbl. In Alaska, the reserves were estimated by DeGolyer MacNaughton at about 10,000,000,000 bbl.

Production. World crude oil production during January–June 1970 rose 7.5% over the first six months of 1969 to 46,650,000 bbl. a day. Significant increases were registered in Nigeria with a production of 902,-000 bbl. a day, an increase of 67%; U.A.R. (excluding Sinai) with 350,000 bbl. a day (20.7%); Indonesia with 835,000 bbl. a day (12.5%). The low-sulfur crude of Indonesia became more attractive because of the pollution problem.

The Middle East maintained its lead as the dominant producing area with an 8% increase, and its production in the first half of 1970 was 13,377,000 bbl. a day, 28.8% of the world total. Iran, with 3,733,-000 bbl. a day, became the third largest world crude oil producer, a little ahead of Venezuela. U.S. production during January–May 1970 was 11,180,000 bbl. a day. The total African production was 5,989,000 bbl. a day, 12.8% of the world total, an increase of 16.4% over 1969.

Australia recorded the largest increase, 98% or 85,000 bbl. a day, when the oil fields in the Bass Strait came into production; they were expected to yield at an accelerating rate throughout 1970. Soviet production for January–June 1970 was estimated at 7,050,000 bbl. a day, or 15.1% of the world total, an increase of 5%. The total production in the Communist bloc was

7.7 million bbl., 16.5% of the world total, an increase of 5.2%.

Consumption. In 1969 the total world consumption of petroleum increased over 1968 by 8.5% (39,130,000 to 42,550,000 bbl. a day). Japan, the second largest consumer, after the U.S., registered the biggest increase (17.7%), from 2.8 million to 3,290,-000 bbl. a day, i.e., 8% of the world total. The Western European increase was 10.8%, from 10,210,000 to 11,340,000 bbl. a day. The U.S. remained the largest consumer at 13,810,000 bbl. a day, 32% of the world total. In the first six months of 1970 world consumption was 16,628,563 bbl. a day, an increase of 8% over the corresponding period in 1969.

Refining. Worldwide crude oil refining capacity in 1969 increased 8.1% over 1968 (43,230,000 to 46,720,000 bbl. a day). The total Western Hemisphere capacity for 1969 was 18,110,000 bbl. a day, a 4.1% increase over 1968 and a 38.8% share of the total; in the Eastern Hemisphere, exclusive of the U.S.S.R., Eastern Europe, and China, it was 21,410,000 bbl. a day, a 10% increase. The U.S. had by far the greatest refining capacity among individual countries in 1969, 11,960,000 bbl. a day, or 25.6% of the world total. In an effort to deal with the problem of air pollution there was considerable activity during the year in desulfurization.

Transportation. The world tanker fleet of 2,000 at the end of 1969 totaled 135.5 million tons deadweight, an increase of 15.7% over 1968. The average size of tankers under construction or on order by 1970 was 145,000 tons deadweight. During the first half of the year, 80 tankers were delivered totaling approximately 10.6 million tons deadweight; by mid-1970 the worldwide total tonnage of tankers was 143.7 million tons deadweight, excluding combined carriers. The total Japanese tonnage at mid-1970 was 14 million and that of the U.S. 9.4 million. Capital costs of the new mammoth tankers had doubled in a year and it was estimated that in the mid-1970s they would reach $120 per hundredweight. Insurance costs increased also, particularly since accidents late in 1969 involved two 100,000-ton and three 200,000-ton vessels, resulting in a total loss of 400,000 tons and extensive damage.

Petrochemicals. In 1969 the production of chemicals from petroleum and natural gas increased by more than 20% over 1969. About 53 million tons of feedstocks were processed in Western Europe, North America, and Japan. Approximately half this total was used in the U.S., where liquid and gaseous feedstocks were used in similar proportions, whereas in Europe and Japan chiefly liquid petroleum products were utilized. Plastic material manufacture grew by more than 20% in Europe and Japan to 8.5 and 3.5 million tons, respectively, and by 17% in the U.S., where 7 million tons were manufactured. Synthetic rubber production advanced by similar rates.

It was estimated that in 1968 approximately 8% of the oil industry's sales revenue came from sales of chemical products and that petrochemicals probably accounted for about one-third of the total industrialized chemical turnover and were increasing, while inorganic chemicals were declining. Prices of petrochemical products remained stable due to economies from building increasingly large-scale plants and extensive substitution, particularly of plastics, for traditional materials, especially in the construction industry.   (R. W. Fᴇ.)

See also Conservation; Engineering Projects; Industrial Review; Mining; Transportation.

Furs

Economic difficulties in the United States in 1970 combined with a fashion upheaval and an aroused conservation movement to spell trouble for the U.S. fur trade. There were reductions in the ranks of mink and chinchilla ranchers, fur dressers, skin merchants, and garment manufacturers. The New York Auction Co. closed its doors after nearly half a century as a pillar of the industry.

The difficulties of the U.S. industry were not fully mirrored elsewhere, however. Demand in Europe was good, and the European fur markets did relatively well. Average prices were somewhat lower because fur prices tend to level out internationally, but the European markets enjoyed far greater financial stability and to a considerable extent were able to turn lower prices to their advantage.

Most of the U.S. trade's problems stemmed from recession; money was tight, credit expensive, and consumers were unwilling to spend for luxuries. This served to aggravate the troubles of the previous year, when similar conditions had depleted the capital of most furriers and forced some out of business. For those that remained, conservatism was the rule; buying at virtually all levels remained at or close to a hand-to-mouth basis.

Further complicating an already difficult situation was a radical change in the women's fashion picture, with fashion leaders decreeing a sharp drop in hemlines. There was some doubt as to whether the new mid-calf and longer lengths would be accepted by American women, and the resulting uncertainty had a deterrent effect on the movement of fur coats.

Finally, the ecology movement, as manifested in animal conservation efforts, also hampered the merchandising of furs. The extensive campaigns by conservationist groups and humane societies were directed primarily against the use of furs from animals considered to be in danger of extinction, but it was believed that many women were influenced to become antifur. In some cases, these campaigns were joined by producers of fake furs, who found the cause to their advantage.

Attention continued to focus on the Alaska fur seal harvesting program, as administered by the U.S. Department of the Interior. The killing of seals in the Pribilof Islands in the Bering Sea again was under

CENTRAL PRESS FROM
PICTORIAL PARADE

A model wears a gray Persian karakul coat from the show of Italian fur fashions held by Eurofur at the Savoy Hotel in London Feb. 4, 1970.

fire from humane societies charging cruelty. In the 60 years that the seal program has been in effect, as part of a treaty between the U.S., the Soviet Union, Canada, and Japan, the Alaska fur seal herd had increased from 215,000 to 1.5 million—a fact hailed by many conservationists. Nevertheless, the methods of slaughter continued to elicit an emotional response, and this appeared to have reduced demand for the item.

During the year the U.S. Congress passed an act prohibiting the importation of skins or products of certain endangered species. However, the three species of leopard and tiger listed had for all practical purposes been discontinued by U.S. furriers, and the reptiles and birds on the list were of no concern to the industry.

Not surprisingly, considering these pressures, retail sales of furs in the U.S. fell in 1970. Although official figures were incomplete, qualified sources estimated the decline at 20% or more. Unit volume was believed to have been close to the previous year, but

CENTRAL PRESS FROM
PICTORIAL PARADE

This midi lynx coat with a "cat's eyes" hat is from "Fashion in Fur," the London Fur Fashion Export Group's most ambitious program.

Furniture:
see Domestic Arts and Sciences

average prices were sharply lower for most furs. Pelt prices had fallen substantially after the first of the year, when it became evident that the wholesale market was not planning as far ahead as it normally would. Most of these price decreases were erased late in the year, but the upturn came too late to affect already established garment prices.

The skin price upturn also came too late to help mink ranchers, many of whom decided to go out of business shortly after selling their pelts in the spring. The U.S. Department of Agriculture estimated the 1971 mink crop at about 4.5 million pelts produced for marketing, a decrease of approximately 20% from the preceding year. During 1970, U.S. ranchers marketed about 5.5 million mink, realizing about $60 million. The average prices were down about one-third from the year before, however, resulting in substantial losses.

Aside from the obvious problems at the wholesale and retail levels, U.S. mink breeders continued to blame many of their difficulties on imports of mink from other countries, particularly Scandinavia. Reflecting poor market demand, imports into the U.S. were running 30% behind the previous year, despite a bumper Scandinavian crop. Nevertheless, efforts by U.S. ranchers to restrict these imports continued.

(S. PA.)

See also Fashion and Dress.

M'ba was restored to power by French paratroops, Ekoh had previously been imprisoned but had returned to favour with the accession of President Bongo.

The Gabonese president, who had been an official guest of the French government in July, declared during celebrations marking the tenth anniversary of his country's independence that Gabon was "no-one's private reservation." Shortly afterward, he issued a warning to private companies in Gabon that had their headquarters abroad.

Relations with Israel became strained in July as a result of Mrs. Bongo's visit to Jerusalem. Dissatisfied with her reception there, the Gabonese government recalled first its ambassador and then Gabonese students and trainees. In October the Gabonese radio denounced the "subversive activities" of certain foreign embassies, declaring that an embassy in Gabon was preparing "Machiavellian plans." Certain embassies had already been the subject of President Bongo's suspicions in August.

A long series of complicated negotiations took place between Gabon and Nigeria on the question of repatriating refugee children from Biafra who had come to Gabon during the Nigerian civil war. An agreement was reached in June to hasten the children's return to Nigeria, and an airlift to that end was begun late in the year.

(PH. D.)

Gabon

A republic of western equatorial Africa and a member of the French Community, Gabon is bounded by Río Muni, Cameroon, the Congo (Brazzaville), and the Atlantic Ocean. Area: 103,100 sq.mi. (267,000 sq.km.). Pop. (1969 est.): 485,000. Cap. and largest city: Libreville (pop., 1969, 73,000). Language: French and Bantu dialects. Religion: traditional tribal beliefs; Christian minority. President in 1970, Albert Bernard Bongo.

In September, Jean-Marc Ekoh, minister of state for agriculture, was arrested, charged with the abduction of a Gabonese official and his wife, and sentenced to ten years' imprisonment. Implicated in the attempted coup of February 1964, following which Léon

PHOTOGRAPHIC NEWS AGENCIES LTD.

Pres. Albert Bongo of Gabon visited England for talks in October 1970.

GABON
Education. (1967–68) Primary, pupils 85,328, teachers 2,139; secondary, pupils 5,603, teachers 297; vocational, pupils 1,539, teachers 140; teacher training, students 136, teachers 17.
Finance. Monetary unit: CFA franc, with a parity of CFA Fr. 50 to the French franc (CFA Fr. 277.71 = U.S. $1; CFA Fr. 666.50 = £1 sterling). Budget (1969 est.) balanced at CFA Fr. 13 billion.
Foreign Trade. (1969) Imports CFA Fr. 20,160,-000,000; exports CFA Fr. 36,830,000,000. Import sources (1968): France 57%; U.S. 10%; West Germany 8%. Export destinations (1968): France 34%; U.S. 12%; Netherlands Antilles 12%; West Germany 9%. Main exports: crude oil 34%; timber 25%; manganese 20%; uranium 5%.
Transport and Communications. Roads (1969) 5,739 km. Motor vehicles in use (1969): passenger 5,921; commercial 4,936. Railways (1968) c. 570 km. Telephones (Jan. 1969) c. 4,300. Radio receivers (Dec. 1968) 50,000. Television receivers (Dec. 1964) 1,200.
Agriculture. Production (in 000; metric tons; 1968; 1967 in parentheses): corn c. 2 (c. 2); coffee c. 2.5 (c. 2.5); cocoa (1968–69) 5.4, (1967–68) 4.6; bananas c. 10 (c. 10); timber (cu.m.; 1967) c. 2,600, (1966) c. 2,500. Livestock (in 000; 1967–68): cattle c. 5; pigs c. 7; sheep c. 47; goats c. 51.
Industry. Production (in 000; metric tons): crude oil (1969) 5,053; manganese ore (metal content; 1968) 640.

Gambia, The

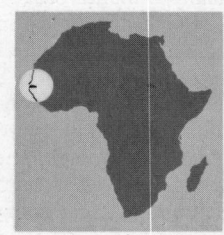

A small independent republic and member of the Commonwealth of Nations, The Gambia extends from the Atlantic Ocean along the lower reaches of the Gambia River in West Africa, and is completely surrounded by Senegal. Area: 4,467 sq.mi. (11,569 sq.km.), including 360 sq.mi. of water. Pop. (1970 est.): 389,447, including (1963) Mandingo 40.8%; Fula 13.5%; Wolof 12.9%; Jola 6.9%; Serahuli 6.8%; non-Africans 1.9%. Cap. and largest city: Bathurst (pop., 1970 est., 35,727). Language: English (official). Religion: predominantly Muslim. To April 24, 1970, queen, Elizabeth II; governor-general Alhaji Sir Farimang Singhateh; prime minister, and, from April 24, president, Sir Dawda Jawara.

In 1970, its fifth year of independence, The Gambia became a republic within the Commonwealth. Its republican constitution was adopted on April 24 after a four-day referendum that sanctioned this change of status by more than the two-thirds majority required (84,968 to 35,683).

Under the new constitution, which established a balance of power among the executive, the judiciary,

THE GAMBIA
Education. (1967–68) Primary, pupils 15,386, teachers 495; secondary, pupils 3,860, teachers 195; vocational, pupils 109, teachers 15; teacher training, students 136, teachers 11.
Finance and Trade. Monetary unit: Gambia pound, at par with the pound sterling (Gam£1 = U.S. $2.40). Budget (1970–71 est.): revenue Gam£3,793,100; expenditure Gam£4,038,350. Foreign trade (1967–68): imports Gam£7,449,808; exports Gam£5,365,794. Import sources: U.K. 41%; Japan 15%; China 6%. Export destinations: U.K. 69%; Netherlands 9%; Portugal 5%; Czechoslovakia 5%. Main exports: peanut oil 45%; peanuts 29%; peanut meal 20%.

and Parliament and retained the "fundamental human rights" provisions of the 1965 independence constitution, Sir Dawda Jawara became president and appointed as vice-president his minister of finance, trade, and development, S. M. Dibba.

The president's term was constitutionally linked to that of the House of Representatives, so that both were to be elected simultaneously every five years.

(W. H. Is.)

Gardening

In Bratislava, Czech., in 1970 police had to be called to restrain enthusiastic crowds wishing to attend a flower show. It had been a long time since such enthusiasm was seen in Britain, where many smaller shows were having to combine or give up altogether, and there were those who saw even major shows like Chelsea threatened. The car, television, and the fact that more and more housewives were employed were given as reasons why gardening was no longer as popular as it had been. A further indication of changing interests in gardening was seen in the results of a survey of the allotments movement in Britain, the providing of small parcels of land rented by individuals for gardens. A committee recommended the movement emulate such countries as Denmark and begin providing ornamental gardens to be used as weekend retreats.

Concern among U.S. gardeners about air pollution, water pollution, noise, and the harmful effects of use of some pesticides appeared to increase sharply during 1970. Pennsylvania's Longwood Gardens reported steadily increasing damage to plant material from air pollutants and forecast that continued pollution buildup would prevent it and similar gardens and arboretums throughout the U.S. from carrying out their objectives by 1974.

The Royal National Rose Society in Britain awarded the President's International Trophy for the best new seedling rose of 1969 to Red Planet, a hybrid tea raised by A. Dickson & Son Ltd., N.Ire. Mullard Jubilee, a cerise-pink hybrid tea, won a gold medal and Alec's Red, also a hybrid tea, won the Henry Edland Memorial Medal for the most fragrant rose on trial. At Courtrai, Belg., the best hybrid tea in the 1970 international trials was, again, Mullard Jubilee and the best floribunda, Satchmo, both raised by S. McGredy, N.Ire. At the 1970 Belfast International Rose Trials, Peer Gynt, raised by Reimer Kordes, W.Ger., was the best hybrid tea; the best floribunda was, most appropriately, City of Belfast (McGredy). The rose with the most fragrance was a hybrid tea, Grand Amore (Kordes). Increasing interest in fragrance as a most desirable attribute for a new rose was notable. In the 1970 trials at The Hague, two hybrid teas, Lily de Gerlache (Rijksstation voor Sierplantenteelt, Melle, Belg.) and Lady Seton (McGredy) won awards for fragrance.

The rose to receive the most attention, however, was a pink grandiflora, Aquarius, raised by Armstrong Nurseries of California. In addition to winning the gold medal for the best large-flowered new rose at the 1970 International Competition in Geneva and the grand prize of the City of Geneva, Aquarius was one of three new roses to win 1971 All-America awards. The others were Redgold, a chrome yellow and red floribunda, and Command Performance, an orange-red hybrid tea. An orange-red hybrid tea rose named Lady

Bird Johnson (with her permission), hybridized by amateur grower Eldon C. Curtis, Dallas, Tex., was introduced by the Texas Rose Research Foundation.

Four flowers and two vegetables were chosen as All-America selections for 1970 introduction. A dwarf marigold, Bolero, was distinguished for its extremely early blooming and profusion of double bright mahogany red and gold flowers. Madame Butterfly, a snapdragon, was a hybrid formula colour mixture of the first double, or azalea-flowered, open-faced blooms. A double-flowered dianthus, China Doll, showed vastly richer colours and more compact and uniform plants than previous forms. The fourth flower was a morning glory, Early Call Rose, with deep rose-coloured flowers that remain open well into the day.

The two vegetables were an F_1 hybrid cherry tomato, Small Fry, a very productive plant bearing bright red fruit in clusters of seven or eight, and a vigorous vining-type winter squash, Waltham Butternut.

"One of the loveliest marigolds we have ever created" was named in honour of the late U.S. Sen. Everett M. Dirksen of Illinois by seedsman David Burpee. Senator Dirksen had advocated making the marigold the national floral emblem of the U.S. A lilac named Lavender Lady, which will grow and bloom in subtropical as well as cold climates, was introduced by a California nursery.

Vegetable growers were becoming increasingly interested in precision growing techniques and, in consequence, in growing only the best strains or stocks in any one cultivar. To meet this need, one U.K. firm intended to hold selected strains of vegetable seeds in store for a year while they were field tested and their performance accurately recorded.

Britain's National Vegetable Research Station showed that, with lettuce, the larger the seed the better chance the plant that follows germination has to grow and develop and that this initial advantage could continue through to maturity. Field trials by the U.K. National Agricultural Advisory Service showed that, if seedling cauliflower plants were subjected to a cold, dark period prior to planting, the cropping period could be predicted and the period over which cutting was to take place reduced. Gibberellic acid, which occurs naturally in plants, was approved in Britain for use on rhubarb. Applied as a spray to the dormant crowns after lifting in the autumn, it broke dormancy artificially and led to earlier, heavier yields of forced rhubarb. In addition, the East Malling Research Station demonstrated that on plum trees sprayed with the growth regulator B_9, crops matured earlier, branches were less liable to break under the weight of the crop, and there was less gumming.

Research at the Maine Agricultural Experiment Station indicated that loss of potatoes through bruising could be reduced about 35% by harvesting them between the hours of 11 A.M. and 11 P.M. instead of the traditional 6 A.M.–6 P.M. schedule. Resistance to bruising was found to be higher when the soil temperature was relatively high. The proportion bruised was greatest when soil temperatures were lowest.

According to research conducted at the Ohio Agricultural Research and Development Center, corn planted with the pointed (proximal) end of the seed down had earlier and more complete germination and more rapid seedling growth, which made it better able to withstand early adverse environmental conditions, than corn planted with the pointed end of the seed upward. A new tomato mutant discovered in the Nether-

FOX PHOTOS FROM PICTORIAL PARADE

Young boy smells daffodils at the 1970 Royal Horticultural Society flower show in London.

lands held promise for minimizing the problem of peeling tomatoes. Discoverers showed that the peeling character is conditioned by a single recessive gene, which could be easily incorporated into varieties grown commercially and in gardens.

The driverless tractor made one of its first commercial appearances in Britain. It used a grid of wires buried in the ground that was followed by the tractor's electronic-sensing head. In West Germany a specialist saintpaulia grower was replacing conventional benches in his greenhouses with large cage wheels called "rotorplants," on which 22 shelves were suspended on free-swinging brackets. The mechanism increased the potential cropping area, reduced heating costs, and facilitated automatic watering and feeding.

As Britain was experiencing the most serious outbreak of Dutch elm disease since the 1930s, researchers at Michigan State University inoculated 30,000 young elm trees from the U.S.S.R., Romania, Czechoslovakia, Japan, Pakistan, India, the Netherlands, and Italy with the disease. (J. G. S. M.; TM. S.)

See also Agriculture; Biological Sciences; Zoos and Botanical Gardens.

ENCYCLOPÆDIA BRITANNICA FILMS. *Plant Through the Seasons (Apple Tree)* (1965); *Flowering Plants and Their Parts* (1966); *Green Plants and Sunlight* (1966); *Gardens for Everyone* (1967).

Geography

Especially noteworthy during 1970 was the publication of *Geography,* one of a series prepared in connection with the Survey of the Behavioral and Social Sciences, conducted between 1967 and 1969 under the auspices of the Committee on Science and Public Policy of the (U.S.) National Academy of Sciences and the Problems and Policy Committee of the Social Science Research Council. The report presented a view of the field of geography in the United States in the late 1960s, stressing geography as a behavioural and social science and the emerging public-policy implications of geographic work.

The report was selective, concerning itself with research rather than educational trends and restricting its coverage to four research subfields—locational analysis, urban study, cultural geography, and environmental perception. The geographic research examined showed a particular concern for socially relevant topics, including such urban problems as changing population patterns, expanding ghettos, and the increasing reach of metropolitan areas. In regional studies, circulation and accessibility patterns were analyzed, and the growth, development, and decline of regional centres were examined. Studies were made of man's perception of his environment, and ways were suggested of organizing and preserving wilderness and other natural resources.

Membership in the geographic professions continued to increase. The *Directory of the Association of American Geographers,* issued in 1970, listed 6,748 members, representing an increase of 2,693 in less than four years. The National Council for Geographic Education listed over 6,000 members, but there was considerable overlap between the two associations. Ph.D. graduates in geography reported no great problems in finding employment, although it was expected that the supply would begin to satisfy the demand in the near future.

Geography in an Urban Age, the completed course of the High School Geography Project of the Asso-

ciation of American Geographers, was published during the year. The six units provide a complete course of study for use in the U.S. high schools. The course utilized the most advanced teaching and learning strategies available and was heavily inquiry-oriented. It emphasized strong student involvement in simulation, gaming, and role-playing activities.

In 1969 the Association of American Geographers, with U.S. Office of Education funds, had launched a comprehensive program to improve the status and teaching of geography at predominantly black colleges. The association's Commission on Geography and Afro-America was administering the program, which provided graduate fellowships in geography for students from predominantly black colleges, a faculty exchange program between black colleges and leading geography departments elsewhere, leadership conferences for black college faculties, and summer and in-service institutes for secondary school teachers in predominantly black schools.

In keeping with geography's quest for social relevance, the National Council for Geographic Education sponsored a new and experimental format for its annual meetings in Detroit in November 1970. The theme of the meetings was "In the Streets, in the Boardrooms, and in the Classrooms—the Geography of Metropolitan America Using Detroit-Windsor as a Case Study." Teachers attending the meetings became participants in field studies, real urban problems, and in discussions of 20 different on-site field experiences dealing with specific urban questions. The results of these experiences would be published in a forthcoming NCGE yearbook.

Planning continued for the Geographic Applications of Remote Sensing program, which was developing guidelines for use of the massive amounts of data expected from the Earth Resources Technical Satellite (ERTS), to be launched in 1972. Using these data, geographers would analyze time-lapse data from instrumented aircraft or satellite overflights and census statistics. As a result, comprehensive lists of environmental factors related to human activities could be translated to maps and graphs and used to study urban, rural, regional, resource, and national spatial changes and trends.

The worldwide concern with the quality of the environment was of utmost interest to geography, which had a traditional and abiding concern with man's environmental relationships. The ecological perspectives needed to understand the problems of the environment stimulated a renewed interest in many fields of physical geography and its connections with geography's social science subfields. High on the list of priorities were the environmental problems associated with offshore oil drilling operations, oil development activities on the North Slope of Alaska, the environmental effects of the Alaska earthquake of 1964, river basin planning, and the overall effects of air, water, soil, and environmental pollution. (*See* CONSERVATION: *Special Report.*)

Preparations continued for the International Geographical Congress, to be held in Montreal in August 1972. As a preliminary activity, a European regional meeting of the International Geographical Union was scheduled for Budapest, Hung., in August 1971.

(S. J. N.)

See also Antarctica; Arctic Regions.

ENCYCLOPÆDIA BRITANNICA FILMS. *Maps for a Changing World* (1960); *The Earth in Change: The Earth's Crust* (1961); *The Language of Maps* (1964); *If You Could See the Earth* (1967); *Earth: Man's Home* (1970).

Geology

Lunar Geology. Lunar samples returned by the Apollo 11 mission from the Sea of Tranquillity were received by laboratories in the United States late in 1969. Additional lunar samples from the Ocean of Storms, brought back by the Apollo 12 mission, were received in the spring of 1970. This initiated a period of intensive analytical activity for which those laboratories had been preparing for a number of years. From the study of the samples more was learned in 1970 about the history of the moon and the processes taking place there than from all previous lunar research.

The lunar samples were collected from a layer of loose rocky debris, commonly called "lunar soil," which covers nearly all of the surface of the moon. Individual pieces of rock and scoops of fine particles were taken from the soil by the astronauts. This soil overlies lava flows at both the Apollo 11 and Apollo 12 landing sites. About half the rock specimens collected from the Apollo 11 site were found to be pieces of basalt, the most common kind of volcanic rock on the earth. Lunar basalt is similar in a general way to the basalt on the earth, but it is richer in the element titanium. The evidence was nearly complete that the so-called seas, or maria, on the moon are vast plains formed by the outpouring of great floods of basaltic lava from the lunar interior.

The most striking discovery obtained from analysis of the lunar samples was the great age of the lunar basalts. Both the rubidium-strontium and the uranium-thorium-lead methods of dating indicated that the lunar basalts ranged from 3,700,000,000 to 4,200,000,000 years old, and, thus, that they were older than any rocks so far discovered on the earth.

Basalts collected by the Apollo 12 astronauts from the Ocean of Storms were about 300 million years younger than the basalts from the Sea of Tranquillity, by both the rubidium-strontium and uranium-thorium-lead dating methods. On the basis of differences in the abundance of small craters observed on their surfaces (fewer on the Ocean of Storms), this was an expected result; the extent of the age difference was much less than expected, however, which indicates that the rate at which craters were being formed on the moon was declining fairly rapidly during the early part of lunar history.

From studies of the distribution of craters on the Sea of Tranquillity and Ocean of Storms, it could be shown that most of the observed features of the lunar soil could be accounted for by repetitive bombardment of the lunar surface by meteoroids and flying bits and pieces of the moon itself. There is a consistent and predictable relationship between the crater abundance, the thickness of the soil, the size distribution of the soil particles, and the exposure history of the coarser rock fragments to cosmic rays.

Many surprises were uncovered in the detailed mineralogic and chemical studies of the fine particles of the lunar soil. About half the soil particles turned out to be glass, and a small percentage of these were in the form of beautiful tiny glass spheres. Such glass was formed by shock from meteorite impacts and was expected to be a constituent of the lunar soil, but not in nearly as great a quantity as was observed.

The study of the lunar samples opened a new chapter in the quest to understand the origin and history of the planets. Scientists looked forward to receiving in 1971 samples collected from a landing site in the lunar highlands. They hoped that these samples might provide some of the clues necessary to unravel the sequence of events that took place at the time the moon and the earth were being formed.

Through the study of lunar geophysics, scientists sought in another way to discover how the moon originated and evolved, and how it is related to the earth's history. The lunar module ascent stage of the Apollo 12 and the third stage of the Saturn V rocket that launched Apollo 13 were impacted on the moon's surface. These impacts generated seismic signals that were recorded by the seismometers placed on the moon by the Apollo 12 astronauts. Unusually long reverberations were notable features of these signals. The seismic data gathered during the impacts caused scientists to believe that the lunar sea near the Apollo 12 landing site consists of material with very low seismic velocities near the surface but with velocities that increase with depth to 5 to 6 km/sec. (for compressional waves) at 20 km. This area of the lunar surface absorbs seismic waves at an extremely low rate compared with typical continental crustal materials on the earth. Scientists concluded that the outer 20 km. of the moon almost certainly do not contain a major boundary similar to the crust-mantle interface on the earth. The long duration of the lunar seismic reverberations was thought to result probably from a combination of dispersion and scattering of surface waves. This scattering indicated that there is a high degree of heterogeneity within the outer zone of the lunar sea.

Deep-Sea Drilling. Advances made during the 1960s in sea-floor exploration brought about a conceptual revolution in the earth sciences. Although a variety of techniques, including both paleomagnetic measurements and seismic surveys of sub-bottom reflecting strata, contributed to the exploration of the sea floor, the climax of this effort was the deep-sea drilling campaign conducted by the ship "Glomar Challenger." Holes were drilled up to 3,300 ft. into the sea floor in water as deep as 20,000 ft. The recovered cores were subjected to shipboard inspection and laboratory work, including paleontological dating, X-ray examination, and measurement of natural radiation. Afterward more detailed investigation was carried out at a variety of shore laboratories.

A widespread layer of chert, or flint, dating from the Eocene Epoch, was found in the North Atlantic sediments. It was among the most surprising discoveries of the project. Although previously found in

This meltwater channel of bedded sandstone in the Sahara Desert was formed by a melting ice cap at the South Pole 450 million years ago. The find indicates that the earth's crust moved about 5,500 mi. during that period.

COURTESY, RHODES FAIRBRIDGE, COLUMBIA UNIVERSITY

marine samples, chert was not expected to occur in such abundance; its presence indicates that the bottom water chemistry in the North Atlantic about 70 million years ago favoured the deposition of opaline skeletons of microorganisms. Usually the skeletons are dissolved, but during that time their silica was redistributed in the sediments to form the layers of chert.

Drilling in the Mediterranean Sea helped scientists to determine the history of that area. One of the noteworthy findings was the presence in the core samples of rock salt and other minerals alien to a marine environment; they were found in a late Miocene layer of sediments devoid of fossils. Scientists sought to explain this finding by noting that the Mediterranean was cut off from the Atlantic 5 to 10 million years ago; this led to extreme evaporation, which apparently concentrated the salt brine. All life was killed, and the rock salt was precipitated. Later movements then opened the Mediterranean to the Atlantic once more.

Plate Tectonics and Sea-Floor Spreading. Plate tectonics became firmly established as a basis for describing the relative horizontal motions of large portions of the earth's crust. The theory of plate tectonics postulates that the sea floor is composed of rigid crustal blocks and that major deformations occur only at their edges or boundaries. The sea-floor spreading hypothesis is based on the assumption that oceanic crust is continuously created by the upwelling of material from the mantle at the mid-ocean ridge and that it is destroyed in the ocean trenches by incorporation into the mantle or by partial incorporation into mountain belts.

One of the main objectives of the deep-sea drilling project was to test the hypothesis of sea-floor spreading. Results confirmed to some degree the ideas developed by the plate tectonic theorists, but the evidence also indicated that the crustal motion is more complicated than had been supposed. It involves substantial vertical motions of the oceanic crust as well as horizontal spreading. The magnitude and rapidity of these motions required a reassessment of the character of the plate movements.

Striking evidence of the continental drift caused by the action of plate tectonics was the discovery in April of the South Pole of 450 million years ago as a flat, rocky formation in the Sahara. Markings on the rock caused by the action of glacial ice and by lines of magnetism, along with the rock's sedimentary nature, convinced the scientists on the expedition of the nature of their find. (L. H. No.)

See also Antarctica; Mining; Oceanography; Seismology; Speleology.

Encyclopædia Britannica Films. *Geological Work of Ice* (1960); *The Earth in Change: The Earth's Crust* (1961); *Erosion—Leveling the Land* (1964); *Evidence for the Ice Age* (1964); *Rocks that Form on the Earth's Surface* (1964); *Waves on Water* (1964); *What Makes Clouds?* (1964); *What Makes the Wind Blow?* (1964); *Why Do We Still Have Mountains?* (1964); *The Beach—A River of Sand* (1965); *Rocks that Originate Underground* (1966); *How Solid Is Rock?* (1968); *Reflections on Time* (1969); *Heartbeat of a Volcano* (1970); *How Level Is Sea Level?* (1970).

Germany

A country of central Europe, Germany was partitioned after World War II into the Federal Republic of Germany (Bundesrepublik Deutschland; West Germany) and the German Democratic Republic (Deutsche Demokratische Republik; East Germany), with a special provisional regime for Berlin. Germany is bordered by Denmark, the Netherlands, Belgium, Luxembourg, France, Switzerland, Austria, Czechoslovakia, and Poland and the North and Baltic seas.

Federal Republic of Germany. Area: 95,974 sq. mi. (248,574 sq.km.). Pop. (1970 est.): 61,194,600. Provisional cap.: Bonn (pop., 1970 est., 299,400). Largest city: Hamburg (pop., 1970 est., 1,817,100). (West Berlin, which is an enclave within East Germany, had a population of 2,134,300 in 1970.) Language: German. Religion (1966): Protestant 47.8%; Roman Catholic 47.8%; Jewish 0.04%. President in 1970, Gustav Heinemann; chancellor, Willy Brandt.

Although the federal chancellor, Willy Brandt (*see* Biography), had said that his coalition government of the Sozialdemokratische Partei Deutschlands (Social Democratic Party, or SPD) and the Freie Demokratische Partei (Free Democratic Party, or FDP) would concentrate on domestic reform, it was the *Ostpolitik*, the policy of improving relations with Eastern Europe, that dominated the government's first year in office. In Moscow in August, Brandt and the Soviet premier, Aleksei N. Kosygin, signed a treaty that recognized the inviolability of existing frontiers. A similar treaty with the Poles was signed in December. (*See* Special Report.)

Domestic Affairs. At state elections in three Länder in June, the FDP was swept out of the parliaments of Saarland and Lower Saxony. In North Rhine-Westphalia the party managed to poll 5.5% of the total votes cast and therefore to stay in the Land Parliament. After the party's poor showing in the federal election of the previous year (when it lost 19 seats), these Länder results were interpreted by right-wing liberals as further proof that the party was heading for disaster because of the leadership's leftish course. At the party congress in Bonn in June, the chairman, Walter Scheel, vice-chancellor and foreign minister in Brandt's government, was reelected with a comfortable majority, and the right-wing rebels were not able to gain much support. But the trouble came to a head in October when a group known as National Liberal Action, formed by FDP dissidents, decided to found a new political party. The chairman of the National Liberals, Siegfried Zoglmann, thereupon left the FDP group in the Bundestag to join the opposition, followed by the former FDP chairman, Erich Mende, and another right-winger, Heinze Starke. All this was a matter of concern for Brandt, who relied upon the FDP's support. The withdrawals meant that his government had an overall majority of only six. In the November elections in Hesse, however, the FDP held its own with about 10% of the vote.

Brandt had two meetings with the East German premier, Willi Stoph—in the East German town of Erfurt on March 19 and in Kassel in West Germany on May 21. They consisted mainly of a reiteration of existing viewpoints, but the fact that, after more than 20 years of stalemate, the meetings took place at all was clearly of political significance. Brandt's line on the German question, laid down in his policy statement on assuming office in October 1969, was that there were two German states within one German nation. Stoph would have none of this. He rejected the concept of "intra-German relations," and said the destruction of the unity of the nation caused by the Nazis and completed after 1945 "by the imperialist forces of West Germany in alliance with U.S. imperialism" could not be undone. At Kassel his tone was exceedingly uncompromising. He said he had come to the Federal Republic to attempt to establish relations based on international law. Again and again

COURTESY, COLORADO HIGHWAY DEPARTMENT

The terraced construction of Interstate 70 through Hogback Ridge in the Rocky Mountains west of Denver includes turnoffs and parking space to allow interested persons a view of 130 million years of geologic history.

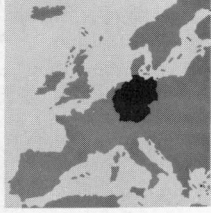

German Literature: *see* Literature

he returned to the theme that only international recognition would suffice.

The Kassel all-German summit ended without arrangements having been made for a third meeting. Both sides said they wanted a pause for thought. Brandt had submitted 20 proposals that could form the basis of a treaty to regulate relations between the two states, including the new proposal that the two states appoint plenipotentiaries for permanent service in each other's states; they would have the rank of minister and would fulfill ambassadorial functions. On his return to Bonn, Brandt said an assessment of his meetings with Stoph could not be made in isolation; they had to be seen in the context of the talks taking place in Moscow and in Warsaw.

By October there were signs that the economic boom, which had been causing difficulties for the government, had passed its peak. The inflationary spiral had slowed down a little, but there was still an acute labour shortage, in spite of the fact that the number of foreign workers reached a record 1.9 million. The finance minister, Alex Möller, introduced a draft budget for 1971 that allowed for a 12% increase in government expenditure. Many thousands of workers in the metal industry took part in warning strikes in the autumn in support of wage claims, a kind of action that was a rarity in the Federal Republic.

Foreign Affairs. The West German-Soviet treaty was signed in Moscow on August 12. Its main article stated that both countries regarded the frontiers of all states in Europe as inviolable, "including the Oder-Neisse Line which forms the western frontier of Poland" and the frontier between the Federal Republic of Germany and the German Democratic Republic. In an accompanying letter, Brandt said that the treaty did not conflict with the political objective of the Federal Republic to work for a state of peace in Europe in which the German nation would recover its unity in free self-determination. In notes to Britain, France, and the United States, the Bonn government stated that the treaty did not affect the rights and responsibilities of the four powers with regard to Germany as a whole and to Berlin.

According to Foreign Minister Scheel, the West German government, in accepting the realities of the situation in Europe, was not saying that matters should rest where they were. Bonn's position, he said, was that it recognized the geographical status quo but

D.P.A. FROM PICTORIAL PARADE

West German Chancellor Willy Brandt (centre) chats with Leonid Brezhnev (left) and Aleksei Kosygin (right) after signing the West German-Soviet nonaggression treaty in Moscow, Aug. 12, 1970.

was working for a political modus vivendi within it.

Brandt clearly told Kosygin that the treaty would not be ratified in the federal Parliament until the four-power talks on Berlin had produced a satisfactory settlement. These talks, in the view of the Western powers, provided the real test of whether the Soviet leaders were willing to work for détente in Europe. The Berlin negotiations began in March between the ambassadors of the four powers and the Soviet ambassador to East Germany, and were designed not to alter the status of Berlin, but solely to improve the situation for the Berliners and the Germans. The Western Allies wished at least to put a stop to the sporadic interference with West German civilian traffic using the surface routes to and from Berlin, to improve communications between West Germany and West Berlin generally, to restore and extend the permits scheme whereby West Berliners were allowed occasionally to visit their relatives in the eastern sec-

continued on page 359

GERMANY: Federal Republic

Education. (1967–68) Primary, pupils 5,700,-490, teachers 213,095; secondary, pupils 1,888,-774, teachers 103,013; vocational, pupils 2,192,837, teachers 102,656; teacher training (1965–66), students 50,134, teachers 2,481; higher (including 36 universities), students 416,-694.

Finance. Monetary unit: Deutsche Mark, with a par value of DM. 3.66 to U.S. $1 (DM. 8.78 = £1 sterling). Gold, SDRs, and foreign exchange, central bank: (June 1970) U.S. $8,443,000,000; (June 1969) U.S. $8,788,000,000. Budget (federal; 1969 est.): revenue DM. 79,410,000,000; expenditure DM. 83,340,000,000. Gross national product: (1969) DM. 601 billion; (1968) DM. 538.5 billion. Money supply: (April 1970) DM. 89.6 billion; (April 1969) DM. 84.7 billion. Cost of living (1963 = 100): (June 1970) 121; (June 1969) 116.

Foreign Trade. (1969) Imports DM. 97.4 billion; exports DM. 113,420,000,000. Import sources: EEC 44% (France 13%, Netherlands 12%, Italy 10%, Belgium-Luxembourg 9%); U.S. 11%. Export destinations: EEC 40% (France 13%, Netherlands 10%, Belgium-Luxembourg 8%, Italy 8%); U.S. 9%; Switzer-land 6%. Main exports: machinery 30%; motor vehicles 14%; chemicals 12%; iron and steel 7%.

Transport and Communications. Roads (1969) 414,673 km. (including 4,110 km. autobahns). Motor vehicles in use (1969): passenger 13,168,560; commercial 1,083,612. Railways: (1968) federal 29,845 km. (including 8,091 km. electrified), private 4,233 km.; traffic (1969) 36,592,000,000 passenger-km., freight 67,195,-000,000 net ton-km. Air traffic (1969): 6,922,-000,000 passenger-km.; freight 465,240,000 net ton-km. Navigable inland waterways in regular use (1968) 4,415 km.; freight traffic 47,932,-000,000 ton-km. Shipping (1969): merchant vessels 100 gross tons and over 2,768; gross tonnage 7,027,384. Telephones (Dec. 1968) 11,248,979. Radio receivers (Dec. 1968) 28 million. Television receivers (Dec. 1968) 14,958,000.

Agriculture. Production (in 000; metric tons; 1969; 1968 in parentheses): wheat 6,000 (6,198); rye 2,886 (3,186); barley 5,130 (4,974); oats 2,976 (2,893); potatoes 15,980 (19,191); sugar, raw value (1969–70) 2,084, (1968–69) 1,980; wine 531 (556); milk 22,269 (22,176); butter c. 522 (537); cheese c. 440 (437); meat 3,373 (3,306); fish catch (1968) 682, (1967) 661. Livestock (in 000; Dec. 1968): cattle 14,061; pigs 18,732; sheep 830; chickens 89,104.

Industry. Index of production (1963 = 100): (1969) 144; (1968) 128. Unemployment: (1969) 0.8%; (1968) 1.6%. Fuel and power (in 000; metric tons; 1969): coal 111,631; lignite 107,-424; crude oil 7,876; coke (1968) 36,306; electricity (kw-hr.) 226,048,000; natural gas (cu.m.) 17,761,000; manufactured gas (cu.m.) 20,139,-000. Production (in 000; metric tons; 1969): iron ore (32% metal content) 6,060; pig iron 33,993; crude steel 45,316; zinc 279; copper 396; lead 306; aluminum 534; cement 35,014; sulfuric acid 4,459; cotton yarn 252; woven cotton fabrics 191; wool yarn 87; rayon, etc., filament yarn 78; rayon, etc., staple fibre 186; nylon, etc., filament yarn 239; nylon, etc., fibre 213; nitrogenous fertilizers (1968–69) 1,598; potash (oxide content; 1968) 2,561; synthetic rubber 288; plastics and resins 3,961; passenger cars (units) 3,312; commercial vehicles (units) 287. Merchant vessels launched (100 gross tons and over; 1969) 1,643,-000 gross tons. New dwelling units completed (1969) 500,000.

WEST GERMANY'S OSTPOLITIK

By Philip Windsor

Throughout much of 1970, the Federal Republic of (West) Germany was conducting three sets of parallel negotiations: with the Soviet Union, with Poland, and with the (East) German Democratic Republic. The somewhat generalized attempt to improve relations with Eastern Europe that had been characteristic of the *Ostpolitik* of the "grand coalition" government during 1966–69 assumed this more distinct form after Willy Brandt had taken office as chancellor in October 1969. But such multilateral negotiations were also a feature of Soviet foreign policy. The Soviet Union was conducting difficult and delicate discussions with its two allies as well as attempting to reach a treaty with the West German government.

An understanding with each of these three countries was an essential element of the Federal Republic's policy, but their own separate interests in reaching such an understanding were not necessarily compatible. Between them, the Federal government and the Soviet government attempted to reconcile the differences, but since they did so from frequently opposed viewpoints, such attempts also complicated their own negotiations. It was this set of interactions that made the negotiations themselves drawn out and complicated, although the actual content of the agreements that the different powers were trying to reach was comparatively simple.

The Changing Soviet Position. Quite apart from the course of the negotiations, the very fact that they had begun raised one fundamental question: why was the Soviet Union, after years of hostility to the Federal Republic, now prepared to work for a treaty? Although the frequent declarations of fundamental hostility had grown more muted in 1969 (except on the part of some military commanders), there had been little indi-

cation of any willingness to work for a more positive relationship. However, during the West German general election campaign in the summer of that year, the Soviet government showed that it was reconsidering its policies by inviting delegations from both the Social Democrats and the Free Democrats to visit Moscow. It also addressed an invitation to the Christian Democrats to do so after the elections. The Soviet government was clearly hoping for a Social Democratic victory in the election, but the fact that the Social Democratic leader, Brandt, won such a victory by maneuver was not in itself enough to account for the rapid development of both Soviet and German policy.

The Soviet interest in developing better relations with the Federal Republic can be accounted for in part by economic necessity. At a time of considerable economic uncertainty in the Soviet Union, and in circumstances where this uncertainty was also producing political divisions, there was an obvious incentive to procure capital loans and investment from the strongest economic power in Europe; *i.e.,* West Germany. But since economic difficulties appear to be endemic in the Soviet system, and since, in the past, political considerations had ruled out any rapprochement with the Federal Republic, some political explanation must also be sought for this change of policy. There is evidence to suggest that the political situation had changed fundamentally in the view of the Soviet government, and that the changes that had come about not only permitted but required a new approach to West Germany.

The changes were of two kinds: first, the change in the situation in Eastern Europe; second, the aggravation of the dispute with China. The situation in Eastern Europe, after the invasion of Czechoslovakia and the promulgation of the various statements that have come to be known collectively as the Brezhnev Doctrine, meant that for the first time in several years—at any rate since the development of the East-West détente—the Soviet Union was able to impose direct limitations on the pattern of relations between Eastern and Western European countries. It no longer needed the more cumbrous methods of diplomacy and, in particular, it could afford to dispense with the German bogey that had hitherto been used to assure the solidarity of the Warsaw Pact. In this sense, the successful development of the Federal Republic's *Ostpolitik* was a direct consequence of the invasion of Czechoslovakia.

At the same time, however, the German Democratic Republic had a direct interest in keeping alive the bogey of West German revanchism, since it could hardly afford an improvement in relations between the Federal Republic and its own allies that did not lead to the recognition of its sovereignty—and this had already been ruled out by the Federal government. For this reason, the same degree of control that enabled the Soviet Union to contemplate a rapprochement with West Germany was bound to be challenged by the state in Eastern Europe that had so far been most distinguished by its loyalty to Soviet policy. One developing paradox of the situation in the following months was that East Germany, which had favoured Soviet repression in Czechoslovakia and the reimposition of tighter control in Eastern Europe generally, now challenged the Soviet government on one of the most important questions of policy.

Moreover, the government of East Germany was not the only one that in one respect or other attempted to either circumvent or challenge Soviet dominance. Romania continued to do so over plans for the future of the Warsaw Pact, and within the Comecon (Council for Mutual Economic Assistance) organization, many Eastern European governments were engaged in a complex diplomacy designed to safeguard their own interests, whatever plans the Soviet Union might have made for them. During 1969, in consequence, the Soviet government made some attempt to use the issue of China as a means of assuring the solidarity of its allies in Europe. In doing so, it met with a double failure: its diplomacy in Eastern Europe came to nothing, and its relations with China continued to deteriorate to the point of open conflict. The question of China led to the breakup of a

West German Chancellor Willy Brandt (left) meets East German Premier Willi Stoph as he arrives for the first of their talks at Erfurt, E.Ger., March 19, 1970.

D.P.A. FROM PICTORIAL PARADE

conference of the Warsaw Pact, to a diplomatic defeat at the Conference of World Communist Parties in Moscow, and to the formation of empirical ad hoc alignments among the Eastern European states.

On the other hand, many governments in Eastern Europe were anxious to improve their relations with the Federal Republic. By the beginning of 1970, Poland, Hungary, and Czechoslovakia had all indicated in Bonn that they would favour closer relations. At the same time, the issue of Germany was bound up with a number of other matters that were occupying an important place in Soviet diplomacy: the Strategic Arms Limitation Talks with the United States and their effects on European security; the European Security Conference that the Soviet Union was attempting to organize—although in doing so it had provided the Federal Republic with a useful bargaining counter; and the Western call for discussions on mutual force reductions. These were the complications of the diplomacy of détente that made it increasingly important to reach some kind of interim settlement of the German problem. On the other side of the Soviet frontiers, the dispute with China made it worthwhile to consider a relaxation in Europe that would reduce the level of military preoccupation and possibly mark the beginning of a transition to a more comprehensive security system.

Complications in Eastern Europe. This combination of circumstances gave the Soviet government a powerful objective interest in a rapprochement with the Federal Republic, and in 1969 both Moscow and Warsaw had shown a desire to begin this process. Movement was slow and cautious—partly because of the complicating factor of East Germany—until after the Federal elections. It was at this point that the Soviet government accepted an offer that had already been made by the previous West German government of the grand coalition: to start talks on the mutual renunciation of the use of force. The diplomatic soundings that followed led to an agreement by the two governments at the end of 1969 to begin negotiations toward a nonaggression pact.

Although it had not yet become clear, the implications of this fact were to dominate the course of the tripartite negotiations for the rest of the period before the German-Soviet treaty was initialed in August. The first implication was that the course of West German-Soviet negotiations would provide the framework for other negotiations between the Federal Republic and Eastern Europe. Specifically, this was against the interests of the Polish government, which in May 1969, at a time when the Soviet government was barely revising its own German policy, had called for a normalization of relations between the Federal Republic and Poland—and though it had obviously done this with the blessing of the Soviet leaders, it nonetheless clearly expected to achieve a greater independence in the conduct of its foreign policy thereby. The agreement to begin talks between Bonn and Moscow at the end of 1969 relegated relations between Bonn and Warsaw to the second rank.

The second implication was that East Germany would soon have to face a decision on whether to join in this process of Eastern rapprochement with West Germany. Here the effects were much more immediately apparent. East Germany, in spite of the approaches to Bonn made by its different allies, had shown no interest in seeking any form of rapprochement with the Federal Republic. But the Federal government was determined to bring East Germany into the process, for reasons of internal domestic politics and also because it had little direct interest in a diplomatic offensive that left out the crucial question of how to improve relations between the two German states. Accordingly, the first weeks of 1970 were dominated by attempts, on the West German side, to maneuver East Germany into a position where it would have to talk and, on the East German side, to avoid any such action, or at least to raise the price beyond what the Federal government was willing to pay.

Thus, in exploratory conversations at the beginning of January, rival proposals for an eventual treaty were put forward.

Walter Ulbricht, the East German president, demanded full international recognition—which the Federal government had ruled out beforehand—as the precondition for any agreement. In doing so, he raised an issue that the Polish government had openly dropped the previous May and that the Soviet government had allowed to lapse. This kind of maneuver was directed, in fact, more toward his allies than to the Federal government. Equally, he asserted the continuing relevance of the Potsdam Agreement to the German situation and that of Berlin in particular.

Such demands and assertions were not strictly compatible; under the Potsdam Agreement, the four powers were expected to work together for a united Germany and, in that case, one German state could hardly demand full international recognition first. But as a means of embarrassing the Soviet government, they were entirely successful. In spite of the initial success of the conversations that went on in Moscow between Brandt's special envoy, Egon Bahr, and the Soviet Foreign Ministry, repeated difficulties were experienced over the very points that Ulbricht had raised.

While two parallel sets of preliminary discussions were going on in Warsaw and Moscow with special representatives of the Federal government, one of the leading figures of the East German Socialist Unity Party (SED), Erich Honecker, delivered a speech in which he made a number of sharp attacks on West German policy, in terms that left no doubt that this was equally a sharp attack on Soviet policy. At almost the same time, however, the East German premier, Willi Stoph, suggested talks between the two German states, and did so as a direct result of the "progress" being made in the other talks that were going on at the time. In this respect, internal divisions in both of the German states not only complicated the course of other negotiations; they also limited beforehand the scope of any concessions that one side might be able to make to the other, and so built into the other negotiations a permanent feature of uncertainty.

Hesitant Progress. Hence, for months it was difficult to discern any real progress. After Brandt's two special envoys, Bahr in Moscow and Georg Ferdinand Duckwitz in Warsaw, had been engaging in discussions for some weeks, the final agreement was made (clearly under considerable Soviet pressure on East Germany) for a meeting between the two German heads of government at Erfurt in East Germany. What this meeting signified was far from clear, however. Its real importance lay in the fact that it was a "historic occasion"—the first such meeting since the division of Germany in 1945. But the only tangible agreement reached was that the two should meet again. In all other respects, the meeting seemed to have been self-defeating even if it was regarded as an attempt on the West German side to draw East Germany into the process of negotiation.

Perhaps because of the enthusiastic public demonstration for Brandt that marked his arrival in Erfurt and that must have alarmed the East German authorities, perhaps because they themselves had little idea of what to do next, the meeting was followed by a sharp downturn in the progress of negotiations in Moscow. Indeed, at the end of March the Soviet ambassador in East Berlin, Pyotr A. Abrasimov, made a speech in which he insisted anew on all the demands that had been quietly dropped over the previous year—in particular, that for full international recognition of East Germany. This was a diplomatic defeat for the Soviet government as much as for Bonn, and it revealed the extent to which the Soviet leaders were vulnerable, not to the threat of East German power, but to that of an East German crisis.

This retraction did not last. It was indicative only of the extent to which West German insistence and Soviet demands had made Ulbricht vulnerable to domestic revolt, and of the extent to which the Soviet government was anxious to avoid the manifestations of such revolt in the leading circles of the SED. But although it did not continue to affect the direct course

KEYSTONE

West German police push back Communist and rightist demonstrators during the second summit talk between East German Premier Willi Stoph and West German Chancellor Willy Brandt in Kassel.

of negotiations between Moscow and Bonn, it did, as it were, let East Germany off the hook. For months thereafter, the East German government made no visible concessions to the imperatives of the Western *Ostpolitik,* and a second meeting in May between the two heads of government, this time in the West German town of Kassel, was so unproductive that not even a date for a subsequent meeting was agreed upon. Thereafter, the East Germans would be able to stall until the approaching success of the Moscow-Bonn negotiations again led to renewed demands from the Soviet government.

Nonetheless, the points raised by the East German government, especially that of Berlin, continued to make the course of Soviet-German negotiations difficult. Although the essence of the proposed treaty was simple—that the two governments should, in renouncing the use of force, provide for recognition of the existing political map of Europe without engaging the Federal government in forms of legal recognition that, either for domestic reasons or for reasons of political principle, it was not willing to accept—the question of Berlin immediately made the situation more complicated. In one sense, the finding of formulas was simple: Bonn could recognize the political reality of East Germany or of the East German-Polish frontier, the Oder-Neisse Line. But if the Soviet Union was asked, by the same token, to recognize the political reality of West German links with West Berlin, it refused categorically. At the same time, the West German representative came under heavy, and not altogether unjustified, domestic attack, because by agreeing to the Soviet search for formulas to cover the political map of Europe, he was also, willy-nilly, recognizing the Soviet right to speak on behalf of what were supposedly fully sovereign states in Eastern Europe. In West Germany this was denounced as a virtual endorsement of the Brezhnev Doctrine. Yet the Soviet Union was not merely safeguarding its own interests; the complex of difficulties it faced in Eastern Europe made it virtually impossible to provoke the East German government into a total boycott of the process of rapprochement by recognizing, as a counterconcession, the West German links with West Berlin.

This knot of difficulties held up the outcome of the negotiations for some weeks. It was finally resolved by direct meetings between the West German and Soviet foreign ministers, Walter Scheel and Andrei A. Gromyko. In reaching a conclusion, the Soviet government made two concessions to the West German government. First, by accepting a reordering of the treaty, putting certain proposed articles into an agreed preamble, and allowing each party to make a separate declaration of what it understood by the treaty, it did much to ensure that the Federal government would not have to face intolerable domestic criticism and possibly risk a rejection of the treaty. Second, it agreed to allow for a delay in the ratification of the treaty until the four-power discussions over Berlin, which were going on simultaneously, had reached an agreed conclusion. This saved the Federal government from domestic embarrassment; it also gave the Soviet Union a direct incentive to reach agreement with the three Western powers over Berlin. At the same time, however, it increased the risk that ratification of the treaty could be delayed to the point where, if the Berlin negotiations should prove to be too drawn out, it would no longer be of great political importance. The treaty was initialed on August 12 but had not been ratified by the end of 1970.

In spite of these concessions and these risks, the Soviet government gained more from the treaty than did West Germany. It secured virtual recognition by a leading Western power that it was competent to negotiate on behalf of other Eastern European governments. It ensured that German-Soviet negotiations would provide the framework for German-Polish and perhaps other subsequent bilateral negotiations. And it immediately acquired considerable resources in capital investment for, concomitantly with the progress of the treaty negotiations, the Federal Republic agreed to give the Soviet Union what was virtually a large measure of economic aid.

In consequence, the German-Polish negotiations were partly held up by the progress of the Soviet round; serious substantive progress was made only after the main Soviet-West German agreements had been reached, and the treaty with Poland was not signed until December 7. But the German gains were also significant. Relations with the Soviet Union were put on a firmer footing than at any time since World War II. Another of the Federal Republic's principal enemies in the East, Poland, was also likely to become a friendly power. And the East German government was confronted with a situation in which— if only because of its own self-interest and the preservation of economic links—it was likely to make more concessions than heretofore.

In July Ulbricht made a speech at Rostock in which he indicated, among other things, that the two German states could exchange ambassadors without full international recognition. It was a measure of how far West German policy had developed in 1970 that this could now be regarded as an East German concession. At the same time, such a concession suggested that the course of relations between the two German states might prove to be one of the most significant elements of international politics in 1971.

continued from page 355

tor, and to reestablish adequate telephone links between the two parts of the city.

The treaty with Poland was signed in Warsaw on December 7. The main difficulty in the negotiations had been the search for a mutually acceptable formula with regard to the Oder-Neisse Line. Even if it wanted to, the Bonn government could not formally recognize this frontier and thus anticipate the decision of an eventual peace treaty, and its recognition of the frontier in principle was accompanied by notes to the Allies explaining that the treaty did not infringe on their rights as victorious powers. The problem of ethnic Germans still living in Poland and desiring to emigrate, which Bonn had been anxious to settle, was not dealt with in the treaty itself, but the Poles gave Brandt an assurance that they would be permitted to leave by 1972. The treaty included a nonaggression clause and normalized relations between the two countries, a step that was expected to lead to an exchange of ambassadors.

Brandt went to Washington in April, and he and U.S. Pres. Richard M. Nixon agreed to revive proposals for a mutual step-by-step reduction of NATO and Warsaw Pact forces. It was made clear to the chancellor, however, that the future strength of United States forces in Europe was to depend almost entirely on how much European governments were prepared to pay for them. Bonn's view was that U.S. forces were not in the Federal Republic merely for the defense of West German territory, but of the whole alliance. The financial burden, Bonn argued, should therefore be shared by the NATO partners.   (N. Cr.)

West Berlin. Almost 22 years to the day after Marshal V. D. Sokolovsky, then Soviet military governor, had left the Allied Control Council building in West Berlin, and one week after the Erfurt meeting between government leaders from the two German states, four-power talks were held again on Berlin on March 26, 1970. These were the first major talks to be held since 1954, when they were at foreign ministry level; this time they were at the ambassadorial level. One day before, the government of East Germany, through a commentary in *Berliner Zeitung,* attacked the "absurd claim" that there was a four-power responsibility for the whole of Berlin.

In contrast to earlier Berlin talks, these were not the result of a crisis but took place in a relatively quiet atmosphere. When the ambassadors parted, after their 12th meeting on December 10, no outline of a Berlin settlement was in sight, but they agreed to go on talking. In the course of one of several visits to the city during the year, Chancellor Brandt stressed at a trade union conference on September 6 that the need for a settlement for the divided city was an "inalienable part" of his Eastern policy.

As a conciliatory gesture at the beginning of the talks, representatives of the three Western powers announced that, as of March 27, they would no longer require East Germans to obtain special permission before visiting member countries of NATO. This announcement meant that the Allied Travel Office in West Berlin, which had issued the necessary documents, suspended its operations. Thenceforth, citizens of East Germany were able to apply for a visa at the consulates in West Berlin.

The West German Bundestag passed new legislation to support Berlin's economy. The new laws, which came into force on June 27, provided for improved income and corporation tax concessions, as well as for special allowances for blue- and white-collar workers, to attract yet more investment and labour from West Germany and elsewhere. Since the building of the Berlin wall in August 1961, 132 new businesses and plants had been established in West Berlin by nonresidents, representing an investment of nearly DM. 600 million ($164 million). The newcomers' share in the total turnover of West Berlin industry amounted to about 8% in 1970.   (S. E. S.)

German Democratic Republic. Area: 41,766 sq. mi. (108,173 sq.km.). Pop. (1970 est.): 17,074,504. Cap. and largest city: East Berlin (pop., 1970 est., 1,083,856). Language: German. Religion (1950): Protestant 81.3%; Roman Catholic 11%. First secretary of the Socialist Unity (Communist) Party (SED) and president in 1970, Walter Ulbricht; minister president (premier), Willi Stoph.

At his meeting with Premier Stoph in Erfurt on March 19, Chancellor Brandt reaffirmed his view that "we must not make it impossible for the German people to decide in free self-determination how they want to live together." A month or so later, on April 29, East Germany's State Council approved a "Declaration on the Implementation of the Principles of Democratic International Law in the GDR (German Democratic Republic) after the Defeat of Hitler Fascism," which said that the founding of the GDR was "an act of popular sovereignty implementing the people's right of self-determination." In spite of the toughness of their confrontation in Kassel on May 21, both Brandt and Stoph made it clear on their return to their respective capitals the next day that they were ready to continue their talks at a later date.

East Germany's Council of Ministers welcomed the Soviet-West German treaty on August 14, saying that its terms now made necessary the establishment of full diplomatic relations between East and West Germany. There was no reason at all for any state to evade diplomatic relations with the GDR. While Bonn had made it clear before and after the signing of the Moscow treaty that its ratification would depend on the normalization of the West Berlin situation, the East German leaders clearly did not share this view. Speaking on October 7 at the 21st anniversary ceremony of the GDR, Stoph, without making a direct

Until the opening of the XX Olympic Games in Munich, this giant ball will be sent rolling through West German cities gathering signatures of those who donate money to finance the games.

AUTHENTICATED NEWS INTERNATIONAL

KEYSTONE

The West German government came under fire from conservationists for failure to spend more money to combat pollution from industries such as these in the Ruhr district.

reference to the Berlin problem, said that anyone trying to establish a link between matters that had nothing to do with one another, and to impose preconditions, could only cause complications.

On October 21 Walter Ulbricht paid a three-day official visit to Czechoslovakia, the first since the military intervention in August 1968 which he described as a "not very pleasant historical episode." The visit came a week after Czechoslovakia's first working contacts with a West German representative to discuss the improvement of relations between Bonn and Prague.

With effect from October 1, every citizen of East Germany, male or female, over the age of 16 could be drafted for "national service" in the event of "crises, war or natural disaster." Compulsory service for men would end at 65, for women at 60. The new law superseded a Civil Defense Act of 1958. The government of West Germany decided on March 12 that the flag and emblems of the GDR could be shown at all sports meetings, exhibitions, and other events.

By the middle of October the GDR was maintaining full diplomatic relations at the ambassadorial level with 26 countries. During 1970 the governments of seven Afro-Asian countries accorded diplomatic recognition to the GDR: the Congo (Brazzaville), Somalia, the Central African Republic, Algeria, Maldives, Ceylon, and Guinea. The Indian government raised the status of its trade mission to that of consulate on February 19. An Office for External Economic Relations, operating in conjunction with the Ministry of Foreign Trade, was set up on February 12 to help further trade relations with those countries that did not accord full diplomatic recognition. A representative office for French industry was opened in East Berlin on February 18. On the same day Austria's Federal Chamber of Commerce agreed to establish an Austrian trade mission in East Berlin. The London Chamber of Commerce announced the formation of an East German section on July 20. According to an ordinance published on October 20, the products of East Germany's industry were no longer to be marked "made in Germany" but "made in the GDR."

The Politburo report to the 12th plenum of the Socialist Unity Party Central Committee spoke of an 8.4% increase in production of industrial goods in 1969 over 1968, a 5% rise in national income, and an 8% increase in productivity. The plan fulfillment report for the first half of 1970 stated that national income advanced by 5% over the corresponding period of 1969. The target for the whole of 1970 was 6.3%. Industrial production grew by 7.5% on average, compared with a plan target of 8%, and labour productivity by more than 6%, against a planned 9.4%. Under an agreement concluded on August 13, trade between East Germany and the U.S.S.R. was planned to increase by 55% in volume in the 1971–75 period. Nearly half of the trade envisaged would be in machines and equipment, with the biggest increase in highly sophisticated machinery. According to the Soviet newspaper *Pravda*, trade between the two countries in 1975 would exceed that of West Germany with the U.S., Britain, or France. In 1970 the Soviet share of East Germany's foreign trade was 43%. On January 29 the French government concluded a five-year trade agreement with East Germany, providing for a doubling of trade between the two countries.

The sensation of the Leipzig Spring Fair was the hour-long conversation of Ulbricht and Stoph with Otto Wolff von Amerongen, president of West Germany's Association of German Chambers of Industry and Commerce, on March 2. Newspapers in East

GERMANY: Democratic Republic

Education. (1967–68) Primary, pupils 2,339,-204; secondary, pupils 100,668; vocational, pupils 508,841; teacher training, students 14,907; primary, secondary, vocational, and teacher training, teachers 127,664; higher (including 7 universities), students 106,534, teaching staff (1966–67) 14,200.

Finance. Monetary unit: "Mark of the German Bank of Issue" (MDN, or Ostmark), with an official exchange rate of MDN.(O.) 2.22 to U.S. $1 (MDN.[O.] 5.33 = £1 sterling) and a general rate (Oct. 1970) of MDN.(O.) 4.20 to U.S. $1 (MDN.[O.] 10.01 = £1 sterling). Budget (actual; 1968): revenue MDN.(O.) 60,939,000,-000; expenditure MDN.(O.) 60,093,000,000. Gross material product: (1967) MDN.(O.) 101.2 billion; (1966) MDN.(O.) 95.7 billion.

Foreign Trade. (1968) Imports MDN.(O.) 15,432,000,000; exports MDN.(O.) 17,285,000,-000. Import sources: U.S.S.R. 41%; Czechoslovakia 9%; West Germany 8%; Poland 6%.

Export destinations: U.S.S.R. 38%; Czechoslovakia 10%; West Germany 8%; Poland 7%; Hungary 5%. Main exports: lignite, chemicals, machinery, transport equipment.

Transport and Communications. Roads (1967) *c.* 160,000 km. (including 46,832 km. main roads and 1,391 km. autobahns). Motor vehicles (1968): passenger 920,200; commercial (including buses) 352,800. Railways (1968): 15,237 km. (including 1,203 km. electrified); traffic 17,098,000,000 passenger-km., freight (1969) 39,445,000,000 net ton-km. Air traffic (1968): 730.1 million passenger-km.; freight 24,090,000 net ton-km. Navigable inland waterways in regular use (1967) 2,519 km.; freight traffic (1968) 2,443,000,000 ton-km. Shipping (1969): merchant vessels 100 gross tons and over 371; gross tonnage 895,932. Telephones (Dec. 1968) 1,896,-151. Radio receivers (Dec. 1968) 5,942,000. Television receivers (Dec. 1968) 4,173,000.

Agriculture. Production (in 000; metric tons;

1969; 1968 in parentheses): potatoes *c.* 9,000 (12,639); wheat (1968) 2,377, (1967) 2,012; rye *c.* 1,480 (1,936); barley *c.* 2,080 (2,131); oats *c.* 810 (864); sugar, raw value (1969–70) *c.* 489, (1968–69) *c.* 495. Livestock (in 000; Dec. 1968): sheep 1,794; cattle 5,109; pigs 9,523; horses used in agriculture 188; poultry 38,802.

Industry. Index of production (1963 = 100): (1969) 144; (1968) 134. Production (in 000; metric tons; 1969): lignite 254,000; coal (1968) 1,579; petroleum products (1968) 9,190; manufactured gas (cu.m.; 1968) 3,868,000; electricity (kw-hr.) 65,463,000; iron ore (metal content; 1968) 354; pig iron 2,097; crude steel 4,826; potash (oxide content; 1968) 2.293; cement (1968) 7,551; sulfuric acid 1,104; synthetic rubber (1968) 102; cotton yarn (1968) 73; rayon filaments and fibres (1968) 158; passenger cars (units; 1968) 115; commercial vehicles (units; 1968) 24.

Germany gave prominent coverage to this event, whereas in the past the presence of exhibitors from West Germany had been consistently ignored.

On September 4 the Potsdam District Court sentenced two young Americans, Jack Strickland, 28, of Santa Barbara, Calif., and Lyle Jenkins, 31, of Norfolk, Va., to 4 years' and 2½ years' imprisonment, respectively, on charges involving East Germans allegedly trying to reach the West. Mark Huess of Jericho, Vt., was sentenced to 7 years by an East Berlin court on September 27, for allegedly saying that the East German government would collapse if Soviet troops were withdrawn. A fourth American, Frank King, 25, of Detroit, was arrested on July 10, together with his British cousin, Michael Woodbridge of London. On October 10 the U.S. authorities in Berlin restricted the granting of visas to East Germans in retaliation for the detention of these four men.

(S. E. S.)

ENCYCLOPÆDIA BRITANNICA FILMS. *Germany—People of the Industrial West* (1957); *Berlin: Test for the West* (1962).

Ghana

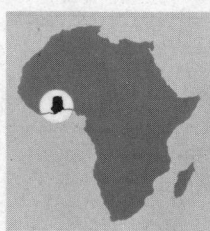

A republic of West Africa, Ghana is on the Gulf of Guinea and is bordered by Ivory Coast, Upper Volta, and Togo. Area: 92,100 sq. mi. (238,539 sq.km.). Pop. (1970): 8,545,561. Cap. and largest city: Accra (pop., 1968 est., 615,800). Language: English (official); local Sudanic dialects. Religion: traditional tribal beliefs; Christian and Muslim minorities. In August 1970 the three-man Presidential Commission was replaced by Pres. Edward Akufo-Addo; prime minister in 1970, Kofi Busia.

The institutional process of Ghana's return to a democratic system of civilian government culminated, on Aug. 31, 1970, in the election by the electoral college of Edward Akufo-Addo (*see* BIOGRAPHY), a former chief justice, as president for a four-year term. Nominated by the ruling Progress Party and elected by a substantial majority, Akufo-Addo took over from the interim three-man Presidential Commission comprising Brig. Akwasi A. Afrifa, J. W. K. Harlley, and Maj. Gen. A. K. Okran. When the commission was constitutionally dissolved on August 7, Afrifa criticized some aspects of the constitution, but the result of the election went unchallenged except by one of the other three presidential candidates—Joe Appiah, president of the Bar Association, whose appeal against its validity was rejected by the Supreme Court.

Toward the end of 1969 Ghana's relations with its West African neighbours were badly jolted by the Busia Cabinet's decision (in the prime minister's absence abroad) to enforce a deportation order against aliens who had failed to ask for residence permits. The order, issued on November 19, gave those without permits two weeks to apply for them or leave the country. Those affected may have numbered more than half of Ghana's two million aliens (comprising almost a quarter of its whole population) and were made up mainly of Nigerians (at least 700,000), about 500,000 immigrants from Upper Volta, and smaller numbers from Dahomey, Togo, Ivory Coast, Niger, and Liberia. Most of these immigrants were engaged in petty trading, and they were widely blamed for the fact that Ghana had 600,000 unemployed. This local

resentment came to the surface when police started to round up aliens during the two-week grace period that expired on December 2. Predictably, the result was panic, confusion, and a mass exodus in circumstances that caused much personal suffering.

Early in 1970 the prime minister clashed with the judiciary following his attempt to cut government spending by reducing the level of the 200,000-strong Civil Service. One of the 568 axed officials sued the government for wrongful dismissal; in April, when the Supreme Court upheld the official's appeal, Busia accused two judges of playing politics. Debates on this issue in the National Assembly underlined the tribal cleavage between the Akan-Ashanti-based government and the mainly Ewe opposition. The political influence of the Ashanti tribal leaders was demonstrated in May when the Asantehene, Nano Opoku II, was enstooled on the death of his uncle and unanimously elected president of the House of Chiefs, which entitled him to a seat on the national Council of State.

In August, when presidential powers were transferred from the three-man commission to President Akufo-Addo, Afrifa, who had headed the commission, was promoted to lieutenant general in recognition of his leading role in restoring civilian rule. Welcoming the emergence of the civilian regime, he stressed its need to tackle the problems reflected in Ghana's external debt and balance of payments deficit, its large-scale unemployment, low productivity, and inflated prices. Also in August, the finance minister, J. H. Mensah, introduced a "hard work" budget. A business promotion act confined a variety of small trading and other activities to Ghanaian citizens.

Seeking a long-term accommodation that would ease

GHANA
Education. (1967–68) Primary, pupils 1,288,383, teachers 49,098; secondary, pupils 179,044, teachers 2,999; vocational, pupils 17,587, teachers 775; teacher training, students 16,782, teachers 1,200; higher (including 3 universities), students 4,768, teaching staff 672.
  Finance. Monetary unit: new cedi, with a par value of 1.02 cedis to U.S. $1 (2.45 cedis = £1 sterling). Gold, SDRs, and foreign exchange, official: (June 1970) U.S. $81.6 million; (June 1969) U.S. $99.9 million. Budget (1970–71 est.): revenue 426.7 million cedis; expenditure 324.4 million cedis. Gross national product: (1968) 2,035,000,000 cedis; (1967) 1,757,000,000 cedis. Money supply: (May 1970) 283.4 million cedis; (May 1969) 236.3 million cedis. Cost of living (Accra; 1963 = 100): (April 1970) 166; (April 1969) 159.
  Foreign Trade. (1969) Imports 354,391,000 cedis; exports 333,264,000 cedis. Import sources: U.K. 27%; U.S. 18%; West Germany 11%; Japan 6%. Export destinations: U.K. 32%; U.S. 14%; Netherlands 10%; West Germany 10%; Japan 8%. Main exports: cocoa 48%; timber 12%; gold 8%.
  Transport and Communications. Roads (1968) c. 31,000 km. Motor vehicles in use (1968): passenger 32,200; commercial (including buses) 21,400. Railways (1968): 1,271 km.; traffic 425 million passenger-km., freight 272 million net ton-km. Air traffic (1969): 134 million passenger-km.; freight 3.5 million net ton-km. Shipping (1969): merchant vessels 100 gross tons and over 61; gross tonnage 165,670. Telephones (Dec. 1968) 35,950. Radio receivers (Dec. 1968) 700,000. Television receivers (Dec. 1968) 6,000.
  Agriculture. Production (in 000; metric tons; 1969; 1968 in parentheses): corn 305 (301); cassava (1968) 1,075, (1967) 1,174; sweet potatoes (1968) 1,351, (1967) 1,134; millet and sorghum (1968) 131, (1967) 164; rice 61 (65); peanuts (1968) 62, (1967) 39; cocoa (exports; 1968–69) 339, (1967–68) 423; timber (cu.m.; 1968) 8,700, (1967) 8,600; fish catch (1968) 102, (1967) 110. Livestock (in 000; 1968–69): cattle c. 690; sheep c. 700; pigs c. 320; goats (1967–68) c. 700.
  Industry. Production (in 000; 1968): gold 727 troy oz.; diamonds 2,447 metric carats; manganese ore (metal content) 198 metric tons; bauxite (1969) 246 metric tons; electricity (1969) 2,772,000 kw-hr.

Gerontology:
see Medicine; Social Services

pressures for the repayment of Ghana's external debts, government delegations visited Western and Communist capitals in April and May. A U.S. loan of up to U.S. $15 million was negotiated in Washington and, aided by an International Development Association credit of U.S. $8.5 million, Ghana embarked on the first stage of a program to rehabilitate the cocoa industry.

At a London conference with 15 major Western creditors on July 7–11, Ghana secured an arrangement that refinanced about £130 million of medium-term debts contracted by the Nkrumah regime. In effect, this ensured a two-year moratorium (July 1970–June 1972) on 50% of the amounts due (both principal and interest). In London, J. H. Mensah, Ghana's chief negotiator, described this relief as "useful" but insisted on the need for a really long-term settlement if Ghana was to recover its prosperity. On July 27 Britain gave Ghana an interest-free 25-year loan of £3.7 million to be used for buying British goods and services and on mutually agreed upon development projects.   (M. Mr.)

WIDE WORLD

Tony Jacklin tosses his putter after sinking his putt for a birdie on the 18th hole to win the U.S. Open championship at the Hazeltine National Golf Club in Chaska, Minn., June 21, 1970.

Jack Nicklaus, in the rough for a moment, went on to win the 1970 British Open at St. Andrews.

Golf

In the history of modern tournament golf 1970 would be memorable as the year when Tony Jacklin became the first British golfer, and only the second from overseas, to win the United States Open championship. His victory by seven strokes was the largest margin except for that of James Barnes in 1921. At the time, Jacklin was British Open champion and for a month held both titles, a distinction previously achieved only by Bobby Jones and Gene Sarazen in the 1930s, Ben Hogan in 1953, and Jack Nicklaus in 1967.

Nicklaus gained his second victory in the British Open at St. Andrews, Scot., bringing his total in the four major championships to eight, more than any other modern golfer save Ben Hogan. Billy Casper redeemed his failure of the previous year by winning the Masters at Augusta, Ga., and eventually was named as the U.S. Professional Golfers' Association (PGA) player of the year. The top money winner of 1970 was Lee Trevino, whose earnings for the season totaled more than $156,000.

On the international scene the United States won the men and women's world amateur team championships in Madrid. The U.S. men were never closely challenged at Puerto de Hierro and finished 12 strokes ahead of New Zealand, which survived a tight contest for second place with South Africa and Australia. A disappointing performance by Great Britain and Ireland left them in seventh place, 25 strokes behind the U.S. The following week at the Club de Campo the U.S. women struggled home by one stroke over France. Their champion, Martha Wilkinson, gained five strokes from Catherine Lacoste de Prado over the last ten holes of the final round.

In World Cup competition at Buenos Aires in November, Australia, with David Graham and Bruce Devlin, won its first championship since 1959. Argentina finished second, and its leading player, Roberto de Vicenzo, won the individual title by one stroke from Graham. Earlier in the summer the U.S. women beat Great Britain and Ireland 11½–6½ at Brae Burn, Mass., and retained the Curtis Cup.

The greatest individual performance of the year was that of Jacklin in the U.S. Open at Chaska, Minn. Many of the leading golfers had expressed their dislike of the course, but Jacklin kept his counsel, took the lead in a strong wind on the first day, and was never caught. While others, notably Arnold Palmer, Gary Player, and Jack Nicklaus, were floundering with first-day scores of around 80, Jacklin came in with a 71. One of his major strengths was his superb putting.

The following day Jacklin maintained a lead of three strokes over Dave Hill, whose criticisms of the course earned him a fine. In the third round Jacklin played with Hill, and once again a masterly short game, at least two wonderful recovery shots, and great holing out enabled him to add another stroke to his lead. For one brief passage before the turn on the final day Jacklin faced crisis, but a great putt hammered home on the 9th steadied him, and he finished the final round with confidence. In the championship he had only 113 putts and was under par in every round, a feat previously achieved only by Lee Trevino in 1968. The impact of his victory on British golf was incalculable. For the first time in a generation the U.K. had produced a competitor of the highest class.

Jacklin made a spirited defense of his British title at St. Andrews. In spite of fears that he was not sufficiently prepared, owing to commercial commitments since his victory in the U.S., he shot to the turn on the Old Course in 29, the lowest ever in a championship there, and was 8 under par playing the 14th when a violent thunderstorm flooded the course and stopped play. The spell was broken although Jacklin finished in 67 the next morning and, with Nicklaus, was only a stroke behind Trevino after two rounds. His challenge continued until the closing holes of the fourth round when the most dramatic finish that even St. Andrews had ever seen was developing.

When Doug Sanders, making a brilliant return to championship contention, played an outstanding bunker shot to the side of the 17th hole and Nicklaus, playing ahead, took three putts on the 18th, Sanders needed only a four on the final hole to win. The 18th measures only 358 yd., with no hazards of any kind except the smooth hollow of the Valley of Sin guarding the green, but Sanders was only able to score five. His first putt was a yard short, and he missed the next. No one within memory had missed a shorter putt to lose a major championship outright. In the play-off of the tie Nicklaus steadily established a four-

POPPERFOTO FROM PICTORIAL PARADE

stroke lead, but Sanders countered with great spirit and in the end Nicklaus, after a monumental drive to the last green, had to sink a six-foot putt to win by a stroke.

The championship was memorable for great golf by Trevino, who had seemed a probable winner until he lost his putting touch in the blustering wind, and by Harold Henning, Neil Coles, and Peter Oosterhuis. Although Christy O'Connor won the £25,000 first prize, the highest ever in Britain, in the John Player tournament, Coles was clearly the finest golfer of the year competing in the U.K., and Oosterhuis the most promising.

After several years' lapse the established professionals took possession of the U.S. Masters tournament again with Billy Casper beating Gene Littler by five strokes in an anticlimactic play-off. The two men had survived a great contest with Player. On the last hole Casper's eight-foot putt for victory circled the hole and stayed out, and Player missed his tie from the same distance. In the play-off everything seemed to run for Casper, but as the most consistent tournament player of the time his success was deserved. Dave Stockton added a further chapter to the continuing frustration of Arnold Palmer in the PGA championship at Tulsa, Okla. Stockton's inspired pitching and putting set a pace that Palmer was unable to match.

In women's professional golf Shirley Englehorn won the Ladies' PGA tournament by four strokes in an 18-hole play-off with Kathy Whitworth. Donna Caponi won her second straight U.S. Women's Open by one stroke over Sandra Haynie and Sandra Spuzich. Miss Haynie was named the player of the year on the basis of two tournament victories and five second-place finishes.

In October the joint committee of the Royal and Ancient Golf Club and the U.S. Golf Association announced their agreement that a uniform-size golf ball of minimum diameter 1.66 in. was feasible for use throughout the world. If further tests confirmed that view, it was to be recommended for adoption by the governing bodies. This would mean that the existing 1.62-in. British- and 1.68-in. U.S.-size balls would be obsolete, and a period of some years would be necessary for existing stocks to be used. The new ball would be confined to a maximum velocity of 250 ft. per sec. as currently permitted in the U.S., and velocity tests would be introduced in Britain.

(P. A. W.-T.)

Government Finance

In 1970 economic stabilization requirements on budget policy (often called fiscal policy) were unusually complicated in most industrialized countries. If aggregate demand in an economy is strong, generating upward pressures on prices and wages, one of the major corrective policies available is to increase the surplus (or decrease the deficit) in the central government budget, either by raising taxes or by curbing expenditures, or by a combination of the two. Conversely, should unemployed labour or unutilized industrial capacity emerge as a result of flagging private demand, it is appropriate to redirect budget policy toward a reduced surplus (or a higher deficit) as a means of bolstering aggregate demand. In many industrialized countries in 1970, however, prices and wages were rising strongly in response to earlier demand pressures,

even though current demand was no longer excessive and, in fact, unemployment was unpleasantly high.

Fiscal policy is not the only stabilization tool available to governments. It has at least an equal partner in monetary policy (*i.e.*, central bank activities affecting the money supply, commercial bank credit, and interest rates). In some countries, still other policies are designed to influence prices and wages through direct government intervention.

United States. The U.S. economy in 1970 exhibited the smallest advance in economic activity and the highest average level of unemployment in several years—by November more than 5% of the labour force was unemployed, compared with less than 4% during 1966–69. This performance was the not unexpected result of extraordinarily restrictive fiscal and monetary policies undertaken in 1969 in an attempt to curb excess demand and inflation. While these policies succeeded in slowing down the economy in 1970, they were notably less successful in stopping inflation, and prices and wages rose rapidly for most of the year.

The budget for the U.S. government for the fiscal year ended June 30, 1970, showed a small deficit, as against a small surplus originally budgeted for the period and a small surplus actually achieved for the preceding year. (*See* Table.) The change from earlier estimates came about as a result of somewhat slower growth of revenues than had originally been forecast, caused, in turn, by slower growth in the economy and in taxable incomes. Regular expenditures were held close to original estimates, and net lending was actually lower than budgeted.

Both receipts and expenditures grew considerably less in 1970 than had been typical for several years. On the expenditure side, this was primarily attributable to the leveling off of defense spending, which was actually a bit lower in 1970 than in 1969. On the receipts side, the slower growth in 1970 resulted from the combined effects of economic slowdown and the first phase of the elimination of the special 10% income tax surtax initiated in 1968.

The budget for fiscal 1971, transmitted to Congress by Pres. Richard Nixon on Feb. 2, 1970, was also planned to show a small surplus, although indications as of late 1970 were that receipts were running considerably lower, and expenditures somewhat higher, than originally budgeted. It thus appeared that 1971 would show a sizable deficit by the time the fiscal year was over. Defense spending was expected to be down sharply in 1971, reflecting the phased withdrawal of troops from Vietnam. Civilian spending appeared to be rising, however, in line with the experience of recent years, even though Congress had failed to approve some of President Nixon's major new expenditure initiatives. Revenue growth in fiscal 1971 was again being retarded by the economic slowdown which began about the middle of 1969, and also by the second phase of surtax elimination and by certain revenue-reducing "reforms" of the tax system enacted in late 1969, notably an increase in personal exemptions, an increase in the minimum standard deduction, and a new ceiling on tax rates applicable to earned income.

Although the federal budget appeared headed for a substantial deficit in 1971, this could not by itself be taken to indicate that fiscal policy was an expansionary influence on the economy. On the contrary, the prospective deficit could be attributed almost entirely to revenue shortfall caused by flagging private incomes and demand. A passive deficit of this kind does not have the same significance for the economy as a comparable deficit reflecting tax cuts or increases in expenditure. For purposes of analyzing the economic effect of the budget, the distinction between "active" and "passive" sources of deficit is sometimes made by reference to a so-called "high employment" budget, in which the surplus or deficit is calculated by comparing expenditures, not with actual revenues, but with the hypothetical level of revenues that would obtain at high employment (generally taken in the case of the U.S. to mean no more than 4% of the civilian labour force unemployed). On this basis, the "high employment" federal budget in 1971 would probably show approximate balance or even a small surplus (although official estimates on this basis are not published), indicating that fiscal policy in fiscal 1971 would be neutral or mildly restraining on the economy, rather than expansionary. In a speech late in 1970, President Nixon indicated that his next budget, while actually in deficit, would be formulated so that it would balance if there were high employment.

A major reform of that portion of the Executive Office of the President responsible for preparation of the federal budget was undertaken during 1970. Under the reform, the Bureau of the Budget—originally created as part of the Treasury Department in the early 1920s and transferred to the Executive Office by Pres. Franklin D. Roosevelt—ceased to exist, and was replaced by a new Office of Management and Budget (OMB). Although the reform at first threatened an unworkable separation of responsibility for policy formulation and budget preparation, this problem was resolved by including the director of OMB as a member of the President's Domestic Council, and the new machinery appeared to be functioning satisfactorily by year's end. The most significant changes appeared to be somewhat enhanced stature and authority for the director of OMB as compared with the budget director under the previous arrangement, and greater attention within the Executive Office to management efficiency throughout the executive branch of government.

State and local governments in the U.S. were pinched financially to an even greater extent than usual. The strong growth of demand for state and local government services, which had been characteristic of the entire period since World War II, continued. Yet the sluggish performance of the national economy held down the growth of taxable sales and incomes and consequently the yields from existing taxes. At the same time, the rather stringent monetary

and credit conditions that prevailed for most of the year severely limited the ability of state and local governments to borrow funds for capital improvements at reasonable interest rates. Moreover, there was evidence of somewhat greater taxpayer resistance to new or increased levies. Some 20 state legislatures did raise rates on one or more of their taxes, including 10 states in which rates were raised on major income, sales, or excise levies. However, both the number of separate tax actions and the amounts of revenue involved were well below the pattern of recent years.

The number of major new state taxes in 1970 was well below the recent pattern. Proposals for new income taxes were defeated by the voters in South Dakota and the state of Washington in November. Proposed income-tax rate increases were rejected in two other states—in California by the legislature and in Missouri by voter referendum. Personal income tax rates were increased in West Virginia and in the District of Columbia, and the personal income tax base was broadened in three states—in Louisiana by eliminating the deduction for federal income taxes; in Michigan by a temporary suspension of certain tax credits; and in New Hampshire by including income earned in the state by nonresidents. New Hampshire enacted a new 6% tax on business profits, and Kansas and Rhode Island increased the rates on their existing corporate income taxes. Of the states levying general retail sales taxes, two—Louisiana and New Jersey—raised rates and three—Colorado, Kansas, and Michigan—broadened the tax base to cover previously untaxed transactions.

West Germany. As in 1969, fiscal policy in West Germany in 1970 aimed at achieving budget surpluses as a means of cooling inflationary pressures in the economy. Expenditures in 1969 were restrained from increasing as fast as revenues, so that public sector debt declined (by contrast with rather sizable increases in public debt in recent years).

The draft federal government budget for 1970 was adopted by the Cabinet and sent to the legislature at the end of January—somewhat later than usual because of the change in government in late 1969. It provided for a 12% increase in spending, to DM. 91.4 billion, and a cash deficit of DM. 2.7 billion. At the same time, DM. 2.7 billion of planned expenditures was temporarily blocked, to be released only if some slackening in the strong pace of economic advance warranted such a move. Moreover, the federal government was to set aside an additional DM. 1.5 billion in contracyclical reserves, to be deposited with the Bundesbank by the end of June; as much federal spending as possible was to be postponed from the first to the second half of the year; and previously planned tax cuts for wage and salary earners were postponed and temporary surtaxes on corporate and individual incomes were extended beyond their scheduled expiration dates. Some special factors contributed to the planned growth of expenditures in 1970, notably increases in pensions to war victims and transfer payments to farmers to compensate for threatened income losses resulting from the revaluation of the mark in 1969. The financial position of the social insurance funds was expected to improve considerably in 1970, partly because of the rapid increase in wage and salary income liable to contributions, and partly because of a further increase of one percentage point—from 16 to 17%—in the contribution rate.

Expenditures of the Länder (states) were also restrained in 1970—DM. 1 billion of their planned ex-

	The Budget of the U.S. Government				

The Budget of the U.S. Government
In $000,000,000

	Fiscal years ending June 30,			
	1969	1970		1971
		(Jan. 1		(Jan. 1
Item	(actual)	est.)	(actual)	est.)
Receipts	187.8	199.4	193.8	202.1
Expenditures	183.1	195.0	195.0	200.1
Expenditure surplus (+) or deficit (−)	+ 4.7	+ 4.4	− 1.1	+ 2.0
Net lending	1.5	2.9	1.8	0.7
Budget surplus (+) or deficit (−)	+ 3.2	+ 1.5	− 2.9	+ 1.3
Composition of expenditures and net lending				
National defense	81.2	79.4	80.3	73.6
Other	103.3	118.5	116.5	127.2
Total	184.6	197.9	196.8	200.8

Note: Detail may not add to totals due to rounding.

penditure was to be set aside in contracyclical reserves on deposit with the Bundesbank. Thus, the public sector as a whole (*i.e.,* local government, social insurance funds, and central government combined) was expected to show a substantial surplus in 1970 for the second year in a row.

The West German economic boom showed more strength than expected in the face of these restrictive fiscal policies. In July the government announced a new 10% temporary income tax surcharge for the period Aug. 1, 1970, to July 1, 1971, and temporary cutbacks in tax depreciation allowances for firms. The recommended surtaxes would have the unusual feature of being repayable in later years.

A major reform of the West German public finance system went into effect on Jan. 1, 1970, as a result of legislation enacted May 12, 1969. By redistributing the shares of the federal government, the Länder, and the municipalities in the various major revenue sources, the Länder were given a more stable (*i.e.,* less cyclically sensitive) mix of revenues, and municipalities were given revenue sources likely to respond more strongly to economic growth in future years. Specifically, the Länder would receive 30% of the revenues accruing under the value-added tax (VAT), in which they previously did not share; the Länder share of individual and corporate income tax was reduced and the federal share increased; and the municipalities would share in the proceeds of the income tax for the first time (previously they had relied principally on local trade taxes). Other less important revenues were also redistributed, and prevailing inequities among municipalities were reduced.

Japan. The Japanese budget outcome in the 1969–70 fiscal year reflected a larger year-to-year growth in revenues than had been forecast initially, thanks to faster than anticipated growth of the national economy. However, expenditures also exceeded initial plans, mainly because of higher payments of rice subsidies following a bumper crop, and larger transfers of tax revenues to local governments (which are treated as expenditures rather than reductions in revenue in the Japanese central government budget).

Because of the general elections at the end of 1969, the budget for the fiscal year beginning in April was delayed a month and was not announced until the beginning of February. Expenditures were budgeted to increase by a large 18%—slightly more than the expected rate of expansion in the national economy. This increase was to be financed by a small increase in corporate tax, together with the growth of revenues under existing taxes. The most rapidly rising expenditure item was again subsidies to rice farmers.

Italy. At the beginning of 1970 the Italian economy was still experiencing the effects of the severe wave of strikes that began in 1969. The disturbances, which involved civil servants, industrial workers, and students, resulted in a marked deterioration in production, sharply rising wages and costs, and a significant deterioration in the balance of payments. The economy resumed its strong growth in 1970, but the civil disturbances had left an aftermath of inflation that contrasted with the rather stable prices experienced for several years.

The 1969 and 1970 budgets were both strongly expansionary. In 1969 expenditures rose faster than revenues, and the government deficit (measured by borrowing needs) rose to 1,590,000,000 lire, compared with 1,192,000,000 lire in 1968; central government expenditures and a large increase in social security

BEN ROTH AGENCY
"You won't feel a thing"
—Liederman, "Long Island Press."

benefits accounted for most of the increase. The expenditure rise would have been even larger if strikes by employees of the revenue service and the postal service had not delayed the recording of both receipts and expenditures in the latter part of the year. Public debt rose 10% in 1969 (to 19.1 billion lire); the interest rate policies being pursued by the central bank made it difficult for the Treasury to sell bonds to the nonbank public, and the share of public debt held by the central bank rose from 17 to 22% of the total.

The deficit for 1970 was expected to be still higher, with regular expenditures scheduled to rise 17%, substantially more than revenues. With inflation threatening Italy's previously favourable balance of trade, however, the budget for 1971, submitted by the government to Parliament in July 1970, aimed at achieving a less expansionary fiscal policy, mainly by holding down expenditure growth. The budgeted 8% increase in expenditures would be mainly for current rather than capital outlays, with higher wages and salaries for civil servants and increased social security pensions accounting for most of the rise. In June 1970, after consultation with the trade unions, the government had agreed to increase income tax exemptions, to be compensated by higher tax rates. The Chamber of Deputies subsequently voted to make this change effective for final 1970 paychecks.

The government proposals for a major reform of the Italian tax and finance system, submitted to Parliament in 1969, were still pending in 1970. The aims of the reform were to simplify the tax structure; improve collection procedures; improve coordination between central government finances and those of local authorities; and permit the financial system to be more responsive to economic stabilization requirements. The proposed reform would provide for a single progressive income tax to replace 16 different taxes and surtaxes levied at various levels of government, and a single company profits tax to replace a variety of enterprise levies.

Proposals were also made to simplify indirect taxation by the adoption of a 10% VAT to replace the present 4% cascade-type sales tax, as well as a number of other national and local taxes. EEC policy was to have member countries rely on VAT as their primary form of indirect taxation, as a step toward tax harmonization in the Community. Italy was supposed to switch over to VAT on Jan. 1, 1970, but it obtained EEC permission to postpone the change to Jan. 1, 1972, in light of the volume of preparatory work required in its case. In December 1969 Italy also reached agreement with the EEC on a two-stage reduction of rates at which Italian exporters could be reimbursed for taxes paid under the present sales tax, pending the switchover to VAT. The reduction, to be completed Jan. 1, 1971, would tend to increase Italian export prices, mainly those for chemicals, textiles, engineering, and automobiles.

United Kingdom. The British budget system is unusual in that expenditure and revenue estimates are presented at different times. Expenditure forecasts for the various ministries and agencies are presented around the turn of the calendar year, well before the start of the fiscal year on April 1. On budget day, which is usually in April, the chancellor of the Exchequer presents the government's tax and borrowing program to Parliament, along with an analysis and forecast of the domestic economy and the balance of international payments.

The stabilization program for fiscal 1969–70 featured stringent restraints on public expenditure and substantial increases in taxation. The resulting large budget surplus, together with tight reins on the extension of bank credit to the private sector, succeeded in holding down import growth while releasing production for export, enabling the U.K. to achieve a large reduction in foreign indebtedness. These same policies of demand restraint served to increase unemployment to about $2\frac{1}{2}\%$—relatively high by British standards—but failed to check price and wage inflation.

On Dec. 4, 1969, the government released a White Paper detailing plans for total public expenditure up to April 1974. Central government expenditures forecast for the 1970–71 fiscal year included increases for social services, roads, and assistance to industry and employment. Defense spending was also expected to show a modest increase, mainly as a result of pay increases for the armed forces.

The chancellor of the Exchequer, Roy Jenkins, presented the budget for fiscal 1970–71 on April 14. Proposed changes in taxation, mainly in income tax, would reduce revenues by an estimated £220 million. The main changes were increases in exemptions and allowances for elderly people and low-income taxpayers. The recommended tax cuts were smaller than had been generally expected in light of the improved trade balance and considering that 1970 was an election year. With revenues for the 1970–71 fiscal year projected to rise at a slightly faster rate than expenditures, the surplus in the central government accounts (adjusted to exclude certain repayable revenues from temporary import deposits) was projected at £1,041 million, up from the already high £392 million achieved in 1969–70. Borrowing by local authorities in 1970–71 was expected to be down slightly. In October Anthony Barber, chancellor of the Exchequer in the new Conservative government, announced a "mini-budget" that included reductions in income and corporation tax, as well as changes in welfare expenditures that were expected to effect a net saving of slightly over £1,000 million by the mid-1970s. (*See* UNITED KINGDOM.)

An important study by W. B. Reddaway, published in March 1970, presented tentative conclusions regarding the effects of the controversial and somewhat unconventional selective employment tax (SET), initiated in 1966. SET had been designed to stimulate national productivity and exports by encouraging the redistribution of labour away from service industries and into manufacturing through the imposition of discriminatory payroll taxes on the former. Reddaway's study indicated that SET probably did have at least some of the intended effects, and the government was encouraged to continue the scheme, at least for the time being.

France. The budget for 1970 was contained in the *Loi de Finances pour 1970,* presented to the National Assembly in October 1969. Among other things, it aimed at achieving restraint on the pace of economic advance. Ordinary budget expenditures were held to the lowest rate of increase in a decade. The projected Fr. 2 billion surplus on ordinary transactions would be offset by projected Treasury loans and advances (*e.g.,* to nationalized industries), and the overall budget was expected to be approximately in balance, requiring no net financing of the Treasury through monetary expansion. Expenditures of almost all government departments were severely curtailed, although the restraint was less severe in the case of education, technical training, social transfers to lower income groups, and investment in telecommunications and roads and for "restructuring" of industry. Subsidies to nationalized industries were scheduled to decline for the first time in years, and agricultural price subsidies were scheduled to show a much smaller increase in 1970 than in the previous year.

On the tax side, there were no major tax rate changes. A special profits tax on banks was introduced and, effective from September 1969, corporate tax payments were accelerated and depreciation allowances reduced. A special increase in taxes on alcohol and automobiles, introduced in November 1968, was extended for an additional year. Tax brackets (although not rates) under the income tax were revised upward to offset the effects of recent general price increases. Some tax relief was granted to low income groups, especially the aged, and an increase in upper-bracket rates, enacted earlier, was reduced.

Later in the year there were some signs that economic expansion was slowing down, and the government announced that, before the end of 1970, it expected to release part of the monies previously frozen in its contracyclical reserve funds. Also, figures became available showing that the budget deficit for 1969 was actually considerably smaller than first estimates, and indicating that the 1970 budget was likely to show a significant surplus.

The government's draft budget for 1971, announced in September, again projected an approximate balance between receipts and expenditures. Further reductions in public support of the nationalized industries was projected, and proposals were put forward for making the tax system more progressive. These would increase income-tax exemptions at the lower end of the scale, raise tax rates on higher incomes, and reduce dependence on indirect taxes (mainly VAT) in the long run. More immediately, reductions in VAT rates on agricultural products were proposed as partial offsets to the inflationary effects of reduced agricultural subsidies. (W. Le.)

Great Britain:
see United Kingdom

See also Economic Planning; Economics; Payments and Reserves, International.

Greece

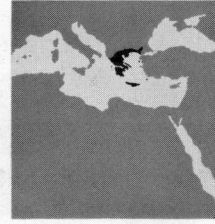

A constitutional monarchy of Europe, Greece occupies the southern part of the Balkan Peninsula. Area: 50,944 sq. mi. (131,944 sq.km.), of which the mainland accounts for 41,-277 sq.mi. Pop. (1969 est.): 8,834,560. Cap. and largest city: Athens (pop., 1961, 627,564). Language: Greek. Religion: Orthodox. King, Constantine II, in exile since Dec. 14, 1967; regent in 1970, Lieut. Gen. Georgios Zoitakis; prime minister, Georgios Papadopoulos.

Domestic Affairs. The resumption of full-scale U.S. military aid to the Army-sponsored Greek regime was by far the most significant domestic event of 1970, chiefly because of its political implications. It demonstrated that the leaders of the 1967 military coup had scored three victories. First, by resisting all pressures for acceleration of the so-called democratization process, they had convinced the U.S. that the heavy arms embargo, imposed after the coup, had been totally ineffective as a political lever. Second, by negotiating purchases of embargoed weapons from France and elsewhere, they aroused misgivings in Washington that a continuation of the embargo might alienate the regime's affections, at a time when the dearth of loyal allies in the Mediterranean was becoming a source of grave concern for the U.S. Third, by underlining the absence of any feasible democratic alternative to their rule, as well as the hazards of an extremist take-over, they induced the U.S. to concentrate on protecting the moderate faction led by Prime Minister Papadopoulos against his less predictable associates.

These developments took place against a background of slow liberalization of the regime, which was becoming less repressive as it consolidated its position at home. Habeas corpus and other constitutional safeguards against arbitrary arrest were restored on April 10. The total number of political prisoners was reduced from about 1,500 to less than 700. One of the most prominent Communist political prisoners, the composer Mikis Theodorakis (*see* BIOGRAPHY), was unexpectedly freed and allowed to go abroad.

The International Committee of the Red Cross had been given free access to all detention sites for Greek political prisoners in November 1969 in order to invalidate accusations of torture, but in April 1970 alarming descriptions of alleged police brutality (prior to the Red Cross visits) were read at the trial of 34 intellectuals charged with sedition and bombing. Trials by special military courts continued; well over 100 opponents of the regime were convicted and some were sent to prison for life.

One of the most spectacular trials involved Ioannis Zigdis, a former minister, and five executives of the aggressively antiregime Athens newspaper *Ethnos*. They were found guilty on April 2 of publishing reports "likely to evoke public alarm," in the form of an interview given by Zigdis. *Ethnos* was compelled to shut down on April 4 after its three publishers and two editors were sent to jail for terms of up to five years. The worldwide outcry that followed induced the regime to grant them a retrial in September, in the course of which the prison sentences for four of the journalists were reduced and one was acquitted. Zigdis, serving a $4\frac{1}{2}$-year term, refused to appeal.

On November 29, 92 candidates for a "consultative committee on legislation" were chosen by 1,240 electors designated by the regime; the prime minister would pick 46 of these candidates and appoint 10 others of his own choosing. The decree establishing the committee, announced on the third anniversary of the coup (April 10), indicated that its functions would be purely academic. It was seen as a "seminar for budding politicians," in keeping with the regime's ultimate aim of breaking completely with the nation's "sinful" political past. When there was a broad Cabinet reshuffle on June 29, all but one of the new government members—a former Athens mayor—were totally unknown to the public. The only former political personality whose services were welcome to the regime, Panayotis Pipinelis, foreign minister since November 1967, died on July 19 (*see* OBITUARIES). His death deprived the king of a strong monarchist influence within the Cabinet.

Papadopoulos personally took over the Ministry of Foreign Affairs and gradually created around him a staff of junior ministers and undersecretaries who acted as a "brain trust." This arrangement was strongly resented by his fellow revolutionaries and precipitated the first major crisis within the junta at the end of August. The rebels called for the prime minister's resignation, which he agreed to sign. The post was then offered to Gen. Odysseus Anghelis, the chief of the armed forces, who declined. The crisis subsided as the rebels realized the magnitude of their own impotence and the need to have as shrewd a leader as Papadopoulos.

Foreign Relations. After withdrawing from the Council of Europe in 1969, Greece kept aloof from its hostile Western European allies, encouraged good

GREPHO FROM PIX

Greek Prime Minister Georgios Papadopoulos on Independence Day.

GREECE

Education. (1966–67) Primary, pupils 979,395, teachers 28,524; secondary, pupils 398,292, teachers 12,111; vocational, pupils 90,211; teacher training (1965–66), students 4,350, teachers 261; higher (including 5 universities), students 64,591, teaching staff 2,541.

Finance. Monetary unit: drachma, with a par value of 30 drachmas to U.S. $1 (72 drachmas = £1 sterling). Gold, SDRs, and foreign exchange, central bank: (June 1970) U.S. $253 million; (June 1969) U.S. $243.1 million. Budget (1970 est.): revenue 57.5 billion drachmas; expenditure 53.8 billion drachmas. Gross national product: (1968) 226.6 billion drachmas; (1967) 211.3 billion drachmas. Money supply: (April 1970) 47,130,000,000 drachmas; (April 1969) 43,310,-000,000 drachmas. Cost of living (1963 = 100): (June 1970) 118; (June 1969) 114.

Foreign Trade. (1969) Imports 47,825,000,000 drachmas; exports 16,609,-000,000 drachmas. Import sources: EEC 42% (West Germany 19%, Italy 9%, France 7%); U.S. 10%; U.K. 9%; Japan 7%. Export destinations: EEC 45% (West Germany 20%, Italy 10%, France 7%, Netherlands 5%); U.S. 10%; Yugoslavia 7%; U.S.S.R. 5%; U.K. 5%. Main exports: tobacco 10%; iron and steel 9%; dried fruit (raisins, currants) 8%; aluminum 7%; fresh fruit 7%; chemicals 6%; cotton 5%. Tourism (1968): visitors 879,500; gross receipts U.S. $120 million.

Transport and Communications. Roads (1969) 34,692 km. Motor vehicles in use (1969): passenger 194,940; commercial 96,904. Railways: (1967) 2,571 km.; traffic (1969) 1,438,000,000 passenger-km., freight 587 million net ton-km. Air traffic (1969): 1,717,000,000 passenger-km.; freight 36.5 million net ton-km. Shipping (1969): merchant vessels 100 gross tons and over 1,700; gross tonnage 8,580,753. Telephones (Dec. 1968) 761,550. Radio receivers (Dec. 1968) 985,000. Television receivers (Dec. 1968) 40,000.

Agriculture. Production (in 000; metric tons; 1969; 1968 in parentheses): wheat c. 1,770 (1,515); barley 540 (465); oats c. 120 (99); corn c. 421 (375); potatoes 1,968 (1,967) 721; rice (1968) 108, (1967) 92; tomatoes (1967) 679, (1966) 611; tobacco (1968) 78, (1967) 114; oranges (1968) 470, (1967) 329; lemons c. 100 (100); cotton, lint c. 107 (98); olive oil 160 (154); wine (1968) 383, (1967) 395; raisins (1968) 188, (1967) 152; currants and sultanas (1967) 149, (1966) 183; figs (1968) 128, (1967) 90. Livestock (in 000; Dec. 1968): sheep 7,804; cattle 1,078; goats (Dec. 1967) 3,791; horses 260; pigs c. 614; chickens 24,500.

Industry. Production (in 000; metric tons; 1969): lignite 6,688; electricity (excluding most industrial production; kw-hr.) 8,012,000; petroleum products (1968) 4,150; bauxite 1,900; magnesite (1968) 446; cement 4,801; cotton yarn 37.

relations with France and the Balkan nations, and made it a point at all times to underline its loyalty to NATO.

Otherwise the regime's principal preoccupation in foreign affairs was the problem of Cyprus. The abortive attempt (March 8) on the life of the Cypriot president, Archbishop Makarios, was attributed by some circles to an Athens plot to eliminate him, as the only obstacle to the drastic solution of partitioning the island between Greece and Turkey and incorporating it into NATO. Although Greek officers serving in Cyprus were apparently implicated in the affair, there was no evidence that such a Machiavellian conspiracy had had the endorsement of Greek government leaders.

Greece's external interests were forcibly drawn to the Middle East conflict in the summer when six Arab commandos hijacked an Olympic Airways jetliner and held its 54 passengers and crew hostage until they had obtained the Greek regime's pledge to free seven Arabs, jailed in Greece for terrorist activity. The seven were released and expelled in August.

The Economy. The economic scene was dominated in 1970 by an anticipated 7% growth rate, combined with relative monetary stability. However, liquidity remained high and the scarcity of foreign capital inflow forced the government to borrow abroad at onerous terms to protect its balance of payments. On a longer-term prospect, the investment contracts signed with the two well-known Greek shipowners, Aristotle Onassis and Stavros Niarchos, in exchange for profitable crude-oil-supply concessions, promised to pump about $750 million into the Greek economy in the next decade.

The regime cultivated trade relations with the Eastern bloc in its effort to increase exports, even concluding a trade agreement with Albania, with which Greece had theoretically been at war since 1940.   (Mo. M.)

WIDE WORLD

Count Karl von Spreti, West German ambassador to Guatemala, was kidnapped by terrorists in Guatemala City March 31, 1970.

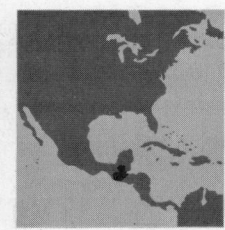

WIDE WORLD

Guatemala City police line up suspects following a shoot-out between political factions Feb. 25, 1970, in which three persons were killed.

political campaigns of three presidential aspirants: Colonel Arana, supported by a right-wing coalition of MLN (National Liberation Movement) and PID (Institutional Democratic Party); Mario Fuentes Pieruccini, supported by the ruling PR (Revolutionary Party); and Jorge Lucas Caballeros of the newly founded PDC (Christian Democratic Party). In the elections of March 1, Arana won a plurality of 43% of the votes as against 35% and 22%, respectively, for Pieruccini and Caballeros. Since no candidate received a majority of the popular vote, the issue remained in doubt until late March when the national

Guatemala

A republic of Central America, Guatemala is bounded by Mexico, British Honduras, Honduras, El Salvador, the Caribbean Sea, and the Pacific Ocean. Area: 42,-042 sq.mi. (108,889 sq.km.). Pop. (1970 est.): 5,172,-000. Cap. and largest city: Guatemala City (pop., 1970 est., 770,000). Language: Spanish, with some Indian dialects. Religion: predominantly Roman Catholic. Presidents in 1970, Julio César Méndez Montenegro and, from July 1, Carlos Manuel Arana Osorio.

The third legal transfer of executive power in the 150-year history of Guatemala's independence took place in July with the assumption of the presidency by Carlos Arana Osorio. Meanwhile, an upsurge of urban terrorism, which had begun in December 1969, continued unabated throughout the first half of 1970. A two-month respite after the inauguration of President Arana was followed by a resumption of terrorist activity in September. On the economic front, a moderately favourable rate of growth was maintained throughout the year in spite of uncertainties surrounding the national elections, the disruptions created in the aftermath of the conflict between El Salvador and Honduras, and in the wake of the devastating hurricane and rains that had struck the nation's southern region during the late summer of 1969.

The first two months of 1970 were focused upon the

GUATEMALA

Education. (1967–68) Primary, pupils 474,919, teachers 12,594; secondary, pupils 43,567, teachers (1965–66) 4,216; vocational, pupils 10,352, teachers (1965–66) 985; teacher training, students 7,601, teachers (1965–66) 1,197; higher (including 4 universities), students 9,388, teaching staff 665.

Finance. Monetary unit: quetzal, at par with the U.S. dollar (2.40 quetzales = £1 sterling). Gold, SDRs, and foreign exchange, central bank: (June 1970) U.S. $90.5 million; (June 1969) U.S. $74.5 million. Budget (1970 est.) balanced at 211 million quetzales. Gross national product: (1968) 1,530,000,000 quetzales; (1967) 1,425,000,000 quetzales. Money supply: (June 1970) 169.2 million quetzales; (June 1969) 157.7 million quetzales.

Foreign Trade. (1968) Imports 247.4 million quetzales; exports 222.4 million quetzales. Import sources: U.S. 41%; El Salvador 11%; West Germany 11%; Japan 9%; U.K. 5%. Export destinations: U.S. 28%; El Salvador 15%; Japan 11%. Main exports: coffee 30%; cotton 14%.

Transport and Communications. Roads (1968) c. 11,200 km. (including 830 km. of Pan-American Highway). Motor vehicles in use: passenger (1967) 33,400; commercial (including buses; 1968) 20,500. Railways: (1967) 1,160 km.; freight traffic (1968) 75 million net ton-km. Air traffic (1968): 77,403,000 passenger-km.; freight 3,850,000 net ton-km. Telephones (Jan. 1969) 36,165. Radio receivers (Dec. 1968) c. 215,000. Television receivers (Dec. 1968) 65,000.

Agriculture. Production (in 000; metric tons; 1969; 1968 in parentheses): corn c. 805 (679); cotton, lint c. 49 (74); cane sugar, raw value (1969–70) c. 190, (1968–69) 154; sugar, panela (1969–70) c. 48, (1968–69) c. 48; dry beans (1968) 69, (1967) 69; coffee c. 111 (c. 99); bananas (1967) c. 76, (1966) c. 74.

Congress declared Arana president. He was formally inaugurated to a four-year term on July 1.

Prior to the inauguration, Guatemala City was subjected to seven months of urban terrorism on an unheard-of scale. Between December 1969 and February 1970 a campaign of arson, bombings, and assassinations reportedly inflicted 20 deaths and $10 million in damages. The FAR (Rebel Armed Forces) was generally credited with most of these attacks. Between late February and April a new dimension of terrorism was witnessed by the successive kidnappings of Guatemalan Foreign Minister Alberto Fuentes Mohr, U.S. embassy aide Sean M. Holly, and Count Karl von Spreti, the West German ambassador. Fuentes Mohr and Holly were both freed in exchange for the release of "political" prisoners. The Guatemalan government, however, refused to negotiate for the release of Spreti in exchange for 22 prisoners and $700,000. The ensuing assassination of Spreti in early April increased tensions between the West German and Guatemalan governments and culminated in the recall of their respective diplomatic missions.

Between April and July terrorism continued unabated, claiming the lives of prominent Guatemalan citizens at both the left and right of the political spectrum. Toward the end of May the Mexican government announced the killing of the Guatemalan guerrilla leader Yon Sosa and several of his companions by an army patrol stationed in the Mexican state of Chiapas near the Guatemalan frontier.

(O. H. H.)

Guinea

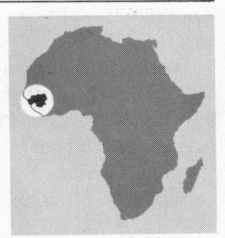

A republic on the west coast of Africa, Guinea is bounded by Portuguese Guinea, Senegal, Mali, Ivory Coast, Liberia, and Sierra Leone. Area: 94,925 sq.mi. (245,856 sq. km.). Pop. (1969 est.): 3,890,000. Cap. and largest city: Conakry (pop., 1967 est., 197,267). Language: French (official). Religion: mostly Muslim. President in 1970, Sékou Touré.

On Nov. 22, 1970, a force of approximately 350 men landed in Conakry from four ships and proceeded to attack parts of the city. The invaders temporarily occupied two army camps and the city's main prison, freeing a number of political prisoners who had opposed President Touré. The raiders ransacked the headquarters of a group that headed the liberation movement in neighbouring Portuguese Guinea and shot up the home neighbourhood of Amilcar Cabral,

the movement's leader. Cabral, however, was not in Conakry at the time. The fighting continued sporadically for about three days. President Touré's summer home was severely damaged, but the president was unhurt. It was estimated that about 100 Guineans were killed. Casualty figures among the invaders were unknown, but about 100 were captured.

President Touré accused Portugal of sponsoring and manning the invasion as an attempt to destroy the movement supporting liberation in Portuguese Guinea. On November 28 he also charged Portugal with an attack on Koundara, near the border with the colony. Portugal denied these accusations.

The UN Security Council on November 24 sent a five-member commission to Guinea to investigate the situation and make recommendations. The commission, consisting of Colombia, Finland, Nepal, Poland, and Zambia, reported to the council on December 4; it concluded that the invasion force in Conakry had consisted mainly of African troops from Portuguese Guinea under the command of white Portuguese Army officers. The Security Council on December 8 voted 11–0 to condemn Portugal for the invasion and demanded that the Portuguese government "pay full compensation to Guinea for the loss of life and property" caused by the attack. Portugal, however, continued to deny any involvement in the raids.

Guyana

A republic and a realm of the Commonwealth of Nations, Guyana is situated between Venezuela, Brazil, and Surinam on the Atlantic Ocean. Area: 83,000 sq.mi. (215,000 sq.km.). Pop. (1969 est.): 741,978, including (1964) East Indian 50.2%; Negro 31.3%; mestizo and mulatto 11.9%; Amerindian 4.6%. Cap. and largest city: Georgetown (pop., 1969 est., 97,190). Language: English (official). Religion: Protestant and Roman Catholic. To Feb. 23, 1970, queen, Elizabeth II; from February 23, president, Arthur Chung; prime minister in 1970, Forbes Burnham.

On Feb. 23, 1970, Guyana became a "cooperative republic" within the Commonwealth of Nations. As president (ceremonial head of state) the governing party, the People's National Congress, chose former Supreme Court Judge Arthur Chung, who was elected on March 17.

The Cooperative Republic of Guyana, said Prime

GUINEA
Education. (1965–66) Primary, pupils 164,119, teachers 3,990; secondary, pupils 16,698, teachers 567; vocational, pupils 5,018, teachers 261; teacher training, students 822, teachers 52; higher, students 376, teachers 95.
Finance. Monetary unit: Guinea franc, with a par value of GFr. 246.85 to U.S. $1 (GFr. 592.45 = £1 sterling). Budget (1969–70 est.) balanced at GFr. 24,386,000,000.
Foreign Trade. (1964) Imports GFr. 11,201,000,000; exports GFr. 16.1 billion. Import sources: U.S. 22%; U.S.S.R. 12%; China 10%. Export destinations: France 16%; U.S. 11%; Cameroon 10%; Poland 8%. Main exports (1962): aluminum 60%; bananas 10%; palm products 7%; coffee 6%; iron ore 6%.

GUYANA
Education. (1967–68) Primary, pupils 138,672, teachers 4,383; secondary, pupils 49,163, teachers 1,741; vocational, pupils 1,717, teachers 115; teacher training, students 561, teachers 39; higher, students 597, teaching staff 63.
Finance. Monetary unit: Guyanan dollar (Guy$2 = U.S. $1; Guy$4.80 = £1 sterling). Budget (1969 rev. est.): revenue Guy$119,414,000; expenditure Guy$105,506,000.
Foreign Trade. (1969) Imports Guy$235.8 million; exports Guy$242 million. Import sources: U.K. 31%; U.S. 21%; Trinidad and Tobago 12%; Canada 8%. Export destinations: U.S. 25%; U.K. 24%; Canada 19%; Trinidad and Tobago 7%; Norway 6%. Main exports: sugar 36%; bauxite 26%; alumina 16%; rice 8%.
Agriculture. Production (in 000; metric tons): sugar, raw value (1969–70) c. 381, (1968–69) 370; rice (1969) c. 210, (1968) 210. Livestock (in 000; 1968–69): cattle 250; sheep 98; pigs (1967–68) 83.
Industry. Production (in 000; metric tons; 1968): manganese ore (metal content) 38; bauxite 4,752; diamonds (metric carats) 66; electricity (kw-hr.) 267,000.

Guiana:
see Dependent States; Guyana

Guided Missiles:
see Defense

Guinea, Portuguese:
see Dependent States

Minister Forbes Burnham in February, had two objectives—to eradicate the people's "colonial mentality" and to harness them into a "self-help program based on a national system of cooperative ventures." This definition was ridiculed by opposition leader Cheddi Jagan; he accused the prime minister of trying to fool the people while creating a new colonial system amenable to bauxite and sugar interests.

In fact, five years of Burnham's "self-help" policies had paid social and economic (as well as political) dividends that gave the new republic's title some relevance to the basic problems of preventing interracial strife and exploiting untapped natural resources. In 1970 racial harmony was broadly maintained, and voluntary ("self-help") labour began to build a 300-mi. road link with Brazil that would also encourage settlement in Guyana's hinterland.

On the industrial front the government's declared aim was full partnership with private enterprise, and the emphasis was on vertical integration (the processing of local raw materials inside Guyana). Burnham's strategy was demonstrated by the growing firmness and precision of his demands for state participation in the expanding bauxite industry, the country's largest export earner.

Agriculture (chiefly sugar and rice) remained the basis of the economy. Rice yields were disappointing, but the 1969 sugar crop, a record 364,465 tons, put Guyana ahead of Jamaica as the largest Commonwealth producer in the Caribbean. Strikes militated against a repetition of this bumper harvest in 1970.

Relations with adjacent countries took a more hopeful turn. In April it was reported that Surinam's claim to 6,000 sq.mi. in eastern Guyana was settled by an agreement to demilitarize the area and make it a zone of mutual cooperation.　　　　　　　　(RA. R.)

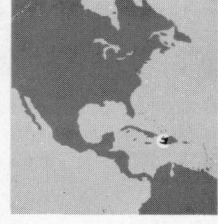

This modern school building under construction in Haiti is part of the republic's effort to upgrade its educational system.

CAMERA PRESS FROM PIX

Haiti

The Republic of Haiti occupies the western one-third of the Caribbean island of Hispaniola, which it shares with the Dominican Republic. Area: 10,714 sq.mi. (27,750 sq.km.). Pop. (1970 est.): 4,867,190, of whom 95% are Negro. Cap. and largest city: Port-au-Prince (pop., 1968 est., 340,175). Language: French and Creole. Religion: Roman Catholic; Voodooism practiced in rural areas. President in 1970, François Duvalier.

During 1970 there were signs of increased political stability and of economic growth. In April 120 dissi-

dents in three coast guard vessels shelled the presidential palace in Port-au-Prince, but this attempt to start a general uprising was quickly suppressed. Among those arrested were Élois Maître, a former head of the Tonton Macoute (secret police); Rameau Estimé, a former justice minister; a previous chief of the Commercial Bank; the Army's quartermaster general; and several congressmen.

Unlike earlier risings, however, the coast guard revolt left no aftermath of violent oppression. In May its leaders were granted political asylum in the U.S., and by September Duvalier's political base appeared stronger than it had ever been during his 13 years of personal rule. Two key officers, the chief of the presidential bodyguard and the commander of the Bataillon Dessalines, the Army's only effective unit, remained loyal during the revolt, while opposition from civilian sources, notably the ambitious finance minister Clovis Dèsinor, was controlled carefully.

Although the government kept a close watch on the church, its last clerical enemies—the Holy Ghost Fathers of the Collège Saint-Martial—had already been expelled and Haiti Progrès, a left-wing group of young priests who had supported an abortive guerrilla uprising in 1969, no longer posed any threat. In 1970 the church's leaders gave the regime their unofficial approval, and the opposition of exiles in New York faded with the disbandment of the Coalition Haïtienne.

After ten years of economic stagnation, 1969 showed a 2.5% growth rate (against the 1963–68 average of 1.5%), chiefly because of higher bauxite exports that more than offset falls in sisal and coffee shipments. A similar rise in the growth rate was forecast for 1970.

Work continued on port improvements at Port-au-Prince (a U.S. contract worth $4 million) and on a new highway from the capital to Cap-Haïtien, but the biggest project under way was the Peligré hydroelectric dam in the Artibonite Valley. This 31,400-kw.-capacity plant, which had cost $8 million since work

HAITI

Education. (1966–67) Primary, pupils 286,187, teachers 6,460; secondary, pupils 21,010, teachers 1,289; vocational, pupils 6,211, teachers 359; teacher training, students 210, teachers 83; higher (at University of Haiti), students 1,527, teaching staff 209.

Finance. Monetary unit: gourde, with a par value of 5 gourdes to U.S. $1 (12 gourdes = £1 sterling). Gold, SDRs, and foreign exchange, central bank: (June 1970) U.S. $5.7 million; (June 1969) U.S. $3.9 million. Budget (1967–68 est.) balanced at 140.2 million gourdes. Money supply: (March 1969) 156.2 million gourdes; (March 1968) 147.8 million gourdes. Cost of living (Port-au-Prince; 1963 = 100): (June 1970) 122; (June 1969) 126.

Foreign Trade. (1968) Imports 187.9 million gourdes; exports 178.2 million gourdes. Import sources: U.S. 61%; Japan 7%; France 6%; Canada 5%. Export destinations: U.S. 61%; France 11%; Italy 7%; Belgium-Luxembourg 5%. Main exports: coffee 38%; bauxite 12%; sugar 9%; sisal 5%.

Transport and Communications. Roads (1968) c. 3,100 km. (including c. 350 km. with improved surface). Motor vehicles in use: passenger (1968) 7,300; commercial (1966) 1,100. Railways (1968) 301 km. Telephones (Jan. 1969) c. 4,450. Radio receivers (Dec. 1968) 80,000. Television receivers (Dec. 1968) 11,000.

Agriculture. Production (in 000; metric tons; 1969; 1968 in parentheses): coffee c. 30 (c. 28); sugar, raw value (1969–70) c. 65, (1968–69) c. 59; bananas (1967) c. 220, (1966) c. 230; sisal 27 (27). Livestock (in 000; 1968–69): pigs c. 1,700; cattle (1967–68) 845; goats (1967–68) 1,295; sheep c. 78.

Industry. Production (in 000; metric tons; 1967): cement 35; bauxite (exports) 370; electricity (kw.-hr.) 115,000.

began in 1957, was expected to go into operation in January 1971 and supply power to the whole country within another ten years.

An International Monetary Fund (IMF) mission in May reported an improvement in the administration of budget and tax funds, and U.S. aid was resumed in June with an Inter-American Development Bank loan of $5.1 million to finance the second stage of a program for improving the water supply facilities of Port-au-Prince and neighbouring towns. This financial aid, of a kind that would have been granted earlier but for the Haitian government's defaulting on the repayment of a U.S. Export-Import Bank loan and Washington's misgivings about the Duvalier regime, was followed in July by an IMF standby credit of $2.2 million. Despite these signs of progress, however, Haiti remained the poorest of the Latin-American countries, with a per capita income of $75.

(Rn. C.)

Encyclopædia Britannica Films. *The West Indies* (1965).

Historical Studies

It was a long-established tradition that historians devote themselves, on the occasion of an anniversary, to the commemoration of the event or figure through their work. Just as the year 1969 had been that of the second centenary of the birth of Napoleon, an occasion that led to the organizing of a number of conferences in France and also outside France, and the publishing of significant new work or of reeditions, so 1970 marked the commemoration of the seventh centenary of the death of the French king St. Louis. The event produced in particular two conferences, one held at Royaumont and the other at the Institut Catholique in Paris, the "acts" of which were to be published, as well as a collective volume, *Le Siècle de Saint Louis* ("The Century of Saint Louis").

The year also saw the publication of the important studies inspired by the celebration in 1967 of the fifth centenary of the birth of Erasmus. A table of these was to be found in the abstract made of them under the title *Erasmus in 1970*, in the *Bibliothèque d'Humanisme et Renaissance*. The two most outstanding studies were those of Roland Bainton, *Erasmus of Christendom,* and two volumes of the *Scrinium Erasmianum*.

But 1970 was marked most of all by the impressive series of conferences and publications throughout the world inspired by the centenary of the birth of Lenin. One might think that the 13th International Congress of Historical Sciences, held in Moscow August 16–23, had met under the aegis of Lenin. Indeed the whole of one afternoon of the congress was devoted to a symposium on "V. I. Lenin and Historical Science." The congress, however, occupied its normal place in the uninterrupted series of great historical congresses organized every five years by the International Committee for Historical Sciences (ICHS). These congresses, for both the themes discussed and the papers presented, stand out as so many milestones along the road of history on the march, and from this point of view the Moscow congress may be seen as an admirable vantage point from which to judge the current directions of historical research, whether in the work of the congress itself, or in that of the different commissions of the committee, all of which met on this occasion.

The first of the major themes on the program of the congress, "The Historian and the Social Sciences," was in itself especially revealing, and the audience that flocked to the sessions at which it was discussed demonstrated the interest of this theme, in relation both to problems concerning the very idea of history as a science and to the application in historical research of the methods of inquiry used by the social sciences. These problems inevitably raised the question of the use of computers.

The second major theme, "Nationalism and Class Struggle in the Process of Modernization in Asia and Africa," showed the concern of historians in lifting history out of its traditional channels, where Europe and the Western world had occupied a privileged position, at the very moment when UNESCO had undertaken the preparation of a *General History of Africa*.

The reports presented to the congress were also a convincing demonstration of the predominance of economic and social history, whatever the historical period being discussed. From this point of view mention must be made of the importance of the work undertaken by the International Commission on Economic History of the ICHS, which met in Leningrad, while another ICHS body, the International Commission for the History of Social Movements and Social Structures, chose as the subject of its discussions in Moscow the study of "Peasant Movements and Agrarian Problems from the End of the XVIIIth Century to the Present." Economic and social questions were also the concern of specialists of World War II when they discussed "The Working Masses in the War Effort During the Second Great World Conflict," of military historians when they dealt with the "Life and Psychology of Combatants and Soldiers," and of specialists in religious history when they studied in Moscow "Social Christianity" or "Church and Revolution" or when they chose as the themes for their Cambridge Conference in 1968 (the publications of which appeared in 1970) "the Missions of the IIIrd to the IXth Centuries," "Recruitment and Training of Catholic and Protestant Clergy in the XVIth Century," and "Dechristianization."

These same preoccupations were revealed in the meeting in Athens (May 1970) of the second Congress of the International Association for the Study of South-East Europe, and in the publication, undertaken in 1970, of a new *Economic and Social History of France* (*Histoire économique et sociale de la France*), under the direction of F. Braudel and E. Labrousse. In this context we may mention the pertinent study by P. Léon, "L'École francaise et l'histoire économique globale" ("The French School and World Economic History"), which appeared in the first issue of the *Revue suisse d'histoire* for 1970. But economic history, like social history, has a necessary extension in the history of technology; a special aspect of this, extremely difficult to elucidate, was chosen as the theme for study at the discussions in Spoleto in April 1970 under the title "Artisan and Technical Skills in the Society of the High Middle Ages in the West."

(Mi. F.)

See also **Literature.**

Encyclopædia Britannica Films. *India: Introduction to Its History* (1957); *Egypt: Cradle of Civilization* (1962); *The Mediterranean World* (1962); *Athens: The Golden Age* (Humanities Course) (1963); *Julius Caesar: Rise of the Roman Empire* (1964); *Life in Ancient Rome* (1964); *Middle Ages: Culture of Medieval Europe* (1965); *Middle Ages: Rise of Feudalism* (1965); *The Spirit of Rome* (1965); *The Medieval Mind* (1969); *Origin of Life—Chemical Evolution* (1969); *Reflections on Time* (1969); *Theories on the Origin of Life* (1969).

Historic Buildings

In 1970 worldwide concern with problems of rapid population expansion, the deleterious effects of industrialization, and pollution of the biosphere extended also to the quality of the urban environment. Problems were posed by the growth of high-rise, high-density housing and by the pressures to remove older neighbourhoods frequently characterized by historically interesting structures. Various factors contributed to this concern: the shift toward a generalized approach that regarded all aspects of the environment as interdependent; the loss of many older neighbourhoods and their replacement by monotonous new constructions of standardized design; and the tendency for new housing developments to attract people of the same age and socioeconomic background, which, instead of promoting stability, seemed to encourage further mobility, anomie, and lack of social cohesion. While recognizing the need for economic development, many countries were also coming to recognize the advantages of preserving historically interesting areas. Programs included the study of pollution problems, analyses of socioeconomic factors to improve the quality of urban living, and the study of the cultural role of cities.

With the aid of UNESCO, the Italian government began a project for the preservation of Venice, which was menaced by gradual subsidence and almost annual flooding. Investigations suggested a number of factors contributing to the subsidence; the deterioration of historic buildings had been due to capillarity as well as to atmospheric pollution and windborne sea salts. The steady migration of the local population to the mainland led to efforts to find a contemporary cultural role and a year-round population for Venice. An international Institute for Germanic Studies was established; the university was expanded to include colleges of letters and of industrial chemistry; and an International University of the Arts was begun in September 1970, in cooperation with the city of Florence. Long-term projects under consideration included a feasibility study on movable gates or locks to prevent inundation of the city; a study of atmospheric and water pollution control; a laboratory for the study of deterioration of monuments and works of art; and an institute to study socioeconomic problems affecting the preservation of historic cities.

New York City, which had undergone extensive redevelopment, was placing greater stress on preservation. A project for an 11-block, 38-ac. area along the waterfront, including the former Fulton Fish Market, old houses, commercial buildings, and warehouses, was sponsored by the South Street Seaport Museum. The plans called for the rehabilitation of some of the historic structures and the revival of commerce in the area, with new shops and restaurants designed to recall the 19th century. A major maritime museum was planned and had already acquired several exhibits, among them the original Ambrose Lightship. Privately financed office and apartment buildings, to be built in keeping with the surroundings, would pay full taxes, thus increasing neighbouring real estate values while providing a low-density recreational and cultural area for tourists and residents of the city.

Another example of this trend in New York was the move to rehabilitate 19th-century residences, initiated by the Brownstone Revival Committee ("brownstone" referring loosely to 19th-century residential buildings built of brick, limestone, or masonry). Privately financed neighbourhood restoration was economically feasible and would avoid the high budgets required for publicly financed urban renewal projects. However, the success of the project depended upon zoning regulations forbidding high-rise structures in the areas to be rehabilitated and imposing lower real estate taxes. The committee published a guide identifying 25 brownstone neighbourhoods and there were waiting lists of prospective purchasers.

The U.S. Congress allocated $1,604,000 for the work of the National Register of Historic Places and operational conservation programs. A National Conference on Architectural Review, Landmarks, and Historic Districts in April 1970 stressed the lack of scientific data on the effects of undirected city growth and the need to understand the implications of current attitudes toward environmental control. Several speak-

The moat and ruins of the 14th-century Scotney Castle, Lamberhurst, Kent, were accepted by England's National Trust.
THE "GUARDIAN"

ers emphasized the need for a dynamic approach to conservation, neither freezing the past nor destroying it indiscriminately.

The British government increased from £575,000 to £700,000 the limit within which the Historic Buildings Council could recommend grants to owners of outstanding individual buildings. Furthermore, a new type of Exchequer grant was available to local councils for the conservation of historic areas. Nevertheless, alarm was expressed at the rate of disappearance of historic buildings. While buildings classified as Category I could be aided by grants from the Ministry of Housing, in practice little aid was granted to owners of Category II and Category III buildings. Since it was not necessary to inform the ministry of the demolition of Category III buildings, it was impossible to know how many had disappeared in recent years; one survey put it at more than 18,000 since the end of World War II. In Bath, for example, monuments and the most important historic buildings were preserved, but the survey reported that the back streets, sections of the main shopping streets, and areas once occupied by the Georgian middle and lower classes were disappearing, and that without them "Bath will be like a forest without undergrowth, robbed of its unique character."

A campaign was launched to raise £500,000 to restore and preserve the Albert Hall in London, and work on the exterior was completed in 1970; the interior remained to be redecorated before the building's centenary in 1971. Projects to adapt historically interesting buildings to new purposes continued. One was the conversion of old malthouses at Bishop's Stortford, Hertfordshire, into a major concert hall and arts complex. The cost of the project was estimated at £250,000 and its completion was scheduled for 1972.

An outstanding example of the restoration of a historic quarter was the project for the Marais in Paris, sparked by the restoration of the Place des Vosges and legislation to aid public and private restoration projects. The coach house of the Hôtel de St. Aignan was restored and adapted for the use of the International Council of Monuments and Sites (ICOMOS) and as an international documentation centre. The *hôtel* itself was cleared of unwanted later additions; reconstruction and adaptation for the Archives of the City of Paris was scheduled to begin in 1971. As a result of this work, it was gradually becoming fashionable to live in the Marais and middle- and upper-class residents were returning.

Conservation projects were not restricted to the older part of Paris; considerable concern was also expressed about changes on the Champs Elysées. In 1969 only a last-minute decision had stopped the demolition of the neo-Baroque buildings surrounding the Rond Point and their replacement by glass curtain-wall structures. Since the end of World War II many apartment buildings had been converted into offices and the avenue had become a major traffic artery. The smart shops and cafés had gradually given way to airline offices, banks, and automobile showrooms, making the avenue less attractive to strollers and visitors. One plan proposed the encouragement of shops by favourable tax rates and the construction of subterranean crossings, underground shopping centres, and arcades off the avenue.

The Japanese National Commission for UNESCO, assisted by a grant from UNESCO, organized a meeting of experts to review the problem of preserving the

"THE TIMES"

Restoration work continues on Anne Hathaway's cottage, which was damaged by arson.

historic quarters of Kyoto and Nara. Besides preservation specialists and town planners, leading Japanese architects and administrators attended. The cities, former capitals of Japan, were also traditional centres of cultural development and contained many of the most important sites and monuments of Japanese civilization. Leading monuments were adequately protected, but population expansion and the growth of commerce and industry placed increasing pressure on historic quarters, such as the Gion in Kyoto, and on the countryside. Various recommendations were made: to amend existing legislation to favour the protection of historic quarters; to obtain national subventions toward maintenance as a form of tourism investment; to analyze sociological factors involved in the maintenance of a viable neighbourhood in historic quarters; and to replace unplanned development with a development plan for the two cities and the surrounding countryside that would encourage aesthetically pleasing construction and meet the needs of the people.

The extension of the Vietnam conflict into Cambodia caused worldwide concern about the great ruins of Angkor. At the request of the Cambodian government, an expert was sent from UNESCO, under the terms of the International Convention for the Protection of Cultural Property in the Event of Armed Conflict (Hague Convention), during June–July 1970. Distinctive emblems were placed on the National Museum, the Angkor Conservancy, the National Library, and the Archives, and guarantees were obtained that they would not be used for military purposes. An expert was sent to plan and supervise defenses for the monuments; other experts were to follow to assist in packaging and storing valuable movable cultural property. (H. Du.)

See also Museums and Galleries.

Hockey

Field Hockey. One of the more surprising and significant events of 1970 in field hockey was the growth of organized competition at all levels of the game in England. It was surprising because competition had long been frowned upon by the Hockey Association, the controlling body, whose rules required the consent of its council before any affiliated association, club, or player could "institute or take part in any hockey challenge cup or prize competition" (rule 14). This rule had restricted competitive events to the county championship, the cup competitions organized by the armed services, and to the universities and similar bodies where entry was restricted and close supervision ensured. In 1970, however, in response to popular demand, the Hockey Association gave general consent to the playing for challenge cups and in prize competitions with only one condition: "that no member of an affiliated club or association shall be offered or accept any personal prize or inducement."

Leagues began operating in the Midlands and London in the 1969–70 season, and a Southern League was formed the following year. In addition, county tournaments sprang up throughout the country. Using these as part of an elimination process, the Hockey Association agreed to organize a national club competition in the 1971–72 season.

England's men's team had a moderate season. In the Home Countries' championship, it lost to Scotland, defeated Wales, and drew with Ireland to finish in third place. Scotland and Ireland shared the championship. In other international matches England drew with Spain at Lord's and beat France at Folkestone, making its overall record: won 2, drawn 2, lost 1, goals for 5, goals against 3. In the Inter-County championship final Lancashire defeated Suffolk 2–1.

Under a newly appointed team manager, W. Vans Agnew, the England team carried out a program of training and match practice throughout the summer in preparation for the European Cup competition at Brussels in September. At first, results were not all that had been hoped for. At Bristol in August, England met with its first defeat ever at the hands of Wales, which was also preparing for the European Cup. Subsequently, however, England won seven internationals in succession, beating Switzerland twice at home before going on a trip around Europe in the course of which victories were scored over Czechoslovakia, West Germany, Denmark (twice), and Belgium. The Netherlands broke England's winning run in the last match of the tour, scoring the only goal registered against the latter in six successive contests.

Three weeks later in the European Cup, England did not quite maintain the level that it had achieved on the European tour. In their pool, the English again lost to the Netherlands by the only goal of the game. In the quarterfinal round they were beaten by West Germany in the fourth period of extra time and again

by the only goal of the game. An exuberant West Germany went on to win the cup, defeating the Netherlands quite comfortably (3–1) in the final. England lost its play-off against Belgium and thus finished in sixth place. This was not high enough to qualify for the World Cup, which was scheduled to be held in Lahore, Pak., in February 1971. Qualification for the World Cup was restricted to the first four in the European Cup: West Germany, the Netherlands, Spain, and France.

At an international tournament held in Bombay, the final placings were: (1) West Germany, (2) the Netherlands, (3) India B, (4) India, (5) Belgium, (6) Japan, (7) Argentina, and (8) Italy.

At the Congress of the International Hockey Federation held in Brussels during the European Cup competition, England and Scotland, Gibraltar, and the U.S.S.R. were admitted to membership. L. S. E. Jones, a vice-president of the U.K. Hockey Association, was elected a member of the council.

At its meeting in June, the International Hockey Rules Board changed rule 14 to provide for a push-in (with the stick) instead of a roll-in (by hand) as a means of bringing the ball back into play after it has gone out of play over a sideline. The board also amended the note to rule 1 so that it stated that substitutes would not be permitted "except as specifically authorized by the International Hockey Federation."

In contrast, the women's International Hockey Rules Board, meeting in July, authorized the use of substitutes to replace injured players, with a limit of two substitutes per match. They also adopted a striking circle of 16-yd. radius, instead of 15 yd. The highlight of the season in women's hockey was England's match against the Australian women's touring team at the White City, London, in March. It was drawn (1–1), as were four of England's five internationals, the other being against the Netherlands, Ireland, and Wales. England's only win was against Scotland.

(R. L. Hs.)

Amateur Ice Hockey. International plans were thwarted in January when Avery Brundage, president of the International Olympic Committee, warned that national teams that participated in a competition that included professionals would not be allowed to compete in the 1972 Winter Olympic Games. As the 1970 world championships had already been allocated to Montreal and Winnipeg, where the host nation, Canada, insisted on taking advantage of the new International Ice Hockey Federation rule permitting up to nine professional players per team, the championships were switched to Stockholm on March 14–30. With Canada declining to compete, the U.S.S.R. won the concurrently decided world and European titles for the eighth successive year.

As in the previous season, six countries contested the championship in Group A, each playing the other five twice. The Soviets won nine of their ten games, losing 2–4 to Sweden, the runners-up, who finished three points behind the Soviet team and four in front of third-place Czechoslovakia. Finland, East Germany, and Poland followed in that order. The leading scorers were Aleksandr Maltsev (U.S.S.R.) with 15 goals and 6 assists (21 points); Vaclav Nedomansky (Czech.), 10 goals and 7 assists (17 points); and the veteran Soviet player Anatoli Firsov, 6 goals and 10 assists (16 points).

The Group B tournament, at Bucharest, Rom., comprised eight teams, each of which played the other once. The United States won convincingly, gaining the

Chicago Black Hawk goalie Tony Esposito slumps as John McKenzie's winning score for Boston hits the twine April 26, 1970. The Bruins won 5–4 to complete a four-game sweep of the NHL Eastern Division play-offs.

UPI COMPIX

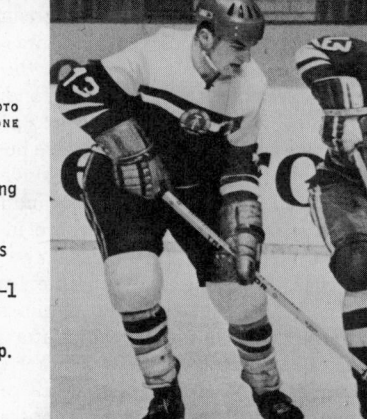

SVENSKT PRESSFOTO
FROM KEYSTONE

East German goalie Klaus Hirche struggles against the Soviets during a seventh-round game of the world ice-hockey championships in Stockholm March 24, 1970. The Soviets won 7–1 and went on to win their eighth consecutive championship.

maximum 14 points. West Germany placed second with Norway third ahead of Yugoslavia, Japan, Switzerland, Romania, and Bulgaria. The Group C competition, with seven teams, was also held in Romania, at Galati. Austria, dropping only one point, finished in front of Italy, Hungary, France, Denmark, the Netherlands, and Belgium.

Although only the six Group A teams had title chances, the subsidiary competitions were spiced by the long-term prospects involving promotion and relegation. As winners of Group B, the U.S. gained promotion to compete in 1971 in Group A, from which the bottom team, Poland, was dropped to Group B. The last two nations in Group B, Romania and Bulgaria, were demoted to Group C and replaced in Group B by Austria and Italy.   (H. B.)

Professional Ice Hockey. Most of the history of the 1969–70 professional hockey season was concentrated in the precocious skills of one player, Robert Gordon Orr (*see* BIOGRAPHY) of the Boston Bruins. The *22-year-old* prodigy won four individual trophies —for most valuable player, scoring, best defenseman, and best player in the play-off tournament—as the Bruins took their first Stanley Cup in the National Hockey League (NHL) in 29 years. With 33 goals and 87 assists, Orr established an NHL scoring record of 120 points, a feat considered startling since his customary position was on defense.

The Bruins lost first place in the Eastern Division to the Chicago Black Hawks on the last night of the schedule. The teams were tied in points, 99 each, but Chicago was awarded the Prince of Wales Trophy on

the basis of more wins, 45 to 40. The St. Louis Blues, dominating the Western Division for the third straight season, were runaway winners of the Clarence S. Campbell Bowl.

The Bruins won the play-offs in their section by eliminating, in successive series, the New York Rangers and the Black Hawks. The Blues qualified for the Stanley Cup final for the third time with play-off conquests of the Minnesota North Stars and the Pittsburgh Penguins.

In the Stanley Cup final, the Blues maintained their record of never having won a cup game, Boston banishing them in four consecutive contests. In the two previous seasons St. Louis had lost eight games in a row to the Montreal Canadiens in the final play-off series.

Tony Esposito, Chicago's agile goalkeeper, won two trophies for individual accomplishment, the Calder Memorial Trophy as the NHL's most proficient freshman and the Vezina Trophy as the netminder who had allowed the fewest number of goals. Phil Goyette, a St. Louis centre later drafted by the Buffalo Sabres, won the Lady Byng Memorial Trophy as the player best combining exemplary conduct with hockey ability. The NHL first-string all-stars, elected by NHL writers and broadcasters, were: goalkeeper, Tony Esposito (Chicago); defensemen, Orr and Brad Park (New York); centre, Phil Esposito (Boston); right wing, Gordie Howe (Detroit); left wing, Bobby Hull (Chicago).

Off the ice, the NHL expanded to 14 teams with the addition of the Vancouver (B.C.) Canucks and Buffalo Sabres (formerly the American Hockey League Bisons), each admitted for $6 million. The divisions were slightly realigned by shifting Chicago to the West and placing Vancouver and Buffalo in the East. The Vancouver Canucks, in their last season in the minors before moving to the NHL, won the Western League championship by beating the Portland (Ore.) Buckaroos four games to one in the final. The Buffalo Bisons, in their last season in the AHL, won the title in their tournament by shutting out the Springfield Kings, four games to nothing. The Omaha Knights won the Jack Adams Trophy as champions of the Central League by defeating the Iowa Stars four games to one in the last round of the play-offs.

(R. H. BE.)

NHL Final Standings						
	Won	Lost	Tied	Goals	Goals against	Pts.
EASTERN DIVISION						
Chicago Black Hawks	45	22	9	250	170	99
Boston Bruins	40	17	19	277	216	99
Detroit Red Wings	40	21	15	246	199	95
New York Rangers	38	22	16	246	189	92
Montreal Canadiens	38	22	16	244	201	92
Toronto Maple Leafs	29	34	13	222	242	71
WESTERN DIVISION						
St. Louis Blues	37	27	12	224	179	86
Pittsburgh Penguins	26	38	12	182	238	64
Minnesota North Stars	19	35	22	224	257	60
Oakland Seals	22	40	14	169	243	58
Philadelphia Flyers	17	35	24	197	225	58
Los Angeles Kings	14	52	10	168	290	38

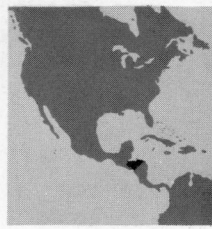

Honduras

A republic of Central America, Honduras is bounded by Nicaragua, El Salvador, Guatemala, the Caribbean Sea, and the Pacific Ocean. Area: 43,277 sq.mi. (112,-088 sq.km.). Pop. (1970 est.): 2,582,000, of which 90% is mestizo. Cap. and largest city: Tegucigalpa (pop., 1970 est., 267,462). Language: Spanish; some Indian dialects. Religion: Roman Catholic. President in 1970, Osvaldo López Arellano.

Efforts were made in 1970 to resolve the hostilities between Honduras and El Salvador that erupted briefly but intensely into open warfare in mid-1969 and resulted in the severing of diplomatic relations and curtailment of trade between the two nations. At the end of January, Honduras and El Salvador each sent three delegates to San José, Costa Rica, for the first of several bilateral peace talks mediated by the former secretary-general of the Organization of American States (OAS), José A. Mora. Finally, at an OAS-sponsored meeting of the Central American foreign ministers in Costa Rica on June 4, Honduras and El Salvador agreed to establish a demilitarized zone (DMZ) 1.8 mi. on either side of their common border. Costa Rica, Guatemala, and Nicaragua were designated "guarantors" of the agreement. On July 16, one year after the war, the DMZ went into effect and, under OAS supervision, Honduras and El Salvador withdrew their armed forces from the zone except for small security patrols in certain speci-

fied locations. Military aircraft of both nations were barred within three miles of the outer edge of the DMZ. The OAS appointed at least 30 military advisers to see that the June agreement was carried out.

The closing of the Honduras-El Salvador border resulted in serious strains on the Honduran economy that remained unresolved. Honduran agricultural exports, which traditionally had a major market in El Salvador, found no alternative buyers among the other Central American nations. Conversely, Honduras was denied access to Salvadoran industrial goods and had to seek such items elsewhere in Central America at unfavourable rates of exchange. This resulted in an ever increasing unfavourable trade balance, and by mid-1970 Honduras' economic situation had so deteriorated that its delegates at a July meeting of Central American Common Market (CACM) representatives in Managua, Nic., were prepared to withdraw from the Market unless cooperative relief measures were taken. The other member nations, including El Salvador, agreed to find some balance of payments relief for Honduras, realizing that the weakening of one member nation further endangered the already precarious health of this decade-old regional economic body.

Equally as devastating as the war in 1969 was the hurricane that struck the north coast west of La Ceiba in September of that year and whose legacy was revealed in decreased agricultural production in 1970. Bananas, corn, and sugarcane along the Caribbean coast and in the Sula Valley bore the brunt of crop losses. To aid Honduras in its recovery in 1970, the World Bank and the International Development Association announced in June the approval of two loans of $5.5 million each.　　(A. D. Bu.)

HONDURAS
Education. (1966–67) Primary, pupils 331,470, teachers 10,881; secondary, pupils 20,388; vocational, pupils 3,121; teacher training, students 4,104; secondary, vocational, and teacher training, teachers 2,296; higher, students 3,006, teaching staff (1963) 302.
Finance. Monetary unit: lempira, with a par value of 2 lempiras to U.S. $1 (4.80 lempiras = £1 sterling). Gold, SDRs, and foreign exchange, central bank: (June 1970) U.S. $28,950,000; (June 1969) U.S. $27,640,000. Budget (1970 est.) balanced at 225.2 million lempiras. Gross national product: (1968) 1,236,000,000 lempiras; (1967) 1,155,000,000 lempiras. Money supply: (May 1970) 167,270,000 lempiras; (May 1969) 146,740,000 lempiras. Cost of living (Tegucigalpa; 1963 = 100): (April 1970) 122; (April 1969) 120.
Foreign Trade. (1968) Imports 371.4 million lempiras; exports 362.9 million lempiras. Import sources: U.S. 46%; El Salvador 13%; Guatemala 8%; Japan 5%; West Germany 5%. Export destinations: U.S. 44%; West Germany 19%; El Salvador 8%; Belgium-Luxembourg 5%. Main exports: bananas 47%; coffee 12%; timber 8%; silver 5%.
Transport and Communications. Roads (1968) c. 3,400 km. (including c. 370 km. paved). Motor vehicles in use (1968): passenger 12,000; commercial (including buses) 11,500. Railways (1968) c. 1,075 km. Air traffic (1968): 109,256,000 passenger-km.; freight 10,210,000 net ton-km. Shipping (1969): merchant vessels 100 gross tons and over 51; gross tonnage 65,659. Telephones (Jan. 1969) 11,150. Radio receivers (Dec. 1968) 140,000. Television receivers (Dec. 1968) 11,000.
Agriculture. Production (in 000; metric tons; 1969; 1968 in parentheses): corn c. 375 (c. 390); coffee c. 26 (c. 24); sorghum (1967) c. 48, (1966) c. 44; sugar, raw value (1969–70) c. 68, (1968–69) c. 59; dry beans (1968) c. 55, (1967) c. 51; bananas (1968) c. 1,509, (1967) c. 1,405; cottonseed c. 14 (14); beef and veal (1968) c. 22, (1967) 22. Livestock (in 000; 1968–69): cattle c. 1,800; pigs (1967–68) c. 930; chickens c. 6,300.
Industry. Production (in 000; metric tons; 1968): silver 0.17; gold (troy oz.) 6.1; lead ore (metal content; exports; 1967) 5.3; zinc ore (metal content; exports; 1967) 9.7; electricity (kw-hr.; 1967) 233,-000.

Honduras, British:
see Dependent States

Hong Kong:
see Dependent States

Horse Racing

Thoroughbred Racing. *U.S.* Two of the highlights of the 1970 Thoroughbred racing season in the United States were jockey Bill Shoemaker's record-setting 6,033rd victory and the four-year-old filly Ta Wee's sprinting prowess under high weights. Shoemaker's historic ride, in his 22nd year of competition, came aboard a two-year-old filly named Dares J. in the fourth race of the Labor Day program at Del Mar, Calif. Coincidentally, it was on Labor Day in 1956 at the same track that Johnny Longden had succeeded Sir Gordon Richards of England as the world's leading jockey in number of winners. Longden, who retired from the saddle in 1966 after a 40-year career, was in the winner's circle to congratulate his successor. Shoemaker had led the national jockey standings five times and in 1963 rode a record number of winners, 485.

Ta Wee, owned and bred in Florida by the Tartan Stable of William L. McKnight and John Nerud, competed in seven stake races. She won five and placed second in two. She opened her campaign in late March at Aqueduct by winning the Correction Handicap under 131 lb. She also triumphed in the Hempstead Handicap (132 lb.), the Regret Handicap (136), the Fall Highweight Handicap (140), and the Interborough Handicap (142). Her defeats came in the Distaff Handicap in April while conceding Process Shot eight pounds (134 to 126), and in the Gravesend Handicap in July while carrying 134 lb., compared with 114 on her victorious male opponent, Distinctive. All of the races were contested at six furlongs except for the seven-furlong Distaff. Ta Wee's other start against male opposition was in the Fall Highweight in which she defeated Towzie Tike (121), Distinctive (134), and others, and carried the most weight ever assigned a filly or mare in that stakes.

Ta Wee was unanimously voted best sprinter in the year-end poll conducted by the *Daily Racing Form* and the *Morning Telegraph* and also had support as horse of the year. That honour, however, was given to Paul Mellon's Fort Marcy, a six-year-old gelding particularly successful on grass courses.

The two major polls agreed on the champions of all divisions except the handicap and three-year-old-filly classifications. Mrs. Stephen C. Clark, Jr.'s Hoist the Flag was named the best two-year-old colt; Aisco Stable's Forward Gal, best two-year-old filly; Mrs. Ethel D. Jacobs' Personality, best three-year-old colt; Mrs. Whitney Stone's Shuvee, best older filly or mare; Fort Marcy, best grass horse; and Mrs. Ogden Phipps' Top Bid, best steeplechase horse. Stephen A. Calder's Office Queen was voted the best three-year-old filly in the *Daily Racing Form-Morning Telegraph* poll, while Jean-Louis Levesque's Canadian homebred Fanfreluche gained the honours in the poll of racing secretaries at racetracks belonging to the Thoroughbred Racing Associations of the U.S. (the TRA poll). Fort Marcy was acclaimed best handicap horse in the *Daily Racing Form-Morning Telegraph* poll, while Gene Goff's Nodouble was voted best handicap horse in the TRA balloting. The latter poll picked Personality as the American champion of the year.

Personality won only one of the Triple Crown races, the Preakness, but he annexed four other stakes, including the prestigious Woodward Stakes at $1\frac{1}{4}$ mi. against older horses in his final start of the season. He also took the Wood Memorial, the Jersey Derby, and the Jim Dandy. In the other two Triple Crown events, Dust Commander won the Kentucky Derby and High Echelon captured the Belmont Stakes.

Fort Marcy closed out his season with consecutive victories in the United Nations Invitational Handicap, the Man o'War Stakes, and the Washington (D.C.) International. Earlier in the year, he won the Dixie and Bowling Green handicaps. Nodouble, idled a good part of the year by a virus, took the Metropolitan and San Pasqual handicaps. Top Bid, a six-year-old gelded son of Olympia, climaxed a successful season by winning the $100,000 Colonial Cup International at Camden, S.C., the richest jump race ever held in the U.S.

Noted trainer Hirsch Jacobs, who (along with long-time partner Isidor Bieber) bred Personality, died in a Florida hospital in February just as the colt, one of his all-time pets, had begun to display the class his mentor knew he possessed. Jacobs left records that probably never would be surpassed. He saddled more winners than any other trainer in history (3,596) and for 11 times in a span of 12 years starting in 1933 ranked as the country's leading trainer in number of races won. With Bieber he bred horses that won 3,513 races and had earned $18,311,412 at the time of his death at 65. Jacobs was probably best remembered for a $1,500 claim he made for a two-year-old named Stymie in June 1943, from King Ranch. When retired six years later, the little chestnut stallion was racing's wealthiest runner, having raced 131 times with 35 victories and earnings of $918,485.

(J. Ag.)

Canada. In 1964, Northern Dancer established himself as Canada's all-time greatest racehorse, winning

UPI COMPIX

Dust Commander (3), with Mike Manganello up, crosses the finish line to win the 96th Kentucky Derby May 2, 1970.

the Kentucky Derby, Queen's Plate, Preakness, and many other top events. In 1970, events on two continents confirmed his excellence in a new role—as a sire of champions.

In Europe, Northern Dancer's three-year-old son Nijinsky became the first English Triple Crown winner in 35 years and was hailed as the horse of the century as he remained undefeated through 11 races. Bred in Ontario by E. P. Taylor (as was Northern Dancer), Nijinsky raced for Charles Englehard of the U.S. until syndicated at a world-record value of $5,440,000 after his tenth victory.

At home in 1970, Northern Dancer's three-year-old daughter Fanfreluche, bred and owned by Jean-Louis Lévesque, became the richest filly in Canadian racing history with lifetime earnings of more than $225,000. Among her achievements were victories over most of the country's best males in the Manitoba Centennial Derby (Winnipeg), Quebec Derby (Montreal), and Benson and Hedges Invitational (Toronto). An overwhelming favourite to gain Canadian horse of the year honours, Fanfreluche also made a strong bid for recognition as North America's champion three-year-old filly when she won the important Alabama Stakes at Saratoga.

The 111th edition of the Queen's Plate, with a record purse of $88,300, went to Parkview Stable's Almoner, a three-year-old son of former Plate winner Victoria Park. Almoner later won the Prince of Wales Stakes at Fort Erie, but failed to become the first Canadian Triple Crown winner since 1963 when he was beaten by Gardiner Farm's filly Mary of Scotland in the Breeders' Stakes at Woodbine in the fall.

Toward the end of the season, attention focused on the two-year-old division. Mrs. A. W. Stollery's giant Kennedy Road and Willow Downs Farm's Great Gabe won the Cup and Saucer Stakes and Coronation Futurity, respectively, to establish themselves as the leading prospects for 1971's Canadian three-year-old classics.

Sandy Hawley of Oshawa, Ont., won the Canadian riding championship by a wide margin in 1970, as he had done in 1969. Hawley had been North America's top apprentice rider in 1969, his first full year of competition. Gardiner Farm was once again Canada's top money-winning stable, while Frank Merrill and Lou Cavalaris engaged in a season-long battle for leadership among the trainers. (ER. AS.)

Europe and Australia. In 1969–70, National Hunt racing in Britain lost one big race, the Schweppes Gold Trophy hurdle handicap, which in mid-February 1970 could not be run because of frost, for the second year in a row. Spanish Steps won the Hennessy Gold Cup at Newbury in November from the previous year's winner, Larbawn, and Titus Oates took the King George VI Steeplechase at Kempton Park from Flyingbolt on December 26. In March, at Cheltenham, Persian War won the Champion Hurdle magnificently for the third running; and two Irish horses, L'Escargot and French Tan, finished first and second, respectively, in the Gold Cup Steeplechase. Gay Trip, carrying top weight, triumphed in the Grand National Steeplechase by 20 lengths from his nearest rival, Vulture, with Miss Hunter, a 33–1 outsider, finishing third. French Excuse won the Welsh Grand National.

On the flat, the 1970 season saw the most brilliant racehorse to be trained in the British Isles for many years: the Canadian-bred Nijinsky, a son of Northern Dancer, who was owned by the U.S. millionaire Charles Engelhard, was trained in Ireland by M. V. O'Brien, and was ridden by L. Piggott in England and France and by L. Ward in Ireland. Outstandingly handsome and commanding in the parade ring, he went out onto the racecourse hardly to be troubled by his opponents in the Two Thousand Guineas (from Yellow God and Roi Soleil), the Derby (from Gyr and Stintino, in the second-fastest time in history), the Irish Sweeps Derby (from Meadowville), the King George VI and Queen Elizabeth Stakes (from Blakeney), and the St. Leger (from Meadowville). Nijinsky thus became the first horse since Bahram in 1935 to win the English Triple Crown. Up to this point he had won all his races, including his two-year-old attempts, and it was confidently expected that he would crown the season by winning the Prix de l'Arc de Triomphe at Longchamp, Paris; but in fact he lost by a head to the French horse Sassafras, in a time that was almost a record for the race. Brought out a fortnight later, he was even more decisively beaten by Lorenzaccio in the Champion Stakes at Newmarket: a great horse had thus apparently passed his peak after a long season of major races over a variety of dis-

tances. Perhaps behind Ribot and Seabird, Nijinsky was nonetheless one of the greatest racehorses of the century; crowds flocked to see him run and his prize money totaled approximately £275,000, a record for a horse trained in the British Isles.

Gyr and Sassafras, both of France, were probably the two next best horses in Europe. Gyr would have been a worthy Derby winner but for Nijinsky, and in France he won the Prix Hocquart and the Grand Prix de Saint-Cloud; Sassafras won the French Derby and St. Leger as well as the Arc. Roll of Honour, who had been second in the French Derby, won the Grand Prix de Paris. Stintino, third in the English Derby, won the Prix Lupin. The Poule d'Essai des Poulains (French equivalent of the Two Thousand Guineas) was won by Caro, the Poule d'Essai des Pouliches (One Thousand Guineas) by the English-trained filly Pampered Miss, and the Prix de Diane (French Oaks) by the Irish filly Sweet Mimosa from the English filly Highest Hopes, who in the latter part of the season triumphed in the valuable Prix Vermeille. British-trained horses carried off an unusual number of notable French prizes. In particular, David Robinson's My Swallow, who was unbeaten and could be considered the outstanding two-year-old in Europe, took the major French two-year-old events—the Prix Robert Papin (by a short head from Mill Reed), the Prix Morny, and the Grand Criterium.

In England, the two fillies' classics, the One Thousand Guineas and the Oaks, were won by Humble Duty and Lupe, respectively. Humble Duty went on to win the Sussex Stakes at Goodwood, and Lupe the Yorkshire Oaks, in which she defeated Highest Hopes. The Ascot Gold Cup was won by Precipice Wood; the Eclipse Stakes by Connaught; the Coronation Cup at Epsom by Caliban from Park Top. Karabas, in a disappointing season, won the Hardwicke Stakes. Welsh Pageant, one of the best English milers, won the Queen Anne Stakes and later the Queen Elizabeth Stakes at Ascot.

Piggott was champion jockey (162 winning rides) in Britain for the eighth time and N. Murless the leading trainer with 53 races won by 35 horses and £199,532 of prize money. Though Engelhard was leading owner with £182,059 and 30 wins from 20 horses, David Robinson's feat in winning £86,369 from 109 races won by 60 horses was hardly less remarkable.

In Australia the $A51,000 (with a $2,000 cup) Melbourne Cup was won by the outsider Baghdad Note, ridden by E. Didham, from Vansittart and Clear Prince. He was the first winner of the cup to be owned, trained, and ridden by New Zealanders. (R. M. GN.)

Harness Racing. Four superb Standardbreds—the seven-year-old trotting mare Fresh Yankee; the three-year-old pacing colt Most Happy Fella; the three-year-old trotting colt Timothy T.; and the two-year-old pacing colt Albatross—were the outstanding harness racing champions of North America in 1970. There were other major stars, including the two-year-old filly trotting queen, Keystone Selene, and the two-year-old colt trotters Quick Pride and Noble Gesture; the three-year-old pacers Columbia George and Truluck; and the older pacers Laverne Hanover and Horton Hanover; but they could not match the brilliance of the dominant quartet, headed by Fresh Yankee, who was voted harness horse of the year.

That incredibly consistent mare, owned by Duncan A. MacDonald of Sydney, N.S., and trained and driven by Joe O'Brien, started 29 times on both sides of the Atlantic during 1970 and never finished

A new track record for the mile and a half on the turf is recorded on the tote board as Fiddle Isle, with Willie Shoemaker up, crosses the finish line to win the San Luis Rey Handicap at Santa Anita March 21, 1970.

UPI COMPIX

worse than second. She won 20 races, including the Grand Prix of Bavaria in Munich, the $125,000 International at Roosevelt Raceway in New York, and the $50,000 United Nations Trot at Yonkers. In the nine races she did not win, Fresh Yankee placed second.

While Fresh Yankee was dominating harness racing's trotting division, pacing headlines were being made by Most Happy Fella, a three-year-old colt that had been purchased early in his two-year-old form for $12,500 by one of the sport's greatest trainer-drivers, Stanley Dancer. The colt had a limited campaign in 1969 because of illness but in 1970 established his superiority over two other outstanding colts, Columbia George and Truluck, in a three-way rivalry that produced some of the finest harness racing of recent years. All three colts were retired to stallion duty at the season's end.

Most Happy Fella swept the Triple Crown of pacing, winning the $123,450 Messenger Stakes, the $102,770 Cane Futurity, and the $100,110 Little Brown Jug, and also captured the $86,740 Adios to account for the Big Four. He also won the $75,000 L. K. Shapiro and four other major events and was sold at the season's end to Blue Chip Farm for $1 million.

Equally impressive in their divisions were Timothy T. and Albatross, both bargain colts as yearlings. Timothy T., purchased privately for $8,500 by John Simpson, Sr., a noted trainer-driver and president of Hanover Shoe Farm, fulfilled his two-year-old promise by winning the $76,351 Kentucky Futurity, the $102,275 Colonial, the $25,000 Vernon Downs Gold Cup, and the sport's most prestigious race for three-year-old trotters, the $143,630 Hambletonian. Two divisional classics that Timothy T. did not contest, the $106,770 Yonkers Futurity and the $111,514 Dexter Cup at Roosevelt Raceway, were won by Victory Star and Marlu Pride, respectively.

Albatross, owned by Canadian Bert James (who twice tried unsuccessfully to sell the colt as a yearling for $7,000), completely dominated the two-year-old pacing ranks. He won stakes both early and late in the year, and included in the 14 victories he registered in 17 starts were the $92,361 Roosevelt Futurity and the $71,030 Fox Stake in Indianapolis. While Albatross ruled the two-year-old pacing colts, a host of good juvenile fillies battled for supremacy in their division, with Keystone Memento, Truthful Waverly, and Betty Hanover winding up with top honours.

There was no doubt which two-year-old trotting filly was best. Breeder Max Hempt's Keystone Selene, like Fresh Yankee a daughter of Hempt's great stallion Hickory Pride, won 19 of 24 races and $118,361 to outdistance all rivals. Quick Pride, a son of Hickory Pride, was the most successful two-year-old trotting colt, winning 13 of 26 races and almost $170,000.

In the speed department, a three-year-old colt named Steady Star paced the fastest mile of the year in a time trial at Lexington, Ky., stopping the electric timer in 1 min. 54 sec. for driver Joe O'Brien. It was the fastest mile ever by a three-year-old and the second fastest in the history of harness racing, surpassed only by Bret Hanover's 1 min. 53.6 sec. in 1966.

The driving star of the year was Herve Filion of Canada. Only driver ever to win 400 races in a single season, Filion shattered his world mark of 407 early in November and set his sights on 500 for the year. In April he added another laurel by winning the first world driving championship, sponsored by Harness Tracks of America. (ST. F. B.)

WIDE WORLD

Timothy T. crosses the finish line to win the first heat of the Hambletonian at Du Quoin, Ill., Sept. 2, 1970.

The $22,700 New Zealand Cup (November 1969) was won by the pacer Spry by disqualification, while the New Zealand Pacers Derby went to Berkleigh. The Dominion Trotting Handicap of $7,700 was won by Tutiri. Garçon Roux and True Averill stamped themselves as the top New Zealand pacers of the year with numerous winning efforts, and Bonnie Frost was the champion filly. The $20,000 Auckland Cup of 2 mi. was won by the pacer Leading Light, the Great Northern Pacing Derby by First Batch, and the New Zealand Messenger Stake (four-year-old pacers) by Western Ridge.

Find of the season in Australia was the pacer Lucky Creed, winner of the Miracle Mile after he had previously established a national record of 24 successive wins. The Inter-Dominion Pacing Championship was raced in Melbourne, and the final was won by Bold David, a pacer from Victoria. The New South Wales Pacing Derby was won by James Darren from the Victoria Derby winner, Welcome Advice.

For France, the trotter Une de Mai (horse of the year for 1969) also swept most of the big international races of 1970 (except the Prix d'Amérique), including the Prix de Sélection, Prix de Paris, and Gran Premio della Ferria in Milan; by the year's end she had earned close to $900,000. In the Prix d'Europe in Paris, Tony M won the $30,000 event by disqualification. The $142,000 Prix d'Amérique went to Toscan and brought his earnings to $460,000.

Italy's top mare, Agaunar, took four major races and won more than $350,000. The Gran Premio dell'Europa went to Vatson. Milan owner-breeder G. Nogara had the distinction of breeding the first, third, and fourth horses in that event. Vatson went on to win the four-year-old "Derby" of $30,000, bringing his earnings to $125,000.

Well-known breeder Count Orsi-Mangelli produced the fastest European-bred three-year-old of 1970 when Tedo won over a mile in 2 min. 5 sec. Tedo went on to capture the $26,000 Premio Italia at Bologna and later won the $52,000 Gran Premio Nazionale. The champion harness horse of West Germany, Simmerl, was beaten by Carolyn Sue in a $5,000 race over one mile at Hamburg in 2 min. 2 sec., a new German record. The $20,000 German Pokal was won by Eskimo, while the $37,500 German Derby went to Maler.

In Sweden the final of the Elite Trot for $45,000 was won by the great U.S.-bred mare Eileen Eden, and the Consolation Event went to Tony M. The prestige $6,000 Göteborg Cup was won by Baron Gruff, and he later won the Lundberg Memorial at Stockholm but unfortunately died the day following his last win. In

1970 a new mile record for two-year-olds was established in Sweden when Garry Hoalerud won in 2 min. 11.4 sec. In Belgium, the International Grand Prix d'Hiver carried $10,500 in prize money and was won by the French horse Tabriz. In the Netherlands, the $30,000 International Trot at The Hague went to the French horse Tatusca d'Avril.

The Danish Trotting Championship of $5,000 at Copenhagen was won by Fox Hanover (a previous winner of the Danish Derby). The $12,000 Criterion for three-year-olds, Danish-bred, went to Newrupin; and the richest race of the season, the Trotting Derby (four-year-olds) of $20,000, went to Max Hanover.

(N. Sī.)

Housing

Throughout 1970 there was little progress in housing construction in either the developed or the less developed countries. According to the UN *Monthly Bulletin of Statistics,* September 1970, a comparison of monthly averages of housing construction activity during the first three to six months of 1970 with those during the full year of 1969 revealed the following: the number of new dwelling units completed, started, or for which building permits were issued increased in Japan (from 112,218 to 115,418 units), South Korea (3,129 to 3,724 units), Norway (2,753 to 2,838 units), Spain (13,178 to 14,610 units), South Africa (958 to 977 units), Switzerland (1,705 to 1,720 units), and Turkey (11,006 to 11,819 units). On the other hand, the number of new dwelling units declined in Czechoslovakia (6,948 to 3,118 units), France (48,261 to 43,900 units), West Germany (41,660 to 15,207 units), Italy (23,596 to 18,724 units), Netherlands (10,260 to 8,469 units), Sweden (9,088 to 8,983 units), Tunisia (758 to 686 units), the U.K. (31,527 to 28,463 units), and the U.S. (125,000 to 100,500 units).

It was feared that this widespread downturn in building, coupled with a population explosion in the 1970s, would lead to a severe housing shortage. The population forecast by the UN Population Commission revealed that the world population would reach 4,934,000,000 in 1985, of which 3,659,000,000 would be in the less developed countries and 1,275,000,000 in the developed countries—almost a 3-to-1 ratio in 1985 compared with a ratio of a little more than 2 to 1

in 1965. In light of this projection there was a strong desire in the less developed countries to establish an international housing finance institution that would help them build the necessary living units.

Recent developments in housing finance were discussed at the 30th World Congress of the International Federation for Housing and Planning in May. It was emphasized at the meeting that the methods of financing housing should be constantly revised. Especially in the less developed countries it was necessary to improve financing methods to promote housing for middle- and low-income groups.

In a report presented to the UN Centre for Housing, Building and Planning by the Stanford Research Institute, the establishment of a new international housing finance corporation was strongly advocated. Its total authorized capital would be $1 billion, $200 million of which would be an initial flow of capital from both public and private sources. It was proposed that 80% of the corporation's funds would be used for seed capital loans at reasonable rates and terms and that the remainder would be employed to insure its own operations and mortgages marketed by recipient institutions in the less developed countries.

The housing situation in the ECAFE (Economic Commission for Asia and the Far East) region worsened, particularly in India, Indonesia, and Pakistan; the exceptions were Australia, New Zealand, Singapore, Hong Kong, and Japan. In Ceylon more than 40% of the 228,230 urban dwellings were in slums, and the situation was becoming even more serious with the increase in the squatter population. Squatter families in Colombo were increasing at the rate of 5,000 per year. In Hong Kong, by contrast, housing construction was very active at 13 units per 1,000 population.

The housing situation in India was grave, with a wide gap between supply and demand for houses. While 6 housing units per 1,000 population per year were required to meet the new demand caused by the population increase, only 3.6 units per 1,000 population had been planned for the 1966–71 period.

In Iran merely to house the increase in population required 6 housing units per 1,000 population, but actual construction had been 3.3 units per 1,000 population in 1961–66 and about 3.6 units in 1966–71. A probable consequence of this was expected to be the rapid deterioration of housing for low-income groups.

While the current home construction rate in Japan was more than 10 units per 1,000 population, an acute housing shortage still existed in large cities such as Tokyo and Osaka. In those cities, housing for low- and middle-income groups was a major problem, and the very high prices for land worsened the situation.

The housing shortage in Pakistan was acute and was estimated at 1,550,000 dwelling units in 1970. The nation's Planning Commission had attempted to build 295,500 urban dwelling units in 1965–70, of which only 80,000 units were to be built by the government. However, the nation's economic difficulties and the large-scale emergency effort to relieve the thousands suffering from the cyclone and tidal wave in East Pakistan compelled the government to curtail its effort temporarily.

In the Philippines it was estimated that an additional 9,430,000 dwelling units would be needed in 1960–80. This amounted to 12 new dwelling units per 1,000 population and represented an annual investment of about 5.7% of the gross national product (GNP). This was a rather high rate compared with

Aase Jepsen sits on her bed in which she had lived for five days outside the Frederiksberg City Hall in Copenhagen. Her sign states that a decent flat is a human right.

KEYSTONE

those in 1965 and 1967: 1.5 and 2.8% of GNP, respectively.

The Housing and Development Board in Singapore had estimated in the early 1960s that a total of 147,-000 houses would have to be built to solve that nation's housing shortage in 1961–70: 80,000 units to cover the existing deficiency, 20,000 units for central area redevelopment needs, and 47,000 units for needs on account of the population increase. The building rate in 1970 was about 9.4 dwelling units per 1,000 population, and it was believed that the target set by the board would be achieved. The next goals of the board included a satellite town development to serve the Jurong industrial estate and the promotion of urban renewal.

In the less developed countries the growing gap between the demand for buildings of all types and the capacity of the construction industry to supply them was a major problem. Being unorganized and unstable, the building industry in the less developed countries suffered from low productivity. Among the ways to modernize it was to introduce prefabrication techniques. There were difficulties, however, in persuading countries to accept prefabrication when construction by those techniques cost more than by the traditional systems, especially at the initial stages. In India, nonetheless, a construction program of prefabricated houses with at least 1,000 units per year for the next 10 to 20 years was recommended for New Delhi, Bombay, Calcutta, Madras, Ahmedabad, and Kanpur by an expert committee on low-cost housing. In Malaysia two of the three pilot low-cost projects using prefabricated housing techniques were completed. Their construction costs were rather high, however, 1.3–1.4 times the cost of traditional methods.

Prefabricated housing was becoming more popular in the developed countries. The rapid rise in wages and the shortage of skilled workers and natural raw materials accelerated the modernization of building construction through industrialization and mechanization. In Britain about 40% of the publicly financed dwellings were being built by industrialized methods. A number of local authorities worked together to make the best use of industrialized systems in their house-building programs. In Japan the industrialization of building was being strongly promoted in both the public and private sectors. The Housing Bureau of the Ministry of Construction took the initiative to unify, systematize, and integrate this industrialization in projects carried out by the Ministry of Construction, the Japan Housing Corporation, the Housing Loan Corporation, and private companies. There were

381

Housing

"TORONTO STAR"
Leaside Towers, under construction in Toronto, was to be Canada's tallest apartment building at 43 stories.

about 60 companies in Japan producing from 1,000 to 2,000 prefabricated houses a year.

In several developed countries a rent subsidy policy was being widely implemented to make decent rental housing available to low-income families and individuals. In the Netherlands, under a new housing plan, low-income tenants of subsidized dwellings could get rent subsidies varying from 120 to 900 guilders a year on the basis of income and rent. To be eligible the tenants had to be paying more than 15 to 17% of their taxable income in rent. In the U.S., under the Department of Housing and Urban Development (HUD) rent supplement program, a total of 6,063 families were receiving assistance by the end of 1968. In the U.K. more than 40% of the housing authorities in England and Wales operated rent rebate schemes, under which tenants with low incomes or with large families were able to claim a reduction in rent.

Slum clearance programs were vigorously undertaken in the U.K. by the public authorities. More than 2.5 million people had been rehoused in Great Britain since the mid-1950s. However, a survey of existing housing in 1967 showed that the number of unfit dwellings in England and Wales was estimated

This four-unit concrete town house in Halifax, Nova Scotia, erected in only 28 hours' actual construction time, was said to be the first of its type in Canada. The price to the buyer is estimated at $14,500 a unit, or $13,000 if mass-produced.

Horticulture:
see Gardening

Household Appliances:
see Domestic Arts and Sciences

ELIHU BLOTNICK
FROM B. B. M. ASSOCIATES

This houseboat community, shown at low tide, is located in Sausalito, Calif. The city was attempting to eliminate the houseboats by forcing the residents to move to more conventional housing.

to be 1.8 million, 11.5% of the existing housing, and that an additional 4.7 million dwellings were structurally sound but in need of repair and improvement work. In this connection residential rehabilitation was considered as an effective and important tool for coping with the problems presented by urban obsolescence. The Housing Act of 1969 aimed to place the economics of housing improvement in a much better relationship to those of redevelopment. The government especially intended to increase the amount of grant aid to improvement works. The Housing Act gave local authorities powers to designate "improvement areas" and to pursue a policy of area-wide improvement. An area could be declared an improvement area if within its bounds 50% or more of the dwellings lacked at least one of the following five standard amenities: a fixed bath or shower, a wash basin, a sink, an inside toilet, and hot and cold running water. The local authorities could encourage householders in the area to improve their dwellings with the aid of grants.

Major financial changes provided in the Housing Act were as follows: an increase from £400 to £1,000 in the maximum improvement grant that might be given at the discretion of the local authority; an increase in the normal total standard grant from £155 to £200; and a new Exchequer grant to local authorities of 50% of the expense for environmental improvement on costs of up to £100 per dwelling in newly designated general improvement areas.

In the U.S. there was no major change in the government's housing policy in 1970. On December 19 Congress approved the Housing and Urban Development Act of 1970, authorizing $2.9 billion for housing and related programs. The principal programs covered by the outlay were urban renewal ($1.5 billion), model cities ($230 million), public housing ($375 million), home ownership and rental assistance ($110 million), open space acquisition ($100 million), neighbourhood facilities ($50 million), and rent supplements ($40

million). The bill also included increased federal aid for new towns and provided for federal insurance against crime in areas where other insurance was unavailable or unreasonably expensive. A provision for aid to mass transportation was passed by the Senate but was deleted in conference committee.

The largest amount of money was allocated to the urban renewal program. In many cities, the lack of subsidy funds had been recognized as the critical factor in retarding construction and development. It was decided also to establish a Community Development Corporation within HUD to encourage the development of new communities and the orderly growth of existing ones.

A simplified structure for housing programs was proposed by HUD. It was generally believed, however, that a broader examination of housing needs and a more complete formulation of U.S. housing policy for the 1970s were needed before such a restructuring could take place. The Senate Banking and Currency Committee reported to the Senate that in 1971 it would examine measures to streamline the legislative authority for housing programs.

Great pressure existed in the U.S. Congress to expand housing and urban development activities, especially urban renewal programs. At the end of 1968 there were 2,038 approved urban renewal projects, of which 450 were in the planning stage, 1,164 under construction, and 424 completed. About 1.3 million new and rehabilitated dwelling units were expected to be provided under the redevelopment program as approved up to June 1969, of which about 860,000 would be for low- and moderate-income families and individuals. (Hr. S.)

See also Architecture; Cities and Urban Affairs; Economy, World; Industrial Review; Money and Banking.

ENCYCLOPÆDIA BRITANNICA FILMS. *The Living City* (1953); *Megalopolis: Cradle of the Future* (1962); *Equality Under Law—The California Fair Housing Cases* (1969); *The House of Man, Part II—Our Crowded Environment* (1969).

Hovercraft:
see Transportation

Hungary

A people's republic of central Europe, Hungary is bordered by Czechoslovakia, the U.S.S.R., Romania, Yugoslavia, and Austria. Area: 35,919 sq.mi. (93,030 sq.km.).

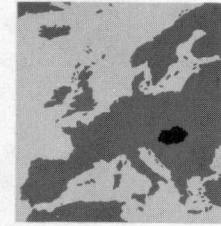

Pop. (1970): 10,314,152, including (1960) Hungarian 98.2%; German 0.5%. Cap. and largest city: Budapest (pop., 1970, 1,939,522). Language (1960): Hungarian 98.2%. Religion (1956): Roman Catholic 67%; Protestant 27.3%; Orthodox 2.5%; Jewish 1.5%. First secretary of the Hungarian Socialist Workers' (Communist) Party in 1970, Janos Kadar; president of the Presidential Council (head of state), Pal Losonczi; president of the Council of Ministers (premier), Jeno Fock.

Visitors to Hungary in 1970 noticed that the tragic memories of the October 1956 uprising had largely died out and that, in spite of a centrally directed society, Hungarians enjoyed a moderately relaxed life. Under the New Economic Mechanism introduced on Jan. 1, 1968, consumer goods were reasonably abundant and the standard of living seemed higher than in the neighbouring countries, Austria excepted. Considering how little room he had for maneuver, Janos Kadar—who had assumed power 14 years earlier in sombre circumstances—could be proud of his country's achievements under his leadership.

On April 4, the 25th anniversary of the liberation of Hungary from German occupation, great celebrations took place in Budapest with the participation of Leonid I. Brezhnev, general secretary of the Soviet Communist Party, Jozef Cyrankiewicz, the Polish premier, Gustav Husak, first secretary of the Czechoslovak Communist Party, and other leaders of the socialist countries. Kadar proclaimed that the Soviet Union was "Hungary's liberator, the first great power in history to treat this small country as an equal, a friend, and an ally." Analyzing the results of the preceding 25 years, Kadar stated that the means of production had doubled during that time; the national income in 1969 was almost four times as high as in 1938; and the volume produced by Hungarian industry had increased seven and a half times in the same period. The manpower in the countryside was one-third below 1938, but the collectivized agriculture produced one-third more.

HUNGARY

Education. (1967–68) Primary, pupils 1,331,079, teachers 62,340; secondary, pupils 129,110, teachers 8,170; vocational, pupils 98,549, teachers 4,413; higher (including 15 universities), students 52,407, teaching staff 8,996.

Finance. Monetary unit: forint, with an exchange rate of 11.74 forints to U.S. $1 (28.18 forints = £1 sterling) and a tourist rate (Oct. 1970) of 30 forints to U.S. $1 (72 forints = £1 sterling). Budget (1969 est.): revenue 154,219,000,000 forints; expenditure 155,929,000,000 forints. National income (net material product): (1969) 244 billion forints; (1968) 221 billion forints.

Foreign Trade. (1969) Imports 22,631,000,000 forints; exports 22,462,000,000 forints. Import sources: U.S.S.R. 37%; East Germany 10%; Czechoslovakia 7%; Poland 6%. Export destinations: U.S.S.R. 35%; East Germany 10%; Czechoslovakia 9%; Poland 6%; Italy 5%. Main exports: machinery 25%; chemicals; iron and steel; fruit and vegetables; meat and products; textiles.

Transport and Communications. Roads (1969) 110,128 km. (including 53 km. expressways). Passenger vehicles in use (1969) 192,300. Railways: (1968) 8,777 km.; traffic (1969) 13,981,000,000 passenger-km., freight 17,736,000,000 net ton-km. Air traffic (1968): 255 million passenger-km.; freight 8,651,000 net ton-km. Telephones (Dec. 1968) 684,389. Radio receivers (Dec. 1968) 2,514,000. Television receivers (Dec. 1968) 1,397,000.

Agriculture. Production (in 000; metric tons; 1969; 1968 in parentheses): corn 4,732 (3,814); wheat (1968) 3,360, (1967) 3,022; rye 236 (238); barley 907 (906); potatoes 1,650 (1,335); sugar, raw value (1969–70) 449, (1968–69) 438; tobacco 27 (27); tomatoes (1968) 434, (1967) 484; sunflower seed *c.* 105 (93); dry peas (1968) 68, (1967) 128; apples (1968) 482, (1967) 675; wine (1968) 484, (1967) 479; beef and veal (1968) 175, (1967) 158; pork (1968) 342, (1967) 297. Livestock (in 000; March 1969): cattle 2,006; pigs 5,334; sheep 3,277; horses 249; chickens 46,204.

Industry. Index of production (1963 = 100): (1969) 135; (1968) 132. Production (in 000; metric tons; 1969): coal 4,133; lignite and brown coal 22,364; crude oil 1,754; natural gas (cu.m.) 3,091,000; electricity (kw-hr.) 14,068,000; iron ore (25% metal content) 680; pig iron 1,758; crude steel 3,031; bauxite 1,936; cement 2,564; sulfuric acid 455; nitrogenous fertilizers (nitrogen content; 1968) 245; cotton yarn 58; wool yarn 15; commercial vehicles (units) 9.

At its July plenary session, the Central Committee of the Hungarian Socialist Workers' Party adopted directives for the fourth five-year plan (1971–75), according to which national income would increase by 30–32%, industrial production by 32–34%, and agricultural output by 15–16%. The real national income, estimated in 1969 at $750 per capita, should reach more than $1,000 in 1975. An indispensable condition for the successful fulfillment of the plan was the use of modern methods of organization and management.

KEYSTONE

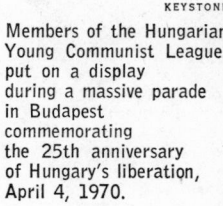

Members of the Hungarian Young Communist League put on a display during a massive parade in Budapest commemorating the 25th anniversary of Hungary's liberation, April 4, 1970.

The supply of fuel and power was a problem of great importance. Hungarian coal production, already insufficient to meet the country's needs, was decreasing. Crude oil extraction was rising, but 3,764,-000 tons had to be imported from the Soviet Union in 1969. Extraction of natural gas had increased fourfold during the preceding five years, reaching 3,096,-000,000 cu.m. in 1969.

On August 20 celebrations began in Budapest marking the thousandth anniversary of the birth of St. Stephen, the first king of Hungary. Members of the government as well as representatives of the various Christian denominations were present at the solemn Mass celebrated by Archbishop Jozsef Ijjas. For the first time since 1947 the reliquary containing St. Stephen's right hand was exposed to public adoration, but not St. Stephen's crown which—inexplicably—was still kept in Washington, D.C.

In his opening speech at the tenth congress of the Hungarian Socialist Workers' Party, held November 23–28 in Budapest, Kadar proclaimed Hungary's loyalty to the Warsaw Pact and Comecon and to the Marxist-Leninist line, although this did not exclude its right to select the kind of internal evolution best suited to its specific needs. Kadar hailed West Germany's treaties with the U.S.S.R. and Poland, adding that Budapest, too, was ready to normalize its relations with Bonn.

Serious floods ravaged eastern Hungary in May and June; some 10,000 homes were destroyed and a further 5,000 badly damaged. Total cost of the losses was estimated at 2.5 billion forints.   (K. Sm.)

Encyclopædia Britannica Films. *Hungary and Communism—Eastern Europe in Change* (1964).

Iceland

Iceland is an island republic in the North Atlantic Ocean. Area: 39,768 sq.mi. (103,000 sq.km.). Pop. (1969 est.): 203,442. Cap. and largest city: Reykjavik (pop., 1969 est., 81,476). Language: Icelandic (similar to Old Norse). Religion: 98% Lutheran. President in 1970, Kristjan Eldjarn; prime ministers, Bjarni Benediktsson and, from July 10, Johann Hafstein.

The events of 1970 were overshadowed by a tragedy that for Icelanders poignantly recalled the medieval saga of Burnt-Njal. On July 10 the prime minister, Bjarni Benediktsson (*see* Obituaries), with his wife and four-year-old grandson, died in a fire at an official summer residence at Thingvellir. Benediktsson, who had led the Independence Party-Social Democratic coalition since 1963, was succeeded by Johann Hafstein, pending parliamentary elections due in the spring of 1971. In municipal elections held on May 30, 1970, the Independence Party maintained the absolute majority in the Reykjavik city council that it had held for 50 years.

On March 1 Iceland became a member of the European Free Trade Association, an event that seemed likely to spur plans to diversify the economy. Meanwhile, progress was made in the export of goods such as wool and skin clothing, in addition to the traditional fish products. Other efforts toward diversification included mink farming and experimental fish farming (salmon and trout). Fish catches were good (except for herring), and high prices led to a favourable trade balance and an overall balance of payments surplus—threatened, however, by the inflationary effects of 15–18% wage increases granted in May.

Hurricanes:
see Disasters;
Meteorology

Hydroelectric Power:
see Engineering
Projects; Fuel and
Power

Ice Hockey:
see Hockey

PRESSENS BILD

Four of the 15 Icelandic students who invaded the Icelandic embassy in Stockholm April 20, 1970, stand on its balcony after confiscating documents and raising the socialist flag.

The volcano Hekla started to erupt on May 5 and was active for several weeks. The lava flow did little damage, but the ash that erupted for the first few hours rendered some pastureland useless.

Tourism was becoming an important economic factor, and arrivals (excluding cruise liners) were expected to reach 53,000 in 1970, a 20% increase over 1969. In February the 18th Nordic Council meeting was held in Reykjavik, with 400 delegates, including 40 ministers, from all five Nordic countries.

(Va. K.)

ICELAND

Education. (1967–68) Primary, pupils 27,500, teachers 1,340; secondary, pupils 14,750, teachers 1,230; vocational, pupils 2,730, teachers (1966–67) 119; teacher training, students 670, teachers (1966–67) 27; higher (at Reykjavik University), students 1,200, teaching staff 135.

Finance. Monetary unit: króna, with a par value of 88 krónur to U.S. $1 (211.20 krónur = £1 sterling). Gold, SDRs, and foreign exchange, central bank: (June 1970) U.S. $52 million; (June 1969) U.S. $32.3 million. Budget (1969 est.): revenue 7,096,482,000 krónur; expenditure 7,000,607,000 krónur. Gross national product: (1968) 25.5 billion krónur; (1967) 24 billion krónur. Money supply: (June 1970) 4,756,-000,000 krónur; (June 1969) 3,505,000,000 krónur. Cost of living (Reykjavik; 1963 = 100): (May 1970) 227; (May 1969) 202.

Foreign Trade. (1969) Imports 10,280,000,000 krónur; exports 8,964,000,000 krónur. Import sources: West Germany 17%; U.K. 13%; Denmark 10%; U.S. 9%; U.S.S.R. 8%; Norway 6%; Netherlands 5%; Sweden 5%. Export destinations: U.S. 28%; U.K. 14%; U.S.S.R. 9%; West Germany 9%; Denmark 7%; Sweden 6%. Main exports: fish and products 67%.

Transport and Communications. Roads (1969) 10,986 km. Motor vehicles in use (1969): passenger 37,304; commercial 5,660. There are no railways. Air traffic (1969): 1,214,000,000 passenger-km.; freight 11.3 million net ton-km. Shipping (1969): merchant vessels 100 gross tons and over 285; gross tonnage 120,460. Telephones (Dec. 1968) 66,267. Radio receivers (Dec. 1968) 60,000.

Agriculture. Fish catch (1968) 601 metric tons, (1967) 898 metric tons. Livestock (in 000; Dec. 1967): cattle 55; sheep 830.

Ice Skating

The world ice figure and dance skating championships were held at the Tivoli Sports Hall, Ljubljana, Yugos., on March 3–7. Fifteen nations were represented by 112 skaters.

Tim Wood (U.S.) impressively retained his men's title after a crucial contest with Ondrej Nepela (Czech.), the European champion, who had led after the compulsory figures. In freestyle, Wood, from Colorado, included a great triple salchow, an extra-high split lutz, a triple toe-loop jump, and an originally positioned jump-parallel spin. Shrewdly conserving his energy between these highlights, Wood displayed a smooth action that made it all look deceptively simple, and he won two sixes for technical merit and another for artistic impression.

Gabriele Seyfert (E.Ger.) successfully defended her women's crown, leaving no doubt about her freestyle supremacy. She gave a flawless display to overhaul with ease the earlier lead established in the figures by Beatrix Schuba (Aus.). Slimmer and more mobile than in the previous season, Miss Seyfert showed all-round strength in difficult jumps and spins, and her skillfully devised program drew a six from the East German judge for artistic impression.

Miss Schuba, runner-up for the second time, was unquestionably the better exponent of the compulsory figures, and her persistent success in this department added weight to a growing conviction that separate titles should be awarded for figures and freestyle, with a combined title for the best overall.

The pairs title was narrowly kept by Aleksei Ulanov and Irina Rodnina (U.S.S.R.) of Moscow, who withstood a spirited challenge from their Leningrad compatriots, Andrei Suraikin and Ludmila Smirnova. The margin would have been more comfortable had Ulanov not fallen during a combination jump, but the champions' wide variety of powerful overhead lifts and several well-matched shadow movements carried the judges' 7–2 verdict.

Aleksandr Gorshkov and Ludmila Pakhomova

(U.S.S.R.) captured the vacant ice dance title, the Soviet Union's first victory in this event. In the closest finish of the meeting, they scored only one-tenth of a point more than James Sladky and Judy Schwomeyer (U.S.).

Memories of Donald Jackson's 1962 amateur triumph were revived in the 14th world professional figure skating championships, at Wembley, Eng., on April 17. Jackson (Canada), the men's winner, proved that at 30 he had lost none of his rare ability to gain spectacular elevation. Hana Maskova (Czech.) scored the first victory for her country in the women's contest. British partnerships, Raymond Wilson with Linda Bernard and Ian Phillips with Yvonne Suddick, won the pairs and ice dance events, respectively.

The year's outstanding speed skating achievements were dominated by performers from the Netherlands. Ard Schenk became overall world men's champion in Oslo on February 14–15, and his compatriot, Atje Keulen-Deelstra, gained the women's title at West Allis, Wis., on February 28 to March 1.

Magne Thomassen (Nor.) won the men's 500-m. sprint, Schenk took the 1,500 m., and another Dutchman, Jan Bols, was first in both 5,000 m. and 10,000 m. Although the best all-rounder, Miss Keulen-Deelstra failed to win any of the four women's events. Ludmila Titova (U.S.S.R.) won the 500 m., repeating her win in the international sprint championships at West Allis a week earlier, and tied for first place in the 1,000 m. with Sigrid Sundby (Nor.). The 1,500 m. and 3,000 m. were both won by yet another Dutch skater, Ans Schut.

Although the championships themselves produced no new records, previous best world times were lowered during the season ten times by men and five times by women. Hasse Bjoerjes (Swed.) raced the fastest-ever 500 m. in 38.46 sec. at Inzell, W.Ger., on March 8. Valeri Muratov (U.S.S.R.) lowered the 1,000-m. record to 1 min. $19\frac{1}{4}$ sec. at Alma Ata, U.S.S.R., on January 25. Kees Verkerk (Neth.) reduced the best 1,500-m. time to 2 min. 1.9 sec. at Inzell on March 8, and Bols became the fastest man over 3,000 m., clocking 4 min. 16.4 sec. at Cortina d'Ampezzo, Italy, on January 27.

WIDE WORLD

Above, the Soviet Union's Ludmila Titova speeds toward victory in the 500-m. event at the international sprint championships in West Allis, Wis., Feb. 22, 1970. Left, Sweden's Hasse Bjoerjes sets a new men's 500-m. record of 38.9 sec. at Davos, Switz., January 18. On March 8 in Inzell, W.Ger., he beat his own record with 38.46 sec. in the fastest 500 ever raced.
KEYSTONE

Three new women's world records were established. Tatiana Sidorova (U.S.S.R.) reduced the 500 m. to 43.22 sec. at Alma Ata on January 17. At the same meeting her compatriot, Nina Statkevich, lowered the 1,500 m. to 2 min. 17.82 sec. after another Soviet skater, Ludmila Fechina, had covered 1,000 m. in 1 min. 29.1 sec. at the same rink.

The Canadian Figure Skating Association reported the world's largest national figure skating membership of 539 clubs, representing more than 100,000 organized participants. This compared with the U.S. Figure Skating Association's membership of 250 clubs and 28,000 skaters. (H. B.)

Income, National

The rate of growth of real gross national product (GNP) in the industrial countries ranged widely in 1969. The United States economy moved into a recessionary phase, which continued into 1970. Canada,

Table I. Growth of Real Gross National Product, 1958–69

Country	Average 1958–67	Percentage real increase 1968 over 1967	1969 over 1968
Industrial countries			
Austria	4.4	4.1	6.4
Belgium	4.4	3.8	6.2
Canada	4.7	4.9	5.0
Denmark	5.0	3.5	7.0
France	5.8	4.9	7.9
Germany, West	4.8	7.2	7.9
Italy	6.0	5.9	4.8
Japan	10.7	14.0	12.2
Luxembourg	3.2	4.0	6.8
Netherlands	5.2	6.2	5.1
Norway	4.9	3.7	3.9
Sweden	4.6	4.1	5.0
Switzerland	4.9	4.0	5.2
United Kingdom	3.3	3.4	1.8
United States	4.7	4.9	2.8
Other developed areas			
Australia*	4.5	8.5	6.5
Finland	5.3	2.2	8.0
Greece	6.7	6.2	...
Iceland	4.1	−6.0	0.0
Ireland	3.7	6.9	4.0
New Zealand†	4.1	1.9	5.5‡
Portugal	6.0	5.7	...
South Africa§	5.9	3.3	7.4
Spain	6.2	4.4	7.8
Turkey	5.0	6.7	6.3
Eastern Europe‖			
Albania	7.5¶	11.7	...
Bulgaria	9.1	6.4	9.9
Czechoslovakia	4.0	8.2	8.4
Germany, East	4.6	5.4	5.1
Hungary	6.2	4.9	7.4
Poland	6.0	9.0	2.9
Romania	9.6	7.0	...
U.S.S.R.	7.1	7.5	...
Yugoslavia	7.0	3.6	...
Less developed areas			
Argentina	2.5	4.7	7.0
Bolivia	4.8	7.2	4.8
Brazil	5.2	8.5	8.9
Ecuador	4.9	5.2	4.9
Ghana	3.1♀	1.4	3.6
Honduras	4.7	7.0	3.1
Iraq	6.3	13.8	4.3
Israel	8.1	16.2	12.5
Kenya	3.8	7.5	5.0
Korea, South	6.7	13.5	16.1
Morocco	2.4	11.3	11.3
Nicaragua	6.3	4.7	4.4
Pakistan*	5.4	5.2	...
Philippines	4.7	4.3	7.7
Puerto Rico*	7.9	6.9	...
Rhodesia	3.9	2.5	4.6
Taiwan	9.3	10.3	8.9
Uganda	4.0	2.3	10.9

*Financial years beginning July 1.
†Financial years beginning April 1.
‡Unofficial estimate.
§Including Botswana, Lesotho, Swaziland, and South West Africa (Namibia).
‖Growth of material product. See text for discussion of comparability with other figures.
¶1960–67.
♀1959–67.

Sources: Publications of United Nations; Organization for Economic Cooperation and Development; International Monetary Fund; official national sources.

however, managed to maintain its growth despite the lower U.S. growth rate. The rate of growth of GNP in the European group of Organization for Economic Cooperation and Development (OECD) countries (mainly developed industrial economies) rose to about 6.1% in 1969, well above the increase of 5% in 1968. It was also above the average growth rate of 5% per year for the preceding decade (1958–67) for the same group of countries. In this group, growth rates generally rose except for Italy, the Netherlands, and the United Kingdom. Some improvement in U.K. growth in 1970 seemed indicated by late quarterly figures, however. In the European Economic Community the six countries improved their growth rate to 7% in 1969, above the 5.9% average achieved in 1968 and well above the 5.4% rate during 1958–67. Japan again maintained its extraordinarily rapid sustained growth during the year.

In the group of other developed countries the rate of growth fell sharply in Australia and Ireland, while Iceland continued in recession. Finland, New Zealand, South Africa, and Spain showed improved growth rates. Among the less developed countries experiences differed widely. Growth was particularly rapid in South Korea, Israel, Morocco, and Uganda. In Latin America output rose most rapidly in Argentina and Brazil.

Comparisons between Eastern European and other countries were made difficult by the formers' exclusion from national income accounts of certain "unproductive services," such as public administration, and personal and professional services. If such items were included, the growth rates in those countries would probably be somewhat lower than those recorded. From the section of Table I which summarizes the recent record of this group, it appears that experience varied widely.

Recent trends in expenditure of the GNP are analyzed for a large number of countries in Table II. The figures are not always completely comparable between countries because of differences in national accounting practices, but they do serve to show major differences. In some cases the original national accounts include a statistical discrepancy between the total and the sum of its components, so that the items shown do not add up to 100%.

The share of private consumption expenditure had fallen since the late 1950s in virtually all countries. This was also generally true for 1969 in relation to 1968, except in a few developing countries and in the U.S., where the share was virtually unchanged. In some countries government current expenditure took a higher share in 1969 than in 1968 (Canada and Norway), but in many the share declined (France, Luxembourg, and the U.K.). During the 1960s the general tendency was for this category to rise faster than total expenditure in nearly every country.

During 1969 the share of fixed investment did not respond everywhere to the generally faster rate of growth. In the U.K. it fell noticeably. Among the less developed countries, as well as in most of the advanced ones, investment's share in the GNP had generally risen during the 1960s and this was largely true in 1969. However, large reductions occurred in Bolivia and the Philippines. Inventory building was modest in the advanced countries, generally the same or somewhat above that of 1968.

The international surplus as shown in Table II includes all transactions in goods and services, and the net effect of factor incomes (payments such as dividends and interest arising in one country, which are paid to residents of another). Thus, the figures are comparable with the current account of the balance of international payments, excluding the effect of current international transfer payments. The largest relative surpluses were recorded in West Germany, Italy, Luxembourg, New Zealand, and Switzerland; the largest deficits by Ireland, Israel, South Korea, Malawi, and several Latin-American countries. The U.K. swung decisively into surplus in 1969.

Table III shows the latest available figures on levels of national income, considered on both a total and per capita basis, in more than 70 countries. The concept of national income is designed to measure the output of the national economy at the cost of producing that output less the value of the depreciation of the capital

stock for that year. The table includes all countries for which 1969 data were available or which had a national income of $1 billion or more in 1963. The national figures at current prices have been converted to U.S. dollars at current exchange rates. Thus, the figures are affected by changes in the price level and do not indicate the growth of real per capita income. Two important qualifications have to be made about the use of this procedure. First, the use of current exchange rates determined for foreign trade and payments purposes may not adequately reflect differences in the purchasing power of the various national currencies. Furthermore, devaluations and revaluations will distort the figures as between different years. Second, the figures in national currencies are themselves estimated in a variety of ways, and there are differences in the definitions used among various

Table II. Disposal of Gross National Product (%)

Country	Year	Private consumption	Public consumption	Gross fixed capital formation	Change in inventory	International surplus	Country	Year	Private consumption	Public consumption	Gross fixed capital formation	Change in inventory	International surplus
Industrial countries							South Africa‡	1967	62.6	11.9	24.1	5.5	—2.8
Austria	1967	59.2	14.7	25.0	2.8	—1.7		1968	64.6	12.4	23.3	—0.1	—0.2
	1968	59.4	15.2	23.6	3.2	—1.3		1969	63.3	12.8	23.0	2.5	—2.3
	1969	57.2	15.5	23.2	3.8	0.3	Spain	1967	69.8	10.2	21.3	2.1	—3.4
Belgium	1967	63.0	13.7	22.1	0.3	0.8		1968	69.3	10.4	20.9	2.1	—2.6
	1968	63.5	14.2	21.1	0.8	0.1		1969	68.6	10.4	22.0	2.3	—3.3
	1969	62.7	14.0	22.4	0.7	0.3	**Less developed areas**						
Canada	1967	59.3	16.6	23.9	0.6	—0.8	Argentina	1967	68.1	11.6	19.3	0.0	1.1
	1968	59.3	17.0	22.1	1.0	—0.3		1968	68.8	10.8	20.4	0.0	—0.1
	1969	59.2	17.5	21.8	1.3	—1.1		1969	68.2	10.2	22.2	0.3	—0.9
Denmark	1967	62.7	17.0	21.5	0.7	—2.0	Bolivia	1967	80.1	11.1	13.1	1.5	—5.8
	1968	63.2	17.8	20.4	0.2	—1.6		1968	77.6	10.8	17.8	0.7	—6.9
	1969	61.9	17.8	22.0	0.8	—2.5		1969	79.9	11.0	14.3	1.6	—6.7
France	1967	60.5	12.3	25.1	1.7	0.4	Costa Rica	1967	71.8	13.9	20.4	2.9	—9.0
	1968	61.0	12.7	25.0	1.2	0.1		1968	70.5	13.8	20.5	2.6	—7.3
	1969	60.4	12.3	25.4	2.5	—0.6		1969	68.8	13.9	20.8	3.6	—7.1
Germany, West	1967	57.5	16.4	23.1	—0.3	3.3	El Salvador	1967	78.6	9.2	14.7	0.1	—4.0
	1968	55.9	15.5	23.2	2.0	3.4		1968	80.1	9.5	10.9	0.3	—2.6
	1969	55.3	15.5	24.4	2.2	2.5		1969	80.1	9.9	11.3	0.6	—3.1
Italy	1967	64.4	13.4	19.0	1.4	1.8	Guatemala	1967	83.2	7.9	13.4	0.8	—5.3
	1968	63.6	13.5	19.4	0.4	3.0		1968	81.7	7.5	14.4	0.2	—3.9
	1969	63.5	13.4	20.5	0.4	2.4		1969	79.9	7.9	14.6	—0.3	—2.2
Japan	1967	53.6	8.7	32.4	5.3	0.0	Honduras	1967	77.1	9.5	17.3	1.9	—5.8
	1968	52.2	8.4	33.8	4.7	0.9		1968	77.0	9.4	17.6	1.0	—5.0
	1969	51.0	8.2	35.2	4.2	1.4		1969	75.2	10.4	19.0	1.1	—5.8
Luxembourg	1967	61.1	12.0	25.1	0.0	1.8	Israel	1967	66.9	29.7	16.4	0.4	—13.4
	1968	61.1	12.0	25.1	—0.5	2.3		1968	64.7	30.8	20.1	2.0	—17.6
	1969	57.0	11.0	27.2	0.0	4.7		1969	65.2	30.5	22.6	0.7	—19.0
Netherlands	1967	57.3	16.1	25.7	2.1	0.1	Jamaica	1967	71.6	12.2	23.3	1.0	—8.0
	1968	56.2	15.6	26.3	1.2	0.6		1968	69.9	13.0	27.4	1.1	—11.3
	1969	55.8	15.7	25.5	2.7	0.3		1969	69.1	13.2	28.3	1.1	—11.7
Norway	1967	54.0	17.2	30.3	1.0	—2.4	Kenya	1967	67.8	14.9	20.2	1.6	—4.5
	1968	53.8	17.7	27.0	—0.1	1.6		1968	68.9	15.7	19.0	0.6	—4.2
	1969	55.7	18.4	25.3	—0.4	1.0		1969	68.5	15.9	18.7	—0.6	—2.5
Switzerland	1967	59.0	11.8	25.4	0.6	3.1	Korea, South	1967	78.4	10.6	21.2	0.7	—9.1
	1968	58.1	11.6	25.0	0.7	4.7		1968	75.6	11.1	25.5	1.2	—11.7
	1969	57.4	11.8	25.5	0.6	4.4		1969	71.9	10.9	26.7	3.3	—11.2
United Kingdom	1967	63.1	18.2	18.1	0.5	0.1	Malawi	1967	84.6	17.5	12.0	2.1	—16.1
	1968	62.9	18.1	18.3	0.5	0.2		1968	85.2	17.3	17.4	—1.1	—19.0
	1969	62.3	17.9	17.3	0.7	1.8		1969	82.0	16.5	17.8	0.8	—17.1
United States*	1967	61.2	20.8	16.5	0.9	0.6	Nicaragua	1967	78.3	11.2	18.9	2.3	—10.8
	1968	61.1	21.0	16.6	1.0	0.3		1968	77.3	11.2	15.8	2.3	—6.6
	1969	61.2	20.9	16.7	0.9	0.2		1969	76.4	11.0	17.1	2.2	—6.7
Other developed areas							Paraguay	1967	80.3	7.9	16.5	0.3	—5.1
Australia	1966–67	62.2	12.0	26.6	2.2	—2.5		1968	82.4	8.5	14.8	0.5	—6.1
	1967–68	63.8	12.8	27.4	0.9	—4.4		1969	79.8	9.3	15.8	0.6	—5.5
	1968–69	60.8	12.5	27.1	3.2	—3.5	Philippines	1967	77.8	9.4	21.2	1.7	—3.3
Finland	1967	57.5	16.2	24.4	3.5	—1.6		1968	75.6	9.3	20.5	1.8	—5.6
	1968	55.2	16.8	23.0	4.2	0.8		1969	76.3	9.7	18.2	1.7	—4.9
	1969	54.3	16.3	23.8	5.6	0.0	Taiwan	1967	60.2	17.3	21.1	4.1	—2.0
Ireland	1967	69.0	12.7	18.9	—0.5	—0.1		1968	59.5	17.7	22.1	3.6	—2.9
	1968	68.7	13.3	19.9	1.3	—3.2		1969	57.7	18.5	23.1	3.3	—2.3
	1969	68.3	13.4	22.5	1.5	—5.6							
New Zealand	1967–68	61.7	14.7	21.9	3.2	—1.5							
	1968–69	60.3	15.2	22.0	1.3	1.2							
	1969–70†	59.0	15.5	22.0	1.1	2.3							

*Government expenditure on equipment is included in public consumption, as is stock building by nonfederal government agencies.
†Unofficial estimate.
‡South African national accounts include Botswana, Lesotho, Swaziland, and South West Africa (Namibia).
Sources: UN, OECD, and IMF publications; official national sources.

Table III. National Income and Income per Head

Country	National income in U.S. $000,000,000 1969	National income per head in U.S. $ 1958	1963	1969	Country	National income in U.S. $000,000,000 1969	National income per head in U.S. $ 1958	1963	1969
Industrial countries					**Caribbean and Latin America**				
Austria	9.3	590	830	1,260	Argentina	17.0	490	480	710
Belgium	18.1	935	1,185	1,875	Bolivia	0.8	85	120	165
Canada	51.4	1,505	1,600	2,435	Brazil	21.0♀	185	245	250♀
Denmark	10.7	890	1,335	2,175	Chile	4.4§	325*	260	465§
France	106.0	1,005	1,270	2,105	Colombia	5.0□	190	270	260□
Germany, West	116.6	840	1,255	1,915	Costa Rica	0.7	300	315	410
Italy	66.7	480*	765*	1,255	Ecuador	1.3	155	160	220
Japan	131.8	285	560	1,290	El Salvador	0.8	210	215	245
Luxembourg	0.6	1,075*	1,340	1,970	Guatemala	1.3§	235	255	275§
Netherlands	23.1	695	995	1,800	Honduras	0.6	170	189	225
Norway	7.4	870	1,200	1,935	Jamaica	0.9	315	375	440
Sweden	21.7†	1,200†	1,730†	2,725†	Mexico	24.2§	270	350	510§
Switzerland	15.3	1,195	1,675	2,450	Nicaragua	0.6	225	265	335
United Kingdom	84.2	1,015	1,300	1,515	Peru	2.9♀	170	210	240♀
United States	775.0	2,115	2,560	3,815	Puerto Rico‡	3.4§	540	825	1,250§
Other developed areas					Uruguay	1.2♀	440	460	425♀
Australia‡	24.0§	1,125	1,485	1,990§	Venezuela	7.8	630*	605	800
Finland	7.2	725	1,130	1,522					
Greece	6.1§	325	460	695§	**Asia, East and Southeast**				
Iceland	0.2§	965	1,270	1,075§	Burma‡	1.5□	55*	60*	60□
Ireland	2.6	465	650	910	Ceylon	1.5§	120*	130	130§
New Zealand‡	4.6†	1,170	1,505	1,640†	Hong Kong	1.0¶	245	300	...
Portugal	4.3§	215	300	455§	India‡	41.1	65*	80	75
South Africa‖	13.2	315	395	675	Indonesia	10.5□	80*	80*	95□
Spain	24.4	300*	440*	740	Iran‡	6.8§	145*	180	250§
Turkey	10.6§	180	225	315§	Korea, South	4.8§	125	130	160§
Less developed areas					Malaysia	2.4♀	195	225	250♀
Africa					Pakistan‡	13.2§	60	80	105§
Algeria	2.3¶	235	205	...	Philippines	6.8	185*	210	180
Congo (Kinshasa)	0.9§	70*	105	55§	Singapore	1.1□	420	480	560□
Ghana	1.8§	140	190	215§	Taiwan	3.7	100	150	270
Kenya	1.1	70	85	105	Thailand	4.2□	80	100	125□
Libya	2.2§	110	430	1,195§	Vietnam, South	1.8♀	90	80	110♀
Morocco	2.8	160	165	185					
Nigeria‡	3.6♀	45	60	60♀	**Middle East**				
Rhodesia	1.2	185	190	240	Iraq	2.3	160	190	250
Sudan‡	1.2♂	80	90	90♂	Israel	3.7	610	835	1,300
Tanzania	0.7♂	50*	60	70♂	Jordan	0.5§	140	185	230§
Tunisia	0.8§	150	190	180§	Kuwait‡	2.1§	1,830	3,430	3,860§
Uganda	0.7§	60	65	85§	Lebanon	1.1□	210	295	430□
United Arab Republic‡	4.8♀	110*	140	160♀	Saudi Arabia‡	2.0♀	125	225	290♀
Zambia	1.0§	110	135	235§	Syria	1.1□	155	165	205□

*Data not strictly comparable with later years.
†Unofficial estimates.
‡Financial year.
§1968.
‖Including Botswana, Lesotho, Swaziland, and South West Africa (Namibia).

¶1963.
♀1966.
♂1965.
□1967.
Sources: UN, OECD, and IMF publications; official national sources.

countries. For these reasons, small differences in per capita national income are insignificant.

Bearing these difficulties in mind, one may draw some tentative conclusions from the data presented. About four-fifths of the aggregate income of the listed countries is accounted for by the 15 industrial countries, while the 52 less developed countries represent between 10–15% of the total. The dominating size of the U.S. economy in relation to all other non-Communist countries is shown in the table; it is roughly six times the size of the two next largest, Japan and West Germany. It is likely, however, that a more sophisticated analysis that allowed for differences in the internal purchasing power of national currencies would show a somewhat different picture. The available evidence suggests that, in comparison with the U.S., real output in several West European countries is relatively higher than suggested by the 1969 figures, particularly so in West Germany and Italy.　(M. F. F.)

See also Economy, World.

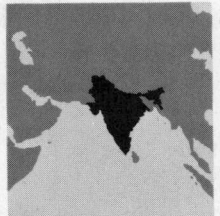

India

A federal republic of southern Asia and a member of the Commonwealth of Nations, India is situated on a peninsula extending into the Indian Ocean with the Arabian Sea to the west and the Bay of Bengal to the east. Area: 1,232,560 sq.mi. (3,192,184 sq.km.). Pop. (1968 est.): 524,080,000; Indo-Aryans and Dravidians are dominant, with Mongoloid, Negroid, and Australoid admixtures. Cap.: New Delhi (pop., 1968 est., 3,470,000). Largest city: Bombay (metro. pop.,

1968 est., 5,368,000). Hindi is the official language; English is an associate language. Religion (1961): Hindu 83.5%; Muslim 10.7%; Christian 2.4%; Sikh 1.8%; Buddhist 0.7%; others 0.9%. President in 1970, Varahagiri Venkata Giri; prime minister, Mrs. Indira Gandhi.

Domestic Affairs. In 1970 there occurred a gradual polarization of the political parties, not around ideology but around support of or opposition to the prime minister, Mrs. Indira Gandhi. The Organization Congress (the faction of the party bosses) drew closer to the Jan Sangh and the Swatantra Party and, with the support of the Samyukta Socialist Party and the Communist Party (Marxist), repeatedly offered battle in Parliament and outside to the Ruling Congress of Mrs. Gandhi, which in turn was backed by the Communist Party of India, the Dravida Munnetra Kazhagam, the Muslim League, and the Akali Dal. Through a series of swift policy initiatives and political moves, Mrs. Gandhi established greater personal ascendancy on the political scene, arousing intense feeling.

Both factions of the Congress Party held plenary sessions just before the year opened. The Ruling Congress elected Jagjivan Ram as its president. Its session, held in Bombay, adopted a radical program involving, among other things, the extension of state trading to more commodities and a government takeover of the sugar industry in Uttar Pradesh.

Nationalization of the country's 14 largest banks, which lit the fuse for the previous year's split in the Congress Party, was declared invalid by the Supreme Court on February 10. In a ten-to-one judgment, the court held that while nationalization was within the

Two rival groups of Sikhs clash outside the Oberoi Intercontinental Hotel, New Delhi, May 18, 1970. The short scuffle occurred an hour before Sant Fateh Singh, chief of Akali Dal and the top authority of Sikhism, was due to arrive for a reception.

LONDON "DAILY EXPRESS" FROM PICTORIAL PARADE

competence of Parliament, the compensation given to the banks under the 1969 act did not fulfill the provisions of art. 31 of the constitution. In March, however, Parliament voted to renationalize the banks.

In his speech to the joint session of Parliament on February 20, the president declared that the government would introduce a bill to amend the constitution to do away with the privy purses and privileges of the rajas and maharajas, the former rulers of princely states. These payments (amounting to more than Rs. 40 million a year) and privileges (such as exemption from taxation, gun salutes, and the right to fly a personal flag) had been agreed to when the princely states were integrated with the rest of the country at the time of independence. Their abolition was one of the items in the ten-point program adopted by the undivided Congress Party. Attempts to find a negotiated settlement failed, the princes maintaining that these were covenants entered into for all time and the government holding them to be political arrangements. Y. B. Chavan, home minister, introduced the 24th Constitution Amendment Bill in the Lok Sabha (House of the People) on May 18 to delete the clauses relating to the princes. The bill was adopted by the Lok Sabha early in September by 339 votes to 154, although it became a rallying point for all groups that opposed the government. But in the Rajya Sabha (Council of States), where the membership of the Ruling Congress was depleted owing to the biennial elections, the voting was 149 for and 75 against,

and the measure thus failed to secure the two-thirds majority required for constitutional amendment. This was perhaps the biggest setback so far for Mrs. Gandhi's government. Within hours, however, the president, on the advice of the Cabinet, signed letters withdrawing recognition of the princes. This action was taken on the opinion of law officers that the president had the power to recognize the princes, and that once the recognition was withdrawn, payments and privileges automatically ceased. Several opposition parties attacked the order as an example of the executive overriding the legislature. Princes filed petitions in the Supreme Court, which on December 15 ruled that the government had acted unconstitutionally and that the president's orders were "inoperative." The court also forbade any further executive action against the princes and ordered that the government should pay the court costs. Mrs. Gandhi announced that the government would continue its efforts to overturn the institution of royalty by "appropriate constitutional means."

On June 26 there was a major Cabinet reshuffle. Mrs. Gandhi transferred the finance portfolio to Y. B. Chavan and took over the home portfolio from him. Jagjivan Ram was made defense minister. Fakhruddin Ali Ahmed was moved to food and agriculture, Swaran Singh to external affairs, and Dinesh Singh to industrial development. At year's end Mrs. Gandhi announced that she had ordered the dissolution of Parliament in order to seek a fresh mandate early in

INDIA

Education. (1965–66) Primary, pupils 49,639,-000, teachers 1,570,000; secondary (1964–65), pupils 6,459,419, teachers 889,800; vocational, pupils 450,101, teachers (1964–65) 24,146; teacher training, students 140,000, teachers 9,477; higher (including 62 universities), students 1,145,554, teaching staff (1963–64) 80,247.

Finance. Monetary unit: rupee, with a par value of Rs. 7.50 to U.S. $1 (Rs. 18 = £1 sterling). Gold, SDRs, and foreign exchange, official: (May 1970) U.S. $1,127,000,000; (May 1969) U.S. $854 million. Budget (1969–70 est.): revenue Rs. 33,020,000,000; expenditure Rs. 32,-620,000,000. National income: (1969–70) Rs. 308 billion; (1968–69) Rs. 281 billion. Money supply: (May 1970) Rs. 65.8 billion; (May 1969) Rs. 58.9 billion. Cost of living (1963 = 100): (May 1970) 166; (May 1969) 157.

Foreign Trade. (1969–70) Imports Rs. 15,-675,000,000; exports Rs. 14,132,000,000. Import sources: U.S. 29%; U.S.S.R. 11%; U.K. 6%;

West Germany 5%; Iran 5%; Canada 5%. Export destinations: U.S. 17%; Japan 13%; U.S.S.R. 12%; U.K. 12%. Main exports: jute manufactures 15%; tea 9%; iron ore 7%; iron and steel 6%; cotton fabrics 6%.

Transport and Communications. Roads (1969) 972,330 km. (including 24,000 km. main roads). Motor vehicles in use (1969): passenger 571,314; commercial 300,653. Railways: (1967) 59,061 km.; traffic (1967–68) 107,513,000,000 passenger-km., freight 101,-181,000,000 net ton-km. Air traffic (1969): 3,-230,000,000 passenger-km.; freight 115.8 million net ton-km. Shipping (1969): merchant vessels 100 gross tons and over 397; gross tonnage 2,238,344. Telephones (Jan. 1969) 1,057,193. Radio receivers (Dec. 1968) 9,275,000. Television receivers (Dec. 1968) 8,000.

Agriculture. Production (in 000; metric tons; 1969; 1968 in parentheses): wheat 18,652 (16,-540); rice c. 63,000 (59,642); barley 2,424

(3,504); corn c. 6,000 (5,701); potatoes 4,773 (4,232); cassava (1968) 4,520, (1967) 3,817; tea (1968) 392, (1967) 382; chick-peas 4,310 (5,972); bananas (1967) 3,155, (1966) 3,412; sugar, raw value (1969–70) c. 4,326, (1968–69) 3,811; millet (1968) 7,254, (1967) 8,976; sorghum (1968) 9,804, (1967) 10,048; tobacco 347 (369); rapeseed and mustard seed (1968) 1,482, (1967) 1,228; linseed 352 (438); peanuts 5,500 (4,476); cotton, lint 1,117 (1,069); jute 1,010 (528). Livestock (in 000; 1968–69): cattle c. 176,200; sheep c. 42,400; buffaloes (1967–68) c. 53,550; goats (1967–68) c. 66,-000; poultry c. 116,000.

Industry. Production (in 000; metric tons; 1969): coal 73,883; iron ore (61% metal content) 28,342; pig iron 7,493; crude steel 6,469; electricity (excluding most industrial production; kw-hr.) 49,475,000; aluminum 132; cement 13,-624; cotton yarn 922; woven cotton fabrics (m.; 1968) 7,896,000.

1971, a year before the five-year term of the existing Parliament expired.

There were important developments in the states. In February, a coalition government headed by Daroga Rai (Ruling Congress) was installed in Bihar, but it collapsed late in December. In Uttar Pradesh, the Ruling Congress wooed Charan Singh and weaned his party, the Bharatiya Kranti Dal (BKD), from the coalition government. The ministry headed by C. B. Gupta (Organization Congress) resigned on February 10, and Charan Singh formed a ministry on February 17 with the support of the Ruling Congress. The Ruling Congress later joined the government but broke with the BKD in September after it refused to merge. No party or combination of parties having a majority, the state was put under president's rule. The Organization Congress and BKD then formed a coalition with three other parties. On October 16 the governor reported to the president that the coalition commanded a majority in the Assembly. President's rule was revoked on October 18, and T. N. Singh formed a ministry.

In West Bengal, the united front government collapsed in March after a long period of feuding between the dominant Communist Party (Marxist) group and the group led by the chief minister, Ajoy Mukherjee. President's rule was promulgated in the state on March 19, and in December it was reported that the prime minister would call for elections in the near future. In Punjab a split in the Akali Dal, the Sikh nationalist party, forced Gurnam Singh out of the chief ministership in March, and a government headed by P. S. Badal was formed. In Kerala, the coalition government headed by Achuta Menon (Communist Party of India) resigned in June, and advised the governor to hold midterm elections. These led to a significant realignment of forces in the state and perhaps in the country. The Ruling Congress reached an electoral accommodation with the Communist Party of India and the Muslim League. Polling took place on September 17. The results showed a sharp increase in the number of seats held by the Ruling Congress (from 5 to 32 in a house of 133), and a decline in the strength of the Communist Party (Marxist) from 49 seats to 30. A coalition government, headed again by Achuta Menon, took office on October 4, with the Ruling Congress remaining outside the coalition but offering it support.

The government decided to grant statehood to the Union Territories of Himachal Pradesh, Manipur, and Tripura. In April, the autonomous state of Meghalaya within Assam came into being, and a government headed by Williamson Sangma was sworn in.

A major interstate dispute was settled in January when the prime minister awarded the disputed city of Chandigarh to Punjab and transferred 110 villages of the Fazilka subdivision and Rs. 200 million to Hariana; the award had not, however, been implemented at the year's end.

The Economy. The budget of the Union government, presented by Mrs. Gandhi on February 28, increased excise duties on luxury articles and direct taxes on incomes and wealth, especially urban property. Holding "growth with social justice" to be its aim, it outlined schemes for helping small farmers while letting off the corporate sector lightly. Revenue for 1970–71 was estimated at Rs. 32,917,000,000 (inclusive of the Union's share of Rs. 1,247,000,000 from new taxation), and expenditure at Rs. 31,526,000,000. Taken with capital expenditure of Rs. 21,884,000,000

UPI COMPIX

Tribesmen march down Calcutta's busiest street Feb. 20, 1970, carrying bows, spears, sticks, and beating drums to protest what they call discrimination by the government.

and capital receipts of Rs. 18,237,000,000, the overall deficit was estimated at Rs. 2,252,000,000. It was decided to increase public outlay under the fourth five-year plan to finance projects to combat unemployment and help small farmers and unirrigated regions. The plan document, presented to Parliament in May, outlined the expenditure on development during the 1969–74 period of Rs. 248,820,000,000, of which Rs. 159,020,000,000 would be in the public sector (compared with Rs. 143,980,000,000 envisaged in the revised draft plan published in 1969).

Agricultural production and prospects during the year were good, despite floods in several states. Grain production in the agricultural year 1969–70 was estimated at about 104 million metric tons. Prices of both food articles and industrial raw materials rose. The general index of wholesale prices stood at 182.7 on October 3 (1961–62 = 100), compared with 173.4 on Oct. 4, 1969, a rise of 5.4%.

Among the measures undertaken in furtherance of the goal of enlarging the public sector and reducing economic concentration and disparities were the appointment of a monopolies commission and a committee to investigate tax evasion, the formation of a cotton corporation to administer the import trade in cotton, and the passage of a long-proposed patents bill, which fixed the royalty payable at 4% and the life of a patent at five years.

The country's first nuclear power station was formally inaugurated at Tarapur, Maharashtra, in January. Offshore oil drilling was undertaken at Cambay from March. An important scientific achievement was the success of the Atomic Energy Commission in separating uranium-233 from thorium.

Foreign Affairs. The prime minister participated in the conference of nonaligned countries in Lusaka, Zambia, in September, and in the silver jubilee ceremonies of the United Nations in New York in October.

It was announced that India would sponsor Bhutan's membership in the UN. The closing of the U.S. cultural

Caravan of migrants rests for an evening meal in India's Jaisalmer District. Eight successive years of drought have forced many residents to move to other areas of the country.

LONDON "DAILY EXPRESS" FROM PICTORIAL PARADE

centres at the behest of the foreign office caused much controversy.

Some progress was made in negotiations with Pakistan to settle the eastern waters dispute. At talks held in July in New Delhi, it was agreed that waters from the Ganges River would be supplied to Pakistan at Farakka, and that the volume would be decided at a separate meeting to be held within six months. There was considerable anxiety over the steady flow of refugees from East Pakistan, estimated at 200,000 during the first nine months of the year. (H. Y. S. P.)

ENCYCLOPÆDIA BRITANNICA FILMS. *Hindu Family* (1952); *India (Pakistan and the Union of India)* (1952); *Mahatma Gandhi* (1955); *Animals of the Indian Jungle* (1957); *India (Customs in the Village)* (1957); *India (Introduction to Its History)* (1957); *Ganges: Sacred River* (1965).

Indonesia

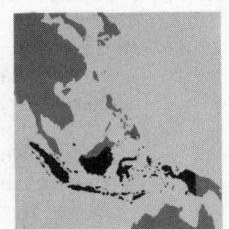

A republic of Southeast Asia, Indonesia consists of the major islands of Sumatra, Java, Kalimantan (Indonesian Borneo), Celebes, and Irian Barat (West New Guinea) and approximately 3,000 smaller islands and islets. Area: 779,675 sq.mi. (2,019,360 sq.km.). Pop. (1970 est.): 121,089,000. Cap. and largest city: Jakarta (pop., 1968 est., 4.5 million). Language: Bahasa Indonesia (official); Javanese; Sundanese; Madurese. Religion: mainly Muslim; some Christian, Buddhist, and Hindu. President and prime minister in 1970, General Suharto.

Indonesia observed the 25th anniversary of its proclamation of independence in 1970, a milestone that found the world's largest archipelago remarkably stable and unified. This state of affairs was in vivid contrast to the almost uninterrupted series of vest-pocket rebellions and political upheavals that had marked the first quarter of a century of independence.

The contrast between then and now was pointed up in 1970 by the death of Sukarno (*see* OBITUARIES), the flamboyant, demagogic former president, who was removed from power following an abortive, Communist-oriented coup in 1965 with which he was associated. Sukarno's death found his presidential successor, General Suharto, a diffident, almost phlegmatic man, caught up in the myriad of problems left by his predecessor, notably widespread corruption, army domination of politics, a disorganized bureaucracy, and a sluggish economy. During the year Suharto pressed his program for a general election in 1971, reorganized the armed forces, and embarked on an active foreign policy for the first time since Sukarno's

deposition. Suharto also found himself confronted by a rising popular clamour that he put an end to corruption at high levels of government.

Domestic Affairs. Sukarno, under house arrest, died on June 21, less than a month after his 69th birthday. He had long been suffering from a kidney ailment, impaired blood circulation, and high blood pressure. He went to his grave bearing with him the intimate details of his role in the abortive 1965 coup. It appeared that the evidence of his involvement, held by the government, might never be made public. The tone was set by Foreign Minister Adam Malik, who, together with Suharto and the sultan of Jogjakarta, filled the power vacuum shortly after the coup. "What is the use," asked Malik, "of questioning someone who is no more?"

Sukarno's plummet from power after the failure of the coup, however, bore mute testimony to the depth of his involvement in the events surrounding the murder of six Indonesian Army generals on the night of Sept. 30–Oct. 1, 1965. Additional silent testimony developed at his funeral. Sukarno was buried at his birthplace in East Java rather than in the cemetery for national heroes at Kalibata, on the outskirts of Jakarta.

In the course of the year the honeymoon between Suharto and the country's student and intellectual groups waned, although he still commanded their strong support. The government was brought under fire for its failure to combat massive corruption. A large part of the corruption allegedly involved the Army, which had assumed operational control of many nationalized mines and plantations during the Sukarno era. Amid demands for action, Suharto established an Advisory Committee to Combat Corruption, which was composed of elder statesmen and was headed by former Prime Minister Wilopo. Former Vice-Pres. Muhammad Hatta, who had co-signed the proclamation of independence with Sukarno, was appointed adviser to the committee, and Maj. Gen. Sutopo Juwono, the director of the National Intelligence Coordination Bureau (BAKIN), was installed as secretary. After six months of inquiry, the committee submitted its report to Suharto. Despite public demands and leaks in the press, the government refused to release the report. It had apparently uncovered large-scale corruption in government departments ranging from Pertamina, the state oil enterprise, to the Department of Religion, where funds for pilgrimages to Mecca had been mislaid.

Suharto was caught in a cross fire, fearful of weakening his position by moving against his fellow army officers and fearful that student discontent would lead

AUTHENICATED NEWS INTERNATIONAL

Pres. Richard M. Nixon receives President Suharto of Indonesia at the White House.

INDONESIA

Education. (1967–68) Primary, pupils 12,574,823, teachers 288,146; secondary, pupils 1,148,502, teachers 64,576; vocational, pupils 325,235, teachers 24,512; teacher training, students 106,575, teachers 7,774; higher, students 192,416, teaching staff 21,309.

Finance. Monetary unit: rupiah, with a free rate (Oct. 1970) of 378 rupiah to U.S. $1 (907.2 rupiah = £1 sterling). Budget (1968 est.) balanced at 97,186,000,000 rupiah. Gross national product (1968): 1,973,900,000,000 rupiah; (1967) 838.2 billion rupiah. Cost of living (Jakarta; 1963 = 100): (May 1970) 68,201; (May 1969) 59,438.

Foreign Trade. (1969) Imports U.S. $697 million; exports U.S. $831.2 million. Import sources: Japan 29%; U.S. 20%; West Germany 8%; China 6%; Netherlands 5%. Export destinations: Japan 33%; Singapore 18%; U.S. 14%; Australia 8%. Main exports: petroleum and products 45%; rubber 22%; coffee 6%; tin ore 5%.

Transport and Communications. Roads (1969) 84,268 km. Motor vehicles in use (1969): passenger 212,123; commercial 95,660. Railways (1967): 6,785 km.; traffic 4,998,000,000 passenger-km., freight 659 million net ton-km. Air traffic (1969): 296.4 million passenger-km.; freight 7,108,000 net ton-km. Shipping (1969): merchant vessels 100 gross tons and over 463; gross tonnage 598,155. Telephones (Dec. 1968) 181,377. Radio receivers (Dec. 1967) c. 1.5 million. Television receivers (Dec. 1968) 72,000.

Agriculture. Production (in 000; metric tons; 1969; 1968 in parentheses): rice 16,197 (15,224); corn c. 3,400 (3,102); cassava 11,140 (c.

11,800); sweet potatoes 1,979 (c. 2,300); sugar, raw value (1969–70) 732, (1968–69) 602; tea (1968) 41, (1967) 33; copra (1968) c. 553, (1967) c. 503; soybeans (1968) 389, (1967) 484; palm oil (estates only; 1968) 188, (1967) 174; peanuts (1968) 455, (1967) 400; coffee c. 120 (c. 120); tobacco c. 130 (c. 110); rubber (1968) c. 752, (1967) c. 762; fish catch (1968) 1,176, (1967) 1,180. Livestock (in 000; Dec. 1968): cattle c. 6,900; pigs c. 2,700; sheep c. 2,500; buffalo (Dec. 1967) 2,732; goats (Dec. 1967) c. 11,300.

Industry. Production (in 000; metric tons; 1969): coal 192; crude oil 39,642; tin concentrates (metal content) 17; bauxite 766; electricity (excluding most industrial production; kw-hr.; 1967) c. 1,677,000.

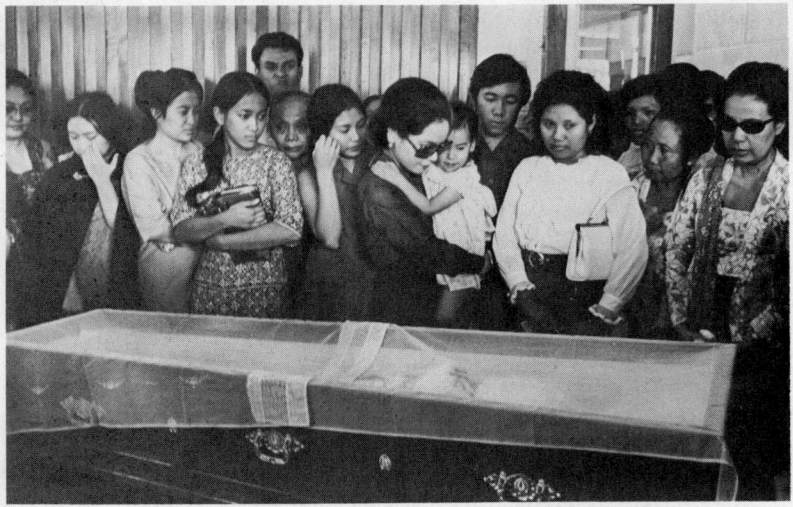

WIDE WORLD

Mourners, including members of the family of former president Sukarno, view Sukarno's body as it lies in state at his mansion in Slipi, June 21, 1970. His widow, Hartini, stands at far right.

to demonstrations of the character that had helped topple Sukarno. Meeting student leaders, Suharto banked the flames with a Javanese phrase that meant let things proceed slowly, provided they are proceeding, and achieve their goal. This, of course, had been Suharto's bedrock philosophy in deposing Sukarno and in dealing with the problems of succession. In October, three months after his conference with the students, Suharto announced a housecleaning of the Army. More than 80 field grade officers were pensioned off. Suharto refused to characterize their removal as a purge. Instead, he said that all officers over the age of 48 were being retired as part of a plan to "rejuvenate" the armed forces. However, he added dryly, the age limit would be waived in special cases.

Throughout the year preparations for the 1971 general election, the second in Indonesian history, proceeded smoothly. About 60 million voters were registered and 172,000 polling places set up. Through a complicated system of appointed members to Parliament and other devices, Suharto and the Army would retain effective power through 1976 and probably into 1978, whatever the electoral outcome. The elections, however, were considered important since they marked another step forward in Suharto's program to restore fully civil liberties and representative government. Once again, it was a case of his making haste slowly.

Foreign Affairs. For the first time in the post-Sukarno era, Indonesia adopted an active foreign policy. Suharto made 11 state visits abroad and attended the conference of nonaligned nations at Lusaka, Zambia. Jakarta also became the site of an Indonesian-sponsored conference on Cambodia, which was attended by 11 Asian and Pacific nations but which accomplished little.

The highlight of Suharto's foreign travel was a visit to the Netherlands. Suharto was the first Indonesian head of state to visit that nation since Indonesia proclaimed its independence from the Dutch in 1945. The Dutch visit was marred when a band of Indonesian exiles attacked and briefly held the Indonesian embassy in The Hague. They hoisted the flag of the separatist Republic of the South Moluccas, which had been proclaimed in 1950 and was subsequently suppressed by Indonesia. Another highlight during his travels was Suharto's first journey to the United States, repaying the state visit Pres. Richard Nixon had made to Indonesia in 1969.

Having restored good relations with the West, as reflected in the Suharto visits to the Netherlands and the U.S., Indonesia moved in 1970 to patch up its relations with the Communist powers. Under the direction of Malik, Indonesia reached an agreement with the U.S.S.R. on the repayment of Indonesia's $1.2 billion debt to the Soviet Union (and Eastern Europe) over a 30-year period. The debt had accumulated during the Sukarno era to pay for Communist arms shipments. The Soviet Union acceded to Indonesian requests to delay repayment only after the non-Communist powers had voluntarily reached a similar accord. Malik also made a bid to reopen diplomatic relations with China, sending a memorandum on the subject to Peking through Romania. Indonesia had suspended diplomatic relations with China in 1967 following Indonesian charges that Peking had had a hand in the attempted 1965 coup. Although Peking moderated its propaganda attacks on Indonesia during 1970, the Chinese Communists did not respond to the Indonesian overture.

The Economy. A notable achievement in 1970 was holding inflationary forces in check and restoring confidence in the rupiah. This, in turn, permitted Indonesia to focus increasingly on the country's five-year plan (1969–74), an economic strategy that called for a 5% annual increase in the gross national product (the equivalent of a per capita growth rate of 2.5%).

In a related development foreign investors, attracted by the country's unexploited natural wealth, cheap labour, and political stability, continued to view Indonesia as a promised land. A ten-nation "Indonesian Consortium" composed of Japan and Western countries extended Jakarta an additional $600 million in new loans and grants. A private group of Japanese and Western banks loaned Indonesia $65 million, and the rate of private Japanese and Western investment in Indonesia accelerated with 210 foreign companies having signed investment agreements with Jakarta totaling $1 billion since the fall of Sukarno. The headlong rush of foreign investors, however, generated concern that the groundwork was being unintentionally laid for the nation to become an economic colony of the West. During the year Suharto took cognizance of the question and expressed the hope that "foreign capital will be able to adapt itself to the interests and aims of our development."

Despite the rate of capital investment, the economy remained basically sluggish. Production was almost stagnant, the Green Revolution had failed to materialize despite the introduction of "miracle rice" technology (in 1970 Indonesia imported 842,000 tons of rice, compared with 579,000 tons the year before), and the gross domestic product was barely keeping ahead of population growth. (Ar. C. B.)

ENCYCLOPÆDIA BRITANNICA FILMS. *Indonesia* (*New Nation of Asia*) (1959).

Industrial Design

As in the previous year, what was said about design in 1970 seemed to be of considerably more value than what was actually designed. And in 1970, too, some of the most outspoken critics of design came from within the ranks of the profession itself.

In particular, the two magazines devoted to design that could reasonably claim to approach international scope—*Design* in Britain and *Industrial Design* in the U.S.—on several occasions carried criticisms of the profession that would have been regarded as destructively outspoken had they not come from designers themselves. *Industrial Design* was even moved by the prevailing mood of uncertainty to devote a lengthy article to attempts by people prominent in various areas of U.S. design to answer the awkward question: "Design: what lies ahead?" Predictably, the results were totally inconclusive.

"I think that designers are in love with design instead of being in love with people." This remark came from James Pilditch, of Allied International Designers, during a seminar organized by *Design* as a spin-off from the sixth international congress of the International Council of Societies of Industrial Design (ICSID), which had been held in September 1969. Pilditch went on, "They [designers] have a much too narrow viewpoint, and I would like them to understand the world they live in." His point was picked up and amplified a few months later in a letter in *Industrial Design,* part of which read: "As designers, all we have proved is that fads can make a few people very rich. . . . I believe that a profession oriented toward the glorification of the department store shelf is not destined for a long history."

"The failure . . . is very specific," wrote Peter Hall in *Design*'s special anniversary issue (1949–70), in an article summing up the deficiencies of postwar planning. "It is the failure to predict, and to devise a series of actions based on those predictions. It is the failure to understand the thing that was being planned, and how it was growing and changing." A few months later, the Association of Finnish Designers' seminar in Helsinki took as its theme, "Is Planning Organized Destruction?"

An Eye on Real Life. But if this apparently despairing near nihilism was one of the most striking aspects of design in 1970, it was not—fortunately—altogether typical. Among other things, 1970 was European Conservation Year, and whether or not this event had any direct influence on the design world, there were plenty of signs that not all designers were "in love with design instead of being in love with people." In some cases, designers seemed to be more than usually involved with life outside the studio.

The 1970 International Design Conference at Aspen, Colo., for example, was built around the theme "Environment by Design," and it proved to be at least as wide-ranging as its title suggested. "It turned out to be about almost everything under the sun," one critic commented—including women's liberation, the revolt of the young, and the protection of minority groups. This sounded refreshing, although not necessarily materially constructive, and accorded well with Buckminster Fuller's definition of environment—which was quoted by one delegate early in the proceedings—as "everything but me."

Another impressive involvement of design with current issues came with the link between the UN's designation of 1970 as International Education Year and the choice of the theme of audiovisual education by the fourth congress of the International Council of Graphic Design Associations (ICOGRADA). Even more interesting than this was ICOGRADA's second contribution to International Education Year: an international student project arranged in association with the International Planned Parenthood Foundation, which gave student designers an opportunity to collaborate with health organizations, sex educationalists, and family planning clinics. Another student project, this time organized in the U.S. as part of Armco

COURTESY, COUNCIL OF INDUSTRIAL DESIGN

The designs for these container transporter cranes (above) by Stothert & Pitt Ltd. of Bath, Eng., and the forklift truck (below) by Lancer Boss Ltd. of Leighton Buzzard won for their creators 1970 Council of Industrial Design Awards (capital goods section).

COURTESY, COUNCIL OF INDUSTRIAL DESIGN

Steel Corp.'s student design program, resulted in design proposals and conceptual thinking on the theme "Tomorrow's Leisure." Students from Illinois Institute of Technology went so far into their subject as to prepare a book and a multimedia presentation focusing on leisure as a way of life rather than a commodity, discussing conflicts inhibiting man in his pursuit of leisure, and outlining methods for planning new life styles.

At the full-fledged professional level, the Royal Institute of British Architects, feeling that the British tradition of public service broadcasting, with its great sympathy for minority culture, was in danger of serious dilution of quality, stepped outside its normal role and decided to organize all dissent into a unanimous voice. This was done by providing the initiative and organization for the radical and effective Campaign for Better Broadcasting. In the U.S. a questionnaire issued by the safety committee of the Industrial Designers Society of America touched directly on the problem of the designer's responsibility to society. "Do you feel industrial designers should share more of the burden of safety responsibility in product design?" one question asked. Happily, 72% of the respondents said they did.

Meanwhile, there was an increasing tendency to make the big design centres—design's shop windows—less like impersonal museums that the public feels privileged to enter. Sweden's Malmö Design Centre turned its exhibitions into events and became almost a community centre. Design shows were transformed into what they should always have been—part of people's enjoyment. At one exhibition, children helped themselves to apples from a vast basket and played with the toys on display; mothers with babies sat alongside old people, taking time off from inspecting the products to gossip with friends or to read newspapers. Meanwhile, in a corner, music students played quartets. West Berlin's new International Design Centre also aimed at participation. It did not so much put on a show as ask questions and urge people to think and argue about their surroundings; visitors were invited to record their comments, either on tape or by scribbling on large sheets of coloured paper supported on blackboard easels.

Simultaneously, the museums themselves, or at any rate a few of them, were beginning to unbend a little. In Sweden the Museum of Modern Art in Stockholm had three designers plan a workshop for children at one end of its main galleries. This consisted of a padded room, a section with ceiling-stored musical instruments and theatrical costumes, and a more formal workshop with benches, tools, and all kinds of usable materials. The workshop offered either relaxation from a tour of the exhibits or a self-sufficient area for play and experimentation. In Austria the Museum of the 20th Century in Vienna got into the act with an exhibition called "Live." This showed the work of Haus-Rucker Co., a group of two architects and a painter whose devices aimed to create an artificial environment that would change man's "normal" state of mind. Examples on display included "Giant Billiard," a 50-ft.-square inflatable mattress-like structure on which visitors could bounce, leap, and roll.

Other exhibitions showed wit and ingenuity in throwing new light on apparently mundane matters. The Camden Arts Centre in London turned its attention to food and put on an exhibition of the visual history of eating. The pièce de résistance was a reproduction of Queen Victoria's wedding cake, while other displays included table settings, menus, china, glass, cutlery, clothes, furniture, and cooking utensils. The matter-of-fact business of eating was thus shown as a matter of style worth thinking about.

Open Minded and Open Ended. Product design, too, showed the influence of this open-minded determination to thrust design into the public view. One example involved New York's portable summer festivals, commissioned by the city's Parks, Recreation, and Cultural Affairs Administration. The design team of Michael Lax & Associates had taken advantage of the local tradition of impromptu fairs by designing a truck carrying basic festival apparatus. Eventually, six street festivals were mounted, each of which involved considerable preparation although they were reported to look spontaneous enough. Each one was serviced by a single truck, carefully designed to include aluminum arches (for decoration and to define the festival boundaries), platforms (for stages), spotlights, loudspeakers, back cloths, and a street fountain to be connected to the nearest hydrant. They had the benefit of expert advice from a professional artist-cum-coordinator, backed up by the truck crew and local community organizers.

The knack of borrowing and adapting existing concepts in this way cropped up fairly frequently in a number of different areas, often in surprising forms. British Rail, for example, looked to space technology for the seating suspension on its proposed 150-mph "advanced passenger trains." For a high-speed train with a weight only half that of conventional trains, a new form of high strength-to-weight ratio was essential. Accordingly, BR's industrial design department acquired an astronaut net from the U.S. National Aeronautics and Space Administration and proved that it could be transformed from a two-dimensional to a three-dimensional form. The final result was an experimental net seat. The aluminum frame provided support without forcing the sitter into a fixed position, and the scalloped shape of the net, which allowed the body to be supported without touching the frame itself, isolated the passenger from carriage vibration.

In Switzerland the Zürich firm Intertip AG developed a programmed reading game, "Tipsi," for three- to five-year-old children. The firm based its thinking on the fact that children normally want to start writing after about 20 reading lessons, but are unable to do so because of their lack of dexterity. Realizing, in ad-

dition to this, that typing was becoming almost as important as writing in many highly developed countries, Intertip came up with a game consisting of sets of cards with words and pictures, used in conjunction with an ordinary portable typewriter that was slightly adapted to take coloured key caps and a projector. The colours were coded to match information on the cards, while the projector illuminated the child's typing and projected it onto a screen in the same dimensions as the typeface on the cards. The simplicity of the basic equipment meant that the adaptations could be progressively reduced as the child's efficiency grew, until the projector and other aids were no longer needed.

A different kind of flexibility, this time cutting across normal industrial specialities, came from West Germany. At the Cologne Fair the firm of Bayer chose as its exhibition piece a showboat designed by Verner Panton of Denmark. The display techniques used were original and fascinating in themselves: in the interior was a sequence of womb-like rooms linked by tube-shaped corridors and offering an environment that appealed to all the senses. But the crucial point was that this chemical and textiles firm was showing some of the year's most ingenious ideas in furniture design. In one room the furniture looked like clusters of tufted trees; in another, seating was formed out of a series of curved ridges running across the floor; and so on.

Future Perfect? Perhaps the most interestingly flexible single design of recent years was one of an increasing number in which a virtue was made of the frank admission that sometimes designers cannot accurately predict future needs. Appropriately enough, the design was for a new college of applied arts and technology, at Kitchener, Ont. The college was one of 20 planned in 1965 to provide courses, flexible in both length and content, for high school students not intending to go on to the university and for adults requiring retraining. When design work started, in 1967, there were no educational or curricular guidelines available upon which to base a master plan; even the future as close as five years ahead could not be foreseen. It was therefore essential that building and equipment should not enforce a rigid method of teaching and learning, and the college—Conestoga College—opened with 20 portable buildings, grouped around a central core that contained vital services such as the library, administration, and cafeteria.

The Toronto designers Muller and Stewart were retained to ensure that an interchangeable furniture system for both permanent and portable buildings could be created—a system, moreover, that would not restrict the use of interior space and that was usable while the college continued to expand around it. They devised a scheme that enabled interior spaces to be shaped by staff and students according to their needs and that was flexible enough to remain essentially a background tool for the training program. Three phases of the building operation were completed in 1969. Phases four and five were undergoing further modification in the light of experience. The emphasis was to be on building up library resources and other communications media in order to distribute knowledge to the remoter parts of the area served by the college. Something like the ultimate in flexibility would eventually be achieved as students began to find the college coming to them.

Other designers devoted themselves to clearing up some of the chaos caused by their less gifted predecessors. In particular, the U.S. designer Henry Dreyfuss,

COURTESY, GEORGE KOVACS

The "Cobra" high intensity lamp, designed by Angelo Lelii of Italy, is a 24-in.-tall polished chrome sculpture containing a magnetized metal ball that swivels to light paintings and sculpture.

allegedly in retirement, began what was likely to be a lengthy process of rationalization. He undertook the compilation of an international dictionary of symbols, which he hoped would eventually become the basis of a major reorganization of the hundreds of thousands of individual symbols in existence—not to mention the several different, allegedly international, symbol agreements that in the past had given rise to conflicting and confusing sign languages.

Finally, an Italian designer offered what seemed to be an opportunity to escape from such a bewildering world. The opportunity came in the form of—a chair. But Gianfranco Fini's "Monade" chair, made by Dimensione of Rome, offered a great deal more than just something to sit on. The armrests contained the following aids to luxurious relaxation: telephone, adjustable reading lamp, radio and stereo speakers, receptacles for glasses, and an ashtray. Moreover, Fini's spherical design had one really special refinement; when the outside world utterly overwhelmed the occupant, he could close the hood and peer at it through a safe barrier of coloured plastic.   (DE. C.)

See also Industrial Review.

Industrial Review

The growth of industrial activity, which after a temporary slowdown in 1967 was resumed in 1968, continued into 1969; the advance achieved was about 7%, comparable to the progress made in 1968. But whereas progress was uninterrupted during 1968, the pattern was different in 1969; industrial output in the Western world started at a high level at the beginning of the year and the rate of expansion slowed down considerably during its course. This was mainly due to developments in North America, which accounted for almost half of world output (without the Soviet bloc and China). There, industrial activity flattened off toward the middle of 1969 and actually fell in the later part of the year. These were important developments for both the U.S. and the world economy which are not reflected by the average annual figures in Table I. In Europe production continued to expand, although some slowdown toward the very end of the year could not be avoided, due partly to the reaction to the U.S. recession, and partly to other factors.

The same trends continued during 1970: the level of output was further reduced in the U.S., but growth in Europe persisted. The total of world industrial output thus remained on an upward trend; the rate of expansion, however, lagged behind that in 1969.

Output in 1969 advanced almost at the same rate in both the less industrialized and the developed industrial countries. The progress in the centrally planned economies of the U.S.S.R. and Eastern Europe was also of the same order.

In the United States industrial production fell in each of the last five months of 1969 and continued on this trend, with minor interruptions until mid-1970, when the level of industrial activity was about 4% lower than a year earlier. This slowing down produced a marked change in the combined output of industrial countries; during the year ended mid-1969 their total industrial production rose about 9% but in the second half of 1969 the annual growth rate was more than halved, largely because of the decline in the U.S. The industrial recession in the U.S. was mainly attributable to the nation's restrictive monetary measures; though principally designed to restrain price

inflation, they had much more impact on the volume of output. A number of industries were hard hit, automobiles being the most noteworthy case. On the whole, appreciable idle capacity began emerging by the end of 1969. There was a mild relaxation of monetary policy in the second half of 1970, but a strike at General Motors and other factors brought industrial production in November to its lowest point since late 1967. The level of activity of Canadian industry, always to some extent dependent on the fortunes of the U.S. economy, reflected the uncertainties across the border; it fell during 1969, and continued to do so in 1970.

In the United Kingdom also, industry began showing signs of near stagnation after the early part of 1969, and this situation did not change until mid-1970. The post-devaluation deflationary measures restricted domestic demand, and industry was further hampered by a multitude of strikes. Exports were the most dynamic element in demand, but they could not entirely balance the stagnation in other sectors.

In continental Western Europe, as in Japan, capacity rather than demand limited the growth of production. West German industry enjoyed a boom. All sectors of demand contributed to the increase, which amounted to about one-seventh over the previous year's level. Output then leveled off during 1970, mainly due to capacity limitations. West German industry was successful in export markets; as a result, it became in 1969 the world's largest supplier of manufactured products, overtaking the U.S.; this leading role was retained in the first half of 1970, despite the revaluation of the mark in October 1969.

In France industry was operating near the ceiling

Table I. Index Numbers of World Production, Employment, and Productivity in Manufacturing Industries
1963 = 100

Area	Relative importance 1963	Relative importance 1969	Production 1967	Production 1968	Production 1969	Employment 1967	Employment 1968	Employment 1969	Productivity* 1967	Productivity* 1968	Productivity* 1969
World†	1,000	1,000	127	136	145	...	...	...	...	...	...
Industrialized countries	876	874	127	135	145	...	...	...	...	...	...
Less industrialized countries	124	126	128	138	148	...	...	...	...	...	...
North America‡	480	460	128	134	139	...	...	...	...	...	...
Canada	28	28	129	135	143	116	115	118	111	117	121
United States	452	432	128	134	139	114	116	118	112	116	118
Latin America§	49	49	128	137	146	...	...	...	...	...	...
Mexico	8	5	146	159	183	...	...	...	...	...	...
East and Southeast Asia‖	88	120	150	173	198	...	...	...	...	...	...
India	16	14	115	121	129	...	...	...	...	...	...
Japan	55	86	164	193	227	111	111	114	148	174	199
Pakistan	3	3	141	151	...	...	...	...	...	...	...
Europe¶	350	338	119	128	140	...	...	...	...	...	...
Austria	7	7	119	129	143	96	95	97	124	136	147
Belgium	11	10	115	123	136	101	99	...	114	124	...
Finland	4	4	125	133	145	103	102	...	121	130	...
France	51	50	121	128	143	98	96	98	123	133	146
Germany, West	89	90	115	129	147	97	98	102	119	132	144
Greece	2	2	141	151	168	109	108	112	129	140	150
Ireland	1	1	125	139	147	104	106	113	120	131	130
Italy	36	35	128	136	141	99	100	104	129	136	136
Netherlands	12	13	126	138	152	98	97	98	129	142	155
Norway	4	4	125	129	136	106	105	107	118	123	127
Portugal	2	2	135	143	154	...	...	...	...	...	...
Sweden	14	14	128	135	146	98	95	97	131	142	151
United Kingdom	73	63	114	121	126	100	99	100	114	122	126
Yugoslavia	13	14	134	142	159	111	110	114	121	129	139
Rest of the world◊	33	...	...	...	...	...	...	...	...	...	...
Australia	14	13	120	129	137	111	114	117	108	113	...
South Africa	5	5	132	137	151	134	138	147	99	99	103
Centrally planned economies◦	...	...	140	152	163	...	...	...	...	...	...

*This is 100 times the production index divided by the employment index, giving a rough indication of changes in output per person employed.
†Excluding Albania, Bulgaria, China, Czechoslovakia, East Germany, Hungary, Mongolia, North Korea, North Vietnam, Poland, Romania, and the U.S.S.R.
‡Canada and the United States.
§South and Central America (including Mexico) and the Caribbean islands.
‖Afghanistan, Brunei, Burma, Ceylon, Hong Kong, India, Indonesia, Iran, Japan, Malaysia, Pakistan, Philippines, South Korea, South Vietnam, Taiwan, Thailand, and Singapore.
¶Excluding Albania, Bulgaria, Czechoslovakia, East Germany, Hungary, Poland, Romania, and the U.S.S.R.
◊Africa, the Middle East, and Oceania.
◦These are not included in the above world total, and consist of Albania, Bulgaria, Czechoslovakia, East Germany, Hungary, Poland, Romania, and the U.S.S.R.
Sources: UN *Monthly Bulletin of Statistics;* U.K. National Institute of Economic and Social Research, *Economic Review.*

Chassis of the last Ford
built in Texas moves
down the assembly line
at the plant in Dallas.
The plant was closed
after 45 years
of operation
because of unfavourable
economic factors.

UPI COMPIX

of capacity in 1969 and made rapid advances; during 1970 some slackening occurred. Industrial export performance improved considerably after the devaluation of the franc in August 1969.

Italian industry was seriously hit by major strikes. During the first eight months of 1969 industrial production was 9% higher than a year earlier, but in the next three it was considerably lower because of the strikes. These continued into 1970, taking a political rather than an industrial character, and had a disruptive impact on industrial development. They also affected export deliveries.

Boom conditions in West Germany and France helped to maintain a fast rate of progress in the Benelux countries. In both Belgium and the Netherlands the output of manufacturing industries was about one-tenth higher in 1969 than a year earlier.

In the smaller European countries, growth of manufacturing activity continued rapidly; the excess over the previous year was 10% or more in Austria, Switzerland, Yugoslavia, and Greece, only a little lower in Sweden and Finland, and about 5–6% in most other countries.

Japanese manufacturing industry followed the path of unprecedented expansion shown in previous years. The domestic element of demand grew strongly in 1969, and exporters were consistently successful in world markets; in 1969 Japan sent overseas about one-ninth of all the manufactured exports of the main industrial countries, and its share equalled that of the U.K.

Although the overall increase of manufacturing activity in the less industrialized countries in 1969 was relatively high, India, the largest of them, had a somewhat lower rate of expansion (6½% over 1968). The growth of manufacturing output in Australia was 6%, whereas South African industry increased production by one-tenth.

Productivity, measured by output per man-hour in manufacturing, continued to grow. In West Germany and the U.K. it lagged somewhat behind the spectacular improvements in 1968, and in Italy remained rather low because of the disturbing effects of strikes.

In the U.S.S.R. industrial output rose 8%, the same rate as in 1968. The other Eastern European countries showed a sharp contrast in industrial growth during 1969: Bulgaria, Poland, and Romania expanded by about 10%, whereas Czechoslovakia and Hungary did so more slowly, by about 2–3%. The reasons, however, were different, namely political troubles in Czechoslovakia, and the transition to a new system of economic management in Hungary. (G. F. R.)

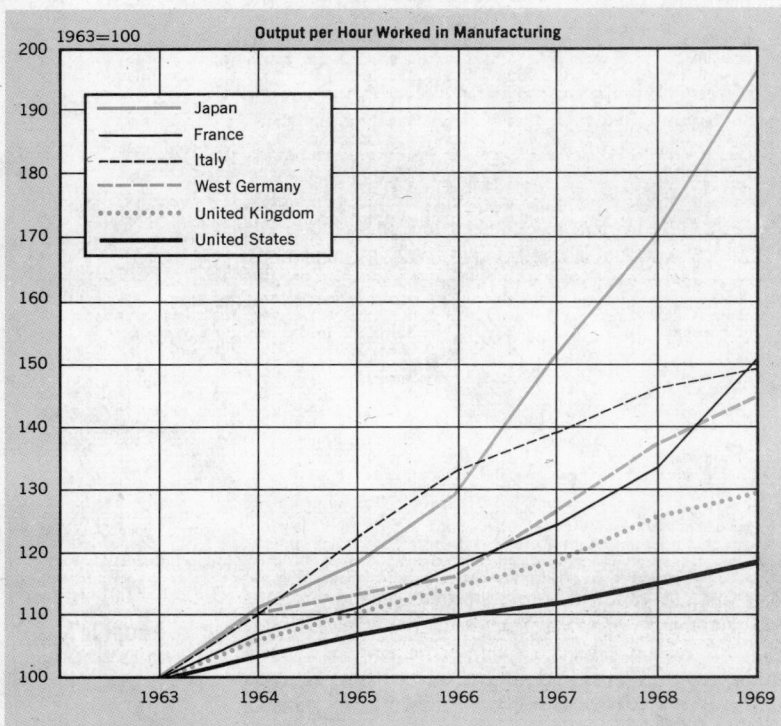

Source: National Institute of Economic and Social Research, *Economic Review.*

Table II. Industrial Production in the U.S.S.R. and Eastern Europe
1963 = 100

Country	1967	1968	1969
Bulgaria	162	181	199
Czechoslovakia	130	137	141
Germany, East	129	136	...
Hungary	134	141	144
Poland	139	152	167
Romania	164	184	205
U.S.S.R.	140	152	164

Source: UN *Monthly Bulletin of Statistics.*

AEROSPACE

Distinctly less sure of its future than in the previous five years, the world's aerospace industry entered into the general recessional trend that was apparent throughout the Western world. Basically this was due to the scarcity of money from both air transport operators and governments. Air transport operators had a particularly poor financial year, largely because of heavy investment costs and interest charges on new equipment.

Among the major companies that felt the chill wind of financial problems was Lockheed, which had a considerable liquidity problem because of contract payments frozen on the Cheyenne helicopter program and because of difficulties with the huge C-5A transport plane. Boeing and McDonnell Douglas were among U.S. manufacturers that cut back on design and manufacturing staff during the year, creating in the process a considerable number of unemployed aerospace technicians. In the U.K. Rolls-Royce had trouble with its finances, which were strained by the need to spend much more on developing the RB.211 engine for the Lockheed TriStar (L-1011) than had been originally scheduled. Two other British airframe manufacturers went into liquidation, Handley Page and Beagle Aircraft.

Although in some cases sales rose, the net earnings of the major U.S. companies were considerably lower, and the number of personnel employed in the industry decreased during the year from 1,295,000 to approximately 1,170,000. New defense equipment for which U.S. government appropriations were gained included $175.1 million for the F-15 air superiority fighter, the prime contract for which was won by McDonnell Douglas. Grumman won the $441.5 million contract to perform the research and development on the F-14 fighter, including the manufacture of nine prototypes. Lockheed obtained $872.6 million (including $225 million overrun on previous years) for the C-5A program, and General Dynamics won an additional $857.2 million for the F-111 project, which was still continuing despite increasing pressure to stop it because of the number of accidents that such planes had suffered.

At the beginning of the year U.S. industry had an order book of 1,234 civil aircraft valued at $8.6 billion. Of these, 608 were commercial transport aircraft worth $8.1 billion, most of the remaining 626 units being for the use of businessmen.

International collaboration in the military field continued to grow, one particularly new aspect being the licensing of the largest U.S. manufacturer, McDonnell Douglas, to make the British Hawker Siddeley Harrier for the U.S. Marine Corps. Ferranti and Northrop also concluded a license agreement for the latter to make the inertial navigation/attack system for the U.S. Harriers, a typical example of the way in which international collaboration was spreading through the entire aircraft systems field.

In other respects the year was notable for three developments in commercial aviation. The first involved the introduction to commercial service of the Boeing 747 and the first flights of the McDonnell Douglas DC-10 and Lockheed TriStar. All three aircraft had the "new-look" wide-bodied fuselage, which was clearly to become an important feature in airline economics because of the greater passenger and freight capacity that it offered for a given aircraft size. The second development was an upsurge in both the U.S. and Europe of the short-haul vertical and short takeoff and landing airliner (V/STOL) concept. The third development was the U.S. government's delay in giving a final approval to a U.S. supersonic transport (SST). It thus appeared that while the British and French Concorde was attaining Mach 2 in test flights, the U.S. was between three to five years behind in civil SST achievement.

The Boeing 747 seemed to have an unusually large number of technical problems following its entry into service. Before the end of its first year its Pratt & Whitney engines were being modified to correct a tendency to "ovalize," i.e., stretch out of true circular shape, thus reducing tolerances between high-speed turbine blades and the casing. It was also found that starting procedures and the use of reverse thrust entailed careful control procedures, and the airlines realized that the step forward in engine technology to the very-large-diameter front-fan high-bypass-ratio designs had not been as smooth as anticipated.

In Europe controversy continued to rage over the two rival "airbus" designs. The French and German governments were still supporting the A-300B, to be built jointly by SNIAS (a new nationalized French airframe company formed by a merger of Sud Aviation, Nord, and Sereb), Dornier, and Hawker Siddeley. The British government was also under strong pressure, helped by political motives arising from Common Market negotiations, to rejoin the A-300B partnership. But the British Aircraft Corp. fielded a strong case for the all-British, Rolls-Royce-powered, Three-eleven airbus. In December the government announced that it would not back either project.

Almost at the other end of the scale, the local short-haul market was rapidly recognizing the advantages of V/STOL aircraft. The West German government launched a design competition in late 1969 which produced five different designs from the three national airframe companies, all with imported engines. Lockheed-Georgia said that it was studying a 100-passenger V/STOL transport that was lighter in weight than any of the West German proposals, and Britain's Hawker Siddeley also announced its designs for a 100-seater.

The SNIAS-BAC Concorde SST prototypes were reportedly achieving design performance during test flying from bases in both Britain and France. Both aircraft had flown at twice the speed of sound, and both had had engine-intake modifications and were fitted with uprated Olympus 593-3B engines. The Soviet Tu-144, in appearance almost identical to Concorde, was also being intensively test-flown, and reports indicated that this SST might see commercial service during 1972.

Public opinion appeared to harden against excessive noise from aircraft of all kinds and the SST sonic boom in particular. There was also a growing movement which complained of the atmospheric pollution by aircraft that deliberately or inadvertently dumped fuel overboard in flight. The money being spent on research into these problems began to be a significant proportion of the research and development funding of the manufacturers. (J. B. Be.)

AUTOMOBILES

Three major preoccupations were shared in varying degrees by vehicle manufacturers of all nationalities during 1970; these were concerned with safety regulations, exhaust gas pollutants, and product quality. Industrial unrest, which interrupted production at intervals in the plants of the vehicle makers and the suppliers of components in the U.K., Italy, the U.S., and other

manufacturing countries, added materially to the problem of quality control as well as having a more obvious impact upon output and cost. Other recurring factors, such as increases in wages and material costs, caused general advances in the prices of passenger cars and commercial vehicles. Few countries other than West Germany and Japan recorded any substantial increase in production figures for the first half of 1970.

U.S. safety standards, both present and projected, continued to set the pace and pattern for legislation in European countries and elsewhere. A decision to share automotive safety technology with the rest of the Western world was announced by the U.S. Department of Transportation in May. The first specific example of this policy was a conference, held in Michigan, organized under the auspices of the NATO Committee for the Challenges of Modern Society. Representatives from America, Europe, and Japan discussed the so-called "air-bag" system of passive restraint for automobile passengers, in which sudden deceleration of the vehicle triggers the rapid inflation of a cushion by gas or air stored at high pressure. A major advantage was that it required no prior action by the car occupants; surveys had shown that no more than 25% used their seat belts. However, the rapid rate at which the bag had to be inflated involved some formidable hazards and technical difficulties.

Early in the year the drive to reduce the harmful constituents present in motor vehicle exhaust gases was given a new direction when Edward N. Cole, president of General Motors Corp., called for the elimination of the lead-based additives used in gasoline for many years to improve its octane rating, i.e., antiknock properties. He claimed that a "crash" program of engineering development would make it possible for General Motors to introduce in its 1971 model lines low-compression engines that could run satisfactorily on low-octane, lead-free gasolines —a program that was, in fact, accomplished. Ford Motor Co. and Chrysler Corp. programmed a more gradual transition to low-compression engines.

Increasing difficulties were encountered by engine designers in trying to meet the proposals of the U.S. Department of Health, Education, and Welfare. These would require further drastic reductions in the permitted emissions of unburned hydrocarbons and carbon monoxide with new and additional restrictions on oxides of nitrogen and particulate matter. Whether lead additives as such were harmful to health was debatable, but the engineers claimed that catalytic afterburners would be needed to destroy the other pollutants, and that lead would seriously reduce the active life of the costly metals used in these devices. The motor industry proposals presented the petroleum industry with many difficult problems, not the least of which was the need to continue to supply high-octane lead gasoline for the millions of cars with high-compression engines already in use. Nevertheless, programs for the progressive phasing out of lead were initiated by the major petroleum companies, and both lead-free and low-lead gasolines became available to the pumps by the fall.

In Europe, modest recommendations for limiting the amounts of carbon monoxide and unburned hydrocarbons in exhaust gases already existed, and the exhaust pollution

COURTESY, FORD MOTOR COMPANY

COURTESY, VOLKSWAGEN OF AMERICA, INC.

COURTESY, GENERAL MOTORS CORP.

COURTESY, AMERICAN MOTORS CORP.

New subcompact automobiles introduced during 1970 included the Ford Pinto (top), the Volkswagen K.70, which features front-wheel drive (above right), the American Motors Gremlin (above), and the Chevrolet Vega (right).

problem was not considered so serious as in the U.S. Another argument against following U.S. policy with regard to lead was the sacrifice in the power and economy involved in the consequent reduction of compression, which would be felt acutely by users of small engines, using heavily taxed gasolines. European governments were seriously endeavouring to reach agreement among themselves on exhaust emissions (as well as safety standards), and negotiations involving many countries were inevitably protracted. The danger that unilateral legislation could form a serious barrier to international trade was stressed by several leaders of the European motor industry.

Of outstanding interest among the new U.S. cars announced in August were the Chevrolet Vega 2300 and Ford Pinto, each backed by manufacturing facilities capable of producing 400,000 such cars a year. Smaller than the "compacts" introduced a

decade earlier, the new models were intended to challenge the increasing share of the market taken by small cars imported into the U.S.; this share was expected to reach 13% in 1970. The Pinto was close to West Germany's Volkswagen Beetle in length and wheelbase, though wider, but the Vega was significantly larger in all basic dimensions. Both cars showed the influence of current European design trends, notably in their use of four-cylinder engines with belt-driven overhead camshafts.

The Vega engine was unique in having an aluminum cylinder block without the usual iron liners; new materials and surface treatments were developed that enabled aluminum pistons to run directly in the block, with savings in weight and cost. Ford announced that the Pinto engine and some other components would be made in its British and West German plants and shipped to U.S. assembly lines. American Motors

entered the small car arena in February with the Gremlin, using an existing six-cylinder engine. This was followed in the same month by Chrysler's new Avenger in the U.K. which, as was announced later, would be imported for sale in the U.S. under the name Cricket. Chrysler's Dodge division introduced the Colt, made in Japan.

Of the many larger U.S. cars introduced in September, Chrysler's Plymouth sport coupé and Buick's new Riviera coupé had particularly attractive lines. In the latter car a novel electronic power control system called the Max Trac, offered as an option, "sensed" the onset of wheelspin and automatically reduced engine power until the tires gripped. The Chevrolet Camaro and Pontiac Firebird were restyled in February and carried through with little change.

The most original of the new cars introduced in Europe during 1970 were the Citroën-Maserati SM sports model, with a V-6 engine and novel speed-sensitive power-assisted steering system, and the Citroën GS sedan, which was introduced at the Paris Show in October. Of about the same over-all size as the Volkswagen Beetle, the GS had an attractively styled fastback sedan body, shaped for low air resistance, a four-cylinder air-cooled engine driving the front wheels, and self-leveling hydropneumatic suspension. Volkswagen's principal exhibit at the Paris show was its entirely new experimental K.70 model, differing from all other Volkswagens in having a water-cooled engine and front-wheel drive.

Several new British models were introduced in the second half of the year. British Leyland was first with a new Triumph GT convertible, named the Stag, equipped with a new overhead-camshaft V-8 engine. This was followed by the Triumph 1500, which was a simplified rear-drive version of the front-drive 1300 model. The versatile four-wheel-drive Land Rover chassis, redesigned and powered by a 3.5-litre V-8 engine, was the basis for a new Range Rover station wagon (estate car).

In October, Ford launched a new Cortina model in the U.K. and a new Taunus in West Germany; each car made use of the Pinto engine, which would be manufactured at Ford plants in both countries. The use of common components extended to many chassis and body parts, and to the configuration, which was conventional.

The Vauxhall Viva, designed and made by General Motors' British subsidiary, acquired entirely new sedan and station wagon bodies, notable for improved quietness and comfort, but there were few mechanical changes. An outstanding new model from Opel was the Manta, a two-door high-performance coupé, appropriately described as "a sports car for the family," with enough rear-seat space to accommodate children in comfort. General Motors announced far-reaching organizational changes for its overseas division in October, directed toward a closer association between the Vauxhall and Opel companies in management and model programs; the company also announced its intention to establish European headquarters in London. In November General Motors announced a deal by which it would acquire manufacturing rights for the Wankel rotary engine from Audi-NSU for $50 million.

The importance of the station wagon was emphasized by new models of this type that were introduced in the fall by Renault, Peugeot, and Fiat. In August the French government authorized Fiat to increase its shareholding in Citroën to 49%, and arrangements were made to market the small front-drive Autobianchi III through Citroën dealers in France. Another important commercial development was an agreement for

Table III. Production and Exports of Motor Vehicles by the Principal Producing Countries

In 000 units

Country	1967 Passenger cars	1967 Commercial vehicles	1968 Passenger cars	1968 Commercial vehicles	1969 Passenger cars	1969 Commercial vehicles
Production						
United States	7,436.7	1,539.4	8,848.6	1,971.8	8,224.3	1,980.7
Germany, West	2,295.7	186.6	2,862.2	244.8	3,312.5	290.0
France	1,776.5	233.2	1,833.0	242.6	2,168.5	290.6
United Kingdom	1,552.1	385.1	1,815.9	409.3	1,717.8	465.7
Japan	1,375.8	1,770.7	2,055.8	2,030.0	2,611.5	2,062.8
Italy	1,439.2	103.5	1,544.9	118.7	1,477.3	185.6
Canada	720.8	226.4	900.9	279.1	1,035.5	317.4
Australia	313.6	76.5	345.0	73.4	371.1	80.7
Sweden	194.0	20.6	223.3	21.4	242.9	27.8
U.S.S.R.*	728.8		801.0		293.6	974.1
Other countries*	1,313.5		1,529.3		1,830	
World total	23,688.7		28,151.0		29,900	
Exports						
Germany, West	1,350.8	104.8	1,801.6	145.6	1,875.1	164.3
United Kingdom	502.6	135.2	676.6	142.0	771.6	181.2
France	547.0	42.7	628.6	47.5	787.5	56.6
Italy	404.4	22.5	557.7	29.5	594.6	35.5
United States	280.6†	82.6†	330.5	92.2	333.4	103.5
Sweden	123.0	15.4	138.8	15.4	141.8	18.8
Japan	223.5	138.8	406.3	206.2	560.4	297.6
Canada	342.4	111.8	522.1	155.0	714.5	409.7

*A reliable breakdown between cars and commercial vehicles was not available for the U.S.S.R. until 1969 and is still not available for "Other countries."
†Excludes unassembled vehicles now recorded only by value.
Source: British Society of Motor Manufacturers and Traders, *The Motor Industry of Great Britain.*

a coordinated development program reached by Dunlop and Pirelli, each company acquiring a capital share in the other.

During the year both Fiat and Renault won extensive contracts for the provision of automobile manufacturing facilities in the U.S.S.R. The growth of Japan's domestic car market continued to be a major factor in the sustained increase in production numbers. Toyo Kogyo (Mazda) increased its output of the controversial Wankel rotary engine that was fitted to about one-sixth of its total car production. A somewhat enlarged version of the engine was developed for its new Capella model RX2. Honda concentrated all its productive capacity on the front-drive 1300 model, with its novel four-cylinder air-cooled power unit, and added an automatic transmission option. Nissan, following the European trend, widened the Datsun range with a high-performance GX model. A new Toyota Corona "1600" was the first Japanese car to offer an electronically controlled automatic transmission.

(M. PL.)

BUILDING AND CONSTRUCTION

During the first seven months of 1970 the value of new construction in the United States was $49,651,000,000, according to the U.S. Department of Commerce. On a seasonally adjusted annual basis this was equal to $89,746,000,000. Compared with the first seven months of 1969, the dollar volume of construction was down approximately 2%. On a constant dollar basis, the physical volume of new construction declined by 8%.

While construction in the U.S. had reached a record level of dollar expenditure in 1969, the industry had been beset with problems. In 1969 the total dollar outlay for construction had increased 8% over the preceding year and equaled the 8% increase in the gross national product. Measured on a constant dollar basis, however, the physical volume of new construction was at about the same level as in 1968, while on this same constant dollar basis the gross national product had increased about 3%. Thus, the data revealed that the inflationary pressures in the construction industry were greater than those in the general economy.

Inflationary problems continued into 1970. In July the construction composite cost index, published monthly by the U.S. Department of Commerce, stood at 151 (1957–59 = 100). It had been 143 in July 1969 and 132 in July 1968. The wholesale price index of all construction materials had moved up 3%, while the average weekly earnings of construction workers had increased 8% during the 12-month period ended July 31, 1970. The other element in construction cost, construction financing, had also moved to new record high levels of cost during 1969, and these conditions had continued into 1970.

During the first seven months of 1970, the dollar outlays for private construction were down 1% while those for public construction were down 5% compared with the same period in 1969. On this same comparative basis, the outlays for all nonfarm residential buildings were down 11%, while those for new housing units were down 15%. In the private sector, the dollar expenditures for construction of nonresidential buildings showed a gain during the first seven months of 1970 over the same period of 1969. While the outlays for industrial buildings declined 2%, the expenditures for commercial buildings rose 11% and those for telephone and telegraph utilities were up 36%. On the same basis, the expenditures for educational buildings were down 14%, while those for hospital and institu-

COURTESY, BROOKHAVEN NATIONAL LABORATORY

Specimens of new concrete polymers are placed in an infrared oven for drying. The new concrete shows great improvement in such physical properties as strength, durability, and freeze-thaw resistance.

tional buildings increased 28%. In the public sector, while, as noted, overall expenditures were down, the changes in expenditures for individual types of construction were not uniform. For example, while the outlays for all types of public buildings combined declined 10%, those for hospitals rose 15%.

In Canada, the outlook for economic growth in 1970 was closely linked to economic developments in the U.S. It was anticipated that there would be a slower rate of growth in output, with the forecast being around 3%. Expenditures for housing were expected to provide a strong stimulus to production because of the pent-up demand for housing and the expected easing of credit.

In Western Europe, combined national outputs in 1969 were reported by the British *National Institute Economic Review* to have been slightly higher than anticipated due to the high levels of output in France and West Germany. In France, industry operated near capacity in 1969, with an increase in output over 1968 of about 8.5%. The forecast for 1970 was an increase of 5%. In Great Britain capital investment in 1969 showed little gain as a result of the 8.5% drop in the investment in dwellings. Private spending for dwellings declined 14%, while public investment also fell. The forecast for 1970 was that public investment in dwellings would continue to decline about 4.5%. On the other hand, it was expected that private investment in that area would rise by about 3.5%. The monthly average number of dwelling units completed in 1969 was 31,527. This was lower than the averages for 1967 and 1968, and it appeared that the average number completed in 1970 would be even lower.

The growth in industrial output in Japan continued throughout 1969 and was expected to continue in 1970. Housing expenditures were expected to rise faster in 1970, and government spending would continue at higher levels. The monthly average number of construction starts was larger in 1970 than in 1969. It appeared, however, that the real growth in national output would not be as high in 1970 as in 1969.

(C. C. O.)

CHEMICALS

The chemical industry moved into the 1970s full of promise for continued growth but also beset with problems and challenges. The U.S. industry, according to the Department of Commerce, increased its value of shipments from $46,465,000,000 in 1968 to $48,698,000,000 in 1969, a 4.8% increase. For the first six months of 1970, shipments totaled $25,434,000,000, a gain of 3.3% over the first six months of 1969. The Federal Reserve index of chemical production rose from 221.7 in 1968 (1957–59 = 100) to 239 in 1969. During the first six months of 1970, it hit a high of 244.4 (seasonally adjusted) in April and then slipped to 240 in June. The growth rates, considerably below those to which the industry had become accustomed, were in large measure a reflection of the general slowdown in the economy.

One encouraging sign for the industry was the trend of chemical prices. Despite inflationary pressures for several years, chemical prices had been falling steadily, partly because of more efficient processing and partly because of overcapacity and increased competition in some important product lines. The combination of higher costs and lower prices had proved an effective damper on profit margins. There were indications during the first half of 1970, however, that the long-term price decline had been halted and reversed. The U.S. Department of Labor's Index of Wholesale Chemical Prices, which had been 98.2 (1957–59 = 100) for 1968 and 98.3 for 1969, climbed steadily during the first half of 1970, reaching 100.9 in June.

There were exceptions to the trend, however. The index for agricultural chemicals, for example, fell from 99.6 in 1968 to 89.8 in 1969 and showed only marginal improvement in the first half of 1970, hitting 91 in June. The fertilizer industry, which makes up an important part of the entire agricultural chemicals field, was particularly hard hit. A survey by the Fertilizer Institute showed that, with about half the industry reporting, producers of primary nutrients (nitrogen, phosphorus, and potassium) lost $70 million in 1969 on sales of $1.6 billion. Indications were that the industry as a whole lost $100 million. But signs for 1970 were more encouraging, said the Institute. Sales for the full year were expected to be higher, and there appeared to be a noticeable improvement in prices.

The chemical industries in other industrialized non-Communist countries recorded some impressive growth rates. Preliminary figures for West Germany indicated chemical sales in 1969 would reach $11.5 billion, at least a 10% rise over 1968. And during the first half of 1970, sales activity increased 10–15%; signs pointed to a 10% increase for the year as a whole. The industry was continuing to expand and modernize at a record pace. It devoted $1.1 billion to capital expenditures in 1969 and was expected to match or surpass that in 1970. Profits were not going up at the same rate as sales, however. Inflationary forces (higher wages, interest rates, and construction costs) were the cause. Also contributing to lower profit margins was the revaluation of the mark in October 1969. This effectively raised the prices of West Germany's chemical exports about 5%; thus, in order to keep competitive, West German chemical companies had to lower prices on exported chemicals.

The Japanese chemical industry continued to grow at a remarkable rate. Chemical sales in 1969 were estimated at $9.4 billion and were expected to approach $11 billion in 1970. Investment was at a high level too. For the fiscal year 1969 (starting in April), the Ministry of International Trade and Industry (MITI) had scheduled an outlay of $1,880,000,000, a 30% increase over 1968. For fiscal 1970, it was looking for a $1,390,000,000 expenditure.

In the United Kingdom, chemical production grew approximately 7% in 1969. Chemical sales registered a comparable increase to hit an estimated $7.6 billion. Profits, which had risen 14% in 1968, were only 8% higher in 1969. The reasons for this decline were higher material costs, higher interest rates, and higher corporate taxes. Chemical exports were, according to preliminary figures, $1.6 billion in 1969. Imports, which had soared 26.4% in 1968, were estimated at $1,090,000,000 in 1969, a 10% increase. British chemical companies were looking toward continued growth in 1970 and 1971 but at a somewhat reduced rate.

The French chemical industry, which had been subject to some major mergers and realignments, posted an enviable record in 1969. Early indications were that production increased 14% and that sales topped $7 billion. This would be the largest growth for the industry since 1960 and appreciably better than the 8.5% increase expected by government planners. French chemical men feared a slowdown during the second half of 1970 in view of the deterioration of the U.S. economy, but it had not materialized well into the third quarter. Leading French chemical makers reported sales increases ranging between 5 and 25% for the first half of 1970 and were also optimistic about second-half prospects. The government remained concerned about long-range prospects, however, and the country's sixth five-year plan (1971–75) called for more consolidations in the fragmented chemical industry.

Chemical companies in industrialized nations throughout the world were beset with a number of problems, epitomized by those the U.S. chemical industry was facing. The troubles for the most part centred on the use of chemicals and their possible effect upon the environment and health. The discovery that the synthetic sweetener cyclamate could cause cancer in rats when injected in massive doses led to the banning of that product in most of its applications. It caused, moreover, a closer scrutiny of chemicals and other additives on the U.S. Food and Drug Administration's GRAS (generally recognized as safe) list. The U.S. Department of Agriculture canceled permission for use of the potent insecticide DDT in control of pests on shade trees, tobacco, lawns and gardens, and wetlands. Six DDT producers challenged the move, however, and during the first three quarters of 1970, they were making and selling the product pending the outcome of statutory proceedings. But state and federal authorities were holding hearings and considering tighter restrictions on DDT and other persistent insecticides (i.e., ones that do not break down into harmless products rapidly).

The use of phosphates in detergents was another centre of controversy. Phosphates played an important role in the composition of synthetic detergents by sequestering the calcium and magnesium ions that make water "hard" and preventing these elements from interfering with the function of the active ingredient. But a number of environmentalists contended that phosphates, being a primary plant nutrient, were causing eutrophication (excessive algae growth) in lakes and streams. Phosphate makers claimed that the amount of phosphates contributed to water bodies by other sources was more than enough to cause eutrophication and that, in effect, removing phosphates from detergents would not accomplish the desired cleaning effect. Nevertheless, U.S. Rep. Henry Reuss (Dem., Wis.), chairman of a congressional subcommittee on conservation and natural resources, was favouring a bill that would ban the use of phosphates in detergents by 1972. Detergent makers, thus, were reducing the amounts of phosphate in their products and searching for substitute materials.

The presence of mercury in fish in some lakes caused considerable concern about the mercury discharged by those who produced caustic soda and chlorine by means of mercury cells. Restrictions that would sharply reduce—perhaps to zero—the allowable discharge of mercury were under consideration. Dow Chemical Corp., the leading producer of chlorine and caustic soda, said it would phase out mercury cells in favour of diaphragm cells, which did not employ mercury. The Chlorine Institute said that it would cost the industry $450 million for a complete changeover to diaphragm cells.

The chemical industry in the U.S. spent $140 million on pollution control equipment in its capital spending for 1969 and planned $226 million for the same purpose in 1970. And it seemed in a position to make important contributions toward improving the environment. One of the big moves in 1970, for example, was the decision by automotive makers and petroleum companies to reduce or eliminate the use of lead in gasoline (see *Automobiles,* above).

(D. P. B.)

ELECTRICAL

The 1970s opened with the expansion of the larger multiproduct companies across national frontiers. Westinghouse Electric Corp. of the U.S. acquired a majority stake in Ateliers de Constructions Électriques de Charleroi (ACEC), Belgium. With products ranging from generators through domestic appliances to electronic capital goods, ACEC, even with an annual turnover of nearly $200 million, found it difficult to remain competitive in world markets. The deal with Westinghouse would give ACEC the opportunity to be more competitive with groups such as General Electric Co.-English Electric of Britain, Siemens of West Germany, Compagnie Générale d'Électricité-Thomson-Brandt of France, and Philips of the Netherlands, and would enable Westinghouse to make its European activities more profitable and effective.

Westinghouse was eager to exploit the expanding European market for nuclear reactors. The Economic Commission for Europe (ECE) was, however, opposed to mergers between European and U.S. nuclear power and electrical engineering companies, and a prior bid by Westinghouse to take over Jeumont-Schneider was vetoed by the French government. The Belgian government, on the other hand, could not see a link between ACEC and another European electrical company producing a group large enough to compete effectively worldwide.

The ECE, in a report on the heavy electrical industry sent to the governments of the European Economic Community (EEC) countries in April, pointed to the increasing competition faced by European companies from the U.S. giants, Westinghouse and General Electric. The Commission did not wish to shut them out of the European market, but instead to build up the European industry to compete successfully with them. In asking the governments of the EEC countries to encourage transnational mergers within the European electrical industry, the Commission sought an ending of the chauvinistic buying policies of supply authorities in Europe. It proposed that no governmental or private agreements should be made in the heavy electrical and nuclear engineering fields that would impede either transnational mergers or opening foreign markets to foreign competition.

Following Westinghouse and General Electric, Philips and Brown Boveri of Switzerland probably went further in making efficient design and production arrangements across frontiers than others, but they were closely followed by such companies as Allmänna Svenska Elektriska Aktiebolaget (ASEA) of Sweden. ASEA and the RTE Corp. of Wisconsin held equal shares in a joint company due to begin production of transformers in Milwaukee in 1971. Another important international agreement was that between Allis-Chalmers of the U.S. and Kraftwerk Union, the company formed in 1969 from the merger of the turbine manufacturing interests of Siemens and Allgemeine Elektricitäts-Gesellschaft of West Germany; the two firms agreed to form a joint company in the U.S. to sell electric power-generating equipment. Reyrolle Parsons of the U.K. and the North American Rockwell Corp. set up a jointly owned company to sell Parsons turbogenerators in America.

With increasing internationalism, more attention was being paid to standardization. In Europe, the changeover to the metric system in the U.K. helped to ease agreement on new international standards. Canada and Australia declared their intention of converting to the metric system, and industry in the U.S. was conscious that it could soon become the only major nation in the world using imperial units. Thus the U.S. National Bureau of Standards, following the 1968 Metric Study Act, was gathering data on possible conversion.

To combat the high cost and price fluctuations of copper, manufacturers increasingly turned to aluminum as a conductor material; however, problems associated with the oxide surface film that forms on aluminum held back applications of aluminum wiring. A U.S. company, Texas Instruments, developed a compromise that was adopted and marketed commercially by cable companies throughout the world. This was "copper-clad" wiring, consisting of conductors drawn from an aluminum rod with a thin copper

Table IV. Exports of Electrical Machinery and Apparatus in 1969 and 1968

Country	1969 Value in U.S. $000,000	1969 Percent increase over 1968	1968 Value in U.S. $000,000	1968 Percent increase over 1967
Germany, West	2,404	23	1,947	11
Belgium-Luxembourg	353	22	291	11
France	833	23	676	14
Italy	838	20	698	18
Netherlands	876	19	733	11
United Kingdom	1,162	14	1,016	3
Sweden	378	15	329	16
Switzerland	355	17	304	22
Canada	427	11	386	25
Japan	1,995	31	1,522	32
United States*	2,678	17	2,286	9

*Excluding special category goods.
Source: U.K. Board of Trade.

layer metallurgically bonded to the outside. The wiring had a somewhat larger cross section, but its behaviour was virtually the same as that of copper wiring, and it was about 15% lower in price. In addition, the handling characteristics of the new conductor were said to be superior to those of copper. It was lighter, less springy, and less likely to tangle.

Of major interest to manufacturers of electrical switchgear was the permanent power fuse developed by the Mitsubishi Electric Corp., Japan. The fuse, which need never be replaced, consisted of a concealed ceramic tube containing sodium. The sodium has a low resistance to the passage of normal full-load current, but a fault current causes it to vaporize, presenting a high resistance. It can therefore be used as a current-limiting device to increase the interrupting capacity of contactors, circuit breakers, and other protective devices.

Following tests on a 80-kilovolt-ampere (kva) superconducting generator, the Massachusetts Institute of Technology was building a 1-Mw. liquid-helium-cooled machine. MIT believed that the prospects for large power station generators with superconducting field windings were attractive.

Feasibility studies on the technical aspects of commercial applications of glow discharges in metal fabrication and heat processing were completed at the Hirst Research Centre of the General Electric Co. in Britain, and potential markets were being investigated. Unlike electron beam welding, this new process was efficient in low-pressure atmospheres. (T. C. J. C.)

GLASS

Glass industries throughout the world reported increasing sales, and their confidence was reflected by the extent to which new production facilities were brought into use. This period of minor boom could be summarized under three main categories of market for glass: construction, containers, and scientific and technical purposes. An example of the construction market was the demand for facilities to make float glass, which caused Pilkington Brothers Ltd. to grant licenses to 11 countries. Also signifi-

cant was the decision by Saint Gobain of France, in conjunction with Pilkington, to build a new flat-glass plant in northern Spain. In Sweden Emmabora Glasverk was building new production facilities for the Saint Gobain continuous horizontal toughening process.

In the developed countries the trend toward convenience packaging continued to grow. In Europe this meant that bottles for beer and carbonated soft drinks, traditionally returned to the bottling plant to be refilled, increasingly became nonreturnable. This followed a strong trend in the U.S. It created boom conditions in the container manufacturing plants, but aroused opposition because of the increase in trash that it caused. There was strong pressure in some countries, notably Norway and Denmark, to ban the one-trip beverage bottle, and in the U.S. the glass container industry had an additional problem in criticism from the National Commission on Product Safety. In each country where the one-trip beverage-bottle market was developing, however, there was strong support from the glass container industry for antilitter campaigns.

Glass container manufacturers throughout the world awaited with considerable interest the next stage in the development of ultralightweight containers by Owens-Illinois, Inc., and this stimulated research by other equipment manufacturers into new systems for making lightweight bottles at increased speeds. A move toward diversification could also be detected.

The third of the markets mentioned at the outset was scientific and technical glass. The West German Schott Co., a leading producer of such specialized glasses, reported considerably increased sales, attributed to the demand for telescope mirrors, cathode-ray tubes, and space exploration uses. A 138-in.-diameter mirror for the Italian National Observatory Commission, for example, was ordered from the Corning Glass Works; it would be the fourth largest produced by Corning.

Interest grew in fibre glass. Apart from the normal growth of the market for textile and industrial purposes, expansion was expected in the supply of fibre glass for impregnating automobile tires.

Labour relations in the U.K. glass industry, trouble free for several decades, received a shock when Pilkington workers called a strike. Settlement was reached only after a bitter dispute and an increase in basic pay, with an agreement to review the negotiating structure.

There was some negotiating activity between Eastern Europe and other regions. The U.S.S.R. was to build a plant for domestic glassware manufacture, with the assistance of Saint Gobain; this was said to constitute the first step toward closer technical cooperation. Installation of Polish-designed glass factories was under way in a number of countries, among them Albania, Cuba, Bulgaria, and Yugoslavia. (Cy. W.)

IRON AND STEEL

World crude steel production rose in 1970 to 595 million metric tons, an increase of 4% over the total for the previous year. Thus, in the 25 years since the end of World War II, annual world steel output had increased more than fivefold. During the same period world trade in steel had developed even more rapidly, rising from an estimated 5 million tons in 1945 to more than 80 million tons in 1970. An important feature of this growth in trade, particularly in the 1970s, was the change from the simple deficit-covering trade of the immediate postwar period to a sophisticated interchange of steel products among industrialized nations.

The early part of 1970 was characterized by a continuation of the boom conditions of 1969, but in the second half of the year uncertainties began to appear in many of the main steel-producing areas. In the U.S., Japan, the European Coal and Steel Community (ECSC), and the U.K. there were signs that demand was beginning to decline, mainly because of the effects of national deflationary policies. Domestic steel price levels, which rose in 1969 and early 1970, partly because of the increasing cost of raw materials and labour and partly for market

Table V. World Production of Pig Iron and Blast Furnace Ferroalloys
In 000 metric tons

Country	1965	1966	1967	1968	1969
World	324,390	335,200	351,630	376,320	407,420
U.S.	80,000	83,010	78,910	80,540	86,620
U.S.S.R.	66,200	70,260	74,810	78,790	81,630
Japan*	27,500	32,020	40,090	46,400	58,150
Germany, West	26,990	25,410	27,270	30,310	33,760
France	15,770	15,590	15,710	16,450	18,210
United Kingdom	17,740	15,960	15,400	16,700	16,650
China†	14,000	14,000	15,000	15,500	16,000
Belgium	8,370	8,230	8,900	10,370	11,210
Italy*	5,500	6,270	7,310	7,840	7,780
India	6,950	7,040	6,890	7,290	7,190
Czechoslovakia	5,870	6,270	6,820	6,920	7,040
Poland	5,380	5,610	6,330	6,640	7,030
Canada*	6,420	6,550	6,310	7,600	6,770
Australia	4,000	4,450	4,970	5,290	5,800
Luxembourg*	4,140	3,960	3,960	4,310	4,870
South Africa	3,320	3,460	3,470	3,830	3,930
Brazil*	2,540	2,890	2,960	3,350	3,700
Romania	2,020	2,200	2,460	2,990	3,490
Netherlands*	2,360	2,210	2,590	2,820	3,460
Spain*	2,330	2,100	2,680	2,780	3,330
Austria*	2,200	2,190	2,140	2,470	2,820
Sweden*	2,290	2,230	2,360	2,490	2,500
Germany, East	2,340	2,450	2,530	2,330	2,100
Korea, North†	1,600	1,800	1,800	1,800	1,800
Hungary*	1,580	1,640	1,670	1,650	1,760
Mexico*	950	1,140	1,290	1,600	1,700
Finland	930	980	1,040	1,140	1,230
Yugoslavia*	1,120	1,140	1,180	1,200	1,200
Bulgaria	700	870	920	1,080	1,120
Norway*	520	630	640	670	680

*Pig iron only.
†Estimated.
Source: British Steel Corporation.

Table VI. World Production of Crude Steel
In 000 metric tons

Country	1965	1966	1967	1968	1969	1970 Year to date	No. of months	1970 Annual rate	Percent change 1970-69
World	456,450	473,110	496,010	528,440	571,620	...	...	595,000*	+ 4.1
U.S.†	119,260	121,660	115,410	119,260	127,980	81,130	8	121,700	− 4.9
U.S.S.R.	91,000	96,910	102,240	106,530	110,290	57,050	6	114,100	+ 3.4
Japan	41,160	47,780	62,150	66,890	82,170	62,380	8	93,560	+13.9
Germany, West	36,820	35,320	36,740	41,160	45,320	31,260	8	46,880	+ 3.4
United Kingdom	27,440	24,710	24,280	26,280	26,850	18,550	8	27,830	+ 3.6
France	19,600	19,590	19,660	20,410	22,510	15,690	8	23,530	+ 4.5
Italy	12,680	13,640	15,890	16,960	16,430	11,680	8	17,520	+ 6.6
China*	12,000	13,000	14,000	15,000	16,000	...	...	17,000	+ 6.3
Belgium	9,160	8,910	9,710	11,570	12,840	8,500	8	12,740	− 0.8
Poland	9,090	9,850	10,410	11,010	11,290	4,800	5	11,520	+ 2.0
Czechoslovakia	8,600	9,130	10,000	10,560	10,820	3,750	4	11,250	+ 4.0
Canada	9,130	9,090	8,800	10,210	9,350	7,400	8	11,100	+18.7
India	6,410	6,610	6,330	6,510	6,500	4,160	8	6,240	− 4.0
Australia	5,270	5,720	6,290	6,470	6,690	4,510	8	6,760	+ 1.0
Sweden	4,730	4,760	4,770	5,090	5,330	3,470	8	5,200	− 2.4
Spain	3,520	3,850	4,510	4,920	5,990	4,840	8	7,260	+21.2
Luxembourg	4,580	4,390	4,480	4,830	5,520	3,770	8	5,660	+ 2.5
Romania	3,430	3,670	4,090	4,750	5,540	2,110	4	6,330	+14.3
Brazil	3,020	3,710	3,670	4,440	4,900	3,530	8	5,290	+ 8.0
Germany, East	4,370	4,540	4,650	4,700	5,140	400	1	4,800	− 6.6
South Africa	3,290	3,290	3,700	4,050	4,620	3,110	8	4,670	+ 1.1
Netherlands	3,150	3,260	3,400	3,710	4,710	3,370	8	5,060	+ 7.4
Austria	3,220	3,190	3,020	3,470	3,930	2,720	8	4,080	+ 3.8
Mexico	2,450	2,790	3,040	3,260	3,420	2,490	8	3,740	+ 9.4
Hungary	2,520	2,650	2,740	2,900	3,030	1,340	5	3,220	+ 6.3
Yugoslavia	1,770	1,860	1,830	2,000	2,220	1,110	6	2,220	...
Argentina	1,370	1,270	1,330	1,550	1,650	1,220	8	1,820	+10.3
Bulgaria	590	700	1,240	1,460	1,510	900	6	1,800	+19.2

*Estimated.
†Excludes production of independent foundries.
Sources: British Steel Corporation; International Iron and Steel Institute.

reasons, were in many cases under increasing pressure from imports in the latter part of the year.

Price levels in international trade began to turn down fairly sharply during the second half of the year, and the reemergence of a surplus of world steelmaking capacity appeared possible, although not, perhaps, of the apparent magnitude that characterized the world market before the beginning of the boom in 1968.

Lower earnings from domestic and export sales and the appearance of surplus steelmaking capacity inevitably raised again questions of capital investment and the desirability of replacing old, and perhaps inefficient, plant. However, producers were likely to be cautious in this regard, since the experience of the 1968–69 boom showed that even an apparently substantial margin of surplus capacity could be illusory.

On Jan. 1, 1970, further reductions in tariffs on steel were made by many countries in accordance with their obligations under the Kennedy Round agreement. Another reduction became due on Jan. 1, 1971. Discussions continued in the UN Conference on Trade and Development (UNCTAD) about the proposal that tariff preferences should be granted by industrialized nations on the manufactures of the less developed countries, and there was general agreement among the major steel-producing countries of the world that such preferences should extend to steel products, subject to certain safeguards.

Steel output in the U.S. in 1970 was estimated at 122 million tons, a decline of nearly 5% from 1969 that was attributable to continuing economic difficulties. Total imports in the first five months of the year were 4,365,000 short tons, compared with 5,185,000 tons in the equivalent period of 1969. Voluntary limitation of steel exports to the U.S. by the ECSC and Japan continued in 1970, and in fact exports under these arrangements did not reach the quota for the year. Protectionist lobbies in Congress nevertheless maintained pressure for a legal restriction of imports.

Japanese output rose in 1970 to an estimated 94 million tons, an increase of approximately 14% over the previous year's output. Despite a tight monetary policy, demand in the home market continued to expand, although toward the end of the year output targets were slightly reduced. Exports increased rapidly except to the U.S. (*see* above), although these also rose in the latter part of the year.

Steel production in the ECSC again increased substantially, the economies of all Community countries continuing to expand throughout the greater part of 1970. Later in the year, however, signs began to appear that domestic demand was leveling out. While this might be attributable in some measure to stock reductions, there were doubts about prospects for 1971. Prices in both domestic and export markets weakened in the second half of the year. Import duties on certain products in short supply in the Community, notably ingots and semis and coils for rerolling, that had been temporarily suspended during the first half of the year, were restored on August 10.

In the U.K., steel production rose by nearly 4% above the 1969 level. Domestic demand continued to be strong throughout the greater part of 1970, and capacity was stretched to its limit. Account was taken of expected future demand in the far-reaching development plans of the British Steel Corporation (BSC).

Production in the Soviet Union and Eastern Europe continued to expand. In the U.S.S.R. itself, output exceeded 114 million tons, 3½% higher than in 1969. In Poland, Czechoslovakia, East Germany, Romania, and Bulgaria output was higher than in the previous year. (L. C. BA.)

MACHINERY AND MACHINE TOOLS

Orders for machine tools in 1970 continued downward in the trend that was established in the last six months of 1969. The first nine months of 1970 reflected the economic uncertainty that prevailed throughout the U.S. economy in most types of manufacturing. Very few industries placed orders for new machinery. There was, therefore, little optimism for the manufacturers of machine tools and allied machinery industries until the economy turned upward.

The tight money market, high interest rates, and a number of work stoppages plagued the industry in 1970. The prolonged General Motors strike caused many customers to use this as an excuse for waiting to place orders for not only metal-forming and metal-cutting tools but also other types of machines. Few industries looked for any increase in orders until 1971, and then only if better interest rates could be obtained. The machine-tool industry met the retreat in capital spending by cutting the work week, employing a no-hiring policy, and taking longer summer vacations; some work forces were cut up to 30%.

During the 1960s the great emphasis in the industry had been on numerical control (NC) and direct numerical control (DNC) manufacturing systems. In 1970, however, tool builders began emphasizing a manufacturing system that was expected to be important for the next decade. This system links the mini-computers in the DNC tool-equipped shops to the computers that are used by accounting departments. This provides management with information that helps solve problems of a company while the manufacturing process is going on. Company officials were expected to be interested in buying this manufacturing system to cut rising costs; however, they were moving slowly and machine-tool builders believed that it would not be a significant trend until the economy took an upswing.

Research in the aerospace industry was aimed at cutting costs on the metal fabrication of new composites and superalloys. Titanium alloys demanded new techniques, leading to the use of the laser beam for drilling, inertia (friction) welding machines, and electrochemical machinery. High-energy forming machines using electrical discharge, explosive charges, and high-pressure water discharge were used to form metal parts.

Competition from European and Japanese machine builders continued to be strong on general purpose machines. The major factors that stimulated tool imports were: prices 25 to 40% lower than those of comparable U.S.-built machines; the rapid progress in machine-tool technology of foreign manufacturers; and the improvement in the marketing, distribution, and servicing organizations in the U.S. of foreign machine-tool builders. In order to cope with this competition, it seemed likely that many domestic builders would reduce their production of standard, general-purpose machines and concentrate on producing the more technically advanced machines.

The only hope for increased orders in the last quarter of 1970 depended on those placed at the National Machine Tool Builder's show in Chicago in September. Some builders expressed optimism, but a significant increase seemed unlikely in the near future. (O. K.)

PAINTS AND VARNISHES

The worldwide urge to combat pollution, intensified in 1970, was expected increasingly to influence the production and utilization of paint. The disposal of factory waste, whether liquid, solid, or volatile, bore on paint manufacture at the production end. The control of solvent vapours and emissions from baking ovens used in paint manufacture required closer technical attention, and official bodies and organized labour became still more aware of fire and health hazards. The industry cooperated closely in stepping up health and safety precautions, such as those required in processing polyurethane and epoxy coatings and in the formulation of solvent mixtures of higher flashpoint. Development of water-based coatings reduced solvent vapour hazards, but it tended to complicate the problem of liquid waste.

In application techniques, the brush and the conventional spray gun lost ground to the hand roller and airless spray for painting ships and buildings. Industrial components were increasingly coated by electropainting or, if in sheet or coil form, by automated roller or curtain coating.

Total production in 1969 in the U.S. was valued at $2,808,000,000, compared with $1,954,000,000 for Western Europe. Among European countries the largest producers were West Germany, with 30% of the continental total at $590 million; the U.K., with 20% at $391 million; and France, with 17% at $338 million. The Netherlands' total of $118 million (6%) was remarkable for a small country. In the Far East, industrial expansion in Japan called for a correspondingly large production of paint.

Profit margins on paint remained extremely low. The industry countered higher labour costs and raw material price rises, sometimes ranging from 10 to 12½%, by seeking greater efficiency. Nevertheless, manufacturers believed that higher paint prices were imperative.

The trend continued in the U.K. toward the combination of paint manufacturers into large groups, and the groups themselves tended to become transnational. Chemical firms supplying raw materials were becoming involved in the industry; for example, Farbwerke Hoechst controlled Berger, Jenson and Nicholson, and British Paints. Some large groups had interests remote from paint: one instance was the Reed Paper Group, which controlled Wallpaper Manufacturers. The large Dutch group AKZO included Sikkens, and through them Astral in France, Lesonal in West Germany, and subsidiaries in Italy, Belgium, and Africa. Some observers criticized such large mergers, alleging inefficiency, poor profitability, and bad staff relations. The full commercial benefits, however, had probably not yet appeared. (R. J. LE.)

PAPER AND PULP

World production of paper and paperboard continued to increase steadily, reaching approximately 140 million short tons in 1969 as compared with 127 million short tons in 1968. Production, doubling about every 15 years, was closely linked to changes in standards of living and population.

The increase in production in 1969 was the largest that had yet occurred, and was considerably above the average annual world increase of just over 5% that was recorded during the previous decade. It reflected rapid economic growth in a number of the leading paper-using nations.

AUTHENTICATED NEWS INTERNATIONAL

New machine built in 1970 by the Georgia-Pacific Corp. converts wastepaper into high-grade face and back papers for gypsum wallboard.

Production in North America increased to 66.2 million tons from 60.1 million in 1968; in Europe to 47.8 million tons from 43.9 million; in Asia to 20.2 million tons from 18.1 million; in Latin America to 3.7 million tons from 3.5 million; and in Africa to 950,000 tons from 900,000. Manufacturing facilities in most countries operated at close to the limits of their capacity, and there was a reasonable balance between demand and available supply for such products as newsprint, linerboard, and wood pulp.

Late in 1969, economic activity in some of the large world markets, among them the U.S. and Canada, slowed considerably as a result of the anti-inflationary policies being enacted by their governments. This led to a reduced rate of increase in paper and paperboard output, with the result that the total rise in world production for 1970 was much smaller than for 1969.

The largest pulp and paper manufacturing nations continued to be the U.S., Canada, Japan, Sweden, Finland, and the Soviet Union, in that order. In 1969 they accounted for more than two-thirds of the total world production. Except for Japan, all had forest resources that were more than adequate to support their present levels of pulp and paper manufacture. Canada, in particular, was using less than one-half of the allowable harvest estimated to be available from its forests, despite a large expansion of its pulp and paper industry in recent years. Japan, on the other hand, supplemented its own supply by the import of substantial quantities of wood and also wood pulp. Of the chief pulp and paper manufacturing nations, Japan had grown most quickly in recent years.

According to the Food and Agriculture Organization of the UN, world capacity for producing paper and paperboard in 1970 was approximately 156 million short tons, an increase of 10 million tons, or 6%, over 1969. The increase was divided as follows: Western Europe 3 million tons; North America 2.4 million; Japan 1.3 million; Soviet Union 800,000; and the balance of the world 2.5 million. About the same growth in total capacity was forecast for 1971 and 1972 with, however, North America rather than Western Europe accounting for the largest share. (Go. M.)

PETROLEUM PRODUCTS

In looking back on 1970, veterans of the petroleum industry could not remember a year that brought more new departures in product demand and specifications. Superimposed on a brisk and rising rate of con-

sumption, world politics and growing concern over the environment sparked a swift succession of changes. Oil was not alone in being affected. Coal, natural gas, and nuclear power underwent changes of position in the total energy field, not only in the U.S. but abroad as well. At the end of the year some fuel shortages threatened.

Some of these changes had been foreseen. The dismal predictions of natural gas economists suddenly came true as demand overtook domestic supply. It had also been long apparent that the nuclear power program was not going to make it on schedule. Then came the unexpected, compounding an energy crisis that focused on power fuels. Electric power companies throughout much of the world were having trouble enough getting the capital to keep up with base load requirements. Many had bet their futures on nuclear power, which was due to begin its take-over in the early 1970s. But the construction of nuclear power plants developed difficulties. Highly sophisticated equipment experienced delivery delays, and costs escalated.

Facing the prospect of brownouts and irate consumers, electric utilities reverted to the old standby—the conventional steam plant fired by coal, heavy fuel oil, or natural gas. Then came another change, brought about in the U.S. by aroused environmentalists. They maintained that sulfur dioxide, a foul-smelling air pollutant, had to be eliminated. Up and down the U.S. East Coast state and local governments reduced the permissible sulfur content of fuels far below expected levels. These new regulations ruled out using a large fraction of the heavy residual fuel oil that had been coming in without restriction from Venezuela and other foreign sources.

Coal was hit much harder. Almost all coal burned at electrical and other power stations in the East failed the sulfur test. And since coal cannot be economically desulfurized, utilities looked elsewhere. Normally, they would have switched to clean-burning natural gas, which in the past had been available in abundance at low prices. But in a prolonged inflationary period, the low gas prices enforced by the U.S. Federal Power Commission had discouraged capital investment in discovery and development of new reserves. Distributors in 1970 were already serving notice on old customers that their future supplies would be restricted, and potential customers got nothing.

Thus, these customers turned to oil. In normal times it was likely that enough low-sulfur fuel oil could have been brought in from Libya and elsewhere to meet the sudden change. But the political upheavals in the Middle East virtually shut off that source of supply. First, the only pipeline moving Arabian oil to the eastern Mediter-

ranean was broken in Syria. Refusing to permit repairs, the Syrian government effectively cut off a major fuel supply to Europe. Libya acted next. Its low-sulfur crude had poured in mounting volume directly across the Mediterranean since the 1967 closing of Suez. In a successful effort to gain price increases, the government heightened the crisis by ordering drastic cutbacks in crude production. During the summer of 1970, Western Europe coped with a shortage of about one million barrels a day in available crude oil. Practically every tanker that could float was pressed into service, at temporary spot charter rates that rose rapidly to very high levels.

These unforeseen events effectively turned back all hopeful U.S. importers of new supplies of low-sulfur fuel oil. At that point, domestic refiners offered a plan for boosting fuel oil production from U.S. crude oils, and the government turned the problem over to them.

While meeting this new challenge, petroleum refiners were making ready for another change in direction, also prompted by concern over the environment. By common agreement, the greatest contributor to air pollution in urban areas was the automobile. Car makers and gasoline manufacturers together were given the job of producing an automobile and fuel that would virtually eliminate this pollution (see *Automobiles*, above). (Ge. We.)

PLASTICS

The plastics industry everywhere maintained the technological impetus of its advance in 1970, with the result that output rose to about 28 million metric tons from the 25 million metric tons of 1969. The slightly lower expansion rate than in the previous year was mainly accounted for by the near recession in the U.S. during the first half of 1970, so that, although conditions improved later, output there rose unusually sluggishly and was unlikely to top 10 million metric tons. Japan, on the other hand, had another year of rapid growth (20% or more) and turned out an estimated 4.9 million metric tons. This confirmed its position as the world's second producer after the U.S., a title it wrested from West Germany in 1969. The 1970 performance of West Germany itself, an estimated 4.7 million metric tons, was scarcely less sparkling. The plastics industries in the other European Economic Community countries also experienced a good year, particularly in France, where production was approximately equal to that of the U.K., previously the Western world's fifth producer (Italy held fourth place). Britain's 8% expansion in 1969 was followed by a similar performance—dull by plastics industry standards—in 1970, to reach approximately 1,450,000 metric tons against a background of general economic stagnation. The output of the U.S.S.R. in 1970 was thought to have been about 1.6 million metric tons.

Materials developments mainly involved the improvement of existing plastics by copolymerization, chemical modification, such as postchlorination, and by the incorporation of fibrous reinforcements and ancillary materials. Materials modified by such techniques included a cross-linked polyethylene that had better performance at elevated temperatures than conventional polyethylene; the first fire-retardant nylon able to conform to stringent specifications such as the British Standard class 1 test;

KEYSTONE

Tubular house built of plastic and fitted with plastic furnishings is intended for weekend and holiday use. The house was designed by Franz Dutler and shown at the 1970 Hanover Fair.

glass-reinforced polyvinyl chloride, hitherto difficult to produce, in which the glass reinforcement resulted in vastly improved low-temperature resistance; an acrylic/polyvinyl chloride alloy combining the benefits of both these classes of polymer to give a tough, easily moldable material; and an ethylene/tetrafluoroethylene copolymer (ETFE) that, unlike conventional fluoroplastics, could be extruded and injection molded by normal methods, but still retained the general properties of fluoroplastics.

Structural foams received considerable attention during 1970. Produced from a variety of polymers, they could be manufactured by several different techniques, but a basic similarity was that all were rigid foams comprising a low-density cellular core with an integral solid skin approximating the normal density of the base material. They fell midway between solid plastics and the more conventional foams, such as expanded polystyrene and polyurethane foams, without an integral skin. The advantage of a foam core enclosed by a skin was that flexural rigidity was much improved, varying in proportion to the density of the structural foam and with the thickness. Certain of these foams also had a characteristic woodlike finish, making them suitable for wood-replacement applications, particularly as they could be stapled, nailed, screwed, glued, and sanded.

Perhaps the most significant materials development of 1970 was in the U.S., where two companies introduced glass-clear resins with high resistance to gas permeation without the necessity for additional coatings. The exact identity of the resins was not revealed, but they were said to be based on acrylonitrile; apart from polymers based on vinylidene chloride, which lacks the required performance characteristics, only plastics containing nitrile radicals could provide the excellent barrier properties of the new resins. This development opened the soft-drink market to the plastics industry; previously, only coated polyvinyl chloride had been even marginally suitable for carbonated drinks. The new resins were

being evaluated by two soft-drink companies and were said to have been completely successful in market trials. If the requirements of such a large market were to be met, blow-molding machinery manufacturers would have to provide extremely high-output machinery, and a number of developments to achieve this were under way.

An additional feature of these new resins was that, unlike polyvinyl chloride, they could be incinerated without producing toxic gases, thus minimizing the problem of waste. The role of plastics in waste was occasionally exaggerated during the year. The percentage by weight of plastics among all solid waste was less than 3% and was not likely to account for much more than 6% by 1980. The industry was, nevertheless, tackling the problem.

"Bigger and faster" would be an apt description of plastics machinery developments in 1970. Design innovations broadened the processing range of existing equipment. Special machinery for structural foams was actively developed, particularly in injection molding. In the U.K., a sandwich molding process, producing moldings comprising a core sandwiched by an outer skin, was developed. The core could be either foamed, providing the advantages of a structural foam, or solid. The major advantage was that the skin could be different from the core, so that an expensive skin could be utilized with a cheap core, resulting in considerable cost savings compared with a conventional solid molding.   (R. C. Pe.)

PRINTING

Throughout the world the printing industry, in common with publishing, was affected by major advances in paper and pulp prices (see *Paper and Pulp,* above) and by substantial wage increases in many European countries and in Japan and Oceania. Technically there were a number of advances during 1970, but no major breakthroughs. In typesetting, where development was concentrated on phototypesetting, the number of keyboard-operated phototypesetting machines working photomechanically or electronically (even with computer-generated character images on cathode-ray tubes) exceeded 2,000 installations throughout the world, some with several machines. As computers became steadily cheaper, computerized hyphenation and line justification, as well as listing and limited page-formatting operations, were gaining ground, and programs for the main languages and special requirements were becoming available more readily at an economical cost. A shortage of keyboarding staff in typesetting encouraged several printers, notably newspapers where typesetting capacity requirements tend to concentrate in a few hours a day, to employ part-time (and mainly female) staff. The Swedish newspaper *Dagens Nyheter* broke new ground by setting up a keyboarding room in suburban Stockholm, linked by cable to the main office, to employ local housewives after short training to set matter for the newspaper, thus relieving pressure on the main-office keyboard staff.

New U.S. low-cost phototypesetting equipment sold well. Machines such as a range from Compugraphic found hundreds of buyers. In Europe interest in such equipment was definite, but awaited a wider range of available typefaces suitable for more exacting typographical demands. While many low-cost phototypesetting machines were from newcomers to the industry, the two largest typesetting machine manufacturers in the world outside the U.S.S.R., Harris-Intertype and Mergenthaler Linotype, both of the U.S., announced new compact and com-

petitive equipment, the Harris-Intertype machine being largely British-designed. The U.S.S.R. made a drive to sell cheap Neotype linecasting machines through newly formed sales companies in Western Europe. Switzerland became the first country outside the U.S. to introduce computerized typesetting services through news agencies, using a system designed by Guettinger AG that was said to surpass its U.S. rivals in potential versatility.

Unlike hot-metal typesetting, photosetting does not normally allow simple proof correction, and to assist editors text editing systems were introduced by Harris-Intertype in the U.S. and by Cossor in the U.K. These systems provided display screens on which computer-stored text matter was displayed; they could be added to or corrected by keyboarding, the alterations being fed back to the computer. The U.S. company envisaged a sale of 100 units during the first production year, the first units having gone to Gannett newspapers in the U.S. The Cossor system was first introduced and field tested by Southwark Offset in London.

A study by Harris-Intertype showed that the cost, albeit heavy, of new sophisticated equipment under the changed conditions of a high wages and materials cost economy accounted for a smaller part of overhead than when machinery expenditure was the heaviest item in a printer's budget. Full machinery utilization round-the-clock was therefore advocated, involving increased automation to reduce human labour and ensure productive use of machinery.

Programmed reproduction systems in black-and-white work using the Gevarex systems found many adherents, bringing about previously unheard of utilization of camera systems at rates of 60–120 shots an hour. Active work by major West German, British, Japanese, and U.S. manufacturers concentrated on providing similarly efficient systems for colour reproduction without scanning. All these systems depended on density reading and standardized automatic processing.

In East Germany the party newspaper *Neues Deutschland* announced plans for a new web offset press for its Berlin edition, the other editions already being printed web offset on Plamag presses via facsimile transmission. In the U.K., the Communist *Morning Star,* with a much smaller circulation, started printing web offset on a press from East Germany. In the U.S. the *Christian Science Monitor* became the first large-circulation daily to print by web offset. Elsewhere, larger newspapers tended to stick to rotary letterpress printing; forecasts that practicable flexible photopolymer and duplicate letterpress plates would become cheap and available during the next few years encouraged management to retain the established printing process.

In terms of volume, letterpress continued static, while offset gained further ground. Rotogravure also grew appreciably, and manufacturers, mainly in West Germany, Italy, and the U.K., reported unusually full order books for both publication and packaging presses. Control of the world's largest manufacturer of sheet-fed offset presses, the Roland works of Faber and Schleicher in West Germany (makers of a range of Miehle presses for the U.S.), passed to their competitors MAN, also of West Germany. Both companies continued to trade as separate units.   (W. P. Ja.)

SHIPBUILDING

Shipbuilding showed a remarkable rate of growth during 1970. For May, June, and July, the net increase in deadweight tonnage was 2½ times that for the February–April quarter. The total order book (*i.e.*, vessels on order and building) in August reached nearly 120 million tons deadweight (dw.), equivalent to approximately 64.6 million gross registered tons (grt). As the greatest number of ships on order were cargo vessels (either dry cargo or tankers), the use of the deadweight figure (the amount of cargo that can be carried) was of special significance.

In Japan more new yards specially designed for building giant tankers became operational. Japanese shipyards had orders for a remarkable total of 22.5 million grt. Although as a shipowner Japan was fourth in the national table of vessels on order, with a total of 175 having an aggregate of 8.2 million tons dw., it continued to lead the world as a shipbuilder in tonnage launched. Second was Sweden, with 5.8 million grt on order and building. The U.K. placed third with just over 5 million tons.

Large tankers over 150,000 tons dw. continued to attract buyers. Vessels in this group represented more than 48% of new ship orders, other than those in the passenger and miscellaneous categories. Tankers of all sizes constituted 58.6% of the total. The next important groups were oil and bulk carriers, making nearly 30%.

In the U.K. the Belfast shipyard of Harland and Wolff built the 250,000-ton-dw. tanker "Esso Ulidia" in a new building dock that had space for the construction of a one million-ton vessel, and the Tyne shipyard of Swan Hunter launched two sister vessels in the same class, the "Esso Northumbria" and the "Esso Hibernia," from specially prepared conventional slipways. There were 30 shipyards in the world capable of building vessels of 250,000 tons dw. and over, of which 8 were in Japan; 4 in West Germany; 3 each in Sweden and the U.K.; 2 each in France, Spain, and the U.S.; and 1 each in Denmark, Italy, the Netherlands, Norway, Portugal, and Yugoslavia.

In nearly all shipbuilding countries the greatest obstacle to production was a shortage of skilled labour. Strenuous efforts were made to speed up the introduction of labour-saving techniques, including prefabrication of larger ship sections, extension of computer-controlled flame-cutting equipment, and greater use of mechanical handling.

Costs continued to rise, however, despite the use of new technologies. Because of the seller's market it was possible for some shipbuilders to include price escalation clauses in their new contracts. Unfortunate as this development was, it could be justified against the comparatively long period, nearly a year, between the confirmation of an order and the completion of a ship. During this period steel prices, labour charges, and the cost of auxiliary machinery could rise at a rate almost impossible to estimate accurately. Many of the orders taken by U.K. shipyards in 1968 proved unprofitable, even when the yards had been modernized and were members of a large group.

A feature of the increase in the number of tankers of more than 150,000 tons dw. on order was the choice of steam turbine propulsion. This was chosen instead of diesel engines for more than 90% of the vessels. The same choice was reflected in the selection of main machinery for the new high-speed container ships on order, where minimum maintenance and very high powers were required. The diesel engine remained the first choice for nearly every dry cargo ship and for most tankers and oil carriers under 150,000 tons dw.

More shipowners and shipbuilders accepted the standard ship concept, which offered both reduction in cost (but not in standards) and quicker delivery. There were more than 60 vessels of the successful Austin and Pickersgill SD.14 14,500-ton design in service and on order, and the standard "Freedom" ship of similar design built in Japan passed the 50 mark. Standard cargo ships were also being built in West Germany and Spain. The principle was also being applied to bulk carriers in the 20,000-to-28,000-ton range.

With the transport of crude oil continuing to increase, and total world cargo movements showing an equally strong upward movement, prospects for world shipbuilding were good. A shortage of shipbuilding capacity by 1975 seemed a definite possibility.

(W. D. E.)

TEXTILES AND FIBRES

Textile Industry. Technical developments in textile machinery and processes were a feature of 1970, and were of both U.S. and European origin. Arrangements were made

for making the Draper shuttleless loom in Switzerland. A well-known spinning and weaving concern installed a new high-speed data processing system which instantly gave minute-by-minute operating efficiencies individually and collectively. Another U.S. company marketed new models of a yarn inspector and an end-break detector. A new print bonding machine for manufacturing lightweight disposable nonwoven fabrics produced at 40 yd. per minute. At the 18th Chemical Finishing Conference, considerable discussion centred on flame-resistant finishes for cotton. Details of the first big breakthrough in research on wool wrinkling were given at the International Wool Textile Research Conference in California.

On the European continent, French, West German, Czechoslovakian, Polish, and Spanish machinery firms came forward with improved spinning, weaving, and finishing machines.

Production of man-made fibres continued to increase, and du Pont expanded polyester capacity to more than double at the Uentrop works. Costing more than $14 million, a new polyester filament yarn plant for Hoechst Fibre Industries was opened at Limavady, N.Ire.

In Australia a new, revolutionary highspeed spinning method discovered by the Commonwealth Scientific and Industrial Research Organization (CSIRO) textile industry division became ready for industrial application. The new machine twisted a short region of a strand of fibres in one direction and reversed the twist in the next region. Two of these strands were then twisted together, on the same machine, to form a yarn.

Australian research showed that, strategically administered, certain dietary additions could be most effective in reducing or increasing crossbred wool shrinkage. The treatment need only be maintained for one-third of the growth of the fibre and not the whole length.

In the U.K., production of man-made fibres was higher, natural fibres showing only slight improvements. Sales of furnishing fabrics improved in the latter part of the year. Management had many problems, including some labour shortages, increased cost of raw materials, rising overhead, and the effects of strikes in other industries. In the jute industry, diversification into synthetic materials affected research. Efforts were made to attain a highly productive bonded fabrics industry, suitable for a fully mechanized fibre-to-fabric system. A new, fully automatic cop winder for the jute industry produced cops of 35 to 50 mm. in diameter and from 240 to 400 mm. in length; a special model made cops 600 mm. long. The jute industry changed completely to the tex yarn-counting system. In Lancashire a notable event was the integration of 12 major textile machinery-making companies into one concern, Platt International Ltd., with headquarters at Helmshore.

The interest shown by manufacturers in producing crimped glass fibres for better bonding and improved insulation properties of fibre glass mats was reflected in the work of development engineers. During the year, Courtaulds Ltd. announced the production of "Teklan Heat Shield" fabrics for protective clothing in fire and other hazards. The fabric was made from core-spun yarns consisting of fine denier fibre glass and modacrylic yarns. Courtaulds and Hercules Inc. of the U.S. also reached an agreement

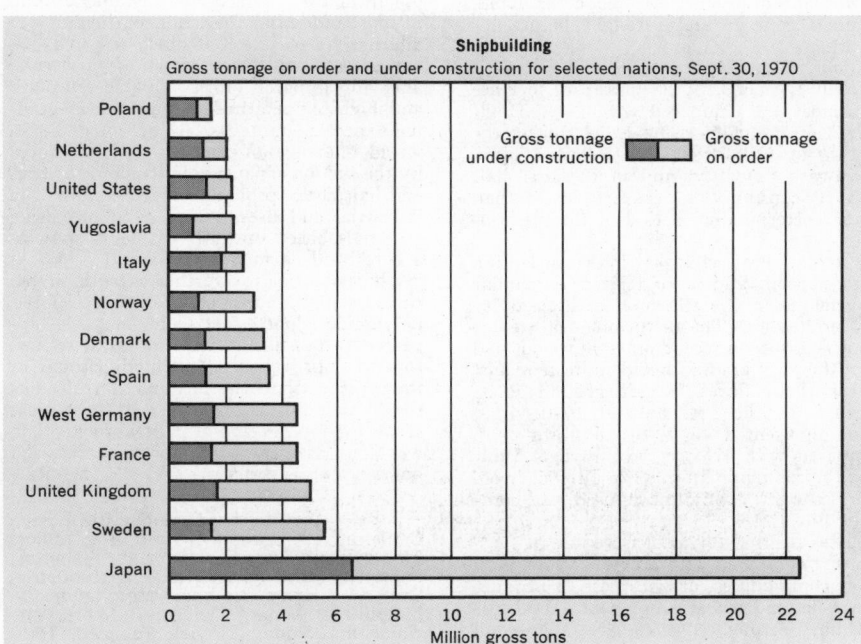

Shipbuilding
Gross tonnage on order and under construction for selected nations, Sept. 30, 1970

Gross tonnage under construction   Gross tonnage on order

Poland
Netherlands
United States
Yugoslavia
Italy
Norway
Denmark
Spain
West Germany
France
United Kingdom
Sweden
Japan

0   2   4   6   8   10   12   14   16   18   20   22   24
Million gross tons

whereby Hercules would set up a plant to make "Grafil" carbon fibre.

In planning new textile mills more attention was being devoted to economies gained by the adoption of high-density storage methods with scientific cleaning systems, and to increasing the use of mobile and planned conveying systems. Advanced quality control instruments included an electronic scanner to detect slubs and the like in warp sheets, and an ultraviolet illuminated bench magnifier for rapid inspection of textile samples. A new electric tachometer offered considerable scope in measuring speeds of spindles, etc. (A. DR.)

Natural Fibres. *Cotton.* World carry-over stocks at the end of the 1969–70 season in July were at a comparatively low level, less than a five-month supply at the current rate of consumption. Throughout the season a feature of the general situation was the stability of prices. This occurred despite a substantial reduction in the outlook for production, which declined due to a variety of causes. It had been expected that supply and demand would be nearer equilibrium than for several years past, but disappointing crops in a number of areas affected the forecast.

Acreage devoted to cotton planting throughout the world increased by nearly 2 million ac. during the season, but available supplies were reduced by much smaller yields than were expected. World cotton production in 1969–70 was 51.9 million bales, compared with 53.7 million in the previous season. A factor in this result was the movement among growers in several important producing countries to turn from cotton harvesting to more remunerative agricultural crops. Much of the decline in prospective output occurred in the U.S. where, despite an increase of nearly 1 million ac. in the area planted, a precipitous drop in yields caused by adverse weather conditions lowered the harvest to barely 10 million bales against initial estimates of 11,750,000.

While this setback was responsible for most of the production problems, output of cotton in other countries also was lower than in the previous season, notably in the U.S.S.R., Mexico, Turkey, Peru, and Spain. Offsetting these figures were better crop returns from Israel, Greece, the United Arab Republic, and Pakistan.

World trade in cotton recovered, with exports estimated at about 17.3 million bales against 16.8 million in 1968–69. As a result of the substantial deterioration in output prospects early in the season, purchasing was stimulated and users tended to anticipate their needs on a freer scale.

Prices based on the Liverpool cost, insurance, and freight index averaging the cost of various American-type cottons of medium staple length were relatively firm during the season, ranging from a low point of 26.95 cents per pound to a peak of 28.7 cents at the end of July. Subsequently, following less favourable information from the U.S. about the progress of the new crop, the quotation advanced sharply to 29.5 cents by late September.

In view of the low level of the current carry-over, traders became more anxious about the outlook. Early reports of the 1970–71 situation in the U.S. were again disappointing after increased plantings and the consequent rise in prices had weakened cotton's competitive position in relation to man-made fibres. (A. TL.)

Silk. During the year there was a rise in the cost of silk from China, which continued as the mainstay of supplies to Europe. A standard grade, known as 3A 20/22, quoted in September 1969 on the British market at 68 shillings ($8.16) per pound was being offered 12 months later at 75 shillings ($9), which represented a rise of 10% and proved to be higher than the market could pay. A serious recession in all textiles had an adverse effect on consumption in all European markets. Prices in China, where silk was a government monopoly, although perhaps not entirely immune from the law of supply and demand, were unlikely to be influenced quickly by falling sales, but the tendency to convert more yarns into fabric might be accentuated.

Japan, with its buoyant economy, stood alone in maintaining a heavy demand for silk and continued to shop abroad to supplement home production. Prices there fluctuated, at times violently, between 78 and 95 shillings. A duty of 15% was payable in Japan on the import of foreign raw silk, which kept price levels always at a premium of 15%, at times rising to as much as 25% above prices in the outside world. How long this would prevail was uncertain, as there were periodic indications of slackening demand.

The U.S. industry was the principal sufferer from the state of affairs in Japan. Unable to buy directly from China, U.S. buyers could obtain raw silk only at the Japanese and Korean price level, and this the U.S. consumer was not prepared to pay. Consumption in the U.S. dropped to about half the 1968 figure and, incidentally, to only one-quarter of the consumption rate in 1965. A similar decline was not experienced by countries where China silk was available during those years at steady and not unreasonable prices, and this seemed to indicate that even a luxury article such as silk could be priced too high for effective marketing.

Equally, there is a level of price below which, in a time of agricultural prosperity, cocoons cannot be economically produced. It was not difficult for most silk farmers to switch to other crops. Silk was in that respect more than usually sensitive to the views of the farming community, because mulberry is a crop that cannot yield for two or three years. This induced caution before uprooting but, on the other hand, required courage and foresight before replanting. (P. W. GA.)

Wool. Consumption of wool in 1969 reached 1,996,600,000 lb. clean, an increase of almost 4% compared with 1968. However, the gradually rising trend during the first half of the year was followed by a downward tendency, and in the first half of 1970 consumption was 6% lower than in the corresponding period of the previous year.

Such cyclical changes in consumption were normal, and were related to similar movements in overall wool textile activity and production. The disturbing feature for wool as a fibre in recent years, however, had been the very gradual but definite tendency for synthetic fibres to gain ground at its expense. In the first half of 1970 virgin wool represented 46½% of all fibres used, compared with 47½% a year earlier. Man-made fibres represented 35%. In 1965 wool represented 53% of all fibres used, and man-made fibres 21%.

Prices realized for wool were low in 1969, whether compared with previous years, with other commodities, or with cost of production. The tendency was downward, and this continued throughout 1970. Australian wool prices in the 1969–70 season were the lowest in more than 20 years, and the decline continued more sharply in the opening months of the 1970–71 selling season. The Australian government provided A$30 million for emergency assistance to woolgrowers hard hit by low prices and drought. Marketing changes were again discussed, though no decision was made.

Three main factors were believed to be the cause of the wool price decline. They were the growing production and use of man-made fibres, at lower prices and involving intense competition not only with natural fibres but between the man-made fibre manufacturers themselves; the downturn in the textile cycle, starting (generally speaking) in the third quarter of 1969 and developing during 1970; and the high level of interest rates throughout the world, which militated against stockholding at every stage. (H. M. F. M.)

Man-Made Fibres. In 1970 the rate of growth of man-made fibres tended to fall below forecasts in most Western countries. There were temporary periods of overproduction, affecting such potentially important sectors as textured synthetic yarns, and in the U.K. there were problems with overproduction of bulk standard lines of woven nylon fabric. Such factors, however, could not detract from the continuous and energetic advance in technological application, which covered virtually every section of the trade.

Long-term forecasts suggested that by the mid-1970s world production of polyester fibres would exceed that of the polyamide fibres, but dogmatism on this score seemed ill-advised, particularly as several advances in polyamide evolution were coming into commercial use. For example, second-generation nylon, with a degree of absorbency that was not obtainable in the original types, and a corresponding elimination of static electrical charges, reached an advanced stage.

The still rather exclusive Qiana nylon, developed by du Pont to compete directly with silk, came into commercial use in several countries for traditional top-quality fashion fabrics. More significant still was a new advanced nylon from Monsanto, developed first in the U.S. but later produced in the U.K., that was only marginally costlier than normal nylon.

Film-based yarns, made by either slitting or fibrillation, gained considerable ground in most industrial countries, particularly as alternatives to jute, but much research was concentrated on the evolution of yarns suitable for apparel fabrics. Flame-retardant and high-temperature-resistant fibres gradually became more widely accepted, but a world shortage of modacrylics, prompted by the sudden expansion in demand for wigs and hairpieces, probably retarded growth in industrial end uses, such as the promising materials based on glass filaments spun as a core inside a modacrylic sheath.

The potential for further growth in the three main groups of man-made fibres, polyamides, polyesters, and acrylics, appeared to be substantial. The trend seemed toward improvements and modifications of these rather than the introduction of completely new fibres. There seemed to be great scope for the development of both dry and wet laid viscose fibres for a variety of bonded fibre fabrics. (P. M. RE.)

See also Advertising; Alcoholic Beverages; Cooperatives; Economy, World; Electronics; Employment, Wages, and Hours; Fisheries; Food; Fuel and Power; Housing; Industrial Design; Labour Unions; Merchandising; Metallurgy; Mining; Prices; Rubber; Television and Radio; Timber; Tobacco; Tourism; Toys and Games; Trade, International.

Insurance

Continued sales growth and financial stability were achieved by private insurance during 1970, in spite of natural and man-made disasters of some consequence. Major losses included European avalanches, the biggest Romanian floods ever experienced, the worst Latin-American earthquake in history in Peru, tornadoes and Hurricane Celia in Texas, brush fires in California, and the destruction of $50 million of jet aircraft by hijackers in the Middle East.

Life and Health Insurance. Assets of U.S. life insurance companies reached the $200 billion mark for the first time in mid-1970. Of the total, approximately 41% was invested in bonds, 37% in mortgages, 8% in policy loans, 6% in stocks, 3% in real estate, and 5% in miscellaneous assets. Major changes in the aggregate portfolio as compared with the previous year included almost a 20% increase in the policy loan amount and a decrease in stockholdings of slightly less than 10%.

Total life insurance in force was expected to exceed one and a half trillion dollars ($1,500 billion) for a new all-time record. The average U.S. family had more than $20,000 of private life insurance protection. Total income neared $50 billion, of which approximately 70% came from premium receipts. Life insurance annuities accounted for most of the premium volume, while health insurance premiums rose beyond $10 billion. Benefits paid exceeded $17 billion, with 60% going to living policyholders and 40% to beneficiaries of policyholders who died.

The interest of the life insurance companies in equity products increased. Mutual funds and/or variable annuities were being sold by 300 or more insurers whose sales forces exceeded 50,000 agents. Holding companies continued to be the typical medium for sales expansion into these areas. Several companies experimented with "variable life insurance" contracts, in which the face value of the policies would change upward with inflation. Prudential Insurance Co., the world's largest life insurer, announced that it would expand into the property-liability field through arrangements with the Kemper Insurance Companies.

Private health insurance continued to be a crucial area of rapid growth for U.S. insurance companies and the Blue Cross-Blue Shield organizations. Medical costs rose sharply and premium rates reacted similarly. Benefit payments exceeded $17 billion. The government Medicare program for the elderly also expanded, and new legislation was proposed for extending its coverage. Approximately $8 billion was paid out under the Medicare programs.

The three British life associations reported new ordinary and industrial (home service) business of £9,401 million in 1969, compared with £8,340 million in 1968; this represented an increase of 13% against 17% in the preceding year. Of the new business, £8,615 million was written in the ordinary branch and £786 million in the industrial branch. New premiums and considerations necessary to secure the new benefits amounted to £353 million. A gross investment yield of 8% was general among offices, and bonus distributions to participating policyholders were at or above previous levels. The total sum in force at the end of 1969, including accrued bonus additions, amounted to £46,100 million, plus £1,660 million a year in annuities.

Property and Liability Insurance. With sales growing approximately 10% to more than $30 billion, U.S. property-liability insurance reached new highs during 1970. Underwriting losses were expected to result for the year, as was also true in 1968–69. Fortunately, investment income of the companies was sufficient to offset them.

Probably the most spectacular insurance loss during the year involved four airliners hijacked and subsequently destroyed by Arab commandos: a Pan American 747 blown up at Cairo airport and three smaller planes destroyed in Jordan. The insurance bill in hull values alone amounted to some $50 million, of which the 747 accounted for more than half. Approximately $31 billion (£13 billion) fell on the London market. Lloyd's subsequently raised its rates sharply, and it was announced that the U.S. government would increase the amount of insurance it would sell to the airlines, as provided under the 1958 Federal Aviation Act.

Automobile insurance, accounting for more than 40% of total premium income in the U.S., was a subject of increasing concern. Massachusetts became the first state to pass compulsory "no fault" legislation, effective in 1971, requiring that all persons involved in automobile accidents be reimbursed by their own companies for medical bills and most lost wages, up to $2,000 per person. This represented a direct change from the tort liability system, in which the injured person must collect his losses from the negligent driver. Other states, including New York, instituted or were considering similar legislation. The intention was to help alleviate the growing costs and problems of automobile liability insurance.

Insured losses resulting from tornado damage in the Lubbock, Tex., area during April and May were estimated at $100 million. Hurricane Celia losses over a much wider area of the state the following month involved predicted losses of more than $200 million. Riot and civil disorder damages increased during 1970, but were not concentrated in the larger urban areas as they had been in 1967–68. Serious crime losses were a major factor in the increased difficulty that some commercial enterprises experienced in obtaining adequate protection.

Increased ties between private and government insurance programs were noted in 1970, and the first federal insurance administrator was appointed to coordinate these efforts. Most states expanded their Fair Access to Insurance Requirements (FAIR) plans, under which property insurance in loss-prone urban areas was obtainable following physical inspection of the buildings. The National Flood Insurers Program, backed by the U.S. Department of Housing (HUD) reinsurance, more than tripled the number of areas in which flood insurance on properties was written.

The worldwide premium income of member companies of the British Insurance Association (BIA) rose 6% in 1969 to a total of £3,313 million, of which short-term (fire, automobile, and miscellaneous) insurance accounted for £1,686 million, and marine, aviation, and transport for £181 million (the remainder was accounted for by life and personal health). Underwriting results on short-term business were the worst in many years, with an overall worldwide loss of £38.4 million: a loss of £39.7 million on automobile business against a profit of £1.3 million on fire and miscellaneous.

The successful development of the Concorde affected the insurance market as a whole. Insurers of

CENTRAL PRESS
FROM PICTORIAL PARADE

Mrs. Margery Hurst, one of the 46 women members newly elected to Lloyd's of London, visits the 300-year-old insurance institution Jan. 1, 1970.

Inland Waterways: see Transportation

nonmarine risks were concerned with the possibility of supersonic commercial aviation and the risk of sonic boom damage as a commonplace occurrence. The position was clarified by the application of a "sonic bangs exclusion clause" to all existing fire, automobile, and general accident policies. The U.K. government undertook to provide compensation for damage resulting from the Concorde's test flights.

Premiums of £469 million received by British companies from business in the U.S. produced an underwriting loss of £16.3 million, which was more than covered by investment income exceeding £30 million. Here again losses resulted principally from automobile and householders' business. Results in Australia and South Africa were marginally profitable. In Canada, where the experience on automobile insurance deteriorated badly and fire business remained generally unprofitable, the U.K. companies suffered an overall loss of $17.2 million.

In Western Europe severe losses resulted from forest fires on the Côte d'Azur and a sharp rise in the number and severity of industrial fires in West Germany and Norway. Heavy weather losses fell on the Swiss insurance market, and two heavy storms in Sweden caused losses of some 200 million kronor. Prolonged labour disturbances in Italy produced a strong demand for strike and malicious damage cover.

The 1960s had been the worst decade ever for marine underwriters. There was some improvement in 1969, but overall the year was disappointing. Casualties to tankers were particularly heavy. In addition, settlements were made in respect of the vessels trapped in the Suez Canal following the Six-Day War of 1967. Premium revenue on aviation account continued to expand, and with a more realistic approach to hull business the market as a whole was profitable.

(D. L. Bɪ.; P. Ss.)

See also Cooperatives; Disasters; Industrial Review; Social Services.

ENCYCLOPÆDIA BRITANNICA FILMS. *Casualty Insurance* (1954).

Intelligence Operations

The year 1970 was marked by Soviet attempts to glamorize their British spies. George Blake (real name Behar), who in 1966 escaped from Britain's Wormwood Scrubs prison while serving a 42-year sentence for espionage, was awarded the Order of Lenin and the military Order of the Red Banner in February. In his reminiscences, published in the Soviet newspaper *Izvestia,* Blake suggested that he first began to consider working as a Soviet agent when he was posted on behalf of the SIS (Special Intelligence Service, the old name for British Intelligence) in Hamburg, Ger., in 1946. Later he was sent to South Korea as a British vice-consul, but this appointment was a blind and his real task was to collect information seeping through Seoul from Vladivostok and Manchuria.

Captured by the North Koreans in 1950, he was freed in 1953, and soon afterward was posted to Berlin as a senior member of MI6 (intelligence). There he was able to disclose to the KGB (the Soviet Committee of State Security) "many" operations jointly undertaken by MI6 and the U.S. Central Intelligence Agency. The biggest of these, he boasted, was "Operation Gold." In December 1953 the British and U.S. intelligence services started building a tunnel from West Berlin to East Berlin so that Soviet and East German

telephones could be tapped. Blake betrayed this plan to his Soviet "contact" in a London street before the building had started, although the Soviet military authorities did not decide to "discover" and destroy the tunnel until 1956.

"Kim" Philby (Harold Adrian Russell Philby), who had been a Soviet agent within British intelligence for more than 20 years before going to the Soviet Union in 1965, was permitted by the KGB to make a film on his life. Rather masochistically, the BBC showed it on July 29. Entitled "Philby, a Ruthless Journey," the film left the impression of a charming man cast up in a milieu he did not really enjoy. Scenes from Philby's life in Moscow with his new wife, formerly Mrs. Melinda Maclean, were shown, but he was not allowed to talk.

Donald Maclean, a high-ranking official in the British Foreign Office who had defected with Guy Burgess to the Soviet Union in 1951, was allowed to write a book in English on *British Foreign Policy Since Suez, 1956–1968.* The book, published in London in May, was a product of Maclean's work in Moscow at the Institute of World Economics and International Relations. Based mainly on published material, it was a melancholic though indirect attempt at self-justification. Maclean wrote with contempt about British rulers "whose capacity to bend other peoples and other nations to their will had sharply diminished"; he considered that British support of U.S. policy in Vietnam was "one of the most shameful pages in the history of British foreign policy." He did not mention the Cuban missile crisis of 1962.

Ethel Gee and her fiancé, Harry Houghton, aides of the Soviet master spy known as Gordon Lonsdale (Konon Trofimovich Molody), who had been sentenced to 15 years' imprisonment in 1961, were released on parole on May 12. They had been members of a spy ring centred around the Underwater Weapons Establishment at Portland, Dorset. Lonsdale, sentenced to 25 years' imprisonment, had been exchanged in 1964 for Greville Wynne, a British businessman convicted of espionage in Moscow.

It was announced in the Soviet press that Lonsdale had died on October 9, after a heart attack suffered while picking mushrooms in a field. His memoirs, full of obvious misrepresentations and concealments, had been published in London in 1965, for which he received £10,000 (free of income tax) from a British publisher. He also became the "star" of a Soviet film, *Krasnaya Zvezda* ("The Dead Season"). In an obituary, the Soviet Defense Ministry newspaper said that Colonel Molody had joined the Soviet security service shortly after World War II. It was, however, intriguing to note that according to *Komsomolskaya Pravda* of November 20 the spy's real name was Georgi Lonov.

William James Owen, Labour MP for Morpeth, Northumberland, was arrested in January by the Special Branch of the London Metropolitan Police and charged under a section of the Official Secrets Act of 1911 relating to collecting and communicating to any other person secrets useful to an enemy. Owen was secretary of the Parliamentary East-West Trade Committee, and in this capacity he had organized many trips to Eastern Europe for MPs. From 1960 to 1964 he served on the House of Commons Select Committee on Estimates. His 13-day trial at the Central Criminal Court ended on May 6, when the jury found him not guilty on all charges. The case had been brought on flimsy evidence, but it was regarded in the London newspaper world as a warning to non-

William Owen, former Labour MP for Morpeth, leaves Old Bailey May 6, 1970, after being acquitted of eight charges made against him under the Official Secrets Act.

KEYSTONE

security-conscious MPs, as well as to diplomatic and defense correspondents.

During the trial, Owen admitted that he was first approached in 1961 by Gustav Husak, a Czechoslovak "diplomat," who had asked him to write an article on economic development in Eastern Europe. For this article, which was never published, Owen was paid £25. Some time after this opening, Husak asked him about the contents of the "blue books"—the reports submitted by the armed services to the Committee on Estimates. Owen tried to wriggle out of the difficulty by passing notices based on hearsay evidence to Husak, while the latter threatened to expose him to MI5 (counterintelligence) unless he cooperated thoroughly. When Husak was recalled to Prague and replaced by Josef Kalina, Owen continued to supply Czechoslovak Intelligence with reports based on published sources. At the trial he firmly denied ever having passed any classified information to his Czechoslovak friends. However, during the eight years that the relationship lasted, he received about £2,300 from Czechoslovak "diplomats."

The fantastic story of the Sidewinder missile, stolen from a NATO base in West Germany in 1967 and delivered by air freight to Moscow, had its epilogue before the Düsseldorf High Court on October 9. Three men accused of the theft were jailed for terms of up to four years: Manfred Ramminger, 39, an architect, and Josef Linowski, 39, a mechanic, were given four years each, and Wolf Diethard Knoppe, 34, a former jet fighter pilot, was sentenced to three years and three months. Ramminger told the court that, having delivered the Sidewinder to Moscow in October 1967, he returned to West Germany with two agreements: one was to build an animal-food factory in the Soviet Union for a fee of DM. 200,000; the other was simply "to be helpful and procure various things which in the Western world can be had by anyone, but could not be legally obtained by the U.S.S.R." Linowski, who ran a construction company with Ramminger, admitted having received DM. 76,000. Knoppe received DM. 29,850 and, in addition, Ramminger offered him a lucrative pilot's job with a private airline.

In May Dieter Blötz, secretary-general of the Social Democratic Party in Hamburg, was installed as vice-president of the West German Intelligence Service. The post had been vacant since its previous holder, Gen. Horst Wendland, shot himself in his office in October 1968. With Gen. Gerhard Wessel, the president, Blötz was responsible for 5,000 employees and an annual budget of more than DM. 100 million.

On March 2 a spokesman for the Karlsruhe office of the West German federal prosecutor general disclosed that three members of an East German spy ring had been arrested in West Germany. Liane Lindner (real name Ingeborg Weber), a 43-year-old psychologist who had "fled" from East Germany, had worked for a publishing house in Cologne, but she was described as a lieutenant colonel in the East German SSD, equivalent to the Soviet KGB. Irene Schultz, 51, a widow, had been chief secretary in the office of three successive West German ministers of scientific research, including the incumbent, Franz Leussink. Heinrich Wiedemann, 80, a former West German judge and former member of the Nazi Party, had resided in Hamburg. The West German press credited the discovery of this ring to the Federal Office for the Protection of the Constitution, with headquarters at Ehrenfeld, near Cologne.

As usual, several "diplomats" were charged with spying and expelled from NATO countries during 1970. Among others they included Aleksandr Vasilievich Tikhomirov, a translator at the UN, who was arrested in Seattle, Wash., in February; Vladimir Aleksandrov, a Soviet embassy official, who was asked to leave Italy in February; Boris Savich, who was caught in March by the security police in Brussels when trying to gain information about NATO bases; and Boris Netrebski and V. S. Sharovatov, two members of the Soviet embassy at The Hague, Neth., who were expelled in May.　　　　　　　　(K. SM.)

Inter-American Affairs

Events in 1970 combined to suggest that a new phase in the Western Hemisphere's internal relations was beginning. In the U.S. Pres. Richard Nixon introduced a cooler approach to Latin America and its problems, while the Latin Americans showed a more general disenchantment over the failure of their relations with the U.S. to solve their difficulties. President Nixon's method of conducting his relations with Latin America became more cautious after the visits of New York Gov. Nelson Rockefeller to several republics in 1969. The president made no comment of substance on the governor's report, on the merits of which opinion was divided.

Among the Latin-American nations themselves, certain trends that had been discernible in 1969 became clearer in 1970. The emergence of more decidedly defined nationalist trends was evident in the governments of Brazil and Peru as each completed another year in office, in Chile as it elected a Marxist to the presidency, and in Bolivia with another change of government. The subregions into which the republics had tended to group themselves, mainly for economic reasons, began in 1970 to acquire more political significance; and there was a concerted current of opinion strongly in favour of restoring commercial and diplomatic relations with Cuba. This latter point became an important question in the Latin Americans' now-firm stand over independent foreign policies, running counter, if need be, to that of the U.S. In the Latin-American context, the concepts of the cold war and of hemisphere solidarity ceased to have much significance.

The changes in the political climate of Latin America reflected a deeply rooted frustration; this was occurring at a national level no less significantly than in universities, in the church, and among individuals. It took the form, in some national policies, of a defiant attitude toward influences that were believed to have made for frustration; the brunt of the resulting action was borne by U.S. private investments and by domestic oligarchies.

The nationalism that was appearing, with a different emphasis in each country, was not in itself right wing or left wing but might be present in either a rightist regime, such as that of Brazil, or the strongly leftist one that Pres. Salvador Allende was expected to introduce in Chile. Common to all the nationalists was a radical, slightly puritan, or at least austere, approach to institutional reforms designed to make government more effective.

Effective government implied a well-managed economy, which in Latin America meant that the executive branch of the government must have complete control of its key factors, sharing no responsibility with the legislature. This was the case in Argentina, Bolivia,

WIDE WORLD

Lieut. Col. Donald Crowley, air attaché for the U.S. embassy in the Dominican Republic, talks to newsmen in Santo Domingo about his kidnapping. He was released on March 26, 1970, after several Dominican political prisoners were freed and flown to Mexico.

CATHERINE LEROY FROM
NANCY PALMER

Earthquake victims rush
to unload food, clothing,
and medical supplies
from U.S. Marine
helicopters in Pira, Peru.

Peru, Ecuador, and, to a great extent, Brazil. Such a policy was seen as requiring effective executive control over the country's natural resources, basic industries, and public and social services. Such ideas had been current in Latin America since the Mexican revolution, but only in 1970 could it be said that they were firmly established virtually throughout the region. Their adoption, and actions derived from them, led to a marked strengthening of the collectively independent attitude of Latin America in relation to the U.S.

Organization of American States. Changes were made in the charter of the Organization of American States (OAS) in February, giving the Inter-American Economic and Social Council (IA-ECOSOC, or CIES, from the initials of its name in Spanish) and the Inter-American Council for Education, Science, and Culture the same permanent status and importance as the political Permanent Council. In June, at the first General Assembly after these changes were adopted, attention was centred on the problems of kidnapping, sabotage, hijacking, and other forms of terrorism, and on the question of restoring relations with Cuba. Although violence in its many forms was recognized as having political consequences and might have been thought to have been within the jurisdiction of the OAS Permanent Council, it was widely seen as having economic and social origins. It was also believed by the ministers at the Assembly that terrorism and violence were spontaneous domestic problems, the product of frustration and lack of opportunity. Few representatives at the Assembly believed that terrorism was inspired by Cuban designs, or indeed by those of any other foreign state. The consensus on the real origins of violence, as being engendered by social and economic conditions in each country, gave the CIES outstanding importance as a body whose deliberations must be, at the very least, highly relevant to that disturbing problem.

The restoration of relations with Cuba and, by inference, the readmission of Cuba into the OAS or into a similar organization that might be formed without U.S. participation, were ideas that rapidly gained wider acceptance in 1970, and not only in countries with markedly left-wing governments. With Chile in the lead, the South American republics were increasingly taking the view, unwaveringly held by Mexico, that Cuba was a Latin-American state first and that a truly independent foreign policy called for a difference of opinion with the U.S. over relations with Cuba.

When U.S. espionage aircraft detected submarine service vessels and what appeared to be the beginnings of a Soviet submarine base at Cienfuegos, in Cuba, the reactions in Washington, in Latin America, and apparently in Moscow were markedly different from the tense atmosphere of the 1962 "missile crisis," although the principles involved were similar. Washington protested, quoting Pres. John F. Kennedy's 1962 statement, and the vessels were withdrawn; Latin-American reactions, however, were cool to the point of indifference.

Another important institutional change in the OAS was made when the CIES decided to make a permanent body of the special committee originally set up in 1969 to discuss with the U.S. government the implications of the matters discussed by the Latin-American foreign ministers at Viña del Mar, Chile, in 1969. The special committee became, after February, the main channel for dialogues between Latin America and the U.S. government on economic, commercial, and social matters; the choice of the special committee for this role was made despite Washington's preference for the Inter-American Committee on the Alliance for Progress (CIAP), which had in effect survived the Alliance itself.

There was in Latin America a growing disappointment that the inter-American system had achieved less than had been hoped for, even after the presentation to President Nixon of the results of the Viña del Mar conference. Nixon's understanding reception of this document, and his subsequent disregard of the Rockefeller report, together with various statements regarding his intentions, had all combined to give the impression that the U.S. would channel more direct aid toward Latin America and, more importantly, would liberalize U.S. trade regulations in favour of Latin-American manufactured goods.

A general deterioration in Latin America's share of the supply of goods imported into the U.S. was noted in a study published in October by the CIAP; Latin America supplied 28.3% of U.S. imports in 1950 but only 11.7% in 1969. In absolute terms, but without allowance for the depreciation of money, Latin America's exports to the U.S. increased over the two decades by approximately 33%, from $3 billion to $4 billion, but total U.S. imports rose over the same period by 300%, from $9 billion to $36 billion. The CIAP explained this trend by the changing pattern of demand in the U.S., which "has moved away from primary products and concentrated more on manufactures." These comments lent point to the claims made by Latin Americans that the U.S. should encourage, or at least not impede, Latin America's export potential in manufactures so as to enable the Latin Americans to export the value added by industry to domestic raw materials.

An important part in attempting to reconcile conflicting economic interests was played over the past ten years by the Inter-American Development Bank, which achieved not only considerable financial success but also a respectable intellectual status as an uncommitted, strictly impartial, institution genuinely involved in the development of Latin America. In mid-1970 the bank published a comprehensive study of the characteristics, problems, aims, policies, and potential of the Latin-American republics, written by Raúl Prebisch, a noted Latin-American economist and director general of the UN Latin American Institute for Economic and Social Planning, in Santiago, Chile. Prebisch showed in his report, entitled *Change and*

Development, that the process of change in Latin America, though extremely rapid, was, nevertheless, impeded by obstacles, both internal and external, that were themselves the result of equally rapid change elsewhere in the world.

Regional and Subregional Integration. The Latin American Free Trade Association (LAFTA) made no more than slow progress toward its ultimate goal of complete trade liberalization and an eventual common market. At the ninth annual meeting held in Caracas, Venezuela, near the end of 1969, it proved impossible to reach agreement on the expansion of the "common list" of liberalized items, and the date by which liberalization should be completed was postponed from 1973 to 1980; the goal of a common market, originally foreseen for 1985, was deferred indefinitely.

It was widely recognized that formal intergovernmental trade concessions had been achieved as extensively as was feasible for the time being, and that further general liberalization, especially since it would increasingly involve industrial goods, would depend on major economic changes within the individual countries. At a less formal level, however, there was an appreciable expansion of intra-LAFTA trade in manufactures derived from private enterprise agreements, such as in the motor vehicle industry, in which there was a notable growth in the interchange of components.

The Central American Common Market (CACM), where progress was halted in mid-1969 by the war between El Salvador and Honduras, began to show signs of a slow recovery; there was a limited resumption of the movement of goods and an improvement in official relations. The five CACM central banks agreed on the formation of a monetary stabilization fund, from which member banks could make short-term borrowings in order to ease temporary balance of payments difficulties.

A growing interest in Central America, both as a trade group and as an area for investment and economic influence, was shown by Mexico. This appeared to be a logical development in light of the uncertain future of LAFTA, of which Mexico was a member and which the CACM would have joined as a single member if its own affairs had been less disturbed. It also seemed logical that both Mexico and the Central American countries should seek at least trade and financial links in the face of the clearer definition acquired by the other subregional groups in South America.

The group that made the greatest impact, both on its component members and on the rest of the Western Hemisphere, was the Andean group, consisting of Bolivia, Chile, Colombia, Ecuador, and Peru. The group acquired formal existence with the ratification by all five countries of the Cartagena Agreement, which came into force on Oct. 16, 1969, and had legal and operational identity from Nov. 24, 1969. The Andean Development Corporation was created in mid-1970, and there were discussions concerning the establishment of a regional investment bank. A round of tariff reductions on intraregional trade, in accordance with LAFTA principles, was concluded later in the year. The Andean group, unlike LAFTA, was already in 1970 working out the broad principles of a common economic policy. In October the board proposed draft regulations to govern foreign investment in the area; not surprisingly, in view of the political convictions of three of the member governments, the document

was of a decidedly nationalist tenor. It was not certain that the proposals would be adopted as they stood, but they unmistakably foreshadowed the direction in which economic and allied policies were tending throughout Latin America.

On the Atlantic side of South America some progress was made in developing the Río de la Plata Basin organization. The member countries—Argentina, Bolivia, Brazil, Paraguay, and Uruguay—pursued their studies of the basin's major natural resources suitable for joint development. The virtue of the principle of joint development between a large country and a small neighbour in the group was virtually the same as the earlier relations between the Northern Hemisphere industrial countries and all those of Latin America. The richer country's financial and technical resources would be mobilized in the development of the less advanced country's resources, leading to exports by the latter; thus, for example, the joint venture between Brazil and Paraguay to harness the hydraulic resources at Acaray enabled Paraguay to export surplus electrical energy to neighbouring areas in Brazil and Argentina. Similarly, Argentina's decision to finance the construction of a pipeline in Bolivia would add substantially to the hydrocarbon fuels that could be fed into the Argentine system, and at the same time would assist Bolivia's exports. The group's annual meeting, held in Asunción, Paraguay, in June, discussed the creation of a regional development bank to finance joint projects; the idea was confirmed at a subsequent meeting in July in Brasília.

The Caribbean Free Trade Association (CARIFTA) continued to make limited progress and, following the example of other economic groups, took the step of setting up a development bank, to which the U.K. made a capital contribution of £4.2 million and made available funds for development loans amounting to £5 million. Colombia also became a shareholder in the Caribbean Development Bank with a subscription of $10 million, and Venezuela was believed to be interested in participating.

Territorial Waters. Brazil, with 4,600 mi. of coastline, adopted the principle, first established by South America's Pacific coast countries, of national jurisdiction over 200 mi. of coastal waters. Chile, Peru, and Ecuador were the first republics to make this claim, and it was at one time a source of many incidents with U.S. fishing boats. The 200-mi. principle was also adopted by Argentina, Uruguay, Panama, Nicaragua, and El Salvador in 1969; those countries, with Brazil, held a conference in Montevideo, Uruguay, in April as a result of which they agreed on the principle that not only the sea, with its life, but also the seabed and all its mineral content pertained to the nation and were part of the national territory. Only Colombia and Venezuela among the South American maritime nations had not yet adopted the principle. Venezuela could not in practice make such a claim with any degree of logic, since the waters concerned would include various Caribbean island territories. Colombia faced the same problem as regards its Caribbean coast, and was therefore unlikely to extend its claim beyond the traditional 12 mi.; it might, however, adopt the 200-mi. limit for its Pacific coast.   (Dd. H.)

ENCYCLOPÆDIA BRITANNICA FILMS. *The Amazon—People and Resources of Northern Brazil* (1957); *Argentina—People of the Pampa* (1957); *Brazil—People of the Highlands* (1957); *Peru: People of the Andes* (1959); *Colombia and Venezuela* (1961); *Guatemala—Nation of Central America* (1961); *Puerto Rico: Past, Present, and Promise* (1965); *The West Indies* (1965); *Siqueiros: "El Maestro"* (*March of Humanity in Latin America*) (1969).

International Organizations

The accompanying table shows the membership of the world's sovereign states in various international organizations as of Sept. 30, 1970. The growing realization that political and economic problems transcended international boundaries led to a proliferation of international organizations after World War II. Of these, the UN and its specialized agencies (some of which, such as the ILO and the UPU, antedated the

Membership in International Organizations

As of Sept. 30, 1970

Country	UN	FAO	IMCO	IAEA	ICAO	ILO	IBRD	IDA	IFC	IMF	ITU	UNESCO	UPU	WHO	WMO	GATT	CE	AL	OAS	WEU	OCAS	C-Plan	Comecon	Euratom	ECSC	EEC	EFTA	IDB	LAFTA	OECD	ANZUS	CENTO	NATO	SEATO	WTO	Antarctic treaty	OAU	SPC
	1	2	3	4	5	6	7	8	9	10	11	12	13	14	15	16	17	18	19	20	21	22	23	24	25	26	27	28	29	30	31	32	33	34	35	36	37	38
Afghanistan																																						
Albania																																						
Algeria																																						
Argentina																																						
Australia																																						
Austria																																						
Barbados																																						
Belgium																																						
Belorussia																																						
Bolivia																																						
Botswana																																						
Brazil																																						
Bulgaria																																						
Burma																																						
Burundi																																						
Cambodia																																						
Cameroon																																						
Canada																																						
Central African Rep.																																						
Ceylon																																						
Chad																																						
Chile																																						
Colombia																																						
Congo (Brazzaville)																																						
Congo (Kinshasa)																																						
Costa Rica																																						
Cuba																																						
Cyprus																																						
Czechoslovakia																																						
Dahomey																																						
Denmark																																						
Dominican Rep.																																						
Ecuador																																						
El Salvador																																						
Equatorial Guinea																																						
Ethiopia																																						
Finland																																						
France																																						
Gabon																																						
Gambia, The																																						
Germany, East																																						
Germany, West																																						
Ghana																																						
Greece																																						
Guatemala																																						
Guinea																																						
Guyana																																						
Haiti																																						
Honduras																																						
Hungary																																						
Iceland																																						
India																																						
Indonesia																																						
Iran																																						
Iraq																																						
Ireland																																						
Israel																																						
Italy																																						
Ivory Coast																																						
Jamaica																																						
Japan																																						
Jordan																																						
Kenya																																						
Korea, South																																						
Kuwait																																						
Laos																																						
Lebanon																																						
Lesotho																																						
Liberia																																						
Libya																																						
Liechtenstein																																						
Luxembourg																																						
Malagasy Rep.																																						
Malawi																																						
Malaysia																																						
Maldives																																						
Mali																																						
Malta																																						

war) aimed at least theoretically at universality. The World Bank, originally established to provide help to war-devastated nations, turned more and more in succeeding years toward concentration on the problems of economic development. Organizations with more restricted membership included regional political groupings (OAS, OAU), military alliances (NATO, the Warsaw Pact), and organizations with a primarily economic orientation (EEC, Comecon). Such groupings as the Colombo Plan and the Alliance for Progress were chiefly vehicles for channeling aid from the developed to the less developed countries.

Membership in International Organizations
As of Sept. 30, 1970

Country	UN 1	FAO 2	IMCO 3	IAEA 4	ICAO 5	ILO 6	IBRD 7	IDA 8	IFC 9	IMF 10	ITU 11	UNESCO 12	UPU 13	WHO 14	WMO 15	GATT 16	CE 17	AL 18	OAS 19	WEU 20	OCAS 21	C-Plan 22	Comecon 23	Euratom 24	ECSC 25	EEC 26	EFTA 27	IDB 28	LAFTA 29	OECD 30	ANZUS 31	CENTO 32	NATO 33	SEATO 34	WTO 35	Antarctic treaty 36	OAU 37	SPC 38
Mauritania	●	●	●		●	●	●	●	●	●	●	●	●	●	●																						●	
Mauritius	●	●	●			●	●	●	●	●	●	●	●	●	●	●																					●	
Mexico	●	●	●	●	●	●	●	●	●	●	●	●	●	●	●				●									●	●									
Monaco	●		●	●							●	●	●	●	●																							
Mongolia	●			●		●					●	●	●	●	●																							
Morocco	●	●	●	●	●	●	●	●	●	●	●	●	●	●	●			●																			●	
Nepal	●	●			●	●	●	●		●	●	●	●	●	●																							
Netherlands	●	●	●	●	●	●	●	●	●	●	●	●	●	●	●	●	●			●				●	●	●		●		●			●			●		
New Zealand	●	●	●	●	●	●	●	●	●	●	●	●	●	●	●	●						●								●	●			●				●
Nicaragua	●	●	●	●	●	●	●	●	●	●	●	●	●	●	●				●		●							●										
Niger	●	●			●	●	●	●	●	●	●	●	●	●	●																						●	
Nigeria	●	●	●		●	●	●	●	●	●	●	●	●	●	●	●																					●	
Norway	●	●	●	●	●	●	●	●	●	●	●	●	●	●	●	●	●										●			●			●			●		
Pakistan	●	●	●	●	●	●	●	●	●	●	●	●	●	●	●	●						●										●		●				
Panama	●	●	●		●	●	●	●	●	●	●	●	●	●	●				●		●							●										
Paraguay	●	●			●	●	●	●	●	●	●	●	●	●	●				●									●	●									
Peru	●	●	●	●	●	●	●	●	●	●	●	●	●	●	●				●									●	●									
Philippines	●	●	●	●	●	●	●	●	●	●	●	●	●	●	●							●												●				
Poland	●	●	●	●	●	●					●	●	●	●	●								●												●			
Portugal	●	●	●		●	●	●	●	●	●	●	●	●	●	●	●											●						●					
Rhodesia											●		●		●																							
Romania	●	●		●	●	●					●	●	●	●	●	●							●												●			
Rwanda	●	●				●	●	●	●	●	●	●	●	●	●																						●	
San Marino											●				●																							
Saudi Arabia	●	●	●		●	●	●	●	●	●	●	●	●	●	●			●																				
Senegal	●	●	●		●	●	●	●	●	●	●	●	●	●	●	●																					●	
Sierra Leone	●	●	●		●	●	●	●	●	●	●	●	●	●	●	●																					●	
Singapore	●	●	●		●	●	●	●	●	●	●	●	●	●	●	●						●																
Somalia	●	●	●			●	●	●	●	●	●	●	●	●	●			●																			●	
South Africa	●	●	●	●	●		●	●	●	●	●		●		●	●																						
Southern Yemen	●	●				●					●	●	●	●	●			●																				
Spain	●	●	●	●	●	●	●	●	●	●	●	●	●	●	●															●								
Sudan	●	●	●		●	●	●	●	●	●	●	●	●	●	●			●																			●	
Swaziland	●	●				●	●	●		●	●	●	●	●	●																						●	
Sweden	●	●	●	●	●	●	●	●	●	●	●	●	●	●	●	●	●										●			●						●		
Switzerland		●	●	●	●	●					●	●	●	●	●	●	●										●			●						●		
Syria	●	●	●		●	●	●	●	●	●	●	●	●	●	●			●																				
Taiwan	●	●	●	●	●	●	●	●	●	●	●	●	●	●	●																							
Tanzania	●	●	●		●	●	●	●	●	●	●	●	●	●	●	●																					●	
Thailand	●	●	●	●	●	●	●	●	●	●	●	●	●	●	●							●												●				
Togo	●	●			●	●	●	●	●	●	●	●	●	●	●																						●	
Trinidad and Tobago	●	●	●		●	●	●	●	●	●	●	●	●	●	●				●									●										
Tunisia	●	●	●		●	●	●	●	●	●	●	●	●	●	●			●																			●	
Turkey	●	●	●	●	●	●	●	●	●	●	●	●	●	●	●	●	●													●		●	●					
Uganda	●	●	●		●	●	●	●	●	●	●	●	●	●	●																						●	
Ukraine	●			●		●					●	●	●	●	●																							
United Arab Republic	●	●	●	●	●	●	●	●	●	●	●	●	●	●	●			●																				
United Kingdom	●	●	●	●	●	●	●	●	●	●	●	●	●	●	●	●	●			●		●					●			●		●	●	●		●		
United States	●	●	●	●	●	●	●	●	●	●	●	●	●	●	●	●			●									●		●	●	●	●	●		●		
Upper Volta	●	●			●	●	●	●	●	●	●	●	●	●	●																						●	
Uruguay	●	●	●		●	●	●	●	●	●	●	●	●	●	●				●									●	●									
U.S.S.R.	●			●	●	●					●	●	●	●	●								●												●	●		
Vatican City				●							●		●		●																							
Venezuela	●	●	●	●	●	●	●	●	●	●	●	●	●	●	●				●									●	●									
Vietnam, South	●	●			●	●	●	●	●	●	●	●	●	●	●							●																
Western Samoa											●				●																							●
Yemen	●	●				●	●	●		●	●	●	●	●	●			●																				
Yugoslavia	●	●	●	●	●	●	●	●	●	●	●	●	●	●	●	●																						
Zambia	●	●	●		●	●	●	●	●	●	●	●	●	●	●																						●	

KEY

UN	1	United Nations.
FAO	2	Food and Agriculture Organization of the United Nations.
IMCO	3	Intergovernmental Maritime Consultative Organization.
IAEA	4	International Atomic Energy Agency.
ICAO	5	International Civil Aviation Organization.
ILO	6	International Labour Organization.
IBRD	7	International Bank for Reconstruction and Development.
IDA	8	International Development Association.
IFC	9	International Finance Corporation.
IMF	10	International Monetary Fund.
ITU	11	International Telecommunication Union.
UNESCO	12	United Nations Educational, Scientific, and Cultural Organization.
UPU	13	Universal Postal Union.
WHO	14	World Health Organization.
WMO	15	World Meteorological Organization.
GATT	16	General Agreement on Tariffs and Trade.
CE	17	Council of Europe.
AL	18	Arab League.
OAS	19	Organization of American States.
WEU	20	Western European Union.
OCAS	21	Organization of Central American States.
C-Plan	22	Colombo Plan for Co-operative Economic Development in South and South-East Asia
Comecon	23	Council for Mutual Economic Assistance.
Euratom	24	European Atomic Energy Community.
ECSC	25	European Coal and Steel Community.
EEC	26	European Economic Community.
EFTA	27	European Free Trade Association.
IDB	28	Inter-American Development Bank.
LAFTA	29	Latin American Free Trade Association.
OECD	30	Organization for Economic Cooperation and Development.
ANZUS	31	Security treaty between Australia, New Zealand, and the United States.
CENTO	32	Central Treaty Organization.
NATO	33	North Atlantic Treaty Organization.
SEATO	34	Southeast Asia Treaty Organization.
WTO	35	Warsaw Treaty Organization.
	36	Antarctic Treaty.
OAU	37	Organization of African Unity.
SPC	38	South Pacific Commission.

Investment, International

Continued expansion in most of the world's economies helped to further increase the flows of international investment in 1969 and 1970. Large corporations were increasingly establishing production facilities in other countries as a means of competing on more favourable terms with both domestic producers and other international competitors. As in previous years the size and direction of international flows of portfolio investment reflected differences between national interest rates, credit, and stock market conditions. West Germany continued to adopt a low interest rate policy, which increased its international investment to such an extent that the outflow of funds reached as high as 75% of the U.S. outflow. The U.S. maintained curbs on the outflow of funds but the Japanese government considerably eased restrictions on foreign direct investment in Japan. Two other features of international investment were worthy of note: the U.K. became a net receiver of capital, and the inflow of capital into the U.S. was greater than into any other economy.

United States. The total value of U.S. long-term assets abroad reached $100 billion during 1970 and at the end of the year amounted to about $104 billion (*see* Table I). Direct investments accounted for 73% of the total and portfolio investments for the remaining 27%. During 1969 the flow of new investment was just over $7 billion; in the first half of 1970 direct investment rose very sharply to an annual rate of $5.5 billion. These early figures suggested that 1970 would be a record year for U.S. investment abroad, particularly direct investment (*see* Table II).

International investment by U.S. corporations was influenced in 1969, as in 1968, by the government's Foreign Direct Investment Program, which aimed at curbing the outflow of funds in order to ease pressure on the balance of payments. The result of this was a much higher level of reinvested profits and increased borrowing abroad by U.S. companies. Table II shows that although direct investment increased in 1969 the outflow of new funds fell a little; reinvested profits financed 45% of direct investment compared with only 30% in 1965. Direct investment reached very high levels in the first half of 1970.

The geographic pattern of U.S. direct investments abroad is shown in Table III. Investments in Canada accounted for about two-thirds of the total, compared with three-quarters in the mid-1960s. Assets in manufacturing industry accounted for 42% of the total and in petroleum for 28%. The major change in the pattern in 1969 was the doubling of investment in the EEC to $1.1 billion, chiefly in the West German manufacturing industry. Investment in the U.K. was $150 million lower, at $435 million, but investment in the rest of Europe increased by a similar amount. Investment in Canada was $160 million higher because of increased investment in transportation equipment, but investment in both Latin America and Africa was about $100 million lower than in 1968. The fall in Latin America was caused by the compulsory purchase by the Chilean government of U.S. interests in two mining companies and the sale of a public utility company to the government in Peru. In the first half of 1970, there were large increases in investment in Canada and Europe; the flow to the U.K. alone was $280 million above a year earlier.

Investment in manufacturing industries accounted for 55% of U.S. international investment in 1969; about half of this was in Western Europe. Manufacturing industry investment in the U.K. fell back from the very high levels of 1968, but the flow of new funds to Canadian manufacturing industry increased by $200 million. Investment in petroleum industries was $1.1 billion in 1969, almost one-fifth of U.S. international investment. This was, however, much lower than the $1.5 billion investment in 1968. U.S. investment in mining was much lower, partly because of the compulsory purchase in Chile and partly because of the completion of several projects in Australia.

Earnings on U.S. international investments reached over $10 billion in 1969; this was an increase of 14% over the 1968 level and very similar to the rate of increase in 1968 (*see* Table IV). Earnings continued to increase in the first half of 1970 but at a slightly slower rate. Considerable increases were recorded in 1969 in both direct and portfolio investment earnings; in the first half of 1970 portfolio investment earnings accelerated but earnings on direct investments grew at an annual rate of little over 5%. The rate of return on direct investments increased to 13% in 1969, compared with an average yield in the 1960s of 12.6%. This increase brought the rate of return on foreign manufacturing investments above that on domestic investments for the first time in a number of years.

Earnings on investment in Europe, particularly in West German manufacturing, accounted for over half the increase in direct investment earnings in 1969, although Canada and Latin America remained the main sources of earnings with 37% of the total between them (*see* Table III). There was a slight drop in U.S. earnings in the U.K., a 65% increase from EEC countries, and a 50% increase from the rest of Western Europe. On the other hand, large losses in petroleum investments in Europe were caused by high exploration and development costs in the North Sea. Earnings from African investments increased by $230 million to $810 million and Asian investments recorded a 10% increase. Petroleum earnings from Asia and Africa increased by $195 million; much of this was related to increased production in new developments in North Africa.

U.S. portfolio investment amounted to almost $1.5 billion in 1969, an increase of 30% over 1968. Purchases of new bonds issued by foreign borrowers in the U.S. amounted to $1.5 billion, but there were net

Table I. U.S. Foreign Assets

In $000,000,000 at end of year

Item	1960	1965	1966	1967	1968	1969
Book value of direct investments	31.9	49.5	54.8	59.5	65.0	70.8
Portfolio investments*	12.5	21.5	21.0	22.2	24.5	25.2
Total	44.4	71.0	75.8	81.7	89.5	96.0

*Book value of foreign bonds and shares held by U.S. residents and U.S. banking claims.
Source: U.S. Department of Commerce, *Survey of Current Business.*

Table II. U.S. Investment Abroad

In $000,000

Item	1965	1966	1967	1968	1969	1st half 1970*
Direct investment						
New funds	3,468	3,661	3,137	3,209	3,070	5,548
Reinvested profits	1,542	1,739	1,598	2,175	2,532	...
Total	5,010	5,400	4,735	5,384	5,602	...
Portfolio investment	1,078	261	1,292	1,133	1,479	138
Total	6,088	5,661	6,027	6,517	7,081	...

*Seasonally adjusted; at annual rate.
Source: U.S. Department of Commerce, *Survey of Current Business.*

sales by U.S. residents of foreign bonds of $500 million. The majority of the new issues placed in the U.S. were Canadian and amounted to almost $1.3 billion, compared with $950 million in 1968. Issues by international organizations and by less developed economies fell sharply to about half their 1968 level. During 1969 it was apparent that high U.S. interest rates were reducing foreign bond placements, and in the first half of 1970 these fell to about two-thirds of the 1969 rate. At the same time, there were net sales of almost $400 million of foreign bonds and stocks by U.S. residents.

In 1969 the U.S., which had been the world's largest exporter of capital, also became the world's largest recipient of international investment. Foreign direct investment in U.S. industry (excluding reinvested profits), which had averaged about $80 million per year in the first half of the 1960s, amounted to over $800 million in 1969 (see Table V). The total value of foreign direct investment assets in the U.S. was about $12 billion, about one-sixth of the value of similar foreign assets held by the U.S. Foreign investment in U.S. manufacturing industry increased very sharply but foreign petroleum investment declined. Investment by Canadian companies increased from $75 million to $320 million, all in new funds. European direct investment in the U.S. increased by $200 million to $870 million, mostly attributable to large investments by West German chemical firms. In the first half of 1970, foreign direct investment fell back from its 1969 peak but remained well above the 1968 level.

Foreign portfolio investment in the U.S. reached a very high level of $4.4 billion in 1968 and fell to $3.1 billion in 1969. This compared with an average of $80 million in 1960–65. About half of this investment in 1968–69 represented new issues by U.S. companies in foreign capital markets in response to the Foreign Direct Investment Program. Foreign purchases of U.S. stocks fell from $2.1 billion in 1968 to $1.6 billion in 1969 as U.S. stock markets weakened. In 1970 there was a further decline in foreign issues of U.S. stocks and a further drop in U.S. stock markets did not encourage purchases by foreign investors.

United Kingdom. Investment abroad by the U.K. fell about 15% in 1969 and provisional estimates for 1970 suggested a further fall to a level equal to only about 75% of the 1968 level (see Table VI). The level of investment in 1968, however, was exceptionally high and investment in 1970 was almost 50% above the 1966–67 average. Within the total, the major change in 1970 was the very sharp 30% fall in direct investment; 1969 had, however, recorded a very high rate, so that the 1970 level was high by comparison with figures for other recent years. The outflow of new funds accounted for about 40% of direct investment in 1969, the remainder being reinvested profits. In recent previous years the proportion of investment financed from profits had been higher and new funds had accounted for about one-third of investment.

Portfolio investment continued its pattern of wide annual fluctuations. After a high level of £236 million in 1968, there was slight net disinvestment in 1969, followed by a return to modest investment in 1970. About £150 million of the fall in investment between 1968 and 1969 was associated with investments in nonsterling-area countries and was accounted for mostly by the decline on Wall Street; the remainder could be attributed to a large reduction in purchases of Australian company securities. There was a recovery in portfolio investment in the first half of 1970,

although this was held back by further falls on Wall Street. Provisional figures for 1970 suggested a sharp increase in oil and miscellaneous investment.

The regional pattern of U.K. direct investment is shown in Table VII (although 1968 was the latest year for which figures were available). The sterling area took about 45% of U.K. direct investment in 1969; this proportion was similar to other recent years but much lower than the share of 55–60% recorded in the early 1960s. This downward trend could be attributed to two factors: the contraction of the sterling area and, more importantly, the slower rate of growth of U.K. investment in sectors such as agriculture and distribution, which are relatively more important among sterling area investments. The nonsterling area was a particularly buoyant field for U.K. investments, receiving twice as much in 1969 as in 1966–67. This increase partly reflected the effect of the devaluation

Table III. U.S. Direct Investment and Earnings by Region, 1969
In $000,000

Area	Total value of assets at end of year	Net investment Reinvested profits	New funds	Total	Earnings Repatriated profits	Total
Canada	47,701	937	619	1,556	762	1,542
Latin America	11,667	362	271	633	1,049	1,401
Other Western Hemisphere	2,144	14	74	88	228	233
EEC	10,194	455	648	1,103	453	888
United Kingdom	7,158	151	284	435	327	488
Other European countries	4,202	239	226	465	246	479
Africa	2,970	117	175	292	684	808
Asia	5,192	162	309	471	1,450	1,613
Australia and New Zealand	3,099	147	147	294	141	266
International shipping	3,061	—52	316	264	298	237
Total	70,763	2,532	3,070	5,602	5,639	7,955

Source: U.S. Department of Commerce, *Survey of Current Business.*

Table IV. U.S. Investment Earnings
In $000,000

Item	1965	1966	1967	1968	1969	1st half 1970*
Direct investment						
Repatriated profits	3,963	4,045	4,517	4,973	5,639	5,990
Reinvested profits†	1,497	1,657	1,516	2,049	2,316	...
Total	5,460	5,702	6,033	7,022	7,955	...
Portfolio investment						
Total income	1,428	1,605	1,717	1,949	2,267	2,602
Total earnings	6,888	7,307	7,750	8,971	10,222	...

*Seasonally adjusted; at annual rate.
†Excluding interest but before deducting foreign withholding taxes.
Source: U.S. Department of Commerce, *Survey of Current Business.*

Table V. Foreign Investment in U.S.
In $000,000

Inflow of funds	1960	1966	1967	1968	1969	1970*
Direct investment	141	86	258	319	832	546
Portfolio investment	282	909	1,016	4,389	3,112	1,158
Total	423	995	1,274	4,708	3,944	1,704
Total earnings†	731	1,593	1,764	2,231	3,686	4,344

*First half of year, seasonally adjusted; at annual rate.
†Excluding undistributed profits, which amounted to $488 million in 1968 and $431 million in 1969.
Source: U.S. Department of Commerce, *Survey of Current Business.*

Table VI. U.K. Investment Abroad
In £000,000

Item	1960	1966	1967	1968	1969	1970*
Direct investment†						
New funds	165	93	91	135	208	...
Reinvested profits	85	183	190	277	323	...
Total	250	276	281	410	531	360
Portfolio investment‡	—37	—83	59	236	—4	60
Oil and miscellaneous	109	110	123	89	90	140
Total	322	303	463	735	617	560

*Estimate based on first half of year.
†Excluding oil and before 1963 insurance.
‡Net disinvestment in 1960, 1966, and 1969.
Sources: *U.K. Balance of Payments, 1970; Economic Trends.*

U.K. exceeded U.K. investment abroad and, for the first time, the U.K. was a net receiver of long-term capital. This net inflow increased to almost £100 million in 1970 as U.K. investment fell and foreign investment in the U.K. continued to increase.

Other Industrial Nations. Trends in the international investments of other countries are reflected in Table VIII. The net inflow of capital to Canada more than doubled between 1967 and 1969, from $1,050,-000,000 to $2,210,000,000. Canadian direct investment abroad increased very sharply. There was only a slight increase in foreign direct investment in Canada and the net inflow of direct investment was reduced by $100 million. Most of the increase in the net capital inflow in 1969 was the result of Canadian investors switching from heavy buying of foreign securities in 1968, mainly U.S. common stock, to net selling of almost $100 million in 1969.

Stringent controls on the outflow of French funds were in force during 1969. As a result, a net outflow of $325 million in 1968 was turned into a net inflow of $440 million in 1969. Almost half of this inflow was accounted for by French issues of securities abroad.

The continued increase in the net outflow of long-term investment capital, from a mere $60 million in 1967 to over $3 billion in 1969, was making West Germany a net lender in international investment comparable only to the U.S. There was further growth in direct investment in 1969 to a level almost double that of 1967, while foreign direct investment in West Germany fell to only one-third of its 1965–66 level. These two movements meant that for the first time since World War II there was a net outflow of direct investment. German portfolio investment rose sharply in 1969 to a level almost double the U.S. rate. Early estimates suggested that the net outflow in 1970 would be considerably below the 1969 record level. The increase in the net outflow of capital from Italy in 1969 was due mainly to increased purchases of foreign investment trusts. The substantial outflow of funds reflected the sizable differential between Italian interest rates and those in other countries.   (A. G. A.)

See also Development, Economic; Payments and Reserves, International; Trade, International.

Table VII. U.K. Direct Investment and Earnings by Region*
In £000,000

Area	Investment				Earnings			
	1966	1967	1968	1969	1966	1967	1968	1969
Nonsterling area								
United States	42	52	84	...	68	73	86	...
EEC	51	30	73	...	25	25	65	...
EFTA	11	−8	19	...	8	11	13	...
Others	54	65	57	...	91	92	118	...
Total	158	139	233	294	192	201	282	324
Sterling area								
Australia	49	54	80	...	55	62	76	...
South Africa	35	47	43	...	60	65	76	...
India	2	11	9	...	18	18	20	...
Others	32	30	45	...	104	92	114	...
Total	118	142	177	237	237	237	286	318
Total	276	281	410	531	429	438	568	642
Of which less developed countries (included above)	61	63	66	85	148	136	170	...

*Excluding oil companies.
Sources: *U.K. Board of Trade Journal; U.K. Balance of Payments, 1970.*

of sterling. Mainly, however, it was due to the buoyancy of the economies and to British firms believing that a good way to compete with international rivals was to establish production facilities overseas.

Earnings on U.K. international investments recorded an increase of 18% in 1969 but provisional figures for 1970 suggested that no further increase took place (*see* Table IX). Well over half the 1969 increase could be attributed to earnings on oil and miscellaneous investments; the remainder was in direct investment earnings; portfolio earnings fell slightly. The trend for an increased proportion of earnings to be reinvested rather than remitted to the U.K. continued in 1969. Earnings from nonsterling-area investments accounted for slightly over half the total earnings in 1969 (*see* Table VII). There was a very sharp increase in earnings from the EEC in 1968–69 after several years of stagnation; it seemed that the high rate of investment was at last bearing fruit. U.K. investment in less developed economies recorded an increase in 1969 in line with the overall increase.

Foreign investment in the U.K. continued to increase in 1969 and 1970 after its very large post-devaluation upsurge in 1968 (*see* Table X). Investment by U.S. companies accounted for about 75% of foreign investment. In 1969, foreign investment in the

---

Table VIII. Other Industrial Countries' International Investment, 1968–69
In $000,000

Country	1968			1969		
	Direct	Portfolio	Total	Direct	Portfolio	Total
Belgium						
Outflow	35	300	335	...	...	290
Inflow	235	5	240	...	...	355
Net	−200	295	95	...	...	−65
Canada						
Outflow	135	470	605	255	−95	160
Inflow	610	1,580	2,190	625	1,745	2,370
Net	−475	−1,110	−1,585	−370	−1,840	−2,210
France						
Outflow	...	...	625	...	...	100
Inflow	...	...	300	...	...	540
Net	...	...	325	...	...	−440
West Germany						
Outflow	430	1,525	1,955	565	2,630	3,195
Inflow	405	0	405	335	−330	5
Net	25	1,525	1,550	230	2,960	3,190
Italy						
Outflow	230	790	1,020	...	...	1,140
Inflow	330	130	460	...	...	435
Net	−100	660	560	...	...	705
Japan						
Outflow	220	0	220	...	...	...
Inflow	80	350	430	...	...	...
Net	140	−350	−210	130	−280	−150
Netherlands						
Outflow	220	260	480	...	240	...
Inflow	135	300	435	...	375	...
Net	85	−40	45	115	−135	−20

Sources: Annual Reports of International Monetary Fund, Bank for International Settlements, and national banks.

Table IX. U.K. Investment Earnings
In £000,000

Item	1960	1966	1967	1968	1969	1970*
Direct investment†						
Repatriated profits	173	246	248	291	319	...
Reinvested profits	85	183	190	277	323	...
Total	258	429	438	568	642	660
Portfolio investment	125	153	145	164	161	155
Oil and miscellaneous	286	377	386	362	489	475
Total	669	959	969	1,094	1,292	1,290

*Estimate based on first half of year.
†Excluding oil and before 1963 insurance.
Sources: *U.K. Balance of Payments, 1970; Economic Trends.*

Table X. Foreign Investment in U.K.
In £000,000

Item	1960	1966	1967	1968	1969	1970*
Direct investment†						
New funds	68	102	73	107	142	...
Reinvested profits	67	93	97	176	131	...
Total	135	195	170	283	273	400
Portfolio investment‡	63	−61	−15	45	140	20
Oil and miscellaneous	55	140	200	245	208	230
Total	253	274	355	573	621	650

*Estimate based on first half of year.
†Excluding oil and before 1963 insurance.
‡Net disinvestment in 1966 and 1967.
Sources: *U.K. Balance of Payments, 1970; Economic Trends.*

Iran

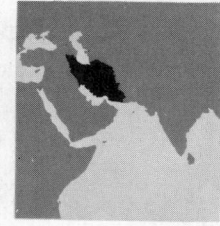

A constitutional monarchy of western Asia, Iran is bounded by the U.S.S.R., Afghanistan, Pakistan, Iraq, and Turkey and the Caspian Sea, the Arabian Sea, and the Persian Gulf. Area: 636,292 sq.mi. (1,648,000 sq.km.). Pop. (1969): 28,165,837. Cap. and largest city: Teheran (metro. pop., 1969 est., 2,980,041). Language: Farsi (Persian). Religion: Muslim; Christian, Jewish, and Zoroastrian minorities. Shah-in-shah, Mohammed Reza Pahlavi; prime minister in 1970, Amir Abbas Hoveida.

Throughout the first quarter of 1970 Iran's main worries concerned foreign affairs. Its relations with Iraq, already soured by their dispute over navigational rights on the Shatt al Arab, had lately worsened with Iraqi allegations of Iranian support for Kurdish insurgents. Teheran denied these charges, but border skirmishes and large-scale expulsions of Iranians from Iraq were followed on January 21 by the Baghdad regime's announcement of a "right wing plot." Accusing Iran of arming and financing the conspirators, Iraq expelled its neighbour's ambassador with four of his staff. They were followed home by the Iranian chargé d'affaires, whose account of his treatment in Baghdad aroused public resentment.

In reply, Prime Minister Hoveida asked Iraq's ambassador to leave, massed troops on the frontier, and,

IRAN
Education. (1967–68) Primary, pupils 2,575,537, teachers 81,127; secondary, pupils 674,059, teachers 22,534; vocational, pupils 16,239, teachers 1,620; teacher training, students 6,693, teachers 362; higher (including 8 universities), students 58,774, teaching staff 3,382.
Finance. Monetary unit: rial, with a par value of 75.75 rials to U.S. $1 (181.80 rials = £1 sterling). Gold, SDRs, and foreign exchange, central bank: (June 1970) U.S. $261 million; (June 1969) U.S. $295 million. Budget (1969–70) balanced at 330.3 billion rials. Money supply: (May 1970) 87,040,000,000 rials; (May 1969) 83,360,000,000 rials. Cost of living (1963 = 100): (June 1970) 112; (June 1969) 112.
Foreign Trade. (1969) Imports 104,830,000,000 rials; exports 159,030,000,000 rials. Import sources (1968): West Germany 22%; U.S. 17%; U.K. 12%; Japan 9%; France 6%; Italy 6%. Export destinations (1968): Japan 31%; U.K. 17%; India 6%; South Africa 5%. Main export crude oil 88%.
Transport and Communications. Roads (1969) 39,122 km. Motor vehicles in use (1969): passenger 187,520; commercial (including buses) 66,803. Railways: (1969) 3,510 km.; traffic (1968) 1,447,000,000 passenger-km., freight 2,225,000,000 net ton-km. Air traffic (1968): 469,056,000 passenger-km.; freight 4,453,000 net ton-km. Shipping (1969): merchant vessels 100 gross tons and over 48; gross tonnage 106,269. Telephones (Jan. 1969) 250,300. Radio receivers (Dec. 1968) 2.5 million. Television receivers (Dec. 1968) c. 200,000.
Agriculture. Production (in 000; metric tons; 1969; 1968 in parentheses): wheat c. 4,500 (4,977); barley (1968) 1,160, (1967) c. 1,020; cotton, lint 170 (160); rice 1,100 (957); sugar, raw value (1969–70) c. 497, (1968–69) c. 473; dates c. 290 (c. 281); grapes (1968) c. 270, (1967) c. 260; raisins c. 35 (c. 60); tobacco 18 (18); tea (1968) c. 18, (1967) c. 18. Livestock (in 000; Oct. 1968): cattle c. 5,700; sheep c. 34,000; goats (Oct. 1967) 13,000; horses (March 1968) c. 420; asses (March 1968) c. 2,200.
Industry. Production (in 000; metric tons; 1968–69): coal 295; crude oil (1969) 166,030; lead concentrates (metal content) c. 15; chrome ore (oxide content) 77; cement 2,000; electricity (kw-hr.) 5,008,000.

presenting the 1970 budget to the Majlis (lower house of Parliament), announced a large increase in defense estimates to protect the country against Iraqi hostility. These moves prompted Iraqi requests to the UN secretary-general and to Iran's close friend Turkey to use their good offices in the interests of peace. The settlement in March of the Kurdish dispute (see IRAQ) induced a calmer mood in Baghdad, and Iranian feelings, though still running high, were restrained by the shah and his government.

The government showed the same restraint in its handling of Iranian reservations about British policy in the Persian Gulf, which centred on the future of Bahrain. Iran had never abandoned its claim to sovereignty over these islands, for the defense of which Britain had been responsible (under a convention with the sheikh of Bahrain) since 1861. With the evolution of London's plans to end British commitments in the area and encourage the Gulf states (the seven Trucial States, Qatar, and Bahrain) to become an independent federation, Iran's attitude hardened to a degree that endangered its friendly relations with Britain.

In March, however, on Iran's initiative, both countries submitted the question to the UN secretary-general and agreed to abide by his findings. In April his representative reported that an overwhelming majority of Bahrainis wanted their islands to be recognized as a sovereign state free to determine its own future. The UN Security Council accepted this verdict, and the Majlis formally renounced the Iranian claim to sovereignty—a decision that settled the question and greatly enhanced the shah's international prestige.

Maintaining its traditional friendship with Communist and non-Communist powers, Iran obtained useful aid from both sides. In 1970 a ten-year agreement (signed in September 1969) came into effect for supplying Romania with crude oil to the value of $100 million in exchange for industrial equipment, including 20,000 tractors, 500 railroad cars, a modern dairy farm, and a timber plant. In March, during a six-day visit to Iran by Soviet Pres. N. V. Podgorny, plans were disclosed to increase Soviet-Iranian trade exchanges and also for the simultaneous inauguration of an oil pipeline to the U.S.S.R. and a hydroelectric plant on the border river, the Aras.

With Pakistan and Turkey, its partners in the Regional Cooperation for Development (RCD), Iran strengthened its links through frequent ministerial and technical conferences, punctuated by summit talks covering external policies as well as economic development. The biggest RCD project was an oil refinery in East Pakistan (established with Iranian help), and the three countries welcomed a report by the UN Conference on Trade and Development (UNCTAD) that suggested the advantages of tariff reductions as a means to increase cooperation. (L. F. R. W.)

ENCYCLOPÆDIA BRITANNICA FILMS. *The Middle East* (1955); *The Mediterranean World* (1961).

CAMERA PRESS FROM PIX
Peasant children line up beneath a portrait of the shah of Iran to enter classes taught by volunteer teachers.

Iraq

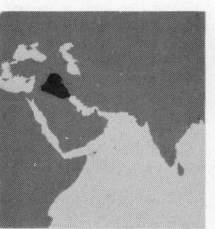

A republic of western Asia, Iraq is bounded by Turkey, Iran, Kuwait, Saudi Arabia, Jordan, Syria, and the Persian Gulf. Area: 169,284 sq.mi. (438,446 sq.km.). Pop. (1970 est.): 9,465,800, including Arabs, Kurds, Turks, Assyrians, Iranians, and others. Cap. and largest city: Baghdad (metro. pop., 1970 est., 2,183,760). Language: Arabic. Religion: mainly Mus-

IRAQ

Education. (1966–67) Primary, pupils 977,582, teachers 42,478; secondary, pupils 243,435, teachers 7,948; vocational, students 8,632, teachers 796; teacher training, students 8,229, teachers 353; higher (including 5 universities; 1965–66), students 28,410, teaching staff 1,002.

Finance. Monetary unit: Iraqi dinar, with a par value of 0.36 dinars to U.S. $1 (0.86 dinars = £1 sterling). Gold, SDRs, and foreign exchange, central bank: (June 1970) U.S. $400.2 million; (June 1969) U.S. $495.1 million. Budget (1969–70 est.) balanced at 379 million dinars. Money supply: (April 1970) 213.6 million dinars; (April 1969) 188.8 million dinars. Cost of living (Baghdad; 1963 = 100): (May 1970) 114; (May 1969) 110.

Foreign Trade. (1968) Imports 144.2 million dinars; exports 372.6 million dinars. Import sources: Japan 9%; U.K. 9%; U.S.S.R. 9%; West Germany 7%; France 5%; Italy 5%. Export destinations: Italy 24%; France 21%; Netherlands 7%; U.K. 5%. Main export crude oil 93%.

Transport and Communications. Roads (1968) 17,893 km. Motor vehicles in use (1968): passenger 75,800; commercial 46,500. Railways: (1967) 1,915 km.; traffic (1967–68) 367 million passenger-km., freight 1,131,000,000 net ton-km. Air traffic (1969): 150 million passenger-km.; freight 1,797,000 net ton-km. Telephones (Jan. 1969) 113,388. Radio receivers (Dec. 1966) c.

1 million. Television receivers (Dec. 1966) 180,-000.

Agriculture. Production (in 000; metric tons; 1969; 1968 in parentheses): wheat 1,189 (1,361); barley 1,250 (931); rice 293 (325); dates (1968) 330, (1967) c. 250; sesame (1968) 12, (1967) 12; linseed (1968) 12, (1967) 13; cotton, lint 12 (13); tobacco 15 (c. 14). Livestock (in 000; 1968–69): sheep 11,040; cattle c. 1,450; horses c. 122; asses c. 542; goats c. 1,800.

Industry. Production: crude oil (1969) 74,-446,000 metric tons; electricity (excluding most industrial production; 1967) 2,142,000,000 kw-hr.

lim, some Christian. President in 1970, Gen. Ahmed Hassan al-Bakr.

For the al-Bakr regime, 1970 was a year of venturesome diplomacy and growing internal strain. A peace settlement in March with the Kurds, whose demands for autonomy had kept Iraq in a state of intermittent civil war for a decade, left the government free not only to step up its territorial claims in the Persian Gulf but also to switch troops from the Kurdish north to the border with Jordan. As the year wore on, however, the U.S. plan for Arab-Israeli peace talks revealed divisions within the Arab world that tempted Iraq to challenge the leadership of the United Arab Republic and side with the Palestinian guerrillas against a negotiated settlement.

In mid-September, when the guerrillas plunged Jordan into civil war, they received no help from the approximately 12,000 Iraqi troops in the area. Baghdad's pretensions to Arab leadership thus lost credibility, with repercussions that caused the dismissal of Air Marshal Hardan Takriti, one of Iraq's two vice-presidents and a key figure in the Baathist regime. The al-Bakr administration continued in control but was plainly split by a power struggle.

Al-Bakr began the year by appointing (Dec. 31, 1969) a Communist, Aziz Sharif, as justice minister, but this bid for popular support failed to impress the Communists, of whom a number were arrested in May. A government statement on June 21 that certain political groups had made unacceptable conditions for joining a national front coalition preceded an officially inspired anti-Communist press campaign.

Relations with Syria were also far from cordial. In February a Pan-Arab Baath Party conference in Baghdad elected a new 16-man command that included four Syrians; the conference also called for a dialogue with the left-wing Baathist regime in Damascus. Despite these moves there was no abatement of Syrian attacks on "the right-wing oppressors of progressive forces in Iraq."

The Kurdish settlement (strongly urged by the U.S.S.R.) was the outcome of negotiations opened in January with the Kurdish nationalist leader Mustafa al-Barzani. On March 11 these produced a 15-point agreement that ended the fighting, declared a general amnesty for all insurgents, gave the Kurdish language equal status with Arabic in Kurdish majority areas (which were to have Kurdish administrators), and stipulated the appointment of a Kurdish vice-president in the Baghdad government. Kurdish rights were to be written into a new constitution (the fourth in 12 years), which was also to provide for a 15-man revolutionary command council, chosen from the Baathists' national command, and create a National Assembly representing both Arabs and Kurds.

WIDE WORLD

An abortive plot to overthrow the Iraqi government of Pres. Ahmed Hassan al-Bakr was reported in January 1970.

On March 29 al-Bakr formed a new government whose 30 members included five Kurds. Two powerful ministers, Takriti (defense) and Saleh Mahdi Ammash (interior), were upgraded to vice-president on April 3; their former posts fell to Gen. Hammad Shehab and Gen. Saadoun Ghaidan. In July the Kurdish Democratic Party reelected al-Barzani as its president. The party's intention was to choose Iraq's first Kurdish vice-president, but this appointment was still unfilled when Takriti fell from grace in October.

In regard to Iraq's relations with neighbouring governments the basic trends were unpromising. Baghdad's announcement on January 21 of an attempted right-wing coup, allegedly with Iranian and U.S. backing, led to the execution (after trial by a revolutionary court) of 44 people, including 7 convicted earlier of spying for the U.S. and Israel. This development brought relations with Iran close to rupture (see IRAN) and prefaced a more ambitious approach—pursued throughout the year—to Iraq's expansionist aims in the Persian Gulf.

On negotiations with Israel, the regime embarked on acrimonious exchanges with Pres. Gamal Abd-al-Nasser of the U.A.R. A top-level Baathist delegation was sent to Moscow on August 4. Although under strong pressure from the Soviet government, heavily committed to the Nasser line, Iraq stood firm and refused to join the U.A.R., Jordan, Syria, Sudan, and Libya at a Tripoli conference of their foreign and defense ministers on August 5–6 because it rejected any solution involving Israel's recognition. (P. Md.)

Ireland

Separated from Great Britain by the North Channel, the Irish Sea, and St. George's Channel, the Republic of Ireland shares its island with Northern Ireland to the northeast. Area: 27,136 sq.mi. (70,283 sq.km.), or 83% of the island. Pop. (1969 est.): 2,921,000. Cap. and largest city: Dublin (pop., 1966, 568,772). Language: English (80%) and Gaelic. Religion: predominantly Roman Catholic (95%). President in 1970, Eamon de Valera; prime minister, John Lynch.

During the early part of 1970 the prime minister, John Lynch (see BIOGRAPHY), was faced with a growing rift in his Cabinet on policy toward Northern Ireland, and on the night of May 5–6 he dismissed two senior ministers, Neil Blaney (agriculture) and Charles Haughey (finance). A third minister, Kevin Boland (local government), resigned in sympathy. In

continued on page 421

THE TWO IRELANDS

By Bruce Arnold

In 1966 the Irish Republic celebrated the 50th anniversary of the Easter Rising. It was treated as an occasion for pride and self-congratulation, and if there was criticism, it came mainly from those who felt that most of the principles for which the heroes of the Easter Rebellion of 1916 had died were not the ones that now guided the government of the country. But in Ireland's economic growth, its industrial expansion, employment, the stemming of emigration, relations with Northern Ireland, and in the reputation the country had earned abroad, there seemed much to be proud of.

A similar atmosphere of progress, enlightenment, and a desire to live at peace together seemed also to prevail in the North. There had been several cross-border meetings between the leaders of the two parts of Ireland, and between Cabinet ministers. In the half-century that divided these rulers from rebellion, the bitterness of the Anglo-Irish War, and the final emergence of the 26-county state, it did seem that maturity, rational government, self-confidence, and a firm belief in the future had come to Ireland, north and south.

Yet the Easter Rising itself had been a heroic failure. It had produced martyrs, but not independence. It had opened the way to seven years of bitterness and bloodshed and to the ultimate compromise of a divided Ireland. And in one of those strange parallels that history occasionally produces, Ireland, 50 years later, seemed to be reaping the sad fruits of that compromise in the troubles in the North and in the crisis provoked by those troubles in the republic.

The Legacy of History. The roots of this compromise lie much further back than the first quarter of the 20th century. In all its recorded history Ireland has witnessed only two successful conquests. The first was a spiritual one, the evangelization of the country by the Church of Rome, properly dating from the coming of St. Patrick in the 5th century. The second was the Plantation of Ulster in the 17th century. And to these two conquests can be traced, specifically and directly, the present troubles in Northern Ireland.

This is not to say that religion is the root cause, only that it provided the historical framework. The conquest begun by St. Patrick was successful because its object was the conquest of souls, not of people, land, or wealth. Other conquests, like that of the Normans, finally failed because the motives of the conquerors did not ultimately impinge on the beliefs of the masses. The Plantation of Ulster was different. Unlike the other intrusions into Ireland, this one was total. Landowners came, bringing with them artisans, labourers, craftsmen—a whole society. The native Irish were pushed out, or up into the hill country, and the roots of a separate state within Ireland were unwittingly laid down long before separation of any kind from England was even considered.

Before independence, the structure of society throughout Ireland was quite blatantly one of first- and second-class citizens. The country was ruled by a Protestant ascendancy, and the inevitable social hierarchy had its roots in the religious distinction between the masses, who were Catholic, and the ruling class, which was predominantly Protestant.

This changed in the republic after independence, but in Northern Ireland the old order of Protestant domination, which in any case had been more reactionary there than anywhere else

and which was backed by a substantial majority of the total Six Counties population, became firmly set. Power in Northern Ireland after the Government of Ireland Act of 1920 remained concentrated in the hands of a Protestant ascendancy, but one rather different from the traditional ruling class that during the 18th and 19th centuries in the other parts of Ireland had slowly learned lessons of religious liberty and religious equality.

The Protestant ascendancy in Northern Ireland traced its roots back to England and the lowlands of Scotland around 1600, when antipopery was having a revival with the rise of the Puritans. The attitudes of the Plantation ancestors of the 20th-century majority in Ulster had been formalized at the end of the 18th century with the formation of the Orange Order, which preserved the religious separateness and much of the bigotry of that time. By the 1960s the Order's divisive and blatantly unfair intrusion into jobs and housing and local government produced the marches, the riots, the violence, and inevitably the deaths that so shocked the world during 1968 and 1969.

Into the Streets. These events really began with the Dungannon March of Aug. 24, 1968, when several thousand demonstrators (among them Bernadette Devlin), led by Austin Currie and Gerry Fitt, marched from Coalisland into Dungannon. They were confronted in Thomas Street by a line of police, while behind them was an angry crowd of Protestants, many armed with clubs and sticks. In spite of some ugly threats and a militant speech by Fitt, the Belfast Republican Labour MP, the confrontation broke up peacefully. But it brought about an important change in the agitation of the numerous groups in Northern Ireland seeking civil rights for everyone in the province. Meetings and the handing out of leaflets were to give way to public, open-air demonstrations and marches. The civil rights campaign was to move out into the streets.

One other legacy of history should be mentioned at this point. The unique comprehensiveness of the Plantation of Ulster at the beginning of the 17th century gave to the Six Counties, and especially to the eastern counties and Belfast, a large Protestant working class. They suffer, like the Catholics, from the high level of unemployment in the province and from the fact that, economically, Northern Ireland has lagged behind the rest of the United Kingdom. But if they fear poverty, they fear Catholics and their traditional link with republicanism much more. In Dungannon working class confronted working class and contemplated violence. Later, this dichotomy was to encourage the sectarian label for the troubles in Northern Ireland, when in fact those troubles have much more to do with the strictly hierarchic structure of power and wealth which places the working-class Catholics at the very bottom.

This structure is nowhere more blatant than in Londonderry, where the discontent and agitation took on the aspects of a major crisis. The city has the highest level of unemployment in Ulster. Through the rigging of wards, its Catholic majority has only minority representation in local government. It has seen few of the benefits of the economic expansion in the province as a whole, and its housing conditions are by any standards wretched. This has bred bitterness and disillusionment, an absence of trust in conventional solutions, and a scorn for the promises of politicians.

It had also produced a number of organizations, with varying degrees of left-wing support, established to better conditions in the city. It was natural, after Dungannon, that the Civil Rights Association should turn its attention to Londonderry and combine with these groups to organize the march of October 5. Out of one of these groups, the Housing Action Committee, there emerged a young militant, Eamonn McCann, who was to give to the march—and to much of the activity of the following weeks—a new, militant, left-wing turn. He was to draw in more young student support and, for a time anyway, he was to frighten off some of the moderates.

There was also a hardening of attitude on the right. Before the October 5 march, protests against it were made by Derry Protestants. In the autumn of 1968 the man in charge of home affairs in Northern Ireland was William Craig, subsequently to emerge as the leading hard-liner among Unionists, a strong critic and opponent of Capt. Terence O'Neill, the prime minister, and equally strongly opposed to O'Neill's successor, Maj. James Chichester-Clark. In response to the protests, Craig banned the march on October 3. The next evening the organizers, led by McCann, decided to go ahead, and the following afternoon about 2,000 people gathered at the Waterside Station, across the Craigavon Bridge from the centre of Londonderry. The police warned the crowd, but the march started, and the inevitable confrontation took place.

This time, however, there was bloodshed. Gerry Fitt and Eddie McAteer, Nationalist leader of the Stormont (Northern Ireland government) opposition, were struck with police batons, and an order to disperse the crowd was given. What followed was short and brutal. The march was broken, but a few hours later, Catholics from the Bogside, bent on revenge, marched into the Protestant Diamond, shouting slogans and waving banners. Again fighting broke out, but this time between Catholics and Protestants, with the police arriving, late and angry, to restore order. The fighting moved down to the Bogside area, and the first of the barricades was raised as the riot squads moved about, forcing people back into their houses. The rioting finally ended two days later. Ulster, the Irish Republic, and the United Kingdom all faced a major crisis, and the whole world knew about it.

Deepening Crisis. The events in Londonderry had given the civil rights movement immense publicity, and the police brutality had provoked great sympathy. Prime Minister Harold Wilson had called on his home secretary, James Callaghan, to prepare a report, and in the republic concern about the border and the fate of the minority in the North, instead of being a talking point for extremist organizations like the Irish Republican Army (IRA), became a Cabinet matter. But the real focus of attention was on the Northern Ireland government. Craig's action in banning the march, and the attempts to whitewash the police, heightened the rift between hard-line Unionism and the more moderate attitude of O'Neill. The hard-liners in the parliamentary party had a powerful ally in Ian Paisley, a self-styled minister of the Free Presbyterian Church, a powerful orator, and the able organizer of many of the Protestant counterdemonstrations during the following months.

Meetings, demonstrations, and marches followed. On December 9, O'Neill appealed for moderation, and was met with widespread expressions of support. Two days later he sacked Craig. Peace, surprisingly, was being maintained, and 1968 ended without further serious disturbance. But on New Year's Day, 1969, a march started that was to change the situation very much for the worse.

There was no doubt, on that cold January morning, when the civil rights movement began a four-day march from City Hall in Belfast to Londonderry, that a new and ominous mood of reaction was abroad among Protestant extremists. They saw the march as doubly provocative in that it followed hard on the defeat which Craig's dismissal represented. And they felt that they could no longer rely on the police to deal with the increasingly outspoken demands for fundamental reform. The new voices from the left, among them that of Bernadette Devlin, spoke a new and powerful language. Their opponents were determined to meet them with a new kind of toughness.

The result was the Burntollet Ambush on January 4. The march was attacked by a Protestant mob not far from Derry, where the Burntollet Bridge crosses the River Faughan. Men, women, and young girls, many of them students at Queen's University, Belfast, were brutally beaten, and the police, who were there in large numbers, did little or nothing to protect them. The remnants of the march entered Derry, and there were more attacks, followed by police assaults on Catholics. Civil law in Londonderry broke down. The Catholics shut themselves into their Bogside ghetto, erected barricades, and even started up an independent radio station, Radio Free Derry.

Again the character of the crisis changed. Catholics throughout

the province cast the police in the role of the enemy. O'Neill, who had tried to introduce some measure of reform but had moved only slowly, was in an untenable position. Two ministers resigned from his Cabinet, and in February he called a general election. It was fought on the issue of civil rights and O'Neill's moderate reform solutions, and within the Unionist Party there was division in many of the constituencies, with hard-line and pro-O'Neill candidates standing in opposition to one another. In the event it was clear that support for hard-line solutions to the civil rights campaign was growing, but so was the strength of that movement.

O'Neill came back weakened after the election, and he was shortly to see 22-year-old Bernadette Devlin capture the Mid-Ulster seat for the British Parliament, with a majority of over 4,000, and carry her campaign for equal rights onto the floor of the House of Commons. He was assailed on both sides. For the civil rights agitators he was far too slow, for his own party he was too fast, and in April he resigned. By a slender majority he was succeeded by the mild, ineffective James Chichester-Clark, who expressed his commitment to the program of reform that had been emerging under O'Neill, but who was untarnished by the dismissals and resignations that had fatally weakened the position of his predecessor.

During the summer, while Chichester-Clark tried vainly to reunite Unionists behind the reform program, Protestant extremists and party hard-liners began a campaign to discredit the civil rights movement and terrorize its supporters. The first was attempted by an old Northern Ireland device—the linking of the left-wing critics of the ruling party with extremist republican elements like the IRA and Sinn Fein which sought to amalgamate the Six Counties with the republic. Rather too conveniently for credibility, a series of alleged IRA outrages started just at the time of O'Neill's resignation. At the same time Paisley stepped up his meetings and rallies, and so did his natural challenger on the civil rights side, Bernadette Devlin. Peace was kept, but at some cost. A large deployment of British troops had taken place since before the Bogside rioting, and the security police, the B Specials, had been mobilized in some areas.

There were two crucial dates facing the province, the anniversary of the Battle of the Boyne on July 12, celebrated by major Protestant demonstrations, and the August 12 celebrations commemorating the siege of Derry, when the militant Protestant organization, the Derry Apprentice Boys, organize a massive march involving people from all over the province. In 1969 both provoked violence, and the second brought death. On the streets there were two ill-disciplined, makeshift armies, one supporting civil rights, the other an extremist Protestant body. There was also a geographic polarization between Londonderry and Belfast. The revolt had begun in the poor, neglected, Catholic west, and the Bogside was already its symbolic capital. The reaction was concentrated in Belfast. And as the violence increased, so did the bemused impotence of Stormont, of the British government, of Dublin, of the police, even of the B Specials. In those weeks of rioting from mid-July to mid-August only one solution presented itself—the British Army.

But it was essentially a stalemate solution, and remained so. The pressures by the British home secretary on the Stormont government, the buildup of military strength under Lieut. Gen. Sir Ian Freeland, the army take-over of police duties in the troubled areas were all admissions of failure to put right grievous wrongs that had been allowed to perpetuate themselves over half a century. They were seen as such by the Irish Republic.

Reaction in the South. Events in the North challenged the republican ideals of the government party in the South, Fianna Fail, and found them wanting. Prime Minister John Lynch made emotional but ill-conceived speeches during the Derry and Belfast troubles, sent his foreign minister to the UN to press for a peace-keeping force, mobilized the army reserve, and set up border hospitals, but his actions were thought out largely in terms of internal party and national considerations. Policy toward the north of Ireland was hollow and sterile. Relations with the British on the delicate question of reunification were virtually nonexistent, and the various cross-border initiatives of the '60s had amounted to nothing more substantial than publicity stunts.

But people were being shot. There was a threat of pogroms. Refugees were crossing into the South, and the demands for help included requests for arms. The Cabinet in the republic was divided and, far worse, there was no really strong hand controlling the individual members. Though the differences between the militants and the prime minister were becoming increasingly public, Lynch declined to dismiss anyone.

Callaghan's arrival in Northern Ireland toward the end of August 1969 brought an atmosphere of sanity after the nightmare of the Falls Road rioting, burning, and looting earlier that month. The British government's pressure for reforms and its backing of Chichester-Clark were spelled out quite precisely by Callaghan, and the ultimate threat of a British take-over became real enough to restrain the hard-line Unionists. But reforms demand time and legislation, and the armies on the streets were impatient and distrustful. As the revelations of injustice and police bias came out in the Cameron and Hunt reports, the bitterness of the extremists was heightened. No violence quite equaled that in the Shankill Road area of Belfast on the night of October 11–12, sparked by the publication of the second of these two reports, recommending the gradual disbanding of the B Specials.

But the superiority of political methods over the gun and the cudgel was learned by many during the winter of 1969–70. Chichester-Clark not only survived but maintained his reform program intact. And both Paisley and Miss Devlin learned political pragmatism as a partial substitute for verbal violence. Belfast itself had returned to a state of comparative quiet when the Cabinet crisis in the republic broke on May 6.

If attention switched from Northern Ireland to the republic, it did so from curiosity rather than concern. The careful, moderate statements of the prime minister during the crisis seemed unreal against the background of alleged illicit arms smuggling. And the mixture of ineffectiveness and irresponsibility that was gradually revealed did widespread damage to a country that had not greatly enhanced its position during the disturbances in the North. Against a background of disaffection, sackings and resignations, party and Dail votes of confidence, the prime minister had to speak out on such occasions as the July 12, 1970, celebrations and the Derry Apprentice Boys' march. It was to his credit that Lynch helped in the unexpected preservation of peace on these occasions, but he did so against a background of deep and bitter division within his own party. The trial and acquittal of the able former minister for finance, Charles Haughey, together with three others, on charges of importing illegal arms brought the rift into the open.

Fianna Fail had been formed with two basic objectives, both of which had become increasingly hollow with the passing of the years. One was the restoration of the Irish language. The other was the unity and independence of Ireland as a republic. The compromises in the republic's attitude toward the North and the uncertainty in Lynch's handling of the problem had not raised the fundamental issue of the aims of Fianna Fail, but the trial did just that. It was seen, with some justice, as a rather shabby political device for getting rid of difficult Cabinet ministers, and Lynch, in the autumn of 1970, was faced with a complicated power struggle within his own party and a much damaged reputation abroad.

It is easy to say of Ireland that what was done a half century ago must be lived with, and that self-determination is the only valid principle. But such a view is at the root of the continued pessimism felt by Irishmen north and south of the border about the future of the country as a whole. Just as the period 1916–23 became an immeasurably complex era of Irish history, so the present period is bringing out the intricate legacies of what happened and was done then. It is difficult to believe that any satisfactory solution to the discord and division is in sight.

continued from page 418

a statement, Lynch said he was satisfied that they did not subscribe fully to government policy on the Northern Ireland situation. In an emergency debate in the Dail the next day, he accused the two men of having been involved in an illegal attempt to import arms into the country. Later in the week he announced that the matter was in the hands of the attorney general. In spite of the crisis, Lynch carried a confidence motion in the Dail with a majority of seven. He refused all calls for a general election, reshuffled his Cabinet, and appointed new ministers to fill the vacancies.

On May 27 three other men were arrested and charged with conspiring to import arms illegally into the republic. The next day the two former ministers were arrested and faced the same charge. That same day Boland called for a conference of the party in order to remove Lynch from the leadership of Fianna Fail and of the government. On June 4 Boland was expelled from the parliamentary party, and on June 22 he resigned from Fianna Fail altogether.

At a preliminary hearing in the district court, Blaney was discharged, but the others were returned for trial. The trial opened in the Central Criminal Court in Dublin on September 22, but a week later the jury was discharged and a new trial ordered after counsel for one of the defendants had accused the president of the High Court, Justice Andreas O'Keefe, of unfairness. A new trial began on October 6 and lasted three weeks. The four men were acquitted.

The result of the trial brought a second crisis, with

IRELAND

Education. (1966–67) Primary, pupils 509,651, teachers 15,850; secondary, pupils 111,111, teachers 7,788; vocational, pupils 72,621, teachers 5,103; teacher training (1965–66), students 1,736; higher, students 20,865, teaching staff (1962–63) 1,208.

Finance. Monetary unit: Irish pound, at par with the pound sterling (U.S. $2.40 = 1£). Gold, SDRs, and foreign exchange, official: (June 1970) U.S. $669 million; (June 1969) U.S. $489 million. Budget (1969–70 est.) balanced at £393,220,000. Gross national product: (1968) £1,269 million; (1967) £1,142 million. Money supply: (Feb. 1970) £365.6 million; (Feb. 1969) £349.9 million. Cost of living (1963 = 100): (May 1970) 144; (May 1969) 133.

Foreign Trade. (1969) Imports £588 million; exports £369.9 million. Import sources: U.K. 53%; U.S. 9%; West Germany 7%. Export destinations: U.K. 65%; U.S. 11%. Main exports: meat 15%; livestock 14%; textiles and clothing 10%; dairy produce 6%; machinery 5%; chemicals 5%; nonferrous metal ores 5%. Tourism (1968): visitors 1,917,000; gross receipts (1967) U.S. $195 million.

Transport and Communications. Roads (1968) 86,427 km. Motor vehicles in use (1968): passenger 340,900; commercial 49,400. Railways: (1968) 2,146 km.; traffic (1969) 520 million passenger-km., freight 466.4 million net ton-km. Air traffic (1969): 1,456,600,000 passenger-km.; freight 60,992,000 net ton-km. Shipping (1969): merchant vessels 100 gross tons and over 90; gross tonnage 164,200. Telephones (Dec. 1968) 274,134. Radio receivers (Dec. 1968) 860,000. Television receivers (Sept. 1968) 441,000.

Agriculture. Production (in 000; metric tons; 1969; 1968 in parentheses): potatoes c. 1,485 (1,625); oats (1968) 286, (1967) 294; barley (1968) 740, (1967) 677; wheat (1968) 412, (1967) 298; sugar, raw value (1969–70) c. 150, (1968–69) 158; milk c. 3,787 (3,671); butter c. 78 (c. 78); cheese c. 29 (c. 28); meat (1968) 500, (1967) 539; fish catch (1968) 53, (1967) 50. Livestock (in 000; June 1969): cattle c. 5,570; sheep c. 4,000; horses 125; pigs c. 1,100; chickens c. 9,500.

Industry. Index of industrial production (excluding power; 1963 = 100): (1969) 153; (1968) 143. Production (in 000; metric tons; 1969): coal 155; cement 1,237; electricity (excluding most industrial production; kw-hr.) 5,125,000; manufactured gas (cu.m.) 205,000; beer (hl.; 1967–68) 3,691; woolen fabrics (sq.m.) 7,800; rayon and acetate fabrics (sq.m.) 10,560.

further calls for Lynch's resignation, both from within his own party and from the opposition. He repudiated accusations that the trial had been a political device and denied any serious rift on policy within his party. But pressure upon him to resign mounted steadily, and the survival of the government became a day-by-day achievement. In December a new crisis arose when the government assumed emergency powers under the Offenses Against the State Act. Lynch announced that he had made the move on the advice of police, who had warned him of a plot to kidnap prominent persons and perpetrate armed bank robberies, probably involving murders. Though the instigators of the alleged plot were not named, it was widely assumed that reference was being made to the Irish Republican Army and the extremist Saor Eire.

Lynch's position was not made easier by the worsening economic situation. Large wage and salary claims from key sectors in the economy, coupled with the third-highest rise in the cost of living in Europe, eventually forced the new minister for finance, George Colley, to introduce a strict 6% wages ceiling, together with stringent controls over other inflationary factors. This was followed, at the end of October, by a second budget, imposing higher taxes in a number of areas.

Throughout these substantial difficulties at home, Lynch and his external affairs minister, P. J. Hillery (*see* BIOGRAPHY), continued to direct Ireland's peaceful coexistence policy toward the North. Hillery visited the Falls Road area of Belfast before the Orange Day parades in July and called on the British foreign secretary in London. Lynch continued to appeal for calm and patience and consideration for the Catholic minority in the Six Counties. (*See* Special Report.)

Early in the year the Springboks Rugby team from South Africa paid a visit to Ireland as part of their controversial British Isles tour. There were protests and scuffles at Dublin airport, and hotel and other services for members of the team were blocked by some trade unions. In the autumn there was another controversial visit, this time by U.S. Pres. and Mrs. Richard Nixon, both of whom traced ancestors back to Ireland. There was strong opposition to Nixon's holding talks on Vietnam on Irish soil.

There were several bank raids in the country, all of them believed to be the work of extremist republican organizations. In the course of one of these, in Dublin on April 3, a policeman was killed. There was also a serious breach among extremist republicans when their political party, Sinn Fein, split at its annual conference, half of the delegates walking out and forming a breakaway party.

A strike of cement workers throughout the country disrupted the building industry during the early part of the year. The banks were shut down for six months because of a pay dispute; during the strike everyday financial transactions were handled informally through pubs and similar establishments, and it was expected to be months before the resulting tangle was straightened out. (B. AR.)

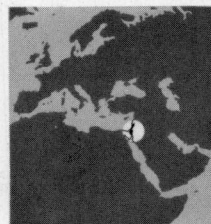

Israel

A republic of the Middle East, Israel is bounded by Lebanon, Syria, Jordan, the U.A.R., and the Mediterranean Sea. Area (not including territory occupied in the June 1967 war): 7,992 sq.mi. (20,700 sq.km.). Pop. (1970 est.): 2,949,100. Cap.: Jerusalem (pop., 1970 est., 283,100). Largest city: Tel Aviv-Jaffa

(pop., 1970 est., 382,900). Language: Hebrew and Arabic. Religion: predominantly Jewish. President in 1970, Schneor Zalman Shazar; prime minister, Mrs. Golda Meir.

Not until the closing weeks of the year did it become evident that 1970 would go down in Israel's history as the year of an emergent new political leadership and the beginning of the first major change in Israeli foreign policy. The central factor in both was the minister of defense, Moshe Dayan (*see* BIOGRAPHY). At the beginning of the year Dayan's influence in the Cabinet council and in the country at large was still overshadowed by the majority of ministers, including the prime minister, Mrs. Golda Meir (*see* BIOGRAPHY), who were arrayed against him. It was against Dayan's advice that the Cabinet majority had supported a decision to embark on deep penetration air attacks against the U.A.R. These attacks continued until mid-April, and the targets included positions in the suburbs of Cairo and industrial objectives in the Nile Delta. The principal military objective, however, was the radar system serving the U.A.R. Air Force, and this was progressively and effectively destroyed during the first ten weeks of the year.

Meanwhile, Israeli casualties on the Suez Canal had been considerably reduced as a result of the more intensive air attack on the U.A.R. positions. In December 1969, Israel had suffered 113 dead and 330 wounded on the canal front; that figure had dropped to 60 dead and 137 wounded in May 1970. But, meanwhile, the event against which Dayan had warned

ISRAEL

Education. (1966–67) Primary, pupils 450,359, teachers 23,729; secondary, pupils 71,401, teachers 6,694; vocational, pupils 42,730, teachers 5,274; teacher training, students 4,408, teachers 411; higher (including 4 universities), students 39,126, teaching staff 5,227.

Finance. Monetary unit: Israeli pound, with a par value of I£3.5 to U.S. $1 (I£8.40 = £1 sterling). Gold, SDRs, and foreign exchange, central bank: (June 1970) U.S. $440.6 million; (June 1969) U.S. $542.5 million. Budget (1969–70 est.): revenue I£4,924 million; expenditure I£4,586 million. Gross national product: (1968) I£14,023 million; (1967) I£12,021 million. Money supply: (May 1970) I£3,101 million; (May 1969) I£3,047 million. Cost of living (1963 = 100): (June 1970) 136; (June 1969) 131.

Foreign Trade. (1968) Imports I£4,616.8 million; exports I£2,534 million. Import sources: U.S. 24%; U.K. 19%; West Germany 12%; Netherlands 5%; Italy 5%. Export destinations: U.S. 19%; U.K. 10%; West Germany 9%; Belgium-Luxembourg 6%; France 5%; Hong Kong 5%; Switzerland 5%. Main exports: diamonds 35%; citrus fruit 16%; textiles and clothing 11%; chemicals 7%.

Transport and Communications. Roads (1968) 9,110 km. (including 1,689 km. main roads). Motor vehicles in use (1969): passenger 136,434; commercial 57,568. Railways (1969): 733 km.; traffic 322 million passenger-km., freight 420 million net ton-km. Air traffic (1969): 2,070,000,000 passenger-km.; freight 84.9 million net ton-km. Shipping (1969): merchant vessels 100 gross tons and over 114; gross tonnage 769,156. Telephones (Dec. 1968) 419,118. Radio receivers (Dec. 1967) 774,000. Television receivers (Dec. 1967) 26.000.

Agriculture. Production (in 000; metric tons; 1969; 1968 in parentheses): oranges *c.* 910 (958); grapefruit *c.* 210 (220); grapes (1968) 72, (1967) 82; wheat (1968) 175, (1967) 222; sorghum (1968) 21, (1967) 24; potatoes (1968) 110, (1967) 93; cotton, lint 39 (33); tomatoes (1968) 132, (1967) 115; olives (1968) *c.* 20, (1967) 10; bananas (1968) 44, (1967) 51; fish catch (1968) 26, (1967) 22. Livestock (in 000; Dec. 1968): cattle 232; sheep 197; chickens 6,550.

Industry. Index of production (1963 = 100): (1969) 185; (1968) 159. Production (in 000; metric tons; 1969): cement 1,308; electricity (kw.-hr.) 6.080,-000; salt (1968) 65; potash (oxide content; 1968–69) 365. New dwelling units completed (1968) 22,200.

when the government had embarked on the deep-penetration raids had materialized. On April 29 an Israeli government communiqué said that Soviet pilots had been flying operational missions near Cairo and Alexandria for some time. It soon became clear that in order not to clash with them the Israelis had halted their attacks on targets outside the immediate Suez Canal zone.

These military events had been accompanied by a seeming deterioration in Israel's relations with the Nixon administration in Washington. It had begun with the formal presentation of a "peace initiative" by U.S. Secretary of State William P. Rogers on Dec. 9, 1969, which set out the political terms and suggested a geographic basis for a possible settlement among Israel, the U.A.R., and Jordan. The Israeli government flatly rejected the Rogers plan, as one that preempted agreements that could be arrived at only as a result of negotiations between Israel and its Arab neighbours.

At the same time, the Israeli Foreign Ministry and other government spokesmen stressed the growing "erosion" of the U.S. position of support for Israel, and the Israeli press and public opinion became noticeably agitated by this development. It was, however, difficult to identify the precise nature of this alleged "erosion," and the concern felt because of it was, significantly, not shared by Dayan or the Department of Defence. It was the first of a series of such divergences in the assessment of current situations between the Department of Defence and the Foreign Ministry.

This critical Israeli position was further confirmed by hostile notes sent by the Soviet Union to the U.S., British, and French governments on February 3, and by U.S. Pres. Richard Nixon's reply four days later. This U.S. response called for a total embargo of arms to the Middle East and said that the U.S. would halt deliveries to Israel if the Soviet Union would stop its supplies to the Arab countries. Israel's worst fears were further reinforced by Secretary of State Rogers' statement on March 23 which indicated that Israel's request to purchase another 25 Phantom and 100 Skyhawk planes would for the time being "remain in abeyance."

Meanwhile, the Israeli air attacks on the U.A.R. had been pressed with increasing intensity. It had become known that U.A.R. Pres. Gamal Abd-al-Nasser had been under great pressure because of them and had paid a three-day secret visit to Moscow on January 28 to seek more direct Soviet aid. By mid-April the implications of the new Soviet commitment were becoming apparent in Washington and Jerusalem. On April 14, the U.S. Department of State's assistant secretary for Near Eastern and South Asian affairs, Joseph J. Sisco, arrived in Israel after having had somewhat fruitless talks with Nasser. On the following day, Sisco met privately with Dayan. This, by all accounts, turned out to be a watershed in the relations between Israel and the United States. It was the beginning of a new appraisal of the Soviet role in the U.A.R.-Israeli confrontation. On the following day Dayan, in an address to Israeli Army cadets, told them that henceforth the main problem they had to be concerned with was the Soviet involvement in the Middle East conflict.

After the Israeli Air Force halted its deep penetration raids into the heart of the U.A.R., it intensified its assault on U.A.R. artillery, missile, and army positions in the canal area. In the course of three months—during May, June, and July—it virtually destroyed all effective U.A.R. air defense and radar installations and

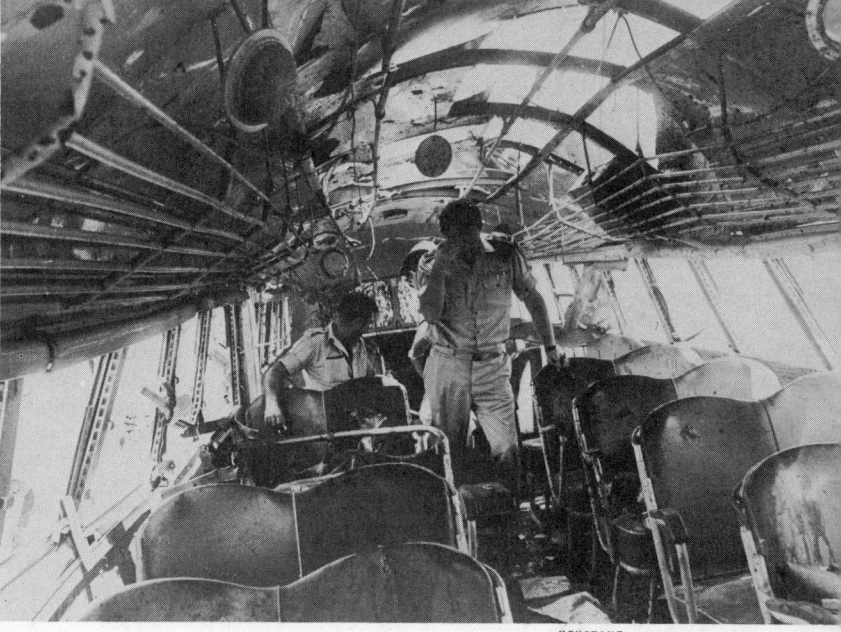

KEYSTONE
Israel's Northern Command chief, Gen. Motta Gur, stands inside the school bus in which eight children and four adults died when Arab terrorists attacked it with bazookas near the Lebanese border, May 22, 1970.

virtually neutralized the U.A.R. Air Force. The introduction of the latest Soviet air defense missile, the SAM-3, qualified the Israeli success somewhat and led to the loss of five Israeli Phantom planes during the attacks, but it served to emphasize that only direct Soviet intervention could turn the tables on the canal front.

The pressure on President Nasser to seek an alternative way out of this losing conflict became considerable. The Israelis, for different reasons, were also becoming anxious to find an alternative to war. The sheer cost of maintaining the attacks was very great. This had already been reflected in the budget estimates announced on February 16, when total expenditure was put at I£9,909 million. Of this total, the defense allocation was put at I£4,500 million, as compared with I£1,200 million in 1967.

With this general situation in mind and in light of the private conversations that Sisco had had with Dayan in April, Rogers addressed in June another initiative to the U.A.R. and Israeli governments that was framed mostly in general terms but did specifically suggest a cease-fire. Nasser formally accepted the Rogers proposals on July 23 and the Israeli government on August 4. The cease-fire, which was to last for 90 days, came into effect at midnight on August 7. It was renewed for another 90 days on November 5.

A critical development for the future of Israel and its relations with the major powers took place during the cease-fire. After some initial confusion and doubt, the U.S. accepted the Israeli charge that the U.A.R., with Soviet help, had utilized the cease-fire standstill agreement to emplace a considerable number of missiles and heavy guns along the canal front and had thus changed the military status quo in its favour. Once President Nixon was convinced that there had been, as he put it, "a breach of faith" on the part of the U.A.R. and the Soviet Union, the U.S. reacted with vigour. Israel received more Phantom planes and a wide range of the most sophisticated electronic equipment and arms.

By the time the cease-fire came to an end and was up for renewal, Israel's military superiority was probably greater than it had ever been. In September, Mrs. Meir was Nixon's guest in Washington and confirmed the new relationship which appeared to be based on total U.S. support for Israel. On Nixon's initiative a bill was presented to Congress that stepped up U.S.

AGENZIA GIORNALISTICA ITALIA
Damaged cars
litter the streets
of Genoa after
an autumn cloudburst
dumped 22 in. of rain
on the coastal city
within 18 hours.

Italian Literature:
see Literature

military and economic aid to Israel for the next fiscal period to $500 million.

These changes in foreign policy approaches and the significant part played in them by Moshe Dayan were also reflected in domestic affairs. Its most dramatic form was the emergence of Dayan as the spokesman for a more flexible foreign policy, in which there would be less insistence on direct negotiations and a peace settlement as the basic Israeli diplomatic objective. Instead, Dayan proposed a more pragmatic approach in order to reach a partial settlement with the U.A.R. To this end, he suggested that Israel would be prepared to withdraw about 20 mi. from the canal to allow it to be reopened and to seek a general demilitarization of the Suez front as a first step. Despite initial opposition from Foreign Minister Abba Eban, Deputy Prime Minister Yigal Allon, and the majority of the Cabinet, Dayan won the support of Prime Minister Meir and also the Cabinet's approval on November 29. He was also authorized to discuss his ideas with President Nixon and other U.S. leaders in Washington on behalf of the Israeli Cabinet. On December 28 the Cabinet agreed to resume the indirect peace talks with the U.A.R., held under the auspices of UN mediator Gunnar Jarring, which Israel had left four months earlier in protest against the Soviet-U.A.R. cease-fire violations. Earlier in December it was reported that the Labour Party had chosen Finance Minister Pinhas Sapir as the eventual successor to Mrs. Meir. Sapir was known as a moderate on the question of Israeli-Arab relations. (J. K.)

ENCYCLOPÆDIA BRITANNICA FILMS. *Major Religions of the World (Development and Rituals)* (1954); *The Middle East* (1955); *Planning Our Foreign Policy (Problems of the Middle East)* (1955); *The Mediterranean World* (1961).

Italy

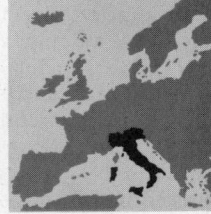

A republic of southern Europe, Italy occupies the Apennine Peninsula, Sicily, Sardinia, and a number of smaller islands. On the north it borders France, Switzerland, Austria, and Yugoslavia. Area: 116,315 sq.mi. (301,255 sq.km.). Pop. (1970 est.): 54,302,019. Cap. and largest city: Rome (pop., 1970 est., 2,731,397). Language: Italian. Religion: predominantly Roman Catholic. President in 1970, Giuseppe Saragat; premiers, Mariano Rumor and, from August 6, Emilio Colombo.

Domestic Affairs. Italy was beset by difficulties in 1970. Two government crises, the election of regional parliaments, and fears of economic setbacks mingled with social unrest to give a dramatic overtone to all major events. On February 7 Premier Rumor offered the resignation of his Christian Democratic government, unable to continue in office without direct participation by the three parties of the previous centre-left coalition, the Socialists, Social Democrats, and Republicans. Although talks had begun with the leaders of those parties in an effort to restore the previous coalition, the crisis dragged on and every possible solution presented great difficulties. On February 28 Rumor gave up the attempt to form a centre-left coalition. On March 3 Pres. Giuseppe Saragat asked former premier Aldo Moro to form a new government, but he also failed; Rumor was again called in, and was successful on March 27. The new government consisted of 17 Christian Democrats, 6 Socialists, 3 Social Democrats, and 1 Republican. On

April 10 the Senate endorsed it by 167 to 117, and on April 17 the Chamber of Deputies accepted it by 348 votes to 239.

On June 7 and 8 Italy voted for the regional parliaments. The four parties of the centre-left coalition showed a 2.8% improvement over the 1968 general election results. Although the Christian Democrat vote dropped by 0.9%, the Socialists and Social Democrats gained 2.6% and the Republicans, 1.1%. Of the opposition parties, the Communists lost 0.1% of their vote and their allies, 1.2%. The right wing gained; the neofascist Movimento Sociale Italiano (MSI) forged ahead by 0.9%. The overall result saw the Christian Democrats in the lead with 37.9% of the votes, followed by the Communist Party (27.9%), Socialists (10.4%), Social Democrats (7%), and the MSI (5.2%).

A second government crisis followed on July 6, when Rumor resigned because of difficulties in bringing the four coalition parties to agree on a common policy. On July 11 Christian Democrat Giulio Andreotti was asked to form a new coalition government, but the refusal of the Social Democrats to accept a "policy of intent" forced him to give up. The finance minister in the previous government, Emilio Colombo (*see* BIOGRAPHY), formed a government on August 6. Its first decisions were aimed at strengthening the economy by arresting inflation, improving the balance of payments, and controlling private expenditure.

On Sept. 20, 1970, Italy celebrated the centenary of the capture of Rome from the Papal States by Italian troops and the restoration of the "Eternal City" as Italy's capital. Pope Paul VI marked the occasion with a speech in which he recognized the existing situation between Vatican City and the republic. Nevertheless, controversy occurred between church and state when Parliament discussed a bill to legalize divorce. The bill, accepted by the deputies, just survived the Senate, and a compromise was reached, giving effect to the law as amended. The articles were soon approved by Parliament, and although the church condemned the measure, the strong lobby in favour of divorce prevailed.

Some 4,500 troops were sent into the southern city of Reggio di Calabria in October, the first time in 25 years that the Army had been used to suppress civil violence. The disorders, which arose from a dispute over whether Reggio or neighbouring Catanzaro should be the capital of the new Calabria region, culminated in several days of rioting and a general strike.

Foreign Affairs. The main aims of Italian policy in 1970 were the effort to preserve peace, a more flexible relationship with Eastern European countries, and the attempt at a realistic contribution to pacification in the Middle and Far East. The Alto Adige problem, which had troubled the country in previous years, seemed finally solved with the presentation, on January 19, of a new bill aimed at modifying the special statute of the Trentino-Alto Adige region. Wider autonomy for the provinces of Bolzano and Trento, a direct financial relationship between the state and the two provinces, and new regulations guaranteeing the welfare of the Italian and German-speaking communities in the region were the main points, and hopes grew that terrorism by minority groups would end.

Italy welcomed the introduction of new Asian, African, and South American countries to the Disarmament Committee in Geneva. Their accession

Education. (1967–68) Primary, pupils 4,594,-033, teachers 209,917; secondary, pupils 2,244,-072, teachers 185,854; vocational, pupils 835,822, teachers 68,650; teacher training, students 249,-676, teachers 17,870; higher (including 35 universities), students 374,486, teaching staff (1966–67) 27,233.

Finance. Monetary unit: lira, with a par value of 625 lire to U.S. $1 (1,500 lire = £1 sterling). Gold, SDRs, and foreign exchange, official: (June 1970) U.S. $3,934,000,000; (June 1969) U.S. $4,422,000,000. Budget (1969 est.): revenue 9,718,000,000,000 lire; expenditure 11,418,149,-000,000 lire. Gross national product: (1968) 46,-741,000,000,000 lire; (1967) 43,553,000,000,000 lire. Money supply: (April 1970) 24,980,000,-000,000 lire; (April 1969) 20,752,000,000,000 lire. Cost of living (1963 = 100): (May 1970) 128; (May 1969) 121.

Foreign Trade. (1969) Imports 7,781,000,-000,000 lire; exports 7,331,000,000,000 lire. Import sources: EEC 39% (West Germany 19%, France 12%); U.S. 11%. Export destinations: EEC 42% (West Germany 20%, France 14%); U.S. 11%. Main exports: machinery 24%; motor vehicles 8%; textile yarns and fabrics 7%; chemicals 7%; clothing 7%; fruit and vegetables 6%; petroleum products 5%. Tourism (1968): visitors 12.6 million; gross receipts U.S. $1,476,-000,000.

Transport and Communications. Roads (1969) 285,484 km. (including 3,502 km. expressways). Motor vehicles in use (1969): passenger 9,028,400; commercial 885,210. Railways: state (1968) 16,351 km.; private (1967) 4,289 km.; traffic (1969) 29,923,000,000 passenger-km., freight 17,222,000,000 net ton-km. Air traffic (1969): 7,102,000,000 passenger-km.; freight 269.1 million net ton-km. Shipping (1969): merchant vessels 100 gross tons and over 1,552; gross tonnage 7,037,846. Telephones (Dec. 1968) 7,752,024. Radio licenses (Dec. 1968) 11,912,000. Television licenses (Dec. 1968) 8,099,000.

Agriculture. Production (in 000; metric tons; 1969; 1968 in parentheses): wheat 9,540 (9,590); corn 4,506 (3,991); barley 292 (258); oats 491 (390); potatoes 3,969 (3,960); rice 862 (639); broad beans 402 (324); onions (1968) 464, (1967) 480; sugar, raw value (1969–70) c. 1,385, (1968–69) 1,296; tomatoes (1968) 3,258, (1967) 3,459; tobacco 79 (74); olives (1968) 1,933, (1967) 2,712; oranges 1,705 (1,676); lemons 790 (849); wine 7,200, (6,524); apples 2,009 (1,932); pears 1,634 (1,395); peaches (1968) 1,315, (1967) 1,125; figs 222 (220); cheese c. 387 (c. 425); beef and veal (1968) 590, (1967) 537; pork (1968) 416, (1967) 348. Livestock (in 000; June 1969): cattle 10,024; sheep 8,206; pigs 7,298; goats (Jan. 1968) 1,124; horses, mules, and asses 820; poultry c. 112,000.

Industry. Index of production (1963 = 100): (1969) 140; (1968) 136. Unemployment: (1969) 3.4%; (1968) 3.5%. Fuel and power (in 000; metric tons; 1969): lignite 1,932; coal 302; crude oil 1,520; natural gas (cu.m.) 11,-984,000; manufactured gas (cu.m.) 2,861,000; electricity (kw-hr.) c. 111,200,000. Production (in 000; metric tons; 1969): iron ore (50% metal content) 763; pig iron 7,947; crude steel 16,365; zinc 130; lead 62; aluminum 145; cement 31,290; cotton yarn 185; rayon, etc., filament yarn 93; rayon, etc., staple fibre 109; nylon, etc., filament yarn 105; nylon, etc., fibre 130; nitrogenous fertilizers (1968–69) 1,088; sulfuric acid 3,201; petroleum products (1968) 83,154; passenger cars (units) 1,477; commercial vehicles (units) 119. Merchant vessels launched (100 gross tons and over; 1969) 634,000 gross tons. New dwelling units completed (1969) 283,000.

underlined the absence of France, and the Italian government appealed to Paris to return to the talks. The U.K.'s efforts to negotiate British entry to the Common Market were viewed with interest. At one ministerial meeting in Brussels, Foreign Minister Moro asserted the possibility of a preferential treaty with Austria while the outcome of negotiations with several other EFTA members was being awaited. Italy regarded the British contribution to building Europe as essential.

Restraint was shown in the face of action by the Libyan government of Muhammad al-Khadafy, who on July 21 announced the expulsion of Italians from Libya, the confiscation of their property, and the freezing of savings deposited in both Italian and Libyan banks in Tripoli. Foreign Minister Moro met his Libyan counterpart, Saleh Busheir, in Beirut, Lebanon, without definite results. By the end of October almost all the 13,000 Italians in Libya had left.

The year was one of intense diplomatic activity. President Saragat received the British minister of state for European affairs, George Thomson; the Irish foreign minister, Patrick Hillery; the Israeli foreign minister, Abba Eban; and Pres. Richard M. Nixon of the U.S. Premier Colombo had a meeting in Rome with UN Secretary-General U Thant. Foreign Minister Moro had a series of meetings with foreign leaders, both in Rome and abroad.

The Economy. On August 27 the government approved a series of measures aimed at averting an economic crisis. These consisted mainly of reducing pressure on home demand, balancing the public accounts while assuring the necessary bases for urgent reforms, and giving new incentives for production and investment through rearranged credits and taxation.

Italy's balance of payments showed a deficit of $6.3 million for July, whereas in July 1969 there had been a $43.3 million surplus. Between January and July 1970 the balance of payments deficit mounted to $581.9 million. The general index for industrial production (1966 = 100) reached 131.5 in June, a reduction of 0.1% compared with June 1969. In the first six months of the year, however, there was an overall increase of 3.8% over the corresponding period of 1969. The retail price index increased by 5% over the index for June 1969.

An important industrial change earlier in the year was the merger between the Italian Pirelli and British Dunlop companies. The two groups decided to maintain their names and separate activities, especially in automobile tires, but to cooperate in research and development.

Following a series of strikes that hit all major Italian manufacturers, the automobile industry showed signs of stress that were reflected in the January–June production figures. In that period, 918,312 units were produced, a reduction of 1.9% from the first six months of 1969, and sales in the home market fell from 82 to 73%. Exports were seriously hit, decreasing by 9.1% from 372,274 to 338,239 units. Fiat, Italy's principal car manufacturer (which during the year increased its interest in the French Citroën company to 49%), was particularly hard hit by strikes. It was calculated that the company lost production of over 98,000 cars in the first six months of the year. As 1970 drew to a close it appeared that the nation was undergoing a repeat of the previous year's unrest. Widespread strikes were called in protest against the government's failure to carry out social reforms, and thousands of students staged marches and demonstrations, some of which resulted in violence.

(F. G.)

Ivory Coast

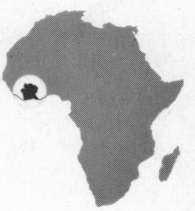

A republic on the Gulf of Guinea, West Africa, the Ivory Coast is bounded by Liberia, Guinea, Mali, Upper Volta, and Ghana. Area: 123,485 sq.mi. (319,-822 sq.km.). Pop. (1969 est.): 4,195,000 including about 15,000 Europeans. Cap. and largest city: Abidjan (pop., 1963 est., 285,000). Language: French and local dialects. Religion: pagan 65%; Muslim 25%; Christian 10%. President and premier in 1970, Félix Houphouët-Boigny.

In May the prime minister of Ghana, Kofi Busia, visited the Ivory Coast. A treaty of friendship was signed and the establishment of a joint commission for mutual cooperation agreed upon. The commission adopted a ten-point program in June for ending border disputes, and a joint technical team was to begin the task of redemarcation of the border.

The fifth congress of the Democratic Party of the

Ivory Coast in October reaffirmed the main objectives of the ruling party: rehabilitation of former political prisoners; speedier promotion of the young intellectual elite to governmental responsibility; and adherence to the principles of a liberal economy. On November 29 President Houphouët-Boigny was re-elected to a third five-year term; a new 100-member National Assembly was also elected.

A rapprochement was under way between Nigeria and the Ivory Coast, in spite of the latter's favourable attitude toward Biafra during the Nigerian civil war. On October 6, the minister of information announced that an interview given to a London newspaper by former Biafran leader Gen. Odumegwu Ojukwu had been a breach of his agreement with the Ivory Coast government, which had granted him political asylum. On October 8 it was announced that Ojukwu had been told to leave the country as soon as possible.

(PH. D.)

IVORY COAST

Education. (1967–68) Primary, pupils 407,609, teachers 8,818; secondary, pupils 37,460, teachers (1965–66) 1,087; vocational, pupils 3,571, teachers (1966–67) 279; teacher training, pupils 1,138, teachers (1966–67) 39; higher, students 2,640.

Finance. Monetary unit: CFA franc, with a parity of CFA Fr. 50 to the French franc (CFA Fr. 277.71 = U.S. $1; CFA Fr. 666.50 = £1 sterling). Gold, SDRs, and foreign exchange, central bank: (April 1970) U.S. $87 million; (April 1969) U.S. $83 million. Budget (1969 est.) balanced at CFA Fr. 46.5 billion. Money supply: (March 1970) CFA Fr. 81,010,000,000; (March 1969) CFA Fr. 65,790,000,000.

Foreign Trade. (1969) Imports CFA Fr. 86,280,-000,000 (46% from France, 9% from West Germany, 8% from U.S., 5% from Italy, 5% from Netherlands); exports CFA Fr. 118,220,000,000 (31% to France, 14% to U.S., 11% to Italy, 10% to West Germany, 9% to Netherlands). Main exports: timber 30%; coffee 26%; cocoa 22%.

Agriculture. Production (in 000; metric tons; 1968; 1967 in parentheses): corn 206 (223); sweet potatoes c. 1,400 (1,371); cassava c. 530 (c. 520); coffee (1969) c. 240, (1968) c. 216; cocoa (1968–69) 144, (1967–68) 147; bananas 184 (186); peanuts 30 (30); cottonseed c. 27 (c. 20); timber (cu.m.; 1967) c. 8,800, (1966) c. 8,300. Livestock (in 000; 1968–69): cattle 392; pigs 169; sheep c. 800; goats (1967–68) 795.

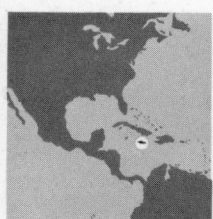

Jamaica

A parliamentary state within the Commonwealth of Nations, Jamaica is an island in the Caribbean Sea about 90 mi. S of Cuba. Area: 4,471 sq.mi. (11,580 sq.km.). Pop. (1970 est.): 1,972,130, predominantly Negro, but including Europeans, Chinese, Indians, and persons of mixed race. Cap. and largest city: City of Kingston (pop., 1969 est., 542,432). Language: English. Religion: Christian, with Anglicans and Baptists in the majority. Queen, Elizabeth II; governor-general in 1970, Sir Clifford Campbell; prime minister, Hugh Lawson Shearer.

The year was marked by considerable concentration on finding the necessary finance for development. Much emphasis was laid on creating an interlocking system of financial institutions, both public and private, to provide capital from at home and abroad. In Jamaica, vigorous efforts were being made to close off all the loopholes that over the years had made possible a fairly substantial amount of tax avoidance. After its admission to membership in the Inter-American Development Bank on Dec. 30, 1969, the nation received a large loan for its farm improve-

Jammu and Kashmir:
see India; Pakistan

JAMAICA

Education. (1965–66) Primary, pupils 323,816, teachers 5,743; secondary, pupils 34,594, teachers 1,429; vocational, pupils 3,524, teachers 218; teacher training, students 212, teachers 10; higher (at University of the West Indies, in Mona; 1966–67), students 2,078.

Finance. Monetary unit: Jamaican dollar, with a par value of Jam$0.83 to U.S. $1 (Jam$2 = £1 sterling). Budget (1969–70 est.): revenue Jam$212,692,-000; expenditure Jam$212,032,000.

Foreign Trade. (1969) Imports Jam$368,490,000; exports Jam$214,010,000. Import sources (1968): U.S. 39%; U.K. 20%; Canada 10%. Export destinations (1968): U.S. 39%; U.K. 24%; Canada 14%; Norway 8%. Main exports: alumina 33%; bauxite 23%; sugar 14%; bananas 6%.

Agriculture. Production (in 000; metric tons; 1968; 1967 in parentheses): sweet potatoes c. 207 (c. 205); cassava c. 10 (c. 10); sugar, raw value (1969–70) 425, (1968–69) 389; bananas c. 280 (c. 300); oranges 62 (72); grapefruit 21 (23); copra 17 (18). Livestock (in 000; 1967–68): cattle c. 240; goats c. 262; pigs c. 160; sheep c. 11.

Industry. Production (in 000; metric tons; 1968): bauxite 8,757; gypsum (1967) 187; cement 408; petroleum products (1967) 1,030; electricity (kw-hr.) 1,068,000.

---

ment scheme. With the announcement in October of an agreement to make available Canadian aid funds up to an amount of $30 million, lines of credit were established with all Jamaica's chief trading partners, Canada, the U.K., and the U.S.

The construction industry continued to prosper. In addition to new hotels, cottages and villas were being built so as to provide more variety in tourist accommodations. Housing developments, both public and private, apartment buildings, shopping plazas, and high-rise office buildings also continued to grow in number. But there were signs that future private developments might be slowed because of government restrictions on credit.

(G. C. Cu.)

ENCYCLOPÆDIA BRITANNICA FILMS. *The West Indies* (1965).

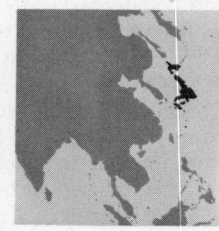

Japan

A constitutional monarchy in the northwestern Pacific Ocean, Japan is an archipelago composed of four major islands (Hokkaido, Honshu, Kyushu, and Shikoku) and minor adjacent islands. Area: 142,871 sq.mi. (370,-036 sq.km.). Pop. (1970 est.): 103,012,811. Cap. and largest city: Tokyo (pop., 1970 est., 9,004,712). Language: Japanese. Religion: primarily Shinto and Buddhist; Christian 1.6%. Emperor, Hirohito; prime minister in 1970, Eisaku Sato.

Domestic Affairs. Following the majority Liberal-Democratic Party's resounding victory in the general election of December 1969, the 63rd session of the Diet was organized on January 14 with the following party standings: House of Representatives (lower): Liberal-Democrats (LDP) 300, Japan Socialists (JSP) 90, Komeito (KMT) 47, Democratic Socialists (DSP) 32, Japan Communists (JCP) 14, independents 3 (total, 486); House of Councillors (upper): LDP 138, JSP 63, KMT 24, DSP 10, JCP 7, Niin Club 4, independents 1, vacancies 3 (total, 250). Thereafter, Prime Minister Sato formed his third Cabinet, retaining five key ministers: Shigeru Hori (chief Cabinet secretary); Kiichi Aichi (foreign affairs); Takeo Fukuda (finance); Michita Sakata (education); and Masuo Araki (public safety). He added former economic planning chief Kiichi Miyazawa (international trade and industry) and Yasuhiro Nakasone (defense; see BIOGRAPHY). On May 13 the Diet finished its session, having passed 98 out of 109 government bills and sanctioned 22 treaties.

Meanwhile, the LDP was looking forward to critical elections. On September 19 Akira Hatano, former Tokyo metropolitan police superintendent, agreed with LDP backing to run in the Tokyo gubernatorial election scheduled for April 1971. He faced the formidable task of opposing the popular incumbent, Gov. Ryokichi Minobe, who had Socialist support. In October Prime Minister Sato was elected to a fourth consecutive term as president of the LDP.

Opposition parties, following the LDP election victory, attempted to regroup. The JSP in its 33rd national convention late in April persuaded Chairman Tomomi Narita, Secretary-General Saburo Eda, and other officers who had been under heavy pressure to resign to continue in their posts. On April 16 Eiichi Nishimura was reelected chairman of the DSP. After its eighth national convention, held June 25–27, the KMT unveiled a new party constitution and a platform, shorn entirely of the Buddhist terms associated with the KMT's parent organization, the Soka Gakkai.

Economic conditions during 1970 were marked by continuing rapid growth, with its attendant advantages and disadvantages. For fiscal 1969 (April 1, 1969–March 31, 1970), according to the Economic Planning Agency, Japan's gross national product (GNP) grew 13% to 62,712,000,000,000 yen ($174.2 billion) with national income per capita at $1,335. Thus, Japan moved up from 20th to 16th in the world in per capita income. Nonetheless, on April 30 the Tokyo Stock Exchange, in a panicky reaction to market trends in the U.S. and in Europe, suffered an average loss of over 200 yen per share, the biggest single-day setback in 17 years.

Japan's growth was attended by heavy social cost. Some Japanese began to refer to GNP as "gross national pollution," and the new word "kogai" ("public nuisance") gained wide currency. In July the Tokyo metropolitan government began to issue public warnings of potential mass poisoning from photochemical smog and sulfuric mist. In August Tokyo began to experiment with one-day "pedestrians' paradises" in the Ginza, Shinjuku, and other congested urban areas.

Most Japanese, however, ignored problems of environment, traveled to Osaka, and enjoyed there the first world exhibition held in Asia, Expo 70. On March 14, in an official inauguration ceremony at the Festival Plaza, Emperor Hirohito expressed words of appreciation for the 77 nations that participated in the fair. (See FAIRS AND SHOWS.)

On February 11, Tokyo University's Institute of Space and Aeronautical Science (ISAS) successfully launched its first artificial satellite. Japan thus became the fourth nation in the world to launch a satellite.

A bizarre incident took place on November 26 when the renowned novelist Yukio Mishima committed sepuku (hara-kiri or ritual suicide) in the office of Lieut. Gen. Kanetoshi Mashita, commander of the Eastern Self-Defense Force. Mishima and four other members of the Shield Society, which he had founded to encourage a revival of the martial samurai spirit, had obtained an appointment with Mashita, apparently with the intention of bringing about a coup. The four took the general prisoner, after which Mishima harangued a hastily assembled group of soldiers from a balcony. When the soldiers proved unresponsive, Mishima returned to Mashita's office where he and one of his followers committed suicide.

Foreign Affairs. Following the Sato-Nixon agreement (November 1969) to return Okinawa to Japan (during 1972) and to "maintain indefinitely" the U.S.-Japan defense treaty, security issues played a less dramatic role in American-Japanese relations. In its annual "Blue Book" surveying Japan's foreign policy, the Foreign Ministry stressed the need to avoid economic friction in U.S. relations, "which are far more important than relations with any other countries." Meanwhile, the ministry maintained the nation's self-defense power should be built up. The settlement of territorial claims over Soviet-held northern islands once belonging to Japan must precede conclusion of a peace treaty with the U.S.S.R. The safety of South Korea, the ministry declared, was crucial to security in the Far East and peace in the Taiwan area was also important. The Japanese government hoped that China would assume a cooperative and constructive attitude in foreign affairs. Finally, according to the ministry, Japan had an obligation to help solve the growing economic gap between developed and less developed countries.

In April formal preparations for the reversion of Okinawa in 1972 began when a commission met in Tokyo. Attending were Ambassador Jiro Takase for Japan; High Commissioner for the Ryukyus Lieut. Gen. James B. Lampert for the U.S.; and Chobyo

KEYSTONE

Helmet-wearing students prepare to demonstrate in Tokyo against the Japan-U.S. security treaty in June 1970. Thousands of students, many armed with steel pipes and Molotov cocktails, later clashed with riot police.

JAPAN

Education. (1967–68) Primary, pupils 9,452,-071, teachers 353,496; secondary, pupils 8,093,-179; vocational, pupils 1,947,207; secondary and vocational, teachers 442,847; higher (including c. 120 universities), students 1,395,173, teaching staff 129,871.

Finance. Monetary unit: yen, with a par value of 360 yen to U.S. $1 (864 yen = £1 sterling). Gold, SDRs, and foreign exchange, official: (June 1970) U.S. $3,250,000,000; (June 1969) U.S. $2,748,000,000. Budget (1969 est.) balanced at 6,739,500,000,000 yen. Gross national product: (1969) 59,902,000,000,000 yen; (1968) 51,077,-000,000,000 yen. Money supply: (June 1970) 18,577,000,000,000 yen; (June 1969) 15,633,-000,000,000 yen. Cost of living (1963 = 100): (June 1970) 142; (June 1969) 133.

Foreign Trade. (1969) Imports 5,408,900,-000,000 yen; exports 5,775,200,000,000 yen. Import sources: U.S. 27%; Australia 8%; Iran 5%. Export destinations: U.S. 31%; South Korea 5%. Main exports: machinery 22%; iron and steel 14%; textile yarns and fabrics 10%.

Transport and Communications. Roads (1969) 1,005,436 km. (including 871 km. expressways). Motor vehicles in use (1969): passenger 6,933,737; commercial 8,334,573. Railways: (1966) 27,949 km.; traffic (1969) 274,271,000,000 passenger-km., freight 59,569,-000,000 net ton-km. Air traffic (1969): 9,000,-000,000 passenger-km.; freight 364.9 million net ton-km. Shipping (1969): merchant vessels 100 gross tons and over 7,665; gross tonnage 23,987,079. Telephones (Dec. 1968) 17,330,791. Radio receivers (Dec. 1968) 25,742,000. Television receivers (Dec. 1968) 21,027,000.

Agriculture. Production (in 000; metric tons; 1969; 1968 in parentheses): rice 17,504 (18,-765); wheat 758 (1,012); barley c. 900 (1,021); sweet potatoes 2,855 (3,594); potatoes 3,572 (4,056); tea (1968) 85, (1967) 85; onions (1968) 1,779, (1967) 1,541; apples 1,078 (1,136); oranges (1968) 2,612, (1967) 1,850; tobacco 174 (193); timber (cu.m.; 1968) 54,500, (1967) 59,300; fish catch (1968) 8,670, (1967) 7,850; whale and sperm oil (1968) 27, (1967)

80. Livestock (in 000; Feb. 1969): cattle 3,458; sheep 64; pigs 5,429; horses 190; goats (Feb. 1968) 223; chickens 157,292.

Industry. Index of production (1963 = 100): (1969) 222; (1968) 190. Fuel and power (in 000; metric tons; 1969): coal 44,657; crude oil 787; natural gas (cu.m.) 2,480,000; electricity (kw.-hr.) 302,107,000. Production (in 000; metric tons; 1969): iron ore (55% metal content) 1,856; pig iron 59,444; crude steel 82,167; petroleum products (1968) 107,970; cement 51,387; cotton yarn 527; woven cotton fabrics (sq.m.) 2,780,000; rayon, etc., filament yarn 142; rayon, etc., staple fibre 373; nylon, etc., filament yarn 360; nylon, etc., fibre 446; sulfuric acid 6,760; cameras (units) 4,801; radio receivers (units) 34,090; television receivers (units) 12,-685; passenger cars (units) 2,609; commercial vehicles (units) 2,080; motorcycles (units) 2,574. Merchant vessels launched (100 gross tons and over; 1969) 9,384,000 gross tons. New dwelling units started (1969) 1,347,000.

Yara, elected chief executive for the Ryukyu government, as adviser. Urgent business included discussion of the U.S. military policy of dismissing Okinawan workers, the total having reached 1,738 in fiscal 1970. The All Okinawa Military Employees' Trade Union (Zengunro) had staged week-long strikes to back up the workers' demands for extension of grace periods and increases in severance allowances. In May opposition parties in Japan protested strenuously against the U.S. cancellation of its initial plan to remove poisonous gas from Okinawa. In December, however, the Pentagon announced that the gas would be taken to Johnson Island, about 715 mi. W of Hawaii.

On May 2 the Japanese government passed a bill providing Diet representation of the Okinawan people for the first time since World War II, and the elections were held in November. Two of the five representatives elected to the lower house were members of the Okinawa Liberal-Democrats (OLDP), while the others belonged, respectively, to the Okinawa Prefecture Socialist, Okinawa Socialist Masses, and Okinawa Peoples parties. Two members were elected to the upper house, one belonging to the OLDP and the other endorsed by Okinawa's four left-wing parties.

Okinawans were shocked by censored testimony, given in the U.S. Congress by former ambassador U. Alexis Johnson and released August 23, to the effect that Japan might not always prohibit the possible introduction of nuclear weapons into Okinawa

A chemical factory near the Japanese village of Minamata discharges waste into the river. Many of the residents who drank water or ate fish from the river contracted what they call a "hurt-hurt" disease, and some died.

KEYSTONE

after the 1972 reversion. Early in September Prime Minister Sato declared that reversion talks were progressing smoothly, that Okinawa would be returned on time, with nuclear weapons removed and bases there placed under the same restrictions as those in Japan proper.

Late in May Prime Minister Sato told U.S. Ambassador Armin Meyer that Japan had no intention of revising the Japan-U.S. security treaty unless the international situation underwent a major change. June 23, the last day of the first ten-year period of the treaty (which had been revised amid a storm of protest in 1960), was an anticlimax as the government declared that "automatic extension" would receive popular endorsement in the 1970s. Opposition parties disputed the declared policy: the JSP, JCP, and KMT reiterated their stands calling for termination of the treaty during the 1970s, while the DSP urged a "comprehensive revision" of the pact. But in rain-dampened Tokyo on June 23 a Socialist-Sohyo (union) demonstration against the treaty was canceled.

Apparently the security treaty was, however, approaching eventual revision. Yasuhiro Nakasone, leader of an important faction within the LDP, continued to call for a "semipermanent" continuation of the U.S. treaty, transfer of U.S. bases to Japanese self-defense forces, and a sweeping revision of security policy. In September, upon his return from Washington, Nakasone reported agreement with U.S. Secretary of Defense Melvin R. Laird on the need to reduce U.S. military installations in Japan.

Japan's relations with the Soviet Union during 1970 revolved first around the "northern territories" issue. Following the 1969 Okinawa reversion agreement with the U.S., Prime Minister Sato renewed his call for the return of the southern Kuril Islands, which had remained under Soviet occupation since the end of World War II. He pressed demands to have the U.S.S.R. acknowledge Japan's "residual sovereignty" over the islands (a formula that had proved successful in Okinawa), and to have the Soviets ultimately return to Japan the islands of Kunashir and Etorofu.

Despite the territorial issue, early in February Japan and the U.S.S.R. signed a trade agreement setting the volume of two-way commerce in 1970 at $720 million on a customs clearance basis. Principal items exported from Japan were to include machinery and equipment, steel products, and textiles.

On April 19 in Peking, Japanese opposition party spokesmen and Chinese delegates concluded trade talks and issued a joint communiqué strongly critical of the Sato Cabinet. Later in April in Tokyo, the LDP's draft statement on the communiqué expressed deep regrets over Peking's criticism, dismissing the accusation of "resurgent militarism" in Japan as "an outrageous distortion of facts" and "malicious slander against the Japanese people." Despite the tension the Japan External Trade Organization (JETRO) estimated that trade between Japan and China during 1970 would exceed $700 million, including 3.5% of Japan's total exports. Meanwhile, protracted talks with the U.S. concerning Japanese textile exports remained stalemated at year's end. The U.S. hoped that Japan would agree to limit voluntarily exports of synthetic fibre and wool products, but there was strong internal opposition to such a move from the Japanese textile industry.

Japan's relations with the two Koreas was dramatized by a bizarre hijacking incident. On March 31 a Japan Air Lines Boeing 727 left Tokyo Haneda airport for Fukuoka. Members of the Red Army (Sekigunha), most militant of ultraleftist Japanese students, seized the aircraft. When ordered to fly to North Korea, Capt. Shinji Ishida responded that the plane did not have sufficient fuel. He was permitted to touch down at Fukuoka, where 23 (of 131) passengers were allowed to disembark. That afternoon the airplane flew to Kimpo airport, outside Seoul in South Korea, where a war of nerves was conducted among hijackers, South Korean authorities, and Japanese officials for the next 48 hours. On April 3 the hijackers accepted the offer of the Japanese vice-minister of transport, Shinjiro Yamamura, that he take the place of the passengers as hostage and accompany the plane to North Korea. The plane then went on to North Korea. On April 4 North Korea abruptly announced that it was returning the crew, Yamamura, and the plane. (A. W. Bs.)

ENCYCLOPÆDIA BRITANNICA FILMS. *Japan—Harvesting the Land and the Sea* (1963); *Japan—Miracle in Asia* (1963).

Jordan

A constitutional monarchy in southwest Asia, Jordan is bounded north by Syria, northeast by Iraq, east and south by Saudi Arabia, and west by Israel. Area (including territory occupied by Israel in the June 1967 war): 37,737 sq.mi. (97,740 sq.km.). Pop. (1969 est.): 2,250,000. Cap. and largest city: Amman (pop., 1969 est., 500,000). Language: Arabic. Religion: Muslim 88%; Christian 12%. King, Husain I; prime ministers in 1970, Bahjat al-Talhouni; from June 28, Abdel Monem Rifai; from September 16, Brig.

JORDAN
Education. (1967–68) Primary, pupils 207,609, teachers 5,066; secondary, pupils 67,283, teachers 2,807; vocational, pupils 2,089, teachers 100; higher (including University of Jordan), students 3,420, teaching staff 308.
Finance. Monetary unit: Jordanian dinar, with a par value of 0.36 dinars to U.S. $1 (0.86 dinars = £1 sterling). Gold, SDRs, and foreign exchange, central bank: (June 1970) U.S. $248.5 million; (June 1969) U.S. $259.3 million. Budget (1970 est.): revenue 84 million dinars; expenditure 88 million dinars. Gross national product: (1968) 197.3 million dinars; (1967) 206 million dinars. Money supply: (June 1970) 101,-760,000 dinars; (June 1969) 92,160,000 dinars. Cost of living (Amman; 1967 = 100): (June 1970) 114; (June 1969) 109.
Foreign Trade. (1969) Imports 67,670,000 dinars; exports 14,750,000 dinars. Import sources (1968): U.K. 12%; West Germany 10%; U.S. 10%; Lebanon 6%; Syria 5%. Export destinations (1968): Kuwait 17%; India 13%; Iraq 13%; Saudi Arabia 11%; Lebanon 8%; Yugoslavia 7%; Syria 6%. Main exports: phosphates 24%; tomatoes 13%; fruit (1968) 9%.
Transport and Communications. Roads (1969) 5,346 km. Motor vehicles in use (1969): passenger 14,165; commercial 5,769. Railways (1968) 366 km. Air traffic (1969): 159,260,000 passenger-km.; freight 1,579,000 net ton-km. Telephones (Jan. 1969) *c.* 34,500. Radio receivers (Dec. 1968) 250,000. Television receivers (Dec. 1968) 17,000.
Agriculture. Production (in 000; metric tons; 1968; 1967 in parentheses): wheat 95 (196); barley 20 (63); cucumbers 3 (28); onions 1 (10); tomatoes 195 (258); olives 13 (22); oranges 17 (42); lemons 8 (15); figs 4 (16); grapes 8 (28); bananas 6 (22). Livestock (in 000; 1967–68): cattle 41; goats 377; sheep (1968–69) 792; camels 11; asses *c.* 96; chickens (1968–69) *c.* 2,400.
Industry. Production (in 000; metric tons; 1968): phosphate rock 1,156; cement 381; electricity (kw-hr.) 156,000.

Gen. Muhammad Daoud; from September 26, Ahmed Toukan; and, from October 28, Wasfi al-Tal.

For Jordan 1970 was overshadowed by the escalation of an internal conflict between the Army, loyal to King Husain (*see* BIOGRAPHY), and the Palestinian guerrilla movement into a brief but bloody civil war that endangered the country's survival as a national entity and the whole future of Arab-Israeli relations.

The guerrilla movement, divided over tactics but united in its opposition to Israel, in February agreed on a "unified command" for its ten main factions—ranging from Al Fatah (the largest and relatively moderate group headed by Yasir Arafat) to the militantly antiroyalist Popular Front for the Liberation of Palestine (PFLP) led by George Habash (*see* BIOGRAPHY).

The guerrillas' first serious encounter with the Army, on February 11–12, followed Husain's attempt to assert his authority by forbidding the former to carry weapons in public. This move, openly defied in Amman, unleashed a battle that left at least half the capital in guerrilla hands. A settlement, announced on February 22, was reached only after the king had "frozen" the ban.

Anti-U.S. riots in Amman on April 13–15 prompted U.S. Assistant Secretary of State Joseph Sisco, then in the Middle East, to cancel a visit to Jordan on the advice of the U.S. ambassador in Amman, Harrison M. Symmes. Husain, mortified by this reflection on his ability to keep order, demanded and obtained the ambassador's immediate recall. Husain yielded to a guerrilla demand for the removal of two "hard-line" army leaders—his uncle, Maj. Gen. Sherif Nasser bin Jamil, and Maj. Gen. Zaid bin Shaker.

This concession, which caused a near mutiny by loyalist units, was followed on June 27 by the formation of a new government under the deputy prime minister and foreign minister, Abdel Monem Rifai. Rifai not only enjoyed the guerrillas' trust but during his previous premiership in 1969 he had won international respect for his handling of Arab-Israeli peace probes. Although the new Cabinet had a pro-guerrilla majority, Husain was clearly supporting U.A.R. Pres. Gamal Abd-al-Nasser's cautious feelers toward a political settlement with Israel.

His domestic dilemma, however, was sharpened by his endorsement on July 26 of U.S. proposals for Arab-Israeli negotiations. Interpreted by the guerrillas as a betrayal of the Palestinian cause, this provoked more anti-U.S. demonstrations in Amman and stiffened the PFLP's determination to wreck any peace initiative.

During September 6–9 the PFLP hijacked to a Jordanian airstrip three airliners (U.S., Swiss, and British) with more than 300 people aboard whom it threatened to blow up with the aircraft unless the governments concerned returned Arab commandos detained in Europe and Israel. All the hostages were freed by September 30 when the PFLP secured its main demands (after destroying the airliners).

This episode, apart from its international repercussions, made civil war inevitable, since the PFLP hijackers had defied the Army's authority. On September 9 Husain (under strong pressure from senior army officers) sanctioned sterner action against the guerrillas. On September 15 he set up a provisional military government under Brig. Gen. Muhammad Daoud, appointing another "hard-liner," Gen. Habis al-Majali, as military governor-general and commander in chief of the armed forces.

PICTORIAL PARADE
Yasir Arafat, leader of Al Fatah, largest of the Palestinian guerrilla organizations.

KEYSTONE
King Husain withstood challenges by the guerrilla movement during 1970.

BRUNO BARBEY FROM MAGNUM

A Jordanian soldier guards the rooftops in Amman during the fighting between government troops and Palestinian guerrillas in September 1970.

By September 17 the fighting was general. It was heaviest in Amman and north Jordan—where the guerrillas, reinforced by Syrian armoured units that crossed the border on September 19, held the towns of Irbid and Ramtha. Formal hostilities ended on September 25 when an inter-Arab mission arranged a cease-fire. This left the guerrillas in control of their two northern strongholds and some districts of Amman. Total casualties in the ten-day civil war (including a high proportion of civilians) were variously estimated at 1,500–5,000 killed and up to 10,000 injured.

Meeting in Cairo on September 27, Husain and Arafat signed a 14-point truce agreement calling for the restoration of civilian rule, and a series of further agreements between the guerrillas and the Jordanian government were negotiated during the fall. On October 16 Husain dismissed Gen. Habis al-Majali. However, the composition of the new government formed on October 28 suggested that the king had no intention of allowing the guerrillas to dictate internal policy. The new civilian prime minister, Wasfi al-Tal, had been one of Husain's closest advisers throughout the civil war. In December Husain visited Washington, where he was reported to have asked for additional military aid.   (P. Md.)

Encyclopædia Britannica Films. *The Middle East* (1955).

Kenya

A republic and a member of the Commonwealth of Nations, Kenya is bordered on the north by Sudan and Ethiopia, east by Somalia, south by Tanzania, and west by Uganda. Area: 224,960 sq.mi. (582,647 sq. km.), including 5,171 sq.mi. of inland water. Pop. (1969 est.): 10,504,000, including (1962) African and Somali 96.9%; Asian 2%. Cap. and largest city: Nairobi (pop., 1969 est., 506,000). Language: English (official); Bantu, especially Swahili; Nilotic. Religion: pagan; Christian and Muslim minorities. President in 1970, Jomo Kenyatta.

Opening the first session of the newly elected Par-

liament on February 6 against a background of recent unrest in the Kisumu area, President Kenyatta stressed the need for a national outlook and declared that Parliament should not harass or oppose the government but should act as a bridge between government and people. He warned of a heavy load of work ahead and announced that the government would be concentrating upon making the country self-sufficient as far as basic foodstuffs were concerned. One of the most important factors contributing to the achievement of this aim was the land reform program, and the minister for lands and settlement took pains in January to explain to the rural population the method of registering titles to land and the importance of doing so. British financial support had been essential to the implementation of the program, and on April 15 Judith Hart, British minister of overseas development, said she had offered to Kenya, subject to the approval of Parliament, £11.5 million to be used for agricultural development.

Early in March Vice-Pres. Arap Moi announced that a more rigorous attitude would be adopted toward Asians holding British passports who became unemployed in Kenya. Previously the government had not pressed its policy of deporting British Asians who had no work permit, but this was now to be enforced. At the same time, the British government strongly resisted pressure to increase the annual quota of East African Asians admitted to Britain and a number of East African Asians consequently found themselves shuttling between airports in an endeavour to find a country willing to accept them.

In October Kenya saw the other side of the picture when many thousands of its subjects were expelled from Uganda as part of the plan of that nation's president, Milton Obote, to find employment for his own citizens. A visit to Uganda by Kenyatta failed to alleviate the trouble, and the Kenya National Chamber of Commerce felt constrained to oppose a proposal by the central organization of trade unions to organize a boycott of goods bound for Uganda in Mombasa on the ground that this would have an adverse effect upon Kenya's economy. A number of Kenyan legislators, however, urged that the country quit the East

African Community as a gesture of disapproval of Uganda's action. The community, indeed, was under some pressure. Ugandan currency was banned in Kenya, while the University of East Africa broke up in the course of the year into its national component parts.

These events seriously weakened the link between the two countries, which only a short time before had seemed strengthened as a result of the two nations' joint aversion to the possibility that Britain might decide to resume arms supplies to South Africa. That news had caused Kenya's foreign minister, Njoroge Mungai, to confer with counterparts in Uganda, Tanzania, and Zambia in July in an attempt to formulate a common policy. Subsequently Mungai tabled a draft resolution at the Council of Ministers of the Organization of African Unity (OAU) in Addis Ababa on August 27, urging the African states to exert maximum pressure to check the supply of arms to South Africa by the Western powers.

On the home front Kenyatta in July ordered the liberation of 12 detainees, members of the banned Kenya Peoples' Union (KPU). Among the 12 were J. M. Nthula, vice-president of the party, and four other former members of Parliament. Kenyatta stated that it was not the government's intention to detain people when it was not absolutely necessary. Oginga Odinga, president of the KPU, was not, however, released. (K. I.)

ENCYCLOPÆDIA BRITANNICA FILMS. *East Africa (Kenya, Tanganyika, Uganda)* (1962); *Youth Builds a Nation in Tanzania* (1970).

KENYA

Education. (1968–69) Primary, pupils 1,209,680, teachers 37,923; secondary, pupils 101,361, teachers 4,644; vocational, pupils 1,872, teachers 161; teacher training, students 6,634, teachers 468; higher (at Nairobi University), students 4,967, teaching staff 395.

Finance. Monetary unit: Kenyan shilling, with a par value of KShs. 7.14 to U.S. $1 (KShs. 17.14 = £1 sterling). Gold, SDRs, and foreign exchange: (June 1970) U.S. $188.4 million; (June 1969) U.S. $130 million. Budget (1969–70 est.): revenue KShs. 1,459,-740,000; expenditure KShs. 1,337,120,000. Gross national product: (1968) KShs. 9,182,000,000; (1967) KShs. 8,652,000,000. Cost of living (Nairobi; 1963 = 100): (May 1970) 113; (May 1969) 110.

Foreign Trade. (Excluding trade with Tanzania and Uganda; 1969) Imports KShs. 2,339,000,000; exports KShs. 1,370,000,000. Import sources: U.K. 31%; West Germany 8%; Japan 8%; U.S. 7%; Iran 7%. Export destinations: U.K. 23%; West Germany 11%; U.S. 8%; Zambia 6%. Main exports: coffee 29%; tea 20%; petroleum products 11%.

Transport and Communications. Roads (1969) 41,856 km. Motor vehicles in use (1968): passenger 80,600; commercial 14,400. Railways: (1967) 2,050 km. (operated under East African Railways Corporation, serving Kenya, mainland Tanzania, and Uganda with a total of 5,870 km.); traffic (total East African; 1966) 4,529,000,000 passenger-km., freight (1968) 4,088,000,000 net ton-km. Air traffic (East African Airways Corporation, including Tanzania and Uganda; 1969): 699.3 million passenger-km.; freight 29,690,000 ton-km. Telephones (Dec. 1968) 65,445. Radio receivers (Dec. 1968) 500,000. Television receivers (Dec. 1968) 15,000.

Agriculture. Production (in 000; metric tons; 1969; 1968 in parentheses): corn 1,682 (1,704); wheat (on farms and estates) 216 (162); coffee (1968) *c.* 50, (1967) 49; tea (1968) 30, (1967) 23; sugar, raw value (1969–70) *c.* 137, (1968–69) 127; sisal 51 (50); cotton, lint (1968) *c.* 6, (1967) 5; fish catch (1968) 31, (1967) 27. Livestock (in 000; 1968–69): cattle *c.* 7,800; sheep *c.* 7,100; pigs *c.* 30; goats (Aug. 1968) *c.* 6,600; camels (1967–68) *c.* 180; poultry *c.* 11,000.

Industry. Production (in 000; metric tons; 1968): salt 33; magnesite 0.1; soda ash 117; gold (troy oz.) 32; cement (1969) 642; electricity (excluding most industrial production; kw-hr.; 1969) 460,000.

Korea

A country of eastern Asia, Korea is bounded by China, the Sea of Japan, the Straits of Korea, and the Yellow Sea. It is divided into two parts at the 38th parallel.

Republic of Korea (South Korea). Area: 38,022 sq.mi. (98,477 sq.km.). Pop. (1969 est.): 31,139,000. Cap. and largest city: Seoul (pop., 1967 est., 3,972,-000). Language: Korean. Religion: Buddhist; Confucian; Tonghak (Chondokyo). President in 1970, Gen. Park Chung Hee; prime ministers, Gen. Chung Il Kwon and, from December 19, Paik Too Chin.

The Nixon Doctrine calling for less U.S. involvement in Asia cast a shadow across South Korea in 1970 and severely strained Seoul-Washington relations. Toward the end of 1969 the U.S. secretary of defense, Melvin R. Laird, had proposed a reduction in the 64,000-man U.S. force in South Korea, moving "in the direction of 'koreanizing' our activities in Korea just as rapidly as we can." Vigorous protests in Seoul and elsewhere led to a freeze on the negotiations, but by May South Korean fears were again at high pitch. Reports from Washington that the U.S. planned to withdraw one army division from Korea by 1971 led to an emergency meeting of the South Korean National Assembly's Foreign Affairs Committee, at which Foreign Minister Choi Kyu Ha warned that the U.S. could not unilaterally withdraw

WIDE WORLD

its troops from Korea. By mid-June the U.S. press reported that secret negotiations on a withdrawal schedule were to begin in Seoul soon. The reports said that as compensation for the proposed troop reduction the U.S. would seek a special congressional outlay of $1 billion spread over five years to modernize the South Korean Army. This was to be in addition to the $140 million a year in military aid already being provided.

The South Korean government's opposition to any change in the status quo obviously stemmed from its realization that its security was dependent on overt and continuous U.S. military involvement in the country. President Park referred to troop cut reports and said in June, "I want to make clear that in view of the existing internal and international situations, it is no time to discuss such a matter." In July the National Assembly unanimously adopted a resolution addressed to the U.S. warning that hasty koreaniza-

A South Korean soldier watches a Japan Air Lines jet under the control of a band of sword-wielding students at Seoul's Kimpo airport, April 1, 1970. Later the aircraft left for P'yongyang, North Korea.

Journalism:
see Publishing
Judaism:
see Israel; Religion
Judo:
see Sporting Record
Karate:
see Sporting Record
Kashmir:
see India; Pakistan

New Samil elevated
highway in Seoul, part
of the modern expressway
system completed in 1970,
carries 65,000
vehicles per day.

There was continued optimism on the economic front. The completion of the 267-mi. Seoul–Pusan expressway marked a major milestone in the ten-year highway development plan begun in 1967. A tentative third five-year plan (1972–76) calling for an annual economic growth rate of 8.5% was outlined in April. In the first six months of the year the growth of the gross national product (GNP) slowed down to 11.6% from the 14.1% registered in the first half of the previous year. The government target for the year was a growth rate of 10%. The per capita GNP was expected to be 91,582 won ($295.40).

Democratic People's Republic of Korea (North Korea). Area: 46,557 sq.mi. (120,583 sq.km.). Pop. (1970 est.): 14 million. Cap.: P'yongyang (pop., 1960 est., 653,100). Language: Korean. Religion: Buddhist; Confucian; Tonghak (Chondokyo). Secretary-general of the Korean Workers' (Communist) Party and chairman of the Council of Ministers (premier) in 1970, Marshal Kim Il Sung; president, Choi Yong Kun.

North Korea's status within the Communist bloc improved considerably in 1970. This followed visits to P'yongyang by the Chinese premier, Chou En-lai; the deposed Cambodian ruler, Norodom Sihanouk; and Communist leaders from North Vietnam, South Vietnam, and Laos. Chou En-lai's unexpected visit on April 5–7 virtually brought about a firm new alliance between the two countries, apparently healing the wounds that Chinese Red Guards had inflicted on North Korea during the Cultural Revolution by ridiculing Marshal Kim Il Sung. The initiative for the rapprochement reportedly came from China, as Peking found common cause with P'yongyang in opposing Japan's growing willingness to serve U.S. interests in Asia.

North Korea was evidently interested in playing an active role in Indochina following the Cambodian coup. It vehemently supported the joint statement issued by the summit conference of Indochinese Communist leaders with Prince Sihanouk in April. Kim Il Sung sent a warm message to Sihanouk, "wholeheartedly greeting" the formation of the "royal government of national union." When Sihanouk went to P'yongyang in June, his reception was truly magnificent. Statements published later suggested that Kim

tion would bring about another major tragedy. There were also threats that South Korea would withdraw its troops from Vietnam.

In the face of such strong South Korean protests, the U.S. seemed willing to make some adjustments without going back on its basic decision. At the third annual defense ministerial meeting between South Korea and the U.S. in Honolulu in July, the American side said that U.S. arms would replace U.S. troops in South Korea. The promise on arms was acceptable to Seoul, which had been persistently asking for increased U.S. military aid. A month after the Honolulu meeting there were reports that South Korea had asked Washington for at least $3 billion in special military aid during the next five years. The Honolulu talks ended on the compromise note that no troops would be withdrawn until modernization of South Korean defenses was completed.

On December 19 Prime Minister Chung Il Kwon resigned in a Cabinet reshuffle looking toward the 1971 elections. He was replaced by a former prime minister, Paik Too Chin.

KOREA: Republic
Education. (1967–68) Primary, pupils 5,382,-500, teachers 89,277; secondary, pupils 1,171,-022, teachers 29,626; vocational, students 203,-997, teachers 8,441; higher (including 18 universities), students 170,941, teaching staff 7,785.

Finance. Monetary unit: won, with an official exchange rate (July 1970) of 312 won to U.S. $1 (745 won = £1 sterling). Gold, SDRs, and foreign exchange, central bank: (June 1970) U.S. $591.3 million; (June 1969) U.S. $412.2 million. Budget (1969 est.) balanced at 324.4 billion won (including defense expenditure 60.3 billion won). Gross national product: (1968) 1,575,700,000,-000 won; (1967) 1,242,400,000,000 won. Money supply: (Sept. 1969) 192.5 billion won; (Sept. 1968) 143.6 billion won. Cost of living (1963 = 100): (June 1970) 246; (June 1969) 219.

Foreign Trade. (1969) Imports 497,730,000,-000 won (including 4,140,000,000 won official aid); exports 179,960,000,000 won. Import sources: Japan 41%; U.S. 29%. Export destinations: U.S. 50%; Japan 21%. Main exports: clothing 26%; plywood 13%; textile yarns and fabrics 11%; electrical machinery and equipment 6%; fish and fish products 5%.

Transport and Communications. Roads

(1967) 34,476 km. Motor vehicles in use (1968): passenger 33,112; commercial 31,582. Railways: (1968) 3,161 km.; traffic (1969) 11,076,000,000 passenger-km., freight 7,118,000,000 net ton-km. Air traffic (1968): 124,341,000 passenger-km.; freight 2,035,000 net ton-km. Shipping (1969): merchant vessels 100 gross tons and over 294; gross tonnage 767,315. Telephones (Dec. 1968) 489,912. Radio receivers (Dec. 1967) 2,258,000. Television receivers (Dec. 1968) 95,000.

Agriculture. Production (in 000; metric tons; 1969; 1968 in parentheses): rice 5,527 (4,438); wheat c. 374 (345); potatoes 599 (617); barley (1968) c. 2,084, (1967) 1,916; sweet potatoes 2,123 (2,049); soybeans (1968) 245, (1967) 201; tobacco c. 80 (70); fish catch (1967) 749, (1966) 701. Livestock (in 000; Dec. 1968): cattle c. 1,240; pigs 1,396; horses 20; goats (Dec. 1967) 133; chickens 25,968.

Industry. Production (in 000; metric tons; 1969): coal 10,274; iron ore (c. 50% metal content) 710; steel 421; cement 4,871; tungsten concentrate (oxide content; 1968) 2.9; kaolin (1967) 103; fluorspar (1967) 57; limestone (1967) 3,916; gold (troy oz.; 1968) 55; silver (troy oz.; 1968) 611; electricity (excluding most industrial production; kw-hr.) 7,700,000.

KOREA: Democratic People's Republic
Education. (1964–65) Primary, pupils 1,113,-000, teachers 25,221; secondary, pupils 704,000, teachers 27,162; vocational, pupils 441,000, teachers 17,176; higher, students 186,000, teaching staff 9,013.

Finance. Monetary unit: won, with an official exchange rate of 2.57 won to U.S. $1 (6.17 won = £1 sterling). Budget (1968 rev. est.) balanced at 5,274,400,000 won.

Foreign Trade. (Excluding trade with China; 1966) Imports c. U.S. $126.5 million (68% from U.S.S.R., 6% from France); exports c. U.S. $148,742,000 (62% to U.S.S.R., 15% to Japan, 7% to Czechoslovakia).

Agriculture. Production (in 000; metric tons; 1968; 1967 in parentheses): rice c. 2,500 (c. 2,500); corn c. 1,700 (c. 1,600); barley c. 250 (c. 250); potatoes c. 955 (c. 955); fish catch (1964) 770, (1963) 640. Livestock (in 000; Dec. 1968): cattle c. 720; pigs c. 1,300; sheep (Dec. 1967) c. 165; goats (Dec. 1967) c. 168.

Industry. Production (in 000; metric tons; 1968): coal c. 18,500; iron ore (metal content) c. 3,500; pig iron c. 2,000; steel c. 1,750; lead c. 55; zinc c. 80; magnesite c. 1,000; cement c. 2,700; tungsten concentrate (oxide content) c. 2.7; electricity (kw-hr.; 1965) 13,300,000.

Il Sung pressed Sihanouk to agree to North Korean volunteers fighting in Cambodia. The idea, however, did not go far, perhaps due to North Vietnam's known opposition to volunteers from outside Indochina. Meanwhile, North Korea established diplomatic relations with Ceylon on July 13, following the electoral victory there of the United Left Front led by Mme Sirimavo Bandaranaike.

Clashes between North Korea and South Korea continued during the year. In early June the North claimed to have sunk a South Korean spy ship. Before the month was over the South reported the capture of a North Korean spy boat. The most spectacular incident was the hijacking of a South Korean airliner with 47 passengers on Dec. 11, 1969. A single man, believed to be a Communist agent, forced the plane, which had taken off from the South Korean coastal town of Kangnung, to land at Yonpo, near Hamhung, in North Korea. North Korea said that the hijacking was the work of the two pilots who were seeking political asylum in the North. Thirty-nine passengers were later released.

Another hijacking, which seemed to embarrass North Korea, occurred on March 31, when a Japan Air Lines Boeing 727 on a domestic flight was seized by nine sword-brandishing students. The plane landed at Seoul airport, which had been hastily disguised to look like P'yongyang, but the students were not fooled. After four days of dramatic bargaining on the Seoul runway, the aircraft was allowed to go to P'yongyang with Shinjiro Yamamura, Japanese vice-minister of transport, on board as hostage, in return for the passengers. P'yongyang later released the plane, the crew, and Yamamura.

On June 24 there was a surprise of a different kind when North Korea said it was ready to set up a "confederation of North and South Korea" as a transitional measure, if necessary, before complete unification of the country. It also proposed mutual troop reductions and a no-war pact. The suggestions were seen by the South and its allies as a propaganda move, though indicative of a softening in the North Korean attitude. (T. J. S. G.)

Kuwait

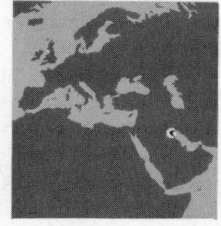

An independent Arab sheikhdom, Kuwait is on the northwestern coast of the Persian Gulf between Iraq and Saudi Arabia. Area: 6,880 sq.mi. (17,820 sq.km.). Pop. (1970): 733,196. Cap.: Kuwait (pop., 1970, 80,008). Largest city: Hawalli (pop., 1970, 106,507). Language: Arabic. Religion: Muslim. Amir in 1970, Sheikh Sabah as-Salim as-Sabah; prime minister, Crown Prince Sheikh Jabir as-Ahmed as-Jabir as-Sabah.

Although Kuwait's oil revenues in 1970 were well over $700 million, it suffered from a sharp economic recession because of the lack of potentialities for further development combined with the deflationary effect of the government's 1969 restrictions on new immigration. Several domestic enterprises, including the Kuwait National Petroleum Company, showed heavy losses. Nevertheless, in February the National Assembly increased Kuwait's grant to the United Arab Republic by 10 million dinars and also granted 5 million dinars to the Palestine Liberation Organization, while Tunisia and Yemen received loans of 3 million

dinars and 700,000 dinars, respectively, from the Kuwait Fund for Arab Economic Development.

In diplomacy, Kuwait's closest concern was the future of the Persian Gulf. During a visit from the Iranian foreign minister in July, the Kuwaiti prime minister announced his country's agreement with the Iranian view that British forces should be withdrawn from the Gulf area by the end of 1971 but Kuwait rejected Iraq's proposal for an Arab military alliance in the area after British withdrawal. (P. Md.)

KUWAIT
Education. (1967–68) Primary, pupils 54,028, teachers 2,425; secondary, pupils 42,286, teachers 2,775; vocational, pupils 1,307, teachers 228; teacher training, students 2,384, teachers 297; higher, students 886, teaching staff 71.
Finance. Monetary unit: Kuwaiti dinar, with a par value of 0.36 dinars to U.S. $1 (0.86 dinars = £1 sterling). Gold and foreign exchange, official: (June 1970) U.S. $191.8 million; (June 1969) U.S. $165.2 million. Budget (1969–70 est.): revenue 302.5 million dinars; expenditure 234.5 million dinars. Money supply: (June 1970) 107.8 million dinars; (June 1969) 125.4 million dinars.
Foreign Trade. (1968) Imports 218.3 million dinars; exports 496.7 million dinars. Import sources: U.S. 17%; Japan 13%; U.K. 13%; West Germany 10%; Italy 5%. Export destinations: U.K. 20%; Italy 18%; Japan 18%; Netherlands 11%; France 7%. Main exports petroleum and products 97%.
Industry. Crude oil production (1969) 129,443,000 metric tons.

Labour Unions

In line with the growing interest in international comparisons of strike activity, the U.K. Ministry of Employment and Productivity published statistics in the November 1969 *Employment and Productivity Gazette* showing the number of days lost through industrial disputes per 1,000 persons employed in a number of countries. The figures are not strictly comparable because the definitions used vary; nonetheless, they show marked and consistent differences. (*See* Table.)

Industrialized Countries. In the U.S., where millions of workers were covered by three-year contracts, major negotiations in 1970 affected about five million workers, roughly twice as many as in 1969. Two strikes of significance that ran into 1970 were settled. The strike of 147,000 production workers in 135 plants owned by General Electric, which began in October 1969, was settled in February, though the machinists' union held out for some weeks longer. One of the most dramatic and widely publicized strikes in recent U.S. history, that involving California grape growers, ended in July. The strike was called in 1965, and by the end of 1969 agreement had been achieved between the United Farm Workers Organizing Committee and the wine grape growers. Meanwhile, a boycott of international dimensions was launched against California table grapes. In April 1970 the table grape growers began to give way, and by July, 37 agreements had been signed. On July 29 a further 26 growers signed contracts with the union, bringing about 85% of California's table grape acreage under union contract. César Chávez (*see* BIOGRAPHY), head of the UFWOC, announced that his next target would be California lettuce growers.

The vital U.S. transportation industry experienced considerable labour unrest. A strike with serious economic consequences occurred in the spring and early

UPI COMPIX

César Chávez, head of the United Farm Workers, ended the five-year grape strike and boycott when contracts with major California growers were signed on July 29, 1970.

JIM ANDERSON
FROM NANCY PALMER

Hard hats march and wave flags outside New York's city hall in May 1970. Several days earlier, many hard hats beat several youths while police stood by.

summer when the Chicago area teamsters stayed out for 12 weeks. A national teamster agreement was achieved on May 15, but the Chicago local, which traditionally carried on its own negotiations, refused to accept it. Chicago teamsters had struck selected truckers early in April, and on April 10 the remaining truckers began a lockout. The strike ended in July with the Chicago local winning substantially better terms than were in the national contract. That contract was then reopened and the settlement revised upward. Throughout the year the nation was threatened by a series of strike deadlines in the railroad industry, but until December strike action was averted by a series of legal maneuvers. A one-day nationwide strike on December 10 ended after Congress passed legislation again postponing the deadline, this time un-

til March 1, 1971. In the spring the federally employed air traffic controllers staged a "sick-out" that led to long delays at airports and some flight cancellations. The controllers' principal complaints involved working conditions.

Postal workers struck in the U.S. and Canada. The U.S. strike, the first in the nation's history, began March 18 in the New York City Post Office and spread rapidly across the country, involving, at its height, more than 200,000 federal employees. Pres. Richard Nixon declared a state of national emergency and sent troops to New York City to move the mail, although the soldiers' lack of training made this largely a symbolic gesture. The agreement between the seven national postal unions and the government, reached on April 2, covered pay raises and reorganization of the postal system. The Canadian strike, which saw sporadic strike action across the nation through most of the year, was settled on September 4.

One of the most prominent union leaders on the contemporary U.S. labour scene, Walter Reuther (*see* OBITUARIES), was killed in an air crash May 9. His place as president of the United Automobile Workers was taken by a union vice-president, Leonard Woodcock (*see* BIOGRAPHY). The negotiations with the three major automobile manufacturers began in July. General Motors was selected as the target firm, and when the old contract expired on September 15 without any settlement having been reached, a strike was called that lasted until November. Major provisions of the new contract included a 13% wage rise in the first year and 3% in each of the next two years; a cost-of-living clause; and improved pension and early retirement benefits.

On August 24 the U.S. Senate decided to cut off the U.S. contribution of $3.7 million due to the International Labour Organization (ILO) for the second half of 1970. This decision, which had immediate effects on the scale and scope of the ILO's activities,

Days Lost Through Strike Action per 1,000 Population in Selected Countries

Country	1964	1965	1966	1967	1968	Average for 5 years (1964–68)	10 years (1959–68)
Australia*	460	390	350	310	450	392	345
Belgium	250	40	320†	90	230‡	186	194
Canada	560	790	1,570†	1,200†	1,670‡	1,158	784
Denmark§	30	400†	30	20	20	100	404
Finland	80	20	150	410	250	182	314
France	280	100	240	430	...	263‖	312¶
Germany, West◊	—	—	—	30	—	6	20
India	560	470	890†	1,270†	1,080†	854	697
Ireland	1,620	1,720†	1,420†	520†	920	1,240	828
Italy	1,270	540	1,710†	580	930	1,006	1,088
Japan	190	360	170	100	160	196	282
Netherlands	20	30	10	—	10	14	37
New Zealand	160	50	230	320	310	214	177
Norway	—	—	—	10	10	4	116
Sweden◊	10	—	110	—	—	24	15
Switzerland	—	—	—	—	—	—	5
United Kingdom	170	220	180†	220	370	232	262
United States	850	860	880†	1,430†	1,590	1,122	1,114

Note: (—) = nil or negligible; (···) = not yet available.
*Including electricity and gas.
†Revised figures (due to revisions of the number of days lost or to more recent bench-mark figures).
‡Preliminary figure.
§Manufacturing only.
‖Average for 1964–67 only.
¶Average for 1959–67 only.
◊Excluding West Berlin.
◊All industries included.
Source: International Labour Office.

followed the appointment of a Soviet Union nominee as an assistant director general of the organization. This appointment was one of the first acts of the newly elected director general, W. Jenks of the U.K., who succeeded David Morse of the U.S. in 1970.

In Great Britain the intensity of strike action in 1970 was greater than in any year since the General Strike of 1926. From January to September there were 3,196 strikes, compared with 2,248 in the corresponding period of 1969. More workers were involved, and the number of working days lost rose from 4,064,000 to 7,399,000. More than half of all the strikes in 1970 were over wage demands, reflecting the relaxation of government constraints on income that had been in force since 1964. The dominant issue in 1969 had been the Industrial Relations Bill, which the government had intended to introduce but had withdrawn under strong trade-union pressure.

Meanwhile, the possibility of antistrike legislation had no effect on the propensity to strike. As in previous years, the vast majority of strikes were not supported officially by the unions, but 1970 was also marked by a number of large-scale union-backed strikes. The first involved schoolteachers. After the teachers' unions rejected a £50 a year increase in November 1969, token strikes were held involving at least 100,000 teachers. On December 1 two-week strikes were organized in about 400 schools, and a second wave of two-week strikes began on January 12. After intervention by the minister of education, £120 of the £135 demanded was offered and accepted on March 3. The culmination was the decision of the National Union of Teachers to seek affiliation with the Trades Union Congress.

A meeting of shop stewards at Ford Motor Co. plants in Britain voted in favour of strike action from February 2 unless the company conceded a £10 a week increase to give parity with automobile workers in other parts of the country. The issue was settled temporarily when Ford agreed to reopen talks about parity. Some vacillation characterized a dispute over a wage demand by British dockers. A national docks delegate conference decided to strike from July 14, but on the 13th the general secretary of the Transport and General Workers' Union appealed to the dockers to remain on the job. The appeal was not successful, and the majority of Britain's dockworkers struck as planned. The next day the strike was made official by the union, and on July 16 the government declared a state of emergency. A court of inquiry was set up which recommended an improvement in the employers' offer. The recommendation was accepted, and the strike ended on August 3. A bitter dispute occurred when workers in 12 Pilkington glass factories throughout Britain struck on April 3 and refused to return to work on the advice of their union. Divisions among the workers led to clashes between pickets and those returning to work. The seven-week strike ended after the general secretary of the Trades Union Congress had intervened, but 4,000 glass workers subsequently resigned from their union and formed a new one.

A dispute with serious national consequences occurred when an official strike of local council employees was called on September 29. By November about 70,000 workers were on strike; street refuse was not collected, and sewage works were not operated properly. The six-week strike ended on November 5. Before it was over, however, attention had been directed to the coal industry, where the miners' union

had demanded an increase of £5 a week but the National Coal Board had offered only half that amount. More than 55% of the miners voted for strike action, but the union required a two-thirds majority before it could call a national strike. The Coal Board improved its offer to £3, and the union executive recommended acceptance. In those areas that had favoured strike action, however, the miners went on strike during the last week of October. By November 10, about 125,000 miners were out. In December four unions in the nationalized electric power industry began working to rule, leading to sporadic blackouts and to the declaration of a state of emergency by the government. Public resentment against the workers was intense, and on December 14 the unions agreed to end their slowdown while a fact-finding committee looked into their wage proposals.

The new Conservative government published its proposals for industrial relations legislation in October. The document proposed to deprive unions of some of the immunities protecting the right to strike; to make strikes for many purposes illegal; and to replace the existing voluntary system of collective bargaining by one involving detailed legal intervention into industrial relations, enforced by means of an extensive apparatus of control. One purpose of the proposals was to reduce the extent of unofficial strikes by giving the government power to impose a 60-day "cooling-off period" and to order secret strike ballots in some cases. The Confederation of British Industry generally welcomed the document, but the General Council of the Trades Union Congress condemned it in its entirety.

Over the years, Italy had lost more working days through industrial disputes than any other country except the U.S. (*See* Table.) Its position was consolidated by an intense strike situation in the autumn of 1969, which continued into 1970. There was a nationwide general strike on November 19 which paralyzed all industries, trades, communications, and public services. A street demonstration of about 100,-000 metal workers took place in Rome on November 28. At the end of January 1970 a 48-hour strike of civilian airport workers was called, while on February 5 the unions called a strike involving 1 million farm workers. These marked the start of a continuing pattern of sporadic strikes that reached a new pitch of intensity late in the year.

In Sweden, where a centralized wage-bargaining system was supported by law, a strike or lockout could not be declared as long as a collective labour agreement had not expired or been revoked. Unofficial strikes occurred regularly, particularly in the metal industry, but they had been of little statistical significance. With the Swedish economy undergoing a relatively rapid structural transformation, however, labour unrest was increasing. In December 1969, 4,700 miners began an unofficial strike that lasted two months. Dockers at Göteborg went on strike, as did workers in the Volvo and Saab automobile plants and a number of other concerns. In total about 15,000 workers had taken part in unofficial strikes by April.

Each year in Spain there were numerous illegal strikes conducted by illegal labour unions, and each year the law was applied against the strikers, but without either a palliative or a deterrent effect. Some 3,000 workers of the Esteban Orbegozo electrical household appliances plant returned to work in mid-January after a two-month strike. In the Asturian coal mines, 30,000 out of 35,000 miners were on strike

One of a task force of 750 French soldiers struggles to clean up the accumulation of trash in Paris during the strike by the city's sanitation workers in April 1970.

UPI COMPIX

in the second half of January. At the same time there were strikes in Madrid and Barcelona and among vineyard workers in Andalusia. A grievance about safety precautions in the state-run Hunosa mining company in June led to a strike of 17,000 miners. Police killed three workers during a demonstration in Granada, and this incident sparked a strike by 12,000 building workers and sympathetic strikes in Madrid, the Asturias, Palma, Gijon, and Barcelona. On July 29, 3,800 workers in Madrid's subway system staged a strike for increased wages and better working conditions, and the government retaliated by threatening to conscript the strikers into the armed forces. The workers returned to work the next day after the authorities had promised partial consideration of their demands. Work stoppages and street demonstrations, especially in the Basque province of Guipúzcoa, took place later in the year, in protest against the court-martial of 16 alleged Basque terrorists. Guipúzcoa was placed under a three-month state of emergency on December 4.

The labour situation in Japan resembled that of previous years. There was a confrontation with the U.S. military employers of Japanese civilian labour when the U.S. military authorities fired about 2,300 employees in October 1969. Zenchuro (the All Japan Garrison Forces Labour Union) planned a 24-hour strike on November 24, but called it off after the government had promised satisfactory safeguards for the workers. The U.S. military authorities in Okinawa also announced firings in December 1969, provoking joint strike action in January by Zenchuro and Zengunro (the All Okinawa Military Employees' Trade Union). Strikes were organized by local and public employees that infringed the terms of art. 18 of the Public Corporation Labor Relations Law, and penalties were meted out. It was estimated that the cost of the disciplinary measures to the locomotive engineers' union would exceed 4 billion yen.

Less Developed Countries. Unions continued to suffer severe repression in Greece. A commission under the chairmanship of Lord Devlin of Britain, appointed by the ILO to investigate complaints about the situation, reported in November that the Greek government had dissolved about 250 trade unions, ostensibly because they had engaged in Communist or political activity. It had deported potential opponents among individual trade unionists, and had renounced officials who would not actively help to further government policies. The commission concluded that the Greek unions' rights had been violated.

The ILO also commented adversely about the attitude of the Portuguese government toward trade-union rights. Strikes occurred in Portugal, but workers were not allowed to form their own unions and did not possess the legal right to strike. The ILO took up the case of seven union leaders of the Chad trade-union federation who had been arrested in December 1968 and detained without trial. In Ecuador the government arrested 88 union leaders in July who, it was claimed, were planning a general strike in Guayaquil. Also in July, the Pakistani government released Rehmatullah-Khan Durrani, a trade-union leader who was arrested in April after a speech calling on the authorities to end a mill lockout in Peshawar. The arrest had occurred despite a relaxation in Martial Law Regulation 18, which made strikes illegal. An Industrial Relations Ordinance, promulgated in November 1969, laid down the rights of association and collective bargaining and restored the right to strike when other means had failed.

In December 1969 the Nigerian federal government imposed a one-year ban on all strikes and lockouts in the country. By the same decree an industrial arbitration tribunal was established and all wage increases were subject to government control. In Kenya a voluntary tripartite agreement between representatives of the government, trade unions, and employers was signed in July. The agreement was for one year and pledged unions to refrain from taking industrial action or making wage demands in return for a commitment by employers to increase their work forces by 10%. A joint agreement incorporating a new code of conduct and an Industrial Relations Charter was signed in Sierra Leone by the Sierra Leone Labour Congress and the Sierra Leone Employers' Federation. Pres. Milton Obote of Uganda announced during May Day celebrations that the Trade Union Act would be amended to outlaw strikes.

Two Philippine trade-union federations announced in February that they would merge into a single central organization with a membership of 400,000. The

Cheered on by fellow union members, a mail truck driver stomps a placard denouncing Postmaster General Eric Kierans at a demonstration in Ottawa, April 7, 1970.

CHARLES MITCHELL
FROM CANADIAN PRESS

first act of the new organization was a demonstration against a proposed antilabour bill and in support of the doubling of the national minimum wage. In Pakistan six major trade-union organizations decided on July 26 to form the All-Pakistan Labour Council. Trade-union divisions in India remained as wide as ever. In August West Bengal was virtually paralyzed by strikes against unemployment, high prices, and continuation of central government rule in the state.

(V. L. A.)

See also Education; Employment, Wages, and Hours; Police; Race Relations.

ENCYCLOPÆDIA BRITANNICA FILMS. *Working Together* (1952); *Walter P. Reuther* ("Dialogue for This Decade") (1962); *The Rise of Labor* (1968); *The Industrial Worker* (1969); *The Rise of Big Business* (1970).

Laos

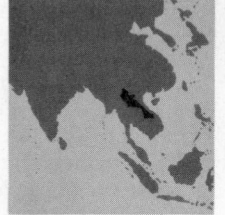

A constitutional monarchy of southeast Asia, Laos is bounded by China, North and South Vietnam, Cambodia, Thailand, and Burma. Area: 91,400 sq.mi. (236,800 sq. km.). Pop. (1969 est.): 2,893,000. Administrative cap. and largest city: Vientiane (pop., 1968 est., 140,000). Royal cap.: Luang Prabang (pop., 1968 est., 25,000). Language: Lao (official); French and English. Religion: Buddhist; tribal. King, Savang Vatthana; premier in 1970, Prince Souvanna Phouma.

The search for a political solution to bring peace to Laos, through mutual concessions, prevailed in 1970 over the military escalation that had been the main concern during the previous year. The governments of the United States and North Vietnam, the parties most responsible for this escalation, accepted that their Laotian allies—Prince Souvanna Phouma (*see* BIOGRAPHY), the prime minister, and his half brother Prince Souphanouvong, president of the pro-Communist Neo Lao Hak Sat (Laotian Patriotic Front)—should enter publicly into discussions that could lead to a cease-fire.

The year began with a move by Prince Souvanna Phouma. While the Laotian Special Forces (a clandes-

LAOS

Education. (1967–68) Primary, pupils 196,751, teachers 5,119; secondary, pupils 6,290, teachers 250; vocational, pupils 1,636, teachers 181; teacher training, students 2,198, teachers 149; higher, students 348, teaching staff (1966–67) 15.

Finance. Monetary unit: kip, with an official exchange rate of 240 kips to U.S. $1 (576 kips = £1 sterling) and a free rate (Oct. 1970) of 500 kips to U.S. $1 (1,200 kips = £1 sterling). Budget (1969–70 est.): revenue (excluding foreign aid) 8,543,000,000 kips; expenditure 17,344,000,000 kips (including military expenditure 8,469,000,000 kips).

Foreign Trade. (1968) Imports 12,878,558,000 kips (26% from Thailand, 21% from U.S., 8% from France, 7% from U.K.); exports 1,448,096,000 kips (56% to Malaysia, 28% to Thailand, 8% to Hong Kong, 7% to Singapore). Main exports: tin 56%; timber 27%.

Transport. Roads (1968) *c.* 5,600 km. (including *c.* 3,000 km. with improved surface). Motor vehicles in use (1968): passenger 10,600; commercial (including buses) 3,400. Air traffic (1968): 24,191,000 passenger-km.; freight 796,000 net ton-km. Inland waterways (main Mekong River routes only; 1968) 1,614 km. Telephones (Dec. 1968) 2,454.

Agriculture. Production (in 000; metric tons; 1968; 1967 in parentheses): rice 932 (784); coffee *c.* 3.5 (*c.* 3.5); corn *c.* 23 (*c.* 22); tobacco 3.8 (4). Livestock (in 000; 1967–68): cattle 390; buffaloes *c.* 900; pigs *c.* 1,000; chickens *c.* 12,000.

PHOTOREPORTERS

Wounded Laotian soldiers are evacuated from camp outside the village of Na Song, south of the Plaine des Jarres, where they were ambushed by Pathet Lao guerrillas in March 1970.

tine army sponsored by the U.S. Central Intelligence Agency) were preparing to evacuate the Plaine des Jarres, which they had taken from their adversaries in the previous year, the premier suggested on January 31 that the plain should be neutralized.

This plan was rejected by the Neo Lao Hak Sat on February 6, but as soon as its forces and those of North Vietnam had reoccupied the Plaine des Jarres, it published (on March 6) a "plan for a political solution to the Laotian problem," proposing in five points the ending of U.S. bombing, the withdrawal of the "pro-American" forces from certain regions, and the formation of a provisional coalition government. A still more significant fact was that Prince Souphanouvong sent a colonel from his "liberation army" to Vientiane to hand over the plan directly to Prince Souvanna Phouma, together with a personal letter from him, on March 22.

The overthrow of Prince Sihanouk in Cambodia on March 18 and the intervention in that country of North Vietnamese forces, the Viet Cong, and then U.S. and South Vietnamese troops impeded the rapprochement that was being worked out in Laos. Prince Souphanouvong's messenger went back to the "liberated zone" empty-handed.

The pro-Communist forces suddenly relaxed their position on July 31, when they sent a new messenger, this time described as a "plenipotentiary," to the Laotian capital. This special envoy was Prince Souk Vongsak, a member of the Neo Lao Hak Sat Central Committee and a cousin of princes Souvanna Phouma and Souphanouvong, belonging, like them, to the Laotian royal family.

He immediately entered into negotiations with the Laotian premier, and on August 11 an agreement was made for talks to begin officially between representatives of Prince Souvanna Phouma and Prince Souphanouvong at Khang Khay, an area situated on the edge of the Plaine des Jarres and controlled by the Neo Lao Hak Sat. The latter thus gave up its precondition of an end to U.S. bombing—although its representative raised the matter again during the talks. Prince Souvanna Phouma offered the Neo Lao Hak Sat the neutralization of the Khang Khay region and of a corridor leading from that area to the nearest government military base, but the offer was rejected.

The initial contact that had been made between Souvanna Phouma and Souk Vongsak became bogged

WIDE WORLD

Laotian Premier Prince Souvanna Phouma called for continued U.S. support in the fight against North Vietnamese troops infiltrating into his country.

Lacrosse: *see* Sporting Record

down in procedural difficulties and was then interrupted for a long period because of a tour of Western capitals by Prince Souvanna Phouma in September and October.

Nonetheless, except on the Ho Chi Minh Trail, used by North Vietnamese troops as a route to South Vietnam, the level of military operations remained lower than in previous years, despite a minor offensive by the Special Forces. At the beginning of October they recaptured the former neutralist base of Muong Soui, situated about 10 mi. NE of the Plaine des Jarres. (M. Cт.)

Law

Court Decisions and Related Developments. Several common problems, some as diverse as the hijacking of aircraft, pornography, the protection of intellectual and industrial property, military law, criminal law, and religion occupied the attention of the courts and legislatures of many countries in 1970. Some of these issues were resolved differently in different countries, but legal scholars were pleased to note that most of the decisions were similar in result or at least in terms of underlying social policy.

Hijacking of Aircraft. In response to a number of acts of air piracy, countries and organizations took firm countermeasures. The French National Assembly enacted a law under which a person could be imprisoned from five to ten years for hijacking an airplane and for life if anyone was killed as a result of such piracy. The Swedish government announced that it would introduce a similar bill. Apparently not content with the efforts of individual states, the International Civil Aviation Organization announced that it had formed a legal committee to prepare a draft treaty covering unlawful interference with civil aviation for presentation in mid-1971 to all commercial nations. The Committee of Ministers of the Council of Europe adopted a formal resolution supporting this action. (See *International Law*, below.)

Narcotics. International concern with the misuse of drugs was exemplified by judicial and legislative ac-

tion in several nations and by the fact that this topic was an important item on the agenda of the sixth conference of European ministers of justice, which met at The Hague in May 1970. Two guidelines were suggested as the starting points in work that hopefully would culminate in the development of common policy: (1) a realization that the solution of drug misuse problems cannot be found through the criminal law alone but requires coordinated action of government, the medical profession, social welfare agencies, and others; and (2) a recognition that distinctions should be made between less harmful forms of drug misuse and those that create significant social problems.

Consistently with many aspects of this resolution, the French National Assembly passed sweeping legislation dealing with the matter of drug addiction. Most drug addicts in France were to be treated as medical rather than criminal cases, but stiff criminal penalties would be imposed on those trafficking in narcotics. The courts were empowered to bar forever from France any foreigner over the age of 21 who was guilty of trafficking in or using drugs. One found to be addicted would be placed in a medical institution for cure and was subject to penal measures only if he repeated his offense after being released from the institution.

In the U.K., the carefully prepared Misuse of Drugs Bill was withdrawn from Parliament because of the general election, but the new (Heath) government announced that it had decided to reintroduce the bill, possibly in early 1971. Sweden extended until June 1971 a special law that permits telephones to be tapped in investigations of crimes involving narcotics.

In *Minor* v. *United States* (90 S.Ct. 284), the U.S. Supreme Court sustained the constitutionality of a law that required anyone selling marihuana to register with the Internal Revenue Service and pay a special occupational tax. The accused was convicted of selling marihuana without complying with these requirements. He contended that if one sought registration for an illicit sale, the registration would be denied in most, if not all, cases and thus the federal government, in effect, had proscribed the sale of marihuana in violation of the Tenth Amendment to the Constitution, which gives this power only to the state governments. He also contended that, if a registration were issued for an illicit sale, the registrant, in effect, would be confessing to a crime, and this forced confession would violate the privilege against self-incrimination found in the Fifth Amendment. The court rejected the first contention, holding that the federal government had power to prohibit the sale of marihuana. It agreed that the Internal Revenue Service would not grant a registration for an illicit sale, and, therefore, there would be no situation in which one attempting to register could incriminate himself.

Military Law. The U.S. Supreme Court handed down two significant decisions respecting the Selective Service law, but avoided on procedural grounds passing on the question of whether a person can be a "conscientious objector," and thus be excused from the duty to perform military service, on the ground that he opposes some, but not all, wars as a matter of conscience. In *Gutknecht* v. *United States* (90 S.Ct. 506), the court held that it was improper for a Selective Service board to accelerate an inductee's time for reporting for active military duty because he had left his draft card and notice of classification on the steps of a federal building in protest of the war in Vietnam.

"Are you kidding—that's my TRIAL date. . !"
—Yardley Jones, "Toronto Telegram."

BEN ROTH AGENCY

In *Welsch* v. *United States* (90 S.Ct. 1792), the court held that one could qualify as a conscientious objector on the basis of moral, as distinguished from religious, beliefs. Three dissenting opinions argued that Congress had provided a draft exemption for conscientious objectors to war only on the basis of religious beliefs and training and that the court should not extend the exemption to cover those that disclaim any religious objection to war.

In *United States* v. *Sisson* (90 S.Ct. 2117), the accused refused to submit to induction into the armed forces on the ground that he had moral objections to the war in Vietnam. He admitted that his objections were not religious in nature and that he was not opposed to all wars. A federal district court jury found him guilty, but the judge "arrested the judgment," stating that under the circumstances the accused could not be found guilty. The prosecution appealed, but the Supreme Court denied the appeal for lack of jurisdiction.

The new law on soldiers (*Soldatengesetz*) promulgated by the West German government required a member of the armed services to recognize the official authority of his superior officers without considering his own sympathies and antipathies, but provided that it was not a breach of duty or a violation of military law for a soldier to criticize the opinion of his superior officers in public, as, for example, in a letter to the editor of a newspaper, so long as the criticism was relevant, realistic, and sensible. The Polish government announced that it would publish new regulations for its armed forces that would reconcile its military law with its new penal code.

Censorship. The Swedish report in 1969 recommending decriminalization of pornography was followed by legislation implementing the proposal. A government bill to the same effect was introduced into the West German Bundestag in the autumn. Similar proposals were in an advanced stage of preparation in the Netherlands and Austria. In the U.S., the Commission on Obscenity and Pornography (appointed by Pres. Lyndon Johnson in 1968 and chaired by William B. Lockhart) presented its report to the same effect, but it was promptly rejected by Congress and the president. Common to all these proposals were two assumptions: that there is no evidence that consumption of pornography is harmful, either socially or individually; and that protection should continue to be given to children and to the nonconsenting adult.

A link with privacy was beginning to be seen, both in the prohibition against indecent displays and mailing embodied in the above-mentioned laws and the new U.S. statute on indecent advertisements by mail, and in the right of a person to consume pornography in private or to have it sent to him by mail if he wants it, which was the subject of court cases in the U.S. and West Germany.

Part of the effort to suppress pornography in the U.S. was a federal law under which a householder may require that the mailer remove his name from its mailing list if, at his sole discretion, he believes the mailings to be erotically arousing or sexually provocative. In 1970 the U.S. Supreme Court sustained this law against constitutional attack in the case of *Rowan* v. *United States Post Office Department* (90 S.Ct. 1484). In West Germany, the federal Supreme Court was called upon to interpret sec. 184 of the Criminal Code under which anyone who exhibits objects designed for the commission of lewd acts, or advertises such objects to the public, is guilty of a crime. The court held that the sale of contraceptives in an automatic vending machine located in a public place did not violate this law.

Film censorship for adults was being abolished in a number of Swiss cantons (Zürich, Aargau, Luzern), and a Dutch bill to that end was introduced in Parliament. Australia was making its film censorship system more flexible by introducing categories and providing for recourse to the courts in certain cases. The Swiss Supreme Court held that the Swedish film *I Am Curious (Yellow)* was not obscene; the U.S. Supreme Court was to give judgment on the same film during the term beginning October 1970.

Protection of Intellectual and Industrial Property. The eighth Congress of Comparative Law, meeting in Pescara, Italy, devoted a number of its sessions to matters of copyright, trademarks, patents, and "know-how," and the International Faculty of Comparative Law held special seminars in Turin, Italy, to consider recent developments in these fields. Additionally, a conference held in Stockholm culminated in the creation of an organization called the World Intellectual Property Organization. The WIPO would involve itself with matters of copyright.

On a more local level, Belgium, the Netherlands, and Luxembourg ratified a treaty that unified their trademark laws. Under this treaty, all existing Belgian, Dutch, and Luxembourg trademarks would be invalid as of Jan. 1, 1971, and would be replaced, if they qualified, with a new Benelux "product mark." The new law provides that rights from trademarks will be based exclusively on registration, and not on use.

Criminal Law. In a case that would have far-reaching effects, the U.S. Supreme Court held, in *State of Illinois* v. *Allen* (90 S.Ct. 1057), that a defendant can lose his right to be present at a trial if, after he has been warned of the consequences by the judge, he insists on conducting himself in a manner so disorderly, disruptive, and disrespectful of the court that his trial cannot be carried on with him in the courtroom. Allen, accused of armed robbery, engaged in such disruptive conduct at his trial that the judge finally removed him from the courtroom and allowed the trial to proceed in his absence. After the prosecution's case had been presented, Allen gave assurances

continued on page 444

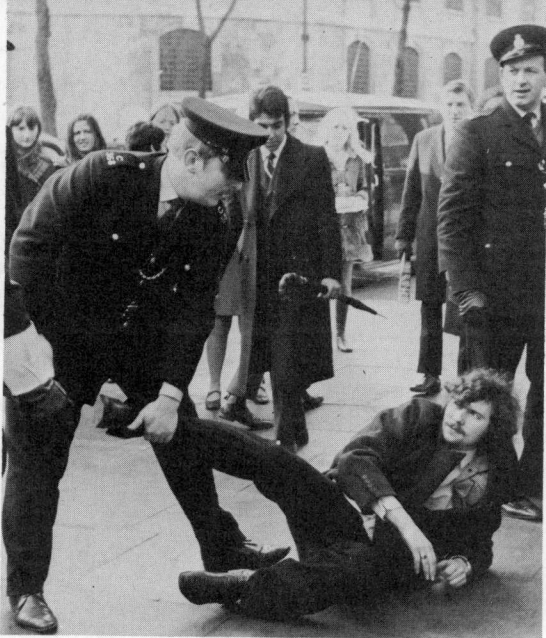

LONDON "DAILY EXPRESS" FROM PICTORIAL PARADE
A policeman arrests one of the demonstrators who stormed into London's High Court in February 1970. Fourteen of the demonstrators were given immediate three-month jail sentences for contempt after an unprecedented courtroom disruption.

THE CHICAGO CONSPIRACY TRIAL

By J. Anthony Lukas

AVEDON

The Chicago 7 are (back row from left) Lee Weiner, David Dellinger, Jerry Rubin, Tom Hayden, and (in front) John Froines, Rennie Davis, and Abbie Hoffman.

T ell me something," Judge Julius J. Hoffman said when I called him that September for press credentials. "Do you think this is going to be the trial of the century?"

Well, I said, "the century" covered a lot of territory. How about the decade? I was thinking of something Rennie Davis, one of the defendants, had told me the day before: "In choosing the eight of us, the government has lumped together all the strands of dissent in the '60s. We respond by saying the movement of the past decade is on trial here."

Dramatis Personae. In that sense, perhaps, the Chicago Conspiracy Trial was the trial of the decade, the government's way of calling to account that tumultuous ten years of protest and disorder—the '60s. Certainly the eight defendants who stood before Judge Hoffman's bench that morning in September 1969 covered a broad spectrum of that decade's dissent:

Tom Hayden: If they were ranked by sheer intelligence, perhaps Hayden would have to come first. He was hardly impressive looking with his acne-scarred face and bulbous nose (which journalist Nicholas von Hoffman said made him look like "a bankrupt, alcoholic pilgrim or English village lout"); but what a policewoman called his "beady eyes" sized up the world with penetrating keenness. Widely regarded as the Movement's chief ideologue, he drafted the founding statement of Students for a Democratic Society ("we regard men as infinitely precious, possessed of unfulfilled capacities for reason, freedom, love"). Since then, this optimistic glow had been seared out of him by beatings in the South where he worked for the Student Non-Violent Coordinating Committee, by the misery he saw in Newark's black ghetto when he ran an SDS project there, by the first-hand evidence of American militarism he picked up on two trips to North Vietnam.

Rennie Davis: An early SDS activist and organizer for the Mobilization Committee to End the War in Vietnam, he had gradually emerged as the Movement's leading organization man. So he was a natural choice to be co-director—with Hayden—of the demonstrations during the 1968 Democratic national convention in Chicago. His wholesome air made him seem like a refugee from a Kansas 4-H club; but beneath those fresh-faced good looks, Rennie was a shrewd, tough-minded radical. After he had been sentenced to prison, he turned to the prosecutor and said, "When I come out of prison it will be to move next door to Tom Foran . . . to organize his kids into the revolution. We are going to turn the sons and daughters of the ruling class in this country into Viet Cong."

David Dellinger: 54, chubby, nearly always dressed in the same green tweed sports jacket and rumpled flannels, Dellinger

looked like an off-duty scoutmaster. Amid that riotous profusion of hair, his few jagged, straw-coloured swatches were folded across his balding dome like a carelessly repaired thatch roof. Politically, too, he was an anachronism: an evangelical Christian socialist among New Leftists who flaunted their agnosticism and celebrated their liberation from outworn dogmas. Yet there was nothing prim about Dave's brand of radicalism. His bedrock convictions made him the most stubbornly intransigent—and least subtle or pragmatic—of all the defendants.

Abbie Hoffman: Who was Abbie? His very identity became an issue in the trial. Was he, as the indictment alleged, Abbott H. Hoffman, a leader of the Youth International Party? Or was he, as he insisted on the witness stand, just Abbie, an orphan of America and a child of the Woodstock Nation? Part of this was a mere word game with the other Hoffman: Abbie called the judge his "illegitimate father" and said he was renouncing the name. But part of it was all too serious, reflecting Abbie's conviction that identity—and reality—are defined by myth artfully propagated through the media. For me, Abbie was the most consistently intriguing figure in the courtroom. There was a touch of genius in his solemn conclusion that one of Judge Hoffman's rulings was the worst he had heard "in all my years on the witness stand" and in his simple admonition to his wife as he was led off to jail: "Water the plant."

Jerry Rubin: Jerry tried hard to be the fighting man's Abbie. He carefully nurtured his Yippie image, buying a bushy wig to cover his prison-sheared head, wearing bright corduroy pants and polo shirts speckled with buttons. But he never quite brought it off. His zany, zonked-out style couldn't cover the hard, knotted roots of Jerry's radicalism, which probably reached back to his childhood days in Cincinnati where, the son of a bakery driver turned teamsters' union official, he grew up feeling snubbed and patronized by his four uncles, the affluent, suburban Katz brothers. "My whole life," he once said, "has been a battle of the Rubins against the Katzes." The battle carried him to Israel where he studied sociology, to Berkeley where he joined the Free Speech Movement, then on to become project director of the march on the Pentagon and a founder of the Yippies.

John Froines: On the day he handed out contempt citations, Judge Hoffman started to deal with the defense attorneys, then looked up and caught himself: "Oh, I beg your pardon, I almost forgot to take care of Mr. Froines." John Froines smiled ruefully as he remarked, "It's part of being a media unknown that even the judge finally forgets you're here." Through most of the trial, John bore his obscurity with good grace. A chemist of some distinction, he was then an assistant professor of chemistry at the University of Oregon. But he was also a co-founder of the Radical Science Information Service, which helped "scientists of a radical bent make explicit connections about science and society." John had made his connections. When the judge finally sentenced him, he stood and read a section from the Oregon constitution, pausing to emphasize the part that said the people "have at all times a right to alter, reform or abolish the government in a manner as they may think proper."

Lee Weiner: Lee was the Conspiracy's odd-man-out, a strangely remote figure who shunned most of the defendants' extracurricular activities. At the defense table, he generally kept his head deep in a book—Lao-tzu's works, the *I Ching,* Matza's *Becoming Deviant,* and a host of science fiction paperbacks. Lee was a doctoral candidate and teaching assistant in sociology at Northwestern. With his bushy black beard and steel-rimmed glasses, he looked as if he had just emerged from the cubicle next to Karl Marx at the British Museum, but he had a nice Jewish sense of the incongruity of his position. He once wrote: "[I have] a tattoo on my forehead that says 'Government Certified Radical.' If I stay in touch with myself and continue to act free, the government has promised to additionally tattoo in 'Bomb Maker and Evil Man.' It makes me happy."

Bobby Seale: When Bobby was led into the courtroom that first morning, several of the defendants barely knew him. For if a conspiracy existed during convention week, he was at most its imported West Coast talent, brought in as a last-minute speaking replacement for Eldridge Cleaver. Those first days in the courtroom I thought I caught a quizzical look in his eyes, as though he were asking himself, "What the hell am I doing here?" He was different: the black son of a Texas carpenter; sheet-metal mechanic; funky jazz drummer; veteran of ghetto skirmishes with the police; co-founder of the Black Panther Party and now (with Cleaver and Huey P. Newton in jail or in flight) the party's national chairman. But I didn't realize just how different he was until he came back later in the trial to testify as a defense witness and the government confronted him with taped recordings of the two speeches he made in Chicago. They contained passages like this: "If the police get in the way of our march, tangle with the blue-helmeted m————s and kill them and send them to the morgue slab."

Prologue. The defendants were tried under the antiriot provisions of the 1968 Civil Rights Act. These provisions originated with Southern congressmen determined to prosecute the "outside agitators" they held responsible for racial unrest. As Rep. William Colmer of Mississippi put it: "Here we are with one Stokeley Carmichael and one Rap Brown, who among others we find traveling from state to state and from city to city, and in their wake comes conflagration, blood-spilling, wholesale pilfering and the loss of life and property."

Federal law did not prohibit rioting or even incitement to riot, for those were state offenses and most states already had ample legislation against them. The new law gave the federal government a legal hook to snag the agitators as they went by: their "intent" to incite a riot as they moved from state to state.

The Justice Department did not want that hook. The then attorney general, Ramsey Clark, felt riots were properly the responsibility of the states and localities. Moreover, he feared that prosecutions for intent might infringe constitutionally protected rights to freedom of speech, assembly, and movement. "Government," he said, "has an absolute duty to do what it can to enlarge the opportunities of its people to speak and a bill like this one does just the opposite. It makes it exceedingly dangerous." Even after Congress passed the provisions, Clark was reluctant to use them. After the violence during the convention, he called U.S. Attorney Thomas Foran and ordered him to proceed cautiously through a "lawyer's investigation" rather than with a grand jury. When word of this got to Chicago's Mayor Richard

J. Daley, he was outraged. Stung by widespread criticism of his hard-line tactics during the convention, he wanted vindication and revenge on the radicals who had dared to challenge him.

So the Daley machine ground smoothly into operation. Chief Federal District Judge William Campbell, long a close friend of the mayor, summoned a grand jury and instructed it to look specifically for violations of the antiriot law. Foran, who owed his appointment directly to the mayor, came up with supporting evidence, and on March 20, 1969, the jury returned indictments against the eight demonstrators both for conspiring and for acting individually to cross state lines with an intent to incite a riot during the Democratic convention (balanced by indictments against eight policemen).

By this time, the Nixon administration was in Washington. The reluctant Clark had been replaced by John Mitchell, who was publicly proclaiming his eagerness to go after the radicals with every instrument at his disposal. Seeing that his interests neatly coincided with Daley's in this case, he gave the final go-ahead for prosecution.

Everything else that followed in those tumultuous five months, I would contend, stemmed from that decision by the Justice Department to carry a political battle into court. Once a political prosecution was launched, it was probably inevitable that it should be met by an aggressive political defense and presided over by an openly political judge.

The defense strategy had been profoundly influenced by the outcome of another political trial: that of Benjamin Spock. The baby doctor and his four co-defendants, accused of conspiring to counsel draft evasion, conducted a cautious, by-the-book defense, sticking to legal questions, eschewing the broad political issues, and making no effort to stir up support outside the courtroom. They were convicted anyway (although the convictions were overturned on appeal).

From the start, the Chicago defendants rejected a narrow Spock defense. If their stance had a precedent, it was far more the Huey P. Newton and Oakland 7 trials, in which the defense staged the fight on openly political grounds.

But here the defendants did more than merely accept the government's challenge to a political trial. They welcomed it. There was not much going on in the radical movement anyway. The SDS was hopelessly splintered and ineffective. Winter was coming on and there would be no campus uprisings for a while. So the defendants determined to make the trial the central radical event of the year. They saw it as an opportunity to radicalize people around the issues of the courts and the law.

The Stage Setting. The scene in that courtroom was a classic tableau. To the left of the aisle, the government's table reproached us all with its cool, efficient order. The gleaming surface was never marred by more than a few neatly stacked memos and a spare pencil or two, but a formidable array of carefully indexed cardboard files stood on a gray steel trolley at one end. The prosecution team always sat in a precise, symmetrical pattern: Tom Foran and his assistant, Dick Schultz, on one side, facing Roger Cubbage, a Justice Department attorney, and Joseph Stanley, an FBI man—all four in neatly creased gray, brown, or olive-drab business suits (never a pattern bolder than a pinstripe), their narrow ties anchored with small gold tacks.

Across the aisle, the defense table was a "liberated zone" right there in the courtroom. The radicals wore blue jeans and sweat shirts that sometimes rode above the waist to expose a hairy belly or a scrawny back. The Yippies wore a dazzling and constantly changing array of brightly striped polo shirts, corduroy or leather pants, sashes, headbands, beads, and buttons. As the proceedings droned on, they read newspapers, books, memos, and mail; wrote speeches and press releases; munched jelly beans; whispered; made faces; snickered; or dozed. The table was littered with papers, candy wrappers, sweaters, boots, and leather jackets—even, one day, a package of marijuana.

But unorthodox grooming and disregard for courtroom protocol are not disruption. And, contrary to the general impression,

441

UPI COMPIX

UPI COMPIX

Left, defense attorney William Kunstler addresses a protest rally in New York. Below, Federal District Judge Julius J. Hoffman, who presided at the trial.

I don't believe there ever was a concerted, premeditated plan to disrupt the court. In fact, there was no single "defense strategy" and, given the differences in style and temperament among the defendants, there could hardly have been one. Those who attended some of the interminable defense meetings say the arguments about strategy and courtroom demeanour often grew fierce.

Some defendants wanted to concentrate on winning the case in the courtroom, which meant a relatively straight legal defense and some respect for courtroom protocol. Others were more concerned with persuading "the jury of the American people," which meant emphasizing the political aspects of the case and keeping the press interested with lots of unorthodox behaviour. By and large, Tom Hayden took the most cautious line and Jerry Rubin the most flamboyant—with the others strung out between them.

But even had they agreed on a consistent, long-term strategy, they probably couldn't have carried it out. For the irreconcilable elements gathered in that courtroom were so volatile that they had a self-generating logic of their own. Much of the time the defendants could only respond to events—or exploit them—as imaginatively as possible.

The most unpredictable element was Judge Hoffman himself. Through it all, the judge looked down from the bench with an air of professorial distaste. At times he reminded me of a spinster schoolteacher in a classroom of unruly children, forever rapping his ruler for order and sending children to stand in the corner, but stirring up more trouble with each new act of discipline.

There were those around the courthouse who attributed the judge's snappishness to his height—barely 5 ft. $4\frac{1}{2}$ in. Indeed, there was a small man's machismo, a feisty defiance about the man. One of his favourite phrases—hurled repeatedly at the defense attorneys—was, "You'll learn I don't frighten very easily." Others said he was a bit of a snob. A confessed anglophile, he had a leather-tooled Chippendale desk in his chambers and the walls were covered with engravings of English jurists—Lord Hardwicke, Lord Thurlow, and Lord Ellenborough. When asked where he travels, the judge said, "Unlike Mr. Justice Douglas, we don't clamber around the Himalayas. I prefer London and

the British Isles." Still others thought he was a pure ham, an egoist who thrived on the reactions he could draw from the other actors below him in the court and the spectators beyond.

The first week of the trial, William Kunstler, one of the defense attorneys, accused him of reading the indictment to the jury "like Orson Welles reading the Declaration of Independence." Feigning indignation, but obviously delighted, the judge said this was the first time in 22 years on the state and federal bench that anybody had complained about his voice. "I do my best to use the vocal facilities the Lord has endowed me with," he said. And those facilities were remarkable. Orson Welles was only one of his many voices. Outraged, he was Lee J. Cobb; garrulous, Lionel Barrymore; insinuating, Vincent Price; cocky, Jimmy Cagney; grandfatherly, pure Edmund Gwenn.

At first, there was something almost endearing about all this. The defendants nicknamed the judge "Mr. Magoo" and thought of designating him "an honorary Yippie," for he was a perfect foil for the courtroom theatre some of them were trying to stage. Yet, as the trial wore on, I felt he was more than an eccentric old curmudgeon. I began to see a pattern in his vocal theatrics and lapses of memory.

Invariably his inflections helped to underline a government point or ridicule the defense—and best of all, they would never show up in the stenographic appellate record. When he asked the court reporter to repeat a word, it was usually something like "erotic" or "vomit," whose emphasis could hardly help the defendants. He mispronounced the name of Leonard Weinglass, a defense attorney, so often—as Weinstein, Weinberg, Feinstein, Fineglass, Weinrob, Weinramer, or Weinruss—that it couldn't have been accidental. And his references to Kunstler as a "New York lawyer" were hardly designed to ingratiate him with a Midwestern jury.

Perplexed by the judge's apparent partisanship, I sought out several Chicago lawyers who had practiced before him. They were not at all surprised. Hoffman, they said, had long shown such a "blind spot for the government" that federal prosecutors often maneuvered to get their weak or sensitive cases before him. "Julius has always regarded himself as the embodiment of everything federal," one lawyer said. "He sees the defense in any criminal case as the enemy, and he thinks it's his duty to help put them away."

The defendants' "disruptions" have been much discussed, but it should be remembered that before they committed any of their 175 "contemptuous" acts, the judge took a step that many lawyers considered extraordinary. On the very first day of the trial, he ordered the arrest of four defense attorneys who failed to show up in court (the defendants had retained them to prepare pretrial motions and had not expected them to appear in court). Lawyers from all over the country came to Chicago to protest; 126 of them filed an amici curiae brief terming his actions "a travesty of justice [which] threatens to destroy the confidence of the American people in the entire judicial process."

Moreover, it ought to be stated clearly that the defendants' contempt when it began was almost exclusively verbal (no other aspect of the trial aroused such widespread confusion—afterward, a friend asked me which of the defendants had defecated in the aisle; I assured him none of them had). The judge spoke several times of the defendants' "violence" in the courtroom. The only violence I witnessed occurred on several occasions when the federal marshals used more than necessary force to seat or lead away defendants (the defendants responded in kind, but they did not attack anyone). The only other physical "actions" I recall were theatrical or symbolic: the attempt to bring a birthday cake into the courtroom on Bobby Seale's birthday; the placing of the National Liberation Front and American flags on the defense table. The rest of the time the contempt was words—irreverent, disrespectful, harsh, and even vulgar—but words.

Finally, as Harry Kalven of the University of Chicago has pointed out, even this verbal contempt (as reflected in the contempt citations) was by no means consistent throughout the trial. It tended to bunch in periods of particular tension or confrontation. Other periods were largely calm, even tedious. Roughly one could divide the trial into five phases.

Tragicomedy in Five Acts. Phase One—or "Jellybeans" as the defendants called it—lasted from the trial's start on September 24 through October 13. During that period, the defendants took a gently mocking stance toward the trial, symbolized by their distribution of jellybeans to the press and spectators. It was so uneventful that the judge found only six contempts during the three weeks—one of them Abbie blowing a kiss to the jury.

Phase Two—which I suppose could be called "Gags and Shackles"—lasted from October 14 through November 5. Some of the increased tension during this period may have stemmed from the defendants' feeling that their mockery had misfired and too many potential sympathizers regarded the trial as a joke. But most of the contempts stemmed directly from Bobby Seale's continuing demand that he either be permitted counsel of his choice or the right to defend himself. The counsel of his choice was Charles R. Garry, a white Californian who had defended many Black Panthers and won their respect. But in August, Garry came down with a gallbladder condition which his doctors said required an immediate operation, and the defense asked a two-month postponement of the trial to permit him to recover. Judge Hoffman refused.

When Seale was brought from California and held in Cook County Jail, Kunstler signed an "appearance" (normally signifying an intention to represent a client) so he could get in to see him. On September 26, when Seale rose to insist he was being denied his constitutional right to counsel, the judge seized on the appearance as evidence that he was adequately represented by Kunstler. Whatever technical points the judge had, the right to be represented by a lawyer you trust or, alternatively, to speak in your own behalf seemed to me so fundamental that I came to admire Seale's dogged persistence. But he and the judge were locked into an increasingly bitter conflict that resulted in Seale being bound and gagged on October 29 and then, on November 5, severed from the case, convicted on 16 counts of contempt, and sentenced to four years in prison.

Phase Three—call it "The Government's Day in Court"—lasted from November 6 until December 10. As Kalven notes, there were only nine contempt citations during this period. This reflected, in part, natural decompression after the pressure cooker tensions of the Seale period; probably an element of caution once the judge had showed how tough he could be; and perhaps a growing recognition of just how weak the government's case was and a feeling that if they "cooled it," the defendants just might squeak through with a hung jury.

Phase Four—"Sing Along with Phil and Judy"—was the early portion of the defense case, from December 11 to January 22. After a lengthy wrangle about whether to present a defense at all (some defendants felt they already had a hung jury), they decided to put on an elaborate political-cultural defense aimed largely at the "big jury out there." The defendants sought to explain and demonstrate their "identity"—through witnesses like Timothy Leary, the high priest of the drug culture, and Jacques Levy, director of *Oh! Calcutta!*, as well as through the songs of Phil Ochs, Judy Collins, Arlo Guthrie, "Country Joe" McDonald, and Pete Seeger. There were relatively few contempts during this period, and many of them grew out of arguments about the admissibility of such evidence.

Phase Five—"The Barnyard Epithet"—lasted from January 23 to February 7 when testimony was completed. This was a time of gradually building tension, culminating in the Epithet (Dave Dellinger's use of the word "b——t" in describing a government witness' testimony) and the revocation of Dellinger's bail. The judge was massively overreacting now, often impulsively and even irrationally. Convinced they had him on the verge of some apocalyptic step, Abbie and Jerry shrugged off all restraints and cut loose with a barrage of grotesque Yippie raillery ("You're a disgrace to the Jews, runt," "Tell him to stick it up his bowling ball," "Mies van der Rohe was a Kraut too"). This period produced a cluster of 48 contempts.

Curtain and Epilogue. When the verdict was in—all seven defendants acquitted of conspiracy, but five of them (Hayden, Davis, Dellinger, Hoffman, and Rubin) convicted on the individual counts—most liberal editorial pages and columnists praised the jury for performing its task well. Time and again the jurors were singled out for their discrimination and dedication in sorting through the maze of charges and defendants to reach a just decision.

And then the jurors began talking about how they had reached their decisions. Those who talked agree that the jury had divided into two camps long before they sat down to deliberate. One group of eight believed all the defendants were guilty on both counts. The other four favoured acquittal for all on both charges.

The deadlock, which lasted almost four days, was broken by Kay Richards, a young computer operator, who later described her own role as follows: "I acted as mediator . . . I went back and forth between the two camps, insisting on a verdict. In the end they agreed to compromise, and it was hard for them to do it. Their beliefs hadn't changed as far as guilt or innocence went, and after the verdict there were some of them who wept in anger and frustration. One was almost ill. I cried too, but only in relief. I hardly realized it, but I think I am probably the only one of the twelve jurors who is really happy or satisfied with our decision."

Ruth Petersen, another juror, said, "If it wasn't for that little Katie Richards, I don't know what we would have done. She was wonderful."

Little Katie Richards sold her story of the trial to the *Chicago Sun-Times* for several thousand dollars. And she deserved it. Mayor Daley could not have pulled off a niftier compromise. Just as the mayor splits the difference between two warring ward bosses, Katie split the difference between the government and the defense. Thanks to her, the verdict was perfectly appropriate: a political end to a political trial.

© Copyright 1970 by J. Anthony Lukas

continued from page 439

of proper conduct and was permitted to return to the courtroom. Allen was convicted, but the United States Court of Appeals for the 7th Circuit reversed the conviction and based its decision on the language of the "confrontation clause" of the Sixth Amendment to the Constitution, which provides that "In all criminal prosecutions, the accused shall enjoy the right . . . to be confronted with the witnesses against him. . . ."

The U.S. Supreme Court, affirming the conviction and overruling the decision of the Court of Appeals, held that Allen by his conduct had relinquished his constitutional right to be present. Justice Hugo Black, writing for the court, established a hard line to protect courts against disruptive tactics and provided "at least three constitutionally permissible ways for a trial judge to handle an obstreperous defendant like Allen: (1) Bind and gag him, thereby keeping him present. (2) Cite him for contempt. (3) Take him out of the courtroom until he promises to conduct himself properly." Justice William O. Douglas, in a separate opinion, pointed out that the case was of the classical criminal type without any political or subversive overtones, and suggested that perhaps different remedies might be more appropriate for the judge in other kinds of cases.

In *Moon* v. *State of Maryland* (90 S.Ct. 1730), the U.S. Supreme Court held that the Constitution does not limit the imposition of a harsher sentence upon retrial. Moon was found guilty of armed robbery by a Maryland jury and sentenced to 12 years' imprisonment. The conviction was set aside on appeal by the Maryland Court of Appeals and, at the second trial for the same offense, Moon was again convicted and the trial judge imposed a sentence of 20 years' imprisonment. The second conviction was affirmed on appeal, and Moon then appealed the case to the Supreme Court on the ground that the Constitution prevents the imposition of a harsher sentence on the retrial than was imposed initially. The court held that there is no absolute constitutional bar to the imposition of a harsher sentence upon retrial, but that due process requires that vindictiveness against a defendant for having successfully attacked his first conviction must play no part in the sentence he receives after a new trial.

Williams v. *Florida* (90 S.Ct. 1893) tested the constitutionality of two special procedures employed in Florida in criminal cases. Both had been under consideration in other states, but constitutional doubts, among other reasons, prevented them from being adopted throughout the U.S. Williams was found

guilty by a 6-man jury of the crime of armed robbery after the court had denied his requests for a 12-man jury and that he be excused from the "notice-of-alibi rule," which requires the defendant prior to a criminal trial to submit to the prosecution the names and addresses of any witnesses he intends to call to establish the defense of alibi. He appealed to the U.S. Supreme Court, asserting that the 6-man jury procedure violated the Sixth Amendment to the Constitution that guarantees a trial by jury, and that the notice-of-alibi procedure compelled him to be a witness against himself contrary to the commands of the Fifth and Fourteenth amendments. The court denied both assertions.

Religion. The British government announced its intention to present to Parliament the much-discussed Prevention of Incitement to Hatred Bill, obviously aimed at conditions that prevailed in Northern Ireland. If passed, the new law would make it an offense to use abusive or insulting language to stir up hatred against any section of the public or arouse the fear of any section of the public on grounds of religious belief, colour, race, or ethnic origin.

The British Court of Appeal held in *Regina* v. *Registrar General, ex parte Segardal,* that a building used for instruction in the tenets of Scientology was not a church for purposes of the privileges conferred by the Places of Worship Registration Act of 1855. The court held that a place of religious worship connotes, among other things, a place of reverence and veneration for a supreme being. The tenets of Scientology, on the contrary, were found to lay stress on man.

The U.S. Supreme Court held in *Walz* v. *Tax Commissioner of the City of New York* (90 S.Ct. 1409) that a New York statute exempting from real property taxation any realty owned by an association organized exclusively for religious purposes was not unconstitutional as an attempt to establish, sponsor, or support religion or as an interference with the free exercise of religion mandated by the Constitution.

(W. D. Hd.)

International Law. *Boundaries and Territory.* Boundary adjustments or disputes settled or under adjustment during the year included a treaty signed between West Germany and Poland in which the Oder-Neisse rivers were accepted as Poland's western boundary. The question of the treatment of the Austrian minorities in the Italian border region of South Tirol, which had been a bone of contention for many years, was settled by an agreement between Italy and Austria. The dispute between Argentina and Chile

Students outside the London Appeals Court protest the sentences of six Cambridge undergraduates who were convicted of mob violence during a protest against the Greek junta.

LONDON "DAILY EXPRESS" FROM PICTORIAL PARADE

over sovereignty in the Beagle Channel was submitted to British arbitration.

By the Protocol of Port of Spain, signed in Trinidad, the 70-year-old border dispute between Guyana and Venezuela was settled for a minimum of 12 years. Under the agreement, Venezuela abandoned its claim to 57,000 sq.mi. of Guyanese territory. The dispute between Guyana and Surinam over some 6,000 sq.mi. of territory was the subject of discussions. Panama formally notified the U.S. that the three draft treaties drawn up in 1967 to create a new status for the Panama Canal were unacceptable as a basis for resuming negotiations.

The dispute between Spain and the U.K. over the British colony of Gibraltar was dormant during most of the year, after the Spanish government closed the frontier. A new factor has been raised, however. Spain concluded a preferential trade agreement with the European Economic Community (EEC) and was working toward an association agreement, which would probably involve freedom of movement for workers. Britain was negotiating for membership in the EEC, and Gibraltar would automatically be brought in under the EEC treaty, either completely or as an associate. The Spanish government protested to the EEC.

Marine boundaries settled or under discussion during the year included the dispute between the Netherlands and Denmark on the one hand and West Germany on the other over the extent of the German sector of the North Sea continental shelf, which the International Court of Justice in 1969 had failed to settle. The three states accepted straight boundary lines that would bring the German sector to the centre line bordering the British area.

Discussions were initiated between legal experts of Norway and the U.S.S.R. concerning the common boundary in the Barents Sea. Sir Gawain Bell, mediator in the territorial waters dispute between the Trucial States of Sharjah, Umm al Qaiwain, and Ajman over the island of Abu Musa (which was also claimed by Iran), submitted his interim report to the parties. An agreement was signed between Malaysia and Indonesia regulating the outer limits of their respective territorial waters in the Strait of Malacca (which is narrower than the sum of their 12-mi. belts of territorial seas). Spain and Portugal signed an agreement providing for close cooperation on fishing problems and defining the areas of exclusive fishing rights. The U.S. Department of State gave notice that the U.S. disputed Canada's claim to sovereignty over part of the seabed in the Gulf of Maine. The two countries, however, negotiated a draft agreement on reciprocal fishing privileges in the exclusive fishery zones set up off the respective coasts in recent years.

The tendency of states to proclaim extensions of their territorial waters, usually to 12 mi., continued and prompted the U.S., with Soviet support, to propose a new universal rule providing a 12-mi. belt. If adopted, such a proposal would obviate the need for states to increase their fishery limits to 12 mi. while retaining their existing territorial water belt, which was done by Poland during the year. Greater fishery control belts were claimed, however, by the U.S.S.R. (30-mi. zone round the Komandorski Islands) and Iceland (coextensive with the continental shelf), and Norway hinted that if international efforts at fisheries conservation had no greater efficacy than previously it might adopt an Icelandic approach.

Canada was adopting an analogous attitude. The claim to a 200-mi. belt of territorial waters, hitherto restricted to certain Pacific coast Latin-American states, was extended to the Atlantic coast when both Brazil and Uruguay made the same claim, and made its first appearance in Africa when Senegal adopted the principle.

The Sea. Major developments in the law of the sea related to the ocean floor and to pollution. The UN's Committee on Disarmament, meeting in Geneva, finally approved a draft, based on U.S. and Soviet proposals, for a treaty prohibiting the use of nuclear weapons on the seabed. The draft, which was adopted by the UN's First Committee of the General Assembly, would ban the placing of nuclear weapons and other means of mass destruction on the ocean floor beyond the 12-mi. limit offshore. It would, therefore, apply to national continental shelves as well as the ocean floor, and in certain cases it would also apply to the seabed under territorial waters.

The other aspect of seabed law was less conclusive. The UN's Committee on the Peaceful Uses of the Sea-Bed and the Ocean Floor Beyond the Limits of National Jurisdiction continued to discuss the status of the seabed outside the continental shelf limits (the 100 fathom isobath). The two schemes that had most support were (1) that coastal states should regulate the exploitation of the ocean floor off their own continental shelves on behalf of the international community, and (2) that the ocean floor should be divided into exploitation squares that would be allotted to all nations, including the landlocked, each state being responsible for regulating exploitation in its own squares, again on behalf of the international community.

But while the seabed was the subject of more articles in the law reviews, marine pollution was continuously before the public eye. The work in the Inter-Governmental Maritime Consultative Organization on oil pollution, after the "Torrey Canyon" ran aground off Cornwall, Eng., in 1967, resulted in an agreement to prohibit ships from discharging on the high seas tank washings of more than 100:1,000,000 oil:water and two conventions (1) authorizing a coastal state to intervene and take measures to protect its coastal interests where a casualty occurs on the high seas, and (2) imposing strict liability on shipowners for causing oil-pollution damage.

But the problem of ocean pollution was more serious than the fouling of beaches. Two remedies would be better policing of the seas against deliberate pollution, and stringent sea traffic control of navigation in busy sea lanes to prevent accidental pollution resulting from collision. Both would require heavy expenditure and interference in the freedom of the high seas, and so had made little progress.

International Adjudication. The International Court of Justice gave judgment in the *Barcelona Traction* case in February, in which it rejected the claim by Belgium (by 15 votes to 1—the Belgian judge ad hoc) on the procedural ground that Belgium lacked *jus standi* to exercise diplomatic protection of Belgian shareholders in a Canadian company with respect to measures taken against that company in Spain. It seemed for a while that the court would thenceforth be out of work, but the UN Security Council asked the court for an advisory opinion on the legal consequences of the continued presence of South Africa in South West Africa, pleadings on which were being exchanged at the end of the year.

WIDE WORLD

U.S. Sen. John Stennis (Dem., Miss.) suggests a constitutional amendment to eliminate the right of trial in some cases such as the Chicago 7 conspiracy trial.

The European Court of Human Rights gave judgment at the end of 1969 in the cases *Matznetter* v. *Austria* and *Stögmüller* v. *Austria,* the latter judgment being given against the defendant state. Its judgment in *Delcourt* v. *Belgium* early in 1970 dismissed the complaint. By the end of the year it had two cases on its docket, *Ringeisen* v. *Austria* (involving detention before trial), and the *Vagrancy Cases* (three applications by vagrants against Belgium over detention under the vagrancy laws), which were consolidated and were being heard by the full court, the first time this had been done. The European Commission of Human Rights gave its opinion in the application by the Scandinavian states against Greece, in which it found that Greece was in violation of several articles of the European Convention on Human Rights. A second application was brought alleging further violations.

The Court of Justice of the European Communities held, inter alia, that the 1969 decision of the Commission fining a number of firms for operating a quinine cartel was valid (although it reduced the fines), and that directives could be enforceable by citizens before their national courts.

International Organizations. A number of new international organizations were created during the year. These included the World Intellectual Property Organization, the Caribbean Development Bank, and the Institute of Human Rights, set up in Strasbourg, France, with the Nobel prize money awarded to René Cassin. The proposed Organization for Nordic Economic Cooperation (Nordek) came to nothing when Finland refused to sign the treaty in view of the forthcoming negotiations for two of the states to join the EEC.

The United Nations celebrated its 25th anniversary, accompanied by articles debating what its future would be, or even whether it had a future. It marked the occasion by mustering a bare majority (but not the requisite two-thirds majority) for acceptance of Communist China's representatives in the organization; but it counterbalanced that by rejecting the credentials of the representatives of South Africa.

The European Communities were absorbed with the opening of negotiations for expansion, and discussions were taking place in parallel with the neutrals (Sweden, Switzerland, and Austria) and with the outer three (Portugal, Iceland, and Finland). In effect, the whole of Western Europe was engaged in political discussions. (*See* EUROPEAN UNITY.) At the same time the U.S. and U.S.S.R. were engaged in the strategic arms limitation talks (SALT) at Helsinki, Fin., and Vienna, and West Germany was taking positive diplomatic initiatives with the U.S.S.R. and Poland. The European Communities themselves continued their policy of concluding preferential trade agreements with Mediterranean countries. (*See* COMMERCIAL POLICIES.)

Hijacking and Kidnapping. Undoubtedly the international law topic with the greatest news value during the year was aircraft hijacking. The problem was not new, especially in relation to Cuba, but it took on a new dimension by spreading to many other countries and by taking on an overt political form in the hands of Palestinian irregulars. For the first time, hijacking of planes was used expressly to exert pressure on governments (successfully) to release prisoners. This new development had a parallel in the activities of "urban guerrillas" operating in many Latin-American countries and in Quebec and Spain, whereby foreign diplomats or indigenous notables were kidnapped and

held for ransom—either money, or release of prisoners, or radio publicity.

No solution had been found to the latter problem, but the Tokyo Convention on Offenses and Certain Other Acts Committed on Board Aircraft came into force just in time for states to use it to overcome the jurisdictional problems that would otherwise apply to hijackings; states of destination rarely had jurisdiction over acts in aircraft registered in another country, and extradition was usually ruled out because the hijackers had a political motive. Nevertheless, many states passed legislation or imposed severe sentences on captured hijackers, and extradition treaties, for example between the U.S. and New Zealand, were revised to exclude hijacking from the political exemptions.

Family Law. Laws came into force in West Germany and Sweden giving illegitimate children the same rights of inheritance, maintenance, etc., as legitimate children; a Finnish committee reported recommendations to the same effect. The principle of breakdown of marriage as the sole ground for divorce was adopted in the English Divorce Reform Act and in the West German bill to reform the marriage law. In Italy, adultery was no longer a crime, and a bill to introduce the concept of divorce into Italian law was passed at the end of the year. Acts to reform the law of adoption in Belgium and the law of husband and wife in France were passed during the year. Laws to permit non-therapeutic abortion were passed in Finland, Denmark, Alaska, Hawaii, New York, and South Australia.

Constitutional and Administrative Law. Laws reducing the voting age or age of majority from 21 to 18 were passed in Bavaria, W.Ger., Canada, Queensland, Austr., West Germany, and Northern Ireland; the U.S. passed a law permitting 18-year-olds to vote in national elections. The principle of publicity in administration was introduced into Denmark and Norway by statutes passed during the year.

Administration of Justice. In England a bill was introduced to implement the recommendation of the Beeching Report on reform of the court structure. Committees were appointed in Sweden to study the matter. In Italy, the growing obsolescence of court administration led to strikes by magistrates and other branches of the legal profession. In France, the minister of justice pursued his policy of persuading the legal profession to accept wide-ranging reforms; one such proposal, that for professional partnerships (*sociétés civiles professionnelles*), which had been authorized by statute, was implemented for the first time in November.

In Eastern European countries a number of major reforms of the law occurred. These included a new penal code in Poland, new labour codes in Czechoslovakia and the U.S.S.R., and a new civil code in Yugoslavia. In the U.S.S.R. the Ministry of Justice was reintroduced at both union and republic levels.

(N. M. H.)

See also Crime; Defense; Police; Race Relations.

ENCYCLOPÆDIA BRITANNICA FILMS. *Understanding the Law —Equal Justice for All* (1953); *The Congress* (1954); *The Supreme Court* (1954); *The Bill of Rights of the United States* (1956); *The Constitution of the United States* (1956); *Magna Carta, Part I* (*Rise of the English Monarchy*) (1959); *Magna Carta, Part II* (*Revolt of the Nobles and the Signing of the Charter*) (1959); *Justice Under Law* (*Gideon Case*) (1966); *Equality Under Law—The Lost Generation of Prince Edward County* (1967); *Freedom to Speak* (*N.Y. v. Feiner*) (1967); *Equality Under Law—California Fair Housing Cases* (1969); *Free Press vs. Fair Trial by Jury—The Sheppard Case* (1969); *The Schempp Case—Bible Reading in Public Schools* (1969).

Lebanon

A republic of the Middle East, Lebanon is bounded by Syria, Israel, and the Mediterranean Sea. Area: 4,015 sq.mi. (10,-400 sq.km.). Pop. (1969 est.): 2,645,000. Cap. and largest city: Beirut (pop., 1965 est., 330,995). Language: Arabic. Religion: approximately 50% Christian, 34% Muslim. Presidents in 1970, Charles Helou and, from September 23, Suleiman Franjieh; prime ministers, Rashid Karami and, from October 5, Saeb Salam.

In 1970 Lebanon's uneasy role as a base for Palestinian guerrillas caused serious disruption in the south and stoked up internal unrest. Political differences, although sharpened by an extension of guerrilla influence, did not harden into a Christian-Muslim confrontation, and civil war was avoided. The government's chief concern was to protect the southern frontier without enmeshing Lebanon in a military alliance against Israel.

Sustained guerrilla actions against Israel brought heavy reprisals, and the Lebanon-Israel border was the most active sector of the Middle East front. In January, after Israeli commandos took from a border village 21 hostages including 10 Lebanese soldiers, the Christian right wing pressed for the guerrillas' expulsion from the country, while the Arab nationalist bloc urged the government to give them a free hand. Steering a middle course, left-wing Interior Minister Kamal Jumblatt sought to contain the activities of the guerrillas on the basis of an agreement pledging mutual cooperation signed in Cairo in November 1969. In March, however, about 40 persons were killed during street fighting in Beirut between the guerrillas and the Katayib, a Christian paramilitary group. This crisis ended when both sides (with Libya mediating) reaffirmed the Cairo agreement. Later, however, the United Arab Republic's acceptance of the U.S. formula

POPPERFOTO FROM PICTORIAL PARADE

Armed troops guard Lebanon's Parliament Building in Beirut as government ministers discuss measures to be taken against the guerrillas who stage raids into Israel across Lebanon's southern border. Thousands of Lebanese were forced to leave their homes there because of Israeli retaliation.

for Arab-Israeli negotiations created local tensions that erupted in August when guerrillas and Nasserites fought a gun battle in the streets of Sidon.

Border defense remained an intractable problem. After a mid-May visit to Damascus (the first to Syria by a Lebanese prime minister since 1964), Karami said that the two countries had reached agreement on all matters discussed. Ten days later he announced, then "temporarily" shelved, a proposal that Moroccan and Tunisian troops should defend southern Lebanon against Israel.

Instead, the government served notice that from June 15 guerrillas would be banned from firing rockets across the frontier and carrying arms in cities. The ban had little effect, but its announcement coincided with a particularly heavy flow of refugees to the north that provoked a threat by Imam Moussa al-Sadr, leader of the predominantly southern Shi'ite Muslims, to paralyze the country's vital services failing adequate defense measures. The government then voted L£30 million to help an estimated 22,000 southerners driven from their homes by Israeli incursions.

On August 17 the National Assembly chose the economy minister, Suleiman Franjieh (see BIOGRAPHY), to succeed President Helou, whose term was expiring. Elected on the third ballot, Franjieh took office on September 23. On October 13 Saeb Salam, appointed prime minister by Franjieh, announced a 12-man Cabinet of "technicians."   (P. Md.)

LEBANON

Education. (1967–68) Primary, pupils 401,776; secondary, pupils 109,767; primary and secondary, teachers 26,465; teacher training, students 2,276, teachers 420; higher (including 4 universities), students 29,138, teaching staff 1,266.

Finance. Monetary unit: Lebanese pound, with a free rate (Oct. 1970) of L£3.25 to U.S. $1 (L£7.76 = £1 sterling). Gold, SDRs, and foreign exchange, central bank: (June 1970) U.S. $348.1 million; (June 1969) U.S. $321.5 million. Budget (1969 est.): revenue L£587 million; expenditure L£661 million.

Foreign Trade. (1968) Imports L£1,881,197,000; exports L£450 million; transit trade L£1,532,938,000. Import sources: U.K. 14%; U.S. 11%; Syria 9%; France 9%; West Germany 8%. Export destinations: Saudi Arabia 21%; Kuwait 9%. Main exports: fruit and vegetables 17%; precious stones and metals 16%; machinery 8%; textiles and clothing 7%.

Transport and Communications. Roads (1969) 7,275 km. Motor vehicles in use (1969): passenger 131,900; commercial 16,050. Railways: (1968) 417 km.; traffic (1969) 7.3 million passenger-km., freight 24.5 million net ton-km. Air traffic (1968): 836,992,-000 passenger-km.; freight 102,620,000 net ton-km. Telephones (Jan. 1969) 150,370. Radio receivers (Dec. 1968) 550,000. Television receivers (Dec. 1968) 375,000.

Agriculture. Production (in 000; metric tons; 1968; 1967 in parentheses): grapes 84 (88); wheat 48 (68); tomatoes 60 (59); oranges 175 (168); lemons 63 (70); apples 163 (157); tobacco 6.6 (6.4). Livestock (in 000; 1967–68): cattle 86; goats 357; sheep 200; poultry 14,980.

Lesotho

A constitutional monarchy of southern Africa, Lesotho is completely surrounded by South Africa. Area: 11,-719 sq.mi. (30,352 sq.km.). Pop. (1968): 1,018,135, almost 99% African. Cap. and largest city: Maseru (pop., 1966 census, 14,077). Language: English (official) and Sesotho. Religion: about 70% Christian. Chiefs of state in 1970, Paramount Chief Moshoeshoe II, in exile from April 3 to December 4; regent from April 3 to December 4, Queen Mamohato Seeiso; prime minister, Chief Leabua Jonathan.

Stormy in both the political and economic spheres, 1970 was marked by the first general elections since independence. They took place on January 27 and were apparently a victory for the opposition Congress

Leeward Islands: see Dependent States

Party. Three days later, Prime Minister Leabua Jonathan (National Party) declared a state of emergency and suspension of the constitution. The reasons given were that thefts of ballot boxes, intimidation, violence, and even murder by the Communist-inspired opposition had made a democratic election impossible, and also that King Moshoeshoe, though prohibited by the 1966 constitution and debarred by personal promises from interfering in party politics, had supported the opposition, and had thus automatically abdicated. The king went into exile and the opposition leader, Ntsu Mokhehle, and his chief supporters were arrested. Calm was restored following an unsuccessful attempt by Congress Party supporters to seize two northern towns. King Moshoeshoe returned on December 4 and resumed the throne after promising to abstain from all political activity.

Under the interim constitution, Chief Jonathan exercised executive power, either directly or through his council of ministers. New elections under a new constitution were promised provided that the democratic process would be guaranteed and that Lesotho could not be made into a Communist base against South Africa. The British Labour government refused recognition to Chief Jonathan and suspended financial aid. Resumption of aid was, however, agreed upon in May, when Chief Jonathan undertook to discuss constitutional problems with the other three political parties and drought made aid urgent.   (M. Mr.)

LESOTHO

Education. (1967) Primary, pupils 167,803, teachers 3,065; secondary, pupils 3,201, teachers 152; vocational, pupils 472, teachers 44; teacher training, students 625, teachers 47; higher (University of Botswana, Lesotho, and Swaziland), students 308, teaching staff 60.

Finance and Trade. Monetary unit: South African rand, with a par value of R 0.71 to U.S. $1 (R 1.71 = £1 sterling). Budget (1970–71 est.) balanced at R 11,704,510 (including R 2,014,000 U.K. grant). Foreign trade (1968): imports R 23,938,000; exports R 3,380,000. Main exports: cattle 33%; wool 26%; mohair 13%; diamonds 11%; wheat 5%. The adverse trade balance is partly offset by receipts from labour working in South Africa (R 2,450,000 in 1968–69).

Agriculture. Production (in 000; metric tons; 1968; 1967 in parentheses): corn 112 (*c.* 110); wheat *c.* 60 (*c.* 50); wool *c.* 2.2 (*c.* 2.2); meat (1967) *c.* 22. Livestock (in 000; Feb. 1968): cattle *c.* 380; goats *c.* 900; sheep (Sept. 1969) *c.* 1,650.

Liberia

A republic on the west coast of Africa, Liberia is bordered by Sierra Leone, Guinea, and Ivory Coast. Area: 43,000 sq.mi. (111,370 sq.km.). Pop. (1970): 1.2 million. Cap. and largest city: Monrovia (pop., 1970, 100,000). Language: English and tribal dialects. President in 1970, William V. S. Tubman.

Liberia's economy experienced robust growth in 1970, thus raising hopes that the country's burden of foreign debt payments—which absorbed about one-third of government revenue—might soon become lighter. Gross national product increased by 5% from $244.9 million in 1969 to approximately $257.2 million in 1970. Production of major Liberian natural resources likewise grew substantially. Iron ore output rose from 22.8 million to approximately 24.4 million metric tons between 1969 and 1970 and natural rubber production increased from 66,000 to about 73,000 metric tons.

U.S. Secretary of State William P. Rogers visited Liberia in February at the end of his tour of Africa. At a state dinner at President Tubman's residence in Monrovia, Rogers jokingly remarked that he knew he was dining "among the establishment." The remark caused some uneasiness among Liberians, who are sensitive to the fact that the approximately 45,000 American-Liberians have constituted an elite class in the country.

Two ships under Liberian registry ran into trouble during 1970. The cargo ship "Deep Freeze" was forced toward a Cuban port by a Cuban gunboat on January 1, but was permitted to proceed to British Honduras the same day. Then, on February 4, the oil tanker "Arrow" ran aground in high winds off Nova Scotia. It broke in two in Chedabucto Bay five days later, releasing large amounts of the 3.8 million gal. of bunker oil it was carrying. A Canadian Transport Department investigation later blamed the accident on "improper navigation."

A major domestic crisis was triggered by the slaying on Nov. 19, 1969, of the American Episcopal missionary bishop of Liberia, the Rt. Rev. Dillard H. Brown. The business manager of Bishop Brown's diocese also was killed and three other persons were wounded in the same incident. President Tubman was granted emergency powers by Congress on November 27 in connection with the killings. He was entitled to suspend habeas corpus for up to 12 months, ban subversive organizations, and arrest persons suspected of sedition. Government spokesmen announced on Dec. 29, 1969, that chemistry professor Justin Obi, 63, had been charged with Brown's murder. Nine others were charged with complicity in the slaying.

It was reported on Nov. 10, 1969, that Tubman had intervened personally to prevent the deportation of 75 black Americans ordered to leave Liberia a week earlier as undesirable aliens. The Americans, who moved to Liberia in 1967, lived together in a colony near Monrovia and were said to have no visible means of support.   (Ri. W.)

LIBERIA

Education. (1968–69) Primary, pupils 120,101, teachers 3,211; secondary, pupils 12,866, teachers 669; vocational, pupils 913, teachers 81; teacher training, pupils 348, teachers 34; higher, students 1,282, teaching staff 163.

Finance. Monetary unit: Liberian dollar, at par with the U.S. dollar (L$2.40 = £1 sterling). Budget (1969 est.): revenue L$58 million; expenditure L$60.1 million.

Foreign Trade. (1968) Imports L$118 million; exports L$169 million. Import sources: U.S. 40%; U.K. 12%; West Germany 9%; Japan 8%. Export destinations: U.S. 26%; West Germany 20%; Netherlands 14%; Italy 11%; Belgium-Luxembourg 9%; U.K. 7%; France 5%. Main exports: iron ore 70%; rubber 15%; diamonds 5%.

Transport and Communications. Roads (1968) *c.* 3,200 km. Motor vehicles in use (1968): passenger 13,400; commercial (including buses) 5,800. Railways (1968) *c.* 570 km. Shipping (1969): merchant vessels 100 gross tons and over 1,731 (mostly owned by U.S. and other foreign interests); gross tonnage 29,215,151. Telephones (Jan. 1969) *c.* 3,600. Radio receivers (Dec. 1966) 152,000. Television receivers (Dec. 1967) 4,600.

Agriculture. Production (in 000; metric tons; 1968; 1967 in parentheses): rice *c.* 152 (*c.* 152); cassava *c.* 430 (*c.* 430); rubber (exports) 59 (62); palm kernels (exports) *c.* 14 (14); cocoa 1.7 (1.9); coffee *c.* 3.8 (*c.* 3.4). Livestock (in 000; August 1968): cattle *c.* 26; pigs *c.* 78; sheep *c.* 145; goats *c.* 135.

Industry. Production (in 000; 1968): iron ore (metal content) 13,292 metric tons; diamonds (exports) 730 metric carats; electricity 573,000 kw-hr.

Libraries

In the international field, libraries joined in the observance of 1970 as International Education Year, as designated by UNESCO. The work of the International Federation of Library Associations (IFLA), a nongovernmental organization in consultative relations with UNESCO, reached its annual climax at the General Council, held in Moscow from August 29 to September 5. This was followed by two days of sessions and visits to libraries in Leningrad and further tours to other parts of the Soviet Union. The main theme of the Moscow meeting was "Libraries as a Force in Education," chosen for International Education Year. At a special plenary session on this theme in the House of Unions, the audience of over 700 participants from some 40 countries was addressed by N. I. Mokhov, deputy minister of culture of the U.S.S.R., and by Malcolm Adiseshiah, deputy director general of UNESCO. The rest of the week's session was devoted to specialized meetings on library techniques and cooperation.

Two weeks later, the International Federation for Documentation (FID), which concentrates on classification, information retrieval, and bibliography, met at Buenos Aires, Arg., to celebrate its 75th anniversary.

UNESCO Department of Documentation, Libraries, and Archives. UNESCO gave subsidies of $10,000 and $20,000, respectively, to the two international organizations in the library field, FID and IFLA. In cooperation with them, UNESCO initiated research projects on the national structure of library services, on library statistics, for a national bibliography of English-speaking countries of Africa, and for a manual on document preservation. The following publications appeared: *A Bibliography of National Directories of Current Periodicals* (with IFLA); *The Planning of Library Services,* revised edition by P. H. Sewell; *Standards for Library Service* by F. N. Withers; *Guide for an Introductory Course of Informatics* by A. I. Mikhailov and R. S. Giliarevsky; and *Guide to National Bibliographical Centres,* third edition.

Work continued on the pilot project on documentation and library services in Ceylon, and a law was passed establishing the Ceylon National Library Services Board. UNESCO financially supported a seminar on automation of libraries at Regensburg, W.Ger., in April 1970; a symposium on national systems of libraries at Prague in October; a symposium on planning national structures of scientific and technical information at Madrid in October; and an experts' meeting on national planning of documentation and library services in Africa, at Kampala, Uganda, in December. Training courses were supported by UNESCO at the Royal School of Librarianship, Copenhagen, for teachers of librarianship from less developed countries, August to November; at the Japan Documentation Society, Tokyo, on documentation techniques, July to August; and at the School of Librarianship of the University of Buenos Aires, also July to August.

Standardized library practices were adopted for UNESCO institutions; special efforts were made to standardize Universal Decimal Classification practice and cataloging by the Anglo-American rules. In Paris a new "Computerized Documentation Service" was set up in UNESCO House, to be operational in 1971. The proposed World Science Information System

COURTESY, MOUNT ANGEL ABBEY

The Mount Angel Abbey library, completed in 1970 near St. Benedict, Ore., was designed by architect Alvar Aalto.

(UNISIST), sponsored by UNESCO and the International Council of Scientific Unions, was discussed at various meetings; the final report was produced as a UNESCO document, to be considered by an intergovernmental Conference on Scientific Information in October 1971.

Europe. *Austria.* The National Library, Vienna, was host to the sixth International Congress of Bibliophiles in October 1969. In the same month an exhibition entitled "England and Austria" was held in connection with British Week. In the summer of 1970, an exhibition entitled "50 Years of Contemporary History" celebrated the acquisition of the Royal Library by the Austrian republic in 1920.

Belgium. The library of the State University at Liège continued the computerization of its cataloging, indexing, and lending procedures. The State University of Ghent published its union catalog of periodicals. A book museum inaugurated in the Royal Library, Brussels, on February 17 offered a permanent exhibition on the history of the book from the 8th to the 20th century.

Finland. By the end of 1969 there were two volumes per inhabitant in the public libraries of Finland, and the number of loans had risen from 27.5 million in 1968 to nearly 30 million (the population of Finland was 4.7 million). As a result of a decision of the Prison Library Committee of the Finnish Library Association, prison libraries were being transferred to the public library authorities. The association carried out a survey of librarians and discovered that 89% were women; among the men 20% were head librarians and among the women, 7%. The sixth Anglo-Scandinavian Public Library Conference was held in Finland in August 1970, with 70 delegates from Britain and Scandinavia.

France. Some new libraries were opened, notably an important addition to the public library and a children's library at Mulhouse, and an annex to the municipal library at Dunkerque to serve the densely populated quarter of the rue de la Paix, far from the

"LONDON (ONT.) FREE PRESS"

Striking employees of the London, Ont., public library system and members of the Canadian Union of Public Employees picket to back up contract demands, June 6, 1970. It was the first time librarians in Canada had gone on strike.

main library. At Troyes a "Discothèque" (library of phonograph records) was inaugurated as a new service of the municipal library. This followed the example and methods of the existing "discothèques" at Bourges, Paris, Saint-Dié, and Tours. A new library for young people was inaugurated at the Saint-Cyprien branch in Toulouse.

Hungary. By the end of 1969, the public libraries of Hungary had over two volumes per head of population. Cooperation of school libraries with the public libraries was to be intensified. The National Szechenyi Library's Centre for Library Science and Methodology issued directives for the technical development of libraries, and also published a *Guide to Special Literature* as part of the organization of subject specialization. In December 1969 there were international meetings in Budapest on library buildings and equipment and on library statistics in the socialist countries. A new periodical, *Konyvtari Figyelo* ("Library Observer"), began publication.

Malta. The Malta Library Association, founded in March 1969, became a member of IFLA in August. A new public lending library service was planned by the Malta Ministry of Education, with £28,000 given by the British government for its first five years. This project would fulfill a great need, since in 1969–70 public libraries in Malta spent only about £4,000 on books, and loans averaged only 1½ books per person per year.

Poland. The Association of Polish Librarians, with over 10,500 members, including more than 6,500 public librarians, was very active in 1970, giving advice to the government on many orders and regulations of the Library Act of 1968, participating in the State Library Council set up under this law, and presenting to it a uniform system of training for librarians.

Spain. The National Association of Archivists, Librarians, and Archaeologists (ANABA) increased its activity in 1970, publishing the proceedings of the third National Congress of Libraries (Las Palmas, 1968), a *Who's Who of Librarians and Archivists,* and a *Bibliography of Children's Books in Catalan;* the *Boletín de ANABA* appeared in improved form. The reconstruction of the National Library in Madrid

continued, and the department of prints and drawings completed its *Catalogo de dibujos.* Some 62 municipal public libraries had been created in 1969, and this movement continued in 1970. By a decree of February 1970, a Spanish bibliographical institute was created, under the General Direction of Archives and Libraries, to coordinate and integrate national bibliographical work.

United Kingdom. Library activity reached record figures; at the end of 1969 the British Library Association had 17,331 members (of whom 16,390 were personal members), and there were 2,559 full-time students in schools of librarianship. The Library Association accepted degree courses offered by the schools at Leeds, Birmingham, and Manchester in lieu of its own examinations. It was anticipated that the annual demand for qualified librarians, estimated in 1968 at 1,100, would rise to about 1,500 by 1980. Expenditure on public libraries rose to £52,717,761 in 1969–70, over £3 million more than in the preceding year. The census of staff taken in April 1969 had revealed 21,491 posts, of which 6,922 were for qualified staff.

Following the recommendations of the Library Advisory Council for England in 1967, a central loan collection for Indian and Pakistani immigrants was organized by the city libraries in Birmingham, where the vast new Central Library building was nearing completion. Other new constructions in 1970 included county libraries in Bedfordshire, Gloucestershire, and the three Welsh counties of Flint, Brecknock, and Pembroke; municipal libraries at Doncaster and Thurock; and three university libraries that received Royal Institute of British Architects awards—Hull University; the Science Library at Queen's University, Belfast; and the History Library at Cambridge University.

Yugoslavia. At the beginning of 1970 there were 1,444 learned and technical libraries with a total of over 15 million volumes; 1,895 public libraries with over 12 million volumes; and 10,690 school libraries with over 14 million volumes. Money was appropriated for a new building for the National and University Library of Bosnia-Hercegovina at Sarajevo; it would hold about a million volumes. In accordance with the usual practice of rotation through the six republics, the Yugoslav Association of Librarians' Societies transferred its office to Zagreb (Croatia) for 1969–71.

Other Countries. *Jordan.* The Jordan Library Association, founded in 1963, had 237 members at the beginning of 1970. It published a pamphlet, *JLA in Six Years, 1964–69.* The new building of the Library of the University of Jordan, for 300,000 volumes and 600 readers, was under construction. A public library was set up at Wadi Seer, bringing the number of public libraries to 13.

Malagasy Republic. At the University of Madagascar in Tananarive, opened in October 1968, an interesting new building for the library was already in operation. The three-story building had a floor area of 1,700 sq.m. Detailed description and plans were published in the *Bulletin des bibliothèques de France* (December 1969).

United States. The American Library Association (ALA) continued to play an important part in international library work. It administered grants from the Ford Foundation to rehabilitate the university library at Algiers and to develop the collections of the university at Addis Ababa, Eth., and of the University of Brasília. The ALA also sent an adviser to Venezuela to help in national and university library planning and development. The work of U.S. consultants at the National Central Library in Florence, Italy, where they had assisted in rehabilitation work following the 1966 flood, was completed. In 1969–70, 46 librarians and libraries in Asia were given complimentary ALA membership.

During the year the ALA took a strong stand upholding the confidentiality of library records. A report by the association's Intellectual Freedom Committee stated that records showing who had withdrawn books should not be surrendered without a court order and promised legal assistance to librarians wishing to contest such orders. The ALA interested itself in the subject after several librarians reported that U.S. Treasury agents had been attempting to discover the names of persons who had withdrawn books on explosives and other "subversive" material.

In the field of children's libraries a bibliography, *1969 Children's Books of International Interest,* was prepared for the August 1970 session of IFLA. Some important 1970 ALA publications on libraries were *Standards for Library Functions at the State Level,* revised edition; *A National Plan for Library Statistics; Library Response to Urban Change: A Study of the Chicago Public Library* by L. A. Martin; *German Exile Literature in America 1933–1950* by R. E. Cazden; *The Undergraduate Library* by I. A. Braden; and *Guide to Reference Books,* eighth edition, by E. P. Sheehy.

The *ALA Bulletin* was replaced in 1970 by *American Libraries.* Important publications of the Special Libraries Association were *Consolidated Index of Translations into English* and *Map Collections in the U.S. and Canada.* (A. TH.)

ENCYCLOPÆDIA BRITANNICA FILMS. *The Library Story* (1952); *The Library: A Place for Discovery* (1965); *Library of Congress* (1969).

Libya

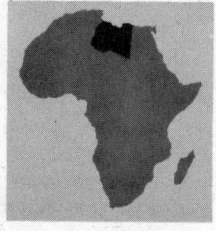

A socialist republic on the north coast of Africa, Libya is bounded by the United Arab Republic, Sudan, Tunisia, Algeria, Niger, and Chad. Area: 686,500 sq.mi. (1,778,000 sq.km.). Pop. (1970 est.): 1,938,000. Co-capitals and largest cities: Tripoli (pop., 1969 est., 255,000) and Benghazi (pop., 1969 est., 164,000); federal administrative centre: al-Bayda (pop., 1968 est., 15,000). Language: Arabic. Religion: predominantly Muslim. Leader of the Revolutionary Command Council in 1970, Col. Muhammad al-Khadafy; prime ministers, Mahmoud Soliman al-Maghreby and, from January 16, Col. Muhammad al-Khadafy.

The new Libyan regime, instituted in September 1969, became increasingly Army-dominated in 1970, and by September the Cabinet had only five civilian members. The trials of former members of the Revolutionary Command Council alleged to have attempted a countercoup in December 1969 continued throughout the year. Another attempted coup, organized in the south of the country, was thwarted in late July.

Colonel al-Khadafy took a leading part in Middle Eastern affairs, organizing a number of high-level meetings of Arab leaders, including the summit meeting at Tripoli in June. He was given strong personal

support by Pres. Gamal Abd-al-Nasser of the United Arab Republic, and there were many reciprocal visits before the latter's death in September. On November 7, Libya, the U.A.R., and Sudan announced their agreement on a program of cooperation looking toward eventual federation. No timetable was given, however, and late in the year Colonel al-Khadafy indicated that consummation of such a federation was probably some years away.

The British and U.S. air bases in Libya were closed down in March and June, respectively, and, following general hostility to the oil companies, the marketing of petroleum products was nationalized in July. That month also brought a ban on the ownership of land by Italian ex-colonists.

Oil exports rose again in 1970 but not as much as the 29.5% average annual rate of increase of the 1964–69 period. Some companies were instructed to cut back production, partly for reasons of conservation but also in an attempt to gain a higher posted price for Libyan oil. In late December the oil companies were ordered to set aside a percentage of their profits for exploration. (Jo. A. A.)

ENCYCLOPÆDIA BRITANNICA FILMS. *Oasis* (1965).

LIBYA

Education. (1966–67) Primary, pupils 215,841, teachers 7,278; secondary, pupils 26,846, teachers 1,807; vocational, pupils 1,064, teachers 121; teacher training, students 4,681, teachers 405; higher (at University of Libya), students 2,215, teaching staff 252.

Finance. Monetary unit: Libyan pound, with a par value of Lib£0.36 to U.S. $1 (Lib£0.86 = £1 sterling). Gold and foreign exchange, central bank: (June 1970) U.S. $1,468,500,000; (June 1969) U.S. $919.1 million. Budget (1969–70 est.) balanced at Lib£426.3 million. Gross national product: (1968) Lib£908.7 million; (1967) Lib£664.1 million. Money supply: (April 1970) Lib£211,130,000; (April 1969) Lib£173,-610,000. Cost of living (Tripoli; 1964 = 100): (March 1970) 138; (March 1969) 131.

Foreign Trade. (1969) Imports Lib£241,290,000; exports Lib£773,940,000. Import sources (1968): Italy 25%; U.S. 17%; U.K. 11%; West Germany 8%; Netherlands 5%; France 5%. Export destinations (1968): West Germany 26%; Italy 20%; U.K. 19%; France 8%; Netherlands 8%; Spain 6%; U.S. 6%. Main export crude oil 99.6%.

Transport and Communications. Roads (with improved surface; 1968) c. 5,200 km. Motor vehicles in use (1968): passenger 77,300; commercial (including buses) 35,200. Railways (1968) 165 km. Air traffic (1968): 210,774,000 passenger-km.; freight 1,934,000 net ton-km. Ships entered (1968) vessels totaling 4,674,000 net registered tons; goods loaded (1968) 124,829,000 metric tons, unloaded 3,049,000 metric tons. Telephones (Jan. 1969) 31,700. Radio receivers (Dec. 1968) 76,000.

Agriculture. Production (in 000; metric tons; 1968; 1967 in parentheses): wheat 52 (62); barley 98 (110); olives 140 (137); dates (1969) 55, (1968) 50. Livestock (in 000; 1967–68): goats 1,336; sheep (1968–69) 1,700; cattle 119; camels 232; asses 118.

Industry. Production (in 000; metric tons; 1968): salt 1; crude oil (1969) 149,188; electricity (excluding industrial and small settlements; kw-hr.) 274,000.

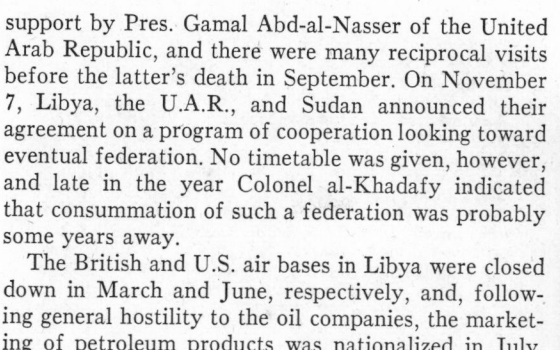

KEYSTONE
Col. Muhammad al-Khadafy, leader of the Revolutionary Command Council, became prime minister of Libya in January 1970.

Liechtenstein

An independent principality between Switzerland and Austria, Liechtenstein is united with Switzerland by a customs and monetary union. Area: 62 sq.mi. (160 sq.km.). Pop. (1969 est.): 21,758. Cap. and largest city: Vaduz (pop., 1969 est., 4,188). Language: German. Religion: 92.3% Roman Catholic. Sovereign prince, Francis Joseph II; chiefs of government in 1970, Gerard Batliner and, from March 18, Alfred Hilbe.

An electorate of slightly more than 4,000 adult

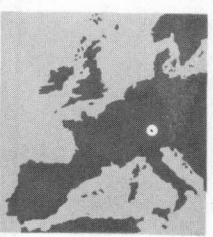

males went to the polls on Feb. 1, 1970. The elections resulted in the defeat of the Progressive Citizens' Party by the Patriotic Union, which gained a total of 8 seats in the 15-member Parliament. This was the first time in 42 years that the PCP had not been the majority party of Liechtenstein. The PCP had furnished the chief of government since 1928. After ruling alone for a decade, in 1938 it became the senior partner in a coalition government with the Patriotic Union. During the period of coalition government, the chief of the PCP served as prime minister while the head of the Patriotic Union was deputy prime minister.

The Patriotic Union plurality was a mere 40 votes. The final tabulation gave the Patriotic Union 2,018 votes; the defeated PCP, 1,978; and the minor Christian Social Party, 65. This was the first national election since the minimum voting age for adult males was reduced from 21 to 20 years in November 1969.

As a result of the loss of its majority, the five-member coalition government of Gerard Batliner submitted its resignation to the prince, who requested Alfred Hilbe, the deputy prime minister and head of the Patriotic Union, to form a new government. Hilbe took office on March 18.   (R. D. Ho.)

Literature

The 1970 Nobel Prize for Literature was awarded to Aleksandr I. Solzhenitsyn, the Soviet novelist, whose works were not being published in the U.S.S.R. (*See* Biography.)

AMERICAN

Fiction. At a time when the figures of the imagination seemed to have run off the page and into the street, when reality seemed often more fantastic and multiform than any fiction, American fiction in 1970 appeared at first glance to have run counter to the stream. The significant novels and books of stories of the year were for the most part traditional in their concerns and cast in the familiar forms of "realism." Where 1969 was marked by such innovative and highly imaginative books as Vladimir Nabokov's *Ada* and Robert Coover's *Pricksongs & Descants,* 1970 seemed almost to have been more attached to the past than to the future, to the securing of some degree of stable truth rather than bright possibility. And two of the most important novels of the year were actually written years before: Ernest Hemingway's *Islands in the Stream,* written in the early 1950s, and Vladimir Nabokov's *Mary,* a new translation into English of his first novel, *Mashenka,* which was published in Russian in 1926.

This reassertion of traditional ways of seeing and writing was most likely merely a coincidence of pub-

lishing schedules, but it may well have been also a reaction against much of the fantastic and revolutionary fiction of the last decade, a fiction that helped produce, in the words of Artur Sammler in Saul Bellow's *Mr. Sammler's Planet,* "More possibility, more actors, apes, copycats, more invention, more fiction, illusion, more fantasy, more despair." That reaction may be seen positively as a continuation of the traditional American commitment to motion and change that has been at the heart of its literature all along, from Cooper to Coover, from Emerson to Ellison. For the writers whose work seems most important in 1970, despite their use of conservative and familiar techniques of fiction, were far from creating "more despair," but rather were committed fully to life itself—painful, dark, and dangerous, but the source of all values and of all possibility.

The question, then, that was at the thematic centre of these novels and stories was simply that of what it is to be a man living and acting in a world that is beyond understanding and in which his values seem so often to drain away even as he lives by them, leaving his beliefs and his accomplishments hollow and absurd. The answers these works of fiction shape are as varied as the men and women who wrote them, but they do share a central understanding that if life itself is the source of all values, then living fully, in the face of all loss and compromise and absurdity, is the one sure moral act in a world without absolute knowing. This understanding is what Heidegger called "letting be," living with and in the flow of life rather than attempting to transcend it, finding freedom in necessity and limitation rather than in the attempt to achieve free action by a "furious motion" that denies necessity and limitation. Bellow's Mr. Sammler states this thematic centre in religious terms:

> The spirit knows that its growth is the real aim of existence.... Besides, mankind cannot be something else. It cannot get rid of itself except by an act of universal self-destruction. But it is not even for us to vote Yea or Nay.... The best, I have found, is to be disinterested. Not as misanthropes disassociate themselves, by judging, but by not judging. By willing as God wills.

The fictional textures of novels that share this com-

Eudora Welty, author of "Losing Battles," which was published in 1970.

ROLLIE MCKENNA

mitment to "letting be," with or without the explicit presence of God, must be woven from the specifics of the day and of direct experience. And out of that commitment, without falling into the traps of social realism or free fantasy, the best writers of fiction in 1970 have managed by the exercise of the imagination to change the "So it goes" of Kurt Vonnegut's recent popular novels to the traditional (and possibly more modern and timely) "So let it be."

The major novel of the year and the one that best exemplified the central methods and concerns of American fiction of the year was Hemingway's *Islands in the Stream*. And, in addition to its own size and strength, the novel is important because it is a vital extension of the structure of Hemingway's work, a body of fiction matched in quality and imaginative vigour only by the work of William Faulkner and Vladimir Nabokov in America in this century.

Islands in the Stream was written shortly after the publication of *Across the River and into the Trees* and was originally intended to be part of a larger work that was also to include *The Old Man and the Sea*. This novel shares many of the elements of both of those books, for it is the story of an aging man, lonely and increasingly alone, aware that even a winner takes nothing but also that a man who loves life and is not afraid to live "all the way up" wins finally beyond all possibility of defeat. Thomas Hudson, the central character of the novel, is, like Joyce Cary's Gulley Jimson, a painter, an artist who before all else *sees* the world and its motions and then creates a visual art not of words but of physical images. This artist's story recapitulates in its structure the thematic progression of Hemingway's earlier fiction and gives substantial form to the development of his imaginative understanding.

The first part of the novel tells of Hudson's son's initiation to the struggle and the attendant failures of successful living, a reenactment of Nick Adams' initiations in *In Our Time* or Jake Barnes's in *The Sun Also Rises*. But Hudson's son is killed soon after his initiation into full life, and the second part of the novel concerns Hudson's coming to terms with the loss of all three of his sons and with them much of his belief in life, with his learning how to live beyond hope, a reenactment of Frederic Henry's painful education in *A Farewell to Arms*. The third part tells of Thomas Hudson's going to sea and to war where he lives fully, beyond the shelter of the land or even of his art, and where he is fatally wounded, not really for his country but for life itself, a reenactment of the defeats and victories unto death of Robert Jordan in *For Whom the Bell Tolls*, Robert Cantwell in *Across the River and into the Trees*, and Santiago in *The Old Man and the Sea*.

Islands in the Stream draws all of these strands together into one structural whole, marred by Hemingway's never giving the book its final, careful rewriting, but nevertheless vital and sound. Thomas Hudson learns that the past must be cut away before it can destroy the future, but also how a dependence on the future can damage the present. The present alone must be lived. Hudson, dying, maintains his love of life, of the sea and the blue hills, of his ship and "the lovely throb of her engines," and "of the sky that he had always loved." The end of the novel looks out and up to the life that renews itself in death, the sun that sets and also rises.

The other most important novels of 1970 develop that same love and understanding in their own various ways. Thomas Berger's *Vital Parts*, the third volume of his Reinhart trilogy, which includes *Crazy in Berlin* and *Reinhart in Love*, is a comic account of Reinhart's aging into a vision of himself as a foolish and guilty failure at living. But Reinhart, because of an encounter with a freeze-therapy scheme right out of Boris Karloff's *The Man with Nine Lives* and his odd, saintly daughter Winona, chooses life beyond his old values and in spite of them. Larry McMurtry's long and subtly complex novel *Moving On* is the story of Patsy Carpenter, a young woman attempting to find her own values in the man's world of Texas. She moves from man to man as her awareness of herself and of life grows, and she finds that a loving commitment to the flesh and the moment opens the future toward which the day always moves. Eudora Welty's long-awaited new novel, *Losing Battles*, takes place on a day in which the past breaks openly into the present, when loss seems to outweigh all that has been gained from the lost past. But the novel ends at high noon when the "sun came out as if for good."

Darker in tone and more directly painful, Saul Bellow's *Mr. Sammler's Planet* is a religious development of the manner and matter of his earlier *Herzog*. Artur Sammler, a Jewish intellectual who literally clawed his way out of the grave in a German concentration camp, finds the values he struggled to live for fading in contemporary America. In a world and life in which reason seems to have failed, Mr. Sammler finds his answer in love and in obligation, in doing "what is required of him" by those who love him, by God. And, in a curious way, James Dickey's raw and violent *Deliverance* offers the same understanding. The past is and must be buried. The worst and deadliest beast in the world lives in each man's heart, and a man is delivered from the horror of that truth perhaps only by knowing it fully, by being fully what he really is with all defenses other than the bared fang gone. In both novels ugliness prevails, but the human heart continues to beat as each new day comes.

And there were other fine novels. Richard Yates's first novel since *Revolutionary Road*, *A Special Providence*, and Sylvia Wilkinson's third novel, *Cale*, are moving and perceptive accounts of a young man's growing into himself in the shadow of a strongly individual mother. James Purdy's *Jeremy's Version* is the first volume of a projected trilogy, *Sleepers in Moon-Crowned Valleys*, in which he abandons the surreal to return to the towns of the Midwest of his youth. And two novels by young writers deserve a place: *Man in Motion*, an unpretentious first novel by Michael Mewshaw, and *Something in the Wind*, a fine second novel by Lee Smith.

No new books of stories could compare to Coover's exciting collection of the year before, but three interesting volumes did appear: David Madden's lively *The Shadow Knows*, Reynolds Price's highly unified studies of the moment of wrong choice in a number of lives, *Permanent Errors*, and W. S. Merwin's curiously dissatisfying collection of Borgesian fictions, *The Miner's Pale Children*.   (R. H. W. D.)

Biography and Memoirs. Of all the biographical and autobiographical writings published in 1970, the most memorable was Philip B. Kunhardt's *My Father's House*, not because it dealt with a world-mover or because the style of the book was "different." Kunhardt's memoir of his father was a frank paean to a good man, and one finished reading it with the sense that the book had been really written (as wood is whittled or stone carved) and not simply typed.

COURTESY, KNOPF

Michael Crichton, author of "Five Patients," published in 1970.

COURTESY, RANDOM HOUSE

Philip Kunhardt, author of "My Father's House," which was published in 1970.

ARTHUR TCHOLAKIAN

William Saroyan published "Days of Life and Death and Escape to the Moon" in 1970.

Similar honesty characterized James V. Bennett's *I Chose Prison*. Based admittedly on Bennett's life as a prison administrator, the book combined anecdotal accounts with pleas for penal reform, including an outright dismissal of the argument that capital punishment is a deterrent to "rape, kidnapping, armed robbery, or most homicides."

Another look at a profession from within the profession by a professional was Michael Crichton's *Five Patients*. More than case histories, Crichton's accounts of the hospitalization of three men and two women are interwoven with such telling comments as: "In fact, the most common early, immediate, direct cause of death from surgery is not the operation but the anesthesia" and "the current administrative structure of medical schools appears incapable of curtailing the curriculum" required for the education of doctors.

Two noteworthy biographies were Nancy Milford's *Zelda*, a long, detailed, and seemingly endless account of the haunted woman who was F. Scott Fitzgerald's wife, and Michael Arlen's *Exiles*, an otherwise incidental book were it not for Arlen's sense of style and his understanding of the torment of his exiled parents.

William Saroyan's *Days of Life and Death and Escape to the Moon* emerged as an elaborate log rather than a perfunctorily kept diary. Regardless, it contained some of Saroyan's best prose. Saroyan's standard for each essay-entry is utter honesty:

> From a swift young man delighting in new clothes, moving everywhere with noise and laughter, I became a sloppy old man in old clothes with a careless posture and a lazy walk going nowhere. . . ; [or] It isn't because I am in my sixty-first year that I take particular interest in the daily dead, some of whom I know (Paul Muni, John Steinbeck, Upton Sinclair), it's simply that noticing death is a fact, and indeed an act, of survival.

Saroyan is at home in this genre, and the result is vintage Saroyan.

James MacGregor Burns's *Roosevelt: The Soldier of Freedom, 1940–1945* is the concluding volume of his biography of Franklin D. Roosevelt. Documenting Roosevelt's leadership from the pre-Pearl Harbor period through the two-ocean war and the various conferences (Cairo, Teheran, and Yalta), Burns tracks the enigma of Roosevelt to the final hours in Warm Springs, Ga. The documentation is definitive and formidable, but suffusing and enlivening it is the steady force of Burns's personality, never intrusive but always sufficiently present to save the prose from becoming "objective." The epilogue (dealing with the death, rites, and burial of the president) is as much a tribute to the poet in Burns as to the historian.

The Princeton University Press's publication of *A Thoreau Gazetteer* appeared not only as a biographical companion to Thoreau's prose but as a harbinger (and a formidable one) of that press's projected 20-volume series of Thoreau's complete works, to be edited by Walter Harding. A deserved biography of Nathanael West was written by Jay Martin with the appropriate subtitle *The Art of His Life*. Each of the plots of the small, tight, and excellent shelf of West's novels receives its long overdue due.

Lawrence Thompson's *Robert Frost: The Years of Triumph, 1915–1938* was a further documentation, if absolutely true, of the cleavage between Robert Frost the poet (wise, tolerant, flinty, and folkishly perceptive) and Robert Frost the man (testy, jealous, vindictive, and egotistical).

World Affairs and General Interest. The most urbane, acerbic, and wittily incisive book on international politics in 1970 was Miles Copeland's *The Game of Nations*. Tracing the pragmatism and shortsightedness of U.S. foreign policy vis-à-vis the U.A.R., Copeland demonstrates the combination of paternalism, moralism, and outright folly (the famous Tower of Cairo, for example, was built because the Egyptians and Americans had nothing more ostentatious to do with $3 million) of our dealings with less developed nations. If Jonathan Swift were alive and writing on foreign affairs today, he would be Miles Copeland, but anyone interested in further investigation of the Middle East would be well advised to consult Jon Kimche's *The Second Arab Awakening* as a companion to Copeland's chapters.

Every occupation needs or creates its devil's disciples, its gadflies, its prods, and Robert Townsend served all these purposes for the American corporation in *Up the Organization*. Perhaps the inherent desire of corporate workers to understand their circumstances contributed to the wide sale of this book, but it is ultimately the *Poor Richard's Almanack* of modern business—no more, not much less. Dale Carnegie flattered readers into opportunistic armies that went out to win friends and influence people; Townsend simply scolds and talks shop, but the desired results are identical—the most lucrative kind of survival.

Two of the best postmortems of the administration of Pres. Lyndon B. Johnson and its Southeast Asia policies were George Christian's *The President Steps Down* and Townsend Hoopes's *The Limits of Intervention*. Christian's book has all the benefits and few of the blind spots of a book written by an administration insider (Christian was Johnson's press secretary from 1966 to 1969). Like many others who worked closely with the former president, Christian insists that the private Johnson was much more personable than the public Johnson—a curious and enigmatic characteristic for such a gregarious public figure. Hoopes's account of the progress (or regress) of U.S. Indochina policy simply and amply documents the obvious, concluding with a postscript that calls complete withdrawal "the only practical course open to the United States."

By far the most challenging book published in 1970 on U.S. domestic problems was Andrew Hacker's *The End of the American Era.* Hacker scrutinizes the benign and malignant tumours of the United States in passing (c. 1950–70), and, what is most important, passes judgment on them. In other words, subjects that most Americans merely think about, Hacker thinks through and, for better or worse, comes to defensible and often disgruntling conclusions about the new American:

> The puritan catechism, with its emphasis on the deferral of gratifications and the avoidance of indulgence, formed the childhood lessons of most modern adults. The difficulty is that the puritan ethic was made for an era of scarcity. Temptation could be avoided if it was seldom available. But affluence encourages promiscuity: not only in sex, but in the accumulation of the amenities which comfort the body and stimulate the senses.

The fact that Hacker's conclusions may or may not conform to what passes for collective thought in America is beside the point. What is undeniable is that this is the result of one man's concentrated attention on some of the most pressing issues on the American agenda, and that is quite enough. There are some books published each year that cannot be ignored; Hacker's is one of them.

ARTHUR SCHATZ, "LIFE" MAGAZINE © TIME INC.

Robert C. Townsend, former Avis executive and top organization man, turned his back on it all with his lampoon of big business, "Up the Organization," published in 1970.

Poetry. It is a truism to say that the test of poetry is neither "timeliness" nor "idiosyncrasy." But there were so many timely and idiosyncratic versifiers writing in 1970 that the truism needed to be said. After all, the significant poet is not a mere information-giver; his test is simply to try to understand his own experience and then express it so that others can feel it as their own. Three collections by poets aware of this criterion appeared in 1970: William Meredith's *Earth Walk,* David Ignatow's *Poems: 1934–1969,* and Philip Booth's *Margins.* Meredith's book includes selections from his out-of-print early works as well as new poems, and the entire collection is prefaced with a brief and modest introduction that should be required reading for all writers to whom talent and egotism are identical. Spanning four decades of poetic effort, Ignatow's book testifies to that kind of artist who aims at consistency of effort rather than a one-shot burst of brilliancy. Booth remains the same spare and accomplished poet he was in his first book, good from the start and able to maintain it.

More of May Swenson's shape-poems appeared in *Iconographs.* Some critics make careful distinctions between Miss Swenson's shape-poems, puzzle-poems, and straight poems, but the only test of poetry is ulti-

mately whether it is poetry and May Swenson's poems, in any shape, are.

The appearance of James Dickey's *The Eye-Beaters, Blood, Victory, Madness, Buckhead and Mercy* was somewhat obscured by the reception given his first novel, *Deliverance,* but his new poems, though below the quality of *Drowning with Others* and some of the best poems in *Buckdancer's Choice,* still proved that Dickey can tell a story poetically rather than writing mere narrative verse.

Of new books by new poets, Shirley Kaufman's *The Floor Keeps Turning* improved with each rereading, not merely because Mrs. Kaufman knows the how of writing a good poem (she does) but because this how does not impede the poetic impulse. These are not feminine poems in the Rossetti-Millay sense, yet they never lose the womanliness of their author. Mrs. Kaufman won the International Poetry Forum's United States Award for this book. Michael Harper's *Dear John, Dear Coltrane* shows how poems by a black American—like Lucille Clifton in *Good Times* —can go beyond racial consciousness, beyond rage, beyond bitterness.

Denise Levertov's *Relearning the Alphabet* maintained the level of *The Sorrow Dance* and her translations of Guillevic. The Wesleyan University poets in 1970 were Clarence Major, William Harmon, Michael Benedikt, Charles Wright, James Seay, and Charles Levendosky.

John Ashbery's *The Double Dream of Spring* testified to his continuing sensitivity to the graceful that is inherent in the fairly commonplace.

To See, To Take was a memorable performance by Mona Van Duyn. If there is such a thing as brave poetry (as opposed to poems calculated merely to shock), then Miss Van Duyn has written a brave book. Mark Strand's *Darker* was notable for his willingness to experiment beyond the good claims he had already established with his earlier *Reasons for Moving.* And W. S. Merwin's *The Carrier of Ladders* was as good as Merwin can be, which, after *The Lice, The Moving Target,* and the earlier books, is very good indeed.

No chronicle of books of poems printed in 1970 could avoid including Louise Bogan's *A Poet's Alphabet* or Stanley Burnshaw's *The Seamless Web.* Miss Bogan's selected criticism proves that she was as judicious a critic as she was a poet, while Burnshaw considers everything from the writer's vision of the world to the importance of the oral presentation of poetry, hopefully by the poets themselves.   (SA. H.)

CANADIAN

English Language. Canadian fiction in 1970 reflected major socioeconomic and political disparities in the country, including the problems of Canada's native Indian and Eskimo minorities and the gulf between the language cultures, French and English. In her novella *Windflower,* Gabrielle Roy gave a compassionate study of a simple Eskimo girl and her blonde, blue-eyed, American-fathered son, who fled his primitive heritage in the North. Mort Forer's *The Humback* was a chilling picture of a Métis settlement in Manitoba whose environment and economy were both out of step with the 20th century. The cultural gulf separating Canada's founding peoples was exemplified in Roch Carrier's *La Guerre, Yes Sir!* (originally published in French), which depicted a confrontation of an Anglo-Saxon honour guard with the French-Canadian family and friends of a dead

COURTESY, VIKING PRESS

Philip Booth is the author of "Margins: A Sequence of New and Selected Poems," published in 1970.

COURTESY, MACMILLAN OF CANADA

Robertson Davies published "Fifth Business" in 1970.

soldier at his brawling wake. Disparity was equally evident in the sordid poverty and brutalized childhood described in Marie-Claire Blais's *The Manuscripts of Pauline Archange.*

In a lighter vein, Robert Kroetsch's *The Studhorse Man* was a ribald safari across Alberta of a man and his stallion, each looking for the perfect mate. Mavis Gallant's *A Fairly Good Time* presented an open-hearted Canadian girl living in Paris who attracts problem people while her own personal life remains an emotional shambles. Richard Wright wrote a funny first novel, *The Weekend Man,* which displayed vigorous imagination. *The Honeyman Festival,* by Marian Engel, was set in Toronto, and Hugh Hood's *A Game of Touch* in Montreal. The first described a woman on the verge of middle age, frustrated by an unsatisfactory marriage; and the second a young man wide-eyed and willing to embrace the whole new big-city world. *Fifth Business,* by Robertson Davies, was a masterly account of how Dunstan Ramsey became attracted to saints and magicians in the course of his eventful life as history master in a boys' private school.

Joan Finnigan's *It Was Warm and Sunny When We Set Out* contained poems that recounted the heart's progress from sorrow to strength, and from despair to hope. Gail Fox, in *Dangerous Season,* presented evocative mood poems of persuasive imagery in which nature translates the poet's experience. John Glassco's *The Poetry of French Canada in Translation* was an anthology of French-Canadian poems translated by English-speaking poets. Harry Howith wrote *Fragments of the Dance,* deeply moving poems of love, loss, time that heals, and time that does not.

The Solitary City by R. A. D. Ford, the Canadian ambassador to the U.S.S.R., contained rich emotional poems in exotic settings and translations of modern Russian and Portuguese poems. Robert Evans collected Canadian songs and poems in *Song to a Seagull.* The poems included some by E. J. Pratt, Al Purdy, Leonard Cohen, and others. The songs, such as those by Gordon Lightfoot, Ian Tyson, and Joni Mitchell, were all chosen for their poetic lyrics. Short notes about the contributors and the songs were given, as well as bibliographies and lists of recordings.

John Glassco's *Memoirs of Montparnasse* described Paris as experienced by a young man. Disarming candour and a graceful style and flair made the book a success.

Robert Speaight's *Vanier: Soldier, Diplomat and Governor General* was written in great detail, interspersing much of Canada's recent history in a thoroughly readable account of Canada's first French-Canadian governor-general. Donald Creighton's interpretation of the last 100 years, *Canada's First Century, 1867–1967,* provided interesting second looks at some of Canada's political figures, and offered an assessment of some of the centrifugal forces at work in Canada leading to its present dilemmas. An interesting companion volume was George Woodcock's *Canada and the Canadians.* Canadians face to face with the physical and political realities of their North American environment, and Canadians seen in socioeconomic and psychological terms were the concerns of this volume. Pierre Berton's *The Great Railway, 1871–1881* was a lively look at the conception and building of the Canadian Pacific Railway.

As with many others in the world, Canadians were becoming concerned with their environment. In many cases, a resurgent nationalism underlay this concern. Donald Waterfield's *Continental Waterboy* was an articulate and sad chronicle of the events preceding and following the signing of the Columbia River Treaty. Jim Lotz, a biologist with St. Paul University in Ottawa, wrote, in *Northern Realities,* an intensely interesting account of Canada's Yukon Territory, its problems of climate, its delicate ecology, and the difficulties of administration in this multiracial, sparsely populated area.

Farley Mowat's *Sibir: My Discovery of Siberia* was a chatty personal account of two recent journeys to Siberia. Well acquainted with Arctic regions, Mowat observed sympathetically, yet objectively, the peoples of Siberia and the Soviet development of the north.

Peter Mellen prepared *The Group of Seven,* a full-length record and critical evaluation of this well-known Canadian group of painters. Moshe Safdie, who designed the pyramidal apartment complex for Expo 67 in Montreal, published his ideas on architecture in *Beyond Habitat. Canadian Art: Vital Decades* by Paul Duval and A. J. Casson dealt with the development of Canadian painting.

Margaret Laurence, a well-known Canadian novelist, wrote her first book for children and young people, *Jason's Quest,* one of few Canadian books of fantasy. Unlikely companions—a mole seeking a cure for the malaise of Molanium, an owl searching for wisdom, and two cats wishing to prove the nobility of their kind—set forth on a quest. The animal world mirroring the human world and "all sorts and condition of men" also reflected human emotions and philosophy, trials, and endeavour.

More Glooscap Stories by Kay Hill was a collection of 18 tales based on the Wabanaki Indians of Eastern Canada. The stories of adventure, magic, and humour were told with simple dignity and could be enjoyed by folklorists and storytellers as well as children.   (H. C. Cl.)

French Language. One remarkable aspect of a very rich year for the novel was the number of well-known novelists who published after a few years of absence: Jean Simard with *La Séparation*, Gabrielle Roy with *La Rivière sans repos*, and Pierre Dagenais with *Le Feu sacré*. Others who continued to publish regularly were Yves Thériault with *Le Dernier havre*, Marie-Claire Blais with *Les Apparences*, Jean Basile with *Les Voyages d'Irkoutsk*, and Jacques Ferron with *L'Amélanchier*. A list of the best novels in these numerous titles would include *L'Amélanchier* and *La Rivière sans repos*, plus the work of a newcomer, Jacques Folch-Ribas, whose *Le Démolisseur* was an indication of a great talent.

The best poetry book of the year was probably *L'Homme Rapaillé*, a "somme" of the poems of Gaston Miron, who had influenced many poets but had never published a book. Yves Préfontaine, after several years of silence, published *Débâcle* and *À l'Orée des travaux*. After a longer silence, Fernand Dumont returned with *Parler de septembre*. Also of interest in 1970 were *Manifeste de l'Infonie* by Raoul Duguay, a poet, musician, and singer; *Suite logique* by Nicole Brossard; and *Les Mangeurs de terre* by Louis-Philippe Hébert. "La nuit de la poésie," an event organized in May by a group of poets from Montreal, where poets from different corners of French Canada recited their poetry before an audience of over 2,000 in the Théâtre du Gesu, did not finish before seven in the morning.

Fewer literary essays were published than in 1969, but of those that were some were outstanding: *Les Actes retrouvés* by Fernand Ouellette, *Jacques Ferron malgré lui* by Jean Marcel, and *Le Réel et le théâtral* by Naïm Kattan. Also significant was Gilles Marcotte's edition of the *Histoire de la littérature française* of Berthelot Brunet.

Other essayists were working in the social sciences and history. French-Canadian history from 1760 to 1840 would not have any secrets from anybody very soon. Following Fernand Ouellette's publication in 1966 of a *Histoire économique et sociale du Québec, 1760–1850*, in 1970 Henri Brun published *La Formation des institutions parlementaires québécoises, 1791–1838*; Maurice Séguin, *La Nation canadienne et l'agriculture, 1760–1850*; Gilles Bourque, *Question nationale et classes sociales, 1760–1840*; and Claude Galarneau, *La France devant l'opinion canadienne, 1760–1815*. One had the impression that only this part of the history was interesting. However, other works in the field were *La Dialectique de l'objet économique* by Fernand Dumont and *L'Histoire de Montréal* by Robert Rumilly.   (AD. T.)

DANISH

An otherwise relatively quiet year for Danish literature provided the background for one literary sensation. When one of the country's most outstanding writers, the virtuoso novelist Klaus Rifbjerg, published his novel *Marts 1970*, eyebrows were raised, less on account of its aesthetic quality than because of its sociological impact. The very opposite of a roman à clef, all the characters in it bore the real names of the models upon whom they were based. Farcical and farfetched, and very funny in parts, it tells how Crown Princess Margrethe, the heir to the Danish throne, and the Swedish prime minister, Olof Palme, embark on a daring love affair in Copenhagen. Various other well-known personalities both great and small figure in the intrigue, though they, too, are

gross caricatures. For a time there was a public debate as to whether this sort of book could be justified.

One person ridiculed in Rifbjerg's novel was a fellow author, Peter Seeberg, who was awarded the critics' prize of the year for his novel *Hyrder*. The title alludes to the idea of self-sacrifice, which appears in many different guises. The action starts with a road accident and describes the various reactions to it on the part of the victim's closest relatives. The book's "message" is a defense of a sober, independent individuality in an age when all sorts of would-be leaders are seeking to herd sheep into their own moral or ideological folds. In contrast to Seeberg's muted pessimism was a book by the older writer William Heinesen. His *Don Juan fra Tranhuset* was a collection of short stories from his native Faeroe Islands, dramatic, demonic, and mythical in nature. There were cosmic overtones to these realistic stories of the strange behaviour of people living in the narrow fishing milieu of Denmark's North Atlantic province. Leif E. Christensen's experimental novel *Drejebogen* took a critical look at the role of the first person and the first-person novel in European tradition.

In contrast to these, Christian Kampmann's novel *Vi elsker mere* represented the new moral realism that had made its mark in recent years. This, too, dealt with the theme of roles, but was not experimental in form. It was concerned with the social roles that modern city dwellers attribute to each other and adopt toward each other. Kampmann portrays modern manners and shows that present-day life with its glossy surface, its facade of liberalism and permissiveness, lacks inner maturity.

Thorkild Hansen, the author of *Det lykkelige Arabien*, finished his vast work on the former Danish colonies with *Slavernes øer*. The concluding volume of this gigantic historical epic on a confused chapter in Danish cultural history was set in the West Indian islands that Denmark sold in 1917.

In the field of poetry, some outstanding modernists of the 1950s and 1960s, such as Thorkild Bjørnvig, Jess Ørnsbo, and Ivan Malinovski, published their collected or selected works. Malinovski, a social revolutionary poet, was awarded the Danish Academy's major prize for 1970.   (NI. B.)

ENGLISH

Prose. It was an inauspicious start to the decade, with life pressing hard on literature, and more than a hint of "Things fall apart; the centre cannot hold." At times the sense of an ending became almost apocalyptic. Two great survivors of the English liberal enlightenment, Bertrand Russell and E. M. Forster (*see* OBITUARIES), finally took their leave. There was a serious outbreak of mourning for the death of the novel; John Wain wrote, in *The Listener* of August 6, the obituary of "the age of criticism," signaling the breakdown of the sense of tradition among the educated young to whom, suddenly, the notion of the present as being nourished by the past no longer seemed natural; and, finally, George Steiner's direly persuasive essay in the *Times Literary Supplement* (*TLS*) on October 2 might almost have been called "The End of the Book," although its actual title was "Classic Culture and Post-Culture," the latter being the condition on whose brink we teeter, since "high culture, in the classic sense, is now becoming obsolete."

All Steiner could foresee for the novel was an "after-life" in which "a nostalgic or parodistic anima-

COURTESY FABER & FABER
Theodore Roszak published "The Making of a Counter-Culture: Reflections on the Technocratic Society and Its Youthful Opposition" in 1970.

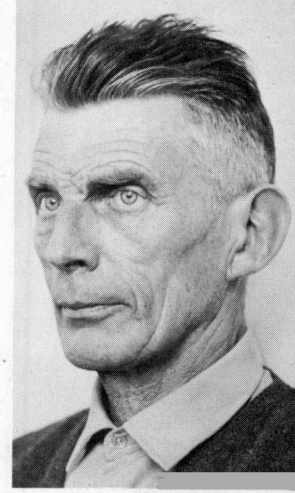

JERRY BAUER
Samuel Beckett, 1969 Nobel Prize winner, published his parable "Lessness" in 1970.

tion may continue." At present it survived most purely in the pungent brevities of Luis Borges and the dry parables of Samuel Beckett (one of which, *Lessness,* a characteristically bleached and enigmatic fragment, appeared in September). Otherwise, one could observe on all hands "the powerful diffusion of fictional techniques into non- and part-fiction." Norman Mailer, the representative case of the writer in all this flux, appropriately appeared in London in the autumn not with a new book but with a film that was itself part parody of the author's narcissistic confusion of his real and imaginary lives. There was thus a widespread and grudging recognition that we were in the middle of a period of major cultural change. Among rearguard actions few fought so intelligently as Storm Jameson in her short, sharply critical survey of the current state of fiction, *Parthian Words.*

Other critics, disposed to see change under a less fearful aspect, considered the "New Romanticism" more optimistically: Alex Comfort, for example, in his review of Theodore Roszak's *The Making of a Counter-Culture: Reflections on the Technocratic Society and Its Youthful Opposition.* "Primitives treat things and animals as human, and experience feedback from them," wrote Comfort. "We treat people as things or animals and attempt to manipulate them." The disparity between humanness and this attitude, he suggested, was at the root of the current revolution in sensibility, and Roszak was a cool, sympathetic, and literate guide to how it was happening.

Fiction. One emblematic ending, C. P. Snow's *Last Things,* the 11th volume in his "Strangers and Brothers" sequence, concluded 30 years of work on the novel. It was received with a certain rather melancholy respect, Snow's novels having been regarded for some time as works of and from history, best when most plainly chronicling; the concluding episode, with some richly plotted student politics and an operation for a detached retina that nearly sees Lewis Eliot off altogether, did not alter the general view. Certainly, one could not imagine novels of this neo-Trollopian kind ever being written with any real success or conviction again.

History, however, provides one refuge from the problem of finding a fictional mode with which to handle contemporary reality. It may be treated directly, as in *Joseph,* Mervyn Jones's cold fictional portrait of Stalin, and Michael Hastings' ambitious

but often tactless attempt on the life of Eleanor Marx, *Tussy Is Me;* or used as Dan Jacobson used a biblical story in *The Rape of Tamar* as a model through which to examine and reflect upon what a writer does in his work. This last was one novel of the year, at least, that would require and repay reading again. Among more conventional historical novels, *Fire from Heaven,* based on the life of the young Alexander the Great, was a fine example of the careful, richly detailed art of Mary Renault.

Three of the *grandes dames* of the English novel produced new works. Iris Murdoch's *A Fairly Honourable Defeat* lacked the depth and density of her previous year's offering (*Bruno's Dream*), and made some readers impatient. Here once more, wrote the *TLS* reviewer, were characters "treated with the interested, speculative, but ultimately neutral attention that is given to acquaintances about whom one gossips but for whom one does not really care." Some reactions to Muriel Spark's new novella, *The Driver's Seat,* seemed compounded of awe at her skill in doing and shock at what was so deliberately done— in this case self-murder (the archaism is apt) with another's hands, the real victim being the instrument of the crime, so carefully chosen, so ruthlessly compelled to act. It is a sickening consummation, obliging the reader to contemplate, with what steadiness he can, the connection between what is consummate and what is sickening. Some critical gazes were steady enough, however, not to say cool. "Muriel Spark," observed Gillian Tindall in the *New Statesman,* "has what one might call a lively interest in death"; and the *TLS* reviewer, after noting that "it will take you 60 minutes to read and cost you sixpence a minute," detected something of Antonioni's planned randomness in the method, and concluded "no doubt it is a great technical triumph to write a brief novel as irritating as a very long film."

The Honours Board, Pamela Hansford Johnson's extended foray into the world of the preparatory school, in spite of its suicidal French mistress and Lesbian matron, provoked no such discomfort and was widely thought to be a good read of a very superior kind, as was *The Backward Shadow,* Lynne Reid Banks's sequel to her immensely successful *The L-Shaped Room.* There was perhaps more real creative originality in *When Did You Last See Your Father,* the second of Margaret Blount's novels to produce scenes from a provincial girlhood with rare tact and emotional intelligence. Edna O'Brien's return to childhood haunts in *A Pagan Place* was a less engrossing journey. What Brigid Brophy once called Miss O'Brien's "Synge-song" went to a tune altogether too fey and fanciful this time; and her "experimental" notion of writing the whole thing in the second person singular gave the *TLS* an opening for one of its notorious punning headlines: "Have done with you."

A very different report of vanished youth was *The Hand-Reared Boy,* Brian Aldiss' bright and breezy first installment of the life and times of Horatio Stubbs, prewar English schoolboy and epic masturbator: England's answer to Portnoy, someone must have said. Two mellowing iconoclasts of the 1950s, John Braine and John Wain, produced novels that were calmly received, the former's *Stay with Me till Morning* confirming its author as the more gifted survivor from the age of late naturalism. Wain's *A Winter in the Hills* was overpopulated with lay figures speaking their Welsh accents like English repertory actors.

Muriel Spark, whose novella "The Driver's Seat" was published in 1970.

JERRY BAUER

From that brilliant creator of imaginary landscapes, J. G. Ballard, there was *The Atrocity Exhibition,* a cut-up representation of contemporary consciousness, ardently of the school of William Burroughs—a mistaken departure, many of his admirers thought, though Ballard said he saw no other way for a novelist with seeing eyes and a mind behind them. *The Bodyguard,* by the poet Adrian Mitchell, projected present disturbances 15 years on, creating with a kind of ruthless puritan energy a very nasty society indeed (yet given the novel's plainly political impulse, there was some point to William Trevor's complaint that Mitchell had a great deal to say about the Fascist Eurocratic Establishment but curiously little about the revolutionaries who seem to have worked i' the earth well enough by the end). C. J. Driver's *Send War in Our Time, O Lord* was a more coolly composed but no less grim vision of the harsh future of southern Africa.

Two other novels generally admired were Paul Bailey's study of personal and social breakdown, *Trespasses,* and Roy Fuller's *The Carnal Island,* a portrait of an aging poet that reflected many of the dominant preoccupations of his own poetry. There were also worthwhile collections of short stories by an old hand, Frank Tuohy (*Fingers in the Door and Other Stories*), and a newcomer, Giles Gordon (*Pictures from an Exhibition*).

Nonfiction. After the series of major autobiographical works that were a feature of the 1960s—most notably Russell's and Leonard Woolf's—1970 seemed a poor year for Lives. The only link with those magisterial records was the first volume of Julian Huxley's *Memories,* a simply written account of the great biologist and educator's family life and work. There was one first-class historical biography, Christopher Hill's brilliantly convincing study of Oliver Cromwell, *God's Englishman,* packed with information and splendid quotations, and an interesting and useful piece of demythologizing by Robert Rhodes James, whose *Churchill: A Study in Failure, 1900–1939* was thought by Robert Skidelsky to be "a formidable indictment of a man repeatedly convicted of erratic judgment and inconsistency of purpose."

The Diplomatic Diaries of Oliver Harvey (Harvey was Eden's and then Halifax's private secretary in the late 1930s) had the great merit, as A. J. P. Taylor said in his *Observer* review, of being an immediate record of events in those miserable years and of Foreign Office reactions to them, and not, like some other diaries, "a demonstration of how much wiser he was than anyone else." A diarist of the latter category, according to Taylor, was the great *Guardian* editor C. P. Scott, whose *Political Diaries* nevertheless presented a remarkably close picture of Lloyd George and of the disintegration of the Liberal Party. John Lewis' engagingly naïve history of *The Left Book Club* had some value as the fullest record yet of that most remarkable episode in the modern history of political education in Britain.

A fine example of the kind of specialized history that laymen can read with pleasure and profit was provided once more by Richard Cobb in his essays on *The Police and the People: French Popular Protest, 1789–1820,* which, as E. J. Hobsbawn said in his *Listener* review, "throws light on the nature of policemen and bureaucracies everywhere" and was compulsively readable in the bargain. A massive and less fashionable piece of specialized history, Arthur J. Marder's study of the Royal Navy in the Lord

Fisher era, *From the Dreadnought to Scapa Flow,* was splendidly concluded with the publication of its fifth volume, *Victory and Aftermath.*

The year's literary-critical focus, the centenary of the death of Charles Dickens, provoked many specialist studies of varying quality, but also one magnificent general critical work and one outstanding novelist's tribute. Angus Wilson paid the personal tribute of a direct heir of Dickens' art in *The World of Charles Dickens,* a work whose most memorable parts, as Raymond Williams said, were essentially a re-creation of his master's imaginative world. Inevitably, the occasion made British intellectual life look more incestuous than usual, with most of the contributors to the celebrations reviewing each other's work. Angus Wilson reviewed *Dickens the Novelist,* by F. R. and Q. D. Leavis, in the *Observer* and thought that it showed more clearly than ever Leavis' "supreme merit" as a critic of novels: "his power to read, to read more carefully and with fewer preconceptions than any other critic I know of (except his wife)." Gabriel Pearson also remarked the emergence of Mrs. Leavis "as a major critic in her own right." The book also contained, however, a measure of the rancorous and selective treatment of other critics which is unfortunately also a recurring feature of Leavis' public style.

Raymond Williams' *The English Novel from Dickens to Lawrence* was a less direct contribution, which Angus Wilson (writing this time in the *Guardian*) thought "a splendid corrective to the widespread academic urge to separate literature from life"; the *TLS* reviewer found it "less a critical study of fiction than a personal proclamation of commitment." Richard Hoggart collected his essays and lectures of the 1960s in two volumes called *Speaking to Each Other,* the first subtitled "About Society" and the second "About Literature." Another excellent reconciler of literature and life, D. J. Enright, took on some of the more schematic academic critics of Shakespeare in *Shakespeare and the Students.*

Other critical works worth recalling were P. N. Furbank's lucid and mind-clearing *Reflections on the World "Image"* and Michael Hamburger's useful international roundup of modern poetry, *The Truth of Poetry.* Two poets of a certain age and eminence produced characteristic prose works coinciding only in a sharp distaste for academic criticism: Geoffrey Grigson's *Notes from an Odd Country* (lively meditations from a second home in central France) and George Barker's *Essays,* often provoking and sententious, but sometimes very funny and pleasurable too.

William Shawcross contributed some interesting details in his biography of *Dubcek.* Anthony Grey's *Hostage in Peking* told a story more interesting on the whole for its revelation of one man's techniques for survival than for the rather restricted view of his captors and their turbulent society. Philip Mason's weighty and wide-ranging study of racial domination, *Patterns of Dominance,* was, wrote V. G. Kiernan, "fascinating as a social study, and urgently practical in its warnings of race problems up and down the globe." Andrew Roth's *Enoch Powell: Tory Tribune* identified the deep strains out of which "Powellism" had emerged, and made plain, as Anthony Howard said in the *New Statesman,* that its subject had not only "bucked the Tory establishment —he also in his own person today threatens the whole established pattern of interparty combat."

It was not fears of racialism, however, that con-

ANTHONY GARRETT

Angus Wilson marked the centenary of the death of Charles Dickens with the publication in 1970 of "The World of Charles Dickens."

CAMERA PRESS FROM PIX

C. P. Snow's "Last Things," the 11th and concluding volume of his "Strangers and Brothers" sequence, was published in 1970.

tributed most to the apocalyptic overtones of much new reading in 1970 but the growing list of works on the dangers of ecological disturbance. The very first day of the year saw the publication of Max Nicholson's *The Environmental Revolution,* bluntly indicating man as "a major and menacing delinquent element in nature." This was rapidly followed by Desmond King-Hele's ambiguously titled *The End of the 20th Century?,* with its quietly appalled computations of likely population levels and its insider's awareness that "scientists are always overcautious and always underestimate the speed with which new knowledge can affect the world." Gordon Rattray Taylor's *The Doomsday Book,* however, left Alex Comfort contemplating the dilemma of "a new danger that public militancy, which we badly need, will be overalarmed and generate mischievous environmental demagogues." Probably the most useful addition to this literature was the admirably ordered assembly of facts and issues coolly identified by Paul and Anne Ehrlich in their book *Population: Resources: Environment.*

Finally there was the huge collaborative enterprise of the *New English Bible,* completed at last, an entirely new translation from the earliest texts. Everyone brought up on the King James Bible would be disturbed by some of the alterations. Although there were immediately things to admire and others to understand for the first time, it would be some time before the common reader could recognize confidently what the *TLS* reviewer found: "a new kind of beauty . . . the beauty of rightness." (*See* RELIGION: *Special Report.*)　　　　　　　　　　　　　　　(W. L. WE.)

Poetry. Liveliness in approach, richness of expression, and variety in ideas and techniques, together with a record number of volumes produced by large and small publishers alike, were undoubtedly the distinguishing features of poetry in 1970. Some remarkably competent first collections, free from any signs of group influences, introduced several promising young poets to the literary scene, as if the beginning of a new decade had opened the way for individual lines of development.

Storm Jameson published "Parthian Words," a critical survey of the present state of fiction, in 1970.

JERRY BAUER

Perhaps the most stimulating of these first volumes were Christopher Pilling's *Snakes and Girls,* which won the New Poets Award sponsored by Leeds University and the *Yorkshire Post,* and Tony Harrison's *The Loiners,* in which sexual wit, controlled energy, lively intelligence, and robustness of outlook combined to offer clear evidence of an exciting new talent. In *Circe* Stuart Montgomery provided an attractively fresh version of Homer's account of the island affair between Ulysses and the enchantress, while in *Neighbours* Glyn Hughes dealt, somewhat sardonically yet without loading the dice unduly against his characters, with the bleaker scene known to the farmers and mill hands of the Yorkshire-Lancashire borderland. Ian Hamilton, who had previously established a reputation for his admirable editorship of *The Review,* displayed his own delicate craftsmanship in *The Visit* by the manner in which he contrived to set up a tension between detachment and personal involvement in such poems as "Funeral" and "Birthday Poems."

More uncertain, but nevertheless worthy of note, were *The Wife of Winter* by Michael Dennis Browne, *My Findings* by Frederick Broadie, and the keenly observed *Poems from Italy* by R. H. Bowden. Mary Wilson, wife of the former British prime minister, was widely praised for the natural simplicity and warmth of her *Selected Poems,* and if her volume could hardly be described as the "best of the year" it was easily the "best selling"—though critics suggested that the extraordinary demand for her book might have been due to its possibilities for private and extraliterary revelations rather than its poetic qualities.

A number of established poets added substantially to their growing reputations. In *A Crow Hymn,* for instance, Ted Hughes created a semi-mythological but monstrous bird protagonist who was represented as having been with God at the Creation, having witnessed the Fall in Eden, and experienced all kinds of catastrophic events to survive as a pessimistic commentator upon the human condition. Donald Davie's *Six Epistles to Eva Hesse* revived and developed an earlier style to comment humorously on explorers in a tone reminiscent of W. H. Auden, and John Wain's *Letters to Five Artists* concentrated his curious mixture of prose and poetry upon the conflict between public and private vision. In *At Thurgarton Church* George Barker continued his search for a more disciplined approach to, and treatment of, his subject (in this case, death); in *The Night Bathers* Ted Walker successfully extended his range beyond the slight descriptive nature poems to which his readers had become accustomed; and in *The Last of England* Peter Porter added a sensuous element to his satirically directed poetry, losing nothing of his vitality and wit in the process.

Among collected editions published were the *Collected Poems* of Clifford Dyment and Burns Singer (a young Scots poet who died in 1964), the *Selected Poems* of Dannie Abse, D. J. Enright, Iain Crichton Smith, and Hugh MacDiarmid, and *The Complete Poems of Walter de la Mare.* An interesting crop of anthologies ranged from such period selections as *Poetry of the 1940s,* edited by Howard Sergeant, and *Poems of the Sixties,* edited by F. E. S. Finn, to *Doves for the Seventies,* edited by Peter Robins, and *The Penguin Book of Socialist Verse,* edited by Alan Bold. Other books deserving attention were *Malcolm Mooney's Land* by W. S. Graham, *The Whispering Roots* by C. Day Lewis, *The Burning Cone* by George

TONY HARRISON

Tony Harrison's first volume of poetry, "The Loiners," was published in 1970.

MacBeth, *A Man in My Position* by Norman Mac-Caig, and *The Way of a World* by Charles Tomlinson.   (Ho. S.)

FRENCH

Fiction. The 1970 Prix Goncourt was awarded to Michel Tournier for his second novel, *Le Roi des aulnes,* thus confirming the continuity of the traditional novel in spite of the extreme originality of the author. Tiffauges, student, garage-owner, and French soldier imprisoned in East Prussia, finds the atmosphere there ideally suited to the flowering of his instincts when, at the side of Göring, the ogre of Reminten, he becomes the ogre of Kaltenborn, charged with the selection and training of Nazi youth. Terrifying but convincing scenes follow one another until finally, at the time of the German collapse, Tiffauges, like the elf king, carries off a child on his shoulders toward deep forests and death. In this powerfully written masterpiece, the story was sufficient in itself, but it was enriched with symbols and Germanic myths that combined to increase its grandeur, in spite of unpleasant and apparently pointless scatological scenes. M. Déon's *Les Poneys sauvages,* a novel of exceptional quality, begins at Cambridge, giving the reader the feeling that he is entering straight into a very good English novel of the turn of the century. The destinies of the four principal characters interweave in different lands, and although the complexity of feminine intrigues detracted from the unity of the work, it remained nonetheless one of the year's best.

In *Isabelle ou l'Arrière-saison,* J. Freustié chose as his hero a thrice-married former Don Juan, who rediscovers the daughter one of his wives bore him 17 years earlier and falls in love with her. This well-written and almost incestuous idyll won its author the Prix Renaudot. In *Le Milliardaire* M. de Saint-Pierre probed the psychology of industrial tycoons—their isolation in the midst of the manifold difficulties created for them by their competitors and even their own children. D. Decoin plunged into an atmosphere of mysticism with *Élisabeth ou Dieu seul le sait,* the story of the daughter of a rich banker who enters a convent, leaves it, and dies with the detachment and serenity of the saints. The old maid heroine of H. Bonnier's *L'Amour des autres,* a telephone operator in a small town in decline, also comes very close to being a saint, while the colourful local characters

enjoy themselves at a dance and a truck driver meets his death in an accident.

The Prix Médicis was won by C. Bourniquel with *Sélinonte ou la chambre impériale.* In this complex story, a writer of many aspirations would have become famous had he not been deprived of the authorship of a book. His feeling of frustration is strangely transformed into renunciation when he writes a second. The ladies of the Femina jury chose F. Nourissier's *La Crève* for their award. The author once again chose a rather unattractive hero, weary of his wife and sons and of his life; an affair with a young girl suddenly prompts him to leave home to join her. In *Kamouraska,* poet and novelist Anne Hébert told a tale of adultery and murder in an atmosphere of mystery. Murder was almost the subject of B. Clavel's *Le Tambour du bief,* which dealt with the problem of euthanasia. *Mort d'un Grec* was a confirmation of the talent of R. Quatrepoint: knowing that he is condemned to imminent death, a Greek meditates upon his life, his island, and his neighbours with serenity and humour. In *Je suis mal dans ta peau,* G. Cesbron chose the character of a Negro whom Western civilization made wretched both in Europe and in Africa. With *L'Entremetteuse,* the title of which revealed the genre, G. des Cars produced a very sound best seller.

Among novels inspired by actual events, R. Merle's *Derrière la vitre* was an exceptional success. Dealing with events at Nanterre on March 22, 1968, from the inside, the book followed the thoughts of characters of differing persuasions, both real and fictitious. The coarseness of the language and the freedom of morals of the students were somewhat staggering. J.-P. Hervé Bazin's *Les Bienheureux de la désolation* did not get beyond the level of mere reportage. The book dealt with the volcanic eruption of Tristan da Cunha and the painful story of its inhabitants and their rejection of Western civilization. No doubt the large quantity of libelous material in *Des Français* led Roger Peyrefitte to dub the work a "novel." In it almost every contemporary figure of importance was attacked. With a more discreet tone, *Virgo et Argo,* a quest for his childhood, led to Georges Guérin's being called a Breton Proust. J. Borel undertook a similar search in *Le Retour;* however, the work seemed too long and detailed in spite of the quality of the style.

Of numerous books published by Romain Gary, *Chien blanc,* a story involving the racial question in the U.S., was both objective and compelling. Christine Aronthy's *Chiche* caricatured life under the reign of technocracy ten years hence. *Fleur d'agonie,* one of the best novels of Christine de Rivoyre, was a gently mocking picture of the bourgeoisie during the events of 1968. About the same period, Hélène Parmelin's *La Manière noire* introduced real-life characters under fictitious names. Intelligent but somewhat incoherent, the work suffered from extravagance and length that made it rather wearisome to read.

In the sphere of the historical novel, Zoë Oldenburg's gigantic fresco of the First Crusade and its atrocities, *La Joie des pauvres,* merited admiration in spite of its length. Closer to modern times, *La Saga des amants séparés,* which centred on the two German occupations of France, was one of the most successful works of the prolific novelist M. Blancpain.

La Folle de Lithuanie by B. Poirot-Delpech evoked hazy memories of a woman in the form of letters addressed to the madwoman of Lithuania, a woman friend—unless the madwoman was the letter-writer herself. Less obscure than his previous novels but nonetheless related to the avant-garde, the book carried off the Grand Prix du Roman of the French Academy—the 40 "immortals" thus breaking the Cartesian logic. Alain Robbe-Grillet's *Projet d'une révolution à New-York* consisted of scenes of eroticism and torture that would have been unbearably crude and harsh but for the talent and irony of the author. In *La Guerre* by J.-M. Le Clézio the war of the title was that of a society harassing the individual, whose stifled humanity seemed without flesh or heart. Samuel Beckett's *Mercier et camier,* written in 1946 but not previously published, prefigured the characters of *En attendant Godot.* Among seven books by M. K. Rezvani in one year, *La Voie de l'Amérique* consisted of a flood of texts—sometimes comprehensible, often pornographic, and always anti-American. In his fourth novel, *Les Gendres,* a social satire, F. Sonkin presented a father obsessed with the idea of his future—or actual—sons-in-law. In *La Fête interrompue* J.-P. Milovanoff captured the fragile enchantment of a Christmas night.

S. Doubrovsky, an important member of the avant-garde critical movement, illustrated in *La Dispersion*

A.F.P. FROM PICTORIAL PARADE

Maurice Frot was awarded the Prix du Roman Populiste in 1970 for his novel "Nibergue."

the explosion of the written word and the breakdown of thought. *Les Commencements* and *Le Troisième Corps* by Hélène Cixous tended toward pure oneirology. Pierre Boulle's collection of short stories, *Quia absurdum,* was a small masterpiece on the logic of the absurd.

Nonfiction. Historical memoirs and biographies of statesmen were the winners among French publications in 1970. At the forefront was the prodigious success of Charles de Gaulle's *Mémoires d'espoir.* A writer as early as 1924, he revealed a command of the written word, culture, and directness of style that led one of the most exacting critics to place him between Montesquieu and Chateaubriand. P. Erlanger's monu-

mental study *Richelieu* presented the minister and cardinal as a desperate fighter and a prey to the spite of his entourage. Far from being unnecessarily cruel, his severity was shown as essential to the unification of France. The numerous petty intrigues, although perhaps described in too much detail, nevertheless shed light upon the great events of history.

In *Bussy-Rabutin* J. Orieux attempted with considerable indulgence to rehabilitate the marquise de Sévigné's cousin, whose wit, pranks, and love affairs were the talk of 17th-century society. The same author also published a masterly *Talleyrand:* backed up by solid documentation, this was an analysis of the character of the brilliant and scheming diplomatist who, whatever the regime in power, remained constant to France and to Europe. Never did the style of the historian better serve his subject. *Les Enragés de Dieu,* written with infectious fervour by G. Blon, portrayed four centuries of bloody confrontation between Catholics and Protestants—studying the frenzied conflicts in all those countries of Europe where they had raged or were still raging. Y. Courrière concluded his trilogy *La Guerre d'Algérie* with *L'Heure des colonels,* a powerful and moving picture presented with captivating style. In his monumental and compelling *Histoire de la douce France,* P. Guth treated even tragic periods with a gentle humour.

J. and P. de Lacretelle collaborated to produce *Le Théâtre et la vie de Racine,* combining penetrating analysis with perfect factual accuracy in dealing with a life of suffering and glory that was not without shortcomings. P. de Boisdeffre's *Vie d'André Gide* was a compelling study, both monumental and exhaustive. Although to a large extent expressed in Gide's books themselves, the step by step reconstruction of the man and his work by a critic unblinded by his own admiration bore comparison with that of Proust by G. D. Painter.

The increasingly marked tendency toward autobiography among French writers again produced many successful works. In a year when he published an expanded version of his *Journal,* Julien Green received the Academy's Grand Prix for the entirety of his works, of which the *Journal* formed one of the most valuable parts. André Maurois' *Mémoires* expressed with simplicity and truthfulness the life of one born to a high position in industry but destined for worldwide fame as a writer. In contrast to the discretion of those volumes, M. Jouhandeau's *Du pur amour* was the rather coarse, lengthy, and complacent story of a 60-year-old author's passion for a boy of 20. Françoise Mallet-Joris maintained her position among the top best sellers for several months with *La Maison de papier,* the story of her family life—both bourgeois and Bohemian—with piquant detail added by the family's Spanish maids. Moving in its courage and reserve was Andrée Martinerie's *Quand finira la nuit?* —the calvary lived through in the long agony of a husband suffering from cancer. Bruno Gay-Lussac's *Introduction à la vie profane,* one of his best works, was a delightfully depraved and enchanting account of the memories and dreams of childhood and adolescence.

Three writers boldly entered the field of satire. With *L'École des jocrisses,* J. Dutourd showed himself equal to the masters of the genre in both style and manner, presenting a merciless but very humorous critique of contemporary bourgeois and academic society. Although the critique was presented from the point of view of a man of the right, Dutourd's talent was so remarkable that one left-wing critic expressed

UPI COMPIX

Michel Tournier signs his book "Le Roi des aulnes" after he was awarded the Prix Goncourt in November 1970.

his regret that the masterpiece had not been written by one of his own persuasion. In *L'Hexagonal tel qu'on le parle,* R. Beauvais attacked the French language, seen as being in the process of destruction due to the vogue for pseudo-scientific and technical terms. J. Cau showed extraordinary virulence in both *L'Agonie de la vieille* (that is, democracy) and in *Tropicanas* (subtitled "de la dictature et de la révolution sous les tropiques").

The experiences of journalists had a particular quality of their own. *La Loi du retour* by J. Dérogy was an odyssey of the 1947 exodus. *Le Manifeste du camp no. 1* by J. Pouget was devoted to the experiences of French officers who were prisoners of war in Vietnam in 1951.

The most remarkable sections of H. de Montherlant's *Le Treizième César* were those devoted to suicide—almost an apology for suicide inspired by the ancient Romans. Montherlant's writing was as remarkable as ever and his attitude haughtier than ever. Maurice Genevoix, disdainful of passing fashions and ages, produced an enchanting book dedicated to nature, *Bestiaire enchanté,* where "he excels the Anglo-Saxons, masters of the literature of the open air." M. Butor's *La Rose des vents* was an esoteric cosmogony inspired by Alain-Fournier in which a period of human history corresponds to each era of the cosmos. In her monumental study *La Vieillesse,* Simone de Beauvoir showed evidence of uncommon historical, scientific, and social knowledge. Although taking a severe attitude toward contemporary society, she nevertheless attacked with less rancour than usual.

Poetry. What had become of poetry after years of hermetism? Those who gave expression to their sensitivity through clear language and obedience to the rules of prosody were condemned as old-fashioned; the technical exercises of the "cliniciens du langage" were accessible only to the initiated. The schism was very well expressed in Alain Bosquet's and Pierre

Seghers' *Poèmes de l'année.* The young poet J. L. Moreau avoided those extremes in *Sous le masque des mots;* the rhythm and warmth of inspiration of his songs of beauty, wonder, and anguish enthrall the reader. J. M. Auzias dedicated a study to *Luc Decaunes,* who in his verse or poetic prose draws images of penetrating fervour from nature itself. L. Brauquier's *Feux d'épaves* reflected his journeys around the world with tenderness and humour.

M. Béalu's *La Nuit nous garde* verged on sheer fantasy, as did M. Leiris' *Mots sans mémoire,* where the author's taste for darkness and blood was comparable with that of Lautréamont. Streams and sea currents abounded in *Incarnada* by M. Manoll, who was termed a modern Alfred de Vigny. C. Le Quintrec's *La Marche des arbres* was a hymn to Father, Son, and Creation in alexandrines and octosyllables, while Vandercammen's *Horizon de la vigie* was a furious attack upon all that is destructive. In *Poèmes à jouer,* J. Tardieu drew his inspiration from everyday life, which he endowed with depth and resonance.

The Prix Max Jacob was awarded to novelist Daniel Boulanger for his first two verse collections: *Tchadiennes* and *Retouches.* Meanwhile, the work of Jean Follain—one of the most undisputed talents—was crowned by the French Academy's Grand Prix de Poésie. (Ae. B.)

GERMAN

In 1970, once again, there was an increasing shift of interest, among both publishers and readers, away from fictional works and toward books on specific subjects, in particular works of popular science, political subjects, or contemporary events, as well as memoirs and autobiographies. This apparently general tendency was obviously closely related to the quality of the most recent works of German literature, which offered no surprises in 1970, the situation being generally somewhat negative.

The first volume of Uwe Johnson's trilogy *Jahrestage,* which had been awaited with high hopes, duly appeared, containing mainly impressions and sketches, commentaries and scenes from New York daily life seen through the eyes of a German just recently arrived and working in a bank. The journal was admittedly based to a large extent upon readings from the much-quoted *New York Times,* but some ironic and parodistic passages offered enjoyable reading. Embedded in the journal was a second plot played out in a small North German town in 1933. This was the story of a petit bourgeois family and was intended to reveal the pressure of social and political conditions on the private life of the individual. However, the saga of family life set in the austere atmosphere of the north was not free from sentimentality. Moreover, to a considerable extent the rather solemn and ponderous language led to stylization and mystification both of the reality of those former times and of the characters presented. There was a rapid evaporation of interest in any further volumes of the trilogy.

By contrast, the Austrian writer Thomas Bernhard's new novel, *Das Kalkwerk,* seemed to provoke no surprise. Bernhard, obliged to struggle against fixed ideas and obsessions but pursuing his goals with a monomaniac single-mindedness although not always with praiseworthy results, presented an unusually sombre and repellent world; the central figure of *Das Kalkwerk* was mentally disturbed and probably mad—a scientist living in monastic seclusion who kills his

CAMERA PRESS FROM PIX   CAMERA PRESS FROM PIX

Above, Heinrich Böll's "Aussatz" appeared in 1970. Above, right, Uwe Johnson's "Jahrestage," the first volume of a trilogy, was published in 1970.

prose pieces of the experimental writer Jürgen Becker, entitled *Umgebungen,* seemed rather arid and sparse. In *Der Stillgelegte Mensch,* the Austrian Herbert Rosendorfer offered amusing and lively stories, often characterized by a high degree of inventive imagination. Another Austrian, G. J. Jonke, born in 1946, showed himself, with *Glashausbesichtigung,* to be an original representative of the newest generation of prose writers in the German language.

In the realm of poetry, the most important—if not the only important—event was the publication of *Lichtzwang,* the last volume of poems of the great lyric poet Paul Celan, who died in April. While admittedly difficult of access and mostly shunning rational meanings, his poems nevertheless captivated through their terseness, musicality, and astonishing richness of imagery.

In the realm of drama, there was no shortage of first performances of works by prominent authors. In *Trotzki im Exil,* Peter Weiss attempted to show the history of Russian Communism from the beginning of the century until World War II. However, his somewhat dilettantish selection merely produced a chaotic piling up of figures, themes, quotations, and documentary episodes. Irritating in its superficiality, the play degraded Trotski and reduced him to the stature of a tedious phrasemonger in spite of the contrary aims of the playwright.

Also undistinguished was Rolf Hochhuth's new drama, *Guerillas,* a naïvely partisan work directed against U.S. imperialism. More favourably received by the critics was Heinrich Böll's *Aussatz,* an unpretentious treatment of problems of Catholicism in West Germany.

The Austrian Wolfgang Bauer, born in 1941, was not undeservedly the most successful stage writer of recent years. Although he was clearly not greatly concerned with new forms, in *Magic Afternoon* and *Change* he drew a sharp and scenically convincing, although admittedly one-sided, picture of the younger generation.   (M. R.-R.)

ITALIAN

Is the art of storytelling alive or dead? When reading enjoyable books, such as *L'attore* by Mario Soldati or *Il dissenso* by Libero Bigiaretti, the question never crosses the mind. Perhaps the critical conscience ought to shudder at their old-fashioned style, their blinkered middle-class outlook, their failure to interpret poetically the central issues of contemporary life; but it lies strangely dormant. The contrast between sophisticated critical tools and their uselessness in justifying the simple pleasure of reading these books is similar to the contrast, in Bigiaretti's first story, between a couple of wealthy left-wing intellectuals and their housekeeper, Filomena. Their "correct" and up-to-date ideology is totally irrelevant to Filomena's reactionary attitudes: they are enlightened, but cannot cope with the housekeeping; she is a near Fascist, but a very good cook. They wish that good cooking and political orthodoxy went together, but alas it is not necessarily so.

This seemed to be true also of many Italian writers: passionately concerned with ideological questions, they tended to forget that good writing does not necessarily flow from "correct" intellectual attitudes. Their novels and stories provided wonderful material for "aware" and sophisticated reviewers, but were often neither enjoyable nor palatable. Proceeding slowly and carefully, the patient reader of G. L. Piccioli's

crippled wife. Many critics felt compelled to ask what reader would voluntarily expose himself to the piercing diction of this extremely painful book.

The young Austrian Peter Handke achieved a considerable success with readers with his little novel *Die Angst des Tormanns beim Elfmeter* ("The Despair of the Goalkeeper"). Nevertheless, many buyers were probably disappointed at finding next to nothing about football in the book, which told the story of a man wandering round in despair after his presumed dismissal, murdering a cinema cashier, and finally fleeing. While the novel was impressively written in parts, Handke's slow-motion tempo rapidly became tedious.

In contrast to Handke, the excellent short-story writer Gabriele Wohmann had little interest in new forms of expression. Her traditionally realistic novel *Ernste Absicht* recounted episodes in the daily life of a woman from an intellectual background. Günter Herburger's futuristic novel *Jesus in Osaka* was not without humour and presented an entirely unconventional Jesus confronted with the world of the 1980s. The poet Helmut Heissenbüttel's first novel, *D'Alembert's Ende,* an attempt to parody the cultural life of the Federal Republic, proved a great disappointment.

Against this uninspiring background, a little book from East Germany created something of a sensation: *Jakob der Lügner,* first novel of Jurek Becker, born in 1937, told an extremely original tale from a Polish ghetto during World War II. The novel proved that even events of the utmost horror could be treated with charm, grace, and humour, without the subject being trivialized or rendered harmless as a result; it found instant acclaim in both German states and placed Becker among the few remarkable prose writers of his generation.

In addition to the novels mentioned above, there were some notable collections of smaller prose works. Elias Canetti published a further volume of aphorisms and diary notes, *Alle vergeudete Verehrung.* Günter Eich's latest collection of short prose texts, *Ein Tibeter in meinem Büro,* fluctuated between the tenderly poetic and the utterly absurd. The most recent

Arnolfini would eventually realize that it is about a boy being educated in a Catholic seminary, and might eventually sift out of the incredibly contrived and contorted syntax a few poetic phrases. But is it worth the effort?

Occasionally the only readable thing about a novel was the publisher's blurb: the praise of Roberto Vigevani's "extraordinary satirical powers" on the cover of *Dalla pancia di un orso bianco,* while semantically clear, was factually inaccurate. Dacia Maraini's *A memoria,* a polyphonic novel combining stream-of-consciousness and epistolary techniques with circular and iterative structures, seemed almost written to suit the subtle interpretive essay by Renato Barilli that preceded it. Alberto Moravia's latest book, *Il paradiso,* a series of existential monologues spoken, always with Moravia's own monotonous drone, by 34 different women, at least managed to arouse the reader's admiration for the difficulty of the feat—as would a set of 34 musical variations on a Baroque theme for percussion and Jew's harp.

Both *Il metodo* by Gaia Servadio and *Super-Eliogabalo* by Alberto Arbasino dealt with sex, pot, pop, and yet more sex. Gaia Servadio seemed to take her subject matter, and herself, rather seriously. Arbasino fortunately did not: however, his spoof lasted too long (322 pages) to be wholly enjoyable. Ercole Patti's *Graziella,* a Sicilian love story, and Ugo Dessy's *L'invasione della Sardegna* had some good points, in spite of the fact that neither book told the reader much about what really goes on in either Sicily or Sardinia.

The protagonist of Guido Piovene's long-awaited novel *Le stelle fredde* suddenly leaves his employment and retires to his house in the country. There he quarrels with his father and is shot at by the husband of his former mistress. Later, accused of murdering the man, he takes to the hills, where he is joined by a philosopher-policeman and by Fedor Dostoevski. The latter explains in a 34-page monologue how he has come back from the dead. They all go to a priest for enlightenment, but fail to be enlightened. Dostoevski disappears again, the real murderer is found, and the protagonist returns home, where he starts building up a card index of literary images. Short summaries do not usually succeed in conveying the real flavour of a novel, but this one does.

Nelo Risi's admirable little book of poems, *Di certe cose,* opened with a quotation from Flaubert: "What a mire of stupidity our age flounders in!" The 1970 poetry vintage was definitely better than the prose. There were beautiful landscapes of the mind in Maria Luisa Spaziani's *L'occhio del ciclone,* and arresting images in *Tutte le poesie* by Sandro Penna, collected in one volume. Alfredo Giuliani's *Il tautofono,* "a sort of poetical Rorschach test," was rather pleasant nonsense. More difficult to catalog were Dino Buzzati's *Poema a fumetti,* a poetic strip-cartoon of some merit; Giovanni Testori's *Erodiade,* a deliberately unperformable dramatic monologue; and Carmelo Bene's *L'orecchio mancante,* a mixture of harsh invective, avant-garde verse, serious criticism, and rubbish.

The year's essays made the most rewarding reading. Pietro Citati's *Goethe* was an imaginative presentation of the great poet's work. Three young postgraduates, Lucia Strappini, Claudia Micocci, and Alberto Abruzzese, produced the best critical analysis to date of Italian culture and society in the first two decades

ARCHIVIO FOTOGRAFICO BOMPIANI

Libero Bigiaretti's "Il dissenso" appeared in 1970.

of the 20th century (*La classe dei colti*). Maria Corti and Cesare Segre edited an important anthology of contemporary Italian literary criticism, *I metodi attuali della critica in Italia.* Ernesto Ragionieri collected, in *Italia giudicata,* the most important writings by contemporary foreign observers on Italian history between 1861 and 1945, making sobering reading. Umberto Eco and Eugenio Battisti wrote the commentary to two stimulating pictorial books on the history of artistic techniques, *L'arte come mestiere* and *L'arte come invenzione.* (G. C.)

JEWISH

Hebrew. The world of Hebrew letters was diminished in 1970 by the death of S. Y. Agnon, co-winner of the 1966 Nobel Prize for Literature with Nelly Sachs, who also died during the year (*see* OBITUARIES).

Despite uncertain political conditions, Hebrew literature in Israel again demonstrated its creativity. P. Sadeh's strangely mythological novel *Mot Abimelech* appeared, as did elder writer Z. Weinberg's *Al Admat Naihar* and the collected writings in four volumes of *Sippurai Yehuda Yaari* ("The Stories of Yehuda Yaari"). Y. Yaoz-Kast's *Halon ha-Bayit ha-Nogea* was an evocation of the Holocaust. H. Bartov's *Shel Mi Atah Yeled* and A. Amir's *Noon* were noteworthy. Volumes of stories by Z. Luz and G. Telpaz were *Onot* and *ha-Epikoires,* respectively.

A volume of critical writings, *Omodot* (translated by its author, Y. Kesheth, as "Appreciations"), drew some attention. Related to this was S. Avneri's *12 Meshorerim* and the late critic M. Feitelsohn's *Behinot ve-Haarahot.* I. Gour's *Nofai Sifrut ve-Tarbut* contained essays on the theatre.

A fine scholarly work was D. Pagis' *Shirat ha-Hol ve-Torat ha-Shir le-Moshe Ibn-Ezra u-Vnai Doro.* A. M. Habermann in *Toledot ha-Shira veha-Piyut* dealt eruditely with the development of post-biblical literature. Centuries removed in time, background, and genre was D. Miron's thorough study entitled *Sholom Aleichem.*

Poetry during 1970 ran the gamut from the relatively simple to the sophisticated. Among the former were a posthumous collection of M. Temkin's *Shirai Yerushalayim,* A. Broides' *Tahana ve-Derech,* Z.

Gilead's *Or Hozer*, and I. Shalev's *Naar Shav Min ha-Tzava*. Abba Kovner's *Hupah ba-Midbar* was a nostalgic statement in modern idiom, while T. Carmi's *Davar Ahed* represented a sharply concrete as well as abstract view of the world. Avot Yeshurun's poems in *Ze Shaim ha-Sefer* were characteristically aphoristic.

In the U.S., Hebrew literature was again at a standstill. Of significance, however, was the publication in Israel of *Iyunim be-Mahashevet Yisrael* by the late scholar Simon Rawidowicz. (G. P.)

Yiddish. The year 1970 marked the 100th anniversary of the founding of the Yiddish press in the U.S. While many Yiddish literary luminaries were missing from the 1970 list, the books issued bore witness to significant accomplishments. In the U.S. Yiddish poetry was enriched by Joseph Rubinstein's *Exodus from Europe*, the last volume of a narrative trilogy; Wolf Pasmanik's *My Poems;* Kadya Molodovsky's *Marzipans*, essentially for children but aimed at adults as well; and Moshe Shifris' *Under One Roof*. Fiction included Ben Gold's *In Those Days*, Paul Rubinstein's popular novel *Upon Strange Ways*, and Wolf Karmiol's *Carts on the Roads to the End of the World*, published in Tel Aviv. To the shelf of essays were added Solomon Simon's *Faith of a Generation*, S. Tenenbaum's *Hunger for the World*, Samuel Margoshes' *In the Process of Generations*, and Jacob Cahan's *In the Struggle of Times*, the latter two issued in Israel.

The revised and enlarged edition of Samuel Niger's *Mendeleh Moikher Sforim*, about the classics of modern Yiddish writing, enriched the field of biography and literary research. The field of autobiography included the two volumes of David Shub's *On the Revolving Stage of History*, Benjamin Laikin's *Memoirs of a Practical Dreamer*, depicting chiefly Jewish life in the Midwest during several decades, and J. B. Beilin's *All in One Life*.

Contributions from Canada included Melekh Ravitch's poetry collection *Post Scriptus* and Ida Maze's autobiographical novel *Dinah*, while Mexico added David Zabludovsky's memoirs *Of Past Years*, and the bilingual, Hebrew-Yiddish literary-scientific collection *Grace to Abraham*, dedicated to writer and educator Abraham Golomb, a resident of Los Angeles, on the occasion of his 80th birthday. Yiddish works from Paris were Mendel Man's collection of short stories *The Black Oak*, Jacob Sternberg's *Poem and Ballad on the Carpathians*, and Moshe Shmulevich's *Warsaw Years*. Moscow's contributions included M. Dobin's *The Power of Life* and Joseph Rabin's *At the Nyeman River*, in fiction, and the collection *With Body and Life* by Izzy Kharik as the most important event in the sphere of poetry.

Yiddish literary activity in Israel resulted in many accomplishments. In poetry these included Abraham Sutzkever's *Ripened Faces*, Yaakov Zvi Shargel's *Sunny Doorsteps*, Aryeh Shamri's *Song in the Barn*, David Rodin's *Young and Younger*, for young readers, and *Thirst for Duration* by Leizer Eichenrand, a resident of Switzerland. Among the outstanding works of fiction were Yekhiel Hoffer's *In Wide Hopelessness*, Joseph Ehrlich's *Sabbath*, and collections of short stories by Israel Kaplan and L. Kheyn-Shimoni. The field of the essay was enriched by Samuel Eisenstadt's *Pioneering Figures*, Malka Locker's monograph *Charles Baudelaire*, and the bilingual Hebrew-Yiddish collection *President and Author*, published on the occasion of the 80th birthday of Israeli Pres. Schneor Zalman Shazar. (M. Sn.)

LATIN-AMERICAN

Latin America continued its literary development in 1970 in a context of repression and guerrillas. Despite censorship and torture, the radical vanguard was again represented by Brazil. Augusto de Campos published *Equivocábulos*, a collection of semantic-visual texts, photo-poems, and "Viagem via linguagem," a collapsible environment-poem resembling an architect's model. He also recalled to public attention, in *Revisão de Kilkerry*, the work of a neglected Brazilian disciple of Mallarmé whose language, despite the time that has elapsed, is remarkably modern. Two poets from the baroque state of Minas Gerais sought a combination of traditional diction and elements of concrete poetry: Affonso Avila (*Código de Minas*) and Silviano Santiago (*Salto*). *Tutaméia: Terceiras estórias,* by the great novelist João Guimarães Rosa, appeared posthumously: one of the stories recounted the metamorphosis of a man into a jaguar and the dissolution of the Portuguese language into an expression based on the indigenous language of Brazil, Tupí-Guaraní.

Among the lucid essays included in Mario da Silva's *Angulo e horizonte* was one devoted to the doyen of the vanguard of the 1920s, Oswaldo de Andrade, whose novel *Os condenados*, with a foreword by Mario da Silva Brito, constituted the first volume of Andrade's *Obras completas*. *O dorso do tigre* brought together Benedito Nunes' literary and philosophical reflections, while *Lingüística, poética, cinema* commemorated Roman Jakobson's visit to Brazil with a collection of his own essays and studies of his work by Haroldo de Campos, Boris Schnaiderman, and J. Mattoso Câmara, Jr.

The wealth of Argentina's literary output defied detailed description. Jorge Luis Borges took the reading public by surprise with his first book of short stories in 17 years, *El informe de Brodie,* in which he confirmed that he was still the contemporary master of Spanish prose writing. These short realistic stories put aside the fictional form that had brought fame to Borges and whose translation, in the opinion of many critics, had initiated a new era in North American literature. Julio Cortázar's miscellany, *Último round,* gathered together stories, poems, essays, and collage-games, while his reprinted play *Los reyes* inverted the Theseus myth and made a hero of the Minotaur. His collection of *Relatos* reached the public at the same time as an exchange published under the title of *La literatura en la revolución y la revolución en la literatura,* in which Cortázar and Mario Vargas Llosa engaged in a polemic with the young Colombian writer Oscar Collazos about the extent of a writer's commitment.

The horrors of power were satirized by H. A. Murena in *Polispuercón* and by Leopoldo Marechal in his novel *Megafón o la guerra*, which appeared posthumously. E. Mallea set his *La penúltima puerta* in Delhi and Buenos Aires. David Viñas gave expression to his concern for the political present and future of Argentina in *Cosas concretas.* H. Constantini (*Háblenme de Funes*), G. L. García (*Cancha rayada*), and H. Romeu (*A bailar esta ranchera*, an expression of the hippie subculture) developed the experimental forms of the narrative. Alberto Girri, an isolated and original poet, published his *Antología temática*, while A. Vanasco assembled in *Canto rodado* the poetry of 20 years. In the second volume of her autobiography, *La vida cotidiana*, M. R. Oliver described the motives that drive a young daughter of the oligarchy to become a socialist militant. In the critical field, Nicolás

Rosa's brilliant *Crítica y significación* earned him a privileged place among the many students of structuralism.

The literature of each of the Central American republics had special characteristics. Guatemalan A. Monterroso, in *La oveja negra,* brought up to date with irony and style the ancient genre of the fable. Costa Rica gave birth to a Caribbean Papillon—*La isla de los hombres solos,* an account of his 20 years in jail by the ex-delinquent J. L. Sánchez. In El Salvador three books were worthy of particular note: short-story writer Salarrué's *Obras escogidas,* Manlio Argueta's novel *El valle de las hamacas,* and I. López Vallecillo's book of poetry *Puro asombro.* P. A. Cuadra, in *El Nicaragüense,* probed deeply into Nicaragua's culture and national character. Ernesto Cardenal rewrote some of the *Salmos* for our time, infusing them with his own political and religious concern.

Gabriel García Márquez continued to dominate the Colombian literary scene. *One Hundred Years of Solitude* was a major success in its English translation, and in France was awarded the annual prize for the best foreign work. In the same field, William Agudelo's *Nuestro lecho no es de flores* gave a frank and impassioned account of the author's struggle between sexuality and the priestly vocation.

R. Fernández Retamar's *Que veremos arder* stood out amid Cuba's abundant and often excellent poetic output, since it showed once again the poet's ability to render poetic the most contradictory experiences.

Poetry and criticism continued to maintain a single high standard in Chile: Nicanor Parra's *Obra gruesa* provided an opportunity to study the evolution of the creator of "antipoetry." In *La musiquilla de las pobres esferas* Enrique Lihn carried to its ultimate consequences a hauntingly sincere and authentic artistic project. José Miguel Ibáñez published the fruits of a rigorous structural analysis in *La creación poética.*

If in *Posdata* Octavio Paz formulated the critique of a Mexican society that had experienced the student rebellion of 1968, in *Conjunciones y Disyunciones* he examined the signs "body" and "no body" through one of the finest expository styles in any language. His poetry, collected in *La centena,* was the object of an able study by Ramón Xirau, *Octavio Paz: El sentido de la palabra.* The same clarity and precision characterized the literary and artistic essays of Carlos Fuentes, *Casa con dos puertas.*

The relations between Mexicans and non-Mexicans, although an unusual theme, occupied a significant place in four new Mexican novels: Sergio Galindo's *Nudo,* J. M. Torres' *Didascalias,* L. J. Hernandez' *Nostalgia de Troya,* and Ulises Carrion's *De Alemania.* Juan García Ponce developed his interpretation of the complexities of love in three new novels, the most noteworthy of which was *La vida perdurable,* and published *El reino milenario,* a study of Robert Musil. Prison experience was movingly described by José Revueltas in *El apando.* The most successful novel of the year was *Hasta no verte, Jesús mío,* in which Elena Poniatowska told the life story of a woman whose experience synthesized the 20th century in Mexico. In *Lo que es del César* Ricardo Garibay borrowed techniques from several of the media; in *Acto propiciatorio* Héctor Manjarrez drew his inspiration from the world of pop culture, while a passion for rock music motivated P. G. Saldaña in *El rey criollo.*

In Peru, Julio Ortega's *Mediodía* was a brilliant novel about the writing of a novel. In the realm of poetry, works by Washington Delgado (*Un mundo dividido*), C. G. Belli (*Sextinas*), J. G. Rose (*Informe al rey*), M. Martos (*Cuaderno de quejas y contentamientos*), and C. Bustamante (*El nombre de las cosas*) were outstanding. The complete works of José Carlos Mariátegui, the Latin-American Gramsci, were further enriched by the addition of five new volumes, including *Peruanicemos el Perú* and *Cartas de Italia.*

Despite the obstacles placed in their way by men and their *machismo* complex, so vigorously denounced by Clara Silva in *Prohibido pasar,* women dominated the literary scene in Uruguay: M. I. Silva Vila satirized the fall of an aristocratic family in *Salto cancán,* and Cristina Peri Rosi gave ample confirmation of her talent in *Los museos abandonados* and *El libro de mis primos.* Sara de Ibáñez described the catastrophes of the age in *Apocalipsis XX,* and L. B. Bejar examined current linguistic procedures in *Análisis de un lenguaje en crisis.* Mario Benedetti brought his indispensable *Literatura uruguaya siglo XX* up to date.

(J. E. Pa.; M. A. G.)

NORWEGIAN

In pride of place was Thor Heyerdahl's *Ra,* a fascinating report on his two transatlantic voyages with papyrus vessels, seen against thousands of years of seafaring history, and with a cornucopia of amazingly well-reproduced photographs.

Several historical novels appeared, foremost among them Kåre Holt's *Hersker og trell.* Concluding a trilogy on the life of King Sverre, this volume covered the period 1179–1202, giving an imaginative and colourful account of the last years of his reign. Asbjørn Øksendal's saga pastiche *Sigrid Ranesdatter og Sigurd Jorsalfare* centred around Sigurd the Crusader's infatuation with a married woman in the early 12th century. Belonging to the middle period of the same century was Ragnhild Magerøy's *Himmelen er gul,* the second volume in a series on Ingerid Ragnvaldsdaughter.

Bergljot Hobæk Haff's *Den sorte kappe* was a strangely innocent account of an elderly businessman's fatal passion for a deformed Italian prostitute. Alcoholism, sex, and manslaughter, seasoned with obscenities, were main ingredients in Gunnar Lunde's first novel, *Drømmekvinnen.* In *Tilfellet Martin,* Solveig Christov juxtaposed a happy holidaying couple and a young murderer on the run. Acid social satire was the basic element in Tor Åge Bringsværd's imaginative *Bazar,* an unusual mixture of pop art, surrealism, and science fiction. In Fredrik Skagen's novel *Jeg vet en deilig have* the social satire was tempered by refreshing baroque humour. Bjørg Vik's first novel, *Gråt elskede mann,* extended the analysis of love relationships dealt with in her earlier short stories. A similar theme, seen from the point of view of three generations of women, was taken up by newcomer Elisabeth Thams in her novel *Tre kvinner.* A touch of *dolce vita* was introduced by another newcomer, Axel Barre, in the thriller *Alle elsket enken.*

The year's principal contributions to Norwegian poetry were the posthumous *Liv ved straumen* by Tarjei Vesaas, Rolf Jacobsen's *Headlines,* Simen Skjønsberg's *Flyttedag,* Stein Mehren's *Aurora,* and Ragnvald Skrede's *Lauvfall.*

In *Tommy* Odd Nansen drew a touching portrait of a Jewish boy he met in the Sachsenhausen concentration camp in 1945, while his *Langs veien* was a series of reminiscences, including fascinating glimpses of his father, Fridtjof Nansen, and of Vidkun Quisling. (To. S.)

GYLDENDAL NORSK FORLAG

Kåre Holt's historical novel "Hersker og trell" completes a trilogy on the life of King Sverre.

SOVIET

To conformist critics and so-called consensus writers in the Soviet Union, the literary landmarks of 1970 were the celebration in April of the centenary of Lenin's birth and in May of the 25th anniversary of victory over Nazi Germany. The first, emphasized at both the plenary session of the Councils for the Creative Arts of the Union Republics (December 1969) and the third Congress of Writers of the Russian Federation (March 1970), provided an opportunity to review the achievements and restate the aims of "the Soviet literature of today"; the second gave writers a chance to reassert the national unity and patriotic fervour that won the "Great Patriotic War" (World War II).

From the viewpoint of the West, however, the main events of the year were: the forced resignation in February of poet and critic Aleksandr Tvardovski (*see* BIOGRAPHY) from editorship of the journal of liberal dissent, *Novy Mir;* publication by Andrei Amalrik, the young essayist and playwright opposed to the political and literary establishment, of two brilliant indictments of the political system, *Will the Soviet Union Survive Until 1984?* and *Involuntary Journey to Siberia,* resulting in his trial and imprisonment in November for "disseminating falsehoods derogatory to the Soviet state and social system"; publication in London in October of the first uncensored revision of *Babii Yar* (1966), by "A. Anatoli," pseudonym of Anatoli Kuznetsov, whose defection had been a sensation of 1969; and, most important of all, acceptance by Aleksandr Solzhenitsyn of the Nobel Prize for Literature, followed by his final refusal to go to Stockholm to receive it.

Not that these events were disregarded in the Soviet Union. An increasingly militant underground greeted Amalrik's essays with enthusiasm; and even while condemning them, "party-line" Soviet writers showed ambivalence in their attitude to Tvardovski and Solzhenitsyn in particular. *Pravda,* a leader in the attack on Tvardovski, in an article celebrating his 60th birthday in June, praised him as "one of the major and most gifted" of contemporary Soviet poets; and speakers in the Writers' Union debate on Solzhenitsyn made it clear that they thought him dangerous because he was "a writer of genius—and a man of principle" and knew that his "courage, integrity, and attachment to the homeland" had won him wide admiration. In the letter written after expulsion from the Writers' Union, Solzhenitsyn struck at the roots of their fear and their failure, reminding them that they looked to the past for their themes, while his were eternal and universal: ". . . the secrets of the human heart and conscience, the confrontation between life and death. Life conquers death, the past is conquered by the future."

It was partly because writers had already too often turned for inspiration to the great days of the Revolution and the Great Patriotic War that the works written to celebrate the Lenin centenary and the Victory Day anniversary fell a little flat. Even Marietta Shaginian, tireless turner-out of stories on roads trodden by Lenin in exile, was forced to retrace her tracks, and, in *Four Lessons by Lenin,* collected essays describing her visits to places where he had lived in Italy, Switzerland, and England. E. Vechtomova's *The Story of Mother* was a life of Lenin's mother, Nikolai Grigoriev's *Ilya Nikolaevich* a study of Lenin's father, and Vladimir Osoysov's *April,* a novel based on the life of Lenin's elder brother, Aleksandr.

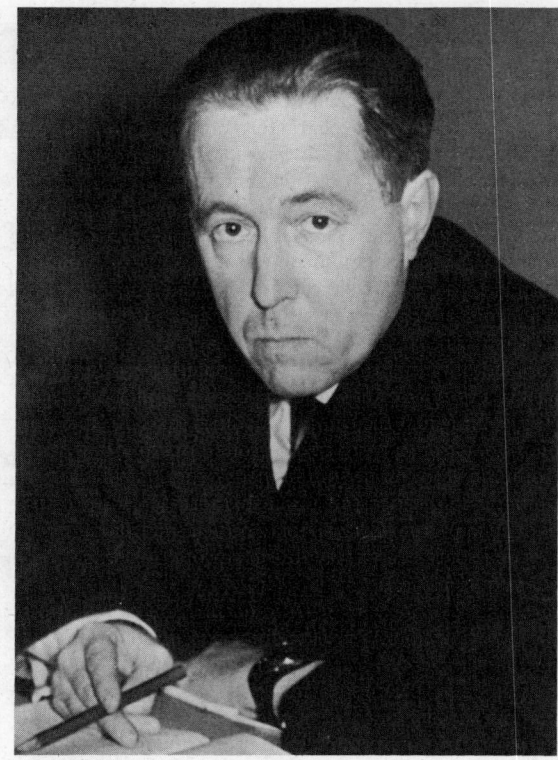

CAMERA PRESS FROM PIX

Aleksandr Solzhenitsyn was awarded the 1970 Nobel Prize for Literature but declined to travel to Stockholm to receive it.

Of books about Lenin himself, most original was *Twelve Roads to Egl,* a penetrating study of the influence on the development of Soviet foreign policy of Lenin's experiences abroad, by Saava Dangulov.

Perhaps the best of the war novels was Yuri Bondarev's *During Snow,* a description, epic in scale, of the critical point in the defense of Stalingrad when Soviet troops turned back the attempt by German tanks to break through to the encircled German Army. Sketches written at the front in 1941 by Konstantin Simonov and published in 1970 as *Notebook of a Young Soldier* had the natural immediacy rarely achieved by attempts to describe from memory what life in the army was like. In *Sister of Sorrow,* a war story of a different kind, V. Shefair evoked the atmosphere of the period immediately before the war, telling with delicate humour, poetry, and poignancy of first love, and the overwhelming grief of a young girl's first experience of irreparable loss.

A novel treating the war from a different viewpoint, the second volume of Grigori Konovolov's *Sources* (the first volume came out in 1959), chronicled the life of a worker's family living in a big industrial city on the Volga in the years leading up to and during the war. It won first prize in an All-Union contest for a novel about the life of the Soviet worker; second prizes went to Mikhail Bubonnov, for *Torrent,* describing the struggles of a group of young workers to clear the bed of the turbulent Argara River in Siberia; and to Vladimir Popov, for *You Will Win the Battle,* set in a vast new metallurgical plant.

Chinghiz Aitmatov, Kirghiz novelist and Lenin Prize winner, regarded as one of the most interesting young Soviet writers for a style and idiom blending modern Russian with the ancient language and form of his people's oral epic poetry, treated a theme very unlike that of his last novel, *Farewell Gul'sary* (1969; trans. 1970), in *White Ship.*

One of the most important of the year's collections of poetry was Andrei Voznesenski's *The Shadow of Sound,* in which, following the English Metaphysicals and the French Symbolists, he plays with words and images, and arranges poems in patterns to suit their subjects. Other new collections included Y. Smelyakov's *December;* Boris Slutski's *Tales for Today; Shows,* by Evgeni Vinokurov, poet of things, who here describes in cerebral, unrhetorical poems the world of theatre, acrobat, circus, banquet, legend, cave art, implying that the whole world is a show; Leonid Martynov's brilliant poems of metamorphosis, *Peoples' Names;* Leonid Vasilyev's *Ognevitsa;* and a retrospective collection by Evgeni Yevtushenko, including some new poems and omitting some controversial earlier ones.

The year's Lenin Prize winners were Nikolai Tikhonov, "elder statesman" of Soviet poetry; and Sergei Mikhalkov, a popular children's writer—the first writer for children to win the Lenin award. (*See* U.S.S.R.: *Special Report.*)   (X.)

SPANISH

The longing for "amputated" Spain, the Spain still in exile, to be reincorporated into the "mother country" was shown with new intensity during the year. The return to Spain of Francisco Ayala, novelist, short-story writer, and critic, elicited a remarkable manifesto, directed only "to public opinion," which expressed "profound joy" at the "recuperation of Francisco Ayala for Spanish cultural life" and was signed by the country's outstanding writers. The novelist Manuel Andujar, born in Andalusia but formed as a writer in Mexico, returned "definitively" to his native country, and a trilogy of his works was published under the general title of *Vísperas,* narrative studies in an apolitical realism. The publishing house Editorial Andorra published the work from Barcelona as well as from Andorra—where it had issued the work of many an exile.

Many of these exiles had other Spanish publication during the year. Max Aub visited fellow-exile Luis Buñuel, who was filming Benito Pérez Galdós' *Tristana* near Saragossa, and wrote a trenchant piece about another amputation, a miraculous one involving Buñuel's family and the Virgin of Saragossa: *De las verdaderas relaciones de Luis Buñuel con la Virgen del Pilar.* Rosa Chacel issued a new novel, *La sinrazón,* in Andorra; Ramón Sender published *El rey y la reina* in Barcelona; and Ayala published his novel *El fondo del vaso,* a critical study *La estructura narrativa,* and a collection of stories, *Los usurpadores,* all in Spain.

The increasing role of Spain as a presence in Hispanic writing was exemplified not only by the return of writers from exile but also by the physical emplacement of Hispano-American writers to the "mother country." The jury for the new Barral Prize for a Spanish novel (offered by the new Barral Editores, a breakaway from Seix Barral) included the leading South American writers Mario Vargas Llosa and Gabriel García Márquez, now resident in Barcelona. García Márquez turned down the position of consul for Colombia, saying that he had "never received a cent not earned at the typewriter," and that any fee foreign to the office of writer compromises the writer's independence, something as important as knowing how to write: "I shall not be one more writer-with-a-tie: I no longer wear one even in real life." Another writer who would not wear a tie, the poet

Diego Jesús Jimenez, who won the Adonais Prize for Poetry in 1964 and the National Literature Prize in 1968, was discovered in a state of actual hunger in Madrid by the newspaper *Pueblo;* he also objected to state aid, on the ground that it "entails an obligated and directed literature, as in Russia."

The historiographer Américo Castro, however, published his new book, *De la España que aún no conocía,* in Mexico, although parts appeared in Spain; one central thesis was that much of the feverish paramilitary activity and feats of the Old Christians in 17th-century Spain were an effort to show that they were not Jews, until the point was reached where "the unanimity of 'clean blood' had reduced Spain to an uncultivated steppe on the margin of a fertile Europe." The philosopher Julian Marías produced an excellent report on Israel, *Israel: una resurrección.* A most valuable contribution was made by the American Paul Ilie in his *Documents of the Spanish Vanguard:* 57 texts from largely unavailable magazines and manifestos. A fascinating work on the world of magic plants was *Botánica oculta o El falso Paracelso* by Juan Perucho, author of books on Antonio Gaudí and Joan Miró.

Undoubtedly the outstanding verse collection published in 1970 was Jorge Guillén's *Obra poética,* a compendium of pure poetry and a marvel of technical skill in which words and message were one. Another fine collection was by the Cuban-Spaniard José Caballero Bonald, whose *Vivir para contarlo* ("Live to Tell It") included "Zauberlehrling."   (AY. K.)

SWEDISH

One of the year's most interesting events was the creation of Författarförlaget (the Author's Publishing Co.), with 145 authors as members and owners of the independent company. The aim was to redress the balance of power in the book trade by giving more influence to writers, and to hold down book prices. Published titles included works by well-known writers: doctor and novelist P. C. Jersild's *Vi ses i Song My,* a political allegory set in Sweden but reflecting a worldwide moral dilemma; veteran writer and academician Artur Lundkvist's prose mosaic *Långt borta, mycket nära;* and the poet Tomas Tranströmer's collection *Mörkerseende.*

The poet Werner Aspenström published the collection *Inre* ("Inner") after a five-year silence. Abandoning the magical and incantatory elements and rich

LUTFI ÖZKÖK
Tore Zetterholm's powerful social satire "666" was published in 1970.

musical allusions of earlier works, he now listened to a still voice from within in the face of threatening global disaster. The younger poet Göran Sonnevi was deeply concerned about injustices and convinced of the need to rebuild society. The title of his latest collection, *Det måste gå* ("It Must Be Possible"), in which most of the poems were socially "involved," reflected this categorical imperative. The style was simple and clear with vivid images, and the intellectual and emotional content was impressive. Maja Ekelöf's award-winning *Rapport från en skurhink* ("Report from a Scrub Bucket") looked on a cleaner's life. In their different ways, both Sonnevi and Miss Ekelöf reflected the importance of human equality as a moral and political issue in Sweden.

The distinguished scholar Henry Olsson published a fine new study of the poet Gustaf Fröding (d. 1911), *Vinlövsranka och hagtornskrans*, and Ole Söderström devoted a semidocumentary novel, *Molnvandring*, to Verner von Heidenstam. Another imaginative documentary novel was *Tegelmästare Lundin och stora världen* by Per Gunnar Evander. Lars Gyllensten's *Palatset i parken* presented a return to a childhood background, but was essentially concerned with human relationships, responsibility, and loneliness, expressed in vigorous and vivid language. Tore Zetterholm's *666* (the Swedish word for the numeral 6 is a homonym for sex) was a social satire of formidable power.   (K. P. P.)

See also Libraries; Philosophy; Theatre.

ENCYCLOPÆDIA BRITANNICA FILMS. *Chaucer's England—With a Special Presentation of The Pardoner's Tale* (1958); *The Theater—One of the Humanities* (Humanities Course) (1959); *Early Victorian England and Charles Dickens* (Humanities Course) (1962); *Great Expectations I: The Story* (Humanities Course) (1962); *Great Expectations II: The Story Interpreted* (Humanities Course) (1962); *The Novel: What It Is, What It's About, What It Does* (Humanities Course) (1962); *Morning on the Lièvre* (1964); *Huckleberry Finn I* (1965); *Huckleberry Finn II* (1965); *Huckleberry Finn III* (1965); *The Odyssey I—The Structure of the Epic* (1965); *The Odyssey II—Return of Odysseus* (1965); *The Odyssey III—Central Themes* (1965); *Bartleby by Herman Melville* (1969); *Dr. Heidegger's Experiment by Nathaniel Hawthorne* (1969); *The Lady, or the Tiger? by Frank Stockton* (1969); *The Lottery by Shirley Jackson* (1969); *Magic Prison* (1969); *My Old Man by Ernest Hemingway* (1969); *James Dickey: Poet* (1970).

Luxembourg

A constitutional monarchy, the Benelux country of Luxembourg is bounded on the east by Germany, on the south by France, and on the west and north by Belgium. Area: 999 sq.mi. (2,587 sq.km.). Pop. (1970 est.): 338,500. Cap. and largest city: Luxembourg (pop., 1970 est., 77,500). Language: French and German. Religion: 97% Roman Catholic. Grand duke, Jean; prime minister in 1970, Pierre Werner.

On March 20, 1970, Luxembourg joined with representatives of 20 other French-language nations of Europe, Africa, Asia, and North America to form an agency for cultural and technical cooperation. The Francophone states chose Paris as the headquarters for the agency and Jean-Marc Léger, a Canadian, as its director.

Colette Flesch, a 32-year-old graduate of Wellesley (Mass.) College, was elected mayor of the capital city, the youngest and only female mayor in its recent history. The mayor was an active athlete, having represented her country in fencing at the last three Olympics. She had also had an active career in Luxembourg's diplomatic service. After serving on the staff of the Common Market in Brussels until 1968, Mlle

Flesch left to stand for Parliament as a Liberal (Democrat). Having been victorious, she was appointed as a Luxembourg representative to the European Parliament in Strasbourg. In 1969 she was elected to the city council of the capital and, as a coalition candidate of the Liberals (Democrats) and Christian Socialists, succeeded to the post of mayor in 1970.

On April 8, 1970, Prince Félix of Luxembourg and Nassau, the Austrian-born consort of Grand Duchess Charlotte and father of Grand Duke Jean, died in his 77th year.

Luxembourg's defense expenditures rose in 1969 to an estimated LFr. 401 million, compared with LFr. 374 million in 1968.   (R. D. Ho.)

Colette Flesch, the first woman mayor of Luxembourg, officially assumed office on Jan. 1, 1970.

WIDE WORLD

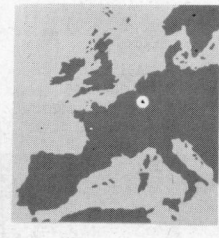

LUXEMBOURG

Education. (1967–68) Primary, pupils 36,625, teachers 1,572; secondary, pupils 8,818, teachers 658; vocational, pupils 6,451, teachers 463; higher, students 667.

Finance. Monetary unit: Luxembourg franc, at par with the Belgian franc (LFr. 50 = U.S. $1; LFr. 120 = £1 sterling). Budget (1969 est.): revenue LFr. 11,003,500,000; expenditure LFr. 11,009,900,000. Gross national product: (1969) LFr. 43,615,000,000; (1968) LFr. 37,926,000,000. Cost of living (1963 = 100): (June 1970) 124; (June 1969) 118.

Foreign Trade. *See* BELGIUM.

Transport and Communications. Roads (1969) 4,440 km. Motor vehicles in use (1969): passenger 88,642; commercial 12,136. Railways: (1968) 328 km.; traffic (1969) 253 million passenger-km., freight 725 million net ton-km. Air traffic (1969): 54.8 million passenger-km.; freight 350,000 net ton-km. Telephones (Dec. 1968) 97,978. Radio licenses (Dec. 1967) 133,000. Television receivers (Dec. 1968) 52,000.

Agriculture. Production (in 000; metric tons; 1969; 1968 in parentheses): oats 34 (34); wheat (1968) 41, (1967) 49; rye 6 (5); potatoes (1968) 60, (1967) 91. Livestock (in 000; May 1969): cattle 191; sheep 4; pigs (May 1968) 105; chickens 440.

Industry. Production (in 000; metric tons; 1969): iron ore (30% metal content) 6,311; pig iron 4,871; crude steel 5,522; electricity (kw-hr.) 2,203,000; manufactured gas (cu.m.; 1968) 16,000.

Malagasy Republic

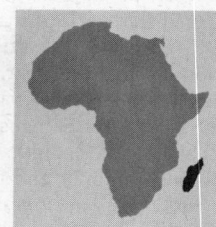

The Malagasy Republic occupies the island of Madagascar and minor adjacent islands in the Indian Ocean off the southeast coast of Africa. Area: 226,660 sq.mi. (587,051 sq.km.). Pop. (1969 est.): 7,198,640. Cap. and largest city: Tananarive (pop., 1970 est., 343,670). Language: French and Malagasy. Religion: Christian (approximately 50%) and traditional tribal beliefs. President in 1970, Philibert Tsiranana.

In 1970 the Malagasy political scene was dominated by three events: the prolonged absence of the head of state because of illness; the formation of a new government; and the signing of economic aid agreements with South Africa. President Tsiranana, suffering from a stroke, was taken to the Salpêtrière hospital in Paris in January and remained under treatment until May.

After various incidents at Tananarive during the electoral campaign, legislative elections took place on September 6 and the election of general councillors a week later. President Tsiranana took the opportunity to accuse the opposition of "subversive activities." The government Social Democratic Party (PSD) gained 104 of the 107 seats in the National Assembly, the 3 remaining seats going to the main opposition party, the Congress for the Independence of

MALAGASY REPUBLIC

Education. (1967–68) Primary, pupils 743,531, teachers (state only) 6,368; secondary, pupils 67,130, teachers (state only) 1,531; vocational, pupils 3,992, teachers (1965–66) 539; teacher training, students 2,600, teachers (1964–65) 118; higher (including University of Madagascar), students 3,449, teaching staff 316.

Finance. Monetary unit: Malagasy franc, at par with the CFA franc (MalFr. 277.71 = U.S. $1; MalFr. 666.50 = £1 sterling). Budget (1969 est.) balanced at MalFr. 43 billion.

Foreign Trade. (1969) Imports MalFr. 46.2 billion (52% from France, 9% from U.S.); exports MalFr. 29,150,000,000 (36% to France, 24% to U.S., 12% to Réunion). Main exports: coffee 28%; vanilla 10%; rice 8%; sugar 6%.

Transport and Communications. Roads (1969) 38,110 km. Motor vehicles in use (1968): passenger 42,925; commercial 27,860. Railways: (1968) c. 880 km.; traffic (1969) 175 million passenger-km., freight 209 million net ton-km. Air traffic (1969): 216 million passenger-km.; freight 8,930,000 net ton-km. Telephones (Dec. 1968) 23,993. Radio receivers (Dec. 1967) 350,000.

Agriculture. Production (in 000; metric tons; 1968; 1967 in parentheses): cassava c. 910 (900); rice (1969) 1,785, (1968) 1,762; corn 88 (97); sweet potatoes 254 (300); potatoes 132 (85); bananas 165 (170); peanuts 43 (48); sugar, raw value (1969–70) c. 115, (1968–69) 99; coffee 67 (71); tobacco 6.1 (4.4); sisal (1969) 25, (1968) 21. Livestock (in 000; Dec. 1968): cattle 9,780; sheep 605; pigs 522; goats (Dec. 1967) 700; chickens c. 11,500.

MALAWI

Education. (1967) Primary, pupils 297,456, teachers 8,104; secondary, pupils 7,964, teachers 424; vocational, pupils 1,096, teachers 114; teacher training, students 1,180, teachers 120; higher, students 644, teaching staff 98.

Finance. Monetary unit: Malawi pound, at par with the pound sterling (Mal£1 = U.S. $2.40). Gold, SDRs, and foreign exchange, official: (June 1970) U.S. $23,980,000; (June 1969) U.S. $21,880,000. Budget (1969 est.): revenue Mal£17,620,000; expenditure Mal£17,620,000.

Foreign Trade. (1969) Imports Mal£30,914,000 (30% from U.K., 17% from Rhodesia, 14% from South Africa, 5% from Japan); exports Mal£22,083,000 (45% to U.K., 11% to Zambia, 7% to Rhodesia, 5% to U.S.). Main exports: tobacco 29%; tea 22%; peanuts 13%.

Transport and Communications. Roads (1968) 10,488 km. Motor vehicles in use (1968): passenger 8,893; commercial 6,240. Railways (1968): c. 820 km.; traffic 49.4 million passenger-km., freight (1969) 152 million net ton-km. Air traffic (1968): 13,652,000 passenger-km.; freight 422,000 net ton-km. Telephones (Dec. 1968) 10,174. Radio receivers (Dec. 1968) 100,000.

Agriculture. Production (in 000; metric tons; 1969; 1968 in parentheses): corn 998 (1,089); cassava (1968) c. 110, (1967) c. 140; sweet potatoes (1968) c. 40, (1967) c. 45; tobacco c. 12 (15); cottonseed 11 (7); peanuts (1968) c. 131, (1967) c. 245; tea (1968) 16, (1967) 17. Livestock (in 000; 1968–69): sheep c. 92; cattle 480; goats (1967–68) c. 700; pigs c. 154.

Madagascar (AKFM). The AKFM won 3 of the 5 seats in the capital, always considered a stronghold of opposition. In the election of general councillors, the PSD gained 92 seats and the AKFM 4, 3 of these in Tananarive.

On November 20 Vice-Pres. Jacques Rabemananjara and the South African foreign minister, Hilgard Muller, signed four economic agreements between the two countries, under which Malagasy would receive loans amounting to $3,240,000. Muller was accompanied by a delegation of some 20 experts, who discussed various possible fields of cooperation with their Malagasy counterparts. (PH. D.)

Malawi

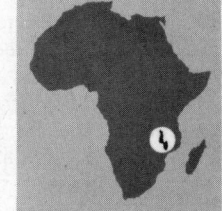

A republic in east central Africa, Malawi is bounded by Tanzania, Mozambique, and Zambia. Area: 45,747 sq.mi. (118,484 sq.km.). Pop. (1970 est.): 4,530,000, nearly all of whom are Africans. Cap.: Zomba (pop., 1966, 19,666). Largest city: Blantyre (pop., 1966, 109,461). Language: English and Nyanja. Religion: predominantly traditional beliefs. President in 1970, H. Kamuzu Banda.

As in the previous year, President Banda rounded off 1969 by appointing a number of new ministers. One of them, however, G. E. Ndema, minister of local government, did not hold office for long and was expelled from the government and from the Malawi Congress Party in April 1970.

Malawi's four British high court judges announced in November 1969 that they planned to relinquish their appointments as a result of legislation which, they believed, seriously undermined the authority of the high court and weakened the safeguards against injustice. An international commission of jurists shared their disquiet, but the minister of finance, Aleke Banda, stated in London that the judges, accustomed to the British system of justice, had failed to understand the significance of superstition in Malawi which could only be dealt with by other methods. The next development came in March when President Banda stated that the police had captured the alleged leader and other members of a gang which since 1968 had been responsible for 28 ritual killings. It was later claimed that among those detained in connection with the killings were three former Cabinet ministers. The president stated that D. D. Bolt, one of the four retiring judges, was partly responsible for four of the deaths which had recently occurred because he had acquitted five men accused of murder during the previous September.

In May South Africa's prime minister, B. J. Vorster, visited Malawi accompanied by his foreign minister, Hilgard Muller. This was Vorster's first visit to an independent black African state. The visitors were followed in July by two senior officials of the South African bureau of standards. They had been invited by J. Z. U. Tembo, minister of trade and industry, to advise the Malawi government on the setting up of a standards bureau.

In September came the surprising news that Zambia, whose relations with Malawi had been far from good, was to open a high commission in Blantyre. This was all the more strange because President Banda had only recently announced his approval of a revival of British arms supplies to South Africa, a policy that Zambia strongly opposed. It was thought that the new move by Zambia might be aimed at countering the influence of South Africa in Malawi. (K. I.)

Malaysia

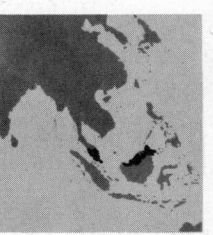

A federation within the Commonwealth of Nations comprising the 11 states of the former Federation of Malaya (known as West Malaysia) and Sabah (formerly North Borneo) and Sarawak (together known as East Malaysia), Malaysia is a federal constitutional monarchy situated in Southeast Asia at the southern end of the Malay Peninsula (excluding Singapore) and on the northern part of the island of Borneo. Area: 128,727 sq.mi. (333,401 sq.km.). Pop. (1969 est.): 10,455,119. Cap. and largest city: Kuala Lumpur (pop., 1968 est., 592,785). Official language: Malay. Religion: Malays are Muslim; Indians mainly Hindu; Chinese mainly Buddhist, Confucian, and Taoist. Supreme heads of state in 1970, with the title of *yang di-pertuan agong,* Tuanku Ismail Nasiruddin Shah ibni al-Marhum Sultan Zainal Abidin and, from September 21, Tuanku Abdul Halim Mu'azzam Shah ibni al-Marhum Sultan Badlishah; prime ministers, Tunku Abdul Rahman and, from September 22, Tun Abdul Razak bin Hussein.

In 1970 Malaysia largely recovered from the tragic setbacks of the May 1969 racial disturbances. The ban on politics and on publications of political parties was lifted in September 1970. Parliament, which had been suspended after the proclamation of a state of emergency after the May 1969 clashes, resumed meeting

WIDE WORLD

Prime Minister Tunku Abdul Rahman greets U.S. Vice-Pres. Spiro Agnew upon his arrival in Kuala Lumpur, one of the stops on Agnew's tour in January.

MALAYSIA

Education. *West Malaysia.* (1967) Primary, pupils 1,297,763, teachers 46,722; secondary, pupils 460,-975, teachers 19,357; vocational, pupils 10,465, teachers 328; higher (including 2 universities), students 15,688, teaching staff 1,650. *East Malaysia: Sabah.* (1968) Primary, pupils 95,979, teachers 3,382; secondary, pupils 21,921, teachers 892; vocational, pupils 188, teachers 9; teacher training, students 509, teachers 40. *East Malaysia: Sarawak.* (1968) Primary, pupils 142,410, teachers 4,374; secondary, pupils 34,-498, teachers 1,397; vocational, pupils 424, teachers 21; teacher training, students 460, teachers (1967) 57; higher, students 291, teaching staff (1965) 11.

Finance. Monetary unit: Malaysian dollar, with a par value of M$3.06 to U.S. $1 (M$7.35 = £1 sterling). Gold, SDRs, and foreign exchange, official: (June 1970) U.S. $651 million; (June 1969) U.S. $581 million. Budget (1969 est.): revenue M$1,961,-800,000; expenditure M$1,925,400,000. Gross national product: (1969) M$11,305,000,000; (1968) M$10,-288,000,000. Money supply: (May 1970) M$1,897,-000,000; (May 1969) M$1,778,000,000. Cost of living (West Malaysia; 1963 = 100): (April 1970) 105; (April 1969) 103.

Foreign Trade. (1969) Imports M$3,596,000,000; exports M$5,085,000,000. Import sources (West Malaysia only): Japan 17%; U.K. 14%; Australia 8%; Singapore 7%; China 6%; Thailand 6%; U.S. 6%; West Germany 5%. Export destinations (West Malaysia only): Singapore 19%; U.S. 18%; Japan 13%; U.K. 6%; U.S.S.R. 6%. Main exports: rubber 40%; tin 18%; timber 15%.

Transport and Communications. Roads (1967) 21,424 km. Motor vehicles in use (1968): passenger 230,000; commercial (including buses) 60,600. Railways: (1968) 1,821 km.; traffic (including Singapore) 583 million passenger-km., freight (1967) 1,080,000,000 net ton-km. Air traffic (Malaysia-Singapore Airlines; 1969): 994 million passenger-km.; freight 17,711,000 net ton-km. Shipping (1969): merchant vessels 100 gross tons and over 85; gross tonnage 38,697. Shipping (1968): vessels entered (excluding Sabah) 27,034,000 net registered tons: goods loaded 20,240,000 metric tons, unloaded 9,236,000 metric tons. Telephones (Jan. 1969) 156,354. Radio receivers (Dec. 1967) 538,000. Television receivers (Dec. 1968) 121,000.

Agriculture. Production (in 000; metric tons; 1968; 1967 in parentheses): rice 1,250 (1,061); rubber (1969) 1,281, (1968) 1,110; copra *c.* 190 (*c.* 180); palm oil (excluding Sarawak; estates only) 277 (234); tea (West Malaysia only) *c.* 3.4 (3.1); bananas (excluding Sarawak) *c.* 339 (*c.* 339); pineapples (West Malaysia only) *c.* 340 (350); pepper (Sarawak only; 1966) 15, (1965) 18; timber (cu.m.) 16,000 (14,200); fish catch (excluding Sarawak) 406 (367). Livestock (in 000; July 1969): cattle *c.* 315; pigs *c.* 965; goats (Dec. 1967) *c.* 335; sheep (West Malaysia only) *c.* 35; buffaloes (Dec. 1967) *c.* 337; poultry (Dec. 1967) *c.* 27,700.

Industry. Production (in 000; metric tons; 1969): tin concentrates (metal content) 73; bauxite 1,073; cement (West Malaysia only) 973; iron ore (West Malaysia only; 60% metal content) 5,236; crude oil (Sarawak only; 1968) 202.

in February. The remaining nationwide curfew was lifted on September 21.

Tunku Abdul Rahman resigned as prime minister on September 21 after 15 years in the post, and his longtime deputy and heir, Tun Abdul Razak bin Hussein (*see* BIOGRAPHY), was sworn in as Malaysia's second prime minister the next day. At the same time, Tuanku Abdul Halim Mu'azzam, the sultan of Kedah, was installed as Malaysia's fifth supreme head of state on September 21.

The elections in Sabah and Sarawak, suspended because of the May 1969 disturbances, were held in July 1970. The Alliance Party won 27 of the 48 seats in Sarawak and 31 of the 32 seats in Sabah. This party, made up of a coalition of the United Malays National Organization (UMNO), the Malaysian Chinese Association (MCA), and the Malaysian Indian Congress (MIC), thus achieved a total of 93 seats in the 144-member Parliament. On the state level, the Alliance commanded eight legislatures; had a narrow, uncertain margin in three; and had lost to the opposition in Penang and Kelantan.

A major threat to the internal security of the country was posed by armed Communist terrorists on the Malaysian-Thai border and in Sarawak. It was necessary to mobilize all efforts and resources to face this challenge, which continued throughout the year. The government thus was forced to divert resources that might otherwise have been used for economic development.

From April to June war exercises involving five nations were held off the east coast of West Malaysia. Taking part were units from Britain, Malaysia, Singapore, New Zealand, and Australia. The operation was designed to train and exercise the combined forces of the five nations under conditions that would prevail after the British military withdrawal from the region.

The Malaysian economy continued to expand and achieved a high rate of growth in 1969 despite some disruption in production caused by the disturbances. The higher rate of growth in gross national product resulted in a steady rise in the per capita gross national product from M$845 in 1963 to M$1,000 in 1968 and

M$1,060 in 1969. The overall balance of payments position showed a great improvement and recorded a surplus of M$530 million in 1969, compared with deficits of M$26 million in 1968 and M$256 million in 1968. Total net external reserves increased to M$2,-471,000,000 at the end of 1969, M$530 million more than in 1968. Despite the satisfactory rate of growth in the economy, the unemployment situation in West Malaysia continued to deteriorate so that it remained the most important single economic and social problem faced during the year.

The 1970 budget envisaged a current account deficit of M$146 million and an overall deficit of M$930 million. Total revenue was expected to increase to M$2,130,000,000, and expenditure was estimated at M$3,076,000,000, of which M$2,276,000,000 was for current expenditure and M$800 million for development. The overall deficit was to be financed through new taxes estimated to yield M$133 million, special receipts of M$22 million from foreign grants, domestic borrowing of M$603 million, foreign borrowing of M$125 million, and a drawing of M$47 million from the federal government's accumulated assets.

(M. S. R.)

ENCYCLOPÆDIA BRITANNICA FILMS. *Malaya, Land of Tin and Rubber* (1957).

Maldives

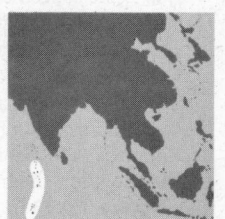

Maldives, a republic in the Indian Ocean, lies southwest of the southern tip of India. Area: 115 sq.mi. (298 sq.km.). Pop. (1969): 110,770. Cap.: Male (pop., 1969, 12,912).

Language: Maldivian. Religion: Muslim. Sultan, Amir Muhammad Farid Didi; president in 1970, Ibrahim Nassir.

Maldives established diplomatic relations with East Germany on May 23, 1970, and later accorded recognition to North Korea, following Ceylon's example after the left-wing election victory there. Its only other overseas diplomatic representation was in Ceylon, as the Maldivian mission in the U.S., which also served as UN representation, closed down.

The importance of work by the British Royal Air Force on Gan Island in Addu Atoll increased with the development of the Skynet satellite communications system and the British government's policy of maintaining a military presence in Asia. As a staging post on the 8,500-mi. route between Singapore and London, the airstrip on the island provided various services for about 400 air movements a month. Apart from the 600 RAF personnel, meals were provided for more than 7,000 transit passengers. Air freight totaled more than one million tons in 1969, and much more was carried by sea.

RAF divers worked during 1970 on the crown-of-thorns starfish menace, which had spread from the

MALDIVES
Education. (State only; 1967–68) Primary, pupils 777, teachers 29; secondary, pupils 190, teachers 22.
Finance and Trade. Monetary unit: Maldivian rupee, with a par value of MRs. 4.76 to U.S. $1 (MRs. 11.43 = £1 sterling). Budget (1968) expenditure MRs. 17,069,488. Foreign trade mainly with Ceylon. Main exports (metric tons; 1968): fish 3,700; copra 53. Fishing accounts for *c.* 95% of exports.

Pacific to the Indian Ocean. The starfish were weakening coral reefs by stripping them of living polyps. A local radio station, largely donated by the Nuffield Trust, was established and staffed by RAF volunteers.

(M. MR.)

Mali

A republic of West Africa, Mali is bordered by Algeria, Niger, Upper Volta, Ivory Coast, Guinea, Senegal, and Mauritania. Area: 478,652 sq.mi. (1,239,710 sq.km.). Pop. (1969 est.): 4,929,000. Cap. and largest city: Bamako (metro. pop., 1967 est., 175,000). Language: French (official); Hamito-Semitic and various tribal dialects. Religion: Muslim 63%; animist 36%. Head of military government in 1970, Lieut. Moussa Traoré.

Two years after the take-over of power by the Army, political unrest persisted in Mali. In March, seven intellectuals were sentenced to imprisonment for defamation of Lieut. Moussa Traoré and other Cabinet ministers.

An important Cabinet reshuffle took place in September. Three civilian members of the government were dismissed, including Louis Nègre, principal engineer of Franco-Malian financial agreements, and were replaced by three army officers. Lieut. Baba Diarra was given the post of finance minister. Capt. Yoro Diakité, a former head of government demoted to minister of transport the previous year, became minister of state in charge of defense, interior, security, and information. Lieut. Joseph Mara was appointed minister of justice. All three new ministers were members of the ruling Military Committee of National Liberation (CMLN). These measures were designed to strengthen the Army's hold on the government; however, owing to disputes among the officers, their authority was, in fact, increased only slightly, if at all. The following month Diakité's replacement as defense minister by Lieut. Kissima Doukara was announced, and M. Diallo became minister of information.

In October, the military leaders came into conflict with the labour unions on the occasion of the second congress of the National Union of Malian Workers (UNTM). An emergency meeting of the CMLN was held. The decision was taken to dissolve the provisional consultative committee of the UNTM, to refuse to recognize the bureau appointed at the congress, and

MALI
Education. (1967–68) Primary, pupils 186,022, teachers 5,324; secondary, pupils 1,841, teachers 171; vocational, pupils 2,301, teachers 304; teacher training, students 2,064, teachers 114; higher, students 345, teaching staff 90.
Finance. Monetary unit: Mali franc, with a par value of MFr. 555.42 to U.S. $1 (MFr. 1,333 = £1 sterling). Budget (1969 est.) balanced at MFr. 23 billion. Money supply: (March 1970) MFr. 29,060,000,000; (March 1969) MFr. 23,870,000,000.
Foreign Trade. (1968) Imports MFr. 22,770,000,000; exports MFr. 9,010,000,000. Import sources: France 32%; U.S.S.R. 19%; China 13%; Ivory Coast 9%; Senegal 7%. Export destinations: Ivory Coast 25%; France 17%; Senegal 16%; Ghana 9%. Main exports: cotton 33%; fish 13%; peanuts 8%.
Agriculture. Production (in 000; metric tons; 1968; 1967 in parentheses): millet and sorghum 757 (881); rice *c.* 150 (160); corn 72 (66); peanuts (1969) *c.* 120, (1968) *c.* 100; sweet potatoes *c.* 65 (*c.* 70); cassava *c.* 220 (*c.* 214); cotton, lint *c.* 15 (*c.* 12). Livestock (in 000; 1968–69): cattle *c.* 5,220; sheep *c.* 5,300; horses *c.* 170; asses *c.* 530.

to reject the statutes proposed there. The minister of information reproached the union in a broadcast for overstepping its rights and setting itself up as a political body. (PH. D.)

Malta

An island in the Mediterranean Sea, between Sicily and Tunisia, Malta is a parliamentary state and a member of the Commonwealth of Nations. Area: 122 sq.mi. (316 sq.km.), including Malta, Gozo, and Comino. Pop. (1969 est.): 322,353. Cap.: Valletta (pop., 1970 est., 15,547). Largest city: Sliema (pop., 1970 est., 21,983). Language: English and Maltese. Religion: mainly Roman Catholic. Queen, Elizabeth II; governor-general in 1970, Sir Maurice Dorman; prime minister, Giorgio Borg Olivier.

The change of government in the U.K. in June 1970 broke the deadlock between the British and Maltese governments on financial aid. Discussions were resumed shortly after the Conservatives were elected, and in October agreement was reached on whether the £22.7 million remaining from the ten-year financial agreement of 1964 was to be considered a grant or a loan. Of this amount, the British government agreed to make available as a gift £1 million for the restoration of historic buildings, £3 million for dockyard development, and 75% of the balance, while the other 25% of the balance would be in the form of a loan.

To check the rising price level, stamp duty on marketable securities was substantially increased, and a new tax on private car ownership came into force. Pending the introduction of an interest equalization tax, exchange control was extended to the movement of capital to the rest of the sterling area. In July agreement was reached with the EEC on the creation of a customs union that would, over a period of ten years, lead to the elimination of tariffs, quotas, and other restrictions between the EEC and Malta, and the adoption by Malta of the Community's common external tariff. Legislation was passed to raise a regular armed force. (A. G.)

MALTA
Education. (1966–67) Primary, pupils 53,456, teachers 2,516; secondary, pupils 10,820, teachers 749; vocational, pupils 2,208, teachers 213; higher (including Royal University of Malta), students 1,266, teaching staff 172.
Finance. Monetary unit: Maltese pound, at par with the pound sterling (M£1 = U.S. $2.40). Budget (1969–70): revenue M£32,399,000; expenditure M£33,394,000.
Foreign Trade. (1969) Imports M£61,516,000 (43% from U.K., 16% from Italy); exports M£15,-957,000 (34% to U.K., 11% to Italy, 5% to Libya, 5% to France, 5% to West Germany, 13% as ship's stores). Main exports: clothing 20%; textile yarns and fabrics 15%; petroleum products 9%; rubber products 8%; textile fibres 6%; transport equipment 6%; meat and products 5%. Tourism (1968): visitors 137,000; gross receipts U.S. $19 million.
Transport and Communications. Roads (1968) 1,110 km. Motor vehicles in use (1968): passenger 31,500; commercial (including buses) 9,300. There are no railways. Air traffic (1969): 236.5 million passenger-km.; freight 2,480,000 net ton-km. Shipping (1969): merchant vessels 100 gross tons and over 25; gross tonnage 58,112. Ships entered (1968) vessels totaling 1,638,000 net registered tons; goods loaded (1968) 66,000 metric tons, unloaded 737,000 metric tons. Telephones (Jan. 1969) 33,092. Radio receivers (Dec. 1967) 87,000. Television receivers (Dec. 1968) 37,000.

Mathematics

In 1924, at the International Congress of Mathematicians in Toronto, Ont., J. C. Fields of the University of Toronto proposed prizes for outstanding work in mathematics. The 1932 congress in Zürich, Switz., endorsed the idea and, by setting an age limit of 40, decided that the awards should go to younger mathematicians who showed unusual promise. The Fields prizes have since had worldwide recognition as the highest honour for mathematical research; in mathematics they are judged equivalent to Nobel prizes.

There were two prizes at the subsequent congresses at Oslo (1936), Cambridge, Mass. (1950), Amsterdam (1954), Edinburgh, Scot. (1958), and Stockholm (1962). The enormous growth of the world mathematical community was recognized at the 1966 congress in Moscow by increasing the number of Fields prizes to four, and four were again awarded at Nice, France, in 1970. The recipients were Alan Baker (U.K.), Heusuke Hironaka (Jap., later in the U.S.), S. P. Novikov (U.S.S.R.), and John Thompson (U.S.). The work of these four young mathematicians reflects important trends in mathematical research.

Alan Baker's Achievements. German mathematician David Hilbert (1862–1943) posed his seventh problem (*see* below) by asking the following question: if a and b are algebraic, a is not 0 or 1, and b is irrational, is a^b necessarily transcendental? This was answered affirmatively by A. Gelfond in 1934, and independently a little later by T. Schneider. The Gelfond-Schneider theorem can be recast as follows: if x and y are algebraic, and $\log x$, $\log y$ are linearly independent over the field of rational numbers, then they are likewise linearly independent over the field of algebraic numbers. Baker made a significant generalization to n numbers, and at the same time strengthened the conclusion by inserting the number 1. In detail: if $x_1, \ldots, x_n$ are algebraic, and $\log x_1, \ldots, \log x_n$ are linearly independent over the rationals, then 1, $\log x_1, \ldots, \log x_n$ are linearly independent over the algebraic numbers. The simplest new transcendental number that Baker obtained was $\pi + \log 2$.

Baker's methods are "effective" in the sense that they yield numerical estimates for the numbers involved. In parallel work on certain diophantine equations (*i.e.*, polynomial equations to be solved in integers), Baker likewise obtained explicit estimates. A remarkable example is the bound:

$$e^{(10^6 M)^{10^6}}$$

for the integral solutions of $y^2 = ax^3 + bx^2 + cx + d$, where M is the largest of the integers $|a|, |b|, |c|, |d|$.

Heusuke Hironaka's Work. An algebraic variety is defined as the set of all solutions of a system of polynomial equations. In the simplest case there is one equation in two variables, and this is graphically represented as a curve in the plane. Certain well-behaved algebraic varieties are called nonsingular; the precise definition is highly technical, but the rough idea is that the variety should not cross itself, as the following curve does:

The problem of the resolution of singularities is posed when it is asked whether any variety is equivalent to one that is nonsingular, in a sense appropriate for algebraic geometry. By a long and delicate analysis,

Mathematics students at Beverley Boys School in New Malden, Eng., use a computer built by three of the school's pupils. The machine can add, subtract, multiply, divide, and evaluate simple logic problems.

UPI COMPIX

Hironaka showed mathematically that the answer to the question was affirmative. His work depended on methods previously developed by O. Zariski, who had in particular given an affirmative answer for varieties with dimension not exceeding three.

S. P. Novikov's Contributions. Novikov was honoured for numerous contributions to topology. His most outstanding work included his extension of rational Pontryagin classes to arbitrary manifolds, plus an accompanying proof of invariance: and his studies of the cohomology and homotopy of Thom spaces of manifolds. The spirit of this work is to assign to manifolds invariants of ever increasing subtlety; the result has been the achievement in recent years of a virtually complete theory of manifolds.

John Thompson's Efforts. The algebraic structure called a group is a basic topic of study in modern algebra. Finite groups are of particular interest, and the major problem is to classify the ultimate building blocks that are called finite simple groups. Thompson made two decisive contributions: in collaboration with Walter Feit he demonstrated that any finite simple group has even order, and he then went on to show that the known list of minimal simple groups is exhaustive.

In Paris at the 1900 congress mathematicians were challenged by Hilbert with a list of 23 problems, the solution of which would be important for 20th-century mathematics. Many of Hilbert's problems have been solved, and each announcement of a solution is a notable event. In 1970 the tenth problem was solved by J. V. Matijasevic of the U.S.S.R. This one asks whether it is possible to give a definite method for solving any diophantine equation. The answer, as expected, was negative; but it is to be noted that for special equations (such as those handled by Baker) it remains conceivable that the answer is affirmative.

Appropriate recognition recently came to Hilbert, by critical agreement the outstanding mathematician of his time. A Soviet book, *Hilbert's Problems* (1969), edited by P. S. Aleksandrov, surveyed the current status of his 23 problems, and a full-length biography of Hilbert by Constance Reid (1970) offered a remarkable picture of his life.

The year saw a vigorous discussion among U.S.

mathematicians concerning the training in that country of Ph.D. candidates in mathematics. Concern was voiced over a possible oversupply of those who hold the doctorate. It was also questioned whether current Ph.D. programs were appropriate for the positions most young mathematicians would be called on to fill. Articles in the *American Mathematical Monthly* grappled with these questions. The consensus seemed to be that there was little probability of more than a marginal oversupply (if any) in the foreseeable future. On the other hand, there were grave reservations on the wisdom of present programs. It was argued that graduate students are exposed to a range of mathematical topics too narrow for general teaching positions and that growing applications of mathematics to other fields (*e.g.*, medicine or business) are being recognized much too slowly. (I. KA.)

Mauritania

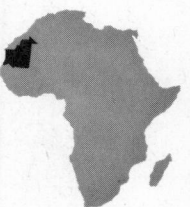

The Islamic Republic of Mauritania is on the Atlantic coast of West Africa, adjoining Spanish Sahara, Algeria, Mali, and Senegal. Area: 397,683 sq.mi. (1,030,-000 sq.km.). Pop. (1969 est.): 1,140,000. Cap.: Nouakchott (pop., 1967 est., 15,000). Language: Arabic (national); French (official). Religion: Muslim. President in 1970, Mokhtar Ould Daddah.

MAURITANIA
Education. (1968–69) Primary, pupils 26,222, teachers (1965–66) 1,025; secondary, pupils 2,663, teachers (1963–64) 61; vocational (1964–65), pupils 197; teacher training (1964–65), students 107.

Finance. Monetary unit: CFA franc, with a parity of CFA Fr. 50 to the French franc (CFA Fr. 277.71 = U.S. \$1; CFA Fr. 666.50 = £1 sterling). Gold, SDRs, and foreign exchange, central bank: (April 1970) U.S. \$4.2 million; (April 1969) U.S. \$6.7 million. Budget (1969 est.): revenue CFA Fr. 7,084,-000,000; expenditure CFA Fr. 6,649,000,000.

Foreign Trade. Imports (1969) CFA Fr. 10,666,-000,000; exports (1968) CFA Fr. 17,920,000,000. Import sources (1968): France 51%; U.S. 16%; Netherlands 11%; Congo (Brazzaville) 5%. Export destinations: U.K. 25%; West Germany 17%; France 17%; Belgium-Luxembourg 14%; Italy 11%; Japan 9%. Main export iron ore 85%.

The reconciliation between Mauritania and Morocco achieved in 1969 began to assume a positive form when the first agreements on cooperation in matters of mutual interest were concluded in February 1970. Shortly before this, the two capitals had agreed to exchange ambassadors.

In June King Hassan II of Morocco received Pres. Mokhtar Ould Daddah in Rabat. The political future of the neighbouring Spanish Sahara was discussed and a treaty of solidarity and cooperation signed. In July commercial agreements were signed at Rabat between Mauritania and Morocco, and shortly afterward an intergovernmental committee was set up. On his return, Ould Daddah received the Spanish minister of foreign affairs, Gregorio López Bravo, at Nouakchott, but no agreement was reached on the future political structure of the Spanish Sahara.

A meeting between Pres. Houari Boumédienne of Algeria, King Hassan, and President Ould Daddah in September resulted in little more than the expression of a hope "to hasten the decolonization of the Spanish Sahara," together with the establishment of a tripartite coordinating committee. (PH. D.)

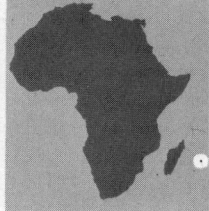

Mauritius

The parliamentary state of Mauritius, a member of the Commonwealth of Nations, lies about 500 mi. E of the Malagasy Republic in the Indian Ocean. Area: 720 sq.mi. (1,865 sq.km.). Pop. (1970 est.): 830,-700, including Indian and Pakistani 67%; Creole (mixed French and African) 29%; others, 4%. Cap. and largest city: Port Louis (pop., 1970 est., 139,300). Queen, Elizabeth II; governor-general in 1970, Sir Leonard Williams; prime minister, Sir Seewoosagur Ramgoolam.

The second year of national independence was marked by the establishment of a coalition "national unity" government in December 1969 between the majority (Indian) Independence Party and the Parti Mauricien. The coalition hoped "to overcome latent hostility between the predominant Hindu community and Muslim, Chinese, Creole, and European minorities." The Cabinet was enlarged from 14 to 20.

The strategic position of Mauritius in the Indian Ocean, in the line of Soviet naval expansion, was emphasized by the visit of India's prime minister, Mrs. Indira Gandhi, in June. For India, Mauritius served as a useful bridge to Africa, and a joint Indian-Mauritian communiqué expressed alarm at the buildup

MAURITIUS
Education. (1968–69) Primary, pupils 142,959, teachers 4,253; secondary, pupils 39,703, teachers 1,706; vocational, pupils 603, teachers 34; teacher training, students 642, teachers 25; higher, students 178, teaching staff 41.
Finance and Trade. Monetary unit: Mauritian rupee, with a par value of MauRs. 5.55 to U.S. $1 (MauRs. 13.44 = £1 sterling). Budget (1968–69 est.): revenue MauRs. 249,025,000; expenditure MauRs. 248,632,000. Foreign trade (1968): imports MauRs. 421 million (24% from U.K., 10% from Burma, 8% from South Africa, 7% from West Germany, 6% from Australia); exports MauRs. 371 million (73% to U.K., 12% to Canada, 6% to U.S.). Main export sugar 91%. Tourism (1967): visitors 14,800; gross receipts U.S. $3 million.
Agriculture. Production (in 000; metric tons): sugar (1969–70) 518, (1968–69) 597; tea (1968) 2.3, (1967) 2.2; tobacco (1968) 0.7, (1967) 0.6. Livestock (in 000; April 1968): cattle 46; pigs 3; sheep c. 3; goats 66; chickens 385.

Meat:
see Agriculture; Food

Medical Education:
see Medicine

of foreign navies in the area. A fishing agreement with the Soviet Union in 1969 was expanded to a trawler landing rights agreement in July, but no naval rights were included.

The high density of population and one-crop (sugar) economy continued to be Mauritius' main problems, despite some attempts at economic diversification. Largely dependent upon British aid and concerned lest the latter's proposed membership in the European Economic Community alter the Commonwealth Sugar Agreement, Mauritius in 1970 accepted £6 million in aid for capital and development purposes. (M. MR.)

Medicine

Attention in medicine and surgery in 1970 was focused largely on long-term results of transplants, development of drugs for treatment of certain major illnesses, and the wide spread of several contagious diseases.

Heart transplants remained a focal point of public interest. When Philip Blaiberg of South Africa continued to live month after month with a donor heart pumping blood through his body, heart transplantation was considered the latest in a series of miracles that started with open-heart surgery. Since December 1967, 164 patients had undergone cardiac transplantation. Of these, 23 were still alive near the end of 1970. When Blaiberg died on Aug. 17, 1969, some 19 months after his operation, and then on May 22, 1970, when Petrus Smith, South Africa's third heart transplant and at that time the world's second-longest-surviving cardiac transplant patient, died of stomach cancer, the miracle lost much of its lustre.

What had not been publicized, however, was that of those 23 still living, 16 had survived for more than a year and were doing well. Louis B. Russell, Jr., a 45-year-old Indianapolis, Ind., schoolteacher who received the heart of a 17-year-old donor on Aug. 24, 1968, was extremely active, with a heavy schedule of teach-

"At last! House calls"—Whitman, "Phoenix Gazette."

BEN ROTH AGENCY

ing, traveling, and lecturing. Donald L. Kaminski of Alpena, Mich., near death from degeneration of the heart muscle, received a heart transplant on Dec. 2, 1968. He claimed that he was the most active of all transplant patients—smoking, drinking, and knowing how to handle a hangover. Joseph E. Murray of Boston, a surgeon who participated in the first successful kidney transplant, was quoted as saying, "It is as reasonable to do heart transplants in the 1970s as it was to do kidney transplants in 1960–65."

With regard to kidney transplants, of 19 patients who received cadaver kidneys at the University of California, San Francisco, in 1969–70, 15 were out of the hospital and back at work by mid-1970. This 80% success as opposed to the 38% average during the previous six years was attributed to an organ-preserving technique and a new cell-matching procedure. Widespread use of cardiac transplantation, however, without some form of effective, albeit short-term, organ preservation system does not appear possible.

Tissue typing has been a source of controversy. Paul I. Teraski pointed out in 1970 that computerized cataloging of antigen matches and kidney survivals will aid in forecasting rejection crises. More than two years earlier Robert A. Good (1970 winner of the Lasker Award in Clinical Medicine) and associates at the University of Minnesota used, instead of the traditional tissue-matching techniques, a horse serum extract so biologically pure that it could be given intravenously in relatively huge amounts. As a result, Minnesota's overall record showed 80% two-year survivals from cadaver donors and a spectacular 90% for related living donors in something under 150 grafts.

Liver transplants have not fared as well. Thomas E. Starzl of the University of Colorado's Medical Center at Denver expressed pessimism over the use of such transplants for hepatic cancer but was less gloomy over the future of his procedure for cases of intractable hepatitis, cirrhosis, and Wilson's disease.

Clinical medicine continued its battles against disease—winning a few against old enemies but discovering new ones immune to the present armamentarium. Sixty-seven percent of those afflicted with Parkinson's disease—an insidious condition affecting the nervous system and causing rigidity, stooped posture, peculiar gait, and early death—considered L-dopa, if not a miracle, certainly something closely akin to it. Relief from symptoms of the disease were remarkable, despite certain side effects, most noticeably involuntary movements, particularly of the mouth and jaw. Increased libido, reported by some investigators, was dismissed by others. Anything that made one feel that much better was bound to increase his libido, they claimed. L-dopa, approved by the U.S. Food and Drug Administration (FDA) on June 4, 1970, for sale by general prescription, remained expensive.

A new oral blood-sugar-lowering agent, glibenclamide, was introduced for the treatment of mild diabetes. In preliminary tests it appeared a potent hypoglycemic drug, effective in a single daily dose of 2.5–20 mg., with no apparent serious side effects. Tolbutamide, once hailed as the end to the search for an "oral insulin" and used by some 1.5 million Americans, was now strongly suspected not only of being ineffective—i.e., no more effective than diet alone—but of increasing the risk of dying from cardiovascular disease. Although it was claimed by many experts, and disputed by as many, that the accumulated data were not statistically significant, one fact appeared indisputable: the drugs had lulled doctors and patients alike

into a false sense of security and many patients were ignoring their diets believing they were protected by the drugs.

Rifamycin is an antibiotic that has been found useful as an antitubercular drug, especially in cases where the patient has developed a resistance to the older, established compounds such as streptomycin, para-aminosalicylic acid, and isoniazid. It took on added significance in 1970 when at least eight persons in Washington, D.C., including two newsmen who died of liver damage, developed jaundice after taking isoniazid.

A British scientist, K. Hellmann, reported the discovery of a drug, known as bio-dioxopipdrazine, which he said controls the spread of cancer in mice. Hellmann said the compound was being tested in human patients in London, Glasgow, and Belfast, but, he warned, results would not be known for some time.

Vitamin C, or ascorbic acid as it is known to the chemist, isolated in 1927, has been known to be essential to man (who cannot synthesize it within his body), for in a diet without it he develops scurvy. Nobel Prize winner Linus Pauling of Stanford University said in 1970 that the vitamin is all that is needed to ward off or treat the common cold or flu. The idea was not a new one, but Pauling said that medical authorities claimed the compound was useless for that purpose because they did not realize that much larger doses than the usually prescribed daily 200 mg. were needed. He pointed out that one to four grams are required each day (four grams is approximately one level teaspoonful of the pure crystalline powder) to be effective. Some dermatologists, however, claimed that some individuals were sensitive to vitamin C in large doses and, as a result, developed warts, papules, and other skin eruptions—all of which subsided when the dosage was decreased or administration stopped.

For the first time since penicillin became available to the general public, the incidence of venereal disease was declared pandemic in the U.S.—having jumped more than 387% in ten years among those in the $9,000 per year income bracket alone. The American Social Health Association at its annual session voted to ask Pres. Richard Nixon to appoint a commission on venereal disease. Only twice before in its 58-year existence had the ASHA declared the prevalence of social disease to be pandemic (pandemic simply means a severe epidemic over an unusually wide geographic area)—once at the end of World War I and once near the end of World War II. Gonorrhea was reported to be out of control with more than two million reported cases in 1970, and there were 250,000 new cases of syphilis. The number of unreported cases was anyone's guess, but experts agreed that it far exceeded the number reported. James McKenzie-Pollock, medical director of the association, estimated that 10% of women between the ages of 18 and 24 may have gonorrhea, be unaware of it, and become sterile because of it.

Asiatic cholera is a highly contagious disease, exclusively of man, that develops in three stages: evacuation, collapse, and reaction. When untreated it is highly fatal. Vibrio cholera prevailed in East Pakistan, and in some parts of India classical biotypes were also isolated. In Laos, Thailand, Indonesia, and Malaysia biotype El Tor, serotype Inaba were identified. In the Philippines, Nepal, India, Burma, and Korea biotype El Tor, serotype Ogawa were found. Cholera (not vibrio) was reported from 15 countries in the Southeast Asian and western Pacific regions. The majority

UPI COMPIX

James Finley of St. Paul, Minn., sued the federal government for $500,000 in damages after medication given him in a veterans' hospital allegedly changed his skin colour from black to white.

of the reported 27,257 cases with 4,422 deaths occurred in India. An outbreak of cholera was reported in a rather obscure manner from the U.S.S.R., at first denied and then confirmed. It is important to note that the worldwide data indicated that either many mild cases were not reported or that facilities for the prompt recognition and effective treatment of the disease were not yet available in many affected countries. In addition, some countries in which there were outbreaks of cholera—even at epidemic proportions—attempted to conceal the presence of the disease. Such an attitude obviously did little to help prevent the spread of cholera to neighbouring countries.

On a worldwide basis the number of cases of smallpox and poliomyelitis definitely declined; the incidence of yellow-fever plague and louse-borne relapsing fever remained about the same; while louse-borne typhus cases showed an increase.

A medical alarm was sounded throughout the world's pharmacodynamic and genetic research laboratories when it was discovered that a large number of pathogenic microbes have developed a "wonder-resistance" against medical science's "wonder drugs." A modern era of medicine was ushered in in the 1940s when the discovery of penicillin and the seemingly endless stream of specific and broad-spectrum antibiotics afforded physicians stunning victories over infectious microbes. It appears that the tide of battle has now turned. The bacteria, gram negative type (so-called because they do not take the usual purple stain when treated with a special dye), appear to have the ability not only to swiftly produce genetic changes that make them immune to antibiotics, but also to pass the immunity on to other bacteria. At the tenth Interscience Conference on Antimicrobial Agents and Chemotherapy held in Chicago in October, medical scientists expressed gravest concern over three principal situations: (1) One of the major hazards to hospitalized patients is infection by gram negative bacteria. These are infections which a patient may contract after hospitalization; they kill an estimated 75,000 patients a year. (2) New York has been suffering from endemic "food poisoning" that could become epidemic. It is being caused by a gram negative salmonella bug against which antibiotics have absolutely no effect. (3) The Shigella dysenterial type 1 bacteria has reappeared in South America. One of the great killers of the past quarter century, it threatens to spread to the southwestern U.S.

A possible case of recovery from rabies was announced in December 1970. A six-year-old boy living in Lima, O., was bitten by a bat, which was subsequently found to be rabid. The boy was given the standard antirabies vaccine treatment. Later admitted to a hospital with what was at first believed to be a reaction to the vaccine, he was found to have active rabies and was given intensive treatment, principally designed to alleviate convulsions and other acute symptoms of the disease. Within a few weeks he began to improve rapidly, and at the end of the year appeared normal except for weakness and some speech difficulty. If the boy indeed survived, it would be the first known case of recovery from rabies in medical history.

(M. Fi.; Al. Pa.; X.)

CANCER

For the first time rational planning of cancer research at the national level in Great Britain was made possible by the formation of a British Cancer Council and by the agreement of the Medical Research Coun-

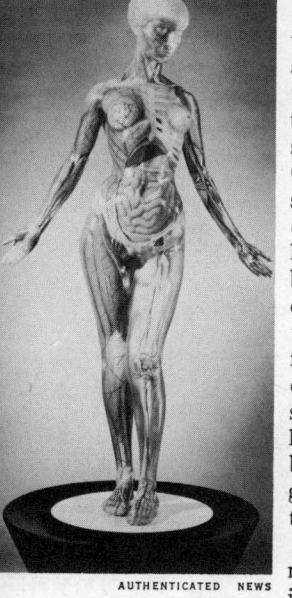

AUTHENTICATED NEWS INTERNATIONAL

TAM (Transparent Anatomical Manikin), a unique new medical education model, is cast of clear epoxy. Each internal organ can be made visible even though obscured by muscle or another organ.

cil, the Imperial Cancer Research Fund, and the Cancer Research Campaign (formerly the British Empire Cancer Campaign for Research) to form a Co-ordinating Committee for Cancer Research. The International Agency for Research on Cancer (IARC), though still waiting to move into new laboratories in Lyons, France, was actively promoting studies of the role of environmental factors in the etiology of human cancers. Recent advances in knowledge most relevant to problems of human cancer, however, stemmed from epidemiological studies. Among the most spectacular of these was a report that when Japanese migrated to the United States from Japan, where cancer of the stomach is prevalent and cancer of the colon rare, their risk of stomach cancer fell and of colon cancer rose. Such studies indicated that environmental factors may be more important than genetic factors in the cause of some forms of human cancer. The IARC hoped, by sponsoring field studies and supporting Regional Cancer Registries, to obtain data concerning cancer risks among various populations, and then, by correlating this information with that of risks in various communities, to identify environmental factors that cause cancer in man.

The discovery in 1969 that prolonged feeding to rats of a 10:1 mixture of sodium cyclamate and sodium saccharin (and in other tests using cyclamate alone) predisposed them to cancer of the bladder led to the banning of the use of cyclamates as artificial sweeteners in food in many countries. It may be relevant that certain gut bacteria can convert cyclamate to cyclohexylamine which is related to dicyclohexylamine previously shown to be carcinogenic in rats. No carcinogenic effect has been observed in mice fed cyclamates in high dosage for periods up to 18 months. The banning of cyclamates marked a turning point in the attitude of legislative authorities and of members of the public toward the use of animal tests for the prediction of cancer hazard for man. The question was raised as to why the carcinogenicity of cyclamates was not discovered in the course of tests reported in 1951. Other questions concerned the justification of withdrawing a valuable product from the market in the light of equivocal laboratory evidence, and pointed out that I. I. Kessler found no excess of bladder cancer in his survey of cancer in diabetics who had been heavily exposed to cyclamates. All he found was the expected excess of cancers of the pancreas known to exist in 1934, ten years before cyclamates were used as sweeteners.

Doubts of the predictive value of carcinogenicity tests on laboratory animals also stemmed from a report from J. R. M. Innes and colleagues that 11 widely used chemical pesticides predispose to the development of tumours of the liver, and in some cases also of the lung and lymphoid systems, in mice; and from the observation that liver tumours and lung tumours tend to occur much later in germ-free mice than in mice carrying a normal gut flora. In one area at least, however, there appeared to be a correlation between what happens in man and what happens in the rat: R. Montesano and Magee showed that human liver can metabolize dimethylnitrosamine at a rate comparable with that of rat liver and that similar levels of methylation of nucleic acids occur in the two species. If the carcinogenicity of this compound depends on such methylation then the results suggest that man is susceptible to its carcinogenic action.

E. D. Acheson and his colleagues reported a greatly increased risk of nasal and nasal sinus cancers in woodworkers and shoemakers in Britain and a report in the *Journal of the National Cancer Institute* suggested that cancer of the pancreas occurs unexpectedly frequently among members of the chemical profession. I. A. Evans and colleagues in Bangor, Wales, reported the induction of cancers in rats fed on the same species of bracken as that eaten by humans in Japan.

The risk of scrotal cancer among tool setters working automatic lathes cooled and lubricated by circulating mineral oils was highlighted by litigation proceedings in Birmingham, Eng. The observation by J. G. Holmes and others that second primary cancers, mostly of the lung and digestive tract, occur significantly more often than expected in men with previous scrotal cancer may point to a hazard from the mineral oil mist frequently generated by automatic cutting machines. The presumption that the carcinogenicity of mineral oil is attributable almost solely to its content of polycyclic aromatic hydrocarbons was seriously questioned by new evidence of the importance of cocarcinogenic straight-chain aliphatic constituents of the oil.

Isoenzyme studies suggested that Burkitt's lymphoma usually arises from a single cell. R. J. Huebner and G. G. Todaro's hypotheses that most vertebrate species have normally "switched-off" C-type RNA virus genomes that are vertically transmitted from parent to offspring and that the derepression of these represents the long-sought final common pathway in carcinogenesis awaited critical evaluation. (See *Occupational Medicine,* below.)   (F. J. C. R.)

CARDIOLOGY

The exploration of the inside of the heart, using fine electrical wires and recording apparatus to improve the definition of the mechanism of the heart rhythm and rate, and refined study under both the light and electron microscope of the tissues forming electrical impulses (pacemaker sites) and of the specialized conduction pathways were actively pursued during 1970. The normal site of the first electrical activity beginning each heartbeat is apparently in a small area called the sinus node. This is connected by three special conducting pathways to an area lower in the heart called the A-V (atrio-ventricular) node. Recent observations indicated this node to be a reception and transmission site and not one that acts as a pacemaker. Below this A-V node are additional conduction pathways that can act as subsidiary pacemaker areas. Further, it was discovered that unusually rapid heart rhythms often represented the passage of an electrical impulse from a subsidiary pacemaker area in the upper portion of the heart down toward the lower portion along these conduction pathways, and then back up a portion of the same route, a phenomenon referred to as "reentry." In other words, the electrical activity of the heart might arise in a number of unusual sites and proceed both down and up the conduction system in an abnormal rapid and circular fashion. Such abnormal heart rhythms were being observed more and more in patients through the increased use of recordings (electrocardiograms or EKGs) of the electrical activity of the heart among cardiac patients.

There was increasing use of computers both in units designed for the care of patients with acute heart attacks and in recovery units for postoperative heart cases. The computers were employed to receive, record, and interpret up to 23 variables, including heart rate, blood pressures, blood oxygen levels, and blood volume. Computers also were being extensively employed in medical centres throughout the world in the interpretation of electrocardiograms that were transmitted directly to the computer by use of special dataphones.

Millions of Americans may have severe coronary disease and not even be aware of it. How to identify them has been one of the biggest diagnostic problems facing physicians in recent years. Only too common is the story of the patient who, after being given a clean bill of health by the electrocardiogram, dropped dead of a heart attack on the way home. Arthur M. Master, of Mt. Sinai School of Medicine of the City University of New York, seemed to have found the key to the diagnosis of so-called silent heart disease with a simple eight-minute test. The test consists of having the patient walk up and down a double-step platform a number of times and then submit to an electrocardiogram. Experience has shown that most individuals with severe heart disease—even with chest pain—will show a relatively normal heartbeat when the EKG is made during a resting position. Under stress, such as during the two-step test, a diseased heart will not receive a sufficient supply of blood and the EKG will produce an abnormal pattern. The test is 95–97% accurate, claims Master, professor emeritus of clinical medicine.

On American Thanksgiving Day, Nov. 26, 1970, a man named Bill Lyons of Port Orchard, Wash., had plenty for which to be thankful. He had "died" four times in the previous 22 months—actually his heart had stopped beating for a total of eight hours during that time. He was probably the only man alive and able to work after having had four open-heart operations, all since February 1969, when he received an artificial heart valve.

Exertion without motion, otherwise known as isometric exercise, may be great for building muscles, but, according to Charles Kivowitz and associates at Cedars-Sinai Medical Center in Los Angeles, it places

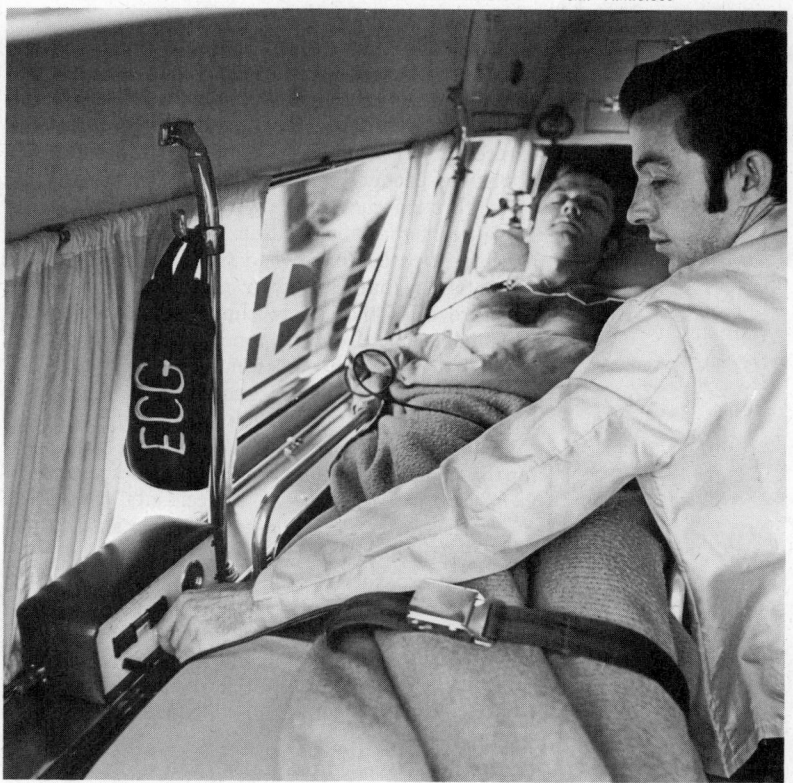

Ambulance attendant attaches leads from the chest of a suspected heart attack victim to a modulator unit. The patient's EKG is then transmitted by radio to a hospital where the information can be interpreted and emergency treatment prescribed.

COURTESY, MOUNT ZION HOSPITAL AND MEDICAL CENTER, SAN FRANCISCO

a severe strain on a diseased heart. In almost all such cases isometric exercise has led to an increase in heart size and oxygen requirement and, at the same time, decreased the cardiac output.

The relationship between dietary fat intake, blood cholesterol level, and cardiovascular disease remained a matter of debate. During the year, however, the (U.S.) Intersociety Commission for Heart Disease Resources recommended, on the basis of available data, that Americans should reduce their current average consumption of cholesterol and saturated fats by 50% and should substantially lower their intake of all fats.

In 1970 nuclear-powered heart pacemakers were successfully implanted in patients in France and Britain. The devices were designed to last some ten years, compared with about a year and a half for battery-powered pacemakers. (*See* NUCLEAR ENERGY.)

M. Harvey Brenner, a specialist in public health research and sociology at the Yale University School of Medicine, reported findings of strong statistical evidence linking increased fatality from heart attacks to the country's economic recessions. After having analyzed the data from the turn of the century on, Brenner stated: "Economic downturns are associated with increased mortality from heart disease, and, conversely, heart disease mortality decreases during economic upturns." (O. PL.)

DERMATOLOGY

In the past few years, dermatologists in the U.S. have established the National Program for Dermatology to coordinate efforts to solve problems that arise from disorders of the skin. One of the first efforts of the program was to increase the number of dermatologists from the present 3,000 to approximately 8,000. Additional plans were to train dermatologic nurse-clinicians and aides to assist the dermatologist. Complementing the program, especially in fund-raising, was the Dermatology Foundation, a national nonprofit, tax-exempt organization established in 1963 by both the practitioners and the teachers of dermatology in the U.S.

The bacillus *Corynebacterium acnes* was implicated as a cause of facial acne. Not only does it grow in normal and abnormal inflamed sebaceous follicles (oil glands of the skin) but the germ produces in test-tube culture a fatty acid that has been identified also in sebum, the product of these follicles. Fatty acids released through the follicle walls are thought to be the cause of the inflammation in acne. *C. acnes* was detected in patients who had responded to the antibiotic tetracycline and then regressed. Subsequent testing revealed that tetracycline, heretofore successful in inhibiting *C. acnes*, appeared to have no bactericidal effect. The role of nutrition in the pathogenesis of acne is unclear; starvation, however, will decrease the production of sebum by 40%.

Milk-white depigmentation of the skin was intentionally achieved by the topical use of derivatives of phenol and catechol, as well as accidentally achieved by a variety of germicidal detergents containing these derivatives and used daily in households.

Chronic exposure to sunlight ages the skin by the disruption of dermal collagen, and also causes epidermal cancers. Experimental radiation in the sunburn spectrum can produce thymine dimers (couplets of the building blocks of DNA) that presumably will lead to genetic misinformation and malformed and malfunctioning cells.

A newly developed oral form of beta carotene was found effective in protecting human skin from ultraviolet and visible radiation. Beta carotene protects the skin from wavelengths of 400 nanometres and was effective in ameliorating the photosensitivity that occurs in erythropoietic protoporphyria, a trait in which there is a congenital and lifelong photosensitivity.

Paramyxovirus-like tubular inclusion bodies were described within the cells of blood vessels in lupus nephritis, polymyositis, and other collagen diseases. They also were seen in active, but not in inactive or healed, skin lesions of discoid lupus erythematosus (DLE), systemic lupus erythematosus (SLE), adult and childhood dermatomyositis, and congenital rubella. These inclusion bodies were not seen in skin lesions of systemic sclerosis or morphea. Whether these are indeed RNA viruses that are causative agents or are degenerated cytoplasmic constituents is not clear.

Lupus erythematosus is an inflammatory, often severe, process, involving many organ systems, particularly the skin, joints, blood vessels, and kidneys. There is speculation that the abnormalities in immunologic patterns signify that lupus erythematosus is an autoimmune disease. Many patients have an inexplicably positive routine serologic test for syphilis without a history of syphilis; the sophisticated FTA-ABS (fluorescent treponemal antibody-absorption) and even TPI (treponemal immobilization) tests, which are extremely sensitive and were thought to be specific for only syphilis, have, on rare occasions, also been found to be falsely positive in SLE.

Almost all patients with SLE and up to 40% of patients with localized cutaneous DLE also have circulating serum antibodies to nuclei of cells. Whether these antibodies are formed to attack nuclei or represent a response to some damage to the nuclear membrane is not clear. Indirect fluorescent techniques reveal that other antibodies and serum complement are attached to the basement membrane (a fine-fibril band in the uppermost portion of the dermis at its border with the epidermis) of the skin.

In DLE these antibodies and serum complement are found only in abnormal skin, whereas in SLE they may be found in both abnormal and normal skin. They may be related specifically to the disease process, as ordinary microscopic examination of skin specimens shows alteration and damage of the basement membrane in lupus erythematosus.

Arsenic, long given generally for a variety of complaints and more specifically for asthma, has been associated with the development of keratoses of the palm and a variety of malignant conditions, especially those affecting the skin. The finding of keratoses on the palms and soles in the absence of exposure to arsenic does not seem to have any relation to the presence of internal or cutaneous malignant conditions.

Chalones are a collection of molecules, which perhaps are protein, that inhibit cellular mitosis and have been reported to be lacking in certain cancers. They have been extracted from normal rat epidermis and have been found to inhibit mitosis in cultures of normal mouse epidermis. Speculation exists as to whether they are absent in psoriasis, where cell mitosis occurs seven times faster than normal.

Methotrexate, an effective inhibitor of mitosis, is useful for control of severe psoriasis. It appears to work by blocking the incorporation of deoxyuridine into DNA and inhibiting DNA synthesis for 12 to 16 hours. Liver toxicity due to methotrexate is a well-acknowledged immediate but reversible side effect; in humans, irreversible liver damage in chronic metho-trexate administration seems to be related more to the concomitant ingestion of alcohol than to the medication. Hydroxyurea, which inhibits mitosis by interfering with the enzyme ribonucleotide reductase, has been noted to thin the skin of patients who are receiving it for the treatment of chronic myelocytic leukemia; it also will slowly bring about a resolution, seen on both clinical and histologic examination, in psoriatic skin. (G. J. Br.; T. B. F.)

ENDOCRINOLOGY

The neurohormones produced in the hypothalamus (a part of the bridge between the brainstem and the cerebral hemispheres) are now considered to be the agents that actually monitor the pituitary gland; they have been called "releasing factors." Although these hormones have been isolated, none was synthesized until 1970 when two teams working independently succeeded in producing thyrotropin-releasing factor (TRF). The credits belong to Roger Guillemin and his associates at Baylor College of Medicine, Houston, Tex., and to Cyril Y. Bowers and Andrew V. Schally of Tulane University School of Medicine, New Orleans, La. With the advent of commercially available synthetic TRF, a convenient means for testing the functional ability of the human pituitary for thyroid-stimulating hormone (TSH) secretion was now possible. Norman Fleischer and his associates at Houston administered synthetic TRF to subjects and were able to obtain in them a rise in plasma TSH levels.

Many bioscientists believed growth hormone and lactogenic hormone (prolactin) to be the same hormone; others were convinced these were individual entities. C. H. Li of the University of California lined up the complete sequence of amino acids in the chain that comprises lactogenic hormone of sheep (OLA). Although he was able to show considerable similarity in amino acid sequences, he nonetheless found that OLA contains ten more amino acid units than human growth hormone (HGH). Whereas, in sheep, two separate hormones are required for growth and lactation, in man, human growth hormone alone seems to perform both functions. Excessive production of HGH, usually by a benign expanding pituitary tumour, causes acromegaly in adults, after the epiphyses of the long bones have closed. The successful treatment of this disorder has long been sought. Surgical hypophysectomy, pituitary implants using gold-198 or yttrium-90, and cryohypophysectomy (a "freezing" probe placed through the nose and sphenoid sinus into the sella turcica) have been used with some success. These methods are, of course, associated with certain risks and dangers, but the results of treatment with conventional radiation have been relatively unsatisfactory. John H. Lawrence and his team at Berkeley, Calif., reported the successful treatment of 120 acromegalics with alpha particles beamed from a cyclotron. They achieved relief of symptoms and signs, and a return to normal of elevated growth hormone levels and other metabolic abnormalities. Another mode of treatment of active acromegaly was the use of hormones. Estrogens have been used in the past with evidence of clinical improvement, but were not associated with lowering of elevated growth hormone levels. However, A. M. Lawrence and Lidia Kirsteins of Chicago induced striking reduction in growth hormone levels and improved cosmetic appearance through oral medroxyprogesterone therapy.

A new family of versatile hormonelike substances called prostaglandins was the subject of much attention during 1970. The first active extracts came from the seminal vesicles. These substances also are found in tiny amounts in a wide variety of animal tissues. Prostaglandins, about 14 in number, are believed to be intracellular metabolic regulators that stimulate or inhibit the action of many hormones and have a wide spectrum of physiologic activity. An English investigator, M. W. Goldblatt, and the Swedish worker U. S. von Euler (see BIOGRAPHY) are considered the co-discoverers, but the first observation was made by Raphael Kurzrok of New York, who in 1930 found that fresh human semen could either contract or relax strips of human uterus. Some of the prostaglandins have been synthesized, allowing extensive laboratory and clinical investigations. S. M. M. Karim of Makerere University Medical School in Uganda, who first discovered prostaglandins in human amniotic fluid, had induced abortions by intravenous infusion of prostaglandin F_2 alpha in 14 of 15 women pregnant from 9 to 22 weeks. The surgical hazards of therapeutic abortion were thus eliminated. M. P. Embrey of Oxford, Eng., found that prostaglandin E_1 and E_2, when infused intravenously in normal saline solution, were effective not only for abortion but also in inducing labour in those women for whom oxytocin was medically contraindicated. N. Wiqvist and M. Bygdeman at the Caroline Institute of Stockholm corroborated the abortifacient properties of certain prostaglandins, and suggested their use to induce uterine cramping and bleeding two to four days following a missed period.

A previously reported new form of thyrotoxicosis caused by excess triiodothyronine was substantiated. The active hormones of the thyroid gland are triiodothyronine (t_3) and thyroxin (t_4). The diagnosis of hyperthyroidism is usually confirmed by elevated protein-bound iodine (PBI) and/or elevated t_4 levels. Gustavo Pinedo and colleagues of Santiago, Chile, presented evidence that an iodine-deficient patient could develop this disorder even though PBI levels were normal. Their studies revealed that a t_3 type of thyrotoxicosis may be present that was detectable by t_3 gas chromatography but not by routine t_3 uptake, PBI, or t_4 assays.

The structure of calcitonin was determined. It is a polypeptide originally isolated from thyroid tissue rather than from the parathyroid gland (actually from the ultimobranchial body from which the hormone is believed to migrate in embryonic life) and has the capacity to reduce serum calcium levels. This polypeptide has now been synthesized, and when assayed biologically in rats had unexpectedly high activity. Armen H. Tashjian and Edward F. Voelkel of Boston found that synthetic human calcitonin was about twice as active as the natural polypeptide on a milligram for milligram basis. Within an hour after injection, the blood calcium of rats drops markedly because of the hormone's basic ability to decrease the rate of bone resorption. This fact, according to Stanley Wallach of New York, laid the groundwork for its possible use in the treatment of human diseases such as Paget's disease and osteoporosis. In the management of the latter, estrogens, fluoride, calcium, and alkaline diets were employed to great advantage. An adequate treatment for Paget's disease has been wanting. Now that calcitonin has been synthesized, it may prove a boon for the treatment of these and possibly other bone disorders.

The unusual finding that an antidiabetic agent,

chlorpropamide, was effective in the treatment of diabetes insipidus resulted in efforts to learn its mechanism of action. While Myron Miller and Arnold Moses of Syracuse, N.Y., believed that chlorpropamide was effective only in the presence of small amounts of endogenous antidiuretic hormone (ADH), Guistina Danisi and confreres of São Paulo, Braz., reported that chlorpropamide had a vasopressin-like effect per se.

Large doses of estrogens have been satisfactorily employed in the treatment of acne, excessive oiliness of the skin, and to modify the rate of sexual hair growth (hirsutism). In selected cases, however, estrogens appeared to aggravate these conditions and, at times, to initiate a mild to moderate degree of hirsutism. These observations posed many unanswerable questions. M. A. Kirschner and colleagues of Bethesda, Md., demonstrated unexpected increases in plasma testosterone concentration in women receiving large doses of estrogens for long periods. They believe that estrogens in these cases caused alterations in the peripheral metabolism by decreasing the metabolic clearance rates of testosterone.

(R. B. Gt.)

GASTROENTEROLOGY

Esophagus. The esophagus was the fourth most common site of malignancy in men past the age of 20, accounting in the United States for 5 to 7% of all cancer in males in 1970. Recovery rate by any method was low, but palliation and even prolonged survival were possible by early diagnosis, and combined surgical and X-ray therapy. Some patients treated by megavoltage irradiation for squamous cell cancer of the esophagus were alive five years after treatment and were leading a normal life.

Stomach, Duodenum. New bioassay and radioimmunoassay were developed for measuring the stomach hormone, gastrin, involved in the production of hydrochloric acid and associated with severe peptic ulcer.

Hemorrhage from the upper gastrointestinal tract remained a serious problem. Early diagnosis as to site and source, essential to successful treatment, was facilitated by prompt fiberoptic endoscopy, demon-

strating erosive gastritis and hiatus hernia as causes additional to peptic ulcer and varicosities of the esophagus. Direct examination of the first portion of the small intestine beyond the stomach (duodenojejunoscopy) also was possible. Drugs were important causes of erosive gastritis, especially acetylsalicylic acid (aspirin), steroids, and other medications taken for the relief of arthritis pain; diuretics; and excessive alcohol and nicotine. For medically uncontrollable bleeding from a duodenal ulcer, vagotomy and resection of the antrum were recommended for the good-risk patient, and vagotomy with pyloroplasty for the poor-risk patient. Nutritional and metabolic problems, including anemia and vitamin B_{12} deficiency, changes in blood sugar, muscle weakness, and calcium deficiency, followed ulcer operations.

A pernicious anemia-like disorder was found in four of ten patients deficient in protective immunoglobulins (absent or very low levels of immunoglobulin G). All patients were relatively young; all suffered from recurrent bacterial infections; many had had diarrhea; one had rheumatoid-like arthritis; another, ulcerative colitis; and a third, severe allergy.

Small Intestine. Poor blood flow to the digestive tract was an increasingly important cause of cramping abdominal pain, nausea, and vomiting, particularly among older people. Predisposing circumstances were arteriosclerosis, heart disease, and the use of diuretics and digitalis preparations. Prompt increase in collateral blood flow by celiac nerve blockade or by extradural anesthesia was recommended.

In September 1969 it was estimated that more than 70,000 men and women of the armed forces returned to the U.S. from Vietnam each month. The elapsed travel time approximated less than 24 hours, emphasizing the potential hazard to the U.S. from enteric infections common to Southeast Asia. The most important of these diseases were shigellosis, amebiasis, hepatitis, malaria, and tropical sprue. *Shigella flexneri* and trophozoites of *Entamoeba histolytica* usually could be recovered from stool cultures. An improved hemagglutination test for amebiasis was helpful in evaluating suspected liver abscess.

Colon. The clinical features of diverticular disease of the colon included pain in the lower abdomen and constipation. Inflammation, bleeding, and perforation were the important complications. The increased pressure within the thickened bowel suggested a new operation, colomyotomy, with initially favourable results.

Cancer of the rectum was highly curable if detected early and removed. For cancer of the colon in the descending and transverse portions, the five-year survival rate approximated 35%. X-ray irradiation, in moderate tumour-doses, helped control symtoms in nonresectable cancer of the rectum and colon. Repeated courses of 5-fluorouracil (5 FU), given as an adjunct to surgery between the time of the initial colon resection and second-look exploration in patients with a high recurrence risk, helped convert some patients to a "cancer-free state." Since the palliative antitumour effect of fluorouracil was limited by its toxic effects, dosage schedules were modified to induce regression of the tumour more safely.

Liver. Despite increasing knowledge of the functions and metabolic activities of the liver, the prevention and treatment of liver disease remained a major unresolved problem. The morbidity and mortality of liver disease increased because alcoholism, adverse reactions from drug use and abuse, and viral

A volunteer at the Clinical Center of the National Institutes of Health in Bethesda, Md., swallows a four-foot tube that collects intestinal tissue samples.

WIDE WORLD

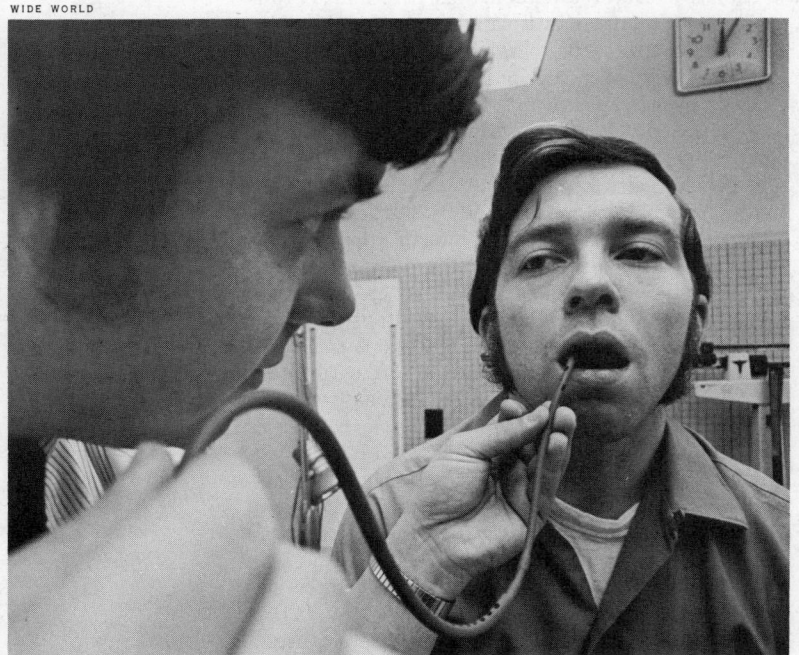

hepatitis were more prevalent in the U.S. Medications damaging the liver either were directly toxic or acted through individual idiosyncrasy. During 1970, drugs found to affect the liver adversely included oxyphenisatin (laxative), oral contraceptives, L-alpha-methyldopa (antihypertensive), and isoniazid (antitubercular). Halothane anesthesia caused necrosis of the liver, jaundice, coma, and death in occasional persons apparently predisposed to this agent. Reactions to halothane were estimated as one in 10,000 subjects but fatal cases were assumed to be one in 800,000 administrations. The clinical features included unexplained fever with chills sometimes progressing to symptoms of liver injury, occurring after relatively mild operations in previously healthy patients. Mitochondrial antibodies were found in the blood serum, with an increased number of eosinophiles and activated lymphocytes, suggesting an immunologic or hypersensitivity mechanism. Repeated exposure to the anesthetic agent was especially important in the development of this complication.

Infectious (viral) hepatitis was an increasing public health problem. Approximately 70,000 such patients were identified in the U.S. each year, with many more unrecognized. The disease caused at least 1,000 deaths annually. The liver involvement varied from minor to fatal. The host response to the infection was influenced by sex, pregnancy, nutritional status, pre-existing diseases, and age. After incubation of the virus in the gastrointestinal tract, its presence in the blood and its elimination in the feces reached peak levels during the pre-jaundice phase and then declined rapidly. Although the severity and duration of the illness were highly variable, most infections appeared to resolve completely, producing lifelong immunity. Semiannual injections of immune serum globulin significantly reduced the incidence of hepatitis among Peace Corps volunteers abroad. Anicteric hepatitis appeared to be more common than icteric hepatitis in patients receiving multiple blood transfusions without gamma globulin prophylaxis during open-heart surgery. The hepatitis virus was highly endemic in some areas, and infants and children served as a continuous reservoir of infection. In many areas, contaminated water supplies and infected food handlers caused large-scale epidemics.

Mounting evidence implicated the Australia antigen with the hepatitis virus. The antigen, first detected in the serum of an Australian aboriginal, could be demonstrated temporarily in the serum of patients with acute viral hepatitis. The antigen persisted for months or years in prolonged viral hepatitis, associated with either unresolved hepatitis or subacute hepatic necrosis progressing to post-hepatic cirrhosis, although presence of the virus did not appear necessary for chronicity of the disease. A further link between the Australia antigen and hepatitis was the high incidence of hepatitis and circulating Australia antigen in patients undergoing chronic renal dialysis. The antigen also was detected in the nuclei of liver cells of six patients who were serologically positive for this antigen, and not in the liver of individuals negative for this substance. In some populations, susceptibility to chronic infection with the Australia antigen appeared to be inherited as a simple autosomal recessive trait.

The Australia antigen, although rare (in 0.1% of normal Americans), occurred commonly and temporarily in patients with acute viral hepatitis; in approximately 60% of persons receiving injections of blood and blood products; and in 30% of those patients who did not. Various epidemiologic observations suggested that this material acted as an infectious agent. The antigen may be observed in the blood very early and it usually disappears within days or weeks of first detection. The period between apparent infection and the time the antigen was found in the blood varied from days to weeks or months. The antigen did not occur in certain other diseases affecting the liver, such as cirrhosis, hepatoma, or infectious mononucleosis. The antigen also was associated with chronic hepatitis. The antigen could be isolated from human serum and purified by various technical procedures. A specific antibody to it could be produced by the appropriate immunization of rabbits. There was considerable evidence that transmission from person to person was possible by the transfusion of donor blood containing the Australia antigen.

Acute diffuse necrosis of the liver with coma resulting from acute fulminating hepatitis was a lethal disease seldom responding to conventional treatment. Vigorous and prolonged plasmapheresis with plasma exchange was occasionally helpful. Exchange transfusions with fresh blood treated with sodium heparin were useful since this provided absent clotting factors, avoided citrate intoxication, and had a lower content of ammonia than banked blood. The underlying principle was the elimination or decrease of circulating toxic factors responsible for the coma, and the replacement of fresh blood or fresh frozen human plasma to support the patient through the critical period required for regeneration of the liver cells.

A chronic disorder characterized by recurrent disturbances of consciousness, impaired intellectual function, neuromuscular abnormalities, and coma, portal systemic encephalopathy was a serious complication in persons with chronic liver disease or after surgical treatment of cirrhosis with portacaval shunts. The condition could be induced or aggravated by excessive intake of protein, gastrointestinal bleeding, constipation, or by intake of ammonium salts. The compound lactulose—by creating an acid environment within the colon, diminishing absorption of ammonia by the colon, and increasing colonic excretion of ammonia and perhaps other "toxic" substances—was helpful.

Gallbladder. Cholesterol gallstones form when excess cholesterol precipitates from bile supersaturated with cholesterol. Either the gallbladder, by changing the composition of normal hepatic bile, or the liver, by the production of an abnormal bile, could be the source of the supersaturated bile. Stones of the bilirubin type were twice as common in patients with cirrhosis of the liver. Gallstones also occurred in children without hemolytic disorders; more commonly in girls during early puberty.   (J. B. Kr.)

GERONTOLOGY

Raymond Harris summarized six current advances in the medical care of the elderly. The primary advance was the recognition that such care required not only the services and concern of physicians but also the full cooperation and personal commitment of other members of the health professions. The second advance was the change from a negative to a positive attitude of health professionals toward actively improving the health care of older people. The third was the improvement of institutions of the aged under the impetus of Medicare. The fourth was the great interest of physicians and paramedical persons concerning the biological factors of aging. The fifth was the extension of rehabilitation to the aged. Last was the recognition that the older person not only has the right to life and good health but also the right to die with dignity.   (B. B. Mo.)

GYNECOLOGY AND OBSTETRICS

Numerous tests were carried out with prostaglandins, a new group of chemically related substances obtainable from the human prostate. (See *Endocrinology*, above.) In Kampala, Uganda, S. M. M. Karim induced labour in 33 out of 35 pregnant women near term with an intravenous infusion of prostaglandin F_2 alpha. He found that the substance caused uterine smooth muscle to contract and was more effective and safer than oxytocin, while M. P. Embrey in Oxford obtained even better results with another member of the group, prostaglandin E_2.

Karim, in collaboration with G. M. Filshie of London, also induced abortion with intravenous prostaglandin E_2 in 50 out of 52 women who were between 9 and 22 weeks pregnant. Abortion was complete within 15 hours in 43 women and no further treatment was necessary. Side effects were few although ten women had vomiting and four had diarrhea. In Stockholm N. Wiqvist and M. Bygdeman induced

abortion by injecting prostaglandin into the uterus. Karim found that the prostaglandins are absorbed from the vaginal mucosa. He suggested that women might prevent themselves from having children by inserting a prostaglandin pessary into the vagina each month in order to bring about an early abortion.

P. C. Steptoe of Oldham Hospital in Lancashire, Eng., caused much public reaction when he announced his intention of creating a test-tube baby with the help of a colleague at Cambridge, R. G. Edwards. Human oocytes were recovered by aspiration from ovarian follicles with the aid of the laparoscope in women who had been treated first with human postmenopausal and chorionic gonadotrophins. These hormones imposed control over the menstrual cycle in order that follicular development and laparoscopy might be accurately timed. Forty-six patients, infertile because of tubal occlusion or absent fallopian tubes, were selected for the experiment. Steptoe planned to place eggs fertilized outside the body into the oviduct of these women or directly into the uterus. He also proposed to use the rabbit oviduct to nourish human fertilized eggs until they were mature enough for implantation. There was no report of a successful pregnancy by the end of 1970.

Following a report by W. H. W. Inman, the U.K. Committee on Safety of Drugs issued a warning to the medical profession on the increased risk of thromboembolism to women who were taking contraceptive pills that contained a high content of estrogen. Inman made a study of 1,305 reports of thromboembolism in the U.K. occurring over a three-and-a-half-year period and probably representing about one in ten of the actual instances of thromboembolism. He also studied 183 Swedish and 122 Danish reports of pulmonary embolism and venous thrombosis of the lower limb. Of the 15 brands of contraceptive pill, those containing 100 micrograms or more of the two estrogens in use, ethinylestradiol and mestranol, were associated with three times as many deaths from pulmonary embolism as the brands of pill containing only 50 micrograms of estrogen. Since the number of women on the two doses was almost equal, a change from the higher to the lower estrogen pill would result in a reduction of total mortality by 50%. A similar association was found for deep vein thrombosis, cerebral thrombosis, and coronary thrombosis.

D. G. Millar investigated the smoking habits of 500 women after confinement and found that smoking was more common in those whose lactation had been suppressed than in those who were breast feeding. Although thrombosis and embolism are three times more common when lactation is suppressed with estrogens, there was not enough evidence to say that smoking was the cause.

S. Campbell and C. J. Dewhurst reported the accurate diagnosis of a quintuplet pregnancy at nine weeks menstrual age (seven weeks after ovulation) by ultrasonic compound B scanning. The five sacs were clearly visible and each was seen to contain a normal fetus. The patient was a 32-year-old woman who had been infertile for eight years because of failure to ovulate. Ovulation had been induced with human pituitary gonadotrophin. She went into spontaneous labour in Queen Charlotte's Hospital, London, at 31 weeks of pregnancy. Five healthy babies weighing 1.10 kg. (2 lb. 7 oz.) to 1.56 kg. (3 lb. 7 oz.) were born by cesarean section and all of them thrived.

Tubal ligation has many advantages for the patient who has completed her family. T. Lippitt reported

Abortion Laws in the U.S.
Amendments as of July 1, 1970

State	1	2	3	4	5	6	7	8	9	10	11	12	13	14
Alaska									1970	30 days	●	●		nvf
Arkansas		●				●	●	●	1969	●			3c	
California						●		●	1967				2-3b	20
Colorado						●	●	●	1967				3b	16
Delaware	●					●	●	●	1969	●			1c-ra	20
Georgia	●					●		●	1968				2c-3b	
Hawaii									1970	90 days	●	●		nvf
Kansas	●					●	●	●	1969				3c	
Maryland				●	●	●		●	1968	●			ra	26
Mississippi	●							●	1966					
New Mexico			●			●	●	●	1969				2b	
New York									1970		●	●		24
N. Carolina			●			●	●	●	1967	●			3c	
Oregon			●			●	●	●	1969	●			1c	150 days
S. Carolina						●	●	●	1970	90 days			3c	
Virginia			●			●	●	●	1970	120 days	●		Board	

Key:

1 Abortion permitted to preserve the life of the mother.
2 Abortion permitted to save the life of the mother.
3 Abortion permitted to preserve the life of the mother or prevent serious bodily injury.
4 Abortion permitted to preserve the life or health of the mother.
5 Abortion permitted to secure the safety of the mother.
6 Abortion permitted to preserve the physical or mental health of the mother.
7 Abortion permitted to prevent birth of child with grave physical or mental defect or deformity.
8 Abortion permitted when pregnancy is result of rape or incest.
9 Date of amendment.
10 Residency period required: ●—yes; or number of days.
11 Done in hospital by licensed physician.
12 At request of mother.
13 Number and kinds of approvals needed: c—consultants; b—therapeutic board members; ra—hospital review authorities.
14 Time limit: weeks of pregnancy (except Oregon—150 days); nvf—non viable fetus

Sources: American Medical Association; New York Times.

JOE BAKER

Exercise classes are part of an expectant mother's preparation for psychophysical analgesia, a technique that is having a marked impact on obstetrical care.

that on visits in the village homes in India of 146 patients following tubal ligation, 98% were delighted with the operation and were advising their friends to have it. W. A. Liston reported the results in 760 Edinburgh patients whose tubes were subjected to electrocoagulation and resection with the aid of a laparoscope. The operation only required the patient to remain in the hospital for 24 hours and the physical disturbance was minimal. Unfortunately, there were nine pregnancies following the procedure, five because the women were already pregnant at the time of the operation and three because one tube had been missed. In six patients, a laparotomy had to be done for bleeding from the area of tubal resection and it was probable that electrocoagulation alone was not enough.

Early in the year R. J. Bench and A. Vass investigated the response of the fetus in utero to external sounds at frequencies of 500 and 4,000 cps from a loudspeaker on the mother's abdomen. They were unable to detect any changes in fetal heart rate but when J. Grimwade of Melbourne, Austr., repeated the experiment to produce an intrauterine sound-pressure level of at least 70 decibels there was a constant increase in the fetal heart rate of at least 15 beats per minute. (T. L. T. L.)

HEMATOLOGY

Although not necessarily a quick killer, sickle-cell anemia has been considered an incurable, hereditary blood disease that affects the Negro population almost exclusively. It results from an abnormality of the red blood cells, which instead of their usual "doughnut" shape become crescent or sickle shaped and clog capillaries, depriving tissues of their normal supply of blood. It is estimated that one in every

500 Negroes has the disease. In both an article and an editorial in an October 1970 issue of the *Journal of the American Medical Association*, the disease with all of its pathological, social, and economic aspects was discussed. The journal pointed out that the kind of research money that might provide a cure for sickle-cell anemia could come only through widespread community volunteer efforts.

Almost coincidentally came the report on November 28 from Detroit that a team of Michigan researchers discovered that urea (an ingredient of human blood and urine) will check and prevent sickle-cell anemia. The discovery appeared to climax two decades of worldwide research in the field, the doctors said. Robert M. Nalbandian of Blodgett Hospital in Grand Rapids, Mich., head of the research team, said that intravenous injections of urea will block the disease, even in its crisis stage, in a matter of a few hours. By itself urea is toxic, but when taken with glucose (dextrose) it becomes nontoxic and therapeutic against sickle-cell anemia. Nalbandian emphasized that the compound should be taken only—and exactly —as prescribed by a physician. The price of commercial urea is only $1 a pound.

In 1926 it was discovered that pernicious anemia was a deficiency disease in which the bone marrow becomes crowded with abnormally large red-cell-forming precursors called "megaloblasts." It could be cured by regular injections of a suitable liver extract. Twenty years later the factor in the liver extracts was isolated, identified, and named vitamin B_{12}. Today the treatment of pernicious anemia is effective and relatively inexpensive. Some patients with megaloblastic marrow and anemia, however, did not respond to liver treatment and were found to be deficient in another substance, identified and named folic acid.

Three types of investigation were being used in 1970 to determine which (or both) of these substances is lacking in a patient with pernicious anemia. (1) In patients with folic-acid deficiency a protein substance called histidine is not completely metabolized and an intermediate product, known shortly as FIGLU, can be detected in the urine in large amounts, whereas patients with B_{12} deficiency show only a small increase. (2) Certain organisms are dependent on B_{12} or folic acid for growth. Media free of B_{12} or folic acid are employed and the growth of the test organism then depends on the amount of B_{12} or folic acid that was present in the blood serum from the patient to be tested. (3) Like so many advances, this one provided a new problem as well. It was found that not all patients with B_{12} deficiency had pernicious anemia. This problem has now been solved by the administration of vitamin B_{12} containing radioactive cobalt. The fate of a test dose of radioactive vitamin B_{12} can be traced quite easily; in pernicious anemia extremely little is absorbed, but if the gastric enzyme that "processes" the B_{12} is added, the absorption is normal.

These new techniques have shown that the megaloblastic anemias are more complex than previously thought, but most of them could be identified and successfully treated. Two interesting points have emerged: folic-acid deficiency is fairly common in elderly people on restricted diets, and a similar deficiency can be serious in persons whose intake of alcohol is excessive. Folic-acid deficiency in the elderly seems to vary with habits and cooking methods. But since it has become simple to detect deficiency, and even more simple to treat it, folic acid is regularly

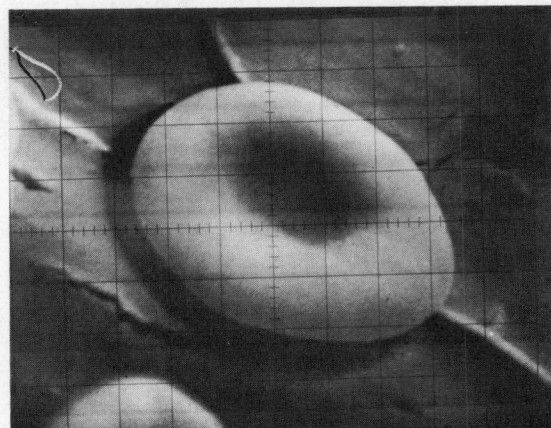

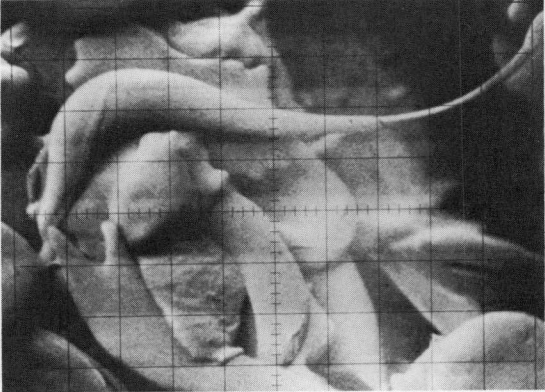

Above, a normal red blood cell magnified 10,000 times. Right, sickled (crescent-shaped) red blood cells, a symptom of sickle-cell anemia, which seriously affects one in 500 Negroes. Using a scanning electron microscope, Barnard College biologist Patricia N. Farnsworth believes she has found the shape-changing step in the disease process.

IRENE PISCOPO, PHILLIPS EM 300 TRANSMISSION ELECTRON MICROSCOPE

checked in chronic infections, chronic illness, and anemia in patients over 65. Persons with chronic alcoholism often have a poor diet, but investigation in the U.S. has shown that even when the diet contains sufficient folic acid, anemia can still occur. This is because chronic alcoholic poisoning actually interferes with the ability of the red-cell-forming tissue to utilize folic acid and iron; the unused iron accumulates in the marrow so that a "rusty" marrow may follow close on the heels of a fatty liver in the alcoholic patient.

Considerable prominence was given during the year to the use of combinations of drugs in the treatment of acute leukemia and the reticuloses like Hodgkin's disease. It is well known that a combination of a steroid, prednisolone, and a cytotoxic drug, mercaptopurine, will produce remission in 80% or more of childhood leukemia cases and a lower percentage of adults. But the remission does not last, and this may be due to drug resistance or to the fact that some of the leukemic cells are unaffected by this combination and eventually proliferate sufficiently to produce a relapse. A theory being tested in 1970 was that if several drugs were used, these causes of relapse would be reduced. Two types of combination have been used; in one, several drugs are given simultaneously in "courses" which are repeated at intervals; in the other, drugs are given in sequence for a definite time, and then the whole sequence is repeated. Most of the current combinations utilize a steroid, such as prednisolone, one or more cytotoxic drugs with different types of action, and sometimes one of the antibiotics that are known to have a damaging effect on tumours. Finally, if remissions are induced and held, an attempt is made to stimulate the patient's immunity by giving either BCG, a vaccine used against tuberculosis, or by giving killed leukemic cells from another patient.   (M. C. G. I.)

IMMUNOLOGY

The immunobiology of the antibody response was greatly clarified in 1970. The problem of antibody production appeared directly related to tolerance. This latter state is one in which an animal, having been previously exposed to a certain dosage of immunogen, will not subsequently respond to the same immunogen by the production of antibody.

In a primary immune response, that is, when the individual is meeting the immunogen for the first time, a cooperative three-cell system seems to be involved in antibody production. The first cell is considered to be a macrophage which apparently "processes" the immunogen for subsequent steps. There are a number of theoretical and experimental objections to this concept, *e.g.*, that for an immunogen to be just that, it must not be deprived of its structure.

Phagocytosis and subsequent breakdown of an immunogen, however, do not necessarily imply that the total structure is obliterated. The macrophage may serve as a sort of "bank" for a certain portion of the immunogen and thus supply the necessary immunogen to drive the proliferative and antibody production phase forward. (The immunogen portion has been extracted from macrophages and shown to be complexed with a low molecular weight ribonucleic acid or RNA.) While the initial thoughts were that the RNA might be a messenger for immunoglobulin synthesis, its low molecular weight would tend to rule out such a possibility. Whether or not the macrophage step is actually essential to the subsequent steps has not been determined.

The next step along the pathway to antibody synthesis is still controversial and it may be that different immunogens follow somewhat different pathways. The cell that synthesizes antibody is of the lymphocytic series and there is disagreement as to whether one or two cells are involved. Two types or classes of lymphocytes have been characterized: those derived from the thymus and those from the bone marrow. The consensus is that the bone-marrow-derived cell is the one that synthesizes the antibody and that the role of the thymus-derived cell is still unknown.

Central to all concepts of antibody production is that there are lymphocytes potentially capable of specific antibody production, and that they carry antigen recognition sites on their cell surfaces. These antigen recognition sites are presumed to have chemical structures potentially similar or identical to those of the antibody that the cell is capable of synthesizing.

In the case of the tolerant animal the question most often asked is whether the tolerant state has led to the death of the cell population involved in the specific antibody production or whether the cell has been silenced, presumably by the presence of the immunogen. Although this question has not been answered, tolerance apparently results from a silent cell. As there is general agreement that the tolerant cell is the potential antibody-synthesizing cell, and that antigen is the element that influences the cell to take one or the other pathway, the question arises as to how the cell is capable of making such a distinction.

Since it is postulated that the antibody-forming cell has on its surface antigen reactive receptors, one possibility is that conformational alterations of the cell surface occur. Tolerance is considered a conse-

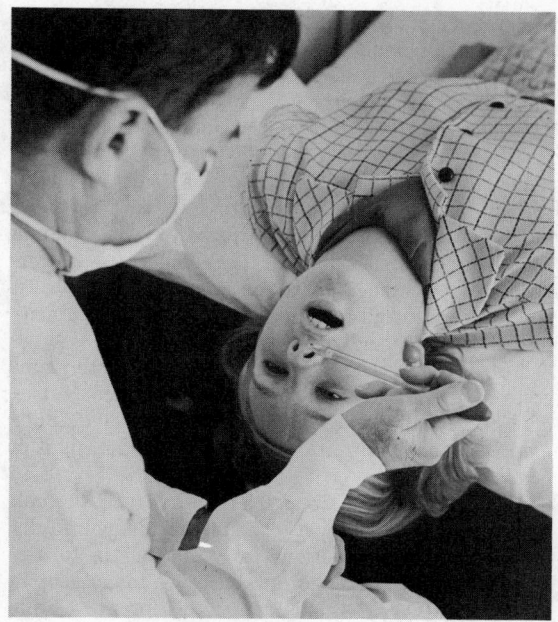

FOX PHOTOS FROM PICTORIAL PARADE

A volunteer at the Medical Research Council's common cold unit at Harvard Hospital in Salisbury, Eng., accepts a dose of a new and promising nasal vaccine against influenza.

quence of receptors that are "stretched" to induce such a conformational change by virtue of immunogen molecules that combine with them. Antibody production occurs when the immunogen molecules have also been complexed with the receptors and further linked with an antibody, thus resulting in a different type of "stretching." (A. S. M.)

MEDICAL EDUCATION

The near-empty coffers of U.S. medical schools have forced many of these institutions almost to the point of bankruptcy, and their dwindling endowments have been drained by expansion programs formulated to help satisfy the need for more physicians. Marquette University School of Medicine in Milwaukee, Wis., for example, sent a distress signal to the state government, which kept the school from closing. Federal funds were being sought by Georgetown and George Washington universities in the District of Columbia to save their medical schools from bankruptcy.

Despite the financial predicament common to all schools, medical school enrollment, in general, sharply increased in 1970, as did the number of minority students admitted in the fall. Of the 11,300 admissions 11% were women, 6.1% were black (an increase of 257 over the previous year), and a relatively comparable increase was shown for American Indians, Puerto Ricans, Americans with Spanish surnames, and Orientals, showing an overall minority student enrollment increase of almost 50% over the 1969–70 freshman class.

At its annual meeting in November the Association of American Medical Colleges reported that it was prepared to act on a program to train 50,000 more M.D.s by the mid-1980s to achieve a goal of 175 doctors per 100,000 population. The program also included plans for the building of 12 new medical schools and the expansion of each freshman class by 15 students. This, the association believed, would allow the U.S. to achieve the world's third highest physician to population ratio, ranking behind the U.S.S.R. and Israel.

The average U.S. medical school in 1970 spent al-

most $20,000 a year educating the average medical student, but charged only an average of about $2,000 a year tuition. The obvious question was: where will the money come from for all of this hoped-for expansion? There appeared to be confidence among medical leaders, administrators, and educators that the federal and state governments would come to their rescue. There was a deep-seated conviction that the people of America wanted more and better medical care and that political leaders must respond to this pressure. At a time when there was a shortage of doctors, and patients' waiting time, in both the doctors' offices and the outpatient clinics, had increased from hours to, sometimes, half-days, it seemed highly unlikely that the national and state capitals would allow even one medical school to close.

John A. D. Cooper, president of the AAMC, while putting the association on record for the 50,000-physician increase, warned that simply increasing the number of M.D.s "will not in itself solve the problems of a more even geographical distribution of physicians or physician services for the rural poor." (X.)

MICROBIOLOGY

The control of poliomyelitis had been known to be most effectively produced in humans following oral immunization with living attenuated virus vaccines. The reason for this was made clear only with the discovery that secretory immunoglobulins (antibody globulins produced by cells present in the mucous membranes) played a key role in neutralizing viruses at the mucous membranes, the points of entry into the human body. Secretory antibodies, in addition to classical antibodies of sera, are stimulated by living virus vaccines. In this situation the attenuated or "weakened" virus is capable of invading host cells and multiplying, thereby increasing the immunizing dose of the virus without producing disease.

When dead virus vaccines, such as the Salk vaccine, are used to immunize by the intramuscular or subcutaneous route, no virus multiplication occurs and only humoral (serum) antibodies result, leaving unprotected the initial site of viral proliferation and entry (the intestinal mucosa). Even if dead virus vaccines were introduced into the intestinal tract by ingestion, as are the attenuated vaccines, little if any secretory antibody would result since the viruses, unable to multiply, would be reduced in number by the physical environment of the stomach and intestinal tracts.

The live vaccine in use the longest was that used for smallpox. In the case of smallpox vaccination, the most significant portion of the host immune response is the population of sensitized lymphoid cells. The host (man) mobilizes a squadron of cells (sensitized lymphocytes), which attack and destroy the cells infected by virus and in the process not only produce more virus but also release virus in the process of dying. This cell-mediated immunity is the same as that mobilized in rejecting incompatible tissue grafts. During recent years this type of immunity has been implicated as the most significant facet of host resistance to infection by other microorganisms (tubercle bacilli, certain salmonella, brucella, some fungi, and some protozoa) that reside for varying periods of time within cells of the reticuloendothelial system and are thereby protected from antibody globulins in the circulation. These recent observations added another chapter to the old discussions of humoral as opposed to cellular immunity.

A blood serum factor termed the Australia antigen was found in 1968 in cases of post-transfusion serum hepatitis. Recent evidence confirmed the fact that detection of the Australia antigen in the serum of hepatitis patients is a valuable diagnostic aid in distinguishing between two major types of viral hepatitis. This antigen appeared to be specific for the virus of serum hepatitis and was rarely found in cases of infectious hepatitis. (See *Gastroenterology*, above.)   (JA. G. S.)

NARCOTICS

Latest available figures on the production of opium in those countries that reported to the United Nations showed an increase to 993 tons in 1968 from 778 tons in 1967. India, the U.S.S.R., and Turkey accounted for 75.8, 11.7, and 12.3%, respectively, of this output—the U.S.S.R. produced somewhat less than in the previous year, but India and Turkey both increased their production. Some 325 tons of opium went into the manufacture of morphine. About 153 tons of morphine were manufactured from opium (61.3%) and from poppy straw (or its concentrate), compared with 143 tons manufactured the previous year. As usual, most of the morphine was converted into codeine.

Bolivia and Peru continued to be the main producers of coca leaves, with harvests in 1968 of 4,203 and 8,756 tons, respectively. Most of the product was used for chewing. In Bolivia the amount produced represented a decrease of 16.9% compared with the previous year, but the production in Peru was increased by 2.9%.

Southeast Asia and the Middle East remained the chief areas of illicit production of opium, morphine, and heroin; South America, of coca leaf and cocaine; and Africa and the Middle East, of cannabis. Total seizure of all these drugs in 1968 amounted to some 1,504 tons, compared with 1,428 tons in 1967. The amount of raw opium seized was some 35 tons, about the same as in 1967, and of cannabis, 1,440 tons, compared with 1,389 tons in 1967. Those countries that had a significant problem of illicit poppy or cannabis cultivation continued to give economic and social assistance to the areas concerned and to pursue programs of crop replacement.

In its second report (1970) to the Economic and Social Council of the United Nations, the International Narcotics Control Board observed that in 1966 its predecessor, the Permanent Central Narcotics Board, had estimated that the total annual yield of opium for illicit purposes was in the region of 1,200 tons. This was a cautious assessment arrived at by careful analysis of the mass of statistical and other material in its possession. The present board was led to believe that the amount currently available for illicit purposes was certainly no less and might well be substantially more. Coca cultivation was similarly huge: even the official figures conceded an annual production of 13,000 tons of coca leaves, of which less than 2% was required for medical purposes and for use as a flavouring agent. (*See* Special Report.)   (PE. B.)

NURSING

For the nursing profession May 12, 1970, had significance as the 150th anniversary of Florence Nightingale's birthday.

The American Nurses Association attracted 8,000 nurses to its convention in Miami Beach, Fla., May 3–8, 1970, with a theme centred on what nursing can do to make quality care available to all people. The delegates passed a resolution supporting a national health insurance program. They supported legislation that approaches drug abuse as a health problem.

Some 1,000 nurses from across Canada attended the Canadian Nurses Association Convention, June 14–19, in Fredericton, N.B. They approved a resolution to ask the Department of National Health and Welfare to call a conference to study health matters affecting Canadians.

Nurses and student nurses who attended the congress of the National Association of Trained Nurses of France called on their government to act immediately on the reform of nursing education in France.

The International Council of Nurses (ICN) took steps to meet the most pressing needs voiced by its 74 member associations for guidelines in formulating or reassessing the laws relating to nursing in each country. With funds from the Florence Nightingale International Foundation, the ICN organized an international seminar on nursing legislation in Warsaw, Pol., July 6–16, 1970. Delegate nurses agreed that the prime purpose of nursing legislation was to secure for society the benefits that come from the services of highly skilled nursing personnel.

(AD. HE.)

NUTRITION

In a study conducted in Denver, Colo., H. P. Chase and H. P. Martin reported results that further suggest that malnutrition during early infancy retards physical and intellectual development. The children in the study group had reduced weight, height, and cranial circumference. The differences were most definite in those children who had been malnourished for more than four months. The findings were similar to those in less developed countries and suggested that conditions existed in urban United States between 1965 and 1970 such that children were exposed to socioeconomic environments that fostered malnutrition and limited growth and development.

Among 40 Western countries, the U.S. ranked 13th in infant mortality rate. In addition, a disproportionate number of infants were born with low birth weight. Because of this evidence, the Committee on Maternal Nutrition was organized by the National Research Council to study the problem. The committee affirmed that medical practice in the U.S. had tended to discourage in many pregnant women the normal physiological gain in weight, which averages about 24 lb. Preventing this gain, the committee reported, was particularly deleterious for underweight women and may also be harmful to pregnant adolescents.

Another report from the U.S. Food and Nutrition Board dealt with a discrepancy between an intake averaging about 11 mg. of iron daily for women between 10 and 55 years of age and a recommended daily allowance of 18 mg. per day. The board recommended that standards of identity for flour and bread fortification be changed to permit the addition of 40–60 mg. iron per pound of flour and 25–40 mg. iron per pound of bread. The board further recommended increased iron enrichment of other cereal products but did not support widespread iron fortifica-

continued on page 492

DRUGS AND YOUTH

By Leonide Goldstein

From time immemorial, man has used plant products capable of changing his moods and feelings, but this was a comparatively rare practice, especially in the Western world, until approximately 20 years ago. Since then both the variety and the quantity of products used have increased in most developed countries to a point where the practice is now considered to have reached epidemic proportions. At the same time, the age range of the users has steadily decreased.

The use of the term "drug" to designate such products is unfortunate, since the word also applies to medicaments—substances employed to counteract or alleviate illnesses. Such remedies are manufactured under controlled conditions, which means, among other things, that the dose is precisely known and is given under medical supervision. By extension, "drug" is applied to the same or other products when they are willfully self-administered for reasons other than to relieve illness. In this case, however, manufacture is most often conducted in secret and purity is not likely to be established, which means that the dose can vary widely. Obviously, the designation of both kinds of products under the same term can be misleading, and it tends to throw suspicion on the most useful medicaments. Although nothing can be done to change this ambiguous terminology, it is important to keep in mind the distinction between "drugs" as medicines and "drugs" as willful mood changers.

We are concerned in this article with the problem of the use of drugs other than for medical need. The first step is to determine which products are so used and the second, to describe their effects. Finally, we will attempt to explain why they are so interesting to young people.

Drugs and What They Do. The table contains a list of the drugs most commonly used in the Western world. Grouping them in classes is more for convenience than for real differentiation, since each class includes compounds that are completely different chemically. Furthermore, some are plant extracts, others are semi-synthetic products (chemically modified plant products), and still others are entirely synthetic.

The effects of certain plant products on the brain have been recognized for an extremely long time. The opium poppy plant, which contains morphine and codeine as well as other chemicals, was used as a sedative by the Sumerians as early as the 4th millennium B.C. Alcohol is mentioned in the Bible as having produced an inebriating effect on Noah—an effect that removed his sense of dignity, to say the least. The history of the other products is much shorter. Morphine was first isolated in 1806, codeine in 1832; heroin was first produced in 1898 (curiously enough as an intended cure for morphine addiction); amphetamine appeared in 1927 and LSD in 1938. Certain derivatives of amphetamine, such as methylene dioxyamphetamine (DOM), have been known only a few years. With a growing market, it is likely that new mood-changing drugs will appear in the future.

In the table these drugs are classified according to certain of their effects, and these must be understood if one is to distinguish the different actions of these agents.

Psychoactivity refers to the main action on the brain, chiefly determined by the change in personal feelings and behaviour. This classification is more apparent than real, since it is almost impossible to catalog the effects of a product with a single designation such as "stimulant" or "depressant." In the first place, the effect can vary widely according to the dose. At small doses LSD is a very strong stimulant; at high doses it is a depressant. Conversely, at relatively small doses morphine can be a sedative while at high doses it can exert excitatory effects. Absorbed in small quantities, marihuana produces an inebriating type of euphoria, while in large doses it brings about overt hallucinations. Second, the effect of a drug depends to a large extent on the state or condition prevailing when it is taken. Alcohol may stimulate its users when they take it in a so-called state of depression, while the same dose may calm them when they are overexcited. For certain drugs, the actions produced in heavy users appear to be quite different from the effects in occasional users.

Heroin addicts shoot up in a Spanish Harlem basement in New York City.

BOB COMBS FROM RAPHO GUILLUMETTE

489

Psychological dependence refers to the development of a state of mind, after exposure to a given drug, that seems to produce a subsequent strong urge to repeat its administration. For class I drugs, the change in the state of mind consists chiefly in relaxation. One of the most widespread ill effects of the technological society is that it creates innumerable sources of irritation, tension, and anxiety in everyday life. Caffeine and nicotine, by virtue of their pharmacological as well as their social effects ("coffee break," for example), help to overcome such conditions. However, the effects are rather mild, and only small changes in mood can be induced. A great many individuals do not need such psychological crutches, either because they are less sensitive to anxiety-producing events or because they can compensate for them in other ways.

For class II and III drugs, the psychological dependence is much more pronounced and generalized. When the drug usually employed is not available, feelings of depression occur, often leading to profound behavioural changes. Irrational irritation appears to be the dominant behavioural feature. In the case of class IV drugs, the psychological dependence becomes overwhelming, and absence of the drugs can lead to overexcitement, rage, and even uncontrolled violence. It is important to point out that for most users of class I drugs, the desired effect is obtained, trial after trial, with approximately the same dose. This is not true of many drugs of the other classes, for which a phenomenon known as *tolerance* develops. As drug use continues, doses must be increased to produce the same effect. The exceptions are cocaine, marihuana, and alcohol in people using small doses.

In contrast to psychological dependence, which is a learned process present only in higher mammals and man and which varies markedly from individual to individual, *physiological dependence* is a generalized phenomenon existing even in single-cell organisms. Physiological dependence is established in man and higher mammals after a series of exposures to a drug, the number varying according to the product. It is marked by an ever growing need to increase the dose in order to obtain a satisfying effect (tolerance) and by dramatic physical upsets when administration is stopped, especially if this is done suddenly. The so-called withdrawal symptoms consist of generalized pain, insomnia, yawning, tearing, running nose, perspiration, pupil dilation with blurred vision, goose pimples, nausea and vomiting, diarrhea, fever, increase in respiratory frequency, increase in blood pressure, abdominal and muscle cramps, dehydration, loss of appetite, and loss of weight. Certain treatments can be used to alleviate these symptoms in drug users wishing to end their dependency, but the therapy is not entirely effective. Drug withdrawal is always a painful process. Furthermore, it is not clear whether it can be completely realized. Some experimental animal findings indicate that even a single exposure to class IV drugs can induce long-lasting changes in the chemical machinery of the body.

Physiological dependence is always accompanied by tolerance, but the opposite is not always true. Amphetamine, for example, produces strong psychological dependence and definite tolerance, although there is no evidence that the typical withdrawal symptoms occur when administration is stopped. The same appears to be true of LSD and the other hallucinogenic drugs. In the case of marihuana there is some evidence that, in contrast to tolerance, smokers obtain greater effects on continued administration of the same dose. This may constitute the only known case of drug sensitization among brain-affecting products.

Turning to *psychotoxicity*, it appears that, in a number of individuals, drugs of class II can precipitate psychotic breakdowns. A fairly large number of patients recently admitted to psychiatric hospitals with symptoms of acute psychosis have been found to have demonstrable amounts of amphetamine, LSD, or other class II drugs in their body fluids. For many such patients, the disturbed mental condition disappears when the drug is eliminated or antidotes are given. There are, however, numerous cases in which the psychosis persists and even worsens

after the drug has disappeared. It is not clear whether such sustained effects are due to the drug itself or to the stressful situation created by its administration. Possibly a number of persons attracted by drugs are indeed borderline psychotics. There are reports of the recurrence of hallucinatory activity weeks and sometimes months after a single administration of LSD, but no precipitating factor has been determined to account for these so-called flashbacks.

For drugs of classes III and IV, psychotoxicity is manifested by a gradual loss of intellectual capacities. The picture of the skid row alcoholic is too well known to warrant description. Heroin users gradually lose interest in their surroundings, to the point where they forget their own names.

An important aspect of drug dependency is that it is often accompanied by *antisocial behaviour*. Except for class I compounds and alcohol, all the drugs listed are illegal. Thus merely obtaining them constitutes antisocial behaviour by definition. Furthermore, drug dependence is expensive, and since drug users are often incapable of holding a job, they may resort to thievery, prostitution, assault, and even murder to obtain funds. Another aspect of the same phenomenon is that, by violating the rules of society, the drug user removes himself from the organized structure of normal interhuman relationships. This can lead to the growth of a drug subculture, with its own rules.

Alcohol is a special case in this regard. It is sold legally and can be obtained quite cheaply in many countries throughout the world. Furthermore, while class III and IV drugs decrease behavioural activity (sometimes to the point of producing completely apathetic individuals), alcohol in high, toxic doses can induce irrational fear, rage, uncoordinated behaviour, and a marked tendency toward agitation and violence. It is estimated that a large proportion of criminal acts are committed by persons under the influence of large doses of alcohol. Nevertheless, misuse of alcohol is widely tolerated in societies that proscribe other drugs.

Finally, drugs, especially those in classes III and IV, produce both *brain and body damage*. Alcohol damages all tissues, especially the liver. The morphine-type compounds can produce a variety of pathological effects, some fatal. An overdose of heroin brings about respiratory arrest which is often irreversible. The use of nonsterile needles and contaminated drug products can produce such conditions as bacterial endocarditis, hepatitis, tetanus, physomycetosis of the brain, cirrhosis of the liver, uremia, myocardial infarct, and pulmonary emboli. Even when the results are not fatal, the constant use of class IV drugs produces brain abscesses and severe constipation with rapid loss of appetite and weight. Irreversible chromosomal damage has been suggested as a toxic side effect of LSD, but the experimental evidence is not conclusive. More studies are needed, especially using the illicit products rather than pure LSD.

Recently a new terminology has been introduced, with "soft drugs" used for drugs of class II, especially marihuana, and "hard drugs" for those of class IV. Such a distinction may be more apparent than actual. For example, marihuana at high doses can induce changes in brain function as great as those produced by LSD and heroin. The drug situation is already so complicated that new, ambiguous terms can only serve to further obscure the facts.

Why Drugs? With this information as background, we can now examine the crucial question of why there is such interest in drugs, especially among young persons. A number of surveys, questionnaires, and studies, conducted in high schools, colleges, and universities as well as in the streets of slum areas of cities, report that the reasons most often cited for drug use are the following:

Curiosity. It is well established that part of the psychic activity of the brain does not come to consciousness unless certain barriers are removed. A familiar example is dreaming, which occurs only during sleep. Under certain conditions, drugs can lift these barriers and bring to consciousness the unknown activity of one's

Commonly Used Drugs and Their Effects

Name	Origin	Common name	Psychoactivity	Psychological dependence	Physiological dependence	Tolerance	Psycho-toxicity	Antisocial behaviour	Brain and/or body damage
Class I									
Nicotine	Plant, *Nicotiana tabacum*	Tobacco, cigarettes, cigars	Mild anti-depressant type	Mild	None	None	None	None	?
Caffeine	Plant, *Coffea arabica*	Coffee	"	"	"	"	"	"	None
Tea	Plant, *Camellia sinensis*	Tea		"	"	"	"	"	"
Class II									
Organic solvents	Synthetic	Airplane glue, nail polish, hair sprays	Stimulant	Strong	None	?	?	?	Definite
Cocaine	Plant, *Erythroxylon coca*	Snuff, snow, the white lady	Strong stimulant	"	"	None	Definite	Severe	?
Amphetamine and derivatives	Synthetic	Speed, bennies, dexies, ups, A's, footballs, STP, DOM	"	"	"	Definite	"	"	?
Mescaline	Plant, *Lophophora williamsii*	Mesc	Hallucinogen	"	"	"	"	"	?
LSD	Semisynthetic, rye ergot	Acid	"	"	"	"	"	"	?
DET—DMT	Synthetic								
Marihuana	Plant, *Cannabis sativa*	Grass, pot, tea, hash, charas, bhang, hemp, THC	Inebriating to hallucinogen	Strong	None	?	?	?	?
Class III									
Ethanol	Plants (fermented cereals, fruits)	Alcohol, whiskey, wine, beer	Depressant	Strong	Strong	Definite	Definite	Severe	Definite
Barbiturates	Synthetic	Downs, blue devils, reds, yellows	"	"	"	"	"	"	"
Class IV									
Opium	Plant, *Papaver somniferum*	Snow	Depressant	Very strong	Strong	Strong	Strong	Severe	Indirect
Morphine	"	M	"	"	"	"	"	"	"
Codeine	"	Coke	"	"	"	"	"	"	"
Heroin	Semisynthetic, *Papaver somniferum*	Smack, dope, junk, stuff, horse, H, scag	"	"	"	"	"	"	"

Note: The entries marked with ? are so identified because presently available information is insufficient to decide whether or not such an effect exists.

own brain. Following the early experimentation with hallucinogenic drugs, it was claimed that fantastic brain capacities were unleashed by these substances, with the "creation of new energy," "discovery of new truths, new insights into oneself," and "new visions of the universe." If anything, hallucinogenic drugs reduce brain function rather than expand it. Yet, these claims have a great appeal, especially among young people searching for a unique identity, a position, a role in the world.

Antidepression. It has often been said that man is a pleasure-seeking creature. But in the last 25 years human society, especially in the West, has produced more apparent sources of struggle, difficulty, and despair than of joy and pleasure. One of the consequences has been that people, especially young people, have lost hope of attaining a pleasurable life through such time-honoured means as work, marriage, raising a family, enjoying good food, and taking vacations. Many drugs are used to replace these rejected sources of enjoyment because they isolate the users from the world's apparent adversity and thus alleviate feelings of hopelessness and depression.

Defiance of Authority. This is a further consequence of the attempt to escape depression. Since society has not produced the joyful world everyone is looking for, society must be wrong and its rules and regulations must be challenged. Illicit drug use appears to be one possible manifestation of such attitudes of defiance—of parents, the law, and established authority in general.

Social Pressure. A number of young people who normally would not become involved with drugs are driven to indulge because they cannot resist the pressures of their peers who do use them. It is quite normal to seek identity with a peer group and also quite normal to emulate the "hero"—in this case the one who has "courageously" tried drugs and has reported his subjective feelings in glowing terms.

Extra Energy for Study. Academic pressures are chiefly responsible for the use of amphetamine and related drugs in schools. The practice derives from the widespread belief that by reducing hours of sleep (which that drug does) one increases the span of time for study and also the brain capacity for storage and sorting of information. As with LSD, the popular claim is contrary to factual knowledge. The amphetamines do increase overall activity in normal, well-rested subjects, but they do so in an uncoordinated manner. Rather than increasing memory storage, they decrease it.

Accidental Drug Dependence. When a patient is in severe pain, the relief produced by a pain-killer such as morphine often amounts to intense feelings of euphoria. In a number of cases this euphoria becomes identified with the morphine rather than with the suppression of pain, to the extent that administration (now illegal self-administration) is continued after the pain has disappeared. Very soon tolerance develops, and with it the early signs of withdrawal pains when the drug is not present in sufficient amounts in the body. An individual with such a drug dependency is no longer a pleasure-seeker; he has become a pain-avoider. This shift from an initial legitimate medicinal use of a drug to its abuse for preventing the pain that follows its withdrawal from the body accounts for a fairly large fraction of drug dependence.

Escape from Slum Conditions. Among youth living in slum areas of the cities, the main reason for drug use and dependence appears to reside in the previously mentioned capacity of a number of compounds to remove the user, as it were, from his surroundings. When living conditions are adverse to the point of being intolerable, such an escape can be a very pleasurable experience. One consequence, however, is that when the effect of the drug wears off, the individual finds himself in a situation that, by contrast with the "artificial paradise" of the drug, appears to be even worse. This provides what psychologists term a reinforcement for more drug use.

A curious aspect of drug use in slum areas is that, regardless of the product administered, a state called a "high" is reached. Thus drugs appear to lose specificity and all produce the same effect. Although it is impossible for a nondrug user to understand what a "high" actually corresponds to, a strong possibility exists that it represents the feelings of escape from reality. The situation may be parallel to that concerning the effects of morphine on patients in pain—removal of pain produces a feeling of elation. If this is the case, one can well understand that removal of the "pains" of terrible living conditions could produce similar feelings of euphoria.

Conclusion. Needless to say, this list of the reasons for drug use is only partial. A great many of the factors involved are not fully known to drug users themselves, much less to the outside observer. Most students of the subject, however, feel that the reasons discussed are among the most important ones.

It will be noted that no mention has been made of the frequency of use or the number of drug users. The main reason is that the drug scene is an illegal one. Statistics can be based only on estimations, conjectures, projections, and other approximations, and these can be grossly misleading. All one can say with certainty is that the use of drugs is increasing rapidly and has already reached an alarming level. It is to be hoped that by a better understanding of what the drugs are and what they do, more effective ways of dealing with the epidemic of illicit nonmedical drug use will be developed.

continued from page 488

tion of a large variety of different foods. Increased iron enrichment of cereal products could be expected to raise the amount of iron in the U.S. diet by approximately 5 mg. per day. (JE. WI.; F. J. SE.)

OCCUPATIONAL MEDICINE

The rapidly changing technology of our society provided a continuous source of new problems in occupational medicine. For example, the manufacture of "biological" detergent washing powders containing proteolytic enzymes was found to be a health hazard to some of the workers involved. M. L. N. Flindt's description of severe allergic respiratory reactions among some employees in one factory was supported and extended by studies at two other locations. All agreed that atopic subjects are more likely to become sensitized, and that the most vulnerable workers were those involved in adding and mixing the enzyme concentrate into the washing powder. The study by M. L. Newhouse and her colleagues showed that vigorous dust control measures installed in the hazardous areas greatly reduced the risk of developing respiratory symptoms. In the third factory, where enzymes had only been handled intermittently, M. Greenberg confirmed the susceptibility of atopic subjects, and showed that impaired ventilatory function could be severe and in several cases had not reverted to normal after three months without exposure to the enzyme. There was no evidence to suggest that the users of these powders were in danger of respiratory disease, but the U.S. Federal Trade Commission was investigating this problem as it applied to the consumer.

The underlying mechanism is the development of a precipitin-mediated immune response, and circulating I_gG antibodies to the protease have been found. Thus detergent enzyme work could join the rapidly enlarging list of occupations causing allergic respiratory disease. Much of the fundamental research into these conditions came from J. Pepys and his colleagues at the Institute of Diseases of the Chest (University of London). Another occupation added to the list in 1970 was that of malting floor workers in whiskey distilleries in Scotland; here, as in farmer's lung, the allergen is fungal. A report from Switzerland described a similar alveolitis in cheese washers.

Sensitization also was found to be of importance in the toxicology of isocyanates. These reactive chemicals used in the preparation of polyurethanes were recognized as highly irritant to the eyes and respiratory tract. The threshold limit value for industrial exposure was set at 0.02 parts per million, but J. M. Peters and his colleagues from Boston demonstrated that levels well below this can have adverse effects on ventilatory capacity.

Byssinosis, a chronic and disabling lung disease of cotton workers, has been known for two centuries but, although recognized as a serious problem in England, it was not considered to be of importance in the U.S. A careful survey in two cotton mills by E. Zuskin and her colleagues from Yale, however, revealed that 25% of cardroom workers and 12% of spinners had the disease. A National Conference on Cotton Dust and Health in Charlotte, N.C., in May 1970 heard evidence that this problem may indeed be serious and that its development could be related to mechanical methods of harvesting, since the raw cotton contains more extraneous matter and bracts, believed to be the etiological agent. The American Textile Manufacturers Institute financed a large-scale survey into this problem to provide a definite answer. Meanwhile, pressure was being exerted in Washington to make the condition ("brown lung disease") compensable under the workmen's compensation acts.

Although an immunological mechanism was suspected in byssinosis it was not confirmed. In 1970 M. Turner-Warwick and W. R. Parkes demonstrated a fourfold increase in the prevalence of antinuclear and rheumatoid factors in persons investigated for asbestosis. More severe radiographic shadowing was related to antibody presence as was also progression of the disease. It seemed possible that some members of the general population could have a genetic tendency to react in an abnormal way to the inhalation of asbestos and perhaps other organic and inorganic dusts. If confirmed, this could lead to such susceptibles being screened before acceptance into hazardous employment.

The new Asbestos Regulations came into effect in Great Britain in May 1970, and required strict control of all processes from which asbestos dust can arise. A threshold value of two fibres/cc. for chrysotile, amosite, and anthophyllite was accepted, above which stringent precautions were obligatory. This level was considered by the British Occupational Hygiene Society as one providing a 1% risk of asbestosis for a man working for 50 years. Crocidolite (blue asbestos) is more hazardous since it definitely causes malignant mesothelial tumours, and its threshold limit was suggested as 0.2 fibres/cc. There were a number of developments in the prevention of other occupational cancers. Many workers in the engineering industry were found to be in danger of scrotal cancer from mineral oil. Screening for this could best be done by the worker himself, and a new leaflet issued free by the U.K. Department of Employment and Productivity included an excellent colour photograph so that the man could see what he must look for. This radical departure from the previous style of notices was expected to help a great deal. (See Cancer, above.) (P. J. T.)

OPHTHALMOLOGY

Continuous exposure of the eye to diffuse light causes damage to the retina, the delicate nervous tissue lining the eye. The retina, however, possesses considerable recuperative ability, and if the nuclei of the cells receiving light are not destroyed, active repair is possible. The topic is of more than theoretical interest because infants born with jaundice are treated with exposure to light. Animal experiments indicated that there should be some protection for the infant's eyes during this procedure.

Light focused on the back of the eye was being used in the treatment of diabetic retinopathy. Focused sunlight causes similar changes and these were also observed following exposure to the light of atomic bomb explosions. Sunlight burns are often observed after an eclipse; despite numerous warnings, most eclipses of the sun are followed by reports of retinal burns in individuals who have viewed the eclipse without adequate eye protection. Some 145 individuals in the United States burned their eyes during a March 7, 1970, eclipse.

During the year, retinal burns were described in patients with acute and senile psychotic disorders. These schizophrenic patients gazed at the sun to see or communicate with God, or to make their eyes stronger. Interest in eye burns was stimulated by

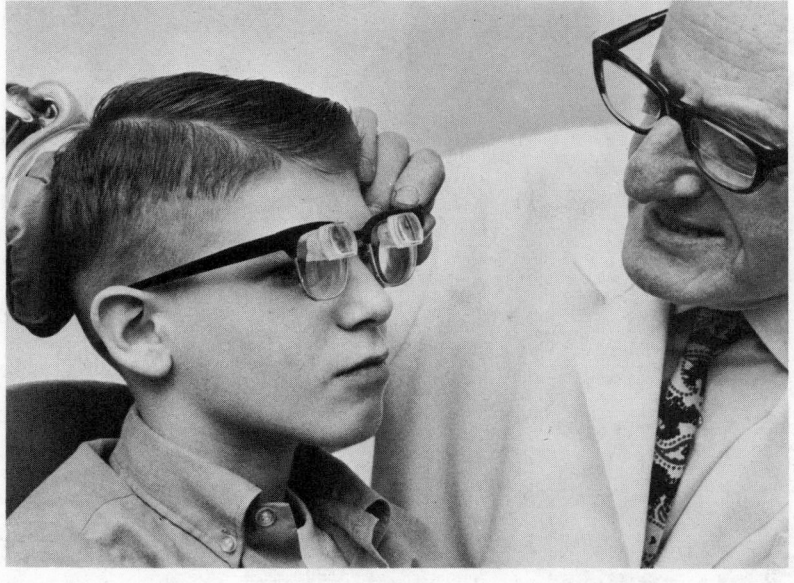

William Feinbloom examines his "bioptic telescopic system" worn by 11-year-old Russell Strayer, who has only 1% vision. The multimicroscopic lens system, which is patterned after the Palomar telescope, raises his vision to 50%.

UPI COMPIX

reports that recruits in the U.S. Marine Corps were avoiding overseas military service by gazing at the sun. Similar injuries were reported after military personnel looked into the sun in search of enemy planes.

A common cause of decreased vision in one eye is failure to use the eye actively before the age of six years. Reasons for this inactivity include conditions in which one eye is markedly more far- or near-sighted than the other, and a number of diseases that prevent image formation at the back of the eye. Many of these conditions, if detected before the age of six years, may be corrected by the use of the eye that had been inactive.

Ordinary spectacles provide significant protection to the eyes even though it is evident that they can break. If plastic lenses (which scratch fairly easily but do not shatter) or case-hardened lenses (lenses in which the surfaces have been particularly hardened) are used, much greater protection is provided for the eyes. In 1970 Alaska approved legislation providing that all lenses sold in the state must be of shatter-resistant construction. This was followed by a similar proposal by the U.S. Food and Drug Administration. This should markedly reduce the some 120,000 accidents arising annually from shattered eyeglasses.

(F. W. N.)

ORTHOPEDICS

In orthopedics in the developed countries of the world a modern scourge was injuries resulting from accidents. In Britain in 1966, while 2.9 million working days were lost from industrial disputes, 22 million working days were lost from industrial accidents. In the case of road accidents it was estimated that in Britain in 1966, of the 8,000 persons who died, 2,000 died on the way to the hospital. At Heidelberg, W.Ger., since 1957, a surgical team from a hospital had been going to the scene of accidents in specially equipped ambulances. In certain country areas of Britain general practitioners were providing "Road Accident After-Care" schemes. The service at the scene of the accident included maintenance of the respiratory airway, artificial respiration, oxygen therapy, external cardiac massage, transfusion, and splintage for limb and spinal injuries. This scheme, pioneered in Britain by K. C. Easton, was fostered by the Medical Commission on Accident Prevention.

In the treatment of limb injuries, A. Sarmiento

in the U.S. reported his further experience in treating fractures of the tibia with an external below-knee splint, enabling the patient to walk with full weight-bearing on the limb, permitting function of the knee and ankle joints. In contrast, a group of Swiss and German surgeons, who practice rigid internal fixation of fractures and early mobilization of the limb without plaster fixation, introduced a new dynamic compression plate. M. Allgöwer and his colleagues in Switzerland reported their experience using this plate in 49 patients, with an average stay in the hospital of 11 days. In a patient who sustained severe injuries to the pelvis and lower limbs, an emergency translumbar amputation (hemicorporectomy) was performed by T. C. Baker and his colleagues in South Africa. At the time of the report, the patient had been fitted with a prosthesis enabling him to stand and use a wheelchair. In the reattachment of severed limbs, J. S. Horn of the U.K. reported considerable experience in China in this type of surgery. In this connection, too, J. R. Cobbett of the U.K. completed the first transfer of a great toe to replace a thumb, lost through injury, involving microvascular techniques to join the appropriate blood vessels.

Congenital dislocation of the hip was widely recognized as a condition that should be looked for, diagnosed, and treated at birth in order to prevent disability later in life. Surveys in Sweden, Britain, and New Zealand indicated that a few cases examined at birth did not become evident until later. In accordance with these observations, the Department of Health and Social Security in London recommended that the hips of all children should be reexamined within three months of birth. By this means it was hoped to prevent the late sequelae resulting from congenital dislocation of the hip.

The rheumatic disorders most commonly needing orthopedic care are osteoarthritis and rheumatoid arthritis. In Britain the mainstay of surgical treatment for the osteoarthritic hip for some years has been juxta-articular osteotomy (surgical division of the bone) and total-joint replacement. In the rheumatoid hip, osteotomy of the lesser trochanter was found to be beneficial in a small group of patients. At the knee, while osteotomy is frequently beneficial for certain types of disease, the total-joint replacements are not, in general, as successful as at the hip. After encouraging experimental research in the canine hip,

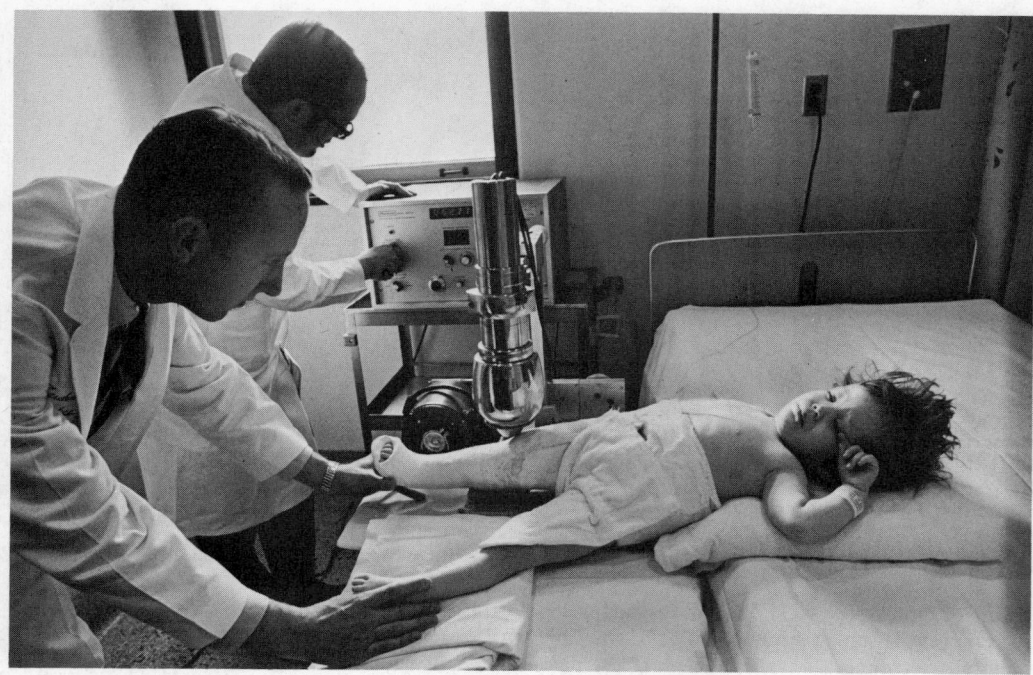

Keith Sheffer (foreground) and C. Conrad Johnston check bone calcium loss in immobilized limbs at Indiana University's research institute, which was scheduled for closing as a result of federal budget cuts.

TOMMY WADLETON FROM BLACK STAR

attempts were being made by Michael Laurence of the U.K. to use biological transplants of articular cartilage to replace diseased cartilage in the human knee joints. The cartilage grafts are procured from the knee joints of cadavers. More massive biological replacements, using frozen cadaveric joints for the surgical treatment of bone tumours and bone infections, were being explored in several countries, particularly the U.S.S.R. In finger joints affected by rheumatoid arthritis, artificial joints, made of metal, plastic, and polypropylene, were being employed. Long-term clinical results were awaited with interest.

The recent progress in North America and Europe in the construction of artificial limbs for amputees was collated on behalf of the British Limbless Ex-Servicemen's Association. In Belgrade, Yugos., R. Tomovic developed an artificial hand utilizing pressure sensors placed in the fingertips and palm to vary the type of grip produced by the hand. In California, V. L. Nickel and his colleagues devised an electrically powered orthotic system to provide patients having severe paralysis of the upper limbs with mobility and voluntary hand movements. The movements are controlled by switches operated by the patient's own tongue. A plastic material called "Plastozote" was finding considerable application for splints.

A report by two staff members of the World Health Organization, W. C. Cockburn and S. G. Drozdov, concluded that in tropical and subtropical less developed countries, the incidence of poliomyelitis, previously low, was increasing. It was recommended that plans be made to combat by local vaccination upsurges of poliomyelitis as they occur. Spinal tuberculosis, a common and crippling disease in Africa and Asia, was the subject of a clinical trial of different forms of treatment in Rhodesia, Hong Kong, and Korea under the aegis of the Tropical Medical Research Board.   (R. G. Bu.)

OSTEOPATHIC MEDICINE

With the cooperation of the U.S. Department of Health, Education, and Welfare, the American Osteopathic Association (AOA) sponsored in Chicago the first two national medical malpractice conferences to which participants came from consumer groups, organized labour, and government departments, as well as from the legal profession, insurance, and medicine.

The year-old Michigan State University College of Osteopathic Medicine at Pontiac became the first of the profession's six schools to be affiliated with a state university. A seventh school, the Texas College of Osteopathic Medicine, opened in Fort Worth.

At its annual meeting in Atlanta, Ga., the AOA House of Delegates went on record supporting the concept of compulsory national health insurance and Peer Review, the policy whereby the performance of hospitals and doctors is monitored by peers.

Georgia enacted a new licensure law giving osteopathic physicians full practice rights and two seats on the board of medical examiners. The osteopathic profession's unlimited practice rights in Georgia were previously based on a ruling by the state attorney general.

The Student Osteopathic Medical Association held its first national convention in Chicago. In 1970, 1,997 students were enrolled in osteopathic colleges and 432 were graduated. Over 200 osteopathic physicians were serving in the medical corps of the armed forces and about a fourth of these were stationed overseas, mostly in Indochina. The American Osteopathic Association counted 13,474 osteopathic physicians and the American Osteopathic Hospital Association listed 254 hospitals with a total of 19,706 beds and 2,096 bassinets.   (R. A. Kl.)

PEDIATRICS

It had been customary for many years to keep premature infants in the hospital until they reached a weight of 5 or $5\frac{1}{2}$ lb. Robert B. Berg, Arthur J. Salisbury, and Richard Kahan of Boston studied the effects of early discharge from the hospital of premature infants who were feeding well and whose mothers were given special training in their care. The infants were discharged after an average stay of 11 days. Follow-up of the infants showed that they thrived and did not develop infections or other difficulties. The savings in cost by shortening the hospital stay were great, and these infants were probably at

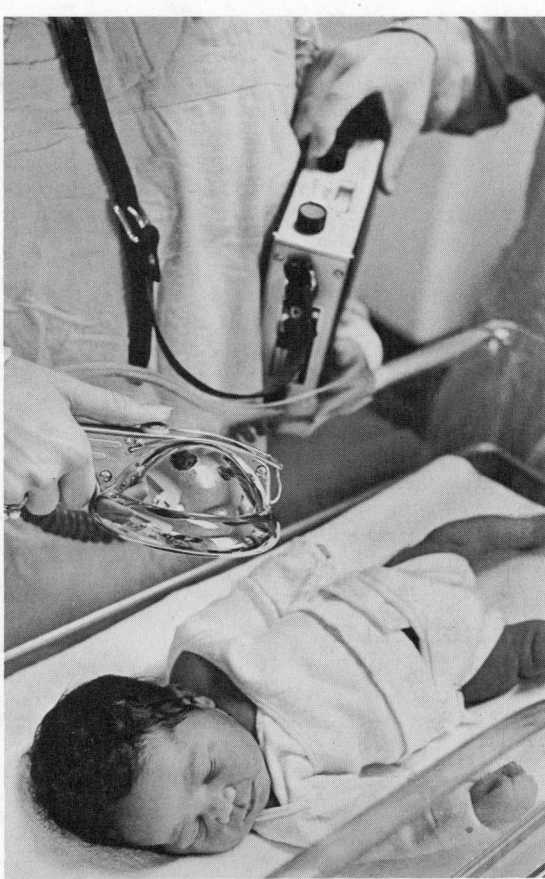

JON BRENNEIS FROM "HOSPITAL PRACTICE"

Using a sound-producing device, a physician prepares to test a day-old baby's hearing. Such early tests for hearing difficulties are urged by specialists to prevent impairment of speech development.

less risk in their own homes than in the hospital. In another study, from Stanford, Calif., C. R. Barnett, P. H. Leiderman, R. Grobstein, and M. Klaus investigated the possible advantages to premature infants whose mothers were allowed to enter the nursery as early as the second day after birth to touch and hold their infants. Preliminary results indicated that the mothers were less depressed than those who were separated from their infants for weeks. Ill effects such as increased incidence of infections were not noted in the infants.

Herpes simplex viruses, to which the common cold-sore virus belongs, were shown to be extremely hazardous for the newborn infant. By 1970 two different strains of herpes simplex virus had been isolated. That associated with lip and mouth infection, type 1, was infrequently related to infection in the newborn. The second agent, type 2, was found to produce genital lesions in the mother and infect her newborn infant as he passed through the birth canal. This virus can penetrate the unbroken skin and produce generalized disease in the baby, injuring brain, liver, and adrenals. The death rate was high. Ordinary human gamma globulin, which contains antibodies to many viruses, is of little help, because there is an antibody to type 1 virus but not against type 2. During 1970 there was successful treatment of several ill infants with the drug idoxuridine, which had previously been used in the treatment of herpes simplex infections of the eye. Several investigators recommended that in mothers known to have herpes infection of the genitalia, cesarean-section delivery be performed to prevent contact of the infant with the virus.

During the years prior to 1970 evidence had been accumulating of a relation between measles virus and the disease known as subacute sclerosing panencephalitis. This devastating disease is a slowly progressive disorder of the brain in childhood, with deterioration of motor and intellectual function, ending in death. Francis E. Payne, J. V. Baublis, and H. H. Itabashi of Ann Arbor, Mich., reported the isolation of a virus agent that appeared to be identical with that of measles from the brain of a six-year-old boy with the disorder. This case confirmed that measles virus can act as a slow virus, staying in nervous tissue for months before giving evidence of its presence and producing a progressively destructive condition. It was not clear whether there is some peculiarity of the measles strain that allows it to act in this manner or whether there is a deficiency in the patient infected with the virus that prevents him from neutralizing the virus as in most cases of infection. The disease appeared in a very small number of children who had received measles vaccine, but it was not known if the agent responsible was the vaccine virus or natural virus.

Frederick L. Day of New London, Conn., called attention in 1970 to the theoretical hazards of exposure to rock music. Fifteen young men whose hearing had been tested and found to be normal were exposed

Guided by a pediatrics resident, a mother administers eye drops to a child shortly after brain surgery. A growing number of parents are allowed to care for their hospitalized children under a care-by-parent system originated by University of Kentucky Medical Center pediatrician Vernon L. James.

TERRY ARMOR

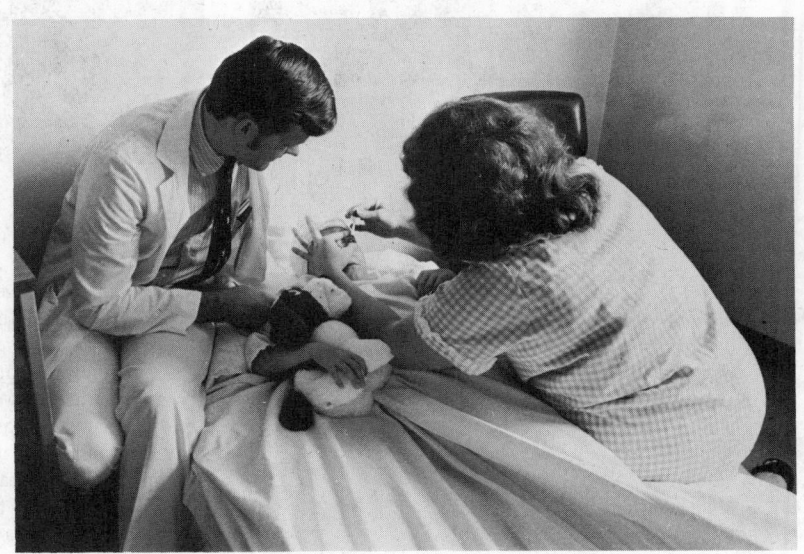

to recordings of music played by a typical rock band in a discotheque for periods of 5 to 120 minutes. Day maintained that after listening to such music for two hours at a sound level of 100 decibels, 16 out of 100 individuals would have deterioration and possible permanent impairment of hearing. More data were needed to confirm the suggestion that the changes are permanent.

Conan Kornetsky, a psychologist at Boston University, reported that an alarming number of babies were born as drug addicts because the mothers passed on their own dependency during pregnancy. His data were confirmed by a number of pediatricians and obstetricians. The infants showed all the typical withdrawal symptoms and frequently had to have methadone added to their formula during withdrawal if the mother was addicted to heroin. (S. S. G.)

PSYCHIATRY

A report containing the collective views of an international group of experts on the present state of biological research in schizophrenia was published by the World Health Organization. The major areas of investigation were genetics, biochemistry, neurophysiology, and psychopharmacology. Geneticists developed a special interest in psychiatric epidemiology—the distribution of mental disorders in populations. Most of the evidence suggested the presence of a genetic factor in schizophrenia, although it seemed to be less potent than had been previously assumed. Geneticists concentrated research on the influence of environmental factors, studying the differences between uniovular twins.

Neurophysiological studies concentrated on the functions of the reticular activating system and the limbic system (or "visceral brain") which were supposed to be involved in schizophrenia. Excessive arousal of the former system, which could be corrected by tranquilizing drugs, was supposed to underlie some schizophrenic phenomena. Conditioning methods were used in the study of schizophrenic behaviour. These methods promised to provide objective criteria for evaluating the quality of remissions and the prognosis of the disorder.

The prophylactic value of antidepressant drugs remained a subject of controversy. There was no definite evidence that continuation of medication after

recovery from depressive illness prevented recurrence of the attack. Lithium was said to have this effect, but convincing proof had been lacking. It was provided by the Danish team of P. C. Baastrup, J. C. Poulsen, M. Schou, K. Thomson, and A. Amdisen, who studied the effect of discontinuation of lithium treatment in manic-depressive and recurrent depressive disorders. They used a double-blind method in which personal bias of the investigators was eliminated. In 50 manic-depressive patients and 34 patients with recurrent endogenous depression, who had been on lithium treatment for at least a year, the drug was substituted by a placebo at random, with a view to establishing whether discontinuation of the drug resulted in relapse. This actually happened in those cases in which lithium was replaced by placebo without either the patient's or the psychiatrist's knowledge. This therapeutic study provided conclusive evidence of the prophylactic effect of lithium carbonate in manic-depressive illness, provided medication continued indefinitely. The action of the drug was described as "mood-normalizing." (E. ST.)

PUBLIC HEALTH

On Jan. 1, 1970, Pres. Richard Nixon said, "The 1970s absolutely must be the years when America pays its debt to the past by reclaiming the purity of its air, its waters, and our living environment. It is literally now or never." Executive and legislative action in 1970 created two new federal environmental agencies. The National Environmental Policy Act established the Council on Environmental Quality

THE "NEW YORK TIMES"

Jefrey Arlen talks with a volunteer staff member at his St. Mark's Clinic, which serves the young people of the "hippie" East Village neighbourhood in New York City.

(CEQ) in the Executive Office of the President. Russell E. Train, former president of the Conservation Foundation, was appointed CEQ chairman. CEQ was to review national policy on environmental quality goals and controls. In July the president issued an executive reorganization order establishing the Environmental Protection Agency (EPA). Several major environmental agencies were transferred from other departments to EPA. These included the National Air Pollution Control Administration, the Bu-

Peter N. Witt, director of research at North Carolina's Department of Mental Health, holds a picture of a normal web while reading computer output on webs spun by spiders on drugs. He hopes to learn whether behaviour patterns are learned or are innate and if they can be changed by environment.

UPI COMPIX

A worker sets out boxes of poisoned cornmeal in a Washington, D.C., alley as part of the War-on-Rats, a $15 million pilot program operating in 20 U.S. cities. At a meeting of urban officials in June 1970, the program was praised, but more money was asked to extend it to all cities on a permanent basis.

THE "NEW YORK TIMES"

reaus of Solid Waste Management, Water Hygiene, and most of Radiological Health, the Federal Water Quality Administration, Pesticides Registration, Environmental Radiation Standards, and the Federal Radiation Council. The EPA had fiscal 1971 budgets totaling $1.4 billion, with a total staff of 5,650.

In 1960 federal natural resource spending was $1.8 billion, 1.9% of total federal spending. In 1970 it was $3.8 billion, 1.9% of total federal spending. For 1971 projections were $4.6 billion, 2.2% of total federal spending. On Feb. 11, 1970, the *New York Times* observed "if the country is really 'to make peace with nature,' he [the president] will have to demand for the purpose, in far greater quantities than he has yet suggested, the chlorophyl of good green cash."

The consequences to society of adding people, products, and power without regard to the environment were seen in many countries. The famed Rhine River, for example, was polluted in Germany, Switzerland, France, and the Netherlands. Its polluters were such industrial giants as Les Mines Domainale de Potasse d'Alsace, CIBA, J. R. Geigy, Sandoz, and Hoffman-La Roche. Pro Agua, a waterways protection trade group in Basel, and the International Commission to Protect the Rhine Against Pollution, an official five-country group to develop uniform policies, sought to reconcile economic and sovereign power with man's needs for safe drinking water.

New Zealand, confronting a doubling of the number of cars in its major cities in ten years, was implementing the report of a research commission with a clean air act based on local enforcement. In the United States, reorganization of environmental functions of health departments was accomplished in several states. (*See* CONSERVATION.)   (E. T. CH.)

REHABILITATION MEDICINE

Mary E. Switzer, the administrator of the U.S. Social and Rehabilitation Service, retired in February 1970

after 48 years of public service, during the last 20 of which she was responsible for the federal-state program for rehabilitation of the disabled. During her tenure the number of disabled persons rehabilitated into employment increased each year.

Although 266,975 persons were rehabilitated in 1970, nearly double that number, or over 500,000, became newly disabled during the year. Nearly 2% of the total U.S. population consists of persons with physical or mental disabilities who need rehabilitation services but are not receiving them.

One of the major technical developments during 1970 was an experimental plastic spiral brace—a unique concept in which no metal joints are required. As compared with the standard metal braces, the new plastic spiral brace is comfortable, permits a nearly normal gait, is more cosmetic, is lighter in weight, permits interchangeability of shoes, and has a built-in foot support.   (H. A. RU.)

SURGERY

Developments in organ transplantation continued in 1970 to be the most newsworthy aspects of surgery (*see* introductory section). Refinements in other surgical techniques and in postoperative care also were significant.

Thrombosis of the deep veins of the leg has been long recognized as a common event in patients a few days after undergoing surgery. Detachment of such a thrombus and its subsequent lodgment in the pulmonary artery (pulmonary embolism) was one of the serious, potentially lethal, complications still associated with modern routine operations. Until recently the incidence of deep vein thrombosis, and therefore the efficacy of measures designed to reduce it, had to rely upon clinical examination of the legs, well known for both false positive and false negative results.

The development of a radioactive scanning technique, however, enormously improved diagnostic ac-

Because he could not use crutches, this 14-month-old triple amputee was fitted with roller skates at the Children's Hospital of Philadelphia. The aim of fitting such children with prostheses at an early age is to let them get used to their artificial aids before they are aware that they are amputees.

ED ECKSTEIN

curacy with a minimum of discomfort or danger to the patient. Fibrinogen labeled with a radioactive iodine isotope, when injected intravenously, gives a "hot spot" of radioactivity in any region in the leg where the fibrinogen is being actively deposited in a thrombus as thrombin. At King's College Hospital, London, a study of 132 patients after an operation demonstrated that 92 had normal counts. In the other 40, the pattern was abnormal and suggested the presence of venous thrombosis. This was confirmed radiologically in all but one patient by injecting radiopaque dye into the deep veins. Only 20 of these patients had clinical signs of thrombosis.

Richard Doll and his colleagues found that 12 of 30 women patients (40%) developing thromboembolism after an operation had taken oral contraceptives in the month before surgery, compared with only 9 of 60 matched controls (15%). They estimated a three- to fourfold increase in the risk of thromboembolism in such patients. Against this must be placed the possibilities (and dangers) of pregnancy if a program of desisting from the contraceptive pill were to be introduced for several weeks before elective surgery.

The first open-heart surgery to be performed on a patient suffering from hemophilia ("bleeder's disease") was reported from Chicago. The patient, a 49-year-old man, received an artificial aortic valve. The 2,500 pints of blood used during the surgery had been collected from some 2,100 persons over seven months.

Modern peripheral reconstructive arterial surgery achieved a high level of effectiveness in limb salvage. Major arteries from the aorta to the popliteal artery at the knee could either be cored out by endarterectomy or short circuited by means of either the patient's own saphenous vein or by a synthetic tube. M. Spiro and L. T. Cotton, for example, reported 46 patients with occlusion of the aortoiliac vessels, 42 of whom survived for between six months and nine years with a 90% patency rate of the endarterectomized vessels. When reconstructive surgery was impossible because of extensive peripheral obstruction (absence of adequate "runoff"), W. Reed and his colleagues of Glasgow report useful palliation from injection of an aqueous phenol solution to destroy the lumbar sympathetic nerve chain.

There was considerable interest in the immediate fitting of an artificial limb on the operating table at the completion of amputation. Originally employed by R. Dederich and by M. Weiss of Warsaw in post-traumatic amputations, the technique had been applied to cases with peripheral vascular disease by E. M. Burgess of Seattle, Wash., and at the Limb Fitting Centre at Queen Mary's Hospital, Roehampton, Eng. Whether immediate or early delayed fitting (carried out as soon as wound healing has been obtained) would prove more effective remained the subject of further trials.

Perhaps the ultimate in surgery was reached in a series of operations reported from a number of centres on patients who had been "sawed in half," a procedure termed hemicorporectomy. Until 1970 the few

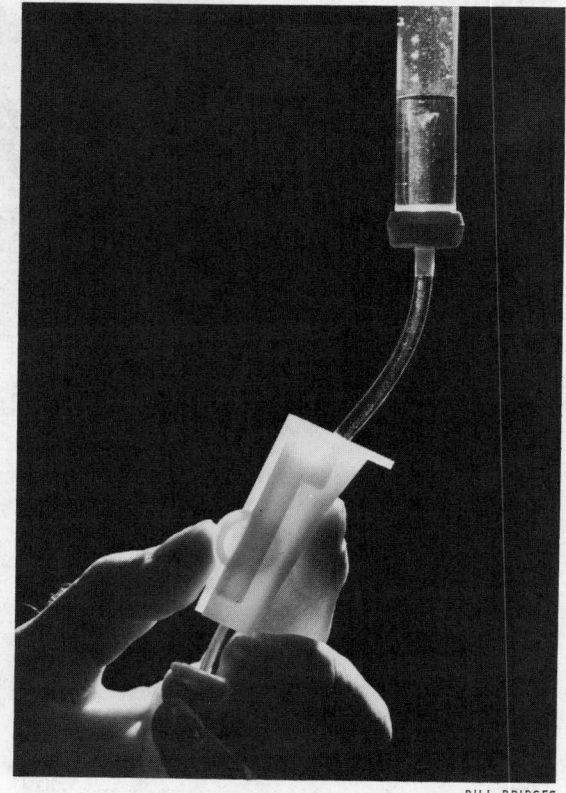

BILL BRIDGES

A new intravenous tubing clamp, which uses an adjustable roller system and maintains the tube's tension for better flow rate, is tested at Massachusetts General Hospital, Boston.

cases reported had been carried out for extensive tumours involving the pelvis and had required the formation of an artificial opening for the large bowel and for the ureters. T. C. Baker and his colleagues from East London, S.Af., performed this formidable procedure in a young man of 21 who was involved in a train accident in which there was extensive and irreparable destruction of the lower part of the body. Nine months after the operation the wounds were healed and the patient's trunk was fitted into a fibre glass prosthesis to which were attached two artificial legs. This, together with intensive physiotherapy to his shoulders and arms, enabled him to stand upright and propel himself between parallel bars and to get about in a wheelchair unaided. (HA. E.)

TROPICAL MEDICINE

Great efforts were being made by tropical countries to improve their medical manpower situation. Whereas in most developed countries there was one doctor to

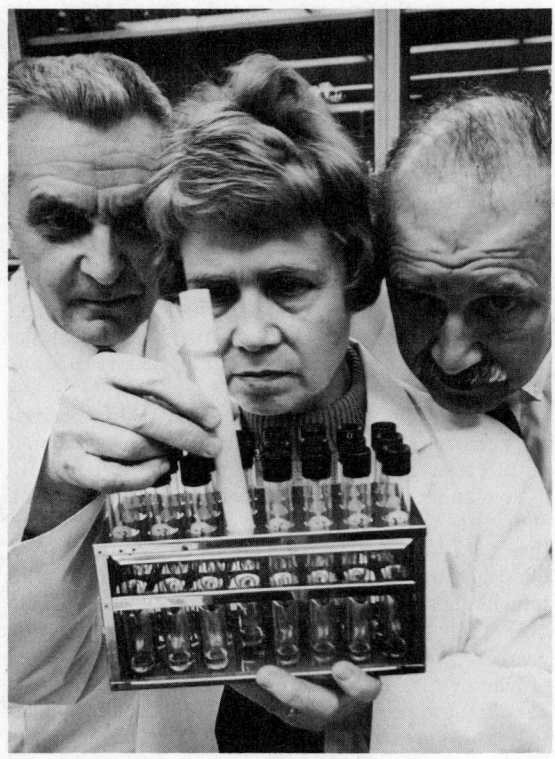

COURTESY, YALE UNIVERSITY NEWS BUREAU

Yale scientists (from left) Jordi Casals, Sonja Buckley, and Wilbur Downs halted research on the deadly Lassa fever virus in February 1970 because it was too dangerous.

every 1,000 or less of the population, in most parts of the tropics the ratio was between one per 20,000 and one per 100,000. An instance of the effort being made, however, was that of the Burmese Ministry of Health and Education, which increased the enrollment of medical students from approximately 50 in 1964 to 550 in 1969.

Increasing attempts were being made to control schistosomiasis (bilharziasis) with the use alone of substances that destroy snails, for it is in snails that the forms of the parasite infective to man develop. At recent meetings of experts in this field, however, it was emphasized that it was unwise to place too great a dependence on snail control by chemical molluscicides. A high degree of control of schistosomiasis was claimed by only a few countries, including Israel and Iran. These were not typical of the majority of countries with a serious schistosomiasis problem in that both have important economic and technical resources and in both the disease was not nearly so serious a problem as elsewhere.

The tropics have long been known as the home of many venereal diseases and have been involved along with many countries of the world in the rise in prevalence of such disease resulting from changes in social and behaviouristic patterns of some sections of modern society. Reports of high prevalence rates have come from all continents and particularly from Ethiopia, Japan, Thailand, and the Americas.

W. M. Hutchinson produced convincing evidence that a coccidian parasite is the causal organism for toxoplasmosis and that *Toxoplasma gondii* may now be placed in the order Eucoccidia, suborder Eimeria.

Nutritional diseases remained among the most important in the tropics, and of these possibly that causing most distress was xerophthalmia in childhood. This disease results in severe damage or destruction of the clear anterior part of the eye and causes blind-

ness. It is now thought that deficiency or absence of vitamin A interferes with formation of mucopolysaccharide in the cornea, leading to keratinizing metaplasia and, with lysosome stability, leading to the opening up of epithelial tissues. Infectious diseases, which often precipitate the disorder with great rapidity, seem to push borderline cases into acute vitamin A deficiency. (A. W. Wo.)

WORLD HEALTH ORGANIZATION

The World Health Assembly, governing body of WHO, met in Geneva in May 1970. The assembly, which brought together delegates of 125 of WHO's 131 member states and associate members, adopted a budget of $73,230,000 to finance the 1971 WHO program.

The assembly unanimously approved a report on chemical and biological weapons and emphasized the need for the rapid prohibition of the development, production, and stockpiling of such weapons, and their destruction as a necessity in the fight for human health.

A WHO pilot project for monitoring adverse reactions to drugs was to be enlarged and established permanently in Geneva. (WHO)

See also Dentistry; Insurance; Molecular Biology; Psychology; Social Services; Vital Statistics.

ENCYCLOPÆDIA BRITANNICA FILMS. *Alcoholism* (1952); *Antibiotics* (1952); *Drug Addiction* (1952); *Mental Health* (1952); *Cancer* (1953); *The Skeleton* (1953); *Bacteria—Friend or Foe* (1954); *Heart Disease—Its Major Causes* (1955); *The Human Brain* (1955); *Immunization* (1955); *The Spinal Column* (1956); *Tuberculosis* (1956); *Work of the Blood* (1957); *The Housefly* (1958); *First Aid on the Spot* (1959); *Health in Our Community* (1959); *DNA—Molecule of Heredity* (1960); *The Blood* (1961); *Mitosis* (1961); *Bacteria* (1962); *Meiosis: Sex Cell Formation* (1962); *Eyes and Vision* (1963); *Gene Action* (1963); *Laws of Heredity* (1963); *Natural Selection* (1963); *The Digestive System* (1965); *The Hospital* (1966); *Chromosomes of Man* (1967); *The Eyes and Seeing* (1968); *The Work of the Heart* (1968); *Ears and Hearing* (1969); *Muscle: Chemistry of Contraction* (1969); *Muscle: Dynamics of Contraction* (1969); *Radioisotopes: Tools of Discovery* (1969); *Respiration in Man* (1969).

Merchandising

In the affluent societies of the West, the consumer revolt joined forces in 1970 with the movement to preserve the environment. According to consumer advocates, not only was the public being brainwashed into buying products it did not really need and cheated by false advertising, inadequate safety standards, and planned obsolescence, but the net result of all this was to pollute the atmosphere (as with automobile exhaust), water (as with phosphates in detergents), and the environment generally (as with indestructible trash).

Concern with the social and environmental consequences of consumer products was much in evidence at the sixth conference of the International Organization of Consumers Unions, held June 29–July 3 at Baden, Aus., and there seemed little doubt that this emphasis would grow. As a priority, however, it was not without its challengers. It had been pointed out that a child born in the U.S. would cause 40 times more pollution during its lifetime than a child born in India, but the reverse of the coin was the deprivation of the Indian child. "The wealthy countries worry about car fumes," said Shankran Kristnamurthy, director of the Consumers Council in India. "We worry about starvation." Delegates representing underprivileged groups in the developed countries agreed, adding that consumer organizations had paid too much

Mental Health:
see Psychology

KEYSTONE

At a Tokyo department store customers, for 500 yen, may take any parts they want from a used car in perfect condition. Tools are provided, and a different car is offered each day. Twenty minutes is allowed for the work.

attention to the relative merits of expensive appliances and not enough to the needs of the poor. In the words of Lillemor Erlander of Sweden, "The young feel frustrated listening to our discussions of washing machines."

In the U.S., consumer advocate Ralph Nader continued his gadfly activities. Early in 1969 he released a 185-page report, bluntly charging the Federal Trade Commission with inadequacy, incompetency, oversensitivity toward politicians, disregard for consumers, and friendliness with big business. The inadequacy of present consumer safeguards was also the theme of the report of the National Commission on Product Safety, issued in June 1970 following a two-year study. The commission, which had been established by Congress, urged the passage of additional safety legislation and the setting up of a Consumer Product Safety Commission to enforce standards. It listed 16 categories of products that it considered hazardous, among them colour television sets, household chemicals, infant furniture, power tools, rotary lawnmowers, and wringer washers. It also criticized lax enforcement in some areas where standards had already been set, claiming, for example, that the Commerce Department had failed to apply "even the weak existing inflammability standard" to blankets and bedding.

The FTC did take some widely publicized actions during the year. It ordered the Coca-Cola Co. to pay the promised $100 prize to several thousand unsuccessful contestants in a promotional game on the ground that they had answered the game questions correctly under any reasonable interpretation of the rules, but that an "undisclosed rule" had been invoked to cut down the number of winners. It further proposed that, in all games of chance in the gasoline and food-retailing industries, the participant should be given a clear definition of his chances of winning. Several cease-and-desist orders were issued against television ads, among them a Campbell soup ad in which marbles were placed in the soup to force the solid ingredients to the top and an ad purporting to show that Zerex antifreeze would seal radiator leaks. Of particular interest in an age of increasing computerization were proposed rules that would safeguard

the secrecy of credit information and would provide on each bill the name, address, and phone number of someone (presumably human) to whom the customer could make complaints. Three days before Christmas, the Food and Drug Administration, acting under the 1969 Toy Safety Act, announced its long-awaited ban on dangerous toys. (*See* Toys and Games.)

In Britain the Consumer Council had done a substantial amount of work in protecting the interests of the consumer, but it suffered from a staid, middle-class image. This seemed likely to change with the appointment of Des Wilson (*see* Biography) as director, but the incoming Conservative government decided to withdraw the council's grant as an economic measure. (*See* Special Report.)

Retail Trade. Whatever the strength of the consumer revolt, economic conditions were at the root of the poor showing of retail sales in the U.S. Inflation and the depressing effects of administration efforts to curb it combined to inhibit consumer enthusiasm, and preliminary indications were that 1970, like 1969, would be a generally poor year. Retail sales totaled approximately $340 billion in 1969, a 4% gain over 1968. However, since commodity prices rose nearly 5%, real consumer demand was down from the previous year. While stores specializing in consumer nondurables reported a 4.5% dollar increase, inflation in this area approached 5.75%, so that there was, in fact, no real gain. Durables as a group experienced the same problem, with demand up 3% and price increases exceeding 3.2%.

The most important determinant in the year's performance was the price level, which rose more than in any year since 1951. Overall, the consumer price index rose 5.75% in 1969, as opposed to 4.75% in 1968. Another factor was personal savings, spurred upward by public uncertainty concerning the economic future and high interest rates offered by savings institutions. During the first two quarters of 1969 savings constituted 5.3% of disposable personal income, but in the last two quarters this figure rose to more than 6.5%— an increase of nearly 23%—and the trend continued into 1970. Viewing the bright side of this phenomenon, a government economist late in 1970 noted that, when economic conditions improved, the consumer would be in a good position to spend. Meanwhile, consumer installment debt continued to rise, but at a generally lower rate than had been the case a year earlier.

Apparel stores reported a dollar gain of more than 5% in 1969, but it was entirely attributable to higher prices. Within the industry, men's and boys' stores, with an increase of 5.5%, outperformed women's stores (3.5%). The outlook for women's clothing was even more bleak in 1970, as the effects of inflation were compounded by consumer resistance to the midiskirt and a general hesitancy to buy when the direction of fashion was so uncertain. (*See* Fashion and Dress.)

Department stores far and away outperformed other sectors in 1969, in both dollar volume and real volume growth. Dollar volume gains averaged in excess of 10%, while estimated price increases averaged slightly less than 5%. The increased volume was partially attributable to the continued growth of discount department stores, which realized a 14.3% gain in sales over 1968. Appliance sales remained steady in 1969, but prices were up approximately 1%. Sales of American-made cars lagged, partly as a result of higher prices. Foreign car sales rose some 10%, however, and in 1970 the American companies began a determined effort to cut into the foreign car market with such new domestic minicars as General Motors' Vega and Ford's Pinto.

In Britain the election of a Conservative government pledged to do away with the selective employment tax had important implications for the retail trade, which was paying 48 shillings a head for each adult male worker. An employment tax of about 25 shillings levied on each worker was suggested as an alternative. This would increase manufacturing costs (in the absence of compensating charges) and lower retailing costs.

Also of concern to retailers was the possibility of a value-added tax being imposed if Britain joined the EEC. The value-added tax, agreed to by the Six as part of their harmonization procedure, had had severely inflationary effects in Belgium, at least in the short run. Somewhat nearer at hand was the switch to decimalization of the British currency, scheduled for Feb. 15, 1971. Many experts predicted that decimalization would cause rises of at least one or two percentage points in the retail price index over a period of several months.

Shoplifting was a growing problem on both sides of the Atlantic. It was estimated that the cost to British retailers would total more than £30 million in 1970. Many reasons were put forward for the increase, but the most obvious was the rise of self-service and the accompanying change in shop layouts, which left the public open to a great deal more temptation. Almost without exception, shopkeepers made no effort to check a customer's bag or basket because it was feared this would frighten customers away.

Trends in Merchandising. Retail trade in the U.S. was becoming increasingly polarized. At one extreme were the mass merchandising operations that successfully implemented the approach already taken by the supermarkets. One example was the large discount department store with a grocery operation. It gained its

appeal by selling food at prices lower than supermarkets were able to offer while providing the convenience of an adjacent or integrated discount department store. Similar in approach were high-volume, rationalized, supermarket-oriented, free-standing specialty stores with "clarity of total offer." Fast-food sellers such as McDonald's, Arby's, and Kentucky Fried Chicken were examples of this type of operation. Others were the home improvement/recreation centres such as Wickes, Handyman, and Gold Triangle, and the "toy supermarkets" like Children's Palace.

At the opposite extreme were the highly specialized boutique-type stores that carried a deep assortment of a very specialized line. The line was often limited to a concept or (as in the case of apparel) a "look" rather than to a commodity type, and it usually appealed to a few or several small market segments. A higher than normal degree of personal selling was involved, together with an emphasis on service. In a seeming contradiction in terms, the boutique concept made its appearance in a number of department stores, especially higher-priced establishments catering particularly to women. Instead of the old-line departments, all or part of the store was divided into small shops, each carrying a single line or a cluster of products grouped around a certain concept. Another incarnation of the boutique idea was the "head shop," a small store catering to the wants of the youth culture and often run by young people. In addition to exotic or "hippie"-type clothing and jewelry, such shops typically carried an assortment of posters, buttons, books on the occult, incense, psychedelic lighting devices, and related exotica. Relatively unimportant in the total retail financial picture, they were not without influence on the decor and merchandising methods of more conventional establishments.

As had been predicted, the high-flying franchise industry was undergoing a shakedown. In this type of

continued on page 505

Patterned after the familiar hot dog cart, new "gourmet pushcarts" stand near New York City's Central Park. They include: the "Oola Cart," which features hot beef burgundy and caviar; the "Bao Cart" with Chinese snacks; the "Fruit 'n' Berries Cart"; and the "Texas Taco Cart."

RUSSELL REIF FROM PICTORIAL PARADE

PROTECTING THE CONSUMER

By Colston E. Warne

False scales are the Lord's abomination;
Correct weights are dear to his heart.
(Prov. 11:1, New English Bible)

In an economy based on consumption, a consumers' revolt is a matter of serious concern. Perhaps "revolt" is too strong a word for what was happening in 1970, but beyond question the consumer was troubled. Prices were rising but products seemed increasingly slipshod. Repairs were hard to obtain and often cost more than the item had originally. Computerization made it difficult to find a human to whom one could complain. Ralph Nader, the young lawyer who had gained fame by charging that General Motors' Corvair was unsafe, regularly brought out new lists of products that he maintained were dangerous or, at best, failed to live up to the claims made for them. Ecologists preached that the consumer was being forced into a pattern of wasteful buying that (if it did not poison the consumer and his environment first) would eventually clog the world with refuse. No wonder that consumers were raising their voices, organizing, and demanding protection.

The idea of consumer protection is hardly a newcomer on the world scene. The shielding of the buyer against fraudulent weights and measures is embedded in the earliest codes of antiquity. In an inconspicuous way, the weights and measures officials of the modern community are carrying out important but long-standing consumer protective functions that constitute the very basis for our exchange system. In the last century, however, economic developments have vastly altered the consumer's competence to judge what he is buying. The limited knowledge that served in a rural technology is lost in a world of additives, preservatives, and synthetics. Today we depend upon packages, labels, guarantees, and, increasingly, upon the functioning of complex but little understood machines. Our heritage of product knowledge has rapidly eroded. We have faith that preservatives and additives are not injurious; that drugs have been adequately tested; that tires are designed for safety. We are surrounded with an abundance of advertising claims for a multiplicity of articles—and by silence concerning their shortcomings.

The result of consumer experience has been the development of a healthy skepticism that demands the establishment of impartial agencies, governmental and nongovernmental, to sift truth from fallacy and to shield the buyer from product hazards or deficiencies. This, in turn, has led to the multiplication of organizations for consumer protection—testing organizations, pressure groups, consumer education programs, consumer centres, consumer councils, government protective agencies, and consumer advisory bodies. Some of the major objectives sought by these consumer groups are:

1. The ensuring of accurate weights and measures and the prominent display of weights on packages.

2. The protection of the health of the consumer through the elimination of dangerous additives and preservatives from foodstuffs and careful control of insecticides and pesticides, as well as pretesting of drugs. (Health protection in recent years has been extended to include the antipollution campaign.)

3. The elimination of unsafe products from the market—for example, unsafe toys, tires, and television sets and flammable carpeting.

4. The strengthening of provisions against fraudulent and misleading advertising—land frauds, advertising frauds, medical frauds.

5. The development of speedy and equitable machinery for handling consumer grievances, with an insistence upon more meaningful product guarantees and warranties.

6. The development of more adequate certification of the basic quality of articles offered on the market through the creation of product standards and grade labels that will indicate performance characteristics and safety.

7. The development of impartial testing services to appraise the performance of competitive goods and services offered on the market and to publish the results, with the clear mention of the brand names involved.

8. The development of consumer education and information services in the schools in order to acquaint future consumers with the nutritive values of foods, the use and misuse of credit, and the rights and responsibilities of buyers in a complex marketing system.

9. The development of adequate and technically competent consumer representation in agencies and commissions dealing with the regulation of consumer prices and consumer services. This would mean that the voice of the consumer would be heard before commissions dealing with such issues as moving costs, television licensing, crop quotas, tariffs, false advertising, product safety, oil imports, and airline rates.

10. Finally, the recognition that consumers have a vital interest in the maintenance of a free competitive system, in which large corporate combines will not have the power to dominate the price structure and minimize the possibility of new and vigorous competitors entering the market.

Ralph Nader, one of the most prominent and effective spokesmen for consumer protection, appears on the CBS television and radio program "Face the Nation," aired Feb. 15, 1970.
WIDE WORLD

The Rise of Consumerism. Behind the new "consumerism" in the United States was the impetus supplied by women's clubs and home economics groups that had become interested in the purity of food and drugs in the days of Harvey Wiley, father of the 1906 Pure Food and Drug Act, and Upton Sinclair, whose novel about the stockyards, *The Jungle* (1906), had led to a demand for stringent meat inspection. The National Consumers League, formed at the turn of the century, also expressed concern over products made with sweatshop labour. The consumer movement still includes some of the state and local groups formed during the period of the New Deal. However, the central thrust for consumer protection has been supplied principally by the consumer testing agencies.

The pioneer in this field was Consumers' Research, Inc., of Washington, N.J., founded in 1929 as the outgrowth of a book, *Your Money's Worth,* by Stuart Chase and F. J. Schlink. The significant contribution of Consumers' Research was to harness the consumer's desire for impartial product advice to create a national consumer organization. Following a protracted internal dispute, Consumers Union of U.S., Inc., was founded in 1936 and quickly overshadowed its competitor. Both organizations continued, but as of 1970 Consumers Union's publication, *Consumer Reports*, went monthly to 1,875,000 families, compared with the 100,000 families who received the *Consumer Bulletin*.

Initially, consumer testing was greeted with hostility from the business community and skepticism from many consumers. This has been largely dispelled by the procedures used: buying samples in the open market; exercising care in testing and in reporting test results; refusing to permit any company to use test results in advertising; and by CU's practice of giving the membership the tasks of electing board candidates and proposing goods and services to be tested. From its inception, Consumers Union has taken vigorous stands on the functioning of consumer protective agencies and pending legislation. It has voiced the complaints of its members over deceptive advertising, watered ham, uninspected drugs, and auto safety. For a considerable period congressional support for these stands was minimal, but in recent years very real gains have been made.

Within government in the U.S., a wide variety of frequently overlapping protective agencies has emerged, largely because the basic jurisdiction over consumer protection has historically been lodged with state or local authorities, while market realities have brought into existence national trademarks as well as national production, packaging, and pricing policies. As a consequence, there is often considerable duplication of national, state, and local legislation. On the federal level the Federal Trade Commission, the Food and Drug Administration, the Department of Agriculture, and many other government agencies share the field of consumer protection. By 1968 approximately 30 states had activated some form of consumer fraud or protection agency, functioning for the most part under the offices of the attorneys general. Three cities, Chicago, New York, and Philadelphia, had adopted consumer representation at the executive level.

The Surge of the '60s. Aided by the initiative of such senators as the late Estes Kefauver, Paul Douglas, Philip Hart, Abraham Ribicoff, and Warren Magnuson, consumer legislation was enacted in unprecedented volume in the 1950s. Yet the great breakthroughs in consumer protection were to come after 1962. Upon his election, Pres. John F. Kennedy formed a Consumer Advisory Council, initially attached to the Council of Economic Advisers. This council gave consumer groups a link with the White House and laid the basis for the appointment by Pres. Lyndon B. Johnson of a special assistant for consumer affairs and the President's Committee on Consumer Interests. It also established the precedent of presidential consumer messages, the first of which was sent to Congress by President Kennedy in March 1962. The result was the establishment of a liaison between some 32 national voluntary organizations and the President's Committee on Consumer Interests. As President Johnson put it in February 1964: "We cannot rest content until [the consumer] is in the front row, not displacing the interest of the producer, yet gaining equal rank and representation with that interest."

With this federal stimulus, consumer organizations designed to tackle consumer problems on the state level emerged in a majority of the states during the late 1960s. On the national level the Consumer Federation of America was formed as an umbrella organization to coordinate the efforts of consumer, cooperative, labour, and agricultural and rural electrification groups interested in promoting a consumer program. This coalition was aided by the emergence of Ralph Nader as a leader in a wide range of consumer reform efforts.

The list of consumer-oriented bills passed since 1962 is impressive, ranging from the Federal Insecticide, Fungicide, and Rodenticide Amendment of 1964 through the Motor Vehicle Safety Act of 1966 and the Wholesome Meat Act of 1967 to the

CHARLES MITCHELL FROM CANADIAN PRESS

Canadian Consumer Affairs Minister Ronald Basford explains new regulations governing labeling of a wide range of hazardous household chemical products during a news conference in Ottawa, March 13, 1970. The regulations were to take effect June 1, 1971.

Truth in Lending Act of 1968 and the Child Protection and Toy Safety Act of 1969. This astounding outpouring of legislation was by no means matched by enforcement, however. Consumer groups soon recognized the political reality that it is far easier to secure the passage of legislation than it is to obtain the appropriations and the dedicated personnel to translate that legislation into effective protection. Thus inadequate enforcement funds in the hands of the Food and Drug Administration had made the Fair Packaging Act largely ineffective. Thus the Federal Trade Commission had for many years failed in its efforts to enforce the mandate of the Wheeler-Lea Act for truth in advertising. The overlapping of the federal enforcement agencies, the pressures brought on them by political groups, the time-consuming legal appeals that ensue when FTC administrative findings are challenged, all contributed to consumer discouragement.

The result was the introduction in Congress of new legislation that would establish a permanent Office of Consumer Affairs in the Executive Office of the President. This office would coordinate the consumer programs and activities in the executive agencies, as well as assisting in the development of such programs and activities throughout the government. In addition, the legislation would provide for the creation of a new independent consumer protective agency to represent the interests of the consumer in proceedings before federal agencies and the courts. This agency would gather and make available the results of tests and analyses of products and would examine the functions of the National Commission on Product Safety. A Consumer Advisory Council of 15 members would be created to advise the heads of the two agencies.

An alternative proposal, preferred by some members of Congress, involved the formation of a Cabinet-level Department of the Consumer, which would include the existing consumer protective agencies, now widely scattered in various government departments, as well as the independent commissions with consumer protective functions, such as the FTC. While the idea of a Cabinet-level department had some support from those who would like to see all these agencies under a single roof, there was a strong feeling among consumer groups that effective enforcement would be facilitated by creating a watchdog agency, rather than by building a new staff that would be subject to the same pressures as the old agencies and would probably receive minimal congressional appropriations.

The Worldwide Consumer Movement. The pattern of consumer protection in Europe bears a remarkable similarity to the U.S. experience. Industrialized nations on both continents generated extensive brand-name advertising and were faced with many of the same problems of packaging and of ensuring the purity of food and drugs. The idea of supplying the consumer with the results of product testing by brand name crossed the Atlantic following World War II. Starting in Great Britain, the Netherlands, and Belgium, it spread to the Scandinavian countries, Austria, West Germany, and France, and was soon exported to Australia, Japan, and Israel.

Initially, European consumer groups feared the legal consequences of publishing adverse test results by brand name, even though this had never proved a problem in the U.S. Nevertheless, the movement, once started, spread so rapidly that in April 1960 the International Organization of Consumers Unions (IOCU) was launched at a conference in The Hague. The charter members were Consumers Union of U.S., Inc.; Consumers' Association, London; Australian Consumers' Association; Consumenten Bond, The Hague; and Association des Consommateurs, Brussels. The IOCU sought to become an authenticating body that would admit to membership only those organizations that accepted no income from advertising and were financially supported by either consumers or governments. The IOCU stimulated the interchange of techniques and test results among its affiliates. It provided an interchange of educational materials and established a technical committee to represent consumers on international standardization bodies. It also moved to assist consumers in less developed nations by obtaining consultative status with the Food and Agriculture Organization, the Economic and Social Council, and UNESCO, agencies of the UN concerned with raising living standards in less developed countries.

In Britain the White Paper of the Maloney Committee formed the basis for a revamping of governmental efforts. The privately operated Consumers' Association assumed the exclusive role of consumer testing. Through its grants, the association established a Research Institute for Consumer Affairs, which conducts investigations into governmental, professional, and commercial services. It also established a National Federation of Consumer Groups to assist local consumer groups with such problems as complaints, store services, and price comparisons, and a Consumer Advice Centre in London. As of 1970, it had a membership of 532,000. A new Consumer Council was created by the government in March 1963 as an independent grant-aided body designed to give advice to the consumer and to initiate reforms on his behalf, but it was abolished in 1970 as an economy measure. Weights and measures controls in Britain remain in the hands of local and county authorities. The body mainly responsible for regulating consumer goods and services is the Board of Trade, although the Home Office deals with most of the safety aspects of consumer protection and the Ministry of Health enforces the Food and Drug Act. The British also created Citizens' Advice Bureaux.

Except for Belgium and the Netherlands, European consumer testing organizations have followed the pattern set by the Scandinavian countries rather than by Britain and the U.S. In Norway substantial government grants are given to a consumer organization, Forbrukerrådet, operated by representatives of seven leading national organizations. The testing agency also handles complaints and publishes a monthly consumer magazine. An Institute of Informative Labeling has also been estab-

lished in Norway to foster the growth of quality marks. In Denmark consumer activities are divided between a governmentally operated Household Advice Centre, which undertakes extensive programs in the field of nutrition and household equipment, and a consumer testing organization supported by its individual members as well as some 21 member organizations and the government. Perhaps the most notable of the European efforts is Austria's Verein für Konsumenten-Information. This organization not only issues a monthly testing publication but also operates a demonstration centre in central Vienna where the consumer may view available brands and receive impartial guidance. Member organizations, including the Chamber of Labour, cover 80% of the organization's budget; the government covers 10% and the individual membership, 10%.

A number of coordinating efforts exist among European groups, among them the European Bureau of Consumers Unions, consisting of nine organizations from the six EEC countries; the Contact Committee of Consumers of the European Economic Community; and the International Labeling Centre, which is linked with the International Organization for Standardization and the International Electrical Technical Commission. These efforts were still weak, but it was expected that the Common Market would inevitably bring increased brand competition between European countries and hence a need for centralized testing. The consumer federations would also enable national groups to act jointly in consultation with the EEC. Similarly, the Scandinavian groups established a Scandinavian Committee on Consumer Matters to coordinate their research and informational efforts. The European consumer protection movement, however, was measurably weakened by the establishment of competitive consumer organizations in many countries, often splitting along political lines. Thus the Belgians had two competing consumer groups, and West Germany had two central organizations, both undertaking consumer testing. The Swiss had four consumer groups until the requirements for obtaining a government subsidy induced coordinated effort.

The development of consumer standards and consumer testing also extended into Eastern Europe. Yugoslavia had a federal board on the family and the household to strengthen the role of consumers. Hungary recently entered the consumer testing field. The Soviet Union established a consumer institute which undertakes comparative testing.

In Asia leadership in the testing field belonged to Japan, where there was competition between the Japan Consumer Association, the Japan Housewives Association, and the Japan Consumers Union. Municipal governments also maintained advice centres in Tokyo and Osaka. A number of embryonic movements had been formed in Korea, the Philippines, Malaysia, and India. Perhaps the strongest organizations in the Pacific area, however, were those in Australia and New Zealand. The Consumers Institute of New Zealand received a heavy government subsidy. The Australian movement was independent in character and received no government money. Local consumer movements existed in leading Australian cities, and New South Wales and Victoria had consumer counsels.

In summary, the world consumer movement has grown most rapidly in more advanced nations that have the discipline of quality control, well-trained government inspection services, and discerning consumers. The unresolved problem in international consumer protection is that of discovering methods of aiding the low-income consumers in nations that have never known an honest civil service and that have low levels of business ethics and consumer competence. Through the Codex Alimentarius, the World Food Organization hopes to assist less developed nations by establishing basic food standards. The IOCU has made a beginning in establishing educational seminars for less developed countries. The problem, nonetheless, was that those with low levels of literacy and minimal income were most likely to be deprived of even the elementary protections of honest weights and measures and of purity in food.

continued from page 501

operation (as distinguished from a chain, in which every store is owned and run by the parent company), the operator of the outlet purchases a franchise to sell the company's product or service in a given territory, under varying degrees of control and with varying amounts of assistance. The concept was not new, but in the past few years it had ballooned. Company after company was founded, many of them using the names of popular entertainment and sports personalities. A few spectacular failures, coupled with overselling (three takeout chicken shops on three corners of an intersection), tended to cool enthusiasm, however. There were also instances where the franchisee was unable to get rid of a failing outlet or did not receive the help he thought he had been promised. Franchise stocks ceased to be the darlings of the stock market, and while this form of selling was undoubtedly a permanent part of the merchandising scene, the attitude toward it was becoming considerably less euphoric.

Nonstore retailing continued to grow in importance. Reversing the direction taken by such companies as Sears, Roebuck, which had gone from purely catalog selling to full-line retail outlets, more and more retail stores were placing greater reliance on catalog and mail-order sales. At the same time, the mail-order industry awaited implementation of the U.S. postal reform with some nervousness, since it seemed almost certain to involve higher third-class rates. At-home selling was exhibiting rapid growth, with Avon reporting a 59% increase in sales between 1965 and 1968. The vending machine industry was also expanding, both in volume and in type of products available.

On the international scene, it was becoming increasingly clear that mass merchandising organizations were taking hold. Among the most significant were the Obs and Wessel operations in Sweden and Carrefour in France. Carrefour was especially noteworthy in that its new stores ranged in size from 200,000 to 300,000 sq.ft. In some ways, all of these operations were more advanced than those found in the U.S.—for example, with regard to the display and storage of high-volume products such as soap and breakfast cereals.

American firms apart, few foreign companies had established themselves in the British market, but in 1970 Carrefour, in partnership with Wheatsheaf Investments, announced that, subject to planning permission, it would open its first out-of-town discount store near Southampton. A number of other stores were planned. Another European entrant into the British market was Marko, a Dutch-German cash-and-carry group, which announced plans to open a number of 150,000-sq.ft. luxury wholesale warehouses, stocking about the same range of goods as a department store. The first would probably be in the Birmingham area.

Planning application was made for a new out-of-town shopping scheme at Almondsbury, which would incorporate a pool for boat sales and a garden centre. The 91-ac. site was about five miles from Bristol. In April planning permission was granted for a vast shopping centre at Brent Cross, North London, to serve an estimated 1.8 million people. Turnover at the unusual Buywell shopping centre at Boston Spa, near the A-1 between York and Leeds, rose 60% in 1969, and sales in 1970 were expected to exceed £750,000. This venture, which utilized former military facilities, had ground-level parking space for 1,000 cars and ten buildings of 11,000 sq.ft. Seven of the buildings were occupied; six were devoted to a single category of

KEYSTONE

Tokyo's department stores, vying with each other for new gimmicks to attract customers, have now gone into used-airplane sales. On the roof of one large store two small planes are for sale.

goods while the seventh was reserved for small shops. The site also had a children's playground, a small zoo, a cafeteria, and a licensed restaurant.

With some 40% of grocery turnover in Britain concentrated in the top 15 food chains, power had largely passed from the food manufacturer to the retailer. One result was that manufacturers probably spent more on promotions to retailers than on direct advertising to the consumer. Others were the heavy cost of promoting new products and the power of retailers to promote their own labels. Not surprisingly, views on these trends differed according to whether the commentator was a manufacturer or a large or small retailer.

An interesting experiment was reported from Switzerland, where four specialized mail-order companies embarked on a joint promotion scheme. The covers and centre pages of the catalog were jointly designed, while the remainder included offers from each of the firms with separate order forms. A West German restaurant chain announced plans to open "entertainment centres" on the franchise principle. To be called Citta 2000, they would start in Germany and be extended to other countries. The aim was to attract customers to the restaurants and then offer them a variety of goods and services such as clothing, accessories, hairdressing, and travel services. A dance floor and other entertainment facilities would also be available.

The year saw considerable activity on resale price maintenance in West Germany. Deutsche Supermarket Co., part of the Weston group, advertised cut prices on goods from seven leading manufacturers and the latter stopped supplies and took legal action. Agfa-Gevaert, Kodak, and Zeiss-Ikon-Voigtländer abandoned price maintenance on the German market in January. There was pressure in several European countries to eliminate resale price maintenance in line with Britain and Switzerland.

The *Parly 2* regional shopping centre in Paris aroused widespread interest. Acclaimed for its quality of design, it included 55,000 sq.m. of shopping space on two levels, enclosed in a landscaped mall with cafes and seating spaces. Shoppers appeared to fear that this luxury would have to be paid for by higher prices, and other retailers were watching the progress of the venture. (A. F. D.; G. C. Ho.)

See also Advertising; Consumer Expenditures; Cooperatives; Domestic Arts and Sciences; Industrial Review; Prices.

Metallurgy

Metallurgy during 1970 was strongly influenced by both economic and social forces. Keen competition, especially in international trade, demanded that production costs and material prices be kept down, while the growing public awareness of environmental problems spurred development in scrap and waste recovery and control of noxious emissions. Development in ore dressing and extractive metallurgy was being encouraged by these and other factors that gave rise to new problems. There was growing awareness of the rapid depletion of many high-grade ore deposits, notably those in the United States. Many new deposits around the world were being opened as it became profitable, due to innovations in transportation and the growing demand for concentrates in newly industrialized areas.

Most new mills were based on fairly conventional practice but showed a strong trend to large machines: grinding mills in which no grinding medium other than the ore itself is used were as large as 40 ft. in diameter and were powered by 4,000-hp. motors, while flotation cells had capacities of 200 and even 300 cu.ft. rather than the previous standard of 30. A high degree of automation was practically universal, as was highly instrumented and often precise process control.

Hydrometallurgy as a means of metal recovery had two advantages of special interest: the potential for economically treating low-grade ore and even waste rock containing a little metal, and the ability to treat sulfide ores without the release of sulfur dioxide. Leaching of waste rock from copper mines was general practice and was often done by using cultures of bacteria that live by oxidizing sulfides into water-soluble sulfates rather than by using chemical solvents. Very-low-grade ore was being crushed and heaped on the ground where runoff could be collected and then sprayed with the leaching solution. Experiments with heap leaching an ore containing 0.02% gold recovered 95% of the metal.

Although not tried in connection with the above experiments, an ion exchange resin developed in the Soviet Union proved selective in removing gold from leaching solutions as the next step in producing pure metal. An ion exchange resin that converted sodium tungstate to ammonium tungstate was being used in an important step in producing pure tungsten from a leaching solution. Finding expanded use was a solvent

extraction that selectively removed the metal of interest from the leaching solution into a second liquid immiscible with it, while leaving the impurities. In these processes purification is carried out before the metal is prepared from its compounds. Leaching of nickel ores at elevated temperature and pressure was being used increasingly, and much development was being done on methods of leaching sulfide copper ores. Many of the processes yielded solid sulfur rather than sulfur dioxide as a by-product.

The use of continuous casting became more extensive, while the cross-section size of a billet continued to decrease, thereby reducing the amount of subsequent mechanical forming. Material for rolling into sheet was being cast into wide billets, some less than an inch thick. Both copper and aluminum for wire were being cast into strands only a few inches square which were fed directly into continuous hot rolling mills to produce rod for drawing into wire. The aluminum rod was being converted to wire by a unique continuous extrusion process.

A shortage of good-grade steel melting scrap and the demand that automobile bodies and other low-grade scrap be cleaned up accelerated investigation of means to utilize the latter material. A continuous run of several hours demonstrated the technical feasibility of using an electric furnace for continuous production of pig iron from automobile scrap. Clean sheet steel scrap was being sintered and rerolled into sheet without remelting.

An alloy of aluminum and silicon made an all-aluminum automobile engine cylinder block practical. Particles of this alloy exposed on the cylinder surfaces by etching after machining gave resistance to wear and seizing. Other new metals included an aluminum-silicon-manganese alloy with properties comparable to 18% chromium-8% nickel stainless steel, a development influenced by the nickel shortage, which continued but was much less severe than in 1969. A new high-strength stainless steel from Japan contained both niobium and titanium and more carbon than usual.

Mechanical alloying, which involves making powder metallurgy parts from pure metal powders that alloy on sintering, was, along with practically all other applications of powder metallurgy (alloying without melting), finding greatly expanded use. The process had been so developed that a great variety of dispersion-strengthened alloys could be made. Copper-clad aluminum electric wire was being made in Britain from billets supplied by a U.S. company. Reliable mechanical and soldered contacts could be made almost as easily as with ordinary copper wire but with an 80% reduction in the amount of the expensive metal needed.

The development of metal composites reinforced by high-strength fibres continued to be strong. Aluminum reinforced with beryllium wire, though not quite as strong as that reinforced with boron, had some ductility which made it more desirable for some applications and less subject to catastrophic failure. A process developed in West Germany for producing fine wire made of maraging steel (steel containing 18 to 25% nickel) with twice the strength of boron fibre was said to have a potential price (if production reached ten tons per year) of about $20 per pound, much lower than that of any of the other high-strength reinforcement fibres. (D. F. C.)

See also Industrial Review; Mining; Physics.

ENCYCLOPÆDIA BRITANNICA FILMS. *The Miner* (1967); *Problems of Conservation—Minerals* (1969).

Meteorology

Many of the common questions about weather and climate were weighed and expounded in the highest forums of the atmospheric sciences during 1970. In his presidential address before the Royal Meteorological Society in April, B. J. Mason, director of the official meteorological organization of the U.K., reviewed the status and prospects up to the year 2000 in the major branches of weather reporting and forecasting services. Of special interest to agriculturalists, industrialists, and others with a practical interest in weather were the remarks and tabulated data Mason presented on applications and limitations of weather forecasting.

Among the many high-level scientific symposia and working groups that reviewed and planned future research in meteorology and kindred fields were several sessions of specialized panels of GARP (the Global Atmospheric Research Program of the World Meteorological Organization or WMO) and the International Union of Geodesy and Geophysics (IUGG), and the joint symposium commemorating the centennial of public weather reporting and forecasting services in the U.S. The consensus of these many studies was that technological wonders such as radar and other optical, radiometric, and acoustical sensing devices, rockets, space satellites, and ultrahigh-speed electronic computers had opened a new era for the atmospheric sciences, and that many of the long-standing problems of meteorology and its applications in weather predicting and storm forecasting could be solved. Nevertheless, the endless complexities of the atmosphere's mechanics and the incredible volume of data to be obtained, analyzed, and interpreted would make for slow progress. As of 1970 reporting and forecasting for periods of 24 to 48 hours had been much improved since 1940, and in most circumstances were reasonably accurate, but long-range weather predictions beyond a general five-day extrapolation were "experimental" and often controversial as to scientific basis. Attempts at weather modification were even more conjectural except in a few limited situations.

In the U.S. a proclamation by Pres. Richard Nixon on January 27 commemorated the centennial of national weather services, established on Feb. 9, 1870, when Pres. Ulysses S. Grant signed a joint congressional resolution inaugurating a weather bureau as part of the U.S. Signal Corps. In proclaiming February 1970 as Weather Services Month, President Nixon urged institutions and science-minded citizens throughout the country to recognize and support constructive programs for the advancement of meteorology and its public-service responsibilities. Accordingly, the local weather bureau offices in most large cities organized technical conferences, symposia, or other suitable events for promoting research and planning improvements in weather forecasting services. The first of these was assembled in Washington, D.C., on February 12–14, under the sponsorship of the American Meteorological Society (AMS) and the U.S. government centennial organizing group (WESCENT). In addition to the centennial, it celebrated the 50th anniversary of the AMS and the beginning of the second decade of full-service meteorological satellites.

Research Results and Prospects. Technical papers delivered at the February symposium gave evidence for the aforementioned consensus. They included reviews of the collection of facts needed to understand air/sea interactions and other flux processes; weather forecasting requirements for synoptic observing systems; air pollution problems and composition of the atmosphere; new opportunities in applied meteorology; and synergisms of life and climate and experiments in modification of clouds and rainfall. The papers attempted to state the significance of scientific and technological advances in meteorology and to examine potential applications to everyday living.

Another feature of the WESCENT celebration was the publication of *A Century of Weather Service— 1870–1970*, which described by word and photograph the evolving weather bureaus in the U.S. and included a 13-page chronology of important events. Other convenient "weather" chronologies were produced during 1970, among them a detailed listing by the Historical Section of the Environmental Science Services Administration (ESSA) and a selection of unusual weather headlines over the century published in *Weatherwise*.

The scope and volume of research reports in the atmospheric sciences during 1970 was exceedingly great. There were numerous technical papers on a wide variety of abstract subjects, but probably the greatest number of research projects were directed toward the more immediate goals of understanding the mechanics

507

Meteorology

Table I. Selected Weather Headlines, 1970

Place	Date	Weather event	Unusual features
Libya	Dec. 1969– Jan. 1970	Prolonged rains caused heavy flooding	Two months recurring rain; much loss of life and property
Peru	January	Heavy rains; flooding	Flooding in usually desert areas
Denmark	Feb. 20	Blizzards; temperature below freezing most of three months	Snarled air and ground traffic; unusually severe for Denmark
Spain	Feb. 21	Smog warnings, Madrid	Increased industrialization and population caused acute pollution
Clarendon, Tex.	April 18	Tornadoes	Over 200-mi. area; 25 persons dead, $5 million damage
Dakotas, U.S.	April 19–20	Heavy snows	Unusually late season snowfall; accumulation 1½ ft. in some areas
Lubbock, Tex.	May 11	Two tornadoes	Destroyed much of city; 26 dead
Washington, D.C.	July 20–30	Frequent days of heavy rain	Rainfall totals 5 in. or more; relieved ten-year deficit in water table
Kew Observatory, Eng.	July 22	Minimum temperature 28°F	Lowest temperature ever recorded at Kew in July (records covering 65 years)
Italy	Sept. 11–12 and in October	Heavy rains; tornado	Venice had tornado killing at least 41; flooding at Genoa, Naples "worst in 100 years"; at least 30 dead
Eastern U.S.	Sept. 20–30	Prolonged heat and humidity	An unusually oppressive heat wave in cities of the eastern U.S.
Puerto Rico	Oct. 4–12	Hurricane	Eight days heavy rain caused disastrous flooding and loss of 50 lives
Italy	Oct. 15–18	A second spell of heavy rain	Central squares in Genoa flooded to 5 ft. depth; 16 drowned on Italian Riviera
Philippine Islands and Vietnam	Oct. 12–20	Typhoons Joan and Kate	Heavy rains (2 ft. in 30 hours); more than 1,000 drowned
Pakistan	Oct. 27	Cyclone (same as hurricane)	Prolonged rain and floods; at least 100 dead, and heavy loss of property
South Vietnam	Oct. 26–30	Floods	Worst in six years; at least 193 dead, more than 200,000 homeless
East Pakistan	Nov. 12–13	Cyclone and tidal wave	Affected more than 3 million persons in a 2,800 sq.mi. area of Ganges-Brahmaputra delta; at least 200,000 persons died

Table II. Selected Weather Satellites in Operation, 1970

Type	Date of launching	Days in operation	Usable photos transmitted	Average altitude (miles)	Orbit or position
Essa 2	Feb. 1966	1,700	Local readouts, probably thousands	860	Near polar orbit
Essa 8	Dec. 1968	700	Local readouts, probably thousands	890	Near polar orbit
Essa 9	Feb. 1969	600	70,000	910	Near polar orbit
ITOS 1	Jan. 1970	250	25,000	890	Near polar orbit
ATS 1	Dec. 1966	530	5,200	22,238	"Stationary" over Equator above mid-Pacific
ATS 3	Nov. 1967	110	2,200	22,232	"Stationary" over Equator above Caribbean

Note: The above list does not include Nimbus-type meteorological satellites, launched primarily for research, and many others which have sensing devices that "observe" meteorological parameters incident to some different primary mission. The Essa, ITOS, and ATS types listed above are designed and used primarily for daily meteorological service operations.

of atmospheric phenomena, improving the reliability and time range of forecasts, and achieving practical methods for modification or "control" of weather, storms, and climate.

Among the many noteworthy scientific contributions were reports of the studies involved in the Global Atmospheric Research Program (GARP), the Barbados Oceanographic and Meteorological Experiment (BOMEX), and the World Weather Watch (WWW). These programs had been conceived and planned during the 1960s, but GARP and WWW would not be in full operation until the mid-1970s and the study of BOMEX data, begun in 1969, would continue for several years. BOMEX had been designed to investigate air/sea interactions and related atmospheric problems in the subtropics, both to promote understanding of the role of tropical atmospheric phenomena in weather and climate over the Western Hemisphere as a whole and as a trial run for GARP. The BOMEX field operations had been performed during mid-1969.

A preliminary report of BOMEX results was published in the *AMS Bulletin* (September–October 1970). Significant new quantitative data vital to the construction of mathematical models of the mechanics of the atmosphere were derived for the sea/air energy flux over the approximately 250,000 sq.km. of the area under study; measurements of evaporation, insolation, wind divergence, and other parameters were also made. These were the type of data that GARP would acquire for the entire globe through an augmented WWW.

The GARP and WWW programs necessitated numerous meetings and study conferences of experts from the many countries participating in this huge international undertaking. Technical reports of subjects under study and detailed analyses and plans were published in several technical journals and monographs, for example in the *WMO Bulletin* for January and April and in the *AMS Bulletin* for January, February, May, June, and September.

Other Basic Research. The sun's radiation holds fundamental interest for scientific study in many different disciplines. For meteorologists its attraction is that solar energy is the initial and by far the greatest source of power to drive the earth's "heat engine," which produces weather and climate. For many years studies of sunspots, fluctuations in measurable received radiation, and related phenomena had sought to determine if there are significant variations in the sun's total energy output that might cause weather changes and even account for the Ice Ages. During the first half of the 20th century assumed variations in the

solar constant were used as a basis for long-range weather forecasts. After many years of testing hypotheses that attempted to predict weather on this basis and much scientific controversy on the subject, however, this method of prediction had fallen more or less into disuse by 1960.

With the invention of very-high-altitude balloons and rockets and, more importantly, space satellites, it became possible to measure solar radiation outside the earth's atmosphere. As a result, during 1960–70 many studies were published regarding relationships between selected portions of the solar spectrum and apparently linked physical or biological phenomena on earth. One such study, published in July 1970 in the *Quarterly Journal* of the Royal Meteorological Society, was by two internationally distinguished scientists of the University of Leningrad. Using data obtained by high-altitude balloons, they found the maximum value of the solar constant to be 1.94 calories per square centimetre per minute. They claimed an accuracy within 1% for this value. They confirmed the fact that volcanic eruptions and nuclear explosions cause a significant decrease in the transparency of the atmosphere and consequently a decrease in the solar radiation that reaches the earth's surface.

Numerical weather prediction—forecasting by the use of electronic computers—had begun on a regular daily-service basis in the 1950s, based on mathematical models designed mostly in England, Norway, and the U.S. By 1970 scientific papers describing the design and use of models of atmospheric phenomena had become an important part of the meteorological literature in the 10 or 15 countries that were most advanced in the atmospheric sciences, notably Australia, Canada, France, West Germany, Japan, Norway, Sweden, the U.S., and the U.S.S.R. Models ranged from simple one or two levels or barometric surfaces to very complex eight levels that aimed to encompass the significant parameters in three dimensions. Most models represented large segments of the general circulation, often the polar hemisphere, but a few dealt with smaller-scale entities such as hurricanes, tornadoes, thunderstorms, or even local convection plumes.

Among the hundreds of technical papers on mathematical models that appeared in 1970 was an extensive study of tropical circulation, published by three researchers at the Geophysical Fluid Dynamics Laboratory, Princeton, N.J., in the AMS *Journal of the Atmosphere*. The paper confirmed that most of the kinetic energy of tropical cyclones and other large-scale tropical depressions comes from conversion of the heat of condensation, as well as that disturbances in the upper troposphere transport angular momentum across the Equator and greatly influence the total budget of this parameter in the model. Other papers dealt with exploratory studies of tornadolike vortex dynamics as simulated by both mathematical models and physical replicas, experiments in localized numerical weather prediction, and parameterization of macroscale heat transport in a mean motion model of the general circulation.

The extraordinary amount of effort, money, and time being devoted to quantitative models of atmospheric motions inevitably led many theoreticians to challenge the ultimate use of such models in predicting changes of weather. The question rested on uncertainty as to whether atmospheric motions over longer periods of time are deterministic, or are random and thus impossible to predict. As of 1970 most scientists in the field expressed hopes that determi-

The wreckage of a village left in the wake of the cyclone and tidal wave that struck the Bay of Bengal and parts of East Pakistan in November 1970.

WIDE WORLD

nistic forecasts of general weather conditions could eventually be developed to cover periods of two to four weeks, but it was recognized that random features and other indeterminable elements might cut the range of accuracy to a few days.

Some insight into the many uncertainties involved, especially for those interested but rather unfamiliar with the vagaries of the earth's three-dimensional ocean of air, was afforded by papers on frontogenesis in the mid-troposphere and cyclones in the intermediate layers of the troposphere over the southwest monsoon regions of the Bay of Bengal and Indian Ocean (*Journal of Applied Meteorology,* June 1970). These were only two of numerous studies of invisible but often controlling cyclones and fronts in the upper air. They added to already conclusive evidence that the endless variety and changes in the atmosphere could be recorded, analyzed, and utilized for weather predictions only through the techniques of high-speed, huge-capacity electronic computers.

Experimental Meteorology. From small beginnings in 1946, the practice of seeding clouds with "dry ice" or silver iodide in order to produce more rain or snow had spread to all continents, and technical literature on this and other methods for modifying weather or climate had become voluminous by 1970. In most cases the results were controversial, but the economic and social implications of successful "control" of the weather were so great that intensive experimentation and serious research were certain to continue. Moreover, there were some circumstances in which meteorological conditions could be artificially modified to very considerable economic advantage, as in clearing some forms of fog from airports. For several years the Soviet Union had reported successes not attained in most other countries, especially in the suppression of destructive hailstorms.

Thousands of experiments in weather modification were made during 1970, both in the research laboratory and in the natural conditions of the free atmosphere. They embraced fundamental phenomena in cloud physics, droplet mechanics, electrical properties and their induced effects on such phenomena as condensation, coalescence, and lightning, and utilization of multiple doppler radar and other advanced techniques and devices for detecting distant elements pertaining to weather modification and storm suppression.

Project Stormfury continued during 1970 in an effort to find ways to weaken the forces of destructive hurricanes. Reports made through ESSA's National Hurricane Research Laboratory and other channels were cautiously optimistic, although informed scientists still considered the idea of seeding hurricane clouds as experimental and unproven. It was somewhat surprising, therefore, that an official announcement by spokesmen for the U.S. Departments of Commerce and Navy, the agencies that jointly supported Project Stormfury, should have featured the results of hurricane seeding in 1969 as a "potential breakthrough."

Some progress was made during the year in devising electronic methods for assimilating and projecting the huge mass of cloud photos and radiation data from satellites, as well as in including other phenomena to be telemetered by satellite, for example, lightning flashes in clouds around the earth. The Nimbus family of experimental meteorological satellites tested new and highly sophisticated parameters designed to solve intricate problems of the atmosphere, such as the various aspects of radiation fluxes and the heat budget of the earth-sun system as a whole. These studies were still largely theoretical, but they might eventually explain vital questions about climate and its changes.

Climate and Air Pollution. Probably one of the most significant developments of 1970 as far as the future welfare of mankind was concerned was the growing awareness that the atmosphere and the oceans have finite dimensions. They are not limitless in their capacity to absorb the contaminants that man pours continuously into the air and the water. Headlines in the daily press and serious scientific articles warned of possible catastrophic consequences in the future—a reversion to the Ice Ages, other major changes in weather and climate, lethal modification of the composition of the atmosphere, or slow but perilous transformations in the relationship of the oceans and the large bays, gulfs, and lakes that are the source of most of the moisture in the air.

For years a few scientists had been trying to measure changes, if any, in the atmosphere. According to tentative reports during 1970, the oxygen content was about 20.9%, indicating that there had been no measurable change over the oceans since 1910. A slight increase in carbon dioxide content seemed to have occurred, however. Another report stated that pollutants in the air over the oceans had doubled in 50 years. These air pollution problems were considered ominous and closer surveillance was planned.

Most of these questions about the atmosphere involved close international cooperation; winds and weather are not confined within national boundaries. WMO continued to be very active in promoting such cooperation. The process of merging related geophysical researches and services also went forward on the national levels. In the U.S., ESSA, established in 1965, was merged into the National Oceanic and Atmospheric Administration. NOAA embraced, among other bodies, the U.S. Weather Bureau, which became the National Weather Service.   (F. W. RR.)

See also Astronautics; Conservation; Disasters; Oceanography.

ENCYCLOPÆDIA BRITANNICA FILMS. *The Climates of North America* (1963): *Origins of Weather* (1963): *Weather Forecasting by Satellite* (1964); *Weather Satellites* (1965); *What Makes Clouds?* (1965): *What Makes the Wind Blow?* (1965); *Whatever the Weather* (1967); *Reflections on Time* (1969).

Mexico

A federal republic of Middle America, Mexico is bounded by the U.S., British Honduras, and Guatemala. Area: 761,600 sq.mi. (1,972,547 sq.km.). Pop. (1970): 48,313,438, including about 70% mestizo and 28% Indian. Cap. and largest city: Mexico City (metro. area pop., 1970, 7,005,855). Language: Spanish. Religion: predominantly Roman Catholic. Presidents in 1970, Gustavo Díaz Ordaz and, from December 1, Luis Echeverría Álvarez.

Domestic Affairs. On Dec. 1, 1970, Luis Echeverría Álvarez, Mexico's 15th constitutional president (*see* BIOGRAPHY), began his six-year term of office. Elected on July 5 as candidate of the Partido Revolucionario Institucional (PRI), Echeverría received 84% of the total vote cast; the rest went to the only other contender, Efraín González Morfín, of the Partido Acción Nacional (PAN). Art. 34 of the constitution had been amended to lower the minimum voting age from 21 to 18; this increased the electorate by approximately 3 million to 21.6 million, of whom only 14 million voted. The election gave the PRI all 60 seats in the Senate and 178 in the Chamber of Depu-

Methodists:
see Religion

WIDE WORLD

Luis Echeverría Álvarez was elected Mexico's new president in July 1970.

WIDE WORLD

Mexico's outgoing president, Gustavo Díaz Ordaz, met with U.S. Pres. Richard M. Nixon at Puerto Vallarta in August 1970.

ties, where the remaining 35 seats were shared by PAN (20), the Partido Popular Socialista (10), and the Partido Auténtico de la Revolución Mexicana (5). Both the elections and transfer of power were peaceful and orderly.

A national census taken in January–February showed that population growth had previously been overestimated. In the 1960s the population actually increased by 38.3% to 48.3 million, of whom women outnumbered men by almost 2.4%; the proportion of illiterates fell to 22% of the total from 35% in 1960. In addition to Mexico City, the country had four cities of more than half a million inhabitants (1960 figures in parentheses): Guadalajara, 1,196,218 (740,394); Monterrey, 830,336 (601,085); Netzahualcóyotl, 571,035 (not available); and Puebla, 521,885 (297,-257). The very rapid development of Netzahualcóyotl, Tlalnepantla, Naucalpan, and Ecatepec, all in the state of México, indicated the growth of industry around the capital, where 40% of the country's total plant was concentrated. This created problems of transport, labour costs, and pollution. Understandably the government announced in midyear that no new manufacturing plants would be allowed in the Federal District after 1975 and on the periphery of Mexico City after 1980.

The Economy. Despite the atmosphere of uncertainty associated with every election year, the economy continued to grow in 1970 at much the same pace as in 1969, when the gross national product showed a real gain of 6.4%. In many respects its performance in 1969 was typical of the 1960s as a whole. During the decade per capita income increased by 46% in real terms, compared with 26% in the 1950s and 39% in the 1940s. Unlike previous governments during their last year in office, the Díaz Ordaz administration refrained from excessive public spending in 1970. Its attitude was largely dictated by the need to keep in reserve a number of large projects that might have had to be activated if a persistent economic recession in the U.S. had spilled over into Mexico. As things were, a moderate rate of public investment was maintained, and in the second half of the year efforts were renewed on some important public works, including those stages of the Mexico City underground railway scheduled by the authorities for completion before the change of government.

Business was further stimulated by a growth of consumer demand attributed to higher minimum wage rates for urban and rural workers (increased by 15% and 16% to 24.90 and 21.20 pesos a day after Jan. 1,

1970) and to marginal benefits for the working class under a new federal labour law implemented on May 1. These factors, together with the effect of more expensive imports from countries with inflationary trends (62% of all Mexican imports in 1969 were from the U.S.), disrupted the price stability that Mexico had enjoyed for many years. In 1969 the official cost-of-living index rose by 3.5%—although many observers thought 7% a truer figure. A succession of price rises affecting steel, newspapers, textiles, restaurant charges, and building costs accelerated the upward trend, and by mid-1970 the wholesale price index showed an increase of 6.4%. Under the circumstances the authorities, intent on handing over to their successors a tidier economic situation than they had inherited six years earlier, took the classic steps to combat inflation and, therefore, credit conditions were difficult in the second half of the year.

In 1970 much attention was paid to the promotion of exports. Foreign trade results for 1969 had shown great promise, with exports rising by 15.7% to $1,-366,300,000 while imports were kept in check and rose by a modest 5.9% to $2,075,900,000; as a result the trade deficit was $70.2 million less than in 1968. Unfortunately, the hopes raised by this performance were not realized in 1970, when statistics for the first six months showed a rise of 2.7% in exports and one of 13.6% in imports; this produced a deficit $118.6 million greater than in January–June 1969. Tourism, however, continued to relieve the pressure on the balance of payments. Fears of a disappointing 1969—after the previous year's boost from the 19th Olympic Games—proved unfounded. In 1969 the number of tourists visiting Mexico increased by 11.5% to 2,097,-801, although the net income from tourism did not increase as much because of an extraordinary rise in expenditure by Mexicans abroad. In the first half of 1970—when attractions included an international automobile rally in May and the World Cup soccer competition in June—Mexicans spent less abroad while the country's foreign visitors increased by 9.3% to 1,063,724.

Relations with the U.S. After a period of strain in the last quarter of 1969, relations with the U.S. improved. On September 21 of that year the U.S. customs authority launched a massive land, sea, and air surveillance of the U.S.-Mexican border in an effort to stamp out contraband in narcotics. Known as Operation Intercept, it involved long delays to travelers, which caused resentment and adversely affected trade along the border. The U.S. did not con-

MEXICO

Education. (1967–68) Primary, pupils 7,772,-257, teachers 158,736; secondary and vocational, pupils 1,063,900, teachers 76,069; teacher training, students 57,845, teachers (1966–67) 6,553; higher (including 38 universities), students 154,-289, teaching staff (1966–67) 16,203.

Finance. Monetary unit: peso, with a par value of 12.50 pesos to U.S. $1 (30 pesos = £1 sterling). Gold, SDRs, and foreign exchange, central bank: (May 1970) U.S. $606 million; (May 1969) U.S. $577 million. Budget (federal government; 1970) balanced at 28.1 billion pesos. Gross national product: (1968) 334.3 billion pesos; (1967) 301.4 billion pesos. Money supply: (Dec. 1969) 48.3 billion pesos; (Dec. 1968) 42,240,000,000 pesos. Cost of living (Mexico City; 1963 = 100): (May 1970) 124; (May 1969) 118.

Foreign Trade. (1969) Imports 25,975,000,-000 pesos; exports 17,874,000,000 pesos. Import sources (1968): U.S. 63%; West Germany 8%. Export destinations (1968): U.S. 57%; Japan

6%. Main exports: cotton 14%; sugar 7%; coffee 5%. Tourism (1968): visitors 1,664,500; gross receipts U.S. $1,137,000,000.

Transport and Communications. Roads (1969) 69,719 km. (including 1,010 km. expressways). Motor vehicles in use (1968): passenger 1 million; commercial (including buses) 465,800. Railways: (1967) 23,826 km.; traffic (1968) 4,398,000,000 passenger-km., freight 20,433,000,-000 net ton-km. Air traffic (1969): 2,620,000 passenger-km.; freight 35,510,000 net ton-km. Shipping (1969): merchant vessels 100 gross tons and over 118; gross tonnage 423,969. Telephones (Dec. 1968) 1,174,885. Radio receivers (Dec. 1967) 10,932,000. Television receivers (Dec. 1968) 2,150,000.

Agriculture. Production (in 000; metric tons; 1969; 1968 in parentheses): corn c. 8,600 (9,360); wheat (1968) 1,894, (1967) 2,058; rice c. 300 (455); potatoes c. 576 (400); coffee (1968) 171, (1967) 165; cotton, lint c. 401 (537); dry beans c. 1,000 (1,035); bananas

(1968) 1,000, (1967) 986; oranges (1968) 892, (1967) 882; lemons (1968) 172, (1967) 171; sugar, raw value (1969–70) c. 2,489, (1968–69) c. 2,394; tobacco c. 62 (62); sisal (1968) 148, (1967) 147; fish catch (1968) 366, (1967) 350. Livestock (in 000; Dec. 1968): cattle c. 34,900; sheep (1968–69) 6,706; pigs c. 15,000; horses c. 5,400; mules c. 2,020; asses c. 3,700; chickens (1968–69) c. 107,000.

Industry. Production (in 000; metric tons; 1969): crude oil 21,415; coal (1967) 1,424; natural gas (cu.m.) 17,217; electricity (kw-hr.) 25,435,000; cement 6,970; iron ore (metal content) 2,066; pig iron 1,701; steel 3,453; sulfur (1968) 1,685; sulfuric acid 1,068; nitrogenous fertilizers (1968–69) 196; lead 144; zinc 88; copper, smelter 66; aluminum 32; manganese ore (metal content; 1968) 27; antimony ore (metal content; 1968) 3.5; silver (1968) 1.2; gold (troy oz.; 1968) 177; cotton yarn (1968) 106; woven cotton fabrics (1968) 95.

sult officially with Mexico before beginning the operation, and this caused particular strain. The U.S. Department of Commerce did its best to repair the damage, and relations were again cordial when Presidents Richard Nixon and Díaz Ordaz met on August 20–21 at Puerto Vallarta to discuss a treaty settlement of boundary disputes between the two countries. Their agreement, besides apportioning tracts of land in the Presidio Valley and about 320 islands in the Rio Grande, proposed maritime demarcations in the Gulf of Mexico and Pacific Ocean, and included provisions for resolving future disputes. No final agreement was reached on the use of the Colorado River waters, but President Nixon proposed an arrangement offering significant advantages to Mexico.

The nationalization of Mexico's railways was completed on June 30 when the federal authorities acquired from the U.S.-owned Southern Pacific Transportation the 44-mi. link between Tijuana and Tecate. A five-year program for the joint development by public and private sectors of the Baja California peninsula was announced in the spring.　　　(M. Pu.)

Middle East

Although a peaceful settlement between Arabs and Israelis still appeared distant at the end of 1970 and the civil war between Jordanians and Palestinians, which had been narrowly avoided for so long, broke out in Jordan, there was some progress toward the fulfillment of some essential conditions for achieving peace. A U.S. peace initiative, which became known as the Rogers peace plan, was accepted in principle by the Soviet Union, the United Arab Republic, Jordan, and Israel, although each country placed its own interpretation on its acceptance. This made possible the relaunching of the mission of Gunnar Jarring, the UN special representative in the Middle East. A cease-fire in the Suez Canal area was declared on August 7 and remained effective despite Israeli accusations that the U.A.R. had violated the military standstill agreement accompanying the cease-fire by installing new surface-to-air missile sites near the canal. For this reason Israel withdrew its delegate from indirect negotiations soon after they had started. However, the U.S. and the Soviet Union agreed that the talks should be resumed, and the U.S. government showed its anxiety that its initiative should not be allowed to lapse.

U.A.R. Pres. Gamal Abd-al-Nasser's death on September 28 was widely expected to cause delay in any renewed peace moves. All Middle Eastern states continued to devote an extraordinarily high proportion of their national incomes and budgets to military expenditure. Only the ending of the civil war in Yemen and of the war with the Kurdish nationalists in Iraq offered some prospect of reducing arms spending in those two countries.

Arab-Israeli Conflict. On January 21 a U.S. Department of State spokesman said that there had been some progress in Big Four talks on the Middle East and that a "settlement was possible." There was agreement on the principle of Israeli withdrawal from occupied Arab territories in return for Arab de facto recognition of Israel, but there was still disagreement over the form of negotiations, the timetable of the Israeli evacuation, the position of the demilitarized zones, and the future of the Palestinian Arab refugees. The principal Palestinian guerrilla organizations—Al

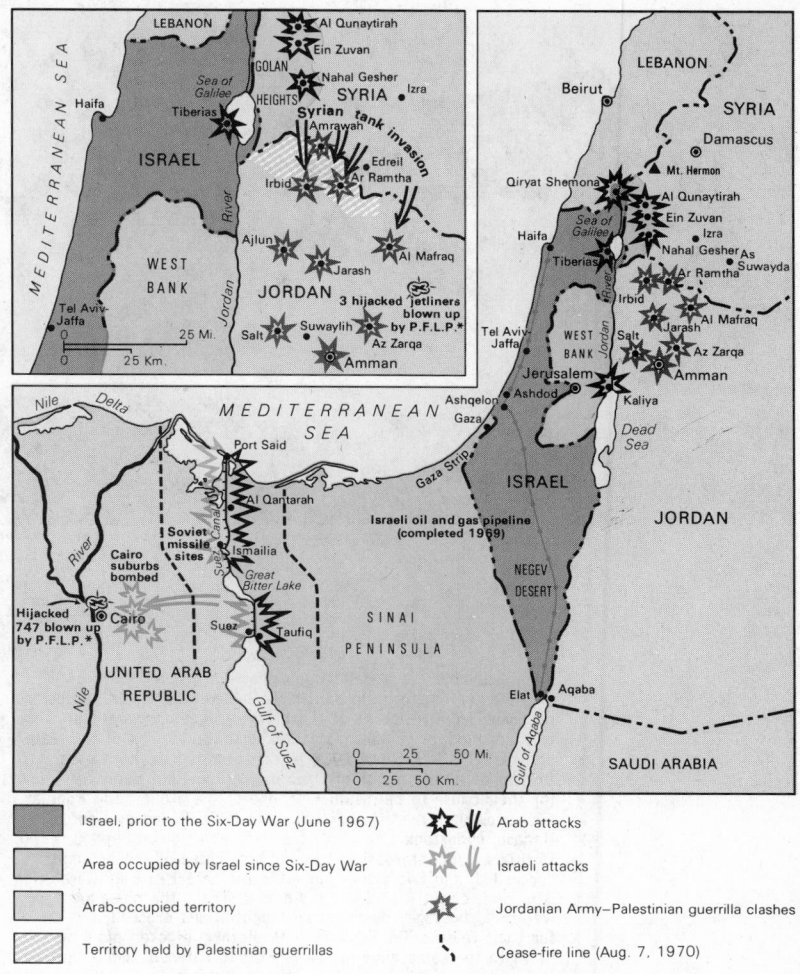

Israel, prior to the Six-Day War (June 1967)　　　✦⬇ Arab attacks

Area occupied by Israel since Six-Day War　　　✦⬇ Israeli attacks

Arab-occupied territory　　　✦ Jordanian Army–Palestinian guerrilla clashes

Territory held by Palestinian guerrillas　　　╱ Cease-fire line (Aug. 7, 1970)

* Popular Front for the Liberation of Palestine

Fatah led by Yasir Arafat (see Biography) and the Popular Front for the Liberation of Palestine (PFLP) led by George Habash (see Biography)—continued to reject any political settlement that did not include the total liberation of Palestine. However, Palestinian spokesmen affirmed that while they aimed at dismantling Israel they had no intention of destroying or expelling the Jews but sought to establish a nonsectarian state in which Jews, Christians, and Muslims could live in equality. In February all the Palestinian organizations linked together in the Palestine Armed Struggle Command announced the formation of a unified command, which for the first time would include the PFLP. However, the PFLP continued to a large extent to act independently.

In January Israel stepped up its air and ground attacks on the U.A.R. Israeli forces occupied for 32 hours the U.A.R.-held Shadwan Island at the southern end of the Suez Gulf. Israel also carried out several air raids close to Cairo with the aim, according to the Israeli defense minister, of making it easier for Israel to hold the Suez Canal line with a minimum of casualties, of convincing the U.A.R. leadership of the futility of launching an all-out war, and of driving home to the Egyptian people that their military and political leadership was doing them harm. The U.A.R. responded by stepping up air raids in the Suez Canal area and the Sinai, and several major air battles took place.

The Arab states were concerned about U.S. arms sales to Israel and especially Israel's request for

Microbiology:
see Medicine; Molecular
Biology

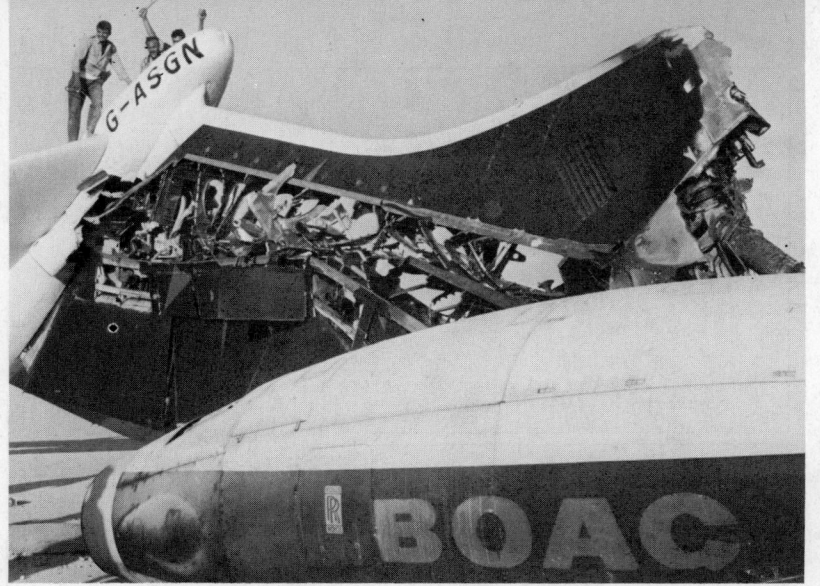

LONDON "DAILY EXPRESS" FROM PICTORIAL PARADE

Young members of a Palestinian guerrilla group
at a training camp in Jordan (right). Members of the groups are
recruited from residents of the many refugee camps set up
to accommodate persons displaced by the formation of the state
of Israel in 1948. Since 1964 terrorist raids have been used
to dramatize the plight of the refugees. Feeling publicity
for their cause to be insufficient, one of the groups, the Popular
Front for the Liberation of Palestine (PFLP), led by George
Habash, undertook a carefully planned operation on Sept. 6, 1970,
to hijack four international jet flights. Three of the attempts
succeeded, and two planes landed in the desert at the "Revolution
Airstrip," about 40 mi. from Amman. There the passengers
were held hostage (below) while negotiations proceeded
for their release. On September 9 another hijacked plane was
flown to the same airstrip. The PFLP threatened to blow up
the passengers with the planes unless guerrillas captured
in earlier hijack attempts were released. Finally, however,
the passengers were moved to other locations
and the planes were destroyed (above).

UPI COMPIX
GORDON CLARK FROM LIAISON AGENCY

STEVE EAGLE FROM
NANCY PALMER AGENCY

Citizens gather in front
of the Knesset in Jerusalem
to protest the peace
plan offered by U.S.
Secretary of State
William Rogers which
called for withdrawal
by Israel from territory
captured in the 1967
war.

25 Phantom and 80 Skyhawk planes. On January 30 U.S. Pres. Richard Nixon announced that a decision on the matter would be declared "within 30 days." Delegations led by the heads of state of the U.A.R., Jordan, Syria, and Sudan, and the Iraqi minister of the interior met in Cairo from February 7 to 9 and warned the U.S. about its "new hostile attitude towards the Arab nation" and its links with Zionism and Israeli expansionism.

On March 10 Jarring was recalled to UN headquarters at New York from his post as Swedish ambassador to the Soviet Union and held talks with the representatives of the U.A.R., Jordan, Israel, and the major powers. Although UN Secretary-General U Thant still saw no sufficient basis for the reactivation of the Jarring mission, he reported some rapprochement among the Big Four in their attitudes toward the Middle East. President Nixon still delayed announcing his decision on Israel's request for Phantoms and Skyhawks, and on March 23 U.S. Secretary of State William Rogers said that the president had decided to grant Israel $100 million in aid instead of the planes. Nixon said that this was "an interim decision," while U.A.R. sources called it a "hoax" and "an attempt to deceive the Arab world." It was widely believed that Nixon was attempting to reach an understanding with the Soviet Union on the Middle East. Exploratory U.S.-Soviet talks on the possibility of resuming Big Four discussions on the Middle East were started on March 25, and in early April the deputy representatives of the Big Four held several meetings to compile a "memorandum of progress" on the Big Four's Middle East discussions.

Heavy artillery and air battles in the Suez Canal area continued throughout mid-1970. The killing of 46 children and the wounding of 20 more in an air raid on the U.A.R. village of Bahr al-Baqar on April 8 was strongly condemned throughout the Arab world, although Israel claimed that there were military targets in the area. On April 28 an Israeli military spokesman described increased U.A.R. military activity as a spring offensive aimed to wrest the initiative from

Israel in the air and on the ground. A special three-member Committee to Investigate Israeli Practices Affecting the Human Rights of the Population of the Occupied Territories set up by the UN General Assembly held hearings in London, Beirut, and Damascus, but Israel refused permission for the committee to enter the occupied territories unless it also investigated the condition of Jews in the Arab countries.

In his May Day speech President Nasser launched a new diplomatic offensive in the form of a "final appeal" to President Nixon. He said that if the U.S. took one more step on the path of securing military superiority for Israel it would affect U.S.-Arab relations for decades or even centuries. He also claimed that with Soviet aid the U.A.R. forces were wresting the initiative from the enemy. On May 30 Israeli forces suffered their worst casualties since the June 1967 war in ground action across the Suez Canal when 13 were killed, 4 wounded, and 2 missing as a result of two U.A.R. commando ambushes.

The Israeli foreign minister said on May 5 that in exchange for true peace Israel would be prepared to make concessions that might surprise the world. His remarks were sharply criticized by Israeli right-wing parties. Big Four discussions remained in a state of stalemate; the U.S. still delayed a decision on Israel's request for Phantoms and Skyhawks, but the U.S. secretary of state said on June 9 that the military situation in the Middle East had deteriorated "largely as a result of increased Soviet involvement in the air defense of the U.A.R." and 73 U.S. senators urged Rogers in a letter on June 1 to "provide Israel with the aircraft so urgently needed for its defense." Israel had abandoned deep penetration raids into U.A.R. territory, but during June and July maintained an almost continuous bombardment of the Suez Canal area with the aim of silencing U.A.R. artillery and preventing establishment of new Soviet-built missile sites.

On June 25 the U.S. secretary of state launched a new peace initiative in the Middle East, which be-

An Israeli Army lieutenant leads a patrol near the Jordanian border.

CAMERA PRESS
FROM PIX

came known as the Rogers plan. He refused to give details on the ground that this would prevent the plan's success, but he said that it was based on the UN Security Council resolution of Nov. 22, 1967, and that the U.S. had decided on the initiative partly in response to President Nasser's appeal to President Nixon of May 1. In order to get negotiations started through the UN mediator, Rogers appealed directly to Jordan, the U.A.R., and Israel to agree to an immediate cease-fire to last at least three months.

The peace initiative made progress when Nasser announced his acceptance of the Rogers proposals on July 23 on his return from a 19-day visit to the Soviet Union. He later told the Arab Socialist Union in Cairo that the U.A.R.'s acceptance was "unconditional." On July 26 Jordan also announced its acceptance but absolved itself from responsibility for Palestinian guerrilla action against Israel. The Palestinian organizations strongly denounced the U.S. initiative and unequivocally rejected it. On August 4 Israel announced its acceptance of the Rogers proposals after receiving assurances from the U.S. that the cease-fire would not be used by the U.A.R. to consolidate its position along the Suez Canal. The cease-fire came into force on August 7, and on the same day the 11 member organizations of the Central Committee for Palestinian Resistance announced that they would not abide by it. Moshe Dayan, Israel's minister of defense, accused the U.A.R. on August 13 of having violated the cease-fire on August 8 by moving surface-to-air missiles into the canal zone. In the following weeks the Israeli government repeated the accusations, which were supported by the U.S.

Indirect negotiations for a settlement began on August 25 in New York when Jarring held separate talks with the permanent UN representatives of the U.A.R., Jordan, and Israel. However, the Israeli government then recalled its delegate to Jerusalem and after a Cabinet meeting on September 6 announced that it was suspending participation in the Jarring peace talks as long as the U.A.R. continued with its alleged breaches of the Middle East cease-fire agreement.

On September 6 members of the Popular Front for the Liberation of Palestine attempted four hijackings of passenger airliners over Western Europe. Of these, an effort to seize a New York-bound El Al plane failed, but a Pan American plane was taken first to Beirut and then to Cairo and a Swissair and a Trans World Airlines (TWA) plane were taken to an unused airstrip in the Jordanian desert near the Iraqi border. The guerrillas released most of the women, children, and elderly among the passengers, but demanded the release of Palestinians held in Israel, Switzerland, West Germany, and Britain in return for the release of the rest whom they held as hostages. On September 9 a BOAC airliner was also hijacked and flown to the same airstrip. Eventually, the hijackers released all of the passengers but destroyed the planes. (*See* Transportation: *Special Report.*)

On September 17 the international crisis caused by the hijackings was overshadowed by the outbreak of civil war in Jordan between the Palestinian organizations and the Jordanian Army. The war began soon after Jordan's King Husain had appointed a new military government and the Palestinians had responded by calling a general strike. Intervention by Syrian armoured units in northern Jordan caused fears that the conflict might spread and the U.S. secretary of state asked the Soviet Union to restrain the Syrians.

On September 21 King Husain appealed to the Big Four to take joint action against the Syrian invasion. The U.S. Sixth Fleet was ordered into the eastern Mediterranean and a division of U.S. paratroops was alerted for the possible evacuation of U.S. citizens from Jordan. The Soviet Union issued a stern warning against the possibility of U.S. intervention.

A hastily summoned Arab summit conference in Cairo failed to end the civil war because neither King Husain nor the principal Palestinian leader, Yasir Arafat, attended. The Arab heads of state then sent a mission to Amman headed by the Sudanese president, Gafaar al-Nimeiry, on September 22, and it presided over a cease-fire agreement between Husain and four leading Palestinian guerrillas who had been captured by the Jordanian Army. But the Nimeiry mission returned to Cairo without having met Arafat, who denounced the agreement. Fighting continued, and General al-Nimeiry accused the Jordanian Army of breaking the cease-fire. The mission returned to Amman, and on September 25 a more effective agreement was reached between Arafat and King Husain.

The agreement was broken on several occasions and sporadic fighting continued, but it gradually died out in the following days. In a message on September 26 Nasser angrily accused Husain of violating the cease-fire and denounced the existence of a plot aimed at liquidating the Palestinian resistance. Husain and Arafat attended a meeting the next day in Cairo with eight Arab heads of state and their representatives; the conference resulted in a 14-point agreement providing for the withdrawal of all Jordanian Army and Palestinian guerrilla forces from every city in Jordan, to be supervised by a three-man inter-Arab committee headed by the Tunisian prime minister.

The death of President Nasser (*see* Obituaries) on September 28 threw the whole Arab world into confusion as it mourned the loss of its only leader of world stature. It was assumed that his death would inevitably cause the postponement of efforts to revive the U.S. peace initiative, although both Israel and the U.A.R. prolonged the cease-fire for three months in November. In a statement issued after Nasser's funeral on October 1, Soviet Premier Aleksei N. Kosygin said that the Soviet government reaffirmed its desire for a peaceful settlement of the Middle East crisis but would continue to supply defensive aid to the Arab states. On December 28 the Israeli Cabinet voted to rejoin the Jarring talks. The U.A.R., meanwhile, indicated that it would not agree to a further extension of the cease-fire unless a definite timetable for Israeli withdrawal was established.

Inter-Arab Relations. The underlying division between conservative pro-Western Arab regimes and the radical republican camp persisted but remained latent during 1970. On the conservative side, King Husain aligned his foreign policy closely with that of the U.A.R., while King Faisal of Saudi Arabia undertook no diplomatic initiatives and finally recognized the republican regime in Yemen. A conference of foreign ministers of Islamic states meeting in Jidda, Saudi Arabia, in March, decided to set up an Islamic secretariat with its headquarters in Jidda, but the decision made little impact in the Middle East. In general, the pro-Western regimes were hampered by what the Arabs regarded as unstinted U.S. support of Israel, while the radical camp was strengthened by the addition of the new regimes in Sudan and Libya, especially the latter with its £500 million a year in oil revenues. However, the radicals were also divided and in 1970

GAMMA
FROM PIX
King Faisal
of Saudi Arabia
(second from left) opens
the Arab summit
conference at Jidda
in March 1970.
On Faisal's left is Sudan
Foreign Minister Omar
Sakkaf, who was elected
president of the meeting.

the most important split in the Arab world was over their attitudes toward the Rogers peace initiative. Both Iraq and Syria denounced it, the latter less vehemently. Iraq, which had 12,000 troops in Jordan and had improved its own military position by the ending of the Kurdish war, declared itself to be the protector of the Palestinian guerrillas and in doing so made a clear bid for Arab leadership. Its claim was largely nullified, however, by its failure to come to the aid of the Palestinians during the Jordanian civil war, in contrast to Syria's intervention. An important factor behind Iraq's inaction was the continuing mistrust and antipathy between the Baathist regimes in Baghdad and Damascus.

Nasser's death seemed certain to reduce the U.A.R.'s dominant position in the Arab world, at least until his successors had established themselves. The U.A.R.'s size and strength, however, meant that it would always be a major factor in the Middle East power balance. In November the U.A.R., Libya, and Sudan entered into an alliance aimed at eventual federation, and later in the month Syria announced that it also was joining.

The Persian Gulf. In the Persian Gulf area little real progress was made toward the establishment of the projected Federation of Arab Amirates because of rivalry and disagreement between the rulers. One of their anxieties was removed, however, by the shah of Iran's acceptance that Iran's claim to Bahrain should be referred to the UN. The UN undersecretary-general, Vittorio Guicciardi, arrived in Bahrain on March 30 to seek the views of the inhabitants, and in his report said that the Bahrainis were virtually unanimous in wanting Bahrain to be a fully independent sovereign state; the great majority added that it should be an Arab state. Iran accepted the verdict but continued to lay claim to three small islands in the Straits of Hormuz, of which one was claimed by Sharjah and two by Ras al-Khaimah.

The advent to power of a Conservative Party government in the U.K. in June held out the possibility that it would reverse the Labour government's decision to withdraw all British forces from the Persian Gulf area by 1971. However, this seemed less likely after Saudi Arabia and Iran had both expressed opposition to a continuing British presence.   (P. Mɒ.)

See also Defense; Migration, International; Refugees; also articles on various political units.

Migration, International

In 1970 economic considerations determined to a greater extent than in the past the volume and direction of migratory movements of European man-

power. In their turn, these movements influenced national labour markets and productivity by increasing or diminishing the available supply of skilled manpower essential to economic growth.

As compared with the overseas emigration of Europeans in the previous 15 years, mobility within Europe, mainly covering the movements of people from the Mediterranean area to the more northerly countries, gained in importance. In 1970 there was only a very small flow of people seeking new opportunities for themselves or their children in the traditional immigration countries overseas.

By 1970, West Germany, Switzerland, Belgium, Sweden, the United Kingdom, and France had become the principal immigration countries of Europe. The Netherlands occupied a halfway position: while maintaining a small flow toward overseas countries, it admitted a relatively sizable contingent of immigrants every year. In Austria, the number of foreign workers had almost saturated the labour market, while in Italy the migratory pattern had been progressively transformed and movements to European countries on a short-term basis predominated over permanent movement to countries overseas.

The demands of the European labour market called for an extension of the recruitment areas to regions farther afield than the Mediterranean. The question arose as to whether the influx of culturally and socially different people was justified or whether it would provoke tensions resulting from the creation of minorities of "second class citizens," due to differences in education, and from the fear of *Überfremdung* (the Swiss term—"overalienization"). Certainly, complex sociopsychological mechanisms were involved.

In Switzerland, as in many European countries, foreign workers had contributed to the creation of a social substratum, which at the same time allowed the local population to rise on the social scale. By 1970, one worker in three in Switzerland was a foreigner, and debate continued on proposals for restrictions on foreign labour. There were fears, however, that such restrictions might lead to an economic crisis, with Swiss workers, mostly in white-collar jobs, being progressively affected by firms having to slow down or halt production due to a shortage of labour.

On June 7, a referendum was held on proposals to reduce the proportion of foreigners to no more than 10% in any one canton, with the exception of Geneva, where the limit would be 25%. Although seasonal workers, workers commuting from neighbouring countries, and various other special groups were excluded, the proposals would nonetheless have meant a very large number of departures. The proposals were rejected by a fairly narrow margin, with 557,000 in favour and 654,000 against. (*See* SWITZERLAND.)

BEN ROTH AGENCY

"It was the overcrowded slums of Calcutta and Delhi that drove us here, officer. . . ."—Cookson, London "Daily Mail."

In Sweden, where one inhabitant in five was a first- or second-generation immigrant, official estimates forecast an additional 10,000 arrivals per year in the near future. By April 1, 1970, there were about 210,000 foreign workers registered in Sweden. The bulk of these were from neighbouring Nordic countries: a total of some 135,000, the Finns alone accounting for 102,000.

The diminishing flow of emigrants from Europe to the traditional immigration countries overseas began to be felt by those countries. In New Zealand, particularly, the decline in the number of immigrants from Great Britain—New Zealand's traditional source of new citizens since the end of World War II—together with the loss of people attracted by higher wages in Australia and by greater opportunities in the arts and professions in Europe, was causing considerable concern. Plans were under consideration to relax the skill requirements for assisted passages, thus allowing unskilled British workers to qualify for entrance.

In the countries of immigration, sociocultural differences sometimes caused difficulties for new arrivals. In the U.K., resources were being mobilized against racial and cultural prejudice and discrimination, and toward cultural pluralism. Nevertheless, immigration continued to be a controversial subject. According to the 1966 sample census in Great Britain, out of a total population of 52.3 million there were 977,720 persons born in the Commonwealth, 885,600 persons born in foreign countries, and 718,010 born in the Republic of Ireland.

A study published in Britain during 1970 threw light on some of the effects of immigrant arrivals. In *The Economic Impact of Commonwealth Immigration,* prepared for the National Institute of Economic and Social Research by K. Jones and A. D. Smith, the authors found that immigrant families made smaller demands on the social services than other families, that immigrants still had lower living standards, but that "indigenous" living standards did not suffer as a result—indeed, rather the opposite appeared to be the case. (*See* RACE RELATIONS.)

A particularly difficult problem for the U.K. was the case of British Asians in East Africa. Under Uganda's Immigration Act, which came into force on May 1, non-Ugandan citizens had to receive specific permission before taking a job, and permits were granted only if the job in question could not be done by a Ugandan. The Kenyan government had introduced similar legislation in 1967. Most of the people affected by these "africanization" measures were U.K. passport holders of Indian and Pakistani origin who had retained their British citizenship after the granting of independence to their countries of residence. But entry into the U.K. was limited by Britain's Commonwealth Immigrants Act of 1968, whereby potential immigrants had to apply for special entry vouchers, limited to 1,500 per year for U.K. citizens from both Kenya and Uganda. Faced with increased pressure from the authorities in Africa and dwindling financial resources, more and more U.K. passport holders left Kenya and Uganda without the necessary permits in the hope of being allowed into Britain. This led to a number of "shuttlecock" Asians being stranded at various European airports, unable to return to Africa or to continue their journey to Britain, and consequently there was growing pressure on the British government to review its annual quota of 1,500 such immigrants. (G. O. K. B.; X.)

In the United States, efforts to revise the immigration laws enacted in 1965 gained momentum during 1970. This movement, which received support in the U.S. Congress and from the executive branch, resulted from unforeseen consequences of the 1965 law. A wholesale alteration of the U.S. immigration laws that had been in effect since the 1920s, the 1965 statute wiped out the old entry quotas based on the country of origin and instead established a system of "preferences" designed to reunite families and favour those in needed occupations.

After a gradual introduction, the new system went into full effect on July 1, 1968, and immediately revealed consequences that set in motion the follow up drive for revision. A clear result of the new law was a shift in the patterns of immigration into the U.S. away from such countries as Britain, Ireland, and West Germany and toward a heavier influx from the Philippines, Italy, Greece, Portugal, and other nations that formerly had not been allowed as many entries under the old national-origin quotas. A ceiling of 120,000 placed on entries from the Western Hemisphere for the first time also radically restricted immigration into the U.S. from that part of the world.

Such patterns emerged as soon as the 1965 laws went into effect and continued into 1970. According to preliminary figures from the Department of State, the number of visas issued during fiscal 1970 for non-Western Hemisphere countries showed that the Philippines led the list of countries of origin for immigrants into the United States with 25,425, followed by Italy with 24,481, Greece with 16,542, Nationalist China (Taiwan) with 16,297, and Great Britain and Northern Ireland with 13,925. They were followed by Portugal, India, Korea, West Germany, and Yugoslavia. This ranking was radically at variance with that of fiscal 1965, the last year the old system was fully in effect. In fiscal 1965 the ranking of non-Western Hemisphere countries showed Great Britain, West Germany, Italy, Poland, Ireland, France, the Netherlands, Japan, the Soviet Union, and Taiwan in that order.

In the Western Hemisphere, the rankings in fiscal 1970 were roughly unchanged from fiscal 1969 or fiscal 1965. The major exceptions were a precipitous decline in the number of entries from Canada, from the 40,013 in fiscal 1965 to 12,263 in fiscal 1970. Also notable was the swelling number of entries from Jamaica and Trinidad and Tobago in recent years. The fiscal 1970 ranking for Western Hemisphere countries was Mexico, Cuba, Jamaica, Canada, the Dominican Republic, Haiti, Colombia, Trinidad and Tobago, Ecuador, and Argentina.

Closer examination of these developments stemming from the 1965 law began in 1968 in the U.S. Congress and continued to generate increasing attention in 1970. Although no major revisions were enacted, the movement seemed to point toward some concrete action in the near future. Especially crucial in this legislative process was the acknowledgment by the federal administration in 1970 that changes were desirable.

Immigration into Canada during 1969 dropped 12.2% to 161,531 from 183,974 in 1968. The number of Europeans and Africans declined, while entries from the Western Hemisphere continued an upward trend. U.S. emigrants to Canada during the year increased 12% from 20,422 in 1968 to 22,785 in 1969. These figures also confirmed a new pattern that had emerged since the introduction three years before of a new point system based on education, skills, language, and age.

Some attention in 1970 was also focused on emigration from the United States. For the first time in the century the number of Americans leaving for Canada exceeded the number of Canadians migrating to the U.S. Although no official statistics were available on U.S. emigration, some figures indicated the situation. In 1968 about 2,500 U.S. citizens either renounced or lost their citizenship, and in 1970 more than 200,000 social security beneficiaries were receiving their checks abroad. Other figures indicated that in the last decade the number of Americans granted permits to work in Britain increased from 517 in 1960 to 1,470 in 1969. Before the June 1967 Middle East war, some 1,000 to 1,200 Americans a year were resettling in Israel, but the figure was up to 6,500 in 1969 and the 1970 monthly rate averaged 30% above that level. Other nations receiving a large number of Americans were reported to be Australia, Mexico, Sweden, Denmark, and West Germany. (D. Fo.)

See also Refugees.

Mining

The upward trend in mineral development and production of recent years was slowed somewhat in 1970. A decline in industrial, construction, and defense activity combined to lessen mineral demand and caused a softening in prices for some minerals and metals. A contrasting picture developed for energy minerals, notably coal. Escalating energy demand was accompanied by a host of uncertainties in production of coal, oil, and natural gas. Prices rose, and there were serious disruptions and readjustments in the supply and demand pattern for fuel minerals. (*See* Fuel and Power.)

Nationalization goals continued to impede mineral development in some of the less developed countries, but such goals often directed intensified commercial mineral resource development efforts in the politically more stable industrial countries. Environmental concern had a widening impact on mining and mineral processing technology, and exerted a growing influence on mineral consumption and recycling patterns. Despite a general high level of unemployment in the U.S., mining companies had difficulty in recruiting workers and engineers. There was a particular shortage of underground miners. Training programs were expanded, and efforts were made to recruit miners from the unemployed labour pools in large cities.

The market for minerals was remarkably steady. Prices of metals drifted downward in the second half of the year, probably in part as a reflection of the slowing of general inflation, but more as a result of a growing supply and diminishing demand. The exceptionally high monetary interest rates during the

year reduced the attractiveness of speculations in silver and gold and their prices fluctuated in a relatively narrow range that, however, turned upward in the last quarter. High interest rates also reduced the availability of capital for mineral exploration and development projects. This undoubtedly contributed to the shortages and high prices of energy minerals, but did not have an immediate influence on the supply of other minerals. One analysis concluded that new outside capital of $40 billion would be required in the next five years to build or replace mine-plant capacity to meet anticipated mineral demand.

The enforcement of U.S. health and safety regulations for metal and nonmetal mines began on July 31. More than 1,000 standards, about half of them mandatory, were applied to ventilation, drilling, blasting, transportation, and other mining procedures.

Formal U.S. Treasury Department sales of silver terminated on November 10. About 300 million oz. of silver had been sold at an average price of $1.85 per ounce from August 1967 until the program ended. Of this, 65 million oz. were sold in 1970. Two-thirds of this was derived from reclaimed coins.

Industry Developments. The main mining event of the year was the worldwide mineral search by major companies and consortia of companies to find and develop mineral and metal supplies for the remaining decades of the century. There was widespread expectation that mineral demand would soar and that known resources would be inadequate. While the physical availability of developed ore loomed as a midterm restraint on supply, the immediate restraints were political uncertainty in some of the less developed countries and the inadequacy of capital for ore searches. In Chile and Peru the governmental policies continued to move toward nationalization of mineral resources, a move that deterred commercial mineral exploration and development of large copper deposits. Mineral exploration in large areas of Africa, Asia, and the Middle East also was discouraged by unfavourable political conditions for business. As a result, the major mining companies concentrated their explorations in Australia, the U.S., Canada, and other countries having stable free-enterprise economies.

Going opposite to the trend in many less developed countries, 1970 was a year of vigorous mineral activity in Indonesia. The most spectacular development was of the huge Ertsberg copper deposit in West Irian—a 33 million-ton monolithic plug projecting out of a mountainside at an elevation of 11,500 ft. The

Military Affairs: *see* Defense

Mineralogy: *see* Geology

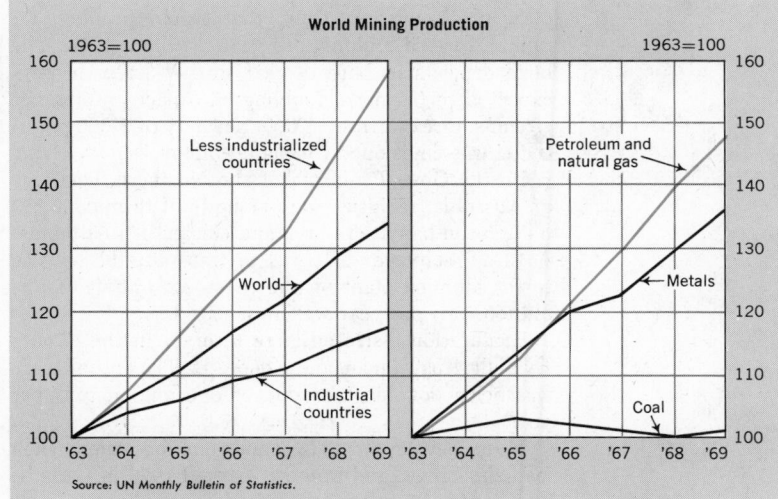

World Mining Production
1963=100
Less industrialized countries
World
Industrial countries
1963=100
Petroleum and natural gas
Metals
Coal
Source: UN *Monthly Bulletin of Statistics.*

deposit contained 2.5% copper and recoverable contents of gold and silver. Freeport Indonesia, Inc., obtained government approval for the $120 million project in June and planned production by 1973 at a rate of 2.5 million tons of ore per year. Approximately two-years' supply of ore was available above ground and could be mined without substantial stripping of waste. In addition to Ertsberg, there were projects under way in Indonesia to develop offshore tin dredging areas, large nickel deposits in Sulawesi and elsewhere, and widespread bauxite deposits.

Active mineral exploration and development continued in Australia. Both sulfide- and lateritic-type nickel deposits were being drilled out. A 45 million-ton, 1.5% nickel reserve was detected by Freeport of Australia, Inc., and a pilot ore-testing plant was to be built in the U.S. A 17-mi.-long zone of ultrabasic rocks favourable for nickel sulfide ores was being explored in Western Australia at Mt. Keith. At Kwinana, Western Australia, a 16,000-ton-per-year ammonia leach nickel refinery started treating sulfide concentrates from the Kambalda mine. Mine output of 33,000 tons of nickel in concentrate was planned. Excess concentrate was to be shipped to Japan for processing.

Plans were made to double the capacity of the world's largest iron ore producer, Hamersley Iron Pty., Ltd., in Western Australia. A new mine was to be opened at Paraburdoo, 32 mi. S of the present Mt. Tom Mine. By 1974 the new mine was expected to add 15 million tons per year of ore to the 22.5 million tons from Mt. Tom.

After seven years of preparation and investigation, a ten million-ton-per-year, $300 million iron ore project at Robe River in Australia reached the development stage. The project was financed by an international consortium, and its output was to be shipped largely to Japan. Mining, processing, pelletizing, and land and harbour shipping facilities were being built, with initial shipments scheduled for 1972 at about 80% of ultimate capacity.

New mines attracted much attention in Australia, but older well-known operations were also the scenes of activity. Mt. Isa Mines, Ltd., was expanding to mine 22,000 tons of ore per day and planned another 16,000 tons of daily output by the mid-1970s. It would become the world's largest lead-zinc-silver mine. A 20-ft.-diameter, 3,400-ft.-deep shaft was sunk to service the mine.

American Metal Climax, Inc., announced its intention to construct a $330 million bauxite-alumina complex in Western Australia that would produce 1.2 million tons of alumina per year by about 1974. The huge deposits of bauxite near Port Warrender were expected to permit a doubling of capacity if market circumstances warranted it. A new city of 3,000 population was envisioned for plant employees.

On the Gove Peninsula of the Northern Territory of Australia, facilities were being built to mine a 250 million-ton bauxite reserve and convert it to alumina. A 13-mi. conveyor belt was to transport the bauxite to the alumina plant on the coast. An output of one million tons per year was anticipated.

Exploration disclosed large reserves in the Groote Eylandt, Austr., manganese deposits. The output there was being doubled to a rate of one million tons per year.

Major developments in copper-molybdenum, nickel, lead-zinc-silver, and iron ore marked 1970 in Canada. The centre of attention shifted to western Canada,

where several huge mines were being developed. In British Columbia, Brenda Mines started its 24,000-ton-a-day open-pit copper-molybdenum mine, and Utah Construction made good progress at its 33,000-ton-per-day copper-molybdenum open-pit mine-mill on Vancouver Island. Production was scheduled to begin in 1972. Valley Copper Mines planned a 25,000-ton-per-day copper-molybdenum mine with good prospects to ultimately mine 75,000 tons per day. The same ore body was expected to yield 30,000 tons per day for Bethlehem Copper. Rio Algom plans for the 38,000-ton-per-day Lornex mine moved ahead but were delayed by the need to meet requirements of new governmental regulations.

The Fox mine of Sherritt Gordon Mines, Ltd., in Manitoba started production in September. About one million tons of ore per year were to be mined, and 84,000 tons of copper concentrate and 18,000 tons of zinc concentrate recovered.

Several developments in various stages of planning or construction were expected to maintain Canada's position as the world's leading nickel producer. International Nickel Co. had a $1 billion expansion program in progress to raise output from 190,000 tons of nickel in 1969 to 300,000 tons by 1972. In the Sudbury district, ten mines were in production, three others were being developed, and three more were being appraised. In the newer Thompson area of northern Manitoba, two mines were in production and two others under development.

Iron Ore Co. of Canada planned expenditures of $270 million to produce high-grade iron pellets and iron concentrate in Newfoundland and Quebec. Mine expansions in the Schefferville area and at Carol were scheduled, and processing and shipping facilities were under construction. The annual output rate of pellets, ore, and concentrate was to be raised from 20 million tons in 1970 to 33 million tons in 1972.

Two copper projects in Arizona, costing nearly $400 million, highlighted mining activity in the U.S. In April the Anaconda Co. reached a full daily ore production rate of 30,000 tons at its Twin Buttes Mine, 25 mi. S of Tucson. Copper production was expected to reach 60,000 tons a year. To uncover the copper deposit, buried 600 to 800 ft. below the surface, it was necessary to remove 266 million tons of waste. The waste was used to build three huge earthfill dams to impound the waste material from which copper and molybdenum had been removed. Careful advance research and planning enabled the company to landscape and plant the waste areas to blend into the desert terrain.

Only a few miles west of Twin Buttes the Duval Corp. began ore output at its Duval Sierrita copper-molybdenum mine. Capacity output of 72,000 tons of ore a day was gradually achieved. The 400 million-ton ore body averaged about 0.35% copper and 0.036% molybdenum, both of which had to be recovered to yield a profit.

Arizona also was the scene of major exploration for copper and of several major mine-plant projects. At Twin Buttes, exploration detected resources adequate to support a doubling of production. More than half a billion tons of ore were found at the Lakeshore mine near Casa Grande. Additional work was being done in order to gather data needed for mine design and general long-term development planning. Exploration in the Miami, Ariz., area disclosed a potential large deposit suitable for surface mining and an underground extension of the long-established Miami-

UPI COMPIX

Elburt Franklin Osborn was named director of the U.S. Bureau of Mines in October 1970.

Inspiration ore body, which produced more than 130 million tons of ore from 1910 to 1960. An 18-ft.-diameter shaft was started in September to explore the vein extension.

Magma Copper Co. began working out details and financing for its $150 million expansion plans at San Manuel and Superior, Ariz. Delineation of the nearby Kalamazoo ore deposit was expected to raise San Manuel copper output from 96,000 tons to 145,000 tons a year. Copper output at Superior would probably be doubled from its 1970 level of 18,000 tons per year. Construction of a new smelter and refinery also was started in March at San Manuel to replace an obsolete plant at Superior.

There was widespread and intensive mineral exploration throughout the U.S. Investigation of copper-nickel occurrences in south-central Montana was promising and, if successful, would lead to the first mines of this type in the U.S. The already productive southwest copper province, eastern zinc area, and mid-continental lead-zinc areas were the scene of geophysical prospecting, followed by drilling when ore targets were identified. Company negotiations continued with the Commonwealth to exploit large copper deposits in west-central Puerto Rico. Environmental considerations and taxation were the principal issues.

Political events again dominated mining news in South America. Nationalization policies in Chile and Peru discouraged private capital from attempting to develop the huge copper resources there and also from searching for other minerals. Nevertheless, projects already well along were expected to raise Chile's copper output to 1.3 million tons by 1972, compared with 750,000 tons in 1969. The government of Peru hoped to more than double that nation's copper output by 1973 to a level of 450,000 tons. Japanese capital was expected to be instrumental in Latin-American mine plans, as that country's industry was actively seeking new supplies of mineral raw materials.

In Brazil the largest current mineral development was in iron ore. By adopting the liberal mineral exporting policies of Australia, Brazil might become a major supplier of iron ore to Western Europe, Japan, and the U.S. A $200 million project at the St. John del Rey mine was expected to produce eight million tons per year for shipment to Japan. U.S. Steel was a partner in a major project in the state of Para, 350 mi. inland. As in Australia, providing land and sea transportation facilities was a large cost element.

Southern and central Africa's role as a major mineral source grew in 1970. Political stability in the Congo resulted in larger copper output in 1970 and invited commercial interest in exploration, which undoubtedly would lead to the development of new mines. Zambia assumed 51% ownership of its copper mines on Jan. 1, 1970. Agreements were reached with private companies to expand present operations and search for new deposits. A massive cave-in at the Mufulira copper mine on September 25 took 89 lives and halted production. Millions of tons of broken rock, old tailings, and water poured into mine openings. Production was resumed slowly, and it was expected to be several years before full recovery was made from the disaster. About 150,000 tons of copper production would be lost in 1970–71.

The Republic of South Africa appeared likely to achieve a record output of gold, reversing the drop that occurred in 1969. Vaal Reefs increased ore production to 336,000 tons per month, becoming the world's largest gold mine. New mines on the Merensky reef were being developed to achieve a 50% rise in platinum output, from 1.1 million to 1,570,000 oz. per year. Consolidated Murchison, principal world antimony mine, raised its capacity substantially on the basis of large reserves of high-grade ore. The discovery of nickel in Rhodesia led to an exploration boom. In adjoining Botswana, copper and nickel exploration showed promising results.

There was increased mining activity outside the principal and traditional metal mining areas of the world. It became increasingly evident that the Papua-New Guinea area might be another major world copper province. The huge Bougainville copper project was well under way there. The port-to-mine access road was opened in October. Kennecott Copper Co. was drilling the area of Ok Tedi in northwest Papua, and its search extended to West Irian, the Indonesian part of the island. A major problem in development was providing the means to transport concentrate to coastal or overseas smelters.

Work continued on the $160 million Marinduque nickel project on Nonoc Island in the Philippines. The lateritic ore was to be treated by a hydrometallurgical process developed by Sherritt Gordon Co. of Canada.

Large nickel deposits in New Caledonia continued to attract interest. A $500 million project was planned by International Nickel Co. of Canada. It included mining, processing, and refining facilities. Patino Mining Corp. joined with Société le Nickel in a $200 million mine and plant to produce 40,000 tons of nickel in ferronickel by 1972.

Nearly a third of the Republic of Ireland was covered by prospecting permits in a geophysical search for lead-zinc-silver-copper ores. Although a nonproducer as recently as 1963, Ireland had since become the leading lead-silver producer in Western Europe.

Technological Developments. Improved and larger equipment accounted for much of the technological advance in mining in 1970. Special attention was given to transportation of ore and waste at the mine and of mine products to processing plants or to consumers. There was increased emphasis on environmental and health and safety research. At underground mines, the trend toward trackless mining and use of load-haul-dump equipment continued. Boring technology steadily improved, and a combined method was proposed of boring a pilot tunnel and enlarging it by conventional drilling and blasting methods. Boring of raises, shafts, and vertical service openings became routine. In South Africa the development of rock cutters to mine the hard and abrasive gold-quartz reefs advanced to the design of prototype equipment. The direct cost of breaking rock was high, but substantial indirect savings were expected to be made. In one test the reef mining width was reduced from 41 to 20 in., saving the high cost of waste handling.

The world's largest continuous underground mining system machine was delivered to Sylvite of Canada. The 230-ton machine was 39 ft. long and was designed to deliver broken potash to a belt conveyor.

The use of pneumatically placed concrete for ground support had a resurgence. In this process concrete layers thick enough to provide strong support are placed over the rock or over reinforced steel networks. Accelerators are needed for high early strength. The technique may be particularly applicable to mechanized rapid excavation systems.

continued on page 522

Select World Mineral and Metal Production in 1969

Metric tons unless otherwise specified; Th. indicates thousands, and Mi. millions of units

	Aluminum (Th.)	Bauxite (Th.)	Antimony* (ore)	Asbestos	Barite (Th.)	Beryl	Bismuth	Cadmium†	Cement, hydraulic	Chromite (Th.)	Coal (Mi.)	Coke (Mi.)	Cobalt	Copper* (in ore)	Copper (smelter)	Diamonds (Th. carats)	Feldspar (Th.)	Fluorspar	Gas, natural (Bi. cu.ft.)	Gold (Th. troy oz.)	Graphite (Th.)	Gypsum (Th.)	Iron Ore* (Mi.)	Pig Iron (Mi.)	Steel, Ingots and Casting (Mi.)	Lead (in ore) (Th.)
North America																										
Canada	995.2	—	384	1,448.0	128.3	—	327	953	7.8	—	9.7	4.5	1,453	500.2	408.8	—	10.7	e>100.0	1,985.3	2,433.5	—	6,234	40.6	7.0	9.4	300.1
Central America			213						.9											126.7		46	NA			14.1
Mexico	32.4	—		—	176.9	—	606	210	6.8	—	2.5	e>1.1	W	4.2	56.7	—	2.0	988.3	283.1	126.7	42.9	1,219	3.5	2.2	3.5	170.9
United States	3,440.6	1,872.4	3,149	114.2	977.2	W	W	5,738	71.1	—	518.0	58.7	1,540	1,401.2	1,438.3	—	83.5	165.6	20,698.2	1,733.2	W	8,964	90.7	88.5	128.2	461.8
West Indies	—	12,257.0		—		—	NA		e>1.9	NA				2.3		—	684.8		53.3	e>3.0		e>374	e>.3			
South America																										
Argentina	e>43.2	—		e>.3	e>16.0	517	NA	—	4.4	—	.5	e>.4	—	8.0	—	—	e>20.0	e>20.0	188.1	e>51.0	e>.1	e>400	e>.3	.6	1.7	31.0
Bolivia	—	—	13,137	—	—	W	607	—	1.2	15.8				3.7	3.5	—				176.9		e>4				e>25.2
Brazil	—	e>348.0		e>4.4	33.9	2,800			1.4		2.4	1.7		697.4	659.1	—	NA	NA	e>8.0	59.1	e>2.5	132	e>33.0	3.8	4.9	27.6
Chile	—	—			4.5			1	2.4	NA	1.7	e>.3					1.0		e>33.5	218.9		151	11.6	.5	.3	
Colombia	—	—			12.2				.5		3.3	.5		.5		—	22.0		44.8	2.3			.4	.2	.2	e>.4
Ecuador	e>.4	—																	e>.5	2.1						
Guyana	—	e>3,760.0																								
Peru	13.8	—	856	.2	e>30.0	27	689	168	1.1		ngl	NA		206.1	168.8	—	1.0		17.5	127.7		NA	9.1	2.5	.2	162.9
Venezuela		—							2.1		.2			.5		52			314.1	19.4		e>82	19.7		.8	
Europe																										
Austria	89.7	—	e>160	12.4	.7			25	4.6		3.8	1.7		2.4	19.3	194	1.8		52.4		25.8	676	4.0	2.8	3.9	6.8
Belgium	—	—						e>850	6.3		13.2	e>7.0			33.9	e>320						79	ngl	11.2	12.8	
Finland	371.7	—			e>100.0		e>58	e>550	1.8	71.3	43.5	e>.1	e>1,650	e>33.3	402.1	—	e>63.0	300.0	229.5	18.9	e>8.0	5,100	55.4	1.2	1.0	4.6
France	262.7	e>3.5			459.2			792	27.5		219.8	13.6		e>.4		—	e>170.0	92.3	289.1	e>48.0	e>12.0	1,362	6.1	18.2	22.5	30.3
Germany, West	80.0	1,940.0			161.0			76.0	35.0	30.0	219.8	41.4	784	1.4		—	290.0			e>1.0		235		33.8	45.3	39.3
Greece	144.2	215.1	1,154	112.5	241.9		e>9	424	4.3		.2			6.0		—	211.2	258.1	416.7		1.7	e>260	.8	.3	e>.3	8.6
Ireland		—							1.3		2.2	7.1		2.4		—						e>3,300	6.3			e>65.0
Italy	72.0	—						e>160	31.3		5.6	NA		20.8	27.9	—	e>115.0		773.2	127.7	e>8.0	e>10	3.8	7.8	16.4	37.0
Luxembourg	502.2	—						86	3.3		.8	2.0		3.7	3.7	—								3.5	e>5.5	
Netherlands	103.1	—	e>45		e>60.0			80	2.5		14.3	.3		4.2	37.6	—	e>50.0					110	6.3	4.8	4.7	3.2
Norway	66.8	—	122				ngl		2.0		ngl	ngl		10.2	51.8	—	33.3	314.7		17.8		4,000	6.3	.7	.7	1.8
Portugal	77.1	e>5.0			17.3		e>15	245	16.0			3.7		25.2		—	e>31.0			42.3		100	33.2	3.4	.4	69.6
Spain	33.8	—	2,037	11.5	71.0	287	102	150	6.0	39.4	153.0	19.9		e>88.0		—	e>45.0	e>200.0	178.7			4,596	12.3	2.8	e>6.0	80.0
Sweden	48.4	—				250			4.5		26.5	1.2			42.0	—			25.8	76.1	e>70.0	100	2.7	ngl	5.3	e>3.0
Switzerland	e>65.0	—		e>2.2	NA			NA	3.6	NA	29.0	.8		e>38.0		—		NA	18.0	NA	NA	e>200	2.7	1.3	.5	123.0
United Kingdom	80.0	—	e>600	NA	e>7.0	144		e>12	6.7		106.5	e>11.7	10,466	e>4.8	362.2	2,022	NA	NA	33.0	NA	NA	e>226	e>1.4	16.7	26.8	e>82.5
Yugoslavia	64.4	1,932.0	18,213	258.2	e>30.0	313	695	420	7.6	1,197.5	249.0	e>9.3	987	e>20.0	126.2	14,116	170.0		109.3	706.6		1,440	22.9	2.1	2.2	e>7.3
Communist nations																										
Bulgaria	96.8	e>20.0	e>3	e>2.5	e>50.0		NA		2.6		26.5	e>1.7		NA	54.7	—	e>23.0	e>80.0	137.3	e>480.0		e>810	2.3	2.1	e>1.5	e>12.0
Czechoslovakia	89.7	e>3.0	e>39	ngl	e>55.0		NA		11.8	e>26.0	164.9	e>16.2		e>4.8	6.2	—	e>23.0	e>39.0	850.6	.3	.5	136	5.2	4.4	10.8	49.0
Germany, East	e>1,100.0	e>20.0	e>82	e>1,000.0	e>280.0	e>1,250	e>50	e>2,300	7.5		19.2	.9		NA		—	35.4	5.5		16.0	73.9	37	1.6	e>.1	4.8	e>40.0
Hungary		e>5,208.0	e>6,600		e>280.0				89.8	1,700.0	e>608.0	73.5	e>1,500	e>900.0	900.0	e>7,500	e>250.0	e>400.0	6,380.0	6,250.0	e>70.0	e>4,700	186.0	e>81.6	e>110.0	e>440.0
Poland																										
Romania																										
U.S.S.R.																										
Africa																										
Algeria	e>.2	—			e>32.0			NA	e>1.0		ngl			e>.6		—			105.4			e>175	2.7	ngl	ngl	e>6.5
Angola			e>60					597	.4					e>.5	362.2	e>2,022				175.8	16		5.5			
Congo (Kinshasa)	113.1	—					250		.3				10,466	362.2		14,116			.9	14.2				.3		
Gabon		269.5	1,407	19.4	.4	3		59	.4	24.8			987			e>2,382	1.6	NA		706.6	17.1	62				
Ghana				9.7		75	3		.7		.4				8.8	e>746				17.9	NA			7.5	ngl	70.6
Kenya			5	.8	86.9	122			.9	370.0	.3			NA		1,937			1.5	.6	.5	1,440				
Liberia		4.4	18,213	21.0		90		191	.6	140.0				120.3		7,862				11.9		2,000	28.3			
Malagasy Republic		NA		NA	NA				NA	29.8	3.3			e>24.0		777			2.3		73.9	560				
Morocco		445.0							5.0		52.8	3.6		e>148.0			22.0	150.3		252.7		359				
Mozambique	568.8				62.3			2,765		216.7	44.6	36.0		27.6	629.2	e>1,937	NA		76.2		1.7		1.9	59.4	82.9	
Nigeria									4.9		10.3			e>1.3	21.5				116.9	50.7						
Rhodesia	6.3	1,073.0	e>27			1,300	695	37	2.7	465.7	e>1.3	e>3.6		e>.3	126.2	—	e>23.0	e>39.0		571.1	73.9	136	5.2	ngl	.5	16.5
Sierra Leone		e>3.0	e>82				115		3.0							7,862				21.5		37	1.6	ngl	e>.1	
South Africa	22.1	1,073.0	e>750	e>3.1		287			2.7	469.7	16.2	.2	1,798	131.4	747.5	757		297.6	31.6	31,275.9			10.9	.9	1.2	60.4
South West Africa			2,550	4.6	33.1				4.6	446.0	4.6			e>2.3	19.3			2.1				92	2.4			23.0
Tanzania									2.1					26.4								5				
Tunisia					8.2				5.8					ngl			3.0									3.0
Uganda															16.6											
United Arab Republic		2,459.0																		e>5.0		470				
Zambia	46.7	—			e>30.0			6	3.6					748.2	747.5	—				e>47.8		e>22	5.5	e>.1	e>.5	e>15.0
Other Africa					.6		2		1.1					e>.8			11.6							.4	ngl	
Asia																										
Burma		e>80							.2	23.5	ngl	ngl		ngl						e>.2	NA	4	e>1.3		ngl	9.0
Cyprus	131.2	—							.3	216.7		e>10.5		19.9	8.8	e>9	34.2	2.2		109.5		16		7.5	6.5	10.1
India	131.2	992.0			51.8				13.3	140.0	77.3	10.5		10.1		20	34.2		25.8	7.6	NA	1,440	28.3	7.5	6.5	2.0
Indonesia		770.3		e>80.0	70.0				e>2.3		.3			e>8.0			e>23.0		30.2			2,000				e>24.0
Iran		—							e>1.3					120.3			60.8		98.2			71				
Israel	568.8	—							51.4		44.6	36.0						11.9	4.9							
Japan		—			62.3		695	2,765	51.4	29.8	44.6	36.0		120.3	629.2	e>1,937	60.8	11.9	76.2	252.7	1.7	560	1.9	59.4	82.9	63.5
Korea, South	6.3	—			3.5		115		4.9		10.3			e>1.3	6.2	7,862	e>23.0	e>39.0		50.7	73.9	37	4.4	ngl	.5	16.5
Malaysia		1,073.0	e>39						e>2.7		e>1.3			e>.3		777	NA			5.7		5	1.6	ngl	e>.1	
Pakistan		e>3.0							3.0	e>26.0	4.6			e>.3			3.0		116.9	21.5		92	.5	ngl	ngl	
Philippines	22.1	—	e>750	3.1					2.7	465.7				131.4	16.6		35.4	297.6	31.6	571.1	73.9	136	1.6	ngl	ngl	ngl
Taiwan		—	2,550	4.6	33.1				4.1	446.0	4.6	.2		e>2.3	19.3			2.1		21.5		5	2.4	ngl	ngl	1.9
Thailand		NA					214		5.8	NA	16.2			26.4		757						92		.9	.3	
Turkey		—	846	.7					4.3				e>300		19.3							220			1.2	2.9
Communist nations																										
China e>	120.0	450.0	12,000	160.0	140.0		250	80	10.0	NA	330.0	17.0		100.0	100.0		e>6.0	250.0		50.0	30.0	550	40.0	20.0	16.0	100.0
Other e>		—		NA	120.0			571	3.4		29.4	2.3		12.0	12.0			105.0		160.0	75.0	25	7.5	2.3	7.0	70.0
Oceania																										
Australia	126.4	7,917.0	846	.7	33.5		214	571	4.3	NA	69.4	e>5.1	e>300	130.0	115.6	.4	e>6.0	250.0	ngl	716.1	30.0	e>920	39.1	6.2	7.0	445.3
New Zealand		—							.8		2.4	ngl						105.0	9.4	10.7	75.0	25				
Pacific Islands		—												.4						e>118.0						
World total e>	9,073.8	52,375.2	65,367	3,304.9	3,630.6	7,178	3,743	17,433	540.1	5,255.7	2,876.6	357.6	20,478	5,999.0	6,620.3	40,718	2,339.7	3,782.7	34,015.5	46,418.3	372.9	51,994	723.8	418.2	573.7	3,211.5

	Lead (smelter) (Th.)	Magnesite, crude (Th.)	Magnesium (Th.)	Manganese ore (Th.)	Mercury (Th. flasks)	Mica (including scrap) (Th.)	Molybdenum	Nickel (Th.)	Nitrogen e>‡ (Th.)	Peat (Th.)
North America										
Canada	169.8	NA	9.6	—	e>20.0	—	13,740	192.7	700.0	285
Central America	.2	—	—	—	—	—	—	—	15.0	—
Mexico	169.0	—	—	133.5	e>22.5	.6	202	—	196.0	—
United States	579.4	W	90.6	5.1	e>29.0	120.7	46,725	14.2	6,778.0	513
West Indies	—	—	—	NA	—	—	—	35.5	133.0	—
South America										
Argentina	e>26.3	—	—	e>31.0	—	e>.7	NA	—	24.0	NA
Bolivia	ngl	—	—	—	ngl	—	—	—	—	—
Brazil	18.7	e>180.0	—	2,149.0	—	e>1.4	—	e>1.1	9.3	—
Chile	—	—	—	23.7	.3	—	4,842	—	116.6	—
Colombia	—	NA	—	—	.3	ngl	—	—	47.0	—
Ecuador	—	—	—	—	—	—	—	—	—	—
Guyana	—	—	—	—	—	—	—	—	—	—
Peru	77.9	—	—	7.3	3.4	—	246	—	25.0	—
Venezuela	—	—	—	—	—	—	—	—	21.0	—
Europe										
Austria	7.5	1,608.0	—	—	—	—	—	—	255.6	—
Belgium	112.4	—	—	—	—	—	—	—	400.0	—
Finland	—	—	—	—	—	—	—	3.8	112.5	e>225
France	108.0	—	4.4	—	—	e>.2	—	—	1,372.0	80
Germany, West	125.8	—	—	—	—	—	—	—	1,597.7	1,432
Greece	11.6	580.0	—	6.4	—	—	—	5.2	126.8	—
Ireland	—	—	—	—	.4	—	—	—	40.0	6,483
Italy	62.3	—	6.4	53.0	48.7	—	—	—	1,088.5	—
Luxembourg	—	—	—	—	—	—	—	—	—	—
Netherlands	—	—	—	—	—	—	—	—	954.2	e>400
Norway	—	—	35.1	—	—	e>3.8	e>243	e>.3	373.7	e>14
Portugal	1.1	—	—	10.0	—	e>2.0	—	—	129.6	—
Spain	81.2	e>200.0	—	23.0	64.5	—	NA	—	494.0	—
Sweden	42.1	—	—	—	—	NA	—	—	143.8	e>125
Switzerland	—	—	—	—	—	—	—	—	36.4	—
United Kingdom	39.1	—	e>4.0	—	—	—	—	—	911.3	—
Yugoslavia	e>120.0	477.0	—	12.3	14.3	e>.1	—	—	119.8	—
Communist nations										
Bulgaria	e>95.2	NA	—	e>41.0	—	—	—	—	504.0	—
Czechoslovakia	e>18.0	e>2,200.0	—	—	.2	—	—	—	263.9	—
Germany, East	e>25.0	—	—	—	—	—	—	NA	351.4	—
Hungary	—	—	—	e>156.0	—	—	—	—	245.1	e>65
Poland	50.7	e>45.0	—	—	—	—	—	e>1.5	758.9	20
Romania	e>40.0	—	—	e>80.0	—	NA	—	—	420.7	—
U.S.S.R.	e>440.0	e>3,100.0	e>45.0	e>7,000.0	e>47.0	37.0	7,500	e>105.0	3,750.0	e>190,000
Africa										
Algeria	—	—	—	—	—	—	—	—	—	—
Angola	—	—	—	29.1	—	—	—	—	—	—
Congo (Kinshasa)	—	—	—	311.4	—	—	—	—	—	—
Gabon	—	—	—	1,363.0	—	—	—	—	—	—
Ghana	—	—	—	349.7	—	—	—	—	—	—
Kenya	—	.5	—	—	—	—	—	—	—	—
Liberia	—	—	—	—	—	—	—	—	—	—
Malagasy Republic	—	—	—	—	—	1.2	—	—	—	—
Morocco	26.8	—	—	130.6	—	—	—	ngl	—	—
Mozambique	—	—	—	—	—	e>.3	—	—	—	—
Nigeria	—	—	—	—	—	—	NA	—	—	—
Rhodesia	—	NA	—	—	—	NA	—	e>8.0	NA	—
Sierra Leone	—	—	—	—	—	—	—	—	—	—
South Africa	—	48.1	—	2,204.1	—	6.4	—	12.0	270.0	—
South West Africa	60.9	—	—	NA	—	NA	NA	—	—	—
Tanzania	—	1.5	—	—	—	.2	—	—	—	—
Tunisia	e>14.0	—	—	—	e>.3	—	—	—	—	—
Uganda	—	—	—	—	—	—	—	—	—	—
United Arab Republic	—	—	—	e>4.0	—	—	—	—	112.0	—
Zambia	23.0	—	—	e>25.0	—	—	—	—	NA	—
Other Africa	—	.5	—	150.4	—	—	—	—	NA	—
Asia										
Burma	10.0	—	—	—	—	—	—	ngl	—	—
Cyprus	—	—	—	—	—	—	—	—	—	—
India	2.0	260.2	—	1,605.0	—	e>27.1	—	—	563.0	—
Indonesia	—	—	—	10.0	—	—	—	e>6.9	47.0	—
Iran	.4	e>6.5	—	35.0	—	—	—	—	25.7	—
Israel	—	—	—	—	—	—	—	—	27.6	e>20
Japan	186.6	—	9.4	301.7	5.6	—	269	—	2,107.0	e>70
Jordan	—	—	—	—	—	—	—	—	—	—
Korea, South	3.5	—	—	2.9	—	—	130	—	315.3	NA
Malaysia	—	—	—	NA	—	—	—	—	—	—
Pakistan	—	e>2.0	—	—	—	—	—	—	135.0	—
Philippines	—	—	—	20.0	3.5	—	16	—	45.6	—
Taiwan	—	—	—	—	—	—	—	—	194.8	—
Thailand	—	—	—	29.9	—	—	—	—	10.0	—
Turkey	e>2.0	219.3	—	13.2	e>4.8	—	—	—	34.5	—
Communist nations										
China e>	100.0	1,000.0	1.0	1,000.0	20.0	NA	1,500	—	NA	—
Other e>	55.0	1,600.0	—	—	—	—	—	—	NA	—
Oceania										
Australia	343.9	e>24.0	—	921.9	—	—	NA	10.8	74.0	—
New Zealand	—	—	—	—	—	—	—	—	—	—
Pacific islands	—	—	—	20.8	—	—	—	90.5	—	—
World Total e>	3,249.2	11,552.6	205.6	18,258.8	284.9	201.8	75,413	487.4	26,600	199,737

	Petroleum, crude (Mi. bbl.)	Phosphate Rock (Th.)	Platinum§ (Th. troy oz.)	Potash‖ (Th.)	Pyrites including cupreous (Th.)	Salt (Th.)	Silver (Mi. troy oz.)	Sulfur (byproduct elemental) (Th.)	Talc (Th.)	Tin* (in ore) (Long tons)	Tin (smelter) (Long tons)	Titanium (ilmenite) (Th.)	Tungsten* Conc.	Uranium¶ (oxides)	Vanadium	Zinc* (in ore) (Th.)	Zinc (smelter) (Th.)
North America																	
Canada	407.5	—	266.1	2,854	293	3,853	41.9	2,707.9	73.9	120	—	679.7	1,440	3,497	—	1,194.2	423.1
Central America	—	—	—	—	—	64	e>4.2	—	—	—	—	—	NA	—	—	16.9	—
Mexico	149.7	33	—	—	—	e>3,000	42.9	58.0	1.3	280	139	—	289	—	—	253.4	80.3
United States	3,371.8	34,224	21.6	2,544	W	40,138	41.9	1,422.8	933.7	W	345	844.8	4,266	10,772	5,059	501.8	944.0
West Indies	58.1	e>85	—	—	NA	e>1,005	ngl	4.3	—	—	—	—	—	—	—	—	—
South America																	
Argentina	130.1	—	—	—	—	e>750	e>2.8	—	e>28.0	700	—	—	e>200	e>45	—	e>31.7	e>24.6
Bolivia	14.8	—	—	—	—	NA	6.0	—	—	29,489	48	—	1,841	—	—	26.2	—
Brazil	e>63.0	e>150	—	—	—	1,630	.4	7.3	e>50.0	e>2,560	1,191	20.3	e>460	—	—	NA	e>6.0
Chile	13.4	17	—	—	—	1,330	3.1	—	.8	—	—	—	—	—	—	1.5	—
Colombia	76.8	12	27.8	—	—	678	ngl	3.8	1.5	—	—	—	—	—	—	e>.4	—
Ecuador	1.6	—	—	—	—	—	ngl	—	—	—	—	—	—	—	—	.2	—
Guyana	—	—	—	—	—	—	—	—	—	—	—	—	—	—	—	—	—
Peru	26.3	e>20	—	—	—	166	34.1	—	7.7	82	—	—	672	—	—	314.8	62.3
Venezuela	1,311.8	e>60	—	—	—	171	—	—	—	—	—	—	—	—	—	—	—
Europe																	
Austria	19.2	—	—	—	—	e>476	.1	41.0	94.1	—	—	—	e>135	—	—	14.2	15.5
Belgium	—	NA	—	—	—	—	—	e>5.0	—	—	4,444	—	—	—	—	—	261.6
Finland	—	—	—	—	e>803	—	.6	111.8	e>30.0	—	—	138.2	—	—	1,346	71.2	1.1
France	18.2	e>30	—	1,938	84	e>4,850	e>2.0	1,732.0	218.6	263	—	—	—	e>1,500	—	19.8	254.5
Germany, West	e>57.1	—	—	2,626	641	8,358	e>1.7	129.2	e>47.9	—	2,415	—	—	NA	—	110.6	218.2
Greece	—	—	—	—	245	75	.3	—	4.5	—	—	—	—	—	—	9.2	—
Ireland	—	—	—	—	—	—	2.0	—	—	—	—	—	—	—	—	105.0	—
Italy	10.1	—	—	e>280	1,475	3,942	1.8	e>3.0	136.5	—	—	—	NA	—	—	132.5	130.3
Luxembourg	—	—	—	—	—	—	—	—	—	—	—	—	—	—	—	—	—
Netherlands	13.8	—	—	—	—	2,669	—	e>43.0	—	—	5,298	—	—	—	—	—	47.0
Norway	—	—	—	—	758	—	—	—	e>70.0	—	—	490.7	—	—	910	11.4	58.9
Portugal	—	—	—	—	531	e>466	.3	e>3.5	1.5	440	496	.1	1,255	e>95	—	1.6	—
Spain	1.4	—	—	636	2,475	e>1,825	e>1.7	e>40.0	e>30.0	121	2,066	29.5	e>70	e>60	—	80.8	80.3
Sweden	—	—	—	—	495	—	3.7	—	28.4	—	—	—	—	e>70	—	90.1	—
Switzerland	—	—	—	—	—	267	—	—	—	—	—	—	—	—	—	—	—
United Kingdom	.6	—	—	—	—	8,604	—	e>47.0	11.0	1,622	25,982	—	—	—	—	—	151.0
Yugoslavia	20.0	—	—	—	272	212	3.5	—	—	—	—	—	—	—	—	e>92.6	81.1
Communist nations																	
Bulgaria	2.8	—	—	—	e>170	120	NA	e>8.7	—	—	—	—	—	—	—	e>63.4	e>77.3
Czechoslovakia	1.5	—	—	—	e>400	e>207	e>1.1	—	—	140	—	—	—	NA	—	e>10.0	—
Germany, East	—	—	—	e>2,300	e>140	e>2,000	e>4.8	e>120.0	—	e>1,000	e>1,200	—	—	NA	—	e>12.0	e>14.0
Hungary	13.2	—	—	—	—	—	NA	e>3.0	—	—	—	—	—	NA	—	NA	—
Poland	3.2	e>100	—	—	e>225	2,817	e>.2	—	—	—	—	—	—	—	—	e>167.0	207.5
Romania	98.7	—	—	—	e>360	e>2,400	e>.8	—	e>130.0	—	—	—	—	—	—	NA	—
U.S.S.R.	2,395.0	e>19,250	e>2,100.0	e>3,180	e>3,500	e>11,500	e>37.0	e>480.0	e>380.0	e>27,000	e>27,000	NA	e>6,500	NA	NA	e>610.0	e>610.0
Africa																	
Algeria	338.0	—	—	—	e>50	e>120	e>.1	e>22.0	—	—	—	—	—	—	—	e>22.2	—
Angola	17.4	—	—	—	—	80	—	—	—	—	—	—	—	—	—	—	—
Congo (Kinshasa)	—	—	—	—	—	—	e>1.9	—	—	6,718	1,882	—	65	e>540	—	e>127.5	63.7
Gabon	36.4	—	—	—	—	—	—	—	—	—	—	—	—	—	—	—	—
Ghana	—	—	—	—	—	34	ngl	—	—	—	—	—	—	—	—	—	—
Kenya	—	—	—	—	—	42	ngl	—	—	—	—	—	—	—	—	—	—
Liberia	—	—	—	—	—	—	—	—	—	—	—	—	—	—	—	—	—
Malagasy Republic	—	—	—	—	—	22	—	—	—	—	—	—	—	—	—	—	—
Morocco	.4	10,662	—	—	392	67	.9	—	—	10	e>12	—	—	—	—	33.9	—
Mozambique	—	—	—	—	—	e>7	—	—	—	ngl	—	—	—	—	—	—	—
Nigeria	197.2	—	—	—	—	ngl	—	—	—	8,606	8,740	—	NA	—	—	—	—
Rhodesia	—	NA	—	—	NA	—	NA	—	NA	e>500	e>500	—	NA	—	—	—	—
Sierra Leone	—	—	—	—	—	—	—	—	—	—	—	9.8	—	—	—	—	—
South Africa	—	1,679	e>964.0	—	837	378	3.3	12.0	8.8	1,847	738	16.5	29	3,610	e>4,700	—	10.7
South West Africa	—	—	—	—	—	e>110	1.3	—	—	e>730	—	—	e>85	—	410	e>70.0	—
Tanzania	—	NA	—	—	—	34	ngl	—	—	178	—	—	NA	—	—	—	—
Tunisia	25.4	3,200	—	—	—	e>350	ngl	—	—	—	—	—	—	—	—	e>5.3	—
Uganda	—	e>145	—	—	—	5	—	—	—	146	—	—	53	—	—	—	—
United Arab Republic	e>95.0	660	—	—	—	385	—	.5	e>30.0	—	—	.2	—	—	—	—	—
Zambia	—	—	—	—	—	—	e>.8	—	2.3	—	—	—	—	—	—	50.5	50.2
Other Africa	e>1,135.1	2,612	.3	NA	—	e>334	—	—	.7	e>1,355	—	—	227	—	—	.9	—
Asia																	
Burma	6.1	—	—	—	—	176	e>1.0	—	—	e>340	—	—	113	—	—	e>4.9	—
Cyprus	—	—	—	—	826	6	—	—	—	—	—	—	—	—	—	—	—
India	51.7	78	—	—	—	6,380	.1	—	186.6	—	—	51.4	21	NA	—	8.7	24.2
Indonesia	271.0	e>10	—	—	—	e>180	.3	—	—	17,146	5,898	—	—	—	—	—	—
Iran	1,231.8	—	—	—	—	e>310	—	e>40.0	—	—	—	—	—	—	—	e>22.5	—
Israel	18.0	987	—	334	—	e>57	—	e>8.0	—	—	—	—	—	—	—	—	—
Japan	5.5	—	7.0	—	4,453	981	10.8	142.1	1,706.0	729	1,377	5.1	607	NA	—	269.9	712.2
Jordan	—	1,087	—	—	—	18	—	—	—	—	—	—	—	—	—	—	—
Korea, South	—	—	—	—	—	289	.9	—	185.5	40	—	—	1,971	—	—	22.1	2.3
Malaysia	3.3	—	—	—	—	—	—	—	—	72,167	88,482	e>132.6	138	—	—	—	—
Pakistan	3.5	—	—	—	—	1,137	—	—	e>2.4	—	—	—	—	—	—	—	—
Philippines	—	NA	—	—	e>96	231	1.6	—	.9	—	—	—	—	—	—	3.3	—
Taiwan	.6	—	—	—	38	383	ngl	e>3.1	24.4	—	—	—	—	—	—	—	—
Thailand	ngl	—	—	—	—	e>200	NA	—	2.0	20,786	22,049	—	653	—	—	e>.7	—
Turkey	e>25.0	2	—	—	130	e>570	NA	—	—	—	—	—	—	—	—	6.8	—
Communist nations																	
China e>	146.0	1,100	—	—	1,800	15,000	.8	130.0	150.0	20,000	20,000	—	8,000	NA	—	100.0	90.0
Other e>	ngl	1,350	—	—	500	708	.7	—	60.0	—	—	—	2,140	—	—	125.0	60.0
Oceania																	
Australia	15.8	e>5	—	—	e>125	e>1,000	24.7	—	41.0	7,873	4,156	712.2	1,250	e>300	—	504.6	246.3
New Zealand	ngl	—	—	—	—	49	ngl	—	—	—	—	—	NA	—	—	—	—
Pacific islands	—	2,762	—	—	—	—	ngl	—	—	—	—	—	—	—	—	—	—
World Total e>	15,219.0	81,897	3,386.9	16,692	22,114	133,963	288.4	7,347.8	4,682.5	223,609	224,458	3,219.1	32,480	20,489	12,425	5,321.3	5,008.1

NOTES: "ngl" indicates negligible production (less than 0.1 unit); NA not available; "W" indicates withheld to avoid disclosing company confidential data. e> indicates an estimate. *Metal content of ore. † to avoid duplication, cadmium exported in concentrates, flue dust, etc., is excluded from the total.
‡ Food and Agricultural Organization of the UN estimated content of nitrogenous fertilizers excluding industrial nitrogen. § Includes all platinum-group metals. ‖ Marketable K_2O equivalent. ¶ U_3O_8. Source: U.S. Department of Interior, Bureau of Mines.

(F. H. Sk.)

continued from page 519

Manganese nodules were mined experimentally from a seabed depth of 3,000 ft. at a site 100 mi. off the coast of South Carolina. The deep-sea dredge used an airlift to raise and transport 1,600 tons of nodules a day to the vessel "Deepsea Miner." The success of the trials led to plans for commercial deep-sea mining, probably off the California coast, by 1975. (P. F. Y.)

Production. The world demand for minerals and mineral products continued to increase during 1969. Output of 55 minerals and mineral commodities increased an average 5.9% over the previous year, with gains for individual minerals ranging from 0.6% (gold) to 11.1% (vermiculite). In a few cases, columbium-tantalum (+7.4%) and selenium (+8.6%), for example, the increase offset and more than compensated for a 1968 decline in production. Only 15 minerals registered a lower output in 1969, for an average decline of 3.8%. Individual decreases varied from 0.2% (potash) to 18.3% (white arsenic). In most cases the decline in production was the result of labour difficulties (cobalt 0.7%, nickel 1.8%, platinum 0.2%) or technical mining difficulties affecting significant producers, as in Moroccan cobalt, rather than the result of an eroding market. The latter affected white arsenic and nonmetallurgical forms of coke (−5%).

Among 56 mineral commodities for which fairly complete worldwide statistics were available, the U.S. led in 1969 in the production of 25, including aluminum, copper, lead, molybdenum, pig iron, steel, natural gas, and petroleum. The Soviet Union led in the production of ten, including iron ore, chromium, platinum, manganese, coal, and coke. Canada led in four; Japan in three; Malaysia, Mexico, South Africa, and the Congo (Kinshasa) in two each; and five other countries in one each.

For the most part, prices for minerals and metals increased during 1969 not only in response to inflationary pressures but also, and more importantly, as a result of the changes taking place in the mineral industries due to the continuing growth of world demand. Beyond a certain point, the available supply of minerals does not expand very quickly in response to enlarged demand because of the long period of time, often from six to eight years, required to find and develop new mineral deposits. Such time and cost requirements increase when, as was true in 1970 for many minerals, the easy-to-find, accessible deposits had been largely exhausted and the search had to turn to remote areas such as within the Arctic Circle or the interior of Africa. Moreover, with a number of minerals, such as copper, iron, nickel, and phosphate, the bulk of production had to come from the large-scale mining of very large but low-grade deposits carrying perhaps six or seven pounds of metal per ton of rock. The capital investment required to develop such a mine was very high, in excess of $100 million in 1970. The end results of these factors were higher metal and mineral prices.

Current new mineral developments in Canada, Australia, and the North Slope of Alaska were particularly good examples of the trend toward the large-scale mining of a considerable variety of minerals. As a result, many traditional aspects of the mining industry were expected to change during the 1970s. In addition to the scale on which new mines were being developed, developments in exploration and production technology caused the search for new mineral deposits to spread to many previously neglected parts of the world. Exploration crews were active throughout the

Arctic region and in the Pacific islands, for example, and a number of countries that had been thought deficient in minerals, such as Ireland, were proving to possess unexpected, sometimes quite rich, mineral resources.

Aluminum. World output of aluminum increased 13% during 1969 for a new record. There were no changes in the relative positions of the five largest producers, led by the U.S. (38%), Soviet Union (12%), and Canada (11%). World output of bauxite, the ore of aluminum, increased by 17% in 1969. As usual, Jamaica (20%) was the leading producer, but its position was threatened by Australia (15%), which spurted from fourth to second place, passing Surinam (11%) and the Soviet Union (10%).

Aluminum consumption increased about 11%, with the greatest gain (about 30%) in Asia, although European demand was also strong. As a result of lowered domestic consumption, U.S. foreign trade in aluminum changed in 1969 from its 1968 position, in which imports amounted to about twice exports, to one in which exports slightly exceeded imports. The U.S. also illustrated the developing change in international aluminum raw material flow patterns. Between 1965 and 1969, U.S. bauxite imports increased by about 7%, but imports of alumina (intermediate between bauxite and aluminum) increased eightfold. Aluminum ingot prices underwent two 1969 price increases of one cent per pound.

Antimony. World antimony production, almost 7% above 1968 levels, reached a new high, exceeding the previous record set in 1964. There were no changes in relative position among the five largest producers: South Africa (28%), Bolivia (20%), China (18%), Soviet Union (10%), and Mexico (5%). Demand for antimony, predominantly for use in automobile batteries, increased in the late 1960s. Thus, supplies were extremely tight in 1969, as reflected by the rise in prices, which in January were about $7 per long ton unit for 60% concentrates (Europe) and 44 cents per pound for metal (U.S. producers and "free market"). The European 60% concentrate price rose to $9 per long ton unit by midyear and $25 per long ton unit by December, while the December U.S. producer price for metal had reached $1.04 per pound and $3 per pound on the free market. The most important cause of the short supply and increased price was the withdrawal of China, formerly a large supplier, from the market. This not only reduced antimony supplies available to the non-Communist countries but also brought China's former customer, the Soviet Union, into the world market as a buyer.

Asbestos. Compared with 1968, world output of asbestos increased almost 11% in 1969, with no change among the largest producers except for Rhodesia dropping from fifth to seventh position in 1969. The three largest producers (Canada 44%, Soviet Union 30%, South Africa 8%) accounted for more than 80% of the estimated world output. Approximately half the asbestos was consumed by the asbestos-cement products industry, where demand was related directly to construction activity. Strengthening demand and limited supplies, particularly in certain grades, pushed prices up somewhat in 1969. Supply and price considerations, together with the usefulness of asbestos in the traditionally localized construction materials industry, were encouraging the exploration and development of asbestos deposits in several countries, including Mexico, Australia, and Afghanistan.

Cement. Estimated world cement production increased about 5.2% in 1969 with no changes in relative ranking among the leading producers (Soviet Union 17%, U.S. 13%, Japan 10%, West Germany 6%, Italy 6%). Most countries produced some cement, but Qatar and Mongolia apparently initiated their first production during 1969. Cement markets were essentially local, and the material was, therefore, locally priced. In the U.S. prices held steady during 1969, but profit margins narrowed as costs of labour, materials, and distribution increased.

Chromium. The output of chromite rose 7% in 1969. Among the leading producers the only change was the Philippines (9%), moving up one place to supplant Turkey (8%) in third place. The Soviet Union (32%) and South Africa (23%) remained first and second, respectively. Demand for chromium, particularly for use in stainless steel, increased in the late 1960s to the extent that it pressed hard on supplies. In 1969 the situation became difficult not only because this second year of UN-imposed sanctions against Rhodesia (which had been the major source of high-grade metallurgical chromite for the U.S.) found stocks depleted but also because the Canadian nickel strike further increased the demand for chromium as a substitute for nickel in stainless steel. As a result, the Soviet Union became a major source of chromite for the U.S. and other countries, and prices rose to new highs. By the end of 1969, prices for Soviet chromite were 80% above those of January 1967, and those for Turkish material were 45% higher.

Cobalt. World cobalt output fell by almost 1% in 1969 for the second consecutive year, although the decline was less than the 3% loss in 1968. Apart from the technical problems that continued to plague cobalt mining in Morocco and smelting in Western Europe, the supply situation was worsened by the nickel strike in Canada, which curtailed the by-product output of cobalt. The Canadian strike still further exacerbated the problem by enhancing the demand for cobalt as a substitute for nickel in stainless steel. Prices reacted predictably, rising in the U.S. (producer) from a first-half, stable $1.85 per pound to $2–$2.10 per pound by the end of the year, and in the European "free market" (mostly Soviet material) to about $2.50 per pound in October and $3.15–$3.50 by the end of the year. Had it not been for the sale of about 3,700 metric tons of surplus material from the U.S. national stockpile, the situation would have been even worse.

Copper. World mine output of copper increased 9.3% in 1969, while smelter output climbed only slightly less (8.5%). There was no change in the relative order among the major copper producers. Fully recovered from the 1967–68 strike, the U.S. (23% of mine output) maintained its traditional lead followed by the Soviet Union (15%), Zambia (12%), Chile (11.5%), and Canada (8%). Mine production increased in most countries except for Canada and Peru, where small declines from 1968 levels were attributable to labour difficulties. Generally strong demand, increasing at more than the historical rate of growth for the third consecutive year, was further enhanced by strong Communist-bloc buying, notably by China.

The pressure on supplies had its effect on prices. The U.S. producer price rose in four steps from 42 cents per pound in April to 52 cents per pound by the end of the year, while the London Metal Exchange price rose, on wirebar copper, for example, from about 54 cents per pound to about 78 cents per pound. Exploration and development of new copper-producing facilities continued throughout the world. The governments of several of the major copper-producing nations continued with their plans to acquire equity participation if not complete control over the copper industries in their countries. Approximately 34% of the 1969 world copper production originated from plants of which the national government owned all or a majority of the capital. This amounted to about 42% of the world's copper production from outside the Communist-bloc countries or 58% of non-Communist copper outside the United States.

Diamonds. Aggregate world diamond output in 1969 showed no significant change from 1968 (down about 0.2%), but while the output of gem diamonds (38% of the total) climbed about 8%, that of industrial diamonds (62%) fell 3% for the second consecutive year of decline. The Congo (Kinshasa) continued to lead the world in aggregate diamond production (35%) because of its immense (46%) output of industrial diamonds, more than twice that of the industrial diamond output of the Soviet Union (20%) or South Africa (15%). The latter led (30%) in gem diamond production and, with 19% of the total, was second in aggregate diamond output. South West Africa (17%) ranked second in gem output, followed by Angola (14%) and the Soviet Union (13%). The decline in industrial diamond production resulted partially from supply equaling or even slightly exceeding demand and partially from the growing availability of synthetic diamonds. Leading synthetic diamond producers included the U.S. with 13 million carats, the Soviet Union with 10 million, South Africa with 7 million, and Ireland with 6 million. The supply of synthetic stones, nearly equal to natural stones in both weight and value, was helping to maintain a stable price, but the value of gemstones rose about 4.5% in the year from July 1968 to July 1969.

Gold. World output of gold rose slightly (0.6%) in 1969, probably as increased by-production from other forms of mining. Some of the increase, however, was possibly in response to the two-tier gold price system in which the free market price usually exceeded the official price of $35 per ounce. There was no change in rank among major producers. South Africa continued in first place with 67% of production followed by the Soviet Union (13%). Canada (5%) might have made a better showing had not by-product gold output declined as a result of the nickel strike. The free market price in January 1969 was about $43 per ounce but rose quickly to the year's peak, $44.25 on March 10. It fell again slightly, although remaining high until September, when it began to decline considerably. By mid-December gold was trading in London and Zürich at less than the $35 official price.

Iron and Steel. World output of iron ore was estimated to have increased by nearly 6% in 1969, production of pig iron and ferroalloys 8%, and that of steel just over 8%. Among iron ore producers, the Soviet Union (25.7%) continued to lead, followed by the U.S. (12.5%); their roles were reversed in the case of pig iron, of which the U.S. accounted for 21.2% and the U.S.S.R. 19.5%. Development of new iron ore deposits continued throughout the world in 1970 but at a rate somewhat slower than that of the previous few years. The trend away from direct shipping of iron ore in favour of pellets continued with the added refinement of metallized pellets. The trend toward replacement of open hearth and even electric furnaces by the basic oxygen process continued unabated.

In the economics of a large-volume, low-unit-value commodity such as iron ore, transportation costs were an extremely important factor, and much effort was being devoted to reducing them. Two transportation events in 1969 were of great potential importance for the iron industry. One was the first transoceanic tanker shipment of an iron ore slurry. The other was the inauguration of the 85-km. Savage River pipeline, the world's first long-distance iron ore slurry pipeline, in Tasmania. The price of iron ore pellets increased about 1.5 cents per

long ton unit and that for natural iron ores about 25 cents per ton.

Lead. Production from the world's lead mines rose about 7.4% in 1969 and that from smelters increased 10%. The U.S., formerly third in lead mine production, was first in 1969 with 14.4% of the total, having displaced the Soviet Union (13.7%), now third, and Australia (13.9%), now second. As before, the U.S. (17.8%) and the Soviet Union (13.5%) were first and second in the smelter production of lead, in which Japan (5.7%) rose from sixth to fourth place. The demand for lead continued strong, 1969 consumption outside the Communist countries having increased about 5%; an important factor was the purchases by China from the world market. The increase in U.S. lead supplies was in part due to the full production achieved by the new Missouri lead mines and smelters as well as to the recovery from the 1968 strike. Despite a good supply situation, 1969 lead prices rose to their highest levels since 1964. In January 1969 the U.S. producer price rose first to 13.5 cents per pound, then to 14 cents. In April it was lifted to 14.5 cents, in June to 15 cents, in August to 15.5 cents, and finally in December to 16.5 cents per pound. London Metal Exchange prices kept pace.

Manganese. World production of manganese increased nearly 5% in 1969. Among the ten largest producers, the Soviet Union (38%) and South Africa (12%) remained first and second. Brazil (11.8%) increased its output by more than half to take third place away from India (9%). Despite increased production, the general market weakness of the preceding few years continued. Supply remained in excess of demand, prices continued to erode, and only the strongest and most efficient producers could continue to compete. As a result of this situation, the Ivory Coast ceased production, and India's position was weakened, primarily because of unfavourable transportation costs arising from poor port facilities. A possible precursor of things to come, the world's first manganese pellet plant was commissioned in Brazil.

Mercury. World output of mercury increased 10.5% in 1969. Spain (23%) retained its traditional lead, followed by Italy (17%), the Soviet Union (16.5%), and the U.S. (10%). Canada, having increased its production approximately three times over 1968 levels, rose to seventh from ninth place among producers, largely on the strength of Cominco's Lake Pinchi Mine in British Columbia. Of interest also was Ireland's appearance among the producers with an estimated 300–400 flasks per year of by-product mercury from Gortdrum Mine. Prices held relatively stable during the year, the availability of surplus material from the U.S. national stockpile being the significant factor. Prices began the year at $530 per flask in January and $540 in February. They began to erode and fluctuate about midyear and then fell off to $480 in October, ending the year at approximately $490.

Molybdenum. World production of molybdenum rose by 13% in 1969, due largely to a 51% increase in Canadian output, although the largest producers (accounting for nearly 98% of production) maintained their relative positions: U.S. (62%), Canada (18%), Soviet Union (10%), Chile (6%). Both production and consumption, up about 7% in the non-Communist countries, set records. Prices were increased about 5% in May 1969, and additional new productive capacity, largely a by-product of copper mining, was being brought into operation.

Nickel. World nickel production declined nearly 2% in 1969, mainly because of strikes against the large Canadian producers. Despite the nearly 20% loss in output, Canada easily maintained its long-term position as the world's largest nickel producer (40%), followed by the Soviet Union (22%) and New Caledonia (19%). The U.S. (3%) ranked fifth after Cuba (9%). The Canadian strike exacerbated an already tight supply situation to the point that some merchant metal was reported to have been sold at about $8 per pound. Producer prices for electrolytic nickel rose from $1.03 per pound to $1.28 in December, while merchant prices, beginning at $1.65–$1.75 per pound in January, rose to more than $3 in July and to $6.65–$7.15 per pound in October; they then declined slightly to $5.50–$5.95 in December. The most significant development, resulting to a considerable extent from the continuing shortness of supply (and limited geographic base of production), was the internationalization of the industry; major new productive facilities were being developed in Australia, Dominican Republic, Botswana, Philippines, Indonesia, Guatemala, Colombia, and Venezuela, many of them by firms new to the nickel industry. In the process, emphasis shifted away from the classical sulfide ores of Canada, source of most of the world's supply for many years, to the lateritic deposits of the tropical countries.

Phosphate. World output of phosphate rock declined about 2.5%, largely in response to deliberately reduced mine output (−8.5% in the U.S., for instance). This reduction resulted from the continued excess of productive capacity over demand, although part of the drop was due to external factors, such as severe flooding in Tunisia (−7%). The U.S. (42%) remained the largest producer followed by the Soviet Union (24%) and Morocco (13%). Because of surplus capacity, prices continued to weaken, a trend not accurately reflected in posted prices since most reductions were made in the form of transportation credits or other rebates. Despite the overcapacity in 1969, plans for bringing the enormous deposits of the Spanish Sahara into production continued.

Platinum Group Metals. World platinum output declined slightly in 1969 (0.2%) due to the curtailment of by-product production by the nickel strike in Canada, the third largest producer (8%). The Soviet Union (62%) and South Africa (28%) maintained their customary positions. Continued pressure upon available supplies from increasing demand among traditional platinum users and unusually strong buying of unmanufactured platinum by China encouraged a year-end rise in the producer price (Rustenberg and Inco), which had been stable for 16 months at $120 per ounce, to $130 per ounce in November. However, the free market price (U.S.S.R. and small producers) fell from $280 (£117) to $175 (£73) per ounce over the course of the year, a considerable retreat from the June 1968 high of $300 (£125). Possibly excepting the new sulfide deposits in Australia, it was not likely that the pending significant increase in world nickel production would add to the platinum supply since the lateritic deposits from which most of the new output would come do not usually contain by-product platinum.

Potash. World output of potash declined approximately 0.2% in 1969 as a result of excess productive capacity. Among the top six producers, led by the Soviet Union (19%) and Canada (17%), the U.S. (15%) dropped from third to fourth place, having been supplanted by West Germany (16%). Although output declined slightly due to the curtailment of production in some mines and the closing of others, world productive capacity actually increased during 1969. Two new mines came into production in Canada where the capacity of a third was increased by half; plants in France, West Germany, and Spain were made more efficient and modernized; a facility was enlarged in Israel; one new mine in the Congo (Brazzaville) and two in the Soviet Union were brought into production; and East German facilities were enlarged. As a consequence of this activity, potash prices reached a new low in 1969 with some North American sales reported at less than $10 per ton of muriate f.o.b. mine. The province of Saskatchewan, centre of Canadian production, announced plans for the imposition of a production quota upon its mines and the maintenance of a floor price equivalent to $18.75 per short ton of muriate ex mine.

Silver. World mine production of new silver increased 5% in 1969. Mexico (15%) regained its lead over Canada (14.5%), while the U.S. (14.5%) ranked third, up from its 1968 fifth position, bypassing both the Soviet Union (13%) and Peru (12%). As usual, those five leading producers accounted for the bulk (69%) of the world's output. The total supply of silver from all sources in 1969, including the release of previously hoarded coins and reclamation of scrap, continued to exceed consumption, but only by about 50 million oz. compared with an estimated 180 million-oz. excess the previous year. The higher mine output in the U.S. marked that nation's recovery from the 1968 strike, which had reduced by-product output. In Mexico, however, the larger output resulted from higher silver prices, which encouraged a mild revival of small-scale silver mining. During 1969, the second year of freedom from government price control, silver prices began high in January ($2.02 per ounce in New York), their highest point for the year, and weakened steadily to a June low ($1.54 per ounce); they then strengthened again, somewhat erratically, to a year-end level of $1.80. This resulted in a 1969 average of $1.79, compared with a $2.14 average in 1968.

Sulfur. World production of native sulfur declined almost 2%, while that of recovered (by-product) sulfur increased 10% for an aggregated sulfur production gain of just over 2%. Both world production and consumption of sulfur in all forms established new records in 1969, but neither gain was large, particularly compared with the annual rates of increase observed since about 1963. Moreover, production exceeded consumption for the second consecutive year in 1969 and by a much larger figure than in the previous year. The critical factor in the world sulfur economy, formerly dominated for many years by U.S. and (later) Mexican producers of elemental sulfur by the Frasch process, had become elemental sulfur recovered as the result of processing sour natural gas for market by removing the hydrogen sulfide as hydrogen and elemental sulfur. This component of supply rose from virtually nothing in 1940 to more than 40% of the 1969 supply of elemental sulfur, or if the sulfur content of pyrite and the sulfur recovered from smelter gases is included, to about 30% of the total 1969 sulfur supply from all sources. Although the output of recovered sulfur in France and the U.S. was far from negligible, Canada was the undisputed leader in this field, having grown from an output of about 1,000 tons in 1953 to an estimated 2.7 million tons in 1969. The most immediate result of this situation in 1969 was a marked weakening in sulfur prices, some falling by as much as 30%, and curtailment of production. The latter bore particularly heavily upon the native sulfur producers and caused Frasch process facilities on the Nash and Caminada domes in the U.S. and the Salinas Dome in Mexico to be closed and placed on standby. Further adjustments were expected.

Tin. Both world mine and smelter production of tin decreased in 1969, the former by nearly 2% and the latter by almost 3%. Among the major mine producers there were no changes in comparative rank. Malaysia, as usual, was first with 32%, followed by Bolivia (13%), Soviet Union (12%), and Thailand (9%). Although relative 1969 smelter output by countries did not change significantly, Bolivia's announced

intention of smelting a significant portion of its own output completed the trend of recent years toward vertical integration of national tin production from mine to metal. Tin remained the only mineral commodity for which production (actually exports) was to a large extent controlled by international agreement among the major producing and consuming countries. Under the workings of the third (five-year) International Tin Agreement, as a result of increases in productive capacity that were outstripping consumption, the International Tin Council in September 1968 imposed mild production (export) quotas upon member countries for the first time since 1960. World consumption increased about 5% during 1969, although demand in the U.S., the largest consumer, tended to be stagnant. Nonetheless, the supply-demand situation as reflected in the London Metal Exchange price for tin improved sufficiently to permit the removal of quotas late in the year.

Titanium. World production of both ilmenite ($FeTiO_2$) and rutile (TiO_2) increased in 1969 by nearly 10% and 3%, respectively. Among the leading producers of ilmenite, the U.S. (26%) retained its lead followed by Australia (22%), which managed to push Canada (21%) down to third place. Australia (95%) and Sierra Leone (3%) continued to be the only significant producers of rutile in 1969. No figures were available for the production of either mineral in the Soviet Union. Demand for rutile (high-grade source of titanium metal, titanium dioxide, and welding rod coatings) continued to rise and appeared to be outstripping productive capacity, with predictable results in terms of increased exploration programs and higher prices. In January, for example, Australian ore was quoted at A$86–$88 per ton f.o.b. Australian ports, but A$140–$150 per ton in December. The demand for ilmenite, more than 90% of which was used for titanium dioxide in pigments, was also increasing, not least because of technical development that enabled the more plentiful mineral to be upgraded into synthetic rutile. Ilmenite prices remained stable in 1969, Australian material, for example, being quoted at about A$9–$12.50 per ton throughout the year.

Tungsten. World output of tungsten concentrates rose approximately 1% in 1969. Among the larger producers, there was no change in relative position except for Portugal supplanting Canada in eighth place. Output among the larger producers appeared to have fallen off or, based upon estimates for the Communist countries, remained static. The increase was due to gains among the smaller producers such as Peru, Thailand, and Japan. The two significant factors in the 1969 tungsten market were the continued absence of China (more than 80% of estimated world reserves) from the market except for insignificant quantities of overpriced material offered at the Canton fairs and the large quantities sold as surplus from the U.S. national stockpile. Because of higher European prices that developed relative to U.S. prices late in the year, exports of tungsten purchased from the stockpile were embargoed in December. Although they were high, tungsten prices remained relatively stable. Average monthly prices, excluding U.S. import duty, ranged from an April low of $41.19 to a December high of $61.04, for a 1969 average of $46.45, compared with $40.88 for 1968.

Uranium. Excluding Communist-bloc countries, for which no information was available, estimated world production of uranium oxide (U_3O_8) declined by almost 1%. There were no relative changes among the larger producers, led by the U.S. (53%), South Africa (18%), and Canada (17%). The downturn was largely due to lagging development in the nuclear electric power generating industry, caused by a variety of factors including untoward delays in plant and component construction and fabrication as well as political controversies interfering with site selection and plant approvals. Long-term prospects appeared brighter, however, if the record level of exploration activity in the U.S. and strong exploration programs elsewhere were any indication. Due to the lagging demand and weak prices in 1969, however, some mines and mills were closed or production was curtailed, and some planned construction was postponed.

Zinc. World mine production of zinc increased almost 4%, but smelter output rose 9%. Among the mine producers, Canada (22%) remained the largest, followed by the Soviet Union (11%). In 1969, Australia (9.5%) managed to edge the United States (9.4%) out of third place, although the latter continued to lead (19%) in smelter production, followed by Japan (14%) and the Soviet Union (12%). Mine and smelter production and world consumption of zinc all rose in 1969, although part of the apparent gain was a return to normal conditions from the 1968 strike in the U.S. Mine productive capacity was fairly evenly and widely distributed, and most of the increased output originated from established properties (Australia +20%), although the new Anvil Point Mine came into production in Canada's Yukon Territory. As a result largely of healthy demand and to a lesser degree of inflation, zinc prices rose from £114 to £131 per long ton on the London Metal Exchange between January and December. During the same period, the U.S. producer price rose from 13.5 cents to 15.5 cents per pound, and the producer price outside North America from £114 to £130 per long ton.

(F. H. Sĸ.)

See also Fuel and Power; Geology; Industrial Review; Metallurgy.

Molecular Biology

Progress in science does not invariably consist of satisfying sequences from one logical step to the next, as was amply demonstrated in 1970 in molecular biology. In addition to some exciting forward progress, there were two major reversals. One of these was the reversal of the cardinal tenet of molecular biology, the central dogma enunciated by Francis Crick, which asserted that the flow of biological information in living systems invariably follows the pattern deoxyribonucleic acid (DNA) → ribonucleic acid (RNA) → protein. The other major reversal concerned DNA polymerase, the enzyme used by A. Kornberg to synthesize DNA in vitro in his Nobel prize-winning experiments, and again in 1967 by M. Goulian and Kornberg to synthesize viral core DNA that was indistinguishable from natural DNA.

A growing suspicion that DNA polymerase is not used to replicate DNA in living cells stemmed mainly from the observation that it replicates single strands of DNA only in one direction, called the 5′ to 3′ direction. But DNA is double-stranded, the two strands have opposite polarities, and in living cells both strands are replicated in the same direction and at the same rate. Searches for an enzyme capable of replicating in the complementary, or 3′ to 5′, direction had been unsuccessful and in 1970 other findings cast more doubt on the Kornberg enzyme's role in replication.

It now appeared that DNA polymerase could function principally in the repair of DNA rather than its replication. R. E. Moses and C. C. Richardson at Harvard University reported the results of studies that allowed DNA replication to be distinguished from DNA repair. They found that cells of the bacterium *Escherichia coli* treated with toluene retained many physiological functions but were permeable to many small molecules such as the precursors of DNA. They used this system to show that DNA replication could differ from repair synthesis in several ways. DNA replication requires the four deoxyribonucleoside triphosphates but does not require exogenous DNA and is markedly stimulated by adenosine triphosphate, a nucleotide not required by DNA polymerase. The rate of synthesis in this system is comparable to that observed in vivo, and synthesis is abolished at the restrictive temperature in DNA temperature-sensitive mutants. In addition, a mutant bacterium was found that has only 1% of the usual DNA polymerase activity but multiplies normally nonetheless. The mutant is extremely sensitive to ultraviolet light and X rays, as would be expected for cells deficient in the ability to repair induced damage to DNA.

Teminism. The most significant story of 1970 was the demonstration that RNA can serve as a template for DNA synthesis. This possibility was first proposed in 1964 by H. Temin, a University of Wisconsin biologist, to account for the persistent cell transformation acquired by cells infected with RNA tumour viruses. Temin suggested that these viruses utilize their single-stranded RNA as a template to direct the synthesis of DNA, and that a DNA copy of the viral genome is integrated into the host genome, which also is DNA, in a fashion similar to that described for lysogeny in bacteria. This could account for the permanent transformation of the host cell, which presumably leads to tumour production.

The evidence to support this proposal came from a number of observations. For example, cell transformation by RNA tumour viruses can be inhibited by compounds that inhibit DNA synthesis, suggestive evidence that transformed cells contained more DNA capable of hybridizing with the virus RNA than non-transformed cells. The fact that the formation of virions, the uncoated viral-RNA molecules, in RNA-tumour-virus transformed cells could be blocked by actinomycin C, a drug known to inhibit the activity of DNA-dependent RNA polymerase, suggested that a DNA template was involved in their formation. The integration of a DNA copy of the viral genome into the host cell's DNA genome could also account for the hereditary transmission of high leukemia frequency to hybrids of strains of mice, if the viral genome became established in the germinal cell line.

A later report, published by Temin in 1970, provided the first direct evidence that such a process does exist and set off a deluge of research activity showing that RNA-dependent DNA-polymerase activity exists in six different RNA tumour viruses: Rauscher murine leukemia virus, Moloney sarcoma virus, mammary tumour virus, feline leukemia virus, monkey mammary tumour virus, and Rous sarcoma virus. It was not certain whether the whole RNA viral molecule is copied and integrated or only part or parts of it. The number and characteristics of the enzymes involved in this process and the exact role of the DNA copy of the viral genome in the viral replication process had yet to be determined. While the finding had an impact on biological theory, it also might have very practical importance for the treatment of tumours caused by these viruses, if it could be found that the RNA-dependent DNA polymerase is specific for these viruses and not generally found in cells.

Gene Synthesis. The year 1970 also was host to some major technical accomplishments. As reported during 1969, the first genes had been isolated by J. Beckwith and his associates at Harvard Medical School. Subsequently, the first synthetic gene was produced from chemical components by H. G. Khorana and his group at the University of Wisconsin. The nucleotide sequence for this gene, which specifies the transfer RNA (tRNA) for alanine in yeast, had been determined earlier at the same institution by R. W. Holley.

A tRNA molecule serves to decode genetic information and translate it from nucleic acid to functional protein. Once the sequence for the tRNA was known, it was possible to determine the base sequence of the gene that coded for it by known base-pairing properties. The actual assembly of the yeast alanine tRNA began with the synthesis of 15 small oligonucleotides, short chains of bases attached together chemically. This was accomplished by successive condensations of nucleotide groups two to four bases in length. The process involved end-to-end additions. To do this, other reactive groups of these molecules had to be blocked chemically to ensure the proper reaction at only the specified site. After each addition the product had to be recovered and purified and protective groups removed. The resulting oligonucleotides were 5–20 bases in length. The single-stranded oligonucleotides were made double-stranded enzymatically by use of DNA polymerase. These segments contained overlapping regions at their ends so that they could be joined end to end by base pairing. The end-to-end joining was made permanent by covalent bonding

WIDE WORLD
Harry Rubin, professor of molecular biology at the University of California at Berkeley, detected a chemical that leaks from malignant cells and temporarily causes normal cells to grow wildly as if cancerous.

Missiles:
see Defense

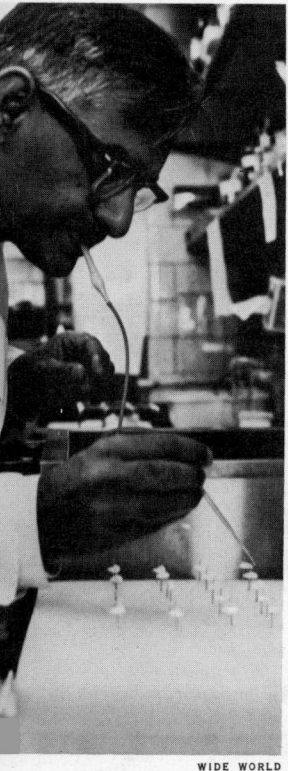

WIDE WORLD

H. Gobind Khorana, 1968 Nobel Prize winner, announced June 2, 1970, that he and his colleagues at the University of Wisconsin had produced the first total synthesis of a gene.

using the enzyme polynucleotide ligase from the bacteriophage T4. The final product was a DNA sequence of 77 base-pairs, one strand of which codes for yeast alanine tRNA. Now that two methods for isolating genes were available, rapid advances in the understanding of biological processes at the molecular genetic level could be expected. Of the two methods, however, the Harvard purifying technique could only be used in bacterial systems with rather specific properties; Khorana's synthetic technique appeared to have more general applicability.

Subcellular Studies. In yet another spectacular advance, bacterial genes in action were visualized by an extension of the electron microscope methods developed earlier by O. Miller at Oak Ridge (Tenn.) National Laboratory to examine genes in larger, more complex cells. Bacteria with fragile cell walls were ruptured osmotically and the cell contents gently extruded. These contents included genes in the act of producing messenger RNA (mRNA). During this transcription, a single active gene, or cistron, which is some one to three microns in length, produces a number of messenger molecules simultaneously. Each messenger strand emanates from an observable enzyme molecule, RNA polymerase, attached to the DNA. The polymerase molecules are irregularly spaced along the DNA, averaging about 0.2 microns apart. As the cistron is transcribed from one end to the other, the lengths of the mRNA strands increase according to the distance traveled by the polymerase.

In addition, each messenger strand is saturated with ribosomes, all presumably translating the RNA message as they synthesize protein. The number of ribosomes increases with the length of each mRNA strand. As many as 40 ribosomes were observed on the longest strands, although the average number was about 20. Because each mRNA molecule is saturated with ribosomes, and because all mRNA molecules are attached to the DNA, the rate of protein synthesis is controlled by the speed of transcription. Only relatively few cistrons, however, appeared to be undergoing transcription at any one time. In addition, some genes contain branching mRNA strands attached by polymerase molecules, but have no ribosomes attached to them. Presumably, these are ribosomal-RNA genes; that is, the RNA that these produce is packaged into ribosomes. The lengths of these genes agreed with earlier estimates for the lengths of RNA cistrons.

An important contribution to our knowledge of the ribosome itself was made in 1970 by S. Mizushima and M. Nomura from the University of Wisconsin. Of the two major components of the bacterial ribosome, the 30S and the 50S particles, the 30S particle was found to consist almost entirely of ribonucleic acid (16S RNA) and protein; 21 different proteins, accounting for all of the protein in the particle, were separated and characterized. The Wisconsin workers were able to reconstitute a 30S particle from the purified proteins and the 16S RNA and found that it was active in protein synthesis. They also found that the reassembly of the particle is cooperative, that is, very few of the proteins bind 16S RNA but once two or three specific proteins bind the RNA, others can then bind; thus, the assembly of a 30S particle requires a specific order of binding reactions.

Also in 1970, other workers examined animal cell membranes using methods similar to those used with the ribosome. J. Leonard at the Sloan-Kettering Institute in New York and J. Gwynne and C. Tanford at Duke University reported that the proteins of red

blood cell membranes fall into several different molecular weight classes ranging from about 15,000 to 200,000. It appeared that perhaps as much as 60% of the proteins have a molecular weight greater than 85,000. One protein that was a major constituent of the membrane had a molecular weight of about 200,000 and was the largest single polypeptide chain noted in mammalian tissue, with the exception of one from myosin of muscle. The problem of understanding how these proteins interact with specific lipids to form the membrane remained unclear.

It was also thought that a new instrument might become particularly valuable in studying macromolecules at the molecular level and, in particular, might permit base sequence determination of nucleic acids from electron micrographs. With a new type of electron microscope, A. Crewe and his associates at the University of Chicago observed images of individual uranium atoms in organic material. This instrument, which used scattered electrons to generate images at a magnification of more than a millionfold, had not yet reached the resolution of conventional electron microscopes, but the technique produced much better image contrast. Because of this contrast it was theoretically possible to mark genetic materials at the molecular level with metal atoms that could be observed.

Protein Analyses. X-ray diffraction analyses of protein structures proceeded at a brisk pace during 1970. Dorothy Hodgkin's group at Oxford determined the three-dimensional structure of the insulin molecule. Their analysis required the use of the method of "isomorphous replacement," in which known sites in the molecule are replaced by a heavy-metal atom, modifying the diffraction image. The three-dimensional structure of a smaller biologically important molecule, adenosine triphosphate, was determined to an exceptionally high resolution of 0.9 angstroms by a group at Cambridge.

The three-dimensional structure of crystalline lactate dehydrogenase, the largest enzyme to be analyzed to date, was reported in 1970 by a group of nine crystallographers at Purdue University under the leadership of M. G. Rossmann. Lactate dehydrogenase is one of the critical enzymes involved in the production of energy from glucose under anaerobic conditions and is present in most animal species. There are two major types of the enzyme, the M form, which predominates in skeletal muscle, and the H form, found in heart muscle. While the M form from dogfish muscle was studied by the Purdue group, it was clear that the structure of the enzyme in higher animals is very similar. The electron density distribution of the crystalline enzyme was established at 2.8 Å resolution by means of X-ray diffraction analysis. Several structural features of the enzyme could now be defined more precisely, including the substrate binding site containing the coenzyme, diphosphopyridine nucleotide, and the exact relationships among the four polypeptide chain subunits.

A major goal for the structure determinations of enzymes is to find out how these function, and X-ray crystallographers were well on their way toward this goal. Each enzyme has an "active site" that controls the reaction it catalyzes. W. N. Lipscomb and his associates (Harvard) showed that carboxypeptidase A changes its conformation extensively when the active site of this enzyme binds the substrate glycyltyrosine. This was the first demonstration of "induced fit," the theory that the necessary alignment of catalytic groups of the enzyme is induced during binding of the substrate. Conformational changes were also observed by other groups in α-chymotrypsin, elastase, and staphylococcal nuclease.

In general, enzyme cores contain pleated sheet structures, backbone chains have points of definite overall folding, and active sites do not lie in any particular cleft, although they do appear to be situated at points of convergence of different segments of the main chain. The substrate also may undergo a configurational change during an enzyme reaction. Each of four enzymes catalyzing the synthesis or cleavage of citrate did so by inversion of the configuration at the methyl or methylene group of the substrate.

The use of cell fusion during the last few years had transformed somatic cell genetics into an experimental discipline. New hybrid cells could be formed during the fusion of two cells, for example from man and mouse, and could be studied for both the relationship between the particular chromosomes they carry and the biochemical properties of the hybrid cells. Using such man-mouse hybrids, two independent groups, at Stanford and at Yale, established that the human genes controlling lactate dehydrogenase B and peptidase B are linked, either structurally or by their control mechanisms. The technique was also extended to study the regulation of DNA synthesis and mitosis by fusion of like cells from different phases in their life cycle. These cells usually were fused by the addition of high multiplicities of inactivated viruses, such as Sendai or Newcastle-disease virus. Although the mechanism leading to fusion was unknown, it was clear that this powerful technique could tell us a good deal about human cells.

Plant cells, too, were fused, by E. C. Cocking and his co-workers at Nottingham. They fused cells by exposing them to sodium nitrate; viruses were not required. The significance of the work with plant cells was that it now permitted the hybridization of plants impossible to hybridize before by greenhouse or conventional methods, and the breeding of more productive and disease-resistant agricultural plants from them. (JA. C. C.; R. L. HI.; H. E. KU.)

See also **Biological Sciences; Medicine.**

Monaco

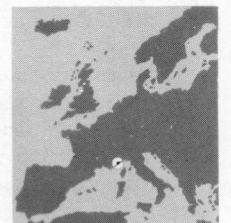

A sovereign principality on the northern Mediterranean coast, Monaco is bounded on all land sides by the French *département* of Alpes-Maritimes. Area: 0.579 sq.mi. (1.51 sq.km.). Pop. (1970 est.): 23,614. Cap.: Monaco-Ville. Language: French. Religion: Roman Catholic. Prince, Rainier III; minister of state in 1970, François-Didier Gregh.

The problems involved in the modernization of Monaco's tourist facilities and appeal continued into

MONACO
Education. (1967–68) Primary, pupils 1,162, teachers 51; secondary, pupils 1,424, teachers 86; vocational, pupils 204, teachers 7.
Finance. Monetary unit: French franc, with a par value of Fr. 5.55 to U.S. \$1 (Fr. 13.33 = £1 sterling). Budget (1969 est.): revenue Fr. 161,804,000; expenditure Fr. 160,664,000. Tourism: visitors (1967) 78,300; gross receipts (1966) U.S. \$6.1 million.

1970. A report stated that "Monaco is full of memories but needs more tourists." In the pre-World War II period the principality had boasted over 70 hotels with nearly 4,000 rooms, but by 1970 the number of hotels had fallen to less than 35 and the number of rooms to under 1,600. Tourists, especially Americans, were flocking to southern France, Italy, and Spain, but the number visiting Monaco showed only a slight gain. Even these visitors were predominantly old or middle-aged.

As part of the effort to remedy this situation, reclamation projects along the Mediterranean shore continued. This work, which had gone on for a decade and was expected to require an additional five years before completion, would increase the area of the principality by nearly 20%. The largest and most promising of the projects involved the Fontvieille Artificial Promontory, where an international group was building a village over the sea. All automobiles were to be banished underground, and the residential centre would include hotels, motels, and parks—even an American-style Holiday Inn—designed to attract younger and more affluent tourists. (R. D. Ho.)

Money and Banking

The dominant note in 1970 was no longer one of recurrent crisis in the exchange markets but rather of the worldwide spread and intensification of price inflation. Indeed, as far as the international monetary system was concerned, the year began in an atmosphere of relative calm.

In little more than two years the realignment of three major currencies had taken place: the devaluation of sterling in November 1967, the devaluation of the French franc in August 1969, and, shortly afterward, the revaluation of the West German mark in October. These developments, combined with the introduction of the "two-tier" gold price in March 1968 and the gold sales agreement reached between South Africa and the International Monetary Fund (IMF) in December 1969, helped to restore tranquillity to the gold and foreign exchange markets. Finally, under the auspices of the IMF, the new system of Special Drawing Rights was inaugurated at the beginning of 1970 with an initial allocation of \$3.5 billion.

This picture of greater international stability was not without blemishes. Most important, protracted domestic inflation had led to a serious deterioration in the U.S. balance of payments position from 1965 to 1969. Moreover, this development, though it had been camouflaged by the extensive borrowing by U.S. banks in the Eurodollar market, had been a prime mover in the propagation of inflation internationally. A lesser cause for concern was Japan's persistently large current-account surplus, which in fact the authorities had managed to offset by encouraging compensating capital outflows.

Nonetheless, the immediate attention of policy makers could now be turned to the problem of combating inflation, which had broadened its grip to include practically all of the Western industrial countries. Particularly disquieting was the fact that the spiraling interaction of wages and prices had seemingly become more difficult to control by means of conventional stabilization instruments. By late 1969 monetary restraint, often backed by restrictive budget policies, was being applied with considerable severity almost everywhere, and interest rates in the principal financial centres had risen to peaks without modern parallel.

The impetus for the international rise in interest rates had come largely from the U.S., where a severely tight monetary policy had led to heavy borrowing in the international money and capital markets. However, by early 1970, after a considerable decline in production, the Federal Reserve authorities were ready to aim at "a modest growth in the monetary aggregates, with about equal weight being given to bank credit and the money stock." This cautious objective appeared to have remained substantially unchanged throughout 1970, but evidence of a slackening of the rate of price inflation was slow to emerge.

Inflationary pressure in Canada, though slightly less severe than in the U.S., made it necessary for restrictive budget and monetary policies to be maintained in early 1970. However, unemployment rose sharply and a growing trade surplus, coupled with capital inflows, resulted in a steep rise in the country's monetary reserves.

To deal with this situation, the authorities on June 1 temporarily ceased intervention to keep the Canadian dollar within its IMF parity margins, with the result that the spot rate soon moved to a premium of about 5%. Among other things this measure gave greater scope for monetary action, and by November the bank rate was brought down to 6%, compared with 8% from July 1969 to May 1970.

In the U.K., against a background of continuing tight budget policy, monetary restraint was made less severe in 1970. In March and April the bank rate was reduced in two stages from 8 to 7%, though this was mainly for external reasons, and in May the quantitative ceiling on bank advances was lifted and replaced by an informal guideline. However, exceptionally large negotiated wage increases soon posed a new threat to stability. By autumn the expansion of bank credit and the money supply was running well above the rate envisaged for the financial year as a whole, and at the end of October new restrictive action was taken.

In the U.S., Canada, and the U.K., demand inflation was effectively brought under control by early 1970. After this, with output relatively stagnant or falling and unemployment reaching quite high levels by past standards, the persistence of inflation was due mainly to the strength of wage pressures and their interaction with prices. In the U.S. the authorities deliberately rejected any direct attempt to curb wage demands, while in the U.K. efforts to apply an incomes policy collapsed toward the end of 1969. Canada sought to formulate such a policy in 1970, but, despite these efforts, wage settlements in industry continued to provide for increases of about 9% a year.

In the continental European countries, both goods and labour markets remained under severe strain over most or the whole of 1970, with the result that demand inflation went hand in hand with a veritable explosion on the wages front.

Compared with year-earlier levels, wage rates (or earnings) by the summer of 1970 had risen by around 10% in Austria, Belgium, France, and the Netherlands, by close to 15% in Germany and Sweden, and by 20% in Italy. One saving feature was that productivity gains were still appreciable, thus helping to keep the rise in consumer prices to a range of about 4–6%, but monetary policy was inevitably called upon to play a major stabilizing role.

On the continent the movement of interest rates in 1970 followed a mixed pattern. Up to the summer, official discount rates either were adjusted further upward or remained fixed at already high levels. In March the Bundesbank raised its rate from 6 to 7½%, while that of the Bank of Italy went up from 4 to 5½%. But in West Germany, after new restrictive fiscal measures had been taken, the official discount rate was lowered in July to 7%. In France, thanks to both devaluation and restrictive domestic policies, the discount rate could be brought down from 8 to 7½% in August. In October 1970, associated with declines in short-term market rates, official discount rates were reduced in Belgium and France from 7½ to 7%. But market rates in other countries, after reaching a peak during the summer, had drifted down only a little by early autumn. Subsequently, on November 17, a few days after the U.S. discount rate had been cut by one fourth of a percentage point, West Germany brought its rate down from 7 to 6½%; on December 4 the West German rate was lowered to 6%.

Long-term interest rates on the continent, after moving up sharply in 1969, generally continued to rise until the summer of 1970, thereafter leveling off or declining somewhat. Italy's abandonment of its policy of interest rate stabilization in the summer of 1969 led to a marked rise in the yield on government bonds, from 5.6 to over 8% within 12 months, while in West Germany the government bond yield went up from only 6.3% in early 1969 to 8.7% by mid-1970. Pronounced increases also occurred in Belgium, the Netherlands, and Switzerland, though Switzerland's long-term rates remained about two percentage points lower than elsewhere. In France, however, long-term yields gradually declined from early 1970 onward.

Eurocurrency and Eurobond Markets. The moderate relaxation of U.S. monetary policy contributed toward a substantial slowdown in the growth of the Eurodollar market in 1970. The U.S. banks' Eurodollar borrowings, the increase in which had been the main impulse behind the extremely rapid expansion of the market in the first three quarters of 1969, reached a peak of $15 billion in November 1969. They subsequently declined to about $12 billion in April 1970 and, following the partial suspension of the Regulation Q ceilings, went below $10 billion in October.

This sharp decline in the demand for Eurodollars by the U.S. banks was reflected in a pronounced easing of market conditions. Although at times there was substantial demand for Eurodollar funds from other areas, the three-month Eurodollar deposit rate in London dropped from over 11% in December 1969 to below 7% in November 1970. The covered interest arbitrage premiums on Eurodollars over investments in national markets, which in the course of 1969 had at times exceeded 6%, narrowed sharply or were even reversed. As a result, the flow of new funds into the Eurodollar market began to peter out. At the same time, however, these developments encouraged the growth of the Euromarkets in Swiss francs and marks.

On the Eurobond market, new-issues activity continued to decline in the first half of 1970 but began to pick up again in the third quarter. For the first nine months as a whole, the volume of international issues with maturities of five years or more came to only $1.7 billion, against $2.2 and $2.6 billion in the corresponding periods of 1969 and 1968, respectively. The yield on outstanding dollar bonds, moving counter to the trend in the Eurodollar market, climbed to

KEYSTONE

The new bank rate of 7½% appears on the wall of London's Stock Exchange, March 5, 1970, the day it was lowered.

more than 10% by mid-1970, whereupon a modest decline set in.

The absorptive capacity of the Eurobond market was limited in 1970 primarily by the tightness of monetary conditions on the continent, particularly in West Germany. Moreover, the practice of encouraging resident borrowers to have recourse to the market, earlier characteristic mainly of the U.S., had in more recent years spread to France, the U.K., and Italy. As a result, the market had become more "European" from the demand side, with the proportion of total issues accounted for by Western European borrowers rising from less than one-quarter in 1968 to over one-half in January–September 1970. Correspondingly, issues by U.S. companies and their subsidiaries declined in both absolute and relative terms.

Coupled with these developments, 1970 saw the introduction of publicly offered variable-interest ten-year notes and the appearance of a substantial volume of five-year notes denominated in Dutch guilders. Convertible dollar issues declined sharply in importance, while straight dollar bond issues made a notable comeback.

United States. When 1970 opened, the policy of monetary restraint had been in force a little more than a year. Its effects were evident in a slowing down in the growth of the money supply (currency plus demand deposits) to $2\frac{1}{2}\%$ from 7.2% in the preceding year. But, in addition, since the ceiling rates payable on time deposits under Regulation Q had been kept unchanged while market interest rates rose, the banks had lost some $13 billion of large time certificates of deposit (CDs) between November 1968 and the end of 1969.

The banks sought to compensate for this loss by turning on a major scale to the Eurocurrency market, where they were free to pay rates above the Regulation Q ceilings. In another circumvention of Regulation Q, they had their affiliates issue large amounts of commercial paper, the proceeds of which were used to finance loans transferred from the parent institutions.

Nonetheless, overall credit restraint had gradually been made effective, and the expansion of the commercial banks' total loans and investments, including those held by domestic subsidiaries, had slowed down considerably by the second half of 1969. This had been achieved, however, only at the cost of record high interest rates. Moreover, although real output had ceased to expand, wage pressures were still strong, the December unemployment rate was no more than $3\frac{1}{2}\%$, and consumer prices were rising at about 6% per year.

The first move toward realignment of monetary policy occurred in January 1970, when Regulation Q ceilings on time deposits were raised across the board. The limit payable, for example, on single-maturity deposits of 60–89 days was increased from $5\frac{3}{4}$ to $6\frac{1}{2}\%$, while that on deposits of 360 days or more went up from $6\frac{1}{4}$ to $7\frac{1}{2}\%$. However, as this action was primarily aimed at correcting previous distortions in financial flows, it could not clearly be interpreted as relaxation of monetary restraint.

A more decisive move came a little later, when the Federal Reserve Open Market Committee decided that policy should aim at modest growth in the "monetary aggregates." This took place against a background of a further decline in industrial production in January, for the sixth consecutive month, and of a marked rise in unemployment. It also coincided with

the presentation of the 1970–71 budget showing a surplus of $1.3 billion.

The shift in policy emphasis to the "monetary aggregates," principally the money supply and bank credit, implied giving such aggregates greater operational weight in short-term monetary management than in the past, when attention had been focused relatively more on the banks' "free" (excess minus borrowed) reserves and on money-market interest rates. On the other hand, the new emphasis did not preclude the possibility that credit-market conditions and interest rates might, on occasion, have to be given priority.

Up to April short-term interest rates fell substantially, with the yield on three-month Treasury bills going down to an average of $6\frac{1}{2}\%$ from 7.87% in January. Toward the end of March the banks reduced their prime lending rate from $8\frac{1}{2}$ to 8%. In late April and early May, however, there was a fairly sharp reversal in the movement of money-market rates.

In part this reflected the market's realization that the intended relaxation of monetary policy was less than had been anticipated, but it was also accentuated in early May by the U.S. intervention in Cambodia and by large Treasury refunding needs. About this time, in order to lend support to the equities market, the authorities reduced cash margin requirements on security purchases.

After going as high as 7% at the end of May, the yield on three-month Treasury bills began to decline. In late June, however, new disturbances threatened, especially in the commercial-paper market, as a result of the failure of the Penn Central railway. To increase alternative means of financing, and thus quell fears of a liquidity crisis, the Federal Reserve suspended Regulation Q ceilings for large, single-maturity deposits with maturities of 30–89 days.

Subsequently, in mid-August, two further measures were announced. With effect from October 1, reserve requirements against time deposits were reduced from 6 to 5% and, in line with earlier proposals, reserve requirements were extended to cover, as from mid-September, commercial paper issued by bank af-

Selected Interest Rates

Country		1968 June	June	1969 Sept.	Dec.	March	1970 June	Sept.
Belgium	A	3.75	6.00	7.50	7.50	7.50	7.50	7.50
	B1	2.64	4.28	7.48	6.07	6.65	6.34	5.30
	C	6.44	7.19	7.37	7.73	7.65	7.77	8.01
France	A	3.50	7.00	7.00	8.00	8.00	8.00	7.50
	B1	5.77	9.46	9.40	10.41	9.42	9.35	8.12
	C	6.63	8.01	8.12	8.51	8.70	8.47	8.42
Germany, West	A	3.00	5.00	6.00	6.00	7.50	7.50	7.00
	B2	2.75	4.75	5.75	5.75	7.00	7.00	6.75
	C	6.40	6.70	7.20	7.60	8.10	8.70	8.50
Italy	A	3.50	3.50	4.00	4.00	5.50	5.50	5.50
	B2	3.63	4.44	4.99	4.99	6.95	6.95	6.95
	C	5.66	5.65	5.90	6.33	7.46	7.95	8.10
Netherlands	A	4.50	5.50	6.00	6.00	6.00	6.00	6.00
	B2	4.68	5.66	6.18	6.18	6.18	6.18	6.18
	C	6.49	7.53	7.98	7.86	8.30	8.52	8.08
Switzerland	A	3.00	3.00	3.75	3.75	3.75	3.75	3.75
	B1	2.69	3.25	4.70	4.75	3.63	2.38	2.00
	C	4.34	4.69	5.37	5.34	5.78	6.03	5.86
United Kingdom	A	7.50	8.00	8.00	8.00	7.50	7.00	7.00
	B2	7.21	7.90	7.80	7.70	7.26	6.87	6.82
	C	7.78	9.38	9.18	8.95	8.55	9.40	9.30
United States	A	5.50	6.00	6.00	6.00	6.00	6.00	6.00
	B2	5.54	6.49	7.13	7.72	6.71	6.74	6.24
	C	5.23	6.06	6.32	6.81	6.39	6.99	6.63
Canada	A	7.50	7.50	8.00	8.00	8.00	7.00	6.50
	B2	6.75	7.03	7.75	7.35	7.35	5.90	5.44
	C	6.62	7.54	7.94	8.33	7.93	8.03	7.88
Japan	A	6.21	5.84	6.25	6.25	6.25	6.25	6.25
	B1	7.67	6.57	8.00	8.25	8.25	8.00	8.25
	C	8.83	8.80	9.01	9.07	9.21	9.38	9.15

A = Central bank's discount rate.
B = Money-market rate.
  B1 = Day-to-day money.
  B2 = 90-day Treasury bills; one-year bills in the case of Italy.
C = Long-term government bond yield.

BEN ROTH AGENCY

—Mahood, © "Punch."

filiates. These changes were followed toward the end of September by a reduction in the banks' prime lending rate from 8 to 7½%.

Meanwhile, money-market rates generally were tending downward, and the banks found themselves increasingly able to compete for time deposits, including CDs, of all maturities. By early November 1970 commercial-bank time deposits had risen 15% above their year-earlier level, while the money supply, narrowly defined, was up by 3.4%. However, a better measure of actual developments is provided by the "adjusted credit proxy," which includes not only bank deposits but also bank-related commercial paper and Eurodollar borrowings. In early November this indicator was 6.8% above the level of a year earlier. By this time the three-month Treasury bill yield had fallen to 5½%.

In the capital market, on the other hand, yields generally kept to high levels in 1970, with those on corporate bonds actually showing an appreciable further increase. While this was in some measure ascribable to the continuing strong demand for capital owing to profit and liquidity strains, inflationary expectations also played a part. In the late summer and early autumn industrial production fell further, partly because of a strike at General Motors. The evidence of a slowing down of the price rise was weak but encouraging. Yet it had become likely that the federal government's budget for fiscal 1970–71 might fall into deficit by as much as $15 billion, mainly because of the slump-induced decline in tax revenue, and that this would put increased pressure on the capital markets.

Toward mid-November, after unemployment had risen to 5.6%, the official discount rate was reduced from 6 to 5¾%, and the banks followed immediately with a cut in their prime lending rate from 7½ to 7¼%. Coincident with these changes, however, the settlement of the strike in the automobile industry, on terms that appeared distinctly inflationary, dampened hopes for a slackening of the wage-price spiral. On November 30 the Federal Reserve announced its second cut in the discount rate in three weeks, from 5¾ to 5½%. At the same time it made certain changes in the reserve requirements against Eurodollar borrowings, designed to reduce the banks' incentive to make repayments. By late December the prime rate had been lowered to 6¾% in the fifth such reduction since March.

In the housing market, long depressed by a shortage of mortgage funds, a sustained recovery got under way early in 1970. This was the result primarily of the relaxation of credit restraint, together with a high rate of personal savings and a continual expansion in capital issues by federal agencies in support of mortgage lending activity. The accelerated flow of mortgage credit took place mainly through the savings and loan associations and the mutual savings banks. Mortgage interest rates edged up somewhat during the year. In a further attempt to encourage construction, the maximum rate on home mortgages backed by the Federal Housing and Veterans administrations was cut from 8½ to 8% in early December.

United Kingdom. The forceful combination of fiscal and monetary policies pursued in 1969 began to yield very favourable results in the second half of the year. The balance of payments on current account shifted into substantial surplus, and this was followed in late 1969 and early 1970 by large inflows of capital. Though by mid-1970 both the current-account surplus and capital inflows had considerably diminished, the external position was still fairly strong, and the authorities had succeeded in reducing their indebtedness to the IMF and other monetary authorities by some £1,900 million.

The monetary impact of the restrictive domestic policies can best be seen in the behaviour of "domestic credit expansion." This aggregate, essentially a money-supply concept adjusted for the effects of the balance of payments surplus or deficit, had recently played a prominent part in U.K. monetary discussion. Domestic credit expansion, after having amounted to £2,300 million in the 1967–68 financial year, dropped to £1,200 million in 1968–69 and then to a negative figure of £610 million in the year ended April 1970.

The turnaround consisted of two main elements: (1) the swing of the public sector from large deficit into a surplus of £535 million in 1969–70; and (2) heavy sales of public-sector debt to the nonbank public (£780 million in 1969–70). Another contributing factor was that bank lending to the private sector was kept under stringent control. The growth of the money supply in 1969–70 dropped to less than 2%, against an increase of nearly 6½% in the preceding year.

In his April 1970 budget speech, the chancellor of the Exchequer announced that the target for domestic credit expansion in the year 1970–71 was to be £900 million, against the net contraction of £610 million in the year just ended. He envisaged a decline in the public sector's net surplus and a reduction in net sales of public debt to the nonbank public.

Moreover, in order to mitigate the liquidity squeeze on industry, the quantitative ceiling on bank advances in effect since devaluation was replaced by an informal guideline allowing for an increase in restricted lending of 5% over the financial year. Finance houses were asked to accept the same guidance. Finally, in view of the previous heavy inflow of funds, the bank rate was cut first in March from 8 to 7½% and again on budget day from 7½ to 7%. For the financial year as a whole, the chancellor foresaw an increase in the money supply of 5%.

This policy strategy, however reasonable in itself, was threatened from the outset by disquieting developments on the wage front. By late 1969 the government's incomes policy had broken down, and the wage settlements negotiated in the first half of 1970 were large and becoming progressively larger. This tendency, together with a weakening of the trade balance and the July dock strike, caused sterling to fall steadily during the summer toward its lower support point. By August the overall wage and salary bill was running almost 12% above the year-earlier level, and retail prices were up by some 6.8%. At the same time, output remained stagnant and unemployment stood at 2.7%.

In consequence, money and credit developments soon ran counter to policy intentions. In the April–June quarter the money supply rose at an unduly high rate, and domestic credit expansion was almost as much as had been envisaged for the whole financial year. Much of the difficulty stemmed from renewed pressures on the capital market. From early April up to the general election in June, the gilt-edged market was hit by fairly heavy net selling, which helped to drive the yield on long-dated government stock to nearly 9.8% in late June.

With the capital market unreceptive to new issues, business firms increasingly turned to bank advances, which had become less costly because of the bank rate reduction in April. The resulting rapid increase in advances prompted the Bank of England in July to ask the banks to exercise greater restraint.

In the autumn of 1970 stabilization policy had clearly reached an impasse. Fiscal and monetary restraint had led to stagnant output and relatively high unemployment without having any perceptible effect on wage inflation. Moreover, the external current-account surplus was no longer adequate to future needs. In late October, in a new departure, the Conservative government introduced a medium-term program designed to curb the growth of government expenditure and make it more selective. At the same time, it proposed a reduction of $2\frac{1}{2}$ percentage points in corporation tax and the standard rate of income tax, and planned to replace investment grants by a system of liberal depreciation allowances. On the other hand, the Bank of England, stating that firm restraint of bank lending was essential, decided at the end of October to make a new call for over £100 million of special deposits from the London clearing and Scottish banks.

EEC Countries. In West Germany the mark revaluation of 9.3%, when it finally came in the autumn of 1969, had been too long delayed to break the momentum of inflation. Moreover, although revaluation was followed by a huge reflux of funds abroad, the banks' liquidity cushion remained big enough to accommodate a large expansion of money and credit. In late January the government announced a stabilization program that sought to limit public expenditure in 1970 to 8.8% and postponed certain tax reliefs. In view of this limited action, the Bundesbank was impelled in early March to raise its discount rate from 6 to $7\frac{1}{2}$%, while simultaneously imposing a marginal reserve requirement on the banks' liabilities to nonresidents so as to discourage inflows of funds.

Nonetheless, with Eurodollar rates having declined, monetary restraint policy was faced with a familiar dilemma. From the spring onward West Germany began to experience large inflows of funds that more than offset its basic deficit and reflected mainly enterprise borrowing abroad. As a partial offset to these inflows, the Bundesbank raised reserve requirements at midyear.

More fundamental, however, were the fiscal measures taken in July, when accelerated depreciation allowances were temporarily suspended, and a one-year refundable surcharge was imposed on income and corporate taxes. This action permitted the Bundesbank, on external grounds, to lower its discount rate from $7\frac{1}{2}$ to 7%. This did not signal any easing of restraint policy, however, and toward mid-August the Bundesbank announced a rather severe set of incremental reserve requirements, related to the growth of liabilities to residents and nonresidents alike.

By late autumn a few signs of easing demand pressures were beginning to appear, but a new round of wage increases threatened a continuation of cost and price pressures well into 1971. In November–December, following the cut in the U.S. discount rate, West Germany brought its official rate down from 7 to 6% to help ward off capital inflows. In addition, the recently imposed set of marginal reserve requirements, which had not proved very effective, was abolished, being replaced by an equivalent increase in average reserve requirements. On the other hand, the special 30% marginal reserve requirement on liabilities to nonresidents, which had been in force up to August, was restored.

BEN ROTH AGENCY

"Looks good! Your temperature's dropping!"—Whitman, "Phoenix Gazette."

In the Netherlands excess aggregate demand and aggressive wage bargaining led—notwithstanding price controls—to a substantial increase in consumer prices and a deterioration in the external current-account position. As in West Germany, a dilemma was posed for monetary policy, and the authorities relied mainly on a quantitative ceiling on short-term bank credit, together with exchange control, to restrict business firms' borrowing abroad. Nevertheless, capital moved in through various channels, including portfolio security transactions, and official reserves increased sharply. In the autumn the Treasury sought to mop up liquidity by means of debt-management operations. A stabilization budget proposed for 1971 laid emphasis on increases in indirect taxation. Moreover, the government sought through a renewal of cooperative action to limit the extent of wage increases in the coming year.

In Italy the "hot autumn" of 1969, characterized

by a wave of strikes that continued into early 1970, resulted in a prolonged disruption of production and a sharp rise in wage rates. In the summer of 1969 monetary policy had shifted toward restraint, since by that time it had become clear that the policy of stabilizing bond prices had caused Italian interest rates to move increasingly out of line internationally, contributing to a massive outflow of capital. The continuation of restraint was underlined in March 1970, when the official discount rate was raised from 4 to $5\frac{1}{2}\%$, and by the summer the yield on long-term government bonds had moved to appreciably above 8%.

Selective measures, including encouragement to semipublic enterprises to borrow in international markets, helped to stem the net outflow of capital. The lira was further strengthened when a new government was formed in August and a stabilization program, consisting mainly of increases in indirect taxes, was announced. Subsequently, monetary restraint policy was relaxed somewhat as a stimulus to investment and output.

In France the devaluation of the franc in August 1969 found reinforcement both in the mark revaluation in October and in stringent domestic fiscal and monetary measures. Immediate steps were taken to reduce the budget deficit and to bring it into balance in 1970, and bank credit was subjected to tight quantitative controls. By late 1969 the external position had already turned around, and in 1970 the net inflow of foreign exchange permitted large debt repayments and a rebuilding of reserves. Over most of 1970 monetary policy remained generally restrictive—in the summer reserve requirements were raised twice to absorb excess liquidity stemming from the external surplus—but medium-term credit was selectively eased to encourage investment. In late August the official discount rate was reduced from 8 to $7\frac{1}{2}\%$, and in October to 7%—mainly to help keep money-market rates in line with those abroad, but also because industrial production had slackened from the spring onward. In October the Bank of France sought to shift to more indirect forms of credit control; quantitative restrictions were lifted, but this was accompanied by a reduction in rediscount ceilings.

In Belgium an external surplus kept monetary conditions fairly comfortable in late 1969 and early 1970. However, with economic overheating still a problem, the official discount rate was held at $7\frac{1}{2}\%$, and quantitative ceilings were adjusted with a view to limiting bank credit expansion in January–September to the same rate as that recorded in the corresponding period of 1969. Over the summer months demand pressures began to ease and wholesale prices flattened out. In September the limits for credit expansion were relaxed for the final quarter so as to permit a 12% increase in controlled credits, and one of 17% for total bank credit, for the year as a whole. By late October, with the balance of supply and demand distinctly better, the discount rate was reduced to 7% to help realign Belgian rates with those abroad.

Canada. The monetary restraint policy in force throughout 1969 had been reinforced by a large swing in the central government's budget from deficit to surplus. Output had slowed down sooner than in the U.S., and by the turn of the year unemployment had begun to rise steeply while the external trade surplus was becoming increasingly large. However, the continuing rapid rise in wages and prices kept budget and monetary policy in a restrictive stance in the early months of 1970. The external current account con-

tinued to gather strength, leading to increased capital inflows and an accelerating growth in official reserves.

In May the official discount rate was reduced from 8 to $7\frac{1}{2}\%$. Then, as a more decisive step to resolve the dilemma between domestic inflation and external surplus, the authorities on June 1 set the Canadian dollar free to float, while at the same time cutting the discount rate to 7%. By late August the Canadian dollar had moved close to parity with the U.S. dollar, and official reserves had recorded a substantial further increase.

From about March onward policy had aimed at a modest rate of monetary expansion. By this time the rate of price inflation had been reduced to some 3% per year. By the summer, however, output was stagnating and unemployment had reached a rate of $6\frac{3}{4}\%$, though bank loans were beginning to expand once again. In these circumstances, the official discount rate was brought down to $6\frac{1}{2}\%$ at the beginning of September and to 6% in November.

Japan. Later than most other countries, Japan shifted to a monetary restraint policy in September 1969. In view of its large, persistent external current account surplus, however, the measures taken were fairly mild, consisting of an increase in the discount rate from 5.84 to 6.25% and a rise in reserve requirements. At the same time, the authorities continued the practice, initiated in April, of using selective measures to encourage outflows of capital and thus a shift to yen financing. In consequence, official reserves grew only slowly, but industrial production went on rising steeply until August. Although the money supply had increased 16% in 12 months, financial markets had gradually become tighter, and there were also signs of a gradual slowdown in industrial production and investment. The upward movement of consumer prices had accelerated to a rate of 6% per annum, but wholesale prices had leveled out. Nonetheless, the authorities decided in early October to ease monetary policy by authorizing the banks to increase their lending relative to the growth recorded a year earlier. This was followed toward the end of the month by a reduction in the official discount rate from 6.25 to 6%.　　　　(W. D. McC.)

See also Cooperatives; Economics; Economy, World; Government Finance; Housing; Investment, International; Merchandising; Payments and Reserves, International; Stock Exchanges.

Mongolia

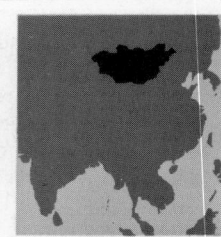

A people's republic of Asia lying between the U.S.S.R. and China, Mongolia occupies the geographic area known as Outer Mongolia. Area: 604,247 sq.mi. (1,565,000 sq.km.). Pop. (1969 est.): 1,290,000. Cap. and largest city: Ulan Bator (pop., 1969 est., 262,600). Language: Mongolian. Religion: Lamaistic Buddhism. First secretary of the Mongolian People's Revolutionary (Communist) Party and chairman of the Council of Ministers (premier) in 1970, Yumzhagiyin Tsedenbal; chairman of the Presidium of the Great People's Khural, Zhamsarangibin Sambuu.

On November 27 Premier Tsedenbal arrived in Moscow to sign with Aleksei N. Kosygin, the Soviet premier, a five-year economic agreement to aid Mongolia's development plan during 1971–75. Similar agreements had already been concluded with East Ger-

MONGOLIA

Education. (1968–69) Primary and secondary, pupils 213,590, teachers (1965–66) 5,721; teacher training, pupils 9,700; higher (including University of Ulan Bator), students 7,034.

Finance. Monetary unit: tugrik, with an official parity of 4 tugriks to U.S. $1 (9.60 tugriks = £1 sterling) and a tourist rate of 6 tugriks to U.S. $1 (14.40 tugriks = £1 sterling). Budget (1969 est.): revenue 1,860,000,000 tugriks; expenditure 1,843,-000,000 tugriks.

Foreign Trade. (1962) Imports U.S. $102.6 million; exports U.S. $68.5 million. Import sources (1960): U.S.S.R. 62%; China 23%; Czechoslovakia 5%. Export destinations (1960): U.S.S.R. 75%; Czechoslovakia 8%; China 5%. Main exports (1960): wool 44%; cattle 34%; butter and meat 8%; hides 6%.

Transport and Communications. Roads (1965) c. 75,000 km. (including c. 8,600 km. motorable). Railways (1967) c. 2,070 km. Telephones (Jan. 1969) 16,220. Radio receivers (Dec. 1968) 90,900.

Agriculture. Production (in 000; metric tons; 1968; 1967 in parentheses): wheat c. 335 (c. 325); barley c. 12 (c. 12); potatoes c. 25 (c. 20). Livestock (in 000; Dec. 1967): cattle c. 2,031; sheep c. 13,059; goats c. 4,800; horses 2,328; camels c. 680.

Industry. Production (in 000; metric tons): coal (1966) 51; crude oil (1967) 10; electricity (kw-hr.; 1968) 342,000.

many, Poland, Czechoslovakia, Hungary, and Bulgaria. Investment in the national economy during this five-year plan was expected to reach about 6 billion tugriks.

Marshal Andrei Grechko, the Soviet minister of defense, paid an official visit to Mongolia from September 9 to 11. Together with other Soviet leaders who had joined him on the visit, he inspected the two Mongolian Army divisions as well as the Soviet units stationed in the country.

Though the Chinese ambassador had been withdrawn from Ulan Bator in 1967, a four-member diplomatic mission remained there. However, work on all Chinese-financed projects had stopped, and unfinished blocks of flats, meant to be a gift of the powerful southern neighbour, continued to tower over the centre of Ulan Bator.

The new industrial town of Darkhan, being built by the Soviets, East Germans, Poles, Czechoslovaks, and Hungarians, continued to grow. It had about 26,000 inhabitants in 1970, but the population was expected to be 50,000 by 1980. (K. SM.)

Morocco

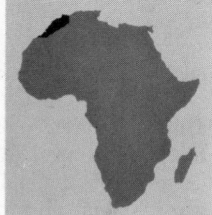

A constitutional monarchy of northwestern Africa, on the Atlantic Ocean and the Mediterranean Sea, Morocco is bordered by Algeria and Spanish Sahara. Area: 174,471 sq.mi. (451,880 sq.km.). Pop. (1969 est.): 15,050,000. Cap.: Rabat (pop., 1970, 325,000). Largest city: Casablanca (pop., 1970, 1,395,000). Language: Arabic; Berber. Religion: Muslim. King, Hassan II; prime minister in 1970, Ahmed Laraki.

After five years of direct rule by decree, King Hassan II decided in 1970 that Morocco should return to a modified form of parliamentary government. On July 24 a revised constitution, strengthening the authority of the king, was approved by 98.7% of the 4.5 million voters in a national referendum; during the following month, elections were held for 240 members of a new single-chamber legislature to be elected for six years.

The new legislature replaced the bicameral Parliament dissolved by the king in June 1965, after it had been in existence for only 18 months. Unlike the first Parliament, which was deeply divided between bickering factions, the new Chamber of Representatives was made up of a large majority of what were described officially as "neutrals." In fact, the elections were boycotted by the established political parties and their trade-union allies, all of whom rejected the constitution.

The elections took place in two stages. In the first, 150 representatives were chosen by five electoral colleges composed of members of existing local assemblies, professional organizations, and wage-earners' delegates. These electors had been themselves elected during the preceding year, for the most part on non-party tickets; these elections also were boycotted by the leftist National Union of Popular Forces (NUPF) and opposed by the old-guard Istiqlal Party. As a consequence, the 150 representatives chosen were practically all "neutrals" or independents.

In the second stage, the remaining 90 members of the chamber were elected by direct universal suffrage. Since the parties had decided to boycott the polls, the result was the election again of mainly "neutral" candidates. Only one party of any consequence—the Mouvement Populaire, representing the rural population—remained in favour of the regime,

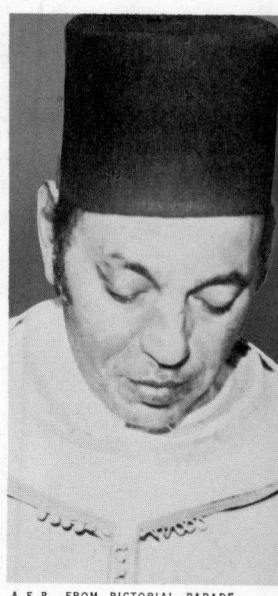

A.F.P. FROM PICTORIAL PARADE

King Hassan II inaugurates the Moroccan Center of Telecommunications in 1970.

MOROCCO

Education. (1967–68) Primary, pupils 1,105,237, teachers (including preprimary) 31,673; secondary, pupils 248,699, teachers 11,020; vocational, pupils 17,768, teachers (1965–66) 886; teacher training, students 1,164, teachers 90; higher (including 4 universities), students 10,505, teaching staff 480.

Finance. Monetary unit: dirham, with a par value of 5.06 dirhams to U.S. $1 (12.15 dirhams = £1 sterling). Gold and foreign exchange, central bank: (June 1970) U.S. $131 million; (June 1969) U.S. $128 million. Budget (1969 est.): revenue 2,620,000,000 dirhams; expenditure 2,770,000,000 dirhams. Money supply: (Dec. 1969) 5,159,000,000 dirhams; (Dec. 1968) 4,723,000,000 dirhams. Cost of living (Casablanca; 1963 = 100): (June 1970) 108; (June 1969) 109.

Foreign Trade. (1969) Imports 2,844,000,000 dirhams; exports 2,455,000,000 dirhams. Main import sources (1968): France 32%; U.S. 14%; West Germany 8%; Italy 5%. Main export destinations (1968): France 38%; West Germany 8%; U.K. 6%; Italy 6%. Main exports: phosphates 22%; citrus fruit 16%; tomatoes 6%; fish 5%. Tourism (1968): visitors 481,100; gross receipts U.S. $84 million.

Transport and Communications. Roads (1969) 24,678 (including 14 km. expressways). Motor vehicles in use (1969): passenger 202,792; commercial 79,242. Railways (1968): 1,788 km.; traffic 416 million passenger-km., freight 2,644,000,000 net ton-km. Air traffic (1969): 365 million passenger-km.; freight 3,380,000 net ton-km. Shipping (1969): merchant vessels 100 gross tons and over 39; gross tonnage 71,757. Telephones (Dec. 1968) 160,326. Radio receivers (Dec. 1968) 826,000. Television receivers (Dec. 1968) 100,-000.

Agriculture. Production (in 000; metric tons; 1969; 1968 in parentheses): wheat 1,469 (2,556); barley 2,030 (3,217); corn 450 (382); potatoes (1968) 160, (1967) 205; oranges 700 (775); dry peas c. 40 (c. 43); dry broad beans (1968) 170, (1967) 97; chickpeas c. 70 (118); wine (1968) c. 150, (1967) 137; olive oil c. 20 (60); figs (1968) c. 65, (1967) 65; dates (1968) c. 90, (1967) 80; tomatoes (1968) c. 277, (1967) 277; fish catch (1968) 219, (1967) 258. Livestock (in 000; 1968–69): cattle c. 3,500; sheep c. 14,400; goats (1967–68) c. 7,787; asses c. 950; horses and mules c. 735; camels (1967–68) c. 216; poultry c. 15,500.

Industry. Production (in 000; metric tons; 1969): coal 396; crude oil 58; cement 902; iron ore (55–60% metal content) 752; phosphate rock (1968) 10,756; manganese ore (metal content; 1968) 80; lead concentrates (metal content) 78; zinc concentrates (metal content; 1968) 32; electricity (public supply; kw-hr.) 1,538,000.

Montserrat: *see* Dependent States

Mormons: *see* Religion

and it joined with the "neutrals" and independents who formed a majority in the legislature.

King Hassan and government supporters asserted that the new chamber was a faithful representation of the Moroccan political reality, characterized in 1970 by a marked drift away from the old, established parties. The latter, meanwhile, joined together in a "National Front" (Al-Koutlah al-Wattania) and issued a manifesto calling for "authentic democracy."

In foreign affairs, King Hassan continued to consolidate his position in northwest Africa by strengthening ties with neighbouring Algeria, whose president, Col. Houari Boumédienne, he met in Tlemcen, Alg., on May 27, and with Mauritania, by conferring with Pres. Mokhtar Ould Daddah in Casablanca in June. The main outcome of those two meetings was the support that both Algeria and Mauritania promised to give to a joint plan for the "liberation" of Spanish Sahara, which bordered on the three states. Strategy for the "liberation" of Spain's sparsely populated desert colony was the main topic of talks at a tripartite summit held in September in Nouadhibou, Mauritania. The Tlemcen meeting also produced accords for economic cooperation between Algeria and Morocco in vast projects in the iron-ore mining and petroleum industries. The visit of the French foreign minister in December marked the resumption of cordial Franco-Moroccan relations following the breach caused by the Ben Barka affair of 1966.   (Sn. H.)

Motor Sports

Automobiles. The year 1970 may have ended the era when vistas seemed unlimited for automobile racing, as the sport found there were limits to the support offered by both sponsors and fans. And also, as if to indicate that there had been overexpansion in the ranks of drivers admitted to major series, the year proved one of the costliest to life in modern history, with at least 29 drivers meeting their deaths.

Three of the drivers who were contesting the world championship were killed in accidents. Bruce McLaren of New Zealand died when a sports racing car that he was testing at Silverstone, Eng., went out of control, while Piers Courage and the posthumous world champion, Jochen Rindt of Austria, were killed in a Grand Prix race and practice, respectively. These accidents underlined the hazards of modern motor racing. The danger stemmed not only from the very high speeds of which the three-litre single-seaters were capable but also from their lightweight construction and the amount of flammable fuel carried.

The Grand Prix Drivers Association (GPDA) was well aware of the increasing dangers and asked for additional safety precautions at most of the race circuits. In 1970 it boycotted the Nürburgring circuit in West Germany, the German Grand Prix normally held there being transferred at the association's request to the less interesting Hockenheim circuit. The use of airfoils in an extreme form, in order to increase tire adhesion, was banned, since these were apt to break off during a race; also, bag tanks for the fuel were introduced as safety measures, along with the previously required oil catch tanks and self-starters, to avoid damaged cars' fouling the track surface or stopping in the path of oncoming competitors.

In spite of these and other precautions and British journalist Louis Stanley's insistence on an efficient trackside hospital service, the three above-mentioned drivers died during the season. By the time of his death at Monza, Italy, which occurred in practice when a brake on his new Lotus 72 appeared to lock up at high speed, Rindt had won the Monaco, Dutch, French, British, and German Grand Prix races for Lotus, and was the rightful world champion. It was only toward the close of the Grand Prix season that Ferrari, with 12-cylinder engines, began to win races against the 8-cylinder cars of other entrants. As the season progressed, the once invincible Keith Duckworth-designed Cosworth-Ford V-8 engines grew notably unreliable, and the early promise of Scotsman Jackie Stewart, the previous year's world champion, in Ken Tyrrell's new March Formula One car faded.

The Spanish Grand Prix was marred by confusion and quarrels but was won by Stewart's March 701/2 from McLaren's M14A/1, with Mario Andretti of the U.S. in third place, driving another March. Only 5 cars finished out of 16 starters. It was in this race that Colin Chapman's interesting new Lotus 72 made its debut, a car with new ideas in body shape and cooling arrangements. It proved its worth in Rindt's hands later in the year. At Monaco, Rindt was driving the older Lotus 49C/R6 and won from Australian Jack Brabham, who made a last-lap error, running into the barriers on the last corner while in the lead, as Rindt closed on him. Prior to this, however, Brabham had won the opening round of the season, in South Africa, and both he and John Surtees, who was at the wheel of a McLaren M7C, set a new lap record of 113.362 mph (182.843 kph). Second place was gained by New Zealander Denis Hulme in a McLaren M14A/2.

Because of the accident to McLaren at Silverstone the McLaren Grand Prix team did not compete in the Belgian Grand Prix, which was held on the very fast Spa circuit in spite of some doubt as to whether the GPDA would go there. The race fully lived up to its exciting reputation, especially as the Cosworth-Ford stranglehold was at last broken by a V 12-cylinder BRM, in which the Mexican driver Pedro Rodriguez won the race. Chris Amon of New Zealand, after setting a fresh Formula One lap record of 155.741 mph (244.744 kph), crossed the finish line in second place in a March 701. The Lotus 72C came into its own at the French Grand Prix at Clermont-Ferrand, when Rindt began his impressive series of consecutive victories. Brabham looked all set to win the British Grand Prix, held in 1970 at Brands Hatch, but yards from victory he was forced to coast over the finish line to take second place, his car having run out of gasoline. This enabled Rindt to score another victory, in a Lotus 72C.

Rindt's winning form had been a feature of the Dutch Grand Prix at sandy Zandvoort, where he came home first ahead of Stewart in a March and Jackie Ickx of Belgium in a Ferrari 312B/001. Piers Courage was killed in this race, when his car left the track and caught fire. In the German Grand Prix at the dull Hockenheim circuit Rindt won for Lotus, but it was Ickx who was second in a Ferrari 312B, ahead of Hulme in a McLaren.

In the Austrian Grand Prix, held at Zeltweg, the superiority of multicylinders became apparent, as Ickx took first place for Ferrari. Amid scenes of delirious Italian enthusiasm, he was followed home by another Ferrari driven by his Swiss teammate Clay Regazzoni. This pattern was followed to the end of the 1970 season, for at Monza in the Italian Grand Prix, where Rindt's fatal accident at practice had cast its shadow, Regazzoni won for Ferrari. It was a similar story in the Canadian Grand Prix, with Ickx the victor in a

Motion Pictures:
see Cinema

Motorboating:
see Motor Sports

Motor Industry:
see Industrial Review

Ferrari 312B and Regazzoni backing him up in second place in another Ferrari.

The Grand Prix circus then moved to Watkins Glen, N.Y., for the U.S. race. In this event Lotus staged a comeback, as its newly recruited driver, the Brazilian Emerson Fittipaldi, finished in first place, driving a Lotus 72. However, the threat of the 12-cylinder cars was still present, because a new Formula One lap record was established by Ickx in a Ferrari and second place went to a BRM 153 V-12 driven by Rodriguez. There remained only the Mexican Grand Prix to end the season, and in this, a race run under dangerous conditions because the spectators refused to keep clear of the course, Ickx concluded a splendid year for Ferrari with outright victory. The drivers' world championship went posthumously to Rindt, who scored 45 points, to the 40 of Ickx and the 33 of Regazzoni. Two new Grand Prix cars appeared during the year. Tyrrell built his own F1 car for Stewart. The car retained a Cosworth-Ford V-8 engine and proved very fast but was apt to develop trouble. John Surtees introduced his Surtees TS7 as the other new automobile, also Cosworth-Ford powered.

Apart from Grand Prix racing, all the various formula cars were active, and long-distance sports-car races provided exciting racing, with Porsche supreme, using 5-litre 12-cylinder cars. Porsche easily captured the 1970 world manufacturers' championship, winning all but one of the premier endurance races. The exception was the Sebring, Fla., 12-hour race where defending United States Auto Club (USAC) champion Mario Andretti gave Ferrari its first endurance triumph in three years by taking over the Nino Vaccarella-Ignazio Giunti team car after his own had broken down and pushing it to a 24-sec. victory over the independent Porsche of actor Steve McQueen and Peter Revson. But the John Wyer Porsche team sent Rodriguez and Leo Kinnunen of Finland to win both the 24 Hours of Daytona and the Watkins Glen Six-Hours, while Hans Herrmann and Dick Attwood won for Porsche at the 24 Hours race at Le Mans, France.

USAC found 1970 a mixed bag. At least six major races were canceled. Moreover, the year witnessed increasing tension between USAC and its fellow members of the Automobile Competition Committee for the U.S., the Sports Car Club of America (SCCA) and the National Association for Stock Car Auto Racing (NASCAR). USAC made it difficult for its drivers to drive in SCCA or NASCAR races and, even more serious, announced that it would not abide by the joint stock car rules for 1971. Even with this dispute, however, Ontario Motor Speedway opened successfully in California with a facsimile of Indianapolis, while the Indianapolis 500, the world's oldest race, paid out its first million dollar purse.

It was Al Unser's year in USAC competition. The 31-year-old New Mexico native, youngest of three racing brothers, won ten Championship Trail races, including the Indianapolis 500 and all five dirt track races, to amass winnings of more than $440,000. The Indianapolis 500-mi. race, which has been run every Memorial Day in the U.S., apart from war years, since 1911, attracted 84 entries in 1970. All but 12 of the 25 different makes of cars entered shared 2.65-litre turbocharged versions of either the old-time Offenhauser design or the later Ford power unit. Unser won the race driving a PJ Colt-Turbo-Ford which averaged 155.749 mph for the 200 laps of the semibanked Indianapolis oval, although the qualifying speeds had been as high as 170 mph and the best race lap, by Joe

UPI COMPIX

The Natural Gas Industry's Blue Flame, driven by Gary Gabelich and using a fuel mixture of liquefied natural gas and hydrogen peroxide, set the new land speed record with a two-run average of 622.407 mph on the Bonneville Salt Flats, Oct. 23, 1970.

Leonard's Johnny Lightning 500 Special, was turned at 167.785 mph. The winner was followed home by Mark Donohue's Lola T153 Turbo-Ford and Dan Gurney's Eagle-Turbo-Offenhauser. Besides Indianapolis, Unser won the five dirt races—the Hoosier 100 in Indianapolis; Sacramento, Calif.; Du Quoin, Ill.; Springfield, Ill.; and Sedalia, Mo.—as well as races at Trenton, N.J., Phoenix, Ariz., and Clermont, Ind.

The other USAC championship triumphs were well spread: Gurney (Sears Point, Calif.); Lloyd Ruby (Trenton); Leonard (Milwaukee); Andretti (Castle Rock, Colo.); Gary Bettenhausen (Michigan Speedway); Bobby Unser, brother of Al Unser (Langhorne, Pa.); Swede Savage (Phoenix); and the veteran Jim McElreath (Ontario). Roger McCluskey repeated for Plymouth as the USAC stock car king, and Larry Dickson became the winningest sprint division driver of all time as he regained that crown.

Part of the reason for the cancellations on the USAC schedule—something unprecedented in such numbers—was the financial problems of American Raceways Inc., the chain of superspeedways assembled by Lawrence LoPatin. Poor crowds at early season races brought in the creditors, and LoPatin was forced out. Les Richter, a former professional football player, was given the job of picking up the pieces of what once had threatened to dominate the sport in America. Races were canceled at Riverside, Calif., and at Texas International because of money problems.

In NASCAR competition it was a Chrysler Corporation year. Not the least of the reasons was the decision of Richard Petty to return to the Plymouth fold, taking on Pete Hamilton, a young college teacher's son from Massachusetts as his number two man. Hamilton made it clear early that on the superspeedways he was more than equal to the task, winning the prestigious Daytona 500 and both races at Talladega, Ala. In the second, the Talladega 500, he averaged 158.157 mph, the fastest stock car 500 ever run there.

Meanwhile, Petty also was winning on the superspeedway trail and at the short track stops of the Grand National circuit. His victories included the Carolina 500 at Rockingham, the Falstaff 400 at Riverside, and the Dixie 500 at Atlanta. He won at least 13 other races, including those at Trenton and Martinsville, Va., en route to another season of earning more than $100,000.

Rocked by the death of Bruce McLaren, the Canadian-American Challenge Cup also faced the problem of promoters who were unhappy because of the runaway victories of Team McLaren in virtually every Can-Am race. Denis Hulme of Team McLaren eventually won the title and was delayed in clinching it only because Dan Gurney, his early season teammate

A.F.P. FROM PICTORIAL PARADE

Giacomo Agostini won the 500-cc. event in the French Grand Prix of motorcyclists at Le Mans in May 1970.

before a sponsor conflict arose, began the competition by driving a McLaren car to victories at St. Jovite and Mosport, Can. Hulme then won three straight, at Watkins Glen, Edmonton, Alta., and Mid-Ohio before an unwanted push cost him a penalty at Road America at Elkhart Lake, Wis., and gave the race to Peter Gethin, the young British Formula 5000 champion who had replaced Gurney on the team. Hulme then won at Donnybrooke in Brainerd, Minn., and at the new Road Atlanta in Georgia, wrapping matters up at Monterey, Calif.

In Britain automobile racing continued to take place every weekend throughout the season, with the Formula Three *Motor Sport*/Shell Championship won by Tony Trimmer, driving a Brabham-Ford. The Tourist Trophy Race degenerated into a two-heat race for Group-two International touring cars, the winner being Brian Muir in a Chevrolet Z28 Camaro with a 5-litre V-8 engine. The Oulton Park Gold Cup Race for Formula One cars backed up by Formula 5000 cars saw Surtees in his Surtees TS7 beat Rindt, who was driving a Lotus 72C. In Europe the oldest motor race, the classic Targa Florio in Sicily, again took place over closed public roads, the victor being a Porsche 3-litre 8-cylinder 908/3 driven by Jo Siffert and Brian Redman.

Gary Gabelich of Long Beach, Calif., set a new world land speed record of 622.407 mph in October over a one-mile stretch of Utah's Bonneville Salt Flats. Driving the rocket-powered 38-ft. Blue Flame, Gabelich broke the mark of 600.601 mph set by Craig Breedlove in 1965.   (R. J. Fe.; W. C. Bo.)

Motorcycles. In the 1970 road-race championship Giacomo Agostini of Italy, riding three-cylinder MV Agusta machines, retained his 350-cc. and 500-cc. titles, although it became noticeable that his once-carefree progress was occasionally threatened by riders of the Japanese Kawasaki two-strokes and the Italian Benellis. The 250-cc. title went to an Englishman, Rod Gould, of Banbury, on a Yamaha, who decided the issue at the Italian Grand Prix by winning by a few yards from Australian Kelvin Carruthers, also on a Yamaha. Dieter Braun of West Germany (Suzuki) was the 125-cc. winner, and Angelo Nieto, a Spaniard riding a Spanish machine, the Derbi, took the 50-cc. title. In the sidecar category it was BMW again, the successful driver being Klaus Enders of West Germany. The TT races in the Isle of Man, marred by no fewer than six fatalities, produced these results: 750 cc. M. Uphill (Triumph), 97.71 mph; 500 cc. F. Whiteway (Suzuki), 89.94 mph; 250 cc. C. Mortimer (Ducati), 84.87 mph; 250-cc. lightweight, Carruthers (Yamaha), 96.13 mph; 350-cc. junior, Agostini (MV Agusta), 101.77 mph; 500-cc. senior, Agostini (MV Agusta), 101.52 mph; 750-cc.

sidecar, S. Schauzu (501 BMW), 90.20 mph; 500-cc. sidecar, Enders (BMW), 92.93 mph.

In international moto cross the 500-cc. championship went for the second successive year to Bengt Åberg of Sweden, riding a Swedish Husqvarna, while Joel Robert of Belgium retained his 250-cc. title. He was riding a Suzuki, and indeed this Japanese firm won the manufacturer's award in that class, the first major honour in motorcycle competition outside road-racing to go to a Japanese manufacturer. In the British Moto Cross Championships Malcolm Davis (AJS) was successful in the 250-cc. class, and Bryan Goss (Husqvarna) in the 500 cc. The European trials champion was S. H. Miller, riding a Bultaco; the world speedway champion, Ivan Mauger; the British league champion, Barry Briggs. The International Six Days Trial, once so prestigious in terms of advertising, took place in the mountains north of Madrid and was won by Czechoslovakia, fielding Jawa machines.   (C. J. Ay.)

Motorboating. Dean Chenoweth began the 1970 unlimited hydroplane racing season with a rough-water victory in the Memorial Day weekend opener at Tampa, Fla. Before the summer-long thunderboat series ended, he had nose-dived his craft in a July race at Pasco, Wash., tearing off the bow and sinking in 20 ft. of water. In the accident Chenoweth suffered a badly bruised left arm and a concussion. Yet in a dramatic comeback, he drove his rebuilt boat to a victory two weeks later at the Seattle Seafair, and finished the season by winning the prestigious Gold Cup and the unlimited national championship at San Diego, Calif., in September.

Chenoweth piloted "Miss Budweiser," owned by Bernie Little and driven to a national championship in 1969 by Bill Sterett. He skippered the speedy hydroplane to victory in the Sun Coast Cup Race at Tampa, the boat's home port, and also won the Indiana Governor's Cup Race at Madison. Between those two events he trailed Bill Muncey's "Myr's Sheet Metal," which collected top honours in the President's Cup at Washington, D.C., the Kentucky Governor's Cup at Owensboro, and the Horace E. Dodge Memorial Race at Detroit.

Their victories put Muncey and Chenoweth into a two-driver race for the national championship going into the Tri-Cities Atomic Cup at Pasco, Wash., on July 19. They had dominated the standings until that time, with Muncey holding a slight edge. But Chenoweth's accident put him in the hospital, and Muncey was sidelined by engine problems. Detroit's Tommy Fults won the Atomic Cup, his only victory of the season. Leif Borgersen's "Notre Dame," a hard-luck contender during the year with three third places, a fourth, and an eighth, was runner-up.

Chenoweth, a 33-year-old racer from Xenia, O.,

Bill Wishnick's powerboat "Boss O'Nova," the 1970 APBA champion, clears the water during the sixth annual Long Beach Hennessy Cup Race, Aug. 15, 1970. He won the event with a record average speed of 62.6 mph.

PICTORIAL PARADE

then bounced back with his battered boat, winning at the Seafair and wrapping up the season with his triumph at the Gold Cup at San Diego. Muncey dropped to a seventh place in the Gold Cup event, allowing Borgersen to finish second and climb on the basis of points earned into the runner-up spot for the season. Muncey could only salvage third place in the season's standings. Chenoweth earned $46,037 in prize money during the eight-race campaign. Borgersen's second-place finish at the end of the year was worth $30,377, and Muncey won $27,498.

International competition for the world offshore powerboat racing championship ended without a clear-cut victory for either of two European sportsmen who had been locked in a year-long struggle for the trophy. Prior to the Miami–Nassau race in October, Britain's Tommy Sopwith nursed a slim lead. He acquired 39 points, largely on the strength of victories at Split, Yugos.; Dauphin d'Or, France; and the important Cowes-Torquay Race in his home waters. He piloted a British-built Avenger hull with a pair of 496 cu.in., naturally aspirated MerCruiser engines.

But 1968 world champion Vincenzo Balestrieri trailed Sopwith by only two points. The diminutive Italian won the Wills International in England, finishing just ahead of Sopwith, and also won races at Naples and Viareggio in Italy. Balestrieri, with a small fleet of boats at his disposal, generally utilized a Bertram hull with large MerCruiser engines.

With scoring based on the best five finishes, Sopwith backed up his three victories with a pair of second places, while Balestrieri had three firsts, a second, and a third. Thus, the Miami–Nassau race was possibly a decisive one, and both men shipped boats to Florida. Sopwith won the race and Balestrieri placed second. However, officials of the Bahamas Power Boat Association disqualified Sopwith for having improper exhausts on his engines and named Balestrieri the winner. Sopwith filed a protest against the decision and the matter was scheduled to be settled by the Union of International Motorboating (UIM), but a binding decision was not expected for months.

The result was that, as the racing year ended, either Sopwith or Balestrieri could be world champion. The year's last event, the Hennessy-Key West, was won by Bob Magoon of Miami as Sopwith's craft caught fire and Balestrieri went to his aid. As a result, the ultimate awarding of the title depended upon the UIM's settlement of the protest.   (JA. E. M.)

Mountaineering

The year 1969–70 was a Himalayan one in mountaineering, a year when Himalayan climbing showed a full revival after the Nepalese ban of previous years.

In the latter part of 1969 two Japanese expeditions in the Mt. Everest region carried out reconnaissances, one of the southwest buttress of Everest and the other for a descent on ski of the South Col; on the latter six Sherpas were killed. A Japanese attempt on Dakura (Peak 29, Nepal) failed, but the first ascents of Gurja Himal and Kande Hiunchuli (Patrasi Himal) were made by Japanese parties. An Austrian expedition failed to climb Dhaulagiri IV, and lost five Austrian members and one Sherpa; an Italian party failed in an attempt on Churen Himal by the south face. Yugoslavs climbed Annapurna II and IV; the latter was also climbed by a Czech party.

In 1970 Everest, Nanga Parbat, Annapurna, and Makalu were among the peaks climbed. After a further reconnaissance of the southwest buttress by a Japanese party, T. Matsuura and N. Uemura climbed Everest by the South Col, the fifth certain ascent; one Japanese climber and one Sherpa were killed on this expedition. The first ascent of Nanga Parbat via the Rupal flank was made by the brothers Messner (one of whom was killed on the descent) of a West German expedition. J. Mayerl and R. Walter of a light Austrian expedition made the first ascent of Lhotse Shar, 27,504 ft. Two British ascents of Annapurna I were achieved: D. Whillans and D. Haston of an Anglo-U.S. expedition made the first one by the south face, one member being killed; Capt. H. Day and Capt. G. Owens of a British Army party repeated the original French route. Annapurna III was climbed by Mrs. J. Tabel and Miss H. Hirakawa of a Japanese women's expedition with two Sherpas, and Annapurna IV by another Japanese party. A Japanese party failed on Dhaulagiri IV but made the first ascent of Dhaulagiri VI. Churen Himal was climbed by Kim Ho Sup and a Sherpa of a South Korean party. A Dutch expedition abandoned an attempt on Dakura and climbed the northeast peak of Himal Chuli on four successive days. Makalu was climbed by H. Tanaka and Y. Ozaki of a Japanese expedition by the southeast ridge. In Kashmir a British women's expedition visited Padar Himal. The ascent of Tukucha was repeated by a Japanese party from Washeda University. In the Lampak group in Garwhal, Indian expeditions made the first ascents of the main peak and of South Lampak in late 1969. The first ascent of Baudda was completed in 1970 by a Japanese party after one member had died on a previous attempt.

In the Alps the most striking feature was the increasing number of solo ascents of very difficult routes. In the autumn of 1969, for example, first solo ascents were made of the south face of the Aiguille de Triolet by M. A. Picconi, of the Pillar and Southeast Crack of the Fleischbank by P. Habeler, and of the Solda Route on the north wall of the Sassolunga and the Philipp-Flamm Route on the Quota IGM (Civetta) by R. Messner. During the winter 1969–70 first winter ascents of the central buttress on the northeast face of the Weisshorn, of the northeast face of the Alphubel, and of the north face of the Studerhorn were made by Swiss parties. The north side of the Col du Plan was climbed by P. Cordier and S. Jouty, while the first winter ascent of the Japanese route on the north face of the Eiger was made by H. P. Trachsel, O. von Allmen, H. Mueller, P. Jangen, and M. Doerflinger. Japanese made the second ascent of the Harlin Route on the same face, and also the second winter ascent of the original route (during which one of the party broke his ankle and was rescued at a cost of £2,000). In the summer of 1970 the weather was bad and accidents were numerous. First ascents were made of the North Pillar of the Eiger by I. MacEacheran, K. Spence, and A. McKeith; of the northwest face of the Olan direct to the middle summit by three Frenchmen; of the north face of the Grandes Jorasses to the Punta Elena by a Polish party; of the west ridge direct of the Wetterhorn by two Swiss guides; and of the west face direct of the Sciora di Fuori by one Swiss and two Italians.

In Norway new routes were made on the southeast face of Setnesfjell in the Romsdal area, and on the west face of Hornindalsrokken in Sunnmøre.

In the Caucasus in 1969 a Kabardino Balkarian

Motor Vehicles:
see Disasters;
Industrial Review;
Motor Sports;
Transportation

UPI COMPIX

WIDE WORLD

Above, Dean Caldwell (left) and Warren Harding refuse the offer of an army helicopter to rescue them from the vertical face of Yosemite National Park's El Capitan. Above, right, Harding hugs his girl friend after he and Caldwell ended their 27-day, 3,000-ft. climb, Nov. 18, 1970.

Mozambique:
see Dependent States

Muhammadanism:
see Religion

Municipal Government:
see Cities and Urban Affairs

Munitions:
see Defense

party led by M. Zalekhanov climbed the southeast face of Tiutiun Bashi. The northeast face of Dalar was climbed by a Leningrad party led by B. Korablin. Climbers from Sverdlovsk led by S. Sorin ascended the northwest face of Kirpich. In the Tien Shan the Soviet tradition of long traverses of numerous peaks was continued with traverses of Jigit, Slonyenok, Karaholsky, Oguzbashi, and Peak 4909 m. by a Kirgiz party led by A. Tustukbayev, and of Kibalchick, Korolev, and Kander by a party from Kaliningrad led by A. Korsun. Two groups of climbers from Krasnoyarsk and Kiev, led by V. Bezzubkin and A. Kutuzovsky, respectively, made routes on the north face of Free Korea Peak. Similar traverses in the Pamirs were of Garmo, Patriot, Russia, Communism, and Pamir by a Leningrad party led by Y. Kuzmin (10 mi. at over 19,700 ft.—with a new route up the "trough" of Garmo) and of Twenty-six Baku Commissars, Revolution, Shipka, and Pamir by a party from Moscow led by V. Logvinov. A Soviet-Polish expedition climbed 14 new peaks in the Matchai area of the Alai-Pamirs.

In 1969 an Austrian expedition went to Khinyang Khish, and Poles made the first ascent of Malubiting North Peak in the Karakoram. K6 was climbed by Koblmueller's party, and Japanese were active in the Baltoro Glacier area. The Hindu Kush saw less activity. In late 1969 the French made the first ascent of the North Pillar of Shakaur. In 1970 various climbs were made, including the first ascent of the west ridge of Koh-i-Marchek by a U.S. party.

In New Zealand climbing continued on a major scale in the 1969–70 summer, but there were no successes on major new routes. In Antarctica a British services expedition went to Elephant Island, and New Zealanders climbed Mt. Minto.

Alaska saw no really big new ascents, though some climbing took place. Mt. McKinley was climbed by a U.S. women's expedition, and Naomi Vemura made the first solo ascent. The most striking climb among the very hard ascents made in the Yosemite area was the first scaling of the sheer 3,000-ft. southeast face of El Capitan by U.S. climbers Warren Harding and Dean Caldwell. Another difficult ascent was a new route on Sentinel, climbed by Royal Robbins solo. Harding, with Galen Rowell, had also previously

made the first ascent of the 2,000-ft. south face of Half Dome.

In South America interest was concentrated in Patagonia rather than the main Andes. In the latter, expeditions went to Huascarán, Rondoy, and Pucarhica; a U.S. party repeated the ascent of Tullingato in the Cordillera Blanca. In Patagonia a New Zealand expedition in 1969–70 climbed numerous peaks on the border of the northern ice cap. The first ascent of Cerro Norte was made by an expedition from the Club Andino Bariloche. An Italian attempt on the west face of the Cerro Torre failed, as did British and Chilean attempts on the Cathedral in the Paine group.

(Jo. N.)

Museums and Galleries

Social radicalism extended its activity to the world of museums in 1970. The Metropolitan Museum of Art and the Museum of Modern Art in New York City and other museums elsewhere were picketed during the year. Twenty-four U.S. artists withdrew their works from the 35th Venice Biennale to protest expansion of the Vietnam war and other U.S. government policies. The annual convention of the American Association of Museums was disrupted and its agenda substantially altered by the appearance of demonstrators.

Even before the convention, however, the association had formed a program under a grant from the U.S. Department of Housing and Urban Development to assist U.S. museums in setting up neighbourhood museums and community centres. To alleviate some of the frustrations of minority group artists and their communities, the Brooklyn Museum established the Community Gallery, the first such gallery within the walls of a major U.S. museum, and the Boston Museum of Fine Arts set up the National Center of Afro-American Artists. Some museum personnel, however, felt that the bureaucratic organization and the "patrician antecedents" of the large central museum worked against its efforts to serve more than a narrow segment of the community. They expected the neighbourhood museum to provide a "role model" of the artist at work and space and materials for creative activity.

New Buildings. The Expo Museum of Fine Arts, designed by K. Kawasaki and Kenzo Tange, opened in Osaka, Jap. Occupying 10,000 sq.m. (108,000 sq.ft.), the building embodied the most advanced techniques in museum architecture. To conserve works on display and permit ease of appreciation, showcases were furnished with a separate air-conditioning system and constant illumination.

In the U.S., the Philadelphia Civic Center announced the establishment of a major Municipal Arts Gallery within the Civic Center Museum, indicating the growing recognition of the museum as a showcase for exhibitions by many major art organizations in the area. The University of Wisconsin opened its new Elvehjem Art Center in September 1970.

The Hudson River Museum at Yonkers, N.Y., housed from 1924 in a Victorian mansion, was extended by very modern new wings, largely hidden belowground, thus showing the possibility of extending historic buildings without defacement. The Sloane-Stanley Museum in Kent, Conn., was opened, as well as a site museum, Old Newgate Prison, at East Granby, and in Pennsylvania preparations began for a new open-air museum in the little coal-mining village of Echley.

The Peabody Museum of Archaeology and Ethnology and the department of anthropology of Harvard University announced the approval of land and architects for the construction of a new wing. A fireproof structure to be attached to the existing museum would provide 18,000 sq.ft. for the Tozzer Memorial Library, 35,000 sq.ft. for a research facility to house the museum's ethnographic collections, and structural capacity for a 40,000-sq.ft. future addition.

During the year the University Art Museum in Berkeley, Calif., the largest university museum building in the U.S., was opened. Major additions opened at the Huntington (W.Va.) Galleries, at the Krannert Pavilion at the Indianapolis (Ind.) Museum of Art, at the Virginia Museum of Fine Arts in Richmond, at the Cleveland (O.) Museum of Art, which tripled the space available for the display of its great collection of Oriental art, and at the American Museum of Natural History in New York City, which displayed 1,000 artifacts in its new Hall of Mexico and Central America. The opening of the Koehler Art Center in Sheboygan, Wis., epitomized the continuing growth of substantial art centres in the smaller U.S. cities.

Yale University announced that Louis I. Kahn had been named the architect of the $6 million Paul Mellon Center for British Art and British Studies. The centre would house Mellon's extensive collection of British paintings, drawings, and rare books. The Archives of American Art, the largest research institution devoted to the study of American art, became a part of the Smithsonian Institution and was to move to Washington, D.C., from its present headquarters in Detroit. The Smithsonian also leased the 64-room Andrew Carnegie mansion in New York City to house the Cooper-Hewitt Museum of Decorative Arts and Design, to be moved from the old Cooper Union Building in the Lower East Side of Manhattan. Building projects in Canada included extensive renovation of the Victoria Memorial Museum in Ottawa and the opening of the Ontario Science Centre in Toronto.

In the U.K., art galleries were completed at Christ Church College, Oxford (architects, Powell and Moya), and the Hayward Gallery, London. At Beamish, near Newcastle upon Tyne, local authorities approved plans to use the 270 ac. of farmland and

grounds of Beamish Hall for the open-air museum showing the development of lead and coal mining and iron and steel working. The Weald and Downland Open-Air Museum was opened for four weekends during September and October before the official opening, planned for April 1971. The main purpose of the museum was the preservation of important buildings in the area, which had a rich tradition of vernacular architecture; many of its smaller timber-frame farm buildings dated from medieval times. Where preservation in situ proved impossible, the museum would dismantle buildings and reerect them at West Dean, a 35-ac. site about six miles from Chichester.

In Montmartre, Paris, the famous painters' atelier Bateau-Lavoir, linked with such names as Picasso, Braque, Apollinaire, Rousseau, and Modigliani, was burned out a few months after becoming the property of the city of Paris. Moreover, La Ruche at Montparnasse, where Chagall, Léger, and Soutine worked, was still in danger of demolition to make space for new constructions.

It was decided to construct the biggest modern art museum in France on the territory occupied until 1969 by the famous Halles of Paris. The museum was to be devoted to 20th-century art, featuring not only paintings and sculpture, but also contemporary music, poetry, architectural plans and models, and other objects characterizing the 20th century.

At Versailles, new exhibition rooms devoted to the Consulate and Empire periods were opened to the public, and a dining room of the Petit Trianon was completely restored and equipped with original wainscots and furniture. All paintings ordered by Louis XV and executed between 1769 and 1777 were assembled. The city of Lyons invited Bernard Zehrfuss, architect of the recently inaugurated UNESCO building in Paris, to prepare plans for a museum.

The National Museum of Pakistan moved to a specially designed new building in the spacious Burns Garden near the Presidential Palace at Karachi. The Stoneham Museum in Kitale, Kenya, housed on Col. H. F. Stoneham's estate, was to be moved to a new building adjacent to the town and designed by Derrick Flatt. Stoneham, who died in 1966, had made provision for the building, and bequeathed his collection as a nucleus for the Western Kenya Museum. A Swaziland National Centre was established at Mbabane, to house a National Museum of Ethnology and Natural History.

Acquisitions. Perhaps the most important acquisition of the year was an early masterpiece by Paul Cézanne purchased by Paul Mellon for the National Gallery in Washington, D.C. The life-sized portrait of Cézanne's father, valued at more than $1.5 million, came from a private French collection, and special authorization from the French government was necessary for its export.

The Museum of Fine Arts, Boston, purchased for $700,000 a painting, from an old European private collection, that had been traditionally ascribed to Raphael but never studied by an expert. The painting was believed to be a portrait of Eleonora Gonzaga, daughter of Isabella d'Este and Francesco Gonzaga, marquis of Mantua, executed by the then 22-year-old Raphael in 1505 on Eleonora's betrothal to Francesco Maria della Rovere, later duke of Urbino. The purchase provoked a protest in Italy, and some legal authorities judged its exportation illegal. The museum also purchased 137 pieces of gold and jewelry from an early Bronze Age royal tomb of the "Eastern Medi-

WIDE WORLD

Rolland O. Hower, chief of exhibits research at the Smithsonian Institution in Washington, D.C., displays a wolf spider preserved by a freeze-dry process that bypasses the conventional mounting procedures.

THE "NEW YORK TIMES"
The helium-filled balloons of Otto Piene perform a "sky ballet" sponsored by the Smithsonian Institution, May 17, 1970.

terranean" for more than $100,000. The very vague information on the origin of the treasure provoked violent discussion.

The problem of illegal export of artifacts from art-rich but capital-poor countries was serious enough that an April meeting of a UNESCO committee in Paris drew up a code for ratification by its members. This code would pledge importing countries to prevent the acquisition by museums of materials illegally exported from the country of origin. The University Museum of the University of Pennsylvania led the way toward a uniform code in the U.S. by announcing that it would no longer consider for acquisition any object that did not have a bona fide pedigree, stating information on previous owners, place of origin, legality of export, and other relevant data. Still another approach to the problem was demonstrated by the Metropolitan Museum in New York, which negotiated a long-term series of loan exhibitions with Mexico.

Important collections donated to U.S. museums during the year included the T. Edward Hanley collection of modern painting, given to the De Young Memorial Museum in San Francisco, and the Stillman collection of Congo sculpture, given to the Dallas (Tex.) Museum of Fine Arts. The Board of Trustees of the Ringling Museum of Art, Sarasota, Fla., approved the sum of $6,500 for the purchase of "A Gothic Tomb" by Monsu Desiderio (1593–c. 1647). The painting was not only one of the most bizarre but also the earliest example of the artist's work, bearing the date 1618.

Among the year's numerous acquisitions by the Louvre, Paris, were G. M. Crespi's "Flea," or "Young Woman Seeking a Flea" (1715–20), a fine example of 18th-century Italian realism; Philippe de Champaigne's "Portrait of the Ten-Year-Old Louis XIV"; Henry Fuseli's "Lady Macbeth"; and Pierre Cécilé Puvis de Chavannes' "Young Girls on the Seashore," dated 1879. The International Museum of Popular Imagery in Épinal received a collection of 200 European and Asian paintings on glass from the 18th and 19th centuries, making the museum one of the richest in Europe in this kind of painting. The most important event in France, however, was a gift to the Dijon museum of 700 works of Impressionists and contemporary painters such as Delacroix, Millet, Manet, Pissarro, Corot, Rousseau, and Picasso.

In the U.K., the National Art Collection Fund reported 1969 as a record year, in which £53,509 was collected, 60% of which went to galleries outside London. Important purchases included five early iron torcs from Ipswich, the Noble Chalice (English, c. 1200), and a self-portrait by John Hamilton Mortimer for the British Museum; a French upright secretaire dating from 1774 and a marble figure of Christ (the

Netherlands, c. 1320) for the Victoria and Albert Museum; "Madonna with Child" by the Italian Alessandro Allori and a marble bust of Nicolas Coustou by Guillaume Coustou for the Walker Art Gallery, Liverpool; and "On the Arno" by Richard Wilson (British) for the City Art Gallery, Manchester. The Art Gallery of York purchased a portrait of William Baynes of Embsay Kirk by Nathan Drake, a scene of "Careless Husband" by Philippe Mercier, and a portrait of a man by M. F. Quadal.

Pablo Picasso donated between 800 and 900 early works to a Barcelona museum. The donation made the museum's Picasso collection one of the most important in the world and put an end to hopes for a Picasso museum in France. On the other hand, Picasso refused a request from the Spanish government that he transfer his famous "Guernica" from the Museum of Modern Art, New York City, to the newly built modern art museum in Madrid. Late in the year Picasso's Paris lawyer revealed that the artist and the museum had agreed that the painting would be returned to Spain when "public liberties [are] re-established in that country." The decision would be made by Picasso or, after his death, by his lawyer.

The French government was strongly criticized by the press for its decision to leave the collection of French paintings permanently at the Musée du Jardin d'Essai in Algiers. The collection, an excellent representation of the French School from the 15th to the 20th centuries, had been sent to Algiers for the centenary of French Algeria in 1930. Budgets for new acquisitions proved largely inadequate to cope with rising prices for art works. One solution being considered was the sale of items duplicated or of secondary importance. The National Museum in Cairo, for example, sold many items that were straining its storage facilities, and the income was to be considered for the construction of new museums in Cairo and Alexandria.

The unearthing in the southern Ukraine of a tomb containing the skeleton of a Scythian warrior, 520 gold objects, and countless other objects of great historical value was the richest find ever made of a 5th-century B.C. Scythian burial. The treasure went to enrich the collection of the Hermitage Museum in Leningrad.

Exhibitions. The problem of degradation of the environment was taken up by the American Museum of Natural History, which organized a provocative, multimedia exhibition, "Can Man Survive?", warning man of his future if serious steps were not taken.

With the loan of the exhibition "200 Years of American Art" to the Mississippi Art Association in Jackson, the Pennsylvania Academy of Fine Arts, the conserver of many of the finest works in the history of American art, inaugurated a long-needed policy of sharing its outstanding collection with other U.S. museums.

The 35th Venice Biennale was organized on a new experimental basis—exhibition and analysis of ideas instead of works of art of individual artists.

Several U.S. museums celebrated birthdays. The Boston Museum of Fine Arts and the Metropolitan were 100 years old. Boston celebrated by displaying various recent acquisitions, and the Metropolitan concluded a two-year plan of major exhibitions with "The Year 1200" and "19th-Century America."

International Cooperation. UNESCO's current biennial program and budget for museum development and protection of cultural heritage terminated in 1970. The number of such projects carried out by UNESCO continued to grow; currently a record 96 projects received direct aid. UNESCO missions, making general evaluations of cultural property and plans toward development of museums and museum laboratories, were carried out for the first time in Bahrain, Qatar, Yemen, Southern Yemen, and Saudi Arabia. More technical missions were being carried out throughout the world by UNESCO experts. In Singapore, for example, a British specialist, James Gardner, established a modern concept of the future Singapore National Museum.

UNESCO invited its member states to participate in a project to encourage the exchange of original works of art and provided a $16,000 budget to assist such cooperation. Six countries, Algeria, Austria, Dahomey, Italy, Niger, and Senegal, expressed interest in participating, but many others informed UNESCO that exchanges were carried on under bilateral programs for which no financial support from UNESCO was necessary. (J. KI.; A. S.)

See also Art Exhibitions; Industrial Design.

Music

At the end of 1969, the New York Philharmonic concerts began with the first performance of Leon Kirchner's *Music for Orchestra,* conducted by the composer. On October 14 *Prometheus,* the last part of Carl Orff's epic trilogy, was given its first U.S. performance by the Little Orchestra Society at New York's Philharmonic Hall, and the Chamber Music Society of Lincoln Center opened its season with the first performance of a trio for violin, cello, and piano by the veteran French composer Darius Milhaud. There were successful visits to the U.S. by two outstanding European orchestras, the Santa Cecilia from Rome and the Royal Philharmonic from London, under their respective conductors, Fernando Previtali and Rudolf Kempe.

In November the Royal Concert in London had a Scottish flavour appropriate to the Scottish National Orchestra. A Macnaghten concert included a number of audiovisual pieces consisting of films associated with electronic music. The London premiere of Iannis Xenakis' *Morsima-Amorsima* was given by the Vesuvius Ensemble on November 2, and the London Sinfonietta premiered Roberto Gerhard's fascinating astrological work *Leo* on November 24. In Paris the Napoleon bicentenary was celebrated with Paisiello's *Mass for the Emperor's Coronation,* given in the Invalides on November 13.

The NHK (Japanese Broadcasting Corporation) Symphony Orchestra visited Carnegie Hall in November under its musical director, Hiryuki Iwaki, playing Beethoven, Tchaikovsky, and Toshiro Mayuzumi's ballet suite *Bugaku.* At the Hunter College Assembly Hall in New York on November 9, the Pro Arte Symphony Orchestra gave the world premiere of Arthur Custer's experimental work *Found Objects II.* The Chamber Music Society of Lincoln Center gave the first performance of Carlos Chavez' Variations for Violin and Piano (December 12). The International Society for Contemporary Music gave George Perle's Fifth String Quartet (December 7), not new but well worth reviving. A concert at Carnegie Hall's Recital Room included new music by Istvan Anhalt, David Jones, Arne Nordheim, and Patric Purswell.

On Jan. 14, 1970, the San Francisco Symphony Orchestra under Josef Krips gave the premiere of William Walton's *Improvisations on an Impromptu of Benjamin Britten,* and on January 20 the Philadelphia Orchestra under Eugene Ormandy gave the first U.S. performance of Shostakovich's Symphony No. 13. The London Symphony Orchestra included the premiere of Wilfred Josephs' *Variations on a Theme of Beethoven* in its Carnegie Hall program on January 23. William Schuman's canticle for orchestra, *In Praise of Shahn,* had its first performance by the New York Philharmonic under Leonard Bernstein on January 29.

In London the premiere of Peter Maxwell Davies' *Vesalii icones* was given by the Pierrot Players on December 9. This unusual piece was "scored" for dancer, cello, and instrumental ensemble and had as its starting point the 14 anatomical engravings of Andreas Vesalius' *De humani corporis fabrica* (1543). Iain Hamilton's *Circus,* a two-movement work for two trumpets and orchestra commissioned by the BBC, had its premiere on January 21 at the Festival Hall with the BBC Symphony Orchestra. During January and February the Guarneri Quartet began the British celebrations of Beethoven's bicentenary with a complete cycle of the string quartets at London's Queen Elizabeth Hall. The Dublin Festival of 20th-century music included one outstanding novelty, Gerard Victory's *Compensations* for English horn and tape recorder.

Luciano Berio's most recent work, *This Means That . . . ,* involving a lecture, ancient folk songs, Gregorian chant, a perfect fifth played continuously on a viola, electronic sounds, and lasting 70 minutes, had its premiere at Carnegie Hall on February 17. George Szell (*see* OBITUARIES) brought his Cleveland Orchestra to Carnegie Hall for two concerts in February, conducting a fine performance of Mahler's *Das Lied von der Erde* with Janet Baker and Richard Lewis as soloists. On February 5 the New York Philharmonic under Bernstein gave the premiere of Elliott Carter's *Concerto for Orchestra,* a superbly organized and well-integrated work.

Leonard Bernstein visited London at the end of February to perform and record Verdi's *Requiem.* Handel's seldom-performed *Brockes Passion* was given at the Victoria and Albert Museum, and Elgar's *The Kingdom,* another rarity, was performed by the London Philharmonic Choir and Orchestra, conducted by veteran Sir Adrian Boult. Another veteran, Otto Klemperer, directed the New Philharmonia Orchestra in a monumental account of Bruckner's Ninth Symphony at the Festival Hall (February 24). At the Queen Elizabeth Hall in February, the stage version of Debussy's *Chansons de Bilitis* was performed in a new edition by Pierre Boulez with choreography by Geoffrey Cauley. In an avant-garde con-

"THE GUARDIAN"
André Previn rehearses with the London Symphony Orchestra, which he conducted for the premiere of Benjamin Frankel's Seventh Symphony at London's Festival Hall, June 4, 1970.

LILIAN TONNAIRE
FROM NANCY PALMER AGENCY
Pablo Casals conducts rehearsals with an all-cello orchestra for a concert in his honour. The concert was given in New York's Philharmonic Hall at Lincoln Center, April 15, 1970.

cert, the Gentle Fire presented John Cage's *Fontana Mix* and Cornelius Cardew's *Solo with Accompaniment* at the Purcell Room (February 4). At Birmingham,. John McCabe's Concerto for piano and wind quartet had its first performance on February 21.

In New York's Alice Tully Hall, the Clarion Concerts Orchestra gave the premiere of Riccardo Malipiero's *Serenata per Alice Tully* on March 10. At Carnegie Hall on March 21 the Baltimore Symphony under Sergiu Comissiona gave the first New York performance of Roger Sessions' *Rhapsody for Orchestra*. Lukas Foss's *Geod* at Buffalo, N.Y., on March 17 brought into play the Buffalo Symphony, five conductors, and a whole lighting scenario. In April, Seiji Ozawa took the Philadelphia Orchestra through the first U.S. performance of Oliver Messiaen's *Sept Haikai*, Gerhard Samuel conducted the Oakland Symphony in Henry Brant's new work, *Kingdom Come*, and Jane Marsh was soloist in the premiere of Alberto Ginastera's *Milena*, for soprano and orchestra, with the New York Philharmonic under Lorin Maazel.

London had a Percy Grainger festival during March, but for all their incidental merits his compositions hardly bore such concentrated examination. Maxim Shostakovich visited the Festival Hall on March 5 to conduct the London Philharmonic Orchestra in his father's eighth and ninth symphonies, with eloquent results. Harry Blech, for 21 years conductor of the popular London Mozart Players, had a 60th birthday concert at the Festival Hall on March 11. Also in March, Alexander Tcherepnin performed some of his own and other composers' music at the Queen Elizabeth Hall, and a Roberto Gerhard Memorial Concert was presented at the Purcell Room. Martin Dalby's First Symphony had its premiere with the Scottish National Orchestra at Aberdeen on March 10, and Thomas Wison's *Missa Pro Mundo Conturbato* had its premiere at Edinburgh on March 1. Birmingham had the first performance of Kenneth Leighton's Third Piano Concerto (March 12).

On April 21 Pierre Boulez gave the first performance of the rediscovered *Waldmärchen*, first part of Mahler's *Das klagende Lied*, in London's Festival Hall; it proved a fascinating piece. The English Bach Festival, despite its title, was most notable for rare Beethoven, including the Joseph II and Leopold II cantatas and the oratorio *Christus am Ölberg*, and for its survey of Karlheinz Stockhausen's music, including *Prozession*, *Spiral*, and *Hymnen*. The Leeds Triennial Festival included the first performance of David Blake's large-scale choral work *Lumina*. The festival at Royan, near Bordeaux, France, included the first performances of Cristobal Halffter's *Antillos*, André Boucourechiliev's *Archipels I* and *IV*, Michel Zbar's *Xenia II*, and Pierre Henry's crazy *Fragments pour Artaud*.

The last of the season's concerts by the New York Philharmonic (May 21) included Schumann's rarely given oratorio *Das Paradies und die Peri*, conducted by Lorin Maazel. During May the Los Angeles Philharmonic gave a cumbrously entitled series, "Contempo '70—20th Century Music: How It Was, How It Is," including first performances of Morton Subotnik's *Play! 4*, Mel Powell's *Immobiles 1–4* (withdrawn at the composer's insistence in mid-performance), and excerpts from Frank Zappa's extravagant *200 Motels*, an attempt to fuse classical and rock in which the Mothers of Invention took part. Schoenberg, Webern, and Stravinsky, conducted by Boulez, provided more considered fare. Boulez also took the orchestra to the Ojai (Calif.) Festival where they gave

Stockhausen's *Kontra–Punkte*, as well as established works of the Second Viennese School.

In May the Beethoven festivities got under way in earnest in Europe. The International Beethoven Festival opened in Bonn; Otto Klemperer began a complete cycle of the symphonies in London with his New Philharmonia Orchestra; and the Vienna Festival began a far-reaching conspectus of his music, as well as offering an absorbing exhibition in the town hall. Klemperer's 85th birthday (May 14) was marked by a New Philharmonia Orchestra concert, in which he conducted *Das Lied von der Erde*, and by the first performance (May 19) of his own Seventh Quartet, given by the Bartok Quartet in St. John's, Smith Square, London. Alexander Goehr's new work, *Symphony in One Movement*, was given by the New Philharmonia Orchestra in the Festival Hall on May 19 (and later at Osaka and Tokyo during the orchestra's Japanese tour). Roger Smalley's *Melody Study II* was performed by the Nash Ensemble at the Purcell Room on May 13.

Pablo Casals, at 93, proved his staying power with an overwhelming performance of Beethoven's Ninth Symphony at his Puerto Rico Festival. The Prague Spring Festival included various excellent chamber music contributions and a new production of Viteslav Novak's ballet *Signorina Gioventa*. The June Gulbenkian Festival in Lisbon, reportedly the last, included the first performance of Cristobal Halffter's *Fibonaciana*, Joly Braga Santos' opera *Trilogia das Barcas*, and Alvaro Cossuta's *Evocacões*, as well as the first modern performance of Domenico Scarlatti's *Laetatus sum*.

The Llandaff Festival included the first performance of John Metcalf's *Sinfonia* and William Matthias' harp concerto. At the Aldeburgh Festival, Hans Werner Henze's *El Cimarrón*, described as a "recital for four musicians," had its premiere. William Pearson, soloist and leader of a quartet, had to perform incredible feats of vocal virtuosity. Shostakovich's 14th Symphony had its first performance outside the U.S.S.R., conducted by its dedicatee, Benjamin Britten. Mstislav Rostropovich gave the first performance of Sir Arthur Bliss's *Concertino* for cello. At the Bath Festival, Joan Sutherland gave a sparkling recital, the Juilliard Quartet played Beethoven, Sir Michael Tippett conducted Tallis' *Spem im Alium* at the Abbey, and Colin Davis revived the whole of Beethoven's incidental music to *Egmont*.

Benjamin Frankel's Seventh Symphony had its premiere at London's Festival Hall on June 4, the London Symphony being conducted by André Previn. Don Banks's *Meeting Place*, given at the Queen Elizabeth Hall on June 15, was another attempt to marry jazz and "serious" music, as was Richard Rodney Bennett's *Jazz Pastoral*, sung by Cleo Laine at the same concert. The Promenade Concerts at the Albert Hall from July to September included the British premiere of Messiaen's *Le Transfiguration* and new works by Elisabeth Lutyens and Sebastian Forbes. The City of London Festival in July was notable for the premiere of Goehr's *Shadowplay–2*, a dramatization of part of Plato's *Republic*. At the Cheltenham Festival, first performances included music by Peter Dickinson, Robin Holloway, Humphrey Searle, and Richard Stoker. There was also a revival of Elgar's rarely heard oratorio *Caractacus*. Beethoven played a large part in the programs of the Edinburgh Festival (August 23–September 12). The Montreux Festival paid homage to Bela Bartok on the 25th anniversary of his death.

Opera. *United States.* The 1969–70 Metropolitan season was seriously curtailed by labour troubles. It finally opened on Dec. 29, 1969, with a performance of *Aida.* In January 1970 came the first new production —*Cavalleria Rusticana* and *Pagliacci,* staged by Franco Zeffirelli, with Grace Bumbry as Santuzza and Franco Corelli as Turiddu in the first work, veteran Richard Tucker as Canio and Sherrill Milnes as a wonderful Tonio in the second. The new production of *Norma* (March 3) had Joan Sutherland in the title role and Marilyn Horne as Adalgisa. The 1970–71 season opened on September 14 with a revival of *Ernani.* It was announced that Göran Gentele, head of the Stockholm Opera, would succeed Rudolf Bing as general manager of the Met when the latter retired in 1972.

The New York City Opera opened its 1970–71 season with a revival of Boito's *Mefistofele.* There followed a new production of Donizetti's *Roberto Devereux,* with Beverly Sills. The 1970–71 season of the San Francisco Opera opened with a new production, by Geraint Evans, of Verdi's *Falstaff,* with Evans in the title role, followed by a new production, by Jean-Pierre Ponnelle, of *Così fan tutte.* The Lyric Opera season in Chicago opened with *Der Rosenkavalier* with Christa Ludwig and Yvonne Minton, and *La Traviata* with Montserrat Caballé in the title role.

On Dec. 2, 1969, Clairion Concerts revived Giovanni Simone Mayr's *Medea in Corinto* at the Alice Tully Hall in New York. The Boston Opera Company opened its 1970 season with *Der fliegende Holländer* (January 28) and turned to *La Fille du Regiment* on February 21. The Hofstra Institute of the Arts (Long Island) presented *Così a Go-Go* (February 6) with Moog Synthesizer, light projections, and the Pershing Rifles Crack Drill Team. The Hartt Opera Theater gave Cherubini's *Medée* for the first time in its original French version with dialogue on February 25, and followed it with Prokofiev's *The Duenna* (April 29).

United Kingdom. The first new production of the 1969–70 season at the Royal Opera, Covent Garden, was *Pelléas et Mélisande* (Dec. 1, 1969), conducted by Pierre Boulez. The premiere of Richard Rodney Bennett's new opera *Victory,* based on Joseph Conrad's novel, took place on April 13 and a new production of *Salome,* conducted by Georg Solti, was staged in June. The company visited Berlin and Munich with great success during April, presenting *Victory, Don Carlos,* and *Falstaff.* The world premiere of Sir Michael Tippett's new opera, *The Knot Garden* (December 2), was the first new production of the 1970–71 season.

The 1969–70 Sadler's Wells season at the Coliseum included new productions of Gilbert and Sullivan's *Patience, Die Walküre,* Beethoven's *Leonora,* and *Carmen* (an exciting production by John Copley, conducted by the company's new musical director, Charles Mackerras). The 1970–71 season opened in August, the first new production being a lively performance of *The Tales of Hoffmann,* followed in October by *Semele,* produced by Filippo Sanjust. Scottish Opera made an outstanding contribution to the Edinburgh Festival with a production of Hans Werner Henze's *Elegy for Young Lovers.* The New Opera Company presented the first British performance of Hindemith's *Cardillac* at Sadler's Wells Theatre (March 11). A gala at Covent Garden in June marked the retirement of Sir David Webster as general administrator. He was succeeded by John Tooley. Peter Hall (*see* BIOGRAPHY) was to become artistic director in 1971.

AUTHENTICATED NEWS INTERNATIONAL

Beethoven's "Fidelio" is performed under the direction of Leonard Bernstein at Vienna's Theater an der Wien May 24, 1970.

Germany. At the end of 1969, the first performance of Forst's *Die Blumen von Hiroshima* was presented in East Berlin (October 10), the Bavarian State Opera gave a new production of *Carmen* (October 24), conducted by Karl Böhm, and Günther Bialas's *Die Geschichte von Aucassin und Nicolette* was given in Munich's Cuvilliés Theatre. On February 4, West Berlin's German Opera mounted a new production of *La Forza del Destino.* Hamburg presented the first performance of Milko Kelemen's *Der Belagerungszustand* (January 13) and Ernst Krenek's *Sardakai* (June 27). Frankfurt gave *Lulu* a new production (January 1) with Anja Silja in the title role.

At the Munich Festival in July and August there were new productions of *Die Zauberflöte,* conducted by Rafael Kubelik; *Die Entführung aus dem Serail,* conducted by Hans Schmidt-Isserstedt; Richard Strauss's *Capriccio,* conducted by Ferdinand Leitner; and Stravinsky's *Oedipus Rex,* conducted by Michael Gielen. At the Bayreuth Festival, Wolfgang Wagner was in charge of a new production of *Der Ring des Nibelungen,* conducted by Horst Stein. Alan Bush's *Joe Hill* had its first performance at the East Berlin Festival (September 29). New productions at the start of the 1970–71 season were *Boris Godunov,* original version (Cologne, September 29), *Der Rosenkavalier,* conducted by Josef Krips (West Berlin, September 24), and *Carmina Burana* (Munich, October 16).

Austria. Toward the end of 1969, Gluck's *Iphigénie en Tauride,* with Sena Jurinac in the name part, was given at the Vienna State Opera, and Cilea's *Adriana Lecouvreur* at the Volksoper. There was a new production of *Macbeth* (April 18), well conducted by Karl Böhm, with Christa Ludwig and Sherrill Milnes giving superb performances as the Macbeths. The producer was Otto Schenk, who was also responsible for the memorable bicentenary production of *Fidelio* (May 24), conducted by Leonard Bernstein, at the Theater an der Wien, where the opera was first performed. The first major new production of the 1970–71 season was *Don Carlos* (October 25).

On March 29, *Götterdämmerung* was produced and conducted by Herbert von Karajan at the Salzburg Easter Festival. At the Salzburg Festival proper in July and August, Karajan produced *Otello,* with Jon Vickers, Peter Glossop, and Mirella Freni in the cast. There was a new production of *Fidelio* by Günther Rennert, conducted by Karl Böhm, in the renovated Felsenreitschule.

Italy. The 1969–70 season at La Scala, Milan, opened with *Ernani,* Placido Domingo in the title role. In March, Beverly Sills was heard as Lucia di Lammermoor in Donizetti's opera and Montserrat Caballé appeared as his Lucrezia Borgia. In April there were two new productions: *Pagliacci* and Prokofiev's *The Fiery Angel.* The Teatro dell' Opera, Rome, gave the premiere of Luciano Chailly's *L'Idiota,* conducted by Nino Sanzongo, on February 14 and the first Italian performance of Gottfried von Einem's *Dantons Tod* on April 30. Other new productions were Bellini's *La Straniera* (February 26) and *Carmen* (March 11) with Grace Bumbry. Other outstanding events during the season included Sills in *Traviata* at Naples; Donizetti's *Le Convenienze ed Inconvenienze Teatrali* (February 3); Rossini's *Armida* (April 3), with Christine Deutekom, at Venice; and *Falstaff,* with Rolando Penerai, at the Florence Maggio Musicale. The Verona Festival opened with Mauro Bolignini's eccentric production of *La Traviata* (July 16), with Renata Scotto as a moving Violetta.

France. In November 1969 Josephine Veasey sang Dido in a new production of Berlioz' *Les Troyens* at the Paris Opéra. At Toulouse on April 10, Alain Vanzo sang the title role in a new production of *Benvenuto Cellini.* Fauré's *Promethée* was revived at the Roman Theatre at Fourvière, Lyons. At the Aix Festival the outstanding production was Rossini's *L'Italiana in Algeri* with Jane Berbié in the title role. The Bolshoi Opera visited Paris in January. The company mounted an outstanding *Eugene Onegin* with Galina Vishnevskaya as Tatiana.

Other Countries. Caballé sang Norma for the first time in a Barcelona production of Bellini's opera on January 8. Hilding Rosenberg's new opera, *The House with Double Entrance,* had its premiere at the Stockholm Opera on May 21. The Netherlands Festival mounted the first modern revival of Haydn's *La Fedeltà Premiata.* Kyril Molchanov's *Russian Women* had its premiere at Saratov (U.S.S.R.). The Wexford (Ire.) Festival opened on October 23 with a double bill of Rossini's *L'Inganno Felice* and Donizetti's *Giovedì Grasso.* (A. G. BL.)

Jazz. The year saw a continuation of those processes by which the energies of jazz music were being dispersed—the denial of all formal logic by the younger school; further attempts to synthesize the jazz art within classical frames; the hopeless, and perhaps deliberate, confusion of aesthetic and political criteria in the so-called revolutionary music of the rising black American musicians; the further blurring of the lines of demarcation, once so strongly drawn, between the fundamentally antipathetic worlds of jazz and pop. All this lent credence to what was not so long ago the great heresy—that jazz might after all prove to be a finite art.

A seminal figure in this context was Miles Davis, a trumpeter and group leader who, ten years before, had created an art of exquisite beauty out of the strict economy of his instrumental style and the mood

GAMMA FROM PIX

Duke Ellington presents a concert of sacred music for 5,000 people in Saint-Sulpice Church in New York City's Harlem.

of melancholia that informed its execution. By 1970 Davis had drifted so far from the old disciplines that the music he produced with the aid of various electronic percussion instruments was beginning to appeal more to the pop followers, leaving some of Davis' contemporaries baffled.

But in spite of the vital importance of such issues as the direction jazz ought to take, whether it was doomed entirely as a method of musical expression, and how to woo audiences away from the world of pop, all such questions were dwarfed in 1970, at least for a period, by junketings all over the world in celebration of the 70th birthday of Louis Armstrong. The unanimity of emotion over this event was quite extraordinary, tempting one to draw parallels between jazz and a declining imperial power with one last opportunity to indulge in a self-congratulatory orgy of nostalgia.

And yet there was a sense in which this slightly hysterical apotheosis of Armstrong was justified. Born in New Orleans, La., on July 4, 1900, Armstrong, more than any other man, had come to personify the jazz spirit. There was little doubt that he had been more influential than any other single figure in the evolution of the art of improvising on a harmonic base against a rhythmic background, which is what jazz is, and through the turbulent years of experimental excess there remained a vague feeling that as long as Armstrong continued to be active, jazz itself must by definition be alive and well.

Under these circumstances, it was perhaps too much to have expected the celebrants to acknowledge publicly the sad fact that it was extremely unlikely that Armstrong the trumpeter would now add anything of significance to his existing body of work. The processes of advancing age had reduced what was once the most heroic of all jazz styles to a very dim echo.

Armstrong's great surviving contemporary and only rival, Duke Ellington, who himself endured fulsome 70th-birthday tributes in 1969, suffered a tragic loss during 1970 with the death of his leading saxophonist, Johnny Hodges (*see* OBITUARIES). A member of the Ellington band since 1928, with one short breach in the early 1950s, Hodges had a spectacular elegiac style on ballads, with unique glissandi effects that had become so intrinsic a part of the Ellington orchestral technique that it was almost impossible to imagine any Ellington band without him. Coupled with the death in 1967 of Ellington's composing alter ego, Billy Strayhorn, the passing of Hodges at the age of 63 was an event that many people felt might prove too much even for Ellington. And yet, soon after the death of Hodges, Ellington toured Europe and staggered audiences with the apparently unaffected power and subtlety of his orchestra.

The death of a man like Hodges (following that of a man like Coleman Hawkins the previous year) underlined the grave problem that was now beginning to be apparent in the jazz world. Since jazz itself was roughly as old as the century, more and more of its founding fathers were dying off. The mortality rate in the jazz world was always high, but in the past there had always been a rising generation to carry on the tradition. Now, for the first time in the music's history, the line of succession seemed about to be broken.

As genuine talent became rarer, an isolated success like that of the Kenny Clarke-Francy Boland band became exaggerated. This group began as a means of relaxation for recording musicians and steadily developed into the only new big band of the past ten years to have any meaning. Clarke-Boland, internationally recruited, represented the musicians' hunger for the larger orchestral effects. The audiences' hunger was reflected in a very different way—in a nostalgic demand for the sounds of the big bands of the golden age of 30 years earlier. The Glenn Miller revival in particular had now reached embarrassing proportions, with groups in every country in Europe, as well as in the U.S., producing facsimiles of the Miller sound. Other veterans, such as Harry James and Benny Goodman, went to Europe to be bowled over by the sheer ferocity of the demand for the sound of the supposedly good old days. Audiences that listen by memory are better than no audiences at all, but current trends strongly hinted that, while the younger musicians continued to dismantle the classical methods of improvisation, the jazz world at large was living off its credit.

(B. GR.)

Popular. During 1969–70 pop music continued to mature, and while no revolution occurred (despite much talk), there were interesting developments. The fast-rising price of single records swayed the market strongly in favour of LPs, many of which were relatively cheap. Artists too were turning away from singles and regarding LPs as the most important aspect of their work. Outstanding among the many excellent albums was The Who's rock-opera "Tommy."

One type of music that kept within the bounds of the single was "reggae," which swept Britain in the autumn of 1969. Imported by West Indian immigrants, reggae was simple, catchy, and very rhythmic; being easy to dance to, it became very popular with younger teen-agers. It was also a style to which many tunes could be adapted, so that, in addition to original West Indian numbers such as Desmond Dekker's "Israelites," "Elizabethan Serenade" appeared in the charts, updated as "Elizabethan Reggae," along with a similar version of the old Everly Brothers' song "Love of the Common People." A year after its arrival reggae's popularity showed no signs of waning.

There was a definite trend toward bigger groups, many of which featured strong brass sections. First of these was Blood, Sweat, and Tears, a nine-piece American "jazz-rock" band whose highly sophisticated music contained both jazz and classical elements. Their first LP was one of the most significant of 1969. During 1970 Blood, Sweat, and Tears concentrated on cabaret work; their place in pop was taken by Chicago, whose exciting music owed more to rock than to jazz.

The most consistently successful group of the year played rock that was pure, simple, and earthy: Creedence Clearwater Revival, four musicians headed by singer-composer John Fogerty. During 1969–70 they produced a string of hit singles and several best-selling LPs, and packed concert halls in the U.S. and Britain.

The most significant event of 1969 had been the Woodstock rock festival, which took place near New York in August 1969; the vast audience and absence of violence made it something of a legend, and a film was made of the three-day "happening." A number of promoters sought to emulate Woodstock in 1970, and the year saw many open-air festivals, the biggest of which was staged on the Isle of Wight at the end of August.

RICHARD BALAGUR FROM
NANCY PALMER
Melanie performs at the three-day Strawberry Fields rock festival at Mosport, Ont., in August 1970.

RICHARD BALAGUR FROM
NANCY PALMER

Sly, of Sly and the Family
Stone, performs
at the Strawberry Fields
rock festival in Canada.

RICHARD BALAGUR FROM
NANCY PALMER

The dynamic Tina, of
the Ike and Tina Turner
Revue, sings at the
Newport (R.I.) Jazz
Festival, July 12, 1970.

In 1970 the term "supergroup" went somewhat out of fashion; Blind Faith, for whom it had been coined, proved to be short-lived and disbanded after their U.S. tour. However, top pop musicians continued to work together in a way similar to their jazz counterparts, teaming up for short periods. Catalysts of this movement were Delaney and Bonnie Bramlett, a couple from the southern U.S., whose brand of "white soul" attracted first Eric Clapton, "god" of the guitarists, and then John Lennon and Yoko Ono. These combined efforts produced some memorable music, and in some cases, notably that of Crosby, Stills, Nash, and Young, the musicians stayed together. On a more commercial level, it became common for session singers to form vocal groups and make their own records, many of which did well in the charts.

By 1970 the Beatles had virtually ceased to exist as a group, although individually they were active—John with the Plastic Ono Band, Paul with a solo album, George with Eastern culture, and Ringo with recording and film acting. No new recordings followed their 1969 LP "Abbey Road"; material for their 1970 single, LP, and promotional film—all entitled "Let It Be"—had been recorded earlier. Many people felt that "Let It Be" was the Beatles' farewell, but their future remained obscure.

Nobody could quite take the place of the Beatles, but much new talent did emerge during the year. Most promising of the new artists were Melanie, a girl singer-composer of Ukrainian origin, and the Jackson 5, a dynamic young family group under the auspices of Tamla Motown. That organization celebrated its tenth anniversary in 1970.

Pop suffered a great loss in September 1970 with the death of Jimi Hendrix, one of the business's most individual guitarists and personalities. Hendrix, who was only 27 when he died, was the inspiration of many young players, among them Ritchie Blackmore, guitarist with the British group Deep Purple. Shortly afterward came the death, at a similarly young age, of Janis Joplin, the spirited jazz-rock singer who had sung with Big Brother and the Holding Company. (See OBITUARIES.)

The year was not without its novelties. In November 1969 the British and U.S. charts were topped by The Archies, a group that did not exist except in a cartoon strip; and over Christmas the British no. 1 slot was held by Australian entertainer Rolf Harris with "Two Little Boys," a song of the Crimean War. The violin became highly popular as a group instrument, being featured by The Band, The Flock, and other rock groups as well as in folk-style ensembles. Simon and Garfunkel scored one of their biggest successes with their single and LP "Bridge Over Troubled Water"; Deep Purple premiered another group-and-orchestra work; and a new British quartet, Mungo Jerry, found overnight fame with their jolly, skiffle-like single "In The Summertime."

Beneath such surface activities, the mainstream of pop flowed steadily on. Artists were becoming increasingly self-sufficient, performing their own material and producing their own records. Outstanding among this new breed of composer-singers were Joni Mitchell from Canada and Elton John, one of Britain's most individual young musicians. It was with artists such as these that the future of pop seemed to lie, at least for the coming year.   (H. R. Mo.)

Folk Music. With the ever increasing tide of commercial popular music emanating from radio and records, there had been a tendency in most parts of the world for the traditional practice of folk music to weaken or even disappear. On the other hand, the growing awareness of the importance of folk music as a cultural component of contemporary life led to increased efforts, not only to encourage its continued practice among the bearers of the tradition, but also to introduce it to a wider circle of the population.

During 1970 many organizations and institutions were actively concerned with folk music in education. A splendid lead was given by the International Library of African Music with the publication of its Codification and Textbook Project, the aim of which was to enable the whole musical tradition of sub-Saharan Africa to take its place in African musical education. The Ford Foundation, which assisted this project, also made an award to the U.S. Bureau of Indian Affairs for work in the field of American Indian music education.

A fruitful means of disseminating songs and dances was through records and films. Of the many records, special mention might be made of those from Czechoslovakia, Hungary, Norway, Romania, Indonesia, Israel, and Ethiopia. Films included a series issued by the National Film Board of Canada on the Natsilek Eskimos. Many archives greatly increased their collections of folk music, some of the richest international collections being those of the Archive of Folk Song at the Library of Congress in Washington, D.C., the British Broadcasting Corporation, and the British Institute of Recorded Sound.

Both radio and television organizations continued to give performances of folk music. Representatives of such organizations and of sound film archives held a conference in Budapest, Hung., under the auspices of the International Folk Music Council (IFMC), where the subject for discussion was "New Approaches to Musical Traditions." Other conferences held under the auspices of the IFMC were on "The History of Folk Music Until 1500" (at Brno, Czech.) and "The Study of Folk Music Instruments" (at Stockholm).

Folk music organizations in all countries increased their activities, whether in collection and research or in instruction and folk song and dance meetings. In particular the Canadian Centre for Folk Culture Studies, attached to the National Museum of Man, carried out extensive field research among its minority communities. The number of people taking part in regional, national, and international festivals grew considerably. The annual festivals given by the English Folk Dance and Song Society at the Royal Albert Hall and elsewhere attracted large numbers. Competitors from some 20 countries took part in the folk song and dance sections of the 24th annual Musical Eisteddfod at Llangollen, Wales.

The year's publications included *Folk Music of Britain and Beyond* by Frank Howes; *Cantrometrics* by Alan Lomax; *T'ang Music and Musical Instruments* by L. E. R. Picken; *La Contredanse et les Renouvellements de la Danse Française* by Jean-Michel Guilcher; *Folk Songs from Newfoundland* by Maud Karpeles; and *The Song Tradition of Tristan da Cunha* by Peter A. Munch.   (MA. KA.)

See also Cinema; Dance; Television and Radio; Theatre.

ENCYCLOPÆDIA BRITANNICA FILMS. *Listening to Good Music (The String Quartet)* (1955); *Playing Good Music (The String Quartet)* (1955); *The Brass Choir* (1956); *Conducting Good Music* (1956); *The Percussion Group* (1956); *The String Choir* (1956); *The Symphony Orchestra* (1956); *The Woodwind Choir* (1956); *Casals Conducts,* 1964 (1965).

Nauru

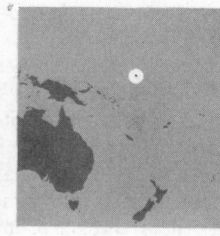

An island republic in the Pacific Ocean, Nauru lies about 1,200 mi. E of New Guinea. Area: 8.2 sq.mi. (21 sq.km.). Pop. (1970 est.): 6,603. President in 1970, Hammer de Roburt.

Improving transport and communication between Nauru and the rest of the Pacific had high priority in 1970. The American Telephone and Telegraph Co. opened a link between Nauru and Guam. Air Nauru, the smallest international airline in the world, carried out its inaugural flight between the island and Brisbane, Austr., in February. The Nauru Local Government Council purchased the "Prinses Margriet" from the Holland-America Line. This 9,336-ton ship had luxury accommodations for 111 people, and was to be used to supplement Nauruan services on the Australia–New Guinea–Fiji route.

In an attempt to facilitate tourism, the government put up for sale a half-completed modern hotel, the former owners of which had gone out of business in October 1969 with unpaid debts of A$130,000. The unfinished hotel, which overlooked Anibare Bay, was well placed to take advantage of Nauru's tourist potential. In another economic development the number of new Australian companies incorporated or registered in Nauru since independence (in order to take advantage of the island's tax-free status) rose to 30.

Because of the menace posed by crown-of-thorns starfish, which threatened to destroy Pacific island coral reefs, the government decided to pay a A$3 bounty for every such starfish caught on Nauru's reef.

(A. R. G. G.)

NAURU
Education. (1967) Primary, pupils 1,419, teachers (1966) 79; secondary, pupils 326, teachers (1966) 19; teacher training, students 18, teachers 1.
Finance and Trade. Monetary unit: Australian dollar (A$0.89 = U.S. $1; A$2.14 = £1 sterling). Budget (1968–69): revenue A$16,447,858; expenditure A$13,368,774. Foreign trade (1968–69): imports A$5,224,924 (72% from Australia, 7% from New Zealand); exports (phosphates) A$24,046,000 (65% to Australia, 24% to New Zealand, 7% to Japan by tonnage).
Industry. Production (in 000): phosphate rock (metric tons; 1967–68) 2,262; electricity (public supply; kw-hr.; 1968) 19,300.

Nepal

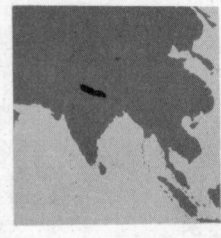

A constitutional monarchy of Asia, Nepal is in the Himalayas between India and Tibet. Area: 54,362 sq.mi. (140,797 sq.km.). Pop. (1970 est.): 11,044,034. Cap. and largest city: Kathmandu (pop., 1968 est., 137,400). Language: Nepali (official); also Newari and Bhutia. Religion: Hindu 85%; Buddhist 8%; Muslim 2%. King, and chairman of the Council of Ministers (prime minister) succeeding Kirti Nidhi Bista in April 1970, Mahendra Bir Bikram Shah Deva.

The resignation of Prime Minister Bista on April 12, 1970, to pave the way for national *panchayat* (village council) elections, due to begin in May, enabled King Mahendra to exercise tighter control over the affairs of state. The king appointed a restricted Cabinet with himself as chairman of the Council of Ministers. The *panchayat* elections were held on May 28 to fill 30 vacancies in the 125-member National Assembly. Bista was defeated, and in the new Cabinet the king assumed the powers of prime minister. In June and July several students were arrested for antigovernment activities and jailed for varying terms.

Nepal's relations with its big northern neighbour, China, were normal during 1970, but ties with India showed signs of strain. Peking sent Kuo Mo-jo, vice-chairman of the Standing Committee of the Chinese People's Congress, as China's official representative to Crown Prince Birendra's wedding in February. Kuo extended his stay in Kathmandu to lead a Chinese goodwill delegation to Nepal and signed a joint statement with Prime Minister Bista at the end of the visit extolling the close ties between the two countries and assuring Nepal of China's continued assistance.

Despite long and protracted discussions during the first half of the year, Indian and Nepalese officials failed to reach agreement on the question of renewing the trade transit treaty between the two countries, due to expire on October 31. In the absence of an agreement, Indian officials said that the treaty might be extended for another three months. Landlocked Nepal was demanding unrestricted passage for its goods through Indian ports.

(G. U.)

NEPAL
Education. (1966–67) Primary, pupils 394,700, teachers 13,960; secondary and vocational, pupils 69,100, teachers 3,500; teacher training, students 217, teachers 19; higher (including university at Kathmandu), students 10,235, teaching staff 751.
Finance. Monetary unit: Nepalese rupee, with a par value of NRs. 10.12 to U.S. $1 (NRs. 24.30 = £1 sterling; NRs. 1.35 = Indian R. 1). Gold, SDRs, and foreign exchange, central bank: (June 1970) U.S. $86.7 million; (June 1969) U.S. $74.7 million. Budget (1968–69): revenue NRs. 641 million (including NRs. 276 million foreign aid); expenditure NRs. 667 million (including NRs. 458.4 million development expenditure).
Foreign Trade. (1968) Imports NRs. 392.9 million (98% from India in 1965–66); exports NRs. 291.6 million (95% to India in 1965–66). Main exports (1965–66): food and livestock 67%; manufactures 23%; crude materials (including timber and jute) 7%.
Agriculture. Production (in 000; metric tons; 1969; 1968 in parentheses): rice c. 2,475 (2,322); jute c. 35 (c. 30). Livestock (in 000; 1968–69): cattle c. 5,980; pigs c. 380; sheep c. 2,100; goats c. 2,350.

Netherlands

A kingdom of northwest Europe on the North Sea, the Netherlands, a Benelux country, is bounded by Belgium on the south and West Germany on the east. Overseas parts of the realm comprise the Netherlands Antilles and Surinam. Area: 14,140 sq.mi. (36,624 sq.km.). Pop. (1970 est.): 12,957,621. Cap. and largest city: Amsterdam (pop., 1970 est., 831,463). Language: Netherlandic (Dutch). Religion (1960): Roman Catholic 40.4%; Dutch Reformed 28.3%; Reformed Churches 9.3%. Queen, Juliana; prime minister in 1970, Piet J. S. de Jong.

Compared with previous years, the Netherlands government underwent only a small change in 1970. The minister of economic affairs, Leo de Block, resigned over the Cabinet's refusal to interfere in labour contracts in the metal industry and was succeeded

Navies:
see Defense

KEYSTONE

Amsterdam police chase "Krakers," young people who occupy uninhabited houses because they cannot find housing elsewhere, after clearing them from a house in May 1970.

by Roelof J. Nelissen. The government continued to consist of six members of the Catholic People's Party, three members of the People's Party for Freedom and Democracy, three members of the Antirevolutionary Party, and two members of the Christian Historical Union.

On March 18 and June 3 the Dutch voters elected their representatives in the Provinciale Staten (roughly equivalent to county councils) and the Gemeenteraden (municipal councils). It was the first time since 1917 that voting in the Netherlands had not been compulsory. The outcome disappointed most politicians. The turnouts of voters were 68.9% (county councils) and 66.6% (municipal councils). Apart from a remarkable success by the Communist Party in both elections, and a successful start for the "Goblin Party"—a new political movement,

mainly supported by young labourers and students— in the elections for the municipal councils, no major changes occurred.

Queen Juliana opened the new session of Parliament on September 15. The queen's speech, prepared by the government, began with a reference to the increasing tensions and conflicts in society. In such a situation, she said, tolerance was of great importance, as was willingness to cooperate and to respect the opinion of others. But she promised that, if necessary, the government would take action against groups that abused freedom. The speech then dealt with ways to improve communication between "the rulers and the ruled" and concluded with a warning against the pollution.

The budget for 1971, presented by the finance minister, Hendrik J. Witteveen, forecast revenue of 30,-663,000,000 guilders and expenditure of 32,725,000,-000 guilders. The deficit amounted to 1.8% of the national income. The minister proposed some measures against the increasing inflation, including a provisional 3% rise in some taxes and a freeze on wages.

At the same time, the Government Planning Office published a survey of economic conditions. As in the previous year, the economic situation in 1970 was unstable. A rapid rise in demand from abroad and a quick growth of national consumption and investments were accompanied by a shortage of labour and of production capacity in some sectors of industry. The price level of imports rose by 5%, and the cost of wages rose by about 11%. The consumption volume increased by 7%, and real income rose by 5%. It was estimated that the prices of consumer goods rose by more than 4%. Investment costs showed an increase of over 8% but, nevertheless, the amount of investments rose by 10%. The average number of unemployed was less than 50,000.

A bill passed in late 1969 gave the government power to intervene in the economy by ordering a freeze on wages or by suspending labour contracts. The bill was opposed by the trade unions and, when it came into force, two of the three national trade unions ceased to cooperate in wage discussions among representatives from the government, trade unions, and employers' organizations.

On Jan. 7, 1970, the Dutch Pastoral Council of the Roman Catholic Church, the only national pastoral council in the world, abolished celibacy. The

NETHERLANDS

Education. (1967–68) Primary, pupils 1,427,-966, teachers 46,008; secondary, pupils 552,087, teachers 29,788; vocational, pupils 559,343; teacher training, students 13,121, teachers 1,149; higher (including 9 universities), students 182,-044.

Finance. Monetary unit: guilder or florin, with a par value of 3.62 guilders to U.S. $1 (8.69 guilders = £1 sterling). Gold, SDRs, and foreign exchange, central bank: (June 1970) U.S. $2,150,-000,000; (June 1969) U.S. $1,965,000,000. Budget (1970 est.): revenue 27,222,000,000 guilders; expenditure 29,397,000,000 guilders. Gross national product: (1968) 91,330,000,000 guilders; (1967) 82,970,000,000 guilders. Money supply: (June 1970) 25,670,000,000 guilders; (June 1969) 23,580,000,000 guilders. Cost of living (1963 = 100): (June 1970) 140; (June 1969) 135.

Foreign Trade. (1969) Imports 39,786,000,-000 guilders; exports 36,073,000,000 guilders. Import sources: EEC 57% (West Germany 27%, Belgium-Luxembourg 18%, France 8%, Italy 5%); U.S. 10%; U.K. 6%. Export destinations: EEC 60% (West Germany 30%, Belgium-Luxembourg 14%, France 12%, Italy 5%);

U.K. 8%; U.S. 5%. Main exports: chemicals 13%; electrical machinery and equipment 9%; textile yarns and fabrics 7%; machinery (non-electrical) 7%; petroleum products 6%; meat products 6%. Tourism (1968): visitors 1,928,-900; gross receipts U.S. $342 million.

Transport and Communications. Roads (1969) 77,770 km. (including 876 km. expressways). Motor vehicles in use (1969): passenger 2,305,700; commercial 326,500. Railways: (1968) 3,147 km. (including 1,645 km. electrified); traffic (1969) 7,533,000,000 passenger-km., freight 3,451,000,000 net ton-km. Air traffic (1969): 4,760,000,000 passenger-km.; freight 373,760,000 net ton-km. Navigable inland waterways (1968): 5,821 km. (including 2,398 km. for ships of 1,000 tons and over); freight traffic 31,044,000,000 ton-km. Shipping (1969): merchant vessels 100 gross tons and over 1,652; gross tonnage 5,254,883. Ships entered (1968) vessels totaling 102,910,000 net registered tons; goods loaded (1969) 48,106,000 metric tons, unloaded 172,576,000 metric tons. Telephones (Dec. 1968) 2,912,384. Radio receivers (Dec. 1968) 3,174,000. Television receivers (Dec. 1968) 2,658,000.

Agriculture. Production (in 000; metric tons; 1969; 1968 in parentheses): wheat 699 (679); rye 207 (239); barley 389 (389); oats 338 (318); potatoes 4,704 (5,045); tomatoes (1968) 343, (1967) 346; apples 460 (340); pears 85 (180); sugar, raw value (1969–70) c. 762, (1968–69) 720; dry peas 38 (36); rapeseed 12 (18); linseed 12 (14); flax fibre 13 (13); beef and veal 286 (285); pork 569 (594); milk 7,848 (7,764); butter 112 (119); cheese c. 260 (245); eggs 228 (223); fish catch (1968) 323, (1967) 315. Livestock (in 000; May 1969): cattle 4,324; pigs 4,780; sheep 554; horses used in agriculture 110; chickens 48,480.

Industry. Index of production (1963 = 100): (1969) 160; (1968) 143. Production (in 000; metric tons; 1969): coal 5,562; crude oil 2,022; natural gas (cu.m.) 21,848,000; manufactured gas (cu.m.) 934,000; electricity (kw-hr.) 37,144,-000; pig iron 3,461; crude steel 4,712; zinc 47; cement 3,296; cotton yarn 55; wool yarn 17; rayon, etc., filament yarn 37. Merchant vessels launched (100 gross tons and over; 1969) 601,-000 gross tons. New dwellings completed (1969) 123,100.

national episcopate adopted this abolition in spite of strong protests from Rome. (*See* RELIGION.)

On March 4 representatives of the United Kingdom, West Germany, and the Netherlands signed an agreement for the joint production of enriched uranium by the gas-ultracentrifuge process in factories at Almelo, Neth., and Capenhurst, Cheshire. To realize this project, Ultra-Centrifuge Nederland NV had been set up in November 1969. The government had a majority of the shares in this limited company.

Late in August the Dutch people were shocked when the Indonesian embassy in The Hague was forcibly occupied by a group of exiles from Amboina in the Moluccas in eastern Indonesia, and a policeman was killed. The object of the action was to draw attention to the claims of the people of the Moluccas, who wanted to be independent of Indonesia. The occupation took place just before the arrival of the president of Indonesia, General Suharto; his visit passed without serious incident but was cut by two days. Also in August police clashed with young demonstrators in Amsterdam after the mayor had prohibited sleeping on the national monument on the Dam. (D. Bo.)

See also Dependent States.

ENCYCLOPÆDIA BRITANNICA FILMS. *People of the Netherlands* (1957); *Holland: Hold Back the Sea* (1967); *Jan—Boy of the Netherlands* (1970); *Rotterdam—Europoort, Gateway to Europe* (1970).

New Zealand

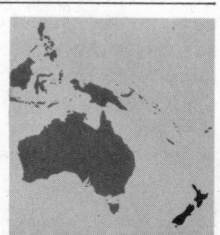

The Dominion of New Zealand, a parliamentary state and member of the Commonwealth of Nations, is in the South Pacific Ocean, separated from southeastern Australia and Tasmania by the Tasman Sea. The country proper consists of North and South islands and Stewart, Chatham, and other minor islands. Area: 103,736 sq.mi. (268,686 sq.km.). Pop. (1970 est.): 2,820,814. Cap.: Wellington (pop., 1970 est., 134,900). Largest city: Christchurch (pop., 1970 est., 166,100). Largest urban area: Auckland (pop., 1970 est., 603,500). Language: English; also Maori. Religion (1966): Church of England 33.7%; Presbyterian 21.8%; Roman Catholic 15.9%. Queen, Elizabeth II; governor-general in 1970, Sir Arthur Porritt; prime minister, Sir Keith J. Holyoake.

New Zealanders tried to pay themselves more than two dollars of extra money for every dollar of extra production, the minister of finance, Robert Muldoon, told Parliament at the end of October 1970, when he introduced emergency measures to stop a cost-price-wage spiral. This followed a warning of a serious economic situation by a government-appointed Monetary and Economic Council. The council chairman, F. W. Holmes, recommended a temporary increase in direct taxation, control of government expenditure, and credit curbs. The government favoured both the income tax rise and increased taxes on cigarettes and gasoline. Post Office charges went up, deposit requirements on installment purchases were stiffened, and provision was made for NZ$60 million more by way of supplementary estimates.

The direct income tax rise was $3\frac{1}{3}\%$, by way of surcharge for 1970–71 and the following year; cigarettes increased in price by 6 cents for 20; gasoline prices went up $2\frac{1}{2}$ cents a gallon, and were to increase again when a price rise granted to the industry and

a local tax authorized by the government became effective. The emergency measures came four months after the normal June budget, which imposed a payroll tax on companies but was otherwise unremarkable.

Most primary exports during the year were to Britain. Meat was a firm seller, wool weakened again, and dairy products were again threatened by U.K. negotiations for entry into the EEC. The new U.K. Conservative government carried out a pledge to place a levy on certain food imports. Freight rates on transport of meat and dairy products to the U.K. increased by $4\frac{1}{2}\%$. Several thousand workers marched on Parliament to protest against price rises. The year bore out the prime minister's New Year message that going for New Zealanders would be tougher in the 1970s. Most promising development was the discovery of oil offshore from New Plymouth-Wanganui (Maui 3), which might boost natural gas resources.

The government suffered a by-election defeat shortly after their general election victory, losing to Labour the seat held until his death by the minister of labour, Tom Shand. MPs during the year adopted a commission's recommendation of a 31% salary increase.

Prime Minister Holyoake was created a knight grand cross of the Order of St. Michael and St. George in the queen's birthday-honours list. His acceptance, unusual for an active politician, increased speculation that he planned retirement, but he denied this.

Prime Minister Holyoake's knighthood followed a

KEYSTONE

Several thousand trade unionists and sympathizers stage a four-hour stopwork meeting on Parliament grounds in Wellington, N.Z., May 12, 1970, to protest the soaring cost of living.

NEW ZEALAND
Education. (1967) Primary, pupils 500,898, teachers 17,983; secondary and vocational, pupils 168,534, teachers 8,356; teacher training, students 6,155, teachers 426; higher (including 6 universities), students 47,516, teaching staff 2,664.
Finance. Monetary unit: New Zealand dollar, with a par value of NZ$0.89 to U.S. $1 (NZ$2.14 = £1 sterling). Gold, SDRs, and foreign exchange, central bank: (June 1970) U.S. $170 million; (June 1969) U.S. $165 million. Budget (1968–69 est.): revenue NZ$1,140,900,000; expenditure NZ$1,146,900,000. Gross national product: (1968–69) NZ$4,341,000,000; (1967–68) NZ$4,055,000,000. Money supply: (June 1970) NZ$812.8 million; (June 1969) NZ$762.1 million. Cost of living (1963 = 100): (2nd quarter 1970) 134; (2nd quarter 1969) 127.
Foreign Trade. (1969) Imports NZ$895.7 million; exports NZ$1,080,900,000. Import sources: U.K. 31%; Australia 20%; U.S. 12%; Japan 8%. Export destinations: U.K. 39%; U.S. 16%; Japan 9%; Australia 7%. Main exports: wool 21%; lamb and mutton 18%; butter 11%.
Transport and Communications. Roads (1969) 93,932 km. Motor vehicles in use (1969): passenger 854,716; commercial 168,057. Railways (state; 1969): 4,929 km.; traffic 516 million passenger-km., freight 2,700,000,000 net ton-km. Air traffic (1968): 1,266,629,000 passenger-km.; freight 34,097,000 net ton-km. Shipping (1969): merchant vessels 100 gross tons and over 124; gross tonnage 180,561. Telephones (Dec. 1968) 1,155,465. Radio receivers (Dec. 1968) 657,000. Television receivers (Dec. 1968) 604,000.
Agriculture. Production (in 000; metric tons; 1969; 1968 in parentheses): wheat 445 (442); barley 202 (219); oats 51 (45); potatoes 258 (300); dry peas (1968) 36, (1967) 32; apples 114 (113); mutton and lamb (1968) 567, (1967) 521; beef and veal (1968) 346, (1967) 302; milk 6,479 (6,157); butter 264 (252); cheese *c.* 98 (112); wool 236 (237); timber (cu.m.; 1968) 7,400, (1967) 6,800; fish catch (1967) 60, (1966) 56. Livestock (in 000; Jan. 1969): cattle 8,557; sheep (June 1969) 60,100; horses *c.* 83; pigs 563; chickens (April 1969) *c.* 5,000.
Industry. Fuel and power (in 000; metric tons; 1969): coal 485; lignite 1,878; manufactured gas (cu.m.) 176,000; electricity (excluding most industrial production; kw-hr.) 12,666,000. Production (in 000; metric tons; 1969): cement 803; superphosphates (1967) 1,358; mechanical wood pulp (1968–69) 235; chemical wood pulp (1968–69) 259; newsprint 207.

AUTHENTICATED NEWS
INTERNATIONAL

Queen Elizabeth II reads
the speech from
the throne at the state
opening of Parliament
during the royal family's
visit to New Zealand.

royal tour in March, timed to honour the bicentenary
of Captain Cook's voyage of discovery. Accompanying
the queen and Prince Philip, the prince of Wales and
his sister Princess Anne made their first tour of the
dominion. During the tour the queen made the Maori
queen, Ariki nui Te Ata-i-Rangikaahu, a dame commander of the British Empire.

Broadcasting control was at the crossroads, with
hearings by a newly appointed broadcasting licensing
authority on the award of a license for a second television channel. During the year the same authority
awarded the first private radio licenses since the nationalization of broadcasting in the late 1930s.

Conservation's biggest issue was a government decision to grant Comalco water rights for a smelter, involving the likely raising of Lake Manapouri and the
drowning of lakeside forest and beaches. A commission
considered a 200,000-signature petition and reported
indecisively. Education had a restless year with the
new minister, Brian Talboys, drawing fire for remarks
made in a TV interview on the status of teachers, and
with salary agitation so sharp that national stopwork
meetings (they were called briefings) were held.

Racial controversy was edgy when a national Rugby
union team was dispatched on a tour of South Africa,
but this time the New Zealanders included nonwhites, and the tour was regarded by many as a foot
in apartheid's door and a morale-raiser for more
liberal elements in South Africa, who were provided
with evidence that mixed sport could be played inside
a country espousing separatism. The agreement on
involvement in Vietnam waned and New Zealand announced in August that an infantry company would be
withdrawn by the end of the year.   (Jo. A. K.)

See also Dependent States.

Nicaragua

The largest country of Central America, Nicaragua
is a republic bounded by Honduras, Costa Rica, the
Caribbean Sea, and the Pacific Ocean. Area: 49,173
sq.mi. (127,358 sq.km.). Pop. (1968 est.): 1,809,477,
including mestizo 70%; white 17%; Negro 9%; Indian 4%. Cap. and largest city: Managua (pop., 1968
est., 380,966). Language: Spanish. Religion: Roman
Catholic. President in 1970, Brig. Gen. Anastasio
Somoza Debayle.

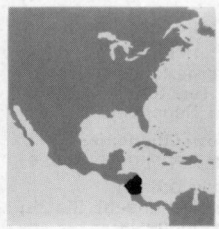

Nickel:
see Mining

The economic recession that had characterized the
second year of President Somoza Debayle's administration continued into the third year. Once again,
cotton, Nicaragua's number one export crop, was responsible for the depressed condition of the nation's
economy. The acreage planted to cotton was greatly
reduced, and poor yields caused increased distress
among the cotton planters.

The rapidly growing beef industry for the first time
surpassed coffee as the nation's second largest foreign
exchange earner, but the future potential for this industry was limited by a restriction on exports to the
U.S., the principal market. High prices on the world
market, an increase in the International Coffee Organization quota, and good weather conditions coincided
to make 1970 a good year for coffee growers. Maintaining its fourth-place position as a major export
crop, sugar, exported exclusively to the U.S., had an
excellent year and more than met its quota; but because of an abundance of sugar throughout the world
there were no plans to increase production. The new
shrimp and lobster industry grew rapidly during the
year. However, the combined total of these expanding
exports was unable to compensate for cotton's decline,
and the result was a 2.2% decrease in total export
earnings over the preceding year.

Imports declined 4.3% from 1969 as a result of the
contraction of the economy. The decline in agricultural production and exports as well as credit controls
and new taxes imposed by the government to conserve foreign exchange had restraining effects.

The construction boom characteristic of the 1960s
continued throughout the year but at a declining rate
as investment in construction decreased. A Japanese-

NICARAGUA

Education. (1966–67) Primary, pupils 224,513, teachers (including preprimary) 6,493; secondary, pupils
20,661, teachers 1,267; vocational, pupils 3,762, teachers 228; teacher training, students 3,917, teachers
472; higher (including 2 universities), students 4,056,
teaching staff 459.

Finance. Monetary unit: córdoba, with a par value
of 7 córdobas to U.S. $1 (16.80 córdobas = £1 ster-
ling). Gold, SDRs, and convertible currency, central
bank: (June 1970) U.S. $56,850,000; (June 1969)
U.S. $39,670,000. Budget (1970 est.) balanced at 686
million córdobas. Gross national product: (1969)
5,097,000,000 córdobas; (1968) 4,806,000,000 córdobas. Money supply: (June 1970) 583.4 million
córdobas; (June 1969) 511.9 million córdobas. Cost
of living (Managua; 1963 = 100): (1969) 117;
(1968) 117.

Foreign Trade. (1968) Imports 1,292,500,000 córdobas; exports 1,100,900,000 córdobas. Import sources:
U.S. 38%; El Salvador 8%; Costa Rica 8%; Japan
8%; Guatemala 7%; West Germany 6%. Export
destinations: U.S. 29%; Japan 26%; West Germany
11%; Costa Rica 7%. Main exports: cotton 38%;
coffee 14%; meat 10%.

Transport and Communications. Roads (1967) *c.*
7,000 km. (including 368 km. of Pan-American Highway). Motor vehicles in use (1967): passenger 12,900;
commercial (including buses) 10,000. Railways:
(1968) 349 km.; traffic (1967) 44 million passenger-
km., freight 14 million net ton-km. Air traffic (1968):
59,430,000 passenger-km.; freight 1,010,000 net ton-
km. Telephones (Jan. 1969) 23,484. Radio receivers
(Dec. 1968) 105,000. Television receivers (Dec. 1967)
25,000.

Agriculture. Production (in 000; metric tons; 1969;
1968 in parentheses): corn *c.* 170 (*c.* 206); rice (1968)
c. 67, (1967) *c.* 64; sorghum (1968) *c.* 60, (1967) *c.*
55; dry beans (1968) *c.* 44, (1967) *c.* 38; cotton, lint
c. 69 (*c.* 91); coffee (1968) *c.* 34, (1967) *c.* 33; sugar,
raw value (1969–70) *c.* 146, (1968–69) *c.* 125. Livestock (in 000; 1967–68): cattle *c.* 1,880; pigs *c.* 485;
chickens *c.* 2,500.

Industry. Production (in 000; 1968): cement
(metric tons) 101; gold (troy oz.) 193; electricity
(kw.-hr.) 484,000.

owned polyvinyl chloride resin plant able to supply the needs of the Central American plastics industry, a textile mill, a cigarette factory, a bag plant utilizing locally grown fibres to produce bags for coffee and cotton, a beef packing plant, and a multistory bank were among the major industrial and commercial projects of the year.

The 54-year-old Bryan-Chamorro Treaty, which gave the U.S. exclusive rights to construct and operate an interoceanic canal across Nicaragua, was terminated during the year. The termination of the treaty also canceled the U.S. lease of the Corn Islands and the option for the U.S. to build and maintain a navy base in Nicaraguan territory on the Gulf of Fonseca.

(A. W. O.)

Niger

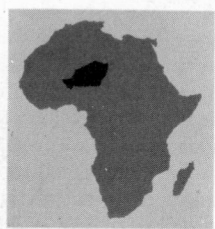

A republic of north central Africa, Niger is bounded by Algeria, Libya, Chad, Nigeria, Dahomey, Upper Volta, and Mali. Area: 458,993 sq.mi. (1,188,794 sq.km.). Pop. (1969 est.): 3,909,372, including (1962) Hausa 49%; Djerma 16%; Peuls 11%; Tuareg 9%. Cap. and largest city: Niamey (pop., 1969 est., 78,991). Language: French and Sudanic dialects. Religion (1960 est.): 1.8 million Muslims; 725,000 animists; 10,000 Christians. President in 1970, Hamani Diori.

The only event of importance in Niger's internal political development in 1970 was the presidential election in the fall. In July the political bureau of the ruling Progressive Party of Niger agreed to appoint President Diori as sole candidate, and on October 1 he was duly reelected with the support of 98.46% of the registered voters (99.9% of those who voted). Legislative elections were held three weeks later on October 22.

In the sphere of economic development, the participation of Italian and West German interests in the SOMAIR mining company marked a new stage in the exploitation of uranium deposits at Arlit. An agreement was also signed in Paris with regard to prospecting and exploiting deposits at Akokan approximately 12 mi. S of Arlit. The agreement was signed by a representative of the Niger government, the president of the Japanese industrial consortium, Overseas

Uranium Resources Development Co., and the administrator of the French Commission for Atomic Energy.

The Agency for Cultural and Technical Cooperation among French-speaking countries was officially founded in Niamey on March 20. The agency would have its headquarters in Paris, and funds for 1971 were expected to be approximately Fr. 9 million. France would provide 45% of this, Canada 33%, and Belgium 12%; the remaining countries would contribute 10%.

(PH. D.)

Nigeria

A federal republic and a member of the Commonwealth of Nations, Nigeria is located in Africa on the north coast of the Gulf of Guinea, bounded by Dahomey, Niger, Chad, and Cameroon. Area: 356,669 sq.mi. (923,774 sq.km.). Pop. (1970 est.): 66,174,000, including (1963 est.): Hausa 18%; Ibo 16%; Yoruba 14%; Fulani 10%. Cap. and largest city: Lagos (pop., 1970 est., 875,000). Language: English (official). Religion: Muslim 48%; Christian 23%. Head of provisional military government in 1970, Maj. Gen. Yakubu Gowon.

After a long period of minor warfare during 1969, the fall of Owerri, headquarters of the Biafran secessionist regime, on Jan. 10, 1970, was followed by the final defeat of Biafra through the federal military government strategy of blockade, bombardment, and land force advance, aided by foreign supplies. Gen. Odumegwu Ojukwu left the last Biafran enclave and was later granted asylum in the Ivory Coast, one of the few states to have recognized Biafra, leaving Maj. Gen. Philip Effiong to negotiate for peace. Formal surrender took place on January 15, the Biafran leaders accepting the existing political and administrative structure of a united Nigeria and whatever constitutional arrangements should be worked out by representatives of the Nigerian people as a whole.

Immediately after the cease-fire, the federal government set about its proclaimed policies of reconciliation, rehabilitation, reconstruction, and reabsorption; predictions of vengeance and genocide proved unwarranted. While accepting offers of aid from many friendly countries (though not from those that supported Biafra, notably France and Portugal), the

Nigerian soldiers escort Ibo refugees into Owerri in fallen Biafra, Jan. 21, 1970.

WIDE WORLD

NIGER
Education. (1967–68) Primary, pupils 77,261, teachers 2,176; secondary, pupils 3,650, teachers 209; vocational (1966–67), pupils 548, teachers 107; teacher training, students 556, teachers 33.
Finance. Monetary unit: CFA franc, with a parity of CFA Fr. 50 to the French franc (CFA Fr. 277.71 = U.S. $1; CFA Fr. 666.50 = £1 sterling). Budget (1969–70 est.) balanced at CFA Fr. 10,799,000,000.
Foreign Trade. (1968) Imports CFA Fr. 10,237,000,000; exports CFA Fr. 9,350,000,000. Import sources: France 65%; Japan 8%; Nigeria 6%; West Germany 5%; Netherlands 5%. Export destinations: France 75%; Italy 9%. Main exports: peanuts 72%; livestock 9%.
Transport and Communications. Roads (1969) 6,746 km. Motor vehicles in use (1969): passenger 3,782; commercial 1,752. Telephones (Dec. 1968) 3,172. Radio receivers (Dec. 1968) 75,000.
Agriculture. Production (in 000; metric tons; 1968; 1967 in parentheses): millet c. 800 (1,000); sorghum c. 260 (342); cassava c. 150 (169); peanuts (1969) c. 290, (1968) c. 268; rice 39 (33); dates c. 5 (c. 5). Livestock (in 000; 1968–69): cattle c. 4,200; sheep c. 2,700; goats (1967–68) c. 5,870.

NIGERIA

Education. (1967–68) Primary, pupils 3,025,-981, teachers 91,049; secondary, pupils 202,638, teachers 11,055; vocational, pupils 26,092, teachers 1,378; teacher training, students 28,673, teaching staff 1,738.

Finance. Monetary unit: Nigerian pound, with a par value of N£0.36 to U.S. $1 (N£0.86 = £1 sterling). Gold, SDRs, and foreign exchange, official: (June 1970) U.S. $146 million; (June 1969) U.S. $124 million. Federal budget (1969–70 est.): revenue N£187 million; expenditure N£186.8 million. Gross domestic product: (1967–68) N£1,474 million; (1966–67) N£1,703 million. Money supply: (May 1970) N£251.8 million; (May 1969) N£172.2 million. Cost of living (Lagos; 1963 = 100): (June 1970) 140; (June 1969) 127.

Foreign Trade. (1969) Imports N£246.8 million; exports N£322.2 million. Import sources: U.K. 35%; U.S. 12%; West Germany 11%; Italy 5%; Netherlands 5%. Export destinations: U.K. 27%; Netherlands 13%; U.S. 12%; France 10%; West Germany 6%. Main exports: crude oil 42%; cocoa 16%; peanuts 14%.

Transport and Communications. Roads (1968) c. 80,000 km. (including c. 12,000 km. with improved surface). Motor vehicles in use (1968): passenger 63,000; commercial (including buses) 30,000. Railways: (1968) 3,505 km.; traffic (1969) 705.6 million passenger-km., freight 1,685,000,000 net ton-km. Air traffic (1969): 190.5 million passenger-km.; freight 6,456,000 net ton-km. Shipping (1969): merchant vessels 100 gross tons and over 45; gross tonnage 98,199. Telephones (Jan. 1969) 75,900. Radio receivers (Nov. 1967) 1,250,000. Television receivers (Nov. 1967) 52,000.

Agriculture. Production (in 000; metric tons; 1968; 1967 in parentheses): millet c. 2,800 (c. 3,000); sorghum c. 3,500 (c. 3,600); corn c. 1,219 (c. 1,219); sweet potatoes c. 12,500 (c. 13,000); cassava c. 6,700 (c. 6,500); peanuts (1969) c. 1,500, (1968) c. 1,375; palm oil c. 350 (c. 325); cocoa 186 (235); cotton, lint (1969) c. 69, (1968) c. 27; rubber (exports) 53 (48). Livestock (in 000; 1967–68): cattle c. 11,410; sheep (1968–69) 7,900; goats c. 23,200; pigs c. 780; horses (Northern Region only) c. 345.

Industry. Production (in 000; metric tons; 1969): crude oil 26,627; tin 8.7; electricity (kw-hr.) 1,235,000.

---

government kept the administration of Biafran relief firmly in its own hands. The British government's offer of an emergency £5 million plus personnel was accepted, and a special emissary was sent to Nigeria to discuss the most effective use of relief aid. The report (January 24) of Lord Hunt's mission noted an improvement in the food situation and the return of people to their homes in a spirit of reconciliation.

Relations between the Ibo, the predominant people of the former Biafran state, and the rest of the population appeared to be improving, though some dissension remained among the Ibos themselves as between those who had and had not supported secession. On August 15 the government published a decree permitting the dismissal of those civil servants and other public officials who had been actively engaged in hostile acts or rebellion against the federation between 1966 and 1970, and the cancelation of their retirement benefits. The decree also covered those who counseled such acts or any officer whose conduct

UPI COMPIX

Biafran children wait for food at a distribution centre in Owerri.

during that period was such that it would not now be in the public interest to employ him.

On October 1, eight months after the end of civil war, Nigeria celebrated the tenth anniversary of its independence, and it was evident that the policy of reconciliation had repaid the country in strength and unity, despite its division into 12 states and differences of tribe, religion, education, and economic potential. In his Independence Day speech, Major General Gowon (*see* BIOGRAPHY) promised a return to civilian rule by 1976. The Nigerian Army, still 200,000 strong, needed time for reorganization to a peacetime basis and was temporarily required to aid the police against the severe crime wave, especially of robbery with violence, that swept the country as an aftermath of war. A nine-point program of national reorganization and development was outlined, including measures to eradicate corruption, the preparation of a new constitution, the organization of political parties, a census in 1973, settlement of the question of the number of states, and the adoption of a nonaligned foreign policy.

Nigeria showed signs of rapid economic recovery. Only a relatively small area had been physically devastated, and valuable oil installations were not completely wrecked. Production of oil had returned to one million barrels a day by June, and exports were estimated at four million tons a month. Losses were largely in overseas markets for agriculture, and in foreign exchange, and they to some extent were balanced by the development of local industry and an internal market. It was estimated that, with normal financial prudence, all 12 states should be economically viable by 1971, though the problems of the East Central State, the heart of Iboland and the area most ravaged by war, were far from settled. The rehabilitation commission was dissolved because of corruption; it was replaced by an interim agency controlled by the military governors of the three eastern states.

(M. Mr.)

ENCYCLOPÆDIA BRITANNICA FILMS. *West Africa (Nigeria)* (1963).

Norway

A constitutional monarchy of northern Europe, Norway is bordered by Sweden, Finland, and the U.S.S.R.; its coastlines are on the North Sea, the Norwegian Sea, and the Arctic Ocean. Area: 125,049 sq.mi. (323,878 sq.km.), excluding the Svalbard Archipelago, 23,957 sq.mi., and

Jan Mayen Island, 144 sq.mi. Pop. (1970 est.) : 3,866,-468. Cap. and largest city: Oslo (pop., 1970 est., 487,-363). Language: Norwegian. Religion: Lutheran (96.2%). King, Olav V; prime minister in 1970, Per Borten.

The main politico-economic theme throughout the year concerned Norway's accession to an extended European Economic Community. The question was complicated by the fact that the coalition government of Conservatives, Agrarians (Centre Party), Christian People's, and Liberals was not uniformly enthusiastic about membership in the EEC. In particular, Prime Minister Borten, while heading an administration that generally supported full membership, derived his position from leadership of the Centre Party, which from time to time expressed doubts about its wisdom.

Until spring, it appeared that the situation might be further complicated by the creation of Nordek, a customs union comprising Norway, Denmark, Finland, and Sweden and embracing a variety of economic institutions aimed at even closer economic cooperation among the Nordic countries. Government experts from the four countries agreed to the draft treaty on February 4, but on March 24 the Finnish government decided not to sign, and the project was shelved.

The first formal negotiating meeting on Norway's membership application took place on September 22. The Norwegian foreign minister, Svenn Stray, made it clear that Norway accepted the political as well as the economic implications of the Treaty of Rome, but he added that certain aspects of EEC policy raised problems that would have to be solved through negotiations. This applied particularly to EEC fisheries policy. He said that Norway could not accept in advance a fisheries policy agreed to by the Six, since the problems relating to such a policy would not be the same in an extended EEC: an enlarged Community would have an export surplus of fish, rather than a deficit. There was condemnation in Norway of the EEC's apparent wish to determine its fishing policy before the entry of Europe's largest fishing nation. There was also concern about agriculture, although government ministers argued that the insignificance of Norwegian agriculture in the European context made it reasonable to expect agreement on special transitional arrangements.

Norway's economic position was good throughout the year, although the balance of payments surplus on current account enjoyed in 1968 and 1969 was not expected to be repeated. Those surpluses, following ten years of deficits, were due largely to special factors, in particular to exceptionally large sales of second-hand ships and low imports of new tonnage. While exports of goods continued to grow, imports grew even faster, and a large trade and payments deficit was forecast. The deficit would have been larger except for an unexpected boom in shipping that occurred during the summer.

A high level of economic activity was maintained during the year, with employment at a record high and unemployment in the best summer months at only 0.5%. Production, and in particular investments, rose to a new peak, resulting in strong pressure on prices and wages. The trend was reinforced by the value-added tax introduced from January 1; it was estimated that this would raise the consumer price index by 5.8% during the year, although there was compensation in the form of reductions in direct income tax

and increased subsidies, children's allowances, and other social measures. Nationwide wage negotiations, affecting several hundred thousand workers, resulted in unanimous approval by workers' and employers' organizations of a new two-year agreement with pay raises averaging 9.5%. A further rise in prices followed, so that by August the consumer price index stood at 111, against 100 in August 1969.

To counter the threat of inflation, Minister of Finance Ole Myrvoll in his 1971 budget, presented to the Storting (parliament) on October 5, proposed higher taxes on cigarettes, tobacco, beer, wine and spirits, mineral oils, and cars. Widespread indignation was aroused, and the Confederation of Trade Unions declared a 15-minute work stoppage.

A cause of mounting excitement and expectation was the confirmation by the U.S. Phillips Petroleum Co. of an important find of oil in the Norwegian sector of the North Sea. It was announced that trial production would start in mid-1971, followed by full-scale production a few years later. The accession of Norway to the ranks of the oil-possessing nations coincided with mounting recognition that Norway's water-power resources were rapidly diminishing and would have to be supplemented by other sources of power before the end of the decade.

A number of ministerial changes were announced, the most important being the resignation in May of the foreign minister, John Lyng, and his replacement by Svenn Stray. The minister of defense, Otto Grieg Tidemand, took over as minister of trade from Kaare Willoch, and Gunnar Hellesen became minister of defense. All were Conservatives.   (O. F. K.)

ENCYCLOPÆDIA BRITANNICA FILMS. *Scandinavia—Norway, Sweden, Denmark* (1962).

NORWAY

Education. (1967–68) Primary, pupils 403,928, teachers 19,784; secondary, pupils 209,715, teachers 16,666; vocational, pupils 71,044, teachers 10,640; teacher training, students 7,870, teachers 871; higher (including 3 universities), students 22,259, teaching staff 2,446.

Finance. Monetary unit: Norwegian krone, with a par value of 7.14 kroner to U.S. $1 (17.14 kroner = £1 sterling). Gold, SDRs, and foreign exchange, central bank: (June 1970) U.S. $572.5 million; (June 1969) U.S. $575.5 million. Budget (1971 est.): revenue 20.7 billion kroner; expenditure 23.7 billion kroner. Gross national product: (1969) 69,530,000,000 kroner; (1968) 64,430,000,000 kroner. Money supply: (June 1970) 16,120,000,000 kroner; (June 1969) 14,-010,000,000 kroner. Cost of living (1963 = 100): (June 1970) 139; (June 1969) 127.

Foreign Trade. (1969) Imports 21,021,000,000 kroner; exports 15,735,000,000 kroner. Import sources: Sweden 19%; West Germany 15%; U.K. 13%; U.S. 8%; Denmark 7%. Export destinations: U.K. 17%; Sweden 16%; West Germany 15%; Denmark 7%; U.S. 7%. Main exports: ships 15%; aluminum 12%; chemicals 8%; machinery 8%; fish 7%; paper 7%; iron and steel 7%.

Transport and Communications. Roads (1969) 71,101 km. Motor vehicles in use (1969): passenger 699,683; commercial 141,297. Railways: (state only; 1968) 4,242 km. (including 2,269 km. electrified); traffic (1969) 1,450,000,000 passenger-km., freight 2,710,000,000 net ton-km. Air traffic (including Norwegian apportionment of international operation of Scandinavian Airlines System; 1969): 1,736,600,000 passenger-km.; freight 72,490,000 net ton-km. Shipping (1969): merchant vessels 100 gross tons and over 2,848; gross tonnage 19,679,094. Ships entered (1968) vessels totaling 14,402,000 net registered tons; goods loaded (1969) 36,756,000 metric tons, unloaded 17,518,000 metric tons. Telephones (Dec. 1968) 1,036,027. Radio receivers (Dec. 1968) 1,152,000. Television receivers (Dec. 1968) 739,000.

Agriculture. Production (in 000; metric tons; 1969; 1968 in parentheses): barley 506 (621); oats c. 130 (176); potatoes 765 (912); apples (1968) 65, (1967) 49; milk (deliveries) 1,596 (1,620); butter 19 (22); cheese (1968) c. 46, (1967) 50; beef and veal (1968) 53, (1967) 53; pork (1968) 61, (1967) 58; timber (cu.m.; 1967–68) 6,700, (1966–67) 7,500; fish catch (1968) 2,804, (1967) 3,269. Livestock (in 000; June 1969): cattle c. 1,050; sheep c. 1,920; pigs c. 630; goats (June 1968) 98; chickens c. 4,700.

Industry. Fuel and power (in 000; 1969): coal (Svalbard mines) 391 metric tons; manufactured gas 30,700 cu.m.; electricity 57,196,000 kw-hr. Production (in 000; metric tons; 1969): iron ore (65% metal content) 3,696; pig iron 1,434; crude steel 824; zinc 59; copper 22; aluminum 511; cement 2,480; sulfur (1968) 309; nitrogenous fertilizers (N content; 1968–69) 374; mechanical wood pulp (1968) 1,127; chemical wood pulp (1968) 854; newsprint 511; other paper (1968) 764. Merchant vessels launched (100 gross tons and over; 1969) 596,000 gross tons. Dwelling units completed (1969) 33,000.

553

Norway

Nuclear Energy

The dynamic international nuclear power industry, by far the most important sector of this complex field, presented a picture of startling contrasts and apparent contradictions in 1970. In the U.S., companies in the business of manufacturing equipment for nuclear-electric generating stations and supplying their fuel had what seemed to be an extremely encouraging year and bright prospects for the future. However, this apparent prosperity masked the fact that the industry as a whole was beset with acute problems, none of them easily solved and many of them discouragingly intractable.

In other countries, the situation generally was even less encouraging. Fragmented and almost frantically competitive, the national nuclear industrial complexes in most industrialized countries faced the fact that the rapidly expanding markets that they had been created to serve had failed once again to materialize.

Nuclear-Electric Power. U.S. utilities ordered 16 nuclear power units with a combined capacity of more than 16 million kw., an output considerably greater than all of the generating capacity already installed in the six New England states. Added to the nuclear plants already operating, under construction, and on order, the new orders brought the nation's nuclear generating potential to 85 million–90 million kw., somewhat more than half of what was available to utilities from all sources, including fossil-fueled and hydroelectric, as recently as 1960.

Together, these nuclear plants—about 100 in 30 states—represented a capital investment of approximately $16 billion, and for suppliers of nuclear fuel they offered an assured market worth about $60 billion–$70 billion over the next 25–30 years. Moreover, the utilities' new commitments, taken together with their announcements of future construction plans, almost guaranteed that in 1980 operable nuclear generating capacity would at least equal the long-standing U.S. Atomic Energy Commission (AEC) forecast of 150 million kw.—something more than a fifth of the probable national total. Despite this sizable investment, however, the industry as a whole found itself under heavy internal and external pressures.

Heading the list of its problems was the determined opposition that a growing number of nuclear power projects encountered from local and national groups concerned that the plants would endanger public health and the quality of the environment. The elaborate preconstruction and preoperating licensing procedures imposed by the AEC gave opponents of individual projects wide latitude for intervention.

Opposition seldom stemmed from fears that a power reactor would explode like a bomb. The many hundreds of safe operating years logged by reactors of many types and sizes had almost eliminated the potentially catastrophic accident as an issue, though it was occasionally revived in sensationalistic books and articles. Instead, when criticism arose, it was usually based on one or both of two concerns: that the plant's small, normal discharges of radioactive effluents would be a health hazard or that discharges of heated water from its steam condensers would degrade the ecology of an adjoining body of water.

Because of these environmental concerns, many utilities planning to build nuclear units—and a few with plants already completed—found themselves embroiled with citizens' groups and also faced pressures from state and federal agencies authorized to regulate heated water discharges. Most of these bodies had only recently been created, and as often as not utilities could not learn what limitations they would be obliged to live with. Thus, several companies with about a dozen big plants under construction on Lake Michigan were confronted with the possibility that federal standards, still to be set, might require them to make extensive modifications, at costs that could easily total more than $100 million.

Ultimately, it was clear, the solution would be to oblige utilities to obtain approval of all power plant sites, long before construction begins, by state or regional authorities following clear guidelines. Legislation to that end was introduced in Congress, but meanwhile the status of plants representing millions of kilowatts of sorely needed generating capacity remained uncertain, at best.

An equally serious problem, one with implications for the nuclear energy industry as a whole, concerned the limits, if any, that should be imposed on nuclear power plants' discharges of low-level radioactivity. The AEC, following the guidance of national and international expert committees, had long enforced regulations requiring that the release of these liquid and gaseous effluents not result in the exposure of large population groups to radiation exceeding an average of 0.17 millirem per year. While no commercial power reactor had ever violated this standard or even closely approached it, and although a large majority of health physics experts considered it conservative, a vocal minority emphatically disagreed. On the basis of studies of existing data, they concluded that incidence of leukemia and other malignancies would rise markedly if the entire population received the "maximum permissible exposure," and that genetic damage also would be considerable.

These conclusions influenced several states to adopt regulations more restrictive than the AEC's, though their legal authority to do so was far from clear. They also had much to do with the introduction in several state legislatures of bills calling for moratoriums on new nuclear power projects.

One of the bright spots for power reactor operators during the year was the fact that the units already in operation generally proved to be reliable electricity producers, often more dependable than coal-fired units of comparable size. On the whole, however, the potential advantages of nuclear power were heavily clouded by the disadvantages, and many of the year's orders were attributed to the fact that building coal, gas, or oil-fueled plants involved even more serious problems.

In Western Europe, generally, the scarcity of nuclear power orders posed an all too familiar problem for most equipment and fuel suppliers. With few exceptions, the companies concerned had gone into the nuclear power business, often with direct government encouragement, primarily to serve their own national markets. However, since it was clear that those markets would be uncomfortably narrow at best, they had counted on being able to widen them through exports. Because they could expect to sell few plants in other industrialized countries, they were obliged to look for export customers elsewhere, and such potential buyers were few.

Public concern about nuclear power plants as sources of radiation hazard and thermal pollution was seldom acute outside the U.S. However, there were some signs that this would become an important issue. In West Germany, suspension of a chemical company's plan to build a large nuclear station to serve a major chemical complex at Ludwigshafen was ordered by the government, pending research to confirm that it could be safely operated in that densely populated area. In Britain, a proposal by the national electricity board to put a nuclear station in a heavily populated area (Stourport) was rejected by regulatory authorities. Several countries, West Germany and Switzerland in particular, showed increasing sensitivity to the threat of thermal pollution.

In the Soviet Union a significant change in nuclear power policy was confirmed. Having chosen the pressurized water reactor (PWR) as its preferred type for central station generation, the U.S.S.R. built and planned few new units during a period of about three years, beginning in 1965–66. In 1969 came signs of intensive new activity, and in 1970 visitors reported that the construction of two new PWR stations was under way, one near Murmansk and the other in Armenia. Standardized Soviet plants were also reported sold to East Germany, Bulgaria, Czechoslovakia, and Hungary.

Meanwhile, Soviet nuclear power development efforts continued to focus on the sodium-cooled, fast-neutron breeder reactor. (A breeder reactor is one able to generate more fuel—usually plutonium—than it consumes. Hence, it will offer utilities almost complete independence of natural fuel resources.) At Beloyarsk, the largest power-producing prototype of this advanced reactor so far begun anywhere in the world was well along in construction. Somewhat smaller prototypes were being built in Britain and France, and a West German-Belgian-Dutch venture, backed by the three governments, planned one for construction in West Germany.

In the U.S., on the other hand, "fast breeder" construction planning faltered. The problem was almost entirely financial: federal budget stringencies and the difficulty utilities encountered in raising money raised serious doubts that the formidable sums required to build even a single prototype could be found.

Nuclear Explosives. Early in the year visitors to the Soviet Union reported that the U.S.S.R. had been carrying out a vigorous program to develop and use nuclear explosives for civil purposes. The report, confirming what knowledgeable observers had long believed, identified not only a number of experimental deep detonations for such purposes as stimulating oil and gas recovery but also excavation shots near the surface, and outlined elaborate plans for the future. Toward the year's end, the U.S.S.R. reported a new achievement: a successful deep detonation to control a wild-flowing oil well.

In the U.S., the pace of the AEC's nuclear explosives program, Project Plowshare, slowed perceptibly, largely because of official sensitivity to public uneasiness about the deliberate or accidental release of small amounts of radioactivity from deep underground or near-surface experiments. On the other hand, private commercial interest in nuclear explosives rose steadily, encouraged by the preliminary results of the AEC- and industry-financed Rulison experiment of 1969 in a submarginal Colorado gas well. Data obtained in 1970 established that the quantity of gas made available by the detonation was impressively large and that residual radioactivity in the gas was far less than the small quantity originally estimated. Whether or when this gas could be fed

COURTESY, BROOKHAVEN NATIONAL LABORATORY

An engineer at Brookhaven National Laboratory, Upton, N.Y., makes final adjustments inside the world's highest energy tandem Van de Graaff accelerator system. Capable of accelerating some heavy ions to 300 MeV (million electron volts), it can fuse one type with another to create new and previously unknown radioactive nuclei.

into the pipeline was far from clear, for no regulatory guidance existed.

Isotopes and Radiation. The year's most significant achievement in the use of isotopes was the successful implantation of a nuclear-powered heart pacemaker in a human patient in France, followed by two similar implantations in Britain. The devices, tiny generators producing a minute current which is passed on to the heart muscles, were used to correct a condition called heart block. Their advantage over conventional battery-powered pacemakers, of which many thousands were in use, was their longevity. The British and French models, and a U.S. model not yet implanted in a human had a design life of at least ten years, while the battery-powered versions required replacement by surgery about every year and a half.

Worldwide, the use of radiopharmaceuticals, chiefly for diagnosis, continued to expand at a dramatic rate: probably at least 25% per year. The sterilization of disposable medical materials, such as hypodermic needles, sutures, and scalpels, by means of intense radiation was established as the preferred technique, and high-volume processing plants were operating or under construction in about a dozen countries to serve this growing market.

Nuclear-Powered Ships. Few nations except Japan showed much interest in the near-term economic potential of nuclear-propelled merchant ships. Japan's first nuclear-propelled vessel, the 8,300-ton freighter "Mutsu," made its first trial voyages under conventional power, and the installation of its reactor-powered propulsion system was begun. West Germany's "Otto Hahn," a 15,000-ton ore carrier, continued to operate in more or less regular service. However, the NS "Savannah" of the U.S., the first nuclear-powered merchant vessel, neared the end of its career. Never expected to operate economically on regular commercial runs, it was considered too expensive to maintain, and its retirement was expected in 1971.   (Jo. H. S.)

See also Defense; Fuel and Power; Physics.

ENCYCLOPÆDIA BRITANNICA FILMS. *Atomic Radiation* (1953); *Carbon Fourteen* (1953); *Atomic Energy—Inside the Atom* (1961); *Electrons at Work* (1961); *Evidence for Molecules and Atoms* (1961).

Obituaries 1970

The following is a selected list of prominent men and women who died during 1970.

ABRAMS, CHARLES, U.S. urban planner (b. Vilna, Pol., Sept. 20, 1901—d. New York, N.Y., Feb. 22, 1970), was a member of several UN housing missions during the 1950s and helped set basic housing policies in a number of countries. He wrote *Man's Struggle for Shelter* (1964).

ACKERMAN, CARL WILLIAM, U.S. journalism educator (b. Richmond, Ind., Jan. 16, 1890—d. New York, N.Y., Oct. 9, 1970), dean of the Columbia University Graduate School of Journalism from 1931 until 1956. He served as a foreign correspondent during World War I and sent the first story to come out of Russia covering the execution of Nicholas II and his family by the revolutionaries.

AGNON, S(HMUEL) Y(OSEF) (Czaczkes), Israeli novelist (b. Buczacz, Galicia, July 17, 1888 —d. Rehovot, Israel, Feb. 17, 1970), recipient of a Nobel Prize for Literature, published his first poems in 1903. An active Zionist at 20, he went to Palestine and there published his short novel *Agunot* ("Forsaken Wives") in 1909. Three years later, in Berlin, he wrote a number of works in Hebrew. Returning permanently to Jerusalem in 1924, he wrote the two-volume *Ha-Khnassat Kallah* (1931; Eng. trans. by I. M. Lask, *The Bridal Canopy*, 1937). Four other works of fiction came out in 1931 under the title *Kol Sippurov* ("Complete Stories"), and in 1935 he added two more. At that time he received the Bialik Prize in Hebrew Literature, which was later to become Israel's highest literary award. Agnon's second major novel, *Oreah Nata la-Lun* (Eng. trans., *A Guest for the Night*), was published in 1937, and *21 Stories* appeared in 1970. Agnon shared the 1966 Nobel Prize for Literature with the Jewish poet and dramatist Nelly Sachs (*q.v.*).

AKERS, MILBURN P., U.S. newspaperman (b. Chicago, May 4, 1900—d. Hopedale, Ill., May 27, 1970), was managing editor (1949–50), executive editor (1950–59), and editor (1959–65) of the *Chicago Sun-Times*.

ALEXII, SERGEI VLADIMIROVICH SIMANSKY, patriarch of Moscow and all Russia (b. Moscow, Russia, 1877—d. Moscow, U.S.S.R., April 17, 1970), head of the Russian Orthodox Church. Ordained priest in 1903, he rose to be successively bishop of Yamburg, archbishop of Novgorod, and, in 1932, metropolitan of Novgorod. In 1933 he was appointed metropolitan of Leningrad and was decorated for his part in the city's defense during World War II. In 1944 he succeeded Sergius on the patriarchal throne. He was loyal to the Communist regime and supported Soviet foreign policy. In July 1969 he opened a conference in Moscow of high churchmen of many denominations, only the second such meeting ever held in Russia.

ALLEN, GEORGE VENABLE, U.S. career ambassador (b. Durham, N.C., Nov. 3, 1903—d. Bahama, N.C., July 11, 1970), held a series of diplomatic and State Department posts including ambassador to Iran (1946–48), to Yugoslavia (1950–53), to India and Nepal (1953), and to Greece (1956–57). In 1966 he was named career ambassador (highest rank in the Foreign Service), and appointed head of the Foreign Service Institute. He retired in 1969.

ARAMBURU, PEDRO EUGENIO, Argentine statesman (b. Río Cuarto, Córdoba Province, Arg., May 21, 1903—d. Timote, Buenos Aires Province, Arg., June 1[?], 1970), who served as president of Argentina from 1955 until 1958, was kidnapped on May 29, 1970, by a Peronist guerrilla group. The guerrillas stated that Aramburu had been executed on June 1 for "crimes" committed during his presidency; the body was found on July 16. In 1950 Aramburu joined three other army officers in a plan to depose Pres. Juan D. Perón, who they felt was undermining Argentina's economy. In 1955 the plotters had gained enough influence to overturn the government and drive Perón from the country. Aramburu became provisional president on Nov. 13, 1955; he restored the 1853 constitution and set a date for

democratic elections, barring himself and members of his government from seeking office. The elections were held in 1958, when Arturo Frondizi won the presidency. Aramburu ran for the office in 1963 but was defeated.

ATCHERLEY, SIR RICHARD LLEWELLYN ROGER, marshal (ret.) of the Royal Air Force (b. Jan. 11, 1904—d. Surrey, Eng., April 18, 1970), a graduate of the RAF College, Cranwell, and an enthusiastic aerobatic flier, became a flying instructor and took part in the 1929 Schneider Trophy race. In 1934 he joined the Royal Aircraft Establishment, Farnborough, as a test pilot. During World War II he held wartime commands in Europe and the Middle East. From 1949 to 1951 he was commander in chief and mentor of the newly formed Pakistan Air Force, returning to command duties in Britain and in Washington.

AYLWARD, GLADYS, British-Chinese missionary (b. 1903—d. T'ai-pei, Taiwan, Jan. 3, 1970), whose life story was the basis for the motion picture *Inn of the Sixth Happiness*, began her missionary work in northern China in 1930.

BARBIROLLI, SIR JOHN, British orchestral conductor (b. London, Eng., Dec. 2, 1899—d. London, July 28, 1970), was conductor of Manchester's Hallé Orchestra from 1943 until 1968, when he was designated the orchestra's "conductor laureate for life." Barbirolli first appeared in public at the age of 11 as soloist in Goltermann's Cello Concerto. He studied at the Royal Academy of Music (1912–17) and after a brief period in the Army became cellist (1919) in the Queen's Hall Orchestra. In 1926 he conducted with the British National Opera Company and in the following year with the Covent Garden Opera Company. From 1933 until 1936 he conducted the Scottish and Northern Philharmonic orchestras and was then appointed to succeed Toscanini as conductor of the New York Philharmonic-Symphony Orchestra. In 1943 Barbirolli took over the Hallé Orchestra. In 1949 he was knighted.

BEAZLEY, SIR JOHN DAVIDSON, British classical scholar (b. Glasgow, Scot., Sept. 13, 1885—d. Oxford, Eng., May 6, 1970) and professor of classical archaeology at Oxford from 1925 to 1956, was a world authority on Greek vase painting.

BEGLEY, ED, U.S. character actor, usually playing a villain (b. Hartford, Conn., March 25, 1901 —d. Hollywood, Calif., April 28, 1970), winner of an Academy Award in 1963 for his role in *Sweet Bird of Youth,* played in about 40 motion pictures including *Twelve Angry Men* (1957) and *The Unsinkable Molly Brown* (1964). He also appeared in more than a dozen Broadway plays, achieving his greatest success in *Inherit the Wind* (1955). On radio he was heard in the title role in "The Adventures of Charlie Chan" series and more than 12,000 other programs; he gave at least 250 performances on television.

BELYAYEV, PAVEL IVANOVICH, colonel, U.S.S.R. Air Force, and cosmonaut (b. Vologda region, U.S.S.R., June 26, 1925—d. Moscow, U.S.S.R., Jan. 10, 1970), was commander of the Voskhod 2 flight—the first journey during which a man left his orbiting craft to "walk" in space. Belyayev received the title of Hero of the Soviet Union for his part in the Voskhod 2 voyage.

BENEDIKTSSON, BJARNI, Icelandic politician (b. Reykjavik, Ice., April 30, 1908—d. Thingvellir, Ice., July 10, 1970), was prime minister of Iceland from 1963 until his death. He entered national politics in 1940 when he became mayor of Reykjavik for the Independence Party, and in

1942 he was elected to the Althing (parliament). In 1946 he was Iceland's representative at the UN and the following year became foreign minister, holding that post until 1953. From 1956 (when his party was defeated in the general election) until 1959 he edited the daily newspaper *Morgunbladid.*

BENHAM, STANLEY, U.S. bobsled champion (b. 1913—d. Miami, Fla., April 22, 1970), who represented the U.S. in more international sledding events than any other bobsledder, won the four-man world championship in 1949 and 1950, and in 1952 took the Winter Olympic silver medal in the four-man competition. He was chosen the 1950 outstanding athlete of the year by the Amateur Athletic Union.

BENZELL, MIMI, U.S. opera singer and entertainer (b. Bridgeport, Conn., 1923—d. Manhasset, L.I., Dec. 23, 1970), soprano with the Metropolitan Opera Company from the time of her debut in 1945 until 1949, when she left opera to follow a career in musical comedy, on radio, and as a nightclub entertainer. She appeared on Broadway in the long-running play *Milk and Honey* during 1961–63.

BERNE, ERIC LENNARD, U.S. psychiatrist and writer (b. Montreal, Que., May 10, 1910—d. Mohterey, Calif., July 15, 1970), founder of the "transactional analysis" method of psychotherapy, was the author of *Games People Play,* published in 1964 and on the best-seller list until 1967.

BLOND, NEVILLE, British industrialist (b. Hull, Eng., Feb. 11, 1896—d. Aug. 4, 1970), was the first chairman of the English Stage Company (1955) and largely responsible for the rebirth the following year of London's Royal Court Theatre. He was in charge of the financial management of the Royal Court and remained chairman of the English Stage Company until his death.

BOARD, LILLIAN, British athlete (b. Durban, S.Af., Dec. 13, 1948—d. Munich, W.Ger., Dec. 26, 1970), was European women's 800-m. champion and a silver medal-winner in the 1968 Olympics 400 m. In a short but brilliant athletic career she competed in the Commonwealth Games in Jamaica in 1966 at the age of 17, beat Judy Pollock, the world women's 440-yd. record holder at Los Angeles in 1967, and scored many successes that brought her titles of "Athlete of the Year" in 1967 and 1969 and "Sportswoman of the Year" in 1968 and 1970.

BOEGNER, MARC, French Protestant clergyman (b. Epinal, France, Feb. 21, 1881—d. Paris, France, Dec. 18, 1970), for many years the leading figure in French Protestantism and a pioneer of the ecumenical movement, was president of the Protestant Federation of France (1929–61), president of the National Council of the Reformed Church of France (1938–50), and president of the World Council of Churches (1948–54).

BOGAN, LOUISE, U.S. poet (b. Livermore Falls, Me., Aug. 11, 1897—d. New York, N.Y., Feb. 4, 1970), poetry critic for *The New Yorker* magazine (1931–69), held the chair of poetry of the Library of Congress in 1945–46. She was the recipient of the 1955 Bollingen Prize in Poetry and of two Guggenheim fellowships. Miss Bogan's work included *Collected Poems, 1923–53* (1954) and *Selected Criticism* (1955).

BORN, MAX, German nuclear physicist (b. Breslau, Ger., Dec. 11, 1882—d. Göttingen, W.Ger., Jan. 5, 1970), recipient of a Nobel Prize for Physics, was educated at the universities of

Sir John Barbirolli   Ed Begley   Mimi Benzell   Eric Lennard Berne

CAMERA PRESS FROM PIX   WIDE WORLD   WIDE WORLD   WIDE WORLD

Breslau, Heidelberg, Zürich, and Göttingen. He received his doctorate at Göttingen in 1907 and returned there as professor of theoretical physics after holding similar positions in the universities at Berlin and Frankfurt. During the Nazi regime Born took up residence in Great Britain, teaching at Cambridge and at Edinburgh; he became a British subject in 1939.

Born returned to Germany in 1954 and, although retired from teaching, continued his scientific studies. He was awarded the Nobel Prize for Physics that same year (co-recipient with Walther Bothe) for his "statistical interpretation of quantum mechanics"—work that he had undertaken 28 years before. In addition to his great contribution to quantum mechanics, Born was a pioneer in the area of solid-state physics and aided in the description of the physical properties of crystals.

BRANNER, MARTIN MICHAEL, U.S. cartoonist (b. New York, N.Y., Dec. 28, 1888—d. New London, Conn., May 19, 1970), was the creator of the "Winnie Winkle" comic strip, first introduced in the *New York Daily News* in 1920 and continued as a syndicated feature in more than 150 daily papers for five decades.

BRUCE LOCKHART, SIR ROBERT HAMILTON, British diplomat and author (b. Berkshire, Eng., Sept. 2, 1887—d. Brighton, Eng., Feb. 27, 1970), was sent as vice-consul to Moscow in 1911, imprisoned in the Kremlin in 1918, and released in exchange for M. M. Litvinov. In 1920 he was appointed commercial secretary at the British legation in Prague. After some years in Fleet Street, he turned his earlier experiences into a book and in 1932 published *Memoirs of a British Agent,* which had an immediate and lasting success. In 1940 he became British representative with the provisional Czechoslovak government-in-exile. A year later he was appointed deputy undersecretary of state in the Foreign Office and took over the direction of the Political Warfare Executive. In 1951 he published a memoir of Jan Masaryk, who had been a personal friend.

BRÜNING, HEINRICH, German chancellor from March 1930 to May 1932 (b. Münster, Westphalia, Ger., Nov. 26, 1885—d. Norwich, Vt., March 30, 1970), held office at a fateful period in history for Germany and the world and subsequently relapsed into obscurity. He entered the Reichstag in 1924, becoming spokesman for the Catholic Centre Party and, in 1929, the party's parliamentary leader. With the breakup of the coalition government under Hermann Müller, Brüning became chancellor. In 1932 he attempted to secure a prolongation of Pres. Paul Hindenburg's term of office, but Hitler quashed the attempt and forced an election. Brüning had to appeal to the left in his campaign for Hindenburg, who, on winning the election, dismissed his chancellor. Brüning retired from political life and left Germany in 1934.

BURKE, BILLIE, U.S. actress (b. Washington, D.C., Aug. 7, 1886—d. Los Angeles, Calif., May 14, 1970), who began her stage career in 1902, starred in many Broadway musicals including the early *Ziegfeld Follies* (in 1914 she was married to Florenz Ziegfeld [d. 1932], the producer of the Follies). Her motion-picture appearances included the role of the good witch in *The Wizard of Oz* (1939), as well as leading parts in the *Topper* series (1937–41) and in *The Man Who Came to Dinner* (1942).

BUTLER, THOMAS, British police officer (b. London, Eng., July 21, 1912—d. London, April 20, 1970), led the hunt for the Great Train Robbers. He became a policeman in 1935 and rose from the beat to be head of the Metropolitan Police Flying Squad. Put in charge of the hunt for the train robbers in 1963, he spent the next five years tracking down and arresting the 13 men who took part in the £2.5 million robbery.

Billie Burke

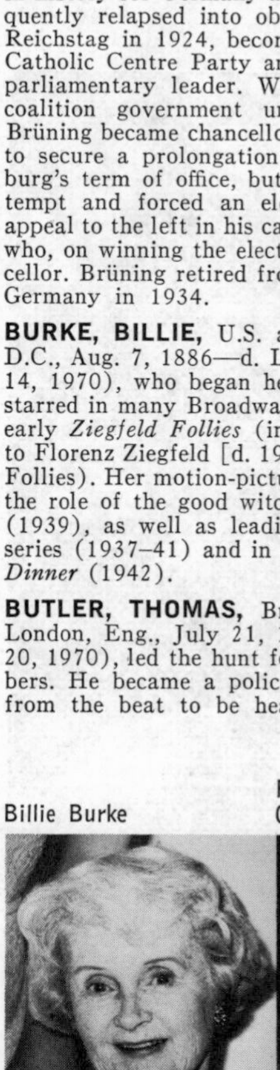

WIDE WORLD

Richard James Cardinal Cushing

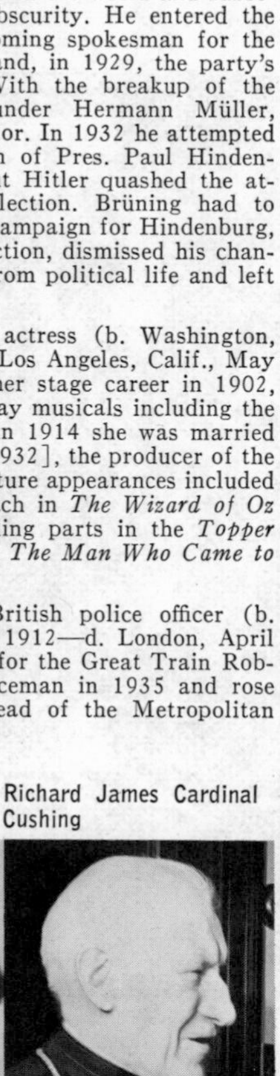

WIDE WORLD

CAFÉ FILHO, JOÃO, Brazilian political figure (b. Natal, Rio Grande do Norte, Braz., Feb. 3, 1899—d. Rio de Janeiro, Braz., Feb. 20, 1970), was president of Brazil from August 1954 until November 1955, having succeeded to that office following Pres. Getúlio Vargas' suicide. Café Filho's brief term was marked by his country's struggle for stability against inflation and the problems of industrialization.

CALDERÓN GUARDIA, RAFAEL ANGEL, Costa Rican statesman (b. March 10, 1900—d. San José, Costa Rica, June 9, 1970), was president of Costa Rica from 1940 until 1944, having served previously in the Congress (1934–40). He was defeated in his second-term bid by the revolutionist José Figueres, and exiled to Mexico. He returned to his country in 1958 as head of the opposition Republican (Calderonista) Party.

CANNON, LESLIE, British trade unionist (b. Wigan, Eng., Feb. 21, 1920—d. Dec. 9, 1970), who opposed fraudulent practices by Communist leaders of the Electrical Trades Union (ETU), became a Communist and in 1945 was elected to the national executive committee of the ETU, which fell increasingly under Communist control. Cannon led an energetic fight to expose Communist malpractices, climaxed by a celebrated 1961 High Court action in which five Communist leaders of the ETU were found guilty of ballot-rigging. Cannon became president of the ETU in 1963 and was elected to the General Council of the Trades Union Congress (TUC) in 1965.

CÁRDENAS, LÁZARO, Mexican political leader (b. Jiquilpan, Mex., May 21, 1895—d. Mexico City, Mex., Oct. 19, 1970), was the 45th president (1934–40) of Mexico. During his term he broke up the large estates of the wealthy landowners and distributed more than 40 million ac. among the poor farmers of Mexico; he seized foreign-owned properties, and nationalized the oil industry (1938). In 1955 he accepted the Stalin Peace Prize, awarded to him by the U.S.S.R.

CARNAP, RUDOLF, U.S. philosopher (b. Wuppertal, Ger., May 18, 1891—d. Santa Monica, Calif., Sept. 14, 1970), was a member of the "Vienna circle," a group of philosophers, mathematicians, and semanticists of the 1920s and 1930s. Carnap was a founder of logical empiricism (or logical positivism), a major school in modern philosophy that rejected the concepts of older philosophers and preferred to believe that philosophy should describe, clarify, and criticize science and language. Carnap was professor of philosophy at the University of Chicago (1936–52) and at the University of California at Los Angeles (1954–62).

CHASSIN, LIONEL, general (ret.), French Air Force (b. Bordeaux, France, April 26, 1902—d. Marseilles, France, Aug. 17, 1970), led an attempted coup d'etat against the Fourth Republic in 1958. He was one of the first French officers to join Gen. Charles de Gaulle in England in 1940. After the war he served at the Defense Ministry, in Indochina, and later commanded French air defenses in Europe. One of the leaders of the secret movement to overthrow the government in 1958, he was first placed on permanent leave, and on May 13, the day of the Algiers putsch, he escaped arrest and went into hiding.

CHRISTMAN, PAUL, U.S. football personality (b. 1919—d. Lake Forest, Ill., March 2, 1970), All-American halfback, played for the University of Missouri from 1938 through the 1940 season. As a professional he starred in the backfield of the old Chicago Cardinals. He was a leading television commentator on background "colour" for both American and National Football League games from 1960 through the 1969 season.

CLARK, FELTON G., U.S. educator (b. Baton Rouge, La., Oct. 13, 1903—d. New Orleans, La., July 5, 1970), was president (1938–69) of Southern University at Baton Rouge, La., when students of Southern staged the first sit-in demonstrations in protest against racially segregated lunch counters in 1960.

CLOUGH, IAN, British mountaineer (b. Yorkshire, Eng., 1937—d. Annapurna, Nepal, May 30, 1970), made numerous first and first British ascents on routes of great severity in the Alps, the Dolomites, the Himalayas, and the Andes, and was classed among the world's greatest mountaineers. He and Christopher Bonington were the first Britons to climb the Eiger north wall. Clough was killed on the south face of Annapurna.

CUSHING, RICHARD JAMES CARDINAL, U.S. prelate of the Roman Catholic Church (b. Boston, Mass., Aug. 24, 1895—d. Boston, Nov. 2, 1970), was archbishop of Boston, second largest diocese in the U.S., from 1944 until October 1970 when he retired because of illness. Cushing attended Boston College, completed his studies at St. John's Seminary, and was ordained a priest on May 26, 1921. He was assigned to the Boston office of the Society for the Propagation of the Faith, fund-raising branch of the church, and six years later became head of the organization. In 1939 he was made an auxiliary bishop; in 1944, on the death of Cardinal O'Connell, he was appointed administrator of the Boston archdiocese, and within months was named an archbishop by Pope Pius XII. Archbishop Cushing introduced a program of modernization within his diocese, building new churches, schools, and hospitals, and streamlining methods of fund raising (it was said he had raised $300 million for the church within his lifetime). He was elevated to cardinal in 1958 by Pope John XXIII. Cardinal Cushing, longtime priest and friend of the Kennedy family, officiated at the funeral of Pres. John F. Kennedy in 1963.

DALADIER, ÉDOUARD, French politician (b. Carpentras, France, June 18, 1884—d. Paris, France, Oct. 10, 1970), was France's premier at the time of the 1938 Munich agreement. Daladier left his lectureship at the Lycée Condorcet in Paris at the outbreak of World War I and joined the Army. After the war he became mayor of his native town and in 1919 was elected a Radical-Socialist deputy for Vaucluse. In 1924 he became minister of the colonies in the Herriot government and in 1933 and 1934 was himself premier for brief periods. His pursuit of a European conciliation met with German demands for further concessions. Nonetheless, the appeasement policy of his third and final premiership, from April 1938, had considerable public support. On the outbreak of war he took over the ministries of war and foreign affairs but resigned his posts by June 1940. He was arrested in September by the Vichy regime and detained throughout the war. Daladier was one of the few Third Republic politicians who were able to resume their careers after the war, and in 1946 was elected to the National Assembly. He was an active supporter of Pierre Mendès-France and in 1956 became president of the Radical parliamentary group.

DARLING, LOUIS, U.S. illustrator and conservationist (b. Stamford, Conn., April 26, 1916—d. Norwich, Conn., Jan. 21, 1970), who, with his wife, Lois, illustrated *Silent Spring* (1962) by Rachel Carson. With camera, brush, and pen, Darling illustrated about 60 other adults' and children's books, 14 of which he also wrote.

DAVIDSON, JOHN COLIN CAMPBELL DAVIDSON, 1st Viscount, British political figure (b. Aberdeen, Scot., Feb. 23, 1889—d. Dec. 11, 1970), played an influential behind-the-scenes role in the country's political affairs during the 1920s and '30s. In 1920 Davidson entered the House of Commons as member for Hemel Hempstead, and then became Andrew Bonar Law's parliamentary private secretary. He held ministerial office in 1923–24 as chancellor of the Duchy of Lancaster and in 1924–27 as Admiralty secretary, but was moved to the chairmanship of the Conservative and Unionist Party in 1926. He resigned this post in 1930 and again held office as chancellor of the Duchy of Lancaster.

DAVIS, BENJAMIN O(LIVER), SR., brigadier general (ret.), U.S. Army (b. Washington, D.C., July 1, 1877—d. North Chicago, Ill., Nov. 26, 1970), first Negro to attain the rank of general in the U.S. armed forces, retired in 1948 after 50 years' service.

DAWSON, WILLIAM L., U.S. congressman (1942–70) from Illinois (b. Albany, Ga., April 26, 1886—d. Chicago, Ill., Nov. 9, 1970), was the first Negro chairman of a major congressional committee, the House Committee on Government Operations.

KEYSTONE

COURTESY, FRENCH EMBASSY PRESS & INFORMATION DIVISION

As a captain in the French Army.

Marching down the Champs-Élysées with other members of the resistance movement after the liberation of Paris, August 1944.

With Winston Churchill after World War II.

HOWARD SOCHUREK, "LIFE" MAGAZINE © TIME INC.

"PARIS MATCH" FROM PICTORIAL PARADE

After taking office as president, January 1959.

FACING PAGE: "PARIS MATCH" FROM PICTORIAL PARADE

DE GAULLE, CHARLES ANDRÉ JOSEPH MA-RIE, general (ret.), French Army, and statesman (b. Lille, France, Nov. 22, 1890—d. Colombey-les-Deux-Églises, France, Nov. 9, 1970), president of France from 1959 until 1969, was one of the greatest figures in recent French history. Born the son of a professor of philosophy and literature, de Gaulle was widely read in the classics as a young man and at the age of 19 entered the École Spéciale Militaire of Saint-Cyr, graduating as a second lieutenant. In 1913 he joined the 33rd Infantry Regiment commanded by Col. (later Marshal) Philippe Pétain. He was wounded three times during World War I and after being taken prisoner at the Battle of Verdun in 1916 made five attempts at escape.

Released after the Armistice, de Gaulle rejoined his old regiment and in 1920 fought under General Weygand in the Polish campaign against the Bolsheviks, returning with a citation and the Polish Cross to take up a lectureship at Saint-Cyr in 1921. After graduating from the École Supérieure de Guerre in 1924 he was called onto the staff of Marshal Pétain, who was then vice-president of the Conseil Supérieur de la Guerre, and in 1927, with the rank of major, served in the army of occupation in the Rhineland. From 1929 until 1931 he served in Lebanon.

His publications, *Le Fil de l'épée* (1931), *Vers l'armée de métier* (1934), and *La France et son armée* (1938), established him as a controversial military theorist arguing in favour of a professional and mechanized army and against the prevailing doctrine of reliance on conscription and the Maginot Line. At the commencement of hostilities in 1939 de Gaulle commanded a tank brigade. In May 1940 he was put in charge of the 4th Armoured Division, becoming the youngest brigadier general in the French Army. He received his first political appointment as undersecretary of state for war from the new premier, Paul Reynaud, on June 6, and twice visited Winston Churchill in London in this capacity. When Pétain sought an armistice de Gaulle returned to London, declared himself head of a new Free French movement, and broadcast an appeal to the French people to continue fighting. He was sentenced to death in absentia on July 7, 1940.

In England, de Gaulle, now the symbol of French resistance to the German occupation, proved a troublesome ally, intransigent in his defense of French prestige and interests, and his relations with other Allied leaders, particularly with Pres. F. D. Roosevelt, were often far from cordial. In 1943, after the Allied landings in North Africa, he moved his headquarters to Algiers, where he headed the French Committee of National Liberation.

Following the liberation of metropolitan France, on Sept. 10, 1944, de Gaulle formed a provisional government but resigned on Jan. 20, 1946, and formed the right-wing Rassemblement du Peuple Français (RPF). After some initial success the party lost ground and was dissolved in 1953, de Gaulle then retiring into private life to write three volumes of his *Mémoires de guerre* (1954–59).

However, when civil war threatened in 1958, following the seizure of power by army leaders in Algeria, the general was called upon to form a national government and was elected president of the Fifth Republic on December 21.

Independence was granted to all 13 French colonies in Africa; a brief revolt by Europeans in Algeria was crushed without bloodshed and by 1962 the Algerian war was over; on Feb. 13, 1960, France exploded its first atomic bomb; in 1966 France withdrew from NATO.

De Gaulle was reelected to the presidency in December 1965 and, following a massive strike and student unrest, again in June 1968. After his proposals for regional reform and the abolition of the Senate had been rejected in a referendum held in April 1969, he resigned from the presidency and again retired from public life. The first volume of his *Mémoires d'espoir* was published in 1970.

DIDDLE, ED(GAR) A(LLEN), SR., U.S. basketball coach (b. 1896—d. Bowling Green, Ky., Jan. 2, 1970), who coached the Western Kentucky University basketball teams for 43 years, spurred his squads to more victories than any other school in college basketball annals—760 games won against only 302 lost. His teams won or shared 32 championships in three different conferences.

DIONNE, MARIE (Mrs. Florian Houle), Canadian quintuplet (b. near Callander, Ont., May 28, 1934—d. Montreal, Que., Feb. 27[?], 1970), smallest of the Dionne quintuplets and second of the five sisters to die (Émilie's death occurred in 1954), she was survived by Annette, Yvonne, and Cécile. At 19 Marie entered the cloistered order of the Servants of the Very Blessed Sacrament in Quebec, but left the convent because of poor health about a year later. For part of 1956 she operated a flower shop and in 1958 she was married.

DOS PASSOS, JOHN RODERIGO, U.S. novelist and historian (b. Chicago, Ill., Jan. 14, 1896—d. Baltimore, Md., Sept. 28, 1970), once considered a literary revolutionary, was the author of more than 30 books, including the *U.S.A.* trilogy. The trilogy, with its theme depicting the decay of American civilization through commercialism and the exploitation of the working man during the 1900–30 era, was made up of *The 42nd Parallel* (1930), *1919* (1932), and *The Big Money* (1936). Other works were *Manhattan Transfer* (1925), *Adventures of a Young Man* (1939), *Most Likely to Succeed* (1954), and *Midcentury* (1961).

DOWDING, HUGH CASWALL TREMENHEERE DOWDING, 1st Baron, air chief marshal of the Royal Air Force (b. Moffat, Dumfries, Scot., April 24, 1882—d. Tunbridge Wells, Eng., Feb. 15, 1970), directed Fighter Command during the Battle of Britain in 1940. An artillery officer before World War I, he was transferred to the Royal Flying Corps in 1914. One of the first to realize the possibilities of the all-metal monoplane fighter and of radar, he was appointed in 1936 to the new post of air officer commanding-in-chief, Fighter Command. In May 1940 his advice that no further squadrons should be committed to France was of crucial significance, the fighters being spared for the struggle against the German Luftwaffe. Criticism of some of his methods led to his being relieved of the post in November 1940, and he retired in 1942. Controversy over his dismissal was revived in 1957 by the publication of his biography and later by the appearance of the film *Battle of Britain* (1969).

FARRAR, CLARENCE B., U.S.-Canadian psychiatrist and editor (b. New York, N.Y., Nov. 27, 1874—d. Toronto, Ont., June 3, 1970), was medical director of the Toronto Psychiatric Hospital and professor of psychiatry at the University of Toronto from 1925 until 1947; he was also editor of the *American Journal of Psychiatry* from 1931 through 1965.

FARREN, SIR WILLIAM SCOTT, British aeronautical engineer (b. Cambridge, Eng., April 3, 1892—d. Kingston, Eng., July 5, 1970), played a major part in the development of aeronautics in the U.K. In 1937 he became deputy director of scientific research at the Air Ministry and from 1941 to 1946 was director of the Royal Aircraft Establishment at Farnborough. Later he saw the Vulcan bomber pass from blueprint to service with the RAF while serving as technical director for A. V. Roe and Co. From 1959 onward he worked with Hawker Siddeley. He was elected to the Royal Society in 1945 and knighted in 1952.

Erle Stanley Gardner

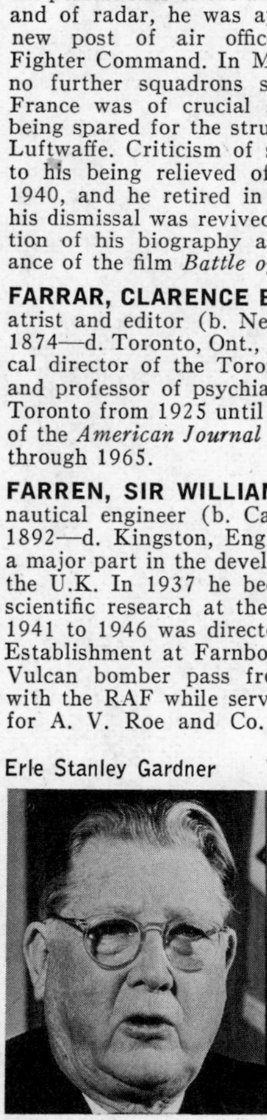

WIDE WORLD

"Rube" Goldberg

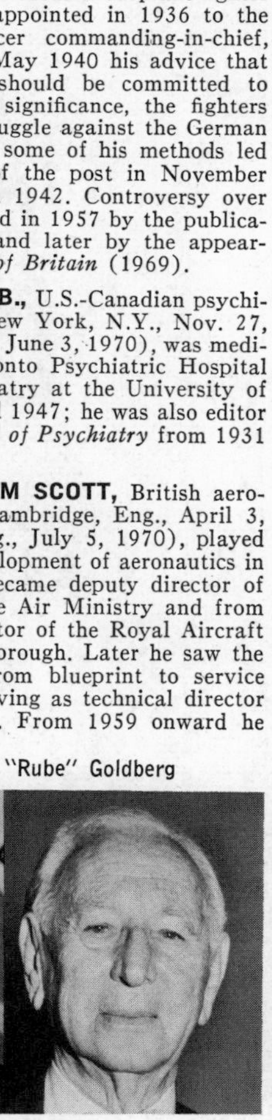

WIDE WORLD

FINLAY, DONALD, British athlete (b. Christchurch, Eng., May 27, 1909—d. April 21, 1970), had a remarkable track career as a high hurdler. He first represented England in 1929 and closed his career by coming in fourth in the 1950 Empire Games. He was Empire champion in 1934, Olympic silver medalist at Berlin in 1936, and European champion in 1938. In 1948 he took the competitors' oath at the London Olympics, and he won his eighth AAA championship in 1949 at the age of 40.

FISHER, JAMES MAXWELL McCONNELL, British naturalist (b. Clifton, Eng., Sept. 3, 1912—d. Hendon, Eng., Sept. 25, 1970), an ornithologist whose work contributed greatly to popularizing the study of birds. He was assistant curator at London Zoo (1936–39), and in 1939 his first book, *Birds as Animals,* appeared. In 1942 he became a co-editor of the "New Naturalist" series.

FLEESON, DORIS, U.S. journalist (b. Sterling, Kan., May 20, 1901—d. Washington, D.C., Aug. 1, 1970), whose stories and syndicated columns on the Washington scene appeared from 1933 until her retirement in 1968.

FORSTER, E(DWARD) M(ORGAN), British novelist and essayist (b. London, Jan. 1, 1879—d. Coventry, Eng., June 7, 1970), held an eminent place among the writers of the first half of the 20th century. He was educated at Tonbridge School in Kent and at King's College, Cambridge. Later he traveled extensively, going to India in 1912. Of his early novels, *Where Angels Fear to Tread* (1905), *The Longest Journey* (1907), *A Room with a View* (1908), and *Howards End* (1910), the latter is considered the most important. In 1924 he published his fifth and best-known novel, *A Passage to India,* an impressive work concerning the barriers existing between persons of different races in India during British colonial rule. His later writing was devoted more to essays, collected in *Abinger Harvest* (1936) and *Two Cheers for Democracy* (1951), although he did collaborate with Eric Crozier on the libretto for B. Britten's opera *Billy Budd* (1951). On Jan. 1, 1969, his 90th birthday, Forster received the Order of Merit from Queen Elizabeth II.

FRANCIS-WILLIAMS, EDWARD FRANCIS WILLIAMS, Baron, British journalist (b. St. Martins, Shropshire, Eng., March 10, 1903—d. Abinger Hammer, Surrey, Eng., June 5, 1970), was a natural publicist whom millions came to know as a frequent television interviewer and debater. After working as city editor and later editor of the *Daily Herald,* in 1941 he became controller of news and censorship at the Ministry of Information. When the Labour Party came to power in 1945, he was appointed adviser on public relations to the prime minister. He edited the Socialist weekly *Forward* from 1956 until it ceased publication four years later. He was made a Labour life peer in 1962.

GAILLARD, FÉLIX, French politician (b. Paris, France, Nov. 5, 1919—d. at sea, July 11[?], 1970), who became Radical Socialist premier in 1957. He worked with the resistance during World War II, and in 1944 became an assistant to Jean Monnet, then at work on the State Plan. In 1946 he became mayor of Barbezieux and deputy for Charente, being reelected from that *département* until his death. His government, one of the last under the Fourth Republic, collapsed in April 1958.

GARCÍA-GODOY CACERES, HÉCTOR, Dominican politician (b. Jan. 11, 1921—d. Santo Domingo, Dominican Republic, April 20, 1970), the National Conciliation Movement candidate in the presidential election scheduled for May 16, 1970, was opposing the reelection of Pres. Joaquín Balaguer. García-Godoy served as provisional president for several months following the U.S. intervention of 1965.

GARDNER, ERLE STANLEY, U.S. lawyer and writer (b. Malden, Mass., July 17, 1889—d. Temecula, Calif., March 11, 1970), was the author of 140 books, including the 80 mystery novels built around his chief character, the lawyer Perry Mason. In the early 1930s he gave up his law practice to devote full time to his writing. Perry Mason made his first appearance in 1933, in a full-length novel entitled *The Case of the Velvet Claws;* after that the standardized title *The Case of the . . .* signaled a Perry Mason courtroom thriller. Another Gardner character, the young district attorney Doug Selby, was the hard-hitting hero of *The D.A. . . .* series. Under the pseudonym A. A. Fair, Gardner also fashioned a third series covering the exploits of a fat, middle-aged private eye called Bertha Cool and her assistant Donald Lam. Gardner supervised the writing of the scripts for the "Perry Mason" television shows (1957–66), which in 1970 were still in reruns in the U.S. and in 16 languages overseas. He founded the Court of Last Resort to investigate possible miscarriages of justice.

GENÉE-ISITT, DAME ADELINE, Danish-born ballerina (b. Hinnerup, Den., Jan. 6, 1878—d. London, Eng., April 23, 1970), was a founder of modern British ballet. Encouraged and trained by her uncle, ballet-master Alexander Genée, Adeline Genée in 1897 came to the Empire Theatre, London, where, with few interruptions, she was to star during the next ten years. After touring the United States and Australia, and further London seasons, she announced her farewell engagement in 1914.

GERHARD, ROBERTO JUAN RENÉ, Spanish-born composer who later became a British citizen (b. Valls, Spain, Sept. 25, 1896—d. Cambridge, Eng., Jan. 5, 1970), was a prolific creative musician. Possibly the greatest Spanish composer since Manuel de Falla, he left Spain after the Spanish Civil War. He acknowledged his native land in *Six Catalan Folksongs* (1928) and in ballet music such as *Don Quixote* (1950). He was one of the first composers to master electronic composition, which in his third symphony he brilliantly combined with live orchestral music.

GILBERT, L. WOLFE, U.S. composer (b. Odessa, Russia, 1887—d. Los Angeles, Calif., July 12, 1970), called "the dean of Tin Pan Alley," wrote more than 250 popular songs, including "Waitin' for the Robert E. Lee" (1912), "Ramona," "Green Eyes," and "My Mother's Eyes."

GINSBERG, MORRIS, British sociologist (b. May 14, 1889—d. London, Eng., Aug. 31, 1970), was professor (1929–54) and emeritus professor of sociology at the London School of Economics. After eight years on the staff of the philosophy department of University College, London, Ginsberg's interest turned to sociology through contact with the great British sociologist Leonard T. Hobhouse. In 1953 he was elected to the British Academy, and he held honorary doctorates from Glasgow and Nottingham. His works included *Studies in Sociology* (1932), *Reason and Unreason in Society* (1947), *Essays on Sociology and Social Philosophy: On the Diversity of Morals* (1956), *Evolution and Progress* (1961), and *Nationalism: A Reappraisal* (1961). Ginsberg was a contributor to *Encyclopædia Britannica*.

GOLDBERG, REUBEN LUCIUS ("Rube"), U.S. cartoonist (b. San Francisco, Calif., July 4, 1883—d. New York, N.Y., Dec. 7, 1970), whose crazy contrivances cartoons became world famous, also excelled in the political cartoon, one of which—"Peace Today"—was awarded a Pulitzer Prize in 1948. Goldberg started his career in 1904 with the *San Francisco Chronicle;* in 1905 he went to the *San Francisco Bulletin,* but by 1907 he was in New York working for the *Evening Mail.* He remained in that job until 1926, creating his characters Boob McNutt, Mike and Ike, and Lala Palooza in the 1920s and '30s. During this time his cartoons were syndicated and appeared in hundreds of dailies until 1964. In 1938 he went to the *New York Sun* as a political cartoonist.

GROSS, ALFRED O., U.S. ornithologist (b. Atwood, Ill., April 8, 1883—d. Greenwich, Conn., May 9, 1970), authority on all sorts of wildlife, was professor emeritus of biology and Josiah Little professor emeritus of natural science at Bowdoin College, Brunswick, Me. In 1934 he was a member of Rear Adm. Donald B. MacMillan's expedition to the Arctic. He was an early conservationist and was instrumental in saving the prairie chicken from extinction in Wisconsin.

GROVES, LESLIE R(ICHARD), lieutenant general (ret.), U.S. Army (b. Albany, N.Y., Aug. 17, 1896—d. Washington, D.C., July 13, 1970), director of the World War II Manhattan Project that developed the atomic bomb. He also planned the military preparations that led to the dropping of the bomb on Hiroshima and Nagasaki, Jap., in August 1945.

GUGGENHEIM, OLGA HIRSH, U.S. philanthropist (b. Cincinnati, O., Sept. 23, 1877—d. New York, N.Y., Feb. 14, 1970), who, with her husband, Simon Guggenheim, in 1925 established the John Simon Guggenheim Memorial Foundation to aid scholars, artists, and scientists in the pursuit of their chosen branches of knowledge. Personally, Olga Guggenheim gave more than $1.5 million to the Museum of Modern Art (New York City) for the purchase of works by Picasso, Matisse, Monet, Braque, and other modern painters. Gifts were also made to the New York Public Library, the Memorial Center for Cancer and Allied Diseases, and to Roosevelt Hospital.

GUNTHER, JOHN, U.S. journalist and author (b. Chicago, Ill., Aug. 30, 1901—d. New York, N.Y., May 29, 1970), was the author of the "Inside" books, which by 1969 had sold more than 3.5 million copies and been translated into 90 languages. Gunther began his foreign journalistic career in Europe in the early 1920s, working for United Press and the *Chicago Daily News* bureau in London. After covering most of the capitals of Europe, in 1930 he was transferred to Vienna where he began his first book, *Inside Europe,* published in 1936. Others followed: *Inside Asia* (1939), *Inside Latin-America* (1941), *Inside U.S.A.* (1947), *Inside Africa* (1955), *Inside Russia Today* (1958), and *Inside South America* (1967); several of the early books were revised a number of times. *Twelve Cities* was published in 1969 and *Indian Sign* in June 1970.

HAYDEN, HENRI, Polish-born French painter (b. Warsaw, Pol., Dec. 24, 1883—d. Paris, France, May 13, 1970), arrived in Paris from Poland in 1907. From 1912 to 1914 the influence of Cubism and of Cézanne became apparent in his work, and he became an important member of the School of Paris. He executed a series of fine paintings, not all in the Cubist manner, culminating in "Les Trois Musiciens" of 1920. Hayden later abandoned Cubism, returning to direct contact with the landscapes of Brittany and the Mediterranean.

HENDRIX, JIMI (JAMES MARSHALL), U.S. rock star (b. Seattle, Wash., Nov. 27, 1942—d. London, Eng., Sept. 18, 1970), a singer-guitarist whose performances appealed to the youth of two continents, formed his own group, the Jimi Hendrix Experience, in London in October 1966. Hendrix returned to the U.S. in 1967 to play to overflow crowds. One of his most successful appearances was at the Woodstock Festival in August 1969. Among his many songs listed on the pop charts were, "Hey Joe," "Purple Haze," "Foxy Lady," and "The Wind Cries Mary."

HODGES, JOHN CORNELIUS ("JOHNNY" or "RABBIT"), U.S. jazz musician (b. Cambridge, Mass., July 25, 1906—d. New York, N.Y., May 11, 1970), who was a member of the "old school" of New Orleans jazz, played alto saxophone with Duke Ellington's band from 1928, except for several years in the early 1950s when he led his own band. As a soloist Hodges was known for his swinging style and slow melodious tone.

HOFSTADTER, RICHARD, U.S. historian (b. Buffalo, N.Y., Aug. 6, 1916—d. New York, N.Y., Oct. 24, 1970), DeWitt Clinton professor of American history at Columbia University from 1959, twice won Pulitzer Prizes for his *The Age of Reform* (in 1956) and for *Anti-Intellectualism in American Life* (in 1964).

HORTON, EDWARD EVERETT, U.S. actor (b. Brooklyn, N.Y., March 18, 1887—d. Encino, Calif., Sept. 29, 1970), whose successful stage and screen career spanned more than 60 years, also made frequent TV appearances.

HUMPHREY, GEORGE M., U.S. financier and executive (b. Cheboygan, Mich., March 8, 1890—d. Cleveland, O., Jan. 20, 1970), served as U.S. secretary of the treasury under Pres. Dwight D. Eisenhower from 1953 until 1957. Before entering the Cabinet he was president (from 1929) and board chairman of the M. A. Hanna Co., a Great Lakes iron and coal shipping company based in Cleveland.

ISHAK, INCHE YUSOF BIN, president of Singapore (b. Aug. 12, 1910—d. Singapore, Nov. 23, 1970), was successively representative of the British crown and then of the Malaysian king before becoming Singapore's president when it became independent in 1965. Before taking public office he was a journalist and managing editor of the Malay-language *Utusan Melayu*.

JACOBS, HIRSCH, U.S. horse trainer (b. New York, N.Y., April 8, 1904—d. Miami, Fla., Feb. 13, 1970), who saddled 3,569 winners in his lifetime, had his best year in 1936 when 177 of his Thoroughbreds won purses. Jacobs' horses earned more than $12 million, with Stymie, a $1,500 claim horse, collecting the largest amount, $918,-485, in the 1940s.

JOHNSON, OSCAR, U.S. skater and producer (b. St. Paul, Minn., 1898—d. Rochester, Minn., March 27, 1970), was one of the three founders of Shipstad's and Johnson's Ice Follies, and chairman of the board.

JOPLIN, JANIS, U.S. rock singer (b. Port Arthur, Tex., Jan. 19, 1943—d. Hollywood, Calif., Oct. 4, 1970), whose performances thrilled thousands of young rock fans, gained prominence at the Monterey Rock Festival in 1967 for her rendition of "Love Is Like a Ball and Chain" and "Summertime," sung with Big Brother and the Holding Company. The group later produced the million-record album *Cheap Thrills.*

KALECKI, MICHAL, Polish economist (b. Lodz, Pol., June 22, 1899—d. Warsaw, Pol., April 17, 1970), had an outstanding career with *An Essay in the Theory of the Business Cycle,* first published in Polish and in 1935 in English. This earned him a Rockefeller scholarship which brought him first to Sweden and subsequently to Great Britain. He worked in the Oxford Institute of Statistics during World War II, and in 1946 was appointed a deputy director in the UN Department of Economic Affairs. In 1955 he returned to Poland to become a vice-chairman of the Planning Commission. From 1961 to 1968 he was professor at the Central School of Planning and Statistics in Warsaw.

KERENSKI, ALEKSANDR FEDOROVICH, Russian political figure (b. Simbirsk [now Ulyanovsk], Russia, April 22, 1881—d. New York, N.Y., June 11, 1970), member of the Social Revolutionary Party who headed the provisional government of Russia for four months (July to November) after the fall of Czar Nicholas II in 1917. On Nov. 6, 1917 (October 24, old style), the Bolsheviks under Lenin overthrew the provisional government and Kerenski was forced to flee to England; he later went to France and in 1940 entered the United States. Kerenski had studied law and participated in the 1905 Revolution that had obtained some concessions from the czar. During this period he gained wide recognition as an eloquent defense lawyer for peasants, workers, and soldiers accused of political crimes. In 1912 he was elected to the fourth Duma. After the outbreak of World War I, Kerenski became actively engaged in the workers' movement that led to the February (1917) Revolution and the formation of the 11-man provisional government. Basically a democrat and a moderate who wished to continue Russia's involvement in the war, Kerenski was unable to control the fast-moving events that led to the Bolshevik seizure of power.

KEYES, FRANCES PARKINSON (WHEELER), U.S. writer (b. Charlottesville, Va., July 21, 1885—d. New Orleans, La., July 3, 1970), novelist, editor, and well-known Washington hostess, was the widow of Henry Wilder Keyes, who was governor of New Hampshire (1917–19) and U.S. senator (1919–37). During the 1920s she was an associate editor of *Good Housekeeping* magazine, for which she also wrote a travel column, and in 1937–39 she was editor of *National History Magazine,* published by the Daughters of the American Revolution. Her many books included *The River Road* (1945), *Came a Cavalier* (1947), *Dinner at Antoine's* (1948), *Joy Street* (1950), and *The Heritage,* published in 1968.

KIRK, PAUL L., U.S. criminologist (b. Colorado Springs, Colo., May 9, 1902—d. Oakland, Calif., June 5, 1970), was a witness in several widely publicized murder cases, including the 1954 Samuel Sheppard trial in Cleveland, O. He established crime laboratories in Chicago, St. Louis, and a number of other U.S. cities. Kirk was the author of *Crime Investigation: Physical Evidence and the Police Laboratory* (1953) and of *Quantitative Ultramicroanalysis,* which was published in 1950.

KNIGHTON-HAMMOND, ARTHUR HENRY, British artist (b. Arnold, Nottinghamshire, Eng., Sept. 18, 1875—d. Feb. 28, 1970), well known as a watercolourist and portrait painter in both Europe and the U.S., where he was elected to the American Watercolor Society, a rare honour for a British artist.

KOENIG, MARIE-PIERRE JOSEPH FRANÇOIS, general (ret.), French Army (b. Caen, France, Oct. 10, 1898—d. Neuilly-sur-Seine, France, Sept. 2, 1970), commanded the Free French forces at the Battle of Bir Hakeim (Libya) in World War II. Koenig was decorated during World War I and saw action in Morocco in the 1930s. In 1940 he served with French troops in Norway, and in 1941, having joined the Free French under Gen. Charles de Gaulle, was sent first to Syria and later to Egypt as commander of the 1st Free French Brigade. He was French commander in chief in Germany (1945–49) and in 1951 entered politics as a Gaullist deputy for Strasbourg. He later served as minister of defense in the governments of Pierre Mendès-France and Edgar Faure.

KRIM, BELKACEM, Algerian politician (b. Kabylie Mountains, Algeria, 1922—d. Frankfurt am Main, W.Ger., Oct. 20, 1970), was one of the chief leaders of the Algerian Front for National Liberation (FLN) in the struggle for independence from France. In 1947 he joined the Algerian nationalist movement and in 1954 became responsible for directing guerrilla operations in the Kabylie region, being five times sentenced to death in absentia by French courts-martial. He was a founder member of the Algerian Revolutionary Committee (CNRA) and in 1958, when a provisional republican government was formed in Cairo, became its vice-president and minister for the armed forces, responsible for all resistance operations within Algeria. As minister for foreign affairs in the rebel government he led the Algerian delegation in peace talks with the French which finally resulted in the Évian agreement of 1962 providing for complete independence. After a violent clash with the rival Algerian leader Ahmed ben Bella, who had been in prison during the Évian negotiations, Krim lost influence and he withdrew from overt political activity. He opposed the Boumédienne regime, which came to power in 1965, and formed a Democratic Movement for Algerian Renewal in Paris in 1967. In April 1969, after an attempt on the life of the FLN party leader Ahmed Kaid, Krim was sentenced to death in absentia for conspiracy against the Algerian government. He was found strangled in Frankfurt.

KRONBERGER, HANS, British physicist (b. Linz, Aus., July 28, 1920—d. Wilmslow, Cheshire, Eng., Sept. 29, 1970), was member for reactor development at the United Kingdom Atomic Energy Authority. In 1956 he became chief physicist at Risley and in 1958 director of research and development.

Jimi Hendrix

Edward Everett Horton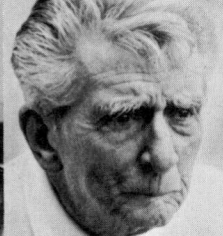

Oscar Johnson

Janis Joplin

CENTRAL PRESS FROM PICTORIAL PARADE

WIDE WORLD

WIDE WORLD

ST. GEORGE TUCKER RANSON FROM PICTORIAL PARADE

KRUG, JULIUS ALBERT ("Cap"), U.S. government official (b. Madison, Wis., Nov. 23, 1907—d. Knoxville, Tenn., March 26, 1970), was U.S. secretary of the interior (1946–49) under Pres. Harry S. Truman. Prior to his service in the Cabinet he had been chairman of the War Production Board (1944–45).

KRUTCH, JOSEPH WOOD, U.S. naturalist, conservationist, and author (b. Knoxville, Tenn., Nov. 25, 1893—d. Tucson, Ariz., May 22, 1970), was drama critic for *The Nation*, a weekly journal, from 1924 until 1952. At the same time he was teaching at Columbia University (where in 1943 he became Brander Matthews professor of dramatic literature), at Brooklyn Polytechic Institute, New York City, Vassar College, in Poughkeepsie, N.Y., and the New School for Social Research, New York City. During this period he also wrote several books, including *The Modern Temper* (1929). In 1948 he published a biography of Henry David Thoreau, and his interests began to turn more to natural history, especially after a respiratory ailment forced him to resign his positions and move to the Southwest. There, living in an adobe home in the desert, he studied the natural beauty and wildlife about him and produced a series of memorable books: *The Desert Year* (1952), *The Measure of Man* (1954, National Book Award for nonfiction), *The Voice of the Desert* (1955), *The Great Chain of Life* (1957), and *Human Nature and the Human Condition* (1959). His autobiography, *More Lives Than One*, appeared in 1962, followed by *A Treasury of Birdlore* (ed. with Paul S. Eriksson, 1962), *Herbal* (1965), and *The Best Nature Writing of Joseph Wood Krutch*, which was published in 1969.

LAMORISSE, ALBERT, French film director (b. Paris, France, Jan. 13, 1922—d. Teheran, Iran, June 2, 1970), displayed a poetic vision in his short fantasies, such as *Bim* (1949), *Le Voyage en ballon* (1960), and *Fifi la Plume* (1964). His most notable films were *Crin Blanc* (1952), which won the Grand Prix at the Cannes festival, and *Le Ballon Rouge* (1955), awarded the Golden Palm at Cannes and a Hollywood Oscar for the best story and screenplay.

LANE, SIR ALLEN, British publisher (b. Bristol, Eng., Sept. 21, 1902—d. Northwood, Eng., July 7, 1970), revolutionized British publishing by introducing low-priced paperback books (Penguins) in the 1930s. He began his career in the family firm of Bodley Head, becoming successively advertising manager and managing director. He and his brothers hit upon the idea of cheap paperbacks, and in 1935 he founded Penguin Books Ltd. The first Penguin was André Maurois' biography of Shelley, *Ariel*. A large order from Woolworth's ensured the Penguin success and further books (mainly biographies and travel, but also fiction) were published by authors such as Shaw, Freud, Julian Huxley, and Virginia Woolf. In 1937 he commissioned the Penguin Specials. These were followed by Penguin Shakespeare, King Penguins, Pelicans, Puffins, and Porpoises. By 1945 over eight million paperbacks a year were being sold. He was knighted in 1952 and made a Companion of Honour in 1969.

LANGE, HALVARD M., Norwegian statesman (b. Kristiania [Oslo], Nor., Sept. 16, 1902—d. Oslo, May 19, 1970), was Norway's foreign minister from 1946 to 1965. It was largely as a result of his efforts that both Norway and Denmark joined NATO in 1949. The son of Christian L. Lange, co-recipient of the 1921 Nobel Peace Prize, he had an international education. After the German occupation of Norway in World War II he became deeply involved in the resistance movement and was arrested in August 1940, but promptly rejoined the resistance on his release in June 1941. In 1942 he was again arrested and sent to Sachsenhausen prison. After the war Lange succeeded Trygve Lie as foreign minister when the latter became the UN's first secretary-general. In 1960 Lange was chairman of the NATO Council.

LAPP, PAUL W., U.S. archaeologist (b. 1931—d. near Kyrenia, Cyprus, April 26, 1970), an authority on the archaeology of the Middle East. Lapp's excavations at Bab ed-Dra, the ancient cemetery near the Lisan in Jordan, uncovered proof of a high-level civilization occupying the area around 2500 B.C. The pottery collection from the site was thought to be the largest yet found from that period.

LE BRUN, PIERRE, French trade unionist (b. Saint-Claude, Jura, France, Oct. 28, 1906—d. Louveciennes, France, Nov. 20, 1970), was confederal secretary of the Confédération Générale du Travail. After graduating as an engineer he was an active member of the resistance during World War II. After the war he left the electrical industry to embark on a political career, becoming an executive member of the CGT, and its confederal secretary in 1948. However, differences between himself and the Communist-dominated leadership, notably over Czechoslovakia, Poland, and the candidacy of the non-Communist left-wing leader François Mitterrand in the 1965 presidential elections, led to his resignation in 1966.

LEE, GYPSY ROSE (Rose Louise Hovick), U.S. ecdysiast (b. Seattle, Wash., Jan. 9, 1914—d. Los Angeles, Calif., April 26, 1970), the "Queen of Burlesque," was a striptease artist, actress, and writer. In 1931 she performed at Minsky's in New York City, and by 1937 was a show girl in the *Ziegfeld Follies*. She appeared in George White's *Scandals* and at the New York World's Fair, 1939–40, in *The Streets of Paris*. She made her first motion picture in 1938. Miss Lee was the author of three popular books: *Gypsy: A Memoir* (1957), which became a Broadway musical and later a movie; *The G-String Murders* (1941); and *Mother Finds a Body* (1942). In 1966 she launched her own nationally syndicated television talk show.

LEWIS, TED ("Kid"), British boxer (b. London, Eng., Oct. 24, 1894—d. London, Oct. 20, 1970), was the only British fighter ever to win a world title in the U.S. He won the British featherweight title at 17, the European featherweight title at 18, and the world welterweight title in Boston in 1915 against Jack Britton, who won it back from him in 1919 after he had successfully defended it four times. Lewis was also British middleweight champion.

LIDDELL HART, SIR BASIL HENRY, British military critic (b. Paris, France, Oct. 31, 1895—d. England, Jan. 29, 1970), was an early and persistent advocate of mechanized warfare. A history student at Cambridge at the outbreak of World War I, he served as a company commander in the King's Own Yorkshire Light Infantry. His experiences convinced him of the need to avoid head-on collisions with the enemy by a combination of surprise and mobility. After his retirement from the Army in 1927 his advocacy of mechanization was continued as military correspondent of the *Daily Telegraph* and *The Times*. In 1937 he became personal adviser to the secretary of state for war, Leslie Hore-Belisha, but withdrew after a year, his reforms still thwarted by opposition within the Army and the War Office. He left *The Times* in 1939 and during World War II wrote war commentaries for the *Daily Mail*. Of his 30 or so books, probably the finest was his history of the tank; in 1969 he completed his one-volume history of World War II, the work of 22 years. Just before his death Liddell Hart completed work on major sections of an important new article, "World Wars," for *Encyclopædia Britannica*.

LISTON, CHARLES ("Sonny"), U.S. boxer (b. near Little Rock, Ark., May 8, 1932 [?]—d. Las Vegas, Nev., Dec. 28[?], 1970), heavyweight champion of the world from September 1962 until February 1964, began his professional career in 1953. He lost only one bout in a series of 34 matches before he battled Floyd Patterson for the heavyweight title in Chicago on Sept. 25, 1962, winning the championship by a knockout in the first round. On Feb. 25, 1964, Cassius Clay (later known as Muhammad Ali) fought Liston for the title and won on a technical knockout when Liston failed to answer the bell for the seventh round because of a shoulder injury. In a return match on May 25, 1965, Liston was KO'd by Clay in the first round. In 1966 Liston began a comeback and won 14 consecutive bouts before being knocked out in the ninth by Leotis Martin on Dec. 6, 1969.

LOCHRIDGE, CHARLES, U.S. contract bridge player (b. 1905—d. Delray Beach, Fla., Nov. 11, 1970), who twice won the Vanderbilt Cup (1937, 1949), was also victorious in the Life Master Mixed Teams (1931), the National Mixed Pairs (1932), and the National Open Pairs. He retired from tournament play in 1949.

LOGINOV, YEVGENY, marshal of the Soviet Air Force (b. Helsinki, Fin., Oct. 23, 1907—d. Moscow, U.S.S.R., Oct. 7, 1970), was Soviet minister of civil aviation from 1964 until relieved in 1970, and a member of the Central Committee of the Communist Party of the Soviet Union. From 1959 he supervised the state airline Aeroflot during a period of rapid growth, involving the introduction of jet aircraft and the development of new routes, including the first Moscow–New York flights by Aeroflot and Pan American. He also signed agreements with Japan Airlines and Air France to fly the short route to Tokyo across Siberia.

LOMBARDI, VINCENT THOMAS ("Vince"), U.S. football coach (b. Brooklyn, N.Y., June 11, 1913—d. Washington, D.C., Sept. 3, 1970), who led the Green Bay Packers to six division titles and five National Football League championships during 1960–67, took over the Washington Redskins in 1969. Lombardi guided the Redskins to their first winning season in 14 years. His own playing career included his years at Fordham University, where he played guard. After graduation from Fordham in 1937, and a season with the Brooklyn Eagles, a minor league team, Lombardi began his coaching career at St. Cecelia High School in Englewood, N.J., in 1939, then coached at Fordham (1947–48) before joining the coaching staff at the U.S. Military Academy at West Point. In 1954 he went with the New York Giants on his first pro assignment, but did not become a head coach until he was offered the post by the Green Bay Packers in 1959. He built the losing Packers into a winning team and captured his first division title the next season. During his nine seasons with Green Bay his team won 141 games, lost 39, and tied 4.

LONDON, HEINZ, British physicist (b. Bonn., Ger., Nov. 7, 1907—d. England, Aug. 3, 1970), was especially interested in low temperature research. After working under Sir Francis Simon at Breslau University on the electrodynamics of superconductivity, London moved to the Clarendon Laboratory in Oxford in 1934 and, with his brother Fritz London, evolved the electrodynamic theory of superconductors. During World War II he joined the U.K. Atomic Energy Project and was principally concerned with the separation of uranium isotopes, discovering the effect on vapour pressure of the symmetry of the molecule. In 1946 he was attached to the Atomic Energy Research Establishment at Harwell, becoming deputy chief scientist in 1958.

LONGMORE, SIR ARTHUR MURRAY, air chief marshal (ret.), Royal Air Force (b. St. Leonards, New South Wales, Austr., 1885—d. Berkshire, Eng., Dec. 10, 1970), was a pioneer of naval aviation. As a naval lieutenant in 1911 he made the first flight from land to water in England, alighting in Sheerness Harbour in a Short biplane fitted with flotation bags. He was an original member of the Naval Wing of the Royal Flying Corps, the Royal Naval Air Service, and the Royal Air Force. Between World Wars I and II he was commandant of the RAF College, Cranwell. In May 1940 he was appointed air officer commanding in the Middle East, and in 1941 inspector general of the RAF. He was knighted in 1935.

LONSDALE, GORDON (Georgi Lonov, or Konon Trofimovich Molody), Soviet intelligence agent (b. 1922[?]—d. near Moscow, U.S.S.R., Oct. 9, 1970), was head of the Portland spy ring uncovered in the U.K. in 1961. Known to the Soviets as "Colonel K," Lonsdale was parachuted behind German lines in 1943 to organize resistance in Minsk. There he met Rudolph Abel (later arrested by the FBI and exchanged for U.S. U-2 spy pilot Gary Powers) and was soon working in Germany as Abel's radio operator. Nothing more was known of him until he went from Canada to New York via Nigeria in 1955, a few weeks before arriving in England, where he set himself up as a businessman. Posing as a U.S. naval commander, he persuaded Harry Houghton, an Admiralty clerk at the secret Portland Underwater Weapons Establishment, and Houghton's girl friend, Ethel Gee, to provide him with information on Britain's nuclear submarine bases and tracking system. This information was then transmitted to Moscow from the Ruislip bungalow of Peter and Helen Kroger. The ring was broken, and in 1961 Lonsdale was sentenced to 25 years' imprisonment. In 1964 he was exchanged for Greville Wynne, a Briton held by the Soviets on spying charges. In 1965 Lonsdale published his autobiography, *Spy.* (*See* INTELLIGENCE OPERATIONS.)

LOUISE, ANITA (ANITA LOUISE FREMAULT), U.S. stage and screen actress (b. New York, N.Y., Jan. 9, 1917—d. Los Angeles, Calif., April 25, 1970), who at age five began a career that was to span five decades and more than 70 motion pictures. Her later work was directed toward television.

LOUW, NICHOLAAS PETRUS VAN WYK, South African poet and critic (b. Sutherland, S.Af., June 6, 1906—d. Johannesburg, S.Af., June 18, 1970), was the most distinguished Afrikaans writer of his day. A lecturer in education at the University of Cape Town for many years, he won the Hertzog Prize for literature five times and was known, apart from his own poetry, for his studies in Afrikaans of contemporary poets such as T. S. Eliot.

McCRACKEN, (EMMETT) BRANCH ("BIG BEAR"), U.S. basketball coach (b. Monrovia, Ind., June 9, 1908—d. Bloomington, Ind., June 4, 1970), whose Indiana University teams twice won the National Collegiate Athletic Association basketball championship—first in 1940 and again in 1953. McCracken's lifetime coaching record was 457 victories and 215 defeats.

McGRAW, JAMES H., JR., U.S. publisher (b. Madison, N.J., May 9, 1893—d. New York, N.Y., Feb. 20, 1970), was president (1937–50) and chairman of the board (1935–50) of McGraw-Hill Publications Co.

McINNES, GRAHAM CAMPBELL, Canadian diplomat and author (b. London, Eng., Feb. 18, 1912—d. Paris, France, Feb. 28, 1970), was educated in Australia and studied art in Europe before going to Canada, where he became art editor of a Toronto newspaper. In 1942 he became a senior producer on the Canadian National Film Board and six years later embarked on a diplomatic career. From 1965 until his death he was Canada's minister and permanent delegate to UNESCO in Paris. McInnes, the son and brother, respectively, of novelists Angela Thirkell and Colin McInnes, was himself the author of numerous novels, articles, short stories, anthologies, and books of art criticism.

MacIVER, ROBERT MORRISON, U.S. sociologist, educator, and writer (b. Stornoway, Scot., April 17, 1882—d. New York, N.Y., June 15, 1970), president (1963–65) and chancellor (1965–66) of the New School for Social Research, New York City, was Lieber professor of political philosophy and sociology at Columbia University (1929–50). He was the author of a number of books, including *The Web of Government* (1947; rev. ed., 1965).

McKAY, DAVID OMAN, U.S. religious leader (b. Huntsville, Utah, Sept. 8, 1873—d. Salt Lake City, Utah, Jan. 18, 1970), who served as president of the nearly three million-member Church of Jesus Christ of Latter-day Saints from 1951, was the ninth head of the Mormon Church since its organization in 1830 by Joseph Smith and his five co-founders. In 1906 he was called to membership in the Council of Twelve Apostles, governing body of the church, with duties in the field of church education, and in 1922 he was placed in charge of worldwide missions. He was appointed second counselor of the First Presidency, highest executive body of the church, in 1934. Upon the death of George Smith in April 1951, McKay, as eldest Apostle in point of service, was accepted as the Mormon Prophet and assumed the presidency of the church. During his tenure the church doubled its membership, with much of its growth in Europe, Latin America, New Zealand, and the South Seas.

McLAREN, BRUCE, New Zealand automobile racing driver (b. Auckland, N.Z., Aug. 30, 1937—d. Goodwood, Eng., June 2, 1970), was a popular and successful figure on the world's racing circuits, as a driver and designer of racing cars and a veteran of 102 world championship Grand Prix events. He joined the British Cooper works team in 1959 and that same year won his first Grand Prix, the United States. After the 1965 season he left Cooper to build his own McLaren cars and in 1968 won the Belgian Grand Prix in a Formula One car of his own design. He established a thriving manufacturing concern, and his death while practicing in one of his own sports cars came just before the announcement by the Royal Automobile Club that he had been awarded the Segrave Trophy for 1969.

MACLEOD, IAIN NORMAN, British politician (b. Skipton, Eng., Nov. 11, 1913—d. London, Eng., July 20, 1970), who was briefly chancellor of the Exchequer in the Conservative government that took office in June 1970. In 1950 he won the seat of West Enfield and also became a member of the One Nation Group which opposed state collectivism. He was appointed minister of health in 1952 and minister of labour in 1955. In 1959 he became colonial minister and until 1961 worked hard to convince his own party of the need for change. Prime Minister Harold Macmillan made him chairman of the Conservative Party and chancellor of the Duchy of Lancaster in October 1961. Later he declined to serve under Sir Alec Douglas-Home and instead worked as editor of the *Spectator.*

MacMILLAN, DONALD BAXTER, rear admiral (ret.), U.S. Navy (b. Provincetown, Mass., Nov. 10, 1874—d. Provincetown, Sept. 7, 1970), last surviving member of the Robert E. Peary expedition that discovered the North Pole in 1909. MacMillan himself made 29 more expeditions into the Arctic. During his almost yearly trips, he made vital contributions to the knowledge of far northern geology, botany, zoology, and geography, and to the understanding of Eskimo culture.

MASLOW, ABRAHAM HAROLD, U.S. psychologist (b. Brooklyn, N.Y., April 1, 1908—d. Menlo Park, Calif., June 8, 1970), Philip Meyers professor of psychology at Brandeis University, Waltham, Mass., was the founder of humanistic psychology. His particular school of psychology, including the concept of the group encounter form of psychotherapy, was outlined by Maslow in 1943; he was still engaged in research in 1970, under a grant from the Laughlin Foundation. His writings included *Motivation and Personality* (1954), *Toward a Psychology of Being* (1962), and *The Psychology of Science* (1966).

MAURIAC, FRANÇOIS CHARLES, French author (b. Bordeaux, France, Oct. 11, 1885—d. Paris, France, Sept. 1, 1970), winner of the Nobel Prize for Literature in 1952, received his higher education in Bordeaux and Paris. Mauriac in 1909 published his first volume of poetry, *Les Mains jointes.* A second volume, *Adieu à l'adolescence,* followed two years later and in 1912 he joined the editorial staff of a literary periodical, *Les Cahiers,* to encourage art of "purely Catholic inspiration." His first novel, *L'Enfant chargé de chaînes,* was published in 1913. In 1922 he published the first novel of which, he said later, he was not ashamed—*Le Baiser au lépreux.* Other major novels followed: *Genitrix* (1923); *Le Désert de l'amour* (1925 Grand Prix of the Académie Française); *Thérèse Desqueyroux* (1927); *Destins* (1928); *Le Noeud de vipères* (1932); and *Le Mystère Frontenac* (1933). With the publication of this last he was elected to the Académie Française.

MAVROGORDATO, JOHN NICOLAS, British classical scholar (b. London, Eng., July 19, 1882—d. July 24, 1970), was Bywater and Sotheby professor of Byzantine and modern Greek language and literature at Oxford University from 1939 to 1947. Apart from his numerous classical publications, he also wrote a standard history of *Modern Greece, 1800–1931* (1931), published a lyrical translation of *The Poems of C. P. Cavafy* (1951), and contributed articles on modern Greece to the 12th and 13th editions of *Encyclopædia Britannica.*

MAY, ERNST, German architect (b. Frankfurt, Ger., July 27, 1886—d. Hamburg, W.Ger., Sept. 14, 1970), who greatly influenced housing programs in Europe. In 1925 he became city architect of Frankfurt, and the model suburban housing estates he built brought him an international reputation. In 1930 he went to the U.S.S.R., where he stayed until 1934. Returning to Nazi Germany, he found himself restricted and emigrated to East Africa. He worked principally in Tanganyika (Tanzania), introducing sophisticated planning and building ideas. After World War II he returned to Europe and was planning consultant to a number of German cities.

MICHELET, EDMOND, French politician (b. Paris, France, Oct. 8, 1899—d. Oct. 9, 1970), who became French minister of culture in 1969, played a leading part in organizing French resistance during World War II. He saw service in World War I and later joined the Catholic Action Movement. In 1940 he published an immediate call to resist the enemy and later helped found two underground networks. In 1943 he was arrested by the Gestapo and imprisoned first at Fresnes, and later at Dachau. He returned actively to French public life, being elected in 1945 as a deputy of the Mouvement Républicain Populaire. Charles de Gaulle made him minister of the armed forces, a post he retained after de Gaulle's resignation in 1946. He was expelled from the party for predicting the general's return. In 1952 he became Gaullist senator for Paris, working closely with de Gaulle. He opposed the Algerian war and as minister of war veterans (1958) and minister of justice (1959–61) worked to conciliate the Algerian nationalists. From 1962 to 1967 he was de Gaulle's nominee on the Constitutional Council, returning to the government as minister in charge of the civil service in 1967. Finally, in 1969, after de Gaulle's resignation, he took over the ministry of cultural affairs from André Malraux.

MIKOYAN, ARTEM IVANOVICH, Soviet aircraft designer (b. Russia, 1905—d. U.S.S.R., Dec. 9, 1970), was co-designer of the MiG-15 jet fighter. A brother of Anastas I. Mikoyan, Soviet head of state (1964–65), he designed the MiG-15 with Mikhail Gurevich, the designation being taken from their two names. The MiG-15 was introduced in 1950 in Korea, piloted by North Korean and Chinese airmen, and was widely used by Communist air forces until its replacement by the MiG-17.

MISHIMA, YUKIO, Japanese novelist (b. Tokyo, Jap., Jan. 14, 1925—d. Tokyo, Nov. 25, 1970), committed seppuku (hara-kiri), ancient suicide ritual, following the failure of an attempt to persuade Japanese soldiers to overthrow the Sato government. The appeal to the soldiers was prompted by Mishima's desire for the people of Japan to throw off the influences of the West and return to the old samurai traditions. Mishima's first successful novel, the autobiographical *Kamen no Kokuhaku,* was published in 1949 (Eng. trans., *Confessions of a Mask,* 1958). Perhaps his best-known novel was *Kinkakuji* (1956; Eng. trans., *The Temple of the Golden Pavilion,* 1959).

MÖLLER, GUSTAV, Swedish politician (b. Malmö, Swed., 1884—d. Stockholm, Swed., Aug. 15, 1970), chief architect of the Swedish welfare state, was minister of social security from 1932 until 1951. President of the Young Social Demo-

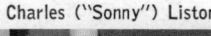

Joseph Wood Krutch   Sir Allen Lane   Charles ("Sonny") Liston   David Oman McKay

WIDE WORLD   CAMERA PRESS FROM PIX   WIDE WORLD   WIDE WORLD

crats from 1911, he was elected to the Riksdag in 1917, and in 1924 first took over the Ministry of Social Security, though his plans clashed with those of the opposition parties and he lost the post. In 1932, however, following the sweeping electoral victory of the Social Democrats, he was reinstated, and between then and 1951 was responsible for introducing a whole series of social reforms.

MOREAU, REGINALD E., British ornithologist (b. London, Eng., 1897—d. Hereford, Eng., May 30, 1970), was a pioneer of modern field ornithology. His interest in birds began in Egypt in 1920. In 1928 he moved to Tanzania (then Tanganyika), where he began his work on African birds. After his retirement from the Colonial Service in 1946, he worked at the Edward Grey Institute at Oxford until 1968. He edited *Ibis,* the journal of the British Ornithologists' Union, from 1947 to 1960, and his own major work, *The Bird Faunas of Africa and Its Islands* (1966), was received with enthusiasm by biologists.

MORRIS, CHESTER, U.S. actor (b. New York, N.Y., Feb. 16, 1901—d. New Hope, Pa., Sept. 11, 1970), created the role of Boston Blackie in a series of 36 detective stories that were favourites among the more than 85 movies he made. His last stage play was *The Subject Was Roses,* in 1967.

MULHOLLAND, JOHN, U.S. magician (b. Chicago, Ill., June 9, 1898—d. New York, N.Y., Feb. 25, 1970), who performed magic tricks at age five and became a professional while still a schoolboy, toured most of the countries of the world demonstrating his illusions and lecturing on his methods. He was editor of the magicians' magazine, *The Sphinx,* for 23 years, and wrote books on magic.

MURPHY, JOHN J. ("Johnny"), U.S. baseball figure (b. New York, N.Y., July 14, 1908—d. New York, Jan. 14, 1970), who was general manager of the New York Mets from 1967, started his major league career as a relief pitcher for the New York Yankees in 1934. During his 11½ seasons with the Yankees he pitched in seven American League pennant races and six World Series championships.

NAGEL, CONRAD, U.S. actor (b. Keokuk, Ia., March 16, 1897—d. New York, N.Y., Feb. 24, 1970), stage and screen star of the 1920s and 1930s, was a founder (1927) and president of the Academy of Motion Picture Arts and Sciences. He received a special Oscar in 1940 for his work with the Motion Picture Relief Fund. He appeared in most of his films (about 150) from 1919 through 1933 and played in many long-run shows on Broadway, including *Skin of Our Teeth* (1943) and *State of the Union* (1946).

NASSER, GAMAL ABD-AL-, Egyptian statesman (b. Beni Mor, Asyut Province, Egypt, Jan. 15, 1918—d. Cairo, U.A.R., Sept. 28, 1970), president of Egypt (later the United Arab Republic) from 1956, was an outstanding leader of his people and the driving force behind the Pan-Arab movement. He embarked early on a military career and graduated from the Staff College of the Cairo Military Academy in 1947. He distinguished himself in the 1948 war against Israel and was wounded at Faluja. With other like-minded junior officers he conspired to put his revolutionary theories into practice, forming in 1948 the Free Officers Committee which planned the coup d'état of July 23, 1952. The coup succeeded without violence and King Faruk abdicated and left Egypt. First the revolutionaries chose as their figurehead Maj. Gen. Muhammad Naguib, but when he began to show signs of sympathy for the old ways he was removed and Nasser emerged as the national hero, becoming prime minister in 1954, president of Egypt in 1956, and of the U.A.R. in 1958. He introduced land reforms, suppressed the Muslim Brotherhood, opposed the Baghdad Pact of 1955, and began looking to the Eastern-bloc countries for arms for his war against Israel, while rigorously suppressing communism in Egypt. He was adept at retaining the goodwill of the West and relied on U.S. and British cooperation in financing the Aswan High Dam project. When this offer was suddenly withdrawn in July 1956 Nasser retaliated by nationalizing the Suez Canal. The fiasco of the

Anglo-French invasion and subsequent withdrawal along with that of Israeli forces from Sinai enhanced Nasser's prestige in the Arab world and left him in control of British assets and of the canal, which was soon reopened to all but Israeli shipping. In February 1958 he established the United Arab Republic of Egypt and Syria; five months later his chief rival, Nuri es-Said, was overthrown in Iraq and the pro-Western union of Iraq and Jordan came to an end. However, although Iraq left the Baghdad Pact, it did not draw nearer to the U.A.R. In 1961 Syria left the U.A.R., and in Nasser's lifetime no state replaced it. The Yemen revolution, which began in 1962 with Egyptian backing but was only partially successful, for several years tied down 50,000 Egyptian troops. Relations with Saudi Arabia, from which Yemeni royalists drew support, became strained, as did those with Britain owing to Egyptian encouragement of terrorism in South Arabia. Nasser also denounced the Tunisian president, Habib Bourguiba, for his attitude to Israel. At home Nasser proclaimed Egypt the Arab Socialist Union and continued to play off the great powers against each other. The Suez Canal was working well, and when in 1964 the Nile was diverted, altering the geographic features of Egypt and north Sudan, N. S. Khrushchev visited the country and Nasser was made a hero of the Soviet Union. In 1965 he broke off relations with West Germany because of its support to Israel. Israel's devastating military defeat of the U.A.R., Jordan, and Syria in June 1967 was provoked by Nasser's request for the withdrawal of the UN Emergency Force from Egyptian territory, the reoccupation of Sharm ash Shaykh, and the threat to close the Gulf of Aqaba to Israeli shipping. Nasser at first blamed the defeat on U.S. and British military intervention, but later took responsibility himself and after a gesture of resignation was reinstated by a show of frenzied popular support. After the June war, Nasser's health deteriorated and he made several visits to the U.S.S.R. both for medical treatment and to obtain further arms

supplies. His agreement in 1970 to a cease-fire along the canal front and apparent willingness for tentative contacts with the Israelis had raised hopes for an end to the Arab-Israeli conflict.

NELSON, ERIK HENNING, brigadier general (ret.), U.S. Army Air Forces (b. Stockholm, Swed., 1889—d. Honolulu, Hawaii, May 9, 1970), who, with Lowell H. Smith, made the first round-the-world airplane flight in 1924 in two Army two-seater, open-cockpit Douglas biplanes.

NEWMAN, ALFRED, U.S. composer-conductor (b. New Haven, Conn., March 17, 1901—d. Hollywood, Calif., Feb. 17, 1970), was the winner of eight Academy Awards for his motion-picture background scores for *The Song of Bernadette* (1943) and *Love Is a Many-Splendored Thing* (1955) and for his scoring of *Alexander's Ragtime Band* (1938), *Tin Pan Alley* (1940), *Mother Wore Tights* (1947), *With a Song in My Heart* (1952), *Call Me Madam* (1953), and *The King and I* (1956).

NOON, MALIK FIROZ KHAN, Pakistani politician (b. India, May 7, 1893—d. Lahore, W.Pak., Dec. 9, 1970), was prime minister during 1957–58, and a prominent leader in the Muslim struggle to create independent Pakistan. He was Indian high commissioner in London before World War II but was recalled to India to serve on the viceroy's council. He represented Indian interests on numerous international bodies, and in the British War Cabinet (1944–45). When Muhammed Ali Jinnah's movement got under way, he took a leading part. However, he received no office in independent Pakistan's first government. In 1956 he became foreign minister and the following year prime minister, continuing as leader of the Republican Party after his resignation.

O'BRIEN, SIR TOM, British trade unionist (b. Llanelly, Wales, Aug. 17, 1900—d. London, Eng., May 5, 1970), was a former chairman of the Trades Union Congress (TUC) and a prominent figure in the international labour movement. In

KARSH, OTTAWA FROM RAPHO GUILLUMETTE

LONDON "DAILY EXPRESS" FROM PICTORIAL PARADE

Gamal Abd-al-Nasser. Right, as a field commander in the 1948 war with Israel. Below, with Soviet Premier Nikita Khrushchev in Cairo, 1964.

LONDON "DAILY EXPRESS" FROM PICTORIAL PARADE

1932 he became general secretary of the National Association of Theatrical and Kine Employees. He was elected to the General Council of the TUC in 1940 and became its chairman in 1952–53. He was MP for Nottingham West (1945–50, 1955–59) and Nottingham Northwest (1950–55). He was knighted in 1956.

O'HARA, JOHN HENRY, U.S. author (b. Pottsville, Pa., Jan. 31, 1905—d. Princeton, N.J., April 11, 1970), who portrayed the lives of the small-town residents of "Gibbsville," counterpart of his own hometown. He was the author of 35 works, beginning with *Appointment in Samarra,* his first novel, in 1934. Among his best-selling novels, many of which were adapted for the stage and screen, were: *Butterfield 8* (1935), *A Rage to Live* (1949), *Ten North Frederick* (1955), and *From the Terrace* (1958). His short-story collections included *Pal Joey* (1940), *The Great Short Stories of John O'Hara* (1956), *The Hat on the Bed* (1963), *Waiting for Winter* (1966), and *And Other Stories* (1968). He also wrote nonfiction (*Sweet and Sour,* 1945), plays (*Five Plays,* 1961), and a newspaper column (collected in *My Turn,* 1966). His last novel, *The Ewings,* was scheduled for publication in February 1971. O'Hara received many honours, including a National Book Award for *Ten North Frederick,* an award for his musical *Pal Joey,* and the American Academy of Arts and Letters Gold Medal in 1964.

OLDENBROEK, JACOBUS HENDRIK, Dutch trade unionist (b. Amsterdam, Neth., Nov. 10, 1897—d. London, Eng., March 8, 1970), was widely known in the international labour movement. In 1938 he was elected assistant general secretary to the International Transport Workers Federation and shortly before World War II helped transfer its headquarters from Amsterdam to London. He became general secretary in 1942. When the anti-Communist International Confederation of Free Trade Unions was formed in London in 1949 Oldenbroek became its first general secretary and served until 1960.

OLSON, CHARLES, U.S. poet (b. Worcester, Mass., Dec. 27, 1910—d. New York, N.Y., Jan. 10, 1970), an influence in post-World War II poetry and leader of the Black Mountain group, taught at Clark University, Worcester, Mass., and at Harvard before joining the faculty at Black Mountain College in North Carolina in 1948. He served as rector of the school from 1951 until 1956. In 1960 two volumes of his major works were published under the titles *The Distances* and *Maximus Poems;* later books were *Human Universe* (1965) and *Selected Writings* (1967).

PETER II, last king of Yugoslavia (b. Belgrade, Yugos., Sept. 6, 1923—d. Los Angeles, Calif., Nov. 5, 1970), was born to the House of Karageorgevich or "Black George." He succeeded to the throne upon the assassination of his father, Alexander I, in Marseilles on Oct. 9, 1934, while on a state visit to France. A Council of Regents, led by his cousin Prince Paul, ruled Yugoslavia until Peter became of age at 18. Almost immediately on the assumption of full responsibility as monarch in 1941 he was forced to leave the throne when the German Army occupied his country. He was evacuated to Britain and there became head of the Yugoslav government-in-exile. With the support of the Allies, Marshal Tito and his Communist-led People's Liberation Army finally gained control of Yugoslavia. Tito was victorious in the November 1945 elections and at the first meeting of the Constituent Assembly the monarchy was abolished and Peter II was formally declared deposed as of 1945.

PHILIP, ANDRÉ, French economist and politician (b. Pont-Saint-Esprit, France, June 28, 1902—d. Paris, France, July 5, 1970), was a member of the French Christian Socialist movement, whose work formed the basis for the Schuman Plan and later for the EEC. He was appointed minister of finance and national economy in the Gouin Cabinet in 1946 and at the end of that year was reappointed to the same post in the Blum ministry. From 1950 to 1964 he was delegate general of the European Movement and president of the Socialist Movement for the United States of Europe.

PICCOLO, (LOUIS) BRIAN, U.S. professional football player (b. Pittsfield, Mass., 1944—d. New York, N.Y., June 16, 1970), was halfback for the Chicago Bears football team for three

seasons (1966–69). He won early recognition at Wake Forest College, Winston-Salem, N.C., where he was named All-American in his senior year, having led all major college players in scoring and in yards gained by rushing. For most of his professional career he was backup man for Gale Sayers. When Sayers injured his knee during the 1968 season, Piccolo played the last five games as a regular, gaining a season record of 450 yd. rushing and 28 passes caught.

PIPER, WILLIAM THOMAS, U.S. aircraft pioneer (b. Knapps Creek, N.Y., Jan. 8, 1881—d. Lock Haven, Pa., Jan. 15, 1970), was the founder (1936) of the giant Piper Aircraft Corp. and developer of the versatile Piper Cub. Graduating from Harvard University in 1903, Piper worked as a construction engineer until 1914 when he became a partner in the Dallas Oil Co. of Bradford, Pa. After service in World War I, he became associated with Taylor Brothers Aircraft Corp. and developed a glider that was the forerunner of the Cub. Originally named the Brownbach Tiger Kitten, the tiny two-cylinder, two-cycle plane was first flown on Sept. 2, 1930. This experimental model was scratched for the improved 37-hp. E-2 Cub, which was approved for flight June 15, 1931. In 1936 Piper bought out the failing Taylor Corp. and finally got into production on his own the following year with a record 687 Cubs. During World War II the U.S. Army used thousands of Cubs in all phases of its operations. In the 1950s a new twin-engine Cub was popular with businessmen, but during the 1960s few Cubs were manufactured. However, by 1970 the company was producing a Super Cub and 16 other aircraft. At the time of his death Piper was credited with having built more planes than anyone else in the world.

PIPINELIS, PANAYOTIS, Greek politician (b. Piraeus, Greece, March 21, 1899—d. Athens, Greece, July 19, 1970), foreign minister of Greece after the 1967 military coup, was briefly prime minister in 1963. He became chief of the Political Bureau under King George II of Greece in 1945. Apart from his service to the royal family, he particularly wished to bring an end to the enmity between Greece and Turkey over Cyprus, but although instrumental in preventing war during the crisis of 1967 he did not achieve a lasting settlement.

POOL, THE REV. DAVID DE SOLA, U.S. leader in Judaism (b. London, Eng., May 16, 1885—d. New York, N.Y., Dec. 1, 1970), rabbi of Shearith Israel, the Spanish and Portuguese synagogue, in New York City from 1907 until his retirement in 1955.

POPHAM, ARTHUR EWART, British art historian (b. Plymouth, Eng., March 22, 1889—d. Dec. 8, 1970), keeper of the Department of Prints and Drawings at the British Museum (1945–54), was a noted authority in the field of old master drawings. After graduating from Cambridge, he joined the staff of the British Museum print room in 1912, becoming in turn deputy keeper (1933) and keeper (1945). He cataloged the Burlington House Italian exhibition (1930), the Phillipps collection (1935), and the 15th- and 16th-century Italian drawings in the Royal Library, Windsor (1949). He was a contributor to *Encyclopædia Britannica.* His later work centred on the 16th-century Parma School and on the drawings of Parmigianino, which he completed cataloging in 1970.

POWDERMAKER, HORTENSE, U.S. anthropologist (b. Philadelphia, Pa., Dec. 24, 1900—d. Berkeley, Calif., June 16, 1970), whose fieldwork covered the culture of the Melanesians, the attitudes and codes of behaviour of Negro and white residents of a small Mississippi town, and the social structure of Hollywood. After graduating from Goucher College, Baltimore, Md., in 1920, she earned a Ph.D. at the University of London in 1928. She began teaching at Queens College, Flushing, N.Y., in 1938 and was professor of anthropology there from 1954 until her retirement in 1967. The results of her many field trips were published in a number of books, including *Life in Lesu* (1933), *After Freedom* (1939), *Hollywood, the Dream Factory* (1950), and *Copper Town: Changing Africa* (1962).

POWELL, PAUL, U.S. politician (b. Vienna, Ill., Jan. 21, 1902—d. Rochester, Minn., Oct. 10, 1970), a powerful but controversial figure in Illinois state politics, served as Illinois secretary of state from Jan. 11, 1965. A Democrat, he was

a member of the Illinois House of Representatives for 30 years, holding the post of speaker three times. In 1966 he appeared voluntarily before a grand jury looking into alleged corruption in his office. After his death an inventory of his effects revealed an unaccounted-for cache of some $800,-000 in cash, part of an estate valued at $3 million, which prompted another official investigation into the conduct of his office.

PRICE, LILIAN NANCY BACHE, British actress and author (b. Kinver, Worcestershire, Eng., Feb. 3, 1880—d. March 31, 1970), began her stage career in 1899 when she left school to join the Theatre Royal, Birmingham, under F. R. Benson. In 1900 she appeared at the Lyceum in London, and in 1902 successfully played in Beerbohm Tree's production of Stephen Phillips' *Ulysses.* She appeared in plays by Pirandello, Ibsen, and Zola during the 1920s, but really made her mark with the foundation of the People's National Theatre in 1930, launched by herself and J. T. Grein at the Fortune. She sustained this enterprise at various theatres for 11 years and in 1950 was awarded the CBE, retiring two years later to devote herself to editing the periodical *Pedlar's Pack* and to writing more than 20 books on nature.

PUSHKIN, ALEKSANDR I., Soviet ballet teacher (b. 1908—d. Leningrad, U.S.S.R., March 20, 1970), taught classical ballet at the Vaganova Choreography School in Leningrad and at the Kirov Theatre, where he had been a distinguished dancer in the 1920s and 1930s. Of Pushkin's students known to the West, Rudolf Nureyev was the most famous.

PYNE, JOE, U.S. television figure (b. Chester, Pa., 1926—d. Hollywood, Calif., March 23, 1970), who conducted a TV talk show that featured constant clashes with his guests. Pyne was known as "Killer Joe" because of his aggressive and abrasive manner toward the persons appearing on his show, which had its largest following during the mid-1960s.

QUEUILLE, HENRI, French politician (b. Neuvic d'Ussel, France, March 31, 1884—d. Paris, France, June 15, 1970), was three times premier of France. A doctor by profession, he obtained his first government post as undersecretary for agriculture in Alexandre Millerand's government in 1920. He was 20 times a minister in the Third Republic under various leaders. During the Vichy period he retired, but resumed his government career under Charles de Gaulle, as acting president of the Comité Français de la Libération Nationale during de Gaulle's absence from Algiers in 1943–44. From July 1948 to June 1954 he served continuously, as either minister or premier, in 12 French governments. As premier in 1948–49, he presided over an uneasy coalition, under fire from both Communists and Gaullists.

RAMAN, SIR CHANDRASEKHARA VENKATA, Indian physicist (b. Trichinopoly, India, Nov. 7, 1888—d. Bangalore, India, Nov. 21, 1970), was awarded the Nobel Prize for Physics in 1930. After initial research in optics and acoustics, Raman became a civil servant, continuing his research in his spare time. In 1917 he became professor of physics at the University of Calcutta, moving in 1933 to the Indian Institute of Science at Bangalore. In 1947 he became director of the Raman Research Institute there. He encouraged the building of many research institutes in India and founded the *Indian Journal of Physics* and the Indian Academy of Sciences. Raman was awarded the Nobel Prize for his discovery that light scattered by any medium is emitted in frequencies equal to the infrared frequencies of that medium, a phenomenon that came to be known as the Raman effect. The use of this effect in determining fine molecular structure was considered a forerunner in the making of laser spectrometers.

RAMBEAU, MARJORIE, U.S. actress (b. San Francisco, Calif., July 15, 1889—d. Palm Springs, Calif., July 6, 1970), whose career on stage and screen spanned almost seven decades, was twice nominated for Academy Awards, in 1940 for *Primrose Path* and in 1953 for *Torch Song.* She became a star in her first Broadway appearance, in 1913 in *Kick In;* she made her film debut in *Her Man,* a 1930 release.

RAPACKI, ADAM, Polish statesman (b. Zwierzyniec, Pol., Dec. 24, 1909—d. Warsaw, Pol., Oct. 10, 1970), as Polish foreign minister (1956–68) put forward in 1957 the Rapacki plan to denuclearize central Europe. After World War II, in which he fought in the Polish Army and was captured by the Germans, he returned to Poland and joined the Polish Socialist Party. In December 1948, when this party fused with the Polish Workers' (Communist) Party, Rapacki was elected to the Politburo of the Polish United Workers' Party. After serving as minister of shipping and later of higher education, he was appointed in April 1956 minister of foreign affairs, retaining this portfolio until 1968, when he resigned to protest the dismissal from his ministry of officials of Jewish extraction.

REED, THE RIGHT REV. ERNEST S., Canadian clergyman (b. Dublin, Ire., 1909—d. Ottawa, Ont., Feb. 28, 1970), Anglican bishop of Ottawa, was vice-president of the Canadian Council of Churches and chairman of the World Council of Churches finance committee.

REMARQUE, ERICH MARIA, German-born writer (b. Osnabrück, Ger., June 22, 1898—d. Locarno, Switz., Sept. 25, 1970), achieved world fame with his novel *Im Westen nichts Neues* (1929; *All Quiet on the Western Front*), a realistic account of the fate of a group of young German "volunteers" in World War I, based on his own experiences as a soldier in the German Army. The book was translated into many languages and was read by millions; the Hollywood screen version of 1930 became a film classic. In the 1920s Remarque worked as a teacher, in advertising, and as a journalist. His books were banned in Nazi Germany and in 1938 he was deprived of German citizenship. The following year he went to the United States, and became a U.S. citizen in 1947, although he lived mainly at Porto Ronco, near Ascona in Switzerland. He wrote a number of other successful novels, all of them strongly antiwar in sentiment, for example *The Road Back* (1931), *Three Comrades* (1937), *Flotsam* (1941), and *Arch of Triumph* (1946).

REUTHER, WALTER PHILIP, U.S. labour leader (b. Wheeling, W.Va., Sept. 1, 1907—d. near Pellston, Mich., May 9, 1970), president of the United Automobile Workers, died with his wife May Wolf Reuther in a plane crash while en route to a union recreation and education centre. Reuther quit school at age 16 to work as a bench hand at the Wheeling Steel Corp. Three years later he went to Detroit and, although working as a well-paid mechanic, decided to finish high school and go on to Detroit's Wayne University. In the early 1930s he and his brother Victor made their way through Europe, touring various auto plants in England and working in one in the U.S.S.R.

Returning to the U.S. in 1935, Reuther went back to the auto plants of Detroit and helped organize the UAW Local 174. He actively participated in the union's demonstrations and sitdown strikes that led to the 1937 recognition by General Motors of the UAW as bargaining agent for its workers; other companies soon followed GM, with only Ford holding out until 1941. During World War II Reuther, by then high in the union leadership, kept the auto workers firm to their no-strike pledge, but after the war he supported their demands for a 30% increase in pay.

Reuther became president of the UAW at the 1946 convention, winning over the incumbent, R. J. Thomas, by 4,444 to 4,320. In 1952 he was elected president of the Congress of Industrial Organizations and in 1955 he led the CIO into a merger with the American Federation of Labor, from which it had split two decades earlier over the question of industrial versus craft unionism. Reuther's relations with George Meany, president of the combined AFL-CIO, were never completely satisfactory, however, and in 1968 the more liberal Reuther took the UAW out of the parent organization. Considered one of the most socially and politically progressive of U.S. labour leaders, Reuther during the 1950s and '60s headed successful drives for improved wages,

better welfare and health benefits, and more liberal retirement plans for the UAW's 1.6 million members.

RICCI, NINA (MARIA NIELLI), Italian-born couturiere (b. Turin, Italy, Jan. 14, 1883—d. Paris, France, Nov. 29, 1970), went to Paris in 1932 and founded one of the most famous French fashion houses. Her Nina Ricci perfumes also became world famous.

RIGGS, ROBERT, U.S. artist (b. Decatur, Ill., Feb. 5, 1896—d. Philadelphia, Pa., April 14, 1970), whose lithographs of circuses and prizefights hang in the Library of Congress in Washington, D.C., the Metropolitan Museum of Art, New York City, and other major U.S. art museums.

RINDT, JOCHEN, Austrian racing driver (b. Mainz, Ger., April 18, 1942—d. Monza, Italy, Sept. 5, 1970), was leading in the 1970 world drivers' championship at the time of his death which occurred during practice for the Italian Grand Prix. He made his racing debut in 1961, his first Formula One race being the South African Grand Prix in 1965. The same year he shared the winning Ferrari with the U.S. driver Masten Gregory in the Le Mans 24-hour race. In 1969 he won the United States Grand Prix.

RIVERS, L(UCIUS) MENDEL, U.S. congressman (from 1941) from South Carolina (b. Gumville, S.C., Sept. 28, 1905—d. Birmingham, Ala., Dec. 28, 1970), assumed the chairmanship of the powerful House Armed Services Committee in 1965, just before the beginning of major escalation in the Vietnam war.

RODRIGUEZ-MOÑINO, ANTÓNIO, Spanish bibliographer (b. Calzadilla de los Caños, Spain, March 14, 1910—d. Madrid, Spain, Aug. 1970), an outstanding figure in contemporary Hispanic studies, was professor at the University of California, Berkeley, from 1960. He published his first article at 15 and throughout his life contributed to the world's most learned literary journals. He edited several collections of Spanish texts and criticism and in 1965, with his wife Maria Brey, published a monumental catalog of manuscripts of Spanish poetry for the Hispanic Society of America, of which he was vice-president.

ROOT, CHARLES ("CHARLIE"), U.S. baseball player (b. Middletown, O., 1899—d. Hollister, Calif., Nov. 5, 1970), Chicago Cub pitcher who threw the ball that Babe Ruth knocked out of the Cubs' ball park at a "predicted" spot during the 1932 World Series. During his 16 years with the Cubs (1926–42), Root won 201 games and lost 160.

ROSSITER, CLINTON L., U.S. historian and political scientist (b. Philadelphia, Pa., Sept. 18, 1917—d. Ithaca, N.Y., July 11[?], 1970), senior university professor of American institutions at Cornell University, was the author of *The American Presidency* (1956), a classic work on the subject. Another book, *Seedtime of the Republic,* published in 1953, won the Bancroft Prize.

ROTH, CECIL, British historian and editor (b. London, Eng., March 5, 1899—d. Jerusalem, Israel, June 21, 1970), an authority on Jewish history, was editor in chief of the almost completed *Encyclopaedia Judaica,* to be one of the most comprehensive works of Jewish scholarship ever published. He wrote more than 30 books on Jewish history, and in 1965 published *The Dead Sea Scrolls: A New Historical Approach.*

ROTHKO, MARK (MARCUS ROTHKOVICH), U.S. painter (b. Dvinsk, Russia, Sept. 25, 1903—d. New York, N.Y., Feb. 25, 1970), a pioneer in abstract expressionism whose monumental canvases were sought by collectors all over the world, received his early art training under Max Weber at the Art Students League in New York City. His realist painting was first exhibited in 1929, and during the mid-1930s he worked on the Federal Arts Project. Surrealist influences crept into his painting in the 1940s and were quite apparent in his first important one-man show, at Peggy Guggenheim's Art of This Century Gallery. From 1946 until 1951 he exhibited at the Betty Parsons Gallery, and in the latter year he showed at the Museum of Modern Art. Success came to Rothko in 1954 with his beginning exhibition at the Sidney Janis Gallery, and in 1958 he was one of four artists chosen to represent the United States at the 29th Venice Biennial.

ROUS, FRANCIS PEYTON, U.S. pathologist and bacteriologist (b. Baltimore, Md., Oct. 5, 1879—d. New York, N.Y., Feb. 16, 1970), research scientist at the Rockefeller University, was co-winner of the 1966 Nobel Prize for Medicine for his discovery of tumour-producing viruses. The research that led to his prize-winning discovery began in 1909 when he examined a hen with cancer of the breast. Rous, endeavouring to determine the cause of the sarcoma, pulverized the diseased tissue, stirred it into a salt solution, and then filtered the mixture. When he injected the cell-free filtrate into healthy hens a number of them developed malignant growths. Rous concluded the cancers were caused by a filterable virus. His findings conflicted with the medical opinions of the day and were dismissed as having resulted from faulty techniques. He was vindicated by later experiments, and more than 50 years afterward was awarded a Nobel Prize for his work.

RUGGLES, CHARLES, U.S. actor (b. Los Angeles, Calif., 1886[?]—d. Santa Monica, Calif., Dec. 23, 1970), appeared in more than 80 motion pictures from his first in 1929 through his last films for the Walt Disney organization. On stage his later work included *The Pleasure of His Company* (Tony Award, 1958). For television he appeared in "The World of Mr. Sweeney," a 1954 series.

RUSSELL, BERTRAND ARTHUR WILLIAM RUSSELL, 3RD EARL, British philosopher (b. Trelleck, Monmouthshire, Wales, May 18, 1872—d. Minffordd, Merionethshire, Wales, Feb. 2, 1970), was the most distinguished philosopher of his age, whose work ranked him with the great English empiricists, Locke, Berkeley, Hume, and Mill. The grandson of Lord John Russell, he was orphaned at the age of three and brought up by his grandmother. He took a first class degree in moral science at Cambridge University in 1894 and in 1896 lectured in the United States on non-Euclidean geometry. In 1900, having eschewed a political career, he produced his first major work, his *Critical Exposition of the Philosophy of Leibnitz,* in whom he recognized a pioneer of mathematical logic. *The Principles of Mathematics* followed in 1903. The conclusions of this work were set out in *Principia Mathematica,* produced with A. N. Whitehead in three volumes (1910–13). This, more completely than ever before, reduced mathematics to a branch of logic. From this standpoint, substituting "logical constructions" for "inferred entities," he critically examined traditional problems and philosophies with a ruthless and polished self-assurance. Empirical and deductive knowledge were the only kinds of knowledge that he was prepared to admit, subject to logical analysis freed from the restrictions of traditional syntax. During World War I his opposition to conscription and advocacy of pacifism brought him six months in jail in 1918. His *Practice and Theory of Bolshevism* (1920) was the first of many attacks on Soviet Communism. *Freedom and Organization* (1934) traced the development of Britain and the United States in the 19th century and foreshadowed his monumental *History of Western Philosophy* (1946). His writings on education, marriage, and morals were revolutionary, witty, and wise. He was profoundly influenced by the irrationality of the rise of Hitler, which led him to abandon pacifism. In 1948 he narrowly escaped death in an air crash in Norway. A fellow of the Royal Society since 1908, he was awarded the Order of Merit in 1949, and the following year he received the Nobel Prize for Literature. From 1958 he carried out a vigorous personal campaign for nuclear disarmament, first through the Campaign for Nuclear Disarmament and later through the Committee of 100, which advocated direct action. He also communicated directly with world leaders. There followed another prison sentence, for breach of the peace, in 1961. In 1963 he gave up his disarmament activities and established two foundations, the Bertrand Russell Peace Foundation and the Atlantic Peace Foundation. During his last years, spent mostly in retirement, he lent his name to the international war crimes tribunal on American activities in Vietnam. His last works returned to the theme of internationalism as the only guarantee of world peace.

SACHS, NELLY, German-born poet (b. Berlin, Ger., Dec. 10, 1891—d. Stockholm, Swed., May 12, 1970), was joint recipient (with S. Y. Agnon; *q.v.*) of the 1966 Nobel Prize for Literature. Nelly Sachs began writing at the age of 16 and her poems of the 1920s gained the attention of Stefan Zweig. Under the threat of Nazi persecution she was enabled by Prince Eugen of Sweden and the Swedish novelist Selma Lagerlöf to escape to Sweden in 1940, and eventually became a Swedish citizen. The experience of hatred and suffering became a new source of inspiration, and the concentration camps and Israel were the central themes of her later work.

SAGENDORPH, ROBB H., U.S. publisher (b. Newton Center, Mass., Nov. 20, 1900—d. Peterborough, N.H., July 4, 1970), was the editor and publisher of *The Old Farmer's Almanac*, an annual assemblage of wit, wisdom, and weather predictions.

SALAZAR, ANTÓNIO DE OLIVEIRA, Portuguese statesman (b. Vimieiro, Port., April 28, 1889—d. Lisbon, Port., July 27, 1970), premier and virtual dictator of Portugal for thirty-six years, came into power in 1932 when the country was in a state of turmoil. Salazar graduated from the University of Coimbra in 1914, became a member of the faculty, and by 1918 had earned a doctorate in law and a full professorship in economics. He helped form the Catholic Centre Party and in 1921 was elected to the Cortes (parliament), although he resigned after one session and returned to the university. In May 1926, after the government had been overthrown in a military coup, Salazar became minister of finance but resigned when he realized he could not introduce his reform measures. Two years later, however, Gen. António Óscar de Fragoso Carmona was elected president and Salazar accepted the finance post with complete control over income and expenditures. He gained in power and on July 5, 1932, became premier, drafting a new constitution for his *Estado Novo* ("New State") that established Portugal as an authoritarian state. While premier, Salazar also served as minister of war (1936–44) and minister of foreign affairs (1936–47). During World War II he maintained Portugal's neutrality, but in 1949 led it into the North Atlantic Treaty Organization. Upon Carmona's death in 1951, Salazar was offered the presidency but chose to remain premier. In the early 1960s colonial problems erupted: the Gôa enclave was incorporated into India; insurrection broke out in Angola, and large numbers of troops had to be stationed in Africa to contain the revolt. In September 1968 Salazar suffered an incapacitating stroke; Marcello Caetano was appointed premier, and Salazar remained unaware of the change at the time of his death.

SAWCHUK, TERRANCE GORDON ("TERRY"), U.S. hockey player (b. Winnipeg, Man., Dec. 28, 1929—d. New York, N.Y., May 31, 1970), winner of four Vezina trophies as the outstanding goaltender in professional hockey and member of seven All-Star teams, held the all-time National Hockey League record of 103 regular-season shutouts. He began his 21-year NHL career with the Detroit Red Wings in 1949, went to the Boston Bruins in 1955 but returned to the Red Wings in 1957. He was traded in 1964 to the Toronto Maple Leafs and played two seasons before joining the Los Angeles Kings for 1967–68 and Detroit again for 1968–69. He finished the 1969–70 season with the New York Rangers. His NHL career goals-against average was 2.52. He died as the result of a freak injury sustained in horseplay with a teammate.

SCHACHT, HORACE GREELEY HJALMAR, German financier (b. Tingleff, Ger., Jan. 22, 1877—d. Munich, W.Ger., June 4, 1970), who directed the economic recovery of Germany under Hitler. He made his name as Reich currency commissioner and president of the Reichsbank from 1923 but resigned from the bank in 1930 in protest against the Young Plan for German reparations. He became an outspoken critic of government policy and in 1933, with the Nazis gaining control, became president of the Reichsbank once more. In the next six years he succeeded in financing the vast rearmament and building program, gaining a worldwide reputation for financial wizardry. His policy was associated with a bilateral trade system with smaller countries that could not afford to neglect their relations with Nazi Germany. He resigned from the bank in 1939 but after the war was brought to trial at Nürnberg, where he was eventually acquitted, a verdict repeated in several German courts. He made a fresh start, founding his own bank in Düsseldorf and acting as financial consultant to several countries.

SCHALK, RAYMOND WILLIAM ("CRACKER"), U.S. major league baseball player (b. Harvel, Ill., Aug. 12, 1892—d. Chicago, Ill., May 19, 1970), was a catcher with the Chicago White Sox from 1912 until 1926. He managed the White Sox in 1927–28 and was catcher-coach for the New York Giants in 1929. His lifetime batting average was .253. Schalk was elected to Baseball's Hall of Fame in 1955.

SCHMIDT, PAUL, German linguist (b. Prussia, June 23, 1899—d. Munich, W.Ger., April 21, 1970), was chief interpreter for Adolf Hitler. After joining the diplomatic service in 1923 he played a considerable part in bringing about the mutual trust between Aristide Briand and Gustav Stresemann that was the basis of Franco-German reconciliation after World War I. Schmidt became a member of the Nazi Party only in 1943. He was arrested by the Americans in 1945 but soon released.

SCHNEIDER CHEREAU, RENÉ, general, Chilean Army (b. Concepción, Chile, Dec. 31, 1913—d. Santiago, Chile, Oct. 25, 1970), who died three days after being struck by an assassin's bullet, was commander in chief of the Chilean Army during 1969–70.

SCHUSTER, MAX LINCOLN, U.S. publisher (b. Kalusz, Aus., March 2, 1897—d. New York, N.Y., Dec. 20, 1970), co-founder of Simon and Schuster, a publishing firm established in 1924.

SCOPES, JOHN THOMAS, U.S. teacher (b. Paducah, Tenn., Aug. 3, 1900—d. Shreveport, La., Oct. 21, 1970), central figure in the famous "monkey trial" of 1925, who was indicted for teaching the theory of evolution in the Dayton, Tenn., public schools. The test case drew wide attention, chiefly because of the court battle between the two attorneys involved—both well-known public figures—Clarence Darrow for the defense and William Jennings Bryan prosecuting the case for the state. The state won, Scopes was convicted and fined $100; however, two years later he won an appeal and the verdict was upset on a technicality. The law itself was not repealed until 1967. After the appeal Scopes became a geologist.

SCOTT, BLANCHE STUART, U.S. pioneer aviatrix (b. 1886—d. Rochester, N.Y., Jan. 12, 1970), who made her first solo flight in September 1910, barnstormed with a daredevil troupe, making 3,000-ft. "death dives." She was for many years a special consultant for the Air Force Museum at Wright-Patterson Air Force Base in Ohio, retiring in 1956.

SHAPIRA, MOSHE HAIM, Israeli government official (b. Grodno, Russia, March 26, 1902—d. Jerusalem, Israel, July 16, 1970), was head of the National Religious Party and a key member of every coalition government after the establishment of the state of Israel in 1948. Shapira was responsible for bringing Moshe Dayan into the Cabinet as minister of defense on the eve of the 1967 Six-Day War.

SHEPPARD, SAMUEL H., U.S. osteopath (b. 1924—d. Columbus, O., April 6, 1970), defendant in a sensational murder trial of the mid-1950s, was granted a new trial and acquitted in 1966 after the U.S. Supreme Court found that "inherently prejudicial publicity" had prevented his receiving a fair first trial.

SHERIDAN, CLARE CONSUELO, British sculptor and writer (b. Sussex, Eng., Sept. 9, 1885—d. May 31, 1970), whose talent was discovered after 1915, when she began exhibiting her work. She did busts of many famous persons of her

time, visiting the U.S.S.R. to sculpt Lenin and Trotski. Her autobiography, *To the Four Winds* (1954), was a best seller.

SHRINER, HERB, U.S. humorist (b. Toledo, O., May 28, 1918—d. Delray Beach, Fla., April 23, 1970), a television star of the 1950s, had appeared also in the Broadway musical *Inside U.S.A.* (1948).

SKELTON, RALEIGH ASHLIN, British cartographic scholar (b. 1906—d. Dec. 7, 1970), superintendent of the Map Room at the British Museum (1950–67), whose exposition of the history of the celebrated Vinland map, published by the Yale University Press in *The Vinland Map and the Tartar Relation* (1965), aroused widespread interest.

SLATER, SIR WILLIAM, British agricultural scientist (b. Shaw, Lancashire, Eng., Oct. 19, 1893—d. Midhurst, Eng., April 19, 1970), was secretary of the Agricultural Research Council (1949–60). After joining the Ministry of Agriculture and Fisheries in 1942, he later helped create the National Agricultural Advisory Service. From 1961 he was U.K. representative on the Central Treaty Organization scientific council; he served on the Royal Society UNESCO committee; and he was largely responsible for developing the Indicative World Plan for agricultural development, the framework for planning in the 1970s.

SLIM, WILLIAM JOSEPH SLIM, 1ST VISCOUNT, field marshal, British Army (b. Bristol, Eng., Aug. 6, 1891—d. London, Eng., Dec. 14, 1970), led the victorious campaign of the British 14th Army in Burma during World War II. At the outbreak of World War I he was commissioned and served in the Dardanelles, France, and Mesopotamia; in 1920 he transferred to the Indian Army and served with the Gurkha Rifles. During 1934–37 he was an instructor at the Staff College at Camberley; in 1940 he commanded the 10th Indian Brigade in the Sudan; in 1941 he commanded the 10th Indian Division in the Middle East, and in 1942 took command of the 1st Burma Corps. In 1943 the new 14th Army was formed under his command. The Japanese were halted at Kohima and Imphal and Slim led the offensive that drove them back. In 1948 he was recalled from retirement to succeed Lord Montgomery as chief of the Imperial General Staff, and received his field marshal's baton in 1949. From 1953 he was governor-general of Australia, holding office until 1960. In that same year he was made a viscount.

SNEDDEN, SIR RICHARD, British industrial negotiator (b. Edinburgh, Scot., 1900—d. March 9, 1970), was chief executive (1936–62) of the British Shipping Federation, general manager of the International Shipping Federation, and a member of the Governing Body of the International Labour Organization (1952–60). He served on various Admiralty, Ministry of Transport, and Ministry of Labour committees and in 1953 became a director of the Monotype Corporation. He was made a CBE in 1942, and was knighted in 1951.

SONNING, LEONIE, Danish property owner (b. Göteborg, Swed., 1895—d. Copenhagen, Den., March 16, 1970), who in 1949 set up an award fund commemorating her husband, author and journalist C. J. Sonning (d. 1937). The Sonning

Walter Philip Reuther   Charles Ruggles   Bertrand Russell   John Thomas Scopes

WIDE WORLD   WIDE WORLD   CAMERA PRESS FROM PIX   WIDE WORLD

Prize, awarded annually, is given for outstanding achievements in the fields of European culture, art, and politics. First recipient of the prize was Sir Winston Churchill (1950); others to whom it was awarded included Albert Schweitzer, Niels Bohr, Bertrand Russell, Alvar Aalto, Boris Christoff, Halldor Laxness, and Max Tau (1970).

SPITALNY, PHIL, U.S. orchestra leader and composer (b. Odessa, Russia, 1890—d. Miami, Fla., Oct. 11, 1970), organized and conducted an all-girl orchestra that appeared on "The Hour of Charm" program on the NBC and CBS radio networks during the 1930s and 1940s.

STEVENS, INGER, U.S. actress (b. Stockholm, Swed., Oct. 18, 1934—d. Hollywood, Calif., April 30, 1970), played the role of the housekeeper in the television series "The Farmer's Daughter" from 1963 until 1966. Before appearing on TV she played on Broadway in *Debut* (1957) and in *Mary, Mary* (1963), and in the films *Man on Fire* (1957), *Cry Terror* (1958), and *The World, the Flesh and the Devil* (1959). Her last motion picture, *A Dream of Kings*, was released in 1969.

STOKES, MAURICE, U.S. basketball player (b. 1934—d. Cincinnati, O., April 6, 1970), was a star with the Cincinnati Royals during the three-year professional career. Chosen All-American centre at St. Francis College (Loretto, Pa.) in 1955, he joined the Royals in 1956 and was named NBA rookie of the year that season. He was a member of the NBA all-star squad in each of his three years, and was among the top 15 scorers with an average of 16.9 points per game when an injury ended his career in 1958.

STRONG, ANNA LOUISE, U.S. leftist writer (b. Friend, Neb., Nov. 24, 1885—d. Peking, China, March 29, 1970), who devoted much of her life to writing books and articles extolling Communism, first wrote for the International News Service, then with the help of the government founded (1930) the *Moscow Daily News,* first English-language newspaper in the Soviet Union. In 1949 she was arrested as a U.S. spy and expelled from the U.S.S.R., but was exonerated six years later. In 1958 Miss Strong went to Peking to live, traveling extensively through China. Glowing descriptions of her observations, especially concerning China's Communist ideology, were written into a monthly four-page "Letter from China."

STURTEVANT, ALFRED HENRY, U.S. geneticist (b. Jacksonville, Ill., Nov. 21, 1891—d. Pasadena, Calif., April 5, 1970), who was Thomas Hunt Morgan professor of biology at the California Institute of Technology from 1947 (emeritus, 1962), graduated from Columbia University in 1912 and received his doctorate in 1914. He became a member of a group of Columbia University men—the "Productive Drosophila Genetics School"—who bred and studied the fruit fly to better understand chromosomes and their part in heredity. Sturtevant joined the staff of the Carnegie Institution, Washington, D.C., in 1915 and in 1928 went to Cal Tech where Morgan had just established the biology division. Sturtevant was a member of the team that first charted the location of specific genes on the chromosomes of fruit flies. He received a National Medal of Science in 1968.

SUKARNO, Indonesian political leader (b. Surabaja, Java, June 6, 1901—d. Slipi, Indon., June 21, 1970), served as the first president of the

Republic of Indonesia after that country became independent in 1949. Sukarno became interested in politics while attending a Dutch-language high school in Surabaja, where the Indonesian Islamic League had been organized. He later went to the Dutch technical college at Bandung and received his degree in civil engineering. In the latter 1920s Sukarno formed the Indonesian Nationalist Party (PNI) and became its chairman. A troublesome nationalist leader by 1929, he was arrested by the Dutch and sentenced to four years' imprisonment. He was released in 1931 and plunged again into party work, was arrested a second time and exiled. In 1942, with the coming of the Japanese, Sukarno returned from exile. After the defeat of Japan in 1945, he declared Indonesia a republic and began a war against the Dutch that lasted four years, ending on Dec. 27, 1949, when the Netherlands, under pressure from world opinion, relinquished administration of the territory. Under Sukarno's leadership Indonesia's 3,000 islands were united; he gave the republic a common language, a national identity, and, especially during the 1950s, a position of international leadership among the nations of the third world. However, his militaristic policy, especially his "confrontation" with Malaysia, brought the country close to economic ruin and his "guided democracy" became increasingly repressive. Not a Communist himself, he attempted to maintain power by balancing Indonesia's large Communist party against other elements, but in time he became increasingly dependent on the Communists. He became increasingly friendly with Peking and took Indonesia out of the UN. In 1965 an attempted Communist coup was aborted by the Army. Sukarno was suspected of complicity, and after a period of unrest, during which several hundred thousand Communists and suspected Communists were massacred, he was deprived of his powers in early 1966 and was succeeded by General Suharto. He was officially deposed March 12, 1967. After leaving office he fell into political obscurity.

SYVERTSEN, GEORGE, U.S. foreign correspondent (b. New York, N.Y., March 22, 1932—d. south of Phnom Penh, Cambodia), who, with seven other newsmen, was captured by North Vietnamese and Viet Cong soldiers while covering the events of the May–June clean-up of Communist sanctuaries in Cambodia. His body was found June 3. Syvertsen was working with the television news section of CBS.

SZELL, GEORGE, U.S. conductor (b. Budapest, Hung., June 7, 1897—d. Cleveland, O., July 30, 1970), who led the Cleveland Orchestra for almost a quarter of a century, began his musical career at age ten when he appeared with the Vienna Symphony as guest pianist. Before he was 20 he was asked to join the staff of the Berlin State Opera, and in 1917 became conductor of the Strasbourg Municipal Theatre. After short stints in Darmstadt and in Düsseldorf, he served as chief conductor for the Berlin State Opera and the Berlin Broadcasting Orchestra from 1924 until 1929. Szell went to Prague in 1929 to direct the German Opera House Orchestra. During the 1930s he also appeared as guest conductor in many of the cities of Europe and the U.S. At the outbreak of World War II Szell was in New York and decided to remain there, making his debut (1941) in that city as guest conductor for the NBC Symphony. He was regular conductor of the Metropolitan Opera from 1942 until 1946, when he took up his post with the Cleveland Orchestra.

TAYLOR, RICHARD, U.S. cartoonist (b. Fort Williams, Ont., Sept. 18, 1902—d. West Redding, Conn., May 25, 1970), whose satirical cartoons appeared in *The New Yorker* and *Playboy* magazines, was also a water colourist whose works

were exhibited in New York's Metropolitan Museum of Art and Museum of Modern Art.

THANH, NGUYEN VIET, major general, South Vietnamese Army (b. 1941—d. Cambodia-Vietnam border, May 2, 1970), close associate of South Vietnamese Pres. Nguyen Van Thieu and commander of the South Vietnamese IV Corps, was killed when his helicopter collided with a U.S. helicopter over Cambodia.

THOMSON, DAVID, British historian (b. Edinburgh, Scot., Jan. 13, 1912—d. Cambridge, Eng., Feb. 24, 1970), was a distinguished academic and writer and a notable university administrator. After a brilliant academic career at Sidney Sussex College, Cambridge University, he became master of the college in 1957. His best-known works are *Democracy in France Since 1870* (1946; 5th ed., revised, 1969), *England in the Nineteenth Century* (first published in 1950 as part of the Pelican History of England), and *Europe Since Napoleon* (1957; 2nd ed., 1962).

THORBORG, KERSTIN, Swedish opera singer (b. Venjan, Swed., May 19, 1896—d. Hedemora, Swed., April 12, 1970), who excelled in the few important mezzo-soprano roles of Wagner's operas, was a member of the New York Metropolitan Opera company, 1938–46 and 1947–50.

THORNHILL, ARTHUR H., U.S. publisher (b. Hyde Park, Mass., Feb. 25, 1895—d. Boston, Mass., Jan. 9, 1970), chairman of the board of Little, Brown and Co., one of the oldest book-publishing companies in the U.S., from 1948, had started with the firm in 1913 as a shipping clerk. He advanced to salesman, New York branch manager (1935), company director (1938), and vice-president (1941) before becoming president and chairman of the board in 1948.

TIMOSHENKO, SEMEN KONSTANTINOVICH, marshal of the Soviet Union (b. Furmanka, Bessarabia [now Odessa, U.S.S.R.], Feb. 18, 1895—d. Moscow, U.S.S.R., March 31, 1970), was credited with halting the German drive on Moscow during World War II. Of peasant stock, he was called up in the Imperial Russian Army in 1915. In 1918 he joined a partisan detachment which, under his command, joined the Red Army and fought at Tsaritsyn. He later joined the 1st Cavalry Army, and his success in the campaign against Denikin in 1919 led to his promotion to divisional commander. During the Russo-Polish war in 1920 he took command of the 4th Cavalry Division; he was severely wounded in the same year when fighting in the Crimea.

After further military training, in 1933 Timoshenko was appointed deputy commander of the Belorussian Military District where the first Soviet experiments with large-scale armoured units were taking place. When Stalin launched the military purge of 1937 he spared Timoshenko and dispatched him as commander of the North Caucasus Military District, later sending him to Kiev. In 1939 Timoshenko took a prominent part in the Soviet occupation of Poland, but it was the storming of the Mannerheim Line against the Finns that won him wider fame. He was made a Hero of the Soviet Union, and Stalin turned to him for help in reorganizing Soviet forces after their bad showing in the "winter war." Timoshenko replaced Kliment Y. Voroshilov as defense commissar and was appointed marshal of the Soviet Union on May 7, 1940. In June 1941, after Hitler had attacked the U.S.S.R., Timoshenko was sent to command the Western Military District. He halted the German advance at Smolensk and moved to the southwestern front where his forces made a successful counterattack. His next offensive, against Kharkov, failed, how-

Inger Stevens   Sukarno   George Szell   Sonny Tufts   Harold Stirling Vanderbilt   Joseph Albert Yablonski

WIDE WORLD   WIDE WORLD   UPI COMPIX   WIDE WORLD   WIDE WORLD   UPI COMPIX

ever, and the Soviet southwestern front was badly mauled. This marked the end of Timoshenko's wartime career as a front commander. In 1943 and 1944 he was "coordinator" of operations in the areas of Leningrad and the Ukraine. Unlike most of his fellow marshals, Timoshenko did not publish detailed memoirs about his military career.

TOBIAS, CHARLES, U.S. songwriter (b. New York, N.Y., Aug. 15, 1897—d. Manhasset, N.Y., July 7, 1970), composed many popular favourites, including "Rose O'Day," "When Your Hair Has Turned to Silver," "The Old Lamplighter," "Lazy, Hazy, Crazy Days of Summer," and the World War II songs "We Did It Before and We Can Do It Again" and "Don't Sit Under the Apple Tree." He was a founding member of the American Guild of Authors and Composers.

TSALDARIS, CONSTANTIN, Greek politician (b. Alexandria, Egypt, 1884—d. Athens, Greece, Nov. 15, 1970), was prime minister from 1946 to 1947 and later foreign minister. He became a deputy under the banner of the Liberal Party but in 1928 went over to the Populists, led by his uncle Panayiotis Tsaldaris. When his uncle died in 1936 he was elected to the governing body of the Populist Party, but all activity was suspended with the advent of the Metaxas dictatorship. After the end of World War II Tsaldaris led the Populist government that ultimately restored the monarchy. From 1947 until 1950 he was minister of foreign affairs and was largely responsible for retaining his country's alliance with the West against violent Communist opposition. He retired from politics in 1958.

TUFTS, SONNY (BOWEN CHARLESTON TUFTS II), U.S. actor (b. Boston, Mass., 1911—d. Santa Monica, Calif., June 4, 1970), who made his first motion picture, *So Proudly We Hail,* in 1943, starred in *Here Come the Waves* (1944), *Bring on the Girls* (1945), *Miss Susie Slagle's* (1946), *The Crooked Way* (1949), and *The Seven Year Itch* with Marilyn Monroe in 1955.

UNGARETTI, GIUSEPPE, Italian poet (b. Alexandria, Egypt, Feb. 2, 1888—d. Milan, Italy, June 2, 1970), was a notable innovator and one of the finest practitioners in modern Italian poetry. He lived as a young man in Paris where his friends included Picasso, Apollinaire, and Valéry, but his first poems were not published until 1916 while he was in the Italian Army. In 1942 he went to Rome University, where he held the chair of modern and contemporary literature until his retirement. *Allegria di naufragi* (1919) was followed by *Sentimento del tempo* (1933), *Il dolore* (1947), and, his most important work, *La terra promessa* (1950).

UNRUH, FRITZ VON, German writer (b. Coblenz, Ger., May 10, 1885—d. Dietz-Lahn, W.Ger., Nov. 30, 1970), a controversial author, whose *Prinz Louis Ferdinand* (1913) fell afoul of the censor because of its attitude toward military duty. His pacifist ideals were reflected in a dramatic poem *Vor der Entscheidung* (1914). In 1916 he wrote a novel, *Opfergang,* published in English in 1928 as *The Way of Sacrifice.* In 1925 he wrote a play to celebrate the 1,000th anniversary of the city of Cologne, *Heinrich aus Andernach,* emphasizing the reconciliation between France and Germany. After the Nazis came to power he left Germany for Italy, and eventually the U.S.

VANDERBILT, HAROLD STIRLING, U.S. financier and yachtsman (b. Oakdale, N.Y., July 6, 1884—d. Newport, R.I., July 4, 1970), a director of the New York Central Railroad from 1913 and the driving force behind the rail network until 1954, when he was defeated in a proxy battle for control of the company. He successfully defended the America's Cup, highest achievement in international yachting competition, with the "Enterprise" in 1930, the "Rainbow" in 1934, and the "Ranger" in 1937. In the 1920s Vanderbilt helped to establish the game of contract bridge, and in 1928 donated the Harold S. Vanderbilt Cup as a trophy for an annual contract bridge tournament, which his team won in 1932.

VINOGRADOV, SERGEI A., Soviet diplomat (b. 1908—d. Moscow, U.S.S.R., Aug. 27, 1970), was appointed to the critical post of Soviet ambassador to Cairo in August 1967, shortly after the Arab-Israeli Six-Day War. Vinogradov joined the Soviet Foreign Service in Turkey in 1940, and was soon appointed ambassador to Ankara. He was present at talks between Churchill and Roosevelt in Cairo in 1943 and in the following September represented the Soviet Union in the peace negotiations with Romania. He remained in Ankara until 1948, when he returned to Moscow to become chief of the Foreign Ministry's department of UN affairs. He attended the Geneva conferences in 1955 and 1959 and the four-power conference in Paris in 1960. From 1953 until 1965 he was highly successful as ambassador to France, his efforts resulting in the Franco-Soviet friendship treaty of 1966.

WAKEHURST, JOHN DE VERE LODER, 2ND BARON, British political administrator (b. London, Eng., Feb. 5, 1895—d. London, Oct. 30, 1970), was governor of Northern Ireland from 1952 until 1964. He was Conservative member of Parliament for East Leicester (1924–29) and for Lewes (1931–36) until resigning from the House when he succeeded to the barony. After two years in the Foreign Office he was appointed governor of New South Wales, Austr., in 1937 and held the post until 1946.

WARBURG, OTTO HEINRICH, German physiologist and biochemist (b. Freiburg im Breisgau, Ger., Oct. 8, 1883—d. West Berlin, Ger., Aug. 1, 1970), winner of the 1931 Nobel Prize for Physiology or Medicine, was a leading cancer researcher. After gaining doctorates in chemistry at Berlin (1906) and in medicine at Heidelberg (1911), he became a prominent figure in the institutes of Berlin-Dahlem. He first became known for his work on the metabolism of various types of ova at the Marine Biological Station in Naples. His Nobel Prize in 1931 was in recognition of his research into respiratory enzymes. In 1944 he was offered a second Nobel Prize, but being Jewish was prevented from accepting the award by the Hitler regime, which nonetheless dared not imprison him because of his international prestige. From 1931 he was head of the Max Planck Institute for Cell Physiology in (West) Berlin.

WATERHOUSE, WALTER LAWRY, Australian agricultural scientist (b. Maitland, Austr., Aug. 31, 1887—d. Australia, Jan. 12, 1970), made plant breeding discoveries that revolutionized wheat growing in Australia. His research, aimed at producing a disease-resistant wheat strain of good quality and high yield, resulted in the Gabo wheat, which was not only successful in Australia but influenced breeding programs in many parts of the world.

WEISS, PIERRE, general (ret.), French Air Force (b. Nancy, France, Oct. 17, 1889—d. Antibes, France, Aug. 8, 1970), played a significant part in the development of aviation in French Africa. He entered the air corps in 1915, and after the war made a series of pioneering flights, including one from France to India in 1930 and another, from France to Ethiopia, in 1931. As a colonel in the French Air Force in North Africa, he made aerial surveys of the Sahara. Recalled to France, he was promoted general in 1938. In 1940 he served in Algeria again, before taking command of the Air Force in Tunisia. In 1944 he was military governor of Algiers, and his action in calling for the death penalty for the former Vichy minister Pierre Pucheu resulted in the Vichy government depriving him of his French citizenship and confiscating his property.

WILDE, JOHANNES, British art historian (b. Budapest, Hung., June 2, 1891—d. Dulwich, Eng., Sept. 13, 1970), was professor of the history of art at the Courtauld Institute, London University, from 1950 to 1961 and afterward emeritus professor. He began his career in Budapest's Museum of Fine Arts, and in 1923 joined the staff of the Kunsthistorisches Museum, Vienna, where he specialized in Italian art. At this time he set up the first efficient X-ray apparatus for examining works of art, publishing his results in a series of notable articles. After the Nazi occupation of Austria in 1938 he went to England. In 1949 he published a catalog of the Windsor Italian Renaissance drawings, and his catalog of the British Museum's Michelangelo drawings appeared in 1953.

WOODS, HARRY MacGREGOR, U.S. composer (b. North Chelmsford, Mass., 1896—d. Phoenix, Ariz., Jan. 13, 1970), wrote more than 350 popular songs during the 1920s and 1930s. Among the best remembered were "When the Moon Comes over the Mountain," "I'm Looking over a Four-Leaf Clover," "Side by Side," "River, Stay 'Way from My Door," "Paddlin' Madelin' Home," and "When the Red Red Robin Comes Bob-Bob-Bobbin' Along."

WRIGHT, MARY CLABAUGH (MRS. ARTHUR F. WRIGHT), U.S. educator and historian (b. Tuscaloosa, Ala., Sept. 25, 1917—d. Guilford, Conn., June 18, 1970), a leading Chinese historian and the first woman to become a full professor at Yale University. Mary Wright and her husband were in Japan at the outbreak of World War II and spent the war years in a prison camp. Returning to the U.S. in 1947, she became a member of the faculty at Stanford University. In 1959 the Wrights went to Yale and in 1964 Mary Wright was named professor of history.

WRIGHT, QUINCY, U.S. authority on the law (b. Medford, Mass., Dec. 8, 1890—d. Charlottesville, Va., Oct. 17, 1970), emeritus professor of international law at the University of Chicago and the University of Virginia, taught at Harvard University and at the University of Minneapolis before joining the faculty of the University of Chicago in 1923. In 1956 he was chosen Carnegie visiting research scholar of the Carnegie Endowment for International Peace, and from 1958 until 1961 he was professor of international law at the University of Virginia.

YABLONSKI, JOSEPH ALBERT, U.S. labour leader (b. Pittsburgh, Pa., March 3, 1910—d. Clarksville, Pa., Jan. 5[?], 1970), was slain in his home, along with his wife and daughter, less than a month after losing a bitter campaign for the presidency of the United Mine Workers of America. Yablonski, who began working in the mines at age 15, became a union organizer and was elected president of his local in 1934. Next elected to the executive board of District 5, he represented the workers in Washington, D.C., until 1942 when he was voted to the international executive board, holding that post through seven elections. He won the presidency of District 5 in 1958, but in 1966 was defeated for reelection by W. A. (Tony) Boyle, the same man whom he attempted to oust from the national presidency in December 1969.

YEOMAN, BERYL BOTTERILL ANTONIA ("ANTON"), British cartoonist (b. Australia, 1914[?]—d. London, Eng., June 29, 1970), whose cartoons showed beminked matrons and large plushy gentlemen, drew regularly for *Punch,* the *New Yorker, Private Eye,* and in earlier days for *Lilliput.*

YEREMENKO, ANDREI, marshal of the Soviet Union (b. Markovka, Ukraine, 1892—d. Moscow, U.S.S.R., Nov. 19, 1970), commanded the Soviet forces at the battle of Stalingrad in 1942. Yeremenko joined the Imperial Russian Army in 1913 and served in the cavalry in World War I, joining the Communist Party in 1918 and the Red Army in 1919. In 1940 he took over the 3rd Mechanized Corps. After a short period in the Soviet Far East he returned to the European theatre, where he commanded the Western front but failed to check Gen. Heinz Guderian's thrust into the Ukraine. After recovering from a severe wound, in August 1942 he took over the southeastern front in the initial stages of the battle for Stalingrad, where he played a vital role in the defensive battle and the subsequent counterattack. He later participated in the capture of Riga. He was appointed marshal in 1955 and general inspector in the Ministry of Defense in 1958.

ZENKEVICH, LEV ALEKSANDROVICH, Soviet oceanographer (b. Russia, June 1889—d. Moscow, U.S.S.R., June 20, 1970), was a notable marine biologist. In the 1920s he helped set up the State Oceanographic Institute and headed a number of Soviet scientific expeditions, particularly in the Pacific. He was the author of many studies of marine life and was awarded a Lenin Prize in 1965.

ZIMMERMANN, BERND ALOIS, German composer and musicologist (b. Bliesheim, Ger., 1918—d. Gross Königsdorf, Cologne, W.Ger., August 1970), taught at Cologne's School of Music from 1953. An avant-garde composer, he produced works that included violin and cello concertos, a symphony, and the ballet *Contrasts.* His opera *Die Soldaten,* based on an 18th-century play by J. M. R. Lenz, was first performed in 1965 and was hailed by some critics as the most significant addition to the operatic repertoire since Alban Berg's *Wozzeck.*

Oceanography

Significant results were reported through 1970 of the work aboard the deep-sea drilling vessel "Glomar Challenger." The findings indicated that the ocean basins are relatively young, perhaps one-tenth to one-twentieth the 3,500,000,000-year age of some of the continental rocks. The concept of sea-floor spreading and the theory that the continents of America, Europe, and Africa drifted apart almost certainly were proved: molten rock appears to come up in midocean from deep in the earth to form a new oceanic crust, and the continents are moved apart as this new crust spreads outward. The half-spreading rate for the crust beneath the ocean is about 1.2 cm. per year in the North Atlantic, 2 cm/year in the South Atlantic, and about 12 cm/year for the equatorial Pacific. The North Atlantic began to form about 200 million years ago, and the South Atlantic about 150 million; thus Europe, Africa, and America had been joined before that time. The North Pacific is an area of very old oceanic sediments and must be a remnant of a basin that existed before the Atlantic had formed. However, some of the western Pacific basins may be much younger.

The large amounts of sedimentary material recovered from the holes drilled by the "Glomar Challenger" allowed detailed studies of the evolution of the microfossils, which showed that the deep ocean waters of the past contained dissolved oxygen, as do those of today. Much of the deep Gulf of Mexico is underlain by salt, some of which has squeezed up as salt domes; it contains oil and gas, the first demonstration that hydrocarbons can form and accumulate in deep-sea conditions. The Mediterranean had deep passages to the Atlantic and Indian oceans 15 million years ago, but when it was closed off for a time by the shifting positions of Africa and Europe it evaporated to strong salt brines and completely sterile muds in which organisms could not live.

One of the most remarkable technological developments of the year was the successful reentry into holes already drilled. Since the drill bits dulled as they penetrated hard rock and the pipe had to be withdrawn from the hole to change bits, before a method of reentry was devised the depth of penetration was limited to what one set of bits could do. A hole that was to be reentered was prepared with an inverted 16-ft. cone to guide the drill. The drill string was lowered to a location near the cone, its position was determined by acoustical sensors, and it was placed exactly into the cone by surface maneuvering of the vessel and water-jet adjustments of the end of the drill pipe. Successful reentry was first made in 10,000 ft. of water in June 1970.

The U.S. National Science Foundation continued to operate the research vessel "Eltanin" in the Antarctic Ocean. In January and February 1970 (Antarctic summer), work was done in the area between Australia and Antarctica. Three instruments were deployed on the ocean bottom at 40°, 50°, and 60° S latitude, at depths ranging from 3,500 to 5,500 m., to measure tides and sea-floor tidal currents in the open ocean. Such open-ocean measurements are of great value in the general study of the propagation of tides. Coastal and island measurements of surface tidal rise and fall show the effects of local conditions and do not correctly represent the oceanic propagation.

Measurements of currents and water characteristics on the same expedition led to another calculation of the water transport of the Antarctic Circumpolar Current. In January 1969 measurements indicated a flow through the Drake Passage of about 270 million tons per second, but the "Eltanin's" work in January 1970 indicated a flow of about 320 million tons per second south of Australia. Later, in Antarctic winter, the "Eltanin" worked to 60° S latitude south of New Zealand, surveying the Macquarie-Balleny Ridge area for water characteristics, depth, gravity, and seismic studies.

Recent investigations in the Weddell Sea led to a new concept for the formation of at least part of the cold water of moderate salinity that fills the deeper parts of the major oceans. Previously it had been thought that the freezing of salt water into sea ice released brine into the underlying water, increasing its density enough to cause it to sink to the bottom. A newer concept was that this freezing may occur at the bottom of the glaciers that extend from Antarctica out into the ocean as ice shelves. The temperature at the tops of these shelves is about −20° C, and freezing

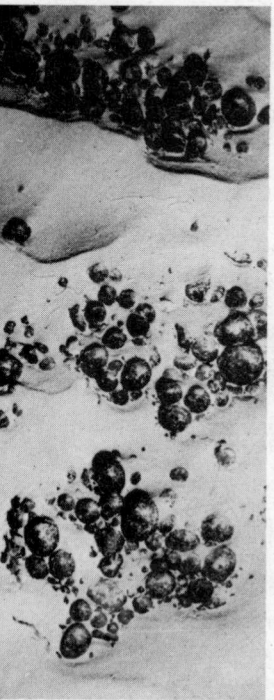

COURTESY, LAMONT-DOHERTY GEOLOGICAL OBSERVATORY OF COLUMBIA UNIVERSITY

Nodules, containing manganese, cobalt, and other metals, that litter the ocean floors were the subject of a meeting in Malta of 260 scientists, June 28–July 3, 1970. The methods and authority under which nodules should be harvested were discussed.

The ocean floor Wilson Tractor Bell, being developed by Wilson Marine Systems, Inc., of Houston, Tex., is powered by a welded steel chain drive that can move the vehicle at a speed of one-half knot at depths up to 600 ft.

AUTHENICATED NEWS INTERNATIONAL

Occupational Medicine:
see Medicine

may occur at the shelf/water interface throughout the year instead of seasonally, as in the case of surface sea ice.

U.S. Pres. Richard M. Nixon reorganized the federal agencies studying the ocean and atmosphere into a single administration, under the Department of Commerce. The various groups making up the new administration were the Environmental Science Services Administration (from Commerce), elements of the Bureau of Commercial Fisheries, the marine sport fish program of the Bureau of Sport Fisheries and Wildlife, and the Marine Minerals Technology Center of the Bureau of Mines (all from Interior), the Office of Sea Grant Programs (from the National Science Foundation), elements of the Army's U.S. Lakes Survey, and the Navy's National Oceanographic Data Center and National Oceanographic Instrumentation Center.

In September 1970 a Joint Oceanographic Assembly was held in Tokyo, under the sponsorship of a number of international organizations. Of the many topics discussed, one of the most important concerned the degree of ocean pollution and its possible consequences on marine life and climate.

A great deal of information was available on the presence and effect of pollutants in lakes, ponds, streams, bays, and estuaries, but little information had been gathered about the open ocean. Previously it had been believed that the ultimate concentrations of pollutants in the ocean might be negligibly small, but the possibility existed that the more persistent substances, such as pesticides, might endure long enough to become concentrated and accumulated in the food chain. Specific evidence of such an effect was found in the livers of many marine fish, particularly in coastal areas near sewage outfalls.

In 1970 the National Marine Fisheries Service (formerly the Bureau of Commercial Fisheries) began a systematic collection of planktonic organisms between the west coast of the U.S. and Hawaii for the purpose of assessing the concentrations of artificially introduced substances. Since the polluting substances may undergo various chemical and biological cycling as well as mixing in the sea, it was not possible to estimate in advance what effects a given substance might have. Some direct measurements would be required before extensive research programs could be properly planned.

Another accidental spillage of oil into the ocean from an offshore oil rig occurred, this time on the continental shelf of the Gulf of Mexico. The company was accused of drilling without the safety valves required by law and was fined $1 million. The spillage was estimated to be as high as 20,000 bbl. Later three other companies were fined $500,000 for similar violations. Local effects of large oil spills were found to be severe in some cases, but the ordinary losses through normal operations of tankers constituted a larger volume spread through broad areas of the ocean. Their effects were less certain and more difficult to assess, but might be more severe in the long run.

Considerable controversy arose over the U.S. Army's decision to dispose of various stocks of nerve gas weapons, which could not be deactivated safely, by placing them at the bottom of the ocean. The weapons consisted of 12,540 rockets, containing in all 66 tons of GB nerve gas, 121 tons of propellant, and 17 tons of explosive. They were loaded aboard a decommissioned Liberty ship, the SS "LeBaron Russell Briggs," which was towed to a point about 300

WIDE WORLD

mi. E of Jacksonville, Fla., flooded, and sunk in water of about 5,000-m. depth. The monitoring vessel reported that the impact on the sea floor was not violent and did not result in any detonation. Monitoring plans included photographing the hulk and collecting water samples from its vicinity at regular intervals. As a result of the strong objections to this method of disposal, however, the Army agreed that it would not dispose of any further chemical warfare agents in this way.

In October President Nixon sent to Congress a report by the Environmental Quality Council detailing the damage caused by ocean dumping and suggesting strict rules to preserve the seas. Nixon called for a total ban on disposal of toxic materials in ocean waters and for strict control of dumping trash and waste at sea. Existing policy prohibited ocean dumping of wastes with a high level of radioactivity. The council recommended cessation of dumping of most other radioactive materials and of industrial wastes and undigested sewage sludge.

For some years aircraft had been used to carry in-

Streams of water are poured onto a Chevron Oil Co. offshore oil platform burning in the mouth of the Mississippi River March 1, 1970. Elaborate precautions were taken to minimize damage from escaping oil after the blaze was extinguished.

struments that could estimate the sea-surface temperature from measurements of the back radiation. The instruments had been considerably improved and adapted for use in satellites, and some success was reported in estimating ocean temperatures over vast areas. Similar instruments, designed to measure sea-surface concentrations of the most abundant photosynthetic pigment, chlorophyll A, had not yet been adapted for satellite use, but aircraft instruments had been able to distinguish between concentrations of 0.1 and 0.2 mg. per cu.mi. from heights of up to 10,000 ft.

(J. L. Re.)

See also Antarctica; Biological Sciences; Geography; Geology; Law; Meteorology; Seismology.

ENCYCLOPÆDIA BRITANNICA FILMS. *Ocean Tides* (*The Bay of Fundy*) (1956); *The Marine Biologist* (1963); *Plankton—Pastures of the Ocean* (1965); *Waves on Water* (1965); *How Level Is Sea Level?* (1970).

POPPERFOTO FROM PICTORIAL PARADE

Oman

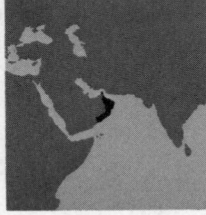

POPPERFOTO FROM PICTORIAL PARADE

An independent sultanate, Oman occupies the southeastern part of the Arabian Peninsula and is bounded by the Trucial States, Saudi Arabia, the Gulf of Oman, and the Arabian Sea. A small part of the country lies to the north of the rest of Oman and is separated from it by the Trucial States. Area: 82,000 sq.mi. (212,000 sq.km.). Pop. (1970 est.): 750,000. Cap.: Muscat (pop., 1969, 9,973). Largest city: Matrah (pop., 1960, 14,119). Language: Arabic. Religion: Muslim. Sultans in 1970, Sa'id bin Taimur and, from July 23, Qabus bin Sa'id.

During 1970 the situation of Muscat and Oman was radically transformed by a coup which replaced Sultan Sa'id bin Taimur by his son Qabus bin Sa'id. Sa'id bin Taimur had kept his country in a state of medieval backwardness, insulated from Western influences despite its growing oil revenues; his son undertook to introduce "modern and forceful" government and hasten development in all fields.

On July 23 the coup, carried out by the palace guard, took place at Salalah; the slightly injured former sultan was then flown to Britain. Amid scenes of great popular enthusiasm, the new sultan announced the removal of his father's ban on smoking, singing, and the wearing of Western dress and permitted the entry of foreign journalists. On August 9 his uncle, Tariq bin Taimur, who had returned from exile, was asked to form a new government. The new sultan announced that in the future the country would be known as the Sultanate of Oman and would apply to join the UN and the Arab League. The sultan released more than 100 prisoners, but the revolutionary opposition was divided in its attitude toward him. Some elements declared their loyalty to the new sovereign, but others described him as being merely an imperialist puppet.

(P. Md.)

Top, Prince Qabus bin Sa'id of Oman took over by force the throne of his father, Sultan Sa'id bin Taimur, above, in July 1970.

Oil:
see Fuel and Power; Industrial Review

Opera:
see Music

Ophthalmology:
see Medicine

Organization for Economic Cooperation and Development:
see Development, Economic

Organization of American States:
see Inter-American Affairs

Ornithology:
see Biological Sciences

OMAN
Finance and Trade. Monetary unit: Saudi riyal, at par with the pound sterling (1 riyal = U.S. $2.40). Budget (oil revenue; 1969 est.) revenue *c.* £30 million. Foreign trade (1968): imports (excluding government and oil company imports of *c.* 3 million riyals) 4,044,761 riyals (mainly from India and U.K.); exports (excluding oil) *c.* 800,000 riyals. Main exports (excluding oil; 1961–62): dates 48%; fruit and vegetables 24%; fish and products 9%.
Industry. Crude oil production (1969) 16,317,000 metric tons.

Pakistan

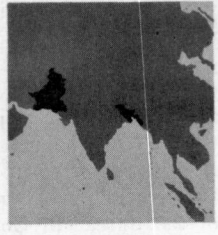

A federal republic and member of the Commonwealth of Nations, Pakistan is divided into two parts, separated by India. West Pakistan, the main part of the country, is bordered on the south by the Arabian Sea and on the west by Afghanistan and Iran; East Pakistan lies on the Bay of Bengal. Total area: 366,041 sq. mi. (948,042 sq.km.), excluding the Pakistani-controlled section of Kashmir. Pop. (1970 est.): 114,-188,612. Cap.: Islamabad (pop., 1967 est., 226,000). Largest city: Karachi (pop., 1970 est., 2,340,042). Language: Urdu, Bengali, English. Religion (1961): Muslim 88.1%; Hindu 10.7%; Christian and Buddhist minorities. President in 1970, Gen. Agha Muhammad Yahya Khan.

One of the worst natural disasters in history struck coastal areas of East Pakistan on Nov. 12–13, 1970. A cyclone and tidal waves ravaged a 3,000-sq.mi. region in the Ganges River delta, leaving about 200,000 dead and 100,000 missing. Governments and other organizations contributed approximately $50 million for the relief of the survivors. (*See* DISASTERS.)

President Yahya Khan, in working out his declared policy of returning power to the people, in 1970 continued to be embarrassed by the highly unstable condition of Pakistan's political life. In East Pakistan the widespread discontent with what was claimed to be the "colonial" status imposed upon the region by the western area caused constant anxiety to the national authorities. The president's primary objectives were to secure the maximum measure of agreement on certain broad governing principles and to hold the country together by convincing East Pakistan that it would henceforth exercise in federal matters the influence to which its predominance in population and its political expertise entitled it; East Pakistan would also be given the maximum amount of control over its own affairs.

According to these principles, the country was to be an Islamic republic in fact as well as name. The future constitution was to be based upon a "one man, one vote" electorate. West Pakistan was to be broken into its original components of Punjab, North-West Frontier Province, Baluchistan, Sind, and the tribal areas (thereby removing East Pakistan's complaint that it had been victimized by an artificial parity of East and West in federal affairs). Maximum autonomy, limited only by the needs of the national government, was to be exercised by every province in administrative, economic, and social affairs (thereby conciliating moderate political opinion on both wings). At the same time, the president announced a plan of action: in March a "legal framework" to enable reforms to take place; in June the completion of the electoral rules; on July 1, the breakup of the West wing; elections for the federal and provincial assemblies in October; and a period of 120 days for the completion of the constitution, failing which a new Federal Assembly would be elected to do the job.

The steps taken to remove corruption and other abuses from the administration, to allay industrial unrest, to reform the educational system, and to remedy the economic grievances of particular sections of the population won growing confidence. No fewer than

303 officials were suspended in December 1969 and brought before six high-level tribunals set up for territorial regions. An Industrial Relations Ordinance of Nov. 3, 1969, gave recognition and negotiating authority to trade unions. To bring the administration closer to the people, decentralization of powers to local levels was begun. Far-reaching educational reforms were planned; autonomy was restored to the universities; the grievances of students were examined; and universal primary education was brought nearer by setting up a National Literacy Corps to work in the villages.

In March the promised "legal framework" was announced; it laid down the composition of the national and of the five provincial assemblies; rules for the conduct of elections; the independence of the judiciary; popular participation in every branch of national activity; and the gradual removal of economic disparities between different areas.

The importance which the central government attached to removing the grievances of East Pakistan was consistently exhibited throughout the year. The president and his ministers toured the East wing frequently, explaining their policies, dealing with complaints, and setting out plans for the future. In addi-

UPI COMPIX
Drowning victim lies in a stream in East Pakistan after the cyclonic storms and floods which devastated the area in November 1970.

tion to ensuring the due representation of East Pakistan in the federal administration, three cadet colleges, an ordnance factory, and improved communications with the West were sanctioned. The oil refinery, to be established with the help of Iran, was to be in East Pakistan. Flood control was given top priority, not only in its claim on the country's resources but also in its call on foreign aid; and when disastrous floods swept the area in August, the entire machinery of government, personally directed by the president, came to the rescue. Because of the dislocation caused by these floods the national elections were postponed from October 5 to December 7.

Despite the cyclone disaster the elections took place on schedule. The Awami League, an East Pakistan-based party that had campaigned on a platform of full regional autonomy for the East, was the big winner, attaining 151 of the 300 National Assembly seats. The other major triumph was registered by the leftist People's Party, based in West Pakistan, which won 81 seats. (L. F. R. W.)

PAKISTAN

Education. (1966–67) Primary, pupils 7,298,321, teachers 178,948; secondary, pupils 2,716,113, teachers 98,345; vocational, pupils 22,675, teachers 1,594; teacher training, students 12,701, teachers 1,113; higher (including 13 universities), students 291,954, teaching staff 11,882.

Finance. Monetary unit: Pakistan rupee, with a par value of PakRs. 4.76 to U.S. $1 (PakRs. 11.43 = £1 sterling). Gold, SDRs, and foreign exchange, central bank: (June 1970) U.S. $291 million; (June 1969) U.S. $316 million. Budget (1969–70 est.): revenue PakRs. 7,533,700,000; expenditure PakRs. 6,120,300,000. National income: (1968–69) PakRs. 63.1 billion; (1967–68) PakRs. 57.4 billion. Money supply: (June 1970) PakRs. 12,597,000,000; (June 1969) PakRs. 11,524,000,000. Cost of living (Karachi; 1963 = 100): (June 1970) 137; (June 1969) 130.

Foreign Trade. (1969) Imports PakRs. 4,798,000,000; exports PakRs. 3,220,000,000. Import sources (1968–69): U.S. 29%; Japan 12%; U.K. 11%; West Germany 9%. Export destinations: U.K. 12%; U.S. 10%; Hong Kong 6%; Singapore 5%; Japan 5%. Main exports: jute manufactures 22%; jute 22%; cotton 8%.

Transport and Communications. Roads (1969) c. 200,000 km. (including 46,289 km. with improved surface). Motor vehicles in use (1969): passenger 88,977; commercial 31,384. Railways: (1966–67) 11,339 km.; traffic (1968–69) 10,221,000,000 passenger-km., freight 7,636,000,000 net ton-km. Air traffic (1969): 1,633,700,000 passenger-km.; freight 71,206,000 net ton-km. Shipping (1969): merchant vessels 100 gross tons and over 172; gross tonnage 530,404. Telephones (Dec. 1968) 176,807. Radio receivers (Dec. 1967) 1,150,000. Television receivers (Dec. 1968) 32,000.

Agriculture. Production (in 000; metric tons; 1969; 1968 in parentheses): rice c. 21,267 (20,065); wheat 6,711 (6,477); barley 115 (121); corn 654 (629); millet 302 (330); sorghum 283 (262); chickpeas (1968) 528, (1967) 578; rapeseed and mustard seed 353 (396); onions (1968) 411, (1967) 397; sugar, raw value (1969–70) c. 736, (1968–69) 506; gur (indigenous raw sugar; 1967–68) 1,881, (1966–67) 1,911; tobacco 166 (170); bananas (1968) 818, (1967) 792; dates (1968) c. 150, (1967) 145; tea (1968) c. 28, (1967) 30; jute 1,265 (1,036); cotton, lint 539 (529); fish catch (1968) 424, (1967) 417. Livestock (in 000; 1968–69): cattle c. 36,200; sheep 11,100; goats c. 11,600; buffaloes c. 8,800; horses 497; asses 925; camels c. 601.

Industry. Production (in 000; metric tons; 1969): cement 2,698; crude oil 478; coal and lignite (1968) c. 1,273; natural gas (cu.m.; 1968) c. 2,230,000; electricity (excluding most industrial production; kwhr.; 1967) 4,991,000; chrome ore (oxide content; 1968) 13; jute manufactures (1967) 490; cotton yarn 286; woven cotton fabrics (m.) 734,000.

Panama

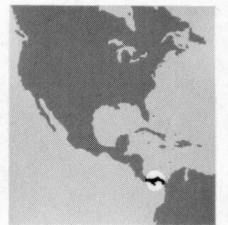

A republic of Central America, bisected by the Panama Canal Zone, Panama is bounded by the Caribbean Sea, Colombia, the Pacific Ocean, and Costa Rica. Area: 29,208 sq.mi. (75,650 sq.km.). Pop. (1970): 1,425,343. Cap. and largest city: Panama (pop., 1970, 418,013). Language: Spanish. Religion: Roman Catholic 93%. Provisional president of the civilian-military government in 1970, Demetrio Lakas Bahas.

During the first week of November 1969, Gen. Omar Torrijos (see BIOGRAPHY), commander of the National Guard of Panama, eased his tight grip on the country to permit greater freedom of speech, assembly, and travel, and to restore the right of habeas corpus and the inviolability of private homes. At about the same time, however, the minister of the presidency, Juan M. Vasquez, announced harsh new decrees. One of these defined the various kinds of activity that constituted subversion and provided specified prison terms for them. Another increased the punishment for the publication of material that the government construed to be libelous.

Despite his efforts to establish a stable, if somewhat ruthless, government, Torrijos had to confront a

Orthodox Churches:
see Religion

Orthopedics:
see Medicine

Osteopathic Medicine:
see Medicine

Painting:
see Art Exhibitions; Art Sales; Museums and Galleries

Paints and Varnishes:
see Industrial Review

Palestine:
see Israel; Jordan

power play designed to remove him. Taking advantage of his absence on a holiday in Mexico, Col. Ramiro Silvera, deputy chief of the National Guard, and Lieut. Col. Amado Sanjur, chief of staff, staged a bloodless coup on Dec. 15, 1969. Various reasons were assigned for the revolt: the fear that Torrijos intended to build a power base like that of former president Juan Perón in Argentina, enmities arising from his drive against corruption, his appointment of leftists to office, apprehensions that he would back compulsory unionism, and the irritations and frustrations among personnel of the National Guard.

Informed of the proceedings in Panama, Torrijos returned to the capital where he received a wild reception of approval. Meantime, pro-Torrijos officers aroused the Guard, and two of them, heavily armed, entered the quarters of the rebellious leaders and arrested them. Thus, the coup of Silvera and Sanjur was ended in a matter of hours and with scarcely a shot. Later, Silvera and Sanjur escaped from jail, finding asylum in the Canal Zone. The figurehead leaders of the governing junta, José M. Pinilla and Bolívar Urrutia, had thrown in their lot with the rebelling colonels and for their misjudgment were removed and also jailed by Torrijos. In their place two civilians were sworn into office on December 19: Demetrio Lakas Bahas and Albert Sucre. Torrijos announced that he would not seek revenge and that plans for a constituent assembly to draft a new constitution would not be changed.

During the year Torrijos launched a program to improve the public vocational school system. The target was to provide facilities for double the number of students in a period of approximately three years.

In the midst of these activities, ships were carrying their cargoes, in record amounts, through the Panama Canal. Neither Panama nor the U.S. indicated much interest in resuming conversations concerning the stalled treaties on building a new waterway and altering the administrative organization. In Washington and in the Canal Zone attention was focused on a plan to double the capacity of the present canal at a cost of perhaps $100 million. On the other hand, the Panamanian government formally rejected in September the draft treaties with the U.S. as a basis of a final accord on administration of the Canal Zone. Furthermore, it reached an agreement with a consortium of British, West German, and Italian interests to build an oil pipeline across the isthmus.   (A. R. W.)

Paraguay

A landlocked republic of South America, Paraguay is bounded by Brazil, Argentina, and Bolivia. Area: 157,047 sq. mi. (406,752 sq.km.). Pop. (1970 est.): 2,386,000. Cap. and largest city: Asunción (pop., 1970 est., 437,136). Language: Spanish (official), though Guaraní is the language of the majority of the people. Religion: Roman Catholic. President in 1970, Gen. Alfredo Stroessner.

In 1970 the Roman Catholic Church continued to provide a focal point for President Stroessner's critics. His earlier reversion to stricter rule (including the banning of opposition newspapers and broadcasts) had failed to silence the opposition of radical priests. In late 1969 the Catholic hierarchy in Paraguay, reacting

PANAMA

Education. (1967–68) Primary, pupils 218,475, teachers 7,488; secondary, pupils 39,811, teachers 2,103; vocational, pupils 22,662, teachers 942; teacher training, students 1,277, teachers 67; higher (including 2 universities), students 9,265, teaching staff 417.

Finance. Monetary unit: balboa, at par with the U.S. dollar (2.40 balboas = £1 sterling). Gold, SDRs, and foreign exchange: (March 1970) U.S. $171 million; (March 1969) U.S. $82.2 million. Budget (1970 est.) balanced at 162.7 million balboas. Gross national product: (1968) 836.1 million balboas; (1967) 778 million balboas. Money supply (deposits only): (March 1970) 94.2 million balboas; (March 1969) 80.3 million balboas. Cost of living (Panama City; 1963 = 100): (1st quarter 1970) 110; (1st quarter 1969) 107.

Foreign Trade. Imports (1968) 266,490,000 balboas; exports (1969) 116,890,000 balboas. Net service receipts from Canal Zone (1969) 124.4 million balboas. Import sources (1968): U.S. 39%; Venezuela 21%. Export destinations (1968): U.S. 79%; Panama Canal Zone 5%. Main exports: bananas 59%; refined petroleum 20%; shrimps 8%.

Transport and Communications. Roads (1968) 6,720 km. Motor vehicles in use (1968): passenger 40,400; commercial (including buses) 12,800. Railways (1968) 538 km. Shipping (1969): merchant vessels 100 gross tons and over 823 (mostly owned by U.S. and other foreign interests); gross tonnage 5,373,722. Telephones (Jan. 1969) 58,608. Radio receivers (Dec. 1965) c. 500,000. Television receivers (Dec. 1967) 77,000.

Agriculture. Production (in 000; metric tons; 1968; 1967 in parentheses): rice 163 (151); sugar, raw value (1969–70) c. 83, (1968–69) 80; bananas c. 600 (592); oranges c. 40 (41); coffee 4.6 (5.2); cocoa (1968–69) 0.4, (1967–68) 0.5. Livestock (in 000; 1968–69): cattle c. 1,210; pigs c. 180; horses c. 160.

Industry. Production (in 000): electricity (Panama and Colón; kw-hr.; 1969) 550,000; manufactured gas (cu.m.; 1968) 19,700; cement (metric tons; 1967) c. 150.

PARAGUAY

Education. (1967) Primary, pupils 385,075, teachers 12,382; secondary (1966), pupils 33,744, teachers 4,680; vocational (1966), pupils 1,940, teachers 507; teacher training (1966), students 3,738; higher (including 2 universities; 1965), students 5,890, teaching staff 780.

Finance. Monetary unit: guaraní, with a free rate (Oct. 1970) of 126 guaranies to U.S. $1 (292.50 guaranies = £1 sterling). Gold, SDRs, and foreign exchange, central bank: (June 1970) U.S. $2,070,000; (June 1969) U.S. $7,110,000. Budget (1970 est.): expenditure 7,662,000,000 guaranies. Gross national product: (1969) 68,360,000,000 guaranies; (1968) 64,160,000,000 guaranies. Money supply: (June 1970) 6,195,000,000 guaranies; (June 1969) 5,628,000,000 guaranies. Cost of living (Asunción; 1964 = 100): (June 1970) 110; (June 1969) 111.

Foreign Trade. (1969) Imports 8,846,300,000 guaranies; exports 6,304,100,000 guaranies. Import sources: U.S. 26%; Argentina 18%; West Germany 14%; U.K. 9%; Italy 5%. Export destinations: Argentina 29%; U.S. 21%; U.K. 7%; Netherlands 7%; France 5%; West Germany 5%. Main exports: timber 23%; meat 22%; tobacco 11%; oilseeds 9%; cotton 6%.

Transport and Communications. Roads (1968) 6,258 km. Motor vehicles in use (1968): passenger 6,900; commercial (including buses) 6,600. Railways (1968): 1,221 km.; traffic 28 million passenger-km., freight 22 million net ton-km. Navigable inland waterways (including Paraguay-Paraná river system; 1966) c. 3,000 km. Telephones (Dec. 1969) 19,128. Radio receivers (Dec. 1968) 164,000.

Agriculture. Production (in 000; metric tons; 1969; 1968 in parentheses): corn 153 (180); peanuts 16 (18); cassava (1968) 1,504, (1967) 1,460; sweet potatoes (1968) 85, (1967) 90; sugar, raw value (1969–70) 46, (1968–69) 37; tobacco 21 (22); oranges 221 (216); bananas (1968) c. 250, (1967) 259; cotton, lint 13 (10). Livestock (in 000; 1968–69): cattle c. 5,600; sheep c. 460; horses c. 730; pigs c. 960; chickens c. 6,550.

Industry. Production (in 000; 1968): cement (metric tons) 24; electricity (kw-hr.) 179,000.

to the breaking up of a peaceful demonstration by priests, nuns, and students in Asunción, excommunicated several high-ranking members of the regime. Despite the president's denial of a conflict between church and state, the clergy maintained its opposition, and the government banned the Roman Catholic charity organization, Caritas.

On the economic front inflation remained negligible, but the real growth of the gross national product was also slow. Measures to reduce the budget deficit included an attempt to introduce an income tax for the first time in Paraguay; this bill met with an unusual display of resistance in Congress.

Paraguay's precarious trade and payments situation was temporarily eased by an export recovery that resulted from higher world prices for the country's traditional products, especially meat. This recovery began in the last quarter of 1969, but the year still ended with an overall deficit of $30 million in Paraguay's goods and services account. In the opinion of an International Monetary Fund economic mission, the main cause of the nation's growing trade deficits was overvaluation of the guaraní (last devalued in 1960). Devaluation was thus one of the IMF's conditions for granting a new standby credit in 1970.

Stroessner, however, refused to devalue, making it a matter of national dignity to maintain the parity of the guaraní; instead, he took measures that included the gradual reduction of export duties. The IMF standby was not renewed when it expired in April, but by then the fortuitous export recovery was in full swing. In the first half of 1970 the trade deficit was reduced to $9 million, compared with $24 million in the same period of 1969.

The debt-servicing element in the balance of payments reached excessive proportions in 1970. At $12 million it represented approximately 20% of projected export earnings. However, with the reduced trade deficit, the continuing inflow of foreign capital attracted by political and economic stability, and the continuing growth of tourism receipts ($15 million in 1969), an overall balance of payments surplus seemed possible for the first time in four years.   (J. J. Sм.)

Parks

Europe. In the United Kingdom in 1970, the Countryside Commission's Committee for Wales began formal consultations to designate approximately 500 sq.mi. of the high spine of central Wales as the Cambrian Mountains National Park. Two new areas of outstanding natural beauty were confirmed: Suffolk Coast and Heaths (151 sq.mi.) and Dedham Vale (22 sq.mi.), in East and West Suffolk and Essex, respectively. At Talybont-on-Usk, on the Monmouthshire and Brecon Canal in the Brecon Beacons National Park, the British Waterways Board replaced an old fixed bridge, an obstacle to craft, by a new drawbridge. After dredging, the canal would again be navigable between Jockey Bridge and Brecon.

A grant from the Countryside Commission enabled the National Trust to purchase, for public access, 921 ac. on Y Gyrn, part of the main Brecon Beacons range above the Tarrell Valley. An Exchequer grant was approved for the Peak District National Park Board's proposed purchase, for public access, of approximately 2 sq.mi. of mostly open moorland, including the popular climbing area of Stanage Edge. In Exmoor National Park the Somerset park authority acquired, with

Exchequer grant aid, approximately 3 sq.mi. of moorland in the wildest and most open part of the park, primarily for public access. An Exchequer grant was authorized for ten parks within easy driving distance of urban centres, and a further 32 schemes were the subject of recommendations by the commission.

In Northern Ireland 11 new nature reserves were declared: Breen Forest, Portrush, Randalstown Forest, and Slieveanorra Forest in County Antrim; Quoile Pondage and Rostrevor Forest in County Down; Castle Archdale Forest, Correl Glen Forest, Lough Naman Bog, and Marble Arch Forest in County Fermanagh; and Killeter Forest in County Tyrone.

The new Doñana National Park (approximately 150 sq.mi.), decreed by the Spanish government, was created. Situated in the Marismas of the Guadalquivir River, it included the Marismillas Down south to the mouth of the Guadalquivir, Las Neuvas and Hinojos, together with the Coto Doñana and Guadiamar nature reserves, established with financial aid from the World Wildlife Fund.

Two new nature parks were established in West Germany: Steinwald, comprising approximately 10 sq.mi. of the southern extension of the Fichtelgebirge, a mainly wooded area interspersed by field patches; and Westensee (over 20 sq.mi.) in Schleswig-Holstein, an area of lake landscape with deciduous woods, the property of landowners and farmers. A Danish Conservation of Nature Act of 1969 provided for the preservation of large areas of fine landscape and areas of scientific interest, as well as for public access facilitating open-air recreation. Visitors to the 15 Swedish parks totaled approximately 69,000 in 1970. In the Netherlands a lookout to enable visitors to view red deer, roebuck, and wild boar was installed in Hoge Veluwe National Park, where 520,000 visitors were recorded.

In Italy the Parco Nazionale della Calabria (approximately 9 sq.mi.) was established. It preserved outstanding landscapes of the Sila Mountains, with fine pinewoods, seminatural beech-fir mixed woods, and rare species of animals.

North America. In Canada agreements were signed for two new parks. One was Kouchibouguac, in New Brunswick, located along the Northumberland Strait between Richibucto Harbour and Portage River, east of Highway 11. The area comprised an open panorama of the Gulf of St. Lawrence, wave-built offshore bars that stretched across the entire ocean front, tidewater lagoons, wetland forests, sandstone marshes, peat

This six-story-high gold dredge, built in 1911, was donated to the Indian Affairs and Northern Development Department by Yukon Consolidated Gold Corp. Ltd. for display at a historic park at Bonanza Creek in the Yukon Territory.

AUTHENTICATED NEWS
INTERNATIONAL

Herodion, the fortress
and tomb of King Herod
near Bethlehem, was
opened to the public
by the Israel National
Parks Authority.

bogs, and extensive inland river drainage systems. The excellent recreational potential of the park included boating, camping, and swimming. The other park, in Quebec's Gaspé region, consisted of approximately 90 sq.mi. of rugged landscape, its highest points 1,800 ft. above sea level. Located on the Forillon Peninsula with main access by car via Highway 6, the park included most of the shoreline areas at the eastern extremity of the peninsula.

The use of persistent herbicides and insecticides was banned by the Canadian national parks administration, and use of nonpersistent chemicals was critically reviewed to restrict their application to a minimum. A program of public hearings to examine the uses and development of Canada's national parks was launched on April 1 with a hearing in Halifax on Nova Scotia's Kejimkujik Park. Potential improvements resulting from each hearing would be incorporated into the master plan for that park. Visitors to the 18 parks totaled 12,586,492 during the year.

The following areas were added to the U.S. National Park System (NPS): Florissant Fossil Beds National Monument, Colorado (approximately 9½ sq.mi.); St. Croix National Scenic Riverway, Wisconsin and Minnesota (approximately 90 sq.mi.); Wolf National Scenic Riverway, Wisconsin (12½ sq.mi.); and Theodore Roosevelt Island, District of Columbia (88.32 ac.). Secretary of the Interior Walter Hickel announced the creation of a new Northwest Region of the NPS, with headquarters at Seattle, Wash., to administer some of the newest and largest NPS areas, including Glacier Bay National Monument (over 4,000 sq.mi.). Legislation to establish a 20,000-ac. Gateway National Recreation Area in New York and New Jersey was introduced in Congress.

The federal government prevented construction of a major international jetport near Everglades National Park, Florida, after a Department of the Interior study had shown that the consequent ecological disruption would destroy the country's only mainland subtropical park. The Endangered Species Act, making it unlawful to transport illegally taken alligator hides across state lines, was expected to end alligator poaching in the Everglades Park and elsewhere in Florida, where alligator extinction had been threatened. Under new legislation, Everglades Park would receive a sufficient flow of fresh water to sustain its normal and viable ecological community, and the water quality would also be protected. The Justice Department brought a legal suit against the Florida Power and Light Co., charging that heated water from the company's existing fossil fuel and planned nuclear power plants would destroy the marine microlife and general ecology of Biscayne Bay, a recreation area for a population expected to reach 2.7 million by 1980.

Africa. Improved internal access roads were constructed in all Kenya's parks, including some all-weather roads, particularly in Tsavo, Meru, Aberdare, and Mount Kenya parks. Visitors to the parks numbered 243,483 in 1970. Hotel-style lodges were opened in Tanzania's Serengeti and Mikumi parks, and in Tarangire Park an animal-viewing track system was developed and a tented camp opened for visitors. Visitors to the parks totaled approximately 106,200, excluding Sunday excursion flights to Serengeti. In Angola the Cangandala Integral Nature Reserve became the Cangandala National Park, and Milando Partial Reserve was disestablished. Improvement works took place in all the parks and game reserves.

Oceania. In South Australia, 12 new parks were dedicated: Carcuma (approximately 11 sq.mi.); Karte (5 sq.mi.); Piccaninnie Ponds (1½ sq.mi.); Sleaford Mere (2½ sq.mi.); Katarapko (12½ sq.mi.); Innes (23½ sq.mi.); Cox's Scrub (almost 2 sq.mi.); Dudley (3½ sq.mi.); Pooginook (11 sq.mi.); Swan Reach (3 sq.mi.); and two unnamed parks covering a total area of approximately 8,236 sq.mi. National park reserves established were White (148 ac.), containing arid shrub community with black oak vegetation and black-faced gray and red kangaroos, and Totness (85½ ac.), an area of stringybark forest with blue gum on the lower slopes. Also dedicated was Gammon Wilderness Park (44 sq.mi.), part of the Gammon ranges.

In Victoria two new parks were dedicated: Captain James Cook (10½ sq.mi.), located on the East Gippsland section of the Victoria coast and containing immense dunes, virgin forest, and unspoiled beaches; and Lower Glenelg Park (35 sq.mi.), encompassing the lower reaches of the Glenelg River in western Victoria and noted for its scenic river features, limestone gorge, and wide variety of native flora and fauna.

Queensland proclaimed 11 new national parks, bringing the total to 271 with a combined area of approximately 3,848 sq.mi. The new parks were: 1357 Russell (227 ac.); 1351 Bellenden Ker (202 ac.); 1353 Bellenden Ker (1½ sq.mi.); 72 Cockenzie (almost 43 sq.mi.); 1359 Parish of Grafton (100 ac.); 56 Southwood (27 sq.mi.); 16 Minnimore (18 sq.mi.); 1392 Bellenden Ker (205 ac.); 155 Whyanbeel (3½ sq.mi.); 1394 Bellenden Ker (over 4 sq.mi.); and 176 Monkhouse (almost 4 sq.mi.).

In New Zealand the value of national parks and other reserves of national importance and the need to develop them for public enjoyment and education was recognized by the appointment of the first director of national parks and reserves, a planning surveyor with major responsibilities in recreational planning, and by an increase in ranger strength. Visitors to the ten parks totaled 1,610,599, an increase of 18.7%.

Asia. In Japan work began on the 812-mi. Tokaido Nature Trail, to run between Tokyo and Osaka, connecting national, quasi-national, and prefectural parks and other reserves. Visitors to the Japanese parks in 1970 numbered 250,671,000. (M. F. B. B.)

See also Conservation; Tourism.

Payments and Reserves, International

On the international monetary scene, the trends, developments, and events of 1970 were marked by two sharply contrasting features. A remarkable calm prevailed in foreign exchange markets—a calm barely disturbed by the floating of the Canadian dollar. Remarkable was, indeed, the word to characterize a truly paradoxical situation—stability of exchange rates in a year when inflation in almost every major country was strong and pervasive, and when the deficit in the U.S. balance of payments resulted in the biggest outflow of dollars ever recorded into the reserves of governments and central banks of Europe, Canada, and Japan.

This state of self-stabilizing confusion will be described, first, by reviewing the position of the U.S. dollar and those of each of the principal currencies, and then by surveying the three elements of "the gold-SDR-dollar complex." The word "complex" is used, not "system," for the world's monetary arrangements at the end of 1970 were far from an orderly, self-correcting, and reliable system—notwithstanding the debut in 1970 of "managed money" in the guise of Special Drawing Rights (SDRs).

The U.S. Dollar. As the result of the U.S. balance of payments deficit, U.S. gold and other international reserve assets were reduced still further and the U.S. indebtedness to foreign governments and central banks was increased (Chart 1 and Table I, accompanied by a note explaining the two ways of calculating the payments deficit, which sometimes cause confusion). The deficit on official settlements was the worst ever—about $10 billion. The worsening was sharp since in the previous two years the U.S. had, on this reckoning, a considerable surplus.

This deterioration was generally received with a feeling of indifference. In part, this feeling reflected past disillusionments with the game of balance of payments statistics. In part, it reflected the knowledge that much of the shifting in these particular statistical measures of surpluses and deficits was, in large part, due merely to big swings in short-term capital flows—large inflows in 1969 and large outflows in 1970. Monetary conditions in 1969 had been far more restrictive in the U.S. than in other industrial countries, but the opposite was true in 1970. Then, as the business slowdown and, in midyear, the threat of a liquidity crisis called for a relaxation of monetary tightness, the Federal Reserve allowed U.S. commercial banks to offer interest rates high enough to attract funds from within the U.S. instead of taking in funds from money markets abroad, as in 1968–69 (*see* MONEY AND BANKING). Furthermore, as short-term interest rates in U.S. markets fell sharply and the holding of Eurodollars became costly, U.S. banks repaid large amounts of Eurodollars; by the end of 1970, their Eurodollar holdings had been whittled down to about $7.5 billion from a peak of $15 billion in November 1969.

Many of these Eurodollars, thus shifted back into the international market, found their way into the hands of West German banks and businesses, which, facing circumstances of extreme monetary tightness, sold them for marks to West Germany's central bank. Other Eurodollars ended up in other central banks. As a result, the U.S. swung from an official settlements surplus to a deficit of record proportions, while West Germany—and, to a lesser extent, Canada, France, and the U.K.—experienced official surpluses. Italy returned to approximate balance in its international payments. Japan managed to hold down the increase in its reserves.

Large shifts of short-term funds are quite normal in a world of convertible currencies in which funds are free to move in response to changing interest rate constellations and varying degrees of tightness in the principal money markets. These swings can be handled by a country so long as they take place within a strong framework consisting of the country's position on foreign trade, income from investments abroad, and long-term capital flows. But there is reason for concern when that very framework also shows signs of continued weakness, as in the U.S. during recent years.

The U.S. deficit on the so-called liquidity basis of measurement showed, it is true, a small improvement in 1970 in comparison with the previous year (Table I). But this end result obscured an improvement on trade account that could not be expected to last, for reasons given below, and a further deterioration on capital accounts other than Eurodollar flows.

During the first 11 months of 1970, U.S. exports, at $43 billion at an annual rate, were 15% above 1969—the best gain since 1964. They exceeded 4% of the gross national product (GNP), the largest figure ever recorded. But imports, at $40 billion, were up by 11%, an even higher rate than the 8.5% increase in 1969 over 1968. They represented 4.1% of GNP, against 3.8% in 1969—a rise indicative of the growing popularity and competitiveness of foreign goods. The 1970 export-import performance thus resulted in an export surplus of $3 billion, more than double the amount recorded in 1969.

The U.S. trade performance in 1970 benefited from the large volume of aircraft deliveries. Basically, however, it reflected the swing in the cyclical positions of the U.S., which experienced a business slowdown, and of continental Europe, Japan, and the primary-producing countries like Australia, where business was buoyant. For the longer run, however, the U.S. could only rely on an unusual cyclical constellation of this sort. Nor could it rely on being outinflated by others. During the second half of the 1960s, the U.S. lost the advantage of the remarkable price-cost stability it had enjoyed during the first half. Over the decade as a whole, unit costs and export unit values in the U.S. increased by about 5–8% more than those of Europe and Japan. The consequences of this will be felt just at the time when the U.S. faces a greater challenge than ever before in those segments of its foreign trade—manufactured goods embodying advanced technology—that have formerly been its greatest strength. European and Japanese automobiles, machine tools, electronic products, and the supersonic airliner Concorde are obvious examples of goods that will pose this challenge.

Income from U.S. private investments in other countries on a net basis, *i.e.*, after allowing for interest payments on the large and costly U.S. short-term indebtedness to money markets abroad, showed only a slight increase from the $5.7 billion in 1969. Military outlays abroad in 1970 were about $3.5 billion, up $1.5 billion from 1964, prior to the war in Vietnam. Of the $3.5 billion total, $2 billion was allocated to Vietnam and elsewhere in Southeast Asia; Western Europe accounted for $1,250,000,000. Savings, including the closings of bases, were offset by increased military and civilian pay. The dollar costs of U.S. government aid programs to other countries remained, on the whole, unchanged. The deterioration of the capital account was partly accounted for by a speedup of long-term fund flows related to direct investment in plant and equipment abroad and by a sharp decrease, for the year as a whole, of foreign purchases of U.S. corporate securities (*see* INVESTMENT, INTERNATIONAL).

The deficit on official settlements was financed only to a very small extent by gold. Some of it was financed through repayments by Britain and France of short-term assistance they had received from the U.S. in earlier years. Another part was covered by the U.S. Treasury through the use of automatic drawing rights in the International Monetary Fund (IMF). For the most part, however, the deficit was financed by increases in short-term indebtedness to governments and central banks, particularly those of Canada, France, West Germany, and Japan (Chart 1). There was room for the rebuilding of foreign official dollar reserves, some of which had been reduced in 1968 and 1969; but, by the end of September 1970, such reserves were, at $18.3 billion, $5.3 billion higher than at the end of 1969.

Currencies of Countries with Payments Surpluses.

The counterparts of the U.S. payments deficit and of the consequent U.S. reserve losses and increases in indebtedness to foreign governments and central banks were the reserve gains of countries with balance of payments surpluses, principally Canada, much of Western Europe, and Japan (Chart 2). Among those countries, Canada showed one of the

most spectacular balance of payments improvements in 1970 as its traditional current account deficit was transformed—mainly because of a sudden upsurge in exports—into a large surplus. Together with capital inflows from the U.S.—long- as well as short-term, partly on the chance of an upward trend in the value of the Canadian dollar in exchange markets—Canada's overall surplus was one of the main counterparts of the U.S. payments deficit.

The payments balance had swung in Canada's favour in late 1969 and even further during the first five months of 1970. Up to that point, however, little of the movement of funds into Canadian dollars was in anticipation of a higher value for the Canadian dollar. The vast bulk was due to the current-account surplus and the capital inflows attracted by high interest rates. At the end of May, in the wake of first inflows of funds motivated by anticipation of an exchange upward valuation, the Canadian authorities found it harmful to the nation's economic and financial interests to hold the exchange rate within its official limits. On May 31, the government of Canada announced that, "for the time being," it would cease buying sufficient U.S. dollars to keep the exchange rate at its par value of U.S. $0.925. Immediately after the Canadian dollar was thus allowed to float, it went up to U.S. $0.97; in September, it almost reached parity with the U.S. dollar, but at the year's end it eased to about U.S. $0.98, or 6.5% above its old par value. Along with the announcement on May 31 that the Canadian dollar would be freed, the government stated that it would intervene in the exchange market to prevent the rate from rising excessively.

For the second time in 20 years, Canada thus

CHART 1.

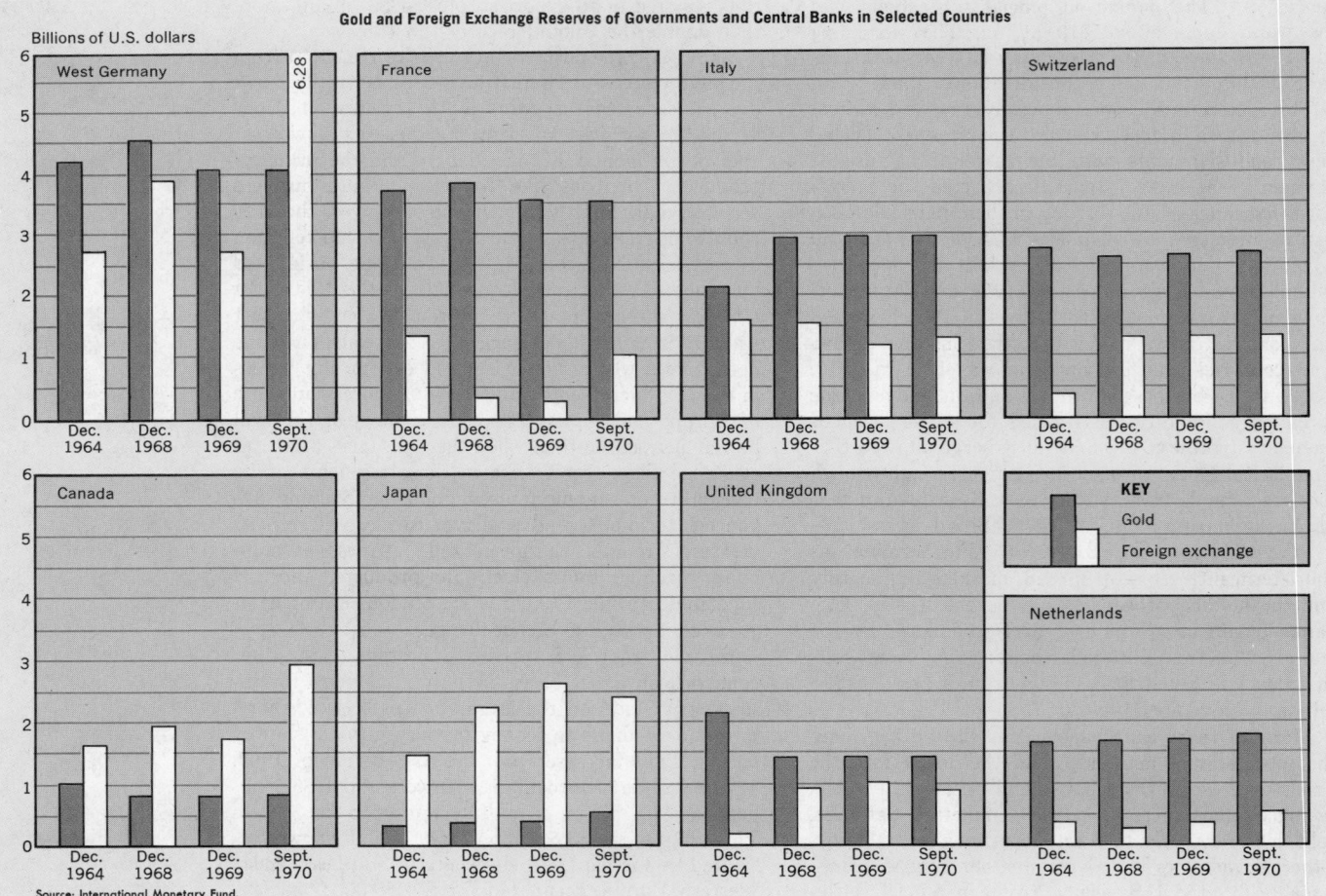

Gold and Foreign Exchange Reserves of Governments and Central Banks in Selected Countries

Source: International Monetary Fund.

placed its dollar on a floating exchange rate basis. After World War II, the exchange rate of the Canadian dollar was fixed at Can$1 = U.S. $1. In the wake of the sterling devaluation in 1949, it was devalued back to its wartime parity of Can$1 = U.S. $0.91. Less than a year later, the Canadian authorities found themselves supporting the U.S. dollar as capital inflows into Canada grew to massive proportions. After one revaluation and one devaluation in four years and faced with great difficulties in avoiding another revaluation, the authorities in 1950 allowed the dollar to float and find its own level. They returned to a fixed parity in 1962—this time at Can$1 = U.S. $0.925—the rate that they abandoned in 1970. Looking backward, it would appear that the period of flotation was economically and financially easier for Canada than the two postwar periods of a fixed exchange rate. A return to a fixed exchange rate obviously depended on the emergence of circumstances that would make such a move plainly in Canada's national interest, including more independence of economic policy in relation to the United States.

Japan had been for most of the past three years one of the principal surplus countries. In 1970, it was true, the overall payments surplus was smaller than in 1969; but the current account surplus was larger than that of any other country. The capital account was in deficit. By and large, Japan's economic and financial strength in South and Southeast Asia, and also in Australia, was one of the most remarkable developments of the late 1960s. It was all the more extraordinary since, as recently as 1967, many observers had thought that Japan might have to devalue the yen.

West Germany's balance of payments experience in 1970 was marked by a persistently high foreign trade surplus, a remarkable result when it is recalled that the revaluation upward of the mark in the fall of 1969 was intended primarily to reduce the trade surplus by slowing exports and speeding up imports. While the mark upvaluation had little impact on trade, it made it less expensive for West Germans to travel abroad and encouraged the two million foreign workers in West Germany to send money home. Other countries' receipts of income from investment in West Germany also rose.

On capital account, the mark revaluation was followed in the last quarter of 1969 by massive outflows of funds to cash in on exchange profits. Early in 1970, however, the capital account was back in surplus. During the second half of 1970, large imports of short-term funds, mainly by West German businesses, were influenced by the fact that continuous monetary stringency in West Germany and a decline in Eurodollar rates turned interest differentials clearly in West Germany's favour. The West German authorities took a variety of steps to stem the inflow of foreign funds, but national interest rates remained above the international level.

France's balance of payments was in substantial surplus in 1970, only two years after the monetary and economic crisis of May–June 1968 and one year after the devaluation of the franc in August 1969 and the accompanying stabilization policies. With the current account in equilibrium, France received a sizable inflow of capital. By April 1970, it had fully repaid the $1.5 billion of central-bank assistance, and during the year it recouped a significant part of earlier losses of its international reserves. Italy's external position, which, together with West Germany's, was

the strongest in Europe during much of the 1960s, weakened in 1969 and deteriorated still further in the first half of 1970. Behind this reversal, two factors were paramount: a marked decline in the current-account surplus as the prolonged industrial unrest had an adverse effect on both imports and exports, and substantial capital outflows seeking refuge abroad.

The United Kingdom's current-account external surplus, which first emerged in 1969, reached the equivalent of $1.4 billion in 1970, the largest in 20 years. This was the combined result of such factors as the devaluation of the pound sterling in November 1967, the slowdown in Britain's domestic economy, and the exceptionally buoyant world trade. Beginning with the last quarter of 1969, Britain also received large amounts of short-term funds attracted by high interest rates. In December 1970, its international reserves were, at $2.8 billion, the highest since November 1967. The bulk of the current and capital surplus was used to repay short- and medium-term international debts. Such indebtedness declined from its $8 billion peak in December 1968 to somewhat below $4 billion in December 1970.

During 1970, Britain's underlying position became gradually less favourable. The foreign trade balance deteriorated as imports rose, while the expansion of exports practically ceased. British prices of manu-

Table I. Main Components of the U.S. Balance of Payments

Item	1967	1968	1969	January–September 1970*
Goods and services				
Exports	30.7	33.6	36.4	31.6
Imports	−26.8	−33	−35.8	−29.6
Trade surplus	3.9	0.6	0.6	2
Income on investments	5.6	6	5.7	4.4
Other services	−2.3	−2.1	−2.3	−1.9
Surplus on goods and services	7.2	4.5	4	4.5
Government outlays				
Military expenditures (net)	−3.1	−3.1	−3.3	−2.6
Government grants and loans	−5.2	−5.4	−5	−3.7
Debt repayments to U.S. government	1	1.4	1.2	1.3
Total government outlays	−7.3	−7.1	−7.1	−5
Private U.S. capital				
Direct investments	−3.1	−3.2	−3.1	−3.6
Portfolio and long-term	−1.3	−1.1	−1.5	−1.1
Short-term	−1.2	−1.1	−0.6	−0.2
Total private U.S. capital	−5.6	−5.4	−5.2	−4.9
Foreign capital				
Purchases of Eurobonds	0.4	2.1	1	0.6
Purchases of U.S. stocks, etc.	0.6	2.2	2.1	0.8
Special official purchases of "nonliquid" U.S. assets	1.3	2.3	−1	−0.1
Other	1	2	2	1.6
Total foreign capital	3.4	8.7	4.1	2.9
Errors and omissions	−1.2	−0.5	−2.8	−1.5
Balance on recorded liquidity basis	−3.5	0.2	−7	−4
Less: Special official purchases of "nonliquid" U.S. assets	−1.3	−2.3	1 }	0 to 0.5
Less: Eurodollar distortions	—	—	1.5 }	
Balance on underlying liquidity basis	−4.8	2.1	−4.5	−3.5 to −4
Plus: Eurodollar takings and increases in "liquid" liabilities to private foreigners	1.4	3.8	7.2	−3.2
Balance on official settlements basis	−3.4	1.7	2.7	−7.2

Note: On both of the two official measurements of the U.S. balance of payments, the resulting surplus or deficit reflects changes in U.S. official reserve assets. From this point on, differences in accounting influence the end result decisively. Most importantly, the official settlements balance records increases in "liquid" liabilities to private foreigners, including Eurodollar takings of U.S. banks, as short-term capital inflows. The liquidity computation of the balance of payments treats increases in "liquid" liabilities to foreigners as financing or settling the overall deficit. However, the recorded liquidity balance has been distorted by special intergovernmental financial transactions and, especially in 1969, by flows of U.S. funds to the Eurodollar market. The underlying liquidity balance adjusts for these distortions.
*Seasonally adjusted and excluding the allocation of Special Drawing Rights.
Source: U.S. Department of Commerce, *Survey of Current Business*.

factured exports increased by nearly 9% during the first nine months of 1970. By the end of the year the roots of price-wage inflation seemed more deeply embedded in Britain than in other industrial nations. The problem of preserving the U.K.'s international competitiveness thus appeared more severe, especially because the benefit of the 1967 devaluation had already been partly eroded. The continued surplus in the balance of payments was the result of the inflow of short-term funds attracted by high interest rates —a lure that could be upset by a weakening of confidence.

The Gold-SDR-Dollar Complex. The ways, just reviewed, in which the large U.S. balance of payments deficit was financed through a substantial accumulation of dollars by governments and central banks of Europe, Canada, and Japan brought about in 1970 an extraordinarily steep addition to international liquidity, amounting to $11.5 billion. Such an increase from this one source was neither planned nor managed by governments. What the governments wanted—and accomplished—was an increase in monetary reserves through the activation of Special Drawing Rights

(SDRs) on Jan. 1, 1970, in the amount of $3.5 billion. But, in the event, SDRs failed to become the largest source of new international monetary reserves in 1970. Ironically enough, the debut of this "paper gold" coincided with the resumption of new flows of South African gold into the monetary stocks of the IMF and of the governments and central banks of Western Europe and Japan—$640 million for the year. Altogether, as Table II shows, as much as $14 billion, or 19%, was added during 1970 to the approximately $74 billion of international monetary reserves of governments and central banks available at the end of 1969.

The resumption of flows of South African gold into the stocks of the IMF and of governments and central banks was a significant development. For, in the aftermath of the gold crisis in 1968, the monetary authorities of seven leading countries "felt" (to use the word of the official communiqué of the Washington conference) that there was enough gold in the world's official reserves and that there was no need to acquire newly mined gold. This understanding was amended, effective Jan. 1, 1970, as a result of new arrangements for the purchase of South African gold by the IMF, which, in turn, sells gold to member countries. Switzerland, which is not an IMF member, made a direct arrangement with South Africa.

The marketing arrangements for South African gold effectively put a floor of $35 an ounce on the price received by South Africa for its gold, but not on the market price. For the IMF buys newly mined South African gold at the monetary price of $35 when the market price falls to or below $35, as was the case in January 1970. Even when the London price exceeds $35, the IMF can buy South African gold provided that South Africa's foreign exchange requirements exceed, over any semiannual period, what can be obtained through the sale on the market of its total current production. This condition existed during most of 1970. From the beginning of February through September, the price fluctuated erratically between $35 and $36 an ounce. It reached a peak of $39.19 on October 27 but fell back three days later to $37.25; on December 31 it stood at $37.43.

Under these arrangements, the IMF purchased during 1970 $640 million of South African gold. During the year, South Africa's monetary stock declined by $449 million. Since output amounted to $1,130,000,-000 (4% more than in 1969), South Africa disposed of about $1,580,000,000 of gold during 1970. On this basis, all placements other than those with the IMF— *i.e.*, in the private market, etc.—were about $940 million, or about 83% of South Africa's output.

The contribution of newly mined gold to international liquidity during 1970 was thus modest, but not negligible (Table III, which also shows a reduction in sales to the private market). In 1970, the governments and central banks of the large industrial countries were willing buyers of South African gold from the IMF. During the year they thus acquired $920 million for their currencies, $280 million more than the IMF itself obtained from South Africa during the period.

Both in the U.S. and in the principal financial powers abroad, gold stocks appeared increasingly to have assumed the character of a heavily defended "last ditch" reserve. In September 1970, the U.S. gold stock stood at $11.5 billion. It thus represented 28% of the $41.2 billion world total, against almost 50% held by continental Europe.

The year 1970 also saw further substantial addi-

CHART 2.

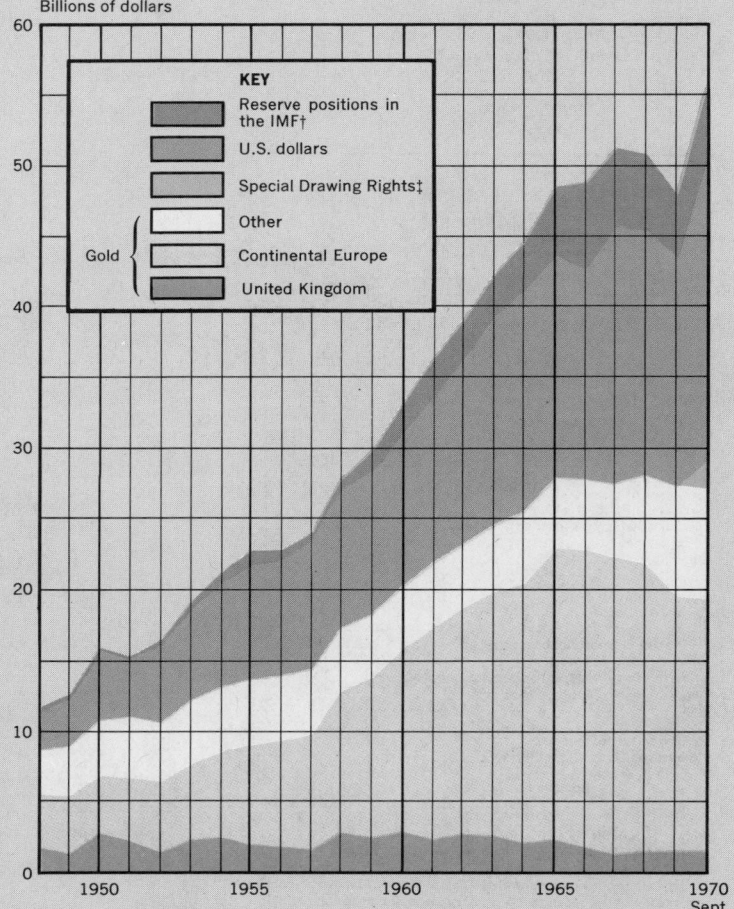

Gold and U.S. Dollar Reserves of Governments and Central Banks Other than the United States*, 1948–70

*Excluding the U.S.S.R., Eastern European countries, China, etc.
†Amounts that can be drawn "essentially automatically" from the IMF, corresponding to members' gold subscriptions plus amounts of their currencies sold by the Fund to other members (net) plus outstanding lendings to the Fund.
‡Special Drawing Rights are unconditional international reserve assets created by the IMF to supplement the total level of world reserves; they are allocated to participating members in proportion to their IMF quotas.

Source: International Monetary Fund.

tions to international monetary facilities to be used, instead of gold or dollars, in the financing of payments deficits and surpluses. The most publicized of these facilities was the scheme for SDRs for a total of $9.5 billion over the three years 1970–72, with $3.5 billion allocated on Jan. 1, 1970, and $3 billion on Jan. 1, 1971. The SDRs were received in 1970 by 105 IMF member countries. These countries were, in turn, obligated to accept SDRs from one another up to specified limits. Within those limits, the SDRs are, in effect, internationally acceptable assets that are usable automatically and unconditionally among governments and central banks.

The advent of SDRs did not, however, change the international monetary scene. The actual use made of such paper gold was moderate. The U.S., despite its large official settlements deficit, was not a user but a receiver of SDRs. Governments of the surplus countries thus preferred dollars to SDRs, although the new instrument, endowed with an absolute gold guarantee, was, in effect, a gold certificate while dollars enjoyed no gold guarantee. Obviously, the authorities in other countries were not insensitive to the high interest rates available in 1970 on short-term investments in the U.S.; SDRs, on the other hand, carry only 1.5% interest. For their part, the U.S. authorities did not seem too eager to redeem in SDRs, the dollars in the hands of foreign governments and central banks, for such redemptions would have shown up in a decline in U.S. official international monetary reserves. At the same time, the governments also did not begin to prefer SDRs to gold.

There was a further substantial addition to international liquidity on October 30 as a result of the fifth general increase in subscriptions (quotas) to the IMF by $7.6 billion to $29 billion. While 1970 thus set a record for the deliberate creation of new international monetary facilities, much of it—above all, and most importantly, the decision to distribute the SDRs —reflected a consensus among the governments of the major countries that there was a global need to supplement international monetary reserves. The decision rested on two specific assumptions: "the attainment of a better balance-of-payments equilibrium" and "the likelihood of a better working of the adjustment process in the future." These assumptions related essentially to the persistent external deficits of the U.S. and the U.K. During the course of 1970, it became evident that these assumptions were not, in fact, fulfilled since the U.S. balance of payments remained heavily in deficit. The SDR scheme was to come up for reconsideration in 1972. If the U.S. balance of payments was still heavily in deficit at that time, there would necessarily be discussion about how a managed growth of global reserves might be achieved if, side by side with further allocations of SDRs, the governments and central banks of the surplus nations continued to accumulate large amounts of dollars.

In 1970, the reemergence of a large deficit in the U.S. balance of payments did not give rise to an open confrontation over the dollar balances. While foreign monetary authorities still had the option of converting unwanted dollars into gold, they refrained from anything like a run on the dollar. Among the Western European countries, only the Netherlands and Switzerland purchased modest amounts of gold from the U.S. Treasury. For a run on the U.S. gold stock to materialize, the political relationships among the financial powers would, obviously, have to undergo deep-seated and dramatic changes. Economic and

financial reasons also were important in avoiding large conversions of dollars into gold. There was some fear that such moves might force disruptive changes in exchange-rate relationships among the major currencies and involve a breach of the cooperative arrangements that protected many of the principal currencies during the crises of recent years. Some students of international monetary affairs concluded from considerations like these that major financial powers other than the U.S. had no option but to learn to live with the U.S. balance of payments deficit and that the U.S. need not be concerned over its balance of payments.

In this domain, much is, evidently, a matter of degree and circumstance. While in the second half of 1970 the U.S. was responding to its business slowdown with an easing of monetary and fiscal policies, foreign governments and central banks undoubtedly realized that they had a vital stake in the maintenance of high and rising levels of business in the country that provides the largest import market in the world. But to stretch considerations like these to the conclusion that the major financial powers abroad would absorb dollars in unlimited amounts and regardless of the circumstances was an oversimplification. Thus, if economic and monetary conditions and policies in the U.S. were to bring about a relapse into inflation, the dollar would undoubtedly lose much of its allure for foreign holders, private as well as official. For the dollar as an international trading and reserve currency could not be sustained for any length of time if its buying power were to be depreciated more than that of other major currencies. Encouragingly—but there was no certainty in these matters —the U.S. at the end of 1970 seemed to be ahead of most other large industrial countries in the world's inflation cycle.

The governments and central banks of Europe, Canada, and Japan were also greatly concerned about the consequences of U.S. economic and monetary conditions and policies for their own economies and their

Table II. Changes in Monetary Reserves of Governments and Central Banks
In $000,000,000

Item	Amounts outstanding December 1969	Annual average 1961–68	Increases or decreases (—) 1969	January–September 1970*	1970†
Gold	39.1	0.1	0.2	−0.5	−0.5
Reserve position in IMF	6.7	0.4	0.2	—	
Special Drawing Rights	—	—	—	3.2	3
Foreign exchange‡	28	0.7	1.1	10.2	11.5
Total	73.9	1.2	1.6	13	14

*Partly estimated.
†Forecast as of December 1970.
‡Adjusted to include dollars created by drawings on intercentral bank credit facilities, but—to avoid double counting—to exclude the foreign currency assets acquired by the lending central banks as the counterpart of such short-term support operations.
Source: Adapted from OECD, *Economic Outlook*, December 1970.

Table III. Flows of Newly Mined Gold*
In $000,000,000

Period	Added to or released from (—) official reserves* World total	Outside of South Africa	Absorbed by the private market
Nine months ended:			
June 1968	−2.4	−2.9	3.5
March 1969	0.5	0.1	0.5
December 1969	−0.1	0.2	1.1
September 1970	0.2	0.4	0.9

*Excluding the U.S.S.R., other countries of Eastern Europe, China, etc.
Source: International Monetary Fund, *International Financial Statistics*.

own policy-making. They felt that the tidal waves of short-term funds to and from the U.S. as a consequence of the changes in U.S. monetary conditions and policies—evidenced in changes in interest rates and expectations—greatly complicated their ability to manage their monetary and economic affairs. They were increasingly aware that, by accumulating dollars in unlimited amounts and for an indefinite period of time, they were, in effect, placing their currencies on a dollar standard. They feared that such a course would be like having two central banks—one at home and the other in Washington—which might, at times, work at cross-purposes.

Not too surprisingly, therefore, much thought was given in 1970 to providing the world with an alternative to the dollar. The European Economic Community (EEC) initiated plans to create, within a decade, a monetary union. A report prepared under the chairmanship of Pierre Werner, prime minister of Luxembourg, not only outlined the long-term goals of monetary union but also set out the first practical steps to be taken in the next three years. The long-term objective was stated to be a monetary union with freely convertible member currencies of irrevocably fixed parities, free movements of capital, and a central body to conduct monetary policy. Harmonization

was called for with regard to fiscal policy, taxation, and financial markets.

These objectives were rather vague; but the first stage of the plan for 1971–73 was precise. It called for the narrowing of allowable fluctuations in exchange rates around parities of the member currencies, a $2 billion pool for mutual assistance, and obligatory consultation. In the second stage of the monetary union, a stabilization fund would be established, looking in the final stage to joint management of international reserves. By 1980, the EEC would have a central banking system modeled somewhat on the U.S. Federal Reserve. It was even said that, sooner or later, a European currency bloc might float against the dollar and that Europe would one day present the world with a challenge to the dollar.

Plans like these assumed full identity of views among the EEC national governments on vital matters affecting not only their economic but also their political interests, including the surrender of a substantial degree of national sovereignty. In any event, a European currency bloc could be achieved only through long-run adjustments in national views, attitudes, and policies. If these processes designed to culminate in a common European currency were to be speeded up by the catalyst of the common concern over the consequences of prolonged and large U.S. payments deficits, the end result would be a sad testimony to the inability of the U.S. to handle its economic and financial affairs, domestically as well as internationally.

The thought was also sometimes expressed during 1970 that countries experiencing unwanted inflows of dollars could turn them off by floating or systematically upvaluing their currencies against the dollar. West Germany and Canada, endeavouring to deal with problems of their own, made moves in this direction in 1969 and 1970. But there were no signs that nations sufficient in number and in economic weight might be willing to float their currencies upward, or to upvalue them outright, merely to help ease the balance of payments position of the U.S. For by doing so, they would weaken their own competitiveness in domestic and foreign markets and correspondingly increase the competitiveness of the U.S., the world's largest, richest, and most productive economy. Nor were the nations abroad likely to increase, through appreciation of their currencies, the value and profitability, in their own currencies, of the large U.S. investments within their borders. Judging from a report, *The Role of Exchange Rates in the Adjustment of International Payments* by the IMF Executive Directors published in September, and from the discussion at the IMF's annual meeting, the governments wanted to maintain the present international monetary arrangements— the fixed exchange rates, which must, of course, be realistic and changed whenever needed (subject to the safeguards built into the IMF statute).

In 1970, there were no islands of monetary stability. But inflation proceeded at an uneven pace. Toward the end of the year it was, hopefully, slowing down in the U.S., but was speeding up in other large industrial countries. For the future of the "gold-SDR-dollar complex," therefore, much depended on how the U.S. dollar might, in the end, fare relative to other currencies. Much also depended on the climate for reasonably free, multilateral, and nondiscriminatory trade and investment across national borders. Finally, monetary cooperation among governments and central banks appeared to be a crucial

CHART 3.

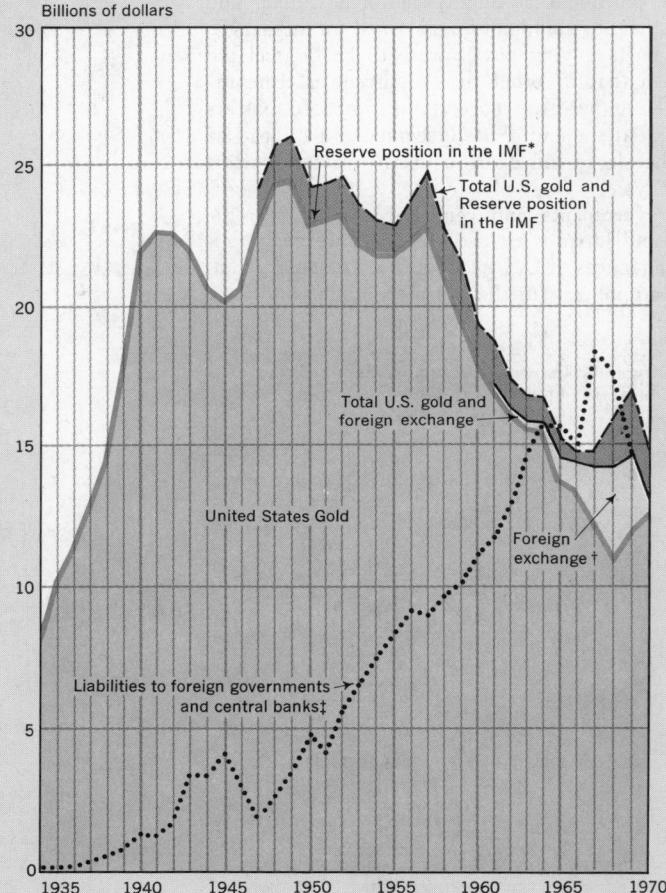

U.S. Monetary Reserves and Liabilities to Foreign Governments and Central Banks, 1935–70

Billions of dollars

Reserve position in the IMF*

Total U.S. gold and Reserve position in the IMF

Total U.S. gold and foreign exchange

United States Gold

Foreign exchange †

Liabilities to foreign governments and central banks‡

*Amounts that can be drawn "essentially automatically" from the IMF, corresponding to the U.S. gold subscription and amounts of U.S. dollars sold by the Fund to other members (net).

†Largely assets acquired as a result of general support in foreign exchange markets for other currencies such as sterling. The United States can, therefore, use such holdings only for bilateral settlements.

‡Deposits, short-term money market instruments, and U.S. government notes and bonds, including special nonmarketable Treasury securities.

Source: *Federal Reserve Bulletin.*

factor. For cooperation could not be maintained if the idea were allowed to gain ground that the condition of a country's balance of payments could be treated as a matter of secondary importance. Reassuringly, it was being increasingly realized that nations need monetary stability not for international considerations but, overwhelmingly, for domestic political, social, and economic reasons.   (M. A. K.)

See also Commercial Policies; Commodities, Primary; Economics; Economy, World; Investment, International; Prices; Trade, International.

Peace Movements

Dramatic new tendencies emerged in 1970, as peace efforts attempted with mixed results to end the conflict in Indochina, de-escalate the arms race between the major powers, stimulate creative methods of prosecuting conflict without violence, and strengthen old coalitions while developing new organizations and forms of protest. Events such as the U.S. incursion into Cambodia, continued revelations concerning the alleged massacre of civilians by U.S. soldiers at My Lai, S.Viet., and the killing of four students at Kent State University by the National Guard during an antiwar demonstration catalyzed the resurgence of a numerically powerful antiwar movement. But the year also witnessed signs of an increasing cultural fragmentation and a sharpening divergence between those committed to nonviolence and those tolerating it as a legitimate tactic.

After the disbanding of the Vietnam Moratorium Committee in mid-April, a swift reappearance of antiwar demonstrations marked the U.S. scene after Cambodia. But the most sustained impulse of 1970 was the development of movements that forged a sophisticated peace-oriented political effort to elect antiwar congressmen. The National Coalition for a Responsible Congress emerged as an effective alliance between the Movement for a New Congress (which worked in 23 primary elections, helping to win 18), the National Petition Committee (which secured over 220,000 signatures on an end-the-war petition), the Universities National Anti-War Fund (sponsored by eight Nobel Prize-winning scientists), the Continuing Presence in Washington (an antiwar lobby), and the Academic and Professional Alliance (representing lawyers, doctors, engineers, and businessmen).

Prominent traditional organizations such as the Council for a Livable World, the Fellowship of Reconciliation (FOR), the American Friends Service Committee (AFSC), SANE, the United World Federalists, and the Americans for Democratic Action continued their efforts to develop peace-oriented constituencies. FOR sponsored an international fact-finding delegation to South Vietnam composed of leaders from the U.S., Australia, New Zealand, and the Netherlands. The mission's report urged withdrawal of support from the Thieu-Ky regime in favour of a "genuine and workable" coalition government. The AFSC published a significant and widely circulated analysis of the dangerous Arab-Israeli confrontation entitled *The Search for Peace in the Middle East*. The American Civil Liberties Union, in a major departure from its traditional domestically oriented policies, adopted a resolution to work for the "immediate termination" of the war in Southeast Asia.

Within the ranks of the military itself, several antiwar groups gained increased visibility during 1970.

WIDE WORLD
On Buddha's birthday monks release a dove of peace at a mass prayer meeting in Saigon's An Quang Pagoda during the 24-hour unilateral cease-fire in effect May 19, 1970.

The oldest and largest was the American Servicemen's Union, initiated in 1967 by Andrew Stapp and claiming 8,000 members. Among its demands were the election of officers by enlisted men, the right to free political association and collective bargaining, and the right to disobey illegal orders, including those to fight in Vietnam. Another group, GIs United Against the War in Vietnam, developed chapters at posts beyond its original base at Ft. Jackson, South Carolina. Such organizations, together with nearly 60 underground antiwar newspapers and the off-base "GI coffeehouses," suggested that the U.S. military confronted a significant peace movement within its own structure.

Peace leaders also pointed to the substantial increase in congressional criticism of foreign and military policies in 1970, especially indicated by the Senate's repeal of the 1964 Gulf of Tonkin resolution and its 58–37 adoption of the Cooper-Church amendment, designed to prohibit the retention of U.S. forces in Cambodia. However, the McGovern-Hatfield "Amendment to End the War" by denying funds for U.S. troops in Southeast Asia after December 1971 was defeated 39–55, and the Hart-Cooper amendment

Vietnam Veterans Against the War are given support by local residents along their 84-mi. march route from Morristown, N.J., to Valley Forge, Pa., Sept. 4–7, 1970.

HOWARD PETRICK FROM NANCY PALMER

UPI COMPIX

Two girls wearing "antiwar paint" take part in the Boston Common demonstration that drew almost 100,000 people, April 15, 1970.

gap between developed and less developed countries, the population problem, and threats to the environment. The group declared its "grave concern" that since its 1969 conference in the Soviet Union there had been "no significant decrease in the threats inherent in the arms race."   (R. Hy.)

Peru

A republic on the west coast of South America, Peru is bounded by Ecuador, Colombia, Brazil, Bolivia, Chile, and the Pacific Ocean. Area: 496,-222 sq.mi. (1,285,215 sq.km.). Pop. (1970 est.): 13,586,300, including approximately 52% whites and mestizos and 46% Indians. Cap. and largest city: Lima (pop., 1970 est., 2,541,300). Language: Spanish; Indians speak Quechuan or Aymaran. Religion: Roman Catholic. President of the military government in 1970, Maj. Gen. Juan Velasco Alvarado.

A major earthquake, the most destructive in the nation's history, struck Andean and coastal areas of Peru on May 31, 1970. Registering 7.75 on the Richter scale, it killed an estimated 50,000 people, injured 100,000, and left 800,000 homeless. (*See* DISASTERS.)

The military government of Major General Velasco celebrated its second year of power on October 3. After taking office, it set about to create in Peru a new socioeconomic structure designed primarily to involve Peruvian citizens more closely in the economic management of their country. The course the government took to do this owed no allegiance to any political or economic ideology; the "revolution" started by the military leaders was an answer to certain problems they regarded as particularly detrimental to their country's future social and economic development, such as excessive foreign participation in national industries, excessive control of domestic wealth by traditional groups, and lack of worker participation.

These problems helped to explain why the government concentrated on reforming industry and banking, and on bringing greater state control to bear upon the more important sectors of the economy. The marketing of fishmeal, fish oil, and minerals—Peru's principal export items—was reserved to the state, and the appropriate agencies were set up to cope with this function. All refining of metals was also to be carried out by the state, beginning with copper.

The state extended its control through the Banco de la Nación, which became very important during the year. In May the government transferred all foreign currency holdings to the state banks and ordered all nationals to repatriate their foreign currency deposits immediately. The Banco de la Nación was given the power to control all exchange transactions which were formerly conducted on the free market. The aim was to stop speculation and the flight of capital from Peru. The measure was successful, and the foreign exchange reserves of the Central Bank had increased by $74 million by the end of May.

The Banco de la Nación also stepped into the banking sphere in May when it fixed the minimum capital of commercial banks in Lima and Callao at 150 million soles. It was hoped that this measure would stimulate mergers of smaller banks, but it was not successful and the requirement was subsequently reduced to 60 million soles. However, the Banco de la Nación

to restrict antiballistic missile deployment to two already-approved sites lost by 47–52. But even in the military-oriented House, peace spokesmen noted the marked increase of votes against military spending from a mere handful to 105 against ABM and 153 against U.S. military intervention in Cambodia.

On the state level, Massachusetts passed a bill giving Massachusetts servicemen the option to refuse combat duty when there was no actual declaration of war by Congress. It was anticipated that the Supreme Court would ultimately be requested to rule on the constitutionality of undeclared wars.

The refusal of Roman Catholic priest Daniel Berrigan to voluntarily surrender himself after being convicted and sentenced to three and one-half years imprisonment for burning draft files in Catonsville, Md., provided the most signal instance of civil disobedience in 1970. For four months Berrigan remained underground, surfacing for TV and newspaper interviews and occasional public appearances, before finally being captured by the FBI in August.

While some peace leaders viewed the increased emphasis on environmental health and ecology (symbolized by the observance of April 22 as Earth Day) as distractions from antiwar efforts, others formulated a radical ecology connecting the issue of planetary health with the peace movement. The Fellowship of Reconciliation, for example, established offices in Brussels to initiate an extensive international Dai Dong The Gioi (The Community of Man) project, designed to stimulate a new transnational peace emphasis.

In related international developments, 37 Soviet dissidents praised the award of the 1970 Nobel Prize for Literature to Aleksandr I. Solzhenitsyn, the Soviet author who had been severely criticized by official government sources. Zinaida Grigorenko, the wife of former Maj. Gen. Pyotr G. Grigorenko, a prominent political dissenter and peace advocate whom the government had declared mentally unbalanced and placed in an asylum, was among the signers of the statement.

The 20th Pugwash Conference met September 8–15 at Fontana, Wis., where the international gathering of scientists focused upon the arms race, the widening

was given authorization to acquire a controlling interest in some of Lima's largest banks.

The main reforms in the industrial sector were included in the Industrial Law, announced in July. By this act the basic industries, such as iron, steel, nonferrous metals, petrochemicals, fertilizers, cement, and paper, were classed as priority industries and were to be supervised closely by the government; important tax and reinvestment allowances were to be granted them, as well as to other industries, in proportion to their contributions to the economy. For assessing these allowances, four categories of industries were established.

The most controversial part of the Industrial Law related to worker participation. "Industrial communities" were established, consisting of employees and workers of companies. Of each company's pre-tax income, 25% was to be allocated to the relevant community, 10% for distribution among the members and 15% toward purchasing company shares.

The Industrial Law also affected foreign investment. Foreign companies wishing to operate wholly owned subsidiaries in Peru had to reduce their shareholding to 33% once they had recovered two-thirds of their original investment plus a "reasonable" profit. Joint ventures between Peru and another country were officially preferred and encouraged by allowing up to 49% foreign capital participation.

The economy was slightly less depressed than in 1969. There were signs of a business recovery in June which coincided with the favourable trade balance of $4.9 million for the first half year.

In foreign relations, Peru looked increasingly toward the Soviet bloc for trade and technical assistance. An agreement was signed with Hungary in February which provided for imports of machinery valued at $15 million, in exchange for Peruvian fishmeal and mineral products. In August the government accepted a credit equivalent to $30 million from the U.S.S.R. for the purchase of agricultural equipment, 30% of which was to be repaid in Peruvian finished and semi-finished products. (D. J. Ro.)

Encyclopædia Britannica Films. *Peru: People of the Andes* (1959).

Philately and Numismatics

Philately. Exciting news in 1970 to all philatelists was the March 24 auction sale of the world's most valuable stamp, the 1856 British Guiana one cent black-on-magenta. The purchasers, a syndicate of professional and business men, included one philatelist. Purchased in 1940 for a reported price of $42,500, this stamp brought $280,000 at the Robert A. Siegel Auction Galleries, Inc., in New York. The identity of the previous owner, Frederick T. Small, had remained a mystery for 30 years.

Other interesting items auctioned in 1970 were three copies of the U.S. 1918 airmail invert stamp, bringing $29,000, $33,000, and $34,000, respectively. Speculative aspects of philately were noted by financial publications, with the *Wall Street Journal* of Feb. 4, 1970, headlining one story "As Other Investments Sour, More Americans Turn to Rare Stamps." The July 1 issue of *Forbes* magazine pointed out that the prices of rare stamps increase each year, never dropping as stocks often do in periods of tight money, increased taxes, and high interest rates.

Two major philatelic appointments changed hands in the United Kingdom. F. Marcus Arman, the founder-curator of the National Postal Museum, retired and was succeeded by A. Rigo de Righi, a well-known philatelist and postal historian. Late in 1969 John B. Marriott, a housemaster at Charterhouse public school and a prominent student of classic stamps, succeeded Sir John Wilson, who had been keeper of

PERU
Education. (1967) Primary, pupils 2,236,397, teachers 65,394; secondary, pupils 424,421, teachers 25,133; vocational, pupils 86,752, teachers 8,254; higher, students 101,099, teaching staff 11,649.
Finance. Monetary unit: sol, with a free exchange rate (Sept. 1970) of 43.38 soles to U.S. $1 (103.50 soles = £1 sterling). Gold, SDRs, and foreign exchange, central bank: (June 1970) U.S. $316 million; (June 1969) U.S. $154.6 million. Budget (1968–69 est.) balanced at 41,844,000,000 soles. Gross national product: (1968) 185.7 billion soles; (1967) 153,-810,000,000 soles. Money supply: (Nov. 1968) 17,-150,000,000 soles; (Dec. 1967) 16,530,000,000 soles. Cost of living (Lima and Callao; 1963 = 100): (June 1970) 205; (June 1969) 197.
Foreign Trade. (1969) Imports 23,382,000,000 soles; exports 33,444,000,000 soles. Import sources (1968): U.S. 34%; West Germany 11%; Argentina 10%; Japan 6%; U.K. 5%. Export destinations (1968): U.S. 39%; Japan 15%; West Germany 11%; Belgium-Luxembourg 7%; Netherlands 6%. Main exports: copper 30%; fish meal 23%; iron ore 8%; cotton 8%; silver 7%; sugar 5%; zinc 5%.
Transport and Communications. Roads (1965) 42,818 km. (including 10,635 km. with improved surface). Motor vehicles in use (1967): passenger 195,100; commercial (including buses) 111,800. Railways: (1965) 3,345 km.; traffic (1967) 211 million passenger-km., freight 625 million net ton-km. Air traffic (1968): 574,204,000 passenger-km.; freight 15,-983,000 net ton-km. Shipping (1969): merchant vessels 100 gross tons and over 366; gross tonnage 338,-080. Telephones (Jan. 1969) 165,121. Radio receivers (Dec. 1968) c. 1,815,000. Television receivers (Dec. 1968) 300,000.
Agriculture. Production (in 000; metric tons; 1969; 1968 in parentheses): rice 417 (208); wheat (1968) 150, (1967) 152; barley c. 175 (c. 170); corn 602 (590); potatoes 1,722 (1,700); cassava 502 (500); dry beans (1968) 70, (1967) 65; sugar, raw value (1969–70) c. 750, (1968–69) c. 630; citrus fruit (1968) c. 300, (1967) 270; cotton, lint c. 98 (101); fish catch (1968) 10,520, (1967) 10,134. Livestock (in 000; 1968–69): cattle c. 3,850; sheep c. 15,000; horses c. 620; pigs c. 1,700; goats c. 4,000; poultry c. 21,000.
Industry. Fuel and power (in 000; metric tons; 1968): coal c. 170; crude oil (1969) 3,420; electricity (kw-hr.) 4,880,000. Production (in 000; metric tons; 1968): cement 1,006; iron ore (metal content) 5,126; pig iron 111; steel 84; lead (1969) 78; zinc (1969) 62; copper (1969) 47; tungsten concentrates (oxide content) 0.6; silver 1.12; gold (troy oz.) 82; fish meal 1,922.

One of three stamps showing paintings from the retable of St. Jean de Caselles Church issued by France for Andorra.

UPI COMPIX

CAMERA PRESS FROM PIX

Above, United States ecology stamps. Above, right, a stamp issued by West Germany to honour the 250th birthday of storyteller Baron Munchausen. Right, a French stamp issued to mark Bordeaux's centennial.

UPI COMPIX

COURTESY, INTERNATIONAL NUMISMATIC AGENCY

Medal honouring
Sir Winston Churchill
and the 25th anniversary
of D-Day.

COURTESY, AMERICAN NUMISMATIC ASSOCIATION

Austria's 25 schilling coin
marking composer Franz
Lehár's 100th birthday.

COURTESY, AMERICAN NUMISMATIC ASSOCIATION

Australia's 50 cent coin
honouring the bicentenary
of Capt. James Cook's
discovery of its east coast.

COURTESY, AMERICAN NUMISMATIC ASSOCIATION

Two riyal coin issued
by Ajman, one
of the Trucial States.

the Royal Philatelic Collections at Buckingham Palace.

In September London was the venue of the year's major international stamp exhibition, Philympia 1970, with exhibits valued at £10 million ($24 million). Attendance during the nine days was 61,000, and the grand award for the best exhibit was won by Roger Loeuillet of Nice, France, for his specialized collection of French stamps from 1849 to 1870. The grand award for the best collection of British stamps went to Harold W. Fisher (U.K.) and that for the best display of British Commonwealth stamps to Hiroyuki Kanai of Osaka, Jap., for classic Mauritius stamps, including an unused example of each of the penny and twopenny "Post Office" stamps of 1847, of which only four were known to exist. Strong support from the British Post Office included the issue of three Philympia postage stamps, the first time a British philatelic exhibition had been so recognized.

The Annual Congress of the Fédération Internationale de Philatélie took place in London for the first time, immediately following Philympia 1970, and attracted a record number of delegates from 42 of the 46 member countries. Two new vice-presidents, Léon Putz (Luxembourg) and Manuel M. Risueno (Argentina), were elected. In the ballot for a vacancy on the executive committee, Ernest Krenkel (U.S.S.R.) was elected.

Those elected in 1970 to be signatories to the Roll of Distinguished Philatelists at the Folkestone meeting of the Philatelic Congress of Great Britain were: Doris M. Green (U.K.), the only living woman signatory; Harrison D. S. Haverbeck (U.S.); Capt. B. J. L. Rogers-Tillstone (U.K.); and Robert Delapierre (Belgium), who died after his election and before being able to sign the roll. The Philatelic Congress Medal was awarded to Richard F. W. Sheraton, of Brighton, Eng.

The market for classic stamps of the world continued to improve, an example being the £112,850 ($269,400) realized by H. R. Harmer Ltd. in London for the Maria de la Queillerie collection of Cape of Good Hope stamps. One of the many records in this sale was the £8,250 ($19,800) paid for the fourpenny "Woodblock" vermilion error of colour in a block of four, this being the highest price ever paid for a single Cape of Good Hope item.

In other developments, at an international exhibition in Calcutta, the Indian Philatelic Society awarded a gold medal to the British Post Office for the best Gandhi centenary stamp issued in 1969.

(R. F. Mi.; K. F. C.)

Numismatics. On August 22 Director of the U.S. Mint Mary T. Brooks announced the establishment of a Numismatic Service there. It was not as extensive a service as the U.S. Post Office Department conducted for philatelists, but there were plans to expand it. The Mint continued not to sell coins, except proof and mint sets of the current year, but it did have various medals which it produced for sale to individuals.

The hobby of coin, paper money, medal, and token-collecting attracted many new devotees during the year, as evidenced by a substantial increase (24,837 to 25,751) in the membership of the American Numismatic Association (ANA). There was some slowdown in commercial activities caused by general economic conditions, yet prices at the 1970 ANA convention were firmer and better than had been expected, indicating an upswing in values. Price changes in the 1971 edition of the standard *A Guide Book of United States*

Coins were erratic in practically all series. The prices of colonial coins, silver dollars prior to 1878, and some commemorative coins advanced, but there were drops in the values of many others.

While the U.S. issued no new commemorative coins, many other countries did so, including Australia (Captain Cook), Austria (Franz Lehár and Innsbruck University), Canada (Manitoba), Czechoslovakia (Bratislava National Theatre), East Germany (Heinrich Hertz and Johann Friedrich Böttger), West Germany (1972 Olympic Games), India (Mohandas Gandhi), Israel (Mikveh Israel), New Zealand (Captain Cook), Norway (liberation from Nazi occupation), Panama (Central American and Caribbean Games), Poland (People's Republic), U.S.S.R. (birth of Lenin), and Western Samoa (Robert Louis Stevenson). Other countries issued new coins for circulation, including the first coinage of Turks and Caicos Islands and a set of decimal coins by Bermuda. A number of countries issued coins under the Food and Agriculture Organization's plan to promote its war against hunger.

In the U.S. the issuance of a dollar coin to honour Dwight D. Eisenhower was held up pending a decision by the Congress on using silver in it. This controversy held up the striking of 1970 regular-issue half-dollars, although the Mint was authorized to strike two million of them for inclusion in the special mint sets of 1970.

The issuance of commemorative and other medals by private concerns continued as techniques were advanced for producing them in high quality at relatively low cost. The Franklin Mint near Philadelphia (not affiliated with the U.S. Mint) was the leader in the field, although others, such as Medallic Art Co. in New York, Presidential Art Medals of Englewood, O., and Wendell's of Minneapolis, were producing a wide variety of medals. Collectors interested in art and historical themes were collecting such works.

During the year two programs of interest to collectors received impetus. One was the formation of an authentication service which was expected to abate the manufacture and sale of false coins. Sponsored by the ANA, the service raised a $50,000 fund to provide facilities for detecting counterfeit and altered coins and, through cooperation with federal agencies, to apprehend the perpetrators.　　(G. B. Sm.)

See also Postal Services.

Philippines

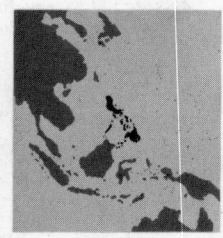

Situated in the western Pacific Ocean off the southeast coast of Asia, the Republic of the Philippines consists of an archipelago of about 7,100 islands. Area: 115,830 sq.mi. (300,000 sq.km.). Pop. (1968 est.): 35,883,000. Administrative capital and largest city: Manila (pop., 1968 est., 1,499,000). Legal capital: Quezon (pop., 1965 est., 545,500). Language: Tagalog or Filipino (official), English, Spanish, and many dialects. Religion: Roman Catholic 84%; Aglipayan 5%; Muslim 5%; Protestant 3%. President in 1970, Ferdinand E. Marcos.

In his state of the nation address to Congress in January, President Marcos referred to the Philippines' balance of payments difficulty as the nation's most pressing problem and described it as having placed the country's economy "in a straitjacket." The national government's deficit the previous year had surpassed $167 million, an increase of more than 165% over that of 1968. The internal debt had reached $764 million late in 1969, while in July 1969 the foreign debt had reached $738 million.

On Feb. 21, 1970, the Central Bank announced a floating rate for the peso as an alternative to devaluation. The peso, formerly traded at 3.90 to $1, was to seek its own level in the foreign market. It was expected to be worth between 5.5 and 6 to $1. The new rate policy was expected to increase the price of imports and make exports worth more in terms of the peso. The resulting cutbacks in imports had an adverse effect upon the nation, however, as they led to shortages of food and clothing.

Corruption in the government and politics was a widely voiced complaint. The 1969 elections, which gave President Marcos an unprecedented second term in office, were followed by reports of fraud, vote manipulation, and terrorism. Government overspending before the elections had taken part of the blame for the economic setback and the weakening of the peso in 1970. Demonstrators voiced the fear that a convention, scheduled for June 1971, to revise the Philippine constitution, would be dominated by Marcos' political allies to such an extent as to ensure his continuance in power.

The first protests were organized by students in January, demanding reform in the political and educa-

UPI COMPIX

A mother feeds one of her children in Manila's poor section where whole families must beg for handouts. A massive study on the problems of family planning was being carried out in the nation, where many families live at poverty levels.

PHILIPPINES

Education. (1966–67) Primary, pupils 5,815,675, teachers 184,938; secondary and vocational, pupils 1,172,695, teachers 31,668; higher (including 34 universities), students 527,284, teaching staff 26,020.

Finance. Monetary unit: peso, with a free rate (Oct. 1970) of 6.43 pesos to U.S. $1 (15.36 pesos = £1 sterling). Gold, SDRs, and foreign exchange, central bank: (June 1970) U.S. $196 million; (June 1969) U.S. $138 million. Budget (1969–70 est.): revenue 3,502,000,000 pesos; expenditure 3,197,000,000 pesos. Gross national product: (1969) 31,740,000,000 pesos; (1968) 28,380,000,000 pesos. Money supply: (June 1970) 4,168,000,000 pesos; (June 1969) 3,525,000,-000 pesos. Cost of living: (Manila; 1963 = 100): (June 1970) 146; (June 1969) 125.

Foreign Trade. (1969) Imports 4,933,000,000 pesos; exports 3,332,000,000 pesos. Import sources (1968): U.S. 32%; Japan 28%; West Germany 6%. Export destinations (1968): U.S. 46%; Japan 34%; Netherlands 5%. Main exports: timber 26%; coconut products 19%; sugar 17%.

Transport and Communications. Roads (1969) 62,203 km. Motor vehicles in use (1968): passenger 232,700; commercial (including buses) 173,300. Railways (state; 1968): 1,026 km.; traffic 894 million passenger-km., freight 117 million net ton-km. Air traffic (1968): 1,320,043,000 passenger-km.; freight 27,404,000 net ton-km. Shipping (1969): merchant vessels 100 gross tons and over 297; gross tonnage 929,317. Telephones (Jan. 1969) 241,496. Radio receivers (Dec. 1966) 639,000. Television receivers (Dec. 1967) 190,000.

Agriculture. Production (in 000; metric tons; 1969; 1968 in parentheses): rice 4,997 (4,445); corn 1,786 (1,733); sweet potatoes (1968) 707, (1967) 708; cassava (1968) 487, (1967) 482; copra (1968) 1,290, (1967) 1,333; sugar, raw value (1969–70) 1,597, (1968–69) 1,612; abaca (1968) 67, (1967) 81; bananas (1968) c. 760, (1967) 781; tobacco 57 (65); rubber 22 (14); pork (1968) c. 295, (1967) 203; timber (cu.m.; 1968) c. 11,500, (1967) c. 10,300; fish catch (1968) 945, (1967) 769. Livestock (in 000; March 1969): pigs c. 6,300; cattle c. 1,700; buffaloes (March 1968) 4,173; goats (March 1968) 624; horses c. 290; chickens c. 69,000.

Industry. Production (in 000; metric tons; 1968): coal 32; chrome ore (oxide content) 161; manganese ore (metal content) 16; copper ore (metal content) 110; iron ore (metal content) 827; gold (troy oz.) 527; silver (troy oz.) 1,511; cement (1969) 2,299; electricity (excluding most industrial production; kw-hr.) 5,644,000.

tional systems. The movement grew rapidly, however, especially after the riots of January 26 and 30. On January 26, President and Mrs. Marcos were pelted with stones and bottles as they left the Congress building in Manila following the president's state of the nation address. The students, along with labour and farmers' groups, were finally dispersed with tear gas.

On January 30, approximately 2,000 demonstrators tried to storm the grounds of Malacanang, the presidential palace. Government forces finally broke up the demonstration in the early morning hours of January 31. Five students were killed, 157 injured, and several hundred arrested. The demonstration had been called to press the allegation of police brutality during the January 26 riot.

The presence of U.S. military bases in the country, long a sore point among nationalists, was also in the demonstrators' list of complaints. A rally to "discuss all the ills of the nation and relate these to the issues of American imperialism, domestic feudalism and the rising fascism of Marcos" was held on February 18 in Manila. From the peaceful demonstration, attended by 25,000, approximately 3,000 militant youths broke off and marched to the U.S. embassy, attacking it with stones and fire bombs. U.S. Marine guards eventually drove them out of the compound with tear gas. The U.S. announced on July 24 that it would withdraw 6,000 of its military personnel from the Philippines.

On March 23 the protest movement had gathered such momentum that an increase in transport fares resulted in rioting in which 90 were injured and thousands of commuters stranded. From March 31 to April 2 riots occurred daily, during which students stoned and overturned vehicles, creating traffic snarls and requiring tear gas squads to disperse them.

Reacting to the demonstrations, President Marcos

assured the people that members of the Nationalist Party, to which he belonged, would not run as delegates to the constitutional convention. Opponents of Marcos among the demonstrators had feared that his supporters would seek election to the 1971 convention so that they could change the constitution and make Marcos eligible for a third term. To quell all doubt, Marcos declared that he would not run for a third term even if the revised constitution allowed it.

In November Pope Paul VI visited Manila, where he was received with great enthusiasm. The visit was marred, however, by an assassination attempt made, during the welcoming ceremonies, by Benjamin Mendoza y Amor Flores, a Bolivian artist.   (RA. PA.)

ENCYCLOPÆDIA BRITANNICA FILMS. *The Philippines: Land and People* (1960).

Philosophy

There was evidence in 1970 that the extreme individualism that had traditionally characterized philosophy was slowly yielding to teamwork and cooperation. Worldwide communication among philosophers and between them and scientists and humanists increased, and joint research projects were becoming common. The growing involvement of philosophy with other disciplines and its continued self-examination and criticism probably had a moderating effect. There was a resurgence of interest in metaphysics, while the techniques of both linguistic and logical analysis were refined. Scholarly and historical interests were high, but the concern for philosophical treatments of contemporary moral and social issues yielded numerous studies. Of special importance was the problem of the relevance of reason to decision and action.

The year was marked by celebrations of the bicentenary of Hegel's birth; international congresses were devoted to this event in Paris, Stuttgart, W.Ger., and East Berlin, as well as special issues of periodicals and a considerable number of other publications. In some countries closer attention was paid to the centenary of Lenin's birth. A congress devoted to his thought was organized by UNESCO in Tampere, Fin.

In January the British Society for Phenomenology published the first issue of its *Journal;* it contained the "Syllabus of the London Lectures" delivered by Edmund Husserl in June 1922, presented by H. Spiegelberg. The second issue was devoted to Jean-Paul Sartre, on the occasion of his 65th birthday. A homage volume, *Durchblicke,* was offered to Martin Heidegger on his 80th birthday, and he published, with Eugen Fink, *Heraklit.*

In logic and the philosophy of science, an excellent résumé of matters under discussion was given in the collective volumes published in 1968 under the direction of R. Klibansky, *Contemporary Philosophy: A Survey.* In the light of studies on induction and quantitative research on problems of scientific methodology, the Synthese Library published first-rate collective volumes: *Induction, Physics and Ethics,* edited by P. Weingartner and G. Zecha; *Induction, Acceptance, and Rational Belief,* edited by M. Swain; *Information and Inference,* edited by J. Hintikka and P. Suppes; and *Philosophical Problems in Logic: Some Recent Developments,* edited by K. Lambert.

In his John Dewey lectures, *Ontological Relativity and Other Essays,* W. V. Quine analyzed the nature of meaning, the meaning of existence, and the nature of natural knowledge. *Margins of Precision* was a compilation of papers on logic and languages by Max Black, which included essays on the theory of language of both Dewey and Ludwig Wittgenstein. Black found areas of agreement in Dewey and Wittgenstein in their opposition to traditional views of logic and meaning, but whereas Wittgenstein "preached the end of all metaphysics," Black saw Dewey as a "metaphysician in the grand manner." Wittgenstein's notes on the problems of knowledge and certainty, composed near the end of his life, were published as *On Certainty. Geometry and Induction* by the French mathematician Jean Nicod was published, with prefaces by Roy Harrod, Bertrand Russell, and André Lalande.

In metaphysics and the theory of knowledge, *The Nature of Philosophical Inquiry,* edited by Joseph Bobik, was a collection of essays by Stephan Körner, Martin Versfel, A. J. Ayer, Stephen Pepper, and O. K. Bowsma arguing the merits of a wide range of conceptions of philosophy. The Oxford philosopher A. J. Ayer examined the method and purpose of philosophy and the relation of philosophical questions to logic and empirical fact in *Metaphysics and Common Sense.*

Defining metaphysics as the study of the relationships between humanity and divinity, and describing it as "the articulation of a path of spiritual experience" and reflections upon that experience, Eliot Deutsch argued that in the depth of his being man is "not different from the divine." Deutsch's *Humanity and Divinity* was a comparative study of metaphysics concerned with both Oriental and Occidental ways of thinking. *Between Philosophy and History* was an argument by Haskell Fain that speculative and analytical philosophy of history are compatible just as narrative and explanation are compatible.

Ethics and social philosophy continued to be an active field. C. Perelman and L. Olbrechts-Tyteca examined the problem of the relationship of reason to action in *The New Rhetoric: A Treatise on Argumentation,* translated by John Wilkinson and Purcell Weaver. They attacked self-evidence as the central dogma of rationalism in their effort to develop a theory that would account for the application of reason to practical decision and action without setting up a dichotomy of the rational and irrational. *Individuality and the New Society,* edited by Abraham Kaplan, was a symposium on youth discontents and the threat to the individual posed by technology and bureaucracy. *The Languages of Criticism and the Sciences of Man,* edited by Richard Macksey and Eugenio Donato, presented the papers of an international symposium at Johns Hopkins University which examined the effect of today's "structuralist" thought on the critical methods of humanistic and social studies.

Scholarly and historical studies included the *Sarva—Darśana—Sangraha* by John C. Plott and Paul D. Mays, a bibliographical guide to the history of philosophy designed to overcome the split between Oriental and Occidental philosophy. In *Jean-Paul Sartre: His Philosophy,* translated by Marina Smyth-Kok, René Lafarge examined Sartre's concepts of nausea, anguish, and bad faith from a Christian standpoint.   (S. M. Mc.; C. H. M. J. W.)

ENCYCLOPÆDIA BRITANNICA FILMS. *Aristotle's Ethics: The Theory of Happiness* (1963); *Athens—The Golden Age* (1963); *Plato's Apology: The Life and Teachings of Socrates* (1963); *Emperor and Slave: The Philosophy of Roman Stoicism* (1965); *The Spirit of Rome* (1965); *The Medieval Mind* (1969).

Photography

A marked trend during 1970 was toward manufacture in the Far East for Western markets. For some time U.S. companies had been licensing production in Japan in order to take advantage of the lower labour costs (a well-known example being some Polaroid cameras). Now, for the first time, the German photographic industry was also looking eastward. Agfa was having some cameras made for it by Minolta, and even Rollei broke with tradition and began to manufacture in Singapore. The wage ratios quoted in the Rollei policy statement were 6:3:1 for Germany, Japan, and Singapore, respectively. This, the firm considered, should allow it to distribute its new single-lens reflex on the export market at a price lower than that of a comparable Japanese product.

Most new products were shown in October at Photokina, the giant trade fair held, at two- or three-year intervals, in Cologne, W.Ger. The changes since 1969 were not great, but they were indicative of definite trends. More roll-film cameras were produced, mostly in the expensive class for professionals or advanced amateurs. Examples were the Fujica G690, a rangefinder camera with interchangeable lenses that took 6 × 9-cm. negatives, and the Mamiya single-lens reflex, producing 6 × 7-cm. negatives and having a revolving back for vertical or horizontal formats. The latter negative size (10 on 120 film), introduced by Linhof and called "Ideal Format," was becoming better known, but the fact that the common enlarger size for a 6 × 6-cm. negative was too small prevented popular acceptance. The Asahi Pentax 6 × 7-cm. single-lens reflex became available for export; it had been heralded over two years earlier, exemplifying the slow rate of acceptance.

Many more cartridge-loading cameras, for 126 or "Instamatic"-size film, were introduced. Most of these were of the "box camera" type, with single-element plastic lenses (of methyl methacrylate) and simple shutters. Electronic shutters, coupled to CdS light cells, were used in the more expensive models, though the combination of poor definition (on large prints) and the expense of sophisticated exposure setting made such models more suitable for the wealthy novice than for the quality-conscious photographer. There were also top-price single-lens reflexes for 126 film, made by famous firms such as Zeiss and Rollei. These had good lenses, but even so the quality of definition was limited by the film flatness and, since 126 cartridges have no proper pressure plate, there was uncertainty in the registration plane. The manufacturers were well aware of this, and investigations were being made by Kodak and Ilford.

No fundamental advances were made in camera design but several small innovations appeared. The trend toward microprism rangefinder spots on focusing screens resulted in the near elimination of the split-image rangefinder, which was more expensive to manufacture. It became more difficult to find new features to add to the modern single-lens reflex with through-the-lens metering, but Ricoh produced a variation by having a waist-level viewing attachment in addition to the usual eye-level system. However, this necessitated the use of a mirror-prism system (Porro prism) instead of the usual type, and the resultant light loss severely diminished the brightness of the screen image.

Increasing numbers of compact cameras for 35-mm. film were produced. The fashion had been set by Rollei about three years previously, closely followed by Petri. Now several firms were producing this type of small, portable camera, though the latest types were not as small as the originals. Another change was the rising popularity of the all-black finish on cameras, as opposed to the conventional bright or satin chrome with black panels. Indeed, several cameras were produced as two models, one chrome and one all black, the latter being considered to look more "professional." The previous drawback to all-black finishes had been their inferior wearing qualities, but the modern types were mainly (though not invariably) better in this respect. A minor change was toward the provision of larger controls; i.e., bigger shutter releases and focusing knobs. With electronic shutters the "release" is really a switch, so the movement could be made as gentle as desired. An interesting novelty was introduced by Canon—the Canodate E, a rangefinder type with an electronic shutter, had a data-printing system that allowed the year, month, and date to be printed on each negative. However, the general trend was for camera systems to become more complex, with greater numbers of accessories, such as motor drives, and a wider range of lenses.

Processes and Equipment. Lens design continued to progress, mainly through the improvement of existing concepts. More firms produced mirror lenses, which gave a long focal length without bulk but had a fixed aperture. Zoom lenses tended to become more compact and the definition continued to improve, though they still could not quite match that of lenses with fixed focal length. The greatest progress was in wide-angle types. The 15-mm. Hologon from Zeiss (an f/8 fixed-focus design with solid glass where the diaphragm would normally be found) gave an angle of 110° with virtually no distortion, and for some time this set the standard at which other firms aimed. In 1970 a 15-mm. lens was announced by Nikon in Japan. Fisheye lenses with quoted angles of 180° became fairly common. The latest introduction, also from Nikon, was a 6.3-mm. f/2.8 fisheye with a quoted angle of 220°, which meant that objects slightly behind the lens were included in the field of view.

LENT BY THE ARTIST, COURTESY, THE MUSEUM OF MODERN ART

Dale Quarterman's photograph construction "Marvella" appeared in the "Photography into Sculpture" exhibition held at the Museum of Modern Art, New York City, April 8–July 5, 1970.

ARTHUR TRESS

"Boy on a Bicycle" by Arthur Tress was included in "The Recreational Potential of the Urban Environment" exhibition at the Sierra Club Gallery in New York City.

KEYSTONE

"In Sian, 500 Kilometres from Peking, in April 1966" by Turkish photographer Goksin Sipahioglu was one of 500 photographs in the exhibition "Woman" at the New York Cultural Center Sept. 2–Nov. 8, 1970.

The greatest advance, which appeared publicly at Photokina, was in lens coating. The almost universally used system involved a thin coating of magnesium fluoride or a similar substance, vacuum deposited on the glass in a thickness corresponding to a fraction of a wavelength of light (obviously, the coating could not be optimum for all colours of light simultaneously). The new technique was based on the use of multiple coatings. The idea was used by Barr & Stroud, Zeiss, and Taylor Taylor & Hobson; Asahi Pentax decided to utilize the technique openly, using the OCLI system. In essence the new system gave more freedom to lens designers, increased light transmission (reducing surface-reflected light to 0.3%), diminished flare, and under certain circumstances could result in better definition of low-contrast objects. Indeed, the difference between multi- and single-coated lenses could be as great as that between single-coated and uncoated optics.

Electronic flashguns continued to evolve. Almost all utilized nickel cadmium batteries in place of the

ELLIOTT ERWITT FROM MAGNUM

A photograph by Elliott Erwitt from an exhibition of his work at the Smithsonian Institution.

previous lead-acid types. The advantage of NiCd types was lighter weight, longer life, greater portability, no maintenance, and simpler charging with no damage from overcharging. The latest introduction was rapid charging. Normally recharging took about 14 hours, but recent developments allowed this to be reduced to about 3 hours or so.

Slide projectors altered little in their primary construction; the fashion was to produce a range, using the same basic body but increasing the price as various refinements were added. For example, the cheapest type might have a simple push-pull carrier for single slides and use a 300-w. main-voltage lamp. In successive stages, a low-voltage lamp, a magazine slide holder, automatic slide changer, and either remote focus control or automatic focus were added, additional features being an automatic timer and facilities for taking a rotary magazine. The latest idea in 1970 was a built-in tape recorder and playback, exemplified by the Agfa 250 AV.

An unexpected development was the Magicube, a flashcube containing four flashbulbs but fired mechanically instead of electrically. The justification for this was the supposedly high rate of failure with the 3-v. batteries used in some cheaper cameras (more expensive types employed a 15- or 22.5-v. battery, firing from a capacitor). The Magicube was ignited when a spring was released as an arm hit an igniter head somewhat like a match head. This acted as the primer to fire a zirconium wire, which burned in an oxygen atmosphere inside the bulb. There was little change in light output, time to peak was a little shorter but not appreciably so, but the price increase of about 25% compared with the previous cube was noticeable. Cameras made to take Magicubes could not employ other kinds of bulbs, and a considerable number of cameras appeared on the market utilizing the new system.

Films did not change appreciably during 1970, though Fuji was introduced in the export market. There was a marked change in the marketing policy of film manufacturers; increasing amounts of film were sold under private labels, with the makers leaving packaging and distribution to others. Examples were Ferrania, owned by 3M, and Ilford, a wholly owned subsidiary of Ciba. Virtually all the Ferrania colour film was sold under private label except for some test marketing in Switzerland; all the Ilford colour material was disposed of in this way, mainly in the U.S.

Photographic chemistry became more stratified. The two main process groups were the conventional developer-fixer types, and the rapid-print processes, where the developing agent is incorporated in the emulsion, to be activated by an alkali at the development stage, followed by stabilization. The combined fixing/development solutions, which had previously showed signs of becoming popular, largely faded from view, mainly because of the lack of control—contrast being "preset" by the solution in conjunction with a particular film—and the lack of hardening of the gelatin, which meant that the films were likely to be mechanically damaged. Moreover, the time saved by the combined processing was lost by the increased drying time necessitated by the swollen emulsion.

In motion-picture photography the previously standard 8 film was virtually eclipsed by the more modern Super 8 size. For a time the Eastern European countries had stayed with the older system, but there were signs that the change was becoming worldwide. In

BRUCE DAVIDSON FROM MAGNUM

One of the photographs from Bruce Davidson's book "East 100th Street." An exhibition of 43 of the photographs was held at the Museum of Modern Art in September 1970.

several cases, motion-picture cameras became smaller and more portable. The trend toward increasingly automated commercial processing techniques continued. A good example was the Colorapid, a processing machine that carried out all the stages automatically and was programmed by a punched card fed into a slot. The whole procedure (perhaps seven stages) could be carried out without any supervision once the film spool was in place, and changing from, say, Kodak to Agfa or Ciba could hardly be more simple.

Trade. World trade in photographic goods in general continued to increase at the same rate as in 1969. The U.K. was an exception; economic restrictions resulted in a smaller rise there than elsewhere although, despite complaints from sections of the retail trade, the overall position was reasonably satisfactory. The abolition of retail price maintenance produced a more fluid price structure, and the small and less enterprising dealers found difficulty in adapting to it. The trade rivalry between Germany and Japan continued, with neither side gaining any great advantage. Some Japanese manufacturers, such as Canon with its new F1, aimed at better quality and a higher price bracket than before, while some German firms made what they described as Japanese-type cameras to sell in the lower price brackets, the Rollei 35-mm. SLR being a good example. Despite this, national tendencies remained, and in general the better German cameras tended to increase in price and quality despite the makers' original intention—as exemplified by the Zeiss Icarex system.

East Germany continued its policy of integrating and rationalizing its production; the obvious ties between Ihagee, which made the Exakta, and Pentacon, which produced the entire range of cameras bearing that name, gave sufficient evidence of this trend. Again, the Meyer lenses (Oreston, etc.) showed strong signs of Zeiss Jena design (the East German firm, as distinct from the West German Zeiss). A recent move by Pentacon was the adoption of the vertical-travel focal-plane shutter employing three blades. This type of construction, pioneered by the Japanese firm of Copal, had a technical advantage over the conventional horizontal-travel style of shutter—which normally, though not invariably, had cloth blinds—in that electronic flash could be synchronized at about 1/125 sec. instead of 1/30 or 1/60 sec.

Other countries produced little of great interest. Various Soviet cameras were made, but apart from the well-known Fed and Zorki ranges there was no serious attempt to export them. China produced cameras that were well finished and consumer oriented, but the design was antiquated and there appeared to be no great desire to export. Switzerland still produced the Alpa SLR and the interesting little Tessina, while Sweden had the famous Hasselblad, but Germany and Japan remained the undisputed centres of the camera manufacturing industry.

Artistic Presentation. Technical expertise was taken for granted, and in many cases the main aim appeared to be novelty in presentation. Increasing use of auxiliary equipment, such as long-focus and wide-angle lenses, resulted in a more flexible approach to pictorial composition, and now that grain-free, sharp prints of large size were comparatively easy to produce, various means of intentionally modifying the image with texture screens and other detail-reducing processes became popular. Manufacturers of photographic printing paper severely curtailed the range of surfaces previously obtainable, preferring to concentrate on the more profitable glossy and stipple lines. Thus the photographer was thrown back on his own resources for means to break up large areas of even tone.

Contrary to the predictions of some firms, colour printing at home did not become more popular. Despite the introduction of three-solution processing and electronic metering with aids to colour balancing, the difficulties and cost deterred most amateurs.

Fashions changed swiftly in some pictorial circles. The use of multifaceted prism attachments, which split the picture into three, four, five, or more replicas of the same scene, was considered somewhat outdated. Much use was made of "twinkler" or "star screen" devices, which produce elongated needles of light emanating from point sources of light—an effect that could be pleasing, especially with a black background.

There was continued experimentation with various systems designed to make electronic recordings of visual data that could be played back through an ordinary domestic television receiver. Progress was insufficient for any commercial exploitation, however.

(V. G. C. B.)

See also Cinema.

Physics

Materials Science. One rapidly expanding topic in materials science at present is the study of composite materials, carbon fibres in particular. After initial announcements (*Nature,* 211:169, 1966; 213:690, 1967) of the preparation of carbon fibres of extremely high Young's modulus (an index of elasticity) and strength equivalent to that of glass fibres, research has been directed toward improving their mechanical properties and reducing production costs.

The carbon fibres initially were produced from synthetic filaments of rayon or polyacrylonitrile (PAN)

WIDE WORLD

Louis Néel
shared the 1970
Nobel Prize for Physics
with Hannes Alfvén.

AUTHENTICATED NEWS
INTERNATIONAL

Scientists at Bell
Laboratories took the first
photograph of the world's
fastest moving object,
a pulse of laser light,
as it passed through
a bottle of water.
A shutter that opens and
closes in 10 trillionths
of a second was used.

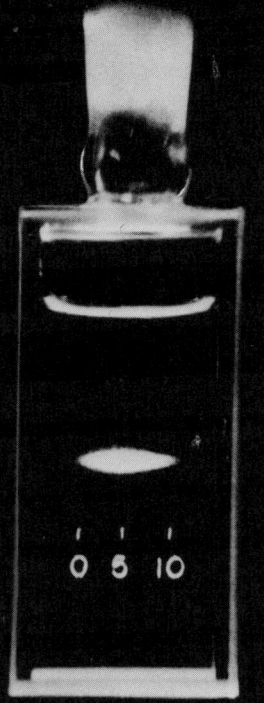

by heat treatments and by stretching up to 300% of original length in rayon or 30% in PAN. This results in small-sized, highly oriented graphite crystallites to produce a fibre with a high Young's modulus (7×10^{12} dynes/cm^2) and a strength of 3.4×10^{10} dynes/cm^2 but with a density of only 1.6; the figures are for PAN (*Nature*, 221:358, 1969).

It has been found that the strength of the carbon fibre can be increased by about 10% if it is bombarded with neutrons (*Nature*, 224:694, 1969). The neutrons displace a small number of atoms in the fibre making slip more difficult. The same report also noted that doping the fibres with boron increased their strength even more significantly, producing the strongest carbon fibre known thus far.

In using carbon fibres to replace metals or plastics, they are embedded in a matrix of some sort. In one novel technique (*Nature*, 227:701, 1970) a resin matrix is used in which the embedded fibres make up 75–80% of the total weight. These composites have a Young's modulus of 2×10^{12} dynes/cm^2 and a strength of 1×10^{10} dynes/cm^2. Unfortunately, above 500° C the material oxidizes rapidly in air and loses about half of its strength in a few hours.

Commercial production of carbon fibres awaited reduction of the high cost of the synthetic rayon or PAN filaments. Toward this end, efforts have been made (*Nature*, 227:947, 1970) to prepare the fibres from crude pitch (asphalt) starter filaments. The resulting carbon fibres have a Young's modulus of 4.4×10^{12} dynes/cm^2 and a strength of 2.6×10^{10} dynes/cm^2, comparable to those made from more expensive starting materials. This was expected to reduce composites considerably.

Lasers. Improvements in laser output to produce increasing levels of power in continuous and pulsed operation were continuing apace. Papers presented at the American Physical Society meeting in Washington, D.C. (*Physics Today,* July 1970), indicate that rapid advances were being made. One report described the use of a rocket engine as a pump for a CO_2 laser; the most powerful thermally pumped gas dynamic laser used in this research produced 60 kw. of multimode power at a wavelength of 10.6 μ, about six times the highest previously reported with the use of electrical pumping on a 200-m. CO_2 laser. At the same meeting it was reported that an 11.5-kw. output was continuously produced (with an efficiency of about 15%) from a CO_2 laser operated at atmospheric pressure, with the gas flowing through the laser tube at a rate of 100–200 m. per sec. This is a development of a recently invented 1-kw. CO_2 gas transport laser (*Appl. Phys. Lett.,* Aug. 1, 1969); the main advantage of this closed-cycle system is that the length of the CO_2 laser can be reduced to 1 m.

A method of pumping a laser from chemical energy also has been developed (*Appl. Phys. Lett.,* 16:55, 1970). The chemical laser is completely self-contained; no external beam of light or outside energy source is required to stimulate the chemical reaction. The excess energy of vibration of hydrogen fluoride molecules produced in the chemical reaction $2F + H_2 \rightarrow 2HF$ is transferred to CO_2 atoms in the gaseous mixture to release this energy as an infrared laser beam. Laser light is produced as long as the correct mixture of chemicals is fed into the device.

A major application of high-powered lasers during the year has been in attempts to initiate nuclear fusion; in particular to trigger off the reaction between two deuterium atoms producing a neutron: $D + D \rightarrow$ $n + He^3$. The aim is to develop practical triggers for thermonuclear-power devices. In one such study (*Phys. Rev.,* 188:300, 1969) a nanosecond pulse of 1 gigawatt from a neodymium-glass laser was used to heat a solid pellet of LiD. On each occasion a powerful burst of neutrons was detected indicating that thermonuclear fusion had taken place. Unfortunately the investigators could not estimate how many neutrons were produced by each pulse of laser light. In another effort (*Phys. Rev.,* 1B:821, 1970) using a Nd-glass laser of 4-gigawatt peak power and 10-nanosecond pulse width, thermonuclear fusion was produced in a deuterium sample; 100–500 neutrons were estimated to have been emitted per laser shot.

Theoretical considerations (*Phys. Rev. Lett.,* 24:92, 1970) have led investigators to predict the production of 10^6 neutrons per square millimetre of target for an absorbed laser energy of 500 joules per square millimetre. Energy of this order of magnitude could be achieved in at least two ways: one would use a Nd-glass laser with peak power of 10^3 gigawatts and with a pulse width of a few nanoseconds; an alternative method would employ a pulsed CO_2 laser with peak power of 10 gigawatts and with a pulse width of 1 microsecond. Both of these lasers were expected to be available shortly. Another alternative seriously being considered is to heat the deuterium with an intense pulse from a Nd-glass laser and then to heat the plasma so formed with a pulse from a high-power CO_2 laser. A major difficulty in employing the long CO_2 pulse is that the plasma would have to be contained magnetically for the duration of the pulse; this would require a magnetic field intensity that exceeds a megagauss.

Before these experiments are ever completely successful, two primary obstacles will have to be overcome: the relatively long delay in energy transfer from laser beam to electrons to deuterium nuclei; and the rapid dissipation of neutrons in the plasma.

High-Energy Physics. A team of researchers led by A. Ghiorso (*Phys. Rev. Lett.,* 24:1498, 1970) reported the discovery of element 105. They proposed that the new substance be named hahnium in honour of Otto Hahn (1879–1968), co-discoverer of nuclear fission. Ghiorso suggested that his results cast doubt on an earlier report of producing element 105 by G. N. Flerov of the Soviet Union. Flerov responded that the Soviets were "deeply convinced" of the reliability of their discovery.

Superconductivity. Recent measurements (*Phys. Lett.,* 31A:349, 1970) on an alloy of niobium, germanium, and aluminum, $Nb_{0.8}(Al_{0.75} Ge_{0.25})_{0.2}$, indicate that it is a superconductor with a transition temperature T_c of 20.7° K and an upper critical field H_{c2} of 410 kilogauss at 4.2° K. These are the highest values of T_c and H_{c2} yet recorded; the previous highest H_{c2} at 4.2° K was 220 kilogauss in Nb_3Sn. If the new alloy can be fabricated into wire form, it should initiate another generation of superconducting magnets. T_c now is of the order of the boiling point of liquid hydrogen (20.4° K); perhaps this achievement will open the way to reducing the cost of practical applications of the phenomena of superconductivity.

General. The 1970 Nobel Prize for Physics was shared by Hannes Alfvén and Louis Néel for their work in magnetohydrodynamics and in antiferromagnetism and ferrimagnetism. (*See* BIOGRAPHY.)

(S. B. P.)

See also Astronautics; Astronomy; Chemistry; Electronics.

Poland

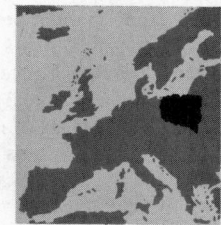

A people's republic of Eastern Europe, Poland is bordered by the Baltic Sea, the U.S.S.R., Czechoslovakia, and East Germany. Area: 120,756 sq. mi. (312,757 sq.km.). Pop. (1970 est.): 32,727,100. Cap. and largest city: Warsaw (pop., 1970 est., 1,289,000). Language: Polish. Religion: predominantly Roman Catholic. First secretaries of the Polish United Workers' (Communist) Party in 1970, Wladyslaw Gomulka and, from December 20, Edward Gierek; chairmen of the Council of State, Marshal Marian Spychalski and, from December 23, Jozef Cyrankiewicz; chairmen of the Council of Ministers (premiers), Jozef Cyrankiewicz and, from December 23, Piotr Jaroszewicz.

The year 1970 ended dramatically for Poland: in foreign relations an era of reconciliation with West Germany was foreshadowed; at home, major cities of the Baltic coast witnessed a violent eruption of popular discontent similar to that of Poznan in 1956. Both the 1956 and 1970 revolts had far-reaching political consequences: that of 1956 brought about Gomulka's (*see* BIOGRAPHY) return to power; that of 1970 swept him away.

The establishment of normal and friendly relations with West Germany on the basis of the existing territorial status quo had been one of the chief aims of Poland's foreign policy, but until 1969 the response from Bonn always was negative. A radical change took place in October 1969 when the new Social Democratic chancellor, Willy Brandt, declared that the West German government was ready to open negotiations with Poland on issues suggested by Gomulka in May 1969. The Polish government acquiesced to this proposal and on Feb. 5, 1970, Polish-West German talks began in Warsaw.

Six preparatory meetings took place, alternately in Warsaw and Bonn, before the final negotiations started in the Polish capital on November 3 between the two foreign ministers, Walter Scheel and Stefan Jedrychowski. The resultant treaty was signed in Warsaw on December 7 by Brandt and Premier Cyrankiewicz. In this historic document the West German government declared that the existing German-Polish border line, determined at Potsdam on Aug. 2, 1945, by the governments of the United States, Great Britain, and the Soviet Union and running from the Baltic Sea to Czechoslovakia along the Oder and Neisse rivers, "forms the western state frontier of Poland." The West German government "affirms the inviolability [of this frontier] now and in the future." (*See* GERMANY: *Special Report.*)

The basic cause of the Polish explosion at home was the new economic mechanism included in the five-year development plan for 1971–75. Adopted by the Communist Party's plenary meeting of May 19–20, 1970, this new system was aimed at ending the wasteful era of extensive growth and beginning a more intensive and selective regime, controlled by a system of economic incentives. The previous policy had resulted in the hasty building of new steelworks, power stations, and industrial plants. Manpower had been signed on freely, and goods produced without due care as to their quality or cost. By intensive growth the socialist planners meant the use, wherever possible, of existing plants with their installed machinery, saving power and raw materials, and fully employing shift labour without overmanning. Selective growth implied —with the balance of trade in mind—increasing production of such goods as machine tools, electrical and electronic equipment, and chemical products.

The May plenary meeting adopted a resolution setting forth the following principles of the new system: (1) wage raises in every enterprise must be directly related to technological advancement; (2) raises for manual and white-collar workers must be even; (3) the norms defining the economic incentives must hold steady for the whole five-year period.

A regulation announced by the government on December 12 raised prices on 46 items of basic foodstuffs, fuel, and clothing by 10 to 30%, while 40 other items—household goods, television sets, and automobiles—became cheaper. This measure was deeply resented by the majority of the Polish people, especially because it came just 12 days before Christmas. On December 14, at a session of the Central Committee, Gomulka justified the new prices, but at the same time bloody riots started in Gdansk, Gdynia, and Szczecin where large Polish shipyards are located. Three days later Premier Cyrankiewicz told the Polish people by radio and television that rioters had been setting fire to public buildings and looting shops, and that police and army units had been authorized to use

POLAND

Education. (1967–68) Primary, pupils 5,706,-270, teachers (full time) 201,382; secondary, pupils 306,135, teachers (full time) 15,044; vocational, pupils 1,398,665, teachers (full time) 53,637; teacher training, pupils 59,787, teachers (full time) 3,928; higher (including 18 universities), students 288,788, teaching staff 25,565.

Finance. Monetary unit: zloty, with an official parity of 4 zlotys to U.S. $1 (9.60 zlotys = £1 sterling) and a tourist rate of 24 zlotys to U.S. $1 (57.60 zlotys = £1 sterling). Budget (1968 est.): revenue 329.7 billion zlotys; expenditure 326.2 billion zlotys. National income (net material product): (1968) 669 billion zlotys; (1967) 605.6 billion zlotys. Cost of living (1963 = 100): (2nd quarter 1970) 108; (2nd quarter 1969) 106.

Foreign Trade. (1969) Imports 12,838,600,-000 zlotys; exports 12,566,100,000 zlotys. Import sources: U.S.S.R. 37%; East Germany 10%; Czechoslovakia 8%; U.K. 6%. Export destinations: U.S.S.R. 36%; East Germany 9%; Czechoslovakia 9%. Main exports (1968): machinery 28%; coal and coke 12%; transport equipment 9%; iron and steel 7%; textiles and clothing 6%; meat and products 5%.

Transport and Communications. Roads (1969) 309,042 km. (including 139 km. expressways). Motor vehicles in use (1969): passenger 423,081; commercial 248,004. Railways: (1968) 26,628 km. (including 3,206 km. electrified); traffic (1969) 36,204,000,000 passenger-km., freight 95,024,000,000 net ton-km. Air traffic (1969): 504 million passenger-km.; freight 7,-149,000 net ton-km. Shipping (1969): merchant vessels 100 gross tons and over 484; gross tonnage 1,536,384. Telephones (Dec. 1968) 1,650,896. Radio receivers (Dec. 1968) 5,598,000. Television receivers (1968) 3,389,000.

Agriculture. Production (in 000; metric tons; 1969; 1968 in parentheses): wheat 4,714 (4,670); rye 8,167 (8,520); barley 1,939 (1,494); oats c. 2,660 (2,891); potatoes 44,925 (50,817); sugar, raw value (1969–70) 1,527, (1968–69) 1,706; rapeseed c. 610 (712); linseed c. 60 (65); dry peas (1968) 61, (1967) 83; apples (1968) 746, (1967) 537; onions (1968) 334, (1967) 306; tobacco 85 (83); butter c. 187 (198); cheese c. 213 (214); beef and veal (1968) 528, (1967) 499; pork (1968) 1,291, (1967) 1,313; fish catch (1968) 407, (1967) 339. Livestock (in 000; June 1969): cattle 11,-049; horses 2,633; pigs 14,337; sheep 3,329; chickens c. 131,000.

Industry. Index of industrial production (1963 = 100): (1969) 164; (1968) 151. Production (in 000; metric tons; 1969): coal 135,010; brown coal 30,865; coke (1968) 14,415; crude oil 438; natural gas (cu.m.) 3,918,000; electricity (kw.-hr.) 60,062,000; manufactured gas (cu.m.; 1968) 6,581,000; iron ore (30% metal content) 2,820; pig iron 7,027; crude steel 11,291; aluminum (1968) 93; zinc (1968) 203; copper (1968) 44; lead (1968) 49; cement 11,831; sulfuric acid 1,517; nitrogenous fertilizers (N content; 1968) 759; superphosphates (1967) 1,569; passenger cars (units) 50; commercial vehicles (units) 46; cotton fabrics (m.) 841,000; woolen fabrics (m.) 99,000; rayon and synthetic fabrics (m.) 121,000. Merchant vessels launched (100 gross tons and over; 1969) 423,000 gross tons. New dwellings completed (1968) 189,260.

arms to restore order. The premier also said that from 10 to 20 had been killed and hundreds wounded.

The riots caused a plenary session of the Central Committee to be assembled in Warsaw on December 20. At the meeting, Gomulka and four of his close associates (Spychalski, Zenon Kliszko, Ryszard Strzelecki, and Boleslaw Jaszczuk) resigned from the 12-man Politburo. Edward Gierek, from 1957 first secretary of the party organization in the country's richest province and a Politburo member from March 19, 1959, succeeded Gomulka as first secretary of the party. On December 23 Cyrankiewicz, premier since February 1947 (except for a period between November 1952 and March 1954 when he was deputy premier), resigned and was elected chairman of the State Council, succeeding Spychalski. Jaroszewicz, deputy premier from 1952, was elected the new premier.

Broadcasting to the Polish people, Gierek said that he would get rid of the "ill-considered economic policies" of the past, and revise the 1971–75 plan in consultation with the workers. There would be no cancellation of the price decree of December 12, but small wage increases to the lowest paid workers were expected partly to offset the higher prices.   (K. Sм.)

Police

Membership of the International Criminal Police Organization (Interpol) in 1970 numbered 105 national police administrations. Reports to the General Assembly, held in Brussels in October, concerned international drug traffic in 1969; currency counterfeiting; theft in ports, airports, and frontier posts; and the unlawful seizure of aircraft and ships. It was unanimously decided that the full resources of Interpol should be available to combat hijacking.

The second Interpol European Regional Conference was held at the General Secretariat in Paris, April 20–24. Twenty European countries sent representatives, and five non-European countries and the Council of Europe sent observers. Interpol was represented at the fifth UN Congress on the Prevention of Crime and the Treatment of Offenders, held in Kyoto, Jap., in August.

As of June 1, the General Secretariat's records comprised 1,451,750 general records of named individuals, 83,781 fingerprint cards, and 6,618 photographs of specialized criminals. Subscribers to the organization's *Counterfeits and Forgeries* numbered 5,713, and during the year June 1969–June 1970 the counterfeit department examined 456 counterfeits and drew up technical reports on 83 genuine notes for comparison purposes.

Europe. *United Kingdom.* During 1970 the Home Office ran a national crime prevention campaign, using extensive advertising on television and in the national and local press. As in previous campaigns, the advertising developed the theme of cooperation with the police, with special reference to reporting suspicious incidents and the protection of property.

The number of indictable offenses known to the police in England and Wales during 1969 was 1,488,-638. At the end of 1969 the strength of the police service in England and Wales was 91,762. General restrictions on increase in police manpower were removed early in 1970, and by the end of the year the strength of the service was about 93,500.

An interim increase in police pay of 8½% was effective from January 1. The normal biennial pay review took place in the autumn, with new rates effective from September 1. The standard workweek was reduced from 42 to 40 hours in April. On September 29 the Police Federation asked the government's Police Council to grant an increase in the starting salary for a constable from £900 ($2,160) to £1,434 ($3,442) plus pay raises ranging from 35 to 56% for higher ranks.

Following the recommendations of an advisory committee headed by Lord Hunt, whose report was published on Oct. 10, 1969, the Northern Ireland government announced several measures to reorganize the province's police during 1970. The controversial Ulster Special Constabulary (the B Specials) was disbanded on April 30, being replaced by the Ulster Defence Regiment (part of the British Army), which became operational on April 1. On the same day a new volunteer force, the Royal Ulster Constabulary Reserve, also came into operation.

As of June 15, the Royal Ulster Constabulary (RUC) had a new district organization and a new rank structure. The commanding officer, previously known as inspector general, became chief constable. On June 19 the governor of Northern Ireland appointed Brig. Sir Ian Fraser to be chairman of the 20-member Police Authority, formed to take over administrative control of the RUC from the Ministry of Home Affairs.

France. A ten-year plan was drawn up by the Ministry of the Interior for the reinforcement of the strength of city police. The 1969 and 1970 budgets of the ministry provided for a marked increase in police strength. There was further progress in the electronic processing of police files. The campaign against drug trafficking, in application since August 1969, showed appreciable results. Close collaboration was established with the U.S. police, and the Franco-U.S. narcotics committee met every three months.

On March 3, 1970, about 125 policemen were injured during a five-hour clash with over 300 leftist students at Nanterre University in a Paris suburb. On May 27–28 Maoist student rioting swept the Latin Quarter in Paris and the police occupied a university building to keep the rioters from smashing the laboratory equipment. During June the Federation of Police Unions, many of whose members were dissatisfied with working conditions, threatened to follow the Swedish example (see *Scandinavia,* below) and report sick en masse.

West Germany. During 1970 there were numerous commitments of police forces at mass meetings and demonstrations in several large cities. This put a great strain on the police because innumerable offenses of the sort likely to be committed by demonstrators were punishable under existing legislation. The incidents furnished grounds for reviewing and mitigating some provisions of the Penal Code.

Radical spokesmen in West Berlin launched particularly vehement attacks on a draft law that would allow police to use truncheons, pistols, tear gas, submachine guns, hand grenades, and machine guns. Up to 1970 no firearms had been used.

Scandinavia. The central Records Bureau of the National Swedish Police Board began its activities on July 1, 1970, when records from the various police departments were transferred to the new office. The 1967 police inquiry, which presented its conclusions in June 1970, proposed that the number of police districts in Sweden be reduced from 119 to 90. In an effort to get higher pay, about 500 Stockholm police reported themselves sick for 50 hours during the weekend of June 6–7.

On Jan. 1, 1970, the total strength of the Danish police was 7,821; during 1969 there were 352 new recruits, and 137 left the force. The number of offenses reported to the police in 1970 was 210,000, an increase of about 7%. Sexual offenses, however, continued to decrease, by nearly 7%.

In Norway the police investigated more than 60,000 crimes in 1969; about 21,000 were cleared up. Almost 60% of the accused persons were under 20 years old.

The Netherlands. About 30 people were injured, three of them by police bullets, in a seven-hour battle between policemen and hippies on Aug. 24, 1970, in what was described as the worst riot in Amsterdam's history. The riot stemmed from a municipal ban against overnight sleeping on the steps of the national war memorial in front of the royal palace, for some time a favourite haunt of hippies. On August 31 police forced the surrender of about 25 rebels, exiles from the Indonesian island of Amboina in the Moluccas, who had killed a Dutch policeman and stormed the Indonesian embassy in The Hague.

U.S.S.R. The Supreme Soviet enacted legislation affecting the corrective labour institutions of the Ministry of the Interior. The act included sections on prisoners' rights and duties and the powers of the institutions. The Soviet militia acquired a new social function, akin to that of the probation officer.

On September 1 the government announced its decision to reestablish a Union-Republican Ministry of Justice, "with corresponding agencies in the localities," as part of an intensified drive against crime, particularly the embezzlement of state property.

Oceania. *Australia.* In a year of social unrest, demonstrations and other forms of public protest resulted in numerous confrontations between police and citizens. The majority of these demonstrations, however, did not result in violence, and no instance was reported in mainland Australia of recourse by police to such crowd-control devices as armed riot squads, gas, or water cannon. In the Australian Trust Territory of New Guinea, however, a massive force of specially trained and armed riot police was used to evict natives squatting on government land in the Gazelle Peninsula of New Britain, the main island in the Bismarck Archipelago. Both state and federal governments moved to enact legislation granting police additional powers to deal with protesters and increasing penalties for a wide range of public-order offenses.

All police forces reported increases in crime in 1970, although the lack of accurate and reliable statistics continued to make assessment of the state of crime difficult. Increases in armed robberies and burglaries appeared particularly significant. The number of persons apprehended for drug offenses rose sharply, the majority of charges relating to possession and sale of marijuana.

Conditions of service for Australian police improved somewhat in 1970 following favourable salary awards in a series of arbitration hearings. A serious setback to police morale and public confidence in police occurred in Victoria in 1970 following a lengthy public inquiry into alleged police involvement in an abortion racket. Criminal charges were brought against a number of police, including the head of the homicide squad. The Victorian government also appointed Sir Eric St. Johnston, chief inspector of constabulary in the U.K., to investigate the operations of the state's police force and to make recommendations for its reform.

North and South America. *United States.* Police personnel strength increased in 1969. Federal Bureau of Investigation (FBI) Uniform Crime Reports revealed that as of Dec. 31, 1969, U.S. cities had an average of 2.2 police employees per 1,000 inhabitants, an increase of 5% over the 2.1 rate in 1968. State police and highway-patrol organizations had a total of 52,812 employees in 1969, an increase of 4% over 1968. *The Municipal Year Book 1970* stated that for 974 reporting cities with a population of 71,531,000, expenditures in 1969 for police department salaries and wages (civilian and uniformed) totaled $1,490,-147,000, a per capita expenditure of $20.83. The median annual police starting salaries, as of July 1, 1969, ranged from $6,318 in cities of 10,000–25,000 population to $7,490 in cities of 250,000–500,000.

Inadequate manpower to handle increasing demands for police services presented serious problems in many cities. In New York City, 50 of the 106 patrolmen assigned to diplomatic posts were to be withdrawn, and protection was to be eliminated at 17 of 37 locations housing foreign interests. Research studies conducted in New York City's 20th precinct revealed that on an average day a patrolman spent six hours patrolling the streets and one hour responding to various calls for service, of which 40 minutes were devoted to noncriminal activities and 20 minutes to criminal matters. The single specific job to which the officer devoted most of his time—15%—was taking care of sick people.

The recruitment of qualified men continued to present a major problem to many departments. In July it was revealed that in New York City the average IQ score for police recruits in 1969, 98.2, was the lowest in recent years. Some departments, such as Los Angeles', would not appoint men with IQ scores under 110. To obtain college-graduate police officers, as recommended by the President's Commission on Law Enforcement and Administration of Justice in 1967, the New York City Police Department announced in February 1970 that more than 125 upperclassmen from such colleges as Princeton, Yale, Harvard, and Union Theological Seminary had been recruited to take the examination to become policemen. In September, however, it was charged that many of the men had gone to Washington, D.C., because of an absence of vacancies in New York. In several cities, organizations of black policemen refused to help recruit black officers, saying that first they "wanted to shape up the department so blacks will be treated fairly when they get in."

U.S. Atty. Gen. John N. Mitchell announced in January 1970 that about $21 million in planning grants and $182,750,000 for action programs had been granted to states by the Law Enforcement Assistance Administration, established under the 1968 Omnibus Crime Control and Safe Streets Act. Seven regional offices were opened by LEAA to assist state and local governments. A nationwide conference on law enforcement education and training was held by LEAA in Jacksonville, Fla., on Feb. 1–3, 1970. Also in compliance with the Omnibus Crime Control Act, Mitchell filed an annual report of all electronic eavesdropping by federal agencies. The report revealed that only 31 electronic eavesdropping surveillances, in 15 cities, were carried out in 1969. Six conducted in Newark, N.J., were instrumental in the arrests of 55 persons on gambling conspiracy charges.

In March Mitchell asked Congress for legislation making it possible to obtain an order from a federal

POPPERFOTO FROM PICTORIAL PARADE

On patrol is one of London's first two mounted policewomen. They patrol streets, parks, and open spaces to watch over mothers and young children.

judge, commissioner, or magistrate requiring suspects in criminal cases to submit to fingerprinting, hand-writing analysis, medical tests, and identification line-ups to determine if they should be charged with a federal crime. One effect of the proposed legislation would be to deal with law enforcement problems created by an April 1969 Supreme Court decision that fingerprints taken from suspects who had been rounded up without probable cause could not be used subsequently in court. In a civil rights suit filed on behalf of three youths detained for six hours by Phil-adelphia police and then forced to appear in a lineup, U.S. Judge Harold K. Wood ruled in September that no citizen who is not a suspect in a crime may be re-quired to participate in a lineup unless he acknowl-edges in writing that he is aware there are no charges against him, that he has not been arrested, and that he is free to leave at any time.

Between 1962 and 1969 assaults on police officers increased 144%. A record high of 86 officers were killed by felonious criminal action in 1969, compared with an average of 53 killed each year between 1960 and 1968. Violence against policemen in 1970 included sniper attacks, terrorist bombings, and assaults, and by August 56 officers had been killed in line of duty. The heads of patrolmen's associations reported that older men were retiring promptly at the end of 20 years' service because of the rising danger involved and that calls for assistance were being handled more slowly because of the fear of ambush.

In New York City on January 25 two police officers responding to a call in Harlem were shot from am-bush, and three hours later a patrolman in Queens was shot at twice by two men in a car; a transit po-liceman handing a summons to a drifter found smok-ing in the subway was shot and killed on February 28; a 23-year-old patrolman was fatally stabbed on May 28 as he sat in a patrol car outside a junior high school; and within a 24-hour period on September 11–12 three New York City policemen were the targets of violence in separate incidents. On June 9 the New York City police headquarters was bombed, and on July 5 Molotov cocktails were found under five police cars in a fenced-in parking area.

In Chicago a policeman, Kenneth G. Kaner, was making out a report in his squad car on the city's South Side on June 19 when he was shot in the head twice with blasts from a sawed-off shotgun and killed. On July 17 two Chicago policemen, James Severin and Anthony Rizzato, were killed by sniper gunfire as they walked across a field near the Cabrini-Green public housing project, where they were assigned to a program intended to improve community relations. On August 13 James A. Alfano became the fourth Chi-cago policeman to be fatally shot from ambush in less than two months. Subsequently, seven members of the Black P. Stone Nation street gang were indicted for Alfano's murder.

In Omaha, Neb., on August 17, a suitcase exploded, killing Patrolman Larry D. Minard and wounding seven other policemen who had responded to an emer-gency call to a vacant house. Two Nebraska leaders of an offshoot of the Black Panther Party were charged with the booby-trap murder. In Detroit, Mich., on June 28, one police officer was seriously wounded and two were slightly injured in an ambush on the city's East Side; two members of a black extremist group were charged with attempted murder. On Detroit's West Side, on October 24, a nine-hour confrontation be-tween 100 policemen and black militants was touched

off by the shotgun slaying of a black patrolman, Glen Smith, while he was on his way to aid policemen answering a complaint that a sidewalk was being blocked.

In February 1970 a bomb detonated in a police station parking lot in Berkeley, Calif., resulted in the injury of two police officers and the destruction of three cars, and an explosion inside a San Francisco police station killed one officer and wounded five others. Subsequently, within a two-month period in the San Francisco Bay area, three policemen were shot and killed while making out traffic tickets.

Brazil. On July 24, 1970, Pres. Emílio G. Médici condemned the vigilante groups known as "death squads," believed to include policemen, which had killed 11 petty criminals in São Paulo and 3 in Rio de Janeiro the preceding week. Médici's public acknowl-edgment of the existence of the squads came after two leading criminal-court judges in São Paulo had linked the squads to the police on a court record and demanded action by the government. A local council of the bar association known as the Order of Lawyers of Brazil delivered a protest on Feb. 26, 1970, to Justice Minister Alfredo Buzaid, charging that a law-yer in Brasília had been tortured during a recent in-terrogation by federal policemen. This was the first publicly documented accusation of police torture of political prisoners in Brazil in 1970. Previously, how-ever, written reports smuggled out of Brazil had ac-cused military and police authorities of systematically torturing political prisoners. In August 1970 Roman Catholic bishops and priests of Maranhão State in northeastern Brazil protested that a young Brazilian priest was tortured by police for two days after his arrest.

Argentina. Deputy Inspector Carlos Benigno Bal-buena of the federal police was allegedly one of four persons involved in an attempt to kidnap Yuri Pivovarov, 40-year-old assistant commercial attaché at the Soviet embassy in Buenos Aires, on March 29, 1970. In May rioting in Córdoba, Rosario, and other Argentine cities resulted in numerous injuries and arrests of over 1,500 persons. On May 23 political police closed Argentina's largest publication, the daily newspaper *Crónica,* charging it had falsely reported the death of a student in clashes with police in the city of Córdoba.

Uruguay. Allegations that the Uruguayan police had regularly tortured political prisoners prompted a three-month congressional investigation and caused a government scandal. The growing harshness of po-lice methods was attributed to efforts to crush a group of left-wing urban guerrillas known as the Tupamaros, which had kidnapped two close friends of Pres. Jorge Pacheco Areco and, on April 5, perpetrated the big-gest robbery in Uruguayan history, carrying off a safe containing 441 lb. of gold valued at $250,000. The po-lice captured thousands of Tupamaro suspects and scores of arms caches. On some occasions the Tupa-maros recaptured their weapons and freed prisoners, thus infuriating the police and the government. On April 13 the head of Uruguay's police intelligence, Hector Moran Charquero, was shot to death by ma-chine gunners, presumably Tupamaros, as he drove to work through Montevideo.   (V. W. P.; X.)

See also **Crime; Law; Prisons and Penology; Race Re-lations.**

ENCYCLOPÆDIA BRITANNICA FILMS. *Canada's Royal Cana-dian Mounted Police* (1960); *The Policeman* (Third Edition, 1966); *Our Community Services* (1969).

THE "NEW YORK TIMES"

Springfield, Mass., is the largest city in which both the fire and police departments cooperate in the use of the "911" emergency number system.

Political Parties

The following table is a general world guide to political parties. All countries that were independent on Dec. 1, 1970, are included; there are a number for which no analysis of political activities is given.

Parties are included in most instances only if represented in parliaments (in the lower house in bicameral legislatures), but the figures in the last column of the table do not necessarily add up to the total number of seats in parliament because independents and certain small political groupings are sometimes omitted. The date of the most recent general election follows the name of the country.

The code letters in the affiliation column show the relative political position of the parties within each country; there is, therefore, no entry in this column for single-party states. There are obvious difficulties involved in labeling parties within the political spectrum of a given country. The key chosen is as follows: F—fascist; ER—extreme right; R—right; CR—centre right; C—centre; L—non-Marxist left; SD—social-democratic; S—socialist; EL—extreme left; and K—communist.

The percentages in the column "Voting strength" indicate proportions of the valid votes cast for the respective parties, or the number of registered voters who went to the polls in single-party states.

COUNTRY AND NAME OF PARTY	Affiliation	Voting strength	Parliamentary representation
Afghanistan (1969)			
Royal government with an elected House of the People (Wolesi Jirga)	—	—	216
Albania (1970)			
Albanian Labour (Communist)	—	100%	214
Algeria			
Military government since June 19, 1965	—	—	—
Andorra (1969)			
No parties	—	—	24
Argentina			
Military government since June 28, 1966	—	—	—
Australia (1969)			
Country (Conservative)	R	...	20
Liberal	CR	...	46
Democratic Labor (DLP)	C	...	—
Australian Labor (ALP)	L	...	59
Austria (1970)			
Freiheitliche Partei Österreichs	R	5.5%	5
Österreichische Volkspartei	C	44.7%	79
Sozialistische Partei Österreichs	SD	48.4%	81
Barbados (1966)			
Barbados National Party	R	...	2
Democratic Labour Party	C	...	14
Barbados Labour Party	L	...	8
Belgium (1968)			
Volksunie (Flemish)	R	9.8%	20
Parti pour la Liberté et le Progrès	CR	20.9%	47
Parti Social-Chrétien	C	31.7%	69
Parti Socialiste Belge	SD	28.0%	59
Parti Communiste Belge	K	3.3%	5
Bhutan			
No parties	—	—	130
Bolivia			
Military government since Sept. 26, 1969	—	—	—
Botswana (1969)			
Botswana Democratic Party	C	...	24
Botswana People's Party	L	...	3
Botswana National Front	EL	...	3
Botswana Independent Party	L	...	1
Brazil (1970)			
Aliança Renovadora Nacional	CR	...	220
Movimento Democratico Brasileiro	L	...	90
Bulgaria (1966)			
Bulgarian Communist / Agrarian Union / Nonparty } Fatherland Front	—	99.8%	416
Burma			
Military government since March 2, 1962	—	—	—
Burundi			
Military government since Nov. 28, 1966	—	—	—
Cambodia			
Military government since Nov. 1, 1970	—	—	—

COUNTRY AND NAME OF PARTY	Affiliation	Voting strength	Parliamentary representation
Cameroon (1969)			
Union Nationale Camérounaise	—	...	50
Canada (1968)			
Social Credit	R	0.7%	—
Progressive Conservative	CR	31.4%	73
Liberal	C	45.5%	154
Rassemblement des Créditistes	C	4.8%	14
New Democratic	L	16.7%	22
Central African Republic			
Military government since Jan. 1, 1966	—	—	—
Ceylon (1970)			
United National	R	34.2%	17
Sri Lanka Freedom	CR	33.0%	91
Federal (Tamil)	C	4.4%	13
Lanka Sama Samaja (Trotskyist)	S	7.9%	19
Communist	K	3.0%	6
Others	—	...	5
Chad (1969)			
Union pour le Progrès du Tchad	—	...	75
Chile (1969)			
Partido Nacional	R	20.9%	34
Partido Radical	C	13.4%	24
Partido Demócrata-Cristiano	C	31.1%	55
Partido Socialista Chileno	S	12.8%	15
Partido Comunista de Chile	K	16.6%	22
China, People's Republic of			
Communist (Kungchan-tang)	—	—	—
China (Taiwan), Republic of			
Nationalist (Kuomintang)	—	—	773
Colombia (1970)			
Alianza Nacional Popular	R	...	72
Partido Conservador	R }	...	} 90
Partido Liberal	C }		
Congo (Kinshasa, 1970)			
Mouvement Populaire de la Révolution	—	98.3%	420
Congo (Brazzaville)			
Military government since September 1968	—	—	—
Costa Rica (1970)			
Partido de Liberación Nacional	R	...	32
Partido de Unificación Nacional	C	...	22
Acción Socialista	L	...	2
Cuba			
Partido Comunista de Cuba	—	—	—
Cyprus (1970)			
Greek-Cypriot			
Progressive Front	R	...	7
Unified Party	C	...	15
Democratic Centre Union	L	...	2
Independents	—	...	2
Progressive Party of Working People	K	...	9
Turkish-Cypriot			
National Solidarity	—	...	15
Czechoslovakia (1964)			
Communist / Socialist } National Front / People's	—	99.9%	300
Dahomey			
Civilian Presidential Council replaced military government on May 1, 1970	—	—	—
Denmark (1968)			
Conservative	R	20.4%	37
De Uafhaengige (Independents)	R	0.5%	—
Venstre (Agrarian)	C	18.6%	34
Centre (Liberal)	C	1.3%	—
Radical-Liberal	C	15.0%	27
Social Democratic	SD	34.0%	62
Socialist People's	S	6.1%	11
Communist	K	1.0%	—
Left Socialists		2.0%	4
Dominican Republic (1966)			
Partido Reformista	R	...	48
Partido Revolucionario Dominicano	C	...	26
Ecuador (1968)			
Alianza Popular	R	...	...
Izquierda Democrática	L	...	...
El Salvador (1970)			
Partido de Conciliación Nacional	R	60.0%	34
Partido Demócrata Cristiano	C	28.8%	16
Partido Popular Salvadoreño	L	1.8%	1
Equatorial Guinea (1968)			
Movimiento por Unión Nacional de Guiné Ecuadorial (MUNGE)			
Idea Popular de Guiné Ecuadorial (IPGE) }	—	...	35
Movimiento Nacional por Liberación de Guiné Ecuadorial (MONALIGE)			
Ethiopia (1965)			
Imperial government with an elected Yeheg Memria (lower chamber)	—	—	250
Fiji (1966)			
Alliance Party (mainly Fijian)	—	...	22
National Federation Party (mainly Indian)	—	...	9
Independents (mainly Chinese)	—	...	3
Finland (1970)			
Kansallinen Kokoomus Puolue (Cons.)	R	18.2%	37
Svenskapartiet (Swedish Party)	R	5.4%	12
Keskusliitto (Centre, ex-Agrarian)	C	18.2%	37
Christian League	C		1
Kansan Puolue (Liberal)	C	5.4%	8
Rural Party	L	10.5%	18
Sosialidemokraatinen Puolue	SD	23.8%	51
People's Democratic League	K	18.1%	36

COUNTRY AND NAME OF PARTY	Affili-ation	Voting strength	Parlia-mentary represen-tation
France (1968)			
Extreme right	ER	0.2%	—
Union des Démocrates pour la République (Gaullists)	CR	38.1%	292
Independent Republicans	CR	5.1%	61
Centre Démocrate	C	10.8%	33
Fédération de la Gauche Démocrate et Socialiste	L	18.0%	57
Parti Socialiste Unifié	EL	4.1%	10
Parti Communiste Français	K	22.1%	34
Gabon (1969)			
Parti Démocratique Gabonais	—	—	—
Gambia, The (1966)			
People's Progressive Party	C	...	24
United Party	L	...	8
German Democratic Republic (1967)			
Sozialistische Einheitspartei			
Christlich-Demokratische Union			
National-Demokratische Partei (National Front)	—	98.82%	434
Liberal-Demokratische Partei			
Demokratische Bauernpartei			
Germany, Federal Republic of (1969)			
Christlich-Demokratische Union	R	46.1%	242
Freie Demokratische Partei	C	5.8%	30
Sozialdemokratische Partei Deutschlands	SD	42.7%	224
Ghana (1969)			
People's Action Party	R	...	2
National Alliance of Liberals	CR	...	29
Progress Party (Busia)	C	...	105
United Nationalist Party	...	...	2
Greece			
Military government since April 21, 1967	—	—	—
Guatemala (1970)			
Movimiento de Liberación Nacional	R	...	31
Partido Institucional Democrático	CR	42.9%	19
Democracia Cristiana Guatemalteca	C	21.5%	5
Partido Revolucionario	L	35.6%	...
Guinea (1968)			
Parti Démocratique de Guinée	—	—	75
Guyana (1968)			
People's National Congress	C	...	30
United Force	L	...	4
People's Progressive Party	EL	...	19
Haiti			
Presidential dictatorship since 1957	—	—	—
Honduras (1965)			
Partido Nacional	R	...	35
Partido Liberal	C	...	29
Hungary (1967)			
Hungarian Socialist Workers' (Patriotic			
National Peasant Party People's	—	99.7%	349
Smallholders' Party Front			
Iceland (1967)			
Independence (Conservative)	R	37.5%	23
Progressive	C	28.1%	18
Social Democratic	SD	15.7%	9
United People's Socialist	K	17.6%	10
India (1967)			
Jan Sangh (Hindu Nationalist)	ER	...	35
Swatantra (Freedom)	R	...	42
Dravida Munnetra Kazhagam	R	...	25
Indian National Congress	C	...	281
Praja Socialist	SD	...	13
Samyukta Socialist	S	...	23
Communist (pro-Soviet)	K	...	23
Communist (pro-Chinese)	K	...	19
Indonesia			
Military government since Oct. 1, 1965	—	—	—
Iran (1967)			
Iran Novin (New Iran)	R	...	180
Mardom (People's) Party	C	...	20
Pan-Iranian Party	C	...	5
Iraq			
Military governments since 1958	—	—	—
Ireland (1969)			
Fianna Fail (Sons of Destiny)	C	...	75
Fine Gael (United Ireland)	C	...	50
Labour	L	...	18
Israel (1969)			
Free Centre	ER	1.2%	2
Gahal (Herut-Liberal Alignment)	C	21.7%	26
National Religious	C	9.7%	12
Agudat Israel	C	3.2%	4
Poalei Agudat Israel	C	1.8%	2
Independent Liberal	C	3.2%	4
State List (Ben-Gurion)	L	3.1%	4
Maarakh (Labour Alignment)	L	46.2%	56
Two Arab lists	L	...	4
Haolam Hazé (Avnery)	L	1.2%	2
Communist (Maki or pro-Israel)	K	1.2%	1
Communist (Rakah or pro-Arab)	K	2.8%	3
Italy (1968)			
Movimento Sociale Italiano	F	4.5%	24
Partito Democratico Italiano di Unitá Monarchica	R	1.3%	6
Partito Liberale Italiano	CR	5.8%	31
Partito Democrazia Cristiana	C	39.1%	266
Partito Socialista Italiano	SD	14.5%	91
Partito Socialista Italiano di Unitá Proletaria	EL	4.5%	23
Partito Comunista Italiano	K	26.9%	177
Südtiroler Volkspartei	—	...	3

COUNTRY AND NAME OF PARTY	Affili-ation	Voting strength	Parlia-mentary represen-tation
Ivory Coast (1970)			
Parti Démocratique de la Côte d'Ivoire	—	...	100
Jamaica (1967)			
Jamaica Labour Party	L	...	33
People's National Party	L	...	20
Japan (1969)			
Komeito	CR	10.91%	47
Liberal-Democratic	CR	47.63%	300
Democratic Socialist	SD	7.74%	32
Socialist	S	21.44%	90
Communist	K	6.81%	14
Jordan			
Royal government, no parties	—	—	60
Kenya (1969)			
Kenya African National Union	—	—	171
Korea, North (1967)			
Korean Workers' (Communist) Party	...	100%	300
Korea, South			
Democratic Republican Party	R	...	130
New Korea Party	C	...	44
Taejung Dang (Party of the Masses)	EL	...	1
Kuwait			
Princely government	—	—	30
Laos			
Royal government; pro-Communist Neo Lao Hak Sat party controls area bordering North Vietnam	—	—	—
Lebanon (1969)			
Chamber of Deputies elected by universal suffrage according to the proportional division between Christians and Muslims	—	—	99
Lesotho (1970)			
Constitution suspended Jan. 30, 1970, following the apparent defeat of the ruling National Party in the Jan. 27 general election.	—	—	—
Liberia (1968)			
True Whig Party	—	...	41
Libya			
Military government since Sept. 1, 1969	—	—	—
Liechtenstein (1970)			
Vaterländische Union	CR	...	8
Fortschrittliche Burgerpartei	C	...	7
Christlich-Soziale Partei	C	...	
Luxembourg (1968)			
Parti Chrétien-Social	CR	35.3%	21
Parti Libéral	C	16.6%	11
Parti Ouvrier Socialiste	SD	32.3%	18
Parti Communiste	K	15.5%	6
Malagasy Republic (1970)			
Parti Social-Démocrate	C	...	104
Parti du Congrès de l'Indépendance de Madagascar (AKFM)	L	...	3
Malawi (1964)			
Malawi Congress Party	CR	...	50
Malawi Constitutional Party	L	...	3
Malaysia			
Malaya (1969)			
Federal Alliance Party	R	...	66
Panmalayan Islamic Party	R	...	12
Gerakan Rakyat Malaysia	C	...	8
Democratic Action (Chinese)	L	...	13
People's Progressive Party	K	...	4
Sarawak (1970)			
Federal Alliance Party	R	...	10
Opposition groups	L	...	14
Sabah (1970)			
Federal Alliance Party	R	...	6
Opposition groups	L	...	10
Maldives (1965)			
Government by the Didi family	—	...	54
Mali			
Military government since Nov. 19, 1968	—	—	—
Malta (1966)			
Nationalist Party	R	...	28
Malta Labour Party	SD	...	22
Mauritania (1965)			
Parti du Peuple Mauritanien	—	92%	40
Mauritius (1967)			
Independence Party (Indian-dominated)	C	...	39
Parti Mauricien Social-Démocrate	L	...	23
Mexico (1970)			
Partido Acción Nacional	CR	13.8%	20
Partido Revolucionario Institucional	C	84.4%	178
Partido Auténtico de la Revolución Mexicana	L	0.9%	5
Partido Popular Socialista	S	0.5%	10
Monaco (1968)			
Union Nationale et Démocratique	—	...	18
Mongolia (1967)			
Mongolian People's Revolutionary Party	—	99%	295
Morocco (1970)			
Independents (pro-government)	CR	...	159
Popular Movement	C	...	60
Istiqlal	C	...	8
National Union of Popular Forces	L	...	1
Others		...	12

COUNTRY AND NAME OF PARTY	Affiliation	Voting strength	Parliamentary representation
Nauru (1968)			
No political parties	—	...	18
Nepal			
Royal government since December 1960	—	—	—
Netherlands (1967)			
Staatkundig Gereformeerde Partij	R	2.01%	3
Boerenpartij (Farmers' Party)	R	4.77%	7
Anti-Revolutionaire Partij	CR	9.90%	15
Christelijk Historische Unie	CR	8.15%	12
Katholieke Volkspartij	C	26.51%	42
"Democraten '66"	C	4.46%	7
Volkspartij voor Vrijheid en Democratie	C	10.74%	17
Partij van de Arbeid	SD	23.55%	37
Pacifistisch Socialistische Partij	S	2.68%	4
Communistische Partij	K	3.61%	5
New Zealand (1969)			
National (Conservative)	CR	...	44
Labour Party	L	...	40
Nicaragua (1967)			
Partido Liberal Nacionalista (Somoza)	R	...	36
Partido Conservador Tradicionalista	R	...	15
Partido Demócrata Cristiano	C	...	2
Partido Liberal Independenta	C	...	1
Niger (1970)			
Parti Progressiste Nigérien	—	...	50
Nigeria			
Military governments since Jan. 15, 1966	—	—	—
Norway (1969)			
Høyre (Conservative)	R	19.4%	29
Kristelig Folkeparti	CR	9.4%	14
Senterpartiet (ex-Agrarian)	C	10.6%	20
Venstre (Liberal)	C	9.3%	13
Arbeiderpartiet (Labour)	SD	46.7%	74
Sosialistisk Folkeparti	S	3.5%	—
Norges Kommunistiske Parti	K	1.0%	—
Oman			
Sultanate	—	—	—
Pakistan (1970)			
People's Party of West Pakistan	C	...	81
Awami League of East Pakistan	L	...	151
Panama			
Civilian-military government since Oct. 11, 1968	—	—	—
Paraguay (1967)			
Partido Colorado (Stroessner)	R	69.4%	80
Partido Liberal Radical	C	21.5%	29
Partido Liberal	C	6.2%	8
Partido Revolucionario (Febrerista)	SD	2.8%	3
Peru			
Military government since Oct. 3, 1968	—	—	—
Philippines (1969)			
Partido Nacionalista	R	...	...
Partido Liberal	CR	...	...
Poland (1969)			
Polska Zjednoczona Partia Robotnicza			255
Zjednoczone Stronnictwo Ludowe	—	97.6%	117
Stronnictwo Demokratyczne			39
Nonparty			49
(Front of National Unity)			
Portugal (1969)			
Acção Nacional Popular	—	...	130
Rhodesia (1970)			
Rhodesian Front (European)	R	70%	50
Centre Party (mainly African)	C	10%	7
National People's Union (African)	L	...	1
Others (elected by councils of chiefs)		...	8
Romania (1969)			
Partidul Comunist Romîn	—	99.75%	465
Nonparty (People's Front)			
Rwanda (1965)			
Parmehutu Party	—	...	47
San Marino (1969)			
Partito Democratico-Cristiano	CR	...	27
Partito Social-Democratico	SD	...	11
Partito Socialista	S	...	7
Partito Communista (pro-Moscow)	K	...	14
Partito Comunista (pro-Peking)	K	...	1
Saudi Arabia			
Royal government	—	—	—
Senegal (1968)			
Union Progressiste Sénégalaise	—	...	80
Sierra Leone (1967)			
All People's Congress	—	...	48
Sierra Leone People's Party	—	...	12
Singapore (1968)			
People's Action Party	C	...	58
United People's Party	EL	...	—
Somalia			
Military government since Oct. 21, 1969	—	—	—
South Africa (1970)			
Nationalist Party	R	...	117
United Party	C	...	47
Progressive Party	L	...	1
Southern Yemen			
National Liberation Front	—	—	—
Spain (1967)			
Movimiento Nacional	—	...	564
Sudan			
Military government since May 25, 1969	—	—	—
Swaziland (1968)			
Imbokodvo Party	...	...	...
Sweden (1970)			
Moderata Samlingspartiet (ex-Höger)	R	11.5%	41
Centerpartiet (ex-Agrarian)	CR	19.9%	71
Folkpartiet (Liberal)	C	16.2%	58
Socialdemokratiska Arbetarepartiet	SD	45.3%	163
Vänsterpartiet Kommunisterna	K	4.8%	17
Switzerland (1967)			
Conservative Christian-Social	R	...	45
Evangelical People's	R	...	3
Liberal Democratic	CR	...	6
Farmers, Artisans, and Middle Class	C	...	21
Radical Democratic	C	...	49
Independents	C	...	16
Social Democratic	SD	...	51
Communist (Partei der Arbeit)	K	...	5
Syria			
Baath and military government	—	—	—
Tanzania (1970)			
Tanganyika African National Union (elected)	C	...	120
Zanzibar Afro-Shirazi Party (nominated)	L	—	52
Thailand			
Royal and military government	—	—	—
Togo			
Military government since Jan. 13, 1967	—	—	—
Tonga (1969)			
Legislative Assembly of seven nobles, seven ministers, and seven elected delegates	—		21
Trinidad and Tobago (1966)			
People's National Movement	C	...	24
Democratic Labour Party	L	...	12
Tunisia (1969)			
Destourian Socialist Party	—	—	101
Turkey (1969)			
Turkish Justice	R	56.9%	257
Republican Nation's	R	1.3%	6
Republican People's	C	31.8%	144
Reliance (breakaway from RPP)	C	3.3%	15
Union	C	1.8%	8
New Turkey	C	1.3%	6
Nationalist Action (Peasants)	L	0.2%	1
Turkish Workers'	EL	0.4%	2
Uganda			
Uganda People's Congress	—	...	...
Union of Soviet Socialist Republics (1970)			
Communist Party of the Soviet Union	—	99.74%	767
United Arab Republic (1968)			
Arab Socialist Union	—	...	350
United Kingdom (1970)			
Conservative and Unionist	R	46.4%	330
Liberal	C	7.4%	6
Labour	L	43.0%	287
Others	—	...	7
United States (1970)			
Republican	CR	...	180
Democratic	C	...	255
Upper Volta (1970)			
Union Démocratique Voltaique	CR	...	37
Parti du Regroupement Africain	C	...	12
Mouvement de Libération Nationale	L	...	6
Uruguay (1967)			
Partido Nacional (Blanco)	R	39.6%	41
Partido Colorado	C	49.8%	50
Partido Demócrata Cristiano	C	3.0%	3
Frente Izquierdista de Liberación	K	5.7%	5
Venezuela (1968)			
Cruzada Cívica Nacional	ER	11.4%	21
Unión Republicana Democrática	R	9.6%	17
Frente Nacional Democrático		2.6%	5
Fuerza Democrática Popular	C	5.5%	10
Comitado Organización Política Electoral Independiente (COPEI; Social Christians)	C	25.4%	57
Acción Democrática	C	28.0%	68
Movimiento Electoral del Pueblo	L	14.5%	27
Unión para Avanzar (Communist)	K	2.8%	5
Vietnam, North (1964)			
Lao Dong (Communist Party)	—	...	366
Vietnam, South (1967)			
National coalition	—	...	137
Western Samoa (1970)			
No political parties	—	...	45
Yemen			
Republican regime since November 1967	—	—	—
Yugoslavia (1969)			
League of Communists of Yugoslavia / Socialist Alliance of the Working People	—		670
Zambia (1968)			
United National Independence Party	—	...	81
African National Congress	—	...	23
Independents	—	...	1

(K. Sm.)

Political Science

Political scientists from throughout the world gathered in Munich, W.Ger., from Aug. 31 to Sept. 5, 1970, for the eighth World Congress of Political Science, convened by the International Political Science Association (IPSA). Attendance at the congress was large: 920 participants, as against 750 at the seventh World Congress (held in Brussels in 1967) and hardly more than 500 at the fifth and sixth congresses (Paris, 1961, and Geneva, 1964). A substantial proportion of delegates came from countries in Asia, Africa, and Latin America, showing that political science was gaining recognition as an academic field of research and teaching in countries where academic and political circumstances had long impeded its progress. Many delegates showed great concern, however, at reports concerning the fate of political science and individual political scientists in several countries where much progress had been achieved previously, such as Greece, Czechoslovakia, and Brazil.

The congress had on its agenda four topics for plenary sessions: quantitative and mathematical methods in political science; the history of political thought: Hegel and Lenin; the church as a political institution; and models and methods in the comparative study of nation-building. In addition, 15 "specialist meetings" were held on the following subjects: European integration; the comparative study of local politics; food and politics; psychology and politics; recent trends in political theory; political finance; biology and politics; the theory of international relations; comparative political recruitment; governmental organization and elite formation in Europe; new approaches to the study of social structure and voting behaviour; political attitudes and opinions of young people; political opposition; political decision-making; and political modernization.

Nearly 200 contributions were written and circulated, and many participants found it difficult to discuss so many in a meaningful way. It was generally agreed that for international congresses to retain their usefulness as intellectual confrontations, new procedures and methods of organization must be found. The ninth World Congress, to be held in 1973 in Montreal, was expected to serve as a testing ground for many new ideas.

No new scientific trends emerged at the Munich congress. The papers and the discussions confirmed that the high level of methodological sophistication reached in most Western countries was not going to be reached rapidly in most of the other countries, where inadequate training and research facilities, the strength of traditional approaches to the subject matter, and, quite often, governmental indifference or hostility to independent political inquiry were hampering progress. The search for greater relevance in the content of studies as opposed to methodological refinement, eloquently expressed by many junior political scientists and some very senior ones in West Germany, Great Britain, and the United States, was not demonstrated as much in the completed research as in private conversations or in criticism of the prevailing trends.

Meeting on the occasion of the congress, the council of IPSA, composed of delegates of 33 national associations of political science, made policy decisions for the following three years. The council elected unanimously a new president—Stein Rokkan, of the University of Bergen, Nor., a leading figure in the field of comparative politics—and also elected a new executive committee. Great concern was expressed at the prospect of UNESCO's discontinuing its support to international scholarly associations.

A new venture in international scientific cooperation was announced at the Munich congress, and attracted great interest: the creation, by eight universities and research institutions, of a European Consortium for Political Science Research, designed to improve the level of information about current research and to provide training at an advanced level. A grant from the Ford Foundation supplementing the member institutions' contributions was made to help the consortium until 1975; it was hoped that by that year it would have a membership of 70–80 schools and research organizations. The chairman of the board of the consortium in 1970 was Stein Rokkan; its executive director was Jean Blondel (University of Essex, Eng.).

Political science in the U.S. continued to be affected by current political events. The previous year had witnessed the failure of the attempt made by the "caucus for a new political science" to gain control of the American Political Science Association (APSA) so as to encourage the development of "a new political science, devoted to radical social criticism and fundamental social change." At the mail ballot conducted in October and November 1969, Robert E. Lane, of Yale University, presented by the APSA nominating committee, was elected president for 1970–71 by 5,474 votes as against 2,816 for Christian Bay of the University of Alberta, the candidate of the caucus.

The reluctance to transform APSA into a political action group thus expressed by most of its members did not mean, however, that APSA's officers and membership were indifferent to political developments. On May 14 a telegram recommending "an immediate and clear commitment to a rapid and orderly withdrawal of all American Armed Forces from Indochina to be substantially underway by December, 1970 and to be completed by July, 1971" was sent to Pres. Richard Nixon by Karl W. Deutsch and Robert Lane, president and president-elect of APSA, and by all six past presidents after 1964. Many political scientists made their opposition to the war in Vietnam and to the Cambodian intervention known to President Nixon and to his advisers, especially to their colleague Henry Kissinger.

A sample survey of opinion among college and university teachers of political science conducted in mid-May by a group of leading scholars produced striking results. Three-fourths of the respondents polled disapproved of the administration's action in Cambodia, over four-fifths thought it was a mistake to have sent combat troops into Vietnam, and two-thirds anticipated a constitutional crisis in the United States if the war continued at its present pace.

(SE. H.)

ENCYCLOPÆDIA BRITANNICA FILMS. *Political Parties* (1952); *Presidential Elections* (1952); *The Presidency—Search for a Candidate* (1970).

Political Security:
see Intelligence Operations

Polo:
see Sporting Record

Populations and Areas

World population reached an estimated 3,672,000,000 in mid-1970, a gain of about 72.6 million over the previous year. This represented a continued growth rate of 2% annually, which meant that the planet's population would double in 35 years if the present trend continued. During the year there were 123.4 million births and 50.8 million deaths. The net addition to the population was 1.4 million per week, 199,014 a day, 8,292 an hour, and 138 a minute. In the period from July 1, 1965, to July 1, 1970, the world grew by a record 343 million people.

The growth of human numbers was not evenly distributed, however. The rich nations continued to grow slowly, at rates of 1% annually or less. The poorest countries, on the other hand, were growing at rates of 2 to 3%, suggesting that they would double their populations in from 24 to 35 years. Oddly enough, the fastest growing country was an exception to the rule. The small, oil-rich sheikhdom of Kuwait was adding to its population at a rate of 8.3% a year, the result of immigration, an extremely high birthrate (61.2 per 1,000), and an extremely low death rate (6.2 per 1,000). If this trend continued, Kuwait would double its 733,000 population in nine years. However, with a per capita gross national product of $3,490, Kuwait had the resources to handle population growth.

Costa Rica was also growing rapidly, but without the influence of immigration. Its population was increasing by 3.8% annually, which could mean doubling in 19 years. In contrast to Kuwait, however, Costa Rica's per capita GNP was $400. In many ways this Central American nation typified the rapidly growing less developed nations. It had a "young" population: about 48% of its people were under 15, in contrast to 30% in the U.S. and 21% in Sweden. Thus its growth potential was much higher than in the "older countries" of Europe and North America or Japan and Israel in Asia. At the other end of the scale were East Germany and Hungary, which were increasing by only 0.3 and 0.4%, respectively. East Germany, with an older population attributed to the loss of youth to West Germany, had a death rate that equaled its birthrate: each was 14.3 per 1,000. Some emigrants were returning to the country, but if the current growth pattern continued, it would take 233 years for East Germany to double its population.

As of 1970, the fastest growth was in Latin America, where people were being added at an average annual rate of 2.9%. The 1970 population was estimated at 293 million. Average birthrates were about 38 and average death rates, 9. Africa, however, had the greatest growth potential. It had the highest vital rates in the world—average birthrates of 47 and high death rates averaging 20. The introduction of improved medical care to Africa would result in an immense increase in the rate of growth, which in 1970 was 2.6%. Within Africa were countries whose birthrates were at the upper physiological limits of reproduction. Dahomey's estimated birthrate, for example, was 54, and Niger, Sudan, and Rwanda each had 52. Guinea had the highest death rate in the world, 40, and Dahomey, Burundi, and Cameroon each had an estimated rate of 26. In most of these countries a high percentage of the population was under 15; the average for the continent was 44%. They also had high infant mortality rates, suggesting that between one-tenth to one-quarter of infants died before they were one year old. In Dahomey the infant mortality rate was 259 per 1,000 live births. In the U.S. it was 20.8 per 1,000 live births and in Norway, 13.7.

Because of increased concern over the implications of a population boom, national birth-control efforts were mounted in a number of the less developed nations of Africa and Asia, some with strong backing from the national governments. In the Latin-American countries, because of the Roman Catholic Church's official opposition to artificial methods of birth control, such programs were proceeding cautiously and quietly.

Low birthrates in the developed countries were the product of decisions by individual families to have fewer children and were not a matter of government policy. Birthrates in these countries ranged from 13.4 in Luxembourg and 16.3 in Poland and in England and Wales to 23.3 in Romania and 26.1 in Israel. Birthrates in the U.S. and the Soviet Union were moderately low, 17.7 and 17.2, respectively. Both countries were growing by 1% annually, and at that rate their populations could double in 70 years.

China, the country with the world's largest population (827 million people), was growing at a rate of 1.8% annually, which meant that its population could double in 39 years. India had 537 million people and the potential for adding an equal number in 27 years if its 2.6% growth rate continued. The next ranking nations were the Soviet Union, 242 million; the U.S., 205 million; Indonesia, 121 million; Pakistan, 114 million; Japan, 103 million; and Brazil, 91 million.

Of the world's largest nations, the richest—the U.S., Japan, and the Soviet Union—were growing most slowly. All had per capita GNPs of approximately $1,000 or more. They would double their populations in no less than 63 years (Japan) and no more than 30% of their populations were under 15 years of age. Among the poorer nations the doubling of population would occur in a quarter of a century or less: per capita GNP was often below $250: and almost one-half the population was under 15.

Preliminary returns from the U.S. decennial census, taken on April 1, 1970, suggested that the nation's population had risen by 25 million since 1960. First reports, which did not include Americans overseas and members of the armed forces, indicated 200 million people, and the final figure was expected to be about 205 million. The fastest growth was reported in the far Western states, Florida, Alaska, Maryland, Delaware, New Hampshire, Hawaii, Connecticut, and New Jersey.

The population trends of the post-World War II period were accentuated as Americans continued to move out of rural areas, small towns, and large, older cities and into suburban areas within large metropolitan centres. Preliminary indications were that suburbia had grown by 28%, or 2½ times faster than the U.S. as a whole. In 1970 about 40% of the nation's popu-

continued on page 607

Table I. The Ten Largest Nations by Area and by Population*

Rank		Area in sq.mi.	Rank		Population
1	U.S.S.R.	8,600,350	1	China	827,000,000
2	Canada	3,851,809	2	India	536,984,000†
3	China	3,691,501	3	U.S.S.R.	241,748,000
4	United States	3,615,210‡	4	United States	204,765,770
5	Brazil	3,286,470	5	Indonesia	121,089,000
6	Australia	2,967,909	6	Pakistan	114,188,612
7	India	1,232,560	7	Japan	103,012,811
8	Argentina	1,072,157	8	Brazil	90,840,000
9	Sudan	967,491	9	Nigeria	66,174,000
10	Algeria	919,590	10	Germany, West	61,194,600

*Areas are latest official data available; populations are 1970 estimates.
†1969 estimate.
‡Excludes Great Lakes waters and territorial sea, 94,485 sq.mi.

Table II. World Census Data

POLITICAL UNIT	Year of census	ENUMERATED POPULATION Total	Male	Percent urban*	AGE DISTRIBUTION 0 to 15	16 to 45	46 and over	ECONOMICALLY ACTIVE Total	Agriculture	Mining and manufacturing
Afars & Issas	1964	82,100	...	57.4	...	...	...	...	...	...
Albania	1960	1,626,315	834,384	30.9	...	...	...	730,800	...	...
Algeria	1966	11,833,126	6,079,900	...	5,947,800	4,387,700	1,744,800	2,335,200	1,300,000	183,500
American Samoa	1970	27,769†	14,450	28.0	13,145‡	10,865‡	2,980‡	14,195	1,218	3,674
Angola	1960	4,830,449†	2,459,015	10.6	2,011,378‡	2,177,631‡	641,440‡	1,421,966	944,716	26,508
Antigua	1960	54,060†	25,230	60.1	23,154	20,964	9,942	16,873	12,564	4,084
Argentina	1960	20,008,945	10,034,544	...	5,772,043§	10,486,674§	3,663,094§	7,599,071	1,460,541	1,959,041
Australia	1966	11,550,462	5,816,359	83.2	3,392,488	4,873,899	3,284,073	4,856,455	...	1,368,468
Austria	1961	7,073,807	3,296,400	50.1	1,660,615	2,729,599	2,683,593	3,369,815	767,604	1,093,046
Bahama Islands	1963	130,220†	63,485	24.0‖	57,452¶	51,924¶	20,844¶	51,948	5,882	...
Bahrain	1965	182,203†	99,384	20.1	83,667	80,589	17,947	50,935	4,348	7,185
Barbados	1960	232,327	105,519	40.3	88,882‡	88,636‡	54,809‡	85,040	22,440	13,468
Belgium	1961	9,189,741	4,496,860	66.4	2,333,846	3,543,729	3,312,166	3,512,463	253,922	1,326,732
Bermuda	1960	42,640	21,233	9.6	14,199	18,179	9,470	19,498	309	322
Botswana	1964	543,105	264,535	...	242,424	204,797	80,198	250,678	227,009	1,800‖
Brazil	1960	70,119,071†	35,010,717	46.3	29,931,481¶	32,976,869¶	7,210,721¶	22,651,263	11,697,798	3,364,232
British Honduras	1960	90,505	44,659	53.7	40,369	34,615	15,521	26,029	8,833	3,329
British Solomon Islands	1959	124,076	65,550	2.3	64,940	43,960	16,140	8,000	3,061	2,508
British Virgin Islands	1960	7,338	3,930	12.1	3,793	2,737	808	2,128	629	107
Brunei	1960	83,877	43,676	43.6	39,109‡	33,059‡	11,709‡	24,830	8,317	5,171
Bulgaria	1965	8,227,866	4,114,167	46.4	2,112,364	3,789,130	2,326,372	4,267,793	1,891,398	1,124,885
Cambodia	1962	5,740,115	2,880,780	16.0	2,513,300‡	2,381,215‡	845,600‡	...	...	...
Canada	1966	20,014,880	10,054,344	73.6	6,591,757‡	8,325,686‡	5,097,437‡	6,458,156	648,910	1,101,553
Canal Zone	1960	42,122†	23,278	31.9	15,204¶	19,888¶	7,030¶	17,085	336	...
Cape Verde Islands	1960	199,661	94,027	23.2	99,023♀	69,816♀	29,358♀	105,570	42,387	1,294
Cayman Islands	1960	8,511†	3,974	41.4	3,020	3,515	1,976	3,132	...	...
Ceylon	1963	10,624,507	5,503,000	18.8	4,616,920	4,408,550	1,564,590	2,542,920	1,272,800◊	258,170
Channel Islands Guernsey	1961	47,099	22,718	33.3	11,262‡	17,410‡	18,427‡	...	...	...
Jersey	1961	63,550	30,715	...	12,534	25,643	25,373	30,696	3,259	2,028
Chile	1960	7,374,115	3,612,807	68.2	3,075,036	3,062,143	1,236,936	2,388,667	662,379	519,974
Christmas Island (Australian)	1966	3,381	2,151	...	...	...	...	...	...	...
Colombia	1964	17,484,508	8,614,652	52.8	8,155,529□	7,022,627□	2,306,508□	5,134,059	2,427,059	81,279
Costa Rica	1963	1,336,274†	668,957	34.5	636,665‡	516,395‡	183,214‡	395,273	194,309	46,459
Cyprus	1960	573,566†	281,983	35.9	221,656‡	226,612‡	125,298‡	241,823	93,287	37,718
Czechoslovakia	1961	13,745,577†	6,704,674	47.6	3,960,752	5,370,682	4,414,143	...	608,000‖	1,282,000‖
Denmark	1965	4,767,597	2,362,000‖	77.1	1,215,000‖	1,957,000‖	1,596,000‖	2,251,000‖	...	...
Dominica	1960	59,916	28,167	25.6	26,802‡	21,599‡	11,515‡	22,477	11,693	2,553
Dominican Republic	1960	3,047,070	1,535,820	30.1	1,440,900‡	1,218,440‡	387,730‡	820,710	504,820	58,890
Ecuador	1962	4,476,007	2,236,476	36.0	2,014,505	1,838,160	623,342	1,442,591	800,390	215,617
El Salvador	1961	2,510,984	1,236,728	38.5	1,176,744	1,011,819	322,421	807,092	486,213	104,227
Equatorial Guinea	1960	245,989	132,293	...	...	...	...	...	...	...
Faeroe Islands	1966	37,122	...	...	...	...	...	...	...	...
Falkland Islands	1962	2,172	1,195	49.4	568°	1,134°	470°	930	359	...
Fiji	1966	476,727	242,747	33.4	232,826	190,543	53,112	125,809	656,921	10,451
Finland	1960	4,446,222†	2,142,263	38.4	1,338,991	1,831,849	1,275,382	2,033,268	720,817	444,516
France	1968	49,654,556†	24,196,528	70.0	11,790,960‡	20,655,544‡	17,208,052‡	19,961,852	3,131,320	7,903,324
French Guiana	1961	33,295†	16,288	75.1	12,127¶	14,296¶	6,872¶	11,981	3,273	...
French Polynesia	1962	84,550	43,106	16.7	45,232	34,591	3,643	25,593	9,484	5,715
Gabon	1960–61	444,264†	204,698	...	135,574	210,611	98,079	311,959	153,414	21,512
Gambia, The	1963	315,486	160,849	8.8	118,586‡	155,834‡	41,066‡	160,000‖	135,000‖	2,500‖
Germany, East	1964	17,011,931†	7,751,862	72.9	4,262,941	6,338,075	6,410,915	7,657,786	1,267,257	3,140,721
Germany, West	1961	56,174,826†	26,413,362	77.8	12,184,784	22,935,570	21,054,478	26,527,328	3,587,000	12,908,000
Ghana	1960	6,726,815	3,400,270	23.1	2,996,506‡	2,894,238‡	836,071‡	2,723,026	1,581,331	282,168
Gibraltar	1961	21,785†	10,436	100.0	5,456	9,336	6,993	9,292	...	783
Gilbert and Ellice Islands	1968	53,517	26,404	14.9	20,323‡	17,130‡	7,187‡	13,121	8,601	496
Greece	1961	8,388,553	4,091,894	43.3	2,392,514	3,710,437	2,285,602	3,638,601	1,960,446	510,087
Greenland	1965	39,600	20,354	...	19,091	15,752	4,757	13,248	3,651	300
Grenada	1960	88,677	40,660	8.2	42,268‡	30,472‡	15,937‡	15,219	10,895	2,657
Guadeloupe	1967	312,724†	159,760	45.8	139,346‡	126,281‡	59,412‡	...	...	...
Guam	1960	67,044	39,211	...	28,014	31,709	7,321	26,304	411	535
Guatemala	1964	4,287,997	2,172,456	33.6	1,949,395‡	1,786,505‡	551,519‡	1,362,669	...	...
Guyana	1960	560,330	279,128	15.5	259,228‡	215,228‡	85,874‡	174,730	59,790	32,371
Honduras	1961	1,884,765	939,029	23.2	940,827	730,153	213,785	567,988	379,125	45,779
Hong Kong	1966	3,716,400	1,880,870	86.9	1,571,440	1,493,630	643,850	1,454,730	27,970	557,300
Hungary	1961	9,961,044	4,804,043	39.7	2,691,036	4,096,392	3,173,616	5,312,831	1,872,730	1,378,987
Iceland	1966	196,933	...	...	...	...	...	...	...	...
India	1961	439,234,771†	226,293,201	18.0	188,500,020	192,142,333	58,294,565	188,675,500	131,142,816	18,561,671
Indonesia	1961	96,318,829	47,493,854	14.8	40,544,678	42,458,049	13,316,102	34,578,234	23,516,197	1,943,546
Iran	1966	25,078,923	12,981,665	38.1	11,639,200▲	9,861,700▲	3,642,800▲	7,584,085	3,168,515	1,293,912
Iraq	1965	8,261,527	4,205,201	44.1	...	...	...	...	...	...
Ireland	1966	2,884,002	1,449,032	49.2	...	...	...	1,106,000	330,000◊	277,000
Isle of Man	1966	50,423	23,226	56.0	10,385	16,450	23,588	13,837	1,829	...
Israel	1961	2,179,491†	1,106,069	77.9	786,196‡	869,045‡	524,250‡	751,230	96,420	168,895
Italy	1961	50,623,569†	24,791,683	47.7	11,549,626‡	22,903,305□	16,170,638□	20,096,693	5,657,446	7,886,181+
Jamaica	1960	1,609,814†	773,439	32.0	662,508‡	646,281‡	301,025‡	677,003	229,718	94,172
Japan	1965	98,274,961†	48,244,445	68.9	27,390,062	48,894,840	21,990,059	48,268,767	10,866,693	12,018,479
Jordan	1961	1,706,226	867,597	47.4	815,910⊕	638,732⊕	251,584⊕	389,978	137,757	41,932
Kenya	1962	8,636,263	4,276,963	7.8	3,975,500‡	3,530,300‡	1,130,400‡	...	...	...
Korea, South	1966	29,207,856	14,700,966	33.5	12,851,456‡	11,975,220‡	4,381,178‡	9,325,000	4,826,000	940,000
Kuwait	1965	467,339	286,312	71.0	184,967	247,905	34,467	179,284	1,983	31,925
Lesotho	1966	969,634	465,784	...	370,390‡	306,208‡	172,756‡	...	...	...
Liberia	1962	1,016,443	503,588	19.7	394,509	471,553	150,381	411,794	298,404	22,913
Libya	1964	1,564,369†	813,386	...	684,831‡	630,379‡	249,160‡	405,258	146,709◊	43,636
Liechtenstein	1960	16,628	8,130	...	4,792	6,267	5,569	7,575	962	3,273
Luxembourg	1966	334,790	164,575	...	75,450‡	138,781‡	120,559‡	164,575	14,554	45,864
Macao	1960	169,299†	83,897	95.2	68,556	60,472	40,271	37,905	1,717	22,000**
Malaysia West Malaysia	1957	6,278,758	3,237,579	26.5	2,752,208‡	2,576,252‡	950,298‡	2,164,861	468,317	58,499
East Malaysia	1960	1,198,950	612,642	15.0‖	197,826‡	199,091‡	57,504‡	470,911	381,941	7,451
Maldives	1965	97,743	51,964	...	49,124††	48,619††	...	...	...	...
Malta	1967	314,216†	150,598	...	93,759‡	136,884‡	83,573‡	94,367	7,109	22,893

Table II. World Census Data *(Continued)*

POLITICAL UNIT	Year of census	ENUMERATED POPULATION Total	Male	Percent urban*	AGE DISTRIBUTION 0 to 15	16 to 45	46 and over	ECONOMICALLY ACTIVE Total	Agriculture	Mining and manufacturing
Martinique	1961	290,679†	140,011	29.1	122,340‡	112,124‡	56,215‡	100,000‖	33,000‖	...
Mauritius	1962	681,619	342,306	34.2	323,007	258,285	100,327	187,401	70,866	27,560
Mexico	1960	34,923,129	17,415,320	50.7	16,205,849	13,999,075	4,718,205	11,332,016	6,144,930	2,147,963
Monaco	1968	23,035†	10,424	100.0	2,979‡	8,273‡	11,783‡	10,093	11	2,170
Mongolia	1963	1,018,800†	508,800	39.5	411,300	378,100	227,700	483,400	279,200	41,900
Montserrat	1960	12,167†	5,407	16.0	5,198	3,946	3,023	4,282	1,881	...
Morocco	1960	11,626,232†	5,809,172	29.3	5,307,824	4,738,350	1,580,058	3,290,950	1,721,000‖	...
Mozambique	1960	6,578,604†	3,149,270	...	...	...	...	...	...	...
Nauru	1966	6,048	3,696	...	...	...	...	...	...	...
Nepal	1961	9,387,661	4,619,973	2.8	3,684,000‖	4,258,000‖	1,445,000‖	...	...	...
Netherlands	1960	11,461,964†	5,706,874	55.4	3,516,623‡‡	6,952,166‡‡	993,175‡‡	4,168,626	446,695	1,306,480
Netherlands Antilles	1960	192,538†	94,811	...	79,683‡	77,069‡	35,786‡	59,806	1,029	16,059
New Caledonia	1969	100,579†	52,591	41.6	34,964‡	46,028‡	19,587‡	39,185	13,357	7,152
New Guinea, Territory of	1966	1,578,650	821,899	47.3	694,633	700,669	183,348	889,287	818,739	9,023
New Zealand	1966	2,676,919	1,343,858	62.4	...	...	...	...	...	...
Nicaragua	1963	1,535,588	757,922	40.9	740,729	603,072	191,787	474,960	283,106	59,644
Nigeria	1963	55,670,046	28,112,118	16.1	25,514,354	25,980,055	4,175,637	18,267,669	10,209,122	2,205,476
Norway	1960	3,591,234†	1,789,406	32.1	989,927	1,396,484	1,204,823	1,406,358	188,431	367,296
Pakistan▲	1961	93,831,982†	49,308,645	13.1	40,178,518	36,322,838	13,781,318	30,205,981	22,441,788	...
Panama	1960	1,075,541	545,774	41.5	491,102	435,207	149,232	336,969	155,690	25,964
Papua	1966	606,336	318,460	87.7	274,873	270,698	60,765	312,748	269,076	4,375
Paraguay	1962	1,816,890	895,551	36.1	866,052	684,563	266,275	596,555	312,647	91,077
Peru	1961	10,420,351§§	4,925,518	47.4	4,290,084¶	4,143,473¶	1,468,200¶	3,124,579	1,555,560	477,393
Philippines	1960	27,087,685†	13,662,869	29.9	12,377,240□	11,310,181□	3,400,264□	10,692,000‖	5,768,000‖	1,120,000‖
Poland▲	1960	29,775,508	14,404,218	47.7	9,935,779‡	11,871,906‡	7,598,044‡	13,907,442	6,636,6328	3,237,814
Portugal	1960	8,889,392†	4,254,373	22.6	2,757,895	3,792,171	2,339,326	3,316,472	1,393,624	717,117
Portuguese Guinea	1960	521,336	260,650	...	...	...	...	...	...	...
Portuguese Timor	1960	517,079	267,783	...	...	...	...	...	...	...
Puerto Rico	1960	2,349,544	1,386,968	44.2	1,058,750	863,849	426,945	551,688	135,100	95,504
Réunion	1967	416,525	203,497	42.8	189,997‡	163,253‡	62,166‡	94,334	27,845	6,910
Rhodesia	1961–62	3,857,470	1,984,050	21.6	1,866,850	1,990,620		713,640	247,030	147,710
Romania	1966	19,103,163†	9,351,075	38.2	4,968,524‡	8,864,512‡	5,253,555‡	10,362,300	5,889,591	2,013,525
Rwanda	1965	3,744,723†	1,493,963	...	1,397,928□	1,235,648□	487,147□	1,136,378	...	...
Ryukyu Islands	1965	934,176†	447,693	...	363,048‡	393,001‡	178,077‡	357,801	108,937	34,934
St. Helena	1966	4,649	2,233	...	1,944¶	1,501¶	1,204¶	1,562	...	...
St. Kitts-Nevis and Anguilla	1960	56,693†	26,149	32.9	25,920	19,378	11,395	32,023	8,565	2,078
St. Lucia	1960	86,108	40,693	24.9	38,109	33,122	14,877	28,544	15,144	3,485
St. Vincent	1960	79,948	37,561	...	39,305‡	28,267‡	12,376‡	23,310	9,954	2,868
São Tomé and Principe	1960	63,485†	35,259	...	...	...	...	...	...	...
Seychelles	1960	41,425	20,289	25.4	15,934	16,491	9,000	17,665	5,910	2,151
Sierra Leone	1963	2,180,355	1,081,123	...	800,404‡	1,016,240‡	363,711‡	...	682,588	88,846
Sikkim	1961	162,189	85,285	4.2	68,019	73,748	20,422	2,728	249	64
South Africa	1960	16,002,797	8,043,493	46.7	6,418,492‡	6,945,380‡	2,638,925‡	5,696,060	1,700,958	1,285,113
South West Africa (Namibia)	1960	526,004	265,312	21.9	217,541	227,238	81,225	203,271	118,996	18,647
Spain	1960	30,430,698	14,763,388	42.5	8,365,000	13,506,800	8,652,900	11,634,214	4,803,316	2,749,419
Spanish Sahara	1960	23,793	13,070	...	...	...	...	...	...	...
Surinam▲	1964	324,211	161,855	40.1	147,927‡	122,897‡	46,668‡	80,199§§	19,922§§	12,713§§
Swaziland	1966	374,571	178,795	12.5	174,455	145,618	54,498	121,063	85,103	23,480
Sweden	1965	7,765,981†	3,879,772	77.4	1,608,528‡	3,158,391‡	2,999,062‡	3,449,897	407,560	1,122,294
Switzerland	1960	5,429,061†	2,663,432	42.0	1,361,210	2,302,312	1,765,539	2,512,411	280,191	1,006,038
Syria	1960	4,565,121	2,344,224	41.9	2,014,509	1,656,452	680,094	1,016,347	518,933	128,954
Taiwan	1966	13,348,096†	7,031,644	59.2	5,775,194‡	5,622,590‡	1,950,312‡	8,619,952	1,437,944	592,082
Tanzania	1967	12,231,342	5,969,107	53.8	...	...	...	...	...	...
Thailand	1960	26,257,916	13,154,149	12.5	11,823,535	10,949,932	3,484,393	13,836,984	11,334,382	500,595
Togo	1958–60	1,439,772	689,556	9.6	695,411	558,839	185,550	566,868	452,889	...
Tonga	1966	77,429	39,157	...	...	...	...	...	...	...
Trinidad and Tobago	1960	827,957	411,580	17.0	351,050‡	336,730‡	140,177‡	262,570	52,528	53,617
Trust Territory of the Pacific	1960	75,836†	38,721	...	33,332	27,139	15,092	...	...	...
Tunisia	1966	4,533,351	2,314,419	40.1	2,191,088	1,678,465	663,798	1,093,735	448,296	103,582
Turkey	1965	31,391,207	15,945,768	...	13,844,128	12,775,996	4,771,083	13,591,822	9,764,652	1,025,022
Turks and Caicos Islands	1960	5,668†	2,667	...	2,557	1,975	1,136	2,034	393	...
Uganda	1959	6,536,616	3,283,230	4.8	2,846,000	2,796,000	895,000	...	...	...
Union of Soviet Socialist Republics	1970	241,748,000	111,300,000	56.3	...	...	...	...	...	...
United Arab Republic	1966	30,053,861	15,168,000	40.5	...	...	...	...	...	...
United Kingdom	1961	52,708,934	25,480,791	79.0	12,335,703‡	20,784,033‡	19,589,198‡	23,616,620	865,129	6,975,166
United States	1960‖‖	179,323,175	88,331,494	69.9	55,786,173‡	70,919,666‡	52,617,336‡	64,639,252	4,256,734	18,167,092
Uruguay	1963	2,592,563	1,289,454	...	721,500‡	1,143,600‡	727,500‡	1,015,500	181,800	213,600
Venezuela	1961	7,523,999§§	3,823,569	62.5	3,538,949	3,022,725	962,325	2,406,725	773,650	1,633,075
Vietnam, North	1960	15,916,955	7,687,814	9.5	7,055,544¶¶	7,556,129¶¶	1,305,282¶¶	8,119,286	6,377,024	537,761
Virgin Islands of the United States	1960	32,099	15,930	57.9	12,768‡	12,510‡	6,821‡	10,845	610	894
Western Samoa	1966	131,379	67,809	19.2	...	...	...	...	...	...
Yugoslavia	1961	18,549,291†	9,043,424	28.8	5,770,817‡	8,168,259‡	4,610,215‡	8,340,400	4,674,856	1,137,848
Zambia	1961–63	3,493,590	1,734,860	21.3	1,492,150	3,092,400	401,190	693,000	220,000	72,000

DEMOGRAPHIC AND/OR SAMPLE SURVEYS

POLITICAL UNIT	Year of census	ENUMERATED POPULATION Total	Male	Percent urban*	AGE DISTRIBUTION 0 to 15	16 to 45	46 and over	ECONOMICALLY ACTIVE Total	Agriculture	Mining and manufacturing
Burundi	1962	2,319,540	1,104,266	...	...	...	...	...	...	...
Central African Republic	1959–60	1,177,000	577,000	6.8	429,000‡	661,000‡	81,000‡	610,000	461,000	52,000
Chad	1964	3,254,000	1,567,000	7.8	...	...	...	950,000	600,000	60,000
Congo (Brazzaville)	1960–61	794,400†	...	...	...	...	...	...	...	...
Cuba	1965	7,630,700	2,895,155	53.0	2,808,190♀♀	4,009,110♀♀	813,400♀♀	2,546,000	838,000	390,000
Dahomey	1961	2,106,000	...	...	...	...	...	...	...	...
Malagasy	1966	6,200,000	3,049,000	...	2,882,000‡	2,326,000‡	992,000‡	2,733,000	2,396,000	337,000
Malawi	1963	3,753,000†	...	...	...	...	...	...	...	...
Mali	1960–61	4,100,000	...	...	1,763,000	2,127,900	209,100	...	...	...
Niger	1959–60	2,556,211	...	...	...	...	...	1,506,490	703,610	4,510
Senegal	1960–61	3,109,840†	1,531,760	23.7	1,320,680	1,641,420	147,720	1,317,580	1,087,020	73,800
Upper Volta	1960–61	4,400,000	2,208,800	4.6	1,830,400	1,892,000	677,600	2,627,000	1,300,000	...

Note: Data reflect results of enumerations conducted 1957 to 1970, as available.
*That population defined as urban by the political unit.
†De jure population.
‡0–14, 15–44, 45 and over.
§0–13, 14–49, 50 and over.
‖Estimate.
¶0–14, 15–49, 50 and over.
♀0–19, 20–49, 50 and over.
δIncludes forestry, hunting, and fishing.
□0–14, 15–45, 46 and over.
○0–15, 16–49, 50 and over.
▲Age distribution excludes unknown. Iran 474,322; Pakistan 3,437,939; Poland 369,779; Surinam 6,719.
+Includes public utilities and construction.
⊕0–15, 16–44, 45 and over.
**Includes transportation.
††0–19, 20–64, 65 and over.
‡‡0–14, 15–64, 65 and over.
§§Excludes Amerindian.
‖‖1970 preliminary 204,765,770
¶¶0–15, 16–55, 56 and over.
♀♀0–14, 15–54, 55 and over.

Table III. Populations and Areas of the Countries of the World

Continent and state	Area in sq.mi.	Population in 000	Persons per sq.mi.
World total	57,911,579	3,647,739	69.6*
AFRICA	11,673,672	350,836	35.0
Algeria	919,590	13,547	14.7
Botswana	220,000	623	2.8
Bouvet Island (Norwegian)	23	—	—
British dependencies	311	58	—
Burundi	10,747	3,475	323.3
Cameroon	183,591	5,680	30.9
Central African Republic	240,540	1,518	6.3
Chad	495,750	3,510	7.1
Congo (Brazzaville)	134,749	880	6.5
Congo (Kinshasa)	905,559	17,100	18.9
Dahomey	43,483	2,718	62.5
Equatorial Guinea	10,830	286	26.4
Ethiopia	471,776	24,140	51.2
French dependencies	10,713	779	—
Gabon	103,100	485	4.7
Gambia, The	4,467	389	87.1
Ghana	92,100	8,546	92.8
Guinea	94,925	3,890	41.0
Ivory Coast	123,483	4,195	34.0
Kenya	224,960	10,506	46.7
Lesotho	11,719	1,018	86.9
Liberia	43,000	1,200	27.9
Libya	686,500	1,938	2.8
Malagasy Republic	226,660	7,199	31.8
Malawi	45,747	4,530	99.0
Mali	478,652	4,929	10.3
Mauritania	397,683	1,140	2.9
Mauritius	788	831	1,054.6
Morocco	174,471	15,050	86.3
Niger	458,993	3,909	8.5
Nigeria	356,669	66,174	185.5
Portuguese dependencies	800,350	13,904	—
Rhodesia	150,820	5,270	34.9
Rwanda	10,169	3,509	345.1
Senegal	76,124	3,822	50.2
Sierra Leone	27,699	2,510	90.6
Somalia	246,155	2,730	11.1
South Africa	471,445	19,618	41.6
South West Africa (Namibia)	317,827	615	1.9
Spanish Sahara (Spanish)	102,700	65	0.6
Sudan, The	967,491	15,186	15.7
Swaziland	6,704	410	61.2
Tanzania	364,900	13,273	36.4
Togo	21,900	1,956	89.3
Tunisia	63,378	5,027	79.3
Uganda	91,076	9,831	107.9
United Arab Republic	386,900	33,329	86.1
Upper Volta	105,869	5,330	50.3
Zambia	290,586	4,208	14.5
ANTARCTICA	5,500,000†	0.3	—
Australian Antarctic Territory	2,472,000	—	—
British Antarctic Territory‡	650,000	0.1	—
French Southern and Antarctic Lands	202,916	0.2	—
Norwegian dependencies	96§	—	—
Ross Dependency (New Zealand)	160,000	—	—
ASIA (exclusive of U.S.S.R.)	10,696,608	2,073,299	193.8
Afghanistan	250,775	17,125	68.3
Australian dependencies	58	4	—
Bahrain‖	256	198	773.4
Bhutan (Indian protected state)	18,000	770	42.8
Brunei‖	2,226	138	62.0
Burma	261,789	27,600	105.4
Cambodia	69,898	6,818	97.5
Ceylon	25,332	11,992	473.4
China	3,691,501	827,000	224.0
Cyprus	3,572	630	176.4
Hong Kong (British)	400	4,089	10,222.5
India (incl. Kashmir)	1,232,560	536,984	435.7
Indonesia	779,675	121,089	155.3
Iran	636,293	27,892	43.8
Iraq¶	169,284	9,466	55.9
Israel	7,992	2,949	369.0
Japan	142,871	103,013	721.0
Jordan	37,737	2,250	59.6
Korea, North	46,557	14,000	300.7
Korea, South	38,022	31,139	819.0
Kuwait	6,880	733	106.5
Laos	91,400	2,893	31.7
Lebanon	4,015	2,645	658.8
Malaysia	128,727	10,455	81.2
Maldives	115	111	965.2
Mongolia	604,247	1,240	2.1
Nepal	54,362	11,044	203.2
Neutral Zone	7,000	...	—
Oman	82,000	750	9.1
Pakistan	366,041	114,189	312.0
Philippines	115,830	37,158	320.8
Portuguese dependencies	5,769	850	—
Qatar‖	4,400	100	22.7
Ryukyu Islands (United States)	848	989	1,166.3
Saudi Arabia¶	873,972	7,200	8.2
Sikkim (Indian protected state)	2,744	191	69.6
Singapore	226	2,034	9,000.0
Southern Yemen	112,000	1,220	10.9
Syria	71,498	5,866	82.0
Taiwan	13,887	14,501	1,044.2
Thailand	198,500	35,814	180.4
Trucial States‖	32,278	135	4.2
Turkey	301,380	35,232	116.9
Vietnam, North	61,293	19,900	324.7
Vietnam, South	67,108	17,903	266.8
Yemen	75,290	5,000	66.4
EUROPE (exclusive of U.S.S.R.)	1,903,048	460,352	241.9
Albania	11,100	2,075	186.9
Andorra	175	20	114.3
Austria	32,374	7,384	228.1
Belgium	11,784	9,661	819.8
British dependencies	298	191	—
Bulgaria	42,823	8,436	197.0
Czechoslovakia	49,371	14,418	292.0
Denmark (incl. Faeroe Islands)	17,169	4,944	—
Finland	130,128	4,695	36.1
France	210,038	50,545	240.6
Germany, East	41,766	17,075	408.8
Germany, West (incl. W. Berlin)	95,974	61,195	637.6
Greece	50,944	8,835	173.4
Hungary	35,919	10,314	287.1
Iceland	39,768	203	5.1
Ireland	27,136	2,921	107.6
Italy	116,315	54,302	466.9
Liechtenstein	62	22	354.8
Luxembourg	999	339	339.3
Malta	122	322	2,639.3
Monaco	0.6	24	40,000.0
Netherlands	14,140	12,958	916.4
Norway (incl. Svalbard and Jan Mayen Land)	149,150	3,869	—
Poland	120,756	32,727	271.0
Portugal	35,553	9,583	269.5
Romania	91,700	20,010	218.2
San Marino	24	17	708.3
Spain	194,884	32,961	169.1
Sweden	173,648	8,014	46.2
Switzerland	15,945	6,184	387.8
United Kingdom	94,216	55,534	589.4
Vatican City	0.2	0.9	4,500.0
Yugoslavia	98,766	20,573	208.3
NORTH AMERICA	9,361,079	315,871	33.7
Barbados	166	254	1,530.1
British dependencies	15,752	880	—
Canada	3,851,809	21,324	5.5
Costa Rica	19,650	1,685	85.8
Cuba	42,827	8,250	192.6
Dominican Republic	18,720	4,174	223.0
El Salvador	8,100	3,480	429.6
French dependencies	1,201	663	—
Greenland (Danish)	840,000	47	.06
Guatemala	42,042	5,172	123.0
Haiti	10,714	4,867	454.3
Honduras	43,277	2,582	59.7
Jamaica	4,471	1,972	441.1
Mexico	761,600	48,313	63.4
Netherlands Antilles (Dutch)	385	220	571.4
Nicaragua	49,759	1,942	39.0
Panama (excl. Canal Zone)	29,208	1,425	48.8
Trinidad and Tobago	1,980	1,040	525.3
United States	3,615,210	204,766	56.6
United States dependencies	4,208	2,815	
OCEANIA	3,291,597	18,939	5.8
Australia	2,967,909	12,295	4.1
Australian dependencies	183,704	2,316	—
British dependencies	11,838	215	—
Canton and Enderbury Islands (U.K.-U.S.)	27	—	—
Fiji	7,071	527	74.5
French dependencies	8,999	213	—
Nauru	8	7	875.0
New Hebrides (Fr.-U.K.)	5,700	83	14.6
New Zealand	103,736	2,821	27.2
New Zealand dependencies	197	28	—
Tonga	269	87	323.4
United States dependencies	1,003	202	—
Western Samoa	1,136	145	127.6
SOUTH AMERICA	6,885,225	186,694	27.1
Argentina	1,072,157	24,352	22.7
Bolivia	424,162	4,931	11.6
Brazil	3,286,470	90,840	27.6
Chile	292,256	9,780	33.5
Colombia	439,735	20,463	46.5
Ecuador	109,483	5,890	53.8
Falkland Islands (British)	6,200	2	0.3
French Guiana (French)	34,750	48	1.4
Guyana	83,000	742	8.9
Paraguay	157,047	2,386	15.2
Peru	496,222	13,586	27.4
Surinam (Dutch)	63,064	389	6.2
Uruguay	68,536	2,886	42.1
Venezuela	352,143	10,399	29.5
U.S.S.R.	8,600,350	241,748	28.1

Note: A dash (—) in the population column indicates none or negligible; a dash in the density column indicates figure not relevant; three dots (...) indicate not available.

*In computing the world density the area of Antarctica is omitted.
†Estimated area, including some unclaimed territory.
‡Includes some territory claimed by Argentina and Chile.
§Insular dependencies only. Norwegian claims to continental Antarctica are undefined.
‖British protected state.
¶Excluding Iraq-Saudi Arabia neutral zone of 7,000 sq.mi.

THE POPULATION CRISIS

By Paul R. Ehrlich and Anne H. Ehrlich

In mid-1970 the earth's human population passed 3,600,000,-000, and if the current growth rate of 2% a year continues, the population will double in 35 years. Such enormous numbers of people and such a rapid growth rate are completely without precedent in human history.

As long as man depended on hunting and gathering for his food, the human population grew extremely slowly, with numerous local and temporary setbacks. About 10,000 years ago there were perhaps five million people scattered around the world, fewer than now live in the Chicago metropolitan area. With the development of agriculture, however, permanent settlements could be established and food could be stored against times of shortage. Death rates, under these more secure conditions, began to fall, although birthrates remained more or less unchanged. Later improvements in agricultural practices, the Industrial Revolution in Europe and North America, and, particularly, the development of modern medicine led to further reductions in death rates, especially in Western countries. But this was followed by some reduction of birthrates in the West over the last century, largely as a result of changing social and economic conditions following industrialization. This so-called demographic transition has partially compensated for the lower death rates and helped to slow growth. Today, the populations in developed countries are growing at an average rate of about 1% per year, which doubles the population every 70 years.

Following World War II modern medical technology was introduced into less developed countries, without any serious effort to introduce birth control techniques. The result was a spectacular drop in death rates and practically no change in birthrates. The less developed areas of the world—most of Africa, Latin America, and Asia—are now growing at an average rate of about 2.5%, doubling every 30 years or less. There is little hope for a spontaneous drop in the birthrates of these nations because the socioeconomic conditions that produced the demographic transition in the West are not present.

The Price of Population Growth. The stress that this burgeoning human population puts on the earth's resources and life-support systems is only beginning to be widely realized, but when such limiting factors as food and nonrenewable resources are considered, it becomes evident that this uncontrolled growth cannot be sustained for long. Our very efforts to produce sufficient food and to expand the industrial society put the earth's ability to support the present population—let alone a much larger one—in serious jeopardy. It is obvious that population growth must soon stop and ultimately be reversed, for if humanity fails to regulate its own numbers, nature will do it for us, sooner or later.

Food and Other Resources. Perhaps as many as half the people in the world today are either undernourished (lacking calories) or, more commonly, malnourished (usually lacking in protein). If all the world's food was equitably distributed, everyone would have enough calories but would be protein deficient. On top of this absolute shortage, however, there are severe problems of inequitable distribution of the available food, both within and between nations. If the human race cannot feed itself adequately today, how can we hope to feed additional hundreds of millions a few years from now? Even our present food supplies are produced at considerable cost to the environment.

Of the various schemes that have been proposed to raise food production or to supplement protein supplies, the most promising, the so-called Green Revolution, involves the introduction into the less developed countries of new high-yield forms of traditional grains together with more "efficient" farming methods. At best, the Green Revolution may enable agricultural production to keep pace with population growth for the next decade or two, but there are numerous social, economic, and environmental obstacles to its success. For example, the new grains require large amounts of fertilizers and irrigation water, and they may require much more protection from pests than naturally resistant traditional crops. To meet these problems, agronomists are trying to introduce into less developed countries the same fertilizing techniques and synthetic insecticides that are causing so many environmental problems in developed countries.

Other panaceas for solving the food crisis have been proposed. Food from the sea, particularly, is promoted as a potential contribution, especially to the supply of protein. If sea life were carefully husbanded, productivity might be doubled by the end of the century (though the population also will have doubled by then). Far from protecting this vital food source, however, we are polluting the oceans with perhaps a half million different substances, including deadly pesticides.

Other resources are running short as well, especially the nonrenewable ones. At the current rates of consumption, presently known reserves of petroleum and many other important minerals will be exhausted within 50 to 150 years. The U.S. and other developed countries consume the overwhelming bulk of these resources, for the technology and way of life of Western countries depend on their use. Now the less developed world is striving to obtain the blessings of Western-style technology, but the consumption of nonrenewable resources in the present wasteful fashion cannot continue much longer in the developed countries alone. The dream of industrializing the entire world can never be realized because the earth simply does not have the resources. Even the consumption of such renewable resources as forests, soils, and fresh water exceeds the rate of replenishment.

The Environment. As a factor in human health and well-being, environmental deterioration is a serious cause for alarm, especially in the developed countries where most pollution is generated. Man's despoliation of his environment has reached a stage where it presents a grave danger to the entire earth—that lovely, lonely planet which nourishes and supports us all. The poisonous substances we are heedlessly releasing into soils, waters, and atmosphere injure not only ourselves, but the ecological systems on which we depend for oxygen to breathe, food to eat, and the recycling of our wastes.

Long-lived chlorinated hydrocarbons, such as DDT, are found in every living plant and animal around the world, on land and in the sea. DDT does not break down readily into harmless substances. It accumulates in the fat of organisms and is concentrated by ecological systems; animals get it from eating plants and pass it on to the predators that devour them. Only about 10% of the food an animal eats is incorporated into its body, but almost 100% of the DDT is. Therefore, concentration of DDT is greatest in such animals as predatory birds and fishes that feed at the upper end of food chains, and many of these predatory species are threatened with extinction today. As the quantity of poisons in the environment increases, species lower in the food chains will be affected—including those involved in the chains that produce human food. Other serious pollutants include the inorganic fertilizers, which not only pollute rivers and lakes—sometimes to the extent of destroying their ability to support life at all—but also appear to interfere with the

OLIPHANT—THE DENVER POST—REPRINTED WITH PERMISSION—LOS ANGELES TIMES SYNDICATE

natural processes of the soil that refresh and renew it. Thus artificially high soil fertility may be achieved temporarily at the cost of lower soil fertility over the long term.

Like DDT, air pollution is no longer a local problem; the entire atmosphere is contaminated. Air pollution damages trees and crops as well as human tissue, but, even more disturbing, it may induce changes in climate. Whether the long-term effect will be to warm or cool the planet remains uncertain, though at the moment there seems to be a general cooling trend. Whichever the direction, accelerated climatic change will inevitably affect agricultural production profoundly and adversely. Another potential influence on climate is the heat generated by the use of power, whether it is the burning of gasoline in a car, the running of a refrigerator, or the generation of electricity by power plants. If power consumption continues to increase at current rates, what is now mainly a local problem of thermal pollution will soon escalate into a worldwide one.

Disease. Medical propaganda to the contrary, man has not been entirely freed from the ravages of epidemic disease. From time to time new forms of old diseases appear, or lethal diseases never before seen in man suddenly transfer from animals to humans. The human population today is the largest, weakest, and most densely packed that has ever existed, and a new virus could be carried around the world by modern transport within hours.

War and Disruption. Population pressure is an important factor in most, if not all, modern wars, appearing most frequently as pressure on resources. As the world's population grows, the potential for conflict will become even greater. War is always undesirable, but the advent of thermonuclear war has provided humanity with a means to achieve self-extinction. Even a limited nuclear exchange could impair the earth's life-support systems enough to prevent survival. And even if war can be avoided (or better, abolished), what about the internal disturbances plaguing so many countries, including the United States? It seems reasonable to suggest that population pressure, especially in our malfunctioning cities, may be contributing to our troubles. It has been shown that crime rates rise as population density rises, and mental disturbance may also be more prevalent in areas of high density. People appear to have very high tolerances for crowding, but our adaptability cannot be limitless.

Optimum Population and Its Achievement. How many people can the earth support? Before answering this question, we must decide what the average standard of living should be in food, shelter, clothing, and other material goods. At the average American standard, the world could temporarily support between 500 million and one billion people (temporarily, because this does not take into account the depletion of nonrenewable resources). By this optimistic measurement, there are already 3.5 to 7 times too many of us. At a much lower standard of living—perhaps the average that prevails worldwide today—we probably could temporarily support more people than now exist, particularly if food and materials are more equitably distributed and less wastefully used. But we could not support so many for long; the environmental stress would be too great. In projecting an ideal population size, thought must also be given to the ideal number of people needed to keep each society functioning efficiently. A primarily industrial area, for example, will naturally require more people than one that is predominately agrarian.

Far more difficult than determining the optimum population size will be achieving it. The ancient, obsolete idea still prevails that there is strength in numbers. Officials and economists in many less developed countries (and some developed ones) still believe that more people are needed to carry out development. They cling to this belief, although high birth- and population-growth rates repeatedly have been shown to hinder economic progress and although most of these countries are suffering from severe unemployment problems.

People in developed countries also mistakenly believe that they have no population problem, because they practice family planning and their populations are growing more slowly than those in less developed countries. However, these slowly growing populations are creating the bulk of the environmental deterioration that is endangering the entire world. These are the people who are consuming most of the world's resources and who are taking an unfair share of food. It is imperative that developed countries, especially the U.S. and the Soviet Union, lead the way in population control. Otherwise, people in less developed countries will consider it simply a new plot to keep them from gaining their share of the world's goods.

Family planning is not equivalent to population control. Family planning serves only to regulate the sizes of individual families; population control is the regulation of population size by a society. Unless a society at least attempts to influence the goals of family planning, there is no control of population. As long as people want and have an average of significantly more than two children per couple, a population will grow. Most of the government-sponsored family-planning programs introduced into less developed countries since 1960 operate as the early birth control centres did in the U.S. and England. They open clinics, provide information and free or low-cost contraceptives. Their propaganda chiefly consists of spelling out the personal advantages of spacing children and avoiding unwanted children. This is socially valuable, but it has had very little effect on birthrates.

The first prerequisite of any form of population control, of course, is that birth control be readily available to all members of each society. Contraceptive information and/or devices are still illegal in many countries, largely because of pressure from the Roman Catholic Church, and abortion—by far the most commonly employed form of birth control in the world—is the subject of a great deal of controversy and is illegal in most countries. The trend, however, seems to be toward liberalization.

But complete availability of contraception and abortion alone will not produce population control. Individuals must be convinced of the need to limit their reproduction. In fully literate, relatively secular societies such as those of North America, Europe, and Japan, this might be achieved simply through an educational campaign to convince society of the consequences of continued population growth and to foster appropriate cultural attitudes, such as social approval of childlessness and non-marriage. Women's roles as wife and mother can be deemphasized and participation in society outside the family encouraged. If family planning, plus an educational campaign, fails to reduce birthrates to the desired level, socioeconomic measures may be required. Tax laws that encourage reproduction can be changed, preferably in a way that will not penalize poor families. There could be special bonuses or tax incentives for childless couples and single persons; encouragement and subsidy for adoption; free or low-cost day care for children, allowing mothers to work; and bonuses for sterilization.

What More Can We Do? Obviously, population control will not solve all human problems. It will, however, provide us with an opportunity to solve them. Without population control, our efforts to solve other problems are ultimately doomed to failure.

There are other steps we can take, however. Besides controlling human numbers, we must cease our abuse of the environmental systems on which we depend for our lives and halt our greedy consumption. This means much more than putting filters in smokestacks and improving sewage-treatment facilities. It means nothing less than that the present Western way of life must be changed fundamentally. The importance of material goods must diminish and wasteful methods of production must be abandoned. All materials should be manufactured with a view to durability and recycling. Agriculture should be practiced in cooperation with nature, not as a war against it. Cities and other human habitations should be planned with human beings in mind, not automobiles. Societies should be rated on the well-being of their citizens rather than their gross national product. This change of basic values must also include the rejection of war, the ending of racism and of the exploitation of poor people and nations.

In generations past, each society had a vision of the future, and it built and planned for that future. Today we seem bent only on continuing to build on past goals, without evaluating their worth or feasibility. What vision of the future remains is out of alignment with reality. Resisting change is useless; our choice now is whether to control and direct the changes of the future toward new goals derived from the hard realities we face, or to continue drifting until the "solutions" find us.

continued from page 601

lation lived in the suburban ring around cities, about 30% lived in the cities, and an equal number lived in small towns and rural areas outside the cities. Major central cities reportedly gained only 750,000 people in the 1960s. They became increasingly black as 2.1 million blacks moved in and 2.7 million whites moved to the suburbs.

Among the states Nevada showed the largest percentage gain, 68.9%, rising from 285,278 to 481,893. California's population increased by almost 4 million (25.4%) to 19.7 million, making it the most populous state in the union. Florida's population increased by 34.7%, or 1.7 million, to 6.7 million. New Jersey, New York, and Texas each gained more than one million people. About 70 million Americans lived in 369 cities with over 50,000 population. New York remained the largest city, with 7,771,730, a loss of 10,000. Chicago, Los Angeles, Philadelphia, and Detroit retained their respective ranks: all had populations above one million. Houston, Tex., grew by more than 250,000 to become the sixth ranking city with 1.2 million.

Despite the national gain, more than half of the 3,042 counties in the U.S. lost population. This confirmed the trend that began in the 1940s when counties in a broad loop of states from the Dakotas and Minnesota south to Texas and east to Georgia registered losses. The Appalachian area of the East recorded a similar pattern. Farm population shrank from 15 million to 10 million, and the predominantly rural states of West Virginia, North Dakota, South Dakota, and Wyoming lost population. In Mississippi there was little overall change, although a shift to urban centres was noted.

The trend toward increasing urbanization manifested itself most strongly in "Megalopolis," the 450-mi.-long by 150-mi.-wide belt from Boston to Washington, D.C., which contained 36.2 million people or one-sixth of the nation. In the 1960s it gained 3.6 million people, growing most rapidly on its fringes by filling in and developing the farmland that lay between its major cities.

According to the 1970 census, the U.S. contained 66 Standard Metropolitan Statistical Areas with more than 500,000 people; 31 had more than one million people. Only two, Pittsburgh, Pa., and Jersey City, N.J., lost population. Anaheim-Santa Ana-Garden Grove in California doubled its population to 1.4 million. Other fast-growing areas were San Jose, Calif.; Phoenix, Ariz.; Fort Lauderdale-Hollywood, Fla.; Washington, D.C.-Maryland-Virginia; San Bernardino-Riverside-Ontario, Calif.; and Dallas, Tex. The U.S. had 150 cities with populations in excess of 150,000. (W. Er.)

See also Food; Migration, International; Vital Statistics; articles on individual political units.

Portugal

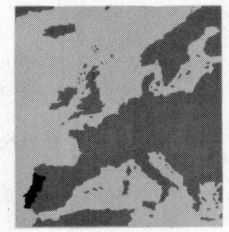

A unitary corporative republic of southwestern Europe, Portugal shares the Iberian Peninsula with Spain. Area: 35,-553 sq.mi. (92,082 sq.km.), including the Azores (893 sq. mi.) and Madeira (308 sq.mi.). Pop. (1969 est.): 9,582,600. Cap. and largest city: Lisbon (pop., 1969

est., 830,600). Language: Portuguese. Religion: Roman Catholic. Portugal has seven overseas provinces (*see* DEPENDENT STATES). President in 1970, Rear Adm. Américo de Deus Rodrigues Tomás; premier, Marcello José das Neves Alves Caetano.

During 1970 Portugal enjoyed political stability and made some economic progress. Premier Caetano's government consolidated its position, especially after the death on July 27 of António Salazar, who had been premier for over 36 years. On January 14 Caetano reorganized his Cabinet and merged several ministries; new ministries of Health and Corporations, Public Works and Communications, and National Defense and Army were headed by Rebelo de Sousa, Rui Sanches, and Gen. Sá Viana Rebelo, respectively. Rui Patrício was appointed foreign minister, replacing Franco Nogueira, who had occupied the post for eight years. The changes, designed to streamline the administration, enabled Caetano to introduce young moderates and technocrats into the government.

The moves toward political liberalization that had been so noticeable in 1969 practically ceased in 1970. On February 21, on being appointed to the presidency of Acção Nacional Popular (the new mass political organization that succeeded the official political party, the União Nacional), Caetano stressed that Salazar's policies would remain largely unaltered, defended the Portuguese presence in Africa and the corporate state, and bitterly attacked socialism. Police forcibly suppressed demonstrations in Coimbra and Lisbon in the late spring, and charges were filed against the exiled opposition leader, Mário Soares.

There were signs during the year that Portugal planned to seek closer ties with the EEC. During an official visit to Lisbon in June, French Foreign Minister Maurice Schumann promised France's support in any negotiations with the EEC that Portugal might undertake. In the following month, the government set up a commission to study the subject. In a speech late in September, Caetano said that Portugal favoured economic links, especially a customs union, but that any form of political federation was unacceptable. A majority of the Cabinet were believed to be in favour of association, but some veteran ministers and large segments of industry and commerce were opposed to it. The chief opposition spokesman was Nogueira, leader of a bloc of deputies who believed that Portugal's future lay in Africa.

Meanwhile, relations with the U.K. and the U.S. improved. The secretary of industry, Rogério Martins, visited London in October, the first official ministerial visit in some years. The U.S. secretary of state, William Rogers, visited Lisbon in May, and it was agreed that talks should begin early in 1971 on renewing the lease on the U.S. base in the Azores. Negotiations had been suspended since 1962 because of Salazar's insistence that the U.S. express official support for Portugal's African policy.

From June there were reports of an intensification of the fighting in Mozambique and Angola. A major Portuguese offensive was launched that resulted in the destruction of several guerrilla bases in Mozambique and the closing of escape routes to Tanzania. It was thought that the Mozambique Liberation Front (FRELIMO) had suffered its worst defeat since fighting began early in the 1960s. In Angola large military operations near the border with the Congo (Kinshasa) resulted in heavy rebel losses. In December Premier Caetano announced proposals for constitutional reforms, the most important of which in-

volved greater administrative autonomy for the African territories, especially Angola and Mozambique. He reiterated his determination to keep the territories, however. Later in the month the UN Security Council condemned Portugal for having backed the invasion of Guinea in November, although Portugal denied any responsibility.

The government continued to pursue highly cautious financial and economic policies aimed at the maintenance of a balanced budget and a strong balance of payments position. However, some attempt was made to introduce economic reforms.

In June there were rumours of an impending devaluation of the escudo, which were officially denied. Despite this, Portugal's persistent trade deficit continued to grow (U.S. $283 million in January–June), and inflationary pressures mounted (the cost of living in Lisbon rose by 10% in January–June). Many foreign observers considered that the escudo was overvalued, and this was confirmed by the virtual standstill in foreign investment during the year.   (RN. C.)

See also Dependent States.

PORTUGAL

Education. (1966–67) Primary, pupils 891,082, teachers 27,666; secondary, pupils 162,561, teachers 7,266; vocational, pupils 167,652, teachers 8,789; teacher training, students 2,867, teachers 323; higher (including 4 universities), students 36,332, teaching staff 2,158.

Finance. Monetary unit: escudo, with a par value of 28.75 escudos to U.S. $1 (69 escudos = £1 sterling). Gold, SDRs, and foreign exchange, official: (June 1970) U.S. $1,352,000,000; (June 1969) U.S. $1,343,-000,000. Budget (1969 rev. est.): revenue 18,503,400,-000 escudos; expenditure 15,286,900,000 escudos. Gross national product: (1968) 144 billion escudos; (1967) 132.1 billion escudos. Money supply: (April 1970) 90,970,000,000 escudos; (April 1969) 80,950,-000,000 escudos. Cost of living (Lisbon; 1963 = 100): (June 1970) 143; (June 1969) 134.

Foreign Trade. (1969) Imports 35,417,000,000 escudos; exports 23,653,000,000 escudos. Import sources: West Germany 16%; U.K. 14%; Angola 9%; France 7%; Italy 6%; U.S. 5%; Mozambique 5%. Export destinations: U.K. 20%; Angola 16%; U.S. 10%; Mozambique 9%; West Germany 7%; Sweden 6%; France 5%. Main exports: textile yarns and fabrics 19%; wine 7%; cork 6%; fruit and vegetables 6%; fish and products 5%. Tourism (1968): visitors 2,510,700; gross receipts U.S. $214 million.

Transport and Communications. Roads (continent; 1968) 37,369 km. (including 77 km. expressways). Motor vehicles in use (1968): passenger 399,-288; commercial 26,212. Railways: (continent; 1968) 3,591 km.; traffic (1969) 3,441,000,000 passenger-km., freight 737 million net ton-km. Air traffic (1969): 1,772,000,000 passenger-km.; freight 34,210,000 net ton-km. Shipping (1969): merchant vessels 100 gross tons and over 364; gross tonnage 825,355. Telephones (Dec. 1968) 653,407. Radio receivers (Dec. 1967) 1,345,000. Television receivers (Dec. 1967) 271,000.

Agriculture. Production (in 000; metric tons; 1969; 1968 in parentheses): wheat 382 (748); barley 57 (94); oats 94 (129); rye 164 (199); corn 570 (550); rice 181 (149); potatoes 1,098 (1,083); dry broad beans 24 (36); other dry beans 48 (50); chick-peas 23 (26); wine 764 (1,169); figs 221 (c. 219); oranges 124 (125); olive oil 62 (53); apples 61 (72); pears 55 (69); meat (1968) 173, (1967) 165; timber (cu.m.; 1968) 5,900, (1967) 5,900; fish catch (1967) 560, (1966) 506. Livestock (in 000; 1968–69): sheep 5,760; cattle (1967–68) c. 920; pigs c. 1,690; horses c. 80; mules c. 140; asses c. 210; goats c. 590; chickens c. 8,100.

Industry. Fuel and power (in 000; metric tons; 1969): coal 360; lignite (1968) 31; electricity (kw-hr.) 6,840,000; manufactured gas (Lisbon only; cu.m.) 114,000. Production (in 000; metric tons; 1969): iron ore (50% metal content) 162; sulfur (1967) 239; cement 2,036; tin concentrates (metal content) 0.4; manganese ore (metal content; 1968) 3.7; tungsten concentrates (oxide content; 1968) 1.7; gold (troy oz.; 1968) 19; cotton yarn 78; woven cotton fabrics 46; preserved sardines (1968) 35; cork products (1968) 337.

Portuguese Overseas Provinces:
see Dependent States

Postal Services

The number of member states in the Universal Postal Union (UPU) rose to 143 with the admission of Swaziland (Nov. 7, 1969) and Equatorial Guinea (July 24, 1970). The 16th Universal Postal Congress, which met in Tokyo from Oct. 1 to Nov. 14, 1969, revised certain acts of the UPU, including the provisions governing operational and financial relations between postal administrations. The revised acts were scheduled to come into force on July 1, 1971. At its annual meeting in Bern, Switz., in May 1970, the UPU's executive council discussed plans for the celebration of the union's centenary in 1974. The UPU continued its activities in the field of technical cooperation during 1970, both at the level of multilateral technical aid (the UN Development Program) and on the basis of its own technical aid in kind or money, under the UPU Special Fund (financed by voluntary contributions).

In the U.K. efforts to improve productivity resulted in further useful savings during 1970. A concept for designing work plans to improve the supervision and organization of sorting offices was developed, and the study of forecasting postal traffic continued. Progress was made with market research and the development of a commercial approach toward postal services. Postal sales forces were introduced experimentally in two regions. The Post Office undertook a massive conversion and training program to ensure that it would be prepared for the decimalization of currency on Feb. 15, 1971.

The mechanized parcel-sorting office opened at Reading, Eng., in October 1969 was the first of 30 new fully mechanized concentration centres that were scheduled to replace the existing 1,200 manual parcel-sorting offices. Instead of the complicated intermovement of parcels between the 1,200 different offices, parcels would be moved in bulk between the 30 concentration centres, where they would be sorted by machines. The machinery used in these modern parcel-sorting offices was described in detail at the British Postal Engineering Conference, held at the Institution of Mechanical Engineers in London in May. This conference, the first of its kind in the world, attracted delegates from about 20 countries.

Many offices were equipped with machines to segregate letters and packets, automatically face the letters, and cancel the stamps. Further machines for code marking and the automatic sorting of letters were installed at five centres, and equipment for nine more offices was on order. Since the automatic letter-sorting machines could read only coded addresses, a coding system, known as the Postcode, was being introduced. By 1970 postcodes had been allocated to over half the 18 million addresses in the U.K., and the remainder were due to be coded by the end of 1972.

In France a study group on the future of the postal services, made up of Post Office employees and others outside the postal administration, submitted its report at the end of 1969. The report highlighted the various elements liable to affect the existing structure of the postal services. It examined the postal market and its expected development up to 1985, as well as analyzing the costs of the postal services. It also tried to describe the "post office of the future," which would have to adapt itself in order to satisfy the needs of the country's economic and social life.

UPI COMPIX

An air force sergeant sorts mail at the Brooklyn General Post Office after military reservists were called in during the postal employees' strike in March 1970.

The expected increase in commercial mailings in the next 15 years would, among other things, result in a threefold increase in the number of large letters and advertising material carried.

The modernization program continued during 1970. New accounting machines and franking machines (155 in all) went into service at Post Office counters, while a considerable number of stamp and other vending machines were installed. In addition to further mechanization of handling services in many sorting centres and major distributing offices, two automatic sorting points for letters were being installed, at Clermont Ferrand and in Arcueil, a suburb of Paris. Motorized delivery increased with the introduction of 1,150 new rural rounds and 450 urban rounds.

In West Germany the reform of legislation affecting postal services, initiated by the new federal government elected in September 1969, was concluded by the promulgation of a law pertaining to posts and the enactment of a new postal giro (for making transfers and payments) and postal savings bank ordinance. The regulations came into force on Jan. 1, 1970, and supplemented ordinances affecting the newspaper service and postal bus services. Total revenue of the Federal Post Office rose by 10.6% in 1969 to DM. 13,746,000,000 but profits were one-third less than in the previous year. The shortage of technical and other staff continued, and training facilities for apprentices were extended. In order to acquaint Post Office executives with modern management methods, a management college, affiliated with the Federal Ministry of Posts and Telecommunications, was inaugurated on March 2, 1970. As from Jan. 1, 1971, the Post Office and the federal railways were to amalgamate their bus services. The proportion of subscriber trunk dialing in international telephone traffic increased to 92.5%. Operations were begun with the second antenna of the earth station in Raisting to cope with increased telecommunications traffic via satellites.

In Sweden rural postmen not only deliver mail to customers, they also function as ambulatory post offices in that they handle money matters, parcels, registered mail, cash on delivery, and similar transactions. In sparsely populated areas in the northern parts of the country, rural postmen in the ordinary sense would be unreasonably expensive in relation to the limited number of customers that each postman could serve during a round. However, in some northern areas bus conductors on the Post Office buslines were acting as rural postmen and counter clerks on an experimental basis. On Oct. 1, 1970, the Swedish Post Office introduced differentiated services in the conveyance of printed matter and sample post. Articles paid for as A-class were handled as fast as sealed letters. B-class matter, in principle sorted only in the daytime, reached the addressee one or two days later. From Jan. 1, 1970, a new law gave the Swedish Post Office Bank, on the whole, the same rights and obligations as other banks. In cooperation with the Association of the Blind, the Swedish Post Office instituted a special giro service for the visually handicapped.

In Pakistan, 2,491 new post offices were added during the third five-year plan (ended June 30, 1970), bringing the total to 14,257. The fourth five-year plan envisaged opening a further 3,000. During 1970 sea mail services between East and West Pakistan were developed further; steamer services utilized for mail transport on the route numbered eight or nine a month in each direction. New regional postal headquarters were established at Peshawar. At the Tokyo Universal Postal Congress, Pakistan was elected to membership in both the executive council and the Consultative Council for Postal Studies.

Two Australian Post Office proposals that attracted international interest were the world's largest and most advanced electronic trunk exchange in Sydney and the Common User Data Network. When complete, the Sydney exchange building would be capable of providing up to 20,000 trunk lines. The Common User Data Network would operate nationally throughout Australia and its facilities would be complementary to those for data transmission over private lines and by the telex and telephone switched network. Equipment valued at about A$4.5 million was on order. About 2,723,000,000 articles of mail were handled during the 12 months to June 30, 1970. After three years of operation, the use of Postcode on letter mail in Australia rose to more than 80% by that date. In July 1970 the Post Office introduced Priority Paid Mail, which provided overnight service between addresses in state capitals and their suburbs and same-day service between neighbouring cities.

In New Zealand, Post Office income for 1969–70 reached a record NZ$119.5 million; expenditure (including NZ$12.2 million in interest on borrowed capital) amounted to NZ$117.1 million. Post Office Bonus Bonds, based on the U.K. premium bonds scheme, were introduced in 1970. On September 7–8 the Post Office staff carried out a "go-slow" in support of a salary claim, creating near chaos for tolls, telegraph, and postal services. It was called off after 48 hours when promises of negotiation from the government were accepted.

Postal service in Canada was disrupted by strikes during much of the year. Rotating strikes were called by the postal unions in May, and late in June the strategy was changed to one of saturation strikes in certain regions. As of August 21, more than 15,000 employees were on strike and 211 post offices were closed. The agreement reached between the government and the unions on September 4 exceeded the government's anti-inflation guidelines.

Figures published in 1970 showed that the Soviet Union's postal service handled nearly 42,000,000,000 items in 1969, including about 7,500,000,000 letters, 31,500,000,000 newspapers and magazines, 167 million

parcels, and 633 million money orders and pension drafts. The Soviet Ministry of Communications and its research organizations continued to work on new or improved mail-processing equipment. One field of research involved mechanization of delivery of newspapers and magazines to subscribers.   (X.)

Postal operations in the U.S. in 1970 were marked by two historic events: the first national postal strike and passage of a reorganization act that made the Post Office an independent agency. The two were closely interconnected. The wildcat strike, which led to the largest walkout ever staged against the federal government, climaxed months of growing resentment among postal employees over low wages and the failure of Congress to enact promised pay increases. When the walkout began in New York on March 18, top scale for a veteran letter carrier was $8,442 a year, well below the $11,236 the government said a family of four required to maintain a moderate standard of living in that city.

While postal union leaders were pushing for pay increases, they were also opposing various aspects of an administration-sponsored bill designed to radically restructure the postal system. The union leaders feared the loss of civil service status and union recognition, as well as their traditional influence over Congress, which historically had set both postal rates and wages. Pres. Richard Nixon insisted he would veto any pay raise bill that was not tied to the reorganization, and the strike erupted as the president, union officials, and congressional leaders were trying to work out a compromise. The walkout spread swiftly across the country, hitting dozens of major cities from coast to coast. It forced a virtual halt to the average daily flow of 270 million pieces of mail and drastically affected the economy as checks, bills, and other legal documents were caught in the logjam. The strike lasted as little as a day in some places, nearly a week in others. Before it was over in New York, 15,000 army reservists were mobilized to help move the mail there.

On August 6 Congress finally approved legislation creating the U.S. Postal Service as an independent agency of the federal government, empowered to approve rates, make its own budget, and bargain directly with employees. With 750,000 employees in 1970, the Postal Service was the government's largest single agency. Its fiscal 1971 budget was $8.3 billion, up $300 million from the previous year, and the fiscal 1972 budget was expected to exceed $9 billion.

The service would be headed by a board of governors and a postmaster general who, unlike his predecessors, would not be a member of the Cabinet. Nine members of the board would be appointed by the president with the advice and consent of the Senate, to serve staggered terms of nine years each. The nine would appoint the postmaster general who would serve, at their pleasure, as the chief operating officer. The 10 together would select a deputy postmaster general, and all 11 would constitute the board of governors. The board itself would not have direct control over rates or classifications of mail; these would be determined by a five-member Postal Rate Commission, appointed by the president. The new corporation had authority to issue up to $10 billion in construction bonds for new facilities, at the rate of up to $2 billion a year. Congress was authorized to appropriate subsidies each year until 1984 on a declining basis to help facilitate the transition. Along with the reorganization, Congress granted the nation's postal workers an 8% pay raise effective April 16, in addition to a 6% raise allotted to most other federal employees as of Dec. 27, 1969.

The new postal corporation, which President Nixon signed into existence on August 12, climaxed years of efforts to streamline the department. Since 1838, Post Office revenue had met costs in only 17 years, with Congress appropriating funds to make up the deficit, which totaled about $1.5 billion in 1970. Historically, whenever deficits topped $1 billion, Congress would react by raising postal rates. Meanwhile, physical plants, many of them built as public works projects during the depression of the 1930s, were decaying, and were poorly suited to handle mail in the 1970s.

(Jy. L.)

See also Philately and Numismatics; Telecommunications.

Encyclopædia Britannica Films. *Our Post Office* (1965).

Prices

In 1970 the industrial countries as a whole experienced what was probably a higher rate of inflation than had occurred at any time during the preceding 20 years. The tendency of price increases to accelerate could be observed in several countries from about the mid-1960s. However, in the period 1969–70 an exceptionally large number of industrial nations were faced with a wage-price spiral of a severity that few had experienced before, so that inflation was regarded widely as the most acute economic problem confronting developed market economies.

The 1970 brand of inflation was unusual not only because of the size of the increases in both wages and prices, but also because it had become an equally serious problem in economies at completely different points of the business cycle. In other words, economies that were passing through a period of recession with unemployment at uncomfortably high levels were affected as much, or even more, than those that had been working for some time near the peak of their capacity and had, therefore, very low rates of unemployment. As a result, it became easier for countries to allow their export prices to rise more or less in step with domestic prices without seriously endangering their balance of payments, at least in the short run. Hence, inflation began to be exported on a scale that was far from insignificant. There were fewer signs of continuing deterioration among less developed countries, even though price rises seemed to be accelerating in a number of them, notably at the wholesale end.

Consumer Prices. The indices and rates given in Table I show that 11 of the 17 developed market economies listed and 19 of the 35 less developed countries experienced, between 1969 and 1970, increases in their cost of living that were above the average for 1960–67. In the case of the less developed countries, the number was almost exactly the same as the year before, but the acceleration was clearly affecting an increasing number of industrial nations.

Among these, the biggest rises in consumer prices took place in Norway (9.5%), Japan (7.5%), and Sweden (6.4%). In Norway the strong growth of domestic demand that started in 1969 continued into 1970, leading to a high degree of capacity utilization and serious pressure on productive resources. However, the exceptionally rapid increase in the cost of living was due mainly to changes in the tax system

and higher import prices. The rate of inflation in Japan was the consequence of a combination of very strong "demand-pull" elements in the industrial sector and pressures on unit labour costs in the rest of the economy. In Sweden, in October 1970, the government imposed a six-month general freeze on prices of both goods and services. Moreover, this direct attack on prices was followed by fiscal measures intended to reduce demand pressure in the economy.

A number of developed market economies experienced very similar increases in the cost of living: the U.S. (5.9%), Denmark (5.8%), France (5.7%), the U.K. (5.6%), and New Zealand (5.6%). In the U.S. the government came under increasing pressure to do something about both high levels of unemployment and rising prices. At the same time, there were growing doubts as to whether the two objectives could be reconciled without something much less conventional than the usual doses of fiscal and monetary measures. The sharp rise in prices in Denmark resulted from a combination of factors: rapid increases in the prices of certain raw materials, the revaluation of the West

Table I. Cost of Living—Selected Countries

Country	Index (1963 = 100) 1968	1969	1970*	Annual percentage changes over preceding year 1960-67 Average	1968	1969	1970†
Developed market economies							
Denmark‡	137	141	147	5.8	8.7	2.9	5.8
Finland	138	141	144	5.0	8.7	2.2	2.9
Japan	129	136	144	5.7	5.7	5.4	7.5
Netherlands	125	134	138	3.7	3.3	7.2	3.0
Norway	123	127	138	4.1	3.4	3.3	9.5
New Zealand	122	128	133	3.2	4.3	4.9	5.6
Sweden	123	126	133	4.2	1.6	2.4	6.4
U.K.	121	127	133	3.4	5.2	5.0	5.6
France	118	124	129	2.9	5.4	5.1	5.7
Belgium‡	119	124	128	2.7	2.6	4.2	4.1
Austria	119	123	126	3.7	2.6	3.4	3.3
Italy	119	122	126	4.5	0.8	2.5	4.1
Canada	117	122	125	2.2	4.5	4.3	4.2
U.S.	114	120	125	1.7	4.6	5.3	5.9
Switzerland	119	122	124	3.5	2.6	2.5	1.6
Australia	116	120	123	2.2	2.6	3.4	3.4
Germany, West	113	116	120	2.7	1.8	2.7	3.4
Centrally planned economies							
Yugoslavia	207	224	247	13.7	5.1	8.2	9.3
Hungary	107	109	108	1.0	0.0	1.9	0.9
Poland	107	108	108	1.3	1.9	0.9	1.9
Less developed countries							
Brazil	714	879	1,005	54.8	24.4	23.1	20.6
Chile	346	452	561	25.1	26.7	30.6	31.1
Argentina	311	335	361	25.4	16.0	7.7	10.1
Korea, South	202	222	244	14.1	11.6	9.9	13.0
Peru	185	196	203	9.3	19.4	5.9	4.1
Colombia	167	184	192	12.8	5.7	10.2	7.9
India	160	160	164	7.8	2.6	0.0	3.1
Spain	144	147	152	6.9	5.1	2.1	4.1
Turkey	138	146	152	6.0	5.3	5.8	5.6
Zambia‡	143	146	145	3.9	10.8	2.1	-1.4
Portugal	126	137	144	3.4	5.9	8.7	7.5
Ireland	125	134	142	3.9	5.0	7.2	7.6
Nigeria	113	124	137	2.9	1.8	9.7	12.3
Pakistan	126	130	136	3.8	0.0	3.2	6.3
Israel	127	130	134	6.5	2.4	2.4	3.9
Ceylon	112	120	127	1.6	5.7	7.1	7.6
Tunisia	122	127	126	2.5	2.5	4.1	0.0
South Africa§	116	119	124	2.5	1.8	2.6	5.1
Mexico‡	116	120	123	2.3	1.8	3.4	4.2
Taiwan	114	119	121	2.4	8.6	4.4	4.3
Cambodia	111	118	117	2.9	5.7	6.3	-0.8
Greece	111	114	117	2.1	0.0	2.7	2.6
Thailand	113	116	116	2.1	1.8	2.7	0.9
Iran	108	111	116	1.6	0.9	2.8	3.6
Costa Rica	108	111	115	1.8	3.8	2.8	4.5
Iraq	103	112	115	1.0	1.9	8.7	2.7
Malta	107	110	113	1.6	1.9	2.8	3.7
Kenya‡	111	110	112	2.3	0.9	-0.9	1.8
Venezuela	107	110	111	1.4	0.9	2.8	1.8
Morocco	106	109	111	2.7	0.0	2.8	1.8
Cyprus	105	107	108	0.4	4.0	1.9	1.9
El Salvador	105	105	108	0.3	1.9	0.0	3.8
Malaysia, West	105	104	106	1.1	0.0	-1.0	1.9
Guatemala	102	104	106	0.3	2.0	2.0	2.9
Dominican Rep.	102	103	104	2.1	0.0	1.0	2.0

*January–June (average).
†First half 1970 over first half 1969.
‡Excluding rent.
§White population only.
Sources: International Monetary Fund, *International Financial Statistics;* United Nations, *Monthly Bulletin of Statistics.*

Poultry:
see Agriculture

Power:
see Engineering Projects; Fuel and Power; Industrial Review

Presbyterians:
see Religion

BEN ROTH AGENCY

"How much did you say
telephone charges
were going up?"
—Franklin,
London "Daily Mirror."

German mark, and the continued upward trend in domestic costs. The government, in addition to another resort to fiscal policy, undertook to compensate enterprises, during a period of several months, for increases in costs resulting from the automatic wage adjustments of September 1970, and imposed a price freeze on services until the end of February 1971.

The U.K., like the U.S., had to cope simultaneously with problems of inflation, high unemployment, and low growth of productivity. Unusually large increases in wage costs made their contribution to the rate of inflation, but so did rises in wholesale prices of basic materials and fuels, as well as the growing pressure on overhead caused by the prolonged underutilization of capacity. New Zealand was another country where the authorities resorted to a price freeze—for two months from November 1970, to be followed by mandatory price controls. Only secondhand goods and those sold by auction were exempt.

As Table I shows, the smallest increases in consumer prices between 1969 and 1970 were, with the exception of Switzerland (1.6%), in the range of 3–3.5%. In Australia deceleration in the rate of inflation toward the end of the year coincided with a reduction in consumer spending and a decrease in demand for labour. The cost of living went up by about 3.4% in West Germany, a remarkably moderate rise given the pace of expansion achieved by the country in recent years and the fact that the unemployment rate in 1970 remained below 1%. However, the rate of inflation began to accelerate toward the end of the year when labour costs were rising faster than at any time since the late 1940s. A similar tendency could be observed in the second part of the year in Austria.

The relative stability of prices in the Netherlands (3%) and Finland (2.9%) was achieved by a direct attack on the problem. The Dutch authorities continued to insist on the strict price policy they had introduced in 1969, even though some of the responsibility for maintaining price stability was transferred in the summer of 1970 from government to trade and industry. In Finland total output expanded very rapidly during 1970—faster than the average for the 1960s. At the same time, the freeze on both incomes and prices continued. Finally, the price stability

achieved by Switzerland was quite exceptional among industrial nations, especially since it was maintained during a period of high levels of demand and very high degrees of capacity utilization.

Most of the centrally planned economies take considerable care to maintain a stable price level, invariably through tight price controls. Consequently, when a serious shortage develops, it tends to lead to rationing rather than soaring prices. Yugoslavia remained an exception; the economy was much more liberal and the controls were not always very successful. For instance, in 1970 prices went up rapidly, not only in the sectors where they were not subject to any controls, but also in those where they were controlled. In the autumn the authorities introduced a number of provisional measures, including a freeze on prices of industrial products, in yet another attempt to arrest the continuing rise in prices and the buoyant demand for imports. Rents and various charges for municipal services, including transport, were to remain fixed.

There were no great changes in the cost of living indices among less developed countries. The situation continued to improve in Latin America, especially in Peru. The notable exception was Chile, where the increase in consumer prices (31.1%) was by far

Table II. Indices of Food Prices in Relation to Cost of Living Index
(1963 = 100)

Country	1967	1968	1969	1970*
Developed market economies				
Japan	102	103	103	105
Finland	102	104	105	103
Belgium	102	101	106	102
Sweden	101	100	101	102
Norway	100	100	101	102
Australia	103	103	101	101
New Zealand	102	101	101	101
Denmark	100	100	101	101
U.S.	101	100	100	100
Austria	101	99	100	100†
Canada	100	100	99	99
Netherlands	100	98	98	99
U.K.	98	97	98	99
France	99	98	98	98
Italy	98	97	97	98‡
Germany, West	98	96	96	95†
Centrally planned economies				
Hungary	105	105	104	104
Yugoslavia	100	99	99	103
Poland	98	99	100	101
Less developed countries				
Vietnam, South	130	135	135	133
Nigeria	98	94	103	111
Thailand	108	109	111	110
India	105	106	108	108‡
Costa Rica	102	103	105	107
Pakistan	105	104	104	106
El Salvador	102	104	104	106
Ceylon	104	105	104	105
Puerto Rico	103	104	105	105
Malta	100	102	103	104
Dominican Republic	99	103	101	104
Kenya	104	104	103	103
South Africa§	104	104	103	102‡
Tunisia	102	102	103	102†
Iran	103	102	100	102‡
Greece	101	101	102	102
Mexico	101	101	101	102‡
Korea, South	95	94	97	102‡
Cyprus	101	102	103	101†
Guatemala	99	101	100	101‡
Morocco	100	99	100	100
Chile	100	99	99	100
Zambia	104	101	99	99‡
Colombia	100	98	98	99
Portugal	101	100	99	98†
Ireland	97	98	97	98‡
Argentina	98	98	96	97
Venezuela	97	96	97	96‡
Spain	96	96	96	94
Israel	95	96	96	94
Cambodia	89	91	94	94
Brazil	94	94	92	92‡

*January–June (average) except where stated otherwise.
†January–July (average).
‡January–May (average).
§White population only.
Source: United Nations, *Monthly Bulletin of Statistics.*

the worst in any of the countries included in Table I. The rate of inflation in South Korea was again near to those experienced in Latin America. Nigeria was not far behind, but there the deterioration was undoubtedly caused by the effects of the civil war. In Cambodia consumer prices declined in the period 1969–70, compared with annual increases of about 6% during the previous two years.

Particularly serious in the case of many less developed countries was the fact that prices of foodstuffs were increasing at even higher rates than consumer prices in general, and in these countries food comprises a very high proportion of total consumer expenditure. The relationship of the index of food prices to the total cost of living index (including food) is shown in Table II. The figures are obtained by dividing index numbers of the first series by the second. Thus the numbers over 100 indicate that food prices rose more rapidly than those of all goods and services, while those below 100 show the opposite.

The two indices went more or less in step in most of the developed market and centrally planned economies. The most noticeable differences were in Japan, Hungary, and West Germany. However, it was among less developed countries that some of the most serious increases in food prices occurred. By far the worst case was that of South Vietnam, which in recent years had had a rate of inflation comparable only to those of Brazil and Chile.

Wholesale Prices. In developed market economies, at least, the index of wholesale prices had tended to be much more stable than that of the cost of living. However, if the rates given in Table III are compared with those in Table I, it will be seen that between 1969 and 1970, price increases were greater at the wholesale level. Since wholesale prices are the first to reflect the pressure from higher costs, and it is only some time later that the pressure is felt by the final consumer, the rates in the last column of Table III might well mean that sizable increases in the cost of living were still to come in most industrial countries.

The worst experiences were those of France (11.5%), Denmark (9.5%), and Italy (8.3%), all of which had to cope with substantial rises in wage and other costs. Moreover, France was feeling the effects of devaluation in the summer of 1969. It is worth noting that wholesale prices in all industrial countries rose faster between 1969 and 1970 than during 1960–67. In many cases the difference was considerable.

On the other hand, in most of the less developed countries wholesale prices went up at what might be called the "customary" rates. The worst deterioration took place in the Philippines, El Salvador, Morocco, and Mexico. With the possible exception of Pakistan, there were no significant improvements over the previous year. (M. Pan.)

See also Commodities, Primary; Economy, World; Employment, Wages, and Hours; Income, National; Industrial Review; Investment, International; Merchandising; Money and Banking; Payments and Reserves, International; Stock Exchanges; Trade, International.

Prisons and Penology

The increasing pressure under which many penal systems operate continued to lead to explosive incidents. In New York inmates of five of the city's correctional institutions rioted over a period of five days in October 1970 in protest against overcrowding and grossly inadequate facilities. At Parkhurst Prison, on the Isle of Wight, Eng., prisoners and staff were injured in violent clashes on Oct. 24, 1969, which led to a trial in May 1970. In 1969 there were serious clashes in the San Vittore prison in the centre of Milan, Italy, and stones were hurled at passersby.

These were not the only problems encountered. As crime increased and more people came before the courts, it took longer for cases to come to trial and more offenders were being remanded to prison. The pressure on centres where accused persons are held waiting for trial, and on penal institutions as a whole, grew alarmingly in some countries in 1970. In England and Wales, for example, the daily average population in prisons, borstals, remand and detention centres was 35,000 at the end of 1969 but had risen to 40,000 by mid-1970. This was about four times the prewar figure, but new buildings erected since World War II had increased the available closed prison facilities by only about one-third. The sheer problem of containing so many in so little space naturally produced tensions, and the fact that among prisoners there is always a proportion of mentally disturbed and potentially violent persons aggravated the difficulties.

In this connection, the authorities in California made an interesting experiment. Realizing that they would be faced with an unprecedented rise in the population of penal institutions, they had asked themselves some years earlier whether a more extensive and intensive use of probation might not succeed with many who would otherwise be sent for custodial treatment. In 1965 the state legislature enacted a probation subsidy law, under which money that would have

Table III. Wholesale Prices for Selected Countries

Country	Index (1963 = 100) 1968	1969	1970*	Annual percentage changes over preceding year Average 1960–67	1968	1969	1970†
Developed market economies							
Finland	131	136	141	3.3	11.0	3.8	5.2
Denmark	113	118	127	2.6	2.7	4.4	9.5
France	106	115	126	1.9	1.0	8.5	11.5
U.K.‡	115	120	125	2.4	3.6	4.3	5.0
New Zealand	115	121	124	1.4	7.5	5.2	3.3
Sweden	113	118	124	2.7	0.9	4.4	6.9
Netherlands	116	117	124	2.3	0.9	0.9	6.9
Austria	114	117	122	2.7	0.9	2.6	5.2
Norway	112	116	121	1.9	0.9	3.6	5.2
Canada	110	115	118	2.0	1.9	4.5	2.6
Belgium	107	113	118	1.4	0.0	5.6	6.3
Italy	107	111	118	2.0	0.9	3.7	8.3
U.S.	108	113	116	0.8	1.9	4.6	3.6
Japan	106	108	112	0.8	1.0	1.9	4.7
Switzerland	104	107	110	1.6	0.0	2.9	3.8
Germany, West	99	101	106	1.0	−4.8	2.0	6.0
Less developed countries							
Vietnam, South	210	251	297	12.4	8.8	19.5	29.1
Argentina	258	274	292	23.1	9.3	6.2	9.8
Korea, South	186	199	214	14.4	8.1	7.0	9.2
India	158	164	172	8.1	−1.2	3.8	7.5
Yugoslavia§	136	142	152	5.3	0.0	4.4	9.4
Turkey	129	137	144	4.9	4.9	6.2	5.9
Philippines	120	121	139	5.0	2.6	0.8	17.8
Pakistan	123	130	131	4.6	−3.9	5.7	2.3
Portugal	117	120	126	1.8	4.5	2.6	5.0
Spain	120	122	125	4.0	2.6	1.7	1.6
Mexico	113	115	122	1.9	1.8	1.8	7.0
Syria	118	114	120	1.0	1.7	−3.4	3.4
South Africa	114	116	118	2.2	1.8	1.8	1.7
Venezuela	112	114	115	3.0	0.9	1.8	1.8
Greece	111	114	115	2.5	−0.9	2.7	0.9
Costa Rica	112	109	114	1.5	7.7	−2.7	3.6
Morocco	106	108	114	3.9	−8.6	1.9	8.6
El Salvador	105	105	113	0.4	0.0	0.0	8.7
Thailand	114	116	110	3.6	−4.2	1.8	−2.7
Dominican Republic	114	109	109	2.3	6.5	−4.4	0.0
Taiwan	105	104	107	2.1	2.9	−1.0	3.9

*January–June (average).
†First half 1970 over first half 1969.
‡Prices of finished goods only.
§Producers' prices of industrial products.
Sources: International Monetary Fund, *International Financial Statistics*; United Nations, *Monthly Bulletin of Statistics*.

Primary Commodities: *see* Commodities, Primary

Printing: *see* Industrial Review

gone to penal institutions and custodial treatment was used to subsidize probation. By 1970 the results were clear: the need to build many costly new institutions had been avoided and the inmate population had been lowered. Follow-up studies showed that the relapse rate into crime had been reduced. It had even become possible to decrease the number of parole staff who deal with discharged prisoners.

The Netherlands also managed to keep its prison population relatively small. Among Western European countries, it had the lowest number of inmates in proportion to its total population. There were about 12,000 voluntary workers involved in preventing former offenders from relapsing into crime. This was a higher proportion of volunteers than in other countries and compared with approximately 2,000 such volunteers in England and Wales.

The use of volunteers in aftercare and crime prevention was one of the subjects discussed at the UN Congress on the Prevention of Crime and Treatment of Offenders, held in Kyoto, Jap., in August 1970. Japan itself had formed an association of young volunteers who set out to help offenders of the same age group, under the general guidance of the probation/parole supervision officers.

Yet another aspect of the pressure on prisons was the increasing length of sentences. Probably the longest sentence ever passed anywhere was imposed in Dallas, Tex., in June 1970, when a young drug pusher was sentenced to 1,500 years in jail. Nothing quite so drastic had happened anywhere else in the world. Nevertheless, the rise in serious professional crime was being met by increasingly stiffer sentences. This meant that cell space was occupied for very long stretches by the same person. It also posed problems in prison management. Prisoners serving very long terms feel they have little to lose. Special security measures were often essential for them and yet the regime somehow had to remain flexible and varied so that individuals did not deteriorate physically and psychologically.

Rules affecting the treatment of Soviet prisoners (specifically those in Uzbekistan) were published in August 1970 in the form of a Corrective Labour Code. Work had always been regarded as the most impor-

tant and effective treatment method in the U.S.S.R., and "good conduct and a conscientious attitude toward labour" were rewarded with the right to spend additional money or to have an extra visit or a parcel. There were a number of different types of labour colonies. There was also a sentence to "exile," often used to banish vagrants from the cities to various specified areas. Exiles were allowed to pick their precise place of residence within the prescribed area and were given ten days in which to pack and arrange their personal affairs. They had to have special identity cards and their freedom of movement was restricted for the duration of the sentence. Finally, there was deportation, mainly used against those who offended against labour laws or the regulations on registration of residence. Deportees might settle in any area from which they had not specifically been excluded. In Moscow and other large towns there was often a floating population without residence permits. People in this category were subject to deportation orders.

Control of residence was used as a penal measure in other countries, as well. France, for example, used the *permis de séjour* as a way of keeping certain types of discharged prisoners out of big cities. This measure was criticized by some because it might make obtaining legitimate employment more difficult.

A number of important major experiments in treatment policy were in progress. The Robert F. Kennedy Youth Center in West Virginia, which opened in 1969, incorporated a training method based on what is called "operant conditioning." Traditionally, punishment has been used not only as a response by the courts to wrongdoing but, more specifically, as a way of controlling and modifying the behaviour of inmates in penal institutions. But pilot tests and experiments in the mental health field had shown that rewards, consistently given for desirable behaviour, could be more effective than punishment for certain types of people.

The Youth Center called the young offenders it housed "students." After careful assessment, the students were classified and allocated into one of five groups. Each group had a different program, corresponding to the needs of its members. Not only was work rewarded, but also such things as participation in leisure activities and acceptance of responsibility. The system was extremely flexible and permitted staff to take into account the degree of effort made by the individual and the particular treatment objective that had been worked out for him. The points earned could be spent on goods such as cigarettes or soap, extra food such as chocolate or soft drinks, on a visit to the movies, or on privileges such as a trip to town. Students could also be fined for misconduct. By the end of 1970 no decisive results were yet available.

Less advanced but nevertheless interesting was the approach used at Coldingley Prison in Surrey, Eng., Britain's first industrial prison. Although its architects did not go quite as far as the Swedish pioneers who, in the 1960s, built factories with prisons around them, it did incorporate some noteworthy features. For example, prisoners were not ordered where to go or told what work to do. Instead, jobs were advertised, as in the outside world, and prisoners could apply for them. They could be hired for a number of relatively interesting and well-paid jobs. They could also be dismissed, in which case they were relegated to low-paying routine cleaning and maintenance tasks. The prison shop contained desirable items such as transistor radios which could be bought by those

In England's Holloway Prison a woman inmate occupies quarters more like a bedroom than a cell.

ASSOCIATED NEWSPAPERS LTD.

who earned enough. Although no follow-up studies had yet been published, by the end of 1970 it was clear that morale was high and that the initial response to the Coldingley regime was good.

Traditionally, prisons are places where the offender has no choice and need accept no responsibility, but merely carries out passively the orders given to him. Since many prisoners are irresponsible, the notion of at least some degree of self-administration involving the development of personal responsibility was being explored further. It underlay the notion of a therapeutic community, and experts in member states of the Council of Europe began to study this question in 1970.

Acquiring a new skill, especially if it can also lead to a well-paid job, can change an offender's often negative self-image and open up the possibility of succeeding lawfully where previously only failure had been experienced or envisaged. In Canada computer training courses were started in the Federal Training Centre, in cooperation with Canadair and IBM of Montreal, and by the Industrial Acceptance Corporation in the Cowansville Institution, Quebec. Some former inmates already had found work in this field.

Of lesser importance were a number of simpler measures which had their uses. New Zealand had a maximum security prison at Auckland, with all the restrictions that this implies. Yet by 1970 it probably had developed more facilities for hobbies than many ordinary prisons with less secure regimes. Apart from the constructive use of leisure as an end in itself, some inmates were able to earn substantial amounts, to be kept for their release.

Turning away from institutions, it was obvious that there was a large gap between probation and the freedom to work and live in the community on the one hand, and confinement in a penal institution on the other. Most countries were in the process of developing a range of intermediate treatment methods. In Denmark gradations ranged from walk-in advice centres where young people in trouble could themselves ask for help, through probation with a condition to attend a centre or clinic, to detention in a penal institution.

Northorpe Hall, in Yorkshire, Eng., presented a different example of this trend. Over weekends and during holidays, urban children, under a probation order, went to this country house which was staffed by qualified social workers. In this residential setting, attempts were made to help the children struggle through to greater maturity. During the week the same team of social workers worked with the parents so that a two-pronged attack on the problem was mounted.

Other simple but useful measures, somewhere between treatment in freedom and in institutions, were taken in ordinary probation hostels where probationers usually work in the community but are required to reside in the hostel at night. These were being used in a growing number of countries. The Curepipe nondenominational probation hostel on Mauritius was a successful example of support and supervision in freedom, with a modicum of more intensive influence and control.

Probation techniques themselves also were undergoing changes. In California it was found useful to try to match different types of probation officers with different types of offenders. In England, group work with probationers gradually was beginning to develop. This enabled one probation officer to deal with up

to a dozen offenders for an hour and a half at a time. It was an economic use of scarce social worker resources, but there were also virtues in the group situation itself.

Many offenders feel they are unacceptable. If they manage to make honest admissions about themselves and continue to be accepted by the group, they are taking the first steps to self-acceptance. Moreover, because pressure to change comes from others like them and not from some outside authority, it can be more effective. In Sweden group work was successfully used in the aftercare of quite difficult discharged prisoners, including alcoholics.

Finally, group work was being used to help the wives of prisoners, particularly in the U.K. At its simplest, this was a way of sharing common problems and giving mutual support. But since such groups were often run by voluntary workers and sometimes had facilities for child care while the mothers discussed their problems together after a prison visit, it was also a way of demonstrating that the community as a whole was not indifferent.   (H. J. KL.)

See also **Crime.**

RUSS REIF FROM
PICTORIAL PARADE

Above, a clenched fist is raised over a bedsheet banner at New York City's House of Detention, better known as the Tombs, Aug. 11, 1970. Below, furniture and mattresses litter Long Island City jail Oct. 6, 1970, during New York's city-wide prison rebellion.

Profits

The widely held view that profits provide a haven against the inroads of inflation was put to a harsh test in 1969 and 1970—at least according to the profit trends in those few countries publishing current data. In the early part of 1970 profits continued the downtrend begun in 1969 in the U.S., the U.K., and Canada, but a turnabout was evident late in the year in the U.S., the only country whose third quarter results were known. In West Germany, where an inflationary boom continued into 1970, profits in the first half of the year barely managed to remain at the same level as in the second half of 1969. In all of these countries, profits represented a smaller share of national income than in the preceding years.

As in 1969, profits in 1970 were conditioned by the interplay between cost and price inflation and the determined efforts by governments to restore stability. A pronounced shift toward policy restraint had begun in 1968 in the U.S. and Canada, where

WIDE WORLD

pressures on capacity had appeared earlier than elsewhere, and in the U.K., where the most pressing reason had been the state of the balance of payments rather than concern over rising prices. By contrast, continental Europe had enjoyed rapid expansion without undue price pressures until late in 1968 because of continuing margins of excess capacity. As these margins shrank and wage pressures mounted, however, these countries were increasingly obliged to orient their policies toward controlling inflation. As a result of this difference in timing, by the early part of 1970 growth had leveled off or actually declined in the U.S., Canada, and the U.K., while it continued at a brisk though moderating rate in continental Europe and Japan.

United States. Profits had been rising in the U.S. in mid-1968 when, to curb the inflation that was still gaining momentum, a 10% surcharge was imposed on personal and business income taxes and a ceiling applied on federal expenditures. Concern at the time that these measures would "overkill" inflation quickly gave way to the conclusion that they were not enough. Accordingly, monetary policy became increasingly more restrictive in 1969. While real growth gave way under the pressure of these policies in 1968, inflationary forces were so deeply rooted that price increases continued their acceleration into 1970.

Corporate profits, both before and after taxes and despite the tax surcharge, continued their expansion until the second quarter of 1969 (*see* Table I). This performance represented the triumph of volume increases over the attrition of rising costs, lower margins, and higher taxes. When the growth of volume did slacken, however, profits were unable to make further headway or even to hold their ground. Their decline, beginning in the third quarter, continued until midyear 1970. Total corporate profits before taxes, including inventory profits, fell 12.2%, and after-tax profits, which benefited from the reduction of the income tax surcharge from 10 to 5% in January 1970 and its total elimination in mid-1970, fell 11.6%. Profits from operations, that is, those deflated for the effect of higher prices on inventories, actually turned about in the second quarter of 1970.

The profits of financial institutions, before taxes and after inventory valuation adjustment, leveled in the final quarter of 1969 and dipped only slightly in the first quarter of 1970 before resuming their growth. But the main impact of the decline in earnings fell on the nonfinancial sector. Within manufacturing, the decline of profits was most pronounced for durables, which in the first quarter of 1970 had dropped almost 30% from their peak a year earlier. In non-

durables, the downtrend that began after the second quarter of 1969 had carried before-tax profits 8.5% below the peak by midyear 1970.

In the third quarter of 1970, total corporate profits before taxes improved at an annual rate of almost 8% over the preceding quarter despite a strike at General Motors, the world's largest manufacturer. A seasonally adjusted diffusion index prepared by the First National City Bank of New York indicated that 54% of manufacturing companies enjoyed higher earnings in the third quarter of 1970, compared with 44% in the second quarter and 50% a year before. Fourth quarter profits were expected to show a temporary decline reflecting the extended General Motors strike.

United Kingdom. The primary objective of public policy following the devaluation of sterling in November 1967 was a lasting improvement in the balance of payments. This effort was rewarded in 1969 and 1970, but at the expense of growth, which declined in real terms to 1.8% in 1969 and came to a virtual halt in the first half of 1970. Labour unrest, always a problem in Britain, was especially disruptive in 1970. Wage and price increases accelerated as unemployment climbed. In the first three quarters of 1970, the cost of living rose around 7%, while basic hourly wage rates in August 1970 were 11% above the levels of the year before. Clearly, inflation had replaced the balance of payments as the economy's most urgent problem.

In this inauspicious environment, company income held up surprisingly well (*see* Table II). The seasonally adjusted official measure of company income, which embraced depreciation allowances, interest expense, and income taxes as well as net income, rose modestly but steadily from after mid-1967 until the third quarter of 1969, when it reached an annual rate some 7% above the results for all of 1968. The ensuing decline slowly and progressively carried total

Table II. United Kingdom: Company Income, Seasonally Adjusted

In £000,000

		Income arising in the United Kingdom		
Period	Total	Gross trading profits*	Rent and non-trading income	Income from abroad
1968: First quarter	2,084	1,267	422	395
Second quarter	2,110	1,261	407	442
Third quarter	2,116	1,218	430	468
Fourth quarter	2,101	1,278	431	392
1969: First quarter	2,137	1,197	456	484
Second quarter	2,141	1,208	458	475
Third quarter	2,254	1,278	485	491
Fourth quarter	2,249	1,265	492	492
1970: First quarter	2,208	1,231	515	462
Second quarter	2,172	1,190	502	480

*Before providing for depreciation and stock appreciation.
Source: *Financial Statistics* (October 1970).

Table III. West Germany: Profit and Income Developments

In DM. 000,000; without adjustment for seasonal variation

Income from entrepreneurial activity and property

Period	Before income taxes	Share of national income (%)	After income taxes	Change from previous corresponding period (%) Before income taxes	After income taxes
1968: First half	67,430	34.8	51,630	15.6	19.4
Second half	81,870	36.9	65,210	19.0	20.8
1969: First half	74,030	34.5	56,740	9.8	9.9
Second half	84,360	34.6	65,460	3.0	0.4
1970: First half	78,310	32.2	61,620	5.8	8.6

Source: *Wirtschaft und Statistik* no. 9 (1970).

Table I. United States Corporate Profits and Related Indicators

Period	Profits (in $000,000,000) Before taxes	Less inventory profits	After taxes	Profits per dollar of sales (cents)*	Ratio of profits to income originating in corporations (%)†	Ratio of price to unit labour cost index‡
1968: First quarter	86.7	81.3	46.9	5.1	11.3	100.6
Second quarter	88.6	86.0	48.3	5.0	11.1	100.2
Third quarter	88.4	87.4	48.0	5.1	10.8	98.9
Fourth quarter	91.3	87.1	49.6	5.1	10.9	98.3
1969: First quarter	93.0	87.1	49.5	5.0	10.7	99.4
Second quarter	93.4	87.4	49.7	4.9	10.5	99.6
Third quarter	89.9	86.8	47.9	4.8	9.9	99.2
Fourth quarter	88.5	82.0	47.1	4.5	9.7	97.9
1970: First quarter	82.6	76.7	44.6	4.1	9.0	97.9
Second quarter	82.0	77.5	43.9	4.2	9.0	98.1
Third quarter	85.0	79.0	45.4	—	—	97.3

*After taxes, all manufacturing.
†All industries.
‡Manufacturing; 1957–59 = 100.
Sources: *Survey of Current Business* (July and November 1970); *Business Conditions Digest* (October 1970).

Table IV. Canada: Corporation Profits Before Taxes, Seasonally Adjusted Annual Rates

In Can$000,000

Period	1968	1969	1970
First quarter	6,960	8,160	7,836
Second quarter	7,316	8,084	7,420
Third quarter	7,568	7,576	
Fourth quarter	7,924	7,588	

Source: *Canadian Statistical Review* (October 1970).

income down some $3\frac{1}{2}\%$ from the peak by the second quarter of 1970. Within this total, operating income (gross trading profits) arising within the U.K. followed the same pattern, reaching a peak in the third quarter of 1969, and declining about 7% by the second quarter of 1970. Rent and nontrading income, however, expanded until the first quarter of 1970 and then declined $2\frac{1}{2}\%$ by midyear. Income from abroad peaked in the final quarter of 1969 and, in the second quarter of 1970, was $2\frac{1}{2}\%$ below the year-end level.

In relation to other income shares, profits fared worse than the changes in their absolute level suggested. In the first half of 1970, the share of gross trading profits, net of inventory appreciation, in total factor income was 30% below the 1964 level. Indeed, the persistent downtrend in the relative position of profits in the past six years had been interrupted only in 1967.

West Germany. Recovery from the 1966–67 recession reached boom dimensions in 1969, as rapid increases in consumption, investment, and exports combined to push output to capacity limits. Although the authorities shifted from a policy of moderate stimulation in 1968 to one of restraint in 1969, inflation proved to be surprisingly durable in West Germany, as elsewhere in the world. The government's progressively tighter restraints included measures directly affecting corporate profits.

West Germany's corporate profits are included in a broader measure called income from entrepreneurial activity and property (IEP), which is published without seasonal adjustment (*see* Table III). In the first half of 1970, IEP before taxes was nearly 6% above its level of a year earlier, but somewhat below the level in the second half of 1969, in line with normal seasonal patterns. The monthly report of the Deutsche Bundesbank of October 1970 noted that, adjusted for seasonal variations and special factors, IEP "probably stagnated in relation to the second half of 1969." After-tax income, however, did somewhat better, partly because of delays in assessing income taxes in the first half of 1970.

While profits failed to keep up with the growth of output, they demonstrated considerable strength in relation to pressures mounted against them. In the 12 months ended in midyear 1970, labour's average earnings rose 14.5%, more than three times as fast as the 4.5% growth of productivity. Unit labour costs consequently expanded around 10% over 1969 levels in both the first and second quarters of 1970, while the price level increased some 7.5% and the growth of output slackened. Depreciation allowances, moreover, rose substantially in the first half of 1970. These adverse developments were partly offset by a leveling off in the rise of indirect taxes and import prices. Still, the seasonally adjusted share of IEP in national income fell in the first half of 1970 to the lowest level since 1945.

Canada. Canada was more successful than the other major countries in the struggle against infla-

tion. In the face of highly restrictive monetary and fiscal policies, rapid rates of expansion and price increase began to subside in 1969. Evidence of success in vanquishing inflation was lacking only on the side of cost pressures.

Corporate profits before taxes had grown rapidly from mid-1967 to an all-time peak in the first quarter of 1969 (*see* Table IV). They fell sharply in the second half of 1969 under the impact of strikes, rising unit labour costs, and slower growth in output and prices. Following a modest rebound in the first quarter of 1970, they resumed their downward course and fell in the second quarter to a level almost 9.5% below the 1969 peak. For all industries, the ratio of profits after taxes to sales was fairly well maintained in 1969, falling only to 4.1 from 4.3% in 1968, but a sharp deterioration to 3.8% was evident by the first quarter of 1970. In manufacturing, the after-tax profit margin actually increased from 4% in 1968 to 4.1% in 1969, but then declined to 3.1% in the first quarter of 1970. (G. A. Po.)

See also Stock Exchanges.

Propaganda

U.S. Pres. Richard Nixon's first annual foreign affairs message in February 1970 postulated that "the postwar period in international relations has ended." This was generally interpreted as notice that the U.S. would limit its commitments abroad, adopt a low-profile posture, and move from the era of confrontation to the era of negotiation. By the end of 1970 it was clear that negotiation itself had become a kind of confrontation and that propaganda on the international scene remained at peak levels.

The year began with a Soviet propaganda extravaganza—the celebration of the hundredth anniversary of Lenin's birth. Later came the 25th anniversary of the dropping of the first atomic bomb and of the founding of the UN. President Nixon's trip to five European countries in September (including Communist Yugoslavia), culminating in a visit to the U.S. 6th Fleet in the Mediterranean, was undoubtedly interpreted as a major propaganda move designed to convey the message of America's great military strength and resolve. It was overshadowed, however, by the sudden death of U.A.R. Pres. Gamal Abd-al-Nasser.

The propaganda of violent acts for political aims accelerated. Guatemalan guerrillas kidnapped and killed a German diplomat; a provincial Cabinet minister was seized and murdered by separatist terrorists in Quebec; a U.S. official was killed by Uruguayan guerrillas. Palestinian commandos resorted to air piracy and the holding of civilian hostages, and political bombings and kidnappings became almost commonplace.

Chilean voters chose Salvador Allende as their president, marking the first time a Communist had been freely elected as a head of state. Soviet media called this "a crushing defeat for the most reactionary, proimperialist circles as well as bourgeois reformism," while the Chinese said that his victory was a reflection of the "mounting struggles of the Chilean people against U.S. imperialism's ruthless oppression, plunder and exploitation."

Although there were signs of increased scientific collaboration during a year marked by the aborting of the U.S. Apollo 13 moon mission and by Soviet emphasis on automated space probes, the propaganda ac-

"'Dear Dayan: Show more
confidence and patience.'
—Nixon"—Behrendt,
"Het Parool."

BEN ROTH AGENCY

companiment was not always reassuring. Though the U.S.-Soviet talks on strategic arms limitation (SALT) continued, and a joint U.S.-Soviet treaty was drafted prohibiting the use of the seabed for nuclear weapons, Soviet propaganda asserted that the U.S. was just going through the motions and that it had always preferred the "mailed fist" approach. The launching of China's first earth satellite was predictably interpreted as a manifestation of the "triumph of the thought of Chairman Mao." East Germany accused West German and U.S. radio stations of inciting the riots that took place in Poland in December.

The Middle East. The year was an especially turbulent one for the Middle East, in terms of both actual events and the propaganda exploitation of them. The Soviet propaganda machine, in high gear from the beginning of the year onward, used U.S. weapons deliveries to the Israelis as an early central theme. They charged that U.S. policy toward Israel was just one piece in the overall mosaic of the "Nixon doctrine," which they claimed "provides for using, as far as possible, U.S. allies and satellites to carry out Washington's expansionist aims." When the U.S. peace proposals in June and July brought prospects for a negotiated settlement, Soviet and U.A.R. propaganda insisted that the U.S. plan was nothing but a rehash of the November 1967 UN Security Council resolution on the Middle East, which both the U.S.S.R. and the U.A.R. had long endorsed. The U.S. and Israel, perceiving that the Arabs could not be conquered, accepted the Security Council's terms.

When the Israelis charged that the U.A.R. had deployed rockets in the truce zone, the Soviets claimed the Israelis had invented the charge as a "maneuver to nullify the first success on the road to a peaceful solution to the Middle-East dispute." The U.A.R., in addition to subscribing to the Soviet line, counter-accused Israel of taking advantage of the cease-fire to build new fortifications of its own. The position of the Voice of America (VOA) was that the Soviets and the U.A.R. had indeed violated the cease-fire agreement and it called their good faith into question. Simultaneously, VOA stressed efforts by the U.S. and others to get talks started.

The eruption of fighting between the Jordanian Army and several of the Palestinian guerrilla organizations caused consternation throughout the Arab world. The U.A.R. deplored the spilling of Arab blood by other Arabs when all should be engaged in the common struggle of "liberating the land and restoring usurped rights." This conflict had barely subsided when Nasser died. In the midst of the general Arab grief, the Soviets spoke with a consoling voice: they also mourned the great leader's death, but the Arab people should not be downcast since they had a strong ally—the U.S.S.R. "The defense of the Arab peoples in the anti-imperialist struggle will go on." U.A.R. propaganda also sounded a militant note: "All of you should become Gamal Abd-al-Nasser in carrying the honourable banner which he held until his last breath—the banner of anti-Zionism and anti-imperialism without bargaining, appeasement, or submission."

Indochina and the Far East. Even before the joint U.S.-South Vietnamese operations in Cambodia began in late April, Soviet propaganda was repeatedly asserting that the U.S. had set military victory in Vietnam as its goal: "By stressing vietnamization, which means a military solution . . . the U.S. has deadlocked the Paris peace talks." The overthrow of Cambodian Prince Sihanouk (which the Soviets claimed was CIA-inspired) and the subsequent U.S.-South Vietnamese Cambodian operations elicited even sharper Soviet condemnation. "Under cover of 'vietnamization' of the war and the 'withdrawal' of American troops from South Vietnam, preparations are going on for an American war against all peoples of the Indochinese peninsula." VOA, meanwhile, stressed that the Cambodian operation had been taken to save American lives by eliminating enemy sanctuaries and gave assurances that U.S. forces would adhere strictly to the preannounced June 30 departure date.

According to Soviet propaganda, not only was the general U.S. policy in Indochina bloodthirsty but the specific methodology of conquest was barbaric. They charged that the "interventionists" in Cambodia were killing women and children and sacking shops. The proceedings against U.S. soldiers accused of massacring Vietnamese civilians at My Lai were termed a whitewash. "In hopes of saving the direct participants of the barbaric reprisal from punishment," they said, "the U.S. authorities are resorting to judicial chicanery and procedural subterfuge." VOA covered the My Lai proceedings fully and commented that, if true, the tragedy was an isolated incident, not typical of U.S. military conduct. Public airing of the incident showed how the processes of an open society were proof against cover-ups.

President Nixon's October proposal for a general cease-fire in Vietnam was denounced by the Soviets, who said there could be no talks while U.S. troops remained in Vietnam and the Thieu-Ky regime held power in Saigon. The Communist delegation at the Paris talks and the Chinese used the same formula. Chinese propaganda with reference to Southeast Asia focused unusual attention on the Japanese. Time and again it accused the Japanese of a revival of militarism and claimed that the Japanese leadership was using books and films to arouse warlike attitudes in the populace.

Sino-Soviet Relations. The year brought little abatement in propaganda hostilities between the U.S.S.R. and China, although the two countries continued to hold talks aimed at reconciling their border dispute. Each side accused the other of provocative troop activities along the borders and of bargaining in bad faith. The Soviets did make several overtures to patch up their ideological differences with the Chinese, but the accent was on Chinese recalcitrance. Applying to the Soviets their standard pejorative of "social imperialism," the Chinese again accused them of supporting a two-Chinas policy (acceptance of both China and Taiwan) and of covertly colluding with the Americans. The Soviets retorted that the Chinese leadership was pushing a war psychosis campaign at home to take the people's minds off the country's internal problems.

The Soviets found the Nixon administration's tentative attempts at rapprochement with the Chinese especially worrisome. They noted that 50% of Lin Piao's report to the ninth Chinese Party Congress was devoted to attacking the U.S.S.R., compared with only 7% attacking America. While both the Soviets and the West Germans hailed their renunciation of force treaty as a positive step, the Chinese said the treaty would "present Soviet mineral deposits and resources as a gift to West German militarism."

Internal Developments: U.S. and U.S.S.R. The attempts by dissident Soviet intellectuals to avoid internal censorship by circulating manuscripts clandestinely or smuggling them to the West continued to bring reprisals from the Soviet government. (*See* UNION OF SOVIET SOCIALIST REPUBLICS: *Special Report*.) Nevertheless, the dissidents persisted in their efforts, and three writers even made secret TV interviews with a CBS correspondent, which they insisted be shown to mass U.S. audiences, even though it meant certain punishment for them. Foreign radios, including VOA, Radio Liberty, and the BBC, made maximum use of the interviews as well as of the illicit manuscripts, broadcasting them back through jamming to Soviet audiences. Meanwhile, late in the year, *Life* magazine began publication of the purported memoirs of Nikita S. Khrushchev, the deposed Soviet premier and Communist party chairman. Moscow, which had not mentioned Khrushchev since his downfall, issued his denial that the memoirs were genuine, while *Life* spokesmen replied that this was only to be expected.

Both the Soviets and the Chinese adhered to their well-established policy of portraying the U.S. as a diseased giant, mortally infected with the plagues of social strife, class exploitation, and economic blundering. They repeatedly spoke of soaring inflation and massive unemployment. When U.S. postal workers struck, Soviet propaganda said that Nixon had called out the Army "to frustrate the growing working-class movement in the U.S."

The violent confrontations between authorities and protesters on college campuses were characterized as fascist suppression of the revolutionary struggle sweeping America. VOA's broadcasts generally reflected the widespread concern in the U.S. over the increasing use of violence and, toward the end of the year, the growing intolerance toward those who would wreck the system rather than work within it for gradual change. VOA pointed out that the great majority of U.S. young people were working for change in positive ways. (H. H. SA.)

Psychology

From 1950 the number of psychologists in the U.S. increased fourfold, and this has been accompanied by an increased range of specialization among faculty members at any given college or university. It long has been asked whether such a diversity of interests should be included under one departmental roof or be divided into separate departments. A conference sponsored by the American Psychological Association examined "The Place of Psychology in the University" (*American Psychologist,* vol. 25, pp. 387-468, May 1970). One of the major speakers held the differences in content and philosophy among the various psychological subspecialities to be so great as to demand the creation of separate, independent institutes. Others felt that, since an underlying body of knowledge pervades all fields of psychology, one should adopt a model of a strong main department, perhaps with closely affiliated sections in other departments; *e.g.,* business, education, psychiatry.

Opinions were similarly divided on the question of how to make the functions of psychology departments more relevant to the problems of society. Most participants followed the traditional view that psychologists must not lose the advantage of scholarly objectivity by becoming directly involved in social issues as active participants. Nevertheless, one speaker maintained that "action and inquiry are mutually related," and that direct social and political involvement by faculty and students is essential.

International attention has been drawn to growing concern over the deteriorating environment and its effect on the quality of human life. Psychologists were challenged (*American Psychologist,* vol. 25, pp. 303-312, April 1970) to apply their knowledge of human behaviour to an understanding of environmental effects. They were urged to participate in planning cities of the future, hopefully to make them more livable places. One response to this challenge was an attempt to explain the characteristic behavioural flavour of cities in terms of city dwellers' reactions to living as members of a large, densely settled, culturally heterogeneous population (*Science,* vol. 167, pp. 1461–68, March 13, 1970). It was held that the sheer number of people with whom the urbanite daily is thrown into contact combines with a bewildering variety of social contexts to impose a psychological "overload" that cannot be tolerated long. The seeming aloofness, unfriendliness, and superficiality of urbanites were interpreted as symptoms of an adaptive mechanism that protects against overstimulation from the social environment. (While the mayor of a small village can keep his doors open to almost everyone who wants to see him, the practice becomes unfeasible in a large metropolis. Administrators of major cities inexorably must establish impersonal institutions to screen demands on their time.) If the flow of population from farm to city to increasingly crowded suburbs continues, it was predicted that the psychological effects of urbanization would become even more severe problems demanding relief.

A series of reports (*e.g., American Journal of Psychiatry,* vol. 125, pp. 1358–69, 1969) gave new endorsement to the long-held theory that hereditary tendencies underlie the psychiatric disorder known as the manic-depressive psychosis. Manic-depressive patients show profoundly severe changes in mood; for example, some sufferers may alternate from exaggerated elation, overactivity, and gregariousness to deep sadness and self-reproach. It was found that manic-depressive men father very few sons with the disorder but that about 40% of the sons of manic-depressive mothers develop the disturbance. It was concluded that the tendency toward manic-depressive

COURTESY, UNIVERSITY OF
CALIFORNIA AT SANTA BARBARA

Sarah, a seven-year-old
chimp with a reading
and writing vocabulary
of 120 "words"
or ideographs, learns
a new lesson with her
trainer at the University
of California at Santa
Barbara.

to the treatment of people who are prone to show violent hostility.

A broad range of emotional expression has been elicited through direct electrical stimulation of different parts of the brain; these include signs of anger, fear, pleasure, and fury, observable in humans as well as in other animals (*Psychology Today,* vol. 3, no. 12, pp. 48–53, May 1970). The discussion included the case of a man who suffered from narcolepsy, a disorder in which the patient suddenly is overcome by a strong tendency to fall asleep (even in the midst of interesting activity). An electrode was implanted in the man's head so that he could activate his own brain by pressing a button. He reported that the narcolepsy was greatly relieved by his ability to rouse his brain cells electrically. (D. L. St.)

See also Medicine.

behaviour is carried by the X chromosome. Since each male receives the X chromosome only from his mother, it was reasoned that sons could not inherit any theorized manic-depressive gene from their fathers. As further evidence, it was reported that some forms of colour blindness (also linked to the X chromosome) are much more prevalent among manic-depressive patients than they are in the general population.

Attempts also were made to verify earlier evidence pointing to a genetic basis for the schizophrenic psychosis. According to one report, a chemical substance was isolated from the perspiration of schizophrenic patients but was not found in that of non-schizophrenic patients or normal people (*Science,* vol. 166, pp. 398–399, Oct. 17, 1969). When this chemical (*trans*-3-methyl-2-hexenoic acid) was added to "normal sweat," observers agreed that it generated a "peculiar" odour distinctive of schizophrenics. In a review of a number of studies (*Science,* vol. 167, pp. 249–256, Jan. 16, 1970), it was concluded that a high incidence of schizophrenia and other psychiatric symptoms among relatives of schizophrenics indicates a hereditary factor.

The same studies were criticized on methodological grounds (*Science,* vol. 165, pp. 1341–42, Sept. 26, 1969). For example, it was observed that they investigated only a small number of cases. It was suggested that, while there may be a genetic predisposition or vulnerability, a person must undergo specific environmental stress to trigger his tendency to develop schizophrenic symptoms.

Techniques for direct electrical or chemical stimulation of the brain continued to be most rewarding in attempts to understand and to control behaviour. In one study (*Science,* vol. 167, pp. 900–901, Feb. 6, 1970) the method was applied to rats, some of which were vigorous mouse killers while others had previously never killed mice. When a small amount of a chemical (carbachol) that triggers specific nerve cells was injected into the brains of the pacifist rats, they soon began to attack mice most aggressively. And when another chemical (methyl atropine) that selectively blocks the activity of cells in the nervous system was injected into the brains of rats that ordinarily were killers, they turned into temporary pacifists. (In both cases the effects waned as the drugs wore off.) Hopefully, such findings may some day be applied

Public Health:
see Medicine

Public Utilities:
see Cooperatives;
Fuel and Power;
Industrial Review;
Transportation

Publishing

Newspapers. The problems of threats to press freedom from big business take-overs and government interference, help for minority papers in their competition for advertising revenues with commercial television and radio, rising costs and falling circulations, and journalists' demands for a share in controlling policy and for better working conditions cut across frontiers in 1970.

Press freedom was by all odds the most important journalistic issue. In the U.S., Vice-Pres. Spiro Agnew's initial criticism late in 1969 that too great a concentration of power over the flow of information resulted in distortion and bias was followed by additional rounds on an irregular basis throughout 1970. Some observers were surprised by the stridency of the vice-president as well as by the reaction of the press.

A rash of subpoenas issued to U.S. newsmen for their notes, film, tapes, and personal testimony in a wide variety of cases raised the question of whether a reporter has immunity from testifying to protect his sources of information. Such reporter privilege, or shield, laws had been passed in several states, but the courts had never recognized the right as being one that existed inherently under the First Amendment to the Constitution. Among those receiving or being threatened with subpoenas during 1970 were the *New York Times,* the Columbia Broadcasting System, and *Time, Newsweek, Life,* and *Fortune* magazines. Most of the action concerned information about militant groups such as the Black Panthers or Weatherman faction of Students for a Democratic Society. Favourable rulings on the rights of newsmen were handed down in New Jersey, New York, and Chicago. A federal Court of Appeals in San Francisco quashed one subpoena against *New York Times* reporter Earl Caldwell, who had been cited for contempt by a federal district judge when he failed to respond to the subpoena.

The controversy was partially laid to rest in August when U.S. Attorney General John Mitchell announced guidelines for his department that recognized the possible limiting effect on First Amendment rights of the subpoena, and promised "all reasonable attempts" to obtain information elsewhere.

Another important event involving the U.S. newspaper industry was passage of the Newspaper Preservation Act in July. The law offered limited exemption from antitrust prosecution to newspapers with joint production, circulation, and advertising sales operations but with independent news staffs. It sanctioned existing arrangements where one of the two newspapers was in financial distress at the time of the agreement; new agreements had to be approved by the U.S. Department of Justice.

U.S. newspaper circulation reached 62,059,589 in 1969 according to *Editor & Publisher Year Book*. A major newspaper strike was averted in New York City, but the city's newspapers claimed that union slowdowns cost them millions of dollars in advertising revenue before contracts were signed. The newspapers in Baltimore were closed for 74 days by a strike of pressmen. The owners of the *Los Angeles Times* bought controlling interest in Long Island's *Newsday* and Cowles Communications, Inc. acquired a 23% interest in the New York Times Co., in exchange for three Florida newspapers, a television station, a book company, a publisher of professional magazines, and *Family Circle* magazine.

Nothing that happened on Fleet Street in 1970 suggested that the terrifying speed at which costs had escalated in the 1960s would be halted. In addition, labour relations, bane of the British newspaper industry for nearly 20 years, seemed to be even more strained. There were other causes, too, for concern. In its annual report, the Press Council expressed anxiety at the widening gap between Parliament and press, and at the use of the Official Secrets Act to prevent papers from performing their duty to probe and to publish—a threat highlighted by a charge under the act against the *Sunday Telegraph,* its editor, and others concerned in publication of a confidential report on the extent of the Labour government's aid to the Federal Army during the Nigerian civil war.

Most managements, and some unions, would have welcomed amalgamation of the six printers' and operatives' unions, but not all union members were willing to forgo their separate interests and powers. Members of the Newspaper Publishers Association (NPA), however, showed a new readiness to tackle difficult situations together. A big step forward was taken in September, when the NPA and the unions set up a joint steering group to provide for maximum security of employment, draw up an agreeable wage structure, and formulate a new procedural agreement to reduce disputes within the industry.

In December 1969, Denis Hamilton, editor in chief (and, from December 1970, chairman) of Times Newspapers Ltd., pointed out, in a letter to all *The Times*'s staff members, that the successes achieved since Lord Thomson took over the paper in 1966 had only been made possible by his investment of more than £5 million. Production costs had risen by 100%, revenue by only 77%. Hamilton proposed that management and union committees draw up new programs for every department. There was an 8% fall in circulation (the first since 1964) during January–June, from 437,270 to 401,750, with rises for the rival "quality" dailies, the *Daily Telegraph,* the *Financial Times,* and *The Guardian* (up by 4%, and for the first time topping the 300,000 mark). In August, control of the management of *The Times,* and responsibility for its losses, were taken over by a privately owned Thomson company, Thomson Scottish Associates Ltd.

Another paper with a big midyear drop in circulation was the *Daily Mirror,* owned by the International Publishing Corporation Ltd. (IPC), down from over 5 million to under 4.5 million. The *Sun,* bought by Rupert Murdoch from IPC in 1969 and relaunched that November as a popular tabloid in direct competition with the *Mirror,* was making spectacular progress.

The biggest single factor in raising costs was newsprint prices, which went up twice during the year and were to reach about £75 a ton in January 1971. Costs were also raised by wage claims and strikes. A dispute at the *Daily Mirror* flared up in April, when the National Graphical Association (NGA) threatened a walkout unless its printing managers got an immediate weekly raise of 48s., to restore parity with managers belonging to the Society of Graphical and Allied Trades (SOGAT). A national stoppage was only averted by intervention of Trades Union Congress general secretary Victor Feather.

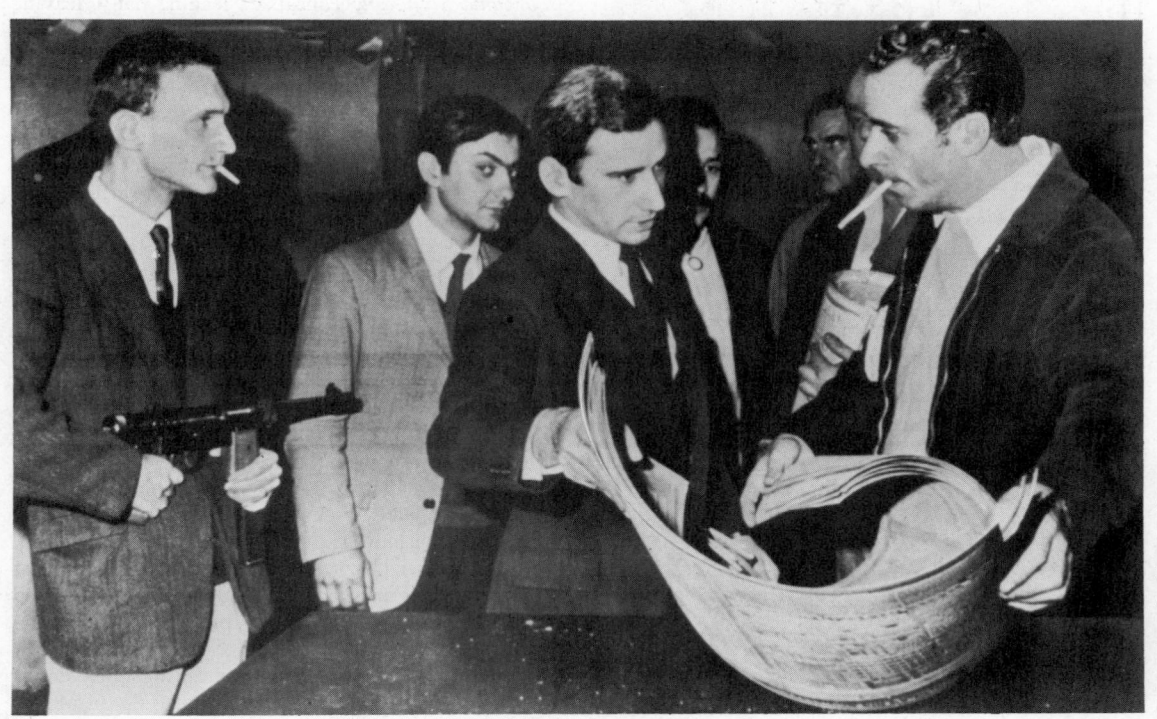

WIDE WORLD
Plainclothes policemen seize matrices of the daily newspaper "Crónica" in Buenos Aires, Arg., May 23, 1970. The government ordered the paper closed on grounds it falsely reported the death of a student in clashes with police during antigovernment demonstrations in Córdoba.

Feather was also instrumental in cutting short the four-day national stoppage in June (when only the Communist Party's *Morning Star* continued to appear) caused by SOGAT's claim for a 25% cost-of-living raise. The strike broke against the unusual solidarity of the NPA, held together by its new chairman, Lord Goodman. A week later a joint SOGAT-NGA claim threatened the provincial press and printing industry. In September, much of Greater London was without national papers for 17 days, when an unofficial overtime ban by members of SOGAT employed as packers and drivers by the Federation of London Wholesale Distributors caused a loss of over 20 million copies, more than half those printed.

A bid for control of the Central London Branch of the National Union of Journalists by a Fleet Street Reform Group was defeated in February, but the group's objectives—reform of the NUJ and radical improvement of journalists' pay and conditions of employment—were taken up in both the national and the provincial press. Throughout the year there were strike threats, unofficial stoppages, disruption, delays in publication, and revolts against NUJ weakness and inactivity. In December the NUJ voted acceptance of an NPA offer of a wage increase of £400 a year with a new minimum Fleet Street wage of £2,500, but many journalists opposed the agreement.

The publishing world was shaken by the take-over of IPC by the Reed group of paper manufacturing industries. IPC owned six major papers, 60 consumer magazines, the most extensive U.K. range of business and trade journals, and a big books division. (See *Magazines; Books,* below.) Reed, an IPC subsidiary and its main supplier of newsprint, had extended its interests to other paper products, and as IPC had declined, it had risen.

In West Germany an agreement gave elected staff committees the right to veto an editor's appointment or dismissal, and to determine with man-

agements the solution of other problems likely to change editorial policy. In Switzerland a statute drawn up by owners and staff of Basel's *National-Zeitung,* guaranteeing editorial independence, came into force on May 1.

On March 16, Paris was deprived of all morning and evening papers by a journalists' strike for a re-evaluation of their professional status (which, they claimed, had been declining since 1935) to include a 12% pay raise, a higher minimum salary, a five-day week, and the establishment of joint commissions on employment conditions. Journalists on *Le Monde,* virtually self-employed as joint owners of 40% of the paper, struck to maintain professional solidarity.

Italian papers, disrupted by stop-and-go printers' strikes in early summer, ran into further trouble in July when journalists claimed a general pay increase. Owners of 18 national papers retaliated by stopping publication of Monday morning editions.

The most violent attack on misuse of press power was launched in West Germany in February when Conrad Ahlers, chief government spokesman and head of the federal press office, accused newspaper magnate Axel Springer of deliberate falsification of the news. The Springer press had mounted a campaign against the government's *Ostpolitik* and Ahlers claimed that the extent to which Springer's editors were under his thumb constituted a threat to democracy and free opinion.

A new Spanish daily, *Nivel,* was closed after only one issue, allegedly for infringement of a technical press regulation. In Greece, one of Athens' oldest dailies, *Ethnos,* suspended publication indefinitely in April, when its two editors and three owners were imprisoned for "spreading false rumours likely to cause alarm and despondency." Two Peruvian papers were confiscated, and varying degrees of censorship were in force in Chile, Argentina, Cuba, Haiti, Brazil, Paraguay, and Panama. In Pakistan, journalists on two Lahore dailies, the *Pakistan Times* and *Daily Imroze,* won a legal victory against dismissal for secretly forming a union and fomenting a strike. In February, Pres. Julius Nyerere nationalized the *Tanzania Standard,* Tanzania's leading daily, leaving the Swahili *Nguromo* as the only independent paper.

Newsday took two Pulitzer Prizes in 1970 for public service and for cartoons (Thomas F. Darcy). Thomas Fitzpatrick of the *Chicago Sun-Times* and William J. Eaton of the *Chicago Daily News* were awarded prizes for national and local reporting, respectively. The international reporting award went to Seymour M. Hersh for his disclosure of the My Lai incident in Vietnam. Anthony Grey, the Reuters correspondent released late in 1969 by China, was given the British Journalist of the Year award. Hubert Beuve-Méry, founder and editor of *Le Monde* for 25 years, who had retired in 1969, received the gold medal of the British Institute of Journalists and his paper was awarded the highest honour of the School of Journalism of the University of Missouri. The Norwegian *Stavanger Aftenblad* received the World Press Achievement Award of the American Newspaper Publishers' Association.

News gathering was risky for reporters during 1970. In Cambodia eight correspondents were killed, at least 17 others were missing, and a number were captured and later released. Reporters were also held hostage during the Jordanian civil war.   (M. D. Bu.; X.)

Magazines. Angry women and Spiro Agnew dominated the 1970 magazine scene in the U.S. On March

Despite the Soviet Union's pro-Arab policies in the Middle East, a folio of sketches on Jewish folk themes by Jewish artist Samuel Rozin was printed in 1970 by a Lithuanian government publishing house. The use of English, Russian, and Lithuanian text suggests that it was intended partly for export.

COURTESY, YIVO INSTITUTE FOR JEWISH RESEARCH

18 some 200 vocal women demanded a chance to put out a liberated issue of the *Ladies' Home Journal;* the editor in chief, John M. Carter, agreed to an eight-page August supplement. *Newsweek* was accused of discrimination against women in editorial jobs and Hugh Hefner at *Playboy* failed to retract a memo leaked by his secretary that began: "These chicks are our natural enemy. . . . It is time to do battle with them." Lacking encouragement from the standard titles, the women turned to a tested solution—they began publishing their own magazines and newspapers. At year's end a good dozen enjoyed moderate success. Clay Felker's *New York Magazine* gave over space regularly to Gail Sheehy, a controversial member of the movement. It was not always flattering, but it built circulation.

Overseas, the U.S.S.R. closed down the *Time* bureau in Moscow. Apparently the Soviets did not care for the continuing stories on the growing dissidence among Soviet intellectuals. Nor did the U.S. Army approve of troops reading dissident magazines and newspapers published by servicemen near bases.

A not-so-free press proved a recurrent complaint of underground press editors. It ranged from a continuing advertising boycott of a weekly newspaper publisher in Port Washington, Wis., who refused to give up printing a Milwaukee underground paper, to harrassment of the two-year-old San Diego, Calif., *Street Journal,* which continued its liberal stance in an essentially conservative community.

Some 270 members of the Committee of Small Magazine Editors and Publishers held their third annual meeting and heard a range of speakers from Allen Ginsberg to George Plimpton. All saw a bright future for the little magazine, although Plimpton reported there would be no more government-supported anthologies of selections from the presses, primarily because congressmen disapproved of the content. The venerable *Kenyon Review,* one of the oldest university-based literary magazines, was slated to go under because it would take an estimated $250,000 to run it over the next four years. Rising costs and diminishing dividends of prestige spelled difficulty for the *South Dakota Review* and the *New Mexico Quarterly.* Academic communities were increasingly questioning the value of their publications.

In keeping with a less than cheerful economic year, commercial magazine publishers were dolefully calculating how much their advertising revenue was likely to be off in 1970. American Business Press, representing some 2,402 publications, forecast an 8% loss in advertising pages. *Look* reported advertising page losses in the first half of 1970 and met the crisis by lowering advertising rates and chopping back circulation. J. Richard Munro, publisher of *Sports Illustrated,* reported newsstand sales up 25% after the price went to 60 cents. Munro thought the reader could and was willing to carry more of the costs of publication.

Another answer to financial woes came from *McCall's Magazine,* which would have a smaller page size in 1971. *Good Housekeeping* had enjoyed a rate advantage because an advertiser spent less for a full page. The most generally accepted buffer against the red ink column was aiming at a specific audience. *National Geographic,* for example, saw at least an 11% jump in advertising pages for 1970. The publishers of *Psychology Today,* a risky venture some three years before, sold it, along with other interests, for $20 million in 1970; the magazine continued to

UPI COMPIX
Georgia Gov. Lester Maddox and about a dozen of his supporters picket the offices of the Atlanta "Journal" and "Constitution," June 4, 1970. The governor was angered by an editorial that opposed his call for a special legislative session on state finances.

gain circulation. *Mad Magazine* also plugged along well enough on subscriptions and newsstand sales.

As *Ebony* approached its 25th year serving the largest Negro audience in the U.S., new publications were launched to meet the needs of specialized black audiences. Making its debut in May, *Essence* represented a major contribution to the women's field. At another level, a new paperback magazine, *Amistad's,* devoted itself to writings on black history and culture. Several comic publishers promised magazines given over entirely to blacks. Social conscience was introduced as Robin of *Batman* became involved with campus skirmishes and other comic immortals promised more awareness of current issues.

The unique needs and whims of the young could make or break a publisher. Jann Wenner, who ran the music magazine *Rolling Stone* into a fortune, split with a partner, Baron Wolman, who tapped a new aspect of the youth market with *Rags,* a fashion monthly. Another effort, the *National Lampoon,* by former editors of the *Harvard Lampoon,* sought to fill a vacuum with a true satirical magazine for the young. Seeking a somewhat broader audience, the muckraking *Ramparts* survived a 1968 bankruptcy crisis with a circulation of well over 130,000. *Scanlan's Monthly,* headed by former *Ramparts* editor Warren Hinckle, opened its guns on much the same target area.

Competition also hit the heretofore unshakable Hugh Hefner of *Playboy.* Adapting much the same formula, layout, and approach, the British magazine *Penthouse* was growing fast, driving for a "younger,

World Daily Newspapers and Circulations, 1969–70*

Country	Daily news-papers	Circulation per 1,000 of popula-tion
AFRICA		
Algeria	4	14
Angola	4	10
Cameroon	1	4
Central African Republic	2	0.6
Ceuta	1	58
Chad	1	0.4
Congo (Brazzaville)	3	1.3
Congo (Kinshasa)	7	2
Dahomey	1	.3
Ethiopia	6	2
Gabon	1	1
Ghana	4	36
Guinea	1	...
Ivory Coast	1	3
Kenya	4	9
Liberia	2	9
Libya	9	20
Malagasy Republic	6	13
Mali	2	0.5
Mauritius	13	96
Melilla	1	60
Morocco	6	14
Mozambique	5	7
Niger	1	0.4
Nigeria	11	7
Portuguese Guinea	1	4
Réunion	1	66
Rhodesia	2	15
Senegal	1	5
Seychelles	2	48
Sierra Leone	2	5
Somalia	2	2
South Africa	21	57
South West Africa	2	12
Sudan	13	5
Tanzania	8	3
Togo	2	6
Tunisia	4	22
Uganda	5	6
United Arab Republic	8	15
Upper Volta	2	...
Zambia	2	9
Total	175	
NORTH AMERICA		
Bahama Islands	3	122
Barbados	2	115
Bermuda	1	228
British Honduras	2	55
Canada	118	212
Costa Rica	5	60
Cuba	9	88
Dominican Republic	7	26
El Salvador	8	51
Guadeloupe	1	9
Guatemala	8	38
Haiti	5	5
Honduras	5	17
Jamaica	1	71
Leeward Islands	3	33
Martinique	1	67
Mexico	157	116
Netherlands Antilles	5	138
Nicaragua	6	49
Panama (incl. Canal Zone)	8	81
Puerto Rico	4	102
Trinidad and Tobago	2	102
United States	1,758	309
Virgin Islands (U.S.)	4	112
Total	2,123	
SOUTH AMERICA		
Argentina	89	128
Bolivia	15	23
Brazil	70	36
Chile	36	118
Colombia	35	53
Ecuador	16	44
French Guiana	1	34
Guyana	2	191
Paraguay	4	37
Peru	72	47
Surinam	5	49
Uruguay	24	314
Venezuela	33	62
Total	402	
ASIA		
Afghanistan	18	7
Burma	8	9
Cambodia	18	11
Ceylon	9	44
China	392	19
Cyprus	9	103
Hong Kong	15	493
India	455	13
Indonesia	73	7
Iran	20	15
Iraq	5	12
Israel	21	188
Japan	114	492
Jordan	2	12
Korea, North	7	†
Korea, South	31	75
Kuwait	5	52
Laos	7	3
Lebanon	33	97
Macao	6	114
Malaysia	34	75
Mongolia	3	16
Nepal	16	3
Pakistan	97	18
Philippines	16	27
Ryukyu Islands	10	269
Saudi Arabia	5	7
Singapore	7	325
Syria	3	15
Taiwan	32	64
Thailand	18	22
Turkey	402	45
Vietnam, North	7	†
Vietnam, South	36	70
Yemen	5	18
Total	1,939	
EUROPE		
Albania	3	53
Austria	27	249
Belgium	56	285
Bulgaria	12	195
Czechoslovakia	24	283
Denmark	94	356
Finland	66	358
France	101	251
Germany, East	17	445
Germany, West	133	328
Gibraltar	3	120
Greece	95	125
Hungary	27	205
Iceland	5	435
Ireland	9	242
Italy	82	112
Luxembourg	6	477
Malta	5	...
Netherlands	88	301
Norway	86	383
Poland	41	199
Portugal	20	71
Romania	9	158
Spain	62	176
Sweden	106	518
Switzerland	125	368
U.S.S.R.	620	305
United Kingdom	122	488
Vatican City (Holy See)	1	‡
Yugoslavia	22	83
Total	2,067	
OCEANIA		
American Samoa	1	65
Australia	56	363
Cook Islands	1	37
Fiji	1	20
French Polynesia	3	68
Guam	1	120
New Caledonia	1	43
New Zealand	39	373
Niue	1	60
Tonga	2	16
Total	106	
Grand total	6,812	

*Only newspapers issued four or more times weekly are included. Areas not listed had no known daily newspapers. †Total circulation less than 1 per 1,000 population. ‡Circulation largely outside territory.
Sources: For numerical count: *Newspaper Press Directory 1970*, *Benn's Guide to Newspapers and Periodicals of the World*; for U.S. and Canada, *Editor & Publisher International Yearbook* (1969); other secondary sources. For circulation estimates: *UN Statistical Yearbook 1969* (1970).

(W. A. Ha.)

more virile" audience. Taking on an even bigger task, the indomitable Ralph Ginzburg (*Eros, Fact, Avant Garde*) challenged the *Consumer Reports* with *Moneysworth*. A reorganized Curtis Publishing Co. announced that the *Saturday Evening Post* would return in 1971 as a quarterly sold only on news-stands.

The President's Commission on Obscenity and Pornography issued its massive report, which proposed repeal of all federal, state, and local laws pertaining to "consenting adults" who wish to get sexually oriented magazines, films, and books. The commission was split on the recommendation, and dissenters filed an opposite opinion.

Another issue interested *Women's Wear Daily*, which singlehandedly deeply divided experts and laymen on the importance of the descending hemline. Individual journalists, also, continued to wield influence. In *Atlantic* Jessica Mitford deflated the much-advertised Famous Writers School. *Esquire* scored a coup with the publication from incomplete manuscripts of one section of Ernest Hemingway's posthumous work *Islands in the Stream*. Late in the year *Life* serialized what it maintained were the authentic reminiscences of former Soviet premier Nikita S. Khrushchev. The oddest story of the year was the total recall of an issue of *Caper* magazine that invited the reader to dissolve two pages of the magazine in methyl alcohol and drink it. The U.S. Food and Drug Administration said the result was possibly deadly. (W. A. Ka.)

In the U.K. magazines generally faced the same problems as newspapers. Women's weeklies were hardest hit, and their slumping circulations added to the troubles of IPC, owner of the four most popular women's weeklies. Such quality weeklies as the *New Statesman* and the *Spectator*, however, managed to increase circulations, even after raising their prices. Underground journals such as the psychedelic *Oz* and the salacious *It* (both in legal trouble during the year) were catering to hippies and dropouts, while the revolutionary could choose *Black Dwarf*, an anarchist fortnightly, the ultra-Marxist *Red Mole*, an English edition of the Parisian *Idiot International*, and a rival *Idiot*. Another sign of the times was the increase in the number of nudes needed to sell a new men-only magazine. *Club*, launched in April by IPC, came out in May with four nudes on its cover, in an attempt to capture a share of the market before the U.S. *Playboy* started its U.K. edition in the fall. Popular weeklies for teen-age girls also followed the permissive trend, with IPC's latest, *Loving*, introducing a pot-smoking heroine.

Mirror Magazine, the *Daily Mirror*'s weekly colour supplement launched in 1969, was the first casualty in the battle of the new company formed by the Reed group's take-over of IPC to turn its losses into profits. (See *Newspapers*, above.) The Reed take-over also lost IPC some 20 key executives, journalists, and salesmen, who left to join the Banner Press Ltd., a new magazine publishing group 85% owned by Rupert Murdoch. The new organization's first venture was a pop music weekly, *Sounds*, a rival to IPC's successful *Melody Maker*. IPC's *Scorcher*, a comic relating spectacular successes by unlikely heroes with whom readers happily identified, was launched in February and was likely to top the circulation table in its first full year.

The bottom seemed suddenly to have fallen out of the part-work publications, book-length topics issued

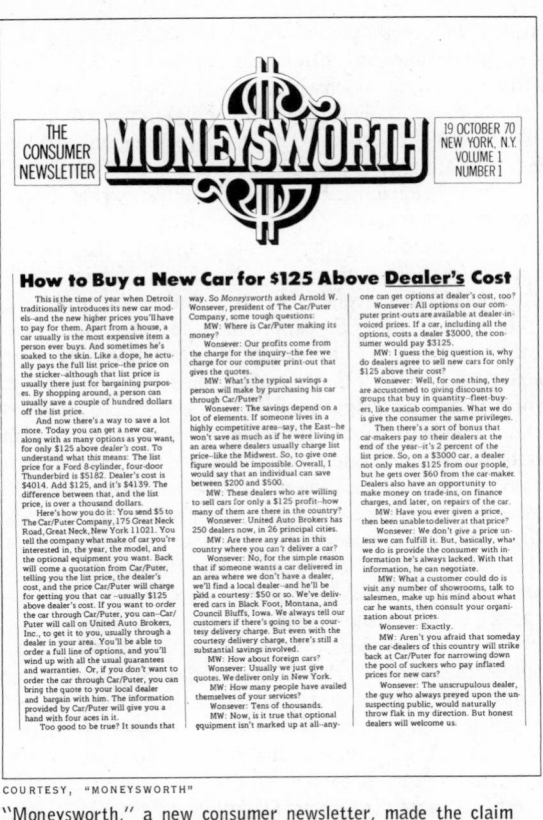

COURTESY, "MONEYSWORTH"

"Moneysworth," a new consumer newsletter, made the claim that it could increase the buying power of its readers by 15%.

in installments. After several years of increasing demand, the market was glutted with new ventures in winter 1970–71, several of which fell well below sales targets.

Both the left-wing *New Statesman* and the conservative *Spectator* changed editors during the year. Richard Crossman, Labour's secretary for health and social security, announced after his party lost the June general election that he had already accepted the editorship of the *New Statesman*. Nigel Lawson, the *Spectator*'s editor, left after a policy disagreement with its owner, and there was a long, rumour-filled gap before George Gale, a professional journalist but with no editorial experience, accepted the post in September. A new left-wing monthly, the *Spokesman*, founded by Bertrand Russell, was begun in February, after his death.

In West Germany, Axel Springer made the headlines with a short-lived linkup with his nearest rival. Bertelsmann, which in 1969 had acquired a 25% interest in Gruner and Jahr, owners of *Stern*, a weekly with political views diametrically opposed to those of Springer, was to have acquired a one-third interest in Springer's empire for $85 million. The deal was canceled by Springer when he found out that Bertelsmann and Gruner and Jahr were plotting for control of his most influential daily, *Die Zeit*.

In France, Jean-Paul Sartre added to his nominal editorship of the extreme left-wing journal *La Cause du peuple*, that of the new *Tout*, founded by Maoist fellow travelers. In Spain, the popular weekly *Sabado Grafico* was banned for four months in April, allegedly for offenses against public morals—publishing photographs of a girl in a bikini—but actually for attacks on the Cabinet as dominated by the Opus Dei technocrats. In September, two weeks after its reappearance, it was banned again, with no reason

given. In December 1969, Yuri Rybakov, editor of the U.S.S.R.'s leading theatre journal, *Teatr*, was replaced, after refusal to heed warnings that the journal was making serious ideological mistakes, while Aleksandr T. Tvardovski (*see* BIOGRAPHY), independent-minded editor of the literary journal *Novy Mir*, resigned in February 1970. Also in the U.S.S.R., the first foreign publication devoted entirely to the U.S. began publication. In October, *Literarni Listy*, former weekly of the Czechoslovak Writers' Union, reappeared, published not from Prague but from "somewhere in Europe." (X.)

Books. More books were being produced in 1970 than ever before and demand was growing for new books, new editions and reprints, and larger editions, especially in English. It was also apparent that the spread of television had, contrary to expectation, increased the demand for books. The worldwide popularity of the British televised version of *The Forsyte Saga*, for instance, had created an unprecedented demand for new editions and translations of all of John Galsworthy's works. In the highly industrialized countries new markets were being opened up by the spread of education and leisure, while in the less developed countries crash literacy and higher education programs created a need for books of all kinds, especially in English, which was becoming securely established as the world's main second language.

Preoccupation with international copyright continued during 1970. New printing techniques and distribution methods were geared to the production, at an economic price, of enough books, in larger editions, to meet the growing demand, and mergers and amalgamations were stimulated by the need to spread overheads and reduce wastage. International publishing operations for the simultaneous production of books in several languages using the same format and illustrations were another aspect of the attempt to provide large quantities of cheap, well-produced books.

Increased production was generally accompanied by increased exports. In 1969, the U.K. published 32,393 titles, topping its 1968 record by nearly 1,000. Of a total turnover of some £142 million, compared with £137 million in 1968, £81 million was in foreign exchange, a £12 million increase over 1968. The value of exports exceeded that of imports for the second straight year and, during October 1968–October 1969, exports represented 47% of total sales.

In both West Germany and France, internal mergers, amalgamations of production and distribution, and take-overs, some by U.S. firms, were increasing. Production in West Germany reached a new record of 35,577 titles and total turnover was up by about 5%. Both exports and imports were up; exports, at DM. 544.7 million, by DM. 54.2 million and imports, at DM. 182.4 million, by DM. 29.6 million. In France, titles produced dropped to about 22,000 but total turnover was up by 8%, with exports up by 5%. French publishing was suffering increasingly from large-scale selling methods, including cut-price offers that undermined sales and price structures, and from the mechanical reproduction by universities and both public and private institutions of whole works or important sections of works. Another problem was the use of mass advertising, which made a book a best seller artificially and forced every other book off the market. For example, Henri Charrière's *Papillon* sold more than a million copies in France alone in 1969 and accounted for 10% of all sales of literary works. By 1970, it was a best seller in several countries.

Of Spain's 1969 total of 125 million volumes (an 11.6% increase over 1968), 35 million were exported, an increase in terms of foreign exchange earned of 24%. Imports rose less steeply, by 13.7%. Although exports were to Latin America, most imports came from other European countries. Titles published—20,031 books and pamphlets—showed only a slight increase over 1968, but numbers of copies per edition were higher.

Production in Switzerland in 1969 rose by 15%, to a record of 6,028 titles, and exports rose, reaching a value of SFr. 129.7 million (1968, SFr. 121.9 million). There was an unusually high increase of 30.7% in books published in Italian and French (up 27%). Italian book production also rose, to 14,-000 titles from 11,000, with the greatest increase for literary works (3,060 new titles, or 26.3% of 1968's total output). In Denmark, production increased by only 6 titles, to 4,978, of which 809 were paperbacks (1968, 959).

There was a fall in production in the U.S.S.R., from more than 75,000 books and pamphlets to about 74,500. An international Book Exhibition in Moscow in April–May 1970, at which books from 35 countries were shown, marked the Lenin centenary. Lenin's complete works were published in 30 languages of the Soviet Union and 22 foreign languages in 1969 and in English, French, and Finnish in 1970. More translated books were published in the U.S.S.R. than in any other country. In 1969, 321 editions of general foreign fiction were produced.

In Australia, where sales were declining and overheads rising, publishing companies reported a sharp drop in profits in 1969, and statistics showed a decline in sales of A$106,000; exports fell steeply. The government set up a tariff board inquiry and, as an interim measure, agreed to pay a 25% bounty, with a ceiling of A$1.5 million, on all books typeset and printed in Australia. The market as a whole, however, was expanding, with imports up from A$38.4 million to A$43.6 million for the year ended June 30, 1970.

International book fairs continued to proliferate. The April International Children's Book Fair at Bologna, Italy, had become a firm date for publishers, with a record of 220 from 22 countries participating in 1970. The lifting of the East German quota restrictions on book imports early in the year made the February Leipzig Spring Book Fair more international than in previous years. The Frankfurt (W.Ger.) Book Fair held its position as main meeting place for the world's publishers, with 3,384 publishers from 66 countries represented in September 1970.

Copyright was again the year's biggest international problem. The differences between the Bern Convention and the Universal Copyright Convention (UCC) had become obvious in 1967 when the Stockholm Protocol was added to the Bern Union copyright convention to help less developed countries acquire more easily the books needed for their education programs. Further difficulties had resulted from infringements of copyright by countries not signatories to either convention, from an increase of unauthorized reproduction of copyright material in the U.S. (a signatory to UCC, while most European countries adhered to the Bern Convention), and from the fact that the U.S.S.R. was not bound by either convention.

A U.S.-U.K. publishers' conference in England in June 1969 had urged union of the two conventions

CAMERA PRESS FROM PIX

Anthony Miles, the new editor of London's "Daily Mirror," was scheduled to take over in the spring of 1971.

and attempts to persuade the U.S.S.R. to sign one of the existing conventions. In October 1969 the joint study group set up by the two conventions, meeting at Washington, D.C., recommended replacement of the Stockholm Protocol by less sweeping relaxations. After prolonged negotiations with the less developed countries, revisions that would help provide books without endangering the basic principle of copyright were accepted in principle in September 1970. A conference of both conventions, to meet in Paris, June–July 1971, was expected to confirm these proposals.

Injections of U.S. capital into British publishing continued in 1970, allowing U.S. publishers to gain a foothold in the rapidly expanding European market for English-language books. At the same time, however, amalgamations and new, independent British publishing companies, often headed by young, unconventional owners, were formed to withstand U.S. take-overs. The year's most interesting take-over in the U.K. was a take-over in reverse, by which, after the death in July of its founder, former chairman, and majority shareholder, Sir Allen Lane (*see* OBITUARIES), Penguin Books, Ltd., world pioneer of quality paperbacks, merged with Pearson Longman, book-publishing subsidiary of S. Pearson & Son. Longman, Britain's second largest book publisher after the Oxford University Press, was willing to guarantee maintenance of the individual character of Penguin Books. The deal, planned by Lane, was announced the day after his death to forestall other offers. The only real danger had been from the U.S. firm McGraw-Hill, which had stepped up its share in Penguin to more than 17%.

The struggle between Leasco Data Processing Equipment Corp. of New York and Robert Maxwell for control of Pergamon Press ended in November after a year of revelations and recriminations. Maxwell, founder of Pergamon, had announced his intention to regain, with U.S. or other backing, the chairmanship he lost in October 1969. He also resisted all attempts to dislodge him as managing director of the U.S. Pergamon Press, Inc., 70% owned by the Pergamon Press. The climax came when a reaudit of Pergamon's profits to September 1969, requested by Leasco, disclosed a £2 million loss; a substantial loss was also forecast for 1970. Leasco, which now owned 35% of Pergamon shares, decided that the position was more complex than when it had made a bid for full control, and withdrew. Meanwhile, Maxwell founded a new specialized publishing company, Sciences, Engineering, Medical and Business Data.

The British Printing Corporation (BPC), which had acquired control of the International Learning Systems Corporation (ILSC) from Pergamon, was also in difficulties. ILSC losses, running at the rate of £1 million, forced BPC to cut its midyear dividends and to downgrade its investment in ILSC. BPC was also suffering from a heavy commitment to part-work publication and the failure of an international part-work venture. (See *Magazines,* above.)

The Reed group's take-over of the IPC led to a shift of power in British book publishing. (See *Newspapers,* above.) Paul Hamlyn, who had become an IPC director and its books division manager, resigned in May, and in September joined Rupert Murdoch's News of the World Organisation Ltd. as joint managing director.

There was a power change, too, in Soviet book

publishing, when the deputy editor of the official Communist Party newspaper, *Pravda,* was appointed chairman of the Committee on the Press, controller of publishing firms throughout the U.S.S.R., and head of the Soviet Union's publishing industry.

Although there was a tendency to relax rules against obscene publications, political censorship continued in 1970. The Oxford University Press had to publish two editions of its *Oxford History of South Africa,* deleting a chapter on the rise of African nationalism from the version distributed in South Africa. Books on Che Guevara and Frantz Fanon were also banned in South Africa. A French edition of a book by Brazilian revolutionary Carlos Manguela, first published in January by Éditions du Seuil and banned by the Interior Ministry, appeared again in July with the imprint of 23 other publishers. Penguin Books' Australian company was prosecuted for publishing Philip Roth's *Portnoy's Complaint.*   (X.)

In the U.S., according to *Publishers' Weekly,* the total number of books published hovered around 30,000 for the third straight year. In 1969, 21,787 new titles and 7,792 new editions were published for a total of 29,579 titles, compared with 30,387 in 1968. These figures did not include government publications or works other than encyclopaedias sold only by subscription. Inflation, however, forced total publishers' receipts for 1969, estimated at $2,765,-000,000, up over 1968 receipts of $2,568,300,000. U.S. titles published in the first three quarters of 1970 totaled 24,629 and included 16,225 new titles and 8,404 new editions.

The Census of Manufacturers report released in October 1969 and covering 1967 showed that publishers' dollar sales had increased 37.3% since 1963, the previous census year. Surveys of publishers indicated that 1968–69 net sales of trade and general books increased 8.9%. Adult trade hardbound books showed increases of 14.9% in dollar sales and 10.9% in the number of copies sold.

The number of corporate mergers and acquisitions declined in 1969 and dropped off sharply in 1970, in contrast to the flurry of such activity that had begun in 1966 when publishing became a good business investment because of increased federal spending on education. Despite anxiety that a publisher's creativity and independence would be threatened in a large, diverse corporate structure, the autonomy of most book divisions involved in such mergers to date continued to be preserved.

In 1969 Dell Publishing purchased the remaining 40% of the Dial Press. Crowell-Collier & Macmillan bought G. Schirmer, Benziger Brothers, and a British house, Cassell. Intext added John Day Co. and Chandler-Davis Publishing. Quadrangle Books was sold to the New York Times Co., while Harper & Row acquired Basic Books. Harcourt, Brace & World acquired Academic Press, Psychological Corp., and Arco Publishing, and in 1970 changed its name to Harcourt Brace Jovanovich. McGraw-Hill bought American Heritage Publishing Co., whose president, James Parton, was named president of Encyclopædia Britannica Educational Corp. in 1970. W. W. Norton sold its children's books department to Grosset and Dunlap. Harrison-Blaine purchased Liveright Publishing, and Meredith Press sold its trade books division to Hawthorn Books.

There were even fewer acquisitions in 1970, perhaps because fewer companies were available. Nonetheless, Atheneum merged with the Lexington, Mass.,

COURTESY, SCANLAN'S LITERARY HOUSE, INC.

The first issue of "Scanlan's," a new monthly magazine of criticism and investigative journalism edited by Warren Hinckle III, former editorial director and president of "Ramparts," and Sidney E. Zion, former "New York Times" reporter.

textbook house D. C. Heath & Co., a division of Raytheon Education Co., and Simon & Schuster first announced a merger with Norton Simon, Inc., but later agreed to join the Kinney National Service, Inc. conglomerate that owned Warner Brothers.

The most interesting aspect of U.S. book publishing in 1969 was the reversal of the 20-year trend for nonfiction to outsell fiction by about two to one. The ten best-selling nonfiction books, usually a list dominated by "how to" books, only outsold the ten top fiction titles by little more than 2%. The 1969 nonfiction list contained only five "how to" titles and was headed by the *American Heritage Dictionary of the English Language,* which recorded 440,000 sales. More copies of the books on the 1969 fiction list were sold than in 1968 and, curiously, more of the books had been panned by the critics. The top fiction title, Philip Roth's *Portnoy's Complaint,* sold 418,000 copies. Other best sellers in 1969 were:

Hard-cover fiction: *The Godfather* by Mario Puzo; *The Love Machine* by Jacqueline Susann; *The Inheritors* by Harold Robbins; *The Andromeda Strain* by Michael Crichton; *The Seven Minutes* by Irving Wallace; *Naked Came the Stranger* by Penelope Ashe; *The Promise* by Chaim Potok; *The Pretenders* by Gwen Davis; and *The House on the Strand* by Daphne du Maurier.

Hard-cover nonfiction: *In Someone's Shadow* by Rod McKuen; *The Peter Principle* by Laurence J. Peter and Raymond Hull; *Between Parent and Teenager* by Haim G. Ginott; *The Graham Kerr Cookbook; The Selling of the President 1968* by Joe McGinniss; *Miss Craig's 21-Day Shape-Up Program for Men and Women* by Marjorie Craig; *My Life and Prophecies* by Jeane Dixon with René Noorbergen; *Linda Goodman's Sun Signs;* and *Twelve Years of Christmas* also by Rod McKuen.

Books that sold well in hard-cover did even better in paperback, an example being *Couples* by John Updike. The demand for publication of black history, culture, and literature paid off in best sellers by such black writers as LeRoi Jones, Malcolm X, and Eldridge Cleaver. Fantasy also did well, particularly among college age readers, as shown by sales of books by Tolkien, of *The Little Prince,* and of Frank Herbert's *Dune.*   (P. B. ST.)

See also Law.

Puerto Rico:
see Dependent States
Qatar:
see Dependent States
Quakers:
see Religion

Race Relations

The worldwide resurgence of nationalism continued in 1970. Dissident minorities increasingly emphasized violence and revolution rather than the manipulation of existing legislative and other peaceful levers. Bombings, hijackings, kidnappings, terrorism, and verbal aggression increased, and small extremist groups within the minorities sought to exploit the grievances of the larger group to achieve a base for continuing revolution against "imperialism" and neo-colonialism. Their activities drew attention to the plight of the minorities concerned, but also provoked repressive countermeasures and sometimes strengthened the opposing extremist factions.

The Soviet Union's approach to the third world remained an uneasy amalgam of expedience and doctrine as Moscow kept one eye cast on competitive Chinese activities, particularly in Africa. While Soviet propaganda in general advocated Pan-African unity, solidarity with the Communist world in an "anti-imperialist" front, and the encouragement of "progressive national" regimes, it also continued its attacks on African forms of socialism. The Soviet Union remained only indirectly concerned with helping the "liberation" forces of Africa and Asia. Meanwhile, China, whose offer of more than $400 million to Tanzania and Zambia to construct their railway was finally accepted in July, continued to accuse the Soviet Union of obstructing the African liberation struggle and of pursuing neo-colonialist policies, especially in Nigeria. On the whole, however, despite some African resentment at outside interference, Soviet influence increased in Africa while that of China waned.

The Organization of African Unity (OAU), meeting in Addis Ababa, Eth., in August, and the summit conference of nonaligned states, which met later in Lusaka, Zambia, both concentrated on the racial conflict in southern Africa. A particular target was the vast Portuguese-inspired Cahorabassa hydroelectric scheme in northern Mozambique, which was regarded as likely to entrench the Portuguese firmly in Mozambique and to help white South Africa economically.

The Nigerian civil war ended in January, and projects for relief, rehabilitation, and reconciliation gradually got under way. In Kenya and Uganda the dispossession of the Asian minority continued. Uganda strained relations with Kenya and Tanzania by dismissing large numbers of their nationals, because of massive unemployment and a serious financial crisis.

Tanzanian Pres. Julius Nyerere's African socialism was marred by bizarre events in Zanzibar, where elderly, much-married government officials were forcibly marrying young girls of Iranian descent on the island and decreeing compulsory intermarriage in the name of racial integration. From his base in Guinea, U.S. black militant Stokely Carmichael made a tour of Guyana in an attempt to import his violent Black Power doctrine and Pan-Africanism into the Caribbean.

In the Soviet Union many national and religious minorities continued to seek greater political and cultural autonomy in opposition to the government's continued campaign against "bourgeois nationalism" (there were no non-Europeans among full members of the central party Politburo). As a result of this unrest, there were frequent government reshuffles in such Soviet republics as Moldavia, Azerbaijan, and the Ukraine, and solidarity among Soviet Jews also was reinforced by official anti-Zionism.

Double standards and overemphasis of black-white conflict were noted in many international councils. Preparations to celebrate the 25th anniversary of the United Nations included the rejection by Soviet-bloc and nonaligned members of the preparatory commission of a proposal to insert in the commemorative address the words: "This Assembly is opposed to oppression and tyranny everywhere."

South Africa. Two important but potentially self-cancelling trends became increasingly discernible in 1970. Certain Afrikaner intellectuals began to criticize the policy of separate development of the races, maintaining that there had arisen a "credibility gap" between the facts and the official statements. These intellectuals displayed a spirit of enlightened utilitarianism similar to that displayed earlier by English-speaking economic liberals. Schalk Pienaar, editor of *Die Beeld,* told the government to stop playing poker with the public and face the fact that "we have a permanent black urban population." The editor of *Dagbreek* also expressed deep concern about the country's manpower shortage, calling on the government to revise the whole question of labour and to determine the "safe margin" for absorbing nonwhites into jobs currently reserved for whites.

Meanwhile, African groups were tending to withdraw from cooperation with white liberal integrationists and to set up separate bodies. African students set up an all-black, independent South African Students' Organization, aimed at crystallizing the needs and aspirations of black students and establishing a solid identity among them. The proliferation of African Independent churches continued, but after a split with the African Independent Churches Association (AICA), attributed to internal leadership disputes, some breakaway churches began to cooperate with the major Dutch Reformed Church (NGK). The number of nonwhite adherents of the NGK in South Africa was reported to be nearly half a million and increasing so fast that it had passed the number of whites.

For the white population, at least, the early months of the year were focused on the general election, called over a year ahead of schedule, largely, it was thought, to enable Prime Minister B. J. Vorster to smoke out and then crush the *verkrampte* ("cramped" or conservative) elements within his party. Many of these, led by Albert Hertzog (*see* BIOGRAPHY), left the party in October 1969 to form the Reconstituted National Party (HNP). Half a year of infighting then

WIDE WORLD

Young Lords, part of a group of 105 arrested for occupying the First Spanish Methodist Church in East Harlem, leave a New York City court building on Jan. 7, 1970. During their 11-day sit-in the group provided hot breakfasts for schoolchildren and taught "liberation" classes stressing Puerto Rican culture.

ensued between the *verligte* ("enlightened") and *verkrampte* elements, and in its successful attempt to crush the HNP challenge the Nationalist establishment went all out to woo the more conservative voters. This campaign resulted in some very tough policy statements and in such measures as the further tightening of the job reservation laws, which excluded urban Africans from an additional range of occupations; the Bantu Laws Amendment Act gave the minister of Bantu administration complete control over the employment of Africans as telephonists, hotel receptionists, shop cashiers, and related urban jobs.

The HNP was soundly defeated, but in achieving this objective the Nationalist Party largely negated Hendrik F. Verwoerd's 1966 breakthrough to the English-speaking voters and lost nine seats to the United Party opposition, while Helen Suzman (*see* BIOGRAPHY), the Progressive Party's sole representative in Parliament, nearly tripled her majority.

A report in September caused political controversy and some alarm. The first figures from the national census in May showed an expected 30% overall population increase from 16 million in 1960 to 21.3 million. But the percentage increase in the different racial groups was not proportional: the African population increased by 36.3%, from 10.9 million to 14.9 million; the Coloured (racially mixed) population from 1.5 million to 2 million; and the Asians from 477,000 to 614,000. By contrast, the white population increased by only 22.4%, from 3.1 million to 3.8 million. The whites thus declined by 1.5% to 17.8% of the total.

Figures were also given for Africans in "white" areas and "homelands," showing that the absolute number of Africans in white areas had risen from 6.8 million to nearly 8 million but had fallen in proportion to the total population (from 62.5 to 53.3%). The number of Africans in the homelands had risen both in percentage and in absolute figures, from 4.1 million (37.5%) to 6.9 million (46.5%). While the government hailed these figures as clear proof that separate development was working, the opposition claimed that the rise of more than a million Africans in white areas was a clear indication of the policy's failure.

The Cape Coloured people lost the last vestiges of their 134-year-old franchise rights when the prime minister announced that Coloured voters were to be removed from the Cape Town municipal voters' roll. The tragic ludicrousness of apartheid was shown in the renewed debate about "honorary white" status for Chinese and Japanese; this was at least a partial result of South Africa extending its trade with China and Japan.

There was little overt evidence of organized resistance or protest from nonwhites within South Africa. However, individuals and groups within the white community continued to utilize the remaining legal opportunities to moderate the inhumanity of the racial policy and to press for changes.

United Kingdom. Immigration was fading as a key political issue in Britain. Official attitudes tended toward "benign neglect" in the field of race relations, and there was a widespread feeling that the subject had been taken over by extremists on both sides.

There was a tendency to look to the second generation of black immigrants for a harmonious solution to current problems, but evidence was accumulating of social alienation, cultural confusion, and disenchantment over jobs and living prospects among black

teenagers. Relations between these teenagers and the police were deteriorating. The latter were criticized for discriminatory and brutal behaviour, but appeared to be making serious efforts to improve matters.

The Race Relations Board's analysis of complaints received during the 12 months to March 31, 1970, showed a total of 1,870 complaints, including 935 from Greater London. Opinions were formed on a total of 432 nonemployment complaints, of which 299 related to the provision of goods, facilities, and services. Unlawful discrimination was found in 56 of these cases. Only 5 complaints concerned the sale of private houses, with three positive opinions. Of 116 complaints of unlawful advertisements, 111 were judged discriminatory. Out of 550 employment complaints on which an opinion was formed, discrimination was adjudged in 68 cases. For the Community Relations Commission, the year was one of consolidation and advance. By the end of March, 47 out of about 80 councils had full-time community relations officers, with an additional 11 approved.

The total number of "new Commonwealth" immigrants (*i.e.,* excluding those from Australia, Canada,

DON NORTH FROM
NANCY PALMER AGENCY

At the formerly all-black West Charlotte High School in North Carolina, the football team begins practice as an integrated team for the first time in August 1970.

and New Zealand) admitted for settlement in 1969 was 33,940, compared with 50,160 in 1968 and 57,648 in 1967. This total was made up of 3,512 holders of work vouchers (4,353 in 1968), 27,984 dependents (42,036), and 2,446 "others" (3,771). For the first six months of 1970 the overall total was 12,747, as compared with 19,658 in 1969. In addition, 6,249 U.K. passport holders from East Africa were admitted in 1969, including 1,672 special voucher holders. Corresponding figures for the first six months of 1970 were 3,005, including 882 special voucher holders. The growing waiting list in East Africa for special vouchers had reached 7,180 by the end of May. A Bow Group memorandum suggested allocating the unused balance (about 4,500) of the overall allocation of work vouchers (8,500) for Commonwealth immigrants to help clear the waiting list in Africa. In October the European Commission on Human Rights decided to hear the complaints of 25 Asian immigrants about degrading treatment and refusal of entry, and a further flood of complaints was expected.

In early June Enoch Powell's election manifesto listed Commonwealth immigration as Britain's greatest danger and called for an end to the automatic

THE "NEW YORK TIMES"

Two members of NEGRO
(the National Economic
Growth and Reconstruction
Organization) stand
on top of the Great Hall
on Ellis Island.
The 62-member group
of former drug addicts
and former convicts took
over on July 20, 1970.
They hoped to turn
the abandoned island
into a rehabilitation
centre for 2,500 people.

entry of dependents, a new law on citizenship, and an emphasis on repatriation. These views were rejected by the Conservative Party leadership. The race issue did not become a central element in the campaign, and the largely unexpected Conservative victory left Edward Heath as victor, not scapegoat, with no commitments to Powell or his followers.

Official Conservative policy was that all citizens should continue to be treated as equal before the law and without discrimination; that the causes of racial tension should be reduced by education, health, and housing policies, and additional funds to local authorities in areas of heavy immigrant settlement. Finally, it was proposed to introduce a new single system of control for all immigrants from overseas; immigrants already in Britain could bring in wives and young children, but in the future work permits would be limited to a specific job in a specific area, usually for 12 months. While assistance would be given to Commonwealth immigrants who might wish to return to their countries of origin, "we will not tolerate any attempt to harass or compel them to go against their will." (SH. P.)

United States. The probable shape of relations between blacks and whites in the United States for the near future began to emerge in 1970, even though it was a year full of apparent paradoxes. Significant drives took place within both the black and white communities, and at local, state, and national levels, for integration of blacks and other minorities into all phases of American life, at a much higher rate of speed than ever before, and on significantly different terms—such as reduced qualifications for admission to schools and jobs. At the same time, it was a year that saw an undeniable increase in militance among that minority of blacks committed to the idea that no decent future could conceivably be achieved within the framework of the American society.

The drive for speedier and deeper integration into the mainstream of opportunity seemed to be due in large part to the increasingly widespread acceptance by the white community of the legitimacy of black demands for first-class citizenship. The year also featured the most sustained drive ever mounted by local and national police authorities against the militant organizations in the black community, most notably the Black Panthers. With Eldridge Cleaver in exile in Algeria, Fred Hampton dead in a so-called shootout in Chicago, and Huey Newton and Bobby Seale both on trial for crimes that could result in their permanent incarceration, or execution, the police authorities in numerous cities, including Chicago, Philadelphia, New York, and New Orleans, seemed determined, with significant encouragement and support from the FBI, to smash the Black Panther leadership and disperse the organization.

The fate of Angela Davis (*see* BIOGRAPHY), a brilliant young black professor of philosophy at the University of California, somehow exemplified the most tragic aspects of thwarted black ambitions in the U.S. An outstanding academic career seemed likely to be destroyed as Miss Davis was indicted for kidnapping and murder resulting from a bizarre shootout in California's Marin County Court House in early August.

The influence of both types of radical groups among the blacks—the Panthers and their allies, and the Nationalists and theirs—seemed to be diminishing in terms of direct recruitment of sympathizers or augmentation of power. But it was evident that they had substantially contributed to the spread of acceptance in the white community of the legitimacy of black claims to first-class citizenship and, with that, of entitlement to some form of compensatory redress for historical grievances and discrimination. Moreover, it was evident that the general run of the black community, though neither radical socialist nor nationalist, was nevertheless much more willing openly to seek, if not demand, new sets of rights and opportunities.

Substantial changes seemed to be occurring even in military life, the traditional bastion of conservative authority and the customary landing place for otherwise dispossessed black youth. Violent confrontations between black and white enlisted men occurred throughout U.S. Army, Navy, and Marine bases at home and abroad, and serious challenges to traditional military authority were made and sustained by black soldiers, including the retention of Afro haircuts and the use of the black solidarity salute. Many blacks claimed they were discriminated against in both promotion to officership and disproportionate exposure to battle risks. Against these assertions, Brigadier Generals Daniel James, Jr., and Frederic E. Davison, the nation's only black generals, declared that "There is no such thing as inequality of opportunity in the armed forces today." Yet it was reported that "studies of military administrative procedures, such as that conducted this year by the Third Division in Germany, do tend to support the charges involving job assignments and promotions."

The drive for interpenetration and intermingling of the two races also was evident in many areas of civilian life, such as education, employment, welfare, politics, and student dissent.

Perhaps nothing seemed so closely to unify black and white as the nomination by Pres. Richard Nixon of G. Harrold Carswell for a post on the U.S. Supreme Court. Patient investigation after the nomination revealed that Carswell, in a 1948 campaign for a seat in the Georgia state legislature, had declared that he would always be governed by principles of white supremacy. Subsequent investigations revealed that he had been an incorporator of a private club apparently particularly designed to evade state laws against segregation of public facilities. Yet it took great effort by some determined senators and leaders in the civil rights community to persuade other senators to vote a second time against Nixon's nominations (Clement F. Haynsworth having been previously defeated). Nixon asserted that while he had not known about Carswell's earlier white supremacy stand, he would have nominated him even if he had known. Such assertions continued to persuade the black community that Nixon was still pursuing the so-called Southern strategy, involving the acceptance of black opposition in an effort to court the favour of the Southern states.

This Southern strategy was said by civil rights spokesmen throughout the year to be most clearly revealed in the volatile shifting of the White House stand on school desegregation. In June Commissioner of Education James Allen, a forthright and admired spokesman for the concept of integrated schools, was fired on the orders of President Nixon, presumably for his outspoken opposition to the war in Vietnam and for his insistence on implementation of the Supreme Court mandate regarding desegregation of the schools.

While some members of the administration seemed determined to press the Supreme Court order, even through law suits against resistant communities, Nixon gave diverse signals, indicating that while he favoured desegregation, he did not intend to send "vigilante" squads to implement the ruling. He also made it clear that he would not move to force desegregation where it was based on residence and was, thus, de facto rather than de jure. At the end of March, Nixon affirmed that he would rely on court orders and efforts of local Southern school officials to comply with such orders and that he would de-emphasize stern desegregation enforcement procedures. He did, however, propose an allocation of $500 million for 1971 and $1 billion for 1972 for technical assistance to public schools throughout the country that wanted to attenuate the effects of de facto segregation with compensatory education programs.

Two major Southern strategies for resisting the desegregation orders emerged. One involved the creation of private schools on a segregated basis. But this method ran into difficulty when the income tax status of such schools and of donations to them was questioned by the Internal Revenue Service. Serious confusion regarding the status of the ruling was created by the filing of a brief in a Mississippi school suit by the U.S. Department of Justice in June, contending that segregated private schools that had developed in the South should be allowed to keep their tax-exempt status. At the same time, the Department of Justice claimed that its action did not constitute government support for segregated schools, all appearances to the contrary notwithstanding.

Some greater clarity regarding the government's position seemed to emerge in July when the Internal Revenue Service revoked the tax-exempt status of schools that continued to practice racial discrimination in admissions, and stated that this loss of exemptions would apply not only to school income and property but also would involve loss of tax deductibility for contributions made to such schools. Yet the commissioner of the Internal Revenue Service would not clarify what his intentions would be in cases involving only token desegregation, or the newly publicized device of segregating black from white within schools.

The second Southern counterthrust to the Supreme Court ruling involved legal efforts through various law suits and through bills introduced in Congress by Mississippi Sen. John Stennis to enforce the desegregation ruling in Northern city schools, on the grounds that they were segregated de facto as much as, if not more than, Southern schools. Stennis was joined by Sen. Abraham Ribicoff of Connecticut, who said that he would support Stennis' amendment in which it was proposed that there should be equal application of the Supreme Court ruling to both de facto and de jure segregation. President Nixon announced his support for the Stennis amendment and for a second amendment the senator had introduced to prevent compulsory bussing designed primarily to produce racial balance.

How effective the drive for school desegregation and the resistance to it had been was not at all clear at the end of 1970. Little credence could be given to Health, Education, and Welfare (HEW) Secretary Elliot Richardson's allegation in December that the job of desegregation of the schools in the South was largely completed and that problems of within-school discrimination would be resolved without serious difficulty over the next few months. To many observers it seemed clear that throughout the South most black children continued to go to schools that were predominantly or all black, and most white children continued to attend schools that were predominantly or all white.

The financial crisis of institutions of higher education became a salient issue in black-white relationships. As the year drew to a close, the word was spreading that numerous scholarship programs would undergo serious cutbacks and that this might seriously affect the admission of blacks. Alternatively, it might mean that the schools, especially "prestigious" private schools that had been conducting vigorous campaigns for recruitment of black students while maintaining their general policy of scholarship sup-

Members of Youth Against War and Fascism protest the prosecution of 21 Black Panthers in New York City.

STEVE ROSE FROM
NANCY PALMER AGENCY

DENNIS BRACK FROM BLACK STAR

The "Liberation Train" of a 110-mi., five-day "march against repression" reaches Atlanta. The march was organized in May 1970 by the Southern Christian Leadership Conference to protest the deaths at Jackson State, Augusta, and Kent State.

port for any needy, qualified student, might be faced with choosing between their needy white and needy black students.

Reviewing the year's developments in education gave credence to the assertion that a major thrust toward fuller incorporation into U.S. life at all levels was central to the stance of the black community, despite the separatist inclinations of one extremist group and the revolutionary denunciations of all things American by another. Most blacks seemed determined to "make it" within American society, rather than outside of it or by revolutionary change of its basic institutions.

This movement into society was also highly evident in U.S. political life. The extension in July by Congress of the 1965 Voting Rights Bill for an additional five years marked a reaffirmation of the relevance of mainstream politics for the black community, however much prejudice and discrimination seemed ever present. Of national prominence was the depletion of the ranks of firm civil rights advocates from the national administration, most notable being the resignation in February of Leon Panetta, director of the Office for Civil Rights, because of what he called "political pressures influencing enforcement of civil rights laws." In March, an unfortunate phrase in a letter from presidential advisor Daniel Moynihan to President Nixon, urging a period of "benign neglect" of racial problems, seemed to persuade the black community even further that the administration did not have its heart in any serious improvement of their fate. The resignation in December of James Farmer as an assistant secretary in HEW, the highest ranking black in government service, did not do much to allay these suspicions about the administration.

Yet blacks continued to accept the challenge of domestic politics, most impressively in the cases of the victorious campaign by Kenneth Gibson for the mayoralty of Newark, N.J., and in the surprising upset of Max Rafferty by W. C. Riles in their contest for the position of superintendent of public instruction in California. Significant numbers of whites joined with blacks to defeat Rafferty, who had epitomized a traditional and conservative position on both public education and race relations within the

state. The same kind of coalition between black and white voters, combined with the trial on charges of corruption of the incumbent mayor, helped achieve victory for Gibson.

Both by a deliberate anti-inflation policy of the government and through the impersonal operations of the economy, unemployment continued to rise throughout the year. As usual, blacks were among the most seriously affected by unemployment at the same time that their incomes were most seriously depreciated by the inflation.

Efforts to combat black unemployment continued to be volatile and varied. Major dimensions included the Philadelphia Plan and others modeled after it, involving the deliberate enforcement of requirements that specified proportions of blacks to be hired, especially in the construction industries, wherever any government financing was involved. Similarly, there were simultaneous efforts to expand the job-training and retraining programs and to open industries of all kinds to black recruits at all levels.

In spite of administration claims of modest success of its various programs, it was stated by various observers that one year after the beginning of Nixon's plan to put significant numbers of minorities into construction jobs, the results were nonexistent. The Philadelphia Plan was said not to have produced even minimal gains in breaking the colour barriers in the construction trades. Yet in at least some cities, the efforts to enforce "hiring plans" by the government seemed more successful than in previous years.

Black capitalism still had its advocates, as newly emerging black businessmen sought financial help to initiate and sustain new business enterprises. Again, the claims of modest success for the administration's efforts in this line were met with vigorous denial by black spokesmen. But debate continued both between white and black and within the black community regarding the feasibility of black capitalism versus job training and retraining for black workers as major avenues to increased black employment and economic well-being.

With both whites and blacks feeling the economic pinch, albeit in disproportionate amounts, the prospect for improved black-white relations became somewhat dimmer. For there had arisen the new dimension of severe competition between black and white for the reduced employment opportunities. Coming at a time when what was most drastically needed was a relatively ample and enriched program of aid to minorities, the economic recession seemed to suggest that the next 12-month period might be one in which there would be less such aid offered.

The most dramatic example of black-white unity occurred in New Haven, Conn., in May in conjunction with the trial of Black Panthers indicted for murder of a so-called Panther renegade. A national call for a demonstration of solidarity resulted in a gathering of 12,000 people at Yale University in New Haven. There, in spite of the governor's summoning of National Guardsmen against possible emergencies, relative quiet prevailed as Yale Pres. Kingman Brewster, Jr., had opened the campus to out-of-town demonstrators and garnered their support with his assertion that members of the Black Panthers probably could not secure a fair trial in the U.S., a statement that brought on great controversy. Among the worst cases of interracial strife was the slaying of two black students by white Mississippi policemen at Jackson State College in May.

The relationships between blacks and other minority groups grew increasingly complex during the year, as Puerto Ricans, Mexican-Americans, and American Indians began to match black militancy with their own. The militant Puerto Rican organization, the Young Lords, commanded special attention by its emulation of Black Panther and other black militant organizational tactics, including the seizure of churches and clashes with the police, especially after instances of presumed police brutality to Puerto Ricans and the suicide of several Puerto Ricans in New York prisons. The Young Lords and other Puerto Ricans began to press for the same kind of "national pride" and "cultural integrity" as had animated the black nationalist movements in previous months. An additional dimension involved the demand for bilingual teachers and instruction in schools where Puerto Rican students were registered, in order to make education more effective and to preserve the Puerto Rican cultural pattern.

Mexican-Americans came in for their share of national attention, partly as a result of the successful union-organizing activities among agricultural workers by César Chávez and accompanying national boycotts of various products, and partly because of new organizational solidarity in various cities and rural areas. The U.S. Civil Rights Commission urged in April that Congress pass legislation to curb widespread patterns of police misconduct against Mexican-Americans in the Southwest, criticizing the inadequacy of Justice Department investigations of civil rights complaints. Similarly, the Immigration Department was criticized for contributing to Mexican-American poverty by permitting 100,000 Mexicans illegally to cross the border daily for agricultural jobs in the U.S., where they were then exploited, it was charged, by being required to work for lower wages, under threat of being expelled for illegal immigration.

American Indians came into public attention during the year, most dramatically as a result of their seizure in November 1969 of Alcatraz Island, but more importantly because of a growing recognition of their rights to compensatory payments for earlier seizure of their tribal lands. In May the Indian Claims Commission awarded $12.3 million to the Seminole Indians for land in Florida taken from them by U.S. military forces in the 19th century, and in December the Senate overwhelmingly agreed to give Taos Indians title to 48,000 ac. of Carson National Forest in New Mexico, including Blue Lake, which is held sacred by the Taos Indians.

The main direction of the new treatment of Indians was indicated by President Nixon, who, in July, denounced centuries of injustice to American Indians and proposed the development of a comprehensive plan that would give them dignity and control over their destinies. He endorsed legislation that would permit tribes to take over control of many present aid programs, criticizing a 17-year-old government policy that fostered dependency of the Indians on the government.

Relationships between blacks and Jews continued in the same vein as in previous years. Significant improvement was noted in some dimensions, such as in invigorated cooperation locally and nationally on important civil rights issues, while some worsening also occurred, especially in relations between Panthers and Jews, as the former developed official liaison with Arab guerrilla movements and secured refuge and

support in Algeria for their exiled leadership. The continuing hostility of extreme portions of the New Left to Israel continued to serve as a source of alienation and hostility between those students and the major portions of American Jewry and led to some instances of physical violence.

No single theme could be said to have been more characteristic of race relations in the U.S. during the year than that of continued demand for and partial success at achieving more adequate and secure places in American society by blacks and other minorities. Yet the gap between ideals and actualities continued to plague the American conscience. Former U.S. Supreme Court Chief Justice Earl Warren sounded the warning for the future when he said, in May, that the United States is in the greatest crisis within the memory of living Americans, stemming from failure to enforce adequately the due process and equal protection sections of the 14th Amendment.

(M. M. Tu.)

See also Crime; Education; Police; South Africa; United States.

Refugees

On the eve of the 20th anniversary of the establishment of the Office of the United Nations High Commissioner for Refugees (UNHCR), the UN General Assembly in November unanimously adopted a resolution on the High Commissioner's 1970 report, which urged governments to lend their support to his humanitarian and constructive task. This unanimity emphasized the assembly's appreciation of the results the high commissioner had achieved. It noted, in particular, the high commissioner's constant efforts, in cooperation with other UN bodies and voluntary agencies, to promote the voluntary repatriation, the integration in countries of asylum, or the resettlement in other countries, of refugees who were his concern.

In 1970 once again the major part of the refugee problem of concern to UNHCR centred on Africa, the UNHCR'S action covering well over a million refugees on that continent. Settlement in a rural environment continued to be the main solution despite the growing number of refugees attracted to the towns, where their presence created new problems. UNHCR also helped in the repatriation to Nigeria of 5,000 children who had been evacuated from the breakaway state of Biafra during the civil war there.

In Asia the UNHCR's concern continued to be essentially with approximately 60,000 Tibetans in India and Nepal and 80,000 Chinese in Macao. Also, however, the governments of Cambodia and of South Vietnam also turned to UNHCR in their attempts to solve the plight of some recently uprooted groups. Approximately 200,000 South Vietnamese who had been living in Cambodia returned to their homeland, mainly because of Cambodia's policy of placing them in camps for "security" purposes. In Latin America UNHCR continued to devote special attention to aged and handicapped refugees, while in Europe most of the 750,000 refugees of concern to UNHCR were already fully integrated in the social and economic sense and measures toward their naturalization were being actively encouraged.

One of the most dramatic refugee incidents of the year occurred off the coast of Massachusetts in November when a Lithuanian seaman on a Soviet fishing trawler tried to defect to the West by jumping aboard

WIDE WORLD

A Palestinian woman
does her wash near her
wrecked home
in the Wahdat refugee
camp near Amman.
Large areas of the camp
were destroyed during
the fighting between
Palestinian guerrillas
and the Jordanian
Army in September 1970.

a U.S. Coast Guard cutter as the two ships drew alongside. After consulting with his superiors on shore the captain of the U.S. ship allowed four Soviet crewmen to come on board and drag the defector off. U.S. Pres. Richard Nixon reacted angrily to the Coast Guard's action, and his press secretary declared that there had been "errors of judgment" on the part of U.S. officials in allowing the defector to be retaken.

(X.)

See also Migration, International.

Religion

There were parts of the world in 1970 where religion was still almost inseparable from political and cultural life, but in the West the churches seemed to be engaged in an ever more frantic search for relevancy. Denomination after denomination addressed itself to such problems as race, poverty, youth rebellion, and war, but the year brought no real assurance that their efforts were effective or even—in some cases—welcome. The question seemed to rest in whether, by renouncing the intense sectarian loyalties that (as in Northern Ireland) could infuse social issues with such virulence, the churches would lose the allegiance they had to have if their attempts to meet those issues were to be meaningful.

Christianity, the dominant religion in the West, seemed to be gaining worldwide, and according to some projections the percentage of Christians in the world population might reach 31.2 in the year 2000, compared with 30.7 in 1965. However, the focus seemed to be shifting away from the traditional homelands to nonwhite regions. David B. Barrett, in the 1970 *International Review of Missions*, pointed out that there were 4 million African Christians in 1900 and 97 million in 1970. By 2000 Africa would have a Christian population of 110 million Protestants,

175 million Roman Catholics, 14 million Orthodox and Copts, and 9 million Independents.

There was a small (1.6%) gain in church membership in the U.S. in 1969. Membership in all churches (226 religious bodies) totaled 128,469,636, according to the 1970 *Yearbook of American Churches*. On the other hand, church attendance dropped from 49% of the adult population in 1958 to 42% in 1970. Slight losses in membership were reported in 1969 by the Presbyterians, Methodists, Episcopalians, and, for the first time, the Lutherans and Roman Catholics. The Mormons and the Southern Baptists had slight gains. Some surveys indicated an upward trend among conservative, fundamentalist-type churches.

More disturbing to organized religion was the annual Gallup survey for 1970, which showed that three adults in every four (75%) thought religion was losing its influence on American life. In 1969 the same Gallup survey showed 70% holding this opinion, while in 1957 the percentage was only 14%.

The amount of money spent on general church and synagogue construction had decreased steadily during the last five years, according to the U.S. Department of Commerce. After an all-time high of $1,207,000,000 in 1965, the total fell to $949 million in 1969 and $900 million in 1970. If the rise in construction costs was taken into account, the physical volume of construction was about one-third less in 1969 than in 1965. One of the biggest factors in this downward trend, according to a Department of Commerce spokesman, was the fact that religious groups could not compete for loan funds. Not mentioned by the department was the growing tendency on the part of many churches not to sink large sums of money into buildings, but rather to expend money on programs of various kinds: poverty programs, inner city ventures, and educational experiments.

Another index of the health of the institutional church is the record for individual giving. In its annual report, *Giving USA*, the American Association of Fund-Raising Counsel said that, while there was a decline in church attendance, giving for religion was up "because the person who goes to church offers more." Among Protestants the local churches were keeping a larger share. As an example, Presbyterian giving was up 11%, but funds to the national body increased by only 1%. In the Roman Catholic Church, the average gift had increased somewhat on the parish level but not on the community and diocesan levels. The financial picture in 1970 was not a healthy one for the denominational bodies. Budget cutting and reductions in manpower and program were commonplace. Interdenominational groups such as the National Council of Churches of Christ in the U.S.A. and the World Council of Churches also had deteriorating financial pictures.

It was a year of crisis generally for the National Council of Churches. The council, representing 33 major church bodies with over 42 million members, was engaged in drafting a major overhaul to meet the criticisms of liberals and conservatives alike. Social activists believed that it was an inefficient vehicle for bringing about social change and that funds could be spent more effectively on the local level. Conservatives said that the council leadership did not reflect local theological perspectives, which tended to be less ecumenical and liberal. The crisis was reflected in the council's deficit of $1.8 million on a budget of $27.3 million in 1969, and the 1970 deficit would be even larger.

Several other developments during the year caused deep concern among churchmen. Abortion reform bills passed in many states raised strong reactions among Roman Catholics and Orthodox Jews. (See *Judaism,* below.) A U.S. district court in Washington, D.C., ruled that compulsory church attendance at the nation's three military academies was constitutional, despite strenuous objections on the part of various church bodies. U.S. Pres. Richard Nixon's appointment of Henry Cabot Lodge to represent him personally at the Vatican brought formal protests from some major Protestant bodies. Church leaders were uncertain how to deal with the so-called neo-Pentecostal movement, emphasizing such mystic practices as speaking in tongues and psychic communication, which had appeared within several mainstream Protestant denominations as well as Roman Catholicism.

The feeling among many theologians, scholars, and other interested persons was that ecumenical progress had slowed down considerably. There were several forward steps, however; for example, 20 Roman Catholic and 20 Baptist scholars, meeting during 1970 to discuss their differences, emerged with an "optimistic consensus" recommending further cooperation, especially on social questions. In May participants in the U.S. Anglican-Catholic dialogue said they had uncovered no theological reason why the two traditions could not eventually reach "full communion and organic union." Dialogue groups involving Catholics, Lutherans, and Orthodox and between Lutherans and Episcopalians reached agreement in many areas.

The outstanding move for church unity occurred in March 1970 when the Consultation on Church Union (COCU) issued its long-awaited draft Plan of Union. COCU, which had its genesis in a 1960 sermon by Eugene Carson Blake, then stated clerk of the United Presbyterian Church in the U.S.A., at Grace Cathedral (Episcopal) in San Francisco, included representatives of nine churches: African Methodist Episcopal Church, African Methodist Episcopal Zion Church, the Christian Church (Disciples of Christ), Christian Methodist Episcopal Church, Episcopal Church, Presbyterian Church in the U.S., United Church of Christ, United Methodist Church, and United Presbyterian Church in the U.S.A. Developed over two years by a commission of theologians, denominational officers, clergy, and laymen, the draft was approved by representatives of the nine denominations at a March meeting in St. Louis, Mo. The churches were to study the plan over a two-year period, after which the document would undergo revision and be submitted to the nine church bodies for approval. It was expected that this would occur before the end of the decade.

If accepted the new church of more than 25 million members would bear the name Church of Christ Uniting. Among other things, the draft:

Affirmed the Lordship of Jesus Christ and the authority of the Bible.
Continued the three historic ordained ministries—presbyters, bishops, and deacons.
Saw as crucial the work and witness of lay men and women and provided for their inclusion at all policy-making levels on a ratio of two laymen to one clergyman.
Stressed that the church at every level must be open to all persons regardless of race, age, sex, wealth, or culture.
Asserted that worship is a key ingredient in renewal of the church and provided for a wide variety in that worship.
Provided for a distinctive new "parish" arrangement for local congregations and task forces.
Declared that the united church would seek communion and union with other churches.
Pledged that the mission of the united church would include the public as well as the private sphere.

Despite the enthusiasm of the delegates at St. Louis, many observers felt that this type of church unity through denominational merger had passed its day. There was a widespread feeling among many younger churchmen that the attempt to reform archaic structures was energy wasted. These younger, anti-Establishment leaders were setting up new ecumenical patterns along other than official lines.

Two important English translations of the Bible appeared during the year. Publication of the Old Testament and Apocrypha, together with a slightly revised New Testament (originally published ten years earlier), completed the New English Bible, the work of British scholars representing most major Protestant denominations. Unlike the Revised Standard Version of 1952, the NEB was translated directly from the ancient texts, with no effort made to preserve the language of the King James. Because of the latter's immense influence on English language and literature, as well as religious thought, the NEB aroused great interest and debate outside strictly religious circles. (*See* Special Report.)

The other translation, the New American Bible, was even more of a departure, being the first full English translation of the Bible directly from original sources to be made under Roman Catholic auspices. The Reims-Douai version, for more than 200 years the standard for English-speaking Catholics, was a retranslation of the Latin Vulgate, while the widely

A series of advertisements prepared for the Interfaith Committee for Religious Careers located in Chicago.

COURTESY, INTERFAITH COMMITTEE FOR RELIGIOUS CAREERS

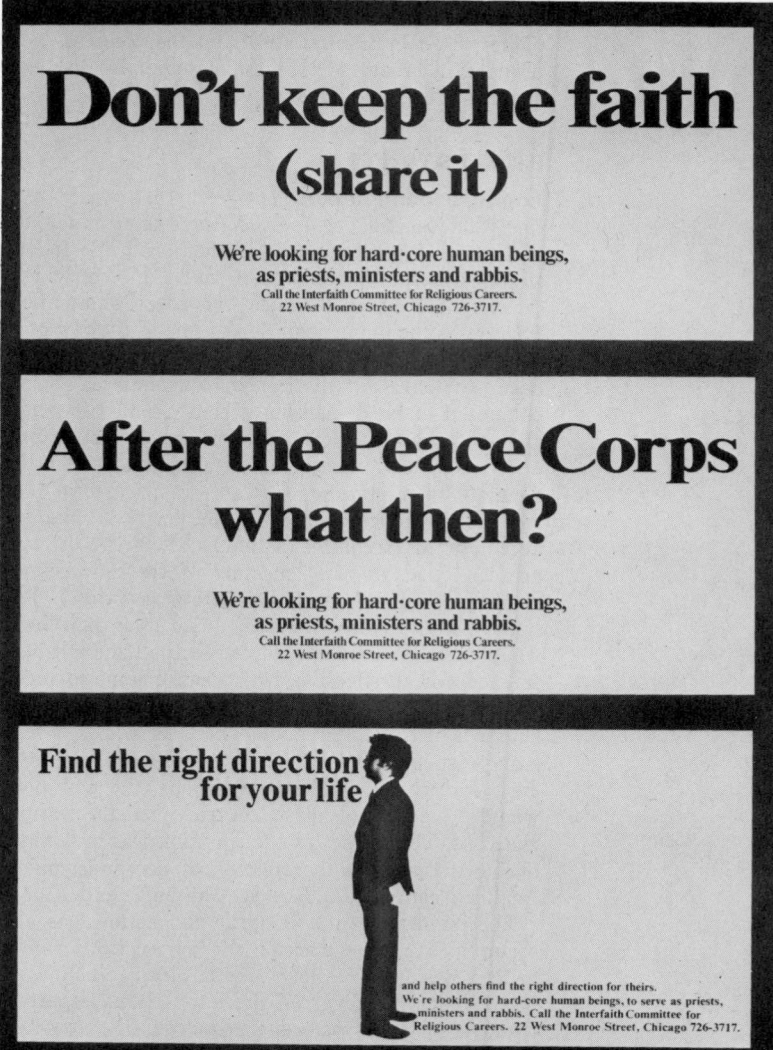

used Jerusalem Bible was based on a modern French translation of the ancient texts. The NAB took more than 25 years to prepare and was the work of 51 scholars, including four Protestants. It was sponsored by the American Bishops' Committee of the Confraternity of Christian Doctrine. The work was begun in 1936 as a modern translation of the Vulgate, which since the Council of Trent in 1546 had been held to be "authentic." After Pope Pius XII encouraged the study of biblical languages, in the 1943 encyclical *Divino Afflante Spiritu,* the already completed portion was put aside and a new start was made using original sources.

Although it was not published in its entirety until September 30, parts of the NAB had been in use for some time in conjunction with the revised Catholic liturgy. Reflecting the increased interest in Bible study among Catholics in recent years, it contained introductions and extensive footnotes designed to help the layman, as well as more than 100 drawings and photographs.

The NAB was well received by scholars of all faiths as accurate, scholarly, and clear. The language was rather more straightforward and less polished than that of the NEB, whose translators, working in the shadow of the King James, had been acutely conscious of that aspect of their work and had been assisted by a panel of literary experts. Unlike the NEB, which kept the archaic and sonorous "thee" and "thou" when the deity was being addressed, the NAB used "you" throughout. The Latin forms of some biblical names, used in translations from the Vulgate, were dropped in favour of the more familiar English versions; for example, Hosea rather than Osee.

(A. P. Kl.)

PROTESTANTS

Anglican Communion. The year 1970 was a relatively uneventful one for the Anglican Communion, with no major conferences of the worldwide fellowship of churches in communion with Canterbury. One development of importance for the Communion's future was the implementation of one of the few positive recommendations of the 1968 Lambeth Conference—the creation of a new Consultative Council composed of elected bishops, clergy, and laity from all the various Anglican churches, which would meet once every two years under the permanent presidency of the archbishop of Canterbury. Late in 1969 an overwhelming majority of the Anglican churches accepted this recommendation, and in 1970 it was arranged that the first meeting of the new council would be held in Uganda the following spring.

High hopes were entertained that this new body would meet the need, pinpointed by the Lambeth Conference, for an effective, permanent channel of communication and cohesion linking all the independent churches of the Communion. There seemed little realistic prospect that it would do more than this, however, for true to Anglican traditions, the new body would have no executive control over the various churches. This aspect of the tradition was underlined during the year by the creation of new independent Anglican churches in Burma, Tanzania, and Kenya.

Local independence of spirit and action was also exemplified by the decision of the Anglican church in New Zealand to follow Canada's lead and allow remarriage of the divorced in church. This departure from Anglican norms was also reflected in New Zealand's formation of an Association of Anglican

"PARIS MATCH" FROM PICTORIAL PARADE

In a meeting that was part of the Christian ecumenical movement, François Cardinal Marty, Roman Catholic archbishop of Paris, is greeted by the Most Rev. Michael Ramsey, Anglican archbishop of Canterbury, at Westminster Abbey, London, on Feb. 17, 1970.

Women, to replace in large measure the Mothers' Union with its opposition to divorce. In England the archbishops appointed a new committee to examine Anglican doctrine and discipline on marriage.

Anglicans remained prominent in the ecumenical field. New Zealand produced a plan for a united church, to embrace Methodists, Congregationalists, Presbyterians, and others along with Anglicans. Similar plans remained under consideration in the U.S. and Canada. In Pakistan, Anglicans formed part of the United Church inaugurated in November. In Britain the archbishops made no secret of their hope that the official scheme for union with the Methodist Church (accepted by the Methodists but rejected by the Anglicans in 1969) would be brought before the Church of England again in the near future.

Relations with Rome remained friendly, in spite of admittedly obstinate differences of doctrine. In July the Anglican authorities at Canterbury gave unprecedented permission for the celebration of the Roman Mass in the cathedral precincts, in honour of St. Thomas à Becket. This was soon followed by a Roman Mass celebrated, for the first time since the Reformation four centuries before, inside an Anglican cathedral, that of Coventry. In October, while proclaiming the sainthood of 40 Roman Catholic martyrs of England and Wales, Pope Paul VI expressed hope for the eventual union of the Roman Catholic and Anglican churches.

After the stormy sessions of recent years, the triennial General Convention of the Episcopal Church (U.S.) in Houston, Tex., in October was almost surprisingly calm and unified, although a projected deficit of some $3 million in the $14 million national budget indicated that not all the laity sympathized with the national church's more advanced social stands. The controversial program of assistance to the disadvantaged was to be continued, but the guidelines were clarified and strengthened. Despite declining revenues (which later in the year led to a 50% cut in the national staff), a $23 million budget was approved for 1971, although only about half was for regular operations.

With women in the House of Deputies for the first time, the convention agreed to permit women to be ordained as deacons, normally a preliminary step toward the priesthood. For the time being, at least, a move to ordain women as priests was rejected. The COCU Plan of Union was to be transmitted to the dioceses for consideration, but without implying approval. Continued liturgical experimentation was encouraged and revisions of about half of the 1928 Prayer Book were authorized for use.　(R. L. R.)

Baptists. Membership in Baptist churches around the world reached 31 million by 1970. The largest Baptist groups outside the U.S. were in India, the U.S.S.R., the Congo (Kinshasa), Brazil, Burma, and Europe.

Representatives from 69 countries attended the 12th Baptist World Congress, held in Tokyo, July 12–18. This was the first time the quinquennial congress had taken place in Asia. William R. Tolbert, Jr., president of the Baptist World Alliance and vice-president of Liberia, presided.

The Baptist European Federation Council held its biennial meeting in Glasgow, Scot., in September. The general secretary of the Romanian Baptist Union, the Rev. Nicolai Kovacs, reported that the government had been greatly impressed by the generous help given by Baptists of the world after the recent floods. The Baptist seminary in Bucharest, closed in 1969, was to be reopened. It was further reported that in Bohemia, Czechoslovakia, where no new church had been opened for 25 years, official permission had been received to build four new churches. In Poland, Baptists obtained permission to produce tapes for the official radio programs.

The Baptist Missionary Society (oldest in the world), with headquarters in London, reported that work had to be restricted because of a shortage of missionaries. The Baptist Union of Great Britain and Ireland and the Baptist Missionary Society were still seeking a site on which to erect joint headquarters. Several schemes had been frustrated because of governmental building restrictions. The Baptist Union of Great Britain and Ireland issued a report on "Ministry Tomorrow." Noting a decline in the number of full-time ministers, it proposed a smaller full-time ministry, highly trained and well paid, supported by a trained supplementary ministry drawn from persons earning their living in trades and professions.

The Southern Baptist Convention observed its 125th anniversary in Denver, Colo., June 1–4, 1970. The messengers attending from local churches resolved to "vigorously oppose every effort to open channels for tax money for support of private church-related elementary and secondary schools." It was also decided to withdraw volume one of the Broadman Bible Commentary, published by the denomination's Sunday School Board, because of its liberal theology and critical approach to the Genesis account of the creation.

The 1970 American (formerly Northern) Convention was held in Cincinnati, O., May 13–17. The program was "designed to encourage examination and response to the issues of revolution, reconciliation and renewal," and the discussion, while spirited, reflected unity in the recognition that the times called for deep and sincere religious concern over contemporary social

conditions. War, especially, was condemned. President Nixon was asked to keep his campaign promises on the war in Vietnam.

In its 90th annual session in New Orleans, La., the National Baptist Convention, U.S.A., Inc. (black), brought together the largest aggregate of delegates and visitors in its history. Some 5,000 college and high school youths participated in a special rally during the session; they were concerned with three aspects of American life—peace on college campuses, the fight against drug addiction, and the unity and the salvation of the nation. In his keynote address, J. H. Jackson, president of the convention, emphasized solving American problems through the American ideology.

Some 500 delegates to the triennial assembly of the Baptist Federation of Canada, meeting in Winnipeg, Man., July 2–5, sent ten young people to Bolivia to study missionary needs there. The federation was formed in 1947 by the Baptist Convention of Ontario and Quebec, the Atlantic Baptist Convention, and the Baptist Union of Western Canada. At Winnipeg a fourth group was added—the Union of the French Baptist Churches of Canada—and a commission was formed to study the possibility of organizing a single national convention.

Conservative (Progressive) Baptists meeting in San Jose, Calif., in June opposed violence but concluded that there should be an attempt to understand why there is rioting. Free Will Baptists, numbering 250,000 in the world, held their 34th annual convention in Fresno, Calif.　(R. E. E. H.; R. W. T.)

Christian Science. The theme of the annual meeting in June—one of the largest in the history of the Mother Church, the First Church of Christ, Scientist, in Boston—was "But What Can I Do?" Those attending saw a documentary film report showing how members on six continents were endeavouring to make a more meaningful Christian response to problems in their communities. First-hand experiences were shared in an associated meeting by Christian Scientists who had been active in the fields of ecology, college administration, politics, and urban affairs.

The denomination's daily newspaper, the *Christian Science Monitor,* published a series "Children in Trouble" that stimulated legislative action in six states to help meet the needs of juveniles. Its series "Crisis in the Courts" was the basis for judicial reform in seven states.

The *Monitor* became the first major U.S. newspaper to change from letterpress to offset printing. Improvements in delivery of the *Monitor* were made possible by use of contract printing plants in Somerset, N.J.; Beverly, Mass.; Chicago; Los Angeles; and London. All of the paper's editions were now printed outside Boston.

Construction went forward on two important building complexes: the Christian Science Center in Boston and the new Christian Science Building in Washington, D.C.

In October a five-day conference held in Boston was attended by committees on publication from many countries. Conferences were held by Christian Science Activities for Armed Services Personnel in Turkey, Vietnam, Thailand, Korea, Japan, England, Germany, and other overseas areas.　(J. B. St.)

Churches of Christ. There were approximately 20,000 congregations with a membership of about 2.5 million in 1970 (because of the independence of each congregation and the lack of central organization,

continued on page 640

THE NEW ENGLISH BIBLE

By Basil Willey

With the publication of the New English Bible in its complete form on March 16, 1970, long-standing problems of biblical translation and criticism once more became matters of popular discussion. Translating the Bible into English raises all the issues involved in the translation of any ancient text, but it raises them in a special form. This is because of the unique part played by Holy Scripture in the spiritual and cultural history of Western civilization. However hard we may try to treat the Bible—in Benjamin Jowett's phrase—"like any other book," the thing can be done only within strict limits.

No other book has been to Christendom what the Bible has been; namely, the "Word of God," the purveyor of saving truth, the rule of faith, the supreme authority in doctrine, a means of grace, a source of comfort, guidance, or admonition. Indeed, it is precisely because the Bible has been all these things, because it has been held to be (or to contain) God's revelation of truths beyond the reach of human reason, that it is considered worthwhile (or indeed essential) to put it into the language of today. Otherwise it might just as well be preserved as a historic monument, a masterpiece of Tudor-Elizabethan prose.

Why Improve Excellence? Even this brief summary indicates the main problem underlying the whole New English Bible project. Was the enterprise necessary or justifiable? We already had, in the King James or Authorized Version (AV) of 1611, a translation whose superlative qualities were universally acknowledged, and whose words, phrases, and rhythms have long enriched the very bloodstream of English language and literature. The excellence of its literary quality is one chief cause of the extraordinary hold exerted by this book over the hearts and minds of Englishmen and, indeed, of all English-speaking peoples. For this excellence we are indebted to the 1611 translators themselves, to William Tyndale and Miles Coverdale, their most notable predecessors, and to the youthful vigour of 17th-century English, of which, as yet, "custom had not bedimmed the lustre nor dried up the sparkle and the dewdrops."

Moreover, the old translators achieved literary distinction largely because they were not self-consciously aiming at it. Convinced that they were dealing with the undoubted word of God, they concentrated upon rendering it faithfully and reverently, and the reward and outcome of their purity of intention was a style that reflected their own nobility. Like all good style, theirs was a by-product; aiming at truth, they achieved beauty without effort or contrivance. Never straining after effect, but imbued with a sense of the momentousness of their task, the translators worked humbly and self-effacingly. The result is a style that, whether simple or elevated, is as genuine as seasoned timber, free from all that is tawdry or meretricious.

To this must be added the good fortune the English translators enjoyed in working when the language had not yet staled into jargon and cliché, when journalese, officialese, and other manifestations of our time were as yet far off. Think, for example, how a modern writer might have strained all his resources to render that supreme moment in the Gospel story

when the disciples recognize their risen Lord. The Authorized Version (John 20:19–20) reads:

> Then the same day at evening, being the first day of the week, when the doors were shut where the disciples were assembled for fear of the Jews, came Jesus and stood in the midst, and saith unto them, Peace be unto you. And when he had so said, he shewed unto them his hands and his side. Then were the disciples glad, when they saw the Lord.

The effect produced by this simplicity is that we are in the presence of something too holy for elaborate utterance. Of course, the simplicity is that of the writer of the Gospel of St. John, but the men of 1611 were transparent to it and let its light shine through. The same authentic quality is to be found, however, when the original demands a loftier style:

> When the morning stars sang together, and all the sons of God shouted for joy. . . . (Job 38:7)
> . . . Hitherto shalt thou come, but no further: and here shall thy proud waves be stayed. . . . (Job 38:11)
> Canst thou bind the sweet influences of Pleiades, or loose the bands of Orion? Canst thou bring forth Mazzaroth in his season? or canst thou guide Arcturus with his sons? (Job 38:31–32)

> And the ransomed of the Lord shall return, and come to Zion with songs and everlasting joy upon their heads: they shall obtain joy and gladness, and sorrow and sighing shall flee away. (Isa. 35:10)

If, then, the old translation is so admirable, and if it has been so dear and so sacred to the hearts of generations, what need was there for a modern version? The onus of demonstrating such a need rested heavily upon those who promoted the New English Bible, and they devoted careful thought to the question. It was not likely, they knew, that any version in 20th-century English, however "timeless," however scholarly, and however free from colloquialism or cliché, would have anything like the literary merit of the AV. Should we not then, by reducing the Bible's style to the level of contemporary speech or writing, reduce its spiritual influence as well? Granted that the Bible has a unique importance for the spiritual life, should we, by modernizing it, enhance that value, bring it home to more people? Or should we in fact cheapen and enervate it by robbing it of its antique patina? Such misgivings were voiced, as expected, when the New Testament, the first part of the New English Bible to be completed, appeared in 1961 (as they had been even in 1611).

Doubts of this kind had been ably expressed in an article by Dwight Macdonald in *The New Yorker* (Nov. 14, 1953) criticizing the American Revised Standard Version of 1952. The new version may make the Bible more "accessible" to the modern reader or listener; it may "slip more smoothly into the modern ear, but it also slides out more easily; the very strangeness and antique ceremony of the old forms made them linger in the mind." Macdonald illustrated his point with some examples: "Thus saith the Lord," for instance, is more impressive and "lordly" than "Thus says the Lord"; "Thou shalt not" more awesome than "Do not"; "Hast thou given the horse strength? hast thou clothed his neck with thunder? . . . the glory of his nostrils is terrible. . . ."—this is wilder, more passionate, more poetic than "Do you give the horse his might? Do you clothe his neck with strength? . . . His majestic snorting is terrible" (Job 39:19–20). Macdonald compares reading the Revised Standard with walking through the streets of a bombed city: "Is this gone? Does that still survive? Surely they might have spared *that*?"

Followed through logically, this line of thought leads to the position that it doesn't much matter what is being said, or whether the translation is accurate, as long as the requisite religious rumble is kept going. For the uninstructed listener, the effect, liturgically speaking, might be almost as good if the language were entirely, instead of partially, unintelligible—that is, not translated at all. It may be said—indeed, something of the sort has been said—that in the AV it sounds as if God were speaking, whereas in the NEB the accents are those of English gentlemen—and dons at that. Such is the prestige of the AV that an extraordinarily large number of people seem to think, or unconsciously feel, that it is The Bible and that God himself spoke in Tudor English. This explains the many complaints that

AUTHENTICATED NEWS INTERNATIONAL

The literary panel for the Old Testament of the New English Bible meets to review new translations.

the NEB translators have "altered" or "tampered with" The Bible. As a matter of fact, the whole translation was made directly from the best ancient texts into modern English, without dependence on the AV at all.

The Advancement of Scholarship. This brings us back to the point raised earlier: what could justify such a project as a translation of the Bible texts directly into modern English? There are two main justifications. First, since the 17th century scholarship had advanced so far in the understanding of Hebrew and Hellenistic linguistic usage and modes of thought, and so many new and important sources had come to light since the 1881 revision, that something more radical than a mere revision of the AV was called for. A great body of new information was now available about what the Bible really means, and it was high time for this to be put into circulation.

Many of those who condemn all modern versions of the Bible as such are themselves familiar only with spot passages and "hallowed phrases." They do not realize, as anyone must who has had to work over the whole AV in minute detail, how much of the old translation is inaccurate or unintelligible. The old translators, when (as often happened) they could not make head or tail of a passage and had no alternative text to check by, fell back upon their belief in "verbal inspiration" and simply "Englished" what was before them, word for word. That is why we get things like:

> Then shall the lambs feed after their manner, and the waste places of the fat ones shall strangers eat. Woe unto them that draw iniquity with cords of vanity, and sin as it were with a cart rope: . . . (Isa. 5:17–18)

or:

> But yet in it shall be a tenth, and it shall return, and shall be eaten: as a teil tree, and as an oak, whose substance is in them, when they cast their leaves: so the holy seed shall be the substance thereof. (Isa. 6:13)

or:

> With clouds he covereth the light; and commandeth it not to shine by the cloud that cometh betwixt. The noise thereof sheweth concerning it, the cattle also concerning the vapour. (Job 36:32–33)

Those who exalt Bible English as the grandest and noblest in our literature ignore this kind of thing. And there is something else they overlook; namely, the constant failure of the old translators to translate, that is, to render Hebrew or Greek idioms, constructions, and modes of speech by English counterparts. Too often they simply transliterate and give us mongrel English, which we tolerate only because we are accustomed to hearing it in church and are conditioned to revering whatever is "in the Bible." I am thinking of Hebraic constructions like:

> Because of the sins of Jeroboam which he sinned, and which he made Israel sin, by his provocation wherewith he provoked the Lord God of Israel to anger. (I Kings 15:30)

or:

> By reason of the multitude of oppressions they make the oppressed to cry: they cry out by reason of the arm of the mighty. (Job 35:9)

In any process of translation, the aim may be primarily to translate the actual words of the original, or it may be to translate its meanings. The former method may yield what is called a faithful translation, and it was the one that the old translators—imbued as they were with rabbinical notions about the inspiration and sanctity of each Hebrew or Greek construction, word, letter, and even squiggle in the holy text—were inclined to follow. Its disadvantage is that, as in the examples just quoted, the results may not be English at all and may be unintelligible. The latter method is the one that must be adopted if the result is to read like something written in English. It is the one followed by the NEB translators who, free at last from fundamentalist presuppositions, saw it as their "most sacred duty to render [the ancient expressions] into their real modern equivalents" (C. F. Moule, *The Listener,* March 23, 1961).

To do this, and to make sense of innumerable obscure passages, it was necessary to go behind the words to the meanings. The result, though far too faithful to be called a paraphrase, can certainly not be used as a crib. But who wants to use his Bible as a crib to the originals? Not the general reader and not the true scholar—only perhaps the embryo theological student, and his needs can be otherwise met.

One of the greatest difficulties facing the translator of Hebrew poetry into modern English is the parallelism on which it is based: the structural principle of saying everything twice over, antiphonally, in slightly varying words:

> Pour out thine indignation upon them,
> and let thy wrathful anger take hold of them.
> Let their habitation be desolate;
> and let none dwell in their tents. (Ps. 69:24–25)
>
> He that worketh deceit shall not dwell within
> my house:
> he that telleth lies shall not tarry in my
> sight. (Ps. 101:7)

This method of poetic utterance is foreign to the English mind and language, and at first the NEB translators struggled hard, whenever they could, to make one statement out of the two without losing whatever was significant in either. In the end, however, they were forced to admit defeat; there was far too much of this kind of thing for even their patience and ingenuity to cope with—it was like trying to change the colour of the Ethiopian's skin. Similarly, many things commonly said and thought and done in ancient times are almost unheard of today: anointing with oil, sacrificing bulls and goats, traveling with camels, possession by evil spirits, rending one's garments. These are all things that have no modern equivalents—or, if they have, those equivalents would be quite inadmissible in a translation (tanks or trucks for camels, psychotherapy for casting out evil spirits).

In a more general sense, as well, the biblical writers, whose world view was so remote from our own, were constantly saying things that we would neither think nor say. Consequently, to say them in the idiom of 20th-century speech may produce new kinds of unreality or absurdity. This, in fact, is one of the most serious objections to the whole project of modernization. Many things that were tolerable when clothed in the dignified archaism or obscurity of AV language may, in the nakedness of current speech, risk perishing of cold. You cannot resuscitate an obsolete thought or an exploded belief merely by stating it in modern terms. You are more likely to kill off, for good and all, various notions that have enjoyed a sort of half-life in the liturgical shadows.

The NEB translators had to face these and other problems, and they recognized, of course, that some of them were insoluble. If they continued and completed their work in good heart—as they did—it was because they were convinced of the need to supplement the old version, often grand but often inaccurate and obscure, with a new translation incorporating all the insights of modern scholarship and intelligible to all readers. But there was also a second main justification for this work, which springs from the first but may be considered separately.

A Bible for Modern Man. Reverting to Dwight Macdonald's image of the tourist revisiting an old bombed city, it is clear that he is presupposing a tourist who had been familiar with the city in its former state and had felt its picturesque charm. But the new translation is intended largely for readers who are not familiar with the AV and have no taste for antiquities. That there are many such people nowadays—indeed, that they form a vast majority—can scarcely be doubted. The new masses have not read or heard the Bible at their mother's knee. It can no longer be assumed that even so-called educated people will understand an allusion to Jephthah's daughter, Naboth's Vineyard, or Jacob's Ladder. Most young people today know as little about the Bible as they do about Homer or Virgil. And this is a disturbing thought, for the combined heritages of biblical and classical antiquity have given Western civilization such ideal purpose or meaning as it has had.

Accordingly, one main hope behind the NEB was that the new translation might reach this new reading public, most of whom were presumably repelled or baffled by the archaic style of the old. It was hoped that, if they found the Bible was no mere special preserve for parsons and pious highbrows but spoke to them in their own language about things that mattered to them, they might be encouraged to read it. As for those who love the AV because they have fed upon it from childhood, because its language has been intermingled with their lives and become inseparable from all that is holy and precious to them—well, here Macdonald's image breaks down. The AV, unlike the bombed city, is still there and still intact. Those who are at home in it can ignore the new satellite town. The NEB was never meant to supersede the AV, but to supplement it by clarifying its meaning in a language intelligible to all.

To sum up: to make a translation of ancient texts that is accurate, up-to-date, and intelligible is not the same thing as to make their contents more credible as history or doctrine— even though many of the NEB's promoters may have unconsciously assumed or hoped that this would be the case. It may even reduce their credibility by rendering them less mysterious. But it must surely be said that the confidence of the translators in the importance and usefulness of their task was justified. Those who talk of loss—loss of mystery, awesomeness, ceremony —should make very certain that they themselves, in responding to the AV, have not mistaken a sort of liturgical trance for true understanding and spiritual discernment.

Much of the Bible has an enduring message for every age; it is hoped that readers, seeing clearly at last what it is saying, may find their consciences disturbed at points formerly protected by the comfortable sonorities of the old version. The new translation was made in the belief that for too long the Bible's message has been embalmed in beautiful or familiar archaism, and that it is time to let it speak to our condition.

(Adapted from *Essays and Studies 1970*, published by John Murray Ltd. for the English Association)

continued from page 637

statistics are only estimates). The church continued to maintain its simplicity of worship with strong emphasis on biblical preaching, Bible classes, and mission work. Youth rallies and seminars were conducted across the U.S. in an effort to maintain the interest of teen-agers. Series of evangelistic meetings continued to be the main organized thrust for evangelism, but growing emphasis was placed on lectureships and seminars to bolster the commitment of the members. Eleven hundred church programs outlined in *Churches of Today*, vol. ii, evidenced growth in budgets, increased interest in mission work and benevolence, and less emphasis on buildings.

"Campaigns for Christ" were held, in which many churches in a city cooperated in an evangelistic effort. One such campaign, in the Dallas-Fort Worth, Tex., area, coordinated by 87 churches, used television preaching, door-to-door visitation, tract distribution, and mass telephoning. Two hundred were baptized, and attendance on the final night was 12,-500. There were similar campaigns in Northern Ireland, Guyana, Switzerland, Germany, Austria, the Netherlands, and Australia. In the U.S., where Churches of Christ were strongest in the South and Southwest, churches in those sections sent groups on evangelistic campaigns to Northern and Northeastern cities. Another missionary outreach was Exodus Guadalajara, in which 40 retirees from California began a movement to Middle America.   (M. N. Y.)

Church of Jesus Christ of Latter-day Saints. Church membership in 1970 totaled approximately 2.9 million. Among the numerous new stakes organized to accommodate the increasing growth of the church were the Tokyo Stake, the first stake in Asia, and the Transvaal Stake, the first in Africa. There were approximately 525 stakes in the church. Convert baptisms numbered 70,010.

David O. McKay, who had served as president of the church for 19 years, died Jan. 18, 1970, at the age of 96. He was succeeded by Joseph Fielding Smith (*see* BIOGRAPHY), president of the Council of the Twelve Apostles. Smith chose as his counselors Harold B. Lee and Nathan Eldon Tanner. These men were sustained as the First Presidency at the General Conference of the church in April. Earlier, in January, the First Presidency issued a statement reaffirming its stand—based on the teachings of the church's founder, Joseph Smith—barring Negroes from the priesthood.

Some 2,500 representative Laurel girls, members of the Young Women's Mutual Improvement Association from the U.S. and Canada, assembled on the Brigham Young University campus, Provo, Utah, August 22, for a conference designed to give leadership training to 16-, 17-, and 18-year-old girls as part of the church's new youth leadership program. On August 27–30 students of the Latter-day Saints Student Association met in the fourth annual LDSSA international conference to consider current social issues and the role of Latter-day Saint students in the modern age. A new Aaronic Priesthood Personal Achievement Program, introduced by the presiding bishopric of the church, was devised to help young men of the church achieve a sense of identity in today's society based on their relationship to God and Christ. An improved primary program for children, introduced in April, emphasized the teachings of Jesus, growth in spiritual knowledge, and homemaking skills.   (Jo. A.)

Disciples of Christ (Christian Church). Additional steps were taken in 1970 away from the former convention-type structure and toward a more formal church organization. By mutual agreement, agencies that had developed independently in the past century related themselves to the General Assembly and general offices of the church as "provisional" divisions and councils.

The largest of these, the United Christian Missionary Society, based in Indianapolis, Ind., agreed to become two divisions—the Division of Church Life and Work (domestic operations) and the Division of World Mission. Five other agencies accepted status as divisions of the church on a provisional basis, pending other changes and the drafting of a constitution. They were the Board of Church Extension, the Board of Higher Education, and the Pension Fund, all based in Indianapolis, and the National Benevolent Association (Division of Social and Health Concerns) and Christian Board of Publication, both of St. Louis, Mo. The Unified Promotion finance unit, Christian Church Foundation, Council on Christian Unity, and Disciples of Christ Historical Society (Nashville, Tenn.), which provided service rather than program, were named councils.

In June, 3,500 women of the Christian Church met in Lafayette, Ind., for their quadrennial assembly. Black Disciples held the first biennial meeting of their National Convocation in Columbia, Mo. The convocation replaced what formerly was the National Christian Missionary Convention. The change represented a merger of the convention with the General Assembly of the church while maintaining a forum for black concerns. (R. L. F.)

Jehovah's Witnesses. During 1970 the society of Christian ministers known as Jehovah's Witnesses carried on its ministry and Bible educational work in 206 lands. This work was organized by 26,524 congregations operating under the supervision of 93 branch offices.

Increased interest in the Bible and the Bible study program offered by Jehovah's Witnesses was reflected in the 164,193 new ministers (members) baptized during 1970, bringing the worldwide total to 1,483,430. During the summer 67 "Men of Good Will" district assemblies were held in the U.S., Canada, the British Isles, and Germany and over 800,000 in these countries heard the public talk "Saving the Human Race—in the Kingdom Way." Continued worldwide growth of Jehovah's Witnesses was evidenced by a total attendance of 3,226,168 at the annual celebration of the Lord's Evening Meal, compared with 2,493,519 in 1969. Peak attendances at congregational meetings necessitated the building of more Kingdom Halls, and there were over 30 such structures being built each month, on the average, in the U.S.

Publication of the Bible study book *The Truth that Leads to Eternal Life* reached a high of 32 million copies in 51 languages. During 1970 the Brooklyn, N.Y., printing plant alone produced 26,232,766 Bibles and bound books and over 212 million magazines. Circulation of *The Watchtower,* the official journal of Jehovah's Witnesses, rose to 6,650,000 in 73 languages, and its companion magazine, *Awake!,* attained a circulation of 6.5 million in 26 languages. (N. H. K.)

Lutherans. In 1970 Lutheran churches had about 75.1 million members on all continents. The 78 member churches of the Lutheran World Federation (LWF) had 53.3 million members. Representatives of virtually all theological factions within Lutheranism met at an international consultation in Vedbaek, Den. Significantly, the participants reached an early consensus that unity should be approached in terms of total Christian—not only Lutheran—unity.

Of great significance to the wider cause of Christian unity were findings on "Eucharist and Ministry" issued by Roman Catholic and Lutheran theologians as they completed their sixth year of doctrinal discussion. The crucial issue of what constitutes an authentic ministry was regarded as a major factor in keeping the two communions apart. A separate Catholic statement asked church authorities "whether the ecumenical urgency flowing from Christ's will for unity" might not dictate recognition of "the validity of the Lutheran ministry and . . . the presence of the body and blood of Christ in eucharistic celebrations of the Lutheran churches." A Lutheran statement urged the Lutheran bodies represented "to declare formally their judgment" that ordained Roman Catholic ministers are "engaged in a valid ministry" and to acknowledge that "the body and blood of our Lord Jesus Christ are truly present in their celebrations of the sacrament of the altar."

A new Joint Committee of the LWF and the World Alliance of Reformed Churches concluded that the dialogue between Lutherans and Reformed Churches should place new stress on those factors that stood in the way of implementing the theological consensus already achieved. Anglican and Lutheran theological delegations, meeting on a worldwide level at Oxford, Eng., for the first time, set as their goal "the establishment of a sufficient and convincing basis for reciprocal recognition and fellowship between the two churches."

Évian-les-Bains, on the French side of Lake Geneva, was finally selected in June as the site for the fifth LWF assembly, as officials regretfully concluded that conditions for a working assembly no longer existed in Pôrto Alegre, Braz. The change had its roots in the alleged use of torture by the Brazilian government. The assembly, the highest forum in Lutheranism, met in July. Youth delegates were present as full delegates for the first time.

Two radical departures from tradition with far-reaching implications for American Lutheranism occurred in 1970. The 3.2 million-member Lutheran Church in America (LCA), largest and most liberal of the nation's three major Lutheran bodies, became the first to allow the ordination of women and to permit communion for children before confirmation. Favourable action on both proposals was also taken by the 2.5 million-member American Lutheran Church (ALC), and both the LCA and the ALC had ordained a woman pastor by the year's end. The conservative 2.8 million-member Lutheran Church-Missouri Synod, holding its next convention in July 1971, might endorse the changes suggested in confirmation and communion practices, but was unlikely to consider the admission of women to the ministry.

A consultation sponsored by the three church bodies and reporting through their common agency, the Lutheran Council in the U.S.A., called upon them to seek increasing theological agreement, congregational fellowship, and unified programs "in awareness" that such efforts "may lead to structural unity."

The LCA and the ALC were moving closer together, but internal problems in the Missouri Synod seemed likely to hinder the achievement of total unity in the foreseeable future. With plans for unified programs in parish education and world mission and joint efforts to restructure church organizations under way, an LCA-ALC merger within a decade loomed as a strong possibility.

The Inter-Lutheran Commission on Worship approved common liturgical texts agreed upon internationally for use by English-speaking Christians. Much of this ecumenical wording was incorporated in a newly developed text for the rite of Holy Communion in modern language and music issued for experimental use in Lutheran churches.

Fredrik A. Schiotz, 69, retired as head of the American Lutheran Church. As his successor, the ALC elected Kent S. Knutson, head of Wartburg Theological Seminary, Dubuque, Ia., who defeated nine other nominees in some of the most open political campaigning in the annals of American Protestantism.

(E. W. M.; W. Vo.)

Methodists. During 1970 the most significant events were once again the demonstrations of unity in which the Methodist Church participated. This was true in many parts of the world and particularly in Britain, where united acts of worship became commonplace. The fourth series of conversations with representatives of the Roman Catholic Church was held in September at the headquarters of the World Methodist Council at Lake Junaluska, N.C. In India the United Church of North India was inaugurated at Nagpur on November 29; it comprised the British Methodist Church, the Baptist Church, the Church of the Brethren, the Disciples of Christ, the Churches of India, Pakistan, Burma, and Ceylon (Anglican), and the United Church of North India (Presbyterian and Congregational). The new Church of Pakistan (United Methodists, Anglicans, and Presbyterians) was inaugurated on November 1.

In December 1969 two new autonomous churches, related to the United Methodist Church (U.S.), came into being—one in Bolivia, the other in Uruguay. It was anticipated that the church in Peru would also become autonomous. The Methodist Church lost two well-known leaders in 1970. Bishop Odd Hagen, president of the World Methodist Council, and Daniel T. Niles, president of the Ceylon Methodist Church. In August Charles C. Parlin (U.S.) succeeded Bishop Hagen; he was the first layman to hold the post.

In London a historic judgment was given in the Chancery Division of the High Court on June 16. Some Methodists had questioned the authority of the Methodist Conference to approve the Anglican-Methodist unity scheme and to appoint ministers to be bishops. After a three-day hearing, Mr. Justice Megarry ruled that the Methodist Conference was the final authority within the Methodist Church on the interpretation of its doctrines, including the doctrinal standards. The ruling gave added significance to the vote that had been taken in the Methodist Conference meeting in Manchester on July 2, 1969, when 79.64% gave approval to the following resolution: "The Conference, affirming its faith that the Holy Spirit will lead us into a new Church, gives approval to the inauguration of Stage One of the Anglican-Methodist proposals."

In the U.S. minorities—ethnic groups, youth, and others—constituted a major focus for United Methodist Church action. This was especially true at a special session of the denomination's General Conference in April, which revised its priorities for 1971–72 to direct funds from ongoing programs into new

support for "self-determination of minority people" and which seated youth delegates for the first time. The conference reduced annual funds appropriated to its agencies by $2 million and allocated this sum to the Commission on Religion and Race. It also raised goals for support of its black colleges to $4 million annually and approved $1 million a year in new scholarship and loan funds for minority students.

Through the year there was a succession of developments concerning ethnic minorities, including some $2 million in loans to minority economic enterprises by the Board of Missions; a $1.3 million contract by the Board of Health and Welfare Ministries to train 700 "hard-core disadvantaged" for health-care careers; and $250,000 from Crusade Scholarships for deprived students at black colleges. The church had collected some $7 million for the four-year Fund for Reconciliation, launched in 1968, and allocated it to meet national and local needs of deprived or minority groups. Part of this also was appropriated for reconstruction and rehabilitation efforts in South Vietnam. Structurally, too, there were changes involving minorities. Two black annual conferences in Texas merged with overlapping white conferences to reduce the remnant of the former segregated Central Jurisdiction from 17 (as of 1964) to 7.

The denomination was the first to receive officially COCU's proposed Plan of Union. The General Conference authorized "thorough study" of the plan. Another ecumenical venture was merger of United Methodist and United Presbyterian mission-oriented magazines into the new *World Outlook.*

The Rhodesia Conference strongly protested that country's segregating Land Tenure Act. A short time later, Bishop Abel T. Muzorewa, first African to head the Rhodesian church, was banned by the government from black tribal areas. This "unwarranted interference" with the ministry was condemned in turn by the executive committee of the World Methodist Council. (M. W. Wo.; W. H. Ta.)

Presbyterian, Reformed, and Congregational. The outstanding event of 1970 was the assembly held at Nairobi, Kenya, on August 20–30, when the World Alliance of Reformed Churches (WARC) and the International Congregational Council (ICC) united to become the new World Alliance of Reformed Churches (Presbyterian and Congregational). On the opening day, two brief separate assemblies were held in the Taifa Hall of Nairobi University. First, ICC representatives were onlookers as delegates to the 20th General Council of the WARC voted for the dissolution of the alliance; then WARC representatives watched delegates to the 11th Assembly of the ICC as they formally recorded their vote to dissolve their organization, formed in 1891. All delegates then jointly voted to agree to the merger, adopting a formal Act of Union and the organization's new constitution. To complete the union, a service of thanksgiving was held at St. Andrew's Church (Presbyterian Church of East Africa).

The first plenary session was addressed by the German theologian Jürgen Moltmann on the assembly theme, "God Reconciles and Makes Free." Themes for subsequent section meetings were: reconciliation and creation; reconciliation and man; reconciliation and society; and reconciliation and the church. In the discussions, the issues of racial justice, concern for less developed countries, the effect of technical change on culture, and the responsibility of affluent nations toward poorer ones received prominence.

With the adoption of the new constitution, the organization was administratively made up of a general secretariat and two departments: of theology and of cooperation and witness. The Rev. Edmond Perret (Switzerland) was appointed general secretary, succeeding Marcel Pradervand, who had been WARC general secretary since 1948, and the Rev. Fred Kaan, minister-secretary of the former ICC. The assembly elected a layman as president, William P. Thompson, a lawyer and the stated clerk of the United Presbyterian Church in the U.S.A.

During the year four new churches were admitted into membership: the Sangir/Talaud Evangelical Church, Indonesia (200,000 members); the Reformed Church of East Africa (300,000 members); the Toradja Church in Indonesia (170,000 members); and the Ethiopian Evangelical Church Bethel (17,000 members). These brought the total membership of the World Alliance of Reformed Churches (Presbyterian and Congregational) to 130. Spread over 75 different countries, they represented some 55 million people, including 3 million in the Congregational Churches. The only constituent members of the ICC not to join in the merger with WARC were the Union of Welsh Independents, the Swedish Mission Covenant Church, and the Free Church of Finland.

During the year 19 of the 25 churches of the Congregational Union of New Zealand were received into the Presbyterian Church of New Zealand while talks continued toward a wider union. Progress continued to be made toward the union of Congregational, Methodist, and Presbyterian churches in Australia. Further steps were taken toward the union of the Congregational Church in England and Wales and the Presbyterian Church of England, planned for 1972. Unexpectedly the proposed union of the Congregational Union of Scotland with the Church of Scotland was finally, though narrowly, rejected by both bodies.

Steps toward union were taken during the year between the United Presbyterian Church in the U.S.A. and the Presbyterian Church in the U.S., separated over 100 years ago. For the third time in recent history, the two bodies held formal reunion conversations, two previous attempts at organic merger having failed in 1931 and 1954. A joint committee of the two denominations (including observers from the Associate Reformed Presbyterian, Cumberland Presbyterian, Hungarian Reformed in America, Reformed Church in America, United Church of Christ, and Second Cumberland Presbyterian Church) began deliberations, and subcommittees were appointed to deal with such subjects as the confessional, polity, mission, strategy, and communications. Plans were under way for presentation of a reunion plan before the assemblies of both churches for study, but not for formal adoption, by the spring of 1971.

Examples of closer cooperation between the two largest Presbyterian denominations in the U.S., pressed by financial necessity, were seen during the year in the merger of the sales organizations of the John Knox and the Westminster presses, in the joint publication of *Church and Society* magazine, and in the establishment of a Joint Department of Worship and Music within their boards of Christian Education.

A major editorial work with a long tradition was produced jointly by the Cumberland Presbyterian Church, the Presbyterian Church in the U.S., and the United Presbyterian Church in the U.S.A. Featuring contemporary English, *The Worshipbook* would be

WIDE WORLD

A policeman speaks with two Protestant clergymen who chained themselves to the railing of Buckingham Palace to protest the church unity talks going on at Windsor in January 1970.

printed initially with services and prayers, with hymns being included in a later edition.

Although decreases in membership faced U.S. churches holding the Presbyterian order, contributions were up. Members of the United Presbyterian Church in the U.S.A. increased total giving to the church by $3.5 million over the preceding year, while members of the Presbyterian Church in the U.S. contributed an all-time high $133,730,777 in 1969.

At the annual assembly of the Congregational Church in England and Wales in May, the Rev. C. S. Duthie, principal of New College, London, was chosen president-elect to succeed Erik Routley in 1971. The Congregational Council for World Mission recorded a substantial financial surplus during the year ended in March, but a decline of 27% in the number of missionaries during the past four years. In response to a general appeal for 1% of income for aid to less developed countries, the Congregational and Presbyterian churches in Britain jointly raised nearly £130,000 during the year. Grants were made to projects sponsored by Christian Aid and the two churches. (See *United Church of Christ*, below.)

(F. H. KA.; R. F. G. C.; W. B. MI.)

Religious Society of Friends. British Friends began the reorganization of their social welfare work by setting up a Social Responsibility Council, to take over the work of committees concerned with race relations, penal reform, temperance and moral welfare, and social and economic affairs. About 2,000 Friends and their families contributed 1% of their net income to a fund to help development projects in poorer countries. British Friends continued to be active in rehabilitation work in Nigeria and in work among refugees in the Middle East. The Peace Committee of London Yearly Meeting, in conjunction with other organizations, pressed the British government not to resume the sale of arms to South Africa.

The Friends World Committee for Consultation met for its 11th triennial session in Sigtuna, Swed., August 1–8. A new African section was created, to parallel the American and the European and Near East sections.

In the U.S. the Friends General Conference held

its biennial gathering at Ocean Grove, N.J., late in June, bringing together 2,000 Quakers from all parts of the nation. "Strategy for Action" was the theme of the first General Conference of the Evangelical Friends Alliance, held in July in Wichita, Kan. A proposal to give more administrative responsibility to the pastor in Friends' churches was discussed. The conference on the "Future of Quakerism" that gathered in St. Louis, Mo., October 5–7, marked the first time representatives from all different groups of Friends had come together since the separations early in the 19th century.

The American Friends Service Committee spent approximately $7.5 million during 1970 on a wide range of programs in the U.S. and some 18 countries overseas. In addition to continuing its rehabilitation centre in South Vietnam, the committee inaugurated a two-year rehabilitation program in Nigeria and a child-care centre program in the Gaza Strip.

(CD. H.; E. B. BR.)

Salvation Army. The Salvation Army maintained and broadened its relief and rehabilitation program in Vietnam in 1970. The ending of hostilities in Nigeria allowed Salvationist medical personnel to enter the former war zones where, throughout the fighting, African Army officers had continued bravely to minister among their own people. Massive resources of manpower and materials were poured into the stricken area when Hurricane Celia struck the Corpus Christi, Tex., area. A Salvation Army officer stationed in Lima and several assistants were among the first rescuers

CENTRAL PRESS FROM PICTORIAL PARADE

The new look in uniforms for women of the Salvation Army (right) is introduced in London, May 12, 1970. The old style is modeled by the woman on the left.

to reach the earthquake-stricken area in Peru; they were speedily joined by other comrades, including well-equipped, highly mobile disaster teams from North America.

The international travels of Gen. Erik Wickberg included Europe, North America, Scandinavia, and the Far East. In Sweden he was made a commander of the Order of Vasa, and Korea's Pres. Park Chung Hee awarded him the nation's highest honour, the Order of Moo-Koong-Wha.

In the U.S. the Salvation Army sponsored a series of seminars on drug use and abuse to "sensitize youth leaders and Salvation Army officers to the new role

that agencies must assume in combating drug use in the neighborhoods."

One of the Army's largest homes for the aging was opened in New York City. The 15-story, nonprofit residence would accommodate nearly 400 men and women. A Spanish-language pilot program to train Salvation Army officers was launched in Puerto Rico, combining classroom study with practical experience.

(C. E. N.; W. P.)

Seventh-day Adventists. A total of 1,782 Seventh-day Adventists from many of the 193 countries in which the church operates met in Atlantic City, N.J., June 11–20, for the 51st General Conference session. The ten-day conference emphasized the imminent return of Christ and how best to proclaim this doctrine to the world. Important features of the session included the adoption of a Declaration on Human Relations, strengthening the commitment of the church to a policy of racial nondiscrimination; the election of three additional blacks to the general headquarters staff in Washington, D.C.; and the formation of the Afro-Mideast Division.

During 1969—the last year for which complete statistics were available—more than 171,000 converts were baptized, bringing the worldwide membership to almost two million; 497 regular workers were sent from home bases to serve overseas, as well as 114 student missionaries. A headquarters committee, the Committee for Inner City Ministry, was coordinating efforts to provide a substantial inner-city program in each major city in North America. Disaster relief work by the Seventh-day Adventist Welfare Service following the Peruvian earthquake of May 31 included the distribution of 1.2 million lb. of food and 30,000 lb. of clothing.

The Youth's Instructor, weekly youth magazine of the church for 118 years, was replaced by a new journal, *Insight,* with a more modern format. The annual Autumn Council, meeting in Washington, D.C., in October, voted a world budget that included appropriations of $49,735,080, an increase of $249,480.61 over the previous year. (K. H. W.)

Unitarians and Universalists. Radical changes in administrative organization, complicated by a new sense of fiscal responsibility that undercut some past ideological commitments, marked institutional developments in North America in 1970. Several years of overspending had exhausted unrestricted capital funds, and severe cutbacks in personnel, grants, and programs became obligatory. North America's 21 administrative districts were reduced to 7, and a $1 million grant voted by two General Assemblies to the Black Affairs Council for Black Empowerment was terminated, 45% fulfilled (the council, however, could raise money directly from the churches). Although this was a year for reflection and retrenchment, the Annual Fund for the support of the Unitarian Universalist Association raised the second highest sum in its history.

Churches, clergy, and laymen continued to be profoundly involved in antiwar activities, racial equality issues, and campus drives for peace, justice, and freedom, and innumerable churches became meeting and planning centres.

The ninth annual General Assembly of the Unitarian Universalist Association met in Seattle, Wash., June 29 to July 4, 1970. It attracted 1,022 delegates from 359 churches and fellowships in 46 states, 6 provinces, and Mexico. Resolutions passed by the assemblage urged withdrawal of troops from Southeast Asia, less federal spending on military activities and more for improving the quality of life, restricting family size to two children except for adoptions, a general and complete program for international disarmament, and a comprehensive program for the protection, compensation, and development of Eskimo and Indian rights and culture.

A National Council of Churches survey revealed that Unitarian Universalist clergymen received a higher median income ($10,412) than their counterparts in the mainstream Christian denominations. A serious oversupply of clergymen existed, dramatized by the fact that only 50 vacant pulpits existed in Canada and the U.S.

The first woman president in the history of the Canadian Unitarian Council, Mrs. Mary Lu MacDonald, was elected at the annual meeting in Toronto, Ont., over the May 8, 1970, weekend. Resolutions were passed dealing with pollution control, Canadian sanctuary for persons fleeing military involvement in Southeast Asia, deactivation and shipment of nerve gas, and the boycott of nonunion grape products. The process of creating an autonomous Canadian organization was under way. Half the moneys raised by the UUA Annual Fund in Canada would henceforth be returned to the Dominion churches and fellowships.

Numerous observances occurred throughout the U.S. in honour of the 200th anniversary of Universalism in America. That movement, which merged with Unitarianism in 1961, dated from September 1770, when the Englishman John Murray landed in New Jersey and preached his first sermon in the New World.

The British General Assembly of Unitarian and Free Christian Churches met in London, April 6–10, 1970. It was decided to form a standing committee to plan and initiate action in support of world development, and a resolution was carried recognizing the need to impress on congregations the urgency of concerted action to conserve and improve the quality of man's environment. Full support was pledged for European Conservation Year.

The assembly decided to affiliate with the National Council for Civil Liberties as an earnest of its traditional and continuing belief in the right to both civil and religious liberty. The Rev. John Kielty resigned as general secretary after 20 years' service to the assembly and was succeeded by the Rev. Brian L. Golland, formerly minister at Mill Hill Chapel, Leeds, Yorkshire.

During the year the assembly was admitted to corporate membership in the World Congress of Faiths and made an increased contribution to the International Association for Religious Freedom, as evidence of its support for the principle of cooperation among all great world religions and its belief in the underlying unity of origin and purpose of every religious faith.   (B. L. Go.; J. N. B.)

United Church of Canada. The rate and extent of change in the United Church of Canada increased in 1970. This was particularly evident in relation to the restructuring of the church. The abolition of administrative boards in favour of divisions had been no mere absorption of the former by the latter. The overlapping of concerns and activities was to be eliminated and all the resources of the boards would come under the control of the divisions. However, the restructuring was taking place primarily from the point of view of mission and not merely as a reorganization.

A new phase of restructuring loomed large in 1970

—an emphasis on regionalism, the extent of which would not be known for some time. It became evident that the various regions of the church must have greater responsibilities, but it was also realized that the unity of the church must be preserved. It appeared that field staff would be related to conferences rather than to the national headquarters, and that the administration of institutions in various regions would be handed over to conferences or other regional authorities.

The involvement of the United Church in ecumenical activity had also increased, through cooperation and cost-sharing with other denominations at the local, regional, and national levels. The United Church cooperated closely with other Protestant churches as well as the Roman Catholic Church in such important areas as community ministries, shared buildings, and theological education. It also extended its cooperation with secular social agencies. In many areas congregations ceased to grow (there was a membership decline of 1% in 1969), but the church's ministry turned up increasingly in crisis, rehabilitation, and drop-in centres, and ministers were appointed as detached or community workers.

In the field of world mission, the United Church continued its policy of cooperating with ecumenical agencies. It also continued to emphasize its role as a helping church, serving, advising, and supporting rather than controlling the autonomous younger churches.

Statistics for 1970 were not yet available, but the decline in church school attendance continued in 1969 with a drop of 14%. In church membership, church attendance, and finances the decline was not nearly so serious, but great concern was felt in 1970 that a further falling off in financial support might mean curtailment of the church's mission at home and abroad.

Union negotiations with the Anglican Church of Canada and the Christian Church (Disciples of Christ) in Canada continued during 1970. While many complained about apathy regarding union in the Anglican and United Churches, a joint commission was diligently at work on a plan of union. In the commission agreement was reached about the administration of baptism and confirmation. While the Doctrinal Commission was still studying the question of the ordination of women (a matter of concern to the United Church, which had ordained women since 1936), there was agreement that "there is no theological reason which would preclude the ordination of women to the ministry of word and sacraments."

(A. G. R.)

United Church of Christ. When the United Church of Christ came into being in 1957 it brought together churches that at the beginning of the 20th century had belonged to four different communions in the U.S. The Congregational and Christian churches had united in 1931, and the Evangelical Synod of North America and the Reformed Church in the United States had merged in 1934. The uniting denominations brought together a membership that in 1970 stood at 6,800 congregations and two million members.

Following directions clearly set by the 1969 General Synod, the national agencies of the church engaged in programs directed toward the empowerment of minorities. The Board for Homeland Ministries put all of its mission work among American Indians under the control of a council composed entirely of Indians. The Commission on Racial Justice placed more than 225 students from black ghettos in colleges

KEYSTONE

Roman Catholic Mass
is celebrated
in the precincts
of England's
Canterbury Cathedral
for the first time
in 400 years,
July 7, 1970.

related to the United Church. The Office of Communication continued its efforts before the Federal Communications Commission to assure fair minority representation in the control and operation of the broadcast media. The Council on Church and Ministry undertook a special program to recruit black college students for the ministry.

Many of the conferences (state bodies) of the church engaged in similar programs. The Massachusetts conference acted to give its unrestricted reserves ($1 million) to the Black Ecumenical Commission of Massachusetts. This action was publicly opposed by Roy Wilkins of the National Association for the Advancement of Colored People, and some of the churches in the Massachusetts conference also were in opposition.

In a somewhat different vein, the Ohio conference passed a resolution condemning the Gulf Oil Corp. for its support of Portuguese colonialism in Angola, Mozambique, and Portuguese Guinea and calling on members of the conference to discontinue the use of Gulf products. Gulf threatened to sue the conference, and the matter was being given further study by the board of directors of the conference as the year ended.

The United Church continued in its commitment to church union, although there was a growing feeling that ecumenical action might offer a more viable way into church union than negotiation. As a full participant in COCU, it prepared during 1970 to engage in conversations among local congregations based on the Plan of Union.

The polarization affecting U.S. society was also evident in the United Church of Christ. As congregations, conferences, and national leadership attempted to address themselves to the problems of racism, war, and the youth culture, signs of conflict in the church became more apparent.

Officers of the church for 1970 were Robert V. Moss, president; Joseph H. Evans, secretary; and Charles H. Lockyear, treasurer. (See *Presbyterian, Reformed, and Congregational,* above.)   (R. V. M.)

ROMAN CATHOLIC CHURCH

The year 1970 saw a growth in the independence of "local churches" (that is, national churches) within the Roman Catholic Church. The visits of Pope Paul VI (*see* BIOGRAPHY) to Australia and the Philippines in November were to preside at meetings of the local

hierarchies. In June the pope referred to local churches as "blossoming branches of the universal Church."

In Latin America there was much discussion on "the theology of revolution." Conflicts between church and state were particularly harsh in Paraguay and Argentina, where many priests were involved in the progressive "third world" movement. Two of them, Father Fernando Carbone and Father Fulgencio Alberto Rojas, were arrested and charged with being accomplices in the murder of the former president of Argentina, Gen. Pedro Eugenio Aramburu.

But the main flash point in Latin America was Brazil. Throughout the year there were well-substantiated reports of torture, with priests and nuns among the victims. At the end of 1969, the bishop of Volta Redonda was accused of "subversive activities": he had supported trade unions and denounced torture. The bishops of Brazil came to his support, the Commission for Justice and Peace in Rome issued protests, and Pope Paul referred to the matter indirectly. Archbishop Helder Camara's visit to Europe in the spring helped to focus attention on Brazil. In June the bishops called on the government to stop using torture and other totalitarian methods, but within a week the government was threatening to take exemplary action against Archbishop Camara for "defaming Brazil" and Agnelo Cardinal Rossi, president of the Bishops' Conference, had backed down and claimed that "one cannot attribute to the government responsibility for several isolated cases of torture."

Another church-state clash occurred in Rhodesia, where the bishops protested vigorously against the Smith government's Land Tenure Act. Their pastoral letter, called *Crisis of Conscience,* ended with these fighting words: "We cannot in conscience and will not in practice accept any limitation of our freedom to deal with all people, irrespective of race, as members of the one human family." This hint of civil disobedience gave the government pause, and it announced that its restrictions would be eased somewhat.

In the U.S. there was continuing polarization among Catholics who were found on all sides in current debates. Some defied the law and went underground, as for example the two priests Daniel and Philip Berrigan, both of whom were arrested in the course of the year. Another novel form of activity for Catholic priests was the attempt to run for Congress. The best known

WIDE WORLD

Mourners fill the Cathedral
of the Holy Cross
in Boston, Nov. 7, 1970,
for the funeral service
of Richard Cardinal
Cushing.

among such candidates were two Jesuits, John J. McLaughlin as a Republican in Rhode Island and Robert F. Drinan as a Democrat in Boston. McLaughlin lost his bid for a Senate seat, but Drinan won election to the House of Representatives.

In Europe the joints were creaking at various points. In France 44 priests left the ministry in June and issued a collective statement declaring that they could "no longer in conscience accept a great many of the present structures of the Church." An international meeting of dissident priests took place in Amsterdam toward the end of September. There was talk of modifying or abolishing the concordats in Portugal and Spain, where many priests involved in the Basque nationalist movement had been arrested. The growing involvement of the church in the social problems of Spain was reflected in a document on poverty issued by the Bishops' Conference in July; it called for freedom of assembly and association and for the creation of "truly representative trade unions." In Italy the Vatican risked a head-on clash with the government by opposing its divorce proposals, which, however, were ultimately adopted.

In June, for the first time in the history of the church in England, a national conference of priests was held. One resolution summed up the spirit of the meeting: "The future survival of the Church in England and Wales demands a radical reappraisal of our evangelical and pastoral mission and for this we are basically unprepared." "Consultation" was the watchword, and in Germany and Switzerland synods, also involving elected members of the laity, were planned for 1971.

Meanwhile, the reverberations of the Dutch Pastoral Council were still being felt. In January it voted for the abolition of compulsory celibacy for priests, and the bishops supported this request. The reply of Rome came indirectly in the form of a papal speech from the balcony in St. Peter's Square and a letter to Jean Cardinal Villot, secretary of state (February 3). The pope rejected the Dutch proposals, though he reluctantly aired the possibility of ordaining men already married, but only in very special circumstances. Léon Cardinal Suenens of Belgium gave a dramatic interview to the French newspaper *Le Monde,* in which he pleaded for openness on this question. There were secret meetings in the nunciature in Paris that led finally to a meeting between Hans Cardinal Alfrink of the Netherlands and the pope. Both sides gave a little. Cardinal Alfrink returned home and his statement concluded: "Without failing to understand the problems explained by the cardinal, the pope considers that the reasons for maintaining the traditional link of priesthood and celibacy in the Latin Church are still valid." On the other hand, the question would be on the agenda for the Synod of the Church that was to meet in Rome in the fall of 1971.

Women were another increasingly rebellious group. Ordination of women to the priesthood remained an extremely unlikely prospect, but a gesture was made when the title "doctor of the church" was conferred on two female saints, St. Catherine of Siena and St. Teresa of Ávila. Heretofore, the title had been given only to men.

Less spectacular questions received attention. New baptismal and funeral rites were promulgated. A *Motu Proprio* on mixed marriages left more room for local hierarchies to make their own arrangements—within a given framework. A draft for a "Constitution for the Church," leaked to the press, met with energetic

UPI COMPIX

Private secretary of Pope Paul VI (center) restrains Benjamin Mendoza y Amor Flores (right), who attempted to assassinate the pope on his arrival at Manila airport on Nov. 27, 1970.

criticism from many theologians. In ecumenism there was a sense that the honeymoon period was over, although there were increasing contacts at the local level. The World Council of Churches was scheduled to discuss possible Roman Catholic membership at its meeting in Addis Ababa, Eth., in January 1971.

Newspaper reports in midsummer described a practice whereby Indian girls from Kerala state were sent to European convents as novices, the convent paying some $700 for each one. The girls, poorly educated and unfamiliar with Western language and customs, could not qualify for the education that had been promised them and frequently ended up doing menial work. A Vatican statement called the press reports "unduly exaggerated," but added that the practice had been under investigation for some time and had been suspended. (*See also* VATICAN CITY STATE.)

(P. A. H.)

EASTERN CHURCHES

The Orthodox Church. On April 10, 1970, Patriarch Alexii of Moscow, together with 14 other bishops, members of the Holy Synod, signed a *tomos* granting total ecclesiastical independence, or autocephaly, to the Orthodox Church in America. First established on American soil by Russian missionaries working in Alaska in the late 18th century, the Orthodox Church, which had gathered into its fold immigrants of various ethnic origins, had been governed since 1870 by a bishop appointed from Russia.

Plans for ecclesiastical independence were drawn up as early as 1905, but the events following the Russian Revolution slowed the process of integration; parallel jurisdictions, organized on a purely ethnic basis (notably the Greek Archdiocese in 1921), and political factiousness brought disunity to the Orthodox in America. The original diocese itself broke with Moscow in 1924 and again in 1931. The action of the Patriarchate of Moscow gave a new start to the cause of Orthodox unity in America: it canceled the former canonical rights of the Russian Church, formally recognized the "Church in America" as a sister church —the 15th autocephalous Orthodox Church in the world—and called on all Orthodox Americans, whatever their ethnic extraction, to join it.

WIDE WORLD

A member of the Orthodox Church in America places a candle near the coffin of Father Herman of Spruce Island during his canonization ceremony in Kodiak, Alaska. He became the first American saint in an Orthodox church.

Positive responses came from the Romanian and the Antiochian dioceses; the first became part of the Church in America, the other was taking appropriate steps through its mother church. Official statements of the Greek Church indicated a more negative attitude. Attempts to raise the problem of American church independence and of adopting English as the liturgical language initially were supported by the Greek archbishop, Iakovos, but they were violently criticized by the Greek press, both in Greece and in America, and were opposed strongly by the Ecumenical Patriarchate of Constantinople.

In a statement addressed to the Greek-American community, the Patriarchate stressed again the importance of ethnic origin, Greek language, and dependence upon higher authority abroad. Patriarch Athenagoras, in two letters addressed to Moscow, protested against American autocephaly and affirmed that it could be granted only by an ecumenical council. In its answers to Constantinople, Moscow pointed out that all the modern autocephalous Orthodox Churches had been established by simple action of the mother church.

Soon after its establishment, the new Orthodox Church in America proceeded with the canonization of the missionary monk Herman (d. 1837), who came to Alaska from the Valamo monastery (presently in Finland) to work among Aleuts, Eskimos, and Indians. The canonization ceremonies took place on Kodiak Island, Alaska, and were attended by the Orthodox archbishop of Finland, Paul.

The Orthodox Church of Japan, originally a Russian mission, which had been in the American jurisdiction since 1945, also acceded to independence as an autonomous church by agreement between the Patriarchate of Moscow and the Church in America. Its founder, Archbishop Nicholas (d. 1913), was also proclaimed a saint.

A few days after having signed the decisive documents concerning America and Japan, Patriarch Alexii died (April 17) at the age of 92 (*see* OBITUARIES). It was announced in Moscow that his successor would be elected at a council of bishops, clergy, and laity on June 2, 1971. This delay in choosing a new patriarch, as well as the legal uncertainty about the composition of the council and the procedure of election, was widely commented upon. It was obvious that the international prestige of the Moscow Patriarchate would

suffer greatly if minimal guarantees of freedom were not formally given by the Soviet government.

The death of Theodosios VI, patriarch of Antioch (September 19), was followed by the rapid election of a successor, Elias IV, formerly metropolitan of Aleppo, Syria. The Orthodox Patriarchate of Antioch exercised jurisdiction over 250,000 Christian Arabs in Syria, Lebanon, Iraq, the U.S., and South America.

An international conference of Orthodox theologians was held at the Hellenic College, Brookline, Mass., September 7–11, with the participation of speakers from France, Romania, Greece, the U.S.S.R., Turkey, and Yugoslavia. It witnessed a great solidarity of concerns and purposes going beyond the tensions on the hierarchical level.

Eastern Non-Chalcedonian Churches. The catholicos of all Armenians, Vasghen I, residing at Echmiadzin in the U.S.S.R., paid a visit to Pope Paul VI in Rome on May 8–12, 1970. The catholicos also visited Armenian communities in France.

Delegates from the churches of Egypt, Syria, Ethiopia, Armenia, and India met for a third informal consultation with theologians of the Orthodox Church in Geneva on August 16–21. The consultation dealt mainly with the problem of the authority of councils and with ecclesiological issues dividing the two communions; it prepared the elements of possible solutions to be considered by the appropriate authorities in the event of formal union. It reaffirmed the agreement, reached at previous consultations, on the "substance" of a common Christology, but registered the persisting disagreement on the formal canonical authority of the Council of Chalcedon (451) and the following councils recognized by the Orthodox Church and rejected by the Non-Chalcedonians. The consultation designated a continuation committee and recommended the appointment of an official joint commission by the churches themselves.   (J. ME.)

JUDAISM

The unresolved Israel-Arab conflict loomed over the diasporic Jewish communities in the year 1970 (5730–31, according to the Jewish calendar). Jews the world over were not only deeply concerned with the problem of Israel's security, but also were directly affected by the events in the Middle East.

Particularly affected were the Jewish communities in the Arab countries. One of the first acts of the revolutionary junta that took over the government in Libya in September 1969 was the sequestration of all Jewish property, and the few hundred Jews who had remained in the country after 1967 were forced to leave. In the U.A.R. the government discreetly allowed all Egyptian Jews to emigrate, and some 90 families left. They were not allowed to take any possessions. Lebanese Jewry, once a thriving and affluent community of some 7,000, dwindled to fewer than 1,000. Although well treated by the authorities, Jews had been leaving steadily because of the unstable political situation and intensified commando activities in Beirut. The 2,000 Jews in Tangier, Mor., were said to be poised to leave, prompted by the incessant anti-Israeli propaganda and by local intimidations.

The position of Jews in the Soviet Union remained a permanent item of world Jewish concern. The tragedy of Soviet Jewry was that its members were not allowed to live fully as Jews within the U.S.S.R. and at the same time they were not allowed to leave the country except in a very few cases. However, in the past year or so, the mood of Soviet Jewry had changed, and like other Soviet dissenters Soviet Jews were now taking active steps to call the world's attention to their plight. Many signed appeals were sent out of the Soviet Union, addressed to the UN secretary-general, the prime minister of Israel, Jewish communities in the West, and international organizations, requesting in unequivocal terms the right to leave the U.S.S.R. The authorities staged a public meeting, attended by many prominent Soviet Jews, to denounce Israel and its "Zionist accomplices," but under the concentrated pressure of world opinion some Jews were given permission to emigrate to Israel. (*See* UNION OF SOVIET SOCIALIST REPUBLICS.)

There were no reliable statistical data relating to the number of Jews who left (or remained in) Poland and Czechoslovakia in the wake of anti-Zionist campaigns. In Czechoslovakia, Jews were accused of being behind the "anti-Soviet and anti-Socialist Dubcek era," but the anticipated anti-Zionist trials did not take place. The position of Jews in Romania and Hungary was generally satisfactory.

The effect of the New Left pro-Arab attitudes was felt within some Western Jewish communities, especially among Jewish students in the U.S., France, and Great Britain, and some of the more radical students did not hesitate to adopt an anti-Israel stance, even supporting some Arab terrorist activities. However, there were signs that Jewish youth in the affluent societies—coming, as many of them did, from a completely assimilated and secularized milieu—were beginning to be more and more aware of their Jewishness and trying to find an outlet for their radical idealism within the Jewish context.

Jews in Great Britain celebrated the centenary of the United Synagogue, their prime congregational union. The British Liberal and Reform congregations were dismayed by the failure of the Board of Deputies to give a formal expression to the de facto existing rights of their religious authorities to be consulted on matters that were their direct concern. The constitutional amendment to that effect was defeated by deputies representing the Federation of Synagogues and the Union of Orthodox Hebrew Congregations. However, the chief rabbi of the United Synagogue declared that he would continue to seek an understanding with the Liberal and Reform religious leaders whereby the existing dichotomy in matters of marriage, divorce, and proselytization could be eliminated or, at least, reduced.

The vexed problem of "who is a Jew?" was again raised by two cases in Israel. One involved an Israeli naval officer and his non-Jewish wife who won a two-year legal fight to have their two children registered as of Jewish nationality. The other case was that of Helen Zeidman, who had been converted from Christianity through the Circle for Progressive Judaism and whose conversion was not recognized by Israeli religious authorities. She was allowed to be registered as Jewish before a formal Orthodox conversion. Jewish religious leaders in Europe and elsewhere lined up behind the Israeli Chief Rabbinate on this issue, stating that "a Jew is only a person born of a Jewish mother or who has been received into Judaism by the proper legal procedure of proselytization, carried out in accordance with the *halacha* by a properly constituted traditional court of Jewish law."

While diplomatic efforts were being made to settle the boundaries of the state of Israel, the concurrent question of Israel's biblical-rabbinical limits was being debated. Chief Rabbi Isaac Nissim of the Sephardic community maintained that it would be a sin for the Israeli Army to withdraw from any area that was part of the traditional Holy Land, and Rabbi Menahem Schneurson, head of the Habad-Hassidic society, issued a similar warning. Actually, the boundaries of the biblical Promised Land are variously described in the Bible and the Talmud. The vast majority of Jewish people, including most Orthodox, were interested only in the maintenance of a viable and secure state.

The passage of abortion reform laws in several U.S. states divided the American rabbinate. The Orthodox rabbis regarded abortion as sinful, while the Conservative and Reform rabbis maintained that in many cases abortion is not immoral and that the parents have to make their own decision in accord with the dictates of their own conscience. In the Talmud, various opinions are given as to whether the soul enters the fetus at conception or at birth. In Jewish law, the baby was considered a human being only after its head had emerged from the birth canal.

The insistence of the Orthodox on limiting the dialogue between Jews and Christians to questions of ethics had cooled the ardour of some Christian ecumenists. During 1970 the ecumenical movement was set back even more decisively by the demand of some Jewish theologians that Christians recognize the religious validity of the state of Israel as a partial fulfillment of biblical prophecy. While some Christians concurred in this view, a great number considered it unacceptable.

A New York state law was enacted providing for state grants to parochial schools to cover expenses mandated by the state, such as maintaining attendance records, administering examinations, and keeping pupil health records. Rabbi Morris Sherer, executive president of the Agudath Israel of America, called this "a first step" in the "battle to obtain government support for the secular educational services offered" by religious day schools. Several states, including New York and New Jersey, moved to eliminate all restrictions against granting aid to students who attend such religious day schools.

The National Jewish Commission on Law and Public Affairs (COLPA) won a judgment against a New York company that had discriminated against a Sabbath observer. The company was found to have violated the New York State Human Rights Law. COLPA was also instrumental in getting the New York State Unemployment Bureau to continue payments to individuals who would not accept jobs that required work on the Sabbath and Jewish holy days. Students at Yeshiva University, the oldest and largest university under Jewish auspices in the U.S., began a massive campaign to end the "threat of strangulation by secularization" at the institution.

(C. U. L.; J. B. A.; P. GL.)

BUDDHISM

Many noteworthy events took place in the world of Buddhism during 1969–70. The unearthing of a five-foot Buddha-like statue, estimated to date from 700–300 B.C., in Mont El Dore in Guatemala by a group of archaeologists stirred speculation that Buddhism had been introduced to the American continent nearly 20 centuries ago. In India remains of a majestic early Buddhist stupa were discovered at Pauni, near Nagpur, and the government announced its decision

WIDE WORLD
Rabbi Abel Respes, one of only a few blacks to hold the position, preaches in his synagogue, Adat Beyt Mosheh, in Elwood, N.J.

to restore Savatthi, where the Buddha spent the rainy season during the last 25 years of his life. Indian authorities also agreed to provide funds and technical assistance for the restoration of the colossal Buddha image in Bamian, Afghanistan.

In 1969 the Dalai Lama and his followers had commemorated the tenth anniversary of their flight from Tibet to India. They had completed the construction of a three-story Tsuglag Khang (cathedral) in Dharamsala, where the Dalai Lama performed the esoteric Vajrayana initiation of Sri Kalachakra for 15,000 Tibetans. Still unknown were the whereabouts of the Panchen Lama, the second-ranking Tibetan leader. There were rumours that he had escaped from China to Mongolia, but it seemed more likely that he had died, probably in Manchuria. In Bombay, P. T. Borale, one of the leaders of scheduled class Indians, became the first Buddhist mayor of a major city in India. (See *Religions of Asia*, below.)

In Ceylon many Buddhist organizations, especially the North-Western Province Sangha Front, the Association of the Chief Incumbents and Trustees of Viharas, and the newly organized Sinhala Buddha Sanvidhanaya, were pressing the government to exempt paddy lands belonging to Buddhist temples and monasteries from the "Paddy Act" on the ground that the loss of income from paddy lands would destroy the economic foundations of Buddhism in that country. Kaled Amer Assrany, a Brazilian citizen and a member of the Druze sect, an offshoot of the Ismailis, was ordained in Colombo and became the first Brazilian monk, with the name Bhikkhu Dhammananda. In Burma the Buddha Sasana reported that it had established 132 Buddhist mission centres in the frontier areas.

In South Vietnam 46 subbranches of the World Buddhist Social Service had been established. They were asking for assistance in setting up hospitals, dispensaries, orphanages, kindergartens, refugee rehabilitation centres, and vocational training schools in the war-torn country. Meanwhile, about 100 monks of Khmer (Cambodian) origin staged a five-day sit-down strike outside the presidential palace in Saigon, demanding the restoration of ethnic minority status for 500,000 Vietnamese of Cambodian origin. Pres. Nguyen Van Thieu rejected this demand, and armed riot police forced the monks to be confined in the Central Saigon Pagoda.

Little was known concerning the activities of Buddhists in China. In Japan, however, the fourth World Shin-shu (True Pure Land sect) Buddhist Women's Convention attracted a large number of Shin-shu women from all parts of Japan as well as from abroad. The largest Buddha statue in Japan, 31.5 m. high, was completed at Mt. Nokogiri, southwest of Tokyo.

In the U.S. a new Buddhist periodical, *Washington Buddhist*, was being published by the Washington Theravada Buddhist Vihara. New Buddhist groups in the West included the Connaissance du Bouddhisme in Paris, a new Buddhist circle in Cape Town, S.Af., and a Buddhist centre in Zürich, Switz. An interesting seminar on Buddhism, family life, and population was held early in 1970 under the joint sponsorship of the East-West Center and the University of Hawaii.

On the organizational side, the World Buddhist Sangha Council and the World Buddhist Social Service had their conferences simultaneously in Saigon in 1969. In June 1970 a conference of world Buddhists, mostly from Communist nations, met in Ulan Bator,

Mongolia. The tenth General Conference of the World Fellowship of Buddhists was to be held in May 1971 in Colombo, Ceylon. (J. M. Ka.)

ISLAM

Again the most notable events of the year were the political developments that affected the concerns and directed the energies of Muslims everywhere. Paramount were the civil war and Syrian intervention in Jordan during September 1970, followed by the death of Pres. Gamal Abd-al-Nasser of the U.A.R. (*see* OBITUARIES) on September 28, both of which further complicated the already unsettled relations among the Arab states and further inhibited relaxation of tensions among them. (*See* JORDAN; MIDDLE EAST.)

The effects of the Middle East political situation were felt throughout the year, however. In the middle of February, Id al-Adha observances in Cairo, marking the end of the formal rites of the annual pilgrimage to Mecca and usually noted for their festive gaiety, were somewhat curtailed by the need to observe blackout precautions against possible Israeli air raids. At the end of February the fifth Ulama Conference, convened in Cairo by the Islamic Research Academy, brought together some 100 Muslim scholars from 38 nations. Its major public pronouncements concerned the Arab-Israeli conflict. Later in March, King Faisal of Saudi Arabia opened a meeting in Jidda of foreign ministers from the Islamic countries; the conference was short but did agree to establish a permanent Islamic secretariat, its announced purpose. It had been called in the wake of the burning of Al Aqsa Mosque in Jerusalem the previous August.

Elsewhere in the Islamic world political upsets and rioting were much less acute than in previous years. Communal riots affecting Muslims in India and clashes in the Kashmir-Jammu area were fewer than in the previous year, and relations between Pakistan and India also seemed less strained. The principal exception was the communal rioting in May in Maharashtra State, where nearly 100 persons were killed and many more injured. This event led to considerable discussion by the Indian press about the wisdom of playing down such occurrences on the theory that wider coverage would lead to an increase of conflicts. But the May riots in Maharashtra were not at all as severe as the previous September's clashes between Muslims and Hindus in India, which were called the worst since 1948. Muslim interests in Pakistan centred on the national elections. Muslim contributions toward relief in East Pakistan following the disastrous cyclone and tidal wave there included $480,000 from Saudi Arabia. (*See* PAKISTAN.)

Prominent among less political events were announcements of mosque-building projects. Early in January the plans and a model of the Islamic Cultural Center in New York City were shown; the project was to include a mosque, school, apartment buildings, and a bazaar. Its establishment had been first announced in February 1967, when the cost was estimated at $6 million. By 1970 this had risen to $15 million, and in March an announcement was made that the centre would appeal to Muslim nations in an effort to raise this sum. It was announced in January that King Faisal of Saudi Arabia had offered to pay for the national mosque Pakistan was planning in its new and rapidly expanding capital of Islamabad. Early in March the Islamic Centre in London announced plans for a $2 million mosque to be built near Regent's Park. Designed by the noted British architect Sir Frederick Gibberd, it would accommodate 2,800 worshipers and would be the largest in Western Europe. Pakistan offered to donate a portion of the cost. Also in March, President Nixon donated a mosque lamp to the Islamic Center in Washington, D.C.

On April 4, Al Azhar university in Cairo, noted as the world's oldest centre for higher learning, celebrated its thousandth anniversary. It was originally built as a mosque and shortly thereafter made a centre of learning by the Fatimid Caliph al-Aziz. In 1970 it had an enrollment of about 8,000 students from all over the world.

In July the Lebanese penal court of appeals acquitted the young Syrian Muslim scholar Sadiq al-Azm and his publisher of charges of criticizing Islam and fomenting religious strife. Al-Azm's book, *Critique of Religious Thought,* questioned whether modern Muslims need accept the literal truth of all the religious stories contained in the Koran and discussed other theological problems such as the Koranic interpretation of Satan.

Following a visit of Muslim leaders to the Vatican, it was agreed to establish regular high-level consultations to promote greater understanding between the two faiths.

(R. W. Sм.)

RELIGIONS OF ASIA

In Asia—probably more than in other parts of the world—religious events continued to have strong political overtones while political events often had religious implications. In India, Hindus and non-Hindus alike found that it was far easier to celebrate the centenary of Mohandas Gandhi (1869–1948) than to practice his teachings. In Ladakh, situated close to the Pakistani and Chinese borders, relations between the predominant Muslim population and the approximately 3,000 Buddhist refugees from Tibet had been strained for some time. Following the alleged desecration of the Buddhist flag by Muslims, the Buddhist Action Committee in Ladakh asked the prime minister of India to intervene on their behalf.

In Aurangabad, Maharashtra, militant Hindus desecrated a statue of Buddha. Leaders of the Republican Party, speaking for the 50 million scheduled class Indians, many of whom were Buddhists, asserted that Buddhists in various villages had been beaten and that many Buddhist women had been molested. In Bhiwandi and Jalgaon, also in Maharashtra, nearly 100 persons were killed in a Hindu-Muslim clash in May 1970. (See *Islam,* above.) Alarmed by widespread social unrest, the government of India urged all state governments to stress moral instruction in educational institutions. The All-India Gandhi Centenary Celebration Committee and other groups started an all-out campaign against liquor. On a more popular level, public debate continued regarding such issues as on-screen kissing and the short "hipster sari."

Ceylon continued to be hard pressed by communal tensions. Among the Hindu-Tamils in the north, the Dravida Munnetra Kazhagam had emerged as a new and aggressive political party, overshadowing the Federal Party which had cooperated with Dudley Senanayake's United National Party government. Following the May 1970 victory of Mme Sirimavo Bandaranaike's United Front, which campaigned for the combined interests of Marxists and Sinhalese Buddhists, militant leftist youths rampaged in the former prime minister's home district.

Former Burmese prime minister U Nu was said

KEYSTONE

Above, his Supreme Holiness Shri Yogiji Maharaj prepares to open Shree Swaminarayan Temple in London, June 14, 1970. Below, members of the Society for Krishna Consciousness dance on and about a 40-ft.-high magenta chariot as they prepare to leave Marble Arch for Trafalgar Square, July 6.

to be determined to go to India as a Buddhist missionary. On the other hand, he still claimed to be Burma's legal prime minister and stated emphatically that he would not rest until Buddhism was reestablished in his country. Rumours persisted that his lieutenants were collecting arms. Prince Norodom Sihanouk of Cambodia, who was deposed as head of state in March, admitted the failure of his brand of Buddhist socialism, saying that it had been unable to solve the problems of corruption, unemployment, and social justice. The United Buddhist Church of South Vietnam, which for some time had been critical of the Saigon regime, accused the Hanoi regime of massacring civilians and demanded the release of monks captured during the 1968 Tet offensive. For its part, Saigon indefinitely suspended the Buddhist daily newspaper *Chan Dao* ("True Religion") on the ground that it nurtured political dissension.

In China after the Cultural Revolution, the cult of Chairman Mao appeared to have become de facto a full-fledged religion, while the traditional religions, such as Buddhism, Taoism, and Islam, had all but lost even their residual influence. In Taiwan and South Korea, both of which were under the rule of strong military leaders, many religious groups were taking on the colouring of patriotic organizations. Komeito, the political branch of the Soka Gakkai-dominated Nichiren Sho sect, now had 47 seats in the lower house of the Japanese Diet, only three short of the number that would give it the right to introduce legislation.

As though to symbolize the aspirations of Asia, a gigantic World Peace Pagoda (Viswa Shanti Stupa) —a joint Indo-Japanese venture—was inaugurated in October 1969 in Rajgir, Bihar, by V. V. Giri, the president of India. Two months later Jesus Vargas, secretary-general of the Southeast Asia Treaty Organization, reiterated the familiar theme of "Asian unity" as a precondition to peace, freedom, and social justice, although the events of 1969–70 indicated that Asia had a long way to go before attaining these goals.

Meanwhile, the influence of Asian religions in the West grew steadily. Those most in evidence ranged from sophisticated versions of Vedanta and Zen to the hypnotic cult of Krishna and the Soka Gakkai.

(J. M. Ka.)

"THE TIMES," LONDON, FROM PICTORIAL PARADE

Estimated Membership of the Principal Religions of the World

Religions	North America*	South America	Europe†	Asia	Africa	Oceania‡	World
Total Christian	214,258,000	150,426,000	442,006,000	61,473,000	42,056,000	14,055,000	924,274,000
Roman Catholic	126,468,000	147,219,000	226,303,000	47,622,000	28,751,000	4,107,000	580,470,000
Eastern Orthodox	3,675,000	47,000	114,103,000	2,819,000	4,956,000	84,000	125,684,000
Protestant§	84,115,000	3,160,000	101,600,000	11,032,000	8,349,000	9,864,000	218,120,000
Jewish‖	6,035,000	705,000	4,025,000	2,460,000	238,000	74,000	13,537,000
Muslim¶	166,000	416,000	13,848,000	374,167,000	104,297,000	118,000	493,012,000
Zoroastrian⌀	—	—	12,000	126,000	—	—	138,000
Shintoδ	31,000	116,000	2,000	69,513,000	—	—	69,662,000
Taoist□	16,000	19,000	12,000	54,277,000	—	—	54,324,000
Confucian□	96,000	109,000	55,000	371,261,000	9,000	57,000	371,587,000
Buddhist⌀	187,000	157,000	8,000	176,568,000	—	—	176,920,000
Hindu▲	55,000	660,000	160,000	434,447,000	1,205,000	218,000	436,745,000
Totals	220,844,000	152,608,000	460,128,000	1,544,292,000	147,805,000	14,522,000	2,540,199,000
Population+	304,439,000	174,246,000	636,993,000	1,907,481,000	328,134,000	18,127,000	3,369,420,000

*Includes Central America and the West Indies.
†Includes communicants claimed by established churches; includes also the U.S.S.R., in which the effect of a half-century of official Marxist ideology upon religious adherence is much disputed among specialists.
‡Includes New Zealand and Australia as well as islands of the South Pacific.
§Protestant statistics usually include "full members" rather than all baptized persons and are not comparable to those of ethnic religions or churches counting all adherents. The World Council of Churches in 1968 constituted a working committee to seek uniform nomenclature and reporting procedures.
‖Based on 1968 estimates of Jewish Statistical Bureau.
¶The chief base of Islam is still ethnic, and the statistics are largely derived from demographic studies. Evangelistic work is now carried on by Muslim renewal movements, and major gains have been made in Europe and the U.S. (viz. Black Muslims).
⌀A declining number of Zoroastrians are found in Iran, Pakistan, and India.
δA Japanese ethnic religion, Shinto has declined in strength since the emperor gave up claim to divinity (1947). Japanese religious statistics are highly problematical because adherents frequently are related to several different religions simultaneously. In 1968 the Japanese government instituted a statistical survey to clarify the status of different religions, cults, and movements, several of which claim millions of new adherents since World War II.
□Figures on China are highly speculative, including the number of remaining Muslims. The effect of Mao's Cultural Revolution upon Taoism and Confucianism is yet to be measured. Moreover, there is a long-standing dispute among scholars as to whether Confucianism should be counted as a "religion" at all.
⌀Buddhism has several modern renewal movements which have won adherents in Europe and the U.S. The shift from an ethnic to a missionary base is evident in some areas not formerly ethnic-Buddhist.
▲Hinduism's strength in India has been enhanced by nationalism, and modern Hinduism has also developed renewal movements that have reached into Europe and the U.S. for converts.
+Source: 1968 United Nations survey.

(F. H. Li.)

World Church Membership. With the expansion of the ecumenical movement, scholarly representatives of world religions, confronting each other, in many cases, for the first time in history, often discovered that they lacked a common language. Nowhere was this more evident than in the matter of religious statistics.

Even in the West there is a wide variety in styles of reckoning. Where religious liberty and voluntary adherence obtain, as in the U.S., the relationship of the religious person to his faith community is termed "membership," comparable to membership in a union or professional association. In European Christendom, where state churches long dominated the religious scene, those in traditional relationship are termed "communicants" or "constituents."

In the Eastern religions, even these terms are too precise. Hinduism, Buddhism, and Islam have "adherents." In Confucianism, Taoism, and Shinto, philosophy and life style are so intertwined that no terms implying a separation of the religious relationship from other functional roles can be used accurately. In the mixed religious situation of modern Japan, for example, the total of religious statistics runs to four times the total population. A considerable number of Japanese "belong" to one or more Buddhist sects, observe festivals at Shinto shrines, and are perhaps counted as adherents of one of the unique universal cults that have sprung up in the Orient since World War II.

Clearly the compilation of reliable religious statistics is severely compromised by the different ways of counting. The membership of the Zen Buddhist Society in Boston can be determined exactly; the number of Buddhist adherents in Burma is often based on estimates of population and population growth. The membership of Lutheran churches in Chicago can be totaled quite precisely; in Sweden and Denmark the state churches reckon over 98% of each population as Lutheran, though official studies show only 3.6 and 3.4%, respectively, in active connection. Similar problems exist for such countries as Spain, Greece, West Germany, Italy, Norway, and other lands where some form of religious establishment still prevails. The problem for totaling Christian statistics reaches its ultimate level of speculation in areas where Marxism is the official ideology. For example, some Orthodox Eastern Church tables still count 100 million Russians as constituents, and even delegations to international assemblies have been determined on a count of 40 million Orthodox in the U.S.S.R.

Accordingly, readers who use the statistics provided in the table are advised to do so with consciousness that mixed styles of reckoning are incorporated.

(F. H. Li.)

ENCYCLOPÆDIA BRITANNICA FILMS. *Major Religions of the World* (*Development and Rituals*) (1954).

Rhodesia

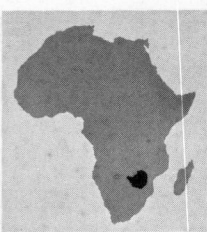

Though Rhodesia declared itself a republic on March 2, 1970, it remained a British colony in the eyes of many other nations. It is bounded by Zambia, Mozambique, South Africa, and Botswana. Area: 150,820 sq.mi. (389,622 sq.km.). Pop. (1970 est.): 5,270,000, of whom 94% are African and 5% white. Cap. and largest city: Salisbury (pop., 1970 est., 93,000). Language: English (official) and Bantu. Religion: predominantly traditional tribal beliefs; Christian minority. President from March 2, 1970, Clifford Dupont; prime minister in 1970, Ian D. Smith.

On New Year's Day 1970, Ian Smith claimed that,

in spite of economic sanctions imposed by the UN, Rhodesia was expected to have achieved a favourable balance of trade for the year 1969 and added that a surge of economic expansion could be anticipated. Accurate figures of Rhodesia's economic position were hard to discover, however, and the British foreign secretary, Michael Stewart, challenged Smith's optimistic view when he affirmed that Rhodesia's declaration of a republic on March 2, with Clifford Dupont as president, was illegal. The U.S. also announced that it would not recognize the Rhodesian government under any circumstances, and after a brief hesitation submitted to British pressure and closed its consulate in Salisbury. A number of other countries closed their consulates, while still others reduced their staff or appointed honorary consuls. Only Portugal and South Africa retained their representation at its former level.

The Council of Ministers of the Organization of African Unity (OAU), meanwhile, called on the major powers to be prepared to use force to achieve a democratic solution in Rhodesia. At a press conference immediately after the declaration of the republic, Prime Minister Smith said that he could not understand why the U.S. and Britain wanted to destroy Rhodesia and maintained that though the black and white races were far apart in their level of civilization, black Africans had been given 16 seats in Parliament which in time might increase to 50. Within Rhodesia itself the multiracial Centre Party offered its loyalty to the sovereign independent state of Rhodesia, but in the elections for Parliament held in April the party failed to win even one of the white seats. All of those were captured by Smith's Rhodesian Front, which did not bother to contest the black seats.

By contrast the Roman Catholic Church in Rhodesia took the lead among the Christian communities in announcing that it would defy all government attempts to impose racial separation. Faced with this clear resolve, the prime minister, after several weeks of protest and petitions, announced in late August that in order to eliminate the need for churches to apply for permits to carry on their work on what was formally mission land the government would amend the Land Tenure Act so that permits would be deemed to have been issued. This was not a great triumph for the churches since the government retained the right to cancel any permit. In November the government announced plans to introduce legislation segregating whites from Asians and persons of mixed race.

Earlier, in January, guerrilla forces from the black African nations to the north carried out raids across the Zambezi River involving attacks on the Victoria Falls airport and on a South African police detach-

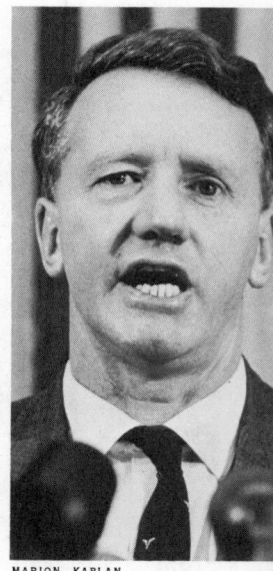

MARION KAPLAN

WIDE WORLD

Top, Ian Smith, prime minister of Rhodesia. Above, students boo and shout "Sieg Heil" as Prime Minister and Mrs. Smith arrive at a Rhodesian Front meeting in Salisbury, April 8, 1970.

RHODESIA

Education. (1969) African: primary, pupils 680,778, teachers 17,498; secondary, pupils 19,817, teachers 926; vocational and teacher training, students 1,824, teachers 122. Non-African: primary, pupils 39,134, teachers 1,619; secondary, pupils 25,444, teachers 1,495; vocational and teacher training, pupils 2,657, teachers 154. African and non-African: higher (University College of Rhodesia), students 857, teaching staff 154.

Finance. Monetary unit: Rhodesian dollar (introduced Feb. 17, 1970, equal to 10 shillings of old currency), with an exchange rate of R$71 to U.S. $1 (R$170 = £1 sterling). Budget (1969–70): revenue R$198.5 million; expenditure R$203.9 million. Gross national product: (1968) R$815.6 million; (1967) R$780.4 million.

Foreign Trade. (1968) Imports R$207 million; exports R$183.4 million. Import sources (1965): U.K. 30%; South Africa 23%; U.S. 7%; Japan 6%. Export destinations (1965): Zambia 29%; U.K. 20%; South Africa 11%; West Germany 8%; Malawi 6%; Japan 5%. Main exports (1965): tobacco 51%; asbestos 12%; machinery 9%; copper 7%; clothing 6%; chemicals 5%.

Transport and Communications. Roads (1968) 78,470 km. Motor vehicles in use (1968): passenger 108,800; commercial (including buses) 42,200. Railways: (1967) 3,330 km.; freight traffic (including Botswana: 1969) 6,050,000,000 net ton-km. Telephones (Dec. 1968) 125,844. Radio receivers (June 1967) 105,078. Television receivers (Dec. 1968) 45,000.

Agriculture. Production (in 000; metric tons; 1969; 1968 in parentheses): tobacco c. 61 (c. 60); corn (1968) c. 610, (1967) c. 600; peanuts (1968) c. 37, (1967) c. 79; tea (1968) c. 2.3, (1967) c. 2.7; sugar, raw value (1969–70) c. 117, (1968–69) c. 117; beef and veal (on farms and estates; 1967–68) c. 68, (1966–67) c. 68. Livestock (in 000; 1968–69): cattle c. 3,800; sheep c. 445; goats (1967–68) c. 660; pigs c. 146.

Industry. Production (in 000; metric tons; 1968): coal 2,969; chrome ore (oxide content; 1965) 281; asbestos (1966) c. 160; iron ore (metal content; 1966) c. 830; gold (troy oz.; 1967) 500; electricity (kw-hr.) 5,576,000.

ment. Smith warned the Zambian government that essential power and transport services might be withheld if Zambia continued to harbour and assist such terrorists and infiltrators. Although the raid caused consternation in Rhodesia, it seemed as if it might mark the end rather than the revival of military activity against Smith's government. Within the Zimbabwe African People's Union (ZAPU), which had organized the attacks from across the Zambian border, divisions were already noticeable when the raid took place, and in March James Chikerema, vice-president of ZAPU, admitted that the defections from his party were numerous. Later in the month Chikerema seized power from jailed ZAPU president Joshua Nkomo and replaced the military command with a new command structure responsible to himself. As a result of the intervention of Zambian Pres. Kenneth Kaunda, the dismissed war council was reinstated, but in April a number of clashes involving violence took place among the members of ZAPU.

In early October the weakness of Rhodesia's financial position was revealed by the government's admission that there was a serious shortage of foreign exchange earnings. This meant that Rhodesia had difficulty in paying for the internal industrial expansion that it so badly needed. Tobacco earnings abroad had been reduced virtually to nothing as a result of the sanctions, and mineral exports also were producing less foreign exchange than had been hoped for. South African aid remained the chief standby, but help from other sources was minimal. An attempt to increase white immigration into Rhodesia had met with little lasting success since many immigrants left soon after entering the country.　(K. I.)

Romania

A socialist republic on the Balkan Peninsula in southeastern Europe, Romania is bordered by the U.S.S.R., the Black Sea, Bulgaria, Yugoslavia, and Hungary. Area: 91,700 sq.mi. (237,500 sq.km.). Pop. (1969 est.): 20,010,178, including (1968) Romanian 87.8%; Hungarian 8.4%. Cap. and largest city: Bucharest (pop., 1969 est., 1,457,802). Religion: Romanian Orthodox 70%; Greek Orthodox 10%. General secretary of the Romanian Communist Party and president of the State Council in 1970, Nicolae Ceausescu; chairman of the Council of Ministers (premier), Ion Gheorghe Maurer.

The worst floods in Romania's history occurred in 1970. From May 12 to 25 one half of the country received between 80 and 100 litres (3–4 in.) of rainfall per square metre, while in the other half the downpour averaged from 35 to 80 litres (1½–3 in.). In not quite one month Romania was ravaged by three successive waves of floods, which caused 170 casualties and great material damage. Farm output on some 1.7 million ac. was affected, and 38,600 cattle were drowned. Production in about 294 industrial establishments was halted for weeks. In towns and villages more than 85,000 dwellings were destroyed, as well as over 3,500 bridges. More than 2,800 km. of roads, several hundred kilometres of railways, and 2,100 km. of electric lines were seriously damaged. The losses exceeded 10 billion lei (about 7% of the yearly state expenditure).

During this catastrophe, Ceausescu was called to Moscow (May 18–19) to attend a lecture on the virtues of "proletarian internationalism." A week before, at the Warsaw meeting of Comecon, Romania had refused to join the newly created International Investments Bank, and for more than two years Bucharest had argued with Moscow about the terms of a new treaty of alliance (the previous one, concluded for 20 years, had been signed on Feb. 4, 1948). Ceausescu stood his ground and refused to incorporate in the new treaty anything smacking of the Brezhnev doctrine. That doctrine justified intervention in the domestic affairs of a socialist state if "the essential common interests" of other socialist countries were threatened.

Both sides made concessions. In the preamble of the new 20-year Soviet-Romanian treaty (signed in Bucharest on July 7 by the two premiers, Aleksei Kosygin and Ion Gheorghe Maurer), the principles of "socialist internationalism" were described with some vagueness. There was, for instance, no mention of the "internationalist duty" to intervene in order to "protect the socialist gains," as was the case in the Soviet-Czechoslovak treaty of May 6. The main pledge taken by Romania was expressed in terms almost identical to those of the Soviet-Czechoslovak treaty, however. In art. 7 Romania expressed its firm determination to take, jointly with other states of

AGIP FROM PICTORIAL PARADE

Romanian Pres. Nicolae Ceausescu speaks at a reception at the Hôtel de Ville in Paris, June 16, 1970.

the Warsaw Pact, "all the measures necessary to prevent aggression. . . , to ensure the inviolability of the frontiers of the Warsaw Treaty member-states, and to repel an aggressor."

Two other similar treaties were renewed by Romania: with Poland on November 12, on the occasion of a visit by Wladyslaw Gomulka and Jozef Cyrankiewicz to Bucharest, and with Bulgaria on November 19 when Ceausescu visited Sofia. During the year Ceausescu paid official visits to France in June and to Austria in September. In October he spent two weeks on a private visit in the United States; on October 19 he addressed the UN General Assembly, and on October 26 he was received by Pres. Richard Nixon.

On November 19 an agreement was signed in Moscow on the coordination of the economic development plans of the U.S.S.R. and Romania during 1971–75. Trade exchanges between the two countries would amount to about $5,880,000,000, 40% above the previous five-year period. A few days later China announced that it had granted Romania a long-term, interest-free loan, the first ever made by China to a Warsaw Pact country. The loan was said to be for the "supply of equipment and installations of whole projects," but the amount was not disclosed.

(K. SM.)

ROMANIA

Education. (1967–68) Primary, pupils 2,879,881, teachers 131,235; secondary, pupils 202,398, teachers 11,338; vocational, pupils 327,642, teachers 17,690; teacher training, students 14,112, teachers 739; higher (including 12 universities), students 141,589, teaching staff 13,792.

Finance. Monetary unit: leu, with an official exchange rate of 6 lei to U.S. $1 (14.40 lei = £1 sterling) and a tourist rate of 18 lei = U.S. $1 (43.20 lei = £1 sterling). Budget (1968 rev. est.): revenue 138,757,-000,000 lei; expenditure 131,921,000,000 lei.

Foreign Trade. (1968): Imports 9,653,800,000 lei; exports 8,811,400,000 lei. Import sources: U.S.S.R. 27%; West Germany 11%; Italy 6%; Czechoslovakia 6%; U.K. 6%; France 5%. Export destinations: U.S.S.R. 31%; Czechoslovakia 8%; West Germany 7%; East Germany 5%; Italy 5%. Main exports: machinery 21%; foodstuffs 14%; raw materials (cereals, timber, etc.) 12%; petroleum products 9%; chemicals 6%.

Transport and Communications. Roads (1968) 77,019 km. (including 10,021 km. with improved surface). Motor vehicles in use: passenger (1965) c. 250,000; commercial (1968) 38,100. Railways: (1968) 11,016 km.; traffic (1969) 16,720,000,000 passenger-km., freight 44,030,000,000 net ton-km. Air traffic (1969): 331.7 million passenger-km.; freight 6,972,-000 net ton-km. Inland waterways in regular use (1967) 1,115 km. Shipping (1969): merchant vessels 100 gross tons and over 64; gross tonnage 338,242. Telephones (Dec. 1968) 568,588. Radio receivers (Dec. 1968) 3,031,000. Television receivers (Dec. 1968) 1,115,000.

Agriculture. Production (in 000; metric tons; 1969; 1968 in parentheses): wheat c. 5,700 (4,848); barley c. 574 (590); oats c. 155 (114); corn 7,680 (7,105); potatoes (1968) 3,665, (1967) 3,085; onions (1968) 148, (1967) 248; tomatoes (1968) 874, (1967) 676; sugar, raw value (1969–70) 484, (1968–69) 417; tobacco (1968) 32, (1967) 35; sunflower seed 795 (730); dry peas (1968) 76, (1967) 183; plums (1968) 562, (1967) 670; apples (1968) 222, (1967) 234; grapes (1968) 1,167, (1967) 910. Livestock (in 000; Jan. 1969): cattle 5,853; sheep 14,-298; horses 703; poultry 47,618.

Industry. Index of production (1963 = 100): (1969) 201; (1968) 182. Production (in 000; metric tons; 1969): coal 5,863; lignite 11,113; coke (1968) 1,133; crude oil 13,345; natural gas (cu.m.) 23,929; electricity (kw-hr.) 31,477,000; iron ore (30–35% metal content) 2,999; pig iron 3,477; crude steel 5,540; cement 7,514; sulfuric acid 838; nitrogenous fertilizers (nitrogen content; 1968) 421; cotton yarn 102; cotton fabrics (sq.m.) 410,000; wool yarn 32; woolen fabrics (sq.m.) 55,300; newsprint 53; other paper (1968) 411; commercial vehicles (units) 33. New dwelling units completed (1968) 110,325.

KEYSTONE

The Cambridge crew leads Oxford as they approach Hammersmith Bridge during the 116th Boat Race, March 28, 1970. Cambridge won by 3½ lengths.

Rowing

The third world rowing championships, held at St. Catharines, Ont., in September 1970, attracted 111 entrants from 29 countries. Canada, East Germany, West Germany, Great Britain, the U.S.S.R., and the United States contested all seven events, and 11 countries shared the medals. East Germany achieved the remarkable distinction of winning a medal in every event, finishing with three gold and four silver medals. West Germany reached four finals and took a gold, a silver, and a bronze medal, but the only other double medalists were the U.S.S.R. with a silver and a bronze and Denmark with a gold and a bronze. The two remaining gold medals went to Argentina and Romania. Poland won a silver medal, and other countries with bronze medals were Czechoslovakia, New Zealand, Norway, and the U.S.

East Germany established a remarkable new record in eights after taking the lead at 500 m. They held off all challenges to win by more than 2 sec. in 5 min. 36.10 sec., breaking the record, which had stood since 1962, by a staggering 14.7 sec. The Soviet Union and New Zealand in second and third places, with only one-fifth of a second separating them, were also well inside the old record. The only other record in any danger was the double sculls, which Denmark missed by only 1.49 sec. in defeating East Germany and the United States by more than 2 sec.

In addition to the East German eight, two other 1969 European champions to win were the West German coxed four and A. Demiddi (Arg.), who again outpaced his rivals in single sculls to finish 1.67 sec. in front of his nearest rival. Although the East Germans could not match their Western neighbours in coxed fours, they gained revenge in coxless fours.

The championships, staged in North America for the first time, were dominated by East and West Germany. That these two were indisputably the world's top rowing countries was due to their policy of introducing the young to the sport early. The East German eight that won the 1970 world title had an average age of 20. Previously, few crews had reached such a standard much before their mid-20s.

East Germany and the U.S.S.R. shared the honours in the Women's European championships, held in Budapest, Hung., in August. Both countries won medals in all five events, East Germany getting three golds, a silver, and a bronze, while the U.S.S.R. took a gold, three silvers, and a bronze. East Germany triumphed in the eights and two sculling events, while Soviet oarswomen beat them in coxed fours; the fifth gold medalist was Romania in the quadruple sculls.

East Germany scored an unprecedented clean sweep in all seven events in the Fédération Internationale Sociétés d'Aviron (FISA) junior championships in Ioannina, Greece, in August. West Germany took three silver and three bronze medals, and the remaining medals were shared by Austria, Czechoslovakia, France, Greece, Italy, and Switzerland.

In the U.K. the five major events at the Henley Royal Regatta went to Germany. East Germany won the Grand Eights, Stewards' fours, and Silver Goblets, and West Germany triumphed in the Prince Philip Cup and Diamond Sculls. The sole U.S. victory was scored by T. McKibbon and J. Van Blom in the Double Sculls. Ridley College, Canada, captured the Princess Elizabeth Cup, while the Wyfold Cup went to Trident Rowing Club of South Africa. In the 116th Boat Race, Cambridge scored its 64th victory over Oxford by 3½ lengths.   (K. L. O.)

Rubber

World production of natural rubber in 1969 was estimated at 2,805,000 long tons, an increase of 205,000 long tons over 1968. Production for the first six months of 1970 was estimated at 1,342,500 metric tons, up 35,000 metric tons from the corresponding period in 1969. (One metric ton = .98 long tons.) The management committee of the International Rubber Study Group (IRSG), meeting in London in June 1970, estimated world production of new rubber in 1970 as follows: natural rubber supplies, 3,030,000 metric tons; synthetic rubber supplies, 4,930,000 metric tons. It was estimated that some 2,950,000 metric tons of natural rubber and 4,930,000 metric tons of synthetic rubber would be consumed (i.e., turned into manufactured goods) in 1970. (Estimates for synthetic rubber production do not include the U.S.S.R., non-IRSG member countries in Eastern Europe, or China.) The New York spot price for no. 1 ribbed smoked sheets was 18 cents per pound at the end of October 1970, compared with 26 cents per pound at the same time in 1969.

West Malaysian production of natural rubber in 1969 totaled 1,279,227 metric tons, representing a new record. The U.S. remained the largest single buyer of natural rubber, taking 572,204 metric tons in 1969. World consumption of natural rubber latex (dry basis) was estimated at 244,750 metric tons in 1969. World consumption figures for synthetic latices (dry basis) were incomplete, but the U.S. consumed 145,278 metric tons (dry basis) of the SBR (styrene-butadiene rubber) type.

World production of all types of synthetic rubber in 1969 (excluding countries not reporting) was estimated at 4,572,000 metric tons, of which the U.S. produced 2,286,301 metric tons. In 1969 synthetic rubber accounted for 77% of total rubber consumed in the U.S. and 66% worldwide. World consumption of both natural and synthetic rubbers in 1969 was estimated at 7,402,500 metric tons. Production of all types of reclaimed rubber amounted to 347,045 metric tons. The area under cultivation of plantation (natural) rubber was estimated at 5,865,000 ha.

As of the March 1970 issue (vol. 24, no. 6) of the *Rubber Statistical Bulletin* published by the IRSG Secretariat, quantities were expressed in metric tons. The Malayan Rubber Exchange and the Rubber Association of Singapore appointed an ad hoc committee to examine the implications of changing both territories to a market based on the metric system (1 metric ton equals 2,204 lb. or 1,000 kg.). The difference between a metric ton (2,204 lb.) and a long ton (2,240 lb.) is small but significant. The whole concept, obviously, would depend on overseas trading and consumer acceptance.

In the spring of 1970, the Firestone Tire and Rubber Co. of Akron, O., announced that their technical people had under development an automobile tire made entirely by an injection process. It carried the regular wire beads to hold the tire on the rims, but it did not need fabric plies and carbon black was not required in the tread. The tire could, therefore, be coloured. The material injected into the mold was referred to as liquid rubber, and the report mentioned

that the total usage of SBR would not be altered. Actual commercial development and customer acceptance were said to be at least several years away. Whether this new tire could compete with currently commercial bias or radial built tires remained to be seen, but the idea was fascinating. Monsanto announced the development of steel wires 3 mils (0.003 in.) in diameter that could be twisted into cords for tires. Such ideas as these could lead to even more intensive competition in tire technology.

(E. B. NN.)

Rwanda

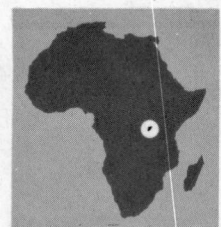

A republic in eastern Africa, Rwanda is bordered by the Congo (Kinshasa), Uganda, Tanzania, and Burundi. Area: 10,169 sq.mi. (26,338 sq.km.). Pop. (1969 est.): 3,509,250; composed of Tutsi (Watutsi), Hutu (Bahutu), and Twa (Batwa) tribes. Cap. and largest city: Kigali (pop., 1967 est., 20,000). Language: French (official); tribal dialects. Religion: traditional or tribal beliefs 50%; Roman Catholic. President in 1970, Grégoire Kayibanda.

A Central African summit conference took place at Gisenyi, Rwanda, on Dec. 19, 1969. President Kayibanda, together with Pres. Joseph Mobutu of the Congo (Kinshasa) and Burundi's Pres. Michel Micombero, adopted a resolution there to establish greater unity and "respond to the profound aspirations of the inhabitants of this region of central Africa." The foreign ministers of the three nations were instructed to establish machinery for economic, technical, and cultural integration, and a conference was scheduled at Bujumbura, Burundi, to inaugurate the Common Organization for Economic Cooperation in Central Africa (OCCEAC).

President Kayibanda, who increased his strength with a 90% unopposed vote at the 1969 elections, welcomed King Baudouin I of the Belgians on his state visit in July as a symbol of Belgium's friendship and aid. The aid agreement with Belgium for 1970 provided not only $4 million but also 261 technicians, to be settled at Murumbi, and 2,500 tons of wheat.

(M. MR.)

Table I. Natural Rubber Production

In 000 long tons

Country	1965	1966	1967	1968	1969
Malaysia	934	983	985	1,092	1,259
Indonesia	706	704	750*	740*	727
Thailand	213	204	211	255	277
Ceylon	116	129	141	146	148
Vietnam	60	48	40	29	26
Cambodia	48	51	53	51	51
India	49	52	62	68	79
Africa	—	—	—	156*	180
Brazil	29	24	21	23	24
Others	187*	202*	189*	56*	33
Total	2,342*	2,397*	2,452*	2,600*	2,805*

*Estimate.

Table II. Synthetic Rubber Production

In 000 long tons

Country	1965	1966	1967	1968	1969
United States	1,814	1,970	1,912	2,131	2,250
Canada	203	200	197	194	196
United Kingdom	172	191	200	233	269
Germany, West	161	182	180	234	287
France	146	161	186	220	271
Japan	159	228	276	375	518
Italy	118*	121*	116*	123*	133
Netherlands	100*	111*	125*	161	210
Brazil	35	53	51	58	61
Czechoslovakia	30*	30*	33*	35*	39
Australia	21	20	26	30	33
Belgium	21*	20*	20*	25*	34*
India	16	15	22	25	24
South Africa	16	18	24	25	24
Argentina	3	10	17	22	35*
Spain	—	—	10*	26	34*
Mexico	—	—	20*	34*	35*
Poland	—	—	—	—	47
Total	3,015*	3,330*	3,415*	3,951*	4,500*

*Estimate.

Source: International Rubber Study Group.

RWANDA
Education. (1967–68) Primary, pupils 372,184, teachers 5,921; secondary, pupils 6,466; vocational, pupils 912; teacher training, students 1,464; secondary, vocational, and teacher training, teachers 580; higher, students 233, teaching staff 59.
Finance and Trade. Monetary unit: Rwanda franc, with a par value of RwFr. 100 to U.S. $1 (RwFr. 240 = £1 sterling) and a free market rate (Oct. 1970) of RwFr. 120 to U.S. $1 (RwFr. 290 = £1 sterling). Gold, SDRs, and foreign exchange, central bank: (June 1970) U.S. $4,010,000; (June 1969) U.S. $1,020,000. Budget (1969 est.): revenue RwFr. 1,636,618,000; expenditure RwFr. 1,664,000,000.
Foreign Trade. (1969) Imports RwFr. 2,362,400,000; exports RwFr. 1,423,500,000. Import sources (1968) Belgium-Luxembourg 18%; Uganda 14%; Japan 14%; West Germany 12%; U.S. 7%. Export destinations: (1966) U.S. 57%; Belgium-Luxembourg 33%. Main exports (1968): coffee 57%; tin 23%.
Agriculture. Production (in 000; metric tons: 1968; 1967 in parentheses): sorghum c. 145 (c. 140); dry beans c. 95 (c. 92); potatoes c. 46 (c. 46); sweet potatoes c. 300 (c. 300); cassava c. 190 (c. 190); coffee c. 12 (c. 11). Livestock (in 000; July 1969): cattle c. 640; sheep c. 133; pigs c. 29.

Sailing

The 604-mi. Middle Sea race organized by the Royal Malta Yacht Club and Royal Ocean Racing Club, the principal offshore racing event in the Mediterranean, started on Nov. 1, 1969, from Malta. Twelve yachts competed, notable for their range of sizes and representing Italy, Malta, the U.K., France, the Netherlands, and Austria. Winds were variable and sometimes highly localized, with a strong breeze in an area only five miles from one of calm. Winner was "Surprise" (N. Puccinelli and N. Violati), an English-designed, Italian-built and owned boat of the one-ton class. Second was the Maltese "Tikka" (J. Ripard), which gained the Farsons Trophy; third was "Spirit of Cutty Sark" (Leslie Williams), a contestant in the 1968 single-handed transatlantic race.

The Sydney to Hobart race, starting on Boxing Day, Dec. 26, 1969, was won by the yacht owned and skippered by Edward Heath (prime minister of Great Britain from June 1970), the "Morning Cloud." The start was attended by an estimated 3,000 boats and 100,000 people. For the first time in this event a team of yachts from the U.K. was entered for the Southern Cross Trophy, the equivalent of the U.S. Onion Patch Trophy and the British Admiral's Cup. This team dominated the Sydney–Hobart race, having the winner and second overall, "Prospect of Whitby" (Arthur Slater), but it failed to accomplish its mission of winning the trophy. This went to the New South Wales team with 419 points, which was closely followed by the U.K. with 387 points. Finishing in third place was the New Zealand team of one-ton boats, with 316 points.

The Bermuda race, alternating annually with the European Fastnet race and Admiral's Cup series, brought the principal offshore events of 1970 to the west side of the Atlantic. A fleet of 149 yachts left Newport, R.I., for a race whose course was slightly modified and lengthened, as compared with former courses, to face a variety of weather conditions ranging for some competitors between calms and moderate winds and for others to winds exceeding 60 knots. Six new yachts lost their masts, while others experienced tiresome windlessness. The overall winner was "Carina" of the U.S. (Richard Nye), the third boat of its famous name. Four boats from the U.K. were racing, and "Lutine" (Lloyd's Yacht Club) was the highest-placed non-U.S. boat and fifth overall.

The Onion Patch Trophy series of races was dominated by the U.S. team, whose boats placed first, second, and third in all four of the races involved— the Astor Trophy, from Oyster Bay, N.Y., to Newport, R.I., the two races on triangular courses off Newport, and the Bermuda race itself. The results gave the U.S. a massive lead of 86 points over the U.K. team, which was 45 points ahead of third-place Argentina.

The Round Britain race, the 1,875 mi. of which were sailed in five legs, clockwise around Great Britain, continued to be an accepted battleground for single- against multihull craft. On July 4 a fleet of 27 craft, comprising 14 single-hull yachts, 6 catamarans, 6 trimarans, and a proa, sailed from Plymouth on the first leg of the course to Crosshaven in Ireland. Conditions over the course brought predominantly head winds as the yachts worked up the coast of Ire-

land to Castle Bay in the Island of Barra, to Lerwick in the Shetland Islands, Lowestoft on the east coast of England, and then on the final leg back to Plymouth.

The 15 boats first home comprised eight single-hulls and seven multihulls. The winner was the large (71 ft. overall) single-hull ketch "Ocean Spirit" (Leslie Williams and Robin Knox-Johnston), which was about as big a boat as two men could handle over such a course. Next to "Ocean Spirit," in the second to sixth places, came multihull craft, while single-hull boats took the last five places. In the middle of the fleet were two single-hull boats and two trimarans.

While the superb seamanship that enabled so large a boat as "Ocean Spirit" to maintain a high speed over such a course was unquestioned, its great length inevitably gave it a built-in advantage. This race, like the first in 1966, was a clear victory for the multihulls, and one that was even more convincing owing to the amount of sailing to windward involved on this occasion. Yet, the capsizing of one catamaran with an experienced crew emphasized the danger inherent in all multihull types of craft, and somewhat lowered the prestige that their performance might have earned.

The year marked the debut of France into America's Cup racing, though its potential challenger "France" failed in the elimination contest for challenger against the Australian "Gretel II." Even more striking than in former America's Cup contests was the intensity of the preparations. In Australia, crew training had been in progress since 1968, with "Gretel," the 1962 challenger, "Dame Pattie," the 1967 challenger, and the old U.S. 12-m. "Vim" engaged. Early in 1970 a new boat, "Gretel II," was launched for the syndicate of Sir Frank Packer. Ini-

Norway's "Christian Radich" takes the lead shortly after the start of the Tall Ships race from Plymouth to the Canary Islands and Spain.

"THE TIMES," LONDON, FROM PICTORIAL PARADE

MICHAEL MAUNEY, "LIFE"
MAGAZINE © TIME INC.

Leaping a breaker
in southern California,
this catamaran
is the latest
among pleasure sailboats.
Designed by custom
surfboard builder Hobie
Alter, the "cat" just skims
the water's surface,
drawing only eight inches
of water fully loaded.

tially its performance was disappointing, and it had difficulty in beating the first "Gretel." However, in the course of tuning up, which included moving the mast, the boat was much improved.

In France the preparations, organized by Marcel Bich, involved the British "Sovereign," challenger in 1964, and "Kurrewa," built for the same contest and renamed "Lévrier des mers"; the U.S. "Constellation"; and a boat built for training, "Chancegger," from designs of the U.S. architect Britton Chance. "France," built for the challenge, was designed by André Mauric of Marseilles.

In the U.S. four yachts were involved: "Intrepid," defender in 1967 against "Dame Pattie"; "Weatherly," defender in 1962; and two new boats, "Heritage" and "Valiant." The two potential challengers and boats against which to tune up were shipped to the U.S. and continued training off Newport, R.I. This led up to the selection races between "Gretel II" and "France," in which the former was victorious, while in the trials for the defense "Intrepid," the defender in the former contest, again won the honour against the newer boats.

The contest itself, held in September off Newport, was one of the closest in the America's Cup history, though the challenger won only a single race. The anxiety of the defense throughout was due to the obvious close matching of the two boats. The first race went to the defender. In the second race the disqualification of "Gretel II," owing to a collision at the start, was the first time in 119 years that an America's Cup race was lost on a foul. "Intrepid" won the third race, but "Gretel II" came back to win the fourth, raising the hopes of the Australians and perhaps adding to the bitterness over the previous disqualification. "Intrepid" won the final race, however, and the cup remained where it had been for so long, in the New York Yacht Club.

The yachtsman of the year, chosen in London, was Robin Knox-Johnston, a tribute to his feat of winning the Golden Globe, first prize in the single-handed, nonstop race around the world, sailed in 1968–69. On Oct. 18, 1970, another prospective single-handed, nonstop circumnavigator set forth from the Hamble River, Eng. He was Chay Blyth, in a steel ketch specially designed for the purpose and sponsored by the British Steel Corp. The particular feature of Blyth's endeavour was that his course was from east to west, which entailed heading the winds

and currents of the southern Atlantic Ocean, through which his course was laid. This voyage was designed to be an endurance test of man and boat.

A test of a different kind was begun in December when Sir Francis Chichester, with a new and larger yacht, "Gipsy Moth V," left Plymouth with the object of sailing 4,000 mi. at an average speed of 200 mi. a day. His first destination was Bissau in Portuguese Guinea, from which a fast passage of 4,000 mi. was planned to be made to San Juan del Norte in Nicaragua, starting in the first week of January 1971. The highest possible sailing speed being the object, the course was planned to provide winds giving a broad reach across the Atlantic, in which the yacht would be able to attain its highest speeds.

"American Eagle" of the U.S. won the Southern Ocean Racing Conference championship series for the third time by triumphing in the Miami–Nassau race and the Venice and Lipton Cup events. In smaller boat competition William Buchanan of Mercer Island, Wash., won the world Star Class championship off the west coast of Sweden in August. Otto Scherer of Laurel, Md., and Gene Miller of Annapolis, Md., sailed "Scimitar" to victory in the world Class C Catamaran championship. The world Tempest Class honours went to John and James Linville of the Larchmont (N.Y.) Yacht Club.   (D. H. C. P.-B.)

San Marino

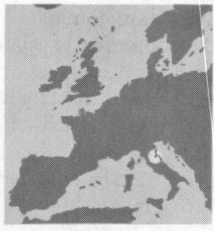

A small republic, San Marino is an enclave in northeastern Italy, 14 mi. SW of Rimini. Area: 24 sq.mi. (61 sq.km.). Pop. (1970 est.): 17,341. Cap. and largest city: San Marino (metro. pop., 1970 est., 4,088). Language: Italian. Religion: Roman Catholic. San Marino is united with Italy by a customs union. The country is governed by two *capitani reggenti*, or coregents, appointed every six months by a Grand and General Council.

Like other small European countries heavily dependent on tourism, San Marino suffered serious economic problems in 1970. Rising demand and the need for modernization, coupled with stable or even declining revenues, produced increasingly serious fiscal problems. The Grand and General Council called for higher taxation on motor travel, land tenancy, liquor, and imported wines. The increased revenue, it was hoped, would offset an estimated $2,289,000 deficit anticipated in fiscal 1970–71.

In June the republic ratified the international agreement on the rescue of astronauts and the return of objects launched into outer space and the nuclear nonproliferation treaty. On July 22, 1970, it became the first country to deposit its ratification of the new international conventions on road traffic and highway signs and signals.   (R. D. Ho.)

SAN MARINO
Education. (1966–67) Primary, pupils, 1,388, teachers 78; secondary, pupils 740, teachers 45.
   Finance. Monetary unit: Italian lira (625 lire = U.S. $1; 1,500 lire = £1 sterling). Budget (1969–70 est.) balanced at 7,391,000,000 lire. Tourism (1968) 2,153,000 visitors.
   Transport and Communications. Roads (1965) c. 100 km. Electric funicular railway 32 km. Telephones (Jan. 1969) 2,022. Radio receivers (Dec. 1967) 3,000. Television receivers (Dec. 1967) 1,900.

Saudi Arabia

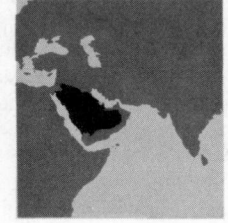

A kingdom occupying four-fifths of the Arabian Peninsula, Saudi Arabia has an area of 873,972 sq.mi. (2,263,587 sq.km.). Pop. (1969 est.): 7.2 million. Cap. and largest city: Riyadh (pop., 1963, 170,000). Language: Arabic. Religion: Muslim. King and prime minister, Faisal ibn 'Abd al-'Aziz ibn 'Abd al-Rahman Al Sa'ud.

In 1970 Saudi Arabia maintained its position as leader of the conservative anti-Communist forces in the Arab world, but politically it was on the defensive and took no diplomatic initiatives. Internal security was an increasing cause for concern. In March a number of prominent civilians were arrested, including the dean of the University of Petroleum and Minerals at Dhahran.

The 5,000 Saudi troops who remained stationed in Jordan suffered their first casualties in January in a clash with the Israelis. King Faisal continued to channel all his financial and diplomatic support for the Palestinian Arabs through the Al Fatah organization and its leader, Yasir Arafat, whom he received on a visit to Jidda on March 9. The king was known to be strongly opposed to the extreme left-wing Popular Front for the Liberation of Palestine.

The Saudi minister of state for foreign affairs, Omar al-Saqqaf, said in Teheran on April 9 that Saudi Arabia and Iran had identical interests in ensuring stability in the Persian Gulf region. This was confirmed when the Iranian foreign minister, Ardeshir Zahedi, visited Saudi Arabia in July. A joint Saudi-Iranian statement said that the two countries wanted Britain to withdraw from the Gulf as planned. On July 3 the British Foreign Office confirmed that Saudi Arabia had renewed its claim to Al Buraymi oasis, at present partitioned between Abu Dhabi and Oman. The Saudi government was reported to be proposing the holding of a plebiscite in the oasis after former Saudi residents had been allowed to return there.

The Syrian government's refusal to allow the repair of the Tapline pipeline after it had been damaged on Syrian territory on May 3 cost the Saudi government an estimated $200,000 a day. The government responded by warning that it might cut off its aid to Jordan, the United Arab Republic, and the Palestinians, and it also banned the entry of Syrian goods and vehicles. The Syrians responded by banning Saudi goods and vehicles. (P. Md.)

SAUDI ARABIA
Education. (1966–67) Primary, pupils 295,823, teachers (including preprimary) 12,429; secondary, pupils 27,907, teachers 1,833; vocational, pupils 1,808, teachers 368; teacher training, students 6,096, teachers 274; higher, students 1,893, teaching staff 286.
Finance. Monetary unit: riyal, with a par value of 4.50 riyals to U.S. $1 (10.80 riyals = £1 sterling). Gold, SDRs, and foreign exchange, official: (June 1970) U.S. $695 million; (June 1969) U.S. $717 million. Budget (1969–70 est.) balanced at 5,966,000,000 riyals. Money supply: (May 1970) 2,352,000,000 riyals; (May 1969) 2,310,000,000 riyals.
Foreign Trade. (1968–69) Imports 2,804,000,000 riyals; exports 8,952,900,000 riyals. Import sources: U.S. 20%; Japan 10%; Lebanon 10%; U.K. 8%; West Germany 7%; Italy 5%; Netherlands 5%. Export destinations: Japan 23%; Italy 10%; U.K. 6%; Spain 6%; Netherlands 6%; Bahrain 5%. Main exports: crude oil 79%; petroleum products 14%.
Transport and Communications. Roads (1969) c. 22,000 km. (including 11,020 km. with improved surface). Motor vehicles in use (1969): passenger 37,561; commercial 27,318. Railways (1968) 606 km. Shipping (1969): merchant vessels 100 gross tons and over 39; gross tonnage 50,694. Telephones (Jan. 1969) 44,250. Radio receivers (Dec. 1964) c. 77,000. Television receivers (Dec. 1964) 30,000.
Agriculture. Production (in 000; metric tons; 1968; 1967 in parentheses): wheat c. 130 (c. 150); barley c. 34 (c. 34); millet c. 16 (c. 16); sorghum c. 52 (c. 52); dates c. 380 (c. 380). Livestock (in 000; 1967–68): cattle c. 160; sheep c. 3,900; goats c. 3,000; camels c. 360; asses c. 125.
Industry. Production: crude oil (1969) 148,532,-000 metric tons; electricity (excluding most industrial production; 1967) 430,000,000 kw-hr.

Savings and Investment

Marked changes in savings and investment in 1970 were associated with and closely followed shifts in the official monetary, fiscal, and exchange rate policies in the principal industrial countries. These changes worked through and affected the financial markets, altering the relative attraction of the various forms of savings and influencing the flow of funds across the national frontiers. They also had a profound effect on the cost of capital needed for investment in real and financial assets.

Following the strong upswing in 1969, which embraced all the major industrial countries except the U.S. and the U.K., in 1970 the pace of growth of economic activity and of investment, both domestic and foreign, was moderated. The moderation was chiefly a result of deliberate government policies designed to reduce inflationary pressures and bring external accounts into better shape.

In the U.S., following the adoption of tight monetary policies, fixed domestic investment fell sharply in 1970 with inventory building contributing to a slowdown in total economic activity. There was, however, an improvement in foreign balance that, because of its small size in relation to gross national product (GNP), had only a minor stimulatory effect (see Table I). Interest rates, which fell very modestly from the peak reached in the first quarter, were pushed up partly as a result of the government policy and, accompanying that, by the process of "disintermediation," the transfer of funds to more profitable users, and, above all, by the need to satisfy the demands of the corporate sector.

With net savings of households lower in 1969 than in 1968 and the requirements for external finance on the part of the corporate sector appreciably higher, the pressure on financial intermediaries and capital markets became very intense. Not only was there a marked switch to different savings media, especially by individuals to the interest-bearing time deposits and by corporations to certificates of deposit, but commercial banks supplemented their reserves by borrowing in the international markets and corporations issued a large volume of shares and bonds overseas. Although this trend continued in the first quarter of 1970, it eased from the second quarter onward.

In the countries of the European Economic Community, after the hectic boom of 1969 when the volume of fixed domestic investment increased by 10% to the highest figure since the end of World War II, there was some slowing down in 1970. Foreign investment showed marked changes as a result of the appreciation of the West German mark and the depreciation of the French franc in the autumn of

Table I. Changes in Gross National Product, Fixed Domestic Investment, Stock Building, and Foreign Balance in Selected Countries
In percent

Country	Year	Increase in GNP	Change in total fixed domestic investment	Change in stock building*	Change in foreign balance
U.S.	1968	4.9	5.5†	0.0	−0.4
	1969	2.8	5.8†	0.0	−0.1
	1970‡	0.25	−0.25†	−0.75	0.25
Canada	1968	4.9	−0.1	0.5	0.6
	1969	5.0	3.1	0.5	−0.9
	1970	3.0	1.5	−0.75	1.0
U.K.	1968	3.5§	3.25	0.25	0.75
	1969	1.75§	−0.75	0.50	1.25
	1970	2.25§	0.25	0.0	0.25
West Germany	1968	7.2	8.0	2.8	0.2
	1969	7.9	12.4	0.4	−0.4
	1970	5.5	8.0	−0.25	−1.25
France	1968	4.9§	6.6	−0.5	−0.3
	1969	7.9§	10.1	1.1	−0.5
	1970	5.5§	6.5	−0.25	1.5
Italy	1968	5.9§	7.7	−0.6	1.4
	1969	4.8§	8.2	−0.2	−0.7
	1970	7.0§	8.0	0.75	−1.25
Japan	1968	14.0	21.3	0.4	1.0
	1969	12.2	18.1	0.2	0.8
	1970	10.75	15.75	0.0	0.25

*As a percentage of GNP in the previous year.
†Private fixed investment.
‡All 1970 figures are estimates.
§Gross domestic product.
Source: Organization for Economic Cooperation and Development, *Economic Outlook* (July 1970).

In West Germany, as in the U.S. in 1969, expansion of investment was very large. The pace moderated in the second half of 1970, however, mainly as a result of a reduction in the additional public spending on fixed assets and some reduction in business investment in the late summer. The outstanding feature of the boom was a large rise in borrowings by the corporate sector, particularly in the form of medium-, long-, and short-term credits from banks, financial institutions, and international markets.

In France the upsurge in investment in 1969 was demanded by the rapid expansion of fixed investment by business, but public sector outlays showed no marked improvement. In the closing months of the year, however, the rate of progress began to slacken because of increasing credit restrictions, whose effects became even more pronounced in 1970. A large part of the funds needed by corporations came from the issue of shares, whose volume doubled as compared with 1968.

In Italy private business investment and housing were the main driving forces behind the investment boom of 1969. This trend was reversed in the closing months of the year, partly as a result of strikes and partly because of restrictive monetary policy, which, along with a rise in the government's own outlays on fixed assets, intensified in early 1970. With private savings showing only a moderate increase and investors preferring to hold their funds in a liquid form or to transfer them overseas, the issues of securities abroad rose in 1969 by over 50% and, in the first six months of 1970, the amount raised abroad was some 150% higher than that raised during the whole of the preceding 12 months.

Belgium and the Netherlands experienced divergent trends. An appreciable rise in fixed investment in Belgium in 1969 was accompanied by a substantial rise in exports and foreign balance and was characterized by large borrowings abroad by the public sector. In the Netherlands, a fractional drop in fixed investment was influenced by the anti-inflationary policy and the defi-

1969. The slowdown in 1970 affected investment by enterprises and the public sector, while housing retained its relative position.

The investment boom of 1969, which continued in the first quarter of 1970, was accompanied by a large increase in the requirements for external finance by business. As the rise in net household savings was moderated, the demands on financial intermediaries and overseas sources increased rapidly, with medium- and short-term borrowings rising very sharply. The issue of bonds, both domestic and foreign, lost in importance because of the rise in interest rates, especially in late 1969. There was some slowing of this trend in the second half of 1970.

Table II. Savings and Investment in U.S., U.K., West Germany, and Japan in 1969

Item	House-holds	Enter-prises	Public sector	Financial institutions	Foreign sector	Total
U.S. (in $000,000,000)						
Gross saving	+147.1	+82.6	+2.0	+2.9	+0.9	+235.5
Gross physical investment	−116.9	−111.5	—	−1.4	—	−235.5
Capital transfers and adjustments	−9.8	−7.2	−0.2	−0.8	+2.8	—
Net financial saving	+20.3	−36.1	—	+0.7	+3.7	—
Financial assets	−50.3	−25.5	−7.9	−78.2	+10.1	−183.4
Indebtedness	+30.0	+61.6	+7.8	+77.5	+6.5	+183.4
U.K. (in £000,000)						
Gross saving	+2,433	+2,838	+6,311	+331	} −366	—
Gross physical investment	−1,687	−3,000	−5,987	−526		—
Capital transfers and adjustments	+1,185	−921	+287	−630	−268	—
Net financial saving	+1,931	−1,083	+611	−825	−634	—
Financial assets	−2,759	−564	−444	−7,273	−4,689	−15,729
Indebtedness	+828	+1,647	−164	+8,098	+5,323	+15,729
West Germany (in DM. 000,000,000)						
Gross saving	+47.32	+74.01	+40.57	+5.79	−7.32	+160.37
Gross physical investment	—	−134.01	−23.21	−3.15	—	−160.37
Capital transfers and adjustments	−5.82	+13.94	−8.39	−4.50	+4.77	—
Net financial saving	+41.52	−46.06	+8.97	−1.86	−2.55	—
Financial assets	−46.03	−21.52	−10.99	−88.75	−10.71	−178.00
Indebtedness	+4.53	+67.58	+2.01	−90.62	+13.26	+178.00
Japan (in 000,000,000 yen)						
Gross saving	+9,732	+9,238	+4,917	—	} −302	—
Gross physical investment	−5,658	−12,629	−5,298	—		—
Capital transfers and adjustments	+1,106	−66	−579	—	−461	—
Net financial saving	+5,180	−3,457	−960	—	−763	—
Financial assets	−9,681	−11,269	−2,957	−13,398	−570	−37,874
Indebtedness	+4,501	+14,726	+3,919	+13,398	+1,333	+37,874

Note: For gross saving, gross physical investment, and capital transfers and adjustments, + means receipts and − means expenditure; for financial assets, − means spending on assets; for indebtedness, + means increase in indebtedness.
For the U.S., public sector includes federal, state, and local governments and financial institutions includes monetary authorities, commercial banks, other private financing institutions, and government-sponsored lending agencies; for the U.K., public sector includes central government, local authorities, and public corporations; for West Germany, enterprises includes housing and public sector includes all social security funds; for Japan, public sector includes central government, local authorities, and public corporations.
Source: Organization for Economic Cooperation and Development, *Financial Statistics*, vol. 1 and supplements 1A and 1B (1970).

cit in the public sector, which had to be financed by borrowings on the capital market.

The U.K. experienced a marked slowing down in fixed investment at home in 1969, particularly in housing. However, inventory building and foreign balance improved. There was a modest acceleration in spending on fixed investment at home in 1970 but a deceleration in inventory outlays, with foreign balance declining a little. This evolution in investment was accompanied by a shift to surplus by the public sector and an increased deficit of the corporate business sector, which resulted in strong pressures on capital markets. The difficulties of raising funds needed for investment at home caused companies to satisfy an increasing proportion of their needs abroad while also reducing their holdings of liquid assets. Tight conditions in the financial markets, associated with the surplus of the public sector, also restricted the ability of private individuals to borrow and induced them to raise their holdings of bonds.

Sweden and Denmark experienced high rates of growth of fixed domestic investment, including housing, in 1969. This development was associated with the reduction in net foreign balance and compelled authorities to tighten fiscal and monetary policies. Private businesses and the public sector had to raise a much greater volume of funds overseas.

In 1970 Japan experienced a modest slackening of the investment boom that started toward the end of 1965. Both fixed domestic investment and inventory building lost some of their momentum, as did also net foreign balance. As in the case of other industrial countries, the requirements for external finance on the part of businesses rose very sharply in 1969. Since household savings advanced quite appreciably, the degree of tightening of monetary conditions that was needed in 1970 to bring investment into equality with saving was relatively small.

Strong advance in output in industrial countries in 1969 had a very favourable effect on prices and volume of exports of the primary producing countries. As a result of this development, and partly because of a rise in absolute terms in the flow of financial resources (in the form of official grants, loans and credits, and private investment credits—*i.e.,* savings) from the more developed countries, the share of investment and savings in total output of most of the less developed countries rose again in 1969.

The broad picture of savings and investment by main types of economic units in four major industrial countries, the U.S., the U.K., West Germany, and Japan, is shown in Table II. A large increase in the requirements for external funds by the corporate sector in the four countries in 1969 was accompanied by changes in external balance, especially in the U.K. and the U.S., and by a shift in financial position of the public and household sectors. All these changes contributed to the tightness of monetary conditions and to the consequent pressure on interest rates, which helped to bring the total of savings and investment together.

Financial intermediaries were playing an increasingly important role in the process of collecting and channeling savings. In 1969–70 their development was marked by a large increase in their numbers, a further rise in the types of savings and lending instruments they made available, and a rapid spread of their involvement in international transactions.

In industrial countries new financial institutions came into being to satisfy the demands of savers and of fund-raising units. Some concentrated their operations in the domestic sphere while others aimed expressly to transact business on an international scale. New types of financial instruments being used were dollar and sterling certificates of deposit, medium-term bonds with floating rates that change every six months in accordance with market conditions, and nonmarketable medium-term loans. Long-term fund-raising instruments included convertible bonds, equity warrants, and securities denominated in more than one currency, such as mark/sterling and sterling/U.S. dollar. (T. M. R.)

See also Money and Banking; Profits; Stock Exchanges.

Seismology

Probably the most disastrous earthquake in Latin-American history occurred on May 31, 1970, off the coast of Peru centred about 12 mi. SW of Chimbote. The tremor, which had a magnitude of 7.8 on the Richter scale, took 66,794 lives and devastated villages in the Callejón de Huaylas, the valley that parallels Peru's Pacific coast. Although a mud- and earthslide (called *huayco*) covered Yungay and a nearby village beneath tons of debris and took thousands of lives, the principal cause of the high death toll was strong earth vibration that led to the collapse of innumerable poorly designed structures.

Seismic signals continued to be recorded more than a year after the Apollo 12 astronauts placed a seismograph on the lunar surface in November 1969. One or more moonquakes occurred every 28.4 days, each time the moon comes closest to the earth. The quakes appeared to centre in the Fra Mauro highland crater, a position only 50 mi. S of the point where Apollo 14 astronauts were scheduled to land in February 1971. They usually occur in pairs, at perigee and a few days later during the lunar month when the face of the moon bulges 20 to 30 in. toward the earth. This bulging, caused by the earth's gravitational pull, ap-

This photograph was taken 6,000 ft. above Yungay, Peru, from a NASA remote sensing aircraft to assess damage and help plan reconstruction after the earthquake and mudslide of May 31, 1970.

PICTORIAL PARADE

parently produces considerable strain within the moon, indicating that, contrary to theories of some scientists, the moon must have some internal heat. The sources of the moonquakes have been estimated to be not more than a mile beneath the surface. They are believed to be generated as are earthquakes, with opposite faces of a fault slipping past one another.

Scientists at the University of Washington were creating miniquakes in order to identify and study the characteristics of various soils subjected to seismic impacts. They developed an instrument, capable of simulating earthquake motions at any level, that shakes a cylinder cell about $6\frac{1}{2}$ in. long and 3 in. in diameter and measures stresses in three directions. The readings indicate what the resonance of ground motion would be in an actual earthquake.

Soviet seismologists reported that hot water reaching the surface from deep-seated layers of the earth's crust can provide advance notice of an impending earthquake. This was first observed during the Tashkent earthquake in 1966 and was verified later by seismologists in Tadzhikistan. Weak disturbances of the earth's crust that precede a sharp earthquake are capable of changing the chemical composition of thermal waters, as well as their temperature. When the crustal rocks shift during an earthquake, the water changes its course to the surface, is enriched by microelements, and becomes hotter or loses some of its heat. Such information could greatly assist seismologists in their search for a solution to the problem of earthquake prediction.

After several years of study, California engineers proposed building multistory structures on ball- or roller-bearing foundations in earthquake zones to eliminate the transfer from foundation to superstructure of lateral forces induced by seismic vibrations. A system of ball bearings, neoprene springs, and horizontal control could be incorporated in the design of a building foundation. The vertical building loads would be transferred to the foundation through a system of ball bearings sandwiched between steel bearing plates. Lateral wind loads would be transferred to the foundation through horizontal control rods set between the building's core and the foundation walls. Neoprene springs between the core floor and the foundation slab would safely arrest any motion of the superstructure under lateral loading.

One characteristic of California earthquakes is that they are shallow, occurring no more than 10 to 20 km.

below the earth's surface. According to recent studies, the motion is most likely taking place on preexisting faults. Though there may be some fracturing of new material, it probably occurs on a small scale in comparison with the area of the fault surface over which the stress drop occurs. The earthquakes may be caused primarily by frictional sliding on fault surfaces. Stable sliding was induced in laboratory experiments using samples of granite and gabbro at 1 to 5 kilobars (1 kilobar = 1,000 times atmospheric pressure) when the temperature rose from 200° to 500° C. Thus, the fact that temperature in the earth increases with depth could account for the absence of earthquakes below shallow depths in California. (L. M. M.)

See also Disasters.

Senegal

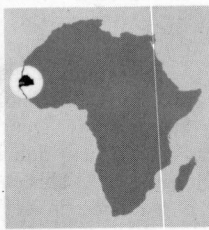

A republic of northwestern Africa, Senegal is bounded by Mauritania, Mali, Guinea, and Portuguese Guinea, and by the Atlantic Ocean. The independent nation of The Gambia forms an enclave within the country. Area: 76,124 sq.mi. (197,161 sq.km.). Pop. (1968 est.): 3,685,000. Cap. and largest city: Dakar (pop., 1965 est., 576,093). Language: French (official); Wolof; Peular (Fulani); other tribal dialects. Religion: Muslim; pagan; Christian minority. President in 1970, Léopold Sédar Senghor; premier from February 26, Abdou Diouf.

On Feb. 22, 1970, an important constitutional reform was submitted to a national referendum and approved by 99.7% of votes cast. It provided for the appointment of a premier for the first time since 1962. President Senghor by this means shed a certain amount of work, but he sacrificed little of his power. He would still decide national policy and would also appoint the premier. A few days later, Abdou Diouf, the former minister of planning and industry, became premier.

On February 28 a new government was formed. All previous holders of important posts retained their portfolios, and Senghor remained in charge of defense and the armed forces. In June Abdoulaye Ly, who had left the government in February, resigned from his post of deputy secretary-general of the governing Senegalese Progressive Union (UPS) Party. He had earlier been a member of the Party of African Regrouping, the main opposition party after independence until its amalgamation with the UPS in 1967.

Earthquake victims gather among the ruins of their homes, destroyed by the massive series of tremors that occurred along the Anatolian fault in western Turkey in March 1970.

CAMERA PRESS FROM PIX

SENEGAL

Education. (1965–66) Primary, pupils 218,795, teachers 5,133; secondary, pupils 25,574, teachers 885; vocational (1966–67), pupils 11,270, teachers 432; teacher training, students 826, teachers 80; higher (including University of Dakar), students 2,755, teaching staff 230.

Finance. Monetary unit: CFA franc, with a parity of CFA Fr. 50 to the French franc (CFA Fr. 277.71 = U.S. $1; CFA Fr. 666.50 = £1 sterling). Budget (1969–70 est.): receipts CFA Fr. 34,953,000,000; expenditure CFA Fr. 37,849,000,000.

Foreign Trade. (1969) Imports CFA Fr. 51.3 billion; exports CFA Fr. 31,910,000,000. Import sources (1968) France 44%; Brazil 7%; West Germany 6%; Ivory Coast 5%; Cambodia 5%. Export destination (1968) France 66%. Main exports (1968): peanuts and peanut oil 72%; phosphates 7%.

Foreign policy continued to be dominated by the conflict between Portuguese troops and nationalists in neighbouring Portuguese Guinea, and relations with Portugal continued to deteriorate. In January Senghor issued a solemn warning to Lisbon after a series of border clashes, and in June the UN held an inquiry into various incidents. Shortly afterward, Senegalese villages in the Casamance region were shelled by Portuguese artillery. In early July attacks on three villages resulted in several civilian deaths and provoked a further Senegalese complaint to the UN with a plea for the convocation of the Security Council. Considerable troop reinforcements were sent into Casamance by the Senegalese authorities. (PH. D.)

Sierra Leone

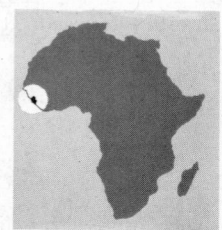

A parliamentary state within the Commonwealth of Nations, Sierra Leone is a West African nation located between Guinea and Liberia. Area: 27,699 sq.mi. (71,740 sq.km.). Pop. (1969 est.): 2,510,000, including (1962 est.) Mende and Temme tribes 60%; other tribes 38.5%; Creole 1.2%. Cap. and largest city: Freetown (pop., 1968 est., 163,000). Language: English (official); tribal dialects; Hausa. Religion: Christian; pagan; Muslim minority. Queen, Elizabeth II; governor-general in 1970, Banja Tejan-Sie; prime minister, Siaka Stevens.

In Sierra Leone 1970 was marked by increasing political instability and violence. Although the prime minister had predicted in January 1969 that the country would be a republic before the end of that year, at the beginning of 1970 the chief justice, Banja Tejan-Sie, was still acting governor-general and on September 29 he was sworn in as substantive governor-general. However, Prime Minister Stevens was believed to favour an executive presidency like that introduced in The Gambia in April.

A number of trials for treason were held during the year, resulting in some death sentences that were under appeal in late 1970. On April 18, after treason trials lasting a year, ten defendants—including the leader of the 1967 coup, David Lansana, former chief of staff of the armed forces—were sentenced to death.

On July 30 Andrew Juxon-Smith, former chairman of the NRC, was also sentenced to death. In October Stevens announced the discovery of an army plot to overthrow the regime and declared a state of emergency. The trial of the first ten officers arrested as a result began late in the year. (W. H. Is.; X.)

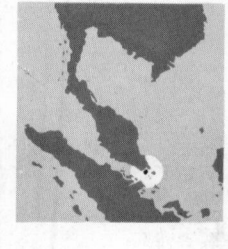

Singapore

The republic of Singapore occupies a group of islands, the largest of which is Singapore, at the southern extremity of the Malay Peninsula. Area: 225.6 sq.mi. (584.3 sq.km.). Pop. (1970 est.): 2,033,500, including approximately 80% Chinese, 12% Malays, and 7% Indians and Pakistanis. Singapore is a city-state, and has no administrative subdivisions. Language: official languages are Malay, Chinese, Tamil, and English. Religion: Malays are Muslim; Chinese, mainly Buddhist; Indians, mainly Hindu. President in 1970, Inche Yusof bin Ishak until November 23; acting president from November 23, Yeoh Ghim Seng; prime minister, Lee Kuan Yew.

Singapore's head of state, Pres. Inche Yusof bin Ishak, died of a heart attack on November 23 (*see* OBITUARIES). He was a pioneer of Malay nationalism and a crusading journalist before being installed as Singapore's first local-born head of state (*yang dipertuan negara*) in 1959 when Singapore attained full self-rule from Britain. Later, when Singapore became independent in 1965 after breaking away from Malaysia, he became its first president. Yeoh Ghim Seng took over as acting president.

Singapore continued to make progress on all fronts in 1970. Economically, it had another successful year, which could be described as a period of transformation from a highly commercialized centre to an industrial base. Unemployment was at an all-time low, and Singapore was able to give work permits more freely to foreign workers. Gross domestic product increased to Sing$4,833,000,000 in 1969, nearly $2\frac{1}{2}$ times that of 1959. Capital investment rose to Sing$919 million, compared with Sing$150 million in 1959.

Prime Minister Lee Kuan Yew made a ten-week tour of the Soviet Union, France, West Germany, Britain, and the United States. One of his main purposes was to interest those countries in investing in

SIERRA LEONE
Education. (1967–68) Primary, pupils 136,824, teachers 4,997; secondary, pupils 22,119, teachers 1,107; vocational, pupils 1,053, teachers 47; teacher training, students 807, teachers 105; higher, students 762, teaching staff 233.
   Finance and Trade. Monetary unit: leone, with a parity of 0.83 leones to U.S. $1 (2 leones = £1 sterling). Budget (1970–71 est.): revenue 51 million leones; expenditure 46.3 million leones. Foreign trade (1969): imports 93,030,000 leones; exports 88,350,000 leones. Import sources (1968): U.K. 28%; Japan 12%; U.S. 9%; France 6%; West Germany 5%. Export destinations (1968): U.K. 67%; Netherlands 12%; West Germany 8%. Main exports: diamonds 69%; iron ore 11%; palm kernels 6%.
   Agriculture. Production (in 000; metric tons; 1968; 1967 in parentheses): rice 426 (468); cassava *c.* 62 (*c.* 60); kernels *c.* 66 (22); palm oil *c.* 42 (*c.* 41); coffee *c.* 5.7 (*c.* 4.8). Livestock (in 000; 1967–68): cattle *c.* 210; sheep *c.* 30; goats *c.* 37; chickens *c.* 2,000.
   Industry. Production (in 000; metric tons; 1968): iron ore (metal content) *c.* 1,800; bauxite *c.* 470; diamonds (metric carats; 1967) *c.* 1,400; electricity (kw-hr.) 144,400.

SINGAPORE
Education. (1967–68) Primary, pupils 368,650, teachers (including preprimary) 12,630; secondary, pupils 124,701, teachers 5,496; vocational, pupils 21,499, teachers 1,041; higher (including 3 universities), students 13,005, teaching staff 933.
   Finance and Trade. Monetary unit: Singapore dollar, with a par value of Sing$3.06 to U.S. $1 (Sing$7.35 = £1 sterling). Budget (1969 est.): revenue Sing$813 million; expenditure Sing$850 million. Foreign trade (1969): imports Sing$6,207,700,000; exports Sing$4,740,900,000. Import sources: Malaysia 22%; Japan 16%; U.S. 8%; U.K. 7%; China 7%; Kuwait 6%. Export destinations: Malaysia 23%; U.S. 11%; South Vietnam 9%; Japan 7%; U.K. 6%. Main exports: rubber 30%; petroleum products 24%; machinery 5%.
   Transport and Communications. Roads (1969) 1,918 km. Motor vehicles in use (1968): passenger 121,106; commercial 27,435. Railways (1968) 45 km. Railway and air traffic: *see* MALAYSIA. Shipping (1969): merchant vessels 100 gross tons and over 112; gross tonnage 233,271. Shipping traffic (1969) goods loaded 15,582,000 metric tons, unloaded 22,932,000 metric tons. Telephones (Dec. 1968) 119,184. Radio receivers (Dec. 1969) 202,000. Television receivers (Dec. 1969) 118,000.

WIDE WORLD

Bernhard Russi
of Switzerland soars
to victory in the downhill
event for men
at the Alpine World Ski
Championships, Feb. 15,
1970, at
Val di Gardena, Italy.

Singapore. He made it clear that the industrial capital and equipment that Singapore wanted must fit in with the nation's new phase of increasing industrialization and that he was interested primarily in skills of which there was a shortage in Singapore.

During the year, the government announced that it was establishing a "watchdog" Presidential Council, headed by the chief justice, Wee Chong Jin. Its purpose was mainly to protect minority interests in the republic.

The ruling People's Action Party (PAP), in search of new talent, retired five members of Parliament and held by-elections. All five new PAP candidates were elected, leaving Parliament again with no opposition member. According to the PAP, the election was held to draw new talent so as to ensure not only the continuity of good and vigorous government but also the capacity of the government to meet changing circumstances and needs. The 18th Commonwealth Prime Ministers' Conference was to take place in Singapore in January 1971.   (M. S. R.)

Skiing

The expansion of skiing as a holiday recreation was accompanied in 1970 by the development of a revolutionary foam-filled ski boot, intended to achieve closer fitting, lighter weight, and improved insulation. Improved facilities at mountain resorts were augmented by an increasing number of artificial training facilities in lowland towns. The longest plastic slope in England, with a skiing surface exceeding 5,500 sq. ft., was to open at Alexandra Palace in London early in 1971.

Alpine Racing. The 21st Alpine World Ski Championships took place at Val di Gardena, Italy, on February 7–15. Approximately 250 competitors represented 31 nations. The eight gold medals went to skiers from France (3), Switzerland (2), Austria, Canada, and the United States. Ideal weather, good courses, and thorough technical organization together provided the best possible conditions.

Without winning any of the three events, Billy Kidd

(U.S.) gained the men's combined title for a consistency that was particularly laudable as a triumph over his frustrating injuries during previous seasons. Patrick Russel (France) was overall runner-up, with Andrzej Bachleda (Pol.) third. Kidd's victory was the first world championship for the U.S. in Alpine combination.

Jean-Noël Augert (France) won the closest finish, in the slalom. His aggregate for the two runs was only 0.04 sec. faster than that of his compatriot Russel. Austrians took revenge in the giant slalom when veteran Karl Schranz dominated both descents to end 0.39 sec. better than his fellow countryman Werner Bleiner. The downhill was won by Bernhard Russi (Switz.), 0.22 sec. quicker than Karl Cordin (Aus.), but a spectacular sensation was Malcolm Milne, whose third-best time gained Australia's first medal in skiing.

Michèle Jacot won the women's combined title for France, ahead of her compatriot Florence Steurer and the U.S. sisters, Marilyn and Barbara Cochran, in that order. It was noteworthy that three racers from non-Alpine countries, Gina Hathorn (U.K.), Karianne Christiansen (Nor.), and Cochita Puig (Spain), finished seventh, eighth, and ninth, respectively. A portent of the future was perhaps the 19th place achieved by Valentina Iliffe (U.K.), at 13 years the youngest girl ever to finish in the top 20.

In a class of their own in the downhill, Anneroesli Zryd (Switz.) beat the favourite, Isabelle Mir (France), by 0.5 sec. Ingrid Lafforgue (France) was superior in the slalom with an aggregate nearly two seconds better than Barbara Cochran. Youth succeeded in the single-run giant slalom when Betsy Clifford (Can.), only 15, outpaced the much more experienced French trio, Mlles Lafforgue, Françoise Macchi, and Jacot, who took the next three places.

The fourth annual Alpine World Cup tournament enjoyed increased interest. Schranz retained the men's trophy in the twilight of a remarkable career spanning 14 years. He scored 3 points more than Russel and 8 more than the third man, Gustavo Thoeni (Italy). The women's trophy went to Mlle Jacot, who was well ahead of the next three, Mlles Macchi, Steurer, and Lafforgue, all also from France. The contests

KEYSTONE

A record 8,695 competitors
take off from Salen, Swed.,
March 1, 1970, in the
annual "Vasa race," the
world's largest ski race.

were decided on a point-scoring basis during 32 events for men and 26 for women held in Europe, Canada, and the U.S. from December 1969 to March 1970. Points were scored by 91 men from 12 countries and 44 women from 9 countries. The same performances also decided the Nations' Cup, won convincingly by France, whose male competitors gained 110 points more than Austria and whose female competitors took 493 points more than the U.S.

Lingering doubts about the retention of Alpine racing in future Winter Olympics were eased when the International Olympic Committee during its congress at Amsterdam in May reached an apparently better understanding with the International Ski Federation concerning control over amateur status.

Nordic Events. The 28th Nordic World Ski Championships took place at Vysoke Tatry, Czech., on February 14–22. Approximately 500 participants represented 25 nations, the ten gold medals being won by the U.S.S.R. (7), Czechoslovakia, Finland, and Sweden. Fine weather with excellent snow happily augmented the much-praised courses and sound organization. The events were attended by about 250,000 spectators. That no title went to Norway emphasized not so much a Norwegian decline as a general rise in the standards among other nations.

The most successful jumper was Gari Napalkov (U.S.S.R.), who won both events. On the smaller 70-m. hill, a great second jump took him from tenth to first, with runner-up Yukio Kasaya (Jap.) demonstrating his country's growing strength. On the big 90-m. hill, Napalkov was only 13th in his first effort, but his second leap of 109.5 m. gained his second gold medal, with the Olympic champion, Jiri Raska (Czech.), taking the silver.

The 30-km. race was won by Vyacheslav Vedenin (U.S.S.R.), with second-place Gerhard Grimmer (E.Ger.) achieving his country's best-ever performance in a men's world cross-country championship. Lars Aslund (Swed.) dominated the 15 km., finishing 34 sec. ahead of the next man, Odd Martinsen (Nor.). The energy-sapping 50 km. found Kalevi Oikarainen (Fin.) the best stayer as he beat Vedenin in a dramatic final spurt. Vedenin also skied the last leg of the 4 × 10-km. relay, to clinch a narrow Soviet victory from East Germany. The Nordic combined event—a 15-km. race and jumping on the 70-m. hill—went to Ladislav Rygl (Czech.).

Soviet skiers won all three women's cross-country races. Galina Kulakova led two team colleagues for a national grand slam in the 5 km. Alevtina Olyunina was 21 sec. faster than runner-up Marjatta Kajosmaa (Fin.) in the 10 km. These two individual gold medalists joined with Nina Fyodorova to outclass the East Germans by 37 sec. in the 3 × 5-km. relay. The East Germans, however, showed a marked improvement in their Nordic racing capabilities.

The individual world biathlon title, contested in March at Östersund, Swed., was retained by Aleksandr Tikhonov (U.S.S.R.). Norway won the team championship. (H. B.)

Social Services

International organizations continued to play an important role in the extension and harmonization of social welfare schemes in 1970. The International Labour Organization (ILO) promulgated a new international standard for the protection of workers and their families in case of sickness, through appropriate social security measures, as an extension of the 1927 convention.

A European social and medicosocial policy for old age was drawn up by the Council of Europe and adopted by its Committee of Ministers. The policy covered resources and income, employment, housing, medical and social services, and scientific research into aging. It was recommended that an adequate share of the national income should be allocated to old people, corresponding to their particular needs as determined by simple and sound criteria. Apart from the question of material support, attention should be drawn to the definition of the place of old people in society through continuous information and education of the active population, the aged themselves, and public opinion as a whole. Old-age protection should be extended to the entire population as far as is necessary; the age of entitlement to the old-age pension should be determined by, among other things, the composition of the population and the financial implications. The pension rates should be as high as possible, bearing in mind the standards laid down in international social security instruments such as the European Code of Social Security and the ILO Social Security Conventions of 1952 and 1967. Both pensions and subsistence allowances should be adjusted at appropriate intervals to take account of changes in the cost of living or the general income level. There should be adequate coordination between statutory pension schemes so as to prevent changes in occupation from entailing loss of pension rights, and to eliminate impediments to occupational mobility. As a general rule, social service arrangements should correspond to the wishes of the elderly and should be carried out in collaboration with as large a section of the local population as possible, especially close relations and neighbours.

The Commission of the European Economic Community (EEC) studied the financial problems of social security between 1958 and 1970—the first study of its kind carried out in the Community. A further study covering 1972–75 was begun. During the previous ten years the member countries had almost reached the goal of extending social security for all the main risks to all categories of the population. It was accepted that more effective and more adequate welfare should be the next aim. The improved and simplified regulations on family allowances, sickness, maternity, and unemployment benefits for workers moving from one Community country to another, adopted in November 1970, were likely to come into force in 1972. Work was still under way regarding social security provisions for the handicapped, the aged, and survivors.

An agreement between the U.K. and the U.S. provided for reciprocal payment of old-age benefits to citizens or residents of the other country under certain conditions. There was also increased collaboration between voluntary organizations in different countries, especially in providing services for the elderly. The activities of the British National Old People's Welfare Council and its 1,500 local committees, particularly with regard to the use of leisure in retirement, continued to interest visitors from overseas. As a result there were similar developments in other countries, for example, France.

United Kingdom. Legislation was passed improving the position of the elderly and others in need in several ways. The Chronically Sick and Disabled Persons Act, 1970, required local authorities to inform themselves of the number of persons in their areas who were substantially and permanently handicapped, including those handicapped by old age, to publish information as to the services available, and to ensure that the persons concerned received this information. They were also required to provide certain practical assistance for such persons, including adaptations of their homes, recreation, traveling facilities, holidays, and telephones where needed.

The Local Authorities Social Services Act, 1970, implemented the recommendation of the Seebohm Committee that each local health and welfare authority should establish a single social services committee and appoint a director. The functions to be discharged by the new committee included all those for which local authorities were responsible under the 1948 National Assistance Act and the 1948 Children Act, as well as certain social service functions that were the responsibility of health committees. The director, whose appointment was mandatory, was to be engaged full-time in the work of the new committee. Central responsibility was assigned to the Department of Health and Social Security.

A somewhat similar act, which already provided for the appointment of social work departments in Scotland, had resulted from the report of another government-sponsored committee. Both committees emphasized the importance of work undertaken by voluntary organizations in cooperation with the local authorities, and this view was accepted by the government. It was significant that the Labour government then in power was just as much in favour of voluntary activity as were the Conservative governments that preceded and followed it. Under both parties, substantial grant-aid was allocated to appropriate national voluntary organizations.

Under the National Insurance (Old Persons' and Widows' Pensions and Attendance Allowances) Act, 1970, provision was made for pensions to be paid to old people who had been excluded from the pre-1948 pension schemes and were accordingly excluded from the comprehensive scheme introduced in 1948. About 100,000 persons were affected, half of whom were receiving supplementary benefit under the social security scheme. This act also made improvements in the widows' pension scheme by introducing a scale that started at 30s. a week for a woman widowed at 40 and rose to the full rate of £5 at age 50. A further improvement brought about by the act was the provision of a £4-a-week attendance allowance for disabled persons needing attention by day and night or who needed continual supervision. However, the allowance was payable only when a disabled person needed attendance for six months. Parents would get the allowance for a severely disabled child living with them. Supplementary benefit rates were increased to compensate for the rise in the cost of living.

During 1969 about 6,688,000 claims for supplementary benefits were received, costing £460 million, compared with £451 million in 1968. At the end of 1969 about 1,875,000 supplementary pensions and 813,000 supplementary allowances were being paid. On average, 7,130,000 retirement pensions were being paid each week, compared with 6,973,000 in 1968. There were 662,000 new claims, compared with 653,000 a year earlier. At the end of 1969 retirement pensions were being paid at the rate of £1,740 million a year, compared with £1,540 million in 1968. During the year there were 11,411,000 claims for sickness benefit, about 803,000 more than in the preceding

LEONARD MCCOMBE, "LIFE" MAGAZINE © TIME INC.

Children share morning snacks at the KLH Child Development Center in Cambridge, Mass. A maker of high-fidelity sound equipment, KLH started the centre in 1968 as an experiment in industrial sponsorship of day-care centres.

year; the rise was mainly due to two epidemics of influenza. There were 3,098,000 claims for unemployment benefit, some 19,000 less than in 1968; 69,000 new claims for widows' pensions and widowed mothers' allowances; and 933,000 claims for maternity benefits, compared with 950,000 the year before.

A bill was introduced to implement the proposals in the government White Paper for fundamental changes in the social security scheme, whereby both contributions and benefits would be related to earnings. The bill had not gone through all its stages in Parliament before the general election, however, and the new Conservative government did not reintroduce it. On October 27 the new government announced its intention to increase the charges for some social services in 1971, including school meals, medical prescriptions, and dental and optical treatment. At the same time the government announced a plan to introduce an "income supplement" for certain low-income families.

In the voluntary sphere, Prince Philip accepted the presidency of the National Council of Social Service. The Pre-Retirement Association received additional support, especially from government departments and the trade unions. It was becoming more generally recognized that retraining for work in later life (discussed with considerable perception in the third report of the Resolutions Committee at the 54th session of the International Labour Conference) was no less important than education for retirement.

Other European Countries. In Belgium the sickness and medical care insurance scheme was extended to the entire population. Family allowances in France were raised with the aim of encouraging young couples to have children; families of three and four children would receive 57 and 92% of the basic wage, respectively, compared with the earlier 55 and 88%. Another improvement was the reform of the sickness and maternity insurance scheme for self-employed persons. In Finland earnings-related pensions were extended to farmers and other self-employed persons for whom the flat-rate pension had been the only retirement protection.

In West Germany the rate of contribution for compulsory pension insurance was raised from 16 to 17%, with a further increase to 18% planned for 1973. Old-age pensions were increased by 6.35% and accident insurance benefits by 6.1%. A new pension system for old age, invalidity, and survivors was introduced in Norway with the aim of simplifying administration. Sickness insurance contributions were reduced for persons with below-average incomes and increased for those with above-average incomes. In Spain a special social security scheme was established for the coal-mining industry.

North America. *Canada.* The age of eligibility for retirement pension and guaranteed income supplement under the Canada pension plan was lowered to 65. An applicant under 70 must be retired from regular employment and must have contributed to the plan. After 70, the pension was payable whether the person was retired or not. Retirement pension and survivor's benefit were increased each year as the cost of living increased, and, beginning in February 1970, this was also true of disability pension. When the plan was introduced in 1966, contributions were based on earnings up to Can$5,000 a year, with the first Can$600 being exempt from contributions. The exempt figure did not change, but the earnings ceiling rose to Can$5,200 in 1969. Old-age security pensions increased to Can

$79.58 a month. Combined with the guaranteed income supplement, the monthly payments totaled Can $111.41.

There were important changes in provincial social assistance programs. In Quebec a new statute, the Social Aid Act, provided for the integration of a number of assistance measures under a comprehensive new program. Newfoundland amended its Social Assistance Act to provide for a decentralized administrative structure. In Nova Scotia needy widows and unmarried women aged 60 to 65 years became eligible for assistance. In other provinces eligibility requirements were modified. Rates of allowances were increased in a number of provinces and other amendments reflected recognition of the importance of preventive and rehabilitative services. In Ontario, Indian groups providing or purchasing home-care services for needy members of the group became eligible for provincial assistance.

Hospital insurance plans administered by the provincial and territorial governments were operative throughout the country, and 99.3% of the population was covered as of 1969. In Saskatchewan and Ontario eligibility for benefit depended on prior payment of a premium, except for recipients of public assistance. By mid-1970 eight provinces were participating in the plan, established by the Canadian Medical Care Act, whereby federal fiscal contributions were made to provincial physicians' care plans meeting certain criteria.

A federal-provincial task force, appointed in 1969 to study various aspects of social welfare programs, recommended that efforts be made to link the administration of public assistance more closely with the provision of employment opportunities. It also recommended the development of some alternative to public assistance that would achieve more effective redistribution of income, particularly for persons fully employed but with inadequate incomes.

As part of the Government Organization Act, 1969, the National Council of Welfare was reconstituted as a citizens' advisory council with the function of advising the minister of national health and welfare. The new council consisted of 21 private citizens, roughly half being drawn from organizations of welfare recipients and half from institutions involved in the provision of welfare services.

Social Security Programs, by Country, 1969* and 1958

Type of program available

Country	Old age, invalidity, survivors 1969	1958	Health, sickness, maternity 1969	1958	Work injury 1969	1958	Unemployment 1969	1958	Family allowances 1969	1958
Afghanistan					X	X				
Albania	X	X	X	X	X	X			X	
Algeria†	X		X		X				X	
Argentina	X	X	X		X		X		X	X
Australia	X	X	X	X	X	X	X	X	X	X
Austria	X	X	X	X	X	X	X	X	X	X
Barbados†	X		X		X					
Belgium	X	X	X	X	X	X	X	X	X	X
Bolivia	X	X	X	X	X	X			X	X
Botswana†					X					
Brazil	X	X	X	X	X	X	X		X	X
Bulgaria	X	X	X	X	X	X	X	X	X	X
Burma			X	X	X	X				
Burundi†	X				X					
Cambodia†					X				X	
Cameroon			X		X				X	
Canada	X	X	X	X	X	X	X	X	X	X
Central African Rep.†	X	X			X				X	
Ceylon	X	X			X		X			
Chad†			X		X				X	
Chile	X	X	X	X	X	X	X	X	X	X
China	X	X	X		X					
Colombia	X		X	X	X	X			X	
Congo (Brazzaville)†	X		X		X				X	
Congo (Kinshasa)†	X		X		X					
Costa Rica	X	X	X	X	X		X			
Cuba	X	X	X	X	X	X				
Cyprus†	X				X		X			
Czechoslovakia	X	X	X	X	X		X	X	X	X
Dahomey†					X				X	
Denmark	X	X	X	X	X	X	X	X	X	X
Dominican Rep.	X	X	X	X	X					
Ecuador	X	X	X	X	X	X	X	X		
El Salvador			X		X					
Ethiopia†			X		X					
Finland	X	X	X		X	X	X		X	X
France	X	X	X	X	X		X	X	X	X
Gabon†	X				X				X	
Gambia, The†					X					
Germany, East	X	X	X	X	X	X	X	X	X	X
Germany, West	X	X	X	X	X	X	X	X	X	X
Ghana	X				X					
Greece	X	X	X	X	X	X	X	X	X	
Guatemala	X		X	X	X	X				
Guinea†	X		X		X				X	
Guyana†	X				X					
Haiti			X		X		X			
Honduras			X		X	X	X	X		
Hungary	X	X	X	X	X		X		X	X
Iceland	X	X	X	X	X	X	X		X	X
India	X	X	X	X	X	X				
Indonesia			X		X					
Iran	X	X	X	X	X	X	X	X		
Iraq	X		X		X					
Ireland	X	X	X	X	X		X	X	X	X
Israel	X		X		X				X	
Italy	X	X	X	X	X	X	X	X	X	X
Ivory Coast†	X		X		X				X	
Jamaica†	X				X					
Japan	X	X	X	X	X	X	X	X	X	
Jordan					X	X				
Kenya†	X				X					
Korea, South					X					
Lebanon	X		X		X	X			X	
Liberia†	X				X					
Libya	X	X	X	X	X	X				
Luxembourg	X	X	X	X	X	X	X	X	X	X
Malagasy Rep.†			X		X				X	
Malawi†					X					
Malaysia	X	X	X		X	X				
Mali†	X		X		X				X	
Malta†	X		X		X		X			
Mauritania†	X		X		X				X	
Mexico	X	X	X	X	X		X			
Morocco	X		X		X				X	X
Nauru	X		X		X				X	
Netherlands	X	X	X	X	X	X	X	X	X	X
New Zealand	X	X	X	X	X	X	X	X	X	X
Nicaragua	X	X	X	X	X	X	X			
Niger†	X		X		X				X	
Nigeria†	X		X		X					
Norway	X	X	X	X	X	X	X		X	X
Pakistan			X		X		X			
Panama	X	X	X	X	X	X	X			
Paraguay	X	X	X	X	X	X				
Peru	X	X	X	X	X	X				
Philippines	X		X		X					
Poland	X	X	X	X	X		X		X	X
Portugal	X	X	X	X	X		X		X	X
Romania	X	X	X	X	X		X		X	X
Rwanda†	X				X					
Saudi Arabia†	X				X					
Senegal†			X		X				X	
Sierra Leone†					X					
Singapore†	X		X		X					
Somalia†					X					
South Africa†	X	X	X		X		X	X	X	X
Spain	X	X	X	X	X	X	X	X	X	X
Sudan†					X					
Swaziland			X		X					
Sweden	X	X	X	X	X	X	X	X	X	X
Switzerland	X	X	X	X	X	X	X	X	X	X
Syria†	X				X					
Taiwan	X	X	X	X	X	X	X			
Tanzania†	X				X					
Thailand					X	X				
Togo†	X		X		X				X	
Trinidad and Tobago†	X				X					
Tunisia			X		X	X			X	X
Turkey	X	X	X	X	X	X	X			
Uganda†	X				X					
U.S.S.R.	X	X	X	X	X		X		X	X
U.A.R.	X	X	X	X	X	X	X			
United Kingdom	X	X	X	X	X	X	X	X	X	X
United States	X	X	X	X	X	X	X	X		
Upper Volta†			X		X				X	
Uruguay	X	X	X	X	X		X		X	X
Venezuela	X		X	X	X	X				
Vietnam, North	X		X		X				X	X
Vietnam, South			X		X				X	X
Western Samoa	X				X					
Yugoslavia	X	X	X	X	X	X	X	X	X	X
Zambia†	X				X					

*Data as of October 1969.
†Country not reported prior to 1964.

Source: U.S. Department of Health, Education, and Welfare, Social Security Administration, Office of Research and Statistics, *Social Security Programs Throughout the World.*

"TORONTO GLOBE AND MAIL"

About 250 students
and faculty members, led
by a group of mothers
carrying babies, occupy
the University of Toronto's
administration building,
March 25, 1970.
The students
wanted a commitment
from the university
on day-care centres
for infants.

Disability pensions, and benefits for the children of those entitled to them, became available in February 1970. To qualify for a disability pension to begin between 1970 and 1975, the applicant must be disabled and must have contributed to the plan during at least five of the years between 1966 and 1975. The pension in 1970 consisted of a flat-rate Can$26.53 a month, plus 75% of the current value of the retirement pension, calculated as though the recipient had reached 65 at the time he became disabled. At age 65 a disability pension would be automatically replaced by a retirement pension. Should a person die while receiving a disability pension, survivor's benefits would be payable to his widow and children.

United States. Pres. Richard Nixon's family assistance proposals were passed by the House of Representatives in 1970, but failed in the Senate despite considerable administration pressure. The proposals, introduced in 1969, would have brought about the first major reform of the U.S. public welfare system since the New Deal era of the 1930s. Basic to the plan was the controversial concept of a minimum income for all U.S. families, including those of the "working poor." A family of four with no employment or other form of income would receive a direct grant of $1,600 yearly and, if a member of the family entered employment, a diminishing portion of the grant could be kept until the family reached a predetermined income level. Any able-bodied person who refused training or a suitable job would lose his benefit. The principal opposition to the measure came from conservatives who felt that it would reduce incentives to work, although some liberals also opposed it on the ground that the benefits were too low. The increasingly militant organizations of welfare recipients also voiced objections, chiefly to the work-requirement provisions. The president announced that he would continue to push for passage of the legislation in 1971. Meanwhile, Daniel Moynihan, the presidential adviser who had been the plan's principal author, left the administration to return to the faculty of Harvard University.

Although generally supported by both the administration and Congress, social security amendments that would have increased cash benefits to recipients failed to pass when conferees from the House and Senate, which had approved somewhat different bills, were unable to compromise their differences before Congress adjourned. It was agreed that priority would be given to a new bill on the subject in the 1971 session.

Approximately 89 million people contributed to social security in 1968. About 95% of mothers and children were protected against risk of loss of income because of the death of the family breadwinner. Some 19 million persons were aged 65 or older at the end of 1968; this was about twice as many as at the end of 1940, and it was anticipated that the figure would reach 25 million by 1985. Approximately 90% of those reaching age 65 were entitled to benefits under the social security program, and practically all persons aged 65 or older were participating in Medicare.

In February 1970 about 342,000 individuals were awarded monthly cash benefits under the Old Age, Survivors, Disability, and Health Insurance (OASDHI) program. About 3,000 persons became entitled to the special benefits for those aged 72 and over, but the number of terminations and suspensions more than offset the number of new awards. Cash benefits were payable at the end of February to more than 25.5 million persons at a monthly cost of $2.2 billion—an increase of 837,000 beneficiaries and $105 million since February 1969. About two-thirds of the new beneficiaries were either retired or disabled workers. In February $25 million was distributed in lump sum payments on the earnings records of 104,-000 deceased workers.

The Social Security Administration received 495,-400 hospital admission notices and 38,200 admission notices for extended care facilities for the month of February. During that month $377.9 million was withdrawn from the hospital insurance trust fund for payments to hospitals, extended care facilities, and home health agencies providing services to beneficiaries. Social security records as of Feb. 6, 1970, showed that 2.8 million claims were approved under the hospital insurance program for the period July–November 1969. Covered days of care per inpatient hospital claim averaged 12.8 days in all hospitals, 12.5 days in short-stay hospitals, and 28.8 days in long-stay hospitals. The average amount reimbursed was $664 per inpatient hospital claim; $76 per home health claim; and $364 per extended care claim.

Expenditure on welfare was increased by a rise in the proportion of the working force that was unemployed. The largest increase was among young people between the ages of 16 and 24 years. Altogether, 4.6 million people (5.8%), out of a labour force of 78.7 million, were out of work in November. Unemployment among blacks was 8.8%, compared with 5.5% for whites.

Other Countries. In Latin America the development of social security in a number of countries was marked by pronounced disparities between the legal provisions applying to different categories of workers and by a proliferation of extremely diverse schemes and of the institutions administering them. In Brazil a basic plan of protection for rural workers against risks of sickness, old age, and disability was enacted; initially it affected only workers in the sugar industry but ultimately it would apply to all agricultural workers. Pension legislation in Costa Rica was reformed.

Social insurance coverage was extended in Cyprus. A social development board was established to coordinate the activities and policies of social welfare and social development and integrate them with overall economic planning, and to coordinate governmental and voluntary action. The Department of Social Welfare Services carried out a survey of the food consumption habits of public assistance recipients.

A report on "untouchability" in India was issued by a committee established by the government in 1965. It covered 65 million persons not belonging to castes. In Pakistan distress caused by widespread flooding continued to be a major problem. Floods in the East during August engulfed an area of 15,000 sq.mi. and affected ten million people, while a tidal wave in November, besides killing at least 200,000, put an estimated 3.3 million people in need of sustained relief. The World Bank agreed to set up a flood consulting group in East Pakistan to advise and assist on the flood problem as a whole. In connection with social services generally, the central government earmarked $2,880,000 to finance schemes for helping the handicapped. Benefit and pension rates were increased in Japan. In Malaysia a new social insurance scheme for invalidity and employment injury benefits was introduced. A retirement scheme was introduced in the Malagasy Republic including a compulsory old-age insurance scheme. Changes were made in the family allowance scheme in Dahomey.   (Jn. M.)

See also Education; Housing; Insurance; Medicine; Migration, International; Race Relations; Refugees.

Sociology

Perhaps the most notable event bearing on sociology in 1970 was the formidable challenge hurled by three British philosophers at the right of sociology to exist as a discipline. According to the philosophers, Peter Winch, A. R. Louch, and Alasdair MacIntyre, its weakness is threefold: sociologists are unable to offer definitive explanations of the differences between the social realities they claim to investigate and other types of realities; sociologists are mistakenly engaged in causal analyses because the concept of cause is applicable only in the natural world; and sociologists are seeking to establish universally applicable social theories by means of cross-cultural analysis, though such analysis cannot bear fruit because of the uniqueness of each society.

Answering these charges, Christopher G. A. Bryant of the University of Southampton noted that, while questions about the type of reality studied by sociologists are now much in the foreground, such problems are not unique to sociology but occur in some degree in all sciences. Further, the concept of cause has its place in many sociological areas: for example, in the study of social stratification, social class depends on occupation, which in turn depends on education, which in turn depends on opportunity to acquire education, etc. Finally, cross-cultural analyses, though difficult, are possible. While all societies have some unique aspects, they also have enough similarities to permit comparison.

Within the discipline, discussion continued between the "traditional" and the "new" sociologists. Traditional sociologists hold that social reality consists of highly stable patterns of behaviour based on consensual arrangements. This view had been criticized by Irving L. Horowitz as approaching an irrational admiration for "imaginary" periods of stability, and Horowitz' appointment as chairman of the department of sociology at Rutgers University was widely acclaimed as a victory for the new sociology. Cooler heads attempted to moderate the conflict. J. H. Robb, president of the Sociological Association of Australia and New Zealand, noted that the new sociology was becoming a vehicle for anti-American sentiment. Jan Szczepanski, president of the International Sociological Association, expressed regrets about the extent to which sociological theories had become pawns in ideological confrontations.

In Canada the influx of Americans led to an awakening of interest in the interrelations among migration, opportunity, and social class. Bernard Blishen of Trent University discovered that, in the Atlantic Provinces and Quebec, immigrants from the U.S., the U.K., and Germany were overrepresented in the three highest classes, while the Canadian born were underrepresented. A study of ethnic penetration into Toronto's elite structure by Merrijoy Kelner of the University of Toronto revealed that the small "core elite" was still almost entirely of Anglo-Saxon ancestry, although non-Anglo Saxons had moved into "strategic elites" as labour leaders, politicians, and academicians.

Concern about the nature of the "new morality" was reflected in Australian sociological research. In a study of premarital pregnancies and ex-nuptial births over a 55-year period, K. G. Basavarajappa of the Australian National University suggested that premarital conceptions had probably more often been a cause of marriages than a result of intercourse in anticipation of marriages already planned. In a critique of Basavarajappa's interpretation published in *The Australian and New Zealand Journal of Sociology,* Geraldine Spencer noted that, compared with 50 years ago, there were now far fewer marriages in which the bride was many months pregnant although confinements five to six months after marriage had become more frequent.

The Soviet sociologists A. S. Gromov, L. B. Gorikova, I. V. Krymskaia, and O. E. Chernetskii focused on the progress of women medical students. In the medical school at Rostov-on-Don, the grades of the women were higher on average than those of the men and, for the most part, the women were better prepared. The lapse of time between completion of secondary school and admission to medical school was usually shorter for the women and the material living conditions of most of the women students were better.   (J. E. McK.)

See also Anthropology; Psychology; Social Services.

Encyclopædia Britannica Films. *The Living City* (1953); *Man and His Culture* (1954); *Megalopolis—Cradle of the Future* (1962); *Population Ecology* (1964); *Operation Bootstrap* (1968); *Heritage in Black* (1969); *The House of Man, Part II—Our Crowded Environment* (1969); *Manuel from Puerto Rico* (1969); *Chicano from the Southwest* (1970); *Linda and Billy Ray from Appalachia* (1970).

THE LARGEST
MINORITY

By Eva Figes

JOHN OLSON, "LIFE" MAGAZINE © TIME INC.

On Aug. 10, 1970, the U.S. House of Representatives (10 women members out of 435) passed an amendment to the Constitution forbidding discrimination on account of sex. Some two weeks later, on August 26, a group of feminist organizations sponsored a nationwide women's strike, urging women to leave their housework and typewriters and demonstrate for equality. The Equal Rights Amendment faced a number of legislative hurdles before it could become law, and August 26 was observed more with rallies and speeches than with strike action. But there could be little doubt that, in the United States at least, women's liberation had become a major and militant movement. The note sounded a few years earlier by Simone de Beauvoir in *The Second Sex* and Betty Friedan in *The Feminine Mystique* had swelled to a full—if occasionally dissonant—chorus.

Noting the movement's sudden rise to prominence, some observers dismissed it as merely the latest in a long series of causes that had provided periodic rallying points for a restless generation. There was a perhaps understandable tendency for the media to concentrate on its more superficial (if symbolic) aspects—the campaign to eliminate brassieres as items of "male chauvinism," the attempts to desegregate men's bars, the hiring of a woman to hold for place kicks on a football team. In the early stages, at least, the eccentric revolutionaries of WITCH (Women's International Terrorist Conspiracy from Hell) received more headline space than the more sober middle-class members of NOW (National Organization for Women).

But in its larger aspects the movement was hardly new. The Equal Rights Amendment had been in committee for 22 years before the House finally passed it, and August 26 had been chosen as women's strike day because it was the 50th anniversary of another amendment (the 19th) that gave American women the right to vote. It was by no means confined to the United States, although its manifestations were undeniably more vocal and colourful there than elsewhere. At midsummer the *New York Times* reviewed rapidly expanding women's rights movements in eight Western European countries. *Time* magazine featured an article on the emergence of African women from tribalism, and in the Middle East Israeli women, descendants of the culture that had given the West its patriarchal tradition, served as soldiers, opposing Arab women guerrillas barely a generation removed from purdah. Nor was the movement superficial. Its roots lay in centuries of development toward

political democracy and in the industrialization and urbanization that had eroded woman's traditional role even while the prevailing social mores denied her a new one.

But Men Are More Equal than Others. The gradual democratization of Western societies during the last 200 years has, by and large, been based on the assumption that "all men are equal," or that men should at least be regarded as equal in the eyes of the law. Ever since J.-J. Rousseau's *Social Contract* appeared in 1762, political and social reformers have rejected the idea of a strictly stratified society and have been motivated by the concept of government by the people for the people as a whole, even if the reality often fell far short of the ideal. But women have never been regarded as equal or been included in the political ideal. Rousseau himself did not include women in the *Social Contract* and elsewhere advocated that they should be educated from birth to be the slaves of men. Marx and Engels were the first really influential political thinkers who did not regard women as merely the subordinate partners of men, and as a result the position of women in the Soviet Union is very different from that of women in most Western countries today, although even in Communist countries the reality does not match up to the official ideal. Fifty years after the Revolution Soviet working women still tend to occupy positions that are more subordinate or more poorly paid, and the lack of adequate childcare and other facilities means that they are often very overworked.

All the available evidence suggests that stereotyped attitudes to sex are more firmly embedded in the human mind than traditional attitudes to, say, race or social class. A man who may learn to accept that differences in skin colour are in themselves merely physical and superficial will find it much more difficult to take the same attitude to the physical differences between the sexes, and he is only rarely encouraged to do so anyhow. Centuries of sex role-playing reinforces the idea that men and women are basically different in character—almost different species—and that they should therefore be treated differently within the social framework. Inevitably the concept of "difference" brings with it implications of inferiority and superiority, and since societies have usually been male dominated, the female has been regarded as inferior. Thus medieval theologians argued that women had no soul and were more prone to sin, and later generations maintained that women were incapable of abstract thought, reasoning, creativity, or taking on the responsibilities of government.

The withholding from women of civil, political, and social rights, as these were gradually extended in Western societies, was justified on the grounds that the family should be regarded as the basic social unit, and throughout the 17th, 18th, and 19th centuries the family was commonly referred to as a microcosm of the state. The husband, it was argued, enjoyed his civil rights on behalf of his family, and this included his wife. On the question of female suffrage, for example, it was maintained that a woman voted "through" her husband. In 1910 one member of the British Parliament opposed a female suffrage bill on grounds which were by no means unusual:

> Innumerable unseen women will guard the entrance to those Division Lobbies tonight, and will be voting through us. It is now proposed, in addition, that they should have votes for themselves, thus practically having two votes, while we have none at all.

Similarly, Rousseau had argued that women had their own, peculiarly feminine rights, and were thus not entitled to usurp those of men into the bargain. These female rights boiled down to "contriving to be ordered to do what she wants."

As John Stuart Mill pointed out, this attitude has to be based on the erroneous assumption that all husbands are models of honour and rectitude. Without this hypocritical assumption, the idea of putting every woman at the legal and economic mercy of her husband could not be tolerated in a society that claimed to be democratic. But, justice apart, this is a system doomed to break down in all kinds of ways and for many differing reasons in a complex urban society. In the 19th century, for instance, agitation among middle-class women for women's rights largely stemmed from the fact that many women in this class were unable to find husbands, since many middle-class men could not afford the economic demands of maintaining a wife and family in the accepted Victorian manner. While her working-class sisters fulfilled the sexual needs of these men as prostitutes, or eked out a miserable existence in the sweatshops, these middle-class "female supernumeraries," as they were called, either had to work as governesses, a humiliating and badly paid form of employment, or to rely on the generosity of their relatives. With both specialized education and the professions closed to women, it is little wonder that the more enterprising turned to novel writing, a lucrative occupation in the 19th century.

The Closed World of Work. Since social and civil rights are closely related to real economic power, it is necessary to consider sexual roles in relation to work and earning power. The situation in a highly developed urban society is very different from that which is likely to exist in a primitive or mainly agrarian community. In such communities both men and women fulfill vital social functions, with mutual interdependence. To find anything approaching this state of affairs in Europe generally we have to go back to the Middle Ages, to an agricultural society of peasants and small craftsmen where the entire household was involved in earning and working for the family livelihood. Small-scale farming always does involve the whole family, and the medieval craftsman lived above his shop, so to speak, so that his wife was actively involved in the business and often took charge if her husband died. In addition, far more specialized skills were needed to run a home—besides cooking and child-rearing, being a housekeeper entailed spinning and weaving, sewing, baking, and brewing beer.

With a growth in industrialization and an increased use of capital came a radical change. After the invention of expensive machinery that had to be housed in special factories, many journeymen never became master craftsmen. All their lives they remained wage earners, and even if greater prosperity often meant that men earned enough to support themselves and their families, it also meant that wives became economically dependent. The gulf between women's work (mainly domestic) and men's work (mainly outside the home and wage-earning) became wider, and women gradually found themselves excluded from

the guilds. Any paid work that women were still able to do, such as spinning at home, was usually adequate for pin money but so badly paid that if they were widowed or otherwise left without male support they and their dependents frequently became paupers. From this time on, poor and uneducated women became a source of cheap, second-class labour, a situation later industrialists were to exploit by employing women in preference to men. Meanwhile, aristocratic and middle-class wives remained at home in comparative idleness, giving birth to ever larger families and cultivating the social graces.

The social position of women has improved gradually during the past 50 years. Women are now able to vote in most countries, and can theoretically concern themselves with politics—although 4% representation in the British House of Commons and 2% in the U.S. House of Representatives is a long way from being proportional. Marriage laws have become less one-sided, although a woman is still regarded as her husband's dependent for the purposes of taxation, pensions, and insurance while, as a housekeeper, she is not protected by the laws governing ordinary employment. Women also have more educational opportunities, although these are by no means equal at an advanced level. The proportion of men to women in universities is unsatisfactory, and women also find it difficult to get places in medical schools or to be accepted for industrial training.

Today the most serious area of remaining discrimination against women is in employment, and although many governments in the Western world are now trying to remedy this situation through legislation, the effect so far has been marginal. In the United States the Civil Rights Act of 1964 made job discrimination on grounds of sex illegal, but it took the U.S. government six years to invoke the act by prosecuting a major company, and it is possible that the act would never have been invoked at all were it not for the increasing "new feminist" militancy. On average, women's salaries in the U.S. were 42% below those of men.

In Europe the Treaty of Rome binds the member countries of the Common Market to introduce equal pay, but this principle on its own does little to improve the position of working women. For example, in the United Kingdom, where equal pay was not yet law, the average hourly earnings in June 1969 were 10s. 9.3d. for men and 6s. 2.0d. for women; in West Germany the average earnings per hour for the same period were DM. 5.56 for men and DM. 3.85 for women, only a very slightly better ratio in a country that claimed to have fulfilled its obligation to implement equal pay. These figures highlight the fact that the most serious aspect of the situation with regard to job discrimination is the selection of men for higher-paid and women for lower-paid jobs. Thus, in the most recent report on equal pay made to the EEC Commission, the West German government comments that equal pay for equal work is not the same as equal pay for equivalent work, and the French government admits a failure to remunerate female manual dexterity at the same rate as masculine muscular strength.

Great Britain was committed to the principle of equal pay by 1975. It seemed a long time to wait for such crudely elementary justice, and showed the extent to which women have been exploited, since employers claimed that to implement this principle any sooner would mean financial ruin. In actual fact, of course, a vast cheap labour force encourages the perpetuation of old-fashioned and wasteful production methods, and is therefore a hindrance to real productivity.

In contrast to the straightforward issue of equal pay, the problem of sex discrimination in job selection is a much more complex one, which cannot be solved by legislation alone. The only remedy is a change in social attitudes, and the problem is complicated by the fact that the attitude of employer and employee interact. Thus an employer may refuse to give a woman a responsible job on the ground that she is likely to leave when she gets married and starts a family, and the woman may do just that, for lack of incentive to go on working. Without a more

JACQUES BURLOT FROM LIAISON AGENCY

basic change in social attitudes to women at work, enforced where necessary by antidiscriminatory legislation, equal pay could simply result in a more total division between what is considered "men's" and "women's work," and could at times result in a high rate of female unemployment.

Looked at in historical perspective, it is clear that women have been allowed to infiltrate professional and semiskilled occupations only as these became less attractive to men in terms of remuneration and social status. Secretarial work is the outstanding example, and it is significant that a secretary remains at that subordinate level—she would rarely if ever be considered an apprentice for promotion to management. Nursing and schoolteaching are also skilled but badly paid professions, particularly nursing, which has become an almost exclusively female occupation. In teaching, we see far more women at the lower-paid levels, such as primary school teaching, with very few women attaining administrative posts at the secondary school level. In medicine, it is very rare for a woman to reach consultancy level. In industry, employers refuse to give further training to women graduates with arts degrees, and the great majority of these women find themselves having to work as secretaries.

The Search for New Attitudes. It is discrimination at the higher levels of employment that has provoked the most vociferous and militant feminist reaction at the present time, combined with the fact that many women feel society does not do enough to help the woman who, out of inclination or necessity, has to fulfill what is regarded as specifically *her* dual role. The simple reason for this is that the educated women who find themselves discriminated against in this way are also the most articulate and the most aware, socially and politically. The generation of educated women who grew up during World War II were restrained from militancy, not only because they formed a much smaller minority but because at the time it was fashionable to emphasize the importance of continuous personal contact between a mother and her young children. A reaction to war-

time conditions also helped to enhance the attractions of family life. But attitudes to family bonds have changed considerably since then, and the people most responsible for changing them are the young adults who were brought up as "Spock babies" by the wartime generation. So the ranks of angry young women are swelled by middle-aged, now redundant mothers who have come to feel that too large a personal sacrifice was demanded of them for those short years of active motherhood, and that they have been cheated of any hope of realizing other ambitions in their middle age.

Two factors are responsible for the particularly rapid growth of feminist militancy in the United States. On the one hand, the gap between male and female roles is particularly wide in the U.S. On the other, the feminist movement is related to a more general mood of political militancy. In this respect it is interesting to note that many of the women's liberationist organizations came into being because women who joined radical and even revolutionary organizations found that there was just as much sexual discrimination within these organizations as in the larger society that they were trying to change. They were simply being used in the age-old way, as handy camp followers.

Many of the new feminist organizations that have recently sprung up in the United States and are beginning to take root in Western Europe are not only concerned with discrimination against women but are trying to promote a totally new concept of male and female roles within society—advocating, in fact, that the whole idea of separate male and female roles should be abandoned. On the one hand women should be able to get out of the home to take an active part in the outside world, and on the other a man should be able to spend less time working and thus be able to take his share in caring for and enjoying his children.

Women's organizations have been as much concerned with the social amenities needed to make it possible for a woman to work outside the home as with the more direct issue of job discrimination and fiscal disincentives. Nursery schools are undoubtedly at the top of the list of priorities, but there is also an awareness that we need different living conditions. The problem of the "captive wife," isolated in a suburban house—probably in a new housing development—with no relatives or friends nearby, has received a good deal of attention in the past few years. Undoubtedly we need a concept of housing which will allow a woman with young children more freedom of movement and action, communities designed to alleviate the practical problems of shopping, cooking, and childminding, and a system of public transport designed for women and children as well as men going into town to work—in other words interresidential transport. Today many young women dream of a home of their own, away from overcrowded slums, out of the reach of interfering parents and in-laws, in which to start their married lives, and this hope is encouraged by manufacturers of consumer goods and by the women's magazines that advertise them. Once the dream is realized, the young woman is liable to find herself trapped inside it, and the interfering mother or mother-in-law who might have acted as babysitter is out of reach.

More than any other factor, reliable birth control has changed the life of modern women, but social organization has failed to keep pace with their suddenly enlarged hopes, choices, and expectations. The choice between marriage and a career, so clear-cut even a generation ago and often so heartbreaking to a woman of intelligence and ambition, is no longer an actual one. In spite of the numerous practical obstacles that still stand in her path, a woman today can obviously have the best of both worlds, and it seems no more than her birthright that she should. Once society has made the necessary, and, on the whole, rather minor adjustments needed to smooth her path, society will surely find itself richly rewarded, not only in terms of increased productivity and national wealth but in terms of general human happiness. And, since no man is an island, this will benefit everybody—men, women, and children.

Somalia

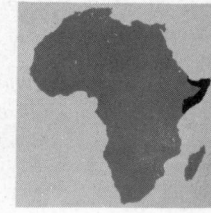

A republic of northeast Africa, the Somali Democratic Republic, or Somalia, is bounded by the Gulf of Aden, the Indian Ocean, Kenya, Ethiopia, and the French Territory of the Afars and Issas. Area: 246,155 sq.mi. (637,541 sq.km.). Pop. (1969 est.): 2,730,000, predominantly Hamitic, with Arabic and other admixtures. Cap. and largest city: Mogadiscio (pop., 1969 est., 200,000). Language: Cushitic Somali with some Arabic influence. Religion: orthodox Muslim. President of the Supreme Revolutionary Council in 1970, Maj. Gen. Muhammad Siyad Barrah.

In 1970 the Supreme Revolutionary Council (SRC) remained in control of Somalia and no date was fixed for the promised elections. On April 27 it was announced that a "counterrevolutionary plot" had been foiled. Among those arrested was the first vice-chairman of the SRC, Maj. Gen. Jama Ali Qorshel, minister of the interior, who was dismissed from the government and charged with treason. The announcement alleged that the plotters intended to provoke an attack from Ethiopia and to use this as a pretext for calling in foreign forces.

Major General Siyad announced in May that certain large foreign-owned firms, including banks and oil companies, would be nationalized. This decision mainly affected Italian interests. Early in June Siyad announced that the U.S. government had suspended all aid to Somalia because of the SRC's trade relations with North Vietnam.

During 1970 the SRC concentrated on "crash programs" to improve agriculture and animal husbandry and to relieve unemployment. In September reductions in the salaries of public and private employees were announced, and rents and prices of essential commodities were fixed by law.

On October 8 the National Security Court in Mog-

adiscio passed a death sentence on Yusuf Ismail, accused of assassinating Pres. Abd-i-Rashid Ali Shermarke on Oct. 15, 1969. Ismail had been working as a security guard for the president. (V. R. Lu.)

South Africa

A republic occupying the southern tip of Africa, South Africa is bounded by South West Africa, Botswana, Rhodesia, Mozambique, and Swaziland. Lesotho forms an enclave within South African territory. Area: 471,445 sq.mi. (1,221,037 sq.km.), excluding Walvis Bay, 372 sq.mi. Pop. (1970): 21,282,000, including Bantu 69.9%; white 17.8%; Coloured 9.4%; Asian 2.9%. Administrative cap.: Pretoria (metro. pop., 1967 est., 523,000); judicial cap.: Bloemfontein (pop., 1967 est., 197,000); legislative cap.: Cape Town (metro. pop., 1967 est., 758,000). Largest city: Johannesburg (metro. pop., 1967 est., 1,309,000). Language: Afrikaans and English. Religion: mainly Christian. State president in 1970, Jacobus J. Fouché; prime minister, Balthazar J. Vorster.

Domestic Affairs. A parliamentary general election was held, a year early, on April 22, 1970, following the formation of the right-wing Herstigte Nasionale Party (HNP, literally Reconstituted National Party) by a dissident Nationalist group under the leadership of Albert Hertzog (*see* BIOGRAPHY), a former Cabinet minister who was expelled from the ruling National Party in 1969. The result of the election for the House of Assembly was: National Party, 117 seats; United Party, 47; Progressive Party, 1. On balance the National Party lost nine seats to the United Party. The 80 HNP candidates were defeated in all the constituencies they contested. The Progressives retained their one seat in Johannesburg, where Helen Suzman (*see* BIOGRAPHY) was reelected. In South West Africa (Namibia) the six seats in the House of Assembly were retained by the National Party.

On October 28 elections took place for the provincial councils in all four provinces. In the overall results the United Party gained 9 seats from the Nationalists, who remained in control of the councils in the Cape, the Transvaal, and the Orange Free State (where they retained all 25 seats). In Natal the United Party increased its previous majority. Neither the Progressives nor the HNP was represented in the provincial councils. A new national Senate was also elected, in which the United Party increased its strength as a result of its gains in parliamentary and provincial elections.

Cabinet changes after the parliamentary election included the appointment of S. L. Muller as minister of economic affairs to succeed J. F. T. Haak, who resigned; J. J. Loots as minister of planning and Coloured affairs; and M. Viljoen as minister of labour and of the interior. T. J. A. Gerdener, administrator of Natal, was appointed deputy minister of Bantu development. New administrators were designated in the Cape Province, Natal, and the Orange Free State.

In July Prime Minister Vorster announced that scientists of the Atomic Energy Board, headed by A. J. A. Roux, had developed a new process for the production of enriched uranium at the Pelindaba nuclear energy centre, at a cost much cheaper than that of any other plants in the Western world. A uranium enrichment corporation costing R 50 million was established. Plans were made for the erection of a nuclear power station near Cape Town.

Soil Conservation:
see Conservation

Sorghum Grains:
see Agriculture

SOMALIA
Education. (1966–67) Primary, pupils 29,043, teachers 973; secondary, pupils 10,250, teachers 510; vocational, pupils 2,093, teachers 135; teacher training, students 476, teachers 61; higher (at University Institute of Somalia; 1965–66), students 791, teaching staff 23.

Finance. Monetary unit: Somali shilling, with a par value of 7.14 Somali shillings to U.S. $1 (17.14 Somali shillings = £1 sterling). Budget (1970 est.) balanced at 409,495,000 Somali shillings. Money supply: (May 1970) 266.6 million Somali shillings; (May 1969) 268.2 million Somali shillings. Cost of living (Mogadiscio; 1963 = 100): (Jan. 1970) 136; (Jan. 1969) 128.

Foreign Trade. (1968) Imports 339.8 million Somali shillings; exports 212 million Somali shillings. Import sources: Italy 33%; Japan 10%; U.S. 10%; U.K. 7%; U.S.S.R. 6%; West Germany 6%. Export destinations: Saudi Arabia 50%; Italy 31%; Southern Yemen 13%. Main exports: livestock 59%; bananas 28%; hides and skins 6%.

Transport and Communications. Roads (1969) 13,396 km. Motor vehicles in use (1968): passenger 5,900; commercial 8,000. There are no railways. Shipping (1969): merchant vessels 100 gross tons and over 58; gross tonnage 295,049. Telephones (Jan. 1969) c. 4,800. Radio receivers (Dec. 1967) 40,000.

Agriculture. Production (in 000; metric tons; 1968; 1967 in parentheses): bananas c. 190 (184); millet and sorghum c. 67 (c. 62); cassava c. 23 (c. 20). Livestock (in 000; 1967–68): cattle c. 1,935; sheep c. 4,400; goats c. 4,050; camels c. 2,300.

LONDON "DAILY EXPRESS"
FROM PICTORIAL PARADE

The Hendrik Verwoerd Dam, under construction on the Orange River at Norvalspont, S.Af., is part of a £265 million project including two more large dams, nine smaller ones, and 20 hydroelectric power stations. The entire project was scheduled to take 30 years to complete.

Minister of Defense P. W. Botha announced that the defense forces had been strengthened by the acquisition of more coastal craft, helicopters, and a replenishment vessel; the establishment of a submarine base to accommodate three submarines commissioned in France; and the opening of new maritime headquarters at the Cape. The reconstructed naval base at Durban was scheduled to be operational in 1971. Estimated defense expenditure in 1970 was R 250 million, a cut of R 14 million from the previous year. It was announced in November 1969 that the Air Force would be reorganized into four commands.

An oil drilling program costing R 17 million and covering 900 mi. of coastline from Cape Agulhas to the Tugela River, Natal, was launched by the government-subsidized Southern Oil Exploration Corporation. A strike of gas, the second, was made at Plettenburg Bay in the eastern Cape. An offshore oil pipeline costing R 20 million was completed at Durban to serve the largest oil tankers. At Sasolburg, the oil-from-coal centre in the Transvaal, an R 50 million oil refinery was built and was scheduled to become operational early in 1971. A government commission was appointed to investigate South Africa's coal resources. The first steps were taken for the erection of what was claimed to be the largest thermal power station in the Southern Hemisphere, at Kriel in the eastern Transvaal. Development of a new platinum mine began in Transvaal.

The minister of transport, B. J. Schoeman, in July announced a new harbour, to be built by the Iron and Steel Corporation (Iscor) at Saldanha Bay, Cape, for the mass export of iron ore, and also a new railway to service it. Negotiations began with Japan for long-term iron-ore sales. Schoeman also announced a new international airport to be constructed near Durban.

Race Relations. Measures for expediting the development of the Bantu homelands were announced by the minister of Bantu administration and development, M. C. Botha, including further special concessions for the establishment of factories on an agency basis, agricultural development, facilities in the white areas bordering the homelands for training Bantu to work in their own areas, and more responsibility for homelands authorities in economic development. Transport services were to be instituted that would enable Bantu workers in white areas to visit their families frequently.

A program for preventive, rehabilitative, and curative health facilities and services in the Bantu homelands was announced by the minister of health, C. de Wet. An economic committee of the Bantu Affairs Commission was set up to advise the government on speeding up homelands development. Official statements indicated that the way to independence for the homelands would not be barred if they desired it and if suitable conditions existed.

The Supreme Court in February acquitted 22 Bantu, charged under the Suppression of Communism Act, but they were then immediately placed under indefinite detention. This led to a series of protests and demonstrations. Most of the detainees were later brought to trial under the Terrorism Act but were discharged on the ground that the charges against them were similar to those heard in the earlier trial. Shortly after their second acquittal and while an appeal by the state was pending, restrictive banning orders were served on them and two were placed under house arrest, including Winifred Mandela, whose husband, Nelson Mandela, a former African National Congress leader, was serving a life sentence under the Suppression of Communism Act. B. Ramotse, who had been tried with the others but had not been acquitted, was found guilty under the Ter-

SOUTH AFRICA

Education. (1967) European: primary, secondary, and vocational, pupils 793,189, teachers 33,-235; teacher training, students 9,985, teachers 772; higher (1966), students 44,184, teaching staff 8,013. African: primary, secondary, and vocational, pupils 2,853,837, teachers 59,000; teacher training, students 8,173; higher (1966), students 4,218, teaching staff 398.

Finance. Monetary unit: rand, with a par value of R 0.71 to U.S. $1 (R 1.71 = £1 sterling). Gold, SDRs, and foreign exchange, official: (June 1970) U.S. $1,271,000,000; (June 1969) U.S. $1,557,000,000. Budget (1969–70 rev. est.): revenue R 1,661,800,000; expenditure R 1,700,-442,000. Gross national product: (1969) R 11,-351,000,000; (1968) R 10,122,000,000. Money supply: (June 1970) R 2,176,000,000; (June 1969) R 2,095,000,000. Cost of living (1963 = 100): (May 1970) 125; (May 1969) 119.

Foreign Trade. (1969) Imports R 2,137,200,-000; exports (excluding gold) R 1,532,700,000 (outflow of gold R 847 million). Import sources: U.K. 23%; U.S. 17%; West Germany 14%; Japan 9%. Export destinations (excluding gold): U.K. 33%; Japan 10%; U.S. 7%; West Germany 7%. Main exports: diamonds 14%; fruit and vegetables 8%; wool 8%; copper 7%; iron and steel 7%; metal ores 5%.

Transport and Communications. Roads (1968) c. 320,000 km. (including c. 12,000 km. main roads). Motor vehicles in use (1968): passenger 1,405,000; commercial 343,000. Railways (1969): 19,798 km. (excluding South West Africa; 2,340 km.); freight traffic (including South West Africa; 1969) 53,018,000,000 net ton-km. Air traffic (1969): 2,168,000,000 passenger-km.; freight 59.3 million net ton-km. Shipping (1969): merchant vessels 100 gross tons and over 241; gross tonnage 498,743. Telephones (Dec. 1968) 1,397,725. Radio receivers (Dec. 1967) 2.7 million.

Agriculture. Production (in 000; metric tons; 1969; 1968 in parentheses): corn (on farms and estates only) 4,799 (5,171); wheat (on farms and estates only) 1,216 (1,270); sorghum (1968) 207, (1967) 844; oats 146 (148); peanuts 361 (227); sunflower seed 94 (86); potatoes 776 (503); sugar, raw value (1969–70) c. 1,615, (1968–69) 1,505; oranges (1968) c. 509, (1967) c. 503; apples (1968) c. 225, (1967) c. 177; wine (1968) c. 481, (1967) 420; tobacco 38 (38); wool (1968) 71, (1967) 68; meat (1968) 570, (1967) 558; milk (1968) c. 2,650, (1967) c. 2,620; fish catch (1968) 1,133, (1967) 905. Livestock (in 000; June 1969): cattle c. 11,700; sheep c. 39,000; horses c. 460; pigs c. 1,800; goats (Aug. 1968) c. 5,450; chickens (on farms and estates; Aug. 1969) c. 12,000.

Industry. Index of manufacturing production (1963 = 100): (1969) 151; (1968) 137. Fuel and power (in 000; 1969): coal (metric tons) 52,293; electricity (kw.-hr.) 44,233,000. Production (in 000; metric tons; 1969): cement 5,104; iron ore (60–65% metal content) 8,787; pig iron 4,356; crude steel 4,628; copper ore (metal content) 126; asbestos (1968) 236; chrome ore (oxide content; 1968) 516; antimony concentrate (metal content; 1968) 17; manganese ore (metal content; 1968) 936; gold (troy oz.) 31,276; diamonds (metric carats) 7,863; fish meal (1968) 256.

rorism Act and sentenced to 15 years' imprisonment. In his defense it was alleged that he had been arrested on Botswana territory.

The government ruled that in practice the Chinese community, some 8,000, would receive across-the-board exemptions from restrictions on access to public facilities open to whites. (*See* RACE RELATIONS.)

Foreign Affairs. The UN Security Council in 1970 decided to seek the World Court's opinion on the legal consequences of South Africa's continued presence in South West Africa (Namibia). The South African government said it would defend its case.

The UN General Assembly, at its 1969 and 1970 sessions, called on member states to break off relations with South Africa and Rhodesia because of their racial policies. A Security Council resolution also requested member states to bar unconditionally the sale of arms to the republic. In July the newly elected Conservative Party government in the U.K. stated that it would consider resuming the sale of arms to South Africa for defense of the Cape sea route under the Simonstown agreement, in view of the growing Soviet naval presence in the Indian Ocean. This statement caused considerable protest, especially in the black African nations. Vorster announced in September that South Africa was prepared to negotiate non-aggression pacts with other southern African states, in answer to the charge that it was planning to attack its neighbours.

By a decision of the International Olympic Committee in May, South Africa was excluded from future Olympic Games, again because of its racial policies. During the year it was also excluded from various other international sports organizations and in some cases withdrew voluntarily to avoid expulsion. A proposed cricket tour of the U.K. by a South African team was canceled at the 11th hour on racial grounds.

The Economy. The budget, presented on August 20 by Minister of Finance N. J. Diederichs, was designed to rectify the imbalance in fixed investment and encourage investment in private manufacturing industries and exports. Domestic consumption had increased too rapidly, stimulated by a relaxation in import controls, and personal savings had fallen. Inflation continued to be a problem, and there were stresses and strains in the banking and monetary systems. Inflationary pressures increased in the second half of the year, with a high degree of consumer spending and of imports. Measures were taken to encourage savings, and the banks and other financial institutions were freed from ceiling limits on interest rates. These moves were balanced by a government subsidy on certain categories of mortgage bonds to relieve the interest burden on owners of smaller houses. Among tax measures, the individual loan levy on incomes was doubled, the sales duty on luxuries was raised, and a number of new items were added to the list of goods on which duties could be imposed. Exporters and manufacturers were given increased tax allowances, and assistance was granted to farmers hit by prolonged drought.

In the first seven months of the year the deficit in the balance of payments, mainly due to the high level of imports, rose to R 514 million, and was running at the annual rate of R 880 million. In October the gold and foreign exchange reserves stood at R 800 million (including R 632 million gold holdings), compared with R 914 million the year before. South Africa reached an agreement in December 1969 with the International Monetary Fund, giving it the right

BEN ROTH AGENCY

"They're not for internal use, but merely to protect South African cricket teams travelling abroad" —Waite, London "Daily Mirror."

to sell gold to the IMF whenever the free market price fell below the official price of $35 an ounce, and to sell such gold as was needed to finance an overall South African balance of payments deficit. South Africa could also sell gold to obtain foreign exchange to buy Special Drawing Rights (SDRs) or for some other Fund-related transactions. The effect of the agreement and of various other international factors was to stimulate the sale of gold to both the IMF and the free market. (L. H.)

ENCYCLOPÆDIA BRITANNICA FILMS. *The Republic of South Africa* (1963).

Southeast Asia

What the Indonesian foreign minister was to call "the most crucial year for Southeast Asia" started with a deceptive calm. On New Year's Day the U.S. vice-president, Spiro Agnew, was in Vietnam, and that seemed about the most exciting event in the region at the time. In a way it also foreshadowed what Southeast Asian countries were expecting for most of the year—continuing efforts by the U.S. to pull out of the region; a sustained Western campaign to reassure Asian allies of future military backing; further maneuvers in the so-called Indian Ocean power vacuum; and a scramble for leverage by Southeast Asian governments themselves in the emerging era of "Asian solutions for Asian problems."

The mood changed with dramatic suddenness following the change of government in Cambodia in March. Communist regimes in the region quickly realized that they were faced with an entirely new situation. Anti-Communist governments saw new serious threats to their own security. Nonaligned elements discovered that, instead of whimpering to a close, the Indochina conflagration was now spreading. All of them had the same instinctive reaction: to get more directly into the act and try to influence the situation more effectively than in the past. For most of the year thereafter, the war and peace issues of Indochina were to be a major preoccupation with Southeast Asian governments.

Communist Summit Meeting. The Communists, already involved in the fighting, were the first to meet for discussions. Their high-level attempt at coordinating their efforts gave an air of urgency to the deliberations of the non-Communist leaders that were

South Arabia: *see* Southern Yemen

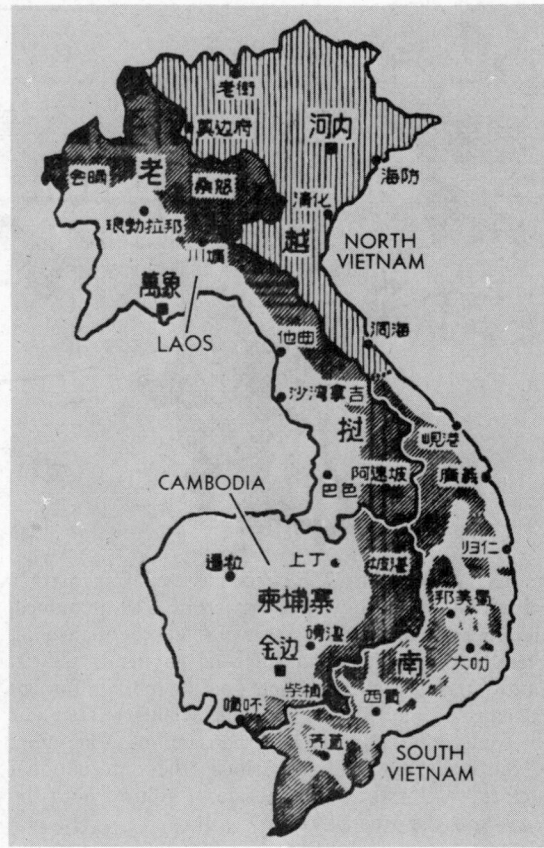

The dark shadings on this map published in the May 1970 issue of "Ta Kong Pao," a major Chinese Communist newspaper, represent areas "liberated" by Communist troops. Washington officials viewed the South Vietnam shadings as highly exaggerated.

A South Vietnamese armoured column moves past a Cambodian Army checkpoint in the heavily damaged town of Tonle Bet in June 1970.

WIDE WORLD

soon to follow. The Communist get-together was in the form of a unique Indochinese summit conference on April 24–25. The exact location was never announced; it was believed to have been somewhere on the China-Vietnam border. The summit was organized in the name of Prince Norodom Sihanouk (*see* BIOGRAPHY), but there was little doubt that the controlling hands were those of Peking and Hanoi. The importance the Communists attached to the conference was clear from the strength of their delegations. Besides Sihanouk, the North Vietnamese premier Pham Van Dong, the Pathet Lao leader Prince Souphanouvong, and Nguyen Huu Tho, chairman of the South Vietnamese Consultative Council of the Provisional Revolutionary Government, addressed the conference. China did not officially participate, but Premier Chou En-lai was present to host a banquet for the leaders.

Perhaps the most important political aspect of the Indochinese summit was the emphasis laid on the responsibility of each country for its own future. The official communiqué said that "the liberation and defense of each country are the business of its people"; one country would go to the help of another only on the basis of "the desire of the party concerned and mutual respect." This was considered a victory for the particular line that North Vietnam had been advocating—that "volunteers" from outside Indochina should not fight there and that within the peninsula each country should be allowed to develop according to its own desires. Outwardly, the summit's insistence on the obligation to refrain from interfering in one another's internal affairs seemed to promise complete autonomy to the different countries. But diplomatic circles were inclined to believe that, in fact, this line was intended to keep China from exerting too much influence in Hanoi's "natural sphere of influence."

Jakarta Conference. In contrast to the smooth Communist summit, the non-Communist governments found both the organization of a conference and the formulation of a common stand difficult. The idea that they should make a unified move for peace in Indochina found its greatest supporter in Adam Malik, Indonesia's foreign minister. For some time past he had been trying to organize a Southeast Asian initiative to bring peace to Vietnam. He and other foreign ministers of the region happened to meet in Manila in April to attend a "One Asia Assembly" sponsored by the Press Foundation of Asia. The crisis in Cambodia figured prominently in their discussions, and a decision was informally made to organize a foreign ministers' conference aimed at finding a solution to the conflict.

Dissensions began as soon as invitations went out to 21 countries. The Chinese government, one of those invited, vehemently denounced the idea and persuaded its allies to boycott the conference. Countries within the Soviet sphere of influence also boycotted it. The crippling blow was the decision of nonaligned countries —India, Pakistan, Ceylon, Burma—to decline the invitation on the ground that they would prefer to be associated with an exclusive conference of nonaligned Asian countries. Eventually only 11 countries participated in the Jakarta conference, including Australia, New Zealand, and South Vietnam. The new Cambodian government was also invited, but at the last moment its status was reduced from participant to "special guest by invitation." The meeting took place on May 16–17.

As soon as it opened, the conference found it necessary to lower its sights, for sharp divisions rose over the question of arms and troop supplies to the Cambodian government. The subsequent shelving of the proposal and the decision to "take the road of a negotiated settlement" helped produce a consensus and a ten-point communiqué calling for Cambodian neutrality, withdrawal of foreign troops, and reactivation of the International Control Commission on Cambodia. Apart from a spate of headlines, nothing concrete came out of the Jakarta conference as far as Indochina was concerned. It was nevertheless of considerable political interest in that it was the first time that members of the Association of Southeast Asian Nations (ASEAN) had made a concerted effort to play an active diplomatic role in regional politics.

ASEAN and SEATO. ASEAN, whose members were Malaysia, Singapore, Indonesia, Thailand, and the Philippines, had started moving in this direction before Cambodia became a war zone. In late 1969 Adam Malik proposed inviting representatives of the participants in the Vietnam conflict to the ASEAN ministerial conference in December. Malik, anxious to make ASEAN a mediator at the Paris peace talks, suggested inviting both North Vietnam and the Viet Cong. He was not against asking South Vietnam, but, in the idiom of nonalignment, he held the view that expansion of ASEAN membership, as and when it came, should be so carried out as to avoid an ideological cast. Invitations to the Communists, in the meantime, were intended to put ASEAN on record as a friendly, nonideological regional bloc.

But Malik was plowing a lonely furrow. The government of Malaysia, the host of the ASEAN conference, was against inviting Communists. Singapore's leaders opposed any move that would extend ASEAN's commitments beyond the economic field. Eventually, the ASEAN meeting at Malaysia's Cameron Highlands ended by inviting only South Vietnam and Laos. The invitations were said to have been unilaterally decided upon by the Malaysian prime minister, Tunku Abdul Rahman, and there were indications that the association, as a body, was embarrassed by them.

It was noteworthy that Rahman himself had earlier taken the initiative in rejecting a suggestion that Australia and New Zealand be invited to join the association. Australian commentators criticized this on the ground that the rejection raised important questions about Australia's will and capacity to play a regional role.

Meanwhile, ASEAN's principal business of promoting economic cooperation in the region kept its uneven pace. The December 1969 ministerial meeting made two specific decisions: to establish a M$15 million ASEAN Fund, and to pay special attention to cooperation in the field of mass communications. The fund, to be created by an equal contribution from each country, was to finance common projects which the ASEAN standing committee would identify. Communications suggestions included broadcasts, film festivals, joint film productions, and seminars on art, literature, the press, and sports. Meanwhile, there was no more progress on specific projects in 1970 than in any previous year.

The other regional alliance, the Southeast Asia Treaty Organization (SEATO), held its 1970 council meeting in Manila in July. It found the Thai government in a highly critical mood. Thailand's foreign minister pledged continued support to the organization, but attacked "the weakening resolve in some quarters" to live up to SEATO obligations and added: "I know SEATO better than to expect collective action against Communist threats." The Thai deputy foreign minister, Sanga Kittikachorn, went so far as to suggest the formation of a new and more effective regional pact in Southeast Asia to take the place of SEATO. The Thai criticism was indicative of some member states' concern over proposed U.S. military disengagement from the region. They seemed unimpressed by U.S. Secretary of State William Rogers' strong reaffirmation at Manila that SEATO was part of "the Nixon doctrine" for Asia and that the U.S. stood fully committed to it. The only announcement that produced some enthusiasm came from Britain's new Conservative government, which said that it would maintain a military presence in the Malaysia-Singapore area beyond 1971, the time set by the previous Labour government for the withdrawal of British forces from the region. If the council meeting produced no evidence of badly needed solidarity among SEATO members, it opened no new fissures either. The best summing up seemed to be the Australian foreign minister's remark that the meeting had dispelled fears of the organization's early demise.

Other Regional Alliances. As SEATO continued its languid existence, there was some new animation in other areas connected with regional defense. During the thick of the Cambodian fighting, South Vietnam projected the idea of an Indochinese anti-Communist defense alliance. In July representatives of South Vietnam and Thailand held talks in Bangkok and agreed that they "might" have to organize a military alliance with Cambodia and Laos, for common protection against future Communist aggression. However, in the briefing given to reporters by the Thai foreign minister, it was significantly emphasized that such an alliance was "a matter for future considera-

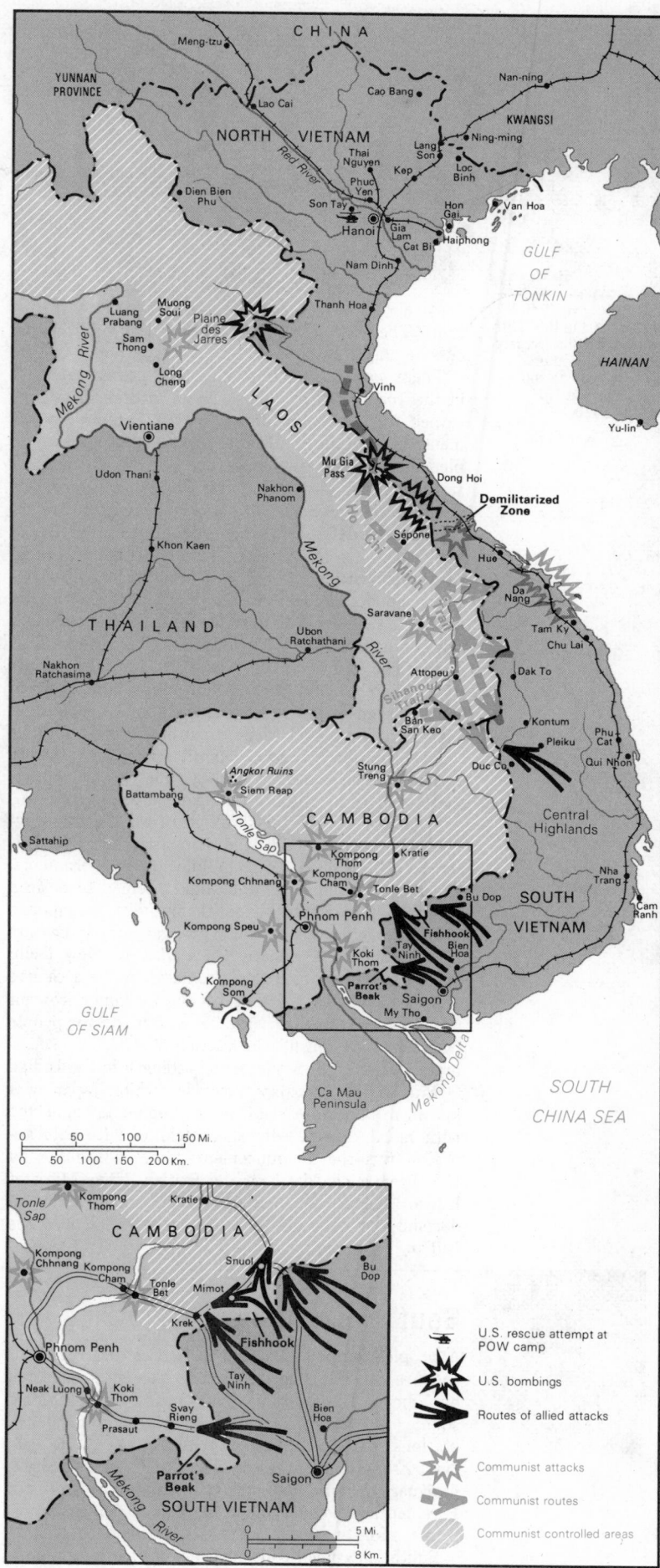

U.S. rescue attempt at POW camp

U.S. bombings

Routes of allied attacks

Communist attacks

Communist routes

Communist controlled areas

Soldiers of the U.S. 25th Infantry Division prepare to board helicopters for a combat assault into Cambodia in May 1970.

WIDE WORLD

tion." The proposal hardly progressed beyond the discussion stage.

There was more action over the "power vacuum" in the Indian Ocean. Those Asian leaders most concerned welcomed the defeat of the Labour government in Britain in June; the Conservatives had pledged themselves to maintain the British military status quo in the area. After assuming power, the Conservative government adopted the policy of working out new defense arrangements for Southeast Asia while allowing the diminishing of British forces to continue. Visiting the region a month after the Conservative victory, Defense Secretary Lord Carrington said that the new arrangements with Malaysia, Singapore, Australia, and New Zealand would be worked out by the end of 1970 or early 1971. The principle of partnership and consultation suited the changed mood, as government leaders in both Malaysia and Singapore were said to be unenthusiastic about ties with Britain by treaty commitments; they would rather be assured of help to "buy time" toward a pragmatic and comfortable buildup of expenditure.

What lay behind the thinking of all the five governments was evidently the demonstrated Soviet interest in the Indian Ocean. While some governments, like those of Indonesia and India, seemed to be in a mood to let events shape themselves, Singapore's prime minister, Lee Kuan Yew, gave an indication of the concern elsewhere. On a visit to New Delhi in September, he said that problems in the area had arisen because of Britain's premature announcement of a pullout together with "moves made by people who feel they can fill the vacuum." Pressed to elaborate, he said that Soviet naval strength in the Indian Ocean would probably increase, while Japan was known to keep abreast of all developments connected with naval design. Almost coinciding with this appraisal was the announcement made in London by U.S. Pres. Richard Nixon and British Prime Minister Edward Heath that their two governments would undertake a joint study of Soviet penetration into the Indian Ocean region.   (T. J. S. G.)

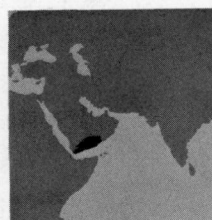

Southern Yemen

A people's republic in the southern coastal region of the Arabian Peninsula, Southern Yemen is bordered by Yemen, Saudi Arabia, and Oman. Area: 112,000 sq.mi. (290,000 sq.km.). Pop. (1968 est.): 1,369,500. National cap. and largest city: Aden (pop., 1968 est., 300,000); administrative cap.: Madinat ash Sha'b. Language: Arabic. Religion: Muslim. Chairman of the Presidential Council in 1970, Salem Ali Rubayyi; prime minister, Muhammad Ali Haitham.

Southern Yemen continued to face acute economic

difficulties and internal dissension in 1970. In January leading members of the Muslim Brotherhood were arrested and charged with conspiracy. On March 11 the government claimed to have forestalled a reactionary coup backed by Saudi Arabia and the U.S. and led by a former governor of the Fifth (Eastern) Governorate. A score of prominent army officers and civilians were arrested; eight were charged with treason before a newly established People's Court, and seven of them were executed on March 20. Further arrests took place from March 30 through April 1, including former president Qahtan al-Shaabi and former prime minister Faisal Abdul Latif. On April 3 it was announced that Latif had been shot while attempting to escape.

The government's foreign policy remained hostile toward the U.S. and Saudi Arabia and friendly toward the Communist countries. President Rubayyi visited China in August. On August 2 the government rejected the U.S. peace plan for the Middle East. There were widespread reports of a Soviet naval base and arms depot established on the Southern Yemeni island of Socotra, 500 mi. from Aden. Relations with the Yemen Arab Republic improved during 1970.

A draft constitution approved by the ruling National Liberation Front and published on August 2 referred to Southern Yemen as a "popular democratic republic" with Islam as its religion. Coming into effect on November 30, it provided for free and direct elections to a 101-member People's Supreme Council, to be held before November 1971. On November 30 the country was officially named the People's Democratic Republic of Yemen.   (P. MD.)

SOUTHERN YEMEN
Education. (1967–68) Primary, pupils 56,267, teachers 1,941; secondary, pupils 17,659, teachers 803; vocational, pupils 232, teachers 32; teacher training, students 294, teachers 38.
Finance and Trade. Monetary unit: South Arabian dinar, at par with the pound sterling (1 dinar = U.S. $2.40). Budget (1968–69 est.): revenue 11 million dinars; expenditure 18 million dinars. Foreign trade (1969): imports 91,010,000 dinars; exports 59,790,-000 dinars. Main exports: petroleum products 74%; ship's bunker oil 6%.
Transport. Roads (1968) c. 4,500 km. (including c. 200 km. in Aden). Motor vehicles in use (1968): passenger 9,000; commercial (including buses) 1,400. There are no railways. Ships entered (1968) vessels totaling 5,912,000 net registered tons; goods loaded (1968) 4,285,000 metric tons, unloaded 5,181,000 metric tons.
Agriculture and Industry. Production (in 000; metric tons): millet and sorghum (1968) c. 35, (1967) c. 35; cotton, lint (1968) c. 2, (1967) 5; dates (1968) c. 8, (1967) c. 8; salt (1968) 90; petroleum products (1968) 4,618; electricity (kw-hr.; 1968) 178,000.

Spain

A nominal monarchy of southwest Europe, Spain is bounded by Portugal, with which it shares the Iberian Peninsula, and by France. Area: 194,884 sq.mi. (504,750 sq.km.), including the Balearic and Canary islands. Pop. (1970 est.): 32,961,028, including the Balearics and Canaries. Cap. and largest city: Madrid (pop., 1970 est., 3,381,406). Language: Spanish. Religion: Roman Catholic. Prince of Spain, Don Juan Carlos de Borbón y Borbón; chief of state and premier in 1970, Gen. Francisco Franco Bahamonde.

SPAIN

Education. (1966–67) Primary, pupils 3,380,-218, teachers 117,067; secondary, pupils 929,589, teachers 31,011; vocational, pupils 330,614, teachers 18,884; teacher training, students 68,-972, teachers 2,638; higher (including 18 universities), students 154,289, teaching staff 9,625.

Finance. Monetary unit: peseta, with a par value of 70 pesetas to U.S. $1 (168 pesetas = £1 sterling). Gold, SDRs, and convertible currencies, official: (June 1970) U.S. $1,052,000,000; (June 1969) U.S. $915 million. Budget (1968) balanced at 237.8 billion pesetas. Gross national product (1969): 2,012,000,000,000 pesetas; (1968) 1,805,000,000,000 pesetas. Money supply: (June 1970) 691.9 billion pesetas; (June 1969) 637 billion pesetas. Cost of living (1963 = 100): (June 1970) 152; (June 1969) 145.

Foreign Trade. (1969) Imports 293.9 billion pesetas; exports 133 billion pesetas. Import sources: EEC 35% (West Germany 13%, France 10%, Italy 6%); U.S. 17%; U.K. 8%. Export destinations: EEC 31% (West Germany 11%, France 10%, Italy 5%); U.S. 15%; U.K. 9%. Main exports: machinery 10%; fruit 10% (citrus 6%); vegetables 6%; chemicals 6%; footwear 5%; petroleum products 5%. Tourism (1968): visitors 6,922,400; receipts U.S. $1,213,000,000.

Transport and Communications. Roads (1968) *c.* 134,000 km. (including 83 km. expressways). Motor vehicles in use (1968): passenger 1,577,200; commercial (including buses) 588,400. Railways: (1968) 17,425 km. (including 3,847 km. electrified); traffic (state system only; 1969) 12,647,000,000 passenger-km., freight 7,889,000,000 net ton-km. Air traffic (1969): 4,835,000,000 passenger-km.; freight 102,005,000 net ton-km. Shipping (1969): merchant vessels 100 gross tons and over 2,119; gross tonnage 3,199,035. Telephones (Dec. 1968) 3,702,244. Radio receivers (Dec. 1968) 6,951,-000. Television receivers (Dec. 1968) 5.3 million.

Agriculture. Production (in 000; metric tons; 1969; 1968 in parentheses): wheat 4,695 (5,315); barley 3,855 (3,441); oats 533 (539); rye 348 (355); corn 1,577 (1,473); potatoes 4,717 (4,570); rice 404 (362); chick-peas 100 (136); dry broad beans (1968) 144, (1967) 130; other dry beans 64 (119); tomatoes (1968) *c.* 1,150, (1967) 1,216; apples (1968) 428, (1967) 308; pears 192 (226); oranges 2,111 (1,812); lemons 104 (82); sugar, raw value (1969–70) *c.* 782, (1968–69) *c.* 734; olive oil *c.* 370 (420); wine 2,583 (2,307); onions (1968) *c.* 760, (1967) *c.* 1,000; bananas (1968) 395, (1967) 373; dates (1968) *c.* 16, (1967) *c.* 16; figs 136 (151); tobacco 25 (26); cotton, lint 64 (78); meat (1968) 818, (1967) 766; fish catch (1968) 1,503, (1967) 1,431. Livestock (in 000; 1968–69): cattle 4,185; horses 306; pigs 6,139; sheep 18,962; goats (1967–68) 2,626; chickens (March 1969) 49,961.

Industry. Index of industrial production (1963 = 100): (1969) 190; (1968) 167. Fuel and power (in 000; metric tons; 1969): coal 11,584; lignite 2,735; electricity (kw-hr.) 52,090,000; manufactured gas (cu.m.) 714,000. Production (in 000; metric tons; 1969): iron ore (50% metal content) 6,253; pig iron 3,544; crude steel 5,950; aluminum 103; zinc 80; copper 76; lead 81; cement 16,012; potash (oxide content; 1968) 616; sulfur (1968) 1,115; cotton yarn 101; cotton fabrics 89; wool yarn 37. Merchant vessels launched (100 gross tons and over; 1969) 566,-000 gross tons.

Probably the most obvious change in Spanish public life during 1970 was the growing outspokenness of dissenters, in many instances former supporters of the regime. General Franco remained the undisputed leader but the nation began to question the validity of his plans to institutionalize a political system notoriously ill-suited to contemporary world trends. The bill on the reform of the syndicates, in particular, met with fierce criticism throughout the nation, including the normally pliant Cortes (parliament).

Labour conflicts (the regime's euphemism for strikes) were a prominent feature in 1970, beginning with a virtual paralysis of the Asturias coal mines early in the year. In Granada on July 21 police trying to disperse a demonstration of construction workers asking for higher wages shot and killed three demonstrators. This action brought general sympathy for the workers' plight as well as explicit support from the Roman Catholic Church. The incident was followed days later by a strike of the Madrid subway workers, which the authorities were particularly anxious to end because of the international attention it was receiving at the peak of the tourist season. The workers were forced to return to work under threat of being drafted into the Army.

The year's end was marked by further strikes and demonstrations in protest against the court-martial of a group of Basque nationalists, as well as by massive counterdemonstrations in support of General Franco. The prisoners, members of a Basque guerrilla organization, were tried on a variety of charges, including banditry and complicity in the murder of a police inspector. Announcement of the sentences was delayed for more than two weeks, possibly because of concern over the fate of Eugen Beihl, the honorary West German consul in San Sebastian, who was kidnapped by Basque terrorists on December 1 and released under mysterious circumstances on Christmas Day. When they came, the sentences were unexpectedly harsh. Six of the prisoners were condemned to death and nine to long prison terms (a 16th defendant, a woman, was acquitted at the request of the prosecution). On December 30 General Franco announced that the death sentences had been commuted to 30 years' imprisonment.

Two pieces of legislation failed to raise as much comment as had been expected. One was a decree conferring upon working women the same legal rights as those of men and entitling them to equal pay; the other was a bill proposing that "political associations" be allowed in Spain. Public apathy probably reflected a general disbelief that the proposals would be implemented in a convincing manner.

The new Cabinet, in office since the end of October 1969, was particularly active in the field of foreign relations. After protracted discussions, on August 6 agreement was reached extending the U.S. use of the military installations in Spain for five years from September 26. U.S. Pres. Richard Nixon visited Madrid on October 2 at the end of his Mediterranean tour and was cordially greeted by General Franco and large crowds that gathered in the streets.

Also outstanding was the development of relations with the Eastern European countries, a trend that suggested some personal influence on foreign policy by Minister of Foreign Affairs Gregorio López Bravo, who in December 1969 had visited Moscow briefly during a flight to Manila. All through the year Spanish newspapers increased their coverage of Soviet news,

Gen. Francisco Franco reviews a military parade marking the 31st anniversary of his Spanish Civil War victory. Prince Juan Carlos (left) is designated by Franco to occupy the throne when the dictator steps down from power or dies.

UPI COMPIX

Southern Rhodesia:
see Rhodesia

South West Africa:
see Dependent States; South Africa

Soviet Literature:
see Literature

Soviet Union:
see Union of Soviet Socialist Republics

Soybeans:
see Agriculture

Spacecraft:
see Astronautics

Space Exploration:
see Astronautics

the Soviet Tass and the Spanish Efe news agencies having agreed to exchange correspondents.

The economy had not found the balance necessary for steady growth. Following two years of recession, national income increased by 7.3% in real terms in 1969, but at the cost of a substantial balance of payments deficit of $306.8 million and a corresponding fall in the gross international reserves, which at the end of the year stood at $886.5 million. To a considerable extent this was caused by a high internal demand for imports, which rose by 20.2% and left a trade deficit of $2,333,000,000 despite a 19.6% rise in exports.

Toward the end of 1969 it was clear that the government's most urgent task was to cool down domestic demand: 10% of all public investment contracts were postponed and banks were instructed to restrict credit. At the same time a 20% prior deposit was imposed on all imports and interest rates were increased to bring them closer to those quoted abroad. The effects of these measures were slow, but after the summer months the picture changed radically. By the end of September 1970, the gold and foreign reserves of the Banco de España had risen to a record $1,569,000,000, an increase of $683 million in nine months, in contrast with the decline of $126 million in January–September 1969. Foreign trade also began to reflect the impact of the prior deposit; the rise in imports slowed to 16.5% for January–September and exports increased 26.4% in the same period.

Less favourable, however, was the question of prices. The moderate increase of 3.5% in the cost of living for the whole of 1969 was soon superseded in 1970 because of rises in goods and services and the partial removal of the freeze on wages and prices that had been implemented in the previous two years. Another even less tractable problem was how to counteract any adverse trends that could develop as a result of a trade agreement signed with the European Economic Community on June 29 that came into force on October 1. The six-year agreement provided for a gradual rise in preferential treatment on imports of a comprehensive range of industrial and agricultural products and many industrialists were anxious about the stronger competition they would have to face. (M. Pu.)

ENCYCLOPÆDIA BRITANNICA FILMS. *People of Spain* (1955); *Spanish Children* (1964).

Speleology

The longest cave in the world was still the Flint Ridge cave system in Kentucky at 72.9 mi. The next longest, though, the Hölloch in Switzerland, was extended significantly by new discoveries in the winter expedition of early 1970 and became 67.2 mi. in length.

The survey of newly discovered passages in Ogof Ffynnon Ddu (Wales) showed that it was the longest (20.3 mi.) and deepest (850 ft.) cave in Britain; it also became the ninth longest in the world. In the same year this cave was threatened with destruction by an expansion of nearby quarrying. In February the Verband Österreichischer Höhlenforscher mounted an eight-day expedition in the Mammuthöhle (Dachstein, Aus.), and their discoveries increased its length to 13 mi.

A shaft in the vicinity of the world's deepest cave, the Gouffre de la Pierre Saint-Martin on the Franco-Spanish border, was found to descend from the surface to just above one of the chambers in the Arumbe inlet of the main cave. At the time of exploration this was blocked with snow at a depth of 650 ft., but it seemed likely to provide a new entrance. In the Sotano de la Golondrinas (Mexico), formerly 1,306 ft. deep, a deep fissure leading downward from the bottom was explored to a new total depth of 1,689 ft., and the cave became the third deepest known in North America. In the second half of 1969 a British group pushed exploration in the Raggejavreraige (Norway) to a depth of 1,885 ft., thus making it the deepest cave in Scandinavia.

Many of the 1970 discoveries in English caves were made by divers. An important new section of Wookey Hole (Somerset) was found in January. The long underwater sump, already partly explored, was penetrated by John Parker and others beyond the ninth chamber to a total length of 300 ft. In the Little Neath River Cave (South Wales), exploration and surveying continued in the passages beyond Sump 4; the total length of the system increased to 4.3 mi., but more than one-third of this was still accessible only to divers. An underwater connection between Peak Cavern and the Speedwell Mine in Derbyshire was discovered by Tom Brown of Manchester University who dived for 140 ft. through the Treasury Sump in Peak and emerged at a pool adjoining the main streamway in Speedwell.

Discovery by members of the Kendal Caving Club of a 170-ft. pitch at the bottom of Long Kin West pothole (Yorkshire) made it one of England's deeper caves at 506 ft. Also in northern England, 2¾ mi. of the new Leck Fell Master Cave were entered from Pippikin Hole and seemed likely to connect in due course with other major cave systems in the area.

In South Devon a greater horseshoe bat was found bearing a numbered ring put on in 1949; it was thus at least 20½ years old. Little was known about the longevity of bats, and this was the oldest yet recorded in Britain.

The centenary of the discovery of the Dobsina Ice Cave in Czechoslovakia was celebrated by a conference on ice caves organized by the Karst Museum there. The fourth National Congress of Speleology, held at Neuchâtel, Switz., in September, dealt particularly with the Jurassic karst.

A study of the caves of Tanga in Tanzania showed that their sequence of formation was related to the fluctuating sea levels in the area. An important find of Pleistocene mammal remains was discovered in one of the Naracoorte caves in South Australia. A skeleton of what might be Neanderthal man was discovered in a cave near Budapest according to Vera Csank of the Budapest Museum of History. Cave paintings of Neolithic age were found in a cave at Porto Badisco, Salento, Italy; their similarity to those of Spain suggested a cultural relationship between the two regions. South African rock paintings by predecessors of the Bushmen were dated for the first time by the radiocarbon method; the paintings were on pebbles found in the Klazies River Mouth Cave, buried with datable organic material of 335 B.C. ± 100 years.

The *Explorations Journal of the University of Leeds Speleological Association* was published in 1970; it gave descriptions and surveys of six miles of discoveries in West Yorkshire. In preparation by the International Union of Speleology was a multilingual glossary of speleological terms. (T. R. Sh.)

Sporting Record

ANGLING

Event	Winner	Country
Alton B. Sharp Trophy (international tuna fishing competition)	T. Naftzger	U.S.

ARCHERY

Event	Winner	Country
WORLD FIELD CHAMPIONS		
Men's bare bow	E. Moore	U.S.
Men's freestyle	S. Lieberman	U.S.
Women's bare bow	E. Schewe	U.S.
Women's freestyle	S. Johansson	Sweden
EUROPEAN FIELD CHAMPIONS		
Men's bare bow	L. Berggren	Sweden
Men's freestyle	D. Gunson	U.K.
Women's bare bow	I. Granquist	Sweden
Women's freestyle	S. Johansson	Sweden
EUROPEAN TARGET CHAMPIONS		
Men	V. Sidoryuk	U.S.S.R.
Men's team	Belgium	
Women	A. Berglund	Sweden
Women's team	U.S.S.R.	

BADMINTON

Event	Winner	Country
EUROPEAN CHAMPIONS		
Men's singles	S. Johnsson	Sweden
Men's doubles	E. Hansen, P. Walsoe	Denmark
Women's singles	E. Twedberg	Sweden
Women's doubles	S. Whetnall, M. Boxall	U.K.
Mixed doubles	D. Eddy, S. Whetnall	U.K.
BRITISH COMMONWEALTH GAMES CHAMPIONS		
Men's singles	J. Paulson	Canada
Men's doubles	Ng Boon Bee, P. Gunalan	Malaysia
Women's singles	M. Beck	England
Women's doubles	S. Whetnall, M. Boxall	England
Mixed doubles	D. Talbot, M. Boxall	England
THOMAS CUP (men's world team championship)		Indonesia
DUTCH OPEN CHAMPIONS		
Men's singles	E. Hansen	Denmark
Men's doubles	R. Powell, D. Eddy	U.K.
Women's singles	S. Whetnall	U.K.
Women's doubles	S. Whetnall, M. Boxall	U.K.
Mixed doubles	D. Talbot, G. Perrin	U.K.
ALL-ENGLAND OPEN CHAMPIONS		
Men's singles	R. Hartono	Indonesia
Men's doubles	T. Bacher, F. Pedersen	Denmark
Women's singles	E. Takenaka	Japan
Women's doubles	S. Whetnall, M. Boxall	U.K.
Mixed doubles	P. Walsoe, P. Moelgaard-Hansen	Denmark

BIATHLON

Event	Winner	Country
WORLD CHAMPIONS		
Individual	A. Tikhonov	U.S.S.R.
Relay	U.S.S.R.	
Junior	G. Buranov	U.S.S.R.

BILLIARDS AND SNOOKER

Event	Winner	Country
BILLIARDS		
European three-pocket championship	R. Ceulemans	Belgium
European 47/2 championship	D. Müller	West Germany
SNOOKER		
World professional championship	J. Spencer	U.K.
World amateur championship	J. Barron	U.K.

BOBSLEDDING

Event	Winner	Country
World two-man champions	H. Floth, P. Bader	West Germany
World four-man champions	N. de Zordo, R. Zandonella, M. Armano, L. de Paolis	Italy
European two-man champions	G. Gaspari, M. Armano	Italy
European four-man champions	W. Zimmerer, W. Steinbauer, S. Geisreiter, P. Utzschneider	West Germany

CANOEING

Event		Winner	Country
WORLD CHAMPIONS—MEN			
Kayak singles	500 m.	I. Tishenko	U.S.S.R.
	1,000 m.	A. Shaparenko	U.S.S.R.
	10,000 m.	Y. Tsarev	U.S.S.R.
Kayak pairs	500 m.	L. Andersson, R. Peterson	Sweden
	1,000 m.	G. Pfaff, G. Seibold	Austria
	10,000 m.	A. Kostyenko, V. Konyonov	U.S.S.R.
Kayak fours	1,000 m.	U.S.S.R.	
	10,000 m.	Norway	
Kayak relay		U.S.S.R.	
Canadian singles	1,000 m.	T. Tatai	Hungary
	10,000 m.	T. Wichmann	Hungary
Canadian pairs	1,000 m.	S. Covaliov, I. Patzaichin	Romania
	10,000 m.	C. Maxim, S. Simionov	Romania
WORLD CHAMPIONS—WOMEN			
Kayak singles	500 m.	L. Pinayeva	U.S.S.R.
Kayak pairs	500 m.	R. Breuer, R. Esser	West Germany
Kayak fours	500 m.	U.S.S.R.	

CROSS-COUNTRY

Event	Winner	Country
INTERNATIONAL CHAMPIONS		
Senior, individual	M. Tagg	U.K.
Senior, team	U.K.	
Junior, individual	J. Hartnett	Ireland
Junior, team	U.K.	
Women, individual	D. Brown	U.S.
Women, team	U.K.	
NATIONAL CHAMPIONS—MEN		
Belgium	G. Roelants	
Canada	D. Ellis	
France	N. Tijou	
Ireland	T. O'Riordan	
Northern Ireland	D. Graham	
Scotland	J. Alder	
Spain	J. Hidalgo	
U.K.	T. Wright	
U.S. (AAU)	J. Bacheler	
U.S.S.R.	N. Sviridov (12 km.)	
	R. Sharafutdinov (8 km.)	
Wales	M. Thomas	
NATIONAL CHAMPIONS—WOMEN		
Ireland	A. O'Brien	
Scotland	M. MacSherry	
U.K.	R. Ridley	
U.S. (AAU)	D. Brown	
U.S.S.R.	L. Bragina	
Wales	T. Bateman	

CURLING

Event	Country
WORLD CHAMPIONS	Canada

CYCLING

Event	Winner	Country
WORLD CHAMPIONS—AMATEUR		
Sprint	D. Morelon	France
Time trial	N. Fredborg	Denmark
Individual pursuit	X. Kurmann	Switzerland
Tandem sprint	J. Barth, R. Müller	West Germany
Team pursuit	West Germany	
Motor-paced	C. Stam	Netherlands
Individual road race	J. Schmidt	Denmark
Team time trial, road	U.S.S.R.	
Women's sprint	G. Careva	U.S.S.R.
Women's individual pursuit	T. Garkushina	U.S.S.R.
Women's road race	A. Konkina	U.S.S.R.
WORLD CHAMPIONS—PROFESSIONAL		
Sprint	G. Johnson	Australia
Pursuit	H. Porter	U.K.
Motor-paced	E. Rudolph	West Germany
Individual road race	J. P. Monseré	Belgium
BRITISH COMMONWEALTH GAMES CHAMPIONS		
Sprint	J. Nicholson	Australia
Time trial	H. Kent	New Zealand
Pursuit	I. Hallam	England
Tandem sprint	G. Johnson, R. Jonker	Australia
10 mi. track	J. Lovell	Canada
Road	B. Biddle	New Zealand
MAJOR ROAD RACE WINNERS		
Paris–Nice	E. Merckx	Belgium
Milan–San Remo	M. Dancelli	Italy
Tour of Flanders	E. Leman	Belgium
Tour of Belgium	E. Merckx	Belgium
Paris–Roubaix	E. Merckx	Belgium
Liège-Bastogne-Liège	R. de Vlaeminck	Belgium
Flèche Wallonne	E. Merckx	Belgium
Tour of Spain	L. Ocana	Spain
Tour of Normandy	G. Pettersson	Sweden
Dunkirk Four Days	W. van Neste	Belgium
Tour of Italy	E. Merckx	Belgium

Event	Winner	Country
Tour of Luxembourg	E. Schutz	Luxembourg
Tour of Switzerland	R. Poggiali	Italy
Tour of France	E. Merckx	Belgium
Paris–Luxembourg	E. de Vlaeminck	Belgium
Tour of Britain	J. Mainus	Czechoslovakia
Tour of Scotland	W. Matusiak	Poland
Prague–Warsaw–Berlin	R. Szurkowski	Poland
Grand Prix des Nations	H. van Springel	Belgium
Tour of Lombardy	F. Bitossi	Italy
Bordeaux–Paris	H. van Springel	Belgium
Paris–Tours	J. Tschan	West Germany
Baracchi Trophy	G. Pettersson, T. Pettersson	Sweden

NATIONAL ROAD RACE CHAMPIONS

Belgium	E. Merckx	
France	P. Gutty	
Italy	F. Bitossi	
Luxembourg	E. Schutz	
Netherlands	P. Kisner	
Portugal	J. Agostinho	
Spain	J. Gonzalez Linares	
Switzerland	K. Rùb	
U.K.	L. West (professional)	
	D. Rollinson (amateur)	
West Germany	R. Altig	

CYCLO-CROSS WORLD CHAMPIONS

Professional, individual	E. de Vlaeminck	Belgium
Professional, team	Belgium	
Amateur, individual	R. Vermeire	Belgium
Amateur, team	Belgium	

EQUESTRIAN SPORTS

Event	Winner	Country
WORLD CHAMPIONS		
Dressage, individual	Elena Petushkova	U.S.S.R.
Dressage, team	U.S.S.R.	
Show jumping, individual	D. Broome	U.K.
Show jumping, women	J. Lefevre	France
Three-day event	Mary Gordon Watson	U.K.
Three-day event, team	U.K.	

FENCING

Event	Winner	Country
WORLD CHAMPIONS		
Men's foil	F. Wessel	West Germany
Men's epée	A. Nikanchikov	U.S.S.R.
Men's sabre	T. Pesza	Hungary
Men's team foil	U.S.S.R.	
Men's team epée	Hungary	
Men's team sabre	U.S.S.R.	
Women's foil	G. Gorokhova	U.S.S.R.
Women's team foil	U.S.S.R.	
WORLD JUNIOR CHAMPIONS		
Men's foil	H. Hein	West Germany
Men's epée	B. Lukomsky	U.S.S.R.
Men's sabre	P. Rensky	U.S.S.R.
Women's foil	V. Nikonova	U.S.S.R.

FOOTBALL, ASSOCIATION

Event	Winner	Country
MAJOR INTERNATIONAL TOURNAMENTS (national teams)		
World Cup	Brazil	
British Isles international championship	England, Scotland, Wales (all tie)	
Central American championship	Costa Rica	
Southeast Asian championship	Burma	
African Nations' Cup	Sudan	
MAJOR INTERNATIONAL TOURNAMENTS (clubs)		
World Champions' Cup	Feijenoord	Netherlands
South American Champions' Cup	Estudiantes de La Plata	Argentina
European Champions' Cup	Feijenoord	Netherlands
European Cup-Winners' Cup	Manchester City	U.K.
European Inter-Cities Fairs' Cup	Arsenal	U.K.
African Champions' Cup	Ismaili Cairo	U.A.R.

NATIONAL LEAGUE CHAMPIONS

Argentina	Boca Juniors
Austria	FC Austria Vienna
Belgium	Standard Liège
Brazil	Palmeiras (National League)
Bulgaria	Levski Sofia
Czechoslovakia	Slovan Bratislava
East Germany	Carl Zeiss Jena
Ecuador	Liga Deportivo Universitario
England	Everton
France	St. Etienne
Greece	Panathinaikos
Hungary	Ujpest Dosza
Ireland	Glentoran (Irish League)
	Waterford (FA of Ireland League)
Italy	Cagliari
Luxembourg	Jeunesse Esch
Mexico	Guadalajara
Netherlands	Ajax Amsterdam
Paraguay	Guaraní
Poland	Legia Warsaw

Event	Winner
Portugal	Sporting Lisbon
Romania	UT Arad
Scotland	Celtic
Spain	Atletico Madrid
Switzerland	FC Basel
Uruguay	Nacional
U.S.S.R.	Moscow Spartak
West Germany	Borussia München-Gladbach
Yugoslavia	Red Star Belgrade

NATIONAL CUP WINNERS

Austria	Wacker Innsbruck
Belgium	F. C. Bruges
Bulgaria	Levski Sofia
England	Chelsea (Football Association Cup)
	Manchester City (Football League Cup)
France	St. Etienne
Greece	Aris Salonika
Hungary	Ujpest Dosza
Ireland	Linfield (Irish Cup)
	Bohemians (Football Association of Ireland Cup)
Italy	Bologna
Luxembourg	Union Luxembourg
Netherlands	Ajax Amsterdam
Poland	Gornik Zabrze
Portugal	Benfica
Romania	Steaua Bucharest
Scotland	Aberdeen
Spain	Real Madrid
Sweden	Atvidaberg
Switzerland	FC Zürich
U.S.S.R.	Dynamo Moscow
Wales	Cardiff City
West Germany	FC Offenbach

GLIDING

Event	Winner	County
WORLD CHAMPIONS		
Open class	G. Moffat	U.S.
Standard class	H. Reichmann	West Germany

GYMNASTICS

Event	Winner	Country
WORLD CHAMPIONS—MEN		
Combined exercises	E. Kenmotsu	Japan
Floor exercises	A. Nakayama	Japan
Pommeled horse	M. Cerar	Yugoslavia
Rings	A. Nakayama	Japan
Long horse vault	M. Tsukahara	Japan
Parallel bars	A. Nakayama	Japan
Horizontal bar	E. Kenmotsu	Japan
Teams	Japan	
WORLD CHAMPIONS—WOMEN		
Combined exercises	L. Turisheva	U.S.S.R.
Floor exercises	L. Turisheva	U.S.S.R.
Beam	E. Zuchold	East Germany
Horse vault	E. Zuchold	East Germany
Asymmetrical bars	K. Janz	East Germany
Teams	U.S.S.R.	

HANDBALL

Event	Winner	Country
World champions (indoor)	Romania	
World champion, individual	P. Kirby	U.S.

JUDO

Event	Winner	Country
EUROPEAN CHAMPIONS		
Lightweight	J. Mounier	France
Light-middleweight	R. Hendel	East Germany
Middleweight	B. Jacks	U.K.
Light-heavyweight	V. Pokatyev	U.S.S.R.
Heavyweight	K. Glahn	West Germany
Unlimited weight	K. Hennig	East Germany
Team	U.S.S.R.	

KARATE

Event	Winner	Country
WORLD CHAMPIONS		
Team	Japan	
EUROPEAN CHAMPIONS		
Individual	D. Valera	France
Team	West Germany	

LACROSSE

Event	Winner
U.S. Club Championship	Long Island Athletic Club

MODERN PENTATHLON

Event	Winner	Country
WORLD CHAMPIONS		
Individual	P. Kelemen	Hungary
Team	Hungary	

MOTORCYCLING

Class	Winner and country	Make
WORLD CHAMPIONS		
50 cc.	A. Nieto, Spain	Derbi
125 cc.	D. Braun, West Germany	Suzuki
250 cc.	R. Gould, U.K.	Yahama
350 cc.	G. Agostini, Italy	MV Agusta
500 cc.	G. Agostini, Italy	MV Agusta
Sidecar	K. Enders, West Germany	BMW

POLO

Event	Winner
U.S. 20-goal championship	Oak Brook (Ill.) Polo Club

RACKETS

Event	Winner	Country
MAJOR TOURNAMENT WINNERS		
World championship	G. Atkins	U.S.
U.K. open championship	C. Swallow	
U.K. amateur championship	M. G. M. Smith	
U.K. amateur championship doubles	M. G. M. Smith, R. M. K. Gracey	

ROLLER HOCKEY

Event	Country
World champions	Spain

ROLLER SKATING

Event	Winner	Country
WORLD SPEED CHAMPIONS		
500 m.	G. Cantarella	Italy
1,000 m.	G. Cantarella	Italy
5,000 m.	D. Hayes	New Zealand
10,000 m.	J. Folley	U.K.
20,000 m.	D. Hayes	New Zealand
Team		U.K.

SAILING

Class	Helmsman	Country
WORLD CHAMPIONS		
Cadet	C. Tillett	Australia
Cherub	R. Bowler	New Zealand
Contender	D. Jobbins	U.K.
Finn	J. Bruder	Brazil
Fireball	J. Caig	U.K.
Flying Dutchman	R. Pattisson	U.K.
Moth	P. Maes	Belgium
O.K.	K. Carlsson	Sweden
Soling	S. Wennerstrom	Sweden
Star	W. Buchanan	U.S.
Tempest	J. Linville	U.S.
Thunderbird	T. Parkes	Australia
Tornado	M. Davies	Australia
Vauriens	R. Meyer	Netherlands
4-2-0	W. Campbell	U.S.
4-7-0	Y. Carre	France
5-0-5	L. Marks	U.K.
5.5. m.	D. Forbes	Australia

AMERICA'S CUP CHALLENGE

Winner	Helmsman	Country
"Intrepid"	J. Hardy	U.S.

SYDNEY-HOBART OCEAN RACE

"Morning Cloud"	E. Heath	U.K.

SNOW-KARTING

Event	Winner	Country
WORLD CHAMPIONS		
Men	M. Schratt	West Germany
Men's team	West Germany	
Women	M. Hoss	West Germany
Women's team	Switzerland	

SPEEDWAY

Event	Winner	Country
World champion, individual	I. Mauger	New Zealand
World champion, pairs	I. Mauger, R. Moore	New Zealand
European champion, individual	I. Mauger	New Zealand
U.K. champion, individual	B. Briggs	New Zealand
World champion, team	Sweden	

SQUASH RACKETS

Event	Winner	Country
British open championship	J. Barrington	U.K.
British amateur championship	G. Hunt	Australia
British women's championship	H. McKay	Australia
Champion of champions (South Africa)	K. Hiscoe	Australia

SURFING

Event	Winner	Country
WORLD CHAMPIONS		
Men	R. Arness	U.S.
Women	S. Weber	U.S.

TABLE TENNIS

Event	Winner	Country
EUROPEAN CHAMPIONS		
Men's singles	H. Alser	Sweden
Men's doubles	A. Stipanek, D. Surbek	Yugoslavia
Women's singles	Z. Rudnova	U.S.S.R.
Women's doubles	Z. Rudnova, S. Grinberg	U.S.S.R.
Mixed doubles	S. Gomozkov, Z. Rudnova	U.S.S.R.
Men's team	Sweden	
Women's team	U.S.S.R.	
EUROPEAN JUNIOR CHAMPIONS		
Men's singles	S. Bengtsson	Sweden
Men's doubles	S. Bengtsson, T. Klampar	Sweden, Hungary
Women's singles	I. Vostova	Czechoslovakia
Women's doubles	E. Johos, H. Lottaler	Hungary
Mixed doubles	M. Orlovsky, I. Vostova	Czechoslovakia
Men's team	Czechoslovakia	
Women's team	Czechoslovakia	

EUROPEAN NATIONS' LEAGUE Sweden

TOBOGGANING

Event	Winner	Country
WORLD CHAMPIONS		
Men	J. Fendt	West Germany
Men's pairs	M. Schmid, E. Walch	Austria
Women	B. Piecha	Poland

TRACK AND FIELD

Event	Winner	Performance
COMMONWEALTH CHAMPIONS—MEN		
100 m.	D. Quarrie, Jamaica	10.2 sec.
200 m.	D. Quarrie, Jamaica	20.5 sec.
400 m.	C. Asati, Kenya	45.0 sec.
800 m.	R. Ouko, Kenya	1 min. 46.8 sec.
1,500 m.	H. K. Keino, Kenya	3 min. 36.6 sec.
5,000 m.	I. Stewart, Scotland	13 min. 22.8 sec.
10,000 m.	I. Stewart, Scotland	28 min. 11.8 sec.
Steeplechase	A. P. Manning, Australia	8 min. 26.2 sec.
110-m. hurdles	D. P. Hemery, U.K.	13.6 sec.
400-m. hurdles	J. Sherwood, U.K.	50.0 sec.
High jump	L. Peckham, Australia	7 ft. 0¼ in.
Pole vault	M. Bull, Northern Ireland	16 ft. 8¾ in.
Long jump	L. Davies, Wales	26 ft. 5¼ in.
Triple jump	P. May, Australia	54 ft. 10 in.
Shot put	D. Steen, Canada	63 ft. 0¼ in.
Discus throw	G. Puce, Canada	193 ft. 7 in.
Hammer throw	A. H. Payne, England	222 ft. 5 in.
Javelin	D. H. Travis, England	260 ft. 9 in.
Decathlon	G. Smith, Australia	7,492 pt.
Marathon	R. Hill, England	2 hr. 9 min. 28 sec.
20-mi. walk	N. Freeman, Australia	2 hr. 33 min. 33 sec.
400-m. relay	Jamaica	39.4 sec.
1,600-m. relay	Kenya	3 min. 3.6 sec.

Event	Winner	Performance
BRITISH COMMONWEALTH CHAMPIONS—WOMEN		
100 m.	R. Boyle, Australia	11.2 sec.
200 m.	R. Boyle, Australia	22.7 sec.
400 m.	M. Neufville, Jamaica	51.0 sec.
800 m.	R. B. Stirling, Scotland	2 min. 6.2 sec.
1,500 m.	R. Ridley, England	4 min. 18.8 sec.
100-m. hurdles	P. Kilborn, Australia	13.2 sec.
High jump	D. Brill, Canada	5 ft. 10 in.
Long jump	S. Sherwood, England	22 ft. 0¼ in.
Shot put	M. B. Peters, Northern Ireland	52 ft. 3 in.
Discus throw	R. B. Payne, Scotland	178 ft. 8 in.
Javelin	P. Rivers, Australia	170 ft. 7 in.
Pentathlon	M. B. Peters, Northern Ireland	5,148 pt.
400-m. relay	Australia	44.1 sec.
EUROPEAN CUP FINAL—MEN		
Overall winner	East Germany	
100 m.	Z. Nowosz, Poland	10.4 sec.
200 m.	S. Schenke, East Germany	20.7 sec.
400 m.	J. Werner, Poland	45.9 sec.
800 m.	Y. Arzhanov, U.S.S.R.	1 min. 47.8 sec.
1,500 m.	F. Arese, Italy	3 min. 42.3 sec.
5,000 m.	H. Norpoth, West Germany	14 min. 25.4 sec.
10,000 m.	J. Haase, East Germany	28 min. 26.8 sec.
Steeplechase	V. Dudin, U.S.S.R.	8 min. 31.6 sec.
110-m. hurdles	G. Drut, France	13.7 sec.
400-m. hurdles	J. C. Nallet, France	50.1 sec.
High jump	K. Lundmark, Sweden	7 ft. 0½ in.
Pole vault	W. Nordwig, East Germany	17 ft. 6¾ in.
Long jump	J. Pani, France	26 ft. 6½ in.
Triple jump	J. Drehmel, East Germany	56 ft. 2½ in.
Shot put	H. Briesenick, East Germany	67 ft. 5 in.
Discus throw	R. Bruch, Sweden	212 ft. 10 in.
Hammer throw	A. Bondarchuk, U.S.S.R.	231 ft. 2 in.
Javelin	W. Nikiciuk, Poland	270 ft. 6 in.
400-m. relay	East Germany	39.4 sec.
1,600-m. relay	Poland	3 min. 5.1 sec.
EUROPEAN CUP FINAL—WOMEN		
Overall winner	East Germany	
100 m.	I. Mickler, West Germany	11.3 sec.
200 m.	R. Meissner, East Germany	23.1 sec.
400 m.	H. Fischer, East Germany	53.2 sec.
800 m.	H. Janze, West Germany	2 min. 4.9 sec.
1,500 m.	E. Tittel, West Germany	4 min. 16.3 sec.
100-m. hurdles	K. Balzer, East Germany	13.1 sec.
High jump	R. Schmidt, East Germany	6 ft. 0½ in.
Long jump	H. Rosendahl, West Germany	22 ft. 3¾ in.
Shot put	N. Chizhova, U.S.S.R.	63 ft. 8½ in.
Discus throw	K. Illgen, East Germany	202 ft. 1 in.
Javelin	R. Fuchs, East Germany	198 ft. 10 in.
400-m. relay	West Germany	43.9 sec.
1,600-m. relay	East Germany	3 min. 37.0 sec.
U.S. NATIONAL AAU CHAMPIONS—MEN (OUTDOORS)		
100 yd.	I. Crockett, Southern Illinois	9.3 sec.
220 yd.	B. Vaughan, U.S. Army	20.8 sec.
440 yd.	J. Smith, UCLA	45.7 sec.
880 yd.	K. Swenson, Kansas State	1 min. 47.4 sec.
1 mi.	H. Michael, William and Mary	4 min. 1.8 sec.
3 mi.	F. Shorter, Florida Track Club	13 min. 24.2 sec.
6 mi.	F. Shorter, Florida Track Club and J. Bacheler, Florida Track Club (tie)	27 min. 24.0 sec.
Steeplechase	W. Reilly, New York Athletic Club	8 min. 34.8 sec.
120-yd. hurdles	T. Hill, Arkansas State	13.3 sec.
440-yd. hurdles	R. Mann, Brigham Young	48.8 sec.
High jump	R. Brown, California Track Club	7 ft. 1 in.
Pole vault	R. Seagren, Southern California Striders	17 ft. 2 in.
Long jump	B. Moore, Oregon	26 ft. 2¾ in.
Triple jump	M. Tiff, unattached	53 ft. 0 in.
Shot put	J. R. Matson, Texas Striders	67 ft. 10¼ in.
Discus throw	L. J. Silvester, unattached	205 ft. 4 in.
Hammer throw	G. Frenn, Pacific Coast Athletic Association	230 ft. 0 in.
Javelin	W. Skinner, Tennessee	276 ft. 7 in.
Decathlon	J. Warkentin, unattached	8,026 pt.
Marathon	R. Fitts, unattached	2 hr. 24 min. 10.6 sec.
U.S. NATIONAL AAU CHAMPIONS—WOMEN (OUTDOORS)		
100 yd.	Chi Cheng, Taiwan	10.1 sec.
220 yd.	Chi Cheng, Taiwan	22.7 sec.
440 yd.	M. Laing	52.9 sec.
880 yd.	C. Toussaint	2 min. 5.1 sec.
1,500 m.	F. Larrieu	4 min. 20.8 sec.
100-m. hurdles	M. Rallins	13.4 sec.
200-m. hurdles	P. Hawkins	26.1 sec.
High jump	A. Plihal	5 ft. 8 in.
Long jump	W. White	21 ft. 1 in.
Shot put	L. Graham	49 ft. 10 in.
Discus throw	C. Frost	172 ft. 3 in.
Javelin	S. Calvert	184 ft. 9 in.
440-yd. relay	Tennessee State	45.2 sec.
1-mi. relay	Atoms Track Club	3 min. 41.3 sec.
U.S. NATIONAL AAU CHAMPIONS—MEN (INDOORS)		
60 yd.	C. Greene, U.S. Army	6.0 sec.
600 yd.	M. McGrady, Sports International	1 min. 7.6 sec.
1,000 yd.	J. Luzins, unattached	2 min. 6.2 sec.
1 mi.	M. Liquori, Villanova	4 min. 0.9 sec.
3 mi.	A. Dulong, Holy Cross	13 min. 19.6 sec.
60-yd. hurdles	W. Davenport, Texas Striders	7.1 sec.
High jump	O. Burrell, Southern California Striders	7 ft. 0 in.
Pole vault	R. Seagren, Southern California Striders	17 ft. 0 in.
Long jump	N. Tate, New York Pioneer Club	26 ft. 4¾ in.
Triple jump	N. Tate, New York Pioneer Club	53 ft. 4½ in.
Shot put	B. Oldfield, University of Chicago Track Club	63 ft. 10¾ in.
35-lb. weight	G. Frenn, Pacific Coast Athletic Association	70 ft. 5½ in.

Event	Winner	Performance
1-mi. relay	Sports International	3 min. 14.0 sec.
2-mi. relay	University of Chicago Track Club	7 min. 30.8 sec.
Medley relay	Rutgers	1 min. 53.4 sec.
1-mi. walk	D. Romansky, unattached	6 min. 14.0 sec.
U.S. NATIONAL AAU CHAMPIONS—WOMEN (INDOORS)		
60 yd.	Chi Cheng, Taiwan	6.7 sec.
220 yd.	J. Kummer	24.9 sec.
440 yd.	K. Hammond	55.2 sec.
880 yd.	F. Johnson	2 min. 10.5 sec.
1 mi.	G. Gibbons	4 min. 58.9 sec.
60-yd. hurdles	Chi Cheng, Taiwan	7.6 sec.
High jump	D. Brill, Canada	5 ft. 11 in.
Long jump	Chi Cheng, Taiwan	21 ft. 0¾ in.
Shot put	M. Jacobson	46 ft. 9 in.

TRAMPOLINE

Event	Winner	Country
WORLD CHAMPIONS		
Men	W. Miller	U.S.
Women	R. Ransom	U.S.
Men's pairs	D. Waters, G. Smith	U.S.
Women's pairs	J. Liebenberg, L. Odendaal	South Africa

VOLLEYBALL

Event	Winner
U.S. Intercollegiate Championship	UCLA

WATER SKIING

Event	Winner	Country
EUROPEAN CUP WINNERS		
Individual	R. Zucchi	Italy
Team	Switzerland	
U.K. CHAMPIONS		
Men's slalom	I. Walker	
Men's tricks	I. Walker	
Men's overall	I. Walker	
Women's slalom	G. Brantingham	
Women's tricks	F. Saunders	
Women's overall	G. Brantingham	
EUROPEAN CHAMPIONS		
Men's slalom	R. Zucchi	Italy
Men's tricks	M. Hofer	Italy
Men's jumps	I. Walker	U.K.
Men's overall	R. Zucchi	Italy
Women's slalom	W. Stahle	Netherlands
Women's tricks	W. Stahle	Netherlands
Women's jumps	W. Stahle	Netherlands
Women's overall	W. Stahle	Netherlands
U.S. CHAMPIONS		
Senior men	M. Suyderhoud	
Senior women	E. Allan	

WEIGHT LIFTING

Event	Winner and country	Performance
WORLD CHAMPIONS		
Flyweight	S. del Rosario, Philippines	710½ lb.
Bantamweight	M. Nassiri, Iran	798¾ lb.
Featherweight	J. Benedek, Hungary	843 lb.
Lightweight	Z. Kaczmarek, Poland	969¾ lb.
Middleweight	V. Kurentsov, U.S.S.R.	1,019¾ lb.
Light-heavyweight	G. Ivanchenko, U.S.S.R.	1,113 lb.
Middle-heavyweight	V. Kolotov, U.S.S.R.	1,184½ lb.
Heavyweight	J. Talts, U.S.S.R.	1,245 lb.
Super-heavyweight	V. Alekseyev, U.S.S.R.	1,323 lb.
Team	U.S.S.R.	

WRESTLING

Event	Winner	Country
WORLD FREESTYLE CHAMPIONS		
Light-flyweight	E. Javadi	Iran
Flyweight	A. Aalan	Turkey
Bantamweight	H. Yamagida	Japan
Featherweight	S. Abassy	Iran
Lightweight	A. Mohaved	Iran
Welterweight	W. Wells	U.S.
Middleweight	Y. Shakhmuradov	U.S.S.R.
Light-heavyweight	G. Stachev	U.S.S.R.
Heavyweight	V. Gulyutkov	U.S.S.R.
Super-heavyweight	A. Medved	U.S.S.R.
WORLD GRECO-ROMAN CHAMPIONS		
Light-flyweight	G. Berceanu	Romania
Flyweight	P. Kirov	Bulgaria
Bantamweight	J. Varga	Hungary
Featherweight	H. Fujimoto	Japan
Lightweight	R. Rurua	U.S.S.R.
Welterweight	V. Igumenov	U.S.S.R.
Middleweight	A. Nazaryenko	U.S.S.R.
Light-heavyweight	V. Rezyanov	U.S.S.R.
Heavyweight	P. Svensson	Sweden
Super-heavyweight	A. Roshchin	U.S.S.R.

(D.K.R.P.)

See also Baseball; Basketball; Bowling and Lawn Bowls; Boxing; Chess; Contract Bridge; Cricket; Cycling; Football; Golf; Hockey; Horse Racing; Ice Skating; Motor Sports; Rowing; Sailing; Skiing; Swimming; Tennis; Track and Field Sports.

Stamp Collecting:
see Philately and Numismatics

Steel Industry:
see Industrial Review

Stock Exchanges

Bear markets in stock prices and record high yields on fixed-income securities dominated the international investment scene during 1970. The rising fear among investors throughout the world that rampant inflation would lead to worldwide recession played an important role in the sharp declines in stock prices from the end of 1969 to the end of December 1970. For the 12 major world stock price indexes for which data were readily available, 10 posted lower prices on the average in 1970 (*see* Table I).

The inability of both businessmen and government officials to cope with the persistent inflation that began during the latter part of the 1960s was a severe disappointment to many investors in securities. To be sure, investor confidence was shaken by a number of unsettling and largely unanticipated developments, the most important of which were the liquidity crisis and near collapse of two of Europe's largest institutional investors, Investors Overseas Services and Gramco International; the U.S. invasion of Cambodia and its inability to disengage itself completely from Vietnam; and the sudden bankruptcy of the largest rail transport company in the U.S., Penn Central Railroad.

Despite these shocks, however, the nature of economic activity within individual countries still tended to be the primary force behind stock price movements. Competitive and political pressures on businessmen to refrain from increasing prices, wage costs in excess of productivity gains, and restrictive monetary policies leading to the highest interest rates in modern times all tended to put a severe squeeze on corporate earnings and dividend payments. Concurrently, government fiscal policies often were designed to collect an ever increasing amount of taxes from both businesses and consumers in order to dampen excess demand.

Taken all together, these economic conditions fostered an environment wherein many long-term investors no longer found sufficient incentives to own shares of stocks. With yields on fixed-income securities offering returns comparable to or greater than what could be reasonably anticipated from common stocks in the immediate future, investors tended to dispose of common stocks. Instead, they either held cash or used the proceeds from stock sales to buy high-yielding corporate bonds and/or invest in short-term government securities, while awaiting the outcome of the battle against rapid inflation. In short, the old market maxim suggesting that higher stock prices invariably follow inflation did not prove to be a reliable principle for equity investors in 1970.   (R. H. TR.)

United States. The worst bear market in eight years touched bottom on May 26, 1970, when the Dow-Jones industrial average dropped to 631, ending a downtrend that had begun in 1968. By the end of 1970 the Dow industrials, which had dropped more than 35% from a 1969 high of 969, were up to 842.

The concurrence of economic recession, very tight money markets, and a smashing of the inflation psychology of investors and businessmen combined to make 1970 the most depressed stock market year in a decade. Paper losses on securities traded on the New York Stock Exchange alone during the early months of 1970 aggregated more than $110 billion; the over-the-counter market virtually collapsed for many days;

and more than 100 stock brokerage firms went bankrupt. Many of the surviving brokerage houses merged in order to shore up their capital positions. The federal government enacted an investor insurance law to protect customers of securities firms against some of the consequences of a firm's insolvency. The failure of the Penn Central Transportation Co., owner of the nation's largest railroad, set a record as the largest bankruptcy in U.S. corporate history and caused a massive run on the commercial paper market which resulted in emergency measures by the Federal Reserve Board to expand the money supply.

The concern of the federal government to control inflation, which had led to restrictive monetary and fiscal policies in 1968 and 1969, continued in 1970 with a growing belief that traditional policy was too slow in meeting the goals of sustained economic growth without inflation or high unemployment. The cost of living gained 5.6% in 1970, while unemployment reached 6% by December 1970, the highest level in nine years. Gradual relaxation of the tight money policy, coupled with an expansionary fiscal policy, began moving the economy into an upswing during the last half of 1970.

In 1969 the Federal Reserve Board fought inflation by virtually stopping the growth of the money supply by midyear. The effect was to restrict bank lending, drive interest rates to their highest level since the

New York Stock Exchange prices and average daily volume, 1970.

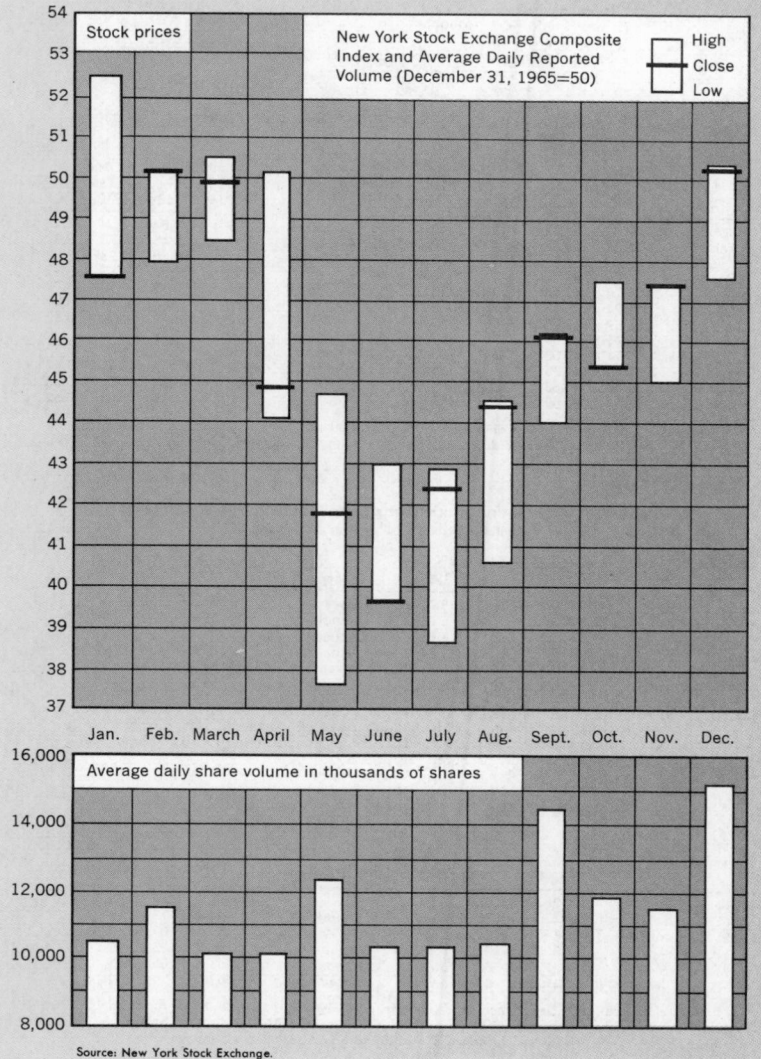

Source: New York Stock Exchange.

Civil War, and ultimately slow down business in general. In 1970 the money supply was permitted to grow at an average rate of 5.4%, compared with the 3% average in 1969. The prime rate of interest, which was 8½% effective June 9, 1969, dropped to 8% on March 25, 1970, to 7½% on September 21, to 7¼% on November 12, and to 7% by the end of 1970. Margin requirements for the purchase of common stocks were dropped on May 6, 1970, from 80 to 65%. On November 11 the Federal Reserve Board discount rate was reduced from 6 to 5¾%, the first such decline since August 1968, and a further reduction to 5½% was made on November 30. On June 24, 1970, the Federal Reserve Board suspended the limits on rates that banks may pay on short-maturity certificates that represented large deposits left with the

banks for a specified time at a specified rate of interest. During the last two months of 1970 long-term interest rates declined more swiftly than at any time in the last century. Rates on average-grade corporate bonds, for example, fell from 9.05 to 7.8%. A smaller drop in mortgage interest rates helped increase housing starts by 59% from January to November 1970.

Despite tight money market conditions and a badly depressed stock market, demands for capital market funds by corporations and by governments at every level were heavy during 1970. Corporate needs for long-term funds to restore liquidity, restructure balance sheets, and maintain projects already under way resulted in a record level of new corporate security offerings. Total gross volume of bonds and stocks issued by corporations during the first three quarters of 1970, valued at $27 billion, was more than one-third larger than in the comparable period of 1969. New stock sold in the first nine months was virtually unchanged from a year earlier despite the slump.

The performance of mutual funds during 1970 was disappointing. A survey of 467 mutual funds showed that 394 trailed the performance of the Dow-Jones industrial average in 1970. Among "growth" funds, the performance was particularly bad with 220 such funds down an average of 20.74% in 1970. Eight funds were down more than 50% for the year.

The average prices of industrial stocks in the Standard and Poor's index declined unevenly from a January 1970 level of 99.4 to a low in June of 82.96 before beginning the climb to a year-end level of 100.9 on 1970's last day of trading. (See Table II.) Public utilities stock prices rose during the early months of 1970 from 55.72 in January to a high of 59.04 in March before dipping to 49.22 in June and then joining in the last half year's rise to a last trading day close of 61.71. Railroad stock prices fell from a level of 37.62 in January to 26.74 in August before recovering to a year-end close of 35.4. The 500 stocks in the composite index reflected the roller-coaster movement of all stocks of larger corporations. The decline that began in June 1969 at a level of 104.62 had dropped the index to 90.31 by January 1970; from there it fell to 75.72 in July before recovering to a year-end level of 92.15, slightly higher at the end of 1970 than at the beginning. In contrast with the price recovery of the listed blue chip stocks, the National Quotation Bureau Index of 35 industrial stocks traded over the counter fell 13.13% between the opening and close of 1970.

Average yields on high-grade common stocks fluctuated within a narrow range during 1970 as profits dipped more than 8% during the year and many corporations cut or deferred dividend distributions. From a January 1970 figure of 3.94%, average yields slipped in February to 3.73%, then rose in March, April, and May to reach a high of 4.51% before dropping off during the remainder of the year. Every month of 1970 reflected substantially higher yields than its corresponding month of 1969.

U.S. government bond prices, as seen in Table III, moved narrowly during the first ten months of the year at levels below the corresponding months of 1969. Yields, which were at all-time high levels for long-term government debt issues, averaged 6.86% in January 1970 and then fell to 6.44% in February and 6.39% in March. They rose in April to 6.53%, in May to 6.94%, and in June to 6.99% before the easing of money following the Penn Central bankruptcy dropped the level of interest rates generally.

Table I. Selected Major World Stock Market Price Indexes*

Country	1970 range High	Low	Year-end indexes 1969	1970	Percent change
Australia	663	474	654	516	−21.1%
Austria	2,154	1,946	1,956	2,049†	+ 4.8
Belgium	93	85	92	92	—
France	86	71	81	75	− 7.4
West Germany	130	94	129	94	−27.1
Italy	76	56	70	56	−20.0
Japan	2,534	1,930	2,359	1,987	−15.8
Netherlands	134	108	122	113	− 7.4
South Africa (gold stocks)	56	45	47	53	+12.8
Sweden	337	231	327	246	−24.8
Switzerland	355	268	347	302	−13.0
United Kingdom	423	316	407	341	−16.2

*Index numbers are rounded, and limited to countries for which full year's data were available.
†As of Dec. 18, 1970.
Sources: *Barron's, The Economist, Financial Times, New York Times,* Swiss Bank Corporation.

Table II. U.S. Stock Market Prices and Yields

Month	Railroads (20 stocks) 1970	1969	Industrials (425 stocks) 1970	1969	Public utilities (55 stocks) 1970	1969	Composite (500 stocks) 1970	1969	Yield (200 stocks; %) 1970	1969
January	37.62	54.11	99.40	110.97	55.72	68.65	90.31	102.04	3.94	3.24
February	36.58	54.78	95.73	110.15	55.24	69.24	87.16	101.46	3.73	3.39
March	37.33	50.46	96.95	108.20	59.04	66.07	88.65	99.30	3.75	3.28
April	36.05	49.53	94.01	110.68	57.19	65.63	85.95	101.26	4.09	3.22
May	31.10	49.97	83.16	114.53	51.15	66.91	76.06	104.62	4.28	3.23
June	28.94	46.43	82.96	108.59	49.22	63.29	75.59	99.14	4.51	3.41
July	26.59	43.00	83.00	103.68	50.91	61.32	75.72	94.71	4.20	3.62
August	26.74	42.04	85.40	103.39	52.62	59.20	77.92	94.18	4.04	3.48
September	29.14	42.03	90.66	103.97	54.44	57.84	82.58	94.51	3.94	3.44
October	31.73	41.75	92.85	105.07	53.37	58.80	84.37	95.52	3.96	3.58
November	30.80	40.63	92.58	105.86	54.86	59.46	84.28	96.21	3.75	3.58
December		36.69		100.48		55.28		91.11		3.62

Source: U.S. Department of Commerce, *Survey of Current Business.* Prices are Standard and Poor's monthly averages of daily closing prices with 1941–43=10. Yield figures are Moody's index of 200 stocks.

Table III. U.S. Government Long-Term Bond Prices and Yields
Average price in dollars per $100 bond

Month	Average 1970	1969	Yield (%) 1970	1969	Month	Average 1970	1969	Yield (%) 1970	1969
January	58.33	67.61	6.86	5.74	July	60.59	64.75	6.57	6.07
February	61.63	66.55	6.44	5.86	August	59.20	65.18	6.75	6.02
March	62.04	64.90	6.39	6.05	September	60.10	62.64	6.63	6.32
April	60.89	67.73	6.53	5.84	October	60.44	63.05	6.59	6.27
May	57.78	66.68	6.94	5.85	November	63.27	61.08	6.24	6.51
June	57.37	64.84	6.99	6.06	December		58.71		6.81

Source: U.S. Department of Commerce, *Survey of Current Business.* Average prices are derived from average yields on the basis of an assumed 3% 20-year taxable U.S. Treasury bond. Yields are for U.S. Treasury bonds that are taxable and due or callable in ten years or more.

Table IV. U.S. Corporate Bond Prices and Yields
Average price in dollars per $100 bond

Month	Average 1970	1969	Yield (%) 1970	1969	Month	Average 1970	1969	Yield (%) 1970	1969
January	62.2	72.5	7.91	6.59	July	59.0	68.2	8.44	7.08
February	62.4	72.1	7.93	6.66	August	60.0	68.4	8.13	6.97
March	62.8	71.0	7.84	6.85	September	60.8	67.2	8.09	7.14
April	62.8	70.1	7.83	6.89	October	61.3	66.5	8.03	7.33
May	61.2	70.2	8.11	6.79	November	61.9	65.6	8.05	7.35
June	59.4	68.8	8.48	6.98	December		62.9		7.72

Source: U.S. Department of Commerce, *Survey of Current Business.* Average prices are based on Standard and Poor's composite index of A1+ issues. Yields are based on Moody's Aaa domestic corporate bond index.

At that time, yields began a steady decline, interrupted only briefly in August.

Yields on three-month Treasury bills began 1970 at about 8%, fell in March to 6½%, rose through June to 7%, dipped to 6% in September, and were under 5% by November. Yields on all maturities of government securities plummeted in November as the growing conviction that interest rates were headed downward bolstered demand for both bills and coupon issues.

U.S. corporate bond prices, as seen in Table IV, rose slightly from a January level of 62.2 to 62.8 in March, then declined to 59 in July, and finally began a rise that gained momentum by the year's end. Yields on high-grade corporate issues were high throughout 1970. From a 7.91% level in January, a record, average yields rose to 7.93% in February, fell in March and April, rose to a new all-time record high of 8.48% in June, and then dropped off during the remaining months of the year. A sharp decline at the end of 1970 brought average yields back to the level of a year earlier.

The economic recession and growing anxiety about continuing inflation, along with rising unemployment, sharply falling profits, high interest rates, and a sharp rise in consumer savings created a bearish climate during the first half of 1970 despite a moderate easing of the growth rate of the money supply and assurances by U.S. Pres. Richard Nixon and his Council of Economic Advisers that the economy was basically sound and inflation was being brought under control.

By the end of 1970 bullish factors were dominant on the stock exchanges. Interest rates were falling sharply, and the prime rate moved downward in small but rapid steps. Fiscal policy was becoming more expansionary with a promise by President Nixon that budget deficits were planned with no new taxes for 1971 and 1972. Monetary policy was loosened, and stock prices were moving forward on a broad front. Customers were beginning to return to the brokers' offices, and speculative interest was reemerging. Unemployment, while abnormally high, was of less concern, and the price level rose more slowly than at the beginning of the year. Most forecasters asserted that the worst was over and that the economy was emerging from a recession, with 1971 to be a good year and 1972 even better.

On the New York Stock Exchange (NYSE) the volume of transactions during 1970 was 2,937,093,020 shares, a slight gain over the 2,850,504,873 recorded in 1969. The number of issues traded was 1,846 in 1970, as compared with 1,794 for the previous year. Aggregate volume in 1970 established an all-time high for the NYSE. Bond volume was also at record levels, with 1970 recording $4,497,260,000 in sales, a gain of 23.2% over the $3,648,741,000 in 1969.

A profit squeeze on brokerage firms, in which high daily volume aggravated their myriad back-office problems and their securities portfolio values declined, caused many to become insolvent and resulted in fundamental changes in the securities marketplace. The special $55 million trust fund of the NYSE was fully committed in the liquidation of ten substantial member firms that closed their doors, and additional contributions to the fund had to be assessed. Acquisitions of troubled firms by stronger members were encouraged, and in the case of Goodbody & Co., taken over by Merrill Lynch, Pierce, Fenner and Smith, Inc., the trust fund agreed to indemnify Merrill Lynch for up to $20 million of losses arising from Goodbody's

WIDE WORLD

Investors check stock prices at a booth of Merrill Lynch, Pierce, Fenner and Smith, Inc., located in New York's Grand Central Station, May 27, 1970. A record Dow-Jones average gain of +32.04 was recorded that day.

operations problems and for up to $10 million of damages stemming from any lawsuits brought against Goodbody.

The enactment of the Securities Investor Protection Act provided a guarantee for an individual investor against cash losses of up to $20,000 and total loss, including securities, of up to $50,000. The insurance fund, backed by a $1 billion line of credit from the U.S. Treasury, was to be financed by assessments against securities firms covered by it.

Stock brokerage commissions were increased in 1970 with a surcharge of up to $15 per transaction on purchases of less than 1,000 shares. On April 2 the Securities and Exchange Commission (SEC) approved the surcharge as an emergency relief measure for the securities industry. Rates on the exchanges' basic minimum fees were increased by $15 or 50% of the minimum fee, whichever was smaller.

A stockholder survey conducted for the NYSE in 1970 revealed that there were 30,850,000 U.S. residents who were shareowners. This was 15% of the population, compared with 10.4% in 1965. Indirectly, through institutions, more than 100 million Americans had interests in stocks. Males accounted for 50.1% of stocks owned by individuals in 1970, displacing the female predominance in this area of wealth ownership.

On the American Stock Exchange, the volume of transactions in 1970 was the lowest since 1966, dropping sharply to 843,116,260 shares, compared with 1,240,742,012 in 1969, a decline of 32%. The number of issues traded on the Amex, however, at 1,234, was the highest ever, a gain of 62 issues over the 1969 number.

Canada. The Canadian stock exchanges in 1970 exhibited patterns similar to those in the U.S. as stock prices declined during the first five months of the year, leveled off, and then rose to their 1970 highs during the last two months. Total 1970 trading vol-

FOX PHOTOS FROM
PICTORIAL PARADE

London's new £10 million
Stock Exchange building
towers over other buildings
at 350-ft. The 26-story
structure was built
by Trollope and Colls Ltd.

ume on the Toronto Stock Exchange was $3.7 billion, off 35% from the 1969 figure but still the third largest on record. At $1,350,000,000, the dollar volume on the Montreal and Canadian stock exchanges was down approximately 17%. Between December 1969 and December 1970 the average yield on 114 stocks on the Toronto Exchange rose 17.8%.

Canadians were proud of the fact that no member firm of a major Canadian stock exchange went bankrupt in 1970. This performance was attributed to strict regulation of minimum capital rules and the conditions for withdrawal of subordinated capital notes of brokerage firms. (I. Pr.)

European Economic Community. Four of the five EEC countries for which current stock market data were available experienced bear markets in 1970. West Germany showed the largest average loss in

stock prices at 27%. Stock prices declined 20% in Italy, while a 7% drop was encountered in both France and the Netherlands. The Belgian stock price index ended 1970 at the same level as at the end of 1969.

For the first time in four years, the West German stock exchanges experienced a bear market. Stock prices began falling in the first week of January, and by March 4 the averages had lost 9%. Mounting pressures on consumer prices in a period of unparalleled prosperity, in part caused by the upward revaluation of the West German mark in October 1969, led to a decision by the Bundesbank to raise the bank rate to a record 7½%. In January the price level for industrial goods was 6% above that of January 1969. The cost of short-term borrowing to prime customers rose from 9.5% in early January to between 11 and 11.5% in March. Following a brief rally in early April, stock prices resumed their decline. From mid-April to May 27, the average decline was 20%.

The Bundestag in mid-July enacted a series of anti-inflationary measures, including a 10% tax increase. In response to these fiscal measures, the Bundesbank sought to ease money market pressures through several reductions in the bank rate. Cuts of a half percentage point each on November 17 and December 4 lowered the rate to 6%.

Average yields on domestic government bonds reached 8.34% in October, only slightly below the 1970 high set in June (8.49%) but substantially above December 1969 (7.38%). The comparable yield on domestic corporate bonds was 8.32%, nearly a full percentage point above the yield that prevailed in January 1970. At the end of December, stock prices were at the year's lowest level, and the overall decline in 1970 was the severest of the major world stock price indexes.

The Italian stock market also took a beating in 1970. After rising 2% in 1968 and 11% in 1969, the Italian stock market dropped 20% from the end of 1969 to the end of 1970. Strikes and production losses were chiefly responsible, and stock prices at the end of December were at their yearly lows.

In France, the price of stocks declined an average of 7% from the end of 1969 to the end of 1970. The first half of 1970 saw prices on the Paris Bourse

Index of industrial
ordinary share prices
on the London Stock
Exchange, 1949–70.

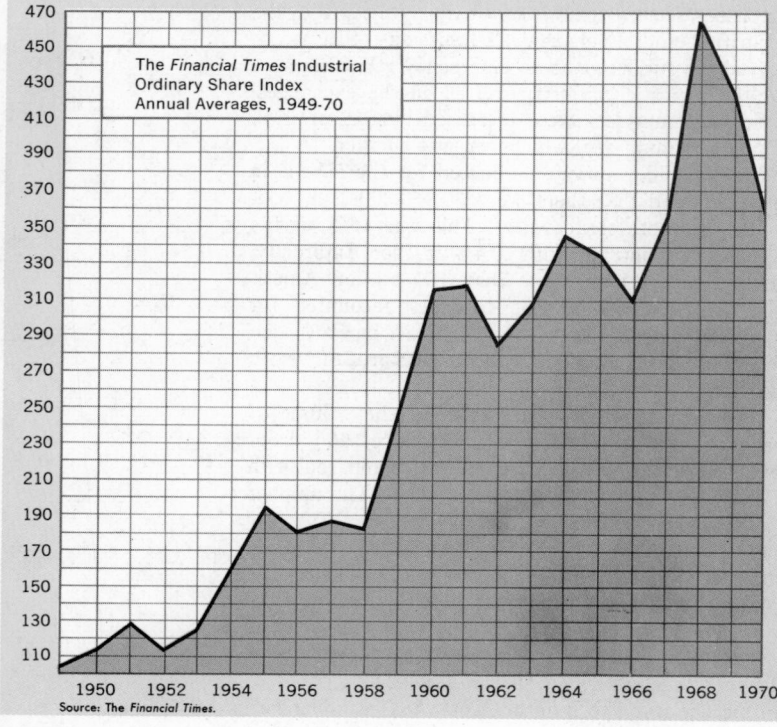

The *Financial Times* Industrial
Ordinary Share Index
Annual Averages, 1949-70

Source: The *Financial Times*.

drop 11%. Prices reached a peak in the last week of January and steadily moved lower until the end of May. The market was adversely affected, particularly in May, by the growing involvement of the U.S. in Southeast Asia. Battle damage to French investments in Cambodia precipitated a sharp decline in share prices. After a brief decline in early July, which carried equity values to the lowest point of the year, the index of stock prices on the Paris Bourse settled into a relatively small trading range, marked by 76 on the upside and 72 on the downside.

The Netherlands stock market in 1970 followed a pattern similar to the one experienced in West Germany. However, the average decline (7%) in stock prices was not as severe. The index of prices on the Amsterdam Stock Exchange moved within a fairly narrow range throughout 1970. The high of 134 was established on April 23, while the lowest reading (108) was recorded on May 26.

In Belgium, stock prices ended 1970 unchanged from the 1969 close. In fact, price performance on the Brussels Bourse was the strongest of the EEC countries, and third best among the selected major stock price indexes. During the first 16 weeks of 1970, the index fluctuated around the December 1969 levels without any apparent trend. The 1970 peak, established on April 6, was 1% above the 1969 close. The subsequent decline (9%) lasted until June 5, which proved to be the year's lowest level. A rebound followed, and prices moved higher until the first week of August. At this point, stock prices were only 1% below the year's high.

European Free Trade Association (EFTA). Current stock price data were available for four of the countries that make up EFTA. Counted among the countries with bear markets were Great Britain, Sweden, and Switzerland. On the bullish side, Austria showed higher stock prices.

In Great Britain, the *Financial Times* index of 30 industrial stocks traded on the London Stock Exchange declined 16% from the end of 1969 to the end of 1970. The index reached its 1970 high on January 14, and the low was established June 15. Stock prices began 1970 on an uptrend. The rally of early January was more or less a continuation of the trend started in mid-December 1969 on news that the November balance of trade had shown a surplus for the fourth consecutive month. However, prices soon started to erode. The market declined on balance from about mid-January to well into June.

The bearish attitude of British investors during this period stemmed from growing apprehension that limited production gains in the face of rising wage costs would severely squeeze corporate profits, and from an uneasy concern that the bear market in New York might be a harbinger of serious economic difficulties for the U.S. that might affect the entire non-Communist world.

The surprise election victory of Edward Heath and the establishment of a Conservative Party government on June 18 touched off a sharp rally on the London Stock Exchange. From the June low to the close of July 1, equity prices rose 10%. However, the market resumed its decline when it became evident to investors that the Conservative government would continue the economic squeeze. A strike by dock workers, which lasted from July 16 to August 3, also contributed to the negative attitude of investors.

Early in September stock prices began to develop strength, in part due to the sharp rally that occurred

in the U.S. after August 20. The *Financial Times* industrial index took off on its most sustained rally of the year between September 14 and 30, rising approximately 8%. A further spurt during the first seven days of October pushed the index 13 points higher, putting it about 20% above the June lows.

In retrospect, this relatively sharp increase in stock prices anticipated, to some limited degree, Prime Minister Edward Heath's October 27 announcement of lower corporate and individual income taxes, effective in April 1971. The Conservative government also proposed to reduce the projected annual growth in public expenditures to 2.8% from 3.5%. At the same time, farm and housing subsidies were lowered. The government sought to restore individual initiative, create incentives for business enterprise, and stimulate the accumulation of savings.

Nevertheless, stock investors sensed that Britain's economic problems were far from solved. Despite the Conservative government's good intentions, the fact remained that the British economy was operating below its productive potential. Unemployment also continued at a very high level by British standards. Consumer prices rose at an annual rate of approximately 8% in the first half of 1970, compared with 3% during the second half of 1969. Strike votes in

Stock trading on the New York Stock Exchange: yearly range of prices and number of shares sold, 1949–70.

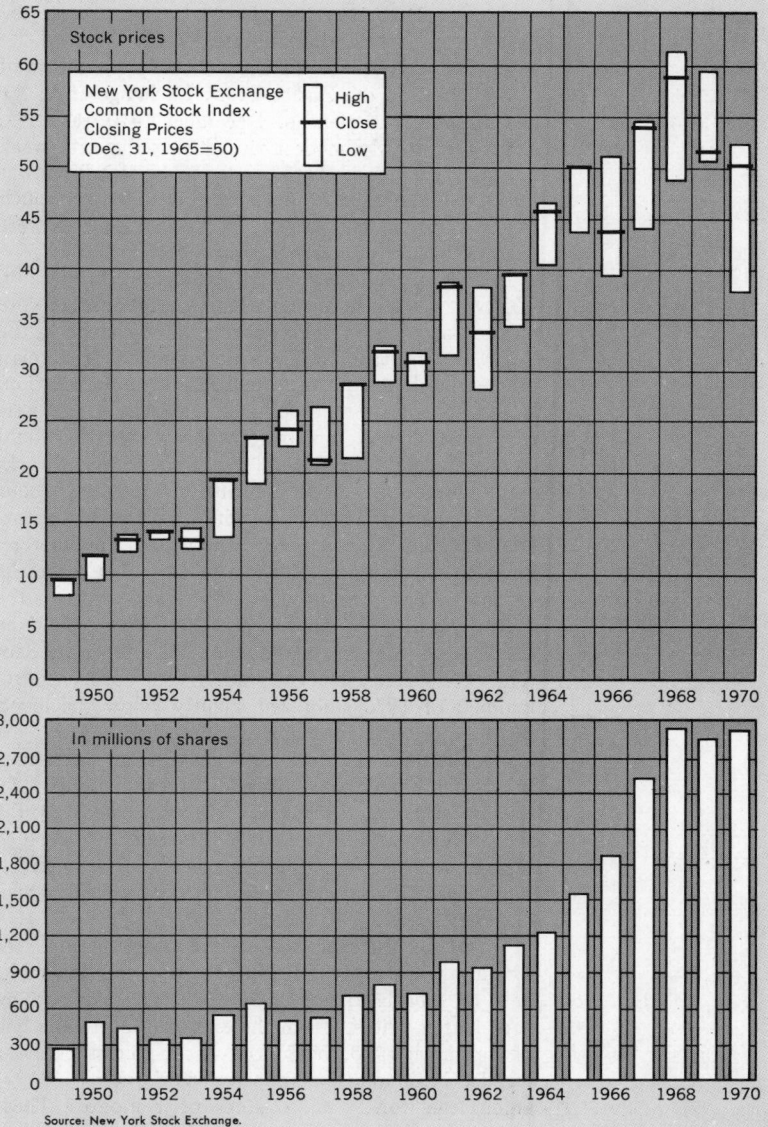

Source: New York Stock Exchange.

early November by British and Scottish miners reminded investors of the country's difficulty in restraining wage demands that exceeded productivity increases. Not surprisingly, the stock market drifted lower throughout November and early December. Share prices at the end of December were about 9% below the October high and 34% below the all-time high reached in January 1969.

The influence of soaring inflation was especially apparent in the Swedish stock market. Average share prices on the Stockholm Stock Exchange declined 25% from the end of 1969 to the end of 1970. The index of prices retreated from the January high of 337 to approximately the 280 level at the end of February before turning upward. The subsequent rally, which carried stock prices back to the 300 level, proved to be of only short duration and before the end of May, the index had declined to less than 240. Average yields on domestic corporate bonds, which were steady at the 8½% level during the first five months of 1970, jumped to 9.3% in May. A summer recovery in stock prices was quite vigorous. September's final prices were 8% above the May lows. This was followed, however, by another wave of selling, and by late October the market had retreated into new low territory. By mid-December the market had recovered some of October's losses, but the overall decline in 1970 was the second largest among the major world stock price indexes.

In Switzerland, the decline in the price index of issues listed on the Zürich Stock Exchange from the end of 1969 to the end of December 1970 was 13%. After a relatively modest rise during the first week of January, average share prices moved steadily lower until the end of April when prices began to drop much faster. Near the end of May, Swiss stock prices were 23% below the December close.

In early June, stock prices managed a brief rally. This was largely in anticipation of a favourable vote on the June 7 referendum asking for a change in the Swiss constitution to limit the number of foreign inhabitants in each canton to 10% of the population. Voters rejected the proposal; the margin was so narrow, however, as to create fears that new curbs would be introduced in the Federal Assembly. Foreign workers accounted for about one-third of the Swiss labour force, and any reduction in their admission into Switzerland would intensify labour shortages and thereby impede the government's plans to control inflation. As a result, stock prices tended to drift lower until the first week of July when there occurred a sustained rise that added 12% to the stock price index by September 4. After a brief decline, prices during the remainder of 1970 stabilized slightly below the levels recorded in early September.

For the third year in a row, the Austrian stock market posted higher share prices. From the end of 1969 to mid-December 1970, the average rise was 5%, the second best increase shown by the major world stock market indexes. This could be traced to the noninflationary growth that had been achieved by the Austrian economy since 1968.

Other Countries. Among the other nations for which current stock price information was available, only the South African gold stocks were able to record higher prices. From the end of 1969 to the end of December 1970, the South African gold stock index (traded in London) was the best performer (+13%) among the world's major stock price indexes. These shares tended to reflect investor views regarding world economic conditions, international monetary prospects, and the price of gold as measured by the bids and offers in the London gold bullion market. In mid-October, gold prices reached $37.43, the highest level in 11 months.

Lower stock markets were experienced by Australia and Japan. The decline on the Sydney Stock Exchange was 21%. In mid-August the government presented its new budget, which called for substantial tax relief in the lower- and middle-income groups. However, the reduction in revenues was to be offset by indirect and corporate taxation. The tax increase on publicly owned corporations, from 45 to 47.5%, was primarily responsible for the depressed hopes of investors for continued gains in per-share earnings.

Japan, with a decline in share prices averaging 16%, also experienced a weak stock market in 1970. The index of 225 common stocks on the Tokyo Stock Exchange reached an all-time high in mid-April, about 100% higher than when the bull market started at the beginning of 1968. A technical correction during the following six weeks dropped prices 24% below the historic peak. After a brief rally in June and early July, the stock price index fluctuated in a relatively narrow range for the rest of the year.   (R. H. Tr.)

See also Economy, World; Investment, International; Money and Banking; Savings and Investments.

Sudan

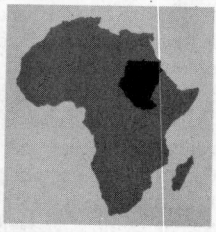

A republic of northeast Africa, the Sudan is bounded by the U.A.R., the Red Sea, Ethiopia, Kenya, Uganda, the Congo (Kinshasa), the Central African Republic, Chad, and Libya. Area: 967,491 sq.mi. (2,505,805 sq.km.). Pop. (1969 est.): 15,186,000, including Arabs in the north and Negroes in the south. Cap.: Khartoum (pop., 1967 est., 188,000). Largest city: Omdurman (pop., 1967 est., 203,000). Language: Arabic; various tribal languages in the south. Religion: Muslim in the north; predominantly pagan in the south. Chairman of the Revolutionary Council and prime minister in 1970, Maj. Gen. Gafaar Muhammad al-Nimeiry.

Sudan moved a stage closer to full cooperation with its Arab neighbour states when the formation of a unified leadership for the United Arab Republic (U.A.R.), Libya, and Sudan was announced in Cairo in mid-November. Collaboration between the three states had been increasing since their three presidents met in Tripoli, Libya, in December 1969, but the drive toward unity was given fresh impetus by the death in September of Pres. Gamal Abd-al-Nasser of the U.A.R. and the consequent need for a united Arab front. During the year joint committees discussed cooperation in foreign affairs, transport, industry, irrigation, agriculture, and trade; and the three presidents met in February, May, and September. A practical aspect of cooperation was the provision by Sudan of air bases and military training camps for the U.A.R.'s armed forces. Sudan was, however, hesitant to rush into complete tripartite unity, preferring to set no timetable even for federation.

The military regime headed by Major General Nimeiry had severe internal political problems during 1970. In March, faced with some provocation during his tour of the central Sudan, Nimeiry decided to suppress the Ansar movement, the country's main Muslim

SUDAN

Education. (1966–67) Primary, pupils 455,765, teachers 10,734; secondary, pupils 108,400, teachers 5,371; vocational, pupils 5,495, teachers 464; teacher training, students 1,355, teachers 156; higher (including 3 universities), students 8,708, teaching staff 1,012.

Finance. Monetary unit: Sudanese pound, with a par value of Sud£0.35 to U.S. $1 (Sud£84 = £1 sterling). Gold, SDRs, and foreign exchange, official: (June 1970) U.S. $39.2 million; (June 1969) U.S. $48.2 million. Budget (1968–69 est.): revenue Sud£113.5 million; expenditure Sud£100 million. Cost of living (1963 = 100): (Dec. 1969) 121; (Dec. 1968) 105.

Foreign Trade. (1969) Imports Sud£89,320,000; exports Sud£86,250,000. Import sources (1968): U.K. 18%; India 10%; Japan 9%; U.S.S.R. 7%; China 7%; Italy 6%; West Germany 5%. Export destinations (1968): West Germany 15%; Italy 12%; India 10%; Japan 8%; China 6%; U.K. 6%; U.S.S.R. 6%; Netherlands 5%. Main exports: cotton 60%; gum arabic 10%; peanuts 6%.

Transport and Communications. Roads (1968) c. 50,000 km. (mainly tracks, including c. 2,500 km. with improved surface). Motor vehicles in use: passenger (1968) 27,400; commercial (including buses; 1967) 18,500. Railways: (1967) 4,749 km.; freight traffic (1968) 2,366,000,000 net ton-km. Air traffic (1968): 151,732,000 passenger-km.; freight 2,476,000 net ton-km. Navigable waterways (1967) 4,068 km. Telephones (Dec. 1968) 45,086. Radio receivers (Dec. 1968) c. 180,000. Television receivers (Dec. 1968) 15,000.

Agriculture. Production (in 000; metric tons; 1969; 1968 in parentheses): millet 427 (278); sorghum 1,417 (710); cotton, lint 225 (184); durra (1967) 880, (1966) 914; sesame 202 (122); dates (1968) c. 70, (1967) c. 68; bananas c. 10 (c. 10); peanuts 383 (197). Livestock (in 000; 1968–69): cattle c. 11,300; sheep 12,678; goats (1967–68) c. 8,400; camels (1967–68) c. 2,500; asses c. 590.

Industry. Production (in 000; 1968): salt (metric tons) 65; electricity (public supply only; kw-hr.) 334,000.

sectarian organization, which had been a major force in politics before the revolution of May 1969. The Ansar resisted in its main strongholds at Omdurman and Aba Island but, with tanks and aircraft, the armed forces achieved a total, if bloody, victory.

In May, on the first anniversary of the revolution, a series of nationalization measures was initiated when all banks and the main British-owned business houses were taken over by the state. Nationalization of other foreign businesses and the cotton trade followed in June, while the grain trade and the press were nationalized in August.

The southern Sudan remained troubled throughout 1970 with clashes between the armed forces and southern rebels reported every month. The Ministry for Southern Affairs sought to restore normal life to those parts of the southern provinces under government control, but there was little or no security in Equatoria Province and the armed forces launched a major offensive against rebel camps there in October. (PR. K.)

ENCYCLOPÆDIA BRITANNICA FILMS. *The Nile Valley and Its People* (1964).

Swaziland

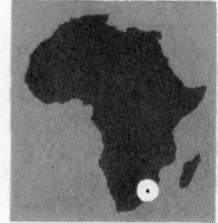

A landlocked constitutional monarchy of southern Africa, Swaziland is bounded by South Africa and Mozambique. Area: 6,704 sq.mi. (17,363 sq.km.). Pop. (1969 est.): 408,609. Cap. and largest city, Mbabane (pop., 1966, 13,803). Language: Swazi. Religion: Christian 60%. King, Sobhuza II; prime minister in 1970, Prince Makhosini Dlamini.

SWAZILAND

Education. (1968) Primary, pupils 62,082, teachers 1,627; secondary, pupils 6,246, teachers 300; vocational, pupils 81, teachers 10; teacher training, students 243, teachers 29; higher, students 69, teaching staff 15.

Finance and Trade. Monetary unit: South African rand (R 0.71 = U.S. $1; R 1.71 = £1 sterling). Budget (1970–71 est.) balanced at R 15,164,000. Foreign trade (1969): imports c. R 38 million; exports c. R 48 million. Main exports: sugar 22%; iron ore 20%; wood pulp 15%; asbestos 13%.

Agriculture. Production (in 000; metric tons; 1968; 1967 in parentheses): corn c. 36 (63); rice 8 (6); sugar, raw value (1969–70) c. 157, (1968–69) 154; cotton, lint c. 2 (2). Livestock (in 000; Sept. 1969): cattle c. 515; sheep c. 42; pigs c. 12; goats (Dec. 1967) c. 240; chickens (Sept. 1968) c. 350.

Industry. Production (in 000; metric tons; 1968): coal 97; iron ore (metal content) 1,292; asbestos 38.

Well endowed with natural resources and racially harmonious, Swaziland continued on its course of political stability and economic development in 1970, attracting large overseas investment and reducing unemployment. The 1970–71 recurrent budget was balanced without external aid for the first time since independence, due to increased revenue from the revised terms of the South African Customs Union and from export returns. The U.K., however, continued to provide R 4.2 million of the R 5 million capital budget.

Economic prospects continued to lie in agricultural development, buttressed by mineral resources and manufacturing diversification. South Africa remained Swaziland's closest trading partner, supplying 91% of its imports as well as considerable capital and technical aid. Anglo-American of South Africa reached record iron ore production at Ngwenya and undertook a mineral survey of the whole country by agreement with King Sobhuza (in whom all mineral rights were vested). Britain continued to finance the R 73.1 million five-year plan, 1969–74, and in January 1970 agreed to contribute £6.4 million for land development projects. The Commonwealth Development Corporation remained Swaziland's biggest single investor with a total investment of about £24 million. (M. MR.)

Sweden

A constitutional monarchy of northern Europe lying on the eastern side of the Scandinavian Peninsula, Sweden has common borders with Finland and Norway. Area: 173,648 sq.mi. (449,750 sq.km.). Pop. (1970 est.): 8,013,696. Cap. and largest city: Stockholm (pop., 1970 est., 747,490). Language: Swedish, with some Finnish and Lapp in the north. Religion: predominantly Lutheran. King, Gustaf VI Adolf; prime minister in 1970, Olof Palme.

Sweden's Social Democratic government held onto office at the general election in September 1970, but its grip was severely shaken. The election, the first for a new one-chamber Riksdag (parliament), wiped out the government's parliamentary majority, leaving it with 45.3% of the vote—a loss of 4.8% compared with the 1968 election. The nonsocialist opposition parties actually came through with 7 seats more than the government, but the latter could rely on the support of the Communists, who unexpectedly gained 17 seats. The government survived against tough odds, including a deteriorating economy, factory closures, unemployment fears, and crumbling labour relations

Sugar: *see* Agriculture
Sulfur: *see* Mining
Surfing: *see* Sporting Record
Surgery: *see* Medicine
Surinam: *see* Dependent States

AUTHENTICATED NEWS INTERNATIONAL

An oil slick resulting from a two-ship collision in April 1970 burns in Trälhavet Bay near Stockholm with the help of a combustion-promoting chemical called Cab-O-Sil ST-2-0.

—to say nothing of Gunnar Hedlund, leader of the Centre Party, who emerged as the "winning loser," since his party's share of the vote showed the largest increase.

In addition, Prime Minister Palme was a sharp contrast to his venerated predecessor, Tage Erlander, a reassuring father figure with a strong personal following. Palme, a clever, courageous, and extremely able politician, displayed a noticeable concern for social injustice—indeed, the linchpin of his idealistic election campaign was the need for more equality— but he lacked the common touch of Erlander. Certainly, the election was to some extent a rebuff, although probably from older voters, since Palme had strong support among younger Social Democrats.

The prime minister had other problems: the economy was faltering badly. Inflationary pressures were high, the balance of payments deficit was worsening, interest rates were climbing, and there was a profits squeeze in industry. Between December 1967 and July 1970 consumer prices had risen by 11.7%, with nearly half the increase in the last six months, and the situation was obviously getting out of hand. The government had imposed restrictions on credit in May and a price freeze on certain categories of food in August, but with the election out of the way, the deflationary arsenal was heftily increased. Early in October, fearful that industry would raise prices to compensate for expected wage increases, the government froze prices on "all goods and services offered on the Swedish market" until April 1, 1971. There was no mention of a wage freeze, which caused glum faces in the business community. A week later certain taxes were raised or extended. This was the first time that

price controls had been used since the emergency controls of World War II.

The budget for 1970–71 reflected a tightening economic policy and restrictive spending, but allowed scope for the government's continuing efforts toward social reform. It was said that a strict application of priorities would ensure security and development toward greater equality between sexes and classes. In connection with the latter, the budget outlined a major tax reform, due to come into force on Jan. 1, 1971, designed to alleviate the burden on low-income groups. The budget revealed a deficit of 799 million kronor (compared with 3,070,000,000 kronor in 1969–70). As usual, the largest slice of the cake went to the Ministry of Social Affairs, followed by education and defense. During 1969 the gross national product rose by a greater percentage than the average for the latter half of the 1960s. Demand was higher than had been predicted, and prices rose sharply. The government's primary task in economic policy, according to the finance bill, was to remove tensions in the economy without departing from the fundamental aims of full employment, continued economic growth, and a more uniform distribution of income. (In April the Organization for Economic Cooperation and Development report on Sweden said that an improvement in the balance of payments must be the major aim of economic policy in 1970.) The budget also showed a 26% increase in aid to less developed countries.

Nordek and the EEC continued to be major points of discussion. Nordek, a proposed economic union of Sweden, Norway, Denmark, and Finland, seemed to have some hope of success toward the end of 1969, but in December of that year the Finns raised the question of whether future growth of the EEC might influence Nordek's structure, a prospect that did not please them. Nevertheless, hope persisted, and in February Nordic leaders expressed their willingness to sign a treaty. A month later, however, the Finns declared themselves unable to be a party to it, due to possible EEC developments. Attention therefore turned to Sweden's efforts to find accommodation within the Treaty of Rome, regarded by many as far more important. The EEC confronted the government with difficult choices; determined to pursue its aims of security and equality, it nonetheless recognized the problems of reconciling them with the EEC's assumption that member countries should adapt themselves to the organization's structure rather than

SWEDEN

Education. (1967–68) Primary, pupils 623,000, teachers 27,700; secondary, pupils 426,400, teachers 37,798; vocational, pupils 242,000, teachers 16,019; teacher training, students 9,740; higher (including 8 universities), students 98,317, teaching staff (1964–65) 2,296.

Finance. Monetary unit: krona, with a par value of 5.17 kronor to U.S. $1 (12.42 kronor = £1 sterling). Gold, SDRs, and foreign exchange, central bank: (June 1970) U.S. $544 million; (June 1969) U.S. $470 million. Budget (1969–70 rev. est.): revenue 39,160,397,000 kronor; expenditure 37,415,012,000 kronor. Gross national product: (1968) 132,290,000,000 kronor; (1967) 124,880,000,000 kronor. Money supply: (June 1970) 15,380,000,000 kronor; (June 1969) 14,760,000,000 kronor. Cost of living (1963 = 100): (June 1970) 134; (June 1969) 126.

Foreign Trade. (1969) Imports 30,401,000,000 kronor; exports 29,425,000,000 kronor. Import sources: West Germany 19%; U.K. 14%; U.S. 9%; Denmark 8%; Norway 6%; Finland 5%. Export destinations: U.K. 13%; West Germany 12%; Denmark 10%; Norway 10%; U.S. 6%; Finland 5%; France 5%. Main exports: machinery 24%; paper 9%; iron and steel 9%; wood pulp 8%; motor vehicles 8%; timber 6%; ships and boats 6%.

Transport and Communications. Roads (1969) 173,582 km. (including 376 km. expressways). Motor vehicles in use (1969): passenger 2,193,634; commercial 142,602. Railways: (1968) 12,812 km. (including 7,547 km. electrified); traffic (state system only; 1969) 4,126,000,000 passenger-km., freight 14,863,000,000 net ton-km. Air traffic (including Swedish apportionment of international routes of Scandinavian Airline System; 1969): 2,124,000,000 passenger-km.; freight 109,959,000 net ton-km. Shipping (1969): merchant vessels 100 gross tons and over; 1,051; gross tonnage 5,029,407. Telephones (Dec. 1968) 3,934,694. Radio receivers (Dec. 1968) 2,927,000. Television receivers (Dec. 1968) 2,345,000.

Agriculture. Production (in 000; metric tons; 1969; 1968 in parentheses): wheat 917 (1,059); barley 1,402 (1,776); oats 1,133 (1,523); rye 178 (210); potatoes 873 (1,424); sugar, raw value (1969–70) 185, (1968–69) 293; rapeseed 198 (263); meat (1968) 397, (1967) 398; butter 62 (66); cheese 58 (59); timber (cu.m.; 1967–68) 51,200, (1966–67) 53,800; fish catch (1968) 315, (1967) 340. Livestock (in 000; June 1969): cattle 2,005; horses c. 67; sheep 332; pigs 2,030; chickens 8,515.

Industry. Index of industrial production (1963 = 100): (1969) 145; (1968) 135. Production (in 000; metric tons; 1969): iron ore (60% metal content) 33,278; coal (1969) 20; electricity (87% hydroelectric in 1968; kw-hr.) 58,004,000; pig iron 2,500; crude steel 5,320; cement 3,957; copper 52; lead (1968) 42; gold (troy oz.; 1968) 50; silver (troy oz.; 1968) 3,524; cotton yarn 13; mechanical wood pulp (1968) 1,320; chemical wood pulp (1968) 5,718; newsprint 934; other paper (1968) 2,826. Merchant vessels launched (100 gross tons and over; 1969) 1,336,000 gross tons. New dwelling units completed (1969) 109,000.

Games at Edinburgh; the World University Games (FISU) at Turin, Italy; and the European championships at Barcelona, Spain, helped spark an onslaught on world records that produced 25 new marks in 1970.

U.S. Competition. U.S. swimmers lowered the individual world marks on 13 occasions and snapped the world standards for relays on three occasions. John Kinsella and Mike Burton engaged in a titanic struggle at the U.S. Amateur Athletic Union (AAU) long-course (outdoor) championships in Los Angeles, and became the first men ever to break the 16-minute barrier for the 1,500-m. freestyle. This was considered an achievement comparable to breaking four minutes for the mile in track.

The AAU meet, August 20–23, produced 12 world and 17 U.S. records. Kinsella, 18, a high-school student from Hinsdale, Ill., defeated Burton, the 1968 Olympic champion and defending world record holder, in the 1,500-m. freestyle (15 min. 57.1 sec.) and also erased the old world mark in the 400-m. freestyle by clocking 4 min. 2.8 sec. Mike Stamm, 18, a high-school senior from San Diego, Calif., erased Roland Matthes' 200-m. backstroke record with a time of 2 min. 6.3 sec.

Gary Hall, 19, a freshman from Indiana University, for the second year in a row lowered three world records. Hall, from Garden Grove, Calif., bettered his own standards in the 200-m. individual medley (2 min. 9.5 sec.) and 400-m. individual medley (4 min. 31 sec.) and showed his versatility by breaking the three-year-old world mark of Mark Spitz in the 200-m. butterfly with a time of 2 min. 5 sec. Earlier in the meet, Spitz had lowered his old mark to 2 min. 5.4 sec., but he was unable to improve on this time in the final and lost to Hall.

Brian Job, 19, a Stanford University freshman, lifted the world mark in the 200-m. breaststroke from the Soviet Union with a time of 2 min. 23.5 sec. The unpredictable Mark Spitz, 19-year-old Indiana University sophomore from Sacramento, Calif., became the world's fastest swimmer when he broke the 100-m. freestyle world record of Australia's Olympic champion Michael Wenden by three-tenths of a second in a preliminary heat at the AAU meet. The new record was 51.9 sec. Spitz could not repeat in the finals and lost the race to a slower time.

Three of the world marks set in the AAU meet in Los Angeles lasted only three weeks. Hall's 200-m. individual medley, Kinsella's 400-m. freestyle, and Stamm's 200-m. backstroke records were lowered in the European championships.

Perennial record smasher Debbie Meyer, a seasoned veteran at 18, showed that she was still the outstanding middle-distance woman swimmer. The Sacramento, Calif., Olympic champion again lowered her 400-m. freestyle mark, to 4 min. 24.3 sec. However, a new threat to Miss Meyer appeared in Australia's Karen Moras, who was less than one second slower than Miss Meyer. At the Australian championships, she lowered Miss Meyer's 800-m. freestyle record to 9 min. 9.1 sec. Subsequently, she broke her own mark in the Commonwealth Games with a time of 9 min. 2.4 sec.

Alice Jones, 18, a student at the University of Cincinnati, lowered one of the oldest marks in the record book when she won the 100-m. butterfly in the time of 1 min. 4.1 sec. The old standard had been set by Ada Kok of the Netherlands in 1965. Earlier in the season, Karen Moe, 17, from Orinda, Calif., erased Miss Kok's 200-m. butterfly mark, but it failed to hold up against the challenge of Miss Jones who

SVENSKT PRESSFOTO FROM KEYSTONE
In Sweden's Parliament Building, Finance Minister Gunnar Sträng answers questions from housewives demonstrating against the new tax reform, which they consider antifamily.

vice versa. Moreover, there was the question of Sweden's neutrality. The government's views on the EEC remained somewhat obscure, but the future path was perhaps indicated by Franco Malfatti, president of the EEC Commission, who in speaking of Sweden's and Switzerland's chances of joining the EEC, said, "It is up to them to evolve, not us."

On the industrial front, Sweden's long-stable labour relations began to show some cracks. Between December 1969 and February 1970 miners at the state-owned iron mines in Swedish Lapland were on strike. Ostensibly about higher pay, the dispute appeared to have other, deeper causes—not least, perhaps, a feeling that the union had fallen into the hands of officials estranged from the rank and file. The strike had much significance for a country increasingly concerned with the concept of industrial democracy. The miners protested, among other things, about a lack of communication among employer, union official, and worker, and there was a strong feeling that the government could ignore them only at its peril. Special in many ways, the strike was nonetheless a timely reminder that even the most successful systems must change and adapt.

Relations between Sweden and the U.S., somewhat cool in recent years, improved slightly with the arrival in April of Jerome Holland as U.S. ambassador to Sweden, a post that had been vacant since his predecessor's departure in January 1969. (A. D. Wi.)

ENCYCLOPÆDIA BRITANNICA FILMS. *Scandinavia—Norway, Sweden, Denmark* (1962).

Swimming

Midway between the 1968 and 1972 Olympic Games, a new set of swimmers emerged with their sights aimed at the 1972 competition. Three international quadrennial tournaments: the British Commonwealth

Swedish Literature:
see Literature

Above, 17-year-old Karen Moe is on her way to a record-breaking time of 2 min. 20.7 sec. in the 200-m. butterfly at the Santa Clara, Calif., international invitational swim meet, July 11, 1970. Above, right, Brian Job edges Rick Colella to set a new 200-m. breaststroke record at the AAU meet in Los Angeles, Aug. 22, 1970.

further lowered the time to 2 min. 19.3 sec. at Los Angeles.

Relays also went through changes, as the men set two world marks and the women one to give the U.S. three of the five new relay marks. A Los Angeles Athletic Club 400-m. freestyle sprint team clocked 3 min. 28.8 sec. at Los Angeles. The U.S. national team competing in Japan lowered the 800-m. freestyle to 7 min. 48 sec., and, also in Japan, the U.S. women's team lowered the 400-m. medley relay to 4 min. 27.4 sec.

European and Commonwealth Competition. The year was one of great success for East Germany. At the European championships the East Germans doubled the medal count of their closest rival, the U.S.S.R., 34 to 17. The East German men won six and the women ten gold medals. Nikolai Pankin, a winner in the 100-m. breaststroke, prevented the Soviets from being shut out in the men's individual races. Roland Matthes set world marks in both the

100-m. and 200-m. backstroke, 56.9 sec. and 2 min. 6.1 sec. His 200-m. time was 0.2 sec. faster than Stamm's set three weeks earlier.

Sweden's Gunnar Larsson, 19, an American-trained athlete, was the surprise of the European meet. Larsson won three gold medals (400-m. freestyle, 200-m. and 400-m. individual medley) and one silver (200-m. freestyle). While winning the 400-m. freestyle, he further lowered the world mark set less than three weeks earlier by Kinsella in Los Angeles to 4 min. 2.6 sec. and then lowered Gary Hall's 200-m. individual medley standard to 2 min. 9.3 sec. West Germany's Hans Fassnacht collected three gold medals (200-m. and 1,500-m. freestyle and 800-m. freestyle relay) and two silver (400-m. freestyle and 400-m. individual medley). East Germany's 400-m. medley relay team took a world record held by the U.S. for ten years when they clipped off one-half second to set the new record at 3 min. 54.4 sec.

Gabriella Wetzko, 16, led a parade of East German women, winning the 100-m. and 200-m. freestyle. For the first time in a decade the U.S. relinquished the women's 400-m. freestyle world record as a quartet of East Germans slashed the mark to 4 min. 0.8 sec.

The World University Games (FISU), generally considered the college Olympics, lost much of its lustre because the East German and the Commonwealth nations' swimmers failed to enter. The U.S. won 19 of the 26 swimming events, capturing 34 gold, 15 silver, and 6 bronze medals.

Australia and Canada dominated the Commonwealth Games, July 17–24. Australia, led by double Olympic gold-medal winner Michael Wenden, won all the men's freestyle events. The Canadians, paced by William Mahoney and George Smith, each winning two events, swept the eight backstroke and breaststroke races. In the women's competition, Karen Moras was the outstanding athlete, winning three individual gold medals (200-m., 400-m., and 800-m. freestyle) as Australia won 10 out of 12 individual events.

Diving. Two U.S. v. Europe diving matches took place in 1970. On April 4–5, at Fort Lauderdale, Fla., the U.S. won. American girls, Cynthia Potter and Debbie Lippman, won the springboard and platform events, while Italy's Giorgio Cagnotto and Klaus Dibiasi won for Europe. In the return match at Bol-

World Records Set in 1970			
Event	Name	Country	Time
MEN			
100-m. freestyle	Mark Spitz	U.S.	51.9 sec.
400-m. freestyle	John Kinsella	U.S.	4 min. 2.8 sec.
400-m. freestyle	Gunnar Larsson	Sweden	4 min. 2.6 sec.
1,500-m. freestyle	John Kinsella	U.S.	15 min. 57.1 sec.
200-m. breaststroke	Brian Job	U.S.	2 min. 23.5 sec.
200-m. butterfly	Mark Spitz	U.S.	2 min. 5.4 sec.
200-m. butterfly	Gary Hall	U.S.	2 min. 5.0 sec.
100-m. backstroke	Roland Matthes	East Germany	56.9 sec.
200-m. backstroke	Mike Stamm	U.S.	2 min. 6.3 sec.
200-m. backstroke	Roland Matthes	East Germany	2 min. 6.1 sec.
200-m. individual medley	Gary Hall	U.S.	2 min. 9.5 sec.
200-m. individual medley	Gunnar Larsson	Sweden	2 min. 9.3 sec.
400-m. individual medley	Gary Hall	U.S.	4 min. 31.0 sec.
400-m. freestyle relay	Los Angeles Athletic Club (D. Frawley, D. Havens, F. Heckl, M. Weston)	U.S.	3 min. 28.8 sec.
800-m. freestyle relay	National team (G. Rogers, W. Devenish, G. White, M. Wenden)	Australia	7 min. 50.8 sec.
800-m. freestyle relay	National team (J. Kinsella, T. McBreen, G. Hall, M. Lampert)	U.S.	7 min. 48.0 sec.
400-m. medley relay	National team (R. Matthes, K. Katzur, U. Poser, L. Unger)	East Germany	3 min. 54.4 sec.
WOMEN			
400-m. freestyle	Debbie Meyer	U.S.	4 min. 24.3 sec.
800-m. freestyle	Karen Moras	Australia	9 min. 9.1 sec.
800-m. freestyle	Karen Moras	Australia	9 min. 2.4 sec.
100-m. butterfly	Alice Jones	U.S.	1 min. 4.1 sec.
200-m. butterfly	Karen Moe	U.S.	2 min. 20.7 sec.
200-m. butterfly	Alice Jones	U.S.	2 min. 19.3 sec.
400-m. freestyle relay	National team (G. Wetzko, I. Komor, E. Sehmisch, C. Schulze)	East Germany	4 min. 00.8 sec.
400-m. medley relay	National team (S. Atwood, K. Brecht, A. Jones, C. Schilling)	U.S.	4 min. 27.4 sec.

zano, Italy, September 19–20, Europe defeated the United States with the Italian men duplicating their Florida victories. The sole U.S. victory was Jerrie Adair's win in the springboard.

At the World University Games, Cynthia Potter won the springboard, and the Soviet Union's Galena Kovalenko took the platform. Dibiasi won both men's titles.

At the European championships, East Germany, which had barred its divers from competing in the U.S.-Europe matches, unveiled two Olympic gold-medal prospects in women's diving. Heidi Becker, 17, and Marina Janicke, 16, placed one-two in the springboard, and Miss Janicke was runner-up to Czechoslovakia's Olympic champion, Milena Duchkova, in the platform. In men's competition Cagnotto won the springboard, while Lothar Matthes of East Germany finished first in the platform event.   (A. SD.)

Switzerland

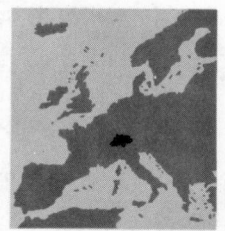

A federal republic in west central Europe consisting of a confederation of 22 cantons, Switzerland is bounded by Germany, Austria, Liechtenstein, Italy, and France. Area: 15,945 sq.mi. (41,297 sq.km.). Pop. (1970 est.): 6,184,000. Cap.: Bern (pop., 1970 est., 166,200). Largest city: Zürich (pop., 1970 est., 427,600). Language (1960): German 69.4%; French 18.9%; Italian 9.5%. Religion (1960): Protestant 52.6%; Roman Catholic 45.6%. President in 1970, Hans Peter Tschudi.

Leisurely discussion of the total revision of the federal constitution continued in 1970. An increasingly important consideration was the effect that possible closer association with the EEC, requiring more centralized government, might have on the federative structure. Around midyear no fewer than 15 "popular initiatives" (each of which required 50,000 signatures to become effective) calling for partial constitutional revisions had been submitted, whereas the total of such initiatives since 1891 was only slightly more than 90.

In April, Valais became the seventh canton to approve the right of women to vote in cantonal matters; Lucerne followed suit soon afterward and Zürich became the ninth on November 15. In June the lower house unanimously approved the federal decree proposing the introduction of the right of women to vote in federal matters by way of revision of art. 74 of the constitution. The issue was expected to be submitted to a nationwide plebiscite in February 1971.

On March 1 citizens of the canton of Bern voted on the new (cantonal) constitutional provisions regarding the Jura, by which the Bernese government opened the way to possible autonomy and separation of the region as a new canton. All political parties recommended approval of the proposal, which was accepted by a vote of 90,000 to 14,086.

The Swiss policy of neutrality was put to a serious test by an explosion in a Tel Aviv-bound Swissair plane over Swiss territory in which 47 people were killed. Sabotage by members of the Popular Front for the Liberation of Palestine (PFLP) was suspected, but could not be proved. There was no possible doubt, however, of the identity of the perpetrators of the hijacking of a New York-bound Swissair craft to

PFLP-occupied territory in Jordan, whereby the PFLP sought to secure the release of a number of its members held for alleged terrorist acts. The government released the three persons imprisoned after their attack on an El Al plane at Zürich airport in 1969. Public opinion was critical of this action, as it was of the federal government's decision, late in the fall, to reject a request for political asylum by the Biafran leader Gen. Odumegwu Ojukwu.

The year was marked by wide discussion of development aid. At a meeting of the Technical Cooperation Department of the federal government in Bern, Pierre Graber, head of the Department of Foreign Affairs, proposed measures to increase the Swiss contribution, including the creation of a new functionary, the "technical cooperator." After publication of statistics showing that Switzerland's 1969 contribution to development aid had dropped to 0.64% (as against 1.41% in 1968) of its gross national product (GNP) —i.e., below the recommended 1%—both public and private efforts were made to remedy the situation. Parliament was to discuss a system of generalized nondiscriminatory trade preferences operating in favour of the less developed countries, together with measures to increase the percentage of government

---

SWITZERLAND

Education. (1966–67) Primary, pupils 465,575, teachers (excluding craft teachers; 1961–62) 23,761; secondary, pupils 249,578, teachers (full time; 1961–62) 6,583; vocational, pupils 148,169; teacher training, students 12,397; higher (including 8 universities; 1967–68), students 35,914, teaching staff 2,773.

Finance. Monetary unit: Swiss franc, with a par value of SFr. 4.37 to U.S. $1 (SFr. 10.50 = £1 sterling). Gold, SDRs, and foreign exchange, central bank: (June 1970) U.S. $3,868,000,000; (June 1969) U.S. $3,220,000,000. Budget (1969 est.): revenue SFr. 6,724,759,000; expenditure SFr. 7,153,058,000. Gross national product: (1969) SFr. 79.8 billion; (1968) SFr. 74 billion. Money supply: (June 1970) SFr. 40,-250,000,000; (June 1969) SFr. 36,560,000,000. Cost of living (1963 = 100): (June 1970) 126; (June 1969) 122.

Foreign Trade. (1969) Imports SFr. 22,712,000,-000; exports SFr. 19,885,000,000. Import sources: EEC 58% (West Germany 29%, France 12%, Italy 10%); U.S. 8%. Export destinations: EEC 37% (West Germany 15%, Italy 9%, France 9%); U.S. 10%; U.K. 7%; Austria 5%. Main exports: machinery 30%; chemicals 21%; watches and clocks 12%; textile yarns and fabrics 7%. Tourism: visitors (1968) 6 million; gross receipts (1967) U.S. $694 million.

Transport and Communications. Roads (1969) 58,550 km. Motor vehicles in use (1969): passenger 1,283,670; commercial 124,569. Railways: federal (1968) 2,914 km. (including 2,897 km. electrified); private (1967) 2,115 (including 2,106 km. electrified); traffic on federal railways (1969) 8,034,000,000 passenger-km., freight 6,072,000,000 net ton-km.; traffic on private railways (1967) 1,143,000,000 passenger-km., freight 386 million net ton-km. Air traffic (1969): 3,835,000,000 passenger-km.; freight 175.3 million net ton-km. Shipping (1969): merchant vessels 100 gross tons and over 32; gross tonnage 193,007. Telephones (Dec. 1968) 2,685,800. Radio receivers (Dec. 1968) 1,752,000. Television receivers (Dec. 1968) 1,011,000.

Agriculture. Production (in 000; metric tons; 1969; 1968 in parentheses): barley c. 135 (112); wheat (including spelt; 1968) 409, (1967) 426; oats 34 (31); rye 44 (64); potatoes 1,210 (1,098); apples (1968) 470, (1967) 580; pears (1968) 194, (1967) 236; sugar, raw value (1969–70) 62, (1968–69) 68; wine (1968) 96, (1967) 89; milk 3,235 (3,322); butter c. 32 (37); cheese 93 (86); meat 319 (312). Livestock (in 000; April 1969): cattle 1,869; horses 56; sheep 290; pigs c. 1,920; chickens 6,345.

Industry. Index of industrial production (1963 = 100): (1969) 136; (1968) 123. Production (in 000; metric tons; 1969): cement 4,530; aluminum 77; rayon, etc., yarn 12; rayon staple fibre (1968) 11; cigarettes (pieces; 1968) 20,510,000; watches (units; 1968) 47,785; electricity (kw-hr.) 29,411,000; manufactured gas (gasworks only; cu.m.; 1968) 378,000.

A technician makes adjustments on the nuclear fuel rods inside Switzerland's first nuclear power plant, Beznau I. It was officially dedicated May 12, 1970, at ceremonies held in nearby Dottingen.

AUTHENTICATED NEWS INTERNATIONAL

as against private industrial and financial assistance.

Statistics published in the spring showed that there were nearly 600,000 foreign workers (more than 500,-000 of them Italians) in Switzerland, which meant that, if their families were included, the proportion of foreigners resident in Switzerland had reached 15.8%. The Federal Council took steps to prevent a further rise. On June 8 a nationwide plebiscite on the second Schwarzenbach initiative, proposing more rigorous restrictions on immigration, was rejected by a narrow margin (654,000 to 557,000). The restrictions were considered to be a potential source of social injustice and likely to harm the extremely labour-short Swiss economy. (*See* MIGRATION, INTERNATIONAL.)

The customary trade deficit reached a record high in January, but was slightly reduced later. According to the Organization for Economic Cooperation and Development, the surplus in the balance of payments was expected to reach some $600 million. The GNP increased by 4.7% during 1969–70.   (M. F. S.)

Syria

A republic in southwestern Asia on the Mediterranean Sea, Syria is bordered by Turkey, Iraq, Jordan, Israel, and Lebanon. Area: 71,498 sq.mi. (185,180 sq.km.). Pop. (1969 est.): 5,866,000. Cap. and largest city: Damascus (pop., 1966 est., 594,426). Language: Arabic (official); also Kurdish, Armenian, Turkish, and Circassian. Religion: predominantly Muslim. Chairman of the Presidency Council and premier until Nov. 13, 1970, Nureddin al-Attassi; president from November 18, Ahmed al-Khatib; premier from November 19, Gen. Hafez al-Assad.

In 1970 Syria's left-wing Baath Party regime maintained both its grip on the country and its uncompromising policies toward the outside world despite an internal power struggle that became acute toward the end of the year and eventually culminated in a military coup.

The minister of the interior and the army chief of staff had represented Syria at the Arab summit meeting in Rabat in December 1969, but the government used the summit's failure to justify its view that such meetings were worthless and that only the "progressive" Arab states could unite effectively against Israel. In early February Premier al-Attassi attended the

limited summit of "front line" Arab states (Iraq, Syria, Jordan, United Arab Republic, and Sudan) in Cairo, which strongly denounced U.S. policy in the Middle East; after the meeting he went on to Algeria for talks with that nation's president.

Syria's refusal to allow the repair of the Tapline pipeline from Saudi Arabia after it was damaged on Syrian territory on May 3 was at least partly a politically motivated action against Western oil companies and the right-wing regime in Saudi Arabia. Saudi retaliatory measures led to a Syrian ban on the overflying of Saudi aircraft, and Syria rejected pressure from the U.A.R., Jordan, and Lebanon to allow the pipeline to be reopened.

The Syrian government repeatedly called for the strengthening of the "eastern front" against Israel, but the chief obstacle remained its own bad relations with Iraq. Throughout the year the Damascus press and radio accused the Iraqi regime of betraying the Baathist and Arab cause. In the summer Gen. Salah al-Jadid, who controlled the Baath Party machine and was especially hostile to Iraq, strengthened his position by gaining control of the Syrian-supported guerrilla organization, Al Saiqa.

In the spring and early summer the Syrians demonstrated their intention to reactivate their front with Israel, which had been relatively dormant since the 1967 war. Their aim was to reduce the pressure on the U.A.R. at the Suez Canal and to reassert their claim to the Golan Heights in the event of a Middle East settlement. In late March and early April Syrian forces made a series of raids on Israeli forces in the Golan Heights, and on May 12–13 Syrian air forces and ar-

Syrian soldiers surrender to an Israeli armoured unit during Israel's raid into the Golan Heights area, June 26, 1970.

WIDE WORLD

SYRIA

Education. (1967–68) Primary, pupils 767,895, teachers 21,228; secondary, pupils 214,536, teachers 8,509; vocational, pupils 7,688, teachers 897; teacher training, students 6,276, teachers 522; higher (including 2 universities), students 33,027, teaching staff 941.

Finance. Monetary unit: Syrian pound, with a par value of S£2.19 to U.S. $1 (S£5.26 = £1 sterling) and an approximate free rate (Oct. 1970) of S£4.40 to U.S. $1 (S£10.50 = £1 sterling). Budget (1968) balanced at S£1,142.7 million. Money supply: (March 1970) S£1,881 million; (March 1969) S£1,724 million. Cost of living (Damascus; 1963 = 100): (June 1970) 116; (June 1969) 115.

Foreign Trade. (1969) Imports S£1,409.1 million; exports S£789.7 million. Import sources: U.S.S.R. 9%; Italy 9%; France 7%; West Germany 7%; Iraq 6%; China 5%; Czechoslovakia 5%; Lebanon 5%; U.K. 5%. Export destinations: U.S.S.R. 17%; Lebanon 14%; Italy 12%. Main exports: cotton 39%; livestock 13%; crude oil 11%; fruit and vegetables 7%; rice 5%.

Transport and Communications. Roads (1969) c. 14,900 km. (including 10,532 km. with improved surface). Motor vehicles in use (1969): passenger 29,379; commercial 16,012. Railways (1968): 543 km.; traffic 85 million passenger-km., freight 122 million net ton-km. Air traffic (1968): 127,470,000 passenger-km.; freight 874,000 net ton-km. Ships entered (1967) vessels totaling 10,451,000 net registered tons; goods loaded (1968) 30,007,000 metric tons, unloaded 1,178,000 metric tons. Telephones (Dec. 1968) 96,613. Radio receivers (Dec. 1969) 1,272,000. Television receivers (Dec. 1969) 106,000.

Agriculture. Production (in 000; metric tons; 1969; 1968 in parentheses): wheat 1,004 (600); barley 627 (512); grapes (1968) 215, (1967) 214; raisins (1968) 8.4, (1967) 8.8; figs (1968) 53, (1967) 52; olive oil c. 21 (22); tobacco (1968) 8.5, (1967) 6; dry broad beans (1968) 8, (1967) 14; chick-peas (1968) 36, (1967) 64; lentils (1968) 48, (1967) 84; cotton, lint 147 (159); wool (1968) 6.4, (1967) 6.7. Livestock (in 000; 1968–69): cattle c. 510; sheep c. 6,000; horses c. 63; asses c. 230; goats (1967–68) 743; chickens (Dec. 1968) 4,247.

Industry. Production (in 000; metric tons; 1968): petroleum products c. 1,100; cement (1969) 934; cotton yarn (1967) 19; electricity (kw-hr.) 773,000.

tillery were engaged against Israeli forces raiding Lebanon. There were further clashes on the Golan Heights between June 1 and 8 in which Syria admitted suffering more than 40 casualties, and more serious engagements between June 24 and 26 with Syria admitting the loss of 45 dead and 75 wounded in addition to the loss of two aircraft. Observers reported that the Syrian forces showed an improved spirit and standard of training.

As the Jordanian crisis deepened in August and September, the Syrians expressed vigorous support for the Palestinian guerrillas. On September 19, after the outbreak of the Jordanian civil war, Syrian armoured units entered northern Jordan; the Syrians claimed that they were all elements of the Palestine Liberation Army. They withdrew a few days later, having suffered severe casualties and also, it was thought, because of Soviet pressure.

This action led directly to a crisis within the regime, with the civilian Baathists criticizing Minister of Defense Gen. Hafez al-Assad, who had opposed the Syrian intervention. General al-Assad took countermeasures to ensure his position and the loyalty of the armed forces. On October 18 it was reported that he had won the power struggle and that his principal rival, General al-Jadid, was in flight.

A Baath Party congress began meeting on October 30 in an attempt to reconcile the differences within the party. That it failed to do so became apparent when General al-Assad placed Premier al-Attassi and General al-Jadid under house arrest on November 13. Under al-Assad's leadership, the more conservative military wing of the Baathists took power, in a bloodless coup, from the political wing, which was blamed for the abortive tank invasion of Jordan. A relatively unknown former teacher, Ahmed al-Khatib, was named president, while al-Assad became the new premier. Although some observers expected the new regime to be more sympathetic to Israel and the West, it soon pledged support to the Palestinian guerrillas and announced that it would work for closer ties with Communist nations. (P. MD.)

ENCYCLOPÆDIA BRITANNICA FILMS. *The Middle East* (1955); *The Mediterranean World* (1961).

Taiwan

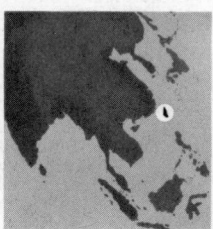

Taiwan, which consists of the islands of Formosa and Quemoy and other surrounding islands, is the seat of the Republic of China (Nationalist China). It is situated north of the Philippines, southwest of Japan and Okinawa, and east of Hong Kong. The island of Formosa has an area of 13,807 sq.mi. (35,760 sq.km.); including its 77 outlying islands (14 in the Taiwan group and 63 in the Pescadores group), the area of Taiwan totals 13,887 sq.mi. Pop. (1970 est.): 14,500,872, excluding armed forces and aliens. Cap. and largest city: T'ai-pei (pop., 1970 est., 1,742,626). President in 1970, Chiang Kai-shek; vice-president and premier (president of the Executive Yuan), C. K. Yen.

In 1970, while economic growth and social advancement in Taiwan continued, the posture and position of the Nationalist government as the sole and legitimate government of all China greatly deteriorated. Factors in this deterioration were moves by Canada and Italy

shifting recognition from Nationalist to Communist China, Peking's renewed interest in bidding for China's seat in the UN, and decisions by the U.S. to reduce its military presence in Asia and to resume Sino-American talks at the ambassadorial level in Warsaw. Particularly threatening to Taiwan was the reiteration by the U.S. of its policy to conciliate Communist China by removing the regular U.S. Navy patrol of the Taiwan Strait and by allowing U.S. companies operating abroad to trade directly with Peking. On the basis of these developments it was generally believed that the United States would no longer resist Peking's obtaining membership in the UN as long as Nationalist China could also remain in the organization. In effect, this subtly became a "two-Chinas" policy, to which both the Communists and the Nationalists openly and strongly objected.

The desire of the U.S. to develop more cordial relations with Communist China was reportedly made clear to the Nationalists by U.S. Vice-Pres. Spiro Agnew on his first goodwill tour of Asia. On his way from Japan to Vietnam, Agnew visited T'ai-pei on January 2–3 and held talks with President Chiang and other high officials. In a statement in T'ai-pei, Agnew declared that the future of Asia lies in the hands of the Asian people themselves but that the U.S. wished to cooperate fully in this Asian effort and intended to honour its commitments to Nationalist China and other allies. The Nationalist reaction was openly affirmed in Premier Yen's report to the Legislative Yuan on February 24 when he said that the U.S.-

TAIWAN
Education. (1967–68) Primary, pupils 2,348,218, teachers 55,683; secondary, pupils 640,447, teachers 23,706; vocational, pupils 143,296, teachers 7,065; teacher training, students 1,570, teachers 88; higher (including 10 universities), students 138,613, teaching staff 15,872.
Finance. Monetary unit: New Taiwan dollar (NT$40 = U.S. $1; NT$96 = £1 sterling). Gold and foreign exchange, official: (June 1970) U.S. $531 million; (June 1969) U.S. $411 million. Budget (1968–69 est.): revenue NT$34,898,000,000; expenditure NT$33,108,000,000. Gross national product: (1968) NT$167,980,000,000; (1967) NT$143,040,000,000. Money supply: (June 1970) NT$30,410,000,000; (June 1969) NT$25,480,000,000. Cost of living (1963 = 100): (June 1970) 121; (June 1969) 116.
Foreign Trade. (1969) Imports U.S. $1,212,800,-000; exports U.S. $1,049,500,000. Import sources: Japan 44%; U.S. 24%. Export destinations: U.S. 38%; Japan 15%; Hong Kong 9%; South Vietnam 5%; West Germany 5%. Main exports: fruit and vegetables 16% (including bananas 5%); textile yarns and fabrics 13%; clothing 12%; telecommunications equipment 9%; plywood 6%; sugar 5%.
Transport and Communications. Roads (1968) 16,885 km. Motor vehicles in use (1968): passenger 30,700; commercial (including buses) 33,400. Railways: (1968) 4,500 km.; traffic (1969) 5,935,000,000 passenger-km., freight 2,595,000,000 net ton-km. Air traffic (1969): 521.2 million passenger-km.; freight 8,385,000 net ton-km. Shipping (1969): merchant vessels 100 gross tons and over 216; gross tonnage 961,-807. Telephones (Jan. 1969) 280,192. Radio receivers (Dec. 1967) 1,402,000. Television receivers (Dec. 1968) 193,000.
Agriculture. Production (in 000; metric tons; 1969; 1968 in parentheses): rice 3,041 (3,299); sweet potatoes (1968) 3,445, (1967) 3,720; cassava (1968) 342, (1967) 299; peanuts 101 (106); oranges 146 (151); tobacco 20 (21); tea (1968) 24, (1967) 24; sugar, raw value (1969–70) 874, (1968–69) 791; bananas (1968) 645, (1967) 654; jute 13 (11). Livestock (in 000; Dec. 1968): cattle 105; pigs 3,011; goats (Dec. 1967) 155; chickens 13,787.
Industry. Production (in 000; metric tons; 1969): coal 4,646; crude oil 82; natural gas (cu.m.) 894,000; electricity (excluding most industrial production; kw-hr.) 11,114,000; cement 4,070; pig iron 72; salt (1968) 311; caustic soda (1967) 91; petroleum products (1968) 3,109; cotton yarn 78; paper (1966) 214.

Table Tennis: *see* Sporting Record

Peking talks in Warsaw were harmful, not beneficial, to the free world, and that "any attempt by a Free World country to establish diplomatic relations or improve its relationship with the Peking regime will not only adversely affect the solidarity and the long-term interests of all the Free World, but also solicit humiliation."

To seek better understanding of all the important issues facing Sino-American relations, Deputy Premier Chiang Ching-kuo (the son of President Chiang) visited the U.S. on April 18–27 at the invitation of Secretary of State William P. Rogers. Before his departure Chiang declared that U.S.-Nationalist relations could be further strengthened by the acceptance of his government's basic premise that it is the government of China and that it intends someday to recover the mainland. During his visit in Washington Chiang conferred with U.S. Pres. Richard Nixon, Agnew, and the secretaries of state and defense. On his way to a hotel in New York City on April 24 to deliver a scheduled address to the Far East-American Council of Commerce and Industry, Chiang was fired upon in the revolving door of the hotel by a student from Taiwan in an assassination attempt. The student later identified himself as a leader of a newly formed organization called the World United Formosans for Independence, with headquarters in New York. Returning to T'ai-pei on May 1, Chiang in a press statement confirmed that during his visit in Washington he had explained the Nationalist basic policy to U.S. officials, and that the U.S. government had renewed its assurance to Taiwan of "unchanged adherence to commitments made under the Sino-American mutual assistance treaty and of continued support of the Republic of China in the United Nations."

Except for sporadic shelling by Communist China around the offshore islands of Quemoy and Matsu, the Taiwan Straits were quiet. Relative national security and continued political stability had led to greater freedom of discussion in the national election held in late December 1969 to fill 11 vacancies in the Legislative Yuan and 15 vacancies in the National Assembly; this was the first national election since 1947. During the election campaigns nonpartisan and independent candidates sharply criticized the ruling Kuomintang for bureaucracy, inefficiency, and expenditure of 70% of the national budget for military purposes. In particular, the independent candidates demanded that the offices of mayor of T'ai-pei and governor of Taiwan should be made elective instead of appointive.

As the fifth four-year economic development plan entered its second year in 1970, the National Security Council, of which President Chiang was ex officio chairman, issued a directive calling for greater efforts to maintain the economic growth rate of 8.5%, as set forth by the plan. The significant industrial development of recent years had caused the economic structure to undergo a notable change from a predominantly agricultural economy to an industrial one. In 1969 agriculture accounted for 20.8% of the net domestic product and industry for 32%, compared with 35 and 20%, respectively, in 1952. To promote industrial development the Executive Yuan adopted in September a set of guiding measures that included financial aid and long-term bank loans to private firms so that they could purchase machines and thereby increase the amount of their exports.

(H.-T. CH.)

See also China.

Tanzania

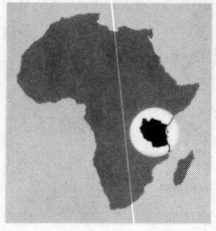

This republic, an East African member of the Commonwealth of Nations, consists of two parts: Tanganyika, on the Indian Ocean, bordered by Kenya, Uganda, Rwanda, Burundi, the Congo (Kinshasa), Zambia, Malawi, and Mozambique; and Zanzibar, just off the coast, including Zanzibar Island, Pemba Island, and small islets. Total area of the united republic: 364,900 sq.mi. (945,100 sq.km.). Total pop. (1970 est.): 13,273,000 (approximately 98% Africans and 1% Arabs). Cap. and largest city: Dar es Salaam (pop., 1967, 272,821), in Tanganyika. Language: primarily Bantu, of which Swahili serves as the lingua franca. Religion: predominantly pagan; many Muslims in coastal areas and in up-country settlements; Christian minority. President in 1970, Julius Nyerere.

Following their arrest in October 1969, seven people, including Bibi Titi Muhammad, one of the founders of the Tanganyika African National Union (TANU), were charged in May 1970 with plotting to overthrow the government and to assassinate President Nyerere and the second vice-president, Rashidi Kawawa. Oscar Kambona, the former foreign minister, was charged in absentia with directing the plot. The accused were brought to trial in June,

TANZANIA

Education. (1966) Primary, pupils 740,991, teachers 14,809; secondary, pupils 23,836, teachers 1,171; vocational, pupils 2,499, teachers 68; teacher training, students 2,473, teachers 230; higher (including Dar es Salaam University; 1965), students 523.

Finance. Monetary unit: Tanzanian shilling, with a par value of TShs. 7.14 to U.S. $1 (TShs. 17.14 = £1 sterling). Gold, SDRs, and foreign exchange: (June 1970) U.S. $68.6 million; (June 1969) U.S. $77.8 million. Budget (1969–70 est.): revenue TShs. 1,505,-719,000; expenditure TShs. 1,502,751,000. National income: (mainland only; 1967) TShs. 5,201,000,000; (1966) TShs. 5,003,000,000. Money supply: (June 1970) TShs. 1,461,000,000; (June 1969) TShs. 1,467,-000,000. Cost of living (Dar es Salaam; 1963 = 100): (May 1970) 124; (June 1969) 120.

Foreign Trade. (Excluding trade with Kenya and Uganda; 1969) Imports TShs. 1,419,000,000; exports TShs. 1,689,000,000. Import sources: U.K. 27%; Japan 9%; West Germany 8%; Iran 7%; U.S. 6%; China 6%; Italy 5%; Netherlands 5%. Export destinations: U.K. 26%; India 8%; U.S. 7%; Zambia 7%; Hong Kong 6%; Japan 5%. Main exports: coffee 15%; cotton 14%; diamonds 11%; sisal 10%.

Transport and Communications. Roads (1969) 16,743 km. Motor vehicles in use (1968): passenger 36,238; commercial 29,788. Railways (1967) 2,970 km. (for traffic *see* KENYA). Construction of a 1,600-km. railway between Dar es Salaam and Zambia began at the end of 1970. Air traffic: *see* KENYA. Shipping traffic (mainland only; 1968) goods loaded 1,378,000 metric tons, unloaded 1,862,000 metric tons. Telephones (Dec. 1968) 29,348. Radio receivers (Dec. 1967) 138,000.

Agriculture. Production (in 000; metric tons; 1968; 1967 in parentheses): corn (mainland) 678 (642); sweet potatoes *c.* 284 (*c.* 259); millet and sorghum *c.* 1,100 (*c.* 1,145); sugar, raw value (mainland; 1969–70) *c.* 98, (1968–69) 100; rice *c.* 222 (212); cassava *c.* 1,205 (*c.* 1,200); cotton, lint (mainland; 1969) *c.* 68, (1968) *c.* 52; sisal (mainland) 197 (220); timber (cu.m.; 1967) *c.* 11,800; (1966) *c.* 11,600; fish catch (1968) 123, (1967) 118. Livestock (in 000; 1968–69): cattle *c.* 11,100; sheep *c.* 3,200; goats (1967–68) *c.* 4,716; asses *c.* 161; pigs *c.* 20.

Industry. Production (in 000; metric tons; 1968): salt *c.* 30; tin concentrates (metal content) 0.3; gold (troy oz.) 17; diamonds (metric carats; 1967) 927; electricity (public supply; kw-hr.) 315,000.

with the exception of Kambona, who, under Tanzanian law, could not be tried in absentia.

In July Kawawa announced that during 1971 he would present to Parliament completed plans for a Tanzanian Air Force. He gave no indication as to the source of any assistance in the project, but observers believed that China, which was already constructing a naval base for Tanzania in Dar es Salaam, was likely to be involved. In July, too, final discussions took place in Peking between members of the Chinese government and ministers and bank governors from Tanzania and Zambia to arrange an interest-free loan of £169 million to finance the 1,100-mi. Tanzam Railway that would link the two countries. Work on the construction of the line, which was scheduled for completion in five years, began officially in October.

Events in Zanzibar continued to cause concern on the mainland, although, under the terms of the interim constitution of 1965, the mainland government could not intervene in questions of law and justice. In May an order that 31 families of Iranian origin must quit Zanzibar had been the precursor of a series of events giving rise to considerable criticism on the mainland. Although at the time no reason was given for the deportation order, which in any case was revoked in June, the families had previously been accused of opposing interracial marriages. In September it was reported that four girls of Iranian origin had been forced by the Revolutionary Council to marry government officials against their will, and it was later claimed that one of the girls had been married to First Vice-Pres. Abeid Karume, while 11 men of Iranian origin, who had refused their consent to the marriages, were sentenced to flogging and imprisonment but were subsequently pardoned.

In September, Nyerere was unanimously nominated as the sole candidate for the presidential election on October 30, when he was reelected by an overwhelming majority. At the same time parliamentary elections were held on the mainland, but not in Zanzibar. Most of the sitting members were reelected, though two ministers lost their seats. (K. I.)

ENCYCLOPÆDIA BRITANNICA FILMS. *East Africa (Kenya, Tanganyika, Uganda)* (1962); *Youth Builds a Nation in Tanzania* (1970).

Telecommunications

Governmental policy makers clearly began in 1970 to take a greater interest in telecommunications. The new spurt of activity was geared toward gaining the greatest possible benefit from modern technology and toward mapping guidelines for the future so that the ideas of scientists and engineers could be exploited to their fullest.

One reason for the heightened interest was the slowly dawning realization that many technologies—not simply telecommunications—were converging and promising revolutionary improvements in the means of transferring information among people. This was most dramatically illustrated by the growing relationship between computers and telecommunications facilities. Working together, computers and telecommunications could greatly increase the flow of information between the users of the information.

To realize their greatest potential, computers had to be linked to users in remote locations. Furthermore, computers linked to other computers could pool their data banks and increase their store of information. In return, computer traffic was expected to add a valuable new source of business for the suppliers of telecommunications services.

Governmental and Research Activities. An encouraging sign in 1970 was that governments began to realize the importance of advance planning so that the continuing growth in telecommunications would not be stifled, as it had been in the past, by a lag in policy making. In the past, issues coming before the policy-making and regulatory bodies had usually been solved by ad hoc decisions. In 1970, however, government officials seemed to step back and take a long-range view in the hope that broad policy formulation would provide a framework that would end the need for ad hoc decisions. In the U.S. the broad policy decisions all seemed to have a common element: the use of competition between the suppliers of telecommunications services as a regulatory tool in itself.

Probably the most important single long-term development in the U.S. was the decision by Pres. Richard Nixon to create a new high-level office to handle the federal government's planning functions for telecommunications. The new agency, called the Office of Telecommunications Policy, was given an extraordinarily broad charter, permitting it a hand in all governmental telecommunications functions except for purely regulatory affairs of the Federal Communications Commission (FCC).

In Britain, traffic over the telephone trunk lines was doubling every seven years and data services were expanding quickly. In response, the Post Office's "Confravision" service was brought to fruition in 1970,

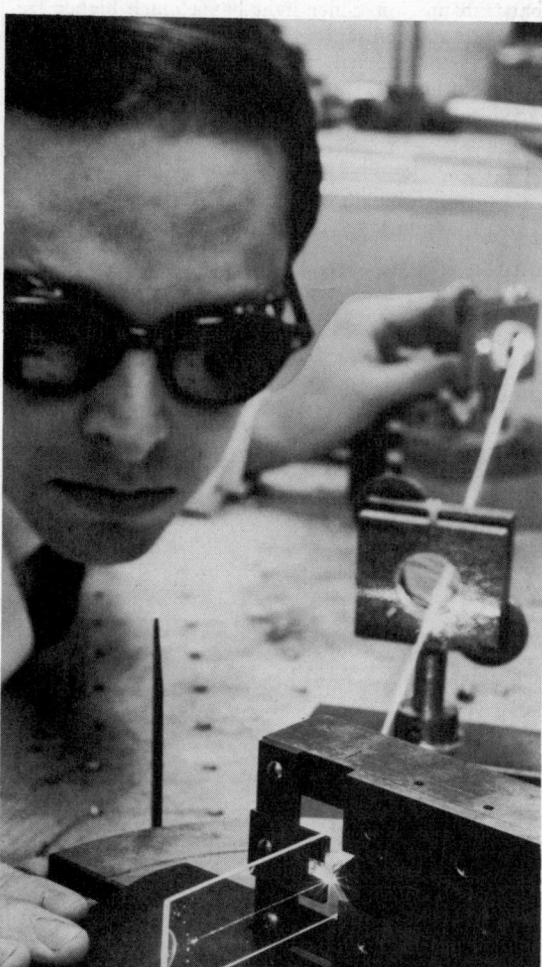

A laser beam is injected into an experimental lightguide at Bell Telephone Laboratories in Murray Hill, N.J. The lightguide, a glass film deposited on a glass plate, may be used to develop a new class of optical circuits for laser communications systems of the future.
AUTHENTICATED NEWS INTERNATIONAL

Tariffs:
see Commercial Policies; Trade, International

Taxation:
see Government Finance

Tea:
see Agriculture

enabling businessmen hundreds of miles apart to participate in face-to-face conferences by television. The Post Office was setting up special studios for the purpose, at first in five cities—London, Glasgow, Manchester, Birmingham, and Bristol—where business leaders were invited to try the service, initially at a nominal fee. Later, larger companies would probably prefer to have their own studios.

In another attempt to solve the growing problem of congestion, the U.K. Post Office in September demonstrated the transmission of colour television by waveguide. The television signal was first converted into digital pulses, and these were transmitted not through the free air but down a carefully constructed long hollow tube. This approach dealt with two problems at once. First, because the beamed signal was completely enclosed by the waveguide, there was no interference from outside. The same equivalent frequencies could therefore be used nearby for different transmissions with no fear of messages becoming intermixed. Second, because high radio frequencies were used, the amount of information that could be transmitted by waveguide was much greater than with a cable of the same physical dimensions. The waveguide developed by the Post Office's Research Department, only two inches in diameter, could carry a third of a million two-way telephone conversations, or 200 television circuits, or other signals, including music and computer data. A 1-km. length of the waveguide was installed at Martlesham Heath near Ipswich, and tests on a 30-km. length were planned for 1973.

The number of messages that can be contained in a transmission is proportional to the frequency of that transmission. Since light has a much higher frequency than even radio, the number of messages that could be transmitted on a light beam is, in theory, extremely high. Many scientific laboratories were engaged in transmitting light along very thin glass fibres with this aim in view, but all had been beaten by the difficulty of building a switchable light source suffi-

ciently powerful yet cool enough to make anything like full use of the transmission capacity theoretically available. Standard Telecommunication Laboratories of Harlow, Essex, successfully developed a small laser made of gallium arsenide which overcame this limitation. A single laser of this kind had the potentiality for enabling millions of television programs to be transmitted along a fibre no thicker than a human hair.

Satellites. Despite technical troubles experienced in both the launching and subsequent operation of communications satellites, the economics of telecommunications encouraged the development of more powerful satellites in 1970. The International Telecommunications Satellite Consortium (Intelsat) 4 system, in which over a period of years eight large satellites would be launched to provide global telecommunications coverage, was scheduled to be launched early in 1971. Whereas Intelsat 1 (Early Bird) weighed 150 lb. at lift-off (87 lb. in orbit), each Intelsat 4 would weigh 2,452 lb. at lift-off (1,075 lb. in orbit). Intelsat 4 would have a greater capacity than any previous satellite, being virtually a 5,000-line telephone exchange floating in space. Alternatively, it would be able to transmit 12 simultaneous television broadcasts in full colour or any equivalent combination of various different kinds of transmissions. The first Intelsat 4 was to be put into synchronous orbit 22,300 mi. above the Atlantic Ocean, and subsequent launchings would eventually provide two Intelsat 4s for the Atlantic and Pacific regions and one for the Indian Ocean, plus spares in orbit. The first five were all to be launched within five years.

This new generation of communications satellites was not only larger and more powerful than its predecessors, but also more sophisticated. For example, a unique feature was to be an ability to focus part of the transmission capacity into two spot beams and direct these at selected areas, providing both a stronger signal and more channel capacity for areas requiring the heaviest communications traffic, such as Western Europe and the eastern U.S. This would be made possible by having two steerable dish aerials on the satellite that could be controlled on command from the earth.

Under the leadership of U.S. Ambassador Abbott Washburn, who succeeded former Pennsylvania governor William Scranton in January, the conference of 75 nations trying to work out a permanent charter for Intelsat remained without firm agreement late in 1970 as delegates debated minute organizational details. As the year ended, Washburn reported that a compromise had been worked out and that he expected approval of the complex agreement early in 1971. Essentially, the agreement would mean a smaller role in the organization for the U.S. and its agent, the Communications Satellite Corporation (Comsat).

At the end of 1970 the U.S. appeared on the brink of a decision concerning which organization or organizations would have the right to operate a domestic satellite system. In September 1965 the first application for a domestic system was filed by the American Broadcasting Company. Approximately 11 months later, Comsat filed its first application. During the following three years a number of organizations, including the Ford Foundation, sought FCC approval to build a system.

Then, late in 1969 when the FCC was about to grant Comsat temporary permission to operate such

		Countries Having More Than 100,000 Telephones				
			Telephones in service, 1969			
Country	Number of telephones	Percentage increase over 1959	Telephones per 100 population	Country	Number of telephones	Percentage increase over 1959	Telephones per 100 population
Algeria	156,038	...	1.19	Lebanon	150,370	255.6	5.76
Argentina	1,599,861	30.8	6.72	Malaysia	156,354	...	1.50
Australia*	3,392,436	65.0	28.20	Mexico	1,174,943	162.3	2.44
Austria	1,242,785	102.0	16.88	Morocco	160,326	25.1	1.08
Belgium	1,847,363	78.3	19.18	Netherlands	2,917,384	108.1	22.80
Brazil	1,560,701	64.4	1.74	New Zealand	1,155,465	80.2	41.56
Bulgaria	378,152	...	4.50	Norway	1,036,027	51.7	27.02
Canada	8,820,770	72.3	42.12	Pakistan	176,811	176.7	0.16
Chile	312,042	87.8	3.30	Peru	165,121	81.0	1.27
China†	244,028	...	0.05	Philippines	241,496	175.9	0.66
Colombia‡	574,700	135.5	2.85	Poland	1,650,896	125.3	5.08
Cuba‡	242,000	42.3	2.97	Portugal	653,407	96.6	6.87
Czechoslovakia	1,789,373	101.1	12.44	Puerto Rico	266,248	247.2	9.73
Denmark	1,516,802	55.3	30.88	Rhodesia	116,973	...	2.47
Finland	1,009,336	85.1	21.50	Romania‡	596,000	127.7	2.99
France	7,503,491	102.6	14.98	Singapore	119,184	137.5	5.95
Germany, East	1,896,151	61.4	11.10	South Africa	1,397,725	57.5	7.29
Germany, West	11,248,979	121.0	18.65	Soviet Union	9,900,000	159.8	4.14
Greece	761,550	350.6	8.63	Spain	3,723,239	149.9	11.44
Hong Kong	426,540	396.0	10.74	Sweden	4,110,579	62.7	51.76
Hungary	684,389	70.7	6.66	Switzerland	2,685,800	82.1	43.42
India	1,057,193	179.3	0.20	Taiwan	280,192	378.7	2.05
Indonesia	181,377	99.4	0.16	Thailand*	114,419	258.4	0.34
Iran	250,300	209.1	0.92	Turkey	451,769	88.9	1.33
Iraq	113,388	155.9	1.30	United Arab Republic‡	365,000	96.8	1.14
Ireland	268,670	95.3	9.20	United Kingdom	12,901,000	71.4	23.26
Israel	401,362	344.1	14.42	United States	109,256,000	63.9	54.02
Italy	7,752,042	143.6	14.37	Uruguay	205,174	51.1	7.23
Japan	20,525,211	302.7	20.12	Venezuela	345,704	118.0	3.51
Korea, South	489,912	626.9	1.60	Yugoslavia	549,019	152.4	2.70

*1968. †1948. ‡Estimate.
Source: American Telephone and Telegraph Co., *The World's Telephones*, 1959 and 1969.

a system, the government asked for and received a delay so that the matter could be studied by a committee from the executive branch. A report by this committee on Jan. 23, 1970, suggested that no single company be allowed to operate a domestic system but that all organizations willing to risk the investment cost should be authorized.

Later in 1970 the FCC adopted a policy largely in line with the committee's suggestions. Its first application under these guidelines came from the Western Union Telegraph Co. Many other firms then announced their plans for filing, including Comsat, American Telephone & Telegraph Co., two special data transmission firms, the broadcasting networks, and a cable television operator.

The logjam seemed to loosen further on October 19, when AT & T and Comsat announced that they had arrived at a plan for a joint system, with Comsat supplying two large satellites and AT & T its vast amount of lucrative business. Most satellite specialists believed that the latter was important for the economic well-being of a system because only AT & T and the television networks had enough business to support a domestic system.

Should the combined AT & T-Comsat system be approved, AT & T would build and own five earth stations. Approval of the arrangement was somewhat in doubt, however, since it would seem to run counter to the philosophy of competition by lumping together two possible competitors. Additional awkwardness and possible antitrust violations might stem from AT & T's ownership of about 22% of Comsat stock. Late in the year there was a movement to pass new legislation to end AT & T's ownership share in Comsat.

Meanwhile, Canada proceeded with its plans for establishing a domestic communications satellite system. In September it awarded a $30 million contract for the system to the Hughes Aircraft Co. of California. A controversy arose over the contract because a Canadian company, RCA Victor of Canada, had also sought the work but said that the cost would be $13 million higher. The Canadian Cabinet chose the lower price over any considerations of nationalism.

Cables and Radio. On March 22 the highest-capacity communications cable ever to be laid across the Atlantic, called TAT5, went into operation, linking Green Hill, R.I., and San Fernando, Spain. The opening of the system led to a series of international rate reductions, including the reduction of transatlantic telephone rates to Spain, Portugal, Italy, and West Germany by as much as 25%. The cable was jointly owned by AT & T, ITT World Communications, Western Union International, RCA Global Communications, Compañia Telefónica Nacional de España, Companhia Portuguesa Radio Marini, and Italcable. The new equipment could handle more than 800 telephone conversations simultaneously.

Early in the year the U.K. Post Office set up one of the first television networks in the world capable of transmitting 22 television pictures simultaneously over one coaxial cable. The network linked the new 26-story London Stock Exchange, which opened in February, to more than 200 of its member's offices within the City of London. At the touch of a button, brokers could display on a television screen in their offices up-to-date prices of more than 700 stocks and shares and the latest news and information on commodities and exchange rates.

The size of the trunk telephone system in Britain had been growing at about 15% annually. In an effort to cope with this, the Post Office developed and in 1970 brought out a "supercable" with a total capacity of 97,200 circuits, six times as many as the largest-capacity coaxial cables previously in use. The cable would be used to link London, Birmingham, and Manchester by the mid-1970s.

Computers and Data Transmission. As mentioned earlier, computers became one of the thorniest problems facing telecommunications policy makers in 1970. There were two elements to the problem: whether or not computers should be regulated as common carriers and if so with what regulatory restrictions; and, second, who should have the government-granted authority to link or provide data transmission for computer users. A corollary to the second issue was whether new firms should be permitted to compete with existing carriers for this lucrative new business.

In 1970 the FCC rendered a tentative decision on these questions. It said that computers and data processing should not be regulated; but, at the same time, it also said that existing communications companies could enter the business only after agreeing to a rigid set of rules. The restrictions on telecommunications companies were made because of the belief that the companies would be unfair competition to other suppliers of computer services.

One reason the telecommunications companies wanted the business was because the message switching systems in their facilities were, in fact, computers. These systems were not used at all times and the companies wanted to sell their services as computers during the off-hours. Restrictions placed on them by the FCC's tentative ruling were expected to hold down their profitability.

The FCC moved to increase competition in the data transmission field when it indicated that it planned to grant operational authority to two companies that had sought permission to crisscross the U.S. with microwave transmission facilities to be used mainly for carrying computer data messages. As 1970 ended, 18 firms affiliated with Microwave Communications of America had filed for authority for a nationwide system. Similarly, the Data Transmission Corp., a University Computing Co. affiliate, had a single nationwide application pending.

Telephones. One of the reasons AT & T and the other telephone companies were faced by vigorous assaults by upstart competitors was that complaints of poor performance of telephone service continued during the year. One of the most criticized, the New York Telephone Co., an affiliate of AT & T, replaced its president in 1970 and chose William M. Ellinghaus to succeed him. Ellinghaus later revealed plans for correcting the service deficiencies.

Nevertheless, the service complaints surely created a climate conducive to the making of many regulatory decisions against the phone companies. Furthermore, the FCC began an extensive program of checking up on these complaints. Until recently, AT & T had never had the commission investigating its management and service responsibilities.

(L. H. Jo.; W. D. Hi.)

International Telecommunication Union. During 1970 membership in the International Telecommunication Union (ITU) increased to 138 with the accession of Equatorial Guinea to the International Telecommunication Convention. The 25th session of the Administrative Council of the ITU took place during May 23–June 11, at ITU headquarters in Geneva.

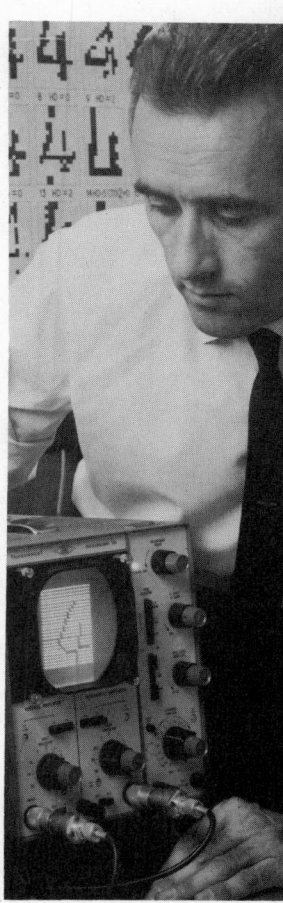

COURTESY, U.K. POST OFFICE

A Post Office technician in Great Britain works on computer stylizing input characters. It is part of the effort to develop an optical character-recognition scanner that could sort typed-addressed mail.

The council decided that the next ITU Plenipotentiary Conference would be held in Geneva in September 1973 and that the next World Administrative Radio Conference for Maritime Services would be held at the beginning of 1974. The latter should establish, on the basis of single side-band operation, a new frequency-allotment plan for high-frequency radiotelephone coast stations, and amend the associated provisions of the Radio Regulations.

The International Radio Consultative Committee (CCIR) held its 12th plenary assembly in New Delhi from January 21 to February 11. Nearly 600 documents concerning radiocommunications were discussed and approved. The subjects included the use of satellites for the transmission of telephony and television, the use of computers to improve the reliability of forecasts of frequencies likely to be usable between various points on earth, reliability of radio services, technical and economic factors related to broadcasting both sound and vision programs from satellites, and the means of facilitating participation in the work of the CCIR by new or less developed countries.   (ITU)

See also Industrial Review; Television and Radio.

ENCYCLOPÆDIA BRITANNICA FILMS. *Development of Communications (From Telegraph to TV)* (1955); *Getting the News* (1967).

Television and Radio

In 1970, according to figures compiled by *Broadcasting* magazine and *Broadcasting Yearbook,* there were an estimated 231 million television sets and 620 million radio sets in use throughout the world. Approximately 85 million of the television sets, or 37% of the world total, were in the United States. According to *Broadcasting,* the U.S.S.R. had more than 25 million, Japan 22.3 million, and the United Kingdom 20 million. *Broadcasting*'s estimates, a few of them revised from earlier accounts, also showed West Germany with 16.2 million sets, Italy with 9.1 million, France 9 million, Canada 6.8 million, Spain 3.6 million, Poland 3.5 million, Argentina 3 million, Czechoslovakia 2.8 million, Australia 2.7 million, Sweden 2.5 million, Belgium 2 million, and Hungary 1.5 million. At the opposite extreme, according to *Broadcasting,* Kuwait had 60,000 sets, Sudan 35,000, Mauritania 15,000, Uganda 10,000, Liberia 6,500, and Sierra Leone 3,000.

Radio was even more universal than television in 1970. Through direct broadcasting stations, boosters, or relays, amplitude modulation (AM) or frequency modulation (FM) stations penetrated virtually every country. About 320.7 million, or a little more than half of the world total of 620 million radio sets, AM and FM, were in the U.S., according to *Broadcasting.*

Approximately 6,360 television stations were on the air or under construction throughout the world in 1970. No area had gained significantly. There were about 2,000 in Western Europe, 2,100 in the Far East, 1,034 in the U.S., 905 in Eastern Europe, 170 in South America, 76 in Canada, and 35 in Africa. Many countries had only one or two program services; others offered multiple choices. In the U.S. it was estimated that virtually all television-equipped homes could receive at least two stations, more than half (53%) could receive at least seven, and almost one-fourth (24%) could receive nine or more.

Radio stations on the air or under construction

throughout the world in 1970 numbered approximately 12,900. Most were AM, but FM was gaining in both number and proportion. More than half of the world total, or 7,134, were in the U.S., and about one-third of these were FM, according to reports published by *Broadcasting* in November.

Organization. One of the biggest disappointments of the year in organization was failure of the international conference on the future organization of the International Telecommunications Satellite Consortium (Intelsat) to reach agreement on what form the administration of international satellite affairs should take. The conference, which had opened in 1969 and then recessed, resumed in Washington, D.C., in February 1970, but after a month was unable to agree on a new system of management for international satellite operations. Since 1964, the U.S. Communications Satellite Corp. (Comsat) had managed Intelsat. When disagreement on future management persisted, the Australian and Japanese delegations at the Washington meeting proposed a compromise that at first seemed likely to succeed. Their plan provided for the establishment of a general assembly in which each nation would have one vote; a board of governors with voting based on use but not to exceed 40% for any one nation (as opposed to the existing system, in which the U.S. had a 53% vote); and a director general to be chosen by the board to serve as chief executive officer of the consortium. Under this plan, the new system would be put into effect over a period of six years, during which Comsat would continue as manager but with gradual diminution of its power. The U.S. called the plan acceptable, but so many amendments were offered from the floor, seeking to change the weight of votes and the authority of the general assembly over the board of governors and its director general, that in the end the conference decided to assign the problem to an "intersessional working group" and consider its proposals at a subsequent conference.

The nations were much more successful in organizing around-the-world distribution of special programs. In one of the most massive coverage efforts in history, an estimated 800 million to 900 million persons in 40 countries witnessed live television coverage, via satellites, of the World Cup soccer championship games played in Mexico City. Between May 31 and June 21, according to Comsat sources, more than 470 hours of satellite time were used to distribute coverage of the games. On April 17, ten hours of satellite time were used to send live coverage of the splashdown of the near-disastrous moon mission of Apollo 13. Satellites were also used extensively to relay to television stations around the world live and taped coverage of, among other events, the funeral of Charles de Gaulle of France and concurrent memorial services attended by many of the world's leaders at Notre Dame Cathedral in Paris in November.

In Canada, work on a satellite system that would provide six television channels to serve the entire nation was scheduled for completion by the end of 1972. In India, ground and airborne facilities were to be meshed with a satellite system for a massive educational program, also effective in 1972. The Soviet Union continued to use its Orbita system of satellites to relay programs from Moscow to remote areas, and the U.S. took the first steps toward establishing a satellite system of its own by inviting and receiving applications from companies seeking to operate domestic satellite services.

BOB PETERSON, LIFE
MAGAZINE © TIME INC.

Draped with sensor wires
attached to a physiograph
recording his responses,
a nine-year-old boy views
filmed violence shown
by Victor Bailey Cline,
a clinical psychologist
at the University of Utah
who wants to determine
to what extent Americans
are influenced
by television violence.

Colour television continued to expand. In Ireland, the state-operated Radio Telefís Eireann provided colourcasts of a British Broadcasting Corp. (BBC) program from the World Cup soccer matches in Mexico City in the spring as a test, then embarked on a program calling for five hours of colour a week starting in the fall and complete conversion to colour in 1974. Österreichischer Rundfunk G.m.b.H. (ÖRF), the Austrian broadcasting agency, ordered $6.1 million worth of colour equipment to be installed in a new television production complex in Vienna.

Introduction of colour was still complicated in most countries by the need to choose between the French SECAM and West German PAL systems. Spain and Sweden had chosen PAL in 1969, followed in 1970 by Italy and Australia (both to begin colour transmissions in 1971). Most Soviet-bloc countries and areas of influence chose SECAM, as did Middle Eastern, African, and other countries formerly part of the French empire.

A boom in colour set sales in Japan was expected to result in colour set ownership by one family in every four by the end of 1970. With set production in 1969 reaching a total of 6 million (more than 3.6 million for export), Japan passed the U.S. to become the world's top producer of colour sets. A new market for Japanese sets was opening in Australia.

Colour set sales reached boom proportions in West Germany, and exports, up by 84% at midyear, showed the extent of Western European demand. Domestic sales in January–June exceeded 465,000, raising ownership to a total of some 800,000. In the U.K., where rental was preferred, especially for colour, both sales and installations rose steadily after a big jump ahead in September 1969, with another in September and October 1970, so that they had passed the total of 560,000 forecast for the year by the end of October. Estimates of total installations for 1970 were raised to 650,000, with expectations of more than 2 million by 1972 and more than 4 million by 1974. Black-and-white sales and rentals also rose, by 20%.

United States. Although most sets still in use produced only black-and-white pictures, most transmissions were in colour. The three national networks—the American Broadcasting Co. (ABC), the Columbia Broadcasting System (CBS), and the National Broadcasting Co. (NBC)—transmitted almost exclusively in colour. So did most stations except in relatively small cities, and these increasingly expanded their colour schedules. And the size of the colour audience was growing steadily. The 26.2 million total of colour-equipped homes on Oct. 1, 1970, represented a gain of 4 million homes, or 18%, since Oct. 1, 1969, according to NBC, the source of the estimates.

A decision on the question of domestic satellites to relay television and radio programming moved a step nearer in January when the White House, after years of uncertainty reaching back into the previous administration, recommended that the Federal Communications Commission (FCC) adopt an open-door policy that would permit virtually any entity with enough financial and technical resources to operate its own system. Although the recommendation was not binding on the FCC, the commission partially accepted it. It announced in March that it was inviting applications from all who were technically and economically qualified and who could show a need for the service. But it also called upon applicants to answer a broad range of questions concerning what future policy on satellites should be. It made clear that it envisioned satellite services transmitting cable, or community antenna television (CATV), as well as broadcast television programming, but it wanted views on questions such as whether it should authorize separate specialized systems for each or a multipurpose system capable of handling both, or perhaps some combination of specialized and multipurpose systems.

The three national commercial television networks, goaded by a 1969 increase of 44% in rates charged by the American Telephone & Telegraph Co. (AT & T), the principal supplier of networking facilities, had already commissioned a study of alternative means of getting programs to their affiliated stations. The study, completed in July, concluded that the networks could save 25 to 35% of their payments to AT & T, which in 1970 would total about $70 million, by setting up either their own domestic-satellite system or their own specialized ground-based microwave system. Over a 20-year period, the study estimated, the total annual cost of either system would range between $50 million and $55 million. Both systems would be equipped to carry not only the television and radio programs of the networks but also the noncommercial programs of the National Educational Network and telecasts of other broadcast users such as Hughes Television Network, which specialized in sports and other occasional programming. Nonbroadcast and common-carrier use was not envisioned for either system.

The networks were later given, at their request, until Dec. 15, 1970, and subsequently were allowed until March 15, 1971, to let the FCC know whether they intended to file a satellite application. Western Union had already filed one, and the FCC gave other potential applicants until March 1, 1971, to do so. Western Union's application was for a multipurpose satellite to handle television transmissions as well as most of the communications services already handled by the company. Comsat and AT & T filed applications in October for a jointly operated multipurpose system, and a number of others, including TelePrompTer Corp. and Hughes Aircraft Co., indicated plans to apply for a system that would include program service to CATV systems.

The pressures upon broadcasters—political, social, and economic—intensified in 1970. In the hope of creating new program sources, the FCC ordered that, beginning Sept. 1, 1971, network-affiliated television stations in the 50 largest markets could carry no more than three hours of network programming between 7 and 11 P.M., Eastern time, on any night. In effect, this meant that stations must produce themselves or buy from non-network sources a half hour of programming each night (they already produced the other half hour). The rule affected network affiliates in all markets, not just the top 50, because it would be uneconomical for networks to produce programs that would be seen only in the smaller markets. *Broadcasting* estimated that loss of the nightly half hour would cost the three networks at least $70 million a year in revenues—in normal times. But the economy was below normal in 1970, and the rule seemed likely to help networks save money by reducing their production costs at a time when advertisers were spending less than usual. Even so, the rule was opposed by CBS and NBC, and by virtually all network affiliates, who protested that suitable substitute programming was not available or would cost much more than they could afford. Court appeals were pending as the year ended but seemed unlikely to be decided in time, even if the rule were overturned, to prevent its going into effect at least for the 1971–72 program season.

After much debate, Congress enacted in 1970 a ban on the broadcast advertising of cigarettes, effective Jan. 2, 1971 (*see* ADVERTISING).

Television stations were increasingly confronted with challenges—and in some cases competing applications for their licenses—filed by local citizens' groups at license-renewal time. Such protests had become more and more widespread after a group of black citizens, assisted by the United Church of Christ, had accused station WLBT-TV in Jackson, Miss., of discriminatory treatment and, in 1969, had made the charge stand up in court.

Another spectre for broadcasters was raised in 1970 when the FCC gave its approval, after 18 years of

consideration, to the Zenith Radio Corp.'s Phonevision system of pay television, the first to win the commission's approval. But by then broadcasters appeared to be more worried by another potential competitor, CATV, which, unlike pay television, had established a foothold and was expanding rapidly. Broadcasters' concern centred on the effect CATV might have upon them by diverting segments of their audiences and, eventually, some of their advertising revenues. *Broadcasting* reported that, after growing at an annual rate of 20% for the past five years, CATV by mid-1970 was serving 3,730,000 U.S. households, more than 6% of the total. Other authorities estimated that by 1980 CATV would be serving more than 28 million homes.

Europe. In most countries in Western Europe broadcasting still faced the need to cut costs while meeting demand for more viewing time and colour programs. In some countries, expansion or introduction of commercial television and radio was controversial; in others, commercial television was fighting a losing financial battle. Evasion of license fees remained a cause of losses, and expensive campaigns were launched to ensure their payment. Accusations of political bias in news presentation and documentary programs about foreign countries, and of the influence of television in encouraging violence, crime, promiscuity, and a general decline in moral standards led to demands for control, and these, in their turn, caused broadcasters to complain of threats to their freedom. Belief in the power of television and radio had been firmly implanted; claims by broadcasters that it had been greatly overstated were hard to swallow, especially when combined with high estimates of the influence of the effects of broadcast advertising. Studies undertaken to provide a basis for a more realistic evaluation of the effects of television on public opinion and action, however, suggested by their preliminary reports that there had been much exaggeration. In the U.K., where charges that television increased aggressive demonstrations and crimes of violence had formed part of the Conservative election campaign's demand for "law and order," studies were undertaken by an Independent Television Authority (ITA) working party and by the University of Leicester's Centre for Research on Mass Communications; their first findings went far to prove that public opinion used what the television screen presented to support its own prejudices, and reduced fears that violence would result from seeing it enacted.

The greatest organizational changes in the U.K. followed the change of government. Within a week of the election the Conservative minister of posts and telecommunications, Christopher Chataway, had given the go-ahead to commercial radio and cut back BBC plans for extension of its local radio program. Although the BBC had been permitted to continue with 12 new local stations, one to be in operation by March 1971, the 20 intended to follow by 1973 were almost certainly doomed. The new stations brought the BBC's total up to 20, giving it a good start against commercial radio's plans for 18 stations by 1973. The BBC, however, was restricted to VHF (very high frequency) transmission, although by 1971 it would be capable of covering 70% of the population, while commercial radio was to use the medium wavelength until 6 P.M. Also, the fact that the 20 BBC stations were in places likely to attract commercial radio caused rumours that a government White Paper might contain plans to sell some BBC local stations to com-

WIDE WORLD

Nicholas Johnson, Federal Communications Commission member, criticized the television networks and the Nixon administration for tactics that he said were intended to stifle dissent.

mercial companies. With support from provincial newspaper and industrial interests, 400 companies had been formed, and were ready to sponsor the new development.

The revival of pirate radio stations caused concern to the Netherlands and other continental European governments as well as to the U.K. In February Radio Nordsee International (RNI) began transmissions from Dutch territorial waters, with plans for 21-hour-a-day programs of pop music and advertising spots aimed at "European listeners in the 15–35 age range," and a high enough power to reach Warsaw, Madrid, Dublin, and Helsinki, Fin. Its biggest potential audience was in the U.K., the Netherlands, and West Germany. Its arrival caused a crisis in the Netherlands coalition Cabinet, and in the U.K. sparked a demand for free radio that had died down with the silencing in 1968 of Radios London and Caroline. The Netherlands, an official signatory to the 1965 Strasbourg Convention against pirate stations on the high seas, had never ratified it because parties in the coalition government feared the effects on young Dutch voters of the banning, in consequence, of popular, commercial, Dutch-owned Radio Veronica, anchored off the Dutch coast since 1960. The Dutch Liberal Party, however, wanted both to ratify the convention and to revise the existing broadcasting legislation. A head-on collision was averted only when RNI moved to the Belgian coast, then toward the North Sea coast of Britain. Meanwhile, despite demonstrations in favour of "free radio," the tabling in the U.K. of a motion by Conservative members of Parliament censoring a Conservative government for suppressing "free enterprise," and a public outcry at the jamming of RNI programs (at a cost of some £1,200 a week), Chataway proved as tough as his Labour predecessor toward illegal commercial competition. A second private station, Radio Capital, began transmission from Dutch territorial waters in July.

Progress in West Germany was hampered by rocketing costs, in part resulting from investment by the first and second television networks in colour program production on their own networks to meet a rise in colour transmission time by 70 to 80% for news programs and by 50% for others. Plans were under way to set up a privately owned commercial station in the Saar; and a group with strong newspaper and magazine interests was negotiating with Yugoslavia's Radio-televizija Ljubljana for rights to transmit programs to West Germany from its station.

In France, the government resisted pressure from industrialists and newspaper owners, led by the director of Radio Monte Carlo, to break the monopoly of the state-controlled Office de Radiodiffusion et Télévision Française (ORTF) by setting up an independent commercial television network. The report in July from a committee of inquiry under former minister of education Lucien Paye pronounced against an independent radio and television system financed by advertising, and recommended that the long-deferred third television channel should be part of the ORTF network, with no extension of the eight minutes a day advertising time introduced in 1968. The necessary money was to be provided by raising the television license fee. In October plans for a third television channel, to be in operation by 1972, were announced; like Channel 2, Channel 3 would transmit in colour.

Television was gaining strength in Spain and Sweden. In Spain, the state-controlled national broadcasting organization, financed by advertising, had raised

COURTESY, CBS NEWS

In a seven-minute film clip aired on CBS in May 1970, a South Vietnamese soldier stabbed to death a North Vietnamese prisoner. The clip was aired in its entirety after rumours were spread that the death scene, which was broadcast in November 1969, was staged.

output on two channels (one carrying colour) to an annual total of more than 4,000 hours with more than 4 million sets in use. A big new production centre at Prado del Rey, Madrid, completed in 1969, was in full operation, and revenue had risen by $4 million since 1968 to top $53 million by mid-1970. Sweden's output was up to approximately 75 hours weekly on two channels, with 50% of all programs in colour and about 25,000 colour sets in use.

Although in a strong financial position (with revenue from license fees and advertising more than trebled since 1959), the Italian broadcasting corporation, Radiotelevisione Italiana (RAI), was facing a crisis. Its monopoly contract was due for renewal in late 1970, and throughout the year it was under attack. Influential northern industrialists and politicians, anxious to set up a privately owned independent broadcasting system, hoped, by discrediting RAI, to prevent renewal of its contract. Accusations by the right-wing press that RAI was staffed at high level by Communists, fellow travelers, radicals, and dissident Catholics, and that stricter controls were needed, forced the resignation after only ten months in office of RAI's president, Aldo Sandulli. With its executive management seriously weakened, and still under fire, RAI seemed unlikely to keep its monopoly.

In Eastern Europe, there were advances in both television and radio. Yugoslavia's plans for a new, centralized broadcasting system began in June, when a construction contract was awarded to Marconi's broadcasting division for an up-to-date radio and television centre for Radio-televizija Zagreb, to bring activities scattered in 19 localities together in a single complex of buildings. In Poland a new radio and television centre under construction in Warsaw was due for completion in 1972. A new Czechoslovak radio station, Hvezda, was opened in August, replacing Czechoslovak I, and transmitting in both Czech and Slovak. With programs scheduled from 8:30 A.M. to 2 A.M. five days a week, it aimed eventually to provide daily around-the-clock service. Emphasis was to be placed on news bulletins (one every hour), magazine programs, and entertainment.

The Soviet Union, with a Central Radio Organization providing seven services, averaged 142.2 hours daily in 1970, and programs for listeners abroad were

Gloria, a patient
in the special adolescent
treatment program
at California's Napa
State Hospital, appeared
on "Cry Help!: An NBC
White Paper on Mentally
Disturbed Youth,"
a 90-minute documentary
aired April 25, 1970.

COURTESY, NBC-TV

transmitted in 70 languages for approximately 215.8 hours a day. The Central Television Organization raised program time to 32 hours a day, with programs seen by about 131.8 million persons. Output of colour sets was increasing to keep pace with rising demand.

Africa. The World Bank was to sponsor a long-term plan for educational television in the Ivory Coast, to begin in 1971. A nationwide instructional television production centre was to be built at Bouaké as part of a $19 million project for expansion and improvement, by use of television, of teacher training, primary and secondary education, and vocational and technical instruction. Eventually it was expected that 700,000 pupils would be taught directly by television, and others by mixed television–correspondence-class methods.

In southern, central, and eastern Africa, radio was being increasingly used for political propaganda. Radio South Africa had increased its external broadcasts, aimed mainly at the white minorities in independent African countries, with emphasis on abuse of native leaders who refused "South Africa's hand of friendship." Powerful transmitters installed in 1968 carried programs in English, Portuguese, French, German, Dutch, Swahili (the lingua franca of East Africa), and Chichewa, widely understood in Malawi and Zambia, throughout the continent.

In December 1969 the UN General Assembly decided to hit back with antiracist programs broadcast from Katanga, in the Congo (Kinshasa), to keep up the morale of Africans in South Africa, South West Africa, Angola, and Mozambique. The station began transmission in 1970. In September Radio Tanzania joined Africa's battle of the air, with an expanded external news service for 6½ hours a day, carried throughout southern and eastern Africa by a Chinese-built 500-kw. transmitter.

Programming. News and sports continued to be the basic services of television and radio broadcasters throughout the world in 1970. Coverage of the aborted moon-landing flight of the U.S. Apollo 13 mission in April and its dramatic return to earth after a nearly disastrous explosion was seen live, via communications satellites, in Europe, Latin America, Puerto Rico, Australia, and Japan and other Far Eastern countries, as well as in the U.S. The midterm elections in the U.S. in November, the events surrounding the hijackings of planes by Palestinian guerrillas in September, and the funeral services for Charles de Gaulle in France in November were also witnessed by audiences throughout the world. One of the biggest cumulative audiences of all time watched telecasts of the World Cup soccer games in Mexico City between May 31 and June 21. It was estimated that between 800 million and 900 million persons viewed coverage of some of the games, with 80 million to 90 million tuned in for the finals between Italy and Brazil on June 21.

Entertainment programs from the U.S. continued to find wide acceptance abroad. U.S. distributors had expected to reach $100 million foreign sales in 1969 but fell short by $6 million, partly because of foreign-import quotas set by some countries and informal but effective resistance to imports, particularly U.S. movies, in others. In 1970, however, reluctance gave way to demand for movies in some countries, notably Japan. Westerns, comedies, and mysteries were the predominant favourites, with "Bonanza," "Gunsmoke," "Carol Burnett Show," "Kraft Music Hall," and "Perry Mason" among those most popular in overseas markets.

United States. Two new trends became apparent in television programming in 1970. One was increased attention to ecology—programs dealing with pollution of atmosphere, rivers and lakes, and the environment in general—and the other was the introduction of many new programs concerned with the problems of minority groups and other social issues. For the most part, ecology was treated in so-called specials, while social and racial problems were dealt with in regular series. The latter were not always too successful in terms of audience response, and a number of the series were scheduled to be replaced, or substantially revised, at the end of the year in an effort to bolster audience ratings. Stations as well as networks, in both radio and television, also devoted substantial amounts of air time to the problem of drug abuse, acting both on their own initiative and in response to government agencies' calls for assistance. A study by the Television Bureau of Advertising found that, among television stations alone, the drug-abuse problem had received on-air scrutiny from more than nine out of every ten stations and had been the subject of 3,800 minutes of editorials alone during the first half of 1970, aside from special programs and spot announcements on the subject.

Despite the failures of some regular series to attract enough audience to justify keeping them on the network schedules, the overall blend of drama, comedy, and musical-variety programs succeeded in winning audiences of unparalleled size. The A. C. Nielsen Co. of Chicago, the principal national rating service, reported that viewing during October averaged a record 6.04 hours per day per television household, up from 5.88 hours in October 1969.

News and special events remained a prime service of both television and radio. Day-to-day news coverage continued to attract huge audiences. R. H. Bruskin & Associates, an independent research firm, found in a nationwide survey commissioned by the Television Information Office and conducted during September that television once again had increased its lead as the primary source of news for most Americans.

But the criticism to which news media had been increasingly subjected since U.S. Vice-Pres. Spiro Agnew's blast at television news in November 1969 was having an effect, though most of it was not apparent to the average viewer. Network news leaders insisted that they were not bowing to political or other pressures in their coverage but acknowledged that the pressures had grown stronger and showed no signs of abating. At the local level, according to a *Broadcasting* study in October 1970, the criticisms and pressures were having some effect, at least to the extent of making radio and television newsmen think twice about their handling of news that might prove controversial.

Some broadcast news operations definitely were affected by another factor. Slackening business, resulting from the general economic slowdown, forced a number of stations to curtail news operations. One of the most dramatic examples was presented by the Kaiser Broadcasting Corp., one of the nation's leading ultrahigh-frequency (UHF) station operators, which notified the FCC in November that economic conditions left it no choice but to reduce news operations at five of its six television stations to a minimum, represented by the maintenance of one experienced newsman at each of the stations. Kaiser officials told *Broadcasting* that "pure" news employees were being laid off.

UPI COMPIX

David Frost (right) confronts Yippies led by Jerry Rubin (extreme left, standing) who disrupted his London Weekend Television program on Nov. 7, 1970. The Yippies invaded the stage, thrust flowers at Frost, and sprinkled him with petals.

Sports continued to attract big audiences and bigger prices. *Broadcasting* reported that in 1970 payments for radio-television rights for professional and college football games came to almost $66.3 million, up $13 million from 1969; baseball commanded more than $38 million, an approximately $1 million increase; basketball brought $5.5 million, as compared with $1.5 million a year in the recent past; ice hockey required a commitment of more than $1 million a year; and lesser but increasing sums were being paid for golf and other sports.

In noncommercial broadcasting, "Sesame Street," produced by the Children's Television Workshop and broadcast over most of the 200-plus noncommercial stations and some commercial outlets, was easily the most highly acclaimed children's television program of the year. While "Sesame Street" continued in 1970–71, a sequel for older children, in the 7-to-10-year-old group, was planned by the Workshop to start in October 1971. It would also be on a daily basis and would be broadcast over the stations of the Public Broadcasting Service, the noncommercial network. In addition to those programs and the regular dramatic, news, documentary, and special programs of National Educational Television (NET), some additional functions were proposed for noncommercial stations. The President's Commission on Obscenity and Pornography proposed, for example, that educational stations could be an excellent mass-media classroom for sex education.

A long-expected reorganization of noncommercial television organizations occurred in mid-1970, when NET, the principal programming source for noncommercial stations, was consolidated with WNDT-TV in New York, a noncommercial station, to form an Educational Broadcasting Corp. (EBC) that would provide "the most comprehensive and best financed public television center in the United States" for all noncommercial stations. EBC was to concentrate on programming, with distribution to be handled by the Public Broadcasting Service, set up for that purpose in late 1969. The Corporation for Public Broadcasting (CPB), the chief funding agency for noncommercial

television, meanwhile received some assurance of continued federal financing. President Nixon signed, in October, a bill authorizing a total of $60 million for CPB financing during fiscal 1971 and 1972, plus $5 million in additional funds each year to be matched equally from nonfederal sources, including donations and grants.   (S. Tf.; R. W. Cr.; Ja. Ma.; X.)

Europe. In general, programming in Western Europe had failed to keep pace with technological advance. Broadcasters' talents had apparently been diverted to the perfecting of new techniques from the more important task of learning how to use them with creative imagination. Colour still too often cloaked mediocrity; stereophonic radio, with its potentialities for experiments with sound, was mainly restricted to classical music and serious speech and drama programs, in which it enhanced, but did not originate, effects; while high audience ratings and wide salability had replaced quality and originality as the criteria of success.

Cutbacks on programming and staff resulted largely from high expenditure on development of new media. Paradoxically, when developed, these failed to make full impact because talented producers had been dispersed by lack of money or of opportunities to develop their talents. As a result, though there were, of course, many memorable programs on both television and radio, few departed far from well-tried formulas.

Only in France, apparently, was it even realized that television called for a new kind of creative writing, using images, not words, and bound neither by literary nor by theatrical conventions. Producers such as Michel Polac, in "Le Fils unique"; Jacques Krier, in "L'Usine un jour" and "La Montée"; Danielle Hunebelle, in "Des Noirs pour voisins"; Dirk Sanders, in "À Contre Soleil"; and Alain D'Hénault, in "Une Heure, une vie," succeeded in creating, from the elements of documentary and topical program, a new medium through which to express contemporary realities in contemporary terms.

Also encouraging was the long-overdue weakening of the association between French television and government policy in news programs. This resulted from

Liza Minnelli presents
her first television
special, "Liza,"
aired on NBC-TV,
June 29, 1970.

COURTESY, NBC-TV

establishment in 1969 of autonomous production units for the two television channels, each its own director of informational production. A series of new programs on both channels won popular and critical acclaim, most notable being the first channel's topical daily "Information première," such magazine programs as "XXe Siècle," with its penetrating analyses of events and tendencies in contemporary and recent history, and the political debates in "À Armes égales"; and the second channel's daily current affairs-cum-magazine, "Vingt-Quatre Heures sur la 2."

General program policy, however, continued to be dominated by anxiety to gain high ratings by providing a continuous output of entertainment and "easy viewing" rather than by concern for cultural and aesthetic standards. Against this general background of mediocrity the few attempts at an experimental approach shone the more brightly. Most successful were Jacques Anjubault and Georgette Elgey's serial production, "La Troisième République," which used original documents and caricatures as well as early film sequences to evoke the atmosphere of a regime that had molded French life for 70 years; and "Les Cents Livres," a monthly program in which Claude Santelli and Françoise Verny presented, in a format combining factual information, academic exposition, and dramatic illustration, the masterpieces of world literature (both on the first channel).

Radiotelevisione Italiana (RAI) kept the flag of culture flying with more programs about the arts, more televised drama, classical music, and opera; an integrated schools and adult education program; and greater participation by writers and journalists in newsmagazines and documentaries. There were few experiments in production methods, and RAI even extended its traditionalist approach by sponsoring co-productions with the national cinema, notably of Roberto Rossellini's "Gli alti degl' Apostoli." Rossellini also directed RAI's most outstanding documentary series of 1970, "La lotta dell'uomo per la sua sopravvivenza," a superbly conceived and executed record of man's evolution from his first appearance on earth to his conquest of space.

West Germany watched the World Cup programs with an excitement approaching frenzy. Interest in sports programs remained high, with boxing the most popular after soccer. The most outstanding, widely seen productions of the year were those commemorating the 25th anniversary of Germany's defeat in World War II, including original sequences from the archives of the Nürnberg rallies, scenes showing Hitler's rise to power, the piles of bodies in the concentration camps, the weary trek home of refugees from the eastern occupied territories, the ruins to which they returned, and the final collapse and disintegration of Nazism. Most effective when shown straight, with scarcely any commentary, these programs provided, for many young Germans, their first realization of what the recent past had been like.

In the Netherlands originality and experiment were concerned with ideas for programs rather than with aesthetics or techniques. A 1970 entry at Montreux that, although not a prizewinner, was sold to several countries, was "Look at That," a mixed filmed-live studio program consisting of interviews and their presentation to a studio audience mainly made up of the people interviewed, who were thus seen watching themselves. An experiment in portrayal of world politics that caused wide interest was "Yes World, No World: A Look into the Future," in which the real world was represented as consisting of 6 countries, each with 14 inhabitants. Of these, 3 "consumers," 3 "investors," and 3 "military tacticians," closely watched by 3 journalists and 3 avant-gardists, decided policy in the context of given historical and economic circumstances. All parts were taken by amateurs, and the program was, to a large extent, unscripted, so that "international" and "national" relations developed spontaneously from character, and from actions representing war, civil strife, trade policies, conference and refusal to confer, etc.

Both culture and experiment were hardest hit in the U.K., where restrictions of radio programs came into effect in April; BBC local radio was more concerned with competition from commercial radio than with programming; and both BBC and Independent Television (ITV) were forced by financial crises to use the maximum number of repeats and cut spending on production to a minimum.

The BBC's new local radio suffered from a need to satisfy mass local interests. Radio Birmingham's manager created an unexciting image with his "first and foremost, people here want information"; a want satisfied, it was to be hoped, by four main news bulletins a day, and shorter news flashes, programs on local issues, up-to-the-minute reports on road congestion, local religious leaders discussing local problems, and a "Phone-a-Groan" complaints department. Radio London's pattern was much the same: news, information, local political and religious discussions, listeners invited to the studio to tell their own news stories and acting as their own disc jockeys, and "Dial-Your-Grumble."

With Radio 3 (the former prestige Third Programme) giving up experiment—its staple in its heyday; Radio 4 passing its livelier programs to Radio 3 and becoming (as its director said) "the middle-aged program"; Radio 2 replacing pop music with more "western, country, and folk," to the disappointment of those who missed the old coziness and syrup; and Radio 1 the teen-age, trendy, all-pop disc jockey program, the central radio network seemed to have disintegrated. But the "repeats policy" provided memorable programs, especially when it dug up, for example, Walter de la Mare from the archives, heard reading his own poems in a frail voice that sounded as if he knew he was dead, but nonetheless effective.

In regard to television, BBC and ITV were engaged in a battle over ratings and sports coverage. ITV accused the BBC of giving exaggerated audience figures for its own programs and lowering those for ITV's; the BBC refused to quote exact figures for listening and stuck to those given for viewing. Independent figures supported neither's claims. Sports had been a source of trouble since 1968, when a fight had broken out between reporters from the two networks at the Wembley Football Association (FA) Cup finals. ITV, forced to take sport seriously to keep audiences and advertisers, tried to break the BBC's monopoly of big sporting events. The BBC, with sole rights in athletics at the White City, amateur boxing, swimming championships, and show jumping, had long-standing contracts with the sporting world. Both claimed top ratings for shared events, and ITV's "World of Sport" program was overtaking the BBC's "Grandstand." Proposals that they should alternate in coverage where neither had sole rights, so saving costly duplication (World Cup coverage had cost the BBC some £750,000 and ITV more than £300,000), were rejected by the BBC.

British television programs ranged from the intellectual opus on the brain, "The Mind of Man" (BBC 2), to BBC 1's serial sweetener for Sunday's tea, "Little Women." In between came BBC 2's Jean-Paul Sartre serial "The Roads to Freedom," acted with brilliant understatement by Michael Bryant and Daniel Massey; London Weekend's monthly arts magazine "Aquarius," introduced by its author, Humphrey Burton, with an engaging air of sharing something he had enjoyed with a group of friends; some excellent programs for children; and London Weekend's new Ronnie Corbett comedy-fantasy series, "No, That's Me Over Here." Otherwise, original comic talent was lacking; so was original drama, although BBC 2 had an interesting, controversial interpretation of *Richard II* by Ian McKellen.

There was little new to report of quality or techniques in Australian television. British programs continued to dominate networks, with a Channel 7 promotion campaign begun late in 1969. It bought a package of British, with a few U.S., programs at a price of A$3 million, the highest ever paid for foreign programs by an Australian network, and such series as "Doctor in the House," "Father, Dear Father," and "Please, Sir" were immediately and spectacularly successful. Popular U.S. imports included "To Catch a Thief," "Mod Squad," and "Ironside." As a protest against this policy a group of television performers led by Bobby Limb, one of Australian television's most popular personalities, began to agitate in March for more home-produced programs.

Programming in Eastern Europe was geared to celebrations: of Lenin's birth centenary and the 25th anniversary of the liberation of the socialist republics. Plans, coordinated by the Communist Party committees and broadcasting organizations of the republics with those of the Soviet Union, were at their most extreme in Czechoslovakia, where the Communist Party Central Committee reminded radio and television of their duty to use the celebrations to inspire the nation to reinstate itself in the Communist world. However, Czechoslovakia's true voice was perhaps more clearly heard in the satirical "The Six Escapers," winner of the 1970 Montreux Gold Rose for the best light entertainment television program—the first time the award had gone to a Communist country. (X.)

Amateur Radio. Radio amateurs throughout the world closely followed a U.S. satellite launch on January 23 from the Western Test Range in California. The reason for the great interest was that a secondary payload of the launch was Australis-Oscar, a satellite designed and built by a group of Australian amateur radio operators. It was fifth in the series of amateur radio satellites and was prepared for launch by Amsat, the Radio Amateur Satellite Corp., a Washington, D.C.-based group. Oscar is an acronym for Orbiting Satellite Carrying Amateur Radio.

Australis-Oscar 5 carried two beacon transmitters, one operating in the high-frequency range and the other in the very-high-frequency range with lifetimes of 46 and 23 days, respectively. The satellite allowed radio amateurs to gain greater knowledge of satellite technology, and also to test several scientific and technological experiments. These included a study of high-frequency and very-high-frequency radio-wave propagation from the satellite, a magnetic attitude stabilization system, and a system to allow ground control of the satellite by amateur stations. A major success of the satellite was the interest it generated among radio amateurs throughout the world. Reports were received from hundreds of stations in at least 27 countries.

The technical and operating competence of amateurs received a real test in May when an earthquake devastated areas of Peru, causing among other things a communications emergency. Following the massive quake, many amateur stations began handling emergency communications traffic, some stations operating around-the-clock to fill the communications void. Improvised amateur stations were moved to disaster sites and were operated from portable electric-power generators. An extensive "National Emergency Net" was operated by the Radio Club of Peru with more than 100 radio amateurs participating. Emergency messages were channeled to the presidential palace, to the Red Cross, and to various government agencies. (WI. D.)

See also Advertising; Astronautics; Cinema; Music; Telecommunications.

ENCYCLOPÆDIA BRITANNICA FILMS. *Development of Communications (From Telegraph to TV)* (1955); *Getting the News* (1967).

Tennis

At the level of top competition 1970 was marked by increased emphasis on commercial sponsorship and bigger prize money. The U.S. Open Championships at Forest Hills, N.Y., for instance, awarded a record $160,000 in prizes, including $20,000 to the men's singles winner; and Rod Laver of Australia, the outstanding player of 1969 with earnings of more than $100,000 in prizes, earned about half as much again in the first nine months of 1970.

Despite his high earnings Laver did not dominate the men's game to the same degree that he had during the previous year. He retained none of the four major championships, those of Australia, France, Wimbledon, and the United States, which had given him in 1969 the traditional Grand Slam for the second time. In 1970 three other Australians, John Newcombe, Tony Roche, and the 35-year-old Ken Rosewall, shared major honours with Laver. The women's game was dominated by Margaret Court of Australia. She became the second woman to ever win the Grand Slam (Maureen Connolly was the first to accomplish this, in 1953).

The administration of the game met with increasing difficulties. Early in the year South Africa was suspended from the Davis Cup competition because so many nations found it difficult or impossible to compete against it in view of its policy of racial separation. Rhodesia, with similar racial policies, withdrew its challenge in the same event to save the embarrassment that its presence might cause. During the year all "contracted" professionals came under the control of one promoter, Lamar Hunt of Texas, the owner of World Championship Tennis (WCT). With 24 leading world players under contract, he signed three prominent Americans, Arthur Ashe, Charles Pasarell, and Bob Lutz, for five-year agreements beginning in 1971. The divergence of interest between Hunt and the amateur world governing body, the International Lawn Tennis Federation (ILTF), grew rather than diminished. During 1970 the ILTF initiated a Grand Prix of individual tournaments with bonus prizes for the players earning the most points. In September WCT announced a similar series of 20 tournaments for 32 men players, worth more than $1 million in

CENTRAL PRESS FROM
PICTORIAL PARADE

Australia's Ken Rosewall,
a top winner in 1970,
is shown in action during
the £10,000 Rothman's
professional tennis
tournament in London's
Royal Albert Hall
in March 1970.

prizes. The ILTF in turn announced its Grand Prix for 1971 with more than $1.5 million in prize money, at least 31 tournaments, and competition for women. At the same time the ILTF stressed its basic policy of keeping its "open" tournaments open to every class of player, including the contract professional not subject to the discipline of the amateur national associations.

New ground was broken in the U.S. by an experimental change in the scoring in some tournaments, notably the U.S. Open. The object was to eliminate long matches. Under the new "tiebreak" method a special game was played when the set score reached six games all. With players serving two serves alternately, the set was decided on the outcome of the best of the next nine points.

Davis Cup. The United States again retained the Davis Cup at Cleveland, O., in August. West Germany was the challenger, and with Arthur Ashe and Cliff Richey in the singles and Stan Smith and Bob Lutz in the doubles the U.S. beat the two-man team of Wilhelm Bungert and Christian Kuhnke 5–0. The last contest, after the outcome had been decided, was notable for Ashe beating Kuhnke 6–8, 10–12, 9–7, 13–11, 6–4. This total of 86 games was the longest singles played in Davis Cup competition and the longest match, singles or doubles, of the challenge round.

It was the 22nd Davis Cup success for the U.S., the same number that had been achieved by Australia. For the second successive year Australia failed at a relatively early stage, losing to India at Bangalore in the final of the Eastern Zone. More than any other nation, Australia had its Davis Cup effort diminished by the ineligibility of contract professionals for team selection.

Brazil joined India as a zone winner by triumphing in the American Zone. Spain won Section "A" of the European Zone when, with Manuel Santana and Manuel Orantes as the principal players, they beat Sweden, Bulgaria, France, and Yugoslavia. West Germany won Section "B" by defeating Denmark, the United Arab Republic, Belgium, and the U.S.S.R. In the interzone contests West Germany beat India 5–0 in Poona, India; Spain defeated Brazil 4–1 in São Paulo, Braz.; and, in the final, West Germany beat Spain 4–1 in Düsseldorf, W.Ger. During the course of the competition Santana brought his number of matches played for Spain to 117, making him the third most seasoned Davis Cup player, behind Jacques Brichant of Belgium (121) and Nicola Pietrangeli of Italy (159).

Men's Competition. *Singles.* The Australian tournament, played in Sydney and combined with the New South Wales championship, brought defeat in the quarterfinals to Roche by Roger Taylor of the U.K. and to Newcombe by Dennis Ralston of the U.S. Semifinal wins by Dick Crealy of Australia over Taylor and by Ashe over Ralston were the prelude to a final victory by Ashe over Crealy 6–4, 9–7, 6–2. Some weeks later a Dunlop-sponsored tournament was staged in Australia that rivaled the traditional national championship in prestige. This was won by Laver with a final victory over Rosewall by 3–6, 6–2, 3–6, 6–2, 6–3 in what was one of the finest matches of the year. Laver also won the South African championship with a quarterfinal win over Ray Moore, a semifinal triumph over Bob Hewitt, and a final 4–6, 6–2, 6–1, 6–2 victory against Frew McMillan.

The French championships in Paris were played without any of the contract professionals participating. Jan Kodes of Czechoslovakia was the winner by 6–2, 6–4, 6–0 in a final against the Yugoslav Zeljko Franulovic. The latter had won 6–3, 3–6, 10–8, 4–6, 6–3 in a quarterfinal match against Ashe and 6–4, 4–6, 1–6, 7–5, 7–5 against Cliff Richey.

Newcombe won the Wimbledon championships for the second time, his previous triumph having occurred in 1967. Laver was beaten in the fourth round by Taylor, and Taylor, in turn, was eliminated in the semifinals by Rosewall, conqueror of Roche in the previous round. Newcombe, quarterfinal victor over Roy Emerson of Australia, beat Andres Gimeno of Spain in the semifinals and went on to win a fluctuating final against Rosewall 5–7, 6–3, 6–2, 3–6, 6–1.

Tom Okker of the Netherlands won the West German title, defeating Ilie Nastase of Romania 4–6, 6–3, 6–3, 6–4. Nastase, however, triumphed in the Italian tournament with a 6–3, 1–6, 6–3, 8–6 victory over Kodes.

The U.S. Open, played under the tiebreak scoring system, brought noteworthy success to Rosewall. Having reached the Wimbledon final 16 years after his first entry onto that stage, he won the U.S. title 14 years after first taking it in 1956. Laver lost in the fourth round to Ralston, who immediately went down in the quarterfinals to Richey. At that stage Rosewall won over Smith, and Newcombe beat Ashe. Both semifinals were one-sided, Roche beating Richey and Rosewall defeating Newcombe. In the finals Rosewall triumphed over Roche 2–6, 6–4, 7–6, 6–3, the third set score demonstrating the application of the tiebreak system.

Doubles. Newcombe and Roche, the outstanding pair of 1969, retained their Wimbledon title. Lutz and Smith took the Australian championship; the South Africans Hewitt and McMillan won in South Africa and West Germany, while Ion Tiriac and Nastase were successful in both Italy and France. Surprisingly, the U.S. Open title fell to Pierre Barthes of France and Nikki Pilic of Yugoslavia, the first European winners since 1937.

Women's Competition. *Singles.* Margaret Court was conspicuously successful, winning not only the championships of Australia, France, Wimbledon, and the United States for the Grand Slam but taking the South African championship as well. She competed in neither the Italian nor West German tournaments. Mrs. Court won the Australian title without losing a set and beat her fellow Australian Kerry Melville 6–3, 6–1 in the final. In the Dunlop event at Sydney, Billie Jean King of the U.S. won the final against Mrs. Court

6–2, 4–6, 6–3. The South African championship went to Mrs. Court with a final win against Mrs. King 6–4, 1–6, 6–3.

Mrs. King won the Italian title after a narrow semifinal victory 3–6, 7–5, 6–3 against Virginia Wade of the U.K. and a final win 6–1, 6–3 against the 1969 champion, Julie Heldman of the U.S. In winning the French title Mrs. Court was taken to three sets only once, by Olga Morozova of the Soviet Union. Mrs. Court defeated Rosemary Casals of the U.S. in the quarterfinals, Miss Heldman in the semifinals, and Helga Niessen of West Germany 6–2, 6–4 in the finals.

The Wimbledon championships saw Mrs. Court a quarterfinal winner against Miss Niessen 6–8, 6–0, 6–0 (the only set she lost) and a semifinal victor against Miss Casals by 6–4, 6–1. She won the championship by beating Mrs. King 14–12, 11–9 in one of the best finals ever played. It was the longest title match of all time with its 46 games. The triumph of Mrs. Court in the U.S. meeting was measured by an easy semifinal win over Nancy Richey of the U.S. and by a 6–2, 2–6, 6–1 final victory over Miss Casals.

Doubles. Mrs. King and Miss Casals had the most success, winning the championships of South Africa, Italy, and Wimbledon. Mrs. Court joined with Judy Dalton to win in Australia and the U.S. Françoise Durr and the Australian-born Gail Chanfreau won the French championship for France.

Wightman Cup. The United States again defeated Great Britain to retain the trophy. They won 4–3 at Wimbledon, represented by Mrs. King, Miss Richey, Miss Heldman, Mary Ann Curtis, and Jane Bartkowicz against Ann Jones, Miss Wade, Winnie Shaw, and Joyce Williams. The match was not settled until the final contest when Mrs. King and Miss Bartkowicz beat Miss Wade and Miss Shaw 7–5, 3–6, 6–2.

Federation Cup. Australia, represented by two players, Mrs. Dalton and Karen Krantzcke, won in Freiburg im Breisgau, W.Ger. They beat West Germany, semifinal victors over the U.S., by 3–0 in the final.   (L. O. T.)

Thailand

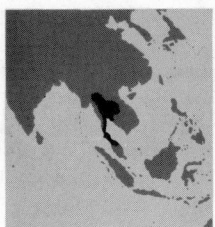

A constitutional monarchy of Southeast Asia, Thailand is bordered by Burma, Laos, Cambodia, and Malaysia. Area: 198,500 sq.mi. (514,000 sq.km.). Pop. (1970 est.): 35,814,000. Cap. and largest city: Bangkok (pop., 1967 est., 2,136,432). Language: Thai. Religion (1964): Buddhist 93.7%; Muslim 3.9%. King, Bhumibol Adulyadej; prime minister in 1970, Field Marshal Thanom Kittikachorn.

Changes in the U.S. administration's Southeast Asian strategy and the enlargement of the Indochina war made 1970 a particularly difficult year for the government of Thailand. It found the security situation deteriorating, and it was hard put to find the money required to meet rising public expenditure.

Toward the end of 1969 the U.S. announced that it would withdraw 6,000 troops from Thailand by July 1. Visiting Bangkok during New Year week, U.S. Vice-Pres. Spiro Agnew reiterated Washington's commitment to Thailand, but the economic effects of the U.S. forces' pullback were already being felt. It became part of Thai government policy thereafter to press the U.S. for increased financial assistance. When the Indo-

china war spilled over into Cambodia, the Thai leaders recognized the need to collaborate with the Cambodian government, but stuck to the line that unless the U.S. rushed substantial financial aid, it would not play any significant role. The resumption of diplomatic relations with Cambodia was announced in May.

Even before the events in Cambodia, the Thai government became concerned about a resurgence of terrorist activities in the northeast and in the south. At the end of 1969 about 1,000 Marines were sent to the south and four provinces were put under martial law. In the northeast the Ubon air base was attacked by guerrilla forces in January. After the start of the war in Cambodia, there were more serious incidents. In June three senior employees of the U.S. Information Service were killed. In September the governor and the police chief of Chiang Rai Province in the far north, along with the information officer of the 3rd Army, were ambushed and killed. Another problem arose along the border with Burma when the former Burmese prime minister, U Nu, who had been granted asylum in Bangkok the previous year, went underground and allegedly slipped into Burma in October.

By midyear the government found it necessary to adopt what appeared to be desperate measures to raise revenue. On June 30 import duties and trade taxes on approximately 200 items were drastically increased.

THAILAND
Education. (1967–68) Primary, pupils 4,983,113, teachers (including preprimary) 119,250; secondary, pupils 358,221, teachers (state only) 10,285; vocational, pupils 57,751, teachers 5,796; teacher training, students 20,534, teachers 2,098; higher (including 7 universities), students 38,204, teaching staff 3,186.
Finance. Monetary unit: baht, with a par value of 20.80 baht to U.S. $1 (49.92 baht = £1 sterling). Gold, SDRs, and foreign exchange, official: (June 1970) U.S. $954 million; (June 1969) U.S. $1 billion. Budget (1967–68 rev. est.): revenue 16,649,900,000 baht; expenditure (including capital account) 19,590,300,000 baht. Gross national product: (1967) 105,630,000,000 baht; (1966) 96.8 billion baht. Money supply: (May 1970) 19,680,000,000 baht; (May 1969) 19,380,000,000 baht. Cost of living (Bangkok; 1963 = 100): (June 1970) 117; (June 1969) 116.
Foreign Trade. (1969) Imports 26,148,000,000 baht; exports 14,782,000,000 baht. Import sources (1968): Japan 34%; U.S. 19%; West Germany 8%; U.K. 7%. Export destinations (1968): Japan 21%; U.S. 13%; Malaysia 9%; Singapore 9%; Netherlands 7%; Hong Kong 7%; India 6%; West Germany 5%. Main exports: rice 20%; rubber 18%; corn 11%; tin 11%; tapioca 6%; kenaf 5%.
Transport and Communications. Roads (1968) c. 10,000 km. Motor vehicles in use (1968): passenger c. 129,500; commercial (including buses) c. 154,600. Railways (1968): 3,855 km.; traffic 3,914,000,000 passenger-km., freight 2,118,000,000 net ton-km. Air traffic (1969): 542.9 million passenger-km.; freight 6,575,000 net ton-km. Shipping (1969): merchant vessels 100 gross tons and over 53; gross tonnage 69,448. Shipping traffic (Bangkok only; 1967) goods loaded 5,225,000 metric tons, unloaded 8,038,000 metric tons. Telephones (Dec. 1968) 114,419. Radio receivers (Dec. 1967) 2,766,000. Television receivers (Dec. 1968) 210,000.
Agriculture. Production (in 000; metric tons; 1968; 1967 in parentheses): rice 10,772 (9,595); peanuts 149 (128); sweet potatoes c. 247 (247); corn (1969) c. 1,700, (1968) 1,500; rubber (1969) c. 283, (1968) c. 259; soybeans c. 51 (51); cassava 2,000 (1,774); sugar, raw value (1969–70) c. 667, (1968–69) c. 575; bananas c. 1,200 (c. 1,200); tobacco 90 (70); cotton, lint 30 (27); kenaf (hard fibre; 1969) 320, (1968) 140; timber (cu.m.; 1968) 4,700, (1967) 4,500; fish catch (1968) 1,089, (1967) 847. Livestock (in 000; 1968–69): cattle c. 5,200; buffaloes (1967–68) c. 6,900; pigs c. 4,200; chickens (1967–68) c. 36,500.
Industry. Production (in 000; metric tons; 1969): cement 2,404; tin concentrates (metal content) 21; tungsten concentrates (oxide content; 1968) 0.6; lead concentrates (metal content; 1968) 2.6; electricity (Bangkok and Thonburi only; kw-hr.) 3,271,000.

Textiles: *see* Industrial Review

So steep was the threatened increase in the cost of living that massive protests broke out. The prime minister went on television to paint a grim picture of the security situation and to explain how it made the new taxes imperative. There was talk about the possibility of dissolving the National Assembly.

The tax bill was passed by the Assembly with a majority of a single vote, but repercussions of the crisis were felt in the government's own ranks. Sixty members of the ruling United Thai People's Party demanded a reorganization of the Cabinet, dismissal of the ministers for national development and finance, and a constitutional amendment to enable Assembly members to become ministers. The dissensions were attributed to "groupism" in the ruling hierarchy, the three significant groups being identified with the prime minister, Field Marshal Thanom Kittikachorn; one of the deputy premiers, Gen. Prapas Charusathiara; and the communications minister, Air Chief Marshal Dawee Chullasapya. The prime minister refused to accept the demands of the dissidents, and the storm had subsided by September. However, the government suffered a major reverse that month when the budget scrutiny committee slashed several items in the 28,646,000,000 baht budget for 1971.

While the Cabinet crisis was still raging, the government published in August a new Press Bill that raised another hornets' nest. The press rebelled against what were described as draconian measures that, among other things, sought to authorize press officers to close newspapers and police officers to screen news whenever they deemed it necessary to maintain peace and order. In protest, the newspapers, with the solitary exception of a U.S. owned and edited English-language daily, jointly boycotted news of Agnew's second visit to Bangkok. Evidently surprised by the vehemence of the press protest, the government shelved consideration of the new bill and promised to water down some of its more objectionable clauses.

(T. J. S. G.)

Theatre

Great Britain and Ireland. On taking office, the new minister with responsibility for the arts, Lord Eccles, stressed the importance of more private support for his domain, but there was little immediate change of policy with regard to the theatre. London's first permanent theatre for young people, the Young Vic, opened under the direction of Frank Dunlop. Dunlop later resigned his administrative but not his artistic duties at the parent Old Vic theatre, and Paul Scofield became assistant there to Sir Laurence Olivier. The Young Vic opened in the autumn with *Scapino,* an updated version of a Molière comedy set in contemporary Naples, and attracted large numbers of young spectators to a series of shows staged mostly "in the open" on its central rectangular platform-stage. The series included a rollicking *Taming of the Shrew* and a colourful revival of Carlo Gozzi's *The King Stag,* the classical comedy with which George Devine had inaugurated the Young Vic's short-lived namesake in 1946.

The National Theatre company took over the Cambridge Theatre as a second West End stage. There, Olivier played Shylock in Jonathan Miller's 19th-century re-siting of *The Merchant of Venice* until ill health forced him to forgo acting for 12 months, and Maggie Smith (*see* BIOGRAPHY) excelled in Ing-

mar Bergman's stylized carbon-copy of the Stockholm *Hedda Gabler* he had taken to the World Theatre Season in 1968. Other National Theatre highlights included: *The Beaux' Stratagem,* with Miss Smith and her husband Robert Stephens as the coy Mrs. Sullen and her fortune-hunting beau Archer; a well-intentioned failure in Simon Gray's over-ambitious stage version of Dostoevski's *The Idiot,* staged by Anthony Quayle with Josef Svoboda sets; Patrick Garland's swashbuckling production of *Cyrano,* his own adaptation of Edmond Rostand's romantic verse-drama; and *Mrs. Warren's Profession,* in which Sarah Badel and Coral Browne made their National Theatre debuts. Visitors included the Dublin Abbey theatre company in Hugh Hunt's well-turned production of John M. Synge's *The Well of the Saints,* and from Nottingham, Stuart Burge's world premiere production of Christopher Fry's first play in ten years, *A Yard of Sun,* as well as Jonathan Miller's *King Lear* and *The Alchemist.*

The Royal Shakespeare Company's growing number of successes both in London and Stratford gave fresh heart to its managing director, Trevor Nunn, when viewing the organization's losses. Extended touring of the company's "theatre-go-round" performances culminated in a two-month season at London's Round House. This included *Arden of Faversham,* starring Dorothy Tutin, and Buzz Goodbody's Marxist production of *King John,* as well as such transfers from Stratford as the sensationally popular circus tent version of *A Midsummer Night's Dream.*

At Stratford, Nunn produced a *Hamlet* (with Alan Howard) of rare modern feel, and a *Tempest* only a shade less highly acclaimed, along with John Barton's *Measure for Measure,* Terry Hands' *Richard III,* and Robin Phillips' *Two Gentlemen of Verona.* At the Aldwych, Phillips made his debut with *Tiny Alice,* starring Irene Worth. Subsequent highlights were: David Mercer's *After Haggerty,* a morose study of an ex-working-class writer; Dion Boucicault's 19th-century farce, *London Assurance;* Günter Grass's *The Plebeians Rehearse the Uprising;* Shaw's *Major Barbara;* and two 1969 Stratford hits, *Twelfth Night* and *The Winter's Tale.* The World Theatre Season broke previous box-office records with the Prague Cinoherni Klub, the Berlin Schiller Theatre (including Martin Held in Samuel Beckett's own production of *Krapp's Last Tape*), the Comédie Française, the Catania Stabile Theatre with Luigi Pirandello's *Liolà,* and the Moscow Art Theatre with *The Seagull.*

The Royal Court Theatre made good use of its studio Theatre Upstairs with new work by Howard Brenton, Heathcote Williams, and Howard Barker. It also gutted its auditorium for an experimental "Come Together" season, bringing together several "anti-theatre" and similar groups of the kind previously seen at the defunct Arts Laboratory. Regular programs included a memorable *Uncle Vanya,* starring Paul Scofield; Christopher Hampton's dark comedy of university life, *The Philanthropist,* later a great success at the Mayfair; *Widowers' Houses;* and, from Nottingham, Peter Barnes's *Lulu,* based on Frank Wedekind's two sex dramas.

Other nonprofit theatres continued to be active. At the Mermaid, Jonathan Miller used black players for the servants' and singers' roles in *The Tempest,* and high standards were attained in Bernard Kops' *Enter Solly Gold, The Apple Cart* (starring John Neville), *Saint Joan* (with Angela Pleasence), and Harold Pinter's Pinteresque revival of James Joyce's

Exiles. The Hampstead Theatre Club discovered David Hare (with his frank exposure of female psychology, *Slag*), and gave to London John Bowen's modern version of the Bacchae legend, *The Disorderly Women*, which had been staged by Bowen in Manchester in 1969. The best offerings at Greenwich comprised: Bowen's *The Corsican Brothers*, adapted from Boucicault; Iris Murdoch's first original drama, *The Servants and the Snow;* and John Mortimer's autobiographical *A Voyage Round My Father*. The Open Space gave John Hopkins's homosexually slanted *Find Your Way Home*, and two quasi-documentaries —one inspired by the Chicago conspiracy trial (with novelist William Burroughs playing the judge), and the other by the self-immolation of Jan Palach in Prague in 1969. Returning to her theatre in London's East End after two years' absence, Joan Littlewood produced two satires on municipal corruption: *Forward up Your End*, dealing with Birmingham; and *The Projector*, based on the 1969 scandal of the Ronan Point disaster in London.

West End hits included: Anthony Shaffer's first play, *Sleuth;* Kevin Laffan's London debut with the anti-Pill *It's a Two-Foot-Six-Inches-Above-the-Ground World;* David Mercer's irreligious *Flint;* David Storey's *The Contractor* and *Home,* both transfers from the Royal Court; Robert Bolt's *Vivat! Vivat Regina!* from the Chichester festival; Ronald Millar's *Abelard and Heloise;* Michael Frayn's *The Two of Us;* Alan Ayckbourn's *How the Other Half Loves;* William Douglas Home's *The Jockey Club Stakes;* Terence Rattigan's 24-year-old *The Winslow Boy* and his latest drama, *A Bequest to the Nation*, about Lord Nelson and Lady Hamilton; and W. Somerset Maugham's hoary *Lady Frederick*. Less successful were Peter Shaffer's *The Battle of Shrivings;* Pinter's two short television plays, *Tea Party* and *The Basement;* and, from the U.S., *1776, Butterflies Are Free, The Square Root of Wonderful, I Never Sang for My Father*, and Morris West's *The Heretic*.

In Dublin, the main events were negative. There were public protests at the Abbey's total failure to use its substage, the Peacock, for its advertised purpose of staging new and unusual plays; for its self-imposed ban on Francis Stuart's historical play about the Irish patriot and martyr Terence MacSwiney, ironically entitled *Who Fears to Speak;* for the closure of the Gate Theatre on grounds of architectural unsafeness; and for the postponement of the Dublin festival until 1971. On the credit side were Hilton Edwards' directorial debut at the Abbey with *The Seagull;* Micheál MacLiammóir's latest one-man show, *Talking About Yeats;* the Abbey's successful tours with *The Hostage* in Europe and the award-winning *Borstal Boy* in New York; Phyllis Ryan's "Gemini Productions" version of Arthur Miller's *The Price;* and the welcome return to Dublin of Cyril Cusack in the title role of *Hadrian VII*. Brian Friel's drama of political corruption, *The Mundy Scheme*, was premiered in Belfast, an unusual occurrence.

France. The death of cultural minister Edmond Michelet did nothing to resolve the growing theatrical crisis or to appease opponents of his "poor theatre" policy, aimed at reducing government aid. Pierre Dux's return as head of the Comédie Française, a post he had held briefly after World War II and then had left because his reforms proved prematurely ambitious, gave hope of better things there. His new policies included a reduced turnover in repertory, higher standards in general, and a forum for untried

playwrights and new one-act plays. Georges Aminel in a brash revival of Henry Montherlant's *Malatesta* paved the way for a new socially oriented *George Dandin,* and a stunning production of Strindberg's *The Dream Play. The Dance of Death*, at the Théâtre National Populaire (TNP), lagged far behind in impact, but the praises awarded to Jacques Rosner's spectacular handling of Witold Gombrowicz's *Operette* on the TNP's substage and to former Comédie Française actresss Cathérine Hubeau, winning all but the hardest of hearts in the final nude sequence, were richly deserved. As shocking to some, in a different sense, was Edward Bond's *Early Morning*, with Maria Casarès as Queen Victoria, which the TNP had introduced during the Avignon festival. Another memorable festival transfer to the Parisian stage was Eugène Schwartz's antidictatorship satire, *The Naked Emperor*. The other subsidized theatres offered stiff competition, with Rafael Rodriguez's unorthodox *Oedipus* and a witty *Italian Straw Hat* at Jean Mercure's Théâtre de la Ville and three notable hits, *Major Barbara, Marie Tudor*, and *The Workhouse Donkey*, at Guy Rétoré's Théâtre de l'Est Parisien.

Roger Planchon continued playing in Paris, both *Bérénice* and his own *L'Infâme* arousing controversy. The latter subsequently achieved a total ban in Nancy for alleged blasphemy. Jean-Louis Barrault exploited the small Récamier for intimate drama, his wife Madeleine Renaud distinguishing herself there in Stanislaw Witkiewicz's early piece, *The Mother*.

Memorable performances in the commercial theatre included: Michel Bouquet as Humpty-Dumpty in Romain Weingarten's whimsical *Alice dans les Jardins du Luxembourg;* Michel Vitold in *Ivanov;* Paul Meurisse in *Un Sale Égoiste* and Edwige Feuillère in *Les Bonhommes*, both by Françoise Dorin; Daniel Ivernel in Françoise Sagan's *Un Piano sur l'Herbe;* and Raymond Gérome and Jean Le Poulain in Francis Veber's *Le Contrat*, and Simone Valère and Jean Dessailly in Robert Thomas's *Double Jeu*, unusual thrillers both. Jean Anouilh was represented by two perfectly fashioned introspective dramas: *Les Poissons d'or*, purporting to sympathize with fascism, and the quasi-autobiographical flashback-studded *Ne Reveillez pas Madame*. Three of Marcel Achard's early plays were revived with success, while Jacques Mauclair made his playwriting debut with the amusing trifle *Zozo*. The U.S. was chiefly represented by *The Beard, Sweet Charity*, and *Butterflies Are Free*, the last presented by Lars Schmidt to follow the un-

A scene from Eugène Ionesco's new play "Jeux de Massacre," which opened at the Paris Théatre Montparnasse in September 1970.

A.F.P. FROM PICTORIAL PARADE

deservedly short run of Jorge Lavelli's eye-catching production of Eugène Ionesco's *Jeux de Massacre*.

Switzerland, Germany, Austria, Belgium, Netherlands. The ferment in the German-speaking theatre continued unabated in 1970. The death of Fritz Kortner was a great loss to the West German theatre. His last production, *Emilia Galotti* at the Vienna Josefstadt, showed his unique talent as a clarifier and innovator of the classics, while his idiosyncratic *Clavigo* in Hamburg was another example of inspired originality in the West German theatre. Heinz Lietzau was accused of neglecting his Hamburg playhouse in favour of the Berlin Schiller theatre, which he was due to take over in 1972, and resigned in December. August Everding was similarly accused of neglecting the Munich Kammerspiele in favour of opera (he was nominated Liebermann's eventual successor at the Hamburg State Opera); however, Claus Peymann's provocative staging there of Harald Mueller's *Great Wolf,* about the brutalizing influence of war, was an undisputed achievement.

In Berlin, Peymann's and Peter Stein's unprecedented "partnership" system of management at the Schaubühne am Halleschen Ufer proved its worth with *The Mother* (Brecht-Gorki), starring Therese Giehse. Outstanding productions at the Schiller and its ancillary stages were Ernst Schröder's production of Gombrowicz's *Yvonne* and both parts of *Henry IV* (adapted by Peter Hacks), both starring the incomparable Martin Held, and Karl Paryla's European premiere of Conor Cruise O'Brien's *Murderous Angels.* After the fiasco of its world premiere in Stuttgart under Peter Palitzsch, Rolf Hochhuth's *Guerrillas* was again fumbled by Hansjörg Utzerath at the Free People's Theatre, but Utzerath's version of Friedrich Dürrenmatt's *Play Strindberg* ranked among his best work. Dürrenmatt's adaptations of *Urfaust* and *Titus Andronicus* were premiered in Zürich and Düsseldorf, respectively, the former staged by the author. *Portrait of a Planet,* a wholly original cartoon satire on mankind, was staged "in the round" by the Polish Erwin Axer at Düsseldorf's new playhouse. Opening festivities there included world premieres of Ionesco's *Jeux de Massacre* and Peter Weiss's *Trotski in Exile.* Palitzsch, aided by Jörg Wehmeier, continued his updated Shakespeare adaptations in Stuttgart with *Henry IV.* He also staged Martin Sperr's study of the Nazi mind, *Koralle Meier,* and gave free rein to Peter Zadek with *The Silver Tassie.*

In Austria, a sudden upsurge of contemporary playwriting centred chiefly on Graz, which had produced Peter Handke, author of the absurdist but thought-provoking trifle, *Quodlibet,* and now boasted Wolfgang Bauer; Thomas Bernhardt, author of the antibourgeois black farce *A Party for Boris;* Harald Sommer; and Harald Mueller. Bauer's *Change* at the Vienna Volkstheater proved a worthy successor to *Magic Afternoon.* The reputedly iconoclastic director, Hans Hollmann, made some impression in Vienna with *Purple Dust* at the Josefstadt, but disappointed his sponsors by losing the appointment of director-designate of the Burgtheater to Gerhard Klingenberg. In Basel, the brilliant Hans Bauer staged a singularly effective *Waiting for Godot* shortly before his untimely death. Heinrich Heinkel's naturalistic first play, *Eisenwichser,* about the drudgery of work, was performed there and subsequently received memorable performances in Brunswick and elsewhere. At Zürich's tiny independent Neumarkt Theatre, the retiring manager Felix Rellstab staged the world premiere of

KEYSTONE

Euripides' tragedy "The Trojan Women" is presented in the Trier, W.Ger., ruins of a Roman bath.

Waclaw, Slawomir Mrozek's "dramatic dirge to exile."

In East Berlin, Hanns Anselm Perten took over the Deutsches, where a new policy of politically conscious theatre was broad enough to admit both Federico García Lorca's *Doña Rosita* (a first production by designer Horst Sagert) and Manfred Wekwerth's production of Hans Magnus Enzensberger's riveting documentary, *Inquiry in Havana.*

Anglo-Saxon importations dominated the Belgian theatre, Flemish writer Hugo Claus once again preferring to have his premieres in the Netherlands. These latter included *Friday,* a drama of incest, and an allegorical satire on Belgian politics, *The Life and Work of Leopold II.* The Dutch touring Centrum Theatre's production of *The Boy Kees,* adapted from Theo Thijssen's novel of adolescence, was the year's undisputed artistic hit.

Italy. Rome, still without a city theatre or Giorgio Strehler to run it, had a bleak theatrical year until the arrival of a sensational version of *Hair,* made palatable by projecting blow-ups of well-known classical nude paintings to balance the stage exposure, and the return of the Proclemer-Albertazzi company in *Four on a Garden.* Strehler's long-awaited *Saint Joan of the Stockyards,* with Valentina Cortese, opened surprisingly at his old Milan Piccolo, after a trial run at the Florence summer festival. The hit of the spring festival there was Nuria Espert's Spanish company in Victor Garcia's production of *The Maids.* Another Strehler premiere was an abstract treatment of Maxim Gorki's *The Lower Depths* in Prato. At the Piccolo, guest-director Patrice Chéreau staged his own adaptation as a play within a play of Pablo Neruda's historical drama of heroic martyrdom in and after the Californian gold rush, originally entitled *Fulgor y Muerte de Joaquin Murieta.* Other notable events included: *The Dream Play* in Turin with guest actress Ingrid Thulin; Luigi Squarzina's *Mother Courage* in Genoa; Giorgio de Lullo's performance in *Victor,* soon after the disbanding of his company, the Giovani; and premieres of Gombrowicz's *Operette* at Aquila and of Eduardo de Filippo's *The Monument* in Florence.

Eastern Europe. The Lenin anniversary year produced a spate of plays about the Soviet leader and political dramas extolling the Revolution and its ideals. Viktor Lavrentyev's *Man and the Globe* at the Maly showed U.S. Pres. Franklin D. Roosevelt and Harry Hopkins planning to unleash the atomic bomb as a weapon for gaining U.S. supremacy over the U.S.S.R. At the Mossoviet, Isidor Shtok's *Leningrad Avenue* praised creative endeavour, and Yuri Zavadsky's cinematic adaptation of *Crime and Punishment,* retitled *Petersburg Dreams,* with Gennadi Bortnikov as Raskolnikov, stressed the social evils that made crime pay. Aleksei Arbuzov's two newest plays were produced during 1970: *Faith, Hope and Charity* at the Komsomol and *Fairy Tales of Old Arbat* at Anatoli Efros' theatre. In an original *Romeo and Juliet* with Olga Yakovleva and Anatoli Grachev, Efros staged the balcony scene against intrusive taped comments by the nurse. At the Moscow Art Theatre, where Oleg Yefremov became principal stage director, Dostoevski's *The Village of Stepanchikovo* proved a popular revival. At the Vakhtangov, the stilled voice of Isaak Babel was heard again in an adaptation of his Red Cavalry stories. At the Taganka, A. A. Voznesenski's *Watch your Faces,* a protest against conformism, was banned after two performances. Highlights at the Gorki Theatre in Leningrad were a revival of Leonid Rakhmanov's *Restless Old Age* and

Erwin Axer's guest production of Jerzy Szaniawski's modern Polish classic, *Two Theatres*. At the Contemporary Theatre in Warsaw, Axer's two outstanding contributions to a lightweight season were *Play Strindberg* and Witkiewicz's *The Mother;* at the National, Adam Hanuszkiewicz appeared as the ghost in his own production of *Hamlet,* wearing the same clothes as Daniel Olbrychski's Hamlet.

In Prague, Otomar Krejca's highly stylized *Ivanov* had the entire cast on stage throughout. In Yugoslavia, Atelje 212 progressed from the nudity of *Hair* to that of *Operette*. Two Slovene playwrights made their mark: Dušan Jovanović, with his first surrealist drama, *Postage-Stamps and Then Emilia,* and Primoš Kozak, with his anticonformist *The Legend of Saint Ché*. In Bucharest, George Constantin scored a double success: as Porfiri in *Crime and Punishment* at the Nottara and in Radu Penciulescu's much-discussed *King Lear* at the National.

Scandinavia. Paavo Haavikko fulfilled the previous year's promise with *The Brotterus Family* at the Helsinki National Theatre. Otherwise, the Finnish theatre was clouded by political controversy. The Helsinki Swedish National Theatre's little substage was closed, and important appointments were denied to those most obviously suitable. Group theatre activity increased most noticeably in Sweden. Successes at the Stockholm City Theatre were three Swedish world premieres and Arnold Wesker's *The Friends,* directed by the author. At the Royal Dramatic, Ingmar Bergman's cleverly imposed stage business in *The Dream Play* left the text to speak for itself.

The threatened closing of the Chat Noir Theatre in Oslo vied in news value with the world premiere of Finn Carling's drama of man's fall from paradise, *The Serpent,* and Espen Skjönberg's performance in the title role of *The Father,* both at the National Theatre. A superb production of Peter Barnes' *The Ruling Class* sold out nightly at the Copenhagen Royal Theatre; in Aalborg, an unusual *Peer Gynt,* using the players as scenery, revealed the bright new directorial talent of Kaspar Rostrup.   (O. Tr.)

U.S. and Canada. Some fruitful alternatives to the traditional predominance of the playwright were being developed during the year in the U.S. theatre. In "performance theatre," as the new kind of work was sometimes called, productions were evolved cooperatively by a company of actors, who either improvised without a written text, or freely adapted an old (dramatic or nondramatic) text, or had a text written to suit their needs by a playwright who worked with them as a member of the company. The last method was extensively employed by the Open Theatre, under the leadership of Joseph Chaikin, which offered during 1970, in New York and elsewhere, two greatly-admired collaborative works: *The Serpent: A Ceremony,* "created by the Open Theatre ensemble, words and structure by Jean-Claude van Itallie, under the direction of Joseph Chaikin," and *Terminal,* "a collective work created by the Open Theatre ensemble, co-directed by Joseph Chaikin and Roberta Sklar, with text by Susan Yankowitz."

One of the great successes of the New York fall season of 1970 was a performance-theatre version of *Alice in Wonderland,* created and performed by the Manhattan Project under Andre Gregory's direction. But perhaps the most promising manifestation of this new kind of work was "Story Theatre," a technique for staging nondramatic texts that used dialogue, narration, mime, and music. Story Theatre

was developed in Chicago by Paul Sills, an important pioneer in improvisational theatre, and was then extensively taken up by the Yale Repertory Theatre. Among the authors whose works formed the basis for Story Theatre productions were Ovid, Gustave Flaubert, I. B. Singer, and Philip Roth. A Story Theatre version of Grimms' *Fairy Tales,* directed by Sills, came to Broadway in October 1970, after a successful engagement in Los Angeles. Story Theatre was distinctive in combining the spontaneity of the new improvisational techniques with the age-old appeal of word and narrative.

Certain other positive tendencies were discernible in the U.S. theatre in 1970, but the major trend was downward, marked by the general paucity of outstanding new works, and in particular by the continuing decline of Broadway. Whatever the reasons—the economic recession, the continuing shift toward the technological media, the theatre's failure to make contact with young people—it was a year, by and large, of diminution and foreboding.

Qualitatively and quantitatively, it was a barren season on Broadway; according to the *New York Times,* there were 34 new shows during the 1969–70 season as against 42 in 1968–69; and the 1970–71 season was slow in getting under way. The Broadway theatre was once a centre of creativity as well as commerce, but each season it seemed more and more given over to the production of bland and superficial entertainment, tailored to the requirements of an ever-shrinking middle-aged, middle-class audience.

In recent years Broadway had largely relied on Britain to provide it with serious drama, but the British imports lately had become fewer and less imposing. After John Osborne's unsuccessful *A Patriot for Me* in the fall of 1969, nothing new came from Britain to Broadway until the fall of 1970, when Barry England's ripely old-fashioned thriller, *Conduct Unbecoming,* arrived; it was followed by David Storey's *Home* (starring Sir John Gielgud and Sir Ralph Richardson), and Anthony Shaffer's *Sleuth,* the former dealing with a group of old people in a mental home, the latter a mystery play. The leading Broadway import of the 1969–70 season came from Ireland: *Borstal Boy,* Frank McMahon's dramatization of Brendan Behan's reform-school reminiscences. It won the New York Drama Critics' Circle Award as the best play of the season.

To replace Britain as a source of supply, Broadway producers began turning to the U.S. resident professional theatres, but nothing from them came close to duplicating the success of *The Great White Hope,* which had come in 1968 from the Arena Stage in Washington, D.C. In the fall of 1969 the Arena Stage sent its production of *Indians* by Arthur Kopit to Broadway, with Stacy Keach in the leading role of Buffalo Bill Cody; it was a critical success but a financial failure. In the spring of 1970 appeared *Inquest* by Donald Freed, a documentary play about Julius and Ethel Rosenberg, who were executed for treason at Sing Sing Prison in 1953; an earlier version of the play had been produced at the Cleveland Play House. On Broadway it aroused some lively controversy, but failed to find an audience.

One new development held out some hope that the Broadway theatre would be substantially enriched by the offerings of the resident professional companies from throughout the country. With a grant from the National Endowment for the Arts (an arm of the U.S. government), the ANTA Theatre, a Broadway

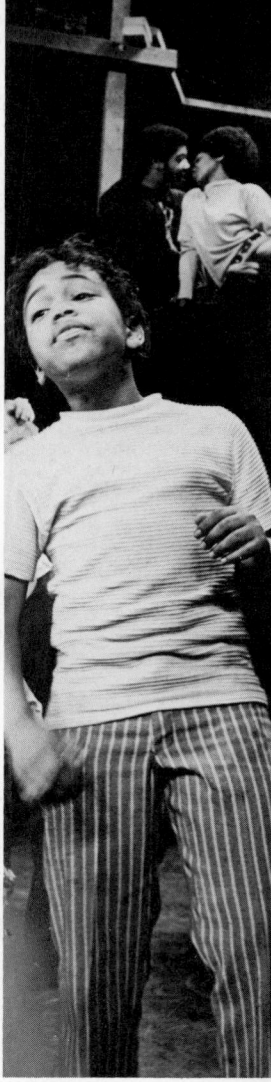

BERT ANDREWS

The musical play "The Me Nobody Knows" opened in New York City in the late spring of 1970 and presented a cast of 12 young people representing children from New York's various ghettos. The story was based on collected writings of black, Puerto Rican, and white ghetto children.

COURTESY,
TYRONE GUTHRIE THEATER

Robert Pastene as Pavel Gai appears in a scene from Aleksandr Solzhenitsyn's "A Play" during its world premiere at the Tyrone Guthrie Theater in Minneapolis, Minn., Oct. 13, 1970.

house, was taken over for use as a showcase for the work of such companies. Its only successes, however, were two revivals of popular plays, both produced by New York-based managements: Thornton Wilder's *Our Town,* with Henry Fonda, produced by the Plumstead Playhouse; and *Harvey* by Mary Chase, with James Stewart and Helen Hayes, presented by the Phoenix Theatre. Among other revivals on Broadway was David Merrick's successful production of Noel Coward's *Private Lives,* with Tammy Grimes and Brian Bedford; it had originally been mounted by the APA Repertory Company during a guest engagement at the University of Michigan.

Prominent among the new U.S. plays that did originate on Broadway was another David Merrick success: *Child's Play,* a thriller about mysterious evil in a Roman Catholic boys' school, by a new playwright named Robert Marasco. Among the comedies, the most successful was *Last of the Red Hot Lovers* by the inevitable Neil Simon. Concerning a middle-aged man struggling unsuccessfully to commit adultery for the first time, it starred a stout, bald, and highly skilled comic actor named James Coco.

When commerce and creativity did join forces successfully on Broadway, the result was usually a musical. In 1970 the prime example of this union was *Company,* an acrid, intelligent, and beautifully crafted musical examination of the liabilities of marriage, and bachelorhood, in the glass-and-steel world of fashionable Manhattan. It was produced and directed by Harold Prince; the music and the brilliant lyrics were by Stephen Sondheim; and the book was by a newcomer, George Furth. On a more conventional level were two shows designed as vehicles for middle-aged stars. *Applause* was a musical version of an old Bette Davis movie, *All About Eve,* made over to fit Lauren Bacall; directed to a hard, sharp fare-thee-well by Ron Field, it was a huge success. *Coco* was based on the life of the celebrated couturière, Coco Chanel; a somewhat heavy, old-fashioned affair, it was notable chiefly for bringing Katharine Hepburn back to Broadway in her first musical-comedy role.

Until an actors' strike in November off-Broadway was somewhat healthier than its uptown neighbour, largely because many plays were being produced there that might once have been staged on Broadway. Producers who despaired of filling 900-seat Broadway theatres with their plays often decided they had a chance with the off-Broadway houses that seated 299 or less; if their play failed, they lost less money. One reason for the economic viability of off-Broadway

was that actors subsidized it by accepting very low salaries. That practice ended on November 16, however, when off-Broadway actors and stage managers went on strike for higher wages. Seventeen shows were forced to close. The strikers and theatre owners agreed on December 16 to submit to binding arbitration and 12 of the closed shows reopened. Of the others, two transferred to Broadway and three closed permanently.

Despite its labour problems, off-Broadway offered hospitality to a certain number of serious plays. In 1969–70 the most successful of these was a grimly compassionate drama of family life entitled *The Effect of Gamma Rays on Man-in-the-Moon Marigolds,* by Paul Zindel; it starred Sada Thompson in a much-admired performance as a neurotic mother and won the New York Drama Critics Circle Award as the best U.S. play of the season. Another family drama was *A Whistle in the Dark* by Thomas Murphy, about a group of Irish immigrants in England; yet another was *Lemon Sky* by Lanford Wilson.

Among off-Broadway comedies, the most notable were *The White House Murder Case* by Jules Feiffer, a bitter satirical attack on governmental lying, and *Steambath* by Bruce Jay Friedman, in which God was represented as a Puerto Rican steambath attendant. In the fall of 1970 came *Happy Birthday, Wanda June,* a first play by the novelist Kurt Vonnegut, Jr., and one of the two that transferred to Broadway after the strike. The late English playwright Joe Orton, who specialized in a peculiarly kinky sort of farce, was represented by two productions. A double bill called *Crimes of Passion* had a short run toward the end of 1969; *What the Butler Saw,* a posthumous work, opened in the spring of 1970 and was Orton's first success in America.

Although the APA Repertory Company closed down, other permanent subsidized theatres remained in New York. The Repertory Theater of Lincoln Center offered a season of U.S. plays during 1969–70, including the world premiere of Sam Shepard's *Operation Sidewinder,* a not-very-successful attempt to put all the elements of the contemporary U.S. malaise (hippies, drugs, Black Panthers, white revolutionaries, computers, the military, etc.) into one play. The Repertory Theatre also offered *Landscape* and *Silence,* two very austere short plays by Harold Pinter.

Joseph Papp's New York Shakespeare Festival experienced its customary financial crisis, which it once again managed to survive. The Festival's indoor Public Theater offered a season of rock musicals during the season of 1969–70; the most successful was a free-form piece in the tradition of *Hair,* entitled *Stomp,* presented by a group of young people from Texas who called themselves The Combine. At the outdoor Delacorte Theatre in Central Park, the Festival offered, in repertory, Shakespeare's rarely performed *Henry VI* plays, plus their sequel *Richard III,* under the overall title of *The Wars of the Roses.*

Outside New York, a tendency toward retrenchment could be seen in some places among the resident theatres, but many seemed more willing than ever to present new or unconventional plays. In Providence, R.I., the Trinity Square Repertory Company presented during its 1969–70 season the world premieres of *Wilson in the Promise Land* by Roland Van Zandt and *Lovecraft's Follies* by James Schevill. Both were written for the company in a sort of historico-politico-satirico-fantastic expressionism that was becoming characteristic of Trinity Square—the only regional theatre that seemed to be developing its own style of playwriting. The Charles Playhouse in Boston offered the U.S. premiere of *Narrow Road to the Deep North*, an enigmatic, Zen-permeated drama, set in Japan, by the British playwright Edward Bond. The Tyrone Guthrie Theatre in Minneapolis, Minn., offered the world premiere of what was billed simply as "A Play by Aleksandr Solzhenitsyn."

In Canada the St. Lawrence Centre, Toronto's Centennial project, opened in February with a resident company under the direction of Mavor Moore. The first season was a disaster; of four productions, only *Striker Schneiderman,* a new play by Jack Gray about the Winnipeg general strike of 1919, won any significant support at all. Moore resigned, and was succeeded by his deputy, Leon Major; the centre's second season began in November, with the North American premiere of *A Yard of Sun* by Christopher Fry.

Meanwhile, *Anne of Green Gables,* a musical version of the famous Canadian story, produced by the Charlottetown Festival on Prince Edward Island, won critical acclaim not only at home, but also in London and at Expo 70. The Manitoba Theatre Centre opened its new home in Winnipeg. The Shaw Festival of Niagara-on-the-Lake, Ont., presented the North American premiere of a London success, *Forty Years On* by Alan Bennett.

The Stratford Festival, also called the Stratford National Theatre of Canada, presented classical repertory (including *Hedda Gabler* with Irene Worth) at the Festival Theatre in Stratford, and devoted its second house, the Avon Theatre, to a season of contemporary plays: *The Friends* by Arnold Wesker, *The Architect and the Emperor of Assyria* by Fernando Arrabal, and *Vatslav* by Slawomir Mrozek. All three were Canadian premieres. This experiment with contemporary plays was not a success, however, and there were no plans to repeat it.   (J. No.)

See also Dance; Literature; Music.

ENCYCLOPÆDIA BRITANNICA FILMS. *The Age of Sophocles* (1959); *The Character of Oedipus* (1959); *Hamlet: The Age of Elizabeth* (1959); *Hamlet: The Poisoned Kingdom* (1959); *Hamlet: The Readiness Is All* (1959); *Oedipus Rex: Man and God* (1959); *Our Town and Ourselves* (1959); *The Recovery of Oedipus* (1959); *The Theatre: One of the Humanities* (1959); *Thornton Wilder: Our Town and Our Universe* (1959); *What Happens in Hamlet?* (1959); *Macbeth: The Politics of Power* (1964); *Macbeth: The Secret'st Man* (1964); *Macbeth: The Themes of Macbeth* (1964); *The Cherry Orchard I—Chekhov: Innovator of Modern Drama* (1967); *The Cherry Orchard II—Comedy or Tragedy?* (1967); *A Doll's House I—The Destruction of Illusion* (1967); *A Doll's House II—Ibsen's Themes* (1967); *Shaw vs. Shakespeare Part I: The Character of Caesar, Part II: The Tragedy of Julius Caesar, Part III: Caesar and Cleopatra* (1970).

Timber

Continuing the steady rise in both volume and value that had been maintained since World War II, the world's output of forest products showed further increases in 1968, the latest year for which figures were available. Estimates by the Forestry Department of the UN Food and Agriculture Organization (FAO), based on reports from most of the world's nations, placed the total value of forest products in 1968 at $45.5 billion, compared with $43.1 billion in 1967. The 1960 figure was $33.9 billion. The estimates were in terms of U.S. dollars based on constant 1960 prices.

The more highly processed products, such as panel and pulp products, showed the greatest gains. The value of panel products (including veneers, plywood, particle board, and fibreboard) was $5.4 billion in 1968, compared with $2.7 billion in 1960, while the value of wood pulp products (paper and paperboard) was $19 billion in 1968, compared with $12.2 billion in 1960. Sawn wood (lumber, railway sleepers, and boxboards) accounted for $15.9 billion. All other wood products had a value of $5.2 billion.

World trade in forest products showed an unprecedented expansion in 1968. Coniferous (softwood) log exports rose 25% over 1967 and broad-leaved (hardwood) log exports, 20%. The expansion in softwood log exports occurred mainly in North America; that in hardwood log exports chiefly in Southeast Asia and Africa. Exports of sawn wood rose about 10%. Of the wood-based panel products, veneer sheet exports, largely from Southeast Asia, rose 20% and plywood exports increased 23%. Wood pulp exports were up 10%, printing and writing papers 24%, and paper and paperboard 14%.

According to FAO estimates, 2,085,826,000 cu.m. of roundwood were cut from the forests of the world in 1968 (1 cu.m. = 35.31 cu.ft.). Of this, 1,188,847,000 cu.m. went for industrial purposes, the remainder being cut for fuel wood, charcoal, and other domestic and nonindustrial uses. For all uses, removals of coniferous and broad-leaved roundwood in 1968 were about equal in volume. For industrial uses, however, coniferous roundwood accounted for nearly 80% of the total.

Sawlogs for lumber and veneer accounted for more than one-third of total roundwood removals and for about three-fourths of removals for industrial purposes. The 1968 total of world lumber production was 388,918,000 cu.m. (1 cu.m., lumber measure = 424 bd-ft.), about 80% of which was coniferous. The FAO's revised estimate for 1967 was 377,509,000 cu.m. Temperate regions of the Northern Hemisphere accounted for approximately 90% of coniferous lumber production and nearly two-thirds of broad-leaved lumber production.

Among individual nations, the U.S.S.R. ranked first in softwood lumber production in 1968, with a reported total of 93,750,000 cu.m. The U.S. was second with 71,116,000 cu.m.; Japan third with 30,940,000 cu.m.; and Canada fourth with 25,162,000 cu.m. Sweden was fifth in the world and first among Western European nations, with 11,291,000 cu.m. Other important European producers were West Germany, Poland, France, Finland, Austria, Czechoslovakia, Romania, Yugoslavia, Norway, Portugal, Spain, Switzerland, and East Germany. China's 1968 output was estimated by the FAO at 8 million cu.m. Brazil reported 3 million cu.m.; New Zealand, 1,673,000 cu.m.; Turkey, 1,632,000 cu.m.; and Mexico, 1,338,000 cu.m.

The U.S.S.R. also led in hardwood lumber production in 1968 with 16,550,000 cu.m., followed closely by the U.S. with 16,426,000 cu.m. Japan's hardwood lumber production was 8,076,000 cu.m. China's output was estimated at 5 million cu.m. Brazil produced 3.1 million cu.m.; Australia, 2,472,000 cu.m.; Romania, 2,479,000 cu.m.; and Malaysia, 2 million cu.m. Other countries producing more than one million cubic metres were France, West Germany, Italy, Yugoslavia, Canada, Indonesia, the Philippines, and Thailand. Among regions, Asia, with 24,861,000 cu.m., was the largest producer. North America was second with 17,464,000 cu.m. and Europe was third with 16,673,000 cu.m.

Preliminary estimates of U.S. lumber production

Theology:
see Religion

Tibet:
see China

were available for 1969, based on information compiled by the National Forest Products Association. The total 1969 output was 37,943,000,000 bd-ft., including 29,481,000,000 bd-ft. of softwood lumber and 8,462,000,000 bd-ft. of hardwood lumber. The combined output of softwood and hardwood lumber was only slightly above the revised 1968 figure, but it was the highest for the decade and approached the postwar high of 38,900,000,000 bd-ft. reached in 1950. U.S. lumber exports totaled 1,135,400,000 bd-ft. and imports, 6,304,400,000 bd-ft. The wholesale price index of lumber in July 1970 was 121.8, down 8.7% from a year earlier (1957–59 = 100).

Canadian lumber production in 1968 was reported at 11,108,800,000 bd-ft., a gain over the 10,489,760,000 bd-ft. (revised figure) of the preceding year. About 95% of the total was softwood lumber. Canada normally exports about two-thirds of its annual lumber production.

World production of wood pulp continued the steady increase of recent years, rising to 90.4 million metric tons in 1968, compared with 86.4 million tons (revised estimate) in 1967. Chemical (including semi-chemical) pulp accounted for about 70% of the total, the remainder being mechanical or groundwood pulp used mainly for newsprint. North America accounted for more than half of 1968 wood pulp production, with the U.S. producing 34.4 million metric tons and Canada, 15 million tons. Among European producers, Sweden led with 7 million tons, followed by Finland (5.9 million), Norway (2 million), West Germany (1.6 million), and France (1.5 million). The U.S.S.R. reported 5 million tons and Japan, 6.9 million tons. Australia and New Zealand together produced slightly more than one million tons.

The FAO reported world production of paper and paperboard in 1968 as 112.3 million metric tons. The 1967 total was 106.7 million tons. The U.S. led in 1968 with 42.4 million tons, followed by Canada with 10.2 million tons and Japan with 9.9 million tons. Other leading producers were the U.S.S.R. (6 million tons), West Germany (4.7 million), the U.K. (4.7 million), Sweden (3.6 million), Finland (3.6 million), France (3.6 million), China (3.4 million), and Italy (3 million). The 1968 total included 19 million tons of newsprint, up slightly from the 1967 output of 18.4 million tons. More than half was produced in North America with Canada accounting for 7.3 million tons and the U.S. for 2.5 million tons.

According to the FAO, world production of plywood increased from 26,348,000 cu.m. in 1967 to 28,061,000 cu.m. in 1968. The U.S. report to the FAO for 1968 was delayed, but in 1967 the U.S., with an output of 13,050,300 cu.m., accounted for nearly half of the world total. Japan produced 4,742,000 cu.m. in 1968; Canada, 1,958,600 cu.m.; the U.S.S.R., 1,832,000 cu.m.; Finland, 614,800 cu.m.; West Germany, 598,500 cu.m.; France, 546,800 cu.m.; Italy, 340,000 cu.m.; Romania, 271,000 cu.m.; Spain, 230,000 cu.m.; Poland, 174,000 cu.m.; Czechoslovakia, 158,900 cu.m.; and Yugoslavia, 134,800 cu.m. Plywood production in a number of Asian countries continued to rise at significant rates. South Korea increased its output from 439,600 cu.m. in 1967 to 703,300 cu.m. in 1968; Taiwan from 334,000 to 390,000 cu.m.; the Philippines from 285,000 to 299,000 cu.m.; and Malaysia from 54,500 to 99,500 cu.m. Brazil ranked first among Latin-American countries with 148,000 cu.m.; Mexico produced 78,200 cu.m. and Colombia, 60,000 cu.m. African output totaled 216,000 cu.m., with

WIDE WORLD

Smog-damaged ponderosa pine is cut down at Lake Arrowhead, California, in April 1970 to make room for healthier, more smog-resistant sugar pines and giant sequoias. The two million board feet harvested were sold at auction.

Timor:
see Dependent States

Tin:
see Mining

Gabon, South Africa, Ghana, and Nigeria the leading producers. Australia's production was 100,100 cu.m.

Particle-board production continued its rapid growth. World output in 1968 was 8,578,000 metric tons, compared with 7,169,000 tons in 1967 and 5,899,000 tons in 1966. The 1966 figure had represented an increase of more than 200% over 1960. The particle-board industry had been expanding rapidly in the U.S. and Canada. Production in the U.S. rose sixfold from 1958 to 1966, while Canada increased its production by nearly 40% between 1965 and 1968. Nevertheless, Europe continued to account for nearly two-thirds of the total, and West Germany, with a 1968 output of 1,698,100 metric tons, was the leading producer. The U.S. accounted for 1,655,000 tons, a substantial increase over the 1,295,200 tons produced in 1967, and the U.S.S.R. ranked third with 979,600 tons. Other leading producers were France (492,900 tons), Italy (444,000), East Germany (330,000), Japan (216,000), Spain (192,000), Finland (189,000), Austria (185,000), the U.K. (182,400), Sweden (173,000), Switzerland (160,000), Romania (158,000), Canada (137,000), Australia (128,200), Czechoslovakia (119,600), Norway (118,000), Poland (117,700), Bulgaria (107,200), and Belgium (100,000).

The U.S. Department of Commerce accepted a new standard for softwood lumber in the United States, which became effective Sept. 1, 1970. The former standard was 16 years old and had become obsolete. The revised standard, recommended in 1968 by an American Lumber Standards Committee, was approved by 87% of the producers, distributors, and users polled by the Commerce Department. It takes account of the fact that lumber shrinks as it dries, and therefore it requires green lumber to be finished to a size sufficiently larger than dry lumber so that both will have the same dimensions after seasoning.

(C. E. R.)

See also Industrial Review.

ENCYCLOPÆDIA BRITANNICA FILMS. *The Temperate Deciduous Forest* (1962); *The Lumberman* (1965); *Trees and Their Importance* (1966); *Science Conserves Forests* (1967); *The Coniferous Forest Biome* (1969): *Problems of Conservation—Forest and Range* (1969); *Problems of Conservation—Our Natural Resources* (1970).

Tobacco

Total world production of tobacco in 1969 was estimated at about 9.9 billion lb. Output was almost the same as in 1968 but was down 4.4% from the record high attained in 1967. There was little change in composition from the previous crop. Production of the American-type cigarette leafs, flue-cured and Burley, rose 3%, balancing a proportional fall in oriental and semioriental types. Production in North America improved by about 6.6% and South America showed an increase of approximately 8.1%. Europe, Asia, and Africa indicated declines of about 5.4, 4, and 0.8%, respectively. The crop in Australia and New Zealand was expected to be almost one-third above the preceding year and about 5 million lb. larger than the 1960–64 average. A total of 25,754 ac. were planted in Australia in 1968–69. This was the largest acreage since 1964–65 and, with a record yield of 1,323 lb. per ac., total production was the highest since the bumper 34.3 million-lb. crop of 1963–64.

Estimates of the total U.S. tobacco crop in 1970 put production of all types at 1,806,000,000 lb., practically the same as that harvested in 1969. The average yield, indicated at 1,997 lb. per ac., was an improvement over 1969. First estimates from India put the area under tobacco in 1969–70 at 5% more than in the previous year. The 1969–70 flue-cured crop was unofficially estimated at some 170 million lb. Pakistan also estimated a small increase in acreage to 262,000.

Attacks on smoking on health grounds continued to intensify all over the world in 1970, eventually finding international expression in a call from the World Health Organization for antismoking campaigns in every member country. Cigarette smoking again received critical attention in Britain in the annual report of the chief medical officer, Department of Health and Social Security. As anxieties about governmental reactions to these pressures grew among tobacco manufacturers, increasing attention was concentrated on the development of possible smoking materials other than tobacco. Work on synthetic materials had been going on for some years. It was believed that research on the subject was more advanced in the U.K. than anywhere else, and this view was strengthened when, in the 1970 budget, the British government brought in legislation allowing the manufacture of tobacco substitutes and their use in smoking products.

Although these regulations cleared the way for research on a larger scale than before, the most optimistic estimate indicated that a marketable product was still two to three years away. Similar research was in progress in other European countries, the U.S., and Japan. It was probable that any practical new smoking material that emerged would be mixed with natural tobacco rather than being sold as a totally synthetic product.

The international significance of these developments was that substitutes, apart from blunting antismoking propaganda, could, with governmental cooperation, considerably reduce manufacturing costs. They could also pose a long-term threat to the leaf-growing industries of the world. Major leaf growers like the United States saw substitutes as a way of diluting tobacco rather than as having any smoking merit of their own, however. Other recent innovations, such as freeze drying, puffing, and making foam sheet, had the same object but differed from substitutes in that they were merely methods of treating tobacco.

Another significant development, noted by the Food and Agriculture Organization of the United Nations, was the emergence of new trade associations and regional integration schemes that led to the formation of new preferential areas, notably the European Economic Community. The Community's tobacco policy, announced early in 1970, tended to favour domestic production and gave preference to associate members (Greece, Turkey, and the African associates). This could lead to substantial limitation of access to the Community for third countries and could in turn considerably affect trade flows.

Exports of unmanufactured tobacco from the U.S. in the first half of 1970 were below those of the previous year, reflecting lower shipments of flue-cured. The total for the first five months of the year reached 168 million lb., 7.2 million lb. more than in the corresponding period of 1969 when shipments were held up by a dockers' strike in the East Coast ports. Imports of unmanufactured tobacco into the U.K. in the first half of 1970 stood at 105 million lb., 15 million lb. less than in the previous year. Even so, supplies from the U.S. were 10.4 million

lb. greater than in 1969, accounting for more than two-thirds of the total from all sources. The main decline was in arrivals from Canada, which were down by more than 50% to 20.8 million lb. Imports from India and Pakistan together showed a drop of over one-third. The most surprising increase was in imports from South Korea. In the first half of 1970 these had already reached 11.5 million lb., four-fifths more than the full year's total for 1969.

Duty-paid imports into the EEC countries, easily the world's largest tobacco-importing area, enjoyed a marked recovery in 1969; the total reached 655 million lb., 117 million lb. more than in 1968. Supplies from the U.S., the main single source, rose by 34 million lb. to 178 million lb. and accounted for 27% of the total. Exports of Canadian unmanufactured tobacco continued their recovery in 1969 to reach 52.4 million lb., one-tenth more than in the previous year. This reflected both the high level of production in 1967 and 1968 and the increased external demand for Canadian leaf, resulting from the sanctions against Rhodesian tobacco.

The partial revival in exports from Turkey was still apparent in the five months to May 1970, with a total of 90 million lb. as against 84 million lb. in the corresponding period in 1969. The quantity of leaf used by the New Zealand tobacco industry declined in 1968–69 to 13.2 million lb. Exports of unmanufactured oriental tobacco in the first half of 1970, at 62 million lb., were 9 million lb. lower than in the corresponding period in 1969, the decline being due to the low level of shipments to the U.S.

(V. F. Ra.)

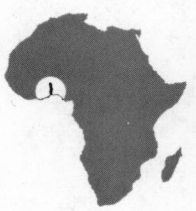

Togo

A West African republic, Togo is bordered by Ghana, Upper Volta, and Dahomey. Area: 21,900 sq.mi. (56,-600 sq.km.). Pop. (1970 est.): 1,955,916. Cap. and largest city: Lomé (metro. area pop., 1970, 148,443). Language: French (official). Religion: pagan; Muslim and Christian minorities. President in 1970, Gen. Étienne Eyadema.

In August, the Togolese authorities announced the discovery of a plot to overthrow President Eyadema's government. Clément Kolor, a former deputy, was killed when he attempted to escape capture, as was the police officer at whose house the conspirators met. A score of people were arrested and accused of plotting to assassinate the president and overthrow the government. It was reported that only three of them were Togolese. A number of ex-soldiers from Ghana and Dahomey were said to have been involved. How-

TOGO

Education. (1966–67) Primary, pupils 157,548, teachers 3,031; secondary, pupils 12,589, teachers 497; vocational, pupils 1,303, teachers 102; teacher training, students 57, teachers 7; higher, students 85, teaching staff 8.

Finance. Monetary unit: CFA franc, with a parity of CFA Fr. 50 to the French franc (CFA Fr. 277.71 = U.S. $1; CFA Fr. 666.50 = £1 sterling). Budget (1970 est.) balanced at CFA Fr. 7,980,000,000.

Foreign Trade. (1969) Imports CFA Fr. 14,564,-000,000; exports CFA Fr. 11,437,000,000. Import sources: France 32%; U.K. 12%; Japan 7%; West Germany 7%; Netherlands 5%; U.S. 5%. Export destinations: France 34%; Netherlands 24%; West Germany 16%; Belgium-Luxembourg 10%. Main exports: cocoa 35%; phosphates 27%; coffee 15%; palm nuts 7%.

Tobogganing:
see Sporting Record

ever, when President Eyadema received the ambassadors of those two countries, he expressly exonerated their governments from any responsibility in the matter.

The presumed instigator of the conspiracy, Noé Kutuklui, a Togolese lawyer in exile, was placed under house arrest by the Dahomean authorities. Kutuklui, who had been a member of the committee of former president Sylvanus Olympio's United Togolese Party, had sought political asylum in Dahomey after the failure of a previous plot in November 1966. However, President Eyadema had asked the Dahomean authorities to release Kutuklui, stating that since the conspiracy had no popular foundation Kutuklui was no danger to his government. On December 1 a newly established permanent Court of National Security passed sentence on 27 accused, including six who were sentenced in absentia. Among the latter was Kutuklui, who was sentenced to a term of 20 years' imprisonment.   (PH. D.)

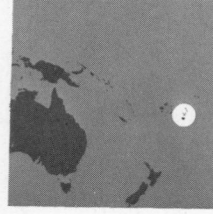

Tonga

An independent monarchy and member of the Commonwealth of Nations, Tonga is an island group in the Pacific Ocean east of Fiji. Area: 269 sq.mi. (697 sq.km.). Pop. (1970 est.): 87,406. Cap.: Nukualofa (pop., 1966, 15,685). Language: English and Tongan. Religion: Christian. King, Taufa'ahau Tupou IV; prime minister in 1970, Prince Tu'ipelehake.

On June 4 the Kingdom of Tonga became the third completely independent South Pacific microstate. Membership in the UN was too expensive a luxury for it to afford, but full membership in the Commonwealth was accepted. Although the four-day independence celebrations were the most lavish ever seen in the islands, actual constitutional changes were few. Revisions of the 1900 Treaty of Friendship and Protection with the U.K. had gradually extended the kingdom's power to conduct its own external affairs, and since World War II it had looked to New Zealand for assistance in defense.

A rigidly stratified society, a narrowly based agricultural economy, a rising population, and a serious land shortage created massive problems. Unemployment was considerable and likely to grow, for 61% of the population was under 21, and the majority faced a landless future. The second five-year development plan, beginning in July, emphasized agriculture with some moves toward small industries, and envisaged an expenditure of about T$5 million (U.S. $5.6 million). The U.K. agreed to continue its financial aid to the tune of T$500,000 annually for the first two years, but there was uncertainty about sources of aid or loan finance thereafter. For the most part, future hopes were pinned on the discovery of offshore oil.   (MY. B. B.)

WIDE WORLD

King Taufa'ahau Tupou IV inspects the guard of honour during independence ceremonies in Tonga, June 4, 1970.

Tornadoes:
see Disasters; Meteorology

TONGA
Education. (1967) Primary, pupils 16,794, teachers 692; secondary, pupils 7,767, teachers 358; teacher training, students 68, teachers 7.
  Finance and Trade. Monetary unit: Tongan dollar or pa'anga, at par with the Australian dollar (T$0.89 = U.S. $1; T$2.14 = £1 sterling). Budget (1968–69 est.) balanced at T$2,397,815. Foreign trade (1969): imports T$5,087,529 (34% from New Zealand, 24% from Australia, 22% from Fiji, 10% from U.K.); exports T$3,398,684. Main exports: copra 62%; bananas 20%; desiccated coconut 9%.

Tourism

The International Union of Official Travel Organizations (IUOTO), at an extraordinary General Assembly held in Mexico City in September, adopted the statutes of a new intergovernmental International Tourism Organization. This was in pursuance of a UN General Assembly recommendation at the end of 1969 that such an organization be established through conversion of the legal status of the Geneva-based IUOTO. Through its recommendation, the UN recognized that the problems faced by international tourism required effective government action and a strong central organization at the intergovernmental level. The new organization would be particularly responsible for the needs of less developed countries and would function as an executive agency of the UN Development Program, helping in the appraisal of technical assistance projects in the field of tourism.

Growth of World Tourism. In the early 1960s, world tourist arrivals and receipts had grown at an average annual rate of 10–12%. In 1968, however, the increase in arrivals was less than 2%, while receipts rose by 4%. But in 1969 international tourism resumed a more accelerated pace: world tourist arrivals grew by 8% and receipts by 9%, with arrivals exceeding 150 million for the first time. Total foreign tourist arrivals reached 153 million, compared with 141 million in 1968. At the same time, world receipts from international tourism, excluding payments for international transportation, reached $15.3 billion, compared with $14 billion in 1968.

Behind these encouraging figures were several trends. One was the high level of economic activity in 1969, with a 13% growth in world trade. A more stable political climate in Europe helped to promote travel there. Renewed U.S. travel spending was another important factor—1968 had witnessed the first net decline in U.S. citizens' travel spending in 20 years. This was largely attributable to the policy of noninterference with foreign travel spending adopted by Pres. Richard M. Nixon's administration. An accelerated rate of finance and development of hotels and tourism infrastructure in Africa, Asia, and the Caribbean allowed more travelers to visit unspoiled and less frequented tourist resorts there. Europe still accounted for more than 70% of international tourist arrivals by volume. In the Middle East there was some improvement in tourism in the main business and commercial centres, with increases in arrivals from Europe and North America.

Travel circles continued to be preoccupied by the fact that world tourism spending grew only marginally faster than arrivals, by 9% at current prices compared with an 8% growth in tourist movements in 1969. This might well result from the continued growth of mass travel, particularly in Europe. In fact, average spending per tourist remained almost constant in money terms, declining in relation to general price indexes. In some cases, for example in Spain, this trend was promoted by government action to stabilize hotel and other tourist prices. In other cases, the growing bargaining power of the major tour operators had a similar effect in stabilizing or even lowering prices paid by the increasing number of tourists who opted for the "inclusive tour" package. The growing practice of fixing by contract the rates paid to hoteliers by tour operators for two to three years in advance also reinforced this trend. There was thus some real justification for the claim that the tourist in 1969 received better value than ever from his holiday spending. Another factor was the growth of foreign travel among students and young people, as well as among lower-income groups.

Most of the principal tourist countries of Europe experienced a very satisfactory year in 1969. In France, arrivals returned to the 12 million level, after a drop to 10.8 million in 1968. In Greece, foreign tourism soared by 30% to reach 1.1 million arrivals in response to an intensive promotional campaign. In Spain, tourist arrivals increased by 13% to 21.7 million, while in the United Kingdom, with more U.S. tourist visits than any other European country, arrivals increased by 21% to 5.9 million. In Italy, another favourite with North American tourists, arrivals increased by 7.5% to 12.1 million. These tourists spent $1,632,000,000, making Italy's earnings from foreign tourism higher than those of any other European country. In comparison, Spain earned $1,311,000,000, France $1,058,000,000, and the United Kingdom— with its first surplus ever—$852 million. The growth of tourism was more modest in Switzerland, where arrivals grew by 4.3% to 6.3 million, and in Belgium, where nights spent by foreign tourists in accommodations grew by only 2.8% to 3.9 million. Tourism in Eastern Europe appeared to develop satisfactorily in 1969. Hungary recorded 41% more foreign visitors, making 6.1 million arrivals. But the saddest story was Czechoslovakia, where arrivals dropped 30% from the 4.3 million of 1968 to 2.9 million, and earnings from foreign tourism dropped by 41% to $36 million.

Outside Europe, Africa saw tourism develop most effectively in 1969. The African continent offered sunshine and sea holidays on a year-round basis at prices more than ever within the budget of the average tourist, particularly the European. This was true from Tunisia in the North to the coasts of Kenya and Tanzania in the East and tiny The Gambia in the West. A traveling public increasingly conscious of the importance of nature conservation was also prepared to pay a rather higher price to visit the great game parks of East Africa. In Kenya, tourist arrivals rose by 12% to 293,000. Arrivals in Morocco increased by 22% to 716,000, and of all African countries Morocco earned most from tourism in 1969, with receipts of $123 million, compared with $47 million in Kenya. Despite severe flooding in September–December, tourism also developed well in Tunisia, where arrivals rose by 13% to 373,000.

In the Americas, the U.S. remained the world's biggest earner from foreign tourism, as well as the biggest spender; 12.3 million foreign tourists spent $2,052,000,000 on holiday or business visits to the U.S. in 1969, arrivals increasing by 14.5% and receipts by 16%. Caribbean tourism continued to thrive on the wealthy neighbouring North American market. Foreign tourists, more than 80% from the U.S., spent $235 million in the Bahamas in 1969; 1.3 million visitors were recorded, 24% more than in 1968. Tourism was also an important source of foreign exchange for Mexico, where 1.8 million foreign tourists, again mainly from the U.S., spent $465 million. Only in South America was the picture still uncertain, with only a small proportion of North American travel spending being earned there. A U.S. Department of Commerce estimate put it lower than receipts in the Bahamas alone.

With the political situation still disturbed, there

KEYSTONE

A monorail car delivers visitors to the underwater observation tower at Shirahama, Jap., where they can view marine life down to seven metres below the surface by descending a circular staircase in the tower's column.

was little progress in Middle East tourism in 1969, despite the region's attractive possibilities and easy access from Europe. Israel recorded a decline of 5% in arrivals, which numbered 409,000 in 1969. However, because 1968 had seen a remarkable flow of foreign tourists celebrating the 20th anniversary of the founding of modern Israel, the decline was not taken too seriously. More serious was the fall in Israel's receipts from $102 million in 1968 to $89 million in 1969. Israel could, however, boast of being the country where tourists stayed the longest; the mean length of stay of foreign tourists (excluding students on working holidays) was calculated as 31 days in 1969. In both Lebanon and the United Arab Republic, tourism progressed satisfactorily in 1969. In Lebanon, arrivals grew by 9.5% to 777,000, while receipts topped $100 million. In the United Arab Republic, arrivals increased by 9% to 345,000.

Tourism developed consistently and well in Asia in 1969. Hong Kong, the crossroads of Far Eastern travel, had 765,000 visitors in 1969, a 24% increase over 1968. In Australia foreign tourism increased by 20% and in Ceylon by 42%, 1969 arrivals being 361,-000 and 40,000, respectively.

Tourism in 1970. At the outset of 1970 the travel trade had reason to take an optimistic view of the prospects for international tourism. From November 1969 the lowest-ever air fares on the North Atlantic route brought increasing numbers of U.S. tourists to

Table I. International Tourist Arrivals and Arrivals Receipts				
	Arrivals		Change	
Region	1968	1969	Absolute	Percent
Europe	104,000,000	112,500,000	+8,500,000	+ 8
North America	26,300,000	28,300,000	+2,000,000	+ 8
Latin America	3,500,000	3,900,000	+ 400,000	+11
Africa	1,600,000	2,000,000	+ 400,000	+25
Asia/Oceania	3,400,000	4,000,000	+ 600,000	+18
Middle East	2,200,000	2,300,000	+ 100,000	+ 4
Total arrivals	141,000,000	153,000,000	+12,000,000	+ 8
Total receipts	$14,000,000,000	$15,300,000,000	+$1,300,000,000	+ 9
Source: International Union of Official Travel Organizations, Geneva.				

KEYSTONE

Tourists stroll
in the newly built
La Grande Motte
in the Camargue district
of southern France,
the first of six tourist
centres the French
government plans
to build in this area
between Montpellier
and Perpignan.

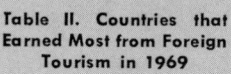

Table II. Countries that Earned Most from Foreign Tourism in 1969

In $000,000

Country	Receipts
United States	2,052
Italy	1,632
Spain	1,311
France	1,058
West Germany	1,026
Canada	1,002
United Kingdom	852
Austria	785
Switzerland	632
Mexico	465

These ten countries alone accounted for 70% of total international tourist receipts in 1969.

Sources: International Union of Official Travel Organizations, Geneva; Organization for Economic Cooperation and Development, Paris.

Europe. Early in 1970 the United Kingdom £50 travel allowance was replaced by an allocation of £300 per trip, which fully accorded with the most liberal internationally approved recommendations, and the French travel allowance was doubled in August to Fr. 3,000. After early 1970 the new Boeing 747 aircraft ensured that seat capacity on world air routes would exceed international travel demands for some time to come. By midyear the 747s had already carried a million passengers, a powerful indication of the new dimension of international tourism in the 1970s.

The year began well for international tourism in Europe. During the first six months, arrivals of foreign tourists in Spain were 8% above those for the corresponding period of 1969. In Greece the increase was about 24% and in the United Kingdom, 21%. This pointed to a growth rate in 1970 that promised to equal, if not exceed, that of 1969.

The shadow of a U.S. recession made some impact upon tourism in the Americas in the early part of 1970, with U.S. government anti-inflation policies affecting consumer spending and borrowing. Early in the year, travel correspondents in Caribbean resorts reported "disappointing" tourist arrivals. A recovery later in the year was perhaps less significant, since the December–March period is the peak season for Caribbean tourism. The U.S. itself, and probably also Canada, made a better showing in the first half of 1970. Arrivals of business and pleasure tourists in the U.S. during January–June 1970 were 17% higher than in the corresponding period of 1969.

Tourism in Africa and Asia, and in the less developed countries generally, progressed satisfactorily in 1970, helped by the further development of "inclusive tour" travel to destinations in Africa and the Far East, especially during the off-peak winter season of European tourism. Balance of payments statistics showed that while tourism accounted for 7% of Europe's exports of goods and services in 1968, it accounted for approximately 4% of Africa's exports in the same year. It could therefore be concluded, subject to the usual reservations inherent in such international comparisons, that Africa was more than halfway toward the achievement of a fully developed international tourist industry. This applied more to the game parks and resorts of East and North Africa, West Africa still being something of a late starter.

The first year of the new decade was not, however, without warning signs of problems that, unless steps were taken, could have serious consequences for inter-

national tourism. Perhaps the most serious was the realization that, in European Conservation Year, the beaches of Europe were often far from clean and, further, that urgent international action was required to keep them safe for bathing. Great publicity surrounded the Italian Riviera, where an 1896 statute was invoked to prohibit bathing on beaches within reach of Rome and Genoa polluted by sewage outfalls, but similar conclusions on pollution hazards could be drawn by other European countries. Tourist arrivals in Italy during January–May 1970 were almost 10% higher than a year earlier, but the lead declined in the peak months of June and July. West German tourists appeared to be particularly sensitive to the pollution issue. Their attendance at certain resorts decreased by 10 to 40% in June.

A second problem concerned prices. While some circles ascribed the smaller numbers of Caribbean tourists in the early months of 1970 to the incipient U.S. recession, others blamed poor service and excessive prices. There was certainly reason to believe that in-season prices at some Caribbean resorts were, relative to European levels, high or even excessive, resulting in many U.S. tourists taking low-priced trips to Europe instead.

For the third successive year, political instability and military hostility severely handicapped tourism in the Middle East, with the spate of hijackings on airliners frightening off all but the most determined tourists.

Promotion of Tourism. Most countries could summarize their objectives in tourism promotion in 1970 as follows: (1) to maintain existing tourist flows; (2) to diversify these flows (by staggering high-season tourism, encouraging winter visitors, organizing off-season conferences and exhibitions, developing "special interest" travel, etc.); and (3) to increase their share of international tourism in a growing world market.

The level of travel publicity and expenditure continued to be highest in the United States: an independent estimate put travel advertising expenditure there at $236 million in 1968. This sum comprised all tourist advertising expenditure by overseas national tourist offices, carriers such as airlines and shipping companies, and hotels and resort complexes. U.S. domestic airlines spent $100 million and international airlines $35 million, these two categories alone amounting to 57% of the total. Certain individual countries spent considerable sums in the U.S. on the promotion of tourism, notably Canada with an expenditure of $4.7 million. In comparison, the Bahamas spent $1.7 million, Mexico $980,000, and the U.K. $770,000 on such promotion in 1968.

Outside the U.S., promotional spending, although more effectively distributed than in the early 1960s, still lagged behind somewhat. However, a growing number of governments began to realize that money spent wisely on tourist promotion was repaid many times over in increased foreign exchange receipts. By aiming suitable advertising at desired markets, smooth and effective, rather than haphazard, development of tourism could be achieved. Some of the traditional tourist countries of Europe were, however, found to be maintaining a comparatively slender budget for tourist publicity. Italy spent only 0.2% of its foreign exchange receipts on tourist publicity, although it was generally acknowledged that up to 3% or more of total receipts could be devoted profitably to such uses.

(P. Sh.; O. Mé.)

See also Parks; Transportation.

Toys and Games

The trends in toys and games in 1970 once again reflected the prevailing interests and concerns of the adult world. In the United States the issue of environmental pollution led to the introduction of new board games, among them "Smog" and "Dirty Water." Interest in the occult and supernatural stimulated "Witch Pitch" from Parker Brothers; the "Mystery Zodiac Game" from Remco Industries; the three-dimensional "Which Witch," complete with cobwebs, spiders, and spells, from Milton Bradley; and a series of "Mystique" games from Mattel. The popularity of professional football and its heroes resulted in a Joe Namath doll.

Two major themes dominated toy production in Europe during 1970, both reflections of events external to the toy trade. These were space and association football (soccer), the latter inspired by World Cup fever. In the miniature space race, Mattel's Major Matt Mason probably took the honours, while those who launched their products after the actual moon landing never reached the target. Soccer, too, suffered the brevity of a craze, although adding a useful midyear stimulus to sales.

A comparatively microscopic bandwagon, but nevertheless of interest, was the public's increasing enthusiasm for golf. This led to many efforts to scale down the sport to board-game size. Louis Marx emerged as the most successful in this field with its "Pre-Shot," promoted by U.S. golfer Arnold Palmer.

Toy sales in the United States set a record in 1969, rising above $2 billion for the first time in history. The final figure reached $2,040,000,000, up 11.9% from 1968. Tight money and the business recession, however, caused toy-makers to worry that 1970 would not approach the previous year. As a result, many manufacturers and retailers decided to concentrate most heavily on those toys and games that had proved most successful in recent years. These included battery-powered slot racing cars, dolls representing characters from the television program "Sesame Street," wooden doll houses, and Mattel's "Barbie" doll series. Among older games experiencing renewed popularity were Parker Brothers' board game "Monopoly," chess, and checkers. Elaborate jigsaw puzzles for adults and the plastic "Frisbee" also enjoyed vigorous sales.

The U.S. Food and Drug Administration (FDA) on December 22 banned 39 toys as dangerous. This was the first such action taken by the FDA under the authority of the Toy Safety Act of 1969. All of the toy manufacturers involved were expected to notify retail stores immediately that the products should be removed from the shelves. The banned toys were of four general types: (1) breakable toy rattles with parts that could cause punctures or be inhaled or swallowed; (2) dolls and stuffed animals that could break and thereby expose sharp parts; (3) noise-making toys with parts that could cut, puncture, or be inhaled or eaten; and (4) caps or toy guns used without caps that produce noise of 138 decibels or higher. The FDA also banned lawn darts as toys but said that they could be sold outside toy departments if they were labeled as being for adult use and bore a warning against use by children.

An important aspect of the industry in 1970 concerned the strides taken by U.S. firms into both European and Far Eastern markets. Britain was a prime target, both for its own market plus the introduction it provided into the European Free Trade Association. For example, at the end of 1969 the U.S. firm Eldon Industries, Inc., acquired Scalecraft Limited. A few months later Eldon Toys was formed in Britain to serve the U.K. and EFTA. In 1970 two U.S. board-game producers, Parker Brothers and Selchow & Righter, agreed on licensing arrangements with Palitoy, Ltd., and the Vic-Toy Division of Invicta Plastics, Ltd., respectively. Another U.S. board-game manufacturer, Milton Bradley, purchased the Fränken-Plastik Group in West Germany to add to its already impressive list of interests in Europe. In Japan, the U.S. Tonka Corp. formed a joint company with the Japanese Bandai Co., Ltd. The new company, Japan Tonka, was based in Tokyo and would market Tonka toys in Japan and Asia. Most recent of the big purchases and mergers was the acquisition by General Mills, the U.S. food giant, of the Denys Fisher Group.

Throughout these acquisitions and mergers Mattel, the largest toy producer of them all, revolutionized—and captured—much of the die-cast model-car business. From the launch of the first Lesney Matchbox toy this had been a British-dominated business, but Mattel's innovative frictionless wheel product, Hot Wheels, changed both the concept and structure of the industry. It quickly became a craze and an interna-

Spiro Agnew wristwatch, introduced in the spring of 1970 by Dirty Time, Inc., of Anaheim, Calif., was a popular novelty item among both liberals and conservatives.

Toys designed by Patrick Rylands for Trendon Ltd. won for him the 1970 Duke of Edinburgh's Prize for Elegant Design.

COURTESY, TRENDÓN LTD.

POPPERFOTO FROM
PICTORIAL PARADE

A new form of skiing called grass skiing uses what looks like a cross between a roller skate and a tractor belt.

Commonwealth marathon silver medalist Jim Alder wins the 30,000-m. race with a world record time of 1 hr. 31 min. 30.4 sec. during the Coca-Cola International Athletics Meet at London's Crystal Palace, Sept. 5, 1970.

CENTRAL PRESS FROM
PICTORIAL PARADE

tional best seller and continued to remain one. It became a bad year for those who could not emulate Mattel's product quickly enough; Lesney closed down four factories in the autumn.

One of the lessons that toy manufacturers appeared to be learning was the need for genuine creative thought to be applied to products they planned. This lesson was often being absorbed the hard way. Many traditionally minded firms, such as Lines Bros., suffered badly in 1970, and the cause was not always the increased competition, updated marketing techniques, and heavy promotion from U.S. competitors. Denys Fisher, with Spirograph, demonstrated that a firm with a good idea could do well internationally.

(J. M. Th.)

Track and Field Sports

The 1970 season would be remembered not for deeds on the track but rather for two superlative jumps—the first high jump over 7½ ft. and the first pole vault over 18 ft. On October 24 in the Karaiskaki Stadium, Athens, in an intercity match between Athens and Belgrade, Christos Papanicolaou, 28, of Greece became the first man in history to vault over 18 ft. This physical education instructor, who had been competing for 11 years, used a fibre-glass pole stressed to 190 lb. in clearing the bar at 5.495 m. (18 ft. ¼ in.) to better the pending world mark of 17 ft. 11 in. by the East German Wolfgang Nordwig. All the stores in Athens closed four days later to mark "Papanicolaou Day."

On November 8 Ni Chih-chin, also 28, was announced to have surpassed the official world high jump record of 2.28 m. (7 ft. 5¾ in.) to achieve a height of 7 ft. 6⅛ in. at Changsha, China. Since China had withdrawn in 1964 as an affiliate member of the world ratifying authority (the 137-nation International Amateur Athletic Federation [IAAF], founded in 1913) in protest against its refusal to expel Taiwan from membership, the performance could not be ratified.

The news agency reports stated that a crowd of 80,000 was on hand to witness Ni clearing 6 ft. 6 in., 6 ft. 8 in., 7 ft., 7 ft. 1¾ in., and 7 ft. 4¼ in., each in his first attempt. He missed on his first try at the record height, whereupon the crowd chanted one of Chairman Mao's thoughts about "Overcoming all obstacles." Ni's second attempt was successful and produced

another chanted thought about "Political victory of the proletarian revolution of the President Mao." The man who would remain the acknowledged and official world record holder, Valery Brumel (U.S.S.R.), who was by curious coincidence born on the same day, commented, "I do not believe him capable of reaching this height. . . . I am skeptical as to the authenticity of this performance."

In a year during which not a single world record for a men's individual dash or middle-distance event was broken, the greatest running deed was that of Ronald Hill (U.K.), who added the British Commonwealth marathon title to his European title by running 26 mi. 385 yd. in 2 hr. 9 min. 28 sec. at Edinburgh, Scot., on July 23. This was the fastest time ever recorded in international competition and underlined the possibility of someone's achieving a time of 2 hr. before the turn of the century.

Drug-taking continued to present problems, particularly because, unlike the amphetamines, the anabolic steroids defied detection procedures. These drugs, which were capable of turning a 150-lb. man into one who could perform as though he weighed 250 lb., had a distorting effect on the four throwing field events: shot put, discus, javelin, and hammer throw. It had become safe to say that any athlete in those four events who had aspirations to the topmost honours had no chance of fulfilling them unless he bulked up his musculature in the way that his opponents were so ostentatiously doing. At the IAAF Congress in Stockholm, on August 29–30, the medical committee extended the definition of illegal doping to include "any attempt to improve the level of performance through the employment of specific substances." Among such substances anabolic steroids were specifically listed but the intake, though not the effect, of them remained undetectable after the lapse of a few days.

Other rule changes included disqualification for the deliberate knocking down of hurdles and the banning of the taping of the hands and wrists of field-event performers unless medically justified.

In declaring electrical timing to be mandatory for all major athletics meetings, the IAAF also decreed that the 0.05-sec. lag now calibrated into the timing mechanisms was to be removed after May 1, 1971. Moves were also afoot, but no decision was taken, to eliminate the rule that javelins must land point first in order for the throw to qualify for measurement.

International Tournaments. Being a season midway between the 1968 Olympic Games in Mexico City and the celebration due in Munich in August–September 1972 and one also without a European championship, 1970 lacked any major occasion in Europe other than the 9th Commonwealth Games in Edinburgh (July 17–25) and the U.S. v. U.S.S.R. match in Leningrad. Among the outstanding performances in the Commonwealth Games were surprise victories by Ian Stewart of Scotland over Ron Clarke of Australia in the 10,000 m. and over Clarke and Kipchoge Keino of Kenya in the 5,000 m.; a 110-m. hurdles win for Olympic champion David Hemery of England; and Keino's triumph in the 1,500 m. In the U.S.-U.S.S.R. meet both the men and women of the Soviet Union were victorious, the former winning 122–114 and the latter 78–59.

The greatest landmark in women's athletics during the year occurred at Portland, Ore., on June 13 when Chi Cheng of Taiwan (see BIOGRAPHY) ran the 100-yd. dash in 10.1 sec. On the same day she lowered the 220-yd. dash record to 22.7 sec. and later in Europe im-

Table I. World 1970 Outdoor Records—Men

Event	Competitor, country, date	Performance
100 yd.	Willie McGee, U.S., May 8	9.1 sec.*
10 mi.	Jerome Drayton, Canada, September 6	46 min. 37.8 sec.
30,000 m.	James Alder, U.K., September 5	1 hr. 31 min. 30.4 sec.
120-yd. hurdles	Thomas Hill, U.S., June 13	13.2 sec.*
440-yd. hurdles	Ralph Mann, U.S., June 20	48.8 sec.
3,000-m. steeplechase	Kerry O'Brien, Australia, July 4	8 min. 22.0 sec.
800-m. relay	Texas A and M, April 24	1 min. 22.1 sec.*
	Texas A and M, April 24	1 min. 21.7 sec.
880-yd. relay	Texas A and M, April 4	1 min. 22.1 sec.*
	Texas A and M, April 24	1 min. 22.1 sec.*
	Texas A and M, April 25	1 min. 21.7 sec.
3,200-m. relay and 2-mi. relay	Kenya national team, September 5	7 min. 11.6 sec.
High jump	Ni Chih-chin, China, November 8	7 ft. 6⅛ in.†
Pole vault	Wolfgang Nordwig, East Germany, June 17	17 ft. 10¾ in.
	Wolfgang Nordwig, East Germany, September 3	17 ft. 11 in.
	Christos Papanicolaou, Greece, October 24	18 ft. 0¼ in.

*Ties record.
†Not ratifiable.

Table II. World 1970 Outdoor Records—Women

Event	Competitor, country, date	Performance
100 yd.	Chi Cheng, Taiwan, June 13	10.1 sec.
100 m.	Chi Cheng, Taiwan, July 18	11.0 sec.*
	Renate Meissner, East Germany, August 2	11.0 sec.*
200 m.	Chi Cheng, Taiwan, July 12	22.4 sec.
220 yd.	Chi Cheng, Taiwan, June 13	22.7 sec.
400 m.	Marilyn Neufville, Jamaica, July 23	51.0 sec.
100-m. hurdles	Chi Cheng, Taiwan, July 12	12.8 sec.
	Karen Balzer, East Germany, July 26	12.7 sec.
	T. Sukniewicz, Poland, September 20	12.7 sec.
200-m. hurdles	Annelie Jahns, East Germany, July 4	25.8 sec.
	T. Sukniewicz, Poland, August 9	25.8 sec.
3,200-m.	U.K. team, June 13	8 min. 27.0 sec.
	U.K. team, September 5	8 min. 25.0 sec.
1-mi. relay	Atoms T. C., U.S., July 4	3 min. 41.3 sec.
Long jump	H. Rosendahl, West Germany, September 3	22 ft. 5¼ in.
Pentathlon	Burglinde Pollak, East Germany, September 5/6	5,406 pt.

*Ties record.

Table III. World 1970 Best Indoor Performances

Event	Competitor, country, date	Performance
MEN		
50 yd.	K. Clayton, U.S., January 10	5.0 sec.
60 yd.	J. W. Carlos, U.S., January 9	5.9 sec.*
	C. Branch, U.S., January 24	5.9 sec.*
	E. Harris, U.S., January 31	5.9 sec.
	J. W. Carlos, U.S., February 7	5.9 sec.*
	H. Washington, U.S., March 14	5.9 sec.*
70 yd.	J. Green, U.S., February 14	6.8 sec.
	C. Highbaugh, U.S., February 14	6.8 sec.
100 yd.	G. Tinker, U.S., February 14	9.4 sec.*
220 yd.	J. W. Carlos, U.S., February 14	21.2 sec.
440 yd.	F. Newhouse, U.S., February 14	45.6 sec.
500 yd.	L. Evans, U.S., February 20	54.5 sec.
500 m.	M. McGrady, U.S., February 20	1 min. 2.9 sec.*
600 yd.	M. McGrady, U.S., February 27	1 min. 7.6 sec.
600 m.	M. Bilham, U.K., Dec. 20, 1969	1 min. 17.7 sec.
1,000 yd.	R. D. Doubell, Australia, January 24	2 min. 5.5 sec.
1,000 m.	T. Von Ruden, U.S., February 20	2 min. 21.0 sec.
3,000 m.	R. Wilde, U.K., March 15	7 min. 47.0 sec.
45-yd. hurdles	W. Davenport, U.S., January 10	5.3 sec.*
50-m. hurdles	G. Nickel, West Germany, February 26	6.2 sec.
60-yd. hurdles	W. Davenport, U.S., January 9	6.8 sec.*
60-m. hurdles	G. Nickel, West Germany, January 31	7.5 sec.
Triple jump	V. Saneyev, U.S.S.R., March 15	55 ft. 7¼ in.
WOMEN		
300 m.	K. Lundgren, Sweden, February 6	38.3 sec.
400 m.	M. Neufville, U.K., March 15	53.0 sec.
600 yd.	C. Toussaint, U.S., February 5	1 min. 22.2 sec.
880 yd.	N. Shafer, U.S., February 1	2 min. 7.2 sec.
1,500 m.	D. Brown, U.S., February 7	4 min. 21.1 sec.
50-yd. hurdles	Chi Cheng, Taiwan, February 5	6.5 sec.
50-m. hurdles	Chi Cheng, Taiwan, February 21	6.9 sec.
60-yd. hurdles	K. Balzer, East Germany, March 1	7.4 sec.
60-m. hurdles	K. Balzer, East Germany, February 21	8.2 sec.
	L. Khitrina, U.S.S.R., March 14	8.2 sec.*
	K. Balzer, East Germany, March 15	8.2 sec.*
	L. Khitrina, U.S.S.R., March 15	8.2 sec.*
High jump	I. Gusenbauer, Austria, March 15	6 ft. 2 in.
Shot put	N. Chizhova, U.S.S.R., March 15	61 ft. 0¼ in.

*Equals existing best performance.

proved the 200-m. record to 22.4 sec. at Munich. Renate Meissner (E.Ger.) equaled the world 100-m. record set by Wyomia Tyus (U.S.) at the 1968 Olympics with 11 sec. on August 2 in East Berlin. Chi Cheng had also equaled this record 15 days earlier in Vienna. Marilyn Neufville, running for her native Jamaica at the Commonwealth Games, took 0.7 sec. off the world's 400-m. record with a highly impressive 51 sec. The record for this event a decade ago was only 53.4 sec., or some 16 yd. slower. (N. D. McW.)

U.S. Competition. In the U.S. two hurdlers were all that prevented a rare occurrence, a track season without an individual world record. In recent years U.S. competitors had accounted for a large share of record-breaking exploits. But record production was off in 1970 with only two entries in the international list, and neither of them actually represented an all-time high. Ralph Mann, a junior at Brigham Young University, climaxed a fine season when he ran the 440-yd. intermediate hurdles in 48.8 sec. in the National Collegiate Athletic Association (NCAA) championships at Des Moines, Iowa. He erased one of the oldest marks, the 49.3-sec. time established in 1960 by Gert Potgieter of South Africa. While no one had ever run the 440-yd. hurdles so fast, the time was rated 0.4 sec. slower than the 48.1 sec. for the slightly shorter 400-m. hurdles achieved by Britain's David Hemery in the 1968 Olympic Games.

The other record entry was by Tom Hill of Arkansas State University. Also a junior, Hill ran the 120-yd. high hurdles in 13.2 sec. in the United States Track and Field Federation (USTFF) championships, tying the oldest of all world records. Martin Lauer of West Germany first ran 13.2 in 1959, a time matched by Lee Calhoun in 1960, Earl McCullouch in 1967, Erv Hall in 1969, and Willie Davenport in 1969. All were from the U.S.

A third world best was achieved by a quartet of sprinters from Texas A and M University. Running on the same fast composition track that later was used by Mann, the relay runners covered 880 yd. in 1 min. 21.7 sec., bettering the standard of 1:22.1 first set by San Jose State College in 1967 and equaled earlier in 1970 by Texas A and M. The occasion was the annual Drake Relays, and Donnie Rogers started with a clocking of 20.9 sec. for his 220-yd. segment,

Erv Hall clears a hurdle to beat Bill High in the 55-m. high hurdles at the U.S. Olympic Invitation track meet at Madison Square Garden, Feb. 20, 1970.

WIDE WORLD

CAMERA PRESS FROM PIX

Heide Rosendahl
sets a new world record
for the women's long jump
with a distance
of 22 ft. 5¼ in.
at the 1970 World
Student Games
in Turin, Italy.

Taiwan's Chi Cheng
breaks the wire to win
at the Portland, Ore.,
Rose Festival meet,
June 13, 1970.
In the one day she set new
world records in the
women's 100-yd. dash
and the 220.

SPORTS ILLUSTRATED PHOTO BY
SHEEDY AND LONG © TIME INC.

The other commonly run middle-distance event, the 1,000-yd. race, saw Ralph Doubell of Australia set a record of 2 min. 5.5 sec. in Albuquerque. It was the second year in a row the Olympic 800-m. titlist had successfully invaded the U.S.

Other indoor bests were achieved in less frequently scheduled events. Kirk Clayton of San Jose State College dashed 50 yd. in 5 sec. flat. Former teammate Lee Evans ran 500 yd. in 54.5 sec.; Earl Harris of Oklahoma State University sprinted 300 yd. in 30.4 sec.; Von Ruden ran 1,000 m. in 2 min. 21 sec.; and William and Mary College had a time of 9 min. 42.6 sec. for the distance medley relay.

A number of indoor best performances were tied, the popular 60-yd. dash alone accounting for six equaling times of 5.9 sec. John Carlos did it twice and Ivory Crockett, Cliff Branch, Harris, and Herb Washington each did it once. Davenport matched the 60-yd. high hurdle mark of 6.8 sec. and the 45-yd. high hurdle standard of 5.3 sec. The 70-yd. dash was run in 6.8 sec. by Larry Highbaugh and Jim Green, the 100-yd. sprint in 9.4 sec. by Gerald Tinker, and the 500-m. event in 1 min. 2.9 sec. by McGrady. In indoor team competition, Kansas annexed the NCAA championship, and the Southern California Striders won the AAU title.

U.S. women had no luck in the world record department during the year, but the outstanding female performer in the world was a resident of and a student in the United States. As mentioned above, Chi Cheng of Taiwan completely dominated the world picture,

followed by Rockie Woods (21.2), Marvin Mills (20), and Curtis Mills (19.6). Marvin and Curtis Mills were brothers, the latter holding the world record at 440 yd.

Five U.S. outdoor records also fell by the wayside. Mark Murro, a junior from Arizona State University, hurled the javelin an even 300 ft., increasing his own national mark by more than 7 ft. Ken Swenson, a senior from Kansas State University, claimed a new 800-m. mark of 1 min. 44.8 sec. against the West German team in Stuttgart. Earlier he had anchored his school's two-mile relay team to a record 7 min. 16.4 sec. clocking. Records in two seldom-run events fell to veteran Tom Von Ruden, who covered 1,000 yd. in 2 min. 6.2 sec. and 1,000 m. in 2 min. 19 sec.

In outdoor team competition it appeared that the University of California had won the NCAA meet. In January 1971, however, the NCAA ruled that California had used an ineligible runner, and awarded the title to Kansas, Oregon, and Brigham Young. California Polytechnic of San Luis Obispo won the NCAA College Division competition, Eastern Michigan led the National Association of Intercollegiate Athletics (NAIA) teams, and Kansas was the USTFF winner. In noncollegiate scoring, the Amateur Athletic Union (AAU) title was won by the Southern California Striders.

By far the biggest oddity of the outdoor season was the setting of a new world indoor pole vault best during the NCAA outdoor championships. Hard rain caused the event to be moved indoors, and when Jan Johnson of the University of Kansas vaulted 17 ft. 7 in. it became the best inside vault on record. There are no official world marks indoors.

Regular indoor competition accounted for a number of other best-of-all-time performances, but only two of them were clear-cut improvements in regularly contested events. Most active was Martin McGrady, a veteran runner with notable success on the indoor board tracks, who lowered the 600-yd. run mark three times. A standard distance indoors, the 600-yd. run was covered by McGrady in 1 min. 8.7 sec., then 1 min. 8.5 sec., and finally in a sensational 1 min. 7.6 sec.

Table IV. NCAA Outdoor Championships

Des Moines, Ia., June 18–20, 1970

Event	Competitor, affiliation	Performance
100 yd.	Eddie Hart, California	9.4 sec.
220 yd.	Willie Turner, Oregon State	20.6 sec.
440 yd.	Larry James, Villanova	45.5 sec.
880 yd.	Ken Swenson, Kansas State	1 min. 46.3 sec.
1 mi.	Marty Liquori, Villanova	3 min. 59.9 sec.
3 mi.	Steve Prefontaine, Oregon	13 min. 22.0 sec.
6 mi.	Bob Bertelsen, Ohio Univ.	27 min. 57.6 sec.
3,000-m. steeplechase	Sid Sink, Bowling Green	8 min. 41.0 sec.
120-yd. hurdles	Paul Gibson, Texas (El Paso)	13.6 sec.
440-yd. hurdles	Ralph Mann, Brigham Young	48.8 sec.
440-yd. relay	California	40.3 sec.
Mile relay	UCLA	3 min. 6.1 sec.
High jump	Pat Matzdorf, Wisconsin	7 ft. 1 in.
Pole vault	Jan Johnson, Kansas	17 ft. 7 in.
Long jump	Arnie Robinson, San Diego State	25 ft. 10½ in.
Triple jump	Mohinder Gill, California Polytechnic	51 ft. 9¼ in.
Shot put	Karl Salb, Kansas	63 ft. 10¼ in.
Discus	John Van Reenen, Washington State	190 ft. 9 in.
Hammer throw	Steve DeAutremont, Oregon State	203 ft. 9 in.
Javelin	Bill Skinner, Tennessee	270 ft. 8 in.
Decathlon	Rick Wanamaker, Drake	7,406 pt.
Team	Kansas, Oregon, Brigham Young	35 pt.

Table V. NCAA Indoor Championships

Detroit, Mich., March 13–14, 1970

Event	Competitor, affiliation	Performance
60 yd.	Herb Washington, Michigan State	5.9 sec.
440 yd.	Larry James, Villanova	48.3 sec.
600 yd.	Rick Wohlhuter, Notre Dame	1 min. 9.5 sec.
880 yd.	Mark Winzenried, Wisconsin	1 min. 51.7 sec.
1,000 yd.	Keith Colburn, Harvard	2 min. 9.9 sec.
1 mi.	Howell Michael, William and Mary	4 min. 3.1 sec.
2 mi.	Jerry Ritchey, Pittsburgh	8 min. 39.2 sec.
60-yd. hurdles	Tom Hill, Arkansas State	6.9 sec.
Mile relay	Villanova	3 min. 15.3 sec.
2-mi. relay	Kansas	7 min. 25.8 sec.
Distance medley relay	Manhattan	9 min. 49.2 sec.
High jump	Ken Lundmark, Brigham Young	7 ft.
Pole vault	Bud Williamson, Maryland	16 ft. 6 in.
Long jump	Bill Lightsey, Kentucky	25 ft. 2¼ in.
Triple jump	Milan Tiff, Miami (O.)	51 ft. 11½ in.
Shot put	Karl Salb, Kansas	67 ft. 2½ in.
35-lb. weight throw	Ed Nosal, Harvard	63 ft. 6¼ in.
Team	Kansas	27½ pt.

breaking sprint records in both the U.S. and Europe. Other outstanding performances included world indoor bests achieved by Kathy Hammond, 1 min. 6.3 sec. for 500 yd.; Cheryl Toussaint, 1 min. 22.2 sec. for 600 yd.; Esther Stroy, 35.7 sec. for 300 yd.; Doris Brown, 4 min. 21.1 sec. for 1,500 m.; and Mamie Rallins, 8.8 sec. for the 70-yd. hurdles. The Mayor Daley Youth Foundation team from Chicago won both the indoor and outdoor AAU championships.

(BE. N.)

Trade, International

The boom in world trade that had begun in 1968 continued throughout 1969 and into 1970, and in the middle of 1970 the value of world trade was 40% higher than it had been three years earlier. A growth in the value of trade of 12% in 1968 was followed by a 14% growth in 1969—the highest annual increase since 1951. There was no sign of moderation in this rate during 1969 and the growth was maintained in the first few months of 1970. The trade of member countries of the Organization for Economic Cooperation and Development (OECD), which accounted for about three-quarters of world trade, was growing at an annual rate of 18% in the first half of 1970. There were, however, signs of moderation during 1970, with the slowing down in the growth of imports into several industrial countries.

The increase in trade in 1969 reflected continued growth in demand and production in the world economy at a much higher rate than the average for the previous decade. The growth in the volume of trade, however, was somewhat less than in the previous year. The average price of goods entering world trade rose by 4%, reflecting inflation in industrial countries and the largest increase in primary product prices since 1963. The pattern of trade in 1969 was dominated by the growth of industrial imports and was notable for the fact that, unlike most previous booms, much of the impetus came from European rather than U.S. demand. Imports into the European Economic Community (EEC), which accounted for 30% of world trade, increased by 21% in 1969, with all member countries except the Netherlands recording increases of over 20%. In the early part of the boom, exports of primary producers had not kept pace with those of industrial countries but during 1969 these exports showed a substantial increase.

Primary Producing Countries. The boom in world trade in 1969 was shared by the primary producers, whose exports increased by 13%, compared with increases of 8 and 4% in the previous two years. (*See* Table I.) This high growth rate was not maintained in 1970 because of some slackening of demand from industrial countries but an increase in exports at least as large as in previous years was expected. Imports of primary producing countries increased by 10% in 1969, considerably more than in 1967 and 1968. This large increase was brought about by the higher growth rate in gross national product (GNP), which averaged 7% in 1969, compared with a 5% per annum average in 1960–67 and 6% in 1968. It was also facilitated by the large increase in export earnings. The primary producing countries taken as a group showed a lower trade deficit in 1969 than in 1968; early indications in 1970, however, suggested that, with imports continuing to rise and export growth slackening somewhat, the trade balance would deteriorate a little.

Exports of the more developed primary producers increased somewhat faster in 1969 than those of the less developed economies: although South African exports failed to grow, exports from Australia and New Zealand increased by 20% and from European primary producers by 17%. Among the less developed economies, there were variations between regions and, more so, between countries. Asian and African economies increased exports by 14 and 15%, respectively; exports from Latin America rose by 11%; and from the Middle East by only 9%. Imports of the more developed producers grew faster than those of the less developed group and, as a result, there was a deterioration of $500 million in the trade balance of the former and an improvement of $1.2 billion in the balance of the latter.

The relative performance of various individual primary producing countries and areas varied and was affected by the geographic pattern of growth in industrial countries and by differential commodity price movements. The growth in national production was much lower in 1969 in North America and the U.K. than in the rest of Europe and Japan. This had a direct influence on demand for primary products, and exports of primary producers to North America and the U.K. rose by only 6% while exports to Japan increased by 18% and to EEC countries by 16%. These factors helped explain the slower export growth in Latin America and some Asian countries dependent on the U.S. or U.K. markets and the large growth in African exports, much of which represented trade with Europe.

Much of the growth in the value of primary producers' exports was due to the 10% increase in the average price of primary commodity exports in 1969. This was by far the largest annual increase since 1963. This growth reached its peak in the first quarter of 1970, at a value some 2–3% above the previous 1964 peak. By the middle of 1970, however, there were definite signs of a fall in the overall price index back to a level similar to that of the latter half of 1969. Within these overall movements, there were variations between commodities. Prices of minerals and metals increased by 17% in 1969 and, in the first half of 1970, reached a peak about 20% higher than a year earlier. The prices of agricultural products, however, rose by only 8% in 1969 and by 3% in the first half of 1970.

Exports from Latin-American countries recorded an 11% increase in 1969 and, although their growth was less than that of African and Asian exports, it was distinctly more rapid than in 1968. Import growth was not so rapid and the trade balance improved. The largest improvement was in Brazil where, despite stagnant coffee exports, the value of exports rose by 22% as exports of cotton, iron ore, and cocoa increased very sharply. A relatively slow import growth brought an improvement of $270 million in the trade surplus. Large export growth was also recorded in Argentina and Mexico and the Mexican trade balance improved by $50 million. Argentine imports, however, increased by over 30% and there was a $130 million reduction in the trade deficit. Exports from Colombia and Peru were less buoyant but import growth was also more modest.

The performances of countries in Asia were influenced by demand in various product markets. Exports from India, Pakistan, and Ceylon grew relatively slowly in the face of unfavourable markets for tea and vegetable fibres, whereas buoyant world demand

Table I. Primary Producing Countries' Foreign Trade
In $000,000

Area	1968 Exports	1968 Imports*	1968 Balance of trade	1969 Exports	1969 Imports*	1969 Balance of trade
More developed countries	14,957	18,451	−3,494	16,921	20,940	−4,019
Less developed countries						
Latin America	12,033	11,554	479	13,410	12,684	726
Asia	9,120	12,565	−3,545	10,352	13,551	−3,199
Middle East	6,228	5,063	1,165	6,811	5,617	1,194
Africa	5,678	4,353	1,325	6,536	4,590	1,946
	33,059	33,635	−576	37,109	36,442	667
All primary producers	48,016	52,086	−4,070	54,030	57,382	−3,352

*Imports in most cases exclude freight and insurance charges.
Source: International Monetary Fund, *Annual Report.*

Table II. World Exports of Manufactured Goods

Year	Total value in $000,000,000*	United States	United Kingdom	West Germany	France	Italy	Japan	Others†
1955	34.0	24.5	19.8	15.5	9.3	3.4	5.1	22.4
1960	52.4	21.6	16.3	19.3	9.7	5.1	6.9	21.0
1965	82.8	20.5	13.5	19.2	8.8	6.8	9.4	21.8
1966	92.4	20.2	12.9	19.5	8.6	6.9	9.8	22.1
1967	99.2	20.5	12.2	19.6	8.5	7.0	9.8	22.5
1968	114.0	20.3	11.3	19.4	8.2	7.3	10.7	22.8
1969	134.0	19.3	11.2	19.5	8.2	7.3	11.2	23.3
1970‡	150.4	19.4	10.7	19.7	8.5	7.0	11.5	23.2

*Excluding arms.
†Belgium, Luxembourg, Canada, Netherlands, Sweden, and Switzerland.
‡First half year (seasonally adjusted); value at annual rate.

and rising prices for rubber and tin brought a large expansion in exports from Indonesia, Malaysia, and Thailand. Exports from China, Hong Kong, and South Korea increased by about 30%—mostly in manufactured goods, including textiles. As a group, the trade balance of Asian countries improved by about $350 million. The continued growth in oil exports from North Africa and the strong world demand for copper were the main factors behind the large growth in African exports and the improved trading balance.

Industrial Countries. The growth in the exports of industrial countries, which had led to the boom in world trade in 1968, continued throughout 1969 and into the first half of 1970. These exports increased by 17% in 1969 and, in the first half of 1970, were 15% above the level of a year earlier. In the middle of 1970 exports of industrial countries were almost 50% higher than three years earlier, but there were signs of a definite slackening after midyear.

The rapid growth of the trade of industrial countries in 1969–70 was based on the large increases in domestic production in many European countries, especially in the EEC, and in Japan. This contrasted with some previous booms, which had been based to a much greater extent on a cyclical upswing in demand in the U.S. economy. Imports into the EEC increased by 21% in 1969, compared with 13% in 1968; and Japanese imports rose by 16% in 1969, compared with 11% in the preceding year. On the other hand, the growth in U.S. imports fell back sharply from 23% in 1968 to 8% in 1969.

The increase in imports of industrial countries in 1969–70 was some 4% higher than the growth in their GNP. This partly reflected a short-term cyclical upswing and was similar to the pattern observed in earlier booms when the average import ratio had tended to rise. Also, however, it reflected a trend, which had prevailed throughout the previous decade in most industrial countries, for foreign trade to increase faster than domestic production because of increased openness in most economies, the formation of customs unions, and a general reduction in tariffs. The growth of imports relative to national production was particularly strong in EEC countries, with the average annual growth rate in imports exceeding that of GNP by about 2% per annum over the decade. In the case of the U.S., increased openness had brought a gap in the growth rates of 2.9%. On the other hand, in Japan, where restrictions were still maintained on imports,

Table III. World Exports by Provenance and Destination, 1969
F.o.b. value in U.S. $000,000

Exports from ↓ / Exports to →	World*	Developed market economies†	Less developed market economies‡	Centrally planned economies§	United States	Canada‖	Latin America	Europe: Developed market economies Total¶♀	EEC♀	EFTA Total	EFTA United Kingdom	Other Northern Europe◊	Other Southern Europe▢
World*	272,050	191,340	51,240	27,700	35,230	12,390	13,110	123,660	72,350	38,980	17,730	3,280	9,050
Developed market economies†	194,080	148,500	37,720	7,170	25,980	11,340	10,230	98,010	57,640	30,900	12,300	2,740	6,730
Less developed market economies‡	48,190	35,950	9,700	2,530	9,060	950	1,900	19,810	12,010	6,200	4,550	185	1,420
Centrally planned economies§	29,470	6,890	3,830	17,990	200	97	980	5,830	2,700	1,880	880	360	890
United States	37,440	26,050	11,140	250	·	8,960	4,810	12,170	6,880	3,860	2,280	205	1,240
Canada‖	13,750	12,770	840	140	9,800	·	410	2,120	790	1,230	1,030	20	88
Latin America	13,100	9,770	2,580	750	3,950	450	1,460	4,490	2,720	1,270	770	71	435
Europe: Developed market economies¶♀	119,320	95,500	17,460	5,800	10,230	1,740	4,140	78,720	47,960	23,340	6,980	2,430	5,000
EEC♀	76,290	62,580	10,250	3,090	6,010	720	2,450	53,770	36,780	12,780	3,380	770	3,440
EFTA	35,620	27,510	6,300	1,650	3,480	960	1,300	20,460	9,050	8,470	2,340	1,610	1,330
United Kingdom	16,890	12,060	4,030	670	2,080	720	580	7,240	3,370	2,250	·	1,010	610
Northern Europe◊	2,950	2,410	155	370	240	25	70	2,090	590	1,420	940	22	59
Southern Europe▢	4,470	3,000	760	700	495	37	325	2,410	1,530	680	310	25	170
Eastern Europe and U.S.S.R.♀◊	27,220	6,110	2,850	17,510	200	72	910	5,370	2,410	1,720	790	350	890
U.S.S.R.	11,660	2,590	1,680	6,810	61	12	650	2,150	860	670	425	270	355
South Africa‖	2,150	1,630	420	1	150	40	13	1,200	400	750	720	19	30
Africa: Less developed market economies	10,950	8,990	1,130	640	750	67	62	7,500	5,060	1,970	1,450	51	415
Northern Africa▲	4,250	3,490	265	480	150	5	25	3,290	2,490	550	405	16	235
Japan	15,990	8,390	6,830	760	5,020	480	800	2,050	970	720	350	51	315
Asia: Less developed market economies Asian Middle East+	9,200	7,130	1,780	215	365	73	145	4,590	2,700	1,430	1,130	35	440
Other Asia	12,870	8,100	3,810	930	2,990	225	135	2,570	1,300	1,130	900	23	115
Asia: Centrally planned economies⊗	2,250	780	980	485	2	25	75	455	290	155	92	10	3
Oceania: Developed market economies**	5,420	4,160	1,030	215	780	125	54	1,740	660	1,000	950	12	68
Rest of world††	2,390	1,970	400	—	1,000	135	105	670	240	405	300	6	18

Note: The data cover world trade with the exception of the trade with one another of: China, Mongolia, North Korea, and North Vietnam. For most countries they represent the official export figures, converted to U.S. dollars. Where official figures are not available, estimates, based on imports reported by partner countries and on other subsidiary data, are used. A dash (—) means magnitude nil or less than $500,000; (.) means not applicable; and (...) means not available.

*The figures for total exports include certain exports which, because their regions of destination could not be determined, are not included elsewhere in the table.
†United States, Canada, developed market economies of Europe, Australia, New Zealand, South Africa, Japan.
‡Sum of regions other than developed market and centrally planned economies.
§Centrally planned economies of Asia, Eastern Europe excluding Yugoslavia, and U.S.S.R.
‖General exports.
¶Includes Turkey and Yugoslavia.

national production had increased faster than imports.

The relative performance of the main industrial countries can be seen in Table II, which shows the countries' shares in the total exports of manufactured goods. (These accounted for almost three-quarters of the exports of industrial countries; the proportion was somewhat smaller for the U.S. and Canada but much higher for Europe.) The halt in the decline of the U.K. share was apparent in 1968 and 1969, following devaluation in 1967. Figures available for the first half of 1970 suggested that a further decline was taking place, bringing the U.K. share down to little more than half its level in 1955. This long-run decline was due partly to the fact that the U.K. was selling its exports in those world markets that were growing relatively slowly. Mainly, however, it reflected a lack of competitiveness for the U.K., which was losing its share in nearly all markets. On the other hand, Italy benefited not only from being a supplier to the fast growing EEC market but also from its price-competitiveness. A noteworthy feature was that West Germany, despite two revaluations, had not lost any of its share in world trade.

As in many other recent years, the most rapidly expanding trade flow in 1969 was that between EEC countries, which was 26% higher than in 1968. Exports by EEC countries to all other countries rose by 18%, with exports to the European Free Trade Association (EFTA) rising by 13% and to North America by only 4%. Japanese exports to the EEC rose by 41% in 1969 and sales to the U.S. by 23%. (See Table III.)

The combined trade balance of industrial countries was a $2.1 billion deficit in 1969, compared with a $1.9 billion deficit in 1968 (see Table IV). This deficit was further reduced to an annual rate of only $300 million in the first half of 1970. The biggest change in 1969 was the reduction of the EEC surplus

Table IV. Trade of Industrial Countries

In U.S. $000,000,000

Country	1969 Exports	1969 Imports†	1969 Balance of trade	1970* Exports	1970* Imports†	1970* Balance of trade
United States	37.99	36.04	1.95	43.07	39.27	3.80
Canada	13.75	13.14	0.61	15.88	13.36	2.52
EEC	75.84	75.74	0.10	86.06	85.99	0.07
EFTA	38.22	43.96	−5.74	42.22	49.74	−7.52
Germany, West	29.05	24.92	4.13	33.16	29.48	3.68
France	15.02	17.39	−2.37	17.48	18.38	−0.90
Italy	11.72	12.46	−0.74	12.79	14.34	−1.55
Netherlands	9.96	10.99	−1.03	11.39	12.81	−1.42
Belgium	10.07	9.98	0.09	11.24	10.98	0.26
United Kingdom	17.52	19.96	−2.44	18.97	21.33	−2.36
Japan	16.00	15.02	0.98	18.71	17.89	0.82
Total	181.80	183.90	−2.10	205.94	206.25	−0.31

*First half of year (seasonally adjusted) at annual rate.
†Imports are valued c.i.f. except for U.S. and Canada; insurance and freight costs on U.S. and Canadian imports are approximately 7% of value of the goods.
Source: Organization for Economic Cooperation and Development, *Main Economic Indicators.*

from $2.4 billion in 1968 to only $100 million in 1969, a level that was maintained in the first half of 1970. This reduction was due largely to increases in the French and Italian deficits and a small reduction in the West German surplus. In 1970, a further worsening in the Italian and West German balances was offset by a considerable reduction in the French deficit. The major industrial countries outside the EEC (U.S., U.K., and Japan) all improved their trading balances substantially in 1969.

The steady decline over the past decade in the U.S. balance of trade surplus was halted in 1969 and 1970. The growth of U.S. industrial production passed its peak in the spring of 1969 and, with this, the growth of imports was checked. Imports in 1969 were 8% higher than in 1968, compared with a growth of 23% between 1967 and 1968. Exports, however, increased by 11%—the largest increase since 1966—and the trading surplus was increased from $1,140,000,000 to $1,950,000,000. Exports continued to grow faster than

Eastern Europe and U.S.S.R.δ◇ Total	U.S.S.R.	South Africa‖	Africa: Less developed market economies Total	Northern Africa▲	Japan	Asia: Less developed market economies Asian Middle East⁺	Other Asia	Centrally planned economies Asia⊕	Oceania: Developed market economies**	Rest of world††	←Exports to Exports from ↓
25,150	9,930	3,000	10,110	3,550	12,490	7,230	17,090	2,550	4,570	3,700	World*
5,990	2,570	2,590	7,770	2,610	6,770	5,440	11,860	1,180	3,800	2,420	Developed market economies†
2,140	1,150	395	1,440	300	5,020	1,120	3,970	390	720	1,260	Less developed market economies‡
17,010	6,210	7	900	640	710	670	1,260	980	55	9	Centrally planned economies§
250	105	510	860	370	3,460	1,250	3,470	—	950	750	United States
28	9	74	42	12	580	39	220	115	190	130	Canada‖
640	305	24	64	33	840	75	120	110	18	860	Latin America
5,280	2,120	1,670	5,590	2,150	1,330	3,250	3,390	520	1,800	1,090	Europe: Developed market economies¶♀
2,740	1,090	790	3,630	1,670	740	1,750	1,830	350	550	590	EEC♀
1,480	480	850	1,720	315	550	1,340	1,470	165	1,210	480	EFTA
540	230	690	1,030	195	295	960	1,030	125	1,040	420	United Kingdom
360	285	18	28	13	13	31	17	6	25	7	Northern Europeδ
690	270	12	210	150	33	135	77	2	20	9	Southern Europe□
16,530	5,980	7	770	590	445	610	550	980	20	6	Eastern Europe and U.S.S.R.♀◇
6,200	.	1	415	350	355	335	280	615	3	—	U.S.S.R.
1	—	.	360	—	210	5	44	—	21	2	South Africa‖
570	320	160	670	91	485	150	225	65	30	30	Africa: Less developed market economies
445	260	—	115	60	44	47	55	34	3	20	Northern Africa▲
340	270	275	880	69		830	4,160	425	560	165	Japan
185	95	165	305	82	1,680	600	650	27	255	74	Asia: Less developed market economies Asian Middle East⁺
740	430	46	370	90	1,920	290	2,940	190	350	80	Other Asia
485	225	—	130	47	265	60	710	...	35	3	Asia: Centrally planned economies⊕
98	60	62	45	7	1,180	60	580	120	280	290	Oceania: Developed market economies**
2	—	1	31	4	100	2	40	—	65	220	Rest of world††

♀The transactions between West Germany and East Germany have been omitted. Based on data reported by the sender, they were $561 million from West Germany to East Germany and $465 million from East Germany to West Germany.
δFinland, Iceland, Ireland.
□Greece, Spain, Turkey, Yugoslavia.
◇Albania, Bulgaria, Czechoslovakia, East Germany, Hungary, Poland, Romania, and U.S.S.R.
▲Algeria, Libya, Morocco, Tunisia, U.A.R.
⁺Including Cyprus and Iran.
⊕China, Mongolia, North Korea, and North Vietnam. Estimates based on import data of trading partners. The intertrade of these countries is excluded.
**New Zealand and Australia, general exports for 1966.
††Consists mainly of islands in the Caribbean and the Pacific areas.
Source: United Nations, *Monthly Bulletin of Statistics.*

(B. N. D.)

imports in 1970 and there was a further improvement in the surplus which, although quite small by comparison with the mammoth surpluses of the early 1960s, was distinctly more healthy than the low and declining surpluses recorded during 1968. U.S. export growth in 1969 was entirely dependent on exports of manufactured goods, which rose by 13%; agricultural exports fell by 5%. With the slackening in industrial production in 1969, imports of industrial raw materials did not increase over the 1968 level. Food imports were also unchanged and the growth of imports of motor vehicles and components slowed down. Imports of other capital and consumer goods increased by 20%, but this growth tailed off considerably in the course of the year.

Although the Canadian trading surplus was lower in 1969 than in the previous year, it was the second best performance in postwar years. A very strong recovery in the first half of 1970 suggested that the year would be a record one. The growth of Canadian exports fell from 19% in 1968 to 10% in 1969; imports, on the other hand, increased by 15%—somewhat faster than in 1968. The main growth in Canadian exports in 1969 was in motors and components to the

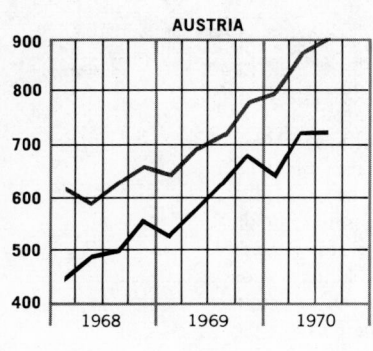

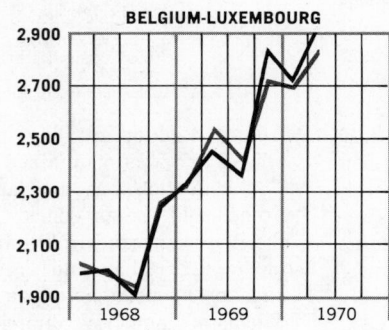

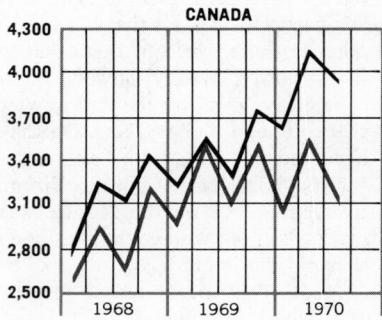

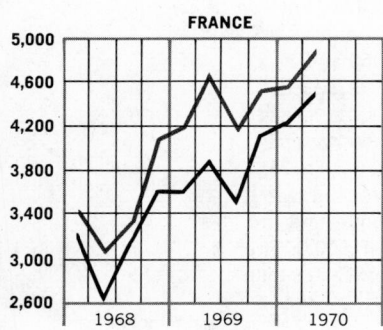

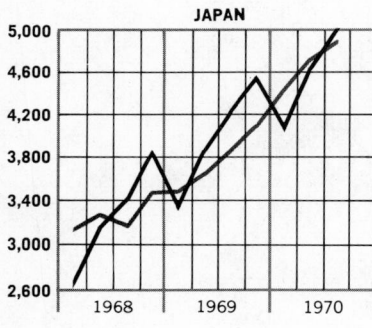

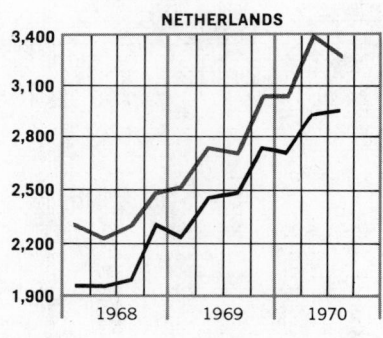

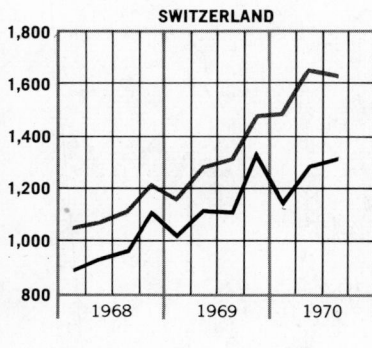

In millions of U.S. dollars

— Exports   — Imports

Source: International Monetary Fund, *International Financial Statistics.*

U.S.; all other exports increased by only 4%. Non-motor exports to the U.S. increased by only 8%, partly because of a Canadian dock strike. Exports to other countries actually declined a little. There was a substantial increase in exports in the first half of 1970 but imports remained at about the same level as at the end of 1969.

The French deficit increased sharply during 1969, by $1.1 billion to $2.4 billion, as France recorded the largest increase in imports of any industrial country. French imports of consumer goods increased by 42% and of capital goods by 33%. In 1970, despite a further increase in imports, French exports fared very well and the trade deficit was sharply reduced.

West German exports benefited from the continued expansion in domestic production in Europe and, in 1969, were some 17% higher than in 1968. Sales to other EEC countries rose by 21% and exports to EFTA countries by 13%. There was a slight decline in exports to the U.S. Such was the buoyancy of the West German economy, however, that imports rose by 23%, including a 27% increase in imports from other EEC countries. In the first half of 1970, the growth in exports slackened but imports accelerated. As a result, there was a further reduction in the trade surplus, which, nonetheless, remained large.

In 1968, Italy had recorded its smallest trade deficit in postwar years but, in 1969 and 1970, the deficit increased from $70 million in 1968 to an annual rate of $1,550,000,000 in the first half of 1970. Italian imports increased by 22% in 1969. Exports were some 20% higher than in 1968 in the first nine months of 1969 but fell back in the fourth quarter, and the increase for the year as a whole was only 15%. In the first half of 1970, exports were growing at an annual rate of 12%, compared with a 20% rate of growth for imports.

The U.K. balance of trade improved somewhat in 1969 and 1970 as the effects of the late-1967 devaluation of sterling were felt. A relatively slow rate of growth of industrial production and a certain amount of surplus capacity prevented imports from rising any faster. Despite this, a considerable deficit remained. In 1969 exports increased by 12% and imports by 5%, compared with increases of 22% in both exports and imports in 1968.

Although U.K. imports were growing faster in 1970 than in the previous year, the growth of exports was maintained and there was a further slight improvement in the trade balance. Much of the deterioration in the trading position in the second quarter seemed to have been made good in the third quarter. The major impetus to U.K. exports in the first half of 1970 came from Europe; exports to EEC countries were 20% higher than a year earlier and exports to EFTA partners were 23% higher. (A. G. A.)

See also Commercial Policies; Commodities, Primary; Payments and Reserves, International.

ENCYCLOPÆDIA BRITANNICA FILMS. *World Trade for Better Living* (1951); *Round Trip: The U.S.A. in World Trade* (1952); *Food and People* (1956); *Britain: World Trader* (1964); *Rotterdam—Europort, Gateway to Europe* (1970).

Transportation

Transportation in 1970 showed continued attention to speedier movement in larger units, and the application of electronics and cybernetics to management and operation. The jumbo jets entered service, and despite teething troubles flew on a growing number of routes.

During tests two prototypes of the Anglo-French Concorde supersonic passenger aircraft approached twice the speed of sound. Civil aviation was harassed by hijacking and sabotage. International action began in the hope of containing this form of piracy. (*See* Special Report.)

At sea the trend toward larger vessels, especially tankers, continued. Containerization and roll-on/roll-off services increased but at a decelerating rate due to fears of overcapacity. The major ports made ambitious plans to meet the requirements of these services. A new element in shipping operations was the entry into service of barge-carrying ships developed in the U.S. They were designed so that barges could go by inland waterway to a seaport, where they were loaded on oceangoing ships, offloaded at the mother ship's port of call, and continued by inland waterway to their destination. One system already operating across the North Atlantic between U.S. Gulf and European ports, and serving the European inland waterway network, was LASH (Lighter Aboard Ship). These vessels carried 76 barges containing 17,500 tons of cargo. The potentialities of container airships were being studied in Britain and elsewhere.

Railways made headway in their fight against road competition. Higher speeds on scheduled services brought more passengers. Research and experimental development of new forms of traction, suspension, and signaling aimed at still higher speeds, notably in North America, the U.K., France, and Japan. Development of container and other unit load services, with improved facilities and phased with road and water transportation, gave encouraging results.

Growing concern over the effect of various modes of transport on environmental standards led to attempts at remedial action nationally and internationally. Measures were introduced or considered to limit noxious exhaust gases and vehicle noise, and to restrict oil discharges at sea. (E. A. J. D.)

AVIATION

The faltering traffic growth, rising costs, and consequent loss of profitability that had plagued the U.S. airlines in 1969 continued to dominate the air transport situation during 1970. Although other countries were not suffering from the effects of a similar general recession, the fact that the U.S. was responsible for 55–60% of the Western world's air traffic, in ton-mile production terms, meant that overall load factors (loads or passengers carried in relation to capacity or seats offered) fell in 1969 and seemed likely to fall still further in 1970. Only cargo carrying continued to show a really healthy growth rate.

Profits dropped sharply, or became losses, for many U.S. carriers. They were consequently wondering seriously how they could afford the cost of reequiping themselves with Boeing 747s and the McDonnell Douglas and Lockheed wide-body, big-capacity trijets, a cost amounting, with ground equipment, to approximately $10 billion during the next five years. Among the giants, Pan American Airways (PAA) lost about $19.6 million in the first six months of 1970 and United Air Lines (the world's biggest carrier apart from the Soviet Union's Aeroflot) returned a fairly heavy loss for the same period. A planned merger between Northeast, a minor domestic airline, and Northwest, a major domestic trunk and transpacific operator, demonstrated a likely trend if the situation did not improve. This merger, together with one between American Airlines and Trans-Caribbean Airways, was approved by

UPI COMPIX

Thousands of would-be Easter travelers jam Chicago's O'Hare Airport as snow added to delays caused by air traffic controller absences.

Pres. Richard Nixon in December. Airlines elsewhere were not suffering to the same extent, however; British Overseas Airways Corp. (BOAC) and British European Airways (BEA), for instance, each reported handsome profits for 1969–70.

The manufacturers of transport aircraft and engines experienced between them a combination of technical success and financial and sales difficulties during 1970. Both the big U.S. trijets already mentioned, the Douglas DC-10 and the Lockheed L-1011 TriStar, were ceremonially rolled out and flown in the second half of the year. The DC-10 made a first flight of 3 hr. 26 min. At that time 15 airlines, including 5 in Europe, had placed firm orders for 119 of these aircraft with 122 more on option. The TriStar, for which orders had been lagging during the previous 12 months (though totaling 178, including options), was rolled out on September 1.

The commercial battle between the manufacturers of these two generally similar airliners was by then causing onlookers elsewhere to wonder whether the day had passed when such head-on competition could be financially worthwhile. Because of cost escalation and other problems with the program for the giant C-5A military transport, Lockheed was in financial trouble during the year, but the situation was improved by government aid for the program and a credit arrangement with a group of banks. Sales success for the TriStar was of great importance for Britain's Rolls-Royce, whose advanced RB.211 turbofan provided the power for the aircraft and whose private-venture expenditure had necessarily to be supplemented by government loans and grants.

Delayed by power plant troubles and modifications in 1969, the Boeing 747 finally entered service with Pan American Airways on Jan. 22, 1970, and suffered initially from a failure to maintain its schedules, mainly because of minor engine ailments. By mid-July, however, things were going fairly well with this first of the wide-body giants; more than 50 were then in service with 11 airlines and about one million passengers had already been carried. Europe's short–medium-haul airbus, the A-300B, to which the French and West German governments and those countries' manufacturers, as well as Hawker Siddeley in Britain and Fokker in the Netherlands, were finally committed, received its first firm airline support in September, when Air France ordered six and took options on another ten. Late in 1969 the decision had been made to use a U.S. engine, the General Electric CF6-50, in the A-300B, but the Rolls-Royce RB.211 could be fitted if specified by buyers. In December the U.K. government, faced with the choice of sharing in the A-300B or providing financial support for the

British Aircraft Corp. (BAC) Three-eleven and its developed RB.211 engines, decided that it would not back either project.

After a four-month grounding for the installation of higher-thrust Anglo-French Olympus engines, fully automatic intake controls, and other changes, the British-built Concorde supersonic transport (SST) prototype 002 was airborne again on August 12 preparatory to starting a series of tests on which the future of the aircraft might depend. These tests, to be made along a north-south track largely over the Irish Sea at speeds up to and over twice that of sound, would help to confirm (or otherwise) the capacity of the production aircraft to operate nonstop over the critical westerly Paris–New York stage with an adequate payload.

Meanwhile, the program for the larger and faster American SST being built by Boeing had been subject to economy cuts by simplifying the plans for air and ground testing of the two prototypes, only one of which would be flown, and deferring some of the work to the stage when (and if) a go-ahead was given for the development of the very different production version that would be airborne toward the end of 1976— or about four years after the first flight of the prototype. At the same time the concept of the SST was under attack from environmentalist groups in the U.S., and in December the Senate voted not to appropriate further funds to the project. SST supporters mounted a counterattack, and a temporary compromise was reached whereby SST development was funded at approximately the current level until March 1971.

In November 1969 and April 1970, respectively, the U.S. and British authorities had each laid down firm and final rules to limit the noise of future aircraft. The U.S. Federal Aviation Administration (FAA) required that all subsonic jets for which application had been made for a type certificate after Jan. 1, 1967, would need to meet specified noise limitations according to weight at different stages of the takeoff, climbaway, and approach to land. The selected date meant that the DC-10 and TriStar, for instance, would have to comply from the start; earlier aircraft with high bypass-ratio turbofan engines such as the Boeing 747, the FAA ruled, would be given time to comply. The U.K. rules laid down similar maximum levels of permitted noise, but involved a somewhat different approach. After Jan. 1, 1971, all new subsonic civil aircraft above a certain weight would be required to hold certificates of quietness when using British airports. The Department of Trade and Industry retained the power to exempt certain types, such as the earlier 747s, and the rules did not apply to existing

continued on page 735

SKYJACKING: CAN IT BE STOPPED?

By Jerry Hannifin

The greatest single problem facing the world's air transport industry in 1970 was aerial piracy, the skyjacking of airliners at the point of a gun. Skyjacking threatened to destroy the delicate instrument of world flight communications systems, and no airline, or country, was invulnerable. Under the category of "crimes against aircraft," which included air piracy, ground sabotage, and all other acts of violence committed during any phase of air transport operations, skyjacking was the subject of urgent discussion and recommendations by airline pilots, their governments, the International Air Transport Association (IATA), and the UN's International Civil Aviation Organization (ICAO).

A consensus arising from these meetings and resolutions was that the only lasting deterrent to "crimes against aircraft" was the adoption of international laws guaranteeing adequate punishment, and/or extradition of accused skyjackers to the country of the aircraft's origination, regardless of the motive for the criminal act. In short, not even a claim of "political asylum" would provide legal immunity for skyjackers.

From 1930 through 1970 there were more than 200 skyjacking attempts. Of them, over 100 involving U.S. aircraft were successful, and approximately 50 succeeded elsewhere. A large proportion occurred in the late 1960s and in 1970. The sum of all available statistical data demonstrated forcefully that skyjacking was not limited by considerations of politics or ideology.

The Tokyo Convention and the 11 Days in September. The public outcry against skyjacking was spectacular, but only after an 11-day sequence involving six attempted skyjackings or acts of air piracy in September was a specific plan of international action to thwart future attempts formulated. Previously, the only formally proposed legal effort to deal with the issue had been the ICAO's Tokyo Convention on Offenses and Certain Other Acts Committed on Board Aircraft, which nominally went into effect on Dec. 4, 1969. Where skyjacking was concerned, the Tokyo Convention proposed only the release of passengers, crew, and aircraft, and had no specific penalties for the skyjacker.

The International Federation of Air Line Pilots Associations opposed the Tokyo Convention as "insufficient and inadequate" to protect passengers and crews, citing a need for international laws guaranteeing punishment or extradition for formal trial of skyjackers. IATA director general Knut Hammarskjöld commented: "If governments do not live up to their responsibilities, public opinion (that is, the people directly affected) will be extremely critical and may express this criticism strongly."

The 11-day sequence of skyjackings in September resulted in the total destruction of a Pan American World Airways Boeing 747 on the ground at Cairo, U.A.R., and the destruction on a desert field near Amman, Jordan, of three other jet transports, one belonging to Trans World Airlines (TWA), one to Swissair, and one to the British Overseas Airways Corporation. The value of the four aircraft was estimated at $50 million. Approximately 300 passengers were held as hostages for a week, and about 50 others were detained in Jordan for an additional fortnight during a violent civil war. The 11 days also saw the apprehension of

one Syrian woman skyjacker and the death of her companion at the hands of a crew of El Al Israel Airlines.

New Preventive Measures. Reviewing events of the 11 days with civil aviation safety experts and others involved in the air transport industry, U.S. Pres. Richard Nixon publicly recognized and spoke out on skyjacking. It was the first time that a leader of one of the world's great powers had made specific public recommendations on coping with criminal acts in the air. In effect, the president ordered federal security procedures to minimize the opportunities for skyjackers, following procedures tried and proved by El Al, by putting armed security guards on all major flights, both domestic and international. The president also asked ICAO to strengthen the Tokyo Convention by requiring extradition or criminal trial for accused air criminals. Following the president's announcement, a group of Federal Aviation Administration (FAA) "sky marshals" began flying aboard U.S. commercial airplanes on unannounced itineraries. In addition, the president ordered "special security force" training to begin immediately for 2,500 additional marshals.

The flying "sky marshals," drawn first from volunteers at the FAA, the armed forces, and the U.S. Secret Service, were to have two additional security tools to enhance their mission. The first was a "behavioural profile" of potential skyjackers, developed by the FAA and the airlines. It was based on a host of personal characteristics common to all known previous skyjackers, and included five basic items.

The second tool was a simple magnetometer examination of each passenger and his hand luggage. The magnetometer in general airline use in the U.S. and at various other places, such as London's Heathrow Airport, consisted of two slender metal poles which generated a magnetic field through which the passenger walked. If he had a ferrous metal object in his pocket or hand luggage, it created an anomaly in the field, and a red light flashed and a needle quivered, alerting the airline agent. The passenger suspect was then asked to submit to a search by a federally deputized airline representative, or an attendant sky marshal if one was available. The passenger could refuse the personal search, but if he did he was not allowed to board the aircraft.

The FAA received thousands of letters from helpful citizens suggesting ways and means to stop skyjackers, and a number of these suggestions had merit, in the judgment of FAA Administrator John Shaffer. The suggestions included pumping an incapacitating gas into the cabin air-conditioning system. Certain El Al flights already had this system available, including injection of strong tear gas into the cabin atmosphere. Other El Al aircraft also had a closed-circuit television camera available to enable the flight deck crew to keep an eye on passengers, and a bullet-resistant steel shield lining the cockpit access door.

By the end of 1970 the U.S. had not ordered the television surveillance system or steel plate reinforcements, although the Air Line Pilots Association (ALPA) formally asked the FAA to require bulletproofing of cockpit doors and bulkheads in all large passenger aircraft. ALPA Pres. Charles H. Ruby said that his pilots wanted a bulletproof partition separating the cockpit from the cabin, a bulletproof window with an electromagnetic-type lock, and a bulletproof window and sliding panel in the door.

The U.S. response to the skyjacking problem was tardy, but effectively pragmatic, along lines pioneered by Israel. Approximately 2,500 of the scheduled airline flights in the world every day were considered by FAA and IATA officials as possibly vulnerable to skyjackers. These flights carried approximately 1.7 million passengers. FAA statisticians estimated that the "probabilities" of being skyjacked somewhere in the world on a daily basis were arithmetically very small, on the order of about one in a million, but nonetheless, more than 3,000 U.S. citizens had made impromptu and unwanted brief visits to Cuba alone in the last ten years with skyjackers in charge of the aircraft. Although there had never been a single fatality or serious injury to passengers during these skyjackings, the pilots said bluntly that this was only by the grace of Providence.

World Transportation

Country	Railways: Route length in 000 km.	Railways Traffic: Passenger in 000,000 pass.-km.	Railways Traffic: Freight in 000,000 net ton-km.	Motor transport: Road length in 000 km.	Motor transport: Vehicles in use, Passenger in 000	Motor transport: Vehicles in use, Commercial in 000	Merchant shipping (Ships of 100 tons and over): Number of vessels	Merchant shipping: Gross reg. tons in 000	Air traffic: Total km. flown in 000	Air traffic: Passenger in 000 pass.-km.	Air traffic: Freight in 000 net ton-km.
EUROPE											
Austria	5.9*	6,294*	8,726*	93.3	1,053.3	107.4	3	1	8,972	428,000	8,925
Belgium	4.3*	8,237*	7,369*	91.8	1,806.5	270.0	228	1,052	38,640	2,206,000	177,710
Bulgaria	4.2	6,062	12,619	29.8	9.3†	20.4†	124	638	4,760	132,910	2,860
Czechoslovakia	13.3	18,570	56,667	145.9	556.4	162.1	10	75	18,579	850,000	12,878
Denmark	2.4*	3,224*	1,380*	61.6†	955.3	254.2	1,194	3,490	25,274‡	1,202,400‡	55,400‡
Finland	5.8	2,201	6,027	71.9	643.1	101.8	388	1,330	14,731	587,000	13,450
France	37.1	39,057*	67,205*	784.7	11,860.0	1,766.0	1,432	5,962	170,449	9,677,793	382,086
Germany, East (excluding Berlin)	15.2	17,098	39,445	c.160.0†	920.2	352.8	371	896	...	730,100	24,090
Germany, West (excluding Berlin)	34.1	36,592	67,195	414.7	13,168.6§	1,083.6§	2,768	7,027	107,945	6,922,000	465,240
Greece	2.6†	1,438	587	34.7	194.9	96.9	1,700	8,581	21,473	1,717,000	36,500
Hungary	8.8	13,981	17,736	110.1	192.3	42.0†	21	34	...	255,000	8,651
Ireland	2.1	520	466	86.4	340.9	49.4	90	164	21,425	1,456,600	60,992
Italy	16.4*	29,923	17,222	285.5	9,028.4	885.2	1,552	7,038	114,949	7,102,000	269,100
Netherlands	3.1	7,533	3,451	77.7	2,305.7	326.5	1,652	5,255	80,757	4,760,000	373,760
Norway	4.2*	1,450*	2,710*	71.1	699.7	141.3	2,848	19,679	36,096‡	1,736,600‡	72,490‡
Poland	26.6	36,204	95,024	309.0	423.1	248.0	484	1,536	13,795	504,000	7,149
Portugal	3.6	3,441	737	37.4	399.3	26.2	364	825	28,826	1,772,000	34,210
Romania	11.0	16,720	44,030	77.0	c.250.0†	38.1	64	338	8,209	331,700	6,972
Spain	17.4	12,647*	7,889*	c.134.0	1,577.2	588.4	2,119	3,199	77,181	4,835,000	102,005
Sweden	12.8	4,126*	14,863*	173.6	2,193.6	142.6	1,051	5,029	45,916‡	2,124,000‡	109,959‡
Switzerland	2.9*	8,034*	6,072*	58.6	1,283.7	124.6	32	193	60,230	3,835,000	175,300
U.S.S.R.	133.6	254,100	2,227,480	1,368.4†	c.1,100.0†	c.4,500.0†	5,622	13,705	...	62,100,000	1,803,000
United Kingdom	20.1‖	28,703‖	24,026‖	331.6‖	11,250.0	1,564.0	3,858	23,844	271,018	16,239,000	614,600
Yugoslavia	10.7	10,120	17,540	88.3	562.5	104.8	349	1,428	12,857	606,000	5,655
ASIA											
Burma	4.3	2,398	802	25.0	28.9	29.1	34	50	4,500	114,600	1,830
Cambodia	0.7	170	71	10.8†	23.1	10.7	3	4	1,417	50,890	1,152
Ceylon	1.5	2,701	336	21.0	84.7	30.4	25	9	2,475	97,118	2,900
China	36.0†	45,670†	265,260†	550.0†	50.0†	300.0†	237	792	...	63,882†	1,967†
India	59.1†	107,513	101,181	972.3	571.3	300.7	397	2,238	61,776	3,230,000	115,800
Indonesia	6.8†	4,998	659	84.3	212.1	95.7	463	598	16,110	296,400	7,108
Iran	3.5	1,447	2,225	39.1	187.5	66.8	48	106	9,771	469,056	4,453
Iraq	1.9†	367	1,131	17.9	75.8	46.5	35	37	3,139	150,000	1,797
Israel	0.7	332	420	9.1	136.4	57.6	114	769	24,356	2,070,000	84,900
Japan	27.9†	274,271	59,569	1,005.4	6,933.7	8,334.6	7,665	23,987	153,371	9,000,000	364,900
Korea, South	3.2	11,076	7,118	34.5†	33.1	31.6	294	767	4,771	124,341	2,035
Malaysia	1.8	583¶	1,080†¶	21.4†	230.0	60.6	85	39	8,657♀	338,383♀	5,146♀
Pakistan	11.3†	10,221	7,636	c.200.0	89.0	31.4	172	530	26,601	1,633,700	71,206
Philippines	1.0	894	117	62.2	232.7	173.3	297	929	34,434	1,320,043	27,404
Syria	0.5	85	122	c.14.9	29.4	16.0	3	1	2,430	127,470	874
Taiwan	4.5	5,935	2,595	16.9	30.7	33.4	216	962	7,745	521,200	8,385
Thailand	3.9	3,914	2,118	c.10.0	c.129.5	c.154.6	53	69	13,180	542,900	6,575
Turkey	8.0	4,538	5,245	c.70.0	128.9	105.9	312	651	13,064	639,600	4,434
Vietnam, South	c.0.7	71	41	20.9	45.6	21.7	27	19	11,662	639,200	5,398
AFRICA											
Algeria	4.0	954	1,337	35.5†	117.0	88	7	19	7,496	362,692	3,747
Central African Republic	—	—	—	c.19.0	c.4.3	c.8.3	...	...	1,511δ	55,659δ	5,129δ
Chad	...	...	...	c.10.0	3.7	6.1	...	...	2,047δ	65,324δ	5,674δ
Congo (Kinshasa)	5.2	619	1,959	141.3	46.1	23.2†	6	29	8,984	330,881	10,727
Dahomey	0.6	63	76	7.2	9.9	6.2	...	...	1,141δ	54,419δ	5,129δ
Gabon	0.6	...	...	5.7	5.9	4.9	3	1	2,671δ	74,119δ	5,289δ
Ghana	1.3	425	272	c.31.0	32.2	21.4	61	166	3,789	134,000	3,500
Ivory Coast	0.6	541	340	24.8	40.6	30.0	21	25	1,546δ	58,953δ	5,239δ
Kenya	2.0†	4,529†□	4,088□	41.9	80.6	14.4	21	16	5,209°	222,188°	8,528°
Malawi	c.0.8	49	152	10.5	8.9	6.2	...	...	801	13,652	422
Mali	c.0.6	66†	110	c.12.0	4.8	5.8	...	...	2,004	26,596	1,548
Morocco	1.8	416	2,644	24.7	202.8	79.2	39	72	6,342	365,000	3,380
Nigeria	3.5	706	1,685	c.80.0	63.0	30.0	45	98	3,905	190,500	6,456
Rhodesia	3.3†	...	6,050▲	78.5	108.8	42.2	...	...	2,834†+	72,112†+	891†+
Senegal	1.2	281	263	10.6†	34.3	18.7	13	4	1,351δ	60,489δ	5,139δ
South Africa	19.8†	...	53,018⊕	c.320.0†	1,405.0	343.0	241	499	29,805	2,168,000	59,300
Tanzania	3.0†	4,529†□	4,088□	16.7	36.2	29.8	10	19	5,209°	222,188°	8,529°
Uganda	0.8†	4,529†□	4,088□	24.2†	32.8	5.0	...	...	5,209°	222,189°	8,529°
United Arab Republic	4.5†	5,512	3,001	c.50.0	115.9	26.7	123	239	14,094	762,400	13,861
Zambia	1.0†	...	...	34.1†	48.2	25.8	...	...	2,380	74,640	930
NORTH AND CENTRAL AMERICA											
Canada	69.5	4,080	139,340	806.3	6,159.6	1,587.2	1,278	2,451	209,757	12,044,454	301,687
Costa Rica	0.7	71	28†	10.0	33.7	17.9	6	3	3,748	122,600	10,650
El Salvador	0.7	...	...	8.4†	31.3	15.9	...	...	...	...	...
Guatemala	1.2†	...	75	c.11.2	33.4†	20.5	2	4	3,751	77,403	3,850
Honduras	c.1.1	...	...	c.3.4	12.0	11.5	51	66	7,832	109,256	10,210
Mexico	23.8†	4,398	20,433	69.7	1,000.0	465.8	118	424	47,854	2,620,000	35,510
Nicaragua	0.3	44†	14†	c.7.0	12.9†	10.0†	8	15	1,570	59,430	1,010
Panama	0.5	...	...	6.7	40.4	12.8	823	5,374	...	...	...
United States	336.4	19,584	1,120,930	5,928.8	83,281.3	16,282.1	3,146	19,550	3,453,611	201,755,000	6,937,629
SOUTH AMERICA											
Argentina	42.0	14,128	12,948	215.3	1,152.3	652.4	319	1,218	44,118	1,748,777	40,058
Bolivia	3.6†	236†	300†	25.0	14.5	24.9	...	...	3,650	61,400	1,380
Brazil	32.0†	13,803	21,974	1,024.0	1,537.0	953.9	414	1,381	89,389	3,932,000	152,375
Chile	8.4	2,085	2,637	54.5	130.2	111.7	133	288	15,759	729,600	39,512
Colombia	3.5†	274	1,166	45.0†	141.1	123.2	47	206	44,755	1,743,000	65,313
Ecuador	1.9	59	60	18.3†	22.0	34.3	16	44	9,867	263,414	5,174
Paraguay	1.2	28	22	6.3	6.9	6.6	26	22	...	...	...
Peru	3.3†	211	625	42.8†	195.1†	111.8†	366	338	16,441	574,204	15,983
Uruguay	3.1	...	...	c.42.0	c.142.0	c.90.3	41	112	2,995	64,660	177
Venezuela	0.8†	39†	17†	37.6	482.0	197.1	90	369	26,104	1,022,900	47,566
OCEANIA											
Australia	40.5*	3,504*†**	20,490*	860.4	3,523.3	949.2	321	894	144,096	7,296,819	217,197
New Zealand	4.9*	516*	2,700*	93.9	854.7	168.1	124	181	34,017	1,266,629	34,097

Note: Data are for 1968 or 1969 unless otherwise indicated.
. . . Indicates not known.
*State system only.
†Data given are the most recent available.
‡Including apportionment of traffic of Scandinavian Airlines System.
§Including West Berlin.
‖Excluding Northern Ireland.
¶Including Singapore.
♀Apportionment of traffic of Malaysia-Singapore Airlines.
δIncluding apportionment of traffic of Air Afrique.
□Total for Kenya, Tanzania, and Uganda (East African Railways Corporation).
°Including apportionment of traffic of East African Airways Corp. and Caspair Ltd.
▲Including traffic for Botswana.
+Including apportionment of traffic of Central African Airways Corp.
⊕Including South West Africa (Namibia).
**Excluding New South Wales and Queensland.

Sources: UN, *Statistical Yearbook 1969*; *Monthly Bulletin of Statistics*; *Annual Bulletin of Transport Statistics for Europe* (1968); Lloyd's Register, *Statistical Tables* (1969); International Road Federation, *World Road Statistics 1970*; *Jahrbuch des Eisenbahnwesens 1969*. (M. C. MacD.)

types still being delivered or to supersonic aircraft.

In May the FAA also introduced more stringent airworthiness rules for all future civil transport aircraft. Among many other requirements, the new standards demanded better protection against impacts by birds, lightning strikes, and fire hazards.

In statistical, if not human-life terms, 1970 was a good year for air transport safety. During the first eight months the average passenger-fatality rate on scheduled operations was well below that for each of the two previous years. Only the death of two passengers in a crash in the Virgin Islands on Dec. 28, 1970, prevented U.S. scheduled airlines from having a fatality-free year. In 1969 a total of 1,123 passengers and 135 crew members had been killed in 32 accidents (2 of them the result of collisions) on scheduled services other than those of the Soviet Union and China. Using the normal yardsticks for safety (or danger) levels, these figures represented a rate of 0.52 passenger fatalities for every 100 million passenger-miles flown, and one of 0.27 fatal accidents for every 100,000 hours. By comparison, the equivalent rates for 1967 (the safest previous year for airline passengers) were 0.40 and 0.29, respectively. Once again, the jet aircraft were shown to be much safer than others, with a fatality rate only about a tenth of that for propeller aircraft. Even when allowance was made for the fact that the jets operate predominantly over medium- and long-haul routes and between well-equipped airports, it was obvious that the introduction of these more reliable aircraft had had a big influence on the improvement of safety levels.

The good safety record of nonscheduled (charter) services in 1968 was maintained in 1969, when 172 passengers were killed. Assuming the total passenger-miles on these services to be 20% of that for scheduled operations, this fatality rate was equivalent to about 0.4 per 100 million passenger-miles—as low as the best-ever figure for scheduled services. Two charter crashes in the U.S. in 1970 involved football teams. In October a Martin 404 crashed in Colorado, killing 31, including 14 members of the Wichita State football team. A month later a DC-9 jetliner crashed in West Virginia; 75 were killed, of whom 43 were members and coaches of the Marshall University team. The FAA charged that the plane involved in the first accident did not have a valid flying certificate but found no irregularities in the second case.

For the aviation insurance organizations 1970 was very far from being a good year. In addition to the accepted and allowed-for losses of aircraft, passengers, and crews in accidents, they were faced with the cost involved in the total destruction of airliners, including a Boeing 747, by Palestinian guerrillas. Within a period of six days in September, four aircraft, valued together at about $50 million, were destroyed on the ground by explosives after being hijacked. Earlier in the year, a Swissair Coronado jet had been destroyed while airborne, killing all 38 passengers and 9 crew members, and an Austrian Caravelle had been landed safely after being similarly sabotaged.

The seriousness for airlines and their passengers and crews of the spate of hijacking and sabotage—no longer, as in previous years, restricted largely to the forced movement of U.S. airliners to Cuba—was underlined at a meeting in Montreal of the International Civil Aviation Organization (ICAO) in the summer of 1970. There it was pointed out that during the 18 months prior to the end of June 1970 there

had been 118 hijackings and 14 sabotage or armed-attack cases in which 96 persons had been killed. The meeting agreed on the detection and other measures that could usefully be taken to forestall attacks and outlined the international action that should be taken by member countries to deal with the persons involved in such crimes. The various proposals were said to have been approved unanimously, but it was later reported that the representatives of two countries, Algeria and Cuba, had "reserved their positions" over the most important document to emerge from the meeting. This contained a six-point manifesto, one item in which called for "concerted action" in suppressing such criminal acts.

After the mass hijackings in September, some governments and airlines were planning to follow the Israeli practice of carrying armed guards, though there was a wide divergence of view on the wisdom of this course—especially in cases where grenades might be carried by the attackers. (See Special Report.)

A prospectively important development during the year was the effect of an earlier agreement that Japan Air Lines (JAL) should be allowed to operate with its own aircraft and flight crews over the Siberian route to Moscow, and on to Paris and London. Previously, the combined Aeroflot/JAL service between Tokyo and Moscow had been operated with Soviet aircraft and flight crews. So as to make the independent JAL (and other airline) services possible over the route, a new airway across Siberia was organized, with about 100 English-speaking air traffic controllers. Trans-Siberian rights were obtained by Air France in December 1969, by BOAC in mid-1970, and later by the Scandinavian Airlines System.

The fares structure over the North Atlantic continued to be the subject of interairline discord. In an effort to combat the competition from charter carriers, a complicated series of time-limited excursion, promotional, and bulk-contract inclusive-tour rates had been agreed upon early in 1969. In October the Italian airline, Alitalia, pulled out of the International Air Transport Association (IATA) agreement because, as

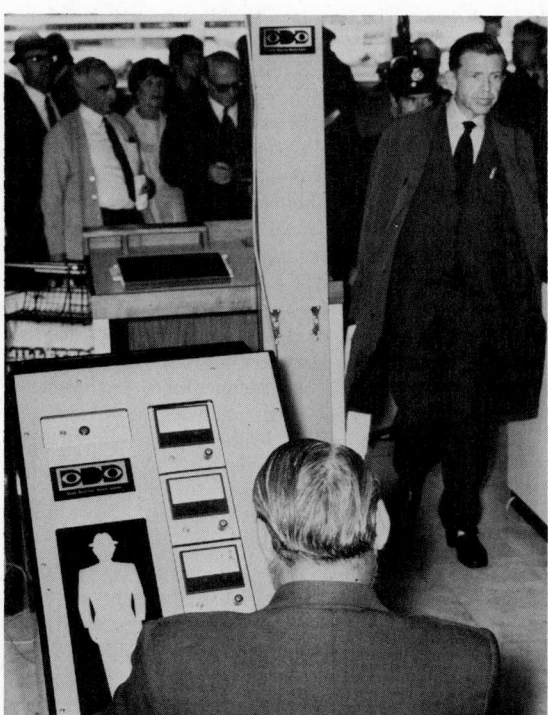

Passengers are screened by a metal-detecting device at London's Heathrow Airport as part of an effort to prevent hijacking that included extra police and preflight baggage inspection.

POPPERFOTO FROM PICTORIAL PARADE

one (non-Italian) observer put it, the whole fares structure was "like a plate of spaghetti"; others later followed. Meetings of the IATA-member airlines at Lausanne, Switz., and (for 14 days) at Caracas, Venez., finally produced agreement, but this did little to reduce the complexity that had been the primary cause of complaint. Some simplification of the tariffs, over the Atlantic and elsewhere, was expected from the regular IATA passenger-traffic conference which was designed to settle world fares for a two-year period beginning April 1, 1971.

Two developments of international interest occurred in Britain during the year. The first was the formation of a third major nonnationalized carrier with the purchase by Caledonian Airways, a British long-haul nonscheduled carrier, of the common stock of British United Airways (BUA) as of the end of November. The second was the completion by the Roskill Commission of the immensely thorough, protracted, and expensive studies and hearings designed to reach a decision on the most effective site for the construction of a third airport to serve the London area. A final report and recommendation by the commission was not expected until 1971.

The May 1969 report of the Edwards Committee on British civil aviation had, among many other recommendations, proposed that two or more private carriers, led by BUA, should merge to form a strong "second-force" airline. For such an airline to be an economic success it would be necessary for it to operate over many more scheduled routes than those already available to BUA. International agreements virtually precluded paralleled ("dual designation") services other than over the very competitive North Atlantic route, so the committee recommended that the necessary routes might be taken from those of the state corporations. In a White Paper published in November 1969, the British Labour government had agreed with most of the recommendations, including the proposed "second-force" airline, but not with that proposing the transfer of routes.

Following the appearance of the Edwards report, BUA and Caledonian had been holding inconclusive talks about a possible merger. Then, early in March 1970, it was learned that BUA was being offered "for sale" to BOAC. The airline's major shareholder, British and Commonwealth Shipping, had seen no prospect of an extended route network or of improved financial results. The proposal was approved by the British Board of Trade, which was not apparently aware that talks between BUA and Caledonian had been continuing. The proposed deal was "put on ice" by the Board of Trade until such time as suitable merger arrangements between Caledonian and BUA might be concluded. There the matter stood when the Conservative government approved, early in August, the transfer of routes, representing perhaps 3–5% of BOAC's revenues, to the second-force airline when it was formed. The situation thus was radically changed, and the merger arrangements were concluded on October 20.   (H. A. Ta.)

COMMERCIAL MOTOR TRANSPORTATION

The main development during the year was the rapid expansion of carrying freight by container and roll-on/roll-off services. Although these were mainly for maritime traffic, except for the long-established railroad piggyback services in the U.S., it was estimated that 85% of this trade originated from, and reached

its destination by, road transport. This applied to both intra- and intercontinental traffic, the latter growing considerably in 1970. In the U.K. about three million tons of freight were carried by roll-on/roll-off services on the short continental routes, both by road vehicles and by containers transported by road, thereby eliminating loading and offloading. Further expansion on these routes was envisaged. The British Rail freightliner services linking the main industrial towns also served the ports and contributed to the container traffic carried by road. Approximately 150,000 trucks and trailers passed through West German Baltic ports on similar services, and Dutch ports handled about three-quarters of a million tons of freight in this way.

This increase in the through carriage of traffic by road across frontiers made urgent the liberalization of international transit in matters such as standardization and simplification of container traffic documents, uniformity of equipment, and greater freedom of access for foreign-based vehicles working international routes. Internationally, further steps were taken to harmonize rules and regulations governing motor transport safety measures and the working conditions of truck crews. The European Conference of Ministers of Transport (ECMT), representing 18 countries of Western Europe, worked for the introduction of a multilateral quota for international road freight transport and combined transport. This liberalization measure was designed to enable quota license holders to handle international hauls between countries taking part in the scheme. An international agreement was being drawn up and was to be given a three-year trial. The ECMT was also studying harmonization of the terms of competition, with special reference to taxation, the existing diversity of which hampered liberalization in road transport.

Many bilateral agreements were made, particularly between the U.K. and European continental countries. Some fixed quotas that limited the number of journeys permitted to or through each country, and exempted them from their respective licensing laws and formalities; this occurred between the U.K. and France and Italy. Others, such as those between the U.K. and the Netherlands and Norway, were more liberal, and allowed haulers of one country to operate freely to or through another country without having to obtain a carrier's or operator's license or a permit locally. Cabotage, *i.e.*, carrying goods by foreign-based vehicles originating from and destined for the country through which they are passing, was generally prohibited, but some agreements permitted the carriage of goods originating in the countries party to the agreement to be carried to a third country.

In the European Economic Community little progress was made toward establishing a common transport policy that would allow free movement and carrying within the six member nations, and the quota system continued. Priority was being given to efforts aimed at harmonizing conditions under which freight vehicles operated. Thus, after October drivers of both passenger and freight vehicles of more than three tons gross weight undertaking journeys to the Common Market countries were required to have a control book recording their hours of work, driving, and rest, with entries for the seven days preceding their arrival. In the U.K. new rules came into force reducing the number of permitted hours of work and fixing minimum rest periods.

Nationally, the only major changes in legislation

affecting commercial motor transport were in the U.K., where, with the change of government in June, it was announced that certain provisions of the Transport Act, 1968, enacted by the previous administration, would not be enforced. They applied mainly to quantity licensing for freight vehicles, which would have required special authorization by an independent licensing authority for vehicles over 16 tons gross weight to carry goods on journeys of more than 100 mi. As of Dec. 1, 1970, the carrier licensing system that controlled the number of vehicles entering road haulage was abolished, leaving entry into the industry unrestricted. The only licensing control over road goods transport remaining would be operators' licenses brought into force at the beginning of 1970 to regulate safety and maintenance standards and working conditions. In West Germany an order was made forbidding heavy vehicle traffic on expressways and certain federal highways, particularly during certain weekends in order to relieve holiday traffic. An attempt to introduce a similar measure in France was frustrated when vehicle drivers demonstrated against it.

Various international organizations were striving to close the gaps in data on commercial motor transport. Statistics were scarce, and there was little uniformity in those available. Such figures as were available concerning road traffic during 1969 showed a general increase in total distances traveled and tonnage carried, and a move toward larger vehicles with greater carrying capacity. In France 1,766,000 freight vehicles, together with 349,000 trailers and 82,000 semitrailers, traveled 124 million vehicle-km. and recorded 61,200,000,000 ton-km. The figures for 1968 were 116,000,000,000 vehicle-km. and 56,000,000,000 ton-km. West Germany, with 1,083,600 vehicles, 414,000 trailers, and 35,700 semitrailers, recorded a substantial increase, from 25,600,000,000 vehicle-km. in 1968 to 26,250,000,000 vehicle-km. in 1969, and from 70,800,000,000 ton-km. to 76,440,000,000 ton-km. The U.K., with 1,564,000 freight-carrying vehicles, reported only a small increase in total distance, 36,500,000,000 vehicle-km. in 1968 and 36,650,000,000 in 1969. Distances traveled per vehicle varied greatly between different countries, West Germany registering 25,000 km. per vehicle per year, the U.K. 22,000 km., and France only 10,900 km. These European figures compared with 40,000 km. per vehicle per year in Canada and 19,000 km. in the U.S. In the U.S.S.R. freight by motor transport, which rose by 6% in 1969, rose further in 1970, with the 1,796,000,000 tons carried in the first six months of 1970 representing an increase of 6% over the same period of 1969. Final figures for the U.S. for 1968 showed that trucks hauled 415,000,000,000 ton-mi. of intercity freight, equal to about 23% of the total for such traffic. A further increase during 1969 was expected.

In commercial road passenger transport, governments attempted to stem the loss of passengers by improved service. In order to accomplish this they sought to give preferential treatment to buses, and to subsidize new equipment and services as well as operation of nonremunerative services. The ECMT sought to liberalize international coach and bus transport.

On a far smaller scale, in the U.K., a bus demonstration program was aimed at raising the quality of service by improving the reliability of scheduled services and journey times. The projects included exemption from one-way street systems and turning bans, reserved lanes for buses, special phases for buses at traffic lights, electronic control of bus fleets, and provision of special express services. Responsibility for the London Transport Board was transferred to the Greater London Council after Jan. 1, 1970. Despite these measures, in most countries the decline in public patronage continued, although at a decelerating rate; consequently, losses were greater, charges were increased, and subsidies became necessary.

A.F.P. FROM PICTORIAL PARADE

At Paris police headquarters television screens show the city's areas of congested traffic. At right is André Ducret, director of traffic.

PIPELINES

The extension of natural-gas pipelines accelerated during 1969–70, far outpacing crude-oil and products line construction. In Western Europe, where 762 km. of crude-oil lines were under construction and another 816 km. planned or under study, 3,606 km. of natural-gas lines were being built and 1,114 km. were planned or being considered. The U.S.S.R. led in both types, total gas lines reaching over 63,000 km. in 1970, through which 45,000,000,000 cu.m. were transmitted during the first quarter of 1970. The Soviet Union's construction plans for 1970 called for the completion of the Astara–Karadag line, the extension of the Transcaucasian network by another 400 km., the completion of the line from Kiev to the western regions of the Ukraine, and the construction of another 500 km. of pipeline in Kirghizstan and Kazakhstan. The program also provided for laying an 830-km. second pipeline from Soviet Central Asia to the centre of the European U.S.S.R., and a 550-km. second line along the Vuktyl–Ukhta–Torzhok trunk route in Siberia. The most ambitious project was the Severny (Northern) system, to be laid over ten years for the transport of Siberian gas and which would consist of four parallel lines running westward for more than 2,000 km. from Nadym in the Tyumen area. Altogether, the total system would have a length of 37,000 km. and cost about $8,640,000,000. Another Soviet project was to transmit gas via Romania to the town of General Toshevo in northeastern Bulgaria and thence to Pleven, Sofia, and Plovdiv. In the reverse direction, gas from Iran was to be transported to the southern provinces of the U.S.S.R. The line was to run 1,127 km. from gas fields in southern Iran to Astara beside the Caspian Sea.

In Europe a 370-km. pipeline from the Czechoslovak border at Bratislava across Austria to Tarvisio in northeastern Italy was to connect with the Ente Nazionale Idrocarburi (ENI) network by 1973. The

87-km. line from Cortemaggiore to La Spezia was completed, linking the Po Valley with Panigaglia, where Libyan gas arrived. In France a 250-km., 24-in. line was planned along the Rhône Valley to an underground storage area at Tersanne, and from there to Lyons to join the Aquitaine gas network. In the Netherlands work started on a 193-km. line from the Bergen gas field to the West German border, and in the U.K. a 827-km. line was being built for gas from the offshore fields.

In North and South America the position was similar. The main concern was the bringing of oil and gas from Alaska to main centres of consumption, but all the major projects of the contenders offering to build crude-oil and gas lines awaited authorization by the U.S. and Canadian governments. In the U.S. the proposed 800-mi. line from Prudhoe Bay via Fairbanks and the Yukon to Valdez was still held up in 1970 by the Department of the Interior, which required satisfaction that it could be constructed without threatening Alaskan ecology. Construction was planned to begin in 1971 on the first section of the proposed Canadian 1,550-mi. natural-gas line from Alaska's North Slope through Canada to U.S. markets.

In Argentina the 570-km., 24-in. line from gas fields in Neuquén to Bahía Blanca to join the existing line from Patagonia to Buenos Aires was under construction. Australia had several gas lines under construction or in the planning stage, but only one project for a new crude-oil pipeline was reported. The largest project was for a gas pipeline from Gippsland to Sydney and Newcastle with branches to Canberra, Wagga Wagga, and Albury.

With the rapid rise in the use of ethylene in Western Europe, the major chemical companies were linking their plants by pipeline to balance fluctuations in supply and demand. The grid was to link major producers and users of ethylene in the Netherlands, West Germany, Belgium, and France. In the U.K. several such lines already served the ethylene plants. In Italy, in the spring, the Ravenna–Chieti methane pipeline came into operation. This directly connected the north-central Italian gas pipeline network with that of the Mezzogiorno and was more than 300 km. long.

Among major crude-oil pipelines scheduled were those for the network from the Mediterranean ports to France, West Germany, and Switzerland. The system had a capacity of 67 million tons a year, estimated to be inadequate by 1972. To meet the future demand the main expansion was to be in the southern European sections, where the overall capacity would ultimately be trebled.

In Yugoslavia negotiations took place for a line from the seaport of Bakar near Rijeka to serve eastern central Europe. Work was scheduled to start in 1970, with completion in 1973. A crude-oil line was also to be built from Salonika to Skopje. A 350-km. line was planned in Bulgaria to serve the refinery at Yasen near Pleven from Shabla on the Black Sea. In Hungary work started on the Hungarian sector of the new Druzhba II pipeline, to bring additional Soviet crude oil to Hungary. Agreement was also reached on the Polish and East German sections. In the U.S.S.R. rapid expansion of crude-oil and products trunk pipelines was under way, with total length approaching 40,000 km.

In the Middle East, Turkey and Iran agreed on the joint construction of 1,707 km. of pipeline to transport crude oil from Ahvaz in Iran to the Turkish port of Iskenderun on the Mediterranean. Israel's line from the Gulf of Aqaba to Ascalon on the Mediterranean came into operation in February.

In Africa, the chief projects were in conjunction with the Nigerian oil fields, where new pipelines were under construction in the Rivers State swamp area to link up with the fields west of the Bonny River.

Japan began a long-term plan for a nationwide pipeline system from the three main terminals of Tateyama, Wakayama, and Aomori to serve the principal refining centres.

In the U.S. approval was given for construction of a 1,300-mi. products line from the Gulf Coast to the Chicago area at a cost of $200 million, with completion scheduled for 1972. In South America, Argentina, Ecuador, Peru, and Chile completed or continued work on a number of crude-oil pipelines.

RAILWAYS

The major progress in 1970 was in the achievement of higher speeds on scheduled routes. Railway investment took place mainly in projects involving better installations and lower labour and equipment costs. These were accomplished by such means as welded rails, replacement of obsolete control boxes by modern centralized units, modernization or replacement of level crossings, modernization and concentration of marshaling yards, and installation of container terminals. Centrally controlled multiple aspect signaling, with its advantages of increased line capacity, higher speeds, increased safety, and saving in manpower, was further extended. British Rail had 11,270 km. of track so controlled.

In Europe, British Rail ran the largest number of high-speed trains, but France led with maximum speeds on particular runs. Gas-turbine trains ran between Paris and Caen and Cherbourg beginning in March 1970, and on two more routes in June, averaging about 130 kmph (80 mph).

Canadian National Railways' Turbotrain was withdrawn because of teething troubles in January 1969, but was reintroduced in May 1970 on the Toronto–Montreal run, covering the 333 mi. in 4 hr. 5 min. Development continued in the U.K. on the Advanced Passenger Train (APT), scheduled for its first test runs in mid-1971 on the 14-mi. test track. This lightweight train, powered by a gas turbine and with a completely new form of suspension, was designed to operate at 125 to 150 mph on existing tracks and within the capabilities of signaling. A U.S. company acquired rights for exploitation in that country. Development continued on tracked air cushion vehicles. A French Hovercraft prototype driven by an airscrew traveled experimentally at 180 mph, and a British system powered by a linear induction motor was being developed.

Automatic coupling for freight trains was scheduled for adoption on European railways before the end of the 1970s. Main advances in freight operation included an increase in block trains between private sidings, giving improved viability and performance of freight-car load traffic, and faster container trains with improved on- and off-loading facilities. For example, British Rail by mid-1970 operated 23 freight-liner terminals connected by 142 services on 61 rail routes serving the principal industrial and port areas.

There were few new construction projects, but in Japan the building of a nationwide high-speed trunk-line network of 7,200 km. was in progress on the 165-km. extension of the Tokaido line from Osaka to Okayama. The line was to be extended to Hakata by 1975, and eventually to Kyushu. Korean National Railways received a $40 million loan for new construction and modernization. The Western Pakistan railway planned construction of five broad-gauge lines of 370 km., and India's 1970 program provided for the conversion of 4,569 km., making 50% of its railways broad gauge.

The principal European project planned was the construction of a high-speed line of 258 km. for speeds up to 250 kmph (155 mph) between Rome and Florence. In the U.S.S.R., 1,250 km. of new track or of doubling existing track, and 37 railroad construction projects with a total length of 4,900 km. were scheduled to go into commission. These included lines of considerable economic importance; for instance, the area between the North Urals and the Ob, where the 370-km. Ivdel–Ob trunk line was built, had previously been inaccessible because of marshy ground in summer and hard frost in winter.

Work was completed in Malawi on the line to the Mozambique border linking with the Mozambique system at Port Nacala. The East African Railway received a loan of $42.4 million to finance in part its 1969–72 development program of $90.8 million. Work was inaugurated on the Tanzam railway in October 1970, to have a 3-ft. 6-in gauge throughout its 1,000 mi. The junction with the Zambia railways, which would be extended right into Dar es Salaam harbour, was to be at Kapiri Mposhi, from where it would go south of the Uluguru Mountains and up the Kilombero Valley to Mbeya, thereby opening up southern Tanzania. China was advancing an interest-free loan repayable over 30 years amounting to about $406 million, and would be responsible for constructing the line.

The change to electric and diesel traction continued. The U.S.S.R. led with 32,000 km. converted by the end of 1969, about 24% of its system. Romania completed electrification of the route via the Iron Gates, Craiova through Filiasi, and Turnu to Orsova. Yugoslavia established full electric service between Zagreb and Belgrade. Austria completed electrification connecting Selzthal, Hieflau, and Eisenerz. In the U.K., British Rail was authorized to spend £25 million electrifying the west coast main line from Crewe, completing the 646-km. route between London and Glasgow and reducing journey time from five to four hours when completed in 1974. France budgeted Fr. 120 million for further electrification of the SNCF network. Sections completed in 1969–70 included the southern end of the Bourg-to-Dijon and the Paris-to-Ventimiglia lines. An indication of the progress of electrification in Europe was provided by figures for the members of the European Economic Community. Between 1953 and 1968 the share of gross ton-kilometres accounted for by steam traction had dropped from 70 to 11%, while electric traction's share rose from 28 to 72%, even though only 30% of the total network was electrified.

The most spectacular conversion to standard gauge was marked by the inauguration of the "Indian-Pacific" train on its Sydney–Perth 3,962-km. run in February 1970. This meant completion of a unified gauge spanning the Australian continent, and was the most ambitious conversion in Australian railway history.

Closings of uneconomic lines, though fewer, continued. The streamlining of systems in Europe was evidenced by the reduction of the overall length in

SOCIÉTÉ DE L'AÉROTRAIN

The first 180-mph hovertrain of the Société de l'Aérotrain makes a trial run near Orléans, France.

ECMT member countries. Their combined networks fell from 196,000 km. in 1953 to 177,344 km. at the end of 1968, of which the U.K. accounted for a reduction of 35%, Sweden 19%, and Belgium 14%.

Rising costs made higher charges general. Some deficits were reduced, and a few systems reported surpluses. In the U.K. the reconstruction of British Rail's finances at the beginning of 1969, with £1,532,-000,000 of accumulated government loans written off, enabled the board to report a working surplus of £56 million. Canadian National's deficit, the smallest since 1966, was $24.6 million. U.S. railways increased their total ton-miles by 3% but were unable to operate profitably; reasons given included inequitable taxation, regulation that strangled enterprise, and rules that required surplus employees. In June the Penn Central Transportation Co., with a loss of $149.4 million for the first six months of 1970, filed a petition in bankruptcy following unsuccessful attempts to persuade Congress to withdraw its opposition to a government loan of $200 million. In February 1970 the merger of the Great Northern Railway and the Northern Pacific Railway (collectively called the Northern Lines) and three of their subsidiaries was approved by the Supreme Court after ten years' legal process and became the largest system (26,509 mi.) in the United States.

Late in November the U.S. government revealed its long-range plan to help shore up the financially ailing intercity passenger network. In the spring of 1971 the new National Railroad Corp., a quasi-governmental organization, would take over the operation and maintenance of intercity service. The number of trains in daily operation would be reduced to about 150, as compared with the nearly 500 at the end of 1969 and the 20,000 in the late 1920s. The plan was submitted to the railroads, railroad unions, and federal and state regulatory bodies for their criticisms. The U.S. railways received another blow when a labour-union strike caused almost all operations to cease for one day, on December 10. Congressional action brought the unions back to work, but the basic issues remained unresolved.   (E. A. J. D.)

WATER TRANSPORTATION

Shipping. The boom in world shipping, which a year or two previously many were predicting would turn into slump in the early 1970s as a result of over-ordering in the late 1960s, continued unabated. Heavy deliveries from the shipyards failed either to bring freight rates down or to dissuade owners from continuing to order new ships at a rate that threatened to book the world shipbuilding industry solid until 1973.

During the height of summer, when oil tanker freights are usually seasonally low, the oil companies were having to pay rates that gave owners of big

250,000-ton tankers up to 700% profit on a voyage. Dry cargo rates, while not matching those for tankers, remained firm, and the glut in cargo liners that was expected to develop in the wake of containerization failed to materialize.

The chief factor that lay behind this unexpected turn of events was a growth in world trade greater than shipowners had budgeted for. The global volume of trade, and actual and likely changes from year to year, were matters about which there was little precise information, and even imprecise information was usually available only some years after the event. Shipowners' estimates of future prospects, on the basis of which they decided to build or not to build new ships, were often based on hunch, or on fairly informed estimates within a particular trade where statistical trends were more easily observable.

With the net addition to world shipping currently approaching 10% a year, the growth in trade volume had evidently been greater than that, taking into account the extra speed and efficiency of new ships over old. According to some calculations, this rate would continue to grow and, on the basis of projections to the year 2000, the world fleet needed to cope with the predicted trade flow could be between five and ten times its existing volume of about 220 million tons.

Turning to more detailed reasons for the flourishing state of shipping, the Suez Canal remained closed (although the prospect of a reopening seemed momentarily nearer at the start of the 1970 canal zone cease-fire), and so did the Trans-Arabian pipeline. For the first time, increasing public objection to pollution had an effect on shipping as some countries, led by the U.S. and Japan, began selective buying of oil with low sulfur content; in some cases this necessitated longer hauls in a period of short supply. The mysterious explosions in three supertankers at the end of 1969 imposed restrictions on tank-washing, and therefore capacity, in those very large ships.

Liberia continued to head the world shipping table, followed by Japan, the U.K., and Norway. Current orders were expected to confirm Liberia's lead, but a noteworthy feature of the previous two years had been the substantial ordering of new tonnage by the traditionally cautious British owners, which could recover for them the second place ceded to Japan in 1969.

Particular growth areas were bulk carriers, short-sea ferries, and passenger ships. Of the last-named, after several years of eclipse, more than 20 were being built or on order, largely for Norwegian owners for operation in the lucrative New York and Caribbean cruise trades.

In the general cargo trades, new container ships continued to predominate, despite overtonnaging on both the Atlantic and Pacific routes. Integrated container services were established between Europe and Australia, and Australia and Japan, and ships were being built for Europe-to-Far East and transpacific use.

Nuclear power for merchant shipping suffered a setback when Japan, after completing one vessel, decided that it was premature to begin work on another. Japan concluded that more land-based research was needed to make nuclear ships economic, thus confirming the view consistently held by Britain during a period when the U.S., West Germany, and Japan all built these vessels experimentally and at considerable cost. (M. By.)

Hovercraft. While the British industry consolidated its position during the year, with no new craft being announced, the U.S. industry began for the first time to develop projects of its own, mainly encouraged by military requirements. In Britain, which retained the monopoly on regularly scheduled Hovercraft services, manufacturers concentrated on improving the performance and economics of their craft. The 165-ton Mountbatten-class craft operating between Britain and France had overall reliability rates of about 96% and carried nearly a million passengers and 100,000 cars during the year. This represented almost one-fifth of cross-Channel car ferry traffic through the two continental ports involved, indicating the popularity of the newer transport medium. On other routes, mainly between the Isle of Wight and the English mainland, older, smaller, Winchester-class craft carrying up to 38 passengers operated with reliability rates better than 99%. The other important British craft, the Vosper Thornycroft VT1, was still being tested during the year, although it was hoped to put two into commercial service in 1971.

U.S. interest in Hovercraft began to burgeon, with a competition between Bell Aerospace and Aerojet-General to build prototypes of two sizes of amphibious assault landing craft on behalf of the U.S. Navy. Bell won both contracts and unveiled a full-scale mock-up of the bigger craft in November. Both companies were also busy working on prototype 100-ton surface-effect-ship (SES) models and were expecting to start trials in 1971. While the SES had rigid sidewalls, the assault landing craft were fully amphibious and both Bell and Aerojet produced designs for a civil version for use primarily on Alaska's North Slope. There the oil industry had a requirement for surface transport for surveying and logistic work over ground that by law could not be traveled over by vehicles having a footprint pressure great enough to break birds' eggs in their nests. Another new U.S. company, Transportation Technology, Inc., based in Texas, also produced designs and a prototype for this work, as well as buying into the British air-cushion vehicle (ACV) industry by taking over the assets of Hovermarine Ltd., the sidewall Hovercraft manufacturer that had technical problems with its originally successful medium-sized passenger ferry craft; the U.S. company worked hard during the year to put Hovermarine back on its feet.

Two other countries, France and Australia, continued to show interest in manufacturing Hovercraft. The French government allocated funds to Sedam to build its N.500 craft, which would be the equivalent of the British Mountbatten class, carrying cars as well as passengers; in Oceania several smaller companies were set up to manufacture utility and light craft in the two- to ten-seat range. (J. B. Be.)

Docks and Harbours. Extensive plans were made by operators in 1970 to cope with larger vessels, especially tankers. Ships up to 500,000 tons deadweight (dwt) were envisaged, and the word "megatonner" was coined to describe them. Provision of berths for the growing proportion of containerized and bulk shipments continued, but on a decreasing scale. A new development was the provision of facilities for barge-carrying oceangoing ships (see above). The Japanese government announced a project for a giant sea berth for oil tankers in the middle of Tokyo Bay with submarine pipelines linked to coastal depots. Le Havre, already receiving tankers of 200,000 dwt, was chosen by the French government as the terminal for the largest tankers yet conceived, from 500,000 to 1 million dwt.

Work began at Rotterdam-Europoort on a new harbour at the Hook of Holland to replace by 1975 the existing "New Waterway" tidal channel. The Port of London Authority made feasibility studies for developments downstream in the Thames estuary to accommodate the largest vessels.

In the Port of New York construction of an additional 3,700 ft. of berth space was authorized to complete the development of the Elizabeth facility. When completed in 1973, 16,850 ft. of berthing space to accommodate 25 container ships would be available. At Long Beach, Calif., one of the largest yet container terminals, to be operational by 1975, was planned. Baltimore produced a revised master plan involving expenditure of $58.9 million for expansion of container facilities during the next seven years.

At Antwerp extensions to dock areas were planned. Another Belgian project was a new maritime lock to accommodate ships up to 125,000 dwt at Zeebrugge, to be begun in 1971. The Italian government approved plans for a new port at Manfredonia on the southeastern coast, able to handle four million tons of dry and liquid cargoes by 1973. In West Germany, at Kiel, a new deepwater port on the Kiel–Ostsee canal was planned, and at Bremerhaven a new container terminal on the outer Weser, with two berths, was under construction. Spain had in construction at Tarragona a new breakwater 1.2 km. long, to increase the port capacity by 25% and accommodate tankers up to 300,000 dwt. A new dock for containers was being built at Seville.

The £35 million U.K. Seaforth project progressed and was scheduled to be operational by 1971 with ten deepwater berths. Nearby, the Tranmere oil terminal was reconstructed to take 200,000-ton tankers. In May Queen Elizabeth II opened at Port Talbot the first new harbour to be completed in Britain in the 20th century. Constructed at a cost of £20 million, it was capable of taking 100,000-ton dry cargo vessels and was designed mainly for iron-ore imports. Greenock, Scot., planned a £1,250,000 extension to the Clydeport container terminal, and at Grangemouth approval was given for a £9 million modernization of the pier.

In Asia major developments in India and Singapore were under way. The new port of Haldi on the Hooghly River, 93 km. from Calcutta, with access for 80,000-ton ships, neared completion. Work at Vishakhapatnam provided for future handling of 100,000-ton ore carriers. In Japan the port of Kashima was opened. It was claimed to be the world's largest man-made harbour, surpassing Rotterdam in size, and upon completion, scheduled for 1973, it would be able to accommodate 100 ships at a time.

Australia's main development was the construction of a new multimillion-dollar port on Darwin's eastern arm. The iron-ore port, Port Hedland, 1,000 mi. N of Perth, became Australia's biggest harbour in terms of cargo weight.

In Africa a new deepwater harbour to cost R 200 million was planned at Richard's Bay in South Africa, for tankers of 200,000 tons. At Durban, S.Af., a new tanker berth at Island View was added to the two existing berths. At Dar es Salaam in Tanzania the extension of deepwater berths and conversion of two of the eight for container traffic was scheduled in anticipation of increased traffic arising from the construction of the Tanzam Railway.

UPI COMPIX

A 35-ft. hydrofoil passes under the Brooklyn Bridge during a test run in April 1970. The craft is to be used by commuters on the waterways surrounding the New York City area.

In terms of trade, the Port of New York Authority handled 10,356,827 long tons of general cargo in 1969 against 9,981,904 in 1968, an increase of 15%. Rotterdam increased its lead with international freight traffic passing through the port totaling 182,646,000 tons in 1969, compared with 158,899,000 in 1968. The first six months of 1970 showed an increase of 15.5 million tons. Antwerp recorded 73,020,300 tons of shipping passing through the port in 1969, against 72,433,113 tons in 1968, and continued to register rises in 1970. Le Havre achieved a record tonnage of 69,870,000. The Port of London Authority experienced a decline in 1969, with shipping tonnage of 30.1 million, compared with 30.2 million in 1968; total trade declined by 3% from 60,080,000 tons in 1968 to 58,020,000 tons in 1969. The Mersey Docks and Harbour Board had a decrease of 2% with 26,835,943 tons in 1969. In December 1970 it faced a financial crisis when the government refused to cover deficiencies of some £20 million over a three-year period.

Inland Waterways. The upward trend in inland waterway traffic continued and extended into 1970, international traffic in Europe rising more steeply than internal. France transported on its inland waterways a record volume of 109,650,000 tons of freight in 1969, up 8% from 1968. Belgium and Italy both increased their carryings, as did the Netherlands, with 52.2 million tons alone passing through Rotterdam to the Rhine during the year. At the West German–Netherlands frontier, Emmerich-Lobith, the annual increase was about 13% during the first six months of 1969. In the U.K. tons carried fell by 7% to 6,370,000. In the U.S.S.R., 3% more tons were carried, and an additional rise of 16% in tons carried and 20% in ton-kilometres took place in the first six months of 1970.

U.S. water transportation expanded in 1969 and 1970, following the record year of 1968. The network of navigable rivers and canals carried about 520 million tons of freight annually. The Mississippi alone was registering approximately 60 ton-mi. a year, and the Ohio carried 145 million tons of freight. The boom continued well into 1970, and for the three months ending March 1970 revenue ton-miles for

Atlantic and Gulf Coast, Great Lakes, Mississippi River and tributaries, Pacific Coast, and Intracoastal Waterways increased from 11,594,000,000 in March 1969 to 15,286,000,000 in 1970. Shipments of iron ore, coal, and grain on the Great Lakes totaled 19 million net tons during July 1970, the largest monthly volume for the three commodities since 1966.

Due largely to labour disputes and lower exports of grain, traffic on the St. Lawrence Seaway was considerably less during the 1969 season than in 1968. On the Montreal–Lake Ontario section transits declined 2.8%, and total cargo tonnage by 14.5%. On the Welland section, transits fell 4.7% and cargo 7.8%. The combined total cargo tonnage for both sections was 60.8 million, carried by 9,094 ship transits. Of this total, 46 million tons were domestic and 14.8 million foreign traffic. Oceangoing ships carried 24.2% and lakers 75.8%. Business improved during the 1970 season, and up to June transits on the Montreal–Lake Ontario section rose by 3.3% and on the Welland section by 2.1%.

Cargo through the Panama Canal established a new record during the first nine months of fiscal 1970 with 87 million long tons carried.

In Europe, on the Dunkerque–Scheldt link and its international extensions, additional improvements were made in 1969, work being done between Denain and Valenciennes and downstream near Condé, while on the Belgian side improvements to the Upper Scheldt continued. On the Scheldt–Rhine link the new lock system from Antwerp to Volkerak Dike came into service. On the Meuse below Liège, and on the Dutch side the widening of the Juliana Canal and several new locks were completed. The canalization of the Moselle as far as the section below Metz was achieved.

The completion of the works on the Arkansas River in the U.S. enabled it to be opened to barge navigation. The cross-Florida canal, which would cut the distance from the Gulf to the Atlantic by 700 mi., neared completion. (E. A. J. D.)

See also Cities and Urban Affairs; Engineering Projects; Industrial Review.

ENCYCLOPÆDIA BRITANNICA FILMS. *The Living City* (1953); *Inland Waterways* (1956); *Development of Transportation* (1958); *The Gasoline Age* (1958); *The Steam Age* (1958); *The St. Lawrence Seaway* (1959); *The Panama Canal* (1961); *The Suez Canal* (1962); *Our Shrinking World—Jet Pilot* (1964); *The Mississippi System: Waterway of Commerce* (1970); *Rotterdam—Europoort, Gateway to Europe* (1970).

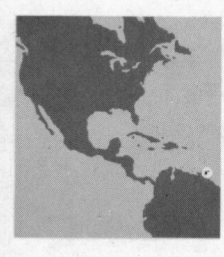

Trinidad and Tobago

A parliamentary state and a member of the Commonwealth of Nations, Trinidad and Tobago consists of two islands off the coast of Venezuela, north of the Orinoco River delta. Area: 1,980 sq.mi. (5,128 sq.km.). Pop. (1968 est.): 1,030,000, including (1960) Negro 43.3%; East Indian 36.5%; mixed 16.3%. Cap. and largest city: Port-of-Spain (pop., 1965 est., 85,-100). Language: English (official); Hindi, French, Spanish. Religion (1960): Christian 66%; Hindu 23%; Muslim 6%. Queen, Elizabeth II; governor-general in 1970, Sir Solomon Hochoy; prime minister, Eric Williams.

From September 1969 there had been signs of impending crisis, sparked off by objections to racial discrimination at home and abroad. The actual outbreaks, which reached their peak between Feb. 26 and April 21, 1970, began with demonstrations on behalf

of citizens deported and fined for antiracial demonstrations at a Canadian university. These spread to many Indians, who joined what started as a young urban Negro protest. Trouble also affected the Army and, following an alleged army mutiny, a state of emergency was proclaimed until November 20. The government sought reinforcement from other Commonwealth Caribbean countries and from Venezuela, which helped to end the crisis, at least on the surface.

Results of the disturbances were apparent in politics and the economy. The ruling People's National Movement drew up a new program meant to give black people a share in the economy reflecting their numbers and political power, and a Public Order Bill was withdrawn after a massive display of public feeling. (Ra. R.)

ENCYCLOPÆDIA BRITANNICA FILMS. *The West Indies* (1965).

TRINIDAD AND TOBAGO
Education. (1966–67) Primary, pupils 227,361, teachers 6,311; secondary, pupils 43,551, teachers 1,174; vocational, pupils 2,139; teachers (1963–64) 122; higher, students 964, teaching staff (1965–66) 120.
Finance and Trade. Monetary unit: Trinidad and Tobago dollar, with an exchange rate of TT$2 to U.S. $1 (TT$4.80 = £1 sterling). Budget (1970 est.): revenue TT$295.2 million; expenditure (recurrent) TT$277.2 million. Foreign trade (1969): imports TT$965.4 million; exports TT$949.2 million. Import sources: Venezuela 36%; U.K. 14%; Saudi Arabia 6%. Export destinations: U.S. 47%; U.K. 10%; Sweden 6%. Main exports: petroleum and products 77%; sugar 6%; ship and aircraft bunkers 5%.
Transport and Communications. Roads (1968) 4,868 km. Motor vehicles in use (1968): passenger 67,600; commercial (including buses) 18,800. Air traffic (1969): 416.8 million passenger-km.; freight 9,259,000 net ton-km. Shipping traffic (1968) goods loaded 20,776,000 metric tons, unloaded 13,762,000 metric tons. Telephones (Jan. 1969) 49,030. Radio receivers (Dec. 1968) 169,000. Television receivers (Dec. 1968) 41,000.
Agriculture. Production (in 000; metric tons; 1968; 1967 in parentheses): rice *c.* 10 (*c.* 10); sweet potatoes *c.* 18 (18); oranges 11 (9); grapefruit 16 (18); sugar, raw value (1969–70) *c.* 216, (1968–69) 244; copra *c.* 13 (*c.* 13). Livestock (in 000; 1967–68): cattle *c.* 59; pigs *c.* 46; sheep 11; goats *c.* 33; poultry *c.* 980.
Industry. Production (in 000; metric tons; 1969): crude oil 8,125; petroleum products 20,545; cement 244; asphalt (1968) 139; electricity (kw-hr.) 1,213,-000.

Tunisia

A republic of North Africa, lying on the Mediterranean Sea, Tunisia is bounded by Algeria and Libya. Area: 63,-378 sq.mi. (164,150 sq.km.). Pop. (1969 est.): 5,027,000. Cap. and largest city: Tunis (pop., 1966, 468,997). Language: Arabic (official). Religion: Muslim; Jewish and Christian minorities. President in 1970, Habib Bourguiba; prime ministers, Bahi Ladgham and, from November 2, Hedi Nouira.

The main political event of the year was the trial of Ahmed ben Salah, former secretary of state for economy, planning, and education and a supporter of socialization of the Tunisian economy, accused of high treason and abuse of authority. The case came before a specially constituted High Court in Tunis on May 19. Witnesses for the prosecution included peasants who gave evidence against Ben Salah's enforced col-

TUNISIA

Education. (1967–68) Primary, pupils 826,069, teachers (state only) 15,188; secondary, pupils 81,717; vocational; pupils 45,595; secondary and vocational (state only; 1965–66), teachers 1,293; teacher training, students 7,297; higher (at University of Tunis), students 7,336.

Finance. Monetary unit: Tunisian dinar, with a parity of 0.52 dinars = U.S. $1 (1.26 dinars = £1 sterling). Gold, SDRs, and foreign exchange, central bank: (June 1970) U.S. $53.3 million; (June 1969) U.S. $29.9 million. Budget (1969 rev. est.) balanced at 132 million dinars. Gross national product: (1968) 550.1 million dinars; (1967) 511.1 million dinars. Money supply: (June 1970) 191,370,000 dinars; (June 1969) 170,320,000 dinars. Cost of living (Tunis; 1963 = 100): (June 1970) 125; (June 1969) 128.

Foreign Trade. (1969) Imports 134,560,000 dinars; exports 86,960,000 dinars. Import sources (1968): France 33%; U.S. 20%; Italy 10%; West Germany 9%. Export destinations (1968): France 23%; West Germany 11%; Italy 11%; Libya 8%; Switzerland 6%; Bulgaria 6%; Poland 5%. Main exports: crude oil 24%; phosphates 20%; olive oil 11%. Tourism (1968): visitors 330,300; gross receipts U.S. $45 million.

Transport and Communications. Roads (1969) 17,786 km. Motor vehicles in use (1969): passenger 62,256; commercial 33,028. Railways: (1967) 2,021 km.; traffic (1969) 446 million passenger-km., freight 1,147,000,000 net ton-km. Air traffic (1968): 177,-773,000 passenger-km.; freight 1,996,000 net ton-km. Telephones (Dec. 1968) 61,923. Radio receivers (Dec. 1968) 450,000. Television receivers (Dec. 1968) 37,-000.

Agriculture. Production (in 000; metric tons; 1969; 1968 in parentheses): wheat *c.* 370 (383); barley (1968) 130, (1967) 70; tomatoes (1968) *c.* 124, (1967) 117; wine (1968) *c.* 95, (1967) 93; dates (1968) *c.* 60, (1967) 39; figs (1968) 19, (1967) 20; olive oil *c.* 26 (59); oranges *c.* 67 (83); lemons *c.* 8 (14). Livestock (in 000; 1968–69): sheep *c.* 3,300; cattle *c.* 600; goats (1967–68) *c.* 480; camels (1967–68) *c.* 220; poultry (1967–68) *c.* 7,000.

Industry. Production (in 000; metric tons; 1969): iron ore (55% metal content) 946; phosphate rock (1968) 3,361; lead 16; cement 602; sulfuric acid (1968) 421; electricity (public supply; kw-hr.) 624,-000.

lectivization policy. He was sentenced to ten years at hard labour.

In June, President Bourguiba returned to Tunisia after six months' medical treatment abroad. Shortly afterward, Prime Minister Ladgham formed a government of national unity. Following Ladgham's appointment as head of the Arab Ceasefire Observer Mission in Jordan, Economics Minister Hedi Nouira became prime minister in the autumn.

U.S. Secretary of State William Rogers' official visit to Tunis in February was marked by hostile student demonstrations. While expressing regret at the demonstrations, Ladgham described the supply of U.S. arms to Israel as a provocation to the Arabs and an encouragement to continued Israeli aggression. However, he also stated that their very different positions with regard to the Middle East situation did not preclude the U.S. and Tunisia from regarding one another as friends. In September, Italian Foreign Minister Aldo Moro paid an official visit to Tunisia.

The work of the joint military commission engaged in solving frontier problems between Tunisia and Algeria was brought to a satisfactory conclusion with the signing on May 17 of the final proceedings on the delineation of the frontier. The document was signed in accordance with the treaty of friendship and co-operation signed in January and an agreement on frontier delineation signed at the same time. The treaty was to be valid for 20 years and would be automatically renewable unless canceled by one or other of the parties by a written request at least one year prior to the date of expiration. (PH. D.)

Turkey

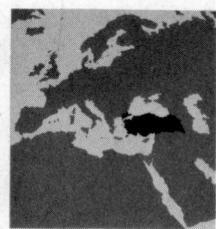

A republic of southeastern Europe and Asia Minor, Turkey is bounded by the Aegean Sea, the Black Sea, the U.S.S.R., Iran, Iraq, Syria, the Mediterranean Sea, Greece, and Bulgaria. Area: 301,380 sq.mi. (780,-576 sq.km.), including 9,158 sq.mi. in Europe. Pop. (1970 est.): 35,232,000. Cap.: Ankara (pop., 1969 est., 1,157,000). Largest city: Istanbul (pop., 1969 est., 1,979,000). Language: Turkish 90.7%; Kurdish 6.7%; Arabic 1.3%. Religion: predominantly Muslim. President in 1970, Gen. Cevdet Sunay; prime minister, Suleyman Demirel.

During 1970 Prime Minister Demirel was assailed from right and left, but he succeeded in reconstituting his administration and went on to carry out major economic and social reforms. The enemies of Demirel's Justice Party and of Parliament were given an opening by the dissatisfaction felt by his right-wing colleagues at their exclusion from the new government, formed after the 1969 election. On January 17, 72 Justice Party parliamentarians signed a memorandum demanding that dissidents not be expelled from the party. When, nevertheless, five deputies and one senator were expelled, seven members of the party executive resigned, and on February 11, 41 Justice Party deputies voted against the budget, securing its rejection by the National Assembly. Demirel resigned on February 14, but was asked by President Sunay to form a new government. After an interval, during which he split the dissidents and recruited another eight deputies into his party, Demirel presented the outgoing administration to the Assembly and, on

TURKEY

Education. (1967–68) Primary, pupils 4,509,433, teachers 102,041; secondary, pupils 755,671, teachers 27,283; vocational, pupils 146,235, teachers 10,867; teacher training, students 57,788, teachers 2,040; higher (including 8 universities), students 125,547, teaching staff 6,726.

Finance. Monetary unit: Turkish pound or lira, with a par value (following devaluation of Aug. 9, 1970) of 15 lire to U.S. $1 (36 lire = £1 sterling). Gold, SDRs, and foreign exchange, central bank: (June 1970) U.S. $218 million; (June 1969) U.S. $149 million. Budget (1969–70 est.): revenue 24,497,364,000 lire; expenditure 25,696,976,000 lire. Gross national product: (1968) 114,750,000,000 lire; (1967) 104 billion lire. Money supply: (May 1970) 13,860,000,000 lire; (May 1969) 12,750,000,000 lire. Cost of living (Istanbul; 1963 = 100): (March 1970) 152; (March 1969) 142.

Foreign Trade. (1969) Imports 6,785,000,000 lire; exports 4,832,000,000 lire. Import sources: West Germany 19%; U.S. 17%; U.K. 12%; Italy 10%. Export destinations: West Germany 21%; U.S. 11%; Italy 8%; U.K. 6%; U.S.S.R. 6%; Switzerland 5%; France 5%. Main exports: cotton 21%; hazelnuts 20%; tobacco 15%.

Transport and Communications. Roads (1968) *c.* 70,000 km. (including *c.* 32,000 km. main roads). Motor vehicles in use (1968): passenger 128,900; commercial 105,900. Railways (1968): 8,008 km.; traffic 4,538,000,000 passenger-km., freight 5,245,000,000 net ton-km. Air traffic (1969): 639.6 million passenger-km.; freight 4,434,000 net ton-km. Shipping (1969): merchant vessels 100 gross tons and over 312; gross tonnage 651,325. Telephones (Dec. 1968) 450,485. Radio receivers (Dec. 1968) 2,933,000. Television receivers (Dec. 1966) 2,500.

Agriculture. Production (in 000; metric tons; 1969; 1968 in parentheses): corn *c.* 1,100 (1,000); rye *c.* 825 (820); wheat (including spelt; 1968) 9,603, (1967) 10,110; barley (1968) 3,560, (1967) 3,800; oats *c.* 480 (450); onions (1968) 525, (1967) 550; potatoes (1968) 1,805, (1967) 1,760; sunflower seed (1968) 230, (1967) 230; chick-peas (1968) 102, (1967) 97; dry beans (1968) 137, (1967) 142; lentils (1968) 96, (1967) 106; oranges (1968) 542, (1967) 451; apples (1968) 700, (1967) 640; pears (1968) 180, (1967) 165; grapes (1968) 3,735, (1967) 3,500; raisins (1968) *c.* 300, (1967) *c.* 300; figs (1968) 215, (1967) 232; sugar, raw value (1969–70) *c.* 545, (1968–69) 707; olive oil *c.* 60 (159); tobacco *c.* 146 (161); cotton, lint *c.* 379 (435). Livestock (in 000; Dec. 1968): cattle 13,761; sheep 36,587; horses 1,151; asses 1,986; buffaloes (Dec. 1967) 1,248; goats (Dec. 1967) 20,659; chickens (Oct. 1968) *c.* 33,000.

Industry. Fuel and power (in 000; metric tons; 1969): crude oil 3,599; coal (1968) 4,769; lignite (1968) 4,101; electricity (kw-hr.) 7,829,000. Production (in 000; metric tons; 1969): iron ore (55–60% metal content) 2,425; pig iron 948; crude steel 1,170; sulfur (1968) 187; sulfuric acid (1968) 28; cement 5,795; superphosphates (1967) 205; manganese ore (metal content; 1968) 10; chrome ore (oxide content; 1968) 235; cotton yarn (1967) 127; woven cotton fabrics (m.; 1967) 694,000; wool yarn (1968) 28.

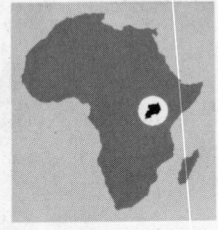

LONDON "DAILY EXPRESS"
FROM PICTORIAL PARADE

Left-wing students rush
to attack
the Turkish-American
trade bank in Ankara
in April 1970. Hundreds
of the students smashed
windows and broke
furniture.

March 15, won a vote of confidence by 232 votes to 172. The budget was passed on May 30 and, on June 25, another 26 dissidents were expelled from the Justice Party.

The assault in Parliament was taken up by the opposition, which demanded an investigation into press allegations that the prime minister had abused his official position to the financial benefit of his brothers. A ruling by the Assembly that it was not competent to go into the matter, while the prime minister's libel suit against the newspapers concerned was being heard by the courts, was quashed by the Constitutional Court on June 18, but on July 31 the Assembly committee of inquiry reported that there was no case to answer.

Outside Parliament, the democratic regime came under fire from student and worker militants. Higher education was largely disrupted, and there were attacks on U.S. property, particularly during "independence week," proclaimed on March 17 by the Federation of Revolutionary Youth. The students forced the Middle East Technical University in Ankara to appoint as rector the candidate of their choice, Erdal Inonu, son of the veteran opposition leader Ismet Inonu. However, student action was weakened by the feud between right- and left-wing militants.

Worker militancy was led by the minority Confederation of Reformist Workers' Unions (DISK). When the National Assembly passed a bill restricting collective bargaining rights to unions representing at least one-third of the work force in a given industry, DISK organized a violent campaign of protest that culminated in riots in Istanbul on June 15–16, in which one policeman and three workers were killed. With the approval of the Assembly, the government imposed martial law, which was subsequently extended until September 16, in the provinces of Istanbul and Kocaeli (Izmit).

Martial law and the widespread backlash against the riots allowed the government to proceed with its planned program. Before Parliament rose on August 3 it had endorsed the controversial trade union law, approved new taxes, increased the pay of the armed forces, and reformed and increased the pay of the civil service. On August 9 the government devalued

Turks and Caicos Islands:
see Dependent States

the Turkish lira, from 9 to 15 to the U.S. dollar, and introduced a package of wide-ranging reforms regulating taxes, prices, credits, export incentives, and imports.

The government's efforts to promote the growth of a Western-style competitive economy were also advanced by the agreement reached on July 22 to proceed with the second stage of Turkey's association with the EEC. However, foreign policy continued to be nicely balanced. By July 1, all U.S. bases and facilities in Turkey, with the exception of the air base at Incirlik near Adana, were handed back to the Turkish authorities. On August 21 an agreement was signed under which the U.S.S.R. would lend Turkey $113.7 million, in addition to the $200 million already promised, for industrial development. President Sunay visited Romania in April and Demirel went to Yugoslavia in September. The Turks refused to hand over to the Soviets two hijackers who forced a Soviet airliner to fly to Turkey. A Turkish officer was held by the Soviets for a time, together with two U.S. generals and a U.S. pilot, after their plane crossed the Soviet border, but all the men were subsequently released. (A. J. A. M.)

See also Cyprus.

ENCYCLOPÆDIA BRITANNICA FILMS. *The Middle East* (1955); *Turkey: Emergence of a Modern Nation* (1963).

Uganda

A republic and a member of the Commonwealth of Nations, Uganda is bounded by the Sudan, the Congo (Kinshasa), Rwanda, Tanzania, and Kenya. Area: 91,076 sq.mi. (235,886 sq.km.), including 16,364 sq.mi. of inland water. Pop. (1970 est.): 9,831,000, about 99% of whom are African. Cap. and largest city: Kampala (pop., 1969, 331,889). Language: Bantu, Nilotic, Nilo-Hamitic, and Sudanic. Religion: pagan, with Hindu, Muslim, and Christian minorities. President and prime minister in 1970, Apollo Milton Obote.

Five of six men, all of the Baganda tribe, charged with an attempt to assassinate President Obote on Dec. 19, 1969, pleaded guilty when brought before a magistrate on March 12, 1970. The sixth claimed that he had been out of the country at the time. Later, in the High Court, all six pleaded guilty and were sentenced on May 6 to life imprisonment.

With the approach of May 1, the day on which the Uganda Immigration Act was due to take effect, concern among the Asian population about their future led to demonstrations in Kampala on March 10 against Britain's immigration policy. The implementation of the act was followed almost immediately by the disappearance of a senior member of the British High Commission, Brian Lea, who had been responsible for the issuance of visas to Asians. He was missing for three days and, when he returned, claimed that he had been kidnapped. Relations between Uganda and Britain were seriously strained, and a commission was appointed to investigate the circumstances of Lea's disappearance. After hearings lasting six weeks, Lea was recalled to Britain and the report of the commission was not made public.

On May 1 Obote announced the immediate nationalization of the import and export trade, with the exception of imports of petroleum products. The gov-

UGANDA

Education. (1966) Primary, pupils 564,190, teachers 17,821; secondary, pupils 90,904, teachers 1,101; vocational, pupils 3,128, teachers 282; teacher training, students 4,097, teachers 281; higher (at Kampala University), students 1,593, teaching staff 216.

Finance. Monetary unit: Uganda shilling, with a par value of UShs. 7.14 to U.S. $1 (UShs. 17.14 = £1 sterling). Gold, SDRs, and foreign exchange: (March 1970) U.S. $52.7 million; (March 1969) U.S. $45 million. Budget (1969–70 rev. est.): revenue UShs. 1,068,-200,000; expenditure UShs. 995 million. Gross domestic product: (1968) UShs. 4,992,000,000; (1967) UShs. 4,962,000,000. Cost of living (Kampala; 1963 = 100): (Dec. 1969) 152; (Dec. 1968) 127.

Foreign Trade. (Excluding trade with Kenya and Tanzania; 1969) Imports UShs. 910 million; exports UShs. 1,412,000,000. Import sources: U.K. 34%; Japan 14%; West Germany 9%; Italy 5%. Export destinations: U.S. 23%; U.K. 22%; Japan 12%. Main exports: coffee 56%; cotton 18%; copper 9%; tea 7%.

Transport and Communications. Roads (1967) 24,173 (including 2,938 km. main roads). Motor vehicles in use (1968): passenger 32,800; commercial 5,000. Railways (1967) 850 km. (for traffic *see* KENYA). Air traffic: *see* KENYA. Telephones (Dec. 1968) 24,874. Radio receivers (Dec. 1967) 509,000. Television receivers (Dec. 1968) 9,000.

Agriculture. Production (in 000; metric tons; 1968; 1967 in parentheses): millet *c.* 430 (*c.* 400); sorghum *c.* 270 (*c.* 270); sweet potatoes *c.* 2,600 (*c.* 2,600); cassava *c.* 2,000 (*c.* 1,800); peanuts *c.* 200 (200); dry beans *c.* 260 (*c.* 252); cotton, lint (1969) *c.* 83, (1968) *c.* 76; coffee *c.* 189 (156); tea 15 (11); sugar, raw value (1969–70) *c.* 156, (1968–69) 146; sesame *c.* 20 (*c.* 20); timber (cu.m.; 1966–67) *c.* 10,900, (1965–66) *c.* 10,800; fish catch 109 (100). Livestock (in 000; Dec. 1968): cattle *c.* 3,800; sheep *c.* 770; goats (Jan. 1968) 1,710; pigs *c.* 45; chickens (1967–68) 9,200.

Industry. Production (in 000; metric tons; 1968): copper, smelter 16; tin concentrates (metal content) 0.17; tungsten concentrates (oxide content) 0.12; salt 4; phosphate rock 159; cement (1969) 175; electricity (public supply; kw-hr.) 731,000.

ernment also acquired a 60% interest in all banks, public transport, manufacturing industries, and plantations, and increased the holdings of the Uganda Development Corporation Ltd. in the Kilembe copper mine to a similar proportion. Obote stated that compensation would be paid out of the government's share of the profits over a period of 15 years.   (K. I.)

ENCYCLOPÆDIA BRITANNICA FILMS. *East Africa (Kenya, Tanganyika, Uganda)* (1962).

Union of Soviet Socialist Republics

The Union of Soviet Socialist Republics is a federal state covering parts of eastern Europe and northern and central Asia. Area: 8,600,350 sq.mi. (22,274,900 sq.km.). Pop. (1970): 241,748,000, including Russians 55%; Ukrainians 18%; Belorussians 4%; Uzbeks 3%; Tatars 2%. Cap. and largest city: Moscow (pop., 1970, 6,942,000). Language: officially Russian, but many others are spoken. Religion: about 40 religions are represented in the U.S.S.R., the major ones being Christian denominations. General secretary of the Communist Party of the Soviet Union in 1970, Leonid I. Brezhnev; chairman of the Presidium of the Supreme Soviet (president), Nikolai V. Podgorny; chairman of the Council of Ministers (premier), Aleksei N. Kosygin.

Domestic Affairs. The struggle of attrition between the Soviet establishment and a small, hetero-geneous group of dissident intellectuals continued throughout 1970. It was difficult to make any exact estimate of the extent and nature of the situation, as most reports about it originated from unconfirmed sources and clandestine news sheets and pamphlets circulating in the Soviet Union. Perhaps the most interesting of these unconfirmed reports concerned an alleged movement for reform on true Communist lines among officers of the Baltic Fleet, culminating in the summary execution of a naval officer in Estonia in June. The writers and poets caused less concern to Soviet authorities than criticism of the system voiced by some scientists, in particular the eminent physicist Andrei Sakharov, whose "open letter" to Soviet leaders reached the West in March. Sakharov, who had first stated his views in 1968, argued again that the U.S.S.R. was falling behind economically and technologically because its "antidemocratic traditions" restricted free circulation of information.

Yet Soviet authorities did not ignore the writers and took steps to assert the official line on the literary front. In February, Aleksandr Tvardovski (*see* BIOGRAPHY) lost his post as editor of *Novy Mir*, the only literary journal of quality in the U.S.S.R. Tvardovski had always stood for high literary standards and he never regarded party orthodoxy as the yardstick for assessing literary values. His dismissal was regarded as a considerable victory for the supporters of strict control over the arts. This was emphasized strongly by the Writers' Congress of the Russian Republic held in Moscow in March and attended by both party leader Brezhnev and Premier Kosygin; the occasion was used to denounce "ideological laxity" in all its forms and to call for more "popular" literature. But in April, the authorities permitted publication of 100,-000 copies of *The Shadow of Sound*, the latest collection of poems by Andrei Voznesenski, who previously had been denounced as "disloyal."

On the whole, however, the official attitude toward intellectual dissent remained firm, and the award of the Nobel Prize for Literature to Aleksandr I. Solzhenitsyn (*see* BIOGRAPHY) officially was regarded as a provocation because of his uncompromising criticism of the less attractive aspects of Soviet society. Solzhenitsyn eventually withdrew his application to be allowed to go to Stockholm in December to receive his prize, but the award nonetheless provided an opportunity for renewed attacks on him that recalled his expulsion from the Writers' Union in November 1969. It was, therefore, most courageous of the famous cellist Mstislav Rostropovich to defend the maligned writer in an open letter to *Pravda* and to recall in this context the cultural terror practiced in Stalin's day. Indeed, the tone of domestic policy in 1970 was typified by the appearance in June of a bust of the dictator on his grave beside the Kremlin wall, signifying Stalin's return to favour.

The literary cause célèbre of the year was that of the young writer Andrei Amalrik, whose book *Will the Soviet Union Survive Until 1984?* had predicted the collapse of what he regarded as the corrupt and inefficient Soviet system and its annihilation at the hands of China. Amalrik was arrested in May, brought to trial in the remote town of Sverdlovsk in November, and sentenced to three years in prison. (*See* Special Report.)

In the light of these pressures, the reorganization of the judicial system in September seemed particularly ominous. The Ministry of Justice, which had been abolished in 1956, was reinstated and given consider-

Unemployment:
see Employment, Wages, and Hours; Social Services

UNESCO:
see United Nations

CAMERA PRESS—
PIX FROM PUBLIX

Workers form a star
in Moscow's Red Square
during May Day
celebrations.

able supervisory powers over the procurators. The procurators, whose function included the safeguarding of the legal rights of all Soviet citizens, had played an important role in the movement for a return to legality made possible by Stalin's death and the fall of Beria and culminating in the reforms introduced in 1956. The judicial clock had now been put back, and *Pravda* was quick to call for "an intensification of the struggle against infringements of law and public discipline, which affect the country's economic performance."

Soviet Jewry represented a special element. At some risk to themselves 39 Jewish intellectuals from Moscow and 21 from Leningrad addressed letters to the United Nations in March asking for their "human rights" and permission to leave for Israel. The official daily *Izvestia* denounced them as "anti-Soviet renegades."

Vague reports in June connecting Jewish groups in the U.S.S.R. with plans to hijack aircraft were followed by more credible reports of fairly widespread arrests among Jews in Leningrad. In December, 11 persons, 9 of them Jews, were tried under art. 64 of the Russian Republic Criminal Code, which made flight abroad treason. They were charged with participating in a plot, organized by a former air force officer, Maj. Mark Dymshits, to seize a plane bound from Leningrad to Tallin, Estonia, and force it to fly them to Finland. On December 24 a Leningrad court found all 11 guilty, sentenced two to death by firing squad, and issued prison camp terms to the others. The severity of the sentences prompted strong international criticism, protest marches in several countries, and appeals for clemency from many quarters. On December 31 the Supreme Court of the Russian Republic commuted the two death sentences, substituting 15-year labour camp sentences, and reduced the prison terms of three other defendants.

The first successful pirating of a Soviet aircraft occurred in October when two Lithuanian dissidents hijacked an Aeroflot AN-24 airliner on an internal flight and forced it to land in Turkey. They were allowed to claim political asylum, even though the Soviet air hostess, Nadezhda Kulchenko, had been killed in the struggle for control of the aircraft. Shortly afterward, a light plane carrying three U.S. army officers and a senior Turkish officer was forced to land in Soviet Armenia after straying across the Turkish-Soviet border. The officers were released in November.

The Economy. The extent of Soviet economic problems became obvious as initially optimistic reports of the Supreme Soviet's discussion of the economy, held in December 1969, were augmented by more analytical examination by the party's Central Committee of results achieved in 1969. Brezhnev addressed the Central Committee on this subject on Dec. 15, 1969, and the contents of his speech were released piecemeal. It appeared that he criticized the relative failure of industry to modernize production and singled out the transport and distribution systems as inefficient and backward. He complained of insufficient financial planning and in general urged the party to exercise tighter controls over planning policies and procedures. *Pravda* reported early in 1970 that industrial production had risen by 7% in 1969 (the plan had stipulated an increase of 7.4%). The party paper criticized a number of industrial ministries for "lethargy" and hinted that the U.S.S.R. was not immune from the worldwide phenomenon of wage inflation as "in some sections of the economy wages have increased at a faster rate than productivity." The five Central Asian union republics all failed to fulfill their industrial production targets.

Agricultural production stood at 3% below the 1968 totals, a disappointing result attributed to poor weather conditions. However, the decline in the actual production total of milk and meat was alarming, as was the failure to meet housing construction targets. The agricultural problems were aired at the Collective Farm Congress, which met in Moscow at the end of November 1969, the first meeting since 1935. An important innovation was announced: a central social insurance fund for collective farmers was set up, thus establishing systematic social insurance for rural workers and extending to them the benefits their comrades in industry had enjoyed virtually since the Revolution. New directives for agriculture were issued in July, providing for immediate cash incentives to increase the production of meat and also calling for improvements in the supply of fruit and vegetables.

The relatively disappointing economic results reported for 1969 became the subject of acrimonious debate in economic journals and the party press. In April, apparently to strengthen the administration of the economy, T. I. Sokolov was named the first vice-president of Gosplan (the central planning authority) and L. N. Yefremov was appointed first vice-president of the State Committee on Science and Technology. Some experts advocated a return to the rigidly centralized economic system of Stalin's day, and in April Brezhnev told a gathering of Communist leaders from all parts of the world, who had come to Moscow for the Lenin centenary, that a "new economic policy" was needed in the U.S.S.R. No new policy, however, had yet emerged.

Khrushchev's boast that by 1970 the Soviet Union would overtake the United States as the world's leading industrial power was not fulfilled. Yet the deficiencies of the Soviet economy were relative, and real progress had been made. The rate of increase in industrial productivity over the last five years—about 4½%—kept pace with Western Europe, and the 1969 harvest of 161.1 million tons of grain, although 9 million tons below 1968, was still the third highest on record. There was little doubt that the results for 1970 would be better than those for the previous year. The harvest was good, and in industry preliminary reports spoke of an 8.2% rise in production. December 1970 marked the end of the five-year plan period, and it seemed that targets would be met—the average annual growth of output over the five years was 7.6%. Consumption was increasing at a faster rate than investment, and it was expected to maintain this trend.

Although efficiency of the Soviet economy improved, there were several persistent problems for which long-term solutions would have to be found. The worst bottleneck was in the manufacture of computers, where the U.S.S.R. lagged far behind. The movement of labour from farming to industry (some 33% of the total labour force was still in agriculture) slowed down. In addition, there was the burden of defense expenditure and the cost of the space program. The 1970 defense estimates stood at 17.9 billion rubles—an increase of 200 million rubles over 1969. In 1969 defense amounted to 13.2% of total expenditures; in 1970 the percentage was down to 12.4%. Published Soviet defense estimates, however, were somewhat misleading; an unknown proportion of defense expenditures was included in the budgets of various industrial sectors and also within the appropriations for space research and development.

Foreign Affairs. Perhaps the most important development in foreign policy was the signing of the Soviet-West German renunciation of force treaty in August. This was the result of new initiatives toward Eastern Europe undertaken by the Brandt government in Bonn, and began with a series of exploratory talks conducted in Moscow by Bonn's special envoy, Egon Bahr, at the beginning of the year. The first sign that the two sides were coming closer together was the conclusion of an agreement in March to exchange consulates general in Leningrad and Hamburg.

On August 12 Willy Brandt, the West German chancellor, signed the treaty in Moscow, expressing the determination of the two countries to "improve and extend cooperation between them, including economic relations as well as scientific, technological, and cultural contacts." Both parties undertook to refrain from the threat or use of force and agreed to accept the "actual situation" existing in Europe, with particular reference to the present frontiers. In effect, this amounted to recognition of Poland's western border and although the treaty was subject to ratification (and this in turn depended on agreement in the four-power talks on the status of Berlin), it was an important contribution toward underpinning the status quo.

Economic cooperation between the U.S.S.R. and West Germany certainly would be of benefit to the Soviet economy. Early in the year an agreement was concluded for the sale of West German wide-bore pipes to be paid for ultimately by supplies of natural gas from the Soviet Union; the bridging finance for the deal was provided by West German banks. Following the signing of the treaty there were reports of negotiations about the possible development of new truck plants in the U.S.S.R. by West German firms. In November Hans Leussink, the West German minister of education and science, visited Moscow for talks on scientific and technological cooperation.

The German question was, of course, of vital concern to the Soviet Union's allies in Eastern Europe, especially to the East German regime which had been rather obdurate in its own contacts with Bonn. The U.S.S.R. apparently kept its Warsaw Pact partners informed about the progress of the Soviet-West German talks. In June the Warsaw Pact powers, meeting in Budapest, issued a memorandum again calling for

continued on page 750

U.S.S.R.

Education. (1968–69) Primary and secondary, pupils 49,195,000, teachers 2,345,000; vocational and teacher training, pupils 4,262,000, teachers (1965–66) 251,000; higher (including 105 universities), students 4,469,700, teaching staff (1965–66) 201,000.

Finance. Monetary unit: ruble, with an exchange rate of 0.90 ruble to U.S. $1 (2.16 rubles = £1 sterling). Budget (1969 est.): revenue 134,098,000,000 rubles; expenditure 133,898,000,000 rubles.

Foreign Trade. (1968) Imports 8,469,000,000 rubles; exports 9,571,000,000 rubles. Import sources: Sino-Soviet area 68% (East Germany 17%, Poland 11%, Czechoslovakia 11%, Bulgaria 9%, Hungary 7%, Romania 5%). Export destinations: Sino-Soviet area 67% (East Germany 14%, Poland 10%, Czechoslovakia 10%, Bulgaria 9%, Hungary 6%, Cuba 6%). Main exports (1967): machinery 21%; crude oil 7%; iron and steel 6%; timber 5%; petroleum products 5%.

Transport and Communications. Roads (1967) 1,368,400 km. (including 433,000 km. surfaced). Motor vehicles in use (1965): passenger *c.* 1.1 million; commercial *c.* 4.5 million. Railways (1968): 133,600 km. (including 30,-800 km. electrified); traffic 254,100,000,000 passenger-km., freight 2,227,480,000,000 net ton-km. Air traffic (1968): 62,100,000,000 passenger-km.; freight 1,803,000,000 net ton-km. Navigable inland waterways (1968) 141,300 km.; traffic 155,400,000,000 ton-km. Shipping (1969): merchant vessels 100 gross tons and over 5,622; gross tonnage 13,704,640. Telephones (Dec. 1968) 10.8 million. Radio receivers (Dec. 1968) 85.5 million. Television receivers (Dec. 1968) 26.8 million.

Agriculture. Production (in 000; metric tons; 1969; 1968 in parentheses): potatoes 91,700 (102,184); wheat (1968) 93,393, (1967) 77,-419; barley (1968) 28,904, (1967) 24,662; oats (1968) 11,639, (1967) 11,581; rye (1968) 14,-120, (1967) 12,986; corn (1968) 8,828, (1967) 9,163; rice (1968) 1,063, (1967) 895; millet (1968) 2,660, (1967) 3,218; sugar, raw value (1969–70) *c.* 8,413, (1968–69) *c.* 10,125; cotton, lint 1,950 (2,031); flax fibre (1968) 402, (1967) 485; tobacco *c.* 259 (*c.* 255); sunflower seed *c.* 6,350 (6,685); linseed (1968) 485, (1967) 519; dry peas (1968) 4,818, (1967) 4,122; soybeans *c.* 580 (528); tea (1968) 56, (1967) 57; wine (1968) 1,913, (1967) 1,800; wool (1968) 248, (1967) 237; eggs (1968) *c.* 1,970, (1967) *c.* 1,880; meat (1968) 8,550, (1967) 8,510; milk 81,550 (82,100); butter *c.* 1,130 (1,165); cheese *c.* 500 (*c.* 460); timber (cu.m.; 1968) *c.* 380,400, (1967) *c.* 383,100; fish catch (1968) 6,082, (1967) 5,777. Livestock (in 000; Jan. 1969): cattle 95,700; pigs 49,000; sheep 140,500; goats (Jan. 1968) 5,580; horses 8,000; poultry 546,-930.

Industry. Index of industrial production (1963 = 100): (1969) 162; (1968) 151. Fuel and power (in 000; metric tons; 1969): coal and lignite 608,000; crude oil 328,000; natural gas (cu.m.) 182,760,000,000; electricity (kw-hr.) 689,-000,000,000. Production (in 000; metric tons; 1969): iron ore (60% metal content) 186,000; pig iron 81,629; steel 110,287; aluminum (1968) *c.* 1,000; copper (1968) *c.* 990; lead (1968) *c.* 400; zinc (1968) *c.* 540; gold (troy oz.; 1968) *c.* 6,040; silver (troy oz.; 1968) *c.* 35,000; manganese ore (metal content; 1968) 2,378; tungsten concentrates (oxide content; 1968) *c.* 7.8; magnesite (1968) *c.* 3,000; superphosphates (1967) 14,760; nitrogenous fertilizers (1968) *c.* 3,750; sulfuric acid 10,664; cement 89,777; newsprint (1968) 1,016; other paper (1968) 4,954; passenger cars (units) 294; commercial vehicles (units) 551; cotton fabrics (sq.m.) 6,207,000; woolen fabrics (sq.m.) 618,000.

INTELLECTUAL DISSENT IN THE SOVIET UNION

By Karel van het Reve

Soviet intellectuals, in common with all citizens of the U.S.S.R., are supposed to express only those opinions held or spread by the government. Whereas in the West almost any issue of any newspaper contains at least some expression of dissatisfaction and disagreement with the actions and intentions of the authorities, this is not so in the Soviet Union. Indeed, such publicly expressed dissent has been possible in Russia only during the second half of the 19th century and the first 17 years of the 20th. Before about 1860 no Russian inside Russia could, with impunity, declare publicly that he disagreed with any official opinion or action, and since 1917 this has been equally true.

The Long History of Suppression. Before 1860 a Russian who expressed an opinion contradicting that of the government ran a very great risk of being rebuked, dismissed, deprived of his income and/or his house, arrested, killed, or put into an asylum for the insane. Thus in 1790 Aleksandr N. Radischev was sentenced to death (the penalty was commuted to ten years' banishment to Siberia by his sovereign, Catherine the Great) for writing and publishing a book in which some moral arguments against serfdom were expressed. In 1836 Petr Y. Chaadaev was declared insane because he disagreed publicly with the official view that "Russia's past is admirable, its present is splendid and as to its future—it surpasses anything the stoutest fantasy can imagine." In 1849 Dostoevski was sentenced to death (the sentence was commuted to four years' penal servitude plus six years' banishment to Siberia by Nicholas I) for reading to a gathering of friends a letter from the critic V. G. Belinsky to Gogol. In 1852 Turgenev was put under arrest and banished to his estate for using the qualification "great writer" in an obituary of Gogol.

Since the 1917 Revolution the penalties for heterodoxy have been no less severe. In 1921 the poet Nikolai Gumilyov was sentenced to death and executed for conspiring against the government, although no proof of conspiracy and no report of his trial were ever published. In 1934 his friend, the great poet Osip Mandelshtam, was arrested, freed, and rearrested (eventually perishing in a concentration camp) for reading his now famous 16-line poem about Stalin to four friends, one of whom informed the police. In 1965 two gifted writers, Yuli Daniel and Andrei Sinyavsky, were arrested and the following year sentenced to five and seven years' hard labour, respectively, for writing, and publishing outside the Soviet Union, a number of short stories and an essay on socialist realism. In 1970 a playwright, poet, memoirist, and historian of great originality, Andrei Amalrik, was sentenced to three years in a labour camp for having written and published in Amsterdam a book entitled *Will the Soviet Union Survive Until 1984?*

Between 1860 and 1917 it was possible, and even customary, for a Russian writer to have his own ideas and to express them more or less freely in his own way—albeit subject to censorship. After 1917, by extensive use of terror and by making all writers completely dependent on the government economically, the au-

thorities succeeded in making the average Soviet intellectual a person who, in his works and in his public statements, enthusiastically and as sincerely as he could, endorsed every government statement or policy. Thousands of writers, musicians, painters, and scholars, every single one of them in daily and especially nightly fear for their lives, extolled with terrible gusto the genius of Stalin and, when asked to do so (and often without being asked), denounced their colleagues, relatives, and friends as they were slandered, arrested, tortured, shot, or put into camps where they died.

All this caused a considerable decline in Russian culture, a demoralization of the whole intelligentsia, and feelings of utter helplessness and despair. This was, intellectually, the situation in the Soviet Union at the time of Stalin's death in 1953. His successors ended the terror, and subsequently the situation differed in many ways from what it had been between 1917 and 1953. There were no more arrests and executions for purely statistical reasons; to be arrested one at least had to say or do something the government disliked intensely. There was greater freedom of (private) speech and opinion than had existed at any time since the Revolution, with a certain relaxation of censorship.

The New Intellectual Ferment. With this relaxation, it became apparent during the 1960s that the official Soviet doctrine of Marxism-Leninism, subscribed to by millions of "true believers" at the height of the Stalin era, had lost its significance for a considerable part of the intelligentsia. Relatively few Soviet historians or sociologists or literary scholars seriously believe today that the teachings of Marx, Engels, Lenin, and X (X standing for Stalin, Khrushchev, Brezhnev, Mao, Castro, or whoever at a given time and place happens to have himself declared the "Lenin of our time," the "faithful brother-in-arms of Lenin," the "true son of the Party," the "great helmsman," the "lider maximo," or the "greatest genius of mankind") are of decisive importance to anyone who wishes to study history, society, or literature. Nor do many Soviet intellectuals believe in the coming (between 1970 and 1980, according to official data) of the "communist" society, in which the citizens of the U.S.S.R. will know a state of material and spiritual bliss never before experienced by the people of any country.

This rather sudden decline in the number of Marxist-Leninists has hardly been studied by Western sovietologists. It may well have been one of the causes that contributed to the development of more or less public expression of dissatisfaction and dissent in the late 1960s. Roughly speaking, the following stages in this development may be discerned:

1. Official declarations were made that all had not been well in the past: Khrushchev's speech at the 20th party congress; official "rehabilitation" of persons who had been "repressed" in the Stalin era; amnesty for most of the remaining prisoners.

2. Nonofficial declarations were made along the same lines: poets repeating the party line in this respect (Evgeni Yevtushenko).

3. Books appeared in print describing the Stalin era or the era of "destalinization": Ilya Ehrenburg's *The Thaw* and later his memoirs, *People and Life; One Day in the Life of Ivan Denisovich* by Aleksandr Solzhenitsyn (*see* BIOGRAPHY); Venyamin Kaverin's *Two Portraits;* Vladimir Dudintsev's *Not by Bread Alone; Tyorkin in Kingdom Come* by Aleksandr Tvardovski (*see* BIOGRAPHY); and many others.

4. A number of books, poems, articles, and scholarly works that had no immediate bearing on the Stalin era or on destalinization "escaped" when the government lifted the lid of the kettle to permit destalinizing works to appear. Some were works that could not have been published under Stalin because of the scholarly approach of the writer (Stepan Veselovsky's book about Ivan the Terrible) or his birth (Gumilyov's son's book about the Mongolians) or because the author had been killed or silenced under Stalin (Isaak Babel, Anna Akhmatova, Boris Pasternak, Andrey Platonov).

5. Manuscripts began to circulate of books, poems, memoirs,

articles, letters, plays, and songs that could not pass censorship (the poetry of Vladislav Khodasevich, Pasternak, Akhmatova, Mandelshtam, Gumilyov; translations of foreign books; the novels of Solzhenitsyn; the songs of Galich). This kind of literature became very popular and is called *samizdat* (short for "do it yourself publishing house").

6. Part of this literature found its way to the West and was printed there. It is estimated that about 10 to 20% of all Russian books printed abroad eventually reach the Soviet Union (Pasternak's *Doctor Zhivago;* the works of Sinyavsky and Daniel; Solzhenitsyn's novels; the memoirs of Evgenia Ginzburg; Andrei D. Sakharov's *Progress, Coexistence and Intellectual Freedom;* Amalrik's *1984?;* Anatoli Marchenko's *My Testimony;* the scholarly Western editions of Akhmatova, Gumilyov, Nikolai Klyuyev, Mandelshtam, Pasternak). This kind of literature, smuggled into the U.S.S.R., is called *tamizdat* ("things published yonder").

The Movement Today. In the late 1960s one could say that a kind of "movement" existed, called by Amalrik the "democratic movement" (not to be confused with the *Program of the Democratic Movement*, which is a document of just one of the opposition groups). We will first discuss the means of this movement, then its aims, and finally its strength.

The Means. Its means are, among others, demonstrations and meetings. These are, as a rule, very small, hardly noticed, often instantly broken up by the police. Frequently only a small group of people know they have happened at all. For example, the demonstration on Pushkin Square in Moscow on Jan. 22, 1967; the meeting dedicated to the memory of the writer Platonov held in the building of the Writers' Union in Moscow on Jan. 31, 1968; the banquet held in a Moscow restaurant on the 72nd birthday of Kosterin on March 17, 1968; the demonstration of Amalrik and his wife at the British embassy in Moscow, in protest against British (and, by implication, Soviet) aid to Gen. Yakubu Gowon during the Nigerian civil war; the demonstration on Red Square by Pavel Litvinov, Larisa Daniel, Vladimir Dremljuga, and others on Aug. 25, 1968, against the occupation of Czechoslovakia; the funeral of Kosterin on Nov. 14, 1968.

Then there are letters to the editors of Soviet newspapers, not published by those newspapers but circulating in manuscript form. Sometimes these letters are also addressed to foreign newspapers, Communist or non-Communist. Other letters are addressed to high Soviet officials or institutions (Brezhnev, Kosygin, the Central Committee, the Supreme Court, the Supreme Soviet). These letters are never answered. They are sometimes signed by well-known public figures of international repute (I. E. Tamm, P. L. Kapitza, Sakharov, K. G. Paustovski, etc.).

During the last few years, several curious periodicals have sprung into existence. The most regular and most famous among these is the *Chronicle of Current Events,* a bimonthly publication of 10,000 to 15,000 words. Since the spring of 1968, 15 issues have reached the West. They give accurate news of arrests, protests, and information about *samizdat.*

The circulation of all these underground publications is not known. It probably does not exceed a few hundred or, at most, a few thousand copies of any one document, for no instruments for the multiplying of texts except typewriters, tape recorders, and cameras can be privately owned in the Soviet Union. On the other hand, the possibilities of manuscript literature should not be underrated. In a *samizdat* article written in January 1969, the author, A. Antipov (probably a pseudonym), urges his fellow intellectuals "to switch from the tea table to the writing desk." "We have learned to talk," he writes, "it is time we learned to write." He thinks it perfectly possible that a rich intellectual life, based on nonprinted literature, will emerge in the Soviet Union. Writers like Euclid and Plato, he argues, were widely read for centuries without benefit of the printing press.

The Aims. What do these dissenters want? Their most important demand is for justice. The end of terror and its official denunciation in the 1950s left many things as they had been before, and the authorities have been very reluctant to change the So-

CAMERA PRESS

Yuli Daniel (left) and Andrei Sinyavsky, accused of secretly publishing anti-Soviet works in the West, at their trial in 1966.

viet state from what it had become under Stalin. Writers and scholars who spent 10 to 20 years in labour camps have been "rehabilitated." If they, or their relatives, insist, they can get an official declaration saying that their arrest, trial (if there was one), and sentence were illegal. But they are not supposed to write or speak about it. The people who denounced them to the political police are in some cases still holding high office. A well-known poet, said to be co-author of the Soviet national anthem (which can only be hummed, not sung, because the text is full of Stalin idolatry), is known to have been, and to be, an informer. Some of his victims have survived. They are not allowed to say anything in public about him.

Millions of peasants are forced by the passport system to stay in their villages, just as the peasants were in the 17th, 18th, and early 19th centuries. Permission to travel abroad is given only to people whom the police think trustworthy, as under Nicholas I. Access to foreign newspapers is as restricted as it was under Paul I. In the whole Soviet Union there is not one single bookshop where a Soviet citizen can freely buy foreign books of his own choice. Even in libraries the *Britannica Book of the Year* is not available to the general reader, and this article can be read in the Soviet Union only by specialists, who have access to special reading rooms. There some of my friends and colleagues will read it, and I salute them from these pages.

Censorship is extremely strict and primitive. In 1967 an edition of Flavius Josephus' *Jewish War,* first published *c.* A.D. 77, was forbidden to appear. There are long lists of persons whose names may not be mentioned in print, among them Khrushchev. In a program of a Soviet performance of the opera *Boris Godunov,* the line "Khrushchev, a nobleman" was altered to read "A nobleman." Some of the best Russian poetry and prose of the 20th century cannot be printed (Gumilyov, Mandelshtam, Khodasevitch, Solzhenitsyn). The children of Jewish parents have to have the word "Jew" in their passports, which on many occasions will bar them from certain jobs and will sometimes hamper their entering an institution of higher learning. Only a trickle of Jews wanting to leave the Soviet Union are allowed out. The law provides the death sentence (art. 64A of the Soviet Criminal Code) for leaving the country without permission or refusing to return. The authorities may put dissident intellectuals into mental asylums, where they are sometimes subjected to terrible treatment.

The "democratic movement" is against all these things. One could call it a movement for civil rights. But its stated aims do not go beyond the demand that the Soviet authorities abide by Soviet law. It is difficult to ascertain whether there are more radical trends in Soviet intellectual dissent. Even in *samizdat* it is dangerous to declare oneself an all-out opponent of the Soviet system. The penalty for criticism of the regime on the basis of existing laws can be up to seven years' penal servitude; denouncing and rejecting the system itself may easily mean a sentence of 15 years. When, in advocating freedom of information or self-determination for Czechoslovakia, a Soviet dissident quotes Lenin, this does not necessarily mean that he seriously believes Lenin to have been an advocate of freedom. From *samizdat* documents that have so far reached the West, however, it cannot be concluded that the authors have any political aims and intellectual convictions other than those stated in their writings.

The Strength. In his brilliant essay *Will the Soviet Union Survive Until 1984?* Amalrik distinguished three groups of dissident intellectuals: the "Marxist-Leninists," people who oppose the regime on the basis of "true Communism"; the "liberals," whose demands go no further than freedom in the Western, liberal sense of the word; and the Christian-nationalists, who envisage some future Russia where Russian culture, the Orthodox religion, and the Russian "people" will produce—and eventually present to the world—something very precious. One might call this third group a latter-day variant of the 19th-century Slavophils. In addition, there is a probably large group of people who disapprove of underground activities and who advocate collaboration with the authorities and pressure from "within" to achieve more freedom. Nor should the religious dissenters be forgotten: Baptists and other sectarian believers who in one way or another clash with the authorities and are therefore persecuted. Important also are non-Russian groups such as Ukrainians who fight against russification or for national self-determination. One of these, the Crimean Tatars, constitutes the only dissident group with large popular support and good organization.

There is no sharp borderline between these groups, nor is it known how numerous they are. To a large extent, knowledge of this whole phenomenon derives from occasional contacts of dissenters with Western scholars, tourists, and journalists. Much of what goes on outside Moscow is hardly known. The whole democratic movement may not have more than a few thousand participants and not more than a few hundred thousand sympathizers. The influence of the opposition on the government is almost nonexistent. Urgent appeals for the democratization of Soviet society by highly placed loyal citizens, like Andrei Sakharov, the famous physicist and member of the Soviet Academy of Sciences, are left unanswered. Sakharov's very name is never mentioned in print, and when Western scholars and journalists in Moscow ask for him they are told that such a person is unknown. The only successes the opposition has had so far are the revocation of some convictions (Amalrik's banishment to Siberia in 1965), the release of scholars from psychiatric clinics after protests by their colleagues (Esenin-Volpin in 1968, Roy Medvedev in 1970), and the fact that some dissidents who lost their jobs have been reinstated after they protested the illegality of their dismissals.

Whether the intellectual opposition in the Soviet Union will have any influence on government policy in the future is uncertain. At present there are no signs that this opposition has acquired any substantial following among other sections of the population. Nevertheless, its significance should not be underestimated. Any government is to some extent dependent on a minimum amount of goodwill among intellectuals, and in this respect the Soviet regime is certainly on the decline. Not only does it have few sympathizers among foreign intellectuals, there are also very few well-known Soviet intellectuals who would publicly defend, say, the arrest of Daniel, Sinyavsky, Maj. Gen. P. G. Grigorenko, Litvinov, and Amalrik, the occupation of Czechoslovakia, or the exclusion of Solzhenitsyn from the Writers' Union. One might say that the Russian word *intelligentsia* has regained its 19th-century meaning: a considerable group of people —writers, musicians, scholars, teachers, engineers, scientists, artists—who have no sympathy whatever with their government.

continued from page 747

a European security conference, but this time advocating full participation of the U.S. and Canada, a reversal of previous Soviet attitudes. Toward the end of August, the leaders of all the U.S.S.R.'s Eastern European allies went to Moscow to discuss the effects of the Soviet-West German treaty.

The status quo in Eastern Europe was further strengthened by cooperation between Moscow and the regime of Gustav Husak in Czechoslovakia; in May, Brezhnev went to Prague to sign yet another Soviet-Czechoslovak treaty of friendship, which formally obliged Czechoslovakia to accept the Brezhnev doctrine justifying the intervention of one socialist country in the affairs of another to safeguard the established socialist order. In the case of Romania, however, the Soviet leaders failed to get the Brezhnev doctrine included in the new Soviet-Romanian treaty of friendship, which renewed the 20-year defense agreement of 1948 that the Romanians had allowed to lapse in 1968. Kosygin went to Bucharest in July to sign the treaty, while Brezhnev remained in Moscow. Romanian Pres. Nicolae Ceausescu replied to this snub by staying away from most of the ceremonies connected with the occasion. Elsewhere in Eastern Europe, the U.S.S.R. signed a new economic cooperative and trade agreement with East Germany, covering the period 1971–75.

Contacts with France developed along the lines of the policy of rapprochement determined by former French Pres. Charles de Gaulle. Soviet Foreign Minister Andrei Gromyko received a warm welcome in Paris in June, and in October French Pres. Georges Pompidou paid a state visit to the U.S.S.R., where he gave general support to the proposal for a European security conference. Later in October, Gromyko went to the UN General Assembly in New York, and on his way back stopped off in West Germany (the first Soviet foreign minister to do so) and in London. His most important contact, however, was with U.S. Pres. Richard Nixon in Washington.

The Soviet-U.S. dialogue was the major concern of Soviet foreign policy in 1970. Recognition that the modus vivendi between the two superpowers had to be developed despite the ritual references to ideological incompatibilities had become one of the fundamental facts of international life. During his visit to Washington, Gromyko eased the tension that had arisen earlier over plans to develop a Soviet submarine base in Cuba. Firm U.S. reaction caused immediate withdrawal of a Soviet submarine tender and a tug, and after talks at the White House, it was agreed that the U.S.S.R. would not construct a base while the U.S. would not object to Soviet ships using Cuba as a port of call.

The great powers continued their dialogue on problems of nuclear disarmament. In September the U.S. and the U.S.S.R. reached agreement on a draft treaty banning the positioning of nuclear devices on the seabed; the draft was endorsed by the UN Disarmament Committee in Geneva. The strategic arms limitation talks (SALT) between the U.S. and the U.S.S.R. reconvened in Vienna in April for an inconclusive session and resumed their slow progress in Helsinki in November, when the head of the Soviet delegation, Vladimir Semyonov, called for "a constructive and businesslike approach." These complex negotiations, hinging on the potential strategic balance between antiballistic missile systems and new powerful offensive missiles equipped with multiple warheads, entered their second year and their outcome remained doubtful. (*See* DEFENSE.)

The most sensitive area of foreign policy was the Middle East, where the U.S.S.R., under increased pressure from Cairo, supplied the United Arab Republic with a more sophisticated system for air defense. First reports confirming installation of the advanced surface-to-air missile (SAM 3) system in the U.A.R. by Soviet technicians appeared in March. In June U.S. Secretary of State William Rogers presented his plan for a three months' cease-fire to provide time for renewed discussions on the basis of the UN Security Council Resolution of November 1967. The Soviet Union gave a cautious welcome to these proposals, which also were accepted by U.A.R. Pres. Gamal Abd-al-Nasser after his return from discussions in Moscow. This peace initiative broke down in August when Israel claimed that the U.A.R. was violating the cease-fire by moving SAM 2 and SAM 3 missile batteries up to the Suez Canal front. The Rogers initiative was overtaken by the hijacking of several airliners by Palestine guerrillas early in September and by the civil war in Jordan that followed. The sudden death of Nasser at the end of September, however, overshadowed the whole Middle East situation.

Soviet diplomacy was presented with a difficult problem in the Middle East. It had to avoid a direct confrontation with the U.S. while consolidating its relations with the Arab governments. Extremists among the Palestine guerrillas did not fit this scenario, and it was not surprising that the Soviet attitude toward their hijacking escapades was unenthusiastic. The Middle East crisis also illustrated some of the differences between China and the U.S.S.R. The Chinese denounced the Rogers plan as an attempt by Washington and Moscow to inflict "a new Munich" on the Arabs, and they gave propaganda support to the Palestinian hijackings.

The U.S.S.R. also was embarrassed in its relations with the U.S. by the need to continue its backing for the North Vietnamese and the Viet Cong in Indochina. In July the Supreme Soviet denounced the U.S. for provoking the coup in Cambodia that drove chief of state Prince Norodom Sihanouk into exile in March, but significantly, the prince located his government-in-exile in Peking, not in Moscow. During the Revolution anniversary celebrations in Moscow in November, the keynote speaker was Mikhail Suslov, one of the most durable members of the Politburo. He expressed Soviet support for the national liberation struggle in Vietnam and also called for a greater degree of normalization in Sino-Soviet relations.

Sino-Soviet relations, despite outbursts of hostile propaganda on both sides, moved toward slightly more pragmatic attitudes, and talks about the frontier issue went on sporadically throughout the year. Despite Chinese troop movements reported in the Soviet press in February, there were no violent clashes along the frontier in 1970. In September a new Soviet ambassador appeared in Peking for the first time in years. He was V. Tolstikov, formerly party chief of the Leningrad area and an important figure in the Soviet hierarchy. The following month Liu Hsin-chuang arrived in Moscow to take up his duties as Chinese ambassador to the U.S.S.R., a post that had remained unfilled since 1966.

The Soviet Union's desire to normalize its relations with Peking might have been prompted partly by China's growing nuclear potential, and Soviet leaders almost certainly would have welcomed creation of a stable modus vivendi in the East, similar to the one they seemed to have achieved in the West. In an important speech in Alma-Ata immediately after the signing of the Soviet-West German treaty, Brezhnev stressed that this pact must not be interpreted as a safeguard for the Soviet western flank because of its difficulties with China; on the contrary, he spoke in most hopeful terms about the negotiations with Peking. The Sino-Soviet Joint Commission for Navigation on Boundary Rivers met from July 10 to December 19. On December 20 the Soviet Union announced that an accord on water navigation along the frontier had been signed, but this subsequently was denied by Peking.

In its foreign policy, the U.S.S.R. tried to combine its quest for stability with determination to play the role of a global power. In particular, its interest in the Indian Ocean might have been motivated by a desire to counter Chinese influence in the Indian subcontinent. The building of a strategic road through Afghanistan, announced in July, was also of interest in this context. Also in July, the U.S.S.R. concluded an agreement with Mauritius on the use of its ports by the Soviet fishing and merchant fleets and on landing rights for the Soviet airline Aeroflot at Plaisance airport.

But quest for stability was complicated by several unpredictable factors, including the situation in Indochina and the chronic crisis in the Middle East. Perhaps the most disturbing problems lay within the Communist world itself: the lethargic condition of the Soviet economy, the slow progress of negotiations with China, and, above all, the relative instability of the Communist regimes in Eastern Europe as demonstrated in December by an outburst in Poland.

(OT. P.)

See also Communist Movement; Propaganda.

ENCYCLOPÆDIA BRITANNICA FILMS. *The Soviet Challenge* (*The Industrial Revolution in Russia*) (1962).

TASS-SOVFOTO

U.S.S.R.'s new Zhiguli cars designed by Fiat roll off the assembly line in Togliatti for the first time in September 1970.

United Arab Republic

A republic of northeast Africa, the United Arab Republic (U.A.R.) is bounded by Israel, Sudan, Libya, the Mediterranean Sea, and the Red Sea. Area: 386,-900 sq.mi. (1,002,000 sq.km.). Pop. (1970 est.): 33,-329,000. Cap. and largest city: Cairo (pop., 1970 est., 4,961,000). Language: Arabic 97%. Religion: Muslim 91%; Christian 8%. President and prime minister until Sept. 28, 1970, Gamal Abd-al-Nasser; president from October 17, Anwar al-Sadat; prime minister from October 20, Muhammad Fawzi.

Unions:
see Labour Unions

Unitarians:
see Religion

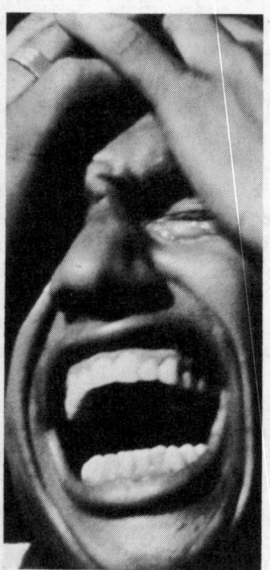

UPI COMPIX

JACK BURLOT—LIAISON

Above, mourners reach out to touch the flag-draped coffin of Gamal Abd-al-Nasser as the funeral cortege passes through the streets of Cairo, Oct. 1, 1970. Above, right, a mourner cries out in grief.

Because of President Nasser's sudden death on September 28 (*see* OBITUARIES), 1970 was a momentous year for the U.A.R. Although every effort was made by his successors to ensure continuity, the passing of a man whose decisions had guided foreign and domestic policy for nearly 18 years transformed the country's situation.

Every aspect of government policy was still dominated by the unresolved conflict with Israel. In January morale suffered from a series of Israeli air raids that penetrated deep into the country and from the 32-hour Israeli occupation of Shadwan Island in the Gulf of Suez on January 22–23. At the end of January Nasser made a secret flight to Moscow (officially denied at the time) and secured a promise of increased Soviet aid for U.A.R. ground and air defenses. In the first half of February, U.A.R. morale improved as its aircraft made several sorties into the Sinai. The heavy civilian casualties caused by an Israeli air raid on a scrap-metal works near Cairo on February 12 created a bitter reaction in the U.A.R. and probably influenced a U.S. decision to refuse, at least temporarily, Israel's request for Phantom and Skyhawk aircraft.

The Soviet deputy foreign minister, Vladimir Vinogradov, visited Cairo February 28 to March 4, and there were persistent reports during that time of

increased Soviet supplies of arms and missiles, including the SAM-3 designed to shoot down low-flying aircraft. The number of Soviet military advisers in the U.A.R. rose from about 3,000 to 8,000–10,000. Nasser said publicly that he had asked for MiG-23 interceptors, but it was uncertain as to whether the U.S.S.R. had agreed; because the U.A.R. had no pilots trained to fly such planes, Soviet pilots would have had to be used. On April 8, 46 children and 1 adult were killed and 20 children and 10 adults injured in an Israeli raid on the village of Bahr al-Baqar; the Israelis claimed the target was in a military camp. Israel made no more deep penetration raids into the U.A.R. after April 18 because of the danger, it was believed, of a direct clash with Soviet military personnel.

The Rabat Arab summit meeting in December 1969 was generally considered a failure from the U.A.R. viewpoint except that Kuwait agreed to provide $24 million in aid for arms purchases. But in 1970 the U.A.R.'s position in the Arab world was greatly strengthened by the support of the new revolutionary regimes in Sudan and Libya. On February 12–13 the Libyan leader Col. Muhammad al-Khadafy and Sudanese Pres. Gafaar Muhammad al-Nimeiry held talks with President Nasser in Cairo. Colonel al-Khadafy returned to Cairo on April 27–28 and June 1–14; on

UNITED ARAB REPUBLIC

Education. (1967–68) Primary, pupils 3,506,-429, teachers 90,773; secondary, pupils 1,031,820, teachers 43,958; vocational, pupils 162,656, teachers 10,800; teacher training, students 34,894, teachers 3,585; higher (including 6 universities), students 179,100.

Finance. Monetary unit: Egyptian pound, with a nominal par value of E£0.35 to U.S. $1 (E£0.84 = £1 sterling) and an effective exchange rate of E£0.43 to U.S. $1 (E£1.04 = £1 sterling). Gold, SDRs, and foreign exchange, central bank: (June 1970) U.S. $136 million; (June 1969) U.S. $209 million. Budget (1969–70 est.) balanced at E£1,661,855,000. Gross national product: (1967–68) E£2,495 million; (1966–67) E£2,459 million. Money supply: (June 1970) E£760.9 million; (June 1969) E£687.2 million. Cost of living (Cairo; 1963 = 100): (Jan. 1970) 143; (Jan. 1969) 137.

Foreign Trade. (1969) Imports E£276.5 million; exports E£324.1 million. Import sources:

U.S.S.R. 14%; France 10%; U.S. 7%; West Germany 7%; Italy 6%; India 6%; Spain 5%; Czechoslovakia 5%. Main exports: cotton 57%; rice 17%.

Transport and Communications. Roads (1969) *c.* 50,000 km. (including 22,142 km. with improved surface). Motor vehicles in use (1968): passenger 115,900; commercial (including buses) 26,700. Railways (1965) 4,508 km.; traffic (1967–68) 5,512,000,000 passenger-km., freight 3,001,000,000 net ton-km. Air traffic (1969): 762.4 million passenger-km.; freight 13,861,000 net ton-km. Shipping (1969): merchant vessels 100 gross tons and over 123; gross tonnage 239,-461. Telephones (Dec. 1968) 365,000. Radio receivers (Dec. 1965) 1,613,000. Television receivers (Dec. 1968) 418,000.

Agriculture. Production (in 000; metric tons; 1969; 1968 in parentheses): corn 2,366 (2,297); wheat (1968) 1,518, (1967) 1,291; barley

(1968) 121, (1967) 100; sorghum 813 (906); potatoes 487 (472); sweet potatoes (1968) 78, (1967) 68; rice (1968) 2,586, (1967) 2,278; sugar, raw value (1969–70) *c.* 471, (1968–69) *c.* 451; tomatoes (1968) 1,486, (1967) 1,230; dry broad beans (1968) 238, (1967) 189; cotton, lint 510 (437); dates 355 (*c.* 330); oranges (1968) 495, (1967) 613; lemons (1968) 99, (1967) 88; bananas (1968) *c.* 68, (1967) 66; grapes (1968) *c.* 120, (1967) 117; onions (1968) 469, (1967) 614; cheese *c.* 266 (*c.* 264); fish catch (1967) 85, (1966) 99. Livestock (in 000; 1967–68): asses 1,209; sheep (1968–69) 2,200; cattle (1968–69) *c.* 1,700; goats 798; buffaloes 1,704; camels 178; chickens 23,930.

Industry. Production (in 000; metric tons; 1969): crude oil 12,966; iron ore (metal content; 1968) 224; cement 3,610; phosphate rock (1968) 1,441; salt (1968) 622; asbestos (1968) 2.6; cotton yarn 157; cotton fabrics (m.) 689,000; electricity (kw-hr.; 1968) 6,735,000.

May 24–29 President Nasser attended a tripartite conference in Khartoum, and he visited Libya on June 20. Libya offered the U.A.R. an undisclosed additional amount of aid, and both Sudan and Libya were ready to provide the U.A.R. with air bases that would be secure from Israeli attack. After Nasser's death a further tripartite conference held in Cairo in early November reached agreement on positive steps toward a political federation of the U.A.R., Libya, and Sudan.

Although Nasser had remained highly critical of the U.S. in all his public pronouncements, blaming it and its continued diplomatic and military support of Israel for the failure to reach a political settlement in the Middle East, he took care not to close the door finally on all contacts with the U.S. He frequently met with the head of the U.S. residual mission in Cairo and had talks with U.S. Assistant Secretary of State Joseph Sisco during the latter's visit to Cairo in April. On May 1 he made what he called his "final appeal" to U.S. Pres. Richard Nixon to withhold support from Israel as long as it occupied Arab lands. After the U.S. launched its peace plan for the Middle East on June 25, Nasser visited the Soviet Union from June 29 to July 17, partly for consultations with the Soviet leaders and partly for treatment for his diabetic condition. After his return he announced on July 23 his acceptance of the U.S. peace proposals. His action was criticized by the Palestinian guerrilla organizations, by Syria, and, most strongly, by Iraq.

After Israel announced its acceptance of the U.S. plan, a 90-day cease-fire in the Suez Canal area went into effect at midnight, August 7. During the previous few weeks the U.A.R. had improved its performance by shooting down at least three Israeli aircraft, but the Israelis were also causing very heavy casualties with regular saturation bombing of U.A.R. positions in the canal zone. After the cease-fire, Israeli accusations that the U.A.R. had violated the military standstill agreement by installing scores of new missile sites in the canal zone were supported by the U.S. government.

Before Nasser's death there had been no important changes in the regime. Anwar al-Sadat (*see* BIOGRAPHY) had been appointed vice-president in December 1969 and Muhammad Hassanein Heikal, editor of the newspaper *Al Ahram,* became minister of national guidance on April 26. In July Ali Sabry became presidential adviser for aviation and air defenses and, it was believed, Nasser's liaison with the Soviet military advisers in the U.A.R.

In September Nasser took a leading role in Arab efforts to reach a settlement of the civil war in Jordan, and it was after the final summit meeting in Cairo at which agreement was reached between the two sides that he died suddenly of a heart attack on September 28. An extraordinary demonstration of national grief followed with millions accompanying his funeral cortege on October 1. Sadat became acting president and after the unanimous approval of his candidature for the presidency by the National Assembly his election was confirmed by a national referendum on October 15 in which 90.04% of the votes cast were affirmative. On October 20 Sadat appointed a 70-year-old former presidential adviser on foreign affairs, Muhammad Fawzi as prime minister. Muhammad Heikal resigned, and on October 31 Husain Shafei and Ali Sabry were appointed vice-presidents by decree. An 11-member National Defense Council was set up to control all aspects of the dispute with Israel.

In 1970 the U.A.R.'s immediate economic situation was fairly satisfactory, and in early November the government cut the prices of some basic commodities. Oil output and exports of agricultural and manufactured goods increased, and the government announced that in 1969–70 the U.A.R. had had its first balance of payments surplus in 30 years. However, future prospects of expansion were sharply affected by the increasing military expenditure. The Aswan High Dam across the Nile was commissioned officially on July 21. On December 28 Sadat ordered the return of property confiscated by the government during the preceding decade, but it was not believed that property taken from non-Egyptians was included in the reform.

(P. MD.)

See also Middle East.

ENCYCLOPÆDIA BRITANNICA FILMS. *Egypt and the Nile* (1954); *The Middle East* (1955); *The Suez Canal* (1962): *The Nile Valley and Its People* (1964).

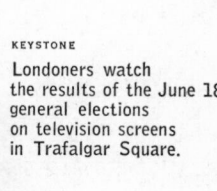

United Kingdom

A constitutional monarchy in northwestern Europe, the United Kingdom comprises the island of Great Britain (England, Scotland, and Wales) and Northern Ireland, together with many small islands. Area: 94,-216 sq.mi. (244,018 sq.km.), excluding 1,188 sq.mi. of inland water, the crown possession of the Isle of Man, and the crown dependencies of the Channel Islands. Pop. (1969 est.): 55,534,000. Cap. and largest city: London (pop. [Greater London], 1969 est., 7,703,410). Language: English is spoken almost universally, but some Welsh and Gaelic are also used. Religion: mainly Protestant. Queen, Elizabeth II; prime ministers in 1970, Harold Wilson and, from June 19, Edward Heath.

Domestic Politics. In a general election on June 18, 1970, the Conservative Party turned out the

KEYSTONE

Londoners watch the results of the June 18 general elections on television screens in Trafalgar Square.

United Church of Canada: *see* Religion

United Church of Christ: *see* Religion

Labour government that had been in office since October 1964. Harold Wilson resigned after being prime minister for more than five years and his place was taken by Conservative leader Edward Heath (*see* BIOGRAPHY)—the U.K.'s first bachelor prime minister since 1905.

Prior to the general election, the Labour Party made substantial local election gains. In elections for the Greater London Council (GLC) on April 9, Labour gained 16 seats, though the Conservatives retained control with 65 of the 100 GLC members. Elections were held between April 6–11 for 59 English and Welsh county councils, but party control remained unchanged. Polling took place on May 7 in 342 English and Welsh boroughs for one third of the seats on the councils. Labour had a net gain of 443 seats and the Conservatives a net loss of 327 seats. In the Scottish burgh council elections on May 5 the Labour Party had a net gain of 57 seats, largely at the expense of the Scottish National Party (SNP). Labour regained control of nine burgh councils. The SNP also suffered a setback in the Scottish county elections on May 13.

During the last few months of the Labour government, several new legislative measures were enacted. Among them was the Local Employment Act, which came into force on March 5. This embodied the government's proposals for assistance to 54 "intermediate" employment exchange areas not classified as full "development areas." Other new measures were enacted on May 29, the day when Parliament was dissolved. These included the Administration of Justice Act, creating a new Family Division of the High Court, and the Equal Pay (No. 2) Act, designed to ensure equal pay for men and women by the end of 1975.

On May 18, encouraged by local election results and opinion poll findings, Harold Wilson announced that the general election would be on June 18. Nominations closed on June 8, with a total of 1,819 candidates for the 630 seats in the House of Commons. Despite most of the pollsters' predictions, the Conservatives were returned to power with a majority of 31 seats over all other parties (excluding the speaker) in the House of Commons, and 43 over Labour. Labour gained 10 seats but lost 70 of the 347 (including one vacancy) they held at the dissolution of the old Parliament, while the Liberals lost 7 of their 13 seats.

KEYSTONE

Conservative Party leader Edward Heath became prime minister of Great Britain in June 1970.

In the new House of Commons there were 330 Conservative members, 287 Labour, 6 Liberals, and 7 others (including the speaker). The percentage of the total votes cast (with 1966 percentages in parentheses) were: Conservative 46.4 (41.9), Labour 43 (47.9), and Liberal 7.4 (8.5). The total Conservative vote increased by about 1.6 million and the Labour vote fell by 900,000. Though the Liberals' vote of 2,109,218 was only about 10% less than in the previous (1966) election, they lost more than half their seats. Among former Labour ministers who were defeated was George Brown, who was deputy leader of the party and a former secretary of state for foreign affairs; he was given a life peerage and took his seat in the House of Lords as Baron George-Brown.

The election campaign centred on Britain's economic performance under the Labour government, with Labour supporters arguing that their party had inherited an £800 million balance of payments deficit from the Conservatives in 1964 and had turned it into a surplus running at an annual rate of £600 million. Conservative tactics concentrated the argument on rising prices and questioned the soundness of Labour's economic policy, particularly as it seemed to be threatened by an outbreak of strikes and inflationary wage awards. The apparent collapse of Labour's incomes policy in the preceding year added force to the argument. Industrial disputes, including a newspaper strike for four days in the middle of the election campaign, gave added point to the Conservative promise of legislation on labour relations.

Conservative persistence in questioning Labour's economic policies was rewarded three days before polling day by the announcement of a £31 million trade deficit for May—a provisional figure which, on recalculation later in the year, turned out to be about twice as large as the actual deficit. The feeling that there was nothing much to choose between the parties was reflected in an unusually low turnout of voters, 72% compared with 75.9% in 1966, and the lowest at a general election since 1935.

The assumption that a change in government would bring no great change to the climate of British political affairs was possibly ill-founded. The policies adopted by the new Conservative administration were regarded by some observers as a watershed in postwar British politics. They involved a decisive turn away from state intervention in the economy and the adoption of the principle that the individual should

---

UNITED KINGDOM

Education. (1966–67) Primary, pupils 4,758,-034; secondary, pupils 3,147,524; primary and secondary, teachers 392,211; vocational, pupils 155,273, teachers (1965–66) 41,042; higher (including 44 universities), students 310,706, teaching staff 31,183.

Finance. Monetary unit: pound sterling, with a par value of £0.42 to U.S. $1 (£1 = $2.40). Gold, SDRs, and convertible currencies, official: (June 1970) U.S. $2,791,000,000; (June 1969) U.S. $2,443,000,000. Budget (1970–71 est.): revenue £16,124 million; expenditure £13,526 million. Gross national product: (1969) £45,650 million; (1968) £42,800 million. Money supply: (June 1970) £16,392 million; (June 1969) £15,-227 million. Cost of living (1963 = 100): (June 1970) 135; (June 1969) 127.

Foreign Trade. (1969) Imports £8,315,141,-000; exports £7,298,008,000. Import sources: EEC 19% (West Germany 6%, Netherlands 5%); U.S. 14%; Canada 6%. Export destinations: EEC 21% (West Germany 6%); U.S. 12%; Ireland 5%. Main exports: machinery 27%; motor vehicles 11%; chemicals 10%; textile yarns and fabrics 5%; precious stones 5%.

Tourism (1968): visitors 4,845,000; gross receipts U.S. $677 million.

Transport and Communications. Roads (1968) 350,802 km. (including 867 km. expressways). Motor vehicles in use (excluding Northern Ireland): (1969): passenger 11,228,000; commercial 1,569,000. Railways (excluding Northern Ireland; 1968): 20,051 km.; traffic 28,703,000,-000 passenger-km., freight 24,026,000,000 net ton-km. Air traffic (1969): 16,239,000,000 passenger-km.; freight 614.6 million net ton-km. Shipping (1969): merchant vessels 100 gross tons and over 3,858; gross tonnage 23,843,799. Ships entered (1968) vessels totaling 122,670,000 net registered tons; goods loaded (1968) 41,027,000 metric tons, unloaded 177,808,000 metric tons. Telephones (Dec. 1968) 12,799,000. Radio licenses (Dec. 1969) 18,184,000. Television licenses (Dec. 1969) 15,809,000.

Agriculture. Production (in 000; metric tons; 1969; 1968 in parentheses): wheat 3,373 (3,469); barley 8,987 (8,271); oats 1,334 (1,224); potatoes 6,215 (6,846); sugar, raw value (1969–70) c. 927, (1968–69) 974; apples (1968) 398, (1967) 337; pears (1968) 82,

(1967) 26; dry peas (1968) 52, (1967) 65; tomatoes (1968) 84, (1967) 86; onions (1968) 120, (1967) 98; eggs (1968) 877, (1967) 870; beef and veal 871 (906); mutton and lamb 206 (246); pork 902 (835); wool 31 (36); milk c. 13,750 (13,509); butter c. 60 (c. 54); cheese c. 119 (120); fish catch (1968) 1,040, (1967) 1,026. Livestock (in 000; June 1969): cattle 12,373; sheep 26,604; pigs 7,804; chickens 121,-318.

Industry. Index of industrial production (1963 = 100): (1969) 123; (1968) 120. Fuel and power (in 000; 1969): coal (metric tons) 151,-300; natural gas (cu.m.) 1,938,000; manufactured gas (cu.m.) 26,100,000; electricity (kw-hr.) 235,972,000. Production (in 000; metric tons; 1969): iron ore (25–30% metal content) 12,300; pig iron 16,670; crude steel 26,844; nitrogenous fertilizers (1968–69) 911; cement 17,420; passenger cars (units) 1,717; commercial vehicles (units) 466; agricultural tractors (units) 180; cotton fabrics (m.) 616,000; woolen fabrics (sq.m.) 239,000; rayon and other synthetic fabrics (m.) 500,000. Merchant vessels launched (1969) 1,053,000 gross tons.

pay, if he could afford it, for more of the services that Labour politicians thought should be provided without charge or at subsidized prices.

In forming his administration, Heath had to make two subsequent reshuffles, one following the death on July 20 of Iain Macleod (*see* OBITUARIES), who had been appointed chancellor of the Exchequer, and one after the reorganization of the departments of government in October. The effect of Macleod's death was to bring Anthony Barber (who, as chairman of the Conservative Party, had played a large part in masterminding the election campaign) to the Treasury as chancellor; to put Geoffrey Rippon in charge of the negotiations for Britain's possible entry into the European Economic Community; and to introduce John Davies, a newly elected member of Parliament but a notable figure in industry as a former director general of the Confederation of British Industries, into the Cabinet as minister of technology. (*See* BIOGRAPHY.*)

The new structure of government, announced in a White Paper on October 15, amalgamated the Ministry of Technology and the Board of Trade into a new Department of Trade and Industry; united the Ministry of Housing and Local Government, the Ministry of Transport, and the Ministry of Public Building and Works in a new Department of the Environment; created for 18 months a Ministry of Aviation Supply; absorbed the Ministry of Overseas Development into the Foreign Office; and renamed the Department of Employment and Productivity the Department of Employment.

After these changes had been completed, the Conservative Cabinet was: Heath (prime minister); Reginald Maudling (home secretary); Sir Alec Douglas-Home (secretary of state for foreign affairs); Barber (chancellor of the Exchequer); Lord Hailsham (lord chancellor); William Whitelaw (leader of the House of Commons); Lord Carrington (defense); Sir Keith Joseph (social services); Rippon (chancellor of the duchy of Lancaster); Robert Carr (employment); Davies (trade and industry); Margaret Thatcher (education and science); Gordon Campbell (Scotland); Earl Jellicoe (leader of the House of Lords); Peter Walker (environment); Peter Thomas (Wales); and James Prior (agriculture). This reduced the Cabinet to 17 ministers, the smallest since 1957.

The Conservative government was elected on an unusually specific manifesto. Among its promises were to reduce rates of personal taxation, including income tax and surtax, and to abolish the selective employment tax; to reduce the number of ministers, the number of civil servants, and the cost of government; to stop unjustified price increases in the public sector of industry; to introduce an industrial relations bill making agreements binding on both unions and employers to reduce state interference in industry; to substitute an import levies system in place of deficiency payments for farming; to concentrate housing subsidies on those who could not afford an economic rent; to leave decisions on comprehensive education to local authorities; to see that pensions retained their purchasing power, and to provide adequate family allowances; to tighten up immigration controls and to assist immigrants to return to their own countries if they wished; to tighten up the law dealing with demonstrations and demonstrators; to remove discrimination in the law against women; to keep a British military presence "east of Suez"; to make further effort to reach agreement with the rebellious

SPORT & GENERAL PRESS AGENCY LTD.

Piles of rubbish line a London street during the strike of municipal workers in September–November 1970.

Controversial Tory MP Enoch Powell speaking during a campaign tour in June 1970.

KEYSTONE

Smith regime in Rhodesia; and to permit commercial local radio.

Some of these pledges were promptly implemented —such as the reduction of the size of the government by cutting down the number of ministers. On June 30, less than two weeks after taking office as minister of education, Margaret Thatcher withdrew the Labour government's circular requiring local authorities to prepare plans for comprehensive secondary schools. Labour's plans to bring the docks into public ownership were abandoned, though the bill to implement the proposals had passed through most of its stages in Parliament before the election.

Legislation mentioned in the program for the new Parliament, announced in the queen's speech on July 2, included provision for pensions for people over 80 who were otherwise excluded from the current pension arrangements (a law to introduce the new pensions was enacted on July 23); an industrial relations bill; an immigration bill; proposals for commercial local radio under the supervision of an independent broadcasting authority; and a bill to abolish the Land Commission (in operation since April 1967).

More substantial developments had to await the return of Parliament after the summer recess on October 27, when Barber announced what came to be called a "mini-budget." His main proposals were: 6*d.* off the standard rate of income tax from April 6, 1971; corporation tax on companies reduced from 45 to 42½% for 1969–70; medical prescription charges to be increased from 2*s.* 6*d.* to 4*s.* on April 1, 1971, with further charges related to the cost of prescriptions to follow; increased charges for eyeglasses; dental charges increased to about half the cost of treatment; cheap welfare milk and school milk for children over seven to cease, but free milk entitlement to continue for some mothers and young children; the cost of school meals to be increased by about one third on April 1, 1971; a new system of housing subsidies and rebates to save between £100 million and £200 million per year; subsidized rail fares for London commuters to end in 1973; charges to be made for admission to national museums and art galleries (formerly free); selective investment grants to industry to be replaced by across-the-board investment allowances; and the Industrial Reorganization Corporation (set up in 1966) to be eliminated.

There was also some provision for extra spending: £28 million more for schools during the four years to 1974–75; £110 million more over the same period

POPPERFOTO FROM
PICTORIAL PARADE

Londonderry
Roman Catholics
attend the military style
funeral of a man and two
of his children who died
when a fire swept through
their home at the height
of the riots
on June 27, 1970.

Bernadette Devlin arrives
at the House of Commons
Oct. 27, 1970, to take
her seat following
the completion of her jail
sentence.

UPI COMPIX

for health and welfare services, including hospitals, particularly for the elderly and mentally handicapped; and legislation was to provide for supplementing low family incomes by up to £3 per week, starting in August 1971. The scale of the economies on the social services was small—setting extra expenditure against the savings and new charges, the net effect was less than 1% on a total expenditure of more than £8,000 million. Over the longer term, the proposals cut back the average annual growth of projected government expenditure between 1971–72 and 1974–75 from 3.5 to 2.8% a year, which was calculated to yield a net saving, on previous forecasts, of £1,040 million by the fiscal year 1974–75.

Details of the proposed new housing subsidies and rebates scheme were given by Environment Minister Walker on November 3. The principle of "fair rents" would operate for privately owned property and for local authority housing, with rebates payable to those who could not afford the full rent. The new arrangements, however, could not come into operation before 1972.

The Labour Party, in opposition, reelected Harold Wilson as leader, unopposed. The former chancellor of the Exchequer, Roy Jenkins, was elected to the post of deputy leader, vacated by George Brown on his defeat at the polls. In the election for 12 members of the parliamentary committee, the order of preference (a measure of ex-ministers' standing with Labour MPs) was: James Callaghan, Denis Healey, Anthony Crosland, Douglas Houghton, Anthony Wedgwood Benn, Michael Foot (not a former minister), Shirley Williams, Harold Lever, Edward Short, Frederick Peart, George Thomson, and Barbara Castle.

Industrial Relations. In Britain, 1970 was the worst year for strikes since 1926, the year of the "general strike." The engineering industry was worst affected. Nearly two-thirds of the 3,491 stoppages in the first ten months of the year arose out of wage disputes (more than three times as many as in 1965). The motor industry was particularly severely hit by strikes in the component-production factories. Notable disputes were the three-week dock strike in July and August, a six-week stoppage of local authority manual workers, and a "work to rule" in the electricity supply industry during December.

This greatly increased readiness by trade unions to resort to strike action encouraged the Conservative government to go ahead with its industrial relations bill, which (opinion polls showed) had widespread popular support in spite of bitter, uncompromising resistance by trade union leaders. The bill was preceded by the publication on October 5 of a consultative document, setting out the government's industrial relations policy. The main proposals were: a code of industrial relations practice; a new system of industrial relations courts; a registrar to supervise the rules of trade unions and employers' associations; a statutory right to belong to a trade union, accompanied by a corresponding right to opt out; statutory safeguards against unfair dismissals; a statutory right to strike, subject to the requirements of contracts; collective agreements to be binding and enforceable; provision to improve inadequate negotiating procedure; provision to oblige employers to disclose specified company information to employees; and provision for "cooling off" periods and a secret ballot in the case of disputes that seriously threatened the national interest.

Local Government. On February 4 the Labour government published a White Paper, *Reform of Local Government in England,* dealing with some of the recommendations made in 1969 by a royal commission on this subject. The government broadly accepted the commission's proposals, but differed on a few conclusions. For example, the government proposed the creation of two additional "metropolitan" areas— West Yorkshire and South Hampshire—in place of seven "unitary" areas proposed by the commission. According to the White Paper, the Labour administration believed that legislation on English local government should be introduced during 1971–72. Another White Paper, published on March 16, contained revised proposals for local government reform in Wales. The new recommendations dealt with the two counties of Glamorgan and Monmouthshire, and envisaged the creation of three "unitary" authorities to replace the numerous existing councils (borough, urban and rural district, and county) in those areas. No specific date for implementing any of the proposed reforms was announced by the Conservative government.

Foreign Policy and Defense. A new emphasis on what were regarded as British interests characterized the foreign policy of the new Conservative government. In the opening debate of the new Parliament, Heath said, "The main aim of our foreign policy must be to make a modern and broadly-based assessment of where British interests lie." This doctrine was a factor in the controversy over the intention to sell maritime arms to South Africa, which was defended as a necessary countermeasure to Soviet naval penetration of the Indian Ocean.

The new government also was determined to keep a small military presence in southeast Asia. However, the main emphasis of its foreign policy, as stated by Foreign Secretary Sir Alec Douglas-Home (*see* BIOGRAPHY), lay in Europe, with a reaffirmation of support for NATO and the opening of negotiations for Britain's entry into the European Economic Community.

The Economy. The balance of payments had been Britain's besetting economic problem ever since Labour took office, but 1969 produced an estimated surplus of £398 million as the reward for the tough economic policies imposed by the Labour chancellor of the Exchequer, Roy Jenkins. To secure a massive switch of resources away from domestic consumption to exports, Jenkins clamped down on demand at home at the expense of economic growth. The opening months of 1970, however, brought the best trade figures for many years, and in May, Jenkins was able to forecast a surplus of £550 million for the year.

Meanwhile, Britain's currency was strong, foreign funds flowed into London, and it was possible to pay off more than half of the £3,000 million borrowed in the deficit years 1964–68. On March 5 the bank rate was reduced from 8 to 7½%. The trends in the early part of 1970 were not entirely satisfactory. From February to April imports were rising faster than exports, which were only 1% up on the previous three months. At home, prices and wages were rising but growth flagged and unemployment remained obstinately high at about 2½%.

Although it was an election year, Jenkins produced a cautious budget on April 14, conceding only minor tax concessions. The bank rate was further reduced to 7% from April 15. Yet inflationary pressures continued to grow, as reflected in an increase of 17% in the money supply from April to June. Jenkins had assumed a 3½% increase in output in the coming year, but output in the first half of 1970 remained virtually static. The visible trade balance slipped back into deficit with the May figures. Trade figures later in the year were distorted by the effects of the dock strike, but it appeared that visible trade would be roughly in balance in the second half of the year, with a surplus of about £40 million a month on "invisibles." Thus the balance of payments situation seemed to have been resolved for the time being, with forecasts of a surplus of at least £300 million in 1971.

But, later in the year, concern for the balance of payments was replaced by growing anxieties over domestic inflation. The rate of increase in wages and prices was rising fast. Hourly wage rates had been rising by between 6 and 7% each year in 1968 and 1969, but in 1970 increases of more than 10% were common, and wage rises in the later part of the year tended to be around 15%. By the end of the year average earnings were 14% higher than a year previously. Prices were rising at a rate of 8% per annum, compared with 5% in 1969. Growth in output since 1968 had been at a general rate of only about 2% per annum, and the rate of growth in productivity was only about 3%. Investment was depressed. Inflation increased the pressure of wage demands and claims for increases as high as 30 to 40% were being made.

The Conservative government's response to inflation was to rely on employers' holding out against excessive wage increases—yet the government had to allow local authorities to concede a 15% pay raise to their manual workers. Manual workers in the national health service received a 15% wage increase. Restrictions were tightened up on money supply, but the government set its face against any form of statutory "freeze" on prices or incomes.

Northern Ireland. The programs of social reform and economic development initiated in 1969 were being implemented against a background of sectarian violence. (*See* IRELAND: *Special Report.*) A local government review body established in December 1969 produced its report on June 25, 1970. A five-year economic development program, published on June 23, proposed an increase of £75 million in public expenditure with a five-year program for building 73,000 houses, an increase of one third on the housing built in the previous five years. The program emphasized employment and industrial training as a way to eradicate some of the root causes of unrest in Northern Ireland.

Unrest persisted, however, both in the Parliament of Northern Ireland at Stormont, in Belfast, and in the streets. Disagreement over the reorganization of the police led to a revolt by five Ulster Unionist backbench members, and this feeling was reflected by the victory of the new and extreme Protestant Unionist Party at by-elections on April 16, when the Rev. Ian Paisley was elected to the Northern Ireland House of Commons for Bannside and the Rev. William Beattie for South Antrim (in the U.K. general election, Paisley also won a seat at Westminster). Nevertheless, Northern Ireland's prime minister, James Chichester-Clark, retained his hold on the province's government.

After a relatively quiet winter, demonstrations

RALPH ERIC SCHNACKENBERG
FROM NANCY PALMER

A woman in the Protestant area of Belfast shouts obscenities at the photographer as he crosses through the barbed wire.

broke out against a new Public Order Act passed on February 5, which strengthened regulations to control processions and demonstrations. Three nights of rioting in Belfast (March 31–April 2) showed some evidence of being supported by the underground Irish Republican Army, which threatened attacks against British troops. This drew from the U.K. government an assurance that troops would stay as long as necessary, and from the commander in chief, Lieut. Gen. Sir Ian Freeland, a warning that rioters using gasoline bombs were liable to be shot. On April 1 a new part-time local force, the Ulster Defence Regiment, became operational, replacing the Ulster Special Constabulary—the controversial B Specials—disbanded on April 30.

The imprisonment on June 26 of Bernadette Devlin, the civil rights MP for Mid-Ulster, on charges of incitement to riot in Londonderry in August 1969, led to three nights of violent clashes in Londonderry, with more than 200 people injured, including 100 soldiers. At the same time the worst riots since 1969 broke out in Belfast, with five shot dead, 200 injured (66 with gunshot wounds), and 100 fires started during the nights of June 27 and 28. The new home secretary, Reginald Maudling (*see* BIOGRAPHY), made his first visit to Northern Ireland on June 30–July 1, giving his backing to the reform program and repeating the Labour government's pledge to make British troops available as long as needed. In another violent outbreak in Belfast on July 3 three people were killed and 60 injured with gunshot wounds. The disturbances also led to official statements of concern by the Irish Republic's prime minister, John Lynch (*see* BIOGRAPHY), and minister for external affairs, Patrick Hillery (*see* BIOGRAPHY), who made a much-criticized visit to Catholic areas in Belfast on July 6. (*See* IRELAND.)

The summer rioting led to the passing of emergency legislation, making it an offense "to use threatening, abusive, or insulting language to stir up hatred against, or arouse the fear of, any section of the community on grounds of religion, belief, colour, race, or ethnic or national origin." On July 23 a six-month ban on marches was imposed. Nevertheless, sporadic rioting, some of it serious, continued to occur.

Clashes with troops in Belfast on July 31–August 4 led Chichester-Clark to blame "sinister elements" operating in the republican cause rather than for civil rights. On August 10 Maudling hinted that if there were a breakdown in the reform program agreed upon by the two governments, there might have to be direct rule from Westminster. Miss Devlin was released from Armagh jail on October 20.   (W. H. Ts.)

ENCYCLOPÆDIA BRITANNICA FILMS. *The British Isles—The Land and the People* (1963); *Britain—Searching for a New Role* (1964).

United Nations

Member nations marked the 25th anniversary of the UN by paying considerable lip service to its purposes and principles, but at the same time they made no greater effort than in recent years to live up to their pledges. In fact, both the U.S. and the U.S.S.R. exploded nuclear test devices at the start of the anniversary celebrations in October.

On the 25th anniversary of the signing of the UN Charter in San Francisco (June 26, 1945), Secretary-General U Thant gave the principal address in San Francisco's War Memorial Opera House. He reminded

delegates of the "crisis of confidence" that the UN faced, and of the need for nations, "especially the great nations," to "improve and change the quality and performance of the United Nations and the way it is used."

UN Day (October 24) festivities were muted, partly because of the unhappy condition of world affairs, partly because neither U.S. Pres. Richard M. Nixon nor Soviet Premier Aleksei N. Kosygin chose to attend the celebrations at UN headquarters. The 25th General Assembly (September 15 to December 17) brought its ten days of special observances to a climax on UN Day by adopting three declarations, one each on international law and international development strategy and a Declaration on the Occasion of the Twenty-Fifth Anniversary, in which members reaffirmed their dedication to the Charter.

Middle East. Private discussions among the Big Four about possible ways of settling the Middle East crisis continued throughout the year. For a short period beginning August 25, talks among three parties to the conflict (Israel, Jordan, and the U.A.R.) were conducted by Ambassador Gunnar V. Jarring, the secretary-general's special representative to the Middle East. He began his work under the sheltering umbrella of a cease-fire, arranged largely by the U.S., which lasted from August 7 to November 5 and was then extended until February 5, 1971. Talks had hardly begun, however, when Israel charged that the U.A.R., with the help of the U.S.S.R., had violated the cease-fire terms by moving surface-to-air missile sites closer to the Suez Canal. Israel left the talks and did not agree to return until late in December.

With peace talks suspended, Middle East tensions rose in September after Palestinian guerrillas carried out several spectacular airplane hijackings and for a time plunged Jordan into virtual civil war. (*See* MIDDLE EAST.) On September 9 the Security Council appealed to "all parties concerned" to release "all passengers and crews without exception, held as a result of hijackings and other interference in international travel." At President Nixon's request, the 27-nation council of the International Civil Aviation Organization held a special meeting September 18 to consider a worldwide aviation boycott against states that harboured hijackers and did not themselves prosecute them. On October 1, by a vote of 14–3–10 (the third figure indicating abstentions), the council approved the U.S. proposal.

Not all the Middle East drama was played out in the last quarter of the year. Earlier there were violations of older cease-fire agreements, especially in the Suez Canal area and on the Lebanese-Israeli frontiers. On February 14–18 U Thant consulted in New York with the chief of staff of the UN Truce Supervision Organization, Norwegian Gen. Odd Bull (succeeded August 1 by Finnish Maj. Gen. Ensio Siilasvuo). The dangers run by UN military observers in the Suez Canal sector were emphasized by the secretary-general in a letter sent June 5 to the permanent representatives of the states whose nationals were serving in that capacity. U Thant praised the observers' courage and dedication, but stated that he was "no longer able to guarantee, to any reasonable degree, the physical safety of the men engaged in the observation operation." His words received tragic emphasis on July 16, when Swedish Maj. J. E. Bogvad was killed while on UN duty.

On May 12 and again on September 5, following complaints by Lebanon about Israeli incursions, the

Security Council demanded the "immediate withdrawal" of Israeli forces from Lebanese territory. In both cases Israel claimed that the "invasion" was an isolated action against guerrilla terrorists and withdrew of its own accord—in September even before the council's resolution had been passed. On May 19 the council condemned Israel for "premeditated military action." On October 21 the council reaffirmed that its November 1967 resolution on the Middle East should be "carried out in all its parts," including the demand that Israeli troops withdraw from occupied Arab territories and the requirement that all parties acknowledge the sovereignty, territorial integrity, and political independence of the others. For the first time in UN history, the council meeting was held at ministerial level under art. 28 (2) of the Charter. The discussion of the Middle East was part of a scheduled "review of the international situation" in which 11 foreign ministers and one president (Anastasio Somoza of Nicaragua) took part.

The continuing plight of the 1.4 million refugees cared for by the UN Relief and Works Agency for Palestine Refugees (UNRWA) remained a critical issue. U Thant warned on August 13 that the agency was $5 million short of meeting its $45 million budget for 1970, and on October 29 UNRWA projected that it was $6 million short of the estimated $47 million needed for 1971. Israel meanwhile alleged that Palestinian guerrillas had taken over some UNRWA installations. On July 14 Israeli security forces announced that they had uncovered a self-styled "Secret Suicide Society" in a UN school in the occupied Gaza Strip. On March 23 the UN Commission on Human Rights condemned Israel's refusal to apply the 1949 Geneva Convention on Protection of Civilians in its conquered territories, and on November 2 a UN investigating committee reported that Israel was violating the human rights of people in Arab territories occupied in the 1967 war. The report was denounced by Israeli officials.

At the request of Arab states, the General Assembly debated the Middle East question. On November 4 it adopted a resolution (57–16–39) calling for an extension of the cease-fire for three months. The resolution also asked Israel to withdraw from occupied territories under threat of Security Council sanctions. Israel, which, like the U.S., opposed the resolution, denounced it as an obstacle to peace.

Peacekeeping and Disarmament. Commenting on peacekeeping problems on July 20, the secretary-general affirmed his view that permanent members of the Security Council had special peacekeeping responsibilities and that, when they vote for peacekeeping missions, they "may reasonably be expected" to help finance them. A UN peacekeeping effort leading the kind of hand-to-mouth existence U Thant deplored was the UN Force in Cyprus. On June 9 and December 10 the council voted unanimously to extend UNFICYP for successive six-month periods.

Speaking about the U.S. incursion into Cambodia in the spring, U Thant on May 5 called for an international conference of all parties to the 1954 and 1962 Geneva agreements on Indochina. For years he had warned that the Vietnam war might spill over its borders. (*See* SOUTHEAST ASIA.)

In Korea, on October 12, seven guards belonging to the UN Command and a Swiss officer of the Neutral Nations Supervisory Commission were injured in a ten-minute fight with North Korean security guards at Panmunjom. The fight apparently started after a North Korean guard pulled an armband off a UN guard protecting several South Korean civilians working in the Military Armistice Commission conference room.

The conference of the 26-member Committee on Disarmament met in Geneva, Switz. (February 17–April 30, June 16–September 3), to revise the text of a draft treaty prohibiting states from placing nuclear

Table I. Member States of the United Nations
Dec. 31, 1970

Afghanistan	Dominican Rep.*	Lebanon*	Senegal
Albania	Ecuador*	Lesotho	Sierra Leone
Algeria	El Salvador*	Liberia*	Singapore
Argentina*	Equatorial Guinea	Libya	Somalia
Australia*	Ethiopia*	Luxembourg*	South Africa*
Austria	Fiji	Malagasy Rep.	Southern Yemen
Barbados	Finland	Malawi	Spain
Belgium*	France*	Malaysia	Sudan
Belorussia*	Gabon	Maldives	Swaziland
Bolivia*	Gambia, The	Mali	Sweden
Botswana	Ghana	Malta	Syria*
Brazil*	Greece*	Mauritania	Tanzania
Bulgaria	Guatemala*	Mauritius	Thailand
Burma	Guinea	Mexico*	Togo
Burundi	Guyana	Mongolia	Trinidad and
Cambodia	Haiti*	Morocco	Tobago
Cameroon	Honduras*	Nepal	Tunisia
Canada*	Hungary	Netherlands*	Turkey*
Central African	Iceland	New Zealand*	Uganda
Rep.	India*	Nicaragua*	Ukraine*
Ceylon	Indonesia	Niger	U.S.S.R.*
Chad	Iran*	Nigeria	United Arab Re-
Chile*	Iraq*	Norway*	public (Egypt*)
China (Taiwan)*	Ireland	Pakistan	United Kingdom*
Colombia*	Israel	Panama*	United States*
Congo (Kinshasa)	Italy	Paraguay*	Upper Volta
Congo (Brazz.)	Ivory Coast	Peru*	Uruguay*
Costa Rica*	Jamaica	Philippines*	Venezuela*
Cuba*	Japan	Poland*	Yemen
Cyprus	Jordan	Portugal	Yugoslavia*
Czechoslovakia*	Kenya	Romania	Zambia
Dahomey	Kuwait	Rwanda	
Denmark*	Laos	Saudi Arabia*	

*Signatories to original charter.

Table II. Council Membership
Years indicate date membership expires

Country	Security Council	Economic and Social Council	Trusteeship Council
China (Taiwan)	Permanent		Permanent
France*	Permanent	1972	Permanent
U.S.S.R.*†	Permanent	1971	Permanent
United Kingdom*†	Permanent	1971	Permanent
United States*†	Permanent	1973‡	Permanent§
Argentina*	1972		
Australia*			§
Belgium	1972	1972	
Brazil*		1972	
Burundi	1971		
Ceylon		1972	
Congo (Kinshasa)		1973	
Ghana		1972	
Greece		1972	
Haiti		1973	
Hungary*		1973	
Indonesia		1971	
Italy*†	1972	1972	
Jamaica		1971	
Japan*	1972		
Kenya		1972	
Lebanon		1973	
Malagasy Republic†		1973	
New Zealand		1973	
Nicaragua	1971		
Niger		1971	
Pakistan*		1971	
Peru		1972	
Poland*†	1971		
Sierra Leone†	1971		
Somalia	1972		
Sudan		1971	
Syria†	1971		
Tunisia†		1972	
Uruguay		1971	
Yugoslavia*†	1971		

*Members of the Conference of the Committee on Disarmament in addition to: Bulgaria, Burma, Canada, Czechoslovakia, Ethiopia, India, Mexico, Mongolia, Morocco, the Netherlands, Nigeria, Romania, Sweden, and the U.A.R. (France does not attend conference meetings.)
†Members of the Committee of 24 on decolonization in addition to: Afghanistan, Bulgaria, Ecuador, Ethiopia, Honduras, India, Iran, Iraq, Ivory Coast, Mali, Norway, Tanzania, and Venezuela. Australia, though formally a member, has withdrawn.
‡Reelected.
§Administering authorities.

WIDE WORLD

Edvard Hambro of Norway was elected president of the UN General Assembly's 25th session.

WIDE WORLD

Diplomats representing Nationalist China watch as the UN General Assembly votes on the admission of Communist China, Nov. 20, 1970. Communist China gained a majority of votes but not the two-thirds majority required.

weapons and other weapons of mass destruction on the seabed. On November 3 the U.S. and the U.S.S.R. joined in recommending the revised draft, which was approved by the General Assembly's First Committee. The Disarmament Committee was also working on a comprehensive nuclear test ban, a program for general and complete disarmament, and the problem of eliminating chemical and bacteriological weapons from national arsenals. (*See* DEFENSE.)

Racial and Colonial Issues. As usual, events in southern Africa occupied the attention of the General Assembly, the Security Council, the Committee of 24 on decolonization, and other UN bodies. On October 14, the assembly called on states to implement the complete arms ban that the council had imposed on South Africa July 23. Only South Africa and Portugal opposed the assembly resolution, but Canada, France, the U.K., and the U.S. were among those that abstained.

The council, in tightening its arms embargo in July, called for the withholding of vehicles and equipment and spare parts for them from South African armed forces and paramilitary organizations, and asked UN members to revoke all licenses and military patents granted to South Africa for manufacturing arms and munitions, aircraft, naval craft, or other military vehicles, to prohibit investments in or technical assistance for manufacturing military hardware, and not to provide military training for any South African military personnel.

The assembly took its most direct action against South Africa on November 13, when it adopted an amendment, introduced by the black African states, declining to accept the credentials of the South African delegation because it did not represent the indigenous black population. Assembly Pres. Edvard Hambro said that the resolution constituted a "very strong condemnation of the policies" of South Africa but would not unseat the state or deny it the right to participate in the assembly.

The council took the first of several actions on Rhodesia on March 18, when it condemned the "illegal proclamation of republican status" by Ian Smith's regime. On July 13 the council's sanctions committee reported that measures against Rhodesia had "not been fully effective," largely because South Africa and Portugal had continued to trade with it. On November 10 the U.K. vetoed a resolution that would have required Britain to ensure majority rule in Rhodesia before granting it independence. On November 17, however, the council unanimously reaffirmed its "condemnation of the illegal declaration of independence" by the Smith regime and urged all states to continue withholding recognition. Britain was again urged to try to end the "illegal rebellion."

Colonialism in general was the subject of an assembly resolution adopted October 24 by a vote of 86–5–15. The text regarded colonialism as an international crime that violates the Charter, reaffirmed "the inherent right of colonial peoples to struggle by all necessary means" for freedom and independence, and requested member states to aid colonial peoples in every possible way. It also asked the council to widen sanctions against Rhodesia and to consider imposing sanctions on South Africa and Portugal.

In December a five-member UN mission, sent to investigate reports of an invasion of Guinea, found that the invading force had been commanded by Portuguese officers and called upon Portugal to compensate Guinea for the loss of life and property sustained in the fighting.

Organizational Matters. Edvard Hambro (*see* BIOGRAPHY) of Norway was elected president of the 25th General Assembly. UN membership rose to 127 on October 13, when the assembly admitted Fiji on recommendation (October 10) of the Security Council. On November 20 the assembly took up the question of Chinese membership and for the first time produced a majority in favour of seating the People's Republic of China. The vote was 51–49 with 25 abstentions. Because the assembly had earlier voted (66–52) to require a two-thirds majority to decide the question, the simple majority did not suffice, however. The vote in 1969 had been 56–48 against the Communist state, with 21 abstentions. (R. N. S.)

UNESCO. Having been principally responsible for the designation of 1970 as International Education Year by the UN, UNESCO was active throughout the year in helping to ensure its success. IEY was aimed at focusing world attention on the present educational crisis and on requirements for the expansion and development of education. Activities included special TV and radio programs, films, publications, exhibitions, and training courses.

A meeting of international experts was convened by UNESCO to consider a first survey on the application of a recommendation concerning the status of teachers, drawn up jointly in 1966 by UNESCO and the International Labour Organization. Reports from 75 states indicated that schoolteachers in many countries still lacked basic social and civil rights, large numbers were poorly paid, and many lacked any clearly defined academic freedom and job security.

The organization continued its active support for the Intergovernmental Oceanographic Commission and the International Hydrological Decade (1965–74), in which 100 countries were taking part. In June UNESCO convened the first conference of ministers responsible for science policy in European member states; 170 delegates from some 30 countries took a strong stand in favour of more fundamental research and urged European countries to put their resources at the service of less advanced regions.

UNESCO called two important meetings in 1970 in the sector of social and human sciences and culture. One, a symposium in June attended by 25 international specialists, was concerned with the general role of social sciences in development. The other, in Venice in August–September, dealt with how best to meet and satisfy the new need for culture.

In collaboration with specialists and lawyers from some 60 of its member states, UNESCO drew up an international convention aimed at preventing the illicit import, export, and transfer of ownership of cultural property, very often through the smuggling of art treasures. (R. D. A. G.)

United States

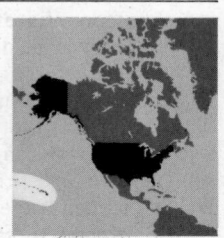

The United States of America is a federal republic composed of 50 states, 49 of which are in North America and one of which consists of the Hawaiian Islands. Area: 3,615,210 sq.mi. (9,363,405 sq.km.), including 66,237 sq.mi. of inland water but excluding the 60,306 sq.mi. of the Great Lakes that lie within U.S. boundaries. Pop. (1970): 204,765,770, including (1960) white 88.6%; Negro 10.5%. Language: English. Religion (1963 est.): Protestant 64,435,000; Roman Catholic 42,-877,000; Jewish 5,365,000; Orthodox 2.8 million. Cap.: Washington, D.C. (pop., 1970, 746,169). Largest city: New York (pop., 1970, 7,771,730). President in 1970, Richard Milhous Nixon.

In 1970 President Nixon (*see* BIOGRAPHY) managed to neutralize the war in Vietnam as a political issue—a feat that his predecessor, Lyndon B. Johnson, never was able to achieve. At the same time, however, Nixon found himself increasingly drawn into conflict with the U.S. Senate on a wide range of issues. Several key measures of the president's legislative program went down to defeat in the Senate, as did his nomination of Judge G. Harrold Carswell of Florida to the Supreme Court. Accordingly, the White House launched an intensive campaign to defeat obstructionist senators in the November 3 general elections. The effort was only partially successful, and the 92nd Congress, like the 91st, would be controlled by the Democrats.

The Omnibus Crime Control Act may have been the most important of the handful of major administration-backed bills that became law in 1970. In signing the measure, Nixon said it would give the federal government the means to wage "a total war against organized crime." He added that it "should be a warning to those who engage in [terrorist] acts that we are not going to tolerate these activities." The crime bill prescribed the death penalty for anyone convicted of a fatal bombing and would permit FBI agents to investigate and federal attorneys to prosecute those accused of bombings and arson on college campuses and at other institutions that receive federal financial aid. To fight organized crime, the measure would permit judges to impose additional sentences of up to 25 years on certain "dangerous and adult special offenders" convicted of crimes that carry lesser penalties.

The administration scored another major legislative victory when Congress approved the Postal Reorganization Act, a measure that had broad bipartisan support. In essence, the reorganization act ended congressional authority to set postal rates, establish preferential classes of mail, determine postal salaries and, through the power of patronage, influence appointments and promotions. These powers would now be exercised by the new United States Postal Service. (*See* POSTAL SERVICES.)

In other legislation passed in 1970, Congress provided for disclosure of consumer credit reporting; revised federal narcotics and drug laws; provided emergency funds for the home-mortgage market; exempted certain operations of newspapers from the antitrust laws; set up a program of long-term financing for urban mass transportation systems; created a semipublic corporation to operate a nationwide rail passenger network (*see* TRANSPORTATION); set a deadline of Jan. 1, 1975, for the virtual elimination of harmful emissions from automobiles; and authorized expansion of federal birth control programs and population research. The president vetoed a bill providing inducements to medical schools to train more general practitioners on grounds that it represented a "wrong approach" and that the administration would present a comprehensive health care program in 1971.

The Senate Finance Committee dealt a stinging setback to the administration when it rejected, on November 20, legislation to overhaul the nation's welfare system. The proposed Family Assistance Plan had been described by President Nixon as the keystone of his domestic legislative program. A further attempt to pass the welfare plan was made after the election, when Congress met in its first lame-duck session in 20 years. Also before the Senate were increases in social security benefits; a trade bill, originally introduced by the administration to establish import quotas on textiles but amended in the House to provide more protection than the president wanted; and continued funding for the supersonic transport, which had been deleted from the Transportation Department appropriation bill by the Senate and reinstated by a conference committee.

Led by Sen. William Proxmire (Dem., Wis.), opponents of the SST staged a series of filibusters that brought Senate business to a standstill during much of the session. In the waning days before adjournment it was agreed that the SST would be funded for three months, during which the matter could be reconsidered. Meanwhile, the welfare, trade, and social security measures—which at one point had been tied into a single legislative package—had been lost in a parliamentary morass, and little other legislation of importance had been passed.

The Senate's rejection of Carswell, Nixon's second choice to fill the Supreme Court seat vacated by former Justice Abe Fortas, was a particularly galling defeat for the president, especially since it came less than five months after the Senate had turned down Nixon's first choice, U.S. District Judge Clement F. Haynsworth, Jr. The two most powerful arguments against confirmation of Carswell were accusations that he was racially biased and had a mediocre record on the bench. Nixon had a different explanation; he accused the Senate of discriminating against the South and pledged that his next nominee to the court would "fulfill the criteria of a strict constructionist [of the Constitution] with judicial experience from either a federal bench or on a state court." That nominee turned out to be Judge Harry A. Blackmun (*see* BIOGRAPHY) of the U.S. Court of Appeals for the 8th Circuit, who was confirmed virtually without dissent.

In a year marked by both economic slowdown and continued inflation, the president and Congress differed often in the field of economic policy. Nixon vetoed

WIDE WORLD

Firemen stand amid the ruins of the Bank of America in Santa Barbara, Calif., after it was burned during rioting at the University of California in February 1970.

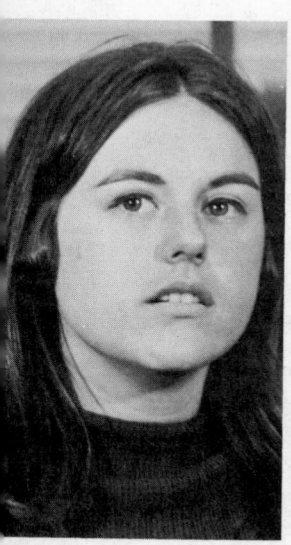

WIDE WORLD

Bernardine Dohrn, fugitive leader of the Weathermen, was believed to have recorded the message heard in New York Oct. 7, 1970, calling for an offensive by dissidents that "will spread from Santa Barbara to Boston, back to Kent and Kansas."

four money bills during the year, and Congress overrode two of the vetoes—those of a hospital construction authorization bill and of the Office of Education appropriation bill. Two vetoes were sustained—those of the fiscal 1970 appropriation bill for the Labor and the Health, Education, and Welfare departments and of the fiscal 1971 appropriation bill for the Department of Housing and Urban Development and independent offices.

Foreign Affairs. In his 1970 state of the union address, President Nixon stated that "the first priority must always be peace for America and the world" and that "the major immediate goal of our foreign policy is to bring an end to the war in Viet Nam." Although no progress was made during the year toward a negotiated settlement of the war, the president continued to reduce U.S. involvement in Vietnam by withdrawing additional troops and encouraging the Saigon government to assume a greater share of the fighting.

In a nationwide television address on April 20, Nixon announced that he planned to have 150,000 more U.S. troops withdrawn from Vietnam by the spring of 1971. "We can now say with confidence," he said, that "pacification is succeeding," that "the South Vietnamese can develop the capability for their own defense," and that "all American combat forces can and will be withdrawn." Only ten days later, however, Nixon announced a major U.S. offensive into Cambodia to clear out sanctuaries used by North Vietnamese and Viet Cong forces in waging the war in South Vietnam. Nixon insisted the U.S. attack was "not an invasion of Cambodia" because the areas were "completely occupied and controlled" by the North Vietnamese. "We will withdraw," he added, once the enemy was driven out and his military supplies destroyed. The announcement sparked a major domestic upheaval (see below), but the operation was officially declared a success, and all U.S. forces were pulled out of Cambodia on June 29, one day before the deadline set by the president.

Nixon proposed a new five-point peace plan for Indochina in a major foreign policy address on October 7. The plan, outlined in a television address, called for: (1) a "cease-fire in place"; (2) an expanded peace conference that would seek to end the fighting in Laos and Cambodia as well as in South Vietnam; (3) U.S. readiness "to negotiate an agreed timetable" for total withdrawal of U.S. troops "as part of an overall settlement"; (4) efforts by the allied and

Communist sides to "search for a political settlement that truly meets the needs of all South Vietnamese"; and (5) the "immediate and unconditional release of all prisoners of war." Communist representatives at the Paris peace talks denounced the Nixon proposal.

The most dramatic development in Vietnam came toward the end of the year. U.S. planes carried out widespread attacks on North Vietnam for a 24-hour period, November 21–22; the raids were described by Defense Secretary Melvin R. Laird as "protective reaction strikes . . . in response to attacks on our unarmed reconnaissance aircraft." News of the bombing mission was followed by disclosure that a U.S. task force had landed 23 mi. from Hanoi on November 21 in an unsuccessful attempt to rescue U.S. prisoners of war believed held captive at a camp there. Laird said the rescue force at Son Tay "successfully returned to safety without suffering a single casualty" after discovering that the prisoners had been removed. In a televised press conference on December 10, Nixon said he would order the bombing of military targets in North Vietnam if the level of fighting was stepped up as U.S. troops withdrew or if U.S. reconnaissance planes were fired upon.

The simmering conflict between Israel and its Arab neighbours provided a second major concern of U.S. foreign policy in 1970. In a television interview on July 1, Nixon said: "I think the Middle East is now terribly dangerous. The two superpowers, the U.S. and the Soviet Union, could be drawn into a confrontation that neither of them wants because of the differences there." The president's remarks came six days after Secretary of State William P. Rogers announced a new U.S. proposal to bring peace to the Middle East. The plan called for a 90-day cease-fire while UN mediator Gunnar V. Jarring resumed indirect peace talks with the U.A.R., Jordan, and Israel. The three countries announced their acceptance of the peace formula at the end of July, and the 90-day truce went into effect on August 7.

The Middle East situation took a dangerous turn in September when civil war broke out in Jordan between Palestinian guerrillas and forces loyal to King Husain. The fighting erupted shortly after guerrillas had hijacked four passenger airliners (including two U.S. planes). By September 19 Syrian tanks were reported to have entered northern Jordan to come to the guerrillas' aid. (See MIDDLE EAST.) In a newspaper interview published the previous day, President Nixon had been quoted as saying that the U.S. was "prepared to intervene in the Jordanian civil war should Syria and Iraq enter the conflict and tip the military balance against the government forces." A direct warning to Syria against intervention in Jordan was issued by the State Department on September 20 and, in the end, the Syrian tanks withdrew—or were forced to retreat—back across the Jordanian border.

Nixon underscored U.S. interest in the Middle East by making an eight-day, five-nation tour of Europe in late September and early October. Three of the nations on his itinerary were in the Mediterranean area—Italy, Spain, and Yugoslavia. A prominent part of the trip—a visit to the U.S. 6th Fleet and conferences with its commanders—served to highlight the president's message, on his arrival in Rome, that a "primary, indispensable" principle of U.S. foreign policy was "to maintain the necessary strength in the Mediterranean to preserve the peace against those who might threaten the peace." The president returned to Europe in November to attend a requiem Mass for Charles de Gaulle at Notre Dame Cathedral in Paris.

In what was described as the first presidential "state of the world" message, Nixon submitted to Congress on February 18 a report entitled "United States Foreign Policy for the 1970s: A New Strategy for Peace." The message stressed two points: the U.S. would maintain its global treaty commitments, but it would also bring into its commitment appraisals a firm assessment of the U.S. interests involved. It emphasized the partnership relationship as opposed to one of domination, and negotiation and multinational cooperation as opposed to great-power rivalry or ideological contention. In Nixon's words: "America cannot—and will not—conceive *all* the plans, design *all* the programs, execute *all* the decisions and undertake *all* the defense of the free nations of the world." The thrust of the Nixon message was sharply at variance with the assertion made by Pres. John F. Kennedy in his inaugural address in 1961: "Let every nation know, whether it wishes us well or ill, that we shall pay any price, bear any burden, meet any hardship, support any friend, oppose any foe to assure the survival and the success of liberty."

Domestic Affairs. The bitterly contested midterm elections for Congress and governorships produced mixed results, and both the Democrats and the Republicans claimed victory. The Democrats scored a net gain of 11 governorships, reversing the Republican margin of 32–18 to 29–21 in favour of the Democrats. The Republicans, on the other hand, lost only nine House seats and gained two Senate seats; usually, the party in power suffers substantial losses in Congress in midterm elections.

Although the Democrats retained control of the Senate after the elections, President Nixon claimed that the voters had given him "a working [ideological] majority of four" in that chamber. The administration was especially pleased with the defeat of three senators it had worked hard to turn out of office—Charles

BEN ROTH AGENCY

". . . and whoever said vaudeville was dead is merely a troglodytic, pusillanimous, pussyfooting radiclib"—Peterson, "Vancover Sun."

E. Goodell (Rep., N.Y.), Albert A. Gore (Dem., Tenn.), and Joseph D. Tydings (Dem., Md.). Goodell's seat was won by James L. Buckley, nominee of the Conservative Party of New York state, who announced during his campaign that he would vote with the Republicans in the organization of the Senate. In Virginia incumbent Harry F. Byrd, Jr., a Democrat running as an independent, won reelection and was expected to continue to vote with the Democrats on Senate organization.

Newcomers to the Senate included Democrats Lawton Chiles (Fla.), Adlai E. Stevenson III (Ill.), and John V. Tunney (Calif.) and Republicans Robert Taft, Jr. (O.), William E. Brock III (Tenn.), and Lowell P. Weicker, Jr. (Conn.). Hubert H. Humphrey (*see* BIOGRAPHY) was reelected to the Senate from

WIDE WORLD

Police guard Disneyland, Aug. 6, 1970, following demonstrations by several hundred Yippies, who put on a radical circus, climbed buildings, and sang the old Mickey Mouse Club song. Some arrests were made, and the park closed early.

WIDE WORLD

Lieut. William Calley, accused of murdering 102 Vietnamese civilians in 1968 at My Lai, approaches the court building at Ft. Benning, Georgia, in December 1970.

The dramatic Democratic upsurge in wresting control of statehouses from the Republicans was the single undisputed trend of the November 3 elections. Democrats replaced Republicans in 13 governorships and lost only 2 (Tennessee and Connecticut) to the GOP. Before November 3, there was only one Democrat (in Texas) in a governorship in the ten most populous states. After the election, there were four—in Pennsylvania, Ohio, and Florida as well as in Texas. Moreover, the Democrats made gains in the state legislatures, winding up with control of both houses in 24 states (previously it had been 20); Republicans won control of both houses in 17 states; and 8 states split control in their legislatures (Nebraska has a nonpartisan unicameral legislature).

Democratic gains in state government were considered particularly important in light of the fact that 1970 was a census year. This meant that district lines for almost all 435 House seats had to be redrawn before the 1972 general election. Final census figures for the 50 states indicated that five states would gain House seats—California (increase of five), Florida (three), and Arizona, Colorado and Texas (one each); and that nine states would lose seats—New York and Pennsylvania (two each) and Alabama, Iowa, North Dakota, Ohio, Tennessee, West Virginia, and Wisconsin (one each). States with no change in House representation but with more than one representative also would have to draw new district boundaries to reflect intrastate population shifts.

The 1970 campaign was notable for the vigorous cross-country electioneering of Nixon and, in particular, Vice-Pres. Spiro T. Agnew (*see* BIOGRAPHY). The vice-president sounded the principal theme of the White House campaign during a six-state tour in mid-September. "The great question for all of us this fall is becoming clearer and clearer," he said at San Diego on September 11. "Will America be led by a

Minnesota after a six-year absence. Prominent incoming House freshmen included Bella Abzug (Dem., N.Y.), an outspoken peace candidate and women's liberation leader; Ronald V. Dellums (Dem., Calif.), a black liberal who won in a predominantly white district; Robert F. Drinan (Dem., Mass.), who would be the first Roman Catholic priest to vote in the House; Louise Day Hicks (Dem., Mass.), who would occupy the seat vacated by House Speaker John W. McCormack; and Jack F. Kemp (Rep., N.Y.), former quarterback of the Buffalo Bills professional football team.

UNITED STATES

Education. (1969–70) Primary (including preprimary), pupils 33,451,000, teachers 1,256,550; secondary and vocational, pupils 19,487,000, teachers 977,400; higher (including junior colleges and teacher-training colleges), students 7,915,417, teaching staff 574,000.

Finance. Monetary unit: U.S. dollar ($2.40 = £1 sterling; $35 = 1 troy oz. of gold). Gold, SDRs, and foreign exchange, official: (June 1970) $13,980,000,000; (June 1969) $14,510,000,000. Federal budget (1969–70 est.): revenue $199.4 billion; expenditure $197.9 billion. Gross national product: (1969) $932.3 billion; (1968) $865.7 billion. Money supply: (June 1970) $198.7 billion; (June 1969) $192.3 billion. Cost of living (1963 = 100): (June 1970) 127; (June 1969) 119.

Foreign Trade. (1969) Imports $36,052,000,000; exports (excluding $674 million military aid) $37,314,000,-000. Import sources: Canada 29%; Japan 9%; West Germany 7%; U.K. 6%. Export destinations: Canada 24%; Japan 13%; U.K. 6%; West Germany 6%. Main exports: machinery 27%; aircraft 10%; motor vehicles 9%; chemicals 9%; cereals 6%.

Transport and Communications. Roads (1968) 3,683,-975 mi. (including 27,244 mi. expressways). Motor vehicles in use (1968): passenger 83,281,300; commercial 16,282,100. Railways (1968): 208,111 mi.; traffic 13,-164,000,000 passenger-mi., freight 750,468,000,000 ton-mi. Air traffic (1969): 125,414,000,000 passenger-mi. (including 95,946,000,000 passenger-mi. on internal services); freight 2,853,000,000 ton-mi. (including 1,762,000,000 ton-mi. on internal services). Inland waterways freight traffic (1968) 291,409,000,000 ton-mi. (including 112,-073,000,000 ton-mi. on Great Lakes system). Shipping (1969): merchant vessels 100 gross tons and over 3,146; gross tonnage 19,550,394. Ships entered (including Great Lakes international traffic; 1968) vessels totaling 172,-744,000 net registered tons; goods loaded (1968) 198,-536,000 short tons, unloaded 309,615,000 short tons. Telephones (Dec. 1968) 109,255,000. Radio receivers

(Dec. 1968) 200.9 million. Television receivers (Dec. 1968) 84,570,000.

Agriculture. Production (in 000; short tons; 1969; 1968 in parentheses): corn 128,180 (122,494); wheat 43,766 (47,113); oats 28,496 (14,872); barley 12,510 (10,035); rye 930 (650); rice 4,565 (5,266); linseed 856 (764); sorghum 20,807 (20,678); soybeans 33,506 (32,390); dry beans 800 (884); dry peas 218 (187); peanuts 1,145 (1,263); potatoes 15,361 (14,709); sweet potatoes (1968) 665, (1967) 683; tobacco 901 (856); sugar, raw value 4,298 (4,395); apples 3,381 (2,727); pears 711 (616); oranges 8,464 (8,459); grapefruit 2,086 (2,238); lemons 601 (759); grapes 3,874 (3,577); raisins 238 (262); cotton, lint 2,520 (2,597); wool 97 (43); beef and veal 10,900 (10,689); pork 6,473 (6,437); milk 58,100 (58,649); butter 560 (590); cheese 1,002 (959); eggs 68,925 (69,270); softwood lumber (bd.-ft.) 37,943,000 (37,450,000); hardwood lumber (bd.-ft.) 8,462,000 (7,227,000); fish catch 2,146 (2,058). Livestock (in 000; Jan. 1969): cattle 112,330; sheep 20,422; horses *c.* 7,300; pigs 56,743; chickens 420,000.

Industry. Index of industrial production (1963 = 100): (1969) 105, (1968) 133; mining (1969) 102, (1968) 117; manufacturing (1969) 105, (1968) 134; electricity, gas, and water (1969) 109, (1968) 145; construction (1968) 111. Unemployment: (1969) 3.5%; (1968) 3.6%. Fuel and power (in 000; short tons; 1968): coal and lignite 556,706; crude oil (bbl.) 3,325,000; natural gas (cu.yd.) 715,670,000; electricity (kw-hr.) 1,436,000,000. Production (in 000; short tons; 1968): iron ore (50–55% metal content) 96,169; pig iron 91,362; crude steel 131,-462; cement (shipments) 76,302; newsprint 3,232; sulfuric acid 29,000; caustic soda 8,865; superphosphates (1969) 1,485; nitrogenous fertilizers (N content; 1968–69) 6,778; plastics and resins 8,100; synthetic rubber 2,250; passenger cars (units) 8,224; commercial vehicles (units) 1,920. Merchant vessels launched (100 gross tons and over; 1969) 418,000 gross tons.

president elected by a majority of the American people or will we be intimidated and blackmailed into following the path dictated by a disruptive radical and militant minority—the pampered prodigies of the radical liberals in the United States Senate?" In virtually every subsequent speech, Agnew included an attack on "radical liberals" or "radic-libs" who, he charged, were pursuing a spendthrift economic policy and a neo-isolationist foreign policy and were overly permissive on such issues as crime and student unrest. Agnew, in turn, was frequently accused of conducting a campaign based on fear and slander.

Many political observers concluded that the economic issue was more decisive in the 1970 elections than the so-called "social issue" stressed by Agnew and Nixon. Although the administration pursued restrictive fiscal and monetary policies in an effort to curb inflation, both prices and unemployment continued to rise throughout the year. The Bureau of Labor Statistics' consumer price index, which stood at 131.8 in January (1957–59 = 100), climbed to 137.4 in October. Unemployment increased from 3.9 to 6% of the civilian labour force between January and December. At the end of the year, Nixon seemed on the verge of applying pressure, for the first time, on labour and business to exercise restraint in seeking wage and price increases.

Unrest on the nation's college campuses, which had been building steadily for five years, reached unprecedented levels in the spring of 1970. News of the Cambodia venture aroused a storm of protest, and there were calls for a nationwide student strike. An antiwar protest at Kent State University in Ohio ended in tragedy on May 4 when four students, two of them women, were killed as 100 National Guardsmen fired their M-1 rifles into a crowd of demonstrators. The Kent State killings gave impetus to a previously planned demonstration in Washington to protest the Cambodia offensive, and a crowd estimated at 60,000–100,000 gathered in the capital on May 9 for what turned out to be a peaceful rally. President Nixon made a surprise pre-dawn trip to the Lincoln

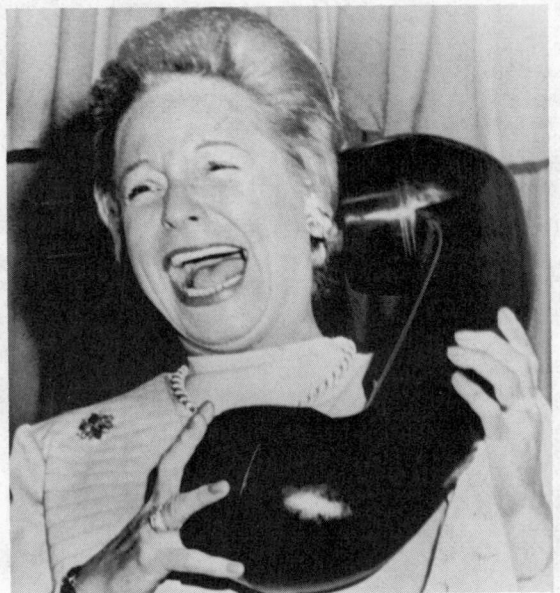

WIDE WORLD
Martha Mitchell, outspoken wife of the U.S. attorney general noted for her telephone calls to newsmen, accepts an oversized, plastic telephone at a reception for Republican candidates in October 1970.

Memorial on the day of the demonstration to talk with student protesters. He said later that he had tried to "relate" to the students "in a way they could feel that I understood their problems." Meanwhile, a student strike centre at Brandeis University in Waltham, Mass., reported that as of May 10, 448 colleges and universities were on strike or closed.

Nixon's difficulties with college students also precipitated a split within his official family. Interior Secretary Walter J. Hickel (see BIOGRAPHY), in a letter to the president that was leaked to the press, stated that "youth in its protest must be heard" and warned that the administration was "embracing a philosophy which appears to lack appropriate concern" for youth. A "vast segment" of young people, Hickel added, felt there was "no opportunity to communicate with government . . . other than through violent confrontation." Hickel ended his letter with an appeal to Nixon to meet "on an individual and conversational basis" with members of the Cabinet. The interior secretary reportedly had talked privately with the president only twice since the inauguration. Publication of the Hickel letter naturally was embarrassing to Nixon; thus, it came as no surprise when Hickel was fired from his job late in the year. Republican National Chairman Rogers C. B. Morton was announced as Nixon's choice to be the new interior secretary.

There were other changes in the president's official family. Earlier in the year Robert Finch had left the Department of Health, Education, and Welfare to become a presidential counselor, and had been succeeded as secretary of HEW by Undersecretary of State Elliot Richardson. Most of the changes, however, came after the election. David Kennedy resigned as secretary of the treasury (he was retained as a presidential adviser on international finance), and former Texas governor John Connally was nominated to the post. Another Texan, defeated senatorial candidate George Bush, was named to succeed career diplomat Charles Yost as chief U.S. representative at the UN, but only after the job had been turned down by presidential counselor Daniel Moynihan, who decided to return to Harvard. Also returning to private life were Bryce Harlow, Nixon's liaison man with Congress, and James Farmer, who, as assistant secretary of health, education, and welfare, had been one

Members of the Gay Activists Alliance demonstrate outside New York Republican State Committee office when they were not allowed to present their demands to Gov. Nelson Rockefeller.

LEONARD FREED FROM MAGNUM

BRUCE ROBERTS FROM RAPHO GUILLUMETTE

WIDE WORLD

Above, about 100 members of PANG (People Against Nerve Gas) stage a "die-in" on a street in downtown Seattle, Wash., May 17, 1970, to protest the shipment of nerve gas through the area. Above, right, a train carrying nerve gas passes through Waxhaw, N.C., Aug. 11, 1970.

of the top black officials in the administration. A new presidential counselor was Donald Rumsfeld, formerly head of the Office of Economic Opportunity.

Two aspects of what some considered to be the national malaise were examined by presidential commissions during the year, but in neither case did the findings gain uncritical acceptance. The President's Commission on Campus Unrest was castigated by Vice-President Agnew as too lenient toward radicals, and the president rejected its suggestion that he bore the principal responsibility for providing leadership in the campus crisis. (*See* EDUCATION.) Even more controversial was the report of the President's Commission on Obscenity and Pornography, which stated that it could find no scientific evidence of a causal relationship between pornography and crime or sexual deviance and urged the repeal of all laws prohibiting the distribution of such materials to consenting adults. It also advocated a massive program of sex education. Several of the commission's members issued a strong dissent. The report was condemned by President Nixon even before its release, and there was no evidence that any action would be taken on its recommendations.

One of the most alarming developments in the U.S. in 1970 was the sharp increase in terrorist bombings, many of them believed to be the work of the Weatherman faction of Students for a Democratic Society. (*See* CRIME.) The bombings appeared to follow no pattern. Among the many buildings damaged by explosions during the year were three Manhattan skyscrapers, the Louisiana capitol at Baton Rouge, four Latin-American embassies in Washington, D.C., the federal building in Minneapolis, and the Army Mathematics Research Center at the University of Wisconsin in Madison.

Many of the major racial incidents of 1970 involved members of black militant groups, particularly the Black Panthers. (*See* RACE RELATIONS.) Following an attempted escape and kidnapping at the San Rafael, Calif., courthouse on August 7, Superior Court Judge Harold J. Haley, two San Quentin convicts, and Jonathan Jackson, the man who had provided the weapons, were killed in a gun battle with law officers. Marin County officials filed charges of murder and kidnapping against Ruchell Magee, 31, a San Quentin convict who was in the courtroom as a witness and who

had been wounded in the gun battle, and Angela Davis (*see* BIOGRAPHY), a black militant and Communist who had recently been ousted from the UCLA faculty. Police said Miss Davis had purchased four guns brought into the courtroom by Jackson, identified as her frequent companion and bodyguard. Miss Davis and Jackson both were involved in raising money for the "Soledad Brothers," three blacks charged with killing a guard at the Soledad state prison. Placed on the FBI's "ten most wanted" list, Miss Davis was apprehended in New York City on October 13 and was subsequently extradited to face trial in California.

Two court cases involving Panthers dragged on for much of the year, and both were still in progress at the end of 1970. In New York City, 13 Panthers went on trial October 19—after months of pretrial hearings—on charges of conspiring to bomb police stations, department stores, and other public places in the city. In New Haven, Conn., eight Panthers faced charges in connection with the 1969 slaying of Alex Rackley, a purported informer. Lonnie McLucas, the first of the eight to stand trial, was convicted on August 31 of conspiracy to murder and was sentenced to a prison term of 12–15 years. The New Haven trial prompted a demonstration at Yale University, May 1–3, in support of the defendants. Yale President Kingman Brewster, Jr. (*see* BIOGRAPHY), stirred a nationwide controversy when he said, on April 23, that he was "skeptical of the ability of black revolutionaries to achieve a fair trial anywhere in the United States." Many observers feared that the Yale rally would lead to violence, but the more than 13,000 youths who attended it conducted themselves in a generally peaceful manner.

Other courtroom proceedings also provided a focus for the nation's divisions and uncertainties. The spectacular Chicago trial of eight (later seven) dissidents in connection with the disorders at the 1968 Democratic national convention ended early in the year when the jury found five defendants guilty of crossing state lines with intent to incite a riot but not of conspiracy. (*See* Law: *Special Report*.) Appeal procedures stemming from the case began with a hearing to determine whether the judge had exerted undue pressure to make the divided jury reach a decision. In the fall proceedings began in the court-martial of army Lieut. William Calley, accused of killing 102

Vietnamese civilians at My Lai during an action in March 1968. The incident, which had come to light only toward the end of 1969, had provoked widespread discussion of the nature of war crimes in general and of the Vietnam war in particular. The prosecution concentrated on proving that there had been a massacre at My Lai and that Calley had taken a leading part in it. As the defense began its presentation late in the year, it appeared that it would concentrate on attempting to show that Calley had acted on higher orders and on demonstrating that, in the peculiar circumstances of the Vietnam war, civilians, including women, children, and old people, often had to be considered as the enemy.

Toward the end of the year the Army became involved in another dispute when a former army intelligence agent assigned to work in Illinois told Sen. Sam Ervin, Jr. (Dem., N.C.), that some 800 persons in that state, including Sen. Adlai Stevenson, Otto Kerner, a federal judge and former governor, and Rep. Abner Mikva, had been subject to surveillance. Other former agents subsequently asserted that the Army's domestic intelligence-gathering role, originally undertaken to prepare for the possible use of troops in quelling civil disturbances, had expanded to include collecting information on anyone considered to be politically deviant. Denials were issued by the Pentagon, and Secretary Laird took steps to strengthen civilian control over military intelligence activities. Senator Ervin announced plans for a full-scale investigation into the matter in 1971.

Two proposed constitutional amendments, one guaranteeing equal rights for women and the other establishing direct election of the president and vice-president, passed the House, but no action on them was taken in the Senate. Attempting to bypass the amending procedure, Congress passed a law giving 18-year-olds the right to vote. The Supreme Court ruled in December that this could apply only in elections for national office (president and vice-president, senators, and congressmen), and local electoral authorities in states that did not grant the vote to 18-year-olds faced the confusion and expense of providing separate ballots for national offices. (RI. W.)

ENCYCLOPÆDIA BRITANNICA FILMS. *People Along the Mississippi* (1952); *Southwestern States* (1954); *Far Western States* (1955); *Northwestern States* (1956); *Southeastern States* (1956); *The Wheat Farmer* (1956); *Hawaii—The 50th State* (1959); *Alaska—The 49th State* (1960); *Corn Farmer* (1960); *Chicago—Midland Metropolis* (1963); *Our Changing Way of Life—The Cotton Farmer* (1963); *Our Changing Way of Life—Cattleman (A Rancher's Story)* (1964); *Our Changing Way of Life—The Dairy Farmer* (1965); *Our Changing Way of Life—The Lumberman* (1965); *Washington D.C.—Capital City U.S.A.* (1965); *The Great Plains—Land of Risk* (1966); *The Interior West—The Land Nobody Wanted* (1966); *Making the Desert Green* (1966); *New England Fisherman* (1967); *The Northeast: Gateway for a Nation* (1967); *The Northeast: Headquarters for a Nation* (1967); *The Northeast: Port of New York* (1967); *The Orange Grower* (1967); *The Sheep Rancher* (1967); *The Industrial Revolution—Beginnings in the United States* (1968); *Midwest—Heartland of the Nation* (1968); *Problems of Conservation—Air* (1968); *Produce—From Farm to Market* (1968); *Heritage in Black* (1969); *The House of Man, Part II—Our Crowded Environment* (1969); *The Pacific West* (1969); *Problems of Conservation—Forest and Range* (1969); *Problems of Conservation—Minerals* (1969); *Problems of Conservation—Soil* (1969); *Problems of Conservation—Water* (1969); *The Rise of Labor* (1969); *The South: Roots of the Urban Crisis* (1969); *Chicano from the Southwest* (1970); *The Garbage Explosion* (1970); *Heartbeat of a Volcano* (1970); *The Industrial City* (1970); *The Industrial Worker* (1970); *Linda and Billy Ray from Appalachia* (1970); *The Mississippi System—Waterway of Commerce* (1970); *The Presidency—Search for a Candidate* (1970); *Problems of Conservation—Our Natural Resources* (1970); *Problems of Conservation—Wildlife* (1970); *The Rise of Big Business* (1970); *The Rise of the American City* (1970).

Upper Volta

A republic of West Africa, Upper Volta is bordered by Mali, Niger, Dahomey, Togo, Ghana, and Ivory Coast. Area: 105,869 sq.mi. (274,200 sq.km.). Pop. (1970 est.): 5,330,000. Cap. and largest city: Ouagadougou (pop., 1970 est., 115,500). Language: French (official). Religion: pagan; Muslim and Christian minorities. President in 1970, Gen. Sangoule Lamizana.

In a referendum on June 15, 1970, 98.41% of the voters accepted the new draft constitution submitted for their approval. Under its terms, for a transitional period of four years the president of the republic would be the oldest army officer of the highest rank. One-third of the government would be military men. The Cabinet-level ministers would have a prime minister at their head and could not number more than 15. After the transitional period, the president would normally be elected for five years by direct universal suffrage, but no president could serve more than two consecutive terms. The president could preside over the Council of Ministers but only when required by exceptional circumstances. All acts of the president were to be countersigned by the prime minister and the relevant ministers. The president would also be commander in chief of the Army and president of the Higher Council of Defense. All the major political parties in Upper Volta had recommended acceptance of the new constitution to their supporters.

In August former president Maurice Yaméogo, deposed in January 1966 and sentenced in May 1969 to a term of hard labour for misappropriation of public funds, was released on the occasion of the tenth anniversary of Upper Volta's independence. Begon Kone, a former president of the National Assembly who was serving a similar sentence, was also released. (PH. D.)

UPPER VOLTA
Education. (1967–68) Primary, pupils 97,364, teachers (including preprimary) 2,142; secondary, pupils 6,666, teachers 406; vocational, pupils 1,186, teachers 106; teacher training, students 1,114, teachers 35; higher, students 58, teaching staff 17.
Finance. Monetary unit: CFA franc, with a parity of CFA Fr. 50 to the French franc (CFA Fr. 277.71 = U.S. $1; CFA Fr. 666.50 = £1 sterling). Budget (1970 est.) balanced at CFA Fr. 9,757,000,000.
Foreign Trade. (1969) Imports CFA Fr. 12,860,-600,000; exports CFA Fr. 5,329,300,000. Import sources: France 44%; Ivory Coast 14%; West Germany 6%. Export destinations: Ivory Coast 40%; France 13%; Ghana 11%; Denmark 6%. Main exports: livestock 37%; cotton 28%; oilseeds 17%; fruit and vegetables 5%.

Uruguay

A republic of South America, Uruguay is on the Atlantic Ocean and is bounded by Brazil and Argentina. Area: 68,536 sq.mi. (177,508 sq.km.). Pop. (1968 est.): 2,818,000, including white 89%; mestizo 10%. Cap. and largest city: Montevideo (pop., 1967, 1,280,-000). Language: Spanish. Religion: mainly Roman Catholic. President in 1970, Jorge Pacheco Areco.

The political scene in Uruguay in 1970 was dominated by three major issues: the maneuvering of President Pacheco to gain support for lengthening the period of his presidency, the activities of the Tupamaro guerrillas, and the troubled state of the economy.

Pacheco's position appeared uncomfortable in the early part of the year, especially during the parliamentary uproar that surrounded the reimposition of security measures in March. It became stronger in May after Pacheco signed an agreement with the supporters of Jorge Battle in the ruling Colorado Party and a large part of the opposition Blanco Party. In return for places on the powerful state trading boards, the two groups would allow Pacheco two years longer in the presidency than constitutionally allowed. The agreement, however, fell apart after a few days.

Maneuvering to bring about Pacheco's reelection in 1971 began again in October but threatened to disrupt the unity of the Unión Colorada y Batllista (UCYB) faction of the Colorado Party. The split to the party became official in November with the Battle group in the UCYB expressing their absolute opposition to the slating of Pacheco for a second term as president.

Pacheco's popularity did not benefit from the activities of the Tupamaros, Uruguay's special type of guerrillas, who continually flouted the authority of the government, Army, and police. In May the government was shaken by a dramatic raid on a naval training centre in Montevideo by Tupamaros who carried off a large quantity of arms. It seemed that some agreement was likely between the guerrillas and the government in June, but such hopes were dissipated by renewed attacks on banks toward the end of the month. The July kidnapping of Judge Daniel Pereira Manelli, who had tried most of the captured

Tupamaros, further embarrassed the Pacheco regime even though he was subsequently released. That incident, however, became insignificant in comparison with the kidnapping in late July of U.S. adviser to the police Dan A. Mitrione, Brazilian diplomat Aloysío Dias Gomide, and, soon afterward, of Claude Fly, a U.S. agronomist. The Tupamaros demanded that captured guerrillas should be released in exchange for the lives of the three men, but the government firmly rejected these demands. Before long the body of the slain Mitrione was found. A combined operation, involving 14,000 members of the police and Army, failed to locate the remaining hostages but did lead to the capture of Raúl Sendic, the most important member of the Tupamaro hierarchy.

The state of the economy was a continuous problem to the government throughout the year. Its anti-inflationary policy had managed to reduce the rise in the cost of living from 66.3% in 1968 to about 12.8% for the first three quarters of 1970. It was claimed, however, that this was at the expense of industrial production and of real wages; the latter appeared to have fallen by 50% since the 1968 wage and price freeze.

(D. K. Da.)

Vatican City State

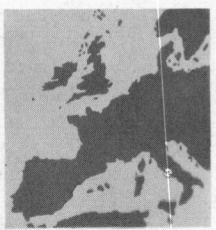

This independent sovereignty is surrounded by but not part of Rome. As a state with territorial limits, it is properly distinguished from the Holy See, which constitutes the worldwide administrative and legislative body for the Roman Catholic Church. The area of Vatican City is 108.7 ac. (44 ha.). Pop. (1970 est.): 847. As sovereign pontiff, Paul VI is the head of state. Vatican City is administered by a pontifical commission of five cardinals, of which the secretary of state, Jean Cardinal Villot, is president.

While emphasizing that the Holy See was not moved by temporal considerations, Pope Paul VI (*see* BIOGRAPHY) continued his efforts for peace during 1970. This side of Paul VI's activity appeared particularly in his meetings with West German Chancellor Willy Brandt in July and with U.S. Pres. Richard M. Nixon in September. President Nixon's appointment of Henry Cabot Lodge to make periodic visits to the Vatican restored the official link between the U.S. and the Holy See that had existed from 1939 to 1950.

The pope's reception in July of a group representing the "national liberation movements" of Portugal's African territories impelled Lisbon to recall its ambassador to the Holy See. When, however, the papal secretary of state confirmed in a letter that Paul VI had received the people in question solely as members of the church, Portugal considered the incident closed.

On September 14, Pope Paul announced the abolition of the Pontifical Military Corps (the Vatican's army) with the exception of the Swiss Guard. Earlier, salary increases had been granted to the staff of the Holy See, where unrest had reached the point of strikes. To demonstrate that the Holy See did not have the resources commonly attributed to it, a communiqué was issued providing for the first time some indication of Vatican finances. It showed that the productive capital of the state was in the neighbourhood of 70–80 billion lire.

(Mx. B.)

See also Religion.

URUGUAY

Education. (1966–67) Primary, pupils 365,597, teachers (including preprimary; 1965–66) 9,152; secondary (·1965–66), pupils 91,371; vocational (1965–66), pupils 26,298; teacher training (1965–66), students 4,947; higher, students (1965–66) 17,087, teaching staff (1963–64) 2,182.

Finance. Monetary unit: peso, with an official rate of 250 pesos to U.S. $1 (600 pesos = £1 sterling). Gold, SDRs, and foreign exchange, central bank: (June 1970) U.S. $195 million; (June 1969) U.S. $184 million. Budget (1968 est.): revenue 46.1 billion pesos; expenditure 56.4 billion pesos. Gross national product: (1968) 376,740,000,000 pesos; (1967) 164,470,000,-000 pesos. Money supply: (June 1968) 37,907,000,000 pesos; (June 1967) 17,506,000,000 pesos. Cost of living (Montevideo; 1963 = 100): (March 1970) 2,225; (March 1969) 1,920.

Foreign Trade. (1968) Imports U.S. $165 million; exports U.S. $179.1 million. Import sources: U.S. 19%; Argentina 12%; Brazil 12%; West Germany 11%; U.K. 5%. Export destinations: U.K. 21%; U.S. 12%; Italy 7%; Spain 7%; West Germany 7%; Greece 6%; Netherlands 6%. Main exports: wool 44%; meat 34%; hides and skins 9%.

Transport and Communications. Roads (1968) c. 42,000 km. (including c. 5,000 km. with improved surface). Motor vehicles in use (1968): passenger c. 142,000; commercial (including buses) c. 90,300. Railways (1968) 3,102 km. Air traffic (1969): 64,660,000 passenger-km.; freight 177,000 net ton-km. Shipping (1969): merchant vessels 100 gross tons and over 41; gross tonnage 112,207. Telephones (Jan. 1969) 205,-174. Radio receivers (Dec. 1968) 1,075,000. Television receivers (Dec. 1965) 200,000.

Agriculture. Production (in 000; metric tons; 1969; 1968 in parentheses): wheat 403 (484); barley (1968) 48, (1967) 14; oats (1968) 73, (1967) 33; sweet potatoes (1968) c. 81, (1967) c. 80; corn 129 (69); linseed 56 (27); sunflower seed 63 (49); rice (1968) 104, (1967) 116; sugar, raw value (1969–70) c. 40, (1968–69) c. 62; oranges c. 60 (c. 65); wine (1968) c. 76, (1967) c. 88; wool (1968) 50, (1967) 48; beef and veal (1968) 339, (1967) 252. Livestock (in 000; May 1969): cattle 8,600; sheep c. 21,600; horses c. 450; pigs c. 390; chickens c. 7,700.

Industry. Production (in 000; metric tons; 1968): cement 506; limestone (1967) 727; electricity (kw-hr.; 1967) 1,944,000.

Venezuela

A republic of northern South America, Venezuela is bounded by Colombia, Brazil, Guyana, and the Caribbean Sea. Area: 352,143 sq.mi. (912,050 sq. km.). Pop. (1968 est.): 9,686,486, including mestizo 69%; white 20%; Negro 9%; Indian 2%. Cap. and largest city: Caracas (metro. pop., 1966 est., 1,764,274). Language: Spanish. Religion: predominantly Roman Catholic. President in 1970, Rafael Caldera.

Because his party, the Comitado Organización Politica Electoral Independiente (COPEI), had a minority of seats in Congress, President Caldera encountered some difficulty in enacting legislation during the year. As a result, important bills, for example those dealing with oil service contracts and the public investment program, were delayed, and during late 1969 and early 1970 Venezuela appeared to lack leadership and to possess no coherent strategy for its future development. This image was altered later in 1970 by a much-publicized working agreement between COPEI and Acción Democrática, the main opposition party in Congress. This agreement was thought to have arisen from a realization within the two parties that the failure of the existing machinery of government to produce effective policies, because of party political differences, was reducing popular support for the whole constitutional structure.

On August 5, therefore, Congress approved the basis of service contracts for the development of oil fields in southern Lake Maracaibo, and by October some 2,194,500,000 bolivares of the 2,915,000,000 bolivares special investment budget had also been authorized.

Little was heard of the guerrilla movement, and its strength was hard to assess. Caldera invited the extraparliamentary opposition to campaign openly within the constitution, and accompanied this announcement with the release of political prisoners. The credibility of this policy to the guerrillas was not clear, however, and its acceptance, therefore, remained in doubt.

In the sphere of foreign relations the two most important events in 1970 were the resumption of diplomatic relations with the U.S.S.R. and the agreement with Guyana on a 12-year standstill period in the territorial dispute between the two countries. This agreement had not, however, secured the ratification of the Venezuelan Congress.

The gross domestic product rose in 1969 by 3.5%, compared with 5.8% in 1968. Few data were available on growth rates in the various sectors of the economy during 1969, but some figures were available for manufacturing, agricultural, iron-ore, and petroleum production. In the manufacturing sector, production increased by 10% between August 1968 and August 1969, against a 5.9% growth for 1968 as a whole. Progress in reducing reliance upon foreign industrial imports was slow, however. Agricultural production increased by 22% in 1969 (at current prices); productivity gains were greater in livestock than in crops, where much of the increase in production was achieved by an extension of the area cultivated. Venezuela remained, however, a net importer of agricultural products. Iron-ore production in 1969 reached 19.4 million tons, an increase of 25% over the 1968 figure of 15.5 million tons, and it continued its rise in 1970. In contrast, petroleum production fell by 0.3%, compared with a 2% increase in 1968. Since petroleum accounted for about 25% of the gross domestic product, Venezuela's overall slow rate of growth in 1969 probably could be attributed to the stagnation in petroleum output. In the second half of the year, however, production was on a rising trend, one that continued in 1970. Thus, production in the first six months of 1970 averaged 3,690,000 bbl. a day against 3,590,000 bbl. for 1969.

The 1970–74 National Plan envisaged an annual

COURTESY, STANDARD OIL COMPANY (NEW JERSEY)

These towers are part of the $120 million desulfurization equipment being installed at the Amuay oil refinery of the Creole Petroleum Corp. on Venezuela's Paraguaná Peninsula. When completed, it would be the largest desulfurization plant in the world.

VENEZUELA

Education. (1967–68) Primary, pupils 1,550,190, teachers 45,530; secondary, pupils 230,333, teachers 10,820; vocational, pupils 115,423, teachers 5,824; teacher training, students 10,943, teachers 1,198; higher (including 8 universities), students 58,747, teaching staff 5,717.

Finance. Monetary unit: bolívar, with an official selling rate of 4.50 bolivares to U.S. $1 (10.80 bolivares = £1 sterling). Gold, SDRs, and foreign exchange, central bank: (June 1970) U.S. $892 million; (June 1969) U.S. $769 million. Budget (1970 est.) balanced at 9,886,000,000 bolivares. Gross national product: (1968) 41,160,000,000 bolivares; (1967) 37,990,000,000 bolivares. Money supply: (June 1970) 6,713,000,000 bolivares; (June 1969) 6,048,000,000 bolivares. Cost of living (Caracas; 1963 = 100): (June 1970) 111; (June 1969) 110.

Foreign Trade. (1968) Imports (f.o.b.) 6,527,000,000 bolivares; exports 12,577,000,000 bolivares. Import sources: U.S. 50%; West Germany 9%; U.K. 6%; Japan 6%; Italy 5%; Canada 5%. Export destinations: U.S. 43%; Canada 12%; Netherlands Antilles 10%; U.K. 7%. Main export crude oil and refined petroleum products 93%.

Transport and Communications. Roads (1968) 37,551 km. (including 494 km. expressways). Motor vehicles in use (1968): passenger 482,000; commercial (including buses) 197,100. Railways (1967): 773 km.; traffic 39 million passenger-km., freight 17 million net ton-km. Air traffic (1969): 1,022,900,000 passenger-km.; freight 47,566,000 net ton-km. Shipping (1969): merchant vessels 100 gross tons and over 90; gross tonnage 369,120. Telephones (Jan. 1969) 345,704. Radio receivers (Dec. 1968) 1,680,000. Television receivers (Dec. 1968) 700,000.

Agriculture. Production (in 000; metric tons; 1968; 1967 in parentheses): corn 736 (633); rice 245 (223); sesame 76 (80); sweet potatoes 115 (111); cassava 341 (316); dry beans 46 (50); coffee 62 (62); tobacco 11 (10); cocoa (1968–69) 25, (1967–68) 25; bananas 949 (859); citrus fruit 102 (93); sugar, raw value (1969–70) c. 435, (1968–69) 386; cotton, lint (1969) c. 18, (1968) 18; beef and veal 192 (184). Livestock (in 000; 1968–69): cattle 7,000; pigs 2,027; sheep 98; horses 419; asses c. 485; poultry c. 14,500.

Industry. Production (in 000; metric tons; 1969): crude oil 188,130; natural gas (cu.m.) 7,977,000; petroleum products (1967) 59,610; iron ore (62% metal content) 19,392; cement (1968) 2,437; gold (troy oz.; 1968) 21; diamonds (metric carats; 1968) 114; electricity (kw-hr.; 1968) 10,814,000.

growth of 6% in the gross domestic product and of 4% in exports, and the creation of 588,000 new jobs. Specific objectives were also set for the petroleum and mining sectors. In petroleum, net investment over the period was projected at 3,613,000,000 bolivares and the value and volume of production in 1974 at 10,633,000,000 bolivares and 1,491,300,000 bbl., respectively (1969: 9,352,300,000 and 1,311,800,000). Policy goals for the mining sector were a gross investment of 1,748,000,000 bolivares and a yearly increase of 9.2% in total production.

In late 1970 there were indications that the high level of petroleum production recorded in the year's first six months would be maintained. The Middle East crisis contributed toward an increased demand for Venezuelan oil, and two companies, Shell and Creole (a subsidiary of Standard Oil of New Jersey), announced that they intended to raise their 1970 investment by 72 million bolivares in order to increase production.

Because of the gain in petroleum, Venezuela's rate of economic growth in 1970 was expected to be higher than that for 1969. Its growth over the next four years appeared to depend most heavily upon developments in government finance and the petroleum industry. The public sector had contributed a third of all new capital formation in recent years, while petroleum accounted not only for 25% of the gross domestic product but for 90% of the country's foreign exchange earnings; these earnings, in turn, helped to finance the import of capital equipment and intermediate industrial products required for the development of other economic sectors. Uncertainty still remained, however, over the nature of these developments. The trend of government finance was not clearly defined, and there was some apprehension over U.S. policy on oil imports, and over the outcome of the service contract negotiations between the Venezuelan government and the oil companies. It appeared, however, that both the production and export of Venezuelan petroleum would increase over the period, despite these uncertainties.   (Ro. E. S.)

ENCYCLOPÆDIA BRITANNICA FILMS. *Colombia and Venezuela* (1961).

Veterinary Medicine

The world animal disease situation during 1970 remained more or less stable. Governments of the less developed nations, in conjunction with veterinarians and livestock specialists of the UN Food and Agriculture Organization, continued to make progress in controlling the more widespread diseases of food-producing animals through vaccination and the development of resistant livestock. The water buffalo was extensively studied as a source of meat, milk, and motive power, especially in tropical Asia and Africa where more conventional animal husbandry was difficult.

To reduce losses from livestock disease, which had been approaching some $100 million annually, the Mexican government established a network of veterinary diagnostic laboratories. There were 18 of these in operation by late 1969, and 15 more were planned. Through the more rapid and precise identification of the causes of disease outbreaks provided by these laboratories, together with stepped-up eradication campaigns, animal losses were expected to be reduced by half as early as 1975.

By the fall of 1970, half of the U.S. states had been declared free of hog cholera (swine fever) or were in the final stages of eradication. A few local outbreaks occurred in areas earlier designated as clean, but concern that prohibition of vaccination might result in large-scale flare-ups proved unfounded. With the cessation of vaccination in 1970, a few veterinarians specializing in swine experienced drastic reductions in income.

In some areas of the U.S., fewer veterinarians were engaged in dairy cattle practice than in previous years, primarily because of the continuing reduction in milk cow numbers. To a considerable extent, however, this decline was being offset by an explosive increase in the horse population, which had tripled during the 1960s.

The discovery of a rapid and simple blood test for equine infectious anemia (swamp fever) by veterinary scientists at Cornell University promised to make control of this disease an economic possibility. Acutely infected animals could be fairly easily identified, but hitherto it had been necessary to inoculate a susceptible horse with blood of a suspect animal to determine whether the latter was a latent carrier. This was too expensive to be practical on a large scale, and along the eastern seaboard the disease had become serious enough to threaten the future of racing.

A means for immunizing poultry against avian leukosis, a form of leukemia, had been sought for several years. In 1970 the apparent discovery of an effective vaccine was announced by scientists at the University of Delaware. The disease had become an increasingly serious problem in most parts of the world with highly developed poultry industries.

The virus of another form of animal leukemia, that of feline lymphosarcoma, was reported by Soviet and British scientists in the spring of 1970 to be transmissible to human cells in tissue culture. Unguarded accounts of this discovery suggested that the disease itself could be transmitted from cats to man, thus causing great alarm among cat owners. Veterinarians at Cornell and the University of California, who earlier had experimentally transmitted the disease from cat to cat and from cat to dog, were quick to point out that the virus could not be passed from animal to animal except under highly artificial conditions.

For some years British and U.S. public health authorities had been concerned over the possibility that residues of antibiotics fed to promote growth of meat animals might have harmful effects on persons who consumed the meat. In Britain the Swann Committee, after an exhaustive study of the problem, issued its report in November 1969, recommending that no animal be fed any antibiotic used for treatment of human disease. Harmless bacteria in animals had been demonstrated to acquire resistance to certain antibiotics fed as growth stimulants and, in a few instances, to transfer this resistance to pathogenic bacteria present in the intestinal tracts of these animals. The primary concern, therefore, was that such resistance might be transferred to human pathogens. Although knowledgeable U.S. scientists expressed doubt that this had in fact occurred, the director of the Bureau of Veterinary Medicine of the U.S. Food and Drug Administration conceded that neither was there evidence to prove it had not. The U.K. implemented the Swann report by ordering that no animals be fed rations containing penicillin, chlortetracycline, or oxytetracycline after March 1, 1971, unless prescribed by a veterinarian.

Another significant development in Great Britain was the apparent finding that established methods of rabies control might be inadequate, although the rigid quarantine of imported animals enforced since 1922 had prevented further cases of the disease in dogs and cats. In 1969 a dog imported from Germany had developed rabies ten days after being released from quarantine, and the period of confinement was increased from six to eight months. In 1970 this was extended to a full year for those animals then in confinement and new imports were banned. (J. F. Ss.)

Vietnam

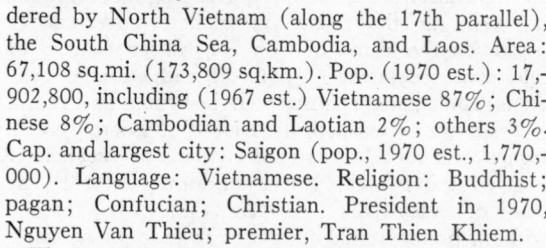

A country comprising the easternmost part of the Indochinese Peninsula, Vietnam, from July 21, 1954, was divided de facto into two republics.

Republic of Vietnam (South Vietnam). This is bordered by North Vietnam (along the 17th parallel), the South China Sea, Cambodia, and Laos. Area: 67,108 sq.mi. (173,809 sq.km.). Pop. (1970 est.): 17,902,800, including (1967 est.) Vietnamese 87%; Chinese 8%; Cambodian and Laotian 2%; others 3%. Cap. and largest city: Saigon (pop., 1970 est., 1,770,000). Language: Vietnamese. Religion: Buddhist; pagan; Confucian; Christian. President in 1970, Nguyen Van Thieu; premier, Tran Thien Khiem.

The long, bitter war in South Vietnam showed signs of winding down in 1970. Not one large-scale military battle took place in the country during the year, although the populace was still subjected to hazards. Action initiated by the North Vietnamese and the Viet Cong was limited to terrorism and harassment, while the armed forces of the United States were being withdrawn from South Vietnam at an accelerated rate.

At the beginning of the year, U.S. troop strength was 475,200. During the 12-month period 130,400 men had been or were scheduled to be withdrawn, and by May 1971 additional forces were to be returned home, reducing the projected troop strength to 284,000. U.S. Secretary of Defense Melvin R. Laird said that by the summer of 1971 he hoped the South Vietnamese "will be capable of assuming responsibility for all ground combat operations."

Vietnamization of the conflict was already placing an increasing burden on Saigon's forces, which had been built up to a strength of more than one million men, an increase of 40% over 1968, when general mobilization was decreed. U.S. officers estimated that about half of South Vietnam's dozen army and marine divisions had been brought up to effective combat-quality levels.

South Vietnamese military activity took the form of active surveillance and reconnaissance to locate North Vietnamese and Viet Cong units and bases, followed by generally more aggressive rapid-reaction operations to exploit contacts and preempt enemy initiatives. These patterns had been established by the U.S. forces, whose own role during much of the year followed a more defensive course.

On the weekend of November 21–22, however, the U.S. Air Force carried out a major attack, as approximately 200 fighter-bombers struck antiaircraft and supply targets in the southern panhandle region of North Vietnam. The U.S. stated that the operation was in retaliation for the downing of a U.S. reconnaissance plane a week earlier. North Vietnam protested these raids but even more vigorously accused the U.S.

of extensive bombing of civilian targets near Hanoi during the same weekend. The U.S. denied any attacks on civilians but admitted that air-to-ground missiles had been fired near Hanoi to support a U.S. commando raid on a prisoner-of-war camp. A small force of U.S. Army and Air Force men successfully reached the camp, about 25 mi. W of Hanoi, but found that all the prisoners had been moved. In the U.S. some criticism was leveled at the government for heating up the war with this raid. The administration responded by maintaining that U.S. prisoners of war were being so badly treated that they were dying and that the rescue attempt was a necessary humane action. In order to build up South Vietnam's 23,000-man Air Force, more than 3,500 pilots and aircraft mechanics were trained in the U.S. Larger numbers were undergoing instruction at the Nha Trang air base, which was turned over to the South Vietnamese as an air training centre. By the end of 1971 the country's air arm was scheduled to include 800 aircraft (about half of them helicopters), which would be double the number being flown at the start of 1970. South Vietnamese pilots during one week in October flew more air strikes in Vietnam than did U.S. fliers (330 sorties to 293). It was the first time that had happened since 1965, the year in which U.S. forces were brought into South Vietnam in strength.

U.S. naval forces were largely withdrawn from combat within South Vietnam during the year. Only 100 of the 660 riverine and other patrol craft were still operated by the Americans, with the remainder turned over to the South Vietnamese. Ships of the U.S. 6th Fleet remained on station in the South China Sea, but

VIETNAM: Republic

Education. (1967–68) Primary, pupils 2,023,893, teachers 34,066; secondary, pupils 499,419, teachers 13,338; vocational, pupils 10,873, teachers 585; teacher training, students 3,118, teachers 95; higher, students 33,929, teaching staff 914.

Finance. Monetary unit: piastre, with an official exchange rate of 80 piastres to U.S. $1 (192 piastres = £1 sterling) and a principal effective rate of 118 piastres to U.S. $1 (283.20 piastres = £1 sterling). Gold, SDRs, and foreign exchange, central bank: (June 1970) U.S. $199 million; (June 1969) U.S. $214 million. Budget (1968 est.) balanced at 95 billion piastres. Money supply: (May 1970) 150,690,000,000 piastres; (May 1969) 133,310,000,000 piastres. Cost of living (Saigon; 1963 = 100): (June 1970) 580; (June 1969) 420.

Foreign Trade. (1969) Imports U.S. $667,840,000; exports U.S. $11,940,000. Import sources (1968): Japan 30%; U.S. 29%; Taiwan 10%; Singapore 5%. Export destinations (1968): France 41%; Japan 18%; U.K. 13%; West Germany 9%; Italy 7%. Main export rubber 79%.

Transport and Communications. Roads (1968) 20,896 km. Motor vehicles in use (1968): passenger 45,599; commercial (including buses) 216,683. Railways (1969): c. 675 km.; traffic 71 million passenger-km., freight 41 million net ton-km. Air traffic (1969): 639.2 million passenger-km.; freight 5,398,000 net ton-km. Telephones (Dec. 1968) 30,964. Radio receivers (Dec. 1968) 1,506,000.

Agriculture. Production (in 000; metric tons; 1968; 1967 in parentheses): sweet potatoes 235 (254); cassava 260 (262); rice (1969) 5,115, (1968) 4,366; peanuts (1969) 34, (1968) 32; dry beans c. 20 (29); rubber (1969) c. 26, (1968) 34; tea 4.8 (4.2); coffee 3 (3.3); fish catch 410 (411). Livestock (in 000; 1968–69): cattle c. 1,030; buffaloes (1967–68) 647; pigs c. 3,150.

Industry. Production (in 000; metric tons; 1968): cement 145; salt (1967) 157; cotton yarn 5.2; woven cotton fabrics (m.) 32,000; electricity (public supply; kw-hr.) 808,000.

VIETNAM: Democratic Republic

Education. (1966–67) Primary and secondary, pupils 4,517,600, teachers 86,495; vocational, pupils 101,880, teachers 4,194; higher (including University of Hanoi), students 48,402, teaching staff 5,004.

Finance and Trade. Monetary unit: dong, with an official exchange rate of 3.70 dong to U.S. $1 (8.80 dong = £1 sterling). Budget (1963) balanced at 1,779,288,000 dong. Foreign trade, total turnover (1965) 780 million dong (85% with China, U.S.S.R., and other Eastern European countries).

Transport. Roads (1965) c. 9,000 km. Railways (1965) 937 km.

Agriculture. Production (in 000; metric tons; 1968; 1967 in parentheses): rice c. 4,920 (c. 4,700); corn 230 (c. 220); sweet potatoes c. 800 (c. 800); cassava c. 700 (c. 720); peanuts c. 25 (c. 25); dry beans c. 15 (c. 15); tobacco c. 4 (c. 4); tea c. 2.7 (c. 2.7); timber (cu.m.; 1964) 10,950; fish catch (1962) 289, (1961) 223. Livestock (in 000; 1967–68): buffaloes c. 1,750; cattle c. 840; pigs c. 6,200.

Industry. Production (in 000; metric tons; 1968): coal c. 3,000; apatite ore (1966) c. 1,000; salt c. 150; cement c. 500; cotton fabrics (m.; 1964) 105,200; paper (1964) 19; electricity (kw-hr.; 1964) 548,000.

WIDE WORLD

South Vietnamese woman
searches through the ruins
of her home in the hamlet
of Thanh My
after an attack
by the Viet Cong,
June 11, 1970.
More than 70 civilians
were killed and over 300
homes were destroyed.

Below, "tiger cage" cells
in the Con Son Island
prison complex.
A U.S. congressional
fact-finding committee
found the cells,
built by the French after
a student uprising in 1907,
were still used to hold
political prisoners.
Right, a woman prisoner
in one of the cells.
Prisoners interviewed
by the congressmen said
they were constantly
shackled and often
had to eat lizards
and insects that they
snared.

THOMAS R. HARKIN

the number of warships was being reduced as part of the U.S. military phase-out.

U.S. Marines were withdrawn from the northernmost part of the country, long their main area of tactical responsibility, and there were plans to keep only one brigade in the country by May 1971. Those Marines remaining would be charged with protecting U.S. installations at the major bases in Da Nang.

Maj. Gen. Dong Van Khuyen, commander of the South Vietnamese Army's Central Supply Command, said that the republic's forces would be logistically self-sufficient by mid-1973. Such support for South Vietnam's combat elements, without primary reliance on the U.S., would complete the military phase of the vietnamization program.

Other allied forces were disengaging from the conflict, or making plans to do so. South Korea indicated that it might pull out part of its 49,000-man force (the second largest foreign contingent fighting in support of the government), but no actual withdrawals took place during the year. Thailand's 11,000 troops in South Vietnam were eventually to be reduced by half, while cuts in the Australian force of 7,500 and New Zealand's 550-man contingent also were planned. Only 100 of the 1,600 civic action troops from the Philippines remained.

North Vietnamese and Viet Cong troop strength in South Vietnam during the year was estimated to be at least 240,000. This included 85,000 North Vietnamese Army regulars (with 19,000 of them serving in Viet Cong units as replacements), 40,000 Viet Cong main and local forces, and 100,000 guerrillas and administrative forces. North Vietnam also maintained 40,000 troops in Cambodia and 67,000 in Laos, some of whom were frequently deployed in South Vietnam to take part in specific military actions.

South Vietnam held more than 35,000 Communist troops in prisoner-of-war camps, with 7,780 identified as "confirmed North Vietnamese soldiers." More than 3,000 South Vietnamese and 1,600 U.S. military personnel were listed as missing or as prisoners of war, held by the Viet Cong or the North Vietnamese. Efforts to free prisoners by an exchange proved unsuccessful, as did the U.S. commando raid described above. Disclosure of the "tiger cages," underground jail cells in the South Vietnamese government's prison on the island of Con Son, raised charges of inhumane treatment of political and criminal prisoners. Some penal reforms were instituted as a result.

Trials connected with the alleged massacre by U.S. troops of South Vietnamese civilians at the hamlet of My Lai in March 1968 began during the year. The chief defendant, Lieut. William Calley, Jr., charged with the premeditated murder of at least 102 civilians, went before a court-martial in November. Meanwhile, on November 21 another military court found Sgt. David Mitchell not guilty of shooting approximately 30 civilians at My Lai.

U.S. officials, using the computerized Hamlet Evaluation System, claimed that 92.8% of the South Vietnamese population lived in areas under governmental control during 1970. The remaining people were said to be in enclaves administered by the Viet Cong or in contested regions. The broadening of governmental control was credited to the expanded pacification program and the general reduction in combat levels.

The most significant military development relating to South Vietnam's defense took place in Cambodia. In April U.S. and South Vietnamese forces launched ten major operations against enemy sanctuaries there, with a troop strength that at one time reached 90,000 men. The U.S. troops (approximately 32,000) were limited in their advance into Cambodia to within 21 mi. of the South Vietnamese frontier. They were withdrawn by July 1, a deadline set by U.S. Pres. Richard Nixon. The invasion caused widespread disapproval in the U.S.

According to President Nixon, the purpose of the incursions into Cambodia were: (1) to reduce allied

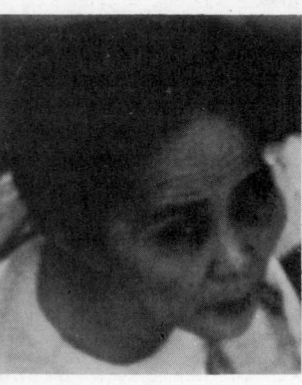

casualties in South Vietnam; (2) to assure the continuing withdrawal of U.S. forces; (3) to permit vietnamization to proceed on a fixed timetable; and (4) to enhance the prospects for peace. Nixon said that "Hanoi left the United States no reasonable option but to move militarily against the Cambodian base areas." Prior to the incursions, North Vietnamese forces reportedly were being resupplied and regrouped for what were assumed to be major military thrusts into the Saigon region and the populous Mekong Delta. Allied intelligence believed that the Communists were preparing to launch an offensive comparable to the Tet campaign of 1968.

When the U.S. forces were pulled out of the Cambodian sanctuaries, Nixon announced the following results in justification of the action: 22,892 individual weapons; 2,509 crew-served weapons; 15 million rounds of ammunition; 143,007 rockets, mortars, and recoilless rifle rounds; 199,552 antiaircraft rounds; 5,482 mines; 62,022 grenades; 83,000 lb. of explosives; 14 million lb. of rice; and 435 vehicles were captured. In addition, 11,688 bunkers and other military structures were destroyed, and 11,349 enemy were killed and 2,328 captured. Nixon declared that "the enemy capacity to mount a major offensive in this vital populated region of the South has been greatly diminished."

While the North Vietnamese could not or chose not to mount any major military actions during 1970, there was a sharp increase in terrorism. Through September nearly 5,000 South Vietnamese were killed by assassination, more than 10,000 were wounded by terrorists, and 6,000 were abducted. These figures represented a significant increase over previous years, about 70% in the number of abductions, for example.

President Thieu early in the year said that he anticipated such actions on the part of the Viet Cong and North Vietnamese while they were deciding on a future course of action. According to Thieu, "What they are doing now . . . is to try to spoil our pacification program in the countryside and to rocket our cities to harass us. They really do not have the capability to do anything as well as they would like to, so they have not yet decided what kind of major measure they will take this year. They must change their strategy because they are so much weaker."

Despite this assessment of their weaknesses, the Viet Cong and the North Vietnamese themselves showed no disposition to move toward concessions in their bargaining positions at the Paris peace talks that might lead to an early end to the hostilities. The revised proposals of the National Liberation Front (NLF) were outlined in an eight-point plan presented in September. They appeared to be essentially the same as the initial formula advanced by the NLF in May 1969. The notable exceptions were an offer not to fire on U.S. and South Vietnamese forces provided Washington would agree to the complete withdrawal of U.S. forces by June 30, 1971, and a willingness to form a coalition government, with the important condition that the new regime not include President Thieu, Vice-Pres. Nguyen Cao Ky, or Prime Minister Khiem.

President Nixon's counteroffer, outlined in October, included a proposal for an immediate cease-fire and military standstill and a "fair political solution [which] should reflect the existing relationship of political forces." The U.S. proposals included plans to end the fighting throughout Indochina.

The South Vietnamese government's position in most ways paralleled the stated attitudes of the U.S., but there were significant shades of difference that indicated less than complete accord. President Thieu, for instance, insisted that a cease-fire would be acceptable to Saigon only under closely supervised conditions and as a prelude to an enforceable general agreement. Thieu insisted that the South Vietnamese government as constitutionally established must be a party to any war-ending agreement in its present makeup and form. Thieu also indicated he did not favour any precipitate U.S. withdrawal and preferred a U.S. residual force in the years ahead. It was Thieu's belief that a military victory could be won by 1972 or 1973.

During the year South Vietnam's deteriorating economy commanded increasing attention. Prices from late 1969 to late 1970 climbed more than 50%. The inflationary spiral was not helped by increases in military and civil service pay, which, while overdue, only exacerbated the situation. More than $800 million in goods were imported into South Vietnam during 1969, while exports amounted to only $20 million. Large-scale importations were planned to absorb some of the currency, in the hope of holding the inflationary rate down to between 25 and 30%.

Economic difficulties fanned political discontent during the year. Demonstrations by disabled veterans living on fixed incomes were common. They were joined by other antigovernment factions, particularly antiwar students and militant Buddhist factions, in subjecting the Thieu administration to one of its most serious challenges since assuming office.

There were, nonetheless, some signs that some of the war-engendered problems were being addressed with various measures of success. Vu Quoc Thuc, minister of state for development, forecast that the national rate of production would be increased by 52% in the 1970s to an equivalent level of more than $600 million annually. He also said that by 1980 the government anticipated rice production would reach 9.2 million tons a year, of which 1.5 million would be for export. In the meantime, the essential food continued to be imported.

In August, South Vietnamese voters cast their ballots for 30 members of the national Senate, one half the total body. Approximately 65% of the eligible voters exercised their franchise, with some surprising

WIDE WORLD

A South Vietnamese soldier demands the surrender of a Viet Cong soldier hiding in a burning bunker during action southwest of Da Nang in November 1970.

results. Of the 16 slates on the ballots (each slate carrying the names of 10 candidates), the one backed by the An Quang faction of the Buddhists polled the heaviest vote. The An Quang Buddhists, as they had always been, were sharply antigovernment in their campaigning. They urged immediate steps to achieve peace through reconciliation with North Vietnam. President Thieu had endorsed three slates, only one of which was elected. One of the tickets that had the president's blessing ended up at the bottom of the list.

A great deal of controversy was generated by the government's actions against National Assemblyman Tran Ngoc Chau. The outspoken political opponent of President Thieu was tried by a military court in March and sentenced to ten years' imprisonment for his alleged pro-Communist activities. The Supreme Court twice ruled that Chau should be released because the military court proceedings against him were unconstitutional. Thieu had sought use of the military tribunals to maintain national security. A law permitting such emergency action was later approved by the Senate and National Assembly.

The issue of military rule in civil matters was expected to be a major point for debate in the 1971 presidential elections. It appeared that Thieu's political future might be jeopardized unless he could broaden his political base. Vice-President Ky's political aspirations, and the extent of his willingness to remain aligned with Thieu, were among the imponderables of an increasingly complex political situation.

(Ro. Go.)

Democratic Republic of Vietnam (North Vietnam). This is bordered by China, the Gulf of Tonkin, the South China Sea, South Vietnam, and Laos. Area: 61,293 sq.mi. (158,750 sq.km.). Pop. (1970 est.): 19.9 million, including (1960) Vietnamese 85.1%. Cap. and largest city: Hanoi (pop., 1965 est., 500,-000). Language: Vietnamese. Religion: Buddhist; pagan; Confucian; Christian. Secretary of the Communist Party in 1970, Le Duan; president, Ton Duc Thang; premier, Pham Van Dong.

The war situation changed suddenly and radically for North Vietnam in early 1970 following the downfall of Prince Norodom Sihanouk in Cambodia. Traditional sanctuaries along the Cambodian border were destroyed and the Ho Chi Minh Trail was disrupted. However, four months later North Vietnam was ready to prove that its strength had not been diminished as a result of the U.S.-led military offensive that destroyed an estimated 60% of Communist supplies stored in Cambodia. In mid-August Hanoi's forces launched what the allies described as the heaviest artillery attacks in more than a year along the demilitarized zone and the Laotian border. The campaign, which lasted more than a week, provoked the U.S. government to commit its entire Pacific force of B-52 bombers against the Communist positions.

Hanoi showed similar firmness on the peace front. It condemned as "a perfidious scheme" President Nixon's April announcement that 150,000 U.S. soldiers would be withdrawn from Vietnam by the spring of 1971. This was consistent with North Vietnamese objections to the U.S. policy of vietnamization—condemned from the start as a policy aimed at making Asians fight Asians. Specifically, Hanoi found it unacceptable that the proposed U.S. troop withdrawals be tied to progress in building up the combat efficiency of the Saigon government's army and reduction in the level of Communist military activity. The deadlock that followed at the Paris peace talks was blamed entirely on the U.S. However, the chief North Vietnamese negotiator at Paris, Xuan Thuy, indicated that he was willing to meet the newly appointed U.S. delegate, David Bruce, for private talks. But in the first week of October, when Nixon offered new peace proposals including a standstill cease-fire and a Geneva-type conference, North Vietnam quickly rejected them as "an electoral gift certificate." On December 17 North Vietnam offered to negotiate a cease-fire if the U.S. suggested a "reasonable date" for complete withdrawal of its forces, but the U.S. refused to agree to withdrawal on Communist terms. On the POW issue, North Vietnam refused to consider an exchange but insisted its prisoners were well treated. Its claim

U.S. troop strength and battle deaths in Vietnam for the years 1965 to 1970. Estimated number of U.S. troops in Vietnam as of Nov. 5, 1970, was 368,000. Battle deaths for the six-year period totaled 43,692.

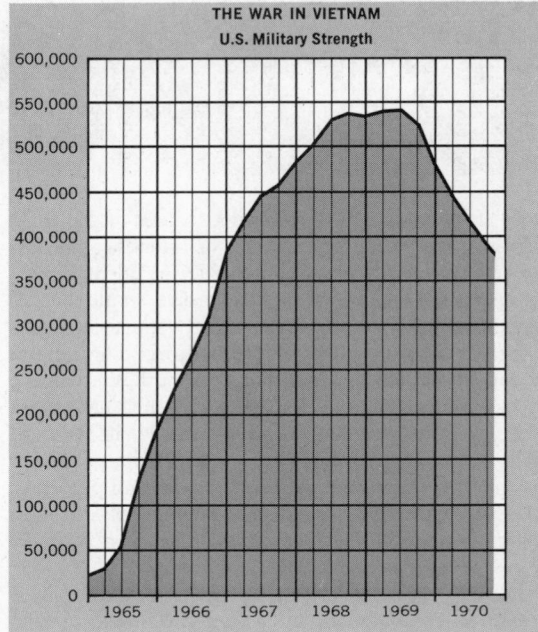

THE WAR IN VIETNAM
U.S. Military Strength

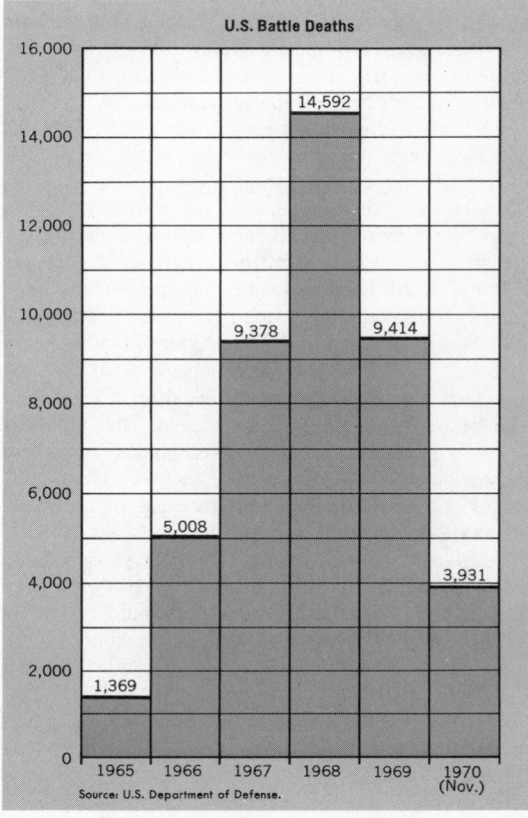

U.S. Battle Deaths

Source: U.S. Department of Defense.

that a list issued in December was "full and complete" was rejected by the U.S.

The expansion of the war had its impact on Sino-Soviet rivalry in North Vietnam. The Chinese government made another shrewd move to draw Hanoi closer to it: a dramatic gesture by Chairman Mao Tse-tung, offering personal support to the Indochinese Communists, was applauded by Hanoi, which referred to the two countries as "both comrades and brothers." At the end of May, China announced a supplementary agreement with North Vietnam providing a gift of economic and military supplies. Though China gave no explanation, Hanoi said the agreement was in fact to replace the supplies captured in the U.S. drive into Cambodia. In June the Soviet Union also signed a new military aid agreement with North Vietnam. Earlier the Kremlin had warned that the Indochinese Communists would be "courting defeat and destruction" if they allowed China to influence their decisions.

Perhaps realizing that the balance had tilted in favour of China during this phase, North Vietnam was soon at pains to show that it was still sticking to its proclaimed policy of strict neutrality between the two Communist "big brothers." In his address to mark the 24th anniversary of North Vietnam's revolution, Premier Pham Van Dong cited the Russian Revolution of 1917 as the turning point in the history of Communism and omitted the usual reference to Mao's victory in China. Also, in mentioning fraternal countries, he put the Soviet Union first and China second. The premier did not fail to refer to the North Vietnamese people's duty "in strengthening the fraternal solidarity and friendship among the brother countries."

There seemed to be a significant shade of difference also in the attitudes of North Vietnam and China to Prince Sihanouk. To all appearances, Hanoi rolled out the red carpet when the deposed Sihanouk arrived for a "state visit" on May 25. But, while Peking had gone all out in support of the prince, Hanoi did not directly offer hard military backing for his restoration to power. On the eve of Sihanouk's visit, Radio Hanoi repeated one of the principles enunciated at the Indochinese Communist summit conference in April: "The liberation of each country is the responsibility of the people in that country alone." This was again reiterated in the joint communiqué issued at the end of Sihanouk's Hanoi visit.

North Vietnam's obvious self-confidence seemed to reflect the consolidation during the year of the post-Ho Chi Minh leadership. Toward the end of May the National Assembly met for the first time since the death of Ho and, among other things, formalized the new power structure. Pres. Ton Duc Thang (see Biography), although apparently a figurehead, ranked first. Next was Le Duan, party secretary and reputedly the inheritor of Ho's mantle. Third in rank was Truong Chinh, National Assembly chairman and chief theoretician, followed by Premier Pham Van Dong, National Assembly Vice-Chairman Hoang Van Hoan, and Defense Minister Gen. Vo Nguyen Giap.

The National Assembly heard a lengthy report by the premier on the political situation and another on the economy by the chairman of the State Planning Commission. Both reflected complete confidence in the ultimate victory of North Vietnam on the military, political, and economic fronts.

To mark the 25th anniversary of the revolution against French control of Indochina, Hanoi issued in August a quarter-century progress report listing

A.F.P. FROM PICTORIAL PARADE

A Red Cross boat carries 86 North Vietnamese war prisoners to North Vietnam in July 1970. The group, liberated by the South Vietnamese forces, included 62 war prisoners and 24 fishermen.

achievements in various fields. Most of the figures in the report conformed to the Communist custom of giving percentage changes only. There were some specific claims too: illiteracy had been completely removed; cholera, smallpox, and polio had been eradicated; infant mortality was down from 30% under French rule to 2.6% in 1968. (T. J. S. G.)

See also Defense.

Vital Statistics

As a decennial census year in the U.S., 1970 was of particular significance for vital statistics. The census provides not only a population count but also data for states and cities by the inhabitants' characteristics, such as age, race, sex, and educational attainment. These furnish the bases for computing vital statistics rates in greater detail than can be done when population estimates cannot be made with precision. The enumeration also provides the checkpoints needed to evaluate the quality of population estimates for intercensal years, thereby allowing the correction of estimates for the previous decade and revision of vital statistics rates. Preliminary data from the 1970 census indicated that some U.S. cities lost population between 1960 and 1970, which meant that birth and death rates estimated on the assumption of continued growth may have understated the true picture.

A number of other countries also conducted population censuses in 1970, among them Argentina, Brazil, Chile, Japan, and Mexico. In England and Wales, Australia, and New Zealand the enumeration was planned for 1971.

In June 1970 the Public Health Conference on Records and Statistics held its 13th national meeting. The conference, a collaborative study program sponsored by the National Center for Health Statistics and other components of the U.S. Public Health Service, provides a forum for representatives of the state and city vital statistics offices and various federal and voluntary agencies. The program centred on forging a closer federal-state-local partnership in health statistics and on strategies for closing the health opportunity gap. At the sessions it became apparent that statistics with greater relevance were needed to bring into focus the entire picture of health status and of disparities between citizens of different income levels, ages, racial groups, and geographic locations.

Birth Statistics. The birthrate in the U.S. turned upward in 1969, following a seven-year decline. The increase was small, however; the provisional rate was 17.7 births per 1,000 population, compared with 17.5 for 1968. The upward trend continued into 1970,

Virgin Islands:
see Dependent States

bringing the rate to an estimated 18 for the 12 months ended August 1970. The change was probably due to the increase in the female population of childbearing ages, especially those in their 20s, rather than to a rise in the rate at which all women in the fertile age span were bearing children. It was estimated that the number of women aged 15–44 years increased 2% between 1968 and 1969, with a larger relative increase (4%) in the 20–29-year-old group. This increase in the potential childbearing population, which stemmed from the high birthrates of the late '40s and early '50s, was expected to continue for the next few years.

The fertility rate for 1969 was 85.8 births per 1,000 women 15–44 years old, or about the same as the rate of 85.7 for 1968. Births in 1969 were estimated to have totaled 3,571,000, or about 2% more than in 1968. Roughly 10% of these registered births in the U.S. were estimated to have been illegitimate. As in previous years, the birthrate among white women was lower than for nonwhites, the rates being, respectively, 16.6 and 24.2.

Birthrates for other countries, as reported to the UN Statistical Office and shown in Table I, were generally higher than the U.S. rate. Exceptions were some European countries, which had recorded rates of 15 to 16 births per 1,000 population in recent years. The provisional rate for England and Wales was 16.3; for France it was 16.7 in 1969. The highest rates, ranging from 40 to 45, were those for the Middle American republics. Data for East and Central African nations were not included in the table because very few of them had national systems for birth and death registration and their estimates had to be based on survey data. In India national legislation requiring the registration of births and deaths became effective in April 1970.

Death Statistics. Mortality in the U.S. was lower in 1969 and the first eight months of 1970 than in

1968. For the 12 months ended August 1970, the death rate was 9.5 per 1,000 population or 2% below the provisional rate of 9.6 for the corresponding period 1968–69. In contrast to 1968 and 1969, the early months of 1970 were relatively free of major outbreaks of influenza, the principal factor contributing to fluctuations in the death rate. Despite these fluctuations, the crude rate had continued on a relatively level course, ranging from 9.3 to 9.7 per 1,000 since 1954, when the steady downward movement ended. Some health experts believed that for many developed countries, where communicable diseases had diminished to negligible importance as causes of death, the death rate had approached an irreducible minimum until there were further medical breakthroughs. Countering this was the experience of Japan, where the death rate dropped from 10.9 in 1950 to 6.7 in 1969.

Influenza was widespread in many European countries in late 1969 and early 1970, thus leading to the expectation of higher death rates, not only for influenza but for other diseases of the older age groups. Provisional crude rates for 1969 were higher than for 1967 and 1968 for many countries in Western Europe, though it was too early to say how much of this was due to influenza.

The provisional number of deaths in the U.S. in 1969 was 1,916,000, 14,000 less than in 1968. (Increased population accounted for part of the lower death rate.) Decreases occurred in death rates for diseases of the heart and cerebrovascular diseases, whereas a slight increase was noted for malignant neoplasms (cancer), due largely to increased mortality from malignant neoplasms of the respiratory system. The death rates for accidents and for influenza combined with pneumonia remained relatively unchanged between 1968 and 1969. The leading causes of death in 1969 and estimated death rates are shown below.

Cause of death	Estimated death rate per 100,000 population
All causes	948.9
Diseases of the heart	364.1
Malignant neoplasms, including neoplasms of lymphatic and hematopoietic tissues	160.1
Cerebrovascular diseases	102.0
Accidents	56.0
Influenza and pneumonia	34.7
All other causes	232.0

These data, which follow the eighth revision of the International Statistical Classification of Diseases, Injuries, and Causes of Death, introduced in the U.S. in 1968, were compiled from a 10% sample of death certificates received monthly during 1969 in state vital statistics offices throughout the U.S. and processed by the National Center for Health Statistics, Public Health Service.

Infant and Maternal Mortality. Infant mortality continued to decline in 1969 and the first part of 1970. From about 60 infant deaths per 1,000 live births in 1934, the U.S. rate had dropped, with only a few interruptions, to 20.1 for the 12 months ended August 1970. This was 4% lower than the rate for the comparable period ended August 1969. Deaths of infants under one year of age numbered 74,100 in calendar 1969, according to provisional reports, resulting in a rate of 20.8 for that year, vis à vis the figure of 21.8 for 1968. Both the neonatal mortality rate (infants under 28 days old) and postneonatal mortality rates (28 days through 11 months) decreased in 1969, having been, respectively, 15.4 and 5.4.

Wide variations are seen to exist in the infant mortality rates shown in Table I. The lowest rates were

Table I. Birthrates and Death Rates per 1,000 Population and Infant Mortality per 1,000 Live Births in Selected Countries, 1969*

Country	Birth-rate	Death rate	Infant mortality	Country	Birth-rate	Death rate	Infant mortality
Africa				Romania	23.3	10.1	54.9
Algeria	40.9†	10.4†	86.3‡	Spain	20.1	9.2	29.8
Sierra Leone†	39.6	17.5	136.3	Sweden	13.5	10.4	12.9§
U.A.R.	36.8	14.4	118.5	Switzerland	16.4	9.2	16.1†
Asia				United Kingdom	16.6	11.9	18.8†
Cyprus	25.5	6.8	28.2†	England & Wales	16.3	11.8	18.3†
Hong Kong	19.9	4.7	21.8	N. Ireland	21.5	10.8	24.0†
Israel	26.1	6.7	23.0	Scotland	17.4	12.3	20.8†
Japan	18.3	6.7	15.3	Yugoslavia	18.8	9.2	56.3
Jordan	33.1†	3.0†	30.7§	**North America**			
Kuwait†	61.2	6.2	35.9	Canada	17.6	7.3	20.8†
Malaysia, West§	35.3	7.5	45.1	Dominican Rep.†	33.9	6.9	72.6
Philippines	25.0†	6.9†	72.0‖	El Salvador	41.9	9.9	59.2†
Singapore	22.2	5.1	20.8	Guatemala	42.5	13.3	89.0‖
Taiwan	25.6	5.3	19.0†	Jamaica†	34.3	7.7	35.2
Europe				Mexico	42.2	9.1	65.7
Albania	35.6†	8.0†	86.8‡	Panama	38.0	7.3	40.8
Austria	16.4	13.3	25.4	Puerto Rico	24.5	5.6	28.3†
Belgium	14.6	12.4	22.9§	Trinidad & Tobago	27.4†	6.8†	35.8§
Bulgaria†	16.9	8.6	28.3	United States	17.7	9.5	20.8
Czechoslovakia	15.5	11.2	22.9	**Oceania**			
Denmark	16.8§	9.7	15.8§	American Samoa	32.6	4.6	17.3
Finland	14.5	9.8	13.9	Australia†	20.0	9.1	17.7
France	16.7	11.3	16.4	Fiji†	30.2	5.2	24.8
Germany, East†	14.3	14.3	20.4	French Polynesia	44.4†	9.1†	52.4§
Germany, West¶	15.0	11.9†	22.8†	Nauru†	32.2	8.3	51.8
Greece	17.4	8.2	31.9	New Zealand	22.5	8.7	16.9
Hungary	15.0	11.3	35.6	Western Samoa†	26.9	4.1	25.5
Iceland†	20.9	6.9	14.1	**South America**			
Ireland	21.5	11.5	20.6	Argentina§	22.3	8.7	58.3
Italy	17.6	10.1	30.3	Chile§	30.9	9.5	91.6
Netherlands, The	19.2	8.3	13.1	Ecuador†	39.6	10.8	87.9
Norway	17.7	9.9	13.7†	Paraguay†	25.9	6.3	51.8
Poland	16.3	8.1	34.3	Venezuela	43.6§	6.7	41.4§
Portugal	19.4	10.4	61.1†	U.S.S.R.†	17.2	7.7	26.4

*Registered births and deaths only.
†1968.
‡1965.
§1967.
‖1966.
¶Not including West Berlin.
Sources: United Nations, *Population and Vital Statistics Report* (July 1, 1970).

recorded by the Scandinavian countries. Australia, New Zealand, and Japan experienced slightly higher rates, but they were still below the rates for the U.K., Canada, and the U.S. The rate for the U.S.S.R. was about one-fourth higher in 1968 than the U.S. rate. Rates for the Central and South American countries were declining, but they continued to be quite high.

Maternal mortality in the U.S. showed no change in 1969; the estimated rate of 27.4 maternal deaths per 100,000 live births was the same as in 1968. This was equivalent to one maternal death from complications of pregnancy, childbirth, and the period immediately following birth for every 3,644 live births. In 1950 the rate had been 83.3. Lower rates were recorded in some countries of Western Europe with more homogeneous populations than the U.S., and Australia and New Zealand also reported low maternal mortality. The rate for nonwhite mothers in the U.S. was about 3.5 times that for white mothers.

Expectation of Life. Babies born in the U.S. in 1969 could be expected to live, on the average, 70.5 years. This equaled the record high for 1967 and exceeded by 0.3 of a year the value for 1968. For males the figure was 66.6 years in 1968, as compared with 74 for females. (Expectation of life at birth is the average number of years that an infant could be expected to live if the age-specific death rates observed during the year of his birth were to prevail throughout his lifetime.) As Table II indicates, life expectancy was much the same among the inhabitants of the various English-speaking countries. For males the values in the mid-1960s were between 66.5 and 68.5 years; for females they ranged from 73 to 74.5 years. The figure for the U.S.S.R. (70 years for the total population in 1967–68) was close to that for the U.S. In the Scandinavian countries, except Finland, males could expect to live to the age of 70 while females could anticipate living to 75.

Marriage and Divorce. Marriages and the marriage rate in the U.S. leveled off during the first eight months of 1970, after increasing through the previous seven years. There were 2,159,000 marriages in the 12 months ended August 1970; the rate for that period was 10.6 per 1,000 population, or the same as for the comparable period ended August 1969.

The principal factor underlying the upward movement in the marriage rate had been the increase in population at the young, marriageable ages, the sequel of the high birthrates of the late 1940s. Since the number of births continued to swell during the 1950s, further increases in the marriage rate were expected, and the reason for the interruption of the rise in 1970 could not be ascertained from the provisional figures.

More marriages in 1969 than in 1968 were reported rather generally throughout the U.S., though the largest increases (5%) occurred in the Northeast and North Central regions. The Southern region experienced only a 3% increase, partly because three of its component states, Georgia, Oklahoma, and Virginia, reported fewer marriages. Brides in 1967 had a median age of 21.4 years as contrasted with the median age of 23.8 for grooms. Three out of every four persons married that year were marrying for the first time. For remarriages, the median age for brides was 35 years and for grooms it was 39.1.

The European countries had marriage rates for 1969 that clustered in the range of 7 to 9.9 per 1,000 population; Australia, Canada, and the U.S.S.R. were also in this group. At the upper end of the scale, Japan, New Zealand, and the U.S. were the major

Table II. Life Expectancy at Birth, in Years, for Selected Countries

Country	Period	Male	Female
Africa			
Gabon	1960–61	25.0	45.0
Liberia	1962	36.1	38.6
Togo	1961	31.6	38.5
United Arab Republic	1960	51.6	53.8
Upper Volta	1960–61	32.1	31.1
Asia			
Cambodia	1958–59	44.2	43.3
Hong Kong	1968	66.7	73.3
India	1951–60	41.9	40.6
Indonesia	1960	47.5	47.5
Israel	1968	69.3	72.9
Japan	1967	68.9	74.2
Jordan	1959–63	52.6	52.0
Korea, South	1955–60	51.1	53.7
Taiwan	1965	65.8	70.4
Thailand	1960	53.6	58.7
Europe			
Albania	1965–66	64.9	67.0
Austria	1968	66.7	73.5
Belgium	1959–63	67.7	73.5
Bulgaria	1965–67	68.8	72.7
Czechoslovakia	1966	67.3	73.6
Denmark	1965–66	70.1	74.7
Finland	1961–65	65.4	72.6
France	1966	68.2	75.4
Germany, East	1965–66	68.7	73.7
Germany, West*	1965–67	67.6	73.6
Greece	1960–62	67.5	70.7
Hungary	1964	67.0	71.8
Iceland	1961–65	70.8	76.2
Ireland	1960–62	68.1	71.9
Italy	1960–62	67.2	72.3
Netherlands, The	1967	71.0	76.5
Norway	1961–65	71.0	76.0
Poland	1965–66	66.9	72.8
Portugal	1959–62	60.7	66.4
Romania	1963	65.4	70.3
Spain	1960	67.3	71.9
Sweden	1967	71.9	76.5
Switzerland	1958–63	68.7	74.1
United Kingdom			
England and Wales	1965–67	68.7	74.9
Northern Ireland	1966–68	68.2	73.5
Scotland	1968	66.9	73.1
Yugoslavia	1961–62	62.4	65.6
North America			
Barbados	1959–61	60.5	64.3
Canada	1960–62	68.4	74.2
Costa Rica	1962–64	61.9	64.8
Guatemala	1963–65	48.3	49.7
Mexico	1959–61	57.6	60.3
Panama	1960–61	57.6	60.9
Puerto Rico	1959–61	67.1	71.9
United States	1967	67.0	74.2
Oceania			
Australia	1960–62	67.9	74.2
New Zealand	1960–62	68.4	73.8
South America			
Argentina	1959–61	63.1	68.9
Chile	1960–61	54.4	59.9
Peru	1960–65	52.6	55.5
Surinam	1963	62.5	66.7
Uruguay	1963–64	65.5	71.6
U.S.S.R.	1967–68	70.0†	—

*Not including West Berlin. †Both sexes.
Source: United Nations, *Demographic Yearbook* (1969).

representatives, while the Central and South American nations fell into the lowest groups; *i.e.*, with rates of less than 8. In countries where the number of consensual marriages is large, the rates based on recorded marriages are correspondingly low.

Countries	Range of marriage rates per 1,000 population, 1969
Colombia*, Dominican Republic, El Salvador	Less than 5
Argentina†, Ireland, Panama, Sweden, Trinidad and Tobago, Venezuela†	5–6.9
Australia*, Austria, Belgium, Canada, Chile†, East* and West Germany, France, Greece, Israel, Italy, Mexico, Norway*, Spain, Switzerland, U.S.S.R.*, United Kingdom*	7–8.9
Japan, New Zealand, Puerto Rico, United States	9–10.9

*1968 data.
†1967 data.
Source: United Nations, *Demographic Yearbook* (1969).

During 1969 and the first eight months of 1970 divorces in the U.S. apparently increased. Divorces and annulments granted were estimated to have numbered 660,000 in 1969, compared with 582,000 in 1968. The provisional rate of 3.3 per 1,000 population for 1969 was 14% higher than the rate of 2.9 for 1968. Detailed divorce data in the U.S. are limited to those states with central, statewide registration, regular reporting, and a standard record form giving the characteristics of couples granted divorces. Because of the differences between states in the legal grounds for divorce and residence requirements, close interstate comparisons of divorce data are not sociologically meaningful.

Divorce rates for countries other than the U.S. were comparatively low, ranging generally from about 0.5 divorces per 1,000 for Canada in 1968 to between 0.8 and 1 for England and Wales, Australia, and New Zealand. Among the European countries the rates for Austria (1.3), East Germany (1.7), and Sweden (1.4) were slightly higher. Only the rate of 2.7 for the U.S.S.R. in 1968 ranked close to the U.S. rate. A marked increase was recorded in the Soviet Union due to relaxing of the divorce laws after 1965, when the rate was 1.6. In some countries of Europe and South America with large Roman Catholic populations (*e.g.*, Spain, Argentina, and Chile) there was no legal provision for divorce. (E. H. HA.)

See also Populations and Areas.

Western Samoa

An independent parliamentary state and member of the Commonwealth of Nations, Western Samoa is an island group in the South Pacific Ocean, about 1,600 mi. E of New Zealand and 2,200 mi. S of Hawaii. Area: 1,136 sq.mi. (2,942 sq.km.), with two major islands, Savai'i (662 sq.mi.) and Upolu (435 sq.mi.), and seven smaller islands. Pop. (1970 est.): 145,000. Cap. and largest city: Apia (pop., 1970 est., 29,400). Language: Samoan and English. Religion: about 80% Protestant, 20% Roman Catholic. Head of state (*O le Ao o le Malo*) in 1970, Malietoa Tanumafili II; prime ministers, Fiame Mata'afa Faumuina Mulinu'u II and, from February 26, Tupua Tamasese Lealofi IV.

The successful adaptation of the "Westminster model" of parliamentary democracy to Samoan custom was demonstrated by the change of government that followed the general elections in February 1970. Tupua Tamasese Lealofi IV was elected prime minister in a secret parliamentary ballot, and selected a completely new Cabinet of eight ministers. A *tama'aiga* (royal son), like his predecessor, Fiame Mata'afa, who had held office since 1959, Tamasese had previously been content to pursue a professional career in medicine and to be a member of the Council of Deputies. His entry into politics and the defeat of Mata'afa may have signified the beginning of party politics. More importantly, it provided a high office

for Sa Tupua (one of the two great families), which it had lost on the death of the new prime minister's uncle, previously joint head of state.

The new Cabinet consisted of younger, more progressive, well-educated titleholders, several of whom had held responsible positions in the public service. More dynamic leadership, rather than radical change, was forecast. Membership in the Commonwealth was obtained on August 28. (My. B. B.)

Words and Meanings, New

European Conservation Year focused attention on the ecological system or **ecosystem** (or, as some would have it, **ecistics** or even **ekistics**). **Environmentalists** deplored what they called **biodegradation** or prolonged spoliation of the natural environment, whereas the self-styled **biocrats** declaimed against the deterioration and misuse of our **livingspace** (echoing the German *Lebensraum*). Clearly **biocides** (blanket term to cover all pesticides, insecticides, etc.) were threatening to exterminate far too many forms of terrestrial life. **Urbanology,** the study of town planning and rehabilitation at a high level of abstraction, was pursued intensively by **urbanologists,** who bewailed, among other things, the new **brutalism** evinced by architects in their misguided endeavours to make buildings banausic and functional.

In the field of cytogenetics **purines** and **pyrimidines** were postulated to be chemical precursors of the raw materials of life. **Sporopollenin** was the name given to one of the most durable of biological materials. Was its suspected presence in meteorites a sign of extraterrestrial life? In Sweden the important new drug **alprenolol** was employed successfully in slowing down the pulse rate. In Africa paleozoologists unearthed the **stegotetrabeledon** or proto-elephant, which flourished some six million years ago. Elsewhere psychologists extended the term **dysrhythmia** to include "the mental fatigue one suffers when making long easterly and westerly flights in which discord arises between external time and the body's biological clock."

Datamation was the new computer term used to cover all forms of data processing. **Cobol,** or **C**ommon **b**usiness **o**riented **l**anguage, and **Fortran,** or **For**mula **tran**slation, spread into almost daily speech. **Videotape cassettes** made a television library a possible reality in every home, whereas the **dex one,** or decision expeditor, promised to speed up business communication by transmitting replicas of documents telephonically to any destination.

Partly, no doubt, under the influence of Lord Robens' book of that name, **human engineering** tended to oust **ergonomics** and **psychotechnology** as terms denoting close connections between humans and machines in the present highly charged field of industrial relations. On the other hand, **terotechnology** was actually invented by Anthony Wedgwood Benn (minister of technology in the British Labour government) to indicate all possible forms of maintenance engineering. The fifth national maintenance engineering conference, which met in London toward the end of the year, was officially renamed the Terotechnologic Conference.

Drift toward the invariable word—that inherent

continued on page 780

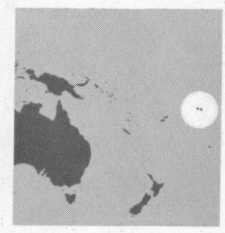

WESTERN SAMOA
Education. (1967) Primary, pupils 24,811, teachers 950; secondary, pupils 7,849, teachers 200; vocational, pupils 131, teachers 16; teacher training, students 227, teachers 15.

Finance and Trade. Monetary unit: Western Samoan dollar (thaler), with a par value of WS$0.71 to U.S. $1 (WS$1.71 = £1 sterling). Budget (1966 rev. est.): revenue WS$4,670,000; expenditure WS$4,824,000. Foreign trade (1968): imports WS$5,450,000; exports WS$3,770,000. Import sources: New Zealand 25%; Australia 22%; Japan 10%; U.K. 9%; U.S. 6%; Fiji 5%. Export destinations: New Zealand 33%; U.K. 14%; West Germany 14%; Norway 12%; Netherlands 11%; Guam 6%; U.S. 5%. Main exports: copra 50%; cocoa 33%; bananas 7%.

The words, phrases, and other forms listed below achieved some currency in the information media during 1970. This list has been prepared by the permanent editorial staff of G. & C. Merriam Company, Springfield, Mass., publishers of *Webster's Third New International Dictionary* and a subsidiary of Encyclopædia Britannica, Inc.

AC/DC *adj* : BISEXUAL

antiversity *n* : an educational institution that offers courses which are outside the traditional disciplines and that emphasizes student involvement

apple *n, specif* : an American Indian who ingratiates himself with white society—called also *Uncle Tomahawk*

aquaspaceman *n* : a scuba diver who lives beneath the surface for an extended period and carries on activities both inside and outside an underwater shelter : OCEANAUT

aquathenics *n pl* : exercises performed in a swimming pool

bells *n pl* : bell-bottom trousers

blahs *n pl* : low spirits : BLUES

bottomless *adj, specif* 1 : NUDE <*bottomless* dancers> 2 : featuring nude entertainers <a *bottomless* nightclub>

brush shoe *n* : a shoe with many small spikes on the sole worn especially by athletes in running events

bubble gum *n, specif* : rock music characterized by simple repetitive phrasings and intended especially for young teen-agers

bump jumper *n* : a stool mounted on a short ski and ridden on a ski slope

burn artist *n* : a narcotics seller who cheats his customers

chopper-copper *n* : a policeman on patrol in a helicopter

club football *n* : intercollegiate football organized and administered by students

communiversity *n* : a conglomerate of educational and cultural institutions (as schools, museums, theaters, and libraries) designed to serve the needs of the residents of a community

computernik *n* : a specialist in the theory and operation of computers

conglomerateur *n* : one who organizes or manages a conglomerate

dartchery *n* : a sports event that combines archery and dart throwing

dial-in *n* : a barrage of phone calls (as to a telephone company) made as a form of organized protest (as against higher rates)

door buster *n* : a widely advertised article designed to attract customers to a store

earthathon *n* : a television program lasting several hours that reports on various events (as teach-ins and demonstrations) relating to the condition and the improvement of the natural environment

ecomanagement *n* : the application of ecological principles to the management of environment and natural resources

ecomodel *n* : a model for the management of environment and natural resources according to ecological principles

ecopolicy *n* : a policy for the management of environment and natural resources according to ecological principles

ecumunity *n* : interchurch cooperation in community projects (as adult education)

elint *adj* : fitted out with electronic intelligence-gathering equipment <fleets of *elint* ships>

fast-food *adj* : specializing in the rapid preparation and service of food (as hamburgers or fried chicken) <a *fast-food* restaurant chain>

flop *vb, specif* : to reassign (a policeman) to a less desirable position—flopping *n*

ghettologist *n* : one who studies ghetto life

guerrilla theater *n* : an informal dramatic presentation that usually depicts episodes of social injustice and is performed in parks and streets by amateurs who are often joined by spectators—called also *street theater*

head shop *n* : a shop that specializes in psychedelic accessories (as hashish pipes, incense, posters, and beads)

hinterurbia *n* : a remote suburb in which city workers reside

hype *n, specif* : ADVERTISEMENT, BLURB <*hypes* on the dust jacket of a novel>

impansion *n* : a reduction in size, extent of operation, or personnel

jawboning *n* : a strong appeal by a chief of state to national business and labor leaders for price and wage restraints

jockette *n* : a female jockey

juice head *n* : a frequent or heavy drinker of alcoholic beverages

kicker *n, specif* : something (as a share in profits or ownership) demanded in addition to interest by mortgage lenders on commercial real estate

kidvid *n* : television programs for children

loading bridge *n* : a covered walkway from an airline terminal to a plane

longuette *adj* : of, relating to, or being a woman's garment (as a skirt or dress) that extends to the mid-calf—longuette *n*

maplaza *n* : a roadside plaza having signs for aiding tourists in locating points of interest and service

marathon *n, specif* : a group session in which members remain together for an extended period (as 24 hours) and interact openly and responsively so as to increase self-understanding

meat packer *n, specif* : a subway worker who is assigned to cram as many passengers as possible into each car during a rush period

megafamily *n* : a group of unrelated adults of both sexes and their children living together communally

noncountry *n* : a country whose size, location, and economic resources are inadequate for economic self-sufficiency and development

no-no *n* : something that is not acceptable

Oreo *n* : a black who ingratiates himself with white society

parochiaid *n* : tax support for nonpublic schools

pigmentocracy *n* : a ruling class made up of individuals of one color

plastic credit *n* : credit obtainable through credit cards

polylogue *n* : a dialogue involving more than two people

psycholog *n* : a written record of one's own mental workings (as images, associations, or feelings)

pudendicity *n* : OBSCENITY; *esp* : an obscenity relating to the sexual organs

rip off *vt* : ROB, STEAL

rockomastics *n* : the study of the names of rock 'n' roll performers

sexploitation *n* : the exploitation of sex especially in motion pictures—sexploitationist *n*

shamburger *n* : a hamburger with a high cereal content

sicknik *n* : one who is emotionally disturbed

sick-out *n* : an unofficial strike in which workers call in sick instead of directly refusing to work

skinhead *n, specif, chiefly Brit.* : a member of a group of young working-class men who militantly hold to conservative views and mores and are distinguishable by their very short haircuts

skytel *n* : a small hotel for passengers of chartered or privately owned planes

slam *n, specif* : PRISON, JAIL

sleep-in *n* : the occupation of a designated area in which protesters sleep en masse as a means of calling attention to their grievances

slug squad *n* : a squad of plainclothesmen assigned to apprehend individuals who use (as in a subway turnstile) a slug instead of a token

snob zoning *n* : the zoning of parcels especially of suburban land so as to prevent ownership by the economically or culturally deprived

sporterize *vb* : to make a military rifle into a hunting rifle by replacing the stock and barrel

taxmobile *n* : a vehicle that serves as an itinerant tax-consultant facility

torpedo *n, specif* : a ballplayer who is specifically assigned to injure a member of the opposing team

zorse *n* : a hybrid between a male horse and a female zebra

continued from page 778

tendency of the English language for a thousand years and more—was partially counterbalanced by an increasing liveliness in the creation of all kinds of derivatives and blends. For instance, new nouns were formed in **-ist, -ant, -ee,** and **-eer: audiotypist,** "one typing direct from tape or other recording," and **discussant,** "one taking part in a formal (often public) discussion or symposium." Derivatives with the prefix **de-** and the suffix **-ization** became well established: **demonetization** (of gold), **depoliticization** (of judges), **detribalization** (of native races), and **desalinization** (of seawater). In this last instance there was regrettable vacillation between **desalinization** (better formed) and **desalination** (shorter and therefore often preferred). Usage had decided quite definitely in favour of **metrication** as applied to weights and measures, however inconsistent this may be when compared with **decimalization** (never decimalation or decimation!) of money.

Among the more notable portmanteau words or blends which showed signs of survival were **slurbs** for slum suburbs and **dormobiles** for dormitory automobiles. Computer booking offices issued **computickets.** Proletarian culture (or rather subculture) was labeled **prolecult.** Top executives saved time and energy by using the unprecedented facilities provided by TV confrontation or **confravision.**

A remarkable semantic twist was given to the vogue word **credibility** in the political world. It came to mean not merely "believability" but also "trustworthiness, confidence, esteem" and then even "plain honesty." It became associated in a somewhat muddled way (although it would be difficult to prove this) with the etymologically related **creditability.** The **credibility gap** came to mean little more than the discrepancy between image and reality. **Sophisticated,** formerly signifying "deprived of primitive simplicity, falsified, not straightforward," was slowly losing that pejorative connotation and was coming to signify little more than "intricate, highly complicated." Moreover, **prestigious,** originally "practicing juggling or legerdemain, cheating, deceptive, illusory," suddenly was popular in the sense of "reputable, esteemed."

There were clear signs that differentiating suffixes were sorting themselves out through usage rather than by any kind of lexicographical edict. Thus, **arbiter** and **arbitrator** ceased to be convertible terms (at least in most parts of the English-speaking world). An arbiter judged in his own right and was answerable to no one. A Parisian stylist, for example, was an arbiter of fashion. An arbitrator was an **ombudsman** deciding a particular issue referred to him by disputants. **Instinctive** meant "determined by natural impulse or innate propensity," whereas **instinctual** meant merely "relating to instinct." **Distributive** meant "engaged in the actual process of sharing out," but **distributional** meant "relating generally to distribution."

In some quarters **amenity** was so overworked that it lost its earlier abstract meaning of "natural pleasantness" and came to denote (especially in the plural) any kind of artificial facility or convenience. **Motivation** moved into daily speech from the technical jargon of psychology and came to mean any kind of urge, drive, inducement, or incentive. **Serendipity,** that faculty of making lucky discoveries by accident possessed by the heroes in Horace Walpole's *The Three Princes of Serendip* (Ceylon), ceased to denote "looking for one thing and finding another" and came to signify more loosely any happy chance. **Synergis-**

tic was frequently used as a stylistic variant of cooperative, and **monolithic** as an impressive epithet describing something solidly uniform.

Occasionally, however, Anglo-Saxon simplicity was preferred. Dress materials were described as **see-through** instead of transparent. The predicative phrase **all about** was done to death by broadcasters. "That is what education is all about," they said, instead of "That is education's main purpose and concern." Instead of the latest maximum or minimum, economists and statisticians talked about an **all-time high** or an **all-time low.**   (Sɪ. P.)

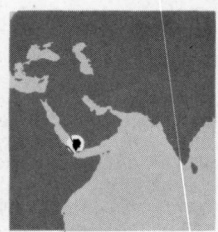

Yemen

A republic situated in the southwestern coastal region of the Arabian Peninsula, Yemen is bounded by Southern Yemen, Saudi Arabia, and the Red Sea. Area: 75,290 sq.mi. (195,000 sq.km.). Pop. (1968 est.): 5 million. Cap. and largest city: San'a' (pop., 1960 est., 60,000). Language: Arabic. Religion: Muslim. Republican Yemen: president in 1970, Qadi Abdul Rahman al-Iryani; premiers, Abdullah Kurshumi until February 1 and, from February 5, Mohsin al-Aini. Royalist Yemen: imam, Muhammad al-Badr.

For Yemen 1970 marked the end of almost eight years of intermittent civil war with a reconciliation between republicans and leading royalists, who were integrated into the republican regime.

In January there was sharp fighting in the north, and in February the key town of Sada, which had changed hands several times in recent months, fell once more to pro-royalist forces. They advanced southward to within 50 mi. of San'a'; their aim was not to restore the former imam but to force the republican regime to include royalist elements. Meanwhile, on February 1 the republican premier, Abdullah Kurshumi, resigned. On February 5 a new government was formed by Mohsin al-Aini.

On March 21 al-Aini arrived in the Saudi Arabian city of Jidda at the head of a delegation to the Saudi-sponsored Islamic foreign ministers' conference. In April it was reported that fighting in the north had ceased and that Saudi Arabia had again cut off aid to the royalists. On May 23 a party of prominent royalists, headed by Ahmed al-Shami, a former royalist foreign minister, arrived in San'a'. He was appointed an additional member of the three-man Republican Council.

On July 21 al-Aini returned to Saudi Arabia. Two days later the latter recognized the San'a' regime, being followed by France, the U.K., and Iran.   (P. Mᴅ.)

YEMEN
Education. (1967–68) Primary, pupils 66,830, teachers (1965–66) 1,726; secondary, pupils 2,718, teachers 115.
Finance and Trade. Monetary unit: riyal, with a value of 1.07 riyal to U.S. $1 (2.57 riyals = £1 sterling). Budget (1967–68) balanced at 50,948,500 riyals. Foreign trade (with U.K. only; 1969): imports £663,000 (but most British goods enter via Southern Yemen); exports £29,000. Main exports: coffee, hides and skins, salt.
Agriculture. Production (in 000; metric tons; 1968; 1967 in parentheses): wheat *c.* 18 (*c.* 18); dates *c.* 60 (*c.* 60); coffee *c.* 3.6 (*c.* 3). Livestock (in 000; March 1968): cattle *c.* 1,300; sheep *c.* 12,000; camels *c.* 56.

Yugoslavia

A federal socialist republic, Yugoslavia is bordered by Italy, Austria, Hungary, Romania, Bulgaria, Greece, and Albania. Area: 98,766 sq.mi. (255,804 sq.km.). Pop. (1970 est.): 20,573,000. Cap. and largest city: Belgrade (pop., 1969 est., 1,083,500). Language: Serbo-Croatian, Slovenian, and Macedonian. Religion (1953): Orthodox 41.4%; Roman Catholic 31.8%; Muslim 12.3%. President of the republic and secretary-general of the League of Communists in 1970, Marshal Tito (Josip Broz); president of the Federal Executive Council (premier), Mitja Ribicic.

The decision to set up a collective presidency of the republic and reshape the federal system was the main political event of 1970, which was characterized in the economic sphere by galloping inflation and a dramatic widening of the foreign trade gap. Yugoslavia moved perceptibly closer to the West in 1970, and improved its relations with China, while its relations with the U.S.S.R. remained cool.

In January Croatia's Central Committee decided by an overwhelming majority to replace Milos Zanko on the League's federal standing conference in Belgrade. Zanko's allegation in November 1969 that nationalist forces were making dramatic progress in Croatia was interpreted by Croatian leaders as part of a plot to overthrow them by conservative party circles. In April the League's Presidium in Belgrade adopted a resolution that affirmed sovereignty of the republics and stressed their need for greater autonomy.

In the Federal Assembly in the spring and summer, advocates of the speedy adoption of the 1971–75 plan clashed repeatedly with those insisting that major changes in the country's economic and political system must come first. No agreement was reached on any of the major economic issues and passage of the economic plan was postponed until the end of 1971.

Agreement was reached on an important political issue. On September 21 President Tito put forward a plan for a collective presidency that would eventually take over the running of the country from him. This presidency, composed of representatives of all the republics and autonomous provinces, would also take over some of the functions of the federal government and the Federal Assembly and would hand over other powers to the governments of the republics. The federal "centre" would only retain the responsibility for defense, foreign policy, and the economic system. Critics of decentralization greeted the plan with open hostility, but it was adopted unanimously at the end of October by the League's national conference.

WIDE WORLD

Yugoslav President Tito and his wife say good-bye to U.S. Pres. and Mrs. Richard Nixon at Belgrade airport as the Nixons complete their state visit, Oct. 2, 1970.

Throughout the year the authorities continued to clash with left-wing Belgrade students. The imprisonment of one student leader, Vlada Mijanovic, in October for "antistate propaganda" sparked a strike at Belgrade University. The authorities also continued to crack down on other critics, including former vice-president Milovan Djilas, whose passport was withdrawn in March for the publication abroad of his book, *The Unperfect Society*.

Industrial production in Yugoslavia increased by 9.5% in the first nine months of 1970. Exports increased 17% over the corresponding period in 1969 while imports jumped 30%. In October Yugoslavia exported 6% less than in October 1969, but imported 60% more than in the same month of the previous year. Retail prices were 10.1% higher in September 1970 than in September 1969. Against this background, on October 29 the federal government imposed a temporary price freeze, a big cash deposit on all imports, and a drastic reduction of consumer credit. The situation was eased somewhat by considerable tourist earnings and by hard currency remittances from Yugoslavs employed in Western countries.

YUGOSLAVIA

Education. (1967–68) Primary, pupils 2,893,624, teachers 109,817; secondary, pupils 181,328, teachers 9,666; vocational, pupils 432.947, teachers 16,191; teacher training, students 25,718, teachers 1,450; higher (including 7 universities), students, 210,810, teaching staff 15,950.

Finance. Monetary unit: dinar, with a par value of 12.50 dinars to U.S. $1 (30 dinars = £1 sterling). Gold, SDRs, and foreign exchange, central bank: (June 1970) U.S. $237 million; (June 1969) U.S. $161 million. Budget (1968 est.): revenue 20,429,000,000 dinars; expenditure 20,167,000,000 dinars. Gross material product: (1968) 112.2 billion dinars; (1967) 103.7 billion dinars. Money supply: (May 1970) 34,660,000,000 dinars; (May 1969) 29,150,000,000 dinars. Cost of living (1963 = 100): (June 1970) 253; (June 1969) 236.

Foreign Trade. (1969) Imports 26.7 billion dinars; exports 18.4 billion dinars. Import sources: West Germany 18%; Italy 15%; U.S.S.R. 8%; Czechoslovakia 6%; U.K. 6%; Austria 5%. Export destinations: Italy 15%; U.S.S.R. 14%; West Germany 11%; U.S. 6%; U.K. 6%. Main exports: machinery 11%; nonferrous metals 11%; meat 7%; ships and boats 7%; clothing 6%; textile yarns and fabrics 5%. Tourism: visitors (1968) 3,887,400; gross receipts U.S. $151 million.

Transport and Communications. Roads (1969) 88,260 km. Motor vehicles in use (1969): passenger 562,509; commercial 104,822. Railways: (1968) 10,688; traffic (1969) 10,120,000,000 passenger-km., freight 17,540,000,000 net ton-km. Air traffic (1969): 606 million passenger-km.; freight 5,655,000 net ton-km. Shipping (1969): merchant vessels 100 gross tons and over 349; gross tonnage 1,427,935. Telephones (Dec. 1968) 549,019. Radio receivers (Dec. 1968) 3,171,000. Television receivers (Dec. 1968) 1,298,000.

Agriculture. Production (in 000; metric tons; 1969; 1968 in parentheses): wheat (including spelt) 4,882 (4,363); barley 459 (450); oats 308 (295); rye 135 (138); corn 7,821 (6,810); potatoes 3,144 (2,890); sunflower seed 390 (309); sugar, raw value (1969–70) 514, (1968–69) 392; dry beans (1968) 175, (1967) 200; onions (1968) 203, (1967) 216; tomatoes (1968) 323, (1967) 322; plums (1968) 721, (1967) 705; apples 483 (304); pears 111 (99); olives (1968) 11, (1967) 40; figs (1968) 22, (1967) 23; wine 706 (617); tobacco 44 (44); beef and veal (1968) 294, (1967) 256; pork (1968) 323, (1967) 309; timber (cu.m.; 1968) 17,000, (1967) 17,400; fish catch (1968) 45, (1967) 48. Livestock (in 000; Jan. 1969): cattle 5,261; sheep 9,730; pigs 5,093; horses 1,109; chickens 33,057.

Industry. Fuel and power (in 000; metric tons; 1969): coal 681; lignite 25,823; crude oil 2,699; natural gas (cu.m.) 730,000; manufactured gas (cu.m.) 86,000; electricity (kw-hr.) 22,947,000. Production (in 000; metric tons; 1969): iron ore (35% metal content) 2,820; pig iron 1,288; crude steel 2,219; bauxite 2,128; antimony ore (metal content; 1968) 2.7; chrome ore (oxide content; 1968) 15; manganese ore (metal content; 1968) 4; copper 75; lead 107; zinc 81; aluminum 48; cement 3,965; sulfuric acid 696; cotton yarn 96; wool yarn 34; wood pulp (1968) 494; newsprint 69; other paper (1968) 438.

Foreign investment in Yugoslavia continued. The most important agreement was a $6.5 million contract signed in July between the West German firm Daimler-Benz and the Yugoslav firm FAP-Famos for the joint production and marketing of commercial vehicles. In March Yugoslavia signed a three-year economic agreement with the European Economic Community, the first Communist country to do so. This agreement provided for preferential treatment for Yugoslav beef exports.

At the end of January, President Tito began a one-month tour of eight African and Middle Eastern countries and, in September, he attended the 54-nation nonaligned summit conference in Lusaka, Zambia. But 1970 was much more of a European year for Yugoslavia. Premier Ribicic visited Britain in February and Tito paid state visits to the Benelux countries in October, stopping en route in Paris and Bonn. On September 30 U.S. Pres. Richard Nixon began a two-day visit to Yugoslavia that was interpreted as an expression of renewed U.S. interest in Yugoslavia's neutrality and a discreet warning to the U.S.S.R. On August 14 Yugoslavia and the Vatican announced the resumption of full diplomatic relations, but Tito's visit to Italy, planned for December 10, when he was to have seen the pope, was postponed because of coolness over the Trieste region border issue. A visit to Moscow in June by Premier Ribicic resulted in the joint reaffirmation of the Belgrade declaration of 1955 recognizing Yugoslavia's right to its own "road to socialism." Of all the Eastern European countries, Hungary and Romania continued to maintain excellent relations with Yugoslavia. Relations with Bulgaria seemed to take a turn for the better in October after an exchange of letters between Bulgarian Premier Todor Zhivkov and President Tito and a visit to Sofia by a Yugoslav delegation that attempted to settle Bulgarian claims that all Macedonians, including those in Yugoslavia, were ethnic Bulgars. Nothing came of these exchanges and relations deteriorated again at the end of the year.

Yugoslavia sent an ambassador to China in April, and a Chinese ambassador arrived in Yugoslavia in August.   (K. F. Cv.)

Zambia

A republic and a member of the Commonwealth of Nations, Zambia is bounded by Tanzania, Malawi, Mozambique, Rhodesia, South West Africa, Angola, and the Congo (Kinshasa). Area: 290,587 sq.mi. (752,621 sq.km.). Pop. (1969 est.): 4,143,700, of whom 99% are Africans. Cap.: Lusaka (pop., 1969 est., 160,500). Language: English and Bantu. Religion: predominantly pagan beliefs; Europeans are Christian. President in 1970, Kenneth Kaunda.

In January 1970 President Kaunda (*see* BIOGRAPHY) accused West Germany, France, Britain, and the U.S. of supplying arms for South Africa to use against black liberation movements and urged the British government to undertake military intervention in Rhodesia to put an end to the Ian Smith regime. He renewed in May his campaign against South Africa's expanding military influence by bringing pressure to bear on a number of European governments to prevent their nationals from taking part in the construction of the Cahorabassa dam in Mozambique. The following month, the victory of the Conservative Party in the British parliamentary elections gave him

ZAMBIA

Education. (1966) Primary, pupils 473,432, teachers 9,325; secondary, pupils 24,005, teachers 1,290; vocational (1965), pupils 3,245, teachers 96; teacher training, students 1,510, teachers 147; higher (1967), students 689, teaching staff 107.

Finance. Monetary unit: kwacha, with a par value of 0.71 kwacha to U.S. $1 (1.71 kwacha = £1 sterling). Gold and foreign exchange, central bank: (June 1970): U.S. $421.2 million; (June 1969) U.S. $145.9 million. Budget (1970 est.): revenue 334 million kwachas; expenditure 244.3 million kwachas. Gross national product: (1968) 919.5 million kwachas; (1967) 840.5 million kwachas. Cost of living (1963 = 100): (May 1970) 144; (May 1969) 148.

Foreign Trade. (1969) Imports 311.8 million kwachas; exports 766.5 million kwachas. Import sources (1968): South Africa 23%; U.K. 23%; U.S. 10%; Rhodesia 7%; Japan 6%. Export destinations (1968): U.K. 30%; Japan 21%; West Germany 13%. Main export copper 95%.

Transport and Communications. Roads (1967) 34,135 km. Motor vehicles in use (1968): passenger 48,200; commercial (including buses) 25,800. Railways (1967) 1,046 km. Construction of a 1,600-km. railway linking Zambia with Dar es Salaam in Tanzania began at the end of 1970. Air traffic (1968): 74,640,000 passenger-km.; freight 930,000 net ton-km. Telephones (Dec. 1968) 47,735. Radio receivers (Dec. 1967) c. 80,000. Television receivers (Dec. 1967) 11,000.

Agriculture. Production (in 000; metric tons; 1968; 1967 in parentheses): corn 375 (c. 380); peanuts c. 20 (c. 20); cassava c. 160 (c. 160); tobacco (1969) 5.4, (1968) 6.1. Livestock (in 000; 1967–68): cattle 1,274; sheep c. 35; goats c. 185; pigs 90.

Industry. Production (in 000; metric tons; 1969): copper 643; zinc 50; lead 23; manganese ore (metal content; 1968) 10; electricity (kw-hr.) 688,000.

further anxiety lest the supply of British arms to South Africa should be resumed.

In October, in his capacity as chairman of the summit meeting of the Organization of African Unity, Kaunda led a mission of ministers from member states of the OAU to a number of Western capitals in an attempt to persuade the governments concerned not to sell arms to South Africa. Edward Heath, the British prime minister, refused to see Kaunda as leader of the OAU mission but had talks with him as president of a Commonwealth country. Their meeting was not entirely amicable, however, and, in the course of a subsequent address to the UN General Assembly Kaunda accused the British government of greed and racism in its dealings with South Africa.

At a secret meeting in April, Kaunda and Sir Seretse Khama, president of Botswana, agreed to resist an attempt by South Africa to prevent the construction of a road link between the two countries. South Africa had claimed that Zambia and Botswana had no common frontier. More important was the official commencement of work on the Tanzania-Zambia (Tanzam) rail link project in October. This was to be financed by a loan from China.

In February the only opposition party, the African National Congress (ANC), was banned after acts of violence in the Livingstone district of southern Zambia. All officeholders in the party were arrested.
                                                    (K. I.)

Zoos and Botanical Gardens

Zoos. The past few years had seen the development of a new type of zoo, known as a safari or wildlife park. These zoos specialized in herds of a few species that were confined in almost natural conditions, where visitors could drive their cars among the animals inside their enclosures. The first zoo of this type to be opened in the U.K. was at Longleat, the Wiltshire estate of the marquess of Bath, which in 1969 attracted over one million visitors. In addition to the main attraction, lions, it exhibited giraffes, zebras, antelopes, cheetahs, and various monkeys. However, a few incidents in such parks in which visitors were attacked by animals pointed to the need for strict observance of safety precautions.

Zoos continued to breed more species of animals in danger of extinction. A world first was a white rhino born at Pretoria, S.Af. The San Diego (Calif.) Zoo received a grant to study a group of ten cheetahs; these animals were becoming increasingly scarce, and there had been only limited success in breeding them in captivity. It was also considered extremely difficult to breed reptiles; Brookfield, Ill., was the first zoo to record the breeding in captivity of the green-crested basilisk. Jersey Zoo, Channel Islands, bred the Szechwan white-eared pheasant, which previously had been bred only in the U.S. Chester (Eng.) Zoo had a first with a Louisiade lorikeet and Frankfurt am Main, W.Ger., with a pigmy kingfisher.

As animal-keeping methods improved, many species were living far longer than they would in the wild state, and therefore frequently required more sophisticated veterinary attention. During the year the oldest gorilla in captivity, a 38-year-old male at Philadelphia, underwent an operation for chronic sinusitis and the removal of bad teeth.

Zoological buildings again showed a trend toward more spacious and natural-looking enclosures, and toward the use of ditches to confine animals rather than wire mesh. At Chester, new lion and tiger enclosures, a spacious flight aviary, a parrot house with 16 modernistic inside and outside aviaries, and a number of ditched antelope enclosures were constructed. West Berlin completed new zebra enclosures and eight barless dry moat paddocks. The first Scandinavian dolphinarium was opened at Kolmarden, Swed., and at Natal, S.Af., a 243-ac. site was purchased for conversion into a modern ditched zoo. A $1 million project announced at Caribbean Gardens, Naples, Fla., would include safari trails and Everglades, Amazonian, Asian, and African exhibits. (G. S. Mo.)

Botanical Gardens. The tercentenary of the Royal Botanic Garden in Edinburgh, Scot., was celebrated in June 1970. Many eminent scientists and horticulturists from various parts of the world attended the ceremonies, which included the opening of an exhibition hall, donated anonymously, to exploit the educational potentialities of the garden. The hall was equipped with a series of imaginative exhibits in which the use of audiovisual equipment played an integral part. In Brussels the Jardin Botanique National de Belgique celebrated its centenary in September with two extensive exhibitions. The theme of one of them, "Botanical Gardens and the Conservation of Nature," was chosen to coincide with European Conservation Year.

Modern methods, automatic systems, and mechanization continued to be introduced at the Royal Botanic Gardens in Kew, Eng. The new fern-propagating house was fully automated, and the modern practice of propagating orchids by germination techniques on nutrient agar enabled many rare species to be grown for the first time. In Munich, W.Ger., the Society of Friends of the Garden, formed in 1955, continued to make donations for the improvement of the botanic garden. A special orchid house, designed for the cultivation of orchids favouring cold humidity, was con-

COURTESY, CHICAGO ZOOLOGICAL SOCIETY

Ziggy, Brookfield Zoo's 53-year-old male elephant, makes his first appearance in 29 years outside his stall, Aug. 27, 1970. He had been confined since 1941 for attempting to kill his trainer. A campaign was under way in the Chicago area to raise $50,000 to build him a new home.

structed over a water tank filled by rainwater collected from the roof.

The Landscape Arboretum of the University of Minnesota had increased to 458 ac. by 1970, more than twice its size when it was donated to the university in 1958 by the Minnesota State Horticultural Society. The State Arboretum of Utah (since 1961 comprising 630 ac. of the university campus) was carrying out research on the cultivated woody flora of the state. Exciting new hybrids of oak were being developed from more than 30 parent species. The George Landis Arboretum was also expanding its educational facilities as a result of a grant by the New York State Council on the Arts. The arboretum had been owned privately until 1966, when it was incorporated as an educational institution under the regents of the University of the State of New York.

About 48 of the 78 ac. under the control of the botanical gardens at the University of British Columbia were being developed. The aim was to provide leadership in the understanding of the green world and to develop a public awareness of plants in relation to man. (F. N. HE.)

Visitors to the New York Zoological Park in the Bronx view one of the large habitat enclosures in the new World of Darkness.

COURTESY, NEW YORK ZOOLOGICAL SOCIETY

continued from page 25

representatives were to be determined, the U.S. delegation submitted an amendment resolution proposing that "Korean delegates duly elected be invited to the discussion of the Korean question" and that a UN Temporary Commission on Korea be established for the purpose of supervising the elections of those delegates. This amendment resolution was approved by the General Assembly, overriding the original Soviet proposal.

Thus, over fierce Soviet objections, the Korean question was accepted by the UN. For a while, a general election for the reunification of Korea seemed to be a possibility. The UN Temporary Commission on Korea began its activities in the beginning of 1948, but, because Soviet opposition made it impossible to hold the election throughout South and North Korea, the committee decided to hold it only where this was feasible. The Soviet Union refused to cooperate with the UN. It was well aware that the Communist organization in North Korea, under the protection of the Soviet military government, would collapse if and when general elections were held in accordance with the UN resolution.

In the face of this intransigence, the first general election ever to be held in Korea was carried out smoothly on May 10, 1948. As had been expected, it resulted in a sweeping victory for the forces supporting Rhee. Some Korean leaders were apathetic to the election, feeling it was premature to hold a general election only in the South. Yet the election was conducted in a democratic way under the supervision of the UN Temporary Commission, and the voter turnout amounted to 95.5%—an eloquent expression of a people's will for early establishment of a sovereign government in any form.

The new National Assembly elected Syngman Rhee as speaker and proclaimed the Constitution of the Republic of Korea. The constitution declared the Korean peninsula and its adjoining islets to be the territory of the republic. The Assembly then elected Rhee president of the country, completing the historic task of founding the government by August 15.

At the same time, the Soviet-backed People's Committee in the North proclaimed a constitution and carried out an election of representatives to the People's Council, with the voters voting only "yes" or "no" on a single and unopposed candidate in each constituency. On Sept. 8, 1948, the so-called Democratic People's Republic of Korea came into being with Kim Il Sung as its chief.

The third UN General Assembly examined a report submitted by the Temporary Commission, which recommended that delegates of the Republic of Korea be invited to the debate on the Korean question before the assembly's Political Committee. It subsequently adopted a resolution confirming the existence of the republic as Korea's only lawful government and recommended that "the occupying Powers should withdraw their occupation forces from Korea as early as practicable." Following adoption of the resolution, the United States offered the Republic of Korea de jure recognition as of Jan. 1, 1949, and a total of 37 countries followed suit.

Even before the UN General Assembly had completed its study of the Korean question, the U.S. began to pull out its troops. President Rhee appealed this action, saying that "any U.S. troop withdrawal before the completion of preparations on the part of Korea to counter a threat of Communist invasion would invite an irreparable misfortune for Korea." The U.S. response was rather cool, and the withdrawal of troops was carried out on schedule. By the end of June 1949 only a small U.S. military advisory group of about 500 men remained in Korea. The only assistance that the U.S. provided was to transfer light weapons worth $110 million to the Republic of Korea's new and inexperienced armed forces. It was quite obvious what was about to happen.

The republic's leaders were at a loss what to do. Depending simply on the UN resolution regarding the unification of Korea, few had the farsightedness to realize the imminent danger confronting them. Nor did they demonstrate a high level of states-manship in countering the oncoming danger. This was another cause of national trial and disgrace. While the people were intoxicated by the republic's establishment and recognition, actually they faced calamity.

The Triumph of Conviction. Preparations for a full-scale invasion southward began in North Korea after the establishment of the regime led by Kim Il Sung. Early in 1949, Kim Il Sung himself led a North Korean delegation to Moscow. While in the Soviet capital, he succeeded in concluding a secret agreement with the Soviet Union, in which he was promised additional equipment to outfit six infantry divisions, three cavalry divisions, and 150 planes, including 100 fighters.

Through the good offices of the Soviet Union, the North Korean regime concluded a mutual defense treaty with Communist China. It also reached an agreement with Peking on the transfer of the "detachment of Korean troops" stationed in Manchuria and mainland China back to North Korean rule. A number of Korean soldiers serving in the Chinese Communist Army had been returned to North Korea by the end of March 1950. By this time, the North Korean regime had formed a 200,000-man combat force with a tank division and an armoured corps—the main military force used in the invasion of South Korea.

On June 7 the Extended Central Committee of the Democratic Front for National Unification adopted an "Appeal for Peaceful Unification," proposing that a general election be held sometime between August 5 and August 8 to set up a supreme legislative organization for reunification, that a session of the body thus elected be held in Seoul on August 15, and that a council of representatives of all political parties and social organizations throughout South and North Korea be convened from June 15 through 17, in either Haeju or Kaesong along the 38th parallel. This false peace offensive on the part of the Communists was a detestable piece of deception.

At dawn on June 25, 1950, the North Korean Army, supported by both the U.S.S.R. and Communist China, launched an all-out attack on the South in all sectors of the 38th parallel with overpowering military strength. The poorly armed forces of the Republic of Korea encountered an invading enemy equipped with heavy weapons and tanks. One by one, the defense lines fell into the hands of the invaders. The R.O.K. forces retreated southward, like men in a tiny boat facing a rising storm.

Fortunately, however, the Korean conflict was quickly brought to the attention of the UN Security Council, thanks to the resolute judgment of U.S. Pres. Harry S. Truman. Without delay, the Security Council approved a set of resolutions calling on the aggressors to stop their act of war, and at the same time recommended that UN member nations render positive assistance to the Republic of Korea to halt the aggression. It also approved the establishment of a UN police force led by the United States. (At the time, the Soviet Union was boycotting the council's sessions.) President Truman ordered General MacArthur to dispatch U.S. forces to check the invasion. Subsequently, 16 member countries sent combat troops to Korea pursuant to the UN resolution.

Because of the strong offensive of the Communist forces, the UN and R.O.K. forces in the early stage of the war had to retreat within a defense perimeter based on Pusan. Early in September, however, they launched an all-out counteroffensive. Seoul was recaptured after a successful landing of UN forces in Inch'on and the consequent collapse of the Communist invasion force. Following the crossing of the 38th parallel by the R.O.K. armed forces, the UN troops also began to march north in accordance with the UN resolution on Korean reunification. It seemed as if the people's cherished dream of national reunification would soon become a reality.

At this point, however, Soviet Premier Joseph Stalin, who had been anxiously observing the situation in the Korean peninsula, dispatched a special emissary to Mao Tse-tung, promising to supply weapons if the Chinese Communists would send reinforcements to Korea. At the beginning of September, the North Korean regime sent a mission to Peking asking for military assistance. Meanwhile, the U.S. Joint Chiefs of Staff sent a directive to General MacArthur telling him to advance to the North provided that the Soviet Union or Communist China would not intervene. Thus it is likely that the U.S. did not intend to have a military showdown with the U.S.S.R. and Communist China over Korea.

Astutely sensing an extraordinary move by the Communists, President Truman met with General MacArthur on Wake Island in the Pacific and asked him about the possibility of Communist China intervening in the situation. MacArthur confidently assured the president that Peking would not intervene. Quite to the contrary, however, Communist China had already moved a large number of troops into North Korea.

The UN forces, some of whom had advanced as far as the Yalu and Tumen rivers on the North Korean border, were forced to retreat due to the mass intrusion of Communist Chinese forces. Although the UN branded Communist China as an aggressor, the Korean War gradually fell into a stalemate following the dismissal of General MacArthur, who had advocated such punitive measures against mainland China as the bombing of Manchuria and a sea blockade.

In July 1951 armistice talks began at the behest of Jakob Malik, the Soviet representative at the UN. By this time, the problem of the disposition of the Korean War had become a political issue in the U.S., where a presidential election was to be held in November 1952. To the people of Korea, it seemed that the U.S. government was making a rather hasty move in entering negotiations prior to the upcoming election, even at the sacrifice of the military and political advantages it had obtained on the battlefield. Fearing that with an armistice they would lose once and for all this ideal opportunity of reunifying their fatherland by driving the Communist aggressors out of the Korean peninsula, the Korean people rose up in opposition to the short-sighted, hasty truce negotiations the U.S. began conducting with the enemy.

Nevertheless, by 1953 the armistice negotiators appeared to be nearing an agreement. In these circumstances, President Rhee suddenly freed all the anti-Communist prisoners of war who had been held in numerous POW camps throughout the country. The abrupt release of the anti-Communist POWs unilaterally by the Korean government was a shocking blow to the U.S., because the prisoners had been detained under the jurisdiction of the UN forces. Deeply annoyed, U.S. Pres. Dwight D. Eisenhower called Korean Ambassador Yang Youchan into his office and assailed the Korean government for its action, asking him, "What would you do if the U.S. forces withdrew from Korea?" Ambassador Yang is said to have replied, "We would all die!"

The U.S. could only try to calm the Korean government with friendly persuasion, and after lengthy negotiations, Korea and the U.S. reached an agreement. Korea undertook not to oppose a truce. In return, a Korea-U.S. mutual defense treaty would be concluded, 20 R.O.K. Army divisions would be equipped and strengthened with U.S. assistance, and U.S. economic aid for the postwar rehabilitation of Korea would be guaranteed.

The Korean War was a hardship unprecedented even in the history of Korea. During the war, which lasted more than three years, the R.O.K. and U.S. forces suffered 212,000 and 75,000 casualties, respectively, while the loss of human life on the part of the Communist enemy totaled more than 1,190,000. Some 700,000 civilians were either killed or listed as missing. The total number of war victims throughout the country exceeded 3,620,-000. The other 15 countries fighting under the UN flag also suffered heavy casualties. (More than 20 other countries gave material and moral support.)

In overcoming the hardships of this war, we once again learned at first hand how precious freedom is, and we felt the pride of a people increasingly identified with the world community. Throughout the period from the liberation to the Korean War, our people, if they made mistakes, nonetheless proved their ability to survive repeated ordeals. They managed to hold onto

right reason, through both the political confusion preceding 1950 and the fire of war in the early 1950s. It must be admitted that the enormous task of filling the political vacuum of the later 1950s was a little too heavy for them to bear, but their patience and gallantry in facing the challenge of a uniquely horrible war proved to be precious capital for the construction of a stronger Korea.

Communist elements have plotted constantly to overthrow the Republic of Korea by subversion and by the instigation of social unrest. Their brutal, well-organized schemes have failed because, once their plots became clear, the masses of innocent people put up a stiff resistance. The people's will to freedom has become stronger as time has passed, despite the long history of foreign threats to their geopolitically fragile country. This national will was the prime factor in enabling us to undergo our harshest trial.

Throughout this fratricidal tragedy, the Koreans felt to the bone the merciless nature of Communism. This one single experience has contributed much more than any amount of theoretical persuasion toward making Korea the most staunchly anti-Communist nation. The Korean people have come to know clearly who their enemy is and what he is like. They have unmistakably realized the emptiness of what is called "peaceful coexistence."

With the nation still divided, the Korean War, which ended in an armistice, brought neither victory nor defeat. It left the remnants and devastation of war, but also a people armed with a new determination and an insight that freedom and peace can be enjoyed only by those who will and can fight for them, and that only those peoples who learn something from confusion and trial and continue to advance can be assured of a bright future.

The miserable aftermath of the Korean War was grave but by no means fatal. Because of the war's destruction, the nation had to endure poverty and hunger for several years. Yet Korea gained through the strong ties of mutual cooperation with friendly countries. Stupefied by the miserable conditions of cities and farming villages that had been reduced to bleak ruins, Korea could not help but rely on the warm assistance of friendly countries. The links of friendship thus forged in the war were firm and enduring, and the hand of help extended by Korea's allies was a prime source of strength.

Just as every Korean has bitter memories of the Korean War, so do the families of those young warriors from friendly nations who were buried in this land. The memories of this terrible experience should lead us to resolve never to repeat past mistakes. In order to apply the war's lessons to the realities of today, the nation must exert itself to prevent the recurrence of Communist provocations that have recently increased both in quantity and intensity. We can best recompense the souls of those who died for the sake of freedom by cultivating our strength and so warning the enemy against resorting to any foolish action.

The stagnancy that prevailed after liberation, and the destruction of the war, caused the nation to lose at least 20 years in its development effort. The national foundation, already weak, was first neglected and then shattered by war. The land reform of 1948, combined with the later confusion and inflation of the war, brought about the downfall of the landowners who had represented the traditional community. Worse yet, the existing strata of organized society underwent drastic change, as millions of uprooted refugees continued to drift about in search of a livelihood. In such circumstances both government and people resembled sufferers from malnutrition, whose physical condition would not permit them to perform as they wished. Frankly speaking, the nation existed entirely on the foreign aid granted us for postwar rehabilitation.

What could be done? Nothing but to prepare for the days to come. In anticipation of improvement, Koreans made it their major task to promote and improve education—the best way any people can develop their inherent potential. It is to our credit

of educational expansion exceeded that of economic expansion many times, to the point where the balance between educational and economic growth could hardly be maintained. Yet the rebuilding of schools, most of which had been destroyed during the war, was a difficult task, and other educational facilities had to be expanded with equal speed. Had the people given up hope for the next generation after their own wartime trials, they would have faced a truly bleak future.

Precedents in other countries indicate that, if a developing country is to achieve modernization, economic development should be achieved parallel with educational development. Korea could hardly have expected the rapid advancement actually attained in the 1960s had it not made such a strenuous effort in the 1950s for the improvement of education.

The Long and Thorny Way to Freedom. The Liberal Party government of President Rhee made repeated mistakes in the disposition of postwar problems, in contrast with its effective and praiseworthy conduct of the war. Its leaders failed to set a real reconstruction in motion, despite the obvious economic and moral necessity of such an effort.

The postwar rehabilitation of Korea was carried out mainly with U.S. aid provided under the Mutual Security Act. By the end of 1957 or 1958, the groundwork was almost completed. Accordingly, U.S. aid, which at its peak in 1957 amounted to $554 million, was decreased year by year. Furthermore, assistance for investment in production facilities was shifted to Development Loan Funds (DLF) in 1958. This caused a major setback to the economy, which had been increasingly dependent on foreign aid since the war.

Even before the shifting of U.S. aid to DLF loans, Foreign Operations Administration (FOA) and International Cooperation Agency (ICA) aid was utilized mainly for the procurement of consumer goods and raw materials. Thus, the importation of production facilities, which Korea urgently needed, amounted to between $75 million and $95 million annually during the period 1954–57. It decreased to an all-time low of $30 million in 1958. Large quantities of surplus agricultural products were imported in accordance with U.S. Public Law 480 (1953), but the money accruing from their sale was allocated mainly to national defense expenditures.

As U.S. policy underwent major changes following the new emphasis on "peaceful coexistence" with the Soviet Union, Korea, which had prepared no independent economic foundation, was compelled to bear the enormous expense of building a self-supporting economy. The problem recalled a man trying to cultivate farmland with his bare hands. The government, nevertheless, continued its desperate attempts to obtain more aid from foreign countries—completely overlooking the changing trends in world affairs. Little effort was made to use wisely the aid that was received, or to actuate an effective policy aimed at making self-reliant economic development possible.

Meanwhile, the labour force expanded day by day, fed by the rapid population growth. The number of new college graduates also continued to increase. The economy of those days could not support enough industry to absorb all these young people, and the steady increase in the number of well-educated unemployed worsened social unrest and dissatisfaction among the nation's youth. Concurrently, a small group of tycoons began to monopolize the booming postwar rehabilitation work. These selfish new rich, in connivance with government officials, neglected both public welfare and private business morals. The result could only be grave social disorder.

The horrible experience of war had given rise to a sort of nihilism, and the extravagant greed for material gains, stimulated by the influx of foreign aid goods, turned the people of Korea in the wrong direction. Social discipline, as well as traditional ethical and moral standards, deteriorated. Yet people were eagerly seeking a national leader and a political force capable of handling state affairs in an impartial manner. The Liberal Party government should have had the wisdom to channel the popular strength

PETER FEBBRORIELLO FROM NANCY PALMER AGENCY

Residents of a small village gather in front of a shop window displaying television sets. Television programming was introduced in 1956, and many citizens, in both urban and rural areas, own sets.

that we lavished keen attention and unique enthusiasm on the development of education, whether or not we recognized its long-range value for our modernization. Since the 17th-century enlightenment period, when our advanced thinkers launched new cultural campaigns under the slogan "Knowledge is power," education in Korea has been linked closely to a sort of "save-the-nation" movement. Our people have never lost the image of education as the "key to the future."

After the war's end, enthusiasm for education began to grow even more intense, due to the people's wartime realization of the value of democracy and the need to be self-reliant. Colleges and middle schools sprouted like mushrooms after a rain. The rate

mustered through its anti-Communist struggle into the task of national modernization. But this it lacked.

The brilliant activities of intellectuals during this period were indeed worthy of admiration. Journalists, especially, displayed a sense of mission similar to that shown by the nation's patriotic leaders during the period of Japanese domination. They infused in the people a sense of resistance against the incumbent government, bravely exposed all sorts of injustices, and roundly criticized governmental corruption. Young students, well aware of democracy's implications, were also ready to devote themselves to the task of establishing national justice. They had learned historical lessons from the various demonstrations their seniors had staged against Japan, often at the cost of their own lives. They knew clearly what justice was.

The illegal elections of March 15, 1960, ignited the spirit of patriotism in those students' hearts. On that day they staged a street demonstration in Masan, a southern port city, protesting against the illegal conduct of the election. Police fired on them, killing and wounding many. On April 19 students in Seoul and throughout the country rose up to clamour for democracy and against the Liberal Party government. When demonstrators swarmed into the official residence of the president, police opened fire again, killing and seriously wounding a large number. Still again, on April 25, a group of college professors staged a street demonstration in Seoul. The huge waves of students and citizens who joined those professors filled the main streets and alleys. Soldiers who were rushed to the scene under martial law were obviously sympathetic with the students and people.

President Rhee was finally compelled to resign his office, bringing to an unhappy end more than 60 years of devotion to the cause of Korean modernization. His efforts in this cause had begun in the closing years of the 19th century when he was a youthful member of the Independence Association. After the loss of Korean independence he had fled abroad to lead the fight for its restoration. In 1919 he was elected president of the provisional government in Shanghai. He had returned to Korea following the liberation from Japanese rule, to become the leader of anti-Communist political forces in the South. In 1948 he was elected first president of the Republic of Korea and was widely hailed as "father of his country" for his efforts to establish a modern democracy and for his successful conduct of the Korean War. In the latter days of his government, however, he was misled by assistants concerned with the extension of their own power. He failed to keep contact with the people and lost his awareness of their needs and desires. This failure led directly to the April 19 student uprising and to the unhappy end of Syngman Rhee's distinguished career.

The uprising was a spontaneous movement launched by the people to overcome the prevailing political crisis, a genuine expression of love of justice by the students, at the risk of their lives. The April 19 uprising, indeed, was a significant civil rights movement aimed at creating a more realistic political climate in which the rights of the people would be guaranteed and the problems of their living conditions would be dealt with.

In our country, a belief in civil rights always has been linked inseparably to a sense of national identity and self-preservation. All our revolutionary movements launched in modern times were founded in nationalist democracy.

Following the April uprising, the second republic came into being and the Democratic Party regime led by Chang Myun (John M. Chang) was established. The Chang government had not come to power through its own efforts, and it turned out to be weak and inefficient. It was not capable of normalizing the social order or of controlling the street demonstrations that became rampant after the April uprising. The nation was driven into an even more chaotic state, nearly beyond control. To make the situation worse, a pro-Communist political force, taking advantage of the confusion, gradually came to the fore. In the spring of 1961, a number of naïve students, unconsciously dancing to the tune played by Communist instigators, rashly advocated the opening of unconditional negotiations between South and North Korea at the Panmunjom truce talks.

The gathering political instability made people seriously concerned for the country's future. Knowing well our demonstrative spirit of nationalism, they must have foreseen that a revolution in one form or another would take place, in the tradition of the great historic popular uprisings. All the people, including myself, felt that if the popular will remained dormant, and the situation worsened, the country would eventually become Communist. The 4,000-year-old history and tradition of the country would then have come to an end. We would have no courage to meet the souls of our forefathers, who had struggled hard so that we and our descendants would live in peace and prosperity through the achievement of a national revival.

When my thoughts reached this point, I was overwhelmed with grief and sorrow that I had been born in this land at such a time of harsh trial and hardship. Yet I stayed awake nights, planning how to save the nation from its crisis by whatever means were available to me. I was a soldier, and I was disinclined to see soldiers get involved in politics. Nevertheless, there is a limit to patience. There is a point beyond which one cannot be simply an onlooker. With the nation on the verge of ruin, with the national economy worsening and the social order deteriorating, my conscience would not allow me to remain concerned with "national defense" only. I could no longer sit idle and indifferent. This was, after all, the nation our soldiers had defended with their lives.

My desire to save the nation from crisis had begun to grow, at the end of the Liberal Party period, long before the April 19 uprising. Actually, the first concrete plan for the military revolution had been drawn up sometime around the March 15 elections, but because of the uprising the plan was not implemented. We took it as rather fortunate that a revolution, aimed at the same goal we had, had been achieved by the students and the public rather than by the military. We also hoped that after the uprising both the political climate and society would be purified, with corruption eliminated.

Contrary to our expectation, however, the national crisis went from bad to worse. It became quite impossible to expect the government to carry out a resolute purification of the armed forces. Finally, on May 16, 1961, my comrades and I staged a military revolution. "The military have risen up," we said, "for the purpose of saving the nation which is wandering on the brink of total collapse, in the belief that the fate of our country and people cannot be left any longer in the hands of the corrupt government and politicians."

We made our future course of action explicitly clear in our revolutionary pledges: to strengthen our anti-Communist postures; to eradicate all corruption; to establish close ties with friendly countries; to build a strong and prosperous country, concentrating our efforts on achieving a self-reliant national economy; and to eventually achieve the territorial reunification long cherished by all our people.

Our prayer for national unification can never be realized with slogans or sentimental theories. The "Let us march north" slogan, prevalent during the days of Liberal Party government, was an imprudent one, which only deepened tensions and was thus detrimental to unification. The idea of holding South-North negotiations so clamorously bandied about on the eve of the May 16 revolution was nothing but a naïve, sentimental plan, easily susceptible to Communist deception and betrayal.

In order to achieve an early unification, the international situation had to be favourable. Equally important, we had first to modernize our country, thus strengthening our capability to deal with unification. The only way to win a victory over Communists is to demonstrate power sufficient to surpass them in the economic, political, social, and all other sectors of life. Devoutly believing this, I and my comrades of the revolutionary government resolved to toil harder under the pledge, "Unification Through Victory over Communism."

All my comrades and I took deep pride from knowing that it was our role to save the country from the hands of aggressors. As most of us had been trained abroad, we felt a strong need for the early modernization of our country and, at the same time, we felt that we could utilize effectively the latest techniques of scientific administration, which we had applied in our military service. We were also confident in our organizing ability and felt we could carry out any undertaking with close unity, however difficult and painstaking it might be. With strong traditional nationalism and positive popular support, we saw ourselves as standard-bearers who would guide the people toward the attainment of their long-cherished hope. Thus we marched forward resolutely to carry out our revolutionary undertaking.

TAKEOFF IN THE 1960s

The Will to Develop. The successful revolutionaries of May 16, 1961, faced complex political, economic, and cultural problems that required immediate settlement, but stress had to be placed on their plan to construct a self-reliant economy by revolutionizing industry. Korea was well aware that this was the key to attaining the revolutionary goal: national reform and reconstruction.

Both the April 19 student revolution and the May 16 military revolution grew out of the chronic poverty of the nation. They were passionate expressions of the people's desire to live better. If poverty had been allowed to weaken the people, as had happened before, they would have faced national collapse. Food comes before politics. Only with a full stomach can one enjoy the arts and talk about social development.

Before May 16 the Korean economy was in disorder. Accumulated political blunders and misguided economic policy had utterly disarranged it. The postwar rehabilitation of the nation was at a near standstill, while the amount of grant-type foreign aid was lessening. Economic stagnation aggravated poverty and unemployment, and farmers' debts rose sharply. On the other hand, a handful of bureaucrats and business profiteers enjoyed luxury at popular expense. Their overconsumption led to an inflow of foreign commodities, making the nation's balance of payments position severely unfavourable.

In its declining days, Syngman Rhee's Liberal Party government lost the opportunity to develop the economy. The brief Democratic Party regime announced an economy-first policy, but it failed to improve the situation. Because of faltering leadership, the climate for economic investment in both government and private sectors took a turn for the worse. As a result, the economy was growing at a rate of only 2.1%, as against a population growth rate of 2.88%.

During the nine-year period after the signing of the armistice in 1953, per capita national income rose a mere 12%. Even this gain was made chiefly during the rehabilitation period of 1953–58. With growth at a standstill at the turn of the 1960s, Korea found itself one of the lowest-income countries in the world.

The industrial structure was not solid. Because a huge amount of foreign aid had gravitated toward them, secondary and tertiary industries seemed excessively swollen in comparison with primary industry. Moreover, the composition of secondary industry contained many unhealthy factors—unbalanced trade, unbalanced development among manufacturing industries, an underdeveloped economic infrastructure, a shortage of industries related to the basic industries—even though the increased value of each industry's products showed some progress, at least on paper.

U.S. grant-type aid had totaled $2.7 billion since the liberation. Yet the Liberal and Democratic Party regimes failed to develop such basic industries as electricity, coal, fertilizer, and cement and such social overhead capital as roads. They lacked a program. They failed also to develop an economic infrastructure involving such sectors as transportation and communications. Private industry alone could not solve such pressing problems as insufficient facilities, lack of raw materials, and financial difficulties resulting from inadequate government assistance. Under these circumstances, industrial production slowed and the supply of commodities fell far short of the demand. The deficit budget and the misdirected monetary policy increased the amount of money in circulation, stimulating a sharp rise in prices. In short, the economy was faced with collapse.

The institutional and moral aspects of the society were no better. People fatalistically took poverty and reliance on foreign aid as unavoidable facts of life. Businessmen and industrialists failed to fulfill their important roles in economic development. Many corrupt government officials and parvenus worked together to amass illegal fortunes. The market, small in scale and lacking vigorous competition, did not function normally. The underdeveloped agricultural system was unable to meet the demand for food, and we were forced to rely on farm products imported from advanced countries. The whole economy was afflicted by inexperience, inefficient and wasteful management, and a lack of desire for economic development.

When I took over power as the leader of the revolutionary group on May 16, 1961, I felt, honestly speaking, as if I had been given a pilfered household or a bankrupt firm to manage. Around me I could find little hope or encouragement. The outlook was bleak. But I had to rise above this pessimism to rehabilitate the household. I had to destroy, once and for all, the vicious circle of poverty and economic stagnation. Only by rehabilitating the economic structure could we lay the foundation for decent living standards. To do all this, and to fulfill our responsibilities in the international economy, would take courage and cooperation.

I soon came to realize the difficulty of achieving our goals of social stability and economic development and of efficient government simultaneously. I was also aware that economic development in the capitalist manner requires not only an immense investment of money and materials but also a stable political situation and competent administrators. To achieve this stability, the military revolutionary government temporarily suspended political activities of students, the press, labour unions, and other social and political organizations, which had caused political crises and social unrest under the Democratic Party regime. We also made it clear that civilian government would be restored in 1963.

As the people came to understand my intentions, we won political stability. Meanwhile, we organized a planning committee of college professors and experts with specialized knowledge in many fields. By mobilizing the maximum available expertise for government administration and policy making, we intended to hold in check the arbitrariness and rashness of the military officers. The establishment of this committee served as a turning point. Korean professors began to show a positive interest in the realities of the country and to present policy recommendations on the basis of scientific analyses of the country's situation. Even though not all of these recommendations could be justified in terms of efficiency and rationality, their advice was of great help to the revolutionary government. Thus the Confucian tradition of Yi Korea, in which scholars played a positive part in government affairs, seems to have revived.

The key to improving a backward economy is the way one uses human resources, for economic development is a human undertaking, impossible without combining the people's potential into a dynamic driving force. This task requires not only strong national willpower, but the ability to translate willpower into achievement. Blueprints must be drawn and explained. If people have a sympathetic understanding of a task, they will voluntarily participate in it.

In 1961 the revolutionary government announced the First Five-Year Economic Development Plan (to start in 1962), the first such overall development program ever prepared for Korea. To prepare it, the revolutionary government mobilized all the wisdom and knowledge available and set clear goals, the primary goal being to found a self-supporting, industrial economy. The principle of free enterprise and respect for the creativity of private industry was adopted, for in this way we believed that the private sector would be encouraged to act voluntarily. Under the plan, however, the economy was not entirely free, since development of basic industries was directed by the government.

Taking into consideration the structural characteristics of the Korean economy, the five-year plan gave priority to the following:

1. Development of energy industries such as coal production and electric power.
2. Expansion of agricultural production aimed at increasing farm income and correcting the structural imbalance of the national economy.
3. Development of basic industries and the economic infrastructure.
4. Maximum utilization of idle resources, increased employment, conservation and utilization of land.
5. Improvement of the balance of payments through export promotion.
6. Promotion of science and technology.

In raising funds for these projects, we tried to draw on domestic resources as much as possible. Self-reliant financing was encouraged.

The five-year plan essayed an annual economic growth of 7.1% and a 40.7% increase of gross national product during the plan period. It would raise the GNP to $2.5 billion and annual per capita income to $112 by the target year of 1966, compared with $94 in 1960. Exports were to rise to $138 million in 1966, a 420% increase over the base year of 1960. The weight of secondary industry in the industrial structure would increase from 19.4% in 1962 to 26.1% in 1966.

The plan's goal of a 7.1% annual growth rate was then considered almost impossible—unprecedented not only in Korea but also in other developing countries. There were those who criticized the plan as too ambitious, but in view of what we needed for future economic development, it was the minimum objective. Some experts also criticized the plan for failing to take into account the possibility of natural catastrophes. Thus, the low agricultural production caused by flood disasters in 1962, the starting year of the plan, was a big blow. Indeed, because of this unexpected catastrophe the plan did not fully achieve its goals in the early years. But there was no alternative other than to push forward—in effect, to try to make something out of nothing.

The past regime had formulated long-term economic development plans, such as the five-year plan recommended in the Nathan Report and the Liberal Party's three-year plan. However, these plans all foundered on incompetent administration and the failure of the people to understand their potential benefit. Thus there was no popular enthusiasm for such efforts. Yet I was convinced that miracles come from concerted effort and action. If we acted with determination to implement the plan, we could achieve a self-supporting economy and a welfare society in Korea.

Success in the first five-year plan could not immediately bring about a self-reliant economy, but it was a landmark that the people had to pass on their long painful journey toward this goal. Indeed, a self-sufficient economy and a welfare society may not be satisfactorily attained during one five-year plan, or even two or more. This underlay our determination and the results, on the whole, were rewarding. The economy sustained a rapid rate of growth and the industrial structure improved.

We are living today in an era of change and competition. Looking back over the achievements of the past decade, we find that the courage with which we met the challenge of modernizing our country has become our primary motivating force. There were many difficulties, however. Long-range policies in themselves were often thought radical by businessmen. Moreover, both the administration and the ruling party lacked knowledge and experience in preparing long-term economic policy and so failed to present a clear vision to the people. Without vision, it is hard to instill confidence.

Some policies were hard to execute. For instance, a set of

PICTORIAL PARADE

Students at the Telecommunications Training Centre in Seoul learn operation, servicing, and maintenance of telecommunications equipment in courses that last from 4 to 12 months.

drastic measures was undertaken during the 1960s to raise interest rates, improve taxation, liberalize trade, encourage the introduction of foreign capital, and place the dollar-won exchange rate under a unitary floating system. These policies drew much criticism, but they eventually contributed much to the rapid development of the economy. The raising of interest rates on both deposits and loans brought a sevenfold increase in bank savings during the ensuing five-year period. Improved taxation enabled the government to formulate a balanced budget. The unitary floating exchange-rate system and trade liberalization sharply increased exports. All these contributed, besides, to an increased inflow of foreign capital, to financial stabilization, and to the strengthening of the nation's international trading power.

One of our big problems in executing these policies concerned the shaky foundations of private industry, which was unable to carry its share of the development burden. Furthermore, the market structure was not modernized. Consequently, the government had to play the leading role in the development plan, though we knew well that, in the long run, such a plan must rely on the creativity and initiative of private industry. In the meantime, the government tried to readjust existing systems to help accumulate private capital, with a view to laying the groundwork of an efficient, competitive market system. We hoped to encourage businessmen who could play leading roles in planning. On the other hand, rigid restrictions were put on business activities that ran against these efforts.

Of course, the government made some mistakes, though these did not have any major effect on the plan as a whole. Because the government's efforts were designed to bring about a policy reform, enterprises that required adaptation to the new pattern of economic activities experienced not a little inconvenience. Also, the government often failed to outline the effects of its policy clearly, thus making it hard to persuade businesses to cooperate.

We now realize, however, the importance of these decisions to rapid economic development. Although hard, they were based on objective reality. To consolidate our gains, we are now confidently moving forward under the second five-year plan. With this second plan, the economy has greatly expanded its infrastructure and has seen a great development of heavy and chemical industry. The economy is continuing to grow rapidly at this moment.

The Groundwork for Self-Sufficiency. In the 1960s Korea changed from a premodern, underdeveloped society to a modern, productive, constantly growing society, moving toward a self-sufficient economy. This was our response to the Development Decade initiated by the UN.

High growth rate and structural improvement made the Korean economy a model of rapid progress in the family of developing nations. Many economists, both Korean and foreign, who have studied the process of growth and development that the Korean economy followed during the past decade, observed that the Korean economic development through its two five-year plans compares favourably with the achievements of West Germany and Japan, which developed into major industrial nations from the ruins of war, and of Israel, which achieved a nearly miraculous development.

As a result of their experience under the two five-year plans, the Korean people have rid themselves of the pessimism that filled their hearts in the 1950s. Furthermore, our augmented economic power permits us to lessen our dependence on foreign aid and to participate as a bona fide competitor in the world market and an earnest partner of less developed nations, thereby taking part in the worldwide effort to expand and equalize the world economy.

What, then, has the Korean economy achieved in concrete terms? First, the economy grew at an annual average of 8.6% during the past ten years. This compares with the 5% set by the UN as the goal for annual growth during the first Development Decade. It engendered a 230% increase in the scale of the economy and a similar increase in national income. Dividing the 1960s in half, we see that an annual growth rate of 5.5% was registered in the first half and an 11.7% growth per annum in the second. Manufactures led this growth, with an annual increase of 16% during the ten-year period. This remarkable development of manufacturing industry was due chiefly to the great expansion of social overhead capital, which rose by an annual average of 17.1%. During the ten-year period, industrial production, including electric power, rose about five times. Per capita GNP climbed from $95 in 1959 to $196 in 1969.

Second, remarkable structural improvement was achieved. Korea lacks natural resources but has a large population. Under these conditions, the government had to improve the economic structure by placing greater emphasis on developing the industrial sector, which had been outweighed by the primary industry. Incidentally, technology was to be furthered and foreign markets exploited. Thus the economic policy gave priority to industrialization and export of manufactured products. As a result, the share of mining and manufacturing industry in GNP rose from 14.1% in 1959 to 25.9% in 1969. Also, the economic infrastructure, including such things as electric power, roads, and harbour facilities, was greatly expanded. Both export-oriented and import-substitute industries emerged. The rapid development of labour-intensive light industries provided a new momentum to exports, while refined oil, cement, steel products, fertilizer, electrical appliances, and pharmaceuticals began to be produced at home, thereby saving foreign exchange.

The third and most amazing achievement of the Korean economy in the 1960s was the increase in exports. Because of Korea's small-scale domestic market and our lack of natural resources, the government adopted financial, monetary, and industrial policies in support of an export-first principle. Exports grew at an annual average of 42% during the 1960s, bringing about a 35-fold increase during the period as a whole. This is the biggest export growth in the world. As exports were increasing, the composition of export commodities began to shift to a preponderance of manufactured goods. In 1959, when the total dollar volume of exports was only $20,436,000, 83% of this consisted of raw materials, primarily tungsten, iron ore, dried seaweed, and fresh fish. In 1969, in contrast, manufactured goods comprised 79% of total exports valued at $702,811,000, and the leading export items were plywood, textiles, human hair, and wigs. In 1961 Korea exported to only 25 nations; in 1969 to 98. Korean exports to the U.S. in 1969 amounted to $341,349,100. Thus the exporting industry now holds the position of a driving force for economic development. The creative efforts of businessmen to expand their markets contributed to the rapid export growth.

Fourth, the inflation that has chronically threatened the Korean economy was considerably curbed over the ten-year period. This was another major economic achievement. A series of price policies such as a financial stabilization program, a commodity supply-and-demand program, the liberalization of imports, an improved income policy, and the elimination of accumulated government deficits helped reduce the annual rate of price rise from 20–30% during the first half of the decade to less than 10% during the latter half. Currently, price rises are being held within a 7% level. With prices stabilized, the groundwork has been laid for achieving lasting economic stability, a prerequisite to sustained, rapid growth. Stabilized prices also helped normalize market functions.

Fifth, the Seoul–Pusan expressway was opened to traffic, heralding the arrival of a transportation revolution. Dedicated on July 7, 1970, the superhighway, which runs the length of the country, was constructed with our own resources and techniques. The 428-km.-long highway took two years and five months to build and its cost of $330,000 per kilometre is probably the lowest in the world. The areas coming under its influence produce 63% of the nation's GNP. The number of vehicles running on it account for 81% of the total number in operation.

In addition to the Seoul–Pusan and Seoul–Inch'on expressways now in operation, construction is under way on a superhighway linking Taejon in the centre of the country with Chonju in the south-central region. In 1971 construction will begin on similar highways along the east and south coasts of the country. When these highways are completed, the major economic areas of the country will be within easy one-day travel distance of each other. This will accelerate urbanization and contribute much to industrial modernization.

When the superhighway program was first announced, some people expressed skepticism about it. I said then that expressways would be a better investment of our limited funds than railroads and harbours for solving our transportation bottleneck. I also said that expressways would contribute by helping to develop industries, by expanding the sphere of economic life, and by promoting regional development. "This is a project symbolic of our modernization task," I added, "so we must carry it out with our own capital, our own technique and our own effort." The successful construction of the Seoul–Pusan expressway, the largest civil engineering project ever launched in Korea's history, gave the Korean people a new confidence that they can do whatever they want to do.

In addition, a fivefold increase in bank savings resulting from the interest-rate reform, the consequent increment in domestic capital for investment, the doubling of agricultural production, the establishment of a foundation for an improved agriculture, and the construction of an industrial complex at Ulsan on the southeast coast can be cited as encouraging achievements made under the two five-year plans.

However, I readily admit that there were several failures in the execution of these plans. There was excessive enthusiasm and too much pressure to attain our goals. We did not correctly evaluate the capital at our disposal and chose inefficient means of implementation.

The currency reform of 1962 can be cited as the representative blunder of the first five-year plan. This reform was intended to prevent inflation and to mobilize idle capital for industrial investment by mopping up excess money in circulation. The result, however, was a fall in the value of the currency and temporary financial confusion.

The measures taken to liquidate usurious loans in rural areas also failed. Designed to cleanse rural society of this obstacle to growth, they attempted to eradicate the centuries-old practice of private money lending at high interest. A huge amount of money was released to farmers to pay off the usurious loans, but the government resorted to coercive methods in re-collecting it. Accordingly, the farmers had to sell their crops, land, and livestock at unreasonably low prices. This, in turn, caused a sharp fall in farm prices, which hardly helped either agricultural production or income.

Furthermore, the growth-oriented policy of the 1960s caused interest rates, the won-dollar exchange rate, tax rates, and the money supply to become excessively fixed and rigid. In an economic development policy, these factors must be considered as variables and adjusted flexibly to meet problems as they arise. In the 1960s they were not kept flexible enough.

I concede that errors were made, also, in the fostering of small and medium industry, the introduction of foreign capital, and in financial and monetary policies. The government, however, gained valuable experience, even through its mistakes.

The development achievements of the Korean economy during the 1960s may seem to some to be either a miracle or an accident. Neither is the case. They are the result of the will to develop, rooted deeply in the minds of the Korean people, of the popular enthusiastic response to the government's policy, the development of education and technology, and the utilization of a skilled labour force.

Efforts Rewarded. Because of limited capital and the shortage of able businessmen, Korea had trouble achieving rapid economic development under a free enterprise system. In the early stage of the development effort, the government had to play the leading role. This made it necessary to improve the government's administrative capability, for without competent administration no successful economic development could be achieved.

The politicians of a developing, modernizing nation, such as Korea, should try to present a realistic policy under systematic leadership. They should not be preoccupied with the pursuit of power or pelf. Because I felt that our cherished desire for national modernization could not be attained by politicians involved in self-serving political struggles, I decided to organize a political party composed of men with fresh political ideas.

I believe that pros and cons can be advanced while policy is being formulated, but once a policy is decided upon, those who participated in the decision should follow it faithfully, whether they approve of it or not. I wanted to see a political party and a parliament of politicians who would do this. Whenever I met objections, I had to renew my decision to dedicate myself to the creation of a fresh and constructive political environment.

Since political ideas must have appropriate administrative support, the revolutionary government began immediately to reform the government administration. We confronted conservative resistance from established politicians, but by using the advanced management techniques employed in our armed forces, the government was able to accomplish its purpose. Particular emphasis was placed on changing the rigid bureaucracy handed down from the days of Japanese colonial rule into a progressive, efficient system.

Rather than assign new functions to the existing government agencies, we established new organizations to provide effective administrative support for the economic development plan. The Economic Planning Board was established immediately after the May 16 military revolution. This was followed by the reorganization of government economic agencies, including the establishment of the Construction Ministry. The government-run enterprises were also reshuffled. So that it could fulfill effectively its function of controlling and supervising the development plan, the Economic Planning Board was made the highest economic planning agency of the government.

The Office of National Tax Administration was set up to ensure fair tax assessment and smooth tax collection. Although some of the increase in tax revenue was due to rapid economic development, the fact that tax collections rose by twice the economic growth rate is attributable to the remarkably improved tax administration. Korea is now ready to formulate its budget with its own revenue, even if foreign aid were to be discontinued.

To implement administrative reform, a system of planning, review, analysis, and control was introduced in all government agencies. The personnel problem was faced squarely. Immediately after the military revolution, the government announced a large-scale reshuffle of ranking government officials, except for those serving in fields requiring specialized knowledge and experience. In addition, it established an expensive training program for government officials to equip them with development-oriented management techniques. The early success of this training program was due partly to the cooperation of scholars and government officials.

Government administration was under my direct control, so the reform program there was relatively easy. However, in other areas, such as education and the press, it took considerable time to realize the reform plans. These areas resist direct political influence. It was not easy for them to rid themselves of the traditions handed down from Yi Korea through Japanese rule. At the same time, in view of the high educational level in Korea as compared with its economic power, the role of education and the press in the national development effort is as important as that of any other sector.

Realizing this, the revolutionary government made an effort to accept their criticism and advice as much as possible. They were left free to raise objections to the government. However, the government could not avoid taking measures against the revival of the tradition of resistance originated in the days of Japanese rule and developed under the corrupt Liberal Party regime. The attitude of "opposing for the sake of opposition" was neither healthy nor constructive, and it had to be done away with in the name of national modernization.

An illustration of this was the political crisis caused by student demonstrations against rapprochement with Japan. The political objective of the revolutionary government was to establish a firm national identity and to prevail over Communism. This objective was not an isolationist one, but aimed at broad cultural contacts with foreign countries, through a positive open-door policy, so as to receive useful stimulation for national development. It was also meant to increase mutual understanding with other countries and thus promote the international status of the republic. Above all, it would speed economic development. Accordingly, the government extended its network of diplomatic missions to neutral nations in Southeast Asia, the Middle East, Africa, and Latin America. Exchanges of visits at the head-of-state level were made with several countries, while goodwill missions were dispatched to others. As a necessary part of this positive diplomacy, immediate efforts were made to normalize relations with Japan, our nearest neighbour.

Japan's former colonial rule had left a strong anti-Japanese feeling in the hearts of the Korean people. They could hardly rid themselves of it quickly after the liberation. Moreover, after the liberation, stress had been placed on anti-Japanese education, thus intensifying the anti-Japanese attitude. Consequently it was only natural that an attempt at normalizing relations with Japan would draw severe opposition. I know that this opposition was motivated by patriotism. However, the force of conservative public opinion could not be allowed to stand in the way of national development. I therefore attempted to convince the people that a changed international situation made normalized relations with Japan a necessity. In spite of my effort, the situation worsened, and a proclamation of martial law was required. This drew heightened criticism from intellectuals and the opposition party, but the government continued its effort toward rapprochement with Japan in view of the far-reaching benefits for the country that it was expected to bring.

Parallel with the open-door policy in diplomacy, efforts were made to infuse in the minds of the people a confident sense of national independence. The unhappy past had caused the Korean

A North Korean delegation (left) and representatives of the U.S. and South Korea meet at Panmunjom near the 38th parallel, the chief point of contact and communication between the North and South.

people to develop a pessimism about life. While they were pre-occupied with such a negative view, no development effort could bear fruit, however hard the government might try. It must be noted that the nonproductive, negative traits of the Korean people are not hereditary; they are the remnants of past invasions and misfortunes. History shows that the Koreans are hardworking, creative, and proud, with a strong sense of achievement. Nevertheless, the government has had to work continually to drive this defeatism away and revive the national pride. Whenever the occasion has arisen, therefore, we have called on educators, journalists, and other opinion-leaders to play a positive role in leading the people toward national modernization. The government itself has promoted our sense of national identity by praising the achievements of national heroes.

All this greatly helped promote the sense of national independence. The Korean people have been used to looking at rulers with a suspicious eye. When I emerged victorious in the 1967 presidential election, enjoying a far greater margin of votes than in the election four years before, I was very happy to have realized my desire to gain the people's confidence.

Students and intellectuals have begun to modify their antagonistic attitude toward the government. They have come to recognize the merits of the government, while criticizing the demerits, and have begun to participate in government affairs, sloughing off their past attitude as fence-sitters. This is very encouraging. Even more encouraging is the fact that the nation is now full of confidence in the future, believing that if one works harder, he can live better. This strong national solidarity has been demonstrated by the unity and courage of the people in facing a series of intensified Communist provocations since 1968. Whenever there has been provocative aggression by North Korea, leaders and people have intensified their opposition to Communism, at the risk of their lives.

This unity is also expressed by the people's faith in democracy. In particular, the generation born after the liberation is being educated in democracy. It is well aware of today's world situation and it has a sense of mission. The young are confident about their future and we are confident in them.

In order to build a capable new generation, the government drew up a Charter of National Education, formulating an educational policy in compliance with its spirit. Traditionally, the Korean people have had a strong desire for learning, but looking back at past education, we find that it lacked objectives. In other words, Korean education in the past was not clear as to its purpose. The government, therefore, sponsored a study to establish clear-cut objectives, mobilizing experts in all fields. The result of the year-long study was presented in the form of the Charter of National Education, designed to see that our rising generation should develop both creativity and the sense of cooperation.

We are still in the process of learning how to apply the ideals set forth in the charter in educating children in schools, at home, and through the mass media. To achieve self-sufficiency in the foreseeable future, the people must positively participate in national activities in the political, economic, and social fields, equipping themselves with a sense of community and a strong national consciousness, rejecting the passive and the pessimistic. While making an effort to achieve peace both at home and abroad, they must move forward toward the national tasks of the 1970s.

THE WAVES OF THE PACIFIC

The Compass of Peace. Some people tend to see this nation as a danger zone bearing the seeds of dispute or as a powder keg a moment before an explosion. In view of the past 25 years, with their record of division, invasion, and open war, these views appear to have some basis. Nearly 20 years after the cease-fire agreement of July 27, 1953, the Communist threat remains especially menacing. The infiltration of armed Communists into the republic, together with the new situation arising from the recent U.S. move toward troop reduction here, has led to the fear that trouble will develop in Korea again.

Some specialists find the source of tension in Korea's very geography, as a bridge between island Japan and the northeastern region of Asia. This view can be justified by historical facts. When the Mongols swept southward to Korea in 1231, their ultimate aim was to secure Korea as a base for an attack on Japan. Contrariwise, when the Japanese invaded Korea in 1592, their intention was to gain a beachhead for advance into the continent. The Chinese-Japanese War of 1894–95 was a struggle between Japan in its effort to advance into the continent and Ch'ing China, which attempted to stop it. The Russo-Japanese War, similarly, arose when czarist Russia's march southward clashed with Japan's march northward toward the Asian continent.

History proves that whenever Korea became a battlefield for the powerful, the peace and security of East Asia was at stake. In this sense, Korea holds the key to peace in East Asia. Japan's invasion of Manchuria in 1931 and the outbreak of the Chinese-Japanese War in 1937 were cases in point. It may rightfully be said that Japan's starting the Pacific War was predictable from its first advance into Korea.

Consider what happened to Korea after World War II. Korea was divided when the Soviet Union forcibly occupied the northern half of the peninsula. Then came the Communist invasion of the republic by the Kim Il Sung regime in 1950. The peninsula became a bloody battlefield and, even after the cease-fire, a target of Communist aggressive acts.

But Korea today is quite different from what it was. A solid foundation of national reconstruction has been laid over the ashes of war. Discarding its past as the "Hermit Kingdom," Korea has marched into the world, contributing to the peace and security of the East Asian region. When Japanese imperialism swept across the Korean peninsula, it destroyed the balance of power in this region and, therefore, peace in Asia. This ultimately led to the tragic Pacific War. It is clear that if this same peninsula should ever become Communist, peace in the Asian and Pacific region would likewise be seriously threatened. Genuine peace in Asia, especially Northeast Asia, was and is dependent on peace in the Korean peninsula, and peace in Korea will be secured when it ceases to be a power vacuum. Korea can fill this vacuum when it builds up its own strength sufficiently to cope with the influence of the big powers.

The Korean people's firm belief in the need for the modernization was not derived from self-centred ultranationalism. Rather, the enthusiasm for modernization was the outcome of their tremendous effort to live peacefully with all the nations in Asia and the Pacific areas. Modernizing the nation is the only possible shortcut to unification of the divided land and is the most valid means of filling the power vacuum. It is no exaggeration to say that the successful modernization of Korea serves as a compass indicating the direction of peace and security in East Asia.

It is true that in the past the Republic of Korea has given the unfavourable impression of being an extremely obstinate and inflexible anti-Communist state, but we continue to try to present a brighter image to world society. We have even decided to establish friendly trade relations with countries in the Communist camp—except, of course, such extremists as the North Korean regime, Communist China, and Cuba. This is a reflection of our desire not to run counter to world trends in this new era of hoped-for détente.

Korea's efforts to ease international tensions have already been demonstrated in its frequent participation in various international conferences and in the many such conferences held in Seoul. Our leading role was exemplified by the creation of the Asian and Pacific Council (ASPAC), an international organ established at Korea's initiative. Since its inception in Seoul in 1966, ASPAC has played a large part in promoting understanding and cooperation among the member nations through its annual ministerial, economic, social, and cultural conferences, and its importance is rapidly increasing. As I emphasized at its inauguration, ASPAC serves as the driving force of the "peaceful revolution," enabling us to make the Asian and Pacific region a community of nations blessed with peace and balanced in prosperity.

The security of Asia, however, depends above all on the honourable conclusion of the war in Vietnam. We feel this acutely, for we sent our troops to Vietnam in the hope of seeing an early and honourable end to this conflict. For even if the Asian and Pacific community is firmly established and the "peaceful revolution" achieved, our efforts will be in vain if Vietnam and the rest of Indochina become Communist as a result of the free world's acceptance of a less than honourable solution. If and when the Vietnam war ends with a just peace settlement, our troops will withdraw from the scene without delay.

The Future of Peaceful Coexistence. World politics in the 1960s has been characterized by peaceful coexistence and multipolarity of power. As the realization deepened that competition in nuclear armament might eventually bring about the near annihilation of mankind, the prevention of an all-out nuclear war became a new issue directly connected with the national interests of both the U.S. and the Soviet Union. The changing attitude of these two giants has not only had a great influence on their respective diplomatic policies and military strategies, but has affected all international politics.

In other words, the military bipolarization, with nuclear weaponry as its basis, has brought about a multipolarization in international politics. America's worldwide alliance structure has gradually undergone a qualitative change. Some believe that, as the nuclear stalemate between the U.S. and the Soviet Union functions to restrict the involvement of the superpowers in overseas conflicts, newly independent countries will be encouraged to attempt autonomous activity. Countries belonging to the third world will capitalize on this trend in international politics but keep themselves aloof from both sides. Others believe that, since nuclear weapons cannot be used in actual war, they have already lost political and psychological efficacy; therefore, the effect of nuclear armament on international politics is limited to deterrence and the maintenance or strengthening of the status quo.

The U.S. has now embarked on a search for a new order in international politics suitable to the new age. The fear arising from recent developments in nuclear weaponry and the reaching of the saturation point in the stockpiling of nuclear weapons has led the U.S. and the Soviet Union to open diplomatic negotiations with a view to easing the armament competition. No notable results have yet been achieved in this direction. Nonetheless, the two powers now exhibit a new tendency of trying to avoid the expansion of, and intervention in, international disputes. The progress of peaceful coexistence has created a thaw among the NATO and Warsaw Pact nations, enabling Western and Eastern

European countries to enter into separate diplomatic relations. In this area, at least, President Nixon's "age of negotiation" seems to have arrived. Even though this new peaceful trend in international politics has its origin in the deterrence capability inherent in nuclear weapons, we should not be reluctant to recognize its affirmative aspects. It is my conviction that peaceful coexistence, whatever its origin, will provide a new momentum for the solidifying of international peace.

Despite the interest of the U.S. and the U.S.S.R. in easing international tensions, however, we must look squarely at the dangers that some parts of the world are still facing. Regional tension still exists in the broad area of East Asia, especially in Southeast Asia. Furthermore, the U.S. disengagement policy as applied to Vietnam is aggravating that tension. In Northeast Asia the trend to multipolarization is being utilized for evil purposes by the North Korean regime. This presents a sharp contrast to the European region, and negates Nixon's age of negotiation and peace.

Since the Nixon administration came to power, U.S. foreign policy has sought a new direction—especially as regards East Asia—including the disposition of the Vietnam war. The Nixon doctrine, seemingly reflecting the new isolationist mood arising in the U.S., is an effort to avoid excessive intervention in, and responsibility for, wars—such as the one in Vietnam—that cannot be brought to a successful conclusion by U.S. military power alone. At the same time, it is a move to urge the countries in East Asia, as yet dependent upon U.S. direct defense support, to step up their own efforts to promote regional security. The problem, of course, is how to fill the power vacuum that will be created in this region if this policy is enforced abruptly.

The Nixon administration has promised that the U.S. will discharge its duty as prescribed in the mutual defense pacts concluded with these countries. In other words, the U.S. is determined to provide the assistance called for in the pacts in case any of its allies in the region are threatened with nuclear war or are attacked on such a massive scale that they cannot repulse the enemy singlehandedly. However, the U.S. will refrain from sending ground forces to the countries in trouble.

As applied to Korea, this doctrine may mean that, even though the U.S. will provide adequate support, including a nuclear deterrent, to Korea in case of large-scale aggression such as the 1950 Korean War or in the event of nuclear attack by Communist China, Korea should assume primary responsibility in coping with such other threats as partial provocations, infiltration, and subversion initiated by North Korea. Viewed in this light, the Nixon doctrine can be regarded as a reconfirmation of the U.S. promise of defense support and, at the same time, a definition of the boundaries of Korean responsibility.

On the other hand, the doctrine, while emphasizing autonomy and self-help in Asian countries and promising economic and other assistance to them, seems to attach heavy importance to the role of Japan in Asia, especially in light of the U.S. domestic situation. The Nixon doctrine presupposes a reevaluation of the economic, political, and military potential of Japan, which has now emerged as the world's third largest industrial country. There is no objection to the U.S. urging self-help on Korea or to its call for the solidification of regional cooperation. However, we must assert that the harmonization of Korea-U.S. and Korea-Japan relations is the key to keeping the Korean peace.

The de-americanization policy in Asia is likely to undergo many trials and face many problems. Peace in the Far East, including Korea, depends ultimately on the construction of a collective security system strong enough to check any aggression attempts. In view of our own experience and from precedents found in the European region, we hold that the possession of power is a prerequisite in any confrontation with Communism. Also, it is most necessary to cultivate a correct recognition of Communism.

The Vietnam war started to assume a different aspect in the latter half of 1969. At present, de-escalation is under way and U.S. troop withdrawals are being carried out. At the same time, the de-americanization and pacification plans are being pushed in accordance with the Nixon doctrine. Although no progress has been made at the Paris negotiations with North Vietnam, the U.S. seems determined to resolve all problems according to its previously established plan. By the time of the U.S. presidential election in 1972, the U.S. plans to have withdrawn about 430,000 troops, that is, the major portion of the U.S. forces stationed in Vietnam.

The ultimate solution to the Vietnam war presupposes a ceasefire, an agreement on the political pattern of Vietnam after the war, international security measures for Laos, Cambodia, and Thailand, and joint international supervision to guarantee the observance of the above agreements—points that were emphasized in President Nixon's peace proposals of October 1970. Since the present state of affairs in Vietnam appears too complicated for an early solution to these problems, it is anticipated that the current stalemate will continue for a considerable period of time. The future of Vietnam depends on how effectively the Vietnamese government operates in replacing the U.S. troops with its own troops and in carrying out the pacification plan, and on how firmly the Vietnamese people can unite.

The Vietnam war, however, cannot remain as a problem limited only to the U.S. and Vietnam. It is a problem common to all Asian countries, including Korea, and is critical to world peace. Although Vietnam, Laos, and Cambodia are separate, independent countries inhabited by different races, the Communists, as has been shown in the Laotian situation, are operating as a unitary, combined front under the leadership of the Indochinese Communist Party, ignoring territorial and racial differences. Therefore, the settlement of a dispute in one area of the Indochinese peninsula is not an ultimate solution. Persistence and strong will are necessary to oppose the Communists until such a solution is found.

That Korea for the first time in its history intervened in a war abroad by dispatching its troops to Vietnam was an outcome of its deep understanding of the significance and nature of the Vietnam war. The bravery displayed by the more than 50,000 Korean troops dutifully discharging their mission in Vietnam has no doubt given strength and encouragement to the dispirited Vietnamese people who are suffering so much from the war devastation.

The Will to Unification. Some 70 km. north of Seoul is a hamlet, an unheard-of backwoods village that suddenly rose to prominence in the summer of 1953 when it became as much a focus of the cold war as Berlin. This is Panmunjom.

Many tourists from abroad make it a rule to visit this place. They consider Panmunjom more or less a sight to be seen, a spot whose unusual atmosphere constitutes a major attraction. To Koreans, however, Panmunjom represents the nation's tragedy and tribulations. Despite changes in the background and conditions of the cold war, Panmunjom remains as grim as ever; it stands as a reminder of national suffering. Panmunjom is the scar of territorial division and national fratricide. What other place on earth can tell such sad tales?

Lying in the middle of the 4-km.-wide and 250-km.-long demilitarized zone that cuts across the Korean peninsula, Panmunjom is the only point of contact and the only avenue of communication between the North and South. But it is a contact point and an avenue in form only; in reality, it does not function as such. Both sides are poles apart even while they meet there. All modes of travel and communication are severed between countrymen of common stock, of common history and language; no one knows what has happened to his or her relatives and friends residing on the other side of this closed gate.

Panmunjom began to attract worldwide attention from the day the guns stopped firing along the Korean War front line. Selected as the truce-signing site, it emerged as the site of negotiations for a peaceful settlement of the Korean question. At that time, a few leaders in the free world were naïve enough to believe that a basis had been established for the peaceful unification of our land. On the contrary, we Koreans soon realized that our long-cherished aspiration for national unification was hopeless. And as the years passed, our dismay and misgiving proved to have been well founded. Our national aspiration for reunification has grown increasingly intense, but the wound of division does not appear any more likely to heal.

The subsequent years did not lack international or domestic endeavours to bring our tragic division to an end. After the conclusion of the armistice on July 27, 1953, the question of Korea's unification was referred to the Geneva political conference which opened on April 26, 1954. The conference was convened on the basis of a UN General Assembly resolution, adopted Aug. 28, 1953, which approved the armistice pact and welcomed the convocation of a political conference under paragraph 60 of the armistice agreement. The Republic of Korea, the 16 UN allies, the Soviet Union, Communist China, and North Korea all took part.

Korea's allies proffered the following bases for a rational settlement of the Korean question: (1) acceptance of UN authority in dealing with the Korean question and a major UN role in the settlement; (2) holding of free general elections in proportion to the populations of North and South Korea; (3) stationing of UN forces in Korea until the establishment of a unified, independent, and democratic Korea. These proposals were fully consistent with the principles the UN had upheld ever since 1947. The Republic of Korea adopted the same policy of free and general all-Korea elections as its official unification formula. On May 22, 1954, a 14-point Korean proposal was put forward.

Turning a deaf ear to our overtures, the North Korean delegates insisted on their three-point proposal calling for the withdrawal of UN forces and elections supervised by a commission drawn from neutral nations. The conference was stalemated, and the allies issued a joint declaration on June 15, restating the joint policy statement on the Korean War that they had made in Washington at the time of the armistice. This declaration affirmed the allies' determination to carry out the terms of the armistice and supported the efforts of the UN to bring about an equitable settlement in Korea. Among other things, it called for genuinely free general elections under UN auspices to achieve a unified, independent, and democratic Korea and for popular representation in proportion to the population of the two zones.

We deeply appreciate and value the UN efforts to solve the Korean question, beginning in 1948 when the third UN General Assembly declared the Republic of Korea to be the only lawful government in the Korean peninsula. In 1950 the UN lost no time in taking a military action against the North Korean aggressor, the first instance of a world organization acting to uphold the principle of collective security. On October 7 military action in North Korea was approved, and the UN Commission for the Unification and Rehabilitation of Korea (UNCURK) was established. Later, the UN Korean Reconstruction Agency was set up to aid in the work of repairing the ravages of war. All these efforts of the UN were frustrated by the obstructionism of Communist China and North Korea. The Korean people regret having allowed all opportunities for unification to pass by.

Subsequent efforts at the UN all seemed to run aground. Before 1960, when the West held an absolute majority in the UN, the Korean unification issue encountered no difficulties. Beginning in that year, however, newly independent Asian and African countries, following the so-called nonaligned course of action, won admission to the UN en masse. Thanks to this change in the power distribution, the number of votes supporting Communist China's admission to the UN began to increase and the Korean question had to undergo many vicissitudes. Since the 15th General Assembly, the number of votes supporting the UN resolutions on Korean unification have decreased in inverse proportion to the increase in the number of the UN member states.

Proposals for the admission of the Republic of Korea into the

UN, first submitted by the Republic of China to the UN Security Council on Dec. 8, 1955, were repeatedly defeated by the Soviet veto. Therefore, Korean unification was approached from a different angle. Each year only the representative of the Republic of Korea was invited to the UN debate on the Korean question. At the 15th General Assembly, U.S. Ambassador Adlai E. Stevenson submitted an amendment calling for the invitation of a North Korean delegation to the UN debate on the Korean question, provided that North Korea first recognize the "authority and competence" of the world body to deal with the Korean unification issue. Since that time, the question of this invitation has become an important procedural issue over and above the unification question itself.

Over the years, a delicate hedging came to the fore. The Indonesian delegate proposed to the 16th General Assembly that "as a new approach to the solution to the Korean question, an international conference of the countries concerned be held in a neutral place such as Geneva under the sponsorship of the United Nations." At the 17th General Assembly, Canada suggested that U.S. forces stationed in Korea be replaced by troops of non-aligned neutral nations and that UNCURK be reorganized in a way acceptable to both the South and North Korean governments. Iraq called for the "convocation of a special conference which will strive to find a consensus on Korean unification." Tunisia and Ceylon expressed the opinion that "in view of the fact that the settlement of the Korean problem has been impossible with the measures worked out in the past, the General Assembly must recognize a new means of solution." At the 18th General Assembly, Indonesia proposed that the question be solved through direct negotiations between South Korea and North Korea, under the sponsorship of neutral nations, outside the UN.

The proposals of some neutral nations became more outspoken at the 22nd General Assembly, reflecting the success of North Korean penetration into the neutral Asian and African bloc after 1967. These countries joined forces with Communist countries in submitting plans for the simultaneous invitation of South and North Korean delegates, the withdrawal of the UN forces, and the disbandment of UNCURK. They proposed convocation of a conference of the countries concerned and the omission of the Korean question from the UN agenda.

To make matters worse, some free world countries—even some that had fought in the Korean War—demonstrated a growing lack of interest in the Korean question. British Commonwealth countries such as Australia, Canada, and New Zealand, for example, spoke against the automatic General Assembly debate on Korea. On Aug. 11, 1966, Chile gave notice of its intention to withdraw from UNCURK. Pakistan, another UNCURK member, also expressed its wish to withdraw. Some Korean War allies withdrew from the group of nations that had jointly submitted the UN resolutions on Korean unification—France and Greece at the 20th General Assembly and Turkey at the 21st. Canada announced its intention of following suit.

The fact remains that the UN, supported by the world's conscience, has made a continuous effort for more than two decades to work out a solution to the question of Korean unification. Korea has maintained solid relations with the UN throughout. It was on these good relations that we Koreans pinned our primary hopes for territorial reunification, but this does not mean that we failed to work toward this end ourselves. The fact is that our persistent efforts have not yet made any marked progress because of the barriers thrown in their way.

The most serious obstacle is Kim Il Sung and his followers, who still control the northern half of the Korean peninsula. This Communist clique has never turned back from its scheme of communizing the whole territory by force. In violation of the armistice agreement of July 27, 1953, the Communists have committed more than 7,800 armed provocations against the South in the past 20 years. Since early spring 1967, they have committed barbarous atrocities in both rural villages and cities, even

YOONG-KI KIM FROM KEYSTONE

R.O.K. troops fight near Da Nang, South Vietnam, in 1968, the result of the 1965 decision by the South Korean government to send in a contingent of armed forces.

killing a little boy who shouted his hatred of Communism. Indeed, they are war criminals who should be put on trial before the bar of history.

Most detestable is the Communists' attempt to throw on others the responsibility for their own crimes. They still assert that the Korean War was provoked by the Republic of Korea. They hurl groundless accusations at the UN side even now, despite their own violations of the truce line and their shooting, killing, and injuring of UN soldiers. Likewise, they fabricated the lie that the South Korean people rose up in rebellion, in order to conceal the destruction, massacre, and arson that armed Communist guerrillas committed in the South. Calculating each turn of events, the Communists repeat their favourite slogans as if chanting a spell—"peaceful unification," "south-north negotiation," "a federal system," "south-north exchange," and even "assistance to the south."

Whenever Kim Il Sung and his party have indulged in criminal acts, they have unfailingly opened a "peace offensive" before and after their atrocities. Their first peace offensive was designed to camouflage the invasion of 1950. On June 25, 1949, the Fatherland Unification Democratic Front was formed in P'yongyang, allegedly with the participation of 71 political parties and social organizations of both North and South Korea. The front immediately proposed a five-point unification formula, which included provision for general elections in both South and North Korea, as well as the evacuation of foreign forces. Less than a year later, Kim Il Sung provoked the Korean War. Their peace offensive was nothing more than an attempt to construct an alibi before committing their crime.

In the 1960s Kim, who since the armistice had advocated general elections in South and North Korea under the supervision of neutral nations, suddenly began to preach autonomous peaceful unification—the so-called three-stage unification formula. The first stage called for the withdrawal of U.S. forces from South Korea, the conclusion of a nonaggression and peace treaty between South and North Korea, the reduction of armed forces in each sector below the 100,000-man level, and the commencement of economic and cultural exchanges. At the second stage a federation would be formed, with each side maintaining its own political and social structure but with a "supreme national commission" established with representatives from the two governments. The third stage would witness general elections, to be held throughout Korea, to form a "unified central government" without the intervention of foreign influence and in an autonomous way.

This unification formula was cannily designed to promote confusion in the South by stirring up the people's sentimental attachment to unification and by capitalizing on the rapidly changing international situation and the chaos caused in South Korea by the April 19, 1960, student uprising. At the same time, the move was aimed at influencing world opinion to the disadvantage of South Korea. Proof that Kim's peace offensive was a falsehood from the start is the fact that, as the Republic of Korea's development became more conspicuous in the latter half of the 1960s and its anti-Communist posture became stronger, the Communists switched to the theory of revolutionary unification.

With the dispatch of a commando team to Seoul on Jan. 21, 1968, Kim Il Sung stripped off his mask of peaceful negotiation completely and exposed his commitment to violence. Busy with war preparations for the past ten years, Kim's cadres have completed the fortification of all North Korea, the armament of the entire population, and the militarization of the party. Watching his chance to reinvade, Kim now publicly announces that the early part of the 1970s is the decisive moment for unification by arms.

This is the barrier hampering unification, our nation's ardent desire. Yet no matter how steep the road to unification, we affirm that we must settle the question by peaceful means, with perseverance and good sense. It should be made crystal clear that the Republic of Korea has not even the slightest intention of seeking unification by war.

What should be done, however, if Kim Il Sung does not abandon his ambition of unifying the country by force and provokes a second Korean War? We will not take a single step backward. Should such a war occur, all the people, be they soldiers or civilians, will fight to the very end. However, we do not want such an emergency to occur.

It is our firm belief that the chief prerequisite for peaceful unification is to ease the present state of tension existing between South and North Korea. We are also firmly convinced that if Korea is to be unified by democratic means, democratic general elections must take place first under the guarantees and supervision of the UN, representing world opinion. But a peaceful approach to unification is impossible as long as Kim Il Sung and his party are entrapped in their own theory of violent revolution. Accordingly, if Kim Il Sung desists immediately from any sort of military provocation, including the dispatch of armed agents into the South, if he makes a public announcement renouncing the policy of communizing the whole of Korea by force, and if we can recognize that the North Korean Communists are proving their sincerity with deeds and the UN verifies this, we would be prepared to suggest realistic means of laying the groundwork for unification—always, of course, on the basis of humanitarian considerations.

We would also earnestly consider the gradual removal of the artificial barriers between the two parts of Korea that presently block commerce, postal service, and traffic, and the opening of doors to mutual exchanges in the fields of education, culture, the arts, sports, the press, and science. If the North Korean regime recognizes the UN's efforts for democracy, unification, independence, and peace in Korea and accepts its competence and authority in this regard, we would not be opposed to the presence of a North Korean Communist at the UN deliberations on the Korean question.

However, I do not think the North Korean Communists will meet these prerequisites in the foreseeable future. In all likelihood, they will, instead, continue and even intensify their slanders against our efforts for peaceful unification, while increasing their provocations to war. The power of Kim Il Sung depends on a dictatorial system that requires war preparation and armed

provocation against the Republic of Korea in order to maintain its existence. Otherwise, Kim could not long divert the attention of the North Korean people from domestic grievances and complaints. Only by keeping the danger of war in the minds of the North Korean people can the regime camouflage its own absurdities. This is proved by their acts such as the capture of the USS "Pueblo" on the high seas and the downing of a U.S. EC-121 reconnaissance plane over international waters—to say nothing of the Korean War itself. The North Korean Communists are trying to create a feeling of danger on the Korean peninsula to maintain their own power.

Politically, Kim Il Sung and his followers have relied on purges and oppression of the North Korean people. The tide of liberalization flowing elsewhere in the Communist world is prevented by Kim from trickling into Korea. The idolization of Kim Il Sung is so strongly pushed that there is practically no chance for a force able to check Kim and his followers to emerge. Only fanaticism remains.

The ultraleft adventurism practiced by Kim Il Sung is very dangerous to the peace of Korea, for no one can say with certainty that he will not unleash another war against the Republic of Korea, especially if his dream of achieving unification by force in his lifetime is taken into consideration. In fact, his fanatic desire for communizing the whole of Korea by force could easily lead to another Korean War by miscalculation. Therefore, as long as Kim Il Sung remains in power in North Korea, the tensions now gripping the Korean peninsula cannot be eased.

Is there, then, no chance for peaceful unification in the near future? I am not pessimistic about this problem. I strongly believe that a breakthrough will soon come. Liberalization will eventually affect North Korea. The liberalizing trend in the Communist world is, I believe, too great a force to be held in check by any one dictator, however tyrannical and powerful he may be. And should Kim Il Sung's dictatorship become shaky in the face of this irresistible force, the war-oriented system he has built on the basis of his idolization will also become shaky. Then the North Korean Communists will have to give up their dream of communizing the whole of Korea by force and opt for a peaceful means of unification.

In such a situation, major efforts toward peaceful and democratic unification of Korea could be made. I hope that, when that time does come, our national strength will have grown and international conditions will have ripened so as to aid our efforts in this cause. The key to unification lies in how much the liberalization process in North Korea can be internally advanced and ultimately directed.

We are earnestly waiting for the arrival of such a time. But this does not mean that, while we are waiting, we will merely busy ourselves maintaining the status quo. We must carry on a bona fide competition that can show the North Korean Communists that democracy provides a better living for the people than Communism. To this end, we must make a continued effort to promote our freedom and expand our prosperity. By so doing, we can call on Kim Il Sung to reflect on what he has done.

But we will never resort to the immoral means of fratricide—as the North Korean Communists did in the Korean War—in order to expedite the collapse of Kim Il Sung's dictatorial system. Instead, we will make a sincere effort to accomplish a democratic and peaceful unification of Korea, while manifesting this resolute attitude toward unification before the world.

I am sure that Kim Il Sung's plan of communizing the whole of Korea by force will fail, for such a plan, requiring the sacrifice of men's lives in a fratricidal war for the achievement of political goals, runs against the traditional philosophy of the Orient. From ancient times, Eastern political philosophy has been based on the virtue of benevolence. This virtue calls for charity and comprehension and completely renounces force and violence. Benevolence is still deeply rooted in the consciousness of the Korean people and exerts an important influence on their ways of thinking. Benevolence remains an indispensable qualification of a leader. I hope that Kim Il Sung may recover this Oriental virtue, but the likelihood is not very great.

Koreans have overcome many national crises with vitality and perseverance. And they should take pride in their spiritual heritage of optimism and in their resistance to despair. Many ordeals are expected to lie along the road to national unification, but with the vitality of our ancestors we must carry out our historic mission. We must continue our march forward to unification, entertaining hope and confidence and displaying courage and patience. We must cross the mountains and hills lying ahead of us, however steep they may be. For the bright morning of unification will surely dawn soon.

WE SHALL NOT GIVE UP HALFWAY

The Continuing Challenge. We are living in the age of national revitalization, in which all of us are called upon to liquidate our unfortunate past, renounce the mistakes of our history, and strive for national revival with renewed resolution. Our past experiences have led us to pursue our ideals with devotion. Our sufferings have given us a zeal for construction.

Our goals are quite clear. They are to establish a politically independent, sovereign state; to build a prosperous society in which all are guaranteed a decent economic life; to enable all to live with pride, wisdom, and love through the further promotion of national culture; and to bring freedom to the enslaved people in the lost half of our land by reunifying the divided country.

In order to complete these tasks, we must first single out the factors that impede our advancement. Rational, persuasive measures will be needed to channel the people's strength into the national endeavour and to overcome negative factors. The advance toward these ideals will be challenged in every case by rugged adversaries, some of them unlooked for. But with composure, we must tackle them one after another. As we pushed ahead with our economic development, we found many problems that had to be solved immediately so that the pace of development could be maintained.

The world economy today is in a state of unprecedented confusion. It is inevitable that the Korean economy, now in the process of transition to a free-economy system as a result of its high growth rate, will relate closely to the world economy. It is presumed that our pace of growth and the character and direction of our development will be greatly affected as a result.

The equilibrium of the world economy is being shifted fundamentally by such phenomena as uncertain business conditions and the deflation policy in the U.S., which is connected with the de-escalation of war in Vietnam; excessive protectionism and a lack of sincerity on the part of advanced countries in solving the problems existing between the "have" and "have-not" nations; and the highly competitive industrialization policies of advancing countries and their change from primary producing to processing. We also have the trend toward the formation of trading blocs and the insecure international financial market. All these constitute grave challenges to the future of the Korean economy, which depends largely on exports, on imports of raw materials, and on the introduction of foreign capital as prerequisites for maintaining a sustained high growth rate.

In our effort to counter these external challenges effectively, we plan to (1) strengthen economic cooperation with neighbouring countries, with the ultimate goal of coordinating development programs and establishing a common market; (2) pursue common development programs through joint investment with major raw-material-supplier nations; and (3) expand the scale of industrial plants, advance technology, and promote labour productivity as a means of improving the nation's international competitiveness.

Four major problems may require action at home. First, the balance of payments situation may become serious. This is attributable to financial pressure on the country's trade, arising from the increased demand for basic raw materials and intermediate materials to supply the industrialization program and

the export drive. Also, consumption has increased with rising incomes and urbanization. When the need to repay debts to foreign capital suppliers is also taken into account, it becomes clear that the improvement of the international payments situation remains one of the most urgent tasks to be accomplished if growth is to continue.

Second, it must be conceded that our drive to attain a high growth rate and to develop strategic sectors with limited resources and capability has brought about an undesirable imbalance in the Korean economy, notably in the differences in income level and development progress between the agricultural and urban regions, resulting from rapid urbanization and industrialization. There is an unhealthy gap between large and small enterprises and between people in the high- and those in the low-income brackets. From the long-range viewpoint, such an imbalance might be a stage in growth toward a new equilibrium, or it might be viewed as the birth pains of development. As part of our endeavour to create a modern, consistent economic structure, we will do our utmost to implement new broad-gauge policies to correct this situation, including, for example, a reform of the taxation system, a national campaign to raise the earnings of farmers and fishermen, the relocation of industrial facilities to rural areas, the expansion of community development programs, and the development of small and medium industry.

Third, we succeeded throughout the 1960s in laying a solid foundation for economic growth by investing enormous amounts of capital and labour in the expansion of social overhead capital, such as electric power, communications, ports, and transportation facilities. Even so, the social overhead sector was unable to keep pace with the overall growth rate, because resources were limited and capital was needed in many sectors. This is one of the factors restricting the acceleration of industrial production and the growth of exports and investment. Mindful of this, we will make stepped-up efforts during the third five-year plan to eliminate bottlenecks arising from the shortage of social overhead capital. We must build a firm base for high economic growth and a self-sufficient economy.

Fourth, the weak management of Korean private enterprises is another major problem. In both developed and developing countries, private enterprises, with their renovation plans, take the initiative in expanding the economy once the primary development plan period is over. The role of government is to maintain conditions under which private enterprise can engage freely in economic activities and to guarantee fair competition. Government must keep down its intervention, restricting its economic activities to extremely strategic sectors. The remarkably rapid economic growth of the Federal Republic of Germany and Japan and the introduction of the principle of free competition in some Eastern European countries illustrate the desirability of this arrangement.

At the outset, the Korean economy followed a government-oriented pattern. In the mid-1960s an attempt was made to transform it into a private-business-oriented economy through the implementation of realistic, liberalized economic policies. Contrary to the original intention of our economic planners, however, private businesses are still unable to play their proper role according to modern business standards, and so remain as barriers to effective economic development. Among others, the deficiencies of private enterprises include their small scale and inefficiency due to the limited domestic market, their weak financial structure, the family ownership system, and a lack of creative management. It goes without saying that economic development in a free, competitive society is attainable only when the private sector is enlightened and is encouraged to take a leading part. This calls for the early start of a dynamic and voluntary campaign for managerial reform in private enterprise.

These are not the only problems. As our economy grows toward

President Park waves to the crowd gathered in Taegu to hear
his platform speech during the 1967 presidential election campaign.
He was returned to office by a wider margin than in the previous election.

self-sufficiency, many others will appear. Rapid industrialization may require more manpower. The demand for capital and prices will continue to move upward. The development of defense-related industries will become urgent if economic development is to be maintained while enormous sums are disbursed for military expenditures. The influx of foreign agricultural goods may necessitate action to protect the people from undue financial burdens. The reform of the agricultural structure and the acceleration of an agricultural revolution will be absolutely necessary to the attainment of a self-sufficient economy. Other problems include the establishment of fair, effective competition; the encouragement of technical renovation; and the prevention of overpopulation, public nuisances, and housing shortages in urban areas.

Such challenges do not dishearten us; rather, they make us stronger. Profiting from the lessons we learned through hardships, we are determined to advance, before this decade ends, to our goals of a completely self-sufficient economy and a welfare society in which the people are assured of an adequate living, the improvement of the environment and labour conditions, and a fairer distribution of income.

I believe strongly that the North Korean Communists pose the gravest possible challenge to the successful accomplishment of national goals. The more our economy develops, the more our people take pride in being members of a free society, strive to enhance their cultural heritage, and aspire with confidence toward territorial unification, the more the North Korean Communists will grow impatient and restless and will try to create tension in the Korean peninsula. As I stressed before, by crushing their reckless provocations promptly and totally, we must make the North Korean Communists realize that their attempts will never succeed. We shall vigilantly maintain sufficient strength and mobility to counter any North Korean challenges, until the regime in the North abandons its schemes and recovers some of its national conscience.

When I look at the realities of international politics, I fully understand that the gathering clouds are not arising solely from the Communist world but also from among some of our friends. Competition and confrontation of conflicting national interests are always present in the relationships of countries. Accordingly, I predict that many difficulties with foreign countries will arise. This will become increasingly true as we bring our economy closer to self-sufficiency, as we take action to secure our political independence, and as we move toward the national goal of reunification.

We have in our hearts and minds the courage of history, which

will enable us to reject any relationship that is not established on mutual trust but instead coerces us into accepting economic subjugation, political control, or ideological regimentation. At the same time, we must pay keen attention to the possibility that challenges to our advancement may come from our own rank and file. Moving toward difficult goals is always accompanied by swift changes and reforms. There is constant danger of a division in national public opinion, unless we create a climate of reasonable dialogue and exercise thoughtfully our power of judgment regarding the common goals of our nation.

My primary objective is to strengthen the forces of independence within society. Hence, I have appreciated well-meant competition and criticism, which make a positive contribution to social development. I am also aware that unproductive confusion can arise, under the pretext of liberty, to the detriment of our advance toward national modernization. What should worry us most is the appearance of a climate in which healthy standards of criticism give way, common ideals are forgotten, and common sense is disregarded as various interests are given priority.

It is my firm conviction that disunity at home should be prevented in advance, through the exercise of wisdom, patience, and self-control. I want to emphasize that democratic ways of forming public opinion should be set in motion, operating not through dogmatism or self-righteousness, but through debate and persuasion, respecting always the people's right to express their thoughts freely and to give a receptive ear to productive and constructive opinions. I ask all the people to abandon factional strife for the sake of achieving the common goals of our national advancement.

The Enhancement of National Identity. The urge to economic development that characterized our national life throughout the 1960s has brought about brilliant results in a once-barren land. These results have become important milestones. Once, when our people had lost their national pride, they lived in indolence and despair. Through their search for something useful, our people have recovered their enthusiasm. Now they believe in the future.

Many have rediscovered their treasured individual potential in the process of executing government policy. The rising tendency to cooperate is felt around us everywhere. The capabilities of those in charge of administration and management have improved markedly. New industrial complexes not only contribute new manufactured goods but also produce a confident and proud people. The educational system produces able, progressive young intellectuals and plays a key role in the formation of national morals by planting in the hearts of people a burning desire to develop their country.

The same is true of the rural people. Actually, farmers benefit less from the modernization program than the urban populace, yet they make unflagging efforts to improve land and labour productivity. Through government community development projects, they seek better methods of cultivation and improved seed. Our farmers further demonstrate their persistent will to raise their living standard through various self-help projects, such as side jobs or off-season work.

Since no development or change can take place without the voluntary participation of citizens, one could not exaggerate the importance of the modern Korean self-awakening. We are now on the threshold of a welfare society with the beginnings of a self-supporting economy. However, we are not satisfied with today's reality. When our national wealth puts us on the level of semi-advanced countries, i.e., when all Koreans have a fairly equal share in economic benefits, we want to go on to help less developed countries.

We firmly believe that the fundamental basis of our goals lies in the construction of a prosperous country and in our dedication to world peace and prosperity. But the ideals of man are by no means limited to the satisfaction of his economic desires. We would not hesitate to live a life of poverty if a life of luxury meant subjugation. Our aspiration to attain a self-sufficient economy arises from a thirst for national identification. In my book *The Country, the Revolution and I,* I interpreted the *hongik ingan,* the fundamental ideal of our nation, as the creation of a free and independent Korea in which simple, diligent, honest, ordinary citizens constitute the backbone of the state, a society of ordinary citizens in which all are guaranteed a free, prosperous, peaceful life with a high level of culture.

In the modernization of the advanced countries, the national leadership emphasized spiritual reform ahead of economic change. Modernization efforts bore fruit only after the energy of a nation was effectively integrated into a single objective by superb leadership from above. In the case of Korea, this process was reversed. Because the emancipation of the people from poverty was most urgent, we began with economic development. But this did not mean that we forgot the need for the balanced improvement in the people's livelihood, the enhancement of ethical values, the prevention of human degradation, and the establishment of sound intellectual life.

While our economic foundation was being put in good shape I proposed an ethical code of conduct and exhorted the people to follow this code in their daily lives. My intention was to help establish the spiritual underpinnings necessary for the creation of a good society. For I realized that no purely welfare society would be able to function without a spiritual revolution, or without diligence, thrift, self-support, and mutual assistance. *Hongik ingan* is the basic slogan by which our ancestors explained this need in a most concise but appealing manner. We embodied this ideal in the Charter of National Education, which advocates the formation of creative, enterprising, and patriotic human beings.

The creative man should accomplish the sublime mission of national modernization by using the proud scientific, cultural, and artistic heritage received from our ancestors, by linking our wisdom and sagacity with the spirit of the Western pioneers, and by our own spiritual posture. This is my personal ideal for the individual citizen and the growth of his originality.

By enterprising man, I mean to stress the need for building a systematic organization on the principle of mutual help that has been part of Korean life from ancient times, although it is not unconnected with the Western ethic of efficiency. This type of man aims at making productive use of good human relations with a view to materializing, in the modern sense, our traditional ideals of national cohesiveness and the spirit of magnanimity.

Patriotic personalities, with a deep-rooted spirit of resistance against intrusion from the outside and a strong love of the nation, should absorb and develop the concepts of citizenship and public service that were the main force of Western nation-building. A new model man should logically develop in a nation that desires to revive cherished national sentiments, that has survived privation so heroically in international competition and the cold war confrontation, and that seeks to protect and enhance the freedom of the individual.

Creativity, cooperation, and patriotism are the supreme aims of life and the major premises on which any value system must be built. They are also the basic values of our historic inheritance. In short, they are *hongik ingan.* They are the spirit of *hwarang* revivified.

It is good to see a consciousness of the need to defend our political as well as our economic independence arising within our society. We must make a thorough, sincere study of our national consciousness, impelling our people to contribute to the national development. As long as we believe that economic development is not an end in itself but a necessary and essential condition to attaining the national ideals, we shall strive to preserve and enhance our political sovereignty through the popular will.

The Pride of a Cultured Nation. Orientals possess a mysterious, unified, and harmonized spiritual culture that can scarcely be understood by Westerners, who have different ways of thinking and different systems of logic. Although it is risky to gen-

eralize, it is clear that Oriental cultures have a certain gentle, mild rhythm and harmony. This characteristic is all the more conspicuous in the culture of a nation with a long history. The 4,000 years of Korean history are the reservoir of our endless national pride, the product of accumulated wisdom that cannot be made or altered overnight.

Our ancestors did not simply imitate the cultures of Asia. They absorbed them with a sense of national identity. The Yi dynasty's *Songrihak,* which expounds a profound theory of human nature and the rule of Heaven, is an excellent example of the superb power of Korea's theoretical imagination. Koreans developed a far more original academic theory than did their Chinese teachers. For we did not regard man and Heaven as being opposed to each other. We took it for granted that they coexisted in one harmonious celestial body. This viewpoint produced a peculiar ethic for the ruler and ruled in Korea, according to which public sentiments were believed to represent heavenly feeling. Moderate ways of thinking—the search for the basic sources of social development and progress in justice and reason—constituted the keynotes of our philosophy.

While adapting their lives to the social order, Koreans thought it most ideal that the order be kept peacefully and developed on a higher plane. They did not believe that conflicts and contradictions in their society would be solved chiefly through struggle and adjustment, as was the case with European nations. Instead, they thought that virtue, and tolerance within the limits of the will of Heaven, solved conflicts and contradictions. Each Korean was proud of his existence in a society where all members were closely tied together by deep affection and respect.

Thus we maintained human relations characterized by mutual trust, honesty, and justice. The highly cultured personality of Koreans and their moral standards were an example to others. The typical Korean had high esteem for his morality. He was a man of integrity. He pursued a moderate course of action, and he loved peace and serenity. Koreans were admired by the Japanese, Chinese, and other neighbouring Asians. We were called "The Country of Courtesy in the East" and "The Land of the Morning Calm." This Korean way of thinking slowed the formation of the individual ego, in the modern sense. The Koreans' ignorance of material civilization hindered technological and scientific development. Yet what we lost in the world of machines we gained in the world of the arts and the spirit.

Of all our inventions, Hangul is the gem. The Korean alphabet is a surprising product of Korean culture and remains its best symbol. It is one of the most rational alphabets in the world, in that the shapes of the 24 phonetic signs indicate the manner of their articulation. In proper combinations, it can be written either vertically or horizontally. It is, in fine, a convenient, superior alphabet and has been adapted to the typewriter. For Koreans, who have always lived within the Chinese cultural sphere, the invention of Hangul was an epoch-making event. We also take great pride in the fact that Hangul is not for a select aristocratic group, but for all the people.

In the past century, this brilliant culture had to face the challenges posed by Western civilization. Western thought and technology, which began to be introduced when Korea adopted an open-door policy in the 1870s, first came as a shock to most Koreans. Even more serious was the later attempt by the Japanese colonialists to destroy Korean culture, as a result of which our culture came to contain fragments of things Japanese, whether we liked it or not. By the time of our national liberation in 1945, a considerable part of the culture had become distorted. It was at this time that the tide of Western ideas and customs hit our land with full force.

Individualism and democracy, which were brought to Korea along with Western civilization after 1945, were accepted blindly by Koreans who were grateful for the liberation and felt friendly toward the West. These new ideologies began to exert a far-reaching influence on our institutions and philosophy. A tendency arose to shift the blame for our national humiliation to the traditional culture. Some cynically held that the stagnation and retardation of the past were due to the meditative, serene inertia that characterizes Oriental culture. And, undeniably, the traditional Korean way of thinking hardly guaranteed individual freedom, ensured the equality of all, or recognized basic, unalienable rights.

Alien social forces unleashed simultaneous attacks on our traditional culture. Inferior elements of Western culture did much to ruin the graceful Korean lyricism that forms the undercurrent of our traditional culture. At the same time, Communist elements, concealing their own ideology, determined to wreck the national traditional culture once and for all. In these circumstances, the new wave of idealism was betrayed by bitter and painful reality. The territorial division and the Korean War were terrible shocks, as was the emergence of an undemocratic, autocratic regime in the postwar era.

Our traditional culture, unable to keep its brighter features intact, exposed its negative side instead, thus lending credence to the constant criticism of its stagnation, indolence, and unreality. The more acutely people felt the gap between ideals and reality, the more strongly was tradition considered an unacceptable remnant of the premodern heritage. Corruption and injustice were often regarded as parts of the heritage. The lethargic spiritual posture of the ruling elite was mistakenly seen as part of its traditional image, instead of as individual corruption and incompetence. Partial defects were exaggerated as if they were representative.

When revolutionary ideas of social improvement began to sweep the country in 1961, I spelled out my views on nationalism in an effort to preserve Korea's cultural and spiritual independence. I did so with the firm conviction that, if we were to ensure sustained development, we must overcome our self-torment and must imbue individuals with a sense of pride. We needed to rediscover our national wisdom and to renew pride in our traditions.

Since then I have devised many institutional guarantees, in the hope of bringing about rejuvenation of the national culture and the development of traditions of our own. To this end, the government erected statues of our great national leaders across the country. A sanctuary was dedicated to Admiral Yi Sunsin, who heroically defended the country from the Japanese invasion in the 16th century. By linking past with present, we tried to interpret our history in such a way as to present vividly the tenaciousness with which Koreans throughout the ages had maintained their lives in the midst of travail.

The effects of this effort are already visible. It seems to me that Koreans are beginning to discover in their cultural tradition what it means to be a Korean. They are beginning to realize that, far from being incompatible with modernization, the traditional culture is a productive force in the modernization process. Furthermore, our people have come to possess a sense of mission. They see themselves as developers of a cultural heritage already full of unique aesthetic values and wisdom. Korean studies have become a vital academic subject. A search for a new sociopsychological approach is also being made. Our task is to accept, resolutely and decisively, the good aspects of newly introduced foreign cultures and to make them ours, attaching them to the foundations of the traditional one. We should not reject unconditionally the rational, efficient cultures of advanced countries. New cultures are created only through constant contacts and exchanges with neighbours. Foreign cultures have already made great contributions to our daily life, and we should begin to incorporate contemporary world currents into our tradition. But they must be assimilated positively and productively. It is urgent that we pay the utmost attention to the possibility that our culture could be destroyed. We must so restructure it that foreign cultures will not dominate us and threaten our heritage.

I feel a strong trend in this direction. We have already decided to use Hangul exclusively. Under a long-range education program, we shall encourage a spirit of creativity by reforming education. The tradition of mutual help, bolstered by fidelity and love, has begun to find its place in the people's consciousness. The creative abilities of individual citizens are developing remarkably. In the arts, Koreans' aesthetic sensitivity is bringing about a graceful revival.

The creativity and wisdom inherent in the Korean people are affecting all walks of contemporary life. No longer do people regard our tradition-rich heritage as something obstinate, premodern, and unscientific. They have begun to realize that it can create as well as conserve. In the next few years, our work to effectuate a spiritual revolution will be steadily carried out. We shall renew in this land the high renaissance of our forefathers. We shall continue our untiring effort to preserve our pride in being a cultured nation, with the inherited ideals of *hongik ingan* and the spirit of *hwarang-do*, by fully developing the talents of our people.

A QUIET REVOLUTION

The seeds for our future have been sown, and the first buds are sprouting. At such a time the responsibility of leadership becomes all the heavier. Yet history is not made by leaders alone. Leaders are but the fertilizer to growth.

One can liken our national ideals to seeds. Only when the seed is good and carefully fertilized will the land bear fruit. Similarly, good ideals and leadership can only be used by a receptive people. Just as flowers wither, a people can become poor without good leadership. Yet in the last analysis, the soil can supply its own nutrients so that plants can at least survive. The people, like the soil, are the ultimate masters.

The people and their leadership must become of one mind in marching toward their goal, so that planned national changes can be made and new, unplanned progress awakened and pursued spontaneously. Backed by the fervour of a united people, a leadership must take the initiative and set the example. In the course of advancing toward our ideals, conflicting views and opinions are bound to arise and national opinion may be divided. Although competition and constructive criticism are a necessary source of fresh creation and reform, we should abstain from the kind of division that is excessive, unproductive, or aimless.

All of us must keep our sense of direction if we are to meet the rapid changes and reforms that are bound to take place. To this end, we must further a realistic dialogue between leadership and people in which they share their common feelings. In so doing, we uphold the democracy which we have accepted and which has taken root deep in our national consciousness.

The prime requisites for achieving modernization, national revival, and the unification of the land are a combination of cooperation, unity, and strength. Mountains of tasks lie ahead. During the 1970s, a decade of great hope, we will have to shift from economic to social development, beginning with the third five-year economic development plan, to be launched in 1972 on successful attainment of the second plan. Our progress must be spread evenly throughout society if we are to attain a happy, prosperous commonwealth.

We will continue in our steady, quiet revolution, founded in democracy. With a joy born of achievement, we will prove that this invisible revolution of ours has something greater than anything before it. While the revolution is ripening within, we can find joy in our realization that our national foundations have become firm and solid.

We must not throw away this rare opportunity. We will continue to march forward courageously in the firm belief that our national revival will contribute to humanity's progress, remembering always that we will be unable to participate in mankind's advance unless we first command our own national destiny. Those who give up halfway can never win. Those who emerge as victors never give up halfway.

Index

The black type entries are article headings in the *Book of the Year*. These black type article entries do not show page notations because they are to be found in their alphabetical position in the body of the book. They show the dates of the issues of the *Book of the Year* in which the articles appear. For example "Agriculture 71, 70, 69, 68, 67" indicates that the article "Agriculture" is to be found in the 1971, 1970, 1969, 1968 and 1967 *Book of the Year*.

The light type headings that are indented under black type article headings refer to material elsewhere in the text related to the subject under which they are listed. The light type headings that are not indented refer to information in the text not given a special article. Biographies and obituaries are listed as cross references to the articles "*Biography*" and "*Obituaries*" for the year in which they appear. References to illustrations are preceded by the abbreviation "il."

All headings, whether consisting of a single word or more, are treated for the purpose of alphabetization as single complete headings. Names beginning with "Mc" and "Mac" are alphabetized as "Mac"; "St." is treated as "Saint." All references below show the exact quarter of the page by means of the letters *a, b, c,* and *d,* signifying, respectively, the upper and lower halves of the first column and the upper and lower halves of the second column. Exceptions to this rule are tables, illustrations, and references from biographies and the articles "*Fuel and Power*" and "*Industrial Review*."

A

Aaltonen, Waeinoe Waldemar: see **Obituaries 67**
Aaron, Hank (athlete) il. 126
AAU (Amateur Athletic Union) 693c
Abaca (agri.) 83b
ABC (American Broadcasting Company) 703c
Abdelsalam, Shadi (movie director) 196d
Abdul Halim Mu'azzam (k., Malaysia) 472a
Abele, L. G. (biol.) 165d
Abernathy, Ralph David: see **Biography 69**
Abid Ali, S. (cricket player) 231b
ABM: see Antiballistic missile system
Abortion 481c
law 232c; 446c
Politics of Change 35a
"Population Crisis, The" (Special Report) 607a
religion 649c
Abrams, Charles: see **Obituaries 71**
Abrams, Creighton Williams, Jr.: see **Biography 69**
Abrasimov, Pyotr A. 357d
Abu Dhabi, sheikhdom, Arabia 254 (table)
Academy of Motion Picture Arts and Sciences (U.S.) 195a
Accidents and safety
industrial design 393d
toys and games 723c
zoos 783a
AC/DC (new word list) 779
Acetylcholine (neurotransmitter) 146
Ackerman, Carl William: see **Obituaries 71**
Ackley, (Hugh) Gardner: see **Biography 68**
"Ada" (Nabokov) 452b
Adam, Karl: see **Obituaries 67**
Adamov, Arthur: see **Obituaries 71**
Adams, John James ("Jack"): see **Obituaries 69**
Adams, Michael: see **Obituaries 68**
Additives 282c
Aden: see Southern Yemen
Adenauer, Konrad: see **Obituaries 68**
ADH (Antidiuretic hormone) 482a
Adiseshiah, Malcolm 449a
Adler, Rabbi Morris: see **Obituaries 67**
Advertising 71, 70, 69, 68, 67
Agnew, Spiro 130
beer 90a
consumer protection 502b
merchandising 499d
publishing 623b
religion il. 635
television and radio 704b
tourism 722d
Advisory Committee to Combat Corruption (Indonesia) 391c
Advisory Council for South East Asia 228c
AEC: see Atomic Energy Commission, U.S.
Aerospace 109a
alcoholic beverages il. 91
cities and urban affairs 198c
defense 254a
disasters 276b
hijacking 438a; 733a
industrial review 397
insurance 407c

labour unions 434c
recovery device il. 244
transportation 731b
see also Astronautics
Afars and Issas, French Territory of the 264 (table)
defense 248b
Afghanistan 71, 70, 69, 68, 67
Buddhism 650a
education 300 (table)
fuel and power 347
internat. organizations 412 (table)
mining 522d
political parties 597 (table)
social services 667 (table)
U.S.S.R. 751c
AFL (American Football League) 337d
Africa 71, 70, 69, 68, 67
agriculture 81c
alcoholic beverages 90a
art exhibitions 106d
Christianity 634b
cinema 196d
commodities, primary 208d
Commonwealth of Nations 211b
defense 253c
engineering projects 315c
fuel and power 345
industrial review 402
Kaunda, Kenneth 146
parks 576c
Politics of Change 38d
"Population Crisis, The" (Special Report) 605b
populations and areas 601b
race relations 628a
refugees 633d
rubber 656 (table)
television and radio 702b
timber 717c
tourism 721a
transportation 738c; 741b
vital statistics 776 (table)
African, Malagasy, and Mauritian Common Organization (OCAMM) 178c; 182d
Africanization 516b
Afro-Americans: see Negroes, American
Afro-Asian Conference 71a
AFSC (American Friends Service Committee) 583b
"After Apollo, What?" (Special Report) 113a
AGA (American Gas Association) 346
"Agaunar" (horse) 379d
Agayants, Ivan Ivanovich: see **Obituaries 69**
Agenbroad, L. D. (archae.) 99b
Agency for International Development (AID) 228b
food 330b
Agnelli, Giovanni: see **Biography 71**
Agnew, Spiro Theodore: see **Biography 71, 70, 69**
elections 764c
Hickel, Walter J. 144
Politics of Change 42d
publishing 620c
Southeast Asia 675d
Taiwan 697c
Thailand 711b
Agnon, S(hmuel) Y(osef) (Czaczkes) (Agnon, Samuel Joseph): see **Obituaries 71.** See **Biography 67**
Agostini, Giacomo (motorcyclist) 536a; il. 535
Agrarian reform 329b
Algeria 93a
Bulgaria 174a
Colombia 78d

European unity 319b
Kenya 430d
Korean history 798a
Mansholt, Sicco L. 149
Agricultural Act of 1970 (U.S.) 209d
Agriculture 71, 70, 69, 68, 67
anthropology 96a
Borlaug, Norman E. 134
commercial policies 205b
commodities, primary 207c
conservation 223a
development, economic 273a
economics 285a
employment, wages, and hours 308d
European unity 319b
gardening 351c
government finance 364d
industrial review 399
Mansholt, Sicco L. 149
Mexican-Americans 633a
molecular biology 527b
"Population Crisis, The" (Special Report) 605a
tobacco 718c
see also under various countries
Agriculture, U.S. Department of (USDA) 74c; 400
Agudelo, William (writ.) 467a
Aguiyi-Ironsi, Johnson Thomas Umunanke: see **Obituaries 67**
Ahidjo, Ahmadou (pres., Cameroon) 178a
Ahmed, Younis (cricket player) 231c
Ahmed Toukan (pr.min., Jordan) 429c
Ahomadegbe, Justin (govt.offi., Dahomey) 240a
AID: see Agency for International Development
Ailleret, Charles-Louis-Marcel: see **Obituaries 69**
Aini, Mohsin al- (premier, Yemen) 780c
Air conditioning 343a
Airlift 350c
Air Line Pilots Association (ALPA) 733d
Air pollution: see Pollution
Aitmatov, Chinghiz (writ.) 468d
Aiyar, Sir Chetpat Pattabhirama Ramaswami: see **Obituaries 67**
Akeley, Mary Jobe: see **Obituaries 67**
Akers, Milburn P.: see **Obituaries 71**
Akhmatova, Anna Andreyevna: see **Obituaries 67**
literature 748d
Akimov, Nikolai: see **Obituaries 69**
Akintola, Samuel Ladoke: see **Obituaries 67**
Akufo-Addo, Edward: see **Biography 71**
Ghana 361b
ALA (American Library Association) 450d
Alam, Intikhab (cricket player) 230d
Alaska (state, U.S.)
archaeology 98d
conservation 220a
disasters 276c
furs 349b
mountaineering 538b
religion 647b
transportation 738a
Alaska, Gulf of 221a
"Alaskan Dilemma" (Special Report) 220a
Albania 71, 70, 69, 68, 67
Central African Republic 183a
China 191c
Communist movement 212c
defense 249 (table)
income, national 386 (table)
industrial review 401
international organizations 412 (table)
political parties 597 (table)
social services 667 (table)
vital statistics 776 (table)
Albareda, (Giocacchino) Anselmo Maria Cardinal: see **Obituaries 67**
Albert, Édouard: see **Obituaries 69**
Albert Hall (London, England) 373a
Alcindor, Ferdinand Lewis, Jr.: see **Biography 69**
basketball 126c; il. 128
Alcoholic Beverages 71, 70, 69, 68, 67
"Drugs and Youth" (Special Report) 489c
industrial review 401
Aldiss, Brian (writer) 458d
Aldrin, Edwin Eugene, Jr.: see **Biography 70**
Alegría, Ciro: see **Obituaries 68**
Alexander, Ben: see **Obituaries 70**
Alexander, Hattie E.: see **Obituaries 69**
Alexander of Tunis, Harold Rupert Leofric George Alexander, 1st Earl: see **Obituaries 70**
Alexandrov, Vladimir 409c
Alexii, Sergei Vladimirovich Simansky: see **Obituaries 71**
Alfalfa 73c
Al Fatah 131; 143
defense 258a
Alfieri, Odoardo Dino: see **Obituaries 67**
Alfrink, Hans Cardinal 647b
Alfvén, Hannes Olof Gösta: see **Biography 71**
Néel, Louis Eugène 151
physics 592d
Algae 163d

Algebra 474c
Algeria 71, 70, 69, 68, 67
agriculture 81d
Canada 178d
commercial policies 205d
commodities, primary 208d
defense 248b; 255d
dependent states 263d
education 300 (table)
France 70a; 342b
fuel and power 347
income, national 388 (table)
international organizations 412 (table)
Mauritania 476a
mining 520 (table)
museums and galleries 541b
political parties 597 (table)
social services 667 (table)
telecommunications 700 (table)
transportation 735c
Tunisia 743b
vital statistics 776 (table)
Alice Tully Hall (New York City) 543a
Alkali metal ion 185b
Allain, Marcel: see **Obituaries 70**
Allen, Sir Carleton Kemp: see **Obituaries 67**
Allen, Florence Ellinwood: see **Obituaries 67**
Allen, George Venable: see **Obituaries 71**
Allen, Henry ("Red"): see **Obituaries 68**
Allen, Herbert Warner: see **Obituaries 69**
Allen, James 631a
Allen, James E., Jr. 301a; il. 297
Allen, Ralph: see **Obituaries 67**
Allen, Terry de la Mesa ("Terrible Terry"): see **Obituaries 70**
Allende Gossens, Salvador: see **Biography 71**
Chile 188b
commodities, primary 210b
Politics of Change 33b
Aller, L. (astron.) 117d
Allgöwer, M. (physician) 493c
Allied International Designers 393a
Alliluyeva, Svetlana: see **Biography 68**
Allingham, Margery (Louise): see **Obituaries 67**
Allport, Gordon Willard: see **Obituaries 68**
Almeida, Guilherme de: see **Obituaries 70**
Almonds 74a
Alonso, José 104c
ALPA (Air Line Pilots Association) 733d
Alpine World Cup (skiing) 664d
Altizer, Thomas Jonathan Jackson: see **Biography 67**
Alumina 518b
Aluminum 398; 520 (table)
casting 506c
commodities, primary 208 (table)
Aluminum-silicon-manganese 506c
Alvarez, Luis W.: see **Biography 69**
Alvaro da Silva, Augusto Cardinal: see **Obituaries 69**
Amalrik, Andrei (writ.) 468a; 745d; 748b
Amateur Athletic Union (AAU) 693c
Amdisen, A. (physician) 496c
Amer, Abdel Hakim: see **Obituaries 68**
American Ballet Company 240d
American Ballet Theatre 240c
American Broadcasting Company (ABC) 703c
American Economic Association 288a
American Football League (AFL) 337d
American Friends Service Committee (AFSC) 583b
American Gas Association (AGA) 346
American League (baseball) 123c
American Library Association (ALA) 450d
American literature 452b
American Lumber Standards Committee 718c
American Meteorological Society (AMS) 507b
American Motors 398
American Numismatic Association (ANA) 586b
American Oil Co. (Texas) il. 347
American Physical Society 592b
American Political Science Association (APSA) 600c
American Samoa, Pac.O. 265 (table)
vital statistics 776 (table)
American Selling Price (ASP) 206a
American Servicemen's Union 583c
American Telephone & Telegraph Co. (AT & T) 701a; 703d
American Textile Manufacturers Institute 492b
Amino acids 119c
Amphetamine 489c
AMS (American Meteorological Society) 507b
ANA (American Numismatic Association) 586b
ANABA (National Association of Archivists, Librarians, and Archaeologists) 450b
Andean Development Corporation 411b
Andean Group (S.Am.) 297b
Anderson, Douglas D. (archaeologist) 98d

H

States Statistical Supplement

ENCYCLOPÆDIA BRITANNICA, INC.

Copyright © 1971

Developments in the states in 1970

Large issues involving the roots of federalism, the availability of financial resources, and the stresses of social change preoccupied the state governments of the United States in 1970. Prominent were pressures for new directions in federal-state relations which, if carried to fruition, would have historic results for the division of responsibilities between the two levels of government. Ever-increasing costs of public services produced a continuing push for more state revenue, from the states' tax resources or from the federal government or both. Slightly more than a fourth of the legislatures increased taxes in some degree. A number of states, meantime, took new steps toward modernizing their governmental structures and operating methods.

In regard to state functions and services, concern and action were outstanding in two fields: control of pollution and protection of the environment; and coping with crime and disorder, including problems on campuses. Action also included measures designed to strengthen education, help deal with urban problems, and protect consumers in their purchases. At the same time, from within state governments and from other sources, there were urgent calls for future state advance.

During the year 33 legislatures met in regular sessions. Five of these and seven others also held special sessions up to autumn.

Election Results. Thirty-two governors were Republicans in 1970, only 18 Democrats. But the political pendulum swung at the state level in the November election, with the result that there would be 29 Democratic and 21 Republican governors in 1971. Democrats captured the governors' offices to replace Republicans in 13 states: Florida, Arkansas, Pennsylvania, Ohio, Wisconsin, Minnesota, Oklahoma, Nebraska, New Mexico, Idaho, South Dakota, Nevada, and Alaska. Republicans elected governors in two states with Democrats in office, Tennessee and Connecticut. In the remaining states that had gubernatorial contests party labels did not change.

Legislators were elected in 45 states, and the Democrats again scored an overall gain. Before the election Republicans controlled both houses of the legislatures of 20 states and Democrats 20; in the remaining states one party controlled the House and the other the Senate except in Nebraska, where the unicameral legislature was elected on a nonparty basis, and Minnesota, where both houses were chosen without party designation. The election gave a majority of the chambers to the Democrats, the precise tallies to depend on checks of totals some time after the voting.

Among noteworthy shifts were those in the most populous and third most populous states, California and Pennsylvania. California's Republican governor was reelected, but the Democrats took control of both legislative houses. In Pennsylvania, besides taking over the governorship, Democrats elected majorities of both houses of the legislature, the first time they had done this in many years. New York's Republicans, however, retained the governorship and majorities in both chambers.

Nationwide, the relative state-level strengths of the two parties were extraordinarily important after this election. This was because the legislatures, except in cases where the task went to courts or other bodies, would need to reapportion legislative seats and in most states congressional districts to meet the requirements of the 1970 census and past court decisions. Governors also would have much influence in this.

Results of the Census. Population counts in the census reflected recent social and economic changes experienced by the states and foreshadowed important alterations of political power within them. California's rise to first rank in population over New York was confirmed. Texas, by a narrow margin, replaced Illinois in fourth place, behind Pennsylvania in third, and thereby moved Ohio down from fifth to sixth. Florida surged ahead of Massachusetts to take ninth place.

Largest gain of any state's in absolute numbers since 1960 was California's, a rise of more than 4 million to 20 million. The largest proportionate gain was Nevada's, 71.3%, followed by Florida,

37.1%; Arizona, 36.1%; Alaska, 33.6%; California, 27%; Maryland, 26.5%; and Colorado, 25.8%. All other states except three gained population. West Virginia was the heaviest loser, down 6.2% during the decade, and it had lost in the 1950s as well. Also recorded were drops of 2.3% for North Dakota, and 2.2% for South Dakota.

As one result, the shifts meant that in coming redistricting more congressional seats would go to some big gainers and reduced representation to some states that slipped in rank. More significant for the tasks of the states and the distribution of power within them were (1) a regional pattern of growth in which most of the West, a few of the southern states, and some of those along the eastern seaboard gained disproportionately and (2) movement within the states from rural to metropolitan areas, and movement to the suburbs. More than three-fourths of the national growth took place in metropolitan areas, and the suburbs showed much the largest share of that growth.

In the fastest-growing states of the West and of the South, the rapid increases of residents, including rising urban concentrations, contributed not only to growing economies and governmental revenues, but also to bigger and costlier problems for state and local governments. Social responsibilities of northern metropolitan areas likewise mounted with their populations. Affecting the intrastate division of political power, the census figures soon would have to be reflected in legislative reapportionment in line with the Supreme Court's one-man, one-vote decisions.

Already, in reapportionments since the *Baker* v. *Carr* decision of 1962, the largest gainers of legislative seats had been urban suburbs. The census results intensified this trend. From 1960 to 1970 populations in what the Census Bureau classified as metropolitan counties gained far more than those in non-metropolitan counties. The farm population, roughly 15 million in 1960, dropped by about one-third. Likewise, populations of many central cities fell in varying degrees, some sharply.

All told, it was clear from the census that what remained of rural domination of state legislatures, once taken as the norm, would be sapped further. At the same time, big city powers in legislatures also faced a decline, in contrast to the assured further increase of suburban representation. Nevertheless, as in all in state government reckoned, the actual wielding of power would continue to involve many and varied alliances among representatives of city, suburban, and rural districts.

Federal-State Relations: "New Federalism." Seldom were federal-state relations examined so widely as in 1970.

President Richard M. Nixon in January renewed his call for a "New Federalism," in which "after 190 years of power flowing from the people and local and state governments to Washington, it will begin to flow from Washington back to the states and to the people." Prominent among related programs were:

(1) The administration's proposal for federal sharing of tax revenue with the states and localities—in amounts that would rise from a relatively small sum to about $5 billion a year after five years. This would be in addition to grants to the states for particular programs.

(2) An administration proposal for welfare reform, centring on a basic innovation: a federally guaranteed minimum income that would total $1,600 a year, aside from food stamps, for a family of four having no other income but registering for work if available. The working poor would be eligible for benefits on a decreasing scale up to a point where wages totaled $3,920. This would mean a sharp reduction in state responsibility for welfare costs.

(3) Legislation to overhaul manpower training programs along lines that would give more latitude to states and cities.

(4) Legislation to authorize the president to consolidate separate grant-in-aid programs, subject to Congressional veto.

In general the "new federalism" received an enthusiastic welcome from state officials, although there were differences on specifics. The National Governors' Conference and other interstate bodies strongly backed revenue sharing. The governors' Committee on Human Resources was encouraged by the family assistance plan but suggested changes. And the Governor's Conference as a whole, for the second year in succession, called for full federal assumption of public welfare costs, with administration, however, to remain in the hands of the states under federal guidelines.

As the year ended, "new federalism" projects continued to receive much attention, but complications abounded. The President's welfare plan passed the House in April, but did not reach a vote in the Senate. Congress passed a bill with manpower training provisions, but the President vetoed it because of features he disapproved. Revenue sharing did not come near a vote in either house. Although grant consolidation provisions cleared one chamber, they did not pass in the other. Thus the issues were handed on to the new Congress.

The president's welfare plan would mean more centralization, as was recognized in the federal administration. The governors' proposal for a total federal take-over of welfare financing would mean still more. Nor was it only the governors and other state officials who called for such financing. The broadly repre-

sentative Advisory Commission on Intergovernmental Relations—created by Congress and composed of members from the national administration, Congress, the states, cities, and counties—recommended federal shouldering of all welfare costs, with the states and localities continuing to administer the program. The Research and Policy Committee of the Committee for Economic Development, a prominent businessmen's organization, urged a federally supported minimum income and phased federal assumption of all financing of public assistance.

Proposals that could result in a flow of powers to the states were opposed by many Congressmen and city officials. The power of mayors and cities in the federal programs of manpower training rose during the year, as did the role of mayors in the federal government's model cities program.

Federal-State Relations: Toward Regional Needs. In 1970 one prestigious body, the Center for the Study of Democratic Institutions, produced as a basis for public study a new draft U.S. constitution that actually would abolish the states. The document was drawn up by Rexford Guy Tugwell, a member of Pres. Franklin D. Roosevelt's "brain trust" in the 1930s, in consultation with resident fellows of the center and many others. It proposed the elimination of the 50 states and the substitution for them of not more than 20 "republics," limited in power, adjustable in size, and subject to redistricting like congressional districts with future changes of population. The center had no illusions that the Tugwell constitution would be adopted or the present states abolished—certainly, at least, for a long time. Vested political interests in the state capitals and Congress, plus the strength of many state governments and traditional public loyalties, would prevent that. But members of the center hoped that the Tugwell document would stimulate a study of the basic problems.

In fact, needs for better regional instruments of government were recognized increasingly and were bringing action. The development of metropolitan areas across state lines was one cause. Problems of large geographic areas, such as multistate river valleys and mountain ranges, were others. Air pollution obviously was stopping at no state lines. The mobility of populations and patterns of transportation and trade, undreamed of when the state boundaries were set, complicated the picture.

In this situation important steps in regional organization stood out in 1970. The national administration began a study of regional commissions, such as one in Appalachia engaged in highway and other development, as a means of distributing federal revenue where needed. Thirteen states and the federal government, with substantial federal funds, cooperated in the Appalachian Commission. The national administration also established standard regional boundaries for five important agencies: Housing and Urban Development; Labor; the Office of Economic Opportunity; the Small Business Administration; and Health, Education, and Welfare. Previously these had operated in regions with varying boundaries.

On a smaller geographic scale, another new set of governmental groupings had emerged: well over 100 regional councils of government, known as "Cogs." These were organizations of municipalities and counties, formed primarily in response to the requirement in the Demonstration Cities and Metropolitan Act of 1966 that applications for certain grants or loans be accompanied by comment from an areawide body authorized to do comprehensive planning. By 1970 the Advisory Commission on Intergovernmental Relations concluded that a number of "Cogs" had progressed far beyond the discussion-type forum "into regional bodies with embryonic powers of general local government."

In conclusion, an evolving change in American federalism could be seen clearly, with increasing responsibilities for each level of government, regardless of the balances of power among them. Federal-state relations were involved in almost all fields of state action. Instances of this appear in summaries of state developments under separate categories below.

Finance. State tax collections in the 1970 fiscal year totaled $47.9 billion, 14.2% above the 1969 figure. Of the 1970 total, $14.1 billion came from general sales and gross receipts taxes; $13.1 billion from selective sales taxes, primarily on motor fuel, tobacco, alcoholic beverages and insurance; $9.2 billion from individual income taxes; $3.7 billion from corporation net income taxes; and $4.6 billion from motor vehicle and other licenses.

Data compiled in 1970 showed that total state revenue reached $77.6 billion in fiscal 1969, compared with $68.5 billion the year before. General revenue—more meaningful for basic government finance since it excluded income of liquor stores in states that had them and receipts of employee retirement and other insurance trust systems—was $67.3 billion, up 13.8% from the year before. Total state expenditures came to $74.2 billion. General expenditure, excluding liquor store and insurance trust outlays, was $68 billion, 12.6% over the figure for the previous 12 months. Of 1969 general revenue, 62.3% came from state taxes, 11.3% from charges and miscel-

laneous state revenue (including tuition at institutions of higher education, highway tolls and other items), and 25.2% from the federal government. A little over 1% was from local governments, including shares of support for state-administered programs and reimbursements for state services.

Budgets were at record highs for 1970 and the year ahead, as they had been year after year with the rise of populations, increased requirements for services —and inflation. Of the legislatures with sessions, some 13 increased taxes. They did so by raising rates, expanding tax bases, adding a new tax, or a combination of those means. Two of those states and one other accelerated collection of certain taxes.

Louisiana's legislature raised its sales tax by adding a 1% levy to the 2% in its basic tax. New Jersey increased its sales tax rate from 3% to 5%. It also expanded the sales tax base, as did Kansas and Michigan. Washington imposed a 1% business and occupation tax on financial institutions. Louisiana and West Virginia raised rates of individual income taxes, and Georgia accelerated their collection. New Hampshire initiated a commuters' income tax applying to nonresidents of the state and a new tax on gross profits of business organizations. Kansas and Rhode Island increased rates on corporation income; Iowa imposed a new income tax on financial institutions alone. In addition to its rate increase, Rhode Island provided for accelerated collection of corporate income taxes, and Pennsylvania did likewise.

Increases of cigarette taxes were the most frequent of all. Legislatures of Arkansas, Kansas, Kentucky, Louisiana, Michigan, New Hampshire, Pennsylvania, and West Virginia raised them, the increases ranging from half a cent to 5 cents a pack. As a result, cigarette taxes in the 50 states ranged from 2 cents in North Carolina to 18 cents in Pennsylvania. Four states—Kansas, Kentucky, Louisiana, and Virginia—boosted rates on alcoholic beverages, while motor fuel taxes went up in Pennsylvania and West Virginia.

Those were legislative enactments. In scattered cases where the issue was referred directly to them, voters did not take kindly to raising their own taxes. In an April referendum Missouri rejected the state income tax increases voted by the 1969 legislature. South Dakota and Washington in November turned down proposed state income taxes. The people of Alabama defeated a proposal to raise the income taxes.

Voter decisions on proposed bond issues were mixed. A number of proposals were rejected, but there were some notable adoptions. These included Alaska's approval of issues totaling $146.2 million

for schools, housing, highways, and other purposes; a $50 million issue for school construction in Maine; and, most notably, $750 million in Illinois, $250 million in California, $173 million in Oregon, and several million in other states for pollution control.

Constitutions and Elections. Voters of Idaho, Arkansas, and Oregon rejected proposed new constitutions, but those of Illinois and Virginia adopted new ones. Both the Illinois and Virginia documents provide for annual legislative sessions, reduce residency requirements for voting and include provisions designed to aid protection of the environment. Features of Virginia's charter include removal of a constitutional prohibition against state lotteries. Among Illinois provisions are some increase in the powers of the governor and strengthened civil rights.

Proposals to reduce the voting age were on the ballot in 17 states. They carried in six—Maine and Nebraska, which cut it from 21 to 20 years old; Minnesota, Montana, and Massachusetts, which reduced it to 19; and Alaska, where it went from 19 to 18. Proposals to lower the voting age failed in 11 states. Colorado, New Jersey, Oregon, South Dakota, Washington, and Wyoming declined to lower it to 19; Connecticut, Florida, Hawaii, Illinois, and Michigan rejected proposals to make it 18. At the time of the November election, a federal act of 1970 to permit voting at 18 was pending before the U.S. Supreme Court. On December 21 the court, in two 5-to-4 decisions, upheld this law as it applies to national elections but ruled that Congress lacked the constitutional authority to extend it to state and local elections. This enfranchised millions of young citizens to vote for president, vice-president, U.S. senators and congressmen. It also would mean complications in procedures at the polls except in states that themselves provide for voting at age 18. Only three states—Alaska, Georgia, and Kentucky—now do so.

Administrative Structure and Powers. Legislatures adopted several important measures for state administrative reorganization. In a particularly comprehensive move, Delaware's session consolidated more than 140 agencies and commissions into 11 Cabinet-level departments. Vermont legislation accomplished extensive consolidation and endorsed the basic idea of developing a Cabinet-type government. It also authorized the governor to reorganize the state government by executive orders subject to legislative veto within 30 days.

One South Dakota enactment created a Department of Administration, which incorporated the State Budget Office and the Department of Finance. The Colorado legislature provided for a new Executive

Budget Office under the governor and implemented a constitutional amendment under which the candidates for governor and lieutenant governor would run as a team. A consolidation measure in Washington established a Department of Social and Health Services to coordinate the work of three existing departments and one division.

The consolidations were in line with others, from broad to narrow, that had been taking place in recent years. In general, the trend was accompanied by a strengthening of the powers of governors. Nevertheless, reform continued to come rather slowly. For example, a large majority of states still had six or more elective state officers. In face of this and the multiplicity of departments and agencies in many states, one governor remarked while hailing the progress made: "We have run our government like a pickup orchestra, where the members meet each other at a dance, shake hands with each other and start to play."

Legislatures of 1970 raised salaries of executives or staff or both in numerous states, including Arizona, Colorado, Delaware, Georgia, Kansas, Nebraska, New York, Rhode Island, Vermont, and Virginia. At the same time, state salaries continued to lag behind those in the federal government. A survey published in 1970 on the basis of Census Bureau figures indicated that in all but six states federal employees in 1968 earned more than state workers in the same states. The average weekly pay of all state employees was recorded as $137.77, but the range was very wide: from $84.69 in Arkansas and $94.38 in Mississippi to $188.08 in California and $213.92 in Alaska.

Voters at the polls adopted several measures to strengthen administration. These included lengthening officials' terms in three states and permitting executive reorganization by the governor subject to legislative veto in four. The new Illinois constitution and constitutional amendments in Kansas, Maryland, Nebraska, and New Mexico provided for election of the governor and lieutenant governor as a team rather than separately.

Also approved by the voters, in at least seven states, were constitutional amendments with the objective of improving the courts. Extensive revisions were voted for Indiana, Missouri and Nebraska.

Legislative Systems. Among actions by legislatures on their own structures and powers, Idaho's session set up the mechanics for annual sessions, already approved by the voters, unrestricted as to subjects for action. To help handle the work of annual sessions which began in 1970, the Mississippi legislature adopted a pre-session system of filing bills and pre-session committee hearings on them.

At the polls the people approved constitutional amendments initiating annual sessions in Connecticut, Indiana, Missouri, Nebraska, and New Hampshire. These, plus the new Illinois and Virginia constitutions, increased to 33 the states with regular annual sessions by constitutional provision. At least two others have them by dividing biennial sessions to meet each year.

Several states improved their legislative facilities. Nevada's legislature moved into a new $4 million building. A hotel annex purchased by Virginia provided private offices for its legislators; previously, only the chief legislative officers had offices in that state, and such a luxury remained rare for members in most states. A New York legislative office building was scheduled for completion in 1971, and plans were under way for new legislative buildings in several other states.

Computers were used increasingly for legislative research. Computerized statutory retrieval systems were implemented in early 1970 by Massachusetts, Oklahoma, and Utah, which raised to 22 the legislatures using these systems. Computers were also used for other research in several additional states.

Legislatures increased their members' pay in Alaska, Colorado, Vermont, and Virginia. Nationwide, these actions continued a marked trend, although liberalizing pay proposals fared badly in most of several cases when submitted to the voters. The Citizens Conference on State Legislatures was able to report in June that state legislative compensation had grown from a biennial countrywide average of $2,460 in 1950–51 to a current $13,256 for the two years. The compensation in question could include salary, per diem pay, and expenses.

Apportionment action was slight, in advance of the nationwide redistricting that loomed as a consequence of the 1970 census. Arizona's legislature, however, adopted new legislative districts in January, after a federal court had directed it to do so. Courts found current apportionments unconstitutional in Iowa and Indiana but did not require the drawing of new plans to apply in the 1970 election.

The once-imposing movement to force a national constitutional convention in order to upset the one-man, one-vote rule received a further setback in March when the Kansas legislature requested Congress to withdraw that state's call for such a convention. Resolutions from 34 states would have been required to make the call effective. The number had reached 33 in earlier years, although the validity of the resolution voted had been challenged in some states. At all events, in 1970 the plan appeared quite dead.

Conflict of Interest Legislation, Ethics. The Kansas legislature increased the number of officials to whom that state's conflict of interest law applied. It also required legislative agents to file annual financial declarations, and created a Committee on Governmental Ethics. Virginia legislation required legislators to file annual disclosures of their economic interests and barred members of state agencies from contractual relations with businesses in which they were materially interested.

In Nebraska the legislature passed a conflict of interest law which included a financial disclosure requirement that applied to state and local government. In Ohio a scandal involving $22 million in loans from the state treasury to companies in need of cash, large fees to a small firm that arranged the loans, and campaign contributions by the members of this firm, complicated government and politics through much of the year.

Pollution and Protection of the Environment. Never had there been so much state action as in 1970 to combat pollution and protect the environment. Legislatures, state officials, and voters all contributed to this. Some of the measures were adopted in the face of strong industrial and commercial opposition.

One of the particularly broad programs was that of Washington's special legislative session. Included were acts that set up a Department of Ecology, imposed unlimited liability on oil companies and shipowners discharging oil in state waters, gave preferential tax treatment for open lands, required reclamation of strip-mined areas, and established procedures to evaluate and certify proposed sites of thermal power plants. Enactments in Maine gave its Environmental Improvement Commission veto power over industrial and commercial development, provided controls over the coastal movement of oil, set up grants for regional planning to control pollution, and allocated bond funds for pollution abatement construction.

New York legislation consolidated three state agencies into a new Department of Environmental Conservation with a commissioner to set minimum acceptable pollution levels. New York's session also authorized the state to pay half the cost of planning solid-waste disposal facilities, and restricted the use of pesticides such as DDT. An impressive Vermont package included a "scenic easements" act permitting state or municipal purchase or lease of land to keep it open; an act to protect lake shorelines from pollution; another setting up environmental commissions, by which any development affecting more than 10 acres must be approved before construction starts; a system under which violators of standards must pay for pollution damage to water; and a pesticide bill which, among other features, banned DDT.

Antipollution programs of varying scope were adopted by the legislatures of Alaska, Colorado, Hawaii, Idaho, Illinois, Kansas, Maryland, Massachusetts, Michigan, New Hampshire, New Jersey, Ohio, Pennsylvania, Rhode Island, and Virginia. Arizona, California, New Mexico, South Carolina, and South Dakota were among states adding new laws relating to air pollution, while Kentucky and Wisconsin banned DDT.

New Jersey's legislature gave that state extensive powers to regulate development of its coastal wetlands. Georgia legislation created a Coastal Marshland Protection Agency to control commercial exploitation. A Delaware enactment required posting of a $1 million bond before exploration or transfer of minerals off that state's shores.

The governor of Alabama in March, citing the danger of oil leaks and slicks, cancelled bids for off-shore drilling for gas and oil. Among the many similar administrative acts in other states, the Florida Cabinet created an environmental safeguard agency which was to review all state development projects for their effect on the environment.

The attorneys general of 15 states—Arizona, Colorado, Hawaii, Illinois, Iowa, Kansas, Maine, Massachusetts, Minnesota, Missouri, Ohio, Rhode Island, Vermont, Virginia, and Washington—sued in the U.S. Supreme Court in an effort to force the nation's four large automobile makers to equip vehicles with effective antipollution devices and to hasten the development of pollution-free engines. The attorney general of Illinois filed many antipollution suits against companies; by autumn a number of positive results were registered, although in a majority of cases results were still to come.

Michigan legislation empowered individual citizens to file suits against anyone, including the state, believed to be seriously polluting water, air, or land resources belonging to all the people. New York's Court of Appeals upheld a new state law prohibiting importation or sale of skins of animals considered near to extinction.

At the polls, the largest bond issues voted were those of Illinois and California—$750 million and $250 million, respectively—for sewage treatment facilities and, in Illinois, some facilities for solid waste disposal. Alaska voted $11 million in sewage facility bonds and Oregon a $173 million issue for sewage control.

Net effects of all the initiatives taken remained to be seen. One reason cited by conservationists for slow progress against the pervasive reality of pollution was the fact that many state boards with key roles for control continued to include prominent representation of industrial and/or agricultural interests that are major polluters themselves.

Campus Disorders. Intensive attention in legislatures and state agencies centred on disturbances at colleges and universities. These had been widespread during the spring with strikes and boycotts involving many campuses, dozens of which temporarily closed down.

A large majority of the legislatures that had sessions in the year adopted laws on campus unrest. Included were provisions to withdraw state scholarship and grant funds from students convicted of participating in illegal demonstrations, dismissal of faculty members at state institutions of higher learning for certain types of protest, strengthening of antitrespass laws, and, in many states, increased powers for campus police. California's legislature provided that any student be ineligible for state aid during two years after conviction for participating in campus violence. The state educational code was amended to require discipline of students or faculty involved in illegal demonstrations, and the criminal code was revised to ban use of physical force to prevent a student or teacher from attending class. A Louisiana antiriot law authorized the governor to declare a state of emergency in the event of campus trouble; it set high penalties for injury or property damage resulting from disorderly conduct.

New York legislation stipulated that to qualify for state aid higher educational institutions must have rules for maintaining order. An Ohio campus riot control act forbade disruptive acts, set misdemeanor penalties for violations, and provided for removal of convicted students or faculty members from campus. Wisconsin measures included one that made it a misdemeanor to refuse to withdraw from an illegal assembly on public university grounds or adjacent highways. New Jersey's session gave campus police the same powers as city or state police to make arrests. A student-expulsion statute was adopted in Kansas, including guarantees of procedural due process.

Following the killing of students by National Guardsmen at Kent State University in Ohio and by police at Jackson State College in Mississippi, President Nixon in June appointed a President's Commission on Campus Unrest, chaired by former governor William W. Scranton of Pennsylvania. The commission, in a report in September, declared that students who bomb and burn are criminals, and that police and National Guardsmen who needlessly shoot or assault students are criminals. It also rebuked ineffective campus officials and the inflammatory language of politicians. The commission recommended that the president offer leadership to reconcile and unite the nation. Among other guidelines it said that governors should develop contacts throughout the school year to further reconciliation, and that state and local officials should plan for handling campus disorders in cooperation with one another and the universities.

In October the commission issued separate reports on "The Killings at Jackson State" and "The Kent State Tragedy." While not absolving students of provocative rhetoric at Jackson State, the commission scored Mississippi police for unjustified overreaction by firing shotgun, machine gun, rifle, and armor-piercing shells at black students in May, when 2 were killed and 12 injured. State and city police both were involved. The commission's report on the Kent State tragedy, in which four students were killed and nine injured, scored many student and non-student protesters for committing and encouraging violence and crime in four days of disorder, including the burning of an R.O.T.C. building and throwing rocks at law enforcement officers; however, it equally charged that national guardsmen's "indiscriminate firing of rifles into a crowd of students and the deaths that followed were unnecessary, unwarranted and inexcusable." It urged that loaded rifles not be issued again as a matter of course to guardsmen confronting student demonstrators. Even if the guardsmen faced danger, said the commission, it was not a danger that called for lethal force. And it noted that the rally which ended in the fatal confrontation began as a peaceful assembly.

In mid-October a special state grand jury at Kent indicted 25 persons in connection with the event, none of them guardsmen. It declared that the guardsmen fired in the belief and under circumstances that would logically cause them to believe they would suffer serious bodily injury unless they did so. The jury charged the university administration with an "attitude of laxity" and permissiveness and, besides blaming students, criticized some faculty members for overemphasizing "the right to dissent." Two weeks later the U.S. Justice Department made public the summary of a Federal Bureau of Investigation (FBI) report that differed sharply with the Kent grand jury's conclusions.

Civil Disorder, Crime, Drugs. Disorder and riots other than on campus, including violence stemming from racial tensions, likewise commanded state attention. An August summary in *State Government News,* published by the Council of State Governments, stated that civil disturbances, including both urban riots and campus disorders, had forced governors to call out the national guard more than 200 times during the preceding two years. In one case, Gov.

5

Richard B. Ogilvie of Illinois late in October sent 24 state police troopers for an indefinite stay in racially troubled Cairo, where there had been confrontation between local police and blacks. Two state troopers had been wounded previously while on emergency duty there.

Laws to curb bombings increased in 1970. Shortly after mid-year, approximately 30 states had some form of license or permit control on the sale of explosives, nearly twice the number of two years before. Reflecting aroused concern, the Midwest Conference of Attorneys General late in the summer asked Congress and the states to set the death penalty, or the maximum allowable, for conviction on charges of bombing buildings, cars, or persons.

In June, at a meeting of the Middle Atlantic Governors' Conference, representatives of New York, New Jersey, Maryland, Pennsylvania, Delaware, and West Virginia set up a regional group to study organized crime, including in particular the feasibility of exchanging state narcotics agents. Organized crime was a target of action in widely separated areas. In Texas the governor established an Organized Crime Prevention Council. New York legislation created a post of statewide prosecutor, while a new Ohio act demanded dissolution of corporations used as "fronts" for crime.

There were many measures to increase effective action against narcotics violations, and especially to distinguish between kinds of offenses. Thus, in Kansas, simple, first-conviction possession of marihuana was reduced from a felony to a misdemeanor; possession with intent to sell remained a felony. Wisconsin reclassified first-offense possession or use of marihuana as a misdemeanor. In Kentucky marihuana was reclassified as a dangerous drug instead of a narcotic, and courts could send first offenders to rehabilitation facilities for a year; the legislature increased penalties for selling dangerous drugs to minors. Virginia made first-offense possession of marihuana and amphetamines a misdemeanor, but possession of LSD and hashish a felony. Iowa legislation forbade hospitals and doctors to report to police the names of persons asking treatment or rehabilitation for drug addiction.

Nebraska, besides reducing first-offense possession of marihuana to a misdemeanor, set the lowest penalty then existing in the country—seven days in jail followed by attendance at a school on effects of drug abuse. A New Jersey enactment cut possession of a small quantity of marihuana from a serious crime, punishable by from 2 to 15 years in prison, to disorderly conduct with a maximum penalty of six months in jail. Later, the New Jersey Supreme Court went farther. It established guidelines eliminating jail or prison sentences for first-time possession or use of marihuana, so long as the convicted person intended it for his use only.

A *New York Times* summary of November 1 indicated that 24 states had cut their penalties for possession of marihuana in the past three years. Usually the reductions were to make the offense a misdemeanor. Nevertheless, great variations remained among the states. Maximum prison terms for simple first-offense possession of marihuana ranged from 7 days to 20 years or even "life"; minimum sentences, although far less, varied widely.

Transportation. Mass transit, with emphasis on urban needs, received unusual attention. In October the states of New York and Connecticut signed contracts to take over the New Haven Division of the Penn Central Railroad serving the New York City metropolitan area. Shortly thereafter the U.S. Department of Transportation granted an additional $11.6 million, to be matched by the states, raising total federal contributions for improvement of the New Haven to $40 million. Signing the contract opened the way for purchase of 144 high-speed cars, modernizing the tracks and other improvements.

A survey by the federal-state relations office of the National Governors' Conference, made public in April, showed that a number of states within the last year had approved or were considering loosening restrictions on highway trust revenues, in order to permit their use for mass transportation or other purposes such as pollution control and airports. However, 28 states still had constitutional restrictions against use of highway revenues for nonhighway purposes, the restrictions stemming largely from a 1934 federal law that granted highway aid. In its annual meeting the Governors' Conference called for gubernatorial powers to exercise more flexibility in use of federal funds for transportation.

Among other acts of the year, Kentucky's legislature authorized cities to take over public transit companies in financial difficulties; an Arizona measure permitted municipal councils to establish mass transit authorities, with powers to include levying a property tax to meet operating deficits; and an Ohio enactment enabled county transit authorities to operate rapid transit systems across county lines. State departments of transportation were established in Delaware, Maryland, Rhode Island, and Pennsylvania.

Education. Largest and much the most expensive of the regular, ongoing state services was education. A 1970 U.S. Census Bureau report showed that in the preceding fiscal year, 1969, the states spent $27.2 billion for education, of which $14.9 billion went to local governments for public schools and $10 billion to state institutions of higher education. A decade before, the corresponding amounts were less than a third as much. The 1969 total amounted to 40% of all state general expenditures. Partly offsetting it was $4.1 billion received for education from the federal government.

Legislative appropriations for education again were up in 1970. Proposals for new directions in financing also were under examination. The National Governors' Conference favoured the assumption of far greater responsibility for financing education by the federal government.

School segregation issues continued to seethe. A survey in the spring showed that Alabama, Georgia, Louisiana, Mississippi, Tennessee, and South Carolina had "freedom of choice" laws on the books, most of them modeled on a New York law of 1969 which forbade appointed school boards or the state commissioner of education to assign pupils to schools in order to achieve racial balance without the consent of the pupils' parents. On October 1, however, a federal court at Buffalo declared the New York act, known as an anti-bussing law, unconstitutional. California legislation of 1970 forbade bussing of pupils for any purpose without the written permission of parent or guardian.

Use of public funds to help support church-related schools was widespread, but there were some setbacks for it. In the November election Michigan's voters adopted a constitutional amendment forbidding such aid, and Nebraska rejected one that would have permitted it. Earlier, the Michigan legislature had approved a $22 million subsidy for nonpublic schools in the year ahead, subject to an advisory opinion by the State Supreme Court. A federal court in Rhode Island ruled unconstitutional a 1969 legislative act under which the state would have provided as much as 15% of the salaries of lay instructors teaching secular subjects in parochial schools. New York's 1970 legislature proposed, subject to passage by next year's session before submission to the voters, repeal of the Blaine Amendment in that state's constitution, which bans aid to parochial schools.

Health and Welfare. Outlays for welfare, health, and hospitals (chiefly mental hospitals) continued to mount. As reported by the Census Bureau in 1970, state welfare expenditures totaled $10.9 billion in 1969, ranking third behind education and highways. Those for hospitals topped $3.7 billion, and those for other health services were almost $1 billion. From the federal government the states received about $6.9 billion for those three purposes. State welfare expenditures were up 25.6% from the year before, much of the rise due to expansion of medical assistance. The states passed $4.4 billion in welfare funds along to local governments.

Before the end of 1970 it was clear that welfare rolls had increased sharply in recent months. This was widely attributed to liberalized regulations on welfare, increased activities of welfare rights groups and related social factors, coupled with a slower economy. One result was a further increase of financial pressure on states and cities.

State legislation included varied measures to provide or improve drug prevention or treatment, aside from the action on penalties summarized in an earlier section. Broad programs included enactments in Delaware, Massachusetts, and New York.

Laws with liberal provisions permitting abortions were enacted in New York, Alaska, Hawaii, and—by the voters—Washington. South Carolina and Virginia acts also authorized them, subject to more restrictive conditions.

Particularly broad health-welfare legislation included that of New York. It raised the state's loan fund for construction of hospitals and nursing homes to $1.75 billion; established a state centre to test drugs, poisons, cosmetics, and medical devices; permitted welfare recipients to keep part of their earnings without sacrificing any welfare benefits; and authorized $50 million in loans to nonprofit companies to build and operate day centres for elderly people. The Massachusetts legislature required doctors to include the generic as well as trade names of drugs in prescriptions; increased the state's meat inspection program; expanded the housing program for the poor, elderly, and handicapped; and adopted an extensive bill of rights for the mentally ill and retarded.

Georgia's legislature appropriated $1.5 million for grants to develop community health programs, and Arizona's initiated a Department of Mental Retardation. Colorado established a division to help localities in housing efforts for people of low income. An Ohio board was set up to make and guarantee housing construction loans. Hawaii legislation authorized issuance of bonds for housing.

Correctional Systems. Several legislatures acted on correctional systems. A Massachusetts bail reform measure guaranteed accused persons, except in capital cases, a speedy hearing to decide whether they should be held to await trial, released on bond, or released without cost on their own recognizance. Persons jailed because of inability to raise bail were given the right of immediate court appeal. A Virginia program was launched enabling prisoners to attend instruction outside prison; for those convicted of misdemeanors, judges were authorized to prescribe access to work-release employment.

Delaware's session set up a professional parole board. The Georgia legislature approved bond funds of $4.7 million for a new women's prison and a work-release facility for prisoners. Measures were adopted in New York to coordinate state and local correctional operations through a Department of Correctional Services.

Conditions in prisons and jails in many parts of the country remained inadequate. Only one evidence of this was the recurrence of prison riots in recent years. Speaking to the National Governors' Conference in August, U.S. Supreme Court Chief Justice Warren Burger pleaded for reform. He declared that the federal and state governments should spend heavily to change the prison systems. With few exceptions, he said, the correctional institutions did not correct, and instead they often aggravated the problem of crime and public safety.

Consumers' Protection. A Massachusetts enactment received more attention than any other in this field—the first "no-fault" auto accident insurance law in the country. Under it a person can collect up to $2,000 from his own insurance company for medical expenses and loss of income arising from injury in an accident, regardless of who was at fault.

The Massachusetts session also passed an anti-loan-shark bill and required many food stores to post prices by the pound, quart, or other measure. Laws to curb the issuance of unsolicited credit cards and to protect people from liability under them were adopted in several states, including Delaware, New York, and Virginia. Among other measures, the Virginia legislature set up a Consumer Counsel Division in the attorney general's office and banned gasoline station giveaway games. Kentucky strengthened penalties for credit card violations and established a Citizens Commission on Consumer Protection.

Labor. Legislation affecting labor included the adoption of a minimum wage standard of $1.25 an hour in Georgia, increase of Delaware's minimum wage to $1.60, and increase of New York's to $1.85. New York exempted the first $85 of weekly salary from garnishment, Ohio exempted $280 per month from garnishment, and a Delaware act forbade firing an employee because his pay was garnisheed. Kentucky's session passed a "black lung" law to facilitate an employee's getting workmen's compensation for job-related lung disease. Arizona removed restrictions on the hours women might work.

Civil Rights and Poverty. Civil rights were much involved, directly or indirectly, in many of the fields reviewed above, notably education, crime and disorder, and welfare. Among additional measures, the Kansas legislature banned discrimination on account of sex in hiring or wages. It also adopted an open housing law, while a New York act required that persons denied housing be given a written statement of the reasons. Antiblockbusting laws were passed in Georgia and New York. Oregon's voters repealed a constitutional provision discriminating against nonwhite foreigners.

The needs of the inner areas of cities, with their poor and disadvantaged citizens, pressed particularly hard, and rural poverty also was much at variance from the general affluence of society. In one response to this situation, the National Governors' Conference, noting that most of America's poverty was in the very urban and very rural areas, asked consideration for launching a model rural area development program patterned after the model cities concept already embodied in federal law. In another response, the Advisory Commission on Intergovernmental Relations said that much dissatisfaction of minority groups in cities had its roots in local government structure and fiscal arrangements—"including the 'white noose' of the suburbs, under-financing of central city schools, inadequate housing, unbalanced patterns of state aid, and repressive restrictions upon the administration of public welfare." These and other sources of unrest, it held, stemmed primarily from state constitutions and statutes. Like the governors, the commission also emphasized areas of rural poverty. And it found that imbalances between well-to-do areas and poor ones had widened in the last decade.

Yet, as all could see, government needs grew among the more affluent neighbourhoods, too. Urban sprawl, burgeoning suburban schools, polluted air and streams, and many other problems requiring governmental action weighed on people of every income group. As the first year of the 1970s came to a close, the states, together with all levels of government, faced monumental and rising tasks.

FRANK SMOTHERS

*Journalist; formerly
Director of Publications
Council of State Governments*

Population

Total population of the United States in 1970 was 204,765,770, an increase of 13.3% over the 1960 total population of 180,697,596.

U.S. Census Data

final 1970 population counts
for urban places of 4,200 or more

Place	1970	1960
Alabama	**3,444,165**	**3,266,740**
Albertville	9,963	8,250
Alexander City	12,358	13,140
Andalusia	10,092	10,263
Anniston	31,533	33,657
Anniston Northwest (U)	6,609	—
Arab	4,399	2,989
Athens	14,360	9,330
Atmore	8,293	8,173
Attalla	7,510	8,257
Auburn	22,767	16,261
Bay Minette	6,727	5,197
Bessemer	33,428	33,054
Birmingham	300,910	340,887
Bluff Park (U)	12,372	—
Boaz	5,621	4,654
Brewton	6,747	6,309
Center Point (U)	15,675	—
Chickasaw	8,447	10,002
Childersburg	4,831	4,884
Clanton	5,868	5,683
Cullman	12,601	10,883
Daleville	5,182	693
Decatur	38,044	29,217
Demopolis	7,651	7,377
Dothan	36,733	31,440
Elba	4,634	4,321
Enterprise	15,591	11,410
Eufaula	9,102	8,357
Fairfield	14,369	15,816
Fairhope	5,720	4,858
Fayette	4,568	4,227
Florence	34,031	31,649
Forestdale (U)	6,091	—
Fort McClellan (U)	5,334	—
Fort Payne	8,435	7,029
Fort Rucker (U)	14,242	—
Fultondale	5,163	2,001
Gadsden	53,928	58,088
Gardendale	6,502	4,712
Geneva	4,398	3,840
Greenville	8,033	6,894
Guntersville	6,491	6,592
Hartselle	7,355	5,000
Homewood	21,245	20,289
Hueytown	7,095	5,997
Huntsville	137,802	72,365
Jackson	5,957	4,959
Jacksonville	7,715	5,678
Jasper	10,798	10,799
Lanett	6,908	7,674
Leeds	6,991	6,162
Marion	4,289	3,807
Midfield	6,399	3,556
Mobile	190,026	194,856
Monroeville	4,846	3,632
Montgomery	133,386	134,393
Mountain Brook	19,474	12,680
Muscle Shoals	6,907	4,084
Northport	9,435	5,245
Oneonta	4,390	4,136
Opelika	19,027	15,678
Opp	6,493	5,535
Oxford	4,361	3,603
Ozark	13,555	9,534
Pell City	5,381	4,165
Phenix City	25,281	27,630
Piedmont	5,063	4,794
Pleasant Grove	5,090	3,097
Prattville	13,116	6,616
Prichard	41,578	47,371
Roanoke	5,251	5,288
Russellville	7,814	6,628
Saraland	7,840	4,595
Scottsboro	9,324	6,449
Selma	27,379	28,385
Sheffield	13,115	13,491
Sylacauga	12,255	12,857
Talladega	17,662	17,742
Tallassee	4,809	4,934
Tarrant City	6,835	7,810
Troy	11,482	10,234
Tuscaloosa	65,773	63,370
Tuscumbia	8,828	8,994
Tuskegee	11,028	7,240
Union Springs	4,324	3,704
Vestavia Hills	8,311	4,029
West End-Cobb Town (U)	5,515	—
Alaska	**302,173**	**226,167**
Anchorage	48,029	44,237
Eielson (U)	6,149	—
Elmendorf (U)	6,018	—
Fairbanks	14,771	13,311
Fort Richardson (U)	8,960	—
Fort Wainwright (U)	9,097	—
Juneau	6,050	6,797
Ketchikan	6,994	6,483
Spenard (U)	18,089	9,074
Arizona	**1,772,482**	**1,302,161**
Ajo (U)	5,881	7,049
Avondale	6,304	6,151
Bisbee	8,328	9,914
Casa Grande	10,536	8,311
Chandler	13,763	9,531
Clifton	5,087	4,191
Coolidge	4,651	4,990
Douglas	12,462	11,925
Eloy	5,381	4,899
Flagstaff	26,117	18,214
Fort Huachuca (U)	6,659	—
Glendale	36,228	15,893
Globe	7,333	6,217
Holbrook	4,759	3,438
Kingman	7,312	4,525
Luke (U)	5,047	—
Mesa	62,853	33,772
Nogales	8,946	7,286
Paradise Valley	7,155	—
Peoria	4,792	2,593
Phoenix	581,562	439,170
Prescott	13,030	12,861
Safford	5,333	4,648
San Manuel (U)	4,332	4,524
Scottsdale	67,823	10,026
Sierra Vista	6,689	3,121
South Tucson	6,220	7,004
Sun City (U)	13,670	—
Superior (U)	4,975	4,875
Tempe	62,907	24,897
Tucson	262,933	212,892
West Yuma (U)	5,552	2,781
Winslow	8,066	8,862
Yuma	29,007	23,974
Arkansas	**1,923,295**	**1,786,272**
Arkadelphia	9,841	8,069
Batesville	7,209	6,207
Benton	16,499	10,399
Bentonville	5,508	3,649
Blytheville	24,752	20,797
Brinkley	5,275	4,636
Camden	15,147	15,823
Clarksville	4,616	3,919
Conway	15,510	9,791
Crossett	6,191	5,370
Dermott	4,250	3,665
Dumas	4,600	3,540
El Dorado	25,283	25,292
Fayetteville	30,729	20,274
Fordyce	4,837	3,890
Forrest City	12,521	10,544
Fort Smith	62,802	52,991
Harrison	7,239	6,580
Helena	10,415	11,500
Hope	8,810	8,399
Hot Springs	35,631	28,337
Jacksonville	19,832	14,488
Jonesboro	27,050	21,418
Little Rock	132,483	107,813
McGehee	4,683	4,448
Magnolia	11,303	10,651
Malvern	8,739	9,566
Marianna	6,196	5,134
Mena	4,530	4,388
Monticello	5,085	4,412
Morrilton	6,814	5,997
Newport	7,725	7,007
North Little Rock	60,040	58,032
Osceola	7,204	6,189
Paragould	10,639	9,947
Pine Bluff	57,389	44,037
Pocahontas	4,544	3,665
Rogers	11,050	5,700
Russellville	11,750	8,921
Searcy	9,040	7,272
Siloam Springs	6,009	3,953
Southwest Little Rock (U)	13,231	—
Springdale	16,783	10,076
Stuttgart	10,477	9,661
Texarkana	21,682	19,788
Trumann	5,938	4,511
Van Buren	8,373	6,787
Warren	6,433	6,752
West Helena	11,007	8,385
West Memphis	25,892	19,374
Wynne	6,696	4,922
California	**19,953,134**	**15,717,204**
Alameda	70,968	63,855
Alamo-Danville (U)	14,059	—
Albany	14,674	14,804
Alhambra	62,125	54,807
Alondra Park (U)	12,193	—
Altadena (U)	42,380	40,568
Alum Rock (U)	18,355	18,942
Anaheim	166,701	104,184
Anderson	5,492	4,492
Antioch	28,060	17,305
Apple Valley (U)	6,702	—
Aptos (U)	8,704	—
Arcadia	42,868	41,005
Arcata	8,985	5,235
Arden-Arcade (U)	82,492	73,352
Arroyo Grande	7,454	3,291
Artesia	14,757	9,993
Arvin	5,090	—
Ashland (U)	14,810	—
Atascadero (U)	10,290	5,983
Atherton	8,085	7,717
Atwater	11,640	7,318
Auburn	6,570	5,586
August School Area (U)	6,293	—
Avocado Heights (U)	9,810	—
Azusa	25,217	20,497
Bakersfield	69,515	56,848
Baldwin Park	47,285	33,951
Banning	12,034	10,250
Barstow	17,442	11,644
Beale East (U)	7,029	—
Beaumont	5,484	4,288
Bell	21,836	19,450
Bellflower	51,454	45,909
Bell Gardens	29,308	—
Belmont	23,667	15,996
Benicia	8,783	6,070
Berkeley	116,716	111,268
Beverly Hills	33,416	30,817
Big Bear (U)	5,268	1,562
Bloomington (U)	11,957	—
Blythe	7,047	6,023
Bonnyview (U)	4,882	4,686
Brawley	13,746	12,703
Brea	18,447	8,487
Broderick-Bryte (U)	12,782	—
Buena Park	63,646	46,401
Burbank	88,871	90,155
Burlingame	27,320	24,036
Calexico	10,625	7,992
Calwa (U)	5,191	—
Camarillo	19,219	—
Camarillo Heights (U)	5,892	1,704
Cambrian Park (U)	5,316	—
Campbell	24,770	11,863
Capitola	5,080	2,021
Cardiff-By-The-Sea (U)	5,724	3,149
Carlsbad	14,944	9,253
Carmel-By-The-Sea	4,525	4,580
Carmichael (U)	37,625	20,455
Carpinteria	6,982	—
Carson	71,150	—
Castro Valley (U)	44,760	37,120
Ceres	6,029	4,406
Cerritos	15,856	3,508
Cherryland (U)	9,969	—
Chico	19,580	14,757
Chico North (U)	6,656	—
Chico West (U)	4,787	—
China Lake (U)	11,105	—
Chino	20,411	10,305
Chowchilla	4,349	4,525
Chula Vista	67,901	42,034
Citrus Heights (U)	21,760	—
Claremont	23,464	12,633

Place	POPULATION 1970	1960
California (continued)		
Clovis	13,856	5,546
Coachella	8,353	4,854
Coalinga	6,161	5,965
Colton	19,974	18,666
Commerce	10,536	9,555
Compton	78,611	71,812
Concord	85,164	36,000
Corcoran	5,249	4,976
Corona	27,519	13,336
Coronado	20,910	18,039
Corte Madera	8,464	5,962
Costa Mesa	72,660	37,550
Covina	30,380	20,124
Cucamonga (U)	5,796	—
Cudahy	16,998	—
Culver City	31,035	32,163
Cupertino	18,216	3,664
Cypress	31,026	1,753
Daly City	66,922	44,791
Dana Point (U)	4,745	1,186
Davis	23,488	8,910
Del Aire (U)	11,930	—
Delano	14,559	11,913
Diamond Bar (U)	12,234	—
Dinuba	7,917	6,103
Dixon	4,432	2,970
Dominguez (U)	5,980	—
Downey	88,445	82,505
East Compton (U)	5,853	—
East La Mirada (U)	12,339	—
East Los Angeles (U)	105,033	104,270
East Palo Alto (U)	17,837	—
Edwards (U)	10,331	—
El Cajon	52,273	37,618
El Centro	19,272	16,811
El Cerrito	25,190	25,437
El Encanto Heights (U)	6,225	—
El Monte	69,837	13,163
El Paso de Robles	7,168	6,677
El Rio (U)	6,173	6,966
El Segundo	15,620	14,219
El Toro (U)	8,654	—
El Toro Station (U)	6,970	—
Encinitas (U)	5,375	2,786
Enterprise (U)	11,486	4,946
Escondido	36,792	16,377
Eureka	24,337	28,137
Exeter	4,475	4,264
Fairfax	7,661	5,813
Fairfield	44,146	14,968
Fair Oaks (U)	11,256	—
Fallbrook (U)	6,945	4,814
Fillmore	6,285	4,808
Florence-Graham (U)	42,895	38,164
Florin (U)	9,646	—
Folsom	5,810	3,925
Fontana	20,673	14,659
Fort Bragg	4,455	4,433
Fortuna	4,203	3,523
Foster City (U)	9,327	—
Fountain Valley	31,826	2,068
Freedom (U)	5,563	4,206
Fremont	100,869	43,790
Fresno	165,972	133,929
Fullerton	85,826	56,180
Gardena	41,021	35,943
Garden Acres (U)	7,870	—
Garden Grove	122,524	84,238
George (U)	7,404	—
Gilroy	12,665	7,348
Glen Avon (U)	5,759	3,416
Glendale	132,752	119,442
Glendora	31,349	20,752
Grand Terrace (U)	5,901	—
Grass Valley	5,149	4,876
Grossmont-Mt. Helix (U)	8,723	—
Grover City	5,939	5,210
Hacienda Heights (U)	35,969	—
Hanford	15,179	10,133
Hawaiian Gardens	8,811	—
Hawthorne	53,304	33,035
Hayward	93,058	72,700
Healdsburg	5,438	4,816
Hemet	12,252	5,416
Hemet East (U)	8,598	1,936
Hermosa Beach	17,412	16,115
Hesperia (U)	4,592	—
Highland (U)	12,669	—
Hillsborough	8,753	7,554
Hollister	7,663	6,071
Home Gardens (U)	5,116	1,541
Huntington Beach	115,960	11,492
Huntington Park	33,744	29,920
Imperial Beach	20,244	17,773
Indio	14,459	9,745
Inglewood	89,985	63,390
Isla Vista (U)	13,441	—
Kensington (U)	5,823	—
La Canada-Flintridge (U)	20,652	18,338
La Crescenta-Montrose (U)	19,594	—
Ladera Heights (U)	6,079	—
Lafayette	20,484	—

Place	POPULATION 1970	1960
Laguna Beach	14,550	9,288
Laguna Hills (U)	13,676	—
Laguna Niguel (U)	4,644	—
La Habra	41,350	25,136
Lakeside (U)	11,991	—
Lakewood	82,973	67,126
La Mesa	39,178	30,441
La Mirada	30,808	22,444
Lamont (U)	7,007	6,177
Lancaster (U)	30,948	26,012
La Palma	9,687	622
La Puente	31,092	24,723
Larkspur	10,487	5,710
La Verne	12,965	6,516
Lawndale	24,825	21,740
Lemon Grove (U)	19,690	19,348
Lemoore	4,219	2,561
Lemoore Station (U)	8,512	—
Lennox (U)	16,121	31,224
Lincoln Village (U)	6,722	—
Linda (U)	7,731	6,129
Lindsay	5,206	5,397
Live Oak (U)	6,443	3,518
Livermore	37,703	16,058
Lodi	28,691	22,229
Loma Linda (U)	9,797	—
Lomita	19,784	—
Lompoc	25,284	14,415
Lompoc Northwest (U)	4,874	—
Long Beach	358,633	344,168
Los Alamitos	11,346	4,312
Los Altos	24,956	19,696
Los Altos Hills	6,865	3,412
Los Angeles	2,816,061	2,479,015
Los Banos	9,188	5,272
Los Gatos	23,735	9,036
Lynwood	43,353	31,614
Madera	16,044	14,430
Manhattan Beach	35,352	33,934
Manteca	13,845	8,242
Marina (U)	8,343	3,310
Martinez	16,506	9,604
Marysville	9,353	9,553
Mather (U)	7,027	—
Maywood	16,996	14,588
Meiners Oaks-Mira Monte (U)	7,025	—
Menlo Park	26,734	26,957
Merced	22,670	20,068
Millbrae	20,781	15,873
Mill Valley	12,942	10,411
Milpitas	27,149	6,572
Mira Loma (U)	8,482	3,982
Mission Viejo (U)	11,933	—
Modesto	61,712	36,585
Monrovia	30,015	27,079
Montclair	22,546	13,546
Montebello	42,807	32,097
Monterey	26,302	22,618
Monterey Park	49,166	37,821
Moraga (U)	14,205	—
Morgan Hill	6,485	3,151
Morro Bay	7,109	—
Mountain View	51,092	30,889
Muscoy (U)	7,091	—
Napa	35,978	22,170
National City	43,184	32,771
Newark	27,153	9,884
Newhall (U)	9,651	4,705
Newport Beach	49,422	26,564
Norco	14,511	—
North Fair Oaks (U)	9,740	—
North Highlands (U)	31,854	21,271
North Island (U)	6,002	—
Norwalk	91,827	88,739
Novato	31,006	17,881
Oakdale	6,594	4,980
Oakland	361,561	367,548
Oak View (U)	4,872	2,448
Oceanside	40,494	24,971
Oildale (U)	20,879	—
Ojai	5,591	4,495
Olivehurst (U)	8,100	4,835
Ontario	64,118	46,617
Opal Cliffs (U)	5,425	3,825
Orange	77,374	26,444
Orangevale (U)	16,493	—
Orcutt (U)	8,500	1,414
Orinda Village (U)	6,790	5,568
Oroville	7,536	6,115
Otay-Castle Park (U)	15,445	—
Oxnard	71,225	40,265
Pacifica	36,020	20,995
Pacific Grove	13,505	12,121
Palmdale	8,511	—
Palm Desert (U)	6,171	1,295
Palm Springs	20,936	13,468
Palo Alto	55,966	52,287
Palos Verdes Estates	13,641	9,564
Palos Verdes Peninsula (U)	39,616	—
Paradise	14,539	8,268
Paramount	34,734	27,249
Parkway-Sacramento South (U)	28,574	—

Place	POPULATION 1970	1960
Pasadena	113,327	116,407
Pendleton North (U)	11,803	—
Pendleton South (U)	13,692	—
Perris	4,228	2,950
Petaluma	24,870	14,035
Pico Rivera	54,170	49,150
Piedmont	10,917	11,117
Pinole	15,850	6,064
Pittsburg	20,651	19,062
Placentia	21,948	5,861
Placerville	5,416	4,439
Pleasant Hill	24,610	—
Pleasanton	18,328	4,203
Pomona	87,384	67,157
Porterville	12,602	7,991
Porterville West (U)	6,200	—
Port Hueneme	14,295	11,067
Portola Valley	4,999	—
Poway (U)	9,422	1,921
Quartz Hill (U)	4,935	3,325
Rancho Cordova (U)	30,451	7,429
Rancho Rinconada (U)	5,149	—
Rancho Santa Clarita (U)	4,860	—
Red Bluff	7,676	7,202
Redding	16,659	12,773
Redlands	36,355	26,829
Redondo Beach	56,075	46,986
Redwood City	55,686	46,290
Reedley	8,131	5,850
Rialto	28,370	18,567
Richmond	79,043	71,854
Ridgecrest	7,629	—
Rio Linda (U)	7,524	2,189
Riverside	140,089	84,332
Rodeo (U)	5,356	—
Rohnert Park	6,133	—
Rolling Hills Estates	6,027	3,941
Roseland (U)	5,105	4,510
Rosemead	40,972	15,476
Roseville	17,895	13,421
Rossmoor (U)	12,922	—
Rowland Heights (U)	16,881	—
Rubidoux (U)	13,969	—
Sacramento	254,413	191,667
Salinas	58,896	28,957
San Anselmo	13,031	11,584
San Bernardino	104,251	91,922
San Bruno	36,254	29,063
San Carlos	25,924	21,370
San Clemente	17,063	8,527
San Diego	696,769	573,224
San Dimas	15,692	—
San Fernando	16,571	16,093
San Francisco	715,674	740,316
San Gabriel	29,176	22,561
Sanger	10,088	8,072
San Jacinto	4,385	2,553
San Jose	445,779	204,196
San Leandro	68,698	65,962
San Lorenzo (U)	24,633	23,773
San Luis Obispo	28,036	20,437
San Marino	14,177	13,658
San Mateo	78,991	69,870
San Pablo	21,461	19,687
San Rafael	38,977	20,460
Santa Ana	156,601	100,350
Santa Barbara	70,215	58,768
Santa Clara	87,717	58,880
Santa Cruz	32,076	25,596
Santa Fe Springs	14,750	16,342
Santa Maria	32,749	20,027
Santa Maria South (U)	7,129	—
Santa Monica	88,289	83,249
Santa Paula	18,001	13,279
Santa Rosa	50,006	31,027
Santee (U)	21,107	—
Saratoga	27,110	14,861
Sausalito	6,158	5,331
Seal Beach	24,441	6,994
Seaside	35,935	19,353
Selma	7,459	6,934
Shafter	5,327	4,576
Sierra Madre	12,140	9,732
Signal Hill	5,582	4,627
Simi Valley	56,464	—
Solana Beach (U)	5,023	—
Soledad	6,843	2,837
Soquel (U)	5,795	—
South El Monte	13,443	4,850
South Gate	56,909	53,831
South Lake Tahoe	12,921	—
South Modesto (U)	7,889	5,465
South Pasadena	22,979	19,706
South San Francisco	46,646	39,418
South San Gabriel (U)	5,051	—
South San Jose Hills (U)	12,386	—
South Whittier (U)	46,641	—
South Yuba City (U)	5,352	3,200
Spring Valley (U)	29,742	—
Stanford (U)	8,691	—
Stanton	17,947	11,163
Stockton	107,644	86,321
Sun City (U)	5,519	—

Place	POPULATION 1970	1960
California (continued)		
Sunnymead (U)	6,708	3,404
Sunnyvale	95,408	52,898
Susanville	6,608	5,598
Taft	4,285	3,822
Tehachapi	4,211	3,161
Temple City	29,673	—
Thermalito (U)	4,217	—
Thousand Oaks	36,334	—
Tiburon	6,209	—
Torrance	134,584	100,991
Tracy	14,724	11,289
Tulare	16,235	13,824
Turlock	13,992	9,116
Tustin	21,178	2,006
Tustin-Foothills (U)	26,598	—
Twentynine Palms (U)	5,667	—
Twentynine Palms Base (U)	5,647	—
Ukiah	10,095	9,900
Union City	14,724	6,618
Upland	32,551	15,918
Vacaville	21,690	10,898
Valencia (U)	4,243	—
Valinda (U)	18,837	—
Vallejo	66,733	60,877
Vandenburg (U)	13,193	—
Ventura (San Buenaventura)	55,797	29,114
Victorville	10,845	—
View Park-Windsor Hills (U)	12,268	—
Visalia	27,268	15,791
Vista	24,688	—
Walnut	5,992	934
Walnut Creek	39,844	9,903
Walnut Creek West (U)	8,330	—
Walnut Park (U)	8,925	—
Wasco	8,269	6,841
Watsonville	14,569	13,293
West Athens (U)	13,286	—
West Carson (U)	15,501	—
West Compton (U)	5,748	—
West Covina	68,034	50,645
West Hollywood (U)	29,448	28,870
Westminster	59,865	25,750
West Modesto (U)	6,135	1,897
Westmont (U)	29,310	—
West Pittsburg (U)	5,969	5,188
West Puente Valley (U)	20,733	—
West Sacramento (U)	12,002	—
West Whittier-Los Nietos (U)	20,845	—
Whittier	72,863	33,663
Willowbrook (U)	28,705	—
Woodland	20,677	13,524
Woodside	4,731	3,592
Yorba Linda	11,856	—
Yreka City	5,394	4,759
Yuba City	13,986	11,507
Yucaipa (U)	19,284	—
Colorado	**2,207,259**	**1,753,947**
Alamosa	6,985	6,205
Applewood (U)	8,214	—
Arvada	46,814	19,242
Aurora	74,974	48,548
Boulder	66,870	37,718
Brighton	8,309	7,055
Broomfield	7,261	—
Canon City	9,206	8,973
Cherry Hills Village	4,605	1,931
Colorado Springs	135,060	70,194
Commerce City	17,407	8,970
Cortez	6,032	6,764
Craig	4,205	3,984
Denver	514,678	493,887
Derby (U)	10,206	10,124
Durango	10,333	10,530
Edgewater	4,866	4,314
Englewood	33,695	33,398
Fort Carson (U)	19,399	—
Fort Collins	43,337	25,027
Fort Morgan	7,594	7,379
Golden	9,817	7,118
Grand Junction	20,170	18,694
Greeley	38,902	26,314
Gunnison	4,613	3,477
La Junta	7,938	8,026
Lakewood	92,787	—
Lamar	7,797	7,369
Leadville	4,314	4,008
Littleton	26,466	13,670
Littleton Southeast (U)	22,899	—
Longmont	23,209	11,489
Loveland	16,220	9,734
Manitou Springs	4,278	3,626
Montrose	6,496	5,044
North Glenn	27,937	—
Orchard Mesa (U)	5,824	4,956
Pueblo	97,453	91,181
Rocky Ford	4,859	4,929
Salida	4,355	4,560
Security-Widefield (U)	15,297	—
Sheridan	4,787	3,559

Place	POPULATION 1970	1960
Sherrelwood (U)	18,868	—
Sterling	10,636	10,751
Stratton Meadows (U)	6,223	—
Thornton	13,326	11,353
Trinidad	9,901	10,691
Walsenburg	4,329	5,071
Welby (U)	6,875	—
Westminster	19,432	13,850
Westminster East (U)	7,576	—
Wheat Ridge	29,795	—
Connecticut	**3,032,217**	**2,535,234**
Ansonia	21,160	19,819
Bethel*	10,945	8,200
Bridgeport	156,542	156,748
Bristol	55,487	45,499
Clinton (U)	5,957	2,693
Conning Towers-Nautilus Park (U)	9,791	3,457
Cromwell*	7,400	6,780
Danbury	50,781	22,928
Danielson	4,580	4,642
Darien*	20,411	18,437
Derby	12,599	12,132
East Hartford*	57,583	43,977
East Haven*	25,120	21,388
Enfield*	46,189	31,464
Fairfield*	56,487	46,183
Greenwich*	59,755	53,793
Groton	8,933	10,111
Hamden*	49,357	41,056
Hartford	158,017	162,178
Madison (U)	4,310	1,416
Manchester*	47,994	42,102
Meriden	55,959	51,850
Middletown	36,924	33,250
Milford	50,858	41,662
Naugatuck	23,034	19,511
New Britain	83,441	82,201
New Canaan*	17,455	13,466
New Haven	137,707	152,048
Newington*	26,037	17,664
New London	31,630	34,182
New Milford*	4,606	3,023
North Haven*	22,194	15,935
Norwalk	79,113	67,775
Norwich	41,433	38,506
Orange*	13,524	8,547
Pawcatuck (U)	5,255	4,389
Plainville*	16,733	13,149
Portland*	8,812	7,496
Prospect*	6,543	4,367
Putnam	6,918	6,952
Ridgefield (U)	5,878	2,954
Rocky Hill*	11,103	7,404
Seymour*	12,776	10,100
Shelton	27,165	18,190
Simsbury (U)	4,994	2,745
Stamford	108,798	92,713
Storrs (U)	10,691	6,054
Stratford*	49,775	45,012
Torrington	31,952	30,045
Trumbull*	31,394	20,379
Wallingford*	35,714	29,920
Waterbury	108,033	107,130
West Hartford*	68,031	62,382
West Haven	52,851	—
Westport*	27,414	20,955
Wethersfield*	26,662	20,561
Willimantic	14,402	13,881
Windsor Locks*	15,080	11,411
Winsted	8,954	8,136
Woodbridge*	7,673	5,182
Delaware	**548,104**	**446,292**
Brookside Park (U)	7,856	—
Claymont (U)	6,584	—
Dover	17,488	7,250
Dover Base (U)	8,106	—
Elsmere	8,415	7,319
Milford	5,314	5,795
Newark	20,757	11,404
New Castle	4,814	4,469
Seaford	5,537	4,430
Smyrna	4,243	3,241
Wilmington	80,386	95,827
Wilmington Manor-Chelsea-Leedom (U)	10,134	—
District of Columbia	**756,510**	**763,956**
Florida	**6,789,443**	**4,951,560**
Altamonte Springs	4,391	1,212
Arcadia	5,658	5,889
Auburndale	5,386	5,595
Avon Park	6,712	6,073
Azalea Park (U)	7,367	—
Bartow	12,891	12,849
Bay Harbor Islands	4,619	3,249
Bayshore Gardens (U)	9,255	2,297
Belle Glade	15,949	11,273
Boca Raton	28,506	6,961
Boynton Beach	18,115	10,467

Place	POPULATION 1970	1960
Bradenton	21,040	19,380
Brandon	12,749	1,665
Broadview Park-Rock Hill (U)	6,049	—
Browardale (U)	17,444	—
Browns Village (U)	23,442	—
Bunche Park (U)	5,773	—
Cape Canaveral	4,258	—
Cape Coral	10,193	—
Carol City (U)	27,361	21,749
Carver Ranch Estates (U)	5,515	—
Casselberry	9,438	2,463
Cedar Hammock-Bradenton South (U)	10,820	—
Chattahoochee	7,944	9,699
Clearwater	52,074	34,653
Cocoa	16,110	12,294
Cocoa Beach	9,952	3,475
Cocoa West (U)	5,779	3,975
Collier Manor-Cresthaven (U)	7,202	—
Combee Settlement (U)	4,963	2,697
Conway (U)	8,642	—
Coral Gables	42,494	34,793
Crestview	7,952	7,467
Cutler Ridge (U)	17,441	7,005
Dade City	4,241	4,759
Dania	9,013	7,065
Daytona Beach	45,327	37,395
Deerfield Beach	17,130	9,573
De Funiak Springs	4,966	5,282
De Land	11,641	10,775
Delray Beach	19,366	12,230
Deltona (U)	4,868	—
Dunedin	17,639	8,444
East Lake-Orient Park (U)	5,697	—
East Naples (U)	6,152	—
Eglin (U)	7,769	—
Egypt Lake (U)	7,556	—
Englewood (U)	5,182	2,877
Eustis	6,722	6,189
Fernandina Beach	6,955	7,276
Florida City	5,133	4,114
Fort Lauderdale	139,590	83,648
Fort Meade	4,374	4,014
Fort Myers	27,351	22,523
Fort Myers Beach (U)	4,305	2,463
Fort Myers Southwest (U)	5,086	—
Fort Pierce	29,721	25,256
Fort Walton Beach	19,994	12,147
Gainesville	64,510	29,701
Gifford (U)	5,772	3,509
Goulds (U)	6,690	5,121
Gulf Gate Estates (U)	5,874	—
Gulfport	9,730	9,730
Haines City	8,956	9,135
Hallandale	23,849	10,483
Hialeah	102,297	66,972
Holden Heights (U)	6,206	—
Holly Hill	8,191	4,182
Hollywood	106,873	35,237
Homestead	13,674	9,152
Homestead Base (U)	8,257	—
Indian Harbour Beach	5,371	—
Jacksonville	528,865	201,030
Kendall (U)	35,497	—
Key West	27,563	33,956
Kissimmee	7,119	6,845
Lake Carroll (U)	5,577	—
Lake City	10,575	9,465
Lake Forest (U)	5,216	—
Lake Holloway (U)	6,227	3,172
Lakeland	41,550	41,350
Lake Magdalene (U)	9,266	—
Lake Park	6,993	3,589
Lake Wales	8,240	8,346
Lake Worth	23,714	20,758
Lantana	7,126	5,021
Largo	22,031	5,302
Lauderdale Lakes	10,577	—
Lauderhill	8,465	132
Leesburg	11,869	11,172
Lehigh Acres (U)	4,394	—
Leto (U)	8,458	—
Lighthouse Point	9,071	2,453
Live Oak	6,830	6,544
Lockhart (U)	5,809	—
Maitland	7,157	3,570
Marathon (U)	4,397	—
Margate	8,867	2,646
Marianna	6,741	7,152
Melbourne	40,236	11,982
Melrose Park (U)	6,111	—
Merritt Island (U)	29,233	3,554
Miami	334,859	291,688
Miami Beach	87,072	63,145
Miami Shores	9,425	8,865
Miami Springs	13,279	11,229
Milton	5,360	4,108
Mims (U)	8,309	1,307
Miramar	23,973	5,485
Mount Dora	4,543	3,756
Myrtle Grove (U)	16,186	—
Naples	12,042	4,655
New Port Richey	6,098	3,520

U.S. Census Data (continued)

Place	POPULATION 1970	1960
Florida (continued)		
New Smyrna Beach	10,580	8,781
North Andrews Terrace (U)	7,082	—
North Bay	4,831	2,006
North Fort Myers (U)	8,798	—
North Miami	34,767	28,708
North Miami Beach	30,723	21,405
North Palm Beach	9,035	2,684
Norwood (U)	14,973	—
Oakland Park	16,261	5,331
Ocala	22,583	13,598
Ocean City (U)	5,267	—
Opa-Locka	11,902	9,810
Orange Park	7,619	2,624
Orlando	99,006	88,135
Ormond Beach	14,063	8,658
Ormond By-The-Sea	6,002	3,476
Pahokee	5,663	4,709
Palatka	9,310	11,028
Palm Bay	6,927	2,808
Palm Beach	9,086	6,055
Palm Beach Gardens	6,102	1
Palmetto	7,422	5,556
Palm River-Clair Mel (U)	8,536	—
Palm Springs	4,340	2,503
Panama City	32,096	33,275
Parker	4,212	—
Pembroke Pines	15,520	1,429
Pensacola	59,507	56,752
Perrine (U)	10,257	6,424
Perry	7,701	8,030
Pine Hills (U)	13,882	—
Pinellas Park	22,287	10,848
Plantation	23,523	4,772
Plant City	15,451	15,711
Pompano Beach	37,724	15,992
Pompano Beach Highlands (U)	5,014	—
Port Charlotte (U)	10,769	3,197
Port St. Joe	4,401	4,217
Quincy	8,334	8,874
Richmond Heights (U)	6,663	4,311
Riverland Village-Lauderdale Isles (U)	5,512	—
Riviera Beach	21,401	13,046
Rockledge	10,523	3,481
St. Augustine	12,352	14,734
St. Cloud	5,041	4,353
St. Petersburg	216,232	181,298
St. Petersburg Beach	8,024	6,268
Sanford	17,393	19,175
Sarasota	40,237	34,083
Sarasota Southeast (U)	6,885	—
Sarasota Springs (U)	4,405	—
Satellite Beach	6,558	825
Sebring	7,223	6,939
Siesta Key (U)	4,460	—
South Daytona	4,979	1,954
South Miami	19,571	9,846
South Miami Heights (U)	10,395	—
South Patrick Shores (U)	10,313	—
Springfield	5,949	4,628
Starke	4,848	4,806
Stuart	4,820	4,791
Sunrise Golf Village	7,403	—
Sweetwater Creek (U)	19,453	—
Tallahassee	71,897	48,174
Tamarac	5,078	—
Tampa	277,767	274,970
Tarpon Springs	7,118	6,768
Temple Terrace	7,347	3,812
Tice (U)	7,254	4,377
Titusville	30,515	6,410
Treasure Island	6,120	3,506
Tyndall (U)	4,248	—
University (U)	10,039	—
Valparaiso	6,504	5,975
Venice	6,648	3,444
Venice South (U)	4,680	—
Vero Beach	11,908	8,849
Vero Beach South (U)	7,330	—
Warrington (U)	15,848	16,752
West Bradenton (U)	6,162	—
West End (U)	5,289	3,124
West Miami	5,494	5,296
West Palm Beach	57,375	56,208
West Pensacola (U)	20,924	—
West Winter Haven (U)	7,716	5,050
Westwood Lakes (U)	12,811	22,517
Wilton Manors	10,948	8,257
Winston (U)	4,505	3,323
Winter Garden	5,153	5,513
Winter Haven	16,136	16,277
Winter Park	21,895	17,162
Georgia	**4,589,575**	**3,943,116**
Adel	4,972	4,321
Albany	72,623	55,890
Americus	16,091	13,472
Ashburn	4,209	3,291
Athens	44,342	31,355
Atlanta	496,973	487,455
Augusta	59,864	70,626

Place	POPULATION 1970	1960
Bainbridge	10,887	12,714
Barnesville	4,935	4,919
Blakely	5,267	3,580
Brunswick	19,585	21,703
Buford	4,640	4,168
Cairo	8,061	7,427
Calhoun	4,748	3,587
Camilla	4,987	4,753
Carrollton	13,520	10,973
Cartersville	9,929	8,668
Cedartown	9,253	9,340
Chamblee	9,127	6,635
Cochran	5,161	4,714
College Park	18,203	23,469
Columbus	154,168	116,779
Conyers	4,890	2,881
Cordele	10,733	10,609
Covington	10,267	8,167
Dalton	18,872	17,868
Dawson	5,383	5,062
Decatur	21,943	22,026
Dock Junction (U)	6,009	5,417
Doraville	9,039	4,437
Douglas	10,195	8,736
Douglasville	5,472	4,462
Dublin	15,143	13,814
Eastman	5,416	5,118
East Point	39,315	35,633
Elberton	6,438	7,107
Fitzgerald	8,015	8,781
Forest Park	19,994	14,201
Fort Benning (U)	27,495	—
Fort Gordon (U)	15,589	—
Fort Stewart (U)	4,467	—
Fort Valley	9,251	8,310
Gainesville	15,459	16,523
Garden City	5,741	5,451
Griffin	22,734	21,735
Hapeville	9,567	10,082
Hartwell	4,865	4,599
Jesup	9,091	7,304
La Fayette	6,044	5,588
La Grange	23,301	23,632
Lawrenceville	5,115	3,804
Macon	122,423	69,764
Manchester	4,779	4,115
Marietta	27,216	25,565
Midway-Hardwick (U)	14,047	16,909
Milledgeville	11,601	11,117
Monroe	8,071	6,826
Moultrie	14,302	15,764
Nashville	4,323	4,070
Newnan	11,205	12,169
Pelham	4,539	4,609
Perry	7,771	6,032
Quitman	4,818	5,071
Rome	30,759	32,226
Roswell	5,430	2,983
St. Simons (U)	5,346	3,199
Sandersville	5,546	5,425
Savannah	118,349	149,245
Smyrna	19,157	10,157
Statesboro	14,616	8,356
Summerville	5,043	4,706
Swainsboro	7,325	5,943
Sylvester	4,226	3,610
Thomaston	10,024	9,336
Thomasville	18,155	18,246
Thomson	6,503	4,522
Tifton	12,179	9,903
Toccoa	6,971	7,303
Valdosta	32,303	30,652
Vidalia	9,507	7,569
Warner Robins	33,491	18,633
Wcycross	18,996	20,944
Waynesboro	5,530	5,359
West Point	4,232	4,610
Winder	6,605	5,555
Windsor Forest (U)	7,288	—
Hawaii	**768,561**	**632,772**
Aiea	12,560	11,826
Ewa Beach	7,765	4,627
Halawa Heights	5,809	—
Hickam Housing	7,352	—
Hilo	26,353	25,966
Honolulu	324,871	294,194
Iroquois Point	4,572	—
Kahului	8,280	4,223
Kailua	33,783	—
Kaneohe	29,903	14,414
Maili	4,397	—
Makaha	4,644	—
Maunawili	5,303	—
Mokapu	7,860	—
Nanakuli	6,506	2,745
Pacific Palisades	7,846	—
Pearl City	19,552	—
Schofield Barracks	13,516	—
Wahiawa	17,598	15,512
Wailuku	7,979	6,969
Waipahu	22,798	—

Place	POPULATION 1970	1960
Idaho	**712,567**	**667,191**
Blackfoot	8,716	7,378
Boise City	74,990	34,481
Burley	8,279	7,508
Caldwell	14,219	12,230
Coeur d'Alene	16,228	14,291
Idaho Falls	35,776	33,161
Lewiston	26,068	12,691
Moscow	14,146	11,183
Mountain Home	6,451	5,984
Mountain Home Base (U)	6,038	—
Nampa	20,768	18,897
Payette	4,521	4,451
Pocatello	40,036	28,534
Rexburg	8,272	4,767
Rupert	4,563	4,153
Twin Falls	21,914	20,126
Illinois	**11,113,976**	**10,081,158**
Addison	24,482	6,741
Alsip	11,141	3,770
Alton	39,700	43,047
Anna	4,766	4,280
Arlington Heights	64,884	27,878
Aurora	74,182	63,715
Barrington	7,701	5,434
Bartonville	7,221	7,253
Batavia	8,994	7,496
Beardstown	6,222	6,294
Belleville	41,699	37,264
Bellwood	22,096	20,729
Belvidere	14,061	11,223
Bensenville	12,833	9,141
Benton	6,833	7,023
Berkeley	6,152	5,792
Berwyn	52,502	54,224
Bethalto	7,074	3,235
Bloomington	39,992	36,271
Blue Island	22,958	19,618
Bolingbrook	7,275	—
Bourbonnais	5,909	3,336
Bradley	9,881	8,082
Bridge View	12,522	7,334
Broadview	9,307	8,588
Brookfield	20,284	20,429
Buffalo Grove	11,799	1,492
Cahokia	20,649	15,829
Cairo	6,277	9,348
Calumet City	32,956	25,000
Calumet Park	10,069	8,448
Canton	14,217	13,588
Carbondale	22,816	14,670
Carlinville	5,675	5,440
Carmi	6,033	6,152
Carol Stream	4,434	836
Carpentersville	24,059	17,424
Cary	4,358	2,530
Centralia	15,217	13,904
Centreville	11,378	12,769
Champaign	56,532	49,583
Charleston	16,421	10,505
Chester	5,310	4,460
Chicago	3,366,957	3,550,404
Chicago Heights	40,900	34,331
Chicago Ridge	9,187	5,748
Chillicothe	6,052	3,054
Cicero	67,058	69,130
Clarendon Hills	6,750	5,885
Clinton	7,570	7,355
Collinsville	17,773	14,217
Country Club Hills	6,920	3,421
Crest Hill	7,460	5,887
Crestwood	5,543	1,213
Crete	4,656	3,463
Creve Coeur	6,440	6,684
Crystal Lake	14,541	8,314
Danville	42,570	41,856
Darien	8,077	—
Decatur	90,397	78,004
Deerfield	18,949	11,786
De Kalb	32,949	18,486
Des Plaines	57,239	34,886
Dixmoor	4,735	3,076
Dixon	18,147	19,565
Dolton	25,937	18,746
Downers Grove	32,751	21,154
Du Quoin	6,691	6,558
East Alton	7,309	7,630
East Chicago Heights	5,000	3,270
East Moline	20,832	16,732
East Peoria	18,455	12,310
East St. Louis	69,996	81,712
Edwardsville	11,070	9,996
Effingham	9,458	8,172
Elgin	55,691	49,447
Elk Grove Village	24,516	6,608
Elmhurst	50,547	36,991
Elmwood Park	26,160	23,866
Evanston	79,808	79,283
Evergreen Park	25,487	24,178
Fairfield	5,897	6,362
Fairview Heights	8,625	—
Flora	5,283	5,331

11

Place	POPULATION 1970	POPULATION 1960
Illinois (continued)		
Flossmoor	7,846	4,624
Forest Park	15,472	14,452
Fox Lake	4,511	3,700
Franklin Park	20,497	18,322
Freeport	27,736	26,628
Gages Lake-Wildwood (U)	5,337	—
Galesburg	36,290	37,243
Geneseo	5,840	5,169
Geneva	9,115	7,646
Glencoe	10,542	10,472
Glendale Heights	11,406	173
Glen Ellyn	21,909	15,972
Glenview	24,880	18,132
Glenwood	7,416	882
Granite City	40,440	40,073
Grayslake	4,907	3,762
Greenville	4,631	4,569
Hanover Park	11,916	451
Harrisburg	9,535	9,171
Harvard	5,177	4,248
Harvey	34,636	29,071
Harwood Heights	9,060	5,688
Havana	4,376	4,363
Hazel Crest	10,329	6,205
Herrin	9,623	9,474
Hickory Hills	13,176	2,707
Highland	5,981	4,943
Highland Park	32,263	25,532
Highwood	4,973	4,499
Hillsboro	4,267	4,232
Hillside	8,888	7,794
Hinsdale	15,918	12,859
Hoffman Estates	22,238	8,296
Hometown	6,729	7,479
Homewood	18,871	13,371
Hoopeston	6,461	6,606
Itasca	4,638	3,564
Jacksonville	20,553	21,690
Jerseyville	7,446	7,420
Joliet	80,378	66,780
Justice	9,473	2,803
Kankakee	30,944	27,666
Ken Rock (U)	5,945	—
Kewanee	15,762	16,324
La Grange	16,773	15,285
La Grange Highlands (U)	6,920	—
La Grange Park	15,626	13,793
Lake Bluff	4,979	3,494
Lake Forest	15,642	10,687
Lansing	25,805	18,098
La Salle	10,736	11,897
Lawrenceville	5,863	5,492
Lemont	5,080	3,397
Libertyville	11,684	8,560
Lincoln	17,582	16,890
Lincolnwood	12,929	11,744
Lisle	5,329	4,219
Litchfield	7,190	7,330
Lockport	9,985	7,560
Lombard	35,977	22,561
Loves Park	12,390	9,086
Lyons	11,124	9,936
McHenry	6,772	3,336
Macomb	19,643	12,135
Madison	7,042	6,861
Marengo	4,235	3,568
Marion	11,724	11,274
Markham	15,987	11,704
Marseilles	4,320	4,347
Mascoutah	5,045	3,625
Matteson	4,741	3,225
Mattoon	19,681	19,088
Maywood	30,036	27,330
Melrose Park	22,706	22,291
Mendota	6,902	6,154
Metropolis	6,940	7,339
Midlothian	15,939	6,605
Milan	4,873	3,065
Moline	46,237	42,705
Monmouth	11,022	10,372
Morris	8,194	7,935
Morrison	4,387	4,159
Morton	10,419	5,325
Morton Grove	26,369	20,533
Mount Carmel	8,096	8,594
Mount Prospect	34,995	18,906
Mount Vernon	15,980	15,566
Mundelein	16,128	10,526
Murphysboro	10,013	8,673
Naperville	23,885	12,933
Niles	31,432	20,393
Normal	26,396	13,357
Norridge	16,880	14,087
North Aurora	4,833	2,088
Northbrook	27,297	11,635
North Chicago	47,275	22,938
Northfield	5,010	4,005
Northlake	14,212	12,318
North Park (U)	15,679	—
North Riverside	8,097	7,989

Place	POPULATION 1970	POPULATION 1960
Oak Forest	17,870	3,724
Oak Lawn	60,305	27,471
Oak Park	62,511	61,093
O'Fallon	7,268	4,018
Olney	8,974	8,780
Orland Park	6,391	2,592
Ottawa	18,716	19,408
Palatine	25,904	11,504
Palos Heights	9,915	3,775
Palos Hills	6,629	3,766
Pana	6,326	6,432
Paris	9,971	9,823
Park Forest	30,638	29,993
Park Ridge	42,466	32,659
Paxton	4,373	4,370
Pekin	31,375	28,146
Peoria	126,963	103,162
Peoria Heights	7,943	7,064
Peru	11,772	10,460
Pittsfield	4,244	4,089
Plano	4,664	3,343
Pontiac	9,031	8,435
Posen	5,498	4,517
Princeton	6,959	6,250
Prospect Heights (U)	13,333	—
Quincy	45,288	43,793
Rantoul	25,562	22,116
Riverdale	15,806	12,008
River Forest	13,402	12,695
River Grove	11,465	8,464
Riverside	10,432	9,750
Robbins	9,641	7,511
Robinson	7,178	7,226
Rochelle	8,594	7,008
Rock Falls	10,287	10,261
Rockford	147,370	126,706
Rock Island	50,166	51,863
Rolling Meadows	19,178	10,879
Romeoville	12,674	3,574
Roselle	4,583	3,581
Rosemont	4,360	978
Round Lake Beach	5,717	5,011
St. Charles	12,928	9,269
Salem	6,187	6,165
Sandwich	5,056	3,842
Sauk	7,479	4,687
Savanna	4,942	4,950
Schaumburg	18,730	986
Schiller Park	12,712	5,687
Scott (U)	7,871	—
Shelbyville	4,597	4,821
Silvis	5,907	3,973
Skokie	68,627	59,364
South Chicago Heights	4,923	4,043
South Elgin	4,289	2,624
South Holland	23,931	10,412
South Stickney (U)	29,900	—
Sparta	4,307	3,452
Springfield	91,753	83,271
Spring Valley	5,605	5,371
Staunton	4,396	4,228
Steger	8,104	6,432
Sterling	16,113	15,688
Stickney	6,601	6,239
Stone Park	4,451	3,038
Streamwood	18,176	4,821
Streator	15,600	16,868
Summit	11,569	10,374
Swansea	5,432	3,018
Sycamore	7,843	6,961
Taylorville	10,644	8,801
Tinley Park	12,382	6,392
Urbana	32,800	27,294
Vandalia	5,160	5,537
Venice	4,680	5,380
Villa Park	25,891	20,391
Washington	6,790	5,919
Washington Park	9,524	6,601
Waterloo	4,546	3,739
Watseka	5,294	5,219
Wauconda	5,460	3,227
Waukegan	65,269	55,719
Westchester	20,033	18,092
West Chicago	10,111	6,854
West End (U)	7,554	—
Western Springs	12,147	10,838
West Frankfort	8,836	9,027
Westmont	8,482	5,997
West Peoria (U)	6,873	—
Wheaton	31,138	24,312
Wheeling	14,746	7,169
Wilmette	32,134	28,268
Wilmington	4,335	4,210
Winfield	4,285	1,575
Winnetka	14,131	13,368
Winthrop Harbor	4,794	3,848
Wonder Lake (U)	4,806	3,543
Wood Dale	8,831	3,071
Woodridge	11,028	542
Wood River	13,186	11,694
Woodstock	10,226	8,897
Worth	11,999	8,196
Zion	17,268	11,941

Place	POPULATION 1970	POPULATION 1960
Indiana	**5,193,669**	**4,662,498**
Alexandria	5,097	5,582
Anderson	70,787	49,061
Angola	5,117	4,746
Attica	4,262	4,341
Auburn	7,337	6,350
Aurora	4,293	4,119
Austin	4,902	—
Bedford	13,087	13,024
Beech Grove	13,468	10,973
Black Oak (U)	9,624	—
Bloomington	42,890	31,357
Bluffton	8,297	6,238
Boonville	5,736	4,801
Brazil	8,163	8,853
Brownsburg	5,186	4,478
Carmel	6,568	1,442
Cedar Lake	7,589	—
Charlestown	5,890	5,726
Chesterton	6,177	4,335
Clarksville	13,806	8,088
Clinton	5,340	5,843
Columbia City	4,911	4,803
Columbus	27,141	20,778
Connersville	17,604	17,698
Crawfordsville	13,842	14,231
Crown Point	10,931	8,443
Decatur	8,445	8,327
Dyer	4,906	3,993
East Chicago	46,982	57,669
East Gary	9,858	9,309
Edinburg	4,906	3,664
Elkhart	43,152	40,274
Elwood	11,196	11,793
Evansville	138,764	141,543
Fort Wayne	177,671	161,776
Frankfort	14,956	15,302
Franklin	11,477	9,453
Garrett	4,715	4,364
Gary	175,415	178,320
Gas City	5,742	4,469
Goshen	17,171	13,718
Greencastle	8,852	8,506
Greenfield	9,986	9,049
Greensburg	8,620	7,492
Greenwood	11,408	7,169
Griffith	18,168	9,483
Grissom (U)	4,963	—
Hammond	107,790	111,698
Hartford City	8,207	8,053
Highland	24,947	16,284
Hobart	21,485	18,680
Huntingburg	4,794	4,146
Huntington	16,217	16,185
Indianapolis	744,624	476,258
Jasper	8,641	6,737
Jeffersonville	20,008	19,522
Kendallville	6,838	6,765
Kokomo	44,042	47,197
Lafayette	44,955	42,330
La Porte	22,140	21,157
Lawrence	16,646	10,103
Lawrenceburg	4,636	5,004
Lebanon	9,766	9,523
Linton	5,450	5,736
Logansport	19,255	21,106
Madison	13,081	10,488
Marion	39,607	37,854
Martinsville	9,723	7,525
Merrillville-Lottaville-Rexville (U)	15,918	—
Michigan City	39,369	36,653
Mishawaka	35,517	33,361
Monticello	4,869	4,035
Mooresville	5,800	3,856
Mount Vernon	6,770	5,970
Muncie	69,080	68,603
Munster	16,514	10,313
New Albany	38,402	37,812
New Castle	21,215	20,349
New Haven	5,728	3,396
New Whiteland	4,200	3,488
Noblesville	7,548	7,664
North Manchester	5,791	4,377
North Vernon	4,582	4,307
Peru	14,139	14,453
Plainfield	8,211	5,460
Plymouth	7,661	7,558
Portage	19,127	11,822
Portland	7,115	6,999
Princeton	7,431	7,906
Rensselaer	4,688	4,740
Richmond	43,999	44,149
Rochester	4,631	4,883
Rushville	6,686	7,264
Salem	5,041	4,546
Scottsburg	4,791	3,810
Seymour	13,352	11,629
Shelbyville	15,094	14,317
South Bend	125,580	132,445
Speedway	15,056	9,624
Sullivan	4,683	4,979
Tell City	7,933	6,609

U.S. Census Data (continued)

Place	POPULATION 1970	POPULATION 1960
Indiana (continued)		
Terre Haute	70,286	72,500
Tipton	5,176	5,604
Valparaiso	20,020	15,227
Vincennes	19,867	18,046
Wabash	13,379	12,621
Warsaw	7,506	7,234
Washington	11,358	10,846
West Glen Park (U)	6,602	—
West Lafayette	19,157	12,680
Whiting	7,247	8,137
Winchester	5,493	5,742
Iowa	**2,825,041**	**2,757,537**
Algona	6,032	5,702
Ames	39,505	27,003
Anamosa	4,389	4,616
Ankeny	9,151	2,964
Atlantic	7,306	6,890
Bettendorf	22,126	11,534
Boone	12,468	12,468
Burlington	32,366	32,430
Carroll	8,716	7,682
Cedar Falls	29,597	21,195
Cedar Rapids	110,642	92,035
Centerville	6,531	6,629
Chariton	5,009	5,042
Charles City	9,268	9,964
Cherokee	7,272	7,724
Clarinda	5,420	5,901
Clear Lake City	6,430	6,158
Clinton	34,719	33,589
Coralville	6,130	2,357
Council Bluffs	60,348	55,641
Creston	8,234	7,667
Davenport	98,469	88,981
Decorah	7,458	6,435
Denison	5,882	4,930
Des Moines	200,587	208,982
Dubuque	62,309	56,606
Eagle Grove	4,489	4,381
Estherville	8,108	7,927
Evansdale	5,038	5,738
Fairfield	8,715	8,054
Fort Dodge	31,263	28,399
Fort Madison	13,996	15,247
Grinnell	8,402	7,367
Hampton	4,376	4,501
Harlan	5,049	4,350
Humboldt	4,665	4,031
Independence	5,910	5,498
Indianola	8,852	7,062
Iowa City	46,850	33,443
Iowa Falls	6,454	5,565
Jefferson	4,735	4,570
Keokuk	14,631	16,316
Knoxville	7,755	7,817
Le Mars	8,159	6,767
Manchester	4,641	4,402
Maquoketa	5,677	5,909
Marion	18,028	10,882
Marshalltown	26,219	22,521
Mason City	30,491	30,642
Mount Pleasant	7,007	7,339
Muscatine	22,405	20,997
Nevada	4,952	4,227
Newton	15,619	15,381
Oelwein	7,735	8,282
Oskaloosa	11,224	11,053
Ottumwa	29,610	33,871
Pella	6,668	5,198
Perry	6,906	6,442
Red Oak	6,210	6,421
Sheldon	4,535	4,251
Shenandoah	5,968	6,567
Sioux City	85,925	89,159
Spencer	10,278	8,864
Storm Lake	8,591	7,728
Urbandale	14,434	5,821
Vinton	4,845	4,781
Washington	6,317	6,037
Waterloo	75,533	71,755
Waverly	7,205	6,357
Webster City	8,488	8,520
West Des Moines	16,441	11,949
Windsor Heights	6,303	4,715
Kansas	**2,249,071**	**2,178,611**
Abilene	6,661	6,746
Arkansas City	13,216	14,262
Atchison	12,565	12,529
Augusta	5,977	6,434
Baxter Springs	4,489	4,498
Chanute	10,341	10,849
Clay Center	4,963	4,613
Coffeyville	15,116	17,382
Colby	4,658	4,210
Concordia	7,221	7,022
Derby	7,947	6,458
Dodge City	14,127	13,520
El Dorado	12,308	12,523
Emporia	23,327	18,190
Fairway	5,133	5,398

Place	POPULATION 1970	POPULATION 1960
Fort Leavenworth (U)	8,060	—
Fort Scott	8,967	9,410
Garden City	14,708	11,811
Goodland	5,510	4,459
Great Bend	16,133	16,670
Hays	15,396	11,947
Haysville	6,483	5,836
Hutchinson	36,885	37,574
Independence	10,347	11,222
Iola	6,493	6,885
Junction City	19,018	18,700
Kansas City	168,213	121,901
Larned	4,567	5,001
Lawrence	45,698	32,858
Leavenworth	25,147	22,052
Leawood	10,349	7,466
Lenexa	5,242	2,487
Liberal	13,471	13,813
Lyons	4,355	4,592
McPherson	10,851	9,996
Manhattan	27,575	22,993
Merriam	10,851	5,084
Mission	8,376	4,626
Newton	15,439	14,877
North Fort Riley (U)	12,469	—
Olathe	17,917	10,987
Osawatomie	4,294	4,622
Ottawa	11,036	10,673
Overland Park	76,623	—
Paola	4,622	4,784
Parsons	13,015	13,929
Pittsburg	20,171	18,678
Prairie Village	28,138	25,356
Pratt	6,736	8,156
Roeland Park	9,974	8,949
Russell	5,371	6,113
Salina	37,714	43,202
Shawnee	20,482	9,072
Topeka	125,011	119,484
Wellington	8,072	8,809
Wichita	276,554	254,698
Winfield	11,405	11,117
Kentucky	**3,219,311**	**3,038,156**
Ashland	29,245	31,283
Bardstown	5,816	4,798
Bellevue	8,847	9,336
Berea	6,956	4,302
Bowling Green	36,253	28,338
Buechel (U)	5,359	—
Campbellsville	7,598	6,966
Cold Spring	5,348	1,095
Corbin	7,317	7,119
Covington	52,535	60,376
Cynthiana	6,356	5,641
Danville	11,542	9,010
Dayton	8,691	9,050
Elizabethtown	11,748	9,641
Elsmere	5,161	4,607
Erlanger	12,676	7,072
Flatwoods	7,380	3,741
Florence	11,457	5,837
Fort Campbell North (U)	13,616	—
Fort Knox (U)	37,608	—
Fort Mitchell	6,982	525
Fort Thomas	16,338	14,896
Fort Wright-Lookout Heights	4,819	—
Frankfort	21,356	18,365
Franklin	6,553	5,319
Georgetown	8,629	6,986
Glasgow	11,301	10,069
Harrodsburg	6,741	6,061
Hazard	5,459	5,958
Henderson	22,976	16,892
Hopkinsville	21,250	19,465
Jeffersontown	9,701	3,431
Lebanon	5,528	4,813
Lexington	108,137	62,810
London	4,337	4,035
Louisville	361,472	390,639
Ludlow	5,815	6,233
Madisonville	15,332	13,110
Mayfield	10,724	10,762
Maysville	7,411	8,484
Middlesborough	11,844	12,607
Morehead	7,191	4,170
Mount Sterling	5,083	5,370
Murray	13,537	9,303
Newport	25,998	30,070
Nicholasville	5,829	4,275
Okolona (U)	17,643	—
Owensboro	50,329	42,471
Paducah	31,627	34,479
Paris	7,823	7,791
Pikeville	4,576	4,754
Pleasure Ridge Park (U)	28,566	10,612
Princeton	6,292	5,618
Providence	4,270	3,771
Radcliff	7,881	3,384
Richmond	16,861	12,168
Russellville	6,456	5,861
St. Matthews	13,152	8,738
Shively	19,223	15,155

Place	POPULATION 1970	POPULATION 1960
Somerset	10,436	7,112
Valley Station (U)	24,471	10,553
Versailles	5,679	4,060
Winchester	13,402	10,187
Louisiana	**3,643,180**	**3,257,022**
Abbeville	10,996	10,414
Alexandria	41,557	40,279
Baker	8,281	4,823
Bastrop	14,713	15,193
Baton Rouge	165,963	152,419
Bayou Cane (U)	9,077	3,173
Bayou Vista (U)	5,121	—
Bogalusa	18,412	21,423
Bossier City	41,595	32,776
Breaux Bridge	4,942	3,303
Bunkie	5,395	5,188
Cooper Road (U)	9,034	—
Covington	7,170	6,754
Crowley	16,104	15,617
Denham Springs	6,752	5,991
De Ridder	8,030	7,188
Donaldsonville	7,367	6,082
Eunice	11,390	11,326
Ferriday	5,239	4,563
Franklin	9,325	8,673
Gonzales	4,512	3,252
Grambling	4,407	3,144
Gretna	24,875	21,967
Hammond	12,487	10,563
Harahan	13,037	9,275
Harvey (U)	6,347	—
Homer	4,483	4,665
Houma	30,922	22,561
Jackson	4,697	1,824
Jeanerette	6,322	5,568
Jefferson Heights (U)	16,489	19,353
Jennings	11,783	11,887
Jonesboro	5,072	3,848
Kaplan	5,540	5,267
Kenner	29,858	17,037
Lafayette	68,908	40,400
Lake Charles	77,998	63,392
Lake Providence	6,183	5,781
Laplace (U)	5,953	3,541
Larose (U)	4,267	2,796
Leesville	8,928	4,689
Little Farms (U)	15,713	—
Mansfield	6,432	5,839
Marksville	4,519	4,257
Marrero (U)	29,015	—
Metairie (U)	135,816	—
Minden	13,996	12,785
Monroe	56,374	52,219
Morgan City	16,586	13,540
Natchitoches	15,974	13,924
New Iberia	30,147	29,062
New Orleans	593,471	627,525
Norco (U)	4,773	4,682
North Fort Polk	7,955	—
Oakdale	7,301	6,618
Opelousas	20,121	17,417
Patterson	4,409	2,923
Pineville	8,951	8,636
Plaquemine	7,739	7,689
Ponchatoula	4,545	4,727
Port Allen	5,728	5,026
Raceland (U)	4,880	3,666
Rayne	9,510	8,634
Reserve (U)	6,381	5,297
Ruston	17,365	13,991
St. Martinville	7,153	6,468
Samtown (U)	4,210	4,008
Scotlandville (U)	22,557	—
Shreveport	182,064	164,372
Slidell	16,101	6,356
South Fort Polk (U)	15,600	—
Springhill	6,496	6,437
Sulphur	13,551	11,429
Tallulah	9,643	9,413
Terry Town (U)	13,832	—
Thibodaux	14,925	13,403
Vidalia	5,538	4,313
Ville Platte	9,692	7,512
West Monroe	14,868	15,215
Westwego	11,402	9,815
Winnfield	7,142	7,022
Winnsboro	5,349	4,437
Zachary	4,964	3,268
Maine	**992,048**	**969,265**
Auburn	24,151	24,449
Augusta	21,945	21,680
Bangor	33,168	38,912
Bath	9,679	10,717
Belfast	5,957	6,140
Biddeford	19,983	19,255
Brewer	9,300	9,009
Brunswick (U)	10,867	9,444
Cape Elizabeth*	7,873	5,505
Caribou	10,419	—
Ellsworth	4,603	4,444
Falmouth*	6,291	5,976

13

Place	POPULATION 1970	1960
Maine (continued)		
Gardiner	6,685	6,897
Houlton (U)	6,760	5,976
Kittery (U)	7,363	8,051
Lewiston	41,779	40,804
Loring (U)	6,266	—
Madawaska (U)	4,452	4,035
Millinocket (U)	7,558	7,318
Old Orchard Beach (U)	5,273	4,431
Old Town	9,057	8,626
Orono (U)	9,146	3,234
Portland	65,116	72,566
Presque Isle	11,452	12,886
Rockland	8,505	8,769
Rumford (U)	6,198	7,233
Saco	11,678	10,515
Sanford (U)	10,457	10,936
Skowhegan (U)	6,571	6,667
South Portland	23,267	22,788
Waterville	18,192	19,001
Westbrook	14,444	13,820
Winslow (U)	5,389	3,640
Maryland	**3,922,399**	**3,100,689**
Aberdeen	12,375	9,679
Aberdeen Proving Ground (U)	7,403	—
Andrews (U)	6,418	—
Annapolis	29,592	23,385
Arbutus (U)	22,745	22,402
Aspen Hill (U)	16,799	—
Avenel-Hillandale (U)	19,520	—
Bainbridge Center (U)	5,257	—
Baltimore	905,759	939,024
Bel Air	6,307	4,300
Beltsville (U)	8,912	—
Bethesda (U)	71,621	56,527
Birchwood City (U)	9,558	—
Bladensburg	7,488	3,103
Bowie	35,028	1,072
Brooklyn (U)	13,896	—
Calverton (U)	6,543	—
Cambridge	11,595	12,239
Camp Springs (U)	22,776	—
Carmody Hills-Pepper Mill Village (U)	6,245	—
Catonsville (U)	54,812	37,372
Chapel Oaks-Cedar Heights (U)	6,049	—
Cheverly	6,696	5,223
Chevy Chase (U)	16,424	—
Chillum (U)	35,656	—
Colesville (U)	9,455	—
College Park	26,156	18,482
Columbia (U)	8,815	—
Coral Hills (U)	7,105	—
Crofton (U)	4,478	—
Cumberland	29,724	33,415
Defense Heights (U)	6,775	—
District Heights	8,424	7,524
Dundalk (U)	85,377	82,428
Easton	6,809	6,337
Edgemere (U)	10,352	11,775
Edgewood (U)	8,551	1,670
Elkton (U)	5,362	5,989
Ellicott City (U)	9,506	—
Essex (U)	38,193	35,205
Ferndale (U)	9,929	—
Forestville (U)	16,152	—
Fort Meade (U)	16,699	—
Frederick	23,641	21,744
Frostburg	7,327	6,722
Gaithersburg	8,344	3,847
Glenarden	4,502	1,336
Glen Burnie (U)	38,608	—
Good Luck (U)	10,584	—
Greenbelt	18,199	7,479
Hagerstown	35,862	36,660
Halfway (U)	6,106	4,256
Halpine (U)	5,912	—
Havre De Grace	9,791	8,510
Hillcrest Heights (U)	24,037	15,295
Hyattsville	14,998	15,168
Joppatowne (U)	9,092	—
Kemp Mill (U)	10,037	—
Kentland (U)	9,649	—
Landover (U)	5,597	—
Langley Park (U)	11,564	11,510
Lanham-Seabrook (U)	13,244	—
Lansdowne-Baltimore Highlands (U)	16,976	13,134
Laurel	10,525	8,503
Lexington Park-Patuxent River (U)	9,136	—
Linthicum (U)	9,830	—
Lutherville-Timonium (U)	24,055	12,265
Maryland City (U)	7,102	—
Middle River (U)	19,935	10,825
Montrose (U)	6,140	—
Mount Rainier	8,180	9,855
New Carrollton	13,395	3,385
North Potomac (U)	12,546	—
North Takoma Park (U)	7,373	—
Odenton (U)	5,989	1,914
Overlea (U)	13,086	10,795

Place	POPULATION 1970	1960
Owings Mills (U)	7,360	3,810
Oxon Hill (U)	11,974	—
Palmer Park (U)	8,172	—
Parkville (U)	33,897	27,236
Perry Hall (U)	5,446	—
Pikesville (U)	25,395	18,737
Potomac Valley (U)	5,094	—
Pumphrey (U)	6,370	—
Randallstown (U)	33,683	—
Randolph (U)	13,233	—
Reisterstown (U)	14,037	4,216
Riverdale	5,724	4,389
Riverdale Heights-East Pines (U)	8,941	—
Riviera Beach (U)	7,464	4,902
Rockville	41,564	26,090
Rosedale (U)	19,417	—
Salisbury	15,252	16,302
Seat Pleasant	7,217	5,365
Severna Park (U)	16,358	—
Silver Spring (U)	77,496	66,348
South Gate (U)	9,356	—
South Kensington (U)	10,289	—
South Laurel (U)	13,345	—
Suitland-Silver Hill (U)	30,355	10,300
Takoma Park (U)	18,455	16,799
Towson (U)	77,809	19,090
Waldorf (U)	7,368	1,048
Walker Mill (U)	6,322	—
West Laurel (U)	4,478	—
Westminster	7,207	6,123
Wheaton (U)	66,247	54,635
White Oak (U)	19,769	—
Woodlawn-Woodmoor (U)	28,811	—
Massachusetts	**5,689,170**	**5,148,578**
Adams (U)	11,256	11,949
Amesbury (U)	10,088	9,625
Amherst (U)	17,926	10,306
Andover*	23,695	17,134
Arlington*	53,524	49,953
Ashland*	8,882	7,779
Athol (U)	9,723	10,161
Attleboro	32,907	27,118
Auburn*	15,347	14,047
Avon*	5,295	4,301
Ayer*	7,393	14,927
Bedford*	13,513	10,969
Bellingham (U)	4,228	—
Belmont*	28,285	28,715
Beverly	38,348	36,108
Boston	641,071	697,197
Braintree*	35,050	31,069
Brockton	89,040	72,813
Brookline*	58,886	54,044
Burlington*	21,980	12,852
Cambridge	100,361	107,716
Canton*	17,100	12,771
Chelsea	30,625	33,749
Chicopee	66,676	61,553
Clinton*	13,383	12,848
Concord*	16,148	12,517
Dalton*	7,505	6,436
Danvers*	26,151	21,926
Dedham*	26,938	23,869
Easthampton*	13,012	12,326
East Longmeadow*	13,029	10,294
Everett	42,485	43,544
Fairhaven*	16,332	14,339
Fall River	96,898	99,942
Falmouth (U)	5,806	3,308
Fitchburg	43,343	43,021
Fort Devens (U)	12,951	—
Framingham*	64,048	44,526
Franklin (U)	8,863	6,391
Gardner	19,748	19,038
Gloucester	27,941	25,789
Greenfield (U)	14,642	14,389
Haverhill	46,120	46,346
Holyoke	50,112	52,689
Hopedale*	4,292	3,987
Hudson (U)	14,283	7,897
Hull*	9,961	7,055
Hyannis (U)	6,847	5,139
Ipswich (U)	5,022	4,617
Lawrence	66,915	70,933
Leominster	32,939	27,929
Lexington*	31,886	27,691
Longmeadow*	15,630	10,565
Lowell	94,239	92,107
Lynn	90,294	94,478
Lynnfield*	10,826	8,398
Malden	56,127	57,676
Manchester*	5,151	3,932
Mansfield*	4,778	4,674
Marblehead*	21,295	18,521
Marlborough	27,936	18,819
Maynard*	9,710	7,695
Medford	64,397	64,971
Melrose	33,180	29,619
Methuen*	35,456	28,114
Middleborough (U)	6,259	6,003
Milford (U)	13,740	13,722
Milton*	27,190	26,375

Place	POPULATION 1970	1960
Natick*	31,057	28,831
Needham*	29,748	25,793
New Bedford	101,777	102,477
Newburyport	15,807	14,004
Newton	91,066	92,384
North Adams	19,195	19,905
Northampton	29,664	30,058
North Andover*	16,284	10,908
North Attleborough*	18,665	14,777
North Reading*	11,264	8,331
North Scituate (U)	5,507	3,421
Norwood*	30,815	24,898
Otis (U)	5,596	—
Oxford (U)	6,109	6,985
Peabody	48,080	32,202
Pinehurst (U)	5,681	1,991
Pittsfield	57,020	57,879
Plainville*	4,953	3,810
Plymouth (U)	6,940	6,488
Quincy	87,966	87,409
Randolph*	27,035	18,900
Reading*	22,539	19,259
Revere	43,159	40,080
Rockland*	15,674	13,119
Salem	40,556	39,211
Saugus*	25,110	20,666
Seekonk*	11,116	8,399
Sharon*	12,367	10,070
Shrewsbury*	19,196	16,622
Somerset*	18,088	12,196
Somerville	88,779	94,697
Southbridge (U)	14,261	15,889
South Yarmouth (U)	5,380	2,029
Spencer (U)	5,895	5,593
Springfield	163,905	174,463
Stoneham*	20,725	17,821
Stoughton*	23,459	16,328
Swampscott*	13,578	13,294
Taunton	43,756	41,132
Turners Falls (U)	5,168	4,917
Wakefield*	25,402	24,295
Waltham	61,582	55,413
Ware (U)	6,509	6,650
Watertown*	39,307	39,092
Webster (U)	12,432	12,072
Wellesley*	28,051	26,071
Westborough (U)	4,474	4,011
Westfield	31,433	26,302
Weston*	10,870	8,261
West Springfield*	28,461	24,924
Weymouth*	54,610	48,177
Whitinsville (U)	5,210	5,102
Whitman*	13,059	10,485
Williamstown (U)	4,285	5,428
Winchester*	22,269	19,376
Winthrop*	20,335	20,303
Woburn	37,406	31,214
Worcester	176,572	186,587
Michigan	**8,875,083**	**7,823,194**
Adrian	20,382	20,347
Albion	12,112	12,749
Allegan	4,516	4,822
Allen Park	40,747	37,494
Alma	9,790	8,978
Alpena	13,805	14,682
Ann Arbor	99,797	67,340
Battle Creek	38,931	44,169
Bay City	49,449	53,604
Belding	5,121	4,887
Benton Central (U)	8,067	—
Benton Harbor	16,481	19,136
Benton South (U)	4,496	—
Berkley	22,618	23,275
Beverly Hills	13,598	8,633
Big Rapids	11,995	8,686
Birmingham	26,170	25,525
Buchanan	4,645	5,341
Cadillac	9,990	10,112
Carrollton (U)	7,300	—
Center Line	10,379	10,164
Charlotte	8,244	7,657
Cheboygan	5,553	5,859
Clawson	17,617	14,795
Coldwater	9,099	8,880
Comstock (U)	5,003	—
Comstock Park (U)	5,766	—
Cutlerville (U)	6,267	—
Davison	5,259	3,761
Dearborn	104,199	112,007
Dearborn Heights	80,069	—
Detroit	1,511,482	1,670,144
Dowagiac	6,583	7,208
Drayton Plains (U)	16,462	—
East Detroit	45,920	45,756
East Grand Rapids	12,565	10,924
East Lansing	47,540	30,198
Eastwood (U)	9,682	—
Eaton Rapids	4,494	4,052
Ecorse	17,515	17,328
Escanaba	15,368	15,391
Essexville	4,990	4,590
Farmington	13,337	6,881

Place	POPULATION 1970	1960
Michigan (continued)		
Fenton	8,284	6,142
Ferndale	30,850	31,347
Flat Rock	5,643	4,696
Flint	193,317	196,940
Flushing	7,190	3,761
Fraser	11,868	7,027
Garden City	41,864	38,017
Gladstone	5,237	5,267
Grand Blanc	5,132	1,565
Grand Haven	11,844	11,066
Grand Ledge	6,032	5,165
Grand Rapids	197,649	177,313
Grandville	10,764	7,975
Greenville	7,493	7,440
Grosse Ile (U)	7,799	—
Grosse Pointe	6,637	6,631
Grosse Pointe Farms	11,701	12,172
Grosse Pointe Park	15,585	15,457
Grosse Pointe Woods	21,878	18,580
Hamtramck	27,245	34,137
Hancock	4,820	5,022
Harper Woods	20,186	19,995
Hastings	6,501	6,375
Hazel Park	23,784	25,631
Highland Park	35,444	38,063
Hillsdale	7,728	7,629
Holland	26,337	24,777
Holly	4,355	3,269
Holt (U)	6,980	4,818
Houghton	6,067	3,393
Howell	5,224	4,861
Huntington Woods	8,536	8,746
Inkster	38,595	39,097
Ionia	6,361	6,754
Iron Mountain	8,702	9,299
Ironwood	8,711	10,265
Ishpeming	8,245	8,857
Jackson	45,484	50,720
Jenison (U)	11,266	—
Kalamazoo	85,555	82,089
Kentwood	20,310	—
Kincheloe (U)	6,331	—
Kingsford	5,276	5,084
K. I. Sawyer (U)	6,679	—
Lakeview (U)	11,391	10,384
Lambertville (U)	5,721	1,168
Lansing	131,546	107,807
Lapeer	6,270	6,160
Lapeer Heights (U)	7,130	—
Lincoln Park	52,984	53,933
Livonia	110,109	66,702
Ludington	9,021	9,421
Madison Heights	38,599	33,343
Manistee	7,723	8,324
Manistique	4,324	4,875
Marine City	4,567	4,404
Marquette	21,967	19,824
Marshall	7,253	6,736
Marysville	5,610	4,065
Mason	5,468	4,522
Melvindale	13,862	13,089
Menominee	10,748	11,289
Midland	35,176	27,779
Milan	4,533	3,616
Milford	4,699	4,323
Monroe	23,894	22,968
Mount Clemens	20,476	21,016
Mount Pleasant	20,504	14,875
Muskegon	44,631	46,485
Muskegon Heights	17,304	19,552
Negaunee	5,248	6,126
Niles	12,988	13,842
North Muskegon	4,243	3,855
Northville	5,400	3,967
Norton Shores	22,271	—
Novi	9,668	6,390
Oak Park	36,762	36,632
Okemos (U)	7,770	—
Owosso	17,179	17,006
Petoskey	6,342	6,138
Plymouth	11,758	8,766
Pontiac	85,279	82,233
Portage	33,590	—
Port Huron	35,794	36,084
Quakertown North (U)	7,101	—
River Rouge	15,947	18,147
Riverview	11,342	7,237
Rochester	7,054	5,431
Rogers City	4,275	4,722
Roseville	60,529	50,195
Royal Oak	85,499	80,612
Saginaw	91,849	98,265
St. Clair	4,770	4,538
St. Clair Shores	88,093	76,657
St. Johns	6,672	5,629
St. Joseph	11,042	11,755
Saline	4,811	2,334
Sault Ste Marie	15,136	18,722
Southfield	69,285	31,501
Southgate	33,909	29,404
South Haven	6,471	6,149
Springfield Place (U)	4,831	5,136

Place	POPULATION 1970	1960
Sterling Heights	61,365	—
Sturgis	9,295	8,915
Swartz Creek	4,928	3,006
Taylor	70,020	—
Tecumseh	7,120	7,045
Three Rivers	7,355	7,092
Traverse City	18,048	18,432
Trenton	24,127	18,439
Troy	39,419	19,402
Walker	11,492	—
Warren	179,260	89,246
Wayne	21,054	16,034
Westland	86,749	—
Westwood (U)	9,143	—
White Lake-Seven Harbors (U)	4,504	2,748
Wolverine Lake	4,301	2,404
Wurtsmith (U)	6,932	—
Wyandotte	41,061	43,519
Wyoming	56,560	45,829
Ypsilanti	29,538	20,957
Zeeland	4,734	3,702
Minnesota	**3,805,069**	**3,413,864**
Albert Lea	19,418	17,108
Alexandria	6,973	6,713
Anoka	13,489	10,562
Apple Valley	8,502	—
Arden Hills	5,628	3,930
Austin	25,074	27,908
Bemidji	11,490	9,958
Blaine	20,640	7,570
Bloomington	81,970	50,498
Brainerd	11,667	12,898
Breckenridge	4,200	4,335
Brooklyn Center	35,173	24,356
Brooklyn Park	26,230	10,197
Burnsville	19,940	—
Chanhassen	4,879	244
Chaska	4,352	2,501
Chisholm	5,913	7,144
Cloquet	8,699	9,013
Columbia Heights	23,997	17,533
Coon Rapids	30,505	14,931
Cottage Grove	13,419	—
Crookston	8,312	8,546
Crystal	30,925	24,283
Detroit Lakes	5,797	5,633
Duluth	100,578	106,884
East Grand Forks	7,607	6,998
Eden Prairie	6,938	—
Edina	44,046	28,501
Ely	4,904	5,438
Eveleth	4,721	5,721
Fairmont	10,751	9,745
Falcon Heights	5,507	5,927
Faribault	16,595	16,926
Fergus Falls	12,443	13,733
Fridley	29,233	15,173
Glencoe	4,217	3,216
Golden Valley	24,246	14,559
Grand Rapids	7,247	7,265
Hastings	12,195	8,965
Hibbing	16,104	17,731
Hopkins	13,428	11,370
Hutchinson	8,031	6,207
International Falls	6,439	6,778
Inver Grove Heights	12,148	—
Lakeville	7,556	924
Litchfield	5,262	5,078
Little Falls	7,467	7,551
Luverne	4,703	4,249
Mankato	30,895	23,797
Maple Grove	6,275	2,213
Maplewood	25,222	18,519
Marshall	9,886	6,681
Mendota Heights	6,165	5,028
Minneapolis	434,400	482,872
Minnetonka	35,776	25,037
Montevideo	5,661	5,693
Moorhead	29,687	22,934
Morris	5,366	4,199
Mound	7,572	5,440
Mounds View	9,988	6,416
New Brighton	19,507	6,448
New Hope	23,180	3,552
New Ulm	13,051	11,114
Northfield	10,235	8,707
North Mankato	7,347	5,927
North St. Paul	11,950	8,520
Oakdale	7,304	—
Orono	6,787	5,643
Owatonna	15,341	13,409
Pipestone	5,328	5,324
Plymouth	17,593	9,576
Red Wing	10,441	10,528
Redwood Falls	4,774	4,285
Richfield	47,231	42,523
Robbinsdale	16,845	16,381
Rochester	53,766	40,663
Roseville	34,518	23,997
St. Anthony	9,239	5,084
St. Cloud	39,691	33,815

Place	POPULATION 1970	1960
St. Louis Park	48,883	43,310
St. Paul	309,980	313,411
St. Paul Park	5,587	3,267
St. Peter	8,339	8,484
Sauk Rapids	5,051	4,038
Shakopee	6,876	5,201
Shoreview	11,034	7,157
Shorewood	4,223	3,197
South St. Paul	25,016	22,032
Spring Lake Park	6,417	3,260
Stillwater	10,191	8,310
Thief River Falls	8,618	7,151
Two Harbors	4,437	4,695
Virginia	12,450	14,034
Wadena	4,640	4,381
Waseca	6,789	5,898
West St. Paul	18,799	13,101
White Bear Lake	23,313	12,849
Willmar	12,869	10,417
Winona	26,438	24,895
Woodbury	6,184	—
Worthington	9,825	9,015
Mississippi	**2,216,912**	**2,178,141**
Aberdeen	6,157	6,450
Amory	7,236	6,474
Bay St. Louis	6,752	5,073
Biloxi	48,486	44,053
Booneville	5,895	3,480
Brookhaven	10,700	9,885
Canton	10,503	9,707
Clarksdale	21,673	21,105
Cleveland	13,327	10,172
Clinton	7,246	3,438
Columbia	7,587	7,117
Columbus	25,795	24,771
Corinth	11,581	11,453
D'Iberville (U)	7,288	3,005
Ellisville	4,643	4,592
Greenville	39,648	41,502
Greenwood	22,400	20,436
Grenada	9,944	7,914
Gulfport	40,791	30,204
Hattiesburg	38,277	34,989
Hazlehurst	4,577	3,400
Holly Springs	5,728	5,621
Indianola	8,947	6,714
Jackson	153,968	144,422
Kosciusko	7,266	6,800
Laurel	24,145	27,889
Leland	6,000	6,295
Long Beach	6,170	4,770
Louisville	6,626	5,066
McComb	11,969	12,020
Meridian	45,083	49,374
Moss Point	19,321	6,631
Natchez	19,704	23,791
New Albany	6,426	5,151
Ocean Springs	9,580	5,025
Oxford	13,846	5,283
Pascagoula	27,264	17,155
Pearl (U)	9,623	5,081
Petal (U)	6,986	4,007
Philadelphia	6,274	5,017
Picayune	10,467	7,834
Senatobia	4,247	3,259
Southaven (U)	8,931	—
Starkville	11,369	9,041
State College (U)	4,595	—
Tupelo	20,471	17,221
Vicksburg	25,478	29,143
Waynesboro	4,368	3,892
West Gulfport (U)	6,996	3,323
West Point	8,714	8,550
Winona	5,521	4,282
Yazoo City	10,796	11,236
Missouri	**4,677,399**	**4,319,813**
Afton (U)	24,067	—
Aurora	5,359	4,683
Ballwin	10,656	5,710
Bellefontaine Neighbors	13,987	13,650
Bel-Ridge	5,561	4,395
Belton	9,783	4,897
Berkeley	19,743	18,676
Blue Springs	6,779	2,555
Bolivar	4,769	3,512
Boonville	7,514	7,090
Breckenridge Hills	7,011	6,299
Brentwood	11,248	12,250
Bridgeton	19,992	7,820
Brookfield	5,491	5,694
Cape Girardeau	31,282	24,947
Carrollton	4,847	4,554
Carthage	11,035	11,264
Caruthersville	7,350	8,643
Charleston	5,131	5,911
Chillicothe	9,519	9,236
Clayton	16,222	15,245
Clinton	7,504	6,925
Columbia	58,804	36,650
Concord (U)	21,217	—

Place	POPULATION 1970	1960
Missouri (continued)		
Crestwood	15,398	11,106
Creve Coeur	8,967	5,122
Dellwood	7,137	4,720
De Soto	5,984	5,804
Des Peres	5,333	4,362
Dexter	6,024	5,519
Ellisville	4,681	2,732
Excelsior Springs	9,411	6,473
Farmington	6,590	5,618
Ferguson	28,915	22,149
Festus	7,530	7,021
Flat River	4,550	4,515
Florissant	65,908	38,166
Fort Leonard Wood (U)	33,799	—
Fulton	12,148	11,131
Gladstone	23,128	14,502
Glendale	6,891	7,048
Grandview	17,456	6,027
Hannibal	18,609	20,028
Harrisonville	4,928	3,510
Hazelwood	14,082	6,045
Higginsville	4,318	4,003
Independence	111,662	62,328
Jackson	5,896	4,875
Jefferson City	32,407	28,228
Jennings	19,379	19,965
Joplin	39,256	38,958
Kansas City	507,087	475,539
Kennett	9,852	9,098
Kinloch	5,629	6,501
Kirksville	15,560	13,123
Kirkwood	31,890	29,421
Ladue	10,491	9,466
Lebanon	8,616	8,220
Lee's Summit	16,230	8,267
Lemay (U)	40,115	—
Lexington	5,388	4,845
Liberty	13,679	8,909
Louisiana	4,533	4,286
Macon	5,301	4,547
Malden	5,374	5,007
Manchester	5,031	2,021
Maplewood	12,785	12,552
Marshall	11,847	9,572
Maryland Heights (U)	8,805	—
Maryville	9,970	7,807
Mexico	11,807	12,889
Moberly	12,988	13,170
Monett	5,937	5,359
Neosho	7,517	7,452
Nevada	9,736	8,416
Normandy	6,306	4,452
North Kansas City	5,183	5,657
Northwoods	4,611	4,701
O'Fallon	7,018	3,770
Olivette	9,341	8,257
Overland	24,949	22,763
Pagedale	5,571	5,106
Perryville	5,149	5,117
Pine Lawn	5,773	5,943
Poplar Bluff	16,653	15,926
Raytown	33,632	17,083
Richmond	4,948	4,604
Richmond Heights	13,802	15,622
Rock Hill	7,275	6,523
Rolla	13,245	11,132
St. Ann	18,215	12,155
St. Charles	31,834	21,189
Ste. Genevieve	4,468	4,443
St. John	8,960	7,342
St. Joseph	72,691	79,673
St. Louis	622,236	750,026
Salem	4,363	3,870
Sappington (U)	10,603	—
Sedalia	22,847	23,874
Shrewsbury	5,896	4,730
Sikeston	14,699	13,765
Spanish Lake (U)	15,647	—
Springfield	120,096	95,865
Sugar Creek	4,755	2,663
Sullivan	5,100	4,098
Trenton	6,063	6,262
Union	5,183	3,937
University City	46,309	51,249
Warrensburg	13,125	9,689
Washington	8,499	7,961
Webb City	6,811	6,740
Webster Groves	26,995	28,990
Wellston	7,050	7,979
West Plains	6,893	5,836
Whiteman (U)	5,040	—
Woodson Terrace	5,936	6,048
Montana	**694,409**	**674,767**
Anaconda	9,771	12,054
Billings	61,581	52,851
Bozeman	18,670	13,361
Butte	23,368	27,877
Deer Lodge	4,306	4,681
Dillon	4,548	3,690

Place	POPULATION 1970	1960
Floral Park (U)	5,113	4,079
Glasgow	4,700	6,398
Glendive	6,305	7,058
Great Falls	60,091	55,244
Havre	10,558	10,740
Helena	22,730	20,227
Kalispell	10,526	10,151
Laurel	4,454	4,601
Lewistown	6,437	7,408
Livingston	6,883	8,229
Malmstrom (U)	8,374	—
Miles City	9,023	9,665
Missoula	29,497	27,090
Missoula South (U)	4,886	—
Missoula West (U)	9,148	—
Sidney	4,543	4,564
Silver Bow Park (U)	5,524	4,798
Nebraska	**1,483,791**	**1,411,330**
Alliance	6,862	7,845
Beatrice	12,389	12,132
Bellevue	19,449	8,831
Blair	6,106	4,931
Chadron	5,853	5,079
Columbus	15,471	12,476
Cozad	4,219	3,184
Crete	4,444	3,546
Fairbury	5,265	5,572
Falls City	5,444	5,598
Fremont	22,962	19,698
Gering	5,639	4,585
Grand Island	31,269	25,742
Hastings	23,580	21,412
Holdrege	5,635	5,226
Kearney	19,181	14,210
La Vista	4,807	—
Lexington	5,618	5,572
Lincoln	149,518	128,521
McCook	8,285	8,301
Millard	7,460	1,014
Nebraska City	7,441	7,252
Norfolk	16,607	13,640
North Platte	19,447	17,184
Offutt East (U)	5,195	—
Offutt West (U)	8,445	—
Ogallala	4,976	4,250
Omaha	347,328	301,598
Papillion	5,606	2,235
Plattsmouth	6,371	6,244
Ralston	4,265	2,977
Scottsbluff	14,507	13,377
Seward	5,294	4,208
Sidney	6,403	8,004
South Sioux City	7,920	7,200
Wayne	5,379	4,217
Nevada	**488,738**	**285,278**
Boulder City	5,223	4,059
Carson City	15,468	5,163
East Las Vegas (U)	6,501	—
Elko	7,621	6,298
Henderson	16,395	12,525
Las Vegas	125,787	64,405
Nellis (U)	6,449	—
North Las Vegas	36,216	18,422
Paradise (U)	24,477	—
Reno	72,863	51,470
Sparks	24,187	16,618
Sunrise Manor (U)	10,886	—
Vegas Creek (U)	8,970	—
Winchester (U)	13,981	—
New Hampshire	**737,681**	**606,921**
Berlin	15,256	17,821
Claremont	14,221	13,563
Concord	30,022	28,991
Derry (U)	6,090	—
Dover	20,850	19,131
Durham (U)	7,221	4,688
Exeter (U)	6,439	5,896
Franklin	7,292	6,742
Hampton (U)	5,407	3,281
Hanover (U)	6,147	5,649
Keene	20,467	17,562
Laconia	14,888	15,288
Lebanon	9,725	9,299
Manchester	87,754	88,282
Milford (U)	4,997	3,916
Nashua	55,820	39,096
Portsmouth	25,717	26,900
Rochester	17,938	15,927
Somersworth	9,026	8,529
Suncook (U)	4,280	2,318
New Jersey	**7,168,164**	**6,066,782**
Absecon	6,094	4,320
Allendale	6,240	4,092
Asbury Park	16,533	17,366
Atlantic City	47,859	59,544
Atlantic Highlands	5,102	4,119
Audubon	10,802	10,440
Barrington	8,409	7,943
Bayonne	72,743	74,215

Place	POPULATION 1970	1960
Beachwood	4,390	2,765
Belleville	34,643	35,005
Bellmawr	15,618	11,853
Belmar	5,782	5,190
Bergenfield	33,131	27,203
Berlin	4,997	3,578
Bernardsville	6,652	5,515
Bloomfield	52,029	51,867
Bloomingdale	7,797	5,293
Bogota	8,125	7,965
Boonton	9,261	7,981
Bordentown	4,490	4,974
Bound Brook	10,450	10,263
Bridgeton	20,435	20,966
Brigantine	6,741	4,201
Browns Mills (U)	7,144	—
Burlington	11,991	12,687
Butler	7,051	5,414
Caldwell	8,719	6,942
Camden	102,551	117,159
Candlewood (U)	5,629	—
Cape May	4,392	4,477
Carlstadt	7,947	6,042
Carteret	23,137	20,502
Chatham	9,566	9,517
Clayton	5,193	4,711
Clementon	4,492	3,766
Cliffside Park	14,387	17,642
Cliffwood-Cliffwood Beach (U)	7,056	—
Clifton	82,437	82,084
Closter	8,604	7,767
Collingswood	17,422	17,370
Cresskill	7,164	7,290
Demarest	6,262	4,231
Dover	15,039	13,034
Dumont	17,534	18,882
Dunellen	7,072	6,840
East Orange	75,471	77,259
East Paterson	22,749	19,344
East Rutherford	8,536	7,769
Eatontown	14,619	10,334
Edgewater	4,849	4,113
Egg Harbor City	4,304	4,416
Elizabeth	112,654	107,698
Emerson	8,428	6,849
Englewood	24,985	26,057
Englewood Cliffs	5,938	2,913
Fairfield	6,731	—
Fair Haven	6,142	5,678
Fair Lawn	37,975	36,421
Fairview	10,698	9,399
Fanwood	8,920	7,963
Florence-Roebling (U)	7,551	—
Florham Park	8,094	7,222
Fort Dix (U)	26,290	—
Fort Lee	30,631	21,815
Franklin	4,236	3,624
Franklin Lakes	7,550	3,316
Freehold	10,545	9,140
Garfield	30,722	29,253
Garwood	5,260	5,426
Gilford Park (U)	4,007	1,560
Glassboro	12,938	10,253
Glen Ridge	8,518	8,322
Glen Rock	13,011	12,896
Gloucester City	14,707	15,511
Guttenberg	5,754	5,118
Hackensack	35,911	30,521
Hackettstown	9,472	5,276
Haddonfield	13,118	13,201
Haddon Heights	9,365	9,260
Haledon	6,767	6,161
Hammonton	11,464	9,854
Harrington Park	4,841	3,581
Harrison	11,811	11,743
Hasbrouck Heights	13,651	13,046
Hawthorne	19,173	17,735
Highland Park	14,385	11,049
Hightstown	5,431	4,317
Hillsdale	11,768	8,734
Hoboken	45,380	48,441
Hohokus	4,348	3,988
Hopatcong	9,052	3,391
Irvington	59,743	59,379
Jamesburg	4,584	2,853
Jersey City	260,545	276,101
Keansburg	9,720	6,854
Kearny	37,585	37,472
Kendall Park (U)	7,412	—
Kenilworth	9,165	8,379
Keyport	7,205	6,440
Kinnelon	7,600	4,431
Lake Hiawatha (U)	11,389	—
Lake Mohawk (U)	6,262	4,647
Lake Parsippany (U)	7,488	—
Lakewood (U)	17,874	13,004
Lambertville	4,359	4,269
Laurence Harbor (U)	6,715	—
Leonia	8,847	8,384
Lincoln Park	9,034	6,048
Linden	41,409	39,931
Lindenwold	12,199	7,335
Linwood	6,159	3,847

Place	POPULATION 1970	POPULATION 1960
New Jersey (continued)		
Little Ferry	9,042	6,175
Little Silver	6,010	5,202
Lodi	25,213	23,502
Long Branch	31,774	26,228
McGuire (U)	10,933	—
Madison	16,710	15,122
Magnolia	5,893	4,199
Manasquan	4,971	4,022
Manville	13,029	10,995
Margate City	10,576	9,474
Marlton (U)	10,180	—
Matawan	9,136	5,097
Maywood	11,087	11,460
Medford Lakes	4,792	2,876
Mercerville-Hamilton Square (U)	24,465	—
Merchantville	4,425	4,075
Metuchen	16,031	14,041
Middlesex	15,038	10,520
Midland Park	8,159	7,543
Milltown	6,470	5,435
Millville	21,366	19,096
Montclair	44,043	43,129
Montvale	7,327	3,699
Moorestown-Lenola (U)	14,179	—
Morris Plains	5,540	4,703
Morristown	17,662	17,712
Mountain Lakes	4,739	4,037
Mountainside	7,520	6,325
Mount Ephraim	5,625	5,447
Neptune City	5,502	4,013
Newark	382,417	405,220
New Brunswick	41,885	40,139
New Milford	20,201	18,810
New Providence	13,796	10,243
New Shrewsbury	5,925	7,313
Newton	7,297	6,563
North Arlington	18,096	17,477
North Caldwell	6,425	4,163
Northfield	8,875	5,849
North Haledon	7,614	6,026
North Plainfield	21,796	16,993
Northvale	5,177	2,892
Norwood	4,398	2,852
Nutley	32,099	29,513
Oakhurst (U)	5,558	4,374
Oakland	14,420	9,446
Oaklyn	4,626	4,778
Ocean City	10,575	7,618
Oceanport	7,503	4,937
Old Bridge (U)	25,176	—
Oradell	8,903	7,487
Orange	32,566	35,789
Palisades Park	13,351	11,943
Palmyra	6,969	7,036
Paramus	29,495	23,238
Park Ridge	8,709	6,389
Passaic	55,124	53,963
Paterson	144,824	143,663
Paulsboro	8,084	8,121
Penns Grove	5,727	6,176
Pennsville (U)	11,014	—
Perth Amboy	38,798	38,007
Phillipsburg	17,849	18,502
Pine Hill	5,132	3,939
Pitman	10,257	8,644
Plainfield	46,862	45,330
Pleasantville	13,778	15,172
Point Pleasant	15,968	10,182
Point Pleasant Beach	4,882	3,873
Pompton Lakes	11,397	9,445
Princeton	12,311	11,890
Princeton North (U)	5,488	4,506
Prospect Park	5,176	5,201
Rahway	29,114	27,699
Ramblewood (U)	5,556	—
Ramsey	12,571	9,527
Raritan	6,691	6,137
Red Bank	12,847	12,482
Ridgefield	11,308	10,788
Ridgefield Park	14,453	12,701
Ridgewood	27,547	25,391
Ringwood	10,393	4,182
River Edge	12,850	13,264
Rockaway	6,383	5,413
Roseland	4,453	2,804
Roselle	22,585	21,032
Roselle Park	14,277	12,546
Rumson	7,421	6,405
Runnemede	10,475	8,396
Rutherford	20,802	20,473
Salem	7,648	8,941
Sayreville	32,508	22,553
Secaucus	13,228	12,154
Somerdale	6,510	4,839
Somers Point	7,919	4,504
Somerville	13,652	12,458
South Amboy	9,338	8,422
South Bound Brook	4,525	3,626
South Orange	16,971	16,175
South Plainfield	21,142	17,879
South River	15,428	13,397

Place	POPULATION 1970	POPULATION 1960
Spotswood	7,891	5,788
Spring Lake Heights	4,602	3,309
Stratford	9,801	4,308
Strathmore (U)	7,674	—
Summit	23,620	23,677
Tenafly	14,827	14,264
Toms River (U)	7,303	6,062
Totowa	11,580	10,897
Trenton	104,638	114,167
Union Beach	6,472	5,862
Union City	58,537	52,180
Upper Saddle River	7,949	3,570
Ventnor City	10,385	8,688
Verona	15,067	13,782
Vineland	47,399	37,685
Waldwick	12,313	10,495
Wallington	10,284	9,261
Wanaque	8,636	7,126
Washington	5,943	5,723
Watchung	4,750	3,312
West Caldwell	11,887	8,314
Westfield	33,720	31,447
West Long Branch	6,845	5,337
West New York	40,627	35,547
West Orange	43,715	39,895
West Paterson	11,692	7,602
Westville	5,170	4,951
Westwood	11,105	9,046
Wharton	5,535	5,006
White Horse-Yardville (U)	18,680	—
White Meadow Lake (U)	8,499	—
Woodbury	12,408	12,453
Woodcliff Lake	5,506	2,742
Wood-Ridge	8,311	7,964
New Mexico	**1,016,000**	**951,023**
Alamogordo	23,035	21,723
Albuquerque	243,751	201,189
Artesia	10,315	12,000
Belen	4,823	5,031
Cannon (U)	5,461	—
Carlsbad	21,297	25,541
Clovis	28,495	23,713
Deming	8,343	6,764
Espanola	4,528	1,976
Farmington	21,979	23,786
Gallup	14,596	14,089
Grants	8,768	10,274
Hobbs	26,025	26,275
Holloman (U)	8,001	—
Las Cruces	37,857	29,367
Las Vegas city	7,528	7,790
Las Vegas town	6,307	6,028
Los Alamos (U)	11,310	12,584
Lovington	8,915	9,660
North Valley (U)	10,366	—
Portales	10,554	9,695
Raton	6,962	8,146
Roswell	33,908	39,593
Sandia (U)	6,867	—
Santa Fe	41,167	33,394
Silver City	7,751	6,972
Socorro	4,687	5,271
South Valley (U)	29,389	—
Truth or Consequences	4,656	4,269
Tucumcari	7,189	8,143
New York	**18,190,740**	**16,782,304**
Albany	114,873	129,726
Albertson (U)	6,792	—
Albion	5,122	5,182
Amityville	9,857	8,318
Amsterdam	25,524	28,772
Ardsley	4,470	3,991
Arlington (U)	11,203	8,317
Auburn	34,599	35,249
Babylon	12,588	11,062
Baldwin (U)	34,525	30,204
Baldwinsville	6,298	5,985
Ballston Spa	4,968	4,991
Batavia	17,338	18,210
Bath	6,053	6,166
Bayport (U)	7,995	—
Bay Shore (U)	11,119	—
Bayville	6,147	3,962
Beacon	13,255	13,922
Bellmore (U)	18,431	12,784
Bethpage (U)	18,555	20,515
Binghamton	64,123	75,941
Blauvelt (U)	5,426	—
Bohemia (U)	8,718	—
Brentwood (U)	27,868	15,387
Briarcliff Manor	6,521	5,105
Brockport	7,878	5,256
Bronxville	6,674	6,744
Buffalo	462,768	532,759
Canandaigua	10,488	9,370
Canastota	5,033	4,896
Canton	6,398	5,046
Carle Place (U)	6,326	—
Catskill	5,317	5,825
Cedarhurst	6,941	6,954
Centereach (U)	9,427	8,524

Place	POPULATION 1970	POPULATION 1960
Central Islip (U)	36,369	—
Clifton Knolls (U)	5,771	—
Cobleskill	4,368	3,471
Cohoes	18,613	20,129
Cold Spring Harbor (U)	5,498	1,705
Colonie	8,701	6,992
Commack (U)	22,507	9,613
Congers (U)	5,928	—
Copiague (U)	19,578	14,081
Corning	15,792	17,085
Cortland	19,621	19,181
Croton-on-Hudson	7,523	6,812
Dansville	5,436	5,460
Deer Park (U)	31,120	16,726
Depew	22,158	13,580
De Witt (U)	10,032	—
Dix Hills (U)	9,840	—
Dobbs Ferry	10,353	9,260
Dunkirk	16,855	18,205
East Aurora	7,033	6,791
Eastchester (U)	21,330	—
East Glenville (U)	5,898	—
East Half Hollow Hills (U)	9,691	—
East Hills	8,675	7,184
East Islip (U)	6,819	—
East Massapequa (U)	15,926	14,779
East Meadow (U)	46,252	46,036
East Neck (U)	5,144	3,789
East Northport (U)	12,392	8,381
East Patchogue (U)	8,092	—
East Rochester	8,347	8,152
East Rockaway	10,323	10,721
East Syracuse	4,333	4,708
East Vestal (U)	10,472	—
Ellenville	4,482	5,003
Elmira	39,945	46,517
Elmira Heights	4,906	5,157
Elmont (U)	29,363	30,138
Elwood (U)	15,031	—
Endicott	16,556	18,775
Endwell (U)	15,999	—
Fairmount (U)	15,317	—
Fairport	6,474	5,507
Fairview (U)	8,517	8,626
Farmingdale	9,297	6,128
Fayetteville	4,996	4,311
Floral Park	18,422	17,499
Flower Hill	4,236	4,594
Franklin Square (U)	32,156	32,483
Fredonia	10,326	8,477
Freeport	40,374	34,419
Fulton	14,003	14,261
Garden City	25,373	23,948
Garden City Park (U)	7,488	—
Gardnertown (U)	4,614	—
Geneseo	5,714	3,284
Geneva	16,793	17,286
Glen Cove	25,770	23,817
Glens Falls	17,222	18,580
Gloversville	19,677	21,741
Goshen	4,342	3,906
Gouverneur	4,574	4,946
Great Neck	10,724	10,171
Great Neck Plaza	5,921	4,948
Greenlawn (U)	8,178	5,422
Half Hollow Hills (U)	12,055	—
Hamburg	10,215	9,145
Hartsdale (U)	12,226	—
Hastings-on-Hudson	9,479	8,979
Hauppauge (U)	13,957	—
Haverstraw	8,198	5,771
Hempstead	39,411	34,641
Herkimer	8,960	9,396
Herricks (U)	9,112	—
Hewlett	6,796	—
Hicksville (U)	48,075	50,405
Highland Falls	4,638	4,469
Hillcrest	5,357	—
Holbrook-Holtsville (U)	12,103	—
Hornell	12,144	13,907
Horseheads	7,989	7,207
Hudson	8,940	11,075
Hudson Falls	7,917	7,752
Huntington	12,130	11,255
Huntington Station (U)	28,817	23,438
Ilion	9,808	10,199
Inwood (U)	8,433	10,362
Irvington	5,878	5,494
Island Park	5,396	3,846
Islip (U)	7,692	—
Ithaca	26,226	28,799
Jamestown	39,795	41,818
Jefferson Valley-Yorktown (U)	9,008	—
Jericho (U)	14,010	10,795
Johnson City	18,025	19,118
Johnstown	10,045	10,390
Kenmore	20,980	21,261
Kings Park (U)	5,555	4,949
Kings Point	5,525	5,410
Kingston	25,544	29,260
Lackawanna	28,657	29,564
Lake Carmel (U)	4,796	2,735
Lake Grove	8,133	—

Place	POPULATION 1970	POPULATION 1960
New York (continued)		
Lakeview (U)	5,471	—
Lancaster	13,365	12,254
Larchmont	7,203	6,789
Latham (U)	9,661	—
Lawrence	6,566	5,907
Le Roy	5,118	4,662
Levittown (U)	65,440	65,276
Liberty	4,293	4,704
Lindenhurst	28,338	20,905
Little Falls	7,629	8,935
Lockport	25,399	26,443
Locust Grove (U)	11,626	11,558
Long Beach	33,127	26,473
Loudonville (U)	9,299	—
Lynbrook	23,776	19,881
Lyons	4,496	4,673
Mahopac (U)	5,265	1,337
Malone	8,048	8,737
Malverne	10,036	9,968
Mamaroneck	18,909	17,673
Manhasset (U)	8,541	—
Manlius	4,295	1,997
Manorhaven	5,710	3,566
Massapequa (U)	26,951	32,900
Massapequa Park	22,112	19,904
Massena	14,042	15,478
Mastic Beach (U)	4,870	3,035
Mattydale (U)	8,292	—
Mechanicville	6,247	6,831
Medina	6,415	6,681
Melville (U)	5,999	—
Merrick (U)	25,904	18,789
Middletown	22,607	23,475
Mineola	21,845	20,519
Monroe	4,439	3,323
Monsey (U)	8,797	—
Monticello	5,991	5,222
Mount Kisco	8,172	6,805
Mount Vernon	72,778	76,010
Nanuet (U)	10,447	—
Nesconset (U)	10,048	1,964
Newark	11,644	12,868
Newburgh	26,219	30,979
New Cassel (U)	8,554	—
New City (U)	27,344	—
New Hyde Park	10,116	10,808
New Paltz	6,058	3,041
New Rochelle	75,385	76,812
New Windsor Center (U)	8,803	4,041
New York	7,867,760	7,781,984
Niagara Falls	85,615	102,394
Nimmonsburg-Chenango Bridge (U)	5,059	—
Niskayuna (U)	6,186	—
North Amityville (U)	11,905	—
North Babylon (U)	39,556	—
North Bellmore (U)	22,893	19,639
North Bellport (U)	5,903	—
North Great River (U)	12,080	—
North Lindenhurst (U)	11,205	—
North Massapequa (U)	23,101	—
North Merrick (U)	13,650	12,976
North New Hyde Park (U)	17,945	17,929
North Patchogue (U)	6,383	—
North Pelham	5,184	5,326
Northport	7,440	5,972
North Syracuse	8,687	7,412
North Tarrytown	8,334	8,818
North Tonawanda	36,012	34,757
North Valley Stream (U)	14,881	17,239
North Wantagh (U)	15,053	—
Norwich	8,843	9,175
Nyack	6,659	6,062
Oakdale (U)	7,334	—
Oceanside (U)	35,028	30,488
Ogdensburg	14,554	16,122
Old Bethpage (U)	7,084	—
Olean	19,169	21,868
Oneida	11,658	11,677
Oneonta	16,030	13,412
Orange Lake (U)	4,348	—
Ossining	21,659	18,662
Oswego	23,844	22,155
Owego	5,152	5,417
Patchogue	11,582	8,838
Pearl River (U)	17,146	—
Peekskill	18,881	18,737
Pelham Manor	6,673	6,114
Penn Yan	5,168	5,770
Perry	4,538	4,629
Plainedge (U)	10,759	21,973
Plainview (U)	32,195	27,710
Plattsburgh	18,715	20,172
Plattsburgh Base (U)	7,078	—
Pleasantville	7,110	5,877
Port Chester	25,803	24,960
Port Jefferson	5,515	—
Port Jefferson Station (U)	7,403	1,041
Port Jervis	8,852	9,268
Port Washington (U)	15,923	15,657
Potsdam	9,985	7,765
Poughkeepsie	32,029	38,330
Rensselaer	10,136	10,506
Riverhead (U)	7,585	5,830
Rochester	296,233	318,611
Rockville Centre	27,444	26,355
Roessleville (U)	5,476	—
Rome	50,148	51,646
Ronkonkoma (U)	7,284	4,220
Roosevelt (U)	15,008	12,883
Roslyn Heights (U)	7,140	—
Rotterdam (U)	25,153	16,871
Rye	15,869	14,225
St. James (U)	10,818	3,524
Salamanca	7,877	8,480
San Remo (U)	8,302	3,160
Saranac Lake	6,086	6,421
Saratoga Springs	18,845	16,630
Sayville (U)	11,680	—
Scarsdale	19,229	17,968
Schenectady	77,859	81,682
Scotia	8,224	7,625
Sea Cliff	5,890	5,669
Seaford (U)	17,379	14,718
Selden (U)	11,613	1,604
Seneca Falls	7,794	7,439
Setauket-South Setauket (U)	6,857	—
Shirley (U)	6,280	—
Sidney	4,789	5,157
Sloan	5,216	5,803
Solvay	8,280	8,732
Southampton	4,904	4,582
South Farmingdale (U)	20,464	16,318
South Holbrook (U)	6,700	—
South Huntington (U)	8,946	7,084
Southport (U)	8,685	—
South Stony Brook (U)	15,329	—
South Valley Stream (U)	6,595	—
South Westbury (U)	10,978	11,977
Spring Valley	18,112	6,538
Springville	4,350	3,852
Stony Brook (U)	6,391	3,548
Stony Point (U)	8,270	3,330
Suffern	8,273	5,094
Syosset (U)	9,970	—
Syracuse	197,208	216,038
Tappan (U)	7,424	—
Tarrytown	11,115	11,109
Thornwood (U)	6,874	—
Tonawanda	21,898	21,561
Troy	62,918	67,492
Tuckahoe	6,236	6,423
Tupper Lake	4,854	5,200
Uniondale (U)	22,077	20,041
Utica	91,611	100,410
Valley Cottage (U)	6,007	—
Valley Stream	40,413	38,629
Vernon Valley (U)	7,925	5,998
Vestal-Twin Orchards (U)	8,303	—
Viola (U)	5,136	—
Walden	5,277	4,851
Wantagh (U)	21,873	34,172
Wappingers Falls	5,607	4,447
Waterloo	5,418	5,098
Watertown	30,787	33,306
Watervliet	12,404	13,917
Waverly	5,261	5,950
Webster	5,037	3,060
Wellsville	5,815	5,967
West Amityville (U)	6,393	—
West Babylon (U)	12,788	—
Westbury	15,362	14,757
West Elmira (U)	5,901	5,763
West Haverstraw	8,558	5,020
West Hempstead (U)	20,375	—
West Islip (U)	16,711	—
Westmere (U)	6,364	—
West Nyack (U)	5,510	—
West Sayville (U)	7,386	—
Westvale (U)	7,253	—
White Plains	50,220	50,485
Whitesboro	4,805	4,784
Williamsville	6,835	6,316
Williston Park	9,154	8,255
Woodmere (U)	19,831	14,011
Wyandanch (U)	14,906	—
Yaphank (U)	5,460	—
Yonkers	204,370	190,634
Yorktown Heights (U)	6,805	2,478
North Carolina	**5,082,059**	**4,556,155**
Ahoskie	5,105	4,583
Albemarle	11,126	12,261
Archdale	6,103	1,520
Asheboro	10,797	9,449
Asheville	57,681	60,192
Balfours (U)	4,836	3,805
Belmont	4,814	5,007
Bessemer City	5,217	4,017
Boone	8,754	3,686
Brevard	5,243	4,857
Burlington	35,930	33,199
Camp Lejeune (U)	34,549	—
Canton	5,158	5,068
Cary	7,430	3,356
Chapel Hill	25,537	12,573
Charlotte	241,178	201,564
Cherry Point (U)	12,029	—
Cherryville	5,258	3,607
Clinton	7,157	7,461
Concord	18,464	17,799
Dunn	8,302	7,566
Durham	95,438	78,302
Eden	15,871	—
Edenton	4,766	4,458
Elizabeth City	14,069	14,062
Farmville	4,424	3,997
Fayetteville	53,510	47,106
Forest City	7,179	6,556
Fort Bragg (U)	46,995	—
Garner	4,923	3,451
Gastonia	47,142	37,276
Goldsboro	26,810	28,873
Graham	8,172	7,723
Greensboro	144,076	119,574
Greenville	29,063	22,860
Hamlet	4,627	4,460
Havelock	5,283	2,433
Henderson	13,896	12,740
Hendersonville	6,443	5,911
Hickory	20,569	19,328
High Point	63,204	60,685
Jacksonville	16,021	13,491
Kannapolis (U)	36,293	34,647
Kernersville	4,815	2,942
Kings Mountain	8,465	8,008
Kinston	22,309	24,819
Laurinburg	8,859	8,242
Lenoir	14,705	10,257
Lexington	17,205	16,093
Lincolnton	5,293	5,699
Lumberton	16,961	15,305
Monroe	11,282	10,882
Mooresville	8,808	6,918
Morehead City	5,233	5,583
Morganton	13,625	9,186
Mount Airy	7,325	7,055
Mount Holly	5,107	4,037
Mount Olive	4,914	4,673
New Bern	14,660	15,717
New River-Gieger (U)	8,699	—
Newton	7,857	6,658
North Belmont (U)	10,759	8,328
Oxford	7,178	6,978
Plymouth	4,774	4,666
Raleigh	121,577	93,931
Reidsville	13,636	14,267
Roanoke Rapids	13,508	13,320
Rockingham	5,852	5,512
Rocky Mount	34,284	32,147
Roxboro	5,370	5,147
Salisbury	22,515	21,297
Sanford	11,716	12,253
Selma	4,356	3,102
Seymour-Johnson (U)	8,172	—
Shelby	16,328	17,698
Siler City	4,689	4,455
Smithfield	6,677	6,117
Southern Pines	5,937	5,198
Statesville	19,996	19,844
Tarboro	9,425	8,411
Thomasville	15,230	15,190
Washington	8,961	9,939
Waynesville	6,488	6,159
West Concord (U)	5,347	5,510
Williamston	6,570	6,924
Wilmington	46,169	44,013
Wilson	29,347	28,753
Winston-Salem	132,913	111,135
North Dakota	**617,761**	**632,446**
Bismarck	34,703	27,670
Devils Lake	7,078	6,299
Dickinson	12,405	9,971
Fargo	53,365	46,662
Grafton	5,946	5,885
Grand Forks	39,008	34,451
Grand Forks Base (U)	10,474	—
Jamestown	15,385	15,163
Mandan	11,093	10,525
Minot	32,290	30,604
Minot Base (U)	12,077	—
Valley City	7,843	7,809
Wahpeton	7,076	5,876
West Fargo	5,161	3,328
Williston	11,280	11,866
Ohio	**10,652,017**	**9,706,397**
Ada	5,309	3,918
Akron	275,425	290,351
Alliance	26,547	28,362
Amberley	5,574	2,951
Amherst	9,902	6,750
Ashland	19,872	17,419
Ashtabula	24,313	24,559
Athens	23,310	16,470
Aurora	6,549	4,049
Austintown (U)	29,393	—

Place	POPULATION 1970	1960
Ohio (continued)		
Avon	7,214	6,002
Avondale (U)	5,195	—
Avon Lake	12,261	9,403
Barberton	33,052	33,805
Barnesville	4,292	4,425
Bay Village	18,163	14,489
Beachwood	9,631	6,089
Bedford	17,552	15,223
Bedford Heights	13,063	5,275
Bellaire	9,655	11,502
Bellefontaine	11,255	11,424
Bellevue	8,604	8,286
Belpre	7,189	5,418
Berea	22,396	16,592
Bexley	14,888	14,319
Blacklick Estates (U)	8,351	—
Blue Ash	8,324	8,341
Boardman (U)	30,852	—
Bowling Green	21,760	13,574
Brecksville	9,137	5,435
Bridgetown (U)	13,352	—
Broadview Heights	11,463	6,209
Brooklyn	13,142	10,733
Brook Park	30,774	12,856
Brookville	4,403	3,184
Brunswick	15,852	11,725
Bryan	7,008	7,361
Bucyrus	13,111	12,276
Cambridge	13,656	14,562
Campbell	12,577	13,406
Canfield	4,997	3,252
Canton	110,053	113,631
Celina	7,779	7,659
Centerville	10,333	3,490
Chagrin Falls	4,848	3,458
Cheviot	11,135	10,701
Chillicothe	24,842	24,957
Churchill (U)	7,457	—
Cincinnati	452,524	502,550
Circleville	11,687	11,059
Cleveland	750,903	876,050
Cleveland Heights	60,767	61,813
Clyde	5,503	4,826
Columbiana	4,959	4,164
Columbus	539,677	471,316
Conneaut	14,552	10,557
Coshocton	13,747	13,106
Covedale (U)	6,639	—
Crestline	5,947	5,521
Crystal Lakes (U)	5,851	1,569
Cuyahoga Falls	49,678	47,922
Dayton	243,601	262,332
Deer Park	7,415	8,423
Defiance	16,281	14,553
Delaware	15,008	13,282
Delphos	7,608	6,961
Dover	11,516	11,300
East Cleveland	39,600	37,991
Eastlake	19,690	12,467
East Liverpool	20,020	22,306
East Liverpool North (U)	6,223	—
East Palestine	5,604	5,232
Eaton	6,020	5,034
Elyria	53,427	43,782
Englewood	7,885	1,515
Euclid	71,552	62,998
Fairborn	32,267	19,453
Fairfield	14,680	9,734
Fairlawn	6,102	—
Fairview Park	21,681	14,624
Findlay	35,800	30,344
Forest Park	15,139	—
Fort McKinley (U)	11,536	—
Fostoria	16,037	15,732
Franklin	10,075	7,917
Fremont	18,490	18,767
Gahanna	12,400	2,717
Galion	13,123	12,650
Gallipolis	7,490	8,775
Garfield Heights	41,417	38,455
Geneva	6,449	5,677
Girard	14,119	12,997
Golf Manor	5,170	4,648
Grandview Heights	8,460	8,270
Greenfield	4,780	5,422
Greenhills	6,092	5,407
Greenville	12,380	10,585
Grove City	13,911	8,107
Hamilton	67,865	72,354
Harrison	4,408	3,878
Heath	6,768	2,426
Highland Heights	5,926	2,929
Hilliard	8,369	5,633
Hillsboro	5,584	5,474
Hubbard	8,583	7,137
Huber Heights (U)	18,943	—
Huron	6,896	5,197
Independence	7,034	6,868
Indian Hill	5,651	4,526
Ironton	15,030	15,745
Jackson	6,843	6,980
Kent	28,183	17,836

Place	POPULATION 1970	1960
Kenton	8,315	8,747
Kenwood (U)	15,789	—
Kettering	69,599	54,462
Kirtland	5,530	—
Knollwood (U)	5,513	—
Lakewood	70,173	66,154
Lancaster	32,911	29,916
Lebanon	7,934	5,993
Lima	53,734	51,037
Lincoln Heights	6,099	7,798
Lincoln Village (U)	11,215	—
Lockbourne Base (U)	5,623	—
Lockland	5,288	5,292
Logan	6,269	6,417
London	6,481	6,379
Lorain	78,185	68,932
Louisville	6,298	5,116
Loveland	7,144	5,008
Lyndhurst	19,749	16,805
Macedonia	6,375	—
Madeira	6,713	6,744
Madison North (U)	6,882	—
Mansfield	55,047	47,325
Maple Heights	34,093	31,667
Mariemont	4,540	4,120
Marietta	16,861	16,847
Marion	38,646	37,079
Martins Ferry	10,757	11,919
Marysville	5,744	4,952
Mason	5,677	4,727
Massillon	32,539	31,236
Maumee	15,937	12,063
Mayfield Heights	22,139	13,478
Medina	10,913	8,235
Mentor	36,912	4,354
Mentor-on-the-Lake	6,517	3,290
Miamisburg	14,797	9,893
Middleburg Heights	12,367	7,282
Middletown	48,767	42,115
Milford	4,828	4,131
Minerva	4,359	3,833
Mingo Junction	5,278	4,987
Montgomery	5,683	3,075
Moraine	4,898	2,262
Mount Healthy	7,446	6,553
Mount Vernon	13,373	13,284
Napoleon	7,791	6,739
Nelsonville	4,812	4,834
Newark	41,836	41,790
New Carlisle	6,112	4,107
New Lebanon	4,248	1,459
New Lexington	4,921	4,514
New Philadelphia	15,184	14,241
Newton Falls	5,378	5,038
Niles	21,581	19,545
North Canton	15,228	7,727
North College Hill	12,363	12,035
North Olmsted	34,861	16,290
Northridge (U)	10,084	—
North Ridgeville	13,152	8,057
North Royalton	12,807	9,290
Northwood	4,222	—
Norton	12,308	—
Norwalk	13,386	12,900
Norwood	30,420	34,580
Oakwood	10,095	10,493
Oberlin	8,761	8,198
Ontario	4,345	3,049
Oregon	16,563	13,319
Orrville	7,408	6,511
Ottawa Hills	4,270	3,870
Overlook-Page Manor (U)	19,596	—
Oxford	15,868	7,828
Painesville	16,536	16,116
Painesville Southwest (U)	5,461	—
Parma	100,216	82,845
Parma Heights	27,192	18,100
Pepper Pike	5,933	3,217
Perrysburg	7,693	5,519
Piqua	20,741	19,219
Port Clinton	7,202	6,870
Portsmouth	27,633	33,637
Ravenna	11,780	10,918
Reading	14,303	12,832
Reynoldsburg	13,921	7,793
Richmond Heights	9,220	5,068
Rittman	6,308	5,410
Rocky River	22,958	18,097
Rossford	5,302	4,406
St. Bernard	6,080	6,778
St. Clairsville	4,754	3,865
St. Marys	7,699	7,737
Salem	14,186	13,854
Sandusky	32,674	31,989
Sandusky South (U)	8,501	4,724
Sebring	4,954	4,439
Seven Hills	12,700	5,708
Shadyside	5,070	5,028
Shaker Heights	36,306	36,460
Sharonville	10,985	3,890
Sheffield Lake	8,734	6,884
Shelby	9,847	9,106
Shiloh (U)	11,368	—

Place	POPULATION 1970	1960
Sidney	16,332	14,663
Silverton	6,588	6,682
Solon	11,519	6,333
South Euclid	29,579	27,569
Springdale	8,127	3,556
Springfield	81,926	82,723
Steubenville	30,771	32,495
Stow	19,847	12,194
Streetsboro	7,966	—
Strongsville	15,182	8,504
Struthers	15,343	15,631
Sylvania	12,031	5,187
Tallmadge	15,274	10,246
Tiffin	21,596	21,478
Tipp City	5,090	4,267
Toledo	383,818	318,003
Toronto	7,705	7,780
Trenton	5,278	3,064
Trotwood	6,997	4,992
Troy	17,186	13,685
Twinsburg	6,432	4,098
Uhrichsville	5,731	6,201
University Heights	17,055	16,641
Upper Arlington	38,630	28,486
Upper Sandusky	5,645	4,941
Urbana	11,237	10,461
Vandalia	10,796	6,342
Van Wert	11,320	11,323
Vermilion	9,872	4,785
Wadsworth	13,142	10,635
Wapakoneta	7,324	6,756
Warren	63,494	59,648
Warrensville Heights	18,925	10,609
Washington	12,495	12,388
Wauseon	4,932	4,311
Waverly	4,858	3,830
Wellston	5,410	5,728
Wellsville	5,891	7,117
West Carrollton	10,748	4,749
Westerville	12,530	7,011
Westlake	15,689	12,906
Whitehall	25,263	20,818
Wickliffe	21,354	15,760
Willard	5,510	5,457
Willoughby	18,634	15,058
Willoughby Hills	5,247	4,241
Willowick	21,237	18,749
Wilmington	10,051	8,915
Wintersville	4,921	3,597
Wooster	18,703	17,046
Worthington	15,326	9,239
Wright-Patterson (U)	10,151	—
Wyoming	9,089	7,736
Xenia	25,373	20,445
Yellow Springs	4,624	4,167
Youngstown	139,788	166,689
Zanesville	33,045	39,077
Oklahoma	**2,559,253**	**2,328,284**
Ada	14,859	14,347
Altus	23,302	21,225
Alva	7,440	6,258
Anadarko	6,682	6,299
Ardmore	20,881	20,184
Bartlesville	29,683	27,893
Bethany	21,785	12,342
Blackwell	8,645	9,588
Bristow	4,653	4,795
Broken Arrow	11,787	5,928
Chickasha	14,194	14,866
Choctaw	4,750	623
Claremore	9,084	6,639
Clinton	8,513	9,617
Cushing	7,529	8,619
Del City	27,133	12,934
Duncan	19,718	20,009
Durant	11,118	10,467
Edmond	16,633	8,577
Elk City	7,323	8,196
El Reno	14,510	11,015
Enid	44,008	38,859
Fort Sill (U)	21,217	—
Frederick	6,132	5,879
Guthrie	9,575	9,502
Guymon	7,674	5,760
Henryetta	6,430	6,551
Hobart	4,638	5,132
Holdenville	5,181	5,712
Hugo	6,585	6,287
Idabel	5,946	4,967
Lawton	74,470	61,697
McAlester	18,802	17,419
Miami	13,880	12,869
Midwest City	48,114	36,058
Moore	18,761	1,783
Muskogee	37,331	38,059
Nichols Hills	4,478	4,897
Norman	52,117	33,412
Oklahoma City	366,481	324,253
Okmulgee	15,180	15,951
Okmulgee	15,180	15,951
Pauls Valley	5,769	6,856
Pawhuska	4,238	5,414
Perry	5,341	5,210

Place	POPULATION 1970	1960
Oklahoma (continued)		
Ponca City	25,940	24,411
Poteau	5,500	4,428
Pryor	7,057	6,476
Purcell	4,076	3,729
Sallisaw	4,888	3,351
Sand Springs	11,519	7,754
Sapulpa	15,159	14,282
Seminole	7,878	11,464
Shawnee	25,075	24,326
Stillwater	31,126	23,965
Sulphur	5,158	4,737
Tahlequah	9,254	5,840
Tecumseh	4,451	2,630
The Village	13,695	12,118
Tulsa	331,638	261,685
Vinita	5,847	6,027
Wagoner	4,959	4,469
Warr Acres	9,887	7,135
Weatherford	7,959	4,499
Wewoka	5,284	5,954
Woodward	8,710	7,747
Yukon	8,411	3,076
Oregon	**2,091,385**	**1,768,687**
Albany	18,181	12,926
Altamont (U)	15,746	10,811
Ashland	12,342	9,119
Astoria	10,244	11,239
Baker	9,354	9,986
Beaverton	18,577	5,937
Bend	13,710	11,936
City of the Dalles	10,423	10,493
Coos Bay	13,466	7,084
Coquille	4,437	4,730
Corvallis	35,153	20,669
Cottage Grove	6,004	3,895
Dallas	6,361	5,072
Eugene	76,346	50,977
Forest Grove	8,275	5,628
Four Corners (U)	6,199	4,743
Gladstone	6,237	3,854
Grants Pass	12,455	10,118
Gresham	9,875	3,944
Hayesville (U)	5,518	4,568
Hermiston	4,893	4,402
Hillsboro	14,675	8,232
Keizer (U)	11,405	5,288
Klamath Falls	15,775	16,949
La Grande	9,645	9,014
Lake Oswego	14,573	8,906
Lebanon	6,636	5,858
McMinnville	10,125	7,656
Medford	28,454	24,425
Milwaukie	16,379	9,099
Monmouth	5,237	2,229
Newberg	6,507	4,204
Newport	5,188	5,344
North Bend	8,553	7,512
Ontario	6,523	5,101
Oregon City	9,176	7,996
Pendleton	13,197	14,434
Portland	382,619	372,676
Roseburg	14,461	11,467
St. Helens	6,212	5,022
Salem	68,296	49,142
Seaside	4,402	3,877
Silverton	4,301	3,081
Springfield	27,047	19,616
Tigard	5,302	—
West Linn	7,091	3,933
Woodburn	7,495	3,120
Pennsylvania	**11,793,909**	**11,319,366**
Abington (U)	8,594	—
Aldan	5,001	4,324
Aliquippa	22,277	26,369
Allentown	109,527	108,347
Altoona	62,900	69,407
Ambler	7,800	6,765
Ambridge	11,324	13,865
Annville (U)	4,704	—
Archbald	6,118	5,642
Ardmore (U)	5,801	—
Arnold	8,174	9,437
Ashland	4,737	5,237
Avalon	7,065	6,859
Baden	5,536	6,109
Bala Cynwyd (U)	6,483	—
Baldwin	26,729	24,489
Bangor	5,425	5,766
Beaver	6,100	6,160
Beaver Falls	14,375	16,240
Bellefonte	6,828	6,088
Bellevue	11,586	11,412
Berwick	12,274	13,353
Bethel Park	34,791	23,650
Bethlehem	72,686	75,408
Blairsville	4,411	4,930
Blakely	6,391	6,374
Bloomsburg	11,652	10,655
Boyertown	4,428	4,067
Brackenridge	4,796	5,697

Place	POPULATION 1970	1960
Braddock	8,682	12,337
Bradford	12,672	15,061
Brandywine Village (U)	11,411	—
Brentwood	13,732	13,706
Bridgeport	5,630	5,306
Bridgeville	6,717	7,112
Bristol	12,085	12,364
Brookhaven	7,370	5,280
Brookville	4,314	4,620
Brownsville	4,856	6,055
Bryn Mawr (U)	5,737	—
Butler	18,691	20,975
California	6,635	5,978
Camp Hill	9,931	8,559
Canonsburg	11,439	11,877
Carbondale	12,808	13,595
Carlisle	18,079	16,623
Carlisle Barracks (U)	4,358	—
Carnegie	10,864	11,887
Carnot-Moon (U)	13,093	—
Castle Shannon	11,899	11,836
Catasauqua	5,702	5,062
Cedarbrook-Melrose Park (U)	9,980	—
Cedar Heights (U)	6,303	—
Chambersburg	17,315	17,670
Charleroi	6,723	8,148
Chatwood (U)	7,168	3,621
Chester	56,331	63,658
Churchill	4,690	3,428
Clairton	15,051	18,389
Clarion	6,095	4,958
Clarks Summit	5,376	3,693
Clearfield	8,176	9,270
Clifton Heights	8,348	8,005
Coatesville	12,331	12,971
Collingdale	10,605	10,268
Columbia	11,237	12,075
Connellsville	11,643	12,814
Conshohocken	10,195	10,259
Coraopolis	8,435	9,643
Corry	7,435	7,744
Crafton	8,233	8,418
Danville	6,176	6,889
Darby	13,729	14,059
Dickson City	7,698	7,738
Donora	8,825	11,131
Dormont	12,856	13,098
Downingtown	7,437	5,598
Doylestown	8,270	5,917
Du Bois	10,112	10,667
Dunmore	17,300	18,917
Duquesne	11,410	15,019
Duryea	5,264	5,626
Easton	30,256	31,955
East Stroudsburg	7,894	7,674
Ebensburg	4,318	4,111
Economy	7,176	5,925
Edgewood	5,101	5,124
Edinboro	4,871	1,703
Edwardsville	5,633	5,711
Elizabethtown	8,072	6,780
Ellwood City	10,857	12,413
Emmaus	11,511	10,262
Ephrata	9,662	7,688
Erie	129,231	138,440
Etna	5,819	5,519
Exeter	4,670	4,747
Farrell	11,022	13,793
Flourtown (U)	9,149	—
Folcroft	9,610	7,013
Ford City	4,749	5,440
Forest Hills	9,561	8,796
Forty Fort	6,114	6,431
Fountain Hill	5,384	5,428
Fox Chapel	4,684	3,302
Frackville	5,445	5,654
Franklin	8,629	9,586
Franklin Park	5,310	—
Freeland	4,784	5,068
Fullerton (U)	7,908	—
General Wayne (U)	5,368	—
Gettysburg	7,275	7,960
Glassport	7,450	8,418
Glenolden	8,697	7,249
Glenside (U)	17,353	—
Greensburg	15,870	17,383
Green Tree	6,441	5,226
Greenville	8,704	8,765
Grove City	8,312	8,368
Hanover	15,623	15,538
Harrisburg	68,061	79,697
Hatboro	8,880	7,315
Hatboro West (U)	13,542	—
Hazleton	30,426	32,056
Hellertown	6,613	6,716
Hershey (U)	7,407	6,851
Highland Park (U)	5,500	—
Hollidaysburg	6,262	6,475
Homeacre-Lyndora (U)	8,415	—
Homestead	6,309	7,502
Honesdale	5,224	5,569
Hummelstown	4,723	4,474
Huntingdon	6,987	7,234

Place	POPULATION 1970	1960
Indiana	16,100	13,005
Ingram	4,902	4,730
Jeannette	15,209	16,565
Jefferson	8,512	8,280
Jefferson-Trooper (U)	13,022	—
Jenkintown	5,990	5,017
Jersey Shore	5,322	5,613
Jessup	4,948	5,456
Jim Thorpe	5,456	5,945
Johnsonburg	4,304	4,966
Johnstown	42,476	53,949
Kane	5,001	5,380
Kennett Square	4,876	4,355
Kingston	18,325	20,261
Kittanning	6,231	6,793
Kutztown	6,017	3,312
Lafayette Hills- Plymouth Meeting (U)	8,263	—
Lancaster	57,690	61,055
Lansdale	18,451	12,612
Lansdowne	14,090	12,601
Lansford	5,168	5,958
Latrobe	11,749	11,932
Laureldale	4,519	4,051
Lebanon	28,572	30,045
Lehighton	6,095	6,318
Lemoyne	4,625	4,662
Lewisburg	6,376	5,523
Lewistown	11,098	12,640
Lititz	7,072	5,987
Lock Haven	11,427	11,748
Lower Burrell	13,654	11,952
Luzerne	4,504	5,118
McChesneytown- Loyalhanna (U)	4,283	3,138
McKeesport	37,977	45,489
McKees Rocks	11,901	13,185
Mahanoy City	7,257	8,536
Manheim	5,434	4,790
Masontown	4,226	4,730
Meadville	16,573	16,671
Mechanicsburg	9,385	8,123
Media	6,444	5,803
Merion (U)	5,686	—
Middletown	9,080	11,182
Midland	5,271	6,425
Millersville	6,396	3,883
Millvale	5,815	6,624
Milton	7,723	7,972
Minersville	6,012	6,606
Monaca	7,486	8,394
Monessen	15,216	18,424
Monongahela	7,113	8,388
Monroeville	29,011	22,446
Montoursville	5,985	5,211
Moosic	4,273	4,243
Morrisville	11,309	7,790
Mount Carmel	9,317	10,760
Mount Joy	5,041	3,292
Mount Oliver	5,487	5,980
Mount Pleasant	5,895	6,107
Munhall	16,674	17,312
Nanticoke	14,632	15,601
Nanty-Glo	4,298	4,608
Narberth	5,151	5,109
Nazareth	5,815	6,209
New Brighton	7,637	8,397
New Castle	38,559	44,790
New Cumberland	9,803	9,257
New Kensington	20,312	23,485
Norristown	38,169	38,925
Northampton	8,389	8,866
North Ardmore (U)	5,856	—
North Braddock	10,838	13,204
North Hills-Ardsley (U)	13,173	—
Norwood	7,229	6,729
Oak Lane (U)	6,192	—
Oakmont	7,550	7,504
Ogontz (U)	5,463	2,254
Oil City	15,033	17,692
Old Forge	9,522	8,928
Olyphant	5,422	5,864
Oreland (U)	9,114	—
Palmerton	5,620	5,942
Palmyra	7,615	6,999
Paoli (U)	5,835	—
Parkville (U)	5,120	4,516
Pencoyd (U)	6,650	—
Penn Square- Plymouth Valley (U)	20,238	—
Penn Wynne (U)	6,038	—
Perkasie	5,451	4,650
Philadelphia	1,948,609	2,002,512
Phoenixville	14,823	13,797
Pitcairn	4,741	5,383
Pittsburgh	520,117	604,332
Pittston	11,113	12,407
Plains (U)	6,606	—
Pleasant Hills	10,409	8,573
Plum	21,932	10,241
Plymouth	9,536	10,401
Port Vue	5,862	6,635
Pottstown	25,355	26,144

U.S. Census Data (continued)

Place	POPULATION 1970	1960
Pennsylvania (continued)		
Pottsville	19,715	21,659
Prospect Park	7,250	6,596
Punxsutawney	7,792	8,805
Quakertown	7,276	6,305
Reading	87,643	98,177
Red Lion	5,645	5,594
Ridgway	6,022	6,387
Ridley Park	9,025	7,387
Rochester	4,819	5,952
Roslyn (U)	18,317	—
Royersford	4,235	3,969
Rydal (U)	5,083	—
St. Clair	4,576	5,159
St. Marys	7,470	8,065
Sayre	7,473	7,917
Schuylkill Haven	6,125	6,470
Scottdale	5,818	6,244
Scranton	103,564	111,443
Selinsgrove	5,116	3,948
Sewickley	5,660	6,157
Shamokin	11,719	13,674
Sharon	22,653	25,267
Sharon Hill	7,464	7,123
Sharpsburg	5,499	6,096
Sharpsville	6,126	6,061
Shenandoah	8,287	11,073
Shillington	6,249	5,639
Shippensburg	6,536	6,138
Slatington	4,687	4,316
Slippery Rock	4,949	2,563
Somerset	6,269	6,347
Souderton	6,366	5,381
South Williamsport	7,153	6,972
Springdale	5,202	5,602
State College	33,778	22,409
Steelton	8,556	11,266
Stroudsburg	5,451	6,070
Sugar Creek	5,944	—
Sunbury	13,025	13,687
Swarthmore	6,156	5,753
Swissvale	13,821	15,089
Swoyersville	6,786	6,751
Tamaqua	9,246	10,173
Tarentum	7,379	8,232
Taylor	6,977	6,148
Throop	4,307	4,732
Titusville	7,331	8,356
Towanda	4,224	4,293
Trafford	4,383	4,330
Turtle Creek	8,308	10,607
Tyrone	7,072	7,792
Uniontown	16,282	17,942
Vandergrift	7,873	8,742
Warren	12,998	14,505
Washington	19,827	23,545
Waynesboro	10,011	10,427
Waynesburg	5,152	5,188
West Chester	19,301	15,705
West Hazleton	6,059	6,278
West Mifflin	28,070	27,289
Westmont	6,673	6,573
West Pittston	7,074	6,998
West Reading	4,578	4,938
West View	8,312	8,079
West York	5,314	5,526
Whitehall	16,551	16,075
White Oak	9,304	9,047
Wilkes-Barre	58,856	63,551
Wilkinsburg	26,780	30,066
Williamsport	37,918	41,967
Willow Grove (U)	16,494	—
Wilson	8,482	8,465
Windber	6,332	6,994
Wyomissing	7,136	5,044
Yeadon	12,136	11,610
York	50,335	54,504
Rhode Island	**949,723**	**859,488**
Barrington*	17,554	13,826
Bristol*	17,860	14,570
Central Falls	18,716	19,858
Cranston	73,037	66,766
East Greenwich*	9,577	6,100
East Providence	48,151	41,955
Johnston*	22,037	17,160
Kingston (U)	5,601	2,616
Newport	34,562	47,049
Newport East (U)	10,285	2,643
North Providence*	24,337	18,220
Pawtucket	76,984	81,001
Providence	179,213	207,498
Wakefield-Peacedale (U)	6,331	5,569
Warren*	10,523	8,750
Warwick	83,694	68,504
Westerly (U)	13,654	9,698
West Warwick*	24,323	21,414
Woonsocket	46,820	47,080
South Carolina	**2,590,516**	**2,382,594**
Abbeville	5,515	5,436
Aiken	13,436	11,243
Anderson	27,556	41,316

Place	POPULATION 1970	1960
Avondale-Moorland (U)	5,236	—
Barnwell	4,439	4,568
Beaufort	9,434	6,298
Belton	5,257	5,106
Bennettsville	7,468	6,963
Berea (U)	7,186	—
Camden	8,532	6,842
Capehart (U)	4,490	—
Cayce	9,967	8,517
Charleston	66,945	65,925
Charleston Base (U)	6,238	—
Charleston Yard (U)	13,565	—
Cheraw	5,627	5,171
Chester	7,045	6,906
Clemson	5,578	1,587
Clinton	8,138	7,937
Columbia	113,542	97,433
Conway	8,151	8,563
Darlington	6,990	6,710
Dillon	5,991	6,173
Easley	11,175	8,283
Florence	25,997	24,722
Forest Acres	6,808	3,842
Fort Mill	4,505	3,315
Gaffney	13,253	10,435
Gantt (U)	11,386	—
Georgetown	10,449	12,261
Greenville	61,208	66,188
Greenwood	21,069	16,644
Greer	10,642	8,967
Hanahan (U)	8,376	—
Hartsville	8,017	6,392
Lake City	6,247	6,059
Lancaster	9,186	7,999
Laurens	10,298	9,598
Marion	7,435	7,174
Mount Pleasant	6,155	5,116
Mullins	6,006	6,229
Myrtle Beach	8,536	7,834
Newberry	9,218	8,208
North Augusta	12,883	10,348
Orangeburg	13,252	13,852
Parris Island (U)	8,868	—
Rock Hill	33,846	29,404
St. Andrews (U)	9,202	—
Saxon (U)	4,807	3,917
Seneca	6,027	5,227
Shannontown (U)	7,491	7,064
Shaw (U)	5,819	—
Spartanburg	44,546	44,352
Sumter	24,435	23,062
Taylors (U)	6,831	1,071
Union	10,775	10,191
Wade-Hampton (U)	17,152	—
Walterboro	6,257	5,417
West Columbia	7,838	6,410
Woodruff	4,576	3,679
York	5,081	4,758
South Dakota	**665,507**	**680,514**
Aberdeen	26,476	23,073
Belle Fourche	4,236	4,087
Brookings	13,717	10,558
Ellsworth (U)	5,805	—
Hot Springs	4,434	4,943
Huron	14,299	14,180
Lead	5,420	6,211
Madison	6,315	5,420
Mitchell	13,425	12,555
Mobridge	4,545	4,391
Pierre	9,699	10,088
Rapid City	43,836	42,399
Sioux Falls	72,488	65,466
Spearfish	4,661	3,682
Sturgis	4,536	4,639
Vermillion	9,128	6,102
Watertown	13,388	14,077
Yankton	11,919	9,279
Tennessee	**3,924,164**	**3,567,089**
Alcoa	7,739	6,395
Athens	11,790	12,103
Bolivar	6,674	3,338
Bristol	20,064	17,582
Brownsville	7,011	5,424
Chattanooga	119,082	130,009
Clarksville	31,719	22,021
Cleveland	20,651	16,196
Clinton	4,794	4,943
Columbia	21,471	17,624
Cookeville	14,270	7,805
Covington	5,801	5,298
Crossville	5,381	4,668
Dayton	4,361	3,500
Dickson	5,665	5,028
Dyersburg	14,523	12,499
Eagleton Village (U)	5,345	5,068
East Ridge	21,799	19,570
Elizabethton	12,269	10,896
Erwin	4,715	3,210
Fayetteville	7,030	6,804
Fort Campbell South (U)	9,279	—
Franklin	9,404	6,977

Place	POPULATION 1970	1960
Gallatin	13,093	7,901
Greater Hendersonville (U)	11,996	—
Greeneville	13,722	11,759
Harriman	8,734	5,931
Hixson (U)	6,188	—
Humboldt	10,066	8,482
Jackson	39,996	34,376
Jefferson City	5,124	4,550
Johnson City	33,770	31,187
Kingsport	31,938	26,314
Kingsport North (U)	13,118	—
Knoxville	174,587	111,827
La Follette	6,902	6,204
Lake Hills-Murray Hills (U)	7,806	—
Lawrenceburg	8,889	8,042
Lebanon	12,492	10,512
Lenoir City	5,324	4,979
Lewisburg	7,207	6,338
Lexington	4,955	3,943
McKenzie	4,873	3,780
McMinnville	10,662	9,013
Manchester	6,208	3,930
Martin	7,781	4,750
Maryville	13,808	10,348
Memphis	623,530	497,524
Milan	7,313	5,208
Millington	21,106	6,059
Morristown	20,318	21,267
Murfreesboro	26,360	18,991
Nashville-Davidson	447,877	170,874
Newport	7,328	6,448
Oak Ridge	28,319	27,169
Paris	9,892	9,325
Pulaski	6,989	6,616
Red Bank	12,715	10,777
Ripley	4,794	3,782
Rockwood	5,259	5,345
Savannah	5,576	4,315
Shelbyville	12,262	10,466
Signal Mountain	4,839	3,413
Smyrna	5,698	3,612
Soddy-Daisy	7,569	—
South Cleveland (U)	5,070	1,512
Sparta	4,930	4,510
Springfield	9,720	9,221
Sweetwater	4,340	4,145
Trenton	4,226	4,225
Tullahoma	15,311	12,242
Union City	11,925	8,837
Winchester	5,211	4,760
Texas	**11,196,730**	**9,579,677**
Abilene	89,653	90,368
Alamo	4,291	4,121
Alamo Heights	6,933	7,552
Alice	20,121	20,861
Alpine	5,971	4,740
Alvin	10,671	5,643
Amarillo	127,010	137,969
Andrews	8,625	11,135
Angleton	9,770	7,312
Aransas Pass	5,813	6,956
Arlington	90,643	44,775
Athens	9,582	7,086
Atlanta	5,007	4,076
Austin	251,808	186,545
Azle	4,493	2,969
Balch Springs	10,464	6,821
Ballinger	4,203	5,043
Bay City	11,733	11,656
Baytown	43,980	28,159
Beaumont	115,919	119,175
Bedford	10,049	2,706
Beeville	13,506	13,811
Bellaire	19,009	19,872
Bellmead	7,698	5,127
Belton	8,696	8,163
Benbrook	8,169	3,254
Biggs (U)	4,226	—
Big Spring	28,735	31,230
Bonham	7,698	7,357
Borger	14,195	20,911
Bowie	5,185	4,566
Brady	5,557	5,338
Breckenridge	5,944	6,273
Brenham	8,922	7,740
Bridge City (U)	8,164	4,677
Brownfield	9,647	10,286
Brownsville	52,522	48,040
Brownwood	17,368	16,974
Bryan	33,719	27,542
Burkburnett	9,230	7,621
Burleson	7,713	2,345
Cameron	5,546	5,640
Canyon	8,333	5,864
Carrizo Springs	5,374	5,699
Carrollton	13,855	4,242
Carthage	5,392	5,262
Castle Hills	5,311	2,622
Center	4,989	4,510
Childress	5,408	6,399
Cleburne	16,015	15,381
Cleveland	5,627	5,838

U.S. Census Data (continued)

Place	POPULATION 1970	1960	Place	POPULATION 1970	1960	Place	POPULATION 1970	1960
Texas (continued)			McGregor	4,365	4,642	East Millcreek (U)	26,579	—
Clute City	6,023	4,501	McKinney	15,193	13,763	Granger-Hunter (U)	9,029	—
Coleman	5,608	6,371	Marlin	6,351	6,918	Granite Park (U)	9,573	—
College Station	17,676	11,396	Marshall	22,937	23,846	Holladay (U)	23,014	—
Colorado City	5,227	6,457	Mathis	5,351	6,075	Kaysville	6,192	3,608
Commerce	9,534	5,789	Mercedes	9,355	10,943	Kearns (U)	17,071	17,172
Conroe	11,969	9,192	Mesquite	55,131	27,526	Layton	13,603	9,027
Copperas Cove	10,818	4,567	Mexia	5,943	6,121	Lehi	4,659	4,377
Corpus Christi	204,525	167,690	Midland	59,463	62,625	Logan	22,333	18,731
Corsicana	19,972	20,344	Mineral Wells	18,411	11,053	Magna (U)	5,509	6,442
Crockett	6,616	5,356	Mission	13,043	14,081	Midvale	7,840	5,802
Crystal City	8,104	9,101	Monahans	8,333	8,567	Moab	4,793	4,682
Cuero	6,956	7,338	Mount Pleasant	8,877	8,027	Mount Olympus (U)	5,909	—
Dalhart	5,705	5,160	Muleshoe	4,525	3,871	Murray	21,206	16,806
Dallas	844,401	679,684	Nacogdoches	22,544	12,674	North Ogden	5,257	2,621
Deer Park	12,773	4,865	Navasota	5,111	4,937	Ogden	69,478	70,197
Del Rio	21,330	18,612	Nederland	16,810	12,036	Orem	25,729	18,394
Denison	24,923	22,748	New Braunfels	17,859	15,631	Payson	4,501	4,237
Denton	39,874	26,844	North Richland Hills	16,514	8,662	Pleasant Grove	5,327	4,772
De Soto	6,617	1,969	Odessa	78,380	80,338	Price	6,218	6,802
Dickinson (U)	10,776	4,715	Orange	24,457	25,605	Provo	53,131	36,047
Dimmitt	4,327	2,935	Palestine	14,525	13,974	Richfield	4,471	4,412
Donna	7,365	7,522	Pampa	21,726	24,664	Roy	14,356	9,239
Dumas	9,771	8,477	Paris	23,441	20,977	St. George	7,097	5,130
Duncanville	14,105	3,774	Pasadena	89,277	58,737	Salt Lake City	175,885	189,454
Eagle Pass	15,364	12,094	Pearland	6,444	1,497	Sandy City	6,438	3,322
Edinburg	17,163	18,706	Pearsall	5,545	4,957	South Ogden	9,991	7,405
Edna	5,332	5,038	Pecos	12,682	12,728	South Salt Lake	7,810	9,520
El Campo	8,563	7,700	Perryton	7,810	7,903	Spanish Fork	7,284	6,472
El Paso	322,261	276,687	Pharr	15,829	14,106	Springville	8,790	7,913
Elsa	4,400	3,847	Plainview	19,096	18,735	Sunset	6,268	4,235
Ennis	11,046	9,347	Plano	17,872	3,695	Tooele	12,539	9,133
Euless	19,316	4,263	Pleasanton	5,407	3,467	Washington Terrace	7,241	6,441
Everman	4,570	1,076	Port Arthur	57,371	66,676	West Jordan	4,221	3,009
Falfurrias	6,355	6,515	Portland	7,302	2,538	White City (U)	6,402	—
Farmers Branch	27,492	13,441	Port Lavaca	10,491	8,864			
Forest Hill	8,236	3,221	Port Neches	10,894	8,696	**Vermont**	**444,330**	**389,881**
Fort Bliss (U)	13,288	—	Randolph (U)	5,329	—	Barre	10,209	10,387
Fort Hood (U)	32,597	—	Raymondville	7,987	9,385	Bennington	7,950	8,023
Fort Sam Houston (U)	10,553	—	Refugio	4,340	4,944	Brattleboro (U)	9,055	9,315
Fort Stockton	8,283	6,373	Richardson	48,582	16,810	Burlington	38,633	35,531
Fort Worth	393,476	356,268	Richland Hills	8,865	7,804	Essex Junction	6,511	5,340
Fredericksburg	5,326	4,629	Richmond	5,777	3,668	Montpelier	8,609	8,782
Freeport	11,997	11,619	Rio Grande City (U)	5,676	5,835	Newport	4,664	5,019
Friendswood	5,675	—	River Oaks	8,193	8,444	Rutland	19,293	18,325
Gainesville	13,830	13,083	Robstown	11,217	10,266	St. Albans	8,082	8,806
Galena Park	10,479	10,852	Rockdale	4,655	4,481	Springfield (U)	5,632	6,600
Galveston	61,809	67,175	Rosenberg	12,098	9,698	Williston Road Section (U)	5,376	3,259
Garland	81,437	38,501	Rusk	4,914	4,900	Winooski	7,309	7,420
Gatesville	4,683	4,626	San Angelo	63,884	58,815			
Georgetown	6,395	5,218	San Antonio	654,153	587,718	**Virginia**	**4,648,494**	**3,966,949**
Gladewater	5,574	5,742	San Benito	15,176	16,422	Abingdon	4,376	4,758
Gonzales	5,854	5,829	San Diego	4,490	4,351	Alexandria	110,938	91,023
Graham	7,477	8,505	San Juan	5,070	4,371	Annandale (U)	27,428	—
Grand Prairie	50,904	30,386	San Marcos	18,860	12,713	Arlington (U)	174,284	—
Grapevine	7,023	2,821	Sansom Park Village	4,771	4,175	Bailey's Crossroads (U)	7,295	—
Greenville	22,043	19,087	Seagoville	4,390	3,745	Bedford	6,011	5,921
Groves	18,067	17,304	Seguin	15,934	14,299	Belleview (U)	8,299	—
Haltom City	28,127	23,133	Seminole	5,007	5,737	Blacksburg	9,384	7,070
Harker Heights	4,216	—	Sherman	29,061	24,988	Bluefield	5,286	4,235
Harlingen	33,503	41,207	Silsbee	7,271	6,277	Bon Air (U)	10,562	—
Hearne	4,982	5,072	Sinton	5,563	6,008	Bristol	14,857	17,144
Henderson	10,187	9,666	Slaton	6,583	6,568	Buena Vista	6,425	6,300
Hereford	13,414	7,652	Snyder	11,171	13,850	Charlottesville	38,880	29,427
Highland Park	10,133	10,411	South Houston	11,527	7,523	Chesapeake	89,580	—
Hillsboro	7,224	7,402	Stamford	4,558	5,259	Chester (U)	5,556	1,290
Hitchcock	5,565	5,216	Stephenville	9,277	7,359	Christiansburg	7,857	3,653
Hondo	5,487	4,992	Sulphur Springs	10,642	9,160	Clifton Forge	5,501	5,268
Houston	1,232,802	938,219	Sweetwater	12,020	13,914	Collinsville (U)	6,015	3,586
Huntsville	17,610	11,999	Taylor	9,616	9,434	Colonial Heights	15,097	9,587
Hurst	27,215	10,165	Temple	33,431	30,419	Covington	10,060	11,062
Iowa Park	5,796	3,295	Terrell	14,182	13,803	Culpeper	6,056	2,412
Irving	97,260	45,985	Terrell Hills	5,225	5,572	Dale City (U)	13,857	—
Jacinto City	9,563	9,547	Texarkana	30,497	30,218	Danville	46,391	46,577
Jacksonville	9,734	9,590	Texas City	38,908	32,065	Emporia	5,300	5,535
Jasper	6,251	4,889	Tulia	5,294	4,410	Fairfax	21,970	13,585
Kermit	7,884	10,465	Tyler	57,770	51,230	Falls Church	10,772	10,192
Kerrville	12,672	8,901	Universal City	7,613	—	Farmville	4,331	4,293
Kilgore	9,495	10,092	University Park	23,498	23,202	Fort Belvoir (U)	14,591	—
Killeen	35,507	23,377	Uvalde	10,764	10,293	Fort Hunt (U)	10,415	—
Kingsville	28,711	25,297	Vernon	11,454	12,141	Fort Lee (U)	12,435	—
Kleberg	4,768	3,572	Victoria	41,349	33,047	Franklin	6,880	7,264
Lackland (U)	19,141	—	Vidor	9,738	—	Fredericksburg	14,450	13,639
Lake Jackson	13,376	9,651	Waco	95,326	97,808	Front Royal	8,211	7,949
Lake Worth Village	4,958	3,833	Waxahachie	13,452	12,749	Galax	6,278	5,254
La Marque	16,131	13,969	Weatherford	11,750	9,759	Groveton (U)	11,750	—
Lamesa	11,559	12,438	Weslaco	15,313	15,649	Hampton	120,779	89,258
Lampasas	5,922	5,061	West Orange	4,787	4,848	Harrisonburg	14,605	11,916
Lancaster	10,522	7,501	West University Place	13,317	14,628	Herndon	4,301	1,960
La Porte	7,149	4,512	Westworth	4,578	3,321	Highland Springs (U)	7,345	—
Laredo	69,024	60,678	Wharton	7,881	5,734	Hopewell	23,471	17,895
League City	10,818	—	White Settlement	13,449	11,513	Huntington (U)	5,559	—
Levelland	11,445	10,153	Wichita Falls	97,564	101,724	Jefferson (U)	25,432	—
Lewisville	9,264	3,956	Woodway	4,819	1,244	Lake Barcroft (U)	11,605	—
Liberty	5,591	6,127	Yoakum	5,755	5,761	Lakeside (U)	11,137	—
Littlefield	6,738	7,236				Leesburg	4,821	2,869
Lockhart	6,489	6,084	**Utah**	**1,059,273**	**890,627**	Lexington	7,597	7,537
Longview	45,547	40,050	American Fork	7,713	6,373	Lincolnia (U)	10,355	—
Lubbock	149,101	128,691	Bountiful	27,853	17,039	Long Branch (U)	21,634	—
Lufkin	23,049	17,641	Brigham City	14,007	11,728	Lynchburg	54,083	54,790
Luling	4,719	4,412	Cedar City	8,946	7,543	McLean (U)	17,698	—
McAllen	37,636	32,728	Clearfield	13,316	8,833	Manassas	9,164	3,555
			Cottonwood (U)	8,431	—	Manassas Park	6,844	5,342

Place	POPULATION 1970	POPULATION 1960
Virginia (continued)		
Mantua (U)	6,911	—
Marion	8,158	8,385
Martinsville	19,653	18,798
Mechanicsville (U)	5,189	—
Newport News	138,177	113,662
Norfolk	307,951	304,869
North Springfield (U)	8,631	—
Petersburg	36,103	36,750
Poquoson	5,441	4,278
Portsmouth	110,963	114,773
Pulaski	10,279	10,469
Quantico Station (U)	6,213	—
Radford	11,596	9,371
Reston (U)	5,723	—
Richlands	4,843	4,963
Richmond	249,621	219,958
Roanoke	92,115	97,110
Rose Hill (U)	14,692	—
Salem	21,982	16,058
Seven Corners (U)	5,590	10,783
South Boston	6,889	5,974
Springfield (U)	11,613	10,783
Staunton	24,504	22,232
Sterling Park (U)	8,321	—
Suffolk	9,858	12,609
Vienna	17,152	11,440
Vinton	6,347	3,432
Virginia Beach	172,106	8,091
Waynesboro	16,707	15,694
West Springfield (U)	14,248	—
Williamsburg	9,069	6,832
Winchester	14,643	15,110
Woodbridge-Marumsco (U)	25,412	—
Wytheville	6,069	5,634
Yorkshire (U)	4,649	—
Washington	**3,409,169**	**2,853,214**
Aberdeen	18,489	18,741
Anacortes	7,701	8,414
Auburn	21,817	11,933
Bellevue	61,102	12,809
Bellingham	39,375	34,688
Bothell	4,883	2,237
Bremerton	35,307	28,922
Camas	5,790	5,666
Centralia	10,054	8,586
Chehalis	5,727	5,199
Cheney	6,358	3,173
Clarkston	6,312	6,209
College Place	4,510	4,031
Dishman (U)	9,079	—
Edmonds	23,998	8,016
Ellensburg	13,568	8,625
Enumclaw	4,703	3,269
Ephrata	5,255	6,548
Everett	53,622	40,304
Fairchild (U)	6,754	—
Fircrest	5,651	3,565
Fort Lewis (U)	38,054	—
Hoquiam	10,466	10,762
Issaquah	4,313	1,870
Kelso	10,296	8,379
Kennewick	15,212	14,244
Kent	21,510	9,017
Kirkland	15,249	6,025
Lacey	9,696	—
Lakes District (U)	48,195	—
Longview	28,373	23,349
Lynnwood	16,919	7,207
McChord (U)	6,515	—
Marysville	4,343	3,117
Mercer Island	19,047	—
Moses Lake	10,310	11,299
Mountlake Terrace	16,600	9,122
Mount Vernon	8,804	7,921
Normandy Park	4,208	3,224
Oak Harbor	9,167	3,942
Olympia	23,111	18,273
Opportunity (U)	16,604	12,465
Parkland (U)	21,012	—
Pasco	13,920	14,522
Port Angeles	16,367	12,653
Port Townsend	5,241	5,074
Pullman	20,509	12,957
Puyallup	14,742	12,063
Redmond	11,031	1,426
Renton	25,258	18,453

Place	POPULATION 1970	POPULATION 1960
Richland	26,290	23,548
Seattle	530,831	557,087
Sedro-Woolley	4,598	3,705
Shelton	6,515	5,651
Shoultes (U)	4,754	3,159
Snohomish	5,174	3,894
Spanaway (U)	5,768	—
Spokane	170,516	181,608
Sumner	4,325	3,156
Sunnyside	6,751	6,208
Tacoma	154,581	147,979
Toppenish	5,744	5,667
Town and Country (U)	6,484	—
Tumwater	5,373	3,885
University Place (U)	13,230	—
Vancouver	42,493	32,464
Walla Walla	23,619	24,536
Wenatchee	16,912	16,726
Yakima	45,588	43,284
West Virginia	**1,744,237**	**1,860,421**
Beckley	19,884	18,642
Bluefield	15,921	19,256
Bridgeport	4,777	4,199
Buckhannon	7,261	6,386
Charleston	71,505	85,796
Clarksburg	24,864	28,112
Dunbar	9,151	11,006
Elkins	8,287	8,307
Fairmont	26,093	27,477
Grafton	6,433	5,791
Hinton	4,503	5,197
Huntington	74,315	83,627
Kenova	4,860	4,577
Keyser	6,586	6,192
Martinsburg	14,626	15,179
Morgantown	29,431	22,487
Moundsville	13,560	15,163
New Martinsville	6,528	5,607
Nitro	8,019	6,894
Oak Hill	4,738	4,711
Parkersburg	44,208	44,797
Point Pleasant	6,122	5,785
Princeton	7,253	8,393
Ravenswood	4,240	3,410
St. Albans	14,356	15,103
South Charleston	16,333	19,180
Vienna	11,549	9,381
Weirton	27,131	28,201
Wellsburg	4,600	5,514
Weston	7,323	8,754
Westover	5,086	4,749
Wheeling	48,188	53,400
Williamson	5,831	6,746
Wisconsin	**4,417,933**	**3,951,777**
Allouez (U)	13,753	—
Antigo	9,005	9,691
Appleton	57,143	48,411
Ashland	9,615	10,132
Ashwaubenon (U)	9,323	—
Baraboo	7,931	7,660
Bayside	4,461	3,181
Beaver Dam	14,265	13,118
Beloit	35,729	32,846
Berlin	5,338	4,838
Brookfield	32,140	19,812
Brown Deer	12,622	11,280
Burlington	7,479	5,856
Cedarburg	7,697	5,191
Chippewa Falls	12,351	11,708
Clintonville	4,600	4,778
Cudahy	22,078	17,975
Delavan	5,526	4,846
De Pere	13,309	10,045
Eau Claire	44,619	37,987
Elm Grove	7,201	4,994
Fond Du Lac	35,515	32,719
Fort Atkinson	9,164	7,908
Fox Point	7,937	7,315
Franklin	12,247	10,006
Germantown	6,974	622
Glendale	13,436	9,537
Grafton	5,998	3,748
Green Bay	87,809	62,888
Greendale	15,089	6,843
Greenfield	24,424	17,636
Hales Corners	7,771	5,549
Hartford	6,499	5,627

Place	POPULATION 1970	POPULATION 1960
Howard	4,911	3,485
Hudson	5,049	4,325
Janesville	46,426	35,164
Jefferson	5,429	4,548
Kaukauna	11,292	10,096
Kenosha	78,805	67,899
Kimberly	6,131	5,322
La Crosse	51,153	47,575
Lake Geneva	4,890	4,929
Little Chute	5,365	5,099
Madison	173,258	126,706
Manitowoc	33,430	32,275
Marinette	12,696	13,329
Marshfield	15,619	14,153
Menasha	14,905	14,647
Menomonee Falls	31,697	18,276
Menomonie	11,275	8,624
Mequon	12,110	8,543
Merrill	9,502	9,451
Middleton	8,286	4,410
Milwaukee	717,099	741,324
Monona	10,420	8,178
Monroe	8,654	8,050
Muskego	11,573	—
Neenah	22,892	18,057
New Berlin	26,937	15,788
New London	5,801	5,288
Oak Creek	13,901	9,372
Oconomowoc	8,741	6,682
Oconto	4,667	4,805
Onalaska	4,909	3,161
Oshkosh	53,221	45,110
Perry Go Place (U)	5,912	4,475
Platteville	9,599	6,957
Plymouth	5,810	5,128
Portage	7,821	7,822
Port Washington	8,752	5,984
Prairie du Chien	5,540	5,649
Racine	95,162	89,144
Reedsburg	4,585	4,371
Rhinelander	8,218	8,790
Rice Lake	7,278	7,303
Richland Center	5,086	4,746
Ripon	7,053	6,163
River Falls	7,238	4,857
St. Francis	10,489	10,065
Shawano	6,488	6,103
Sheboygan	48,484	45,747
Sheboygan Falls	4,771	4,061
Shorewood	15,576	15,990
South Milwaukee	23,297	20,307
Sparta	6,258	6,080
Stevens Point	23,479	17,837
Stoughton	6,081	5,555
Sturgeon Bay	6,776	7,353
Sun Prairie	9,935	4,008
Superior	32,237	33,563
Tomah	5,647	5,321
Two Rivers	13,553	12,393
Watertown	15,683	13,943
Waukesha	40,258	30,004
Waupaca	4,342	3,984
Waupun	7,946	7,935
Wausau	32,806	31,943
Wausau West (U)	6,399	4,105
Wauwatosa	58,676	56,923
West Allis	71,723	68,157
West Bend	16,555	9,969
West Milwaukee	4,405	5,043
Whitefish Bay	17,394	18,390
Whitewater	12,038	6,380
Wisconsin Rapids	18,587	15,042
Wyoming	**332,416**	**330,066**
Casper	39,361	38,930
Cheyenne	40,914	43,505
Cody	5,161	4,838
Evanston	4,462	4,901
Gillette	7,194	3,580
Lander	7,125	4,182
Laramie	23,143	17,520
Powell	4,807	4,740
Rawlins	7,855	8,968
Riverton	7,995	6,845
Rock Springs	11,657	10,371
Sheridan	10,856	11,651
Torrington	4,237	4,188
Warren (U)	4,527	—
Worland	5,055	5,806

*Town (township) population.
Dash (—) indicates place did not exist at time
of the 1960 Census, or data not available.
(U) indicates unincorporated urban place.
Source: U.S. Department of Commerce publications PC(V1)-2
through PC(V1)-52 (Advance Reports of Final Population Counts).

Population change

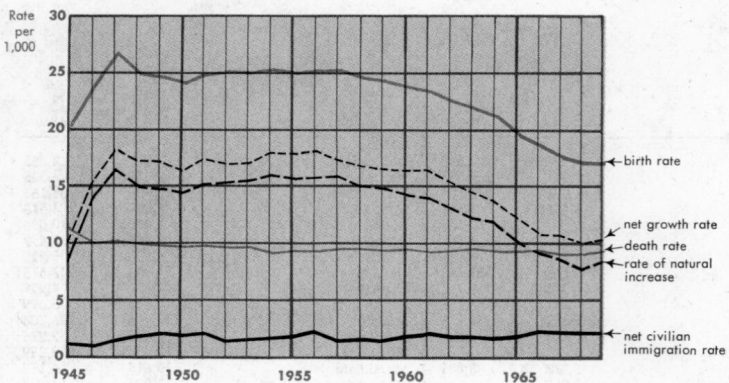

Rate per 1,000

→ birth rate
→ net growth rate
→ death rate
→ rate of natural increase
→ net civilian immigration rate

1945 1950 1955 1960 1965

Source: U.S. Department of Commerce, Bureau of the Census.

Immigration and naturalization

year ending June 30, 1969

Country or region	Total immigrants admitted	Quota immigrants	NONQUOTA IMMIGRANTS Total	Families of U.S. citizens	Aliens naturalized
Europe*	120,086	94,813	25,273	23,046	51,847
France	2,024	1,252	772	736	1,416
Germany	9,289	3,919	5,370	5,275	10,618
Greece	17,724	15,534	2,190	2,120	3,029
Hungary	1,795	1,322	473	380	1,725
Ireland	1,989	1,579	410	285	2,626
Italy	23,617	18,494	5,123	4,926	8,773
Netherlands	1,303	882	421	386	1,930
Poland	4,052	3,253	799	702	3,643
Portugal	16,528	15,490	1,038	1,007	1,543
Spain	3,916	2,869	1,047	907	721
United Kingdom	15,014	11,327	3,687	3,442	7,979
Yugoslavia	8,868	7,850	1,018	553	1,808
North America	132,426	111,948	20,478	16,898	24,831
Canada	18,582	14,954	3,628	2,778	6,387
Mexico	44,623	31,951	12,672	10,400	5,111
Cuba	13,751	13,286	465	435	9,654
Dominican Republic	10,670	9,933	737	612	522
Jamaica	16,947	16,266	681	620	481
South America	23,928	22,295	1,633	1,325	3,758
Argentina	3,938	3,770	168	106	1,014
Brazil	1,713	1,510	203	183	366
Colombia	7,627	7,291	336	266	742
Ecuador	5,086	4,913	173	122	444
Asia	73,621	55,322	18,299	17,084	15,362
China†	15,440	12,312	3,128	2,640	3,399
Hong Kong	5,453	4,946	507	468	—
India	5,963	5,532	431	384	384
Israel	2,049	1,724	325	304	1,836
Japan	3,957	1,588	2,369	2,307	2,067
Korea	6,045	2,904	3,141	3,106	1,646
Philippines	20,744	16,208	4,536	4,142	3,877
Africa	5,876	4,925	951	776	671
Australia and Oceania	2,639	1,691	948	885	384
Total	358,579	290,995	67,584	60,016	98,709

Immigrants listed by country of birth; aliens naturalized by country of former allegiance.
*Includes Turkey and the U.S.S.R. †Includes Taiwan.
Source: U.S. Department of Justice, Immigration and Naturalization Service.

Marriage and divorce rates

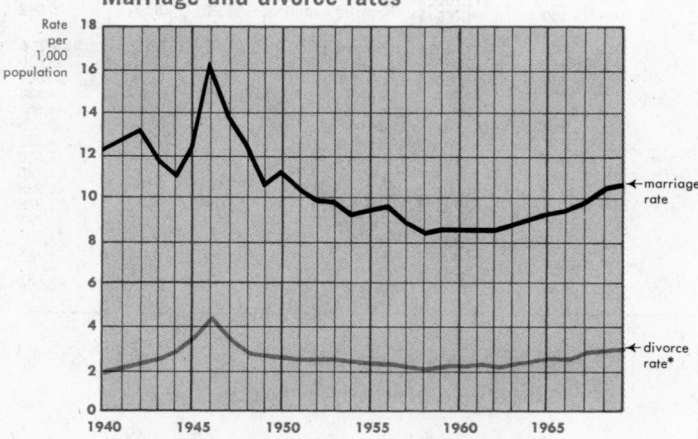

Rate per 1,000 population

→ marriage rate
→ divorce rate*

1940 1945 1950 1955 1960 1965

All rates are based on population excluding Armed Forces abroad, except 1941-46 divorce rates which include Armed Forces abroad.
*Includes annulments.
Source: U.S. Department of Health, Education, and Welfare, Public Health Service, Monthly Vital Statistics Report.

Church membership

Religious body	Total clergy	Inclusive membership
Adventists, Seventh-day	3,151	407,766
Apostolic Overcoming Holy Church of God	350	75,000
Armenian Apostolic Church of America	37	125,000
Armenian Church of North America	64	300,000
Baptist Bodies		
American Baptist Association	3,512	786,536
American Baptist Convention	7,352	1,454,965
Baptist General Conference	1,006	101,226
Baptist Missionary Association of America	3,000	183,342
Conservative Baptist Association of America	...	300,000
Free Will Baptists	3,372	200,000
General Baptists	1,045	65,000
National Baptist Convention of America	28,574	2,668,799
National Baptist Convention, U.S.A., Inc.	27,500	5,500,000
National Baptist Evangelical Life and Soul Saving Assembly of U.S.A.	137	57,674
National Primitive Baptist Convention, Inc.	597	1,523,000
North America Baptist General Conference	445	55,080
Primitive Baptists	...	72,000
Progressive National Baptist Convention, Inc.	863	521,692
Regular Baptist Churches	...	192,495
Southern Baptist Convention	...	11,487,708
United Baptists	1,100	63,641
United Free Will Baptist Church	784	100,000
Brethren (German Baptists)		
Church of the Brethren	2,027	185,198
Buddhist Churches of America	100	100,000
Christian and Missionary Alliance	1,137	120,330
Christian Church (Disciples of Christ)	7,306	1,444,465
Church of God (Anderson, Ind.)	2,763	147,752
Church of God in Christ	6,000	425,000
Church of the Nazarene	6,481	372,943
Churches of Christ	6,200	2,400,000
Congregational Christian Churches, National Association of	478	110,000
Eastern Churches		
American Carpatho-Russian Orthodox Greek Catholic Church	64	104,600
Antiochian Orthodox Christian Archdiocese of New York and All North America	110	100,000
Bulgarian Eastern Orthodox Church	13	86,000
Exarchate of the Russian Orthodox Church in North and South America	98	152,973
Greek Orthodox Archdiocese of North and South America	585	1,875,000
Orthodox Church in America	362	1,000,000
Romanian Orthodox Episcopate of America	50	50,000
Russian Orthodox Church Outside Russia	168	55,000
Serbian Eastern Orthodox Diocese for the U.S.A. and Canada	64	65,000
Ukranian Orthodox Church in America	131	87,475
Episcopal Church	11,041	3,330,272
Evangelical Covenant Church of America	654	67,522
Evangelical Free Church of America	807	63,735
Friends United Meeting	459	69,149
Independent Fundamental Churches of America	901	122,388
Jehovah's Witnesses	None	359,146
Jewish Congregations	6,200	5,780,000
Latter-Day Saints		
Church of Jesus Christ of Latter-day Saints	13,205	1,930,811
Reorganized Church of Jesus Christ of Latter Day Saints	16,007	200,113
Lutherans		
American Lutheran Church	6,009	2,559,588
Lutheran Church in America	7,295	3,135,684
Lutheran Church-Missouri Synod	6,758	2,786,102
Wisconsin Evangelical Lutheran Synod	923	376,319
Mennonite Church	1,895	85,343
Methodists		
African Methodist Episcopal Church	7,089	1,166,301
African Methodist Episcopal Zion Church	5,500	940,000
Christian Methodist Episcopal Church	2,259	466,718
Free Methodist Church of North America	1,771	64,394
United Methodist Church	34,651	10,824,010
Moravian Church in America	226	59,415
North American Old Roman Catholic Church	116	59,422
Pentecostal Assemblies		
Assemblies of God	11,677	625,027
Church of God	2,698	75,290
Church of God (Cleveland, Tenn.)	6,900	257,995
International Church of the Foursquare Gospel	2,690	89,215
Pentecostal Church of God of America, Inc.	1,325	115,000
Pentecostal Holiness Church, Inc.	2,997	66,790
United Pentecostal Church, Inc.	2,300	200,000
Polish National Catholic Church of America	144	282,411
Presbyterians		
Cumberland Presbyterian Church	709	92,368
Presbyterian Church in the U.S.	4,395	957,569
United Presbyterian Church in the U.S.A.	12,955	3,165,490
Reformed Bodies		
Christian Reformed Church	934	284,737
Reformed Church in America	1,281	380,133
Roman Catholic Church	59,525	47,872,089
Salvation Army	5,443	331,711
Spiritualists, International General Assembly of	190	164,072
Triumph the Church and Kingdom of God in Christ	1,315	50,080
Unitarian Universalist Association	868	265,408
United Church of Christ	10,171	1,997,898
Wesleyan Church	3,309	82,358

Table includes churches reporting a membership of 50,000 or more and represents the latest information available.
Source: National Council of Churches, *Yearbook of American Churches, 1971.* (C. H. J.)

National Government

The national executive

December 31, 1970

Department, bureau, or office	Executive officer and official title

DEPARTMENT OF STATE
William P. Rogers, secretary
John N. Irwin II, undersecretary
- Political Affairs — U. Alexis Johnson, undersecretary
- Public Affairs — Michael Collins, asst. secretary
- Economic Affairs — Philip H. Trezise, asst. secretary
- Educational and Cultural Affairs — John Richardson, Jr., asst. secretary
- African Affairs — David D. Newsom, asst. secretary
- Inter-American Affairs — Charles A. Meyer, asst. secretary
- European Affairs — Martin J. Hillenbrand, asst. secy.
- East Asian and Pacific Affairs — Marshall Green, asst. secretary
- Near Eastern, South Asian Affairs — Joseph J. Sisco, asst. secretary
- International Organization Affairs — Samuel DePalma. asst. secretary
- Peace Corps — Joseph H. Blatchford, director

DEPARTMENT OF THE TREASURY
John B. Connally*, secretary
Charles E. Walker, undersecretary
- Monetary Affairs — Paul A. Volcker, undersecretary
- Bureau of Customs — Myles J. Ambrose, commissioner
- Bureau of Engraving and Printing — James A. Conlon, director
- Bureau of the Mint — Mary T. Brooks, director
- Internal Revenue Service — Randolph W. Thrower, commissioner
- U.S. Savings Bonds Division — Elmer L. Rustad, national director
- U.S. Secret Service — James J. Rowley, director

DEPARTMENT OF DEFENSE
Melvin R. Laird, secretary
David Packard, deputy secretary
- Joint Chiefs of Staff — Adm. Thomas H. Moorer, chairman
  - Chief of Staff, U.S. Army — Gen. W. C. Westmoreland
  - Chief of Naval Operations — Adm. Elmo R. Zumwalt, Jr.
  - Chief of Staff, U.S. Air Force — Gen. John D. Ryan
  - Commandant, Marine Corps — Gen. Leonard F. Chapman, Jr.
- Department of the Army — Stanley R. Resor, secretary
  Thaddeus R. Beal, undersecretary
- Department of the Navy — John H. Chafee, secretary
  John W. Warner, undersecretary
  - Marine Corps — Gen. L. F. Chapman, Jr., commandant
- Department of the Air Force — Robert C. Seamans, Jr., secretary
  John L. McLucas, undersecretary

DEPARTMENT OF JUSTICE
John N. Mitchell, attorney general
R. G. Kleindienst, deputy atty. gen.
- Solicitor General — Erwin N. Griswold
- Federal Bureau of Investigation — J. Edgar Hoover, director
- Bureau of Prisons — Norman A. Carlson, director
- Narcotics, Dangerous Drugs — John E. Ingersoll, director
- Immigration and Naturalization — Raymond F. Farrell, commissioner

DEPARTMENT OF THE INTERIOR
Rogers C. B. Morton*, secretary
Fred J. Russell, undersecretary
- Fish and Wildlife, and Parks — (vacancy)
  - National Park Service — George B. Hartzog, Jr., director
- Mineral Resources — Hollis Dole, asst. secretary
  - Bureau of Mines — Elburt F. Osborn, director
  - Geological Survey — William T. Pecora, director
- Public Land Management — Harrison Loesch, asst. secretary
  - Indian Affairs — Louis R. Bruce, commissioner
  - Bureau of Outdoor Recreation — G. Douglas Hofe, Jr., director
- Water and Power Development — James R. Smith, asst. secretary
- Water Quality and Research — (vacancy)

DEPARTMENT OF AGRICULTURE
Clifford M. Hardin, secretary
J. Phil Campbell, undersecretary
- Rural Development, Conservation — Thomas K. Cowden, asst. secretary
  - Farmer Co-op Service — Eric Thor, administrator
  - Forest Service — Edward P. Cliff, chief
  - Rural Electrification — David W. Hamil, administrator
  - Soil Conservation Service — Kenneth E. Grant, administrator
- International Affairs — C. D. Palmby, asst. secretary

DEPARTMENT OF COMMERCE
Maurice H. Stans, secretary
R. C. Siciliano, undersecretary
- Economic Development — Robert A. Podesta, asst. secretary
- Domestic, Internat'l Business — William R. McLellan, asst. secretary
- Science and Technology — Myron Tribus, asst. secretary
- Economic Affairs — Harold C. Passer, asst. secretary
- Tourism — C. L. Washburn, asst. secretary
- Maritime Affairs — Andrew E. Gibson, asst. secretary
- Bureau of the Census — George Hay Brown, director
- Environmental Science Services — Robert M. White, administrator
- National Bureau of Standards — Lewis M. Branscomb, director
- Patent Office — W. E. Schuyler, Jr., commissioner

DEPARTMENT OF HEALTH, EDUCATION, AND WELFARE
Elliott L. Richardson, secretary
John G. Veneman, undersecretary
- Community and Field Services — Patricia Reilly Hitt, asst. secretary
- Education — (vacancy)
- Health and Scientific Affairs — (vacancy)
- Public Health Service — C. C. Johnson, Jr., administrator
- Food and Drug Administration — Charles C. Edwards, commissioner
- Social Security Administration — Robert M. Ball, commissioner

DEPARTMENT OF LABOR
James D. Hodgson, secretary
Laurence H. Silberman, undersecretary
- Manpower — Malcolm R. Lovell, Jr., asst. secretary
- Labor-Management Relations — W. J. Usery, Jr., asst. secretary
- Wage and Labor Standards — A. A. Fletcher, asst. secretary
  - Women's Bureau — Elizabeth D. Koontz, director
  - Employees' Compensation — John Ekeberg, director

POST OFFICE DEPARTMENT
W. M. Blount, postmaster general
E. T. Klassen, deputy postmaster gen.
- Bureau of Operations — Frank J. Nunlist, asst. post. gen.
- Bureau of Personnel — Kenneth A. Housman, asst. post. gen.
- Chief Postal Inspector — William J. Cotter

DEPARTMENT OF HOUSING AND URBAN DEVELOPMENT
George W. Romney, secretary
R. C. Van Dusen, undersecretary
- Research and Technology — Harold B. Finger, asst. secretary
- Housing Production, Mortgage Credit — Eugene A. Gulledge, asst. secretary
- Model Cities — Floyd H. Hyde, asst. secretary
- Renewal and Housing Management — Lawrence M. Cox, asst. secretary

DEPARTMENT OF TRANSPORTATION
John A. Volpe, secretary
James M. Beggs, undersecretary
- U.S. Coast Guard — Adm. Chester R. Bender, commandant
- Federal Aviation Administration — John H. Shaffer, administrator
- Federal Highway Administration — F. C. Turner, administrator
- Federal Railroad Administration — R. N. Whitman, administrator
- Urban Mass Transportation — C. C. Villarreal, administrator
- St. Lawrence Seaway — David W. Oberlin, administrator
- National Transportation Safety — John H. Reed, board chairman

INDEPENDENT OFFICES AND ESTABLISHMENTS

- Atomic Energy Commission — Glenn T. Seaborg, chairman
- Civil Aeronautics Board — Secor D. Browne, chairman
- Commission of Fine Arts — William Walton, chairman
- District of Columbia — Walter E. Washington, commissioner
- Environmental Protection Agency — William D. Ruckelshaus, director
- Equal Employment Opportunity Commission — William H. Brown III, chairman
- Export-Import Bank of the U.S. — Henry Kearns, pres. and chairman
- Federal Communications Commission — Dean Burch, chairman
- Federal Deposit Insurance Corp. — Frank Wille, chairman
- Federal Maritime Commission — Helen Delich Bentley, chairman
- Federal Mediation and Conciliation Service — J. Curtis Counts, director
- Federal Power Commission — John N. Nassikas, chairman
- Federal Reserve System — Arthur F. Burns, chairman
- Federal Trade Commission — Miles W. Kirkpatrick, chairman
- General Services Administration — Robert L. Kunzig, administrator
- Interstate Commerce Commission — George M. Stafford, chairman
- National Aeronautics and Space Administration — (vacancy)
- National Labor Relations Board — Edward B. Miller, chairman
- National Science Foundation — William D. McElroy, director
- Railroad Retirement Board — H. W. Habermeyer, chairman
- Securities and Exchange Commission — (vacancy)
- Selective Service System — Curtis W. Tarr, director
- Small Business Administration — Hilary Sandoval, Jr., administrator
- Smithsonian Institution — S. Dillon Ripley, secretary
- Tennessee Valley Authority — Aubrey J. Wagner, chairman
- U.S. Arms Control and Disarmament Agency — Gerard Smith, director
- U.S. Civil Service Commission — Robert E. Hampton, chairman
- U.S. Information Agency — Frank Shakespeare, director
- U.S. Tariff Commission — Glenn W. Sutton, commissioner
- Veterans Administration — Donald E. Johnson, administrator

EXECUTIVE OFFICE OF THE PRESIDENT

- Counsellor to the President — Robert H. Finch
- Counsellor to the President — Donald Rumsfeld
- Counsellor to the President — Robert P. Mayo
- Assistant, Domestic Affairs — John D. Ehrlichman
- Assistant, National Security — Henry A. Kissinger
- Spec. Asst., Consumer Affairs — Virginia H. Knauer
- Director, Office of Management and Budget — George P. Shultz
- Director, Office of Science and Technology — Edward E. David, Jr.
- Chairman, Council on Environmental Quality — Russell E. Train

QUASI-OFFICIAL AGENCIES

- American National Red Cross — E. Roland Harriman, chairman
- National Academy of Sciences — Philip Handler, president
- National Academy of Engineering — Eric A. Walker, president

*Nominated, subject to congressional approval.

House of Representatives

membership in 1970, and new members elected Nov. 3, 1970

State, district, name, and party	Residence
Ala.—1. Edwards, W. J. (R)	Mobile
2. Dickinson, W. L. (R)	Montgomery
3. Andrews, George W. (D)	Union Springs
4. Nichols, William (D)	Sylacauga
5. Flowers, W. W. (D)	Tuscaloosa
6. Buchanan, John H., Jr. (R)	Birmingham
7. Bevill, Tom (D)	Jasper
8. Jones, Robert E., Jr. (D)	Scottsboro
Alaska—Pollock, H. W. (R)	Anchorage
*Begich, Nick J. (D)	
Ariz.—1. Rhodes, John J. (R)	Mesa
2. Udall, Morris K. (D)	Tucson
3. Steiger, Sam (R)	Prescott
Ark.—1. Alexander, Bill (D)	Osceola
2. Mills, Wilbur D. (D)	Kensett
3. Hammerschmidt, J. P. (R)	Harrison
4. Pryor, David (D)	Camden
Calif.—1. Clausen, Don H. (R)	Crescent City
2. Johnson, Harold T. (D)	Roseville
3. Moss, John E. (D)	Sacramento
4. Leggett, Robert L. (D)	Vallejo
5. Burton, Phillip (D)	San Francisco
6. Mailliard, William S. (R)	San Francisco
7. Cohelan, Jeffery (D)	Berkeley
*Dellums, R. V. (D)	Berkeley
8. Miller, George P. (D)	Alameda
9. Edwards, W. Donlon (D)	San Jose
10. Gubser, Charles S. (R)	Gilroy
11. McCloskey, Paul N., Jr. (R)	Portola Valley
12. Talcott, Burt L. (R)	Salinas
13. Teague, Charles M. (R)	Ojai
14. Waldie, Jerome R. (D)	Antioch
15. McFall, John J. (D)	Manteca
16. Sisk, B. F. (D)	Fresno
17. Anderson, Glenn M. (D)	Torrance
18. Mathias, Robert B. (R)	Visalia
19. Holifield, Chet (D)	Montebello
20. Smith, H. Allen (R)	Glendale
21. Hawkins, Augustus F. (D)	Los Angeles
22. Corman, James C. (D)	Van Nuys
23. Clawson, Del M. (R)	Compton
24. Rousselot, John H. (R)	San Marino
25. Wiggins, Charles (R)	El Monte
26. Rees, Thomas (D)	Beverly Hills
27. Goldwater, Barry, Jr. (R)	Burbank
28. Bell, Alphonzo (R)	Beverly Hills
29. Brown, George E., Jr. (D)	Monterey Park
*Danielson, George E. (D)	Los Angeles
30. Roybal, Edward R. (D)	Los Angeles
31. Wilson, Charles H. (D)	Los Angeles
32. Hosmer, Craig (R)	Long Beach
33. Pettis, Jerry (R)	Loma Linda
34. Hanna, Richard T. (D)	Fullerton
35. Schmitz, John G. (R)	Tustin
36. Wilson, Bob (R)	San Diego
37. Van Deerlin, Lionel (D)	San Diego
38. Tunney, John V. (D)	Riverside
*Veysey, Victor A. (R)	Brawley
Colo.—1. Rogers, Byron G. (D)	Denver
*McKevitt, James D. (R)	Denver
2. Brotzman, D. G. (R)	Boulder
3. Evans, Frank (D)	Pueblo
4. Aspinall, Wayne N. (D)	Palisade
Conn.—1. Daddario, Emilio Q. (D)	Hartford
*Cotter, William R. (D)	Hartford
2. (vacancy)	
*Steele, Robert H. (R)	
3. Giaimo, Robert N. (D)	North Haven
4. Weicker, Lowell P., Jr. (R)	Greenwich
*McKinney, Stewart B. (R)	Fairfield
5. Monagan, John S. (D)	Waterbury
6. Meskill, Thomas J. (R)	New Britain
*Grasso, Ella T. (D)	Windsor Locks
Del.—Roth, William V., Jr. (R)	Wilmington
*duPont, Pierre S., IV (R)	Rockland
Fla.—1. Sikes, Robert L. F. (D)	Crestview
2. Fuqua, Don (D)	Altha
3. Bennett, Charles E. (D)	Jacksonville
4. Chappell, William, Jr. (D)	Ocala
5. Frey, Louis, Jr. (R)	Winter Park
6. Gibbons, Sam (D)	Tampa
7. Haley, James A. (D)	Sarasota
8. Cramer, William C. (R)	St. Petersburg
*Young, C. William (R)	Seminole
9. Rogers, Paul G. (D)	West Palm Beach
10. Burke, J. Herbert (R)	Hollywood
11. Pepper, Claude (D)	Miami
12. Fascell, Dante B. (D)	Miami
Ga.—1. Hagan, G. Elliott (D)	Sylvania
2. O'Neal, M. (D)	Bainbridge
*Mathis, Dawson (D)	
3. Brinkley, Jack (D)	Columbus
4. Blackburn, B. B. (R)	Atlanta
5. Thompson, S. F. (R)	East Point
6. Flynt, J. J., Jr. (D)	Griffin
7. Davis, John W. (D)	Summerville
8. Stuckey, W. S., Jr. (D)	Eastman
9. Landrum, Phil M. (D)	Jasper
10. Stephens, Robert G., Jr. (D)	Athens
Hawaii—Mink, Patsy (D)	Waipahu
Matsunaga, Spark M. (D)	Honolulu
Ida.—1. McClure, James A. (R)	Payette
2. Hansen, Orval (R)	Idaho Falls
Ill.—1. Dawson, William L. (D)	Chicago
*Metcalfe, Ralph (D)	Chicago
2. Mikva, Abner (D)	Chicago
3. Murphy, William T. (D)	Chicago
*Murphy, Morgan (D)	Chicago
4. Derwinski, Edward J. (R)	Chicago
5. Kluczynski, John C. (D)	Chicago
6. Collins, George W. (D)	Chicago
7. Annunzio, Frank (D)	Chicago
8. Rostenkowski, Dan (D)	Chicago
9. Yates, Sidney R. (D)	Chicago
10. Collier, Harold R. (R)	Berwyn
11. Pucinski, Roman C. (D)	Chicago
12. McClory, Robert (R)	Lake Bluff
13. Crane, Philip M. (R)	Arlington Heights
14. Erlenborn, J. N. (R)	Elmhurst
15. Reid, Charlotte T. (R)	Aurora
16. Anderson, John B. (R)	Rockford
17. Arends, Leslie C. (R)	Melvin
18. Michel, Robert H. (R)	Peoria
19. Railsback, Thomas F. (R)	Moline
20. Findley, Paul (R)	Pittsfield
21. Gray, Kenneth J. (D)	West Frankfort
22. Springer, William L. (R)	Champaign
23. Shipley, George E. (D)	Olney
24. Price, Melvin (D)	East St. Louis
Ind.—1. Madden, Ray J. (D)	Gary
2. Landgrebe, Earl F. (R)	Valparaiso
3. Brademas, John (D)	South Bend
4. Adair, E. Ross (R)	Fort Wayne
*Roush, J. Edward (D)	Huntington
5. Roudebush, Richard L. (R)	Noblesville
*Hillis, Elwood H. (R)	Kokomo
6. Bray, William G. (R)	Martinsville
7. Myers, John (R)	Covington
8. Zion, Roger (R)	Evansville
9. Hamilton, L. H. (D)	Columbus
10. Dennis, David (R)	Richmond
11. Jacobs, A., Jr. (D)	Indianapolis
Iowa—1. Schwengel, Fred (R)	Davenport
2. Culver, J. C. (D)	Marion
3. Gross, H. R. (R)	Waterloo
4. Kyl, John H. (R)	Bloomfield
5. Smith, Neal (D)	Altoona
6. Mayne, Wiley (R)	Sioux City
7. Scherle, W. J. (R)	Henderson
Kan.—1. Sebelius, Keith G. (R)	Norton
2. Mize, C. L. (R)	Atchison
*Roy, William R. (D)	
3. Winn, Larry, Jr. (R)	Leawood
4. Shriver, Garner E. (R)	Wichita
5. Skubitz, Joseph (R)	Pittsburg
Ky.—1. Stubblefield, Frank A. (D)	Murray
2. Natcher, William H. (D)	Bowling Green
3. Cowger, William O. (R)	Louisville
*Mazzoli, Romano L. (D)	Louisville
4. Snyder, Gene (R)	Jeffersontown
5. Carter, Tim L. (R)	Tompkinsville
6. Watts, John C. (D)	Nicholasville
7. Perkins, Carl D. (D)	Hindman
La.—1. Hébert, F. Edward (D)	New Orleans
2. Boggs, Hale (D)	New Orleans
3. Caffery, Patrick (D)	New Iberia
4. Waggonner, Joe D., Jr. (D)	Plain Dealing
5. Passman, Otto E. (D)	Monroe
6. Rarick, John R. (D)	St. Francisville
7. Edwards, Edwin W. (D)	Crowley
8. Long, Speedy O. (D)	Jena
Me.—1. Kyros, Peter (D)	Portland
2. Hathaway, W. D. (D)	Auburn
Md.—1. Morton, Rogers C. B. (R)	Easton
2. Long, Clarence D. (D)	Ruxton
3. Garmatz, Edward A. (D)	Baltimore
4. Fallon, George H. (D)	Baltimore
*Sarbanes, Paul S. (D)	Baltimore
5. Hogan, Lawrence J. (R)	Hyattsville
6. Beall, J. Glenn, Jr. (R)	Frostburg
*Byron, Goodloe E. (D)	Frederick
7. Friedel, Samuel N. (D)	Baltimore
*Mitchell, Parren J. (D)	Baltimore
8. Gude, Gilbert (R)	Bethesda
Mass.—1. Conte, Silvio O. (R)	Pittsfield
2. Boland, Edward P. (D)	Springfield
3. Philbin, Philip J. (D)	Clinton
*Drinan, Robert F. (D)	Brighton
4. Donohue, Harold D. (D)	Worcester
5. Morse, F. Bradford (R)	Lowell
6. Harrington, M. J. (D)	Beverly
7. Macdonald, Torbert H. (D)	Malden
8. O'Neill, Thomas P., Jr. (D)	Cambridge
9. McCormack, John W. (D	Dorchester
*Hicks, Louise Day (D)	Boston
10. Heckler, Margaret (R)	Wellesley Hills
11. Burke, James A. (D)	Milton
12. Keith, Hastings (R)	West Bridgewater
Mich.—1. Conyers, John, Jr. (D)	Detroit
2. Esch, Marvin (R)	Ann Arbor
3. Brown, Garry E. (R)	Schoolcraft
4. Hutchinson, Edward (R)	Fennville
5. Ford, Gerald R., Jr. (R)	Grand Rapids
6. Chamberlain, Charles E. (R)	East Lansing
7. Riegle, D. W., Jr. (R)	Flint
8. Harvey, James (R)	Saginaw
9. Vander Jagt, Guy (R)	Cadillac
10. Cederberg, Elford A. (R)	Bay City
11. Ruppe, Philip (R)	Houghton
12. O'Hara, James G. (D)	Utica
13. Diggs, Charles C., Jr. (D)	Detroit
14. Nedzi, Lucien N. (D)	Detroit
15. Ford, W. D. (D)	Taylor
16. Dingell, John D. (D)	Detroit
17. Griffiths, Martha W. (D)	Detroit
18. Broomfield, William S. (R)	Royal Oak
19. McDonald, J. H. (R)	Detroit
Minn.—1. Quie, Albert H. (R)	Dennison
2. Nelsen, Ancher (R)	Hutchinson
3. MacGregor, Clark (R)	Plymouth Village
*Frenzek, William (R)	Minneapolis
4. Karth, Joseph E. (D)	St. Paul
5. Fraser, Donald M. (D)	Minneapolis
6. Zwach, John M. (R)	Walnut Grove
7. Langen, Odin (R)	Kennedy
*Bergland, Bob S. (D)	Roseau
8. Blatnik, John A. (D)	Chisholm
Miss.—1. Abernethy, Thomas G. (D)	Okolona
2. Whitten, Jamie L. (D)	Charleston
3. Griffin, Charles (D)	Utica
4. Montgomery, G. V. (D)	Meridian
5. Colmer, William M. (D)	Pascagoula
Mo.—1. Clay, William (D)	St. Louis
2. Symington, James W. (D)	Clayton
3. Sullivan, Leonor K. (D)	St. Louis
4. Randall, William J. (D)	Independence
5. Bolling, Richard (D)	Kansas City
6. Hull, W. R., Jr. (D)	Weston
7. Hall, Durward G. (R)	Springfield
8. Ichord, Richard H. (D)	Houston
9. Hungate, W. L. (D)	Troy
10. Burlison, Bill D. (D)	Cape Girardeau
Mont.—1. Olsen, Arnold (D)	Helena
*Shoup, Richard G. (R)	
2. Melcher, John (D)	Billings
Neb.—1. Denney, Robert V. (R)	Fairbury
*Thone, Charles (R)	
2. Cunningham, Glenn (R)	Omaha
*McCollister, John Y. (R)	
3. Martin, David (R)	Kearney
Nev.—Baring, Walter S. (D)	Reno
N.H.—1. Wyman, Louis C. (R)	Manchester
2. Cleveland, James C. (R)	New London
N.J.—1. Hunt, John E. (R)	Pitman
2. Sandman, Charles W., Jr. (R)	Cape May
3. Howard, J. J. (D)	Wall Township
4. Thompson, Frank, Jr. (D)	Trenton
5. Frelinghuysen, Peter, Jr. (R)	Morristown
6. (vacancy)	
*Forsythe, Edwin B. (R)	Moorestown
7. Widnall, William B. (R)	Saddle River
8. Roe, Robert A. (D)	
9. Helstoski, Henry (D)	E. Rutherford
10. Rodino, Peter W., Jr. (D)	Newark
11. Minish, Joseph G. (D)	West Orange
12. Dwyer, Florence P. (R)	Elizabeth
13. Gallagher, Cornelius E. (D)	Bayonne
14. Daniels, Dominick V. (D)	Jersey City
15. Patten, Edward J. (D)	Perth Amboy
N.M.—1. Lujan, Manuel, Jr. (R)	Albuquerque
2. Foreman, Ed (R)	Las Cruces
*Runnels, Harold L. (D)	Lovington
N.Y.—1. Pike, Otis G. (D)	Riverhead
2. Grover, James R., Jr. (R)	Babylon
3. Wolff, L. L. (D)	Great Neck
4. Wydler, John W. (R)	Garden City
5. Lowenstein, A. K. (D)	Long Beach
*Lent, Norman F. (R)	New York City
6. Halpern, Seymour (R)	Forest Hills
7. Addabbo, Joseph P. (D)	Ozone Park
8. Rosenthal, Benjamin S. (D)	Elmhurst
9. Delaney, James J. (D)	Long Island City
10. Celler, Emanuel (D)	Brooklyn
11. Brasco, Frank J. (D)	Brooklyn
12. Chisholm, Shirley (D)	Brooklyn
13. Podell, B. L. (D)	Brooklyn
14. Rooney, John J. (D)	Brooklyn
15. Carey, Hugh L. (D)	Brooklyn
16. Murphy, John M. (D)	Staten Island
17. Koch, Edward I. (D)	New York City
18. Powell, Adam C. (D)	New York City
*Rangel, Charles B. (D)	New York City
19. Farbstein, Leonard (D)	New York City
*Abzug, Bella (D)	New York City
20. Ryan, William Fitts (D)	New York City
21. Badillo, Herman (D)	Bronx
22. Scheuer, James (D)	Bronx
23. Bingham, J. B. (D)	Bronx
24. Biaggi, Mario (D)	Bronx
25. Ottinger, R. (D)	Pleasantville
*Peyser, Peter A. (R)	Irvington
26. Reid, Ogden R. (R)	Purchase
27. McKneally, M. B. (R)	Newburgh
*Dow, John G. (D)	Grand View
28. Fish, Hamilton, Jr. (R)	Millbrook
29. Button, Daniel E., Jr. (R)	Albany
*Stratton, Samuel S. (D)	Amsterdam
30. King, Carleton J. (R)	Saratoga Springs
31. McEwen, Robert (R)	Ogdensburg
32. Pirnie, Alexander (R)	New Hartford
33. Robison, Howard W. (R)	Oswego
34. Terry, John H. (R)	Syracuse
35. Hanley, James M. (D)	Syracuse
36. Horton, Frank J. (R)	Rochester
37. Conable, B., Jr. (R)	Alexander
38. Hastings, James F. (R)	Allegany
39. McCarthy, R. D. (D)	Buffalo
*Kemp, Jack F. (R)	Buffalo
40. Smith, H. P., III (R)	N. Tonawanda
41. Dulski, Thaddeus J. (D)	Buffalo
N.C.—1. Jones, Walter B. (D)	Farmville
2. Fountain, L. H. (D)	Tarboro
3. Henderson, David N. (D)	Wallace
4. Galifianakis, Nick (D)	Durham
5. Mizell, Wilmer (R)	Winston-Salem
6. Preyer, L. R. (D)	Greensboro

State, district, name, and party	Residence
7. Lennon, Alton (D)	Wilmington
8. Ruth, Earl B. (R)	Salisbury
9. Jonas, Charles Raper (R)	Lincolnton
10. Broyhill, James T. (R)	Lenoir
11. Taylor, Roy A. (D)	Black Mountain
N.D.—1. Andrews, Mark (R)	Mapleton
2. Kleppe, Thomas S. (R)	Bismarck
*Link, Arthur A. (D)	Alexander
Ohio—1. Taft, Robert A., Jr. (R)	Cincinnati
*Keating, William J. (R)	
2. Clancy, Donald D. (R)	Cincinnati
3. Whalen, Charles W., Jr. (R)	Dayton
4. McCulloch, William M. (R)	Piqua
5. Latta, Delbert L. (R)	Bowling Green
6. Harsha, William H., Jr. (R)	Portsmouth
7. Brown, Clarence J., Jr. (R)	Urbana
8. Betts, Jackson E. (R)	Findlay
9. Ashley, Thomas L. (D)	Waterville
10. Miller, Clarence E. (R)	Lancaster
11. Stanton, John W. (R)	Painesville
12. Devine, Samuel L. (R)	Columbus
13. Mosher, Charles A. (R)	Oberlin
14. Ayres, William H. (R)	Akron
*Seiberling, John F., Jr. (D)	Akron
15. Wylie, Chalmers P. (R)	Columbus
16. Bow, Frank T. (R)	Canton
17. Ashbrook, John M. (R)	Johnstown
18. Hays, Wayne L. (D)	Flushing
19. (vacancy)	
*Carney, Charles J. (D)	
20. Feighan, Michael A. (D)	Cleveland
*Stanton, James V. (D)	Cleveland
21. Stokes, Louis (D)	Shaker Heights
22. Vanik, Charles A. (D)	Cleveland
23. Minshall, William E. (R)	Cleveland
24. Lukens, Donald E. (R)	Middletown
*Powell, Walter E. (R)	Fairfield
Okla.—1. Belcher, Page (R)	Enid
2. Edmondson, Ed (D)	Muskogee
3. Albert, Carl (D)	McAlester
4. Steed, Tom (D)	Shawnee
5. Jarman, John (D)	Oklahoma City
6. Camp, J. N. H. (R)	Waukomis
Ore.—1. Wyatt, Wendell (R)	Astoria
2. Ullman, Al (D)	Baker
3. Green, Edith (D)	Portland
4. Dellenback, John R. (R)	Medford
Penn.—1. Barrett, William A. (D)	Philadelphia
2. Nix, Robert N. C. (D)	Philadelphia
3. Byrne, James A. (D)	Philadelphia
4. Eilberg, Joshua (D)	Philadelphia
5. Green, William J., III (D)	Philadelphia
6. Yatron, Gus (D)	Reading
7. Williams, L. G. (R)	Springfield
8. Biester, E. G., Jr. (R)	Furlong
9. (vacancy)	
*Ware, John H., III (R)	Oxford
10. McDade, Joseph M. (R)	Scranton
11. Flood, Daniel J. (D)	Wilkes-Barre
12. Whalley, J. Irving (R)	Windber
13. Coughlin, R. L. (R)	Villanova
14. Moorhead, William S. (D)	Pittsburgh
15. Rooney, Fred B. (D)	Bethlehem
16. Eshleman, Edwin D. (R)	Lancaster
17. Schneebeli, Herman T. (R)	Williamsport
18. Corbett, Robert J. (R)	Pittsburgh
19. Goodling, George A. (R)	Loganville
20. Gaydos, Joseph (D)	McKeesport
21. Dent, John H. (D)	Jeannette
22. Saylor, John P. (R)	Johnstown
23. Johnson, Albert W. (R)	Smethport
24. Vigorito, J. P. (D)	Erie
25. Clark, Frank M. (D)	Bessemer
26. Morgan, Thomas E. (D)	Fredericktown
27. Fulton, James G. (R)	Pittsburgh
R.I.—1. St Germain, Fernand J. (D)	Woonsocket
2. Tiernan, Robert O. (D)	Warwick
S.C.—1. †Rivers, L. Mendel (D)	Charleston
2. Watson, Albert W. (R)	Columbia
*Spence, Floyd D. (R)	Lexington
3. Dorn, W. J. Bryan (D)	Greenwood
4. Mann, James R. (D)	Greenville
5. Gettys, Thomas S. (D)	Rock Hill
6. McMillan, John L. (D)	Florence
S.D.—1. Reifel, Ben (R)	Aberdeen
*Denholm, Frank E. (D)	
2. Berry, E. Y. (R)	McLaughlin
*Abourezk, James (D)	Rapid City
Tenn.—1. Quillen, James H. (R)	Kingsport
2. Duncan, John J. (R)	Knoxville
3. Brock, W. E., III (R)	Chattanooga
*Baker, LaMar E. (R)	Chattanooga
4. Evins, Joseph L. (D)	Smithville
5. Fulton, Richard (D)	Nashville
6. Anderson, W. R. (D)	Waverly
7. Blanton, Ray (D)	Adamsville
8. Jones, Edward (D)	Yorkville
9. Kuykendall, Dan (R)	Memphis
Tex.—1. Patman, Wright (D)	Texarkana
2. Dowdy, John (D)	Athens
3. Collins, James M. (R)	Grand Prairie
4. Roberts, Ray (D)	McKinney
5. Cabell, Earle (D)	Dallas
6. Teague, Olin E. (D)	College Station
7. Bush, George (R)	Houston
*Archer, William R. (R)	Houston
8. Eckhardt, Robert C. (D)	Houston
9. Brooks, Jack (D)	Beaumont
10. Pickle, J. J. (D)	Austin
11. Poage, W. R. (D)	Waco
12. Wright, James C., Jr. (D)	Fort Worth
13. Purcell, Graham (D)	Wichita Falls
14. Young, John (D)	Corpus Christi
15. de la Garza, E. (D)	Mission
16. White, Richard C. (D)	El Paso
17. Burleson, Omar (D)	Anson
18. Price, Robert (R)	Pampa
19. Mahon, George (D)	Lubbock
20. Gonzalez, Henry B. (D)	San Antonio
21. Fisher, O. C. (D)	San Angelo
22. Casey, Robert R. (D)	Houston
23. Kazen, Abraham, Jr. (D)	Laredo
Utah—1. Burton, Laurence J. (R)	Ogden
*McKay, Koln G. (D)	Huntsville
2. Lloyd, Sherman P. (R)	Salt Lake City
Vt.—Stafford, Robert T. (R)	Rutland City
Va.—1. Downing, Thomas N. (D)	Newport News
2. Whitehurst, G. W. (R)	Norfolk
3. Satterfield, D. E., III (D)	Richmond
4. Abbitt, Watkins M. (D)	Appomattox
5. Daniel, W. C. (D)	Danville
6. Poff, Richard H. (R)	Radford
7. Marsh, John O., Jr. (D)	Strasburg
*Robinson, James K. (R)	Winchester
8. Scott, William L. (R)	Fairfax
9. Wampler, William C. (R)	Bristol
10. Broyhill, Joel T. (R)	Arlington
Wash.—1. Pelly, Thomas M. (R)	Seattle
2. Meeds, Lloyd (D)	Everett
3. Hansen, Julia Butler (D)	Cathlamet
4. May, Catherine (R)	Yakima
*McCormack, Mike (D)	Richland
5. Foley, Thomas S. (D)	Spokane
6. Hicks, Floyd V. (D)	Tacoma
7. Adams, B. (D)	Seattle
W.Va.—1. Mollohan, R. H. (D)	Fairmont
2. Staggers, Harley O. (D)	Keyser
3. Slack, John M., Jr. (D)	Charleston
4. Hechler, Ken (D)	Huntington
5. Kee, James (D)	Bluefield
Wis.—1. Schadeberg, H. C. (R)	Burlington
*Aspin, Leslie (D)	Racine
2. Kastenmeier, Robert W. (D)	Watertown
3. Thomson, Vernon W. (R)	Richland Center
4. Zablocki, Clement J. (D)	Milwaukee
5. Reuss, Henry S. (D)	Milwaukee
6. Steiger, William A. (R)	Oshkosh
7. Obey, David R. (D)	Wausau
8. Byrnes, John W. (R)	Green Bay
9. Davis, Glenn R. (R)	New Berlin
10. O'Konski, Alvin E. (R)	Mercer
Wyo.—Wold, John (R)	Casper
*Roncalio, Teno (D)	Cheyenne

*Elected to replace member listed immediately above.
†Died December 28, 1970.

Senate

membership in 1970, and new members elected Nov. 3, 1970.

State, name, and party	Residence	Term expires
Ala.—Allen, James B. (D)	Gadsden	1975
Sparkman, John (D)	Huntsville	1973
Alaska—Gravel, Mike (D)	Anchorage	1975
*Stevens, Theodore F. (R)	Anchorage	1977
Ariz.—Goldwater, Barry (R)	Phoenix	1975
*Fannin, Paul J. (R)	Phoenix	1977
Ark.—Fulbright, J. W. (D)	Fayetteville	1975
McClellan, John (D)	Little Rock	1973
Calif.—Cranston, Alan (D)	Los Angeles	1975
Murphy, George (R)	Beverly Hills	1971
†Tunney, John V. (D)	Riverside	1977
Colo.—Dominick, Peter (R)	Englewood	1975
Allott, Gordon (R)	Lamar	1973
Conn.—Ribicoff, Abraham (D)	Hartford	1975
Dodd, Thomas J. (D)	West Hartford	1971
†Weicker, Lowell P., Jr. (R)	Greenwich	1977
Del.—*Williams, John J. (R)	Millsboro	1977
Boggs, J. Caleb (R)	Wilmington	1973
†Roth, William V., Jr. (R)	Wilmington	1977
Fla.—Gurney, Edward (R)	Winter Park	1975
Holland, Spessard L. (D)	Bartow	1971
†Chiles, Lawton (D)	Lakeland	1977
Ga.—Talmadge, Herman (D)	Lovejoy	1975
Russell, Richard B. (D)	Winder	1973
Hawaii—Inouye, Daniel K. (D)	Honolulu	1975
*Fong, Hiram L. (R)	Honolulu	1977
Ida.—Church, Frank (D)	Boise	1975
Jordan, Len B. (R)	Boise	1973
Ill.—Smith, Ralph T. (R)	Alton	1971
†Stevenson, Adlai, III (D)	Chicago	1977
Percy, Charles H. (R)	Kenilworth	1973
Ind.—Bayh, Birch E., Jr. (D)	Terre Haute	1975
*Hartke, Vance (D)	Evansville	1977
Ia.—Hughes, Harold (D)	Ida Grove	1975
Miller, Jack R. (R)	Sioux City	1973
Kan.—Dole, Robert (R)	Russell	1975
Pearson, James B. (R)	Prairie Village	1973
Ky.—Cook, Marlow W. (R)	Louisville	1975
Cooper, John S. (R)	Somerset	1973
La.—Long, Russell (D)	Baton Rouge	1975
Ellender, Allen J. (D)	Houma	1973
Me.—*Muskie, Edmund S. (D)	Waterville	1977
Smith, Margaret Chase (R)	Skowhegan	1973
Md.—Mathias, C. M., Jr. (R)	Frederick	1975
Tydings, Joseph D. (D)	Havre de Grace	1971
†Beall, J. Glenn, Jr. (R)	Frostburg	1977
Mass.—*Kennedy, Edward M. (D)	Boston	1977
Brooke, Edward W. (R)	Newton Center	1973
Mich.—*Hart, Philip A. (D)	Mackinac Island	1977
Griffin, Robert P. (R)	Traverse City	1973
Minn.—McCarthy, Eugene (D)	St. Paul	1971
†Humphrey, Hubert H. (D)	Minneapolis	1977
Mondale, Walter F. (D)	Minneapolis	1973
Miss.—*Stennis, John (D)	DeKalb	1977
Eastland, James (D)	Doddsville	1973
Mo.—Eagleton, T. F. (D)	St. Louis	1975
*Symington, Stuart (D)	St. Louis	1977
Mont.—*Mansfield, Mike (D)	Missoula	1977
Metcalf, Lee (D)	Helena	1973
Neb.—*Hruska, Roman L. (R)	Omaha	1977
Curtis, Carl T. (R)	Minden	1973
Nev.—Bible, Alan (D)	Reno	1975
*Cannon, Howard W. (D)	Las Vegas	1977
N.H.—Cotton, Norris (R)	Lebanon	1975
McIntyre, Thomas J. (D)	Laconia	1973
N.J.—*Williams, Harrison, Jr. (D)	Westfield	1977
Case, Clifford P. (R)	Rahway	1973
N.M.—Anderson, Clinton (D)	Albuquerque	1973
*Montoya, Joseph M. (D)	Santa Fe	1977
N.Y.—Javits, Jacob K. (R)	New York	1975
Goodell, Charles E. (R)	Jamestown	1971
†Buckley, James L. (C)	New York	1977
N.C.—Ervin, Sam J., Jr. (D)	Morganton	1975
Jordan, B. Everett (D)	Saxapahaw	1973
N.D.—Young, Milton R. (R)	La Moure	1975
*Burdick, Quentin N. (D)	Fargo	1977
Ohio—Saxbe, William (R)	Mechanicsburg	1975
Young, Stephen M. (D)	Shaker Heights	1971
†Taft, Robert, Jr. (R)	Cincinnati	1977
Okla.—Bellmon, Henry (R)	Red Rock	1975
Harris, Fred R. (D)	Lawton	1973
Ore.—Packwood, Robert (R)	Portland	1975
Hatfield, Mark O. (R)	Salem	1973
Penn.—Schweiker, R. S. (R)	Worcester	1975
*Scott, Hugh (R)	Philadelphia	1977
R. I.—*Pastore, John O. (D)	Providence	1977
Pell, Claiborne (D)	Newport	1973
S.C.—Hollings, Ernest F. (D)	Charleston	1975
Thurmond, Strom (R)	Aiken	1973
S.D.—McGovern, George (D)	Mitchell	1975
Mundt, Karl E. (R)	Madison	1973
Tenn.—Gore, Albert (D)	Carthage	1971
†Brock, William E., III (R)	Chattanooga	1977
Baker, Howard, Jr. (R)	Knoxville	1973
Tex.—Yarborough, Ralph (D)	Austin	1971
†Bentsen, Lloyd M., Jr. (D)	Houston	1977
Tower, John G. (R)	Wichita Falls	1973
Utah—Bennett, Wallace (R)	Salt Lake City	1975
*Moss, Frank E. (D)	Salt Lake City	1977
Vt.—Aiken, George D. (R)	Putney	1975
*Prouty, Winston L. (R)	Newport	1977
Va.—*Byrd, Harry F., Jr. (D)	Winchester	1977
Spong, William, Jr. (D)	Portsmouth	1973
Wash.—Magnuson, Warren (D)	Seattle	1975
*Jackson, Henry M. (D)	Everett	1977
W.Va.—*Byrd, Robert C. (D)	Sophia	1977
Randolph, Jennings (D)	Elkins	1973
Wis.—Nelson, Gaylord (D)	Madison	1975
*Proxmire, William (D)	Madison	1977
Wyo.—*McGee, Gale W. (D)	Laramie	1977
Hansen, Clifford P. (R)	Jackson	1973

*Incumbent, reelected.
†Elected to replace member listed immediately above.

Supreme Court

Chief Justice of the United States: Warren Earl Burger

Associate Justices:

Hugo L. Black	Potter Stewart
William O. Douglas	Byron R. White
John M. Harlan	Thurgood Marshall
William J. Brennan, Jr.	Harry A. Blackmun

Act	House vote	Senate vote	Date of enactment
Voting Rights Bill (Extended for five years the Voting Rights Act of 1965. Lowered voting age in all federal elections to 18.)	224–183 Yeas: D. 165, R. 59 Nays: D. 66, R. 117 (June 17)	64–12 Yeas: D. 31, R. 33 Nays: D. 11, R. 1 (March 13)	Signed June 22
Emergency Home Finance Act of 1970 (Provided additional funds for home mortgage market. Intended also to reduce interest rates for home buyers.)	322–2 Yeas: D. 187, R. 135 Nays: D. 1, R. 1 (June 25)	72–0 Yeas: D. 38, R. 34 Nays: D. 0, R. 0 (April 16)	Signed July 24
Postal Reorganization Act of 1970 (Established independent U.S. Postal Service. Granted eight percent pay raise to postal employees. Permitted new postal service to issue revenue-raising bonds.)	359–24 Yeas: D. 204, R. 155 Nays: D. 16, R. 8 (June 18)	76–10 Yeas: D. 42, R. 34 Nays: D. 4, R. 6 (June 30)	Signed Aug. 12
Military Procurement Authorization (Authorized $19.2 billion for military procurement, research, and construction of antiballistic missile sites, for fiscal 1971.)	326–69 Yeas: D. 167, R. 159 Nays: D. 55, R. 14 (May 6)	84–5 Yeas: D. 46, R. 38 Nays: D. 3, R. 2 (Sept. 1)	Signed Oct. 7
Organized Crime Control Act of 1970 (Permitted wider gathering of wiretap evidence in organized crime cases; made it a crime for money gained from organized crime to be used to buy or begin a business; expanded federal jurisdiction in large gambling cases.)	341–26 Yeas: D. 181, R. 160 Nays: D. 26, R. 0 (Oct. 7)	73–1 Yeas: D. 45, R. 28 Nays: D. 1, R. 0 (Jan. 23)	Signed Oct. 15
Urban Mass Transportation Act of 1970 (Authorized $3.1 billion over six years for larger urban mass transit systems.)	327–16 Yeas: D. 188, R. 139 Nays: D. 8, R. 8 (Sept. 29)	84–4 Yeas: D. 47, R. 37 Nays: D. 3, R. 1 (Feb. 3)	Signed Oct. 15
Foreign Bank Account and Transaction Act (Required federally-insured banks to maintain records and report certain international monetary transactions to Treasury Department, to prevent foreign bank transactions designed to avoid U.S. taxes.)	302–0 Yeas: D. 161, R. 141 Nays: D. 0, R. 0 (May 25)	Passed by voice vote (Sept. 18)	Signed Oct. 26
Credit Reporting (an amendment to above Foreign Bank Bill.) (Restricted circumstances in which credit reporting agencies may provide credit information about individuals.)	Passed by voice vote (Oct. 13)	Passed by voice vote (Nov. 6)	Signed Oct. 26
Legislative Reform Act of 1970 (Required that roll call votes in committees of House of Representatives be made public. Required that names be recorded on teller votes.)	326–19 Yeas: D. 186, R. 140 Nays: D. 13, R. 6 (Sept. 17)	59–5 Yeas: D. 30, R. 29 Nays: D. 5, R. 0 (Oct. 6)	Signed Oct. 26
Comprehensive Drug Abuse Prevention and Control Act of 1970 (Revised federal narcotics laws. Eased penalties for marihuana users. Increased programs for drug abuse rehabilitation and education.)	341–6 Yeas: D. 187, R. 154 Nays: D. 6, R. 0 (Sept. 24)	82–0 Yeas: D. 47, R. 35 Nays: D. 0, R. 0 (Jan. 28)	Signed Oct. 27
Railroad Passenger and Service Act of 1970 (Established semi-public corporation to run basic nationwide network of railroad passenger service. Provided federal grants and loans to establish the network.)	Passed by voice vote (Oct. 14)	78–3 Yeas: D. 42, R. 36 Nays: D. 3, R. 0 (May 6)	Signed Oct. 30
Agricultural Act of 1970 (Established three-year program of price supports for farmers, for: wheat, feed grain, cotton, wool. Limited subsidy payments to farmers, to $55,000 per crop.)	212–171 Yeas: D. 126, R. 86 Nays: D. 85, R. 88 (Aug. 5)	65–7 Yeas: D. 41, R. 24 Nays: D. 1, R. 6 (Sept. 15)	Signed Nov. 30
Occupational Health and Safety Act of 1970 (Authorized Secretary of Labor to establish safety standards for most of U.S.'s 80 million jobs. Established commission to enforce these standards.)	383–5 Yeas: D. 215, R. 168 Nays: D. 3, R. 2 (Nov. 24)	83–3 Yeas: D. 48, R. 35 Nays: D. 2, R. 1 (Nov. 17)	Signed Dec. 29

(Ro. P. H.),

Ambassadors and envoys

Country	From the U.S.	To the U.S.
Afghanistan	Robert G. Neumann	Abdullah Malikyar
Algeria	(Embassy closed June 6, 1967)	
Argentina	John Davis Lodge	Pedro E. Real
Australia	Walter L. Rice	Sir James Plimsoll
Austria	John P. Humes	Karl Gruber
Barbados	Eileen R. Donovan	Valerie T. McComie
Belgium	John S. D. Eisenhower	Walter Loridan
Bolivia	Ernest V. Siracusa	*Antonio Cespedes
Botswana	†Charles H. Pletcher	Linchwe II Molefi Kgafela
Brazil	William M. Rountree	Mozart G. Valente
Bulgaria	Horace G. Torbert, Jr.	Luben Nikolov Guerassimov
Burma	Arthur W. Hummel	U San Maung
Burundi	Thomas P. Melady	Terence Nsanze
Cambodia	Emory C. Swank	Sonn Voeunsai
Cameroon	Lewis Hoffacker	Joseph Owono
Canada	Adolph W. Schmidt	Marcel Cadieux
Central African Republic	Melvin L. Manfull	Roger Guerillot
Ceylon	Robert Strausz-Hupé	Neville T. D. Kanakaratne
Chad	Terence A. Todman	Lazare Massibe
Chile	Edward M. Korry	Domingo Santa Maria
China (Formosa)	Walter P. McConaughy	Chow Shu-kai
Colombia		Douglas Botero-Boshell
Congo (Brazzaville)	(Embassy closed Aug. 13, 1965)	
Congo (Kinshasa)	Sheldon B. Vance	Pierre Ileka
Costa Rica	Walter C. Ploeser	Rafael Alberto Zuniga
Cuba	(Embassy closed Jan. 3, 1961)	
Cyprus	David H. Popper	Zenon Rossides
Czechoslovakia	Malcolm Toon	Ivan Rohal-Ilkiv
Dahomey	Matthew J. Looram, Jr.	Wilfred de Souza
Denmark	Guilford Dudley, Jr.	Torben Rønne
Dominican Republic	Francis E. Meloy, Jr.	S. Salvador Ortiz
Ecuador	Findlay Burns, Jr.	Carlos Mantilla-Ortega
El Salvador	William G. Bowdler	Julio A. Rivera
Equatorial Guinea	Lewis Hoffacker	
Estonia	(Legation at Tallinn closed)	†Ernst Jaakson
Ethiopia	William O. Hall	Minasse Haile
Finland	Val Peterson	Olavi Munkki
France	Arthur K. Watson	Charles E. Lucet
Gabon	John A. McKesson III	G. Bouckat-Bou-Nziengui
Gambia	G. Edward Clark	
Germany, West	Kenneth Rush	Rolf Pauls
Ghana	Thomas W. McElhiney	Ebenezer Moses Debrah
Greece	Henry J. Tasca	Basil George Vitsaxis
Guatemala	Nathaniel Davis	Julio Asensio
Guinea	Albert W. Sherer, Jr.	Fadiala Keita
Guyana	Spencer M. King	Rahman B. Gajraj
Haiti	Clinton E. Knox	Arthur Bonhomme
Honduras	Hewson A. Ryan	Roberto Galvez Barnes
Hungary	Alfred Puhan	János Nagy
Iceland	Luther I. Replogle	Magnus V. Magnusson
India	Kenneth B. Keating	Lakshmi Kant Jha
Indonesia	Francis J. Galbraith	R. M. Soedjatmoko
Iran	Douglas MacArthur II	Amir Aslan Afshar
Iraq	(Embassy closed June 7, 1967)	
Ireland	John D. J. Moore	William Warnock
Israel	Walworth Barbour	Yitzhak Rabin
Italy	Graham A. Martin	Egidio Ortona
Ivory Coast	John F. Root	Timothée N'Guetta Ahoua
Jamaica	Vincent de Roulet	Sir Egerton R. Richardson
Japan	Armin H. Meyer	Nobuhiko Ushiba
Jordan	L. Dean Brown	Abdul Hamid Sharaf
Kenya	Robinson McIlvaine	Leonard Oliver Kibinge
Korea, South	William J. Porter	Dong Jo Kim
Kuwait	John Patrick Walsh	Talat al-Ghoussein
Laos	G. McMurtrie Godley	*Lane Pathemmavong
Latvia	(Legation at Riga closed)	*Anatol Dinbergs
Lebanon	William B. Buffum	Najati Kabbani
Lesotho	—	Mothusi T. Mashologu
Liberia	Samuel Z. Westerfield, Jr.	S. Edward Peal

Country	From the U.S.	To the U.S.
Libya	Joseph Palmer II	*Abdalla Suwesi
Lithuania	(Legation at Kaunas closed)	*Joseph Kajeckas
Luxembourg	Kingdon Gould, Jr.	Jean Wagner
Malagasy Republic	Anthony D. Marshall	Jules A. Razafimbahiny
Malawi	William C. Burdett	Nyemba Wales Mbekeani
Malaysia	Jack W. Lydman	Tan Sri Ong Yoke Lin
Maldive Islands	Robert Strausz-Hupé	Abdul Sattar
Mali	Robert O. Blake	Seydou Traoré
Malta	John C. Pritzlaff, Jr.	Arvid Pardo
Mauritania	*Robert A. Stein	*Ismael Ould Mouloud
Mauritius	William D. Brewer	Pierre G. G. Balancy
Mexico	Robert H. McBride	Emilio O. Rabasa
Morocco	Stuart W. Rockwell	*Abdeslam Tadlaoui
Nepal	Carol C. Laise	Kul Shekhar Sharma
Netherlands	William J. Middendorf II	Baron R. B. Van Lynden
New Zealand	Kenneth Franzheim II	Frank Corner
Nicaragua	Turner B. Shelton	Guillermo Sevilla-Sacasa
Niger	Roswell D. McClelland	Georges M. Condat
Nigeria	William C. Trueheart	Joe Iyalla
Norway	Philip K. Crowe	Arne Gunneng
Pakistan	Joseph S. Farland	Agha Hilaly
Panama	Robert M. Sayre	José A. de la Ossa
Paraguay	J. Raymond Ylitalo	Roque J. Avila
Peru	Taylor G. Belcher	Fernando Berckemeyer
Philippines	Henry A. Byroade	Ernesto V. Lagdameo
Poland	Walter J. Stoessel, Jr.	Jerzy Michalowski
Portugal	Ridgway B. Knight	Vasco Vieira Garin
Romania	Leonard C. Meeker	Corneliu Bogdan
Rwanda	Leo G. Cyr	Fidèle Nkundabagenzi
Saudi Arabia	Nicholas G. Thacher	Ibrahim al-Sowayel
Senegal	G. Edward Clark	Cheikh Ibrahima Fall
Sierra Leone	Robert G. Miner	John J. Akar
Singapore	Charles T. Cross	Ernest Steven Monteiro
Somali Republic	Fred L. Hadsel	Abdullahi Ahmed Addou
South Africa	John G. Hurd	Harold L. T. Taswell
Southern Yemen	(Embassy closed Oct. 26, 1969)	
Spain	Robert C. Hill	Jaime Arguelles
Sudan	(Embassy closed June 7, 1967)	
Swaziland	—	Msindazwe Sukati
Sweden	Jerome H. Holland	Hubert de Besche
Switzerland	Shelby Davis	Felix Schnyder
Syria	(Embassy closed June 6, 1967)	
Tanzania	Claude G. Ross	Gosbert M. Rutabanzibwa
Thailand	Leonard Unger	Sunthorn Hongladarom
Togo	Dwight Dickinson	Alexandre Ohin
Trinidad and Tobago	J. Fife Symington, Jr.	Sir Ellis E. I. Clarke
Tunisia	John A. Calhoun	Slaheddine el Goulli
Turkey	William J. Handley	Melih Esenbel
Uganda	Clarence C. Ferguson, Jr.	E. Otema Allimadi
U.S.S.R.	Jacob D. Beam	Anatoliy F. Dobrynin
United Arab Republic	(Embassy closed June 6, 1967)	
United Kingdom	Walter H. Annenberg	Lord Cromer
Upper Volta	William E. Schaufele, Jr.	Paul Rouamba
Uruguay	Charles W. Adair, Jr.	Hector Luisi
Venezuela	Robert McClintock	Julio Sosa-Rodriguez
Vietnam, South	Ellsworth Bunker	Bui Diem
Yemen	(Embassy closed June 7, 1967)	
Yugoslavia	William Leonhart	Bogdan Crnobrnja
Zambia	Oliver L. Troxel, Jr.	Andrew B. Mutemba

U.S. AMBASSADORS TO INTERNATIONAL ORGANIZATIONS

Ambassador at Large	David M. Kennedy
European Office of the UN and other International Organizations—Geneva	Idar Rimestad
International Atomic Energy Agency	T. Keith Glennan
North Atlantic Treaty Organization	Robert Ellsworth
Organization of American States	Joseph J. Jova
United Nations	George H. Bush

*Charge d'affaires.   †Consul general.

The federal government dollar

estimates for year ending June 30, 1971

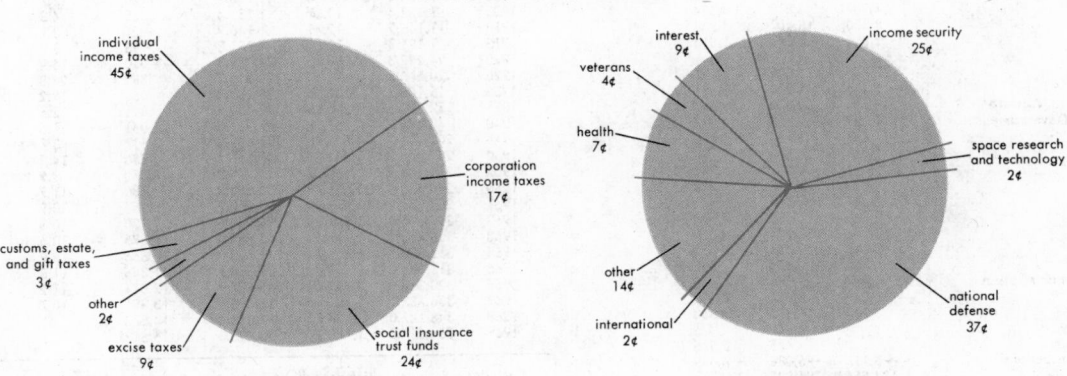

where it comes from

individual income taxes 45¢
corporation income taxes 17¢
social insurance trust funds 24¢
excise taxes 9¢
other 2¢
customs, estate, and gift taxes 3¢

where it goes

income security 25¢
interest 9¢
veterans 4¢
health 7¢
other 14¢
international 2¢
national defense 37¢
space research and technology 2¢

Data are based on federal administrative budget and trust fund receipts and expenditures.
Source: Executive Office of the President, Bureau of the Budget, *The Budget in Brief.*

The federal administrative budget

in millions of dollars

Source and function	1969	1970 estimate	1971 estimate
Budget receipts	187,792	199,386	202,103
Individual income taxes	87,249	92,200	91,000
Corporation income taxes	36,678	37,000	35,000
Social insurance and tax contributions:			
Employment taxes and contributions	34,236	38,914	42,842
Unemployment insurance	3,328	3,340	3,335
Contributions for other insurance and retirement	2,353	2,551	2,931
Excise taxes:			
Federal funds	10,585	10,872	12,059
Trust funds (highway)	4,637	5,068	5,461
Estate and gift taxes	3,491	3,500	3,600
Customs duties	2,319	2,260	2,260
Miscellaneous receipts	2,916	3,681	3,614
Budget expenditures*	184,556	197,885	200,771
National defense*	81,240	79,432	73,583
Department of Defense—Military†	77,877	76,505	71,191
Atomic energy†	2,450	2,461	2,411
Military assistance†	789	495	600
Defense-related activities	260	119	−51
International affairs and finance*	3,785	4,113	3,589
Economic and financial assistance	2,420	2,746	2,357
Food for Peace	975	971	852
Conduct of foreign affairs	371	396	412
Foreign information and exchange activities	237	237	241
Space research and technology*	4,247	3,886	3,400
Manned space flight	2,781	2,355	1,937
Space science and application	569	634	612
Space technology	344	337	306
Aircraft technology	168	180	184
Supporting space activities	390	387	376
Agricultural and rural development*	6,221	6,343	5,364
Farm income stabilization	5,000	4,485	4,467
Agricultural land and water resources	343	344	317
Rural housing and public facilities	318	830	−176
Research and other agricultural services	645	726	799
Natural resources*	2,129	2,485	2,503
Water resources and power	2,256	2,325	2,940
Land management	643	746	771
Recreational resources	372	447	546
Mineral resources	71	116	110
Other natural resources programs	160	178	183
Commerce and transportation*	7,873	9,436	8,785
Ground transportation	4,413	4,810	4,881
Air transportation	1,042	1,290	1,668
Water transportation	864	919	938

Source and function	1969	1970 estimate	1971 estimate
Area and regional development	584	717	710
Postal service	920	1,247	382
Advancement and regulation of business	260	597	425
Community development and housing*	1,961	3,046	3,781
Low- and moderate-income housing aids	871	1,153	1,499
Community environment	632	1,122	1,173
Community facilities	146	200	237
Concentrated community development	684	960	1,242
Community planning and administration	47	82	95
Maintenance to the housing mortgage market	−406	−469	−464
Education and manpower*	6,825	7,538	8,129
Elementary and secondary education	2,480	2,668	2,710
Higher education	1,230	1,395	1,449
Science education and basic research	490	490	490
Vocational education	262	266	329
Other education aids	373	434	411
Manpower training	1,193	1,368	1,720
Other manpower aids	810	929	1,034
Health*	11,696	13,265	14,957
Providing or financing medical services	9,315	10,582	12,106
Development of health resources	1,918	2,142	2,235
Prevention and control of health problems	465	542	618
Income security*	37,399	43,832	50,384
Retirement and social insurance	32,240	37,106	41,895
Public assistance	4,272	5,381	7,035
Social and individual services	888	1,347	1,454
Veterans benefits and services*	7,640	8,681	8,475
Income security	5,528	5,950	6,018
Hospital and medical care	1,556	1,787	1,796
Education, training, and rehabilitation	701	1,000	1,206
Housing	102	162	−315
Other veterans benefits and services	237	266	269
General government*	2,866	3,620	4,084
Central fiscal operations	1,094	1,257	1,345
Law enforcement and justice	534	772	1,027
General property and records management	567	631	632
Legislative and judicial functions	302	364	377
National Capital region	162	256	414
Central personnel management	146	166	184
Executive direction and other general government	299	426	360
Interest	15,791	17,821	17,799
Allowances for revenue sharing, pay increases, contingencies	...	475	2,575
Undistributed intragovernmental transactions	−5,117	−6,088	−6,639

Data are for years ending June 30. *Totals reflect interfund and intragovernmental transactions and applicable receipts not shown separately.
†Entries net of offsetting receipts.
Source: Executive Office of the President, Bureau of the Budget, *The Budget in Brief.*

Budget expenditures of government agencies

in millions of dollars

Agency	1969	1970 estimate	1971 estimate
Legislative Branch	277	341	368
The Judiciary	109	125	130
Executive Office of the President	31	39	45
Funds appropriated to the President	4,967	4,818	4,184
Department of Agriculture	8,330	8,407	7,953
Department of Commerce	854	1,078	1,014
Department of Defense			
Military	77,877	76,505	71,191
Civil	1,268	1,270	1,411
Department of Health, Education, and Welfare	46,594	52,670	59,653
Department of Housing and Urban Development	1,529	2,776	3,317
Department of the Interior	837	1,164	913
Department of Justice	515	743	985
Department of Labor	3,475	4,232	5,563
Post Office Department	920	1,247	382
Department of State	437	447	473
Department of Transportation	5,970	6,673	7,048
Department of the Treasury	16,924	19,107	19,066
Atomic Energy Commission	2,450	2,461	2,411
General Services Administration	425	454	28
National Aeronautics and Space Administration	4,247	3,886	3,400
Veterans Administration	7,669	8,657	8,455
Other independent agencies	3,969	6,397	6,844
Allowances for revenue sharing, pay increases, and contingencies	...	475	2,575
Undistributed intragovernmental transactions	−5,117	−6,088	−6,639
TOTAL BUDGET OUTLAYS	184,556	197,885	200,771

Years ending June 30. Source: Executive Office the President, Bureau of the Budget, *The Budget in Brief.*

Debt of the federal government

	DEBT OUTSTANDING* on June 30			INTEREST PAID on public debt for fiscal year	
Year	Total in $000,000†	Per capita	Gross public debt in $000,000	Total in $000,000	Percent of federal expenditures
1900	1,263.4	$ 16.60	1,263.4	40	7.7
1905	1,132.4	13.51	1,132.4	25	4.3
1910	1,146.9	12.41	1,146.9	21	3.1
1915	1,191.3	11.85	1,191.3	23	3.0
1920	24,299.3	228.23	24,299.3	1,020	15.9
1925	20,516.2	177.12	20,516.2	882	28.8
1930	16,185.3	131.51	16,185.3	659	19.2
1935	32,823.6	257.95	28,700.9	821	12.6
1940	48,496.6	367.08	42,967.5	1,041	11.5
1945	259,115.3	1,851.70	258,682.2	3,617	3.7
1950	257,376.9	1,696.80	257,357.4	5,750	14.5
1955	274,418.4	1,660.37	274,374.2	6,370	9.9
1960	286,470.6	1,585.48	286,330.8	9,180	11.9
1961	289,211.2	1,573.89	288,970.9	8,957	10.9
1962	298,645.0	1,599.98	298,200.8	9,120	10.3
1963	306,466.2	1,617.94	305,859.6	9,895	10.6
1964	312,525.9	1,626.72	311,712.9	10,666	10.9
1965	317,864.2	1,633.63	317,273.9	11,346	11.8
1966	320,368.6	1,627.54	319,907.1	12,014	11.2
1967	326,733.1	1,640.90	326,220.9	13,391	10.7
1968	348,147.0	1,730.77	347,578.4	14,573	...
1969	354,317.3	1,743.37	353,720.3	16,613‡	...

*Includes certain securities not subject to statutory limitation. †Gross public debt plus guaranteed debt of U.S. government agencies held outside the Treasury. ‡Preliminary.
Source: U.S. Department of the Treasury, *Annual Report of the Secretary of the Treasury.*

State Government

State finance

Major sources of revenue
in billions of dollars

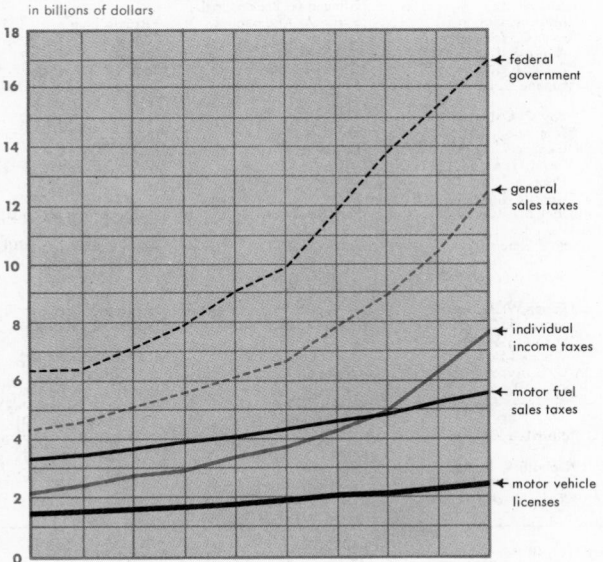

Major expenditures
in billions of dollars

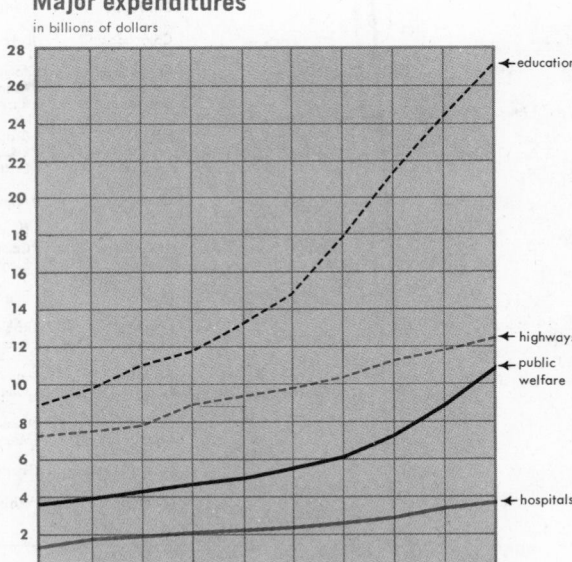

Source: U.S. Department of Commerce, Bureau of the Census, *State Government Finances.*

State legislatures

State	Name of house	Composition before November 1970 election			Composition after November 1970 election†		
		Total seats*	Democrats	Republicans	Total seats*	Democrats	Republicans
Alabama	Senate	35	33	0	35	35	0
	House of Representatives	106	105	1	106	104	2
Alaska	Senate	20	9	11	20	10	10
	House of Representatives	40	22	18	40	31	9
Arizona	Senate	30	13	17	30	12	18
	House of Representatives	60	26	34	60	26	34
Arkansas	Senate	35	34	1	35	34	1
	House of Representatives	100	96	4	100	98	2
California	Senate	40	19	21	40	20	19
	Assembly	80	39	40	80	43	37
Colorado	Senate	35	11	24	35	14	21
	House of Representatives	65	27	38	65	27	38
Connecticut	Senate	36	24	12	36	19	17
	House of Representatives	177	110	67	177	99	78
Delaware	Senate	19	6	13	19	6	13
	House of Representatives	39	14	25	39	15	24
Florida	Senate	48	32	16	48	33	15
	House of Representatives	119	77	42	119	81	38
Georgia	Senate	56	49	7	56	50	6
	House of Representatives	195	168	27	195	175	20
Hawaii	Senate	25	17	8	25	17	7
	House of Representatives	51	38	13	51	34	17
Idaho	Senate	35	14	21	35	16	19
	House of Representatives	70	32	38	70	41	29
Illinois	Senate	58	19	38	58	29	29
	House of Representatives	177	81	92	177	87	90
Indiana	Senate	50	15	35	50	21	29
	House of Representatives	100	27	72	100	46	53
Iowa	Senate	61	17	44	50	12	38
	House of Representatives	124	38	86	100	37	63
Kansas	Senate	40	8	32	‡	—	—
	House of Representatives	125	38	87	125	41	84
Kentucky‡	Senate	38	23	14	—	—	—
	House of Representatives	100	72	28	—	—	—
Louisiana‡	Senate	39	38	0	—	—	—
	House of Representatives	105	103	0	—	—	—
Maine	Senate	32	14	18	32	14	18
	House of Representatives	151	66	85	151	71	80
Maryland	Senate	43	35	8	43	33	10
	House of Delegates	142	117	25	142	121	21
Massachusetts	Senate	40	27	13	40	30	10
	House of Representatives	240	170	68	240	178	62
Michigan	Senate	38	18	20	38	19	19
	House of Representatives	110	57	53	110	58	52
Minnesota§	Senate	67	—	—	67	—	—
	House of Representatives	135	—	—	135	—	—
Mississippi‡	Senate	52	48	3	—	—	—
	House of Representatives	122	119	2	—	—	—
Missouri	Senate	34	23	11	34	25	9
	House of Representatives	163	108	55	163	112	51
Montana	Senate	55	29	26	55	30	25
	House of Representatives	104	46	58	104	49	55
Nebraska§	Unicameral	49	—	—	49	—	—
Nevada	Senate	20	11	9	20	13	7
	Assembly	40	18	22	40	19	21
New Hampshire	Senate	24	9	15	24	9	15
	House of Representatives	400	143	255	400	148	252
New Jersey‡	Senate	40	9	31	—	—	—
	General Assembly	80	21	59	—	—	—
New Mexico	Senate	42	25	17	42	27	14
	House of Representatives	70	44	26	70	48	22
New York	Senate	57	24	33	57	25	32
	Assembly	150	69	78	150	71	79
North Carolina	Senate	50	38	12	50	44	6
	House of Representatives	120	94	26	120	97	23
North Dakota	Senate	49	6	43	49	12	37
	House of Representatives	98	17	81	98	40	58
Ohio	Senate	33	12	21	33	13	20
	House of Representatives	99	35	64	99	45	54
Oklahoma	Senate	48	38	10	48	39	9
	House of Representatives	99	76	23	99	78	21
Oregon	Senate	30	14	14	30	16	14
	House of Representatives	60	21	34	60	26	34
Pennsylvania	Senate	50	24	26	50	27	23
	House of Representatives	203	108	95	203	113	90
Rhode Island	Senate	50	37	13	50	41	9
	House of Representatives	100	76	24	100	75	24
South Carolina	Senate	46	43	3	‡	...	...
	House of Representatives	124	119	4	...	...	...
South Dakota	Senate	35	8	27	35	11	24
	House of Representatives	75	16	59	75	31	44
Tennessee	Senate	33	19	14	33	19	13
	House of Representatives	99	49	49	99	55	44
Texas	Senate	31	29	2	31	29	2
	House of Representatives	150	142	8	150	139	10
Utah	Senate	28	8	20	28	12	16
	House of Representatives	69	21	48	69	38	31
Vermont	Senate	30	8	22	30	8	22
	House of Representatives	150	50	98	150	54	96
Virginia‡	Senate	40	33	7	—	—	—
	House of Delegates	100	76	24	—	—	—
Washington	Senate	49	27	22	49	29	20
	House of Representatives	99	43	56	99	48	51
West Virginia	Senate	34	22	12	34	23	11
	House of Delegates	100	63	37	100	68	32
Wisconsin	Senate	33	10	22	33	12	20
	Assembly	100	47	53	100	66	34
Wyoming	Senate	30	12	18	30	11	19
	House of Representatives	61	16	45	61	19	41

*The total number of seats is not always equal to the number of Democrats plus Republicans because of vacancies and seats held by independents. †Preliminary. ‡No election held. §Nonpartisan election. Sources: State governments.

State	Governor	Lieutenant Governor	Secretary of State	Treasurer
Alabama	Albert P. Brewer(D) / *George C. Wallace(D)	(vacancy) / *Jere Beasley(D)	†Mabel Amos(D)	†Agnes Baggett(D)
Alaska	Keith H. Miller(R) / *William A. Egan(D)	Robert W. Ward(R) / *H. A. Boucher(D)	—	—
Arizona	†Jack Williams(R)	—	†Wesley Bolin(D)	Morris A. Herring(R) / *Ernest Garfield(R)
Arkansas	Winthrop Rockefeller(R) / *Dale Bumpers(D)	Maurice Britt(R) / *Bob Riley(D)	†Kelly Bryant(D)	†Nancy Hall(D)
California	†Ronald Reagan(R)	†Ed Reinecke(R)	H. P. Sullivan(R) / *Edmund G. Brown, Jr.(D)	†Ivy Baker Priest(R)
Colorado	†John A. Love(R)	Mark A. Hogan(D) / *John D. Vanderhoof(R)	†Byron A. Anderson(R)	Virginia Blue(R) / *Palmer Burch(R)
Connecticut	John N. Dempsey(D) / *Thomas J. Meskill(R)	Attilio R. Frassinelli(D) / *T. Clark Hull(R)	Ella T. Grasso(D) / *Gloria Schaffer(D)	John A. Iorio(D) / *Robert I. Berdon(R)
Delaware	Russell W. Peterson(R)	†Eugene D. Bookhammer(R)	†Eugene Bunting(R)	Daniel Ross(R) / *Emily Womach(D)
Florida	Claude R. Kirk(R) / *Reubin O'D. Askew(D)	Ray C. Osborne(R) / *Tom Adams(D)	Tom Adams(D) / *Richard B. Stone(D)	Broward Williams(D) / *Thomas D. O'Malley(D)
Georgia	Lester G. Maddox(D) / *James Earl Carter(D)	George T. Smith(D) / *Lester G. Maddox(D)	†Ben W. Fortson, Jr.(D)	Jack B. Ray(R) / *William H. Burson(D)
Hawaii	†John A. Burns(D)	Thomas P. Gill(D) / *George R. Ariyoshi(D)	—	—
Idaho	Don Samuelson(R) / *Cecil D. Andrus(D)	†Jack M. Murphy(R)	†Pete Cenarrusa(R)	†Marjorie Ruth Moon(D)
Illinois	Richard B. Ogilvie(R)	Paul Simon(D)	John Lewis(R)	Adlai E. Stevenson III(D) / *Alan J. Dixon(D)
Indiana	Edgar D. Whitcomb(R)	Richard E. Folz(R)	William N. Salin(R) / *Larry A. Conrad(D)	John K. Snyder(R) / *Jack New(D)
Iowa	†Robert D. Ray(R)	†Roger W. Jepsen(R)	†Melvin D. Synhorst(R)	†Maurice E. Baringer(R)
Kansas	†Robert B. Docking(D)	James H. DeCoursey(R) / *Reynolds Shultz(R)	†Elwill M. Shanahan(R)	†Walter H. Peery(R)
Kentucky	Louie B. Nunn(R)	Wendell H. Ford(D)	Elmer Begley(R)	Thelma L. Stovall(D)
Louisiana	John J. McKeithen(D)	C. C. Aycock(D)	Wade O. Martin, Jr.(D)	A. P. Tugwell(D) / *Mary Evelyn Parker(D)
Maine	†Kenneth M. Curtis(D)	—	Joseph T. Edgar(R)	Norman K. Ferguson(R)
Maryland	†Marvin Mandel(D)	*Blair Lee III(D)	Blair Lee III(D)	John Leutkemeyer(D)
Massachusetts	†Francis W. Sargent(R)	*Donald R. Dwight(R)	†John F. X. Davoren(D)	†Robert Q. Crane(D)
Michigan	†William G. Milliken(R)	Thomas F. Schweigert(R) / *James Brickley(R)	James M. Hare(D) / *Richard Austin(D)	Allison Green(R)

Party affiliations are indicated by (D) for Democrat, (R) for Republican, and (DFL) for Democratic Farmer Labor Party.
*Winner, replacing official listed immediately above. †Incumbent re-elected.
Source: State governments: The Council of State Governments.

State	FISCAL YEAR TOTALS				GENERAL REVENUE, FISCAL 1969				Liquor store revenue fiscal 1969
	Revenue		Expenditure		Total	State taxes	Intergovernmental	Charges and other	
	1960	1969	1960	1969					
Alabama	543,686	1,169,105	565,342	1,167,542	1,030,432	575,154	339,379	115,899	69,209
Alaska	74,646	250,910	56,109	285,144	228,553	71,828	105,602	51,123	—
Arizona	296,060	767,776	261,986	693,405	655,719	410,723	160,703	84,293	—
Arkansas	278,621	600,913	261,687	575,905	562,700	317,602	194,355	50,743	—
California	3,752,919	10,263,202	3,583,197	9,633,346	8,502,417	5,243,537	2,564,053	694,827	—
Colorado	358,008	827,827	332,201	757,464	749,526	408,092	225,433	116,001	—
Connecticut	420,958	993,650	446,898	1,082,933	861,416	541,573	196,927	122,916	—
Delaware	113,116	247,892	120,107	283,091	241,656	156,999	39,110	45,547	—
Florida	812,496	1,962,094	764,831	1,846,760	1,784,558	1,269,436	360,808	154,314	—
Georgia	613,748	1,459,773	564,300	1,402,368	1,340,637	828,109	390,300	122,228	—
Hawaii	204,909	528,135	192,088	534,314	473,247	289,033	128,642	55,572	—
Idaho	140,271	294,539	131,137	258,205	248,623	150,532	71,748	26,343	19,339
Illinois	1,452,061	3,268,185	1,362,598	3,205,940	3,004,678	1,927,422	821,504	255,752	—
Indiana	683,221	1,559,994	668,466	1,517,739	1,448,647	881,725	325,774	241,148	—
Iowa	526,688	1,072,608	483,789	1,091,901	937,658	588,599	239,525	109,534	66,150
Kansas	353,168	706,858	335,321	669,999	662,586	385,077	178,897	98,612	—
Kentucky	431,776	1,230,376	439,419	1,208,439	1,150,963	654,900	372,384	123,679	—
Louisiana	815,037	1,571,325	829,944	1,493,032	1,457,889	776,704	412,951	268,234	—
Maine	187,742	340,557	181,352	340,043	272,519	158,221	76,529	37,769	36,550
Maryland	524,786	1,355,481	491,234	1,284,778	1,251,672	862,770	249,953	138,949	—
Massachusetts	852,001	2,108,540	914,283	2,039,549	1,905,010	1,233,510	514,384	157,116	—
Michigan	1,652,216	3,875,188	1,641,812	3,554,717	3,324,099	2,248,779	684,015	391,305	263,652
Minnesota	628,990	1,606,759	631,621	1,452,911	1,465,859	914,569	353,260	198,030	—
Mississippi	339,277	783,010	350,718	779,157	696,867	400,390	214,218	82,259	42,408
Missouri	587,514	1,295,737	561,443	1,298,333	1,175,328	711,110	354,644	109,574	—
Montana	165,614	292,771	159,118	287,336	238,563	111,822	91,241	35,500	22,583
Nebraska	182,125	424,457	176,582	395,904	408,892	217,329	117,526	74,037	—
Nevada	87,239	255,211	80,186	226,316	210,089	125,561	65,532	18,996	—
New Hampshire	128,109	251,947	122,774	238,854	171,541	83,247	59,503	28,791	55,972
New Jersey	811,011	2,282,695	698,699	2,005,316	1,843,975	1,181,308	425,471	237,196	—
New Mexico	240,940	543,028	221,381	478,325	506,286	237,423	166,190	102,673	—
New York	3,303,310	9,174,323	3,317,205	9,028,225	7,934,671	5,329,946	1,877,312	727,413	—
North Carolina	734,712	1,680,438	643,510	1,552,274	1,517,166	1,009,568	329,930	177,668	—
North Dakota	154,290	269,264	155,833	260,098	254,939	105,421	71,396	78,122	—
Ohio	1,841,221	3,531,732	1,686,780	3,153,022	2,547,763	1,540,503	673,541	333,719	301,564
Oklahoma	471,373	1,004,268	457,316	982,933	966,342	472,562	327,927	165,853	—
Oregon	485,498	938,935	443,697	831,047	737,448	405,808	219,251	112,389	76,242
Pennsylvania	2,065,941	4,171,754	2,131,883	4,313,831	3,350,374	2,265,832	822,542	262,000	340,038
Rhode Island	158,249	380,024	153,308	411,625	323,843	200,104	84,095	39,644	—
South Carolina	381,898	801,027	329,748	780,772	726,642	465,146	175,044	86,452	—
South Dakota	121,683	225,733	117,284	225,536	218,992	91,889	84,347	42,756	—
Tennessee	517,311	1,127,971	494,351	1,113,043	1,044,018	645,758	312,333	85,927	—
Texas	1,419,751	3,137,863	1,304,665	2,870,111	2,938,809	1,710,686	810,188	417,935	—
Utah	209,357	463,102	191,534	455,415	401,398	203,314	139,162	58,922	22,388
Vermont	92,315	230,266	94,239	243,911	196,409	100,892	72,446	23,071	19,966
Virginia	622,126	1,649,760	576,246	1,484,863	1,420,595	924,229	313,692	182,674	146,363
Washington	829,161	1,830,675	767,069	1,710,277	1,471,254	980,715	320,327	170,212	125,750
West Virginia	364,187	758,991	345,956	739,448	636,686	346,556	224,792	65,338	44,994
Wisconsin	686,891	1,803,630	645,248	1,780,770	1,620,996	1,090,826	334,119	196,051	—
Wyoming	119,391	214,007	109,260	191,788	190,925	77,858	82,154	30,913	10,330
All states	32,837,660	77,584,306	31,595,755	74,218,085	67,311,875	41,930,697	17,775,159	7,606,019	1,663,498

Source: U.S. Department of Commerce, Bureau of the Census, State Government Finances.

State	Governor	Lieutenant Governor	Secretary of State	Treasurer
Minnesota	Harold LeVander(R)	James B. Goetz(R)	Joseph L. Donovan(DFL)	†Val Bjornson(R)
	*Wendell R. Anderson(DFL)	*Rudolph G. Perpich(DFL)	*Arlen I. Erdahl(R)	
Mississippi	John Bell Williams(D)	Charles L. Sullivan(D)	Heber A. Ladner(D)	Evelyn Gandy(D)
Missouri	Warren E. Hearnes(D)	Thomas F. Eagleton(D)	James Kirkpatrick(D)	M. E. Morris(D)
		*William S. Morris(D)		*William E. Robinson(R)
Montana	Forrest Anderson(D)	Thomas Judge(D)	Frank Murray(D)	Alex Stephenson(R)
Nebraska	Norbert T. Tiemann(R)	John E. Everroad(R)	Frank Marsh(D)	†Wayne Swanson(R)
	*J. J. Exon(D)	*Frank Marsh(R)	*Allen Beermann(R)	
Nevada	Paul Laxalt(R)	Ed Fike(R)	†John Koontz(D)	†Michael Mirabelli(D)
	*Donal O'Callaghan(D)	*Harry M. Reid(D)		
New Hampshire	†Walter Peterson(R)	—	Robert L. Stark(R)	Robert Flanders(R)
New Jersey	William T. Cahill(R)		Paul J. Sherwin(R)	Joseph T. McCrane, Jr.(R)
New Mexico	David F. Cargo(R)	E. Lee Francis (R)	Ernestine D. Evans(D)	†Jesse D. Kornegay(D)
	*Bruce King(D)	*Robert A. Mondragon(D)	*Betty Fiorina(D)	
New York	†Nelson A. Rockefeller(R)	†Malcolm Wilson(R)	John P. Lomenzo(R)	†Arthur Levitt(D)
North Carolina	Robert Scott(D)	H. Patrick Taylor, Jr.(D)	Thad Eure(D)	Edwin Gill(D)
North Dakota	William L. Guy(D)	Richard Larsen(D)	Ben Meier(R)	Bernice Asbridge(R)
Ohio	James A. Rhodes(R)	†John W. Brown(R)	†Ted W. Brown(R)	John D. Herbert(R)
	*John J. Gilligan(D)			*Gertrude Donahey(D)
Oklahoma	Dewey F. Bartlett(R)	†George Nigh(D)	†John Rogers(D)	†Leo Winters (D)
	*David Hall(D)			
Oregon	†Tom McCall(R)	—	Clay Meyers(R)	Robert Straub(D)
Pennsylvania	Raymond P. Shafer(R)	Raymond Broderick(R)	Joseph Kelley, Jr.(R)	Grace M. Sloan(D)
	*Milton Shapp(D)	*Ernest P. Kline(R)		
Rhode Island	†Frank Licht(D)	†J. Joseph Garrahy(D)	†August P. LaFrance(D)	†Raymond H. Hawksley(D)
South Carolina	Robert E. McNair(D)	John C. West(D)	†O. Frank Thornton(D)	†Grady L. Patterson, Jr.(D)
	*John C. West(D)	*Earle Morris, Jr.(D)		
South Dakota	Frank L. Farrar(R)	James Abdnor(R)	†Alma Larson(R)	†Neal Strand(R)
	*Richard Francis Kneip(D)	*William Dougherty(D)		
Tennessee	Buford Ellington(D)	Frank C. Gorrell(D)	†Joe C. Carr(D)	Charles Worley(D)
	*Winfield Dunn(R)	...		...
Texas	†Preston Smith(D)	†Ben Barnes(D)	Martin Dies, Jr.(D)	†Jesse James(D)
Utah	Calvin L. Rampton(D)		Clyde L. Miller(D)	Golden L. Allen(D)
Vermont	†Deane C. Davis(R)	Thomas L. Hayes(R)	†Richard C. Thomas(R)	†Frank H. Davis(R)
		*John S. Burgess(R)		
Virginia	A. Linwood Holton(R)	J. Sargeant Reynolds(D)	Cynthia Newman(R)	Walter F. Craigie, Jr.(R)
Washington	Daniel J. Evans(R)	John A. Cherberg(D)	A. Ludlow Kramer(R)	Robert S. O'Brien(D)
West Virginia	Arch A. Moore, Jr.(R)		John D. Rockefeller IV(D)	John H. Kelly(D)
Wisconsin	Warren P. Knowles(R)	Jack B. Olson(R)	†Robert C. Zimmerman(R)	Harold W. Clemens(R)
	*Patrick J. Lucey(D)	*Martin J. Schreiber(D)		*Charles Smith(D)
Wyoming	†Stanley K. Hathaway(R)	—	†Thyra Thomson(R)	Minnie A. Mitchell(R)
				*James Griffith(R)

GENERAL EXPENDITURES, FISCAL 1969					Liquor store expenditure fiscal 1969	INSURANCE TRUST FUND, FISCAL 1969				DEBT, FISCAL 1969		
Total	Education	Highways	Public welfare	Hospitals		Revenue	Total	Employee retirement	Unemployment compensation	Gross debt outstanding at end of year	Long-term debt issued	Long-term debt retired
1,065,695	495,635	219,249	154,189	47,121	61,046	69,464	40,801	20,298	20,496	634,768	60,820	34,630
275,691	86,265	63,167	11,323	5,194	—	22,357	9,453	1,895	7,528	190,168	34,325	5,131
649,766	333,134	128,185	40,223	10,758	—	112,057	43,639	9,821	8,588	90,238	8,450	1,173
552,243	222,524	138,601	87,800	25,988	—	38,213	23,662	12,085	11,568	111,346	2,748	8,831
8,560,998	2,659,967	1,211,893	2,132,763	277,517	—	1,760,785	1,072,348	340,899	394,398	5,506,375	445,458	189,978
719,864	326,827	126,078	115,451	48,304	—	78,301	37,600	17,622	6,525	126,380	1,000	17,325
990,243	310,340	169,480	165,895	92,548	—	132,234	92,690	33,056	59,445	429,198	86,467	26,083
276,138	131,053	34,884	24,381	16,127	—	6,236	6,953	789	6,162			
1,773,394	959,361	262,631	152,452	76,869	—	177,536	73,396	52,177	20,484	941,238	159,300	42,027
1,359,936	673,854	174,240	206,426	83,745	—	119,136	42,432	28,195	14,237	876,989	79,484	39,609
504,867	209,764	56,007	35,928	20,130	—	54,888	29,447	22,897	6,550	448,820	122,355	16,941
231,325	82,551	61,334	22,762	6,990	13,948	26,577	12,932	4,327	6,906	30,505	10,350	791
3,008,087	1,166,256	693,680	504,515	218,311	—	263,507	197,853	111,591	86,165	1,305,484	120,800	79,424
1,451,734	740,893	333,463	71,367	83,237	—	111,347	66,005	40,694	25,239	570,731	26,735	15,849
1,008,611	462,270	222,721	115,967	47,886	49,462	68,800	33,828	18,584	15,241	100,224	14,425	3,770
643,898	279,339	131,743	89,596	45,771	—	44,272	26,101	13,201	12,813	236,525	7,575	7,563
1,162,328	444,189	321,564	164,013	38,662	—	79,413	46,111	21,876	19,829	1,247,920	115,730	26,299
1,417,296	550,707	238,672	250,207	95,578	—	113,436	75,736	38,652	37,084	783,667	52,211	25,728
290,374	104,277	66,130	43,293	15,063	24,002	31,488	25,667	15,545	10,122	200,901	35,685	10,654
1,225,489	436,043	208,318	183,358	85,515	—	103,809	59,289	26,463	30,083	966,341	118,140	79,841
1,869,839	430,045	228,182	566,358	138,205	—	203,530	169,710	75,299	94,299	1,864,594	150,125	93,763
3,158,499	1,514,137	466,454	448,717	179,480	213,178	287,437	183,040	66,957	109,508	930,273	11,010	59,028
1,399,339	590,772	278,377	149,884	84,638	—	140,590	53,572	29,969	23,200	360,955	33,770	29,656
723,128	313,380	130,764	82,286	30,091	36,757	43,735	19,272	11,695	7,564	447,011	42,579	17,840
1,241,364	500,174	253,212	233,485	85,511	—	120,409	56,969	21,547	35,298	148,833	10,079	7,181
249,901	92,500	78,136	23,291	10,085	18,345	31,625	19,090	9,897	4,994	81,993	—	4,602
386,413	152,030	90,924	49,469	29,783	—	15,565	9,491	3,268	6,216	54,655	—	1,069
200,872	76,797	49,308	18,379	3,548	—	45,122	25,444	8,170	8,378	29,203	—	1,193
189,944	63,912	54,002	18,641	11,460	41,947	24,434	6,963	4,789	2,174	150,660	125	11,291
1,692,167	574,483	445,299	219,397	106,448	—	438,720	313,149	107,802	155,060	1,408,431	277,969	58,162
459,416	240,708	80,507	57,049	12,646	—	36,742	18,909	12,968	5,941	130,621	16,564	22,188
8,444,670	3,045,040	888,574	1,878,005	605,134	—	1,239,652	583,555	217,101	283,817	6,744,795	797,013	158,447
1,500,022	768,780	277,889	119,515	93,647	—	163,272	52,252	30,289	21,951	582,484	70,894	39,940
249,407	93,284	52,478	26,568	9,603	—	14,325	10,691	2,237	4,053	34,639	3,530	662
2,558,729	963,032	729,576	337,506	120,817	209,473	682,405	384,820	199,762	60,771	1,403,396	285,890	98,302
951,960	353,451	190,805	224,623	44,120	—	37,926	30,973	16,989	11,029	685,935	29,065	9,408
717,437	280,994	152,302	77,469	30,251	48,602	125,245	65,000	12,940	23,471	596,450	127,360	25,542
3,705,903	1,495,218	882,431	510,382	229,199	282,357	481,342	325,571	161,776	120,598	2,903,580	556,960	82,527
366,969	123,465	65,105	73,491	24,771	—	56,181	44,656	12,684	16,693	351,850	54,770	12,335
750,728	360,959	112,300	52,671	45,015	—	74,385	30,044	16,531	12,573	326,896	34,670	19,054
221,171	81,225	67,800	24,422	7,595	—	6,741	4,365	745	3,620	28,821	1,345	358
1,069,282	467,739	253,763	117,917	53,554	—	83,953	43,761	16,508	27,148	370,193	293	19,600
2,751,503	1,356,421	571,608	376,571	145,773	—	199,054	118,608	91,643	26,925	938,621	105,593	30,361
418,541	226,400	85,463	40,550	14,488	16,416	39,316	20,458	7,314	9,158	103,091	102	6,844
217,278	76,850	61,749	28,489	6,859	19,388	13,891	7,245	2,803	4,442	169,995	36,470	6,330
1,330,132	605,970	330,928	64,567	94,061	123,801	82,802	30,930	22,633	8,297	344,085	103,060	18,082
1,480,245	691,094	275,269	195,324	57,381	91,206	233,671	138,826	41,004	43,559	676,020	96,975	47,032
655,884	266,305	181,728	74,195	28,141	33,085	77,311	50,479	17,973	12,926	460,631	40,375	12,200
1,709,113	621,062	253,105	197,733	89,613	—	182,634	71,657	31,857	39,141	513,579	98,030	8,528
176,296	60,922	67,887	7,213	4,970	9,632	12,752	5,860	1,792	1,713	52,995	190	733
68,014,129	27,162,098	12,517,965	10,866,076	3,738,201	1,292,645	8,608,933	4,911,311	2,087,609	1,983,980	39,333,344	4,638,704	1,604,362

Taxation

City taxes, 1968-69

in thousands of dollars

City	Per capita total tax	TAX in $000 Total	Property	General sales and gross receipts	Income
Baltimore, Maryland	$201	186,346	141,828	—	26,300
Boston, Massachusetts	326	200,855	197,808	—	—
Chicago, Illinois	98	347,879	200,003	48,998	—
Cleveland, Ohio	103	80,749	56,356	—	21,637
Columbus, Ohio	46	27,317	5,857	—	20,014
Dallas, Texas	82	70,953	59,103	3,665	—
Denver, Colorado	110	58,701	31,837	20,848	—
Detroit, Michigan	129	202,306	119,543	—	78,729
Houston, Texas	69	86,862	66,558	10,740	—
Jacksonville, Florida	...	...	...	...	...
Kansas City, Missouri	82	50,373	18,744	—	12,469
Los Angeles, California	110	322,635	164,591	89,878	—
Memphis, Tennessee	77	43,470	31,657	—	—
Milwaukee, Wisconsin	78	60,967	58,727	—	—
New Orleans, Louisiana	80	56,622	24,198	23,135	—
New York, New York	358	2,861,063	1,697,358	444,880	495,766
Philadelphia, Pennsylvania	140	287,491	113,337	—	141,303
Phoenix, Arizona	62	33,683	13,501	16,441	—
Pittsburgh, Pennsylvania	106	58,695	37,113	—	11,958
St. Louis, Missouri	147	98,605	36,001	—	35,728
San Antonio, Texas	34	25,373	23,754	—	—
San Diego, California	57	40,078	21,685	12,825	—
San Francisco, California	248	185,670	150,270	28,266	—
Seattle, Washington	63	37,480	20,225	—	—
Washington, D.C.	414	341,286	120,334	58,163	84,362

Source: U.S. Department of Commerce, Bureau of the Census, *City Government Finances in 1968–69.*

Internal revenue collections

in millions of dollars

Type of tax	1968	1969
Corporation income tax	29,896	38,338
Individual income and employment taxes	106,338	130,509
Withheld	82,377	99,958
Not withheld	22,495	28,973
Railroad retirement	858	939
Unemployment insurance	607	640
Estate tax	2,710	3,137
Gift tax	372	393
Alcohol taxes	4,287	4,554
Distilled spirits	3,197	3,390
Wines	127	157
Beer	963	1,007
Tobacco taxes	2,122	2,138
Cigarettes	2,066	2,082
Cigars	55	54
Stamp taxes on documents, other instruments, and playing cards*	49	1
Manufacturers' excise taxes	5,714	6,501
Gasoline	3,031	3,186
Lubricating oils	92	97
Tires and tubes	462	604
Passenger cars, chassis, bodies, etc.	1,531	1,864
Trucks and buses, chassis, bodies, etc.	448	589
Parts and accessories for cars, trucks, etc.†	76	81
Fishing rods, creels, etc.	9	12
Firearms (except pistols and revolvers), shells, cartridges	31	33
Pistols and revolvers	5	6
Retailers' excise taxes‡	1	§
Miscellaneous excise taxes	1,859	2,147
Admissions taxes‖	1	§
Club dues and initiation fees‖	1	1
Telephone, wire, etc., and equipment services¶	1,105	1,316
Air transportation of persons	199	224
Sugar	102	108
Diesel and special motor fuels	202	225
Use tax on highway motor vehicles weighing over 26,000 lb.	109	124
Coin-operated gaming devices ♀	15	12
Narcotics and marijuana	2	2
Unclassified excise taxes	288	200
Total	153,637	187,920

Years ending June 30.
*Tax on playing cards and issues and transfers of stock repealed effective June 22, 1965, and January 1, 1966, respectively. †Tax on auto parts and accessories repealed effective January 1, 1966. ‡Repealed effective June 22, 1965. §Less than $1,000,000. ‖Repealed effective noon December 31, 1965. ¶Tax on local and toll telephone and typewriter service reduced to 3% and tax on private communications services, telegraph service, and wire equipment service repealed effective January 1, 1966. Tax on general and toll telephone service and typewriter exchange service is increased from 3% to 10% on bills paid after April 1, 1966 for services rendered after January 31, 1966. ♀ Repealed effective July 1, 1965.
Source: U.S. Department of the Treasury, Internal Revenue Service.

Tax collections

State	STATE TAX COLLECTIONS fiscal 1969 Total in $000,000	Per capita	FEDERAL TAX COLLECTIONS Total in $000,000, fiscal 1969	Individual income and employment tax in $000,000 fiscal 1969	Per capita*, fiscal 1970	LOCAL TAX COLLECTIONS fiscal 1969 Total in $000,000	Per capita
Alabama	575	$163	1,333	1,040	$ 567	218	$ 62
Alaska	72	255	132	121	894	38	136
Arizona	411	243	717	620	735	244	144
Arkansas	318	159	652	524	533	123	62
California	5,244	270	16,777	13,051	1,059	5,256	270
Colorado	408	194	2,243	1,878	815	402	191
Connecticut	542	181	3,478	2,567	1,268	635	212
Delaware	157	291	1,319	648	1,203	44	81
District of Columbia	—	—	†	†	1,152	341	428
Florida	1,269	200	3,626	2,844	814	826	130
Georgia	828	178	2,615	1,905	657	423	91
Hawaii	289	364	527	413	862	92	116
Idaho	150	210	380	311	654	85	118
Illinois	1,927	174	14,286	9,990	1,092	2,191	198
Indiana	882	172	3,410	2,278	863	829	162
Iowa	589	212	1,442	1,136	784	492	177
Kansas	385	166	1,185	951	792	419	180
Kentucky	655	203	2,541	1,029	614	242	75
Louisiana	777	207	1,640	1,291	655	339	90
Maine	158	162	470	376	700	143	146
Maryland	863	229	5,425†	4,470†	1,054	683	181
Massachusetts	1,234	226	5,455	3,948	1,049	1,241	227
Michigan	2,249	257	13,872	7,374	983	1,505	172
Minnesota	915	247	3,196	2,341	814	588	159
Mississippi	400	170	620	492	451	171	72
Missouri	711	153	4,783	3,414	849	689	148
Montana	112	$161	273	227	$ 728	132	$190
Nebraska	217	150	1,032	796	796	307	212
Nevada	126	275	351	284	1,065	88	192
New Hampshire	83	116	448	371	881	131	183
New Jersey	1,181	165	6,670	4,592	1,077	1,721	241
New Mexico	237	239	368	322	653	84	85
New York	5,330	291	33,245	10,200	1,156	5,214	285
North Carolina	1,010	194	4,066	1,963	613	338	65
North Dakota	105	171	202	178	645	102	167
Ohio	1,540	143	12,407	2,407	922	1,744	162
Oklahoma	473	184	1,598	1,056	695	265	103
Oregon	406	200	1,288	1,029	843	381	187
Pennsylvania	2,266	192	11,111	1,667	909	1,742	148
Rhode Island	200	220	891	676	950	145	159
South Carolina	465	173	963	779	549	140	52
South Dakota	92	139	219	185	629	141	213
Tennessee	646	162	1,868	1,442	643	360	90
Texas	1,711	153	7,615	1,180	771	1,373	123
Utah	203	195	435	361	656	139	133
Vermont	101	230	212	174	740	68	154
Virginia	924	198	2,829	1,875	765	540	116
Washington	981	288	2,472	1,980	933	414	122
West Virginia	347	191	630	513	605	132	72
Wisconsin	1,091	258	3,354	2,364	869	768	181
Wyoming	78	243	145	119	789	54	170
Total U.S.	41,931‡	208	187,920§	130,509§	893	34,781‡	172

*Federal tax burden is estimated by Tax Foundation, Inc. by a special formula designed for this purpose, since data on Federal tax collections do not accurately reflect the tax burden by state.
†District of Columbia included with Maryland. ‡Data not equal to total due to rounding. §Includes some collections not allocated by state.
Sources: Tax Foundation, Inc. U.S. Department of Commerce, Bureau of the Census, *Governmental Finances* and *State Tax Collections.*
U.S. Department of the Treasury, Internal Revenue Service.

Income and Expenditures

Disposable personal income
in billions of dollars

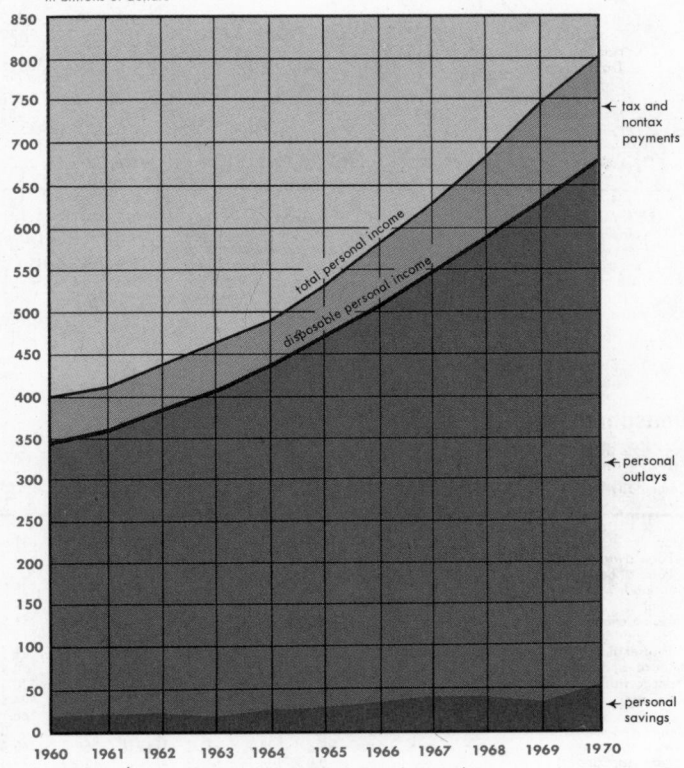

Labels on chart: total personal income; disposable personal income; tax and nontax payments; personal outlays; personal savings

1970 data are for the second quarter, seasonally adjusted at annual rates.
Source: U.S. Department of Commerce, Office of Business Economics, *Survey of Current Business.*

Average employee earnings
September figures

Industry	AVERAGE WEEKLY EARNINGS		AVERAGE HOURLY EARNINGS	
	1969	1970	1969	1970
MANUFACTURING	$132.84	$135.43	$3.24	$3.42
Durable goods	143.45	145.16	3.44	3.62
Ordnance and accessories	140.48	146.37	3.46	3.65
Lumber and wood products	114.45	120.69	2.84	3.04
Furniture and fixtures	109.08	108.92	2.68	2.80
Stone, clay, and glass products	137.80	143.24	3.25	3.46
Primary metal industries	162.93	167.69	3.87	4.08
Fabricated metal products	143.14	145.08	3.40	3.60
Nonelectrical machinery	155.00	152.00	3.63	3.80
Electrical equipment and supplies	127.39	131.93	3.13	3.34
Transportation equipment	166.66	167.26	3.94	4.14
Instruments and related products	131.34	134.30	3.19	3.40
Nondurable goods	118.00	122.15	2.95	3.14
Food and kindred products	124.15	131.29	2.97	3.21
Tobacco manufactures	97.89	109.91	2.51	2.90
Textile mill products	98.81	96.43	2.41	2.46
Apparel and related products	83.77	83.69	2.34	2.44
Paper and allied products	143.32	147.55	3.31	3.53
Printing and publishing	144.75	150.40	3.75	4.00
Chemicals and allied products	147.14	158.76	3.52	3.78
Petroleum and coal products	172.10	187.49	4.04	4.32
Rubber and plastics products	129.90	130.98	3.13	3.25
Leather and leather products	87.58	90.50	2.38	2.50
NONMANUFACTURING				
Metal mining	160.33	169.15	3.72	3.98
Coal mining	167.22	180.67	4.17	4.45
Oil and gas extraction	151.20	153.19	3.46	3.63
Contract construction	193.36	193.14	4.92	5.35
Local and suburban transportation	134.83	146.86	3.18	3.48
Telephone communication	134.64	138.00	3.30	3.45
Electric, gas, and sanitary services	164.74	174.72	3.96	4.21
Wholesale trade	132.18	137.76	3.28	3.47
Retail trade	79.69	83.82	2.33	2.48
Hotels, tourist courts, and motels*	64.73	68.26	1.86	1.99

*Excludes tips.
Source: U.S. Department of Labor, Bureau of Labor Statistics, *Employment and Earnings.*

Employment

Civilian labor force: employment status
percent of labor force

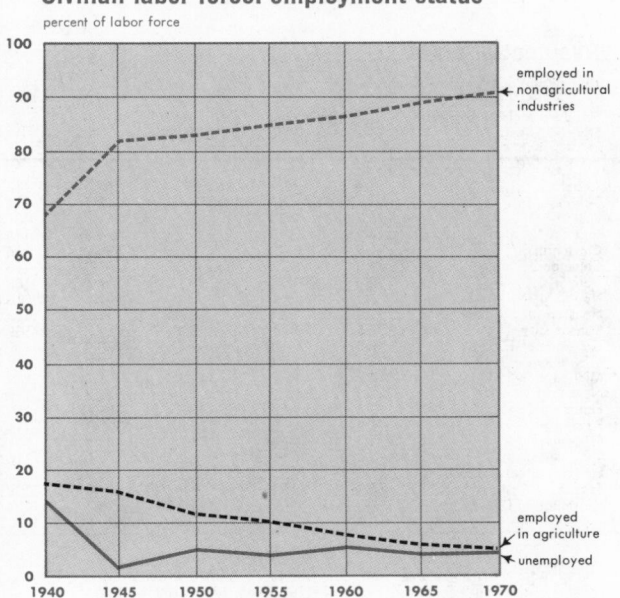

Labels: employed in nonagricultural industries; employed in agriculture; unemployed

1970 data are average of first 6 months.
Source: U.S. Department of Labor, Bureau of Labor Statistics, *Employment and Earnings.*

Labor force by age and sex
Percent

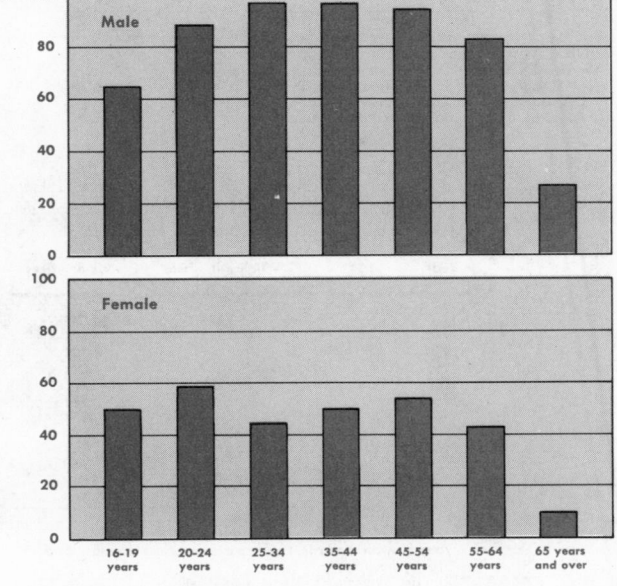

Male; Female; 16-19 years; 20-24 years; 25-34 years; 35-44 years; 45-54 years; 55-64 years; 65 years and over

Data as of September 1970.
Source: U.S. Department of Labor, Bureau of Labor Statistics, *Employment and Earnings.*

Prices

Mortgage loan interest rates
conventional mortgages on single-family homes

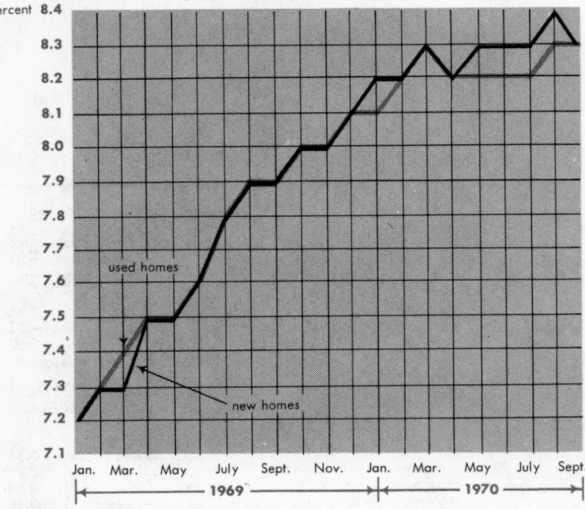

Source: Federal Home Loan Bank Board.

Annual cost of living for an urban family of four, 1969
based on spring prices in dollars

Item	LOWER BUDGET		INTERMEDIATE BUDGET		HIGHER BUDGET	
	Metro-politan areas	Nonmetro-politan areas*	Metro-politan areas	Nonmetro-politan areas*	Metro-politan areas	Nonmetro-politan areas*
Total budget†	6,673	6,092	10,273	9,204	14,959	12,942
Family consumption	5,364	4,935	7,968	7,151	11,064	9,645
Food	1,803	1,663	2,322	2,135	2,876	2,572
Housing‡	1,418	1,237	2,426	2,012	3,677§	2,954§
Transportation	457	603	925	1,006	1,214	1,217
Clothing and personal care	796	713	1,113	1,023	1,628	1,527
Medical care	557	460	561	464	584	482
Other	333	261	621	511	1,085	893
Personal taxes	638	536	1,387	1,176	2,618	2,101

Refers to a family comprising a 38-year-old employed husband, a wife not employed outside the home, an 8-year-old girl, and a 13-year-old boy.
*Places with 2,500 to 50,000 inhabitants. †Includes allowances for gifts and contributions, life insurance, occupational expenses, and social security, disability, and unemployment compensation taxes. ‡Includes shelter, household operations, and house furnishings. §Includes an allowance for lodging away from home city.
Source: U.S. Department of Labor, Bureau of Labor Statistics, *Monthly Labor Review.*

Retail food prices
in cents per pound, except as indicated

Commodity and unit	1940	1950	1960	1970*
Cereals and bakery products				
Flour, wheat	4.3	9.8	11.1	11.9
Corn flakes (12 oz.)	10.7	18.5	25.8	31.5
Bread, white	8.0	14.3	20.3	23.9
Meats, poultry, and fish				
Steak, round	36.4	93.6	105.5	133.3
Hamburger	...	56.6	52.4	66.3
Pork chops, center cut	27.9	75.4	85.8	117.2
Bacon, sliced	27.3	63.7	65.5	97.6
Frying chickens	...	59.5	42.7	40.9
Ocean perch, fillet, frozen	...	...	47.4	63.2
Dairy products				
Milk, fresh (grocery) (qt.)	11.5	19.3	24.7	57.2†
Butter	36.0	72.9	74.9	86.0
Cheese, Am. process	25.9	51.8	34.3‡	50.3‡
Fruits and vegetables				
Apples	5.2	12.0	16.2§	20.7
Oranges, size 200 (doz.)	29.1	49.3	74.8	79.2
Potatoes	2.4	4.6	7.2	9.0
Tomatoes	...	24.3	31.6	48.2
Peas, green, No. 303 can	13.6	...	20.7	25.1
Other				
Eggs, Grade A, large (doz.)	33.1	60.4	57.3	57.3
Margarine	15.9	30.8	26.9	29.2
Sugar	5.2	9.7	11.6	12.8
Coffee‖	21.2	79.4	75.3	88.7

Prior to 1965, data exclude Alaska and Hawaii. *April, 1970. †½ gal. ‡½ lb. §11-month average. ‖Beginning 1960, vacuum-pack can only.
Source: U.S. Department of Commerce, Bureau of the Census, *Statistical Abstract of the United States.* Data compiled by the U.S. Department of Labor, Bureau of Labor Statistics, *Retail Food Prices by Cities* and *Estimated Retail Food Prices by Cities.*

Purchasing power of the dollar
1957-59 = $1.00

Year	Wholesale prices	Consumer prices
1940	$2.326	$2.048
1945	1.727	1.595
1950	1.152	1.194
1955	1.073	1.071
1960	.993	.971
1965	.976	.910
1966	.945	.884
1967	.943	.860
1968	.919	.825
1969	.885	.783
1970*	.858	.749

Prior to 1960, wholesale prices exclude data for Alaska and Hawaii; prior to 1965, consumer prices exclude data for those states.
*Data are average of first six months only.
Source: U.S. Department of Commerce, Office of Business Economics, *Survey of Current Business.*

Consumer prices by commodity groups
1957-59 = 100

Commodity	1950	1955	1960	1965	1968	1969	1970*
Food	85.8	94.0	101.4	108.8	119.3	125.5	131.8
Food away from home	...	91.8	105.5	117.8	136.3	144.6	153.1
Food at home	85.8	94.4	100.6	107.2	115.9	121.5	127.4
Housing	83.2	94.1	103.1	108.5	119.1	126.7	133.7
Rent	79.1	94.8	103.1	108.9	115.1	118.8	122.4
Home ownership	...	92.6	103.7	111.4	127.0	139.4	151.0
Fuel and utilities	...	92.8	104.5	107.2	110.4	112.9	115.7
Household furnishings and operation	...	97.3	101.5	103.1	113.0	117.9	121.6
Apparel and upkeep	90.1	95.9	102.2	106.8	120.1	127.1	130.8
Transportation	79.0	89.7	103.8	111.1	119.6	124.2	128.5
Private	82.6	89.9	103.2	109.7	117.3	121.3	124.5
Public	64.6	89.0	107.0	121.4	138.2	148.9	166.1
Health and recreation	...	91.4	105.4	115.6	130.0	136.6	141.8
Medical care	73.4	88.6	108.1	122.3	145.0	155.0	162.0
Personal care	78.9	90.0	104.1	109.9	120.3	126.2	129.6
Reading and recreation	89.3	92.1	104.9	115.2	125.7	130.5	134.3
Other goods and services	82.6	94.3	103.8	111.4	123.6	129.0	135.2
All items	83.8	93.3	103.1	109.9	121.2	127.7	133.6

Prior to 1960, data exclude Alaska and Hawaii. *6-month average.
Sources: U.S. Dept. of Commerce, Bureau of the Census, *Statistical Abstract of the United States;* U.S. Dept. of Labor, Bureau of Labor Statistics, *Monthly Labor Review.*

Residential rents
1957-59 = 100, except as indicated

Standard Metropolitan Statistical Area	1950	1955	1960	1965	1969
Atlanta	82.6	97.0	102.3	105.2	114.6
Baltimore	81.4	93.7	103.7	108.7	116.1
Boston	75.1	87.4	108.4	121.3	137.1
Chicago*	66.9	92.3	102.5	105.8	113.2
Cincinnati	73.9	93.2	101.7	103.2	106.0
Cleveland	67.5	90.7	101.3	101.0	106.9
Detroit	72.6	96.4	97.1	95.9	108.7
Honolulu†	...	...	...	102.4	116.8
Houston	91.0	99.4	99.7	99.7	106.3
Kansas City	79.6	98.1	102.3	104.7	109.4
Los Angeles-Long Beach	78.3	95.8	102.4	110.2	119.4
Milwaukee	71.8	96.4	100.8	102.7	111.2
Minneapolis-St. Paul	72.1	93.1	103.2	108.6	119.3
New York*	82.0	92.9	105.9	117.3	129.1
Philadelphia	83.6	92.5	103.3	109.6	120.1
Pittsburgh	81.0	95.8	103.6	107.7	115.6
St. Louis	73.4	93.8	103.3	105.8	111.7
San Diego‡	...	...	...	100.0	117.2
San Francisco-Oakland	72.3	91.5	107.1	122.9	144.5
Seattle	75.2	94.6	103.9	108.5	126.7
Washington, D.C.	84.3	96.9	103.9	113.7	123.2

Through 1960, indexes applied only to families of 2 persons or more in urbanized area. Beginning 1964, indexes represent entire urban area.
*Standard Consolidated Area. †Dec. 1963=100. ‡Feb. 1965=100.
Source: U.S. Department of Commerce, Bureau of the Census. *Statistical Abstract of the United States.* Data compiled by the U.S. Department of Labor, Bureau of Labor Statistics.

Health and Welfare

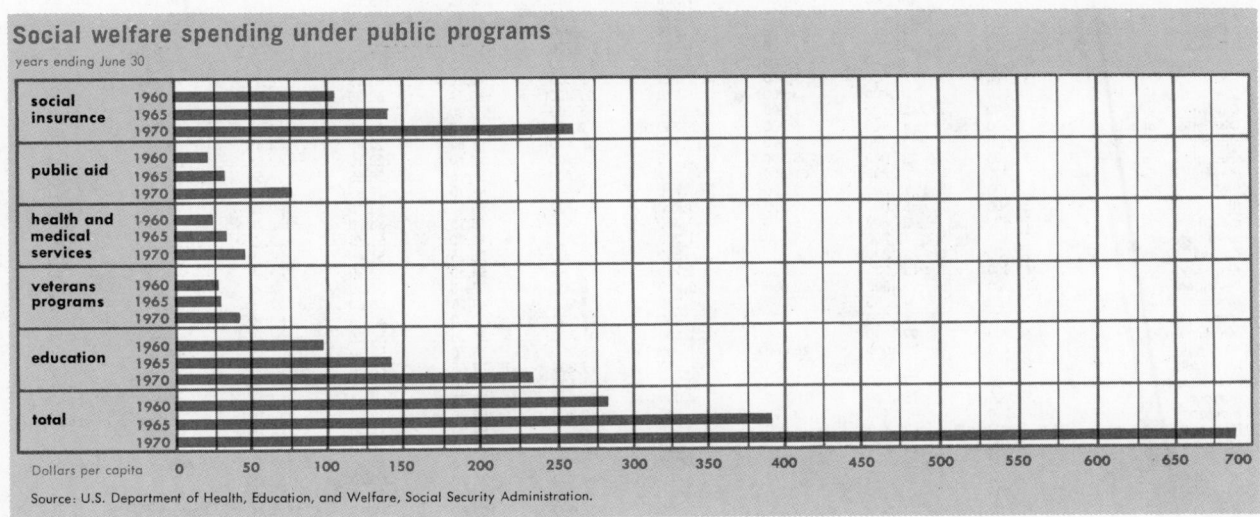

Social welfare spending under public programs
years ending June 30

			Dollars per capita 0 ... 700
social insurance	1960 / 1965 / 1970		
public aid	1960 / 1965 / 1970		
health and medical services	1960 / 1965 / 1970		
veterans programs	1960 / 1965 / 1970		
education	1960 / 1965 / 1970		
total	1960 / 1965 / 1970		

Dollars per capita 0   50   100   150   200   250   300   350   400   450   500   550   600   650   700

Source: U.S. Department of Health, Education, and Welfare, Social Security Administration.

Social insurance beneficiaries and benefits

State	OLD-AGE AND SURVIVORS INSURANCE Beneficiaries Jan. 1, 1970	Benefits for year ending Jan. 1, 1970 in $000	DISABILITY INSURANCE Beneficiaries Jan. 1, 1970	Benefits for year ending Jan. 1, 1970 in $000	Medicare enrollment* July 1, 1969	UNEMPLOYMENT INSURANCE State programs Beneficiaries† June 30, 1970	Benefits for year ending June 30, 1970 in $000
Alabama	384,956	335,587	64,001	57,551	320,478	15,195	24,141
Alaska	10,321	10,699	1,074	1,087	6,377	3,389	9,058
Arizona	183,730	192,894	24,208	25,481	150,163	6,128	9,658
Arkansas	268,293	222,540	43,945	37,294	233,396	9,323	17,230
California	1,956,884	2,168,235	226,480	259,583	1,759,299	221,851	498,108
Colorado	205,676	212,958	20,180	20,609	186,481	3,998	10,155
Connecticut	313,139	386,663	23,135	27,756	284,690	36,491	86,265
Delaware	52,077	57,645	5,433	5,934	44,312	2,822	7,622
District of Columbia	68,705	68,992	7,652	7,748	69,386	4,602	10,206
Florida	999,439	1,047,716	96,894	100,081	884,647	19,543	26,133
Georgia	427,146	377,490	77,977	68,305	359,508	14,193	21,341
Hawaii	57,057	57,822	5,767	6,071	43,350	4,141	9,784
Idaho	80,748	82,089	8,205	8,349	67,658	2,841	8,080
Illinois	1,194,630	1,383,222	96,096	111,135	1,092,009	69,866	131,904
Indiana	570,916	633,677	51,525	56,068	490,163	26,723	41,908
Iowa	383,094	400,328	25,974	26,913	353,051	10,857	22,301
Kansas	283,132	293,549	20,267	20,933	265,663	12,809	22,422
Kentucky	391,601	352,177	67,807	57,957	338,105	12,977	28,519
Louisiana	343,086	308,419	64,486	54,383	298,897	23,274	47,142
Maine	132,539	135,377	12,292	11,813	119,113	6,419	13,824
Maryland	330,215	358,116	31,617	34,849	287,351	16,854	36,520
Massachusetts	661,031	774,274	50,355	56,393	632,019	61,558	122,976
Michigan	919,578	1,056,687	91,767	106,210	755,970	83,813	178,079
Minnesota	454,142	464,363	29,294	30,323	410,391	17,926	35,887
Mississippi	264,291	202,105	45,766	36,348	220,406	7,402	11,250
Missouri	596,870	614,604	59,711	59,921	557,380	32,270	57,120
Montana	81,619	84,737	8,443	8,526	69,256	2,683	7,074
Nebraska	195,645	199,454	12,691	12,813	182,994	3,299	7,297
Nevada	35,462	40,595	3,898	4,661	29,872	4,365	9,318
New Hampshire	88,740	99,849	6,750	7,270	80,531	1,984	4,064
New Jersey	766,743	923,558	66,591	78,601	684,464	71,824	190,955
New Mexico	88,976	81,420	15,387	12,888	70,462	4,586	8,295
New York	2,137,995	2,584,127	192,489	222,768	1,956,568	173,489	381,199
North Carolina	520,326	460,360	78,832	70,551	404,747	23,335	34,370
North Dakota	78,331	74,773	6,014	5,247	67,190	1,146	3,856
Ohio	1,115,985	1,247,642	110,163	121,181	990,782	51,451	94,551
Oklahoma	312,138	302,107	41,872	39,593	293,086	9,484	14,571
Oregon	257,907	281,057	25,136	28,277	222,112	20,508	41,357
Pennsylvania	1,419,336	1,610,915	136,439	157,136	1,264,207	79,144	152,866
Rhode Island	113,301	129,735	10,816	11,850	103,399	11,271	22,577
South Carolina	247,648	214,577	47,154	41,734	188,540	12,097	18,656
South Dakota	91,997	88,298	6,787	6,194	80,986	716	3,255
Tennessee	443,269	391,618	63,712	57,222	379,480	24,312	40,490
Texas	1,096,361	1,044,826	124,615	117,201	965,379	27,563	40,897
Utah	89,168	96,273	8,137	8,566	75,146	4,529	11,385
Vermont	54,088	56,483	5,503	5,350	48,984	2,748	5,451
Virginia	428,523	406,606	64,238	60,146	358,675	7,315	12,723
Washington	361,971	401,912	31,512	35,788	318,212	63,182	89,170
West Virginia	239,821	233,025	55,477	53,279	197,038	8,791	13,871
Wisconsin	541,577	588,058	41,796	45,576	471,088	23,902	56,989
Wyoming	34,806	36,567	3,127	3,176	30,548	572	1,890
Total U.S.	22,826,288‡	24,208,637‡	2,487,519	2,542,204‡	20,102,741‡	1,361,560	2,754,762

*Includes hospital and/or medical insurance. †Weekly average. ‡Includes data for American Samoa, Guam, Puerto Rico, Virgin Islands, and for beneficiaries or enrollees living abroad.
Source: U.S. Department of Health, Education, and Welfare, Social Security Administration.

Public assistance
June 1970

State	NUMBER OF RECIPIENTS					AVERAGE MONEY PAYMENTS				
	Old-age assistance	Aid to dependent children*	Aid to the permanently and totally disabled	Aid to the blind	General assistance	Old-age assistance	Aid to dependent children, per recipient	Aid to the permanently and totally disabled	Aid to the blind	General assistance
Alabama	112,000	137,000	18,400	1,900	100	$66.10	$15.15	$50.05	$70.40	$12.50
Alaska	1,600	8,500	730	89	780	96.45	48.10	133.60	133.65	32.60
Arizona	13,800	57,800	8,100	540	5,100	72.20	32.30	79.30	79.55	26.40
Arkansas	56,800	51,200	11,300	1,700	530	59.35	22.75	67.25	74.50	5.25
California	317,000	1,322,000	174,000	13,600	80,100	109.85	52.95	135.50	159.80	52.10
Colorado	37,100	75,600	9,600	220	2,100	76.40	43.45	78.65	79.75	18.55
Connecticut	8,000	89,600	6,900	240	22,800†	90.30	60.95	116.25	95.60	37.00
Delaware	2,300	21,600	1,300	360	5,300	73.80	34.45	110.90	104.60	29.50
District of Columbia	3,300	46,800	6,400	210	2,100	89.35	54.85	101.25	100.00	95.65
Florida	61,500	224,000	20,800	2,300	20,400†	51.85	22.80	64.45	66.15	—
Georgia	91,200	224,000	33,200	3,200	2,900	52.70	28.10	63.85	66.65	21.30
Hawaii	2,300	26,800	1,800	69	5,700	89.75	58.65	126.55	112.70	63.75
Idaho	3,500	17,600	2,700	100	—	63.30	49.85	79.65	83.85	—
Illinois	37,600	406,000	42,100	1,700	87,100	73.65	53.75	99.30	95.00	62.25
Indiana	15,900	87,600	5,200	1,300	—	55.15	36.10	56.70	70.35	—
Iowa	23,400	68,700	3,100	1,200	8,300†	112.70	51.75	142.25	122.45	—
Kansas	13,500	58,300	6,100	340	7,600	78.35	51.40	96.45	81.95	47.20
Kentucky	62,800	133,000	16,800	2,100	—	54.50	30.30	73.05	74.00	—
Louisiana	117,000	225,000	22,000	2,400	8,200	67.40	22.30	54.90	76.85	48.30
Maine	10,500	43,200	3,600	230	7,200	61.25	40.60	97.35	89.65	15.05
Maryland	8,300	142,000	16,000	360	7,900	58.60	42.65	80.20	89.70	79.20
Massachusetts	52,200	227,000	16,700	2,800	41,700	99.20	70.85	128.10	152.05	59.90
Michigan	37,400	296,000	26,800	1,400	85,400	75.70	52.90	101.35	99.75	47.95
Minnesota	21,100	86,400	11,300	830	19,300	72.65	73.30	115.65	95.55	40.20
Mississippi	73,400	122,000	21,800	2,100	1,600	50.40	12.05	59.30	59.15	14.75
Missouri	94,000	155,000	18,800	4,000	13,800	75.95	30.05	76.55	91.60	57.30
Montana	3,500	15,400	2,100	180	2,300	58.20	39.55	79.15	82.60	18.80
Nebraska	7,800	33,700	4,500	340	—	59.20	41.20	68.45	92.75	—
Nevada	3,400	13,500	—	180	—	64.50	31.10	—	89.10	—
New Hampshire	4,200	10,400	810	220	2,800	122.90	49.35	109.05	125.65	24.90
New Jersey	17,100	355,000	12,900	970	10,100	75.20	60.70	102.55	97.95	120.75
New Mexico	9,000	55,800	8,300	360	720	57.95	32.60	75.85	79.90	41.40
New York	97,700	1,103,000	80,200	3,600	207,000	102.00	69.60	121.65	121.10	68.40
North Carolina	35,600	134,000	27,500	4,500	3,900	64.85	30.60	75.95	82.60	11.20
North Dakota	3,800	11,300	3,100	84	710	84.80	54.20	92.75	96.25	15.60
Ohio	56,400	292,000	30,800	2,600	81,700	60.70	42.60	76.45	75.95	37.55
Oklahoma	73,200	101,000	21,700	1,300	2,500	69.60	36.80	96.60	106.00	7.95
Oregon	7,100	86,700	5,600	540	4,300	63.55	46.15	92.05	111.25	35.30
Pennsylvania	48,400	488,000	43,000	8,200	96,100	101.75	60.70	90.55	119.00	76.65
Rhode Island	3,900	40,100	4,000	120	14,900	54.25	54.10	89.40	81.35	—
South Carolina	18,600	61,500	10,400	1,900	1,100	48.70	19.55	55.70	67.25	32.75
South Dakota	4,200	17,200	1,500	110	660	59.55	49.95	64.55	88.55	11.75
Tennessee	53,100	150,000	25,100	1,800	4,900	50.40	29.20	67.95	71.05	10.05
Texas	231,000	264,000	23,500	4,100	...	62.65	28.05	64.85	78.85	—
Utah	3,300	36,300	5,200	160	1,500	52.95	44.20	70.20	82.95	47.75
Vermont	4,300	12,500	1,900	100	—	72.90	55.60	99.60	94.90	—
Virginia	12,100	99,600	7,700	1,100	9,300	61.90	43.05	74.60	80.30	42.30
Washington	22,400	127,000	16,400	460	7,900	66.65	57.85	95.70	94.35	69.25
West Virginia	12,900	98,700	10,100	560	1,200	70.55	27.50	63.60	70.00	12.20
Wisconsin	18,500	82,200	6,900	680	20,800	99.20	54.00	88.60	86.10	34.20
Wyoming	1,600	5,700	900	34	500	60.95	43.55	66.25	...	21.45
Total U.S.§	2,052,000	8,291,000	874,000	80,100	926,000‡	74.75	47.20	94.50	102.05	53.85

*Includes children and parents or caretaker relatives in families in which these adults were included in determining amount of assistance.
†Estimated. ‡Partly estimated. Excludes Idaho, Indiana, Kentucky, Nebraska, Nevada, Puerto Rico. §Includes Guam, Puerto Rico, and the Virgin Islands.
Source: U.S. Department of Health, Education, and Welfare, Social Security Administration, *Social Security Bulletin*.

Physicians and hospital facilities

State	PRACTICING PHYSICIANS* Jan. 1, 1970			HOSPITALS 1969		State	PRACTICING PHYSICIANS Jan. 1, 1970			HOSPITALS 1969	
	Total	Engaged in patient care	In other professional activity†	Number	Beds		Total	Engaged in patient care	In other professional activity†	Number	Beds
Alabama	2,827	2,627	200	137	28,464	Montana	644	624	20	64	4,624
Alaska	188	181	7	26	1,840	Nebraska	1,541	1,413	128	116	12,910
Arizona	2,070	1,955	115	80	9,339	Nevada	462	441	21	22	2,787
Arkansas	1,581	1,482	99	93	11,012	New Hampshire	885	802	83	36	6,593
California	33,699	30,794	2,905	641	133,043	New Jersey	9,405	8,630	775	142	52,454
Colorado	3,459	3,067	392	93	16,118	New Mexico	954	862	92	58	5,938
Connecticut	5,241	4,650	591	65	24,356	New York	39,995	35,317	4,678	433	201,215
Delaware	654	604	50	14	5,093	North Carolina	5,082	4,541	541	164	35,361
District of Columbia	2,731	2,314	417	21	15,187	North Dakota	544	517	27	65	6,129
Florida	8,043	7,451	592	190	44,974	Ohio	13,081	12,018	1,063	245	80,858
Georgia	4,470	4,106	364	164	34,664	Oklahoma	2,376	2,197	179	150	16,860
Hawaii	1,022	934	88	32	6,134	Oregon	2,712	2,484	228	88	15,069
Idaho	603	578	25	54	3,895	Pennsylvania	16,506	14,815	1,691	323	115,869
Illinois	14,127	12,884	1,243	312	98,511	Rhode Island	1,286	1,195	91	24	8,725
Indiana	4,831	4,483	348	136	38,306	South Carolina	2,071	1,951	120	84	18,553
Iowa	2,692	2,492	200	147	21,724	South Dakota	501	483	18	61	6,341
Kansas	2,361	2,173	188	165	19,900	Tennessee	4,312	3,910	402	160	32,899
Kentucky	3,082	2,832	250	134	23,007	Texas	11,868	11,018	850	556	75,685
Louisiana	4,048	3,723	325	153	26,318	Utah	1,324	1,195	129	39	4,988
Maine	931	868	63	58	9,307	Vermont	734	644	90	25	4,508
Maryland	6,402	5,423	979	83	33,284	Virginia	5,026	4,602	424	130	38,716
Massachusetts	10,670	8,995	1,675	206	63,672	Washington	4,497	4,045	452	128	18,677
Michigan	10,240	9,379	861	251	69,000	West Virginia	1,697	1,599	98	89	16,298
Minnesota	5,331	4,794	537	206	33,736	Wisconsin	4,821	4,444	377	200	37,750
Mississippi	1,692	1,609	83	103	16,657	Wyoming	284	273	11	33	3,853
Missouri	5,528	4,950	578	145	38,462	Total U.S.	300,595‡	268,597	31,998	7,144	1,649,663

*Excludes data for physicians temporarily abroad, or whose addresses are unknown.
†Includes medical school faculty, administration, and research.
‡Includes 29,464 physicians in government service not allocated by state.
Sources: American Hospital Association, American Medical Association.

Law Enforcement

Arrests, 1969

Offense charged	UNDER 18		18 AND OVER		ALL AGES	
	Persons arrested	Percent change from 1968	Persons arrested	Percent change from 1968	Persons arrested	Percent change from 1968
Murder and nonnegligent manslaughter	985	+ 3.8	9,133	+10.4	10,118	+ 9.7
Manslaughter by negligence	221	+ 9.4	2,544	−10.3	2,765	+10.2
Forcible rape	2,601	+ 9.2	9,898	−13.9	12,499	−12.9
Robbery	23,709	+12.9	43,581	+12.7	67,290	+12.8
Aggravated assault	16,701	+ 4.9	80,244	+ 4.4	96,945	+ 4.5
Other assaults	41,999	+ 9.0	195,516	+ 9.6	237,515	+ 9.5
Burglary—breaking or entering	124,314	− 0.3	100,903	+ 1.7	225,217	+ 0.6
Larceny—theft	252,278	+ 5.4	214,888	+13.9	467,166	+ 9.1
Auto theft	64,330	− 3.4	43,970	+ 6.0	108,300	+ 0.2
Arson	4,941	− 6.1	2,895	+ 0.3	7,836	− 3.8
Forgery and counterfeiting	3,714	+ 1.7	27,423	+ 9.0	31,137	+ 8.0
Fraud	2,842	+22.9	53,645	+11.9	56,487	+12.4
Embezzlement	220	+10.0	5,529	+12.7	5,749	+12.6
Stolen property; buying, receiving, possessing	13,503	+15.8	29,028	+33.4	42,531	+27.2
Vandalism	71,254	− 5.1	25,162	+ 4.7	96,416	− 2.7
Weapons; carrying, possessing, etc.	14,049	+ 3.3	67,560	+ 8.4	81,609	+ 7.5
Prostitution and commercialized vice	864	+12.4	41,998	+12.5	42,862	+12.5
Sex offenses (except forcible rape and prostitution)	10,237	− 0.9	33,342	+ 9.1	43,579	+ 6.6
Narcotic drug laws	46,612	+32.9	144,308	+49.5	190,920	+45.1
Gambling	1,531	−16.4	72,612	+ 3.5	74,143	+ 3.0
Offenses against family and children	724	+32.6	44,281	+ 2.3	45,005	+ 2.7
Driving while intoxicated	3,216	+28.4	282,294	+15.5	285,510	+15.6
Liquor law violations	64,066	+ 8.0	127,246	+ 1.5	191,312	+ 3.6
Drunkenness	38,892	+16.0	1,234,431	− 0.5	1,273,323	− 0.1
Disorderly conduct	109,191	− 9.5	428,973	+ 0.3	538,164	− 1.9
Vagrancy	10,187	+ 5.0	87,637	+ 7.6	97,824	+ 7.3
All other offenses, except traffic	187,261	+ 2.8	408,633	+ 5.6	595,894	+ 4.7
Suspicion	20,165	− 4.3	64,734	†	84,899	− 1.1
Curfew and loitering law violations	93,243	+ 6.4	—		93,243	+ 6.4
Runaways	146,091	+ 7.1	—		146,091	+ 7.1
TOTAL ARRESTS*	1,349,776	+ 3.7	3,817,674	+ 5.6	5,167,450	+ 5.1

Data are from 3,999 agencies reporting on estimated population of 128,095,000.
*Excludes arrests for suspicion.   †Decrease of less than one-tenth of 1 percent.
Source: U.S. Department of Justice, Federal Bureau of Investigation, *Uniform Crime Reports.*

Public expenditures and employment for law enforcement

Expenditure (in 000,000)	1955	1960	1965	1968
All governments	2,231	3,349	4,573	...
Police protection	1,359	2,030	2,792	3,700
Judicial	409	597	748	...
Correction*	463	722	1,033	1,335
Federal Government	206	291	377	445
Police protection	129	173	243	290
Judicial	49	74	75	90
Correction*	28	44	59	65
State governments	475	769	1,135	1,559
Police protection	139	245	348	516
Judicial	68	99	155	205
Correction*	268	425	632	838
Local governments	1,550	2,289	3,062	...
Police protection	1,091	1,612	2,201	2,894
Judicial	292	424	518	...
Correction*	167	253	343	432
Employees (in 000)				
Police protection, all governments	265	363	420	489
Federal	...	22	23	26
State	...	32	41	52
Local	244	309	357	412
Correction, all governments	...	...	117	137
Federal	...	...	3	5
State	...	...	71	81
Local	...	...	43	51

1955 and 1960 expenditures for fiscal years closing during calendar year; 1965 and 1967 are for years closing during 12 months ending June 30. Employees as of October. *Includes capital outlay.
Source: U.S. Department of Commerce, Bureau of the Census, *Statistical Abstract of the United States.*

Rearrests

Age, and type of release	Within 30 months of 1963 release	Within 6 years of 1963 release
Age	Percent	
Under 20	65	74
20–24	64	72
25–29	59	69
30–39	55	66
40–49	46	56
50 and over	34	43
All ages	55	65
Type of release		
Fine and probation	30	38
Suspended sentence and probation	47	57
Parole	57	63
Fine	63	78
Mandatory release	67	76
Acquitted or dismissed	83	92
All types	55	65

Source: U.S. Department of Justice, Federal Bureau of Investigation, *Uniform Crime Reports.*

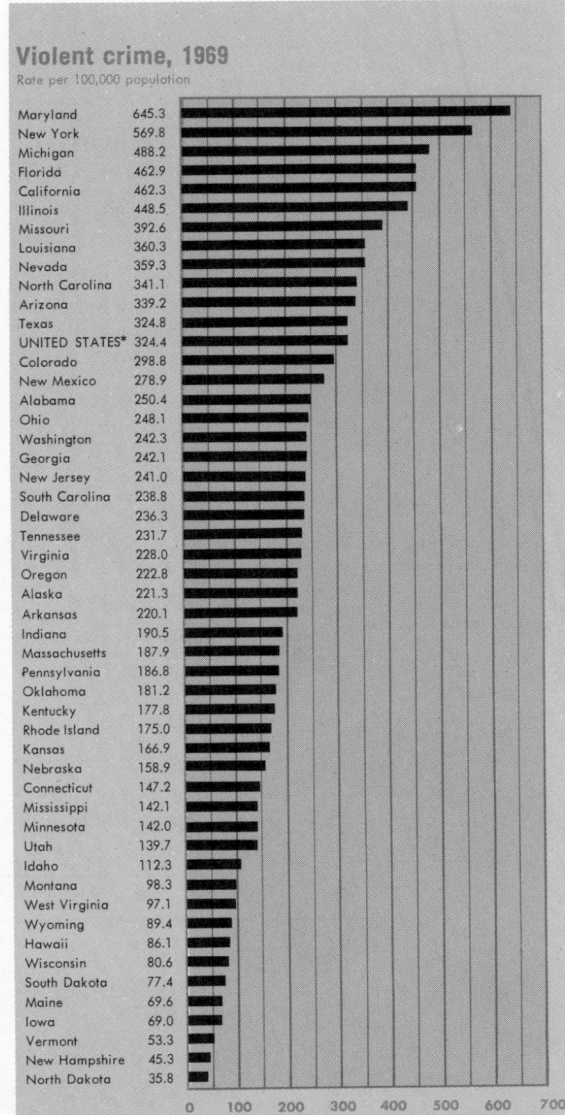

Violent crime, 1969
Rate per 100,000 population

Maryland	645.3
New York	569.8
Michigan	488.2
Florida	462.9
California	462.3
Illinois	448.5
Missouri	392.6
Louisiana	360.3
Nevada	359.3
North Carolina	341.1
Arizona	339.2
Texas	324.8
UNITED STATES*	324.4
Colorado	298.8
New Mexico	278.9
Alabama	250.4
Ohio	248.1
Washington	242.3
Georgia	242.1
New Jersey	241.0
South Carolina	238.8
Delaware	236.3
Tennessee	231.7
Virginia	228.0
Oregon	222.8
Alaska	221.3
Arkansas	220.1
Indiana	190.5
Massachusetts	187.9
Pennsylvania	186.8
Oklahoma	181.2
Kentucky	177.8
Rhode Island	175.0
Kansas	166.9
Nebraska	158.9
Connecticut	147.2
Mississippi	142.1
Minnesota	142.0
Utah	139.7
Idaho	112.3
Montana	98.3
West Virginia	97.1
Wyoming	89.4
Hawaii	86.1
Wisconsin	80.6
South Dakota	77.4
Maine	69.6
Iowa	69.0
Vermont	53.3
New Hampshire	45.3
North Dakota	35.8

Violent crime includes murder, nonnegligent manslaughter, forcible rape, robbery, and aggravated assault.
*Includes the District of Columbia.
Source: U.S. Department of Justice, Federal Bureau of Investigation, *Uniform Crime Reports.*

Crime rates per 100,000 population

Unit	MURDER* 1960	1969	FORCIBLE RAPE 1960	1969	ROBBERY 1960	1969	AGGRAVATED ASSAULT 1960	1969	BURGLARY 1960	1969	LARCENY† 1960	1969	AUTO THEFT 1960	1969
STATE														
Alabama	12.9	**13.7**	8.3	14.0	26.9	41.0	123.2	181.7	368.6	655.8	183.2	498.5	95.6	171.2
Alaska	10.2	10.6	**20.8**	29.4	28.3	67.4	45.1	113.8	332.1	870.6	352.4	959.2	242.3	591.5
Arizona	6.1	6.0	16.1	23.0	54.6	99.9	120.1	210.2	687.1	1,302.6	415.0	1,004.8	339.6	438.6
Arkansas	8.6	9.9	8.7	17.4	25.0	44.4	56.7	148.4	273.9	587.3	160.2	509.7	46.5	101.3
California	3.9	7.1	18.3	**36.3**	98.0	201.8	120.2	217.0	913.3	**1,676.1**	494.5	**1,293.5**	328.1	678.6
Colorado	4.2	5.3	13.3	28.8	80.0	110.7	41.0	154.0	579.7	1,133.2	317.3	1,086.3	217.5	507.0
Connecticut	1.7	2.9	4.2	8.7	9.5	56.5	21.9	79.1	330.7	987.5	179.0	772.5	131.1	427.8
Delaware	6.5	7.2	8.3	12.4	34.5	113.7	21.1	103.0	557.0	813.1	179.3	708.1	162.7	458.3
Florida	10.5	11.3	8.4	21.2	81.1	162.8	114.7	267.5	829.6	1,358.3	366.1	961.8	198.6	382.9
Georgia	12.0	11.9	7.6	17.1	26.6	62.4	98.9	150.7	408.1	701.5	179.4	566.4	153.7	273.0
Hawaii	2.4	3.4	3.3	12.2	10.9	35.5	5.2	35.0	525.9	1,304.8	284.9	981.7	269.9	535.9
Idaho	2.4	1.9	7.0	10.0	13.9	16.7	14.7	83.6	301.3	590.0	265.0	680.8	100.0	131.5
Illinois	5.1	8.6	12.4	19.1	**159.7**	236.7	94.2	184.0	521.4	738.7	340.1	566.6	307.5	474.5
Indiana	4.4	4.9	4.7	15.2	34.4	91.2	37.4	79.2	429.7	760.7	182.8	612.1	162.2	375.7
Iowa	0.6	1.4	3.7	6.4	11.2	22.4	8.7	38.8	233.5	489.1	181.9	535.1	77.1	177.5
Kansas	3.2	3.5	5.3	15.1	20.8	54.8	29.0	93.5	355.4	693.3	168.6	676.5	91.0	228.0
Kentucky	6.8	10.4	5.5	11.4	33.7	69.2	51.8	86.7	376.8	569.3	211.5	570.0	125.7	345.9
Louisiana	8.7	9.5	9.5	22.1	52.8	102.6	78.0	226.0	411.2	694.6	242.8	584.8	225.3	324.2
Maine	1.7	1.6	5.0	5.9	7.9	11.3	10.7	50.7	246.0	510.7	150.7	317.8	117.9	137.5
Maryland	5.5	9.3	7.3	29.9	37.9	294.4	90.1	**311.7**	366.8	1,114.7	239.7	929.0	184.3	592.6
Massachusetts	1.5	3.5	5.0	10.8	21.2	90.6	20.1	82.9	309.9	1,032.6	185.1	661.0	215.6	**858.8**
Michigan	4.3	8.3	12.4	27.4	73.7	266.5	96.0	186.0	592.1	1,250.8	273.9	958.1	178.5	495.7
Minnesota	1.3	1.9	2.5	11.5	29.4	81.5	10.8	47.1	360.1	779.4	218.0	717.1	141.8	384.3
Mississippi	10.0	8.1	5.1	9.1	15.0	14.6	66.0	110.3	205.3	316.9	89.8	208.5	48.4	73.0
Missouri	4.6	10.4	11.0	27.3	76.2	182.4	71.6	172.5	523.4	1,118.8	231.9	642.8	177.0	578.5
Montana	3.9	3.6	7.3	11.1	28.0	22.2	24.5	61.4	401.3	561.8	269.3	612.5	248.1	215.9
Nebraska	2.3	2.5	4.2	6.8	18.0	51.8	16.5	97.8	231.8	482.3	125.6	490.6	125.8	284.5
Nevada	8.8	9.0	12.6	20.6	74.0	170.9	50.5	158.9	**913.5**	1,366.5	**541.9**	1,263.5	**391.9**	560.2
New Hampshire	1.3	2.5	4.1	4.0	3.0	10.5	4.9	28.3	182.6	463.3	88.5	329.4	57.7	143.2
New Jersey	2.9	5.2	7.9	12.8	46.0	135.1	59.8	87.9	438.6	953.0	236.7	743.3	201.9	521.0
New Mexico	7.3	6.1	12.0	24.3	38.7	63.7	89.0	184.7	434.9	1,174.2	378.4	1,017.2	371.1	403.1
New York	2.9	7.2	6.3	15.6	44.1	**351.2**	73.8	195.8	336.3	1,304.5	403.3	1,070.2	178.2	622.0
North Carolina	10.1	10.7	7.3	11.6	17.0	40.6	**182.1**	278.3	258.2	565.4	140.2	485.2	78.2	149.4
North Dakota	0.5	0.2	2.2	4.1	6.3	7.2	5.2	24.4	199.2	249.3	93.4	368.1	68.5	95.1
Ohio	3.3	6.4	6.0	15.3	41.6	126.7	34.2	99.8	350.4	740.1	195.4	608.1	138.1	482.1
Oklahoma	7.5	5.8	12.8	14.3	40.2	48.6	36.0	112.5	536.7	687.6	261.0	565.2	199.4	241.3
Oregon	2.4	4.0	9.3	18.3	31.9	86.6	26.0	113.9	406.3	1,124.7	317.3	985.5	130.9	318.5
Pennsylvania	2.8	4.1	9.0	11.5	36.1	88.4	53.7	82.8	308.8	572.4	149.6	341.0	128.2	300.2
Rhode Island	1.0	3.1	2.3	4.0	14.5	73.4	19.8	94.5	517.3	982.4	419.2	812.8	317.3	823.2
South Carolina	**13.3**	12.5	9.4	13.4	20.4	50.0	102.2	163.0	371.4	716.7	205.4	507.7	104.7	228.5
South Dakota	2.1	2.0	5.4	11.1	9.1	12.9	16.0	51.4	247.9	425.0	198.8	412.6	86.6	105.9
Tennessee	8.5	9.6	5.2	12.7	27.8	75.2	50.4	134.3	469.4	715.0	153.5	437.2	132.2	281.6
Texas	8.7	11.3	9.3	19.4	32.8	114.6	111.8	179.4	613.8	1,083.9	233.1	679.4	168.1	376.0
Utah	1.6	2.5	9.5	14.1	28.1	49.0	34.5	74.2	517.7	848.5	320.1	892.2	207.3	297.7
Vermont	0.3	2.5	2.3	9.1	2.3	9.3	4.6	32.3	242.1	599.5	201.9	261.3	87.7	113.0
Virginia	10.0	5.9	7.3	14.8	25.3	78.1	102.1	129.2	346.3	669.7	212.0	562.7	120.0	276.1
Washington	2.1	3.6	5.9	19.4	31.5	113.0	15.5	106.3	488.7	1,296.5	331.5	1,064.3	158.0	380.7
West Virginia	4.4	5.6	4.4	5.1	13.5	19.1	35.5	67.3	239.0	322.7	198.4	259.5	71.5	85.4
Wisconsin	1.3	2.1	2.8	7.2	8.5	28.3	16.9	43.1	199.6	498.5	378.1	579.6	106.4	223.9
Wyoming	4.8	10.3	7.0	11.6	53.6	15.9	51.5	51.6	300.2	565.0	331.8	679.1	114.8	177.2
METROPOLITAN AREA														
Baltimore	7.2	13.4	8.5	41.6	56.5	467.6	132.1	**499.8**	424.7	1,347.7	319.2	1,125.9	245.6	760.3
Boston	1.8	4.2	5.2	13.3	29.4	122.1	28.4	89.7	313.5	982.4	203.0	669.0	262.8	953.8
Chicago	6.7	11.6	17.0	24.7	**237.5**	340.4	134.9	241.8	640.8	807.8	451.4	609.4	442.3	644.6
Cleveland	5.3	13.8	5.3	17.9	81.7	289.8	33.0	131.1	265.0	835.9	125.6	578.9	196.3	**1,294.7**
Detroit	5.1	13.0	14.6	35.7	130.6	477.0	159.6	220.2	746.3	1,565.7	303.8	1,182.6	256.1	788.4
Houston	**10.9**	**16.8**	16.1	26.6	53.7	289.3	149.9	186.2	877.8	1,508.6	312.3	786.6	261.7	697.2
Los Angeles—Long Beach	4.4	9.7	**29.0**	**51.8**	143.9	286.0	**199.1**	355.2	**1,200.9**	1,902.0	**657.3**	1,386.0	**444.3**	861.5
Minneapolis—St. Paul	1.8	3.2	3.9	20.1	62.5	164.5	19.0	80.4	585.7	1,205.7	345.2	1,067.3	258.2	689.4
Newark	3.8	7.3	12.7	19.9	95.4	269.2	121.0	169.5	663.5	1,249.8	411.9	864.9	332.7	680.6
New York	4.0	9.4	8.4	19.4	64.2	521.7	106.9	266.7	414.2	1,674.3	565.0	**1,392.1**	228.4	847.9
Philadelphia	4.8	7.5	16.5	16.1	62.3	130.6	119.4	111.2	430.3	701.1	184.7	369.5	135.9	417.0
Pittsburgh	2.4	3.2	10.6	14.8	47.9	143.0	34.0	107.4	354.9	765.7	212.6	557.6	261.4	533.4
St. Louis	5.7	14.3	17.4	34.2	152.8	247.9	133.0	207.3	785.9	1,360.0	350.7	607.5	279.7	831.0
San Francisco—Oakland	3.5	9.5	11.9	46.1	102.8	383.1	92.9	226.8	739.9	**2,241.5**	335.7	1,361.9	320.8	1,172.1
Washington, D.C.	6.9	12.5	10.2	27.6	67.3	**524.1**	183.6	216.9	455.1	1,495.7	270.8	1,003.0	192.6	739.0

Boldface type indicates highest rate for that crime among the states or the listed metropolitan areas.
*Includes nonnegligent manslaughter.   †$50 and over.
Source: U.S. Department of Justice, Federal Bureau of Investigation, *Uniform Crime Reports*.

Prisoners

Year	PRISONERS PRESENT AT END OF YEAR — All institutions Number	Rate	Federal institutions Number	Rate	State institutions Number	Rate	PRISONERS RECEIVED FROM COURTS — All institutions Number	Rate	Federal institutions Number	Rate	State institutions Number	Rate
1940	173,706	132.0	19,260	14.6	154,446	117.3	73,104	55.5	15,109	11.5	57,995	44.1
1945	133,649	100.5	18,638	14.0	115,011	86.5	53,212	40.0	14,171	10.7	39,041	29.4
1950	166,123	110.3	17,134	11.4	148,989	98.9	69,473	46.1	14,237	9.5	55,236	36.7
1955	185,780	113.4	20,088	12.3	165,692	101.1	78,414	47.9	15,286	9.3	63,128	38.5
1960	212,957	118.6	23,218	12.9	189,739	105.7	88,575	49.3	13,723	7.6	74,852	41.7
1961	220,149	120.8	23,696	13.0	196,453	107.8	93,513	51.3	13,517	7.4	79,996	43.9
1962	218,830	118.3	23,944	12.9	194,886	105.3	89,082	48.1	13,514	7.3	75,568	40.8
1963	217,283	115.7	23,128	12.1	194,155	103.4	87,826	46.8	12,882	6.9	74,944	39.9
1964	214,336	112.6	21,709	11.4	192,627	101.2	87,578	46.0	12,482	6.6	75,096	39.4
1965	210,895	109.5	21,040	10.9	189,855	98.6	87,505	45.4	12,781	6.6	74,724	38.8
1966	199,654	102.7	19,245	9.9	180,409	92.8	77,857	40.0	11,508	5.9	66,349	34.1
1967	194,896	99.1	19,579	10.0	175,317	89.2	77,850	39.6	11,447	5.8	66,403	33.8

Rate per 100,000 estimated civilian population, excluding Alaska and, prior to 1960, Hawaii. Excludes state institutions in Alaska and, prior to 1960, those in Hawaii.
Source: U.S. Department of Justice, Bureau of Prisons, *National Prisoner Statistics*.

Education

State expenditure on education

public elementary and secondary, year ending June 30, 1970

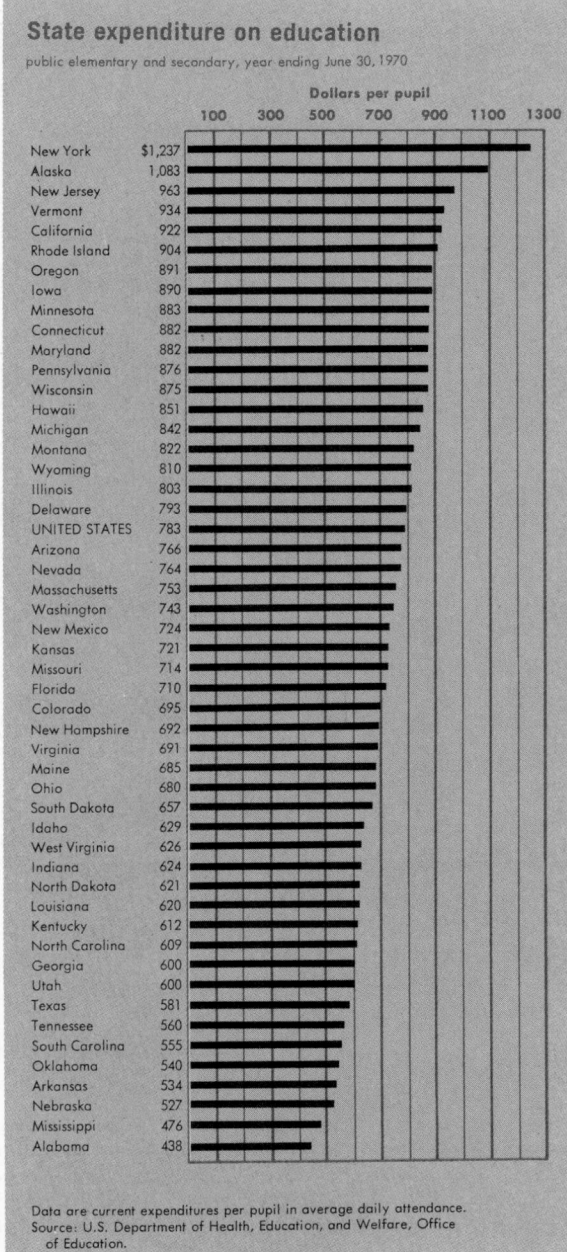

Dollars per pupil

		100	300	500	700	900	1100	1300
New York	$1,237							
Alaska	1,083							
New Jersey	963							
Vermont	934							
California	922							
Rhode Island	904							
Oregon	891							
Iowa	890							
Minnesota	883							
Connecticut	882							
Maryland	882							
Pennsylvania	876							
Wisconsin	875							
Hawaii	851							
Michigan	842							
Montana	822							
Wyoming	810							
Illinois	803							
Delaware	793							
UNITED STATES	783							
Arizona	766							
Nevada	764							
Massachusetts	753							
Washington	743							
New Mexico	724							
Kansas	721							
Missouri	714							
Florida	710							
Colorado	695							
New Hampshire	692							
Virginia	691							
Maine	685							
Ohio	680							
South Dakota	657							
Idaho	629							
West Virginia	626							
Indiana	624							
North Dakota	621							
Louisiana	620							
Kentucky	612							
North Carolina	609							
Georgia	600							
Utah	600							
Texas	581							
Tennessee	560							
South Carolina	555							
Oklahoma	540							
Arkansas	534							
Nebraska	527							
Mississippi	476							
Alabama	438							

Data are current expenditures per pupil in average daily attendance.
Source: U.S. Department of Health, Education, and Welfare, Office of Education.

Vocational education

Type of program	NUMBER OF STUDENTS		
	1959–60	1964–65	1968–69
Agriculture	796,237	887,529	850,705
Distributive occupations	303,784	333,342	563,431
Home economics	1,588,109	2,098,520	2,449,052
Trades and industry	938,490	1,087,807	1,720,859
Health occupations	40,250	66,772	175,101
Technical education	101,279	225,737	315,311
Office occupations	—	730,904	1,835,124
Total	3,768,149	5,430,611	7,979,366*

Data refer to vocational programs receiving federal aid.
*Includes 69,783 enrollees not classified by type of program.
Source: U.S. Department of Health, Education, and Welfare,
Office of Education, *Digest of Educational Statistics*.

Enrollment in special education

programs for exceptional children

Type	1958	1963	1966 estimate
Visually handicapped	12,000	21,531	23,300
Deaf and hard of hearing	20,000	45,594	51,400
Speech impaired	490,000	802,197	989,500
Crippled and special health problems	52,000	64,842	69,400
Emotionally and socially maladjusted	29,000	79,587	87,900
Mentally retarded	223,000	431,890	540,100
Other handicapped conditions	12,000	22,039	32,500
Gifted	52,000	214,671	312,100
Total	890,000	1,682,351	2,106,200

Data are for February of years reported.
Beginning 1963, includes public and private residential schools;
1958 includes public day schools only.
Source: U.S. Department of Health, Education, and Welfare,
Office of Education.

Universities and colleges

state statistics

State	NUMBER OF INSTITUTIONS fall, 1969		ENROLL-MENT fall, 1969	EARNED DEGREES CONFERRED 1968-1969		
	Total	Public		Bachelor's and first professional	Master's, except first professional	Doctor's
Alabama	47	27	97,846	11,772	1,996	212
Alaska	3	1	7,445	285	121	4
Arizona	16	12	97,018	7,283	2,778	277
Arkansas	20	10	50,961	6,626	1,005	99
California	195	110	1,136,657	63,301	18,017	2,806
Colorado	28	20	111,490	11,210	3,214	543
Connecticut	46	17	115,775	10,230	4,155	479
Delaware	6	3	21,768	1,389	383	56
District of Columbia	22	3	74,174	7,476	3,869	418
Florida	61	34	220,571	16,783	3,957	550
Georgia	60	27	114,578	13,213	2,648	290
Hawaii	7	1	33,628	2,172	982	58
Idaho	10	6	23,157	2,396	315	51
Illinois	132	43	419,711	36,731	11,657	1,744
Indiana	43	5	180,411	21,563	7,734	1,165
Iowa	52	15	105,883	14,107	2,255	563
Kansas	53	27	98,794	11,889	2,765	331
Kentucky	35	7	97,130	12,157	2,192	155
Louisiana	23	12	114,854	12,846	2,850	310
Maine	16	2	29,067	3,842	587	16
Maryland	47	22	135,858	11,995	2,498	500
Massachusetts	110	29	282,442	30,413	9,728	1,509
Michigan	89	40	366,569	33,263	11,892	1,355
Minnesota	56	24	155,486	17,537	2,511	484
Mississippi	43	25	67,377	7,800	1,408	170
Missouri	67	20	173,232	18,598	4,670	507
Montana	12	9	28,461	3,369	505	51
Nebraska	26	11	65,256	8,953	1,194	155
Nevada	4	3	11,743	923	179	12
New Hampshire	20	4	27,835	3,942	532	55
New Jersey	57	22	186,658	17,751	4,790	510
New Mexico	11	8	41,215	3,509	1,132	152
New York	218	72	724,049	69,953	24,334	3,046
North Carolina	96	51	157,002	18,194	3,288	556
North Dakota	12	9	28,799	3,671	567	78
Ohio	88	20	356,695	40,587	7,927	1,056
Oklahoma	35	23	104,744	11,536	2,844	413
Oregon	39	20	103,656	9,737	2,629	419
Pennsylvania	142	29	392,405	47,402	10,396	1,314
Rhode Island	14	3	40,123	4,415	1,004	160
South Carolina	44	19	63,689	7,061	756	92
South Dakota	17	7	30,607	4,358	762	43
Tennessee	53	15	127,506	15,692	2,834	380
Texas	122	69	406,268	37,921	7,989	1,053
Utah	13	9	79,413	8,207	1,739	315
Vermont	17	5	21,660	2,703	602	18
Virginia	59	25	136,190	13,565	2,271	259
Washington	39	27	167,122	13,611	2,675	456
West Virginia	22	11	60,792	7,402	1,156	73
Wisconsin	64	33	188,911	18,834	4,356	797
Wyoming	7	7	13,440	1,102	318	65
Total U.S.	2,525	1,060	7,916,991	764,185	193,756	26,188

All totals exclude data for service academies.
Source: U.S. Department of Health, Education, and Welfare, Office of Education.

State	Operating school districts	Instruction rooms in use	ENROLLMENT Elementary	ENROLLMENT Secondary	High school graduates	INSTRUCTIONAL STAFF Total*	Principals and supervisors	Teachers, elementary Total	Teachers, elementary Men	Teachers, secondary Total	Teachers, secondary Men	TEACHERS' AVERAGE ANNUAL SALARIES Elementary	TEACHERS' AVERAGE ANNUAL SALARIES Secondary
Alabama	118	31,750	464,130	389,207	45,300	35,932	1,669	16,755	935	17,508	6,493	$ 6,745	$ 6,887
Alaska	28	3,017	62,345	27,346	3,220	3,889	194	2,154	476	1,360	729	10,598	10,499
Arizona	294	16,940	335,016	126,148	22,500	19,850	810	12,850	3,265	5,300	3,300	8,435	9,390
Arkansas	384	18,532	253,913	209,445	25,300	20,790	662	10,166	686	9,444	4,297	6,193	6,476
California	1,082	171,700	3,176,000	1,868,000	285,000	210,750	12,750	115,000	23,000	75,000	53,000	9,775	10,825
Colorado	181	21,889	325,000	240,000	30,800	26,550	1,700	12,400	2,000	11,000	6,000	7,400	7,800
Connecticut	173	26,468	436,000	240,000	34,000	35,638	2,567	17,720	3,796	13,035	7,592	8,900	9,320
Delaware	26	5,355	76,500	57,700	7,150	6,244	237	2,857	463	2,872	1,548	8,663	9,137
District of Columbia	1	5,224	99,000	59,000	5,400	8,990	600	4,150	500	3,560	1,270	...	...
Florida	67	49,417	852,974	682,185	72,000	70,600	3,170	32,930	3,790	29,200	14,310	8,180	8,440
Georgia	190	43,908	751,120	406,177	57,059	49,030	2,479	28,131	2,299	18,420	7,414	7,134	7,216
Hawaii	1	7,362	103,000	78,000	10,500	8,603	600	4,415	264	2,943	1,295	9,420	9,500
Idaho	115	7,701	98,000	92,000	12,400	8,567	513	3,808	495	4,159	2,342	6,480	7,240
Illinois	1,221	89,760	1,504,000	814,000	131,033	109,456	3,300	61,227	12,745	42,729	24,004	9,250	10,200
Indiana	322	55,639	716,400	560,000	71,824	56,810	3,700	25,610	4,010	25,000	14,500	8,891	9,402
Iowa	453	31,000	485,526	203,508	43,859	37,770	1,563	17,824	2,317	15,249	9,150	8,079	8,987
Kansas	311	25,129	402,383	161,681	33,646	26,799	1,396	12,328	1,365	11,838	6,904	7,485	7,745
Kentucky	193	27,454	519,000	200,000	37,700	32,478	1,600	17,978	2,467	10,900	4,900	7,220	7,880
Louisiana	66	37,387	559,650	350,350	46,500	42,050	2,050	22,300	2,650	17,700	7,350	6,810	7,220
Maine	239	10,057	173,500	65,500	12,500	11,895	585	7,335	1,520	3,725	2,250	7,380	7,950
Maryland	24	31,930	538,669	390,264	46,300	45,396	2,552	21,335	2,451	19,347	9,142	9,235	9,547
Massachusetts	388	34,166	648,000	487,000	65,300	54,400	3,111	26,137	3,737	22,552	13,000	8,600	8,800
Michigan	635	95,020	1,234,000	963,000	123,000	98,756	4,739	41,740	5,958	51,677	26,626	9,572	10,024
Minnesota	858	38,492	521,000	424,000	63,000	46,500	2,200	21,000	2,730	21,300	13,680	8,450	8,900
Mississippi	148	22,214	345,000	249,224	30,550	24,934	1,320	12,354	954	10,275	4,575	5,747	6,020
Missouri	651	40,491	789,000	279,000	55,300	47,991	2,941	29,719	5,647	13,175	7,440	7,745	7,917
Montana	701	8,387	115,000	66,000	11,000	9,300	410	5,400	900	3,060	1,930	7,300	8,150
Nebraska	1,420	16,806	201,000	139,000	21,100	17,334	720	8,989	500	7,400	3,900	7,074	8,052
Nevada	17	4,972	89,000	56,000	5,700	5,700	340	2,650	510	2,400	1,380	9,213	9,472
New Hampshire	158	6,575	95,400	61,970	8,790	7,687	345	3,720	540	2,981	1,697	7,617	7,837
New Jersey	572	57,210	996,200	500,500	87,200	78,800	4,366	39,700	8,300	27,300	15,600	8,950	9,330
New Mexico	89	11,668	165,000	133,000	15,700	13,346	965	6,355	1,176	5,416	3,087	7,840	7,820
New York	735	143,000	2,030,300	1,550,000	194,100	200,586	15,187	88,389	14,036	84,584	42,630	9,400	10,000
North Carolina	152	52,735	863,348	357,274	67,100	54,012	2,620	33,192	4,412	15,642	6,360	7,284	7,842
North Dakota	375	7,336	106,500	47,500	10,710	7,565	310	4,475	799	2,536	1,710	6,300	7,580
Ohio	639	93,028	1,544,900	926,870	146,300	107,100	5,600	53,500	7,800	42,900	24,000	7,680	8,100
Oklahoma	685	28,296	345,622	269,116	36,000	28,438	1,509	14,146	2,320	12,463	7,749	6,884	7,105
Oregon	345	21,369	298,079	198,720	33,134	25,750	1,550	12,300	2,800	9,500	5,700	8,500	9,100
Pennsylvania	600	89,245	1,280,200	1,089,000	151,200	117,600	5,700	52,000	9,600	53,000	30,600	8,600	8,000
Rhode Island	40	6,937	103,567	78,671	10,652	9,555	507	4,260	724	4,215	2,411	8,778	8,838
South Carolina	93	24,999	400,000	269,000	35,700	31,022	1,347	14,900	900	12,425	4,250	6,550	7,000
South Dakota	663	7,643	119,000	52,000	11,700	9,720	475	5,900	700	2,975	1,975	5,670	7,060
Tennessee	149	34,050	581,585	338,915	48,000	37,950	1,750	20,650	2,450	13,600	5,700	6,935	7,600
Texas	1,208	115,790	2,015,000	754,000	145,000	129,900	6,837	62,625	7,452	55,153	27,080	7,215	7,335
Utah	40	11,274	188,226	140,839	18,500	13,000	750	5,850	1,080	5,400	3,350	7,580	7,650
Vermont	253	5,477	67,867	39,746	5,400	6,430	422	3,053	422	2,501	1,417	7,680	8,320
Virginia	134	47,000	717,500	383,900	58,800	54,150	3,250	30,000	2,700	20,900	8,100	7,700	8,400
Washington	323	33,661	460,000	376,700	50,500	39,100	2,650	17,900	3,680	15,300	5,865	8,700	9,420
West Virginia	55	16,554	233,271	182,873	27,100	18,585	1,700	8,633	794	7,760	3,259	7,490	7,730
Wisconsin	455	38,564	617,440	411,627	64,697	50,743	3,747	25,424	4,831	21,572	13,375	8,750	9,200
Wyoming	154	4,548	48,000	41,000	5,114	4,974	295	2,260	351	2,191	1,389	8,108	8,380
Total U.S.	18,224	1,835,626	29,151,131	18,086,956	2,640,338	2,219,015	122,360	1,106,494	170,297	892,442	477,625	$ 8,310	$ 8,831

Kindergartens are included in the elementary schools; junior high schools, in the secondary schools.
Enrollment data show cumulative count of pupils registered at any time during the school year in each state.
All dollar amounts for Alaska should be reduced by about one-fourth to make purchasing power generally more comparable to data reported for other areas.
*Includes librarians, guidance and psychological personnel, and related instructional workers.
Sources: National Education Association, Research Division, *Estimates of School Statistics, 1969–70* (Copyright 1969. All rights reserved. Used by permission).
U.S. Department of Health, Education, and Welfare, Office of Education, *Fall 1969 Statistics of Public Schools.*

Private elementary and secondary day schools
fall 1970 estimates

State	ENROLLMENT Elementary	ENROLLMENT Secondary	CLASSROOM TEACHERS Elementary	CLASSROOM TEACHERS Secondary	State	ENROLLMENT Elementary	ENROLLMENT Secondary	CLASSROOM TEACHERS Elementary	CLASSROOM TEACHERS Secondary
Alabama	17,100	8,800	650	510	Montana	10,100	3,800	370	250
Alaska	1,200	500	70	60	Nebraska	32,300	13,100	1,200	830
Arizona	17,100	7,700	660	500	Nevada	3,900	1,200	140	50
Arkansas	7,600	3,300	330	210	New Hampshire	22,100	11,000	810	790
California	307,200	101,800	10,650	5,930	New Jersey	242,200	71,100	7,550	4,150
Colorado	27,600	10,400	1,110	740	New Mexico	14,900	3,200	610	200
Connecticut	75,500	41,300	2,900	2,980	New York	639,800	197,200	20,700	10,550
Delaware	14,000	3,600	520	250	North Carolina	15,700	4,000	730	320
District of Columbia	13,600	8,100	570	540	North Dakota	10,300	4,200	460	230
Florida	79,000	30,200	3,110	1,900	Ohio	276,000	87,700	8,480	4,300
Georgia	18,500	10,000	870	750	Oklahoma	9,100	3,000	430	190
Hawaii	17,400	10,700	640	600	Oregon	24,800	8,800	920	560
Idaho	5,800	1,600	220	100	Pennsylvania	418,400	146,200	12,940	7,530
Illinois	367,700	114,700	11,780	5,670	Rhode Island	35,000	10,100	1,350	590
Indiana	97,200	26,200	3,370	1,430	South Carolina	15,500	5,900	780	400
Iowa	61,600	22,400	2,440	1,150	South Dakota	9,700	3,200	410	240
Kansas	33,100	9,900	1,350	600	Tennessee	21,600	12,800	1,060	910
Kentucky	54,800	21,100	2,100	1,240	Texas	87,200	23,800	3,910	1,580
Louisiana	97,300	31,600	3,670	1,720	Utah	3,300	1,000	120	70
Maine	15,500	10,000	650	740	Vermont	8,500	7,200	360	530
Maryland	96,200	31,200	3,510	2,100	Virginia	39,500	18,100	1,850	1,360
Massachusetts	162,900	71,700	5,690	3,930	Washington	38,200	14,400	1,410	820
Michigan	193,400	57,900	6,200	3,030	West Virginia	9,300	4,200	340	260
Minnesota	101,900	27,600	3,920	1,650	Wisconsin	186,700	38,300	6,970	2,200
Mississippi	15,200	4,900	720	320	Wyoming	2,700	4,000	120	20
Missouri	124,200	38,900	4,280	2,420	Total U.S.	4,200,000	1,400,000	146,000	80,000

Data exclude subcollegiate departments of institutions of higher education and residential schools for exceptional children.
Source: U.S. Department of Health, Education, and Welfare, Office of Education, *Digest of Educational Statistics.*

Universities and colleges

Selected list of four-year schools, 1970

Institution	Location	Year founded	Total students	Faculty	Bound library volumes	Endowment fund
ALABAMA						
Alabama, U. of	University	1831	13,034	673	819,000	$ 7,773,000
Alabama A. & M.	Normal	1875	1,288	121	...	—
Alabama State	Montgomery	1874	2,340	100	115,000	—
Athens	Athens	1822	1,273	57	46,000	1,354,868
Auburn U.	Auburn	1856	14,525	840	670,000	4,563,000
Birmingham-Southern	Birmingham	1856	1,005	86	88,000	5,482,000
Florence State U.	Florence	1873	3,114	142	99,000	—
Huntingdon	Montgomery	1854	832	54	78,000	2,606,000
Jacksonville State U.	Jacksonville	1883	5,651	146	150,000	—
‡Judson	Marion	1838	454	33	38,000	1,000,000
Livingston U.	Livingston	1835	1,775	70	60,000	—
Montevallo, U. of	Montevallo	1896	2,225	120	109,000	678,000
Oakwood	Huntsville	1896	689	35	48,000	—
St. Bernard	St. Bernard	1892	715	51	61,185	—
Samford U.	Birmingham	1842	2,676	169	238,000	2,861,000
Spring Hill	Mobile	1830	970	80	112,000	2,500,000
Stillman	Tuscaloosa	1876	654	46	40,000	400,000
Talladega	Talladega	1867	550	55	60,000	1,413,000
Troy State U.	Troy	1887	2,779	100	40,000	250,000
Tuskegee Inst.	Tuskegee Institute	1881	3,062	227	177,542	9,903,514
ALASKA						
Alaska, U. of	College	1917	2,225	170	250,000	1,918,000
Alaska Methodist U.	Anchorage	1957	844	51	47,500	300,000
ARIZONA						
Arizona, U. of	Tucson	1885	24,726	1,533	1,415,344	3,358,000
Arizona State U.	Tempe	1885	23,341	1,013	927,000	787,000
Grand Canyon	Phoenix	1949	756	34	56,000	175,000
Northern Arizona U.	Flagstaff	1899	8,700	400	230,000	3,000,000
ARKANSAS						
Arkansas	Batesville	1872	353	26	50,000	818,000
Arkansas, State Col. of	Conway	1907	4,620	175	116,000	—
Arkansas, U. of	Fayetteville	1871	10,600	780	560,000	—
at Little Rock	Little Rock	1927	3,527	150	82,000	6,000,000
Arkansas A. & M.	College Heights	1909	1,950	100	50,000	—
Arkansas A. M. & N.	Pine Bluff	1873	3,463	202	47,455	—
Arkansas Polytech.	Russellville	1909	2,540	104	57,057	—
Arkansas State U.	State University	1909	6,357	282	237,000	—
Harding	Searcy	1924	1,888	106	97,000	12,660
Henderson State	Arkadelphia	1929	3,383	132	115,000	—
Hendrix	Conway	1884	902	50	75,000	7,100,000
John Brown U.	Siloam Springs	1919	768	55	40,000	12,000,000
Ouachita Baptist U.	Arkadelphia	1886	1,281	94	78,000	1,842,000
Ozarks, Col. of the	Clarksville	1834	539	32	62,000	596,222
Philander Smith	Little Rock	1877	672	38	55,676	408,661
Southern State	Magnolia	1909	2,243	123	57,200	—
CALIFORNIA						
Armstrong	Berkeley	1918	400	30	13,000	—
Azusa Pacific	Azusa	1899	912	51	54,000	360,000
Biola	La Mirada	1908	1,571	98	86,000	...
Brooks Inst.	Santa Barbara	1945	535	31	2,000	—
California Baptist	Riverside	1950	677	32	80,000	264,000
California Arts & Crafts	Oakland	1907	1,212	92	16,000	78,000
†California Inst. of Tech.	Pasadena	1891	1,537	575	220,000	105,485,000
California Inst. of Arts	Los Angeles	1961	630	86	40,000	350,000
California Lutheran	Thousand Oaks	1959	1,254	69	58,000	152,000
Calif. State Col. System	Los Angeles					
California State	Dominguez Hills		2,645	150	—	55,000
California State	Fullerton	1959	12,890	544	279,000	—
California State	Hayward	1959	9,588	525	300,000	—
California State	Long Beach	1949	26,891	1,150	425,000	36,814,106
California State	Los Angeles	1947	22,300	998	456,000	—
California State	San Bernardino	1967	1,723	105	125,000	—
Calif. State Polytech.	Pomona	1956	8,073	400	160,000	—
Calif. State Polytech.	San Luis Obispo	1901	11,279	628	266,934	—
Chico State	Chico	1887	9,134	561	260,000	1,432,000
Fresno State	Fresno	1911	12,906	793	300,000	...
Humboldt State	Arcata	1913	5,173	297	126,161	—
Sacramento State	Sacramento	1947	14,877	604	250,000	—
San Diego State	San Diego	1897	23,770	1,500	680,000	—
San Fernando Vy. St.	Northridge	1958	21,363	1,349	500,000	—
San Francisco State	San Francisco	1899	17,857	1,138	400,000	99,822
San Jose State	San Jose	1857	23,889	1,200	515,000	150,000
Sonoma State	Rohnert Park	1960	3,500	185	110,000	—
Stanislaus State	Turlock	1960	2,069	112	80,000	—
Chapman	Orange	1861	3,519	270	77,000	1,120,000
Claremont Col. System	Claremont					
†Claremont Men's	Claremont	1946	800	97	622,000	10,000,000
Claremont U. Ctr.	Claremont	....	1,151	50	785,000	15,421,786
Harvey Mudd	Claremont	1955	365	50	650,000	2,644,000
Pitzer	Claremont	1963	647	50	625,000	—
Pomona	Claremont	1887	1,257	123	652,000	23,901,000
‡Scripps	Claremont	1926	526	52	67,000	9,656,000
‡Dominican	San Rafael	1890	756	60	64,000	—
Golden Gate	San Francisco	1901	3,099	150	54,000	502,000
‡Holy Names	Oakland	1880	1,002	75	66,000	143,000
‡Immaculate Heart	Los Angeles	1916	829	86	130,000	130,000
La Verne	La Verne	1891	662	46	36,000	1,105,000
Loma Linda U.	Loma Linda	1905	2,922	1,200	282,000	2,894,000
Lone Mountain	San Francisco	1921	776	44	146,000	—
Loyola U.	Los Angeles	1911	3,086	154	254,108	2,461,500
†Menlo	Menlo Park	1915	547	30	35,000	—
Mills	Oakland	1852	833	74	152,000	11,633,000
‡Mt. St. Mary's	Los Angeles	1925	1,459	77	99,000	519,000
Northrop Inst. of Tech.	Inglewood	1942	2,082	104	77,000	—
Notre Dame	Belmont	1851	1,370	56	69,000	—
Occidental	Los Angeles	1887	1,832	120	234,000	$18,600,000
Pacific Union	Angwin	1882	1,906	135	76,000	—
Pasadena	Pasadena	1902	1,232	59	104,000	—
Pepperdine	Los Angeles	1937	2,042	140	100,000	2,500,000
Redlands, U. of	Redlands	1907	1,880	102	165,000	12,500,000
St. Mary's	St. Mary's College	1863	929	79	90,000	1,819,000
San Diego, U. of (Men)	San Diego	1949	840	56	75,000	100,000
San Diego, U. of (Wmn.)	San Diego	1949	558	48	70,000	100,000
San Francisco, U. of	San Francisco	1855	6,835	303	302,000	3,160,000
San Francisco Art Inst.	San Francisco	1871	915	64	24,000	460,000
Santa Clara, U. of	Santa Clara	1851	5,683	274	266,000	11,630,079
Southern California	Costa Mesa	1920	516	27	34,000	—
Southern Calif., U. of	Los Angeles	1880	20,016	2,450	1,290,862	36,568,512
Stanford U.	Stanford	1885	12,385	1,267	3,275,000	243,545,000
West Coast U.	Los Angeles	1909	1,750	72	6,500	—
Westmont	Santa Barbara	1940	846	53	75,000	346,000
Whittier	Whittier	1901	2,247	125	75,000	4,500,000
Woodbury	Los Angeles	1884	2,143	76	16,000	—
COLORADO						
Adams State	Alamosa	1921	3,555	124	122,000	—
Colorado	Colorado Springs	1874	1,761	135	232,000	9,834,000
Colorado, U. of	Boulder	1876	31,874	1,575	1,190,000	7,750,000
Colorado Sch. of Mines	Golden	1874	1,685	135	133,000	400,000
Colorado State	Greeley	1890	9,413	412	300,000	175,000
Colorado State U.	Fort Collins	1870	15,361	949	455,000	1,067,000
Denver, U. of	Denver	1864	9,309	530	594,000	15,387,000
Fort Lewis	Durango	1911	1,851	95	60,000	86,000
Loretto Heights	Denver	1918	936	63	91,000	198,000
Regis	Denver	1877	1,232	80	80,000	750,000
Southern Colorado State	Pueblo	1933	6,757	283	102,000	—
‡Temple Buell	Denver	1888	1,064	81	83,000	800,000
†U.S. Air Force Academy	USAF Academy	1954	3,860	656	290,000	—
Western State	Gunnison	1901	3,088	134	107,000	—
CONNECTICUT						
‡Albertus Magnus	New Haven	1925	584	61	63,000	200,000
‡Annhurst	Woodstock	1941	497	40	31,740	—
Bridgeport, U. of	Bridgeport	1927	8,838	388	173,000	4,200,000
Central Connecticut State	New Britain	1849	11,472	501	167,379	—
Connecticut, U. of	Storrs	1881	21,845	1,125	880,000	1,518,000
Connecticut	New London	1911	1,695	175	258,095	6,728,000
Eastern Connecticut State	Willimantic	1889	1,613	110	59,000	—
†Fairfield U.	Fairfield	1942	3,148	180	102,000	—
Hartford, U. of	West Hartford	1877	8,107	385	170,000	3,960,000
New Haven	West Haven	1920	4,319	240	57,000	125,000
Quinnipiac	Hamden	1929	2,753	151	70,000	—
‡St. Joseph	West Hartford	1932	904	78	63,000	292,000
Southern Connecticut St.	New Haven	1893	11,194	526	240,000	—
Trinity	Hartford	1823	1,875	156	485,000	17,404,000
†U.S. Coast Guard Acad.	New London	1876	940	114	80,000	...
Wesleyan U.	Middletown	1831	1,825	235	620,000	115,802,000
Western Connecticut St.	Danbury	1903	3,605	235	81,212	—
Yale U.	New Haven	1701	8,665	2,725	5,300,000	482,897,000
DELAWARE						
Delaware State	Dover	1891	1,336	83	59,000	99,000
Delaware, U. of	Newark	1833	14,373	553	670,000	60,800,000
DISTRICT OF COLUMBIA						
American U.	Washington	1893	15,347	464	377,000	4,482,000
Catholic U. of America	Washington	1887	6,161	492	789,000	7,743,000
Dist. of Columbia Tchrs.	Washington	1851	2,856	121	96,000	—
Gallaudet	Washington	1864	640	97	102,000	—
Georgetown U.	Washington	1798	7,730	1,796	704,000	15,019,000
George Washington U.	Washington	1821	14,556	918	495,000	12,973,000
Howard U.	Washington	1867	8,852	1,169	575,357	8,074,000
‡Trinity	Washington	1897	822	75	118,000	1,518,120
FLORIDA						
Barry	Miami	1940	1,339	103	74,000	50,000
Bethune Cookman	Daytona Beach	1872	1,160	57	53,000	1,385,000
Florida, State U.	Tallahassee	1857	17,010	1,060	807,000	80,000
Florida A. & M. U.	Tallahassee	1887	4,248	256	180,000	—
Florida Atlantic U.	Boca Raton	1961	5,057	220	225,000	696,340
Florida, U. of	Gainesville	1853	20,769	2,042	1,400,000	4,639,000
South Florida, U. of	Tampa	1960	15,635	684	262,432	188,000
Florida Inst. of Tech.	Melbourne	1958	1,929	93	49,000	30,000
Florida Memorial	St. Augustine	1892	850	45	50,000	500,000
Florida Presbyterian	St. Petersburg	1958	958	75	86,000	1,632,318
Florida Southern	Lakeland	1885	1,539	105	112,480	8,259,566
Jacksonville U.	Jacksonville	1934	2,963	150	130,000	1,327,000
Miami, U. of	Coral Gables	1925	18,026	974	901,000	28,113,000
Rollins	Winter Park	1885	2,736	132	152,000	8,600,000
Stetson U.	DeLand	1883	2,596	140	189,595	5,234,949
Tampa, U. of	Tampa	1931	2,448	95	102,000	1,000,000
GEORGIA						
‡Agnes Scott	Decatur	1889	736	86	112,000	12,800,000
Albany State	Albany	1903	1,816	96	50,000	—
Armstrong State	Savannah	1935	2,200	97	62,000	—
Atlanta U.	Atlanta	1865	1,025	98	239,000	11,651,437
Augusta	Augusta	1925	2,672	93	91,000	...
Berry	Mount Berry	1926	1,174	70	67,000	11,178,511
‡Brenau	Gainesville	1878	486	53	33,000	1,287,700
Clark	Atlanta	1869	1,007	98	39,491	—
Emory U.	Atlanta	1836	5,041	742	897,219	75,063,000
Fort Valley State	Fort Valley	1895	2,247	105	91,000	85,442
Georgia, U. of	Athens	1785	21,590	1,500	1,000,000	4,200,000

†Men's schools, ‡women's schools; the others are coeducational.

Universities and colleges (continued)

Institution	Location	Year founded	Total students	Faculty	Bound library volumes	Endowment fund
Georgia	Milledgeville	1889	1,732	97	100,000	—
Georgia Inst. of Tech.	Atlanta	1885	7,113	469	560,000	$ 2,329,000
Georgia Southern	Statesboro	1908	5,178	287	160,000	—
Georgia Southwestern	Americus	1926	2,089	119	42,000	—
Georgia State U.	Atlanta	1913	12,197	569	270,000	19,000
LaGrange	LaGrange	1831	584	40	47,000	4,253,000
Mercer U.	Macon	1833	1,932	110	180,000	9,610,000
†Morehouse	Atlanta	1867	982	80	252,326	4,278,466
Morris Brown	Atlanta	1881	1,142	96	22,000	1,004,000
North Georgia	Dahlonega	1873	1,135	65	85,000	—
Oglethorpe	Atlanta	1835	1,042	46	39,000	1,700,000
Paine	Augusta	1883	689	51	45,917	402,519
Piedmont	Demorest	1897	488	29	40,000	1,500,000
Savannah State	Savannah	1890	2,331	91	72,000	—
Shorter	Rome	1873	639	46	60,000	1,500,000
‡Spelman	Atlanta	1881	1,004	80	28,515	—
‡Tift	Forsyth	1847	654	29	39,000	1,764,000
Valdosta State	Valdosta	1906	2,888	153	97,000	—
‡Wesleyan	Macon	1836	517	62	89,000	4,448,000
West Georgia	Carrollton	1933	5,049	235	102,000	—
GUAM						
Guam, U. of	Agana	1952	2,400	126	58,000	—
HAWAII						
Chaminade	Honolulu	1955	870	51	34,000	12,056
Church Col. of Hawaii	Laie	1955	1,192	60	75,000	20,000
Hawaii, U. of	Honolulu	1907	19,335	1,245	722,000	780,000
IDAHO						
Boise State	Boise	1932	5,157	283	100,000	—
Idaho	Caldwell	1891	915	63	150,000	1,721,549
Idaho, U. of	Moscow	1889	6,354	468	650,000	12,739,000
Idaho State U.	Pocatello	1901	5,818	261	200,000	17,000
Lewis-Clark Normal	Lewiston	1955	1,165	58	10,000	161,000
Northwest Nazarene	Nampa	1913	1,101	67	61,000	150,000
ILLINOIS						
Augustana	Rock Island	1860	2,030	102	144,000	3,761,000
Aurora	Aurora	1893	1,329	59	65,000	261,282
‡Barat	Lake Forest	1863	663	56	68,000	—
Blackburn	Carlinville	1837	612	37	54,000	3,955,000
Bradley U.	Peoria	1897	6,057	391	182,000	4,803,000
Chicago, U. of	Chicago	1892	10,137	1,157	2,854,000	233,343,000
Chicago State	Chicago	1869	5,911	309	149,000	—
Concordia Teachers	River Forest	1864	1,459	103	90,000	427,000
De Paul U.	Chicago	1898	8,581	393	277,000	2,390,000
Eastern Illinois U.	Charleston	1895	7,887	475	182,000	—
Elmhurst	Elmhurst	1871	1,520	112	86,000	990,000
Eureka	Eureka	1855	535	48	60,000	1,386,000
George Williams	Downers Grove	1890	834	84	51,000	—
Greenville	Greenville	1892	772	75	68,000	350,000
Illinois	Jacksonville	1829	920	48	64,000	4,200,000
Illinois, U. of	Urbana	1868	51,926	18,000	4,743,205	11,631,368
Illinois Inst. of Tech.	Chicago	1892	8,164	709	1,100,000	12,315,000
Illinois State U.	Normal	1857	14,687	1,047	430,000	—
Illinois Wesleyan U.	Bloomington	1850	1,524	145	10,000	5,281,000
Knox	Galesburg	1837	1,425	100	141,000	8,920,000
Lake Forest	Lake Forest	1857	1,357	116	113,000	6,843,000
Lewis	Lockport	1930	2,321	114	50,800	—
Loyola U.	Chicago	1870	13,548	1,484	485,000	14,537,000
Millikin U.	Decatur	1901	1,493	124	109,000	3,680,000
Monmouth	Monmouth	1853	1,302	92	123,000	2,203,000
‡Mundelein	Chicago	1930	1,245	73	82,000	392,934
National Col. of Ed.	Evanston	1886	1,720	102	56,000	541,000
North Central	Naperville	1861	842	66	107,000	2,377,500
Northeastern Illinois St.	Chicago	1869	7,510	341	150,000	—
Northern Illinois U.	DeKalb	1895	22,519	1,594	463,000	—
North Park	Chicago	1891	1,702	89	105,000	1,772,000
Northwestern U.	Evanston	1851	16,259	1,302	2,021,261	174,885,000
Olivet Nazarene	Kankakee	1907	1,826	93	70,000	57,000
Principia	Elsah	1910	744	60	100,000	14,000,000
Quincy	Quincy	1860	1,810	213	150,000	865,000
Rockford	Rockford	1847	1,360	124	68,000	2,847,000
Roosevelt U.	Chicago	1945	6,752	237	240,000	1,326,000
Rosary	River Forest	1901	1,334	106	131,000	700,000
St. Procopius	Lisle	1887	969	75	70,000	—
St. Xavier	Chicago	1847	844	101	92,000	—
Shimer	Mt. Carroll	1853	312	27	31,000	330,000
Southern Illinois U.	Carbondale	1869	35,154	2,468	1,000,000	—
Western Illinois U.	Macomb	1899	11,112	770	260,555	—
Wheaton	Wheaton	1860	1,927	144	153,000	10,771,105
INDIANA						
Anderson	Anderson	1917	1,707	104	108,000	518,000
Ball State U.	Muncie	1918	15,750	700	398,000	—
Butler U.	Indianapolis	1855	4,184	170	201,000	26,000,000
De Pauw U.	Greencastle	1837	2,439	162	286,000	14,530,000
Earlham	Richmond	1847	1,098	76	168,000	6,978,368
Evansville, U. of	Evansville	1854	5,369	224	106,000	3,200,000
Franklin	Franklin	1834	780	63	77,000	6,523,000
Goshen	Goshen	1894	1,254	75	98,000	394,000
Hanover	Hanover	1827	1,025	72	125,000	7,655,000
Huntington	Huntington	1897	528	34	45,000	568,000
Indiana Central	Indianapolis	1902	2,333	84	59,000	819,000
Indiana Inst. of Tech.	Fort Wayne	1930	942	47	45,000	—
Indiana State U.	Terre Haute	1870	13,319	735	422,625	—
Indiana U.	Bloomington	1820	54,433	3,974	2,800,000	10,200,000
Manchester	North Manchester	1889	1,489	71	101,000	1,500,000
Marian	Indianapolis	1851	1,105	80	60,000	120,000
Marion	Marion	1920	848	39	48,000	66,000
†Notre Dame, U. of	Notre Dame	1842	7,924	727	918,000	$62,000,000
Purdue U.	Lafayette	1869	37,338	2,188	950,000	18,045,000
†Rose Polytech. Inst.	Terre Haute	1874	1,220	65	30,000	3,173,000
St. Francis	Fort Wayne	1890	2,325	80	64,000	—
St. Joseph	Rensselaer	1889	1,454	100	140,000	1,050,077
‡St. Mary's	Notre Dame	1844	1,473	131	102,000	905,000
Taylor U.	Upland	1846	1,409	79	89,000	682,000
Tri-State	Angola	1884	1,947	108	42,000	498,000
Valparaiso U.	Valparaiso	1859	4,549	274	220,000	2,034,000
Wabash	Crawfordsville	1832	868	74	189,000	16,600,000
IOWA						
Briar Cliff	Sioux City	1930	1,067	61	58,000	123,000
Buena Vista	Storm Lake	1891	930	52	60,000	516,150
Central U. of Iowa	Pella	1853	1,283	87	77,000	1,263,701
‡Clarke	Dubuque	1843	942	99	72,000	641,000
Coe	Cedar Rapids	1851	1,100	83	121,000	7,346,000
Cornell	Mount Vernon	1853	995	96	150,000	7,704,000
Drake U.	Des Moines	1881	7,431	300	294,000	4,521,320
Dubuque, U. of	Dubuque	1852	1,274	77	156,000	3,075,265
Graceland	Lamoni	1895	1,274	78	69,000	472,650
Grinnell	Grinnell	1846	1,174	122	187,000	12,150,000
Iowa, U. of	Iowa City	1847	20,236	1,622	1,491,000	4,548,000
Iowa State U.	Ames	1858	19,172	1,080	680,000	2,951,000
Iowa Wesleyan	Mt. Pleasant	1842	984	61	67,000	1,304,725
†Loras	Dubuque	1839	1,558	106	170,000	—
Luther	Decorah	1861	1,983	139	171,000	1,700,000
Marycrest	Davenport	1939	1,103	69	78,000	336,000
Morningside	Sioux City	1894	1,312	99	98,000	2,179,000
Mt. Mercy	Cedar Rapids	1928	613	38	34,000	—
Northwestern	Orange City	1928	708	51	56,943	470,000
St. Ambrose	Davenport	1882	1,374	79	72,000	1,230,154
Simpson	Indianola	1860	926	68	77,000	3,387,102
Upper Iowa U.	Fayette	1857	1,032	72	83,833	960,000
Wartburg	Waverly	1852	1,381	82	89,000	—
Westmar	La Mars	1890	1,123	65	75,000	686,000
William Penn	Oskaloosa	1873	902	54	63,000	606,000
KANSAS						
Baker U.	Baldwin City	1858	803	70	100,000	3,103,000
Bethany	Lindsborg	1881	664	42	48,000	1,100,000
Bethel	North Newton	1887	549	34	62,000	1,071,000
Emporia	Emporia	1882	1,116	52	57,000	376,000
Fort Hays Kansas State	Hays	1902	5,578	236	210,000	582,000
Friends U.	Wichita	1898	1,030	59	42,000	950,000
Kansas, U. of	Lawrence	1866	19,108	1,040	1,510,000	27,021,000
Kansas State	Pittsburg	1903	5,879	345	308,000	357,000
Kansas State Tchrs.	Emporia	1863	6,763	376	320,000	1,000,000
Kansas State U.	Manhattan	1863	13,149	705	575,000	4,682,000
Kansas Wesleyan U.	Salina	1886	717	42	59,000	1,605,000
Marymount	Salina	1922	590	56	37,000	—
McPherson	McPherson	1887	745	47	45,000	1,377,000
Ottawa U.	Ottawa	1865	1,024	58	71,000	1,397,000
Sacred Heart	Wichita	1933	705	48	46,000	—
†St. Benedict's	Atchison	1858	1,099	72	170,000	—
St. Mary of the Plains	Dodge City	1952	656	50	39,000	—
Southwestern	Winfield	1885	666	49	70,000	3,875,000
Sterling	Sterling	1887	549	37	58,000	1,151,000
Tabor	Hillsboro	1908	432	29	37,000	242,000
Washburn U.	Topeka	1865	4,635	232	103,000	466,577
Wichita State U.	Wichita	1895	12,296	391	276,000	1,530,000
KENTUCKY						
Asbury	Wilmore	1890	1,032	62	78,000	5,000,000
Bellarmine-Ursuline	Louisville	1968	1,876	102	61,000	—
Berea	Berea	1855	1,399	111	166,000	43,000,000
Brescia	Owensboro	1925	1,007	61	49,000	300,000
Campbellsville	Campbellsville	1906	882	846	55,000	436,000
Centre	Danville	1819	749	55	85,000	5,447,000
Cumberland	Williamsburg	1889	1,117	63	23,000	915,000
Eastern Kentucky U.	Richmond	1906	9,664	495	287,000	—
Georgetown	Georgetown	1829	1,478	89	94,000	1,539,000
Kentucky State	Frankfort	1886	1,620	89	56,080	—
Kentucky Wesleyan	Owensboro	1858	901	56	55,000	784,000
Louisville, U. of	Louisville	1798	9,049	775	521,000	9,370,000
Morehead State U.	Morehead	1922	6,460	287	227,000	—
Murray State U.	Murray	1922	7,255	405	200,000	—
Pikeville	Pikeville	1889	932	53	60,000	1,332,000
Thomas More	Ft. Mitchell	1921	2,224	92	62,000	61,852
Transylvania	Lexington	1780	879	68	75,000	1,218,400
Union	Barbourville	1879	807	54	53,000	2,112,779
Western Kentucky U.	Bowling Green	1906	11,069	495	390,000	270,000
LOUISIANA						
Dillard U.	New Orleans	1869	898	91	88,000	6,547,000
Francis T. Nicholls State	Thibodaux	1948	4,837	158	101,000	—
Grambling	Grambling	1901	3,706	184	80,000	1,500,000
Louisiana	Pineville	1906	904	50	65,000	2,692,000
Louisiana Polytech. Inst.	Ruston	1894	7,709	435	155,000	—
Louisiana State U.	Baton Rouge	1860	31,828	1,918	1,614,000	650,000
Loyola U.	New Orleans	1912	4,923	265	245,000	. . .
McNeese State	Lake Charles	1939	4,632	230	101,000	—
Northeast Louisiana St.	Monroe	1931	7,616	318	130,000	—
Northwestern State	Natchitoches	1884	6,017	321	170,000	—
Southeastern Louisiana	Hammond	1925	5,552	264	120,000	—
Southern U.	Baton Rouge	1880	7,232	353	218,000	—
Southwestern La., U. of	Lafayette	1898	10,217	508	350,000	—
Tulane U.	New Orleans	1834	8,234	894	1,027,697	40,960,000
Xavier U.	New Orleans	1925	1,207	87	98,000	—
MAINE						
Bates	Lewiston	1864	1,079	78	139,121	974,200

Institution	Location	Year founded	Total students	Faculty	Bound library volumes	Endowment fund
†Bowdoin	Brunswick	1794	967	89	420,000	$31,600,000
Colby	Waterville	1813	1,531	150	300,000	15,589,000
Maine, U. of	Bangor					
at Presque Isle	Presque Isle	1903	556	33	50,000	—
at Farmington	Farmington	1864	1,144	68	38,000	262,000
Gorham State	Gorham	1878	2,400	90	65,000	9,713,000
at Orono	Orono	1865	13,743	748	472,000	5,101,000
Portland-Gorham	Portland	1957	5,100	140	...	...
Nasson	Springvale	1912	801	56	60,000	520,641
Ricker	Houlton	1848	643	43	33,000	—
St. Francis	Biddeford	1953	608	37	31,000	—

MARYLAND

Institution	Location	Year founded	Total students	Faculty	Bound library volumes	Endowment fund
Bowie State	Bowie	1867	793	75	60,000	—
Columbia Union	Takoma Park	1904	915	90	77,000	—
Coppin State	Baltimore	1900	647	57	55,000	—
Frostburg State	Frostburg	1898	1,932	130	80,000	—
‡Goucher	Baltimore	1885	1,064	91	137,000	9,256,000
‡Hood	Frederick	1893	654	66	93,000	3,562,000
Johns Hopkins U.	Baltimore	1876	10,211	956	1,766,000	91,928,240
Loyola	Baltimore	1852	3,066	104	80,000	2,219,417
Maryland, U. of	College Park	1807	48,203	2,955	1,169,000	8,860,528
Maryland State	Princess Anne	1886	776	58	64,000	—
Morgan State	Baltimore	1867	4,653	225	116,000	—
‡Mt. St. Agnes	Baltimore	1867	355	33	44,775	179,513
†Mt. St. Mary's	Emmitsburg	1808	1,064	84	79,000	546,000
‡Notre Dame	Baltimore	1873	990	66	56,000	1,209,517
Peabody Inst.	Baltimore	1857	466	77	275,000	—
‡St. Joseph	Emmitsburg	1809	528	56	59,000	495,000
St. Mary's	St. Mary's City	1839	471	39	24,000	23,500
†St. Mary's Sem. & U.	Baltimore	1791	733	84	155,511	—
Salisbury State	Salisbury	1925	1,081	61	83,000	—
Towson State	Baltimore	1866	5,401	337	131,000	—
Washington	Chesterton	1782	635	56	89,000	2,839,000
Western Maryland	Westminster	1867	1,755	93	74,000	3,383,000

MASSACHUSETTS

Institution	Location	Year founded	Total students	Faculty	Bound library volumes	Endowment fund
American International	Springfield	1885	1,841	99	80,000	800,140
†Amherst	Amherst	1821	1,217	145	405,000	51,000,000
‡Anna Maria	Paxton	1946	647	58	30,000	—
†Assumption	Worcester	1904	1,232	64	93,000	613,000
Atlantic Union	South Lancaster	1882	754	63	63,000	—
Babson	Babson Park	1919	1,464	39	52,000	5,000,000
Boston	Chestnut Hill	1863	10,214	625	752,050	5,689,857
Boston U.	Boston	1869	23,806	2,141	782,000	21,057,000
Brandeis U.	Waltham	1947	2,286	340	416,000	19,859,000
Clark U.	Worcester	1887	3,259	260	300,000	10,520,000
Eastern Nazarene	Wollaston	1918	783	58	53,000	397,000
Emerson	Boston	1880	1,300	115	284,000	35,000
‡Emmanuel	Boston	1919	1,543	110	81,000	—
Gordon	Wenham	1889	685	42	65,000	803,772
Harvard U.	Cambridge	1636	15,350	7,953	8,087,000	696,803,000
‡Radcliffe	Cambridge	1879	1,226		160,000	23,883,000
†Holy Cross	Worcester	1843	2,557	180	275,000	4,000,779
‡Lesley	Cambridge	1909	728	41	54,000	179,000
Lowell Tech. Inst.	Lowell	1895	6,544	230	125,000	159,000
Massachusetts, U. of	Amherst	1863	17,805	1,065	841,000	1,231,000
Mass. Inst. of Tech.	Cambridge	1861	8,024	1,050	1,133,000	142,447,000
Mass. State Col. System						
Boston State	Boston	1852	7,455	394	69,000	—
Bridgewater State	Bridgewater	1840	3,005	192	70,000	—
Fitchburg State	Fitchburg	1894	3,293	166	60,000	—
Framingham State	Framingham	1839	3,700	130	75,000	—
Lowell State	Lowell	1894	2,030	141	65,000	...
North Adams State	North Adams	1894	943	53	52,000	—
Salem State	Salem	1854	5,989	212	71,000	—
Westfield State	Westfield	1839	3,457	144	55,000	—
Worcester State	Worcester	1874	3,266	132	70,000	—
Merrimack	North Andover	1947	1,906	110	64,000	420,000
‡Mt. Holyoke	South Hadley	1837	1,829	11	308,100	31,627,000
New England Conservatory	Boston	1867	589	80	42,000	4,000,000
Northeastern U.	Boston	1898	37,134	1,120	259,000	22,525
‡Our Lady of Elms	Chicopee	1928	621	61	44,218	374,000
‡Regis	Weston	1927	953	93	90,000	234,023
‡Simmons	Boston	1899	2,216	304	143,000	9,754,000
‡Smith	Northampton	1871	2,491	250	716,000	61,588,000
Southeastern Mass. U.	North Dartmouth	1895	3,084	202	120,000	115,000
Springfield	Springfield	1885	2,396	102	92,000	3,834,000
Stonehill	North Easton	1948	1,423	81	63,786	—
Suffolk U.	Boston	1906	4,743	128	103,726	2,500,000
Tufts U.	Medford	1852	5,010	1,650	480,000	25,043,000
‡Wellesley	Wellesley	1870	1,771	162	470,000	83,706,000
Western New England	Springfield	1919	3,319	116	47,000	180,000
‡Wheaton	Norton	1834	1,111	100	132,000	5,692,000
‡Wheelock	Boston	1889	665	48	45,000	291,000
†Williams	Williamstown	1793	1,380	162	350,000	50,043,000
Worcester Polytech. Inst.	Worcester	1865	2,183	271	75,000	23,300,000

MICHIGAN

Institution	Location	Year founded	Total students	Faculty	Bound library volumes	Endowment fund
Adrian	Adrian	1859	1,478	94	82,000	2,420,000
Albion	Albion	1835	1,870	123	162,000	11,132,000
Alma	Alma	1886	1,265	72	78,000	2,008,000
Andrews U.	Berrien Springs	1874	2,024	160	215,295	362,000
Aquinas	Grand Rapids	1923	1,473	73	75,000	9,000
Calvin	Grand Rapids	1876	3,572	180	215,000	—
Central Michigan U.	Mt. Pleasant	1892	12,883	596	315,000	134,000
Detroit, U. of	Detroit	1877	9,319	569	344,000	3,487,000
Detroit Inst. of Tech.	Detroit	1891	1,212	80	40,000	91,000
Eastern Michigan U.	Ypsilanti	1849	16,670	990	70,000	200,000
Ferris State	Big Rapids	1884	8,439	400	148,264	—
General Motors Inst.	Flint	1919	2,931	230	28,000	—
Grand Valley State	Allendale	1960	2,718	125	105,000	—
Hope	Holland	1866	2,033	137	129,000	2,200,000
Kalamazoo	Kalamazoo	1833	1,331	80	157,800	13,530,000
Lawrence Inst. of Tech.	Southfield	1932	3,929	110	26,000	—
‡Madonna	Livonia	1947	611	33	55,000	—
‡Marygrove	Detroit	1910	967	79	142,000	$ 687,000
Mercy	Detroit	1941	1,118	100	62,000	—
Michigan, U. of	Ann Arbor	1817	38,328	2,930	4,084,000	58,926,000
Michigan State U.	East Lansing	1855	40,820	2,467	1,500,000	9,000,000
Michigan Tech. U.	Houghton	1885	4,728	320	219,000	551,000
Lake Superior State	Sault Ste. Marie	1946	1,830	85	35,000	—
Northern Michigan U.	Marquette	1899	7,839	341	129,842	—
Oakland U.	Rochester	...	5,811	282	160,000	357,000
Olivet	Olivet	1844	823	57	59,000	514,000
Siena Heights	Adrian	1919	548	53	68,000	—
Spring Arbor	Spring Arbor	1873	708	43	35,000	45,000
Wayne State U.	Detroit	1868	34,924	1,632	1,195,000	3,121,000
Western Michigan U.	Kalamazoo	1903	20,125	851	609,987	33,107

MINNESOTA

Institution	Location	Year founded	Total students	Faculty	Bound library volumes	Endowment fund
Augsburg	Minneapolis	1869	1,786	101	100,000	...
Bemidji State	Bemidji	1913	4,734	217	127,000	—
Bethel	St. Paul	1871	1,034	66	60,000	409,455
Carleton	Northfield	1866	1,450	125	238,000	18,600,680
Concordia	Moorhead	1891	2,405	155	130,000	1,001,000
Concordia	St. Paul	1893	800	57	61,000	12,000
Gustavus Adolphus	St. Peter	1862	1,782	126	125,000	1,689,954
Hamline U.	St. Paul	1854	1,272	85	120,000	10,500,000
Macalester	St. Paul	1885	1,980	176	192,000	27,732,000
Mankato State	Mankato	1867	12,700	715	285,000	—
Minnesota, U. of	Minneapolis	1851	66,824	3,621	2,690,000	80,703,000
Moorhead State	Moorhead	1887	5,260	300	100,000	—
‡St. Benedict	St. Joseph	1913	627	56	80,000	209,000
‡St. Catherine	St. Paul	1905	1,337	113	170,000	1,713,000
St. Cloud State	St. Cloud	1869	9,274	557	226,000	12,000
†St. John's U.	Collegeville	1857	1,544	116	200,000	5,336,000
St. Mary's	Winona	1912	1,043	62	96,000	628,000
St. Olaf	Northfield	1874	2,593	182	236,000	2,853,000
St. Scholastica	Duluth	1912	661	70	62,000	4,300
‡St. Teresa	Winona	1907	1,188	120	102,000	866,000
†St. Thomas	St. Paul	1885	2,411	120	140,000	6,400,000
Winona State	Winona	1858	4,080	231	98,000	—

MISSISSIPPI

Institution	Location	Year founded	Total students	Faculty	Bound library volumes	Endowment fund
Alcorn A. & M.	Lorman	1871	2,440	120	59,054	—
Belhaven	Jackson	1883	633	47	40,000	1,100,000
Delta State	Cleveland	1924	2,535	117	75,000	—
Jackson State	Jackson	1877	3,686	176	59,000	—
Millsaps	Jackson	1892	979	84	76,000	4,722,987
Mississippi, U. of	University	1848	6,639	318	478,000	1,534,415
Mississippi	Clinton	1826	2,358	105	121,000	2,126,000
‡Mississippi State	Columbus	1884	2,633	144	151,000	—
Mississippi State U.	State College	1878	8,730	563	340,000	414,131
Southern Miss., U. of	Hattiesburg	1910	7,538	450	250,000	—
Tougaloo	Tougaloo	1869	743	57	60,000	360,000

MISSOURI

Institution	Location	Year founded	Total students	Faculty	Bound library volumes	Endowment fund
Avila	Kansas City	1916	547	41	53,000	59,000
Central Methodist	Fayette	1854	872	66	74,000	4,250,000
Central Missouri State	Warrensburg	1871	12,168	573	260,000	—
Culver-Stockton	Canton	1853	844	43	85,000	1,008,859
Drury	Springfield	1873	2,344	175	106,000	3,549,000
Evangel	Springfield	1955	977	55	57,000	—
‡Fontbonne	St. Louis	1917	826	78	65,000	—
Harris Teachers	St. Louis	1857	1,470	70	41,000	...
Lincoln U.	Jefferson City	1866	2,250	131	90,000	—
Lindenwood	St. Charles	1827	660	56	63,000	5,492,000
Missouri, U. of	Columbia	1839	21,082	1,403	1,497,000	5,858,000
at Kansas City	Kansas City	1929	9,674	546	361,000	6,222,000
at Rolla	Rolla	1870	6,088	413	153,000	658,000
at St. Louis	St. Louis	1963	9,598	328	125,000	2,000
Missouri Southern	Joplin	1949	3,120	120	58,000	—
Missouri Valley	Marshall	1888	899	48	70,000	1,763,000
Missouri Western	St. Joseph	1915	2,536	95	30,000	—
Northeast Missouri State	Kirksville	1867	5,718	210	140,000	—
Northwest Missouri State	Maryville	1905	4,365	230	110,000	—
Park	Kansas City	1875	708	50	79,000	3,082,115
Rockhurst	Kansas City	1910	2,327	133	83,000	879,000
St. Louis U.	St. Louis	1818	11,232	1,278	911,000	21,713,000
Southeast Missouri State	Cape Girardeau	1873	7,082	331	152,000	—
Southwest Baptist	Bolivar	1878	1,131	65	60,000	80,693
Southwest Missouri State	Springfield	1906	8,104	411	160,000	—
‡Stephens	Columbia	1833	1,867	174	80,000	1,700,000
Tarkio	Tarkio	1883	735	39	55,000	500,000
Washington U.	St. Louis	1853	11,259	1,149	1,144,000	114,118,000
Webster	St. Louis	1915	1,317	75	30,000	—
†Westminster	Fulton	1851	860	59	69,000	3,253,000
William Jewell	Liberty	1849	906	72	102,000	6,302,420
‡William Woods	Fulton	1870	889	52	105,000	752,000

MONTANA

Institution	Location	Year founded	Total students	Faculty	Bound library volumes	Endowment fund
Carroll	Helena	1909	1,029	72	50,000	550,000
Eastern Montana	Billings	1927	3,771	154	122,000	—
Great Falls	Great Falls	1932	1,174	52	41,000	428,000
Montana, U. of	Missoula	1893	8,030	468	500,000	1,225,000
Montana Min. Sc. & Tech.	Butte	1893	909	47	37,000	50,000
Montana State U.	Bozeman	1893	7,718	371	495,000	3,190,903
Northern Montana	Havre	1929	1,193	86	45,000	—
Rocky Mountain	Billings	1883	534	43	49,000	878,307

NEBRASKA

Institution	Location	Year founded	Total students	Faculty	Bound library volumes	Endowment fund
Chadron State	Chadron	1911	2,332	95	95,000	—
Concordia Tchrs.	Seward	1894	1,569	115	66,000	116,000
Creighton U.	Omaha	1878	4,234	403	285,000	7,703,000

Institution	Location	Year founded	Total students	Faculty	Bound library volumes	Endowment fund
Dana	Blair	1884	978	50	66,000	$ 250,000
Doane	Crete	1872	741	48	56,000	4,047,000
Hastings	Hastings	1882	853	59	75,000	2,900,000
Kearney State	Kearney	1905	5,869	240	117,970	187,000
Midland Lutheran	Fremont	1883	906	50	62,000	753,000
Nebraska, U. of	Lincoln	1869	19,618	963	952,000	9,047,000
at Omaha	Omaha	1908	12,120	353	250,000	—
Nebraska Wesleyan U.	Lincoln	1887	1,326	110	85,000	3,800,000
Peru State	Peru	1867	1,261	53	90,000	63,000
Union	Lincoln	1891	954	88	87,000	—
Wayne State	Wayne	1891	3,006	135	85,000	—

NEVADA

Nevada-Reno, U. of	Reno	1874	8,838	341	386,000	5,508,000
Nevada-Las Vegas	Las Vegas	1964	5,241	190	200,000	—

NEW HAMPSHIRE

†Dartmouth	Hanover	1769	3,146	491	1,000,000	139,682,000
New England	Henniker	1946	938	83	27,000	106,541
New Hampshire, U. of	Durham	1866	7,729	512	535,000	4,665,016
Keene State	Keene	1909	1,697	115	74,000	—
Plymouth State	Plymouth	1870	1,977	103	65,000	—
‡Rivier	Nashua	1933	908	46	65,000	129,000
†St. Anselm's	Manchester	1889	1,587	141	90,000	—

NEW JERSEY

Drew U.	Madison	1866	1,490	119	305,000	11,609,000
Fairleigh Dickinson U.	Rutherford	1941	19,192	788	330,000	6,659,461
‡Georgian Court	Lakewood	1908	704	60	51,000	—
Glassboro State	Glassboro	1923	9,140	328	155,000	—
Jersey City State	Jersey City	1927	8,362	450	100,000	—
Monmouth	West Long Branch	1933	5,856	232	110,000	1,244,969
Montclair State	Upper Montclair	1908	9,054	438	145,000	185,000
Newark Engineering	Newark	1881	6,205	315	64,000	229,000
Newark State	Union	1855	10,934	273	100,000	—
Paterson State	Wayne	1855	5,858	325	150,000	—
Princeton U.	Princeton	1746	4,432	708	2,200,000	245,496,146
Rider	Trenton	1865	5,951	203	185,000	3,135,813
Rutgers, State U. of	New Brunswick	1766	31,096	2,375	1,655,964	34,757,449
‡St. Elizabeth	Convent Station	1899	817	68	90,000	503,000
St. Peter's	Jersey City	1872	4,716	221	110,000	500,000
Seton Hall U.	South Orange	1856	9,696	600	274,000	3,767,000
†Stevens Inst. of Tech.	Hoboken	1870	2,725	203	75,000	40,000,000
Trenton State	Trenton	1855	9,652	353	185,000	—
Upsala	East Orange	1893	1,843	98	109,000	1,298,000

NEW MEXICO

Albuquerque, U. of	Albuquerque	1940	1,651	70	60,000	—
Eastern New Mexico U.	Portales	1934	4,015	161	143,000	—
New Mexico, U. of	Albuquerque	1889	15,692	522	672,000	11,555,000
N. Mexico Highlands U.	Las Vegas	1893	2,376	100	100,000	—
N. Mexico Inst. of M. & T.	Socorro	1889	788	52	45,000	1,250,000
New Mexico State U.	Las Cruces	1889	7,356	359	237,000	2,054,000
Santa Fe	Santa Fe	1947	1,366	60	54,000	—
Western New Mexico U.	Silver City	1893	1,438	63	85,000	—

NEW YORK

Adelphi U.	Garden City	1896	7,793	361	180,000	2,706,278
Alfred U.	Alfred	1857	1,866	174	169,437	5,452,000
Bard	Annandale	1860	678	56	105,000	311,000
‡Briarcliff	Briarcliff Manor	1903	668	58	52,000	1,724,000
Canisius	Buffalo	1870	3,861	239	145,000	1,507,089
Clarkson Tech.	Potsdam	1895	2,757	185	91,000	5,985,000
Colgate U.	Hamilton	1819	2,090	173	261,000	25,720,000
Columbia U.	New York	1754	17,040	4,723	4,000,000	227,000,000
Cooper Union	New York	1859	1,161	180	82,000	34,526,255
Cornell U.	Ithaca	1865	14,706	2,544	3,250,000	190,952,000
‡D'Youville	Buffalo	1908	1,287	103	81,500	215,000
‡Elmira	Elmira	1855	1,183	79	103,000	3,300,000
‡Finch	New York	1900	398	77	57,000	—
Fordham U.	Bronx	1841	10,261	624	818,000	4,567,000
†Good Counsel	White Plains	1923	446	51	55,000	—
†Hamilton	Clinton	1793	893	81	284,000	22,700,000
Hartwick	Oneonta	1928	1,692	116	91,000	4,383,000
Hobart & William Smith	Geneva	1822	1,520	127	136,000	3,405,000
Hofstra U.	Hempstead	1935	12,373	534	330,000	7,191,733
Houghton	Houghton	1883	1,170	78	73,000	400,000
Iona	New Rochelle	1940	3,198	180	92,000	515,000
Ithaca	Ithaca	1892	3,545	280	130,000	377,000
Juilliard Sch. of Music	New York	1905	1,057	104	40,000	...
‡Keuka	Keuka Park	1892	844	65	54,000	1,025,000
Ladycliff	Highland Falls	1933	532	44	55,500	—
Le Moyne	Syracuse	1946	1,720	86	84,000	1,080,000
Long Island U.	Greenvale	1926	20,064	980	391,000	3,235,000
†Manhattan	Bronx	1853	4,714	255	125,000	1,770,000
‡Manhattanville	Purchase	1841	1,479	101	175,000	2,904,000
Marist	Poughkeepsie	1929	1,714	75	67,000	124,000
‡Marymount	Tarrytown	1918	1,111	85	78,000	—
Medaille	Buffalo	1937	471	30	60,000	80,000
Mercy	Dobbs Ferry	1950	1,001	75	60,000	12,500
‡Molloy Catholic	Rockville Centre	1955	1,143	78	47,000	22,901
Mt. St. Mary	Newburgh	1959	687	44	46,000	—
‡Nazareth	Rochester	1924	1,417	91	100,000	—
‡New Rochelle	New Rochelle	1904	940	91	99,000	1,000,000
New School	New York	1919	13,873	464	60,000	—
New York, City U. of	New York	1847	172,730	7,400	2,677,000	—
Brooklyn	Brooklyn	1930	24,768	1,820	500,000	298,600
City	New York	1847	20,153	1,402	833,000	2,270,000
Hunter	New York	1870	19,401	1,055	325,000	1,500,000
Lehman	Bronx	1968	10,147	697	150,000	1,200,000
Queens	Flushing	1937	23,844	1,154	282,000	138,000

Institution	Location	Year founded	Total students	Faculty	Bound library volumes	Endowment fund
Richmond	Staten Island	1965	2,507	131	135,000	—
York	Flushing	1966	1,260	107	40,000	—
New York, St. U. System	Albany	1948	116,656	6,932	5,487,000	—
SUNY at Albany	Albany	1844	12,143	643	508,000	—
SUNY at Binghamton	Binghamton	1946	5,946	365	369,000	—
SUNY at Buffalo	Buffalo	1846	22,629	1,370	1,155,000	—
SUNY at Stony Brook	Stony Brook	1957	8,825	589	382,000	—
Downstate Med. Ctr.	Brooklyn	1858	1,042	343	333,000	—
Upstate Medical Ctr.	Syracuse	1834	682	145	96,000	—
†Maritime	Bronx	1874	747	51	69,000	—
State U. College						
at Brockport	Brockport	1867	5,575	320	175,000	—
at Buffalo	Buffalo	1867	9,872	472	210,000	—
at Cortland	Cortland	1868	4,715	270	170,000	—
at Fredonia	Fredonia	1867	4,254	215	167,000	—
at Geneseo	Geneseo	1871	4,687	252	192,000	—
at New Paltz	New Paltz	1885	6,604	348	197,000	—
at Oneonta	Oneonta	1887	5,336	291	202,000	—
at Oswego	Oswego	1861	7,238	345	249,000	—
at Plattsburgh	Plattsburgh	1889	4,776	246	160,000	—
at Potsdam	Potsdam	1867	3,791	237	162,000	—
New York U.	New York	1831	40,711	5,503	1,815,000	$71,542,000
Niagara U.	Niagara University	1856	3,013	205	109,000	476,000
Pace	New York	1906	9,794	371	180,000	3,156,000
Polytechnic Inst.	Brooklyn	1854	4,427	366	200,000	6,300,000
Pratt Inst.	Brooklyn	1887	4,445	302	233,000	17,696,000
Rensselaer Polytech.	Troy	1824	5,244	295	180,000	68,847,000
Roberts Wesleyan	North Chili	1866	766	78	46,000	—
Rochester Inst. of Tech.	Rochester	1829	13,962	793	125,000	22,167,000
‡Rosary Hill	Buffalo	1948	1,375	90	62,000	12,000
‡Russell Sage	Troy	1916	1,418	100	106,000	6,000,000
St. Bonaventure U.	St. Bonaventure	1859	2,458	185	149,649	411,000
St. Francis	Brooklyn	1884	2,345	126	70,000	374,000
†St. John Fisher	Rochester	1948	1,350	75	65,000	615,000
St. John's U.	Jamaica	1870	13,207	565	448,000	1,031,000
St. Joseph's	Brooklyn	1916	589	75	68,000	64,000
St. Lawrence U.	Canton	1856	2,111	152	211,000	9,600,000
St. Rose	Albany	1920	1,349	95	77,000	369,481
Sarah Lawrence	Bronxville	1926	725	90	103,000	2,058,000
Siena	Loudonville	1937	1,873	119	125,170	800,402
Syracuse U.	Syracuse	1870	22,667	1,136	1,432,000	54,149,000
Union Col. & U. System						
Albany Col. of Pharm.	Albany	1881	444	21	5,000	—
Union	Schenectady	1795	1,700	134	264,000	29,333,000
†U.S. Merch. Marine Acad.	Kings Point	1938	1,030	88	58,000	—
†U.S. Military Acad.	West Point	1802	3,762	524	300,000	—
Vassar	Poughkeepsie	1861	1,650	216	404,000	51,912,260
Wagner	Staten Island	1883	3,124	137	130,000	1,436,587
‡Wells	Aurora	1868	647	70	154,000	5,200,000
Yeshiva U.	New York	1886	5,356	1,850	500,000	3,500,000

NORTH CAROLINA

Appalachian State U.	Boone	1903	6,833	338	203,000	638,000
Atlantic Christian	Wilson	1902	1,544	77	61,000	979,678
Barber-Scotia	Concord	1867	560	49	42,000	140,000
Belmont Abbey	Belmont	1878	775	40	54,000	600,000
‡Bennett	Greensboro	1873	658	73	63,000	1,884,882
Campbell	Buie's Creek	1887	2,306	126	81,000	925,000
Catawba	Salisbury	1851	1,046	76	75,000	5,048,000
†Davidson	Davidson	1837	1,033	93	153,000	15,665,000
Duke U.	Durham	1838	7,948	1,060	2,100,000	68,868,000
East Carolina U.	Greenville	1907	9,788	572	357,000	113,000
Elizabeth City State	Elizabeth City	1891	1,011	72	62,000	—
Elon	Elon College	1889	1,843	90	71,616	1,515,000
Fayetteville State U.	Fayetteville	1877	1,332	77	67,565	—
Greensboro	Greensboro	1838	674	52	55,000	1,806,488
Guilford	Greensboro	1837	1,782	105	130,000	3,678,672
High Point	High Point	1924	1,131	63	78,000	2,641,070
Johnson C. Smith U.	Charlotte	1867	1,248	73	82,000	681,753
Lenoir Rhyne	Hickory	1891	1,314	97	70,000	1,933,616
Livingstone	Salisbury	1879	825	66	66,000	518,000
Mars Hill	Mars Hill	1856	1,257	93	70,000	750,000
‡Meredith	Raleigh	1891	946	65	53,000	1,468,000
Methodist	Fayetteville	1956	894	54	48,000	594,000
North Carolina, U. of	Chapel Hill	1795	40,923	2,900	2,696,384	29,000,000
N. Carolina A.&T. St. U.	Greensboro	1891	3,714	252	284,000	...
N. Carolina at Durham	Durham	1910	3,042	255	191,000	—
N. Carolina Wesleyan	Rocky Mount	1956	644	46	40,000	—
Pembroke State	Pembroke	1887	1,696	106	65,000	—
Pfeiffer	Misenheimer	1885	834	70	57,000	1,807,000
‡Queens	Charlotte	1857	708	68	65,000	2,789,000
St. Andrews Presbyterian	Laurinburg	1858	898	71	76,000	500,000
St. Augustine's	Raleigh	1867	740	51	25,000	479,000
‡Salem	Winston-Salem	1772	557	55	75,000	3,372,000
Shaw U.	Raleigh	1865	1,203	81	45,000	525,000
Wake Forest U.	Winston-Salem	1834	3,210	498	400,000	22,500,000
Warren Wilson	Swannanoa	1894	401	34	38,000	1,000,000
Western Carolina U.	Cullowhee	1889	5,178	285	100,000	217,242
Winston-Salem State U.	Winston-Salem	1892	1,346	102	72,000	276,507

NORTH DAKOTA

Dickinson State	Dickinson	1916	1,640	90	60,000	—
Jamestown	Jamestown	1884	638	45	39,503	2,147,092
Mayville State	Mayville	1889	970	50	66,000	545,000
Minot State	Minot	1913	3,144	130	100,000	—
North Dakota, U. of	Grand Forks	1883	7,925	472	315,000	1,202,000
North Dakota State U.	Fargo	1890	6,591	320	235,000	2,860,000
Valley City State	Valley City	1889	1,355	70	72,000	880,000

OHIO

†Air Force Inst. of Tech.	Wright-Patterson AFB	1919	561	111	100,000	—
Antioch	Yellow Springs	1852	2,100	120	166,000	6,197,000
Ashland	Ashland	1878	2,612	242	115,000	1,421,000
Baldwin-Wallace	Berea	1845	3,153	143	141,967	5,521,000
Bluffton	Bluffton	1900	750	54	54,350	1,110,945

Institution	Location	Year founded	Total students	Faculty	Bound library volumes	Endowment fund
Bowling Green State U.	Bowling Green	1910	15,559	640	650,000	—
Capital U.	Columbus	1850	1,989	143	100,000	$ 1,974,000
Case Western Reserve U.	Cleveland	1826	9,951	1,200	1,491,000	88,000,004
Central State U.	Wilberforce	1887	2,657	120	97,000	—
Cincinnati, U. of	Cincinnati	1819	35,440	1,596	1,068,000	42,289,000
Cleveland State U.	Cleveland	1964	13,073	423	250,000	—
Dayton, U. of	Dayton	1850	9,770	441	295,000	3,487,000
Defiance	Defiance	1850	1,096	77	60,000	960,000
Denison U.	Granville	1831	2,131	164	172,000	14,351,000
‡Edgecliff	Cincinnati	1935	894	59	66,000	—
Findlay	Findlay	1882	1,294	54	57,000	681,000
Heidelberg	Tiffin	1850	1,264	101	102,000	4,153,822
Hiram	Hiram	1850	1,148	84	100,000	6,885,000
John Carroll U.	Cleveland	1886	4,143	211	185,000	4,460,000
Kent State U.	Kent	1910	24,599	1,225	562,000	—
Kenyon	Gambier	1824	970	94	181,000	8,000,000
‡Lake Erie	Painesville	1856	794	64	60,000	2,090,000
Malone	Canton	1892	953	52	55,000	616,000
Marietta	Marietta	1835	2,223	138	164,000	5,000,000
‡Mary Manse	Toledo	1922	757	54	70,000	560,000
Miami U.	Oxford	1809	11,878	538	537,000	1,546,000
‡Mt. St. Joseph on-the-Ohio	Mt. St. Joseph	1854	907	91	80,000	266,000
Mt. Union	Alliance	1846	1,255	88	135,000	4,404,000
Muskingum	New Concord	1837	1,426	107	103,000	6,997,000
‡Notre Dame	Cleveland	1922	586	50	51,000	—
Oberlin	Oberlin	1833	2,727	220	670,000	76,200,000
Ohio Dominican	Columbus	1911	985	63	51,906	174,338
Ohio Northern U.	Ada	1871	2,314	156	91,000	3,296,000
Ohio State U.	Columbus	1870	49,132	5,754	2,245,957	26,638,000
Ohio U.	Athens	1804	17,870	925	475,000	1,551,885
Ohio Wesleyan U.	Delaware	1842	2,633	188	400,000	9,518,000
Otterbein	Westerville	1847	1,362	95	90,000	2,213,000
‡St. John	Cleveland	1928	902	68	48,000	—
‡Steubenville	Steubenville	1946	1,333	70	70,000	—
‡Toledo, U. of	Toledo	1872	14,489	835	740,060	597,000
‡Ursuline	Cleveland	1871	519	47	52,050	—
Wilberforce U.	Wilberforce	1856	858	41	34,000	95,000
Wilmington	Wilmington	1870	945	57	71,852	1,867,139
Wittenberg U.	Springfield	1845	3,199	188	190,000	13,246,623
Wooster	Wooster	1806	150		199,000	14,000,000
Wright State U.	Dayton	1967	8,946	254	191,000	5,000
Xavier U.	Cincinnati	1831	6,054	203	168,326	2,831,000
Youngstown State U.	Youngstown	1908	14,762	527	190,000	—

OKLAHOMA

Institution	Location	Year founded	Total students	Faculty	Bound library volumes	Endowment fund
Bethany Nazarene	Bethany	1899	1,440	87	78,000	—
Cameron State Ag.	Lawton	1909	3,684	143	43,612	—
Central State	Edmond	1890	10,572	323	181,000	—
East Central State	Ada	1909	3,003	106	90,000	—
Langston U.	Langston	1897	1,225	70	108,218	—
Northeastern State	Tahlequah	1846	5,336	216	147,000	—
Northwestern State	Alva	1897	2,507	98	127,000	...
Oklahoma, U. of	Norman	1890	21,589	691	1,065,779	27,732,912
Oklahoma Baptist U.	Shawnee	1911	1,457	103	85,000	3,113,000
Oklahoma Christian	Oklahoma City	1950	1,100	30	30,000	1,141,000
Oklahoma City U.	Oklahoma City	1904	2,401	95	125,000	2,340,617
Oklahoma Liberal Arts	Chickasha	1908	980	47	64,000	—
Oklahoma Panhandle St.	Goodwell	1909	1,267	63	42,000	—
Oklahoma State U.	Stillwater	1890	17,492	850	962,000	10,471,000
Phillips U.	Enid	1906	1,346	97	163,000	3,817,000
Southeastern State	Durant	1909	2,456	106	100,000	—
Southwestern State	Weatherford	1901	5,174	195	114,000	—
Tulsa, U. of	Tulsa	1894	6,567	318	350,000	9,000,000

OREGON

Institution	Location	Year founded	Total students	Faculty	Bound library volumes	Endowment fund
Eastern Oregon	La Grande	1929	1,712	102	69,000	—
George Fox	Newberg	1891	422	43	39,000	1,300,000
Lewis and Clark	Portland	1867	2,001	111	96,000	2,373,000
Linfield	McMinnville	1849	1,067	74	67,000	2,600,000
‡Marylhurst	Marylhurst	1893	675	52	76,000	179,066
Northwest Christian	Eugene	1895	445	16	35,000	—
Oregon, U. of	Eugene	1872	15,355	781	1,158,823	3,636,160
Oregon Col. of Education	Monmouth	1856	3,719	209	101,000	...
Oregon State U.	Corvallis	1868	15,244	882	615,000	...
Oregon Technical Inst.	Klamath Falls	1947	1,353	132	27,028	—
Pacific U.	Forest Grove	1849	1,209	84	85,000	6,918,864
Portland, U. of	Portland	1901	1,878	131	125,777	79,000
Portland State U.	Portland	1955	11,146	602	274,000	—
Reed	Portland	1908	1,388	112	200,000	5,686,000
Southern Oregon	Ashland	1926	4,432	250	153,000	—
Warner Pacific	Portland	1937	378	35	40,000	—
Willamette U.	Salem	1842	1,637	106	122,000	9,996,000

PENNSYLVANIA

Institution	Location	Year founded	Total students	Faculty	Bound library volumes	Endowment fund
Albright	Reading	1856	1,524	114	130,000	2,867,000
Allegheny	Meadville	1815	1,655	112	191,500	8,129,800
Alliance	Cambridge Springs	1912	609	47	50,000	—
Beaver	Glenside	1853	903	70	71,000	...
‡Bryn Mawr	Bryn Mawr	1885	1,328	132	370,000	33,587
Bucknell U.	Lewisburg	1846	2,845	200	280,000	20,000,000
‡Carlow	Pittsburgh	1929	1,101	81	91,500	209,457
Carnegie-Mellon U.	Pittsburgh	1967	5,254	593	342,032	111,010,000
‡Cedar Crest	Allentown	1867	786	60	71,000	2,182,000
‡Chatham	Pittsburgh	1869	620	64	78,000	10,810,635
Chestnut Hill	Philadelphia	1871	1,038	78	79,000	601,000
†Delaware Valley	Doylestown	1896	1,168	74	42,000	2,291,000
Dickinson	Carlisle	1773	1,611	107	181,873	11,052,208
Drexel U.	Philadelphia	1891	10,206	466	281,000	12,647,000
Duquesne U.	Pittsburgh	1878	7,527	312	280,000	—
Eastern Baptist	St. Davids	1952	562	44	50,000	919,000
Elizabethtown	Elizabethtown	1899	1,584	120	81,000	—
Franklin and Marshall	Lancaster	1787	2,566	175	200,000	10,295,000
Gannon	Erie	1944	3,728	178	92,000	575,000
Geneva	Beaver Falls	1848	1,754	87	81,000	3,219,335
Gettysburg	Gettysburg	1832	1,893	148	180,000	3,180,000

Institution	Location	Year founded	Total students	Faculty	Bound library volumes	Endowment fund
Grove City	Grove City	1876	2,051	107	113,000	$ 4,867,000
‡Gwynedd-Mercy	Gwynedd Valley	1948	1,020	83	35,000	—
†Haverford	Haverford	1833	670	70	275,000	18,236,562
‡Immaculata	Immaculata	1920	1,448	75	88,000	257,100
Indiana U.	Indiana	1875	10,240	578	367,000	—
Juniata	Huntingdon	1876	1,132	90	103,000	3,373,000
King's	Wilkes-Barre	1946	2,038	106	102,000	572,000
Lafayette	Easton	1826	2,070	144	242,000	27,700,000
Lebanon Valley	Annville	1866	974	68	87,698	2,339,000
Lehigh U.	Bethlehem	1865	5,035	394	519,000	34,288,000
Lincoln U.	Lincoln University	1854	1,131	101	118,000	1,582
Lycoming	Williamsport	1812	1,530	92	90,000	1,450,000
‡Marywood	Scranton	1915	1,818	129	91,835	304,519
Mercyhurst	Erie	1926	689	64	53,000	424,000
Messiah	Grantham	1909	582	50	56,000	587,200
†Misericordia	Dallas	1924	1,016	89	65,000	268,000
Moravian	Bethlehem	1807	1,196	81	100,000	5,097,000
Muhlenberg	Allentown	1848	1,564	112	150,000	5,000,000
Pennsylvania, U. of	Philadelphia	1740	19,021	2,112	2,271,000	198,182,000
Penn. State Col. System						
Bloomsburg State	Bloomsburg	1839	4,125	278	136,000	...
California State	California	1852	6,626	385	127,000	—
Cheyney State	Cheyney	1837	1,932	182	85,000	—
Clarion State	Clarion	1866	4,037	280	184,000	—
East Stroudsburg State	East Stroudsburg	1893	2,550	174	150,000	—
Edinboro State	Edinboro	1857	6,849	426	228,000	—
Kutztown State	Kutztown	1866	4,891	266	110,000	—
Lock Haven State	Lock Haven	1870	2,360	172	168,866	—
Mansfield State	Mansfield	1857	2,625	203	86,000	—
Millersville State	Millersville	1855	5,600	321	160,000	—
Shippensburg State	Shippensburg	1871	3,650	298	203,000	—
Slippery Rock State	Slippery Rock	1889	4,931	352	206,000	—
West Chester State	West Chester	1812	6,742	460	206,500	...
Pennsylvania State U.	University Park	1855	43,697	3,190	1,294,000	517,000
Philadelphia Col. of Art	Philadelphia	1876	1,676	83	30,000	1,020,264
Phila. Col. of Tex. & Sci.	Philadelphia	1884	1,511	74	30,000	2,184,000
Pittsburgh, U. of	Pittsburgh	1787	24,299	2,269	1,302,611	82,977,856
PMC	Chester	1821	3,027	147	78,000	837,000
‡Rosemont	Rosemont	1921	701	58	100,000	—
St. Francis	Loretto	1847	1,630	110	100,000	—
St. Joseph's	Philadelphia	1851	6,839	293	108,000	581,000
†St. Vincent	Latrobe	1846	942	53	236,000	360,091
†Scranton, U. of	Scranton	1888	2,971	136	117,052	2,393,000
‡Seton Hill	Greensburg	1883	879	66	63,000	579,385
Susquehanna U.	Selinsgrove	1858	1,223	95	80,000	1,363,000
Swarthmore	Swarthmore	1864	1,114	118	315,000	31,485,000
Temple U.	Philadelphia	1884	32,973	2,489	975,149	7,052,348
Thiel	Greenville	1866	1,341	77	77,000	1,072,000
Ursinus	Collegeville	1869	2,060	94	90,000	6,042,000
‡Villa Maria	Erie	1925	635	50	38,500	6,000
Villanova U.	Villanova	1842	8,769	485	380,600	553,000
Washington & Jefferson	Washington	1781	812	80	128,000	6,584,848
Waynesburg	Waynesburg	1849	1,090	67	78,000	2,000,000
Westminster	New Wilmington	1852	1,955	108	110,000	3,231,000
Wilkes	Wilkes-Barre	1933	3,122	85	100,000	3,500,000
‡Wilson	Chambersburg	1869	620	64	105,000	7,271,622
York	York	1941	2,247	72	58,000	1,094,000

PUERTO RICO

Institution	Location	Year founded	Total students	Faculty	Bound library volumes	Endowment fund
Catholic U.	Ponce	1948	6,343	363	128,000	440,000
Inter American U.	San German	1912	8,557	308	130,800	883,000
Puerto Rico, U. of	Rio Piedras	1903	37,839	2,560	1,766,000	61,000
‡Sacred Heart	Santurce	1935	556	34	46,000	50,000

RHODE ISLAND

Institution	Location	Year founded	Total students	Faculty	Bound library volumes	Endowment fund
Barrington	Barrington	1900	617	43	45,000	749,000
Brown U.	Providence	1764	5,545	1,333	1,235,000	98,293,000
Bryant	Providence	1863	3,260	80	44,000	—
†Providence	Providence	1917	2,344	196	111,000	1,292,000
Rhode Island	Providence	1854	3,209	238	120,000	...
Rhode Island, U. of	Kingston	1892	7,292	745	367,000	66,390
‡Salve Regina	Newport	1934	744	64	53,000	101,000

SOUTH CAROLINA

Institution	Location	Year founded	Total students	Faculty	Bound library volumes	Endowment fund
Benedict	Columbia	1870	1,340	79	50,000	451,112
Charleston	Charleston	1770	548	28	45,000	1,911,066
†The Citadel	Charleston	1842	2,521	147	106,974	—
Claflin	Orangeburg	1869	772	49	38,000	556,000
Clemson U.	Clemson	1889	6,839	392	394,000	620,000
Coker	Hartsville	1908	339	32	46,000	5,000,000
‡Columbia	Columbia	1854	875	57	66,000	2,000,000
‡Converse	Spartanburg	1889	872	75	86,000	1,500,000
Erskine	Due West	1839	747	55	52,000	1,432,000
Furman U.	Greenville	1826	2,011	140	164,000	8,773,000
Lander	Greenwood	1872	591	48	55,000	—
Limestone	Gaffney	1845	738	45	38,000	930,000
Newberry	Newberry	1856	815	61	62,000	982,000
Presbyterian	Clinton	1880	777	52	57,000	2,628,000
South Carolina, U. of	Columbia	1801	15,607	753	928,674	2,500,000
South Carolina State	Orangeburg	1896	2,191	120	103,420	1,000,000
Voorhees	Denmark	1897	725	53	33,000	137,000
‡Winthrop	Rock Hill	1886	3,753	177	268,000	—
†Wofford	Spartanburg	1854	961	62	100,000	2,456,571

SOUTH DAKOTA

Institution	Location	Year founded	Total students	Faculty	Bound library volumes	Endowment fund
Augustana	Sioux Falls	1860	2,078	125	91,000	851,000
Black Hills State	Spearfish	1883	3,001	114	50,000	411,865
Dakota State	Madison	1881	1,473	64	55,000	—
Dakota Wesleyan U.	Mitchell	1885	761	43	51,600	1,252,000
Huron	Huron	1883	713	40	45,000	—
Northern State	Aberdeen	1901	3,474	158	120,000	—
Sioux Falls	Sioux Falls	1883	1,000	52	48,000	521,468
S. Dakota Mines & Tech.	Rapid City	1885	1,868	135	66,000	525,000

Universities and colleges (continued)

Institution	Location	Year founded	Total students	Faculty	Bound library volumes	Endowment fund
South Dakota State U.	Brookings	1883	5,790	345	200,000	$ 3,440,000
Southern State	Springfield	1881	1,086	82	60,000	518,000
Yankton	Yankton	1881	634	52	52,000	1,390,142
TENNESSEE						
Austin Peay State U.	Clarkville	1929	3,421	139	107,000	—
Belmont	Nashville	1951	986	52	48,000	650,000
Bethel	McKenzie	1842	685	41	50,000	1,028,876
Carson-Newman	Jefferson City	1851	1,764	101	95,000	1,886,000
Christian Brothers	Memphis	1871	1,116	72	61,000	190,000
David Lipscomb	Nashville	1891	2,205	100	65,000	3,153,139
East Tennessee State	Johnson City	1911	9,181	467	264,000	—
Fisk U.	Nashville	1867	1,126	119	167,000	8,945,000
George Peabody Tchrs.	Nashville	1875	1,800	170	1,000,000	13,000,000
King	Bristol	1867	317	35	54,000	1,523,000
Knoxville	Knoxville	1875	918	75	50,000	—
Lambuth	Jackson	1843	773	56	65,000	3,378,000
Lane	Jackson	1882	964	49	55,000	1,410,318
Lee	Cleveland	1918	1,006	48	4,000	40,000
LeMoyne-Owen	Memphis	1870	703	40	50,000	1,245,000
Lincoln Memorial U.	Harrogate	1897	741	40	59,000	2,819,861
Maryville	Maryville	1819	714	59	90,000	4,000,000
Memphis State U.	Memphis	1909	17,449	696	397,000	60,942
Middle Tennessee State U.	Murfreesboro	1911	7,425	386	178,000	285,000
Milligan	Milligan College	1882	863	52	55,000	—
Scarritt	Nashville	1892	203	25	25,000	2,296,000
South, U. of the	Sewanee	1858	906	73	201,136	18,906,000
Southern Missionary	Collegedale	1892	1,250	107	53,000	—
Southwestern	Memphis	1848	1,058	96	125,000	6,737,000
Tennessee, U. of	Knoxville	1794	30,771	2,879	1,075,000	4,646,000
Tennessee State U.	Nashville	1909	4,543	276	120,000	36,450,270
Tennessee Tech. U.	Cookeville	1915	6,046	256	307,000	—
Tennessee Wesleyan	Athens	1857	752	45	55,000	843,000
Tusculum	Greeneville	1794	595	40	46,500	2,200,000
Union U.	Jackson	1825	778	52	49,000	798,087
Vanderbilt U.	Nashville	1872	5,963	1,236	1,203,000	93,159,164
TEXAS						
Abilene Christian	Abilene	1906	3,110	...	152,000	7,080,000
Angelo State U.	San Angelo	1928	3,482	121	79,105	—
Austin	Sherman	1849	1,080	88	90,000	4,300,000
Baylor U.	Waco	1845	6,176	335	453,000	26,000,000
Bishop	Dallas	1881	1,968	143	77,000	614,000
Corpus Christi, U. of	Corpus Christi	1947	624	26	67,000	190,248
Dallas, U. of	Irving	1956	1,210	87	75,000	7,500,000
Dallas Baptist	Dallas	1898	1,310	73	50,000	325,000
‡Dominican	Houston	1945	440	70	49,000	—
East Texas Baptist	Marshall	1912	762	36	59,000	1,035,000
East Texas State U.	Commerce	1889	8,782	402	412,000	—
Hardin-Simmons U.	Abilene	1891	1,723	97	114,000	5,000,000
Houston, U. of	Houston	1927	24,383	749	521,000	6,068,000
Howard Payne	Brownwood	1889	1,429	75	89,000	3,091,000
Houston-Tillotson	Austin	1876	641	48	48,000	305,579
‡Incarnate Word	San Antonio	1881	1,303	102	79,000	1,060,787
Jarvis Christian	Hawkins	1912	554	40	44,500	578,896
Lamar State Tech.	Beaumont	1923	9,790	402	197,000	285,146
‡Mary Hardin-Baylor	Belton	1845	799	51	71,000	3,500,000
McMurry	Abilene	1922	1,591	80	90,000	3,288,000
Midwestern U.	Wichita Falls	1922	4,008	139	122,000	—
North Texas State U.	Denton	1890	15,015	911	720,000	—
Our Lady of the Lake	San Antonio	1911	1,664	121	88,850	1,235,550
Pan American	Edinburg	1927	4,612	139	83,000	62,000
Rice U.	Houston	1891	3,163	450	550,000	—
St. Edward's U.	Austin	1885	825	68	61,000	—
St. Mary's U.	San Antonio	1852	4,278	129	110,000	733,000
St. Thomas, U. of	Houston	1947	1,147	101	42,000	—
Sam Houston State U.	Huntsville	1879	8,602	310	350,000	—
Southern Methodist U.	Dallas	1911	9,830	642	1,000,000	26,000,000
Southwestern Union	Keene	...	428	54	40,000	259,000
Southwestern U.	Georgetown	1840	863	63	92,419	10,068,152
Southwest Texas State U.	San Marco	1899	9,372	348	264,463	33,000
Stephen F. Austin State U.	Nacogdoches	1923	8,740	379	390,000	...
Sul Ross State U.	Alpine	1920	2,300	110	142,000	—
Texas, U. System of	Austin	1883	62,275	3,302	3,063,759	585,641,097
U. of Texas at Arlington	Arlington	1895	13,869	444	336,000	290,000
U. of Texas at Austin	Austin	1881	35,678	1,714	2,195,434	23,002,448
U. of Texas at El Paso	El Paso	1913	10,485	350	290,000	3,650,000
Texas A & I U.	Kingsville	1925	7,254	250	200,000	—
Texas A & M U.	College Station	1876	14,034	790	550,000	3,767,000
Prairie View A. & M.	Prairie View	1876	4,325	218	116,000	619,450
Tarleton State	Stephenville	1899	2,665	123	99,000	—
Texas Christian U.	Fort Worth	1873	6,463	385	683,000	23,385,000
Texas Lutheran	Seguin	1891	821	51	70,000	887,000
Texas Southern U.	Houston	1947	4,754	195	189,000	34,000
Texas Tech U.	Lubbock	1923	19,490	923	649,000	1,232,000
Texas Wesleyan	Fort Worth	1891	1,900	70	70,000	—
‡Texas Women's U.	Denton	1901	5,500	300	379,000	500,000
Trinity U.	San Antonio	1869	2,641	192	181,497	42,000,000
Wayland Baptist	Plainview	1908	692	41	50,000	3,404,000
West Texas State U.	Canyon	1910	6,727	296	142,000	—
Wiley	Marshall	1873	500	42	30,000	1,000,000
UTAH						
Brigham Young U.	Provo	1875	23,549	1,099	803,000	34,796,000
Southern Utah State	Cedar City	1897	1,716	88	55,000	—
Utah, U. of	Salt Lake City	1850	23,111	975	1,157,529	12,833,108
Utah State U.	Logan	1888	7,712	472	541,000	956,000
Weber State	Ogden	1889	10,661	341	150,000	75,000
Westminster	Salt Lake City	1875	827	44	34,000	250,000
VERMONT						
Bennington	Bennington	1925	554	68	60,000	1,221,000
Castleton State	Castleton	1867	1,150	74	28,000	—
Goddard	Plainfield	1938	883	68	35,000	—
Johnson State	Johnson	1867	691	48	29,000	—
Lyndon State	Lyndonville	1911	647	50	43,000	...
Marlboro	Marlboro	1946	125	25	27,000	$ 39,000
Middlebury	Middlebury	1800	1,625	135	188,851	14,969,119
†Norwich U.	Northfield	1819	1,217	125	98,000	7,400,000
St. Michael's	Winooski	1903	1,219	92	70,539	162,201
‡Trinity	Burlington	1925	454	43	38,000	—
Vermont	Montpelier	1834	494	43	25,000	248,000
Vermont, U. of	Burlington	1791	6,221	607	500,000	14,100,000
Windham	Putney	1951	886	68	56,000	18,000
VIRGINIA						
Bridgewater	Bridgewater	1880	852	67	75,000	1,329,000
Eastern Mennonite	Harrisonburg	1917	955	67	55,000	490,000
Emory & Henry	Emory	1836	826	76	90,000	3,175,000
†Hampden-Sydney	Hampden-Sydney	1776	641	51	80,000	4,500,000
Hampton Inst.	Hampton	1868	2,265	199	130,000	32,000,000
‡Hollins	Hollins College	1842	1,047	91	112,000	4,382,977
‡Longwood	Farmville	1839	1,956	133	113,000	—
Lynchburg	Lynchburg	1903	1,928	124	63,000	2,038,000
Madison	Harrisonburg	1908	3,818	245	148,208	—
‡Mary Baldwin	Staunton	1842	709	57	89,000	2,000,000
Old Dominion U.	Norfolk	1930	8,991	462	170,000	—
‡Radford	Radford	1910	3,959	220	114,595	—
†Randolph-Macon	Ashland	1830	847	65	81,000	3,727,238
‡Randolph-Macon Wmn's	Lynchburg	1891	827	81	117,000	4,476,708
Richmond, U. of	Richmond	1830	4,606	239	210,000	47,764,000
Roanoke	Salem	1842	1,524	88	81,000	1,708,000
St. Paul's	Lawrenceville	1888	537	44	40,000	779,000
Shenandoah	Winchester	1875	536	61	18,000	110,000
‡Sweet Briar	Sweet Briar	1901	740	73	139,000	6,400,000
Virginia, U. of	Charlottesville	1819	9,735	1,155	1,527,903	59,224,772
‡Mary Washington	Fredericksburg	1908	2,166	157	203,000	14,000
George Mason	Fairfax	1957	1,936	110	...	...
Virginia Commonwealth U.	Richmond	1838	13,737	926	233,900	6,272,000
†Virginia Military Inst.	Lexington	1839	1,222	127	166,000	7,226,000
Virginia Polytech. Inst.	Blacksburg	1872	9,427	934	485,000	875,000
Virginia State	Petersburg	1882	2,739	173	105,000	183,275
Virginia Union U.	Richmond	1865	1,280	79	67,000	1,490,000
†Washington & Lee U.	Lexington	1749	1,450	129	289,000	15,667,000
William & Mary	Williamsburg	1693	4,100	383	503,000	5,151,000
WASHINGTON						
Central Washington State	Ellensburg	1891	6,927	359	143,000	—
Eastern Washington State	Cheney	1890	6,345	314	177,879	9,000
Gonzaga U.	Spokane	1887	2,710	256	187,931	—
Pacific Lutheran U.	Tacoma	1890	2,831	160	119,000	744,171
Puget Sound, U. of	Tacoma	1888	3,985	191	160,000	5,679,000
St. Martin's	Olympia	1895	1,407	79	57,223	—
Seattle Pacific	Seattle	1891	1,927	120	78,000	509,000
Seattle U.	Seattle	1891	3,468	234	135,000	1,000,000
Walla Walla	College Place	1892	1,715	95	110,000	—
Washington State U.	Pullman	1890	13,150	675	900,000	44,400,000
Western Washington St.	Bellingham	1899	8,634	541	225,000	58,848
Whitman	Walla Walla	1859	1,121	82	146,000	12,412,000
Whitworth	Spokane	1890	1,630	74	60,000	—
WEST VIRGINIA						
Alderson-Broaddus	Philippi	1871	943	61	50,000	850,000
Bethany	Bethany	1840	1,016	76	100,000	7,784,000
Bluefield State	Bluefield	1895	1,248	74	45,000	—
Concord	Athens	1872	2,030	103	99,000	—
Davis and Elkins	Elkins	1904	791	58	60,000	822,300
Fairmont State	Fairmont	1867	3,289	154	100,000	—
Glenville State	Glenville	1872	1,698	88	59,000	—
Marshall U.	Huntington	1837	8,041	375	165,000	—
Morris Harvey	Charleston	1888	3,135	96	60,000	2,250,000
Salem	Salem	1888	1,582	98	65,000	1,000,000
Shepherd	Shepherdstown	1871	1,395	80	60,000	—
West Liberty State	West Liberty	1837	4,047	182	80,000	—
West Virginia	Montgomery	1895	2,480	146	62,000	—
West Virginia State	Institute	1891	3,710	147	100,000	...
West Virginia U.	Morgantown	1867	15,921	1,420	888,000	1,875,000
West Virginia Wesleyan	Buckhannon	1890	1,796	108	90,000	2,159,000
Wheeling	Wheeling	1954	804	58	70,000	43,000
WISCONSIN						
‡Alverno	Milwaukee	1936	884	69	75,000	250,000
Beloit	Beloit	1846	1,777	150	220,000	8,360,000
‡Cardinal Stritch	Milwaukee	1937	660	47	44,000	—
Carroll	Waukesha	1846	1,247	88	93,000	2,689,000
Carthage	Kenosha	1847	1,933	91	95,000	3,587,000
Dominican	Racine	1935	689	49	37,000	—
Edgewood	Madison	1927	581	55	42,000	—
Lakeland	Sheboygan	1862	665	40	40,000	186,000
Lawrence U.	Appleton	1847	1,342	132	183,000	23,332,000
Marian	Fond du Lac	1936	431	42	40,000	—
Marquette U.	Milwaukee	1864	10,636	809	500,000	7,019,000
Milton	Milton	1848	689	40	48,000	140,000
‡Mt. Mary	Milwaukee	1872	919	93	70,000	450,000
Northland	Ashland	1892	679	49	45,000	1,098,000
Ripon	Ripon	1850	1,082	86	85,000	2,200,000
St. Norbert	West De Pere	1898	1,651	107	85,000	1,415,163
Stout State U.	Menomonie	1893	4,910	316	108,000	110,000
‡Viterbo	La Crosse	1931	449	48	51,000	—
Wisconsin, U.	Madison	1848	68,109	...	3,013,172	—
Wisconsin-Milwaukee	Milwaukee	1956	18,978	...	516,560	—
Wisconsin State U. System	8 campuses	—	54,514	3,353	1,528,000	364,235
WYOMING						
Wyoming, U. of	Laramie	1886	7,924	574	390,000	12,381,000

Defense

Army personnel

Military status	1960	1965	1970
Personnel on active duty	873,078	968,313	1,322,549*
Officers	101,236	111,541	166,722
Enlisted	771,842	856,772	1,155,827
Reserve personnel not on active duty†	703,000	641,000	717,308
National Guard	402,000	379,000	409,192
Officers	37,000	34,000	29,391
Enlisted	365,000	345,000	379,801
Army Reserve	301,000	262,000	308,116
Officers	50,000	40,000	45,185
Enlisted	251,000	221,000	262,931

Data are for June 30 of years reported.
*Includes cadets and officer candidates.
†Paid status only; excludes personnel in inactive reserve.
Source: U.S. Department of Defense.

Navy and Marine Corps personnel

Military status	1960	1965	1970
Personnel on active duty	788,605	861,196	952,397*
Navy	617,984	671,009	692,660
Officers	69,559	77,720	80,761
Enlisted	548,425	593,289	611,899
Marine Corps	170,621	190,187	259,737
Officers	16,203	17,234	24,941
Enlisted	154,418	172,953	234,796
Reserve personnel not on active duty†	165,000	169,000	181,392
Naval Reserve	120,000	123,000	131,723
Officers	26,000	23,000	23,416
Enlisted	94,000	100,000	108,307
Marine Corps Reserve	45,000	46,000	49,669
Officers	4,000	3,000	3,566
Enlisted	41,000	43,000	46,103

Data are for June 30 of years reported.
*Includes cadets and officer candidates.
†Paid status only; excludes personnel in inactive reserve.
Source: U.S. Department of Defense.

Air Force personnel

Military status	1960	1965	1970
Personnel on active duty	814,752	823,633	791,349*
Officers	129,689	131,141	129,803
Enlisted	685,063	692,492	661,546
Reserve personnel not on active duty†	129,000	123,000	142,118
Air National Guard	71,000	76,000	89,847
Officers	9,000	10,000	10,872
Enlisted	62,000	66,000	78,975
Air Force Reserve	58,000	46,000	52,271
Officers	22,000	11,000	12,732
Enlisted	37,000	36,000	39,539

Data are for June 30 of years reported.
*Includes cadets and officer candidates.
†Paid status only; excludes personnel in inactive reserve.
Source: U.S. Department of Defense.

Coast Guard personnel

Military status	1960	1965	1970
Personnel on active duty	31,406†	31,792†	37,942*
Officers	4,011	4,492	5,553
Enlisted	26,991	26,860	31,736
Reserve personnel not on active duty†	14,144	16,578	26,433
Officers	1,712	1,943	3,193
Enlisted	12,432	14,635	23,240

Data are for June 30 of years reported.
*Includes cadets.
†Paid status only; excludes personnel in inactive reserve.
Source: U.S. Department of Transportation,
U.S. Coast Guard.

The Selective Service, 1970

State	Registrants classified 1-A and 1-A-O as of June 30	Registrants forwarded to Armed Forces year ending June 30*	Inductions year ending June 30	ENLISTMENTS† year ending June 30 Regular	Reserves or National Guard
Alabama	34,337	25,550	4,232	8,912	5,885
Alaska	1,814	1,063	181	454	477
Arizona	15,967	11,486	1,996	3,526	1,571
Arkansas	18,456	14,426	2,189	5,178	3,069
California	175,926	114,770	16,428	32,788	17,141
Colorado	15,890	11,397	1,845	4,628	1,796
Connecticut	20,510	20,516	1,921	5,226	4,250
Delaware	3,785	3,539	460	1,093	1,145
District of Columbia	14,903	3,814	588	1,520	478
Florida	46,498	35,863	4,843	13,982	6,581
Georgia	40,621	35,075	5,465	10,366	5,039
Hawaii	5,623	4,736	462	2,594	910
Idaho	7,251	5,835	763	1,958	1,028
Illinois	109,647	73,444	13,806	18,684	8,756
Indiana	43,756	34,691	6,456	10,378	5,745
Iowa	31,651	17,863	3,367	6,851	3,388
Kansas	18,408	12,940	2,189	5,863	3,154
Kentucky	39,800	25,762	4,796	6,659	2,986
Louisiana	32,223	32,882	5,402	7,418	4,503
Maine	8,961	7,045	849	3,146	1,151
Maryland	28,004	24,658	3,219	7,332	4,641
Massachusetts	38,867	35,782	2,773	11,968	10,189
Michigan	79,571	64,871	12,542	15,107	6,533
Minnesota	40,678	21,786	4,561	7,856	4,920
Mississippi	18,218	17,368	2,500	4,959	3,521
Missouri	39,975	27,296	6,708	10,108	4,920
Montana	6,227	3,916	734	1,830	1,524
Nebraska	12,312	11,712	1,927	3,431	2,410
Nevada	4,501	1,842	432	805	493
New Hampshire	5,132	3,929	368	1,853	830
New Jersey	42,902	40,244	3,914	11,146	9,058
New Mexico	9,337	6,266	1,095	2,684	1,151
New York	131,816	120,652	11,610	27,981	19,678
North Carolina	42,545	38,925	7,351	12,529	4,138
North Dakota	7,595	4,554	1,166	1,485	1,049
Ohio	82,209	68,716	10,837	21,164	10,298
Oklahoma	21,103	14,959	2,761	7,082	4,416
Oregon	21,910	13,252	1,887	5,386	2,651
Pennsylvania	92,379	75,368	8,730	24,777	14,811
Rhode Island	6,721	7,162	588	1,921	1,670
South Carolina	20,099	17,232	2,820	6,983	3,791
South Dakota	5,257	4,870	835	1,805	1,407
Tennessee	40,335	25,980	5,426	9,025	4,337
Texas	110,092	73,949	11,487	23,761	9,838
Utah	11,539	7,708	1,206	1,876	2,743
Vermont	4,131	2,555	213	1,195	773
Virginia	38,607	28,383	4,998	10,347	5,005
Washington	26,358	18,717	2,404	8,127	3,863
West Virginia	16,252	14,222	2,483	5,850	1,840
Wisconsin	33,688	32,381	5,469	8,414	5,045
Wyoming	3,770	3,155	542	931	538
TOTAL U.S.‡	1,758,062	1,347,336	203,707	413,270	229,000

*For preinduction examinations.
†Estimated.
‡Includes Canal Zone, Guam, Puerto Rico, and Virgin Islands.
Source: Selective Service System and Department of Defense.

Vietnam

U.S. armed forces and casualties

	1961	1962	1963	1964	1965	1966	1967	1968	1969	1970*
Military forces	3,200	11,300	16,300	23,300	184,300	385,300	485,600	536,100	475,200	414,900
Army	2,100	7,900	10,100	14,700	116,800	239,400	319,500	359,800	331,100	298,600
Navy†	100	500	800	1,100	8,400	23,300	31,700	36,100	30,200	25,700
Marine Corps	—	500	800	900	38,200	69,200	78,000	81,400	55,100	39,900
Air Force	1,000	2,400	4,600	6,600	20,600	52,900	55,900	58,400	58,400	50,500
Coast Guard	—	—	—	—	300	500	500	400	400	200
Casualties‡										
Battle deaths	11	31	78	147	1,369	5,008	9,378	14,592	9,414	2,896
Killed	1	19	53	112	1,130	4,179	7,482	12,588	8,119	2,471
Died of wounds	—	1	5	6	87	517	981	1,636	1,170	346
Died while missing	10	11	20	28	151	309	911	367	120	57
Died while captured	—	—	—	1	1	3	4	1	5	2
Wounded, nonfatal										
Hospital care required	2	41	218	522	3,308	16,526	32,371	46,799	32,940	9,899
Hospital care not required	1	37	193	517	2,806	13,567	29,654	46,021	37,276	10,005

Data are for December 31 of years reported, except as indicated.
*As of June 30.
†Excludes personnel on ships off Vietnam's shores.
‡Represents casualties from enemy action. Deaths exclude servicemen who died in accidents or from disease.
Source: U.S. Department of Defense.

Production

Gross national product and national income

in billions of dollars

Item	1960	1965	1969	1970*
Gross national product	503.7	684.9	931.4	971.1
By type of expenditure				
Personal consumption expenditures	325.2	432.8	577.5	614.4
Durable goods	45.3	66.3	90.0	91.9
Nondurable goods	151.3	191.1	245.8	262.6
Services	128.7	175.5	241.6	259.9
Gross private domestic investment	74.8	108.1	139.8	134.3
Fixed investment	71.3	98.5	131.4	131.2
Changes in business inventories	3.6	9.6	8.5	3.1
Net exports of goods and services	4.0	6.9	1.9	4.1
Exports	27.2	39.2	55.5	62.8
Imports	23.2	32.3	53.6	58.7
Government purchases of goods and services	99.6	137.0	212.2	218.4
Federal	53.5	66.9	101.3	99.7
State and local	46.1	70.1	110.8	118.7
By major type of product				
Goods output	256.0	337.6	451.6	471.8
Durable goods	97.4	133.0	183.9	188.5
Nondurable goods	158.6	204.7	267.7	283.3
Services	187.3	262.9	377.6	405.8
Structures	56.8	74.8	93.8	90.4

Item	1960	1965	1969	1970*
National income	414.5	564.3	769.5	797.4
By type of income				
Compensation of employees	294.2	393.8	564.2	596.4
Proprietors' income	46.2	57.3	66.8	67.8
Rental income of persons	15.8	19.0	22.0	22.6
Corporate profits and inventory valuation adjustment	49.9	76.1	85.8	77.5
Net interest	8.4	18.2	30.7	33.1
By industry division				
Agriculture, forestry, and fisheries	16.9	21.0	24.3	24.8
Mining and construction	26.5	35.2	47.4	49.1
Manufacturing	125.8	172.6	226.2	222.9
Nondurable goods	52.2	66.5	87.0	88.7
Durable goods	73.6	106.1	139.3	134.2
Transportation	18.2	23.2	29.2	30.5
Communications and public utilities	17.1	22.7	30.1	29.4
Wholesale and retail trade	64.4	84.3	115.2	121.5
Finance, insurance, and real estate	45.9	61.9	83.5	87.4
Services	44.4	64.1	95.3	103.4
Government and government enterprises	52.9	75.2	114.1	124.6
Other	2.4	4.2	4.3	3.9

*Second quarter, seasonally adjusted at annual rates.

Source: U.S. Department of Commerce, Office of Business Economics, *Survey of Current Business.*

Agriculture

Farming trends

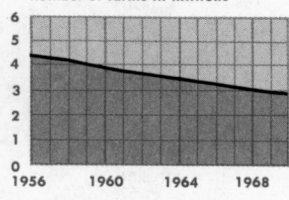

number of farms in millions

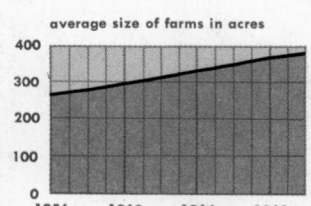

average size of farms in acres

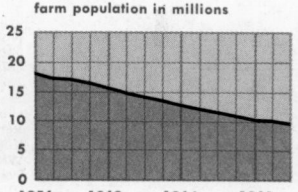

farm population in millions

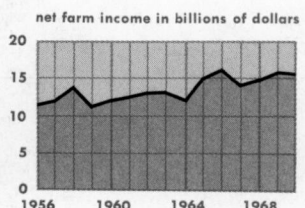

net farm income in billions of dollars

Sources: U.S. Department of Agriculture, Economic Research Service.

Farms and farm income

State	Number of farms 1970*	Land in farms 1970* in 000 acres	CASH INCOME, 1969, IN $000 Crops	CASH INCOME, 1969, IN $000 Livestock and products	Government payments	Realized net income per farm 1969
Alabama	85,000	14,800	195,695	526,859	82,032	$ 3,558
Alaska	310	1,835†	861	2,935	123	461
Arizona	5,900	43,300	292,606	369,398	47,850	26,692
Arkansas	74,000	17,900	504,902	534,006	82,488	5,135
California	57,000	36,800	2,605,440	1,765,820	123,206	17,428
Colorado	30,500	39,000	219,978	795,830	66,492	4,943
Connecticut	4,600	590	61,515	104,606	808	10,302
Delaware	3,700	700	43,881	107,039	2,161	14,146
Florida	34,000	16,200	960,974	382,141	19,284	16,953
Georgia	75,000	16,900	407,432	740,445	86,089	6,227
Hawaii	4,600	2,340	158,571	39,986	10,954	8,849
Idaho	28,500	15,500	352,436	278,892	46,086	7,725
Illinois	126,000	29,600	1,360,758	1,342,199	195,374	6,630
Indiana	96,000	17,200	670,518	816,595	132,164	6,024
Iowa	140,000	34,400	930,299	2,857,721	206,351	8,914
Kansas	86,000	50,000	573,360	1,144,393	235,247	5,587
Kentucky	120,000	16,800	398,386	487,748	52,513	3,594
Louisiana	52,000	12,200	317,827	254,374	52,266	4,479
Maine	9,700	2,300	81,065	158,434	1,901	7,076
Maryland	17,700	3,200	123,793	265,532	8,602	7,348
Massachusetts	6,000	710	74,999	91,001	639	7,162
Michigan	85,000	13,000	383,154	480,162	73,394	3,174
Minnesota	125,000	32,200	615,756	1,341,693	171,156	5,247
Mississippi	93,000	17,500	325,737	481,509	133,611	4,003
Missouri	142,000	33,000	413,975	1,031,985	156,259	3,886
Montana	26,300	67,100	181,464	352,740	80,081	7,128
Nebraska	73,000	48,100	534,158	1,399,187	200,603	$8,106
Nevada	2,100	9,000	13,458	62,702	1,884	7,822
New Hampshire	3,500	700	12,877	44,222	581	2,485
New Jersey	8,700	1,010	146,633	102,934	4,889	7,672
New Mexico	13,600	48,200	91,451	298,871	41,647	9,119
New York	57,000	11,500	292,419	788,376	25,453	6,150
North Carolina	157,000	16,100	812,034	594,127	69,757	4,266
North Dakota	41,000	42,000	479,260	264,997	162,966	6,376
Ohio	111,000	17,400	483,867	769,955	103,424	3,571
Oklahoma	90,000	37,200	261,258	678,021	115,214	2,836
Oregon	39,500	20,900	289,963	256,212	24,343	3,312
Pennsylvania	73,000	10,585	236,880	752,264	27,866	4,411
Rhode Island	900	90	10,003	11,018	69	3,452
South Carolina	51,000	8,200	234,634	165,512	56,189	3,164
South Dakota	46,500	45,500	183,251	802,766	94,361	7,731
Tennessee	125,000	15,400	259,256	414,176	73,724	2,305
Texas	187,000	145,000	1,122,738	1,782,523	505,248	5,529
Utah	14,500	13,200	42,969	166,482	11,810	3,442
Vermont	7,200	2,250	14,331	137,497	1,444	6,008
Virginia	71,000	11,400	248,258	328,440	19,654	2,851
Washington	45,500	18,100	491,683	282,874	56,889	6,077
West Virginia	29,000	5,100	25,784	80,012	3,877	817
Wisconsin	112,000	20,400	211,632	1,313,149	56,346	4,932
Wyoming	8,400	37,000	36,216	188,404	14,349	4,615
Total U.S.	2,895,210	1,119,410	18,790,395	28,438,764	3,793,718	5,437

*Preliminary. †Includes about 1,765,000 acres of grazing land leased from the U.S. government.
Source: U.S. Department of Agriculture, Economics Research Service, Statistical Reporting Service.

Principal crops
of the United States and each state

Crops (unit of production)	Amount produced in 000 1970	Acreage harvested in 000 acres 1970	VALUE OF PRODUCTION in $000 1969	1970
UNITED STATES				
Corn, grain (bu.)	4,109,792	57,359	5,289,754	5,478,958
Hay (tons)	127,899	63,234	2,984,426	3,072,213
Soybeans for beans (bu.)	1,135,769	42,447	2,647,499	2,203,958
Wheat (bu.)	1,378,464	44,306	1,815,732	1,870,428
Tobacco (lb.)	1,905,751	899	1,295,700	1,376,157
Cotton lint (bales)	10,270	11,168	1,054,981	1,155,347
Sorghum grain (bu.)	697,050	13,751	791,153	784,989
Potatoes (cwt.)	324,861	1,425	693,974	711,651
Oats (bu.)	909,481	18,580	564,629	577,130
Rice (cwt.)	82,859	1,815	449,940	420,530
Alabama				
Cotton lint (bales)	510	540	48,617	57,375
Peanuts harvested for nuts (lb.)	313,740	189	33,365	40,159
Soybeans for beans (bu.)	14,312	609	34,056	40,074
Hay (tons)	791	494	21,392	22,544
Corn, grain (bu.)	12,535	545	23,572	19,805
Alaska				
Hay (tons)	10,500	8,900	532	788
Potatoes (cwt.)	105	1	471	643
Silage (tons)	20	4	257	355
Barley (bu.)	56	2	59	100
Arizona				
Cotton lint (bales)	489	275	70,866	59,025
Hay (tons)	1,318	243	30,688	40,858
Sorghum grain (bu.)	12,670	181	20,489	17,485
Barley (bu.)	10,640	140	12,576	12,768
Cottonseed (tons)	203	...	10,467	12,180
Arkansas				
Soybeans for beans (bu.)	97,043	4,313	208,884	276,573
Cotton lint (bales)	1,075	1,080	124,629	120,938
Rice (cwt.)	21,024	438	130,143	109,325
Hay (tons)	1,348	788	25,313	31,004
Wheat (bu.)	10,725	325	10,565	13,192
California				
Hay (tons)	7,744	1,907	206,140	229,333
Grapes (tons)	2,760	...	234,205	227,769
Cotton lint (bales)	1,165	662	152,861	145,726
Oranges (tons)	1,463	...	105,587	108,268
Rice (cwt.)	18,205	331	103,162	89,205
Peaches (bu.)*	38,167	...	96,997	80,476
Potatoes (cwt.)	29,760	87	26,967	29,893
Barley (bu.)	61,776	1,188	65,571	69,807
Colorado				
Wheat (bu.)	68,944	2,420	51,427	83,407
Hay (tons)	3,364	1,723	84,686	82,418
Corn, grain (bu.)	31,872	332	32,963	41,115
Sugar beets (tons)	2,416	146	28,094	35,998
Potatoes (cwt.)	13,590	53	22,045	24,183
Connecticut				
Tobacco (lb.)	7,884	5	23,259	23,697
Hay (tons)	203	102	7,763	8,120
Apples (bu.)†	1,200	...	3,784	3,377
Potatoes (cwt.)	1,127	5	3,402	3,043
Delaware				
Corn, grain (bu.)	13,690	185	16,575	19,987
Soybeans for beans (bu.)	3,402	162	10,852	9,866
Potatoes (cwt.)	1,512	7	3,696	3,599
Hay (tons)	76	35	2,993	2,698
Florida				
Oranges (tons)	6,197	...	321,692	271,431
Grapefruit (tons)	1,590	...	65,428	88,009
Sugarcane for sugar (tons)	5,762	172	53,238	62,345
Tobacco (lb.)	28,923	15	31,554	30,712
Corn, grain (bu.)	8,050	322	17,871	12,880
Georgia				
Peanuts harvested for nuts (lb.)	1,133,145	507	115,445	145,043
Tobacco (lb.)	133,305	67	75,665	102,390
Corn, grain (bu.)	44,206	1,426	64,469	71,172
Soybeans for beans (bu.)	11,880	528	27,348	34,452
Cotton lint (bales)	290	380	27,837	31,175
Hawaii				
Papayas (lb.)	24,960	1	2,385	2,521
Macadamia nuts (lb.)	11,500	4	2,474	2,496
Coffee (lb.)	4,900	3	1,562	1,715
Taro (lb.)	8,400	§	671	714
Bananas (lb.)	5,590	1	580	598
Idaho				
Potatoes (cwt.)	73,195	327	140,834	144,350
Hay (tons)	3,957	1,398	80,862	85,076
Wheat (bu.)	42,734	929	60,127	59,069
Sugar beets (tons)	3,087	170	48,909	45,996
Barley (bu.)	36,300	660	27,939	33,033
Illinois				
Corn, grain (bu.)	744,884	10,066	1,121,477	1,020,491
Soybeans for beans (bu.)	212,815	6,865	536,583	606,523
Hay (tons)	3,378	1,260	78,420	82,761
Wheat (bu.)	35,748	993	55,579	46,472
Oats (bu.)	34,272	612	24,872	21,591
Indiana				
Corn, grain (bu.)	371,998	5,027	523,517	502,197
Soybeans for beans (bu.)	104,297	3,311	246,422	292,032
Hay (tons)	2,204	932	54,611	56,202
Wheat (bu.)	29,799	774	38,680	39,037
Oats (bu.)	15,423	291	11,139	10,025
Iowa				
Corn, grain (bu.)	859,140	9,990	1,034,933	1,099,699
Soybeans for beans (bu.)	186,624	5,832	424,446	522,547
Hay (tons)	6,910	2,502	146,880	138,200
Oats (bu.)	92,394	1,711	55,366	57,284
Sorghum grain (bu.)	2,368	32	2,863	2,463
Kansas				
Wheat (bu.)	299,013	9,061	363,330	382,737
Sorghum grain (bu.)	145,960	3,560	181,067	159,096
Corn, grain (bu.)	79,670	1,285	103,354	103,571
Hay (tons)	4,102	2,384	107,373	96,397
Soybeans for beans (bu.)	15,075	1,005	43,503	40,703
Kentucky				
Tobacco (lb.)	411,201	157	297,010	288,829
Hay (tons)	3,059	1,585	87,276	87,182
Corn, grain (bu.)	49,400	988	99,900	75,088
Soybeans for beans (bu.)	15,066	558	31,506	42,185
Wheat (bu.)	6,120	170	7,591	8,078
Louisiana				
Soybeans for beans (bu.)	37,890	1,688	72,103	108,243
Rice (cwt.)	20,397	523	94,409	100,965
Sugarcane for sugar (tons)	7,209	267	54,830	71,153
Cotton lint (bales)	530	455	54,377	59,625
Sweet potatoes (cwt.)	4,165	49	13,393	10,829
Maine				
Potatoes (cwt.)	35,700	150	77,220	64,260
Hay (tons)	408	290	11,104	13,872
Apples (bu.)†	1,476	...	3,886	3,844
Oats (bu.)	1,485	33	1,032	1,040
Maryland				
Corn, grain (bu.)	40,172	484	49,275	59,053
Hay (tons)	735	328	21,945	23,520
Tobacco (lb.)	27,040	26	21,028	20,307
Soybeans for beans (bu.)	5,112	213	15,560	14,825
Wheat (bu.)	4,181	113	5,521	5,477
Massachusetts				
Cranberries (bbl.)	957	11	12,307	15,599
Tobacco (lb.)	3,230	2	10,524	10,192
Hay (tons)	239	126	8,610	9,082
Apples (bu.)†	2,567	...	6,980	6,899
Potatoes (cwt.)	1,046	5	2,565	2,929
Michigan				
Corn, grain (bu.)	114,076	1,444	106,800	148,299
Hay (tons)	3,260	1,425	70,554	71,720
Beans, dry edible (cwt.)	6,269	1,050	51,150	52,033
Soybeans for beans (bu.)	13,624	524	27,545	38,147
Wheat (bu.)	22,035	565	30,144	31,069
Apples (bu.)†	17,857	...	26,928	28,650
Cherries (tons)	100	...	20,692	15,440
Minnesota				
Corn, grain (bu.)	390,490	4,594	369,406	472,493
Soybeans for beans (bu.)	82,919	3,129	178,143	228,027
Hay (tons)	8,155	3,231	172,221	159,023
Oats (bu.)	167,700	3,354	106,248	102,297
Wheat (bu.)	22,882	830	35,545	37,731
Mississippi				
Cotton lint (bales)	1,635	1,190	146,555	179,850
Soybeans for beans (bu.)	56,064	2,336	120,408	162,586
Cottonseed (tons)	676	...	23,717	37,518
Hay (tons)	1,061	642	25,398	27,056
Corn, grain (bu.)	6,944	248	13,505	10,833
Missouri				
Soybeans for beans (bu.)	90,896	3,496	190,008	254,509
Corn, grain (bu.)	173,057	2,837	216,830	242,280
Hay (tons)	5,535	3,008	123,640	127,305
Wheat (bu.)	31,222	932	39,082	39,652
Cotton lint (bales)	225	275	35,740	25,875
Montana				
Wheat (bu.)	85,167	3,383	118,864	115,928
Hay (tons)	4,112	2,495	93,168	92,520
Barley (bu.)	65,132	1,714	48,219	47,546
Sugar beets (tons)	922	58	16,763	13,738
Potatoes (cwt.)	1,388	7	5,233	4,442
Nebraska				
Corn, grain (bu.)	367,275	4,897	468,329	466,439
Hay (tons)	6,237	4,418	142,496	130,977
Wheat (bu.)	97,204	2,558	102,457	119,561
Sorghum grain (bu.)	76,449	1,499	113,891	81,036
Soybeans for beans (bu.)	17,864	812	57,481	49,126
Nevada				
Hay (tons)	834	448	22,932	22,101
Barley (bu.)	930	15	1,344	1,060
Wheat (bu.)	810	14	876	1,116
New Hampshire				
Hay (tons)	204	124	6,100	7,548
Apples (bu.)†	1,236	...	2,580	3,322
Potatoes (cwt.)	184	1	510	515

Boldface type indicates states which lead in the value of production for the ten leading crops in the United States.
*48 lb. equivalents. †42 lb. equivalents.
§Less then 1,000 ac.
Source: U.S. Department of Agriculture, Statistical Reporting Service, Crop Reporting Board, *Crop Production and Crop Values*, December 1970.

Principal crops (continued)

Crops (unit of production)	Amount produced in 000 1970	Acreage harvested in 000 acres 1970	Value of production in $000 1969	1970
New Jersey				
Hay (tons)	331	136	11,573	12,909
Potatoes (cwt.)	3,207	12	7,865	8,499
Peaches (bu.)*	1,875	...	7,733	8,460
Corn, grain (bu.)	5,070	65	6,572	7,656
Apples (bu.)†	2,357	...	6,344	5,297
New Mexico				
Hay (tons)	1,044	300	28,701	30,798
Sorghum grain (bu.)	17,499	307	19,553	20,124
Cotton lint (bales)	135	142	19,886	17,184
Wheat (bu.)	5,520	184	5,538	7,452
Cottonseed (tons)	55	...	2,912	3,410
New York				
Hay (tons)	5,798	2,652	143,598	159,445
Potatoes (cwt.)	16,861	65	47,349	42,416
Apples (bu.)†	22,738	...	39,929	34,858
Corn, grain (bu.)	22,041	279	24,824	32,180
Grapes (tons)	140	...	22,385	25,900
Oats (bu.)	22,554	358	15,126	18,494
North Carolina				
Tobacco (lb.)	814,603	390	516,233	583,932
Corn, grain (bu.)	67,250	1,345	112,369	102,893
Soybeans for beans (bu.)	21,024	876	55,584	60,970
Peanuts harvested for nuts (lb.)	442,800	164	44,257	59,335
Hay (tons)	602	410	20,328	20,769
North Dakota				
Wheat (bu.)	152,826	6,486	277,907	235,446
Hay (tons)	4,414	3,400	62,946	68,417
Oats (bu.)	115,541	2,687	74,426	61,237
Barley (bu.)	68,705	1,963	69,246	57,712
Flaxseed (bu.)	16,440	1,644	47,471	38,634
Ohio				
Corn, grain (bu.)	232,078	3,014	274,822	313,305
Soybeans for beans (bu.)	69,483	2,438	160,423	198,027
Hay (tons)	2,913	1,460	71,222	72,825
Wheat (bu.)	35,927	971	46,980	51,016
Oats (bu.)	29,870	515	19,813	20,312
Oklahoma				
Wheat (bu.)	98,202	3,777	145,478	128,645
Hay (tons)	2,806	1,737	69,414	74,359
Sorghum grain (bu.)	23,306	542	27,767	26,336
Peanuts harvested for nuts (lb.)	206,500	118	24,888	25,813
Cotton lint (bales)	185	450	26,380	18,963
Oregon				
Hay (tons)	2,369	1,129	61,230	60,410
Wheat (bu.)	30,216	728	39,339	44,706
Potatoes (cwt.)	16,056	58	26,967	29,893
Pears (tons)	95	...	17,898	11,020
Cherries (tons)	40	...	12,186	13,915
Pennsylvania				
Hay (tons)	4,396	2,019	120,263	131,880
Corn, grain (bu.)	80,155	943	104,378	118,629
Potatoes (cwt.)	8,280	34	24,914	21,528
Oats (bu.)	24,795	435	16,530	18,844
Wheat (bu.)	9,834	298	14,743	13,768
Rhode Island				
Potatoes (cwt.)	1,323	5	3,448	3,572
Hay (tons)	25	13	1,053	1,075
Apples (bu.)†	162	...	322	483
South Carolina				
Tobacco (lb.)	141,075	67	99,487	101,292
Soybeans for beans (bu.)	20,439	997	51,140	59,273
Cotton lint (bales)	215	290	21,881	24,188
Peaches (bu.)*	6,042	...	17,576	22,040
Corn, grain (bu.)	10,854	402	25,129	17,041
Hay (tons)	378	218	11,682	11,529
South Dakota				
Corn, grain (bu.)	102,336	2,496	143,663	123,827
Hay (tons)	5,795	4,555	104,861	104,310
Oats (bu.)	105,329	2,569	60,281	60,038
Wheat (bu.)	2,835	81	58,380	59,154
Flaxseed (bu.)	7,392	704	25,337	18,110
Tennessee				
Tobacco (lb.)	117,864	54	78,478	80,355
Soybeans for beans (bu.)	28,267	1,229	66,140	77,734
Hay (tons)	2,036	1,337	57,159	60,062
Cotton lint (bales)	390	390	45,047	43,875
Corn, grain (bu.)	22,760	569	36,736	34,823
Texas				
Sorghum grain (bu.)	329,616	5,886	340,780	369,170
Cotton lint (bales)	3,247	4,851	267,207	351,440
Rice (cwt.)	20,782	467	105,632	108,066
Hay (tons)	4,037	2,210	88,001	106,981
Cottonseed (tons)	1,356	...	49,951	72,546
Wheat (bu.)	54,408	2,267	86,070	70,730
Peanuts harvested for nuts (lb.)	435,000	300	46,299	53,070
Utah				
Hay (tons)	1,592	579	37,320	39,004
Wheat (bu.)	5,976	207	8,020	8,281
Barley (bu.)	7,353	129	7,327	7,647
Sugar beets (tons)	480	30	7,700	7,152
Potatoes (cwt.)	1,088	6	3,463	2,829
Vermont				
Hay (tons)	904	506	26,264	30,736
Apples (bu.)†	905	...	2,945	2,660
Maple sirup (gal.)	305	...	1,856	2,288
Potatoes (cwt.)	240	1	737	696
Virginia				
Tobacco (lb.)	126,015	68	94,533	87,437
Hay (tons)	1,778	1,054	59,500	61,341
Corn, grain (bu.)	31,144	458	42,578	46,093
Peanuts harvested for nuts (lb.)	306,000	102	31,067	41,616
Soybeans for beans (bu.)	6,441	339	21,389	18,679
Apples (bu.)†	10,714	...	17,936	17,505
Washington				
Wheat (bu.)	100,731	2,258	123,815	149,081
Apples (bu.)†	32,619	...	49,078	77,816
Hay (tons)	2,335	927	61,828	59,543
Potatoes (cwt.)	33,590	87	47,286	53,474
Pears (tons)	140	...	10,423	17,556
Sugar beets (tons)	1,260	63	25,380	18,774
West Virginia				
Hay (tons)	873	595	27,145	27,500
Apples (bu.)†	5,762	...	11,830	12,826
Corn, grain (bu.)	3,120	52	4,198	4,555
Tobacco (lb.)	3,145	2	2,433	2,217
Wheat (bu.)	462	14	533	651
Wisconsin				
Hay (tons)	10,601	4,016	197,082	196,119
Corn, grain (bu.)	143,520	1,794	162,136	193,752
Oats (bu.)	104,594	1,687	65,860	74,262
Potatoes (cwt.)	12,768	52	33,304	31,703
Soybeans for beans (bu.)	3,213	153	7,769	8,836
Wyoming				
Hay (tons)	1,853	1,213	40,296	44,472
Sugar beets (tons)	956	59	17,180	14,244
Barley (bu.)	5,922	126	5,739	5,271
Wheat (bu.)	6,259	221	5,039	7,409
Beans, dry edible (cwt.)	501	30	3,580	3,707

Increased efficiency per man-hour in agriculture

selected activities; 1957-59 = 100

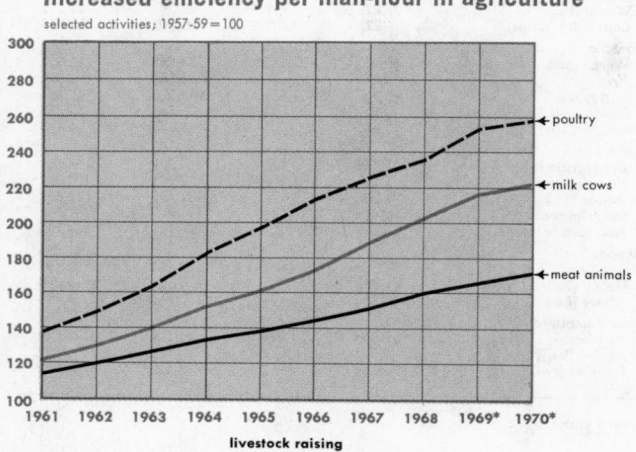

livestock raising

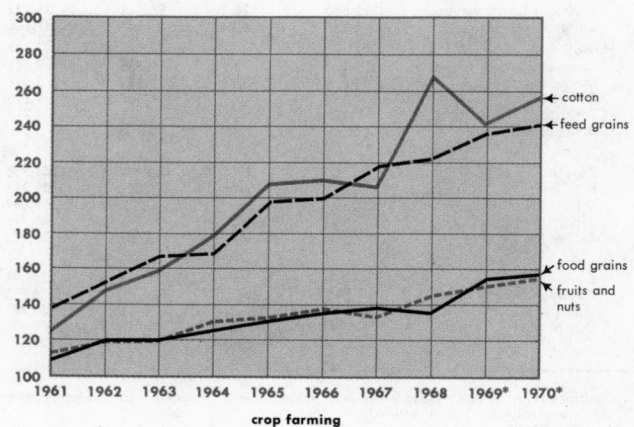

crop farming

*Preliminary. Source: U.S. Department of Agriculture, Economic Research Service.

Mining
Principal minerals produced
in the United States and each state

Mineral (unit of production)	1960 Quantity	1960 Value in $000	1969 Quantity	1969 Value in $000
UNITED STATES		18,032,000		26,928,000
Mineral fuels		12,142,000		17,965,000
Petroleum, crude (000 42-gal. bbl.)	2,574,933	7,420,181	3,371,751	10,426,680
Natural gas (000,000 cu.ft.)	12,771,038	1,789,970	20,698,240	3,455,615
Coal (000 short tons)				
Bituminous and lignite*	415,512	1,950,425	560,505	2,795,509
Pennsylvania anthracite	18,817	147,116	10,473	100,769
Natural-gas liquids (000 gal.)				
Natural gasoline and cycle products	5,842,507	416,819	8,474,928	603,084
Liquefied petroleum gases	8,444,074	391,566	15,895,194	498,927
Nonmetallic minerals, except fuels		3,868,000		5,625,000
Cement				
Portland (000 376-lb. bbl.)	321,646	1,089,134	400,883	1,284,600
Masonry (000 280-lb. bbl.)			23,253	69,106
Natural and slag (000 376-lb. bbl.)			§	
Stone† (000 short tons)	616,784	952,555	862,895	1,424,694
Sand and gravel (000 short tons)	709,792	720,432	936,906	1,070,302
Lime (000 short tons)	12,935	172,731	20,209	280,736
Salt (000 short tons)	25,479	161,140	44,245	287,680
Clays (000 short tons)	49,069	162,411	58,694	264,415
Phosphate rock (000 short tons)	19,620	117,041	37,725	208,689
Sulfur, Frasch-process mines (000 long tons)	5,003	115,494	6,551	176,659
Potassium salts, K₂O equivalent (000 short tons)	2,638	89,676	2,804	73,572
Bromine (000 lb.)	175,010	44,637	391,883	87,990
Boron minerals (000 short tons)	641	47,550	1,020	81,261
Metals		2,022,000		3,338,000
Copper, recoverable (000 short tons)	1,080	693,468	1,545	1,468,400
Iron ore, usable (000 long tons)	82,963	724,131	89,854	929,293
Zinc, recoverable (000 short tons)	435	112,365	553	161,512
Uranium (recoverable U₃O₈) (000 lb.)	7,970‡	152,188‡	23,748	142,161
Molybdenum, content of concentrate (000 lb.)	69,941	87,406	103,009	173,819
Lead, recoverable (000 short tons)	247	57,722	509	151,635
Gold (troy oz.)	1,666,772	58,336	1,733,176	71,944‖
Silver, recoverable (000 troy oz.)	30,766	27,846	41,906	75,040
Alabama [22]		221,802		284,736
Coal, bituminous (000 short tons)	13,011	92,439	17,456	130,405
Cement†				
Portland (000 376-lb. bbl.)	12,931	42,706	16,527	51,251
Masonry (000 280-lb. bbl.)			2,600	8,520
Stone (000 short tons)	13,503	19,970	19,854	37,512
Petroleum, crude (000 42-gal. bbl.)	7,329	§	7,701	20,793
Sand and gravel (000 short tons)	4,359	4,759	8,323	9,427
Iron ore, usable (000 long tons)	4,068	23,511	1,125	6,435
Lime (000 short tons)	536	6,593	747	9,870
Clays† (000 short tons)	1,840	2,170	3,097	7,083
Alaska [24]		21,860		257,776
Petroleum, crude (000 42-gal. bbl.)	559	1,230	73,953	214,464
Sand and gravel (000 short tons)	6,013	5,483	16,205	18,615
Natural gas (000,000 cu.ft.)	246	30	50,864	12,665
Arizona [8]		417,225		859,303
Copper, recoverable (000 short tons)	346	345,784	801	761,840
Sand and gravel (000 short tons)	14,490	14,235	16,481	18,066
Molybdenum (000 lb.)	4,359	5,211	12,699	20,947
Silver, recoverable (000 troy oz.)	4,775	4,322	6,141	10,992
Stone (000 short tons)	4,249	5,107	2,827	5,812
Petroleum, crude (000 42-gal. bbl.)	73	§	2,433	7,056
Arkansas [27]		159,519		208,126
Petroleum, crude (000 42-gal. bbl.)	30,117	83,424	18,049	51,079
Stone (000 short tons)	10,939	13,555	16,463	23,134
Bauxite (000 long tons)	1,932	20,469	1,755	24,706
Bromine (000 lb.)	§	§	145,100	28,287
Sand and gravel (000 short tons)	8,192	10,262	12,674	14,949
Natural gas (000,000 cu.ft.)	55,451	6,599	169,257	26,743
California [3]		1,422,087		1,850,517
Petroleum, crude (000 42-gal. bbl.)	305,352	751,166	375,291	920,060
Natural gas (000,000 cu.ft.)	517,535	138,182	677,689	207,440
Cement (000 376-lb. bbl.)	39,712†	128,826†	50,610	170,612
Sand and gravel (000 short tons)	87,679	107,503	124,718	155,883
Natural-gas liquids¶ (000 gal.)	1,203,035	83,978	890,064	57,590
Stone (000 short tons)	33,075	49,842	38,033	57,757
Boron minerals (000 short tons)	641	47,550	1,020	81,261
Mercury (76-lb. flasks)	18,764	3,955	18,480	9,333
Lime (000 short tons)	345	5,628	585	9,666
Colorado [17]		345,418		368,494
Petroleum, crude (000 42-gal. bbl.)	47,469	137,660	28,294	88,277
Molybdenum (000 lb.)	51,615	65,448	62,411	105,346
Coal, bituminous (000 short tons)	3,607	21,090	5,530	29,121
Sand and gravel (000 short tons)	19,053	16,882	19,877	27,266
Zinc, recoverable (000 short tons)	31	8,070	54	15,685
Natural gas (000,000 cu.ft.)	107,404	12,781	118,754	17,219
Uranium (recoverable U₃O₈) (000 lb.)	1,150‡	23,462‡	2,736	16,935‖
Connecticut [45]		15,353		27,767
Stone (000 short tons)	5,057	8,313	7,562	15,325
Sand and gravel (000 short tons)	6,575	5,960	8,857	10,359
Delaware [50]		989		2,086
Sand and gravel (000 short tons)	1,084	907	2,257	2,074
Florida [21]		180,286		295,377
Phosphate rock (000 long tons)	12,321	82,530	§	§
Stone† (000 short tons)	27,629	37,419	42,332	56,611
Sand and gravel (000 short tons)	6,757	5,559	14,409	13,988
Clays (000 short tons)	252†	6,357†	907	13,627
Titanium concentrate (000 short tons)	286	7,489	§	§
Georgia [29]		92,305		190,902
Clays (000 short tons)	3,519	40,160	5,670	98,462

Mineral (unit of production)	1960 Quantity	1960 Value in $000	1969 Quantity	1969 Value in $000
Georgia (continued)				
Stone (000 short tons)	14,297	37,033	27,755	59,451
Sand and gravel (000 short tons)	3,338	3,047	3,824	4,709
Hawaii [44]		9,367		29,539
Cement (000 376-lb. bbl.)	113	571	2,075	10,544
Stone (000 short tons)	3,535	6,443	6,534	16,059
Idaho [32]		57,606		118,309
Silver, recoverable (000 troy oz.)	13,647	12,351	18,930	33,897
Lead, recoverable (000 short tons)	43	10,040	66	19,541
Zinc, recoverable (000 short tons)	37	9,495	56	16,323
Phosphate rock (000 long tons)	2,177	11,044	§	§
Sand and gravel (000 short tons)	7,088	6,594	8,555	7,583
Illinois [10]		589,874		659,815
Coal, bituminous (000 short tons)	45,977	184,087	64,722	279,712
Petroleum, crude (000 42-gal. bbl.)	77,341	228,929	50,724	161,302
Stone (000 short tons)	41,721	55,593	54,857	81,318
Sand and gravel (000 short tons)	33,138	36,255	44,138	56,688
Cement				
Portland (000 376-lb. bbl.)	9,139	30,732	8,720	29,996
Masonry (000 280-lb. bbl.)			603	2,137
Natural-gas liquids (000 gal.)	374,862	21,254	16,380‖	16,760
Fluorspar (000 short tons)	134,529	6,936	88	4,676
Indiana [26]		210,932		241,871
Coal, bituminous (000 short tons)	15,538	61,570	20,086	82,902
Cement (000 bbl.)	14,052	48,310	14,497	45,264
Stone (000 short tons)	18,956	34,920	25,559	45,400
Petroleum, crude (000 42-gal. bbl.)	12,054	35,439	7,841	25,013
Sand and gravel (000 short tons)	20,752	18,377	26,218	27,438
Iowa [31]		99,319		119,930
Cement				
Portland (000 376-lb. bbl.)	12,517	44,204	14,084	47,265
Masonry (000 280-lb. bbl.)			606	1,912
Stone (000 short tons)	23,185	30,321	26,233	40,895
Sand and gravel (000 short tons)	14,692	13,516	18,391	17,867
Gypsum (000 short tons)	1,283	5,428	1,169	5,274
Kansas [15]		486,534		577,815
Petroleum, crude (000 42-gal. bbl.)	113,453	329,014	88,716	283,891
Natural gas (000,000 cu.ft.)	634,410	74,226	883,156	122,759
Helium¶ (000,000 cu.ft.)	21,696	350	2,999	40,245
Cement				
Portland (000 376-lb. bbl.)	8,162	26,373	9,764	29,365
Masonry (000 280-lb. bbl.)			348	1,023
Stone (000 short tons)	11,814†	15,031†	15,828	22,645
Natural-gas liquids¶ (000 gal.)	243,138	13,037	1,026,018	38,077
Salt (000 short tons)	1,213	14,109	1,270†	17,090†
Kentucky [13]		414,553		591,048
Coal, bituminous (000 short tons)	66,846	282,395	109,049	450,950
Petroleum, crude (000 42-gal. bbl.)	21,147	60,268	12,924	40,194
Stone (000 short tons)	15,810	21,493	30,158†	44,644†
Natural gas (000,000 cu.ft.)	75,329	18,380	81,304	20,407
Sand and gravel (000 short tons)	5,113	5,763	8,364	9,628
Louisiana [2]		1,990,895		4,685,326
Petroleum, crude (000 42-gal. bbl.)	400,832	1,258,138	844,603	2,791,269
Natural gas (000,000 cu.ft.)	2,988,414	511,019	7,227,826	1,387,743
Natural-gas liquids				
Natural gasoline (000 gal.)	875,567	66,214	2,249,730	171,434
Petroleum gases, liquefied (000 gal.)	606,023	28,147	3,018,414	96,302
Sulfur, Frasch-process mines (000 long tons)	2,256	52,639	3,999	108,299
Salt (000 short tons)	4,792	21,959	12,435	61,102
Sand and gravel (000 short tons)	14,319	19,106	18,131	21,895
Maine [47]		14,108		20,188
Sand and gravel (000 short tons)	9,833	3,892	11,275	6,026
Stone (000 short tons)	1,012	3,851	1,101	3,798
Maryland [36]		57,697		83,483
Stone (000 short tons)	7,944	16,962	15,067	30,504
Sand and gravel (000 short tons)	10,076	13,221	14,230	21,226
Coal, bituminous (000 short tons)	748	2,799	1,368	5,261
Massachusetts [43]		28,245		49,843
Sand and gravel (000 short tons)	14,789	13,013	19,456	22,950
Stone (000 short tons)	5,247	12,782	7,847	22,521
Michigan [9]		437,598		668,247
Iron ore, usable (000 long tons)	10,792	95,791	14,058	169,756
Cement				
Portland (000 376-lb. bbl.)	22,361	77,694	30,373	98,425
Masonry (000 280-lb. bbl.)			1,904	5,473
Copper, recoverable (000 short tons)	56	36,199	75	71,516
Sand and gravel (000 short tons)	46,910	39,304	58,092	58,968
Petroleum, crude (000 42-gal. bbl.)	15,899	46,266	12,213	37,494
Stone (000 short tons)	31,256	32,274	39,186	43,572
Salt (000 short tons)	4,088	33,759	4,819	45,961
Magnesium compounds, MgO equivalent (000 short tons)	§	§	328	30,604
Lime (000 short tons)	1,177	15,730	1,589	20,372
Minnesota [12]		515,521		635,636
Iron ore, usable (000 long tons)	54,723	470,874	56,957	570,446
Sand and gravel (000 short tons)	30,302	24,611	48,121	40,191
Stone (000 short tons)	4,234	10,034	5,035	14,253
Manganiferous ore (000 short tons)	441	§	381	§
Mississippi [25]		199,210		243,184
Petroleum, crude (000 42-gal. bbl.)	51,673	146,235	64,283	187,514
Natural gas (000,000 cu.ft.)	172,478	32,426	131,234	23,097
Sand and gravel (000 short tons)	6,181	5,568	11,484	12,263
Missouri [18]		162,244		367,232
Stone (000 short tons)	27,180	37,878	41,977	63,251

Principal minerals produced (continued)

Mineral	(unit of production)	1960 Quantity	1960 Value in $000	1969 Quantity	1969 Value in $000
Missouri (continued)					
Cement					
Portland	(000 376-lb. bbl.)	12,183	42,330	21,325	74,368
Masonry	(000 280-lb. bbl.)			427	1,319
Lead, recoverable	(000 short tons)	112	26,196	355	105,889
Iron ore, usable	(000 long tons)	365	3,760	2,622	35,826
Lime	(000 short tons)	1,254	14,701	§	§
Sand and gravel	(000 short tons)	10,207	11,601	10,940	14,574
Coal, bituminous	(000 short tons)	2,890	12,450	3,301	14,283
Montana [23]			179,406		282,631
Petroleum, crude	(000 42-gal. bbl.)	30,240	72,878	43,954	118,359
Copper, recoverable	(000 short tons)	92	59,046	103	98,219
Sand and gravel	(000 short tons)	12,589	11,657	16,595	14,383
Stone	(000 short tons)	1,183	1,576	7,667	10,579
Silver, recoverable	(000 troy oz.)	3,607	3,265	3,429	6,141
Nebraska [39]			103,942		78,030
Petroleum, crude	(000 42-gal. bbl.)	23,825	68,378	12,106	36,075
Sand and gravel	(000 short tons)	10,876	8,746	12,758	13,592
Stone	(000 short tons)	3,336	5,651	4,665	9,494
Natural gas	(000,000 cu. ft.)	15,258	2,670	6,989	1,209
Natural-gas liquids¶	(000 gal.)	§	§	22,512	1,125
Nevada [30]			80,892		168,295
Copper, recoverable	(000 short tons)	77	49,745	105	99,749
Sand and gravel	(000 short tons)	4,085	5,224	8,447	10,834
Iron ore, usable	(000 long tons)	740	3,683	§	§
Gold	(troy oz.)	58,187	2,037	456,294	18,941
Mercury	(76-lb. flasks)	7,821	1,648	8,165	4,124
New Hampshire [48]			5,439		8,120
Sand and gravel	(000 short tons)	6,621	3,687	6,310	5,149
Stone	(000 short tons)	104	594	320	2,888
New Jersey [37]			56,469		83,107
Stone	(000 short tons)	10,202	22,814	15,162	34,034
Sand and gravel	(000 short tons)	11,594	19,511	20,325	33,977
Zinc, recoverable	(000 short tons)	—	—	25	7,322‖
Clays	(000 short tons)	664	1,597	327	1,123
New Mexico [7]			653,766		935,746
Petroleum, crude	(000 42-gal. bbl.)	107,380	305,895	129,227	404,441
Potash, K_2O equivalent	(000 short tons)	2,440	82,645	2,327	62,034
Natural gas	(000,000 cu.ft.)	798,928	85,485	1,138,133	155,924
Copper, recoverage	(000 short tons)	67	43,199	120	114,040
Natural-gas liquids¶	(000 gal.)	966,783	49,200	1,426,866	54,790
Uranium (U_3O_8)	(000 lb.)	3,793‡	61,827‡	11,811	69,887‖
Coal, bituminous	(000 short tons)	295	1,747	4,471	16,376
New York [20]			260,922		302,339
Stone	(000 short tons)	29,802	46,955	37,561	66,839
Sand and gravel	(000 short tons)	30,687	35,152	39,806	42,518
Salt	(000 short tons)	4,008	30,763	5,582	45,561
Zinc, recoverable	(000 short tons)	66	17,122	59	17,149
North Carolina [34]			45,096		90,455
Stone	(000 short tons)	14,721	23,296	26,812	47,829
Sand and gravel	(000 short tons)	8,801	7,453	10,562	11,437
Feldspar	(000 long tons)	271	2,781	§	§
Clays†	(000 short tons)	2,476	1,548	3,342	2,610
Mica, scrap	(000 short tons)	47	1,100	67	1,513
North Dakota [33]			78,378		91,048
Petroleum, crude	(000 42-gal. bbl.)	21,992	59,598	22,703	63,568
Sand and gravel	(000 short tons)	8,648	6,904	7,039	7,274
Natural gas	(000,000 cu.ft.)	19,483	2,221	33,587	5,441
Coal, lignite	(000 short tons)	2,525	5,790	4,704	8,696
Natural-gas liquids	(000 gal.)	§	§	103,278	4,214
Ohio [14]			406,142		580,667
Coal, bituminous	(000 short tons)	33,957	130,877	51,242	210,082
Stone	(000 short tons)	35,856	59,479	51,792	86,570
Cement					
Portland	(000 376-lb. bbl.)	17,480	61,478	15,100	50,071
Masonry	(000 280-lb. bbl.)			1,123	3,527
Lime	(000 short tons)	3,117	44,403	4,159	60,975
Petroleum, crude	(000 42-gal. bbl.)	5,405	16,053	10,972	36,098
Sand and gravel	(000 short tons)	37,943	44,979	49,160	63,361
Salt	(000 short tons)	3,108	24,149	5,844	43,519
Clays	(000 short tons)	5,165	14,325	4,587	11,693
Natural gas	(000,000 cu.ft.)	36,074	8,477	49,793	12,837
Oklahoma [4]			782,579		1,090,809
Petroleum, crude	(000 42-gal. bbl.)	192,913	563,306	224,729	701,115
Natural gas	(000,000 cu.ft.)	824,266	98,088	1,523,715	233,128
Natural-gas liquids					
Natural gasoline	(000 gal.)	531,995	33,074	614,082	38,931
Petroleum gases, liquefied	(000 gal.)	762,258	32,409	1,146,768	34,403
Stone	(000 short tons)	14,054†	16,098†	18,799	23,650
Helium¶	(000 cu.ft.)	289,068	4,691	353,400	8,840
Coal, bituminous	(000 short tons)	1,342	9,113	1,838	10,662
Oregon [40]			55,772		60,164
Sand and gravel	(000 short tons)	17,673	16,170	15,740	20,491
Stone	(000 short tons)	16,913	19,721	11,662	18,897
Nickel, content of ore	(000 short tons)	13	5,246	17	§
Lime	(000 short tons)	§	§	115	2,337
Pennsylvania [5]			838,146		976,367
Coal					
Bituminous	(000 short tons)	65,425	345,971	78,631	461,579
Anthracite	(000 short tons)	18,817	147,116	10,473	100,769
Cement					
Portland	(000 376-lb. bbl.)	38,320	131,763	44,893	126,941
Masonry	(000 280-lb. bbl.)			3,085	8,504
Pennsylvania (continued)					
Stone	(000 short tons)	42,136	74,168	66,992	117,726
Sand and gravel	(000 short tons)	13,011	21,204	18,105	31,451
Natural gas	(000,000 cu.ft.)	113,928	36,229	79,134	21,841
Petroleum, crude	(000 42-gal. bbl.)	6,009	27,341	4,448	20,086
Lime	(000 short tons)	1,120	16,277	2,008	28,952
Clays†	(000 short tons)	3,557	16,536	2,727	19,637
Rhode Island [49]			5,727		4,433
Sand and gravel	(000 short tons)	1,535	1,355	§	4,433
Stone	(000 short tons)	1,810	4,372		
South Carolina [41]			30,987		55,864
Stone	(000 short tons)	7,327	10,593	8,846	13,506
Clays	(000 short tons)	1,297	6,201	2,444	10,911
Sand and gravel	(000 short tons)	3,029	3,048	5,692	8,229
South Dakota [42]			47,675		54,921
Gold	(troy oz.)	554,771	19,417	593,146	24,621
Stone	(000 short tons)	3,149	7,909	2,092	10,839
Sand and gravel	(000 short tons)	13,548	9,359	11,158	10,807
Cement					
Portland	(000 376-lb. bbl.)	§	§	1,556	5,715
Masonry	(000 280-lb. bbl.)	§	§	49	181
Tennessee [28]			145,538		205,451
Stone	(000 short tons)	20,074	29,942	33,265†	46,192†
Zinc, recoverable	(000 short tons)	91	23,579	125	36,363
Cement					
Portland	(000 376-lb. bbl.)	8,246	27,384	9,159	29,403
Masonry	(000 280-lb. bbl.)			1,331	3,587
Coal, bituminous	(000 short tons)	5,930	21,154	8,082	30,687
Phosphate rock	(000 short tons)	2,172	15,424	§	§
Sand and gravel	(000 short tons)	6,293	7,655	6,175	9,709
Copper, recoverable	(000 short tons)	13	8,168	15	14,596
Texas [1]			4,126,419		5,769,970
Petroleum, crude	(000 42-gal. bbl.)	927,479	2,748,735	1,151,755	3,696,328
Natural gas	(000,000 cu.ft.)	5,892,704	665,876	7,853,199	1,075,888
Natural-gas liquids					
Natural gasoline	(000 gal.)	2,880,906	207,583	4,058,376	289,042
Petroleum gases, liquefied	(000 gal.)	4,476,142	200,478	8,173,158	237,411
Cement					
Portland	(000 376-lb. bbl.)	23,365	76,577	36,037	117,989
Masonry	(000 280-lb. bbl.)			1,110	3,873
Sulfur, Frasch-process mines	(000 long tons)	2,747	62,855	2,552	68,360
Stone	(000 short tons)	39,029	45,088	46,638	64,986
Sand and gravel	(000 short tons)	29,844	30,754	29,972	39,756
Salt	(000 short tons)	4,756	18,222	9,261	43,012
Lime	(000 short tons)	821	9,087	1,633	22,107
Helium¶	(000 cu.ft.)	120,921	2,044	1,130,800	17,970
Utah [16]			432,712		543,282
Copper, recoverable	(000 short tons)	218	139,987	297	282,066
Petroleum, crude	(000 42-gal. bbl.)	37,594	103,008	23,295	65,320
Coal, bituminous	(000 short tons)	4,955	31,458	4,657	29,396
Iron ore, usable	(000 long tons)	3,334	23,862	1,921	12,552
Lead, recoverable	(000 short tons)	39	9,219	41	12,313
Gold	(troy oz.)	368,255	12,889	433,385	17,990
Sand and gravel	(000 short tons)	6,848	6,182	19,151	16,835
Vermont [46]			22,903		27,759
Stone	(000 short tons)	2,114	17,444	2,151	19,810
Sand and gravel	(000 short tons)	1,809	1,218	3,336	3,028
Virginia [19]			208,880		317,527
Coal, bituminous	(000 short tons)	27,838	122,723	35,555	192,802
Stone	(000 short tons)	19,358	33,019	33,461	58,713
Sand and gravel	(000 short tons)	7,666	11,432	12,140	15,954
Lime	(000 short tons)	711	8,028	1,072	13,653
Zinc, recoverable	(000 short tons)	20	5,142	19	5,462‖
Washington [35]			72,404		88,626
Sand and gravel	(000 short tons)	25,594	19,459	34,245	31,046
Cement					
Portland	(000 376-lb. bbl.)	§	§	6,356	22,724
Masonry	(000 280-lb. bbl.)	§	§	58	204
Stone	(000 short tons)	13,897	15,796	15,742	21,069
Zinc, recoverable	(000 short tons)	21	5,500	10	2,843
Lead, recoverable	(000 short tons)	8	1,808	9	2,577
West Virginia [6]			722,628		948,430
Coal	(000 short tons)	118,944	597,222	141,011	807,811
Natural gas	(000,000 cu.ft.)	208,757	54,694	231,759	62,575
Natural-gas liquids	(000 gal.)	353,085	18,040	§	§
Stone	(000 short tons)	8,001	14,001	9,031†	15,801†
Petroleum, crude	(000 42-gal. bbl.)	2,300	9,361	3,104	11,888
Sand and gravel	(000 short tons)	4,506	9,802	5,890	12,666
Wisconsin [38]			78,760		79,792
Sand and gravel	(000 short tons)	35,681	25,648	42,815	35,414
Stone	(000 short tons)	16,486	22,302	18,954	27,571
Zinc, recoverable	(000 short tons)	18	4,750	23	6,687
Wyoming [11]			439,256		647,443
Petroleum, crude	(000 42-gal. bbl.)	133,910	336,114	154,945	433,846
Natural gas	(000,000 cu.ft.)	181,610	21,793	303,517	44,617
Uranium (U_3O_8)	(000 lb.)	1,357‡	27,387‡	6,716	40,318‖
Iron ore, usable	(000 long tons)	§	§	2,048	20,751
Clays	(000 short tons)	788	9,571	1,992	18,970
Coal, bituminous	(000 short tons)	2,024	6,992	4,602	15,443

Figure in brackets is the rank of the state by value of 1969 mineral production.
Boldface type indicates the state that leads in value of production for that mineral.
Production is measured by mine shipments, sales, or marketable production (including consumption by producers).
*Includes small quantity of anthracite mined in states other than Pennsylvania. †Excludes certain varieties.

‡Short tons of uranium ore. §Figure withheld to avoid disclosing confidential data. ‖Estimated.
¶For cement, portland and masonry figures combined; for helium, grade A and crude figures combined; for natural-gas liquids, natural gasoline, cycle products, and liquefied petroleum gases combined.
Source: U.S. Department of the Interior, Bureau of Mines.

(F. H. Sk.)

Forestry and Fisheries

Lumber production

in millions of board feet

Kind of wood	1960	1965	1968*
Softwoods	26,672	29,295	30,223
Cedar	...	633	618
Douglas fir	8,832	8,783	8,955
Hemlock	2,032	2,576	2,408
Ponderosa pine	3,169	3,776	3,981
Redwood	1,000	1,087	1,051
Southern yellow pine	5,660	6,628	6,901
Spruce	471	641	757
White fir	2,224	2,422	2,591
White pine	...	1,151	1,111
Other softwoods	675	1,134	1,284
Hardwoods†	6,254	7,467	7,227
Ash	125	141	132
Basswood	92	87	68
Beech	195	182	157
Cottonwood and aspen	206	198	190
Elm	195	206	210
Maple	602	786	700
Oak	2,789	3,356	3,318
Sweet (red and sap) gum	331	387	364
Tupelo and black gum	292	385	335
Yellow poplar	592	681	662
Other hardwoods†	709	788	996
TOTAL	32,926	36,762	37,450

*Preliminary.
†Includes estimate for western hardwoods, not reported by species.
Source: U.S. Department of Commerce, Bureau of the Census, *Current Industrial Reports*; and U.S. Department of Agriculture, Forest Service.

Power

Electric utilities

State	Number of utilities having generating plants	Number of generating plants*	Total generating capacity in kw.	SALES OF ELECTRIC ENERGY in 000 kw-hrs. 1968	1969
Alabama	5	31	9,614,718	28,182,704	32,541,291
Alaska	26	53	335,883	842,247	948,878
Arizona	10	32	3,942,500	10,699,490	12,463,311
Arkansas	14	31	2,721,812	11,578,308	12,624,314
California	26	220	27,646,580	104,561,271	111,392,223
Colorado	31	73	2,760,083	9,039,350	9,892,026
Connecticut	10	46	3,625,850	13,818,177	15,068,065
Delaware	4	13	822,733	3,872,299	4,304,866
District of Columbia	2	4	1,114,550	†	†
Florida	26	81	12,139,638	39,716,115	44,811,037
Georgia	6	41	5,649,865	25,609,757	28,590,237
Hawaii	6	16	865,087	3,132,081	3,445,770
Idaho	10	42	1,260,570	9,863,484	10,211,025
Illinois	41	99	16,003,618	61,206,358	66,342,325
Indiana	21	55	9,930,613	33,187,166	36,490,116
Iowa	94	176	3,435,859	13,197,301	14,360,106
Kansas	80	125	3,401,829	11,895,690	12,945,139
Kentucky	10	29	7,960,674	28,322,251	29,966,468
Louisiana	29	63	6,576,956	24,025,994	26,984,301
Maine	15	66	886,223	4,459,407	4,805,851
Maryland	11	28	4,274,127	22,959,102†	25,250,079†
Massachusetts	23	71	5,946,657	21,250,915	22,924,211
Michigan	48	161	10,830,259	49,939,202	53,935,627
Minnesota	73	161	3,845,611	17,378,637	19,187,318
Mississippi	10	23	2,125,586	12,300,928	13,497,652
Missouri	62	94	6,836,112	22,345,190	24,201,234
Montana	8	29	1,831,930	7,433,147	8,786,595
Nebraska	66	96	2,010,148	6,777,808	8,592,581
Nevada	7	26	1,519,245	4,749,775	5,398,883
New Hampshire	6	27	1,144,312	3,028,745	3,310,857
New Jersey	8	34	8,198,048	32,600,535	35,636,828
New Mexico	16	27	2,705,988	4,771,017	5,207,773
New York	29	196	19,934,862	77,482,342	83,590,370
North Carolina	22	74	8,901,100	33,749,162	37,294,223
North Dakota	14	39	1,116,948	2,389,225	2,569,319
Ohio	35	92	15,616,090	77,273,583	82,200,598
Oklahoma	27	65	4,230,898	13,510,030	15,169,143
Oregon	19	60	5,008,023	22,857,588	24,592,350
Pennsylvania	19	95	16,534,343	66,167,918	71,744,920
Rhode Island	6	11	397,125	3,412,938	3,686,411
South Carolina	9	54	3,339,499	18,148,322	19,924,045
South Dakota	30	57	1,717,830	2,431,287	2,591,239
Tennessee	5	35	9,437,838	48,083,103	50,432,509
Texas	58	169	22,095,230	77,642,102	88,909,161
Utah	25	76	792,929	4,430,232	4,932,881
Vermont	12	60	303,265	2,059,077	2,345,533
Virginia	18	48	6,256,004	25,493,740	28,445,983
Washington	21	66	12,068,105	42,175,078	47,646,633
West Virginia	9	20	5,814,134	14,190,093	15,308,447
Wisconsin	45	161	5,948,166	21,641,395	23,323,273
Wyoming	15	39	1,136,184	3,261,661	3,581,771
TOTAL U.S.	1,105†	3,490	312,612,237	1,199,143,327	1,312,405,796

Figures for number of utilities and plants and total capacity are preliminary as of Jan. 1, 1970. *Each prime mover at combination plants is counted as a plant. †District of Columbia included with Maryland. ‡Adjusted to exclude duplications because of utilities with generating plants in more than one state.
Source: Federal Power Commission.

Commercial fishing

1969 catch, by states

State	Quantity in 000 lb.	Value in $000	State	Quantity in 000 lb.	Value in $000
Alabama*	34,200	11,100	Montana	...	...
Alaska	346,800	71,100	Nebraska	...	...
Arizona	...	...	New Hampshire	1,500	900
Arkansas	...	...	New Jersey	92,500	10,900
California	575,900	62,100	New Mexico	...	...
Connecticut	4,900	1,800	New York*	39,900	13,600
Delaware	600	200	North Carolina	219,000	12,100
Florida	181,400	40,900	North Dakota	...	...
Georgia	15,400	6,300	Ohio*	9,600	900
Hawaii	9,700	3,400	Oklahoma	...	...
Idaho	...	...	Oregon	82,600	16,000
Illinois	...	...	Pennsylvania	...	...
Indiana	...	...	Rhode Island	81,700	5,200
Iowa	...	...	South Carolina	20,900	5,400
Kansas	...	...	South Dakota	...	...
Kentucky	...	...	Tennessee	...	...
Louisiana*	1,016,500	56,700	Texas*	160,800	46,900
Maine	191,300	27,500	Utah	...	...
Maryland	72,000	17,900	Virginia	277,700	17,800
Massachusetts	280,000	41,900	Washington	142,400	26,200
Michigan	20,800	2,700	Wisconsin	41,800	2,400
Minnesota	...	...	—†	62,600	5,700
Mississippi*	310,000	10,900			
Missouri	...	...	Total U.S.	4,292,500	518,500

Preliminary data. *Catch in interior waters estimated. †Estimated catch for states for which data not available. Source: U.S. Department of the Interior, Fish and Wildlife Service.

Commercial fishing

principal species caught

Species	QUANTITY in 000 lb. 5-year average 1963–67	1968	1969
TOTAL	4,517,019	4,116,100	4,292,500
Menhaden	1,516,654	1,380,900	1,547,700
Tuna	308,774	293,840	323,041
Shrimp*	248,555	291,600	317,100
Salmon, Pacific	315,808	327,700	246,200
Crabs	307,064	238,500	234,800
Flounder	125,662	112,900	117,500
Alewives	76,951	88,000	85,200
Herring, sea	120,878	107,500	82,700
Clams†	65,687	66,200	75,500
Cod, Atlantic	41,063	48,600	58,100
Ocean perch, Atlantic	86,826	61,500	55,800
Jack mackerel	66,179	57,400	51,900
Oysters†	59,117	55,600	51,900
Whiting	85,880	77,900	46,300
Haddock	124,405	71,300	46,200
Lobsters	34,498	39,800	39,500
Halibut, Pacific	40,423	25,700	33,400
Mullet	39,641	30,500	31,400

Preliminary data. *Heads-on. †Weight of meats, excluding shell. Source: U.S. Department of the Interior Fish and Wildlife Service.

Mineral fuels and electricity production

in trillions of British thermal units

Year	Total production	MINERAL FUELS Bituminous coal and lignite	Anthracite	Crude petroleum	Natural gas, wet (unprocessed)	ELECTRICITY* Hydro-power	Nuclear power
1960	41,704	10,886	478	14,935	13,822	1,578	5
1961	42,499	10,558	443	15,185	14,691	1,605	17
1962	44,146	11,060	429	15,495	15,365	1,774	23
1963	46,274	12,024	464	15,741	16,271	1,741	33
1964	47,836	12,759	436	15,690	17,056	1,861	34
1965	49,467	13,417	378	15,930	17,652	2,051	39
1966	52,256	13,988	329	16,925	18,894	2,062	58
1967	55,400	14,479	311	18,098	20,087	2,344	81
1968§	57,379	14,279	291	18,953	21,372	2,352	132
1969†	59,226	14,569	277	18,780	22,772	2,687	141

The fuel equivalent of hydropower and nuclear power is calculated from the kilowatt-hours of power produced, converted to coal input equivalent, at the prevailing average pounds of coal per kilowatt-hour each year at central electric plants, using 12,000 BTU per pound.
*Includes installations owned by manufacturing plants and mines, as well as government and privately owned public utilities. †Preliminary. §Revised.
Source: U.S. Department of the Interior, Bureau of Mines. (F. H. Sk.)

Manufacturing

Principal manufacturing industries

in the United States and each state

Industry	EMPLOYEES 1963	EMPLOYEES 1967	VALUE ADDED BY MANUFACTURE* in $000 1963	VALUE ADDED BY MANUFACTURE* in $000 1967
United States§	16,960,983	19,398,000	192,103,102	259,301,000
Transportation equipment	1,601,158	1,890,000	22,765,674	28,901,000
Motor vehicles and equipment	693,821	781,000	12,780,577	14,266,000
Aircraft and parts	679,385	824,000	7,867,349	11,602,000
Nonelectrical machinery	1,459,377	1,872,000	17,310,599	27,697,000
Metalworking machinery	259,002	347,000	3,037,659	5,154,000
General industrial machinery	233,143	283,000	2,812,672	4,212,000
Construction machinery	210,959	260,000	2,732,269	3,854,000
Office and computing machines	137,138	197,000	1,633,690	3,644,000
Food and kindred products	1,643,111	1,654,000	21,825,516	26,352,000
Beverages	204,621	221,000	3,724,834	4,848,000
Canned and frozen foods	244,824	263,000	2,778,810	3,627,000
Bakery products	280,144	269,000	3,030,822	3,475,000
Dairy products	256,828	238,000	3,184,867	3,517,000
Meat products	299,576	305,000	2,882,580	3,414,000
Electrical machinery	1,511,819	1,884,000	17,010,665	24,855,000
Communication equipment	476,849	523,000	5,341,463	6,913,000
Electronic components	288,527	396,000	2,508,117	4,517,000
Electrical industrial apparatus	160,953	215,000	1,889,181	2,865,000
Chemicals and allied products	737,414	854,000	17,586,138	23,440,000
Industrial chemicals	236,652	252,000	6,171,182	7,685,000
Plastics materials and synthetics	144,713	177,000	2,865,399	3,887,000
Drugs	99,001	119,000	2,807,331	3,999,000
Cleaning and toilet goods	85,572	97,000	2,866,446	3,848,000
Primary metal industries	1,126,536	1,283,000	15,261,089	20,148,000
Blast furnace and basic steel products	568,849	619,000	8,617,266	10,424,000
Nonferrous rolling and drawing	167,005	195,000	2,127,688	3,291,000
Iron and steel foundries	199,635	237,000	1,959,949	2,701,000
Fabricated metal products	1,082,102	1,307,000	11,791,081	17,054,000
Structural metal products	325,470	374,000	3,219,813	4,513,000
Printing and publishing	913,243	1,064,000	10,476,433	14,155,000
Newspapers	306,439	350,000	3,201,872	4,291,000
Commercial printing	300,309	351,000	2,961,069	3,919,000
Paper and allied products	588,014	643,000	7,395,677	9,676,000
Apparel and related products	1,279,534	1,363,000	7,861,011	9,693,000
Women's and misses' outerwear	405,466	425,000	2,459,739	3,137,000
Stone, clay, and glass products	573,859	605,000	7,043,987	8,408,000
Textile mill products	863,246	931,000	6,122,982	8,003,000
Rubber and plastics products†	414,959	504,000	4,653,953	6,474,000
Instruments and related products	305,452	377,000	3,992,131	6,063,000
Lumber and wood products	563,135	563,000	4,020,600	4,828,000
Petroleum and coal products	153,486	140,000	3,713,231	5,356,000
Petroleum refining	119,297	106,000	3,137,603	4,685,000
Furniture and fixtures	376,548	429,000	3,068,287	4,041,000
Ordnance and accessories‡	245,934	377,000	2,882,521	5,044,000
Leather and leather products	327,489	332,000	2,078,572	2,577,000
Tobacco manufactures	77,330	75,000	1,680,594	2,011,000
Alabama§	243,800	289,300	2,518,314	3,508,200
Primary metal industries	40,078	44,600	693,292	630,200
Blast furnace and basic steel products	21,774	22,500	494,292	364,600
Textile mill products	35,474	40,200	219,338	322,700
Chemicals and allied products	8,490	11,800	216,531	412,700
Paper and allied products	11,675	15,000	165,574	319,200
Food and kindred products	22,420	23,200	203,421	256,000
Alaska	5,809	7,600	84,954	130,400
Food and kindred products	2,860	3,800	39,819	52,600
Arizona	57,039	76,800	627,141	995,300
Electrical machinery	9,131	19,000	86,431	234,200
Electronic components	5,776	13,000	48,687	147,300
Nonelectrical machinery	5,771	13,600	51,324	199,000
Arkansas§	113,658	143,400	960,886	1,524,300
Food and kindred products	17,878	21,500	155,929	260,800
Lumber and wood products	21,198	19,600	119,830	140,300
Paper and allied products	7,224	7,400	118,853	150,100
Electrical machinery	7,619	11,600	79,169	150,700
California§	1,398,611	1,584,600	17,162,564	23,416,000
Transportation equipment	202,090	. . .	2,665,830	. . .
Food and kindred products	155,731	160,600	2,412,559	2,996,300
Canned and frozen foods	51,619	51,500	656,233	789,800
Electrical machinery	187,965	213,800	2,192,114	2,960,100
Communication equipment	96,738	97,500	1,166,416	1,464,400
Ordnance and accessories‡	136,447	. . .	1,743,355	. . .
Nonelectrical machinery	93,308	122,400	1,086,421	1,778,400
Fabricated metal products	88,535	108,000	1,036,525	1,556,100
Chemicals and allied products	35,703	42,400	809,488	1,118,500
Printing and publishing	74,407	82,300	846,820	1,180,900
Colorado	93,722	104,000	1,193,828	1,509,200
Nonelectrical machinery	5,172	11,200	65,722	254,100
Food and kindred products	18,597	18,700	252,251	310,700
Primary metal products	7,642	8,200	91,813	109,500
Electrical machinery	3,486	8,000	43,322	105,700
Connecticut	419,412	477,700	4,495,878	6,389,800
Transportation equipment	84,784	103,200	898,047	1,444,300
Aircraft and parts	65,193	. . .	706,556	. . .
Nonelectrical machinery	58,587	68,800	684,061	974,200
Electrical machinery	43,302	48,800	483,694	639,000
Fabricated metal products	40,334	49,000	422,235	627,200
Primary metal industries	25,865	28,100	321,769	474,600
Nonferrous rolling and drawing	15,250	15,900	192,859	292,500
Delaware	58,395	70,700	658,189	958,400
Food and kindred products	6,124	8,700	54,634	156,500
Fabricated metal products	1,617	1,800	20,768	22,700
Primary metal industries	2,282	2,500	19,371	23,100
District of Columbia	22,147	23,100	256,813	332,800
Printing and publishing	13,153	14,800	162,058	229,000
Newspapers	4,789	4,900	55,591	69,800
Florida	215,447	285,100	2,351,973	3,682,700
Food and kindred products	39,593	44,300	499,694	627,200
Chemicals and allied products	18,143	20,700	346,897	466,100
Paper and allied products	13,594	16,300	204,604	290,900
Electrical machinery	15,125	24,400	153,347	280,100
Fabricated metal products	14,459	19,600	137,556	225,500
Transportation equipment	16,667	25,000	132,541	265,600
Georgia	354,023	423,100	3,254,007	4,683,600
Textile mill products	93,482	109,200	618,226	990,600
Transportation equipment	30,357	43,900	514,266	741,800
Food and kindred products	41,949	45,700	441,953	557,400
Paper and allied products	20,484	22,800	339,327	436,700
Apparel and related products	57,145	66,500	323,163	413,300
Hawaii	25,144	25,400	261,147	326,200
Food and kindred products	15,231	14,200	166,986	185,400
Canned and frozen foods	7,502	7,100	63,012	69,600
Idaho§	30,487	37,400	366,411	510,300
Food and kindred products	9,881	12,200	111,086	143,500
Lumber and wood products	10,288	11,000	88,581	122,300
Illinois§	1,210,802	1,397,200	14,640,121	20,004,700
Nonelectrical machinery	178,573	224,800	2,264,672	3,445,200
Construction and like equipment	52,590	63,100	735,987	1,022,900
Electrical machinery	167,834	211,200	1,806,838	2,455,700
Food and kindred products	116,063	120,500	2,059,037	2,521,600
Fabricated metal products	121,879	146,200	1,366,458	1,997,500
Primary metal industries	97,851	108,300	1,176,747	1,644,600
Printing and publishing	95,476	106,900	1,197,739	1,581,700
Chemicals and allied products	47,468	53,500	1,218,465	1,544,000
Indiana	609,840	710,200	7,726,942	10,308,000
Primary metal industries	93,613	110,000	1,456,412	1,817,900
Blast furnace and basic steel products	59,295	66,900	1,056,396	1,123,000
Electrical machinery	91,105	118,600	1,125,703	1,601,600
Transportation equipment	91,203	96,000	1,119,585	1,361,000
Motor vehicles and equipment	60,226	58,000	775,522	889,100
Nonelectrical machinery	54,501	71,000	678,261	1,005,800
Chemicals and allied products	22,185	24,700	597,366	833,300
Iowa	178,199	210,100	2,287,001	3,250,900
Food and kindred products	50,356	49,200	653,155	816,800
Meat products	25,659	25,300	281,560	338,800
Nonelectrical machinery	35,496	46,400	476,926	753,100
Farm machinery and equipment	21,605	24,200	287,319	387,000
Electrical machinery	19,635	26,900	252,644	373,500
Kansas	114,288	143,800	1,460,374	2,112,400
Transportation equipment	34,610	49,000	446,673	625,800
Food and kindred products	21,225	18,800	239,227	277,800
Chemicals and allied products	6,224	10,100	179,704	276,300
Petroleum and coal products	3,954	3,600	115,621	179,700
Nonelectrical machinery	8,486	14,200	97,032	174,000
Kentucky	180,460	224,600	2,548,531	3,636,000
Food and kindred products	23,849	23,000	444,202	513,300
Beverages	10,003	10,500	288,516	338,800
Electrical machinery	21,319	31,400	350,172	549,100
Nonelectrical machinery	16,156	22,500	231,352	467,500
Chemicals and allied products	11,189	13,300	273,669	391,600
Louisiana	139,511	164,500	1,915,625	2,790,300
Chemicals and allied products	15,629	19,100	435,387	679,500
Industrial chemicals	10,865	13,600	308,005	509,800
Food and kindred products	29,588	29,600	367,891	455,000
Petroleum and coal products	11,126	9,900	273,562	345,500
Petroleum refining	10,004	9,000	258,454	326,900
Maine	99,926	110,800	785,730	1,069,500
Paper and allied products	16,537	18,100	232,399	276,800
Paper mills, except building	13,526	14,600	190,688	224,600
Leather and leather products	24,699	28,000	135,204	197,900
Maryland	263,672	287,600	3,001,468	3,781,300
Primary metal industries	36,035	36,900	509,289	524,600
Food and kindred products	35,881	35,400	419,836	525,600
Chemicals and allied products	14,227	17,600	298,182	422,500
Transportation equipment	31,671	30,700	403,388	460,500
Electrical machinery	26,871	32,200	312,625	367,200
Massachusetts	674,023	713,600	6,403,789	8,715,000
Electrical machinery	96,183	106,900	985,805	1,337,000
Nonelectrical machinery	67,673	78,700	714,596	1,237,800
Fabricated metal products	39,608	43,700	450,999	622,400
Instruments and related products	28,431	35,000	343,078	612,800
Printing and publishing	40,578	44,700	439,640	589,200
Michigan§	961,090	1,137,600	13,090,328	17,243,700
Transportation equipment	281,870	313,400	5,090,843	5,825,100
Motor vehicles and equipment	263,442	292,800	4,906,456	5,571,100
Nonelectrical machinery	134,256	165,500	1,794,126	2,746,900
Metalworking machinery	49,673	64,200	661,570	1,094,300
Primary metal industries	81,807	97,000	1,155,577	1,489,000
Fabricated metal products	86,619	132,700	1,025,281	1,969,300
Chemicals and allied products	33,595	37,200	761,996	1,039,700
Food and kindred products	52,472	52,200	729,211	917,300

Industry	EMPLOYEES 1963	1967	VALUE ADDED BY MANUFACTURE* in $000 1963	1967
Minnesota§	245,931	300,200	2,806,116	4,077,800
Nonelectrical machinery	37,532	53,000	482,493	911,700
Food and kindred products	48,619	48,300	587,507	759,100
Electrical machinery	18,953	25,100	225,256	333,700
Printing and publishing	21,879	23,600	206,341	237,200
Paper and allied products	13,505	14,500	177,998	232,200
Stone, clay, and glass products	10,961	10,200	158,740	212,400
Chemicals and allied products	5,646	6,000	166,551	217,100
Mississippi§	128,506	161,000	1,016,962	1,635,100
Lumber and wood products	20,914	20,700	130,696	166,900
Food and kindred products	14,641	14,700	130,946	159,200
Apparel and related products	31,435	35,700	131,465	174,600
Missouri§	391,254	452,400	4,296,036	5,891,400
Transportation equipment	58,206	79,500	998,328	1,234,400
Motor vehicles and equipment	23,467	...	632,520	...
Food and kindred products	48,188	48,800	629,933	804,400
Chemicals and allied products	19,558	22,300	395,319	545,600
Nonelectrical machinery	26,449	31,200	275,562	413,800
Printing and publishing	27,643	32,200	286,952	436,700
Montana§	20,247	20,500	236,230	312,000
Primary metal industries	3,261	...	47,795	...
Lumber and wood products	8,297	8,500	70,670	85,500
Nebraska	64,882	77,000	746,597	1,150,000
Food and kindred products	26,698	26,000	316,634	428,700
Meat products	12,613	13,100	115,537	186,200
Electrical machinery	5,348	7,200	64,379	80,500
Nevada	6,768	7,000	106,278	133,800
Chemicals and allied products	849	700	22,273	24,300
New Hampshire§	84,107	95,000	636,088	935,000
Electrical machinery	11,508	15,900	100,912	183,200
Nonelectrical machinery	8,002	10,900	78,269	129,200
Leather and leather products	20,137	19,600	104,325	132,500
New Jersey§	829,201	886,700	9,957,333	12,797,500
Chemicals and allied products	84,490	96,900	2,103,260	2,825,000
Industrial chemicals	30,209	31,400	654,206	787,100
Drugs	16,775	21,500	539,611	892,500
Electrical machinery	127,564	131,500	1,315,329	1,738,000
Communication equipment	57,898	54,800	612,512	823,200
Food and kindred products	61,098	60,200	1,034,623	1,248,800
Nonelectrical machinery	57,384	69,600	703,081	1,016,200
Fabricated metal products	57,451	63,500	687,255	897,200
New Mexico	15,324	16,900	149,641	204,500
Food and kindred products	3,595	3,500	34,537	40,500
Stone, clay, and glass products	1,353	1,000	19,264	16,400
New York§	1,853,050	1,937,300	19,559,120	25,331,300
Printing and publishing	171,593	187,800	2,576,592	3,426,800
Nonelectrical machinery	134,680	151,300	1,541,141	2,302,700
Office machines	36,466	33,600	324,940	475,000
Apparel and related products	316,522	290,800	2,472,531	2,881,700
Electrical machinery	185,978	213,900	1,964,932	2,679,600
Transportation equipment	99,811	104,800	1,342,730	1,746,300
Instruments and related products	75,499	92,400	1,259,704	1,997,800
Photographic equipment	39,401	...	882,624	...
Food and kindred products	128,774	113,000	1,846,827	1,972,600
North Carolina	530,646	643,800	4,566,547	6,606,500
Textile mill products	220,769	257,200	1,425,377	2,022,500
Knitting mills	68,203	80,600	385,621	591,600
Yarn and thread mills	47,992	58,800	312,216	470,700
Tobacco manufactures	29,187	27,300	849,989	975,900
Cigarettes	19,507	18,500	792,928	898,700
Furniture and fixtures	47,994	58,500	337,299	516,700
Household furniture	44,371	53,800	311,142	470,300
Electrical machinery	23,195	34,300	279,179	449,600
North Dakota	6,507	7,500	72,445	112,800
Food and kindred products	3,063	3,200	36,747	39,900
Ohio	1,239,515	1,397,000	15,506,118	20,435,400
Transportation equipment	164,408	170,800	2,459,304	2,593,800
Motor vehicles and equipment	112,368	105,900	1,895,276	1,724,300
Nonelectrical machinery	167,277	215,300	2,036,679	3,253,800
Primary metal industries	155,047	169,600	2,197,734	2,679,800
Blast furnace and basic steel products	92,152	95,500	1,441,640	1,691,100
Electrical machinery	117,182	129,900	1,547,622	1,979,100
Fabricated metal products	115,296	149,900	1,345,844	2,212,200
Chemicals and allied products	43,323	47,700	956,050	1,358,600
Rubber and plastics products†	80,471	93,400	968,715	1,330,600
Oklahoma	97,691	117,700	978,774	1,346,200
Food and kindred products	14,212	13,800	148,173	176,400
Nonelectrical machinery	11,032	15,000	120,244	184,300
Transportation equipment	7,801	13,900	67,542	156,900
Oregon	145,164	163,100	1,574,816	2,060,500
Lumber and wood products	69,975	70,600	700,535	770,600
Millwork and related products	27,982	30,200	284,488	317,300
Sawmills and planing mills	27,199	25,100	252,005	269,800
Food and kindred products	19,938	20,900	234,720	299,500
Pennsylvania	1,392,922	1,549,500	14,043,602	19,276,800
Primary metal products	210,388	233,100	2,663,777	3,540,700
Blast furnace and basic steel products	161,235	177,200	2,155,134	2,815,400
Electrical machinery	107,010	135,800	1,190,613	1,884,300
Nonelectrical machinery	112,607	138,300	1,257,664	1,946,500
Food and kindred products	107,508	108,500	1,355,664	1,638,300
Fabricated metal products	104,800	118,800	1,085,860	1,538,700
Chemicals and allied products	45,805	49,500	987,162	1,361,100
Transportation equipment	66,339	81,800	733,011	1,233,400
Apparel and related products	173,130	173,900	876,008	1,057,700
Rhode Island	113,940	122,300	958,575	1,350,900
Miscellaneous manufacturing	21,239	24,200	152,303	240,400
Jewelry and silverware	8,467	10,700	71,953	123,100
Textile mill products	22,863	22,000	155,023	188,200
Nonelectrical machinery	9,106	10,900	88,643	138,600
Primary metal industries	9,096	9,700	94,983	162,000
Nonferrous rolling and drawing	6,425	6,800	60,568	117,500
South Carolina§	261,655	304,200	2,111,117	3,020,000
Textile mill products	130,371	138,400	941,238	1,884,000
Weaving mills, cotton	67,371	62,100	426,634	523,400
Weaving mills, synthetics	23,087	29,900	170,690	253,600
Chemicals and allied products	16,181	19,900	342,833	475,700
Fibers, plastics, rubbers	5,625	9,800	141,351	231,400
South Dakota	13,234	15,500	140,042	171,300
Food and kindred products	7,905	7,800	94,923	95,000
Meat products	4,922	5,000	59,676	48,600
Tennessee	339,108	418,000	3,302,688	4,921,100
Chemicals and allied products	39,820	52,100	826,807	1,155,500
Industrial chemicals	16,299	16,600	403,979	522,400
Fibers, plastics, rubbers	16,582	21,800	300,809	391,600
Electrical machinery	17,530	31,600	230,442	478,200
Food and kindred products	31,928	32,400	349,348	457,600
Apparel and related products	52,140	68,100	251,859	412,500
Texas	513,802	657,500	7,086,283	10,922,400
Chemicals and allied products	43,538	47,900	1,644,714	2,076,700
Industrial chemicals	27,130	27,200	1,215,258	1,454,100
Petroleum and coal products	35,963	33,400	1,016,211	1,800,500
Petroleum refining	33,700	31,000	986,911	1,765,100
Food and kindred products	75,351	78,700	929,542	1,172,300
Transportation equipment	50,099	80,400	615,617	1,248,100
Aircraft and parts	34,341	58,400	362,289	1,059,900
Utah	53,504	47,000	710,627	777,900
Food and kindred products	8,463	7,600	99,108	102,900
Nonelectrical machinery	3,150	4,400	33,689	53,300
Fabricated metal products	2,639	2,600	28,851	47,300
Vermont	33,740	42,500	309,253	515,000
Nonelectrical machinery	6,398	7,600	68,140	101,800
Electrical machinery	1,871	...	19,939	...
Virginia	302,084	339,800	3,046,268	4,067,500
Chemicals and allied products	35,106	40,900	609,341	762,000
Fibers, plastics, rubbers	21,888	24,500	395,447	486,200
Tobacco manufactures	13,740	13,700	308,014	421,800
Cigarettes	8,744	...	271,637	...
Food and kindred products	32,048	31,500	326,468	392,700
Textile mill products	35,961	38,400	260,606	328,300
Washington§	224,375	271,500	3,028,577	3,776,800
Transportation equipment	72,402	...	1,058,202	...
Lumber and wood products	42,440	41,700	360,706	433,200
Food and kindred products	26,704	29,200	360,950	466,200
Paper and allied products	17,985	18,900	330,262	377,700
Primary metal industries	9,768	13,500	202,202	286,400
Primary nonferrous metal	4,234	5,300	138,061	172,800
West Virginia	117,026	124,000	1,887,148	2,169,500
Chemicals and allied products	22,573	22,500	783,235	836,300
Industrial chemicals	14,915	13,900	606,027	583,400
Primary metal industries	21,652	23,300	389,749	488,200
Blast furnace and basic steel products	14,771	15,200	272,193	302,800
Wisconsin	461,807	512,200	5,363,153	7,014,100
Nonelectrical machinery	85,113	107,500	1,004,641	1,590,200
Food and kindred products	58,714	56,700	754,500	910,300
Electrical machinery	49,762	51,900	596,348	697,300
Paper and allied products	36,339	39,800	501,795	663,500
Transportation equipment	42,975	32,900	734,560	558,100
Motor vehicles and equipment	37,721	27,100	692,595	492,300
Wyoming	6,797	5,900	81,678	86,200
Petroleum and coal products	2,127	1,800	37,222	36,900

Sum of state totals may not add to United States total because figures were independently derived.
Boldface type indicates the state which leads in the value added by manufacture for that industry.
*Adjusted. Represents value of products shipped less cost of materials, supplies, fuel, electric energy, and contract work plus the net change in finished products and work-in-process inventories.
†Excludes certain products.　‡Excludes government-owned and operated establishments.　§1967 figures are preliminary.
Source: U.S. Department of Commerce, Bureau of the Census, 1963 Census of Manufactures and 1967 Census of Manufactures.

Distribution and Services

Services

Kind of service	NUMBER OF SERVICES* First quarter 1968	1969	EMPLOYEES Mid-March pay period 1968	1969
Hotels and other lodging places	52,033	51,885	737,050	752,439
Hotels, tourist courts, and motels	35,527	35,220	617,173	624,027
Rooming and boarding houses	6,885	6,915	84,501	90,419
Personal services	184,255	183,207	1,037,043	1,029,887
Laundries and dry cleaning plants	48,928	48,073	490,270	521,728
Photographic studios	6,891	6,948	33,686	34,320
Beauty shops	69,275	71,050	271,346	280,380
Barber shops	29,158	27,176	62,654	59,124
Funeral service, crematories	13,435	13,309	64,945	66,630
Miscellaneous business services	83,569	88,722	1,365,505	1,506,963
Advertising	7,755	8,028	112,221	116,824
Credit reporting and collection	5,556	5,579	61,385	63,028
Duplicating, mailing, stenographic	5,024	5,065	61,971	62,813
Services to buildings	14,107	15,033	241,302	266,944
Private employment agencies	4,344	4,913	38,925	45,691
Research, development laboratories	1,823	1,946	80,828	77,610
Business consulting services	14,983	16,836	199,749	238,662
Detective and protective services	2,981	3,145	118,451	133,238
Equipment rental and leasing	6,189	6,868	46,725	55,511
Temporary help supply service	1,960	1,973	136,218	162,170
Auto repair, services, and garages	68,417	69,612	348,833	368,054
Auto rentals, without drivers	4,912	5,113	52,181	58,437
Auto parking	3,945	4,025	36,169	38,430
Auto repair shops	53,395	53,854	200,023	208,751
Auto laundries	3,900	4,213	42,976	46,521
Miscellaneous repair services	37,795	38,355	196,360	197,940
Electrical repair shops	12,791	12,964	55,815	60,718
Motion pictures	10,880	10,970	177,688	184,832
Picture filming and distributing	2,461	2,672	50,212	52,456
Motion picture theaters	7,949	7,820	113,608	119,046
Other amusement, recreation services	39,109	38,694	408,469	414,801
Producers, orchestras, entertainers	6,428	6,392	59,196	59,746
Bowling, billiard establishments	10,374	9,715	96,128	94,469
Golf clubs and country clubs	4,454	4,547	80,774	81,949
Medical and other health services	210,045	213,435	2,572,012	2,724,626
Offices of physicians, surgeons	103,814	104,696	337,495	355,412
Offices of dentists, dental surgeons	62,028	63,172	140,840	150,344
Hospitals	5,215	5,180	1,586,502	1,654,724
Medical and dental laboratories	6,606	6,847	44,592	47,935
Sanatoria, convalescent, rest homes	11,030	11,096	350,645	394,009
Legal services	67,899	68,313	214,671	225,634
Educational services	29,625	31,521	816,673	834,854
Elementary and secondary schools	20,971	22,346	268,570	284,967
Colleges and universities	1,765	1,807	451,406	444,211
Correspondence, vocational schools	3,148	3,292	46,894	50,167
Museums, botanical gardens, zoos	746	791	16,211	17,135
Nonprofit membership organizations	119,454	122,226	1,054,116	1,107,102
Business associations	11,841	11,920	69,619	71,035
Labor organizations	20,235	20,234	133,862	134,150
Civic and social associations	28,344	28,298	235,687	241,055
Religious organizations	41,501	43,538	270,483	284,636
Charitable organizations	6,644	6,524	138,397	137,653
Miscellaneous services	56,901	59,188	517,015	553,765
Engineering, architectural services	21,171	22,031	242,785	257,531
Nonprofit research agencies	3,372	3,505	99,021	101,158
Accounting, auditing, bookkeeping	27,918	28,846	151,514	169,158
TOTAL†	963,485	979,581	9,517,738	9,974,335

*Each business is counted as only one service in each county for each kind of service it performs, regardless of the number of establishments it operates.
†Includes administrative and auxiliary businesses not shown separately.
Source: U.S. Department of Commerce, Bureau of the Census, *County Business Patterns.*

Sales of merchant wholesalers

in millions of dollars

Kind of business	1960 total	1965 total	1969 total	1970 1st half
Durable goods	56,803	76,232	109,578	54,799
Motor vehicles, automotive equipment	7,883	10,945	18,493	9,885
Electrical goods	8,660	11,248	15,748	7,490
Furniture, home furnishings	2,910	3,392	5,422	2,553
Hardware, plumbing, heating equipment, supplies	6,422	7,947	10,748	5,115
Lumber, construction materials	6,680	7,747	11,750	5,162
Machinery, equipment, supplies	14,287	20,279	28,093	14,122
Metals, metalwork (except scrap)	5,708	8,796	11,794	6,412
Scrap, waste materials	3,296	4,590	5,542	3,229
Jewelry	960	1,294	...	...
Nondurable goods	80,477	101,354	127,130	65,142
Groceries and related products	27,661	36,478	47,771	24,904
Beer, wine, distilled alcoholic beverages	7,424	9,496	11,913	5,889
Drugs, chemicals, allied products	5,370	6,859	9,369	4,750
Tobacco, tobacco products	4,164	4,856	5,752	2,930
Dry goods, apparel	6,675	8,614	10,157	4,881
Paper, paper products (excluding wallpaper)	4,153	5,234	7,296	3,621
Farm products (raw materials)	11,683	12,808	13,357	6,875
Other nondurable goods	13,346	17,008	21,514	11,292
Total	137,281	177,587	236,708	119,942

Source: U.S. Department of Commerce, Bureau of the Census, *Monthly Wholesale Trade Report.*

Retail sales

in millions of dollars

Kind of business	1960 total	1965 total	1969 total	1970 1st half
Durable goods stores	70,733	93,718	112,779	54,300
Automotive group	39,509	56,266	66,911	32,763
Passenger car, other automotive dealers*	36,981	53,217	62,048	30,372
Tire, battery, accessory dealers	2,528	3,049	4,863	2,391
Furniture and appliance group	10,598	13,737	16,719	7,930
Furniture, home furnishings stores	6,770	8,538	10,439	4,923
Household appliance, TV, radio stores	3,828	4,223	5,223	2,438
Lumber, building, hardware, farm-equipment group	14,819	16,274	19,246	9,026
Lumberyards, building-materials dealers†	8,618	9,302	11,278	5,184
Hardware stores	2,693	2,813	3,284	1,442
Nondurable goods stores	148,796	190,232	238,854	119,201
Apparel group	13,708	15,752	20,158	9,014
Men's, boys' wear stores‡	2,619	3,258	4,761	2,083
Women's apparel, accessory stores§	5,329	6,243	7,606	3,402
Family clothing stores	2,728	2,981	3,631	1,597
Shoe stores	2,450	2,571	3,505	1,623
Drug and proprietary stores	7,530	9,335	11,863	6,059
Eating and drinking places	16,096	21,423	25,849	13,257
Food group	53,837	66,920	75,866	39,608
Grocery stores	48,339	61,068	70,955	36,990
Meat and fish markets	1,560	1,552	1,851	1,020
Bakery products stores	1,034	1,142	1,082	555
Gasoline service stations	17,594	21,765	25,116	12,921
General merchandise group	24,007	35,840	58,615	26,970
Department stores and dry goods general merchandise stores	16,994	27,939	43,016	19,586
Variety stores	3,899	5,320	6,548	2,994
Mail-order houses (department store merchandise)	1,857	2,581	5,319	1,641
Liquor stores	4,880	6,305	7,403	3,684
Total	219,529	283,950	351,633	173,501

*Includes both franchised and nonfranchised car dealers. †Includes lumberyards, building materials dealers; paint, plumbing, and electric stores. ‡Includes men's, boys' clothing, furnishings stores, and custom tailors. §Includes women's ready-to-wear; other apparel, accessory, specialty shops; and furriers.
Source: U.S. Department of Commerce, Bureau of the Census, *Monthly Retail Trade Report.*

Business activity in wholesaling, retailing, and services

Item	WHOLESALING 1960	1965	1968*	RETAILING 1960	1965	1968*	SERVICES 1960	1965	1968*
Number of businesses (in 000)									
Sole proprietorships	306	265	268	1,548	1,554	1,623	1,966	2,208	2,390
Active partnerships	41	32	32	238	202	175	159	169	176
Active corporations	117	147	153	217	288	316	121	188	230
Business receipts (in $000,000)									
Sole proprietorships	17,061	17,934	20,432	65,439	77,760	85,490	23,256	29,789	36,548
Active partnerships	12,712	10,879	10,973	24,787	23,244	22,940	9,281	12,442	16,220
Active corporations	130,637	171,414	203,277	125,787	183,925	233,903	22,106	36,547	47,549
Net profit (less loss) (in $000,000)									
Sole proprietorships	1,305	1,483	1,796	3,869	5,019	5,778	8,060	11,008	13,645
Active partnerships	587	548	556	1,612	1,654	1,688	3,056	4,402	5,824
Active corporations	2,130	3,288	4,385	2,225	4,052	5,793	849	1,505	1,956

Data cover accounting periods which ended between July 1 of the year shown and June 30 of the following year.
*Preliminary figures.
Source: U.S. Department of the Treasury, Internal Revenue Service, *Statistics of Income, U.S. Business Tax Returns and Corporation Income Tax Returns.*

Foreign Aid and Commerce

Major recipients of foreign assistance

in millions of dollars

Program and country	1962	1963	1964	1965	1966	1967	1968	1969	1970*
Total	6,208	6,488	5,812	5,662	6,495	6,598	6,160	5,200	5,834
By program									
Economic assistance programs	4,681	4,502	4,276	4,352	5,102	5,117	4,695	4,102	4,745
Agency for International Development	2,509	2,300	2,141	2,033	2,554	2,253†	1,892†	1,449†	1,663†
Loans	1,330	1,346	1,333	1,129	1,228	1,091	929	570	686
Grants	1,180	954	808	904	1,326	1,162	963	879	977
Food for Peace	1,403	1,455	1,503	1,372	1,610	982	1,386	1,230	1,197
Export-Import Bank long-term loans	317	255	334	376	389	1,329	820	774	1,221
Other economic programs‡	452	492	298	572	549	553	597	649	664
Military assistance programs	1,527	1,986	1,536	1,309	1,392	1,480	1,465	1,098	1,089
By country									
Africa									
Ethiopia	26	25	19	28	63	27	26	11	18§
Ghana	119	3	3	3	9	37	29	39	32§
Morocco	48	72	46	36	61	52	84	50	38
Nigeria	25	29	50	35	30	18	22	58	45§
Tunisia	48	63	47	50	21	54	48	42	47§
Asia									
India	744	685§	664§	698§	902§	588	619	451	462
Indonesia	41	49	19	−1	22	58	106	249	215
Iran	100	111	53	91	114	181	127	170	140
Israel	80	74	38	70	39	12	76§	75§	51§
Japan	124	119	71	72	46	112	94	109	170
Korea, South	327	364	342	355	415	331	386	451	396
Laos	64	38§	42§	48§	55§	55§	63§	50§	53§
Pakistan	416§	350§	371§	342§	142§	234	359	86	214
Philippines	44	116	28	45	40	66	47	59	56
Ryukyu Islands	17	11	11	17	15	38	14	17	22
Taiwan	157	162	171	132	136	92	124	75	142
Thailand	87	94	68	78	101	82	49‖	36‖	29‖
Turkey	156	172	102	118	100	118	131	109	211
Vietnam, South	287	384	401	542	897	541‖	440‖	349‖	421‖
Canada	—	—	—	—	—	—	10	6	21
Europe									
France	41	24	17	13	13	9	1	1	59
Greece	81	141	108	131	78	46	46	56	38
Italy	105	135	78	88	21	64	80	51	160
Netherlands	15	19	11	50	¶	3	—	—	49
Spain	66	54	73	99	153	177	20	70	190
Switzerland	—	—	—	—	—	—	—	—	45
United Kingdom	27	12	¶	¶	86	407	396	100	73
Latin America									
Argentina	60	134	13	16	34	12	46	77	35
Brazil	247	152	354	287	367	286	354	50	212
Chile	182	109	136	138	113	290	114	112	44
Colombia	83	134	130	38	102	145	117	135	133
Costa Rica	10	15	17	16	14	14	11	18	19
Dominican Republic	35	52	16	77	110	62	67	33	24
Ecuador	39	41	30	25	32	8	16	16	32
Guatemala	11	16	15	14	5	22	20	80	34
Mexico	50	46	106	105	33	102	86	18	40
Uruguay	9	20	9	2	9	5	39	5	21
Venezuela	64	54	55	47	18	45	79	8	22
Oceania									
Australia	1	12	18	19	118	242	171	182	167
New Guinea (Papua)	—	—	—	—	—	—	—	—	23
Trust Territory of the Pacific Islands	6	11	16	18	18	24	38	40	55
Nonregional	464	642	548	345	618	520	473	620	640

Years ending June 30. Economic assistance data on net obligation and loan authorization basis, rather than expenditure basis. Military assistance data represent value of goods delivered. A minus figure indicates deobligations in excess of new obligations.
*Preliminary. †Excludes $43 million in 1967, $35 million in 1968, $35 million in 1969 and $54 million in 1970 in reimbursements by the Department of Defense for grants to Vietnam. ‡Principal programs include contributions to international lending organizations and the Peace Corps. §Economic assistance only; military assistance data classified. Values are included in overall total. ‖Economic assistance only. Military assistance transferred to the Department of Defense. ¶ Less than $500,000.
Source: U.S. Department of State, Agency for International Development.

Trade by commodity groups

in millions of dollars

Commodity group	EXPORTS								IMPORTS							
	1960	1963	1964	1965	1966	1967	1968	1969	1960	1963	1964	1965	1966	1967	1968	1969
Food and live animals	2,684	3,657	4,076	4,003	4,562	4,061	3,890	3,733	2,996	3,401	3,487	3,460	3,948	4,003	4,577	4,531
Beverages and tobacco	483	531	554	517	624	649	702	713	396	462	535	553	642	698	786	778
Crude materials, inedible, except fuels	2,805	2,494	2,978	2,856	3,071	3,284	3,541	3,570	2,752	2,726	2,880	3,103	3,310	2,997	3,346	3,460
Mineral fuels and related materials	842	978	953	947	976	1,104	1,050	1,131	1,587	1,924	2,030	2,221	2,262	2,248	2,527	2,794
Animal and vegetable oils and fats	295	303	414	472	357	338	274	308	95	105	119	116	146	122	158	137
Chemicals	1,776	2,009	2,364	2,402	2,675	2,802	3,287	3,383	807	701	702	769	955	958	1,129	1,232
Machinery and transport equipment	6,992	8,243	9,369	10,147	11,155	12,574	14,447	16,380	1,466	1,823	2,216	2,948	4,823	5,794	7,987	9,768
Other manufactured goods	3,815	4,046	4,795	4,890	5,388	5,468	6,084	7,001	4,572	5,546	6,188	7,528	8,668	9,004	11,508	12,021
Other transactions	718	841	794	954	1,187	959	924	1,227	401	518	591	730	866	1,065	1,208	1,331
Total	20,408	23,102	26,297	27,187	29,994	31,238	34,199	37,444	15,073	17,207	18,749	21,429	25,618	26,889	33,226	36,052

Export data exclude reexports. Import data show commodities released for domestic consumption during each year. Source: U.S. Department of Commerce, Bureau of the Census. *Statistical Abstract of the United States.* Data compiled by U.S. Department of Commerce, Bureau of International Commerce.

Principal trading partners

by exports and imports, in millions of dollars

EXPORTS

Country	1955	1960	1965	1969
Africa	642	793	1,229	1,392
Libya	6	43	65	134
South Africa	272	288	438	505
Asia	2,581	4,186	6,012	8,265
Hong Kong	51	125	191	363
India	194	650	928	517
Indonesia	83	100	42	201
Iran	84	156	195	352
Israel	92	130	224	457
Japan	683	1,447	2,080	3,490
Korea, South	145	231	274	699
Lebanon	43	45	75	90
Pakistan	59	182	336	195
Philippines	373	307	349	374
Saudi Arabia	84	46	137	154
Singapore*	—	—	—	152
Taiwan	361	277	234	393
Thailand	73	71	107	148
Vietnam, South	—	—	—	285
Australia and Oceania	295	514	956	998
Australia	231	423	797	855
New Zealand and Western Samoa	56	78	133	99
Europe	5,126	7,399	9,364	12,619
Belgium and Luxembourg	407	467	650	960
Denmark	97	146	209	205
Finland	42	56	76	76
France	536	699	971	1,195
Germany, West	607	1,272	1,650	2,118
Greece	120	103	172	255
Ireland	42	43	69	118
Italy	473	715	891	1,262
Netherlands	581	817	1,088	1,447
Norway	129	108	140	198
Soviet Union	§	39	45	106
Spain	182	208	472	580
Sweden	165	332	336	477
Switzerland	166	263	369	605
Turkey	200	178	205	299
United Kingdom	1,006	1,487	1,615	2,335
Yugoslavia	198	88	149	86
North America	5,160	5,506	7,742	11,900
Bahamas	15	49	107	179
Canada	3,404	3,810	5,643	9,138
Costa Rica	45	45	61	77
Dominican Republic	64	42	76	124
Guatemala	59	64	96	84
Jamaica	23	48	87	175
Mexico	719	831	1,106	1,450
Netherlands Antilles	65	65	75	99
Panama	78	90	125	164
South America	1,743	2,177	2,175	2,814
Argentina	155	359	268	378
Brazil	273	464	348	672
Chile	99	203	237	315
Colombia	354	253	198	303
Ecuador	51	57	80	98
Peru	135	147	282	168
Venezuela	577	567	626	708
Total	**15,547**	**20,575**	**27,478**	**37,988**

IMPORTS

Country	1955	1960	1965	1969
Africa	619	534	878	1,045
Libya	§	§	30	111
South Africa	96	108	226	243
Asia	1,876	2,721	4,528	8,276
Hong Kong	15	139	343	815
India	221	228	348	344
Indonesia	212	216	165	194
Iran	34	51	88	87
Israel	17	27	62	129
Japan	432	1,149	2,414	4,888
Korea, South	6	5	54	291
Malaysia†	—	—	212	307
Pakistan	30	36	45	73
Philippines	253	307	369	423
Taiwan	6	20	93	388
Thailand	105	56	41	92
Australia and Oceania	174	266	453	828
Australia	126	142	311	588
New Zealand and Western Samoa	44	119	130	216
Europe	2,453	4,268	6,292	10,336
Austria	34	49	66	115
Belgium and Luxembourg	242	364	494	684
Denmark	58	98	147	258
Finland	44	52	84	120
France	202	396	615	843
Germany, West	366	897	1,341	2,603
Ireland	6	28	58	123
Italy	180	393	620	1,204
Netherlands	147	213	251	467
Norway	61	66	124	150
Poland	27	39	66	98
Portugal	27	35	56	86
Spain	59	88	133	304
Sweden	85	170	243	355
Switzerland	147	198	306	452
Turkey	57	60	83	68
United Kingdom	616	993	1,405	2,121
Yugoslavia	26	41	61	102
North America	4,038	4,429	6,579	12,912
Canada	2,653	2,901	4,832	10,390
Costa Rica	28	35	57	101
Dominican Republic	62	110	111	165
Guatemala	71	59	67	76
Honduras	23	34	72	94
Jamaica	22	54	125	151
Mexico	397	443	638	1,029
Netherlands Antilles	217	265	319	392
Panama	20	24	60	75
Trinidad and Tobago	6	55	142	232
South America	2,224	2,435	2,624	2,643
Argentina	126	98	122	156
Brazil	633	570	512	616
Chile	201	193	209	151
Colombia	442	299	277	240
Ecuador	53	65	106	81
Peru	111	183	241	313
Venezuela	576	948	1,018	940
Total ‖	**11,384**	**14,654**	**21,366**	**36,052**

For security reasons, exports of Special Category commodities are excluded from totals for certain countries. They are, however, included in the continent totals.

*Part of Malaysia prior to Aug. 1965. †Became independent Aug. 1957.

§Less than $500,000. ‖Includes estimates for low-valued shipments from countries which could not be identified because of illegible reporting on import entries.

Source: U.S. Department of Commerce, Bureau of the Census, *Statistical Abstract of the United States.*

Transactions in the balance of payments

in millions of dollars

Type of transaction	1960	1965	1967	1968	1969	1970 1st quarter	1970 2nd quarter
Exports of goods and services	29,253	41,027	47,108	51,426	56,273	15,174	16,494
Merchandise, excluding military	19,650	26,447	30,681	33,588	36,473	10,129	11,027
Military sales and grants	2,100	2,458	2,145	2,199	2,274	403	709
Transportation	1,782	2,414	2,790	2,969	3,131	810	945
Travel	919	1,380	1,646	1,775	2,058	490	617
Fees and royalties from direct investments	403	924	1,136	1,246	1,369	337	386
Other private and U.S. Government services	1,051	1,512	1,837	1,962	2,129	567	586
Income on U.S. investments abroad	3,349	5,893	6,872	7,687	8,838	2,438	2,224
Imports of goods and services	−23,355	−32,278	−40,990	−48,129	−53,564	−13,837	−14,975
Merchandise, excluding military	−14,744	−21,496	−26,821	−32,964	−35,835	−9,458	−10,015
Military expenditures	−3,087	−2,952	−4,378	−4,535	−4,850	−1,178	−1,247
Transportation	−1,915	−2,675	−2,993	−3,269	−3,608	−890	−1,111
Travel	−1,750	−2,438	−3,195	−3,022	−3,390	−618	−970
Payments for other private and U.S. Government services	−795	−989	−1,241	−1,406	−1,419	−353	−353
Income on foreign investments in U.S.	−1,063	−1,729	−2,362	−2,933	−4,463	−1,340	−1,279
Net unilateral transfers (to foreigners [−])	−4,025	−4,386	−3,874	−3,632	−3,594	−903	−1,050
Private remittances	−382	−581	−726	−715	−784	−210	−263
Military grants of goods and services	−1,765	−1,628	−905	−804	−759	−149	−222
Other U.S. Government grants	−1,664	−1,808	−1,802	−1,707	−1,644	−444	−446
U.S. Government pensions and other transfers	−214	−369	−441	−406	−406	−101	−118
Net transactions in U.S. private assets (increase [−])	−3,878	−3,794	−5,638	−5,412	−5,233	−1,806	−1,981
Net transactions in U.S. Government assets (increase [−])*	−1,104	−1,598	−2,421	−2,268	−2,184	−485	−461
Net transactions in U.S. official reserve assets (increase [−])	2,145	1,222	52	−880	−1,187	−386	1,022
Net transactions in foreign assets in the U.S. (increase [+])	2,120	383	6,852	9,410	12,330	1,489	1,489
Net errors and omissions	−1,156	−576	−1,088	−514	−2,841	−114	−538

*Excluding transactions in official reserve assets.

Source: U.S. Department of Commerce, Office of Business Economics, *Survey of Current Business.*

Finance

Stock dividends

July data, at annual rates per share in dollars

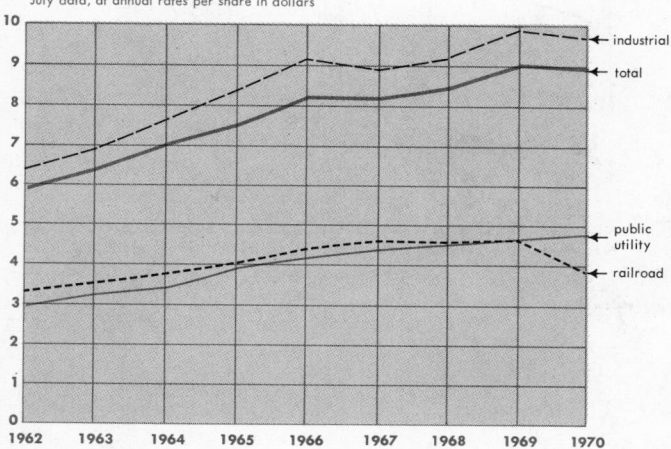

Source: U.S. Department of Commerce, Office of Business Economics, *Survey of Current Business.* Data compiled by Moody's Investors Service, Inc.

Money stock and money in circulation

in millions of dollars, except per capita

Year	Stock of money in U.S.*	MONEY HELD IN TREASURY			MONEY OUTSIDE OF TREASURY		
		In trust against gold and silver certificates	Treasury cash	For federal reserve banks and agents	Held by federal reserve banks and agents	In circulation† Amount	Per capita
1960	53,071	(21,455)	395	16,213	4,398	32,065	177.46
1961	51,947	(19,662)	379	14,440	4,724	32,405	176.35
1962	52,195	(18,435)	379	13,342	4,705	33,770	180.92
1963	53,335	(17,585)	369	12,641	4,855	35,470	187.30
1964	55,451	(16,997)	391	12,369	4,957	37,734	196.46
1965	56,690	(14,559)	747	13,669	2,554	39,720	204.33
1966	60,362	(13,595)	1,049	12,992	3,768	42,554	213.99
1967	61,408	(13,006)	1,472	12,607	2,616	44,712	225.97
1968	61,506	(10,026)	838	10,024	3,003	47,640	238.37
1969	64,387	(10,027)	633	10,026	2,792	50,936	252.26
1970	68,783	(11,045)	439	11,044	2,949	54,351	264.64

Data are for June 30 of each year.
*Does not include duplications, which are shown in parentheses.
†Includes any paper currency held outside the U.S. and currency and coin held by banks.
Source: Board of Governors of the Federal Reserve System, *Federal Reserve Bulletin.*

Banks

December 31, 1969

State	Number of banks	Total assets Total liabilities in $000,000	SELECTED ASSETS in $000,000 Loans*	Investments	Reserves, cash, and bank balances	SELECTED LIABILITIES in $000,000 Deposits Total	Domestic Inter-bank	Other Demand	Time	Capital accounts
Alabama	268	5,068	2,660	1,485	786	4,428	191	2,248	1,989	417
Alaska‡	10	539	265	181	72	490	3	234	253	33
Arizona	12	3,522	2,324	631	420	3,111	17	1,400	1,694	219
Arkansas	249	3,122	1,560	896	585	2,784	146	1,468	1,170	257
California	155	53,809	32,443	10,465	8,226	43,501	1,120	18,898	23,483	3,491
Colorado	267	4,685	2,663	977	880	3,959	233	2,000	1,726	352
Connecticut	131	10,822	7,568	2,135	884	9,489	96	2,659	6,734	883
Delaware‡	19	1,380	701	440	205	1,205	20	715	470	124
District of Columbia	14	3,065	1,607	813	565	2,692	64	1,602	1,025	246
Florida	475	13,949	6,691	4,406	2,430	12,327	804	6,078	5,444	1,002
Georgia	433	8,159	4,783	1,679	1,356	6,648	407	3,463	2,778	668
Hawaii	11	1,740	1,027	406	207	1,488	19	720	749	153
Idaho	26	1,379	807	343	191	1,235	8	605	622	93
Illinois	1,088	37,943	20,593	10,945	5,164	31,042	1,844	14,603	14,595	3,040
Indiana	414	11,759	6,287	3,223	2,011	10,247	296	5,001	4,950	798
Iowa	668	6,943	3,507	2,249	1,075	6,186	319	2,810	3,057	553
Kansas	603	5,270	2,611	1,763	784	4,641	188	2,355	2,097	468
Kentucky	345	5,561	2,841	1,650	967	4,929	328	2,570	2,032	437
Louisiana	231	6,715	3,369	1,988	1,189	5,842	410	3,000	2,432	538
Maine†	75	2,235	1,421	563	200	1,965	26	536	1,404	197
Maryland	127	6,569	3,964	1,569	834	5,690	168	2,679	2,843	543
Massachusetts†	335	24,375	15,926	5,344	2,462	20,113	744	6,256	13,113	2,027
Michigan	332	22,703	13,297	5,846	2,977	19,197	435	6,922	11,840	1,481
Minnesota‡	724	9,761	5,273	2,792	1,468	8,331	559	3,561	4,211	684
Mississippi	181	3,261	1,705	988	483	2,863	124	1,610	1,128	242
Missouri	668	12,681	6,421	3,809	2,181	10,861	988	5,539	4,334	1,054
Montana	136	1,680	868	543	229	1,486	36	663	787	116
Nebraska	442	3,789	1,975	1,045	687	3,323	247	1,713	1,363	304
Nevada	8	1,135	665	285	142	998	5	457	535	79
New Hampshire	107	2,220	1,592	426	163	1,930	13	429	1,488	201
New Jersey	249	18,583	10,845	5,247	2,062	16,362	170	6,493	9,699	1,396
New Mexico	64	1,471	785	400	243	1,298	28	676	594	109
New York	442	154,918	96,759	25,314	26,162	121,184	9,243	48,623	63,319	11,184
North Carolina	109	7,675	4,247	1,927	1,237	6,477	349	3,187	2,942	574
North Dakota	169	1,617	797	638	154	1,441	18	611	811	129
Ohio‡	521	24,012	13,507	6,627	3,355	20,354	548	8,944	10,862	1,916
Oklahoma	426	5,632	2,872	1,629	1,002	4,878	291	2,582	2,005	493
Oregon‡	51	4,419	2,622	990	601	3,752	47	1,566	2,139	278
Pennsylvania	499	35,665	21,689	8,678	4,293	29,750	885	12,047	16,817	2,921
Rhode Island	20	2,958	2,079	613	196	2,480	12	681	1,786	249
South Carolina	105	2,466	1,318	678	405	2,142	38	1,414	691	203
South Dakota	163	1,611	822	560	194	1,440	18	633	788	118
Tennessee	305	7,683	4,217	1,909	1,353	6,607	593	2,961	3,053	614
Texas	1,166	27,869	14,924	6,522	5,486	23,758	2,122	12,219	9,416	2,096
Utah	51	1,901	1,120	428	296	1,657	74	730	853	140
Vermont	50	1,177	845	226	84	1,057	2	277	778	86
Virginia	233	8,347	4,900	2,088	1,125	7,211	209	3,081	3,920	627
Washington	101	7,413	4,694	1,503	888	6,385	90	2,490	3,804	533
West Virginia	195	2,904	1,466	992	362	2,496	52	1,159	1,284	267
Wisconsin	607	10,026	5,467	2,900	1,397	8,762	327	3,577	4,858	715
Wyoming	70	834	428	244	140	741	25	340	376	69
Other areas‡	28	5,012	2,973	782	304	4,301	59	1,031	3,211	269
TOTAL U.S.	14,178	610,029	356,791	140,783	91,159	507,530	25,058	218,119	264,353	45,687

Columns may not add to totals due to rounding. *Includes Federal Funds sold and securities purchased under agreement to resell.
†Massachusetts figures include two noninsured mutual savings banks in Maine. ‡Figures for mutual savings banks in Alaska (2), Delaware (2), Minnesota (1), Ohio (1), and Oregon (1) are included in "Other areas."
Source: Federal Deposit Insurance Corporation, *Assets and Liabilities. Commercial and Mutual Savings Banks. December 31, 1969.*

Consumer credit outstanding

in billions of dollars

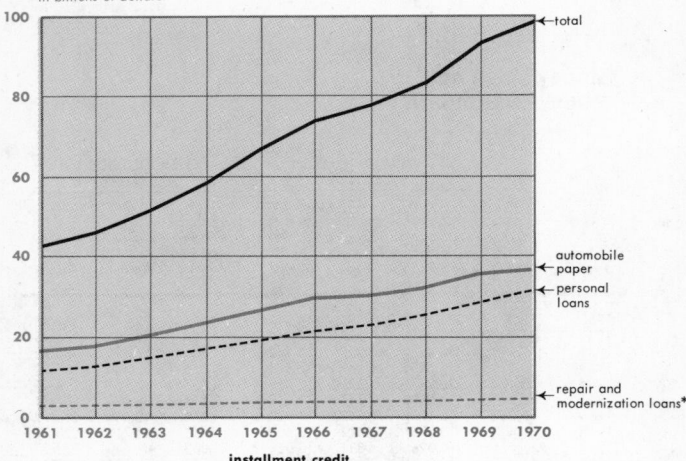

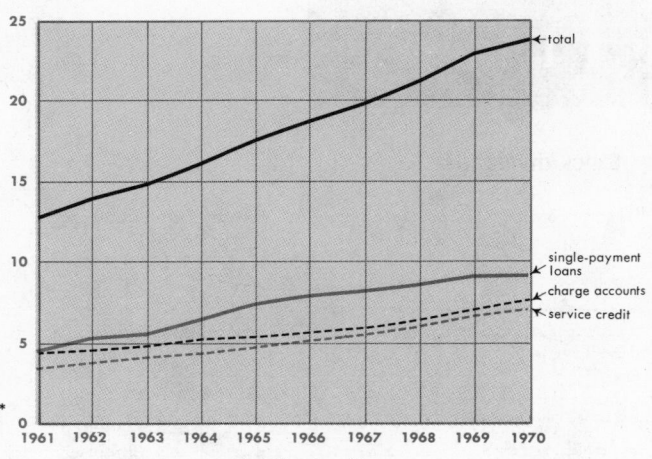

installment credit

non installment credit

Graphs cover loans outstanding as of June 30 to individuals for household, family, and other personal expenditures, except real estate mortgage loans
*Holdings of financial institutions only.
Source: Board of Governors of the Federal Reserve System, *Federal Reserve Bulletin*.

Health insurance

Item	1960	1965	1969
Premiums received (in $000,000)	7,485	12,130	17,285
Insurance companies	4,671	7,352	10,197
Other*	2,814	4,778	7,088
Benefit payments (in $000,000)	5,688	9,617	14,187
By type of insurer			
Insurance companies	3,069	5,160	7,495
Other*	2,619	4,457	6,692
By type of benefit			
Hospital expense†	3,207	5,695	8,256
Surgical and medical expense†	1,642	2,876	4,439
Loss of income	839	1,046	1,572
Number of persons covered, Dec. 31 (in 000)			
Insurance companies‡			
Hospital expense	78,885	97,042	108,508
Surgical expense	75,305	93,717	99,576
Regular medical expense	41,312	58,398	72,286
Blue Cross, Blue Shield, and Medical Society			
Hospital expense	58,050	64,495	74,009
Surgical expense	50,281	55,420	65,673
Regular medical expense	45,017	52,042	60,820
Independent plans§			
Hospital expense	5,542	7,376	8,030
Surgical expense	6,573	8,974	10,250
Regular medical expense	6,773	8,718	10,050

*Blue Cross, Blue Shield, and other insuring organizations.
†Includes benefits from major medical expense policies.
‡Persons covered by more than one insurance company are counted
  only once.
§Industrial plans, community plans, private group clinics, college health
  plans, and consumer-sponsored plans.
  Source: Health Insurance Institute.

Life insurance

dollar figures in millions

Item	1960	1965	1968	1969	1970
Number of companies	1,442	1,610	1,758	1,812	...
Amount in force	$560,000	$849,000	$1,140,000	$1,240,000	$1,345,000*
Value of purchases†	72,989	108,989	147,546	154,439	165,216
Ordinary	52,382	78,122	98,989	107,833	115,830
Group	13,706	23,506	41,672	40,048	40,020
Industrial	6,901	7,361	6,885	6,558	6,366
Benefit payments					
Death payments	3,253	4,643	5,976	6,478	6,898
Matured endowments	652	933	994	969	960
Policy dividends	1,541	2,416	2,995	3,265	3,419

Years ending June 30.
*Estimated.
†Exclusive of revivals, increases, dividend additions, and reinsurance acquired.
 Source: Institute of Life Insurance.

Stock market prices, 1970

1941-43=10

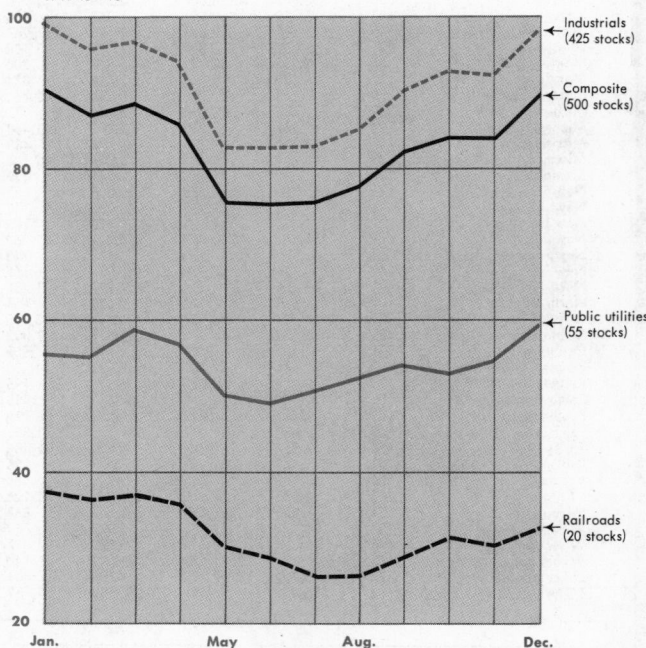

Source: U.S. Department of Commerce, Office of Business Economics, *Survey of Current Business.* Data compiled by Standard & Poor's Corporation.

Sales of stocks and bonds

in millions

Year and month	Market value of all sales	STOCKS* Market value	STOCKS* Number of shares	BONDS† Market value	BONDS† Principal amount
1969					
October	$17,628	$17,152	488	$397	$466
November	13,722	13,352	376	318	376
December	14,385	13,951	430	382	527
1970					
January	13,363	12,958	396	363	485
February	12,294	11,980	349	283	366
March	11,735	11,374	346	314	405
April	11,474	11,130	341	310	384
May	11,068	10,704	387	300	465
June	10,699	10,025	402	646	824
July	8,937	8,554	338	371	537
August	8,436	8,026	299	312	442
September	11,522	11,027	427	401	517

*Includes voting trust certificates, certificates of deposit for stocks, American
 depository receipts for stocks; excludes rights and warrants.
†Excludes U. S. Government bonds.
 Source: U.S. Securities and Exchange Commission, *Statistical Bulletin*.

Transport and Communications

Automobile ownership

Unit	1955	1960	1965	1969
Total number of families in the U.S. (000,000)	49.1	53.4	58.4	62.1
Percent of families owning automobiles	70	77	79	79
Owning 1 automobile	60	62	55	52
Owning 2 or more automobiles	10	15	24	27
Age of automobiles owned, by percent				
Less than 2 years old	12	14	16	15
2 and 3 years old	22	20	21	22
4 to 7 years old	43	41	33	41
8 years old and over	23	25	30	22
Total automobiles purchased (000,000)	13.6	14.1	18.3	20.5
New cars (000,000)	4.4	5.2	7.2	7.5
Average price paid	$2,730	$3,140	$3,140	$3,510
Used cars (000,000)	9.2	9.1	11.1	13.0
Average price paid, gross	$ 780	$ 980	$ 920	$1,000
Method of financing purchases, by percent				
Full cash (including trade-in allowance)	38	38	48	47
Installment credit and other borrowing	60	62	52	53

Source: U.S. Department of Commerce, Bureau of the Census, *Statistical Abstract of the United States*. Data compiled by The University of Michigan, Survey Research Center, *Survey of Consumer Finances*.

Transportation accident death rates
per 100,000,000 passenger-miles

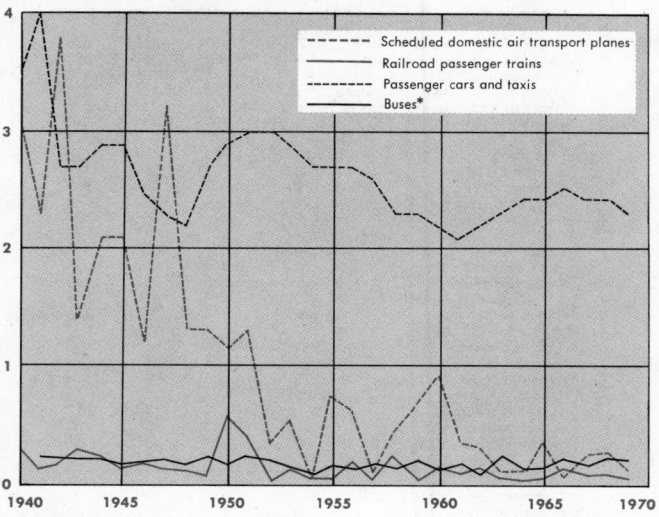

- ---- Scheduled domestic air transport planes
- —— Railroad passenger trains
- ------ Passenger cars and taxis
- —— Buses*

*1940 data included with passenger cars and taxis.
Source: National Safety Council.

Transportation

State	ROAD AND STREET MILEAGE Jan. 1, 1970 Total*	Total surfaced	Municipal mileage	Rural mileage State controlled	Rural mileage Locally controlled	AUTOMOBILES, TRUCKS, AND BUSES registrations, in 000, 1969 Total	Private and commercial Auto-mobiles	Private and commercial Trucks and buses	Publicly owned†	RAILROAD MILEAGE OWNED Jan. 1, 1970 Total	RAILROAD MILEAGE OWNED Class 1	AIRPORTS‡ Jan. 1, 1970 Total	AIRPORTS‡ Private	CIVIL AIRCRAFT Jan. 1, 1970 Total	CIVIL AIRCRAFT Eligible
Alabama	78,080	68,172	11,403	19,877§	46,800	1,860	1,466	364	30	4,567	3,888	131	48	3,156	2,262
Alaska	7,123	3,538	693	4,381	1,507	131	90	36	5	20	—	691	196	3,671	2,272
Arizona	41,773	20,515	6,166	5,212	17,465	1,024	776	228	20	2,052	1,879	207	107	3,330	2,197
Arkansas	78,861	59,568	8,698	12,913	55,307	950	654	284	12	3,584	3,318	135	68	2,391	1,588
California	162,223	118,040	44,080	13,839	70,955	11,601	9,627	1,811	163	7,447	6,636	720	467	25,926	17,643
Colorado	81,999	49,504	7,108	8,282	66,558	1,374	1,042	308	24	3,510	3,393	185	115	3,126	2,236
Connecticut	18,251	18,105	12,906	1,511	3,834	1,677	1,483	175	20	688	633	74	61	1,601	1,140
Delaware	4,847	4,829	1,401	3,446§	—	297	248	44	5	287	—	24	19	724	561
District of Columbia	1,086	1,086	1,086	—	—	254	227	18	9	31	12	5	—	1,089	813
Florida	87,654	60,504	19,979	16,800	49,823	3,895	3,365	476	54	4,290	3,814	296	183	8,289	5,454
Georgia	98,901	67,955	14,507	15,444	68,608	3,487	1,993	468	26	5,436	3,807	192	88	3,953	2,891
Hawaii	3,512	3,343	964	884	1,573	375	330	39	6	—	—	59	34	408	226
Idaho	55,065	30,602	2,912	4,730	26,372	477	323	140	13	2,668	2,478	168	47	1,607	1,102
Illinois	129,388	122,840	26,805	13,219	89,364	5,162	4,487	617	58	10,868	9,091	585	507	8,220	5,800
Indiana	90,957	85,965	12,713	10,305	67,939	2,975	2,418	531	26	6,441	3,424	180	119	4,652	3,373
Iowa	112,320	105,356	12,769	9,149	90,376	1,754	1,361	364	29	8,127	7,866	240	143	3,270	2,588
Kansas	134,117	98,154	10,830	10,026	113,261	1,515	1,104	387	25	7,801	7,777	272	163	4,012	2,896
Kentucky	69,615	58,972	5,366	23,821§	39,992	1,713	1,338	352	22	3,518	3,097	69	21	1,319	980
Louisiana	52,512	47,388	10,424	14,266‖	27,536	1,750	1,380	347	23	3,793	3,482	218	152	3,065	2,082
Maine	21,341	19,712	2,388	10,958¶	7,833	496	396	93	6	1,679	1,523	140	97	868	596
Maryland	26,114	26,042	4,097	4,933	16,939	1,795	1,561	216	19	1,127	564	82	67	2,161	1,549
Massachusetts	28,897	28,243	21,539	1,214	6,095	2,426	2,172	223	31	1,462	1,258	117	91	2,663	1,919
Michigan	114,562	97,122	19,795	7,972	86,793	4,488	3,833	588	67	6,301	4,217	302	176	7,312	5,356
Minnesota	127,578	115,137	16,796	11,476	97,458	2,144	1,710	406	28	7,908	7,787	259	132	4,804	3,447
Mississippi	66,655	64,019	6,435	9,735	49,956	1,085	798	271	17	3,653	3,170	153	86	2,160	1,393
Missouri	114,816	107,046	14,945	30,092	69,106	2,313	1,825	465	24	6,355	5,726	287	192	4,678	3,395
Montana	78,253	41,312	2,325	11,753	53,492	478	310	158	10	4,925	4,888	180	64	1,962	1,461
Nebraska	101,749	75,376	6,350	9,541	85,296	929	672	241	16	5,498	5,496	260	180	2,366	1,763
Nevada	48,829	15,575	2,022	6,146§	40,660	329	246	71	11	1,635	1,474	107	55	1,444	972
New Hampshire	14,785	12,151	4,736	3,049	6,880	377	317	54	6	816	679	51	35	635	445
New Jersey	31,579	30,835	16,493	1,804	13,277	3,490	3,113	321	56	1,762	932	167	146	4,084	2,798
New Mexico	67,574	19,944	4,537	11,596	45,862	611	436	161	13	2,120	2,046	124	60	1,744	1,181
New York	104,716	100,368	21,276	14,036	69,369	6,505	5,792	614	99	5,662	4,743	409	347	8,749	6,130
North Carolina	85,460	77,492	13,569	70,078§	—	2,717	2,126	516	75	4,463	2,947	209	155	3,420	2,445
North Dakota	106,671	67,917	3,094	6,512	95,788	420	264	147	8	5,164	5,096	175	98	1,394	1,005
Ohio	108,644	106,926	23,311	16,720	68,613	5,875	5,218	602	56	7,884	4,564	451	352	8,008	5,619
Oklahoma	107,809	78,415	13,677	11,390	82,712	1,650	1,172	453	25	5,439	5,347	226	120	4,178	2,972
Oregon	93,139	58,310	6,150	8,962	35,004	1,335	1,080	227	27	3,075	2,774	206	112	3,735	2,684
Pennsylvania	114,683	95,258	23,478	44,180	46,303	5,760	5,007	693	59	8,444	5,595	453	389	5,998	4,244
Rhode Island	5,397	5,181	4,362	514	521	470	415	50	5	146	103	14	7	265	202
South Carolina	59,825	39,415	6,678	30,923	21,731	1,311	1,061	227	23	3,102	2,115	108	51	1,422	1,051
South Dakota	84,355	58,990	2,958	8,644	71,080	418	286	122	10	3,721	3,721	112	46	1,277	892
Tennessee	77,495	75,448	9,376	8,146	58,766	1,971	1,576	365	30	3,237	2,783	105	43	2,539	1,933
Texas	243,450	177,199	45,185	60,385	136,937	6,506	4,994	1,417	95	13,888	13,210	960	718	14,442	10,055
Utah	39,439	22,392	4,363	4,671	21,298	601	464	125	13	1,749	1,685	82	24	1,085	772
Vermont	14,320	12,356	946	2,468	10,773	215	178	33	4	770	325	44	31	356	267
Virginia	60,705	59,526	8,206	49,652§	805	2,161	1,801	321	39	3,932	3,278	161	115	2,474	1,727
Washington	74,570	61,191	9,940	10,940	39,537	2,106	1,638	430	38	4,931	4,815	235	134	4,882	3,323
West Virginia	35,820	26,352	3,557	31,299§	—	836	659	165	13	3,547	3,161	49	28	800	586
Wisconsin	102,299	96,840	13,900	10,760	77,560	2,075	1,726	311	38	5,970	5,675	250	151	3,394	2,432
Wyoming	40,486	17,605	1,279	5,687	20,996	238	152	80	6	1,812	1,805	87	45	839	600
Total U.S.	3,710,299	2,914,131	548,573	704,341	2,274,709	105,404	86,710	17,155	1,539	207,005	178,099	11,016	6,885	189,947	133,316

*Includes federally controlled rural roads. †Excludes vehicles owned by military services. ‡Includes seaplane bases, heliports, and military fields having joint civil-military use. §Includes mileage of state-controlled county roads. ‖Includes mileage designated as farm-to-market. ¶Includes the state-aid system.
Sources: Interstate Commerce Commission; U.S. Department of Transportation, Federal Aviation Administration; Federal Highway Administration, Bureau of Public Roads.

Railroads

years ending December 31

Item		1960	1965	1968
Number of operating companies*		407	372	360
Miles of road owned, first track†		217,552	211,384	208,111
Total miles operated		381,745	370,636	366,238
Number of locomotives in service		31,178	30,061	29,448
Number of passenger-train cars in service‡		25,746	20,022	14,816
Operating revenues	($000,000)	9,642	10,425	11,062
Operating expenses	($000,000)	7,657	8,003	8,724
Net income§	($000,000)	473	866	623‖
Passenger revenue	($000,000)	641	556	447
Passengers carried	(000,000)	327	306	301
Passenger-miles	(000,000)	21,284	17,454	13,164
Revenue per passenger-mile	(cents)	3.014	3.185	3.393
Average journey per passenger	(miles)	65.05	57.07	43.68
Freight revenue	($000,000)	8,152	9,037	9,942
Freight revenue-tons originated	(000,000)	1,301	1,479	1,515
Tons carried one mile	(000,000)	575,360	705,705	750,468
Revenue ton-miles per mile of road	(000)	2,497	3,121	3,386
Revenue per ton-mile	(cents)	1.417	1.281	1.325
Haul per ton				
U.S. as a system	(miles)	442.14	477.15	495.37
Individual railroad	(miles)	238.83	257.40	270.47
Revenue per ton				
U.S. as a system	(dollars)	6.26	6.11	6.56
Individual railroad	(dollars)	3.38	3.30	3.58
Average number of employees	(000)	793	655	602
Compensation of employees	($000,000)	4,957	4,887	5,197

All data are for Classes I and II.
*Includes unofficial companies.
†Includes lessors, proprietary and unofficial companies.
‡Includes switching and terminal companies.
§Includes lessors.
‖After extraordinary and prior period items.
Source: Interstate Commerce Commission.

Aviation

Item		1960	1969
CIVIL FLYING			
Total aircraft		111,580	179,285*
Hours flown†	(000)	13,121	24,053*
Miles flown†	(000,000)	1,769	3,701*
Aircraft accidents†		4,883	4,995
Aircraft accident fatalities†		787	1,388
Pilot licenses		348,062	720,028
SCHEDULED AIR CARRIERS			
Aircraft operating‡		1,867	2,363
Fixed wing		1,842	2,345
Four-engine		1,160	865
Twin-engine		677	867
Express and freight flown§	(000,000 ton-mi)	579	2,853
Mail flown	(000,000 ton-mi)	239	1,265
Domestic operations‖			
Number of operators§		39	35*
Route miles in operation¶		101,414	116,567*
Revenue passengers carried	(000,000)	56	154
Revenue passenger-miles flown	(000,000)	30,567	95,946
International operations‖			
Number of operators§		10	7*
Route miles in operation		148,303	154,120*
Revenue passengers carried	(000,000)	6	17
Revenue passenger-miles flown	(000,000)	8,306	29,468

*1968. †Excludes civil flying performed by public carriers.
‡Excludes aircraft used for crew training and general utility purposes, those held for disposal, and those operated by the scheduled all-cargo carriers.
§Excludes all-cargo operators. ‖Operations between conterminous U.S. and Hawaii and Alaska included with international. ¶Excludes intra-Alaska.
Source: U.S. Department of Commerce, Bureau of the Census, *Statistical Abstract of the United States*. Data compiled by U.S. Department of Transportation, Federal Aviation Administration, *FAA Statistical Handbook of Aviation*.

Communication facilities

State	Post offices July 1, 1970	RADIO STATIONS Jan. 1, 1969 AM	FM	TV STATIONS March 1, 1970 Commercial	Educational	TELEPHONES Jan. 1, 1970 Total	Residence	NEWSPAPERS Daily Number Feb. 1, 1970	Circulation Oct. 1, 1969	Weekly March 1, 1970 Number	Circulation	Sunday Number Feb. 1, 1970	Circulation Oct. 1, 1969
Alabama	674	133	45	15	8	1,501,400	1,120,500	20	703,009	102	324,095	14	615,681
Alaska	203	18	3	7	—	85,300	49,500	6	67,721	6	9,238	2	19,291
Arizona	216	58	14	10	2	879,200	602,100	13	423,807	55	126,876	5	351,098
Arkansas	711	83	28	6	1	806,800	599,500	35	427,168	124	272,441	11	368,908
California	1,171	230	142	48	9	12,891,900	9,035,000	134	5,814,217	441	4,874,017	39	4,832,912
Colorado	428	66	24	11	1	1,292,100	895,500	26	698,204	125	258,728	9	732,660
Connecticut	253	37	18	5	3	1,956,500	1,430,100	28	951,199	48	255,143	7	607,058
Delaware	57	10	3	—	1	360,300	262,800	3	156,266	12	53,854	—	—
Dist. of Columbia	1	6	6	6	1	863,200	443,200	3	1,000,102	...	...	2	982,470
Florida	473	189	75	25	9	3,828,200	2,688,000	49	1,986,712	131	445,577	30	1,842,288
Georgia	661	169	50	15	10	2,266,500	1,634,700	31	972,528	183	504,780	12	912,200
Hawaii	80	25	4	10	2	424,000	267,000	5	227,663	2	15,817	2	180,116
Idaho	277	42	6	7	1	336,700	240,400	15	172,772	58	100,894	5	138,520
Illinois	1,299	121	88	23	5	6,876,900	4,948,000	93	3,958,825	585	2,551,834	19	2,921,086
Indiana	770	83	70	18	3	2,766,800	2,078,000	83	1,703,154	192	453,272	20	1,188,332
Iowa	975	72	33	12	2	1,557,500	1,194,400	43	1,003,895	361	689,057	9	876,459
Kansas	736	57	22	12	2	1,251,300	944,500	50	649,941	252	389,458	14	436,848
Kentucky	1,364	99	55	9	13	1,364,100	1,018,200	27	762,030	131	385,744	13	568,199
Louisiana	553	89	36	15	1	1,701,200	1,270,400	23	763,933	86	243,146	10	674,297
Maine	518	36	12	7	4	460,000	343,200	9	269,097	35	128,184	1	110,790
Maryland	433	52	31	6	1	2,330,700	1,698,800	12	751,766	60	410,850	4	723,358
Massachusetts	456	62	37	10	2	3,399,500	2,374,700	46	2,345,451	139	697,629	12	1,609,036
Michigan	889	124	72	20	4	4,957,300	3,691,500	55	2,414,693	289	1,431,152	12	2,079,653
Minnesota	893	82	35	13	4	2,134,600	1,589,700	31	1,135,703	328	667,683	7	1,018,287
Mississippi	491	95	29	9	1	833,000	628,200	26	315,177	100	231,338	7	187,600
Missouri	1,017	103	38	22	2	2,659,200	1,945,800	54	1,781,512	284	628,120	14	1,511,322
Montana	394	41	4	10	—	340,100	246,700	15	189,415	72	117,157	9	179,574
Nebraska	567	47	15	14	9	838,800	627,800	19	481,489	200	416,312	5	363,094
Nevada	100	19	8	7	1	306,600	187,600	7	143,470	15	28,523	4	130,473
New Hampshire	255	25	10	2	5	396,600	297,400	9	159,516	33	120,149	1	51,694
New Jersey	525	32	25	1	—	4,585,000	3,399,000	31	1,752,875	211	1,142,398	8	1,272,800
New Mexico	347	54	16	7	1	467,900	307,500	19	207,810	25	62,215	12	177,354
New York	1,652	154	89	28	8	12,199,700	8,363,500	80	7,625,010	412	1,789,949	15	6,485,631
North Carolina	799	191	68	18	6	2,205,800	1,639,500	48	1,260,591	127	416,375	18	906,779
North Dakota	484	27	9	12	1	306,200	226,800	10	184,811	94	159,225	3	102,237
Ohio	1,092	114	105	28	8	6,034,600	4,490,800	96	3,522,257	251	1,300,793	20	2,326,344
Oklahoma	665	63	32	10	3	1,394,100	1,002,500	52	846,449	210	364,795	41	790,355
Oregon	372	80	16	13	2	1,128,000	810,100	21	654,101	98	298,568	5	530,444
Pennsylvania	1,866	168	105	24	8	7,201,000	5,429,500	109	4,036,704	228	1,255,309	10	2,843,903
Rhode Island	59	15	7	3	1	506,800	369,500	7	318,917	13	66,776	2	215,566
South Carolina	401	100	33	11	5	1,093,400	810,600	17	556,855	76	224,292	7	436,930
South Dakota	438	28	5	10	3	319,700	239,700	12	170,589	143	179,295	4	120,852
Tennessee	610	138	60	16	4	1,845,900	1,369,200	33	1,148,380	122	362,269	14	916,547
Texas	1,582	283	115	51	6	5,995,300	4,251,500	112	3,197,538	491	1,115,063	83	3,115,396
Utah	231	31	10	3	5	563,700	405,000	5	255,625	50	104,811	4	252,343
Vermont	296	18	1	2	4	221,200	157,200	9	112,916	14	30,658	—	—
Virginia	975	122	51	13	5	2,336,300	1,668,400	32	1,002,634	97	395,324	13	716,416
Washington	503	96	37	13	6	1,920,700	1,376,200	23	1,045,544	144	812,976	12	962,145
West Virginia	1,087	58	20	9	2	740,800	555,700	31	492,887	83	237,152	9	391,312
Wisconsin	803	93	70	16	3	2,281,200	1,623,700	38	1,221,377	246	649,392	7	851,610
Wyoming	183	29	1	3	—	187,300	131,000	9	72,990	28	58,629	3	46,579
Total U.S.	32,002*	4,167	1,888	665	188	115,200,700	82,980,100	1,758†	62,059,589†	7,612‡	27,857,332‡	585†	49,674,847†

*Includes 117 post offices in U.S. territories.
†Total has been adjusted to account for double listings of Covington, Ky. edition of Ohio newspaper.
‡Excludes District of Columbia.
Sources: American Newspaper Representatives, Inc. American Telephone and Telegraph Co. Federal Communications Commission.
Television Digest, Inc., *Television Factbook* (Copyright 1970. All rights reserved. Used by permission.). The Editor & Publisher Co., Inc., *International Year Book* (Copyright 1970. All rights reserved. Used by permission.). U.S. Post Office Department.

Printed in U.S.A. by R. R. Donnelley & Sons Company